collecting WORLD COINS

A CENTURY OF CIRCULATING ISSUES
1901 - PRESENT

George S. Cuhaj
Managing Editor

Tom Michael
Market Analysist

Elizabeth Burgert
Coordinating Editor

Fred Borgmann
New Issues Editor

Robert Wilhite
US Market Analysist

Sherry Dopp
Production Coordinator

Randy Thern
Numismatic Cataloging Supervisor

UNCIRCULATED VALUATIONS

The uncirculated valuations represented in this edition are for typical quality specimens; for some of the more popularly collected series. Brilliant uncirculated (BU), or superior quality examples may easily command 10% to 50% premiums, or even greater where particularly popular or rare types or dates are concerned.

BULLION VALUE (BV) MARKET VALUATIONS

Valuations for all platinum, gold, palladium or silver coins of the more common, basically bullion types, or those possessing only modest numismatic premiums are presented in this edition based on market levels of $350 per ounce for platinum, $295 for gold, $275 for palladium and $5.00 per ounce for silver. Wherever the letters "BV" – Bullion Value – appear in a value column, that particular issue in the condition indicated generally trades at or near the bullion value of its precious metal content. Further information on using this catalog to evaluate platinum, gold, palladium or silver coins amid fluctuating precious metal market conditions is presented in the users guide section of the Introduction.

collecting WORLD COINS

A CENTURY OF CIRCULATING ISSUES
1901 - PRESENT

EIGHTH EDITION

Published in the United States by Krause Publications, Inc.

krause publications

700 E. State Street, Iola, WI 54990
Telephone: 715-445-2214 • FAX: 715-445-4087
Internet: www.krause.com

COPYRIGHT 1999 by KRAUSE PUBLICATIONS INC.
Library of Congress Catalog Card Number: 86-82722
International Standard Book Number: 0-87341-765-8

Printed in the United States of America

INTRODUCTION

Collecting World Coins is designed to offer a focused approach to collecting world coins, catering to the needs of a particular section of the hobby. The beginner, novice on casual collector. This reference is not intended as an enhancement to other numismatic catalogs—rather a response to a specific need.

The scope of this volume embraces only 20th century monetary coin issues circulated by nations around the globe. The coverage of silver and non-precious metal coinages is broad based, generally speaking, while the coverage of gold coinages is limited to those which enjoyed currency status at the time of issue, or have been popularly traded in later years at bullion issues. The period spanned is a rich one stretching from the era of full flower for the colonial empires, outside the Spanish realm, through the modern phenomenon of emerging nations.

The presentation of listings is detailed and comprehensive. The needs of the audience to which this volume is aimed can no longer be adequately served by a catalog that presents the world's coin issues as simple type listings. This catalog presents detailed listings of all issues which fall within its scope of coverage, including dates and mints of issue, along with mintage figures where available, and valuations in up to four grades of preservation.

Not intended as the ultimate reference, however, this handbook provides thorough, but not absolute coverage of its broad sweeping range. What you will not find listed are those coin issues expressly created for non-monetary purposes, including most limited issue commemorative coinages. You will also find few gold coin issues, as few were produced to serve circulating monetary purposes.

This volume has been designed, then, to provide the user with a comprehensive, compact, user friendly handbook that documents a century of the world's monetary issue coins.

The objective of this volume, then, is to provide users with accurate, reliable and instructive information on 20th century monetary issue coins—coins of great historical value, which attribute is drawn from the people, events and symbols emblazoned on them, or because they provide a tangible tie to historic eras—enabling those individuals to fully understand the heritage they represent and encourage them to deeper involvement in the collecting realm.

This handbook is keyed to enabling all who reach beyond its cover, be they possessed of novice or more advanced knowledge, to easily and quickly identify coins which require attribution to country or valuation. Two key features facilitate this purpose; an INSTANT IDENTIFIER guide that focuses on dominant design characteristics, including monograms, which when coupled with a comprehensive COUNTRY INDEX documenting the variable forms of country names that appear on subject coins, enables the novice user to quickly attribute any monetary world coin issue of this century to its country of origin.

The keystone feature of the country listings is the integration of actual size coin illustrations which accord quick identification, by type, of all denominations and design changes of an issue. All listings are accompanied by not only complete documentation of dates of issue and mintages, but also metals of issue, with the addition of ACTUAL SILVER WEIGHT (ASW) and ACTUAL GOLD WEIGHT (AGW) figures for all listed coins struck of silver or gold alloys.

From Afghanistan to Zimbabwe, the listings are cataloged according to a historic-geographical criteria which group under singular headings the various coinages circulated in historically continuous areas. Thus, the issues of the old Belgian Congo and its successor entities will be found listed under Zaire, and the coins of both North Korea and South Korea will be found entered under the heading of Korea.

The country listings are arranged, generally, in the ascending denomination and date of issue cataloging style popularly employed in American coin catalogs, sequences that have been broken only when major monetary reforms of coinage standard conversions have transpired. Catalog numbers accompany each coin of issue type listing cataloged, which designators are those that prevail in the marketplace; principally they are the designators (KM #) carried in the *Standard Catalog of World Coins* authored by Chester L. Krause and Clifford Mishler.

Users of this catalog seeking to advance their collecting pursuit of many countries listed herein are referred to the complete listings offered for many countries in the more detailed and comprehensive *Standard Catalog of World Coins, 20th Century*, a volume published annually providing coverage of all countries from 1900 to present. Companion 17th, 18th, and 19th century editions present in four volumes total, world coin issues from 1601 to the present.

Collectors seriously interested in expanding their pursuit of world coins should consider subscribing to "World Coin News," another Krause Publications product, the only monthly hobby newspaper devoted exclusively to world numismatic subjects. In addition to presenting a wide range of news reports covering various aspects of the world coin collecting realm, each issue also features "World Coin Roundup," a detailed presentation of timely information on newly released issues from around the globe, plus newly discovered varieties unearthed by scholars from many countries.

Krause Publications offers collectors in the U.S. the opportunity to receive, a special offer to World Coin News as noted on page 20. All requests should be submitted in writing to: World Coin News, Dept. CGW, 700 East State St., Iola, WI 54990. Overseas collectors may obtain a free sample copy of a current issue by directing their requests to the same address and including one (1) International Postal Reply Coupon for surface mail delivery, or two (2) coupons for airmail dispatch. Internet users can access a complete listing of numismatic books and periodicals at www.krause.com

COUNTRY INDEX

HOW TO USE THIS CATALOG

This catalog series is designed to serve the needs of both the novice and advanced collectors. It provides a comprehensive guide to 20th Century world coinage. It is generally arranged so that persons with no more than a basic knowledge of world history and a casual acquaintance with coin collecting can consult it with confidence and ease. The following explanations summarize the general practices used in preparing this catalog's listings. However, because of specialized requirements which may vary by country and era, these must not be considered ironclad. Where these standards have been set aside, appropriate notations of the variations are incorporated in that particular listing.

ARRANGEMENT

All coin listings are alphabetically arranged in a historical-geographic approach according to the current identity of the sovereign government concerned. Thus, the coins of Persia can be located by referring to the listings for Iran, or the now defunct Union of Soviet Socialist Republics (U.S.S.R.) by turning to Russia. This approach has also resulted in combining the coin listings for such issuing entities as Annam, French Cochin China, Tonkin, North and South Viet Nam as sub-groupings under the identity of Viet Nam. Likewise, coins of North and South Korea will be found under Korea, and those of the Congo Free State, Belgian Congo, Congo Democratic Republic, Katanga and Zaire, under the latter identity.

Coins of each country are generally arranged by denomination from lowest to highest, except where arrangement by ruler, mint of issue, type or period makes a series easier to understand. Exceptions which are not readily adaptable to this traditional North American cataloging style are generally found in the more complicated series, most notably those encompassing the early issues of Afghanistan, Mughal issues of India, Indian Princely States, Iran, Nepal and the areas under the influence of the late Ottoman Empire, which are listed by ruler or by mint.

Strict date sequence of listings is also interrupted in a number of countries which have been subjected to major monetary reforms or conversion to decimal or other new currency systems. Where these considerations apply, appropriate headings are incorporated to introduce the change from one standard to another.

IDENTIFICATION

The most important step in the identification of a coin is the determination of the nation of origin. This is generally easily accomplished where English-speaking lands are concerned, however, use of the country index is sometimes required. The coins of Great Britain provide an interesting challenge. For hundreds of years the only indication of the country of origin was in the abbreviated Latin legends. In recent times there have been occasions when there has been no indication of origin. Only through the familiarity of the monarchical portraits, symbols and legends or indication of currency system are they identifiable.

The coins of many countries beyond the English-language realm, such as those of French, Italian or Spanish heritage, are also quite easy to identify through reference to their legends, which appear in the national languages based on Western alphabets. In many instances the name is spelled exactly the same in English as in the national language, such as France; while in other cases it varies only slightly, like Italia for Italy, Belgique or Belgie for Belgium, Brasil for Brazil and Danmark for Denmark.

This is not always the case, however, as in Norge for Norway, Espana for Spain, Sverige for Sweden and Helvetia for Switzerland. Some other examples include:

DEUTSCHES REICH - Germany 1873-1945

BUNDESREPUBLIK DEUTSCHLAND - Federal Republic of Germany.

DEUTSCHE DEMOKRATISCHE REPUBLIK - German Democratic Republic.

EMPIRE CHERIFIEN MAROC - Morocco.

ESTADOS UNIDOS MEXICANOS - United Mexican States (Mexico).

ETAT DU GRAND LIBAN - State of Great Lebanon (Lebanon).

Thus it can be seen there are instances in which a little schooling in the rudiments of foreign languages can be most helpful. In general, colonial possessions of countries using the Western alphabet are similarly identifiable as they often carry portraits of their current rulers, the familiar lettering, sometimes in combination with a companion designation in the local language.

Collectors have the greatest difficulty with coins that do not bear legends or dates in the Western systems. These include coins bearing Cyrillic lettering, attributable to Bulgaria, Russia, the Slavic states and Mongolia, the Greek script peculiar to Greece, Crete and the Ionian Islands; The Amharic characters of Ethiopia, or Hebrew in the case of Israel. Dragons and sunbursts along with the distinctive word characters, attribute a coin to the Oriental countries of China, Japan, Korea, Tibet, Viet Nam and their component parts.

The most difficult coins to identify are those bearing only Persian or Arabic script and its derivatives, found on the issues of nations stretching in a wide swath across North Africa and East Asia, from Morocco to Indonesia, and the Indian subcontinent coinages which surely are more confusing in their vast array of Nagari, Sanskrit, Ahom, Assamese and other local dialects found on the local issues of the Indian Princely States. Although the task of identification on the more modern issues of these lands is often eased by the added presence of Western alphabet legends, a feature sometimes adopted as early as the late 19th Century, for the earlier pieces it is often necessary for the uninitiated to laboriously seek and find.

Except for the cruder issues, however, it will be found that certain characteristics and symbols featured in addition to the predominant legends are typical on coins from a given country or group of countries. The toughra monogram, for instance, occurs on some of the coins of Afghanistan, Egypt, the Sudan, Pakistan, Turkey and other areas of the late Ottoman Empire. A predominant design feature on the coins of Nepal is the trident; while neighboring Tibet features a lotus blossom or lion on many of their issues.

To assist in identification of the more difficult coins, we have assembled the *Instant Identifier* and *Monogram* sections presented on the following pages. They are designed to provide a point of beginning for collec-

tors by allowing them to compare unidentified coins with photographic details from typical issues.

We also suggest reference to the *Index of Coin Denominations* presented here and also the comprehensive *Country Index*, where the inscription will be found listed just as it appears on the coin for nations using the Western alphabet.

DATING

Coin dating is the final basic attribution consideration. Here, the problem can be more difficult because the reading of a coin date is subject not only to the vagaries of numeric styling, but to calendar variations caused by the observance of various religious eras or regal periods from country to country, or even within a country. Here again with the exception of the sphere from North Africa through the Orient, it will be found that most countries rely on Western date numerals and Christian (AD) era reckoning, although in a few instances, coin dating has been tied to the year of a reign or government. The Vatican, for example dates its coinage according to the year of reign of the current pope, in addition to the Christian-era date.

Countries in the Arabic sphere generally date their coins to the Muslim era (AH), which commenced on July 16, 622 AD (Julian calendar), when the prophet Mohammed fled from Mecca to Medina. As their calendar is reckoned by the lunar year of 354 days, which is about three percent (precisely 2.98%) shorter than the Christian year, a formula is required to convert AH dating to its Western equivalent. To convert an AH date to the approximate AD date, subtract three percent of the AH date (round to the closest whole number) from the AH date, then add 622. A chart for converting all AH years from 1010 (July 2, 1601) to 1421 (April 6, 2000) is presented on the last page of this volume.

The Muslim calendar is not always based on the lunar year (AH), however, causing some confusion, particularly in Afghanistan and Iran, where a calendar based on the solar year (SH) was introduced around 1920. These dates can be converted to AD by simply adding 621. In 1976 the government of Iran implemented a new solar calendar based on the foundation of the Iranian monarchy in 559 BC. The first year observed on the new calendar was 2535 (MS), which commenced March 20, 1976. A reversion to the traditional SH dating standard occurred a few years later.

Several different eras of reckoning, including Christian and Muslim (AH), have been used to date coins of the Indian subcontinent. The two basic systems are the Vikrama Samvat (VS), which dates from Oct. 18, 58 BC, and the Saka era, the origin of which is reckoned from March 3, 78 AD. Dating according to both eras appears on various coins of the area.

Coins of Thailand (Siam) are found dated by three different eras. The most predominant is the Buddhist era (BE) which originated in 543 BC. Next is the Bangkok or Ratanakosindsok (RS) era, dating from 1781 AD; followed by the Chula-Sakarat (CS) era, dating from 638 AD. The latter era originated in Burma and is used on that country's coins.

Other calendars include that of the Ethiopian era (EE) which commenced seven years, eight months after AD dating; and that of the Jewish people, which commenced on Oct. 7, 3761 BC. Korea claims a legendary dating from 2333 BC, which is acknowledged in some of its coin dating. Some coin issues of the Indonesian area carry dates determined by the Javanese Aji Saka

era (AS), a calendar of 354 days (100 Javanese years equal 97 Christian or Gregorian calendar years) which can be matched to AD dating by comparing it to AH dating.

The following table indicates the year dating for the various eras which correspond to 1997 in Christian calendar reckoning, but it must be remembered that there are overlaps between the eras in some instances.

Christian era (AD) —	1999
Muslim era (AH) —	AH1420
Solar year (SH) —	SH1378
Monarchic Solar era (MS) —	MS2558
Vikrama Samvat (VS) —	VS2056
Saka era (SE) —	SE1921
Buddhist era (BE) —	BE2542
Bangkok era (RS) —	RS218
Chula-Sakarat era (CS) —	CS1361
Ethiopian era (EE) —	EE1991
Jewish era —	5759
Korean era —	4332
Javanese Aji Saka era (AS) —	AS1932
Fasli era (FE) —	FE1409

Coins of Oriental origin — principally Japan, Korea, China, Turkestan and Tibet and some modern gold issues of Turkey — are generally dated to the year of the government, dynasty, reign or cyclic eras, with the dates indicated in Oriental characters which usually read from right to left. In recent years, however, some dating has been according to the Christian calendar and in Western numerals. In Japan, Oriental character dating was reversed to read from left to right in Showa year 23 (1948 AD).

More detailed guides to less prevalent coin dating systems which are strictly local in nature are presented with the appropriate listings.

Some coins carry dates according to both locally observed and Christian eras. This is particularly true in the Arabic world, where the Hejira date may be indicated in Arabic numerals and the Christian date in Western numerals, or both dates in either form.

The date actually carried on a given coin is generally cataloged here in the first column (Date) to the right of the catalog number. If the date is not by AD reckoning, the next column (Year) indicates the date by the conventional calendar which applies, generally Christian. If an AD date appears in either column, the AD is not necessarily indicated. Era abbreviations in the dating table in this section are generally shown in conjunction with the listings of coins dated in those eras.

Dates listed in either column which does not actually appear on a given coin is generally enclosed by parentheses. Undated coins are indicated by the letters ND in the date column and the estimated year of issue in parentheses.

Timing differentials between some era of reckoning particularly the 354-day Mohammedan and 365-day Christian years, cause situations whereby coins which carry dates for both eras exist bearing two year dates from one calendar combined with a single date from another.

NUMBERING SYSTEM

Some catalog numbers assigned in this volume are based on established references. This practice has been observed for two reasons: First, when world coins are listed chronologically they are basically self-cataloging; second, there was no need to confuse collectors with

totally new numeric designations where appropriate systems already existed. As time progressed we found many of these established systems incomplete and inadequate and are now replaced with new KM numbers with appropriate cross-referencing.

Some of the coins listed in this catalog are identified or cross-referenced by numbers assigned by R.S. Yeoman (Y#), or slight adaptations thereof, in his *Modern World Coins,* and *Current Coins of the World.*

In some countries, listings are cross-referenced to Robert Friedberg's (FR#) *Gold Coins of the World* or *Coins of the British World* or W.H. Valentine's (V#) reference on the *Modern Copper Coins of the Muhammadan States.* Coins issued under the Chinese sphere of influence are assigned numbers from E. Kann's (K#) *Illustrated Catalog of Chinese Coins* and T.K. Hsu's (Su) work of similar title.

DENOMINATIONS

The second basic consideration to be met in the attribution of a coin is the determination of denomination. Since denominations are usually expressed in numeric, rather than word form on a coin, this is usually quite easily accomplished on coins from nations which use Western numerals, except in those instances where issues are devoid of any mention of face value, and denomination must be attributed by size, metallic composition or weight. Coins listed in this volume are generally illustrated in actual size. Where size is critical to proper attribution, the coin's millimeter size is indicated.

The sphere of countries stretching from North Africa through the Orient, on which numeric symbols generally unfamiliar to Westerners are employed, often provide the collector with a much greater challenge. This is particularly true on nearly all pre-20th Century issues. On some of the more modern issues, and increasingly so as the years progress, Western style numerals, usually presented in combination with the local numeric system, are becoming more commonplace on these coins.

Determination of a coin's currency system can also be valuable in attributing the issue to its country of origin. A comprehensive alphabetical index of currency names, applicable to the countries as cataloged in this volume, with all individual nations of use for each, is presented in this section.

The included table of *Standard International Numeral Systems* presents charts of the basic numeric designations found on coins of non-Western origin. Although denomination numerals are generally prominently displayed on coins, it must be remembered that these are general representations of characters which individual coin engravers may have rendered in widely varying styles. Where numeric or script denominations designation forms peculiar to a given coin or country apply, such as the script used on some Persian (Iranian) issues, they are so indicated or illustrated in conjunction with the appropriate listings.

MINTAGES

Quantities minted of each date are indicated where that information is available, generally stated in millions, rounded off to the nearest 10,000 pieces. On quantities of a few thousand or less, actual mintages are generally indicated, a fact that can be determined by the presence of a comma, rather than a decimal point, in the stated figure. The following mintage conversion formulas have been observed:

10,000,000 - 10.000
1,000,000 - 1.000
100,000 - .100
10,000 - .010
9,999 - 9,999
1,000 - 1,000
842 - 842 pcs. (Pieces)
27 - 27 pcs.

The abbreviation "Inc. Ab." or "I.A." means Included Above, while "Inc. Be." or "I.B." means Included Below. An "*" beside a mintage figure indicates the number given is an estimate or mintage limit.

MINT AND PRIVY MARKS

The presence of distinctive, but frequently inconspicuously placed, mint marks indicates the mint of issue for many of the coins listed in this catalog. An appropriate designation in the date listings notes the presence, if any, of a mint mark on a particular coin type by incorporating the letter or letters of the mint mark adjoining the date, i.e., 1950D or 1927R.

The presence of mint and/or mintmaster's privy marks on a coin in non-letter form is indicated by incorporating the mint letter in lower case within parentheses adjoining the date; i.e. 1927(a). The corresponding mark is illustrated or identified in the introduction of the country.

A listing format by mints of issue has been adopted for some countries — including France, Spain and Mexico — to allow for a more logical arrangement. In these instances, the name of the mint and its mint mark letter or letters is presented at the beginning of each series.

Where listings incorporate mintmaster initials, they are always presented in capital letters separated from the date; i.e., 1850 MF. The different mint mark and mintmaster letters found on the coins of any country, state or city of issue are always shown at the beginning of listings.

METALS

At the beginning of each date listing, the metallic composition of each coin denomination is listed, and thereafter, whenever a change in metal occurs. The traditional coinage metals and their symbolic chemical abbreviations used in this catalog are:

Platinum - (PT)	Copper - (Cu)
Gold - (Au)	Brass -
Silver - (Ag)	Copper-nickel - (CN)
Billion -	Lead - (Pb)
Nickel - (Ni)	Steel -
Zinc - (Zn)	Tin - (Sn)
Bronze - (Ae)	Aluminum - (Al)

During the 18th and 19th centuries, most of the worlds coins were struck of copper or bronze, silver and gold. Commencing in the early years of the 20th century, however, numerous new coinage metals, primarily non-precious metal alloys, were introduced. Gold has not been widely used for circulation coinages since World War I, although silver remained a popular coinage metal in most parts of the world until after World War II. With the disappearance of silver for circulation coinage, numerous additional compositions were introduced to coinage applications.

Most recent is the development of clad or plated planchets in order to maintain circulation life and extend the life of a set of production dies as used in the production of the copper-nickel clad copper 50 centesimos of Panama or in the latter case to reduce produc-

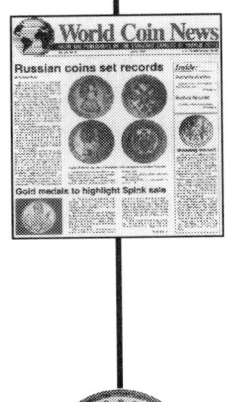

tion costs of the planchets and yet provide a coin quite similar in appearance to its predecessor as in the case of the copper plated zinc core United States 1983 cent.

PRECIOUS METAL WEIGHTS

Listings of weight, fineness and actual silver (ASW), gold (AGW), platinum or palladium (APW) content of most machine-struck silver, gold, platinum and palladium coins are provided in this edition. These designations will be found incorporated in the listings immediately beneath illustrations or in conjunction with type changes wherever these factors could be determined.

The ASW, AGW and APW figures were determined by multiplying the gross weight of a given coin by its known or tested fineness and converting the resulting gram or grain weight to troy ounces, rounded to the nearest ten-thousandth of an ounce. A silver coin with a 24.25 gram weight and .875 fineness, for example, would have a fine weight of approximately 21.2188 grams, or a .6822 ASW, a factor that can be used to accurately determine the intrinsic value for multiple examples.

The ASW, AGW or APW figure can be multiplied by the spot price of each precious metal to determine the current intrinsic value of any coin accompanied by these designations.

WEIGHTS AND FINENESSES

Coin weights are indicated in grams (abbreviated "g") along with fineness where the information is of value in differentiating between types. These weights are based on 31.103 grams per troy (scientific) ounce, as opposed to the avoirdupois (commercial) standard of 28.35 grams. Actual coin weights are generally shown in hundredths or thousands of a gram; i.e., .500 SILVER 2.9200g.

As the silver and gold bullion markets have advanced and declined sharply in recent years, the fineness and total precious metal content of coins has become espe-cially significant where bullion coins — issues which trade on the basis of their intrinsic metallic content rather than numismatic value — are concerned. In many instances, such issues have become worth more in bullion form than their nominal collector values or denominations indicate.

Establishing the weight of a coin can also be valuable for determining its denomination. Actual weight is also necessary to ascertain the specific gravity of the coin's metallic content, an important factor in determining authenticity.

TROY WEIGHT STANDARDS
24 Grains = 1 Pennyweight
480 Grains = 1 Ounce
31.103 Grams = 1 Ounce

UNIFORM WEIGHTS
15.432 Grains = 1 Gram
0.0648 Gram = 1 Grain

AVOIRDUPOIS STANDARDS
27-11/32 Grains = 11 Dram
437-1/2 Grains = 1 Ounce
28.350 Grams = 1 Ounce

BULLION VALUE CHARTS

Universal silver, gold, and platinum bullion value charts are provided for use in combination with the ASW, AGW and APW factors to determine approximate intrinsic values of listed coins. By adding the component weights as shown in troy ounces on each chart, the approximate intrinsic value of any silver, gold or platinum coin's precious metal content can be determined.

Again referring to the examples presented in the above section, the intrinsic value of a silver coin with a .6822 ASW would be indicated as $4.43 + based on the application of the silver bullion chart. This result is obtained by moving across the top to the $6.50 column, then moving down to the line indicated .680 in

Coin Alignment

Medal Alignment

COIN vs MEDAL ALIGNMENT

Coins are traditionally struck with obverse and reverse aligned at a rotation of 180 degrees from each other. When a coin is held for vertical viewing with the obverse design aligned upright and the index finger and thumb at the top and bottom, upon rotation from left to right for viewing the reverse, the latter will be upside down. Such alignment is called "coin rotation." Some coins are struck with the obverse and reverse designs mated on an alignment of zero or 360 degrees. If such a piece is held and rotated as described, the reverse will appear upright. This is the alignment which is generally observed in the striking of medals, and for that reason coins produced in this manner are termed to have been struck in "medal rotation." In some instances, usually through error, certain coin issues have been struck to both alignment standards, creating interesting collectible varieties which will be found noted in some listing.

the far left hand corner which reveals a bullion value of $4.420. To determine the value of the remaining .0022 of ASW, return up the same column to the .002 line, the closest factor available, where a $ .0130 value is indicted. The two factors total to $4.433, which would be slightly less than actual value.

The silver bullion chart provides silver values in thousandths from .001 to .009 troy ounce, and in hundredths from .01 to 1.00 in 50¢ value increments from $3.00 to $10.50. If the market value of silver exceeds $10.50, doubling the increments presented will provide valuations in $1 steps from $6.00 to $21.00.

The gold/platinum bullion chart is similarly arranged in $10 increments from $350 to $490, and by doubling the increments presented, $20 steps from $700 to $980 can be determined.

Valuations for most of the silver, gold, platinum and palladium coins listed in this edition are based on assumed market values of $5.00 per troy ounce for silver, $295. for gold, $350. for platinum, and $275. for palladium. To arrive at accurate current market indications for these issues, increase or decrease the valuations appropriately based on any variations in these indicated levels.

COUNTERMARKS/COUNTERSTAMPS

There is some confusion among collectors over the terms "countermark" and "counterstamp" when applied to a coin bearing an additional mark or change of design and/or denomination.

To clarify, a countermark might be considered similar to the "hall mark" applied to a piece of silverware, by which a silversmith assured the quality of the piece. In the same way, a countermark assures the quality of the coin on which it is placed.

Countermarks are generally applied singularly and in most cases indiscriminately on either side of the "host" coin.

Counterstamped coins are more extensively altered. The counterstamping is done with a set of dies, rather than a hand punch. The coin being counterstamped is placed between the new dies and struck as if it were a blank planchet as found with the Manila 8 reales issue of the Philippines. A more unusual application where the counterstamp dies were smaller than the host coin in the revalidated 50 centimos and 1 colon of Costa Rica issued in 1923.

PHOTOGRAPHS

To assist the reader in coin identification, every effort has been made to present actual size photographs of every coinage type listed. Obverse and reverse are illustrated, except when a change in design is restricted to one side, and the coin has a diameter of 39mm or larger, in which case only the side required for identification of the type is generally illustrated. All coins up to 60mm are illustrated actual size, to the nearest 1/2mm up to 25mm, and to the nearest 1mm thereafter. Coins larger than 60mm diameter are illustrated in reduced size, with the actual size noted thereunder. Where slight change in size is important to coin type identification, actual millimeter measurements arestated.

TRADE COINS

From approximately 1750-1940, a number of nations, particularly European colonial powers and commercial traders, minted trade coins to facilitate commerce with the local populace of Africa, the Arab countries, the Indian subcontinental, Southeast Asia and the Far East. Such coins generally circulated at a value based on the weight and fineness of their silver or gold content, rather than their stated denomination. Examples include the sovereigns of Great Britain and the gold ducat issues of Austria, Hungary and the Netherlands. Trade coinage will be found listed at the end of the domestic issues.

VALUATIONS

Values quoted in this catalog represent the current market and are compiled from recommendations provided and verified through various source documents and specialized consultants. **It should be stressed, however, that this book is intended to serve only as an aid for evaluating coins, actual market conditions are constantly changing and additional influences,** such as particularly strong local demand for certain coin series, fluctuation of international exchange rates and worldwide collection patterns must also be considered. Publication of this catalog is not intended as a solicitation by the publisher, editors or contributors to buy or sell the listed coins at the prices indicated.

All valuations are stated in U.S. dollars, based on careful assessment of the varied international collector market. Valuations for coins priced below $1,000.00 are generally stated in full amounts — i.e. 37.50 or 950.00 — while valuations at or above that figure are rounded off in even dollars — i.e. $1250.00 is expressed 1250. A comma is added to indicate tens of thousands of dollars in value.

For the convenience of overseas collectors and for U.S. collectors doing business with overseas dealers, the base exchange rate for the national currencies of approximately 180 countries are presented in the Foreign Exchange Table.

It should be noted that when particularly select uncirculated or proof-like examples of uncirculated coins become available they can be expected to command proportionately high premiums. Such examples in reference to choice Germanic Thalers are referred to as "erst schlage" or first strikes.

NEW ISSUES

All newly released coins that have been physically observed by our staff and those that have been confirmed by press time have been incorporated in this edition. Exceptions exist in some countries where current date coin production lags far behind and other countries whose fiscal year actually begins in the latter half of the current year.

Collectors and dealers alike are kept up to date with worldwide new issues having newly assigned catalog reference numbers and releases of mintage figures of previous years presented in the monthly feature "World Coin Roundup" in *World Coin News*. Direct ordering instructions from worldwide mints and authorized institutions is also provided through new releases and the "Mint Data" column in *World Coin News*. A free sample copy will be sent upon request. Overseas requests should include 1 international postal reply coupon for surface mail or 2 international postal reply coupons for air mail dispatch: Write to *World Coin News,* 700 East State St., Iola, WI 54990 USA. Contact us on the web: www.krause.com

STANDARD INTERNATIONAL GRADING TERMINOLOGY AND ABBREVIATIONS

	PROOF	UNCIRCULATED	EXTREMELY FINE	VERY FINE	FINE	VERY GOOD	GOOD	POOR
U.S. and ENGLISH SPEAKING LANDS	PRF	UNC	EF or XF	VF	F	VG	G	PR
BRAZIL	—	(1)FDC or FC	(3) S	(5) MBC	(7) BC	(8) BC/R	(9) R	UT GeG
DENMARK	M	0	01	1+	1	1÷	2	3
FINLAND	00	0	01	1+	1	1?	2	3
FRANCE	FB Flan Bruni	FDC Fleur de Coin	SUP Superbe	TTB Très très beau	TB Très beau	B Beau	TBC Très Bien Conservée	BC Bien Conservée
GERMANY	PP Polierte Platte	STG Stempelglanz	VZ Vorzüglich	SS Sehr schön	S Schön	S.G.E. Sehr gut erhalten	G.E. Gut erhalten	Gering erhalten
ITALY	FS Fondo Specchio	FDC Fior di Conio	SPL Splendido	BB Bellissimo	MB Molto Bello	B Bello	M	—
JAPAN	—	未 使 用	極 美 品	美 品	並 品	—	—	—
NETHERLANDS	Proef	FDC Fleur de Coin	Pr. Prachtig	Z.f. Zeer fraai	Fr. Fraai	Z.g. Zeer goed	G	—
NORWAY	M	0	01	1+	1	1÷	2	3
PORTUGAL	—	Soberba	Bela	MBC	BC	MREG	REG	MC
SPAIN	Prueba	SC	EBC	MBC	BC+	BC	RC	MC
SWEDEN	Polerad	0	01	1+	1	1?	2	—

CONDITIONS/GRADING

Wherever possible, coin valuations are given in four grades of preservation. The following standards have been observed to provide continuity in grouping grade ranges in this catalog. However, because they cannot be universally applied, appropriate variations have been incorporated and noted: 1) Good, Very Good, Fine and Very Fine — used for crude "dump" or similar issues: 2) Very Good, Very Fine and Extremely Fine — used for early machine-minted issues of Europe (early 1800s), Latin America (up to the mid-1800s), the present. Listings in three grades of preservation will also be found, usually in cases of modern issues.

There are almost no grading guides for world coins. What follows is an attempt to help bridge that gap until a detailed, illustrated guide becomes available.

In grading world coins, there are two elements to look for: 1) Overall wear, and 2) loss of design details, such as strands of hair, feathers on eagles, designs on coats of arms, etc.

The age, rarity or type of a coin should not be a consideration in grading.

Grade each coin by the weaker of the two sides. This method appears to give results most nearly consistent with conservative American Numismatic Association standards for U.S. coins. Split grades, i.e., F/VF for obverse and reverse, respectively, are normally no more than one grade apart. If the two sides are more than one grade apart, the series of coins probably wears differently on each side and should then be graded by the weaker side alone.

Grade by the amount of overall wear and loss of detail evident in the main design on each side. On coins with a moderately small design element which is prone to early wear, grade by that design alone. For example, the 5-ore (KM#554) of Sweden has a crown above the monogram on which the beads on the arches show wear most clearly. So, grade by the crown alone.

For **Uncirculated** (Unc.) grades there will be no visible signs of wear or handling, even under a 30-power microscope. Bag marks may be present.

For **Almost Uncirculated** (AU), all detail will be visible. There will be wear only on the highest point of the coin. There will often be half or more of the original mint luster present.

On the **Extremely Fine** (XF or EF) coin, there will be about 95% of the original detail visible. Or, on a coin with a design with no inner detail to wear down, there will be a light wear over nearly all the coin. If a small design is used as the grading area, about 90% of the original detail will be visible. This latter rule stems from the logic that a smaller amount of detail needs to be present because a small area is being used to grade the whole coin.

The **Very Fine** (VF) coin will have about 75% of the original detail visible. Or, on a coin with no inner detail, there will be moderate wear over the entire coin. Corners of letters and numbers may be weak. A small grading area will have about 66% of the original detail.

For **Fine** (F), there will be about 50% of the original detail visible. Or, on a coin with no inner detail, there will be fairly heavy wear over all of the coin. Sides of letters will be weak. A typically uncleaned coin will often appear as dirty or dull. A small grading area will have just under 50% of the original detail.

On the **Very Good** (VG) coin, there will be about 25% of the original detail visible. There will be heavy wear on all of the coin.

The **Good** (G) coin's design will be clearly outlined but with substantial wear. Some of the larger detail may be visible. The rim may have a few weak spots of wear.

On the **About Good** (AG) coin, there will be typically only a silhouette of a large design. The rim will be worn down into the letters if any.

Strong or weak strikes, partially weak strikes, damage, corrosion, attractive or unattractive toning, dipping or cleaning should be described along with the above grades. These factors affect the quality of the coin just as do wear and loss of detail, but are easier to describe.

In the case of countermarked/counterstamped coins, the condition of the host coin will have a bearing on the end valuation. The important factor in determining the grade is the condition, clarity and completeness of the countermark itself. This is in reference to countermarks/counterstamps having raised design while being struck in a depression.

Incuse countermarks cannot be graded for wear. They are graded by the clarity and completeness including the condition of the host coin which will also have more bearing on the final grade/valuation determined.

Silver Bullion Chart

FRACTION OF ONE OUNCE

Price $	3.00	3.50	4.00	4.50	5.00	5.50	6.50	7.00	7.50	8.00	8.50	9.00	9.50	10.00
0.001	0.003	0.004	0.004	0.005	0.005	0.006	0.007	0.007	0.008	0.008	0.009	0.009	0.010	0.010
0.002	0.006	0.007	0.008	0.009	0.010	0.011	0.013	0.014	0.015	0.016	0.017	0.018	0.019	0.020
0.003	0.009	0.011	0.012	0.014	0.015	0.017	0.020	0.021	0.023	0.024	0.026	0.027	0.029	0.030
0.004	0.012	0.014	0.016	0.018	0.020	0.022	0.026	0.028	0.030	0.032	0.034	0.036	0.038	0.040
0.005	0.015	0.018	0.020	0.023	0.025	0.028	0.033	0.035	0.038	0.040	0.043	0.045	0.048	0.050
0.006	0.018	0.021	0.024	0.027	0.030	0.033	0.039	0.042	0.045	0.048	0.051	0.054	0.057	0.060
0.007	0.021	0.025	0.028	0.032	0.035	0.039	0.046	0.049	0.053	0.056	0.060	0.063	0.067	0.070
0.008	0.024	0.028	0.032	0.036	0.040	0.044	0.052	0.056	0.060	0.064	0.068	0.072	0.076	0.080
0.009	0.027	0.032	0.036	0.041	0.045	0.050	0.059	0.063	0.068	0.072	0.077	0.081	0.086	0.090
0.010	0.030	0.035	0.040	0.045	0.050	0.055	0.065	0.070	0.075	0.080	0.085	0.090	0.095	0.100
0.020	0.060	0.070	0.080	0.090	0.100	0.110	0.130	0.140	0.150	0.160	0.170	0.180	0.190	0.200
0.030	0.090	0.105	0.120	0.135	0.150	0.165	0.195	0.210	0.225	0.240	0.255	0.270	0.285	0.300
0.040	0.120	0.140	0.160	0.180	0.200	0.220	0.260	0.280	0.300	0.320	0.340	0.360	0.380	0.400
0.050	0.150	0.175	0.200	0.225	0.250	0.275	0.325	0.350	0.375	0.400	0.425	0.450	0.475	0.500
0.060	0.180	0.210	0.240	0.270	0.300	0.330	0.390	0.420	0.450	0.480	0.510	0.540	0.570	0.600
0.070	0.210	0.245	0.280	0.315	0.350	0.385	0.455	0.490	0.525	0.560	0.595	0.630	0.665	0.700
0.080	0.240	0.280	0.320	0.360	0.400	0.440	0.520	0.560	0.600	0.640	0.680	0.720	0.760	0.800
0.090	0.270	0.315	0.360	0.405	0.450	0.495	0.585	0.630	0.675	0.720	0.765	0.810	0.855	0.900
0.100	0.300	0.350	0.400	0.450	0.500	0.550	0.650	0.700	0.750	0.800	0.850	0.900	0.950	1.000
0.110	0.330	0.385	0.440	0.495	0.550	0.605	0.715	0.770	0.825	0.880	0.935	0.990	1.045	1.100
0.120	0.360	0.420	0.480	0.540	0.600	0.660	0.780	0.840	0.900	0.960	1.020	1.080	1.140	1.200
0.130	0.390	0.455	0.520	0.585	0.650	0.715	0.845	0.910	0.975	1.040	1.105	1.170	1.235	1.300
0.140	0.420	0.490	0.560	0.630	0.700	0.770	0.910	0.980	1.050	1.120	1.190	1.260	1.330	1.400
0.150	0.450	0.525	0.600	0.675	0.750	0.825	0.975	1.050	1.125	1.200	1.275	1.350	1.425	1.500
0.160	0.480	0.560	0.640	0.720	0.800	0.880	1.040	1.120	1.200	1.280	1.360	1.440	1.520	1.600
0.170	0.510	0.595	0.680	0.765	0.850	0.935	1.105	1.190	1.275	1.360	1.445	1.530	1.615	1.700
0.180	0.540	0.630	0.720	0.810	0.900	0.990	1.170	1.260	1.350	1.440	1.530	1.620	1.710	1.800
0.190	0.570	0.665	0.760	0.855	0.950	1.045	1.235	1.330	1.425	1.520	1.615	1.710	1.805	1.900
0.200	0.600	0.700	0.800	0.900	1.000	1.100	1.300	1.400	1.500	1.600	1.700	1.800	1.900	2.000
0.210	0.630	0.735	0.840	0.945	1.050	1.155	1.365	1.470	1.575	1.680	1.785	1.890	1.995	2.100
0.220	0.660	0.770	0.880	0.990	1.100	1.210	1.430	1.540	1.650	1.760	1.870	1.980	2.090	2.200
0.230	0.690	0.805	0.920	1.035	1.150	1.265	1.495	1.610	1.725	1.840	1.955	2.070	2.185	2.300
0.240	0.720	0.840	0.960	1.080	1.200	1.320	1.560	1.680	1.800	1.920	2.040	2.160	2.280	2.400
0.250	0.750	0.875	1.000	1.125	1.250	1.375	1.625	1.750	1.875	2.000	2.125	2.250	2.375	2.500
0.260	0.780	0.910	1.040	1.170	1.300	1.430	1.690	1.820	1.950	2.080	2.210	2.340	2.470	2.600
0.270	0.810	0.945	1.080	1.215	1.350	1.485	1.755	1.890	2.025	2.160	2.295	2.430	2.565	2.700
0.280	0.840	0.980	1.120	1.260	1.400	1.540	1.820	1.960	2.100	2.240	2.380	2.520	2.660	2.800
0.290	0.870	1.015	1.160	1.305	1.450	1.595	1.885	2.030	2.175	2.320	2.465	2.610	2.755	2.900
0.300	0.900	1.050	1.200	1.350	1.500	1.650	1.950	2.100	2.250	2.400	2.550	2.700	2.850	3.000
0.310	0.930	1.085	1.240	1.395	1.550	1.705	2.015	2.170	2.325	2.480	2.635	2.790	2.945	3.100
0.320	0.960	1.120	1.280	1.440	1.600	1.760	2.080	2.240	2.400	2.560	2.720	2.880	3.040	3.200
0.330	0.990	1.155	1.320	1.485	1.650	1.815	2.145	2.310	2.475	2.640	2.805	2.970	3.135	3.300
0.340	1.020	1.190	1.360	1.530	1.700	1.870	2.210	2.380	2.550	2.720	2.890	3.060	3.230	3.400
0.350	1.050	1.225	1.400	1.575	1.750	1.925	2.275	2.450	2.625	2.800	2.975	3.150	3.325	3.500
0.360	1.080	1.260	1.440	1.620	1.800	1.980	2.340	2.520	2.700	2.880	3.060	3.240	3.420	3.600
0.370	1.110	1.295	1.480	1.665	1.850	2.035	2.405	2.590	2.775	2.960	3.145	3.330	3.515	3.700
0.380	1.140	1.330	1.520	1.710	1.900	2.090	2.470	2.660	2.850	3.040	3.230	3.420	3.610	3.800
0.390	1.170	1.365	1.560	1.755	1.950	2.145	2.535	2.730	2.925	3.120	3.315	3.510	3.705	3.900
0.400	1.200	1.400	1.600	1.800	2.000	2.200	2.600	2.800	3.000	3.200	3.400	3.600	3.800	4.000
0.410	1.230	1.435	1.640	1.845	2.050	2.255	2.665	2.870	3.075	3.280	3.485	3.690	3.895	4.100
0.420	1.260	1.470	1.680	1.890	2.100	2.310	2.730	2.940	3.150	3.360	3.570	3.780	3.990	4.200
0.430	1.290	1.505	1.720	1.935	2.150	2.365	2.795	3.010	3.225	3.440	3.655	3.870	4.085	4.300
0.440	1.320	1.540	1.760	1.980	2.200	2.420	2.860	3.080	3.300	3.520	3.740	3.960	4.180	4.400
0.450	1.350	1.575	1.800	2.025	2.250	2.475	2.925	3.150	3.375	3.600	3.825	4.050	4.275	4.500
0.460	1.380	1.610	1.840	2.070	2.300	2.530	2.990	3.220	3.450	3.680	3.910	4.140	4.370	4.600
0.470	1.410	1.645	1.880	2.115	2.350	2.585	3.055	3.290	3.525	3.760	3.995	4.230	4.465	4.700
0.480	1.440	1.680	1.920	2.160	2.400	2.640	3.120	3.360	3.600	3.840	4.080	4.320	4.560	4.800
0.490	1.470	1.715	1.960	2.205	2.450	2.695	3.185	3.430	3.675	3.920	4.165	4.410	4.655	4.900
0.500	1.500	1.750	2.000	2.250	2.500	2.750	3.250	3.500	3.750	4.000	4.250	4.500	4.750	5.000
0.510	1.530	1.785	2.040	2.295	2.550	2.805	3.315	3.570	3.825	4.080	4.335	4.590	4.845	5.100
0.520	1.560	1.820	2.080	2.340	2.600	2.860	3.380	3.640	3.900	4.160	4.420	4.680	4.940	5.200
0.530	1.590	1.855	2.120	2.385	2.650	2.915	3.445	3.710	3.975	4.240	4.505	4.770	5.035	5.300
0.540	1.620	1.890	2.160	2.430	2.700	2.970	3.510	3.780	4.050	4.320	4.590	4.860	5.130	5.400
0.550	1.650	1.925	2.200	2.475	2.750	3.025	3.575	3.850	4.125	4.400	4.675	4.950	5.225	5.500
0.560	1.680	1.960	2.240	2.520	2.800	3.080	3.640	3.920	4.200	4.480	4.760	5.040	5.320	5.600
0.570	1.710	1.995	2.280	2.565	2.850	3.135	3.705	3.990	4.275	4.560	4.845	5.130	5.415	5.700
0.580	1.740	2.030	2.320	2.610	2.900	3.190	3.770	4.060	4.350	4.640	4.930	5.220	5.510	5.800
0.590	1.770	2.065	2.360	2.655	2.950	3.245	3.835	4.130	4.425	4.720	5.015	5.310	5.605	5.900
0.600	1.800	2.100	2.400	2.700	3.000	3.300	3.900	4.200	4.500	4.800	5.100	5.400	5.700	6.000
0.610	1.830	2.135	2.440	2.745	3.050	3.355	3.965	4.270	4.575	4.880	5.185	5.490	5.795	6.100
0.620	1.860	2.170	2.480	2.790	3.100	3.410	4.030	4.340	4.650	4.960	5.270	5.580	5.890	6.200
0.630	1.890	2.205	2.520	2.835	3.150	3.465	4.095	4.410	4.725	5.040	5.355	5.670	5.985	6.300
0.640	1.920	2.240	2.560	2.880	3.200	3.520	4.160	4.480	4.800	5.120	5.440	5.760	6.080	6.400
0.650	1.950	2.275	2.600	2.925	3.250	3.575	4.225	4.550	4.875	5.200	5.525	5.850	6.175	6.500
0.660	1.980	2.310	2.640	2.970	3.300	3.630	4.290	4.620	4.950	5.280	5.610	5.940	6.270	6.600
0.670	2.010	2.345	2.680	3.015	3.350	3.685	4.355	4.690	5.025	5.360	5.695	6.030	6.365	6.700
0.680	2.040	2.380	2.720	3.060	3.400	3.740	4.420	4.760	5.100	5.440	5.780	6.120	6.460	6.800
0.690	2.070	2.415	2.760	3.105	3.450	3.795	4.485	4.830	5.175	5.520	5.865	6.210	6.555	6.900
0.700	2.100	2.450	2.800	3.150	3.500	3.850	4.550	4.900	5.250	5.600	5.950	6.300	6.650	7.000
0.710	2.130	2.485	2.840	3.195	3.550	3.905	4.615	4.970	5.325	5.680	6.035	6.390	6.745	7.100
0.720	2.160	2.520	2.880	3.240	3.600	3.960	4.680	5.040	5.400	5.760	6.120	6.480	6.840	7.200
0.730	2.190	2.555	2.920	3.285	3.650	4.015	4.745	5.110	5.475	5.840	6.205	6.570	6.935	7.300
0.740	2.220	2.590	2.960	3.330	3.700	4.070	4.810	5.180	5.550	5.920	6.290	6.660	7.030	7.400
0.750	2.250	2.625	3.000	3.375	3.750	4.125	4.875	5.250	5.625	6.000	6.375	6.750	7.125	7.500
0.760	2.280	2.660	3.040	3.420	3.800	4.180	4.940	5.320	5.700	6.080	6.460	6.840	7.220	7.600
0.770	2.310	2.695	3.080	3.465	3.850	4.235	5.005	5.390	5.775	6.160	6.545	6.930	7.315	7.700
0.780	2.340	2.730	3.120	3.510	3.900	4.290	5.070	5.460	5.850	6.240	6.630	7.020	7.410	7.800
0.790	2.370	2.765	3.160	3.555	3.950	4.345	5.135	5.530	5.925	6.320	6.715	7.110	7.505	7.900
0.800	2.400	2.800	3.200	3.600	4.000	4.400	5.200	5.600	6.000	6.400	6.800	7.200	7.600	8.000
0.810	2.430	2.835	3.240	3.645	4.050	4.455	5.265	5.670	6.075	6.480	6.885	7.290	7.695	8.100
0.820	2.460	2.870	3.280	3.690	4.100	4.510	5.330	5.740	6.150	6.560	6.970	7.380	7.790	8.200
0.830	2.490	2.905	3.320	3.735	4.150	4.565	5.395	5.810	6.225	6.640	7.055	7.470	7.885	8.300
0.840	2.520	2.940	3.360	3.780	4.200	4.620	5.460	5.880	6.300	6.720	7.140	7.560	7.980	8.400
0.850	2.550	2.975	3.400	3.825	4.250	4.675	5.525	5.950	6.375	6.800	7.225	7.650	8.075	8.500
0.860	2.580	3.010	3.440	3.870	4.300	4.730	5.590	6.020	6.450	6.880	7.310	7.740	8.170	8.600
0.870	2.610	3.045	3.480	3.915	4.350	4.785	5.655	6.090	6.525	6.960	7.395	7.830	8.265	8.700
0.880	2.640	3.080	3.520	3.960	4.400	4.840	5.720	6.160	6.600	7.040	7.480	7.920	8.360	8.800
0.890	2.670	3.115	3.560	4.005	4.450	4.895	5.785	6.230	6.675	7.120	7.565	8.010	8.455	8.900
0.900	2.700	3.150	3.600	4.050	4.500	4.950	5.850	6.300	6.750	7.200	7.650	8.100	8.550	9.000
0.910	2.730	3.185	3.640	4.095	4.550	5.005	5.915	6.370	6.825	7.280	7.735	8.190	8.645	9.100
0.920	2.760	3.220	3.680	4.140	4.600	5.060	5.980	6.440	6.900	7.360	7.820	8.280	8.740	9.200
0.930	2.790	3.255	3.720	4.185	4.650	5.115	6.045	6.510	6.975	7.440	7.905	8.370	8.835	9.300
0.940	2.820	3.290	3.760	4.230	4.700	5.170	6.110	6.580	7.050	7.520	7.990	8.460	8.930	9.400
0.950	2.850	3.325	3.800	4.275	4.750	5.225	6.175	6.650	7.125	7.600	8.075	8.550	9.025	9.500
0.960	2.880	3.360	3.840	4.320	4.800	5.280	6.240	6.720	7.200	7.680	8.160	8.640	9.120	9.600
0.970	2.910	3.395	3.880	4.365	4.850	5.335	6.305	6.790	7.275	7.760	8.245	8.730	9.215	9.700
0.980	2.940	3.430	3.920	4.410	4.900	5.390	6.370	6.860	7.350	7.840	8.330	8.820	9.310	9.800
0.990	2.970	3.465	3.960	4.455	4.950	5.445	6.435	6.930	7.425	7.920	8.415	8.910	9.405	9.900
1.000	3.000	3.500	4.000	4.500	5.000	5.500	6.500	7.000	7.500	8.000	8.500	9.000	9.500	10.000

Foreign Exchange Table

The latest foreign exchange fixed rates below apply to trade with banks in the country of origin. The left column shows the number of units per U.S. dollar at the official rate. The right column shows the number of units per dollar at the free market rate.

Country	Official #/$	Market #/$
Afghanistan (Afghan)	4,750	20,200
Albania (Lek)	140.45	–
Algeria (Dinar)	64.463	75.00
Andorra uses French Franc and Spanish Peseta		
Angola (Readjust Kwanza)	257,128	
Anguilla uses E.C. Dollar	2.70	–
Antigua uses E.C. Dollar	2.70	–
Argentina (New Peso)	.9999	–
Armenia (Dram)	420.0	–
Aruba (Florin)	1.79	–
Australia (Dollar)	1.6123	–
Austria (Schilling)	12.4821	–
Azerbaijan (Manat)	3,950	–
Bahamas (Dollar)	1.00	–
Bahrain Is. (Dinar)	.38	–
Bangladesh (Taka)	48.40	–
Barbados (Dollar)	2.00	–
Belarus (Ruble)	11,500	–
Belgium (Franc)	36.593	–
Belize (Dollar)	2.00	–
Benin uses CFA Franc West	595.03	–
Bermuda (Dollar)	1.00	–
Bhutan (Ngultrum)	42.72	–
Bolivia (Boliviano)	5.70	–
Bosnia-Herzegovina (New Dinar)	141.00	195.0
Botswana (Pula)	4.6544	–
British Virgin Islands uses U.S. Dollar	1.00	–
Brazil (Real)	2.045	–
Brunei (Ringgit)	1.722	–
Bulgaria (Lev)	1,765	–
Burkina Faso uses CFA Fr. West	595.03	–
Burma (Kyat)	6.3411	–
Burundi (Franc)	511.69	–
Cambodia (Riel)	3,770	–
Cameron uses CFA Franc	595.03	–
Canada (Dollar)	1.5136	–
Cape Verde (Escudo)	94.71	–
Cayman Is. (Dollar)	0.8333	–
Central African Rep.	595.03	–
CFA Franc Central	595.03	–
CFA Franc West	595.03	–
CFP Franc	102.23	–
Chad uses CFA Franc Central	595.03	–
Chile (Peso)	498.74	–
China, P.R. (Renminbi Yuan)	8.279	–
Colombia (Peso)	1,577	–
Comoros (Franc)	446.23	–
Congo uses CFA Franc Central	595.03	–
Cook Islands (Dollar)	1.47	–
Costa Rica (Colon)	275.92	–
Croatia (Kuna)	6.8677	–
Cuba (Peso)	23.00	35.00
Cyprus (Pound)	.5262	–
Czech Republic (Koruna)	34.403	–
Denmark (Danish Krone)	6.7412	–
Djibouti (Franc)	177.72	–
Dominica uses E.C. Dollar	2.70	–
Dominican Republic (Peso)	15.75	–
East Caribbean (Dollar)	2.70	–
Ecuador (Sucre)	7,610	–
Egypt (Pound)	3.4188	–
El Salvador (Colon)	8.755	–
England (Sterling Pound)	.6249	–
Equatorial Guinea uses CFA Franc Central	595.03	–
Eritrea, see Ethiopia		
Estonia (Kroon)	14.19	–
Ethiopia (Birr)	6.9875	7.25
Euro	.9070	–
Falkland Is. (Pound)	.6249	–
Faroe Islands (Krona)	6.7412	–
Fiji Islands (Dollar)	1.9912	–
Finland (Markka)	5.3934	–
France (Franc)	5.9503	–
French Polynesia uses CFP Franc	102.23	–
Gabon (CFA Franc)	595.03	–
Gambia (Dalasi)	11.05	–
Georgia (Lari)	1.30	–
Germany (D. Mark)	1.7742	–
Ghana (Cedi)	2,403	–
Gibraltar (Pound)	.6249	–
Greece (Drachma)	291.94	–
Greenland uses Denmark Krone	6.7412	–
Grenada uses E.C. Dollar	2.70	–
Guatemala (Quetzal)	6.8348	–
Guernsey uses Sterling Pound	.6249	–
Guinea Bissau (CFA Franc)	595.03	–
Guinea Conakry (Franc)	1,300	–
Guyana (Dollar)	162.80	–
Haiti (Gourde)	16.797	–
Honduras (Lempira)	14.01	–
Hong Kong (Dollar)	7.7477	–
Hungary (Forint)	229.82	–
Iceland (Krona)	72.18	–
India (Rupee)	42.72	–
Indonesia (Rupiah)	8,840	–
Iran (Rial)	3,000	4,800
Iraq (Dinar)	1,200	1,690
Ireland (Punt)	.7144	–
Isle of Man uses Sterling Pound	.6249	–
Israel (New Sheqalim)	4.0473	–
Italy (Lira)	1,756	–
Ivory Coast uses CFA Franc West	595.03	–
Jamaica (Dollar)	36.65	–
Japan (Yen)	119.95	–
Jersey uses Sterling Pound	.6249	–
Jordan (Dinar)	.709	–
Kazakhstan (Tenge)	65.00	–
Kenya (Shilling)	63.80	–
Kiribati uses Australian Dollar	1.6123	–
Korea-PDR (Won)	2.20	170.0
Korea-Rep. (Won)	1,224	–
Kuwait (Dinar)	.3047	–
Kyrgyzstan (Som)	11.05	–
Laos (Kip)	4,203	–
Latvia (Lat)	.5842	–
Lebanon (Pound)	1,508	–
Lesotho (Maloti)	6.185	–
Liberia (Dollar)	1.00	30.00
Libya (Dinar)	.45	2.00
Liechtenstein uses Swiss Franc	1.4411	–
Lithuania (Litas)	4.0018	–
Luxembourg (Franc)	36.593	–
Macao (Pataca)	8.0034	–
Macedonia (New Denar)	54.94	–
Madagascar (Franc)	5,220	–
Malawi (Kwacha)	43.88	–
Malaysia (Ringgit)	3.80	–
Maldives (Rufiya)	11.77	–
Mali uses CFA Franc West	595.03	–
Malta (Lira)	.3794	–
Marshall Islands uses U.S. Dollar	1.00	–
Mauritania (Ouguiya)	204.4	–
Mauritius (Rupee)	24.95	–
Mexico (Peso)	9.975	–
Moldova (Leu)	4.55	–
Monaco uses French Franc	5.9503	–
Mongolia (Tugrik)	817.61	–
Montenegro uses Yugoslavia	10.6349	–
Montserrat uses E.C. Dollar	2.70	–
Morocco (Dirham)	9.6504	10.50
Mozambique (Metical)	11,495	12,100
Myanmar (Burma) (Kyat)	6.2481	202.0
Namibia (Rand)	6.185	–
Nauru uses Australian Dollar	1.6123	–
Nepal (Rupee)	67.68	–
Netherlands (Gulden)	1.999	–
Netherlands Antilles (Gulden)	1.79	–
New Caledonia uses CFP Franc	102.23	–
New Zealand (Dollar)	1.9102	–
Nicaragua (Cordoba Oro)	11.3443	–
Niger uses CFA Franc West	595.03	–
Nigeria (Naira)	87.0	–
Northern Ireland uses Sterling Pound	.6249	–
Norway (Krone)	7.8955	–
Oman (Rial)	.385	–
Pakistan (Rupee)	51.25	–
Palau uses U.S. Dollar	1.00	–
Panama (Balboa) uses U.S. Dollar	1.00	–
Papua New Guinea (Kina)	2.2371	–
Paraguay (Guarani)	2,900	–
Peru (Nuevo Sol)	3.4725	–
Philippines (Peso)	39.07	–
Poland (Zloty)	3.9035	–
Portugal (Escudo)	181.86	–
Qatar (Riyal)	3.641	–
Romania (Leu)	12,816	–
Russia (Ruble)	22.86	–
Rwanda (Franc)	320.3	370.0
St. Helena (Pound)	.6249	–
St. Kitts uses E.C. Dollar	2.70	–
St. Lucia uses E.C. Dollar	2.70	–
St. Vincent uses E.C. Dollar	2.70	–
San Marino uses Italian Lira	1,756	–
Sao Tome e Principe (Dobra)	2,390	–
Saudi Arabia (Riyal)	3.7523	–
Scotland uses Sterling Pound	.6249	–
Senegal uses CFA Franc West	595.03	–
Seychelles (Rupee)	5.301	–
Sierra Leone (Leone)	1,475	–
Singapore (Dollar)	1.722	–
Slovakia (Sk. Koruna)	39.865	–
Slovenia (Tolar)	155.64	–
Solomon Is. (Dollar)	4.7915	–
Somalia (Shilling)	2,620	–
Somaliland (Somali Shilling)	1,800	3,000
South Africa (Rand)	6.185	–
Spain (Peseta)	150.9	–
Sri Lanka (Rupee)	69.53	–
Sudan (Dinar)	196.0	–
Surinam (Guilder)	401	–
Swaziland (Lilangeni)	6.185	–
Sweden (Krona)	8.166	–
Switzerland (Franc)	1.4411	–
Syria (Pound)	46.25	–
Taiwan (NT Dollar)	33.08	–
Tajikistan uses Russian Ruble	22.86	–
Tanzania (Shilling)	692.25	–
Thailand (Baht)	37.365	–
Togo uses CFA Franc West	595.03	–
Tonga (Pa'anga)	1.6054	–
Transdniestra (New Ruble)	630,000	675,000
Trinidad & Tobago (Dollar)	6.2525	–
Tunisia (Dinar)	1.1542	–
Turkey (Lira)	354,830	–
Turkmenistan (Manat)	195	6,500
Turks & Caicos uses U.S. Dollar	1.00	–
Tuvalu uses Australian Dollar	1.6123	–
Uganda (Shilling)	1,233	–
Ukraine (Hryvnia)	3.85	–
United Arab Emirates (Dirham)	3.673	–
Uruguay (Peso Uruguayo)	10.995	–
Uzbekistan (Som)	24.00	–
Vanuatu (Vatu)	129.25	–
Vatican City uses Italian Lira	1,756	–
Venezuela (Bolivar)	5861.0	–
Vietnam (Dong)	13,892	–
Western Samoa (Tala)	3.0157	–
Yemen (Riyal)	141.34	–
Yugoslavia (Novikh Dinar)	10.6349	–
Zaire (Noveaux Zaire)	245,000	–
Zambia (Kwacha)	2,175	–
Zimbabwe (Dollar)	38.3	–

Gold & Platinum Bullion Chart

FRACTION OF ONE OUNCE

Price $	270.00	280.00	290.00	300.00	310.00	320.00	330.00	340.00	350.00	360.00	370.00	380.00	390.00	400.00	410.00
0.001	0.27	0.28	0.29	0.30	0.31	0.32	0.33	0.34	0.35	0.36	0.37	0.38	0.39	0.40	0.41
0.002	0.54	0.56	0.58	0.60	0.62	0.64	0.66	0.68	0.70	0.72	0.74	0.76	0.78	0.80	0.82
0.003	0.81	0.84	0.87	0.90	0.93	0.96	0.99	1.02	1.05	1.08	1.11	1.14	1.17	1.20	1.23
0.004	1.08	1.12	1.16	1.20	1.24	1.28	1.32	1.36	1.40	1.44	1.48	1.52	1.56	1.60	1.64
0.005	1.35	1.40	1.45	1.50	1.55	1.60	1.65	1.70	1.75	1.80	1.85	1.90	1.95	2.00	2.05
0.006	1.62	1.68	1.74	1.80	1.86	1.92	1.98	2.04	2.10	2.16	2.22	2.28	2.34	2.40	2.46
0.007	1.89	1.96	2.03	2.10	2.17	2.24	2.31	2.38	2.45	2.52	2.59	2.66	2.73	2.80	2.87
0.008	2.16	2.24	2.32	2.40	2.48	2.56	2.64	2.72	2.80	2.88	2.96	3.04	3.12	3.20	3.28
0.009	2.43	2.52	2.61	2.70	2.79	2.88	2.97	3.06	3.15	3.24	3.33	3.42	3.51	3.60	3.69
0.010	2.70	2.80	2.90	3.00	3.10	3.20	3.30	3.40	3.50	3.60	3.70	3.80	3.90	4.00	4.10
0.020	5.40	5.60	5.80	6.00	6.20	6.40	6.60	6.80	7.00	7.20	7.40	7.60	7.80	8.00	8.20
0.030	8.10	8.40	8.70	9.00	9.30	9.60	9.90	10.20	10.50	10.80	11.10	11.40	11.70	12.00	12.30
0.040	10.80	11.20	11.60	12.00	12.40	12.80	13.20	13.60	14.00	14.40	14.80	15.20	15.60	16.00	16.40
0.050	13.50	14.00	14.50	15.00	15.50	16.00	16.50	17.00	17.50	18.00	18.50	19.00	19.50	20.00	20.50
0.060	16.20	16.80	17.40	18.00	18.60	19.20	19.80	20.40	21.00	21.60	22.20	22.80	23.40	24.00	24.60
0.070	18.90	19.60	20.30	21.00	21.70	22.40	23.10	23.80	24.50	25.20	25.90	26.60	27.30	28.00	28.70
0.080	21.60	22.40	23.20	24.00	24.80	25.60	26.40	27.20	28.00	28.80	29.60	30.40	31.20	32.00	32.80
0.090	24.30	25.20	26.10	27.00	27.90	28.80	29.70	30.60	31.50	32.40	33.30	34.20	35.10	36.00	36.90
0.100	27.00	28.00	29.00	30.00	31.00	32.00	33.00	34.00	35.00	36.00	37.00	38.00	39.00	40.00	41.00
0.110	29.70	30.80	31.90	33.00	34.10	35.20	36.30	37.40	38.50	39.60	40.70	41.80	42.90	44.00	45.10
0.120	32.40	33.60	34.80	36.00	37.20	38.40	39.60	40.80	42.00	43.20	44.40	45.60	46.80	48.00	49.20
0.130	35.10	36.40	37.70	39.00	40.30	41.60	42.90	44.20	45.50	46.80	48.10	49.40	50.70	52.00	53.30
0.140	37.80	39.20	40.60	42.00	43.40	44.80	46.20	47.60	49.00	50.40	51.80	53.20	54.60	56.00	57.40
0.150	40.50	42.00	43.50	45.00	46.50	48.00	49.50	51.00	52.50	54.00	55.50	57.00	58.50	60.00	61.50
0.160	43.20	44.80	46.40	48.00	49.60	51.20	52.80	54.40	56.00	57.60	59.20	60.80	62.40	64.00	65.60
0.170	45.90	47.60	49.30	51.00	52.70	54.40	56.10	57.80	59.50	61.20	62.90	64.60	66.30	68.00	69.70
0.180	48.60	50.40	52.20	54.00	55.80	57.60	59.40	61.20	63.00	64.80	66.60	68.40	70.20	72.00	73.80
0.190	51.30	53.20	55.10	57.00	58.90	60.80	62.70	64.60	66.50	68.40	70.30	72.20	74.10	76.00	77.90
0.200	54.00	56.00	58.00	60.00	62.00	64.00	66.00	68.00	70.00	72.00	74.00	76.00	78.00	80.00	82.00
0.210	56.70	58.80	60.90	63.00	65.10	67.20	69.30	71.40	73.50	75.60	77.70	79.80	81.90	84.00	86.10
0.220	59.40	61.60	63.80	66.00	68.20	70.40	72.60	74.80	77.00	79.20	81.40	83.60	85.80	88.00	90.20
0.230	62.10	64.40	66.70	69.00	71.30	73.60	75.90	78.20	80.50	82.80	85.10	87.40	89.70	92.00	94.30
0.240	64.80	67.20	69.60	72.00	74.40	76.80	79.20	81.60	84.00	86.40	88.80	91.20	93.60	96.00	98.40
0.250	67.50	70.00	72.50	75.00	77.50	80.00	82.50	85.00	87.50	90.00	92.50	95.00	97.50	100.00	102.50
0.260	70.20	72.80	75.40	78.00	80.60	83.20	85.80	88.40	91.00	93.60	96.20	98.80	101.40	104.00	106.60
0.270	72.90	75.60	78.30	81.00	83.70	86.40	89.10	91.80	94.50	97.20	99.90	102.60	105.30	108.00	110.70
0.280	75.60	78.40	81.20	84.00	86.80	89.60	92.40	95.20	98.00	100.80	103.60	106.40	109.20	112.00	114.80
0.290	78.30	81.20	84.10	87.00	89.90	92.80	95.70	98.60	101.50	104.40	107.30	110.20	113.10	116.00	118.90
0.300	81.00	84.00	87.00	90.00	93.00	96.00	99.00	102.00	105.00	108.00	111.00	114.00	117.00	120.00	123.00
0.310	83.70	86.80	89.90	93.00	96.10	99.20	102.30	105.40	108.50	111.60	114.70	117.80	120.90	124.00	127.10
0.320	86.40	89.60	92.80	96.00	99.20	102.40	105.60	108.80	112.00	115.20	118.40	121.60	124.80	128.00	131.20
0.330	89.10	92.40	95.70	99.00	102.30	105.60	108.90	112.20	115.50	118.80	122.10	125.40	128.70	132.00	135.30
0.340	91.80	95.20	98.60	102.00	105.40	108.80	112.20	115.60	119.00	122.40	125.80	129.20	132.60	136.00	139.40
0.350	94.50	98.00	101.50	105.00	108.50	112.00	115.50	119.00	122.50	126.00	129.50	133.00	136.50	140.00	143.50
0.360	97.20	100.80	104.40	108.00	111.60	115.20	118.80	122.40	126.00	129.60	133.20	136.80	140.40	144.00	147.60
0.370	99.90	103.60	107.30	111.00	114.70	118.40	122.10	125.80	129.50	133.20	136.90	140.60	144.30	148.00	151.70
0.380	102.60	106.40	110.20	114.00	117.80	121.60	125.40	129.20	133.00	136.80	140.60	144.40	148.20	152.00	155.80
0.390	105.30	109.20	113.10	117.00	120.90	124.80	128.70	132.60	136.50	140.40	144.30	148.20	152.10	156.00	159.90
0.400	108.00	112.00	116.00	120.00	124.00	128.00	132.00	136.00	140.00	144.00	148.00	152.00	156.00	160.00	164.00
0.410	110.70	114.80	118.90	123.00	127.10	131.20	135.30	139.40	143.50	147.60	151.70	155.80	159.90	164.00	168.10
0.420	113.40	117.60	121.80	126.00	130.20	134.40	138.60	142.80	147.00	151.20	155.40	159.60	163.80	168.00	172.20
0.430	116.10	120.40	124.70	129.00	133.30	137.60	141.90	146.20	150.50	154.80	159.10	163.40	167.70	172.00	176.30
0.440	118.80	123.20	127.60	132.00	136.40	140.80	145.20	149.60	154.00	158.40	162.80	167.20	171.60	176.00	180.40
0.450	121.50	126.00	130.50	135.00	139.50	144.00	148.50	153.00	157.50	162.00	166.50	171.00	175.50	180.00	184.50
0.460	124.20	128.80	133.40	138.00	142.60	147.20	151.80	156.40	161.00	165.60	170.20	174.80	179.40	184.00	188.60
0.470	126.90	131.60	136.30	141.00	145.70	150.40	155.10	159.80	164.50	169.20	173.90	178.60	183.30	188.00	192.70
0.480	129.60	134.40	139.20	144.00	148.80	153.60	158.40	163.20	168.00	172.80	177.60	182.40	187.20	192.00	196.80
0.490	132.30	137.20	142.10	147.00	151.90	156.80	161.70	166.60	171.50	176.40	181.30	186.20	191.10	196.00	200.90
0.500	135.00	140.00	145.00	150.00	155.00	160.00	165.00	170.00	175.00	180.00	185.00	190.00	195.00	200.00	205.00
0.510	137.70	142.80	147.90	153.00	158.10	163.20	168.30	173.40	178.50	183.60	188.70	193.80	198.90	204.00	209.10
0.520	140.40	145.60	150.80	156.00	161.20	166.40	171.60	176.80	182.00	187.20	192.40	197.60	202.80	208.00	213.20
0.530	143.10	148.40	153.70	159.00	164.30	169.60	174.90	180.20	185.50	190.80	196.10	201.40	206.70	212.00	217.30
0.540	145.80	151.20	156.60	162.00	167.40	172.80	178.20	183.60	189.00	194.40	199.80	205.20	210.60	216.00	221.40
0.550	148.50	154.00	159.50	165.00	170.50	176.00	181.50	187.00	192.50	198.00	203.50	209.00	214.50	220.00	225.50
0.560	151.20	156.80	162.40	168.00	173.60	179.20	184.80	190.40	196.00	201.60	207.20	212.80	218.40	224.00	229.60
0.570	153.90	159.60	165.30	171.00	176.70	182.40	188.10	193.80	199.50	205.20	210.90	216.60	222.30	228.00	233.70
0.580	156.60	162.40	168.20	174.00	179.80	185.60	191.40	197.20	203.00	208.80	214.60	220.40	226.20	232.00	237.80
0.590	159.30	165.20	171.10	177.00	182.90	188.80	194.70	200.60	206.50	212.40	218.30	224.20	230.10	236.00	241.90
0.600	162.00	168.00	174.00	180.00	186.00	192.00	198.00	204.00	210.00	216.00	222.00	228.00	234.00	240.00	246.00
0.610	164.70	170.80	176.90	183.00	189.10	195.20	201.30	207.40	213.50	219.60	225.70	231.80	237.90	244.00	250.10
0.620	167.40	173.60	179.80	186.00	192.20	198.40	204.60	210.80	217.00	223.20	229.40	235.60	241.80	248.00	254.20
0.630	170.10	176.40	182.70	189.00	195.30	201.60	207.90	214.20	220.50	226.80	233.10	239.40	245.70	252.00	258.30
0.640	172.80	179.20	185.60	192.00	198.40	204.80	211.20	217.60	224.00	230.40	236.80	243.20	249.60	256.00	262.40
0.650	175.50	182.00	188.50	195.00	201.50	208.00	214.50	221.00	227.50	234.00	240.50	247.00	253.50	260.00	266.50
0.660	178.20	184.80	191.40	198.00	204.60	211.20	217.80	224.40	231.00	237.60	244.20	250.80	257.40	264.00	270.60
0.670	180.90	187.60	194.30	201.00	207.70	214.40	221.10	227.80	234.50	241.20	247.90	254.60	261.30	268.00	274.70
0.680	183.60	190.40	197.20	204.00	210.80	217.60	224.40	231.20	238.00	244.80	251.60	258.40	265.20	272.00	278.80
0.690	186.30	193.20	200.10	207.00	213.90	220.80	227.70	234.60	241.50	248.40	255.30	262.20	269.10	276.00	282.90
0.700	189.00	196.00	203.00	210.00	217.00	224.00	231.00	238.00	245.00	252.00	259.00	266.00	273.00	280.00	287.00
0.710	191.70	198.80	205.90	213.00	220.10	227.20	234.30	241.40	248.50	255.60	262.70	269.80	276.90	284.00	291.10
0.720	194.40	201.60	208.80	216.00	223.20	230.40	237.60	244.80	252.00	259.20	266.40	273.60	280.80	288.00	295.20
0.730	197.10	204.40	211.70	219.00	226.30	233.60	240.90	248.20	255.50	262.80	270.10	277.40	284.70	292.00	299.30
0.740	199.80	207.20	214.60	222.00	229.40	236.80	244.20	251.60	259.00	266.40	273.80	281.20	288.60	296.00	303.40
0.750	202.50	210.00	217.50	225.00	232.50	240.00	247.50	255.00	262.50	270.00	277.50	285.00	292.50	300.00	307.50
0.760	205.20	212.80	220.40	228.00	235.60	243.20	250.80	258.40	266.00	273.60	281.20	288.80	296.40	304.00	311.60
0.770	207.90	215.60	223.30	231.00	238.70	246.40	254.10	261.80	269.50	277.20	284.90	292.60	300.30	308.00	315.70
0.780	210.60	218.40	226.20	234.00	241.80	249.60	257.40	265.20	273.00	280.80	288.60	296.40	304.20	312.00	319.80
0.790	213.30	221.20	229.10	237.00	244.90	252.80	260.70	268.60	276.50	284.40	292.30	300.20	308.10	316.00	323.90
0.800	216.00	224.00	232.00	240.00	248.00	256.00	264.00	272.00	280.00	288.00	296.00	304.00	312.00	320.00	328.00
0.810	218.70	226.80	234.90	243.00	251.10	259.20	267.30	275.40	283.50	291.60	299.70	307.80	315.90	324.00	332.10
0.820	221.40	229.60	237.80	246.00	254.20	262.40	270.60	278.80	287.00	295.20	303.40	311.60	319.80	328.00	336.20
0.830	224.10	232.40	240.70	249.00	257.30	265.60	273.90	282.20	290.50	298.80	307.10	315.40	323.70	332.00	340.30
0.840	226.80	235.20	243.60	252.00	260.40	268.80	277.20	285.60	294.00	302.40	310.80	319.20	327.60	336.00	344.40
0.850	229.50	238.00	246.50	255.00	263.50	272.00	280.50	289.00	297.50	306.00	314.50	323.00	331.50	340.00	348.50
0.860	232.20	240.80	249.40	258.00	266.60	275.20	283.80	292.40	301.00	309.60	318.20	326.80	335.40	344.00	352.60
0.870	234.90	243.60	252.30	261.00	269.70	278.40	287.10	295.80	304.50	313.20	321.90	330.60	339.30	348.00	356.70
0.880	237.60	246.40	255.20	264.00	272.80	281.60	290.40	299.20	308.00	316.80	325.60	334.40	343.20	352.00	360.80
0.890	240.30	249.20	258.10	267.00	275.90	284.80	293.70	302.60	311.50	320.40	329.30	338.20	347.10	356.00	364.90
0.900	243.00	252.00	261.00	270.00	279.00	288.00	297.00	306.00	315.00	324.00	333.00	342.00	351.00	360.00	369.00
0.910	245.70	254.80	263.90	273.00	282.10	291.20	300.30	309.40	318.50	327.60	336.70	345.80	354.90	364.00	373.10
0.920	248.40	257.60	266.80	276.00	285.20	294.40	303.60	312.80	322.00	331.20	340.40	349.60	358.80	368.00	377.20
0.930	251.10	260.40	269.70	279.00	288.30	297.60	306.90	316.20	325.50	334.80	344.10	353.40	362.70	372.00	381.30
0.940	253.80	263.20	272.60	282.00	291.40	300.80	310.20	319.60	329.00	338.40	347.80	357.20	366.60	376.00	385.40
0.950	256.50	266.00	275.50	285.00	294.50	304.00	313.50	323.00	332.50	342.00	351.50	361.00	370.50	380.00	389.50
0.960	259.20	268.80	278.40	288.00	297.60	307.20	316.80	326.40	336.00	345.60	355.20	364.80	374.40	384.00	393.60
0.970	261.90	271.60	281.30	291.00	300.70	310.40	320.10	329.80	339.50	349.20	358.90	368.60	378.30	388.00	397.70
0.980	264.60	274.40	284.20	294.00	303.80	313.60	323.40	333.20	343.00	352.80	362.60	372.40	382.20	392.00	401.80
0.990	267.30	277.20	287.10	297.00	306.90	316.80	326.70	336.60	346.50	356.40	366.30	376.20	386.10	396.00	405.90
1.000	270.00	280.00	290.00	300.00	310.00	320.00	330.00	340.00	350.00	360.00	370.00	380.00	390.00	400.00	410.00

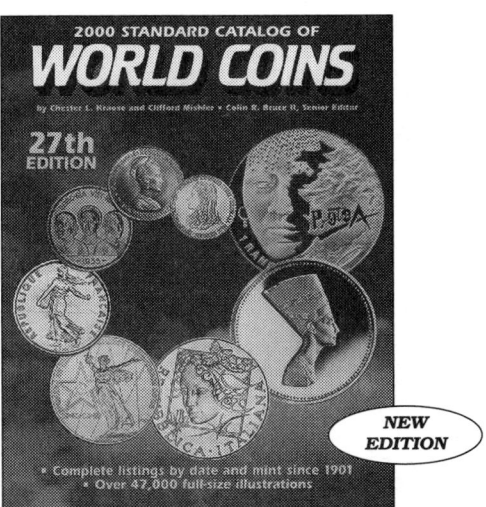

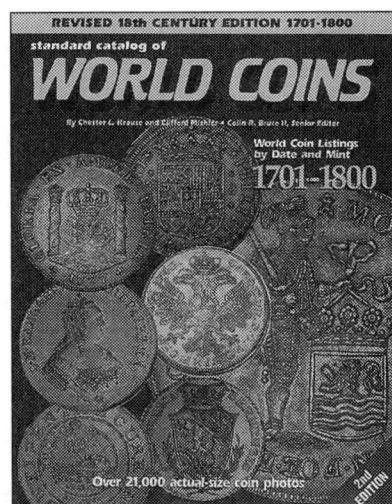

STANDARD INTERNATIONAL NUMERAL SYSTEMS

PREPARED ESPECIALLY FOR THE **STANDARD CATALOG OF WORLD COINS** ©1997 BY KRAUSE PUBLICATIONS

	0	½	1	2	3	4	5	6	7	8	9	10	50	100	500	1000
WESTERN	0	½	1	2	3	4	5	6	7	8	9	10	50	100	500	1000
ROMAN			I	II	III	IV	V	VI	VII	VIII	IX	X	L	C	D	M
ARABIC-TURKISH	٠	١/٢	١	٢	٣	٤	٥	٦	٧	٨	٩	١٠	٥٠	١٠٠	٥٠٠	١٠٠٠
MALAY—PERSIAN	٠	١/٢	١	٢	٣	۴	۵	۶	٧	٨	٩	١٠	۵٠	١٠٠	۵٠٠	١٠٠٠
EASTERN ARABIC	0	½	١	٢	٣	ٯ	٤	٥	٧	٦	9	١0	٤١٠	١00	٤١00	١000
HYDERABAD ARABIC	0	١/٢	١	٢	٣	ﻋ	ﻉ	ﻍ	<	٨	٩	١٠	٨٠	١٠٠	٨٠٠	١٠٠٠
INDIAN (Sanskrit)	०	½	१	२	३	४	५	६	७	८	९	१०	५०	१००	५००	१०००
ASSAMESE	০	৹/২	১	২	৩	৪	৫	৬	৭	৮	৯	১০	৫০	১০০	৫০০	১০০০
BENGALI	০	১/২	১	২	৩	৪	৫	৬	৭	৮	৯	১০	৫০	১০০	৫০০	১০০০
GUJARATI	૦	૧/૨	૧	૨	૩	૪	૫	૬	૭	૮	૯	૧૦	૫૦	૧૦૦	૫૦૦	૧૦૦૦
KUTCH	0	½	૧	૨	૩	૪	૫	૬	૭	૮	૯	10	40	100	400	1000
DEVAVNAGRI	0	१/२	१	२	३	४	५	६ or	७	८	९ or	१०	५०	१००	४००	१०००
NEPALESE	0	¹/२	११ or	२	३	४	४५ or	६	७	८ or	९ or	१०	५०	१००	४००	१०००
TIBETAN	༠	༡/༢	༡	༢	༣	༤	༥	༦	༧	༨	༩	༡༠	༥༠	༡༠༠	༤༠༠	༡༠༠༠
MONGOLIAN	᠐	᠑/᠒	᠑	᠒	᠓	᠔	᠕	᠖	᠗	᠘	᠙	᠑᠐	᠕᠐	᠑᠐᠐	᠕᠐᠐	᠑᠐᠐᠐
BURMESE	၀	၁/၂	၁	၂	၃	၄	၅	၆	၇	၈	၉	၁၀	၅၀	၁၀၀	၅၀၀	၁၀၀၀
THAI-LAO	๐	๑/๒	๑	๒	๓	๔	๕	๖	๗	๘	๙	๑๐	๕๐	๑๐๐	๕๐๐	๑๐๐๐
JAVANESE	0		꧑	꧒	꧓	꧔	꧕	꧖	꧗	꧘	꧙	꧑꧐	꧕꧐	꧑꧐꧐	꧕꧐꧐	꧑꧐꧐꧐
ORDINARY CHINESE JAPANESE-KOREAN	零	半	一	二	三	四	五	六	七	八	九	十	十五	百	百五	千
OFFICIAL CHINESE			壹	貳	叄	肆	伍	陸	柒	捌	玖	拾	拾伍	佰	佰伍	仟
COMMERCIAL CHINESE			〡	〢	〣	〤	〥	〦	〧	〨	〩	十	〥十	〡百	〥百	〡千
KOREAN		반	일	이	삼	사	오	육	칠	팔	구	십	오십	백	오백	천

GEORGIAN

	1	2	3	4	5	6	7	8	9	10	50	100	500	1000
	ა	ბ	გ	დ	ე	ვ	ზ	თ	ი	კ	ნ	რ	ჳ	ჰ

	11	20	30	40	50	60	70	80	90	100	200	300	400	600	700	800
	ლ	მ	ნ	ო	პ	ჟ	რ	ს	ტ	უ	ფ	ქ	ღ	ყ	შ	ჩ

ETHIOPIAN

	½	1	2	3	4	5	6	7	8	9	10	50	100	500	1000
	◆	፩	፪	፫	፬	፭	፮	፯	፰	፱	፲	፶	፻	፭፻	፲፻

	20	30	40	60	70	80	90
	፳	፴	፵	፷	፸	፹	፺

HEBREW

	1	2	3	4	5	6	7	8	9	10	50	100	500	1000
	א	ב	ג	ד	ה	ו	ז	ח	ט	י	נ	ק	תק	תת

	20	30	40	60	70	80	90	200	300	400	600	700	800
	כ	ל	מ	ס	ע	פ	צ	ר	ש	ת	תר	תש	תת

GREEK

	1	2	3	4	5	6	7	8	9	10	100	500	1000
	Α	Β	Γ	Δ	Ε	Σ	Ζ	Η	Θ	Ι	Ν	Ρ	Φ	Α

	20	30	40	50	60	70	80	200	300	400	600	700	800
	Κ	Λ	Μ	Ξ	Ο	Π	Σ	Τ	Υ	Χ	Ψ	Ω

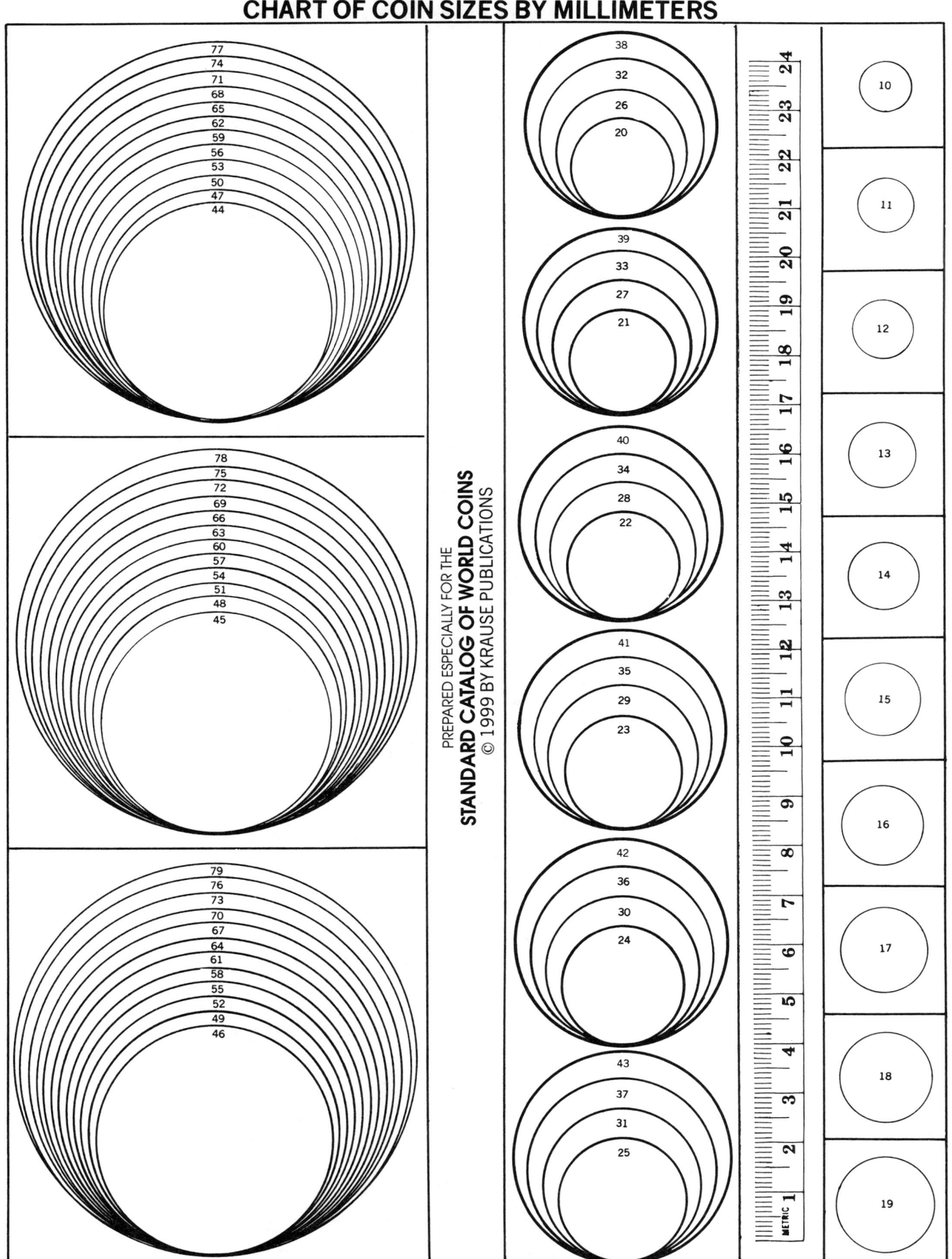

PREPARED ESPECIALLY FOR THE
STANDARD CATALOG OF WORLD COINS
© 1999 BY KRAUSE PUBLICATIONS

COIN SIZE CHART

COIN DENOMINATIONS

A

ABBASI - Afghanistan
ADHIO - India-IPS
AFGHANI - Afghanistan
AGORAH - Israel
AGOROT - Israel
AHMADI RIYAL - Yemen Republic
AKSHA - Tannu Tuva
AMANI - Afghanistan
ANGEL - Isle of Man
ANNA - India-British, IPS, Republic; Muscat & Oman, Pakistan
ARIARY - Madagascar Dem. Rep., Malagasy Republic
ASARFI - Nepal
ASHRAFI - India-IPS, Iran, Nepal
ASHRAPHI - Nepal
ATT - Laos, Thailand
AURAR - Iceland
AUSTRAL - Argentina
AUSTRALES - Argentina, Catamarca, LaRioja
AVOS - Macao, Timor
AZADI - Iran

B

BAHT - Thailand
BAISA - Muscat & Oman
BAIZA - Oman (Sultanate of)
BALBOA - Panama
BAN - Moldova, Romania
BANI - Moldova, Romania
BELGA - Belgium
BESA - Ethiopia, Italian Somaliland
BESE - Italian Somaliland
BIN LIRA - Turkey
BIPKWELE - Equatorial Guinea
BIRR - Ethiopia
BIT - Danish West Indies
BOLIVAR - Bolivia, Venezuela
BOLIVIANO - Bolivia
BRITANNIA - Great Britain
BUQSHA - Yemen Republic
BUTUT - Gambia

C

CANDAREENS - China
CASH - China, India-IPS, Viet Nam
CAURIS - Guinea
CEDI - Ghana
CENT - American Samoa, Antigua & Barbuda, Aruba, Australia, Bahamas, Barbados, Belize, Bermuda, Botswana, British Honduras, British East Caribbean Territories, British North Borneo, British Virgin Islands, Canada, Cayman Islands, Ceylon, China, Cook Islands, Curacao, Cyprus, Danish West Indies, Dominica, East Africa & Uganda Protectorate, East Africa, East Caribbean States, Eritrea, Ethiopia, Fiji, French Indo-China, Guyana, Hong Kong, Indonesia, Jamaica, Keeling-Cocos, Kenya, Kiribati, Laos, Liberia, Malaya, Malaya & British Borneo, Malta, Mauritius, Montserrat, Nauru, Netherlands, Netherlands Antilles, Netherlands East Indies, New Zealand, Newfoundland, Rhodesia, Palo Seco, Sarawak, Saint Kitts & Nevis, St. Lucia, St. Vincent, Seychelles, Sierra Leone, Singapore, Solomon Islands, South Africa, Sri Lanka, Straits Settlement, Surinam, Swaziland, Taiwan, Trengganu, Trinidad & Tobago, Tuvalu, Uganda, United States of America, Zanzibar, Zimbabwe
CENTAI - Lithuania
CENTAS - Lithuania
CENTAVO - Angola, Argentina, Bolivia, Brazil, Cape Verde, Chile, Colombia, Costa Rica, Cuba, Culion Island Dominican Republic, Ecuador, El Salvador, Guatemala, Guinea-Bissau, Honduras, India-Portuguese, Mexico, Mozambique, Nicaragua, Paraguay, Peru, Philippines, Portugal, Portuguese Guinea, St. Thomas & Prince Is., Timor
CENTESIMI - Italy, San Marino, Somali Republic, Somalia, Vatican City
CENTESIMO - Chile, Italy, Panama, Somalia, Uruguay
CENTIME - Algeria, Belgian Congo, Belgian Congo Ruanda-Urundi, Burundi, Cambodia, Cameroon, Central Af. Rep., Central Af. States, Comoros, Congo Free State, Djibouti, Eq. Af. States, France, French Equatorial Africa, French Oceania, French Polynesia, French West Africa, Ghent, Guadeloupe, Guinea, Haiti, Luxembourg, Madagascar, Martinique, Monaco, Morocco, New Caledonia, Reunion, Rwanda-Burundi, St. Pierre & Miquelon, Senegal, Togo, Tunisia
CENTIMO - Costa Rica, Mozambique, Paraguay, Peru, St. Thomas & Prince Is., Spain, Venezuela
CENTIMS - Andorra
CENTU - Lithuania
CHERVONETZ - Russia, CCCP, RSFSR
CHETRUM - Bhutan
CHHERTUM - Bhutan
CHIAO - China, Hong Kong, Japanese Puppet States
CHI'EN - China, Hong Kong
CHITRA RUPEE - India-IPS
CHON - Korea, Korea-North, Korea-South
CHUCKRAM - India-IPS
COLON - Costa Rica, El Salvador
COLONES - Costa Rica, El Salvador
CONDOR - Ecuador
CORDOBA - Nicaragua
CORONA - Austria
CROWN - Alderney, Ascension Island, Australia, Bermuda, Biafra, Ghana, Gibraltar, Great Britain, Ireland Republic, Isle of Man, Malawi, New Zealand, Rhodesia & Nyasaland, St. Helena & Ascension, Southern Rhodesia, Turks & Caicos Island, Tristan da Cunha
CRUZADO - Brazil
CRUZEIRO - Brazil
CRUZEIROS REALS - Brazil

D

DALASI - Gambia
DALER - Aland Islands, Danish West Indies
DAM - Nepal
DECIME - Monaco
DECIMO - Chile, Ecuador
DENAR - Macedonia
DENARI - Macedonia
DENGA - Russia, Empire
DENI - Macedonia
DEUTSCHE MARK - Germany
DHABU - India-IPS
DHINGLO - India-IPS
DHOFARI RIAL - Muscat & Oman
DIME - United States of America
DINAR - Algeria, Bahrain, Hejaz, Iran, Iraq, Jordan, Kuwait, Libya, Nejd, Serbia, Sudan, Tunisia, Yemen Republic, Yugoslavia
DINARA - Bosnia-Herzegovina, Serbia, Yugoslavia
DINAR HASHIMI - Hejaz
DINER - Andorra
DINERO - Peru
DIRHAM - Gambia, Iraq, Jordan, Libya, Morocco, Ras Al-Khaima, Sudan, United Arab Emirates
DIRHEM - Qatar, Qatar & Dubai
DOBRA - St. Thomas & Prince Is.
DOKDA - India-IPS
DOKDO - India-IPS
DOLLAR - American Samoa, Anguilla, Antigua, Antigua & Barbuda, Australia, Bahamas, Barbados, Belize, Bermuda, British Virgin Islands, Brunei, Canada, Cayman Islands, China, Cook Islands, Dominica, East Caribbean States, East Caribbean Territories, Eritrea, Ethiopia, Fiji, Great Britain, Grenada, Guyana, Hong Kong, Jamaica, Kiribati, Liberia, Malaya, Malaya and British North Borneo, Marshall Islands, Montserrat, Namibia, Nauru Island, New Zealand, Niue, Palau, Palo Seco, Pitcairn Islands, Rhodesia, Sarawak, St. Kitts, St. Lucia, St. Vincent, Sierra Leone, Singapore, Solomon Islands, Straits Settlements, Taiwan, Turks & Caicos Islands, Tuvalu, Trinidad & Tobago, United States of America, Zimbabwe
DOLYA - Russia, Empire
DONG - Viet Nam, Viet Nam-South
DOUBLE - Guernsey
DRACHMA - Crete, Greece
DRACHMAI - Crete, Greece
DRACHMES - Greece
DRAM - Armenia
DUCAT - Austria, Czech Republic, Netherlands, Netherlands East Indies
DUITOLA ASARPHI - Nepal
DUKAT - Bosnia-Herzegovina, Bulgaria, Croatia, Czechoslovakia, Yugoslavia
DUKATA - Yugoslavia
DUKATU - Czechoslovakia
DUKATY - Czechoslovakia

E

ECU - Andorra, Belgium, Bosnia-Herzegovina, Finland, France, Gibraltar, Ireland Republic, Isle of Man, Luxembourg, Malta, Norway, Saharawi Arab D.R., St. Thomas & Prince Is., Spain
EEN POND - South Africa
EKUELE - Equatorial Guinea
EKWELE - Equatorial Guinea
EMALANGENI - Swaziland
ESCALIN - Martinique
ESCUDO - Angola, Azores, Cape Verde, Chile, India-Portuguese, Madeira Islands, Martinique, Mozambique, Portugal, Portuguese Guinea, St. Thomas & Prince Is., Timor
EURO Bosnia-Herzegovina, Finland, France, Isle of Man
EYRIR - Iceland

F

FALUS - Uzbekistan
FANAM - India-IPS
FARTHING - Gibraltar, Great Britain, Ireland Republic, Jamaica, Malta
FEN - China, Japanese Puppet States
FENIG - Poland
FENIGOW - Poland
FILS - Bahrain, Iraq, Jordan, Kuwait, South Arabia, United Arab Emirates, Yemen Republic
FILLER - Hungary
FLORIN - Aruba, Australia, East Africa, Fiji, Gibraltar, Great Britain, Ireland Republic, Malawi, New Zealand, South Africa
FORINT - Hungary
FRANC - Algeria, Belgian Congo, Belgian Congo Ruanda-Urundi, Belgium, Benin, Burundi, Cameroon, Central African States, Central African Republic, Chad, Comoros, Congo Dem. Rep., Congo Free State, Dahomey, Danish West Indies, Djibouti, Equatorial African States, France, French Afars & Issas, French Somaliland, French Equatorial Africa, French Polynesia, French West Africa, Gabon, Guadeloupe, Guinea, Ivory Coast, Katanga, Luxembourg, Madagascar, Malagasy Republic, Mali, Martinique, Mauritania, Monaco, Morocco, New Caledonia, New Hebrides, Niger, Reunion, Rwanda, Rwanda & Burundi, St. Pierre & Miquelon, Senegal, Switzerland, Togo, Tunisia, West African States
FRANCO - Equatorial Guinea
FRANG AR - Albania
FRANGA AR - Albania
FRANK - Belgium, Liechtenstein
FRANKEN - Belgium; Ghent, Liechtenstein, Saarland
FUANG - Thailand
FUN - Korea

G

GAUCHO - Uruguay
GERSH - Ethiopia
GHIRSH - Hejaz & Nejd, Saudi Arabia, Sudan
GOLD KORI - India-IPS
GOLD MISCAL - China
GOLD RIYAL - Yemen Republic
GOLDE - Sierra Leone
GOURDE - Haiti
GRAMO - Bolivia
GRAMS - Afghanistan
GRANI - Malta (Order of)
GROAT - Great Britain
GROSCHEN - Austria
GROSZ - Poland
GROSZE - Poland
GROSZY - Poland
GUARANI - Paraguay
GUARANIES - Paraguay
GUILDER - Surinam
GUINEA - Saudi Arabia
GULDEN - Curacao, Danzig, Indonesia, Netherlands, Netherlands Antilles, Netherlands East Indies, Surinam

H

HABIBI - Afghanistan
HALALA - Saudi Arabia, Yemen Republic
HALER - Czechoslovakia
HALERE - Czechoslovakia
HALERU - Bohemia & Moravia, Czech Republic, Czechoslovakia
HALFPENNY - Ghana, Nigeria
HALF DOLLAR - United States of America
HALIER - Slovakia
HALIEROV - Slovakia
HAO - Viet Nam
HARF - Yemen Republic
HAU - Tonga, Viet Nam
HELLER - Austria, German East Africa, Liechtenstein
HRYVEN - Ukraine
HRYVNA - Ukraine
HRYVNIA - Ukraine
HSIEN - Hong Kong
HWAN - Korea-South

I

IMADI RIYAL - Yemen Republic
INTI - Peru

J

JIAO - China

K

KABIR - Yemen Republic
KAPEEK - Belarus
KARBOVANETS - Ukraine
KARBOVANTSIV - Ukraine
KEPING - Kelantan
KHOUMS - Mauritania
KHUMSI - Quaiti State of Hadhramau
KINA - Papua New Guinea
KIP - Laos
KLEINGELDERSATZMARKE - Germany
KOBO - Nigeria
KOPEJEK - Tannu Tuva
KOPEK - Germany; Russia: Empire, PCOCP (RSFSR), CCCP (USSR); Spitzbergen
KOPIJA - Ukraine
KOPIJOK - Ukraine
KORI - India-IPS
KORONA - Hungary
KORUN - Czech Republic, Czechoslovakia, Slovakia
KORUNA - Bohemia & Moravia, Czech Republic, Czechoslovakia, Slovakia
KORUNY - Czechoslovakia, Slovakia
KOULA - Tonga
KRAN - Iran
KRIEGSGELD - Germany
KRIEGSMUNZE - Germany
KRONA - Iceland, Sweden
KRONE - Denmark, Greenland, Liechtenstein, Norway
KRONEN - Austria, Liechtenstein
KRONER - Denmark, Greenland, Norway, Thule Yap York
KRONOR - Sweden
KRONUR - Iceland
KROON - Estonia
KROONI - Estonia
KRUGERRAND - South Africa
KUNA - Croatia
KUNE - Croatia
KURUS - Turkey
KURUSH - Turkey
KWACHA - Malawi, Zambia
KWANZA - Angola
KYAT - Myanmar

L

LAARI - Maldive Islands
LANG - Viet Nam-Annam
LARI - Georgia
LARIAT - Maldive Islands
LARIN - Maldive Islands
LATI - Latvia
LATS - Latvia
LATU - Latvia

LEI - Moldova, Romania
LEK - Albania
LEKE - Albania
LEKU - Albania
LEMPIRA - Honduras
LEONE - Sierra Leone
LEPTA - Crete, Greece
LEPTON - Crete
LEU - Moldova, Romania
LEV - Bulgaria
LEVA - Bulgaria
LI - China, Japanese Puppet States
LIANG - China, French Indo-China
LIBERTAD - Mexico
LIBERTY DOLLAR - Anguilla
LIBRA - Peru
LICENTE - Lesotho
LIKUTA - Congo Democratic Republic
LILANGENI - Swaziland
LIP - Slovenia
LIPA - Croatia, Slovenia
LIPE - Croatia, Slovenia
LIRA - Albania, Italy, San Marino, Syria, Turkey, Vatican City, Yemen Republic
LIRAH - Israel
LIRE - Italian Somaliland, Italy, San Marino, Vatican City
LIROT - Israel
LISENTE - Lesotho
LITAI - Lithuania
LITAS - Lithuania
LITU - Lithuania
LIVRE - Lebanon, Martinique
LOTI - Lesotho
LOWE - Bophuthatswana, South Africa
LUHLANGA - Swaziland
LUMA - Armenia
LWEI - Angola

M

MACE - China
MACUTA - Angola
MAKUTA - Congo Democratic Republic, Zaire
MALOTI - Lesotho
MANAT - Azerbaijan, Turkmenistan
MARK - Danzig, Estonia, German States, Germany, Poland-Lodz Ghetto
MARKA - Bosnia-Herzegovina, Estonia, Poland
MARKKA - Finland
MARKKAA - Finland
MAT - Myanmar
MATONA - Ethiopia
MAZUNA - Morocco
METICA - Mozambique
METICAIS - Mozambique
METICAL - Mozambique
MIL - Cyprus, Hong Kong, Israel, Malta, Palestine
MILLIEME - Egypt, Libya
MILLIM - Sudan, Tunisia
MILREIS - Brazil
MISCAL - China
MOHAR - Nepal
MOHUR - India British, India-IPS
MOMME - Japan
MONGO - Mongolia
MU - Myanmar, Union of Burma

N

NAIRA - Nigeria
NAYA PAISA - Bhutan, India-Republic
NAYE PAISE - India-Republic
NAZARANA MOHUR - India-IK, India-IPS
NAZARANA NEW PAISA - India-IPS
NAZARANA PAISA - India-IPS
NAZARANA RUPEE - India-IK, India-IPS
NEW AGORAH - Israel
NEW AGOROT - Israel
NEW PENCE - Alderney, Gibraltar, Great Britain, Guernsey, Isle of Man, Jersey
NEW PENNY - Great Britain, Guernsey, Isle of Man, Jersey
NEW PESO - Mexico
NEW SHEQALIM - Israel
NEW SHEQEL - Israel
NGULTRUM - Bhutan
NGWEE - Zambia
NICKEL - United States of America
NKWE - Bophuthatswana, South Africa
NOBLE - Isle of Man
NOTGELD - Germany
NOTSTANDSGELD - Germany
NOUVEAUX ZAIRES - Zaire
NOVO CRUZADO - Brazil
NOVI DINAR - Yugoslavia
NUEVO PESO - Mexico, Uruguay
NUEVO SOL - Peru

O

OMANI RIAL - Muscat & Oman, Oman (Sultanate of)
ONZA - Chile, Cuba, Dominican Republic, Mexico
ORE - Denmark, Faeroe Islands, Greenland, Iceland, Norway, Sweden, Thule Yap York
OUGUIYA - Mauritania
OUNCE - China, South Africa

P

PA'ANGA - Tonga
PAGODA - India-IPS
PAHLAVI - Iran
PAI - India-IPS
PAISA - Afghanistan; Bhutan; India-IPS, Republic; Nepal; Pakistan
PAISE - Afghanistan; India-IPS, Republic
PARA - Bosnia-Herzegovina, Hejaz, Montenegro, Nejd,

Serbia, Turkey, Yugoslavia
PARE - Montenegro, Serbia
PATACA - Macao
PAYALO - India-IPS
PE - Myanmar
PENCE - Ascension Island, Australia, Biafra, British Guiana, British Guiana & West Indies, British West Africa, Falkland Islands, Fiji, Gambia, Ghana, Gibraltar, Great Britain, Guernsey, Ireland Republic, Isle of Man, Jamaica, Jersey, Malawi, New Guinea, New Zealand, Nigeria, Rhodesia, Rhodesia & Nyasaland, St. Helena & Ascension, South Africa, Southern Rhodesia, Tristan da Cunha
PENGO - Hungary
PENNI - Finland
PENNIA - Finland
PENNY - Australia, British West Africa, Falkland Islands, Fiji, Gambia, Ghana, Gibraltar, Great Britain, Guernsey, Ireland Republic, Isle of Man, Jamaica, Jersey, Malawi, Malta, New Guinea, New Zealand, Nigeria, Rhodesia & Nyasaland, St. Helena & Ascension, South Africa, Southern Rhodesia, Zambia
PENNY FARTHING - South Africa
PERPER - Montenegro
PERPERA - Montenegro
PESETA - Andorra, Equatorial Guinea, Saharawi Arab D.R., Spain
PESEWA - Ghana
PESO - Argentina, Chile, Colombia, Cuba, Dominican Republic, Culion Island, El Salvador, Guatemala, Guinea-Bissau, Honduras, Mexico, Nicaragua, Paraguay, Philippines, Uruguay
PESO BOLIVIANO - Bolivia
PESO P/M - Colombia
PFENNIG - Danzig, Germany, Poland-Lodz Ghetto
PHAN - Viet Nam-Annam
PIASTRE - Cyprus, Egypt, Ethiopia, French Indo-China, Hejaz, Jordan, Laos, Lebanon, Libya, Nejd, Sudan, Syria, Viet Nam-Tonkin
PICE - Bhutan; India: British, IPS, Republic; Pakistan
PIE - India British, India-IPS, Pakistan
PISO - Philippines
PITIS - Kelantan
POISHA - Bangladesh
POLUSHKA - Russia, Empire
POND - South Africa
POUND - Alderney, Ascension Island, Australia, Biafra, Cyprus, Egypt, Falkland Islands, Fiji, Gambia, Ghana, Gibraltar, Great Britain, Guernsey, Iraq, Ireland Republic, Isle of Man, Israel, Jersey, Libya, Malawi, Malta, New Guinea, New Zealand, Nigeria, Rhodesia, St. Helena-Ascension, Saudi Arabia, South Africa, Sudan, Syria, Tristan da Cunha, Uganda
PROTEA - South Africa
PRUTA - Israel
PRUTAH - Israel
PUFFIN - Lundy
PUL - Afghanistan
PULA - Botswana
PUNT - Ireland
PYA - Myanmar

Q

QAPIK - Azerbaijan
QINDAR AR - Albania
QINDARKA - Albania
QINDAR LEKU - Albania
QIRAN - Afghanistan
QIRSH - Egypt, Jordan
QUARTER DOLLAR - United States of America
QUETZAL - Guatemala
QUETZALES - Guatemala

R

RAND - Namibia, South Africa
RAPPEN - Liechtenstein, Switzerland
REAIS - Brazil
REAL - Brazil, El Salvador, Guatemala
REALES - Jamaica
REICHSMARK - Germany
REICHSPFENNIG - Germany
REIS - Azores, Brazil, India Portuguese, Martinique, Portugal
RENTENPFENNIG - Germany
RIAL - Iran, Morocco, Muscat & Oman, Sudan, Yemen Republic
RIEL - Cambodia, Kampuchea, Khmer Republic
RIN - Japan
RINGGIT - Brunei, Malaysia
RIYAL - Ajmam, Al-Fujairah, Hejaz & Nejd, Iraq, Qatar, Qatar & Dubai, Ras Al-Khaima, Saudi Arabia, Sharjah, Umm Al-Qaiwain, Yemen Republic
ROB'I - Iran
ROUBLE - Belarus; Russia: Empire, PCOCP (RSFSR), CCCP (USSR), CIS; Russian Caucasia, Spitzbergen, Uzbekistan
ROYAL - Gibraltar
RUFIYAA - Maldive Islands
RUPEE - Afghanistan; Bhutan; Ceylon; India: British, IPS, Republic, Keeling Cocos, Mauritius, Muscat & Oman, Nepal, Pakistan, Seychelles, Sharjah, Sri Lanka, Tibet, Zanzibar
RUPIA - India-Portuguese, Italian Somaliland
RUPIAH - Indonesia
RUPIE - German East Africa
RUPIEN - German East Africa
RYALS - Oman

S

SAIDI RIAL - Muscat & Oman
SALUNG - Thailand
SANAR - Afghanistan
SANTEEM - Ethiopia

SANTIM - Morocco
SANTIMAT - Morocco
SANTIMI - Latvia
SANTIMS - Latvia
SANTIMU - Latvia
SAPEQUE - French Indo-China
SAR - China
SATANG - Thailand
SCELLINO - Somali Republic
SCHILLING - Austria
SCUDI - Malta (Order of), San Marino
SCUDO - Malta (Order of), San Marino
SEN - Brunei, Cambodia, Indonesia, Irian Barat, Japan, Kampuchea, Malaysia, Riau Archipelago, Thailand
SENE - Western Samoa
SENGIS - Congo Dem. Republic
SENITI - Tonga
SENT - Estonia
SENTE - Lesotho
SENTI - Estonia, Somalia, Tanzania
SENTIMO - Philippines
SERTUM - Bhutan
SHAHI - Afghanistan, Iran
SHAHI SEFID - Iran
SHEQALIM - Israel
SHEQEL - Israel
SHILINGI - Tanzania
SHILLING - Alderney, Australia, Biafra, British West Africa, Cyprus, East Africa, Fiji, Gambia, Ghana, Gibraltar, Great Britain, Guernsey, Ireland Republic, Isle of Man, Jamaica, Jersey, Kenya, Malawi, New Guinea, New Zealand, Nigeria, Rhodesia, Rhodesia & Nyasaland, Sierra Leone, Somali Republic, South Africa, Southern Rhodesia, Uganda, Zambia
SHO - Tibet
SIXPENCE - Australia, Fiji, Zambia
SKAR - Tibet
SOL - Martinique, Peru
SOLES - Peru
SOM - Kyrgyzstan, Uzbekistan
SOMALO - Somalia
SOVEREIGN - Andorra, Australia, Canada, Cyprus, Gibraltar, Great Britain, India-British, Isle of Man, Saudi Arabia, South Africa
SOVRANO - Malta (Order of)
SRANG - Tibet
STOTINKA - Bulgaria
STOTINKI - Bulgaria
STOTINOV - Slovenia
STRAITS DOLLAR - British North Borneo
SU - Viet Nam-South
SUCRE - Ecuador
SUVERENA - Bosnia-Herzegovina
SYLI - Guinea

T

TAEL - China, French Indo-China
TAKA - Bangladesh
TALA - Tokelau, Western Samoa
TALLERO - Eritrea
TAMBALA - Malawi
TAMLUNG - Thailand
TANGA - India-Portuguese
TARI - Order of Malta
TENE - Cook Islands
TENGA - Uzbekistan
TENGE - Kazakhstan
TENNESI - Turkmenistan
TETRI - Georgia
THALER - Austria, Ethiopia
THEBE - Botswana
THREEPENCE - Australia, Fiji
TIEN - Viet Nam-Annam
TILLA - Afghanistan, Uzbekistan
TIYIN - Uzbekistan
TOEA - Papua New Guinea
TOLA - India-British, Nepal
TOLAR - Slovenia
TOLARJA - Slovenia
TOLARJEV - Slovenia
TOMAN - Iran, Russian Caucasia
TRAMBIYO - India-IPS
TUGRIK - Mongolia
TYIN - Kazakhstan

V

VAN - Viet Nam-Annam
VATU - Vanuatu
VINAR - Slovenia

W

WAN - Hong Kong
WERK - Ethiopia
WHAN - Korea
WON - Korea, Korea-North, Korea-South

X

XU - Viet Nam-North, Viet Nam-South, Viet Nam

Y

YANG - Korea
YEN - Japan
YUAN - China, Hong Kong

Z

ZAIRE - Congo Democratic Republic, Zaire
ZALAT - Yemen Republic
ZLOTE - Poland
ZLOTY - Poland
ZLOTYCH - Poland
ZOLOTNIK - Russia, Empire

INSTANT IDENTIFIER

Austria

Finland

German Empire

Montenegro
(Yugoslavia)

Russia (Czarist)

Serbia
(Yugoslavia)

United Arab
Republic
(Egypt, Syria)

Yemen
Arab Republic

Bulgaria

Burma

Finland

Norway

Nepal

Morocco
(AH1320=1902AD)

Morocco
(AH1371=1951AD)

Sri Lanka
(Ceylon)

Japan

Japan

Iran
(Persia)

Morocco

Japan

African States

Greenland

German New
Guinea (Papua
New Guinea)

Maldive Islands

Ireland

Israel

Lebanon

Sweden

North Korea

CCCP-USSR

CCCP-USSR

Yugoslavia

Formosa
(Rep. of China)

French Colonial

French Colonial

French Colonial

Brazil

Hungary

Portugal

Slovakia
(Czechoslovakia)

Iraq

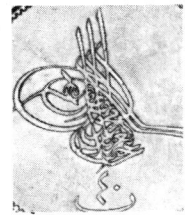
Turkey, Egypt,
Sudan

Saudi Arabia

Tunisia

China, Japan,
Annam, Korea
(All holed 'cash' coins look quite similar.)

Japan

Korea

Greece

Serbia
(Yugoslavia)

Switzerland

Albania

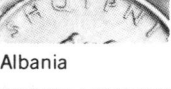
Thailand
(Siam)

Israel

Japan
(Dai Nippon)

South Korea
(Korea)

Guernsey

MONOGRAMS

FF8
Frederick VIII
Denmark

F IX R
Frederick IX
Denmark

HVII
Haakon VII
Norway

LL III
Leopold III
Belgium

M 2 R
Margrethe II Regina
Denmark

NII
Nicholas II
Russia

OII
Oscar II
Norway

O V
Olav V
Norway

R
Rainier III
Monaco

OII
Oscar II
Sweden

CC99
Christian IX
Danish West Indies

H7
Haakon VII
Norway

A
Albert I
Belgium

GRI
Georgius Rex
Imperator
New Guinea

L
Leopold II
Belgium

CX
Christian X
Denmark

A
Albert I
Belgium

B
Baudouin I
Belgium

CIX
Christian IX
Denmark

CCX
Christian X
Denmark

EP
Elizabeth-Philip
Great Britain

ERI
Edward Rex
Imperator
New Guinea

EIIR
Elizabeth II Regina
Cook Isl.

FJI
Franz Joseph I
Austria

NII
Nicholas II
Russia-Empire
(U.S.S.R.)

AIII
Alexander III
Russia-Empire
(U.S.S.R.)

HEJIRA DATE CONVERSION CHART

HEJIRA DATE CHART

HEJIRA (Hijra, Hegira), the name of the Muslim era (A.H. = Anno Hegirae) dates back to the Christian year 622 when Mohammed "fled" from Mecca, escaping to Medina to avoid persecution from the Koreish tribemen. Based on a lunar year the Muslim year is 11 days shorter.

*= Leap Year (Christian Calendar)

AH Hejira	AD Christian Date
1010	1601, July 2
1011	1602, June 21
1012	1603, June 11
1013	1604, May 30
1014	1605, May 19
1015	1606, May 19
1016	1607, May 9
1017	1608, April 28
1018	1609, April 6
1019	1610, March 26
1020	1611, March 16
1021	1612, March 4
1022	1613, February 21
1023	1614, February 11
1024	1615, January 31
1025	1616, January 20
1026	1617, January 9
1027	1617, December 29
1028	1618, December 19
1029	1619, December 8
1030	1620, November 26
1031	1621, November 16
1032	1622, November 5
1033	1623, October 25
1034	1624, October 14
1035	1625, October 3
1036	1626, September 22
1037	1627, September 12
1038	1628, August 31
1039	1629, August 21
1040	1630, July 10
1041	1631, July 30
1042	1632, July 19
1043	1633, July 8
1044	1634, June 27
1045	1635, June 17
1046	1636, June 5
1047	1637, May 26
1048	1638, May 15
1049	1639, May 4
1050	1640, April 23
1051	1641, April 12
1052	1642, April 1
1053	1643, March 22
1054	1644, March 10
1055	1645, February 27
1056	1646, February 17
1057	1647, February 6
1058	1648, January 27
1059	1649, January 15
1060	1650, January 4
1061	1650, December 25
1062	1651, December 14
1063	1652, December 2
1064	1653, November 22
1065	1654, November 11
1066	1655, October 31
1067	1656, October 20
1068	1657, October 9
1069	1658, September 29
1070	1659, September 18
1071	1660, September 6
1072	1661, August 27
1073	1662, August 16
1074	1663, August 5
1075	1664, July 25
1076	1665, July 14
1077	1666, July 4
1078	1667, June 23
1079	1668, June 11
1080	1669, June 1
1081	1670, May 21
1082	1671, May 10
1083	1672, April 29
1084	1673, April 18
1085	1674, April 7
1086	1675, March 28
1087	1676, March 16*
1088	1677, March 6
1089	1678, February 23
1090	1679, February 12
1091	1680, February 2*
1092	1681, January 21
1093	1682, January 10
1094	1682, December 31
1095	1683, December 20
1096	1684, December 8*
1097	1685, November 28
1098	1686, November 17
1099	1687, November 7
1100	1688, October 26*
1101	1689, October 15
1102	1690, October 5

AH Hejira	AD Christian Date
1103	1691, September 24
1104	1692, September 12*
1105	1693, September 2
1106	1694, August 22
1107	1695, August 12
1108	1696, July 31*
1109	1697, July 20
1110	1698, July 10
1111	1699, June 29
1112	1700, June 18
1113	1701, June 8
1114	1702, May 28
1115	1703, May 17
1116	1704, May 6*
1117	1705, April 25
1118	1706, April 15
1119	1707, April 4
1120	1708, March 23*
1121	1709, March 18
1122	1710, March 2
1123	1711, February 19
1124	1712, February 9*
1125	1713, January 28
1126	1714, January 17
1127	1715, January 7
1128	1715, December 27
1129	1716, December 16*
1130	1717, December 5
1131	1718, November 24
1132	1719, November 14
1133	1720, November 2*
1134	1721, October 22
1135	1722, October 12
1136	1723, October 1
1137	1724, September 29*
1138	1725, September 9
1139	1726, August 29
1140	1727, August 19
1141	1728, August 7*
1142	1729, July 27
1143	1730, July 17
1144	1731, July 6
1145	1732, June 24*
1146	1733, June 14
1147	1734, June 3
1148	1735, May 24
1149	1736, May 12*
1150	1737, May 1
1151	1738, April 21
1152	1739, April 10
1153	1740, March 29*
1154	1741, March 19
1155	1742, March 8
1156	1743, February 25
1157	1744, February 15*
1158	1745, February 3
1159	1746, January 24
1160	1747, January 13
1161	1748, January 2
1162	1748, December 22*
1163	1749, December 11
1164	1750, November 30
1165	1751, November 20
1166	1752, November 8*
1167	1753, October 29
1168	1754, October 18
1169	1755, October 7
1170	1756, September 26*
1171	1757, September 15
1172	1758, September 4
1173	1759, August 25
1174	1760, August 13*
1175	1761, August 2
1176	1762, July 28
1177	1763, July 12
1178	1764, July 1*
1179	1765, June 20
1180	1766, June 9
1181	1767, May 30
1182	1768, May 18*
1183	1769, May 7
1184	1770, April 27
1185	1771, April 16
1186	1772, April 4*
1187	1773, March 25*
1188	1774, March 14
1189	1775, March 4
1190	1776, February 21*
1191	1777, February 9
1192	1778, January 30
1193	1779, January 19
1194	1780, January 8*
1195	1780, December 28*
1196	1781, December 17
1197	1782, December 7
1198	1783, November 26
1199	1784, November 14*
1200	1785, November 4
1201	1786, October 24
1202	1787, October 13
1203	1788, October 2*
1204	1789, September 21
1205	1790, September 10
1206	1791, August 31
1207	1792, August 19*
1208	1793, August 9

AH Hejira	AD Christian Date
1209	1794, July 29
1210	1795, July 18
1211	1796, July 7*
1212	1797, June 26
1213	1798, June 15
1214	1799, June 5
1215	1800, May 25
1216	1801, May 14
1217	1802, May 4
1218	1803, April 23
1219	1804, April 12*
1220	1805, April 1
1221	1806, March 21
1222	1807, March 11
1223	1808, February 28*
1224	1809, February 16
1225	1810, February 6
1226	1811, January 26
1227	1812, January 16*
1228	1813, January 4
1229	1813, December 24
1230	1814, December 14
1231	1815, December 3
1232	1816, November 21*
1233	1817, November 11
1234	1818, October 31
1235	1819, October 20
1236	1820, October 9*
1237	1821, September 28
1238	1822, September 18
1239	1823, September 7
1240	1824, August 26*
1241	1825, August 16
1242	1826, August 5
1243	1827, July 25
1244	1828, July 14*
1245	1829, July 3
1246	1830, June 22
1247	1831, June 12
1248	1832, May 31*
1249	1833, May 21
1250	1834, May 10
1251	1835, April 29
1252	1836, April 18*
1253	1837, April 7
1254	1838, March 27
1255	1839, March 17
1256	1840, March 5*
1257	1841, February 23
1258	1842, February 12
1259	1843, February 1
1260	1844, January 22*
1261	1845, January 10
1262	1845, December 30
1263	1846, December 20
1264	1847, December 9
1265	1848, November 27*
1266	1849, November 17
1267	1850, November 6
1268	1851, October 27
1269	1852, October 15*
1270	1853, October 4
1271	1854, September 24
1272	1855, September 13
1273	1856, September 1*
1274	1857, August 22
1275	1858, August 11
1276	1859, July 31
1277	1860, July 20*
1278	1861, July 9
1279	1862, June 29
1280	1863, June 18
1281	1864, June 6*
1282	1865, May 27
1283	1866, May 16
1284	1867, May 5
1285	1868, April 24*
1286	1869, April 13
1287	1870, April 3
1288	1871, March 23
1289	1872, March 11*
1290	1873, March 1
1291	1874, February 18
1292	1875, February 7
1293	1876, January 28*
1294	1877, January 16
1295	1878, January 5
1296	1878, December 26
1297	1879, December 15
1298	1880, December 4*
1299	1881, November 23
1300	1882, November 12
1301	1883, November 2
1302	1884, October 21*
1303	1885, October 10
1304	1886, September 30
1305	1887, September 19
1306	1888, September 7*
1307	1889, August 28
1308	1890, August 17
1309	1891, August 7
1310	1892, July 26*
1311	1893, July 15
1312	1894, July 5
1313	1895, June 24
1314	1896, June 12*

AH Hejira	AD Christian Date
1315	1897, June 2
1316	1898, May 22
1317	1899, May 12
1318	1900, May 1
1319	1901, April 20
1320	1902, April 10
1321	1903, March 30
1322	1904, March 18*
1323	1905, March 8
1324	1906, February 25
1325	1907, February 14
1326	1908, February 4*
1327	1909, January 23
1328	1910, January 13
1329	1911, January 2
1330	1911, December 22
1331	1912, December 11*
1332	1913, November 30
1333	1914, November 19
1334	1915, November 9
1335	1916, October 28*
1336	1917, October 17
1337	1918, October 7
1338	1919, September 26
1339	1920, September 15*
1340	1921, September 4
1341	1922, August 24
1342	1923, August 14
1343	1924, August 2*
1344	1925, July 22
1345	1926, July 12
1346	1927, July 1
1347	1928, June 20*
1348	1929, June 9
1349	1930, May 29
1350	1931, May 19
1351	1932, May 7*
1352	1933, April 26
1353	1934, April 16
1354	1935, April 5
1355	1936, March 24*
1356	1937, March 14
1357	1938, March 3
1358	1939, February 21
1359	1940, February 10*
1360	1941, January 29
1361	1942, January 19
1362	1943, January 8
1363	1943, December 28
1364	1944, December 17*
1365	1945, December 6
1366	1946, November 25
1367	1947, November 15
1368	1948, November 3*
1369	1949, October 24
1370	1950, October 13
1371	1951, October 2
1372	1952, September 21*
1373	1953, September 10
1374	1954, August 30
1375	1955, August 20
1376	1956, August 8*
1377	1957, July 29
1378	1958, July 18
1379	1959, July 7
1380	1960, June 25*
1381	1961, June 14
1382	1962, June 4
1383	1963, May 25
1384	1964, May 13*
1385	1965, May 2
1386	1966, April 22
1387	1967, April 11
1388	1968, March 31*
1389	1969, March 20
1390	1970, March 9
1391	1971, February 27
1392	1972, February 16*
1393	1973, February 4
1394	1974, January 25
1395	1975, January 14
1396	1976, January 3*
1397	1976, December 23*
1398	1977, December 12
1399	1978, December 2
1400	1979, November 21
1401	1980, November 9*
1402	1981, October 30
1403	1982, October 19
1404	1983, October 8
1405	1984, September 27*
1406	1985, September 16
1407	1986, September 6
1408	1987, August 26
1409	1988, August 14*
1410	1989, August 3
1411	1990, July 24
1412	1991, July 13
1413	1992, July 2*
1414	1993, June 21
1415	1994, June 10
1416	1995, May 31
1417	1996, May 19*
1418	1997, May 9
1419	1998, April 28
1420	1999, April 17
1421	2000, April 6*

A Guide To International Numerics

	ENGLISH	CZECH	DANISH	DUTCH	ESPERANTO	FRENCH
1/4	one-quarter	jeden-ctvrt	én kvart	een-kwart	unu-kvar' ono	un-quart
1/2	one-half	jeden-polovicni or pul	én halv	een-half	unu-du'one	un-demi
1	one	jeden	én	een	unu	un
2	two	dve	to	twee	du	deux
3	three	tri	tre	drie	tri	trois
4	four	ctyri	fire	vier	kvar	quatre
5	five	pet	fem	vijf	kvin	cinq
6	six	sest	seks	zes	ses	six
7	seven	sedm	syv	zeven	sep	sept
8	eight	osm	otte	acht	ok	huit
9	nine	devet	ni	negen	nau	neuf
10	ten	deset	ti	tien	dek	dix
12	twelve	dvaná ct	tolv	twaalf	dek du	douze
15	fifteen	patná ct	femten	vijftien	dek kvin	quinze
20	twenty	dvacet	tyve	twintig	du'dek	vingt
24	twenty-four	dvacet-ctyri	fire og tyve	twintig-vier	du'dek kvar	vingt-quatre
25	twenty-five	dvacet-pet	fem og tyve	twintig-vijf	du'dek kvin	vingt-cinq
30	thirty	tricet	tredive	dertig	tri'dek	trente
40	forty	ctyricet	fyrre	veertig	kvar'dek	quarante
50	fifty	padesát	halvtreds	vijftig	kvin'dek	cinquante
60	sixty	sedesát	tres	zestig	ses'dek	soizante
70	seventy	sedmdesát	halvfjerds	zeventig	sep'dek	soizante-dix
80	eighty	osemdesát	firs	tachtig	ok'dek	quatre-vingt
90	ninety	devadesát	halvfems	negentig	nau'dek	quatre-vingt-dix
100	one hunded	jedno sto	et hundrede	een-honderd	unu-cento	un-cent
1000	thousand	tisí c	tusind	duizend	mil	mille

	GERMAN	HUNGARIAN	INDONESIAN	ITALIAN	NORWEGIAN	POLISH
1/4	einvertel	egy-negyed	satu-suku	uno-quarto	en-fjerdedel	jeden-c wierc
1/2	einhalb	egy-fél	satu-setengah	uno-mezzo	en-halv	jeden-polowa
1	ein	egy	satu	uno	en	jeden
2	zwei	kettö	dud	due	to	dwa
3	drei	három	tiga	tre	tre	trzy
4	vier	négy	empot	quattro	fire	cztery
5	fünf	öt	lima	cinque	fem	piec´
6	sechs	hat	enam	sei	seks	szes´ c´
7	sieben	hét	tudjuh	sette	sju	siedem
8	acht	nyolc	delapan	otto	atte	osiem
9	neun	kilenc	sembilan	nove	ni	dziewiec´
10	zehn	tí z	sepuluh	dieci	ti	dziesiec´
12	zwolf	tizenketto	dua belas	dodici	tolv	dwanas´ cie
15	fünfzehn	tizenöt	lima belas	quindici	femten	pietnas´ cie
20	zwanzig	húsz	dua pulah	venti	tjue or tyve	dwadzies´ cia
24	vierundzwanzig	húsz-négy	dua pulah-empot	venti-quattro	tjue-fire or tyve-fire	dwadzies´ cia-cztery
25	fünfundzwanzig	húsz-öt	dua-pulah-lima	venti-cinque	tjue-fem or tyve-fem	dwadzies´ cia-piec
30	dreissig	harminc	tigapulah	trenta	tredve	trzydzies´ ci
40	vierzig	negyven	empat pulah	quaranta	forti	czterdries´ ci
50	fünfzig	otven	lima pulah	cinquanta	femti	piec´ dziesiat
60	sechzig	hatvan	enam pulah	sessanta	seksti	szes´ c´ dziesiat
70	siebzig	hetven	tudjuh pulu	settanta	sytti	siedemdziesiat
80	achtzig	nyolvan	delapan puluh	ottanta	atti	osiemdziesiat
90	neuzig	kilencven	sembilan puluh	novanta	nitty	dziewiec´ dziesiat
100	ein hundert	egy-száz	satu-seratus	uno-cento	en-hundre	jeden-sto
1000	tausend	ezer	seribu	mille	tusen	tysiac

	PORTUGUESE	ROMANIAN	SERBO-CROATIAN	SPANISH	SWEDISH	TURKISH
1/4	um-quarto	un-sfert	jedan-ceturtina	uno-cuarto	en-fjärdedel	bir-ceyrek
1/2	un-meio	o-jumatate	jedan-polovina	uno-medio	en-hälft	bir-yarim
1	um	un	jedan	uno	en	bir
2	dois	doi	dva	dos	tva	iki
3	três	trei	tri	tres	tre	üc
4	quatro	patru	cetiri	cuatro	fyra	dört
5	cinco	cinci	pet	cinco	fem	bes
6	seis	sase	sest	seis	sex	alti
7	sete	sapte	sedam	siete	sju	yedi
8	oito	opt	osam	ocho	atta	sekiz
9	nove	noua	devet	nueve	nio	dokuz
10	dez	zece	deset	diez	tio	on
12	doze	doisprezece	dvanaest	doce	tolv	on iki
15	quinze	cincisprezece	petnaest	quince	femton	on bes
20	vinte	douazeci	dvadset	veinte	tjugu	yirmi
24	vinte-quatro	douazeci-patru	dvadesel-cetiri	veinte-cuarto	tjugu-fyra	yirmi-dört
25	vinte-cinco	douazeci-cinci	dvadeset-pet	veinte-cinco	tjugu-fem	yirmi-bes
30	trinta	treizeci	trideset	treinta	trettio	otuz
40	quarenta	patruzeci	cetrdeset	cuarenta	fyrtio	kirk
50	cinqüenta	cincizeci	padeset	cincuenta	femtio	elli
60	sessenta	saizeci	sezdeset	sesenta	sextio	altmis
70	setenta	saptezeci	sedamdeset	setenta	sjuttio	yetmis
80	oitenta	optzeci	osamdeset	ochenta	attio	seksen
90	noventa	novazeci	devedeset	noventa	nittio	doksan
100	un-cem	o-suta	jedan-sto	uno-ciente	en-hundra	bir-yüz
1000	mil	mie	hiljada	mil	tusen	bin

AFGHANISTAN

The Islamic State of Afghanistan, which occupies a mountainous region of Southwest Asia, has an area of 251,773 sq. mi. (652,090 sq. km.) and a population of 21.3 million. Presently about a fifth of the total population lives (mostly in Pakistan) in exile as refugees. Capital: Kabul. It is bordered by Iran, Pakistan, Turkmenistan, Uzbekistan, Tajikistan, and China's Sinkiang Province. Agriculture and herding are the principal industries; textile mills and cement factories add to the industrial sector. Cotton, wool, fruits, nuts, oil, sheepskin coats and hand-woven carpets are normally exported but foreign trade has been interrupted since 1979.

The last king, Muhammed Zahir Shah, became a constitutional, though still autocratic, monarch in 1964. In 1973 a coup d'etat displaced him and created the Republic of Afghanistan. A subsequent military coup established the pro-Soviet Democratic Republic of Afghanistan in 1978. Mounting resistance in the countryside and violence within the government led to the Soviet invasion of late 1979, a brutal civil war ensued, which continues to the present.

Afghanistan's traditional coinage was much like that of its neighbors Iran and India. There were four major mints: Kabul, Qandahar, Balkh and Herat. The early Durranis also controlled mints in Iran and India. On gold and silver coins, the inscriptions in Persian (called *Dari* in Afghanistan) included the name of the mint city and, normally, of the ruler recognized there, but some issues were anonymous. The arrangement of the inscriptions, and frequently the name of the ruler, was different at each mint. Copper coins were controlled locally and usually did not name any ruler. For these reasons the coinage of each mint is treated separately. The relative values of gold, silver, and copper coins were not fixed but were determined in the marketplace.

In 1890 Abdur Rahman had a modern mint set up in Kabul using British minting machinery and the help of British advisors. The other mints were closed down, except for the issue of local coppers. The new system had sixty paisa to the rupee; intermediate denominations also had special names. In 1901 the name Afghanistan appeared on coins for the first time. A decimal system, 100 puls to the rupee, was introduced in 1925. The gold amani, rated at 20 afghanis, was a bullion coin.

The national symbol on most coins of the kingdom is a stylized mosque, within which is seen the *mihrab*, a niche indicating the direction of Mecca, and the *minbar*, the pulpit, with a flight of steps leading up to it. Inscriptions in Pashtu were first used under the rebel Habibullah, but did not become standard until 1950.

Until 1919, coins were dated by the lunar Islamic Hijri calendar (AH), often with the king's regnal year as a second date. The solar Hijri (SH) calendar was introduced in 1919 (1337 AH, 1298 SH). The rebel Habibullah reinstated lunar Hijri dating (AH 1347-50), but the solar calendar was used thereafter. The solar Hijri year begins on the first day of spring, about March 21. Adding 621 to the SH year yields the AD year in which it begins.

RULERS

Names of rulers are shown in Perso-Arabic script in the style usually found on their coins; they are not always in a straight line.

BARAKZAI DYNASTY

Abdur Rahman, عبدالرحمن

AH1297-1319/1880-1901AD

Habibullah, حبيب الله

AH1319-1337/1901-1919AD

Amanullah, امان الله

AH1337, SH1298-1307/1919-1929AD

Habibullah (rebel, known as
Baccha-i-Saqao), حبيب الله
١٣٤٧(٥٣٨)

AH1347-1348/1929AD

Muhammed Nadir Shah, محمد نادرشاه

AH1348-1350, SH1310-1312
1929-1933AD

Muhammad Zahir Shah, محمد ظاهرشاه

SH1312-1352/1933-1973AD

Republic, SH1352-1358/1973-1979AD
Democratic Republic, SH1358-1373/1979-1994 AD
Islamic Republic, SH1373-/1994AD

MINTNAME

Kabul

'Dar al-Mulk'
Abode of the King   افغانستان

MILLED COINAGE

MONETARY SYSTEM

10 Dinar = 1 Paisa
5 Paise = 1 Shahi
2 Shahi = 1 Sanar
2 Sanar = 1 Abbasi
1-1/2 Abbasi = 1 Qiran
2 Qiran = 1 Kabuli Rupee

PAISA

BRONZE or BRASS

KM#	Date	Mintage	VG	Fine	VF	XF
848	AH1329	—	6.00	12.00	20.00	30.00
	1329/17 on KM#828 obverse die					
		—	8.00	15.00	30.00	50.00

21mm

KM#	Date	Mintage	VG	Fine	VF	XF
849	AH1329	—	2.00	4.00	7.50	15.00
	1331	—	2.00	4.00	7.50	15.00
	1332	—	2.50	4.75	9.00	16.00
	1334	—	3.00	6.00	11.50	20.00

Thick flan, reduced size: 19mm

KM#	Date	Mintage	VG	Fine	VF	XF
854	AH1336	—	2.50	5.00	10.00	25.00

Thin flan

KM#	Date	Mintage	VG	Fine	VF	XF
855	AH1336	—	1.75	3.00	5.00	12.50
	1337	—	1.75	3.00	5.00	12.50

Thick flan, 20mm

KM#	Date	Mintage	VG	Fine	VF	XF
857	AH1337	—	6.50	10.00	20.00	35.00

Thin flan, 19-20mm

KM#	Date	Year	VG	Fine	VF	XF
858	AH1337	—	3.00	6.00	10.00	20.00
	SH1298	(1919)	4.50	8.00	15.00	32.50

NOTE: 3 varieties are known dated AH1337.

KM#	Date	Year	VG	Fine	VF	XF
880	SH1299	(1920)	1.75	4.00	8.00	12.50
	1300	(1921)	2.50	5.00	9.00	15.00
	1301	(1922)	2.50	5.00	9.00	15.00
	1302	(1923)	1.75	4.00	8.00	12.50
	1303	(1924)	1.75	4.00	8.00	12.50

NOTE: 2 varieties are known dated SH1301.

SHAHI
(5 Paisa)

COPPER or BRASS
Thick flan

KM#	Date	Mintage	VG	Fine	VF	XF
859	AH1337	—	9.00	16.00	25.00	55.00

Thin flan

KM#	Date	Mintage	VG	Fine	VF	XF
860	AH1337	—	8.00	15.00	22.50	40.00

SANAR
(10 Paisa)

1.5500 g, .500 SILVER, .0249 oz ASW

KM#	Date	Mintage	VG	Fine	VF	XF
846	AH1325	—	10.00	20.00	35.00	60.00
	1326	—	5.00	7.50	12.50	20.00
	1328	—	5.00	7.50	12.50	20.00
	1329	—	5.75	8.50	14.00	25.00

KM#	Date	Mintage	VG	Fine	VF	XF
850	AH1329	—	4.00	7.00	11.00	16.00
	1330	—	3.00	6.00	10.00	15.00
	1331	—	3.00	6.00	10.00	15.00
	1332	—	3.00	6.00	10.00	15.00
	1333	—	3.00	5.00	9.00	14.00
	1335	—	3.00	5.00	9.00	14.00
	1337	—	3.00	6.00	10.00	15.00

NOTE: Coins dated AH1333 and 1337 are known in 2 varieties.

COPPER or BRASS
Thick flan

KM#	Date	Mintage	VG	Fine	VF	XF
861	AH1337	—	10.00	17.50	30.00	55.00

Thin flan

KM#	Date	Mintage	VG	Fine	VF	XF
862	AH1337	—	9.00	14.00	20.00	35.00

10 PAISE

COPPER

KM#	Date	Mintage	VG	Fine	VF	XF
901	AH1348	—	6.00	10.00	18.00	32.00

3 SHAHI
(15 Paisa)

COPPER, 32-33mm
Obv: W/o *Al-Ghazi*.

Rev: Mosque in 8-pointed star.

KM#	Date	Year	VG	Fine	VF	XF
863	AH1337	—	3.00	7.00	14.00	20.00

NOTE: 3 varieties are known.

Obv: Shamsi left and below date.

869	SH1298	(1919)	2.00	4.00	8.00	15.00

NOTE: *Shamsi* (= Solar) is an additional word written on some of the coins dated SH1298, to show the change from a lunar to solar calendar.

Obv: Al-Ghazi, w/o Shamsi by date.
Rev: Mosque in 8-pointed star.

870	SH1298	(1919)	3.00	5.00	8.00	15.00
	1299	(1920)	3.00	5.00	8.00	15.00
	1300	(1921)	—	Reported, not confirmed		

Thick flan, 11.5 g.
Obv: Al-Ghazi, Shamsi.

871.1	SH1298	(1919)	10.00	14.00	18.00	24.00

Thin flan, 9 g.

871.2	SH1298	(1919)	2.00	4.00	8.00	15.00

Obv: Shamsi.
Rev: Mosque in 7-pointed star.

872	SH1298	(1919)	2.00	4.00	8.00	15.00

Obv: W/o Shamsi.

881	SH1298	(1919)	4.00	15.00	22.00	25.00
	1299	(1920)	1.50	3.50	7.00	15.00
	1300	(1921)	1.50	3.50	7.00	15.00
	1302	(1923)	1.50	3.50	7.00	15.00

NOTE: 4 varieties for date SH1299 and 3 varieties for date SH1300 are known.

BRASS

881a	SH1300	(1921)	4.00	8.00	12.00	20.00
(892)						

Obv. and rev: 8 stars around perimeter.

891	SH1300	(1921)	—	—	—	

COPPER

KM#	Date	Year	VG	Fine	VF	XF
893	SH1300	(1921)	1.00	2.00	5.00	10.00
	1301 (2 vars.)					
		(1922)	1.00	2.00	5.00	10.00
	130x(error)				—	—
	1303	(1924)	1.00	2.00	5.00	10.00

ABBASI
(20 Paisa)

3.1100 g, .500 SILVER, .0499 oz ASW

KM#	Date	Mintage	VG	Fine	VF	XF
837	AH1320	—	12.50	22.50	35.00	50.00
845	AH1324	—	7.00	12.00	18.00	30.00
	1328	—	7.00	12.00	18.00	30.00

851	AH1329	—	6.00	11.00	16.00	22.50
	1330	—	4.00	7.00	10.00	15.00
	1333	—	3.00	6.00	9.00	14.00
	1334	—	3.00	6.00	9.00	14.00
	1335	—	3.00	5.00	8.00	13.00
	1337	—	3.00	5.00	8.00	13.00

COPPER or BILLON

KM#	Date	Year	VG	Fine	VF	XF
874	SH1298	(1919)	50.00	75.00	90.00	150.00

25mm

882	SH1299	(1920)	15.00	30.00	50.00	75.00

883	SH1299	(1920)	2.00	5.00	10.00	20.00
	1300	(1921)	2.00	5.00	10.00	20.00
	1301	(1922)	2.00	5.00	10.00	20.00
	1302	(1923)	2.00	5.00	10.00	20.00
	2031(error)					
	1303	(1924)	2.00	5.00	10.00	20.00

NOTE: 2 varieties for date SH1301 exist.

20 PAISE

BRONZE or BRASS

KM#	Date	Mintage	VG	Fine	VF	XF
895	AH1347	—	3.00	5.00	7.50	17.50

1/2 RUPEE
(Qiran)

4.6500 g, .500 SILVER, .0747 oz ASW
Obv: Toughra. Rev: Crossed cannons

below mosque.

KM#	Date	Mintage	VG	Fine	VF	XF
831	AH1319	—	14.00	25.00	40.00	65.00

Obv: Date below toughra.

838	AH1320	—	8.00	14.00	22.50	35.00
	1325	—	7.00	11.00	18.00	27.50

Obv: Date at upper right of toughra.
Rev. dated: AH1320

841	AH1321	—	7.00	10.00	14.00	22.50

Obv: Inscription. Rev: Date at upper right of mosque.

844	1323	—	4.00	6.00	10.00	18.00
	1324	—	4.00	6.00	9.00	16.00
	1326	—	4.00	6.00	9.00	16.00
	1327/6	—	4.00	6.00	9.00	16.00
	1327	—	4.00	6.00	9.00	16.00
	1328	—	4.00	6.00	9.00	16.00
	1329	—	4.00	6.00	10.00	19.00

NOTE: 2 varieties are known.
NOTE: Varieties exist w/1326 on obverse and reverse.

4.6000 g, .500 SILVER, .0739 oz ASW

852	AH1329	—	3.50	5.50	8.50	14.00
	1333	—	3.50	5.50	8.50	14.00
	1334	—	4.50	7.50	12.50	20.00
	1335	—	4.50	7.50	12.50	20.00
	1337	—	3.50	5.50	8.50	14.00

5.00 g
Obv. leg: Name of *Habibullah*.
Rev: Star of Solomon.

864	AH1335	—	—	300.00	500.00	—

Obv: Uncircled inscription.

KM#	Date	Year	VG	Fine	VF	XF
865	AH1337	—	4.00	9.00	13.00	20.00

NOTE: 5 varieties are known.

25mm
Obv. leg: Within circle and wreath.

866	AH1337	—	150.00	300.00	500.00	725.00

4.7500 g, .500 SILVER, .0763 oz ASW
Obv: Star above inscription, *Shamsi*.

875	SH1298	(1919)	3.00	5.00	8.00	14.00

NOTE: 2 varieties are known.

Obv: *Al-Ghazi* above inscription, *Shamsi*.

KM#	Date	Year	VG	Fine	VF	XF
876	SH1298	(1919)	15.00	30.00	50.00	75.00

Obv: W/o *Shamsi*.

KM#	Date	Year	VG	Fine	VF	XF
884	SH1299	(1920)	3.00	4.00	7.00	12.00
	1300	(1921)	3.00	4.00	7.00	12.00

NOTE: 2 varieties are known dated 1299.

KM#	Date	Year	VG	Fine	VF	XF
894	SH1300	(1921)	2.00	4.00	7.00	11.00
	1301	(1922)	2.00	4.00	7.00	10.00
	1302	(1923)	2.00	4.00	7.00	10.00
	1303	(1924)	2.00	4.00	7.00	10.00

4.7000 g, .500 SILVER, .0755 oz ASW

KM#	Date	Mintage	VG	Fine	VF	XF
896	AH1347	—	4.00	7.00	12.00	20.00

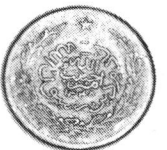 

| 902 | AH1348 | — | 14.00 | 25.00 | 35.00 | 50.00 |

RUPEE

9.2000 g, .500 SILVER, .0755 oz ASW
Obv: Toughra of Habibullah in wreath, star above.

| 832 | AH1319 | — | 8.00 | 12.00 | 25.00 | 70.00 |

NOTE: 2 varieties are known.

Obv: *Afghanistan* above small toughra, star at right. Rev: Large inverted pyramid dome.

833.1	AH1319	—	4.00	5.50	10.00	25.00
	1320	—	4.00	5.50	8.50	20.00
	1325	—	5.00	8.00	15.00	40.00

Obv: W/o star.

| 833.2 | AH1319 | — | 4.00 | 5.50 | 10.00 | 25.00 |
| | 1325 | — | 5.00 | 8.00 | 15.00 | 40.00 |

Obv: *Afghanistan* divided by a star above large toughra.

| 839 | AH1320 | — | 4.00 | 6.00 | 10.00 | 20.00 |

Rev: Small dome mosque.

KM#	Date	Mintage	VG	Fine	VF	XF
840.1	AH1320	—	5.00	8.00	15.00	35.00

Obv: Date in loop of toughra.

| 840.2 | AH1321 | — | 10.00 | 15.00 | 25.00 | 50.00 |

Rev: *Afghanistan* above mosque, crossed swords and cannons.

| 842.1 | AH1321 | — | 4.00 | 7.00 | 10.50 | 22.00 |
| | 1322 | — | 4.00 | 7.00 | 10.50 | 22.00 |

NOTE: 2 varieties exist for AH1321 date.

Rev: Crossed cannons.

842.2	AH1322	—	4.00	5.00	8.00	18.00
	1324	—	4.00	5.00	8.00	18.00
	1325	—	5.00	8.00	12.00	25.00
	1326	—	4.00	6.00	10.00	19.00
	1327	—	4.00	6.00	10.00	20.00
	1328	—	6.00	8.00	15.00	30.00
	1329	—	5.00	7.50	12.50	25.00

NOTE: 2 varieties exist for AH1328 date.

**Obv: Date divided 13 Arabic *j* 28.
Rev: Large dome mosque w/o *Afghanistan*.**

| 847.1 | AH1328 | — | 7.00 | 12.00 | 20.00 | 40.00 |

Obv: Date divided 132 Arabic *j* 8.

| 847.2 | AH1328 | — | 10.00 | 20.00 | 28.00 | 50.00 |

**Obv: Name and titles of Habibullah in wreath.
Rev: Mosque within sunburst.**

853	AH1329	—	4.00	6.00	10.00	18.50
	1330	—	4.00	6.00	9.00	15.00
	1331	—	4.00	6.00	9.00	15.00
	1332	—	4.00	6.00	9.00	15.00
	1333	—	4.00	6.00	9.00	15.00
	1334	—	4.00	6.00	9.00	15.00
	1335	—	4.00	6.00	9.00	15.00
	1337	—	4.00	6.00	10.00	18.50

NOTE: 2 varieties exist for AH1330, 1331 and 1337 and 3 varieties exist for AH1333. Thickness of obverse inscription and size of mosque dome on rev. vary.

Obv: Name and titles of Amanullah, star above inscription.

KM#	Date	Year	VG	Fine	VF	XF
867	AH1337	—	6.00	10.00	18.00	30.00

NOTE: 7 varieties are known.

**9.0000 g, .900 SILVER, .2604 oz ASW
Obv: *Al-Ghazi* above inscription.**

| 877 | SH1298 | (1919) | 4.50 | 6.50 | 10.00 | 18.50 |
| | 1299 | (1920) | 4.50 | 6.50 | 10.00 | 18.50 |

NOTE: 4 varieties are known for date SH1298. 2 varieties are known for date SH1299.

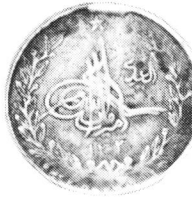 

**9.2500 g, .900 SILVER, .2676 oz ASW
Obv: Toughra of Amanullah.**

885	SH1299	(1920)	4.00	5.00	7.50	15.00
	1300	(1921)	4.00	5.00	7.50	15.00
	1301	(1922)	4.00	5.00	7.50	15.00
	1302	(1923)	4.00	5.00	7.50	15.00
	1303	(1924)	4.00	5.00	7.50	15.00

**9.1000 g, .900 SILVER, .2633 oz ASW
Obv: Name and titles of Amir Habibullah
(The Usurper).**

KM#	Date	Mintage	VG	Fine	VF	XF
897	AH1347	—	4.00	8.00	16.00	32.00

Obv: Title in circle.

| 898 | AH1347 | — | 25.00 | 35.00 | 55.00 | 90.00 |

2-1/2 RUPEES

22.9200 g, .900 SILVER, .6632 oz ASW

KM#	Date	Year	VG	Fine	VF	XF
878	SH1298	(1919)	12.50	16.50	20.00	40.00
	1299	(1920)	8.50	12.50	16.50	37.50
	1300	(1921)	8.50	12.50	16.50	37.50
	1301	(1922)	8.50	12.50	15.00	32.50
	1302	(1923)	8.50	12.50	15.00	32.50
	1303	(1924)	8.50	12.50	15.00	32.50

NOTE: 2 varieties each are known for dates SH 1298-1300.

5 RUPEES

45.6000 g, .900 SILVER, 1.3194 oz ASW
Rev: Similar to KM#826.

KM#	Date	Mintage	VG	Fine	VF	XF
834.1	AH1319	—	25.00	45.00	85.00	160.00

Obv: Date at left of toughra.

| 834.2 | AH1319 | — | 25.00 | 45.00 | 85.00 | 160.00 |

843	AH1322	—	20.00	25.00	38.00	80.00
	1323	—	Reported, not confirmed			
	1324	—	15.00	20.00	32.00	75.00
	1326	—	15.00	20.00	32.00	75.00
	1327/6	—	15.00	20.00	32.00	75.00
	1328	—	22.50	30.00	45.00	90.00
	1329	—	25.00	40.00	60.00	115.00

NOTE: Most dates are recut dies. 2 varieties are known for each date, AH1324 and 1327.

1/2 AMANI
(5 Rupees)

2.3000 g, .900 GOLD, .0665 oz AGW

KM#	Date	Year	VG	Fine	VF	XF
886	SH1299	(1920)	BV	45.00	65.00	100.00

TILLA
(10 Rupees)

4.6000 g, .900 GOLD, 19mm, .1331 oz AGW
Obv: Star above toughra.

KM#	Date	Mintage	VG	Fine	VF	XF
835	AH1319	—	70.00	95.00	140.00	240.00

Obv. leg: *Afghanistan* divided by star above toughra.

| 836.1 | AH1319 | — | 75.00 | 100.00 | 150.00 | 250.00 |

Obv. leg: *Afghanistan* above toughra w/star to right.

| 836.2 | AH1320 | — | 75.00 | 100.00 | 150.00 | 250.00 |

Obv: Date divided.

| A856 | AH1325 | — | 450.00 | 650.00 | 900.00 | |

Obv. leg: Name of *Habibullah.*

856	AH1335	—	170.00	200.00	260.00	330.00
	1336	—	100.00	120.00	175.00	240.00
	1337	—	110.00	130.00	180.00	220.00

Obv. leg: Name of *Amanullah.*
Rev: Crossed swords below mosque.

| 868.1 | AH1337 | — | 100.00 | 125.00 | 160.00 | 225.00 |

Rev: 6-pointed star below mosque.

| 868.2 | AH1337 | — | 100.00 | 135.00 | 175.00 | 250.00 |

AMANI
(10 Rupees)

4.6000 g, .900 GOLD, 22mm, .1331 oz AGW

KM#	Date	Year	VG	Fine	VF	XF
887	SH1299	(1920)	BV	60.00	80.00	140.00

2 TILLAS
(20 Rupees)

9.2000 g, .900 GOLD, 22mm, .2661 oz AGW

KM#	Date	Year	Fine	VF	XF	Unc
879	SH1298	(1919)	BV	140.00	240.00	380.00

2 AMANI
(20 Rupees)

9.2000 g, .900 GOLD, .2662 oz AGW

KM#	Date	Year	VG	Fine	VF	XF
888	SH1299	(1920)	BV	140.00	200.00	275.00
	1300	(1921)	BV	140.00	200.00	275.00
	1301	(1922)	BV	140.00	200.00	275.00
	1302	(1923)	BV	140.00	200.00	275.00
	1303	(1924)	BV	140.00	200.00	275.00

HABIBI
(30 Rupees)

4.6000 g, .900 GOLD, .1331 oz AGW

KM#	Date	Mintage	VG	Fine	VF	XF
899	AH1347	—	75.00	125.00	200.00	325.00

Obv: Small star replaces '30 Rupees' in leg.

| 900 | AH1347 | — | 75.00 | 125.00 | 200.00 | 325.00 |

5 AMANI
(50 Rupees)

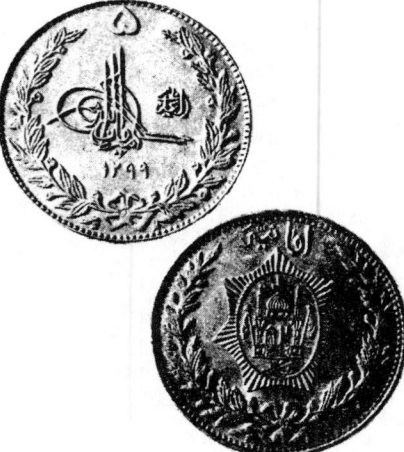

23.0000 g, .900 GOLD, 34mm, .6656 oz AGW
Obv: Persian *5* above toughra; *Al Ghazi* at right. Rev. leg: *Amaniya* above mosque.

KM#	Date	Year	VG	Fine	VF	XF
889	SH1299	(1920)	BV	400.00	675.00	1500.

Obv: Star above toughra. Rev: Persian *5* above mosque.

| 890 | SH1299 | (1920) | BV | 400.00 | 675.00 | 1500. |

60 RUPEES

6.9000 g, .900 GOLD, .1997 oz AGW

| 903 | AH1337 | — | — | 550.00 | 800.00 | 1600. |

DECIMAL COINAGE
100 Pul = 1 Afghani
20 Afghani = 1 Amani

PUL

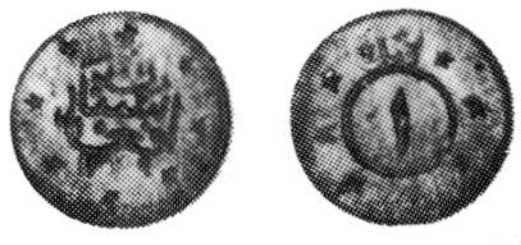

BRONZE or BRASS

KM#	Date	Year	Fine	VF	XF	Unc
A922	AH1349	—	.75	1.25	1.75	2.50

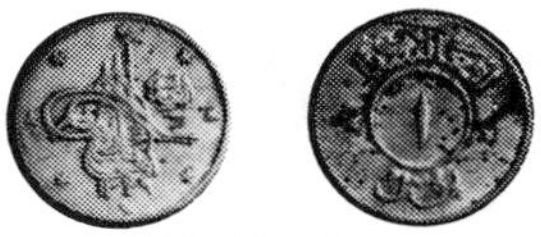

Obv: Toughra.

KM#	Date	Year	Fine	VF	XF	Unc
922	AH1349	—	100.00	250.00	300.00	400.00

NOTE: On these and many other Afghan copper coins, various alloys were used quite indiscriminately, depending upon what was immediately at hand. Thus one finds bronze, brass, and various shades in between. For this reason, bronze and brass coins are not given separate types, but are indicated as a single listing.

2 PUL

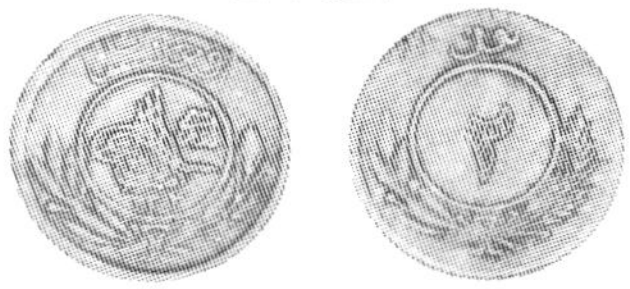

BRONZE or BRASS, 2.00 g

KM#	Date	Year	Fine	VF	XF	Unc
905	SH1304	(1925)	2.00	3.00	4.50	10.00
	1305	(1926)	2.00	3.00	4.50	10.00

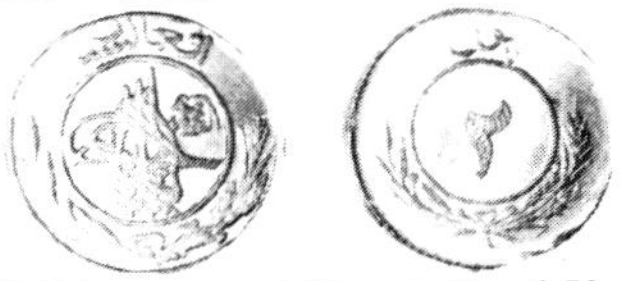

KM#	Date	Year	Fine	VF	XF	Unc
917	AH1348	—	1.25	2.50	3.50	8.00
	1349/8	—	1.25	2.50	3.50	8.00

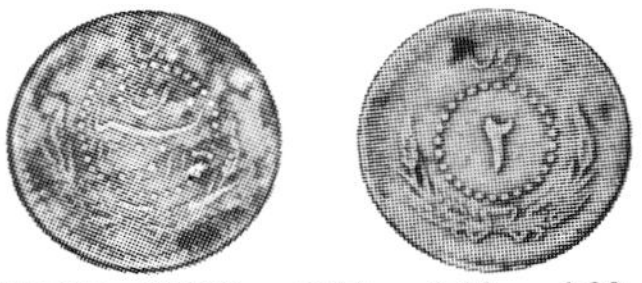

KM#	Date	Year	Fine	VF	XF	Unc
928	SH1311	(1932)	2.00	3.00	4.00	12.00
	1312	(1933)	1.50	2.25	3.00	10.00
	1313	(1934)	1.75	2.75	3.75	10.00
	1314	(1935)	2.00	3.00	4.00	12.00

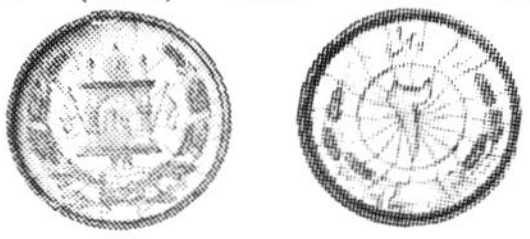

BRONZE

KM#	Date	Year	Fine	VF	XF	Unc
936	SH1316	(1937)	.15	.20	.35	1.00

3 PUL

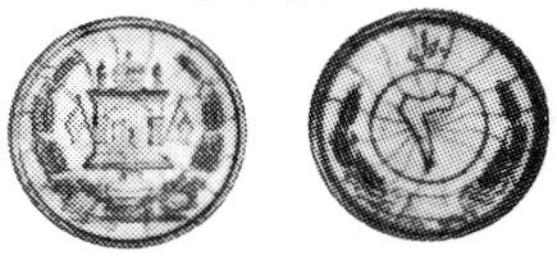

BRONZE

KM#	Date	Year	Fine	VF	XF	Unc
937	SH1316	(1937)	.35	.50	.75	2.00

5 PUL

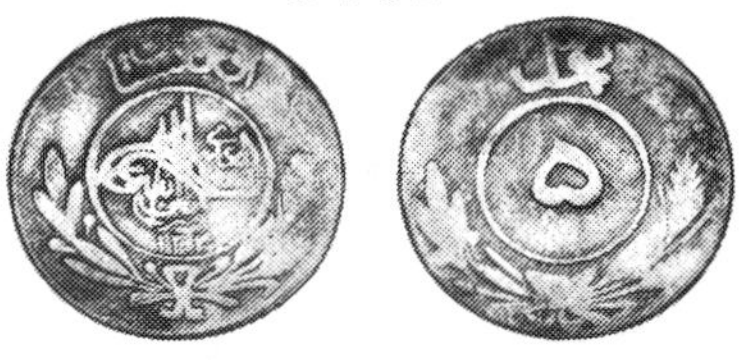

BRONZE or BRASS, 3.00 g

KM#	Date	Year	Fine	VF	XF	Unc
906	SH1304	(1925)	1.75	3.50	6.00	14.00
	1305	(1926)	1.50	3.00	5.50	14.00

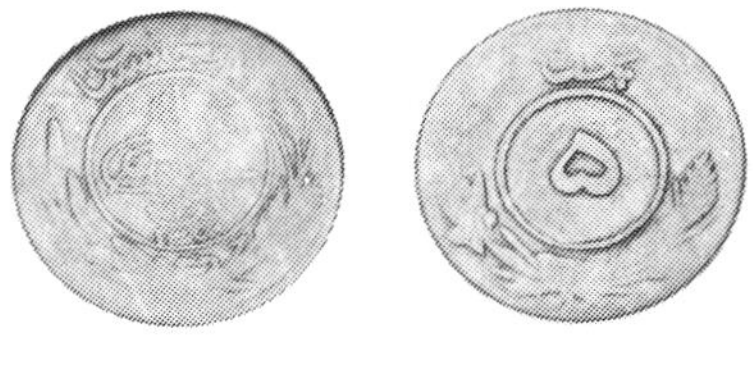

KM#	Date	Year	Fine	VF	XF	Unc
923	AH1349	—	1.75	2.75	4.50	12.50
	1350	—	1.25	2.25	3.50	12.50

NOTE: 2 varieties are known dated AH1350.

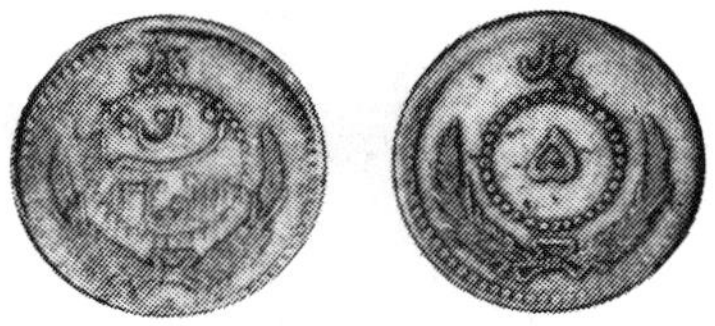

KM#	Date	Year	Fine	VF	XF	Unc
929	SH1311	(1932)	2.00	3.50	6.00	18.50
	1312	(1933)	2.00	3.50	6.00	18.50
	1313	(1934)	2.00	3.50	6.00	18.50
	1314	(1935)	2.00	3.50	6.00	18.50

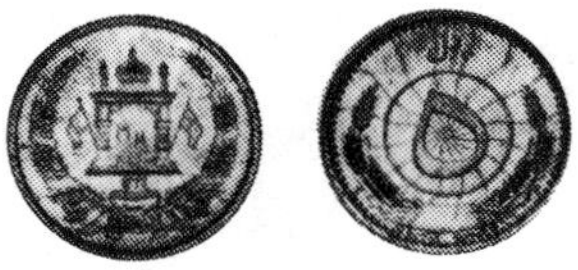

BRONZE

KM#	Date	Year	Fine	VF	XF	Unc
938	SH1316	(1937)	.35	.50	.75	2.00

10 PUL

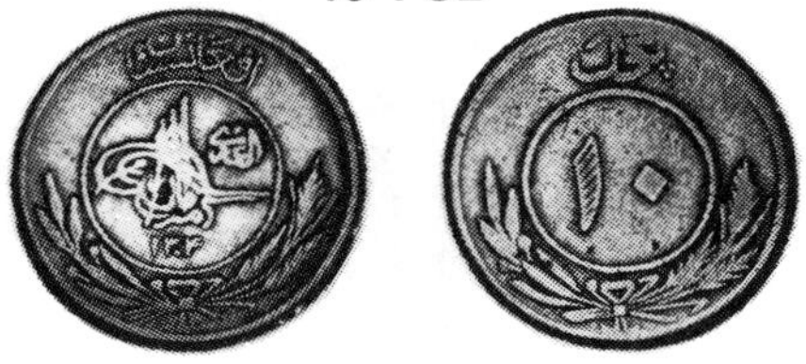

COPPER, 6.00 g

KM#	Date	Year	Fine	VF	XF	Unc
907	SH1304	(1925)	2.00	3.50	5.50	15.00
	1305	(1926)	2.50	4.00	6.00	20.00
	1306	(1927)	2.50	4.00	6.00	20.00
	ND	—	— Reported, not confirmed			

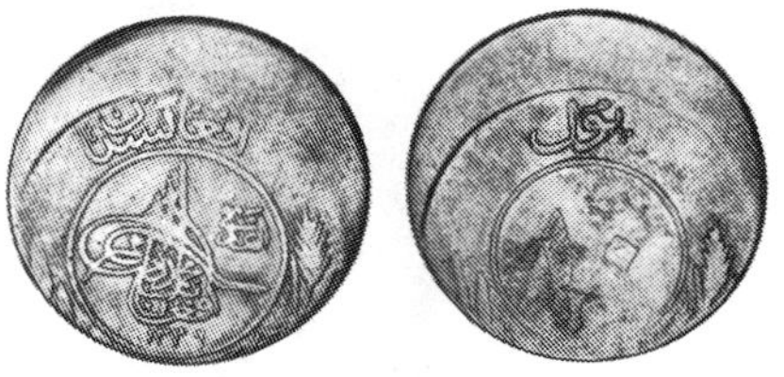

COPPER or BRASS

KM#	Date	Year	Fine	VF	XF	Unc
918	AH1348	—	2.00	3.50	5.00	15.00
	1349(2 vars.)		2.25	4.00	5.50	15.00

NOTE: Illustration shows an example struck off-center; prices are for properly struck specimens.

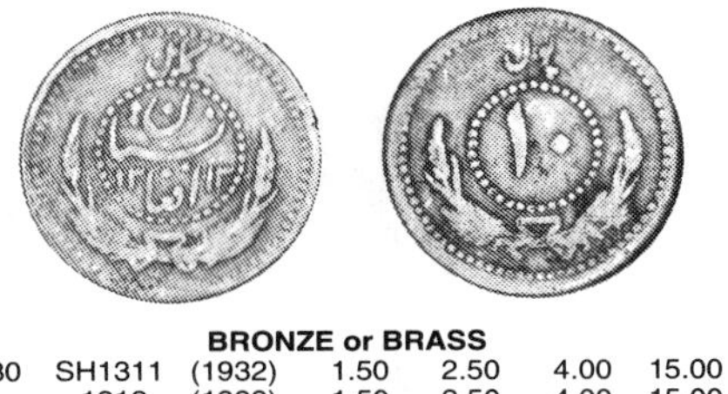

BRONZE or BRASS

KM#	Date	Year	Fine	VF	XF	Unc
930	SH1311	(1932)	1.50	2.50	4.00	15.00
	1312	(1933)	1.50	2.50	4.00	15.00
	1313	(1934)	1.50	2.50	4.00	15.00
	1314	(1935)	1.50	2.50	4.00	15.00

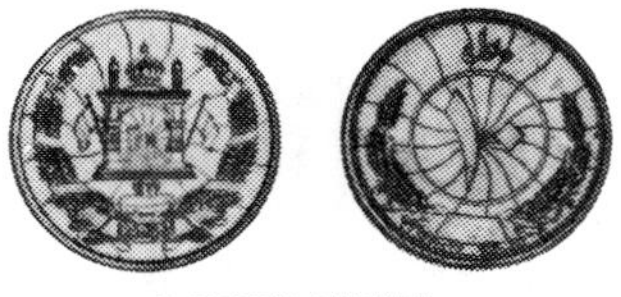

COPPER-NICKEL

KM#	Date	Year	Fine	VF	XF	Unc
939	SH1316	(1937)	.40	.65	1.00	3.00

20 PUL

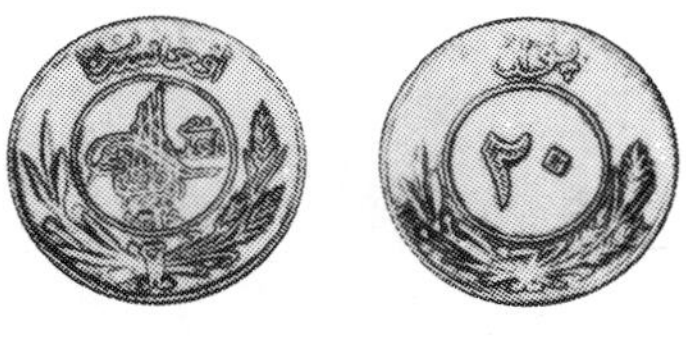

BILLON, 2.00 g

KM#	Date	Year	Fine	VF	XF	Unc
908	SH1304	(1925)	75.00	95.00	125.00	170.00
	134 (error)	—	—	—	—	—
	ND	—	60.00	85.00	110.00	160.00

NOTE: Varieties exist.

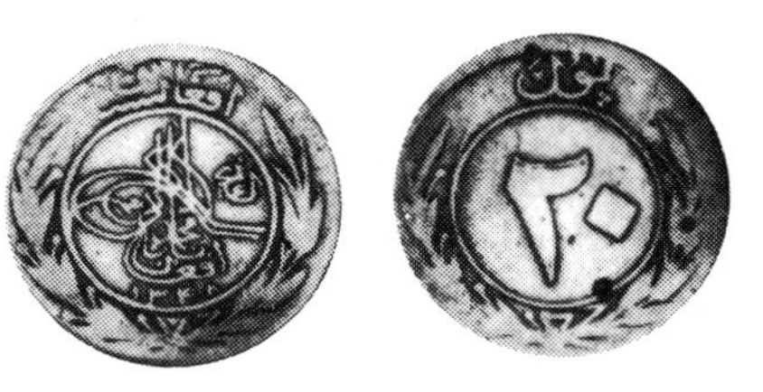

COPPER or BRASS

KM#	Date	Year	Fine	VF	XF	Unc
919	AH1348	—	2.00	4.00	10.00	22.00
	1349	—	3.00	5.00	12.00	25.00

25 PUL

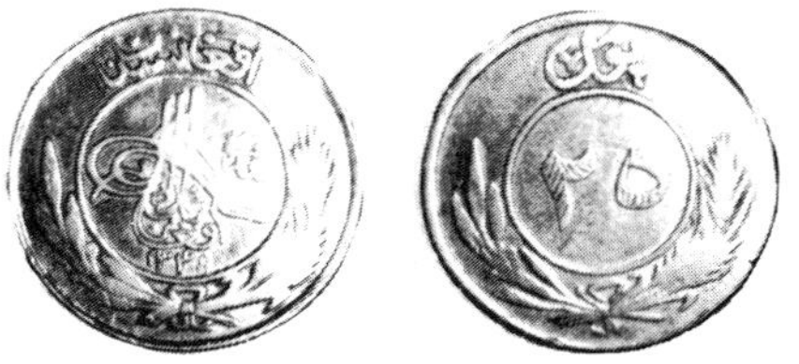

COPPER or BRASS

KM#	Date	Mintage	Fine	VF	XF	Unc
924	AH1349	—	2.00	3.50	9.00	18.00

NOTE: 2 varieties are known dated AH1349.

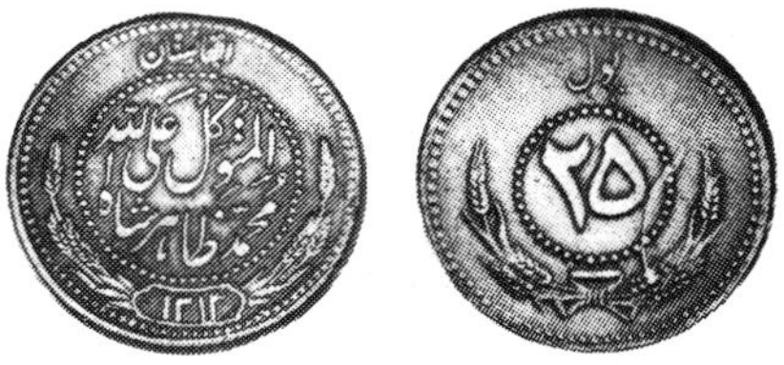

BRONZE or BRASS

KM#	Date	Year	Fine	VF	XF	Unc
931	SH1312	(1933)	1.50	2.50	9.00	15.00
	1313	(1934)	1.50	2.50	9.00	15.00
	1314	(1935)	1.75	2.75	12.00	17.50
	1315	(1936)	— Reported, not confirmed			
	1316	(1937)	1.75	2.75	4.00	17.50

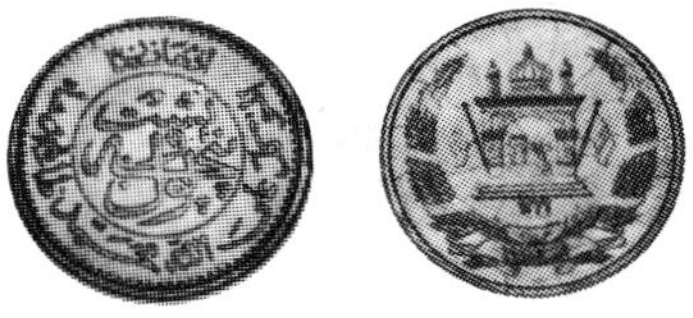

COPPER-NICKEL

KM#	Date	Year	Fine	VF	XF	Unc
940	SH1316	(1937)	.60	.75	1.25	3.00

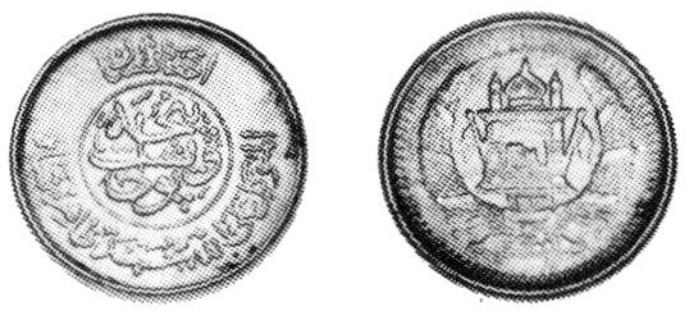

BRONZE

KM#	Date	Year	Fine	VF	XF	Unc
941	SH1330	(1951)	.15	.25	.50	1.00
	1331	(1952)	.15	.25	.50	1.00
	1332	(1953)	.15	.25	.50	1.00

NICKEL CLAD STEEL, 20mm, reeded edge

KM#	Date	Year	Fine	VF	XF	Unc
943	SH1331	(1952)	1.00	2.00	3.50	6.00
	1332	(1953)	1.50	3.00	5.00	7.50

Plain edge

KM#	Date	Year	Fine	VF	XF	Unc
944	SH1331	(1952)	.30	.50	.60	1.00
	1332	(1953)	.30	.50	.60	1.00
	1333	(1954)	.30	.50	.60	1.00
	1334	(1955)	.30	.50	.60	1.50

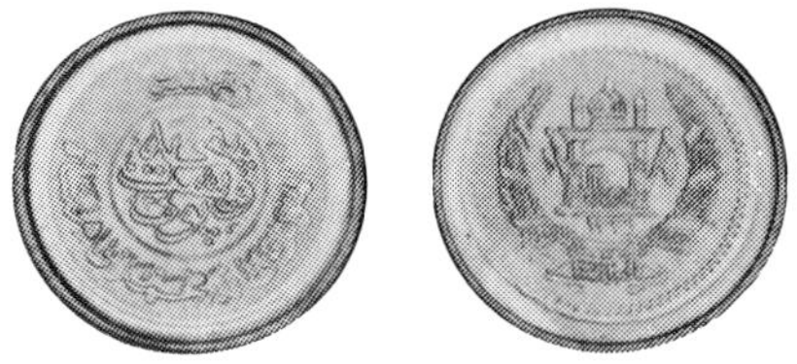

ALUMINUM

KM#	Date	Year	Fine	VF	XF	Unc
945	SH1331	(1952)	.50	1.00	3.00	10.00

NOTE: Struck on oversize 2 Afghani KM#949 planchets in 1970.

1/2 AFGHANI

(50 Pul)

5.0000 g, .500 SILVER, .0803 oz ASW
Obv: Date below toughra.

KM#	Date	Year	Fine	VF	XF	Unc
909	SH1304	7	2.00	3.50	6.50	18.50
	1305	8	2.00	3.50	6.50	18.50
	1306	9	2.00	3.50	6.50	18.50

NOTE: 2 varieties are known dated SH1304.

Rev: Date below mosque.

915	SH1307	10	3.00	5.50	10.00	30.00

920	AH1348	1	1.50	2.25	4.50	12.00
(919)	1349	2	1.50	2.25	4.50	12.00
	1350	3	1.50	2.25	4.50	12.00

4.7500 g, .500 SILVER, .0763 oz ASW

926	SH1310	(1931)	1.50	2.25	4.50	12.00
	1311	(1932)	1.50	2.25	4.50	12.00
	1312	(1933)	1.50	2.25	4.50	12.00

Obv: Smaller dotted circle.

932.1	SH1312	(1933)	1.75	2.50	5.00	12.50

Obv: Larger dotted circle.

932.2	SH1313	(1934)	1.75	2.50	5.00	12.50
	1314	(1935)	1.75	2.50	5.00	12.50
	1315	(1936)	1.50	2.25	4.50	12.00
	1316	(1937)	1.50	2.25	4.50	12.00

BRONZE, 22.5mm
Obv: Denomination in numerals.

942.1	SH1330	(1951)	.35	.55	.85	2.00
	133x	(195x)	.35	.55	.85	2.00

24mm

942.2	SH1330	(1951)	20.00	30.00	40.00	50.00

NICKEL CLAD STEEL

946	SH1331	(1952)	.20	.35	.65	2.00
	1332	(1953)	.20	.35	.65	2.00
	1333	(1954)	.30	.50	.85	3.00
	1334	(1955)	.20	.35	.65	2.00

Obv: Denomination in words.

KM#	Date	Year	Fine	VF	XF	Unc
947	SH1331	1952	.40	.65	.85	2.50

AFGHANI
(100 Pul)

10.0000 g, .900 SILVER, .2893 oz ASW
Obv: Date below toughra.

910	SH1304	7	3.00	6.00	12.00	28.00
	1305	8	3.00	6.00	12.00	28.00
	1305	9	3.00	6.00	12.00	28.00
	1306	9	3.00	6.00	12.00	28.00

NOTE: 3 varieties are known for date SH1304. 2 varieties each are known for dates SH1305-06.

Rev: Date below mosque.

916	SH1307	(1928)	— Reported, not confirmed

9.9500 g, .900 SILVER, .2879 oz ASW

921	AH1348	1	3.00	5.00	9.00	16.50
	1349	2	3.00	5.00	9.00	16.50
	1350	3	3.00	5.00	9.00	16.50

10.0000 g, .900 SILVER, .2893 oz ASW

927.1	SH1310	(1931)	50.00	65.00	80.00	115.00
	1311	(1932)	110.00	160.00	180.00	260.00

Thick flan, 22.5mm

927.2	SH1310	(1931)	250.00	375.00	500.00	700.00

NICKEL CLAD STEEL

953	SH1340	(1961)	.15	.20	.30	.50

2 AFGHANI

ALUMINUM

KM#	Date	Year	Fine	VF	XF	Unc
949	SH1337	(1958)	.60	1.00	1.50	2.00

NOTE: The above issue was withdrawn and demonetized due to extensive counterfeiting.

NICKEL CLAD STEEL
Coin type

954.1	SH1340	(1961)	.20	.30	.50	1.00

Medallic die orientation

954.2	SH1340	(1961)	.20	.30	.50	1.00

2-1/2 AFGHANI

25.0000 g, .900 SILVER, .7234 oz ASW

913	SH1305	8	15.00	25.00	50.00	125.00
	1306	9	15.00	20.00	40.00	80.00

NOTE: 2 varieties are known for each date.

5 AFGHANI

ALUMINUM

950	SH1337	(1958)	1.00	1.75	2.25	3.00

NOTE: The above issue was withdrawn and demonetized due to extensive counterfeiting.

NICKEL CLAD STEEL
Shah Mohammed Sahir

955	SH1340					
	AH1381		.25	.40	.75	1.50

10 AFGHANI

ALUMINUM

KM#	Date	Year	Fine	VF	XF	Unc
948	SH1336	(1957)	—	—	—	900.00

1/2 AMANI

3.0000 g, .900 GOLD, .0868 oz AGW

KM#	Date	Year	Fine	VF	XF	Unc
911	SH1304	7	BV	40.00	60.00	100.00
	1305	8	BV	40.00	60.00	100.00
	1306	9	BV	40.00	60.00	100.00

4 GRAMS

4.0000 g, .900 GOLD, .1157 oz AGW

KM#	Date	Year	Fine	VF	XF	Unc
935	SH1315	(1936)	BV	75.00	100.00	160.00
	1317	(1938)	BV	75.00	100.00	160.00

AMANI

6.0000 g, .900 GOLD, .1736 oz AGW

KM#	Date	Year	Fine	VF	XF	Unc
912	SH1304	7	BV	90.00	110.00	160.00
	1305	8	BV	90.00	130.00	200.00
	1306	9	BV	90.00	110.00	160.00

20 AFGHANI

6.0000 g, .900 GOLD, .1736 oz AGW

KM#	Date	Year	Fine	VF	XF	Unc
925	AH1348	—	125.00	175.00	200.00	300.00
	1349	2	BV	110.00	165.00	240.00
	1350	3	BV	110.00	165.00	240.00

TILLA

6.0000 g, .900 GOLD, .1736 oz AGW

KM#	Date	Year	Fine	VF	XF	Unc
933	SH1313	(1934)	125.00	150.00	175.00	250.00

8 GRAMS

8.0000 g, .900 GOLD, .2314 oz AGW

KM#	Date	Year	Fine	VF	XF	Unc
934	SH1314	(1935)	BV	130.00	175.00	240.00
	1315	(1936)	BV	130.00	175.00	240.00
	1317	(1938)	BV	130.00	175.00	240.00

KM#	Date	Year Mintage	VF	XF	Unc
952	SH1339				
		AH1380 200 pcs.	—	300.00	800.00

NOTE: Struck for royal presentation purposes. Specimens struck with the same dies (including the "8 grams", the "8" having been effaced after striking), but on thin planchets weighing 3.9-4 grams, exist. They are regarded as "mint sports". Market value $300.00 in unc.

2-1/2 AMANI

15.0000 g, .900 GOLD, .4340 oz AGW

KM#	Date	Year	Fine	VF	XF	Unc
914	SH1306	9	1500.	2000.	2750.	3500.

REPUBLIC

SH1352-1357/1973-1978AD

25 PUL

BRASS CLAD STEEL

KM#	Date	Mintage	Fine	VF	XF	Unc
975	SH1352					
		45.950	.25	.50	1.00	2.00

50 PUL

COPPER CLAD STEEL

KM#	Date	Mintage	Fine	VF	XF	Unc
976	SH1352					
		24.750	.50	1.00	2.00	4.00

5 AFGHANI

COPPER-NICKEL CLAD STEEL

KM#	Date	Mintage	Fine	VF	XF	Unc
977	SH1352					
		34.750	1.75	3.50	5.00	10.00

DEMOCRATIC REPUBLIC

SH1358-1371/1979-1992

MINT MARK
(K) - Key/* = Havana, Cuba

25 PUL

ALUMINUM-BRONZE

KM#	Date	Year	Fine	VF	XF	Unc
990	SH1357	(1978)	.25	.50	1.00	2.00

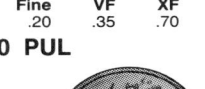

KM#	Date	Year	Fine	VF	XF	Unc
996	SH1359	(1980)	.20	.35	.70	1.50

50 PUL

ALUMINUM-BRONZE, 3.00 g

KM#	Date	Year	Fine	VF	XF	Unc
992	SH1357	(1978)	.50	.80	1.50	2.50

| 997 | SH1359 | (1980) | .25 | .50 | 1.00 | 2.00 |

AFGHANI

COPPER-NICKEL

KM#	Date	Year	Fine	VF	XF	Unc
993	SH1357	(1978)	.60	1.00	2.00	4.00

| 998 | SH1359 | (1980) | .50 | .80 | 1.50 | 2.50 |

2 AFGHANIS

COPPER-NICKEL

KM#	Date	Year	Fine	VF	XF	Unc
994	SH1357	(1978)	1.00	1.50	2.00	4.00
	1358	(1979)	1.00	1.50	2.00	4.00

Obv: Similar to 1 Afghani, KM#998.

| 999 | SH1359 | (1980) | .60 | 1.00 | 1.50 | 3.00 |

5 AFGHANIS

COPPER-NICKEL, 7.40 g

KM#	Date	Year	Fine	VF	XF	Unc
995	SH1357	(1978)	1.00	2.00	4.00	6.50

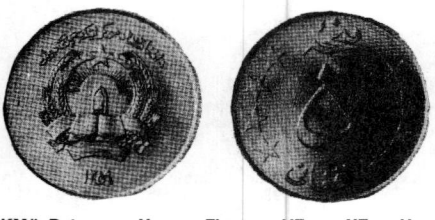

KM#	Date	Year	Fine	VF	XF	Unc
1000	SH1359	(1980)	1.00	1.50	2.00	4.00

BRASS
F.A.O. Issue - World Food Day

| 1001 | SH1360 | (1981) | .25 | .50 | 1.00 | 1.50 |

10 AFGHANIS

BRASS
70th Anniversary of Independence

KM#	Date	Mintage	Fine	VF	XF	Unc
1015	1989	—	—	—	—	3.50

50 AFGHANIS

COPPER-NICKEL
100 Years of the Automobile

| 1016 | ND(1986) | — | — | — | — | 14.00 |

World Wildlife Fund - Leopard

| 1006 | 1987 | .028 | — | — | — | 12.00 |

ALBANIA

The Republic of Albania, a Balkan republic bounded by Macedonia, Greece, Montenegro, and the Adriatic Sea, has an area of 11,100 sq. mi. (28,748 sq. km.) and a population of 3.4 million. Capital: Tirane. The country is predominantly agricultural, although recent progress has been made in the manufacturing and mining sectors. Petroleum, chrome, iron, copper, cotton textiles, tobacco and wood products are exported.

Since it had been part of the Greek and Roman empires little is known of the early history of Albania. After the disintegration of the Roman Empire, Albania was overrun by Goths, Byzantines, Venetians, and Turks. Skanderbeg, the national hero, resisted the Turks and established an independent Albania in 1443, but in 1468 the country again fell to the Turks and remained part of the Ottoman Empire for more than 400 years.

Independence was re-established by revolt in 1912, and the present borders established in 1913 by a conference of European powers which, in 1914, placed Prince William of Wied on the throne; popular discontent forced his abdication within months. In 1920, following World War I occupancy by several nations, a republic was set up. Ahmed Zogu seized the presidency in 1925, and in 1928 proclaimed himself king with the title of Zog I. King Zog fled when Italy occupied Albania in 1939 and enthroned King Victor Emanuel of Italy. Upon the surrender of Italy to the Allies in 1943, German troops occupied the country. They withdrew in 1944, and communist partisans seized power, naming Gen. Enver Hoxha provisional president. In 1946, following a victory by the communist front in the 1945 elections, a new constitution modeled on that of the USSR was adopted. In accordance with the constitution of Dec. 28, 1976, the official name of Albania was changed from the Peoples Republic of Albania to the Peoples Socialist Republic of Albania.

Albania's former Communists were routed in elections. March, 1992, amid economic collapse and social unrest. Sali Berisha was elected as the first non-communist president since World War II. Rexhep Mejdani, elected president in 1997, succeeds him.

RULERS
Ahmed Bey Zogu - King Zog I, 1928-1939
Vittorio Emanuele III, 1939-1943

MINT MARKS
L - London
R - Rome
V - Vienna

MONETARY SYSTEM
100 Qindar Leku = 1 Lek
100 Qindar Ari = 1 Franga Ari = 5 Lek

KINGDOM
5 QINDAR LEKU

BRONZE

KM#	Date	Mintage	Fine	VF	XF	Unc
1	1926R	.512	18.00	40.00	70.00	140.00

QINDAR AR

BRONZE

| 14 | 1935R | 2.000 | 2.50 | 6.00 | 12.00 | 20.00 |

10 QINDAR LEKU

BRONZE

KM#	Date	Mintage	Fine	VF	XF	Unc
2	1926R	.511	12.00	27.00	60.00	120.00

2 QINDAR AR

BRONZE

| 15 | 1935R | 1.500 | 3.50 | 10.00 | 17.00 | 30.00 |

1/4 LEKU

 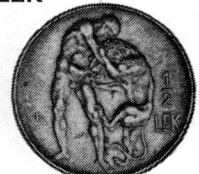

NICKEL

| 3 | 1926R | .506 | 3.50 | 8.00 | 17.00 | 32.00 |
| | 1927R | .756 | 3.50 | 8.00 | 15.00 | 30.00 |

1/2 LEK

NICKEL

| 4 | 1926R | 1.002 | 3.00 | 6.00 | 14.00 | 25.00 |

13	1930V	.500	3.00	5.50	11.00	20.00
	1931L	.500	3.00	5.50	11.00	20.00
	1931L	—	—	—	Proof	—

LEK

NICKEL

5	1926R	1.004	2.00	4.00	10.00	25.00
	1927R	.506	3.00	7.00	16.00	32.00
	1930V	1.250	1.50	3.00	6.00	22.00
	1931L	1.000	2.00	4.00	10.00	25.00
	1931L	—	—	—	Proof	—

FRANG AR

5.0000 g, .835 SILVER, .1342 oz ASW

6	1927R	.100	60.00	100.00	160.00	300.00
	1927V	.050	—	Reported, not confirmed		
	1928R	.060	60.00	110.00	170.00	300.00

| 16 | 1935R | .700 | 6.00 | 12.00 | 25.00 | 65.00 |
| | 1937R | .600 | 6.00 | 14.00 | 30.00 | 75.00 |

25th Anniversary of Independence

KM#	Date	Mintage	Fine	VF	XF	Unc
18	1937R	.050	8.00	16.00	35.00	80.00

2 FRANGA AR

10.0000 g, .835 SILVER, .2684 oz ASW

7	1926R	.050	50.00	115.00	230.00	320.00
	1927R	.050	60.00	140.00	250.00	350.00
	1928R	.060	50.00	115.00	230.00	320.00

17	1935R	.150	10.00	30.00	70.00	120.00

25th Anniversary of Independence

19	1937R	.025	13.00	28.00	55.00	110.00

5 FRANGA AR

25.0000 g, .900 SILVER, .7234 oz ASW

8.1	1926R	.060	80.00	190.00	390.00	550.00
	1927V	*.040	—	—	—	—

*NOTE: Only exist as provas.

Obv: Star below bust.

8.2	1926R	Inc. Ab.	120.00	290.00	470.00	650.00

ITALIAN OCCUPATION WW II
MONETARY SYSTEM
1 Lek = 1 Lira

0.05 LEK

ALUMINUM-BRONZE

KM#	Date	Mintage	Fine	VF	XF	Unc
27	1940R	1.400	3.00	6.00	14.00	25.00
	1941R	.200	—	—	Rare	—

0.10 LEK

ALUMINUM-BRONZE

28	1940R	.550	4.00	8.00	18.00	30.00
	1941R	.250	18.00	47.00	85.00	140.00

NOTE: 1939 dated coins of KM#29-32 exist in 2 varieties, magnetic and non-magnetic.

0.20 LEK

STAINLESS STEEL

29	1939R	.900	1.00	4.00	8.00	14.00
	1940R	.700	1.00	2.00	4.00	12.00
	1941R	1.400	1.00	2.00	4.00	12.00

0.50 LEK

STAINLESS STEEL

30	1939R	.100	1.50	4.00	8.00	20.00
	1940R	.500	1.50	3.00	6.00	16.00
	1941R	.900	1.50	3.00	7.00	18.00

LEK

STAINLESS STEEL

31	1939R	2.100	1.00	2.00	4.00	14.00
	1940R	—	—	—	Rare	—
	1941R	—	—	—	Rare	—

NOTE: Coins dated after 1939 were not struck for circulation.

2 LEK

STAINLESS STEEL

32	1939R	1.300	2.00	4.00	8.00	18.00
	1940R	—	—	—	Rare	—
	1941R	—	—	—	Rare	—

NOTE: Coins dated after 1939 were not struck for circulation.

5 LEK

5.0000 g, .835 SILVER, .1342 oz ASW

KM#	Date	Mintage	Fine	VF	XF	Unc
33	1939R	1.350	6.00	12.00	30.00	65.00

10 LEK

10.0000 g, .835 SILVER, .2684 oz ASW

34	1939R	.175	40.00	80.00	125.00	235.00

PEOPLES SOCIALIST REPUBLIC
MONETARY SYSTEM
100 Qindarka = 1 Lek

5 QINDARKA

ALUMINUM

39	1964	—	.10	.25	.50	1.25

25th Anniversary of Liberation

44	ND(1969)	—	.10	.20	.30	.85

Plain edges.

71	1988	—	—	—	—	.50

10 QINDARKA

ALUMINUM

40	1964	—	.15	.30	.60	1.50

25th Anniversary of Liberation

45	ND(1969)	—	.10	.20	.35	1.00

60	1988	—	—	—	—	.60

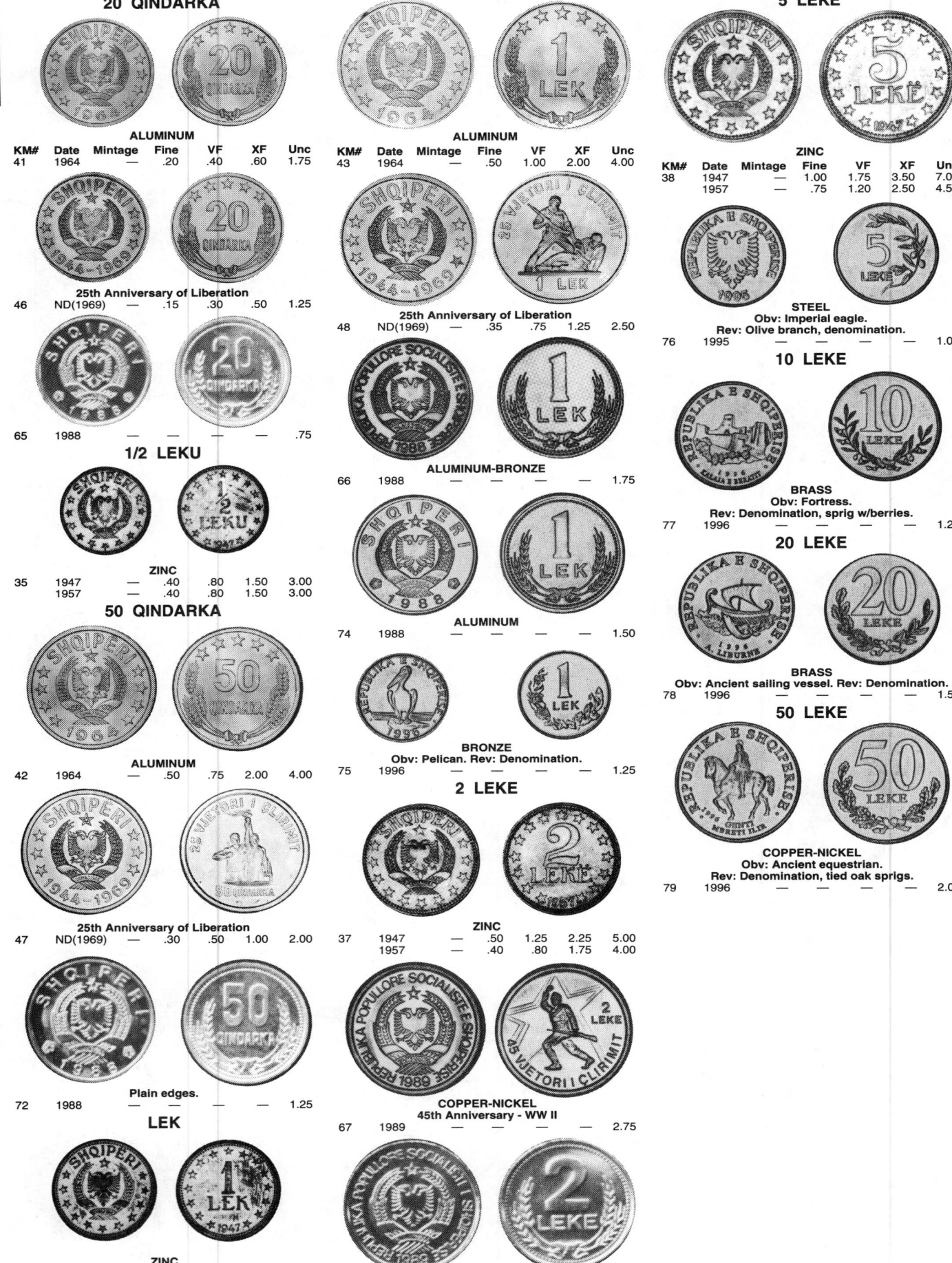

20 QINDARKA

ALUMINUM

KM#	Date	Mintage	Fine	VF	XF	Unc
41	1964	—	.20	.40	.60	1.75

25th Anniversary of Liberation

| 46 | ND(1969) | — | .15 | .30 | .50 | 1.25 |
| 65 | 1988 | — | — | — | — | .75 |

1/2 LEKU

ZINC

| 35 | 1947 | — | .40 | .80 | 1.50 | 3.00 |
| | 1957 | — | .40 | .80 | 1.50 | 3.00 |

50 QINDARKA

ALUMINUM

| 42 | 1964 | — | .50 | .75 | 2.00 | 4.00 |

25th Anniversary of Liberation

| 47 | ND(1969) | — | .30 | .50 | 1.00 | 2.00 |

Plain edges.

| 72 | 1988 | — | — | — | — | 1.25 |

LEK

ZINC

| 36 | 1947 | — | .60 | 1.00 | 2.00 | 4.50 |
| | 1957 | — | .50 | 1.00 | 1.75 | 4.00 |

ALUMINUM

KM#	Date	Mintage	Fine	VF	XF	Unc
43	1964	—	.50	1.00	2.00	4.00

25th Anniversary of Liberation

| 48 | ND(1969) | — | .35 | .75 | 1.25 | 2.50 |

ALUMINUM-BRONZE

| 66 | 1988 | — | — | — | — | 1.75 |

ALUMINUM

| 74 | 1988 | — | — | — | — | 1.50 |

BRONZE
Obv: Pelican. Rev: Denomination.

| 75 | 1996 | — | — | — | — | 1.25 |

2 LEKE

ZINC

| 37 | 1947 | — | .50 | 1.25 | 2.25 | 5.00 |
| | 1957 | — | .40 | .80 | 1.75 | 4.00 |

COPPER-NICKEL
45th Anniversary - WW II

| 67 | 1989 | — | — | — | — | 2.75 |
| 73 | 1989 | — | — | — | — | 2.50 |

5 LEKE

ZINC

KM#	Date	Mintage	Fine	VF	XF	Unc
38	1947	—	1.00	1.75	3.50	7.00
	1957	—	.75	1.20	2.50	4.50

STEEL
Obv: Imperial eagle.
Rev: Olive branch, denomination.

| 76 | 1995 | — | — | — | — | 1.00 |

10 LEKE

BRASS
Obv: Fortress.
Rev: Denomination, sprig w/berries.

| 77 | 1996 | — | — | — | — | 1.25 |

20 LEKE

BRASS
Obv: Ancient sailing vessel. Rev: Denomination.

| 78 | 1996 | — | — | — | — | 1.50 |

50 LEKE

COPPER-NICKEL
Obv: Ancient equestrian.
Rev: Denomination, tied oak sprigs.

| 79 | 1996 | — | — | — | — | 2.00 |

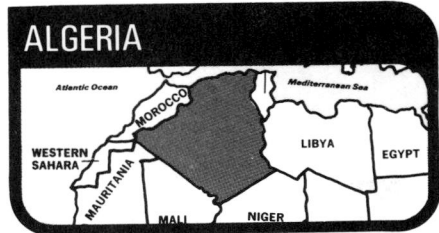

ALGERIA

The Democratic and Popular Republic of Algeria, a North African country fronting on the Mediterranean Sea between Tunisia and Morocco, has an area of 919,595 sq. mi. (2,381,740 sq. km.) and a population of 28.5 million. Capital: Algiers (Alger). Most of the country's working population is engaged in agriculture although a recent industrial diversification, financed by oil revenues, is making steady progress. Wines, fruits, iron and zinc ores, phosphates, tobacco products, liquified natural gas, and petroleum are exported.

Algiers, the capital and chief seaport of Algeria, was the site of Phoenician and Roman settlements before the present Moslem city was founded about 950. Nominally part of the sultanate of Tilimsan, Algiers had a large measure of independence under the amirs of its own. In 1492 the Jews and Moors who had been expelled from Spain settled in Algiers and enjoyed an increasing influence until the imposition of Turkish control in 1518. For the following three centuries Algiers was the headquarters of the notorious Barbary pirates as Turkish control became more and more nominal. The French took Algiers in 1830, and after a long and wearisome war completed the conquest of Algeria and annexed it to France, 1848. Following the armistice signed by France and Nazi Germany on June 22, 1940, Algeria fell under Vichy Government control until liberated by the Allied invasion forces under the command of Gen. D.D. Eisenhower on Nov. 8, 1942. The inability to obtain equal rights with Frenchmen led to an organized revolt which began on Nov. 1, 1954 and lasted until a ceasefire was signed on July I, 1962. Independence was proclaimed on July 5, 1962, following a self-determination referendum, and the Republic was declared on September 25, 1962.

FRENCH OCCUPATION

Until July, 1962

MINT MARKS

(a) Paris - Privy marks only

MONETARY SYSTEM

100 Centimes = 1 Franc

20 FRANCS

COPPER-NICKEL

KM#	Date	Mintage	Fine	VF	XF	Unc
91	1949(a)	25.556	.50	1.00	3.50	8.50
	1956(a)	7.500	.50	1.00	5.00	12.50

50 FRANCS

COPPER-NICKEL

KM#	Date	Mintage	Fine	VF	XF	Unc
92	1949(a)	18.000	1.50	3.00	9.00	18.00

100 FRANCS

COPPER-NICKEL

KM#	Date	Mintage	Fine	VF	XF	Unc
93	1950(a)	22.189	1.50	3.00	10.00	20.00
	1952(a)	12.000	2.00	4.00	12.00	25.00

NOTE: During World War II homeland coins were struck at the Paris Mint and the French 2 Francs, Y#89 were struck at the Philadelphia Mint for use in French African Territories.

REPUBLIC

MONETARY SYSTEM

100 Centimes = 1 Dinar

CENTIME

ALUMINUM

KM#	Date	Year Mintage	VF	XF	Unc
94	AH1383	1964 35.000	.10	.20	.45

2 CENTIMES

ALUMINUM

KM#	Date	Year Mintage	VF	XF	Unc
95	AH1383	1964 50.000	.10	.20	.60

5 CENTIMES

ALUMINUM

KM#	Date	Year Mintage	VF	XF	Unc
96	AH1383	1964 40.000	.15	.30	.75

1st Four Year Plan and F.A.O. Issue

KM#	Date	Mintage	VF	XF	Unc
101	ND(1970)	10.000	.10	.20	.50

NOTE: Varieties exist.

2nd Four Year Plan and F.A.O. Issue

KM#	Date	Mintage	VF	XF	Unc
106	ND(1974)	10.000	.10	.20	.50

1st Five Year Plan and F.A.O. Issue

KM#	Date	Mintage	VF	XF	Unc
113	ND(1980)	—	.20	.50	1.50

2nd Five Year Plan and F.A.O. Issue

KM#	Date	Mintage	VF	XF	Unc
116	ND(1985)	—	.10	.25	.70

NOTE: Varieties exist.

10 CENTIMES

ALUMINUM-BRONZE

KM#	Date	Year Mintage	VF	XF	Unc
97	AH1383	1964 —	.10	.20	.65

ALUMINUM

KM#	Date	Mintage	VF	XF	Unc
115	1984	—	.10	.25	.60

NOTE: Varieties exist.

20 CENTIMES

ALUMINUM-BRONZE

KM#	Date	Year Mintage	VF	XF	Unc
98	AH1383	1964 —	.20	.50	1.50

BRASS

Agricultural Revolution and F.A.O. Issue

KM#	Date	Mintage	VF	XF	Unc
103	1972	20.000	.10	.25	.75

ALUMINUM-BRONZE
F.A.O. Issue

107.1	1975	50.000	.15	.30	1.50

Obv: Small flower above 20.

107.2	1975	Inc. Ab.	.15	.30	1.50

F.A.O. Issue

118	1987	60.000	.15	.30	1.50

50 CENTIMES

ALUMINUM-BRONZE

KM#	Date	Year Mintage	VF	XF	Unc
99	AH1383	1964 —	.20	.35	1.00

COPPER-NICKEL-ZINC

KM#	Date	Year	Mintage	VF	XF	Unc
102	AH1391	1971	10.000	.15	.30	1.00
	1393	1973	—	.15	.30	1.00

BRASS
30th Anniversary French-Algerian Clash

KM#	Date	Mintage	VF	XF	Unc
109	ND(1975)	18.000	.20	.50	2.00

ALUMINUM-BRONZE
1400th Anniversary of Mohammad's Flight

KM#	Date	Year	Mintage	VF	XF	Unc
111	AH1400	1980	—	.20	.50	2.50
	1401	1981	—	.20	.50	2.50

25th Anniversary of Constitution

KM#	Date	Mintage	VF	XF	Unc
119	1988	—	.15	.35	2.00

1/4 DINAR

ALUMINUM
Fennec Fox

KM#	Date	Year	Mintage	VF	XF	Unc
127	AH1413	1992	—	.50	1.00	2.00
	1413	1992	—	—	Proof	12.00

1/2 DINAR

STEEL
Barbary Horse

128	AH1413	1992	—	.65	1.25	2.50
	1413	1992	—	—	Proof	12.00

DINAR

COPPER-NICKEL

100	AH1383	1964	15.000	.40	.80	1.75

F.A.O. Issue

KM#	Date	Mintage	VF	XF	Unc
104.1	1972	20.000	.45	.85	2.50

Legend touches inner circle.

104.2	1972	Inc. Ab.	.45	.85	2.50

20th Anniversary of Independence

112	ND(1983)	—	.75	1.50	4.50

25th Anniversary of Independence - Monument

117	1987	—	.65	1.25	4.00

STEEL
Prehistoric Buffalo

KM#	Date	Year	Mintage	VF	XF	Unc
129	AH1413	1992	—	1.00	2.00	4.50
	1413	1992	—	—	Proof	15.00
	1417	1997	—	—	2.00	4.50

2 DINARS

STEEL
Camel's Head

130	AH1413	1992	—	1.00	2.50	5.00
	1413	1992	—	—	Proof	18.00

5 DINARS

12.0000 g, .750 SILVER, .2893 oz ASW
Privy mark: Owl
10th Anniversary & F.A.O. Issue

KM#	Date	Mintage	VF	XF	Unc
105	ND(1972)(a)	—	5.00	10.00	16.50

NICKEL

KM#	Date	Mintage	VF	XF	Unc
105a.1	ND(1972)(a)	—	3.50	7.00	12.50

Privy mark: Dolphin

105a.2	ND(1972)(a)	—	3.50	7.00	12.50
	ND(1974)(a)	—	3.50	7.00	12.50

20th Anniversary of Revolution

108	ND(1974)	—	3.50	7.00	12.50

30th Anniversary of Revolution

114	ND(1984)	—	3.50	7.00	12.50

 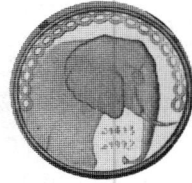

STEEL
Obv: Denomination. Rev: Elephant.

KM#	Date	Year	Mintage	VF	XF	Unc
123	AH1413	1992	—	1.50	3.50	6.50
	1413	1992	—	—	Proof	20.00

10 DINARS

ALUMINUM-BRONZE, 11.37 g

KM#	Date	Mintage	VF	XF	Unc
110	1979	25.001	3.00	5.00	9.00
	1981(a)	40.000	3.00	5.00	9.00

ALUMINUM center in STEEL ring
Obv: Denomination. Rev: Falcon.

KM#	Date	Year	Mintage	VF	XF	Unc
124	AH1413	1992	—	2.00	5.00	8.50
	1413	1992	—	—	Proof	22.00

20 DINARS

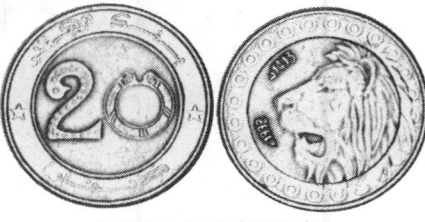

BRASS center in STEEL ring

Obv: Denomination. Rev: Lion.

KM#	Date	Year	Mintage	VF	XF	Unc
125	AH1413	1992	—	3.00	7.00	12.50
	1413	1992	—	—	Proof	28.00
	1417	1997	—	—	7.00	12.50

50 DINARS

STEEL center in BRASS ring
Obv: Denomination. Rev: Gazelle.

126	AH1413	1992	—	4.00	9.00	16.50
	1413	1992	—	—	Proof	35.00
	1416	1996	—	4.00	9.00	16.50

40th Anniversary - Revolution

131	ND(1994)	—	—	5.00	10.00	17.50

100 DINARS

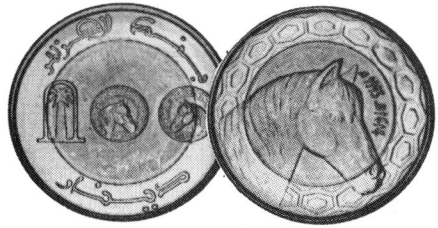

**ALUMINUM-BRONZE center
in STAINLESS STEEL ring
Obv: Denomination stylized w/rev. design.
Rev: Horse head.**

132	AH1413	1992	—	7.00	15.00	25.00
	1414	1993	—	7.00	15.00	25.00
	1417	1997	—	7.00	15.00	25.00

ANGOLA

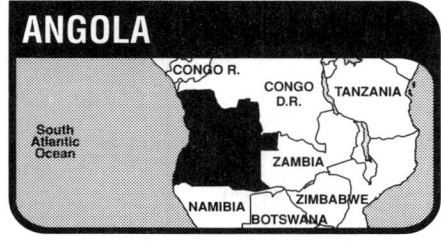

The Republic of Angola, a country on the west coast of southern Africa bounded by Zaire, Zambia, and Namibia (South-West Africa), has an area of 481,354 sq. mi. (1,246,700 sq. km.) and a population of 10.1 million, predominantly Bantu in origin. Capital: Luanda. Most of the people are engaged in subsistence agriculture. However, important oil and mineral deposits make Angola potentially one of the richest countries in Africa. Iron and diamonds are exported.

Angola was discovered by Portuguese navigator Diogo Cao in 1482. Portuguese settlers arrived in 1491, and established Angola as a major slaving center which sent about 3 million slaves to the New World.

A revolt, characterized by guerrilla warfare, against Portuguese rule began in 1961 and continued until 1974, when a new regime in Portugal offered independence. The independence movement was actively supported by three groups, the National Front, based in Zaire, the Soviet-backed Popular Movement, and the moderate National Union. Independence was proclaimed on Nov. 11, 1975, and the Portuguese departed, leaving the Angolan people to work out their own political destiny. Within hours, each of the independence groups proclaimed itself Angola's sole ruler. A bloody intertribal civil war erupted in which the Communist Popular Movement, assisted by Soviet arms and Cuban mercenaries, was the eventual victor.

RULERS
Portuguese until 1975

MINT MARKS
KN - King's Norton

MONETARY SYSTEM
100 Centavos = 20 Macutas = 1 Escudo
100 Centavos = 1 Escudo

CENTAVO

BRONZE

KM#	Date	Mintage	Fine	VF	XF	Unc
60	1921	1.360	7.50	12.50	30.00	60.00

2 CENTAVOS

BRONZE

61	1921	.530	10.00	15.00	50.00	100.00

5 CENTAVOS
(1 Macuta)

BRONZE

62	1921	.720	5.00	10.00	30.00	75.00
	1922	5.680	4.00	8.00	20.00	50.00
	1923	5.840	4.00	8.00	20.00	50.00
	1924	—	12.00	25.00	60.00	125.00

NICKEL-BRONZE

66	1927	2.002	2.50	6.00	12.00	22.50

10 CENTAVOS
(2 Macutas)

COPPER-NICKEL

KM#	Date	Mintage	Fine	VF	XF	Unc
63	1921	.160	10.00	17.50	45.00	90.00
	1922	.340	7.50	15.00	35.00	75.00
	1923	2.960	3.50	8.00	20.00	45.00

67	1927	2.003	2.00	4.00	15.00	30.00
	1928	1.000	2.00	4.00	15.00	30.00

BRONZE
300th Anniversary - Revolution of 1648

70	1948	10.000	.50	1.00	3.50	7.00
	1949	10.000	.35	.75	3.00	6.00

ALUMINUM

82	1974	4.000	—	—	—	10.00

NOTE: Not released for circulation, but relatively available.

20 CENTAVOS
(4 Macutas)

COPPER-NICKEL

64	1921	2.115	4.00	9.00	18.00	40.00
	1922	1.730	6.50	14.50	28.00	65.00

68	1927	2.001	2.50	4.00	8.00	17.50
	1928	.500	3.50	6.00	12.00	22.00

BRONZE
300th Anniversary - Revolution of 1648

71	1948	7.850	.50	1.00	2.00	4.00
	1949	2.150	4.00	7.50	12.50	20.00

78	1962	3.000	—	.25	.65	1.75

50 CENTAVOS

NICKEL

KM#	Date	Mintage	Fine	VF	XF	Unc
65	1922	6.000	3.00	8.00	15.00	40.00
	1923 KN	6.000	—	—	225.00	375.00
	1923	Inc. Ab.	3.00	8.00	15.00	40.00

NICKEL-BRONZE

69	1927	1.608	5.00	18.00	35.00	70.00
	1928/7	1.600	5.00	18.00	40.00	75.00
	1928	Inc.Ab.	5.00	18.00	30.00	65.00

300th Anniversary - Revolution of 1648

72	1948	4.000	.35	.75	2.00	4.50
	1950	4.000	.35	.75	2.00	4.50

BRONZE

KM#	Date	Mintage	VF	XF	Unc
75	1953	5.000	.25	.65	2.25
	1954	11.731	.20	.40	1.50
	1955	1.126	3.00	5.00	15.00
	1957	8.873	.20	.45	1.75
	1958	17.520	.15	.35	1.25
	1961	8.750	.20	.45	1.75

ESCUDO

BRONZE

76	1953	2.001	.75	1.75	6.50
	1956	2.989	.75	1.50	6.00
	1963	5.000	.75	1.50	5.00
	1965	5.000	.75	1.50	5.00
	1972	10.000	.75	1.50	4.00
	1974	6.214	.75	1.50	4.00

COPPER-NICKEL

76a	1972	—	—	Rare	—
	1974	—	—	Rare	—

NOTE: Not released for circulation.

2-1/2 ESCUDOS

COPPER-NICKEL

77	1953	6.008	.40	1.20	5.00

KM#	Date	Mintage	VF	XF	Unc
77	1956	9.992	.25	.50	3.00
	1967	6.000	.35	.75	4.00
	1968	5.000	.35	.75	4.00
	1969	5.000	.35	.75	4.00
	1974	19.999	.25	.50	3.00

5 ESCUDOS

COPPER-NICKEL

81	1972	8.000	10.00	20.00	45.00
	1974	*3.343	—	100.00	200.00

*NOTE: Not released for circulation.

10 ESCUDOS

5.0000 g, .720 SILVER, .1157 oz ASW

73	1952	2.023	2.50	5.00	9.00
	1955	1.977	2.50	5.00	9.00

COPPER-NICKEL

79	1969	3.022	1.50	3.00	6.00
	1970	.978	2.00	4.00	7.00

20 ESCUDOS

10.0000 g, .720 SILVER, .2315 oz ASW

74	1952	1.003	2.50	6.00	12.50
	1955	.997	2.50	5.00	10.00

NICKEL

80	1971	1.572	.75	2.00	4.00
	1972	.428	2.50	5.00	10.00

PEOPLES REPUBLIC

MONETARY SYSTEM
100 Lwei = 1 Kwanza

---

50 LWEI

COPPER-NICKEL

KM#	Date	Mintage	VF	XF	Unc
90	ND	—	.15	.35	.1.25
(82)	1979	—	.10	.30	.1.00

KWANZA

COPPER-NICKEL

83	ND	—	.30	.50	1.50
	1978	—	.25	.40	1.50
	1979	—	.25	.40	1.50

2 KWANZAS

COPPER-NICKEL

84	ND		.40	.60	1.75

5 KWANZAS

COPPER-NICKEL

85	ND	—	.65	1.25	2.50

10 KWANZAS

COPPER-NICKEL
Rev: Small date, dots near rim.

86.1	ND	—	1.25	2.00	3.50
	1978	—	1.50	2.50	4.50

Rev: Large date, dots away from rim.

86.2	1978	—	1.50	2.50	4.50

20 KWANZAS

COPPER-NICKEL

87	1978	—	2.25	3.50	6.50

50 KWANZAS

COPPER
Obv: State emblem. Rev: Denomination.

KM#	Date	Mintage	VF	XF	Unc
91	ND	—	2.50	4.50	9.00

100 KWANZAS

COPPER
Obv: State emblem. Rev: Denomination.

92	ND	—	3.50	6.50	14.00

ARGENTINA

The Argentine Republic, located in southern South America, has an area of 1,073,518 sq. mi. (3,761,274 sq. km.) and a population of 35 million. Capital: Buenos Aires. Its varied topography ranges from the subtropical lowlands of the north to the towering Andean Mountains in the west and the wind-swept Patagonian steppe in the south. The rolling, fertile pampas of central Argentina are ideal for agriculture and grazing, and support most of the republic's population. Meat packing, flour milling, textiles, sugar refining and dairy products are the principal industries. Oil is found in Patagonia, but most mineral requirements must be imported.

Argentina was discovered in 1516 by the Spanish navigator Juan de Solis. A permanent Spanish colony was established at Buenos Aires in 1580, but the colony developed slowly. When Napoleon conquered Spain, the Argentines set up their own government on May 25, 1810. Independence was formally declared on July 9, 1816. A strong tendency toward local autonomy, fostered by difficult transportation, resulted in a federalized union with much authority left to the states or provinces, which resulted in the coinage of 1817-1867.

Internal conflict through the first half century of Argentine independence resulted in a provisional national coinage, chiefly of crown-sized silver. This was supplemented by provincial issues, mainly of minor denominations.

MONETARY SYSTEM
100 Centavos = 1 Peso
10 Pesos = 1 Argentino

REPUBLIC
CENTAVO

BRONZE

KM#	Date	Mintage	Fine	VF	XF	Unc
12	1939	3.488	.15	.35	.75	1.75
	1940	3.140	.15	.35	.75	1.75
	1941	4.572	.15	.35	.75	1.75
	1942	.496	.30	.75	1.50	7.50
	1943	1.294	.20	.50	1.00	2.50
	1944	3.104	.10	.25	.55	1.50

COPPER
Cruder diework.

12a	1945	.420	.20	.50	1.00	4.00
	1946	4.450	.15	.35	.50	1.25
	1947	5.630	.15	.35	.50	1.25
	1948	4.420	.15	.35	.50	1.25

2 CENTAVOS

BRONZE

13	1939	5.490	.10	.25	.55	1.35
	1940	4.625	.10	.25	.55	1.85
	1941	4.567	.10	.25	.55	1.85
	1942	2.082	.10	.25	.55	1.85
	1944	.387	.25	.50	1.00	6.50

KM#	Date	Mintage	Fine	VF	XF	Unc
13	1945	4.585	.10	.25	.55	1.85
	1946	3.395	.10	.25	.55	1.85
	1947	4.395	.10	.25	.55	1.65

COPPER
Cruder diework.

13a	1947	Inc. Ab.	.15	.30	.60	2.00
	1948	3.645	.15	.30	.60	2.00
	1949	7.290	.15	.30	.55	1.85
	1950	.903	.25	.65	1.25	3.50

5 CENTAVOS

COPPER-NICKEL

9	1903	2.502	.25	.50	3.00	12.00
	1904	2.518	.25	.50	3.00	12.00
	1905	4.359	.25	.50	3.00	12.00
	1906	3.939	.25	.50	3.00	12.00
	1907	1.682	.50	1.00	5.00	20.00
	1908	1.693	.50	1.00	5.00	20.00
	1909	4.650	.25	.50	3.00	12.00
	1910	1.469	.75	2.00	6.00	22.00
	1911	1.431	.25	.75	4.00	15.00
	1912	2.377	.25	.75	4.00	15.00
	1913	1.477	.25	.75	4.00	15.00
	1914	1.097	.50	1.00	5.00	20.00
	1915	1.903	.30	.75	3.50	15.00
	1916	1.310	.30	.75	3.50	15.00
	1917	1.009	.75	1.50	4.00	15.00
	1918	2.287	.25	.50	3.00	8.00
	1919	2.476	.25	.50	3.00	8.00
	1920	5.235	.25	.50	3.00	8.00
	1921	7.040	.20	.35	2.00	7.00
	1922	9.427	.20	.35	2.00	7.00
	1923	6.256	.20	.35	2.00	7.00
	1924	6.355	.20	.35	2.00	7.00
	1925	3.955	.20	.35	2.00	7.00
	1926	3.560	.20	.35	2.00	7.00
	1927	5.650	.20	.35	2.00	7.00
	1928	6.380	.20	.35	2.00	7.00
	1929	11.831	.20	.35	2.00	7.00
	1930	7.110	.20	.35	2.00	7.00
	1931	.506	2.00	4.00	8.00	20.00
	1933	5.537	.10	.25	1.00	3.00
	1934	1.288	.25	.50	3.00	7.00
	1935	3.052	.10	.25	1.00	3.00
	1936	7.175	.10	.25	1.00	3.00
	1937	7.063	.10	.25	1.00	3.00
	1938	10.252	.10	.25	1.00	3.00
	1939	7.171	.10	.25	1.00	3.00
	1940	10.191	.10	.25	1.00	3.00
	1941	.951	.50	1.00	3.00	12.00
	1942	8.692	.10	.25	1.00	3.00

NOTE: Earlier dates (1896-1899) exist for this type.

ALUMINUM-BRONZE

15	1942	2.130	.15	.35	1.00	3.00
	1943	15.778	.10	.25	.50	1.75
	1944	21.081	.10	.25	.50	1.75
	1945	21.600	.10	.25	.50	1.75
	1946	20.460	.10	.25	.50	1.75
	1947	22.520	.10	.25	.50	1.75
	1948	42.790	.10	.25	.50	1.75
	1949	35.470	.10	.25	.50	1.75
	1950	13.500	.10	.25	.50	1.75

COPPER-NICKEL
Jose de San Martin
Reeded edge.

18	1950	3.460	.20	.40	.60	2.00

21	1951	34.994	—	.20	.30	.50

KM#	Date	Mintage	Fine	VF	XF	Unc
21	1952	33.110	—	.20	.30	.50
	1953	20.129	—	.20	.30	.50

COPPER-NICKEL CLAD STEEL
Plain edge.

KM#	Date	Mintage	Fine	VF	XF	Unc
21a	1953	56.300	—	.15	.20	.35

Rev: Smaller head.

KM#	Date	Mintage	Fine	VF	XF	Unc
25	1954	50.640	—	.15	.20	.35
	1955	42.200	—	.15	.20	.35
	1956	36.870	—	.15	.20	.35
28	1957	26.930	—	.15	.20	.35
	1958	13.108	—	.15	.20	.35
	1959	14.971	—	.15	.20	.35

10 CENTAVOS

COPPER-NICKEL

KM#	Date	Mintage	Fine	VF	XF	Unc
10	1905	3.785	.50	1.00	3.50	8.00
	1906	3.854	.50	1.00	3.50	8.00
	1907	2.355	.50	1.00	4.50	10.00
	1908	2.280	.50	1.00	4.50	10.00
	1909	3.738	.50	1.00	3.50	8.00
	1910	3.026	.50	1.00	3.50	8.00
	1911	2.142	.75	2.00	5.00	12.00
	1912	2.993	.75	2.00	5.00	12.00
	1913	1.828	1.00	2.50	5.50	15.00
	1914	.751	1.00	2.50	5.50	15.00
	1915	2.607	.50	1.00	3.50	8.00
	1916	.835	1.00	2.50	5.50	15.00
	1918	3.897	.50	1.00	3.50	8.00
	1919	2.517	.50	1.00	3.50	8.00
	1920	7.509	.25	.75	2.50	7.00
	1921	11.564	.25	.60	2.00	3.75
	1922	6.542	.20	.50	1.50	3.50
	1923	5.301	.20	.50	1.50	3.50
	1924	3.489	.20	.50	1.50	3.50
	1925	5.415	.20	.50	1.50	3.50
	1926	5.055	.15	.35	1.00	3.00
	1927	5.205	.15	.35	1.00	3.00
	1928	8.255	.15	.35	1.00	3.00
	1929	2.501	.15	.35	1.00	3.00
	1930	14.586	.15	.35	1.00	2.50
	1931	.893	.50	1.00	2.50	7.50
	1933	5.394	.15	.35	1.00	2.50
	1934	3.319	.15	.35	1.00	2.50
	1935	1.018	.30	.75	2.00	5.00
	1936	3.000	.15	.35	1.00	4.50
	1937	11.766	.15	.35	1.00	2.00
	1938	10.494	.15	.35	1.00	2.00
	1939	5.585	.15	.35	1.00	3.00
	1940	3.955	.15	.35	1.00	3.00
	1941	4.101	.15	.35	1.00	3.00
	1942	2.962	.15	.25	1.00	3.00

NOTE: Earlier dates (1896-1899) exist for this type.

ALUMINUM-BRONZE

KM#	Date	Mintage	Fine	VF	XF	Unc
16	1942	15.541	.15	.25	.75	1.75
	1943	13.916	.15	.25	.75	1.75
	1944	16.411	.15	.25	.75	.1.75
	1945	12.500	.15	.25	.75	1.75
	1946	15.790	.15	.25	.75	1.75
	1947	36.430	.15	.25	.75	1.75
	1948	54.685	.15	.25	.75	1.75
	1949	57.740	.15	.25	.75	1.75
	1950	42.825	.15	.25	.75	1.75

COPPER-NICKEL
Jose de San Martin
Reeded edge.

KM#	Date	Mintage	Fine	VF	XF	Unc
19	1950	17.505	.20	.40	.60	1.75

KM#	Date	Mintage	Fine	VF	XF	Unc
22	1951	98.521	—	.20	.30	.50
	1952	67.328	—	.20	.30	.50

NICKEL CLAD STEEL
Plain edge.

KM#	Date	Mintage	Fine	VF	XF	Unc
22a	1952	33.240	—	.10	.15	.25
	1953	106.685	—	.10	.15	.25

Obv: Smaller head.

KM#	Date	Mintage	Fine	VF	XF	Unc
26	1954	117.200	—	.10	.15	.25
	1955	97.045	—	.10	.15	.25
	1956	122.630	—	.10	.15	.25
29	1957	52.810	—	.10	.15	.25
	1958	41.916	—	.10	.15	.25
	1959	29.183	—	.10	.15	.25

20 CENTAVOS

KM#	Date	Mintage	Fine	VF	XF	Unc
11	1905	4.455	.75	2.00	5.00	20.00
	1906	4.331	.75	2.00	5.00	20.00
	1907	3.730	1.00	3.00	7.00	25.00
	1908	.719	2.25	5.00	10.00	30.00
	1909	1.329	.50	1.50	4.00	15.00
	1910	1.845	.50	1.50	4.00	15.00
	1911	1.110	.50	1.50	4.00	15.00
	1912	2.402	.50	1.50	4.00	15.00
	1913	1.579	.50	1.00	2.50	10.00
	1914	.527	2.25	5.00	10.00	45.00
	1915	1.921	.50	1.00	2.50	7.50
	1916	.985	.50	1.25	2.50	17.50
	1918	1.638	.40	.75	2.00	7.50
	1919	2.280	.40	.75	2.00	7.50
	1920	7.572	.40	.75	2.00	6.25
	1921	5.286	.25	.60	1.75	5.00
	1922	2.324	.25	.60	1.75	5.00
	1923	4.416	.25	.60	1.75	5.00
	1924	3.676	.25	.60	1.75	5.00
	1925	3.799	.25	.60	1.75	5.00
	1926	3.250	.25	.50	1.25	3.75
	1927	2.880	.25	.50	1.25	3.75
	1928	2.886	.25	.50	1.25	3.75
	1929	8.361	.25	.50	1.25	3.00
	1930	8.281	.25	.50	1.25	3.00
	1931	.315	2.25	5.00	10.00	20.00
	1935	1.127	.25	.60	1.75	5.00
	1936	.855	.50	1.25	2.50	12.50
	1937	3.314	.25	.50	1.50	3.75
	1938	6.449	.25	.50	1.25	3.00
	1939	3.555	.25	.50	1.25	3.00
	1940	4.465	.25	.50	1.25	3.00
	1941	.600	.50	1.00	2.00	10.00
	1942	4.844	.25	.50	1.25	3.00

NOTE: Earlier dates (1896-1899) exist for this type.

ALUMINUM-BRONZE

KM#	Date	Mintage	Fine	VF	XF	Unc
17	1942	10.255	.15	.25	.75	1.75
	1943	13.775	.15	.25	.75	1.75
	1944	12.225	.15	.25	.75	1.75
	1945	13.340	.15	.25	.75	1.75
	1946	14.625	.15	.25	.75	1.75
	1947	23.165	.15	.25	.75	1.75
	1948	32.245	.15	.25	.75	1.75
	1949	67.115	.15	.25	.75	1.75
	1950	40.071	.15	.25	.75	1.75

COPPER-NICKEL
Jose de San Martin
Reeded edge.

KM#	Date	Mintage	Fine	VF	XF	Unc
20	1950	86.770	.15	.25	.60	1.50
23	1951	85.782	.10	.20	.30	.50
	1952	69.796	.10	.20	.30	.50

NICKEL CLAD STEEL
Plain edge.

KM#	Date	Mintage	Fine	VF	XF	Unc
23a	1952	12.863	—	.15	.40	1.00
	1953	36.893	—	.15	.25	.50

Head size reduced slightly.

KM#	Date	Mintage	Fine	VF	XF	Unc
27	1954	52.563	—	.15	.20	.25
	1955	46.952	—	.15	.20	.25
	1956	35.995	—	.15	.20	.25
30	1957	89.365	—	.15	.20	.25
	1958	52.710	—	.15	.20	.25
	1959	56.585	—	.15	.20	.25
	1960	21.254	—	.15	.20	.25
	1961	2.083	—	.25	.50	1.50

50 CENTAVOS

NICKEL
Reeded edge.

KM#	Date	Mintage	Fine	VF	XF	Unc
14	1941	10.961	.40	1.00	1.50	2.75

NICKEL CLAD STEEL
Jose de San Martin
Plain edge.

KM#	Date	Mintage	Fine	VF	XF	Unc
24	1952	29.736	.10	.20	.35	.75
	1953	62.814	.10	.20	.35	.75
	1954	132.224	.10	.20	.35	.75
	1955	75.490	.10	.20	.35	.75
	1956	19.120	.10	.20	.45	1.00
31	1957	18.139	—	.10	.25	.30
	1958	51.750	.10	.20	.30	.40
	1959	13.997	—	.10	.20	.30

KM#	Date	Mintage	Fine	VF	XF	Unc
31	1960	26.038	.10	.20	.30	.40
	1961	11.106	—	.10	.20	.35

PESO

NICKEL CLAD STEEL

32	1957	118.118	.10	.20	.40	.85
	1958	118.151	.10	.20	.40	.85
	1959	237.733	.10	.20	.30	.60
	1960	75.048	.10	.30	.50	1.00
	1961	76.897	.10	.30	.50	1.00
	1962	30.006	.10	.30	.50	1.00

150th Anniversary - Removal of Spanish Viceroy

33	ND(1960)					
		98.751	.20	.50	.75	1.25

5 PESOS

NICKEL CLAD STEEL
Sailing Ship - Presidente Sarmiento

34	1961	37.423	.10	.20	.30	.60
	1962	42.362	.10	.20	.30	.60
	1963	71.769	.10	.20	.30	.60
	1964	12.302	.15	.25	.40	.80
	1965	19.450	.10	.20	.30	.60
	1966	17.259	.10	.20	.30	.60
	1967	17.806	.10	.20	.30	.60
	1968	12.634	.10	.20	.30	.60

10 PESOS

NICKEL CLAD STEEL
Gaucho

35	1962	57.401	.10	.20	.30	.65
	1963	136.792	.10	.20	.30	.65
	1964	46.576	.10	.20	.30	.65
	1965	40.640	—	.15	.30	.65
	1966	50.733	.10	.20	.30	.65
	1967	43.050	.10	.20	.30	.75
	1968	36.588	—	.15	.30	.65

150th Anniversary - Declaration of Independence

37	ND(1966)					
		29.336	.10	.15	.35	1.00

25 PESOS

NICKEL CLAD STEEL

1st Issue of National Coinage in 1813

KM#	Date	Mintage	Fine	VF	XF	Unc
36	1964	20.485	.10	.25	.50	1.35
	1965	14.884	.10	.25	.50	1.35
	1966	16.426	.10	.25	.50	1.35
	1967	15.734	.10	.25	.50	1.35
	1968	4.446	.10	.25	.75	1.75

80th Anniversary - Death of D. Faustino Sarmiento

38	1968	15.804	.25	.60	.85	1.65

MONETARY REFORM
1970 - 1983
100 Old Pesos = 1 New Peso

CENTAVO

ALUMINUM

39	1970	47.801	—	—	.10	.30
	1971	44.644	—	—	.10	.30
	1972	92.430	—	—	.10	.30
	1973	29.515	—	—	.10	.30
	1974	5.162	—	—	.15	.35
	1975	3.840	—	.10	.20	.50

5 CENTAVOS

ALUMINUM

40	1970	56.174	—	.10	.15	.40
	1971	3.798	.10	.20	.35	.65
	1972	84.250	—	.10	.15	.40
	1973	113.912	—	.10	.15	.40
	1974	18.150	—	.10	.15	.40
	1975	6.940	.10	.20	.35	.65

10 CENTAVOS

BRASS

41	1970	52.903	—	.10	.15	.35
	1971	135.623	—	.10	.15	.35
	1973	19.930	—	.10	.15	.35
	1974	79.156	—	.10	.15	.35
	1975	31.270	—	.10	.15	.35
	1976	.730	.10	.20	.35	1.00

20 CENTAVOS

BRASS

42	1970	27.029	—	.10	.15	.35
	1971	32.211	—	.10	.15	.35
	1972	.220	2.00	6.00	10.00	20.00
	1973	9.676	—	.10	.15	.35
	1974	41.024	—	.10	.15	.35
	1975	26.540	—	.10	.15	.35
	1976	.960	—	.10	.15	.35

50 CENTAVOS

BRASS

43	1970	44.748	.10	.15	.30	.60

KM#	Date	Mintage	Fine	VF	XF	Unc
43	1971	34.947	.10	.15	.30	.60
	1972	40.960	.10	.15	.30	.60
	1973	69.472	.10	.15	.30	.60
	1974	63.063	.10	.15	.30	.60
	1975	64.859	.10	.15	.30	.60
	1976	9.768	.10	.15	.30	.60

PESO

ALUMINUM-BRASS

44	1974	77.292	—	.10	.25	.75
	1975	423.000	—	.10	.20	.50
	1976	100.075	—	.10	.20	.50

NOTE: Wide and narrow rim varieties exist.

5 PESOS

ALUMINUM-BRONZE

46	1976	118.353	—	.10	.20	.65
	1977	64.738	—	.10	.20	.65

Admiral G. Brown Bicentennial

48	1977	Inc. Ab.	.10	.15	.25	.50

10 PESOS

ALUMINUM-BRONZE

47	1976	128.965	.10	.15	.35	1.00
	1977	113.400	.10	.15	.35	1.00
	1978	253.863	.10	.15	.35	1.00

Admiral G. Brown Bicentennial

49	1977	Inc. Ab.	.10	.20	.50	1.25

20 PESOS

ALUMINUM-BRONZE
1978 World Soccer Championship

50	1977	1.506	.10	.20	.40	.80
	1978	2.000	.10	.20	.40	.80

50 PESOS

ALUMINUM-BRONZE
1978 World Soccer Championship

51	1977	1.506	.10	.20	.40	.80
	1978	2.000	.10	.20	.40	.80

200th Anniversary - Birth of Jose de San Martin

KM#	Date	Mintage	Fine	VF	XF	Unc
56	1978	40.601	.20	.50	1.00	2.00

Jose de San Martin

58	1979	103.491	.10	.25	.65	1.50
	1980		.10	.25	.65	1.50

BRASS CLAD STEEL

58a	1980	94.730	.10	.25	.65	1.25
	1981	4.372	.10	.25	.65	1.25

ALUMINUM-BRONZE
Conquest of Patagonia Centennial

59	1979	Inc. Ab.	.10	.25	.65	1.50

100 PESOS

ALUMINUM-BRONZE
1978 World Soccer Championship

52	1977	1.506	.15	.30	.75	1.25
	1978	2.000	.15	.30	.75	1.25

200th Anniversary - Birth of Jose de San Martin

57	1978	113.826	—	.50	1.00	2.00

Jose de San Martin

60	1979	207.572	.15	.30	.75	1.25
	1980	154.260	.15	.30	.75	1.25
	1981	145.680	.15	.30	.75	1.25

BRASS CLAD STEEL

60a	1980	Inc. Ab.	.15	.30	.75	1.50
	1981	Inc. Ab.	.15	.30	.75	1.50

ALUMINUM-BRONZE
Conquest of Patagonia Centennial

KM#	Date	Mintage	Fine	VF	XF	Unc
61	1979	Inc. Ab.	.15	.30	.75	1.50

MONETARY REFORM
1983 - 1985
10,000 Pesos = 1 Peso Argentino
100 Centavos = 1 Peso Argentino

CENTAVO

ALUMINUM

62	1983	19.959	—	—	—	.10

5 CENTAVOS

ALUMINUM

63	1983	59.870	—	—	—	.15

10 CENTAVOS

ALUMINUM

64	1983	307.513	—	—	—	.15

50 CENTAVOS

ALUMINUM

65	1983	243.909	—	—	—	.25

PESO

ALUMINUM
National Congress

66	1984	785.791	—	—	—	.25

5 PESOS

BRASS
Buenos Aires City Hall

67	1984	11.206	—	—	—	.35
	1985	14.168	—	—	—	.35

10 PESOS

BRASS
Independence Hall at Tucuman

KM#	Date	Mintage	Fine	VF	XF	Unc
68	1984	16.528	—	—	—	.60
	1985	14.618	—	—	—	.60

50 PESOS

ALUMINUM-BRONZE
50th Anniversary of Central Bank

69	1985	26.400	—	—	—	.85

MONETARY REFORM
1985 - 1992
1000 Pesos Argentinos = 1 Austral
100 Centavos = 1 Austral

1/2 CENTAVO

BRASS
Rufous Hornero Bird

70	1985	7.490	—	—	—	.35

CENTAVO

BRASS
Common Rhea
Thick flan.

71.1	1985	76.082	—	—	—	.50

Thin flan.

71.2	1986	18.934	—	—	—	.50
	1987	87.315	—	—	—	.50

5 CENTAVOS

BRASS
Pampas Cat
Thick flan.

72.1	1985	36.924	—	—	—	.75

Thin flan.

72.2	1986	66.414	—	—	—	.75
	1987	56.181	—	—	—	.75
	1988	23.895	—	—	—	.75

10 CENTAVOS

BRASS

73	1985	23.268	—	—	—	.65
	1986	158.427	—	—	—	.65
	1987	184.330	—	—	—	.65
	1988	174.003	—	—	—	.65

50 CENTAVOS

BRASS

KM#	Date	Mintage	Fine	VF	XF	Unc
74	1985	13.884	—	—	—	1.50
	1986	59.074	—	—	—	1.50
	1987	64.525	—	—	—	1.50
	1988	62.388	—	—	—	1.50

NOTE: Varieties exist.

AUSTRAL

ALUMINUM
Buenos Aires City Hall

| 75 | 1989 | | — | — | — | .15 |

5 AUSTRALES

ALUMINUM
Independence Hall at Tucuman

| 76 | 1989 | | — | — | — | .25 |

10 AUSTRALES

ALUMINUM
Casa del Acuerdo

| 77 | 1989 | | — | — | — | .35 |

100 AUSTRALES

ALUMINUM

| 78 | 1990 | | — | — | — | .25 |
| | 1991 | | — | — | — | .25 |

500 AUSTRALES

ALUMINUM

| 79 | 1990 | | — | — | — | .35 |
| | 1991 | | — | — | — | .35 |

1000 AUSTRALES

ALUMINUM

| 80 | 1990 | | — | — | — | .60 |
| | 1991 | | — | — | — | .60 |

MONETARY REFORM
1992 -
10,000 Australes = 1 Peso

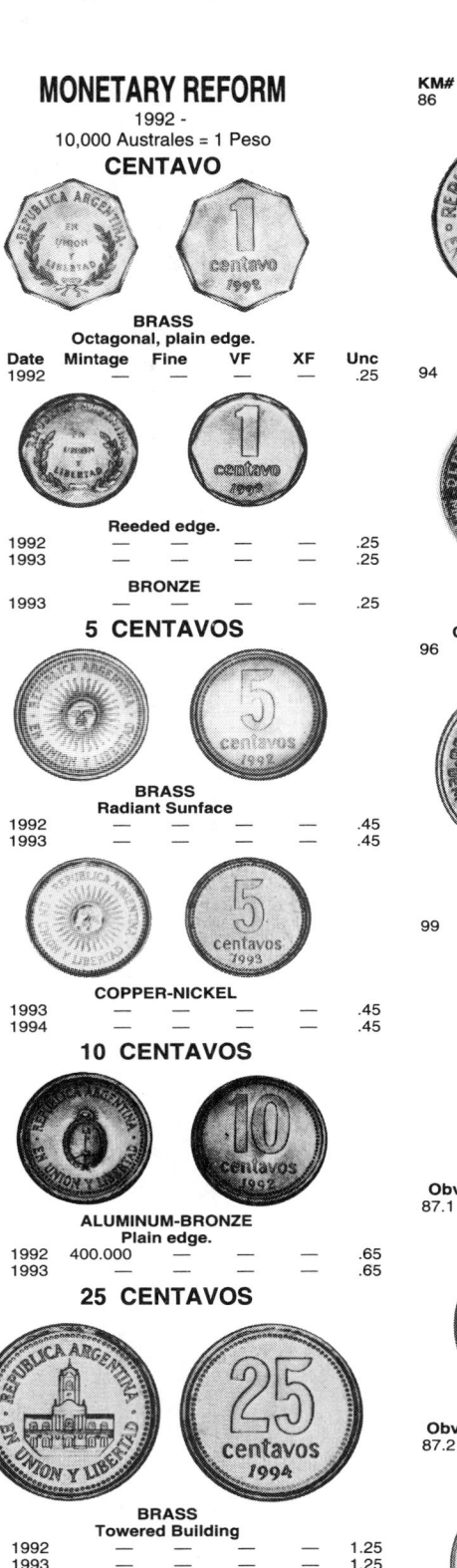

CENTAVO

BRASS
Octagonal, plain edge.

KM#	Date	Mintage	Fine	VF	XF	Unc
83	1992		—	—	—	.25

Reeded edge.

| 88 | 1992 | | — | — | — | .25 |
| | 1993 | | — | — | — | .25 |

BRONZE

| 88a | 1993 | | — | — | — | .25 |

5 CENTAVOS

BRASS
Radiant Sunface

| 84 | 1992 | | — | — | — | .45 |
| | 1993 | | — | — | — | .45 |

COPPER-NICKEL

| 84a | 1993 | | — | — | — | .45 |
| | 1994 | | — | — | — | .45 |

10 CENTAVOS

ALUMINUM-BRONZE
Plain edge.

| 82 | 1992 | 400.000 | — | — | — | .65 |
| | 1993 | | — | — | — | .65 |

25 CENTAVOS

BRASS
Towered Building

| 85 | 1992 | | — | — | — | 1.25 |
| | 1993 | | — | — | — | 1.25 |

COPPER-NICKEL

85a	1993		—	—	—	1.25
	1994		—	—	—	1.25
	1995		—	—	—	1.25

50 CENTAVOS

BRASS
Tucuman Province Capital Building

| 86 | 1992 | | — | — | — | 1.75 |
| | 1993 | | — | — | — | 1.75 |

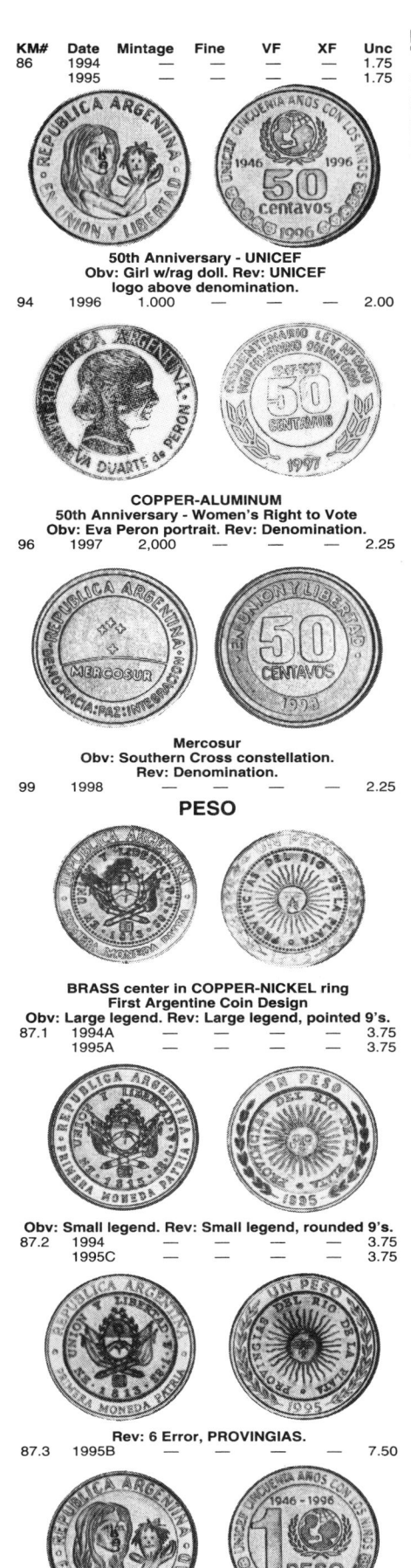

KM#	Date	Mintage	Fine	VF	XF	Unc
86	1994		—	—	—	1.75
	1995		—	—	—	1.75

50th Anniversary - UNICEF
Obv: Girl w/rag doll. Rev: UNICEF logo above denomination.

| 94 | 1996 | 1.000 | — | — | — | 2.00 |

COPPER-ALUMINUM
50th Anniversary - Women's Right to Vote
Obv: Eva Peron portrait. Rev: Denomination.

| 96 | 1997 | 2,000 | — | — | — | 2.25 |

Mercosur
Obv: Southern Cross constellation.
Rev: Denomination.

| 99 | 1998 | | — | — | — | 2.25 |

PESO

BRASS center in COPPER-NICKEL ring
First Argentine Coin Design
Obv: Large legend. Rev: Large legend, pointed 9's.

| 87.1 | 1994A | | — | — | — | 3.75 |
| | 1995A | | — | — | — | 3.75 |

Obv: Small legend. Rev: Small legend, rounded 9's.

| 87.2 | 1994 | | — | — | — | 3.75 |
| | 1995C | | — | — | — | 3.75 |

Rev: 6 Error, PROVINGIAS.

| 87.3 | 1995B | | — | — | — | 7.50 |

50th Anniversary - UNICEF
Obv: Girl w/rag doll. Rev: UNICEF logo above denomination.

| 95 | 1996 | 1.000 | — | — | — | 3.75 |

50th Anniversary - Women's Right to Vote
Obv: Eva Peron portrait. Rev: Denomination.

KM#	Date	Mintage	Fine	VF	XF	Unc
97	1997	1.000	—	—	—	3.75

Mercosur
Obv: Southern Cross constellation.
Rev: Denomination.

100	1998	—	—	—	—	3.75

ARMENIA

The Republic of Armenia (formerly Armenian S.S.R.) is bounded in the north by Georgia, to the east by Azerbaijan and to the south and west by Turkey and Iran. It has an area of 11,490 sq. mi. (29,800 sq. km) and a population of 3.5 million. Capital: Yerevan. Agriculture including cotton, vineyards and orchards, hydroelectricity, chemicals - primarily synthetic rubber and fertilizers, and vast mineral deposits of copper, zinc and aluminum and production of steel and paper are major industries.

Russia occupied Armenia in 1801 until the Russo-Turkish war of 1878. British intervention excluded either side from remaining although the Armenians remained more loyal to the Ottoman Turks, but in 1894 the Ottoman Turks sent in an expeditionary force of Kurds fearing a revolutionary movement. Large massacres were followed by retaliations, then amnesty was proclaimed which led right into WW I and once again occupation by Russian forces in 1916. After the Russian revolution the Georgians, Armenians and Azerbaijanis formed the short lived Transcaucasian Federal Republic on Sept. 20, 1917 which broke up into three independent republics on May 26, 1918. Communism developed and in Sept. 1920 the Turks attacked the Armenian Republic; the Russians soon followed suit from Azerbaijan routing the Turks. On Nov. 29, 1920 Armenia was proclaimed a Soviet Socialist Republic. On March 12, 1922, Armenia, Georgia and Azerbaijan were combined to form the Transcaucasian Soviet Federated Socialist republic, which on Dec. 30, 1922, became a part of U.S.S.R. On Dec. 5, 1936, the Transcaucasian federation was dissolved and Armenia became a constituent Republic of the U.S.S.R. A new constitution was adopted in April 1978. Elections took place on May 20, 1990. The Supreme Soviet adopted a declaration of sovereignty in Aug. 1991, voting to unite Armenia with Nagorno - Karabakh. This newly constituted "Republic of Armenia" became fully independent by popular vote in Sept. 1991. It became a member of the CIS in Dec. 1991.

Fighting between Christians in Armenia and Muslim forces of Azerbaijan escalated in 1992 and continued through early 1994. Each country claimed the Nagorno-Karabakh, an Armenian ethnic enclave, in Azerbaijan. A temporary cease-fire was announced in May, 1994.

MONETARY SYSTEM
50 Luma = 1 Dram

10 LUMA

ALUMINUM

KM#	Date	Mintage	VF	XF	Unc
51	1994	—	—	—	.25

20 LUMA

ALUMINUM

52	1994	—	—	—	.25

50 LUMA

ALUMINUM

53	1994	—	—	—	.45

DRAM

ALUMINUM

KM#	Date	Mintage	VF	XF	Unc
54	1994				.65

3 DRAMS

ALUMINUM

55	1994	—	—	—	.85

5 DRAMS

ALUMINUM

56	1994	—	—	—	1.20

10 DRAMS

ALUMINUM

58	1994	—	—	—	2.00

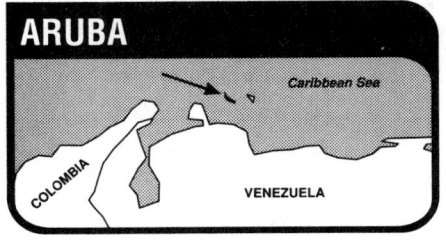

ARUBA

Caribbean Sea

COLOMBIA

VENEZUELA

Aruba, formerly a part of the Netherlands Antilles, achieved on Jan. 1, 1986 a special status "status aparte" as the third state under the Dutch crown, together with the Netherlands and the remaining five islands of the Netherlands Antilles. On Dec. 15, 1954 the Netherlands Antilles were given complete domestic autonomy and granted equality within the Kingdom of the Netherlands. The separate constitution put in place for Aruba in 1986 established it as an autonomous government within the Kingdom of the Netherlands. In 1990 Aruba opted to remain a part of the Kingdom without the promise of future independence.

The second largest island of the Netherlands Antilles, Aruba is situated near the Venezuelan coast. The island has an area of 74-1/2 sq. mi. (193 sq. km.) and a population of *63,000. Capital: Oran jestad, named after the Dutch royal family. Aruba was important in the processing and transportation of petroleum products in the first part of the twentieth century, but today the chief industry is tourism.

For earlier issues see Curacao and the Netherlands Antilles.

RULERS
Dutch

MINT MARKS
(u) Utrecht - Privy marks only
Anvil, 1986-1988
Bow and Arrow, 1989-

MONETARY SYSTEM
100 Cents = 1 Florin

5 CENTS

NICKEL BONDED STEEL

KM#	Date	Mintage	Fine	VF	XF	Unc
1	1986(u)	.276	—	.10	.25	.50
	1987(u)	.232	—	.10	.25	.50
	1988(u)	.656	—	—	—	.30
	1989(u)	.770	—	—	—	.30
	1990(u)	.612	—	—	—	.30
	1991(u)	.411	—	—	—	.30
	1992(u)	.810	—	—	—	.25
	1993(u)	.709	—	—	—	.25
	1994(u)	.709	—	—	—	.25
	1995(u)	.809	—	—	—	.25
	1996(u)	.590	—	—	—	.25
	1997(u)	.536	—	—	—	.25
	1998(u)	.920	—	—	—	.25
	1999(u)	—	—	—	—	.25

10 CENTS

NICKEL BONDED STEEL

KM#	Date	Mintage	Fine	VF	XF	Unc
2	1986(u)	.356	—	.10	.30	.60
	1987(u)	.222	—	.10	.30	.60
	1988(u)	.986	—	—	.10	.40
	1989(u)	.610	—	—	.10	.40
	1990(u)	.762	—	—	.10	.40
	1991(u)	.511	—	—	.10	.40
	1992(u)	.610	—	—	.10	.40
	1993(u)	1.009	—	—	—	.35
	1994(u)	.409	—	—	—	.35
	1995(u)	.919	—	—	—	.35
	1996(u)	.458	—	—	—	.35
	1997(u)	.424	—	—	—	.35
	1998(u)	.954	—	—	—	.35
	1999(u)	—	—	—	—	.35

25 CENTS

NICKEL BONDED STEEL

KM#	Date	Mintage	Fine	VF	XF	Unc
3	1986(u)	.356	—	.15	.35	.70
	1987(u)	.222	—	.15	.35	.70
	1988(u)	.116	—	.15	.35	.70
	1989(u)	.360	—	—	—	.50
	1990(u)	.512	—	—	—	.50
	1991(u)	.611	—	—	—	.50
	1992(u)	.460	—	—	—	.50
	1993(u)	.609	—	—	—	.50
	1994(u)	.109	—	—	—	.50
	1995(u)	.609	—	—	—	.50
	1996(u)	.288	—	—	—	.50
	1997(u)	.468	—	—	—	.50
	1998(u)	.741	—	—	—	.50
	1999(u)	—	—	—	—	.50

50 CENTS

NICKEL BONDED STEEL

KM#	Date	Mintage	Fine	VF	XF	Unc
4	1986(u)	.236	—	—	.50	1.00
	1987(u)	.122	—	—	.50	1.00
	1988(u)	.216	—	—	.50	1.00
	1989(u)	.110	—	—	.50	1.00
	1990(u)	.262	—	—	.50	1.00
	1991(u)	.311	—	—	.40	.80
	1992(u)	.311	—	—	.40	.80
	1993(u)	.459	—	—	.40	.80
	1994(u)	.308	—	—	.40	.80
	1995(u)	.259	—	—	.40	.80
	1996(u)	.393	—	—	.40	.80
	1997(u)	.028	—	—	.60	1.25
	1998(u)	.197	—	—	.40	.80
	1999(u)	—	—	—	.40	.80

FLORIN

NICKEL BONDED STEEL

KM#	Date	Mintage	Fine	VF	XF	Unc
5	1986(u)	.336	—	—	.75	1.75
	1987(u)	.222	—	—	.75	1.75
	1988(u)	.566	—	—	.75	1.75
	1989(u)	.410	—	—	.75	1.75
	1990(u)	.412	—	—	.75	1.75
	1991(u)	.161	—	—	.75	1.75
	1992(u)	.611	—	—	.75	1.75
	1993(u)	.409	—	—	.75	1.75
	1994(u)	.108	—	—	.75	1.75
	1995(u)	.209	—	—	.75	1.75
	1996(u)	.133	—	—	.75	1.75
	1997(u)	.416	—	—	.75	1.75
	1998(u)	.300	—	—	.75	1.75
	1999(u)	—	—	—	.75	1.75

2-1/2 FLORIN

NICKEL BONDED STEEL

KM#	Date	Mintage	Fine	VF	XF	Unc
6	1986(u)	.086	—	—	1.75	2.50
	1987(u)	.032	—	—	—	2.50
	1988(u)	.026	—	—	—	2.50
	1989(u)	.015	—	—	—	2.50
	1990(u)	.017	—	—	—	2.50
	1991(u)	.016	—	—	—	2.50
	1992(u)	.013	—	—	—	2.50
	1993(u)	.011	—	—	—	2.50
	1994(u)	.011	—	—	—	2.50
	1995(u)	.011	—	—	—	2.50
	1996(u)	.008	—	In set only		3.00
	1997(u)	.008	—	In set only		3.00
	1998(u)	.008	—	—	—	3.00
	1999(u)	—	—	—	—	2.50

5 FLORIN

NICKEL BONDED STEEL

KM#	Date	Mintage	Fine	VF	XF	Unc
12	1995(u)	.200	—	—	—	6.00
	1996(u)	.376	—	—	—	6.00
	1997(u)	.028	—	—	—	6.50
	1998(u)	.162	—	—	—	6.00
	1999(u)	—	—	—	—	6.00

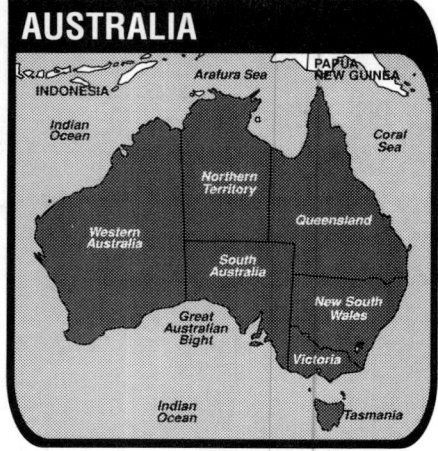

AUSTRALIA

The Commonwealth of Australia, the smallest continent and largest island in the world, is located south of Indonesia between the Indian and Pacific oceans. It has an area of 2,966,200 sq. mi. (7,686,850 sq. km.) and a population of 18.3 million. Capital: Canberra. Due to its early and sustained isolation, Australia is the habitat of such curious and unique fauna as the kangaroo, koala, platypus, wombat, echidna and frilled-necked lizard. The continent possesses extensive mineral deposits, the most important of which are iron ore, coal, gold, silver, nickel, uranium, lead and zinc. Livestock raising, mining and manufacturing are the principal industries. Chief exports are wool, meat, wheat, iron ore, coal and nonferrous metals.

The first caucasians to see Australia probably were Portuguese and Spanish navigators of the late 16th century. In 1770, Captain James Cook explored the east coast and annexed it for Great Britain. New South Wales was founded as a penal colony, following the loss of British North America, by Capt. Arthur Phillip on January 26, 1788, a date now celebrated as Australia Day. Dates of creation of the six colonies that now comprise the states of the Australian Commonwealth are: New South Wales, 1823; Tasmania, 1825; Western Australia, 1838; South Australia, 1842; Victoria, 1851; Queensland, 1859. A constitution providing for federation of the colonies was approved by the British Parliament in 1900; the Commonwealth of Australia came into being in 1901. Australia passed the Statute of Westminster Adoption Act on October 9, 1942, which officially established Australia's complete autonomy in external and internal affairs, thereby formalizing a situation that had existed for years. Australia is a member of the Commonwealth of Nations. Elizabeth II is Head of State as Queen of Australia.

Australia's currency system was changed from Pounds-Shillings-Pence to a decimal system of Dollars and Cents on Feb. 14, 1966.

RULERS

British

MINT MARKS

Abbr.	Mint	Mint Marks and Locations
A	Adelaide	—
(b)	Bombay	"I" below bust; dots before and after HALF PENNY, 1942-43
(b)	Bombay	"I" below bust dots before and after PENNY, 1942-43
B	Brisbane	—
(c)	Calcutta	"I" above date, 1916-18
(c)	Canberra	None, 1966 to date
C	Canberra	—
D	Denver	"D" above date 1/-& 2/-, below date on 3d
D	Denver	"D" below date on 6d
H	Heaton	"H" below date on silver coins, 1914-15
H	Heaton	"H" above date on bronze coins
(L)	London	None, 1910-1915, 1966
M	Melbourne	"M" below date on silver coins, 1916-21
M	Melbourne	"M" above date on the ground on gold coins w/St. George
M	Melbourne	—
(m)	Melbourne	Dot below scroll on penny, 1919-20
(m)	Melbourne	Two dots; below lower scroll and above upper, 1919-20
(m)	Melbourne	None, 1922-1964
P	Perth	"P" above date on the ground on gold coins w/St. George
(p)	Perth	Dot between KG (designer's initials), 1940-44
(p)	Perth	Dot after PENNY, 1941-51 1954-64
(p)	Perth	Dot after AUSTRALIA, 1952-53
(p)	Perth	Dot before SHILLING, 1946
(p)	Perth	None, 1922 penny, 1966
P	Perth	Nuggets, 1986
PL	London	"PL" after PENNY in 1951
PL	London	"PL" on bottom folds of ribbon, 1951 threepence
PL	London	"PL" above date on sixpence,

Abbr.	Mint	Mint Marks and Locations
PL		1951
S	San Francisco	"S" above or below date, 1942-44
S	Sydney	"S" above date on the ground on gold coins w/St. George
S	Sydney	—
(sy)	Sydney	Dot above bottom scroll on penny 1920
(sy)	Sydney	None, 1919-1926

Mint designations are shown in ( ). Ex. 1978(m).
Mint marks are shown after date. Ex. 1978M.

MONETARY SYSTEM
(Until 1966)

12 Pence = 1 Shilling
2 Shillings = 1 Florin
5 Shillings = 1 Crown
20 Shillings = 1 Pound

(Commencing 1966)

100 Cents = 1 Dollar

1/2 PENNY

BRONZE

KM#	Date	Mintage	Fine	VF	XF	Unc
22	1911(L)	2.832	.35	2.00	20.00	85.00
	1911(L)	—	—	—	Proof	1600.
	1912H	2.400	.35	2.25	25.00	120.00
	1912H	—	—	—	Proof	1600.
	1913(L)	2.160	.40	3.25	28.00	160.00
	1914(L)	1.440	2.00	4.50	40.00	250.00
	1914H	1.200	2.50	5.50	45.00	250.00
	1915H	.720	12.50	35.00	200.00	900.00
	1916-I(c)	3.600	.30	1.25	13.50	100.00
	1916-I(c)	—	—	—	Proof	1600.
	1917-I(c)	5.760	.30	1.25	13.50	100.00
	1918-I(c)	1.440	3.00	18.00	120.00	950.00
	1919(sy)	3.326	.20	1.50	13.50	100.00
	1919(sy)	—	—	—	Proof	1600.
	1920(sy)	4.114	.65	2.75	25.00	150.00
	1920(m)	—	—	—	Proof	1600.
	1921(sy)	5.280	.30	1.75	16.00	80.00
	1922(sy)	6.924	.30	1.75	16.00	80.00
	1923(sy)	*1.113				
			400.00	550.00	2000.	10,000.
	1923(sy)	—	—	—	Proof	25,000.
	1924(m)	.682	2.00	5.50	65.00	320.00
	1924(m)	—	—	—	Proof	1600.
	1925(m)	1.147	1.00	2.50	28.00	250.00
	1925(m)	—	—	—	Proof	2750.
	1926(m&sy)					
		4.139	.20	1.25	17.50	100.00
	1926(m)	—	—	—	Proof	1550.
	1927(m)	3.072	.20	.75	17.50	100.00
	1927(m)	50 pcs.	—	—	Proof	1500.
	1928(m)	2.318	1.25	3.25	25.00	250.00
	1928(m)	—	—	—	Proof	1500.
	1929(m)	2.635	.20	.75	17.50	115.00
	1929(m)	—	—	—	Proof	1600.
	1930(m)	.638	2.25	4.50	32.00	250.00
	1930(m)	—	—	—	Proof	10,000.
	1931(m)	.370	2.25	4.50	32.00	250.00
	1931(m)	—	—	—	Proof	1500.
	1932(m)	2.554	.20	.75	10.00	65.00
	1932(m)	—	—	—	Proof	1500.
	1933(m)	4.608	.20	.75	8.00	50.00
	1933(m)	—	—	—	Proof	1250.
	1934(m)	3.816	.20	.75	8.00	50.00
	1934(m)	100 pcs.	—	—	Proof	750.00
	1935(m)	2.916	.20	.75	4.75	32.00
	1935(m)	100 pcs.	—	—	Proof	750.00
	1936(m)	2.562	.20	.75	4.75	32.00
	1936(m)	—	—	—	Proof	1000.

*NOTE: Dies dated 1922 were used for the majority of the calendar year 1923, leaving only a small portion of this mintage figure as 1923 dated coins.

Mule. Obv. India 1/4 Anna, KM#511. Rev: KM#22.

KM#	Date	Mintage	Fine	VF	XF	Unc
30	1916-I(c)	*10	4000.	7500.	—	—

KM#	Date	Mintage	Fine	VF	XF	Unc
35	1938(m)	3.014	.20	.50	2.00	16.00
	1938(m)	250 pcs.	—	—	Proof	650.00
	1939(m)	4.382	.20	.50	4.00	25.00
	1939(m)	—	—	—	Proof	1400.

KM#	Date	Mintage	Fine	VF	XF	Unc
41	1939(m)	.504	4.50	7.50	50.00	245.00
	1939(m)	100 pcs.	—	—	Proof	1500.
	1940(m)	2.294	.20	1.00	6.00	32.00
	1940(m)	—	—	—	Proof	900.00
	1941(m)	5.011	.20	.75	3.50	18.00
	1941(m)	—	—	—	Proof	1000.
	1941(p)	—	—	—	Proof	1000.
	1942(m)	.720	2.00	4.50	25.00	100.00
	1942(m)	—	—	—	Proof	900.00
	1942(p)	4.334	.20	.50	2.00	16.00
	1942(p)	—	—	—	Proof	1000.
	1942-I(b)	6.000	.15	.25	2.00	20.00
	1942-I(b)	—	—	—	Proof	800.00
	1943(m)	33.989	.15	.25	1.50	8.00
	1943(p)	—	—	—	Proof	1000.
	1943-I(b)	6.000	.20	.35	3.25	16.00
	1943-I(b)	—	—	—	Proof	800.00
	1944(m)	.720	2.00	3.50	25.00	115.00
	1944(m)	—	—	—	Proof	1200.
	1945(m)	3.033	1.50	3.00	14.50	65.00
	1945(p) w/o dot					
	Inc. Ab.	1.50	3.00	14.50	65.00	
	1945(p)	—	—	—	Proof	850.00
	1946(m)	13.747	.15	.25	1.50	7.00
	1946(m)	—	—	—	Proof	850.00
	1947(p)	9.293	.15	.25	1.50	7.00
	1947(p)	—	—	—	Proof	850.00
	1948(m)	4.608	.25	.50	3.25	16.00
	1948(m)	—	—	—	Proof	1000.
	1948(p)	25.553	.15	.25	1.50	8.00
	1948(p)	—	—	—	Proof	850.00

Obv. leg: IND:IMP: dropped.

KM#	Date	Mintage	Fine	VF	XF	Unc
42	1949(m)	—	—	—	Proof	1000.
	1949(p)	22.310	.15	.25	2.25	12.00
	1949(p)	—	—	—	Proof	1000.
	1950(p)	12.014	.15	.50	4.00	15.00
	1950(p)	—	—	—	Proof	850.00
	1951(p)	29.422	.15	.25	1.50	7.50
	1951(p)	—	—	—	Proof	850.00
	1951(p) w/o dot					
	Inc. Ab.	.15	.35	1.50	7.50	
	1951PL	*17.040	.15	.35	1.50	8.00
	1951PL	—	—	—	Proof	1000.
	1952(p)	1.832	.50	2.75	8.00	28.00
	1952(p)	—	—	—	Proof	850.00

*NOTE: 5.040 Struck at the Birmingham Mint.

KM#	Date	Mintage	Fine	VF	XF	Unc
49	1953(p)	23.967	.15	.25	1.00	5.50
	1953(p)	16 pcs.	—	—	Proof	850.00
	1954(p)	21.963	.15	.25	1.00	6.50
	1954(p)	—	—	—	Proof	850.00
	1955(p)	9.343	.15	.25	1.00	6.50
	1955(p) w/o dot					
	301 pcs.	—	—	—	Proof	600.00

Obv. leg: F:D: added.

KM#	Date	Mintage	Fine	VF	XF	Unc
61	1959(m)	10.166	.10	.15	.25	3.50
	1959(m)	1.506	—	—	Proof	65.00
	1960(m)	17.812	.10	.15	.25	1.25
	1960(p)	1.030	—	—	Proof	85.00
	1961(p)	20.183	.10	.15	.25	1.25
	1961(p)	1.040	—	—	Proof	85.00
	1962(p)	10.259	.10	.15	.25	1.00
	1962(p)	1.064	—	—	Proof	75.00

KM#	Date	Mintage	Fine	VF	XF	Unc
61	1963(p)	16.410	.10	.15	.25	1.00
	1963(p)	1,060	—	—	Proof	75.00
	1964(p)	18.230	.10	.15	.25	1.00
	1964(p)	1 known	—	—	Proof	3000.

PENNY

Bronze

KM#	Date	Mintage	Fine	VF	XF	Unc
23	1911(L)	3.768	1.00	3.50	20.00	100.00
	1911(L)	—	—	—	Proof	1800.
	1912H	3.600	1.00	3.50	25.00	150.00
	1912H	—	—	—	Proof	1800.
	1913(L)	2.520	1.50	9.00	32.00	200.00
	1914(L)	.720	3.50	10.00	75.00	475.00
	1915(L)	.960	2.50	18.00	90.00	650.00
	1915H	1.320	2.00	10.00	65.00	550.00
	1916-I(c)	3.324	.50	1.75	17.50	115.00
	1916-I(c)	—	—	—	Proof	1800.
	1917-I(c)	6.240	.40	1.25	15.00	110.00
	1918-I(c)	1.200	4.50	18.00	85.00	520.00
	1919(m) w/o dots	5.810	.50	2.75	25.00	160.00
	1919(m) dot below bottom scroll	Inc. Ab.	1.50	4.50	40.00	180.00
	1919(m) dots below bottom scroll and above upper	I.A.	11.50	32.00	130.00	—
	1919(m)	—	—	—	Proof	1800.
	1920(m&sy) w/o dots	8.250	.75	8.00	200.00	1650.
	1920(m) dot below bottom scroll	Inc. Ab.	2.25	9.00	50.00	350.00
	1920(m)	—	—	—	Proof	1800.
	1920(sy) dot above bottom scroll	Inc. Ab.	3.50	9.00	50.00	520.00
	1920(m) dots below bottom scroll and above upper	I.A.	6.50	35.00	130.00	—
	1921(m&sy)	7.438	.25	3.50	32.00	250.00
	1922(m&p)	12.697	.25	3.00	32.00	250.00
	1923(m)	5.654	.25	3.00	28.00	250.00
	1923(m)	—	—	—	Proof	1600.
	1924(m&sy)	4.656	.25	1.75	22.50	210.00
	1924(m)	—	—	—	Proof	1500.
	1925(m)	1.639	13.50	27.50	200.00	3000.
	1925(m)	—	—	—	Proof	8000.
	1926(m&sy)	1.859	1.25	4.50	40.00	350.00
	1926(m)	—	—	—	Proof	1800.
	1927(m)	4.922	.30	2.75	15.00	120.00
	1927(m)	50 pcs.	—	—	Proof	1200.
	1928(m)	3.038	.30	4.00	25.00	250.00
	1928(m)	—	—	—	Proof	1800.
	1929(m)	2.599	.30	3.00	25.00	320.00
	1929(m)	—	—	—	Proof	1750.
	1930(m)	*3,000	4500.	7500.	20,000.	40,000.
	1930(m)	—	—	—	Proof	75,000.
	1931(m)	.494	2.00	5.50	40.00	650.00
	1931(m)	—	—	—	Proof	1750.
	1932(m)	2.117	.30	3.00	25.00	150.00
	1933/2(m)	5.818	3.50	13.50	55.00	300.00
	1933(m)	Inc. Ab.	.25	1.75	16.00	75.00
	1933(m)	—	—	—	Proof	1400.
	1934(m)	5.808	.25	1.00	12.00	65.00
	1934(m)	100 pcs.	—	—	Proof	900.00
	1935(m)	3.725	.25	1.00	8.00	60.00
	1935(m)	100 pcs.	—	—	Proof	900.00
	1936(m)	9.890	.25	1.00	6.50	50.00
	1936(m)	—	—	—	Proof	1000.

KM#	Date	Mintage	Fine	VF	XF	Unc
36	1938(m)	5.552	.25	.50	4.50	25.00
	1938(m)	250 pcs.	—	—	Proof	750.00
	1939(m)	6.240	.25	.50	4.50	30.00
	1939(m)	—	—	—	Proof	1250.
	1940(m)	4.075	.30	1.25	7.50	50.00
	1940(p)K.G	1.114	1.75	3.50	40.00	280.00
	1941(m)	1.588	.30	1.25	10.00	50.00
	1941(p)K.G	12.794	1.00	2.25	25.00	100.00
	1941(p)	—	—	—	Proof	1600.
	1941(p)Y.	I.A.	.25	1.00	7.50	50.00
	1941(p) high dot after 'Y'	Inc. Ab.	.50	1.50	10.00	48.00
	1942(p)	12.245	.15	.75	5.00	32.00
	1942(p)	—	—	—	Proof	1200.
	1942-I(b)	9.000	.15	.50	4.00	25.00
	1942(b) w/o 'I'	Inc. Ab.	2.00	4.50	12.00	60.00

KM#	Date	Mintage	Fine	VF	XF	Unc
36	1942(b)	—	—	—	Proof	1200.
	1943(m)	11.112	.20	.50	6.00	25.00
	1943(p)	33.086	.15	.50	6.50	28.00
	1943(p)	—	—	—	Proof	1000.
	1943-I(b)	9.000	.20	.50	5.00	22.50
	1943-I(b) w/o (I)	Inc. Ab.	2.00	4.50	12.00	60.00
	1943(b)	—	—	—	Proof	800.00
	1944(m)	2.112	.50	4.50	25.00	110.00
	1944(p)	27.830	.15	.50	4.00	28.00
	1944(p)	—	—	—	Proof	1200.
	1945(p)	15.173	.20	1.00	5.50	35.00
	1945(p)	—	—	—	Proof	1400.
	1945-I(b)	6 pcs.	—	—	Rare	—
	1945(m)	—	—	—	—	15,000.
	1946(m)	.240	6.50	18.00	50.00	520.00
	1947(m)	6.864	.15	.40	2.50	13.50
	1947(p)	4.49	.50	1.50	7.50	50.00
	1947(p)	—	—	—	Proof	1400.
	1948(m)	26.616	.15	.40	2.50	13.50
	1948(p)	1.534	1.00	3.50	32.00	175.00
	1948(p)	—	—	—	Proof	1500.

Obv. leg: IND:IMP. dropped.

KM#	Date	Mintage	Fine	VF	XF	Unc
43	1949(m)	27.065	.15	.25	2.25	12.00
	1949(m)	—	—	—	Proof	2000.
	1950(m)	36.359	.15	.25	2.25	16.00
	1950(m)	—	—	—	Proof	2000.
	1950(p)	21.488	.20	.30	7.50	40.00
	1950(p)	—	—	—	Proof	1200.
	1951(m)	21.240	.15	.20	1.25	10.00
	1951(p)	12.888	.20	.40	6.00	25.00
	1951(p)	—	—	—	Proof	1200.
	1951PL	18.000	.15	.25	1.00	8.00
	1951PL	—	—	—	Proof	1250.
	1952(m)	12.408	.15	.30	1.25	8.00
	1952(m)	—	—	—	Proof	2500.
	1952(p)	45.514	.15	.30	1.25	7.50
	1952(p)	—	—	—	Proof	1250.

KM#	Date	Mintage	Fine	VF	XF	Unc
50	1953(m)	6.936	.20	1.00	3.50	16.00
	1953(m)	—	—	—	Proof	800.00
	1953(p)	6.203	.20	.75	1.75	18.00
	1953(p)	16 pcs.	—	—	Proof	1400.

Obv. leg: F:D: added.

KM#	Date	Mintage	Fine	VF	XF	Unc
56	1955(m)	6.336	.25	1.25	3.00	16.00
	1955(m)	1,200	—	—	Proof	90.00
	1955(p)	11.110	.10	.20	1.00	10.00
	1955(p)	301 pcs.	—	—	Proof	900.00
	1956(m)	13.872	.10	.20	1.00	8.00
	1956(m)	1,500	—	—	Proof	65.00
	1956(p)	12.121	.10	.20	1.00	7.50
	1956(p)	417 pcs.	—	—	Proof	750.00
	1957(p)	15.978	.10	.20	1.00	6.50
	1957(p)	1,112	—	—	Proof	120.00
	1958(m)	10.012	.10	.20	1.00	6.50
	1958(m)	1,506	—	—	Proof	65.00
	1958(p)	14.428	.10	.20	1.00	7.50
	1958(p)	1,028	—	—	Proof	110.00
	1959(m)	1.617	.50	1.50	8.00	32.00
	1959(m)	1,506	—	—	Proof	65.00
	1959(p)	14.428	.10	.20	1.00	6.00
	1959(p)	1,030	—	—	Proof	100.00
	1960(p)	20.515	.10	.20	1.00	2.00
	1960(p)	1,030	—	—	Proof	90.00
	1961(p)	30.607	.10	.20	.40	1.50
	1961(p)	1,040	—	—	Proof	90.00
	1962(p)	34.851	.10	.20	.40	1.50
	1962(p)	1,064	—	—	Proof	85.00

KM#	Date	Mintage	Fine	VF	XF	Unc
56	1963(p)	10.258	.10	.20	.40	1.50
	1963(p)	1,100	—	—	Proof	85.00
	1964(m)	49.130	.10	.20	.50	1.25
	1964(p)	54.590	.10	.20	.50	1.25
	1964(p)	1 known	—	—	Proof	4000.

THREEPENCE

1.4100 g, .925 SILVER, .0419 oz ASW

KM#	Date	Mintage	Fine	VF	XF	Unc
18	1910(L)	4.000	2.00	4.50	10.00	40.00
	1910(L)	—	—	—	Proof	700.00

KM#	Date	Mintage	Fine	VF	XF	Unc
24	1911(L)	2.000	5.00	12.50	50.00	200.00
	1911(L)	—	—	—	Proof	2000.
	1911(L) reeded edge	—	—	—	Proof	10,000.
	1912(L)	2.400	6.50	60.00	200.00	900.00
	1914(L)	1.600	10.00	32.00	120.00	650.00
	1915(L)	.800	15.00	65.00	210.00	1000.
	1916M	1.913	6.00	12.00	65.00	450.00
	1916M	25 pcs.	—	—	Proof	1000.
	1917M	3.808	2.00	6.50	22.00	150.00
	1918M	3.119	2.00	6.50	25.00	130.00
	1919M	3.201	3.00	10.00	32.00	150.00
	1919M	—	—	—	Proof	1000.
	1920M	4.196	7.50	18.00	65.00	400.00
	1920M	—	—	—	Proof	1000.
	1921M	7.378	2.00	5.00	20.00	125.00
	1921(m)plain	I.A.	9.00	16.00	100.00	600.00
	1922/1(m)	5.531	2250.	5000.	10,000.	17,500.
	1922(m)	Inc. Ab.	2.00	9.00	25.00	185.00
	1922(m)	—	—	—	Proof	1000.
	1923(m)	.815	13.50	35.00	150.00	850.00
	1924(m&sy)	2.014	6.50	13.50	60.00	350.00
	1924(m)	—	—	—	Proof	900.00
	1925(m&sy)	4.347	.50	4.00	17.50	120.00
	1925(m)	—	—	—	Proof	900.00
	1926(m&sy)	6.158	.50	2.25	16.00	115.00
	1926(m)	—	—	—	Proof	900.00
	1927(m)	6.720	.50	2.25	15.50	85.00
	1927(m)	50 pcs.	—	—	Proof	900.00
	1928(m)	5.000	.50	2.25	16.00	110.00
	1928(m)	—	—	—	Proof	900.00
	1934/3(m)	1.616	22.50	45.00	180.00	675.00
	1934(m)	Inc. Ab.	.50	2.25	16.00	90.00
	1934(m)	100 pcs.	—	—	Proof	450.00
	1935(m)	2.800	.50	2.25	16.00	100.00
	1935(m)	—	—	—	Proof	550.00
	1936(m)	3.600	.30	1.50	8.00	40.00
	1936(m)	—	—	—	Proof	650.00

KM#	Date	Mintage	Fine	VF	XF	Unc
37	1938(m)	4.560	.30	1.50	7.50	16.00
	1938(m)	250 pcs.	—	—	Proof	300.00
	1939(m)	3.856	.30	1.75	8.00	32.00
	1939(m)	—	—	—	Proof	450.00
	1940(m)	3.840	.30	1.75	8.00	40.00
	1941(m)	7.584	.30	1.25	4.50	25.00
	1942(m)	.528	10.00	40.00	175.00	750.00
	1942D	16.000	BV	.40	1.25	4.00
	1942S	8.000	BV	.75	1.50	5.00
	1943(m)	24.912	BV	.40	1.00	3.50
	1943D	16.000	BV	.40	1.25	4.00
	1943S	8.000	BV	.75	1.50	5.00
	1944S	32.000	BV	.40	1.00	4.00

1.4100 g, .500 SILVER, .0226 oz ASW

KM#	Date	Mintage	Fine	VF	XF	Unc
37a	1947(m)	4.176	1.00	2.25	8.00	25.00
	1948(m)	26.208	—	BV	2.00	6.00

Obv. leg: IND:IMP. dropped.

KM#	Date	Mintage	Fine	VF	XF	Unc
44	1949(m)	26.400	—	BV	2.00	6.00
	1949(m)	—	—	—	Proof	700.00
	1950(m)	35.456	—	BV	2.00	8.00
	1951(m)	15.856	—	.50	3.00	12.00
	1951PL	40.000	—	BV	1.25	3.50
	1951PL	—	—	—	Proof	500.00
	1952(m)	21.560	—	BV	2.00	10.00

KM#	Date	Mintage	Fine	VF	XF	Unc
51	1953(m)	7.664	BV	2.00	5.50	20.00
	1953(m)	—	—	—	Proof	500.00
	1954(m)	2.672	1.00	3.00	6.50	35.00
	1954(m)	—	—	—	Proof	600.00

Obv. leg: F:D: added.

KM#	Date	Mintage	Fine	VF	XF	Unc
57	1955(m)	27.088	—	BV	1.50	5.00
	1955(m)	1,040	—	—	Proof	40.00
	1956(m)	14.088	—	BV	1.50	6.00
	1956(m)	1,500	—	—	Proof	35.00
	1957(m)	26.704	—	BV	1.00	3.50
	1957(m)	1,256	—	—	Proof	35.00
	1958(m)	11.248	—	BV	2.00	5.00
	1958(m)	1,506	—	—	Proof	35.00
	1959(m)	19.888	—	BV	1.00	3.00
	1959(m)	1,506	—	—	Proof	35.00
	1960(m)	19.600	—	BV	.75	1.50
	1960(m)	1,509	—	—	Proof	30.00
	1961(m)	33.840	—	BV	.75	1.50
	1961(m)	1,506	—	—	Proof	30.00
	1962(m)	15.968	—	BV	.75	1.50
	1962(m)	2,016	—	—	Proof	30.00
	1963(m)	44.016	—	BV	.50	1.50
	1963(m)	5,042	—	—	Proof	20.00
	1964(m)	20.320	—	BV	.50	1.50

SIXPENCE

2.8200 g, .925 SILVER, .0838 oz ASW

KM#	Date	Mintage	Fine	VF	XF	Unc
19	1910(L)	3.046	6.00	15.00	40.00	90.00
	1910(L)	—	—	—	Proof	800.00

KM#	Date	Mintage	Fine	VF	XF	Unc
25	1911(L)	1.000	8.50	25.00	100.00	600.00
	1911(L)	—	—	—	Proof	2000.
	1912(L)	1.600	16.00	60.00	175.00	1000.
	1914(L)	1.800	6.50	14.50	80.00	400.00
	1916M	1.769	9.00	25.00	140.00	675.00
	1916M	25 pcs.	—	—	Proof	1750.
	1917M	1.632	9.00	22.50	120.00	520.00
	1918M	.915	22.50	75.00	275.00	1250.
	1919M	1.521	9.00	22.50	75.00	350.00
	1919M	—	—	—	Proof	1600.
	1920M	1.476	10.00	30.00	140.00	675.00
	1920M	—	—	—	Proof	2500.
	1921(m)	—	—	—	Proof	2000.
	1921(m&sy)	3.795	6.00	12.00	40.00	200.00
	1922(sy)	1.488	16.00	45.00	175.00	950.00
	1922(sy)	—	—	—	Proof	2500.
	1923(m&sy)	1.458	10.00	25.00	140.00	650.00
	1924(m)	—	—	—	Proof	2000.
	1924(m&sy)	1.038	10.00	25.00	180.00	900.00
	1925(m)	—	—	—	Proof	900.00
	1925(m&sy)	3.266	.75	10.00	50.00	200.00
	1926(m)	—	—	—	Proof	900.00
	1926(m&sy)	3.609	.75	8.00	32.00	125.00
	1927(m)	3.592	.75	7.00	25.00	120.00
	1927(m)	50 pcs.	—	—	Proof	900.00
	1928(m)	2.721	.75	7.00	25.00	130.00
	1928(m)	—	—	—	Proof	900.00
	1934(m)	1.024	3.00	8.00	35.00	200.00
	1934(m)	100 pcs.	—	—	Proof	700.00
	1935(m)	.392	5.00	12.00	60.00	285.00
	1935(m)	—	—	—	Proof	1000.
	1936(m)	1.800	.75	3.50	12.00	100.00
	1936(m)	—	—	—	Proof	900.00

KM#	Date	Mintage	Fine	VF	XF	Unc
38	1938(m)	2.864	.65	2.25	8.00	28.00
	1938(m)	250 pcs.	—	—	Proof	400.00
	1939(m)	1.600	.65	3.00	16.00	140.00
	1939(m)	—	—	—	Proof	900.00
38	1940(m)	1.600	.65	3.00	12.00	75.00
	1941(m)	2.912	.65	2.25	6.50	32.00
	1942(m)	8.968	BV	1.50	4.00	18.00
	1942D	12.000	BV	.75	2.50	12.00
	1942S	4.000	BV	.75	2.50	16.00
	1943D	8.000	BV	.75	2.50	12.00
	1943S	4.000	BV	.75	2.50	15.00
	1944S	4.000	BV	1.25	2.75	14.00
	1945(m)	10.096	BV	1.25	2.75	12.00

2.8200 g, .500 SILVER, .0453 oz ASW

KM#	Date	Mintage	Fine	VF	XF	Unc
38a	1946(m)	10.024	BV	1.00	4.00	22.00
	1946(m)	—	—	—	Proof	900.00
	1948(m)	1.584	BV	1.00	4.00	25.00

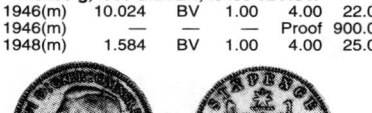

Obv. leg: IND:IMP. dropped.

KM#	Date	Mintage	Fine	VF	XF	Unc
45	1950(m)	10.272	BV	2.25	4.00	22.00
	1950(m)	—	—	—	Proof	1500.
	1951(m)	13.760	BV	1.75	3.25	18.00
	1951PL	20.024	BV	.50	2.00	8.00
	1951PL	—	—	—	Proof	650.00
	1952(m)	2.112	.75	5.00	25.00	200.00

KM#	Date	Mintage	Fine	VF	XF	Unc
52	1953(m)	1.152	.75	4.00	12.00	100.00
	1953(m)	—	—	—	Proof	700.00
	1954(m)	7.672	BV	1.00	1.75	5.50
	1954(m)	—	—	—	Proof	750.00

Obv. leg: F:D: added.

KM#	Date	Mintage	Fine	VF	XF	Unc
58	1955(m)	14.248	BV	.75	2.00	10.00
	1955(m)	1,200	—	—	Proof	60.00
	1956(m)	7.904	BV	2.75	5.00	25.00
	1956(m)	1,500	—	—	Proof	50.00
	1957(m)	13.752	BV	.50	1.00	5.00
	1957(m)	1,256	—	—	Proof	50.00
	1958(m)	17.944	BV	.50	1.00	3.50
	1958(m)	1,506	—	—	Proof	45.00
	1959(m)	11.728	BV	.50	1.25	6.00
	1959(m)	1,506	—	—	Proof	45.00
	1960(m)	18.592	BV	.50	1.00	5.00
	1960(m)	1,509	—	—	Proof	40.00
	1961(m)	9.152	BV	.50	1.00	3.00
	1961(m)	1,506	—	—	Proof	40.00
	1962(m)	44.816	BV	.50	.75	2.00
	1962(m)	2,016	—	—	Proof	40.00
	1963(m)	25.056	BV	.50	.75	2.00
	1963(m)	5,042	—	—	Proof	25.00

SHILLING

5.6500 g, .925 SILVER, .1680 oz ASW

KM#	Date	Mintage	Fine	VF	XF	Unc
20	1910(L)	2.536	4.50	18.00	75.00	150.00
	1910(L)	—	—	—	Proof	900.00

KM#	Date	Mintage	Fine	VF	XF	Unc
26	1911(L)	1.700	11.50	32.50	80.00	650.00
	1911(L)	—	—	—	Proof	5000.
	1912(L)	1.000	22.50	110.00	200.00	2000.
	1913(L)	1.200	13.50	55.00	160.00	1500.
	1914(L)	3.300	7.50	20.00	50.00	400.00
	1915(L)	.800	22.50	125.00	280.00	1800.
	1915H	.500	35.00	135.00	400.00	3750.
	1916M	5.141	1.50	6.50	25.00	115.00
	1916M	25 pcs.	—	—	Proof	1750.
	1917M	5.274	1.50	6.50	25.00	115.00
26	1918M	3.761	4.50	16.00	50.00	180.00
	1919M	—	—	—	Proof	20,000.
	1920M	.520	6.50	25.00	120.00	1000.
	1920M	—	—	—	Proof	6000.
	1921star(sy)	1.641	18.00	90.00	285.00	2500.
	1921star(m)	—	—	—	Proof	7500.
	1922(m)	2.040	9.00	22.50	100.00	400.00
	1922(m)	—	—	—	Proof	2700.
	1924(m&sy)	.674	18.00	50.00	250.00	1100.
	1924(m)	—	—	—	Proof	4000.
	1925/3(m&sy)	1.448	1.50	12.00	40.00	145.00
	1925(m)	—	—	—	Proof	1500.
	1926(m&sy)	2.352	1.50	12.00	50.00	150.00
	1926(m)	—	—	—	Proof	2000.
	1927(m)	1.146	4.50	12.00	35.00	140.00
	1927(m)	50 pcs.	—	—	Proof	1850.
	1928(m)	.664	11.50	28.00	160.00	850.00
	1928(m)	—	—	—	Proof	3000.
	1931(m)	1.000	4.50	12.00	50.00	160.00
	1931(m)	—	—	—	Proof	—
	1933(m)	.220	40.00	145.00	850.00	2000.
	1933(m)	—	—	—	Proof	10,000.
	1934(m)	.480	9.00	22.00	90.00	275.00
	1934(m)	100 pcs.	—	—	Proof	900.00
	1935(m)	.500	6.00	12.00	28.00	145.00
	1935(m)	—	—	—	Proof	1000.
	1936(m)	2.000	3.00	9.00	28.00	150.00
	1936(m)	—	—	—	Proof	1250.

KM#	Date	Mintage	Fine	VF	XF	Unc
39	1938(m)	1.484	2.75	5.50	10.00	35.00
	1938(m)	250 pcs.	—	—	Proof	500.00
	1939(m)	1.520	2.75	5.50	12.00	90.00
	1939(m)	—	—	—	Proof	2000.
	1940(m)	.760	6.00	13.50	40.00	250.00
	1941(m)	3.040	BV	4.50	8.00	35.00
	1942(m)	1.380	BV	3.50	7.00	25.00
	1942S	4.000	BV	1.50	3.50	12.00
	1943(m)	2.720	2.75	6.00	16.00	75.00
	1943S	16.000	BV	1.50	2.75	10.00
	1944(m)	14.576	BV	2.75	7.00	32.00
	1944S	8.000	BV	1.50	3.00	12.00

5.6500 g, .500 SILVER, .0908 oz ASW

KM#	Date	Mintage	Fine	VF	XF	Unc
39a	1946(m)	10.072	BV	3.00	5.50	15.00
	1946(p)	1.316	5.50	13.50	32.00	90.00
	1948(m)	4.132	BV	3.50	6.50	18.00

Obv. leg: IND:IMP. dropped.

KM#	Date	Mintage	Fine	VF	XF	Unc
46	1950(m)	7.188	BV	3.00	5.00	12.00
	1952(m)	19.644	BV	2.75	4.00	9.00

KM#	Date	Mintage	Fine	VF	XF	Unc
53	1953(m)	12.204	BV	2.25	4.00	8.00
	1953(m)	—	—	—	Proof	700.00
	1954(m)	16.188	BV	2.25	4.00	9.00
	1954(m)	—	—	—	Proof	800.00

Obv. leg: F:D: added.

KM#	Date	Mintage	Fine	VF	XF	Unc
59	1955(m)	7.492	BV	1.75	4.00	15.00
	1955(m)	1,200	—	—	Proof	60.00
	1956(m)	6.064	BV	1.00	3.00	20.00
	1956(m)	1,500	—	—	Proof	50.00
	1957(m)	12.668	BV	.75	1.50	6.50
	1957(m)	1,256	—	—	Proof	50.00
	1958(m)	7.412	BV	.75	1.50	6.50
	1958(m)	1,506	—	—	Proof	45.00
	1959(m)	10.876	BV	.75	1.25	5.00
	1959(m)	1,506	—	—	Proof	45.00
	1960(m)	14.512	—	BV	1.00	3.50
	1960(m)	1,509	—	—	Proof	40.00

KM#	Date	Mintage	Fine	VF	XF	Unc
59	1961(m)	31.864	—	BV	.75	2.00
	1961(m)	1,506	—	—	Proof	40.00
	1962(m)	6.592	—	BV	.75	2.00
	1962(m)	2,016	—	—	Proof	40.00
	1963(m)	10.072	—	BV	.75	2.00
	1963(m)	5,042	—	—	Proof	30.00

FLORIN

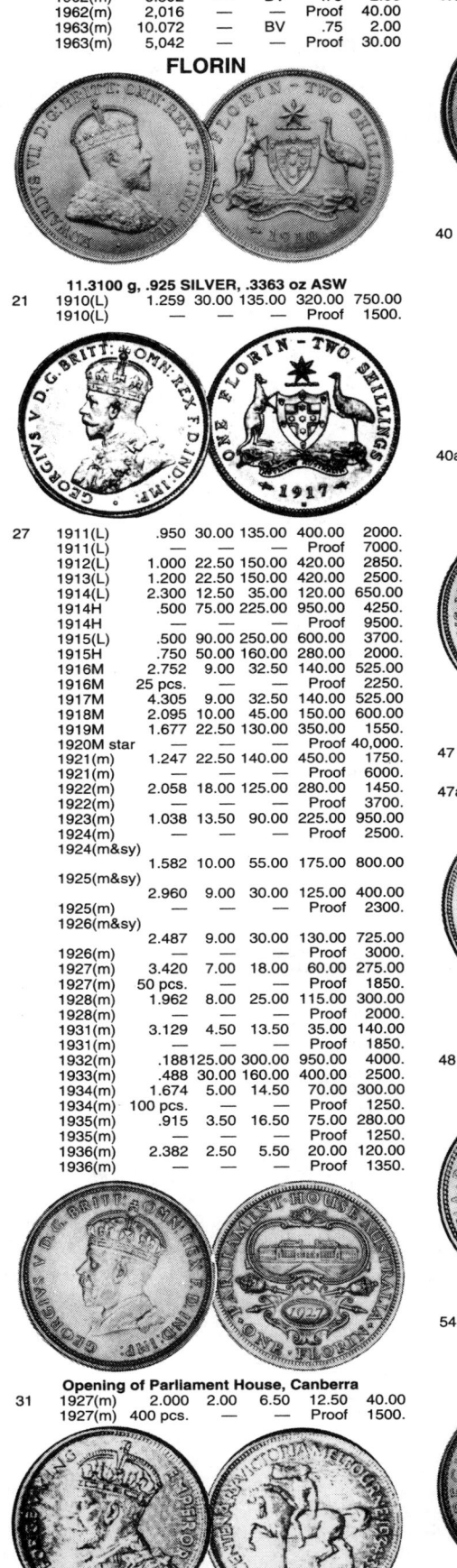

11.3100 g, .925 SILVER, .3363 oz ASW

KM#	Date	Mintage	Fine	VF	XF	Unc
21	1910(L)	1.259	30.00	135.00	320.00	750.00
	1910(L)	—	—	—	Proof	1500.

KM#	Date	Mintage	Fine	VF	XF	Unc
27	1911(L)	.950	30.00	135.00	400.00	2000.
	1911(L)	—	—	—	Proof	7000.
	1912(L)	1.000	22.50	150.00	420.00	2850.
	1913(L)	1.200	22.50	150.00	420.00	2500.
	1914(L)	2.300	12.50	35.00	120.00	650.00
	1914H	.500	75.00	225.00	950.00	4250.
	1914H	—	—	—	Proof	9500.
	1915(L)	.500	90.00	250.00	600.00	3700.
	1915H	.750	50.00	160.00	280.00	2000.
	1916M	2.752	9.00	32.50	140.00	525.00
	1916M	25 pcs.	—	—	Proof	2250.
	1917M	4.305	9.00	32.50	140.00	525.00
	1918M	2.095	10.00	45.00	150.00	600.00
	1919M	1.677	22.50	130.00	350.00	1550.
	1920M star	—	—	—	Proof	40,000.
	1921(m)	1.247	22.50	140.00	450.00	1750.
	1921(m)	—	—	—	Proof	6000.
	1922(m)	2.058	18.00	125.00	280.00	1450.
	1922(m)	—	—	—	Proof	3700.
	1923(m)	1.038	13.50	90.00	225.00	950.00
	1924(m)	—	—	—	Proof	2500.
	1924(m&sy)	1.582	10.00	55.00	175.00	800.00
	1925(m&sy)	2.960	9.00	30.00	125.00	400.00
	1925(m)	—	—	—	Proof	2300.
	1926(m&sy)	2.487	9.00	30.00	130.00	725.00
	1926(m)	—	—	—	Proof	3000.
	1927(m)	3.420	7.00	18.00	60.00	275.00
	1927(m)	50 pcs.	—	—	Proof	1850.
	1928(m)	1.962	8.00	25.00	115.00	300.00
	1928(m)	—	—	—	Proof	2000.
	1931(m)	3.129	4.50	13.50	35.00	140.00
	1931(m)	—	—	—	Proof	1850.
	1932(m)	.188	125.00	300.00	950.00	4000.
	1933(m)	.488	30.00	160.00	400.00	2500.
	1934(m)	1.674	5.00	14.50	70.00	300.00
	1934(m)	100 pcs.	—	—	Proof	1250.
	1935(m)	.915	3.50	16.50	75.00	280.00
	1935(m)	—	—	—	Proof	1250.
	1936(m)	2.382	2.50	5.50	20.00	120.00
	1936(m)	—	—	—	Proof	1350.

Opening of Parliament House, Canberra

KM#	Date	Mintage	Fine	VF	XF	Unc
31	1927(m)	2.000	2.00	6.50	12.50	40.00
	1927(m)	400 pcs.	—	—	Proof	1500.

Centennial of Victoria and Melbourne

KM#	Date	Mintage	Fine	VF	XF	Unc
33	"1934-35"	*.054	90.00	115.00	155.00	225.00
	"1934-35"	—	—	—	Proof	2500.

*NOTE: 21,000 pcs. were melted.

KM#	Date	Mintage	Fine	VF	XF	Unc
40	1938(m)	2.990	2.50	5.50	20.00	55.00
	1938(m)	—	—	—	Proof	700.00
	1939(m)	.630	9.00	18.00	55.00	520.00
	1939(m)	—	—	—	Proof	2500.
	1940(m)	8.410	BV	4.50	10.00	32.00
	1941(m)	7.614	BV	4.50	9.00	30.00
	1942(m)	17.986	BV	4.00	6.00	28.00
	1942S	6.000	BV	4.50	7.00	28.00
	1943(m)	12.762	BV	3.50	5.00	22.00
	1943S	11.000	BV	3.50	5.00	20.00
	1944(m)	22.440	BV	3.50	5.00	25.00
	1944S	11.000	BV	3.50	5.00	20.00
	1945(m)	11.970	BV	4.50	9.00	40.00

11.3100 g, .500 SILVER, .1818 oz ASW

KM#	Date	Mintage	Fine	VF	XF	Unc
40a	1946(m)	22.154	BV	2.00	4.00	14.50
	1946(m)	—	—	—	Proof	600.00
	1947(m)	39.292	BV	2.00	4.00	14.50
	1947(m)	—	—	—	Proof	600.00

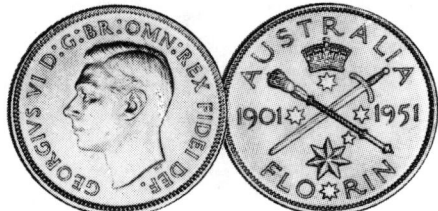

50th Year Jubilee

KM#	Date	Mintage	Fine	VF	XF	Unc
47	1951(m)	2.000	BV	2.75	4.00	10.00

COPPER-NICKEL

KM#	Date	Mintage	Fine	VF	XF	Unc
47a	1951(L)	—	—	—	Proof	5000.

11.3100 g, .500 SILVER, .1818 oz ASW
Obv. leg: IND:IMP. dropped.

KM#	Date	Mintage	Fine	VF	XF	Unc
48	1951(m)	10.068	2.75	6.00	12.00	37.50
	1952(m)	10.044	3.00	6.50	12.50	38.00

KM#	Date	Mintage	Fine	VF	XF	Unc
54	1953(m)	12.658	BV	3.50	6.00	12.00
	1953(m)	—	—	—	Proof	900.00
	1954(m)	15.366	BV	3.50	6.00	16.00
	1954(m)	—	—	—	Proof	1000.

Royal Visit

KM#	Date	Mintage	Fine	VF	XF	Unc
55	1954(m)	4.000	BV	2.25	4.00	12.00

Obv. leg: F:D: added.

KM#	Date	Mintage	Fine	VF	XF	Unc
60	1956(m)	8.090	2.75	4.50	12.00	40.00
	1956(m)	1,500	—	—	Proof	75.00
	1957(m)	9.278	BV	2.75	3.25	6.50
	1957(m)	1,256	—	—	Proof	50.00
	1958(m)	8.972	BV	2.75	3.25	6.50
	1958(m)	1,506	—	—	Proof	45.00
	1959(m)	3.500	BV	2.75	3.25	7.00
	1959(m)	1,506	—	—	Proof	40.00
	1960(m)	15.760	BV	2.25	2.75	4.50
	1960(m)	1,509	—	—	Proof	35.00
	1961(m)	9.452	BV	2.25	3.00	5.00
	1961(m)	1,506	—	—	Proof	35.00
	1962(m)	13.748	BV	2.25	2.75	4.50
	1962(m)	2,016	—	—	Proof	35.00
	1963(m)	12.002	BV	2.25	2.75	4.50
	1963(m)	5,042	—	—	Proof	25.00

CROWN

28.2800 g, .925 SILVER, .8411 oz ASW

KM#	Date	Mintage	Fine	VF	XF	Unc
34	1937(m)	1.008	6.00	9.00	18.00	50.00
	1937(m)	100 pcs.	—	—	Proof	2000.
	1938(m)	.102	20.00	45.00	90.00	320.00
	1938(m)	250 pcs.	—	—	Proof	2500.

TRADE COINAGE

MINT MARKS

M - Melbourne
P - Perth
S - Sydney
(sy) - Sydney

1/2 SOVEREIGN

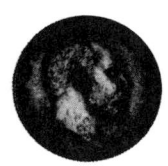
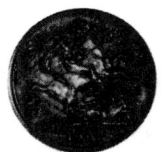

3.9940 g, .917 GOLD, .1177 oz AGW
Obv: Older veiled head. Rev: Mintmark above date.

KM#	Date	Mintage	Fine	VF	XF	Unc
14	1902S	.084	65.00	100.00	190.00	600.00
	1902S	—	—	—	Proof	7500.
	1903S	.231	65.00	100.00	220.00	600.00
	1904P	.060	125.00	325.00	900.00	2400.
	1906S	.308	60.00	80.00	130.00	440.00
	1906M	.082	60.00	80.00	170.00	650.00
	1907M	.400	60.00	75.00	100.00	480.00
	1908S	.538	60.00	75.00	100.00	480.00
	1908M					
		Inc. 1907M	60.00	75.00	110.00	440.00
	1908M	.025	200.00	450.00	1000.	2400.
	1909M	.186	60.00	75.00	140.00	550.00
	1909P	.044	125.00	275.00	640.00	1600.
	1910S	.474	60.00	75.00	110.00	320.00

KM#	Date	Mintage	Fine	VF	XF	Unc
28	1911S	.252	50.00	60.00	80.00	100.00
	1911S	—	—		Matte Proof	11,500.
	1911P	.130	75.00	100.00	150.00	270.00
	1912S	.278	BV	60.00	80.00	100.00
	1914S	.322	BV	60.00	80.00	100.00
	1915S	.892	BV	40.00	70.00	90.00
	1915M	.125	BV	60.00	80.00	110.00
	1915P	.138	75.00	100.00	150.00	250.00
	1916S	.448	BV	50.00	70.00	100.00
	1918P	*200-250 pcs.	300.00	450.00	650.00	1200.

SOVEREIGN

7.9881 g, .917 GOLD, .2354 oz AGW
Obv: Older veiled head.

KM#	Date	Mintage	Fine	VF	XF	Unc
13	1901S	3.012	—	BV	100.00	130.00
	1901M	3.987	—	BV	100.00	130.00
	1901M	—	—	—	Proof	10,000.
	1901P	2.889	—	BV	120.00	225.00
	1901P	—	—	—	Proof	12,500.

NOTE: Earlier dates (1893-1900) exist for this type.

KM#	Date	Mintage	Fine	VF	XF	Unc
15	1902S	2.813	—	—	BV	110.00
	1902S	—	—	—	Proof	12,500.
	1902M	4.267	—	—	BV	110.00
	1902P	4.289	—	—	BV	115.00
	1902P	—	—	—	Proof	12,500.
	1903S	2.806	—	—	BV	110.00
	1903M	3.521	—	—	BV	110.00
	1903P	4.674	—	—	BV	115.00
	1904S	2.986	—	—	BV	110.00
	1904M	3.743	—	—	BV	110.00
	1904M	—	—	—	Proof	12,500.
	1904P	4.506	—	—	BV	110.00
	1905S	2.778	—	—	BV	110.00
	1905M	3.633	—	—	BV	110.00
	1905P	4.876	—	—	BV	110.00
	1906S	2.792	—	—	BV	110.00
	1906M	3.657	—	—	BV	110.00
	1906P	4.829	—	—	BV	110.00
	1907S	2.539	—	—	BV	110.00
	1907M	3.332	—	—	BV	110.00
	1907P	4.972	—	—	BV	110.00
	1908S	2.017	—	—	BV	110.00
	1908M	3.080	—	—	BV	110.00
	1908P	4.875	—	—	BV	110.00
	1909S	2.057	—	—	BV	110.00
	1909M	3.029	—	—	BV	110.00
	1909P	4.524	—	—	BV	110.00
	1910S	2.135	—	—	BV	110.00
	1910M	3.054	—	—	BV	110.00
	1910M	—	—	—	Proof	12,500.
	1910P	4.690	—	—	BV	110.00

KM#	Date	Mintage	Fine	VF	XF	Unc
29	1911S	2.519	—	—	BV	120.00
	1911S	—	—	—	Proof	12,500.
	1911M	2.851	—	—	BV	120.00
	1911M	—	—	—	Proof	12,500.
	1911P	4.373	—	—	BV	120.00
	1912S	2.227	—	—	BV	120.00
	1912M	2.467	—	—	BV	120.00
	1912P	4.278	—	—	BV	120.00
	1913S	2.249	—	—	BV	120.00
	1913M	2.323	—	—	BV	120.00
	1913P	4.635	—	—	BV	120.00
	1914S	1.774	—	—	BV	120.00
	1914S	—	—	—	Proof	11,500.
	1914M	2.012	—	—	BV	120.00
	1914P	4.815	—	—	BV	120.00
	1915S	1.346	—	—	BV	120.00
	1915M	1.637	—	—	BV	120.00
	1915P	4.373	—	—	BV	120.00
	1916S	1.242	—	—	BV	120.00
	1916M	1.277	—	—	BV	120.00
	1916P	4.906	—	—	BV	120.00
	1917S	1.666	—	—	BV	120.00
	1917M	.934	—	—	BV	120.00
	1917P	4.110	—	—	BV	120.00
	1918S	3.716	—	—	BV	120.00
	1918M	4.969	—	—	BV	120.00

KM#	Date	Mintage	Fine	VF	XF	Unc
29	1918P	3.812	—	—	BV	120.00
	1919S	1.835	—	—	BV	120.00
	1919M	.514	—	BV	110.00	155.00
	1919P	2.995	—	—	BV	110.00
	1920S	.360	20,000.	30,000.	50,000.	120,000.
	1920M	.530	1000.	1500.	2000.	4400.
	1920P	2.421	—	—	BV	120.00
	1921S	.839	1000.	1500.	2000.	4400.
	1921M	.240	1500.	3400.	5000.	10,000.
	1921P	2.314	—	—	BV	120.00
	1922S	.578	3000.	8000.	12,000.	20,000.
	1922M	.608	1000.	3000.	5500.	10,000.
	1922P	2.298	—	—	BV	120.00
	1923S	.416	1000.	2800.	5500.	10,000.
	1923M	.510	100.00	150.00	200.00	4000.
	1923P	2.124	100.00	150.00	200.00	2000.
	1924S	.394	200.00	750.00	1200.	2000.
	1924M	.278	BV	105.00	120.00	140.00
	1924P	1.464	BV	135.00	190.00	300.00
	1925S	5.632	—	—	BV	120.00
	1925M	3.311	—	—	BV	120.00
	1925P	1.837	BV	175.00	200.00	400.00
	1926S	1.031	7000.	12,000.	17,000.	24,000.
	1926S	—	—	—	Proof	22,500.
	1926M	.211	—	BV	120.00	145.00
	1926P	1.131	200.00	500.00	800.00	1500.
	1927M	.310	—	—	—	—
	1927P	1.383	BV	150.00	200.00	400.00
	1928M	.413	750.00	1250.	2000.	3200.
	1928P	1.333	BV	150.00	200.00	325.00

Obv: Smaller head.

KM#	Date	Mintage	Fine	VF	XF	Unc
32	1929M	.436	700.00	1200.	1850.	3200.
	1929M	—	—	—	Proof	10,000.
	1929P	1.606	—	BV	120.00	145.00
	1930M	.077	100.00	150.00	225.00	300.00
	1930M	—	—	—	Proof	10,000.
	1930P	1.915	—	BV	120.00	145.00
	1931M	.057	150.00	250.00	450.00	650.00
	1931M	—	—	—	Proof	10,000.
	1931P	1.173	—	BV	120.00	145.00

DECIMAL COINAGE

100 Cents = 1 Dollar

CENT

BRONZE
Ring-tailed Opossum

KM#	Date	Mintage	Fine	VF	XF	Unc
62	1966(c)	146.457	—	—	.15	.50
	1966(c)	.018	—	—	Proof	3.00
	1966(m) blunted whisker on right	238.990	—	.15	.25	1.50
	1966(p) blunted 2nd whisker from right	26.620	.15	.30	1.50	8.00
	1967	110.055	—	.15	.25	2.00
	1968	19.930	—	.15	.55	7.00
	1969	87.680	—	—	.15	.60
	1969	.013	—	—	Proof	3.00
	1970	72.560	—	—	.15	.55
	1970	.015	—	—	Proof	3.00
	1971	102.455	—	—	.15	.50
	1971	.010	—	—	Proof	3.00
	1972	82.400	—	—	.10	.50
	1972	.010	—	—	Proof	3.00
	1973	140.710	—	—	.10	.30
	1973	.010	—	—	Proof	3.00
	1974	131.720	—	—	.10	.30
	1974	.011	—	—	Proof	3.00
	1975	134.775	—	—	—	.20
	1975	.023	—	—	Proof	.75
	1976	172.935	—	—	—	.20
	1976	.021	—	—	Proof	1.75
	1977	153.430	—	—	—	.20
	1977	.055	—	—	Proof	.75
	1978	97.253	—	—	—	.15
	1978	.039	—	—	Proof	.75
	1979	130.339	—	—	—	.15
	1979	.036	—	—	Proof	.75
	1980	137.892	—	—	—	.15
	1980	.068	—	—	Proof	.75
	1981	223.900	—	—	—	.15
	1981	.086	—	—	Proof	.75
	1982	134.290	—	—	—	.15
	1982	.100	—	—	Proof	.75
	1983	205.625	—	—	—	.15
	1983	.080	—	—	Proof	.75
	1984	74.735	—	—	—	.15
	1984	.061	—	—	Proof	.75

KM#	Date	Mintage	Fine	VF	XF	Unc
78	1985	38.300	—	—	—	.10
	1985	.075	—	—	Proof	.50
	1986	.180		In sets only		2.50
	1986	.067	—	—	Proof	.50
	1987	127.000	—	—	—	.10
	1987	.070	—	—	Proof	.50
	1988	56.910	—	—	—	.10
	1988	.106	—	—	Proof	.50
	1989	—	—	—	—	.10
	1989	—	—	—	Proof	.50
	1990	—	—	—	—	.10
	1990	—	—	—	Proof	.50
	1991	—	—	—	—	.10
	1991	—	—	—	Proof	.50

2 CENTS

BRONZE
Frilled Lizard

KM#	Date	Mintage	Fine	VF	XF	Unc
63	1966(c)	145.226	—	—	.10	.50
	1966(c)	.018	—	—	Proof	6.00
	1966(m) blunted 3rd left claw	66.575	—	.15	.35	2.50
	1966(p) blunted 1st right claw	217.735	—	.15	.25	1.50
	1967	73.250	—	.15	.30	4.00
	1968	17.000	—	.15	.55	5.00
	1969	12.940	—	.15	.30	2.50
	1969	.013	—	—	Proof	5.50
	1970	39.872	—	—	.15	1.00
	1970	.015	—	—	Proof	5.50
	1971	60.735	—	—	.15	1.00
	1971	.010	—	—	Proof	5.50
	1972	77.570	—	—	.10	.75
	1972	.010	—	—	Proof	5.00
	1973	94.058	—	—	.10	.60
	1973	.010	—	—	Proof	5.00
	1974	177.723	—	—	.10	.60
	1974	.011	—	—	Proof	5.00
	1975	100.045	—	—	.10	.50
	1975	.023	—	—	Proof	1.00
	1976	121.882	—	—	.10	.50
	1976	.021	—	—	Proof	2.50
	1977	102.000	—	—	.10	.50
	1977	.055	—	—	Proof	1.00
	1978	128.253	—	—	.10	.50
	1978	.039	—	—	Proof	1.00
	1979	69.705	—	—	.10	.50
	1979	.036	—	—	Proof	1.00
	1980	145.603	—	—	.10	.50
	1980	.068	—	—	Proof	1.00
	1981	219.176	—	—	.10	.50
	1981	.086	—	—	Proof	1.00
	1982	121.770	—	—	.10	.50
	1982	.100	—	—	Proof	1.00
	1983	177.227	—	—	.10	.50
	1983	.080	—	—	Proof	1.00
	1984	57.963	—	—	.10	.50
	1984	.061	—	—	Proof	1.00

KM#	Date	Mintage	Fine	VF	XF	Unc
79	1985	34.500	—	—	.10	.30
	1985	.075	—	—	Proof	.50
	1986	.180		In sets only		1.00
	1986	.067	—	—	Proof	.50
	1987	.200		In sets only		1.00
	1987	.070	—	—	Proof	.50
	1988	28.905	—	—	.10	.30
	1988	.106	—	—	Proof	.50
	1989	—	—	—	.10	.30
	1989	—	—	—	Proof	.50
	1990	—	—	—	.10	.30
	1990	—	—	—	Proof	.50
	1991	—	—	—	.10	.30
	1991	—	—	—	Proof	.50

5 CENTS

COPPER-NICKEL
Short-beaked Spiny Ant-eater

KM#	Date	Mintage	Fine	VF	XF	Unc
64	1966(c)	45.427	—	.15	.25	1.50
	1966(c)	.018	—	—	Proof	9.00
	1966(L)	30.000	—	.15	.25	1.50
	1966(L)	—	—	—	Proof	15.00
	1967	62.144	—	.15	.35	2.50
	1968	67.336	—	.15	.40	3.50
	1969	38.170	—	.15	.20	2.50
	1969	.013	—	—	Proof	12.00
	1970	46.058	—	—	.15	2.50
	1970	.015	—	—	Proof	12.00
	1971	39.516	—	.15	.25	3.00
	1971	.010	—	—	Proof	11.50
	1972	8.256	.15	.30	1.30	9.00
	1972	.010	—	—	Proof	10.00
	1973	48.816	—	.15	.20	1.00
	1973	.010	—	—	Proof	10.00
	1974	64.248	—	.15	.20	1.00
	1974	.011	—	—	Proof	10.00
	1975	44.256	—	—	.10	.40
	1975	.023	—	—	Proof	2.00
	1976	113.180	—	—	.10	.30
	1976	.021	—	—	Proof	4.50
	1977	108.800	—	—	.10	.30
	1977	.055	—	—	Proof	2.00
	1978	25.210	—	—	.10	.25
	1978	.039	—	—	Proof	2.25
	1979	44.533	—	—	.10	.25
	1979	.036	—	—	Proof	2.00
	1980	115.042	—	—	.10	.25
	1980	.068	—	—	Proof	1.50
	1981	162.264	—	—	.10	.25
	1981	.086	—	—	Proof	1.50
	1982	139.468	—	—	.10	.25
	1982	.100	—	—	Proof	1.50
	1983	131.568	—	—	.10	.25
	1983	.080	—	—	Proof	2.00
	1984	35.436	—	—	.10	.25
	1984	.061	—	—	Proof	2.00

KM#	Date	Mintage	Fine	VF	XF	Unc
80	1985	.170	In Mint sets only			4.00
	1985	.075	—	—	Proof	3.00
	1986	.180	In Mint sets only			1.00
	1986	.067	—	—	Proof	1.00
	1987	73.500	—	—	—	.20
	1987	.070	—	—	Proof	1.00
	1988	65.424	—	—	—	.20
	1988	.106	—	—	Proof	1.00
	1989	—	—	—	—	.20
	1989	—	—	—	Proof	1.00
	1990	1.446	—	—	—	.20
	1990	—	—	—	Proof	1.00
	1991	29.889	—	—	—	.20
	1991	—	—	—	Proof	1.00
	1992	3.000	—	—	—	.20
	1992	—	—	—	Proof	1.00
	1993	—	—	—	—	.20
	1993	—	—	—	Proof	1.00
	1994	—	—	—	—	.20
	1994	—	—	—	Proof	1.00
	1995	—	—	—	—	.20
	1995	—	—	—	Proof	1.00
	1996	—	—	—	—	.20
	1996	—	—	—	Proof	1.00
	1997	—	—	—	—	.20
	1997	—	—	—	Proof	1.00

10 CENTS

COPPER-NICKEL
Superb Lyre-bird

KM#	Date	Mintage	Fine	VF	XF	Unc
65	1966(c)	10.984	—	.15	.30	2.00
	1966(c)	.018	—	—	Proof	8.00
	1966(L)	30.000	—	.15	.30	2.00
	1966(L)	—	—	—	Proof	12.00
	1967	51.032	—	.15	.55	7.00
	1968	57.194	—	.15	.45	5.00
	1969	22.146	—	.15	.25	2.50
	1969	.013	—	—	Proof	8.50
	1970	22.306	—	.15	.25	2.50
	1970	.015	—	—	Proof	8.50
	1971	20.726	—	.10	.25	3.50
	1971	.010	—	—	Proof	8.00
	1972	12.502	—	.10	.25	4.00
	1972	.010	—	—	Proof	7.00
	1973	27.320	—	.10	.15	1.50
	1973	.010	—	—	Proof	7.00
	1974	46.550	—	.10	.15	1.50
	1974	.011	—	—	Proof	7.00
	1975	50.900	—	.10	.15	.80
	1975	.023	—	—	Proof	1.75
	1976	57.060	—	.10	.15	.80
	1976	.021	—	—	Proof	3.75
	1977	10.940	—	.10	.15	1.00
	1977	.055	—	—	Proof	1.75
	1978	48.400	—	.10	.15	.45
	1978	.039	—	—	Proof	1.75
	1979	36.950	—	.10	.15	.45
	1979	.036	—	—	Proof	1.75
	1980	55.084	—	.10	.15	.45
	1980	.068	—	—	Proof	1.50
	1981	116.060	—	.10	.15	.40
	1981	.086	—	—	Proof	1.50
	1982	61.492	—	.10	.15	.35
	1982	.100	—	—	Proof	1.50
	1983	82.318	—	.10	.15	.35
	1983	.080	—	—	Proof	1.75
	1984	25.728	—	.10	.15	.30
	1984	.061	—	—	Proof	1.75

NOTE: One 1981 coin was struck on a Sri Lanka 50 cents planchet, KM#135.1. It carries an approximate value of $600.

KM#	Date	Mintage	Fine	VF	XF	Unc
81	1985	2.100	—	—	.10	.20
	1985	.075	—	—	Proof	1.25
	1986	.180	In sets only			1.00
	1986	.067	—	—	Proof	3.00
	1987	.200	In sets only			1.00
	1987	.070	—	—	Proof	1.25
	1988	35.095	—	—	—	.20
	1988	.106	—	—	Proof	1.25
	1989	—	—	—	—	.20
	1989	—	—	—	Proof	1.25
	1990	5.452	—	—	—	.20
	1990	—	—	—	Proof	1.25
	1991	3.174	—	—	—	.20
	1991	—	—	—	Proof	1.25
	1992	5.589	—	—	—	.20
	1992	—	—	—	Proof	1.25
	1993	—	—	—	—	.20
	1993	—	—	—	Proof	1.25
	1994	—	—	—	—	.20
	1994	—	—	—	Proof	1.25
	1995	—	—	—	—	.20
	1995	—	—	—	Proof	1.25
	1996	—	—	—	—	.20
	1996	—	—	—	Proof	1.25
	1997	—	—	—	—	.20
	1997	—	—	—	Proof	2.25

20 CENTS

COPPER-NICKEL
Duckbill Platypus

KM#	Date	Mintage	Fine	VF	XF	Unc
66	1966(c)	28.223	—	.20	1.00	10.00
	1966(c)	.018	—	—	Proof	12.50
	1966(L) wave on base of 2					
			—	—	—	185.00
	1966(L)	30.000	—	.20	.75	8.00
	1966(L)	—	—	—	Proof	15.00
	1967	83.848	—	.20	1.35	15.00
	1968	40.537	—	.20	1.10	13.00
	1969	16.502	—	.20	1.10	13.00
	1969	.013	—	—	Proof	13.50
	1970	23.271	—	.20	.65	5.50
	1970	.015	—	—	Proof	13.50
	1971	8.947	—	.15	.75	12.50
	1971	.010	—	—	Proof	12.50
	1972	16.643	—	.15	.50	7.00
	1972	.010	—	—	Proof	12.00
	1973	23.356	—	.15	.45	8.00
	1973	.010	—	—	Proof	12.00
	1974	33.548	—	.15	.45	7.50
	1974	.011	—	—	Proof	12.00
	1975	53.300	—	.15	.20	2.00
	1975	.023	—	—	Proof	2.50
	1976	59.774	—	.15	.20	.90
	1976	.021	—	—	Proof	4.50
	1977	41.272	—	.15	.20	.80
	1977	.055	—	—	Proof	2.00
	1978	38.781	—	.15	.20	.80
	1978	.039	—	—	Proof	2.00
	1979	22.300	—	.15	.20	1.00
	1979	.036	—	—	Proof	2.00
	1980	77.673	—	.15	.20	.40
	1980	.068	—	—	Proof	1.50
	1981	164.500	—	.15	.20	.40
	1981	.086	—	—	Proof	1.50
	1982	76.600	—	.15	.20	.40
	1982	.100	—	—	Proof	1.50
	1983	55.113	—	.15	.20	.40
	1983	.080	—	—	Proof	2.00
	1984	27.820	—	.15	.20	.35
	1984	.061	—	—	Proof	2.00

NOTE: Some 1981 dated coins were struck on a Hong Kong 2 Dollar planchet, KM#37. 6 pcs. are reported. Each carries an approximate value of $800.

KM#	Date	Mintage	Fine	VF	XF	Unc
82	1985	27.000	—	.15	.20	.30
	1985	.075	—	—	Proof	2.00
	1986	.180	In sets only			1.00
	1986	.067	—	—	Proof	3.00
	1987	.200	In sets only			1.00
	1987	.070	—	—	Proof	1.50
	1988	.240	In sets only			1.00
	1988	.106	—	—	Proof	1.50
	1989	—	—	—	—	.30
	1989	—	—	—	Proof	1.50
	1990	—	—	—	—	.30
	1990	—	—	—	Proof	1.50
	1991	—	—	—	—	.30
	1991	—	—	—	Proof	1.50
	1992	—	—	—	—	.50
	1992	—	—	—	Proof	1.50
	1993	—	—	—	—	.50
	1993	—	—	—	Proof	1.50
	1994	—	—	—	—	.50
	1994	—	—	—	Proof	1.50
	1995	—	—	—	—	.50
	1995	—	—	—	Proof	1.50
	1996	—	—	—	—	.50
	1996	—	—	—	Proof	1.50
	1997	—	—	—	—	.50
	1997	—	—	—	Proof	1.50

50th Anniversary - United Nations

KM#	Date	Mintage	Fine	VF	XF	Unc
295	1995	—	—	—	—	1.50

50 CENTS

13.2800 g, .800 SILVER, .3416 oz ASW

KM#	Date	Mintage	Fine	VF	XF	Unc
67	1966	36.454	—	—	BV	6.50
	1966	.018	—	—	Proof	75.00

COPPER-NICKEL

KM#	Date	Mintage	Fine	VF	XF	Unc
68	1969	14.015	—	.45	1.25	8.50
	1969	.013	—	—	Proof	60.00
	1971	21.056	—	.45	2.00	9.00
	1971	.010	—	—	Proof	40.00
	1972	5.586	—	.45	2.25	10.00
	1972	.010	—	—	Proof	40.00
	1973	4.009	—	.45	2.50	17.50
	1973	.010	—	—	Proof	40.00
	1974	8.962	—	.45	.85	8.50
	1974	.011	—	—	Proof	35.00
	1975	19.025	—	.40	.50	3.50

KM#	Date	Mintage	Fine	VF	XF	Unc
68	1975	.023	—	—	Proof	11.50
	1976	27.280	—	.40	.50	2.50
	1976	.021	—	—	Proof	22.00
	1978	25.765	—	.40	.50	1.00
	1978	.039	—	—	Proof	7.50
	1979	24.886	—	.40	.50	1.00
	1979	.036	—	—	Proof	8.50
	1980	38.681	—	.40	.50	1.00
	1980	.068	—	—	Proof	6.00
	1981	24.168	—	.40	.50	.80
	1981	.086	—	—	Proof	6.00
	1983	48.923	—	—	.40	.75
	1983	.080	—	—	Proof	8.50
	1984	26.281	—	—	.40	.75
	1984	.061	—	—	Proof	8.50

200th Anniversary - Cook's Australian Voyage
Obv: Similar to KM#68.

69	1970	17.100	—	.40	1.50	4.00
	1970	.015	—	—	Proof	55.00

Queen's Silver Jubilee

70	1977	25.076	—	.40	.50	1.25
	1977	.055	—	—	Proof	7.50

Mule. Obv: KM#70. Rev: Fiji 50 Cent KM#36.

A72	1978	—	—	—	—	—

Wedding of Prince Charles and Lady Diana

72	1981	44.100	—	—	.40	.50	1.25

XII Commonwealth Games - Brisbane

74	1982	23.287	—	—	.40	.50	1.25
	1982	.100	—	—	—	Proof	6.00

KM#	Date	Mintage	Fine	VF	XF	Unc
83	1985	1.000	—	—	.40	.60
	1985	.075	—	—	Proof	4.00
	1986	.180	—	In sets only		3.50
	1986	.067	—	—	Proof	4.00
	1987	.200	—	In sets only		3.50
	1987	.070	—	—	Proof	4.00
	1989	—	—	—	—	2.50
	1989	—	—	—	Proof	4.00
	1990	—	—	—	—	2.50
	1990	—	—	—	Proof	4.00
	1992	—	—	—	—	2.50
	1992	—	—	—	Proof	4.00
	1993	—	—	—	—	2.50
	1993	—	—	—	Proof	4.00
	1996	—	—	—	—	2.50
	1996	—	—	—	Proof	4.00
	1997	—	—	—	—	2.50
	1997	—	—	—	Proof	4.00

Australian Bicentennial

99	1988	2.793	—	—	—	2.50
	1988	.106	—	—	Proof	4.00

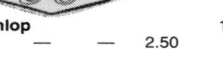

25th Anniversary of Decimal Currency - Merino Ram

139	1991	4.364	—	—	—	2.50
	1991	—	—	—	Proof	12.00

18.0000 g, .925 SILVER, .5353 oz ASW
International Year of the Family

257	1994	—	—	—	—	2.25
	1994	—	—	—	Proof	12.00

"Weary" Dunlop

294	1995	—	—	—	—	2.50

George Bass and Matthew Flinders
Obv: Queen's portrait. Rev: Portraits of Bass and Flinders.

KM#	Date	Mintage	Fine	VF	XF	Unc
364	1998	—	—	—	—	2.50
	1998	—	—	—	Proof	12.00

DOLLAR

NICKEL-ALUMINUM-COPPER
Kangaroos

77	1984	185.985	—	—	.85	3.25
	1984	.159	—	—	Proof	10.00

84	1985	91.400	—	—	.85	3.25
	1985	.075	—	—	Proof	10.00
	1987	.200	—	In sets only		3.50
	1987	.070	—	—	Proof	10.00
	1989	—	—	—	—	3.00
	1989	—	—	—	Proof	10.00
	1990	—	—	—	—	3.00
	1990	—	—	—	Proof	10.00
	1991	—	—	—	—	3.00
	1991	—	—	—	Proof	10.00
	1994	—	—	—	—	3.00
	1994	—	—	—	Proof	10.00
	1995	—	—	—	—	3.00
	1995	—	—	—	Proof	10.00

ALUMINUM-BRONZE
International Year of Peace

87	1986	25.100	—	—	.85	3.00
	1986	.067	—	—	Proof	21.50

Aboriginal Art

100	1988	1.564	—	—	—	3.00
	1988	.106	—	—	Proof	20.00

Olympics - Female Javelin Thrower
Edge: Alternating reeded and plain sections.

175.1	1992	.016	—	—	—	4.00
	1992	.046	—	—	Proof	20.00

Landcare Australia - Stylized Tree

KM#	Date	Mintage	Fine	VF	XF	Unc
208	1993	15.000	—	—	—	3.00
	1993	—	—	—	Proof	18.00
	1993C	.092	—	—	—	3.50
	1993M	.060	—	—	—	3.50
	1993S	.088	—	—	—	3.50

NOTE: Visitors at mints and coin shows were allowed to strike a coin for a fee at the following: C - Canberra, M - Hall of Manufacturers Pavilion Coin Show, Melbourne and S - Sydney International Coin Fair.

10th Anniversary - Introduction of Dollar Coin

258	1994C	.123	—	—	—	March	3.50
	1994M	.065	—	—	—		4.00
	1994S	.074	—	—	—		4.00

NOTE: Coin show issues: A - Adelaide, B - Brisbane, C - Canberra, M - Melbourne, S - Sydney.

A.B. "Banjo" Paterson - Waltzing Matilda

269	1995B	.074	—	—	—	5.50
	1995C	.156	—	—	—	4.50
	1995M	.074	—	—	—	5.50
	1995S	.083	—	—	—	5.50

NOTE: Coin show issues: A - Adelaide, B - Brisbane, C - Canberra, M - Melbourne, S - Sydney.

Sir Henry Parks

310	1996	—	—	—	—	4.00
	1996	—	—	—	Proof	—
	1996A	—	—	—	—	5.00
	1996B	—	—	—	—	5.00
	1996C	.025	—	—	—	6.00
	1996M	—	—	—	—	5.00
	1996S	.064	—	—	—	5.00

NOTE: Coin show issues: A - Adelaide, B - Brisbane, C - Canberra, M - Melbourne.

Sir Charles Kingsford Smith
Obv: Queen's portrait.
Rev: Pilot above airplane, dates.

327	1997	—	—	—	—	4.00

Howard Florey

Obv: Queen's portrait. Rev: Portrait of Florey.

KM#	Date	Mintage	Fine	VF	XF	Unc
366	1998A	—	—	—	—	4.50
	1998B	—	—	—	—	4.50
	1998M	—	—	—	—	4.50
	1998S	—	—	—	—	4.50

2 DOLLARS

ALUMINUM-BRONZE
Male Aborigine

101	1988	59.679	—	—	—	4.50
	1988	.106	—	—	Proof	10.00
	1989	—	—	—	—	4.50
	1989	—	—	—	Proof	10.00
	1990	.339	—	—	—	4.50
	1990	—	—	—	Proof	10.00
	1991	—	—	—	—	4.50
	1991	—	—	—	Proof	10.00
	1992	—	—	—	—	4.50
	1992	—	—	—	Proof	10.00
	1993	—	—	—	—	4.50
	1993	—	—	—	Proof	10.00
	1994	—	—	—	—	4.50
	1994	—	—	—	Proof	10.00
	1995	—	—	—	—	4.50
	1995	—	—	—	Proof	10.00
	1996	—	—	—	—	4.50
	1996	—	—	—	Proof	10.00
	1997	—	—	—	—	4.50
	1997	—	—	—	Proof	10.00

AUSTRIA

The Republic of Austria, a parliamentary democracy located in mountainous central Europe, has an area of 32,378 sq. mi. (83,850 sq. km.) and a population of 8 million. Capital: Vienna. Austria is primarily an industrial country. Machinery, iron, steel, textiles, yarns and timber are exported.

The territories later to be known as Austria were overrun in pre-Roman times by various tribes, including the Celts. Upon the fall of the Roman Empire, the country became a margravate of Charlemagne's Empire. Premysl Otaker, King of Bohemia, gained possession in 1252, only to lose the territory to Rudolf of Habsburg in 1276. Thereafter, until World War I, the story of Austria was conducted by the ruling Habsburgs.

During World War I, the Austro-Hungarian Empire was one of the Central Powers with Germany, Bulgaria and Turkey. At the end of the war, the Empire was dismembered and Austria established as an independent republic. In March, 1938, Austria was incorporated into Hitler's short-lived Greater German Reich. Allied forces of both East and West occupied Austria in April 1945, and subsequently divided it into 4 zones of military occupation. On May 15, 1955, the 4 powers formally recognized Austria as a 'sovereign independent democratic state.'

RULERS

Franz Joseph I, 1848-1916
Karl I, 1916-1918

MINT MARKS

(a) - Vienna

MONETARY SYSTEM

100 Heller = 1 Corona, 1892-1918

TRADE COINAGE
DUCAT

3.4909 g, .986 GOLD, .1106 oz AGW

KM#	Date	Mintage	Fine	VF	XF	Unc
2267	1901	.349	60.00	100.00	125.00	175.00
	1902	.311	60.00	100.00	125.00	175.00
	1903	.380	60.00	100.00	125.00	175.00
	1904	.517	60.00	100.00	125.00	175.00
	1905	.392	60.00	125.00	150.00	200.00
	1906	.492	60.00	125.00	150.00	200.00
	1907	.554	60.00	125.00	175.00	250.00
	1908	.409	60.00	80.00	125.00	175.00
	1909	.366	60.00	80.00	100.00	150.00
	1910	.440	60.00	80.00	100.00	150.00
	1911	.591	60.00	80.00	100.00	125.00
	1912	.495	60.00	80.00	100.00	125.00
	1913	.320	60.00	80.00	100.00	125.00
	1914	.378	60.00	80.00	100.00	125.00
	1915 (restrike)*	—	—			BV + 10%
	1951 (error for 1915)					
		—	75.00	125.00	150.00	225.00

NOTE: 996,721 pieces were struck from 1920-1936.
NOTE: Earlier dates (1872-1900) exist for this type.

4 DUCAT

13.9636 g, .986 GOLD, .4430 oz AGW

KM#	Date	Mintage	Fine	VF	XF	Unc
2276	1901	.052	225.00	250.00	450.00	600.00
	1902	.069	225.00	250.00	400.00	600.00
	1903	.073	225.00	250.00	400.00	600.00
	1904	.080	225.00	250.00	400.00	600.00
	1905	.091	225.00	250.00	400.00	550.00
	1906	.123	225.00	250.00	300.00	450.00
	1907	.104	225.00	250.00	300.00	500.00
	1908	.080	225.00	250.00	450.00	600.00
	1909	.084	225.00	250.00	375.00	500.00
	1910	.101	225.00	250.00	275.00	400.00
	1911	.142	225.00	250.00	275.00	350.00
	1912	.151	225.00	250.00	275.00	350.00
	1913	.119	225.00	250.00	275.00	350.00
	1914	.102	225.00	250.00	275.00	350.00
	1915 (restrike)*	—	—		BV + 8%	

NOTE: 496,501 pieces were struck from 1920-1936.
NOTE: Earlier dates (1872-1900) exist for this type.

THALER

An unofficial trade dollar, the final date of the famous Maria Theresa Thaler has been restruck intermittently since 1781 to modern times at many world mints. It has been used in many areas that lacked a firm local coinage, particularly in north and east Africa and the Near East. Gunzburg Mint was where the original talers were struck. (Listings for these can be found under Burgau-Austrian States, KM#23). Since then the thalers have been restruck at the following mints: Vienna, Prague, Milan, Venice, Gunzburg, London, Paris, Brussels, Kremnitz, Karlsburg, Rome, Bombay and Florence with an estimated 800 million struck to date.

Period	Mintage	Mint
1920-1937	52,069,465	Vienna
1935-1939	19,496,729	Rome
1935-1957	11,809.956	Paris
1936-1961	20,159,070	London
1937-1957	10,995,024	Brussels
1940-1941	18,864,576	Bombay
1949-1955	3,428,500	Birmingham
1956-1975	9,924,151	Vienna

HELLER

BRONZE

KM#	Date	Mintage	Fine	VF	XF	Unc
2800	1901	52.096	.20	.35	.50	2.00
	1902	20.553	.20	.50	1.25	3.00
	1903	13.779	.20	.35	.50	2.50
	1909	12.668	.20	.35	.50	2.50
	1910	21.900	.20	.35	.50	2.50

KM#	Date	Mintage	Fine	VF	XF	Unc
2800	1911	18.387	.20	.35	.50	2.50
	1912	27.053	.20	.35	.50	2.50
	1913	8.782	.20	.35	.50	2.50
	1914	9.906	.20	.35	.50	2.50
	1915	5.670	.20	.35	.50	2.50
	1916	12.484	.35	.75	1.50	4.00

NOTE: Earlier dates (1892-1900) exist for this type.

Obv: Austrian shield on eagle's breast.

2823	1916	Inc. Ab.	4.00	6.00	10.00	17.50

2 HELLER

BRONZE

KM#	Date	Mintage	Fine	VF	XF	Unc
2801	1901	12.157	2.00	3.00	6.00	25.00
	1902	18.760	.15	.50	1.50	3.00
	1903	26.983	.50	1.50	3.00	8.00
	1904	12.863	.15	.50	1.75	7.00
	1905	6.679	.75	2.75	5.50	15.00
	1906	20.104	.50	1.50	3.00	8.00
	1907	23.804	.15	.25	.75	3.00
	1908	21.984	.15	.25	.75	3.00
	1909	25.975	.15	.25	.75	3.00
	1910	28.406	.50	1.50	3.00	8.00
	1911	50.007	.15	.25	.50	2.00
	1912	74.234	.15	.20	.35	2.00
	1913	27.432	.35	.75	2.25	6.00
	1914	60.674	.15	.20	.35	2.00
	1915	7.870	.15	.20	.35	2.00

NOTE: Earlier dates (1892-1900) exist for this type.

IRON
Obv: Austrian shield on eagle's breast.

2824	1916	61.909	.50	1.00	2.00	7.50
	1917	81.186	.25	.50	1.00	5.00
	1918	66.353	.25	.50	1.00	4.00

10 HELLER

NICKEL

2802	1907	8.662	.25	.50	1.00	4.00
	1908	7.772	.75	1.50	2.50	6.00
	1909	20.462	.15	.25	.75	2.50
	1910	10.100	.15	.25	.75	2.50
	1911	3.634	1.00	2.00	3.50	8.00

NOTE: Earlier dates (1892-1895) exist for this type.

COPPER-NICKEL-ZINC

2822	1915	18.366	.15	.25	.50	2.00
	1916	27.487	.15	.25	.50	2.00

Obv: Austrian shield on eagle's breast.

2825	1916	14.804	.50	1.00	2.00	5.00

20 HELLER

NICKEL

KM#	Date	Mintage	Fine	VF	XF	Unc
2803	1907	7.650	.75	1.50	3.00	12.00
	1908	7.469	.75	1.25	2.50	9.00
	1909	7.592	1.00	2.00	4.00	15.00
	1911	19.560	.25	.35	1.00	5.00
	1914	2.342	5.00	15.00	25.00	50.00

NOTE: Earlier dates (1892-1895) exist for this type.

IRON
Obv: Austrian shield on eagle's breast.

2826	1916	130.770	.50	1.25	2.00	6.50
	1917	127.420	.50	1.25	2.00	5.50
	1918	48.985	.25	.65	1.25	4.50

CORONA

5.0000 g, .835 SILVER, .1342 oz ASW

2804	1901	10.387	1.75	2.75	5.00	10.00
	1902	2.947	2.00	4.25	7.50	15.00
	1903	2.198	2.00	4.25	8.00	25.00
	1904	.993	4.00	8.50	17.50	40.00
	1905	.505	10.00	25.00	45.00	85.00
	1906	.165	80.00	125.00	200.00	450.00
	1907	.244	30.00	60.00	100.00	300.00

NOTE: Earlier dates (1892-1900) exist for this type.

60th Anniversary of Reign

2808	ND(1908)	4.784	2.00	3.00	5.00	10.00

2820	1912	8.457	1.50	2.00	3.00	8.00
	1913	9.345	1.50	2.00	3.00	7.00
	1914	37.897	1.50	2.00	3.00	6.00
	1915	23.000	1.50	2.00	3.00	6.00
	1916	12.415	1.50	2.00	3.00	6.00

2 CORONA

10.0000 g, .835 SILVER, .2684 oz ASW

2821	1912	10.245	3.50	5.00	7.00	10.00
	1913	7.256	3.50	5.00	7.00	10.00

5 CORONA

24.0000 g, .900 SILVER, .6945 oz ASW

KM#	Date	Mintage	Fine	VF	XF	Unc
2807	1907	1.539	10.00	15.00	35.00	100.00
	1907	—	—	—	Proof	650.00

NOTE: Earlier date (1900) exists for this type.

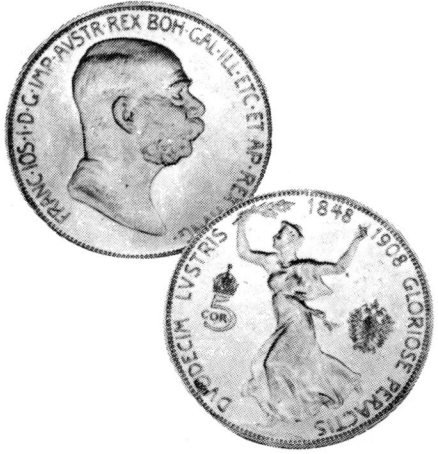

60th Anniversary of Reign

2809	ND(1908)	5.090	7.00	11.50	25.00	60.00
	ND(1908)	—	—	—	Proof	650.00

Obv: Head w/o wreath.

2813	1909	1.709	10.00	16.00	40.00	125.00

Obv: Similar to KM#2809.
Rev: Similar to KM#2807.

2814	1909	1.776	10.00	15.00	35.00	90.00

10 CORONA

3.3875 g, .900 GOLD, .0980 oz AGW
Obv: Laureate head of Franz Joseph I right.
Rev: Eagle w/value and date below.

2805	1905	1.933	BV	55.00	60.00	90.00
	1906	1.081	BV	55.00	60.00	90.00

NOTE: Earlier dates (1892-1897) exist for this type.

60th Anniversary of Reign
Obv: Small plain head of Franz Joseph I right.
Rev: Eagle, value below, 2 dates above.

KM#	Date	Mintage	Fine	VF	XF	Unc
2810	1908	.654	BV	60.00	70.00	100.00

Rev: Eagle, value and date below.

2815	1909	2.320	BV	55.00	60.00	80.00

Obv: Large head.

2816	1909	.192	55.00	60.00	80.00	100.00
	1910	1.005	BV	50.00	60.00	80.00
	1911	1.286	BV	50.00	60.00	80.00
	1912	(restrike)				BV + 10%

20 CORONA

6.7751 g, .900 GOLD, .1960 oz AGW

2806	1901	.049	150.00	225.00	325.00	400.00
	1902	.441	BV	110.00	140.00	160.00
	1903	.323	BV	110.00	140.00	160.00
	1904	.494	BV	110.00	140.00	160.00
	1905	.146	100.00	120.00	150.00	170.00

NOTE: Earlier dates (1892-1900) exist for this type.

60th Anniversary of Reign
Rev: 2 dates above eagle.

2811	1908	.188	100.00	125.00	150.00	200.00

2817	1909	.228	450.00	750.00	1250.	1750.

2818	1909	.102	575.00	850.00	1250.	1750.
	1910	.386	120.00	150.00	250.00	350.00
	1911	.059	125.00	175.00	275.00	375.00
	1912	4,460	250.00	325.00	400.00	500.00
	1913	.028	350.00	500.00	750.00	1000.
	1914	.082	135.00	225.00	300.00	500.00
	1915	(restrike)	—	—		BV + 5%
	1916	.072	2500.	3500.	5500.	7500.

Rev: Austrian shield on eagle.

2827	1916	Inc. Ab.	450.00	550.00	900.00	1200.

Obv: Head of Kaiser Karl I. Rev: Similar to KM#2818.

2828	1918	*2,000	—	—	Unique	—

*NOTE: All but one specimen were remelted.

---

100 CORONA

33.8753 g, .900 GOLD, .9803 oz AGW
60th Anniversary of Reign

KM#	Date	Mintage	Fine	VF	XF	Unc
2812	1908	.016	500.00	600.00	900.00	1400.
	1908	—	—	—	Proof	1850.

2819	1909	3,203	500.00	650.00	950.00	1500.
	1910	3,074	500.00	650.00	950.00	1500.
	1911	11,165	500.00	650.00	950.00	1500.
	1912	3,591	550.00	850.00	1150.	2000.
	1913	2,696	500.00	800.00	1200.	1700.
	1914	1,195	500.00	650.00	1000.	1600.
	1915	(restrike)	—	—		BV + 2%
	1915	(restrike)	—	—	Proof	—

REPUBLIC
MONETARY SYSTEM
10,000 Kronen = 1 Schilling
20 KRONEN

6.7751 g, .900 GOLD, .1960 oz AGW

2830	1923	6,988	650.00	1400.	1850.	2500.
	1924	10,337	650.00	1400.	1850.	2500.

100 KRONEN

33.8753 g, .900 GOLD, .9802 oz AGW

KM#	Date	Mintage	Fine	VF	XF	Unc
2831	1923	617 pcs.	750.00	1550.	2250.	3500.
	1923			—	Proof	4000.
	1924	2,851	750.00	1550.	2250.	3500.

BRONZE

2832	1923	6.404	4.00	8.00	15.00	30.00
	1924	43.014	.25	.50	1.50	4.50

200 KRONEN

BRONZE

2833	1924	57.160	.50	1.00	2.00	6.50

1000 KRONEN

COPPER-NICKEL

2834	1924	72.353	.75	1.50	3.00	8.00

PRE WWII DECIMAL COINAGE
100 Groschen = 1 Schilling

GROSCHEN

BRONZE

2836	1925	30.465	.10	.20	.50	2.00
	1926	15.487	.10	.30	.75	2.00
	1927	9.318	.10	.30	.75	2.50
	1928	17.189	.10	.30	.75	2.50
	1929	11.400	.10	.30	.75	2.50
	1930	8.893	.10	.30	.75	2.50
	1931	.971	10.00	20.00	30.00	60.00
	1932	3.040	1.00	2.50	5.00	7.50
	1933	3.940	.50	1.00	2.00	6.00
	1934	4.232	.15	.50	1.00	4.00
	1935	3.740	.15	.50	1.00	4.00
	1936	6.020	.50	1.00	3.00	9.00
	1937	5.830	.50	1.00	2.00	7.50
	1938	1.650	2.00	3.00	6.00	15.00

2 GROSCHEN

BRONZE

2837	1925	29.892	.10	.25	.50	1.50
	1926	17.700	.10	.30	.75	2.00
	1927	7.757	.20	.75	2.00	5.00
	1928	19.478	.10	.30	.75	2.00
	1929	16.184	.10	.30	.75	2.00
	1930	5.709	.20	.60	1.50	4.00
	1934	.812	7.00	12.00	15.00	25.00
	1935	3.148	.20	.60	1.50	4.00
	1936	4.410	.15	.30	1.00	3.00
	1937	3.790	.20	.40	1.25	3.50
	1938	.860	2.50		6.50	12.50

5 GROSCHEN

COPPER-NICKEL

KM#	Date	Mintage	Fine	VF	XF	Unc
2846	1931	16.631	.15	.40	.80	2.00
	1932	4.700	.25	1.00	2.00	5.00
	1934	3.210	.30	1.00	2.50	6.00
	1936	1.240	.50	4.00	7.50	15.00
	1937	1.540	20.00	30.00	45.00	80.00
	1938	.870	125.00	175.00	250.00	425.00

10 GROSCHEN

COPPER-NICKEL

2838	1925	66.199	.10	.25	.50	3.00
	1928	11.468	.50	1.00	4.00	12.00
	1929	12.000	.40	.75	1.50	4.50

1/2 SCHILLING

3.0000 g, .640 SILVER, .0617 oz ASW

2839	1925	18.370	1.00	2.00	3.00	8.00
	1926	12.943	2.00	4.00	6.00	12.00

50 GROSCHEN

COPPER-NICKEL

2850	1934	8.225	20.00	35.00	50.00	90.00
	1934	Inc. Ab.	—	—	Proof	125.00

2854	1935	11.435	.75	1.25	2.50	5.00
	1935	Inc. Ab.	—	—	Proof	80.00
	1936	1.000	30.00	40.00	60.00	115.00
	1936	Inc. Ab.	—	—	Proof	140.00

SCHILLING

7.0000 g, .800 SILVER, .1800 oz ASW

2835	1924	11.086	1.50	2.50	4.50	10.00

6.0000 g, .640 SILVER, .1235 oz ASW

2840	1925	38.209	1.25	2.00	3.50	7.00
	1926	20.157	1.25	2.00	4.00	8.00
	1932	.700	30.00	40.00	60.00	100.00

COPPER-NICKEL

KM#	Date	Mintage	Fine	VF	XF	Unc
2851	1934	30.641	1.00	2.00	3.50	7.50
	1934			—	Proof	150.00
	1935	11.987	3.00	6.00	12.50	30.00

2 SCHILLING

12.0000 g, .640 SILVER, .2469 oz ASW
Centennial - Death of Franz Schubert

2843	1928	6.900	4.00	5.00	10.00	20.00
	1928	Inc. Ab.	—	—	Proof	400.00

100th Anniversary - Birth of Dr. Theodor Billroth

2844	1929	2.000	6.00	9.00	18.00	37.50

**7th Centennial - Death
of Walther von der Vogelweide**

2845	1930	.500	5.00	6.00	9.00	18.00
	1930	Inc. Ab.	—	—	Proof	125.00

175th Anniversary Birth of Wolfgang Mozart

2847	1931	.500	8.00	16.00	25.00	50.00
	1931	Inc. Ab.	—	—	Proof	300.00

200th Anniversary - Birth of Joseph Haydn

2848	1932	.300	20.00	40.00	90.00	150.00
	1932	Inc. Ab.	—	—	Proof	500.00

Death of Dr. Ignaz Seipel

KM#	Date	Mintage	Fine	VF	XF	Unc
2849	ND(1933)	.400	10.00	20.00	37.50	70.00
	1933	Inc. Ab.	—	—	Proof	400.00

Death of Dr. Engelbert Dollfuss

2852	1934	1.500	7.00	12.00	20.00	32.50
	1934	Inc. Ab.	—	—	Proof	275.00

25th Anniversary - Death of Dr. Karl Lueger

2855	1935	.500	8.00	16.00	25.00	45.00
	1935	Inc. Ab.	—	—	Proof	285.00

Bicentennial - Death of Prince Eugen of Savoy

2858	1936	.500	6.00	9.00	18.00	30.00
	1936	Inc. Ab.	—	—	Proof	225.00

Bicentennial - Completion of St. Charles Church

2859	1937	.500	6.00	9.00	18.00	30.00
	1937	Inc. Ab.	—	—	Proof	185.00

5 SCHILLING

15.0000 g, .835 SILVER, .4027 oz ASW
Madonna of Mariazell

2853	1934	3.066	12.50	18.50	32.00	55.00
	1934	—	—	—	Proof	200.00
	1935	5.377	12.50	18.50	32.00	55.00
	1936	1.557	42.50	75.00	115.00	220.00

25 SCHILLING

5.8810 g, .900 GOLD, .1702 oz AGW

KM#	Date	Mintage	Fine	VF	XF	Unc
2841	1926	.276	—	—	P/L	135.00
	1927	.073	—	—	P/L	145.00
	1928	.134	—	—	P/L	135.00
	1929	.243	—	—	P/L	135.00
	1930	.130	—	—	P/L	145.00
	1931	.169	—	—	P/L	135.00
	1933	4,944	—	—	P/L	2000.
	1934	.011	—	—	P/L	700.00

St. Leopold

2856	1935	2,880	—	—	P/L	1000.
	1936	7,260	—	—	P/L	850.00
	1937	7,660	—	—	P/L	850.00
	1938	1,360	—	—	P/L	25,000.

100 SCHILLING

23.5245 g, .900 GOLD, .6806 oz AGW

2842	1926	.064	—	—	P/L	525.00
	1927	.069	—	—	P/L	525.00
	1928	.040	—	—	P/L	650.00
	1929	.075	—	—	P/L	525.00
	1930	.025	—	—	P/L	525.00
	1931	.102	—	—	P/L	525.00
	1933	4,700	—	—	P/L	1650.
	1934	9,383	—	—	P/L	700.00

Madonna of Mariazell

2857	1935	951 pcs.	—	—	P/L	5500.
	1936	.012	—	—	P/L	2000.
	1937	2,900	—	—	P/L	2250.
	1938	1,400	—	—	P/L	25,000.

GERMAN OCCUPATION
1938-1945
MONETARY SYSTEM
150 Schillings = 100 Reichsmark
NOTE: During this time period German Reichsmark coins and banknotes circulated.

POST WWII DECIMAL COINAGE
100 Groschen = 1 Schilling
GROSCHEN

ZINC

KM#	Date	Mintage	Fine	VF	XF	Unc
2873	1947	23.758	.15	.25	.75	2.50

2 GROSCHEN

ALUMINUM

KM#	Date	Mintage	VF	XF	Unc
2876	1950	21.600	.15	.60	4.00
	1950	—	—	Proof	28.00
	1951	7.370	.25	1.00	4.50
	1951	—	—	Proof	300.00
	1952	37.851	.15	.50	2.50
	1952	—	—	Proof	25.00
	1954	49.879	.15	.50	2.50
	1954	—	—	Proof	50.00
	1957	23.211	.15	.50	3.00
	1957	—	—	Proof	45.00
	1962	6.692	.15	.50	2.50
	1962	—	—	Proof	28.00
	1964	.173	—	Proof	6.50
	1965	11.865	.10	.30	1.50
	1965	—	—	Proof	2.50
	1966	7.454	.10	.30	1.50
	1966	—	—	Proof	7.50
	1967	.013	—	Proof	100.00
	1968	.176	.10	.30	1.50
	1968	.022	—	Proof	10.00
	1969	.062	—	Proof	6.00
	1970	.277	—	Proof	2.50
	1971	.145	—	Proof	2.50
	1972	2.763	—	.20	.50
	1972	.132	—	Proof	1.00
	1973	5.883	—	.20	.50
	1973	.149	—	Proof	1.00
	1974	1.387	—	.20	.50
	1974	.093	—	Proof	1.00
	1975	1.096	—	.20	.50
	1975	.052	—	Proof	1.00
	1976	2.755	—	.20	.50
	1976	.045	—	Proof	1.00
	1977	1.837	—	.20	.50
	1977	.047	—	Proof	1.00
	1978	1.527	—	.20	.50
	1978	.044	—	Proof	1.00
	1979	2.434	—	.20	.50
	1979	.044	—	Proof	1.00
	1980	1.893	—	.20	.50
	1980	.048	—	Proof	10.00
	1981	.950	—	.20	.50
	1981	.049	—	Proof	10.00
	1982	3.950	—	.20	.50
	1982	.050	—	Proof	3.00
	1983	2.665	—	.20	.50
	1983	.065	—	Proof	2.00
	1984	.500	—	.20	.50
	1984	.065	—	Proof	2.00
	1985	1.060	—	.20	.50
	1985	.045	—	Proof	5.00
	1986	1.800	—	.20	.50
	1986	.042	—	Proof	10.00
	1987	.958	—	.20	.50
	1987	.042	—	Proof	6.00
	1988	1.061	—	.20	.50
	1988	.039	—	Proof	2.00
	1989	.950	—	.20	.50
	1989	.038	—	Proof	2.00
	1990	.035	—	Proof	25.00
	1991	2.600	—	.20	.50
	1991	.027	—	Proof	5.00
	1992	.025	—	In sets only	20.00
	1993	.035	—	In sets only	20.00
	1994	—	—	In sets only	25.00

5 GROSCHEN

ZINC

KM#	Date	Mintage	VF	XF	Unc
2875	1948	17.200	.20	.75	12.00
	1950	19.400	.20	.75	8.00
	1950	—	—	Proof	200.00
	1951	12.400	.20	.75	12.00
	1951	—	—	Proof	35.00
	1953	84.900	.15	.75	8.00
	1955	17.000	.15	.75	12.00
	1957	22.260	.15	.75	6.00
	1957	—	—	Proof	50.00
	1961	3.429	.20	.75	8.00
	1961	—	—	Proof	25.00
	1962	5.999	.20	.75	8.00
	1963	13.295	.15	.75	8.00
	1963	—	—	Proof	40.00
	1964	4.659	.15	.75	4.00
	1964	—	—	Proof	2.50
	1965	9.481	.10	.50	3.00
	1965	—	—	Proof	2.50
	1966	9.348	.10	.50	3.00
	1966	—	—	Proof	8.00
	1967	4.404	.10	.50	3.00
	1967	—	—	Proof	10.00
	1968	7.372	.10	.50	3.00
	1968	.016	—	Proof	8.00
	1969	—	—	—	—
	1969	.044	—	Proof	10.00
	1970	—	—	—	—
	1970	*.179	—	Proof	2.50
	1971	*.066	—	—	—
	1971	.125	—	Proof	2.50
	1972	10.979	—	.20	.75
	1972	.116	—	Proof	1.00
	1973	10.336	—	.20	.75
	1973	.120	—	Proof	1.00
	1974	2.911	—	.20	.75
	1974	.087	—	Proof	1.00
	1975	7.102	—	.20	.75
	1975	.051	—	Proof	1.00
	1976	8.079	—	.20	.75
	1976	.045	—	Proof	1.00
	1977	1.600	—	.20	.75
	1977	.045	—	Proof	1.00
	1978	2.657	—	.20	.75
	1978	.044	—	Proof	1.00
	1979	4.927	—	.20	.75
	1979	.044	—	Proof	1.00
	1980	3.100	—	.20	.75
	1980	.048	—	Proof	8.00
	1981	.450	—	.20	.75
	1981	.049	—	Proof	8.00
	1982	3.950	—	.20	.75
	1982	.050	—	Proof	2.50
	1983	.501	—	.20	.75
	1983	.065	—	Proof	2.50
	1984	.988	—	.20	.75
	1984	.065	—	Proof	2.50
	1985	1.915	—	.20	.75
	1985	.045	—	Proof	4.00
	1986	1.008	—	.20	.75
	1986	.042	—	Proof	7.00
	1987	1.048	—	.20	.75
	1987	.042	—	Proof	4.00
	1988	1.261	—	.20	.75
	1988	.039	—	Proof	3.00
	1989	2.604	—	.20	.75
	1989	.038	—	Proof	2.00
	1990	2.608	—	.20	.75
	1990	.035	—	Proof	7.00
	1991	2.400	—	.20	.75
	1991	.027	—	Proof	5.00
	1992	.670	—	.20	.75
	1993	.035	—	In sets only	12.00
	1994	.025	—	In sets only	15.00

10 GROSCHEN

ZINC

KM#	Date	Mintage	Fine	VF	XF	Unc
2874	1947	6.845	.75	2.00	4.00	20.00
	1947	—	—	—	Proof	55.00
	1948	66.205	.20	.50	1.00	3.00
	1948	—	—	—	Proof	65.00
	1949	51.202	.20	.50	1.00	3.00
	1949	—	—	—	Proof	75.00

ALUMINUM

KM#	Date	Mintage	VF	XF	Unc
2878	1951	9.573	.20	.75	8.00
	1951	—	—	Proof	85.00
	1952	45.911	.10	.50	4.00
	1952	—	—	Proof	50.00
	1953	39.002	.10	.50	4.00
	1953	—	—	Proof	175.00
	1955	27.525	.10	.50	4.00
	1955	—	—	Proof	28.00
	1957	33.509	.10	.50	4.00
	1957	—	—	Proof	150.00
	1959	80.719	.10	.35	3.50
	1959	—	—	Proof	45.00
	1961	11.183	.20	.75	8.00
	1961	—	—	Proof	—
	1962	24.635	.10	.35	3.50
	1962	—	—	Proof	40.00
	1963	38.062	.10	.35	3.50
	1963	—	—	Proof	45.00
	1964	34.928	.10	.20	2.00
	1964	—	—	Proof	1.50
	1965	37.025	.10	.20	2.00
	1965	—	—	Proof	1.50
	1966	24.991	.10	.20	2.00
	1966	—	—	Proof	6.00
	1967	32.553	.10	.20	2.00
	1967	—	—	Proof	12.00
	1968	42.412	.10	.20	2.00
	1968	.016	—	Proof	8.00
	1969	19.953	.10	.20	2.00
	1969	.027	—	Proof	5.00
	1970	36.998	—	.10	.45
	1970	.102	—	Proof	1.00
	1971	57.450	—	.10	.45
	1971	.082	—	Proof	1.00
	1972	75.661	—	.10	.45
	1972	.081	—	Proof	1.00
	1973	60.244	—	.10	.45
	1973	.097	—	Proof	.75
	1974	55.924	—	.10	.45
	1974	.078	—	Proof	.75
	1975	60.576	—	.10	.45
	1975	.049	—	Proof	.75
	1976	39.367	—	.10	.45
	1976	.044	—	Proof	.75
	1977	53.610	—	.10	.45
	1977	.044	—	Proof	.75
	1978	57.857	—	.10	.45
	1978	.043	—	Proof	.75
	1979	103.686	—	—	.45
	1979	.044	—	Proof	.75
	1980	79.848	—	—	.45
	1980	.048	—	Proof	2.00
	1981	92.268	—	—	.45
	1981	.049	—	Proof	2.00
	1982	99.950	—	—	.45
	1982	.050	—	Proof	.75
	1983	93.768	—	—	.45
	1983	.065	—	Proof	.75
	1984	86.603	—	—	.45
	1984	.065	—	Proof	.75
	1985	86.304	—	—	.45
	1985	.045	—	Proof	.75
	1986	108.910	—	—	.45
	1986	.042	—	Proof	1.50
	1987	114.058	—	—	.45
	1987	.042	—	Proof	.75
	1988	114.461	—	—	.45
	1988	.039	—	Proof	.75
	1989	127.784	—	—	.45
	1989	.038	—	Proof	.75
	1990	182.050	—	—	.45
	1990	.035	—	Proof	1.50
	1991	140.000	—	—	.45
	1991	.027	—	Proof	1.50
	1992	125.000	—	—	.45
	1993	120.000	—	—	.45
	1994	110.000	—	—	.45
	1995	110.000	—	—	.45
	1996	—	—	—	.45
	1997	—	—	—	.45

20 GROSCHEN

ALUMINUM-BRONZE

KM#	Date	Mintage	Fine	VF	XF	Unc
2877	1950	1.610	.20	.50	2.00	12.00
	1950	—	—	—	Proof	40.00
	1951	7.781	.10	.25	.75	2.50
	1951	—	—	—	Proof	25.00
	1954	5.343	.10	.25	.75	2.50
	1954	—	—	—	Proof	275.00

50 GROSCHEN

ALUMINUM

KM#	Date	Mintage	Fine	VF	XF	Unc
2870	1946	13.058	.20	.50	1.75	10.00
	1946	—	—	—	Proof	75.00
	1947	26.990	.15	.35	1.25	7.00
	1947	—	—	—	Proof	35.00
	1952	7.455	.40	1.00	2.50	8.00
	1952	—	—	—	Proof	55.00
	1955	16.919	.20	.40	1.25	5.00
	1955	—	—	—	Proof	55.00

ALUMINUM-BRONZE

KM#	Date	Mintage	VF	XF	Unc
2885	1959	14.122	.50	2.00	15.00
	1959	—	—	Proof	25.00
	1960	22.404	.20	1.50	12.00
	1960	—	—	Proof	100.00
	1961	19.891	.50	2.00	15.00
	1961	—	—	Proof	75.00
	1962	10.008	.40	1.75	15.00
	1962	—	—	Proof	40.00
	1963	9.483	.50	2.00	18.00
	1963	—	—	Proof	40.00
	1964	5.331	.10	.75	3.00
	1964	—	—	Proof	1.50
	1965	7.849	.10	.75	3.00
	1965	—	—	Proof	1.50
	1966	7.322	.10	.75	3.00
	1966	—	—	Proof	10.00
	1967	8.237	.10	.75	3.00
	1967	—	—	Proof	15.00
	1968	7.757	—	.75	3.00
	1968	.015	—	Proof	10.00
	1969	7.070	.10	.75	3.00
	1969	.026	—	Proof	5.00
	1970	2.994	.10	.50	2.00
	1970	.129	—	Proof	3.00
	1971	14.217	—	.25	1.50
	1971	.084	—	Proof	2.50
	1972	17.367	—	.25	1.50
	1972	.080	—	Proof	2.00
	1973	17.902	—	.25	1.50
	1973	.090	—	Proof	2.00
	1974	15.852	—	.25	1.50
	1974	.076	—	Proof	2.00
	1975	7.726	—	.15	1.00
	1975	.049	—	Proof	1.50
	1976	11.150	—	.15	1.00
	1976	.044	—	Proof	1.50
	1977	7.258	—	.15	1.00
	1977	.044	—	Proof	1.50
	1978	12.407	—	.15	1.00
	1978	.043	—	Proof	1.50
	1979	16.351	—	.15	1.00
	1979	.044	—	Proof	1.50
	1980	29.884	—	.15	1.25
	1980	.048	—	Proof	3.50
	1981	12.993	—	.15	1.25
	1981	.049	—	Proof	3.50
	1982	9.950	—	.15	1.00
	1982	.050	—	Proof	1.50
	1983	15.182	—	.15	1.00
	1983	.065	—	Proof	1.50
	1984	20.742	—	.15	1.00
	1984	.065	—	Proof	2.00
	1985	15.654	—	.15	1.00
	1985	.045	—	Proof	2.00
	1986	17.016	—	.15	.75
	1986	.042	—	Proof	2.00
	1987	7.258	—	.15	.75
	1987	.042	—	Proof	2.00
	1988	16.267	—	.15	.75
	1988	.039	—	Proof	2.00
	1989	17.352	—	.15	.75
	1989	.038	—	Proof	2.00
	1990	29.653	—	.15	.75
	1990	.035	—	Proof	2.00
	1991	44.990	—	.15	.75
	1991	.027	—	Proof	2.00
	1992	20.000	—	—	.45
	1993	15.000	—	—	.45
	1994	10.000	—	—	.45
	1995	20.000	—	—	.45
	1996	—	—	—	.45
	1997	—	—	—	.45

SCHILLING

ALUMINUM

KM#	Date	Mintage	Fine	VF	XF	Unc
2871	1946	27.336	.30	1.00	2.50	20.00
	1946	—	—	—	Proof	500.00
	1947	35.838	.20	.50	1.50	6.00
	1947	—	—	—	Proof	35.00
	1952	23.231	.25	.75	1.65	7.00
	1952	—	—	—	Proof	50.00
	1957	28.649	.25	.75	1.65	7.00
	1957	—	—	—	Proof	145.00

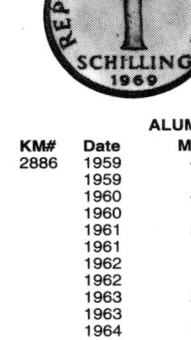

ALUMINUM-BRONZE

KM#	Date	Mintage	VF	XF	Unc
2886	1959	46.726	.25	.75	12.00
	1959	—	—	Proof	15.00
	1960	46.111	.25	1.50	20.00
	1960	—	—	Proof	200.00
	1961	51.115	.25	1.50	15.00
	1961	—	—	Proof	400.00
	1962	9.303	.25	1.50	15.00
	1962	—	—	Proof	65.00
	1963	20.863	.25	1.50	20.00
	1963	—	—	Proof	45.00
	1964	15.651	.25	1.25	3.50
	1964	—	—	Proof	2.00
	1965	21.290	.20	.75	3.50
	1965	—	—	Proof	8.00
	1966	18.688	.20	.75	3.50
	1966	—	—	Proof	8.00
	1967	22.214	.20	.75	3.50
	1967	—	—	Proof	12.00
	1968	30.860	.20	.75	3.50
	1968	.017	—	Proof	8.00
	1969	10.285	.20	.75	3.50
	1969	.028	—	Proof	4.00
	1970	10.679	.15	.50	2.50
	1970	.100	—	Proof	1.75
	1971	27.974	.15	.50	2.50
	1971	.082	—	Proof	1.75
	1972	54.577	.10	.25	1.50
	1972	.078	—	Proof	1.25
	1973	41.332	.10	.25	1.50
	1973	.090	—	Proof	1.25
	1974	43.712	.10	.25	1.50
	1974	.077	—	Proof	1.25
	1975	13.989	.10	.25	1.50
	1975	.049	—	Proof	1.25
	1976	28.748	.10	.25	1.50
	1976	.044	—	Proof	1.25
	1977	19.584	.10	.25	1.50
	1977	.044	—	Proof	1.25
	1978	35.632	.10	.25	1.50
	1978	.043	—	Proof	1.25
	1979	64.802	.10	.25	1.50
	1979	.044	—	Proof	1.25
	1980	49.855	—	.15	.75
	1980	.048	—	Proof	2.50
	1981	37.502	—	.15	.75
	1981	.049	—	Proof	2.50
	1982	29.950	—	.15	.75
	1982	.050	—	Proof	1.50
	1983	38.186	—	.15	.75
	1983	.065	—	Proof	1.50
	1984	31.891	—	.15	.75
	1984	.065	—	Proof	1.50
	1985	49.150	—	.15	.75
	1985	.045	—	Proof	1.50
	1986	57.618	—	—	.65
	1986	.042	—	Proof	1.50
	1987	44.158	—	—	.65
	1987	.042	—	Proof	1.50
	1988	51.561	—	—	.65
	1988	.039	—	Proof	1.50
	1989	62.821	—	—	.65
	1989	.038	—	Proof	1.50
	1990	103.710	—	—	.50
	1990	.035	—	Proof	1.56
	1991	117.700	—	—	.50
	1991	.027	—	Proof	1.50
	1992	55.000	—	—	1.25
	1993	60.000	—	—	1.25
	1994	50.000	—	—	1.25
	1995	70.000	—	—	1.25
	1996	—	—	—	1.25
	1997	—	—	—	1.25
	1998	—	—	—	1.25

2 SCHILLING

ALUMINUM

KM#	Date	Mintage	Fine	VF	XF	Unc
2872	1946	10.082	.45	1.25	2.75	25.00
	1946	—	—	—	Proof	700.00
	1947	20.140	.45	1.25	2.50	20.00
	1947	—	—	—	Proof	40.00
	1952	.149	55.00	100.00	200.00	350.00
	1952	—	—	—	Proof	900.00

5 SCHILLING

ALUMINUM

KM#	Date	Mintage	Fine	VF	XF	Unc
2879	1952	29.873	1.00	2.00	5.00	15.00
	1952	—	—	—	Proof	45.00
	1957	.240	100.00	200.00	300.00	500.00
	1957	—	—	—	Proof	700.00

5.2000 g, .640 SILVER, .1070 oz ASW
Reeded edge

KM#	Date	Mintage	Fine	VF	XF	Unc
2889	1960	12.618	—	BV	2.50	6.00
	1960	1,000	—	—	Proof	65.00
	1961	17.902	—	BV	2.50	5.00
	1961	—	—	—	Proof	25.00
	1962	6.771	—	BV	2.50	5.00
	1962	—	—	—	Proof	50.00
	1963	1.811	BV	2.00	4.00	15.00
	1963	—	—	—	Proof	120.00
	1964	4.030	—	BV	2.00	3.50
	1964	—	—	—	Proof	3.50
	1965	3.030	—	BV	2.00	3.50
	1965	—	—	—	Proof	3.50
	1966	4.481	—	BV	2.00	3.50
	1966	—	—	—	Proof	8.00
	1967	1.900	BV	2.00	4.00	6.00
	1967	—	—	—	Proof	15.00
	1968	4.792	—	BV	2.00	3.50
	1968	.020	—	—	Proof	8.00

COPPER-NICKEL
Plain edge

KM#	Date	Mintage	VF	XF	Unc
2889a	1968	2.075	1.00	2.50	5.00
	1969	41.222	.75	1.50	4.00
	1969	.021	—	Proof	6.00
	1970	15.771	—	1.00	4.00
	1970	.092	—	Proof	2.00
	1971	14.408	—	1.00	4.00
	1971	.084	—	Proof	2.00
	1972	12.444	—	1.00	4.00
	1972	.075	—	Proof	2.00
	1973	8.259	—	1.00	4.00
	1973	.087	—	Proof	1.50
	1974	17.956	—	1.00	4.00
	1974	.076	—	Proof	1.50
	1975	6.849	—	.75	4.00
	1975	.049	—	Proof	1.50
	1976	1.458	—	1.00	5.00
	1976	.044	—	Proof	4.00
	1977	6.423	—	.65	2.00
	1977	.044	—	Proof	1.75
	1978	9.907	—	.65	2.00
	1978	.043	—	Proof	1.75
	1979	11.607	—	.65	2.00
	1979	.044	—	Proof	1.75
	1980	14.448	—	.65	2.00
	1980	.048	—	Proof	3.50
	1981	13.837	—	.65	2.00
	1981	.049	—	Proof	3.50
	1982	4.950	—	.65	1.50
	1982	.050	—	Proof	2.50
	1983	9.268	—	.65	1.50
	1983	.065	—	Proof	2.50
	1984	13.763	—	.65	1.50

KM#	Date	Mintage	VF	XF	Unc
2889a	1984	.065	—	Proof	2.50
	1985	12.750	—	.60	1.25
	1985	.045	—	Proof	3.00
	1986	16.560	—	.60	1.25
	1986	.042	—	Proof	3.00
	1987	9.758	—	.60	1.25
	1987	.042	—	Proof	3.00
	1988	10.161	—	.60	1.25
	1988	.039	—	Proof	3.00
	1989	24.043	—	.60	1.25
	1989	.038	—	Proof	3.00
	1990	36.512	—	.60	1.25
	1990	.035	—	Proof	2.50
	1991	24.000	—	.60	1.25
	1991	.027	—	Proof	2.50
	1992	20.000	—	—	1.25
	1993	20.000	—	—	1.25
	1994	10.000	—	—	1.25
	1995	20.000	—	—	1.25
	1996	—	—	—	1.25
	1997	—	—	—	1.25
	1998	—	—	—	1.25

10 SCHILLING

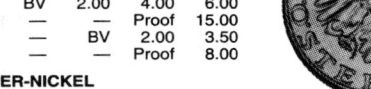

7.5000 g, .640 SILVER, .1543 oz ASW

KM#	Date	Mintage	Fine	VF	XF	Unc
2882	1957	15.636	BV	1.50	3.00	8.00
	1957	—	—	—	Proof	80.00
	1958	27.280	BV	1.50	3.00	8.00
	1958	—	—	—	Proof	700.00
	1959	3.923	BV	1.50	3.50	12.00
	1959	—	—	—	Proof	40.00
	1964	.195	7.00	10.00	25.00	45.00
	1964	.027	—	—	Proof	15.00
	1965	1.896	BV	1.50	3.50	12.00
	1965	—	—	—	Proof	5.00
	1966	3.392	BV	1.50	3.50	10.00
	1966	—	—	—	12.00	7.00
	1967	1.394	BV	1.50	3.50	12.00
	1967	—	—	—	Proof	15.00
	1968	1.525	BV	1.50	3.50	10.00
	1968	.015	—	—	Proof	9.00
	1969	1.316	BV	1.50	3.50	12.00
	1969	.020	—	—	Proof	12.00
	1970	4.493	—	BV	2.50	6.50
	1970	.089	—	—	Proof	5.00
	1971	7.320	—	BV	2.50	5.50
	1971	.080	—	—	Proof	5.00
	1972	14.210	—	BV	2.50	4.50
	1972	.075	—	—	Proof	5.00
	1973	14.559	—	BV	2.50	4.50
	1973	.080	—	—	Proof	5.00

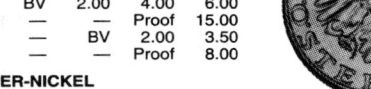

COPPER-NICKEL

KM#	Date	Mintage	VF	XF	Unc
2918	1974	59.877	—	2.00	6.00
	1974	.075	—	Proof	4.00
	1975	16.869	—	2.00	6.00
	1975	.049	—	Proof	3.00
	1976	13.459	—	2.00	6.00
	1976	.044	—	Proof	3.00
	1977	3.804	—	2.00	6.00
	1977	.044	—	Proof	3.00
	1978	6.813	—	2.00	6.00
	1978	.043	—	Proof	3.00
	1979	11.691	—	2.00	6.00
	1979	.044	—	Proof	2.50
	1980	10.884	—	2.00	6.00
	1980	.048	—	Proof	6.50
	1981	9.470	—	2.00	6.00
	1981	.049	—	Proof	6.50
	1982	3.470	—	2.00	5.00
	1982	.050	—	Proof	2.50
	1983	8.993	—	1.50	4.00
	1983	.065	—	Proof	2.50
	1984	7.936	—	1.50	4.00
	1984	.065	—	Proof	2.50
	1985	9.009	—	1.50	4.00
	1985	.045	—	Proof	2.50
	1986	8.768	—	1.50	4.00
	1986	.042	—	Proof	2.50
	1987	9.258	—	1.50	4.00
	1987	.042	—	Proof	2.50
	1988	9.011	—	1.50	4.00
	1988	.039	—	Proof	4.50

KM#	Date	Mintage	VF	XF	Unc
2918	1989	16.233	—	1.25	3.00
	1989	.038	—	Proof	2.50
	1990	27.150	—	1.25	3.00
	1990	.035	—	Proof	2.50
	1991	18.000	—	1.25	3.00
	1991	.027	—	Proof	2.50
	1992	11.000	—	—	2.00
	1993	12.500	—	—	2.00
	1994	15.000	—	—	2.00
	1995	12.500	—	—	2.00
	1996	—	—	—	2.00
	1997	—	—	—	2.00

20 SCHILLING

COPPER-ALUMINUM-NICKEL

KM#	Date	Mintage	VF	XF	Unc
2946.1	1980	9.850	—	2.50	3.50
	1980	.048	—	Proof	20.00
	1981	.450	—	4.50	7.50
	1981	.049	—	Proof	22.50
	Plain edge				
2946.2	1991	.140	—	2.25	5.00
	1992	.100	—	2.25	6.00
	1993	.180	—	2.25	5.00

250th Anniversary - Birth of Joseph Haydn

KM#	Date	Mintage	VF	XF	Unc
2955.1	1982	3.100	—	2.25	3.50
	1982	.050	—	Proof	9.00
	1991	—	—	—	—
	Plain edge				
2955.2	1991	.140	—	2.25	5.00
	1992	.100	—	2.25	6.00
	1993	.180	—	2.25	5.00

Hochosterwitz Castle

KM#	Date	Mintage	VF	XF	Unc
2960.1	1983	1.002	—	2.25	3.50
	1983	.065	—	Proof	7.50
	Plain edge				
2960.2	1991	.140	—	2.25	4.50
	1992	.100	—	2.25	5.00
	1993	.180	—	2.25	4.50

Grafenegg Palace

KM#	Date	Mintage	VF	XF	Unc
2965.1	1984	1.203	—	2.25	3.50
	1984	.065	—	Proof	7.50
	Plain edge				
2965.2	1991	.140	—	2.25	4.50
	1992	.100	—	2.25	5.00
	1993	.180	—	2.25	4.50

ALUMINUM-BRONZE
200th Anniversary - Diocese of Linz

KM#	Date	Mintage	VF	XF	Unc
2970.1	1985	.814	—	2.25	4.50
	1985	.045	—	Proof	11.50
	Plain edge				
2970.2	1991	.140	—	2.25	4.50
	1992	.100	—	2.25	5.00
	1993	.180	—	2.25	4.50

800th Anniversary - Georgenberger Treaty

KM#	Date	Mintage	VF	XF	Unc
2975.1	1986	.801	—	2.25	4.50
	1986	.042	—	Proof	16.50
	Plain edge				
2975.2	1991	.140	—	2.25	4.50
	1992	.100	—	2.25	5.00
	1993	.180	—	2.25	4.50

COPPER-ALUMINUM-NICKEL
300th Anniversary - Birth of Salzburg's Archbishop Thun

KM#	Date	Mintage	VF	XF	Unc
2980.1	1987	.508	—	2.25	4.50
	1987	.042	—	Proof	11.50
	Plain edge				
2980.2	1991	.140	—	2.25	4.50
	1992	.100	—	2.25	5.00
	1993	.180	—	2.25	4.50

Tyrol

KM#	Date	Mintage	VF	XF	Unc
2988.1	1989	.242	—	2.25	4.50
	1989	.038	—	Proof	8.00
	Plain edge				
2988.2	1991	.140	—	2.25	4.50
	1992	.100	—	2.25	5.00
	1993	.180	—	2.25	4.50

Martinsturm in Bregenz Vorarlberg

KM#	Date	Mintage	VF	XF	Unc
2993.1	1990	.250	—	2.25	4.50
	1990	.035	—	Proof	11.50
	1991	—	—	—	—
	Plain edge				
2993.2	1991	.140	—	2.25	4.50
	1992	.100	—	2.25	6.50
	1993	.180	—	2.25	4.50

200th Anniversary - Birth of Franz Grillparzer

KM#	Date	Mintage	VF	XF	Unc
2995.1	1991	.610	—	2.25	4.50
	1991	.027	—	Proof	10.00
	Plain edge				
2995.2	1992	.100	—	2.25	5.00
	1993	.180	—	2.25	4.50

800th Anniversary - Vienna Mint

3016	1994	2.000	—	—	4.50

1000th Anniversary - Krems

3022	1995	2.000	—	—	4.50

Anton Bruckner

3033	1996	—	—	—	4.50

St. Stephen's Cathedral
Obv: Denomination. Rev: Cathedral, dates.

3041	1997	—	—	—	4.50

Michael Pacher
Obv: Denomination.
Rev: Pacher's altar at St. Wolfgang.

3048	1998	—	—	—	4.50

50 SCHILLING

COPPER-NICKEL plated NICKEL center in BRASS ring
Austrian Millenium
Obv: Circle of provincial arms around denomination. Rev: Arms below Heinrich I as knight on horse back.

KM#	Date	Mintage	VF	XF	Unc
3038	1996	.900	—	—	7.50
	1996	.100	—	BU	25.00

100th Anniversary - Wiener Secession
Obv: Circle of provincial arms. Rev: Vienna secession building portal.

3044	ND(1997)	1.400	—	—	6.50
	ND(1997)	.100	—	BU	11.50

Austrian Presidency of the European Union
Obv: Denomination. Rev: New Hofburg palace w/logo.

3050	1998	1.200	—	—	6.50
	1998	.100	—	BU	11.50

AZERBAIJAN

The Republic of Azerbaijan (formerly Azerbaijan S.S.R.) includes the Nakhichevan Autonomous Republic and Nagomo-Karabakh Autonomous Region (which was abolished in 1991). Situated in the eastern area of Transcaucasia, it is bordered in the west by Armenia, in the north by Georgia and Dagestan, to the east by the Caspian Sea and to the south by Iran. It has an area of 33,430 sq. mi. (86,600 sq. km.) and a population of 7.8 million. Capital: Baku. The area is rich in mineral deposits of aluminum, copper, iron, lead, salt and zinc, with oil as its leading industry. Agriculture and livestock follow in importance.

Until the Russian Revolution of 1905, there was no political life in Azerbaijan. A Mussavat (Equality) party was formed in 1911 by Mohammed Emin, Rasulzade, a former Social Democrat. After the Russian Revolution of March 1917, the party started a campaign for independence. Baku, however, the capital with its mixed population, constituted an alien enclave in the country While a national Azerbaijani government was established at Gandzha (Elizavetpol), a Communist-controlled council assumed power at Baku with Stepan Shaumian, an Armenian, at its head. The Gandzha government joined first, on Sept. 20, 1917, a Transcaucasian federal republic, but on May 28, 1918, proclaimed the independence of Azerbaijan. On June 4, 1918, at Batum, a peace treaty was signed with Turkey. Turko-Azerbaijani forces started an offensive against Baku, occupied since Aug. 17, 1918 by 1,400 British troops coming by sea from Anzali, Persia. On Sept. 14 the Briish evacuated Baku, returning to Anzali, and three days later the Azerbaijan government, headed by Fath Khoysky, established itself at Baku.

After the collapse of the Ottoman empire, the British returned to Baku, at first ignoring the Azerbaijan government. A general election with universal suffrage for the Azerbaijan constituent assembly took place on Dec. 7, 1918 and out of 120 members there were 84 Mussavat supporters. On Jan. 15, 1920, the Allied powers recognized Azerbaijan de facto, but on April 27 of the same year the Red army invaded the country, and a Soviet republic of Azerbaijan was proclaimed the next day. Later it became a member of the Transcaucasian Federation joining the U.S.S.R. on Dec. 30, 1922, it became a self-constituent republic in 1936.

The Azerbaijan Communist party held its first congress at Baku in Feb. 1920. From 1921 to 1925 its first secretary was a Russian, S.M. Kirov, who directed a mass deportation to Siberia of about 120,000 Azerbaijani "nationalist deviationists," among them the country's first two premiers.

In 1990 it adopted a declaration of republican sovereignty and in Aug. 1991 declared itself formally independent. This action was approved by a vote of referendum in Jan. 1992. It announced its intention of joining the CIS in Dec. 1991, but a parliamentary resolution of Oct. 1992 declined to confirm its involvement. On Sept. 20, 1993, Azerbaijan became a member of the CIS. Communist President Mutaibov was relieved of his office in May 1992. On June 7, in the first democratic election in the country's history, a National Council replaced Mutaibov with Abulfez Elchibey. Surat Huseynov led a military coup against Elchibey and seized power on June 30, 1993. Huseynov became prime minister with former communist Geidar Aliyev, president.

Fighting commenced between Muslim forces of Azerbaijan and Christian forces of Armenia in 1992 and continued through early 1994. Each faction claimed the Nagorno-Karabakh, an Armenian ethnic enclave, in Azerbaijan. A cease-fire was declared in May 1994.

MONETARY SYSTEM
100 Qapik = 1 Manat

5 QAPIK

		BRASS			
KM#	Date	Mintage	VF	XF	Unc
31	1992	—	—	1.50	3.00
		ALUMINUM			
31a	1993	—	—	—	1.00

10 QAPIK

		ALUMINUM			
KM#	Date	Mintage	VF	XF	Unc
32	1992	—	—	—	.50

20 QAPIK

		BRASS			
33	1992	—	—	.75	1.50
	1993	—	—	.75	1.50
		ALUMINUM			
33a	1992	—	—	—	.75
	1993	—	—	—	.75

NOTE: Varieties in spelling of Respublikas exist.

50 QAPIK

		COPPER-NICKEL			
34	1992	—	—	1.25	2.50
	1994	—	—	1.25	2.50
		ALUMINUM			
34a	1992	—	—	—	1.25
	1993	—	—	—	.75

AZORES

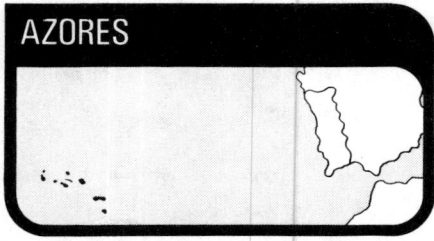

The Azores, an archipelago of nine islands of volcanic origin, are located in the Atlantic Ocean 740 miles (1,190 km.) west of Cape de Roca, Portugal. They are the westernmost region of Europe under the administration of Portugal and have an area of 902 sq. mi. (2,305 sq. km.) and a population of 236,000. Principal city: Ponta Delgada. The natives are mainly of Portuguese descent and earn their livelihood by fishing, wine making, basket weaving and the growing of fruit, grains and sugar cane. Pineapples are the chief item of export. The climate is particularly temperate, making the islands a favorite winter resort.

The Azores were discovered about 1427 by the Portuguese navigator Diogo de Sevill. Portugal secured the islands in the 15th century and established the first settlement, on Santa Maria, about 1439. From 1580 to 1640 the Azores were subject to Spain.

The Azores' first provincial coinage was ordered by law of August 19, 1750. Copper coins were struck for circulation in both the Azores and Madeira Islands. Keeping the same technical specifications, but with different designs. In 1795 a second provincial coinage was introduced but the weight was reduced by 50 percent.

Angra on Terceira Island became the capital of the captaincy-general of the Azores in 1766 and it was here in 1826 that the constitutionalists set up a pro-Pedro government in opposition to King Miguel in Lisbon. The whole Portuguese fleet attacked Terceira and was repelled at Praia, after which Azoreans, Brazilians and British mercenaries defeated Miguel in Portugal. Maria de Gloria, Pedro's daughter, was proclaimed queen of Portugal on Terceira in 1828.

A U.S. naval base was established at Ponta Delgada in 1917.

After World War II, the islands acquired a renewed importance as a refueling stop for transatlantic air transport. The United States maintains defense bases in the Azores as part of the collective security program of NATO.

In 1976 the archipelago became the Autonomous Region of Azores.

RULERS
Portuguese

MONETARY SYSTEM
1000 Reis (Insulanos) = 1 Milreis

PROVINCIAL COINAGE
5 REIS

COPPER
Carlos I

KM#	Date	Mintage	Fine	VF	XF	Unc
16	1901	.800	1.50	3.00	8.00	20.00

10 REIS

COPPER
Carlos I

| 17 | 1901 | .600 | 1.75 | 3.50 | 9.00 | 22.00 |

BAHAMAS

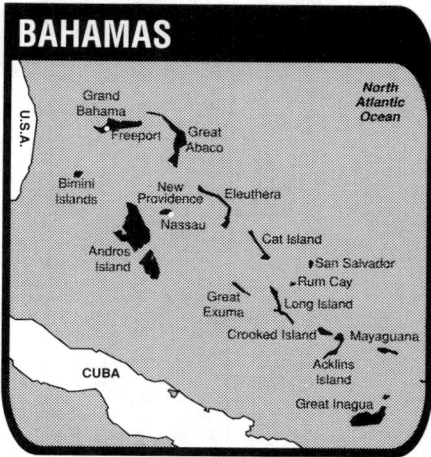

The Commonwealth of the Bahamas is an archipelago of about 3,000 islands, cays and rocks located in the Atlantic Ocean east of Florida and north of Cuba. The total land area of the 800 mile (1,287 km.) long chain of islands is 5,382 sq. mi. (13,935 sq. km.). They have a population of 256,616. Capital: Nassau. The Bahamas import most of their food and manufactured products and export cement, refined oil, pulpwood and lobsters. Tourism is the principal industry.

The Bahamas were discovered by Columbus in October, 1492, upon his sighting of the island of San Salvador, but Spain made no attempt to settle them. British influence began in 1626 when Charles I granted them to the lord proprietors of Carolina, with settlements in 1629 at New Providence by colonists from the northern territory. Although the Bahamas were temporarily under Spanish control in 1641 and 1703, they continued under British proprietors until 1717, when, as the result of political and economic mismanagement, the civil and military governments were surrendered to the King and the islands designated a British Crown Colony. Full international agreement on British possession of the islands resulted from the Treaty of Versailles in 1783. The Bahamas obtained complete internal self-government under the constitution of Jan. 7, 1964. Full independence was achieved on July 10, 1973. The Bahamas is a member of the Commonwealth of Nations. Elizabeth II is Head of State, as Queen at Bahamas.

The coinage of Great Britain was legal tender in the Bahamas from 1825 to the issuing of a definitive coinage in 1966.

RULERS
British

MINT MARKS
Through 1969 all decimal coinage of the Bahamas was executed at the Royal Mint in England. Since that time issues have been struck at both the Royal Mint and at the Franklin Mint (FM) in the U.S.A. While the mint mark of the latter appears on coins dated 1971 and subsequently, it is missing from the 1970 issues.

JP - John Pinches, London
None - Royal Mint
(t) - Tower of London
FM - Franklin Mint, U.S.A.*

*NOTE: From 1975-1985 the Franklin Mint produced coinage in up to 3 different qualities. Qualities of issue are designated in ( ) after each date and are defined as follows:

(M) MATTE - Normal circulation strike or a dull finish produced by sandblasting special uncirculated (polish finish) or proof quality dies.

(U) SPECIAL UNCIRCULATED - Polished or proof-like in appearance without any frosted features.

(P) PROOF - The highest quality obtainable having mirror-like fields and frosted features.

MONETARY SYSTEM
100 Cents = 1 Dollar
100 Cents = 1 Dollar

CENT

NICKEL-BRASS
Starfish

KM#	Date	Mintage	VF	XF	Unc
2	1966	7.312	—	.10	.30
	1968	.800	—	.25	.75
	1969	4.036	—	.30	.30
	1969	.010	—	Proof	.50

BRONZE

KM#	Date	Mintage	VF	XF	Unc
15	1970	.125	.10	.25	.50
	1970	.023	—	Proof	.50

NOTE: Proof specimens of this date are struck in 'special brass' which looks like a pale bronze.

16	1971FM	1.007	—	.10	.25
	1971FM(P)	.031	—	Proof	.50
	1972FM	1.037	—	.10	.25
	1972FM(P)	.035	—	Proof	.50
	1973	7.000	—	.10	.25
	1973FM	1.040	—	.10	.25
	1973FM(P)	.035	—	Proof	.50

BRASS

59	1974	.011	—	.20	.40
	1974FM	.071	—	.10	.25
	1974FM(P)	.094	—	Proof	.50
	1975FM(M)	.060	—	.10	.25
	1975FM(U)	3,845	—	.10	.50
	1975FM(P)	.029	—	Proof	.50
	1976FM(M)	.060	—	.10	.25
	1976FM(U)	1,453	—	.10	.50
	1976FM(P)	.023	—	Proof	.50
	1977	3.000	—	.10	.25
	1977FM(M)	.060	—	.10	.25
	1977FM(U)	713 pcs.	—	.50	1.50
	1977FM(P)	.011	—	Proof	.50
	1978FM(M)	.060	—	.10	.25
	1978FM(U)	767 pcs.	—	.50	1.50
	1978FM(P)	6,931	—	Proof	.75
	1979	—	—	.10	.25
	1979FM(P)	2,053	—	Proof	1.00
	1980	4.000	—	.10	.25
	1980FM(P)	2,084	—	Proof	1.00
	1981	5.000	—	.10	.25
	1981FM(M)	—	—	.10	.25
	1981FM(P)	1,980	—	Proof	1.00
	1982	5.000	—	.10	.25
	1982FM(M)	—	—	.10	.25
	1982FM(P)	1,217	—	Proof	1.00
	1983	8.000	—	.10	.25
	1983FM(P)	1,020	—	Proof	1.00
	1984	—	—	.10	.25
	1984FM(P)	7,500	—	Proof	.75
	1985	12.000	—	.10	.25
	1985FM(P)	7,500	—	Proof	.50

COPPER PLATED ZINC

59a	1985	—	—	.10	.25
	1987	12.000	—	.10	.25
	1989	12.000	—	.10	.25
	1989	—	—	Proof	.75
	1990	—	—	.10	.25
	1991	—	—	.10	.25
	1992	—	—	.10	.25
	1995	—	—	.10	.25

5 CENTS

COPPER-NICKEL
Pineapple

3	1966	2.571	—	.10	.25
	1968	.600	—	.10	.30
	1969	2.026	—	.10	.25
	1969	.075	—	Proof	.50
	1970	.026	—	.30	.60
	1970	.023	—	Proof	.75

NOTE: The obverse of the above also comes muled with the reverse of a New Zealand 2-cent piece KM#32. The undated 1967 error is listed as New Zealand KM#33.

KM#	Date	Mintage	VF	XF	Unc
17	1971FM	.013	—	.15	.40
	1971FM(P)	.031	—	Proof	.50
	1972FM	.011	—	.15	.40
	1972FM(P)	.035	—	Proof	.50
	1973FM	.021	—	.15	.40
	1973FM(P)	.035	—	Proof	.50

Obv. leg: THE COMMONWEALTH OF THE BAHAMAS

38	1973	1.000	—	.10	.65

60	1974FM	.023	—	.10	.25
	1974FM(P)	.094	—	Proof	.50
	1975	—	—	.10	.30
	1975FM(M)	.012	—	.10	.25
	1975FM(U)	3,845	—	.15	.50
	1975FM(P)	.029	—	Proof	.50
	1976FM(M)	.012	—	.10	.25
	1976FM(U)	1,453	—	.15	.75
	1976FM(P)	.023	—	Proof	.50
	1977FM(M)	.012	—	.10	.35
	1977FM(U)	713 pcs.	—	.50	1.50
	1977FM(P)	.011	—	Proof	.50
	1978FM(M)	.012	—	.10	.35
	1978FM(U)	767 pcs.	—	.50	1.50
	1978FM(P)	6,931	—	Proof	.50
	1979FM(P)	2,053	—	Proof	.75
	1980FM(P)	2,084	—	Proof	.75
	1981	—	—	.10	.25
	1981FM(P)	1,980	—	Proof	.75
	1982FM(P)	1,217	—	Proof	.75
	1983	2.000	—	.10	.25
	1983FM(P)	1,020	—	Proof	.75
	1984	—	—	.10	.25
	1984FM(P)	1,036	—	Proof	.75
	1985FM(P)	7,500	—	Proof	.75
	1987	4.000	—	.10	.25
	1989	—	—	.10	.25
	1989	—	—	Proof	.75
	1991	—	—	.10	.25
	1992	—	—	.10	.25

10 CENTS

COPPER-NICKEL
Bone Fish

4	1966	2.198	—	.10	.30
	1968	.550	—	.50	4.00
	1969	2.026	—	.10	.30
	1969	.010	—	Proof	.50
	1970	.027	—	.15	.40
	1970	.023	—	Proof	.50

18	1971FM	.013	—	.15	.50
	1971FM(P)	.031	—	Proof	.50
	1972FM	.011	—	.15	.50
	1972FM(P)	.035	—	Proof	.50
	1973FM	.015	—	.15	.50
	1973FM(P)	.035	—	Proof	.50

Obv. leg: THE COMMONWEALTH OF THE BAHAMAS

KM#	Date	Mintage	VF	XF	Unc
39	1973	1.000	—	.15	.85

61	1974FM	.017	—	.10	.35
	1974FM(P)	.094	—	Proof	.75
	1975	3.000	—	.10	.25
	1975FM(M)	6,000	—	.15	.50
	1975FM(U)	3,845	—	.15	.50
	1975FM(P)	.029	—	Proof	.75
	1976FM(M)	6,000	—	.15	.50
	1976FM(U)	1,453	—	.25	1.00
	1976FM(P)	.023	—	Proof	.75
	1977FM(M)	6,000	—	.15	.50
	1977FM(U)	713 pcs.	—	.50	1.50
	1977FM(P)	.011	—	Proof	.75
	1978FM(M)	6,000	—	.15	.50
	1978FM(U)	767 pcs.	—	.50	1.50
	1978FM(P)	6,931	—	Proof	1.00
	1979FM(P)	2,053	—	Proof	1.25
	1980	2.500	—	.10	.35
	1980FM(P)	2,084	—	Proof	1.25
	1981FM(P)	1,980	—	Proof	1.25
	1982	2.000	—	.10	.35
	1982FM(P)	1,217	—	Proof	1.25
	1983FM(P)	1,020	—	Proof	1.25
	1984FM(P)	1,036	—	Proof	1.25
	1985	2.000	—	.10	.35
	1985FM(M)	—	—	.15	.50
	1985FM(P)	7,500	—	Proof	1.00
	1987	3.000	—	.15	.50
	1989	—	—	.15	.50
	1989	—	—	Proof	1.00
	1991	—	—	.15	.50
	1992	—	—	.15	.50

15 CENTS

COPPER-NICKEL
Hibiscus

5	1966	.930	—	.20	.75
	1969	1.026	—	.20	.75
	1969	.010	—	Proof	1.00
	1970	.028	—	.25	.75
	1970	.023	—	Proof	.75

19	1971FM	.013	—	.15	.50
	1971FM(P)	.031	—	Proof	.75
	1972FM	.011	—	.15	.50
	1972FM(P)	.035	—	Proof	.75
	1973FM	.014	—	.15	.50
	1973FM(P)	.035	—	Proof	.75

62	1974FM	.015	—	.20	.50
	1974FM(P)	.094	—	Proof	.75
	1975FM(M)	3,500	—	.20	1.00
	1975FM(U)	3,845	—	.20	1.00

KM#	Date	Mintage	VF	XF	Unc
62	1975FM(P)	.029	—	Proof	.50
	1976FM(M)	3,500	—	.20	1.00
	1976FM(U)	1,453	—	.25	1.50
	1976FM(P)	.023	—	Proof	.50
	1977FM(M)	3,500	—	.20	1.00
	1977FM(U)	713 pcs.	—	.50	2.00
	1977FM(P)	.011	—	Proof	.50
	1978FM(M)	3,500	—	.20	1.00
	1978FM(U)	767 pcs.	—	.50	2.00
	1978FM(P)	6,931	—	Proof	.75
	1979FM(P)	2,053	—	Proof	1.00
	1980FM(P)	2,084	—	Proof	1.00
	1981FM(P)	1,980	—	Proof	1.00
	1982FM(P)	1,217	—	Proof	1.25
	1983FM(P)	1,020	—	Proof	1.25
	1984FM(P)	1,036	—	Proof	1.25
	1985FM(P)	7,500	—	Proof	.75
	1989	—	—	.15	.50
	1989	—	—	Proof	1.00
	1991	—	—	.15	.50
	1992	—	—	.15	.50

25 CENTS

NICKEL
Bahaminian Sloop

6	1966	3.685	—	.25	.50
	1969	1.026	—	.25	.50
	1969	.010	—	Proof	.75
	1970	.026	—	.35	.75
	1970FM	.023	—	Proof	1.00
	1970FM(M)	—	—	—	—

20	1971FM	.013	—	.25	.50
	1971FM(P)	.031	—	Proof	.75
	1972FM	.011	—	.25	.50
	1972FM(M)	—	—	.25	.50
	1972FM(P)	.035	—	Proof	.75
	1973FM	.012	—	.25	.50
	1973FM(P)	.035	—	Proof	.75

63	1974FM	.013	—	.25	.50
	1974FM(P)	.094	—	Proof	.75
	1975FM(M)	2,400	—	.25	1.00
	1975FM(U)	3,845	—	.25	1.00
	1975FM(P)	.029	—	Proof	.75
	1976FM(M)	2,400	—	.25	1.00
	1976FM(U)	1,453	—	.30	1.25
	1976FM(P)	.023	—	Proof	.75
	1977	—	—	.25	.50
	1977FM(M)	2,400	—	.25	1.00
	1977FM(U)	713 pcs.	—	.50	3.00
	1977FM(P)	.011	—	Proof	.75
	1978FM(M)	2,400	—	.25	1.00
	1978FM(U)	767 pcs.	—	.50	3.00
	1978FM(P)	6,931	—	Proof	1.00
	1979	—	—	.25	.50
	1979FM(P)	2,053	—	Proof	1.25
	1980FM(P)	2,084	—	Proof	1.25
	1981	1.600	—	.25	.50
	1981FM(P)	1,980	—	Proof	1.25
	1982FM(P)	1,217	—	Proof	1.50
	1983FM(P)	1,020	—	Proof	1.50
	1984FM(P)	1,036	—	Proof	1.50
	1985	2.000	—	.25	.50
	1985FM(P)	7,500	—	Proof	1.00
	1987	—	—	.25	.50
	1989	—	—	.25	.50
	1989	—	—	Proof	1.25
	1991	—	—	.25	.50
	1992	—	—	.25	.50

50 CENTS

10.3700 g, .800 SILVER, .2667 oz ASW
Blue Marlin

KM#	Date	Mintage	VF	XF	Unc
7	1966	.701	BV	1.50	2.00
	1969	.026	BV	1.75	2.50
	1969	.010	—	Proof	3.00
	1970	.025	BV	1.75	2.50
	1970	.023	—	Proof	3.00

KM#	Date	Mintage	VF	XF	Unc
21	1971FM	.014	BV	1.75	2.50
	1971FM(P)	.031	—	Proof	3.00
	1972FM	.012	BV	1.75	2.50
	1972FM(P)	.035	—	Proof	3.00
	1973FM	.011	BV	1.75	2.50
	1973FM(P)	.035	—	Proof	3.00

COPPER-NICKEL

KM#	Date	Mintage	VF	XF	Unc
64	1974FM	.012	—	.50	2.00
	1975FM(M)	1,200	—	1.00	8.00
	1975FM(U)	3,828	—	.65	4.00
	1976FM(M)	1,200	—	.75	5.00
	1976FM(U)	1,453	—	.65	4.00
	1977FM(M)	1,200	—	.75	5.00
	1977FM(U)	713 pcs.	—	1.25	10.00
	1978FM(M)	1,200	—	1.00	8.00
	1978FM(U)	767 pcs.	—	1.25	10.00
	1981FM(P)	1,980	—	Proof	3.00
	1982FM(P)	1,217	—	Proof	3.50
	1983FM(P)	1,020	—	Proof	3.50
	1984FM(P)	1,036	—	Proof	3.50
	1985FM(P)	7,500	—	Proof	2.50
	1989	—	—	.75	2.00
	1989	—	—	Proof	2.50
	1991	—	—	.75	2.00
	1992	—	—	.75	2.00

DOLLAR

KM#	Date	Mintage	VF	XF	Unc
8	1970	.027	BV	3.00	5.00
	1970	.023	—	Proof	6.00

	Date	Mintage	VF	XF	Unc
22	1971FM	.015	BV	3.00	5.00
	1971FM(P)	.031	—	Proof	6.00
	1972FM	.018	BV	3.00	5.00
	1972FM(P)	.035	—	Proof	6.00
	1973FM	.010	BV	3.00	5.00
	1973FM(P)	.035	—	Proof	6.00

COPPER-NICKEL

	Date	Mintage	VF	XF	Unc
65	1974FM	.012	—	1.00	3.50
	1975FM(M)	600 pcs.	—	7.50	20.00
	1975FM(U)	3,845	—	1.00	3.50
	1976FM(M)	600 pcs.	—	7.50	20.00
	1976FM(U)	1,453	—	1.00	3.75
	1977FM(M)	600 pcs.	—	7.50	20.00
	1977FM(U)	713 pcs.	—	5.00	15.00
	1978FM(U)	1,367	—	2.00	10.00

COPPER-NICKEL, 32mm

	Date	Mintage	VF	XF	Unc
65b	1981FM(P)	1,980	—	Proof	12.00
	1989	—	—	1.50	3.50
	1989	*2,000	—	Proof	12.00
	1991	—	—	1.50	3.50
	1992	—	—	1.50	3.50

2 DOLLARS

29.8000 g, .925 SILVER, .8863 oz ASW
National Bird - Flamingos

	Date	Mintage	VF	XF	Unc
9	1966	.104	BV	5.00	7.00
	1969	.026	BV	5.00	7.00
	1969	.010	—	Proof	9.00
	1970	.032	BV	5.00	7.00
	1970	.023	—	Proof	9.00

KM#	Date	Mintage	VF	XF	Unc
23	1971FM	.088	BV	5.00	8.00
	1971FM(P)	.060	—	Proof	9.00
	1972FM	.065	BV	5.00	8.00
	1972FM(P)	.059	—	Proof	9.00
	1973FM	.043	BV	5.00	8.00
	1973FM(P)	.050	—	Proof	9.00

COPPER-NICKEL

	Date	Mintage	VF	XF	Unc
66	1974FM	.037	—	2.00	5.00
	1975FM(M)	300 pcs.	—	9.00	25.00
	1975FM(U)	8,810	—	2.00	5.00
	1976FM(M)	300 pcs.	—	9.00	25.00
	1976FM(U)	4,381	—	2.00	5.50
	1977FM(M)	300 pcs.	—	9.00	25.00
	1977FM(U)	946 pcs.	—	3.00	15.00
	1978FM(U)	1,067	—	3.00	15.00
	1979FM(U)	300 pcs.	—	7.50	25.00
	1980FM(U)	—	—	—	—

18.1400 g, .800 SILVER, .4666 oz ASW
Conch Shell

	Date	Mintage	VF	XF	Unc
8	1966	.406	BV	3.00	5.00
	1969	.026	BV	3.00	5.00
	1969	.010	—	Proof	6.00

BAHRAIN

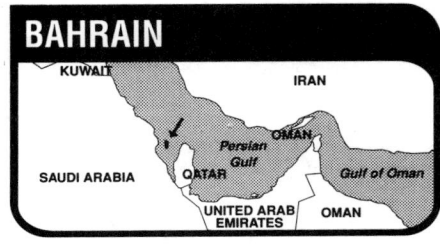

The State of Bahrain, a group of islands in the Persian Gulf off Saudi Arabia, has an area of 268 sq. mi. (622 sq. km.) and a population of 575,925. Capital: Manama. Prior to the depression of the 1930's, the economy was based on pearl fishing. Petroleum and aluminum industries and transit trade are the vital factors in the economy today.

The Portuguese occupied the islands in 1507 but were driven out in 1602 by Arab subjects of Persia. They in turn were ejected by Arabs of the Ataiba tribe from the Arabian mainland who have maintained possession up to the present time. The ruling sheikh of Bahrain entered into relations with Great Britain in 1805 and concluded a binding treaty of protection in 1861. In 1968 Great Britain decided to terminate treaty relations with the Persian Gulf sheikhdoms. Unable to agree on terms of union with the other skeikhdoms, Bahrain decided to seek independence as a separate entity and became fully independent on August 14, 1971.

Bahrain took part in the Arab oil embargo against the U.S. and other nations. The government bought controlling interest in the oil industry in 1975.

The coinage of the State of Bahrain was struck at the Royal Mint, London, England.

RULERS
Al Khalifa Dynasty

Isa Bin Ali, 1869-1932
Hamad Bin Isa, 1932-1942
Salman Bin Hamad, 1942-1961
Isa Bin Salman, 1961-

MINT MARKS

Bahrain

بحرين

al-Bahrain
= of the two seas

البحرين

MONETARY SYSTEM

فلساً   فلس   فلوس

Falus, Fulus   *Fals, Fils*   *Falsan*

1000 Fils = 1 Dinar

FILS

BRONZE

KM#	Date	Year	Mintage	VF	XF	Unc
1	AH1385	1965	1.500	.10	.20	.40
	1385	1965	.012	—	Proof	1.00
	1386	1966	1.500	.10	.20	.40
	1386	1966	—	—	Proof	2.00

5 FILS

BRONZE

2	AH1385	1965	8.000	.10	.20	.40
	1385	1965	.012	—	Proof	1.00

BRASS
Palm Tree

16	AH1412	1992	—	—	—	.50

10 FILS

BRONZE

KM#	Date	Year	Mintage	VF	XF	Unc
3	AH1385	1965	8.500	.10	.25	.50
	1385	1965	.012	—	Proof	1.50

BRASS
Palm Tree

17	AH1412	1992	—	—	—	.75

25 FILS

COPPER NICKEL

4	AH1385	1965	11.250	.20	.35	.75
	1385	1965	.012	—	Proof	2.00

Ancient Painting

18	AH1412	1992	—	—	—	1.25

50 FILS

COPPER-NICKEL

5	AH1385	1965	6.909	.25	.55	1.25
	1385	1965	.012	—	Proof	2.50

Stylized Sail Boats

19	AH1412	1992	—	—	—	1.50

100 FILS

COPPER-NICKEL

6	AH1385	1965	8.300	.35	.75	1.50
	1385	1965	.012	—	Proof	3.00

COPPER-NICKEL center in BRASS ring
Coat of Arms

20	AH1412	1992	—	—	—	2.50

KM#	Date	Year	Mintage	VF	XF	Unc
20	AH1415	1995	—	—	—	2.50
	AH1417	1997	—	—	—	2.50

250 FILS

COPPER-NICKEL
F.A.O. Issue

7	AH1389	1969	.050	1.50	2.50	6.00
	1389	1969	—	—	Proof	8.00
	1403	1983	3,000	1.75	3.00	8.50

500 FILS

18.3000 g, .800 SILVER, .4707 oz ASW
Opening of Isa Town

8	AH1385	1965	.012	—	Proof	17.50
	1388	1968	.050	2.00	4.00	10.00
	1388	1968	—	—	Proof	17.50

BANGLADESH

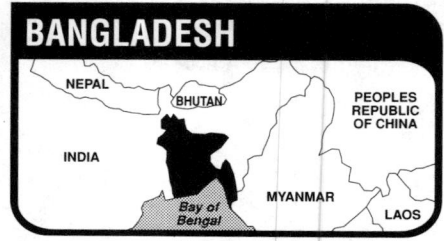

The Peoples Republic of Bangladesh (formerly East Pakistan), a parliamentary democracy located on the Bay of Bengal bordered by India and Burma, has an area of 55,295 sq. mi. (143,998 sq. km.) and a population of 128.1 million. Capital: Dhaka. The economy is predominantly agricultural. Jute products, jute and tea are exported.

British rule over the vast Indian sub-continent ended in 1947 when British India attained independence and was partitioned into the two successor states of India and Pakistan. Pakistan consisted of East and West Pakistan, two areas united by the Moslem religion but separated by culture and 1,000 miles of Indian territory. Restive under the de facto rule of the militant but fewer West Pakistanis, the East Pakistanis unsuccessfully demanded greater economic benefits and political reforms. The inability of the leaders of East and West Pakistan to resolve a political breakdown occasioned by the East Pakistan success in the general elections of 1970 precipitated massive civil disobedience in East Pakistan which West Pakistan sought to suppress militarily. East Pakistan seceded from Pakistan, March 26, 1971, and with the support of India declared an independent Peoples Republic of Bangladesh.

Bangladesh is a member of the Commonwealth of Nations. The president is the Head of State and of the Government.

MONETARY SYSTEM
100 Poisha = 1 Taka

DATING
Christian era using Bengali numerals.

POISHA

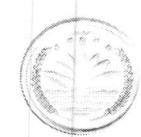

ALUMINUM

KM#	Date	Mintage	VF	XF	Unc
5	1974	300.000	—	.10	.15

5 POISHA

ALUMINUM

KM#	Date	Mintage	VF	XF	Unc
1	1973	*47.088	—	.10	.20
	1974	—	—	.10	.20

F.A.O. Issue

KM#	Date	Mintage	VF	XF	Unc
6	1974	5.000	—	.10	.20
	1975	3.000	—	.10	.20
	1976	3.000	—	.10	.20
	1977	—	—	.10	.20

F.A.O. Issue

KM#	Date	Mintage	VF	XF	Unc
10	1977	90.000	—	.10	.15
	1978	52.432	—	.10	.25
	1979	120.096	—	.10	.15
	1980	127.008	—	.10	.15
	1981	72.992	—	.10	.15

10 POISHA

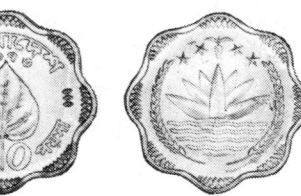

ALUMINUM

KM#	Date	Mintage	VF	XF	Unc
2	1973	*21.500	—	.10	.35
	1974	—	—	.10	.35

F.A.O. Issue

KM#	Date	Mintage	VF	XF	Unc
7	1974	5.000	—	.15	.35
	1975	4.000	—	.15	.35
	1976	4.000	—	.15	.35
	1977	4.000	—	.15	.35
	1978	141.744	—	.15	.30
	1979	—	—	.15	.40

F.A.O. Issue

KM#	Date	Mintage	VF	XF	Unc
11.1	1977	48.000	—	.15	.30
	1978	77.518	—	.15	.30
	1979	170.112	—	.15	.30
	1980	200.000	—	.15	.30

21.9 mm

KM#	Date	Mintage	VF	XF	Unc
11.2	1981	—	—	.25	.50
	1983	142.848	—	.15	.30
	1984	57.152	—	.15	.30

25 POISHA

STEEL
Rohy

KM#	Date	Mintage	VF	XF	Unc
3	1973	*25.072	—	.25	.75

F.A.O. Issue

KM#	Date	Mintage	VF	XF	Unc
8	1974	5.000	—	.20	.50
	1975	6.000	—	.20	.50
	1976	6.000	—	.20	.50
	1977	51.300	—	.15	.35
	1978	66.750	—	.15	.35
	1979	—	—	.15	.35

F.A.O. Issue

KM#	Date	Mintage	VF	XF	Unc
12	1977	45.300	—	.15	.40
	1978	66.750	—	.15	.40
	1979	56.704	—	.15	.40
	1980	228.992	—	.15	.40
	1981	45.072	—	.15	.40
	1983	96.128	—	.15	.35
	1984	203.872	—	.15	.35
	1991	50.002	—	.15	.35

50 POISHA

STEEL

KM#	Date	Mintage	VF	XF	Unc
4	1973	18.000	—	.50	2.00

F.A.O. Issue

KM#	Date	Mintage	VF	XF	Unc
13	1977	12.700	—	.20	.75
	1978	37.300	—	.20	.75
	1979	2.208	—	.20	.75
	1980	124.512	—	.20	.50
	1981	36.680	—	.20	.75
	1983	31.392	—	.20	.75
	1984	168.608	—	.20	.50

TAKA

COPPER-NICKEL
F.A.O. Issue
Obv: Stylized family. Rev: Shapla flower.

KM#	Date	Mintage	VF	XF	Unc
9.1	1975	4.000	.15	.45	1.00
(9)	1976	—	.15	.45	1.00
	1977	—	.15	.45	1.00

Smaller size, 25mm

KM#	Date	Mintage	VF	XF	Unc
9.2	1993	—	.15	.45	1.00

5 TAKKA

STEEL, 7.87 g
Obv: Shapla flower. Rev: Bridge.

KM#	Date	Mintage	VF	XF	Unc
18.1	1994	—	—	—	1.25

8.12 g
Thicker design on obverse.

KM#	Date	Mintage	VF	XF	Unc
18.2	1996	—	—	—	2.00

BARBADOS

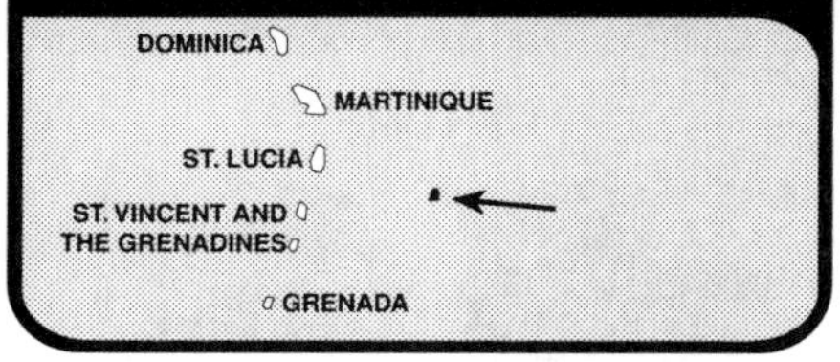
DOMINICA
MARTINIQUE
ST. LUCIA
ST. VINCENT AND
THE GRENADINES
GRENADA

Barbados, an independent state within the British Commonwealth, is located in the Windward Islands of the West Indies east of St. Vincent. The coral island has an area of 166 sq. mi. (430 sq. km.) and a population of 256,395. Capital: Bridgetown. The economy is based on sugar and tourism. Sugar, petroleum products, molasses, and rum are exported.

Barbados was named by the Portuguese who achieved the first landing on the island in 1563. British sailors landed at the site of present-day Holetown in 1624. Barbados was under uninterrupted British control from the time of the first British settlement in 1627 until it obtained independence on Nov. 30, 1966. It is a member of the Commonwealth of Nations. Elizabeth II is Head of State, as Queen of Barbados.

Unmarked 'side cut' pieces of Spanish and Spanish Colonial 1, 2 and 8 reales were the principal coinage medium of 18th-century Barbados. The "Neptune" tokens issued by Sir Phillip Gibbs, a local plantation owner, circulated freely but were never established as legal coinage. The coinage and banknotes of the British Caribbean Territories (Eastern Group) were employed prior to 1973 when Barbados issued a decimal coinage.

RULERS

British, until 1966

MINT MARKS

FM - Franklin Mint, U.S.A.*

None - Royal Mint

***NOTE:** From 1975-1985 the Franklin Mint produced coinage in up to 3 different qualities. Qualities of issue are designated in ( ) after each date and are defined as follows:

(M) MATTE - Normal circulation strike or a dull finish produced by sandblasting special uncirculated (polish finish) or proof quality dies.

(U) SPECIAL UNCIRCULATED - Polished or proof-like in appearance without any frosted features.

(P) PROOF - The highest quality obtainable having mirror-like fields and frosted features.

MONETARY SYSTEM

100 Cents = 1 Dollar

CENT

19 73
BARBADOS
ONE CENT

BRONZE

KM#	Date	Mintage	VF	XF	Unc
10	1973	5.000	—	.10	.25
	1973FM(M)	7,500	—	—	1.00
	1973FM(P)	.097	—	Proof	.50
	1974FM(M)	8,708	—	—	1.00
	1974FM(P)	.036	—	Proof	.50
	1975	8.000	Reported, not confirmed		
	1975FM(M)	5,000	—	—	.75
	1975FM(U)	1,360	—	—	1.00
	1975FM(P)	.020	—	Proof	.50
	1977FM(M)	2,102	—	—	.75
	1977FM(U)	468 pcs.	—	—	3.00
	1977FM(P)	5,014	—	Proof	.50
	1978	4.807	—	—	—
	1978FM(M)	2,000	—	—	1.00
	1978FM(U)	2,517	—	—	1.50
	1978FM(P)	4,436	—	Proof	1.00
	1979	5.606	—	.10	.25
	1979FM(M)	1,500	—	—	1.00
	1979FM(U)	523 pcs.	—	—	2.50
	1979FM(P)	4,126	—	Proof	1.00
	1980	14.400	—	.10	.25
	1980FM(M)	1,500	—	—	1.00
	1980FM(U)	649 pcs.	—	—	2.00
	1980FM(P)	2,111	—	Proof	1.50
	1981	10.160	—	.10	.25
	1981FM(M)	1,500	—	—	1.00
	1981FM(U)	327 pcs.	—	—	2.00
	1981FM(P)	943 pcs.	—	Proof	1.50
	1982	5.040	—	.10	.25
	1982FM(U)	1,500	—	—	1.25
	1982FM(P)	843 pcs.	—	Proof	1.50
	1983FM(M)	1,500	—	—	1.00
	1983FM(U)	—	—	—	1.25
	1983FM(P)	459 pcs.	—	Proof	1.50
	1984	5.008	—	.10	.25
	1984FM(M)	868 pcs.	—	—	1.25
10	1984FM(P)	—	—	Proof	1.50
	1985	—	—	.10	.25
	1986	—	—	.10	.25
	1987	10.000	—	.10	.25
	1988	12.136	—	.10	.25
	1989	—	—	.10	.25
	1990	—	—	.10	.25
	1991	—	—	.10	.25

COPPER PLATED ZINC

KM#	Date	Mintage	VF	XF	Unc
10a	1992	—	—	.10	.25
	1993	—	—	.10	.25
	1995	—	—	.10	.25
	1996	—	—	.10	.25

5 CENTS

19 73
BARBADOS
FIVE CENTS

BRASS
South Point Lighthouse

KM#	Date	Mintage	VF	XF	Unc
11	1973	3.000	.10	.15	.35
	1973FM(M)	7,500	—	—	1.25
	1973FM(P)	.097	—	Proof	.75
	1974FM(M)	8,708	—	—	1.25
	1974FM(P)	.036	—	Proof	.75
	1975FM(M)	5,000	—	—	1.00
	1975FM(U)	1,360	—	—	1.25
	1975FM(P)	.020	—	Proof	.75
	1977FM(M)	2,100	—	—	2.00
	1977FM(U)	468 pcs.	—	—	3.00
	1977FM(P)	5,014	—	Proof	.75
	1978FM(M)	2,000	—	—	.75
	1978FM(U)	2,517	—	—	2.75
	1978FM(P)	4,436	—	Proof	1.25
	1979	4.800	.10	.15	.35
	1979FM(M)	1,500	—	—	.75
	1979FM(U)	523 pcs.	—	—	2.75
	1979FM(P)	4,126	—	Proof	1.25
	1980FM(M)	1,500	—	—	1.00
	1980FM(U)	649 pcs.	—	—	2.25
	1980FM(P)	2,111	—	Proof	1.75
	1981FM(M)	1,500	—	—	1.00
	1981FM(U)	327 pcs.	—	—	2.25
	1981FM(P)	943 pcs.	—	Proof	1.75
	1982	2.100	.10	.15	.35
	1982FM(U)	1,500	—	—	1.50
	1982FM(P)	843 pcs.	—	Proof	1.75
	1983FM(M)	1,500	—	—	1.50
	1983FM(U)	—	—	—	1.50
	1983FM(P)	459 pcs.	—	Proof	1.75
	1984FM	1,737	—	—	1.50
	1984FM(P)	—	—	Proof	2.00
	1985	—	—	—	.25
	1986	—	—	—	.25
	1988	4.200	—	—	.25
	1989	—	—	—	.25
	1991	—	—	—	.25
	1994	—	—	—	.25
	1996	—	—	—	.25

10 CENTS

19 73
BARBADOS
TEN CENTS

COPPER-NICKEL
Bonaparte Tern

KM#	Date	Mintage	VF	XF	Unc
12	1973	4.000	.10	.15	.50
	1973FM(M)	5,000	—	—	1.50
	1973FM(P)	.097	—	Proof	1.00
	1974FM(M)	6,208	—	—	1.50
	1974FM(P)	.036	—	Proof	1.00
	1975FM(M)	2,500	—	—	1.00
	1975FM(U)	1,360	—	—	1.50
	1975FM(P)	.020	—	Proof	1.00
	1977FM(M)	2,100	—	—	1.00
	1977FM(U)	468 pcs.	—	—	4.00
	1977FM(P)	5,014	—	Proof	1.00
	1978FM(M)	2,000	—	—	1.00
	1978FM(U)	2,517	—	—	3.00
	1978FM(P)	4,436	—	Proof	1.50
	1979	2.500	.10	.20	.60
	1979FM(M)	1,500	—	—	2.50
	1979FM(U)	523 pcs.	—	—	3.00
	1979FM(P)	4,126	—	Proof	1.50
	1980	3.500	.10	.15	.50
	1980FM(M)	1,500	—	—	1.00
	1980FM(U)	649 pcs.	—	—	2.50
	1980FM(P)	2,111	—	Proof	2.00
	1981FM(M)	1,500	—	—	1.00
	1981FM(U)	327 pcs.	—	—	2.50
	1981FM(P)	943 pcs.	—	Proof	2.00
	1982FM(U)	1,500	—	—	1.75
	1982FM(P)	843 pcs.	—	Proof	2.00
	1983FM(M)	1,500	—	—	1.75
	1983FM(U)	—	—	—	1.75
	1983FM(P)	459 pcs.	—	Proof	2.00
12	1984	3.400	.10	.15	.50
	1984FM(P)	—	—	Proof	2.25
	1985	—	.10	.15	.50
	1986	—	.10	.15	.50
	1987	3.500	.10	.15	.50
	1988	—	.10	.15	.50
	1989	—	.10	.15	.50
	1990	—	.10	.15	.50
	1992	—	.10	.15	.50
	1995	—	.10	.15	.50

25 CENTS

19 73
BARBADOS
TWENTY FIVE CENTS

COPPER-NICKEL
Morgan Lewis Sugar Mill

KM#	Date	Mintage	VF	XF	Unc
13	1973	6.000	.15	.30	.60
	1973FM(M)	4,300	—	—	1.75
	1973FM(P)	.097	—	Proof	1.25
	1974FM(M)	5,508	—	—	1.75
	1974FM(P)	.036	—	Proof	1.25
	1975FM(M)	1,800	—	—	1.25
	1975FM(U)	1,360	—	—	1.75
	1975FM(P)	.020	—	Proof	1.25
	1977FM(M)	2,100	—	—	1.00
	1977FM(U)	468 pcs.	—	—	4.25
	1977FM(P)	5,014	—	Proof	1.25
	1978	2.407	.20	.40	.80
	1978FM(M)	2,000	—	—	1.00
	1978FM(U)	2,517	—	—	3.25
	1978FM(P)	4,436	—	Proof	1.75
	1979	1.200	.20	.40	.80
	1979FM(M)	1,500	—	—	1.00
	1979FM(U)	523 pcs.	—	—	3.00
	1979FM(P)	4,126	—	Proof	1.75
	1980	2.700	.15	.30	.60
	1980FM(M)	1,500	—	—	3.00
	1980FM(U)	649 pcs.	—	—	2.75
	1980FM(P)	2,111	—	Proof	2.25
	1981	4.365	.15	.30	.60
	1981FM(M)	1,500	—	—	3.00
	1981FM(U)	327 pcs.	—	—	2.75
	1981FM(P)	943 pcs.	—	Proof	2.25
	1982FM(U)	1,500	—	—	2.00
	1982FM(P)	843 pcs.	—	Proof	2.25
	1983FM(M)	1,500	—	—	2.00
	1983FM(U)	—	—	—	2.00
	1983FM(P)	459 pcs.	—	Proof	2.25
	1984FM	868 pcs.	—	—	2.00
	1984FM(P)	—	—	Proof	2.50
	1985	—	.15	.30	.60
	1986	—	.15	.30	.60
	1987	3.150	—	—	2.00
	1988	—	.15	.30	.60
	1989	—	.15	.30	.60
	1990	—	.15	.30	.60
	1994	—	.15	.30	.60

DOLLAR

19 73
BARBADOS
ONE DOLLAR

COPPER-NICKEL
Flying Fish

KM#	Date	Mintage	VF	XF	Unc
14.1	1973	3.955	.60	.75	1.00
	1973FM(M)	3,000	—	—	2.00
	1973FM(P)	.097	—	Proof	1.00
	1974FM(M)	4,208	—	—	2.00
	1974FM(P)	.036	—	Proof	1.00
	1975FM(M)	500 pcs.	—	—	3.50
	1975FM(U)	1,360	—	—	2.00
	1975FM(P)	.020	—	Proof	1.00
	1977FM(M)	600 pcs.	—	—	5.00
	1977FM(U)	468 pcs.	—	—	4.50
	1977FM(P)	5,014	—	Proof	1.50
	1978FM(U)	1,017	—	—	3.50
	1978FM(P)	4,436	—	Proof	2.00
	1979	2.000	.75	1.25	1.75
	1979FM(M)	600 pcs.	—	—	3.00
	1979FM(U)	523 pcs.	—	—	3.50
	1979FM(P)	4,126	—	Proof	2.00
	1980FM(M)	600 pcs.	—	—	3.50
	1980FM(U)	649 pcs.	—	—	3.50
	1980FM(P)	2,111	—	Proof	2.50
	1981FM(M)	600 pcs.	—	—	3.00
	1981FM(U)	327 pcs.	—	—	3.50

KM#	Date	Mintage	VF	XF	Unc
14.1	1981FM(P)	943 pcs.	—	Proof	3.00
	1982FM(U)	600 pcs.	—	—	3.00
	1982FM(P)	843 pcs.	—	Proof	3.00
	1983FM(M)	600 pcs.	—	—	3.00
	1983FM(U)	—	—	—	3.00
	1983FM(P)	459 pcs.	—	Proof	4.00
	1984FM	469 pcs.	—	—	3.50
	1984FM(P)	—	—	Proof	4.50
	1985	—	—	—	1.00
	1986	—	—	—	1.00
		25.5mm			
14.2	1988	3.145	—	—	2.25
	1989	—	—	—	2.25
	1994	—	—	—	2.25

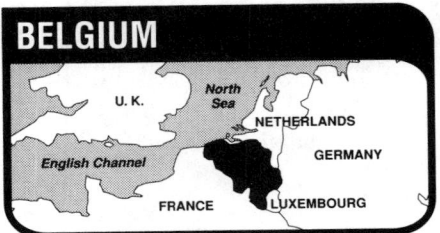

BELGIUM

The Kingdom of Belgium, a constitutional monarchy in northwest Europe, has an area of 11,787 sq. mi. (30,519 sq. km.) and a population of 10.1 million, chiefly Dutch-speaking Flemish and French-speaking Walloons. Capital: Brussels. Agriculture, dairy farming, and the processing of raw materials for re-export are the principal industries. Beurs voor Diamant in Antwerp is the world's largest diamond trading center. Iron and steel, machinery motor vehicles, chemicals, textile yarns and fabrics comprise the principal exports.

The Celtic tribe called 'Belgae', from which Belgium derived its name, was described by Caesar as the most courageous of all the tribes of Gaul. The Belgae eventually capitulated to Rome and the area remained for centuries as a part of the Roman Empire known as Belgica.

As Rome began its decline Frankish tribes migrated westward and established the Merovingian, and subsequently, the Carolingian empires. At the death of Charlemagne Europe was divided among his three sons Karl, Lothar and Ludwig. The eastern part of today's Belgium lies in the Duchy of Lower Lorraine while much of the western parts eventually became the County of Flanders. After further divisions the area came under the control of the Duke of Burgundy from whence it passed under Hapsburg control when Marie of Burgundy married Maximilian of Austria. Phillip I (the Fair), son of Maximilian and Marie then added Spain to the Hapsburg empire by marrying Johanna, daughter of Ferdinand and Isabella. Charles and Ferdinand, sons of Phillip and Johanna, began the separate Spanish and Austrian lines of the Hapsburg family. The Burgundian lands, along with the northern provinces which make up present day Netherlands, became the Spanish Netherlands. The northern provinces successfully rebelled and broke away from Hapsburg rule in the late 16th century and early 17th century. The southern provinces along with the Duchy of Luxembourg remained under the influence of Spain until the year 1700 when Charles II, last of the Spanish Hapsburg line, died without leaving an heir and the Spanish crown went to the Bourbon family of France. The Spanish Netherlands then reverted to the control of the Austrian line of Hapsburgs and became the Austrian Netherlands. The Austrian Netherlands along with the Bishopric of Liege fell to the French Republic in 1794.

At the Congress of Vienna in 1815 the area was reunited with the Netherlands, but in 1830 independence was gained and the constitutional monarchy of Belgium was established. A large part of the Duchy of Luxembourg was incorporated into Belgium and the first king was Leopold I of Saxe-Coburg-Gotha. It was invaded by the German Army in August, 1914 and the German forces carried on a devastating occupation of most of the territory until the Armistice. Belgium joined the League of Nations. On May 10, 1940 it was invaded again by Nazi German armies. The Belgian and Allied forces were quickly overwhelmed and were evacuated through Dunkirk. Allied troops reached Belgium again in Sept. 1944. Prince Charles, Count of Flanders, assumed King Leopold's responsibilities until liberation by the U.S. Army in Austria on May 8, 1945. As of January 1, 1989, Belgium became a federal kingdom.

RULERS

Leopold II, 1865-1909
Albert I, 1909-1934
Leopold III, 1934-1950
Baudouin I, 1951-1993
Albert II, 1993

MINT MARKS

Angel head - Brussels

MINTMASTERS INITIALS & PRIVY MARKS

(b) - bird - Vogelier
Lamb head - Lambret

MONETARY SYSTEM

100 Centimes = 1 Franc
43 Francs = 1 Ecu

LEGENDS

Belgian coins are usually inscribed either in Dutch, French or both. However some modern coins are being inscribed in Latin and German. The language used is best told by noting the spelling of the name of the country.

(Fr) French: BELGIQUE or BELGES
(Du) Dutch: BELGIE or BELGEN
(La) Latin: BELGICA
(Ge) German: BELGICA

Many Belgian coins are collected by what is known as Position A and Position B edges. Some dates command a premium depending on the position which are as follows:

Position A: Coins with portrait side down having upright edge lettering.
Position B: Coins with portrait side up having upright edge lettering.

CENTIME

COPPER
Obv. French leg: DES BELGES.

KM#	Date Mintage	Fine	VF	XF	Unc
33.1	1901/801 near 1				
	3.743	.50	1.50	3.50	10.00
	1901/801 far 1				
	Inc. Ab.	.50	1.50	3.50	10.00
	1901 Inc. Ab.	.25	.50	1.50	7.00
	1902/802 near 2				
	2.847	1.00	2.00	7.50	20.00
	1902/802 far 2				
	Inc. Ab.	1.00	2.00	7.50	20.00
	1902/801 I.A.	1.00	2.00	7.50	20.00
	1902/1 I.A.	1.00	2.00	7.50	20.00
	1902 Inc. Ab.	.20	.50	1.50	7.00
	1907 3.967	.20	.50	1.50	7.00

NOTE: Earlier dates (1869-1899) exist for this type.

Thin flan.

33.2	1901 Inc. Ab.	1.00	1.50	4.00	12.50
	1902 Inc. Ab.	1.00	1.50	6.00	15.00

NOTE: Earlier date (1882) exists for this type.

Rev: Additional stop in signature. . . BRAEMT.F.

33.3	1902 Inc. Ab.	1.00	2.00	10.00	30.00

Obv. Dutch leg: DER BELGEN.

34.1	1901/899 I.A.	.75	2.25	4.50	10.00
	1901 Inc. Ab.	.25	.50	1.50	6.00
	1902/1 2.482	1.25	3.50	9.00	15.00
	1902 Inc. Ab.	.25	.75	2.00	8.00
	1907 3.966	.25	.75	1.50	7.00

NOTE: Earlier dates (1882-1899) exist for this type.

Thin flan.

34.2	1901 Inc. Ab.	1.00	1.50	8.00	20.00
	1902 Inc. Ab.	1.00	1.50	8.00	20.00

NOTE: Earlier date (1887) exists for this type.

Obv. French leg: DES BELGES.

76	1912 2.540	.20	.50	2.50	5.00
	1914 .870	.25	.75	3.50	6.00

Obv. Dutch leg: DER BELGEN.

77	1912 2.542	.20	.50	1.50	4.00

2 CENTIMES

COPPER
Obv. French leg: DES BELGES.

35.1	1902 2.490	.15	.50	4.00	10.00
	1902 2.490	.15	.50	4.00	10.00
	1905 4.981	.15	.35	2.00	6.00
	1909/5 4.983	.15	1.50	8.00	20.00
	1909 Inc. Ab.	.15	.35	2.00	6.00

NOTE: Earlier dates (1869-1876) exist for this type.

Thin flan.

35.2	1902 Inc. Ab.	3.00	5.00	35.00	100.00

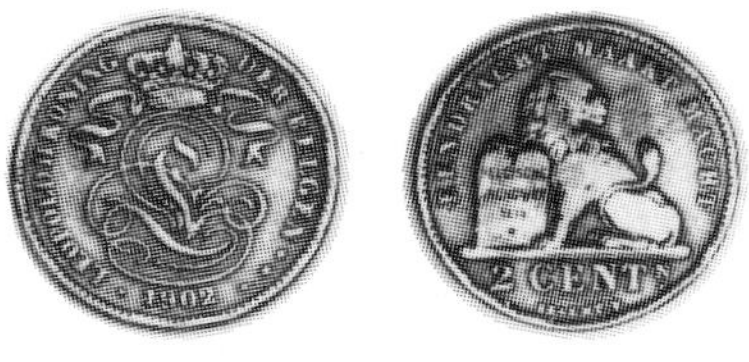

Obv. Dutch leg: DER BELGEN.

KM#	Date	Mintage	Fine	VF	XF	Unc
36	1902	2.488	.15	1.50	3.00	10.00
	1905/2	4.986	1.50	3.00	15.00	40.00
	1905	Inc. Ab.	.15	1.00	2.00	6.00
	1909	.565	.50	2.00	12.00	25.00

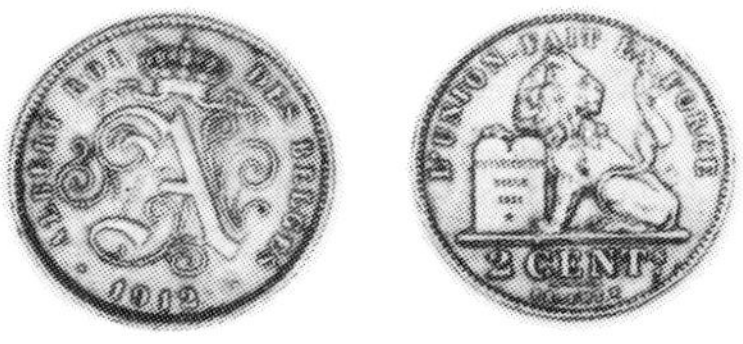

Obv. French leg: DES BELGES.

KM#	Date	Mintage	Fine	VF	XF	Unc
64	1911	.645	1.50	3.00	14.00	30.00
	1912/1	4.928	1.00	2.00	8.00	20.00
	1912	Inc. Ab.	.15	.50	2.00	5.00
	1914	.491	1.00	2.50	12.00	25.00
	1919/4	5.000	.75	1.00	5.00	15.00
	1919	Inc. Ab.	.15	.25	1.00	3.00

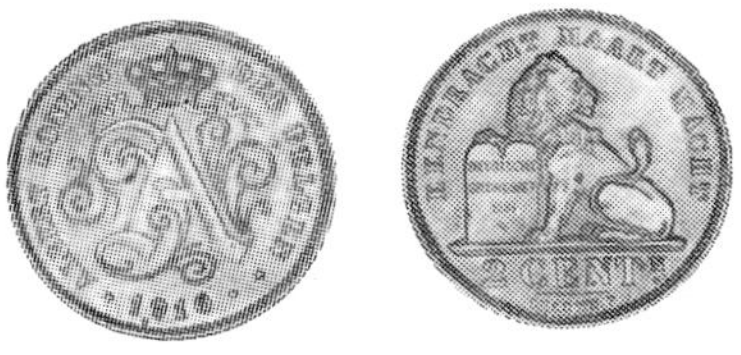

Obv. Dutch leg: DER BELGEN.

KM#	Date	Mintage	Fine	VF	XF	Unc
65	1910	1.248	.25	.50	3.00	8.00
	1911 large date	6.441	.15	.35	1.50	4.50
	1911 small date	Inc. Ab.	.15	.35	1.50	4.50
	1912	1.602	.35	.50	2.00	7.00
	1919	4.998	.15	.35	.75	3.00

5 CENTIMES

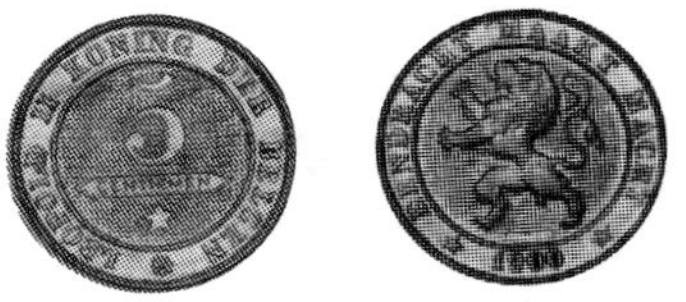

COPPER-NICKEL

Obv. French leg: DES BELGES.

KM#	Date	Mintage	Fine	VF	XF	Unc
40	1901	—	10.00	16.00	65.00	140.00

NOTE: Earlier dates (1894-1900) exist for this type.

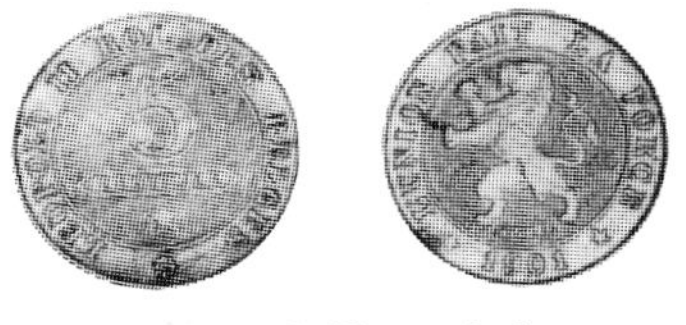

Rev: Lion of different design.

KM#	Date	Mintage	Fine	VF	XF	Unc
44	1901	2.494	3.00	8.00	35.00	70.00

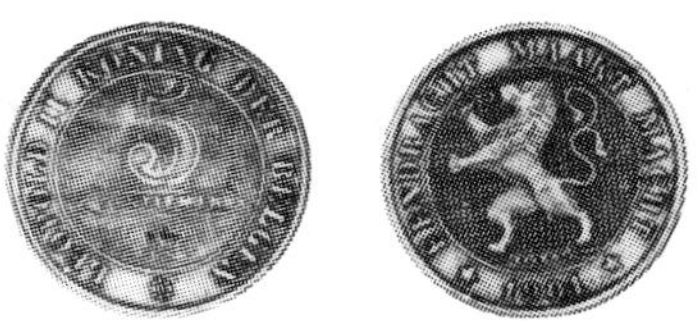

Obv. Dutch leg: DER BELGEN.

Rev: Lion of different lower design.

KM#	Date	Mintage	Fine	VF	XF	Unc
45	1901	2.491	3.00	8.00	35.00	70.00

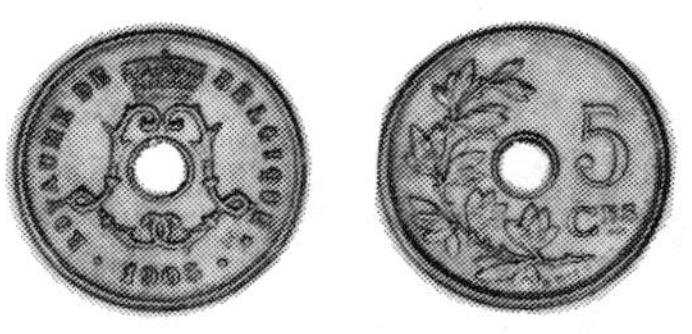

Obv. French leg: BELGIQUE, small date.

KM#	Date	Mintage	Fine	VF	XF	Unc
46	1901	.202	15.00	30.00	75.00	150.00
	1902/1	1.416	.50	2.00	9.00	20.00
	1902	Inc. Ab.	.25	1.50	6.00	14.00
	1903	.864	1.00	4.00	15.00	30.00

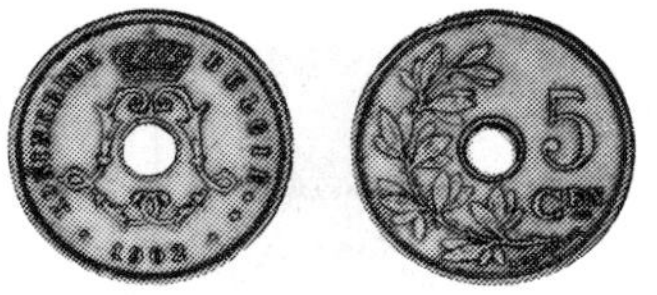

Obv. Dutch leg: BELGIE, small date.

KM#	Date	Mintage	Fine	VF	XF	Unc
47	1902/1	1.485	1.75	5.50	22.50	55.00
	1902	Inc. Ab.	.15	1.50	7.00	20.00
	1903	1.002	1.00	5.00	15.00	40.00

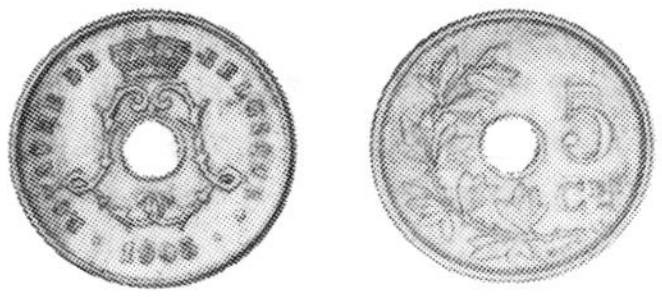

Obv: Large date.

KM#	Date	Mintage	Fine	VF	XF	Unc
54	1904	5.814	.15	.35	2.00	10.00
	1905/4	9.575	.30	1.00	3.00	15.00
	1905	Inc. Ab.	.15	.35	2.00	10.00
	1905 WICHAUX (error)	Inc. Ab.	2.00	5.00	25.00	60.00
	1905 A. MICHAUX	Inc. Ab.	1.00	3.50	15.00	35.00
	1906/5	8.463	.30	1.50	5.00	15.00
	1906	Inc. Ab.	.15	.35	2.00	7.00
	1907	.993	1.00	3.00	12.00	30.00

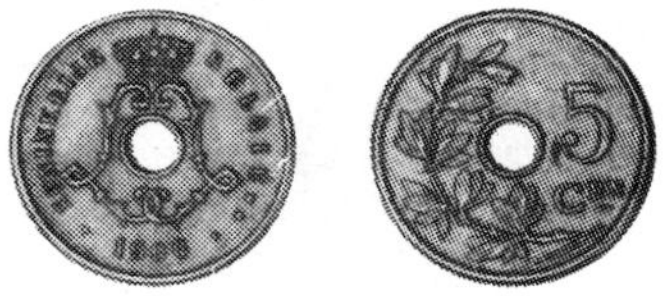

Obv: Large date.

KM#	Date	Mintage	Fine	VF	XF	Unc
55	1904	5.812	.15	.35	2.00	10.00
	1905/3	7.002	.35	2.50	15.00	35.00
	1905/4	I.A.	.30	1.50	10.00	25.00
	1905	Inc. Ab.	.15	.35	2.00	10.00
	1905 w/o cross	Inc. Ab.	—	1.50	12.50	25.00
	1906	11.016	.15	.35	2.00	10.00
	1906 w/o cross	Inc. Ab.	—	—	—	—
	1907	.998	1.00	2.00	10.00	25.00

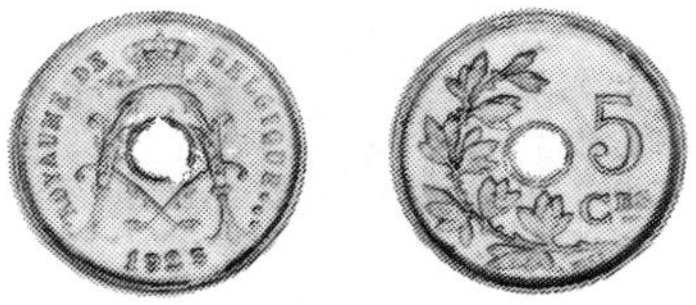

Obv. French leg: BELGIQUE.

KM#	Date	Mintage	Fine	VF	XF	Unc
66	1910	8.011	.10	.35	1.25	6.00
	1913/0	5.005	.20	.75	2.25	10.00
	1913	Inc. Ab.	.10	.40	1.50	7.00
	1914	1.004	1.00	3.00	8.00	20.00
	1920/10	10.040	.10	1.00	3.00	7.00
	1920	Inc. Ab.	.10	.35	1.25	4.00
	1922/0	12.640	.10	1.00	2.50	8.00
	1922/1	I.A.	.10	1.50	3.50	9.00
	1922	Inc. Ab.	.10	.35	1.25	4.00
	1923/13	9.000	.10	.75	2.50	8.00
	1923	Inc. Ab.	.10	.35	1.25	4.00
	1925/13	15.860	.10	.50	2.00	8.00
	1925	Inc. Ab.	.10	.35	1.25	4.00
	1926/5	7.000	.10	1.00	2.50	8.00
	1926	Inc. Ab.	.10	.35	1.25	4.00
	1927	2.000	.10	1.00	2.50	9.00
	1928	12.507	.10	.35	1.25	5.00
	1932	Inc. KM93	5.00	15.00	50.00	150.00

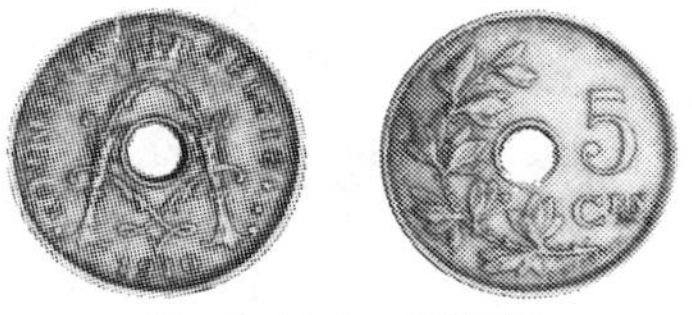

Obv. Dutch leg: BELGIE.

KM#	Date	Mintage	Fine	VF	XF	Unc
67	1910	8.033	.10	.35	1.25	8.00
	1914	6.040	.10	.35	1.25	6.00
	1920/10	10.030	.10	.50	3.00	12.00
	1920	Inc. Ab.	.10	.35	1.25	5.00
	1921/11	4.200	.10	1.00	2.50	12.00
	1921	Inc. Ab.	.10	1.00	2.00	9.00
	1922/12	13.180	.10	1.00	2.50	8.00
	1922/0	I.A.	.10	1.00	3.00	9.00
	1922	Inc. Ab.	.10	.35	1.25	4.00
	1923/13	3.530	.10	1.00	3.00	14.00
	1923	Inc. Ab.	.10	.75	2.00	7.00
	1924/11	5.260	.10	1.00	2.50	9.00
	1924/14	I.A.	.10	.50	1.75	8.00
	1924	Inc. Ab.	.10	.35	1.25	5.00
	1925/13	13.000	.10	1.00	2.50	8.00
	1925/15 high 2	Inc. Ab.	.10	1.00	2.00	9.00
	1925/15 level 2	Inc. Ab.	.10	1.00	2.00	9.00
	1925/3	I.A.	.10	.60	2.00	9.00
	1925	Inc. Ab.	.10	.35	1.25	4.00
	1927	6.938	.10	.35	1.25	6.00
	1928/3	6.252	.10	.75	2.50	9.00
	1928	Inc. Ab.	.10	.35	1.25	4.00
	1930	Inc. KM94	5.00	15.00	50.00	150.00
	1931	Inc. KM94	7.50	18.00	60.00	170.00

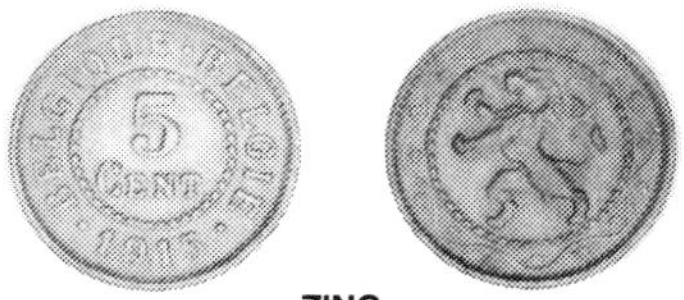

ZINC

German Occupation WW I

Obv. French leg: BELGIQUE-BELGIE.

KM#	Date	Mintage	Fine	VF	XF	Unc
80	1915	10.199	.15	2.00	4.00	15.00
	1916	45.464	.10	.60	2.00	5.00

NICKEL-BRASS

Obv. French leg: BELGIQUE.

Rev: Star added above 5.

KM#	Date	Mintage	Fine	VF	XF	Unc
93	1932	5.520	.10	.20	.35	3.00

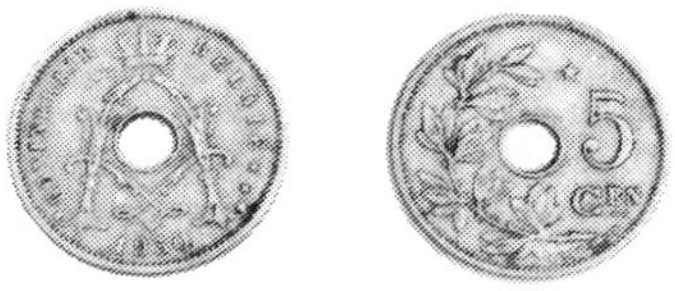

Obv. Dutch leg: BELGIE.

KM#	Date	Mintage	Fine	VF	XF	Unc
94	1930	3.000	.10	.20	.35	3.00
	1931	7.430	.10	.20	.35	3.00

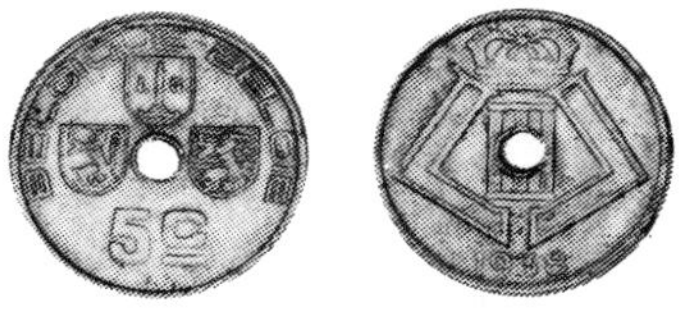

Obv. French leg: BELGIQUE-BELGIE.

KM#	Date	Mintage	Fine	VF	XF	Unc
110.1	1938	4.970	.10	.20	.75	2.00
	1939 (restrike)		—	—	—	—

Medal alignment.

KM#	Date	Mintage	Fine	VF	XF	Unc
110.2	1938	Inc. Ab.	1.25	3.00	8.00	30.00

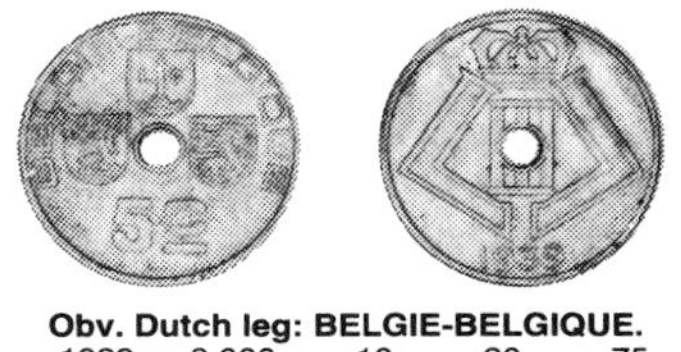

Obv. Dutch leg: BELGIE-BELGIQUE.

KM#	Date	Mintage	Fine	VF	XF	Unc
111	1939	3.000	.10	.20	.75	2.00
	1940	1.970	.20	.50	1.50	5.00

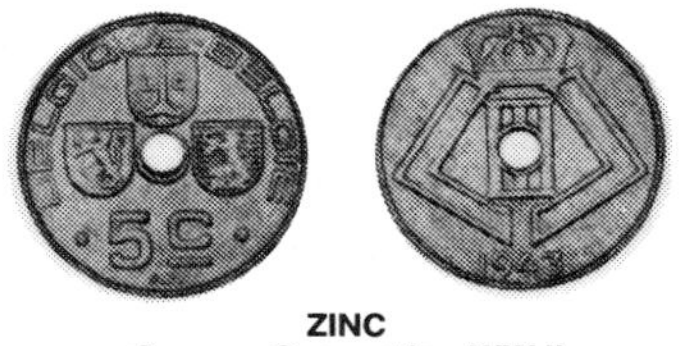

ZINC

German Occupation WW II

Obv. French leg: BELGIQUE-BELGIE.

KM#	Date	Mintage	Fine	VF	XF	Unc
123	1941	10.000	.10	.20	1.00	4.00
	1943	7.606	.10	.20	1.00	4.00

Obv. Dutch leg: BELGIE-BELGIQUE.

KM#	Date	Mintage	Fine	VF	XF	Unc
124	1941	4.000	.15	.75	2.50	8.00
	1942	18.430	.10	.20	.50	3.00

10 CENTIMES

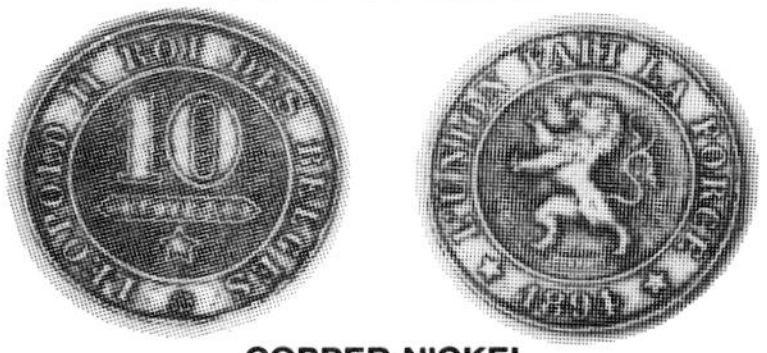

COPPER-NICKEL

Obv. French leg: DES BELGES.

KM#	Date	Mintage	Fine	VF	XF	Unc
42	1901	.551	30.00	50.00	110.00	275.00

NOTE: Earlier dates (1894-1898) exist for this type.

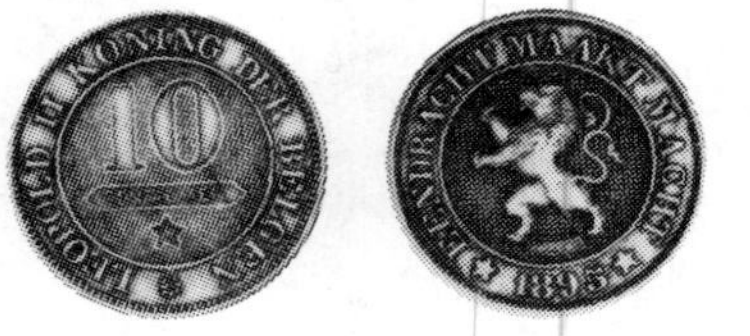

Obv. Dutch leg: DER BELGEN.

KM#	Date	Mintage	Fine	VF	XF	Unc
43	1901	.556	30.00	50.00	110.00	250.00

NOTE: Earlier dates (1894-1898) exist for this type.

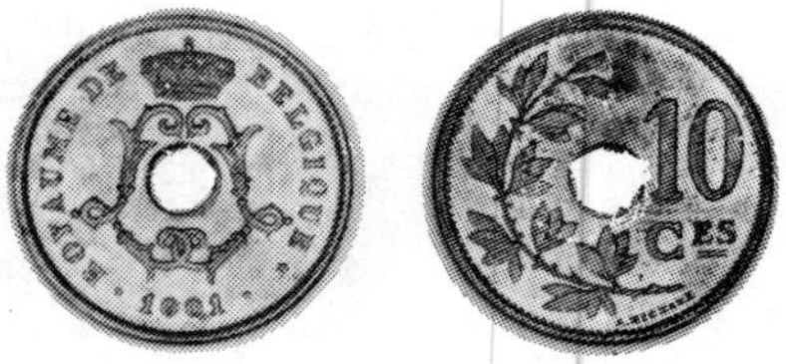

Obv. French leg: BELGIQUE, small date.

KM#	Date	Mintage	Fine	VF	XF	Unc
48	1901	.582	6.00	15.00	30.00	100.00
	1902/1	5.866	.50	3.00	7.00	18.00
	1902	Inc. Ab.	.15	1.00	2.50	9.00
	1903	.763	1.00	4.00	10.00	30.00

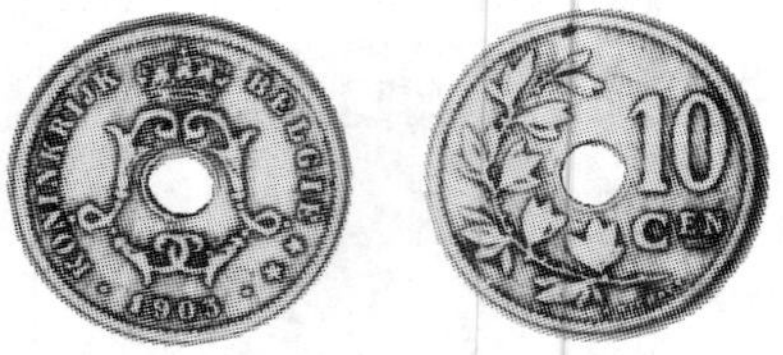

Obv. Dutch leg: BELGIE, small date.

KM#	Date	Mintage	Fine	VF	XF	Unc
49	1902	1.560	.20	1.00	5.00	15.00
	1903/2	—	.50	1.25	7.00	18.00
	1903	5.658	.15	.50	2.00	7.00

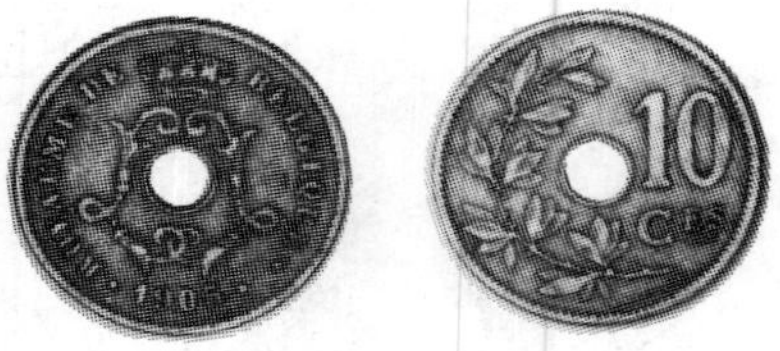

Obv: Large date.

KM#	Date	Mintage	Fine	VF	XF	Unc
52	1903	Inc. Ab.	2.00	7.00	17.00	40.00
	1904	16.354	.15	.60	2.00	7.50
	1905/4	14.392	.25	1.00	5.00	18.00
	1905	Inc. Ab.	.15	.60	2.00	7.00
	1906/5	1.483	.50	1.50	5.00	18.00
	1906	Inc. Ab.	.25	.75	2.50	10.00

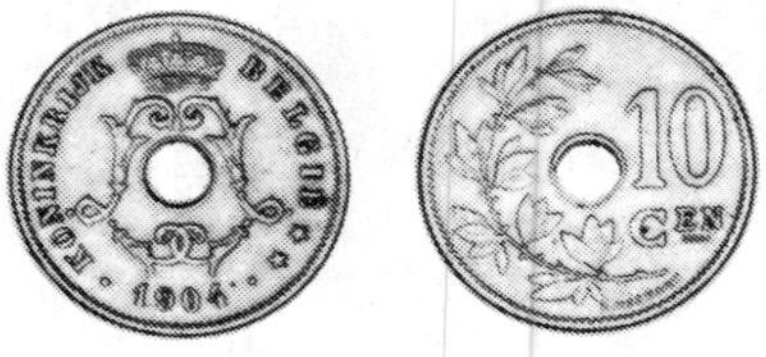

Obv: Large date.

KM#	Date	Mintage	Fine	VF	XF	Unc
53	1903	Inc. Ab.	1.00	4.00	10.00	20.00
	1904	16.834	.20	.50	2.00	7.00
	1905/3	13.758	.35	1.00	3.00	15.00
	1905/4	I.A.	.30	1.00	3.00	15.00
	1905	Inc. Ab.	.20	.50	2.00	7.00
	1906/5 point above center of 6	2.017	.50	1.25	4.00	15.00
	1906/5 point above right side of 6	Inc. Ab.	.50	1.25	4.00	15.00
	1906	Inc. Ab.	.10	.75	2.50	8.00

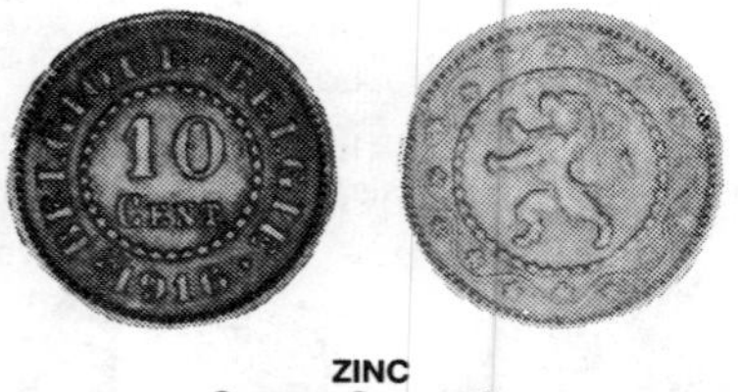

ZINC
German Occupation
Obv. French leg: BELGIQUE-BELGIE.

KM#	Date	Mintage	Fine	VF	XF	Unc
81	1915	9.681	.25	1.50	4.00	12.00
	1916	37.382	.15	.75	3.00	9.00
	1916.	Inc. Ab.	10.00	17.50	70.00	150.00
	1917	1.447	17.50	25.00	85.00	200.00

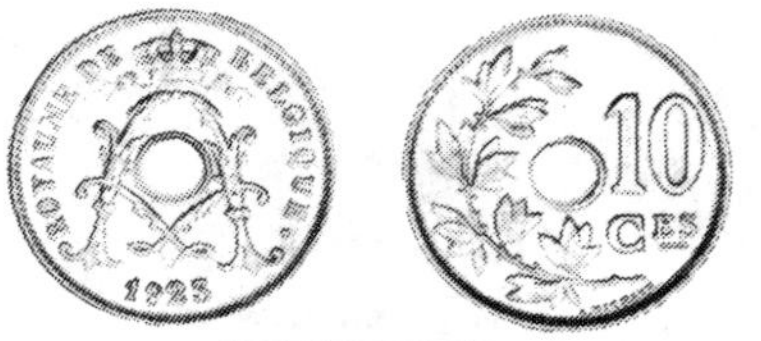

COPPER-NICKEL
Obv. French leg: BELGIQUE.

KM#	Date	Mintage	Fine	VF	XF	Unc
85.1	1911	(restrike)	—	—	—	—
	1920	6.520	.15	.40	1.50	8.00
	1921	7.215	.15	.20	1.00	7.00
	1923	20.625	.10	.20	1.00	6.00
	1926/3	6.916	.20	.75	3.00	12.00
	1926/5	I.A.	.20	.75	3.00	12.00
	1926	Inc. Ab.	.15	.20	1.00	7.00
	1927	8.125	.15	.20	1.00	6.00
	1928/3	6.895	.20	1.00	4.50	16.00
	1928	Inc. Ab.	.15	.20	1.00	7.00
	1929	12.260	.15	.20	1.00	6.00

Rev: Single line below ES of CES.

KM#	Date	Mintage	Fine	VF	XF	Unc
85.2	1920	Inc. Ab.	.50	1.00	3.00	10.00
	1921	Inc. Ab.	1.00	2.50	9.00	30.00

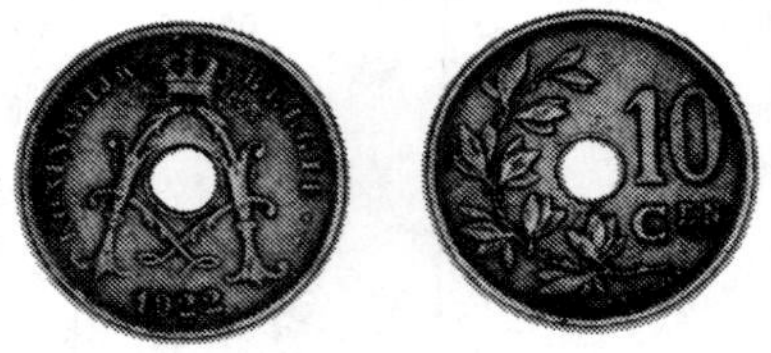

Obv. Dutch leg: BELGIE.

KM#	Date	Mintage	Fine	VF	XF	Unc
86	1920	5.050	.15	.20	1.00	7.00
	1921	7.580	.15	.20	1.00	6.00
	1922	6.250	.15	.20	1.00	6.00
	1924	5.825	.15	.20	1.00	7.00
	1925/4	8.160	.20	.40	2.00	9.00
	1925	Inc. Ab.	.10	.20	1.00	6.00
	1926/5	6.250	.20	.40	2.00	9.00
	1926	Inc. Ab.	.15	.20	1.00	6.00
	1927	10.625	.15	.20	1.00	6.00
	1928/5	6.750	.20	.40	2.00	9.00
	1928	Inc. Ab.	.15	.20	1.00	6.00
	1929	4.668	.15	.20	1.00	8.00
	1930	—	15.00	30.00	100.00	250.00

NICKEL-BRASS
Obv. French leg: BELGIQUE.
Rev: Star added above 10.

KM#	Date	Mintage	Fine	VF	XF	Unc
95.1	1930/20	2.000	50.00	75.00	200.00	375.00
	1930	Inc. Ab.	20.00	30.00	100.00	250.00
	1931	6.270	1.00	2.00	8.00	20.00
	1932	1.270	35.00	50.00	175.00	350.00
	1932 A instead of signature	Inc. Ab.	50.00	100.00	240.00	500.00

Rev: Single line below ES of CES.

KM#	Date	Mintage	Fine	VF	XF	Unc
95.2	1931	Inc. Ab.	2.00	5.00	15.00	40.00
	1932	Inc. Ab.	45.00	90.00	200.00	500.00

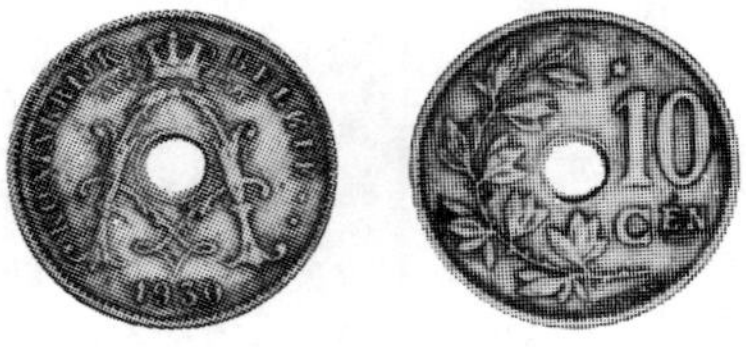

Obv. Dutch leg: BELGIE.

KM#	Date	Mintage	Fine	VF	XF	Unc
96	1930	1.581	.30	.75	3.00	10.00
	1931	5.000	25.00	40.00	125.00	250.00

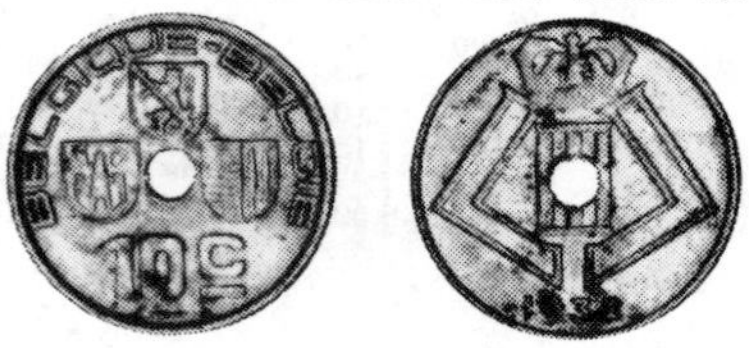

Obv. French leg: BELGIQUE-BELGIE.

KM#	Date	Mintage	Fine	VF	XF	Unc
112	1938	6.000	.10	.25	.50	1.50
	1939	7.000	.50	1.00	3.00	8.00

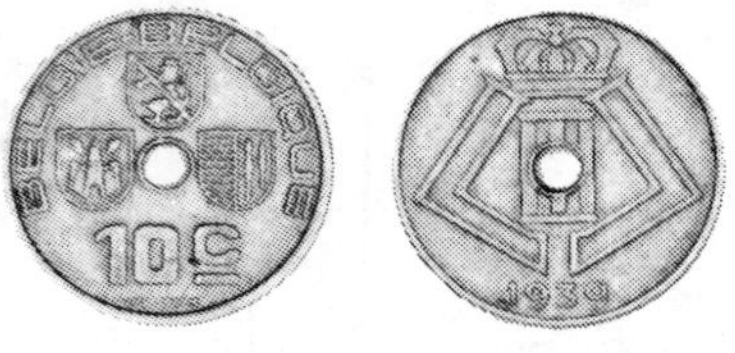

Obv. Dutch leg: BELGIE-BELGIQUE.

KM#	Date	Mintage	Fine	VF	XF	Unc
113.1	1939	8.425	.10	.25	.50	1.50

Thin flan.

KM#	Date	Mintage	Fine	VF	XF	Unc
113.2	1939	Inc. Ab.	1.25	3.00	10.00	35.00

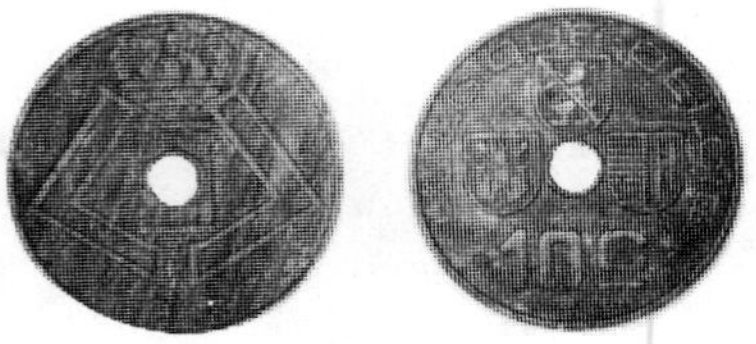

ZINC
German Occupation WW II
Obv. French leg: BELGIQUE-BELGIE.

KM#	Date	Mintage	Fine	VF	XF	Unc
125	1941	10.000	.15	.25	1.50	4.00
	1942	17.000	.15	.25	1.50	4.00
	1943	22.500	.15	.25	1.50	4.00
	1945	(restrike)	—	—	—	—
	1946	*10.370	—	—	—	—

***NOTE:** Not released for circulation.

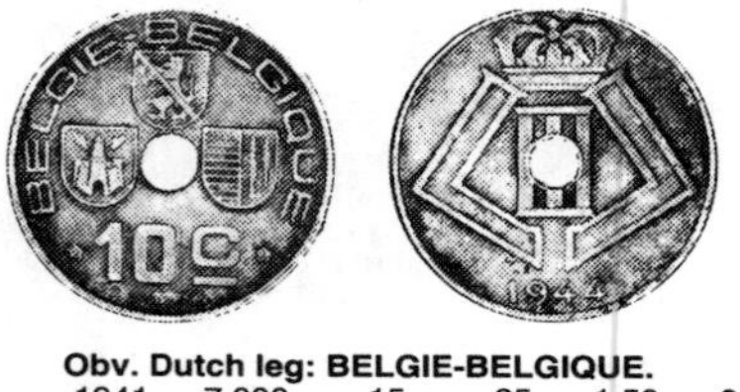

Obv. Dutch leg: BELGIE-BELGIQUE.

KM#	Date	Mintage	Fine	VF	XF	Unc
126	1941	7.000	.15	.25	1.50	6.00
	1942	21.000	.15	.25	1.50	4.00
	1943	22.000	.15	.25	1.50	4.00
	1944	28.140	.15	.25	1.50	4.00
	1945	8.000	.15	.50	2.00	6.00
	1946	5.370	.15	.50	2.00	6.00

20 CENTIMES

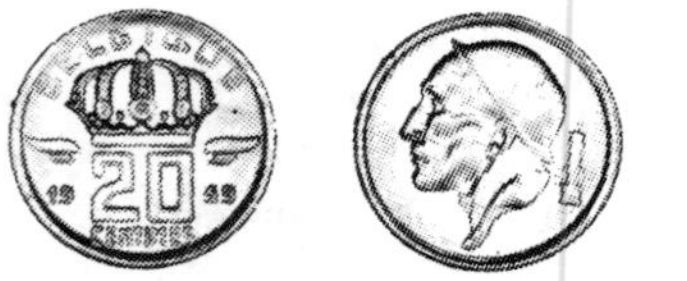

BRONZE
Obv. French leg: BELGIQUE.

KM#	Date	Mintage	Fine	VF	XF	Unc
146	1953	14.150	—	.10	.20	.50
	1953 CENTIMES not touching rim	—	—	.10	.75	2.50
	1954	—	—	400.00	600.00	800.00
	1957	13.300	—	—	.10	.25
	1958	8.700	—	—	.10	.25
	1959	19.670	—	—	.10	.25
	1962	.410	—	6.00	10.00	12.50
	1963	2.550	.10	.20	.50	1.00

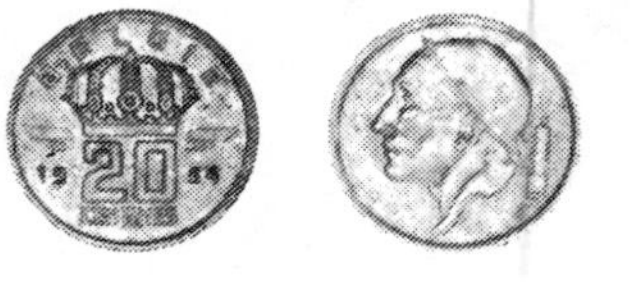

Obv. Dutch leg: BELGIE.

KM#	Date	Mintage	Fine	VF	XF	Unc
147.1	1954	50.130	—	—	.10	.20
	1960	7.530	—	—	.10	.25

Obv: CENTIMES touching rim.

KM#	Date	Mintage	Fine	VF	XF	Unc
147.2	1954	Inc. Ab.	—	.15	.75	2.50
	1960	Inc. Ab.	—	.15	.75	2.50

25 CENTIMES

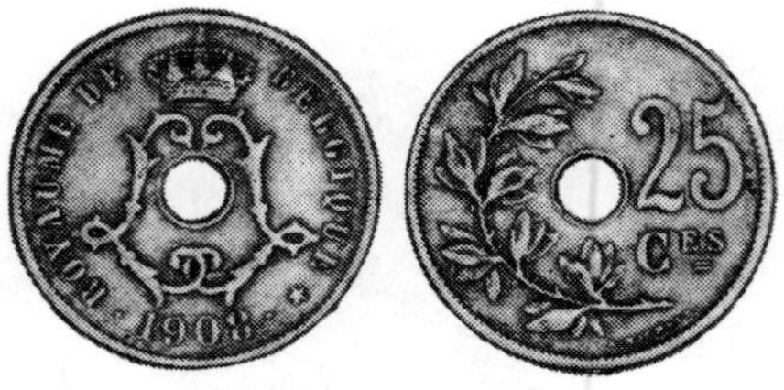

COPPER-NICKEL
Obv. French leg: BELGIQUE.

KM#	Date	Mintage	Fine	VF	XF	Unc
62	1908	4.007	.50	2.50	20.00	65.00
	1909/8	1.998	4.00	30.00	100.00	200.00
	1909	Inc. Ab.	1.00	3.50	25.00	80.00

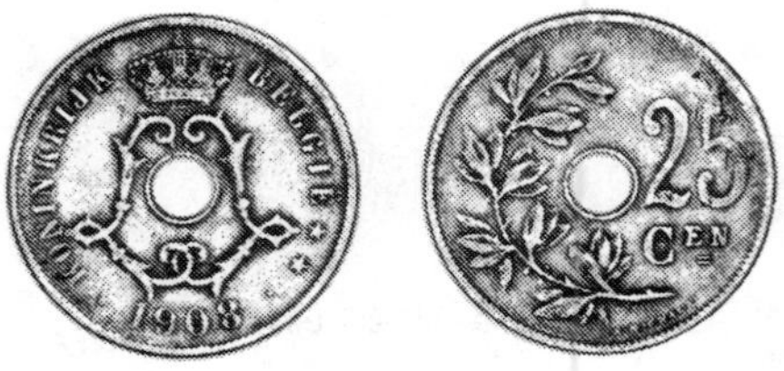

Obv. Dutch leg: BELGIE.

KM#	Date	Mintage	Fine	VF	XF	Unc
63	1908	4.011	.50	2.50	20.00	65.00

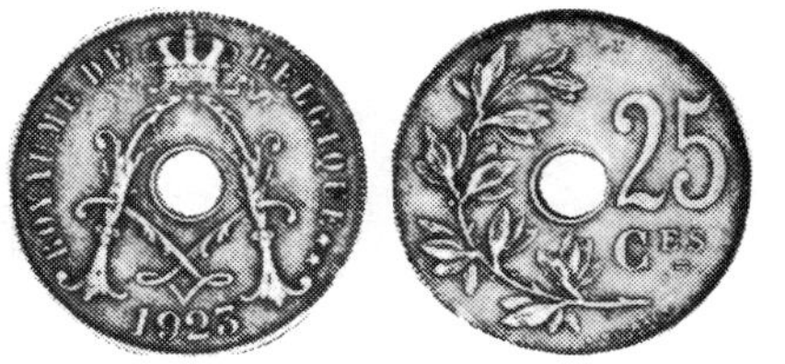

Obv. French leg: BELGIQUE.

KM#	Date	Mintage	Fine	VF	XF	Unc
68.1	1913	2.011	.15	.75	4.00	18.00
	1920	2.844	.15	.50	3.00	14.00
	1921	7.464	.10	.25	1.50	6.00
	1922	7.600	.10	.25	1.50	6.00
	1923	11.356	.15	.25	1.25	6.00
	1926/3	1.300	1.00	2.00	12.00	30.00
	1926	Inc. Ab.	.50	1.00	7.00	25.00
	1927/3	8.800	.20	.75	3.00	12.00
	1927	Inc. Ab.	.10	.25	1.50	6.00
	1928	4.351	.10	.25	1.50	8.00
	1929	9.600	.10	.25	1.00	6.00

Rev: Single line below ES of CES.

KM#	Date	Mintage	Fine	VF	XF	Unc
68.2	1920	Inc. Ab.	.50	1.00	8.00	25.00
	1921	Inc. Ab.	.35	.75	5.00	15.00

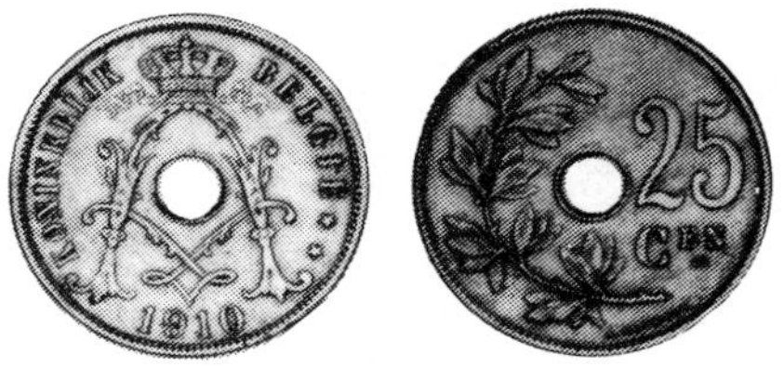

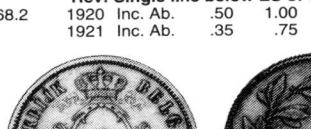

Obv. Dutch leg: BELGIE.

KM#	Date	Mintage	Fine	VF	XF	Unc
69	1910	2.006	.15	1.00	5.00	18.00
	1911 (restrike)		—	—	—	—
	1913	2.010	.15	1.00	5.00	15.00
	1921	11.173	.15	.25	1.50	6.00
	1922/1	14.200	.20	1.00	3.00	12.00
	1922	Inc. Ab.	.15	.25	1.50	6.00
	1926/3	6.400	.25	.50	3.00	12.00
	1926	Inc. Ab.	.10	.40	1.25	6.00
	1927/3	3.799	.20	.60	4.00	14.00
	1927	Inc. Ab.	.10	.25	1.50	8.00
	1928	9.200	.10	.25	1.25	6.00
	1929	8.980	.10	.25	1.25	6.00

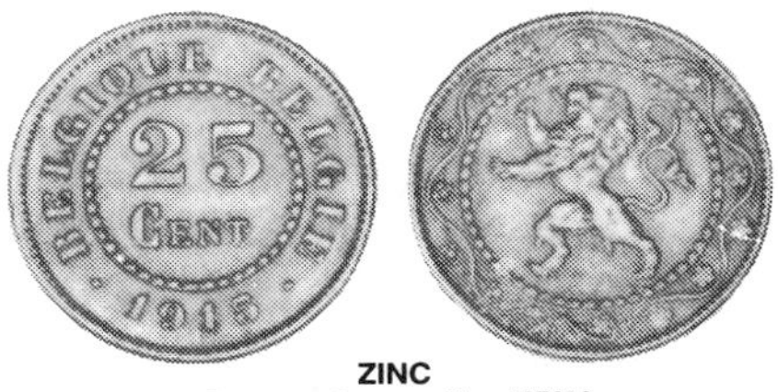

ZINC
German Occupation WW I
Obv. French leg: BELGIQUE-BELGIE.

KM#	Date	Mintage	Fine	VF	XF	Unc
82	1915	8.080	.50	2.00	7.00	18.00
	1916	10.671	.50	2.00	7.00	18.00
	1917	3.555	2.00	4.00	15.00	35.00
	1918	5.489	1.00	3.00	10.00	25.00

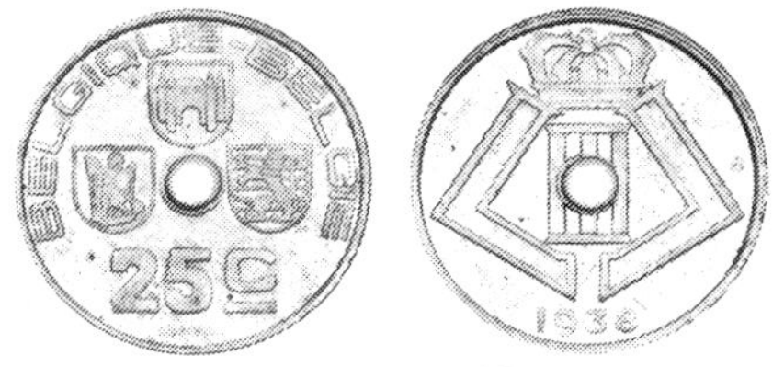

NICKEL-BRASS
Obv. French leg: BELGIQUE-BELGIE.

KM#	Date	Mintage	Fine	VF	XF	Unc
114.1	1938	7.200	—	.25	1.00	4.00
	1939	7.732	—	.25	1.00	4.00

Medal alignment.

KM#	Date	Mintage	Fine	VF	XF	Unc
114.2	1939	Inc. Ab.	1.75	3.00	10.00	30.00

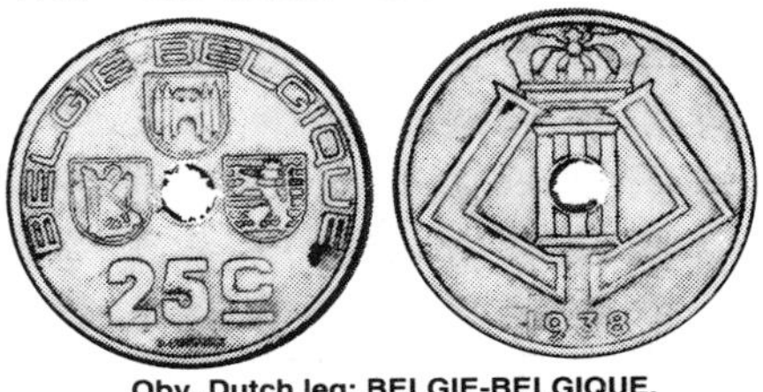

Obv. Dutch leg: BELGIE-BELGIQUE.

KM#	Date	Mintage	Fine	VF	XF	Unc
115.1	1938	14.932	—	.25	1.00	3.00

Medal alignment.

KM#	Date	Mintage	Fine	VF	XF	Unc
115.2	1938	Inc. Ab.	1.75	3.00	10.00	30.00

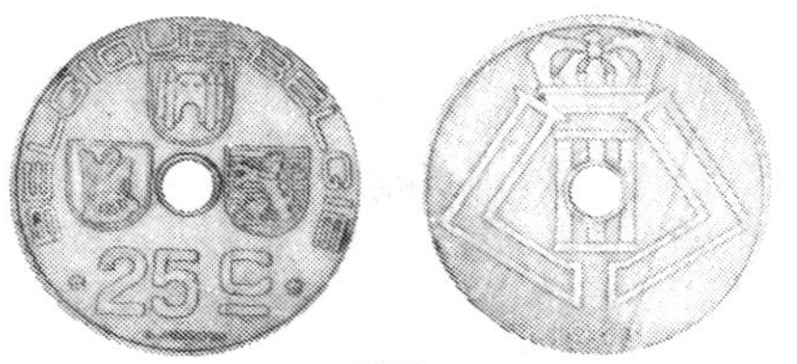

ZINC
German Occupation WW II
Obv. French leg: BELGIQUE-BELGIE.

KM#	Date	Mintage	Fine	VF	XF	Unc
131	1941	—	—	—	Rare	—
	1942	14.400	—	.20	.75	3.00
	1943	21.600	—	.20	.75	3.00
	1945 (restrike)		—	—	—	—
	1946	21.428	—	.20	.75	3.00
	1947	*.300	—	—	—	—

***NOTE:** Not released for circulation.

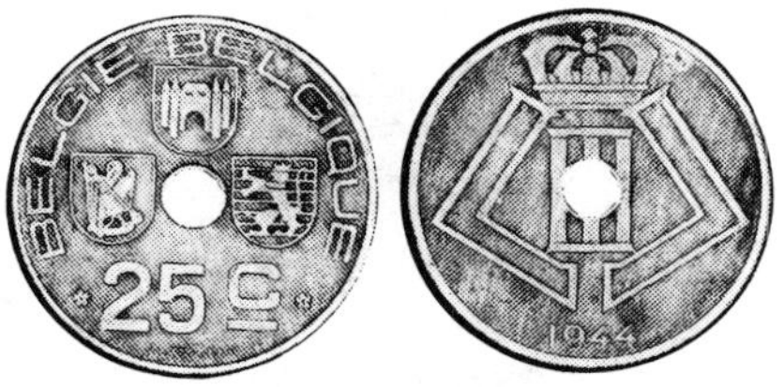

Obv: Dutch leg: BELGIE-BELGIQUE.

KM#	Date	Mintage	Fine	VF	XF	Unc
132	1942	14.400	—	.20	.75	3.00
	1943	21.600	—	.20	.75	3.00
	1944	25.960	—	.20	.75	3.00
	1945	8.200	—	.25	1.25	4.00
	1946	11.652	—	.20	.75	3.00
	1947	*.316	—	—	—	—

***NOTE:** Not released for circulation.

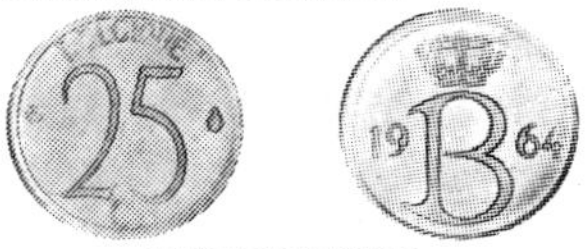

COPPER-NICKEL
Obv. French leg: BELGIQUE.

KM#	Date	Mintage	Fine	VF	XF	Unc
153.1	1964	21.770	—	—	.10	.15
	1965	11.440	—	—	.10	.15
	1966	19.990	—	—	.10	.15
	1967	6.820	—	—	.10	.15
	1968	25.250	—	—	.10	.15
	1969	7.670	—	—	.10	.15
	1970	27.000	—	—	.10	.15
	1971	16.000	—	—	.10	.15
	1972	20.000	—	—	.10	.15
	1973	12.500	—	—	.10	.15
	1974	20.000	—	—	.10	.15
	1975	12.000	—	—	.10	.15

Medal alignment.

KM#	Date	Mintage	Fine	VF	XF	Unc
153.2	1964	Inc. Ab.	—	—	5.00	12.00
	1965	Inc. Ab.	—	—	10.00	25.00
	1967	Inc. Ab.	—	—	10.00	25.00
	1970	Inc. Ab.	—	—	5.00	12.00
	1971	Inc. Ab.	—	—	5.00	12.00
	1974	Inc. Ab.	—	—	10.00	25.00

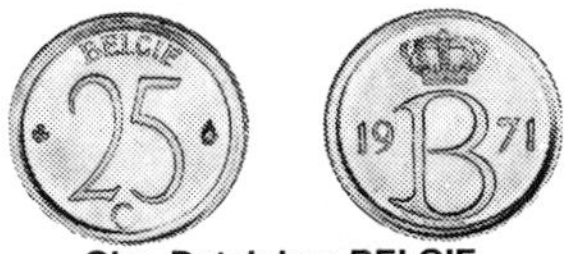

Obv. Dutch leg: BELGIE.

KM#	Date	Mintage	Fine	VF	XF	Unc
154.1	1964	21.300	—	—	.10	.15
	1965	7.900	—	—	.10	.15
	1966	23.420	—	—	.10	.15
	1967	7.720	—	—	.10	.15
	1968	22.750	—	—	.10	.15
	1969	25.190	—	—	.10	.15
	1970	12.000	—	—	.10	.15
	1971	16.000	—	—	.10	.15
	1972	20.000	—	—	.10	.15
	1973	12.500	—	—	.10	.15
	1974	20.000	—	—	.10	.15
	1975	12.000	—	—	.10	.15

Medal alignment.

KM#	Date	Mintage	Fine	VF	XF	Unc
154.2	1964	Inc. Ab.	—	—	5.00	12.00
	1965	Inc. Ab.	—	—	5.00	15.00
	1966	Inc. Ab.	—	—	5.00	12.00
	1967	Inc. Ab.	—	—	6.00	15.00
	1969	Inc. Ab.	—	—	5.00	12.00
	1971	Inc. Ab.	—	—	6.00	15.00
	1972	Inc. Ab.	—	—	5.00	12.00

50 CENTIMES

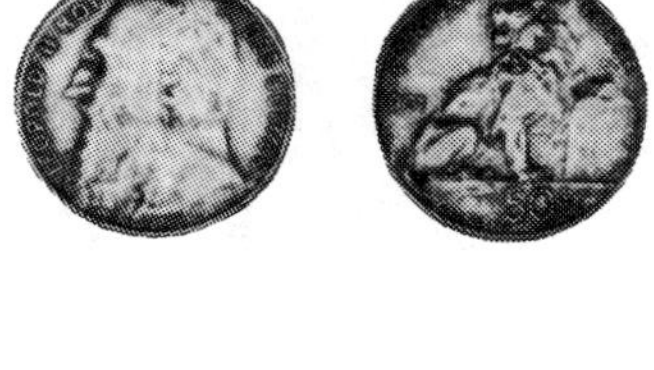

2.5000 g, .835 SILVER, .0671 oz ASW
Obv. French leg: DES BELGES.

KM#	Date	Mintage	Fine	VF	XF	Unc
50	1901	3.000	1.00	10.00	30.00	75.00

Obv. Dutch leg: DER BELGEN.

KM#	Date	Mintage	Fine	VF	XF	Unc
51	1901	3.000	1.00	10.00	30.00	75.00

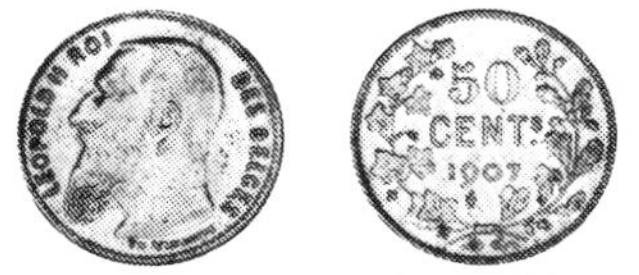

Obv. French leg: DES BELGES.

KM#	Date	Mintage	Fine	VF	XF	Unc
60.1	1907	.545	3.00	5.00	18.00	50.00
	1909	2.503	1.00	2.50	10.00	27.00

Obv: W/o period in signature.

KM#	Date	Mintage	Fine	VF	XF	Unc
60.2	1907	Inc. Ab.	4.00	10.00	25.00	75.00
	1909	Inc. Ab.	2.00	5.00	12.00	35.00

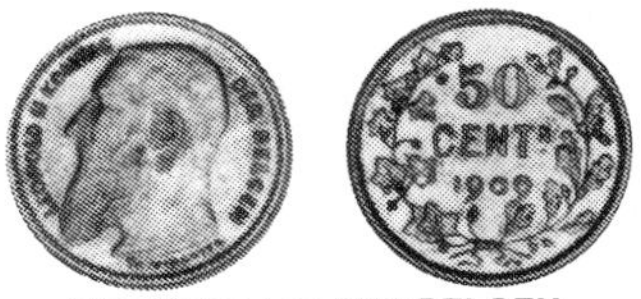

Obv. Dutch leg: DER BELGEN.

KM#	Date	Mintage	Fine	VF	XF	Unc
61.1	1907	.545	3.00	10.00	25.00	45.00
	1909	2.510	1.00	2.50	9.00	25.00

Medal alignment.

KM#	Date	Mintage	Fine	VF	XF	Unc
61.2	1909	Inc. Ab.	12.50	15.00	40.00	125.00

Obv: W/o periods in signature.

KM#	Date	Mintage	Fine	VF	XF	Unc
61.3	1907	Inc. Ab.	4.00	10.00	25.00	70.00
	1909	Inc. Ab.	2.00	6.00	17.50	50.00

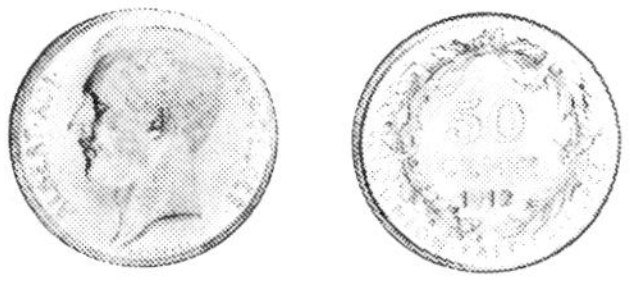

Obv. French leg: DES BELGES.

KM#	Date	Mintage	Fine	VF	XF	Unc
70	1910	1.900	1.00	2.00	9.00	25.00
	1911	2.063	1.00	3.00	10.00	30.00
	1912	1.000	.50	1.00	1.50	6.00
	1914	.240	2.50	5.00	15.00	45.00

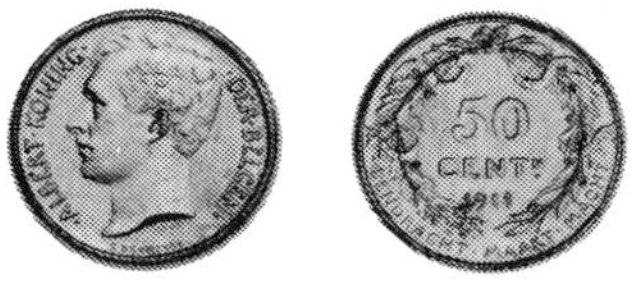

Obv. Dutch leg: DER BELGEN.

KM#	Date	Mintage	Fine	VF	XF	Unc
71	1910	1.900	1.00	3.00	10.00	30.00
	1911	2.063	.50	1.00	1.50	6.00
	1912	1.000	.50	1.00	1.50	6.00

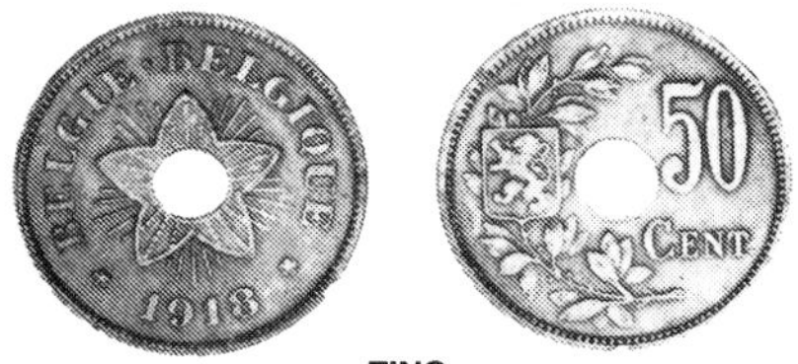

ZINC
German Occupation WW I
Obv. Dutch leg: BELGIE-BELGIQUE.

KM#	Date	Mintage	Fine	VF	XF	Unc
83	1918	7.394	.50	3.00	10.00	25.00

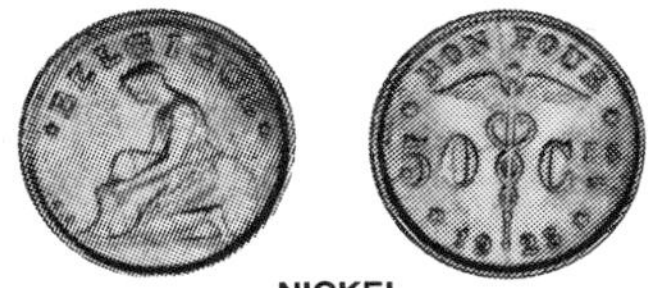

NICKEL
Obv. French leg: BELGIQUE.

KM#	Date	Mintage	Fine	VF	XF	Unc
87	1922	6.180	.15	.25	.50	3.00
	1923	8.820	.15	.25	.50	3.00
	1927	1.750	.15	.30	.50	3.00
	1928	3.000	.15	.35	1.00	4.00
	1929	1.000	.25	.50	3.00	10.00
	1930	1.000	.25	.50	3.00	10.00
	1932/23	2.530	1.00	3.00	10.00	25.00
	1932	Inc. Ab.	.15	.50	1.00	4.00
	1933	2.861	.15	.25	.75	4.00

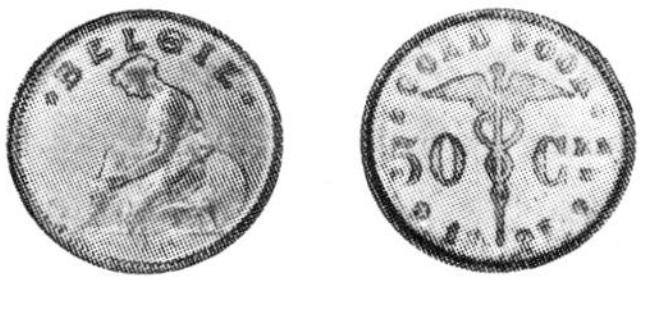

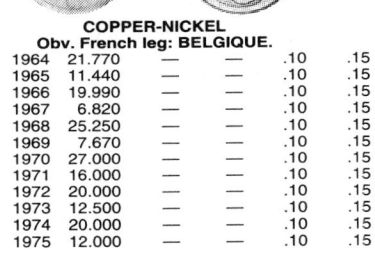

Obv. Dutch leg: BELGIE.

KM#	Date	Mintage	Fine	VF	XF	Unc
88	1922	(restrike)	—	—	—	—
	1923	15.000	.20	.25	.50	3.00
	1928/3	10.000	.25	.50	3.00	10.00
	1928	Inc. Ab.	.20	.25	.50	3.00
	1930/20	2.252	.50	2.00	3.50	12.00
	1930	Inc. Ab.	.20	.75	2.50	6.00
	1932	2.000	.20	.50	1.00	4.00
	1933	1.189	1.00	2.00	4.00	12.00
	1934	.935	50.00	80.00	140.00	250.00

Obv. French leg: BELGIQUE-BELGIE.

KM#	Date	Mintage	Fine	VF	XF	Unc
118	1939	15.500	200.00	400.00	800.00	1200.

NOTE: Striking interrupted by the war. Seems to have never been officially released into circulation.

BRONZE

Obv. French leg: BELGIQUE. Rev: Large head.

KM#	Date	Mintage	Fine	VF	XF	Unc
144	1952	3.520	—	.10	.25	1.00
	1953	22.620	—	—	.10	.35

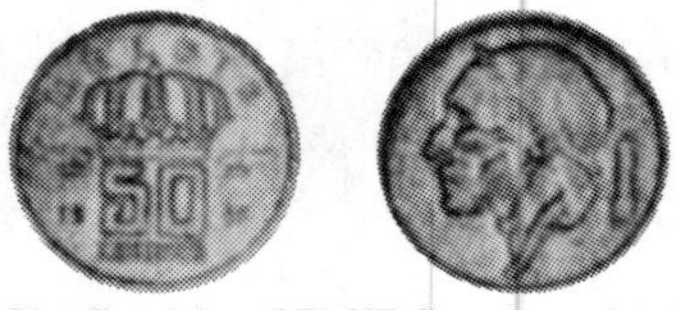

Obv. Dutch leg: BELGIE. Rev: Large head.

KM#	Date	Mintage	Fine	VF	XF	Unc
145	1952	5.830	—	.10	.25	1.00
	1953	22.930	—	—	.10	.35
	1954	15.730	—	—	.10	.35

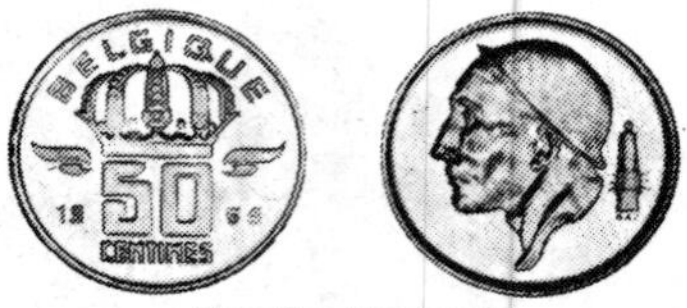

Rev: Smaller head.

KM#	Date	Mintage	Fine	VF	XF	Unc
148.1	1955	29.160	—	—	.10	.25
	1958	9.750	—	—	.10	.25
	1959	17.350	—	—	.10	.20
	1962	6.160	—	—	.10	.15
	1964	5.860	—	—	.10	.15
	1965	10.320	—	—	.10	.15
	1966	11.040	—	—	.10	.15
	1967	7.200	—	—	.10	.15
	1968	2.000	—	—	.10	.20
	1969	10.000	—	—	.10	.15
	1970	16.000	—	—	.10	.15
	1971	1.250	—	—	.10	.20
	1972	3.000	—	—	.10	.15
	1973	3.000	—	—	.10	.15
	1974	5.000	—	—	.10	.15
	1974 wide rim	Inc. Ab.	—	—	.10	.15
	1975	7.000	—	—	.10	.15
	1976	8.000	—	—	.10	.15
	1977	13.000	—	—	.10	.15
	1978	2.500	—	—	.10	.15
	1979	20.000	—	—	.10	.15
	1980	20.000	—	—	.10	.15
	1981	2.000	—	—	.10	.15
	1982	7.000	—	—	.10	.15
	1983	14.100	—	—	.10	.15
	1985	6.000	—	—	.10	.15
	1987	9.000	—	—	.10	.15
	1988	4.500	—	—	.10	.15
	1989	.060	—	—	—	.50
	1990	.060	—	—	—	.50
	1991	.060	—	—	—	.50
	1992	7.060	—	—	.10	.15
	1994	10.000	—	—	.10	.15
	1995	.060	—	—	—	.50
	1996	4.320	—	—	—	.50
	1997	—	—	—	—	.50
	1998	—	—	—	—	.50

Medal alignment.

KM#	Date	Mintage	Fine	VF	XF	Unc
148.2	1953	Inc. Ab.	—	—	2.00	6.50
	1959	Inc. Ab.	—	—	2.00	5.00
	1965	Inc. Ab.	—	—	2.00	4.00
	1966	Inc. Ab.	—	—	2.00	4.00
	1967	Inc. Ab.	—	—	2.00	4.00
	1969	Inc. Ab.	—	—	2.00	4.00
	1974	Inc. Ab.	—	—	2.00	4.00
	1976	Inc. Ab.	—	—	2.00	4.00
	1980	—	—	—	2.00	4.00

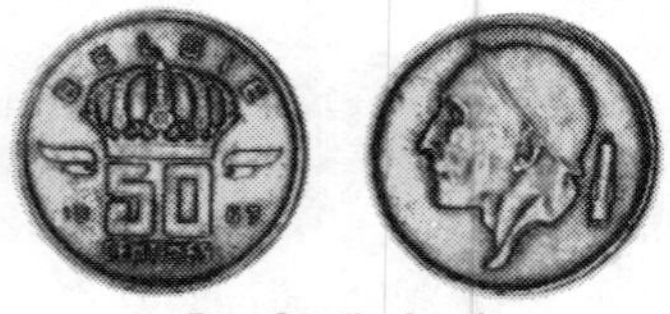

Rev: Smaller head.

KM#	Date	Mintage	Fine	VF	XF	Unc
149.1	1956	5.640	—	—	.10	.25
	1957	13.800	—	—	.10	.25
	1958	19.480	—	—	.10	.20
	1962	4.150	—	—	.10	.15
	1963	1.110	—	—	.10	.15
	1964	10.340	—	—	.10	.15

KM#	Date	Mintage	Fine	VF	XF	Unc
149.1	1965	9.590	—	—	.10	.15
	1966	6.930	—	—	.10	.15
	1967	6.970	—	—	.10	.15
	1968	2.000	—	—	.10	.20
	1969	10.000	—	—	.10	.15
	1970	12.000	—	—	.10	.15
	1971	1.250	—	—	.10	.20
	1972	7.000	—	—	.10	.15
	1973	3.000	—	—	.10	.15
	1974	5.000	—	—	.10	.15
	1975	7.000	—	—	.10	.15
	1976	8.000	—	—	.10	.15
	1977	13.000	—	—	.10	.15
	1978	2.500	—	—	.10	.15
	1979	40.000	—	—	.10	.15
	1980	20.000	—	—	.10	.15
	1981	2.000	—	—	.10	.15
	1982	7.000	—	—	.10	.15
	1983	14.100	—	—	.10	.15
	1985	6.000	—	—	.10	.15
	1987	9.000	—	—	.10	.15
	1988	9.000	—	—	.10	.15
	1989	.060	—	—	—	.50
	1990	.060	—	—	—	.50
	1991	.060	—	—	—	.50
	1992	7.060	—	—	.10	.15
	1993	1.040	—	—	.10	.15
	1994	10.000	—	—	.10	.15
	1995	.060	—	—	—	.50
	1996	.060	—	—	—	.50
	1997	—	—	—	—	.50
	1998	—	—	—	—	.50

Medal alignment.

KM#	Date	Mintage	Fine	VF	XF	Unc
149.2	1953	Inc. Ab.	—	—	2.00	6.50
	1958	Inc. Ab.	—	—	2.00	6.50
	1967	Inc. Ab.	—	—	2.00	6.50
	1969	Inc. Ab.	—	—	2.00	6.50
	1977	Inc. Ab.	—	—	2.00	6.50
	1979	Inc. Ab.	—	—	2.00	6.50
	1981	Inc. Ab.	—	—	2.00	6.50

FRANC

5.0000 g, .835 SILVER, .1342 oz ASW

Obv. French leg: DES BELGES.

KM#	Date	Mintage	Fine	VF	XF	Unc
56.1	1904	.803	4.00	20.00	50.00	75.00
	1909	2.250	2.00	15.00	35.00	45.00

Obv: W/o period in signature.

KM#	Date	Mintage	Fine	VF	XF	Unc
56.2	1904	Inc. Ab.	7.00	25.00	60.00	80.00
	1909	Inc. Ab.	2.50	15.00	35.00	45.00

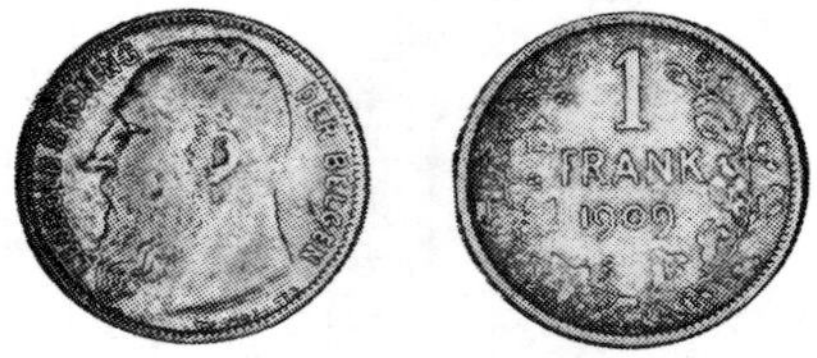

Obv. Dutch leg: DER BELGEN.

KM#	Date	Mintage	Fine	VF	XF	Unc
57.1	1904	.803	5.00	20.00	60.00	80.00
	1909	2.250	2.00	15.00	35.00	45.00

Obv: W/o period in signature.

KM#	Date	Mintage	Fine	VF	XF	Unc
57.2	1904	Inc. Ab.	10.00	60.00	140.00	200.00
	1909	Inc. Ab.	3.00	15.00	35.00	45.00

Obv. French leg: DES BELGES.

KM#	Date	Mintage	Fine	VF	XF	Unc
72.1	1910	2.190	1.00	3.00	8.00	25.00
	1911	2.810	.75	1.50	5.00	12.00
	1912	3.250	.75	1.50	2.50	7.00
	1913	3.000	.75	1.50	2.50	7.00
	1914	10.563	.75	1.50	2.50	7.00
	1917	8.540	350.00	700.00	1500.	2000.
	1918	1.469	300.00	600.00	1400.	2000.

Medal alignment.

KM#	Date	Mintage	Fine	VF	XF	Unc
72.2	1914	Inc. Ab.	4.50	12.50	50.00	125.00

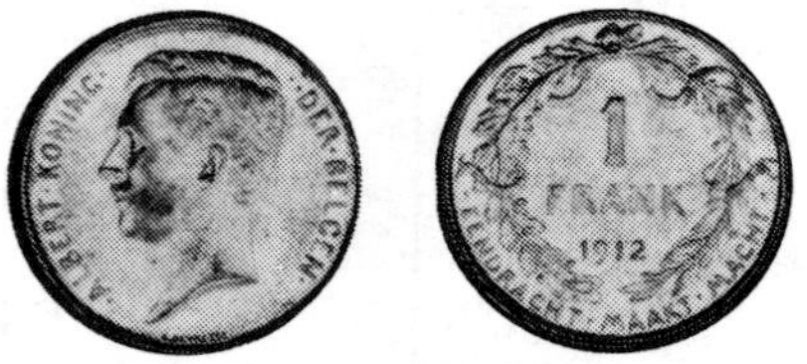

Obv. Dutch leg: DER BELGEN.

KM#	Date	Mintage	Fine	VF	XF	Unc
73.1	1910	2.750	1.00	4.00	15.00	35.00
	1911	2.250	.75	1.50	5.00	12.00
	1912	3.250	.75	1.50	2.50	7.00
	1913	3.000	.75	1.50	2.50	7.00
	1914	10.222	.75	1.50	2.50	7.00
	1918	—	300.00	600.00	1400.	2000.

Medal alignment

KM#	Date	Mintage	Fine	VF	XF	Unc
73.2	1914	Inc. Ab.	4.50	12.50	50.00	125.00

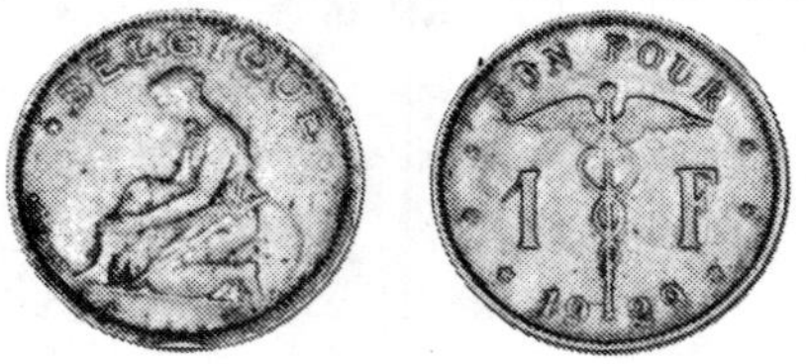

NICKEL

Obv. French leg: BELGIQUE.

KM#	Date	Mintage	Fine	VF	XF	Unc
89	1922	14.000	.15	.25	1.00	3.00
	1923	22.500	.15	.25	1.00	3.00
	1928/3	5.000	.25	1.50	5.00	15.00
	1928/7	I.A.	.25	1.50	5.00	15.00
	1928	Inc. Ab.	.15	.25	1.00	4.00
	1929	7.415	.15	.25	1.00	3.50
	1930	5.365	.15	.25	1.00	3.50
	1931	—	250.00	500.00	1000.	1800.
	1933	1.998	.25	1.50	5.00	12.00
	1934/24	10.263	.50	2.00	7.00	20.00
	1934	Inc. Ab.	.15	.25	1.00	3.00

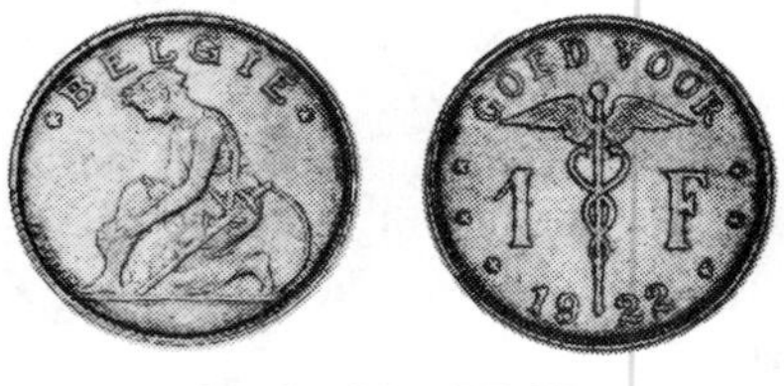

Obv. Dutch leg: BELGIE.

KM#	Date	Mintage	Fine	VF	XF	Unc
90	1922	19.000	.15	.25	1.00	3.00
	1923/2	17.500	.20	1.50	4.00	14.00
	1923	Inc. Ab.	.15	.25	1.00	3.00
	1928/3	4.975	.20	2.00	7.00	15.00
	1928/7	I.A.	.20	2.00	7.00	15.00
	1928	Inc. Ab.	.15	.50	2.00	7.00
	1929	10.365	.15	.25	1.00	3.00
	1933	.786	200.00	400.00	600.00	1200.
	1934/24	8.025	.35	2.50	7.00	20.00
	1934	Inc. Ab.	.15	.50	1.00	3.00
	1935/23	2.238	.35	1.25	4.00	14.00
	1935	Inc. Ab.	.25	.75	2.00	6.00

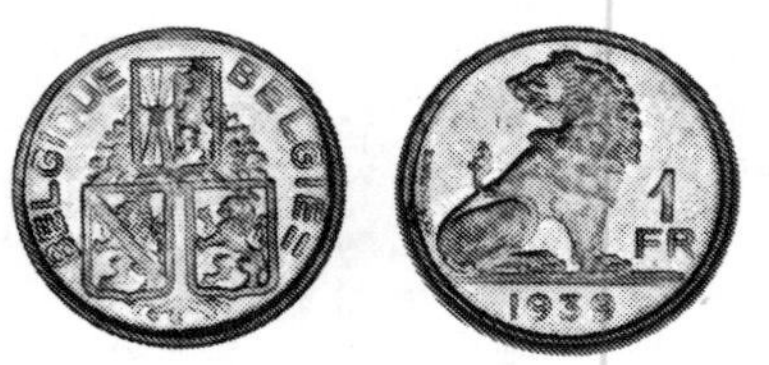

Obv. French leg: BELGIQUE-BELGIE.

KM#	Date	Mintage	Fine	VF	XF	Unc
119	1939	46.865	.15	.25	.50	1.50
	1940	(restrike)	—	—	—	—

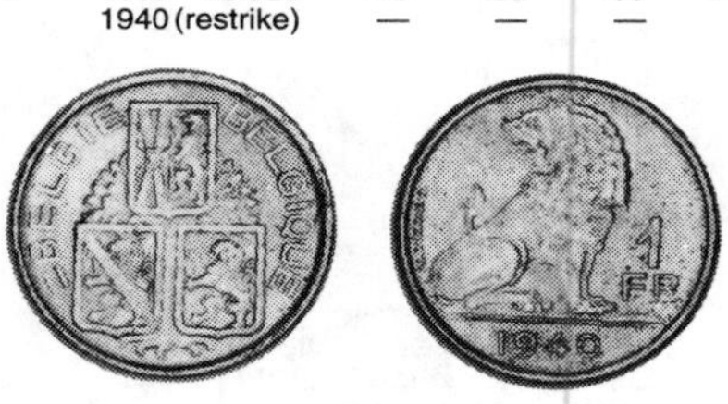

Obv. Dutch leg: BELGIE-BELGIQUE.

KM#	Date	Mintage	Fine	VF	XF	Unc
120	1939	36.000	.15	.25	.50	1.50
	1940	10.865	.20	.40	.75	2.50

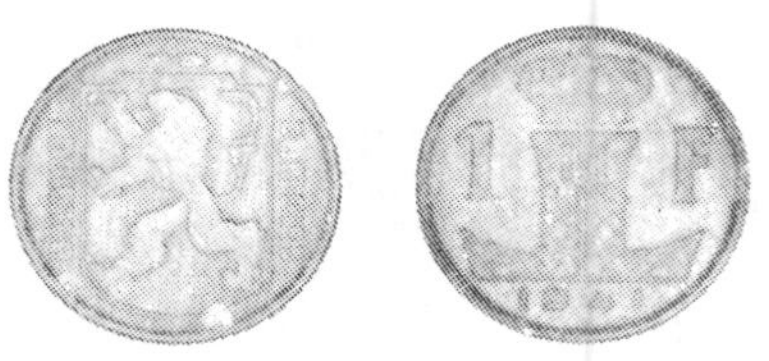

ZINC

German Occupation WW II

Obv. French leg: BELGIQUE-BELGIE.

KM#	Date	Mintage	Fine	VF	XF	Unc
127	1941	16.000	.20	.75	1.50	6.00
	1942	25.000	.20	.75	1.50	4.00
	1943	28.000	.20	.75	1.50	4.00
	1947	3.175	60.00	125.00	400.00	700.00

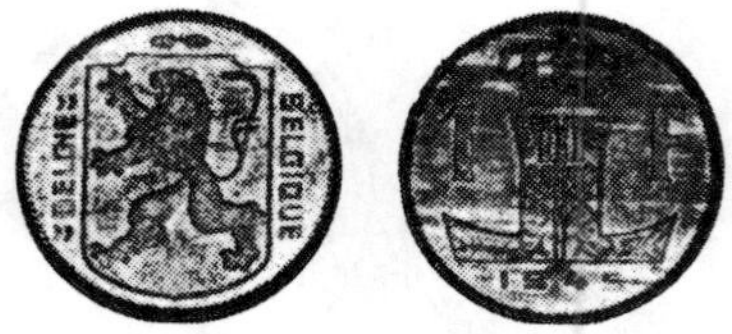

Obv. Dutch leg: BELGIE-BELGIQUE.

KM#	Date	Mintage	Fine	VF	XF	Unc
128	1942	42.000	.20	.75	1.50	4.00
	1943	28.000	.20	.75	1.50	4.00
	1944	24.190	.20	.75	1.50	4.00
	1945	15.930	.20	1.00	2.00	7.00
	1946	36.000	.20	.75	1.50	4.00
	1947	3.000	25.00	40.00	100.00	200.00

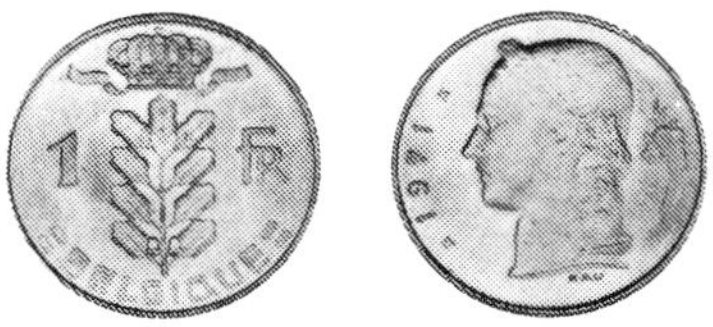

COPPER-NICKEL
Obv. French leg: BELGIQUE.

KM#	Date	Mintage	Fine	VF	XF	Unc
142.1	1950	13.630	—	—	.10	3.00
	1951	51.025	—	—	.10	2.00
	1952	53.205	—	—	.10	2.00
	1954	4.980	—	.10	.25	3.00
	1955	3.960	—	.10	.25	3.00
	1956	10.000	—	—	.10	1.00
	1958	31.750	—	—	.10	1.00
	1959	9.000	—	—	.10	1.00
	1960	10.000	—	—	.10	.50
	1961	5.030	—	—	.10	.50
	1962	12.250	—	—	.10	.50
	1963	18.700	—	—	.10	.50
	1964	10.110	—	—	.10	.50
	1965	10.185	—	—	.10	.50
	1966	16.430	—	—	.10	.50
	1967	32.945	—	—	.10	.30
	1968	8.000	—	—	.10	.30
	1969	21.950	—	—	.10	.30
	1970	35.500	—	—	.10	.30
	1971	10.000	—	—	.10	.30
	1972	35.000	—	—	.10	.30
	1973	42.500	—	—	.10	.30
	1974	30.000	—	—	.10	.30
	1975	80.000	—	—	.10	.30
	1976	18.000	—	—	.10	.30
	1977	68.500	—	—	.10	.30
	1978	47.500	—	—	.10	.30
	1979	25.000	—	—	.10	.30
	1980	66.500	—	—	.10	.30
	1981	2.000	.10	.20	.50	.75
	1988	17.500	—	—	.10	.30

Medal alignment.

KM#	Date	Mintage	Fine	VF	XF	Unc
142.2	1952	Inc. Ab.	—	3.00	9.00	20.00
	1956	Inc. Ab.	—	3.00	9.00	20.00
	1958	Inc. Ab.	—	3.00	9.00	20.00
	1959	Inc. Ab.	—	3.00	9.00	20.00
	1963	Inc. Ab.	—	3.00	9.00	20.00
	1965	Inc. Ab.	—	3.00	9.00	20.00
	1966	Inc. Ab.	—	3.00	9.00	25.00
	1969	Inc. Ab.	—	3.00	9.00	25.00
	1970	Inc. Ab.	—	3.00	9.00	25.00
	1974	Inc. Ab.	—	3.00	9.00	25.00
	1975	Inc. Ab.	—	3.00	9.00	25.00
	1977	Inc. Ab.	—	3.00	9.00	25.00
	1978	Inc. Ab.	—	3.00	9.00	25.00
	1979	Inc. Ab.	—	3.00	9.00	25.00
	1988	Inc. Ab.	—	3.00	9.00	25.00

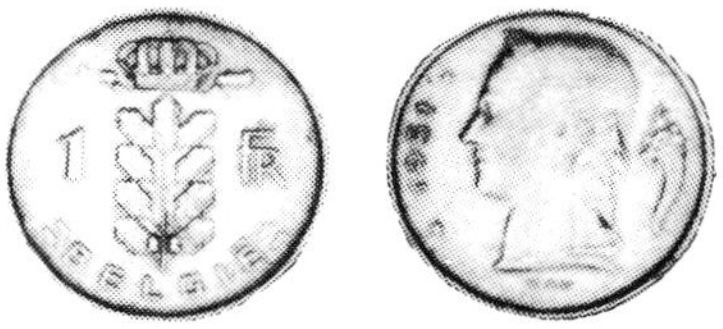

Obv. Dutch leg: BELGIE.

KM#	Date	Mintage	Fine	VF	XF	Unc
143.1	1950	10.000	—	—	.10	3.00
	1951	53.750	—	—	.10	2.00
	1952	49.145	—	—	.10	2.00
	1953	9.915	—	—	.10	2.00
	1954	4.940	—	.10	.25	3.00
	1955	3.960	—	.10	.25	3.00
	1956	10.040	—	—	.10	1.00
	1957	18.315	—	—	.10	1.00
	1958	17.365	—	—	.10	1.00
	1959	5.830	—	—	.10	1.00
	1960	5.555	—	—	.10	.50
	1961	9.350	—	—	.10	.50
	1962	10.720	—	—	.10	.50
	1963	23.460	—	—	.10	.50
	1964	7.430	—	—	.10	.50
	1965	11.190	—	—	.10	.50
	1966	20.990	—	—	.10	.50
	1967	27.470	—	—	.10	.50
	1968	8.170	—	—	.10	.30
	1969	21.730	—	—	.10	.30
	1970	35.730	—	—	.10	.30
	1971	10.000	—	—	.10	.30
	1972	35.000	—	—	.10	.30
	1973	42.500	—	—	.10	.30
	1974	30.000	—	—	.10	.30
	1975	80.000	—	—	.10	.30
	1976	18.000	—	—	.10	.30
	1977	68.500	—	—	.10	.30
	1978	47.500	—	—	.10	.30
	1979	50.000	—	—	.10	.30
	1980	66.500	—	—	.10	.30
	1981	2.000	—	—	.10	.50
	1988	17.500	—	—	.10	.30

Medal alignment.

KM#	Date	Mintage	Fine	VF	XF	Unc
143.2	1951	Inc. Ab.	—	3.00	9.00	20.00
	1952	Inc. Ab.	—	3.00	9.00	20.00
	1956	Inc. Ab.	—	3.00	9.00	20.00
143.2	1957	Inc. Ab.	—	3.00	9.00	20.00
	1958	Inc. Ab.	—	3.00	9.00	20.00
	1964	Inc. Ab.	—	3.00	9.00	20.00
	1970	Inc. Ab.	—	3.00	9.00	20.00
	1971	Inc. Ab.	—	3.00	9.00	20.00
	1973	Inc. Ab.	—	3.00	9.00	20.00
	1976	Inc. Ab.	—	3.00	9.00	20.00
	1977	Inc. Ab.	—	3.00	9.00	20.00
	1979	Inc. Ab.	—	3.00	9.00	20.00
	1981	Inc. Ab.	—	3.00	9.00	20.00

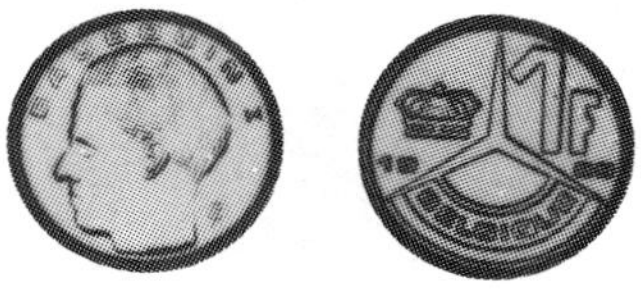

NICKEL-PLATED IRON
Rev. French legend: BELGIQUE.

KM#	Date	Mintage	Fine	VF	XF	Unc
170	1989	200.060	—	—	—	.35
	1990	200.060	—	—	—	.35
	1991	200.060	—	—	—	.35
	1992	.060	—	—	—	1.25
	1993	15.060	—	—	—	.35

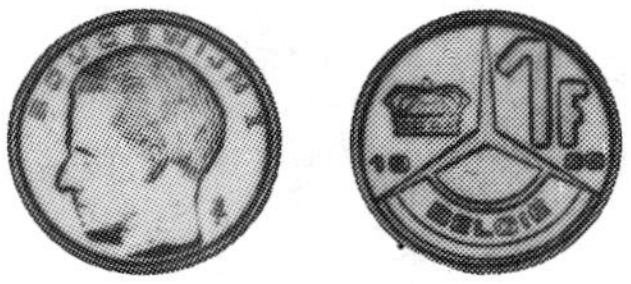

Rev. Dutch legend: BELGIE.

KM#	Date	Mintage	Fine	VF	XF	Unc
171	1989	200.060	—	—	—	.35
	1990	200.060	—	—	—	.35
	1991	200.060	—	—	—	.35
	1992	.060	—	—	—	1.25
	1993	15.060	—	—	—	.35

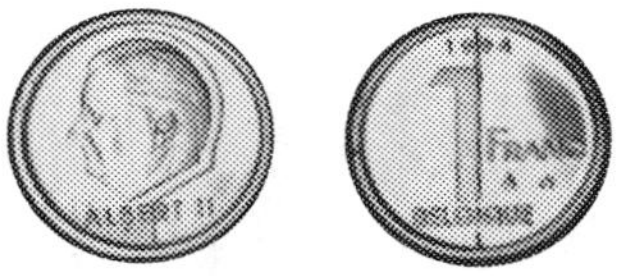

Albert II
Rev. French leg: BELGIQUE.

KM#	Date	Mintage	Fine	VF	XF	Unc
187	1994	75.060	—	—	—	.25
	1995	75.060	—	—	—	.25
	1996	75.060	—	—	—	.25
	1997	—	—	—	—	.25
	1998	—	—	—	—	.25

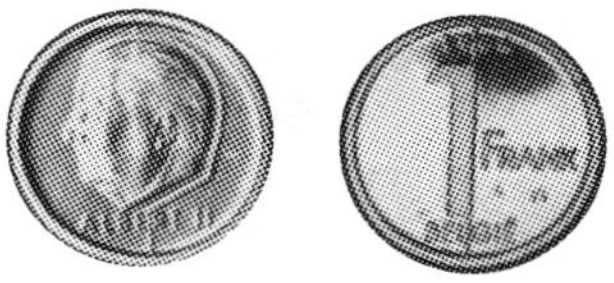

Rev. Dutch leg: BELGIE.

KM#	Date	Mintage	Fine	VF	XF	Unc
188	1994	75.060	—	—	—	.25
	1995	75.060	—	—	—	.25
	1996	75.060	—	—	—	.25
	1997	—	—	—	—	.25
	1998	—	—	—	—	.25

2 FRANCS/2 FRANK

10.0000 g, .835 SILVER, .2685 oz ASW
Obv. French leg: DES BELGES.

KM#	Date	Mintage	Fine	VF	XF	Unc
58.1	1904	.400	6.00	9.00	35.00	100.00
	1909	1.088	2.50	4.00	15.00	50.00

Obv: W/o period in signature.

KM#	Date	Mintage	Fine	VF	XF	Unc
58.2	1904	Inc. Ab.	9.00	12.00	50.00	125.00
	1909	Inc. Ab.	10.00	20.00	75.00	200.00

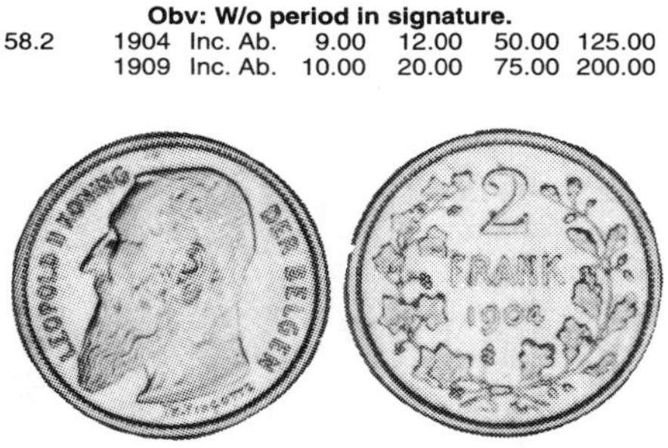

Obv. Dutch leg: DER BELGEN.

KM#	Date	Mintage	Fine	VF	XF	Unc
59.1	1904	.400	5.00	9.00	35.00	100.00
	1909	1.088	2.50	4.00	15.00	50.00

Obv: W/o period in signature.

KM#	Date	Mintage	Fine	VF	XF	Unc
59.2	1904	Inc. Ab.	12.50	45.00	90.00	210.00
	1909	Inc. Ab.	7.00	15.00	50.00	110.00

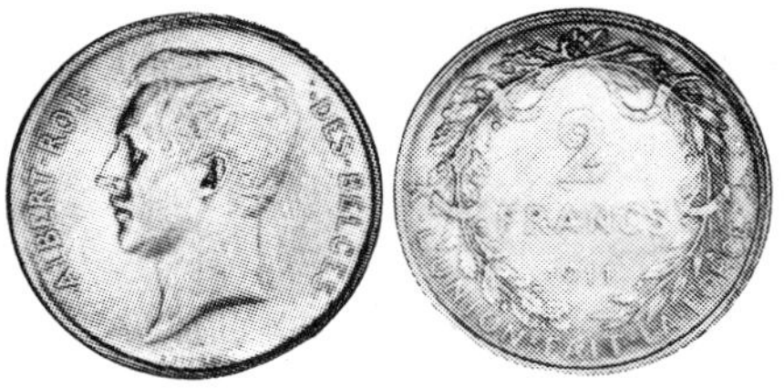

Obv. French leg: DES BELGES.

KM#	Date	Mintage	Fine	VF	XF	Unc
74	1910	.800	2.50	4.00	15.00	50.00
	1911	1.000	2.00	3.00	10.00	30.00
	1912	.375	3.00	5.00	20.00	55.00

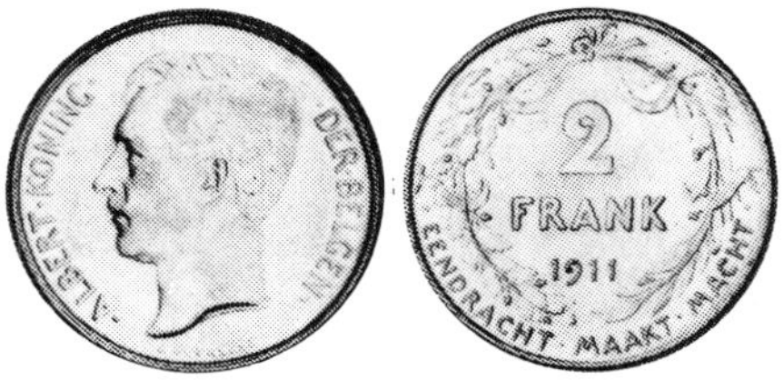

Obv. Dutch leg: DER BELGEN.

KM#	Date	Mintage	Fine	VF	XF	Unc
75	1911	1.775	2.00	3.00	10.00	30.00
	1912	.375	2.50	4.00	15.00	45.00

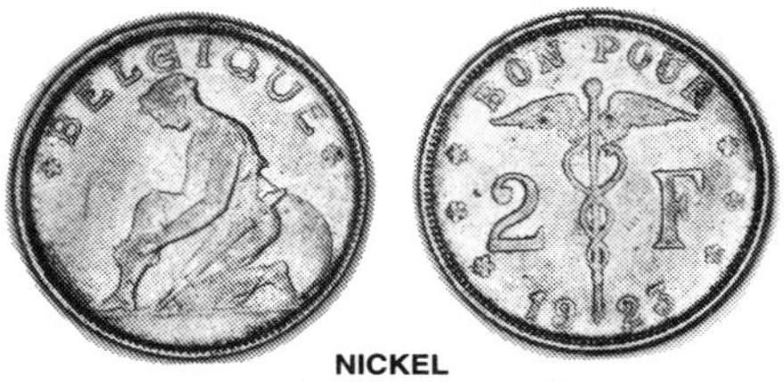

NICKEL
Obv. French leg: BELGIQUE.

KM#	Date	Mintage	Fine	VF	XF	Unc
91.1	1923	7.500	.50	1.50	8.00	15.00
	1930/20	1.250	12.00	20.00	140.00	250.00
	1930	Inc. Ab.	10.00	17.00	100.00	200.00

Medal alignment.

KM#	Date	Mintage	Fine	VF	XF	Unc
91.2	1923	Inc. Ab.	5.00	8.00	45.00	110.00

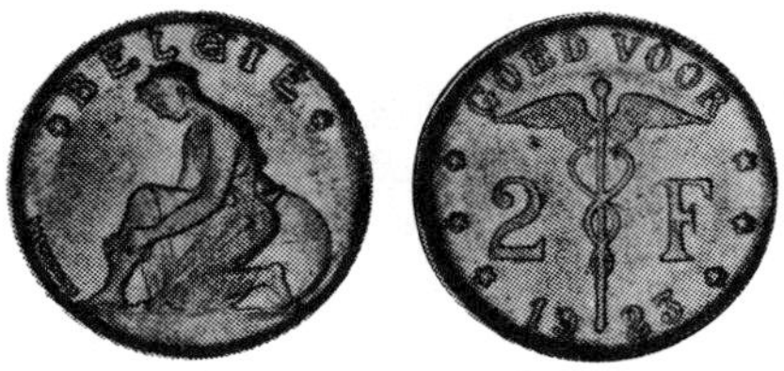

Obv. Dutch leg: BELGIE.

KM#	Date	Mintage	Fine	VF	XF	Unc
92	1923	6.500	.25	1.50	7.00	15.00
	1924	1.000	5.00	10.00	65.00	125.00
	1930/20	1.252	10.00	20.00	125.00	250.00
	1930	Inc. Ab.	8.00	15.00	100.00	200.00

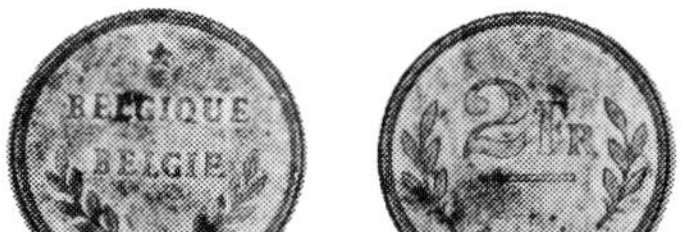

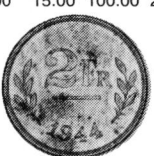

ZINC COATED STEEL
Allied Occupation Issue
Obv. French leg: BELGIQUE-BELGIE.

KM#	Date	Mintage	Fine	VF	XF	Unc
133	1944	25.000	.25	.50	1.50	3.50

NOTE: Made in U.S.A. on blanks for 1943 cents.

5 FRANCS/5 FRANK

Un or Een (1) Belga

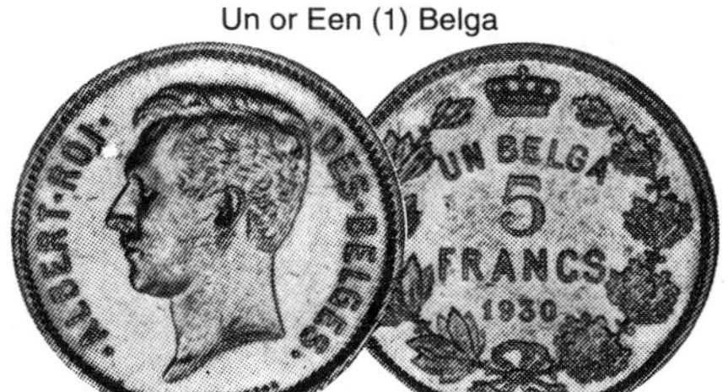

NICKEL
Obv. French leg: DES BELGES.
Rev. value: UN BELGA.

KM#	Date	Mintage	Fine	VF	XF	Unc
97.1	1930	1.600	1.50	6.00	12.00	20.00
	1931	9.032	1.00	4.00	10.00	15.00
	1932	3.600	1.50	7.00	14.00	25.00
	1933	1.387	6.00	15.00	35.00	50.00
	1934	1.000	30.00	75.00	160.00	250.00

NOTE: All dates exist in position A and B, values are the same.

Medal alignment.

KM#	Date	Mintage	Fine	VF	XF	Unc
97.2	1930	Inc. Ab.	17.50	50.00	150.00	300.00

NOTE: Edge varieties exist.

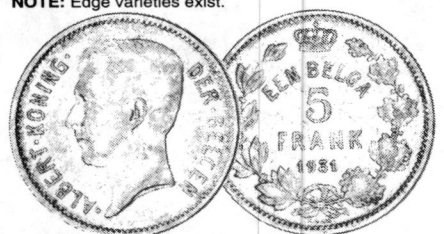

Obv. Dutch leg: DER BELGEN.
Rev. value: EEN BELGA.

98	1930	5.086	2.00	8.00	16.00	25.00
	1931	5.336	1.50	6.00	12.00	20.00
	1932	3.683	1.50	7.00	14.00	25.00
	1933	2.514	8.00	20.00	40.00	60.00

NOTE: All dates exist in position A and B, values are the same.

Rev. French leg: BELGIQUE.

108.1	1936	.650	6.00	20.00	50.00	85.00
	1937	1.848	6.00	17.50	40.00	70.00

NOTE: Both dates exist in position A and B, values are the same.

Medal alignment.

108.2	1936	Inc. Ab.	17.50	55.00	150.00	350.00

NOTE: Edge varieties exist.

Rev. Dutch leg: BELGIE.

109.1	1936	2.498	4.00	15.00	35.00	60.00
	1937					

NOTE: Both dates exist in position A and B, values are the same.

Medal alignment.

109.2	1936	Inc. Ab.	15.00	45.00	130.00	300.00

NOTE: Edge varieties exist.

Obv. French leg: BELGIQUE-BELGIE.
Milled edge, lettering w/crown.

116.1	1938 Pos. A					
		11.419	.20	.75	3.00	6.00
	1938 Pos. B					
		Inc. Ab.	.30	1.00	4.00	7.00

Milled edge, lettering w/star.

116.2	1939 Pos. A					
		Inc. Ab.	200.00	500.00	900.00	1750.
	1939 Pos. B					
		Inc. Ab.	200.00	500.00	900.00	1750.

Milled edge, w/o lettering (error).

116.3	1938	Inc. Ab.	40.00	70.00	135.00	300.00

Obv. Dutch leg: BELGIE-BELGIQUE.

Milled edge, lettering w/crown.

KM#	Date	Mintage	Fine	VF	XF	Unc
117.1	1938 Pos. A					
		3.200	7.00	15.00	50.00	125.00
	1938 Pos. B					
		Inc. Ab.	7.00	15.00	50.00	125.00
	1939 Pos. A					
		8.219	7.50	20.00	80.00	175.00
	1939 Pos. B					
		Inc. Ab.	7.50	20.00	80.00	175.00

Milled edge, lettering w/star.

117.2	1938 Pos. A					
		Inc. Ab.	6.00	20.00	70.00	160.00
	1938 Pos. B					
		Inc. Ab.	6.00	20.00	70.00	160.00
	1939 Pos. A					
		Inc. Ab.	.15	.50	1.25	4.00
	1939 Pos. B					
		Inc. Ab.	.15	.50	1.25	4.00

Milled edge, w/o lettering (error).

117.3	1939	Inc. Ab.	30.00	60.00	175.00	350.00

ZINC
German Occupation WW II
Obv. French leg: DES BELGES.

129.1	1941	15.200	.35	.75	2.50	10.00
	1943	16.236	.35	.75	2.00	10.00
	1944	1.868	.75	3.00	12.00	35.00
	1945	3.200	.50	1.00	6.00	15.00
	1946	4.452	1.00	4.50	15.00	40.00
	1947	3.100	20.00	40.00	110.00	300.00

Medal alignment.

129.2	1943	Inc. Ab.	5.00	15.00	50.00	130.00

Obv. Dutch leg: DER BELGEN.

130	1941	27.544	.30	.50	2.50	10.00
	1945	3.200	15.00	30.00	75.00	200.00
	1946	4.000	—	—	Rare	—
	1947	.036	75.00	150.00	375.00	750.00

COPPER-NICKEL
Obv. French leg: BELGIQUE.

134.1	1948	5.304	—	—	.20	4.00
	1949	38.752	—	—	.20	2.00
	1950	23.948	—	—	.20	2.00
	1958	9.088	—	—	.20	1.00
	1961	6.000	—	—	.20	.50
	1962	6.576	—	—	.20	.50
	1963	11.144	—	—	.20	.35
	1964	3.520	—	—	.20	.40
	1965	11.988	—	—	.20	.35
	1966	6.772	—	—	.20	.40
	1967	13.268	—	—	.20	.35
	1968	5.192	—	—	.20	.40
	1969	22.235	—	—	.20	.35
	1969 w/o engravers name					
		Inc. Ab.	—	2.50	9.00	20.00
	1970	2.000	—	—	.20	.45
	1971	15.000	—	—	.20	.35
	1972	17.500	—	—	.20	.35
	1973	10.000	—	—	.20	.35
	1974	25.000	—	—	.20	.35
	1975	34.000	—	—	.20	.35
	1976	7.500	—	—	.20	.40
	1977	22.500	—	—	.20	.35
	1978	27.500	—	—	.20	.35
	1979	5.000	—	—	.20	.40
	1980	11.000	—	—	.20	.35
	1981	2.000	—	—	.20	.40

Medal alignment.

134.2	1949	Inc. Ab.	—	4.00	10.00	30.00
	1950	Inc. Ab.	—	4.00	10.00	30.00
	1958	Inc. Ab.	—	4.00	10.00	30.00
	1962	Inc. Ab.	—	4.00	10.00	30.00
	1963	Inc. Ab.	—	4.00	10.00	30.00

KM#	Date	Mintage	Fine	VF	XF	Unc
134.2	1965	Inc. Ab.	—	4.00	10.00	30.00
	1966	Inc. Ab.	—	4.00	10.00	30.00
	1969	Inc. Ab.	—	4.00	10.00	30.00
	1975	Inc. Ab.	—	4.00	10.00	30.00
	1977	Inc. Ab.	—	4.00	10.00	30.00

Obv. Dutch leg: BELGIE.

135.1	1948	4.800	—	—	.20	4.00
	1949	31.500	—	—	.20	2.00
	1950	34.728	—	—	.20	2.00
	1958	2.672	—	—	.20	4.00
	1960	5.896	—	—	.20	.75
	1961	4.120	—	—	.20	.50
	1962	7.624	—	—	.20	.50
	1963	6.136	—	—	.20	.40
	1964	8.128	—	—	.20	.40
	1965	9.956	—	—	.20	.40
	1966	7.136	—	—	.20	.40
	1967	16.132	—	—	.20	.35
	1968	3.200	—	—	.20	.40
	1969	21.500	—	—	.20	.35
	1970	2.000	—	—	.20	.45
	1971	15.000	—	—	.20	.35
	1972	17.500	—	—	.20	.35
	1972 w/o engravers name					
		Inc. Ab.	—	2.50	9.00	20.00
	1973	10.000	—	—	.20	.35
	1974	25.000	—	—	.20	.35
	1975	34.000	—	—	.20	.35
	1976	7.500	—	—	.20	.40
	1977	22.500	—	—	.20	.35
	1978	27.500	—	—	.20	.35
	1979	10.000	—	—	.20	.35
	1980	11.000	—	—	.20	.35
	1981	2.000	—	—	.20	.40

Medal alignment.

135.2	1950	Inc. Ab.	—	4.00	10.00	30.00
	1962	Inc. Ab.	—	4.00	10.00	30.00
	1963	Inc. Ab.	—	4.00	10.00	30.00
	1965	Inc. Ab.	—	4.00	10.00	30.00
	1966	Inc. Ab.	—	4.00	10.00	30.00
	1969	Inc. Ab.	—	4.00	10.00	30.00
	1974	Inc. Ab.	—	4.00	10.00	30.00

BRASS or ALUMINUM-BRONZE
Rev. French leg: BELGIQUE.

163	1986	208.400	—	—	.35	.65
	1987	22.500	—	—	.35	.65
	1988	26.500	—	—	.35	.65
	1989	.060	—	—	—	2.00
	1990	.060	—	—	—	2.00
	1991	.060	—	—	—	2.00
	1992	5.060	—	—	.35	.65
	1993	15.060	—	—	.35	.65

Rev. Dutch leg: BELGIE.

164	1986	208.400	—	—	.35	.65
	1987	22.500	—	—	.35	.65
	1988	26.500	—	—	.35	.65
	1989	.060	—	—	—	2.00
	1990	.060	—	—	—	2.00
	1991	.060	—	—	—	2.00
	1992	5.060	—	—	.35	.65
	1993	15.060	—	—	.35	.65

ALUMINUM-BRONZE
Albert II
Rev. French leg: BELGIQUE.

KM#	Date	Mintage	Fine	VF	XF	Unc
189	1994	30.060	—	—	—	.50
	1995	.060	—	—	—	2.00
	1996	.060	—	—	—	2.00
	1997	—	—	—	—	2.00
	1998	—	—	—	—	2.00

Rev. Dutch leg: BELGIE.

KM#	Date	Mintage	Fine	VF	XF	Unc
190	1994	30.060	—	—	—	.50
	1995	.060	—	—	—	2.00
	1996	2.430	—	—	—	2.00
	1997	—	—	—	—	2.00
	1998	—	—	—	—	2.00

10 FRANCS/10 FRANK

Deux or Twee (2) Belgas.

NICKEL
Independence Centennial
Rev. French leg: BELGIQUE.

KM#	Date	Mintage	Fine	VF	XF	Unc
99	1930	2.699	25.00	70.00	120.00	150.00

NOTE: Exists in position A and B, values are the same.

Rev. Dutch leg: BELGIE.

KM#	Date	Mintage	Fine	VF	XF	Unc
100	1930	3.000	30.00	75.00	130.00	170.00

NOTE: Exists in position A and B, values are the same.

Rev. French leg: BELGIQUE.

KM#	Date	Mintage	Fine	VF	XF	Unc
155.1	1969	22.235	—	—	.40	.70
	1970	9.500	—	—	.40	.70
	1971	15.000	—	—	.40	.70
	1972	10.000	—	—	.40	.70
	1973	10.000	—	—	.40	.70
	1974	5.000	—	—	.40	.70
	1975	5.000	—	—	.40	.70
	1976	7.500	—	—	.40	.70
	1977	7.000	—	—	.40	.70
	1978	2.500	—	—	.60	1.50
	1979	5.000	—	—	.60	1.50

Medal alignment.

KM#	Date	Mintage	Fine	VF	XF	Unc
155.2	1969	Inc. Ab.	—	6.00	12.00	35.00
	1974	Inc. Ab.	—	6.00	12.00	35.00
	1977	Inc. Ab.	—	6.00	12.00	35.00
	1978	Inc. Ab.	—	6.00	12.00	30.00

Rev. Dutch leg: BELGIE.

KM#	Date	Mintage	Fine	VF	XF	Unc
156.1	1969	21.500	—	—	.40	.70
	1970	10.000	—	—	.40	.70
	1971	15.000	—	—	.40	.70
156.1	1972	10.000	—	—	.40	.70
	1973	10.000	—	—	.40	.70
	1974	5.000	—	—	.40	.70
	1975	5.000	—	—	.40	.70
	1976	7.500	—	—	.40	.70
	1977	7.000	—	—	.40	.70
	1978	2.500	—	—	.60	1.50
	1979	10.000	—	—	.60	1.50

Medal alignment.

KM#	Date	Mintage	Fine	VF	XF	Unc
156.2	1971	Inc. Ab.	—	6.00	12.00	35.00
	1976	Inc. Ab.	—	6.00	12.00	35.00

20 FRANCS/20 FRANK

6.4516 g, .900 GOLD, .1867 oz AGW
Obv. French leg: DES BELGES.

KM#	Date	Mintage	Fine	VF	XF	Unc
78	1914 Pos. A	.125	—	BV	115.00	135.00
	1914 Pos B	Inc. Ab.	125.00	250.00	400.00	550.00

Obv. Dutch leg: DER BELGEN.

KM#	Date	Mintage	Fine	VF	XF	Unc
79	1914 Pos. A	.125	—	BV	115.00	135.00
	1914 Pos. B	Inc. Ab.	BV	110.00	135.00	150.00

Vier or Quatre (4) Belgas.

NICKEL
Obv. French leg: DES BELGES

KM#	Date	Mintage	Fine	VF	XF	Unc
101.1	1931	3.957	30.00	50.00	80.00	140.00
	1932	5.472	25.00	45.00	75.00	130.00
	1934 (restrike)	—	—	—	—	

NOTE: All dates exist in position A and B, values are the same.

Medal alignment.

KM#	Date	Mintage	Fine	VF	XF	Unc
101.2	1932	Inc. Ab.	65.00	175.00	400.00	600.00

NOTE: Edge varieties exist.

Obv. Dutch leg: DER BELGEN.

KM#	Date	Mintage	Fine	VF	XF	Unc
102	1931	2.600	30.00	50.00	85.00	140.00
	1932	6.950	25.00	45.00	75.00	130.00
	1934 (restrike)	—	—	—	—	

NOTE: All dates exist in position A and B, values are the same.

11.0000 g, .680 SILVER, .2405 oz ASW

Obv. French leg: DES BELGES.

KM#	Date	Mintage	Fine	VF	XF	Unc
103.1	1933 Pos. A	.200	22.50	40.00	90.00	175.00
	1933 Pos. B	Inc. Ab.	25.00	45.00	100.00	200.00
	1934 Pos. A	12.300	BV	2.00	4.00	8.00
	1934 Pos. B	Inc. Ab.	1.50	2.50	4.50	9.00

Medal alignment.

KM#	Date	Mintage	Fine	VF	XF	Unc
103.2	1934	Inc. Ab.	35.00	80.00	190.00	400.00

Obv. Dutch leg: DER BELGEN.

KM#	Date	Mintage	Fine	VF	XF	Unc
104.1	1933 Pos. A	.200	14.00	30.00	60.00	110.00
	1933 Pos. B	Inc. Ab.	16.00	32.50	65.00	125.00
	1934 Pos. A	12.300	BV	2.00	4.00	8.00
	1934 Pos. B	Inc. Ab.	1.50	2.50	4.50	9.00

Medal alignment.

KM#	Date	Mintage	Fine	VF	XF	Unc
104.2	1934	Inc. Ab.	30.00	70.00	170.00	350.00

KM#	Date	Mintage	Fine	VF	XF	Unc
105	1934	1.250	2.00	4.00	8.00	15.00
	1935	10.760	BV	2.50	5.00	7.00

NOTE: Both dates exist in position A and B, values are the same. Coins dated 1934 exist w/and w/o umlauts above E in BELGIE.

8.0000 g, .835 SILVER, .2148 oz ASW
Obv. French leg: BELGIQUE.

KM#	Date	Mintage	Fine	VF	XF	Unc
140.1	1949	4.600	BV	1.50	3.50	5.00
	1950	12.957	BV	1.50	3.00	5.00
	1953	3.953	BV	2.00	4.00	7.00
	1954	4.835	12.00	20.00	60.00	100.00
	1955	1.730	150.00	250.00	650.00	900.00

Medal alignment.

KM#	Date	Mintage	Fine	VF	XF	Unc
140.2	1949	Inc. Ab.	15.00	35.00	75.00	125.00
	1950	Inc. Ab.	15.00	35.00	75.00	125.00

Obv. Dutch leg: BELGIE.

KM#	Date	Mintage	Fine	VF	XF	Unc
141.1	1949	5.545	BV	1.50	3.50	5.00
	1950	—	150.00	400.00	600.00	1000.
	1951	7.885	BV	1.50	3.00	5.00
	1953	6.625	BV	1.50	3.00	7.00
	1954	5.323	8.00	15.00	50.00	80.00
	1955	3.760	8.00	15.00	50.00	125.00 200.00

Medal alignment.

KM#	Date	Mintage	Fine	VF	XF	Unc
141.2	1949	Inc. Ab.	20.00	35.00	85.00	135.00
	1951	Inc. Ab.	15.00	40.00	95.00	150.00

BRONZE
Rev. French leg: BELGIQUE.

KM#	Date	Mintage	Fine	VF	XF	Unc
159	1980	60.000	—	—	.70	1.00
	1981	60.000	—	—	.70	1.00
	1982	54.000	—	—	.70	1.00
	1989	.060	—	—	—	3.50
	1990	.060	—	—	—	3.50
	1991	.060	—	—	—	3.50
	1992	2.610	—	—	.70	1.00
	1993	7.540	—	—	.70	1.00

Rev. Dutch leg: BELGIE.

	Date	Mintage	Fine	VF	XF	Unc
160	1980	60.000	—	—	.70	1.00
	1981	60.000	—	—	.70	1.00
	1982	54.000	—	—	.70	1.00
	1989	.060	—	—	—	3.50
	1990	.060	—	—	—	3.50
	1991	.060	—	—	—	3.50
	1992	2.610	—	—	.70	1.00
	1993	7.540	—	—	.70	1.00

NICKEL-BRONZE
Albert II
Rev. French leg: BELGIQUE.

	Date	Mintage	Fine	VF	XF	Unc
191	1994	12.560	—	—	.70	1.00
	1995	.060	—	—	—	3.75
	1996	.060	—	—	—	3.75
	1997	—	—	—	—	3.75
	1998	—	—	—	—	3.75

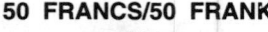

Rev. Dutch leg: BELGIE.

	Date	Mintage	Fine	VF	XF	Unc
192	1994	12.560	—	—	.70	1.00
	1995	.060	—	—	—	3.75
	1996	11.352	—	—	—	3.75
	1997	—	—	—	—	3.75
	1998	—	—	—	—	3.75

50 FRANCS/50 FRANK

22.0000 g, .680 SILVER, .4810 oz ASW
Brussels Exposition And Railway Centennial
Obv. leg: DE BELGIQUE.
Rev. French leg: DE FER BELGES.

KM#	Date	Mintage	Fine	VF	XF	Unc
106.1	1935	.140	40.00	80.00	140.00	210.00

NOTE: Exists in position A and B, values are the same.

Medal alignment.

| 106.2 | 1935 | Inc. Ab. | 250.00 | 500.00 | 900.00 | 1800. |

NOTE: Exists in position A and B, values are the same.

Obv. leg: BELGIE.
Rev. Dutch leg: DER BELGISCHE.

| 107.1 | 1935 | .140 | 50.00 | 100.00 | 175.00 | 250.00 |

NOTE: Exists in position A and B, values are the same.

Medal alignment.

| 107.2 | 1935 | Inc. Ab. | 400.00 | 800.00 | 1500. | 2500. |

NOTE: Exists in position A and B, values are the same.

20.0000 g, .835 SILVER, .5369 oz ASW
Rev. French leg: BELGIQUE: BELGIE.

	Date	Mintage	Fine	VF	XF	Unc
121.1	1939	1.000	BV	8.00	12.00	18.00
	1940	.631	BV	10.00	18.00	27.50

NOTE: Both dates exist in position A and B, values are the same.

Rev: W/o cross on crown.

| 121.2 | 1939 | Inc. Ab. | 7.50 | 15.00 | 22.00 | 35.00 |
| | 1940 | Inc. Ab. | 10.00 | 20.00 | 30.00 | 50.00 |

NOTE: Both dates exist in position A and B, values are the same.

Rev. Dutch leg: BELGIE: BELGIQUE.

| 122.1 | 1939 | 1.000 | BV | 8.00 | 12.00 | 18.00 |
| | 1940 | .631 | BV | 10.00 | 20.00 | 30.00 |

NOTE: Both dates exist in position A and B, values are the same.

Rev: W/o cross on crown.

| 122.2 | 1939 | Inc. Ab. | 6.00 | 15.00 | 20.00 | 35.00 |
| | 1940 | Inc. Ab. | 20.00 | 40.00 | 60.00 | 80.00 |

NOTE: Both dates exist in position A and B, values are the same.

Rev: Triangle in 3rd arms from left, cross on crown.

KM#	Date	Mintage	Fine	VF	XF	Unc
122.3	1940	Inc. Ab.	20.00	35.00	50.00	75.00

NOTE: Exists in position A and B, values are the same.

Rev: W/o cross on crown.

| 122.4 | 1940 | Inc. Ab. | 30.00 | 60.00 | 100.00 | 150.00 |

NOTE: Exists in position A and B, values are the same.

12.5000 g, .835 SILVER, .3356 oz ASW
Obv. French leg: BELGIQUE.

	Date	Mintage	Fine	VF	XF	Unc
136.1	1948	2.000	BV	2.00	3.00	6.00
	1949	4.354	BV	2.00	3.00	6.00
	1950	—	200.00	400.00	800.00	1750.
	1951	2.904	BV	2.00	3.00	7.00
	1954	3.232	BV	6.00	12.00	25.00

Medal alignment.

| 136.2 | 1949 | Inc. Ab. | 10.00 | 30.00 | 90.00 | 175.00 |

Obv. Dutch leg: BELGIE.

	Date	Mintage	Fine	VF	XF	Unc
137	1948	3.000	BV	2.00	3.00	6.00
	1950	4.110	BV	2.00	3.00	6.00
	1951	1.698	BV	2.00	3.00	7.00
	1954	2.978	BV	2.00	3.00	7.00

Brussels World Fair
Obv. French leg: DES BELGES.

	Date	Mintage	Fine	VF	XF	Unc
150.1	1958	.476	BV	4.00	7.50	10.00

Medal alignment.

| 150.2 | 1958 | Inc. Ab. | 18.00 | 45.00 | 100.00 | 180.00 |

Obv. Dutch leg: DER BELGEN.

| 151.1 | 1958 | .382 | BV | 4.00 | 7.50 | 10.00 |

Medal alignment.

| 151.2 | 1958 | Inc. Ab. | 15.00 | 35.00 | 75.00 | 125.00 |

King Baudouin Marriage

	Date	Mintage	Fine	VF	XF	Unc
152.1	1960	.500	BV	4.00	6.00	9.00

Medal alignment.

| 152.2 | 1960 | Inc. Ab. | 12.50 | 30.00 | 60.00 | 120.00 |

NICKEL
Rev. French leg: BELGIQUE.

KM#	Date	Mintage	Fine	VF	XF	Unc
168	1987	30.000	—	—	2.00	4.00
	1988	3.500	—	—	2.00	4.00
	1989	15.060	—	—	2.00	4.00
	1990	15.060	—	—	2.00	4.00
	1991	3.500	—	—	2.00	4.00
	1992	15.060	—	—	2.00	4.00
	1993	15.060	—	—	2.00	4.00

Rev. Dutch leg: BELGIE.

169	1987	30.000	—	—	2.00	4.00
	1988	3.500	—	—	2.00	4.00
	1989	15.060	—	—	2.00	4.00
	1990	15.060	—	—	2.00	4.00
	1991	3.500	—	—	2.00	4.00
	1992	15.060	—	—	2.00	4.00
	1993	15.060	—	—	2.00	4.00

Albert II
Rev. French leg: BELGIQUE.

193	1994	5.000	—	—	—	3.00
	1995	.060	—	—	—	4.50
	1996	.060	—	—	—	4.50
	1997	—	—	—	—	4.50
	1998	—	—	—	—	4.50

Rev. Dutch leg: BELGIE.

194	1994	5.000	—	—	—	4.50
	1995	.060	—	—	—	4.50
	1996	.060	—	—	—	4.50
	1997	—	—	—	—	4.50
	1998	—	—	—	—	4.50

100 FRANCS/100 FRANK

18.0000 g, .835 SILVER, .4832 oz ASW
Obv. French leg: BELGIQUE.

138.1	1948	1.000	BV	2.75	4.00	7.00
	1949	.106	12.50	25.00	40.00	60.00
	1950	2.807	BV	2.75	4.00	7.00
	1954	2.517	BV	2.75	4.00	7.00

Medal alignment.

KM#	Date	Mintage	Fine	VF	XF	Unc
138.2	1948	Inc. Ab.	10.00	40.00	90.00	220.00
	1950	Inc. Ab.	10.00	40.00	90.00	200.00

Obv. Dutch leg: BELGIE.

139.1	1948	1.000	BV	2.75	4.00	7.00
	1949	2.271	BV	2.75	4.00	7.00
	1950	—	300.00	500.00	850.00	1200.
	1951	4.691	BV	2.75	4.00	7.00

Medal alignment.

139.2	1948	Inc. Ab.	10.00	40.00	90.00	200.00
	1949	Inc. Ab.	7.50	30.00	75.00	160.00
	1951	Inc. Ab.	10.00	40.00	90.00	200.00

BELIZE (British Honduras)

Belize, formerly British Honduras, but now an independent member of the British Commonwealth, is situated in Central America south of Mexico and east and north of Guatemala, with an area of 8,867 sq. mi. (22,960 sq. km.) and a population of 214,061. Capital: Belmopan. Tourism now augments Belize's economy, in addition to sugar, citrus fruits, chicle and hardwoods which are exported.

The area, site of the ancient Mayan civilization, was sighted by Columbus in 1502, and settled by ship-wrecked English seamen in 1638. British buccaneers settled the former capital of Belize in the 17th century. Britain claimed administrative right over the area after the emancipation of Central America from Spain. In 1825, Imperial coins were introduced into the colony and were rated against the Spanish dollar and Honduran currency. It was declared a colony subordinate to Jamaica in 1862 and was established as the separate Crown Colony of British Honduras in 1884. In May, 1885 an order in Council authorized coins for the colony, with the first shipment arriving in July. While the Guatemalan peso was originally the standard of value, in 1894 the colony changed to the gold standard, based on the U.S. gold dollar. The anti-British Peoples United Party, which attained power in 1954, won a constitution, effective in 1964 which established self-government under a British appointed governor. British Honduras became Belize on June 1, 1973, following the passage of a surprise bill by the Peoples United Party, but the constitutional relationship with Britain remained unchanged.

In Dec. 1975, the U.N. General Assembly adopted a resolution supporting the right of the people of Belize to self-determination, and asking Britain and Guatemala to renew their negotiations on the future of Belize. Independence was obtained on Sept. 21, 1981. Elizabeth II is Head of State, as Queen of Belize.

RULERS

British, until 1981

MINT MARKS

H - Birmingham Mint
No mm - Royal Mint

MONETARY SYSTEM

100 Cents = 1 Dollar

BRITISH HONDURAS
CENT

BRONZE

KM#	Date	Mintage	Fine	VF	XF	Unc
11	1904	.050	6.00	15.00	35.00	70.00
	1904	' —	—	—	Proof	200.00
	1904	—	—	Matte Proof		1550.
	1906	.050	12.00	27.50	65.00	225.00
	1906	—	—	Matte Proof		1050.
	1909	.025	35.00	80.00	150.00	300.00

15	1911	.050	60.00	100.00	180.00	400.00
	1912H	.050	85.00	160.00	225.00	500.00
	1913	.025	90.00	175.00	250.00	600.00

KM#	Date	Mintage	Fine	VF	XF	Unc
19	1914	.175	3.00	7.50	25.00	120.00
	1916H	.125	3.50	8.50	27.50	125.00
	1918	.040	7.00	15.00	40.00	95.00
	1919	.050	7.00	15.00	40.00	150.00
	1924	.050	7.00	15.00	40.00	125.00
	1924	—	—	—	Proof	250.00
	1926	.050	5.00	12.00	35.00	125.00
	1926	—	—	—	Proof	225.00
	1936	.040	2.00	5.00	20.00	65.00
	1936	50 pcs.	—	—	Proof	170.00

21	1937	.080	.75	4.00	12.00	75.00
	1937	—	—	—	Proof	170.00
	1939	.050	2.00	7.00	20.00	150.00
	1939	—	—	—	Proof	100.00
	1942	.050	2.00	7.00	20.00	150.00
	1942	—	—	—	Proof	125.00
	1943	.100	1.00	5.00	15.00	125.00
	1943	—	—	—	Proof	150.00
	1944	.100	2.00	7.00	20.00	150.00
	1944	—	—	—	Proof	200.00
	1945	.130	.75	2.00	7.50	50.00
	1945	—	—	—	Proof	120.00
	1947	.100	.75	2.50	10.00	70.00
	1947	—	—	—	Proof	150.00

Obv. leg: W/o EMPEROR OF INDIA.

24	1949	.100	.60	1.50	4.00	15.00
	1949	—	—	—	Proof	135.00
	1950	.100	.40	1.00	2.50	5.00
	1950	—	—	—	Proof	135.00
	1951	.100	.60	1.50	4.00	15.00
	1951	—	—	—	Proof	135.00

27	1954	.200	.50	.75	1.00	5.00
	1954	—	—	—	Proof	100.00

30	1956	.200	.10	.25	.50	3.50
	1956	—	—	—	Proof	80.00
	1958	.400	.50	1.00	5.00	30.00
	1958	—	—	—	Proof	80.00
	1959	.200	1.00	2.50	10.00	100.00
	1959	—	—	—	Proof	80.00
	1961	.800	—	.15	.25	.50
	1961	—	—	—	Proof	80.00
	1964	.300	—	.10	.30	.90
	1965	.400	—	—	.10	.50
	1966	.100	—	—	.10	.50
	1967	.400	—	—	.10	.50
	1968	.200	—	—	.10	.50
	1969	.520	—	—	.10	.40
	1970	.120	—	—	.10	.40
	1971	.800	—	—	.10	.40
	1972	.800	—	—	.10	.40
	1973	.400	—	—	.10	.40

5 CENTS

COPPER-NICKEL

KM#	Date	Mintage	Fine	VF	XF	Unc
14	1907	.010	25.00	50.00	100.00	250.00
	1909	.010	25.00	50.00	100.00	250.00

16	1911	.010	20.00	40.00	75.00	200.00
	1912H	.020	10.00	25.00	55.00	175.00
	1912H	—	—	—	Proof	550.00
	1916H	.020	10.00	25.00	55.00	175.00
	1918	.020	10.00	25.00	55.00	175.00
	1919	.020	8.00	20.00	50.00	160.00
	1936	.060	2.50	5.00	20.00	75.00
	1936	50 pcs.	—	—	Proof	450.00

22	1939	.020	3.00	6.00	25.00	75.00
	1939	—	—	—	Proof	275.00

NICKEL-BRASS

22a	1942	.030	5.00	15.00	65.00	200.00
	1942	—	—	—	Proof	300.00
	1943	.040	2.00	12.00	60.00	190.00
	1944	.050	1.50	10.00	50.00	175.00
	1944	—	—	—	Proof	275.00
	1945	.065	1.00	5.00	15.00	75.00
	1945	—	—	—	Proof	150.00
	1947	.040	1.50	5.00	15.00	85.00
	1947	—	—	—	Proof	185.00

Obv. leg: W/o EMPEROR OF INDIA.

25	1949	.040	1.50	3.00	10.00	50.00
	1949	—	—	—	Proof	150.00
	1950	.225	.40	1.00	4.00	30.00
	1950	—	—	—	Proof	200.00
	1952	.100	.50	2.00	6.00	35.00
	1952	—	—	—	Proof	250.00

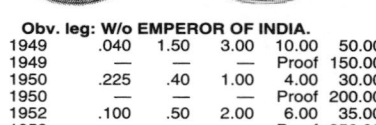

31	1956	.100	.20	.50	3.00	75.00
	1956	—	—	—	Proof	125.00
	1957	.100	.30	.75	1.50	10.00
	1957	—	—	—	Proof	175.00
	1958	.200	.30	1.00	7.50	90.00
	1958	—	—	—	Proof	125.00
	1959	.100	.40	2.00	8.00	80.00
	1959	—	—	—	Proof	185.00
	1961	.100	.30	.75	2.50	35.00
	1961	—	—	—	Proof	120.00
	1962	.200	.15	.35	.65	2.00
	1962	—	—	—	Proof	115.00
	1963	.100	.10	.20	.50	1.50
	1963	—	—	—	Proof	175.00
	1964	.100	.10	.15	.35	1.00
	1965	.150	—	.10	.25	.75
	1966	.150	—	.10	.20	.60
	1968	.200	—	.10	.15	.50
	1969	.540	—	.10	.15	.50
	1970	.240	—	.10	.15	.50
	1971	.450	—	.10	.15	.50
	1972	.200	—	.10	.15	.50
	1973	.210	—	.10	.15	.75

10 CENTS

2.3240 g, .925 SILVER, .0691 oz ASW

KM#	Date	Mintage	Fine	VF	XF	Unc
20	1918	.010	15.00	25.00	100.00	350.00
	1919	.010	15.00	25.00	100.00	350.00
	1936	.030	6.00	12.00	25.00	100.00
	1936	50 pcs.	—	—	Proof	300.00

23	1939	.020	3.00	7.00	20.00	60.00
	1939	—	—	—	Proof	300.00
	1942	.010	4.00	12.00	45.00	200.00
	1943	.020	3.00	6.00	30.00	250.00
	1944	.030	2.50	5.00	35.00	150.00
	1944	—	—	—	Proof	250.00
	1946	.010	5.00	12.00	45.00	200.00
	1946	—	—	—	Proof	450.00

COPPER-NICKEL

32	1956	.100	.40	1.00	2.00	7.50
	1956	—	—	—	Proof	200.00
	1959	.100	.60	1.50	2.00	37.50
	1959	—	—	—	Proof	135.00
	1961	.050	.30	.75	1.25	3.00
	1961	—	—	—	Proof	135.00
	1963	.050	.20	.50	.75	2.00
	1963	—	—	—	Proof	135.00
	1964	.060	.15	.25	.50	1.00
	1965/6	.200	5.00	10.00	20.00	40.00
	1965	Inc. Ab.	—	—	.10	.15	.50
	1970	—	—	.10	.15	.75

25 CENTS

5.8100 g, .925 SILVER, .1728 oz ASW

9	1901	.020	20.00	35.00	125.00	400.00
	1901	30 pcs.	—	—	Proof	600.00

NOTE: Earlier dates (1894-1897) exist for this type.

12	1906	.030	15.00	30.00	110.00	375.00
	1907	.060	10.00	25.00	95.00	325.00

17	1911	.014	25.00	55.00	150.00	400.00
	1919	.040	8.00	17.50	75.00	250.00

COPPER-NICKEL

26	1952	.075	1.40	3.50	35.00	175.00
	1952	—	—	—	Proof	250.00

KM#	Date	Mintage	Fine	VF	XF	Unc
29	1955	.075	.40	1.00	3.50	15.00
	1955	—	—	—	Proof	150.00
	1960	.075	.40	1.00	5.00	100.00
	1960	—	—	—	Proof	250.00
	1962	.050	.30	.50	1.00	2.50
	1962	—	—	—	Proof	150.00
	1963	.050	.30	.50	2.00	7.50
	1963	—	—	—	Proof	150.00
	1964	.100	.30	.50	.75	1.50
	1965	.075	—	.50	1.00	2.00
	1966	.075	.40	1.00	2.00	8.00
	1968	.125	.25	.50	1.00	2.00
	1970	—	.20	.35	.75	1.50
	1971	.150	.20	.30	.50	1.50
	1972	.200	.20	.30	.50	1.50
	1973	.100	.20	.30	.60	1.75

50 CENTS

11.6200 g, .925 SILVER, .3456 oz ASW

10	1901	.010	35.00	80.00	350.00	1000.
	1901	30 pcs.	—	—	Proof	1000.

NOTE: Earlier dates (1894-1897) exist for this type.

13	1906	.015	20.00	60.00	225.00	600.00
	1907	.019	18.00	55.00	170.00	500.00

18	1911	.012	30.00	75.00	250.00	850.00
	1919	.040	20.00	40.00	150.00	850.00
	1919	—	—	—	Proof	1250.

COPPER-NICKEL

28	1954	.075	.30	.50	1.00	3.00
	1954	—	—	—	Proof	175.00
	1962	.050	.30	.50	1.50	3.50
	1962	—	—	—	Proof	200.00
	1964	.050	.30	.50	1.50	2.50
	1965	.025	1.00	3.00	5.00	25.00
	1966	.025	.75	2.00	4.00	15.00
	1971	.030	.30	.50	1.50	2.50

BELIZE

MINT MARKS

No mm - Royal Mint
FM - Franklin Mint, U.S.A.*

***NOTE:** From 1975-1985 the Franklin Mint produced coinage in 3 different qualities. Qualities of issue are designated in ( ) after each date and are defined as fol-

---

lows:

(M) MATTE - Normal circulation strike or a dull finish produced by sandblasting special uncirculated (polish finish) or proof quality dies.

(U) SPECIAL UNCIRCULATED - Polished or proof-like in appearance without any frosted features.

(P) PROOF - The highest quality obtainable having mirror-like fields and frosted features.

CENT

BRONZE

KM#	Date	Mintage	VF	XF	Unc
33	1973	.400	—	.10	.25
	1974	2.000	—	.10	.20
	1975	Inc. Ab.	—	.10	.15
	1976	3.000	—	.10	.15

ALUMINUM

33a	1976	2.050	—	.10	.15
	1979	2.505	—	.10	.15
	1980	1.505	—	.10	.15
	1982	—	—	.10	.15
	1983	—	—	.10	.15
	1986	—	—	.10	.15
	1987	—	—	.10	.15
	1989	—	—	.10	.15
	1991	—	—	.10	.15
	1996	—	—	.10	.15

BRONZE
Swallow-tailed Kite

38	1974FM(M)	.225	—	.40	.75
	1974FM(P)	.021	—	Proof	1.25

BRONZE

46	1975FM(M)	.118	—	.10	.75
	1975FM(U)	1,095	—	.20	1.00
	1975FM(P)	8,794	—	Proof	1.00
	1976FM(M)	.126	—	.10	.75
	1976FM(U)	759 pcs.	—	.20	1.00
	1976FM(P)	4,893	—	Proof	1.00

ALUMINUM

46b	1977FM(U)	.126	—	.10	.20
	1977FM(P)	2,107	—	Proof	1.00
	1978FM(U)	.125	—	.10	.20
	1978FM(P)	1,671	—	Proof	1.00
	1979FM(U)	808 pcs.	—	.15	.75
	1979FM(P)	1,287	—	Proof	1.00
	1980FM(U)	761 pcs.	—	.15	.75
	1980FM(P)	920 pcs.	—	Proof	1.00
	1981FM(U)	297 pcs.	—	.15	.75
	1981FM(P)	643 pcs.	—	Proof	1.00

83	1982FM(U)	—	—	.15	.75
	1982FM(P)	—	—	Proof	1.00
	1983FM(U)	—	—	.15	.75
	1983FM(P)	—	—	Proof	1.00

90	1984FM(P)	—	—	Proof	1.00
	1984FM(U)	—	—	—	1.00

Obv: New portrait of Queen Elizabeth II.

KM#	Date	Mintage	VF	XF	Unc
114	1992	—	—	.10	.15
	1994	—	—	.10	.15
	1996	—	—	.10	.15

5 CENTS

NICKEL-BRASS

34	1973	.210	—	.10	.40
	1974	.210	—	.10	.40
	1975	.420	—	.10	.40
	1976	.570	—	.10	.40
	1979	—	—	.10	.40

ALUMINUM

34a	1976	1.000	—	.10	.20
	1979	.960	—	.10	.20
	1980	1.040	—	.10	.20
	1986	—	—	.10	.20
	1987	—	—	.10	.20
	1989	—	—	.10	.20
	1991	—	—	.10	.20
	1994	—	—	.10	.20

NICKEL-BRASS
Fork-tailed Flycatcher

39	1974FM(M)	.050	—	.25	1.25
	1974FM(P)	.021	—	Proof	1.50

47	1975FM(M)	.024	—	.25	1.50
	1975FM(U)	1,095	—	.25	1.50
	1975FM(P)	8,794	—	Proof	1.25
	1976FM(M)	.025	—	.25	1.50
	1976FM(U)	759 pcs.	—	.25	1.50
	1976FM(P)	4,893	—	Proof	1.25

ALUMINUM

47b	1977FM(U)	.026	—	.10	.50
	1977FM(P)	2,107	—	Proof	1.50
	1978FM(U)	.025	—	.10	.50
	1978FM(P)	1,671	—	Proof	1.50
	1979FM(U)	808 pcs.	—	.15	.75
	1979FM(P)	1,287	—	.25	1.75
	1980FM(U)	761 pcs.	—	.15	.75
	1980FM(P)	920 pcs.	—	Proof	1.75
	1981FM(U)	297 pcs.	—	.15	.75
	1981FM(P)	643 pcs.	—	Proof	1.75

84	1982FM(U)	—	—	.15	.75
	1982FM(P)	—	—	Proof	1.75
	1983FM(U)	—	—	.15	.75
	1983FM(P)	—	—	Proof	1.75

World Food Day

64	1981	—	—	.10	.35

KM#	Date	Mintage	VF	XF	Unc
91	1984FM(P)	—	—	Proof	1.75
	1984FM(U)	—	—	—	1.75

Obv: New portrait of Queen Elizabeth II.

115	1992	—	—	.10	.20
	1993	—	—	.10	.20

10 CENTS

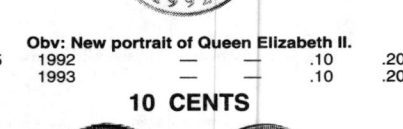

COPPER-NICKEL

35	1974	.100	.15	.30	.60
	1975	.200	.10	.20	.50
	1976	.700	.10	.15	.45
	1979	.800	.10	.15	.35
	1980	—	.10	.15	.35
	1981	—	.10	.15	.35

Long-tailed Hermit

40	1974FM(M)	.027	—	.50	2.00
	1974FM(P)	.021	—	Proof	1.75

48	1975FM(M)	.012	—	.25	1.50
	1975FM(U)	1,095	—	.30	2.00
	1975FM(P)	8,794	—	Proof	1.50
	1976FM(M)	.013	—	.25	1.50
	1976FM(U)	759 pcs.	—	.35	2.50
	1976FM(P)	4,893	—	Proof	1.50
	1977FM(U)	.014	—	.25	1.50
	1977FM(P)	2,107	—	Proof	2.00
	1978FM(U)	.013	—	.25	1.50
	1978FM(P)	1,671	—	Proof	2.00
	1979FM(U)	808 pcs.	—	.25	1.50
	1979FM(P)	1,287	—	Proof	2.50
	1980FM(U)	761 pcs.	—	.25	1.50
	1980FM(P)	920 pcs.	—	Proof	2.50
	1981FM(U)	297 pcs.	—	.25	1.50
	1981FM(P)	643 pcs.	—	Proof	2.50

85	1982FM(U)	—	—	.25	1.50
	1982FM(P)	—	—	Proof	2.50
	1983FM(U)	—	—	.25	1.50
	1983FM(P)	—	—	Proof	2.50

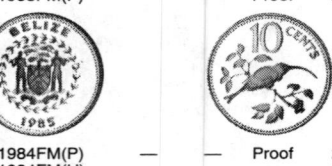

92	1984FM(P)	—	—	Proof	2.50
	1984FM(U)	—	—	—	2.50

Obv: New portrait of Queen Elizabeth II.

KM#	Date	Mintage	VF	XF	Unc
116	1992	—	—	.15	.40

25 CENTS

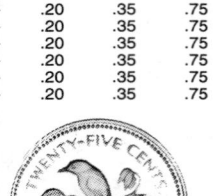

COPPER-NICKEL

36	1974	.100	.35	.65	1.25
	1975	.200	.20	.35	.75
	1976	.790	.20	.35	.75
	1979	.500	.20	.35	.75
	1980	—	.20	.35	.75
	1981	—	.20	.35	.75
	1986	—	.20	.35	.75
	1987	—	.20	.35	.75
	1988	—	.20	.35	.75
	1989	—	.20	.35	.75
	1991	—	.20	.35	.75

Blue-crowned Motmot

41	1974FM(M)	.013	—	1.00	3.50
	1974FM(P)	.021	—	Proof	2.50

49	1975FM(M)	4,716	—	.40	3.00
	1975FM(U)	1,095	—	.40	3.00
	1975FM(P)	8,794	—	Proof	2.50
	1976FM(M)	5,000	—	.50	4.00
	1976FM(U)	759 pcs.	—	.45	3.50
	1976FM(P)	4,893	—	Proof	2.50
	1977FM(U)	5,520	—	.30	2.00
	1977FM(P)	2,107	—	Proof	2.75
	1978FM(U)	5,458	—	.30	2.00
	1978FM(P)	1,671	—	Proof	2.75
	1979FM(U)	808 pcs.	—	.40	3.00
	1979FM(P)	1,287	—	Proof	3.00
	1980FM(U)	761 pcs.	—	.40	3.00
	1980FM(P)	920 pcs.	—	Proof	3.00
	1981FM(U)	297 pcs.	—	.40	3.00
	1981FM(P)	643 pcs.	—	Proof	3.00

86	1982FM(U)	—	—	.40	3.00
	1982FM(P)	—	—	Proof	3.00
	1983FM(U)	—	—	.40	3.00
	1983FM(P)	—	—	Proof	3.00

93	1984FM(P)	—	—	Proof	3.00
	1984FM(U)	—	—	—	3.00

World Forestry Congress

KM#	Date	Mintage	VF	XF	Unc
77	1985	—	—	.15	.25	.85

Obv: New portrait of Queen Elizabeth II.

117	1991	—	.20	.35	.75
	1992	—	.20	.35	.75
	1993	—	.20	.35	.75

50 CENTS

COPPER-NICKEL

37	1974	.123	.40	.75	2.00
	1975	Inc. Ab.	.40	.75	2.00
	1976	.312	.40	.75	2.00
	1979	.125	.40	.75	1.75
	1980	—	.40	.75	1.75
	1989	—	.40	.75	1.75
	1991	—	.40	.75	1.75

Frigate Bird

42	1974FM(M)	8,806	—	.40	4.00
	1974FM(P)	.021	—	Proof	3.50

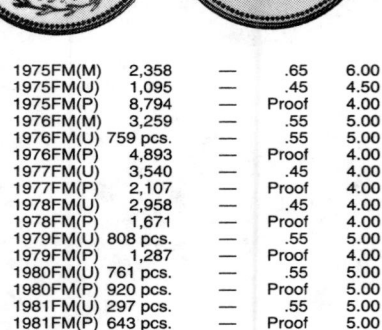

50	1975FM(M)	2,358	—	.65	6.00
	1975FM(U)	1,095	—	.45	4.50
	1975FM(P)	8,794	—	Proof	4.00
	1976FM(M)	3,259	—	.55	5.00
	1976FM(U)	759 pcs.	—	.55	5.00
	1976FM(P)	4,893	—	Proof	4.00
	1977FM(U)	3,540	—	.45	4.00
	1977FM(P)	2,107	—	Proof	4.00
	1978FM(U)	2,958	—	.45	4.00
	1978FM(P)	1,671	—	Proof	4.00
	1979FM(U)	808 pcs.	—	.55	5.00
	1979FM(P)	1,287	—	Proof	4.00
	1980FM(U)	761 pcs.	—	.55	5.00
	1980FM(P)	920 pcs.	—	Proof	5.00
	1981FM(U)	297 pcs.	—	.55	5.00
	1981FM(P)	643 pcs.	—	Proof	5.00

87	1982FM(U)	—	—	.55	5.00
	1982FM(P)	—	—	Proof	5.00
	1983FM(U)	—	—	.55	5.00
	1983FM(P)	—	—	Proof	5.00

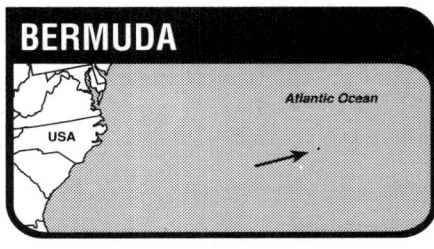

KM#	Date	Mintage	VF	XF	Unc
94	1984FM(P)	—	—	Proof	5.00
	1984FM(U)	—	—	—	5.00

Obv: New portrait of Queen Elizabeth II.

118	1992	—	.40	.75	1.75
	1993	—	.40	.75	1.75

DOLLAR

COPPER-NICKEL
Scarlet Macaw

43	1974FM(M)	6,656	—	1.00	5.00
	1974FM(P)	.021	—	Proof	4.50
	1975FM(M)	1,182	—	1.50	8.00
	1975FM(U)	1,095	—	.75	5.00
	1975FM(P)	8,794	—	Proof	4.50
	1976FM(M)	1,250	—	1.50	8.00
	1976FM(U)	759 pcs.	—	1.25	6.00
	1976FM(P)	4,893	—	Proof	5.00
	1977FM(U)	1,770	—	1.00	5.00
	1977FM(P)	2,107	—	Proof	6.00
	1978FM(U)	1,708	—	1.00	5.00
	1978FM(P)	1,671	—	Proof	6.00
	1979FM(U)	808 pcs.	—	1.25	5.50
	1979FM(P)	1,287	—	Proof	6.00
	1980FM(U)	761 pcs.	—	1.25	5.50
	1980FM(P)	920 pcs.	—	Proof	6.00
	1981FM(U)	297 pcs.	—	1.50	7.50
	1981FM(P)	643 pcs.	—	Proof	8.50

88	1982FM(U)	—	—	1.50	3.50
	1982FM(P)	—	—	Proof	4.50
	1983FM(U)	—	—	1.50	3.50
	1983FM(P)	—	—	Proof	4.50

KM#	Date	Mintage	VF	XF	Unc
95	1984FM(P)	—	—	Proof	7.50
	1984FM(U)	—	—	—	7.50

NICKEL-BRASS
Columbus' Three Ships

99	1990	—	—	—	2.25
	1991	—	—	—	2.25
	1992	—	—	—	2.25

The Parliamentary British Colony of Bermuda, situated in the western Atlantic Ocean 660 miles (1,062 km.) east of North Carolina, has an area of 20.6 sq. mi. (53 sq. km.) and a population of 61,600. Capital: Hamilton. Concentrated essences, beauty preparations, and cut flowers are exported. Most Bermudians derive their livelihood from tourism.

Bermuda was discovered by Juan de Bermudez, a Spanish navigator, in about 1503. British influence dates from 1609 when a group of Virginia-bound British colonists under the command of Sir George Somers was shipwrecked on the islands for 10 months. The islands were settled in 1612 by 60 British colonists from the Virginia Colony and became a crown colony in 1684. The earliest coins issued for the island were the "Hogge Money" series of 2, 3, 6 and 12 pence, the name derived from the pig in the obverse design, a recognition of the quantity of such animals then found there. The next issue for Bermuda was the Birmingham coppers of 1793; all locally circulating coinage was demonetized in 1842, when the currency of the United Kingdom became standard. Internal autonomy was obtained by the constitution of June 8, 1968.

In February, 1970, Bermuda converted from its former currency, which was sterling, to a decimal currency, the dollar unit which is equal to one U.S. dollar. On July 31, 1972, Bermuda severed its monetary link with the British pound sterling and pegged its dollar to be the same gold value as the U.S. dollar.

RULERS
British

MINT MARKS
CHI - Valcambi, Switzerland
FM - Franklin Mint, U.S.A.*
*NOTE: From 1975-1985 the Franklin Mint produced coinage in up to 3 different qualities. Qualities of issue are designated in ( ) after each date and are defined as follows:

(M) MATTE Normal circulation strike or a dull finish produced by sandblasting special uncirculated (polish finish) or proof quality dies.
(U) SPECIAL UNCIRCUALTED - Polished or proof-like in appearance without any frosted features.
(P) PROOF - The highest quality obtainable having mirror-like fields and frosted features.

MONETARY SYSTEM
12 Pence = 1 Shilling
20 Shillings = 1 Pound

CROWN

28.2800 g, .925 SILVER, .8411 oz ASW
350th Anniversary - Founding of the Colony

KM#	Date	Mintage	Fine	VF	XF	Unc
13	1959	.100	BV	5.00	7.00	12.50
	1959	6-10 pcs.	—	Matte Proof		1000.

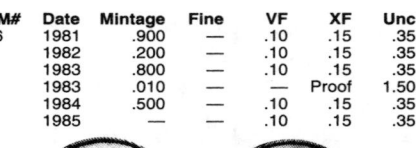

KM#	Date	Mintage	Fine	VF	XF	Unc
16	1981	.900	—	.10	.15	.35
	1982	.200	—	.10	.15	.35
	1983	.800	—	.10	.15	.35
	1983	.010	—	—	Proof	1.50
	1984	.500	—	.10	.15	.35
	1985	—	—	.10	.15	.35

45	1986	.700	—	.10	.15	.35
	1986	Inc. Ab.	—	—	Proof	2.50
	1987	—	—	.10	.15	.35
	1988	—	—	.10	.15	.35
	1990	—	—	.10	.15	.35
	1993	—	—	.10	.15	.35
	1994	—	—	.10	.15	.35
	1995	—	—	.10	.15	.35
	1997	—	—	.10	.15	.35

10 CENTS

COPPER-NICKEL
Bermuda Lily

17	1970	2.500	—	.10	.15	.35
	1970	.011	—	—	Proof	.50
	1971	2.000	—	.10	.15	.35
	1978	.500	—	.10	.15	.40
	1979	.800	—	.10	.15	.40
	1980	1.100	—	.10	.15	.35
	1981	1.300	—	.10	.15	.35
	1982	.400	—	.10	.15	.40
	1983	1.000	—	.10	.15	.35
	1983	.010	—	—	Proof	2.00
	1984	.500	—	—	.15	.40
	1985	—	—	.10	.15	.40

46	1986	.350	—	.10	.15	.40
	1986	Inc. Ab.	—	—	Proof	3.50
	1987	—	—	.10	.15	.40
	1988	—	—	.10	.15	.40
	1990	—	—	.10	.15	.40
	1993	—	—	.10	.15	.40
	1994	—	—	.10	.15	.40
	1997	—	—	.10	.15	.40

25 CENTS

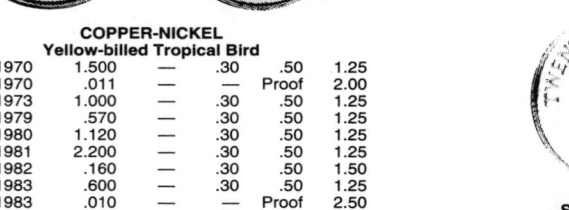

COPPER-NICKEL
Yellow-billed Tropical Bird

18	1970	1.500	—	.30	.50	1.25
	1970	.011	—	—	Proof	2.00
	1973	1.000	—	.30	.50	1.25
	1979	.570	—	.30	.50	1.25
	1980	1.120	—	.30	.50	1.25
	1981	2.200	—	.30	.50	1.25
	1982	.160	—	.30	.50	1.50
	1983	.600	—	.30	.50	1.25
	1983	.010	—	—	Proof	2.50
	1984	.400	—	.30	.50	1.25
	1985	—	—	.30	.50	1.25

375th Anniversary of Bermuda
Arms of the Bermudas
Obv: Similar to KM#18.

32	1984	—	—	—	.75	2.50

City of Hamilton
Obv: Similar to KM#18.

KM#	Date	Mintage	Fine	VF	XF	Unc
33	1984	—	—	—	.75	2.50

Town of St. George
Obv: Similar to KM#18.

34	1984	—	—	—	.75	2.50

Warwick Parish
Obv: Similar to KM#18.

35	1984	—	—	—	.75	2.50

Smith's Parish
Obv: Similar to KM#18.

36	1984	—	—	—	.75	2.50

Devonshire Parish
Obv: Similar to KM#18.

37	1984	—	—	—	.75	2.50

Sandy's Parish
Obv: Similar to KM#18.

38	1984	—	—	—	.75	2.50

Hamilton Parish
Obv: Similar to KM#18.

39	1984	—	—	—	.75	2.50

22.6200 g, .500 SILVER, .3636 oz ASW

KM#	Date	Mintage	Fine	VF	XF	Unc
14	1964	.470	—	—	BV	4.00
	1964	.030	—	—	Proof	6.00

DECIMAL COINAGE

100 Cents = 1 Dollar

CENT

BRONZE
Wild Boar

15	1970	5.500	—	—	.10	.20
	1970	.011	—	—	Proof	.50
	1971	4.256	—	—	.10	.20
	1972	—	—	Reported, not confirmed		
	1973	2.144	—	—	.10	.20
	1974	.856	—	—	.10	.25
	1975	1.000	—	—	.10	.20
	1976	1.000	—	—	.10	.20
	1977	2.000	—	—	.10	.20
	1978	3.160	—	—	.10	.20
	1980	3.520	—	—	.10	.20
	1981	3.200	—	—	.10	.20
	1982	.320	—	—	.10	.20
	1983	.800	—	—	.10	.20
	1983	.010	—	—	Proof	1.00
	1984	.800	—	—	.10	.20
	1985	—	—	—	.10	.20

44	1986	.960	—	—	.10	.20
	1986	Inc. Ab.	—	—	Proof	2.00
	1987	—	—	—	.10	.20
	1988	—	—	—	.10	.20
	1990	—	—	—	.10	.20
	1991	—	—	—	.10	.20

COPPER COATED STEEL

44a	1988	—	—	—	—	2.50

COPPER PLATED ZINC

44b	1991	—	—	—	.10	.20
	1993	—	—	—	.10	.20
	1994	—	—	—	.10	.20
	1995	—	—	—	.10	.20
	1997	—	—	—	.10	.20

5 CENTS

COPPER-NICKEL
Queen Angel Fish

16	1970	2.190	—	.10	.15	.35
	1970	.011	—	—	Proof	.50
	1974	.310	—	.10	.15	.35
	1975	.500	—	.10	.15	.35
	1977	.500	—	.10	.15	.35
	1979	.500	—	.10	.15	.35
	1980	1.100	—	.10	.15	.35

Southampton Parish
Obv: Similar to KM#18.

KM#	Date	Mintage	Fine	VF	XF	Unc
40	1984	—	—	—	.75	2.50

Pembroke Parish
Obv: Similar to KM#18.

41	1984	—	—	—	.75	2.50

Paget Parish
Obv: Similar to KM#18.

42	1984	—	—	—	.75	2.50

KM#	Date	Mintage	Fine	VF	XF	Unc
47	1986	.560	—	.30	.40	.75
	1986	Inc. Ab.	—	—	Proof	5.00
	1987	—	—	.30	.40	.75
	1988	—	—	.30	.40	.75
	1993	—	—	.30	.40	.75
	1994	—	—	.30	.40	.75
	1995	—	—	.30	.40	.75
	1997	—	—	.30	.40	.75

50 CENTS

COPPER-NICKEL

19	1970	1.000	—	.60	.75	1.00
	1970	.011	—	—	Proof	2.00
	1978	.200	—	.60	.85	1.25
	1980	.060	—	.60	.85	1.50
	1981	.100	—	.60	.85	1.25
	1982	.080	—	.60	.85	1.50
	1983	.060	—	.60	.85	1.50
	1983	.010	—	—	Proof	4.50
	1984	.040	—	.60	.85	1.50
	1985	—	—	.60	.85	1.50

48	1986	.060	—	.60	.85	1.50
	1986	Inc. Ab.	—	—	Proof	7.50
	1988	—	—	.60	.85	1.50

DOLLAR

NICKEL-BRASS
Cahow over Bermuda

KM#	Date	Mintage	Fine	VF	XF	Unc
30	1983	.250	—	—	—	3.00
	1983	.010	—	—	Proof	5.00

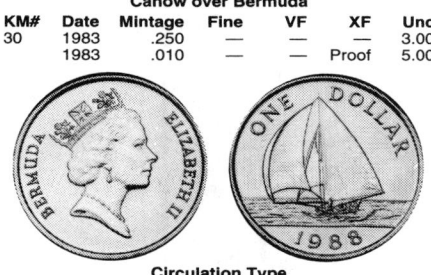

Circulation Type

56	1988	—	—	—	—	2.25
	1993	.015	—	—	Mint Sets only	5.00
	1997	—	—	—	—	2.25

BHUTAN

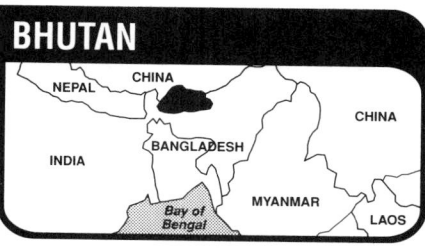

The Kingdom of Bhutan, a landlocked Himalayan country bordered by Tibet and India, has an area of 18,150 sq. mi. (47,000 sq. km.) and a population of 1.8 million. Capital: Thimphu. Virtually the entire population is engaged in agricultural and pastoral activities. Rice, wheat, barley, and yak butter are produced in sufficient quantity to make the country self-sufficient in food. The economy of Bhutan is primitive and many transactions are conducted on a barter basis.

Bhutan's early history is obscure, but is thought to have resembled that of rural medieval Europe. The country was conquered by Tibet, in the 9th century, and a dual temporal and spiritual rule developed which operated until the mid-19th century, when the southern part of the country was occupied by the British and annexed to British India. Bhutan was established as a hereditary monarchy in 1907, and in 1910 agreed to British control of its external affairs. In 1949, India and Bhutan concluded a treaty whereby India assumed Britain's role in subsidizing Bhutan and guiding its foreign affairs. In 1971 Bhutan became a full member of the United Nations.

RULERS

Ugyen Wangchuck, 1907-1926
Jigme Wangchuck, 1926-1952
Jigme Dorji Wangchuck, 1952-1972
Jigme Singye Wangchuck, 1972-

MODERN COINAGE

64 Pice (Paisa) = 1 Rupee

CYCLICAL DATES

Earth-Dragon	Iron-Tiger

(1928)	(1950)

OBVERSE LEGENDS

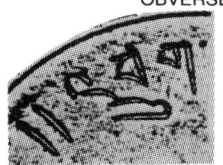 

Normal	Modified

PICE

BRONZE, 7.00 g, 26.5mm
Similar to KM#23.2.

KM#	Date	Mintage	Fine	VF	XF	Unc
23.1	1928	—	22.50	40.00	65.00	100.00

BRONZE, 4.90 g, 25.1mm

23.2	1928	.010	20.00	35.00	60.00	90.00
	1928	—	—	—	Proof	100.00

NOTE: Actually struck in 1931.

3.30 g

A27	ND	—	—	—	—	—

2.90 g

KM#	Date	Mintage	Fine	VF	XF	Unc
27	ND	*1.260	.75	1.00	1.50	2.25

*NOTE: Actually struck in 1951 and 1955. Later strikes of 1955 dates differ in detail due to recut dies.

1/2 RUPEE

SILVER, 5.83-5.85 g

24	ND(1928)*	.050	10.00	15.00	22.50	35.00
	ND(1928)			—	Proof	100.00

NOTE: Actually struck in 1929.

Obv: Leg. modified.

25	ND(1928)	I.A.	10.00	15.00	22.50	35.00

NOTE: Actually struck in 1930.

NICKEL, 5.78-5.90 g
Obv: Leg. normal.

26	ND(1928)*	.020	2.00	3.00	4.50	7.00
	ND(1950)**	.202	1.50	2.50	3.00	4.50

*NOTE: Actually struck in 1951.
**NOTE: Actually struck in 1955.

NICKEL, reduced wgt., 5.08 g
Obv: Leg. normal.

28	ND(1950)***					
		10.000	.75	1.00	1.50	2.25

***NOTE: Actually struck in 1967/68.

DECIMAL COINAGE
1957-1974
100 Naye Paisa = 1 Rupee
100 Rupees = 1 Sertum

25 NAYA PAISA

COPPER-NICKEL
40th Anniversary Accession of Jigme Wangchuk

KM#	Date	Mintage	VF	XF	Unc
29	1966	.010	.20	.40	.75
	1966	6,000	—	Proof	1.00

50 NAYA PAISA

COPPER-NICKEL
40th Anniversary Accession of Jigme Wangchuk

30	1966	.010	.25	.50	1.00
	1966	6,000	—	Proof	1.50

RUPEE

COPPER-NICKEL
40th Anniversary Accession of Jigme Wangchuk

KM#	Date	Mintage	VF	XF	Unc
31	1966	.010	.50	.75	1.50
	1966	6,000	—	Proof	1.50

3 RUPEES

COPPER-NICKEL
40th Anniversary Accession of Jigme Wangchuk

32	1966	5,826	—	—	4.00
	1966	6,000	—	Proof	4.00

MONETARY REFORM
Commencing 1974
100 Chetrums (Paisa) =
1 Ngultrum (Rupee)
100 Ngultrums = 1 Sertum

5 CHETRUMS

ALUMINUM

37	1974	—	.10	.20	.50
	1974	1,000	—	Proof	1.25
	1975	—	.10	.15	.20
	1975	—	—	Proof	1.25

5 CHHERTUM

BRONZE

45	1979	—	.10	.20	.50
	1979	—	—	Proof	1.00

10 CHETRUMS

ALUMINUM

38	1974	—	.15	.25	.50
	1974	1,000	—	Proof	1.50

F.A.O. Issue and International Women's Year

KM#	Date	Mintage	VF	XF	Unc
43	1975	4.000	.15	.25	.65
	1975		—	Proof	2.50

10 CHHERTUM

BRONZE

46	1979	—	.15	.30	1.00
	1979	—	—	Proof	2.00

20 CHETRUMS

ALUMINUM-BRONZE
F.A.O. Issue

39	1974	1.194	.15	.25	.50
	1974	*	—	P/L	1.50
	1974	1,000	—	Proof	2.00

*NOTE: In mint set only.

25 CHETRUMS

COPPER-NICKEL
Rev. I

40.1	1974	—	.10	.20	.75
	1974	1,000	—	Proof	3.00

Rev. II

40.2	1974	—	.10	.20	.75
	1975	—	.10	.20	.75
	1975	—	—	Proof	3.00

25 CHHERTUM

COPPER-NICKEL

47	1979	—	.25	.50	1.25
	1979	—	—	Proof	4.00

50 CHHERTUM

COPPER-NICKEL

48	1979	—	.25	.65	1.50
	1979	—	—	Proof	5.00

NGULTRUM

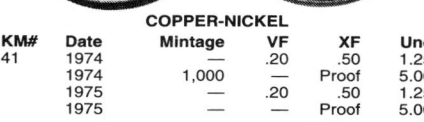

COPPER-NICKEL

KM#	Date	Mintage	VF	XF	Unc
41	1974	—	.20	.50	1.25
	1974	1,000	—	Proof	5.00
	1975	—	.20	.50	1.25
	1975	—	—	Proof	5.00

49	1979	—	.30	.75	2.00
	1979	—	—	Proof	5.50

3 NGULTRUMS

COPPER-NICKEL

50	1979	—	1.00	2.00	4.00
	1979	—	—	Proof	7.50

Bohemia, a western province in the Czech Republic, was combined with the majority of Moravia in central Czechoslovakia (excluding parts of north and south Moravia which were joined with Silesia in 1938) to form the German protectorate in March, 1939, after the German invasion. Toward the end of war in 1945 the protectorate was dissolved and Bohemia and Moravia once again became part of Czechoslovakia.

MONETARY SYSTEM
100 Haleru = 1 Koruna

10 HALERU

			ZINC		
KM#	Date	Mintage	Fine	VF	XF	Unc
1	1940	82.114	.25	.50	1.00	6.00
	1941	Inc. Ab.	.25	.50	1.00	7.50
	1942	Inc. Ab.	.25	.50	1.00	7.50
	1943	Inc. Ab.	.50	.75	1.50	10.00
	1944	Inc. Ab.	.75	1.50	2.50	12.00

20 HALERU

			ZINC		
2	1940	106.526	.25	.50	1.00	7.50
	1941	Inc. Ab.	.25	.50	1.00	7.50
	1942	Inc. Ab.	.25	.50	1.00	7.50
	1943	Inc. Ab.	.50	.75	1.50	10.00
	1944	Inc. Ab.	.50	1.00	1.75	12.00

50 HALERU

			ZINC		
3	1940	53.270	.35	.75	1.25	10.00
	1941	Inc. Ab.	.35	.75	1.25	10.00
	1942	Inc. Ab.	.35	.75	1.25	10.00
	1943	Inc. Ab.	.75	1.50	3.00	15.00
	1944	Inc. Ab.	.35	.75	1.25	10.00

KORUNA

			ZINC		
4	1941	102.817	.50	.75	1.50	12.50
	1942	Inc. Ab.	.50	.75	1.50	12.50
	1943	Inc. Ab.	.50	.75	1.50	12.50
	1944	Inc. Ab.	.50	.75	1.50	12.50

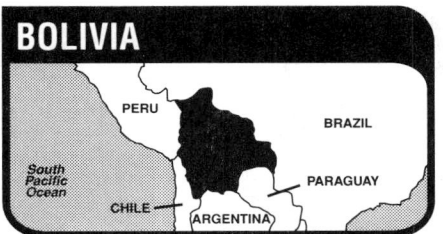

The Republic of Bolivia, a landlocked country in westcentral South America, has an area of 424,165 sq. mi. (1,098,580 sq. km.) and a population of 7.9 million. Its capitals are: La Paz (administrative) and Sucre (constitutional). Principal exports are tin, zinc, antimony, tungsten, petroleum, natural gas, cotton and coffee.

Much of present day Bolivia was first dominated by the Tiahuanaco Culture ca.400 BC. It had in turn been incorporated into the Inca Empire by 1440AD prior to the arrival of the Spanish, in 1535, who reduced the Indian population to virtual slavery. When Joseph Napoleon was placed upon the throne of occupied Spain in 1809, a fervor of revolutionary activity quickened throughout Alto Peru - culminating in the 1809 Proclamation of Liberty. Sixteen bloody years of struggle ensued before the republic, named for the famed liberator Simon Bolivar, was established on August 6, 1825. Since then Bolivia has survived more than 16 constitutions, 78 Presidents, 3 military juntas and over 160 revolutions.

The Imperial City of Potosi, founded by Villaroel in 1546, was established in the midst of what is estimated to have been the world's richest silver mines (having produced in excess of 2 billion dollars worth of silver).

The first mint, early in 1574, used equipment brought over from Lima; before that it had been used at La Plata where the operation failed. The oldest type was a cob with the Hapsburg arms on the obverse and cross with quartered castles and lions on the reverse. To the heraldic right of the shield (at the left as one faces it) is a "p" and, under it, the assayer's initial. While production at the "Casa de Moneda" was enormous, the quality of the coinage was at times so poor that some 50 were condemned to death by their superiors.

Therefore, by royal decree of February 17, 1651, the design was changed to the quartered castles and lions for the obverse and two crowned pillars of Hercules floating above the waves of the sea for the reverse. This new design began in 1652 and as the last cob type continued on for several years along with the milled pillars and bust pieces from 1767 through 1773. In the final years under Charles III the planchet is compact and dumpy, very irregular and of poor style, contrasting sharply with their counterpart denominations of the pillar and bust types.

Rarely, and at very high prices, we may be offered almost perfectly round cobs, with the dies well-centered, showing the legend and date completely. These have gained importance in the last decades and are known as "royal" or "presentation" pieces. Every year a few of these specimens were coined, using dies in good condition and a regular and round planchet, to prove the quality of the mintage to the Viceroy or even to the King. Most surviving specimens are holed or plugged. The rest of the production was of primitive quality due to the shortage of skilled laborers and the volume to be struck.

Most pre-decimal coinage of independent Bolivia carries the assayers' initials on the reverse near the rim to the left of the date, in 4 to 5 o'clock position. The mint mark or name appears in the 7 to 8 o'clock area.

MONETARY SYSTEM
100 Centavos = 1 Boliviano

5 CENTAVOS

COPPER-NICKEL

KM#	Date	Mintage	Fine	VF	XF	Unc
173.1	1909	4.000	.50	1.00	4.00	15.00
	1918	.530	1.25	2.00	6.00	15.00
	1919	4.370	3.00	5.00	10.00	25.00

NOTE: Earlier dates (1893-1899) exist for this type.
NOTE: Coins dated 1893, 1918 and 1919 medal rotation strike at Heaton Mint.

173.3	1902	2.000	.50	1.25	5.00	15.00
	1907	2.000	1.75	3.75	7.50	20.00
	1908	3.000	.50	1.00	4.00	15.00
	1909	—	2.00	4.00	9.00	25.00

NOTE: Earlier date (1897) exists for this type.

178	1935	5.000	.50	1.00	3.00	9.00

10 CENTAVOS

COPPER-NICKEL
Rev: W/o privy marks.

KM#	Date	Mintage	Fine	VF	XF	Unc
174.1	1918	1.335	2.50	5.00	7.50	15.00
	1919	6.165	.50	1.00	3.00	10.00

NOTE: Earlier dates (1893-1899) exist for this type.
NOTE: Coins dated 1893, 1918 and 1919 medal rotation strike at the Heaton Mint.

Rev: Cornucopia and torch flank date.

KM#	Date	Mintage	Fine	VF	XF	Unc
174.3	1901	—	17.50	27.50	45.00	75.00
	1902	8.500	.50	1.00	4.00	15.00
	1907/2	4.000	1.25	2.50	7.00	20.00
	1907	Inc. Ab.	.50	1.00	4.00	15.00
	1908	6.000	.50	1.00	4.00	15.00
	1909	8.000	.50	1.00	4.00	15.00

NOTE: Earlier date (1897) exists for this type.

Rev: Wide 0 in value.

KM#	Date	Mintage	Fine	VF	XF	Unc
179.1	1935	10.000	.50	1.00	2.50	10.00
	1936	10.000	.50	1.00	2.50	10.00

Rev: Narrow 0 in value.

KM#	Date	Mintage	Fine	VF	XF	Unc
179.2	1939	—	.50	1.00	2.50	10.00

180	1937	20.000	.50	1.00	2.50	10.00

ZINC

179a	1942(p)	10.000	.50	1.00	2.50	10.00

20 CENTAVOS

4.6000 g, .900 SILVER, .1331 oz ASW

KM#	Date	Mintage	VG	Fine	VF	XF
159.2	1901 MM	.040	2.50	5.00	13.50	20.00
	1901 MM/MW					
		—	2.50	5.00	16.50	25.00
	1902 MM	—	6.50	10.00	20.00	40.00

KM#	Date	Mintage	VG	Fine	VF	XF
159.2	1903 MM	.010	10.00	15.00	30.00	50.00
	1904 MM	—	7.00	12.00	20.00	40.00
	1907 MM	—	45.00	90.00	150.00	300.00

NOTE: Earlier dates (1895-1900) exist for this type.
NOTE: The small bar usually found below "S" in "9 DS" is missing in 1902 date.

4.0000 g, .833 SILVER, .1071 oz ASW

KM#	Date	Mintage	Fine	VF	XF	Unc
176	1909H	1.500	2.50	5.00	12.50	20.00

ZINC

183	1942(p)	10.000	1.00	2.50	6.50	15.00

NOTE: Medal rotation strike.

50 CENTAVOS
(1/2 Boliviano)

11.5000 g, .900 SILVER, .3328 oz ASW

KM#	Date	Mintage	VG	Fine	VF	XF
175.1	1901/0 MM					
		2.000	BV	7.00	18.00	35.00
	1901 MM	I.A.	BV	3.50	7.50	15.00
	1902 MM	1.530	BV	3.50	7.50	15.00
	1903/2 MM	.690	BV	5.00	15.00	35.00
	1903 MM	I.A.	BV	3.50	7.50	15.00
	1904 MM	1.290	BV	3.50	7.50	15.00
	1905 MM	1.690	BV	3.50	7.50	15.00
	1905 AB	I.A.	BV	3.50	7.50	15.00
	1906 MM	.630	BV	4.50	8.50	20.00
	1906 AB	5.500	BV	3.50	7.50	15.00
	1907 MM	.050	BV	4.00	8.50	20.00
	1908 MM	—	BV	3.50	7.50	15.00
	1908 MM inverted 8					
		—	BV	10.00	25.00	45.00

NOTE: Earlier date (1900) exists for this type.
NOTE: Date varieties exist for this type.

10.0000 g, .833 SILVER, .2678 oz ASW

177	1909H	1.400	BV	4.50	9.00	20.00
	1909H	—	—	—	Proof	400.00

COPPER-NICKEL

KM#	Date	Mintage	Fine	VF	XF	Unc
181	1937	8.000	10.00	25.00	45.00	75.00

NOTE: Most melted upon receipt in Bolivia. Medal rotation strike.

KM#	Date	Mintage	Fine	VF	XF	Unc
182	1939	—	.25	.50	1.00	4.50

NOTE: Medal rotation strike.

BRONZE

182a.1	1942(p)	10.000	.35	.60	1.25	5.00

NOTE: Medal rotation strike.

Restrike-poor detail.

182a.2	1942	5.310	.25	.50	1.00	4.00

NOTE: Medal rotation strike.

BOLIVIANO

BRONZE

184	1951	10.000	.10	.20	.40	1.50
	1951	10 pcs.	—	—	Proof	200.00
	1951H	15.000	.10	.20	.40	1.50
	1951KN	15.000	.25	.50	1.00	3.00

NOTE: Medal rotation strike.

5 BOLIVIANOS

BRONZE

185	1951	7.000	.25	.50	.75	2.50
	1951	—	—	—	Proof	150.00
	1951H	15.000	.25	.50	.75	2.50
	1951KN	15.000	.60	.90	1.25	3.50

NOTE: Medal rotation strike.

10 BOLIVIANOS
(1 Bolivar)

BRONZE

186	1951	40.000	.60	1.00	1.75	3.50
	1951	—	—	—	Proof	—

NOTE: Medal rotation strike.

MONETARY REFORM
100 Centavos = 1 Peso Boliviano

5 CENTAVOS

KM#	Date	Mintage	Fine	VF	XF	Unc
		COPPER CLAD STEEL				
187	1965	10.000	.20	.30	.65	1.50
	1970	.100	.20	.30	.65	2.00

10 CENTAVOS

		COPPER CLAD STEEL				
188	1965	10.000	.10	.25	.50	1.50
	1967	—	.10	.20	.40	1.00
	1969	5.700	.10	.20	.40	1.00
	1971	.200	.15	.25	.50	1.00
	1972	.100	.20	.40	.80	1.50
	1973	6.000	.10	.20	.40	1.00

20 CENTAVOS

		NICKEL CLAD STEEL				
189	1965	5.000	.20	.40	.70	2.00
	1967	—	.20	.40	.65	1.75
	1970	.400	.20	.40	.80	2.50
	1971	.400	.20	.40	.80	2.50
	1973	5.000	.20	.40	.60	1.50

25 CENTAVOS

		NICKEL CLAD STEEL				
193	1971	—	.15	.30	.60	1.00
	1972	9.998	.15	.30	.60	1.00

50 CENTAVOS

		NICKEL CLAD STEEL				
190	1965	10.000	—	.25	.65	1.50
	1967	—	—	.25	.65	1.25
	1972	—	—	.25	.65	1.25
	1973	5.000	—	.25	.65	1.25
	1974	15.000	—	.25	.65	1.25
	1978	5.000	—	.25	.65	1.25
	1980	3.600	—	.25	.65	1.25

PESO BOLIVIANO

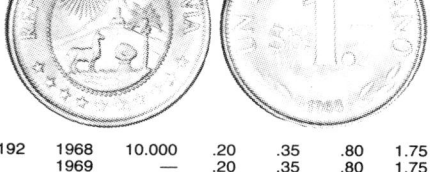

		NICKEL CLAD STEEL				
		F.A.O. Issue				
191	ND(1968)	.040	—	2.50	3.50	6.50

192	1968	10.000	.20	.35	.80	1.75
	1969	—	.20	.35	.80	1.75
	1970	10.000	.15	.20	.80	1.75
	1972	—	.20	.35	.80	1.75

KM#	Date	Mintage	Fine	VF	XF	Unc
192	1973	5.000	.15	.25	.80	1.75
	1974	15.000	.15	.25	.80	1.75
	1978	10.000	.15	.25	.80	1.75
	1980	2.993	.15	.25	.80	1.75

5 PESOS BOLIVIANOS

		NICKEL CLAD STEEL				
197	1976	20.000	.65	1.25	2.50	5.00
	1978	10.000	.65	1.25	2.50	5.00
	1980	5.231	.65	1.25	2.50	5.00

MONETARY REFORM

1,000,000 Peso Bolivianos = 1 Boliviano
100 Centavos = 1 Boliviano

2 CENTAVOS

		STAINLESS STEEL				
200	1987	20.000	—	—	—	.50

5 CENTAVOS

		STAINLESS STEEL				
201	1987	20.000	—	—	—	.50

10 CENTAVOS

		STAINLESS STEEL				
202	1987	20.000	—	—	—	.75
	1991	23.000	—	—	—	.75
	1995	14.000	—	—	—	.75
	1997	33.000	—	—	—	.75
		COPPER-CLAD STEEL				
202a	1997	—	—	—	—	.75

20 CENTAVOS

		STAINLESS STEEL				
203	1987	20.000	—	—	—	.75
	1991	20.000	—	—	—	.75
	1995	14.000	—	—	—	.75
	1997	19.000	—	—	—	.75

50 CENTAVOS

		STAINLESS STEEL				
204	1987	15.000	—	—	—	1.00
	1991	20.000	—	—	—	1.00
	1995	14.000	—	—	—	1.00
	1997	15.000	—	—	—	1.00

BOLIVIANO

KM#	Date	Mintage	Fine	VF	XF	Unc
		STAINLESS STEEL				
205	1987	10.000	—	—	—	2.00
	1991	20.000	—	—	—	1.25
	1995	9.000	—	—	—	1.25
	1997	17.000	—	—	—	1.25

2 BOLIVIANOS

		STAINLESS STEEL				
206	1991	18.000	—	—	—	1.50
(207)						

NOTE: The 1995 date previously listed here has not yet been released into circulation.

BOTSWANA

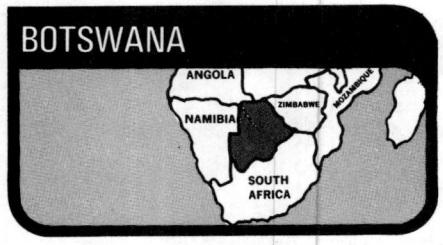

The Republic of Botswana (formerly Bechuanaland), located in south central Africa between Namibia and Zimbabwe, has an area of 224,607 sq. mi. (600,370 sq. km.) and a population of 1.4 million. Capital: Gaborone. Botswana is a member of a Customs Union with South Africa, Lesotho, and Swaziland. The economy is primarily pastoral with a rapidly developing mining industry, of which diamonds, copper and nickel are the chief elements. Meat products and diamonds comprise 85 percent of the exports.

Little is known of the origin of the peoples of Botswana. The early inhabitants, the Bushmen, did not develop a recorded history and are now dying out. The ancestors of the present Botswana residents probably arrived about 1600AD in Bantu migrations from the north and east. Bechuanaland was first united early in the 19th century under Chief Khama III to more effectively resist incursions by the Boer trekkers from Transvaal and by the neighboring Matabeles. As the Boer threat intensified, appeals for protection were made to the British Government, which proclaimed the whole of Bechuanaland a British protectorate in 1885. In 1895, the southern part of the protectorate was annexed to Cape Province. The northern part, known as the Bechuanaland Protectorate, remained under British administration until it became the independent Republic of Botswana on Sept. 30, 1966. Botswana is a member of the Commonwealth of Nations. The president is Chief of State and Head of government.

MINT MARKS

B - Berne

MONETARY SYSTEM

100 Cents = 1 Thebe

THEBE

ALUMINUM
Turako

KM#	Date	Mintage	VF	XF	Unc
3	1976	15.000	.10	.15	.25
	1976	.026	—	Proof	.75
	1981	.010	—	Proof	1.00
	1983	5.000	.10	.20	.35
	1984	5.000	.10	.20	.35
	1985	—	.10	.20	.35
	1987	—	.10	.20	.30
	1988	—	.10	.20	.30
	1989	—	.10	.20	.30
	1991	—	.10	.20	.30

2 THEBE

BRONZE
World Food Day - Millet

KM#	Date	Mintage	VF	XF	Unc
14	1981	9.990	.15	.25	.50
	1981	.010	—	Proof	1.00
	1985	—	.15	.25	.50

5 THEBE

BRONZE
Toko

KM#	Date	Mintage	VF	XF	Unc
4	1976	3.000	.15	.25	.50
	1976	.026	—	Proof	1.00
	1977	.250	.15	.25	.50
	1979	.200	.15	.25	.50
	1980	1.000	.15	.25	.50
	1981	4.990	.15	.25	.50
	1981	.010	—	Proof	1.25
	1984	2.000	.15	.25	.50
	1985	—	.15	.25	.50
	1988	—	.15	.25	.50
	1989	—	.15	.25	.50

BRONZE CLAD STEEL

KM#	Date	Mintage	VF	XF	Unc
4a	1991	—	.15	.25	.50

10 THEBE

COPPER-NICKEL
South African Oryx

KM#	Date	Mintage	VF	XF	Unc
5	1976	1.500	.25	.40	.75
	1976	.026	—	Proof	1.50
	1977	.500	.25	.40	.75
	1979	.750	.25	.40	.75
	1980	—	.25	.40	.75
	1981	2.590	.25	.40	.75
	1981	.010	—	Proof	1.75
	1984	4.000	.20	.30	.60
	1985	—	.20	.30	.60
	1989	—	.20	.30	.60

NICKEL CLAD STEEL

KM#	Date	Mintage	VF	XF	Unc
5a	1991	—	.20	.30	.60

25 THEBE

COPPER-NICKEL
Zebu

KM#	Date	Mintage	VF	XF	Unc
6	1976	1.500	.25	.55	1.50
	1976	.026	—	Proof	2.00
	1977	.265	.25	.60	1.75
	1980	—	.25	.60	1.30
	1981	.740	.25	.60	1.30
	1981	.010	—	Proof	2.50
	1982	.400	.25	.60	1.75
	1984	2.000	.25	.55	1.30
	1985	—	.30	.60	1.30
	1989	—	.30	.60	1.30

NICKEL CLAD STEEL

KM#	Date	Mintage	VF	XF	Unc
6a	1991	—	.30	.60	1.30

50 THEBE

COPPER-NICKEL
African Fish Eagle

KM#	Date	Mintage	VF	XF	Unc
7	1976	.266	.65	1.35	2.25
	1976	.026	—	Proof	3.00
	1977	.250	.65	1.35	2.25
	1980	—	.65	1.35	2.25
	1981	—	Reported, not confirmed		
	1981	.010	—	Proof	3.50
	1984	2.000	.65	1.35	2.25
	1985	—	.65	1.35	2.25

NICKEL CLAD STEEL

KM#	Date	Mintage	VF	XF	Unc
7a	1991	—	.65	1.35	2.25

PULA

COPPER-NICKEL
Zebra

KM#	Date	Mintage	VF	XF	Unc
8	1976	.166	1.50	2.50	5.00
	1976	.026	—	Proof	6.00
	1977	.500	1.50	2.50	4.00
	1981	—	1.50	2.50	4.00
	1981	.010	—	Proof	6.50
	1985	—	1.50	2.50	4.00
	1987	—	1.50	2.50	4.00

NICKEL-BRASS
Zebra

KM#	Date	Mintage	VF	XF	Unc
24	1991	—	.75	1.50	3.00

2 PULA

NICKEL - BRASS
Rhinoceros

KM#	Date	Mintage	VF	XF	Unc
25	1994	—	—	—	4.50

The Federative Republic of Brazil, which comprises half the continent of South America and is the only Latin American country deriving its culture and language from Portugal, has an area of 3,286,488 sq. mi. (8,511,965 sq. km.) and a population of 160.7 million. Capital: Brasilia. The economy of Brazil is as varied and complex as any in the developing world. Agriculture is a mainstay of the economy, while only 4 percent of the area is under cultivation. Known mineral resources are almost unlimited in variety and size of reserves. A large, relatively sophisticated industry ranges from basic steel and chemical production to finished consumer goods. Coffee, cotton, iron ore and cocoa are the chief exports.

Brazil was discovered and claimed for Portugal by Admiral Pedro Alvares Cabral in 1500. Portugal established a settlement in 1532 and proclaimed the area a royal colony in 1549. During the Napoleonic Wars, Dom Joao VI established the seat of Portuguese government in Rio de Janeiro. When he returned to Portugal, his son Dom Pedro I declared Brazil's independence on Sept. 7, 1822, and became emperor of Brazil. The Empire of Brazil was maintained until 1889 when the federal republic was established. The Federative Republic was established in 1946 by terms of a constitution drawn up by a constituent assembly. Following a coup in 1964 the armed forces retained overall control under a dictatorship until civilian government was restored on March 15, 1985. The current constitution was adopted in 1988.

MINT MARKS

(a) - Paris, privy marks only
A - Berlin 1913
P - Pernambuco

MONETARY SYSTEM

(1833-1942)
1000 Reis = 1 Milreis
(1942-1967)
100 Centavos = 1 Cruzeiro

REPUBLIC

20 REIS

BRONZE

KM#	Date	Mintage	Fine	VF	XF	Unc
490	1901	.713	1.00	5.00	10.00	20.00
	1904	.850	1.00	5.00	10.00	20.00
	1905	1.075	4.00	8.00	15.00	50.00
	1906	.215	2.00	6.00	12.00	30.00
	1908	4.558	1.00	5.00	10.00	20.00
	1909	1.215	5.00	10.00	22.00	100.00
	1910	.828	1.00	5.00	10.00	20.00
	1911	1.545	1.00	5.00	10.00	20.00
	1912	.480	1.00	5.00	10.00	25.00

NOTE: Earlier dates (1889-1900) exist for this type.

COPPER-NICKEL

KM#	Date	Mintage	Fine	VF	XF	Unc
516	1918	.373	.25	.50	2.00	5.00
	1919	2.870	.25	.50	1.00	4.00
	1920	.825	.25	.50	1.25	5.00
	1921	1.020	.25	.50	1.25	5.00
	1927	.053	5.00	10.00	30.00	80.00
	1935	100 pcs.	200.00	450.00	900.00	1500.

40 REIS

BRONZE
Rev: FC above star.

KM#	Date	Mintage	Fine	VF	XF	Unc
491	1901	.525	.75	2.00	3.50	15.00
	1907	.218	.75	2.00	3.50	15.00
	1908	4.639	.75	2.00	3.50	15.00
	1909	4.226	.75	2.00	3.50	17.50
	1910	.848	.75	2.00	4.00	20.00
	1911	1.660	.75	2.00	4.00	20.00
	1912	.819	1.00	2.50	4.50	22.50

NOTE: Earlier dates (1889-1900) exist for this type.

50 REIS

COPPER-NICKEL

KM#	Date	Mintage	Fine	VF	XF	Unc
517	1918	.558	.15	.35	.75	6.00
	1919	.558	.15	.35	.75	6.00
	1920	.072	.40	1.00	4.00	16.00
	1921	.682	.15	.35	.75	6.00
	1922	.176	.40	1.00	4.00	16.00
	1925	.128	.40	1.50	5.00	20.00
	1926	.194	.40	1.50	5.00	20.00
	1931	.020	2.00	10.00	40.00	80.00
	1935	100 pcs.	125.00	300.00	800.00	1500.

100 REIS

Date: MCMI = 1901.

KM#	Date	Mintage	Fine	VF	XF	Unc
503	1901	15.775	.40	1.50	3.50	20.00

KM#	Date	Mintage	Fine	VF	XF	Unc
518	1918	.600	.40	1.50	3.50	17.50
	1919	1.219	.40	1.50	3.50	17.50
	1920	1.251	.40	1.50	3.50	17.50
	1921	.853	.40	1.50	3.50	17.50
	1922	.347	.40	1.50	5.00	20.00
	1923	.956	.40	1.50	5.00	20.00
	1924	1.478	1.00	2.50	9.00	25.00
	1925	2.502	.30	1.25	3.00	17.50
	1926	1.807	.50	1.50	5.00	20.00
	1927	1.451	.30	1.25	3.00	17.50
	1928	1.514	.30	1.25	3.00	17.50
	1929	2.503	.30	1.25	3.00	17.50
	1930	2.398	.30	1.25	3.00	17.50
	1931	2.500	.25	1.00	2.50	17.50
	1932	.948	.25	1.00	2.50	17.50
	1933	1.314	.25	1.00	2.50	17.50
	1934	3.614	.25	1.00	2.50	17.50
	1935	3.442	.25	1.00	2.50	17.50

Cazique Tibirica
400th Anniversary of Colonization

KM#	Date	Mintage	Fine	VF	XF	Unc
527	1932	1.012	.50	1.00	2.50	7.00

Admiral Marques Tamandare

KM#	Date	Mintage	Fine	VF	XF	Unc
536	1936	3.928	.20	.50	1.50	3.00
	1937	7.905	.10	.35	1.00	2.50
	1938	8.618	.10	.35	1.00	2.50

Dr. Getulio Vargas
Fluted edge.

KM#	Date	Mintage	Fine	VF	XF	Unc
544	1938	8.106	.10	.20	.50	1.50
	1940	8.797	.10	.20	.50	1.50
	1942	1.285	.10	.20	.50	1.50

NOTE: The 1942 issue has a deeper yellow cast due to higher copper content.

200 REIS

COPPER-NICKEL
Date: MCMI = 1901.

KM#	Date	Mintage	Fine	VF	XF	Unc
504	1901	12.625	.60	1.50	2.00	13.50

KM#	Date	Mintage	Fine	VF	XF	Unc
519	1918	.625	.35	1.25	2.25	15.00
	1919	.882	.35	1.25	2.25	15.00
	1920	1.657	.35	1.25	2.25	15.00
	1921	1.135	.35	1.25	2.25	15.00
	1922	.678	.35	1.25	2.25	15.00
	1923	1.655	.35	1.25	2.25	15.00
	1924	1.750	.35	1.25	2.25	15.00
	1925	2.082	.35	1.25	2.25	15.00
	1926	.324	1.00	3.00	8.00	22.50
	1927	1.806	.35	1.25	2.25	15.00
	1928	.782	.35	1.25	2.25	15.00
	1929	2.440	.25	1.00	2.00	15.00
	1930	1.697	.25	1.00	2.00	15.00
	1931	1.830	.25	1.00	2.00	15.00
	1932	.761	.25	1.00	2.00	15.00
	1933	.173	.35	1.25	2.25	15.00
	1934	.612	.25	1.00	2.00	15.00
	1935	1.329	.25	1.00	2.00	15.00

400th Anniversary of Colonization

KM#	Date	Mintage	Fine	VF	XF	Unc
528	ND(1932)	.596	.75	1.75	5.00	17.50

Viscount de Maua

KM#	Date	Mintage	Fine	VF	XF	Unc
537	1936	2.256	.30	.75	2.25	9.00
	1937	6.506	.30	.75	2.25	9.00
	1938	5.787	.30	.75	2.25	9.00

Dr. Getulio Vargas
Fluted edge.

KM#	Date	Mintage	Fine	VF	XF	Unc
545	1938	7.666	.20	.50	1.00	3.00
	1940	10.161	.15	.40	.60	2.50
	1942	1.966	.15	.40	.60	2.50

NOTE: The 1942 issue has a yellow cast due to higher copper content.

300 REIS

COPPER-NICKEL
Antonio Carlos Gomes

KM#	Date	Mintage	Fine	VF	XF	Unc
538	1936	3.029	.30	1.50	4.50	12.50
	1937	4.507	.30	1.50	4.50	12.50
	1938	3.753	.30	1.50	4.50	12.50

Dr. Getulio Vargas
Fluted edge.

546	1938	12.080	.20	.35	.50	2.50
	1940	8.124	.20	.35	.50	2.50
	1942	2.020	.25	.40	.75	3.50

NOTE: The 1942 issue has a yellow cast due to higher copper content.

400 REIS

COPPER-NICKEL
Obv: Date: MCMI = 1901.

505	1901	5.531	1.25	2.50	6.50	27.50

515	1914	.646	15.00	35.00	75.00	150.00

NOTE: This is considered a pattern by many authorities.

520	1918	.491	.75	2.00	6.00	18.00
	1919	.891	.75	2.00	6.00	18.00
	1920	1.521	.75	2.00	6.00	18.00
	1921	.871	.50	1.75	6.00	18.00
	1922	1.275	.50	1.75	6.00	18.00
	1923	.764	.50	1.75	6.00	18.00
	1925	2.048	.50	1.75	6.00	18.00
	1926	1.034	.50	1.75	6.00	18.00
	1927	.738	.50	1.75	6.00	18.00
	1929	.869	.50	1.75	6.00	18.00
	1930	1.031	.50	1.75	6.00	18.00
	1931	1.431	.50	1.75	6.00	18.00
	1932	.588	.50	1.75	6.00	18.00
	1935	.225	.50	1.75	6.00	18.00

400th Anniversary of Colonization

KM#	Date	Mintage	Fine	VF	XF	Unc
529	ND(1932)	.416	1.00	3.00	5.00	12.00

539	1936	2.079	.50	1.00	3.00	10.00
	1937	3.111	.50	1.00	3.00	10.00
	1938	2.681	.50	1.00	3.00	10.00

Oswaldo Cruz

Dr. Getulio Vargas
Fluted edge.

547	1938	10.620	.25	.50	1.00	2.50
	1940	7.312	.25	.50	1.00	2.50
	1942	1.496	.25	.50	1.00	3.50

NOTE: The 1942 issue has a yellow cast due to higher copper content.

500 REIS

5.0000 g, .900 SILVER, .1446 oz ASW

506	1906	.352	BV	3.00	5.00	15.00
	1907	1.282	BV	3.00	5.00	15.00
	1908	.498	BV	3.00	5.00	15.00
	1911	8,000	20.00	35.00	70.00	150.00
	1912	*.222	20.00	40.00	80.00	200.00

509	1912	*Inc. Ab.	3.50	7.50	15.00	40.00

512	1913A	—	1.25	2.50	5.00	16.50

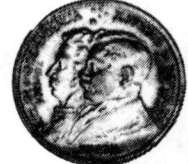 

ALUMINUM-BRONZE
Independence Centennial

521.1	ND(1922)					
		13.744	.25	.60	1.25	5.00

Error: BBASIL instead of BRASIL

KM#	Date	Mintage	Fine	VF	XF	Unc
521.2	ND(1922)					
		Inc. Ab.	17.50	35.00	55.00	120.00

 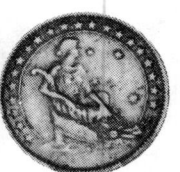

524	1924	7.400	.30	.75	1.50	7.50
	1927	2.725	.30	.75	1.50	7.50
	1928	9.432	.30	.75	1.50	7.50
	1930	.146	1.00	2.00	4.00	10.00

Joao Ramalho
400th Anniversary of Colonization

530	ND(1932)	.034	1.50	4.50	12.50	20.00

Diogo Feijo
4.00 g
Rev: CB on truncation.

533	1935	.014	2.00	9.00	25.00	45.00

5.00 g

540	1936	1.326	.60	1.25	5.00	10.00
	1937	Inc. Ab.	.60	1.25	5.00	10.00
	1938	—	.60	1.25	5.00	10.00

Joaquim Machado de Assis

549	1939	5.928	.50	1.00	4.00	9.00

1000 REIS

10.0000 g, .900 SILVER, .2894 oz ASW
Reeded edge.

507	1906	.420	BV	5.00	9.00	25.00
	1907	1.282	BV	5.00	9.00	25.00
	1908	1.624	BV	5.00	9.00	25.00
	1909	.816	BV	5.00	9.00	25.00
	1910	2.354	BV	5.00	9.00	25.00
	1911	2.810	BV	5.00	9.00	25.00
	1912	*1.570	BV	5.00	9.00	25.00

KM#	Date	Mintage	Fine	VF	XF	Unc
510	1912	*Inc. Ab.	4.00	6.00	10.00	35.00
	1913	2.525	4.00	6.00	10.00	35.00

| 513 | 1913A | — | BV | 3.50 | 6.50 | 18.50 |

ALUMINUM-BRONZE
Independence Centennial

522.1	ND(1922)					
		16.698	.40	.60	2.00	6.00

Error: BBASIL instead of BRASIL

522.2	ND(1922)					
		Inc. Ab.	2.50	6.00	12.50	20.00

Obv: Monogram left of knot.

525	1924	9.354	.50	1.25	2.50	8.00
	1925	6.205	.50	1.25	2.50	8.00
	1927	35.817	.50	1.25	2.50	8.00
	1928	1.899	.50	1.25	2.50	8.00
	1929	.083	3.50	15.00	45.00	100.00
	1930	.045	3.50	15.00	45.00	100.00
	1931	.200	1.00	5.00	8.50	15.00

Martim Affonso da Sousa
400th Anniversary of Colonization

| 531 | ND(1932) | .056 | 2.50 | 4.50 | 8.00 | 16.00 |

Jose de Anchieta

Rev: CB under chin.

KM#	Date	Mintage	Fine	VF	XF	Unc
534	1935	.138	1.00	3.00	5.00	12.00

Size reduced.
Rev: LGCB under chin.

541	1936	.926	.50	1.00	3.00	8.00
	1937	Inc. Ab.	.50	1.00	3.00	8.00
	1938 LGCB under chin					
	—		.50	1.00	3.00	8.00
	1938 CB under chin					
	—		.50	1.00	3.00	8.00

Tobias Barreto de Menezes
Rev: BR monogram right of bust.

| 550 | 1939 | 9.586 | .25 | .75 | 2.50 | 7.50 |

2000 REIS

20.0000 g, .900 SILVER, .5787 oz ASW

508	1906	.256	5.00	10.00	17.50	60.00
	1907	2.863	BV	6.50	12.00	50.00
	1908	1.707	BV	6.50	12.00	50.00
	1910	.585	5.00	10.00	17.50	60.00
	1911	1.929	BV	6.50	12.00	50.00
	1912	.741	5.00	10.00	17.50	60.00

511	1912	Inc. Ab.	6.50	12.50	25.00	60.00
	1913	.395	6.50	12.50	25.00	65.00

KM#	Date	Mintage	Fine	VF	XF	Unc
514	1913A	—	5.00	10.00	15.00	45.00

7.9000 g, .900 SILVER, .2285 oz ASW
Independence Centennial

| 523 | ND(1922) | 1.560 | BV | 3.00 | 4.00 | 9.00 |

7.9000 g, .500 SILVER, .1269 oz ASW

523a	ND(1922)					
		Inc. Ab.	BV	3.00	4.00	9.00

*NOTE: Struck in both .900 and .500 fine silver, but can only be distinguished by analysis (and color, on worn specimens).

526	1924	9.147	BV	1.50	4.00	13.00
	1925	.723	BV	1.50	4.00	13.00
	1926	1.787	BV	1.50	4.00	13.00
	1927	1.009	BV	2.50	5.00	15.00
	1928	1.250	BV	1.50	4.00	13.00
	1929	1.744	BV	1.50	4.00	13.00
	1930	1.240	BV	1.50	4.00	13.00
	1931	.546	BV	1.50	4.00	13.00
	1934	.938	BV	1.50	4.00	13.00

John III
400th Anniversary of Colonization

| 532 | ND(1932) | .695 | 2.00 | 2.50 | 5.00 | 15.00 |

Duke of Caxias
Rev: CB below chin.

| 535 | 1935 | 2.131 | BV | 1.50 | 4.00 | 13.00 |

ALUMINUM-BRONZE
Duke of Caxias
Reeded edge.

KM#	Date	Mintage	Fine	VF	XF	Unc
542	1936	.665	.50	1.00	2.00	6.00
	1937	Inc. Ab.	.50	1.00	2.00	6.00
	1938	—	2.50	5.00	12.50	30.00

Plain edge, polygonal planchet.

548	1937	—	25.00	50.00	125.00	300.00
	1938	—	.75	1.50	3.50	8.00

Floriano Peixoto

551	1939	5.048	.50	1.00	2.50	6.00

5000 REIS

10.0000 g, .600 SILVER, .1929 oz ASW
Alberto Santos Dumont

543	1936	1.986	BV	2.00	3.50	9.00
	1937	.414	BV	2.00	3.50	9.00
	1938	.994	BV	2.00	3.50	9.00

10,000 REIS

8.9645 g, .917 GOLD, .2643 oz AGW

496	1901	111 pcs.	150.00	250.00	550.00	1100.
	1902	—	—	—	Unique	—
	1903	391 pcs.	150.00	250.00	700.00	1150.
	1904	541 pcs.	150.00	250.00	700.00	1150.
	1906	572 pcs.	150.00	250.00	700.00	1150.
	1907	878 pcs.	150.00	250.00	600.00	1100.
	1908	689 pcs.	150.00	250.00	600.00	1100.
	1909	1,069	150.00	250.00	600.00	1100.
	1911	137 pcs.	175.00	350.00	800.00	1350.
	1914	969 pcs.	250.00	500.00	1500.	2400.
	1915	4,314	250.00	500.00	1400.	2000.
	1916	4,720	150.00	250.00	700.00	1150.
	1919	526 pcs.	150.00	250.00	700.00	1150.
	1921	2,435	150.00	250.00	600.00	1000.
	1922	6 pcs.	—	—	Rare	—

NOTE: Earlier dates (1889-1899) exist for this type.

20,000 REIS

17.9290 g, .917 GOLD, .5286 oz AGW

497	1901	784 pcs.	BV	350.00	700.00	1350.
	1902	884 pcs.	BV	350.00	700.00	1350.
	1903	675 pcs.	BV	350.00	700.00	1350.
	1904	444 pcs.	BV	350.00	700.00	1350.
	1906	396 pcs.	BV	500.00	900.00	1600.
	1907	3,310	BV	300.00	550.00	1100.
	1908	6,001	BV	300.00	550.00	1100.
	1909	4,427	BV	300.00	550.00	1100.

KM#	Date	Mintage	Fine	VF	XF	Unc
497	1910	5,119	BV	300.00	550.00	1100.
	1911	8,467	BV	300.00	550.00	1100.
	1912	4,878	BV	300.00	550.00	1100.
	1913	5,182	BV	300.00	600.00	1200.
	1914	1,980	BV	350.00	700.00	1400.
	1917	2,269	BV	400.00	800.00	1550.
	1918	1,216	BV	400.00	800.00	1550.
	1921	5,924	BV	300.00	800.00	1200.
	1922	2,681	BV	400.00	800.00	1550.

NOTE: Earlier dates (1889-1900) exist for this type.

MONETARY REFORM
1942-1967
100 Centavos = 1 Cruzeiro
10 CENTAVOS

COPPER-NICKEL
Getulio Vargas

KM#	Date	Mintage	VF	XF	Unc
555	1942	3.826	.35	.50	1.00
	1943	13.565	.25	.35	.75

ALUMINUM-BRONZE

555a	1943	Inc. Ab.	.25	.35	.75
	1944	12.617	.25	.60	1.00
	1945	24.674	.25	.60	1.00
	1946	35.159	.25	.60	1.00
	1947	20.664	.25	.35	.75

NOTE: KM#555 has a very light yellowish appearance while KM#555a is a deeper yellow.

Jose Bonifacio de Andrada e Silva

561	1947	Inc. Ab.	.15	.20	.35
	1948	45.041	.15	.20	.35
	1949	21.763	.15	.20	.35
	1950	16.330	.15	.20	.35
	1951	15.561	.10	.15	.35
	1952	10.966	.15	.20	.50
	1953	25.883	.10	.15	.35
	1954	17.031	.10	.15	.35
	1955	25.172	.10	.15	.35

ALUMINUM
National Arms

564	1956	.741	.10	.15	.50
	1957	25.311	.10	.15	.25
	1958	5.813	.10	.15	.25
	1959	2.611	.10	.15	.25
	1960	.624	.10	.15	.50
	1961	.951	.10	.15	.50

20 CENTAVOS

COPPER-NICKEL
Getulio Vargas

556	1942	3.007	.25	.50	1.00
	1943	13.392	.15	.40	.75

NOTE: KM#556 has a very light yellowish appearance while KM#556a is a deeper yellow.

ALUMINUM-BRONZE

556a	1943	Inc. Ab.	.15	.35	.75
	1944	12.673	.15	.35	.75
	1945	61.632	.15	.35	.60
	1946	31.526	.15	.35	.60
	1947	36.422	.15	.35	.75
	1948	39.671	.15	.35	.75

NOTE: Coins dated 1944 exist w/and w/o designer's initials and straight or curved backed 9 in date.

Ruy Barbosa

KM#	Date	Mintage	VF	XF	Unc
562	1948	Inc. Ab.	.15	.25	.50
	1949	24.805	.15	.25	.50
	1950	15.145	.15	.25	.50
	1951	14.964	.15	.25	.50
	1952	10.942	.15	.25	.50
	1953	25.585	.15	.25	.50
	1954	16.477	.15	.25	.50
	1955	25.122	.15	.25	.50
	1956	6.716	.15	.25	.50

ALUMINUM
National Arms

565	1956	Inc. Ab.	.10	.25	.50
	1957	27.110	.10	.20	.40
	1958	8.552	.10	.20	.40
	1959	4.810	.10	.20	.40
	1960	.510	.10	.25	.50
	1961	2.332	.10	.20	.40

NOTE: Varieties exist in the thickness of the planchet for year 1956.

50 CENTAVOS

COPPER-NICKEL
Getulio Vargas

557	1942	2.358	.40	.75	1.50
	1943	13.392	.35	.50	1.00

NOTE: KM557 has a very light yellowish appearance while KM#557a is a deeper yellow.

ALUMINUM-BRONZE

557a	1943	Inc. Ab.	.30	.50	1.00
	1944	12.102	.30	.50	1.00
	1945	73.222	.30	.50	1.00
	1946	13.941	.30	.50	1.00
	1947	23.588	.20	.50	1.00

General Eurico Gaspar Dutra

563	1948	32.023	.15	.25	.50
	1949	11.392	.15	.25	.50
	1950	7.804	.15	.35	.75
	1951	7.523	.15	.35	.75
	1952	6.863	.15	.35	.75
	1953	17.372	.15	.25	.50
	1954	11.353	.15	.25	.50
	1955	27.150	.15	.25	.50
	1956	32.130	.15	.25	.50

National Arms

566	1956	Inc. Ab.	.15	.25	.50

ALUMINUM

569	1957	49.350	.10	.20	.35
	1958	59.815	.10	.20	.35
	1959	32.891	.10	.20	.35
	1960	15.997	.10	.20	.35
	1961	18.456	.10	.20	.35

CRUZEIRO

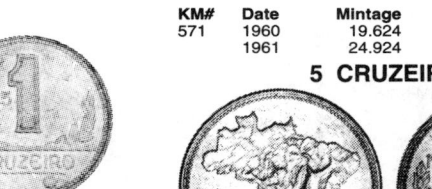

ALUMINUM-BRONZE

KM#	Date	Mintage	VF	XF	Unc
558	1942	.381	.50	1.00	3.50
	1943	2.728	.25	.50	1.00
	1944	3.820	.25	.50	1.00
	1945	32.544	.25	.50	.75
	1946	49.794	.25	.50	1.00
	1947	15.391	.25	.50	1.00
	1949	7.889	.25	.50	1.00
	1950	5.163	.25	.50	1.00
	1951	3.757	.25	.50	1.00
	1952	1.769	.50	1.00	3.50
	1953	5.195	.25	.50	1.00
	1954	1.145	.25	.50	1.50
	1955	1.758	.25	.50	1.00
	1956	.668	6.00	12.00	20.00

567	1956	Inc. Ab.	.20	.35	.65

ALUMINUM

570	1957	11.849	.20	.75	2.50
	1958	15.443	.20	1.00	3.00
	1959	25.010	.20	.75	2.50
	1960	35.267	.20	.75	2.50
	1961	22.181	.20	1.00	3.00

2 CRUZEIROS

ALUMINUM-BRONZE

559	1942	.276	.75	1.50	4.00
	1943	1.929	.25	.50	1.00
	1944	3.820	.25	.50	1.00
	1945	32.544	.20	.40	1.00
	1946	33.650	.20	.40	1.00
	1947	9.908	.20	.40	1.00
	1949	11.252	.20	.40	1.00
	1950	7.754	.25	.50	1.00
	1951	.390	.40	1.00	3.00
	1952	1.456	1.00	2.00	5.00
	1953	3.582	.20	.40	1.00
	1954	1.197	.25	1.00	2.00
	1955	1.838	.20	.50	1.00
	1956	—	2.00	4.00	10.00

568	1956	Inc. Ab.	.20	.40	1.50

ALUMINUM

571	1957	.194	.20	.30	1.25
	1958	13.687	.15	.25	1.00
	1959	20.894	.15	.25	1.00

KM#	Date	Mintage	VF	XF	Unc
571	1960	19.624	.15	.25	1.00
	1961	24.924	.15	.25	1.00

5 CRUZEIROS

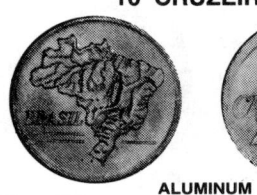

ALUMINUM-BRONZE

560	1942	.115	1.00	3.00	8.00
	1943	.222	.75	2.00	6.50

10 CRUZEIROS

ALUMINUM

572	1965	19.656	.10	.20	.50

20 CRUZEIROS

ALUMINUM

573	1965	25.930	.15	.25	.75

50 CRUZEIROS

COPPER-NICKEL

574	1965	18.001	.15	.35	1.00

MONETARY REFORM

1967-1985
1000 Old Cruzeiros = 1 Cruzeiro Novo (New)
100 Centavos = 1 (New) Cruzeiro

CENTAVO

STAINLESS STEEL

575.1	1967	57.499	—	—	.15

Thinner planchet.

575.2	1969	243.855	—	—	.15
	1975	—	—	.15	.30
	1976	—	—	.15	.30

F.A.O. Issue - Sugar Cane

585	1975	31.700	—	.15	.30
	1976	18.355	—	—	.20
	1977	.100	—	—	.20
	1978	.050	—	.15	.30

F.A.O. Issue - Soja

589	1979	.100	.15	.35	1.00
	1980	.060	.15	.35	1.00
	1981	.100	.15	.35	1.00
	1982	.100	.15	.35	1.00
	1983	—	.15	.35	1.00
	1984	—	.15	.35	1.00

---

2 CENTAVOS

STAINLESS STEEL

KM#	Date	Mintage	VF	XF	Unc
576.1	1967	65.226	—	—	.25

Thinner planchet.

576.2	1969	*134.298	—	—	.50
	1975	—	—	.25	.75
	1976	—	—	.25	.75

*NOTE: Mintage figure includes coins struck through 1974 dated 1969.

F.A.O. Issue - Soja

586	1975	31.400	—	—	.25
	1976	18.754	—	—	.25
	1977	.100	—	—	.25
	1978	.050	—	.20	.50

5 CENTAVOS

STAINLESS STEEL

577.1	1967	69.304	—	.20	.50

Thinner planchet.

577.2	1969	*345.071	—	.20	.50
	1975	—	—	.20	.50
	1976	—	—	.20	.50

*NOTE: Mintage figure includes coins struck through 1974 dated 1969.

F.A.O. Issue - Zebu
Rev: Plain 5.

587.1	1975	44.500	—	.20	.50
	1976	134.267	—	.20	.50
	1977	85.360	—	.20	.50
	1978	34.090	—	.20	.65

Rev: 5 over wavy lines.

587.2	1975	Inc. Ab.	—	.20	.50
	1976	Inc. Ab.	—	.20	.50
	1977	Inc. Ab.	—	.20	.50
	1978	Inc. Ab.	—	.20	.65

10 CENTAVOS

COPPER-NICKEL

578.1	1967	22.420	—	.20	.50

Thinner planchet.

578.2	1970	*134.070	—	.20	.40

*NOTE: Mintage figure includes coins struck through 1974 dated 1970.

STAINLESS STEEL

578.1a	1974	114.598	—	.20	.40
	1975	—	—	.20	.40
	1976	—	—	.20	.40
	1977	225.213	—	.20	.40
	1978	225.000	—	.20	.40
	1979	.100	—	.20	.40

20 CENTAVOS

COPPER-NICKEL

KM#	Date	Mintage	VF	XF	Unc
579.1	1967	123.610	—	.20	.50
	1970	—	—	.20	.50

Thinner planchet.

| 579.2 | 1970 | *384.894 | — | .20 | .60 |

*NOTE: Mintage figure includes coins struck through 1974 dated 1970.

STAINLESS STEEL

579.1a	1975	102.367	—	.20	.50
	1976	—	—	.20	.50
	1977	240.001	—	.20	.50
	1978	255.000	—	.20	.50
	1979	.116	—	.20	.50

50 CENTAVOS

NICKEL

580	1967	12.987	.25	.50	1.25

COPPER-NICKEL

580a	1970	503.895	.20	.35	1.00
	1975	—	.20	.35	1.00

STAINLESS STEEL

580b	1975	79.062	.20	.35	1.00
	1976	—	.20	.35	1.00
	1977	160.019	.20	.35	1.00
	1978	200.000	.20	.35	1.00
	1979	.104	.20	.35	1.00

CRUZEIRO

NICKEL

581	1970	*48.930	.25	.50	1.00
	1970	.018	—	Proof	3.00
	1974	24.135	.20	.45	1.00

*NOTE: Mintage figure includes coins struck through 1972 dated 1970.

COPPER-NICKEL

581a	1975	21.613	.20	.45	1.00
	1976	—	.20	.45	1.00
	1977	.098	.20	.45	1.00
	1978	.077	.20	.45	1.00

NICKEL
150th Anniversary of Independence

582	1972 lettered edge				
		5.600	.35	.85	1.65
	1972 plain edge				
		Inc. Ab.	.35	.85	1.65
	1972 lettered edge				
		—	—	Proof	3.00
	1972 plain edge				
		—	—	Proof	3.00

NOTE: Coins w/plain edge are believed by some to be errors.

STAINLESS STEEL
Sugar Cane

KM#	Date	Mintage	VF	XF	Unc
590	1979	.596	.15	.25	.65
	1980	690.497	.15	.25	.65
	1981	560.000	.15	.25	.65
	1982	300.000	.15	.25	.65
	1983	.100	.15	.25	.65
	1984	62.100	.15	.25	.65

F.A.O. Issue - Sugar Cane

598	1985	10.000	—	.20	.50

5 CRUZEIROS

STAINLESS STEEL
Coffee Plant

591	1980	288.200	.20	.35	.75
	1981	82.000	.20	.35	.75
	1982	108.000	.20	.35	.75
	1983	113.400	.20	.35	.75
	1984	243.000	.20	.35	.75

F.A.O. Issue - Coffee

599	1985	10.000	.20	.40	.85

10 CRUZEIROS

11.3000 g, .800 SILVER, .2906 oz ASW
10th Anniversary of Central Bank

588	1975	.020	—	—	55.00

STAINLESS STEEL

592.1	1980	100.010	—	.50	.75
	1981	200.000	—	.50	.75
	1982	331.000	—	.50	.75
	1983	390.000	—	.50	.75
	1984	390.000	—	.50	.75

Reduced weight.

592.2	1985	201.000	—	.50	.75
	1986	—	—	.50	.75

20 CRUZEIROS

STAINLESS STEEL
Francis of Assisi Church

KM#	Date	Mintage	VF	XF	Unc
593.1	1981	88.297	—	.25	.85
	1982	158.200	—	.20	.65
	1983	312.000	—	.20	.65
	1984	226.000	—	.20	.65

Reduced weight.

593.2	1985	205.000	—	.20	.65
	1986	—	—	.20	.65

50 CRUZEIROS

STAINLESS STEEL

594.1	1981	57.000	—	.35	1.00
	1982	134.000	—	.20	.65
	1983	181.800	—	.20	.65
	1984	292.418	—	.20	.65

Reduced weight.

594.2	1985	180.000	—	.20	.65
	1986	—	—	.20	.65

100 CRUZEIROS

STAINLESS STEEL

595	1985	162.000	—	.20	.40
	1986	—	—	—	.35

200 CRUZEIROS

STAINLESS STEEL

596	1985	55.000	—	.25	.50
	1986	—	—	—	.40

500 CRUZEIROS

STAINLESS STEEL

597	1985	74.000	—	.35	1.00
	1986	—	—	—	.65

MONETARY REFORM

1986-1989
1,000 Cruzeiros Novos = 1 Cruzado
100 Centavos = 1 Cruzado

CENTAVO

STAINLESS STEEL

600	1986	100.000	—	—	.15
	1987	1.000	—	—	.20
	1988	1.000	—	—	.20

5 CENTAVOS

STAINLESS STEEL

KM#	Date	Mintage	VF	XF	Unc
601	1986	99.282	—	—	.15
	1987	1.000	—	—	.20
	1988	1.000	—	—	.20

10 CENTAVOS

STAINLESS STEEL

602	1986	200.000	—	—	.15
	1987	245.628	—	—	.15
	1988	21.293	—	—	.20

20 CENTAVOS

STAINLESS STEEL

603	1986	140.000	—	—	.20
	1987	157.500	—	—	.20
	1988	16.000	—	—	.25

50 CENTAVOS

STAINLESS STEEL

604	1986	200.000	—	—	.35
	1987	201.884	—	—	.35
	1988	131.255	—	—	.35

CRUZADO

STAINLESS STEEL

605	1986	—	—	—	1.00
	1987	383.087	—	—	.45
	1988	321.216	—	—	.45

5 CRUZADOS

STAINLESS STEEL

606	1986	—	—	—	1.50
	1987	141.000	—	—	.65
	1988	291.906	—	—	.65

10 CRUZADOS

STAINLESS STEEL

607	1987	131.500	—	—	1.75
	1988	457.977	—	—	.85

100 CRUZADOS

STAINLESS STEEL
Abolition of Slavery Centennial - Male

KM#	Date	Mintage	VF	XF	Unc
608	ND(1988)	.200	—	1.00	3.00

Abolition of Slavery Centennial - Female

609	ND(1988)	.200	—	1.00	3.00

Abolition of Slavery Centennial - Child

610	ND(1988)	.200	—	1.00	3.00

MONETARY REFORM

1989 - 1990
1,000 Old Cruzados = 1 Novo Cruzado

CENTAVO

STAINLESS STEEL

611	1989	—	—	—	.35
	1990	—	—	—	.35

5 CENTAVOS

STAINLESS STEEL

612	1989	—	—	—	.35
	1990	—	—	—	.35

10 CENTAVOS

STAINLESS STEEL

613	1989	—	—	—	.45
	1990	—	—	—	.45

50 CENTAVOS

STAINLESS STEEL

614	1989	—	—	—	.60
	1990	—	—	—	.60

NOVO CRUZADO

STAINLESS STEEL
Centennial of the Republic

KM#	Date	Mintage	VF	XF	Unc
615	ND(1989)	—	—	—	1.75

MONETARY REFORM

1990 - 1993
100 Centavos = 1 Cruzeiro
1 Novo Cruzado = 1 Cruzeiro

CRUZEIRO

STAINLESS STEEL

617	1990	—	—	—	.35
	1991	—	—	—	.35
	1992	—	—	—	.35

5 CRUZEIROS

STAINLESS STEEL

618	1990	—	—	—	.45
	1991	—	—	—	.45
	1992	—	—	—	.45

10 CRUZEIROS

STAINLESS STEEL

619	1990	—	—	—	.50
	1991	—	—	—	.50
	1992	—	—	—	.50

50 CRUZEIROS

STAINLESS STEEL

620.1	1990	—	—	—	.65

Thinner planchet.

620.2	1991	—	—	—	.60
	1992	—	—	—	.60

100 CRUZEIROS

STAINLESS STEEL
Manatee

623	1992	—	—	—	.65
	1993	—	—	—	.65

500 CRUZEIROS

STAINLESS STEEL
Loggerhead Sea Turtle

KM#	Date	Mintage	VF	XF	Unc
624	1992	—	—	—	.75
	1993	—	—	—	.75

1000 CRUZEIROS

STAINLESS STEEL
Fish - Acara

626	1992	—	—	—	.85
	1993	—	—	—	.85

5000 CRUZEIROS

STAINLESS STEEL
200th Anniversary of Tiradentes' Death

625	ND(1992)	—	—	—	2.50

MONETARY REFORM
1993 - June 30, 1994
1,000 Cruzeiros = 1 Cruzeiro Real

5 CRUZEIROS REALS

STAINLESS STEEL
Macaw Parrots - Arara

627	1993	—	—	—	.60
	1994	—	—	—	.60

10 CRUZEIROS REALS

STAINLESS STEEL
Anteater - Tamandua

628	1993	—	—	—	.75
	1994	—	—	—	.75

50 CRUZEIROS REALS

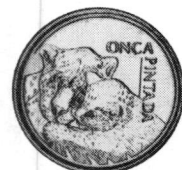

STAINLESS STEEL
Mother Jaguar and Cub

629	1993	—	—	—	.85
	1994	—	—	—	.85

100 CRUZEIROS REALS

STAINLESS STEEL
Maned Wolf

KM#	Date	Mintage	VF	XF	Unc
630	1993	—	—	—	1.50
	1994	—	—	—	1.50

MONETARY REFORM
July 1, 1994 -
2,750 Cruzeiros Reals = 1 Real
100 Centavos = 1 Real

CENTAVO

STAINLESS STEEL

631	1994	—	—	—	.25
	1995	—	—	—	.25
	1996	—	—	—	.25
	1997	—	—	—	.25

COPPER-PLATED STEEL
Cabral
Obv: Cabral's portrait. Rev: Denomination.

647	1998	—	—	—	.20

5 CENTAVOS

STAINLESS STEEL

632	1994	—	—	—	.30
	1995	—	—	—	.30
	1996	—	—	—	.30
	1997	—	—	—	.30

COPPER-PLATED STEEL
Tiradentes
Obv: Tiradente's portrait. Rev: Denomination.

648	1998	—	—	—	.25

10 CENTAVOS

STAINLESS STEEL

633	1994	—	—	—	.40
	1995	—	—	—	.40
	1996	—	—	—	.40
	1997	—	—	—	.40

F.A.O. - Seedling in Hand

KM#	Date	Mintage	VF	XF	Unc
641	1995	10.000	—	—	.50

BRASS-PLATED STEEL
Pedro I
Obv: Pedro's portrait and Horseman.
Rev: Denomination.

649	1998	—	—	—	.35

25 CENTAVOS

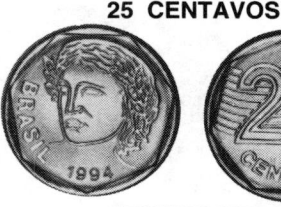 

STAINLESS STEEL

634	1994	—	—	—	.60
	1995	—	—	—	.60

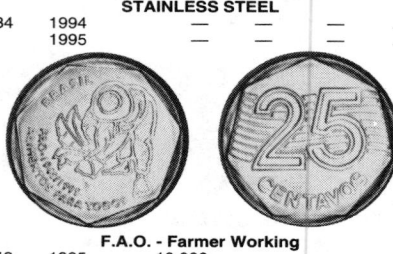

F.A.O. - Farmer Working

642	1995	10.000	—	—	.65

BRASS-PLATED STEEL
Deodoro
Obv: Deodoro's portrait and national emblem.
Rev: Denomination.

650	1998	—	—	—	.50

50 CENTAVOS

STAINLESS STEEL

635	1994	—	—	—	1.00
	1995	—	—	—	1.00

COPPER-NICKEL
Rio Branco
Obv: Rio Branco's portrait. Rev: Denomination.

651	1998	—	—	—	1.00

REAL

STAINLESS STEEL

636	1994	—	—	—	2.00
	1997	—	—	—	2.00

COPPER-NICKEL center in BRASS ring
Obv: Allegorical portrait. Rev: Denomination.

KM#	Date	Mintage	VF	XF	Unc
652	1998	—	—	—	2.50

BRITISH VIRGIN IS.

The Colony of the Virgin Islands, a British colony situated in the Caribbean Sea northeast of Puerto Rico and west of the Leeward Islands, has an area of 59 sq. mi. (155 sq. km.) and a population of 13,000. Capital: Road Town. The principal islands of the 36-island group are Tortola, Virgin Gorda, Anegada, and Jost Van Dyke. The chief industries are fishing and stock raising. Fish, livestock and bananas are exported.

The Virgin Islands were discovered by Columbus in 1493, and named by him, Las Virgienes, in honor of St. Ursula and her companions. The British Virgin Islands were formerly part of the administration of the Leeward Islands but received a separate administration as a Crown Colony in 1950. A new constitution promulgated in 1967 provided for a ministerial form of government headed by the Governor.

The Government of the British Virgin Islands issued the first official coinage in its history on June 30, 1973, in honor of 300 years of constitutional government in the islands. U.S. coins and currency continue to be the primary medium of exchange, though the coinage of the British Virgin Islands is legal tender.

RULERS

British

MINT MARKS

FM - Franklin Mint, U.S.A.*

*NOTE: From 1975-1985 the Franklin Mint produced coinage in up to 3 different qualities. Qualities of issue are designated in ( ) after each date and are defined as follows:

(M) MATTE - Normal circulation strike or a dull finish produced by sandblasting special uncirculated (polish finish) or proof quality dies.

(U) SPECIAL UNCIRCULATED - Polished or proof-like in appearance without any frosted features.

(P) PROOF - The highest quality obtainable having mirror-like fields and frosted features.

MONETARY SYSTEM

100 Cents = 1 Dollar

CENT

BRONZE
Green-throated Carib and Antillean Crested Hummingbird

KM#	Date	Mintage	VF	XF	Unc
1	1973FM	.053	—	.10	.50
	1973FM(P)	.181	—	Proof	1.00
	1974FM	.022	—	.10	.50
	1974FM(P)	.094	—	Proof	1.00
	1975FM(M)	6,000	—	.10	.75
	1975FM(U)	2,351	—	.10	.50
	1975FM(P)	.032	—	Proof	1.00
	1976FM(M)	.012	—	.10	.50
	1976FM(U)	996 pcs.	—	.10	.50
	1976FM(P)	.015	—	Proof	1.00
	1977FM(M)	500 pcs.	—	.25	2.00
	1977FM(U)	782 pcs.	—	.10	.50
	1977FM(P)	7,218	—	Proof	1.00
	1978FM(U)	1,443	—	.10	.50
	1978FM(P)	7,059	—	Proof	1.00
	1979FM(U)	680 pcs.	—	.10	.50
	1979FM(P)	5,304	—	Proof	1.00
	1980FM(U)	1,007	—	.10	.50
	1980FM(P)	3,421	—	Proof	1.00
	1981FM(U)	472 pcs.	—	.10	.50
	1981FM(P)	1,124	—	Proof	1.50
	1982FM(U)	—	—	.10	.50
	1982FM(P)	—	—	Proof	1.50
	1983FM(U)	—	—	.10	.50
	1983FM(P)	—	—	Proof	1.50
	1984FM(P)	—	—	Proof	1.50

5 CENTS

COPPER-NICKEL
Zenaida Dove

KM#	Date	Mintage	VF	XF	Unc
2	1973FM	.026	—	.15	.75
	1973FM(P)	.181	—	Proof	1.25
	1974FM	.018	—	.15	.75
	1974FM(P)	.094	—	Proof	1.25
	1975FM(M)	3,800	—	.20	1.00
	1975FM(U)	2,351	—	.15	.75
	1975FM(P)	.032	—	Proof	1.25
	1976FM(M)	4,800	—	.20	1.00
	1976FM(U)	996 pcs.	—	.15	.75
	1976FM(P)	.015	—	Proof	1.25
	1977FM(M)	500 pcs.	—	.35	3.50
	1977FM(U)	782 pcs.	—	.15	.75
	1977FM(P)	7,218	—	Proof	1.25
	1978FM(U)	1,443	—	.15	.75
	1978FM(P)	7,059	—	Proof	1.25
	1979FM(U)	680 pcs.	—	.15	.75
	1979FM(P)	5,304	—	Proof	1.25
	1980FM(U)	1,007	—	.15	.75
	1980FM(P)	3,421	—	Proof	1.25
	1981FM(U)	472 pcs.	—	.15	.75
	1981FM(P)	1,124	—	Proof	1.25
	1982FM(U)	—	—	.15	.75
	1982FM(P)	—	—	Proof	1.25
	1983FM(U)	—	—	.15	.75
	1983FM(P)	—	—	Proof	1.25
	1984FM(P)	—	—	Proof	1.25

10 CENTS

COPPER-NICKEL
Ringed Kingfisher

KM#	Date	Mintage	VF	XF	Unc
3	1973FM(U)	.023	—	.20	1.00
	1973FM(P)	.181	—	Proof	1.50
	1974FM(U)	.013	—	.20	1.00
	1974FM(P)	.094	—	Proof	1.50
	1975FM(M)	2,000	—	.20	1.25
	1975FM(U)	2,351	—	.20	1.00
	1975FM(P)	.032	—	Proof	1.50
	1976FM(M)	3,000	—	.20	1.00
	1976FM(U)	996 pcs.	—	.20	1.00
	1976FM(P)	.015	—	Proof	1.50
	1977FM(M)	500 pcs.	—	.45	4.00
	1977FM(U)	782 pcs.	—	.20	1.00
	1977FM(P)	7,218	—	Proof	1.50
	1978FM(U)	1,443	—	.20	1.00
	1978FM(P)	7,059	—	Proof	1.50
	1979FM(U)	680 pcs.	—	.20	1.00
	1979FM(P)	5,304	—	Proof	1.50
	1980FM(U)	1,007	—	.20	1.00
	1980FM(P)	3,421	—	Proof	1.50
	1981FM(U)	472 pcs.	—	.20	1.00
	1981FM(P)	1,124	—	Proof	1.50
	1982FM(U)	—	—	.20	1.00
	1982FM(P)	—	—	Proof	1.50
	1983FM(U)	—	—	.20	1.00
	1983FM(P)	—	—	Proof	1.50
	1984FM(P)	—	—	Proof	1.50

25 CENTS

COPPER-NICKEL
Mangrove Cuckoo

KM#	Date	Mintage	VF	XF	Unc
4	1973FM	.021	—	.30	1.50
	1973FM(P)	.181	—	Proof	1.75
	1974FM	.012	—	.30	1.50
	1974FM(P)	.094	—	Proof	1.75
	1975FM(M)	1,000	—	.35	3.00
	1975FM(U)	2,351	—	.30	1.50
	1975FM(P)	.032	—	Proof	1.75
	1976FM(M)	2,000	—	.30	2.00
	1976FM(U)	996 pcs.	—	.30	1.50
	1976FM(P)	.015	—	Proof	1.75
	1977FM(M)	500 pcs.	—	.50	5.00
	1977FM(U)	782 pcs.	—	.30	1.50
	1977FM(P)	7,218	—	Proof	1.75
	1978FM(U)	1,443	—	.30	1.50
	1978FM(P)	7,059	—	Proof	1.75
	1979FM(U)	680 pcs.	—	.30	1.50
	1979FM(P)	5,304	—	Proof	1.75
	1980FM(U)	1,007	—	.30	1.50
	1980FM(P)	3,421	—	Proof	1.75
	1981FM(U)	472 pcs.	—	.30	1.50
	1981FM(P)	1,124	—	Proof	1.75
	1982FM(U)	—	—	.30	1.50
	1982FM(P)	—	—	Proof	1.75
	1983FM(U)	—	—	.30	1.50
	1983FM(P)	—	—	Proof	1.75
	1984FM(P)	—	—	Proof	1.75

50 CENTS

KM#	Date	Mintage	VF	XF	Unc
6a	1974FM(P)	.094	—	Proof	9.00
	1975FM(P)	.032	—	Proof	11.00
	1976FM(P)	.015	—	Proof	11.00
	1977FM(P)	7,218	—	Proof	12.00
	1978FM(P)	7,059	—	Proof	12.00
	1979FM(P)	5,304	—	Proof	12.50
	1980FM(P)	3,421	—	Proof	13.50
	1981FM(P)	1,124	—	Proof	14.50
	1982FM(P)	1,865	—	Proof	15.00
	1983FM(P)	478 pcs.	—	Proof	22.00
	1984FM(P)	—	—	Proof	15.00

COPPER-NICKEL
Brown Pelican

KM#	Date	Mintage	VF	XF	Unc
5	1973FM	.020	—	.75	2.50
	1973FM(P)	.181	—	Proof	2.50
	1974FM	.012	—	.75	2.00
	1974FM(P)	.094	—	Proof	2.50
	1975FM(M)	1,000	—	1.00	5.00
	1975FM(U)	2,351	—	.75	2.50
	1975FM(P)	.032	—	Proof	2.50
	1976FM(M)	2,000	—	.75	3.00
	1976FM(U)	996 pcs.	—	.75	2.50
	1976FM(P)	.015	—	Proof	2.50
	1977FM(M)	600 pcs.	—	1.00	6.00
	1977FM(U)	782 pcs.	—	.75	2.50
	1977FM(P)	7,218	—	Proof	2.50
	1978FM(U)	1,543	—	.75	2.50
	1978FM(P)	7,059	—	Proof	2.50
	1979FM(U)	680 pcs.	—	.75	2.50
	1979FM(P)	5,304	—	Proof	2.50
	1980FM(U)	1,007	—	.75	2.50
	1980FM(P)	3,421	—	Proof	2.50
	1981FM(U)	472 pcs.	—	.75	2.50
	1981FM(P)	1,124	—	Proof	2.50
	1982FM(U)	—	—	.75	2.50
	1982FM(P)	—	—	Proof	2.50
	1983FM(U)	—	—	.75	2.50
	1983FM(P)	—	—	Proof	2.50
	1984FM(P)	—	—	Proof	2.50

DOLLAR

COPPER-NICKEL
Magnificent Frigate

6	1974FM(M)	.012	—	2.50	6.50
	1974FM(U)	—	—	—	—
	1975FM(M)	800 pcs.	—	2.50	8.00
	1975FM(U)	2,351	—	2.50	6.50
	1976FM(M)	1,800	—	2.50	6.50
	1976FM(U)	996 pcs.	—	2.50	8.00
	1977FM(M)	800 pcs.	—	2.50	8.00
	1977FM(U)	782 pcs.	—	2.50	8.00
	1978FM(U)	1,743	—	2.50	6.50
	1979FM(U)	680 pcs.	—	2.50	8.00
	1980FM(U)	1,007	—	2.50	6.50
	1981FM(U)	472 pcs.	—	2.50	8.00
	1982FM(U)	—	—	2.50	8.00
	1983FM(U)	—	—	2.50	8.00

25.7000 g, .925 SILVER, .7643 oz ASW

6a	1973FM(M)	.020	—	8.00	11.00
	1973FM(P)	.181	—	Proof	9.00

BRITISH WEST AFRICA

British West Africa was an administrative grouping of the four former British West African colonies of Gambia, Sierra Leone, Nigeria and Gold Coast (now Ghana). All are now independent republics and members of the British Commonwealth of Nations. See separate entries for individual statistics and history.

The Bank of British West Africa became the banker to the Colonial Government in 1894 and held this status until 1912. As such they were responsible for maintaining a proper supply of silver coinage for the colonies.

Through the subsidiary efforts of the Governor of Lagos, Nigeria a specific British West African coinage was put into use between 1907 and 1911. These coins bear the inscription, NIGERIA-BRITISH WEST AFRICA.

The four colonies were supplied with a common coinage and banknotes by the West African Currency Board from 1912 through 1958. This coinage bore the inscription BRITISH WEST AFRICA. The coinage, which includes three denominations of 1936 bearing the name of Edward VIII, is obsolete.

For later coinage see Gambia, Ghana, Sierra Leone and Nigeria.

RULERS
British, until 1958

MINT MARKS
G-J.R. Gaunt & Sons, Birmingham
H - Heaton Mint, Birmingham
K, KN - King's Norton, Birmingham
SA - Pretoria, South Africa
No mm - Royal Mint, London

MONETARY SYSTEM
12 Pence = 1 Shilling
20 Shillings = 1 Pound

1/10 PENNY

ALUMINUM

KM#	Date	Mintage	Fine	VF	XF	Unc
1	1907	1.254	2.00	4.00	10.00	20.00
	1908	8.363	1.00	3.00	6.00	15.00
	1908	—	—	—	Proof	250.00

COPPER-NICKEL

3	1908	9.600	.30	.50	1.00	2.00
	1909	4.800	.40	.75	1.50	5.00
	1910	7.200	.50	1.00	2.00	7.50

4	1911H	7.200	1.50	3.50	7.50	15.00

Rev. leg: W/o NIGERIA.

7	1912H	10.800	.30	.75	1.50	4.00
	1913	4.632	1.00	2.00	3.50	6.50
	1913H	1.080	.30	.75	1.50	3.50
	1914	1.200	3.00	5.00	10.00	22.50
	1914H	20.088	.50	1.25	2.00	5.00

KM#	Date	Mintage	Fine	VF	XF	Unc
7	1915H	10.032	.30	.75	1.50	5.00
	1916H	.480	25.00	50.00	75.00	150.00
	1917H	9.384	2.00	3.00	5.00	15.00
	1919H	.912	1.25	2.00	4.00	7.50
	1919KN	.480	10.00	25.00	50.00	75.00
	1920H	1.560	2.00	3.00	5.00	10.00
	1920KN	12.996	.40	1.00	3.00	5.00
	1920KN	—	—	—	Proof	125.00
	1922KN	7.265	1.00	1.75	4.50	12.00
	1923KN	12.000	.30	.75	1.50	5.00
	1925	2.400	5.00	10.00	20.00	40.00
	1925H	12.000	2.00	3.00	5.00	12.00
	1925KN	12.000	.75	1.50	3.00	8.00
	1926	12.000	.75	1.50	2.50	6.00
	1927	3.984	.20	.50	1.50	3.00
	1927	—	—	—	Proof	150.00
	1928	11.760	.20	.50	1.50	3.00
	1928	—	—	—	Proof	150.00
	1928H	2.964	.20	.50	1.50	3.00
	1928KN	3.151	2.00	3.00	6.00	15.00
	1930	9.600	2.00	3.00	6.00	15.00
	1930	—	—	—	Proof	150.00
	1931	9.840	.20	.50	1.00	3.00
	1931	—	—	—	Proof	150.00
	1932	3.600	.20	.50	1.50	5.00
	1932	—	—	—	Proof	150.00
	1933	7.200	.20	.50	1.50	3.50
	1933	—	—	—	Proof	150.00
	1934	4.800	.75	1.50	3.00	6.00
	1934	—	—	—	Proof	150.00
	1935	13.200	.75	1.50	3.00	7.50
	1935	—	—	—	Proof	150.00
	1936	9.720	.20	.50	1.00	3.00
	1936	—	—	—	Proof	150.00

KM#	Date	Mintage	Fine	VF	XF	Unc
14	1936	5.880	.25	.50	1.00	2.50
	1936	—	—	—	Proof	200.00
	1936H	1.404	50.00	75.00	125.00	250.00
	1936H	—	—	—	Proof	275.00
	1936KN	3.000	1.00	2.00	3.50	9.00
	1936KN	—	—	—	Proof	200.00

KM#	Date	Mintage	Fine	VF	XF	Unc
20	1938	12.000	.10	.25	.50	1.50
	1938	—	—	—	Proof	125.00
	1938H	1.596	5.00	8.00	12.00	22.50
	1938H	—	—	—	Proof	100.00
	1939	9.840	.25	.50	1.00	3.50
	1939	—	—	—	Proof	200.00
	1940	13.920	.25	.50	1.00	2.00
	1940	—	—	—	Proof	125.00
	1941	16.560	1.00	2.00	4.00	8.00
	1941	—	—	—	Proof	125.00
	1942	12.360	1.00	2.50	4.50	10.00
	1942	—	—	—	Proof	125.00
	1943	22.560	1.00	2.50	5.00	10.00
	1944	10.440	1.00	2.50	5.00	10.00
	1945	25.706	.50	1.00	1.75	6.00
	1945	—	—	—	Proof	125.00
	1946	2.803	1.00	2.00	4.00	9.00
	1946	—	—	—	Proof	125.00
	1946H	5.004	1.00	2.00	4.00	9.00
	1946KN	1.152	.25	.50	1.00	3.00
	1946KN	—	—	—	Proof	125.00
	1947	4.202	.25	.50	1.00	3.50
	1947	—	—	—	Proof	125.00
	1947KN	3.900	200.00	300.00	500.00	600.00

Obv. leg: W/o IND: IMP:

KM#	Date	Mintage	Fine	VF	XF	Unc
26	1949H	3.700	1.00	2.00	3.00	6.00
	1949KN	3.036	1.00	2.00	3.00	5.00
	1950KN	13.200	.25	.50	1.00	2.50

BRONZE

KM#	Date	Mintage	Fine	VF	XF	Unc
26a	1952	15.060	.50	1.00	2.00	6.00
	1952	—	—	—	Proof	150.00

KM#	Date	Mintage	Fine	VF	XF	Unc
32	1954	4.800	.50	1.00	2.00	4.00
	1954	—	—	—	Proof	150.00
	1956	2.400	75.00	150.00	300.00	600.00
	1956	—	—	—	Proof	750.00
	1957	7.200	60.00	120.00	220.00	325.00
	1957	—	—	—	Proof	600.00

1/2 PENNY

COPPER-NICKEL

KM#	Date	Mintage	Fine	VF	XF	Unc
5	1911H	3.360	4.00	12.00	25.00	40.00

Rev. leg: W/o NIGERIA.

KM#	Date	Mintage	Fine	VF	XF	Unc
8	1912H	3.120	2.00	5.00	7.00	20.00
	1913	—	200.00	300.00	400.00	600.00
	1913H	.216	5.00	10.00	17.50	30.00
	1914	1.622	10.00	20.00	35.00	60.00
	1914H	.586	15.00	25.00	40.00	75.00
	1914K	3.360	3.00	6.00	17.50	30.00
	1914K*	—	—	—	Proof	225.00
	1915H	3.577	1.00	2.00	4.00	15.00
	1916H	4.046	1.00	3.00	5.00	15.00
	1917H	.214	6.00	12.00	28.00	50.00
	1918H	.490	2.50	5.00	10.00	30.00
	1919H	4.950	1.25	2.50	6.00	20.00
	1919KN	3.861	1.25	2.50	7.50	25.00
	1920H	26.285	1.50	3.00	7.50	15.00
	1920KN	13.844	.50	3.00	8.50	16.50
	1922KN	5.817	300.00	500.00	750.00	1200.
	1927	.528	20.00	30.00	65.00	135.00
	1927	—	—	—	Proof	225.00
	1929	.336	6.00	22.00	47.50	95.00
	1929	—	—	—	Proof	225.00
	1931	.096	500.00	800.00	1200.	1500.
	1931	—	—	—	Proof	225.00
	1932	.960	2.50	15.00	35.00	55.00
	1932	—	—	—	Proof	225.00
	1933	2.122	12.00	23.50	55.00	110.00
	1933	—	—	—	Proof	225.00
	1934	1.694	2.50	15.00	35.00	75.00
	1934	—	—	—	Proof	225.00
	1935	3.271	1.00	3.00	18.00	35.00
	1935	—	—	—	Proof	225.00
	1936	5.400	2.50	5.00	18.00	32.00
	1936	—	—	—	Proof	225.00

***NOTE:** The 1914K was issued with East Africa KM#11 in a double (4 pc.) specimen set.

KM#	Date	Mintage	Fine	VF	XF	Unc
15	1936	14.760	.25	.50	1.00	2.50
	1936	—	—	—	Proof	200.00
	1936H	2.400	1.00	2.00	5.00	12.50
	1936H	—	—	—	Proof	200.00
	1936KN	2.298	.65	1.25	2.25	4.00
	1936KN	—	—	—	Proof	200.00

KM#	Date	Mintage	Fine	VF	XF	Unc
18	1937H	4.800	.40	.85	1.50	4.00
18	1937H	—	—	—	Proof	125.00
	1937KN	5.577	.40	.85	3.00	5.00
	1940KN	2.410	2.00	4.00	6.00	15.00
	1940KN	—	—	—	Proof	125.00
	1941H	2.400	.40	2.00	4.00	12.00
	1942	4.800	.40	.85	2.00	8.50
	1943	3.360	.50	1.00	5.00	10.00
	1944	3.600	1.00	3.00	7.00	20.00
	1944	—	—	—	Proof	125.00
	1946	3.600	.25	1.00	3.00	7.00
	1946	—	—	—	Proof	125.00
	1947H	15.218	.35	.75	1.25	5.00
	1947KN	12.000	.40	.85	2.00	6.00

Obv. leg: W/o IND: IMP:

KM#	Date	Mintage	Fine	VF	XF	Unc
27	1949H	5.909	1.50	3.50	8.00	22.00
	1949KN	3.413	1.50	3.50	8.00	25.00
	1951	3.468	1.50	3.50	9.00	25.00
	1951	—	—	—	Proof	250.00

BRONZE

KM#	Date	Mintage	Fine	VF	XF	Unc
27a	1952	11.332	.25	.50	1.50	5.50
	1952	—	—	—	Proof	150.00
	1952H	27.603	.20	.35	.75	2.00
	1952KN	4.800	.50	1.00	3.00	7.50

PENNY

COPPER-NICKEL

KM#	Date	Mintage	Fine	VF	XF	Unc
2	1907	.863	2.00	5.00	9.00	20.00
	1908	3.217	2.00	4.00	8.00	17.50
	1909	.960	3.50	9.00	18.00	45.00
	1910	2.520	2.75	7.00	12.00	25.00

KM#	Date	Mintage	Fine	VF	XF	Unc
6	1911H	1.920	10.00	30.00	70.00	125.00

Rev. leg: W/o NIGERIA.

KM#	Date	Mintage	Fine	VF	XF	Unc
9	1912H	1.560	1.50	3.00	7.50	22.50
	1913	1.680	7.50	15.00	30.00	75.00
	1913H	.144	5.00	10.00	17.50	35.00
	1914	3.000	2.50	5.00	10.00	22.50
	1914H	.072	35.00	50.00	100.00	200.00
	1915H	3.295	1.25	2.00	5.00	15.00
	1916H	3.461	1.25	2.00	7.00	14.00
	1917H	.444	5.00	7.00	15.00	45.00
	1918H	.994	7.50	15.00	35.00	75.00
	1919H	21.864	1.25	2.50	5.00	15.00
	1919KN	.264	7.50	15.00	25.00	50.00
	1920H	37.870	1.00	1.75	3.50	12.50
	1920KN	20.685	1.00	2.00	5.00	17.50
	1922KN	3.971	350.00	700.00	1000.	1500.
	1926	8.040	2.00	4.00	10.00	30.00
	1927	.792	25.00	45.00	85.00	200.00
	1927	—	—	—	Proof	225.00
	1928	6.672	2.00	4.00	10.00	25.00
	1928	—	—	—	Proof	225.00
	1929	.636	15.00	30.00	50.00	100.00
	1929	—	—	—	Proof	225.00
	1933	2.806	2.00	14.00	32.50	65.00
	1933	—	—	—	Proof	225.00
	1934	2.640	3.00	14.00	30.00	55.00

KM#	Date	Mintage	Fine	VF	XF	Unc
9	1934	—	—	—	Proof	225.00
	1935	8.551	1.25	12.50	27.50	45.00
	1935	—	—	—	Proof	225.00
	1936	7.368	1.00	2.00	8.50	16.00
	1936	—	—	—	Proof	225.00

16	1936	7.992	.50	1.00	3.50	7.00
	1936	—	—	—	Proof	250.00
	1936H	12.600	.35	.75	1.00	2.25
	1936H	—	—	—	Proof	250.00
	1936KN	12.512	.35	.75	1.00	2.25
	1936KN	—	—	—	Proof	250.00

Mule. Obv: East Africa, KM#24. Rev: KM#16.

17	1936H	—	125.00	150.00	225.00	350.00

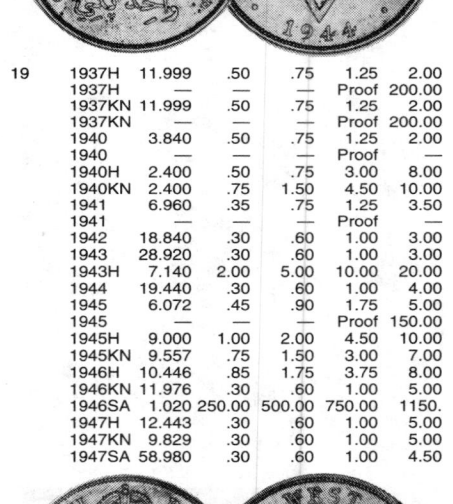

19	1937H	11.999	.50	.75	1.25	2.00
	1937H	—	—	—	Proof	200.00
	1937KN	11.999	.50	.75	1.25	2.00
	1937KN	—	—	—	Proof	200.00
	1940	3.840	.50	.75	1.25	2.00
	1940	—	—	—	Proof	
	1940H	2.400	.50	.75	3.00	8.00
	1940KN	2.400	.75	1.50	4.50	10.00
	1941	6.960	.35	.75	1.25	3.50
	1941	—	—	—	Proof	
	1942	18.840	.30	.60	1.00	3.00
	1943	28.920	.30	.60	1.00	3.00
	1943H	7.140	2.00	5.00	10.00	20.00
	1944	19.440	.30	.60	1.00	4.00
	1945	6.072	.45	.90	1.75	5.00
	1945	—	—	—	Proof	150.00
	1945H	9.000	1.00	2.00	4.50	10.00
	1945KN	9.557	.75	1.50	3.00	7.00
	1946H	10.446	.85	1.75	3.75	8.00
	1946KN	11.976	.30	.60	1.00	5.00
	1946SA	1.020	250.00	500.00	750.00	1150.
	1947H	12.443	.30	.60	1.00	5.00
	1947KN	9.829	.30	.60	1.00	5.00
	1947SA	58.980	.30	.60	1.00	4.50

Mule. Obv: KM#16. Rev: KM#19.

25	1945H	—	1500.	2000.	3000.	5000.

Obv. leg: W/o IND: IMP:

KM#	Date	Mintage	Fine	VF	XF	Unc
30	1951	1.258	7.50	12.50	27.50	45.00
	1951	—	—	—	Proof	250.00
	1951KN	2.692	6.00	10.00	20.00	35.00

BRONZE

30a	1952	10.542	.75	1.50	3.00	8.50
	1952	—	—	—	Proof	175.00
	1952H	30.794	.20	.40	.60	3.00
	1952KN	45.398	.20	.40	.60	3.00
	1952KN	—	—	—	Proof	175.00

33	1956	—	.75	1.50	3.50	12.00
	1956H	13.503	.75	1.50	3.50	9.00
	1956KN	13.500	.30	.60	2.00	8.00
	1957	9.000	.75	1.50	6.00	13.50
	1957	—	—	—	Proof	150.00
	1957H	5.340	1.00	2.50	8.00	20.00
	1957KN	5.600	1.00	2.50	6.00	16.00
	1958	12.200	.75	1.50	4.00	13.50
	1958	—	—	—	Proof	125.00
	1958KN	Inc. Ab.	.75	1.50	3.00	10.00

34	1956H	—	60.00	90.00	150.00	250.00

Mule. Obv: KM#30. Rev: KM#33.

3 PENCE

1.4138 g, .925 SILVER, .0420 oz ASW

10	1913	.240	3.50	7.50	12.50	30.00
	1913	—	—	—	Proof	250.00
	1913H	.496	2.00	4.00	7.50	25.00
	1914H	1.560	1.00	2.00	7.50	25.00
	1915H	.270	18.00	25.00	50.00	100.00
	1916H	.820	10.00	15.00	30.00	65.00
	1917H	3.600	1.50	2.50	7.50	25.00
	1918H	1.722	1.75	3.50	8.00	20.00
	1919H	19.826	1.00	2.00	6.00	15.00
	1919H	—	—	—	Proof	200.00

1.4138 g, .500 SILVER, .0227 oz ASW

10a	1920H	3.616	25.00	50.00	75.00	125.00

TIN-BRASS

10b	1920KN	19.000	1.00	5.00	12.50	25.00
	1920KN	—	—	—	Proof	75.00
	1920KN*	—	—	—	Unique	
	1925	8.800	1.50	5.00	20.00	40.00
	1926	1.600	10.00	25.00	50.00	85.00
	1927	.800	20.00	40.00	100.00	200.00
	1928	1.760	10.00	35.00	70.00	125.00
	1928	—	—	—	Proof	175.00
	1933	2.800	2.00	4.50	18.00	40.00
	1933	—	—	—	Proof	200.00
	1934	6.400	1.00	12.50	20.00	35.00
	1934	—	—	—	Proof	200.00
	1935	11.560	1.00	12.50	20.00	35.00
	1935	—	—	—	Proof	200.00
	1936	17.160	1.00	3.50	15.00	28.00
	1936	—	—	—	Proof	200.00
	1936H	1.000	15.00	25.00	45.00	85.00
	1936H	—	—	—	Proof	200.00
	1936KN	2.038	10.00	15.00	30.00	65.00

*NOTE: Mint mark on obverse below bust.

COPPER-NICKEL

21	1938H	7.000	.30	.60	2.50	7.50
	1938H	—	—	—	Proof	200.00
	1938KN	9.056	.35	.75	2.50	8.00

KM#	Date	Mintage	Fine	VF	XF	Unc
21	1938KN	—	—	—	Proof	300.00
	1939H	16.500	.30	.60	2.00	5.00
	1939H	—	—	—	Proof	300.00
	1939KN	15.500	.30	.60	2.00	8.00
	1939KN	—	—	—	Proof	200.00
	1940H	3.862	.50	1.00	2.50	7.50
	1940KN	10.000	.30	.60	2.00	5.00
	1941H	5.032	.40	.85	3.50	9.00
	1943H	5.106	.40	.85	6.00	15.00
	1943KN	9.502	.40	.85	3.50	9.00
	1944KN	2.536	.40	.85	6.50	15.00
	1945	.998	3.00	5.00	10.00	20.00
	1945KN	3.000	.40	.85	5.00	12.50
	1946KN	7.488	.40	.85	3.50	9.00
	1947H	10.000	.35	.75	3.50	8.00
	1947KN	11.248	.40	.85	3.50	8.00

35	1957H	.800	35.00	75.00	165.00	375.00

6 PENCE

2.8276 g, .925 SILVER, .0841 oz ASW

11	1913	.560	3.00	5.00	12.00	35.00
	1913	—	—	—	Proof	350.00
	1913H	.400	3.00	5.00	15.00	37.50
	1914H	.952	2.75	5.00	17.50	40.00
	1916H	.400	5.00	10.00	30.00	60.00
	1917H	2.400	3.00	5.00	16.50	37.50
	1918H	1.160	2.00	5.00	16.50	37.50
	1919H	8.676	2.00	3.50	11.50	22.00
	1919H	—	—	—	Proof	200.00

2.8276 g, .500 SILVER, .0454 oz ASW

11a	1920H	2.948	12.50	30.00	50.00	175.00
	1920H	—	—	—	Proof	275.00

TIN-BRASS

11b	1920KN	12.000	1.00	5.00	20.00	37.50
	1920KN	—	—	—	Proof	125.00
	1923H	2.000	5.00	12.50	50.00	95.00
	1924	1.000	15.00	30.00	80.00	150.00
	1924H	1.000	15.00	30.00	80.00	150.00
	1924KN	1.000	15.00	30.00	80.00	150.00
	1925	2.800	3.50	7.00	30.00	60.00
	1928	.400	25.00	50.00	150.00	250.00
	1928	—	—	—	Proof	180.00
	1933	1.000	20.00	40.00	120.00	180.00
	1933	—	—	—	Proof	225.00
	1935	4.000	5.00	12.50	25.00	50.00
	1935	—	—	—	Proof	225.00
	1936	10.400	7.50	15.00	25.00	50.00
	1936	—	—	—	Proof	225.00
	1936H	.480	25.00	50.00	125.00	200.00
	1936H	—	—	—	Proof	225.00
	1936KN	2.696	15.00	25.00	35.00	70.00
	1936KN	—	—	—	Proof	225.00

NICKEL-BRASS

22	1938	12.114	.50	1.00	2.00	8.00
	1938	—	—	—	Proof	200.00
	1940	17.829	.75	1.50	3.00	10.00
	1940	—	—	—	Proof	200.00
	1942	1.600	2.50	4.00	10.00	20.00
	1943	10.586	.75	1.75	5.00	11.00
	1944	1.814	2.00	3.00	15.00	30.00
	1945	4.000	1.00	2.00	12.50	25.00
	1945	—	—	—	Proof	200.00
	1946	4.000	2.50	5.00	25.00	50.00
	1946	—	—	—	Proof	225.00
	1947	6.120	.50	1.50	5.00	15.00
	1947	—	—	—	Proof	175.00

Obv. leg: W/o IND: IMP:

31	1952	2.544	10.00	20.00	55.00	90.00
	1952	—	—	—	Proof	300.00

SHILLING

5.6552 g, .925 SILVER, .1682 oz ASW

KM#	Date	Mintage	Fine	VF	XF	Unc
12	1913	8.800	2.75	4.00	12.50	22.50
	1913	—	—	—	Proof	400.00
	1913H	3.540	2.75	4.00	12.50	30.00
	1914	3.000	2.75	4.00	15.00	35.00
	1914H	11.292	2.75	4.00	12.50	30.00
	1915H	.254	15.00	35.00	75.00	150.00
	1916H	11.838	2.75	4.00	15.00	35.00
	1917H	15.018	2.75	4.00	15.00	35.00
	1918H	9.486	2.75	5.50	17.50	40.00
	1918H	—	—	—	Proof	200.00
	1919	2.000	10.00	15.00	30.00	55.00
	1919H	.992	15.00	30.00	65.00	100.00
	1919H	—	—	—	Proof	200.00
	1920	.828	22.50	40.00	85.00	150.00

TIN-BRASS

KM#	Date	Mintage	Fine	VF	XF	Unc
12a	1920G	.016	1500.	2200.	3000.	4000.
	1920KN	38.800	1.50	5.00	12.50	32.50
	1920KN	—	—	—	Proof	200.00
	1920KN*	—	—	—	Unique	—
	1922KN	32.324	2.00	6.50	35.00	70.00
	1923H	24.384	4.00	7.50	25.00	45.00
	1923KN	5.000	8.00	15.00	50.00	90.00
	1924	17.000	2.00	6.50	30.00	60.00
	1924H	9.567	10.00	20.00	65.00	125.00
	1924KN	7.000	7.50	15.00	40.00	80.00
	1925	19.800	4.00	8.00	18.00	45.00
	1926	19.952	2.00	5.00	10.00	40.00
	1927	22.248	1.50	4.00	8.50	35.00
	1927	—	—	—	Proof	250.00
	1928	10.000	20.00	35.00	75.00	225.00
	1928	—	—	—	Proof	300.00
	1936	70.200	3.00	6.50	11.00	32.50
	1936	—	—	—	Proof	225.00
	1936H	10.920	12.50	22.50	35.00	75.00
	1936KN	14.962	2.00	5.00	15.00	42.50
	1936KN	—	—	—	Proof	200.00

*NOTE: Mint mark on obverse below bust.

NICKEL-BRASS

KM#	Date	Mintage	Fine	VF	XF	Unc
23	1938	57.806	.50	1.25	4.50	12.00
	1938	—	—	—	Proof	200.00
	1939	55.472	.50	1.25	6.50	18.00
	1939	—	—	—	Proof	200.00
	1940	40.311	.50	1.25	5.50	15.00
	1940	—	—	—	Proof	200.00
	1942	42.000	.50	1.25	6.50	18.00
	1943	133.600	.50	1.25	5.50	15.00
	1945	8.010	1.00	1.50	12.00	25.00
	1945	—	—	—	Proof	200.00
	1945H	12.864	2.00	3.50	15.00	35.00
	1945KN	11.120	1.00	2.00	12.00	25.00
	1946	37.350	1.00	2.00	15.00	35.00
	1946	—	—	—	Proof	200.00
	1946H	—	750.00	1000.	2000.	4000.
	1947	99.200	.50	1.00	4.50	12.00
	1947	—	—	—	Proof	200.00
	1947H	10.000	1.50	3.00	15.00	30.00
	1947KN	10.384	.50	1.00	6.50	16.50

TIN-BRASS
Obv. leg: W/o IND: IMP:

KM#	Date	Mintage	Fine	VF	XF	Unc
28	1949	70.000	.50	2.50	12.00	25.00
	1949	—	—	—	Proof	175.00
	1949H	10.000	1.25	4.00	12.50	27.50
	1949KN	10.016	1.25	4.00	12.50	27.50
	1949KN	—	—	—	Proof	200.00
	1951	35.346	1.25	5.00	15.00	30.00
	1951	—	—	—	Proof	175.00
	1951H	10.000	1.25	5.00	15.00	30.00
	1951KN	16.832	1.25	5.00	15.00	30.00
	1952	98.654	.50	1.00	3.00	9.00
	1952	—	—	—	Proof	200.00
	1952H	44.096	.50	1.00	2.00	7.50
	1952KN	41.653	.50	1.00	2.00	6.00
	1952KN	—	—	—	Proof	175.00

2 SHILLINGS

11.3104 g, .925 SILVER, .3364 oz ASW

KM#	Date	Mintage	Fine	VF	XF	Unc
13	1913	2.100	5.00	8.00	16.50	45.00
	1913	—	—	—	Proof	500.00
	1913H	1.176	6.00	15.00	27.50	55.00
	1914	.330	15.00	50.00	125.00	200.00
	1914H	.637	10.00	25.00	35.00	75.00
	1915H	.066	20.00	50.00	100.00	175.00
	1916H	9.824	5.00	15.00	30.00	60.00
	1917H	1.059	15.00	40.00	85.00	150.00
	1917H	—	—	—	Proof	300.00
	1918H	7.294	5.00	12.00	27.50	55.00
	1919	2.000	6.00	20.00	40.00	85.00
	1919H	10.866	4.50	10.00	32.00	65.00
	1919H	—	—	—	Proof	200.00
	1920	.683	30.00	60.00	175.00	250.00

11.3104 g, .500 SILVER, .1818 oz ASW

KM#	Date	Mintage	Fine	VF	XF	Unc
13a	1920H	1.926	30.00	55.00	100.00	275.00

TIN-BRASS

KM#	Date	Mintage	Fine	VF	XF	Unc
13b	1920KN	15.856	2.50	5.00	15.00	40.00
	1920KN	—	—	—	Proof	250.00
	1922	10.000	3.00	9.00	17.50	55.00
	1922KN	5.500	6.00	15.00	30.00	75.00
	1922KN	—	—	—	Proof	250.00
	1923H	12.696	4.00	12.00	22.50	65.00
	1924	1.500	7.50	15.00	35.00	90.00
	1925	3.700	4.00	12.00	25.00	70.00
	1926	11.500	4.50	15.00	45.00	80.00
	1927	11.100	6.00	20.00	60.00	100.00
	1927	—	—	—	Proof	250.00
	1928	7.900	1500.	2000.	3000.	5000.
	1928	—	—	—	Proof	3000.
	1936	32.940	5.00	12.00	35.00	60.00
	1936	—	—	—	Proof	250.00
	1936H	8.703	6.00	18.00	45.00	75.00
	1936KN	8.794	6.00	18.00	45.00	75.00

NICKEL-BRASS

KM#	Date	Mintage	Fine	VF	XF	Unc
24	1938H	32.000	1.00	2.00	3.50	15.00
	1938KN	27.852	1.00	2.00	3.50	15.00
	1939H	5.750	2.00	5.00	15.00	35.00
	1939KN	6.250	1.00	4.00	12.00	30.00
	1939KN	—	—	—	Proof	200.00
	1942KN	10.000	1.25	4.50	14.00	30.00
	1946H	10.500	1.25	4.00	12.00	27.50
	1946KN	4.800	1.25	7.00	22.00	42.50
	1947H	5.055	1.00	6.00	20.00	40.00
	1947KN	4.200	1.25	7.00	22.00	42.50

NOTE: Grained edge variety of 1938KN exists.

Obv. leg: W/o IND: IMP:

KM#	Date	Mintage	Fine	VF	XF	Unc
29	1949	7.500	1.25	7.00	22.00	40.00
	1949KN	7.576	1.25	6.00	20.00	35.00
	1951H	6.566	1.25	7.00	22.00	40.00
	1951H	—	—	—	Proof	250.00
	1952H	4.410	2.00	8.00	22.50	42.00
	1952KN	1.236	5.00	15.00	35.00	60.00

BRUNEI

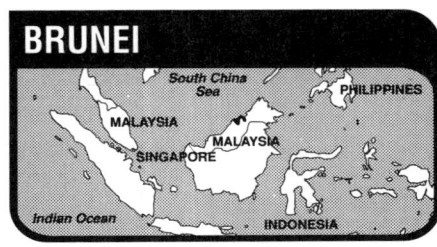

Negara Brunei Darussalam (State of Brunei), an independent sultanate on the northwest coast of the island of Borneo, has an area of 2,226 sq. mi. (5,765 sq. km.) and a population of 292,266. Capital: Bandar Seri Begawan. Crude oil and rubber are exported.

Magellan was the first European to visit Brunei in 1521. It was a powerful state, ruling over northern Borneo and adjacent islands from the 16th to the 19th century. Brunei became a British protectorate in 1888 and a British dependency in 1905. The Constitution of 1959 restored control over internal affairs to the sultan, while delegating responsibility for defense and foreign affairs to Britain. On January 1, 1984 it became independent.

RULERS

Sultan Hashim Jelal, 1885-1906
British 1906-1950
Sultan Sir Omar Ali Saifuddin III, 1950-1967
Sultan Hassanal Bolkiah I, 1967-

MONETARY SYSTEM

100 Sen = 1 Dollar (Ringgit)

SEN

BRONZE

KM#	Date	Mintage	VF	XF	Unc
4	1967	1.000	.10	.20	.50

KM#	Date	Mintage	VF	XF	Unc
9	1968	.060	.25	.50	1.50
	1970	.140	.10	.20	.50
	1970	4,000	—	Proof	2.50
	1971	.400	.10	.15	.40
	1973	.120	.10	.30	1.25
	1974	.640	—	.10	.30
	1976	.140	—	.10	.30
	1977	.140	—	.10	.30

Obv. leg: W/o numeral 'I' in title.

KM#	Date	Mintage	VF	XF	Unc
15	1977	.280	—	.10	.20
	1978	.269	—	.10	.15
	1979	.250	.10	.20	.50
	1979	.010	—	Proof	.90
	1980	.260	—	.10	.15
	1981	.540	—	.10	.15
	1982	.100	—	.30	1.50
	1983	.500	—	.10	.15
	1984	.400	—	.10	.15
	1984	3,000	—	Proof	1.00
	1985	.200	—	.10	.15
	1985	—	—	Proof	1.00
	1986	.101	—	—	.15
	1986	7,000	—	Proof	1.00

COPPER CLAD STEEL

KM#	Date	Mintage	VF	XF	Unc
15a	1986	.102	—	—	.30
	1987	.390	—	—	.30
	1988	.500	—	—	.30
	1989	.601	—	—	.30
	1990	.680	—	—	.30
	1991	.680	—	—	.30
	1992	.887	—	—	.30
	1993	.948	—	—	.30

2.9200 g, .925 SILVER, .0869 oz ASW

KM#	Date	Mintage	VF	XF	Unc
15b	1987	2,000	—	Proof	3.00
	1988	2,000	—	Proof	3.00
	1989	2,000	—	Proof	3.00
	1990	2,000	—	Proof	3.00
	1991	2,000	—	Proof	3.00
	1992	2,000	—	Proof	3.00
	1995	2,000	—	Proof	3.00

COPPER CLAD STEEL

KM#	Date	Mintage	VF	XF	Unc
34	1993	.948	—	—	.50
	1994	—	—	—	.50
	1995	—	—	—	.50

5 SEN

COPPER-NICKEL

5	1967	1.160	.20	.40	1.00

10	1968	.320	.10	.35	.80
	1970	.760	.10	.30	.60
	1970	4,000	—	Proof	2.50
	1971	.320	.10	.20	.70
	1973	.128	.10	.45	1.85
	1974	.576	.10	.15	.40
	1976	.384	.10	.15	.45
	1977	.384	.10	.15	.45

Obv. leg: W/o numeral 'I' in title.

16	1977	.920	—	.10	.30
	1978	.640	—	.10	.30
	1979	.650	.10	.20	.50
	1979	.010	—	Proof	1.25
	1980	.640	—	.10	.30
	1981	.960	—	.10	.30
	1982	.240	—	.45	1.75
	1983	1.280	—	.10	.30
	1984	.800	—	.10	.30
	1984	3,000	—	Proof	1.25
	1985	.800	—	.10	.30
	1985	—	—	Proof	1.25
	1986	.189	—	—	.30
	1986	7,000	—	Proof	1.25
	1987	.960	—	—	.30
	1988	.820	—	—	.30
	1989	1.504	—	—	.30
	1990	1.340	—	—	.30
	1991	1.340	—	—	.30
	1992	1.900	—	—	.30
	1993	1.951	—	—	.30

1.6500 g, .925 SILVER, .0490 oz ASW

16a	1987	2,000	—	Proof	3.00
	1988	2,000	—	Proof	3.00
	1989	2,000	—	Proof	3.00
	1990	2,000	—	Proof	3.00
	1991	2,000	—	Proof	3.00
	1992	2,000	—	Proof	3.00
	1993	2,000	—	Proof	3.00

COPPER-NICKEL

35	1993	1.951	—	—	.50
	1994	—	—	—	.50

10 SEN

COPPER-NICKEL

6	1967	3.510	.10	.20	.50

KM#	Date	Mintage	VF	XF	Unc
11	1968	.580	.10	.25	.60
	1970	1.360	.10	.20	.50
	1970	4,000	—	Proof	2.50
	1971	.420	.10	.20	.50
	1973	.300	.10	.25	.60
	1974	1.410	.10	.20	.50
	1976	.920	.10	.20	.50
	1977	.920	—	.15	.40

Obv. leg: W/o numeral 'I' in title.

17	1977	1.800	.10	.15	.40
	1978	1.080	—	.10	.30
	1979	2.050	—	.10	.30
	1979	.010	—	Proof	1.35
	1980	2.840	—	.10	.25
	1981	.976	—	.10	.25
	1983	1.080	—	.10	.25
	1984	1.400	—	.10	.25
	1984	3,000	—	Proof	1.50
	1985	1.540	—	.10	.25
	1985	—	—	Proof	1.50
	1986	2.181	—	—	.25
	1986	7,000	—	Proof	1.50
	1987	2.560	—	—	.25
	1988	.960	—	—	.25
	1989	1.000	—	—	.25
	1990	1.800	—	—	.25
	1991	1.800	—	—	.25
	1992	3.839	—	—	.25
	1993	3.973	—	—	.25

3.3500 g, .925 SILVER, .0996 oz ASW

17a	1987	2,000	—	Proof	6.00
	1988	2,000	—	Proof	6.00
	1989	2,000	—	Proof	6.00
	1990	2,000	—	Proof	6.00
	1991	2,000	—	Proof	6.00
	1992	2,000	—	Proof	6.00
	1993	2,000	—	Proof	6.00

COPPER-NICKEL

36	1993	3.973	—	—	.75
	1994	—	—	—	.75
	1996	—	—	—	.75

20 SEN

COPPER-NICKEL

7	1967	2.130	.25	.75	1.50

12	1968	.510	.20	.50	1.00
	1970	.850	.15	.35	.85
	1970	4,000	—	Proof	2.50
	1971	.450	.20	.50	1.00
	1973	.450	.20	.50	1.00
	1974	.700	.15	.35	.85
	1976	.640	.15	.35	.85
	1977	.640	.15	.35	.85

Obv. leg: W/o numeral 'I' in title.

18	1977	1.200	.10	.25	.75
	1978	.720	.15	.40	1.00
	1979	1.060	.20	.50	1.25
	1979	.010	—	Proof	2.00
	1980	1.540	.10	.20	.50

KM#	Date	Mintage	VF	XF	Unc
18	1981	2.140	.10	.20	.50
	1982	.120	1.00	4.00	8.00
	1983	1.350	.10	.15	.40
	1984	.750	.10	.15	.40
	1984	3,000	—	Proof	2.25
	1985	1.000	.10	.15	.40
	1985	—	—	Proof	2.25
	1986	2.639	—	—	.40
	1986	7,000	—	Proof	2.25
	1987	2.400	—	—	.40
	1988	.560	—	—	.40
	1989	.500	—	—	.40
	1990	.720	—	—	.40
	1991	.725	—	—	.40
	1992	2.432	—	—	.40
	1993	2.521	—	—	.40

6.5100 g, .925 SILVER, .1936 oz ASW

18a	1987	2,000	—	Proof	10.00
	1988	2,000	—	Proof	10.00
	1989	2,000	—	Proof	10.00
	1990	2,000	—	Proof	10.00
	1991	2,000	—	Proof	10.00
	1992	2,000	—	Proof	10.00
	1993	2,000	—	Proof	10.00

COPPER-NICKEL

37	1993	—	—	—	1.25
	1994	—	—	—	1.25

50 SEN

COPPER-NICKEL

8	1967	.788	.50	1.25	2.50

13	1968	.212	.30	1.00	1.75
	1970	.300	.30	1.00	1.75
	1970	4,000	—	Proof	5.00
	1971	.320	.30	1.00	1.75
	1973	.140	.50	2.50	4.00
	1974	.244	.30	1.00	1.75
	1976	.240	.30	1.00	1.75
	1977	.240	.30	1.00	1.75

Obv. leg: W/o numeral 'I' in title.

19	1977	.499	.30	.85	1.65
	1978	.264	.30	.85	1.65
	1979	.730	.30	.85	1.65
	1979	.010	—	Proof	3.50
	1980	.536	.30	.45	.85
	1981	.960	.30	.40	.75
	1982	.136	.50	2.50	6.00
	1983	.408	.30	.40	.75
	1984	.320	.30	.40	.75
	1984	3,000	—	Proof	4.00
	1985	.450	.30	.40	.75
	1985	—	—	Proof	4.00
	1986	1.067	—	—	.75
	1986	7,000	—	Proof	4.00
	1987	1.120	—	—	.75
	1988	.250	—	—	.75
	1989	.500	—	—	.75
	1990	.472	—	—	.75
	1991	.508	—	—	.75
	1992	1.072	—	—	.75
	1993	1.102	—	—	.75

10.8200 g, .925 SILVER, .3218 oz ASW

19a	1987	2,000	—	Proof	15.00
	1988	2,000	—	Proof	15.00
	1989	2,000	—	Proof	15.00
	1990	2,000	—	Proof	15.00
	1991	2,000	—	Proof	15.00
	1992	2,000	—	Proof	15.00
	1993	2,000	—	Proof	15.00

COPPER-NICKEL

KM#	Date	Mintage	VF	XF	Unc
38	1993	—	—	—	2.25
	1994	—	—	—	2.25

DOLLAR

COPPER-NICKEL

14	1970	5,000	—	Proof	35.00

Obv. leg: W/o numeral 'I' in title.

20	1979	.010	—	Proof	15.00
	1984	5,000	—	—	10.00
	1984	3,000	—	Proof	20.00
	1985	.015	—	—	8.00
	1985	.010	—	Proof	15.00
	1986	.010	—	—	8.00
	1986	7,000	—	Proof	20.00
	1987	2,000	—	—	10.00
	1988	2,000	—	—	10.00
	1989	2,000	—	—	10.00
	1990	3,000	—	—	10.00
	1991	3,000	—	—	10.00
	1992	—	—	—	10.00
	1993	—	—	—	10.00

BULGARIA

The Republic of Bulgaria, formerly the Peoples Republic of Bulgaria, a Balkan country on the Black Sea in southeastern Europe, has an area of 42,855 sq. mi. (110,910 sq. km.) and a population of 8.8 million. Capital: Sofia. Agriculture remains a key component of the economy but industrialization, particularly heavy industry, has been emphasized since the late 1940s. Machinery, tobacco and cigarettes, wines and spirits, clothing and metals are the chief exports.

The area now occupied by Bulgaria was conquered by the Bulgars, an Asiatic tribe, in the 7th century. Bulgarian kingdoms continued to exist on the Bulgarian peninsula until it came under Turkish rule in 1395. In 1878, after nearly 500 years of Turkish rule, Bulgaria was made a principality under Turkish suzerainty. Union seven years later with Eastern Rumelia created a Balkan state with borders approximating those of present-day Bulgaria. A Bulgarian kingdom, fully independent of Turkey, was proclaimed Sept. 22, 1908. During WWI Bulgaria had been aligned with Germany. After the Armistice certain land concessions were given to Greece and Romania. In 1934 King Boris III suspended all political parties and established a dictatorial monarchy. In 1938 the military began rearming through the aide of the Anglo-French loan. As WW II developed, Bulgaria again supported the Germans but protected their Jewish community. Boris died mysteriously in 1943 and Simeon II became King at the age of six. The country was then ruled by a pro-Nazi regency until it was liberated by Soviet forces in 1944.

The monarchy was abolished and Simeon was ousted by plebiscite in 1946 and Bulgaria became a Peoples Republic on the Soviet pattern. After democratic reforms in 1989 the name was changed to the Republic of Bulgaria.

Coinage of the Peoples Republic features a number of politically oriented commemoratives.

RULERS
Ferdinand I, as Prince, 1887-1908
    As King, 1908-1918
Boris III, 1918-1943

MINT MARKS
A - Berlin
(a) Cornucopia & torch - Paris
BP - Budapest
H - Heaton Mint, Birmingham
KB - Kormoczbanya
(p) Poissy - Thunderbolt

MONETARY SYSTEM
100 Stotinki = 1 Lev

STOTINKA

BRONZE
Rev: Privy marks and designer name below denomination.

KM#	Date	Mintage	Fine	VF	XF	Unc
22.1	1901	20.000	1.00	2.00	6.00	12.50

Rev: W/o privy marks and designer name.

22.2	1912	20.000	.50	1.00	3.00	6.00

2 STOTINKI

BRONZE
Rev: Privy marks and designer name below denomination.

23.1	1901(a)	40.000	1.00	2.00	5.00	10.00

Rev: W/o privy marks and designer name.

23.2	1912	40.000	.50	1.00	2.00	5.00

5 STOTINKI

COPPER-NICKEL

KM#	Date	Mintage	Fine	VF	XF	Unc
24	1906	14.000	.20	.60	2.00	5.00
	1912	14.000	.20	.40	1.00	3.00
	1913	20.000	.20	.40	1.00	3.00
	1913	—	—	—	Proof	—

ZINC

24a	1917	53.200	.60	1.00	2.50	6.00

10 STOTINKI

COPPER-NICKEL

25	1906	13.000	.50	1.00	2.50	6.00
	1912	13.000	.20	.40	1.00	3.00
	1912	—	—	—	Proof	—
	1913	20.000	.20	.40	1.00	3.00

ZINC

25a	1917	59.100	.40	1.00	2.00	5.00
	1917	—	—	—	Proof	125.00

20 STOTINKI

COPPER-NICKEL

26	1906	10.000	.50	1.50	3.50	10.00
	1912	10.000	.20	.50	1.25	5.00
	1913	5.000	.20	.50	1.50	5.50
	1913	—	—	—	Proof	—

ZINC

26a	1917	40.000	.50	1.75	4.00	8.50
	1917	—	—	—	Proof	125.00

KINGDOM
50 STOTINKI

2.5000 g, .835 SILVER, .0671 oz ASW

27	1910	.400	1.75	3.50	6.00	14.00

30	1912	2.000	1.00	2.00	4.50	10.00
	1913	3.000	1.00	2.00	3.50	8.00
	1916	4.562	50.00	100.00	175.00	275.00

ALUMINUM-BRONZE

46	1937	60.200	.25	.50	1.00	2.50

LEV

5.0000 g, .835 SILVER, .1342 oz ASW

28	1910	3.000	2.00	4.00	7.00	16.00

KM#	Date	Mintage	Fine	VF	XF	Unc
31	1912	2.000	2.00	3.00	5.50	12.50
	1913	3.500	2.00	3.00	5.00	10.00
	1916	4.569	100.00	200.00	350.00	600.00

ALUMINUM

35	1923	40.000	2.50	5.00	12.00	35.00
	1923H	3 pcs.	—	—	Rare	—

COPPER-NICKEL

37	1925	35.000	.20	.50	1.00	2.50
	1925(p)	34.982	.25	.60	1.25	3.00

NOTE: The Poissy issue bears the thunderbolt mint mark.

IRON

37a	1941	10.000	3.00	6.00	15.00	40.00

2 LEVA

10.0000 g, .835 SILVER, .2685 oz ASW

29	1910	.400	4.50	7.50	16.00	45.00

32	1912	1.000	4.00	6.00	12.00	20.00
	1913	.500	4.00	6.00	12.00	20.00
	1916	2.286	200.00	400.00	700.00	1150.

ALUMINUM

36	1923	20.000	3.00	6.00	15.00	50.00
	1923H	2 pcs.	—	—	Rare	—

COPPER-NICKEL

38	1925	20.000	.40	.80	1.75	4.00
	1925(p)	20.000	.50	1.00	2.00	4.50

NOTE: The Poissy issue bears the thunderbolt privy mark.

IRON

38a	1941	15.000	.75	1.50	3.50	10.00

KM#	Date	Mintage	Fine	VF	XF	Unc
49	1943	35.000	.75	1.50	4.50	15.00

5 LEVA

COPPER-NICKEL

39	1930	20.001	.60	1.25	2.50	6.00

IRON

39a	1941	15.000	1.00	3.00	6.00	20.00

NICKEL CLAD STEEL

39b	1943	36.000	.50	1.00	2.00	5.00

10 LEVA

COPPER-NICKEL

40	1930	15.001	.75	1.50	3.50	8.00

IRON

40a	1941	2.200	6.00	12.00	25.00	65.00

NICKEL CLAD STEEL

40b	1943	25.000	.60	1.25	3.00	7.00

20 LEVA

6.4516 g, .900 GOLD, .1867 oz AGW
Declaration of Independence

33	1912	.075	100.00	125.00	200.00	350.00
	1912	—	—	—	Proof	1500.

4.0000 g, .500 SILVER, .0643 oz ASW

41	1930BP	10.016	1.00	2.00	3.50	8.50

COPPER-NICKEL

47	1940A	6.650	.50	1.00	2.00	5.00

50 LEVA

10.0000 g, .500 SILVER, .1607 oz ASW

KM#	Date	Mintage	Fine	VF	XF	Unc
42	1930BP	9.028	1.50	3.00	5.50	14.00

44	1934	3.001	2.00	4.00	7.00	16.00
	1934	—	—	—	Proof	—

COPPER-NICKEL

48	1940A	12.340	.75	1.50	3.00	7.50

NICKEL CLAD STEEL

48a	1943A	15.000	1.00	2.00	4.00	9.00

100 LEVA

20.0000 g, .500 SILVER, .3215 oz ASW

43	1930BP	1.556	BV	5.00	9.00	25.00

45	1934	2.506	BV	4.00	6.00	11.50
	1934	—	—	—	Proof	—
	1937	2.207	BV	4.00	6.00	11.50

PEOPLES REPUBLIC
STOTINKA

BRASS

50	1951	—	—	—	.10	.25

59	1962	—	—	—	.10	.25
	1970	—	—	.20	.50	2.00

Obv: 2 dates on arms, '681-1944'.

KM#	Date	Mintage	Fine	VF	XF	Unc
84	1974	—	—	—	.10	.15
	1979	2,000	—	—	Proof	1.50
	1980	2,000	—	—	Proof	1.50
	1981	137 pcs.	—	—	—	2.00
	1988	—	—	—	.10	.15
	1989	—	—	—	.10	.15
	1990 lg. dt.	—	—	—	.10	.15

NOTE: Edge varieties exist.

1300th Anniversary of Bulgaria

111	1981	—	—	.10	.20	.50
	1981	—	—	—	Proof	2.00

2 STOTINKI

BRASS

60	1962	—	—	—	.10	.25

Obv: 2 dates on arms, '681-1944'.

85	1974	—	—	—	.10	.25
	1979	2,000	—	—	Proof	2.00
	1980	2,000	—	—	Proof	2.00
	1981	20 pcs.	—	—	Rare	—
	1988	—	—	—	.10	.25
	1989	—	—	—	.10	.25
	1990 lg. dt.	—	—	—	.10	.25

1300th Anniversary of Bulgaria

112	1981	—	—	.10	.20	.60
	1981	—	—	—	—	Proof	2.50

3 STOTINKI

BRASS

51	1951	—	—	—	.10	.25	.75

5 STOTINKI

BRASS

52	1951	—	.10	.15	.25	.75

61	1962	—	—	—	.10	.20	.50

Obv: 2 dates on arms '681-1944'.

KM#	Date	Mintage	Fine	VF	XF	Unc
86	1974	—	—	.10	.15	.25
	1979	2,000	—	—	Proof	2.00
	1980	2,000	—	—	Proof	2.00
	1988	—	—	—	.15	.25
	1989	—	—	—	.15	.25
	1990 lg. dt.	—	—	—	.15	.25

1300th Anniversary of Bulgaria

113	1981	—	—	.10	.25	.75
	1981	—	—	—	Proof	2.50

10 STOTINKI

COPPER-NICKEL

53	1951	—	—	.10	.20	.40

NICKEL-BRASS

62	1962	—	—	.10	.20	.40

Obv: 2 dates on arms, '681-1944'.

87	1974	—	—	.10	.15	.25
	1979	2,000	—	—	Proof	3.50
	1980	2,000	—	—	Proof	3.50
	1988	—	—	—	.15	.25
	1989	—	—	—	.15	.25
	1990 lg. dt.	—	—	—	.15	.25

COPPER-NICKEL
1300th Anniversary of Bulgaria

114	1981	—	—	.20	.50	1.50
	1981	—	—	—	Proof	3.50

20 STOTINKI

COPPER-NICKEL

55	1952	—	1.00	2.50	7.50	20.00
	1954	—	.10	.25	.75	1.50

NICKEL-BRASS

63	1962	—	.10	.20	.30	.75

Obv: 2 dates on arms, '681-1944'.

KM#	Date	Mintage	Fine	VF	XF	Unc
88	1974	—	.10	.20	.30	.60
	1979	2,000	—	—	Proof	3.50
	1980	2,000	—	—	Proof	3.50
	1988	—	—	—	.30	.60
	1989	—	—	—	.30	.60
	1990 lg. dt.	—	—	—	.30	.60

COPPER-NICKEL
1300th Anniversary of Bulgaria

115	1981	—	—	.25	.65	2.00
	1981	—	—	—	Proof	4.00

25 STOTINKI

COPPER-NICKEL

54	1951	—	.10	.20	.50	1.00

50 STOTINKI

COPPER-NICKEL

56	1959	—	.10	.20	.40	.80

NICKEL-BRASS

64	1962	—	.10	.40	.65	1.00

Obv: 2 dates on arms, '681-1944'.

89	1974	—	.10	.40	.65	1.50
	1979	2,000	—	—	Proof	4.00
	1980	2,000	—	—	Proof	4.00
	1988	—	—	—	.50	1.00
	1989	—	—	—	.50	1.00
	1990 lg. dt.	—	—	—	.50	1.00

COPPER-NICKEL
University Games at Sofia

98	1977	2,000	.20	.40	.75	1.50

1300th Anniversary of Bulgaria

116	1981	—	—	.30	.60	1.80
	1981	—	—	—	Proof	4.00

LEV

COPPER-NICKEL
Obv: Date 9 • IX • 1944 on ribbon.

KM#	Date	Mintage	Fine	VF	XF	Unc
57	1960	—	.10	.25	.60	1.00

NICKEL-BRASS

| 58 | 1962 | — | — | .50 | 1.00 | 1.50 |

25th Anniversary of Socialist Revolution

| 74 | 1969 | 3.700 | .35 | .60 | 1.25 | 2.50 |

90th Anniversary Liberation From Turks

| 76 | 1969 | 2.150 | .35 | .65 | 1.50 | 2.75 |

Obv: 2 dates '681-1944' on ribbon.

90	1974	—	—	.50	1.00	2.00
	1979	2,000	—	—	Proof	6.00
	1980	2,000	—	—	Proof	6.00
	1988	—	—	—	.75	2.00
	1989	—	—	—	.75	2.00
	1990 lg. dt.	—	—	—	.75	2.00

BRONZE
100th Anniversary of the "April Uprising" Against the Turks

| 94 | 1976 | .300 | .35 | .60 | 1.25 | 2.50 |
| | 1976 | — | — | — | Proof | 4.00 |

COPPER-NICKEL
World Cup Soccer Games in Spain

| 107 | 1980 | .220 | — | .60 | 1.25 | 2.50 |
| | 1980 | .030 | — | — | Proof | 3.50 |

1300th Anniversary of Bulgaria

KM#	Date	Mintage	Fine	VF	XF	Unc
117	1981	—	—	.50	1.00	2.00
	1981	—	—	—	Proof	

International Hunting Exposition

| 118 | 1981 | .250 | — | .60 | 1.25 | 2.50 |
| | 1981 | .050 | — | — | Proof | 3.50 |

Russo-Bulgarian Friendship

| 119 | 1981 | .250 | — | .60 | 1.25 | 2.50 |
| | 1981 | .050 | — | — | Proof | 3.50 |

1988 Winter Olympics - Hockey

| 175 | 1987 | — | — | — | — | 2.50 |
| | 1987 | .300 | — | — | Proof | 3.50 |

Summer Olympics - Sprinters

| 176 | 1988 | — | — | — | — | 2.50 |
| | 1988 | .300 | — | — | Proof | 3.50 |

REPUBLIC

10 STOTINKI

NICKEL-BRASS
Ancient Lion Sculpture

KM#	Date	Mintage	VF	XF	Unc
199	1992	—	—	—	.25

20 STOTINKI

NICKEL-BRASS
Ancient Lion Sculpture

| 200 | 1992 | — | — | — | .35 |

50 STOTINKI

NICKEL-BRASS
Ancient Lion Sculpture

KM#	Date	Mintage	VF	XF	Unc
201	1992	—	—	—	.50

LEV

NICKEL-BRASS
Madara Horseman

| 202 | 1992 | — | — | — | .75 |

2 LEVA

NICKEL-BRASS
Madara Horseman

| 203 | 1992 | — | — | — | 1.25 |

5 LEVA

NICKEL-BRASS
Madara Horseman

| 204 | 1992 | — | — | — | 1.75 |

10 LEVA

COPPER-NICKEL
Madara Horseman

| 205 | 1992 | — | — | — | 2.50 |

BRASS
Reduced size and metal change.

| 224 | 1997 | — | — | — | 1.25 |

20 LEVA

BRASS
Obv: Madara Horseman. Rev: Denomination.

| 228 | 1997 | — | — | — | 1.50 |

50 LEVA

BRASS
Obv: Madara Horseman. Rev: Denomination.

KM#	Date	Mintage	VF	XF	Unc
225	1997	—	—	—	1.75

BURUNDI

The Republic of Burundi, a landlocked country in central Africa, was a kingdom with a feudalistic society, caste system and Mwami (king) for more than 400 years before independence. It has an area of 10,740 sq. mi. (27,830 sq. km.) and a population of 6.3 million. Capital: Bujumbura. Plagued by poor soil, irregular rainfall and a single-crop economy, coffee, Burundi is barely able to feed itself. Coffee and tea are exported.

Although the area was visited by European explorers and missionaries in the latter half of the 19th century, it wasn't until the 1890s that it, together with Rwanda, fell under European domination as part of German East Africa. Following World War I, the territory was mandated to Belgium by the League of Nations and administered with the Belgian Congo. After World War II it became a U.N. Trust Territory. Limited self-government was established by U.N.-supervised elections in 1961. Burundi gained independence as a kingdom under Mwami Mwambutsa IV on July 1, 1962. The republic was established by military coup in 1966.

NOTE: For earlier coinage see Belgian Congo, and Rwanda and Burundi. For previously listed coinage dated 1966, coins of Mwambutsa IV and Ntare V, refer to *UNUSUAL WORLD COINS,* 3rd edition, Krause Publications, 1992.

RULERS
Mwambutsa IV, 1962-1966
Ntare V, 1966

MINT MARKS
PM - Pobjoy Mint
(b) - Privy Marks, Brussels

MONETARY SYSTEM
100 Centimes = 1 Franc

KINGDOM
1962-1966
FRANC

BRASS

KM#	Date	Mintage	Fine	VF	XF	Unc
6	1965	10.000	—	.75	1.50	3.00

REPUBLIC
1966
FRANC

ALUMINUM

18	1970	10.000	2.00	4.50	7.50	17.50

19	1976	5.000	—	.30	.75	1.50
	1980	—	—	.15	.50	1.25
	1990PM	—	—	.15	.50	1.25
	1993	—	—	.15	.50	1.25

5 FRANCS

ALUMINUM

KM#	Date	Mintage	Fine	VF	XF	Unc
16	1968(b)	2.000	—	.25	.85	2.00
	1969(b)	2.000	—	.25	.85	2.00
	1971(b)	2.000	—	.25	.85	2.00

20	1976	2.000	—	.25	.75	1.50
	1980	—	—	.25	.75	1.50

10 FRANCS

COPPER-NICKEL
F.A.O. Issue

17	1968	2.000	—	.75	1.50	3.00
	1971	2.000	—	.75	1.50	3.00

CAMBODIA

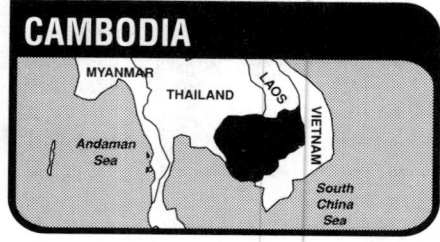

The State of Cambodia, formerly Democratic Kampuchea and the Khmer Republic, a land of paddy fields and forest-clad hills located on the Indo-Chinese peninsula, fronting on the Gulf of Thailand, has an area of 70,238 sq. mi. (181,040 sq. km) and a population of 10.6 million. Capital: Phnom Penh. Agriculture is the basis of the economy, with rice the chief crop. Native industries include cattle breeding, weaving and rice milling. Rubber, cattle, corn, and timber are exported.

The region was the nucleus of the Khmer empire which flourished from the 5th to the 12th century and attained an excellence in art and architecture still evident in the magnificent ruins at Angkor. The Khmer empire once ruled over much of Southeast Asia, but began to decline in the 13th century as the Thai and Vietnamese invaded the region and attached its territories. At the request of the Cambodian king, a French protectorate attached to Cochin-China was established over the country in 1863, saving it from dissolution, and in 1885, Cambodia was included in the French Union of Indo-China. France established a constitutional monarchy for Cambodia within the French Union in 1949. The 1954 Geneva Convention resulted in full independence for the Kingdom of Cambodia. King Sihanouk abdicated to his father and won the office of Prime Minister.

Prince Sihanouk was toppled by a bloodless coup led by Lon Nol in March of 1970. Sihanouk moved to Peking to head a government-in-exile. On Oct. 9, 1970, Cambodia became the Khmer Republic, and Lon Nol its President. The government of Lon Nol was in turn toppled, April 17, 1975, by the Khmer Rouge insurgents who took control of the government and renamed the country Democratic Kampuchea.

The Khmer Rouge completely eliminated the economy and created a state without money, exchange or barter while exterminating about 2 million Cambodians. These atrocities were finally halted at the beginning of 1979 when the Vietnamese regulars and Cambodian rebels launched an offensive that drove the Khmer Rouge out of Phnom Penh and the country acquired another new title - The Peoples Republic of Kampuchea.

In 1993 Prince Norodom Sihanouk returned to Kampuchea to lead the Supreme National Council.

RULERS
Kings of Cambodia
Norodom I, 1835-1904
Sisowath, 1904-1927
Sisowath Monivong, 1927-1941
Norodom Sihanouk, 1941-1955
Norodom Suramarit, 1955-1960
Norodom Sihanouk, 1960-1970, 1993—

MINT MARKS
(a) - Paris, privy marks only
(k) - Key, Havana, Cuba

INDEPENDENT KINGDOM
MONETARY SYSTEM
100 Centimes = 1 Riel
100 Sen = 1 Riel (Commencing 1959)

10 CENTIMES

ALUMINUM
KM#	Date	Mintage	Fine	VF	XF	Unc
51	1953(a)	4.000	.25	.45	.85	2.00

10 SEN

ALUMINUM
KM#	Date	Mintage	Fine	VF	XF	Unc
54	1959(a)	1.000	.10	.20	.35	.65

20 CENTIMES

ALUMINUM
KM#	Date	Mintage	Fine	VF	XF	Unc
52	1953(a)	3.000	.25	.65	1.50	3.00

20 SEN

ALUMINUM
KM#	Date	Mintage	Fine	VF	XF	Unc
55	1959(a)	1.004	.15	.25	.60	1.00

50 CENTIMES

ALUMINUM
KM#	Date	Mintage	Fine	VF	XF	Unc
53	1953(a)	3.170	.45	.85	2.00	4.00

50 SEN

ALUMINUM
KM#	Date	Mintage	Fine	VF	XF	Unc
56	1959(a)	3.399	.20	.35	.75	1.50

KHMER REPUBLIC
1970-1975
RIEL

COPPER-NICKEL
F.A.O. Issue
59	1970	5.000	—	—	7.50	16.50

NOTE: According to the Royal Mint of Great Britain, this coin was minted at the Llantrissant Branch Mint in 1972 but dated 1969. According to the FAO, the coin was to have been dated 1971, but was "not minted" due to the fall of the Cambodian government in 1970. However, this coin was released in limited numbers in 1983. The photograph of the coin, supplied by the FAO, is dated 1970.

PEOPLE'S REPUBLIC OF KAMPUCHEA
1979-1990
5 SEN

ALUMINUM
KM#	Date	Mintage	VF	XF	Unc
69	1979		.60	1.25	2.50

NOTE: Exists w/thick and thin flan.

KINGDOM OF CAMBODIA
1994—
50 RIELS

STEEL
Ancient Tower
KM#	Date	Year Mintage	VF	XF	Unc
92	BE2538	(1994)	—	—	.25

100 RIELS

STEEL
3 Towered Building
93	BE2538	(1994)	—	—	.50

200 RIELS

STEEL
2 Ceremonial Bowls
94	BE2538	(1994)	—	—	1.00

500 RIELS

STEEL center in BRASS ring
Royal Emblem
95	BE2538	(1994)	—	—	3.00

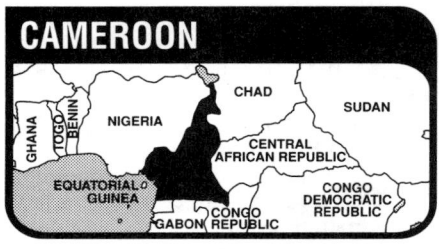

CAMEROON

The Republic of Cameroon, located in west-central Africa on the Gulf of Guinea, has an area of 183,569 sq. mi. (475,445 sq. km.) and a population of 13.5 million. Capital: Yaounde. About 90 percent of the labor force is employed on the land; cash crops account for 80 percent of the country's export revenue. Cocoa, coffee, aluminum, cotton, rubber, and timber are exported.

European contact with what is now the United Republic of Cameroon began in the 16th century with the voyage of Portuguese navigator Fernando Po. The following three centuries saw continuous activity by Spanish, Dutch, and British traders and missionaries. The land was spared colonial rule until 1884, when treaties with tribal chiefs brought German domination. In 1919, the League of Nations divided the Cameroons between Great Britain and France, with the larger eastern area going to France. The French and British mandates were converted into United Nations trusteeships in 1946. French Cameroon became the independent Cameroon Republic on Jan. 1, 1960. The federation of East (French) and West (British) Cameroon was established in 1961 when the southern part of British Cameroon voted for reunification with the Cameroon Republic, and the northern part for union with Nigeria Cameroon joined the Commonwealth of Nations in November 1995.

Coins of French Equatorial Africa and of the monetary unions identified as the Equatorial African States and Central African States are also current in Cameroon.

MINT MARKS
(a) - Paris, privy marks only
SA - Pretoria, 1943

MONETARY SYSTEM
100 Centimes = 1 Franc

FRENCH MANDATE
50 CENTIMES

ALUMINUM-BRONZE

KM#	Date	Mintage	Fine	VF	XF	Unc
1	1924(a)	4.000	1.50	3.50	22.00	80.00
	1925(a)	2.500	2.00	5.00	25.00	85.00
	1926(a)	7.800	1.00	2.00	12.00	50.00

BRONZE

| 4 | 1943SA | 4.000 | 2.00 | 3.50 | 7.00 | 18.00 |

Obv. leg: LIBRE added.

| 6 | 1943SA | 4.000 | 2.50 | 5.50 | 12.00 | 25.00 |

FRANC

ALUMINUM-BRONZE

2	1924(a)	3.000	2.00	4.00	20.00	90.00
	1925(a)	1.722	3.00	6.00	30.00	125.00
	1926(a)	11.928	1.00	2.00	12.00	60.00

BRONZE

KM#	Date	Mintage	Fine	VF	XF	Unc
5	1943SA	3.000	2.50	4.50	17.50	40.00

Obv. leg: LIBRE added.

| 7 | 1943SA | 3.000 | 3.50 | 6.50 | 20.00 | 45.00 |

ALUMINUM

| 8 | 1948(a) | 8.000 | .10 | .25 | .75 | 1.50 |

2 FRANCS

ALUMINUM-BRONZE

| 3 | 1924(a) | .500 | 5.00 | 15.00 | 65.00 | 185.00 |
| | 1925(a) | .100 | 8.00 | 25.00 | 100.00 | 275.00 |

ALUMINUM

| 9 | 1948(a) | 5.000 | .50 | 1.00 | 1.50 | 5.00 |

NOTE: 5, 10 and 25 Francs dated 1958 previously listed here are now listed in Equatorial African States, KM#24-26.

REPUBLIC
50 FRANCS

COPPER-NICKEL
Independence Commemorative
Obv: Three Giant Eland. Rev: Denomination.

| 13 | 1960(a) | 1.154 | 2.00 | 3.50 | 5.50 | 10.00 |

100 FRANCS

NICKEL
Obv: Three Giant Eland. Rev: Denomination.

KM#	Date	Mintage	Fine	VF	XF	Unc
14	1966(a)	9.950	1.00	2.00	4.50	10.00
	1967(a)	10.000	1.00	2.00	4.50	10.00
	1968(a)	11.000	1.00	2.00	4.50	10.00

NOTE: KM#14 was issued double thick and should not be considered a piefort.

| 15 | 1971(a) | 15.000 | 2.00 | 3.00 | 6.00 | 12.50 |
| | 1972(a) | 20.000 | 2.00 | 3.00 | 6.00 | 12.50 |

NOTE: Refer also to Equatorial African States and Central African States.

Obv: KM#17. Rev: KM#15.

| 16 | 1972(a) | — | 7.00 | 15.00 | 25.00 | 50.00 |

Obv: Three Giant Eland. Rev: Denomination.

17	1975(a)	—	1.00	2.00	3.00	5.50
	1980(a)	—	1.00	2.00	3.00	5.50
	1982(a)	—	.75	1.50	2.50	4.50
	1983(a)	—	.75	1.50	2.50	4.50
	1984(a)	—	.75	1.50	2.50	4.50
	1986(a)	—	.75	1.50	2.50	4.50

500 FRANCS

COPPER-NICKEL

23	1985(a)	—	2.00	3.50	5.50	10.00
	1986(a)	—	2.00	3.50	5.50	10.00
	1988(a)	—	2.00	3.50	5.50	10.00

CANADA

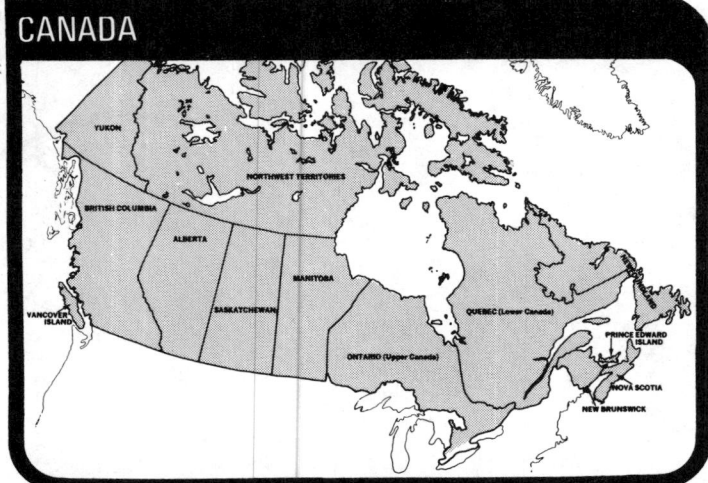

The history of Canadian coinage parallels that of the United States in many respects, although in several aspects it also contrasts quite sharply. Canadian coins are widely collected in the U.S., particularly in the northern tier of states, where at times the issues of our northern neighbors have been encountered in substantial circulating quantities.

This is a most logical situation, as when the dollar was established as the monetary unit of Canada, in 1857 it was given the same intrinsic value as the U.S. dollar. Through the years the Canadian dollar has traded on an approximate par with the U.S. dollar, although from time to time one or the other units has traded at a slight premium.

The first Canadian decimal coins were issued in 1858 — 1, 5, 10 and 20 cents — in the name of the Province of Canada (Upper and Lower Canada, or the provinces of Ontario and Quebec as we know them today). The first truly Canadian coinage was offered in 1870 — 5, 10, 25 and 50 cents — following the confederation of these provinces with Nova Scotia and New Brunswick in 1867. Both of the latter had offered their own distinctive coinages in the early 1860s.

Prince Edward Island also offered a single issue of a one cent coin in 1871, prior to its 1873 entry into the confederation. A coinage of Newfoundland was also initiated during this period, in 1865, which continued through 1947, with the British dependency moving into the confederation in 1949.

In contrast to the .900 fine standard of American silver coins, Canada's coinage was originally launched with a .925 fine silver content, and as a result slightly smaller coin sizes. In 1920 the standard was reduced to .800 fine, remaining there until mid-1967 when it was lowered to .500 fine, then abandoned in favor of pure nickel a year later. Another contrast with U.S. coinage was evident in the issue of the large cent from 1858 to 1920, when a small cent of similar size, content and weight to the U.S. cent was introduced.

When Canada's dominion coin issue of 1870 was introduced, the 1858 provincial issue of a decimal 20 cent piece was abandoned in favor of a quasi-decimal 25 cent piece. This move was made, in part, because of the confusion between the 20 cent piece and the U.S. 25 cent piece, which also circulated in Canada, forecasting the similar fate which would befall the U.S. 20 cent piece a few years later. Although tentative steps aimed at the creation of a dollar coin were instituted in 1911, it was not until 1935, the year the issue of silver dollars was halted in the U.S., that Canada launched the issue of a silver dollar.

The first dollar was a commemorative of the silver jubilee of the reign of George V, while the other George V dollar coin (1936) utilized dies which had been prepared at the Royal Mint in London in anticipation of the 1911 dollar which did not materialize. From the beginning, Canada's dollar series has been frequently employed as a vehicle for the commemoration of national events. In addition, a 1951 nickel commemorated the 200th anniversary of the isolation of nickel, of which Canada is the world's leading producer, while the entire 1967 series commemorates the centennial of Canadian confederation.

In the early years, Canada's coins were struck in England at London's Royal Mint or at the Heaton Mint in Birmingham. Issues struck at the Royal Mint do not bear a mintmark, but those produced by Heaton carry an "H". All Canadian coins have been struck since January 2, 1908, at the Royal Canadian Mints at Ottawa and recently at Winnipeg except for some 1968 pure nickel dimes struck at the U.S. Mint in Philadelphia, and do not bear mint marks. Ottawa's mintmark (C) does not appear on some 20th century Newfoundland issues, however, as it does on English type sovereigns struck there from 1908 through 1918.

Canadian coins are graded on standards similar to those used for the U.S. series. The points of greatest wear are generally found on the obverses in the bands of the crowns, the sprays of laurel around the head and in the hairlines above or over the ear. The susceptibility of these varying points to wear has decreed that Canadian coins are almost exclusively graded accordingly, with little concentration on the reverses, unless they are abnormally worn.

LARGE CENTS

BRONZE

KM#	Date	Mintage	VG-8	F-12	VF-20	XF-40	MS-60	MS-63
7	1901	4,100,000	1.50	2.50	3.00	5.00	22.00	65.00

NOTE: Earlier dates (1876-1900) exist for this type.

KM#	Date	Mintage	VG-8	F-12	VF-20	XF-40	MS-60	MS-63
8	1902	3,000,000	1.25	1.50	2.00	5.00	16.00	45.00
	1903	4,000,000	1.25	1.50	2.00	4.00	20.00	50.00
	1904	2,500,000	1.50	2.00	3.25	5.00	25.00	75.00
	1905	2,000,000	2.50	4.00	6.00	8.50	35.00	95.00
	1906	4,100,000	1.25	1.50	2.00	4.00	22.00	75.00
	1907	2,400,000	2.50	3.50	4.25	5.00	30.00	85.00
	1907H	800,000	7.00	10.00	16.00	30.00	80.00	275.00
	1908	2,401,506	2.25	3.75	4.50	6.00	26.00	80.00
	1909	3,973,339	1.25	1.50	2.00	4.00	20.00	55.00
	1910	5,146,487	1.25	2.25	2.50	3.00	18.00	55.00

KM#	Date	Mintage	VG-8	F-12	VF-20	XF-40	MS-60	MS-63
15	1911	4,663,486	1.00	1.25	1.75	3.50	18.50	60.00

KM#	Date	Mintage	VG-8	F-12	VF-20	XF-40	MS-60	MS-63
21	1912	5,107,642	.75	1.00	1.50	2.50	15.00	50.00
	1913	5,735,405	.75	1.00	1.50	2.50	15.00	50.00
	1914	3,405,958	1.25	1.40	2.00	3.50	28.00	90.00
	1915	4,932,134	.80	1.10	1.75	2.75	18.00	65.00
	1916	11,022,367	.50	.65	.90	2.00	12.00	45.00
	1917	11,899,254	.50	.65	.90	1.50	9.00	45.00
	1918	12,970,798	.50	.65	.90	1.50	9.00	45.00
	1919	11,279,634	.50	.65	.90	1.50	9.00	45.00
	1920	6,762,247	.50	.75	1.00	2.00	12.00	50.00

SMALL CENTS

Dot

BRONZE, 3.24 g

KM#	Date	Mintage	VG-8	F-12	VF-20	XF-40	MS-60	MS-63
28	1920	15,483,923	.25	.50	1.00	2.00	9.00	40.00
	1921	7,601,627	.50	.75	1.75	4.00	18.00	70.00
	1922	1,243,635	8.75	10.00	14.50	22.00	120.00	300.00
	1923	1,019,002	14.25	16.25	23.00	34.00	200.00	600.00
	1924	1,593,195	4.00	4.75	6.25	11.50	85.00	200.00
	1925	1,000,622	12.00	14.25	18.75	28.00	130.00	400.00
	1926	2,143,372	2.25	3.00	4.50	8.75	65.00	200.00
	1927	3,553,928	.90	1.25	2.25	4.00	30.00	95.00
	1928	9,144,860	.15	.25	.65	1.50	10.00	40.00
	1929	12,159,840	.15	.25	.65	1.50	10.00	40.00
	1930	2,538,613	1.35	1.80	2.50	5.00	30.00	90.00
	1931	3,842,776	.55	1.00	1.75	3.50	25.00	80.00
	1932	21,316,190	.15	.25	.50	1.50	9.00	35.00
	1933	12,079,310	.15	.25	.50	1.50	9.00	35.00
	1934	7,042,358	.20	.30	.50	1.50	9.00	35.00
	1935	7,526,400	.20	.30	.50	1.50	9.00	35.00
	1936	8,768,769	.15	.25	.50	1.50	9.00	35.00
	1936 dot below dt	678,823	—	—	—	—	Rare	—
	1936 dot below dt	3 known	—	—	—	*Specimen	—	—

*NOTE: David Akers, John Jay Pittman sale 10-97 Gem Specimen realized $110,000.

Maple Leaf

KM#	Date	Mintage	VG-8	F-12	VF-20	XF-40	MS-60	MS-63
32	1937	10,040,231	.50	.90	1.25	1.60	2.50	6.00
	1938	18,365,608	.30	.50	.65	1.00	2.00	6.50
	1939	21,600,319	.30	.50	.60	1.00	2.00	5.00
	1940	85,740,532	—	.20	.40	1.00	2.00	6.00
	1941	56,336,011	—	.20	.40	1.00	5.00	35.00
	1942	76,113,708	—	.10	.20	.75	4.50	25.00
	1943	89,111,969	—	.10	.20	.75	3.00	12.00
	1944	44,131,216	.20	.30	.40	1.00	5.00	32.00
	1945	77,268,591	—	.10	.25	.50	2.00	5.00
	1946	56,662,071	—	.20	.30	.60	2.00	5.00
	1947	31,093,901	—	.10	.25	.50	2.00	6.00
	1947ML	47,855,448	—	.10	.25	.50	2.00	5.00

Modified Obverse Legend

KM#	Date	Mintage	VG-8	F-12	VF-20	XF-40	MS-60	MS-63
41	1948	25,767,779	.10	.20	.40	.80	2.50	8.00
	1949	33,128,933	—	.10	.25	.50	2.00	4.00
	1950	60,444,992	—	.10	.20	.40	1.75	4.00
	1951	80,430,379	—	.10	.20	.40	1.75	4.00
	1952	67,631,736	—	.10	.20	.40	1.50	4.00

Elizabeth II Effigy by Gillick

KM#	Date	Mintage	VG-8	F-12	VF-20	XF-40	MS-60	MS-63
49	1953 w/o strap	67,806,016	—	.10	.15	.25	.65	2.00
	1953 w/strap	Inc. Ab.	.75	1.50	2.00	3.00	10.00	35.00

KM#	Date	Mintage	VG-8	F-12	VF-20	XF-40	MS-60	MS-63
	1954 w/strap	22,181,760	.10	.15	.30	.50	2.00	4.00
	1954 w/o strap	Inc. Ab.	Proof-Like Only		—	150.00	250.00	
	1955 w/strap	56,403,193	—	—	.10	.15	.45	1.00
	1955 w/o strap	Inc. Ab.	75.00	100.00	150.00	250.00	500.00	950.00
	1956	78,658,535	—	—	—	.10	.50	.90
	1957	100,601,792	—	—	—	.10	.30	.70
	1958	59,385,679	—	—	—	.10	.30	.70
	1959	83,615,343	—	—	—	.10	.25	.50
	1960	75,772,775	—	—	—	.10	.25	.50
	1961	139,598,404	—	—	—	—	.15	.40
	1962	227,244,069	—	—	—	—	.10	.25
	1963	279,076,334	—	—	—	—	.10	.25
	1964	484,655,322	—	—	—	—	.10	.25

Elizabeth II Effigy by Machin

KM#	Date	Mintage	VG-8	F-12	VF-20	XF-40	MS-60	MS-63
59.1	1965 sm. beads, pointed 5	304,441,082	—	—	—	.10	.45	.75
	1965 sm. beads, blunt 5	I.A.	—	—	—	—	.10	.25
	1965 lg. beads, pointed 5	I.A.	—	—	1.50	4.25	18.00	30.00
	1965 lg. beads, blunt 5	I.A.	—	—	—	.10	.20	.35
	1966	184,151,087	—	—	—	—	.10	.20
	1968	329,695,772	—	—	—	—	.10	.20
	1969	335,240,929	—	—	—	—	.10	.20
	1970	311,145,010	—	—	—	—	.10	.20
	1971	298,228,936	—	—	—	—	.10	.20
	1972	451,304,591	—	—	—	—	.10	.20
	1973	457,059,852	—	—	—	—	.10	.20
	1974	692,058,489	—	—	—	—	.10	.20
	1975	642,318,000	—	—	—	—	.10	.20
	1976	701,122,890	—	—	—	—	.10	.20
	1977	453,762,670	—	—	—	—	.10	.20
	1978	911,170,647	—	—	—	—	.10	.20

Smaller Bust

KM#	Date	Mintage	VG-8	F-12	VF-20	XF-40	MS-60	MS-63
59.2	1979	754,394,064	—	—	—	—	.10	.20

Reduced Weight, 2.80 g

KM#	Date	Mintage	VG-8	F-12	VF-20	XF-40	MS-60	MS-63
127	1980	912,052,318	—	—	—	—	.10	.15
	1981	1,209,468,500	—	—	—	—	.10	.15
	1981	199,000	—	—	—	—	Proof	1.00

Reduced Weight, 2.50 g
Edge: Multi-sided.

KM#	Date	Mintage	VG-8	F-12	VF-20	XF-40	MS-60	MS-63
132	1982	911,001,000	—	—	—	—	.10	.15
	1982	180,908	—	—	—	—	Proof	1.50
	1983	975,510,000	—	—	—	—	.10	.15
	1983	168,000	—	—	—	—	Proof	1.50
	1984	838,225,000	—	—	—	—	.10	.15
	1984	161,602	—	—	—	—	Proof	1.50
	1985 pointed 5	771,772,500	—	—	—	4.50	12.50	18.50
	1985 blunt 5	I.A.	—	—	—	—	.10	.15
	1985	157,037	—	—	—	—	Proof	1.50
	1986	740,335,000	—	—	—	—	.10	.15
	1986	175,745	—	—	—	—	Proof	2.25
	1987	774,549,000	—	—	—	—	.10	.15
	1987	179,004	—	—	—	—	Proof	2.25
	1988	482,676,752	—	—	—	—	.10	.15
	1988	175,259	—	—	—	—	Proof	2.25
	1989	1,077,347,200	—	—	—	—	.10	.15
	1989	170,928	—	—	—	—	Proof	2.25

Elizabeth II Effigy by dePedery-Hunt

KM#	Date	Mintage	VG-8	F-12	VF-20	XF-40	MS-60	MS-63
181	1990	218,035,000	—	—	—	—	.10	.15
	1990	140,649	—	—	—	—	Proof	2.50
	1991	831,001,000	—	—	—	—	.10	.15
	1991	131,888	—	—	—	—	Proof	3.50
	1993	752,034,000	—	—	—	—	.10	.15
	1993	145,065	—	—	—	—	Proof	2.00
	1994	639,516,000	—	—	—	—	.10	.15
	1994	146,424	—	—	—	—	Proof	2.50
	1995	559,047,000	—	—	—	—	.10	.15
	1995	—	—	—	—	—	Proof	2.50

COPPER PLATED STEEL

KM#	Date	Mintage	VG-8	F-12	VF-20	XF-40	MS-60	MS-63
181a	1996	445,746,000	—	—	—	—	.10	.15
	1996	—	—	—	—	—	Proof	2.50

BRONZE PLATED STEEL

Edge: Round and plain.

KM#	Date	Mintage	VG-8	F-12	VF-20	XF-40	MS-60	MS-63
289	1997	506,928,000	—	—	—	—	.10	.15
	1997	—	—	—	—	—	Proof	1.50
	1998	—	—	—	—	—	.10	.15
	1998O	—	—	—	—	In Proof sets only		1.50
	1998W	—	—	—	—	In Mint sets only		.20

COMMEMORATIVE CENTS

BRONZE

KM#	Date	Mintage	VG-8	F-12	VF-20	XF-40	MS-60	MS-63
65	1967 Confederation Centennial							
		345,140,645	—	—	—	—	.10	.20
204	1992 Confederation 125							
		673,512,000	—	—	—	—	.10	.15
		147,061	—	—	—	—	Proof	1.00

5.6700 g, COPPER-PLATED .925 SILVER, .1677 oz ASW

KM#	Date	Mintage	VG-8	F-12	VF-20	XF-40	MS-60	MS-63
309	ND(1998) 90th Anniversary Royal Canadian Mint							
		.025	—	—	—	—	In Unc sets only	16.50

322	ND(1998) 90th Anniversary Royal Canadian Mint							
		.025	—	—	—	—	Proof	16.50

FIVE CENTS

1.1620 g, .925 SILVER, .0346 oz ASW

KM#	Date	Mintage	VG-8	F-12	VF-20	XF-40	MS-60	MS-63
2	1901	2,000,000	2.75	4.00	8.00	18.00	90.00	265.00

NOTE: Earlier dates (1858-1900) exist for this type.

KM#	Date	Mintage	VG-8	F-12	VF-20	XF-40	MS-60	MS-63
9	1902	2,120,000	1.50	2.00	3.25	7.00	30.00	50.00
	1902 lg. broad H	2,200,000	2.00	2.75	4.50	8.00	40.00	70.00
	1902 sm. narrow H	Inc. Ab.	5.00	10.00	20.00	35.00	130.00	225.00
13	1903	1,000,000	4.00	7.00	14.00	30.00	120.00	280.00
	1903H	2,640,000	1.75	3.00	7.00	13.00	90.00	200.00
	1904	2,400,000	1.75	3.00	7.00	18.00	140.00	400.00
	1905	2,600,000	1.75	3.00	6.00	12.00	85.00	200.00
	1906	3,100,000	1.50	2.00	4.00	8.00	70.00	175.00
	1907	5,200,000	1.50	2.00	4.00	7.00	60.00	125.00
	1908	1,220,524	4.00	6.50	12.00	25.00	95.00	175.00
	1909 round leaves	1,983,725	2.00	2.50	7.00	15.00	125.00	350.00
	1909 pointed leaves	Inc. Ab.	8.00	11.00	27.50	55.00	275.00	800.00
	1910 pointed leaves	3,850,325	1.50	1.75	3.25	7.00	45.00	85.00
	1910 round leaves	Inc. Ab.	10.00	15.00	30.00	75.00	325.00	900.00

KM#	Date	Mintage	VG-8	F-12	VF-20	XF-40	MS-60	MS-63
16	1911	3,692,350	1.75	2.50	5.00	11.00	65.00	120.00
22	1912	5,863,170	1.50	2.00	3.00	6.00	45.00	125.00
	1913	5,488,048	1.25	2.00	5.00	24.00	45.00	
	1914	4,202,179	1.50	2.20	3.50	7.00	55.00	125.00
	1915	1,172,258	6.50	12.00	20.00	40.00	400.00	475.00
	1916	2,481,675	2.75	4.00	5.50	12.50	90.00	200.00
	1917	5,521,373	1.25	1.75	2.00	4.00	30.00	70.00
	1918	6,052,298	1.25	1.75	2.00	4.00	24.00	60.00
	1919	7,835,400	1.25	1.75	2.00	4.00	27.50	60.00

KM#	Date	Mintage	VG-8	F-12	VF-20	XF-40	MS-60	MS-63
	1.1664 g, .800 SILVER, .0300 oz ASW							
22a	1920	10,649,851	1.25	1.75	2.00	4.00	24.00	45.00
	1921	2,582,495	1500.	2000.	2500.	5000.	11,500.	20,000.

NOTE: Approximately 460 known, balance remelted.
NOTE: Stack's A.G. Carter Jr. Sale 12-89 Choice BU finest known realized $57,200.

Near 6   Far 6

NICKEL

KM#	Date	Mintage	VG-8	F-12	VF-20	XF-40	MS-60	MS-63
29	1922	4,794,119	.25	.75	1.75	7.00	40.00	80.00
	1923	2,502,279	.40	1.25	3.50	12.00	90.00	225.00
	1924	3,105,839	.30	.70	2.50	7.00	75.00	165.00
	1925	201,921	25.00	36.00	60.00	150.00	900.00	2000.
	1926 near 6	938,162	2.25	6.00	14.00	45.00	275.00	900.00
	1926 far 6	Inc. Ab.	65.00	95.00	160.00	300.00	1200.	2200.
	1927	5,285,627	.25	.65	1.75	6.50	45.00	120.00
	1928	4,577,712	.25	.65	1.75	6.50	40.00	80.00
	1929	5,611,911	.25	.65	1.75	6.50	45.00	120.00
	1930	3,704,673	.25	.65	1.75	6.50	70.00	150.00
	1931	5,100,830	.25	.65	2.00	10.25	75.00	200.00
	1932	3,198,566	.25	.65	2.25	10.50	75.00	150.00
	1933	2,597,867	.40	2.75	4.00	11.50	150.00	400.00
	1934	3,827,304	.25	.65	1.75	10.75	80.00	200.00
	1935	3,900,000	.25	.65	1.75	6.50	70.00	160.00
	1936	4,400,450	.25	.65	1.75	6.50	40.00	85.00

33	1937 dot	4,593,263	.20	.35	1.25	2.50	9.00	22.00
	1938	3,898,974	.20	1.00	2.00	7.00	65.00	135.00
	1939	5,661,123	.20	.50	1.75	4.50	40.00	70.00
	1940	13,920,197	.15	.30	.75	1.50	14.00	40.00
	1941	8,681,785	.10	.30	.75	1.50	17.00	42.00
	1942 round	6,847,544	.10	.30	.75	1.75	14.00	40.00

Tombac (BRASS)

39	1942 - 12 sided	3,396,234	.40	.65	1.25	1.75	3.00	9.00

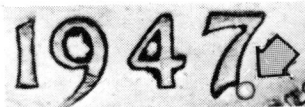 

Dot   Maple leaf

NICKEL

39a	1946	6,952,684	.15	.25	.50	2.00	10.00	25.00
	1947	7,603,724	.15	.25	.50	1.25	10.00	20.00
	1947 dot	Inc. Ab.	12.00	15.00	22.00	50.00	220.00	425.00
	1947 maple leaf	9,595,124	.15	.25	.50	1.25	8.00	16.00

Modified Obverse Legend

42	1948	1,810,789	.50	.80	1.00	2.00	15.00	25.00
	1949	13,037,090	.15	.20	.40	.75	4.00	7.00
	1950	11,970,521	.15	.20	.40	.75	4.00	7.00

CHROMIUM and NICKEL-PLATED STEEL

42a	1951 low relief*	4,313,410	.15	.25	.50	1.00	2.50	4.50
	1951 high relief* *	Inc. Ab.	325.00	450.00	600.00	1100.	2700.	3800.
	1952	10,891,148	.15	.25	.50	1.00	3.00	5.00

*NOTE: A in GRATIA points between denticles.
* *NOTE: A in GRATIA points to a denticle.

Elizabeth II Effigy by Gillick - 12 Sided Coinage

50	1953 w/o strap	16,635,552	.15	.25	.40	1.00	3.00	4.50
	1953 w/strap	Inc.Ab.	.15	.25	.45	1.00	3.50	7.00
	1954	6,998,662	.15	.25	.50	1.00	4.50	8.00

KM#	Date	Mintage	VG-8	F-12	VF-20	XF-40	MS-60	MS-63
						NICKEL		
50a	1955	5,355,028	.15	.25	.40	.75	3.00	4.50
	1956	9,399,854	—	.20	.30	.45	1.75	3.25
	1957	7,387,703	—	—	.25	.30	1.50	3.00
	1958	7,607,521	—	—	.25	.30	1.50	3.00
	1959	11,552,523	—	—	—	.20	.65	1.25
	1960	37,157,433	—	—	—	.15	.25	.75
	1961	47,889,051	—	—	—	—	.20	.40
	1962	46,307,305	—	—	—	—	.20	.40

Round Coinage

KM#	Date	Mintage	VG-8	F-12	VF-20	XF-40	MS-60	MS-63
57	1963	43,970,320	—	—	—	—	.20	.40
	1964	78,075,068	—	—	—	—	.20	.40
	1964 XWL	—	8.75	11.00	14.00	16.00	23.00	35.00

Elizabeth II Effigy by Machin

KM#	Date	Mintage	VG-8	F-12	VF-20	XF-40	MS-60	MS-63
60.1	1965	84,876,018	—	—	—	—	.20	.30
	1966	27,976,648	—	—	—	—	.20	.30
	1968	101,930,379	—	—	—	—	.20	.30
	1969	27,830,229	—	—	—	—	.20	.30
	1970	5,726,010	—	—	—	.25	.55	.75
	1971	27,312,609	—	—	—	—	.20	.30
	1972	62,417,387	—	—	—	—	.20	.30
	1973	53,507,435	—	—	—	—	.20	.30
	1974	94,704,645	—	—	—	—	.20	.30
	1975	138,882,000	—	—	—	—	.20	.30
	1976	55,140,213	—	—	—	—	.20	.30
	1977	89,120,791	—	—	—	—	.20	.30
	1978	137,079,273	—	—	—	—	.20	.30

Smaller bust

KM#	Date	Mintage	VG-8	F-12	VF-20	XF-40	MS-60	MS-63
60.2	1979	186,295,825	—	—	—	—	.20	.30
	1980	134,878,000	—	—	—	—	.20	.30
	1981	99,107,900	—	—	—	—	.20	.30
	1981	199,000	—	—	—	—	Proof	1.00

COPPER-NICKEL

KM#	Date	Mintage	VG-8	F-12	VF-20	XF-40	MS-60	MS-63
60.2a	1982	64,924,400	—	—	—	—	.20	.30
	1982	180,908	—	—	—	—	Proof	1.00
	1983	72,596,000	—	—	—	—	.20	.30
	1983	168,000	—	—	—	—	Proof	1.00
	1984	84,088,000	—	—	—	—	.20	.30
	1984	161,602	—	—	—	—	Proof	2.00
	1985	126,618,000	—	—	—	—	.20	.30
	1985	157,037	—	—	—	—	Proof	2.00
	1986	156,104,000	—	—	—	—	.20	.30
	1986	175,745	—	—	—	—	Proof	2.00
	1987	106,299,000	—	—	—	—	.10	.15
	1987	179,004	—	—	—	—	Proof	2.00
	1988	75,025,000	—	—	—	—	.10	.15
	1988	175,259	—	—	—	—	Proof	2.00
	1989	141,570,538	—	—	—	—	.10	.15
	1989	170,928	—	—	—	—	Proof	2.00

Elizabeth II Effigy by dePedery-Hunt

KM#	Date	Mintage	VG-8	F-12	VF-20	XF-40	MS-60	MS-63
182	1990	42,537,000	—	—	—	—	.10	.15
	1990	140,649	—	—	—	—	Proof	2.50
	1991	10,931,000	—	—	—	—	.20	.35
	1991	131,888	—	—	—	—	Proof	3.50
	1993	86,877,000	—	—	—	—	.10	.15
	1993	143,065	—	—	—	—	Proof	2.50
	1994	99,352,000	—	—	—	—	.10	.15
	1994	146,424	—	—	—	—	Proof	3.00
	1995	78,528,000	—	—	—	—	.10	.15
	1995	50,000	—	—	—	—	Proof	2.50
				NICKEL PLATED STEEL				
182a	1996	36,686,000	—	—	—	—	.10	.15
	1997	26,573,000	—	—	—	—	.10	.15
	1998	—	—	—	—	—	.10	.15
	1998W	—	—	—	—	In Unc sets only		.20

5.3500 g, .925 SILVER, .1591 oz ASW

KM#	Date	Mintage	VG-8	F-12	VF-20	XF-40	MS-60	MS-63
182b	1996	—	—	—	—	—	Proof	5.50
	1997	—	—	—	—	—	Proof	5.50
	1998O	—	—	—	—	In Proof sets only		4.00

COMMEMORATIVE FIVE CENTS

KM#	Date	Mintage	VG-8	F-12	VF-20	XF-40	MS-60	MS-63
40	1943 Victory, Tombac (Brass)							
		24,760,256	.20	.30	.40	1.00	2.00	7.00
	1944	8,000	—	—	—	—	Rare	—
			CHROMIUM-PLATED STEEL					
40a	1944	11,532,784	.15	.25	.50	1.00	2.25	4.50
	1945	18,893,216,	.15	.25	.50	1.00	2.25	4.50

KM#	Date	Mintage	VG-8	F-12	VF-20	XF-40	MS-60	MS-63
48	1951 Nickel Bicentennial, Nickel							
		9,028,507	.15	.20	.25	.75	2.00	4.00

KM#	Date	Mintage	VG-8	F-12	VF-20	XF-40	MS-60	MS-63
66	1967 Confederation Centennial, Copper-Nickel							
		36,876,574	—	—	—	—	.20	.30
205	1992 Confederation 125							
		53,732,000	—	—	—	—	.10	.15
		147,061	—	—	—	—	Proof	5.25

KM#	Date	Mintage	VG-8	F-12	VF-20	XF-40	MS-60	MS-63
310	ND(1998) 90th Anniversary Royal Canadian Mint							
		.025	—	—	—	In Unc sets only		2.75
		.025	—	—	—	In Proof sets only		2.75

TEN CENTS

2.3240 g, .925 SILVER, .0691 oz ASW

KM#	Date	Mintage	VG-8	F-12	VF-20	XF-40	MS-60	MS-63
3	1901	1,200,000	6.75	10.50	25.00	50.00	150.00	390.00

NOTE: Earlier dates (1858-1900) exist for this type.

KM#	Date	Mintage	VG-8	F-12	VF-20	XF-40	MS-60	MS-63
10	1902	720,000	3.50	8.00	18.00	45.00	235.00	475.00
	1902H	1,100,000	2.75	5.00	12.50	28.00	100.00	235.00
	1903	500,000	8.00	20.00	60.00	125.00	800.00	1900.
	1903H	1,320,000	3.00	7.00	15.00	42.00	200.00	450.00
	1904	1,000,000	4.50	9.00	20.00	65.00	250.00	500.00
	1905	1,000,000	4.00	8.00	25.00	70.00	350.00	800.00
	1906	1,700,000	2.75	5.00	14.00	40.00	200.00	400.00
	1907	2,620,000	2.75	5.00	12.50	30.00	160.00	350.00
	1908	776,666	5.00	10.00	27.00	65.00	220.00	425.00
	1909 Victorian leaves, similar to 1902-1908 coinage							
		1,697,200	3.50	9.00	20.00	50.00	285.00	700.00
	1909 broad leaves similar to 1910-1912 coinage							
		Inc. Ab.	5.50	12.00	25.00	70.00	375.00	800.00
	1910	4,468,331	2.75	5.00	12.50	28.00	125.00	275.00
17	1911	2,737,584	4.00	9.00	15.00	40.00	110.00	250.00

| | Small leaves | | Broad leaves |

KM#	Date	Mintage	VG-8	F-12	VF-20	XF-40	MS-60	MS-63
23	1912	3,235,557	1.75	2.50	6.00	22.00	160.00	400.00
	1913 sm. leaves	3,613,937	1.50	2.25	5.00	17.50	125.00	350.00
	1913 lg. leaves	Inc. Ab.	75.00	140.00	275.00	650.00	3850.	6700.
	1914	2,549,811	1.50	2.50	5.50	18.50	135.00	400.00
	1915	688,057	4.00	10.00	22.00	80.00	340.00	700.00
	1916	4,218,114	1.00	1.50	4.00	11.00	80.00	225.00
	1917	5,011,988	.75	1.25	3.00	8.75	50.00	110.00
	1918	5,133,602	.75	1.25	3.00	8.75	45.00	90.00
	1919	7,877,722	.75	1.25	3.00	8.75	45.00	90.00

2.3328 g, .800 SILVER, .0600 oz ASW

KM#	Date	Mintage	VG-8	F-12	VF-20	XF-40	MS-60	MS-63
23a	1920	6,305,345	.75	1.25	3.00	9.00	50.00	110.00
	1921	2,469,562	1.25	2.00	4.00	12.50	65.00	200.00
	1928	2,458,602	1.00	1.75	4.00	10.00	55.00	130.00
	1929	3,253,888	1.00	1.50	3.50	9.50	55.00	130.00
	1930	1,831,043	1.25	2.00	4.50	14.00	55.00	150.00
	1931	2,067,421	1.00	1.75	4.00	10.00	55.00	125.00
	1932	1,154,317	1.50	2.50	6.00	20.00	75.00	160.00
	1933	672,368	2.00	3.00	9.00	25.00	175.00	400.00
	1934	409,067	3.00	6.00	18.00	55.00	250.00	500.00
	1935	384,056	3.00	6.00	18.00	55.00	250.00	500.00
	1936	2,460,871	.60	1.25	3.00	8.75	45.00	85.00
	1936 dot on rev.	4 known	—	—	—	*Specimen		—

*NOTE: David Akers, John Jay Pittman sale 10-97 Gem Specimen realized $120,000.

Maple Leaf

KM#	Date	Mintage	VG-8	F-12	VF-20	XF-40	MS-60	MS-63
34	1937	2,500,095	1.00	1.75	3.00	4.50	10.00	16.00
	1938	4,197,323	1.25	2.00	3.50	7.00	40.00	70.00
	1939	5,501,748	BV	1.50	2.50	6.00	35.00	60.00
	1940	16,526,470	BV	.75	1.25	3.00	14.00	25.00
34	1941	8,716,386	BV	1.00	2.50	6.00	35.00	70.00
	1942	10,214,011	BV	.75	1.25	4.00	25.00	40.00
	1943	21,143,229	BV	.75	1.25	4.00	12.00	25.00
	1944	9,383,582	BV	.75	1.50	4.50	20.00	40.00
	1945	10,979,570	BV	.75	1.25	4.00	12.00	22.00
	1946	6,300,066	BV	1.00	2.00	4.50	20.00	40.00
	1947	4,431,926	BV	1.25	2.50	6.00	32.00	45.00
	1947 maple leaf	9,638,793	BV	.75	1.50	3.00	10.00	16.00

Modified Obverse Legend

KM#	Date	Mintage	VG-8	F-12	VF-20	XF-40	MS-60	MS-63
43	1948	422,741	2.00	3.50	8.00	17.00	40.00	60.00
	1949	11,336,172	—	BV	1.25	2.00	7.00	12.00
	1950	17,823,075	—	BV	1.00	1.50	6.00	10.00
	1951	15,079,265	—	BV	.75	1.50	5.00	9.00
	1952	10,474,455	—	BV	.75	1.50	5.00	9.00

Elizabeth II Effigy by Gillick

KM#	Date	Mintage	VG-8	F-12	VF-20	XF-40	MS-60	MS-63
51	1953 w/o straps	17,706,395	—	—	BV	1.25	3.00	6.00
	1953 w/straps	Inc. Ab.	—	—	BV	1.25	3.50	6.50
	1954	4,493,150	—	BV	1.00	1.50	6.00	11.00
	1955	12,237,294	—	—	BV	.75	3.00	5.00
	1956	16,732,844	—	—	BV	.75	2.25	3.50
	1956 dot below date	Inc. Ab.	1.00	2.00	3.00	5.00	12.50	22.50
	1957	16,110,229	—	—	—	BV	1.25	2.00
	1958	10,621,236	—	—	—	BV	1.25	2.00
	1959	19,691,433	—	—	—	BV	1.00	1.50
	1960	45,446,835	—	—	—	BV	.75	1.00
	1961	26,850,859	—	—	—	BV	.75	1.00
	1962	41,864,335	—	—	—	BV	.75	1.00
	1963	41,916,208	—	—	—	BV	.75	1.00
	1964	49,518,549	—	—	—	BV	.75	1.00

KM#	Date	Mintage	VG-8	F-12	VF-20	XF-40	MS-60	MS-63
		Elizabeth II Effigy by Machin						
61	1965	56,965,392	—	—	—	BV	.75	1.00
	1966	34,567,898	—	—	—	BV	.75	1.00

| OTTAWA | | PHILADELPHIA |

Reeding

| 72 | 1968 Ottawa | 70,460,000 | — | — | — | BV | .60 | .75 |

NICKEL

72a	1968 Ottawa	87,412,930	—	—	—	.15	.25	.40
73	1968 Philadelphia	85,170,000	—	—	—	.15	.25	.40
	1969 lg.date, lg.ship	4 known	—	—	6500.	10,000.	—	—

Redesigned Smaller Ship

KM#	Date	Mintage	VG-8	F-12	VF-20	XF-40	MS-60	MS-63
77.1	1969	55,833,929	—	—	—	.15	.25	.40
	1970	5,249,296	—	—	—	.25	.65	.95
	1971	41,016,968	—	—	—	.15	.25	.40
	1972	60,169,387	—	—	—	.15	.25	.40
	1973	167,715,435	—	—	—	.15	.25	.40
	1974	201,566,565	—	—	—	.15	.25	.40
	1975	207,680,000	—	—	—	.15	.25	.40
	1976	95,018,533	—	—	—	.15	.25	.40
	1977	128,452,206	—	—	—	.15	.25	.40
	1978	170,366,431	—	—	—	.15	.25	.40
77.2	1979	237,321,321	—	—	—	.15	.25	.40
		Smaller bust						
	1980	170,111,533	—	—	—	.15	.25	.40
	1981	123,912,900	—	—	—	.15	.25	.40
	1981	199,000	—	—	—	—	Proof	1.50
	1982	93,475,000	—	—	—	.15	.25	.40
	1982	180,908	—	—	—	—	Proof	1.50
	1983	111,065,000	—	—	—	.15	.25	.40
	1983	168,000	—	—	—	—	Proof	2.00
	1984	121,690,000	—	—	—	.15	.25	.40
	1984	161,602	—	—	—	—	Proof	2.00
	1985	143,025,000	—	—	—	.15	.25	.40
	1985	157,037	—	—	—	—	Proof	2.00
	1986	168,620,000	—	—	—	.15	.25	.40
	1986	175,745	—	—	—	—	Proof	2.00
	1987	147,309,000	—	—	—	.15	.25	.40
	1987	179,004	—	—	—	—	Proof	2.00
	1988	162,998,558	—	—	—	.15	.25	.40
	1988	175,259	—	—	—	—	Proof	2.00
	1989	199,104,414	—	—	—	.15	.25	.40
	1989	170,528	—	—	—	—	Proof	2.00

Elizabeth II Effigy by dePedery-Hunt

KM#	Date	Mintage	VG-8	F-12	VF-20	XF-40	MS-60	MS-63
183	1990	65,023,000	—	—	—	.15	.25	.40
	1990	140,649	—	—	—	—	Proof	3.00
	1991	50,397,000	—	—	—	.15	.25	.40
	1991	131,888	—	—	—	—	Proof	6.50
	1993	135,569,000	—	—	—	.15	.25	.40
	1993	143,065	—	—	—	—	Proof	3.00
	1994	145,800,000	—	—	—	.15	.25	.40
	1994	146,424	—	—	—	—	Proof	3.00
	1995	145,800,000	—	—	—	.15	.25	.40
	1995	50,000	—	—	—	—	Proof	3.00

NICKEL PLATED STEEL

183a	1996	51,814,000	—	—	—	.15	.25	.40
	1997	42,882,000	—	—	—	.15	.25	.40
	1998	—	—	—	—	.15	.25	.40
	1998W	—	—	—	—	In Mint sets only		.50

2.4000 g, .925 SILVER, .0713 oz ASW

183b	1996	—	—	—	—	—	Proof	5.50
	1997	—	—	—	—	—	Proof	5.50
	1998O	—	—	—	—	In Proof sets only		4.00

COMMEMORATIVE TEN CENTS

2.3328 g, .800 SILVER, .0600 oz ASW

| 67 | 1967 Confederation Centennial | 62,998,215 | — | — | — | BV | .75 | 1.50 |

2.3328 g, .500 SILVER, .0372 oz ASW

KM#	Date	Mintage	VG-8	F-12	VF-20	XF-40	MS-60	MS-63
	2.3328 g, .800 SILVER. .0600 oz ASW							
67	1967 Confederation Centennial							
		62,998,215	—	—	—	BV	.75	1.50

2.3328 g, .500 SILVER, .0372 oz ASW

KM#	Date	Mintage	VG-8	F-12	VF-20	XF-40	MS-60	MS-63
67a	1967 Confederation Centennial							
		Inc. Ab.	—	—	—	BV	.75	1.50
	NICKEL							
206	1992 Confederation 125							
		174,476,000	—	—	—	.15	.25	.40
		147,061	—	—	—	—	Proof	3.00

2.4000 g, .925 SILVER, .0714 oz ASW

KM#	Date	Mintage	VG-8	F-12	VF-20	XF-40	MS-60	MS-63
299	ND(1997) John Cabot							
		*.050	—	—	—	—	Proof	16.25
	2.3200 g, .925 SILVER, .0690 oz ASW							
311	ND(1998) 90th Anniversary Royal Canadian Mint							
		.025	—	—	In Matte sets only			5.50
		.025	—	—	In Proof sets only			5.50

TWENTY-FIVE CENTS

5.8100 g, .925 SILVER, .1728 oz ASW

KM#	Date	Mintage	VG-8	F-12	VF-20	XF-40	MS-60	MS-63
5	1901	640,000	6.00	9.75	27.00	80.00	375.00	975.00

NOTE: Earlier dates (1870-1900) exist for this type.

KM#	Date	Mintage	VG-8	F-12	VF-20	XF-40	MS-60	MS-63
11	1902	464,000	7.00	15.00	40.00	110.00	500.00	1450.
	1902H	800,000	4.00	6.50	32.00	60.00	225.00	475.00
	1903	846,150	5.00	9.00	30.00	110.00	475.00	1100.
	1904	400,000	9.75	27.00	95.00	250.00	1150.	3000.
	1905	800,000	5.50	15.00	65.00	200.00	1250.	3250.
	1906 lg. crown	1,237,843	5.00	7.00	27.00	70.00	325.00	1100.
	1906 sm. crown	Inc. Ab.	—	—	—	—	Rare	—
	1907	2,088,000	4.00	7.00	27.00	70.00	325.00	1000.
	1908	495,016	6.00	12.00	45.00	125.00	350.00	825.00
	1909	1,335,929	5.00	9.00	40.00	150.00	485.00	1350.
	5.8319 g, .925 SILVER. .1734 oz ASW							
11a	1910	3,577,569	3.00	7.00	26.00	65.00	210.00	475.00

KM#	Date	Mintage	VG-8	F-12	VF-20	XF-40	MS-60	MS-63
18	1911	1,721,341	6.00	14.00	30.00	75.00	250.00	500.00
24	1912	2,544,199	2.25	3.50	10.00	40.00	285.00	1000.
	1913	2,213,595	2.25	3.50	10.00	40.00	265.00	850.00
	1914	1,215,397	2.50	4.00	15.00	50.00	500.00	1500.
	1915	242,382	8.00	22.00	100.00	350.00	2000.	4000.
	1916	1,462,566	2.00	3.00	10.00	30.00	200.00	550.00
	1917	3,365,644	1.50	3.00	9.00	20.00	110.00	200.00
	1918	4,175,649	1.50	3.00	9.00	18.00	75.00	185.00
	1919	5,852,262	1.50	3.00	9.00	18.00	75.00	185.00

5.8319 g, .800 SILVER, .1500 oz ASW

KM#	Date	Mintage	VG-8	F-12	VF-20	XF-40	MS-60	MS-63
24a	1920	1,975,278	1.50	3.00	10.00	22.00	140.00	425.00
	1921	597,337	7.00	16.00	65.00	180.00	800.00	1800.
	1927	468,096	16.00	30.00	75.00	200.00	800.00	1500.
	1928	2,114,178	1.50	3.00	9.00	22.00	110.00	320.00
	1929	2,690,562	1.50	2.75	8.00	22.00	110.00	320.00
	1930	968,748	2.00	3.50	10.00	25.00	185.00	500.00
	1931	537,815	2.00	3.50	12.00	27.50	235.00	550.00
	1932	537,994	2.25	4.00	12.00	30.00	200.00	475.00
	1933	421,282	3.00	4.50	16.50	40.00	190.00	400.00
	1934	384,350	3.50	6.00	22.00	55.00	250.00	450.00
	1935	537,772	3.50	5.00	17.50	42.00	200.00	400.00
	1936	972,094	1.50	3.00	9.00	20.00	80.00	200.00
	1936 dot	153,322	27.50	60.00	130.00	275.00	700.00	1700.

Maple Leaf Variety

KM#	Date	Mintage	VG-8	F-12	VF-20	XF-40	MS-60	MS-63
35	1937	2,690,176	BV	1.25	4.00	5.00	10.00	25.00
	1938	3,149,245	BV	1.25	4.50	6.50	55.00	100.00
	1939	3,532,495	BV	1.25	3.00	6.50	50.00	85.00
	1940	9,583,650	BV	1.25	2.50	4.50	10.00	25.00
	1941	6,654,672	BV	1.00	2.50	4.50	12.00	26.00
	1942	6,935,871	BV	1.00	2.50	4.50	12.00	26.00
	1943	13,559,575	BV	1.00	2.50	4.00	15.50	30.00
	1944	7,216,237	BV	1.00	2.50	4.50	17.00	36.00
	1945	5,296,495	BV	1.00	2.50	4.00	10.00	26.00
	1946	2,210,810	BV	1.25	3.00	5.00	35.00	60.00
	1947	1,524,554	BV	1.25	3.00	6.00	40.00	75.00
	1947 dot after 7	Inc. Ab.	24.00	40.00	65.00	115.00	200.00	450.00
	1947 maple leaf	4,393,938	BV	1.00	2.75	4.00	12.00	25.00

Modified Obverse Legend

KM#	Date	Mintage	VG-8	F-12	VF-20	XF-40	MS-60	MS-63
44	1948	2,564,424	BV	1.50	3.00	5.00	40.00	90.00
	1949	7,988,830	—	BV	1.50	2.00	9.00	18.00
	1950	9,673,335	—	BV	1.50	2.25	9.00	15.00
	1951	8,290,719	—	BV	1.50	2.25	6.00	12.00
	1952	8,859,642	—	BV	1.50	2.25	6.00	12.00

Elizabeth II Effigy by Gillick

KM#	Date	Mintage	VG-8	F-12	VF-20	XF-40	MS-60	MS-63
52	1953 NSS	10,546,769	—	BV	1.25	2.00	4.00	7.00
	1953 SS	Inc. Ab.	—	BV	1.25	2.00	6.00	12.00
	1954	2,318,891	BV	1.25	2.00	6.00	20.00	30.00
	1955	9,552,505	—	—	BV	1.50	3.50	6.00
	1956	11,269,353	—	—	BV	1.25	3.00	5.00
	1957	12,770,190	—	—	BV	1.00	2.00	4.00
	1958	9,336,910	—	—	BV	1.00	2.00	4.00
	1959	13,503,461	—	—	—	BV	1.50	2.50
	1960	22,835,327	—	—	—	BV	1.50	2.50
	1961	18,164,368	—	—	—	BV	1.50	2.50
	1962	29,559,266	—	—	—	BV	1.50	2.25
	1963	21,180,652	—	—	—	BV	1.25	1.75
	1964	36,479,343	—	—	—	BV	1.25	1.75

Elizabeth II Effigy by Machin

KM#	Date	Mintage	VG-8	F-12	VF-20	XF-40	MS-60	MS-63
62	1965	44,708,869	—	—	—	BV	1.25	1.75
	1966	25,626,315	—	—	—	BV	1.25	1.75
	5.8319 g, .500 SILVER, .0937 oz ASW							
62a	1968	71,464,000	—	—	—	BV	1.00	1.75
	NICKEL							
62b	1968	88,686,931	—	—	—	.30	.50	.75
(74.1)	1969	133,037,929	—	—	—	.30	.50	.75
	1970	10,302,010	—	—	—	.30	1.00	1.50
	1971	48,170,428	—	—	—	.30	.50	.75
	1972	43,743,387	—	—	—	.30	.50	.75
	1974	192,360,598	—	—	—	.30	.50	.75
	1975	141,148,000	—	—	—	.30	.50	.75
	1976	86,898,261	—	—	—	.30	.50	.75
	1977	99,634,555	—	—	—	.30	.50	.75
	1978	176,475,408	—	—	—	.30	.50	.75

KM#	Date	Mintage	VG-8	F-12	VF-20	XF-40	MS-60	MS-63
		Smaller bust						
74	1979	131,042,905	—	—	—	.30	.50	.75
	1980	76,178,000	—	—	—	.30	.50	.75
	1981	131,580,272	—	—	—	.30	.50	.75
	1981	199,000	—	—	—	—	Proof	2.00
	1982	171,926,000	—	—	—	.30	.50	.75
	1982	180,908	—	—	—	—	Proof	2.00
	1983	13,162,000	—	—	—	.30	.75	1.50
	1983	168,000	—	—	—	—	Proof	3.00
	1984	121,668,000	—	—	—	.30	.50	.75
	1984	161,602	—	—	—	—	Proof	2.00
	1985	158,734,000	—	—	—	.30	.50	.75
	1985	157,037	—	—	—	—	Proof	2.00
	1986	132,220,000	—	—	—	.30	.50	.75
	1986	175,745	—	—	—	—	Proof	3.00
	1987	53,408,000	—	—	—	.30	.75	1.50
	1987	179,004	—	—	—	—	Proof	3.00
	1988	80,368,473	—	—	—	.30	.75	1.50
	1988	175,259	—	—	—	—	Proof	3.50
	1989	119,796,307	—	—	—	.30	.50	.75
	1989	170,928	—	—	—	—	Proof	3.50

Elizabeth II Effigy by dePedery-Hunt

KM#	Date	Mintage	VG-8	F-12	VF-20	XF-40	MS-60	MS-63
184	1990	31,258,000	—	—	—	.30	.75	1.50
	1990	140,649	—	—	—	—	Proof	3.50
	1991	459,000	—	—	2.00	4.00	8.00	12.00
	1991	131,888	—	—	—	—	Proof	25.00
	1993	73,758,000	—	—	—	.30	.75	1.50
	1993	143,065	—	—	—	—	Proof	3.00
	1994	77,670,000	—	—	—	.30	.75	1.50
	1994	146,424	—	—	—	—	Proof	5.00
	1995	89,210,000	—	—	—	.30	.75	1.50
	1995	50,000	—	—	—	—	Proof	5.00

NICKEL PLATED STEEL

184a	1996	28,106,000	—	—	—	.30	.75	1.50
	1997	—	—	—	—	.30	.75	1.50
	1998	—	—	—	—	—	—	1.75
	1998W	—	—	—	—	—	In Mint sets only	2.00

5.9000 g, .925 SILVER, .1754 oz ASW

184b	1996	—	—	—	—	—	Proof	6.50
	1997	—	—	—	—	—	Proof	6.50
	1998O	—	—	—	—	In Proof sets only		5.00

COMMEMORATIVE TWENTY-FIVE CENTS

68	1967 Confederation Centennial, .800 Silver							
		48,855,500	—	—	—	BV	1.25	1.75
68a	1967 Confederation Centennial, .500 Silver							
		Inc. Ab.	—	—	—	BV	1.25	1.75

81.1	1973 RCMP Centennial, 120 beads, Nickel							
		134,958,587	—	—	—	.30	.50	.80
81.2	1973 RCMP Centennial, 132 beads, Nickel							
		Inc. Ab.	35.00	55.00	65.00	75.00	100.00	130.00
207	1992 Confederation 125, Nickel							
		442,986	—	—	—	—	—	12.50
		147,061	—	—	—	—	Proof	20.00

125th Anniversary of Confederation

203	1992 New Brunswick, Nickel							
		12,174,000	—	—	—	—	—	.80
203a	1992 New Brunswick, .925 Silver							
		149,579	—	—	—	—	Proof	7.50
212	1992 North West Territories, Nickel							
		12,582,000	—	—	—	—	—	.80
212a	1992 North West Territories, .925 Silver							
		149,579	—	—	—	—	Proof	7.50

KM#	Date	Mintage	VG-8	F-12	VF-20	XF-40	MS-60	MS-63
213	1992 Newfoundland, Nickel							
		11,405,000	—	—	—	—	—	.80
213a	1992 Newfoundland, .925 Silver							
		149,579	—	—	—	—	Proof	7.50
214	1992 Manitoba, Nickel							
		11,349,000	—	—	—	—	—	.80
214a	1992 Manitoba, .925 Silver							
		149,579	—	—	—	—	Proof	7.50
220	1992 Yukon, Nickel	10,388,000	—	—	—	—	—	.80
220a	1992 Yukon, .925 Silver							
		—	—	—	—	—	Proof	7.50

221	1992 Alberta, Nickel	12,133,000	—	—	—	—	—	.80
221a	1992 Alberta, .925 Silver	—	—	—	—	—	Proof	7.50
222	1992 Prince Edward Island, Nickel							
		13,001,000	—	—	—	—	—	.80
222a	1992 Prince Edward Island, .925 Silver							
		149,579	—	—	—	—	Proof	7.50
223	1992 Ontario, Nickel							
		14,263,000	—	—	—	—	—	.80
223a	1992 Ontario, .925 Silver	—	—	—	—	—	Proof	7.50

231	1992 Nova Scotia, Nickel							
		13,600,000	—	—	—	—	—	.80
231a	1992 Nova Scotia, .925 Silver							
		149,579	—	—	—	—	Proof	7.50
232	1992 British Columbia, Nickel							
		14,001,000	—	—	—	—	—	.80
232a	1992 British Columbia, .925 Silver							
		149,579	—	—	—	—	Proof	7.50
233	1992 Saskatchewan, Nickel							
		14,165,000	—	—	—	—	—	.80
233a	1992 Saskatchewan, .925 Silver							
		149,579	—	—	—	—	Proof	7.50

234	1992 Quebec, Nickel							
		13,607,000	—	—	—	—	—	.80
234a	1992 Quebec, .925 Silver							
		149,579	—	—	—	—	Proof	7.50
312	ND(1998) 90th Anniversary Royal Canadian Mint							
		.025	—	—	—	—	In Matte sets only	16.50
								In Proof sets only	16.50

FIFTY CENTS

11.6200 g, .925 SILVER, .3456 oz ASW

KM#	Date	Mintage	VG-8	F-12	VF-20	XF-40	MS-60	MS-63
6	1901	80,000	42.00	70.00	165.00	365.00	4200.	10,500.

Victorian Leaves   Edwardian Leaves

KM#	Date	Mintage	VG-8	F-12	VF-20	XF-40	MS-60	MS-63
12	1902	120,000	11.00	22.50	75.00	200.00	1100.	3000.
	1903H	140,000	18.00	35.00	110.00	225.00	1250.	3500.
	1904	60,000	80.00	165.00	300.00	650.00	2800.	7000.
	1905	40,000	100.00	225.00	435.00	1000.	5000.	10,000.
	1906	350,000	10.00	25.00	70.00	190.00	1150.	3250.
	1907	300,000	10.00	25.00	70.00	200.00	1250.	3850.
	1908	128,119	14.75	45.00	120.00	275.00	1150.	2250.
	1909	302,118	13.00	40.00	120.00	325.00	2175.	6000.
	1910 Victorian lvs.	649,521	9.00	22.00	65.00	180.00	950.00	3150.

11.6638 g, .925 SILVER, .3461 oz ASW

	Date	Mintage	VG-8	F-12	VF-20	XF-40	MS-60	MS-63
	1910 Edwardian lvs.	Inc. Ab.	9.00	22.00	65.00	180.00	1000.	3150.

	Date	Mintage	VG-8	F-12	VF-20	XF-40	MS-60	MS-63
19	1911	209,972	9.00	70.00	225.00	475.00	1300.	2900.

Modified Obverse Legend

KM#	Date	Mintage	VG-8	F-12	VF-20	XF-40	MS-60	MS-63
25	1912	285,867	4.50	16.00	75.00	200.00	1100.	2500.
	1913	265,889	4.50	16.00	85.00	210.00	1400.	4000.
	1914	160,128	10.00	45.00	135.00	400.00	2250.	5000.
	1916	459,070	3.00	14.00	50.00	125.00	700.00	2000.
	1917	752,213	3.00	12.00	35.00	90.00	500.00	1200.
	1918	754,989	3.00	8.00	22.00	70.00	425.00	1000.
	1919	1,113,429	3.00	8.00	22.00	70.00	425.00	1000.

11.6638 g, .800 SILVER, .3000 oz ASW

	Date	Mintage	VG-8	F-12	VF-20	XF-40	MS-60	MS-63
25a	1920	584,691	3.00	8.50	30.00	110.00	500.00	1250.
	1921	75 to 100 pcs.known	12,300.	17,000.	20,750.	25,000.	35,850.	45,300.

NOTE: Bowers and Merena Victoria Sale 9-89 MS-65 realized $110,000.

	Date	Mintage	VG-8	F-12	VF-20	XF-40	MS-60	MS-63
	1929	228,328	3.00	8.00	30.00	100.00	550.00	1100.
	1931	57,581	7.00	22.00	65.00	200.00	900.00	2000.
	1932	19,213	32.00	100.00	200.00	500.00	2400.	5500.
	1934	39,539	10.00	25.00	75.00	200.00	650.00	1200.
	1936	38,550	8.50	20.00	65.00	150.00	500.00	1000.

KM#	Date	Mintage	VG-8	F-12	VF-20	XF-40	MS-60	MS-63
36	1937	192,016	2.50	3.00	6.00	10.00	25.00	60.00
	1938	192,018	3.00	5.00	10.00	28.00	100.00	300.00
	1939	287,976	3.00	4.50	8.00	16.50	70.00	220.00
	1940	1,996,566	BV	2.00	3.00	5.00	22.00	60.00
	1941	1,714,874	BV	2.00	3.00	5.00	22.00	60.00
	1942	1,974,164	BV	2.00	3.00	5.00	22.00	60.00
	1943	3,109,583	BV	2.00	3.00	5.00	22.00	60.00
	1944	2,460,205	BV	2.00	3.00	5.00	22.00	60.00
	1945	1,959,528	BV	2.00	3.00	5.00	22.00	60.00
	1946	950,235	BV	4.00	6.00	9.00	60.00	110.00
	1946 hoof in 6	Inc. Ab.	12.00	22.50	45.00	110.00	975.00	1800.
	1947 straight 7	424,885	2.00	4.50	6.00	12.00	80.00	175.00
	1947 curved 7	Inc. Ab.	2.00	4.50	6.00	12.00	80.00	190.00
	1947ML straight 7	38,433	14.00	18.00	30.00	60.00	160.00	225.00
	1947ML curved 7	Inc. Ab.	875.00	1200.	1650.	2000.	3000.	5000.

Modified Obverse Legend

KM#	Date	Mintage	VG-8	F-12	VF-20	XF-40	MS-60	MS-63
45	1948	37,784	35.00	50.00	65.00	90.00	145.00	225.00
	1949	858,991	2.00	3.00	6.00	10.00	35.00	90.00
	1949 hoof over 9	Inc. Ab.	5.00	12.00	22.00	60.00	350.00	700.00
	1950	2,384,179	3.00	4.50	9.00	20.00	175.00	275.00
	1950 lines in 0	Inc. Ab.	BV	2.50	3.00	4.00	11.00	20.00
	1951	2,421,730	BV	1.75	2.50	3.50	8.00	17.00
	1952	2,596,465	BV	1.75	2.50	3.50	8.00	16.00

Elizabeth II Effigy by Gillick

KM#	Date	Mintage	VG-8	F-12	VF-20	XF-40	MS-60	MS-63
53	1953 sm. date	1,630,429	—	BV	2.00	2.50	5.50	12.00
	1953 lg.dt,straps	Inc. Ab.	—	BV	3.50	5.00	20.00	30.00
	1953 lg.dt,w/o straps	I.A.	BV	3.00	5.00	12.00	70.00	110.00
	1954	506,305	BV	2.50	4.75	7.00	20.00	30.00
	1955	753,511	BV	2.00	3.00	5.00	12.00	22.00
	1956	1,379,499	—	BV	2.00	3.00	4.50	9.00
	1957	2,171,689	—	—	BV	2.00	3.50	6.00
	1958	2,957,266	—	—	BV	2.00	3.00	5.50

New Reverse Shield

KM#	Date	Mintage	VG-8	F-12	VF-20	XF-40	MS-60	MS-63
56	1959	3,095,535	—	—	BV	2.00	2.50	4.50
	1960	3,488,897	—	—	—	BV	2.25	3.25
	1961	3,584,417	—	—	—	BV	2.00	3.00
	1962	5,208,030	—	—	—	BV	2.00	3.00
	1963	8,348,871	—	—	—	BV	2.00	3.00
	1964	9,377,676	—	—	—	BV	2.00	3.00

Elizabeth II Effigy by Machin

KM#	Date	Mintage	VG-8	F-12	VF-20	XF-40	MS-60	MS-63
63	1965	12,629,974	—	—	—	BV	2.00	3.00
	1966	7,920,496	—	—	—	BV	2.00	3.00

| | 1968-76 | | 1977 | | 1978- | | |

NICKEL

KM#	Date	Mintage	VG-8	F-12	VF-20	XF-40	MS-60	MS-63
75.1	1968	3,966,932	—	—	—	.50	.65	1.00
	1969	7,113,929	—	—	—	.50	.65	1.00
	1970	2,429,526	—	—	—	.50	.65	1.00
	1971	2,166,444	—	—	—	.50	.65	1.00
	1972	2,515,632	—	—	—	.50	.65	1.00
	1973	2,546,096	—	—	—	.50	.65	1.00
	1974	3,436,650	—	—	—	.50	.65	1.00
	1975	3,710,000	—	—	—	.50	.65	1.00
	1976	2,940,719	—	—	—	.50	.65	1.00

Smaller bust

75.2	1977	709,839	—	—	.50	.75	1.50	2.00
75.3	1978 square jewels	3,341,892	—	—	—	.50	.75	1.00
	1978 round jewels	Inc. Ab.	—	—	.50	2.50	3.00	4.00
	1979	3,425,000	—	—	—	.50	.65	1.00
	1980	1,574,000	—	—	—	.50	.65	1.00
	1981	2,690,272	—	—	—	.50	.65	1.00
	1981	199,000	—	—	—	—	Proof	3.00
	1982 small beads	2,236,674	—	—	—	.50	.65	1.00
	1982 small beads	180,908	—	—	—	—	Proof	3.00
	1982 large beads	Inc. Ab.	—	—	—	.50	.65	1.00
	1983	1,177,000	—	—	—	.50	.65	1.00
	1983	168,000	—	—	—	—	Proof	3.00
	1984	1,502,989	—	—	—	.50	.65	1.00
	1984	161,602	—	—	—	—	Proof	3.00
	1985	2,188,374	—	—	—	.50	.65	1.00
	1985	157,037	—	—	—	—	Proof	3.50
	1986	781,400	—	—	—	.50	.85	1.25
	1986	175,745	—	—	—	—	Proof	3.50
	1987	373,000	—	—	—	.50	.85	1.35
	1987	179,004	—	—	—	—	Proof	4.00
	1988	220,000	—	—	—	.50	1.50	2.20
	1988	175,259	—	—	—	—	Proof	4.00
	1989	266,419	—	—	—	.50	.85	1.60
	1989	170,928	—	—	—	—	Proof	4.50

Elizabeth II Effigy by dePedery-Hunt

185	1990	207,000	—	—	—	.50	2.00	3.00
	1990	140,649	—	—	—	—	Proof	7.50
	1991	490,000	—	—	—	.50	.85	1.60
	1991	131,888	—	—	—	—	Proof	10.00
	1993	393,000	—	—	—	.50	.85	1.25
	1993	143,065	—	—	—	—	Proof	5.00
	1994	987,000	—	—	—	.50	.75	1.00
	1994	146,424	—	—	—	—	Proof	6.00
	1995	626,000	—	—	—	.50	.75	1.00
	1995	50,000	—	—	—	—	Proof	6.00

NICKEL PLATED STEEL

185a	1996	458,000	—	—	—	.50	.65	1.00

.925 SILVER

185b	1996	—	—	—	—	—	Proof	7.50
	1997	—	—	—	—	—	Proof	7.50
290	1997 Redesigned Arms, Nickel plated Steel							
		387,000	—	—	—	.50	.65	1.00
	1998	—	—	—	—	.50	.65	1.00
	1998W	—	—	—	—	In Mint sets only		1.75
290a	1997 Redesigned Arms, .925 Silver							
		—	—	—	—	—	Proof	7.00
	1998O	—	—	—	—	In Proof sets only		6.00

COMMEMORATIVE FIFTY CENTS

KM#	Date	Mintage	VG-8	F-12	VF-20	XF-40	MS-60	MS-63
69	1967 Confederation Centennial, .800 Silver							
		4,211,392	—	—	—	3.00	4.00	4.50

KM#	Date	Mintage	VG-8	F-12	VF-20	XF-40	MS-60	MS-63
208	1992 Confederation 125, Nickel							
		445,000	—	—	—	.50	1.25	1.50
		147,061	—	—	—	—	Proof	8.50
261	1995 Atlantic Puffin, .925 Silver							
		—	—	—	—	—	Proof	11.50
262	1995 Whooping Crane, .925 Silver							
		—	—	—	—	—	Proof	11.50

263	1995 Gray Jays, .925 Silver							
		—	—	—	—	—	Proof	11.50
264	1995 White Tailed Ptarmigans, .925 Silver							
		—	—	—	—	—	Proof	11.50
283	1996 Moose Calf, .925 Silver							
		—	—	—	—	—	Proof	12.00
284	1996 Wood Ducklings, .925 Silver							
		—	—	—	—	—	Proof	12.00
285	1996 Cougar Kittens, .925 Silver							
		—	—	—	—	—	Proof	12.00
286	1996 Black Bear Cubs, .925 Silver							
		—	—	—	—	—	Proof	12.00
292	1997 Duck Tolling Retriever, .925 Silver							
		—	—	—	—	—	Proof	12.50

293	1997 Labrador Retriever, .925 Silver							
		—	—	—	—	—	Proof	13.50
294	1997 Newfoundland, .925 Silver							
		—	—	—	—	—	Proof	13.50
295	1997 Eskimo Dog, .925 Silver							
		—	—	—	—	—	Proof	12.50

313	ND(1998) 90th Anniversary Royal Canadian Mint, .925 Silver							
		.025	—	—	—	In Matte sets only		32.25
		.025	—	—	—	In Proof sets only		32.25
314	ND(1998) 110 Years Canadian Speed and Figure Skating, .925 Silver							
		—	—	—	—	—	Proof	12.00
315	ND(1998) 100 Years Canadian Ski Racing and Jumping, .925 Silver							
		—	—	—	—	—	Proof	12.00

318	1998 Killer Whales, .925 Silver							
		—	—	—	—	—	Proof	12.00
319	1998 Humpback whale, .925 Silver							
		—	—	—	—	—	Proof	12.00
320	1998 Beluga Whale, .925 Silver							
		—	—	—	—	—	Proof	12.00
321	1998 Blue Whale, .925 Silver							
		—	—	—	—	—	Proof	12.00
327	ND(1998) 110 Years Canadian Soccer, .925 Silver							
		—	—	—	—	—	Proof	12.00
328	ND(1998) 20 Years Canadian Auto Racing, .925 Silver							
		—	—	—	—	—	Proof	12.00

VOYAGEUR DOLLARS

23.3276 g, .800 SILVER, .6000 oz ASW

KM#	Date	Mintage	F-12	VF-20	XF-40	AU-50	MS-60	MS-63
31	1936	339,600	10.00	14.50	18.50	22.50	36.00	85.00

KM#	Date	Mintage	F-12	VF-20	XF-40	AU-50	MS-60	MS-63
37	1937	207,406	9.00	10.50	13.50	18.00	26.00	70.00
	1937	1,295	—	—	Proof		—	450.00
	1937	I.A.	—	—	Matte Proof		—	250.00
	1938	90,304	25.00	40.00	55.00	60.00	75.00	215.00
	1945	38,391	65.00	115.00	145.00	165.00	200.00	475.00
	1945	—	—	—	—	Specimen		2750.
	1946	93,055	15.00	27.00	42.00	47.00	75.00	220.00

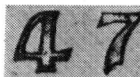
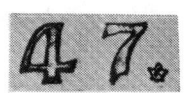

Pointed 7	Blunt 7	Maple Leaf (blunt 7 only)

KM#	Date	Mintage	F-12	VF-20	XF-40	AU-50	MS-60	MS-63
	1947 pointed 7	Inc. Bl.	60.00	90.00	120.00	160.00	285.00	950.00
	1947 blunt 7	65,595	40.00	75.00	100.00	120.00	140.00	245.00
	1947 maple leaf	21,135	100.00	140.00	165.00	220.00	270.00	550.00

Modified Left Legend

KM#	Date	Mintage	VF-20	XF-40	AU-50	MS-60	MS-63	
46	1948	18,780	450.00	525.00	615.00	685.00	785.00	1150.
	1950 w/4 water lines	261,002	5.00	8.00	11.00	12.00	18.00	32.00
	1950 w/4 water lines, (1 known)				Matte Proof			—
	1950 Arnprior w/1-1/2 w.l.	I.A.	7.00	10.00	13.50	20.00	36.00	100.00
	1951 w/4 water lines	416,395	4.00	5.00	7.00	8.50	11.50	26.00
	1951 w/4 water lines	—	—	—	—	Proof		400.00
	1951 Arnprior w/1-1/2 w.l.	I.A.	25.00	34.00	47.00	65.00	105.00	275.00
	1952 w/4 water lines	406,148	4.00	5.00	7.00	8.00	11.50	26.00
	1952 Arnprior	I.A.	35.00	55.00	70.00	120.00	175.00	375.00
	1952 Arnprior	—	—	—	—	Proof		Rare
	1952 w/o water lines	I.A.	5.00	6.50	9.00	10.00	16.50	40.00

Elizabeth II Effigy by Gillick

KM#	Date	Mintage	F-12	VF-20	XF-40	AU-50	MS-60	MS-63
54	1953 w/o strap, wire rim	1,074,578	3.85	4.50	5.00	8.00	16.00	
	1953 w/strap, flat rim	Inc. Ab.	3.85	4.50	5.00	8.00	16.00	

KM#	Date	Mintage	VF-20	XF-40	AU-50	MS-60	MS-63
54	1954	246,606	7.00	10.00	12.00	16.50	32.50
	1955 w/4 water lines	268,105	7.00	10.00	12.00	16.50	29.00
	1955 Arnprior w/1-1/2 w.l.*	I.A.	60.00	75.00	95.00	110.00	165.00
	1956	209,092	9.00	13.50	15.50	19.00	40.00
	1957 w/4 water lines	496,389	BV	4.75	6.00	8.00	13.50
	1957 w/1 water line	I.A.	5.50	7.50	8.50	12.00	26.50
	1959	1,443,502	—	—	BV	5.00	7.50
	1960	1,420,486	—	—	BV	5.00	7.50
	1961	1,262,231	—	—	BV	5.00	7.50
	1962	1,884,789	—	—	BV	5.00	7.50
	1963	4,179,981	—	—	BV	5.00	7.50

*NOTE: All genuine circulation strike 1955 Arnprior dollars have a die break running along the top of TI in the word GRATIA on the obverse.

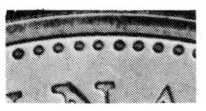
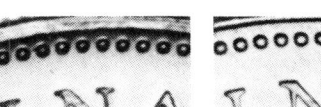

Small Beads	Medium Beads	Large Beads

Elizabeth II Effigy by Machin

KM#	Date	Mintage	VF-20	XF-40	AU-50	MS-60	MS-63
64.1	1965 sm. beads, pointed 5	10,768,569	—	—	BV	4.75	6.50
	1965 sm. beads, blunt 5	Inc. Ab.	—	—	BV	4.75	6.50
	1965 lg. beads, blunt 5	Inc. Ab.	—	—	BV	7.50	10.00
	1965 lg. beads, pointed 5	Inc. Ab.	—	—	BV	4.75	6.50
	1965 med. beads, pointed 5	Inc. Ab.	6.75	8.75	10.75	14.00	27.50
	1966 lg. beads	9,912,178	—	—	BV	4.50	6.50
	1966 sm. beads	*485 pcs.	—	750.00	1250.	1400.	1700.

23.3276 g, .500 SILVER, .3750 oz ASW, 36mm

Smaller bust

KM#	Date	Mintage	MS-63	Mintage	P/L	Spec.
64.2a	1972	—	—	341,598		8.00

NICKEL, 32mm

Large bust

KM#	Date	Mintage	MS-63	Mintage	P/L	Spec.
76.1	1968	5,579,714	1.65	1,408,143	3.00	—
	1969	4,809,313	1.65	594,258	3.50	—
	1972	2,676,041	2.00	405,865	3.75	—

Smaller bust

KM#	Date	Mintage	MS-63	Mintage	P/L	Spec.
76.2	1975	3,256,000	2.00	322,325	3.75	—
	1976	2,498,204	2.50	274,106	4.00	—
76.3	1975 mule w/1976 obv.	Inc. Ab.	—	—	*	—

*NOTE: Only known in proof-like sets w/1976 obv. slightly modified.

Modified Reverse

KM#	Date	Mintage	MS-63	Mintage	P/L	Spec.
117	1977	1,393,745	2.50	—	3.50	—

KM#	Date	Mintage	MS-63	Mintage	P/L	Spec.
120.1	1978	2,948,488	2.00	—	3.50	—
	1979	2,954,842	2.00	—	3.50	—
	1980	3,291,221	2.00	—	4.50	—

Modified Design

	1981	2,778,900	2.00	—	5.00	6.50
	1982	1,098,500	2.00	—	5.00	6.50
	1983	2,267,525	2.00	—	5.00	8.00

KM#	Date	Mintage	MS-63	Mintage	P/L	Proof
120.1	1984	1,223,486	2.00	—	5.00	
	1984	161,602	—	—	—	8.00
	1985	3,104,092	2.00	—	5.00	
	1985	157,037	—	—	—	7.50
	1986	3,089,225	2.00	—	6.00	
	1986	175,259	—	—	—	10.00
	1987	287,330	2.00	—	7.00	
	1987	179,004	—	—	—	10.00
120.2	1985 mule w/New Zealand 50 cent, KM-37 obverse	—	—	—	—	—

LOON DOLLARS

AUREATE-BRONZE PLATED NICKEL

Elizabeth II Effigy by Machin

KM#	Date	Mintage	MS-63	P/L	Proof
157	1987	205,405,000	2.75	—	—
	1987	178,120	—	—	8.00
	1988	138,893,539	2.75	4.75	—
	1988	175,259	—	—	7.50
	1989	184,773,902	2.75	4.75	—
	1989	170,928	—	—	7.50

Elizabeth II Effigy by dePedery-Hunt

KM#	Date	Mintage	MS-63	P/L	Proof
186.1	1990	68,402,000	2.25	4.75	—
	1990	140,649	—	—	9.00
	1991	23,156,000	2.50	6.50	—
	1991	—	—	—	18.00
	1993	33,662,000	2.50	5.50	—
	1993	—	—	—	9.00
	1994	36,237,000	2.00	5.50	—
	1994	—	—	—	9.00
	1995	41,813,000	2.00	6.50	—
	1995	—	—	—	9.00
	1996	17,101,000	2.00	4.75	—
	1996	—	—	—	7.50
	1997	—	2.50	—	—
	1998	—	2.50	—	—
	1998O	—	In Proof sets only		10.00
	1998W	—	In Mint sets only		3.50

COMMEMORATIVE DOLLARS

23.3276 g, .800 SILVER, .6000 oz ASW

KM#	Date	Mintage	F-12	VF-20	XF-40	AU-50	MS-60	MS-63
30	1935 Jubilee	428,707	13.50	20.00	30.00	32.50	38.00	65.00
38	1939 Royal Visit	1,363,816	5.00	6.00	7.00	8.50	11.50	25.00
	1939 Royal Visit	—	—	—	—	Specimen		475.00
	1939 Royal Visit	—	—	—	—	—	Proof	2500.

KM#	Date	Mintage	F-12	VF-20	XF-40	AU-50	MS-60	MS-63
47	1949 Newfoundland	672,218	9.00	12.00	18.50	22.00	25.00	31.50
	1949 Newfoundland	—	—	—	—	Specimen		725.00
55	1958 Br. Columbia	3,039,630	BV	4.50	5.00	5.50	6.50	10.50

KM#	Date	Mintage	F-12	VF-20	XF-40	AU-50	MS-60	MS-63
58	1964 Charlottetown	7,296,832	—	—	—	BV	4.50	7.50
70	1967 Goose, Confederation Centennial	6,767,496		6.00		9.00		450.00

KM#	Date	Mintage	MS-63	P/L	Spec.
78	1970 Manitoba (Nickel, 32mm)	4,140,058	2.00	—	—
		645,869	—	2.50	—
79	1971 Br. Columbia (Nickel, 32mm)	4,260,781	2.00	2.50	—
		468,729	—	(c) 2.50	—

KM#	Date	Mintage	MS-63	P/L	Spec.
80	1971 Br. Columbia (.500 Silver, 36mm)	585,674	—	—	7.50

*NOTE: All silver dollars dated 1971 to date are minted to this standard.

82	1973 Pr. Edward Island (Nickel, 32mm)				
		3,196,452	2.00	—	—
		466,881	—	(c) 2.50	—

KM#	Date	Mintage	MS-63	P/L	Spec.
83	1973 Mountie (.500 Silver, 36mm)	1,031,271	—	—	5.00
83v	1973 Mountie, with metal crest on case	Inc. Ab.	—	—	12.00
88	1974 Winnipeg (Nickel, 32mm)	2,799,363	2.00	—	—
		363,786	—	(c) 3.00	—
88a	1974 Winnipeg (.500 Silver, 36mm)	728,947	—	—	5.00

KM#	Date	Mintage	MS-63	P/L	Spec.
97	1975 Calgary (.500 Silver, 36mm)	930,956	—	—	4.25
106	1976 Parliament Library (.500 Silver, 36mm)	578,708	—	—	6.00

KM#	Date	Mintage	MS-63	P/L	Spec.
118	1977 Silver Jubilee	744,848	—		5.00
121	1978 XI Games (.500 Silver, 36mm)	709,602	—		5.00

KM#	Date	Mintage	MS-63	P/L	Proof
143	1985 National Parks - Moose	163,314	14.50	—	
	(.500 Silver, 36mm)	733,354	—	—	6.00
149	1986 Vancouver	125,949	21.50	—	
	(.500 Silver, 36mm)	680,004	—	—	7.00

KM#	Date	Mintage	MS-63	P/L	Spec.
124	1979 Griffon (.500 Silver, 36mm)	826,695	—		10.00
128	1980 Arctic Territories				
	(.500 Silver, 36mm)	539,617	—		20.00

KM#	Date	Mintage	MS-63	P/L	Proof
154	1987 John Davis	118,722	16.50	—	
	(.500 Silver, 36mm)	602,374	—	—	9.50
161	1988 Ironworks	106,872	25.00	—	
	(.500 Silver, 36mm)	255,013	—	—	20.00

KM#	Date	Mintage	MS-63	P/L	Proof
130	1981 Railroad (.500 Silver, 36mm)	699,494	16.00	—	15.50
133	1982 Regina	144,930	14.25	—	
	(.500 Silver, 36mm)	758,958	—	—	5.00

KM#	Date	Mintage	MS-63	P/L	Proof
168	1989 MacKenzie River	99,774	25.00	—	
	(.500 Silver, 36mm)	244,062	—	—	22.00
170	1990 Henry Kelsey	99,455	14.50	—	
	(.500 Silver, 36mm)	254,959	—	—	15.00

KM#	Date	Mintage	MS-63	P/L	Proof
134	1982 Constitution (Nickel, 32mm)	9,709,422	3.00	—	6.00
138	1983 Edmonton University Games	159,450	8.50	—	
	(.500 Silver, 36mm)	506,847	—	—	6.50

KM#	Date	Mintage	MS-63	P/L	Proof
179	1991 S.S. Frontenac	73,843	15.00	—	
	(.500 Silver, 36mm)	195,424	—	—	20.00
210	1992 Stagecoach Service	78,160	14.50	—	
	(.925 Silver, 36mm)	187,612	—	—	15.00

KM#	Date	Mintage	MS-63	P/L	Proof
140	1984 Toronto Sesquicentennial	133,610	22.50	—	—
	(.500 Silver, 36mm)	732,542	—	—	5.50
141	1984 Cartier (Nickel, 32mm)	7,009,323	2.25	—	—
		87,760	—	—	6.50

KM#	Date	Mintage	MS-63	P/L	Proof
186.2	ND(1992) Loon, Aureate	4,242,085	2.50	—	—
(209)					10.50
218	ND(1992) Parliament, Aureate	23,915,000	2.50	—	—
		24,227	—	—	11.50

KM#	Date	Mintage	MS-63	P/L	Proof
235	1993 Stanley Cup Hockey	88,150	12.50	—	—
	(.925 Silver, 36mm)	294,314	—	—	18.50
251	1994 Last RCMP Sled Dog Patrol	61,561	17.50	—	—
	(.925 Silver, 36mm)	170,374	—	—	20.00

KM#	Date	Mintage	MS-63	P/L	Proof
248	1994 War Memorial	15,000,000	2.50	—	—
	Aureate, 26mm	54,524	—	—	12.50
258	1995 Peacekeeping Monument in Ottawa,	—	2.50	—	—
	Aureate, 26mm	50,000	—	—	12.50

KM#	Date	Mintage	MS-63	P/L	Proof
259	1995 Hudson Bay Company,	—	14.50	—	—
	(.925 Silver, 36mm)	—	—	—	15.00
274	1996 McIntosh Apple	—	17.50	—	—
	(.925 Silver, 36mm)	—	—	—	18.50

KM#	Date	Mintage	MS-63	P/L	Proof
282	ND(1997) 25th Anniversary Hockey Victory	—	14.50	—	—
	(.925 Silver, 36mm)	—	—	—	19.50
291	1997 10th Anniversary - Loon Dollar				
	Aureate, 26mm	—	9.50	—	—

KM#	Date	Mintage	MS-63	P/L	Proof
296	1997 10th Anniversary - Loon Dollar				
	(.925 Silver, 36mm)	*.025	—	—	60.00
306	120th Anniversary Royal Canadian				
	Mounted Police	—	—	15.00	—
	(.925 Silver, 36mm)	—	—	—	22.50

*NOTE: (c) Individually cased Proof-likes (P/L), Proofs or Specimens are from broken up Proof-like or specimen sets.

2 DOLLARS

ALUMINUM-BRONZE center in NICKEL ring

KM#	Date	Mintage	MS-63	P/L	Proof
270	1996 Polar Bear	375,483,000	3.50	9.00	15.75
	1997	16,942,000	3.50		
	1998		3.50		
	1998W	—	In Mint sets only		4.00

5.7456 g, GOLD, .1847 oz AGW center within 5.0958 g, SILVER, .1638 oz ASW ring

KM#	Date	Mintage	MS-63	P/L	Proof
270a	1996	5,000			365.00

25.0000 g, GOLD plated .925 SILVER center in .925 SILVER ring, .7434 oz ASW

KM#	Date	Mintage	MS-63	P/L	Proof
270b	1996	*.015			80.00

8.8300 g, GOLD plated center, .925 SILVER in .925 SILVER ring, .2626 oz ASW

KM#	Date	Mintage	MS-63	P/L	Proof
270c	1997	—		—	23.50
	1998O	—	In Proof sets only		20.00

5 DOLLARS

8.3592 g, .900 GOLD, .2419 oz AGW

KM#	Date	Mintage	F-12	VF-20	XF-40	AU-50	MS-60	MS-63
26	1912	165,680	135.00	160.00	190.00	200.00	325.00	725.00
	1913	98,832	135.00	160.00	190.00	200.00	325.00	825.00
	1914	31,122	200.00	300.00	375.00	500.00	800.00	2300.

Olympic Commemoratives

24.3000 g, .925 SILVER, .7227 oz ASW

Series I

KM#	Date	Mintage	MS-63	Proof
84	1973 Sailboats (Kingston)	—	5.25	—
		165,203	—	6.50
85	1973 North America Map	—	5.25	—
		165,203	—	6.50

Series II

KM#	Date	Mintage	MS-63	Proof
89	1974 Olympic Rings	—	5.25	—
		97,431	—	6.50
90	1974 Athlete with torch	—	5.25	—
		97,431	—	6.50

16.7185 g, .900 GOLD, .4838 oz AGW

KM#	Date	Mintage	F-12	VF-20	XF-40	AU-50	MS-60	MS-63
27	1912	74,759	250.00	350.00	400.00	500.00	750.00	2500.
	1913	149,232	250.00	350.00	400.00	500.00	775.00	3300.
	1914	140,068	275.00	375.00	425.00	600.00	925.00	3100.

Olympic Commemoratives

Series III

KM#	Date	Mintage	MS-63	Proof
91	1974 Rowing	—	5.25	—
		104,684	—	6.50
92	1974 Canoeing	—	5.25	—
		104,684	—	6.50

Series IV

KM#	Date	Mintage	MS-63	Proof
98	1975 Marathon	—	5.25	—
		89,155	—	6.50
99	1975 Ladies' Javelin	—	5.25	—
		89,155	—	6.50

48.6000 g, .925 SILVER, 1.4454 oz ASW

Series I

KM#	Date	Mintage	MS-63	Proof
86.1	1973 World Map	103,426	10.25	—
		165,203	—	13.00
86.2	1974 World Map (Error-Mule)	320 pcs.	235.00	—
87	1973 Montreal Skyline	—	10.25	—
		165,203	—	13.00

Series V

KM#	Date	Mintage	MS-63	Proof
100	1975 Swimmer	—	5.25	—
		89,155	—	6.50
101	1975 Diver	—	5.25	—
		89,155	—	6.50

Series II

KM#	Date	Mintage	MS-63	Proof
93	1974 Head of Zeus	—	10.25	—
		104,684	—	13.00
94	1974 Temple of Zeus	—	10.25	—
		104,684	—	13.00

Series VI

KM#	Date	Mintage	MS-63	Proof
107	1976 Fencing	—	5.25	—
		82,302	—	7.00
108	1976 Boxing	—	5.25	—
		82,302	—	7.00

Series III

KM#	Date	Mintage	MS-63	Proof
95	1974 Cycling	—	10.25	—
		97,431	—	13.00
96	1974 Lacrosse	—	10.25	—
		97,431	—	13.00

Series IV

KM#	Date	Mintage	MS-63	Proof
102	1975 Men's Hurdles	—	10.25	—
		82,302	—	13.00
103	1975 Ladies' Shot Put	—	10.25	—
		82,302	—	13.00

Series VII

KM#	Date	Mintage	MS-63	Proof
109	1976 Olympic Village	—	5.25	—
		76,908	—	7.00
110	1976 Olympic Flame	—	5.25	—
		79,102	—	7.00

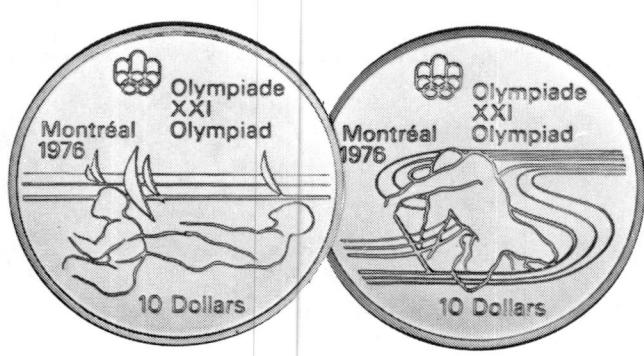

KM#	Date	Series V Mintage	MS-63	Proof
104	1975 Sailing	—	10.25	—
		89,155	—	13.50
105	1975 Canoeing	—	10.25	—
		89,155	—	13.50

KM#	Date	Series VI Mintage	MS-63	Proof
111	1976 Football	—	10.25	—
		76,908	—	14.00
112	1976 Field Hockey	—	10.25	—
		76,908	—	14.00

KM#	Date	Series VII Mintage	MS-63	Proof
113	1976 Olympic Stadium	—	10.25	—
		79,102	—	14.00
114	1976 Olympic Velodrome	—	10.25	—
		79,102	—	14.00

15 DOLLARS

Olympic Commemoratives

33.6300 g, .925 SILVER, 1.0000 oz ASW

KM#	Date	Mintage	MS-63	Proof
215	1992 Coaching Track	*275,000	—	28.00
216	1992 High Jump, Rings, Speed Skating	*275,000	—	28.00

33.6300 g, .925 SILVER, 1.0000 oz ASW and
0.3700 g, .9999 GOLD insert, .0118 oz AGW

KM#	Date	Mintage	MS-63	Proof
304	1998 Year of the Tiger	.069	—	55.00
331	1999 Year of the Rabbit	—	—	70.00

20 DOLLARS

18.2733 g, .900 GOLD, .5288 oz AGW

KM#	Date	Mintage	MS-63	Proof
71	1967 Centennial	337,688	—	210.00

Olympic Commemoratives
33.6300 g, .925 SILVER, 1.0000 oz ASW

KM#	Date	Mintage	MS-63	Proof
145	1985 Winter Olympics, Downhill Skier, lettered edge			
		406,360	—	22.50
	1985 Plain edge	Inc. Ab.	—	180.00
146	1985 Winter Olympics, Speed Skater, lettered edge			
		354,222	—	22.50
	1985 Plain edge	Inc. Ab.	—	180.00

KM#	Date	Mintage	MS-63	Proof
147	1986 Winter Olympics, Biathlon, lettered edge			
		308,086	—	22.50
	1986 Plain edge	Inc. Ab.	—	180.00
148	1986 Winter Olympics, Hockey, lettered edge			
		396,602	—	22.50
	1986 Plain edge	Inc. Ab.	—	180.00

KM#	Date	Mintage	MS-63	Proof
150	1986 Winter Olympics, Cross Country Skier	303,199	—	22.50
151	1986 Winter Olympics, Free Style Skier, lettered edge			
		294,322	—	22.50
	1986 Plain edge	Inc. Ab.	—	180.00

34.1070 g, .925 SILVER, 1.0000 oz ASW

KM#	Date	Mintage	MS-63	Proof
155	1987 Winter Olympics, Figure Skater	334,875	—	22.50
156	1987 Winter Olympics, Curling	286,457	—	22.50

KM#	Date	Mintage	MS-63	Proof
236	1993 Fairchild 71C Float plane	32,199	—	45.00
237	1993 Lockheed 14	32,550	—	45.00

KM#	Date	Mintage	MS-63	Proof
159	1987 Winter Olympics, Ski Jumper	290,954	—	22.50
160	1987 Winter Olympics, Bobsled	274,326	—	22.50

KM#	Date	Mintage	MS-63	Proof
246	1994 Curtiss HS-2L Seaplane	31,242	—	45.00
247	1994 Vickers Vedette	30,880	—	45.00

Aviation Commemoratives

31.1030 g, .925 SILVER, .9743 oz ASW,
w/.0257 oz AGW GOLD Cameo, 1.0000 oz ASW

KM#	Date	Mintage	MS-63	Proof
172	1990 Lancaster/Fauquier	43,596	—	190.00
173	1990 Anson and Harvard	41,844	—	60.00

KM#	Date	Mintage	MS-63	Proof
271	1995 C-FEA1 Fleet Cannuck	17,438	—	50.00
272	1995 DHC-1 Chipmunk	17,722	—	50.00

KM#	Date	Mintage	MS-63	Proof
196	1991 Silver Dart	28,791	—	45.00
197	1991 de Haviland "Beaver"	29,399	—	45.00

KM#	Date	Mintage	MS-63	Proof
276	1996 CF-100 Cannuck	18,508	—	50.00
277	1996 CF-105 Arrow	27,163	—	50.00

KM#	Date	Mintage	MS-63	Proof
224	1992 Curtiss JN-4 Canuck ("Jenny")	33,105	—	45.00
225	1992 de Haviland Gypsy Moth	32,537	—	45.00

KM#	Date	Mintage	MS-63	Proof
297	1997 Canadair F-86 Sabre	*.050	—	45.00
298	1997 Canadair CT-114 Tutor	15,669	—	50.00

KM#	Date	Mintage	MS-63	Proof
329	1998 CP-107 Argus	*.050	—	45.00
330	1998 CP-215 Waterbomber	*.050	—	45.00

100 DOLLARS

13.3375 g, .583 GOLD, .2500 oz AGW

KM#	Date	Mintage	MS-63	Proof
115	1976 Olympics, beaded borders, 27mm	650,000	90.00	—

16.9655 g, .917 GOLD, .5000 oz AGW

KM#	Date	Mintage	MS-63	Proof
116	1976 Olympics, reduced size, 25mm, plain borders	337,342	—	190.00
119	1977 Queen's Silver Jubilee	180,396	—	190.00

KM#	Date	Mintage	MS-63	Proof
122	1978 Canadian Unification	200,000	—	190.00
126	1979 Year of the Child	250,000	—	190.00
129	1980 Arctic Territories	300,000	—	190.00

KM#	Date	Mintage	MS-63	Proof
131	1981 National Anthem	102,000	—	190.00
137	1982 New Constitution	121,708	—	190.00
139	1983 St. John's, Newfoundland	83,128	—	190.00

KM#	Date	Mintage	MS-63	Proof
142	1984 Jacques Cartier	67,662	—	195.00
144	1985 National Parks - Big horn sheep	61,332	—	195.00
152	1986 Peace	76,409	—	190.00

13.3375 g, .583 GOLD, .2500 oz AGW

KM#	Date	Mintage	MS-63	Proof
158	1987 1988 Olympics - Torch and logo, lettered edge	142,750	—	105.00
	1987 Plain edge	Inc. Ab.	—	350.00
162	1988 Whales	52,594	—	122.50
169	1989 Sainte-Marie	59,657	—	115.00

KM#	Date	Mintage	MS-63	Proof
171	1990 Intl. Literacy Year	49,940	—	115.00
180	1991 S.S. Empress of India	*33,966	—	135.00
211	1992 Montreal	28,162	—	145.00

KM#	Date	Mintage	MS-63	Proof
245	1993 Antique Automobiles	25,971	—	160.00
249	1994 WWII Home Front	16,201	—	175.00
260	1995 Louisbourg	16,916	—	175.00

KM#	Date	Mintage	MS-63	Proof
273	1996 Klondike Gold Rush	17,973	—	170.00
287	1997 Alexander Graham Bell	*25,000	—	190.00

7.7801 g, .999 GOLD, .2501 oz AGW plus
5.5570 g, .999 SILVER, .1787 oz ASW

KM#	Date	Mintage	MS-63	Proof
307	1998 Discovery of Insulin	.025	—	195.00

175 DOLLARS

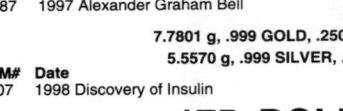 

16.9700 g, .917 GOLD, .5000 oz AGW

KM#	Date	Mintage	MS-63	Proof
217	1992 Olympics - Passing the Torch	22,092	—	325.00

200 DOLLARS

17.1060 g, .917 GOLD, .5042 oz AGW

KM#	Date	Mintage	MS-63	Proof
178	1990 Canada Flag Silver Jubilee	20,980	—	200.00
202	1991 Hockey	10,215	—	245.00
230	1992 Niagara Falls	9,465	—	265.00

17.1350 g, .917 GOLD, .5500 oz AGW

KM#	Date	Mintage	MS-63	Proof
244	1993 Mounted Police	10,807	—	235.00
250	1994 Novel: Anne of Green Gables	8,017	—	235.00
265	1995 Maple Syrup Production	7,621	—	260.00

KM#	Date	Mintage	MS-63	Proof
275	1996 Transcontinental Canadian Railway	7,508	—	265.00
288	1997 Haida Mask	*.025	—	295.00
317	1998 Legendary White Buffalo	*.025	—	305.00

350 DOLLARS

38.0500 g, .9999 GOLD, 1.2233 oz AGW

KM#	Date	Mintage	MS-63	Proof
308	1998	1,998	—	745.00

SOVEREIGN

1908-1910   **7.9881 g, .917 GOLD, .2354 oz AGW**   **1911-1919**

C mint mark below horse's rear hooves

KM#	Date	Mintage	F-12	VF-20	XF-40	AU-50	MS-60	MS-63
14	1908C	636 pcs.	1000.	1750.	2350.	2850.	3450.	4250.
	1909C	16,273	155.00	220.00	285.00	400.00	650.00	1900.
	1910C	28,012	125.00	175.00	250.00	300.00	600.00	1900.
20	1911C	256,946	105.00	115.00	125.00	145.00	200.00	245.00
	1911C	—	—	—	—	Specimen		6500.
	1913C	3,715	400.00	550.00	750.00	1000.	1650.	2800.
	1914C	14,871	175.00	250.00	325.00	550.00	675.00	1400.
	1916C	*About 20 known	7920.	12,500.	14,000.	16,750.	20,000.	31,000.

NOTE: Stacks's A.G. Carter Jr. Sale 12-89 Gem BU realized $82,500.

	1917C	58,845	110.00	120.00	130.00	160.00	200.00	465.00
	1918C	106,516	110.00	120.00	130.00	160.00	200.00	945.00
	1919C	135,889	110.00	120.00	130.00	160.00	200.00	660.00

SILVER BULLION ISSUES
5 DOLLARS

31.1000 g, .9999 SILVER, 1.0000 oz ASW

KM#	Date	Mintage	MS-63	Proof
163	1988 Maple leaf	1,155,931	8.00	—
	1989 Maple leaf	3,288,235	7.25	—
	1989 Maple leaf	43,965	—	28.50
	New Elizabeth II Effigy			
187	1990 Maple leaf	1,708,800	8.00	—
	1991 Maple leaf	644,300	10.00	—
	1992 Maple leaf	343,800	10.00	—
	1993 Maple leaf	889,946	7.50	—
	1994 Maple leaf	1,133,900	7.75	—
	1995 Maple leaf	326,244	7.75	—
	1996 Maple leaf	250,445	9.50	—
	1997 Maple leaf	100,970	9.50	—
	1998 Maple leaf	—	7.50	—
	1999 Maple leaf	—	7.50	—

50 DOLLARS

311.0350 g, .9999 SILVER, 10.0000 oz ASW

KM#	Date	Mintage	MS-63	Proof
326	1998 10th Anniversary Silver Maple Leaf	*.025	—	150.00

GOLD BULLION ISSUES
1 DOLLAR

1.5551 g, .9999 GOLD, .0500 oz AGW

KM#	Date	Mintage	MS-63	Proof
238	1993 Maple leaf	37,080	BV + 37%	—
	1994 Maple leaf	78,860	BV + 37%	—
	1995 Maple leaf	85,920	BV + 37%	—
	1996 Maple leaf	56,520	BV + 37%	—
	1997 Maple leaf	59,720	BV + 37%	—

2 DOLLARS

2.0735 g, .9999 GOLD, .0666 oz AGW

KM#	Date	Mintage	MS-63	Proof
256	1994 Maple leaf	7,815	55.00	—

5 DOLLARS

3.1200 g, .9999 GOLD, .1000 oz AGW

Elizabeth II Effigy by Machin

KM#	Date	Mintage	MS-63	Proof
135	1982 Maple leaf	246,000	BV + 14%	—
	1983 Maple leaf	304,000	BV + 14%	—
	1984 Maple leaf	262,000	BV + 14%	—
	1985 Maple leaf	398,000	BV + 14%	—
	1986 Maple leaf	529,516	BV + 14%	—
	1987 Maple leaf	459,000	BV + 14%	—
	1988 Maple leaf	506,500	BV + 14%	—
	1989 Maple leaf	539,000	BV + 14%	—
	1989 Maple leaf	16,992	—	75.00

Elizabeth II Effigy by dePedery-Hunt

KM#	Date	Mintage	MS-63	Proof
188	1990 Maple leaf	476,000	BV + 14%	—
	1991 Maple leaf	322,000	BV + 14%	—
	1992 Maple leaf	384,000	BV + 14%	—
	1993 Maple leaf	248,630	BV + 14%	—
	1994 Maple leaf	313,150	BV + 14%	—
	1995 Maple leaf	294,890	BV + 14%	—
	1996 Maple leaf	179,220	BV + 14%	—
	1997 Maple leaf	188,540	BV + 14%	—

10 DOLLARS

7.7850 g, .9999 GOLD, .2500 oz AGW
Elizabeth II Effigy by Machin

KM#	Date	Mintage	MS-63	Proof
136	1982 Maple leaf	184,000	BV + 10%	—
	1983 Maple leaf	308,800	BV + 10%	—
	1984 Maple leaf	242,400	BV + 10%	—
	1985 Maple leaf	620,000	BV + 10%	—
	1986 Maple leaf	915,200	BV + 10%	—
	1987 Maple leaf	376,000	BV + 10%	—
	1988 Maple leaf	436,000	BV + 10%	—
	1989 Maple leaf	328,800	BV + 10%	—
	1989 Maple leaf	6,998	—	175.00

Elizabeth II Effigy by dePedery-Hunt

KM#	Date	Mintage	MS-63	Proof
189	1990 Maple leaf	253,600	BV + 10%	—
	1991 Maple leaf	166,400	BV + 10%	—
	1992 Maple leaf	179,600	BV + 10%	—
	1993 Maple leaf	158,452	BV + 10%	—
	1994 Maple leaf	148,792	BV + 10%	—
	1995 Maple leaf	127,596	BV + 10%	—
	1996 Maple leaf	89,148	BV + 10%	—
	1997 Maple leaf	98,104	BV + 10%	—

20 DOLLARS

15.5515 g, .9999 GOLD, .5000 oz AGW
Elizabeth II Effigy by Machin

KM#	Date	Mintage	MS-63	Proof
153	1986 Maple leaf	529,200	BV + 7%	—
	1987 Maple leaf	332,800	BV + 7%	—
	1988 Maple leaf	538,400	BV + 7%	—
	1989 Maple leaf	259,200	BV + 7%	—
	1989 Maple leaf	6,998	—	275.00

Elizabeth II Effigy by dePedery-Hunt

KM#	Date	Mintage	MS-63	Proof
190	1990 Maple leaf	174,400	BV + 7%	—
	1991 Maple leaf	96,200	BV + 7%	—
	1992 Maple leaf	108,000	BV + 7%	—
	1993 Maple leaf	99,492	BV + 7%	—
	1994 Maple leaf	104,766	BV + 7%	—
	1995 Maple leaf	103,162	BV + 7%	—
	1996 Maple leaf	66,246	BV + 7%	—
	1997 Maple leaf	63,354	BV + 7%	—

50 DOLLARS

31.1030 g, .999 GOLD, 1.0000 oz AGW
Rev: 999. Maple Leaf. 999.

KM#	Date	Mintage	MS-63	Proof
125.1	1979 Maple leaf	1,000,000	BV + 4%	—
	1980 Maple leaf	1,251,500	BV + 4%	—
	1981 Maple leaf	863,000	BV + 4%	—
	1982 Maple leaf	883,000	BV + 4%	—

31.1030 g, .9999 GOLD, 1.0000 oz AGW
Rev: 9999 Maple Leaf 9999

KM#	Date	Mintage	MS-63	Proof
125.2	1983 Maple leaf	843,000	BV + 4%	—
	1984 Maple leaf	1,067,500	BV + 4%	—
	1985 Maple leaf	1,908,000	BV + 4%	—
	1986 Maple leaf	779,115	BV + 4%	—
	1987 Maple leaf	978,000	BV + 4%	—
	1988 Maple leaf	826,500	BV + 4%	—
	1989 Maple leaf	856,000	BV + 4%	—
	1989 Maple leaf	17,781	—	450.00

Elizabeth II Effigy by dePedery-Hunt

KM#	Date	Mintage	MS-63	Proof
191	1990 Maple leaf	815,000	BV + 4%	—
	1991 Maple leaf	290,000	BV + 4%	—
	1992 Maple leaf	368,900	BV + 4%	—
	1993 Maple leaf	321,413	BV + 4%	—
	1994 Maple leaf	180,357	BV + 4%	—
	1995 Maple leaf	208,729	BV + 4%	—
	1996 Maple leaf	143,682	BV + 4%	—
	1997 Maple leaf	465,298	BV + 4%	—

KM#	Date	Mintage	MS-63	Proof
305	1997 Guaranteed Gold Mountie	12,913	335.00	—

PLATINUM BULLION ISSUES
1 DOLLAR

1.5552 g, .9995 PLATINUM, .0500 oz APW

KM#	Date	Mintage	MS-63	Proof
239	1993 Maple Leaf	2,120	BV + 35%	—
	1994 Maple Leaf	4,260	BV + 35%	—
	1995 Maple Leaf	460 pcs.	BV + 35%	—
	1996 Maple Leaf	1,640	BV + 35%	—
	1997 Maple Leaf	1,340	BV + 35%	—

2 DOLLARS

2.0735 g, .9995 PLATINUM, .0666 oz APW

KM#	Date	Mintage	MS-63	Proof
257	1994 Maple leaf	1,470	395.00	—

5 DOLLARS

3.1203 g, .9995 PLATINUM, .1000 oz APW
Elizabeth II Effigy by Machin

KM#	Date	Mintage	MS-63	Proof
164	1988 Maple leaf	74,000	BV + 18%	—
	1989 Maple leaf	18,000	BV + 18%	—
	1989 Maple leaf	11,999	—	90.00

Elizabeth II Effigy by dePedery-Hunt

KM#	Date	Mintage	MS-63	Proof
192	1990 Maple leaf	9,000	BV + 18%	—
	1991 Maple leaf	13,000	BV + 18%	—
	1992 Maple leaf	16,000	BV + 18%	—
	1993 Maple leaf	14,020	BV + 18%	—
	1994 Maple leaf	19,190	BV + 18%	—
	1995 Maple leaf	8,940	BV + 18%	—
	1996 Maple leaf	8,820	BV + 18%	—
	1997 Maple leaf	7,050	BV + 18%	—

10 DOLLARS

7.7857 g, .9995 PLATINUM, .2500 oz APW
Elizabeth II Effigy by Machin

KM#	Date	Mintage	MS-63	Proof
165	1988 Maple leaf	93,600	BV + 13%	—
	1989 Maple leaf	3,200	BV + 13%	—
	1989 Maple leaf	1,999	—	175.00

Elizabeth II Effigy by dePedery-Hunt

KM#	Date	Mintage	MS-63	Proof
193	1990 Maple leaf	1,600	BV + 13%	—
	1991 Maple leaf	7,200	BV + 13%	—
	1992 Maple leaf	11,600	BV + 13%	—
	1993 Maple leaf	8,048	BV + 13%	—
	1994 Maple leaf	9,456	BV + 13%	—
	1995 Maple leaf	6,524	BV + 13%	—
	1996 Maple leaf	6,160	BV + 13%	—
	1997 Maple leaf	4,552	BV + 13%	—

20 DOLLARS

15.5519 g, .9995 PLATINUM, .5000 oz APW

KM#	Date	Mintage	MS-63	Proof
	Elizabeth II Effigy by Machin			
166	1988 Maple leaf	23,600	BV + 9%	—
	1989 Maple leaf	4,800	BV + 9%	—
	1989 Maple leaf	1,999	—	350.00
	Elizabeth II Effigy by dePedery-Hunt			
194	1990 Maple leaf	2,600	BV + 9%	—
	1991 Maple leaf	5,600	BV + 9%	—
	1992 Maple leaf	12,800	BV + 9%	—
	1993 Maple leaf	6,022	BV + 9%	—
	1994 Maple leaf	6,710	BV + 9%	—
	1995 Maple leaf	6,308	BV + 9%	—
	1996 Maple leaf	5,490	BV + 9%	—
	1997 Maple leaf	3,990	BV + 9%	—

30 DOLLARS

3.1100 g, .999 PLATINUM, .1000 oz APW

KM#	Date	Mintage	MS-63	Proof
174	1990 Polar bear swimming	2,629	Proof	90.00
198	1991 Snowy Owl	*3,500	Proof	90.00
226	1992 Cougar head and shoulders	*3,500	Proof	100.00

KM#	Date	Mintage	MS-63	Proof
240	1993 Arctic fox	*3,500	Proof	90.00
252	1994 Sea otter	1,500 sets only	Proof	95.00
266	1995 Canadian lynx	620 pcs.	Proof	100.00

KM#	Date	Mintage	MS-63	Proof
278	1996 Falcon portrait	489 pcs.	Proof	130.00
300	1997 Bison head	5,000	Proof	115.00
322	1998 Gray wolf	*2,000	Proof	120.00

50 DOLLARS

31.1030 g, .9995 PLATINUM, 1.0000 oz APW

KM#	Date	Mintage	MS-63	Proof
	Elizabeth II Effigy by Machin			
167	1988 Maple leaf	37,500	BV + 4%	—
	1989 Maple leaf	10,000	BV + 4%	—
	1989 Maple leaf	5,965	—	700.00
	Elizabeth II Effigy by dePedery-Hunt			
195	1990 Maple leaf	15,100	BV + 4%	—
	1991 Maple leaf	31,900	BV + 4%	—
	1992 Maple leaf	40,500	BV + 4%	—
	1993 Maple leaf	17,666	BV + 4%	—
	1994 Maple leaf	36,245	BV + 4%	—
	1995 Maple leaf	25,829	BV + 4%	—
	1996 Maple leaf	62,273	BV + 4%	—
	1997 Maple leaf	25,480	BV + 4%	—

75 DOLLARS

7.7760 g, .999 PLATINUM, .2500 oz APW

KM#	Date	Mintage	MS-63	Proof
175	1990 Polar bear resting	2,629	Proof	200.00
199	1991 Snowy Owls perched on branch	*3,500	Proof	220.00
227	1992 Cougar prowling	*3,500	Proof	220.00

KM#	Date	Mintage	MS-63	Proof
241	1993 2 Arctic foxes	*3,500	Proof	230.00
253	1994 Sea otter eating urchin	1,500 sets only	Proof	235.00
267	1995 2 lynx kittens	*1,500	Proof	250.00

KM#	Date	Mintage	MS-63	Proof
279	1996 Peregrine falcon - diving falcon	*1,500	Proof	210.00
301	1997 Two bison calves	1,500	Proof	215.00
323	1998 Gray wolf	1,000 sets only	Proof	210.00

150 DOLLARS

15.5520 g, .999 PLATINUM, .5000 oz APW

KM#	Date	Mintage	MS-63	Proof
176	1990 Polar bear walking	2,629	Proof	360.00
200	1991 Snowy Owl flying	*3,500	Proof	375.00
228	1992 Cougar mother and cub	*3,500	Proof	375.00

KM#	Date	Mintage	MS-63	Proof
242	1993 Arctic fox by lake	*3,500	Proof	400.00
254	1994 Sea otter mother carrying pup	1,500 sets only	Proof	435.00
268	1995 Prowling lynx	226 pcs.	Proof	450.00

KM#	Date	Mintage	MS-63	Proof
280	1996 Peregrine falcon - falcon on branch	100 pcs.	Proof	445.00
302	1997 Bison bull	4,000	Proof	420.00
324	1998 2 gray wolf cubs	*2,000	Proof	420.00

300 DOLLARS

31.1035 g, .999 PLATINUM, 1.0000 oz APW

KM#	Date		Mintage	MS-63	Proof
177	1990 Polar bear mother and cub		2,629	Proof	700.00
201	1991 Snowy Owl w/chicks		*3,500	Proof	650.00
229	1992 Cougar resting in tree		*3,500	Proof	650.00

KM#	Date		Mintage	MS-63	Proof
243	1993 Mother fox and 3 kits		*3,500	Proof	800.00
255	1994 2 otters swimming			Proof	850.00
269	1995 Female lynx and 3 kittens		*1,500	Proof	875.00

KM#	Date		Mintage	MS-63	Proof
281	1996 Peregrine falcon feeding nestlings		*1,500	Proof	825.00

31.1600 g, .9995 PLATINUM, 1.0013 oz APW

KM#	Date		Mintage	MS-63	Proof
303	1997 Bison family		1,500	Proof	820.00
325	1998 Gray wolf and 2 cubs		1,000 sets only	Proof	820.00

PROOF-LIKE DOLLARS

23.3276 g, .800 SILVER, .6000 oz ASW

KM#	Date	Mintage	Identification	Issue Price	Mkt Value
D3	1953	1,200	KM54, Canoe w/shoulder fold	—	275.00
D4	1954	5,300	KM54, Canoe	1.25	150.00
D5	1955	7,950	KM54, Canoe	1.25	125.00
D5a	1955	Inc. Ab.	KM54, Arnprior	1.25	185.00
D6	1956	10,212	KM54, Canoe	1.25	65.00
D7	1957	16,241	KM54, Canoe	1.25	35.00
D8	1958	33,237	KM55, British Columbia	1.25	32.00
D9	1959	45,160	KM54, Canoe	1.25	14.50
D10	1960	82,728	KM54, Canoe	1.25	9.50
D11	1961	120,928	KM54, Canoe	1.25	9.00
D12	1962	248,901	KM54, Canoe	1.25	7.50
D13	1963	963,525	KM54, Canoe	1.25	6.50
D14	1964	2,862,441	KM58, Charlottetown	1.25	6.50
D15	1965	2,904,352	KM64, Canoe	—	6.50
D16	1966	672,514	KM64, Canoe	—	6.50
D17	1967	1,036,176	KM70, Confederation	—	8.50

MINT SETS (MS)
Olympic Commemoratives

KM#	Date	Mintage	Identification	Issue Price	Mkt Value
MS1	1973(4)	—	KM84-87, Series I	45.00	31.00
MS2	1974(4)	—	KM89-90,93-94, Series II	48.00	31.00
MS3	1974(4)	—	KM91-92,95-96, Series III	48.00	31.00
MS4	1975(4)	—	KM98-99,102-103, Series IV	48.00	31.00
MS5	1975(4)	—	KM100-101,104-105, Series V	60.00	31.00
MS6	1976(4)	—	KM107-108,111-112, Series VI	60.00	31.00
MS7	1976(4)	—	KM109-110,113-114, Series VII	60.00	31.00

SPECIMEN SETS (SS)

NOTE: Some authorities list these as proof sets. However, the Canadian Mint does not. The coins are double struck with higher than usual pressure, but are considered to have the same quality as proof issue from the Royal Mint, London.

KM#	Date	Mintage	Identification	Issue Price	Mkt Value
SS1	1858(4)	—	KM1-4 Reeded Edge	—	6000.
SS2	1858(4)	—	KM1-4 Plain Edge	—	6000.
SS3	1858(8)	—	KM1-4 Double Set	—	12,500.
SS4	1858(8)	—	KM1(overdate),2-4 Double Set	—	14,000.
SS5	1870(4)	100*	KM2,3,5,6 (reeded edges)	—	12,500.
SS6	1870(8)	—	KM2,3,5,6 Double Set (plain edges)	—	25,000.
SS7	1872H(4)	—	KM2,3,5,6	—	12,500.
SS8	1875H(3)	—	KM2(Large Date),3,5	—	20,000.
SS9	1880H(3)	—	KM2,3,5(Narrow 0)	—	7000.
SS10	1881H(5)	—	KM7,2,3,5,6	—	12,000.
SS11	1892(2)	—	KM3,5	—	10,000.
SS12	1902(5)	100*	KM8-12	—	10,000.
SS13	1902H(3)	—	KM9(Large H),10,11	—	6500.
SS14	1903H(3)	—	KM10,12,13	—	7000.

NOTE: A 1903H double set has been reported on display in Bombay, India.

KM#	Date	Mintage	Identification	Issue Price	Mkt Value
SS15	1908(5)	1,000*	KM8,10-13	—	2200.
SS16	1911(5)	1,000*	KM15-19	—	5500.
SS17	1911/12(8)	5	KM15-20,26-27	—	52,250.
SS18	1921(5)	—	KM22-25,28	—	80,000.
SS19	1922(2)	—	KM28,29	—	800.00
SS20	1923(2)	—	KM28,29	—	800.00
SS21	1924(2)	—	KM28,29	—	800.00
SS22	1925(2)	—	KM28,29	—	1800.
SS23	1926(2)	—	KM28,29 (Near 6)	—	1800.
SS24	1927(3)	—	KM24a,28,29	—	3200.
SS25	1928(4)	—	KM23a,24a,28,29	—	2800.
SS26	1929(5)	—	KM23a-25a,28,29	—	10,000.
SS27	1930(4)	—	KM23a,24a,28,29	—	6500.
SS28	1931(5)	—	KM23a-25a,28,29	—	8500.
SS29	1932(5)	—	KM23a-25a,28,29	—	10,000.
SS30	1934(5)	—	KM23-25,28,29	—	8500.
SS31	1936(5)	—	KM23-25,28,29	—	8500.
SS32	1936(5)	—	KM23a(dot),24a(dot),25a,28(dot),29,30	—	Rare
SS33	1937(6)	1025*	KM32-37 Matte Finish	—	750.00
SS34	1937(4)	—	KM32-35 Mirror Fields	—	500.00
SS35	1937(6)	75*	KM32-37 Mirror Fields	—	1550.
SS36	1938(6)	—	KM32-37	—	25,000.
SS-A36	1939(6)	—	KM32-35,38 Matte Finish	—	—
SS-B36	1939(6)	—	KM32-35,38 Mirror Fields	—	—
SS-C36	1942(2)	—	KM32,33	—	300.00
SS-D36	1943(2)	—	KM32,40	—	300.00
SS37	1944(5)	3	KM32,34-37,40a	—	11,300.
SS-A37	1944(2)	—	KM32,40a	—	300.00
SS38	1945(6)	6	KM32,34-37,40a	—	6500.
SS-A38	1945(2)	—	KM32,40a	—	300.00
SS39	1946(6)	15	KM32,34-37,39a	—	4000.
SS40	1947(6)	—	KM32,34-36(7 curved),37(pointed 7),39a	—	8500.
SS41	1947(6)	—	KM32,34-36(7 curved),37(blunt 7),39a	—	6200.
SS42	1947ML(6)	—	KM32,34-36(7 curved right),37,39a	—	4250.
SS43	1948(6)	30	KM41-46	—	7500.
SS44	1949(6)	20	KM41-45,47	—	3200.
SS44A	1949(2)	—	KM47	—	1550.
SS45	1950(6)	12	KM41-46	—	2300.
SS46	1950(6)	—	KM41-45,46(Arnprior)	—	4500.
SS47	1951(7)	12	KM41,48,42a,43-46 (w/water lines)	—	2725.
SS48	1952(6)	2,317	KM41,42a,43-46 (water lines)	—	3175.
SS48A	1952(6)	—	KM41,42a,43-46 (w/o water lines)	—	—
SS49	1953(6)	28	KM49 w/o straps,50-54	—	1850.
SS50	1953(6)	—	KM49 w/straps,50-54	—	1250.
SS51	1964(6)	—	KM49,51,52,56-58	—	450.00
SS52	1965(6)	—	KM59.1-60.1,61-63,64.1	—	450.00

Double Dollar Prestige Sets

KM#	Date	Mintage	Identification	Issue Price	Mkt Value
SS56	1971(7)	66,860	KM59.1-60.1,62b-75.1,77.1,79(2 pcs.)	12.00	10.00
SS57	1972(7)	36,349	KM59.1-60.1,62b-75.1,76.1,(2 pcs.),77.1	12.00	15.00
SS58	1973(7)	119,819	KM59.1-60.1,75.1,77.1,81.1,82,83	12.00	10.00
SS59	1973(7)	Inc. Ab.	KM59.1-60.1,75.1,77.1,81.2,82,83	—	135.00
SS60	1974(7)	85,230	KM59.1-60.1,62b-75.1,77.1,88,88a	15.00	10.00
SS61	1975(7)	97,263	KM59.1-60.1,62b-75.1,76.2,77.1,97	15.00	10.00
SS62	1976(7)	87,744	KM59.1-60.1,62b-75.1,76.2,77.1,106	16.00	10.00
SS63	1977(7)	142,577	KM59.1-60.1,62b,75.2,77.1,117.1,118	16.50	10.00
SS64	1978(7)	147,000	KM59.1-60.1,62b,75.3,77.1,120,121	16.50	10.00
SS65	1979(7)	155,698	KM59.2-60.2,74,75.3,77.2,120,124	18.50	12.50
SS66	1980(7)	162,875	KM60.2,74-75.3,77.2,120,127,128	30.50	25.00

Regular Specimen Sets Resumed

KM#	Date	Mintage	Identification	Issue Price	Mkt Value
SS67	1981(6)	71,300	KM60.2,74,75.3,77.2,120,123	10.00	6.00
SS68	1982(6)	62,298	KM60.2a,74,75.3,77.2,120,123	11.50	6.00
SS69	1983(6)	60,329	KM60.2a,74,75.3,77.2,120,132	12.75	6.00
SS70	1984(6)	60,400	KM60.2a,74-75.3,77.2,120,132	10.00	6.00
SS71	1985(6)	61,553	KM60.2a,74,75.3,77.2,120,132	10.00	6.50

KM#	Date	Mintage	Identification	Issue Price	Mkt Value
SS73	1986(6)	67,152	KM60.2a,74,75.3,77.2,120,132	10.00	6.50
SS72	1987(6)	75,194	KM60.2a,74,75.3,77.2,120,132	11.00	7.00
SS73	1988(6)	70,205	KM60.2a,74,75.3,77.2,132,157	12.30	8.00
SS74	1989(6)	75,306	KM60.2a,74,75.3,77.2,132,157	14.50	14.50
SS75	1990(6)	76,611	KM181-186	15.50	14.50
SS76	1991(6)	68,552	KM181-186	15.50	32.50
SS77	1992(6)	78,328	KM204-209	16.25	21.50
SS78	1993(6)	77,351	KM181-186	16.25	16.50
SS79	1994(6)	77,349	KM181-186	*16.50	19.50
SS80	1995(6)	—	KM181-186	13.95	19.50
SS81	1996(6)	—	KM181-186	—	20.00
SS82	1996(6)	—	KM181a-185a,186	18.95	20.00
SS83	1997(7)	—	KM182a-184a,270,289-291	19.95	22.50
SS84	1998(7)	—	KM182-184,186,270, 289,290	19.95	20.00

NOTE: *Estimated.

V.I.P. SPECIMEN SETS (VS)

NOTE: A very limited number of cased Specimen sets were produced by the Mint beginning in 1969 for presentation to dignitaries visiting the Royal Canadian Mint or other parts of Canada. (A small quantity of 1970 cased Specimen sets were sold to the public for $13.00 each.) The coins, 1¢ to $1.00 were cased in long narrow leather cases (black and other colors).

KM#	Date	Mintage	Identification	Issue Price	Mkt Value
VS1	1969	4 known	—	—	1700.
VS2	1970	100	KM59.1-60.1,74.1-75.1,77.1,78	—	350.00
VS3	1971	69	KM59.1-60.1,74.1-75.1,77.1,79(2 pcs.)	—	375.00
VS4	1972	25	KM59.1-60.1,74.1-75.1,76.1,(2 pcs.),77.1	—	435.00
VS5	1973	26	KM59.1-60.1,75.1,77.1,81.1,82,83	—	435.00
VS6	1974	72	KM59.1-60.1,74.1-75.1,77.1,88,88a	—	375.00
VS7	1975	94	KM59.1-60.1,74.1-75.1,76.2,77.1,97	—	375.00
VS8	1976	—	KM59.1-60.1,74.1-75.1,76.2,77.1,106	—	375.00

PROOF-LIKE SETS (PL)

NOTE: These sets do not have the quality of the Proof or Specimen Set, but are specially produced and packaged.

KM#	Date	Mintage	Identification	Issue Price	Mkt Value
PL1	1953(6)	1,200	KM49 w/o straps, 50-54	2.20	1250.
PL2	1953(6)	Inc. Ab.	KM49-54	2.20	760.00
PL3	1954(6)	3,000	KM49-54	2.50	205.00
PL4	1954(6)	Inc. Ab.	KM49 w/o straps, 50-54	2.50	475.00
PL5	1955(6)	6,300	KM49,50a,51-54	2.50	145.00
PL6	1955(6)	Inc. Ab.	KM49,50a,51-54,Arnprior	2.50	225.00
PL7	1956(6)	6,500	KM49,50a,51-54	2.50	80.00
PL8	1957(6)	11,862	KM49,50a,51-54	2.50	50.00
PL9	1958(6)	18,259	KM49,50a,51-53,55	2.50	40.00
PL10	1959(6)	31,577	KM49,50a,51,52,54,56	2.50	18.00
PL11	1960(6)	64,097	KM49,50a,51,52,54,56	3.00	13.50
PL12	1961(6)	98,373	KM49,50a,51,52,54,56	3.00	12.00
PL13	1962(6)	200,950	KM49,50a,51,52,54,56	3.00	9.00
PL14	1963(6)	673,006	KM49,51,52,54,56,57	3.00	7.50
PL15	1964(6)	1,653,162	KM49,51,52,56-58	3.00	7.50
PL16	1965(6)	2,904,352	KM59.1-60.1,61-63,64.1	4.00	7.50
PL17	1966(6)	672,514	KM59.1-60.1,61-63,64.1	4.00	7.50
PL18	1967(6)	961,887	KM65-70 (pliofilm flat pack)	4.00	12.00
PL18A	1967(6)	70,583	KM65-70 and Silver Medal (red box)	12.00	16.50
PL18B	1967(7)	337,688	KM65-71 (black box)	40.00	250.00
PL19	1968(6)	521,641	KM59.1-60.1,62b,72a,75.1-76.1	4.00	2.50
PL20	1969(6)	326,203	KM59.1-60.1,62b,75.1-77.1	4.00	2.50
PL21	1970(6)	349,120	KM59.1-60.1,62b-75.1,77.1,78	4.00	3.25
PL22	1971(6)	253,311	KM59.1,60.1,62b-75.1,77.1,79	4.00	2.50
PL23	1972(6)	224,275	KM59.1-60.1,62b-75.1,77.1	4.00	2.50
PL24	1973(6)	243,695	KM59.1-60.1,62b-75.1 obv. 120 beads, 77.1,81.1,82	4.00	2.50
PL25	1973(6)	Inc. Ab.	KM59.1-60.1,62b-75.1 obv. 132 beads, 77.1,81.2,82	4.00	125.00
PL26	1974(6)	213,589	KM59.1,60.1,62b-75.1,77.1,88	5.00	2.75
PL27.1	1975(6)	197,372	KM59.1,60.1,62b-75.1,76.2,77.1	5.00	2.75
PL27.2	1975(6)	Inc. Ab.	KM59.1,60.1,62b-75.1,76.3,77.1	5.00	—
PL28	1976(6)	171,737	KM59.1,60.1,62b-75.1,76.2,77.1	5.15	3.00
PL29	1977(6)	225,307	KM59.1,60.1,62b-75.2,77.1,117.1	5.15	2.50
PL30	1978(6)	260,000	KM59.1,60.1,62b,75.3,77.1,120	5.25	2.50
PL31	1979(6)	187,624	KM59.2-60.2,74,75.3,77.2,120	6.25	3.00
PL32	1980(6)	410,842	KM60.2,74,75.3,77.2,120,127	6.50	4.50
PL33	1981(6)	186,250	KM60.2,74,75.3,77.2,120,123	5.00	3.75
PL34	1982(6)	203,287	KM60.2,74,75.3,77.2,120,123	6.00	2.75
PL36	1983(6)	190,838	KM60.2a,74,75.3,77.2,120,132	5.00	6.00
PL37	1984(6)	181,249	KM60.2a,74,75.3,77.2,120,132	5.25	5.50
PL38	1985(6)	173,924	KM60.2a,74,75.3,77.2,120,132	5.25	6.50
PL39	1986(6)	167,338	KM60.2a,74,75.3,77.2,120,132	5.25	7.50
PL40	1987(6)	212,136	KM60.2a,74,75.3,77.2,120,132	5.25	5.50
PL41	1988(6)	182,048	KM60.2a,74,75.3,77.2,132,157	6.05	6.75
PL42	1989(6)	173,622	KM60.2a,74,75.3,77.2,132,157	6.60	9.00
PL43	1990(6)	170,791	KM181-186	7.40	9.00
PL44	1991(6)	147,814	KM181-186	7.40	25.00
PL45	1992(6)	217,597	KM204-209	8.25	12.50
PL46	1993(6)	171,680	KM181-186	8.25	6.00
PL47	1994(6)	141,676	KM181-185,258	*8.50	7.00
PL48	1994(6)	18,794	KM181-185,258 (Oh Canada holder)	—	12.00
PL49	1995(6)	143,892	KM181-186	6.95	7.00
PL50	1995(6)	50,927	KM181-186 (Oh Canada holder)	14.65	15.00
PL51	1995(6)	36,443	KM181-186 (Baby Gift holder)	—	13.50
PL52	1996(6)	116,736	KM181-186	—	12.50
PL53	1996(6)	29,747	KM181-186 (Oh Canada holder)	—	15.00
PL54	1996(6)	—	KM181a-185a,186	8.95	10.00
PL55	1996(6)	—	KM181a-185a,186 (Oh Canada holder)	14.65	15.00
PL56	1996(6)	—	KM181a-185a,186 (Baby Gift holder)	—	15.00
PL57	1997(7)	—	KM182a-184a,209, 270,289-290	10.45	11.50
PL58	1997(7)	—	KM182a-184a,270, 289-291 (Oh Canada holder)	16.45	16.50

KM#	Date	Mintage	Identification	Issue Price	Mkt Value
PL59	1997(7)	—	KM182a-184a,209,270 289-290 (Baby Gift holder)	18.50	17.50
PL60	1998W(7)	—	KM182-184,186,270,289-290	10.45	10.50
PL61	1998W(7)	—	KM182-184,186,270,289-290, (Oh Canada holder)	16.45	16.50
PL62	1998W(7)	—	KM182-184,186,270,289-290, (Tiny Treasures holder)	16.45	16.50

CUSTOM PROOF-LIKE SETS (CPL)

KM#	Date	Mintage	Identification	Issue Price	Mkt Value
			Each set contains two 1 cent pieces.		
CPL1	1971(7)	33,517	KM59.1(2 pcs.),60.1,62b-75.1,77.1,79	6.50	5.25
CPL2	1972(7)	38,198	KM59.1(2 pcs.),60.1,62b-75.1-77.1	6.50	5.25
CPL3	1973(7)	35,676	KM59.1(2 pcs.),60.1,75.1, 77.1,81.1 obv. 120 beads, 82	6.50	5.25
CPL4	1973(7)	Inc. Ab.	KM59.1(2 pcs.),60.1,75.1, 77.1,81.1 obv. 132 beads,82	6.50	140.00
CPL5	1974(7)	44,296	KM59.1(2 pcs.),60.1,62b-75.1,77.1,88	8.00	5.25
CPL6	1975(7)	36,851	KM59.1(2 pcs.),60.1,62b-75.1,76.2,77.1	8.00	5.25
CPL7	1976(7)	28,162	KM59.1(2 pcs.),60.1,62b-75.1,76.2,77.1	8.00	6.00
CPL8	1977(7)	44,198	KM59.1(2 pcs.),60.1,62b,75.2,77.1,117.1	8.15	6.00
CPL9	1978(7)	41,000	KM59.1(2 pcs.),60.1,62b,75.3,77.1,120	—	6.00
CPL10	1979(7)	31,174	KM59.2(2 pcs.),60.2,74,75.3,77.2,120	10.75	6.00
CPL11	1980(7)	41,447	KM60.2,74,75.3,77.2,120,127(2 pcs.)	10.75	6.75

PROOF SETS (PS)

KM#	Date	Mintage	Identification	Issue Price	Mkt Value
PS1	1981(7)	199,000	KM60.2,74,75.3,77.2,120,123,130	36.00	20.00
PS2	1982(7)	180,908	KM60.2a,74,75.3,77.2,120,123,133	36.00	10.00
PS3	1983(7)	166,779	KM60.2a,74,75.3,77.2,120,132,138	36.00	15.00
PS4	1984(7)	161,602	KM60.2a,74,75.3,77.2,120,132,140	30.00	15.00
PS5	1985(7)	157,037	KM60.2a,74,75.3,77.2,120,132,143	30.00	15.50
PS6	1986(7)	175,745	KM60.2a,74,75.3,77.2,120,132,149	30.00	15.00
PS7	1987(7)	179,004	KM60.2a,74,75.3,77.2,120,132,154	34.00	17.50
PS8	1988(7)	175,259	KM60.2a,74,75.3,77.2,132,157,161	37.50	26.50
PS9	1989(7)	170,928	KM60.2a,74,75.3,77.2,132,157,168	40.00	26.50
PS10	1989(4)	6,823	KM125.2,135-136,153	1190.	1000.
PS11	1989(4)	1,995	KM164-167	1700.	1325.
PS12	1989(3)	2,550	KM125.2,163,167	1530.	1225.
PS13	1989(3)	9,979	KM135,163-164	165.00	155.00
PS14	1990(7)	158,068	KM170,181-186	41.00	26.50
PS15	1990(4)	2,629	KM174-177	1720.	1175.
PS16	1991(7)	14,629	KM179,181-186	—	80.00
PS17	1991(4)	873	KM198-201	1760.	1275.
PS18	1992(13)	84,397	KM203a,212a-214a,218,220a-223a, 231a-234a	—	95.00
PS19	1992(7)	147,061	KM204-210	42.75	32.50
PS20	1992 (4)	*3,500	KM226-229	1680.	1275.
PS21	1993(7)	143,065	KM181-186,235	42.75	25.00
PS22	1994(7)	47,303	KM181-186,248	47.50	45.00
PS23	1994(7)	99,121	KM181-186,251	*43.00	38.50
PS24	1994(4)	1,500	KM252-255	915.00	1295.
PS25	1995(7)	—	KM181-186,259	37.45	32.50
PS26	1995(7)	50,000	KM181-185,258,259	49.45	55.00
PS27	1995(4)	—	KM261-264	42.00	42.00
PS28	1995(4)	682	KM266-269	1555.	1550.
PS29	1995(2)	—	KM261-262	22.00	21.00
PS30	1995(2)	—	KM263-264	22.00	21.00
PS31	1996(7)	423	KM278-286	1555.	1625.
PS32	1996(7)	—	KM181a,182b-185b,186,274	49.00	50.00
PS33	1996(7)	—	KM283-286	44.45	50.00
PS34	1997(8)	—	KM182b-184b,209,270c,282,289,290a	60.00	65.00
PS35	1997(4)	—	KM292-295	44.45	50.00
PS36	1997(4)	—	KM300-303	1530.	1605.
PS37	1998(8)	—	KM182b-184b,186,270b,289,290a, 306	59.45	60.00
PS38	ND(1998)(5)	.025	KM309-313	73.50	73.50
PS39	ND(1998)(2)	*.080	KM316 w/China Y-727	72.50	72.50
PS40	1998(4)	—	KM318-321	44.45	45.00
PS41	1998(4)	1,000	KM322-325	1552.	1555.
PS42	ND(1998)(5)	.025	KM310-313,332	73.50	73.50

Olympic Commemoratives (OCP)

KM#	Date	Mintage	Identification	Issue Price	Mkt Value
OCP1	1973(4)	—	KM84-87,Series I	78.50	40.00
OCP2	1974(4)	—	KM89,90,93,94,Series II	88.50	40.00
OCP3	1974(4)	—	KM91,92,95,96,Series III	88.50	40.00
OCP4	1975(4)	—	KM98,99,102,103,Series IV	88.50	40.00
OCP5	1975(4)	—	KM100,101,104,105,Series V	88.50	40.00
OCP6	1976(4)	—	KM107,108,111,112,Series VI	88.50	42.00
OCP7	1976(4)	—	KM109,110,113,114,Series VII	88.50	42.00

NEWFOUNDLAND
LARGE CENTS

BRONZE

KM#	Date	Mintage	VG-8	F-12	VF-20	XF-40	MS-60	MS-63
9	1904H	100,000	5.00	10.00	20.00	35.00	275.00	650.00
	1907	200,000	1.50	2.50	4.00	12.00	110.00	375.00
	1909	200,000	1.50	2.50	4.00	10.50	100.00	200.00
	1909	—	—	—	—	—	Proof	400.00

KM#	Date	Mintage	VG-8	F-12	VF-20	XF-40	MS-60	MS-63
16	1913	400,000	.75	1.50	2.00	4.00	40.00	100.00
	1917C	702,350	.75	1.50	2.00	4.00	65.00	185.00
	1919C	300,000	.75	1.50	2.25	5.00	90.00	275.00
	1919C	—	—	—	—	—	Proof	220.00
	1920C	302,184	.75	1.50	3.50	12.00	145.00	650.00
	1929	300,000	.75	1.50	2.00	4.00	55.00	150.00
	1929	—	—	—	—	—	Proof	185.00
	1936	300,000	.75	1.25	1.75	3.00	28.00	75.00
	1936	—	—	—	—	—	Proof	250.00

SMALL CENTS

BRONZE

KM#	Date	Mintage	VG-8	F-12	VF-20	XF-40	MS-60	MS-63
18	1938	500,000	.50	.75	1.50	2.50	16.00	40.00
	1938	—	—	—	—	—	Proof	125.00
	1940	300,000	1.25	2.00	3.00	7.00	35.00	175.00
	1940 re-engraved date	—	16.00	27.50	40.00	70.00	230.00	400.00
	1941C	827,662	.40	.50	.70	1.50	13.50	120.00
	1941C re-engraved date	—	13.00	22.00	32.50	50.00	165.00	400.00
	1942	1,996,889	.40	.50	.70	1.50	13.50	70.00
	1943C	1,239,732	.40	.50	.70	1.50	13.50	70.00
	1944C	1,328,776	.75	2.00	3.00	4.50	60.00	335.00
	1947C	313,772	.75	1.50	2.25	4.50	40.00	200.00

FIVE CENTS

1.1782 g, .925 SILVER, .0350 oz ASW

KM#	Date	Mintage	VG-8	F-12	VF-20	XF-40	MS-60	MS-63
7	1903	100,000	3.00	6.00	18.00	50.00	465.00	1200.
	1904H	100,000	2.00	5.00	14.00	35.00	220.00	475.00
	1908	400,000	1.75	3.50	11.50	25.00	200.00	335.00

KM#	Date	Mintage	VG-8	F-12	VF-20	XF-40	MS-60	MS-63
13	1912	300,000	1.00	2.00	5.00	20.00	125.00	275.00
	1917C	300,319	1.00	2.00	4.00	14.00	200.00	450.00
	1919C	100,844	2.00	3.00	10.00	30.00	750.00	1250.
	1929	300,000	1.00	1.75	3.25	12.00	165.00	350.00
	1929	—	—	—	—	—	Proof	750.00
19	1938	100,000	.85	.90	1.50	4.00	75.00	200.00
	1938	—	—	—	—	—	Proof	350.00
	1940C	200,000	.85	.90	1.50	4.00	60.00	200.00
	1941C	621,641	.60	.90	1.50	3.00	15.00	30.00
	1942C	298,348	.85	.90	2.50	3.00	25.00	45.00
	1943C	351,666	.60	.90	1.50	3.00	15.00	27.50

1.1664 g, .800 SILVER, .0300 oz ASW

KM#	Date	Mintage	VG-8	F-12	VF-20	XF-40	MS-60	MS-63
19a	1944C	286,504	.85	1.25	2.50	3.00	30.00	65.00
	1945C	203,828	.60	.90	1.50	3.00	18.00	26.00
	1945C	—	—	—	—	—	Proof	250.00
	1946C	2,041	200.00	275.00	355.00	435.00	1100.	1750.
	1946C	—	—	—	—	—	Proof	4000.
	1947C	38,400	3.25	4.50	6.75	15.00	60.00	125.00
	1947C	—	—	—	—	—	Proof	400.00

TEN CENTS

2.3564 g, .925 SILVER, .0701 oz ASW

KM#	Date	Mintage	VG-8	F-12	VF-20	XF-40	MS-60	MS-63
8	1903	100,000	5.00	10.00	35.00	110.00	850.00	2000.
	1904H	100,000	2.50	6.50	20.00	65.00	275.00	400.00

KM#	Date	Mintage	VG-8	F-12	VF-20	XF-40	MS-60	MS-63
14	1912	150,000	1.50	3.00	9.00	30.00	275.00	400.00
	1917C	250,805	1.00	3.00	6.50	24.00	350.00	1250.
	1919C	54,342	1.50	3.00	9.00	25.00	170.00	325.00
20	1938	100,000	1.00	1.50	2.50	7.00	90.00	225.00
	1938	—	—	—	—	—	Proof	500.00
	1940	100,000	.60	1.20	2.50	5.00	80.00	225.00
	1941C	483,630	.55	1.50	2.00	3.25	27.00	85.00
	1942C	293,736	.55	1.50	2.00	3.25	27.00	90.00
	1943C	104,706	.60	1.20	2.50	5.00	50.00	165.00

2.3328 g, .800 SILVER, .0600 oz ASW

KM#	Date	Mintage	VG-8	F-12	VF-20	XF-40	MS-60	MS-63
20a	1944C	151,471	1.00	1.25	3.00	5.00	70.00	225.00
	1945C	175,833	.60	1.00	2.00	3.25	27.00	90.00
	1946C	38,400	3.00	5.00	10.00	20.00	65.00	200.00
	1947C	61,988	1.75	3.00	7.00	12.00	60.00	175.00

TWENTY CENTS

4.7127 g, .925 SILVER, .1401 oz ASW

KM#	Date	Mintage	VG-8	F-12	VF-20	XF-40	MS-60	MS-63
10	1904H	75,000	9.00	16.00	50.00	175.00	2000.	4250.
	1904H	—	—	—	—	—	Proof	4550.
15	1912	350,000	2.00	3.00	10.00	40.00	350.00	900.00

TWENTY-FIVE CENTS

5.8319 g, .925 SILVER, .1734 oz ASW

KM#	Date	Mintage	VG-8	F-12	VF-20	XF-40	MS-60	MS-63
17	1917C	464,779	1.50	2.00	4.00	9.00	120.00	250.00
	1919C	163,939	1.50	2.25	4.25	12.00	220.00	700.00

FIFTY CENTS

11.7818 g, .925 SILVER, .3504 oz ASW

KM#	Date	Mintage	VG-8	F-12	VF-20	XF-40	MS-60	MS-63
11	1904H	140,000	3.25	5.00	16.00	40.00	300.00	850.00
	1907	100,000	4.00	7.00	20.00	45.00	325.00	1000.
	1908	160,000	3.25	4.50	12.50	32.50	175.00	625.00
	1909	200,000	3.25	4.50	12.50	35.00	200.00	700.00

KM#	Date	Mintage	VG-8	F-12	VF-20	XF-40	MS-60	MS-63
12	1911	200,000	2.75	3.25	8.00	20.00	210.00	500.00
	1917C	375,560	2.75	3.25	6.00	16.50	125.00	285.00
	1918C	294,824	2.75	3.25	6.00	16.50	125.00	285.00
	1919C	306,267	2.75	3.25	6.00	16.50	125.00	380.00

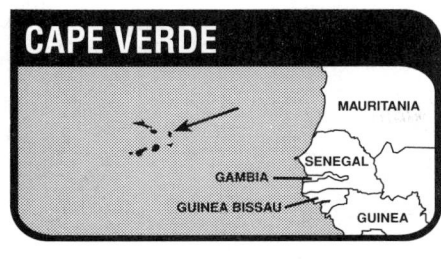

CAPE VERDE

(map: MAURITANIA, SENEGAL, GAMBIA, GUINEA BISSAU, GUINEA)

The Republic of Cape Verde, Africa's smallest republic, is located in the Atlantic Ocean, about 370 miles (595 km.) west of Dakar, Senegal, off the coast of Africa. The 14-island republic has an area of 1,557 sq. mi. (4,033 sq. km.) and a population of 435,983. Capital: Praia. The refueling of ships and aircraft is the chief economic function of the country. Fishing is important and agriculture is widely practiced, but the Cape Verdes are not self-sufficient in food. Fish products, salt, bananas, and shellfish are exported.

The date of discovery of the islands is uncertain. Possibly they were visited by Venetian captain Alvise Cadamosto in 1456. Portuguese navigator Diogo Gomes claimed them for Portugal in May of 1460. Settlement began two years later. The early importance and wealth of the islands, which caused them to be attacked by Sir Francis Drake and the Dutch, resulted from the monopoly of the Guinea slave trade granted the inhabitants in 1466. Poverty and famine occasioned by frequent periods of severe drought have marked the history of the country since abolition of the slave trade in 1876.

After 500 years of Portuguese rule, the Cape Verdes became independent on July 5, 1975. At the first general election, all seats of the new national assembly were won by the Party for the Independence of Guinea-Bissau and Cape Verde (PAIGC). The PAIGC linked the two former colonies into one state. Antonio Mascarenhas Monteiro won the first free presidential election in 1991.

RULERS
Portuguese, until 1975

MONETARY SYSTEM
100 Centavos = 1 Escudo

COLONIAL COINAGE
5 CENTAVOS

BRONZE

KM#	Date	Mintage	Fine	VF	XF	Unc
1	1930	1.000	.75	1.50	3.00	7.00

10 CENTAVOS

BRONZE

2	1930	1.500	.75	1.50	3.50	10.00

20 CENTAVOS

BRONZE

3	1930	1.500	1.00	2.00	4.00	11.50

50 CENTAVOS

NICKEL-BRONZE

4	1930	1.000	7.00	15.00	50.00	275.00

KM#	Date	Mintage	Fine	VF	XF	Unc
6	1949	1.000	.50	1.00	2.50	6.00

BRONZE

11	1968	1.000	.25	.50	1.00	2.50

ESCUDO

NICKEL-BRONZE

5	1930	.050	15.00	35.00	85.00	350.00

7	1949	.500	1.25	2.50	5.50	12.50

BRONZE

8	1953	.250	1.00	2.00	4.50	10.00
	1968	.500	.50	1.00	2.00	5.00

2-1/2 ESCUDOS

NICKEL-BRONZE

9	1953	.500	1.50	3.00	8.00	25.00
	1967	.400	.50	1.00	2.50	8.00

5 ESCUDOS

NICKEL-BRONZE

12	1968	.200	.75	1.50	3.50	10.00

10 ESCUDOS

5.0000 g, .720 SILVER, .1158 oz ASW

KM#	Date	Mintage	Fine	VF	XF	Unc
10	1953	.400	1.50	3.00	6.00	18.00

REPUBLIC
20 CENTAVOS

ALUMINUM

15	1977	—	.10	.20	.30	.50
	1980	—	.10	.20	.30	.50

50 CENTAVOS

ALUMINUM

16	1977	—	.15	.25	.40	.75
	1980	—	.15	.25	.40	.75

ESCUDO

NICKEL-BRONZE
F.A.O. Issue

17	1977	1.000	.25	.50	.85	1.75
	1980	—	.25	.50	.85	1.75

BRASS PLATED STEEL
10th Anniversary of Independence

23	1985	—	—	—	.75	1.50
	1985	—	—	—	Proof	—

BRASS PLATED STEEL
Tartaruga Sea Turtle

27	1994	—	—	—	—	.75

2-1/2 ESCUDOS

NICKEL-BRONZE
F.A.O. Issue

18	1977	1.200	.25	.50	.85	1.75

KM#	Date	Mintage	Fine	VF	XF	Unc
18	1980	—	.25	.50	.85	1.75
	1982	—	.25	.50	.85	1.75

5 ESCUDOS

COPPER PLATED STEEL
Guincho Bird

28	1994					1.00

Flowers - Contra Bruxas

31	1994					1.00

Sailboat - Belmira

36	1994					1.00

10 ESCUDOS

COPPER-NICKEL
Eduardo Mondlane

19	1977	—	.25	.50	1.00	2.00
	1980	—	.25	.50	1.00	2.00
	1982	—	.20	.40	.75	1.50

10th Anniversary of Independence

24	1985	—	—	—	—	2.00
	1985	—	—	—	Proof	

NICKEL PLATED STEEL
Passarinha Bird

29	1994					1.50

Flowers - Lingua De Vaca

32	1994					1.25

Carvalho
Obv: National emblem. Rev: Sail ship.

KM#	Date	Mintage	Fine	VF	XF	Unc
41	1994					1.25

20 ESCUDOS

COPPER-NICKEL
Domingos Ramos

20	1977	—	.35	.65	1.25	2.75
	1980	—	.35	.65	1.25	2.75
	1982	—	.25	.50	.85	1.75

NICKEL PLATED STEEL
Alcatraz Bird

30	1994					2.25

Flowers - Carqueja

33	1994					2.00

Novas de Alegria
Obv: National emblem. Rev: Sail ship.

42	1994					2.00

50 ESCUDOS

COPPER-NICKEL
Amilcar Lopes Cabral

21	1977		1.00	1.50	2.50	4.50
	1980		1.00	1.50	2.50	4.50

F.A.O. World Fisheries Conference

KM#	Date	Mintage	Fine	VF	XF	Unc
22	1984	*.115	—	—	—	7.50

Pardal De Terra Bird

37	1994					5.00

NICKEL PLATED STEEL
Senhor das Areias
Obv: National emblem. Rev: Sail ship.

43	1994	—	—	—	—	4.50

100 ESCUDOS

COPPER-NICKEL
Papal Visit

25	1990	—	—	—	—	8.00

COPPER-NICKEL center in BRONZE ring
Saiao Flowers

38	1994					8.00

COPPER-NICKEL center in BRASS ring

38a	1994	—	—	—	—	8.00

COPPER-NICKEL center in BRONZE ring
Calhandra Do Ilheu Raso Bird

39	1994					8.00

COPPER-NICKEL center in BRASS ring

39a	1994	—	—	—	—	8.00

COPPER-NICKEL center in BRONZE ring
Sailship Madalan

KM#	Date	Mintage	Fine	VF	XF	Unc
40	1994	—	—	—	—	8.00

COPPER-NICKEL center in BRASS ring

| 40a | 1994 | — | — | — | — | 8.00 |

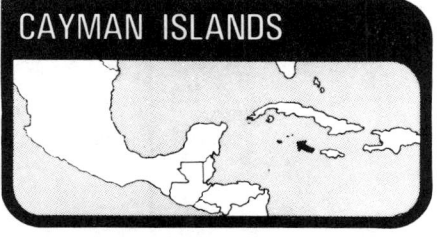

CAYMAN ISLANDS

The Cayman Islands, a British colony situated about 180 miles (290 km.) northwest of Jamaica, consists of three islands: Grand Cayman, Little Cayman, and Cayman Brac. The islands have an area of 102 sq. mi. (259 sq. km.) and a population of 33,200. Capital: Georgtown. Seafaring, commerce, banking, and tourism are the principal industries. Rope, turtle shells, and shark skins are exported.

The islands were discovered by Columbus in 1503, and named by him Tortugas (Spanish for 'turtles') because of the great number of turtles in the nearby waters. Ceded to Britain in 1670, they were colonized from Jamaica by the British and remained dependencies of Jamaica until 1959, when they became a unit territory within the Federation of the West Indies. They became a separate colony when the Federation was dissolved in 1962. Since 1972 a form of self-government has existed, with the Governor responsible for defense and certain other affairs.

While the islands used Jamaican currency for much of their history, the Caymans issued its first national coinage in 1972. The $25 gold and silver commemorative coins issued in 1972 to celebrate the silver wedding anniversary of Queen Elizabeth II and Prince Philip are the first coins in 300 years of Commonwealth coinage to portray a member of the British royal family other than the reigning monarch.

RULERS

British

MINT MARKS

CHI - Valcambi
FM - Franklin Mint, U.S.A.*

MONETARY SYSTEM

100 Cents = 1 Dollar

CENT

BRONZE
Great Caiman Thrush

KM#	Date	Mintage	VF	XF	Unc
1	1972	2.155	—	.10	.25
	1972	.011	—	Proof	.50
	1973	9,988	—	Proof	.50
	1974	.030	—	Proof	.50
	1975	7,175	—	Proof	.50
	1976	3,044	—	Proof	.50
	1977	1.800	—	.10	.25
	1977	1,970	—	Proof	1.00
	1979FM	4,247	—	Proof	.50
	1980FM	—	—	.10	.25
	1980FM	1,215	—	Proof	1.25
	1981FM	865 pcs.	—	Proof	1.50
	1982FM	589 pcs.	—	Proof	1.50
	1982	—	—	.10	.25
	1983FM	—	—	Proof	1.50
	1984FM	—	—	Proof	1.50
	1986	1,000	—	Proof	1.50

87	1987	—	—	.10	.25
	1987	*500 pcs.	—	Proof	3.00
	1988	*500 pcs.	—	Proof	3.00
	1990	—	—	.10	.25

BRONZE CLAD STEEL

87a	1992	—	—	.20	.50
	1996	—	—	.10	.25

5 CENTS

COPPER-NICKEL
Prawn

2	1972	.300	—	.10	.25

KM#	Date	Mintage	VF	XF	Unc
2	1972	.012	—	Proof	.50
	1973	.200	—	.10	.25
	1973	9,988	—	Proof	.50
	1974	.030	—	Proof	.50
	1975	7,175	—	Proof	.50
	1976	3,044	—	Proof	.50
	1977	.600	—	.10	.20
	1977	1,980	—	Proof	.50
	1979FM	4,247	—	Proof	.50
	1980	—	—	Proof	2.00
	1981FM	—	—	Proof	2.50
	1982	—	—	.10	.20
	1982FM	—	—	Proof	2.50
	1983FM	—	—	Proof	2.50
	1984FM	—	—	Proof	2.50
	1986	1,000	—	Proof	2.50

NOTE: 1973 Uncs. were not released to circulation.

88	1987	—	—	.10	.25
	1987	*500 pcs.	—	Proof	4.50
	1988	*500 pcs.	—	Proof	4.50
	1990	—	—	.10	.25

NICKEL CLAD STEEL

88a	1992	—	—	.20	.50
	1996	—	—	.10	.25

10 CENTS

COPPER-NICKEL
Green Turtle

3	1972	.550	.15	.20	.50
	1972	.011	—	Proof	.75
	1973	.200	.15	.20	.50
	1973	9,988	—	Proof	.75
	1974	.030	—	Proof	.75
	1975	7,175	—	Proof	.75
	1976	3,044	—	Proof	.75
	1977	.960	.15	.20	.50
	1977	1,980	—	Proof	.75
	1979FM	4,247	—	Proof	.75
	1980FM	1,215	—	Proof	3.00
	1981FM	865 pcs.	—	Proof	3.00
	1982	—	.15	.20	.50
	1982FM	589 pcs.	—	Proof	3.00
	1983FM	—	—	Proof	3.00
	1984FM	—	—	Proof	3.00
	1986	1,000	—	Proof	3.00

NOTE: 1973 Uncs. were not released to circulation.

89	1987	—	.15	.20	.50
	1987	*500 pcs.	—	Proof	5.00
	1988	*500 pcs.	—	Proof	5.00
	1990	—	.15	.20	.50

NICKEL CLAD STEEL

89a	1992	—	.25	.40	1.00
	1996	—	.20	.30	.75

25 CENTS

COPPER-NICKEL

4	1972	.350	.30	.50	1.00
	1972	.011	—	Proof	1.00
	1973	.100	.30	.50	1.00
	1973	9,988	—	Proof	1.00
	1974	.030	—	Proof	1.00
	1975	7,175	—	Proof	1.00
	1976	3,044	—	Proof	1.00
	1977	.520	.30	.50	1.00
	1977	1,980	—	Proof	1.00
	1979FM	4,247	—	Proof	1.00
	1980FM	1,215	—	Proof	3.50
	1981FM	865 pcs.	—	Proof	4.00
	1982	—	.30	.50	1.00
	1982FM	589 pcs.	—	Proof	4.00

KM#	Date	Mintage	VF	XF	Unc
4	1983FM	—	—	Proof	4.00
	1984FM	—	—	Proof	4.00
	1986	1,000	—	Proof	4.00

NOTE: 1973 Uncs. were not released to circulation.

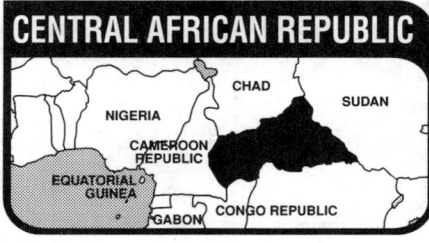

90	1987	—	.30	.50	1.00
	1987	*500 pcs.	—	Proof	6.00
	1988	*500 pcs.	—	Proof	6.00
	1990	—	.30	.50	1.00

NICKEL CLAD STEEL

90a	1992	—	.45	.75	1.50
	1996	—	.35	.60	1.25

CENTRAL AFRICAN REPUBLIC

The Central African Republic, a landlocked country in Central Africa, bounded by Chad on the north, Cameroon on the west, Congo (Brazzaville) and Congo Democratic Republic, (formerly Zaire) on the south and the Sudan on the east, has an area of 240,324 sq. mi. (622,984 sq. km.) and a population of 3.2 million. Capital: Bangui. Deposits of uranium, iron ore, manganese and copper remain to be developed. Diamonds, cotton, timber and coffee are exported.

The area that is now the Central African Republic was constituted as the French territory of Ubangi-Shari in 1894. It was united with Chad in 1905 and joined with Middle Congo and Gabon in 1910, becoming one of the four territories of French Equatorial Africa. Upon dissolution of the federation on Dec. 1, 1958, the constituent territories became fully autonomous members of the French Community. Ubangi-Shari proclaimed its complete independence as the Central African Republic on Aug. 13, 1960.

On Jan. 1, 1966, Col. Jean-Bedel Bokassa, Chief of Staff of the Armed Forces, overthrew the government of President David Dacko and assumed power as president of the republic. President Bokassa abolished the constitution of 1959 and dissolved the National Assembly. In 1975 the Congress of the sole political party appointed Bokassa president for life. The republic became a constitutional monarchy on Dec. 4, 1976; President Bokassa was named Emperor Bokassa I. Bokassa was ousted as Central African emperor in a bloodless takeover of the government led by former president David Dacko on Sept. 20, 1979, and the African nation proclaimed once again a republic.

NOTE: For earlier coinage see French Equatorial Africa and Equatorial African States including later coinage as listed in Central African States.

RULERS

French, until 1960
Marshal Jean-Bedel Bokassa,
  1976-1979

MINT MARKS

(a) - Paris, privy marks only

MONETARY SYSTEM

100 Centimes = 1 Franc

100 FRANCS

NICKEL
Obv: Three Giant Eland. Rev: Denomination.

KM#	Date	Mintage	Fine	VF	XF	Unc
6	1971(a)	3.500	5.00	8.00	13.50	28.00
	1972(a)	—	5.00	8.00	13.50	28.00
	1974(a)	—	6.00	12.00	20.00	40.00

7	1975(a)	—	4.50	7.50	12.50	22.50
	1976(a)	—	2.00	3.50	6.00	10.00
	1979(a)	—	6.00	13.50	20.00	35.00
	1982(a)	—	2.75	4.50	8.00	15.00
	1983(a)	—	2.75	4.50	8.00	15.00
	1984(a)	—	2.50	4.00	7.00	11.50
	1985(a)	—	2.50	4.00	7.00	11.50
	1988(a)	—	2.50	4.00	7.00	11.50
	1990(a)	—	2.00	3.50	6.00	10.00

EMPIRE
100 FRANCS

NICKEL
Obv: Three Giant Eland,
leg: EMPIRE CENTRAFRICAIN.

KM#	Date	Mintage	Fine	VF	XF	Unc
8	1978(a)	—	30.00	75.00	185.00	375.00

REPUBLIC
500 FRANCS
COPPER-NICKEL

11	1985(a)	—	7.50	15.00	30.00	55.00
	1986(a)	—	7.50	15.00	30.00	55.00

CENTRAL AFRICAN STATES

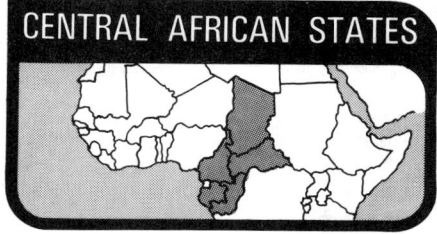

The Central African States, a monetary union comprised of Equatorial Guinea (a former Spanish possession), the former French possessions and now independent states of the Republic of Congo (Brazzaville), Gabon, Central African Republic, Chad and Cameroon, issues a common currency for the member states from a common central bank. The monetary unit, the African Financial Community franc, is tied to and supported by the French franc.

In 1960, an attempt was made to form a union of the newly independent republics of Chad, Congo, Central Africa and Gabon. The proposal was discarded when Chad refused to become a constituent member. The four countries then linked into an Equatorial Customs Unit, to which Cameroon became an associate member in 1961. A more extensive cooperation of the five republics, identified as the Central African Customs and Economic Union, was entered into force at the beginning of 1966.

In 1974 the Central Bank of the Equatorial African States, which had issued coins and paper currency in its own name and with the names of the constituent member nations, changed its name to the Bank of the Central African States. Equatorial Guinea converted to the CFA currency system issuing its first 100 Franc in 1985.

For earlier coinage see French Equatorial Africa.

EQUATORIAL AFRICAN STATES

MINT MARKS
(a) - Paris, privy marks only

MONETARY SYSTEM
100 Centimes = 1 Franc (C.F.A.)

FRANC

ALUMINUM
Obv: Three Giant Eland. Rev: Denomination.

KM#	Date	Mintage	Fine	VF	XF	Unc
6	1969(a)	2.500	.25	.65	1.00	2.25
	1971(a)	3.000	.25	.65	1.00	2.25

5 FRANCS

ALUMINUM-BRONZE
Obv: Three Giant Eland. Rev: Denomination.

24	1958(a)	30.000	.25	.50	1.00	3.00

1	1961(a)	10.000	.35	1.00	1.50	2.50
	1962(a)	5.000	.35	1.00	1.50	2.50

ALUMINUM-NICKEL-BRONZE

1a	1965(a)	2.010	.35	1.00	1.50	3.00
	1967(a)	5.795	.35	1.00	1.25	2.50
	1968(a)	5.000	.35	1.00	1.25	2.50
	1969(a)	—	.35	1.00	1.25	2.50
	1970(a)	9.000	.35	1.00	1.25	2.50
	1972(a)	31.010	.35	1.00	1.25	2.50
	1973(a)	5.010	.35	1.00	1.25	2.50

10 FRANCS

ALUMINUM-BRONZE
Obv: Three Giant Eland. Rev: Denomination.

KM#	Date	Mintage	Fine	VF	XF	Unc
25	1958(a)	25.000	.25	.50	1.50	4.00

2	1961(a)	10.000	.40	1.00	1.75	3.00
	1962(a)	5.000	.40	1.00	1.75	3.00

ALUMINUM-NICKEL-BRONZE

2a	1965(a)	7.000	1.00	1.75	2.75	5.00
	1967(a)	8.000	.40	1.00	1.75	3.00
	1968(a)	2.000	1.50	2.25	3.50	6.00
	1969(a)	10.000	.40	1.00	1.75	3.00
	1972(a)	23.500	.40	1.00	1.75	3.00
	1973(a)	5.000	.75	1.50	2.50	4.50

25 FRANCS

ALUMINUM-BRONZE
Obv: Three Giant Eland. Rev: Denomination.

26	1958(a)	12.000	.50	1.00	2.00	6.00

NOTE: KM#24-26 were previously listed in French Equatorial Africa and Cameroon.

4	1962(a)	6.000	.50	1.25	2.25	4.00

ALUMINUM-NICKEL-BRONZE

4a	1968(a)	—	1.25	2.50	4.00	7.50
	1969(a)	—	1.25	2.50	4.00	7.50
	1970(a)	3.019	.50	1.25	2.25	4.00
	1972(a)	18.516	.50	1.25	2.00	3.00
	1973(a)	—	1.25	2.50	4.00	7.50

50 FRANCS

COPPER-NICKEL
Obv: Three Giant Eland. Rev: Denomination.

3	1961(a)	5.000	2.00	4.00	6.00	10.00
	1963(a)	5.000	2.00	4.00	6.00	10.00

100 FRANCS

NICKEL
Obv: Three Giant Eland. Rev: Denomination.

KM#	Date	Mintage	Fine	VF	XF	Unc
5	1966(a)	9.948	2.00	4.00	7.00	12.00
	1967(a)	11.000	2.00	4.00	7.00	12.00
	1968(a)	—	2.00	4.00	7.00	12.00

NOTE: For later issues see individual listings under Central African Republic, Congo Peoples Republic, Gabon, Chad, Cameroon and Equatorial Guinea.

CENTRAL AFRICAN STATES

COUNTRY CODE LETTERS

The country in which the coin is intended to circulate in is designated by the following additional code letters.

A = Chad
B = Central African Republic
C = Congo
D = Gabon
E = Cameroon

FRANC

ALUMINUM
Obv: Three Giant Eland. Rev: Denomination.

8	1974(a)	—	.30	.60	1.00	2.50
	1976(a)	—	.30	.60	1.00	2.50
	1978(a)	—	.20	.40	.80	1.75
	1979(a)	—	.20	.40	.80	1.75
	1982(a)	—	.20	.40	.80	1.75
	1985(a)	—	.20	.40	.80	1.75
	1986(a)	—	.20	.40	.80	1.75
	1988(a)	—	.20	.40	.80	1.75
	1990(a)	—	.20	.40	.80	1.75
	1992(a)	—	.20	.40	.80	2.00

5 FRANCS

ALUMINUM-BRONZE
Obv: Three Giant Eland. Rev: Denomination.

7	1973(a)	—	.15	.30	.60	1.50
	1975(a)	—	.15	.30	.60	1.50
	1976(a)	—	.15	.30	.60	1.50
	1977(a)	—	.15	.30	.60	1.50
	1978(a)	—	.15	.30	.60	1.50
	1979(a)	—	.15	.30	.60	1.50
	1980(a)	—	.15	.30	.60	1.25
	1981(a)	—	.15	.30	.60	1.25
	1982(a)	—	.15	.30	.60	1.25
	1983(a)	—	.15	.30	.60	1.25
	1984(a)	—	.15	.30	.60	1.25
	1985(a)	—	.15	.30	.60	1.25
	1992(a)	—	.15	.30	.60	1.25

10 FRANCS

ALUMINUM-BRONZE
Obv: Three Giant Eland. Rev: Denomination.

9	1974(a)	—	.20	.35	.75	1.85
	1975(a)	—	.20	.35	.75	1.85
	1976(a)	—	.20	.35	.75	1.85
	1977(a)	—	.20	.35	.75	1.85
	1978(a)	—	.20	.35	.75	1.85
	1979(a)	—	.20	.35	.75	1.85
	1980(a)	—	.20	.35	.65	1.25
	1981(a)	—	.20	.35	.65	1.25
	1982(a)	—	.20	.35	.65	1.25
	1983(a)	—	.20	.35	.65	1.25
	1984(a)	—	.20	.35	.65	1.25
	1985(a)	—	.20	.35	.65	1.25
	1992(a)	—	.20	.35	.65	1.25
	1996(a)	—	.20	.40	.75	1.50

25 FRANCS

ALUMINUM-BRONZE
Obv: Three Giant Eland. Rev: Denomination.

KM#	Date	Mintage	Fine	VF	XF	Unc
10	1975(a)	—	.50	1.00	1.75	2.75
	1976(a)	—	.50	1.00	1.50	2.50
	1978(a)	—	.50	1.00	1.50	2.50
	1982(a)	—	.35	.75	1.25	2.25
	1983(a)	—	.35	.75	1.25	2.25
	1984(a)	—	.35	.75	1.25	2.25
	1985(a)	—	.35	.75	1.25	2.25
	1986(a)	—	.35	.75	1.25	2.25
	1996(a)	—	.35	.75	1.25	2.25

50 FRANCS

NICKEL
Obv: Three Giant Eland. Rev: Denomination.

KM#	Date	Mintage	Fine	VF	XF	Unc
11	1976A(a)	10.000	2.00	3.50	7.50	12.00
	1976B(a)	I.A.	2.00	3.50	7.50	12.00
	1976C(a)	I.A.	1.00	2.00	4.00	7.00
	1976D(a)	I.A.	1.00	2.00	4.00	7.00
	1976E(a)	I.A.	1.00	2.00	4.00	7.50
	1977A(a)	—	2.00	3.50	7.50	12.00
	1977B(a)	—	2.00	3.50	7.50	12.00
	1977C(a)	—	1.00	2.00	4.00	7.00
	1977D(a)	—	1.00	2.00	4.00	7.00
	1977E(a)	—	1.00	2.00	4.00	7.50
	1978A(a)	—	2.00	3.50	7.50	12.00
	1978B(a)	—	2.00	3.50	7.50	12.00
	1978C(a)	—	1.00	2.00	4.00	7.00
	1978D(a)	—	1.00	2.00	4.00	7.00
	1979E(a)	—	1.00	2.00	4.00	7.50
	1980A(a)	—	1.50	2.75	5.50	11.50
	1980C(a)	—	.75	1.50	3.50	6.00
	1981C(a)	—	.75	1.50	3.50	6.00
	1981D(a)	—	.85	1.75	3.75	6.50
	1982A(a)	—	1.50	2.75	5.50	11.50
	1983D(a)	—	.75	1.50	3.50	6.00
	1983E(a)	—	.75	1.50	3.50	6.00
	1984A(a)	—	1.50	2.75	5.50	11.50
	1984B(a)	—	1.50	2.75	5.50	11.50
	1984C(a)	—	.75	1.50	3.50	6.00
	1984D(a)	—	.75	1.50	3.50	6.00
	1985A(a)	—	1.50	2.75	5.50	11.50
	1985B(a)	—	1.50	2.75	5.50	11.50
	1985D(a)	—	.75	1.50	3.50	6.00
	1986B(a)	—	1.50	2.75	5.50	11.50
	1986E(a)	—	.85	1.75	3.75	6.50
	1988B(a)	—	1.50	2.75	5.50	11.50
	1989A(a)	—	1.50	2.75	5.50	11.50
	1990B(a)	—	1.50	2.75	5.50	11.50
	1991A(a)	—	1.50	2.75	5.50	11.50
	1996(a)	—	.75	1.50	3.50	6.00

100 FRANCS

NICKEL
Obv: Three Giant Eland. Rev: Denomination.

KM#	Date	Mintage	Fine	VF	XF	Unc
13	1996(a)	—	—	—	—	4.00

500 FRANCS

COPPER-NICKEL

KM#	Date	Mintage	Fine	VF	XF	Unc
12	1976A(a)	4.000	5.50	8.50	15.00	25.00
	1976B(a)	I.A.	5.50	8.50	15.00	25.00

KM#	Date	Mintage	Fine	VF	XF	Unc
12	1976C(a)	I.A.	4.50	8.00	12.50	20.00
	1976D(a)	I.A.	4.50	8.00	12.50	20.00
	1976E(a)	I.A.	4.50	8.00	12.50	20.00
	1977A(a)	—	5.50	8.50	15.00	25.00
	1977B(a)	—	5.50	8.50	15.00	25.00
	1977C(a)	—	4.50	8.00	12.50	25.00
	1977D(a)	—	4.50	8.00	12.50	20.00
	1977E(a)	—	3.00	6.00	10.00	16.50
	1979D(a)	—	3.50	7.00	12.00	18.50
	1982D(a)	—	3.50	7.00	12.00	18.50
	1984A(a)	—	3.50	7.00	12.00	18.50
	1984B(a)	—	3.50	7.00	12.00	18.50
	1984C(a)	—	3.50	7.00	12.00	18.50
	1984E(a)	—	3.50	7.00	12.00	18.50

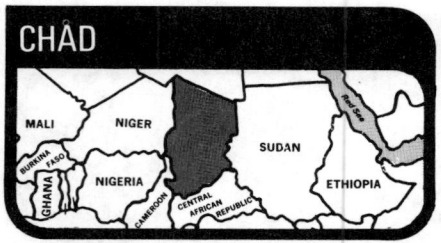

CHAD

The Republic of Chad, a landlocked country of central Africa, is the largest country of former French Equatorial Africa. It has an area of 495,755 sq. mi. (1,284,000 sq. km.) and a population of 5.6 million. Capital: N'Djamena. An expanding livestock industry produces camels, cattle and sheep. Cotton (the chief product), ivory and palm oil are important exports.

Although supposedly known to Ptolemy, the Chad area was first visited by white men in 1823. Exaggerated estimates of its economic importance led to a race for its possession (1890-93) which resulted in the territory being divided by treaty between Great Britain, France and Germany. As a consequence of World War I, the German area was mandated to France in 1919. Chad was absorbed into the colony of French Equatorial Africa, as part of Ubangi-Shari, in 1910 and became a separate colony in 1920. Upon dissolution of French Equatorial Africa in 1959, the component states became autonomous members of the French Union. Chad became an independent republic on Aug. 11, 1960.

NOTE: For earlier and related coinage see French Equatorial Africa and the Equatorial African States. For later coinage see Central African States.

MINT MARKS
(a) - Paris, privy marks only

100 FRANCS

NICKEL
Obv: Three Giant Eland. Rev: Denomination.

KM#	Date	Mintage	Fine	VF	XF	Unc
2	1971(a)	5.000	10.00	17.50	27.50	45.00
	1972(a)	5.000	10.00	17.50	27.50	45.00

KM#	Date	Mintage	Fine	VF	XF	Unc
3	1975(a)	—	9.00	15.00	22.00	35.00
	1978(a)	—	12.00	20.00	28.00	45.00
	1980(a)	—	10.00	17.50	25.00	40.00
	1982(a)	—	9.00	15.00	22.00	35.00
	1984(a)	—	9.00	15.00	22.00	35.00
	1985(a)	—	7.00	12.00	20.00	30.00
	1988(a)	—	7.00	12.00	20.00	30.00
	1990(a)	—	7.00	12.00	20.00	30.00

500 FRANCS

COPPER-NICKEL

KM#	Date	Mintage	Fine	VF	XF	Unc
13	1985(a)	—	15.00	22.00	35.00	50.00

CHILE

The Republic of Chile, a ribbon-like country on the Pacific coast of southern South America, has an area of 292,135 sq. mi. (756,950 sq. km.) and a population of 14.2 million. Capital: Santiago. Historically, the economic base of Chile has been the rich mineral deposits of its northern provinces. Copper has accounted for more than 75 percent of Chile's export earnings in recent years. Other important mineral exports are iron ore, iodine and nitrate of soda. Fresh fruits and vegetables, as well as wine are increasingly significant in inter-hemispheric trade.

Diego de Almargo was the first Spaniard to attempt to wrest Chile from the Incas and Araucanian tribes in 1536. He failed, and was followed by Pedro de Valdivia, a favorite of Pizarro, who founded Santiago in 1541. When the Napoleonic Wars involved Spain, leaving the constituent parts of the Spanish Empire to their own devices, Chilean patriots formed a national government and proclaimed the country's independence, Sept. 18, 1810. Independence however, was not secured until Feb. 12, 1818, after a bitter struggle led by Bernardo O'Higgins and San Martin. Despite a long steady history of monetary devaluation - reflected in declining weight and fineness in its currency, Chile developed a strong democracy. This was displaced when rampant inflation characterized chaotic and subsequently repressive governments in the mid to late 20th century.

MINT MARKS

So - Santiago

MONETARY SYSTEM

10 Centavos = 1 Decimo
10 Decimos = 1 Peso
10 Pesos = 1 Condor

UN (1) CENTAVO

COPPER

KM#	Date	Mintage	VG	Fine	VF	XF
161	1904	.970	.50	1.00	2.00	6.00
	1908	.174	.65	1.25	3.00	9.00
	1919	.173	.50	1.00	2.50	8.50

DOS (2) CENTAVOS

COPPER

KM#	Date	Mintage	Fine	VF	XF	Unc
164	1919	.147	1.50	3.00	5.50	16.50

DOS I MEDIO
2-1/2 CENTAVOS

COPPER

KM#	Date	Mintage	Fine	VF	XF	Unc
162	1904	.277	2.75	7.50	20.00	50.00
	1906	.161	3.50	10.00	22.00	55.00
	1907	.262	2.75	7.50	20.00	45.00
	1908	.201	2.50	7.00	19.00	45.00

NOTE: Varieties exist for 1907 dated coins.

CINCO (5) CENTAVOS

1.0000 g, .500 SILVER, .0160 oz ASW
Obv: 0.5 below condor.

KM#	Date	Mintage	Fine	VF	XF	Unc
155.2	1901/801	2.109	3.00	5.00	8.50	20.00
	1901/891	I.A.	3.00	5.00	8.50	20.00
	1901	Inc. Ab.	2.00	3.00	5.00	15.00
	1904/894	2.527	—	—	—	—
	1904/1	I.A.	3.50	7.00	12.50	27.50
	1904	Inc. Ab.	2.00	3.00	5.00	15.00
	1906/4	.713	—	—	—	—
	1906	Inc. Ab.	2.00	3.00	6.00	17.00
	1907.	2.791	2.00	3.00	5.00	15.00
	1909/899	—	2.50	4.00	7.00	18.50

NOTE: Earlier date (1899) exists for this type.
NOTE: Varieties exist w/0.5, 0.5., 0,5 or 05. below condor.

1.0000 g, .400 SILVER, .0128 oz ASW

KM#	Date	Mintage	Fine	VF	XF	Unc
155.2a	1908	3.642	2.00	3.00	5.00	10.00
	1909/1	1.177	2.00	4.00	6.00	12.50
	1909/8	I.A.	2.00	4.00	6.00	12.50
	1909	Inc. Ab.	2.00	4.00	6.00	12.50
	1910/01	1.587	2.00	3.00	5.00	10.00
	1910	Inc. Ab.	2.00	3.00	5.00	10.00
	1911	.847	2.00	4.00	6.00	12.50
	1913/2	2.573	2.00	5.00	10.00	20.00
	1913	Inc. Ab.	2.00	3.00	5.00	10.00
	1919	Inc. Be.	1.50	3.00	5.00	10.00

NOTE: Varieties exist with a dot below 1 in date for 1913.

1.0000 g, .450 SILVER, .0144 oz ASW
Obv: 0.45 below condor.

KM#	Date	Mintage	Fine	VF	XF	Unc
155.3	1915	2.250	1.50	3.00	5.00	10.00
	1916/1	4.337	1.50	3.50	6.00	12.00
	1916/5	I.A.	1.50	3.50	6.00	12.00
	1916	Inc. Ab.	1.50	3.00	5.00	10.00
	1919/1	1.494	3.00	5.00	10.00	20.00
	1919/5	I.A.	3.00	5.00	10.00	20.00
	1919	Inc. Ab.	2.00	4.00	6.00	12.00

NOTE: 1915 exists w/flat and curved top on 5.

COPPER-NICKEL
Obv: O. ROTY deleted.

KM#	Date	Mintage	Fine	VF	XF	Unc
165	1920	.718	1.00	1.50	3.00	6.50
	1921	2.406	.50	1.25	2.00	5.00
	1922	3.872	.50	1.25	2.00	5.00
	1923	2.150	.50	1.25	2.00	5.00
	1925	.994	.50	1.25	2.00	5.00
	1926	.594	1.50	2.50	3.00	6.50
	1927	1.276	.50	1.00	2.00	5.00
	1928	5.197	.50	1.00	2.00	5.00
	1933	3.000	5.00	10.00	17.50	35.00
	1934	Inc. Ab.	.25	.50	1.00	2.00
	1936	2.000	.25	.50	1.00	2.00
	1937	2.000	.25	.50	1.00	2.00
	1938	2.000	.25	.50	1.00	2.00

NOTE: Varieties exist.

DIEZ (10) CENTAVOS

2.0000 g, .500 SILVER, .0321 oz ASW
Obv: 0.5 below condor.

KM#	Date	Mintage	Fine	VF	XF	Unc
156.2	1901/801	—	15.00	25.00	35.00	60.00
	1901/891	—	15.00	25.00	35.00	60.00
	1901	Inc. Ab.	10.00	20.00	30.00	50.00
	1904/899	.779	2.00	3.00	6.00	15.00
	1904	Inc. Ab.	2.00	3.50	7.00	16.50
	1906	.139	2.50	4.50	8.50	18.00
	1907	3.151	2.00	3.50	7.00	16.50

NOTE: Earlier dates (1899-1900) exist for this type.
NOTE: Varieties exist for dated coins w/0.5, 0,5, 0.5. or 0.5/9 below condor.

1.5000 g, .400 SILVER, .0192 oz ASW

KM#	Date	Mintage	Fine	VF	XF	Unc
156.2a	1908	4.149	1.00	2.00	4.50	12.00
	1908/inverted 6	—	1.50	3.00	6.00	15.00
	1909/8	2.964	1.50	3.00	6.00	15.00
	1909	Inc. Ab.	1.00	2.00	4.50	12.00
	1913	1.269	1.50	3.00	6.00	15.00
	1919	.883	2.50	5.00	9.00	18.50
	1920	2.109	1.00	2.00	4.50	12.00

NOTE: Varieties exist.

1.5000 g, .450 SILVER, .0217 oz ASW
Obv: 0.45 below condor.

KM#	Date	Mintage	Fine	VF	XF	Unc
156.3	1915	1.620	1.00	1.50	3.00	6.50
	1916	2.855	1.00	1.50	3.00	6.50
	1917	.736	1.50	2.50	5.00	12.50
	1918	Inc. Ab.	1.50	2.50	5.00	12.50

COPPER-NICKEL
Obv: O. ROTY deleted.
Plain edge.

KM#	Date	Mintage	Fine	VF	XF	Unc
166	1920	.451	1.50	3.50	5.00	10.00
	1921	2.654	.50	.75	1.50	3.00
	1922	4.017	.50	.75	1.50	3.00
	1923	3.356	.50	.75	7.00	16.50
	1924	1.445	.50	.75	1.50	3.00
	1925	2.665	.50	.75	1.50	3.00
	1927	.523	1.00	2.00	3.00	6.00
	1928	3.052	.50	.75	1.50	3.00
	1932	1.500	.75	1.00	2.00	4.00
	1933/2	5.800	—	—	—	—
	1933	Inc. Ab.	.25	.50	1.00	2.00
	1934	.900	.50	.75	1.50	3.00
	1935	1.500	.50	.75	1.50	3.00
	1936	3.300	.25	.50	1.00	2.00
	1937	2.000	.25	.50	1.00	2.00
	1938	5.000	.25	.50	1.00	2.00
	1939	1.200	.25	.50	1.00	2.00
	1940	6.100	.25	.50	1.00	2.00
	1941	.900	1.00	2.00	3.00	6.00

VEINTE (20) CENTAVOS

4.0000 g, .835 SILVER, .1073 oz ASW
Obv: O. ROTY below condor.
Rev: Hammer and sickle.

KM#	Date	Mintage	VG	Fine	VF	XF
151.1	1895	.146	12.50	20.00	30.00	70.00

4.0000 g, .500 SILVER, .0643 oz ASW
Obv: 0.5 below condor.

KM#	Date	Mintage	Fine	VF	XF	Unc
151.2	1906/896	.866	—	—	—	—
	1906	Inc. Ab.	2.00	3.50	4.50	9.00
	1907/895	7.625	2.00	3.00	4.00	8.50
	1907	Inc. Ab.	1.00	2.00	3.00	7.50

NOTE: Earlier dates (1899-1900) exist for this type.
NOTE: Varieties with 0.5 or 0.5. exist.

3.0000 g, .400 SILVER, .0385 oz ASW
Obv: W/o 0.5 below condor.

KM#	Date	Mintage	Fine	VF	XF	Unc
151.3	1907	1.201	1.00	1.50	3.00	7.50
	1908	5.869	.75	1.25	2.50	6.50
	1909	1.080	.75	1.25	2.50	6.50
	1913/1	3.507	1.50	2.50	4.00	9.00
	1913/50	I.A.	—	—	—	—
	1913	Inc. Ab.	.75	1.25	2.50	6.50
	1919	3.749	.75	1.25	2.50	6.50
	1920	4.189	.75	1.25	2.50	6.50

3.0000 g, .450 SILVER, .0434 oz ASW
Obv: 0.45 below condor.

KM#	Date	Mintage	Fine	VF	XF	Unc
151.4	1916	3.377	2.00	3.00	5.00	10.00

COPPER-NICKEL
Obv: W/o designer's name. Rev: Large 20.
Plain edge.

KM#	Date	Mintage	Fine	VF	XF	Unc
167.1	1920	.499	1.00	2.50	5.00	12.00
	1921	6.547	.35	.75	1.25	3.50
	1922	8.261	.35	.75	1.25	3.50
	1923	5.439	.35	.75	1.25	3.50
	1924	16.096	.35	.75	1.25	3.50
	1925	9.830	.35	.75	1.25	3.50
	1929	9.685	.35	.75	1.25	3.50

NOTE: Varieties exist with dot under 5 in date for 1925.

Obv: O.ROTY.

167.4	1929	Inc. Ab.	1.00	2.50	5.00	10.00

Obv: W/o designer's name. Rev: Small 20.

167.2	1925	—	—	—	—	—
	1932	—	.50	1.00	2.00	4.50
	1933/reversed 33	5.900	—	—	—	—
	1933	Inc. Ab.	.35	.75	1.25	3.50
	1937	—	.50	1.00	2.00	4.50

Obv: O. ROTY.

167.3	1932	—	.35	.75	1.25	3.50
	1933/reversed 33	1.000	1.00	1.50	2.50	6.00
	1933	Inc. Ab.	.35	.75	1.25	3.50
	1937	—	.35	.75	1.25	3.50
	1938	3.043	.35	.75	1.25	3.50
	1939 3/reversed 3		1.00	1.50	2.50	6.00
	1939	5.283	.35	.75	1.25	3.50
	1940	9.300	.35	.75	1.25	3.00
	1941	3.000	.35	.75	1.25	3.00

COPPER
General Bernardo O'Higgins
Obv: Thenot on truncation.

177	1942	30.000	.15	.25	.50	1.50
	1943	39.600	.15	.25	.50	1.50
	1944	29.100	.15	.25	.50	1.50
	1945	11.400	.15	.25	.50	1.50
	1946	13.800	.15	.25	.50	1.50
	1947	15.700	.15	.25	.50	1.50
	1948	15.200	.15	.25	.50	1.50
	1949	14.700	.15	.25	.50	1.50
	1950	15.200	.15	.25	.50	1.50
	1951	14.700	.15	.25	.50	1.00
	1952	15.500	.15	.25	.50	1.00
	1953	7.800	.15	.25	.50	1.00

40 CENTAVOS

6.0000 g, .400 SILVER, .0771 oz ASW

KM#	Date	Mintage	Fine	VF	XF	Unc
163	1907	.056	15.00	25.00	50.00	100.00
	1908	1.452	2.50	6.00	10.00	20.00

50 CENTAVOS

10.0000 g, .700 SILVER, .2250 oz ASW

160	1902	2.022	3.50	6.00	10.00	25.00
	1903	1.111	3.50	6.00	10.00	25.00
	1905	1.075	3.50	6.00	10.00	25.00
	1906	.142	—	Reported, not confirmed		

NOTE: Varieties with 0.7 or 0.7. exist.

COPPER
General Bernardo O'Higgins
Obv: Thenot on truncation. Plain edge.

178	1942	4.715	.50	1.00	2.00	5.00

UN (1) PESO

20.0000 g, .700 SILVER, .4501 oz ASW
Obv: 0.7 below condor.

152.2	1902	.178	8.00	17.50	35.00	65.00
	1903	.372	6.00	12.50	16.50	40.00
	1905	.429	6.00	12.50	16.50	40.00

12.0000 g, .900 SILVER, .3472 oz ASW
Obv: 0.9 below condor.

152.3	1910	2.166	4.00	6.00	12.00	22.50

9.0000 g, .720 SILVER, .2083 oz ASW
Obv: 0.72 below condor.

152.4	1915	6.032	3.75	5.00	6.50	15.00
	1917	3.033	4.00	5.50	8.00	17.50

9.0000 g, .500 SILVER, .1446 oz ASW
Obv: 0.5 below condor.

KM#	Date	Mintage	Fine	VF	XF	Unc
152.5	1921	2.287	2.25	3.50	5.00	10.00
	1922	2.718	2.25	3.50	5.00	10.00
152.6	1924	1.748	2.25	3.50	5.00	10.00
	1925	2.037	2.25	3.50	5.00	10.00

NOTE: Struck with medal rotation. Varieties of 1925 dated coins exist w/flat and curved tops.

W/o mint mark.
Mule. Obv: KM#152.5. Rev: KM#171.

A171.1	1927	—	15.00	30.00	45.00	90.00

Rev: Thin 1 in denomination.

171.1	1927So	3.890	4.00	6.00	10.00	18.00

Rev: Thick 1 in denomination.

171.2	1927So	—	4.00	6.00	10.00	18.00

NOTE: Varieties 0.5 and 0,5 exist. Total of 2,431,608 pieces dated 1921-1927 were melted down in 1932.

6.0000 g, .400 SILVER, .0771 oz ASW

174	1932	4.000	1.75	2.75	3.50	6.50

COPPER-NICKEL

176.1	1933	29.976	.20	.50	1.00	2.00

Obv: O ROTY incuse on rock base.

176.2	1940	.150	1.50	2.00	2.50	4.00

COPPER
General Bernardo O'Higgins

179	1942	15.150	.10	.35	1.00	4.00
	1943	16.900	.10	.35	1.00	4.00
	1944	12.050	.10	.35	1.00	5.00
	1945	7.600	.10	.35	1.00	5.00
	1946	2.050	.10	.35	1.50	7.50

KM#	Date	Mintage	Fine	VF	XF	Unc
179	1947	2.200	.10	.35	1.50	7.50
	1948	5.900	.10	.25	.75	3.75
	1949	7.100	.10	.20	.45	2.25
	1950	7.250	.10	.20	.45	2.25
	1951	8.150	.10	.20	.45	2.25
	1952	10.400	.10	.20	.45	2.25
	1953 short top 5					
		17.200	.10	.20	.40	1.50
	1953 long top 5					
		Inc. Ab.	.10	.20	.40	1.50
	1954	7.566	.10	.20	.40	1.50
	ALUMINUM					
179a	1954	43.550	.10	.15	.25	.40
	1955	69.050	.10	.15	.25	.40
	1956	58.250	.10	.15	.25	.40
	1956	—	—	—	Proof	—
	1957	49.250	.10	.15	.25	.40
	1958	29.900	.10	.15	.25	.40

DOS (2) PESOS

18.0000 g, .500 SILVER, .2893 oz ASW

172	1927	1.060	BV	4.00	8.00	17.50

NOTE: Varieties 0.5 and 0,5 w/curved top and flat top 5 exist. 459,510 pieces were melted down in 1932.

CINCO (5) PESOS

2.9955 g, .917 GOLD, .0883 oz AGW

159	1911	1,399	—	—	200.00	350.00

NOTE: Earlier dates (1897-1900) exist for this type.

25.0000 g, .900 SILVER, .7234 oz ASW
Rev: Wide 5.

173.1	1927	.965	10.00	12.50	18.50	40.00

Rev: Narrow 5.

173.2	1927	Inc. Ab.	10.00	12.50	18.50	40.00

NOTE: Varieties 0.9 and 0,9 exist. 436,510 pieces of the above 2 coins were melted down in 1932.

ALUMINUM

180	1956	1.600	.15	.35	.50	.75

DIEZ (10) PESOS

5.9910 g, .917 GOLD, .1766 oz AGW

KM#	Date	Mintage	Fine	VF	XF	Unc
157	1901	1.651	BV	100.00	125.00	200.00

NOTE: Earlier dates (1896-1900) exist for this type.

ALUMINUM

181	1956	13.100	.15	.35	.50	.75
	1957	28.800	.15	.35	.50	.75
	1958	44.500	.15	.35	.50	.75
	1959	10.220	.25	.50	1.00	1.50

VEINTE (20) PESOS

11.9821 g, .917 GOLD, .3532 oz AGW

158	1906	.041	—	BV	185.00	290.00
	1907	.012	—	BV	185.00	290.00
	1908	.026	—	BV	185.00	290.00
	1910	.028	—	BV	185.00	290.00
	1911	.017	—	BV	185.00	290.00
	1913/11	.018	—	BV	185.00	290.00
	1913	Inc. Ab.	—	BV	185.00	290.00
	1914	.022	—	BV	185.00	290.00
	1915	.065	—	BV	185.00	290.00
	1916	.036	—	BV	185.00	290.00
	1917	.717	—	BV	185.00	290.00

NOTE: Earlier date (1896) exists for this type.

168	1926	.085	—	BV	65.00	90.00
	1958	500 pcs.	BV	65.00	125.00	200.00
	1959	.025	—	—	BV	70.00
	1961	.020	—	—	BV	70.00
	1964	—	—	—	BV	70.00
	1976	.099	—	—	BV	70.00
	1977	.038	—	—	BV	70.00
	1979	.030	—	—	BV	70.00
	1980	.030	—	—	BV	70.00

Rev: Coat of arms on ornamental vines.

188	1976	Inc. Ab.	—	BV	65.00	90.00

CINCUENTA (50) PESOS

10.1698 g, .900 GOLD, .2943 oz AGW

169	1926	.126	—	BV	140.00	175.00
	1958	.010	—	—	BV	175.00
	1961	.020	—	—	BV	175.00
	1962	.030	—	—	BV	175.00
	1965	—	—	—	BV	175.00
	1966	—	—	—	BV	175.00
	1967	—	—	—	BV	175.00
	1968	—	—	—	BV	175.00
	1969	—	—	—	BV	175.00
	1974	—	—	—	BV	175.00

CIEN (100) PESOS

20.3397 g, .900 GOLD, .5886 oz AGW

KM#	Date	Mintage	Fine	VF	XF	Unc
170	1926	.678	—	BV	250.00	325.00

175	1932	9,315	—	BV	325.00	425.00
	1946	.260	—	—	BV	300.00
	1947	.540	—	—	BV	300.00
	1948	.420	—	—	BV	300.00
	1949	.310	—	—	BV	300.00
	1950	.020	—	—	BV	300.00
	1951	.145	—	—	BV	300.00
	1952	.245	—	—	BV	300.00
	1953	.175	—	—	BV	300.00
	1954	.190	—	—	BV	300.00
	1955	.150	—	—	BV	300.00
	1956	.060	—	—	BV	300.00
	1957	.040	—	—	BV	300.00
	1958	.157	—	—	BV	300.00
	1959	.090	—	—	BV	300.00
	1960	.200	—	—	BV	300.00
	1961	.295	—	—	BV	300.00
	1962	.260	—	—	BV	300.00
	1963	.210	—	—	BV	300.00
	1964	—	—	—	BV	300.00
	1968	—	—	—	BV	300.00
	1969	—	—	—	BV	300.00
	1970	—	—	—	BV	300.00
	1971	—	—	—	BV	300.00
	1972	—	—	—	BV	300.00
	1973	—	—	—	BV	300.00
	1974	—	—	—	BV	300.00
	1976	.172	—	—	BV	300.00
	1977	.025	—	—	BV	300.00
	1979	.100	—	—	BV	300.00
	1980	.050	—	—	BV	300.00

MONETARY REFORM

10 Pesos = 1 Centesimo
100 Centesimos = 1 Escudo

1/2 CENTESIMO

ALUMINUM

KM#	Date	Mintage	VF	XF	Unc
192	1962	3.750	.10	.30	.50
	1962	—	—	Proof	—
	1963	8.100	.10	.30	.50

CENTESIMO

ALUMINUM

189	1960	20.160	.35	.75	1.25
	1961	Inc. Ab.	.15	.30	.50
	1962	26.320	.15	.30	.50
	1963	27.100	.15	.30	.50

2 CENTESIMOS

ALUMINUM-BRONZE

KM#	Date	Mintage	VF	XF	Unc
193	1960*	—	—	—	50.00
	1964	2.050	—	.10	1.00
	1965	32.550	—	.10	1.00
	1966	31.800	—	.10	1.00
	1967	34.750	—	.10	1.00
	1968	29.400	—	.10	1.00
	1969	—	—	—	2.50
	1969	—	—	Proof	50.00
	1970	20.250	—	.10	1.00

*NOTE: Not released for circulation.

5 CENTESIMOS

ALUMINUM-BRONZE

KM#	Date	Mintage	VF	XF	Unc
190	1960	—	—	Proof	100.00
	1961	.012	2.50	5.00	10.00
	1962	Inc. Be.	.10	.15	1.00
	1963	17.280	.10	.15	1.00
	1964	16.628	.10	.15	1.00
	1965	27.680	.10	.15	1.00
	1966	32.360	.10	.15	1.00
	1967	19.680	.10	.15	1.00
	1968	4.400	.10	.15	1.00
	1968	—	—	Proof	50.00
	1969	13.200	—	—	3.50
	1969	—	—	Proof	50.00
	1970	30.680	.10	.15	1.00
	1971	16.080	.10	.15	1.00

10 CENTESIMOS

ALUMINUM-BRONZE

KM#	Date	Mintage	VF	XF	Unc
191	1960	—	2.00	3.50	6.50
	1961	1.915	.10	.20	1.00
	1962	1.480	.10	.20	1.00
	1963 sm. date	10.980	.10	.20	1.00
	1964	27.070	.10	.20	1.00
	1965	49.480	.10	.20	1.00
	1966	60.680	.10	.20	1.00
	1967	27.520	.10	.25	1.00
	1968	8.040	.10	.20	1.00
	1969	15.660	—	—	3.50
	1970 lg. date	42.080	.10	.20	1.00

Bernardo O'Higgins

KM#	Date	Mintage	VF	XF	Unc
194	1971	99.700	—	.10	.15

20 CENTESIMOS

ALUMINUM-BRONZE
Jose Manuel Balmaceda

KM#	Date	Mintage	VF	XF	Unc
195	1971	89.200	—	.10	.20
	1972	—	.10	.20	1.00

50 CENTESIMOS

ALUMINUM-BRONZE
Manuel Rodriguez

KM#	Date	Mintage	VF	XF	Unc
196	1971	58.300	.10	.15	.25

ESCUDO

COPPER-NICKEL
Jose Miguel Carrera

	1971	160.900	.10	.20	.40
197	1972	Inc. Ab.	.10	.20	.40
	1972	—	—	Proof	50.00

2 ESCUDOS

COPPER-NICKEL
Caupolican, Chief of Araucanian Indians

198	1971*	106 pcs.	—	—	125.00
	1971	—	—	Proof	50.00

*NOTE: Not released for circulation.

5 ESCUDOS

COPPER-NICKEL

	1971	—	.10	.25	.75
199	1972	—	.10	.25	.75
	1972	—	—	Proof	50.00

ALUMINUM

199a	1972	—	.10	.15	.20

10 ESCUDOS

ALUMINUM

	1974	33.750	.10	.15	.20
200	1974	—	—	Proof	50.00
	1975	31.600	.10	.15	.20

50 ESCUDOS

NICKEL-BRASS

	1974	5.700	.15	.25	.60
201	1975	20.300	.15	.20	.50

100 ESCUDOS

NICKEL-BRASS

KM#	Date	Mintage	VF	XF	Unc
202	1974	32.100	.20	.35	.75
	1975	65.600	.20	.35	.75

MONETARY REFORM

100 Centavos = 1 Peso
1000 Old Escudos = 1 Peso

CENTAVO

ALUMINUM

203	1975	2.000	.10	.15	.50

5 CENTAVOS

ALUMINUM-BRONZE

204	1975	5.400	—	.10	.15
	1976	6.600	—	.10	.15

ALUMINUM

204a	1976	5.000	—	.10	.15

10 CENTAVOS

ALUMINUM-BRONZE

205	1975	8.600	—	.10	.15
	1976	9.000	—	.10	.15

ALUMINUM

205a	1976	6.600	—	.10	.20
	1977	57.800	—	.10	.15
	1978	58.050	—	.10	.15
	1979	101.950	—	.10	.15

50 CENTAVOS

COPPER-NICKEL

206	1975	38.000	—	.10	.20
	1976	1.000	.50	1.00	2.00
	1977	10.000	—	.10	.20

ALUMINUM-BRONZE

206a	1978	19.250	—	.10	.20
	1979	28.000	—	.10	.20

PESO

COPPER-NICKEL
Obv. leg: BERNARDO O'HIGGINS.

207	1975	51.000	.10	.15	.25

Obv. leg: LIBERTADOR. B.O'HIGGINS.

KM#	Date	Mintage	VF	XF	Unc
208	1976	30.000	—	.10	.25
	1977	20.000	—	.10	.25

ALUMINUM-BRONZE

208a	1978	39.706	—	.10	.25
	1979	63.000	—	.10	.25

Reduced size, 17mm. Wide date.

216.1	1981	40.000	—	.10	.20
	1984	60.000	—	.10	.20
	1985	20.000	—	.10	.20
	1986	45.000	—	.10	.20
	1987	80.000	—	.10	.20

Narrow date.

216.2	1988	105.000	—	.10	.20
	1989	205.000	—	.10	.20
	1990	140.000	—	.10	.20
	1991	140.000	—	.10	.20
	1992	—	—	.10	.20

ALUMINUM

231	1992	—	—	—	.10
	1993	—	—	—	.10
	1994	—	—	—	.10
	1995	—	—	—	.10

NOTE: Varieties exist.

5 PESOS

COPPER-NICKEL
3rd Anniversary of New Government

209	1976	2.100	.15	.25	2.00
	1977	28.300	.15	.25	2.00
	1978	11.704	.15	.25	2.00
	1980	8.200	.15	.25	2.00

NICKEL-BRASS, 19mm. Wide date.

217.1	1981	17.000	—	.10	.50
	1982	20.000	—	.10	.50
	1984	12.000	—	.10	.50
	1985	16.000	—	.10	.50
	1986	16.000	—	.10	.50
	1987	8.000	—	.10	.50

Narrow date.

217.2	1988	27.000	—	.10	.50
	1989	32.000	—	.10	.50
	1990	23.000	—	.10	.50

Obv: O'Higgins right. Rev: Denomination, date.

229	1990	8.000	—	.10	.50
	1991	2.000	—	.10	.50
	1992	—	—	.10	.50

ALUMINUM-BRONZE

232	1992	—	—	.10	.50
	1993	—	—	.10	.50
	1994	—	—	.10	.50
	1995	—	—	.10	.50

NOTE: Varieties exist.

10 PESOS

COPPER-NICKEL
3rd Anniversary of New Government

KM#	Date	Mintage	VF	XF	Unc
210	1976	2.100	.10	.20	1.25
	1977	30.000	.10	.20	1.00
	1978	20.004	.10	.20	1.00
	1979	7.000	.10	.20	1.00
	1980	20.000	.10	.20	1.00

NICKEL-BRASS
Wide date, narrow rim.

218.1	1981	55.000	.10	.20	.50
	1982	45.000	.10	.20	.50
	1984	30.000	.10	.20	.50
	1985	.400	.50	1.50	3.50
	1986	25.000	.10	.20	.50
	1987	8.000	.10	.20	.50

Narrow date.

218.2	1988	45.000	.10	.20	.50
	1989	73.000	.10	.20	.50

Wide rim.

218.3	1990	10.000	.10	.20	.50

Obv: Small bust of Higgins right, wide rim.

228.1	1990	5.000	.10	.20	.50
	1993	—	.10	.20	.50

Obv: Large bust of Higgins right, normal rim.

228.2	1990	25.000	.10	.20	.50
	1991	—	.10	.20	.50
	1992	—	.10	.20	.50
	1993	—	.10	.20	.50
	1994	—	.10	.20	.50
	1995	—	.10	.20	.50
	1996	—	.10	.20	.50

50 PESOS

ALUMINUM-BRONZE
Wide date.

219.1	1981	12.000	.25	.50	1.25
	1982	14.000	.25	.50	1.25
	1985	.400	.60	1.50	3.50
	1986	1.000	.25	.50	1.25
	1987	4.000	.25	.50	1.25

Narrow date.

219.2	1988	4.800	.25	.50	1.25
	1989	4.000	.25	.50	1.25
	1991	10.845	.25	.50	1.25
	1992	—	.25	.50	1.25
	1993	—	.25	.50	1.25
	1994	—	.25	.50	1.25
	1995	—	.25	.50	1.25

---

100 PESOS

ALUMINUM-BRONZE
Wide date w/pointed 9.

KM#	Date	Mintage	VF	XF	Unc
226.1	1981	10.000	.50	.75	2.50
	1983	—	.50	.75	2.50
	1984	8.000	.50	.75	2.50
	1985	15.000	.50	.75	2.50
	1986	11.000	.50	.75	2.50
	1987	15.000	.50	.75	2.50

Narrow date w/curved 9.

226.2	1988	—	.50	.75	2.50
	1989	20.000	.50	.75	2.50
	1991	4.320	.50	.75	2.50
	1992	—	.50	.75	2.50
	1993	—	.50	.75	2.50
	1994	—	.50	.75	2.50
	1995	—	.50	.75	2.50

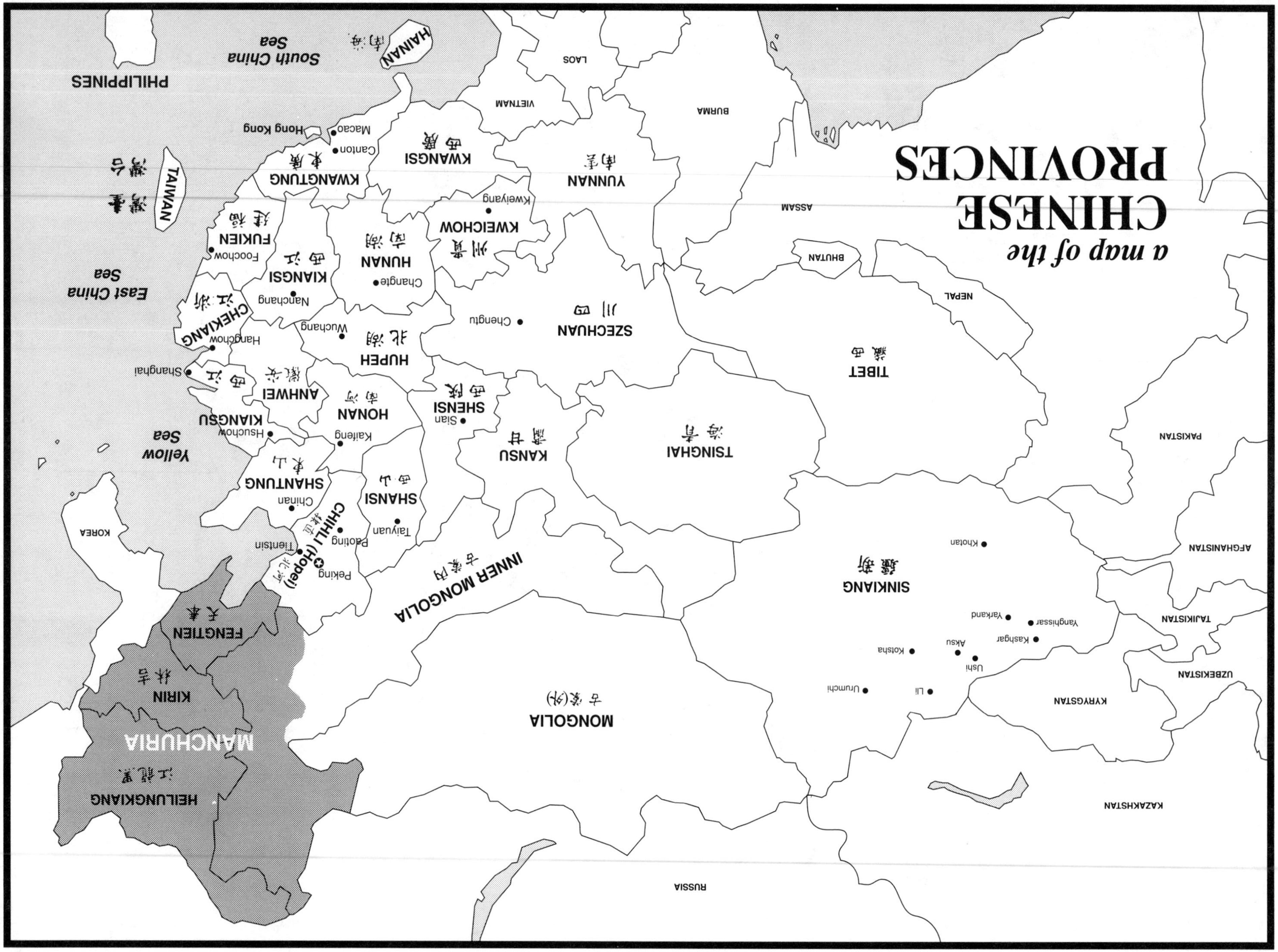

a map of the
CHINESE PROVINCES

AFGHANISTAN

UZBEKISTAN

TAJIKISTAN

KYRYGSTAN

KAZAKHSTAN

PAKISTAN

NEPAL

BHUTAN

ASSAM

BURMA

RUSSIA

Yanghissar •
• Kashgar
• Yarkand
• Khotan

Ushi •
Aksu •
• Kołsha
• Lii
• Urumchi

SINKIANG
蕴新

TIBET
藏西

TSINGHAI
海青

MONGOLIA
古蒙(外)

INNER MONGOLIA
古蒙内

SZECHUAN
川四

• Chengtu

KANSU
滿甘

YUNNAN
南言

Kweiyang •

KWEICHOW
州貴

KWANGSI
西廣

HAINAN
南海

• Sian
SHENSI
西陝

Changte •

HUNAN
南湖

HUPEH
北湖

• Wuchang

HONAN
南河

Kaifeng •

SHANSI
西山

Taiyuan •

Paoting •

Peking •
CHIHLI (Hopei)
捷直北河

Tientsin •

Chinan •

SHANTUNG
東山

Hsuchow •

ANHWEI
徽安
西女

KIANGSU
建江

Shanghai •

Yellow
Sea

East China
Sea

Nanchang •

KIANGSI
西江

Hangchow •

CHEKIANG
江浙

Foochow •

FUKIEN
建福

KWANGTUNG
東廣

Canton •
Macao •
Hong Kong

South China
Sea

PHILIPPINES

TAIWAN
灣臺

VIETNAM

LAOS

PHILIPPINES

KOREA

MANCHURIA
FENGTIEN
天奉

KIRIN
林吉

HEILUNGKIANG
江龍黑

CHINA

Before 1912, China was ruled by an imperial government. The republican administration which replaced it was itself supplanted on the Chinese mainland by a communist government in 1949, but it has remained in control of Taiwan and other offshore islands in the China Sea with a land area of approximately 14,000 square miles and a population of more than 14 million. The People's Republic of China administers some 3.7 million square miles and an estimated 1.19 billion people. This communist government, officially established on October 1, 1949, was admitted to the United Nations, replacing its nationalist predecessor, the Republic of China, in 1971.

Cast coins in base metals were used in China many centuries before the Christian era, but locally struck coinages of the western type in gold, silver, copper and other metals did not appear until 1888. In spite of the relatively short time that modern coins have been in use, the number of varieties is exceptionally large.

Both Nationalist and Communist China, as well as the pre-revolutionary Imperial government and numerous provincial or other agencies, including some foreign-administered agencies and governments, have issued coins in China. Most of these have been in dollar (yuan) or dollar-fraction denominations, based on the internationally used dollar system, but coins in tael denominations were issued in the 1920's and earlier. The striking of coins nearly ceased in the late 1930's through the 1940's due to the war effort and a period of uncontrollable inflation while vast amounts of paper currency were issued by the Nationalist, Communist and Japanese occupation institutions.

EMPERORS
OBVERSE TYPES

NOTE: Obverse Type B, *Chung-pao* and Type C *Yuan-pao* were normally used for multiple-cash issues.

TE TSUNG 德宗
1875-1908

Type A

Reign title: Kuang-hsu 光緒

Kuang-hsu T'ung-pao 光緒通寶

Type B

Kuang-hsu Chung-pao 光緒重寶

Type C

Kuang-hsu Yuan-pao 光緒元寶

HSUAN T'UNG 宣統
1908-1911

Type A

Reign title: Hsuan-t'ung 宣統

Hsuan-t'ung T'ung-pao 宣統通寶

Although Hsuan-t'ung became Emperor in 1908, all the coins of his reign are based on an Accession year of 1909.

YUAN SHIH KAI
Dec. 15, 1915 - March 21, 1916

Reign title: Hung-hsien 洪憲

Hung-hsien T'ung-pao 洪憲通寶

Hung-hsien (more popularly known as Yuan Shih Kai).

NUMERALS

NUMBER	CONVENTIONAL	FORMAL	COMMERCIAL
1	一 元	壹 弌	〡
2	二	弍 貳	〢
3	三	叁 弎	〣
4	四	肆	〤
5	五	伍	〥
6	六	陸	〦
7	七	柒	〧
8	八	捌	〨
9	九	玖	〩
10	十	拾 什	十
20	十 二 or 廿	拾貳	〢十
25	五 十 二 or 五廿	伍拾貳	〢十〥
30	十 三 or 卅	拾叁	〣十
100	百 一	佰壹	〡百
1,000	千 一	什壹	〡千
10,000	萬 一	萬壹	〡万
100,000	萬 十 億 一	萬拾 億壹	十万
1,000,000	萬百 一	萬佰壹	〡万百

NOTE: This table has been adapted from *Chinese Bank Notes* by Ward Smith and Brian Matravers.

MONETARY UNITS

Dollar Amounts		
DOLLAR (Yuan)	元 or 員	圓 or 圜
HALF DOLLAR (Pan Yuan)	圓 半	元 中
50¢ (Chiao/Hao)	角伍	毫伍
10¢ (Chiao/Hao)	角壹	毫壹
1¢ (Fen/Hsien)	分壹	仙壹
Copper and Cash Coin Amounts		
COPPER (Mei)	枚	
CASH (Wen)		文
Tael Amounts		
1 TAEL (Liang)	兩	
HALF TAEL (Pan Liang)	兩半	
5 MACE (Wu Ch'ien)	錢伍	
1 MACE (I Ch'ien)	錢壹	
1 CANDEREEN (I Fen)	分壹	
Common Prefixes		
COPPER (T'ung)	銅	
GOLD (Chin)		金
SILVER (Yin)	銀	
Ku Ping (Tael)*		平庫

NOTE: This table has been adapted from *Chinese Bank Notes* by Ward Smith and Brian Matravers.

DATING

Most struck Chinese coins are dated by year within a given period, such as the regnal eras or the republican periods. A 1907 issue, for example, would be dated in the 33rd year of the Kuang Hsu era (1875 + 33 - 1 = 1907) or a 1926 issue is dated in the 15th year of the Republic (1912 + 15 - 1 = 1926). The mathematical discrepancy in both instances is accounted for by the fact that the first year is included in the elapsed time. Modern Chinese Communist coins are dated in western numerals using the western calendar, but earlier issues use conventional Chinese numerals. The coins of the Republic of China (Taiwan) are also dated in the year of the Republic, which is added to equal the calendar

year. Still another method is a 60-year, repeating cycle, outlined in the table below. The date is shown by the combination of two characters, the first from the top row and the second from the column at left. In this catalog, when a cyclical date is used, the abbreviation CD appears before the AD date.

Dates not in parentheses are those which appear on the coins. For undated coins, dates appearing in parentheses are the years in which the coin was actually minted. Undated coins for which the year of minting is unknown are listed with ND (No Date) in the date or year column.

CYCLICAL DATES

	庚	辛	壬	癸	甲	乙	丙	丁	戊	己
戌	1850 1910		1862 1922		1874 1934		1886 1946		1838 1898	
亥		1851 1911		1863 1923		1875 1935		1887 1947		1839 1899
子	1840 1900		1852 1912		1864 1924		1876 1936		1888 1948	
丑		1841 1901		1853 1913		1865 1925		1877 1937		1889 1949
寅	1830 1890		1842 1902		1854 1914		1866 1926		1878 1938	
卯		1831 1891		1843 1903		1855 1915		1867 1927		1879 1939
辰	1880 1940		1832 1892		1844 1904		1856 1916		1868 1928	
巳		1881 1941		1833 1893		1845 1905		1857 1917		1869 1929
午	1870 1930		1882 1942		1834 1894		1846 1906		1858 1918	
未		1871 1931		1883 1943		1835 1895		1847 1907		1859 1919
申	1860 1920		1872 1932		1884 1944		1836 1896		1848 1908	
酉		1861 1921		1873 1933		1885 1945		1837 1897		1849 1909

NOTE: This table has been adapted from *Chinese Bank Notes* by Ward Smith and Brian Matravers.

GRADING

Chinese coins should not be graded entirely by western standards. In addition to Fine, Very Fine, Extremely Fine (XF), and Uncirculated, the type of strike should be considered weak, medium or sharp strike. China had no rigid minting rules as we know them. For instance, Kirin (Jilin) and Sinkiang (Xinjiang) Provinces used some dies made of iron - hence, they wore out rapidly. Some communist army issues were apparently struck by crude hand methods on soft dies (it is hard to find two coins of the same die!). In general, especially for some minor coins, dies were used until they were worn well beyond western standards. Subsequently, one could have an uncirculated coin struck from worn dies with little of the design or letters still visible, but still uncirculated! All prices quoted are for well-struck (sharp struck), well-centered specimens. Most silver coins can be found from very fine to uncirculated. Some copper coins are difficult to find except in poorer grades.

REFERENCES

The following references have been used for this section:

K - Edward Kann - **Illustrated Catalog of Chinese Coins.**

Hsu - T.K. Hsu - **Illustrated Catalog of Chinese Coins, 1981 edition.**

W - A.M. Tracey Woodward - **The Minted Ten-Cash Coins of China.**

NOTE: The die struck 10 and 20 Cash coins are often found silver plated. This was not done at the mint. They were apparently plated to be passed to the unwary as silver coins.

GENERAL ISSUE

EMPIRE

Peking Hu Pu Mint
(Board of Revenue)

CASH

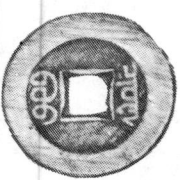

CAST BRASS
Obv. leg: *Kuang-hsu T'ung-pao.*

C#	Date	Emperor	Good	VG	Fine	VF
1-16	ND(1875-1908)					
		Kuang-hsu	1.50	2.00	2.75	4.00

CAST BRASS, 19mm
Obv. leg: *Hsuan-t'ung T'ung-pao.*

C#	Date	Emperor	Good	VG	Fine	VF
1-19.1	ND(1909-11)					
		Hsuan-t'ung	5.50	7.00	10.00	15.00

24mm
1-19.2	ND(1909-11)					
		Hsuan-t'ung	10.00	15.00	25.00	30.00

IRON, 23mm
1-19a	ND(1909-11)					
		Hsuan-t'ung	12.00	20.00	30.00	50.00

10 CASH

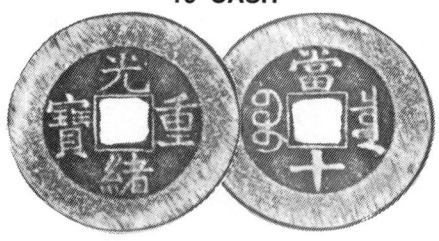

CAST BRASS, 30mm
Obv. leg: *Kuang-hsu Chung-pao.*
Rev: Normal character for 10 below.

1-17	ND(1875-1908)					
		Kuang-hsu	3.00	5.00	8.00	10.00

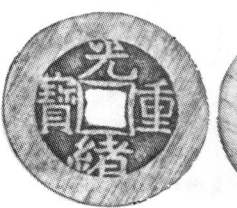

28mm
Rev: Official character for 10 below.
1-18	ND(1875-1908)					
		Kuang-hsu	4.50	7.50	10.00	15.00

22mm
1-18.1	ND(1875-1908)					
		Kuang-hsu	6.00	9.00	15.00	20.00

Peking Kung Pu Mint
(Board of Public Works)

CASH

CAST BRASS
Obv. leg: *Kuang-hsu T'ung-pao.*
2-15	ND(1875-1908)					
		Kuang-hsu	1.50	3.00	6.00	7.00

10 CASH

CAST BRASS
Obv. leg: *Kuang-hsu T'ung-pao.*
Rev: Normal *Shih* (10) below.

C#	Date	Emperor	Good	VG	Fine	VF
2-17	ND(1875-1908)					
		Kuang-hsu	4.50	7.50	10.00	25.00

Rev: Official *Shih* (10) below.
2-18	ND(1875-1908)					
		Kuang-hsu	6.00	10.00	15.00	35.00

Standard Unified General Issues

A Central mint opened at Tientsin in 1905, was made responsible for producing most of the dies for the Tai Ch'ing "Hupoo" coinage and for the 1910 and 1911 unified coinage. The mint was burned down in 1912 but resumed operations in 1914 with Yuan Shih-kai dollar issues. It continued producing dies for selected branch mints until 1921. It was superseded as the Central mint of China by Nanking in 1927 and by the new Nationalist Government mint at Shanghai in 1933.

CASH

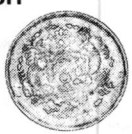

BRASS, struck
Y#	Date	Mintage	VG	Fine	VF	XF
7	CD1908	—	1.00	3.00	6.00	12.00

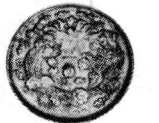

18	CD1909					
		Inc. Y25	25.00	50.00	85.00	135.00

| 25 | ND | 92.126 | 1.00 | 1.50 | 2.00 | 3.00 |

2 CASH

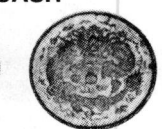

COPPER
8	CD1905	—	2.50	4.50	10.00	17.50
	CD1906	—	3.00	6.00	10.00	25.00

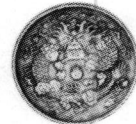

Obv: 4 dots divide leg.
8.1	CD1907	—	7.00	18.00	25.00	40.00
A18	CD1909	13.353	—	—	Rare	—

5 CASH

COPPER
3	ND(1903-05)					
		3.671	7.00	14.00	21.00	35.00

Rev. leg: Smaller English letters.
3.1	ND(1903-05)	—	—	Reported, not confirmed		

9	CD1905	—	5.00	10.00	20.00	35.00
	CD1906	—	—	—	Rare	—

Obv: 4 dots divide leg.

Y#	Date	Mintage	VG	Fine	VF	XF
9.1	CD1907	—	16.50	40.00	75.00	125.00

Obv: leg: *Hsuan Tung*.

Y#	Date	Mintage	VG	Fine	VF	XF
19	CD1909	2.170	—	—	850.00	1200.

10 CASH

COPPER

Y#	Date	Mintage	Fine	VF	XF	Unc
4	ND(1903-05)	281.171	2.00	3.50	6.00	25.00

Rev: Smaller English letters and different rosettes.

Y#	Date	Mintage	Fine	VF	XF	Unc
4.1	ND(1903-05)	Inc. Ab.	1.00	2.00	5.00	20.00

Y#	Date	Mintage	Fine	VF	XF	Unc
10	CD1905	Inc. Ab.	1.50	3.00	5.00	25.00

Rev: Larger English letters and different dragon.

Y#	Date	Mintage	Fine	VF	XF	Unc
10.1	CD1905	—	25.00	65.00	110.00	200.00

Y#	Date	Mintage	Fine	VF	XF	Unc
10.2	CD1906	—	.75	1.50	3.00	20.00

Obv: W/o dots. Rev. leg: W/o dot after KUO.

Y#	Date	Mintage	Fine	VF	XF	Unc
10.3	CD1907	—	1.00	2.00	4.50	18.00

Rev. leg: Dot after KUO.

Y#	Date	Mintage	Fine	VF	XF	Unc
10.4	CD1907	—	1.00	2.00	4.50	18.00

BRASS
Obv: W/o dots.

Y#	Date	Mintage	Fine	VF	XF	Unc
10.4a	CD1907	—	5.50	20.00	35.00	80.00

COPPER
Obv: 4 dots divide leg.

Y#	Date	Mintage	Fine	VF	XF	Unc
10.5	CD1907	—	1.00	2.00	4.50	18.00

BRASS

Y#	Date	Mintage	Fine	VF	XF	Unc
10.5a	CD1907	—	5.50	15.00	30.00	85.00

COPPER
Rev: Waves below dragon.

Y#	Date	Mintage	Fine	VF	XF	Unc
20	CD1909	—	1.00	2.00	4.00	22.50

Rev: Rosette below dragon, U of KUO inverted A.

Y#	Date	Mintage	Fine	VF	XF	Unc
20.1	CD1909	—	5.50	12.00	25.00	60.00

NOTE: Although this coin bears no indication of its origin, it was minted in the Manchurian Provinces ca. 1922.

Y#	Date	Mintage	Fine	VF	XF	Unc
20x	CD1909	—	10.00	20.00	30.00	80.00

NOTE: Although this coin bears no indication of its origin, it was minted in Kirin Province.

BRONZE

Y#	Date	Mintage	Fine	VF	XF	Unc
27	Yr.3(1911)	95.585	2.50	4.00	8.00	40.00
	Yr.3(1911)	—	—	—	Proof	Rare

BRASS

Y#	Date	Mintage	Fine	VF	XF	Unc
27a	Yr.3(1911)	—	30.00	45.00	95.00	150.00

20 CASH

COPPER

Y#	Date	Mintage	VG	Fine	VF	XF
5	(1917)	—	.50	1.00	2.00	3.00

NOTE: This coin was struck at the Wuchang Mint in 1917 from unused dies prepared in 1903.

Obv: 4-point rosette in center.

Y#	Date	Mintage	VG	Fine	VF	XF
5.1	ND(restrike)	—	2.50	6.00	12.00	25.00

Rev: Head of dragon and clouds redesigned.

Y#	Date	Mintage	VG	Fine	VF	XF
5.2	ND(restrike)	—	2.50	6.00	12.00	25.00

Rev: Dragon in circle of dots.

Y#	Date	Mintage	VG	Fine	VF	XF
5a	ND(1903-05)	—	30.00	50.00	85.00	125.00

Y#	Date	Mintage	VG	Fine	VF	XF
11	CD1905	—	12.50	30.00	50.00	75.00

Y#	Date	Mintage	VG	Fine	VF	XF
11.1	CD1906	—	12.50	30.00	50.00	75.00

Obv: Dots around date, 1.2-1.7mm thick.

Y#	Date	Mintage	VG	Fine	VF	XF
11.2	CD1907	—	.60	1.50	2.00	4.00

2.0-2.3mm thick

| 11.3 | CD1907 | — | 2.50 | 6.00 | 12.00 | 25.00 |

BRASS

| 11.3a | CD1907 | — | 3.50 | 8.00 | 15.00 | 30.00 |

COPPER
Obv: W/o dots around date.

| 11.4 | CD1907 | — | | Reported, not confirmed | | |

Rev. leg: Dot between KUO and COPPER,
6 waves beneath dragon.

| 21 | CD1909 | — | 1.00 | 2.50 | 5.00 | 10.00 |

1.2-1.7mm thick
Rev. leg: W/o dot between KUO and COPPER,
6 waves beneath dragon.

| 21.1 | CD1909 | — | 1.25 | 3.00 | 6.00 | 10.00 |

2.0-2.3mm thick

| 21.2 | CD1909 | — | 1.25 | 3.00 | 6.00 | 10.00 |

Rev: Rosette beneath dragon.

| 21.3 | CD1909 | — | 6.00 | 15.00 | 40.00 | 70.00 |

NOTE: Although this coin bears no indication of its origin, it was minted in the Manchurian Provinces ca. 1922.

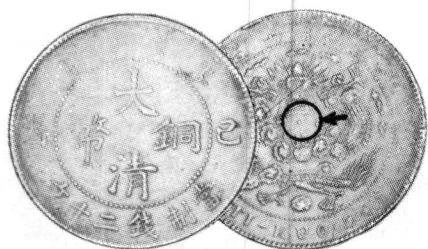

Rev: Dot below dragon's chin.

| 21.4 | CD1909 | — | 3.50 | 8.50 | 16.00 | 30.00 |

NOTE: Although this coin bears no indication of its origin, it was minted in the Manchurian Provinces ca. 1922.

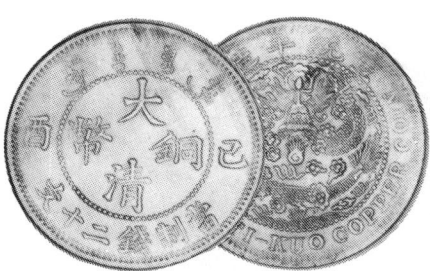

Rev: 5 crude waves beneath dragon w/
redesigned forehead.
Inner circle of large dots on obv. and rev.

Y#	Date	Mintage	VG	Fine	VF	XF
21.5	CD1909	—	1.20	3.00	6.00	16.00

10 CENTS

2.7000 g, .820 SILVER, .0712 oz ASW
Similar to Y#12.

Kann#	Date	Mintage	Fine	VF	XF	Unc
215	CD1907	—	85.00	150.00	250.00	400.00

Y#	Date	Mintage	Fine	VF	XF	Unc
12	ND(1908)	—	30.00	40.00	90.00	200.00

3.2000 g, .650 SILVER, .0669 oz ASW
Similar to 50 Cents, Y#23.

Kann#	Date	Mintage	Fine	VF	XF	Unc
222	ND(1910)	—	85.00	150.00	250.00	500.00
	ND(1910)	—	—	—	Proof	750.00

SILVER, 2.70 g

Y#	Date	Mintage	Fine	VF	XF	Unc
28	Yr.3(1911)	—	15.00	30.00	75.00	180.00

NOTE: Refer to Hunan Republic 10 Cents, K#762.

20 CENTS

5.5000 g, .820 SILVER, .1450 oz ASW

Kann#	Date	Mintage	Fine	VF	XF	Unc
214	CD1907	—	100.00	150.00	250.00	450.00

5.30 g

Y#	Date	Mintage	Fine	VF	XF	Unc
13	ND(1908)	—	60.00	100.00	150.00	260.00

(Error) Rev. leg: "COPPER COIN"

Kann#	Date	Mintage	Fine	VF	XF	Unc
217w	ND(1908)	—	—	—	Rare	—

SILVER, 5.40 g

Y#	Date	Mintage	Fine	VF	XF	Unc
29	Yr.3(1911)	—	50.00	100.00	175.00	350.00

25 CENTS

6.7000 g, .800 SILVER, .1724 oz ASW

Kann#	Date	Mintage	Fine	VF	XF	Unc
221	ND(1910)	1.410	200.00	400.00	750.00	1200.
	ND(1910)	—	—	—	Proof	2000.

50 CENTS

13.6000 g, .860 SILVER, .3761 oz ASW

	Date	Mintage	Fine	VF	XF	Unc
213	CD1907	—	125.00	300.00	550.00	1000.

13.4000 g, .800 SILVER, .3447 oz ASW

Y#	Date	Mintage	Fine	VF	XF	Unc
23	ND(1910)	1.571	40.00	70.00	150.00	450.00
	ND(1910)	—	—	—	Proof	750.00

| 30 | Yr.3 (1911) | I.A. | 250.00 | 500.00 | 800.00 | 1500. |
| | Yr.3 (1911) | — | — | — | Proof | 2000. |

DOLLAR

26.9000 g, .900 SILVER, .7785 oz ASW

Kann#	Date	Mintage	Fine	VF	XF	Unc
212	CD1907	—	200.00	350.00	700.00	1400.

Y#	Date	Mintage	Fine	VF	XF	Unc
14	ND(1908)	—	20.00	35.00	75.00	300.00

Kann#	Date	Mintage	Fine	VF	XF	Unc
219	ND(1910)	—	125.00	300.00	600.00	1000.
	ND(1910)	—	—	—	Proof	2100.

Y#	Date	Mintage	Fine	VF	XF	Unc
31	Yr.3 (1911)					
		77.153	18.00	25.00	50.00	300.00

NOTE: Struck at the Tientsin, Nanking and Wuchang Mints without distinctive marks.

Rev: Mint mark "dot" after DOLLAR.

31.1	Yr.3 (1911) I.A.	25.00	40.00	75.00	350.00

REPUBLIC
1/2 CENT

 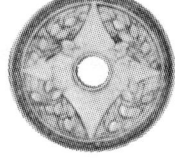

BRONZE
Mint: Tientsin

323	Yr.5 (1916)					
		1.789	5.00	10.00	20.00	45.00

Y#	Date	Mintage	Fine	VF	XF	Unc
346	Yr.25 (1936)					
		64.720	.75	1.50	3.00	7.50

10 CASH
(1 CENT OR 1 FEN)

NOTE: Some sources date these 10 Cash pieces bearing crossed flags ca. 1912, but many were not struck until the 1920's.

COPPER
Mint: Nanking
Rev: Double circle w/small rosettes separating leg.

301	ND	—	.50	.75	1.50	15.00

BRASS

301a	ND	—	—	—	—	—

COPPER
Mint: Unknown
Obv: 2nd character from right in bottom leg. is rounded. Rev: Double circle w/3 dots separating leg.

301.1	ND	—	1.00	2.00	5.00	22.00

Obv: 2nd character from right in bottom leg. rounded. Rev: Double circle w/2 dots separating leg.

301.2	ND	—	.50	1.00	2.50	16.00

Mint: Nanking
Obv: Small star on flag. Rev: Double circle w/6-pointed stars separating leg.

301.3	ND	—	.75	1.50	3.00	18.00

Obv: Large star on flag extending to edges of flag. Rev: Double circle w/6-pointed stars separating leg.

301.4	ND	—	10.00	15.00	25.00	65.00

BRASS

Y#	Date	Mintage	Fine	VF	XF	Unc
301.4a	ND	—	—	—	—	—

COPPER
Obv: Flower w/many stems. Rev: Single circle.

301.5	ND	—	.75	1.50	3.00	20.00

Obv: Flower w/fewer stems. Rev: Single circle.

301.6	ND	—	.75	1.50	3.00	20.00

Mint: Anhwei
Rev: Vine above leaf at 12 o'clock. Wreath tied at bottom. M-shaped leaves at base of wheat ears.

302	ND(ca.1920)	—	.75	1.50	3.00	18.00

BRASS

302a	ND(ca.1920)	—	—	—	—	—

COPPER
Rev: Larger wheat ears.

302.1	ND(ca.1920)	—	1.00	3.50	6.50	20.00

Rev: Vine beneath leaf at 12 o'clock. Wreath not tied at bottom. W/o M-shaped leaves at base of wheat ears.

302.2	ND(ca.1920)	—	1.60	4.00	8.00	20.00

Rev: Leaves pointing clockwise.

302.3	ND(ca.1920)	—	30.00	40.00	60.00	100.00

Obv: Small star-shaped rosettes.
Rev: Small 4-petalled rosettes separating leg.

Y#	Date	Mintage	Fine	VF	XF	Unc
303	ND		.50	1.00	2.00	15.00

Obv: Left flag's star in relief.

| 303.1 | ND | | .50 | 1.00 | 2.00 | 15.00 |

BRASS
Obv: Stars replace rosettes.

| 303a | ND | — | 1.60 | 4.00 | 10.00 | 22.50 |

COPPER
Obv: Large rosettes replace stars.
Rev: Stars separating leg.

| 303.3 | ND | — | 3.00 | 6.25 | 12.50 | 25.00 |

Obv: Very small pentagonal rosettes.

| 303.4 | ND | — | .75 | 1.50 | 3.00 | 15.00 |

BRASS

| 303.4a | ND | — | 3.00 | 6.25 | 12.50 | 25.00 |

Obv: Large rosettes.
Similar to Y#307a.1.

| 303.5 | ND | — | — | — | — | — |

COPPER
Mint: Anhwei
Obv: Circled flag flanked by pentagonal rosettes.

| 304 | ND(ca.1920) | — | 11.50 | 21.50 | 42.50 | 85.00 |

Mint: Changsha, Hunan
Rev: Chrysanthemum.

Y#	Date	Mintage	Fine	VF	XF	Unc
305	ND		15.00	25.00	50.00	115.00

Mint: Changsha, Hunan

| 306.1 | ND(ca.1920) | — | .50 | 1.25 | 3.00 | 14.00 |

BRASS

| 306b | ND(ca.1920) | — | 1.00 | 2.50 | 5.00 | 18.00 |

COPPER
Obv: Y#306.1, Rev: Y#306.4

| 306.1b | ND(ca.1920) | — | 5.00 | 7.50 | 14.00 | 30.00 |

Obv: Dot on either side of upper legend.

| 306.2 | ND(ca.1920) | — | 1.00 | 2.00 | 3.50 | 15.00 |

BRASS

| 306.2b | ND(ca.1920) | | 1.25 | 3.00 | 5.00 | 15.00 |

COPPER
Obv: Star between flags.

| 306.3 | ND(ca.1920) | — | 20.00 | 40.00 | 75.00 | — |

Obv: Elongated rosettes, different characters in bottom leg. Rev: Thin leaf blade between lower wheat ears.

| 306.4 | ND(ca.1920) | — | 27.50 | 55.00 | 85.00 | 210.00 |

Obv: 5 characters in lower leg.

| 306a | ND(ca.1920) | — | 5.00 | 12.00 | 25.00 | 65.00 |

Mint: Taiyuan, Shensi
Obv: 1 large rosette on either side.
Rev: Slender leaves and short ribbon.

Y#	Date	Mintage	Fine	VF	XF	Unc
307	ND(1919)					
		421.138	.50	1.00	3.00	14.00

Rev: Larger leaves and longer ribbon.

| 307.1 | ND(1919) | I.A. | 10.00 | 20.00 | 40.00 | 100.00 |

Obv: 3 rosettes on either side, ornate right flag.
Rev: Long ribbon.

| 307a | ND(1919) | I.A. | 1.00 | 2.00 | 4.00 | 12.50 |

BRASS

| 307b | ND(1919) | — | — | — | — | — |

COPPER
Rev: Short ribbon and smaller wheat ears.

| 307a.1 | ND(1919) | I.A. | 10.00 | 20.00 | 40.00 | 100.00 |

Mint: Tientsin

| 309 | ND(1914-17) | — | 10.00 | 20.00 | 40.00 | 120.00 |

NOTE: Pieces w/L. GIORGI near rim are patterns.

BRONZE
Mint: Tientsin

Y#	Year	Date	Fine	VF	XF	Unc
324	5	(1916)	5.00	10.00	20.00	50.00

NOTE: Pieces w/L. GIORGI near rim are patterns.

COPPER
Mint: Kalgan

Y#	Year	Date	Fine	VF	XF	Unc
311	13	(1924)	175.00	350.00	500.00	850.00

BRONZE

Y#	Year	Date	Fine	VF	XF	Unc
324a	22	(1933)	8.00	15.00	30.00	100.00

COPPER

Y#	Date	Mintage	Fine	VF	XF	Unc
347	Yr.25 (1936)					
		311.780	.40	.75	1.75	2.50
	Yr.26 (1937)					
		307.198	.45	1.00	1.50	3.00
	Yr.27 (1938)					
		12.000	3.00	5.00	8.00	16.00
	Yr.28 (1939)					
		75.000	2.00	4.00	7.00	15.00

BRASS
Shi Kwan Cent

Y#	Year	Date	Fine	VF	XF	Unc
353	28	(1939)	40.00	80.00	150.00	250.00

ALUMINUM

Y#	Date	Mintage	Fine	VF	XF	Unc
355	Yr.29 (1940)					
		150.000	.10	.25	.50	1.50

BRASS

Y#	Date	Mintage	Fine	VF	XF	Unc
357	Yr.29 (1940)					
		50.000	.75	1.00	2.00	4.00

BRONZE

Y#	Year	Date	Fine	VF	XF	Unc
363	37	(1948)	4.00	10.00	15.00	20.00

RED COPPER

363a	38	(1949)	—	—	—	—

NOTE: Circulated in Shansi where it was minted.

---

20 CASH
(2 CENTS or 2 FEN)

COPPER
Mint: Taiyuan, Shansi

Y#	Date	Mintage	Fine	VF	XF	Unc
308	Yr.8 (1919)					
		200.861	1.50	3.00	7.50	30.00

CAST BRASS

Y#	Date	Mintage	Good	VG	Fine	VF
308b	Yr.8	—	10.00	15.00	18.50	25.00

NOTE: A "warlord" issue. Refer to note under Szechuan - Republic.

COPPER
Obv: 4 rosettes added between legends.

Y#	Date	Mintage	Fine	VF	XF	Unc
308a	Yr.10 (1921)I.A.		1.00	2.50	6.00	30.00

Mint: Tientsin

310	ND	—	15.00	30.00	70.00	135.00

NOTE: Some sources date these 20 Cash pieces bearing crossed flags ca. 1912, but many were not struck until the 1920's. This coin is usually found weakly struck and lightweight.

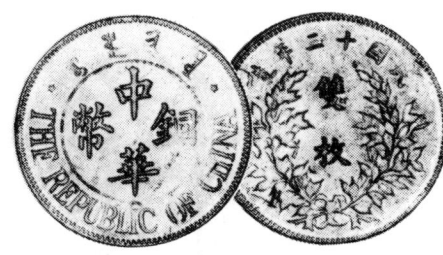

Mint: Kaigan

Y#	Year	Date	Fine	VF	XF	Unc
312	13	(1924)	10.00	30.00	70.00	135.00

NOTE: This coin is usually found weakly struck.

Nationalist Commemorative

Hsu#	Date	Mintage	Fine	VF	XF	Unc
9	ND(1927/8)	—	225.00	400.00	650.00	900.00

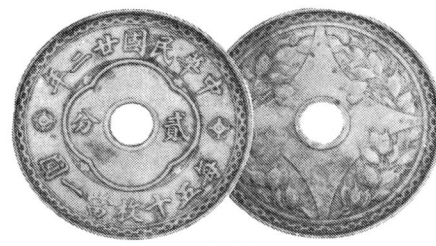

BRONZE

Y#	Date	Mintage	Fine	VF	XF	Unc
325a	Yr.22 (1933)	—	40.00	60.00	95.00	150.00

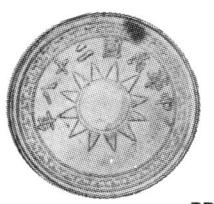

BRASS

Y#	Date	Mintage	Fine	VF	XF	Unc
354	Yr.28 (1939)					
		300.000	10.00	15.00	25.00	50.00

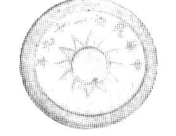

358	Yr.29 (1940)	—	.50	1.00	1.50	2.00
	Yr.30 (1941)	—	—	—	Rare	—

NICKEL

Y#	Date	Mintage	Fine	VF	XF	Unc
348	Yr.25 (1936)					
		72.844	1.00	1.50	3.00	6.00
	Yr.27 (1938)					
		34.325	2.50	4.50	8.00	15.00
	Yr.28 (1939)					
		6.000	10.00	15.00	25.00	50.00

Rev: A mint mark below spade (Vienna).

348.1	Yr.25 (1936)					
		20.000	1.00	2.00	3.50	15.00

Obv: Character P'ing on both sides of portrait.

Y#	Year	Date	Fine	VF	XF	Unc
348.2	25	(1936)	50.00	80.00	125.00	175.00

Obv: Character Ch'ing on both sides of portrait.

348.3	25	(1936)	50.00	80.00	125.00	175.00

ALUMINUM

Y#	Date	Mintage	Fine	VF	XF	Unc
356	Yr.29 (1940)					
		350.000	.50	1.00	2.50	4.00

COPPER-NICKEL

Y#	Date	Mintage	Fine	VF	XF	Unc
359	Yr.29 (1940)					
		57.000	.25	1.50	2.50	5.00
	Yr.30 (1941)					
		96.000	.25	1.50	2.50	6.00

RED COPPER

Y#	Date	Mintage	Fine	VF	XF	Unc
359a	Yr.38 (1949)	—	—	—	—	—

10 CENTS
(10 FEN or 1 CHIAO)

SILVER, 2.30 g
Similar to 1 Dollar, Y#318, vertical reeding.

Kann#	Date	Mintage	Fine	VF	XF	Unc
602	ND(1912)	—	200.00	500.00	700.00	1250.

Edge engrailed w/circles.

602b	ND(1912)	—	—	700.00	850.00	1500.

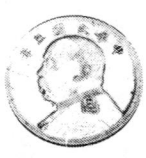 

2.7000 g, .700 SILVER, .0607 oz ASW

Y#	Year	Date	Fine	VF	XF	Unc
326	3	(1914)	5.00	10.00	17.50	50.00
	5	(1916)	20.00	35.00	50.00	100.00

SILVER
Pu Yi Wedding

334	15	(1926)	5.00	12.00	25.00	65.00

SILVER, 2.50 g
Death of Sun Yat-sen

339	16	(1927)	25.00	40.00	70.00	135.00

NICKEL

Y#	Date	Mintage	Fine	VF	XF	Unc
349	Yr.25 (1936)					
		73.866	.60	1.00	3.00	7.50
	Yr.27 (1938)					
		110.203	2.00	4.25	8.00	20.00
	Yr.28 (1939)					
		68.000	1.50	3.50	10.00	27.50

NON-MAGNETIC NICKEL ALLOY

349a	Yr.25 (1936)					
		1.000	18.00	30.00	35.00	65.00

NOTE: All of the Y#349 coins were supposed to have been minted in pure nickel at the Shanghai Mint. However in 1936 the Tientsin Mint produced about one million 10 Cent pieces of heavily alloyed nickel. The result is that the Shanghai pieces are attracted to a magnet while the Tientsin pieces are not.

NICKEL
Rev: A mint mark below spade (Vienna Mint).

349.1	Yr.25 (1936)A					
		60.000	1.00	2.00	8.00	25.00

COPPER-NICKEL
Reeded edge.

Y#	Date	Mintage	Fine	VF	XF	Unc
360	Yr.29 (1940)					
		68.000	.50	2.50	8.00	15.00
	Yr.30 (1941)					
		254.000	.50	1.50	2.50	5.00
	Yr.31 (1942)					
		10.000	25.00	60.00	80.00	120.00

Plain edge.

360.1	Yr.29(1940) I.A.	—	—	Rare	—	
	Yr.30(1941) I.A.	—	2.00	7.50	10.00	15.00

20 CENTS
(20 FEN or 2 CHIAO)

SILVER, 5.20 g
Founding of the Republic

317	ND(1912)	.155	15.00	20.00	35.00	80.00

5.4000 g, .700 SILVER, .1215 oz ASW

Y#	Year	Date	Fine	VF	XF	Unc
327	3	(1914)	3.00	5.00	10.00	35.00
	5	(1916)	3.00	5.00	12.00	50.00
	9	(1920)	100.00	250.00	300.00	500.00

SILVER, 5.20 g
Pu Yi Wedding

335	15	(1926)	10.00	15.00	30.00	80.00

SILVER, 5.30 g
Death of Sun Yat-sen

340	16	(1927)	15.00	25.00	40.00	100.00

 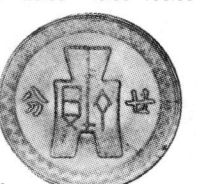

NICKEL

Y#	Date	Mintage	Fine	VF	XF	Unc
350	Yr.25 (1936)					
		49.620	.50	2.50	6.00	10.00
	Yr.27 (1938)					
		61.248	1.00	2.00	7.00	12.00
	Yr.28 (1939)					
		38.000	2.00	5.00	10.00	15.00

Rev: A mint mark below spade (Vienna Mint).

Y#	Date	Mintage	Fine	VF	XF	Unc
350.1	Yr.25 (1936)					
		40.000	1.00	2.00	3.50	6.00

COPPER-NICKEL

361	Yr.31 (1942)					
		32.300	.40	1.00	2.25	4.00

500 CASH

COPPER
Nationalist Commemorative

Hsu#	Date	Mintage	Fine	VF	XF	Unc
445a	ND(1927/8)					
	12 pcs. (8 known)		—	—	Rare	—

50 CENTS

13.6000 g, .700 SILVER, .3060 oz ASW

Y#	Year	Date	Fine	VF	XF	Unc
328	3	(1914)	20.00	30.00	50.00	100.00

COPPER-NICKEL

Y#	Date	Mintage	Fine	VF	XF	Unc
362	Yr.31 (1942)					
		57.000	1.50	3.00	7.50	15.00
	Yr.32 (1943)					
		4.000	3.50	9.50	17.50	30.00

DOLLAR (YUAN)

26.9000 g, .900 SILVER, .7785 oz ASW
Sun Yat-sen Founding of the Republic
Rev: 2 five-pointed stars dividing leg. at top.

Y#	Date	Mintage	Fine	VF	XF	Unc
318	ND(1912)	—	100.00	150.00	300.00	650.00

Obv: Dot below ear.

318.1	ND		—	—	—	—

NOTE: For similar issue w/rosettes see Y#318a.1 (1927).

27.3000 g, .900 SILVER, .7900 oz ASW
Obv: Similar to Y#318.

319	ND(1912)	—	80.00	125.00	200.00	450.00

SILVER, 26.50 g
Li Yuan-hung Founding of Republic
Rev: Similar to Y#319.

320	ND(1912)	—	125.00	250.00	400.00	700.00

Rev. leg: OE for OF.

320.1	ND(1912)	—	150.00	275.00	450.00	750.00

Rev. leg: CIIINA for CHINA.

320.2	ND(1912)	—	150.00	275.00	450.00	750.00

Li Yuan-hung Founding of Republic
Rev: Similar to Y#319.

321	ND(1912)	—	50.00	100.00	150.00	250.00

Rev. leg: H of 'THE' engraved as I I.

Y#	Date	Mintage	Fine	VF	XF	Unc
321.1	ND(1912)	—	60.00	125.00	175.00	275.00

26.7000 g, .900 SILVER, .7474 oz ASW
39.1mm, thickness 2.8mm
Yuan Shih-kai Founding of Republic

322	ND(1914)	.020	—	125.00	250.00	375.00

39.5mm, thickness 3.25mm

322.1	ND	—	—	125.00	250.00	375.00

NOTE: A restrike made about 1918 for collectors.

26.4000 g, .890 SILVER, .7555 oz ASW
Yuan Shih-kai
Obv: 6 characters above head.
Vertical reeding.

Y#	Year	Date	Fine	VF	XF	Unc
329	3	(1914)	8.00	12.50	16.00	30.00

Edge engrailed w/circles.

329.1	3	(1914)	30.00	80.00	500.00	1000.

Edge ornamented w/alternating T's.

329.2	3	(1914)	30.00	80.00	500.00	1000.

Plain edge.

329.3	3	(1914)	20.00	40.00	300.00	500.00

Tiny circle in ribbon bow. This is a mint mark, but it is not clear what mint is indicated.

329.4	3	(1914)	15.00	30.00	70.00	125.00

Obv: 7 characters above head.

Y#	Year	Date	Fine	VF	XF	Unc
329.6	8	(1919)	10.00	15.00	35.00	100.00
	9	(1920)	7.50	10.00	15.00	30.00
	10	(1921)	7.50	10.00	15.00	30.00

Oblique edge reeding.

329.5	10	(1921)	17.50	30.00	35.00	50.00

NOTE: Although bearing dates of Yr. 3 (1914) and Yr. 8-10 (1919-21), these Yuan Shi-Kai Dollars were struck for years afterwards. Coins dated Yr. 3 (1914) were struck continuously through 1929 and were also later restruck by the Chinese Communists. Later again in the 1950's this coin was struck for use in Tibet. Coins with dates Yr. 9 and 10 (1920 and 1921) were struck at least until 1929. The total mintage of all four dates of Y#329 is estimated at more than 750 million pieces.

27.0000 g, .890 SILVER, .7727 oz ASW
Incuse edge reeding.
Rev: 2 rosettes dividing leg. at top.

Y#	Date	Mintage	Fine	VF	XF	Unc
318a.1	ND(1927)	—	7.50	10.00	15.00	25.00

Edge reeding in relief.

318a.2	ND(1927)	—	7.50	10.00	15.00	25.00

NOTE: Varieties exist with errors in the English legend. For similar coins with 5 pointed stars dividing legends, see Y#318 (1912). In 1949 the Canton Mint restruck Memento dollars.
NOTE: There are modern restrikes in red copper and brass.

26.7000 g, .880 SILVER, .7555 oz ASW
Rev: Birds above junk, rising sun.

Y#	Date	Mintage	Fine	VF	XF	Unc
344	Yr.21 (1932)					
		2.260	125.00	200.00	300.00	600.00

Rev: W/o birds above junk or rising sun.

345	Yr.22 (1933)					
		46.400	12.00	15.00	20.00	50.00
	Yr.23 (1934)					
		128.740	10.00	12.50	15.00	25.00

NOTE: In 1949, three U.S. mints restruck a total of 30 million "Junk Dollars" dated Year 23.

CHINA-JAP. PUPPET STATES

Shortly after World War I the greatest external threat to the territorial integrity of China was posed by Japan, which urgently needed room for an expanding population and raw materials for its industrial and military machines, and which recognized the necessity of controlling all of China if it was to realize its plan of dominating the rest of the Asiatic and South Sea countries. The Japanese had large investments in Manchuria (a name given by non-Chinese to the three northeastern provinces of China) which allowed them privileges that compromised Chinese sovereignty. The educated of China remained unreconciled to Japan's growing power in Manchuria, and the resultant friction occasioned a series of vexing incidents which Japan decided to circumvent by direct action. On the night of Sept. 18-19, 1931, with a contrived incident for an excuse, Japanese forces seized the city of Mukden (Shenyang), and within a few weeks completely demolished Chinese power north of the Great Wall.

In Feb. 1932, after the Japanese occupation of Manchuria, they set up Manchoukuo as an independent republic. Jehol (Rehe) was occupied by the Japanese in 1933 and added to Manchoukuo. Manchoukuo was established as an empire in 1934 with the deposed Manchu emperor Hsuan T'ung (the late Henry Pu Yi) as the puppet emperor K'ang Te. Lacking the means to face the Japanese armies in the field, the Chinese could only trade space for time.

Not content with confining its control of China to the areas north of the Great Wall, the Japanese launched a major campaign in 1937, and by the fall of 1938 had occupied in addition to Manchuria the provinces of Hopei (Hebei) and Chahar, most of the port cities, and the major cities as far west as Hankow (Hankou), now part of Wuhan. In addition, they dominated or threatened the provinces of Suiyuan, Shansi (Shanxi) and Shantung (Shandong).

Still the Chinese did not yield. The struggle was prolonged until the advent of World War II, which brought about the defeat of Japan and the return of the puppet states to Chinese control.

As the victorious Japanese armies swept deeper into China, Japan established central banks under control of the Bank of Japan in the conquered provinces for the purpose of establishing control over banking and finance in the puppet states, and eventually in all of China. These included the Chi Tung Bank which had its main office in Tientsin (Tianjin) with branches in Peking (Beijing), Chinan (Jinan) and Tangshan, the Federal Reserve Bank of China with its main office in Peking (Beijing) and branches in 37 other cities; and the Hua Hsing Bank with its main office in Shanghai and two branches. The puppet states of Manchukuo, previously detailed in this introduction, and Mengchiang, which comprised a greater part of Inner Mongolia, were also major coin-issuing entities.

EAST HOPEI

AUTONOMOUS

Obv: Japanese character "first".

Chi Tung Bank

The Chi Tung Bank was the banking institution of the "East Hopei Anti-Comintern Autonomous Government" established by the Japanese in 1936 to undermine the political position of China in the northwest provinces. It issued both coins and notes between 1937 and 1939 with a restraint uncharacteristic of the puppet banks of the China-Japanese puppet states.

5 LI

Y#	Year	Date	Fine	VF	XF	Unc
		COPPER				
516	26	(1937)	7.50	12.50	25.00	75.00

FEN

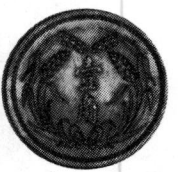

		COPPER				
517	26	(1937)	3.00	6.00	9.00	30.00

5 FEN

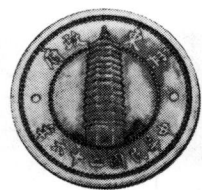 

		COPPER-NICKEL				
518	26	(1937)	2.50	4.50	6.50	25.00

CHIAO

		COPPER-NICKEL				
		Obv: T'ien Ning Pagoda in Peking.				
519	26	(1937)	2.50	4.50	6.50	20.00

2 CHIAO

		COPPER-NICKEL				
520	26	(1937)	3.00	6.00	9.00	30.00

MANCHOUKUO

The former Japanese puppet state of Manchoukuo (largely Manchuria), comprising the northeastern Chinese provinces of Fengtien (Liaoning), Kirin (Jilin), Heilungkiang (Heilongjiang) and Jehol (Rehe), had an area of 503,143 sq. mi. (1,303,134 sq. km.) and a population of 43.3 million. Capital: Changchun, renamed Hsinking. The area is rich in fertile soil, timber and mineral resources, including coal, iron and gold.

Until the closing years of the 19th century when Chinese influence became predominant, Manchuria was chiefly a domain of the tribal Manchus and their Mongol allies. Coincident with the rise of Chinese influence, foreign imperialistic powers began to appreciate the value of the area to their expansionist philosophy. Japan, overpopulated and poor in resources, desired it as a source of raw materials and for increased living area. Russia wanted it as the eastern terminus of the Trans-Siberian railway that was to unite its Asian empire. The inevitable conflict of Japanese, Chinese and Russian interests required that one or more of the powers be eliminated. After eliminating Russia in their war of 1904-05, Japan eliminated China on the night of Sept. 18, 1931, when, on the pretext of a contrived incident, it moved militarily to seize control of the Three Eastern Provinces. Early in 1932 Japan declared Manchuria independent by virtue of a voluntary separatist movement and established the state of Manchoukuo. To give the puppet state an aura of legitimacy, the deposed emperor of the former Manchu dynasty was recalled from retirement and designated "chief executive". The area was restored to China at the end of World War II.

RULERS

Ta T'ung, 1932-1934
K'ang Te, 1934-1945

The puppet emperor under the assumed name of K'ang Te was previously the last emperor of China (P'u-yi, or Hsuan T'ung, 1909-11).

MONETARY SYSTEM

10 Li = 1 Fen
10 Fen = 1 Chiao

IDENTIFICATION OF REIGN CHARACTERS

'Nien' Year   1932-1934   Ta T'ung

'Nien' Year   1934-1945   K'ang Te

DATE ABBREVIATIONS

TT - Ta T'ung
KT - K'ang Te

NOTE: Uncirculated aluminum coins without any planchet defects are worth up to twice the market valuations given.

5 LI

BRONZE

Y#	Year	Date	Fine	VF	XF	Unc
1	TT 2	(1933)	20.00	35.00	50.00	100.00
	TT 3	(1934)	4.00	9.00	15.00	30.00

Obv: Character Yuan for "first".

5.1	KT 1	(1934)	3.00	7.50	10.00	25.00

5.2	KT 2	(1935)	3.00	7.50	10.00	25.00
	KT 3	(1936)	17.50	27.50	40.00	70.00
	KT 4	(1937)	4.00	10.00	12.50	27.50
	KT 6	(1939)	150.00	200.00	275.00	375.00

FEN

BRONZE

2	TT 2	(1933)	2.00	4.00	8.00	25.00
	TT 3	(1934)	1.50	3.00	5.00	20.00

Obv: Character Yuan for "first".

6.1	KT 1	(1934)	1.00	3.00	6.00	15.00

6.2	KT 2	(1935)	1.00	3.00	5.00	10.00
	KT 3	(1936)	1.00	3.00	5.00	10.00
	KT 4	(1937)	1.00	3.00	5.00	10.00
	KT 5	(1938)	1.00	3.00	5.00	10.00
	KT 6	(1939)	1.00	3.00	6.00	15.00

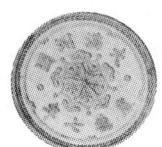 

ALUMINUM

Y#	Year	Date	Fine	VF	XF	Unc
9	KT 6	(1939)	.40	.75	2.00	5.00
	KT 7	(1940)	.40	.75	2.00	5.00
	KT 8	(1941)	.40	.75	2.00	5.00
	KT 9	(1942)	.40	.75	2.00	5.00
	KT 10	(1943)	.40	.75	2.00	5.00

 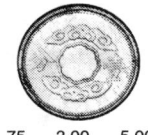

13	KT 10	(1943)	.75	2.00	5.00	10.00
	KT 11	(1944)	.75	2.00	5.00	10.00

RED FIBER

Y#	Year	Date	VG	Fine	VF	XF
13a	KT 12	(1945)	.50	1.25	3.00	4.50

BROWN FIBER

13a.1	KT 12	(1945)	1.50	4.00	10.00	15.00

5 FEN

 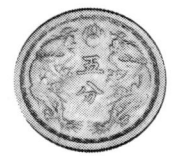

COPPER-NICKEL

Y#	Year	Date	Fine	VF	XF	Unc
3	TT 2	(1933)	.75	2.00	5.00	15.00
	TT 3	(1934)	.40	1.00	2.00	10.00

GREEK RIM BORDER VARIETIES

Narrow Design   Wide Design

Obv: Character Yuan for "first".

7.1	KT 1	(1934)	.60	1.50	3.00	6.00

7.2	KT 2	(1935)	.60	1.50	3.00	6.00
	KT 3	(1936)	narrow border design			
			.60	1.50	3.00	6.00
	KT 3	(1936)	wide border design			
			1.25	3.00	6.00	12.00
	KT 4	(1937)	1.00	2.00	4.00	7.50
	KT 6	(1939)	1.00	2.00	4.00	7.50

ALUMINUM

11	KT 7	(1940)	.60	1.50	3.00	6.00
	KT 8	(1941)	.40	.75	2.00	4.00
	KT 9	(1942)	.40	.75	2.00	4.00
	KT 10	(1943)	.40	.75	2.00	4.00

 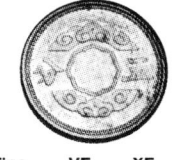

Y#	Year	Date	Fine	VF	XF	Unc
A13	KT 10	(1943)	1.00	2.50	5.00	12.50
	KT 11	(1944)	1.00	2.50	5.00	12.50

 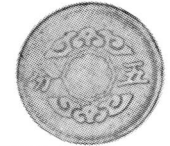

RED FIBER

Y#	Year	Date	VG	Fine	VF	XF
A13a						
	KT 11	(1944)	1.00	2.00	3.50	6.00
	KT 12	(1945)	—	—	Rare	—

BROWN FIBER

A13a.1						
	KT 11	(1944)	4.00	10.00	15.00	20.00

CHIAO
(10 Fen)

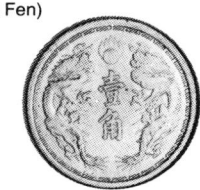

COPPER-NICKEL

Y#	Year	Date	Fine	VF	XF	Unc
4	TT 2	(1933)	1.50	3.00	7.00	15.00
	TT 3	(1934)	.80	2.00	3.75	12.50

Obv: Character Yuan for "first".

8.1	KT 1	(1934)	.80	2.00	3.00	7.50

8.2	KT 2	(1935)	.80	2.00	3.00	7.50
	KT 5	(1938)	.80	2.00	3.00	7.50
	KT 6	(1939)	.80	2.00	3.00	7.50
	KT 6	(1939)	—	—	Proof	—

10	KT 7	(1940)	1.00	3.00	5.00	12.50

ALUMINUM

12	KT 7	(1940)	.80	2.00	3.00	7.50
	KT 8	(1941)	.80	2.00	3.00	7.50
	KT 9	(1942)	.80	2.00	3.00	7.50
	KT 10	(1943)	275.00	400.00	500.00	600.00

 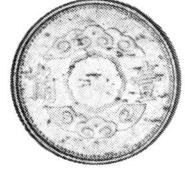

14	KT 10	(1943)	1.50	3.00	5.00	12.50

MENG CHIANG

As Japanese troops moved into North China in 1937,

the political situation became fluid in several provinces bordering on Manchoukuo, which were sometimes referred to as Inner Mongolia. On September 27, 1937, the Chanan Bank was established. As the situation became more settled the Japanese effected the merger of two local banks with the Bank of Chanan under a new title, Meng Chiang (Mongolian Borderlands or Mongol Territory) Bank. The Meng Chiang Bank was organized on November 27 and opened on December 1, 1937, with headquarters in Kalgan (Zhangjiakou) and branch offices in about a dozen locations throughout the region. Its notes were declared the exclusive currency for the area. The bank closed at the end of the war.

5 CHIAO

COPPER-NICKEL

Y#	Date	Mintage	Fine	VF	XF	Unc
521	Yr.27 (1938)					
		10.800	3.50	6.50	10.00	25.00

PROVISIONAL GOVT. OF CHINA

In late 1937 the Japanese North China Expeditionary Army established the "Provisional Government of China" at Peking (Beijing).

FEDERAL RESERVE BANK

The Federal Reserve Bank of China was opened in 1938 by Japanese military authorities in Peking (Beijing). It was the puppet financial agency of the Japanese in northeast China. This puppet bank issued both coins and currency, but in modest amounts.

FEN

ALUMINUM

Y#	Year	Date	Fine	VF	XF	Unc
523	30	(1941)	.50	1.00	2.00	6.00
	31	(1942)	.50	1.00	2.00	6.00
	32	(1943)	3.00	6.00	10.00	30.00

5 FEN

ALUMINUM

	524	30	(1941)	.75	2.00	4.00	10.00
		31	(1942)	.75	2.00	4.00	10.00
		32	(1943)	2.00	4.00	8.00	20.00

NOTE: The 5 Fen pieces were struck on thick (1.3g) and thin (1.0g) planchets.

CHIAO

ALUMINUM

	525	30	(1941)	.40	1.00	2.00	6.00
		31	(1942)	.40	1.00	2.00	6.00
		32	(1943)	1.50	3.00	6.00	15.00

NOTE: The 1 Chiao pieces were struck on thick (1.5g) and thin (1.2g) planchets.

CHINA/Peoples Republic

The Peoples Republic of China, located in eastern Asia, has an area of 3,696,100 sq. mi. (9,596,960 sq. km.) (including Manchuria and Tibet) and a population of *1.20 billion. Capital: Peking (Beijing). The economy is based on agriculture, mining, and manufacturing. Textiles, clothing, metal ores, tea and rice are exported.

China's ancient civilization began in east-central Henan's Huayang county, 2800-2300 B.C. The warring feudal states comprising early China were first united under Emperor Ch'in Shih (246-210 B.C.) who gave China its name and first central government. Subsequent dynasties alternated brilliant cultural achievements with internal disorder until the Empire was brought down by the revolution of 1911, and the Republic of China installed in its place. Chinese culture attained a pre-eminence in art, literature and philosophy, but a traditional backwardness in industry and administration ill prepared China for the demands of 19th century Western expansionism which exposed it to military and political humiliations, and mandated a drastic revision of political practice in order to secure an accommodation with the modern world.

The Republic of 1911 barely survived the stress of World War I, and was subsequently all but shattered by the rise of nationalism and the emergence of the Chinese Communist movement. Moscow, which practiced a policy of cooperation between Communists and other parties in movements for national liberation, sought to establish an entente between the Chinese Communist Party and the Kuomintang ('National Peoples Party') of Sun Yat-sen. The ensuing cooperation was based on little more than the hope each had of using the other.

An increasingly uneasy association between the Kuomintang and the Chinese Communist Party developed and continued until April 12, 1927, when Chiang Kai-shek, Sun Yat-sen's political heir, instituted a bloody purge to stamp out the Communists within the Kuomintang and the government and virtually paralyzed their ranks throughout China. Some time after the mid-1927 purges, the Chinese Communist Party turned to armed force to resist Chiang Kai-shek and during the period of 1930-34 acquired control over large parts of Kiangsi (Jiangxi), Fukien (Fujian), Hunan and Hupeh (Hubei). The Nationalist Nanking government responded with a series of campaigns against the soviet power bases and, by October of 1934, succeeded in driving the remnants of the Communist army to a refuge in Shensi (Shaanxi) Province. There the Communists reorganized under the leadership of Mao Tse-tung, defeated the Nationalist forces, and on Sept. 21, 1949, established the Peoples Republic of China. Thereafter relations between Russia and Communist China steadily deteriorated until 1958, when China emerged as an independent center of Communist power.

MONETARY SYSTEM
Before 1949
10 Cash (Wen) = 1 Cent (Fen)
100 Cents (Fen) = 1 Dollar (Yuan)

SOVIET PERIOD

Prior to 1949, the Peoples Republic of China did not exist as such, but the Communists did control areas known as Soviets. Most of the Soviets were established on the borders of two or more provinces and were named according to the provinces involved. Thus there were such soviets as the Kiangsi-Hunan Soviet, the Hunan-Hupeh-Kiangsi Soviet, the Hupeh-Honan-Anhwei Soviet and others. In 1931 some of the soviets in the southern Kiangsi area were consolidated into the Chinese Soviet Republic, which lasted until the Long March of 1934.

CHINESE SOVIET REPUBLIC

In November, 1931, the first congress of the Chinese Soviet proclaimed and established the "Chinese Soviet Republic" under the Chairmanship of Mao Tse-Tung.

CENT

COPPER

Y#	Date	Mintage	VG	Fine	VF	XF
506	ND	—	10.00	20.00	30.00	50.00

Rev: Sharp star.

Y#	Date	Mintage	Fine	VF	XF	Unc
506a	ND	(restrike)	—	—	8.00	20.00

5 CENTS

COPPER
Plain edge.

Y#	Date	Mintage	VG	Fine	VF	XF
507	ND	—	20.00	30.00	50.00	80.00

NOTE: Varieties exist.

Reeded edge.

507.1	ND	—	20.00	30.00	50.00	80.00

NOTE: Varieties exist.

Y#	Date	Mintage	Fine	VF	XF	Unc
507a	ND	(restrike)	—	—	10.00	25.00

20 CENTS

SILVER, 5.50 g

Y#	Date	Mintage	VG	Fine	VF	XF
508	1932	—	15.00	25.00	40.00	65.00
	1933	—	10.00	20.00	30.00	55.00

NOTE: Many minor varieties exist.

DOLLAR

SILVER
Obv: Crude facing portrait of Lenin.
Rev: Hammer, sickle and value within wreath.

KM#	Date	Mintage	VG	Fine	VF	XF
5	1931	—	—	—	Rare	

NOTE: For previously listed KM#6 refer to North Shensi-Soviet, KM#2.

PEOPLES REPUBLIC

MONETARY SYSTEM
10 Fen (Cents) = 1 Jiao
10 Jiao = 1 Renminbi Yuan

FEN

ALUMINUM

Y#	Date	Mintage	Fine	VF	XF	Unc
1	1955	—	.20	.50	1.50	5.00
	1956	—	.40	1.00	2.50	7.50
	1957	—	.60	1.50	3.50	10.00
	1958	—	.10	.25	.75	2.50
	1959	—	.10	.25	.75	2.50
	1961	—	.10	.25	.75	2.50
	1963	—	.10	.25	.50	1.50
	1964	—	.10	.25	.50	1.00
	1971	—	.10	.25	.50	1.00
	1972	—	.10	.25	.50	1.00
	1973	—	.10	.25	.50	1.50
	1974	—	.10	.25	.50	1.00
	1975	.500	.10	.25	.50	1.00
	1976	—	—	.10	.25	.50
	1977	—	—	.10	.25	.50
	1978	—	—	.10	.25	.50
	1979	—	—	.10	.25	.50
	1980	—	—	.10	.25	.50
	1980	—	—	—	Proof	1.00
	1981	—	—	.10	.25	.50
	1981	—	—	—	Proof	1.00
	1982	—	—	.10	.25	.50
	1982	—	—	—	Proof	1.00
	1983	—	—	—	.10	.25
	1983	2.412	—	—	Proof	1.00
	1984	—	—	—	.10	.25
	1984	3.283	—	—	Proof	1.00
	1985	—	—	—	.10	.25
	1985	—	—	—	Proof	1.00
	1986	—	—	—	.10	.25
	1986	—	—	—	Proof	1.00
	1987	—	—	—	.10	.25
	1991	—	—	—	.10	.25
	1991	—	—	—	Proof	1.00
	1992	—	—	—	.10	.25
	1992	—	—	—	Proof	1.00
	1993	—	—	In sets only		.75
	1993	—	—	—	Proof	1.00
	1994	—	—	In sets only		.75
	1994	—	—	—	Proof	1.00
	1995	—	—	In sets only		.75
	1995	—	—	—	Proof	1.00
	1996	—	—	In sets only		.75
	1996	—	—	—	Proof	1.00

2 FEN

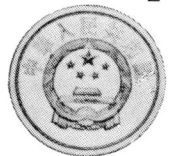 

ALUMINUM

Y#	Date	Mintage	Fine	VF	XF	Unc
2	1956	—	.10	.25	.75	1.50
	1959	—	.20	.50	1.00	4.00
	1960	—	.20	.50	1.00	4.00
	1961	—	.10	.25	.75	1.50
	1962	—	.10	.25	.75	1.50
	1963	—	.10	.25	.75	1.50
	1964	—	.10	.25	.50	1.25
	1974	—	.10	.25	.50	1.50
	1975	—	.10	.25	.50	1.00
	1976	—	.10	.25	.50	1.00

Y#	Date	Mintage	Fine	VF	XF	Unc
2	1977	.360	.10	.25	.50	.75
	1978	—	.10	.20	.40	.60
	1979	—	.10	.20	.40	.60
	1980	—	.10	.20	.40	.60
	1980	—	—	—	Proof	1.00
	1981	—	.10	.20	.40	.60
	1981	—	—	—	Proof	1.00
	1982	—	.10	.20	.40	.60
	1982	—	—	—	Proof	1.00
	1983	—	—	—	.10	.20
	1983	1.790	—	—	Proof	1.00
	1984	—	—	—	.10	.20
	1984	1.963	—	—	Proof	1.00
	1985	—	—	—	.10	.20
	1985	—	—	—	Proof	1.00
	1986	—	—	.15	.35	.75
	1986	—	—	—	Proof	1.00
	1987	—	—	—	.10	.20
	1988	—	—	—	.10	.20
	1989	—	—	—	.10	.20
	1990	—	—	—	.10	.20
	1991	—	—	—	.10	.20
	1991	—	—	—	Proof	1.00
	1992	—	—	—	.10	.20
	1992	—	—	—	Proof	1.00
	1993	—	—	In sets only		.75
	1993	—	—	—	Proof	1.00
	1994	—	—	In sets only		.75
	1994	—	—	—	Proof	1.00
	1995	—	—	In sets only		.75
	1995	—	—	—	Proof	1.00
	1996	—	—	In sets only		.75
	1996	—	—	—	Proof	1.00

5 FEN

ALUMINUM

Y#	Date	Mintage	Fine	VF	XF	Unc
3	1955	—	.30	.75	2.00	10.00
	1956	—	.15	.35	.75	2.00
	1957	—	.15	.35	.75	2.50
	1974	—	.15	.25	.50	1.50
	1975	—	.15	.25	.50	1.50
	1976	.350	.15	.25	.50	.75
	1979	—	—	—	—	2.00
	1980	—	.15	.25	.50	.75
	1980	—	—	—	Proof	1.00
	1981	—	.15	.25	.50	.75
	1981	—	—	—	Proof	1.00
	1982	—	.15	.25	.50	.75
	1982	—	—	—	Proof	1.00
	1983	—	—	.15	.25	.45
	1983	.484	—	—	Proof	1.00
	1984	—	—	.15	.25	.45
	1984	.600	—	—	Proof	1.00
	1985	—	—	.15	.25	.45
	1985	—	—	—	Proof	1.00
	1986	—	—	.15	.25	.45
	1986	—	—	—	Proof	1.00
	1987	—	—	.15	.25	.45
	1988	—	—	.15	.25	.45
	1989	—	—	.15	.25	.45
	1990	—	—	.15	.25	.45
	1991	—	—	.15	.25	.45
	1991	—	—	—	Proof	1.00
	1992	—	—	.15	.25	.45
	1992	—	—	—	Proof	1.00
	1993	—	—	In sets only		.75
	1993	—	—	—	Proof	1.00
	1994	—	—	In sets only		.75
	1994	—	—	—	Proof	1.00
	1995	—	—	In sets only		.75
	1995	—	—	—	Proof	1.00
	1996	—	—	In sets only		.75
	1996	—	—	—	Proof	1.00

JIAO

COPPER-ZINC

Y#	Date	Mintage	Fine	VF	XF	Unc
24	1980	—	—	—	—	.50
	1980	—	—	—	Proof	1.00
	1981	—	—	—	—	.50
	1981	—	—	—	Proof	1.00
	1982	—	—	—	Proof	1.00
	1983	3.100	—	—	Proof	1.00
	1984	3.500	—	—	Proof	1.00
	1985	—	—	—	Proof	1.00
	1986	—	—	—	Proof	1.00

BRASS
6th National Games - Gymnast

Y#	Date	Mintage	Fine	VF	XF	Unc
148	1987	10.530	—	—	1.00	2.00

6th National Games - Soccer

149	1987	10.530	—	—	1.00	2.00

6th National Games - Volleyball

150	1987	10.530	—	—	1.00	2.00

ALUMINUM

	Date	Mintage	Fine	VF	XF	Unc
328	1991	—	—	—	—	.50
	1991	—	—	—	Proof	1.00
	1992	—	—	—	—	.50
	1992	—	—	—	Proof	1.00
	1993	—	—	—	—	.50
	1993	—	—	—	Proof	1.00
	1994	—	—	—	—	.50
	1994	—	—	—	Proof	1.00
	1995	—	—	—	—	.50
	1995	—	—	—	Proof	1.00
	1996	—	—	—	—	.50
	1996	—	—	—	Proof	1.00
	1997	—	—	—	—	.50

2 JIAO

COPPER-ZINC

	Date	Mintage	Fine	VF	XF	Unc
25	1980	—	—	—	—	.60
	1980	—	—	—	Proof	1.25
	1981	—	—	—	—	.60
	1981	—	—	—	Proof	1.25
	1982	—	—	—	Proof	1.25
	1983	4.200	—	—	Proof	1.25
	1984	2.500	—	—	Proof	1.25
	1985	—	—	—	Proof	1.25
	1986	—	—	—	Proof	1.25

5 JIAO

COPPER-ZINC

	Date	Mintage	Fine	VF	XF	Unc
26	1980	—	—	—	—	.75
	1980	—	—	—	Proof	1.50
	1981	—	—	—	—	.75
	1981	—	—	—	Proof	1.50
	1982	—	—	—	Proof	1.50
	1983	3.000	—	—	Proof	1.50
	1984	3.500	—	—	Proof	1.50
	1985	—	—	—	—	.75
	1985	—	—	—	Proof	1.50
	1986	—	—	—	Proof	1.50

BRASS

Y#	Date	Mintage	Fine	VF	XF	Unc
329	1991	—	—	—	—	1.00
	1991	—	—	—	Proof	1.50
	1992	—	—	—	—	1.00
	1992	—	—	—	Proof	1.50
	1993	—	—	—	—	1.00
	1993	—	—	—	Proof	1.50
	1994	—	—	—	—	1.00
	1994	—	—	—	Proof	1.50
	1995	—	—	—	—	1.00
	1995	—	—	—	Proof	1.50
	1996	—	—	—	—	1.00
	1996	—	—	—	Proof	1.50
	1997	—	—	—	—	1.00
	1998	—	—	—	—	1.00

YUAN

COPPER-NICKEL

Y#	Date	Mintage	Fine	VF	XF	Unc
27	1980	—	—	—	—	2.00
	1980	—	—	—	Proof	3.00
	1981	—	—	—	—	2.00
	1981	—	—	—	Proof	3.00
	1982	—	—	—	Proof	3.00
	1983	3.100	—	—	Proof	3.00
	1984	4.100	—	—	Proof	3.00
	1985	—	—	—	—	2.00
	1985	—	—	—	Proof	3.00
	1986	—	—	—	Proof	3.00

NICKEL CLAD STEEL

Y#	Date	Mintage	Fine	VF	XF	Unc
330	1991	—	—	—	—	1.50
	1991	—	—	—	Proof	2.50
	1992	—	—	—	—	1.50
	1992	—	—	—	Proof	2.50
	1993	—	—	—	—	1.50
	1993	—	—	—	Proof	2.50
	1994	—	—	—	—	1.50
	1994	—	—	—	Proof	2.50
	1995	—	—	—	—	1.50
	1995	—	—	—	Proof	2.50
	1996	—	—	—	—	1.50
	1996	—	—	—	Proof	2.50

REPUBLIC OF CHINA

The Republic of China, comprising Taiwan (an island located 90 miles (145 km.) off the southeastern coast of mainland China), the offshore islands of Quemoy and Matsu and nearby islets of the Pescadores chain, has an area of 14,000 sq. mi. (35,980 sq. km.) and a population of 20.2 million. Capital: Taipei. During the past decade, manufacturing has replaced agriculture in importance. Fruits, vegetables, plywood, textile yarns and fabrics and clothing are exported.

Chinese migration to Taiwan began as early as the sixth century. The Dutch established a base on the island in 1624 and held it until 1661, when they were driven out by supporters of the Ming dynasty who used it as a base for their unsuccessful attempt to displace the ruling Manchu dynasty of mainland China. After being occupied by Manchu forces in 1683, Taiwan remained under the suzerainty of China until its cession to Japan in 1895. It was returned to China following World War II. On Dec. 8, 1949, Taiwan became the last remnant of Sun Yat-sen's vast Republic of China. Chiang Kai-Shek had quickly moved his government and nearly exhausted army from the mainland leaving the Communist forces under Mao Tse-Tung victorious.

The coins of Nationalist China do not carry A.D. dating, but are dated according to the year of the republic, which was established in 1911. However, republican years are added to 1911 to find the western year. Thus republican year 38 plus 1911 equals Gregorian calendar year 1949AD.

MONETARY SYSTEM
10 Cents = 1 Chiao
10 Chiao = 1 Dollar (Yuan)

10 CENTS

BRONZE
Sun Yat-sen

Y#	Date	Mintage	Fine	VF	XF	Unc
531	Yr.38 (1949)					
		157.600	.10	.30	1.00	4.00

ALUMINUM

Y#	Date	Mintage	Fine	VF	XF	Unc
533	Yr.44 (1955)					
		583.980	—	.10	.15	1.00

	Date	Mintage	Fine	VF	XF	Unc
545	Yr.56 (1967)					
		89.999	—	.10	.15	.75
	Yr.59 (1970)					
		30.000	—	.10	.25	1.00
	Yr.60 (1971)					
		19.925	—	.20	.40	1.50
	Yr.61 (1972)					
		11.141	.10	.40	.60	2.00
	Yr.62 (1973)					
		111.400	—	—	.10	.75
	Yr.63 (1974)					
		71.930	—	.10	.25	1.00

20 CENTS

ALUMINUM
Sun Yat-sen

Y#	Date	Mintage	Fine	VF	XF	Unc
534	Yr.39 (1950)					
		327.495	—	.10	.50	3.00

50 CENTS

5.0000 g, .720 SILVER, .1157 oz ASW
Sun Yat-sen

	Date	Mintage	Fine	VF	XF	Unc
532	Yr.38 (1949)	—	1.50	2.00	3.50	5.00

BRASS

	Date	Mintage	Fine	VF	XF	Unc
535	Yr.43 (1954)					
		279.624	—	.10	.25	1.00

	Date	Mintage	Fine	VF	XF	Unc
546	Yr.56 (1967)					
		109.999	—	.10	.15	.50
	Yr.59 (1970)					
		6.010	.15	.30	.60	1.25
	Yr.60 (1971)					
		4.434	.20	.40	.80	1.50
	Yr.61 (1972)					
		21.171	—	.10	.20	1.00
	Yr.62 (1973)					
		88.840	—	.10	.20	1.00
	Yr.69 (1980)					
		3.972	—	.10	.20	1.00
	Yr.70 (1981)					
		100.000	—	.10	.20	1.00

BRONZE

	Date	Mintage	Fine	VF	XF	Unc
550	Yr.70 (1981)					
		103.800	—	.10	.20	1.00
	Yr.70 (1981)	—	—	—	Proof	10.00
	Yr.75 (1986)					
		22.000	—	.10	.20	1.00
	Yr.77 (1988)					
		10.000	—	.15	.30	1.25

DOLLAR (YUAN)

COPPER-NICKEL-ZINC

	Date	Mintage	Fine	VF	XF	Unc
536	Yr.49 (1960)					
		321.717	—	.10	.20	.50
	Yr.59 (1970)					
		48.800	.10	.20	.50	1.00
	Yr.60 (1971)					
		41.532	.10	.20	.50	1.00
	Yr.61 (1972)					
		105.309	—	.10	.20	.50
	Yr.62 (1973)					
		353.924	—	.10	.20	.50
	Yr.63 (1974)					
		535.605	—	.10	.20	.50
	Yr.64 (1975)					
		456.874	—	.10	.20	.50
	Yr.65 (1976)					
		634.497	—	.10	.20	.50
	Yr.66 (1977)					

Y#	Date	Mintage	Fine	VF	XF	Unc
536	Yr.67 (1978)	116.900	—	.10	.20	.50
	Yr.68 (1979)	104.245	—	.10	.20	.50
	Yr.69 (1980)		.10	.20	.50	.80
		113.900	—	.10	.20	.50

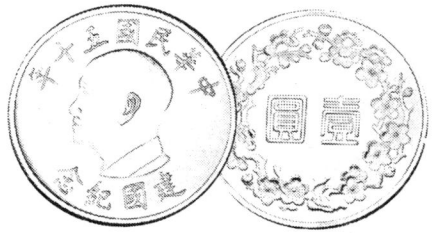

SILVER
50th Anniversary of the Republic
Chiang Kai-shek
A537 Yr.50 (1961) — 280.00
NOTE: This coin was released accidentally or was released and quickly withdrawn and is very scarce today.

COPPER-NICKEL
80th Birthday of Chiang Kai-shek
543 Yr.55 (1966) — .15 .25 .40 1.00

COPPER-NICKEL-ZINC
F.A.O. Issue
547 Yr.58 (1969) 10.000 .15 .25 .40 1.00

BRONZE
Chiang Kai-shek

Y#	Date	Mintage	Fine	VF	XF	Unc
551	Yr.70 (1981)	1,080.000	—	—	.10	.15
	Yr.70 (1981)	—	—	— Proof		12.50
	Yr.71 (1982)	780.000	—	—	.10	.15
	Yr.72 (1983)	420.000	—	—	.10	.15
	Yr.73 (1984)	110.000	—	—	.10	.15
	Yr.74 (1985)	200.000	—	—	.10	.15
	Yr.75 (1986)	200.000	—	—	.10	.15
	Yr.76 (1987)	110.000	—	—	.10	.15
	Yr.77 (1988)	40.000	—	—	.20	.50
	Yr.81 (1992)	—	—	—	.15	.25
	Yr.82 (1993)	—	—	—	.15	.25
	Yr.83 (1994)	—	—	—	.15	.25

5 DOLLARS

COPPER-NICKEL
Sun Yat-sen
537 Yr.54 (1965) — .25 .75 1.50 5.00

Chiang Kai-shek

Y#	Date	Mintage	Fine	VF	XF	Unc
548	Yr.59 (1970)	12.360	.15	.40	.80	1.50
	Yr.60 (1971)	20.575	.15	.35	.50	1.00
	Yr.61 (1972)	27.998	.15	.35	.50	1.00
	Yr.62 (1973)	50.122	.15	.35	.50	.80
	Yr.63 (1974)	418.068	.15	.35	.50	.80
	Yr.64 (1975)	39.520	.15	.35	.50	.80
	Yr.65 (1976)	140.000	.15	.35	.50	.80
	Yr.66 (1977)	50.260	.15	.35	.50	.80
	Yr.67 (1978)	78.082	.15	.35	.50	.80
	Yr.68 (1979)	—	.15	.35	.50	.80
	Yr.69 (1980)	273.000	.15	.35	.50	.80
	Yr.70 (1981)	162.000	.15	.35	.50	.80

		Mintage	Fine	VF	XF	Unc
552	Yr.70 (1981)	522.432	—	.15	.20	.50
	Yr.70 (1981)	—	—	— Proof		12.50
	Yr.71 (1982)	66.000	—	.15	.20	.50
	Yr.72 (1983)	34.000	—	.15	.20	.50
	Yr.73 (1984)	280.000	—	.15	.20	.50
	Yr.77 (1988)	200.000	—	.15	.20	.50
	Yr.78 (1989)	—	—	.15	.20	.50

10 DOLLARS

COPPER-NICKEL
Sun Yat-sen
538 Yr.54 (1965) — .50 1.00 2.00 6.00

Chiang Kai-shek

		Mintage	Fine	VF	XF	Unc
553	Yr.70 (1981)	123.000	—	.30	.40	.65
	Yr.70 (1981)	—	—	— Proof		15.00
	Yr.71 (1982)	361.000	—	.30	.40	.65
	Yr.72 (1983)	196.000	—	.30	.40	.65
	Yr.73 (1984)	220.000	—	.30	.40	.65
	Yr.74 (1985)	200.000	—	.30	.40	.65
	Yr.75 (1986)	100.000	—	.30	.40	.65
	Yr.76 (1987)	90.000	—	.30	.40	.65
	Yr.77 (1988)					

Y#	Date	Mintage	Fine	VF	XF	Unc
553		100.000	—	.30	.40	.65
	Yr.78 (1989)	—	—	.30	.40	.65
	Yr.79 (1990)	—	—	.30	.40	.65
	Yr.80 (1991)	—	—	.30	.40	.65
	Yr.81 (1992)	—	—	.30	.40	.65
	Yr.82 (1993)	—	—	.30	.40	.65

50th Anniversary - Taiwan's Liberation from Japan
555 Yr.84 (1995) — — — — 2.25

50 DOLLARS

17.1000 g, .750 SILVER, .4123 oz ASW
Sun Yat-sen
539 Yr.54 (1965) — — — 10.00 20.00

BRASS

Y#	Date	Year	Mintage	VF	XF	Unc
554	1992	81	—	.50	1.00	3.50
	1993	82	—	.50	1.00	3.50

BRASS center in COPPER-NICKEL ring
Parliament Building
556 1996 85 — — — 5.75
1997 86 — — — 5.75

COLOMBIA

The Republic of Colombia, in the northwestern corner of South America, has an area of 440,831 sq. mi. (1,138,910 sq. km.) and a population of 36.2 million. Capital: Bogota. The economy is primarily agricultural with a mild, rich coffee being the chief crop. Colombia has the world's largest platinum deposits and important reserves of coal, iron ore, petroleum and limestone; other precious metals and emeralds are also mined. Coffee, crude oil, bananas, sugar and emeralds are exported.

The northern coast of present Colombia was one of the first parts of the American continent to be visited by Spanish navigators. At Darien in Panama is the site of the first permanent European settlement on the American mainland in 1510. New Granada, as Colombia was known until 1861, stemmed from the settlement of Santa Marta in 1525. New Granada was established as a Spanish colony in 1549. Independence was declared in 1810, and secured in 1819 when Simon Bolivar united Colombia, Venezuela, Panama and Ecuador as the Republic of Gran Colombia. Venezuela withdrew from the Republic in 1829; Ecuador in 1830; and Panama in 1903.

RULERS

Spanish, until 1819

MINT MARKS

A, M - Medellin (capital), Antioquia (state)
B - Bogota
H - Heaton (Birm. England)
(m) - Medellin, w/o mint mark
(Mo) - Mexico City
NI - Numismatica Italiana, Arezzo, Italy
  mint marks stylized in wreath
(P) - Philadelphia
(W) - Waterbury, CT (USA, Scoville mint)
caduceus - Bogota
floral spray - Popayan

REPUBLIC

CENTAVO

COPPER-NICKEL
Plain edge.

KM#	Date	Mintage	Fine	VF	XF	Unc
275	1918	.989	4.00	12.00	20.00	40.00
	1919	.496	15.00	25.00	37.50	65.00
	1920	7.540	2.50	7.50	12.50	27.50
	1921	12.460	1.25	6.00	12.00	21.50
	1933(P)	3.000	.50	2.25	3.75	8.00
	1935	5.000	.50	3.00	5.00	10.00
	1936	1.540	1.50	5.00	7.50	13.50
	1938(P)	7.920	.15	.25	1.00	3.00
	1941B	1.000	.35	.75	2.00	6.00
	1946B	2.096	.30	.55	1.50	4.00
	1947/17B	1.835	1.00	3.50	6.00	12.00
	1947/37B	I.A.	1.00	3.50	6.00	12.00
	1947/6B	I.A.	1.00	3.50	6.00	12.00
	1947B	Inc. Ab.	.35	.75	1.50	3.75
	1948/38B	1.139	1.00	3.50	6.00	12.00
	1948B	Inc. Ab.	.35	.75	2.00	4.50

NOTE: Erratically punched final two digits of date are common on these issues, esp. 1935-48.

NICKEL CLAD STEEL

KM#	Date	Mintage	Fine	VF	XF	Unc
275a	1952	8.697	— Reported, not confirmed			
	1952B	Inc. Ab.	.10	.15	.25	1.00
	1954B	5.080	.10	.15	.25	1.00
	1956	1.315	.10	.15	.40	1.50
	1957	.900	.15	.25	.50	2.50
	1958/48	—	.35	.75	1.50	5.00
	1958	1.596	.10	.15	.40	2.00

NOTE: Erratically punched final two digits of date are common on these issues.

BRONZE

KM#	Date	Mintage	Fine	VF	XF	Unc
205	1942	1.000	.20	.50	1.50	3.50
	1942B	Inc. Ab.	.25	.75	2.00	5.00
	1943	—	.15	.35	1.00	3.00
	1943B	4.515	.15	.35	1.00	3.00
	1944B	4.515	.15	.35	1.00	3.00
	1945	3.769	.15	.35	1.00	3.00
	1945B	—	.15	.35	1.00	3.00
	1948B	.585	.30	1.00	2.50	6.50
	1949B	4.255	.15	.35	1.00	3.50
	1950B	5.827	.15	.35	1.00	3.50
	1951B	Inc. Ab.	.20	.60	1.75	4.50
	1957	2.500	—	.10	.20	1.00
	1958	.590	.10	.25	.50	2.00
	1959	2.677	—	.10	.20	1.00
	1960	2.500	—	.10	.20	1.00
	1961 wide spaced date					
		3.673	.10	.15	.30	1.50
	1961 narrow spaced date					
		Inc. Ab.	—	.10	.20	1.00
	1962	4.065	—	.10	.20	1.00
	1963	1.845	.10	.15	.30	2.00
	1964/44	3.165	.10	.30	.75	2.50
	1964	Inc. Ab.	.10	.15	.30	1.50
	1965 large date					
		5.510	—	.10	.20	1.00
	1965 sm. dt.	I.A.	—	.10	.20	1.00
	1966	3.910	.10	.15	.30	1.50

NOTE: Several date varieties exist.

COPPER CLAD STEEL

KM#	Date	Mintage	Fine	VF	XF	Unc
205a	1967	5.730	—	.10	.15	.25
	1968	7.390	—	.10	.15	.25
	1969	6.870	—	.10	.15	.25
	1970	3.839	—	.10	.15	.25
	1971	3.020	—	.10	.20	.50
	1972	3.100	—	.10	.15	.25
	1973	—	—	—	.10	.20
	1974	2.000	—	—	.10	.20
	1975	1.000	—	—	.10	.20
	1976	1.000	—	—	.10	.20
	1977	.900	—	—	.10	.20
	1978	.224	—	.10	.20	.40

NOTE: Several date varieties exist.

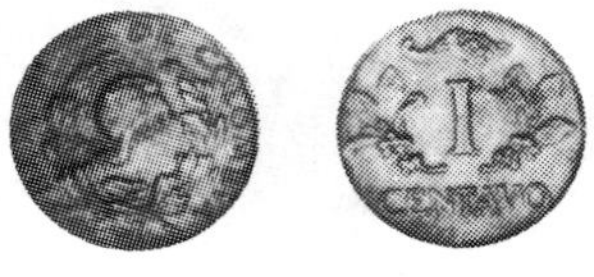

BRONZE
Uprising Sesquicentennial

KM#	Date	Mintage	Fine	VF	XF	Unc
218	ND(1960)	.500	.60	1.50	3.00	5.00

NOTE: This and the other issues in the uprising commemorative series offer the usual design of the period with the dates 1810-1960 added at the bottom of the obverse.

DOS, II (2) CENTAVOS

COPPER-NICKEL

KM#	Date	Mintage	Fine	VF	XF	Unc
198	1918	.745	2.50	6.00	15.00	45.00
	1919	.930	10.00	20.00	45.00	110.00
	1920	3.855	1.00	2.25	7.50	15.00
	1921	11.145	.25	.75	2.50	9.00
	1922	10 pcs.	known	—	—	400.00
	1933(P)	3.500	.25	.75	3.00	6.00
	1935(P)	2.500	.25	.75	3.00	6.00
	1938(P)	3.872	.20	.50	2.00	5.00
	1941B	.500	.75	1.50	2.75	6.50
	1942B	.500	1.50	2.50	3.75	7.50
	1946/36B	2.593	1.25	2.50	6.00	12.00
	1946B	Inc. Ab.	1.25	2.50	5.75	11.50
	1947/3B	1.337	1.00	2.00	4.50	10.00
	1947/36B	I.A.	1.00	2.00	4.50	10.00
	1947B	Inc. Ab.	.50	1.00	2.50	5.50

NOTE: Erratically punched final two digits exist for 1946-47.

BRONZE

KM#	Date	Mintage	Fine	VF	XF	Unc
210	1948B	2.648	.50	1.00	4.00	7.50
	1949B	1.278	.50	1.00	4.50	8.50
	1950B	2.285	.50	1.00	4.00	8.50

ALUMINUM-BRONZE

Obv: Divided legend.

KM#	Date	Mintage	Fine	VF	XF	Unc
211	1952B small date					
		5.038	—	.10	.25	1.00
	1965/3	1.830	—	.15	.20	.35
	1965 large date					
		Inc. Ab.	—	.10	.20	.85

Obv: Continuous legend.

KM#	Date	Mintage	Fine	VF	XF	Unc
214	1955 large date					
		2.513	.10	.20	.75	3.00
	1955B large date					
		Inc. Ab.	—	.10	.20	.85
	1959 small date					
		4.609	—	.10	.15	.50

Uprising Sesquicentennial

KM#	Date	Mintage	Fine	VF	XF	Unc
219	ND(1960)	.250	1.00	1.65	2.25	5.00

2-1/2 CENTAVOS

COPPER-NICKEL

KM#	Date	Mintage	Fine	VF	XF	Unc
190	1902(W)	.400	50.00	120.00	175.00	225.00

NOTE: Earlier date (1900) exists for this type.

CINCO (5) CENTAVOS

COPPER-NICKEL

KM#	Date	Mintage	Fine	VF	XF	Unc
184	1902(W)	.400	40.00	65.00	125.00	165.00

NOTE: Earlier date (1886, 1886/5) exists for this type.

1.2500 g, .666 SILVER, .0268 oz ASW
Plain edge.

KM#	Date	Mintage	Fine	VF	XF	Unc
191	1902(P)	.400	.35	1.00	2.25	5.50

COPPER-NICKEL

KM#	Date	Mintage	Fine	VF	XF	Unc
199	1918	.767	6.50	10.00	15.00	35.00
	1919	1.926	2.50	4.00	9.00	22.50
	1920	2.062	3.50	6.00	10.00	25.00
	1920H	—	3.50	6.00	10.00	25.00
	1921	1.574	1.50	3.00	6.00	17.50
	1921H	—	1.50	3.00	6.00	17.50
	1922	2.623	3.50	5.00	10.00	20.00
	1922H	—	3.50	5.00	10.00	20.00
	1924	.120	8.00	17.50	27.50	60.00
	1933(P)	2.000	.75	1.50	2.50	5.00
	1933B	—	— Reported, not confirmed			
	1935/24	11.616	—	—	—	—
	1935	Inc. Ab.	.50	1.50	2.00	4.00
	1936	—	4.50	7.50	12.50	27.50
	1938B	2.000	1.50	3.50	5.00	10.00
	1938	3.867	.50	1.35	2.00	5.00
	1938 large 8 in date					
		Inc. Ab.	.75	2.00	3.50	8.00
	1939/5	2.000	.75	1.75	3.50	8.00
	1939	Inc. Ab.	.50	1.35	2.50	5.50
	1941	—	2.75	5.00	7.50	18.00
	1941B	.500	1.25	2.50	3.50	7.00
	1946 small date					
		40.000	.20	.50	.75	2.00
	1946 large date					
		3.330	2.00	4.00	7.50	15.00
	1949B	2.750	.45	1.00	2.00	4.00
	1949	—	1.75	3.00	4.50	10.00
	1950B large 50 in date					
		3.611	.45	1.00	2.00	4.00
	1950B small 50 in date					
		Inc. Ab.	.45	1.00	2.00	4.00

NOTE: Varieties exist.
NOTE: Erratically punched final two digits of date are common on these issues, esp. 1935-50.

BRONZE

KM#	Date	Mintage	Fine	VF	XF	Unc
206	1942	—	1.25	2.50	4.00	12.00
	1942B	.800	.50	1.25	2.00	7.00
	1943	—	1.00	1.75	3.50	10.00
	1943B	6.053	.20	.60	1.00	4.00
	1944	—	.25	.75	1.25	7.00
	1944B	9.013	.25	.75	1.50	8.00
	1945/4	—	.50	1.25	2.50	9.00
	1945	—	.50	1.25	2.50	9.00
	1945B	11.101	.25	.75	1.25	4.00
	1946/5	—	1.25	2.50	3.50	10.00
	1946	—	.50	1.25	2.00	7.00
	1952	—	1.25	2.50	3.50	10.00
	1952B	3.985	.15	.40	.75	1.25
	1953B	5.180	.10	.25	.50	1.00
	1954B	1.159	.10	.25	.50	1.00
	1955B	6.819	.10	.25	.50	1.00
	1956	8.772	.10	.25	.50	1.00
	1956B	—	.35	1.25	2.50	6.50
	1957	8.912	.10	.25	.50	1.00
	1958	15.016	.10	.25	.40	.80
	1959	14.271	.10	.25	.40	.80
	1960/660	11.716	.25	.75	1.00	2.00
	1960/70	I.A.	.25	.75	1.00	2.00
	1960	Inc. Ab.	.10	.25	.40	.80
	1961	11.200	.10	.25	.40	.65
	1962	10.928	—	.10	.20	.35
	1963/53	15.113	—	—	—	—
	1963	Inc. Ab.	—	.10	.20	.40
	1964	9.336	—	.10	.20	.35
	1965	6.460	—	.10	.20	.40
	1966	7.170	—	.10	.35	1.00

NOTE: Some coins of 1942-56 have weak "B".

COPPER CLAD STEEL

KM#	Date	Mintage	Fine	VF	XF	Unc
206a	1967	10.280	—	—	.10	.25
	1968	8.900	—	—	.10	.25
	1969	17.800	—	—	.10	.25
	1970	14.842	—	—	.10	.25
	1971	10.730	—	—	.10	.25
	1972	10.170	—	—	.10	.25
	1973	10.525	—	—	.10	.25
	1974	5.310	—	—	.10	.20
	1975	5.631	—	—	.10	.20
	1976	3.009	—	—	.10	.20
	1977	2.000	—	—	.10	.20
	1978	.468	—	.10	.15	.30
	1979	8.087	—	—	.10	.20

NOTE: Date varieties exist for 1967, 1970 and 1973.

BRONZE
Uprising Sesquicentennial

KM#	Date	Mintage	Fine	VF	XF	Unc
220	ND(1960)	.400	1.75	3.50	7.50	25.00

DIEZ (10) CENTAVOS

2.5000 g, .900 SILVER, .0723 oz ASW
Simon Bolivar

KM#	Date	Mintage	Fine	VF	XF	Unc
196.1	1911	5.065	1.00	1.75	5.00	25.00
	1913	8.305	1.00	1.75	4.00	20.00
	1914	3.840	1.00	1.75	5.00	25.00
	1920	2.149	1.00	1.75	5.00	25.00
	1934B on obv.	.140	2.50	4.00	8.00	35.00
	1934/24	I.A.	—	—	—	—
	1934	Inc. Ab.	15.00	25.00	35.00	75.00
	1937	—	8.00	18.50	27.50	50.00
	1938/7	2.055	1.75	3.75	6.50	20.00
	1938 wide date	I.A.	.75	1.25	3.00	7.50
	1938 narrow date	Inc. Ab.	.75	1.25	3.00	7.50
	1940	.450	1.50	2.50	4.50	15.00
	1941	4.415	.75	1.25	3.00	7.50
	1942	3.140	5.00	10.00	16.50	37.50
	1942B on rev.	I.A.	.75	1.25	3.00	7.50

NOTE: Varieties exist.

Rev: National arms re-cut.

KM#	Date	Mintage	Fine	VF	XF	Unc
196.2	1920	I.A.	1.50	2.50	7.00	27.50

2.5000 g, .500 SILVER, .0401 oz ASW
Francisco de Paula Santander
Rev: Mint mark at bottom.

KM#	Date	Mintage	Fine	VF	XF	Unc
207.1	1945B	4.830	.50	1.25	2.50	6.00
	1945 B-B	—	—	—	—	—
	1945 backwards B	—	1.00	2.00	4.00	9.00
	1946/5B	—	.60	1.50	3.00	8.00
	1946B	—	.60	1.50	3.00	8.00
	1947/5B	7.366	1.50	3.00	5.00	10.00
	1947/6B	I.A.	1.50	3.00	5.00	10.00
	1947B	I.A.	1.50	3.00	5.00	10.00

Rev: Mint mark at top.

KM#	Date	Mintage	Fine	VF	XF	Unc
207.2	1947/5B	I.A.	2.00	4.00	7.50	20.00
	1947B	Inc. Ab.	2.00	4.00	7.50	20.00
	1948/5B	3.629	.60	1.50	3.00	8.00
	1948B	Inc. Ab.	.50	1.00	2.25	6.00
	1949/5B	5.923	2.00	4.00	7.50	20.00
	1949B	Inc. Ab.	.50	1.00	2.00	5.00
	1950B	6.783	.50	1.00	2.25	6.00
	1951/5B	5.185	.50	1.00	2.25	6.00
	1951B	Inc. Ab.	.50	1.00	2.00	5.00
	1952B	1.060	1.00	1.50	3.00	8.00

NOTE: Varieties exist.

COPPER-NICKEL 18mm
Chief Calarca

KM#	Date	Mintage	Fine	VF	XF	Unc
212.1	1952B	6.035	.10	.25	.60	2.25
	1953B	6.985	.10	.25	.60	2.25

18.5mm

KM#	Date	Mintage	Fine	VF	XF	Unc
212.2	1954B	13.006	.10	.20	.30	2.00
	1955B	9.968	.10	.20	.30	1.75
	1956	36.010	.10	.20	.30	1.00
	1956B	—	.10	.20	.30	1.00
	1958	41.695	.20	.50	1.00	3.00
	1959	36.653	.10	.20	.30	1.00
	1960	32.290	.10	.20	.30	2.00
	1961	17.780	.10	.20	.30	2.00
	1962	8.930	.10	.20	.30	1.50
	1963	37.540	.10	.20	.30	1.00
	1964	61.672	.10	.20	.30	.75
	1965	12.804	.10	.20	.30	1.50
	1966 large date	23.544	.10	.20	.30	.50

NOTE: Varieties exist.

Uprising Sesquicentennial

KM#	Date	Mintage	Fine	VF	XF	Unc
221	ND(1960)	1.000	.75	1.25	2.50	8.00

NICKEL CLAD STEEL
Francisco de Paula Santander

KM#	Date	Mintage	Fine	VF	XF	Unc
226	1967	26.980	—	.10	.15	.50
	1968	23.670	—	.10	.15	.50
	1969	29.450	—	.10	.15	.50

Obv. leg: Divided after REPUBLICA DE.

KM#	Date	Mintage	Fine	VF	XF	Unc
236	1969	Inc. Ab.	—	—	.10	.15
	1970	—	—	—	.10	.15
	1971	—	—	.10	.15	.20

Obv. leg: Divided after REPUBLICA.

KM#	Date	Mintage	Fine	VF	XF	Unc
243	1970	38.935	—	.10	.15	.20
	1971	53.314	—	.10	.15	.20

Obv. leg: Continuous.

KM#	Date	Mintage	Fine	VF	XF	Unc
253	1972	58.000	—	.10	.15	.20
	1973	46.549	—	.10	.15	.20
	1974	49.740	—	.10	.15	.20
	1975	46.037	—	.10	.15	.20
	1976	46.084	—	.10	.15	.20
	1977	8.127	—	.10	.15	.20
	1978	97.081	—	.10	.15	.20
	1980	18.929	—	.10	.15	.20

NOTE: Varieties exist.

VEINTE (20) CENTAVOS

5.0000 g, .900 SILVER, .1446 oz ASW
Simon Bolivar

KM#	Date	Mintage	Fine	VF	XF	Unc
197	1911	1.206	1.50	3.50	7.50	17.50
	1913	1.630	1.50	3.50	7.50	22.50
	1914	2.560	1.50	3.50	9.00	25.00
	1920 wide date	1.242	1.75	4.00	10.00	27.50
	1920 narrow date	Inc. Ab.	1.75	4.00	10.00	27.50
	1921	.372	4.00	10.00	22.50	55.00
	1922	.045	13.50	30.00	57.50	135.00
	1933B on obv.	.330	2.00	5.00	9.00	25.00
	1933B on rev.	Inc. Ab.	12.50	25.00	45.00	125.00
	1933B both sides	Inc. Ab.	3.00	6.00	10.00	30.00
	1938/1	1.410	—	—	—	—
	1938	Inc. Ab.	1.25	2.50	5.00	15.00
	1941	—	1.50	3.50	7.50	22.50
	1942	.155	9.00	20.00	32.50	65.00
	1942B on rev.	Inc. Ab.	1.50	3.50	7.50	20.00

5.0000 g, .500 SILVER, .0803 oz ASW
Rev: Mint mark in field below CENTAVOS.

KM#	Date	Mintage	Fine	VF	XF	Unc
208.1	1945B	1.675	1.00	2.50	5.00	10.00
	1945BB*	I.A.	4.25	8.00	15.00	32.50
	1946/5B	6.599	1.00	2.50	5.00	10.00
	1946B	Inc. Ab.	1.50	3.00	5.50	12.00
	1947/5B	9.708	2.50	4.50	8.00	20.00
	1947B	—	2.50	4.50	8.00	20.00

NOTE: 1945BB has extra B on wreath at bottom.

Rev: Mint mark on wreath at top.

KM#	Date	Mintage	Fine	VF	XF	Unc
208.2	1947/5B	I.A.	5.00	10.00	20.00	50.00
	1948/5B	I.A.	1.50	3.00	5.00	12.00
	1948B	Inc. Ab.	1.50	3.00	5.00	14.00
	1949/5B	.403	3.75	8.50	17.50	45.00
	1949B	Inc. Ab.	2.50	5.00	10.00	32.50
	1950/45B	1.899	2.75	6.75	15.00	50.00
	1950B	Inc. Ab.	2.75	6.00	13.50	37.50
	1951/45B	7.498	.75	2.00	4.00	9.00
	1951B	Inc. Ab.	.75	2.00	3.50	7.00

NOTE: Almost all dies for 1946-51 show at least faint traces of overdating from 1945. Coins with absolutely no underdate, and those with very bold underdate, are generally worth more to advanced specialists. Varieties exist.

Rev: W/o mint mark.

KM#	Date	Mintage	Fine	VF	XF	Unc
208.3	1946/5(m)	—	3.75	9.50	16.50	37.50
	1946(m)	—	3.00	7.50	15.00	32.50
	1947(m)	1.748	5.00	8.50	15.00	35.00

5.0000 g, .300 SILVER, .0482 oz ASW

Simon Bolivar

KM#	Date	Mintage	Fine	VF	XF	Unc
213	1952B	3,887			Rare	
	1953B	17.819	.40	.60	1.25	3.50

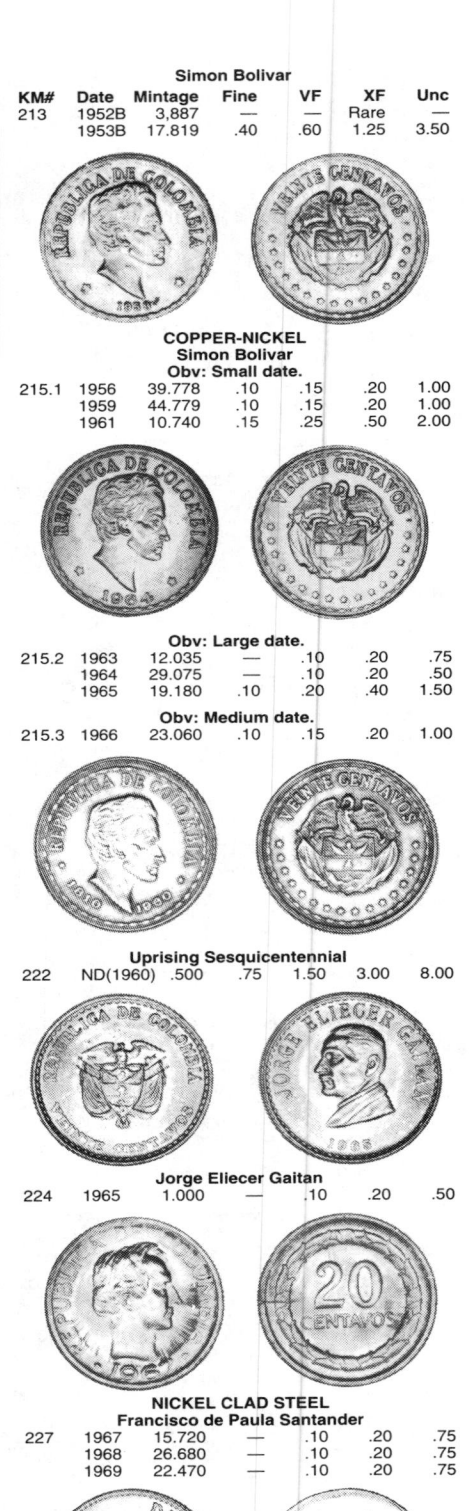

COPPER-NICKEL
Simon Bolivar
Obv: Small date.

KM#	Date	Mintage	Fine	VF	XF	Unc
215.1	1956	39.778	.10	.15	.20	1.00
	1959	44.779	.10	.15	.20	1.00
	1961	10.740	.15	.25	.50	2.00

Obv: Large date.

215.2	1963	12.035	—	.10	.20	.75
	1964	29.075	—	.10	.20	.50
	1965	19.180	.10	.20	.40	1.50

Obv: Medium date.

215.3	1966	23.060	.10	.15	.20	1.00

Uprising Sesquicentennial

222	ND(1960)	.500	.75	1.50	3.00	8.00

Jorge Eliecer Gaitan

224	1965	1.000	—	.10	.20	.50

NICKEL CLAD STEEL
Francisco de Paula Santander

227	1967	15.720	—	.10	.20	.75
	1968	26.680	—	.10	.20	.75
	1969	22.470	—	.10	.20	.75

Obv. leg: Divided after REPUBLICA.

237	1969	Inc.KM227	—	.10	.20	.30
	1970	44.358	—	—	.10	.20

Obv. leg: Divided after REPUBLICA DE.

245	1971	77.526	—	—	.10	.20

Obv. leg: Continuous.

KM#	Date	Mintage	Fine	VF	XF	Unc
246.1	1971	Inc. Ab.	—	—	.10	.20
	1972	41.891	—	—	.10	.20
	1973/1	41.440	—	—	.10	.20
	1973	Inc. Ab.	—	—	.10	.25
	1974/1	45.941	—	—	—	
	1974	Inc. Ab.	—	—	.10	.20
	1975	28.635	—	—	.10	.20
	1976	29.590	—	—	.10	.20
	1977	2.054	—	—	.10	.25
	1978	10.630	—	—	.10	.20

NOTE: Varieties exist w/ and w/o dots.

Obv: Smaller letters in legend.
Rev: Wreath with larger 20 and smaller CENTAVOS.

246.2	1979	16.655	—	—	.10	.20

25 CENTAVOS

ALUMINUM-BRONZE
Francisco de Paula Santander

267	1979	88.874	—	.10	.15	.25
	1980	46.168	—	.10	.15	.25

50 CENTAVOS

12.5000 g, .835 SILVER, .3356 oz ASW
Mint: Bogota
Edge: DIOS LEI LIBERTAD.
Obv: Incuse lettering on head band.

KM#	Date	Mintage	VG	Fine	VF	XF
186.2	1906	.446	6.00	12.50	22.50	50.00
	1907	1.126	5.00	10.00	18.50	40.00
	1908/7	.871	17.50	37.50	70.00	145.00
	1908	Inc. Ab.	8.00	15.00	25.00	55.00

Reduced size, 29.6mm.
Obv: Tip of cap points to right side of
A in REPUBLICA.

KM#	Date	Mintage	Fine	VF	XF	Unc
192	1902(P)	.960	7.00	13.50	27.50	100.00

12.5000 g, .900 SILVER, .3617 oz ASW
Mints: Birmingham and Bogota
Simon Bolivar
Obv: Sharper featured bust.
Rev: Left wing and flags far from legend.

KM#	Date	Mintage	Fine	VF	XF	Unc
193.1	1912	1.207	5.00	9.00	22.50	55.00
	1912				Proof	Rare
	1913	.417	5.00	9.00	22.50	55.00
	1914 closed 4					
		.769	BV	6.50	20.00	75.00
	1915 sm. dt.					
		.946	5.00	7.50	15.00	48.00
	1915 lg. dt.					
		Inc. Ab.	5.00	7.50	15.00	48.00
	1915		—	—	Proof	Rare
	1916 sm. dt.					
		1.060	5.00	10.00	22.50	50.00
	1917 normal 7					
		.099	10.00	20.00	30.00	65.00
	1917 foot on 7					
		Inc. Ab.	5.00	10.00	25.00	50.00
	1917 curved top					
		Inc. Ab.	5.00	10.00	25.00	50.00
	1918	.400	5.00	10.00	25.00	50.00
	1919	Inc. Ab.	15.00	25.00	35.00	80.00
	1922	.150	10.00	15.00	30.00	75.00
	1923	.150	10.00	15.00	30.00	75.00
	1931/21B					
	1931B	.700	BV	5.00	15.00	30.00
	1931	Inc. Ab.	40.00	75.00	120.00	350.00
	1932/12B	.300	8.00	14.00	25.00	50.00
	1932/22B	I.A.				
	1932B	Inc. Ab.	BV	5.00	15.00	30.00
	1932 flat top 3, w/o B					
		Inc. Ab.	20.00	30.00	40.00	80.00
	1933/13B					
		1.000	5.00	10.00	20.00	45.00
	1933/23B	I.A.	5.00	10.00	25.00	50.00
	1933B	Inc. Ab.	BV	5.00	10.00	25.00

NOTE: Many date varieties exist.

Mint: Medellin
Rev: Larger letters, left wing and flags
close to legend.

193.2	1914 open 4	—	5.00	10.00	25.00	75.00
	1915/4 lg.dt.	—	25.00	55.00	85.00	175.00
	1915 lg.dt.	—	35.00	65.00	95.00	175.00
	1918/4	—	10.00	20.00	35.00	75.00
	1918	—	BV	6.00	25.00	50.00
	1919/8	—	7.50	15.00	30.00	70.00
	1919	—	7.50	15.00	30.00	70.00
	1921	.300	7.50	15.00	30.00	70.00
	1922	—	5.00	10.00	25.00	65.00
	1932/22M					
		1.200	Inc. Ab.	10.00	15.00	25.00	50.00
	1932M	Inc. Ab.	BV	5.00	10.00	25.00
	1932 round top 3, no M					
		Inc. Ab.	20.00	35.00	60.00	125.00
	1933M	.800	BV	7.50	25.00	50.00
	1933/23 round top 3's, no M					
		Inc. Ab.	15.00	25.00	35.00	75.00

NOTE: Many date varieties exist.

Obv: Rounded feature bust.

274	1916	1.300	BV	7.50	25.00	50.00
	1917	.142	15.00	30.00	60.00	125.00
	1921	1.000	BV	5.00	20.00	45.00
	1922	3.000	BV	5.00	15.00	40.00
	1934	10.000	BV	4.00	10.00	25.00

12.5000 g, .500 SILVER, .2009 oz ASW

Simon Bolivar

KM#	Date	Mintage	Fine	VF	XF	Unc
209	1947/6B	1.240	3.00	6.00	20.00	50.00
	1947B	Inc. Ab.	5.00	10.00	20.00	50.00
	1948/6B	.707	3.00	6.00	20.00	50.00
	1948B/B	I.A.	5.00	10.00	20.00	50.00
	1948B	Inc. Ab.	5.00	10.00	20.00	50.00

COPPER-NICKEL
Simon Bolivar

217	1958	3.596	.15	.30	.50	2.00
	1959	13.466	.15	.30	.45	1.50
	1960	4.360	.15	.30	.75	2.00
	1961	3.260	.15	.30	.75	2.00
	1962	2.336	.15	.30	.75	2.00
	1963	4.098	.15	.30	.50	1.50
	1964	9.274	.15	.20	.40	1.50
	1965	5.800	.10	.15	.25	1.00
	1966	2.820	.15	.30	.50	1.50

NOTE: Various sizes of date exist.

Uprising Sesquicentennial

223	ND(1960)	.200	1.50	3.00	7.50	15.00

Jorge Eliecer Gaitan

225	1965	.600	.10	.20	.30	.60

NICKEL CLAD STEEL
Francis de Paula Santander

228	1967	3.460	.10	.15	.25	.65
	1968	5.460	.10	.15	.25	.65
	1969	1.590	.10	.15	.25	.65

244.1	1970	30.906	—	.10	.15	.35
	1971	32.650	—	.10	.15	.30
	1972	25.290	—	.10	.15	.30
	1973	8.060	—	.10	.15	.30
	1974	19.541	—	.10	.15	.25
	1975	4.325	—	.10	.15	.30
	1976	13.181	—	.10	.15	.25
	1977	10.413	—	.10	.15	.25
	1978	10.736	—	.10	.15	.25

NOTE: Date varieties exist.

KM#	Date	Mintage	Fine	VF	XF	Unc
244.2	1979	22.584	—	.10	.15	.25
	1980	16.433	—	.10	.15	.25
	1982	10.107	—	.10	.15	.25

NOTE: Various sizes of dates exist.

Rev: Larger 50.

244.3	1979	—	—	.10	.15	.25

PESO

25.0000 g, .900 SILVER, .7234 oz ASW
200th Anniversary of Popayan Mint

216	ND(1956)(Mo)					
		.012	6.00	9.00	15.00	22.50

COPPER-NICKEL
Simon Bolivar

229	1967	4.000	.15	.30	.50	1.00

Simon Bolivar
Obv: Small date.

258.1	1974	56.020	—	.10	.15	.40
	1975	117.714	—	.10	.15	.35
	1976	98.728	—	.10	.15	.35

Obv: Large date.

KM#	Date	Mintage	Fine	VF	XF	Unc
258.2	1976	Inc. Ab.	—	.10	.15	.35
	1977	62.083	—	.10	.15	.35
	1978	48.624	—	.10	.15	.35
	1979	83.908	—	.10	.15	.35
	1980	93.406	—	.10	.15	.35
	1981	65.219	—	.10	.15	.35

2 PESOS

BRONZE
Simon Bolivar

263	1977	76.661	.10	.15	.25	.50
	1978	69.575	.10	.15	.25	.50
	1979	56.537	.10	.15	.25	.50
	1980	108.521	.10	.15	.25	.50
	1981	40.368	.10	.15	.25	.50
	1983	8.358	.10	.15	.25	.50
	1987		.10	.15	.25	.50
	1988	16.200	.10	.15	.25	.50

NOTE: Varieties exist.

2-1/2 PESOS

3.9940 g, .917 GOLD, .1177 oz AGW

194	1913	.018	—	BV	75.00	125.00

Simon Bolivar
Obv: Large head.

200	1919A	—	—	BV	60.00	100.00
	1919B	—	—	—	—	—
	1919	.034	—	BV	60.00	100.00
	1920/19A	—	—	BV	60.00	100.00
	1920A	—	—	BV	60.00	100.00
	1920	.034	—	BV	85.00	150.00

Simon Bolivar
Obv: Small head, MEDELLIN below bust.

203	1924	—	—	BV	60.00	100.00
	1925	—	—	Reported, not confirmed		
	1927	—	—	BV	75.00	125.00
	1928	.014	—	BV	100.00	175.00
	1929	—	—	Reported, not confirmed		

5 PESOS

7.9881 g, .917 GOLD, .2355 oz AGW

195.1	1913	.017	BV	150.00	200.00	250.00
	1918/3	.423	BV	125.00	175.00	225.00
	1918	Inc. Ab.	BV	125.00	175.00	225.00
	1919	2.181	—	BV	120.00	150.00
	1919 longtail 9					

KM#	Date	Mintage	Fine	VF	XF	Unc
195.1	1913	Inc. Ab.	—	BV	125.00	160.00
	1919 dot over 9					
		Inc. Ab.	100.00	125.00	175.00	225.00

NOTE: Various rotations of dies exist.

Medallic reverse.

KM#	Date	Mintage	Good	VG	Fine	VF
195.2	1913	Inc. Ab.	BV	110.00	150.00	200.00
	1917	.043	BV	110.00	150.00	200.00
	1918	Inc. Ab.	BV	125.00	175.00	225.00
	1919	Inc. Ab.	BV	110.00	150.00	200.00

NOTE: Various rotations of dies exist.

Simon Bolivar
Obv: Large head.

KM#	Date	Mintage	Fine	VF	XF	Unc
201.1	1919 longtail 9					
		Inc. Ab.	—	BV	110.00	150.00
	1919A	Inc. Ab.	BV	110.00	135.00	150.00
	1919B	—		BV	125.00	150.00	175.00
	1920	.870	—		BV	110.00	150.00
	1920A	Inc.Ab.	—		BV	110.00	150.00
	1920B	.108	BV	110.00	135.00	175.00
	1921A	—				—
	1922B	.029	—		BV	110.00	150.00
	1923B	.074	—		BV	110.00	150.00
	1924	—	Reported, not confirmed			
	1924B	.705	—		BV	110.00	150.00

NOTE: 1920A dated coins come with mint mark centered or on right side of coat of arms, and 1923B dated coins come with B on the left or right of coat of arms. The 1923B mint mark to right carries a 25" premium in value.

NOTE: Various rotations of dies exist.

Medallic reverse

KM#	Date	Mintage	Good	VG	Fine	VF
201.2	1920	Inc. Ab.	BV	125.00	150.00	175.00

Simon Bolivar
Obv: Small head, MEDELLIN below bust.

KM#	Date	Mintage	Fine	VF	XF	Unc
204	1924 lg. 2	.120	BV	100.00	145.00	175.00
	1924 lg. 4	I.A.	—	BV	100.00	125.00
	1924 sm. 4	I.A.	BV	100.00	125.00	150.00
	1925/4	.668	—	BV	110.00	135.00
	1925	Inc. Ab.	—	BV	110.00	135.00
	1926	.383	BV	100.00	125.00	150.00
	1927	.365	BV	100.00	125.00	150.00
	1928	.314	—	BV	110.00	135.00
	1929	.321	BV	100.00	145.00	175.00
	1930	.502	BV	100.00	125.00	150.00

NOTE: 1924 dated coins have several varieties in size of 2 and 4. 1925 dated coins exist with an Arabic and a Spanish style 5. 1930 dated coins have three varieties in size and placement of 3.

COPPER-NICKEL
International Eucharistic Congress

230	1968B	.660	.25	.50	.75	1.75

NICKEL CLAD STEEL
6th Pan-American Games

KM#	Date	Mintage	Fine	VF	XF	Unc
247	1971	2.000	.15	.35	.60	1.50

BRONZE

KM#	Date	Mintage	Fine	VF	XF	Unc
268	1980	146.268	.15	.35	.60	1.25
	1.981 (1981)					
		9.148	.15	.35	.60	1.25
	1.982 (1982)					
		—	.15	.35	.75	1.50
	1983	84.107	.15	.35	.60	1.25
	1985	—	.15	.35	.60	1.25
	1986	14.700	.15	.35	.60	1.25
	1987	—	.15	.35	.60	1.25
	1988 small date					
		45.000	.15	.35	.60	1.25
	1988 large inverted date					
		Inc. Ab.	.15	.35	.60	1.25
	1989	—	.15	.35	.60	1.25

COPPER-ALUMINUM-NICKEL

280	1989	—	—	—	—	.35
	1990					.35
	1991					.35
	1992					.35
	1993					.35

NOTE: Varieties exist.

10 PESOS

15.9761 g, .917 GOLD, .4710 oz AGW
Simon Bolivar

202	1919	.101	—	BV	250.00	350.00
	1924B	.055	—	BV	250.00	350.00

COPPER-NICKEL-ZINC
Cordoba, San Andreas Island and Providencia

270	1.981(1981)					
		104.554	—	.15	.25	1.25
	1.982(1982)					
		83.605	—	.15	.25	1.25
	1983	104.051	—	.15	.25	1.25
	1985	80.000	—	.15	.25	1.25
	1988	50.700	—	.15	.25	1.25
	1989	—	—	.15	.25	1.25

NOTE: Date varieties exist.

KM#	Date	Mintage	Fine	VF	XF	Unc
281	1989	—	—	—	—	.50
	1990					.50
	1991					.50
	1992					.50
	1993					.50

NOTE: Varieties exist.

20 PESOS

ALUMINUM-BRONZE

271	1982	—	—	.15	.20	.30
	1984	64.066	—	.15	.20	.30
	1985	100.690	—	.15	.20	.30
	1986	18.300	—	.15	.20	.30
	1987	—	—	.15	.20	.30
	1988	72.000	—	.15	.20	.30
	1989	—	—	.15	.20	.30

NOTE: 1985 and 1988 coins exist with large and small dates.

COPPER-ALUMINUM-NICKEL
Obv: 72 beads circle around rim.

282.1	1989	—	—	—	—	.50
	1990					.50
	1991					.50
	1992					.50
	1993					.50
	1994					.50

NOTE: Varieties exist.

Obv: 66 beads circle around rim.

282.2	1994	—	—	—	—	.50

50 PESOS

COPPER-NICKEL
National Constitution

272	1986	14.900	—	—	—	1.25
	1987 lg. dt.	—	—	—	—	1.25
	1988 small date					
		100.000	—	—	—	1.25
	1989	—	—	—	—	1.25

COPPER-NICKEL-ZINC
Obv: 66 beads circle around rim.

283.1	1989	—	—	—	—	1.00
	1990					1.00
	1991					1.00
	1992					1.00
	1993					1.00
	1994					1.00

NOTE: Varieties exist.

Obv: 72 beads circle around rim.

283.2	1994	—	—	—	—	1.00

100 PESOS

BRASS
Rev: Numerals 4.5mm tall.

KM#	Date	Mintage	VF	XF	Unc
285.1	1992	—	—	—	1.75

KM#	Date	Mintage	VF	XF	Unc
285.1	1993	—	—	—	1.75
	1994	—	—	—	1.75
	1995	—	—	—	1.75

Rev: Numerals 6mm tall.

285.2	1994	—	—	—	1.75
	1995	—	—	—	1.75

200 PESOS

COPPER-ZINC-NICKEL
Quimbaya Artwork

287	1994	—	—	—	1.50
	1995	—	—	—	1.50

500 PESOS

ALUMINUM-BRONZE center in
COPPER-NICKEL ring
Guacari Tree

286	1993	—	—	—	3.25
	1994	—	—	—	3.25
	1995	—	—	—	3.25
	1996	—	—	—	3.25

1000 PESOS

COPPER-ALUMINUM-NICKEL
Edge: Reed and inscribed CULTURA.
SINU MIL PESOS

288	1996	—	—	—	3.75

COMOROS

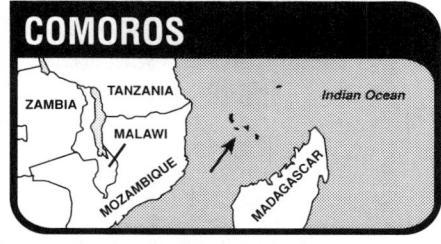

The Federal Islamic Republic of the Comoros, a volcanic archipelago located in the Mozambique Channel of the Indian Ocean 300 miles (483 km.) northwest of Madagascar, has an area of 719 sq. mi. (2,171 sq. km.) and a population of 549,338. Capital: Moroni. The economy of the islands is based on agriculture. There are practically no mineral resources. Vanilla, essence for perfumes, copra, and sisal are exported.

Ancient Phoenician traders were probably the first visitors to the Comoro Islands, but the first detailed knowledge of the area was gathered by Arab sailors. Arab dominion and culture were firmly established when the Portuguese, Dutch, and French arrived in the 16th century. In 1843 a Malagasy ruler ceded the island of Mayotte to France; the other three principal islands of the archipelago-Anjouan, Moheli, and Grand Comore came under French protection in 1886. The islands were joined administratively with Madagascar in 1912. The Comoros became partially autonomous, with the status of a French overseas territory, in 1946, and achieved complete internal autonomy in 1961. On Dec. 31, 1975, after 133 years of French association, the Comoro Islands became the independent Republic of the Comoros.

Mayotte retained the option of determining its future ties and in 1976 voted to remain French. Its present status is that of a French Territorial Collectivity. French currency now circulates there.

TITLES
Daulat Anjazanchiyah

دولة انجزنجية

RULERS
French, 1886-1975

MINT MARKS
(a) - Paris, privy marks only
A - Paris

MONETARY SYSTEM
100 Centimes = 1 Franc

COLONIAL COINAGE
FRANC

ALUMINUM

KM#	Date	Mintage	Fine	VF	XF	Unc
4	1964(a)	.500	.15	.25	.40	.75

2 FRANCS

ALUMINUM

5	1964(a)	.600	.15	.25	.50	1.00

5 FRANCS

ALUMINUM

6	1964(a)	1.000	.20	.40	.65	1.25

10 FRANCS

ALUMINUM-BRONZE

KM#	Date	Mintage	Fine	VF	XF	Unc
7	1964(a)	.600	.20	.50	1.00	2.00

20 FRANCS

ALUMINUM-BRONZE

8	1964(a)	.500	.30	.65	1.25	2.50

REPUBLIC
Banque Central
5 FRANCS

ALUMINUM
World Fisheries Conference - Coelacanth Fish

15	1984(a)	1.010	.25	.50	1.00	2.50
	1992(a)	—	.25	.50	1.00	2.50

10 FRANCS

ALUMINUM-BRONZE

17	1992(a)	—	—	—	—	1.65

25 FRANCS

NICKEL
F.A.O. Issue - Chickens

14	1981(a)	1.000	1.50	3.00	6.00	15.00
	1982(a)	2.007	.20	.40	.80	1.75

50 FRANCS

NICKEL PLATED STEEL

16	1990(a)	—	.50	.80	1.50	2.50
	1994(a)	—	.50	.80	1.50	2.50

Institut D'Emission

50 FRANCS

NICKEL
Independence of Republic

KM#	Date	Mintage	Fine	VF	XF	Unc
9	1975(a)	1.200	.40	.75	1.25	2.25

100 FRANCS

NICKEL
F.A.O. Issue

KM#	Date	Mintage	Fine	VF	XF	Unc
13	1977(a)	1.500	.60	1.00	2.00	3.75

CONGO REPUBLIC

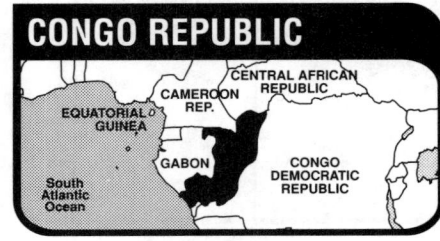

The Republic of the Congo (formerly the Peoples Republic of the Congo), located on the equator in west-central Africa, has an area of 132,047 sq. mi. (342,000 sq. km.) and a population of 2.5 million. Capital: Brazzaville. Agriculture forestry, mining, and food processing are the principal industries. Timber, industrial diamonds, potash, peanuts, and cocoa beans are exported.

The Portuguese were the first Europeans to explore the Congo (Brazzaville) area, 14th century. They conducted a slave trade with the tribal kingdoms of Teke, Loango, and Kongo without attempting developmental colonization. French influence was established in 1883 when the king of Teke signed a treaty with Savorgnan de Brazza, thereby placing his kingdom under the protection of France. While a French protectorate, the area was known as Middle Congo. In 1910 Middle Congo became a part of French Equatorial Africa, which also included Gabon, Ubangi-Shari (now the Central African Republic), and Chad. Following World War II, during which it was an important center of Free French activities, the Middle Congo was given a large measure of internal autonomy, and its inhabitants were made French citizens. Upon approval of the constitution of the Fifth French Republic, 1958, it became a member of the new French Community. On Aug. 15, 1960, Middle Congo became the independent Republic of the Congo-Brazzaville. In Jan. 1970 the country's name was changed to Peoples Republic of the Congo. A new constitution which asserts the government's advocacy of socialism was adopted in 1973.

In June and July of 1992, a new 125-member National Assembly was elected. Later that year a new president, Pascal Lissouba was elected. In November, President Lissouba dismissed the previous government and dissolved the National Assembly. A new 23-member government, including members of the opposition, was formed in December, 1992, and the name was changed to Republique du Congo.

NOTE: For earlier and related coinage see French Equatorial Africa and the Equatorial African States. For later coinage see Central African States.

RULERS
French

MINT MARKS
(a) - Paris, privy marks only

MONETARY SYSTEM
100 Centimes = 1 Franc

100 FRANCS

NICKEL

KM#	Date	Mintage	Fine	VF	XF	Unc
1	1971(a)	2.500	8.00	15.00	25.00	40.00
	1972(a)	—	8.00	15.00	25.00	40.00

2	1975(a)	—	4.00	8.00	16.50	30.00
	1982(a)	—	2.50	4.50	8.00	12.50
	1983(a)	—	2.50	5.00	8.00	12.50
	1985(a)	—	2.00	3.00	6.00	10.00
	1990(a)	—	2.00	3.00	4.00	6.00

500 FRANCS

COPPER-NICKEL

KM#	Date	Mintage	Fine	VF	XF	Unc
4	1985(a)	—	3.50	6.50	10.00	18.50
	1986(a)	—	3.50	6.50	10.00	18.50

CONGO DEMOCRATIC REPUBLIC

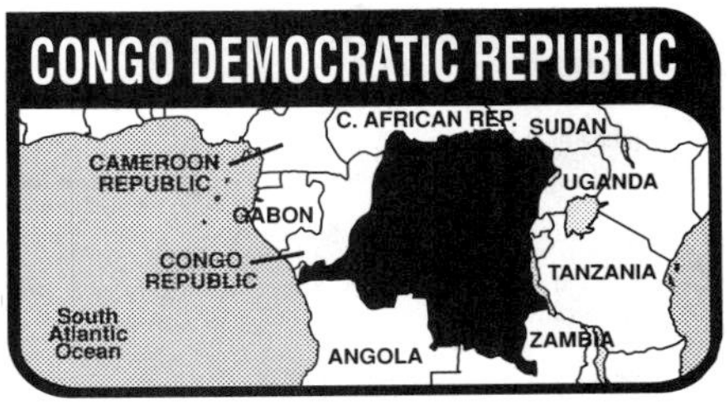

The Democratic Republic of the Congo (formerly the Republic of Zaire, and earlier the Belgian Congo), located in the south-central part of Africa, has an area of 905,568 sq. mi. (2,345,410 sq. km.) and a population of *47.4 million. Capital: Kinshasa. The mineral-rich country produces copper, tin, diamonds, gold, zinc, cobalt and uranium.

In ancient times the territory comprising former Zaire was occu-pied by Negrito peoples (Pygmies) pushed into the mountains by Bantu and Nilotic invaders. The interior was first explored by the American correspondent Henry Stanley, who was subsequently commissioned by King Leopold II of Belgium to conclude development treaties with the local chiefs. The Berlin conference of 1885 awarded the area to Leopold, who administered and exploited it as his private property until it was annexed to Belgium in 1908. Belgium received the man-date for the German territory of Ruanda-Urundi as a result of the international treaties after WWI. During World War II, Belgian Congolese troops fought on the side of the Allies, notably in Ethiopia. Following the erup-tion of bloody inde-pendence riots in 1959, Belgium granted the Belgian Congo independence as the Republic of the Congo on June 30, 1960. The nation offi-cially changed its name to Zaire on Oct. 27, 1971, and following a Civil War in 1997 changed its name to the "Democratic Republic of the Congo."

CONGO FREE STATE

RULER

Leopold II

5 CENTIMES

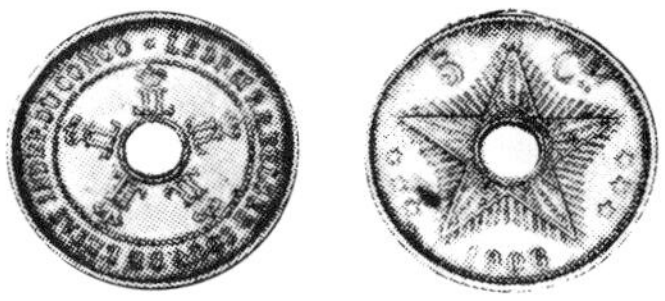

COPPER-NICKEL

KM#	Date	Mintage	Fine	VF	XF	Unc
9	1906	.100	5.00	10.00	25.00	60.00
	1908	.180	4.00	8.00	20.00	50.00

10 CENTIMES

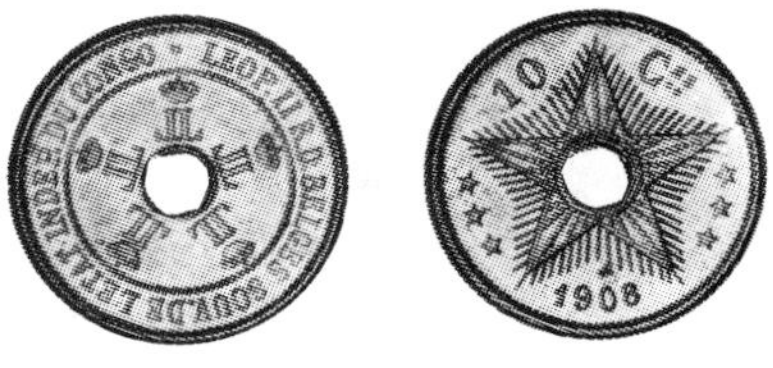

COPPER-NICKEL

10	1906	.100	5.00	12.00	35.00	85.00
	1908	.800	3.00	8.00	30.00	80.00

20 CENTIMES

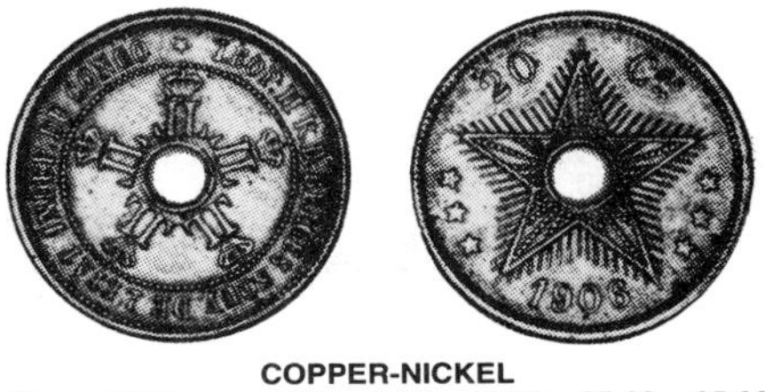

COPPER-NICKEL

11	1906	.100	5.00	12.00	35.00	85.00
	1908	.400	4.00	8.00	30.00	80.00

BELGIAN CONGO

The Belgian Congo attained independence (as Republic of Zaire) with the distinction of being the most ill-prepared country to ever undertake self-government. Without a single doctor, lawyer or engineer, with no organized unit capable of maintaining law and order, independence disintegrated into an orgy of anarchy. Provinces seceded. Intertribal warfare erupted. Belgian troops intervened to protect Belgian citizens from retri-butive massacre. By 1961 four groups were fighting for political dominance. The most serious threat to the viabi-lity of the country was posed by the secession of mineral-rich Katanga province on July 11, 1960. After two and one-half years of sporadic warfare with a U.N. military force, Katanga's leaders capitulated, Jan. 14, 1963, and the rebellious province was partitioned into three provinces.

RULERS

Belgian, until 1960

MINT MARKS

H - Heaton, Birmingham

MONETARY SYSTEM

100 Centimes = 1 Franc

CENTIME

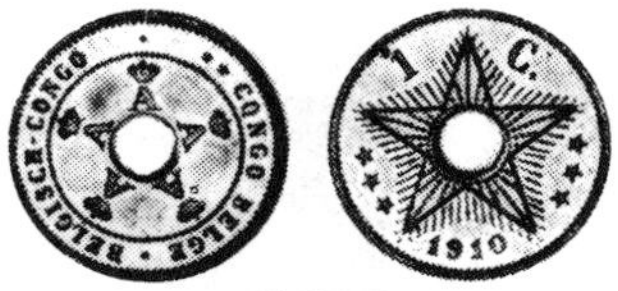

COPPER

KM#	Date	Mintage	Fine	VF	XF	Unc
15	1910	2.000	1.00	2.00	3.00	9.00
	1919	.500	1.00	2.00	3.00	10.00

2 CENTIMES

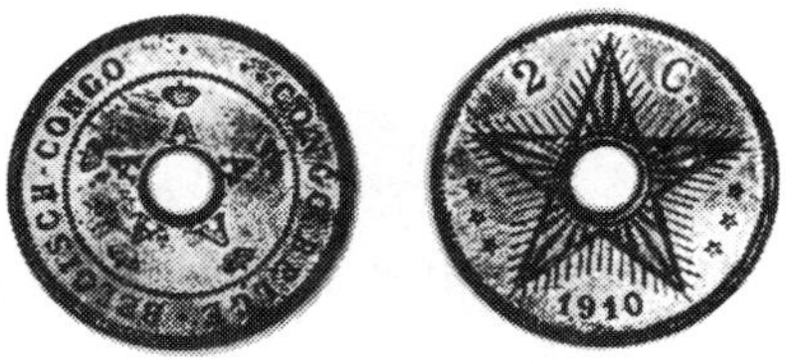

COPPER

16	1910	1.500	1.00	3.00	7.00	25.00
	1919	.500	1.50	3.50	10.00	30.00

5 CENTIMES

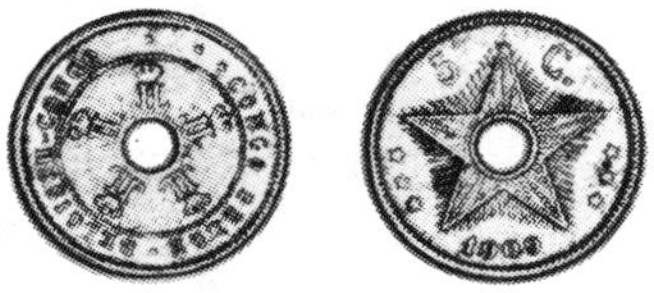

COPPER-NICKEL

12	1909	1.800	5.00	12.50	40.00	90.00

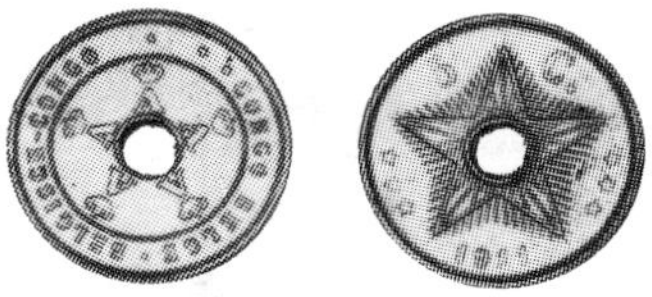

17	1910(H)	6.000	.75	1.50	2.50	10.00
	1911(H)	5.000	.75	1.50	2.50	10.00
	1917(H)	1.000	3.00	7.00	15.00	50.00
	1917(H)	—	—	—	Proof	175.00
	1919(H)	3.000	1.50	3.00	6.00	20.00
	1919	6.850	.50	1.00	2.00	10.00
	1920	2.740	.50	1.00	3.00	11.00
	1921	17.260	.25	.75	1.50	9.00
	1921(H)	3.000	1.00	2.00	5.00	15.00
	1925	11.000	.25	.75	2.00	9.00
	1926/5	5.770	2.25	4.50	—	—
	1926	Inc. Ab.	.25	1.00	2.00	9.00
	1927	2.000	.50	1.00	2.50	10.00
	1928/6	1.500	2.00	4.00	8.00	20.00
	1928	Inc. Ab.	.75	1.25	3.00	10.00

10 CENTIMES

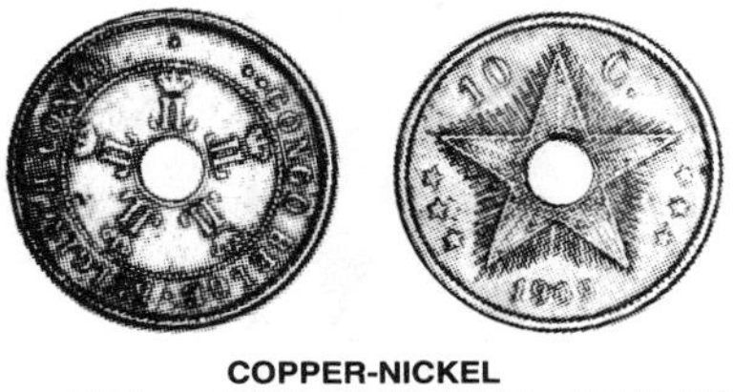

COPPER-NICKEL

13	1909	1.500	8.00	20.00	60.00	140.00

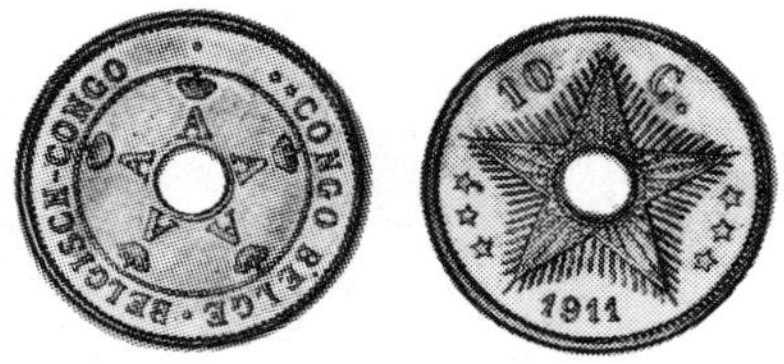

18	1910	5.000	.50	1.00	3.00	10.00
	1911	5.000	.50	1.00	3.00	10.00
	1917(H)	.500	5.00	10.00	25.00	75.00
	1919	3.430	.50	1.00	3.50	11.00
	1919(H)	1.500	.75	1.25	4.00	12.00
	1920	1.510	.75	1.25	4.00	12.00
	1921	13.540	.25	.75	2.00	9.00

KM#	Date	Mintage	Fine	VF	XF	Unc
18	1921(H)	3.000	.75	1.50	3.50	10.00
	1922	14.950	.25	1.00	2.50	9.00
	1924	3.600	.50	1.50	3.00	10.00
	1925/4	4.800	2.00	4.00	8.00	50.00
	1925	Inc. Ab.	.25	1.00	3.00	10.00
	1927	2.020	.25	1.00	3.00	9.00
	1928/7	5.600	1.00	3.00	8.00	40.00
	1928	Inc. Ab.	.25	1.00	3.00	9.00

20 CENTIMES

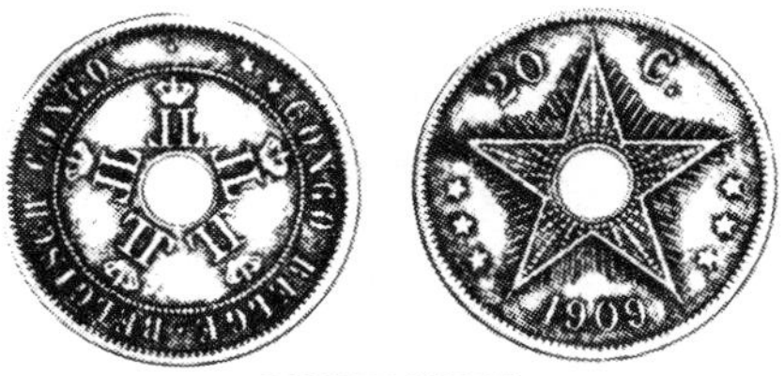

COPPER-NICKEL

14	1909	.300	10.00	25.00	65.00	175.00

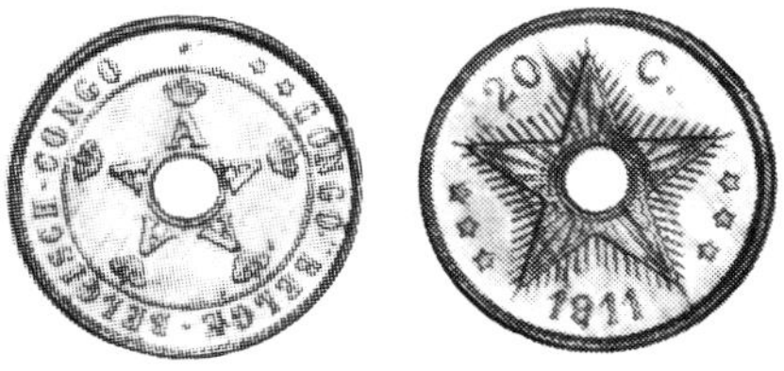

19	1910	1.000	2.00	5.00	10.00	30.00
	1911	1.250	1.50	4.00	8.00	25.00

50 CENTIMES

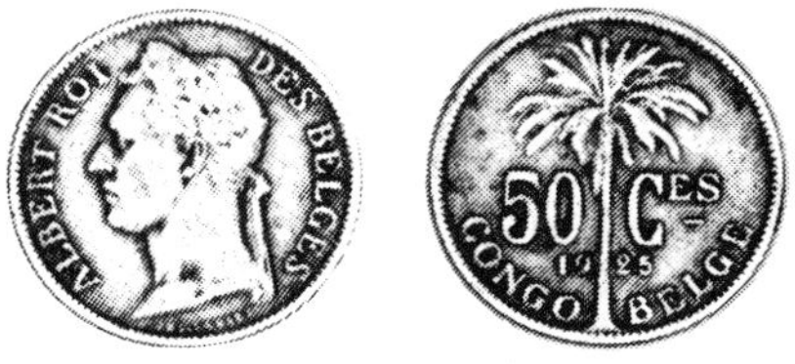

COPPER-NICKEL
Rev: French leg. CONGO BELGE

22	1921	4.000	.60	2.00	8.00	27.50
	1922	6.000	.60	2.00	8.00	27.50
	1923	7.200	.60	2.00	8.00	27.50
	1924	1.096	.75	3.00	10.00	32.50
	1925	16.104	.60	2.00	7.00	25.00
	1926/5	16.000	1.00	4.00	12.00	45.00
	1926	Inc. Ab.	.60	2.00	8.00	25.00
	1927	10.000	.60	2.00	8.00	27.50
	1929/7	7.504	.60	2.00	9.00	32.00
	1929/8	Inc. Ab.	1.00	4.00	15.00	90.00
	1929	Inc. Ab.	.60	2.00	7.00	25.00

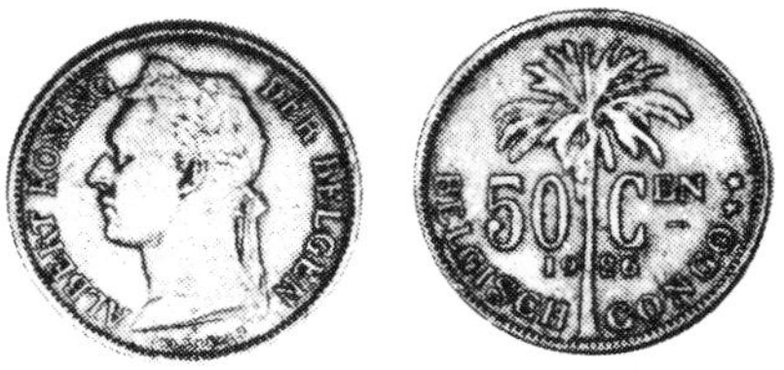

Rev: Flemish leg. BELGISCH CONGO

23	1921	4.000	.60	2.00	8.00	32.00
	1922	5.592	.60	2.00	7.00	27.50
	1923/1	7.208	1.00	5.00	16.50	70.00
	1923	Inc. Ab.	.60	2.00	7.00	25.00
	1924	7.000	.60	2.00	8.00	27.50
	1925/4	10.600	1.50	7.00	20.00	90.00
	1925	Inc. Ab.	.60	2.00	7.00	27.50
	1926	25.200	.60	2.00	7.00	25.00
	1927	4.800	.60	2.00	8.00	27.50
	1928	7.484	.60	2.00	7.00	25.00
	1929/8	.116	25.00	50.00	75.00	120.00
	1929	Inc. Ab.	20.00	40.00	70.00	100.00

FRANC

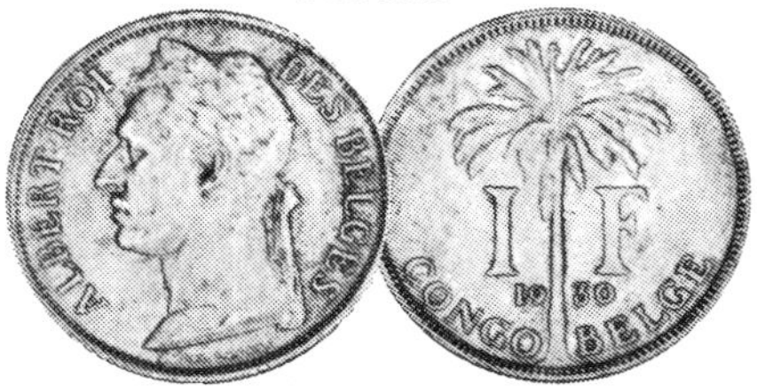

COPPER-NICKEL
Rev: French leg. CONGO BELGE

20	1920	4.000	.85	2.75	10.00	37.50
	1922	5.000	.85	2.75	9.00	32.00
	1923/2	5.000	2.00	7.00	16.00	45.00
	1923	Inc. Ab.	.85	2.75	9.00	32.00
	1924	6.030	.85	2.75	9.00	35.00

KM#	Date	Mintage	Fine	VF	XF	Unc
20	1925	10.470	.85	2.75	9.00	32.00
	1926/5	12.500	2.00	7.00	16.50	50.00
	1926	Inc. Ab.	.85	2.75	8.00	30.00
	1927	15.250	.85	2.75	8.00	30.00
	1929	5.763	.85	2.75	9.00	32.00
	1930	5.000	.85	2.75	10.00	40.00

Rev: Flemish leg. BELGISCH CONGO

21	1920	.475	2.00	5.00	16.50	50.00
	1921	3.525	.85	3.00	9.00	37.50
	1922	5.000	.85	3.00	9.00	37.50
	1923/2	7.362	2.00	5.00	17.00	55.00
	1923	Inc. Ab.	.85	2.75	9.00	32.00
	1924	4.608	.85	3.00	10.00	37.50
	1925	9.530	.85	2.75	9.00	32.00
	1926/5	17.000	2.00	5.00	17.00	55.00
	1926	Inc. Ab.	.85	2.75	9.00	32.00
	1928	9.250	.85	2.75	9.00	32.00
	1929	4.250	.85	3.00	10.00	37.50

BRASS

26	1944	25.000	.50	1.00	3.00	7.00
	1946	15.000	.75	1.50	3.50	8.00
	1949	15.000	.75	1.50	3.00	7.50

2 FRANCS

BRASS

25	1943	25.000	2.50	4.50	9.00	40.00

28	1946	13.000	1.00	2.00	3.50	12.00
	1947	12.000	1.00	2.00	4.00	15.00

5 FRANCS

NICKEL-BRONZE

24	1936	2.600	5.00	10.00	20.00	110.00
	1937	11.400	4.00	12.00	25.00	125.00

BRASS

KM#	Date	Mintage	Fine	VF	XF	Unc
29	1947	10.000	3.00	7.00	15.00	50.00

50 FRANCS

17.5000 g, .500 SILVER, .2814 oz ASW

27	1944	1.000	20.00	50.00	90.00	165.00

BELGIAN CONGO RUANDA-URUNDI

The Belgian Congo and Ruanda-Urundi were united administratively from 1925 to 1960. Ruanda-Urundi was made a U.N. Trust territory in 1946. Coins for these 2 areas were made jointly between 1952 and 1960. Ruanda-Urundi became the Republic of Rwanda on June 1, 1962.

For later coinage refer to Rwanda and Burundi, Rwanda, and Burundi.

MONETARY SYSTEM

100 Centimes = 1 Franc

50 CENTIMES

ALUMINUM

KM#	Date	Mintage		VF	XF	Unc
2	1954 DB	4.700		.35	.75	2.00
	1955 DB	20.300		.15	.60	1.50

FRANC

ALUMINUM

4	1957	10.000		.50	1.00	2.00
	1958	20.000		.50	1.00	2.00
	1959	20.000		.50	1.00	2.00
	1960	20.000		.50	1.00	2.00

5 FRANCS

BRASS

1	1952	10.000		2.50	5.00	10.00

ALUMINUM

KM#	Date	Mintage		VF	XF	Unc
3	1956 DB	10.000	1.00	2.00	4.00
	1958 DB	26.110	.75	1.75	3.50
	1959 DB	3.890	1.00	2.50	5.00

CONGO DEM REP.

Democratic Republic of the Congo achieved independence on June 30, 1960. It followed the same monetary system as when under the Belgians. Monetary Reform of 1967 introduced new denominations and coins. The name of the country was changed to Zaire in 1971.

MINT MARKS

(b) - Brussels, privy marks only

10 FRANCS

ALUMINUM

KM#	Date	Mintage	Fine	VF	XF	Unc
1	1965(b)	*100.000	.60	1.50	3.00	7.00

*NOTE: Most recalled and melted down.

MONETARY REFORM

100 Sengis = 1 Likuta
100 Makuta (plural of Likuta) = 1 Zaire

10 SENGIS

ALUMINUM

7	1967	90.996	—	.15	.45	1.00

LIKUTA

ALUMINUM

8	1967	49.180	—	.15	.50	1.25

5 MAKUTA

COPPER-NICKEL

9	1967	2.470	.25	.50	1.00	3.00

KATANGA

Katanga, the southern province of the former Belgian Congo, had an area of 191,873 sq. mi. (496,951 sq. km.) and was noted for its mineral wealth.

MONETARY SYSTEM

100 Centimes = 1 Franc

FRANC

BRONZE

KM#	Date	Mintage		VF	XF	Unc
1	1961	—		1.00	1.75	3.50

5 FRANCS

BRONZE

KM#	Date	Mintage	VF	XF	Unc
2	1961	—	2.00	3.75	7.50

REPUBLIC OF ZAIRE

Under the command of Laurent Kabila, rebel forces overthrew ruler Sese Seko Mobutu in May of 1997. Self appointed President Kabila has officially renamed the country the Democratic Republic of Congo. While coins minted for this new republic still bare the word Zaire, they will be found here.

MONETARY SYSTEM
100 Makuta = 1 Zaire
1993 -
3,000,000 old Zaires = 1 Nouveau Zaire

5 MAKUTA

COPPER-NICKEL

KM#	Date	Mintage	VF	XF	Unc
12	1977	8.000	.50	1.00	3.50

10 MAKUTA

COPPER-NICKEL

KM#	Date	Mintage	VF	XF	Unc
7	1973	5.000	2.25	4.00	8.00
	1975	—	2.25	4.00	8.00
	1976	—	2.50	4.50	9.00
	1978	—	2.50	4.50	9.00

20 MAKUTA

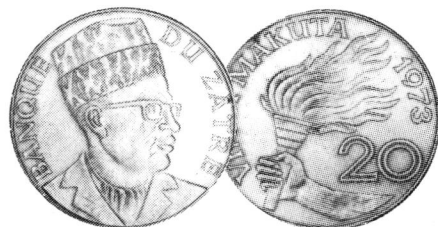

COPPER-NICKEL

KM#	Date	Mintage	VF	XF	Unc
8	1973	—	3.00	5.50	10.00
	1976	—	3.50	6.50	12.00

ZAIRE

BRASS

KM#	Date	Mintage	VF	XF	Unc
13	1987	—	.50	1.00	2.00

5 ZAIRES

BRASS

KM#	Date	Mintage	VF	XF	Unc
14	1987	—	.65	1.25	2.50

10 ZAIRES

BRASS

KM#	Date	Mintage	VF	XF	Unc
19	1988	—	2.00	4.00	8.00

COOK ISLANDS

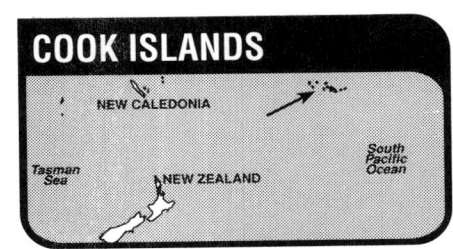

Cook Islands, a political dependency of New Zealand consisting of 15 islands, is located in the South Pacific Ocean about 2,000 miles (3,218 km.) northeast of New Zealand. It has an area of 93 sq. mi. (234 sq. km.) and a population of 17,185. Capital: Avarua. The United States claims the islands of Danger, Manahiki, Penrhyn, and Rakahanga atolls. Citrus and canned fruits and juices, copra, clothing, jewelry, and mother-of-pearl shell are exported.

The islands were first sighted by Spanish navigator Alvaro de Mendada in 1595. Portuguese navigator Pedro Fernandes de Quieros landed on Rakahanga in 1606. English navigator Capt. James Cook sailed to the islands on three occasions: 1773, 1774 and 1777. He named them Hervey Islands, in honor of Augustus John Hervey, a lord of the Admiralty. The islands were declared a British protectorate in 1888, and were annexed to New Zealand in 1901. They were granted internal self-government in 1965. New Zealand provides an annual subsidy and retains responsibility for defense and foreign affairs.

RULERS
British

MINT MARKS
(b) - British Royal Mint
FM - Franklin Mint, U.S.A. *
PM - Pobjoy Mint

*NOTE: From 1975-1985 the Franklin Mint produced coinage in up to three different qualities. Qualities of issue are designated in () after each date and are defined as follows:

(M) MATTE - Normal circulation strike or a dull finish produced by sandblasting special uncirculated (polish finish) or proof quality dies.

(U) SPECIAL UNCIRCULATED - Polished or proof-like in appearance without any frosted features.

(P) PROOF - The highest quality obtainable having mirror-like fields and frosted features.

MONETARY SYSTEM
(Until 1967)
12 Pence = 1 Shilling
20 Shillings = 1 Pound
(Commencing 1967)
100 Cents = 1 Dollar

CENT

BRONZE
Taro Leaf

KM#	Date	Mintage	VF	XF	Unc
1	1972	.117	—	.10	.20
	1972	.017	—	Proof	.50
	1973	8,500	—	.10	.20
	1973	.013	—	Proof	.50
	1974	.300	—	.10	.20
	1974	7,300	—	Proof	.50
	1975	.429	—	.10	.20
	1975FM(M)	1,000	—	—	.50
	1975FM(U)	2,251	—	—	.20
	1975FM(P)	.021	—	Proof	.50
	1976FM(M)	1,001	—	—	.50
	1976FM(U)	1,066	—	—	.20
	1976FM(P)	.018	—	Proof	.50
	1977FM(M)	1,171	—	—	.50
	1977FM(U)	1,002	—	—	.20
	1977FM(P)	5,986	—	Proof	.50
	1979FM(M)	1,000	—	—	.50
	1979FM(U)	500 pcs.	—	—	1.00
	1979FM(P)	4,058	—	Proof	.50
	1983	—	—	.10	.20
	1983	.010	—	Proof	.50

Edge: 1728 CAPTAIN COOK 1978.

1a	1978FM(M)	1,000	—	—	1.00
	1978FM(U)	767 pcs.	—	—	1.00
	1978FM(P)	6,287	—	Proof	.50

Wedding of Prince Charles and Lady Diana
Edge: THE ROYAL WEDDING 29 JULY 1981.

1b	1981FM(M)	1,000	—	—	.50
	1981FM(U)	1,100	—	—	.50
	1981FM(P)	9,205	—	Proof	.40

2 CENTS

BRONZE
Pineapple

KM#	Date	Mintage	VF	XF	Unc
2	1972	.063	.10	.15	.30
	1972	.017	—	Proof	.75
	1973	8,500	.15	.20	.40
	1973	.013	—	Proof	.75
	1974	.120	.10	.15	.30
	1974	7,300	—	Proof	.75
	1975	.129	.10	.15	.25
	1975FM(M)	1,000	—	—	.75
	1975FM(U)	2,251	—	—	.30
	1975FM(P)	.021	—	Proof	.75
	1976FM(M)	1,001	—	—	.75
	1976FM(U)	1,066	—	—	.30
	1976FM(P)	.018	—	Proof	.75
	1977FM(M)	1,171	—	—	.75
	1977FM(U)	1,002	—	—	.30
	1977FM(P)	5,986	—	Proof	.75
	1979FM(M)	1,000	—	—	.75
	1979FM(U)	500 pcs.	—	—	.30
	1979FM(P)	4,058	—	Proof	.75
	1983	—	.10	.15	.25
	1983	.010	—	Proof	.75

Edge: 1728 CAPTAIN COOK 1978.

KM#	Date	Mintage	VF	XF	Unc
2a	1978FM(M)	1,000	—	—	.75
	1978FM(U)	767 pcs.	—	—	.75
	1978FM(P)	6,287	—	—	.50

Wedding of Prince Charles and Lady Diana
Edge: THE ROYAL WEDDING 29 JULY 1981.

KM#	Date	Mintage	VF	XF	Unc
2b	1981FM(M)	1,000	—	—	.75
	1981FM(U)	1,100	—	—	.75
	1981FM(P)	9,205	—	Proof	.50

5 CENTS

COPPER-NICKEL
Hibiscus

KM#	Date	Mintage	VF	XF	Unc
3	1972	.032	.10	.20	.40
	1972	.017	—	Proof	1.00
	1973	8,500	.15	.25	.50
	1973	.013	—	Proof	1.00
	1974	.080	.10	.20	.40
	1974	7,300	—	Proof	1.00
	1975	.089	.10	.20	.40
	1975FM(M)	1,000	—	—	1.00
	1975FM(U)	2,251	—	—	.40
	1975FM(P)	.021	—	Proof	1.00
	1976FM(M)	1,001	—	—	1.00
	1976FM(U)	1,066	—	—	.40
	1976FM(P)	.018	—	Proof	1.00
	1977FM(M)	1,171	—	—	1.00
	1977FM(U)	1,002	—	—	.40
	1977FM(P)	5,986	—	Proof	1.00
	1979FM(M)	1,000	—	—	1.00
	1979FM(U)	500 pcs.	—	—	.40
	1979FM(P)	4,058	—	Proof	1.00
	1983	—	.10	.20	.40
	1983	.010	—	Proof	1.00

Edge: 1728 CAPTAIN COOK 1978.

KM#	Date	Mintage	VF	XF	Unc
3a	1978FM(M)	1,000	—	—	1.00
	1978FM(U)	767 pcs.	—	—	.75
	1978FM(P)	6,287	—	Proof	.50

Wedding of Prince Charles and Lady Diana
Edge: THE ROYAL WEDDING 29 JULY 1981.

KM#	Date	Mintage	VF	XF	Unc
3b	1981FM(M)	1,000	—	—	1.00
	1981FM(U)	1,100	—	—	1.00
	1981FM(P)	9,205	—	Proof	.50

KM#	Date	Mintage	VF	XF	Unc
33	1987	—	—	.10	.25
	1987	—	—	Proof	1.25
	1988	—	—	.10	.25
	1988	—	—	Proof	1.25
	1992	—	—	.10	.25
	1992	—	—	Proof	1.25
	1994	.020	—	.10	.25
	1994	200 pcs.	—	Proof	1.50

10 CENTS

COPPER-NICKEL
Orange

KM#	Date	Mintage	VF	XF	Unc
4	1972	.035	.10	.20	.50
	1972	.017	—	Proof	1.25
	1973	.059	.10	.20	.50
	1973	.013	—	Proof	1.25
	1974	.050	.10	.20	.50
	1974	7,300	—	Proof	1.25
	1975	.059	.10	.20	.50
	1975FM(M)	1,000	—	—	1.25
	1975FM(U)	2,251	—	—	.50
	1975FM(P)	.021	—	Proof	1.25
	1976FM(M)	1,001	—	—	1.25
	1976FM(U)	1,066	—	—	.50
	1976FM(P)	.018	—	Proof	1.25
	1977FM(M)	1,171	—	—	1.25
	1977FM(U)	1,002	—	—	.50
	1977FM(P)	5,986	—	Proof	1.25
	1983	—	.10	.20	.50
	1983	.010	—	Proof	1.25

Edge: 1728 CAPTAIN COOK 1978.

KM#	Date	Mintage	VF	XF	Unc
4a	1978FM(M)	1,000	—	—	1.25
	1978FM(U)	767 pcs.	—	—	1.25
	1978FM(P)	6,287	—	Proof	1.00

F.A.O. Issue

KM#	Date	Mintage	VF	XF	Unc
4b	1979FM(M)	9,000	—	—	1.00
	1979FM(U)	500 pcs.	—	—	1.50
	1979FM(P)	4,058	—	Proof	1.25

Wedding of Prince Charles and Lady Diana
Edge: THE ROYAL WEDDING 29 JULY 1981.

KM#	Date	Mintage	VF	XF	Unc
4c	1981FM(M)	1,000	—	—	1.25
	1981FM(U)	1,100	—	—	1.25
	1981FM(P)	9,205	—	Proof	.75

KM#	Date	Mintage	VF	XF	Unc
34	1987	—	—	.15	.25
	1987	—	—	Proof	1.25
	1988	—	—	.15	.25
	1988	—	—	Proof	1.25
	1992	—	—	.15	.25
	1992	—	—	Proof	1.25
	1994	.020	—	.15	.25
	1994	200 pcs.	—	Proof	1.50

20 CENTS

COPPER-NICKEL
Fairy Tern

KM#	Date	Mintage	VF	XF	Unc
5	1972	.031	.20	.40	.75
	1972	.017	—	Proof	1.50
	1973	.049	.20	.40	.75
	1973	.013	—	Proof	1.50
	1974	5,500	.20	.45	.85
	1974	7,300	—	Proof	1.50
	1975	.060	.20	.40	.75
	1975FM(M)	1,000	—	—	1.50
	1975FM(U)	2,251	—	—	.85
	1975FM(P)	.021	—	Proof	1.50
	1983	—	.20	.40	.85
	1983	.010	—	Proof	1.50

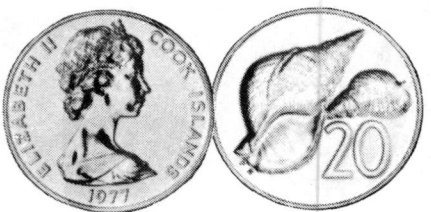

Pacific Triton Shell

KM#	Date	Mintage	VF	XF	Unc
14	1976FM(M)	1,001	—	—	1.50
	1976FM(U)	1,066	—	—	1.00
	1976FM(P)	.018	—	Proof	1.50
	1977FM(M)	1,171	—	—	1.50
	1977FM(U)	1,002	—	—	1.00
	1977FM(P)	5,986	—	Proof	1.50
	1979FM(M)	1,000	—	—	1.50
	1979FM(U)	500 pcs.	—	—	2.00
	1979FM(P)	4,058	—	Proof	1.50

Edge: 1728 CAPTAIN COOK 1978.

KM#	Date	Mintage	VF	XF	Unc
14a	1978FM(M)	1,000	—	—	1.50
	1978FM(U)	767 pcs.	—	—	2.00
	1978FM(P)	6,287	—	Proof	1.00

Wedding of Prince Charles and Lady Diana
Edge: THE ROYAL WEDDING 29 JULY 1981.

KM#	Date	Mintage	VF	XF	Unc
14b	1981FM(M)	1,000	—	—	1.50
	1981FM(U)	1,100	—	—	1.50
	1981FM(P)	9,205	—	Proof	1.00

KM#	Date	Mintage	VF	XF	Unc
35	1987	—	—	.25	.35
	1987	—	—	Proof	1.50
	1988	—	—	.25	.35
	1988	—	—	Proof	1.50
	1992	—	—	.25	.35
	1992	—	—	Proof	1.50
	1994	.020	—	.25	.35
	1994	200 pcs.	—	Proof	2.00

50 CENTS

COPPER-NICKEL
Bonito Fish
Obv: Youthful portrait of Queen Elizabeth.
Rev: Fish, denomination.

KM#	Date	Mintage	VF	XF	Unc
6.1	1972	.031	.40	.75	1.50
(6)	1972	.017	—	Proof	3.00
	1973	.019	.40	.75	1.50
	1973	.013	—	Proof	3.00
	1974	.010	.40	.75	1.50
	1974	7,300	—	Proof	3.00
	1975	.019	.40	.75	1.50
	1975FM(M)	1,000	—	—	2.00
	1975FM(U)	2,251	—	—	1.50
	1975FM(P)	.021	—	Proof	3.00
	1976FM(M)	1,001	—	—	2.00
	1976FM(U)	1,066	—	—	1.50
	1976FM(P)	.018	—	Proof	3.00
	1977FM(M)	1,171	—	—	2.00
	1977FM(U)	1,002	—	—	1.50
	1977FM(P)	5,986	—	Proof	3.00
	1983	—	.40	.75	1.50
	1983	.010	—	Proof	3.50

Edge: 1728 CAPTAIN COOK 1978.

KM#	Date	Mintage	VF	XF	Unc
6.2	1978FM(M)	1,000	—	—	2.00
(6a)	1978FM(U)	767 pcs.	—	—	2.00
	1978FM(P)	6,287	—	Proof	2.00

F.A.O. Issue
Rev: FAO logo, fish, denomination.

KM#	Date	Mintage	VF	XF	Unc
6.3	1979FM(M)	9,000	.50	1.00	2.00
(6b)	1979FM(U)	500 pcs.	—	—	2.50
	1979FM(P)	4,058	—	Proof	2.25

Wedding of Prince Charles and Lady Diana
Edge: THE ROYAL WEDDING 29 JULY 1981.

6.4	1981FM(M)	1,000	—	—	2.00
	1981FM(U)	1,100	—	—	2.00
	1981FM(P)	9,205	—	Proof	1.50

Obv: Mature portrait of Queen Elizabeth.
Rev: Fish, denomination.

36	1987	—	.40	.75	1.50
	1987	—	—	Proof	2.00
	1992	—	.40	.75	1.50

50 TENE

COPPER-NICKEL
Turtle

41	1988	.060	—	—	1.50
	1988	1,000	—	Proof	2.50
	1992	—	—	—	1.50
	1992	—	—	Proof	2.50
	1994	.020	—	—	1.50
	1994	200 pcs.	—	Proof	3.00

DOLLAR

COPPER-NICKEL
Tangaroa, Polynesian God of Creation

7	1972	.031	1.25	2.00	4.00
	1972	.027	—	Proof	5.00
	1973	.049	1.25	2.00	4.00
	1973	.013	—	Proof	6.00

KM#	Date	Mintage	VF	XF	Unc
7	1974	.020	1.25	2.00	4.00
	1974	7,300	—	Proof	6.00
	1975	.029	1.25	2.00	4.00
	1975FM(M)	1,000	—	—	5.00
	1975FM(U)	2,251	—	—	4.00
	1975FM(P)	.021	—	Proof	6.00
	1976FM(M)	1,001	—	—	5.00
	1976FM(U)	1,066	—	—	5.00
	1976FM(P)	.018	—	Proof	6.00
	1977FM(M)	1,171	—	—	5.00
	1977FM(U)	1,002	—	—	5.00
	1977FM(P)	5,986	—	Proof	8.00
	1979FM(M)	1,000	—	—	5.00
	1979FM(U)	500 pcs.	—	—	6.00
	1979FM(P)	4,058	—	Proof	8.00
	1983	—	1.25	2.00	4.00
	1983	.010	—	Proof	6.00

Edge: 1728 CAPTAIN COOK 1978.

7a	1978FM(M)	1,000	—	—	6.00
	1978FM(U)	767 pcs.	—	—	6.00
	1978FM(P)	6,287	—	Proof	5.00

Wedding of Prince Charles and Lady Diana
Edge: THE ROYAL WEDDING 29 JULY 1981.

7b	1981FM(M)	1,000	—	—	6.00
	1981FM(U)	1,100	—	—	6.00
	1981FM(P)	9,205	—	Proof	5.00

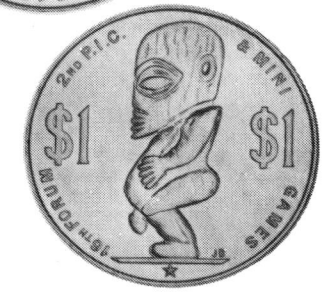

16th Forum, 2nd P.I.C. and Mini Games

30	1985	—	—	—	4.00

37	1987	—	—	1.50	3.00
	1987	—	—	Proof	5.00
	1988	—	—	1.50	3.00
	1988	—	—	Proof	5.00
	1992	—	—	1.50	3.00
	1992	—	—	Proof	5.00
	1994	.020	—	1.50	3.00
	1994	200 pcs.	—	Proof	6.00

2 DOLLARS

COPPER-NICKEL

38	1987	—	—	2.25	3.50
	1987	—	—	Proof	7.50
	1988	—	—	2.25	3.50
	1988	—	—	Proof	7.50
	1992	—	—	2.25	3.50
	1992	—	—	Proof	7.50
	1994	.020	—	2.25	3.50
	1994	200 pcs.	—	Proof	8.50

5 DOLLARS

ALUMINUM-BRONZE
Conch Shell

KM#	Date	Mintage	VF	XF	Unc
39	1987	—	—	5.00	10.00
	1987	—	—	Proof	15.00
	1988	—	—	5.00	10.00
	1988	—	—	Proof	15.00
	1992	—	—	5.00	10.00
	1992	—	—	Proof	15.00
	1994	.020	—	5.00	10.00
	1994	200 pcs.	—	Proof	16.00

COSTA RICA

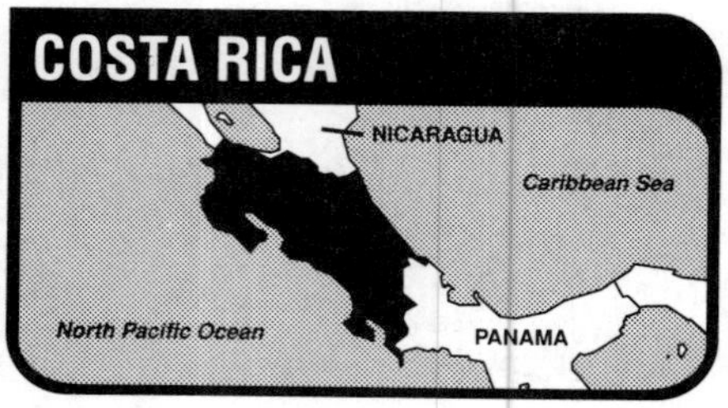
NICARAGUA
Caribbean Sea
North Pacific Ocean
PANAMA

The Republic of Costa Rica, located in southern Central America between Nicaragua and Panama, has an area of 19,730 sq. mi. (51,100 sq. km.) and a population of 3.4 million. Capital: San Jose. Agriculture predominates; tourism and coffee, bananas, beef and sugar contribute heavily to the country's export earnings.

Costa Rica was discovered by Christopher Columbus in 1502, during his last voyage to the New World, and was a colony of Spain from 1522 until independence in 1821. Columbus named the territory Nueva Cartago; the name Costa Rica wasn't generally applied until 1540. Bartholomew Columbus attempted the first settlement but was driven off by Indian attacks and the country wasn't pacified until 1530. After centuries as part of the Spanish Captaincy-General of Guatemala, Costa Rica was absorbed into the Mexican Empire of Augustin de Iturbide from 1821-1823. From 1823 to 1848, it was a constituent state of the Central American Republic (q.v.). Established as a republic in 1848, Costa Rica adopted democratic reforms in the 1870's and 80's. Today, Costa Rica remains a model of orderly democracy in Latin America, although, like most of the hemisphere - its economy is in stress.

NOTE: Also see Central American Republic.

MINT MARKS

CR - San Jose 1825-1947

ISSUING BANK INITIALS - MINTS

BCCR - Philadelphia 1951-1958,1961
BICR - Philadelphia 1935
BNCR - London 1937,1948
BNCR - San Jose 1942-1947
GCR Philadelphia 1905-1914,1929
GCR - San Jose 1917-1941

ASSAYERS INITIALS

CY - 1902
JCV - 1903

MONETARY SYSTEM

100 Centimos = 1 Colon

2 CENTIMOS

COPPER-NICKEL
Plain edge.

KM#	Date	Mintage	Fine	VF	XF	Unc
144	1903	.360	.50	1.00	2.25	5.00

5 CENTIMOS

1.0000 g, .900 SILVER, .0289 oz ASW
Reeded edge.

KM#	Date	Mintage	Fine	VF	XF	Unc
145	1905	.500	BV	.75	2.00	8.00
	1910	.400	BV	.75	2.00	9.00
	1912	.540	BV	.75	1.50	5.00
	1914	.510	BV	.75	1.50	5.50

10 CENTIMOS

2.0000 g, .900 SILVER, .0578 oz ASW

KM#	Date	Mintage	Fine	VF	XF	Unc
146	1905	.400	BV	1.00	3.00	10.00
	1910	.400	BV	1.00	3.00	10.00
	1912	.270	BV	1.00	3.00	10.00
	1914	.150	BV	1.25	3.50	12.00

50 CENTIMOS

10.0000 g, .900 SILVER, .2893 oz ASW

KM#	Date	Mintage	Fine	VF	XF	Unc
143	1902CY	.120	15.00	25.00	40.00	85.00
	1903JCV	.380	10.00	17.50	30.00	65.00
	1914GCR	.200	300.00	500.00	850.00	1200.

NOTE: Most coins dated 1914 were later counterstamped UN COLON/ 1923. See KM#164.

DOS (2) COLONES

1.5560 g, .900 GOLD, .0450 oz AGW
Christopher Columbus

KM#	Date	Mintage	Fine	VF	XF	Unc
139	1915	5,000	40.00	60.00	75.00	90.00
	1916	5,000	40.00	60.00	75.00	90.00
	1921	3,000	50.00	75.00	95.00	125.00
	1922	.013	30.00	40.00	60.00	75.00
	1926	.015	30.00	40.00	60.00	75.00
	1928	.025	30.00	40.00	60.00	75.00

NOTE: Earlier dates (1897-1900) exist for this type.

MONETARY REFORM

100 Centavos = 1 Colon

5 CENTAVOS

BRASS
Plain edge.

KM#	Date	Mintage	Fine	VF	XF	Unc
147	1917	.400	2.25	4.50	10.00	30.00
	1918	1.000	1.25	3.75	9.00	26.50
	1919	.500	2.25	4.50	10.00	30.00

10 CENTAVOS

2.0000 g, .500 SILVER, .0321 oz ASW
Reeded edge.

KM#	Date	Mintage	Fine	VF	XF	Unc
148	1917	.100	1.00	1.75	2.75	6.50

BRASS
Rev: GCR at lower right.

KM#	Date	Mintage	Fine	VF	XF	Unc
149.1	1917	.500	1.75	3.75	8.50	30.00

Rev: GCR at bottom center.

KM#	Date	Mintage	Fine	VF	XF	Unc
149.2	1917	Inc. Ab.	2.75	5.00	12.50	35.00
	1918	.900	1.25	2.75	6.50	25.00
	1919	.250	1.75	4.50	10.00	32.50

50 CENTAVOS

10.0000 g, .500 SILVER, .1607 oz ASW

KM#	Date	Mintage	Fine	VF	XF	Unc
150	1917GCR	9,400	—	—	800.00	1000.
	1918GCR	.030	—	—	—	—

NOTE: All but 10 examples of the 1917 issue and the complete 1918 mintage were counterstamped UN COLON/1923. See KM#165.

MONETARY REFORM

100 Centimos = 1 Colon

5 CENTIMOS

BRASS
Plain edge.

KM#	Date	Mintage	Fine	VF	XF	Unc
151	1920	.500	1.25	3.25	8.00	18.50
	1921	.500	1.25	3.25	7.50	17.50
	1922	.500	1.75	3.75	10.00	22.50
	1936	1.500	.40	.75	1.50	5.50
	1938	1.000	.50	1.25	3.00	9.00
	1940	1.300	.40	.75	1.50	6.00
	1941	1.000	.40	.85	2.00	10.00

BRONZE

KM#	Date	Mintage	Fine	VF	XF	Unc
169	1929	1.500	.60	1.25	3.50	10.00

COPPER-NICKEL

KM#	Date	Mintage	Fine	VF	XF	Unc
178	1942	.274	.55	1.25	2.50	5.25

NOTE: Struck over 2 Centimos, KM#144.

BRASS

KM#	Date	Mintage	Fine	VF	XF	Unc
179	1942	1.730	.20	.60	1.25	4.50
	1943	1.000	.20	.60	2.00	6.00
	1946	1.000	.35	.90	2.25	6.50
	1947	3.000	.15	.45	.75	3.00

COPPER-NICKEL
Rev: Large lettering B.C. - C.R. divided.

KM#	Date	Mintage	Fine	VF	XF	Unc
184.1	1951	3.000	.35	.75	1.50	3.75

Obv: Small ships, 5 stars in shield.
Rev: Small lettering B.C.C.R. not divided.

KM#	Date	Mintage	Fine	VF	XF	Unc
184.2	1951	7.000	.10	.15	.40	1.00

STAINLESS-STEEL

KM#	Date	Mintage	Fine	VF	XF	Unc
184.2a	1953	9.040	—	—	.10	.25
	1958	19.940	—	—	.10	.15
	1967	6.020	—	—	.10	.20

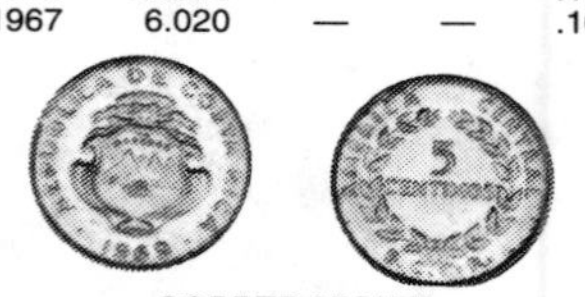

COPPER-NICKEL
Obv: Small ships, 7 stars in shield.

KM#	Date	Mintage	Fine	VF	XF	Unc
184.3	1969	20.000	—	—	.10	.15
	1976	—	—	—	.10	.15
	1976	—	—	—	Proof	.75
	1978	7.520	—	—	.10	.15

NOTE: Varieties exist.

Obv: Large ships, 7 stars in shield.

KM#	Date	Mintage	Fine	VF	XF	Unc
184.4	1972	12.550	—	—	.10	.15
	1973	20.000	—	—	.10	.15
	1976	33.270	—	—	.10	.15

NOTE: Dies vary for each date.

BRASS

KM#	Date	Mintage	Fine	VF	XF	Unc
184.4a	1979	3.060	—	—	.10	.15

10 CENTIMOS

BRASS
Rev: GCR at lower right.

152	1920	.850	.75	2.00	4.50	15.00
	1921	.750	1.00	2.50	6.00	16.50
	1922	.750	.75	2.00	3.75	13.50

BRONZE
Rev: GCR at bottom.

170	1929	.500	1.25	2.75	6.00	16.00

BRASS

174	1936	.750	.35	.65	1.75	9.00
	1941	.500	.50	1.25	3.25	12.00

Rev: BN - CR divided at bottom.

180	1942	1.000	.30	.60	1.75	6.00
	1943	.500	.35	.75	2.25	7.50
	1946	.500	.50	1.00	2.75	8.00
	1947	1.500	.25	.50	1.50	5.50

NOTE: Edge varieties exist on 1947 strikes.

COPPER-NICKEL
Obv: Small ships, 5 stars in shield.
Rev: BCCR at bottom.

185.1	1951	2.500	.10	.20	.70	1.25

STAINLESS STEEL

185.1a	1953	5.290	—	—	.10	.75
	1958	10.470	—	—	.10	.25
	1967	5.500	—	—	.10	.25

COPPER-NICKEL
Obv: Small ships, 7 stars in field. Rev: Small 10.

185.2	1969	10.000	—	—	.10	.15
	1976	40.000	—	—	.10	.15
	1976	—	—	—	Proof	.75

NOTE: Dies vary for each date.

ALUMINUM
Obv: Small ships, 7 stars in field.

185.2a	1982	40.000	—	—	.10	.15

NICKEL CLAD STEEL

KM#	Date	Mintage	Fine	VF	XF	Unc
185.2b	1979	10.000	—	—	.10	.15

COPPER-NICKEL
Obv: Large ships, 7 stars in field. Rev: Large 10.

185.3	1972	20.000	—	—	.10	.15
	1975	5.000	—	—	.10	.15

25 CENTIMOS

3.4500 g, .650 SILVER, .0721 oz ASW
Reeded edge.

168	1924	1.340	1.25	2.25	4.50	12.50

COPPER-NICKEL
Lettered edge.
Rev: BICR at bottom.

171	1935	1.200	.25	.75	2.00	12.00

Rev: BNCR at bottom.

175	1937	1.600	.25	.75	1.75	8.00
	1937	—	—	—	Proof	100.00
	1948	9.200	.10	.20	.40	1.25
	1948	—	—	—	Proof	

BRASS
Edge: Reeded.
Rev: BN * CR at bottom.

181	1944	.800	.50	1.25	3.50	14.50
	1945	1.200	.50	1.00	2.75	12.50
	1946	1.200	.50	1.00	2.50	10.00

BRONZE
Edge: Reeded.

181a	1945	Inc. Ab.	1.00	2.00	4.00	20.00

COPPER-NICKEL
Obv: Small ships, 7 stars in shield.
Rev: BCCR at bottom.

188.1	1967	4.000	—	—	.10	.50
	1969	4.000	—	—	.10	.50
	1974	—	—	—	.10	.30
	1976	—	—	—	.10	.30
	1976	12.000	—	—	Proof	1.00
	1978	—	—	—	.10	.30

NOTE: Dies vary for each date.

Obv: Large ships, 7 stars in shield.

KM#	Date	Mintage	Fine	VF	XF	Unc
188.2	1972	8.000	—	—	.10	.20

NICKEL CLAD STEEL
Obv: Small ships.

188.1a	1980	30.000	—	—	.10	.20

ALUMINUM

188.1b	1982	30.000	—	—	.10	.20

Reeded edge. Reduced size, 17mm.

188.3	1983	—	—	—	.10	.20
	1986	—	—	—	.10	.20
	1989	—	—	—	.10	.20

NOTE: Dies vary for each date.

50 CENTIMOS

COPPER-NICKEL
Rev: BICR at bottom.

172	1935	.700	.50	1.25	4.00	22.50

Rev: BNCR at bottom.

176	1937	.600	.30	1.00	3.00	14.00
	1937	—	—	—	Proof	125.00

182	1948	4.000	.15	.25	.50	2.00
	1948	—	—	—	Proof	

Obv: Small ships, 7 stars in shield, small 50.

KM#	Date	Mintage	Fine	VF	XF	Unc
189.1	1965	1.000	—	.10	.25	1.00

Rev: Large 50.

189.3	1968	2.000	—	.10	.15	.50
	1970	4.000	—	.10	.15	.35
	1976	6.000	—	.10	.15	.35
	1976	—	—	—	Proof	1.50
	1978	—	—	.10	.15	.35

NOTE: Dies vary for each date.

Obv: Large ships, 7 stars in shield.

189.2	1972 lg.dt.	4.000	—	.10	.15	.35
	1972 sm.dt. I.A.		—	.10	.15	.35
	1975 lg.dt.	.524	—	.10	.15	.35
	1975 sm.dt. I.A.		—	.10	.15	.35

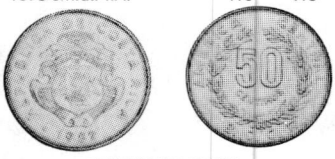

STAINLESS STEEL
Obv: Large ships, letters incuse on ribbon.

209.1	1982	12.000	—	—	.10	.20
	1983	—	—	—	.10	.20
	1990	—	—	—	.10	.20

Obv: Small ships, letters in relief on ribbon.

| 209.2 | 1984 | — | — | — | .10 | .20 |

UN (1) COLON

COPPER-NICKEL
Plain edge.

| 173 | 1935 | .350 | .75 | 2.00 | 6.50 | 35.00 |

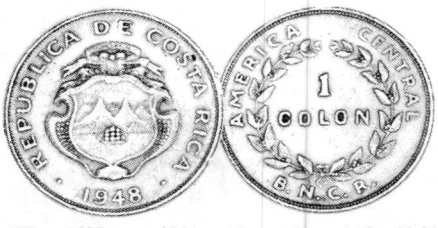

177	1937	.300	.50	1.25	4.50	20.00
	1937	—	—	—	Proof	150.00
	1948	1.350	.20	.40	.75	2.00
	1948	—	—	—	Proof	—

STAINLESS STEEL

| 186.1 | 1954 | .990 | .20 | .35 | 1.00 | 7.50 |

COPPER-NICKEL
Obv: Small ships, 5 stars in shield.

KM#	Date	Mintage	Fine	VF	XF	Unc
186.1a	1961	1.000	.10	.20	.50	2.00

Obv: Small ships, 7 stars in shield. Rev: Small 1.

186.2	1965	1.000	.10	.20	.35	1.00
	1968	2.000	.10	.20	.25	.50
	1970	2.000	.10	.20	.25	.50
	1974	—	.10	.20	.25	.50
	1978	—	.10	.20	.25	.50

Rev: Large 1.

186.4	1976	12.000	.10	.20	.25	.50
	1976	—	—	—	Proof	2.50
	1977	22.000	.10	.20	.25	.50

NOTE: Dies vary for each date.

Obv: Large ships, 7 stars in shield.

| 186.3 | 1972 | 2.000 | .10 | .20 | .25 | .50 |
| | 1975 | 1.028 | .10 | .20 | .25 | .50 |

STAINLESS STEEL
Obv: Letters incuse on ribbon.

210.1	1982	12.000	—	—	.10	.25
	1983	—	—	—	.10	.25
	1984	—	—	—	.10	.25
	1991	—	—	—	.10	.25

Obv: Small ships, letters in relief on ribbon.

210.2	1984	—	—	—	.10	.25
	1989	—	—	—	.10	.25
	1993	—	—	—	.10	.25
	1994	—	—	—	.10	.25

2 COLONES

COPPER-NICKEL

| 183 | 1948 | 1.380 | .50 | .75 | 1.25 | 3.00 |
| | 1948 | — | — | — | Proof | — |

STAINLESS STEEL
Obv: Small ships, 5 stars in shield.

KM#	Date	Mintage	Fine	VF	XF	Unc
187.1	1954	1.030	.25	.50	2.00	10.00

COPPER-NICKEL

| 187.1a | 1961 | 1.000 | .15 | .30 | .50 | 1.25 |

Obv: Small ships, 7 stars in shield.

187.2	1968	2.000	.15	.30	.40	.90
(187.3)	1970	1.000	.15	.30	.50	1.00
	1972	2.000	.15	.30	.40	.90
	1976	—	.15	.30	.40	.90
	1978	—	.15	.30	.40	.90

NOTE: Dies vary for each date.

STAINLESS STEEL
Obv: Letters incuse on ribbon.

| 211.1 | 1982 | 12.000 | — | — | .10 | .50 |
| | 1983 | — | — | — | .10 | .50 |

Obv: Letters in relief on ribbon.

| 211.2 | 1984 | — | — | — | .10 | .50 |

5 COLONES

NICKEL
25th Anniversary of the Central Bank

| 203 | 1975 | 2.000 | — | .15 | .35 | 1.25 |
| | 1975 | 5,000 | — | — | Proof | 2.00 |

STAINLESS STEEL
Obv: Letters in relief on ribbon.

214.1	1983	—	—	.10	.15	.50
	1989	—	—	.10	.15	.50
	1993	—	—	.10	.15	.50

Obv: Letters incuse on ribbon.

| 214.2 | 1985 | — | — | .10 | .15 | .50 |

BRASS PLATED STEEL

Obv: National arms. Rev: Denomination.

KM#	Date	Mintage	Fine	VF	XF	Unc
227	1995	—	—	—	—	.75

10 COLONES

NICKEL
25th Anniversary of the Central Bank

204	1975	.500	.25	.50	1.00	2.00
	1975	5,000	—	—	Proof	4.00

STAINLESS STEEL
Obv: Letters in relief on ribbon.

215.1	1983	—	—	.20	.30	1.00
	1992	—	—	.20	.30	1.00

Obv: Letters incuse on ribbon.

215.2	1985	—	—	.20	.30	1.00

BRASS PLATED STEEL
Obv: National arms. Rev: Denomination.

228	1995	—	—	—	—	1.00
	1996	—	—	—	—	1.00

20 COLONES

NICKEL
25th Anniversary of the Central Bank

205	1975	.250	.50	1.00	2.00	4.00
	1975	5,000	—	—	Proof	9.00

STAINLESS STEEL
Obv: Letters in relief on ribbon.

KM#	Date	Mintage	Fine	VF	XF	Unc
216.1	1983	—	—	.35	.60	1.50
	1989	—	—	.35	.60	1.50
	1994	—	—	.35	.60	1.50

Obv: Letters incuse on ribbon.

216.2	1985	—	—	.35	.60	1.50
	1994	—	—	.35	.60	1.50
	1996	—	—	.35	.60	1.50

25 COLONES

BRASS PLATED STEEL
Obv: National arms. Rev: Denomination.

229	1995	—	—	—	—	2.00

50 COLONES

BRASS
Obv: National arms. Rev: Denomination.

231	1997	—	—	—	—	2.50

100 COLONES

BRASS PLATED STEEL
Obv: National arms. Rev: Denomination.

230	1995	—	—	—	—	4.50

BRASS

230a	1997	—	—	—	—	4.50

COUNTERSTAMPED COINAGE
50 CENTIMOS
1923

Type VIII
Obv. c/s: 1923 in 11mm circle.
Rev. c/s: 50 CENTIMOS in 11mm circle.

SILVER
c/s: Type VIII on 25 Centavos, KM#105.

KM#	Date	Year	VG	Fine	VF	XF
155	1923	1864 GW	325.00	550.00	900.00	—

c/s: Type VIII on 25 Centavos, KM#106.

156	1923	1864 GW	225.00	400.00	650.00	—
		1865 GW	28.50	48.00	80.00	125.00
		1875 GW	22.50	40.00	65.00	100.00

c/s: Type VIII on 25 Centavos, KM#127.1.
Rev: GW 9Ds.

KM#	Date	Year	VG	Fine	VF	XF
157	1923	1886 GW	3.00	5.00	9.00	15.00
		1887 GW	3.00	5.00	9.00	15.00

c/s: Type VIII on 25 Centavos, KM#127.2.
Rev: 9Ds GW.

158	1923	1886 GW	4.00	8.00	15.00	25.00
		1887 GW	3.00	5.00	9.00	15.00

c/s: Type VIII on 25 Centavos, KM#130.

159	1923	1889H	1.50	2.75	5.00	8.50
		1890/80H	2.50	3.75	7.00	10.00
		1890H	1.50	2.75	5.00	8.50
		1892H	1.50	2.75	5.00	8.50
		1893H	1.25	2.50	4.50	7.50

NOTE: For KM#155-159 the entire mintage of 1,866,000 was created by counterstamping the above coins.

UN (1) COLON
1923

Type IX
Obv. c/s: 1923 in 14mm circle.
Rev. c/s: UN COLON in 14mm circle.

SILVER
c/s: Type IX on 50 Centavos, KM#112.

162	1923					
		1865 GW	30.00	45.00	70.00	125.00
		1866/5GW	32.50	55.00	85.00	150.00
		1867 GW	—	—	Rare	—
		1870 GW	—	—	Rare	—
		1872 GW	—	—	Rare	—
		1875 GW	30.00	45.00	70.00	125.00

c/s: Type IX on 50 Centavos, KM#124.

163	1923	1880 GW	6.50	10.00	25.00	50.00
		1885 GW	6.50	10.00	25.00	50.00
		1886 GW	9.00	17.50	30.00	60.00
		1887 GW	6.50	10.00	27.50	55.00
		1890 GW	6.50	10.00	27.50	55.00

c/s: Type IX on 50 Centimos, KM#143.

164	1923	1902 CY	4.00	8.00	13.50	22.50
		1903 JCV	3.00	6.00	10.00	17.50
		1914 GCR	4.00	8.00	13.50	20.00

c/s: Type IX on 50 Centimos, KM#150.

KM#	Date	Year	VG	Fine	VF	XF
165	1923	1917GCR	4.50	8.50	13.50	20.00
		1918GCR	6.00	12.00	17.50	25.00

NOTE: For KM#165, a total of 9,390 of 50 Centimos, KM#150 dated 1917 and 28,800 dated 1918 were counterstamped. For KM#162-165 the entire mintage of 460,000 was created by counterstamping the above coins.

CROATIA

The Republic of Croatia, (Hrvatska) bordered on the west by the Adriatic Sea and the northeast by Hungary, has an area of 21,829 sq. mi. (56,538 sq. km.) and a population of 4.7 million. Capital: Zagreb.

The country was attached to the Kingdom of Hungary until Dec. 1, 1918, when it joined with the Serbs and Slovenes to form the Kingdom of the Serbs, Croats and Slovenes, which changed its name to the Kingdom of Yugoslavia on Oct. 3, 1929. On April 6, 1941, Hitler, angered by the coup d'etat that overthrew the pro-Nazi regime of regent Prince Paul, sent the Nazi armies crashing across the Yugoslav borders from Germany, Hungary, Romania and Bulgaria. Within a week the army of the Balkan Kingdom was prostrate and broken. Yugoslavia was dismembered to reward Hitler's Balkan allies. Croatia, reconstituted as a nominal kingdom, was given to the administration of an Italian princeling, who wisely decided to remain in Italy. By 1947 it was again totally part of the 6 Yugoslav Socialist Republics.

Croatia proclaimed their independence from Yugoslavia on Oct. 8, 1991.

Local Serbian forces, supported by the Yugoslav Federal Army, had developed a military stronghold and proclaimed an independent "SRPSKEKRAJINA" State in the area around Knin, located in southern Croatia having an estimated population of 350,000 Croat Serbs. In September, 1995, Croat forces overwhelmed Croat Serb forces ending the short life of their proclaimed Serbian Republic.

MONETARY SYSTEM
100 Banica = 1 Kuna

The word 'kunas', derived from the Russian 'cunica' which means marten, reflects the use of furs for money in medieval eastern Europe.

KUNA

ZINC
Similar to 2 Kune, KM#2.

KM#	Date	Mintage	Fine	VF	XF	Unc
1	1941	—	—	—	Rare	—

2 KUNE

ZINC

2	1941	—	4.00	8.00	16.00	32.00
	1941	—	—	—	Proof	80.00

50 KUNA

NOTE: Dated 1934, this coin is found struck in various metals, 2 sizes - 25 and 26mm - as well as 2 thicknesses. It is considered a modern fantasy issue.

500 KUNA

9.9500 g, .900 GOLD, .2821 oz AGW, 23mm

KM#	Date	Mintage	VF	XF	Unc
B3	1941	—	—	—	3000.

KM#	Date	Mintage	VF	XF	Unc
A3	1941	170 pcs.	1750.	2250.	3000.

MONETARY REFORM

May 30, 1994
1000 Dinara = 1 Kuna
100 Lipa = 1 Kuna

LIPA

ALUMINUM
Ears of Corn

3	1993	—	—	.10	.20
	1993	.025	—	Proof	.50
	1995	—	—	.10	.20
	1995	—	—	Proof	.50

ALUMINUM
Rev: Ears of corn, leg: ZEA MAYS.

12	1994	—	—	—	.25
	1994	—	—	Proof	.55
	1996	—	—	—	.25

Rev: Ears of corn, leg: FAO.

13	ND(1995)	1.000	—	—	.35
	ND(1995)	—	—	Proof	12.00

2 LIPE

ALUMINUM
Grape Vine

4	1993	—	—	.20	.35
	1993	—	—	Proof	.80
	1995	—	—	.20	.35
	1995	—	—	Proof	.80

ALUMINUM
Rev: Grape vine, leg: VIIIS VINIFERA.

14	1994	—	—	—	.40
	1994	—	—	Proof	.85
	1996	—	—	—	.40

Olympics
Obv: Denomination. Rev: Olympic rings, flame.

36	1996	—	—	—	.25
	1996	—	—	Proof	.75

5 LIPA

BRASS PLATED STEEL
Oak Leaves

KM#	Date	Mintage	VF	XF	Unc
5	1993	—	—	.25	.45
	1993	.025	—	Proof	1.20
	1995	—	—	.25	.45
	1995	—	—	Proof	1.20
	1995 w/dot	—	—	.25	.50

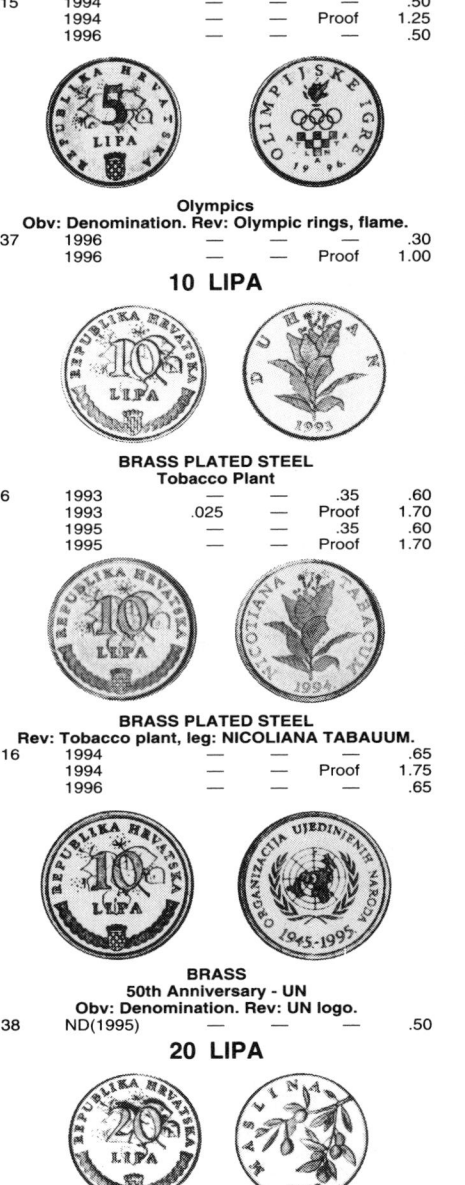

BRASS PLATED STEEL
Rev: Oak leaves, leg: QUERCUS ROBUR.

15	1994	—	—	—	.50
	1994	—	—	Proof	1.25
	1996	—	—	—	.50

Olympics
Obv: Denomination. Rev: Olympic rings, flame.

37	1996	—	—	—	.30
	1996	—	—	Proof	1.00

10 LIPA

BRASS PLATED STEEL
Tobacco Plant

6	1993	—	—	.35	.60
	1993	.025	—	Proof	1.70
	1995	—	—	.35	.60
	1995	—	—	Proof	1.70

BRASS PLATED STEEL
Rev: Tobacco plant, leg: NICOLIANA TABAUUM.

16	1994	—	—	—	.65
	1994	—	—	Proof	1.75
	1996	—	—	—	.65

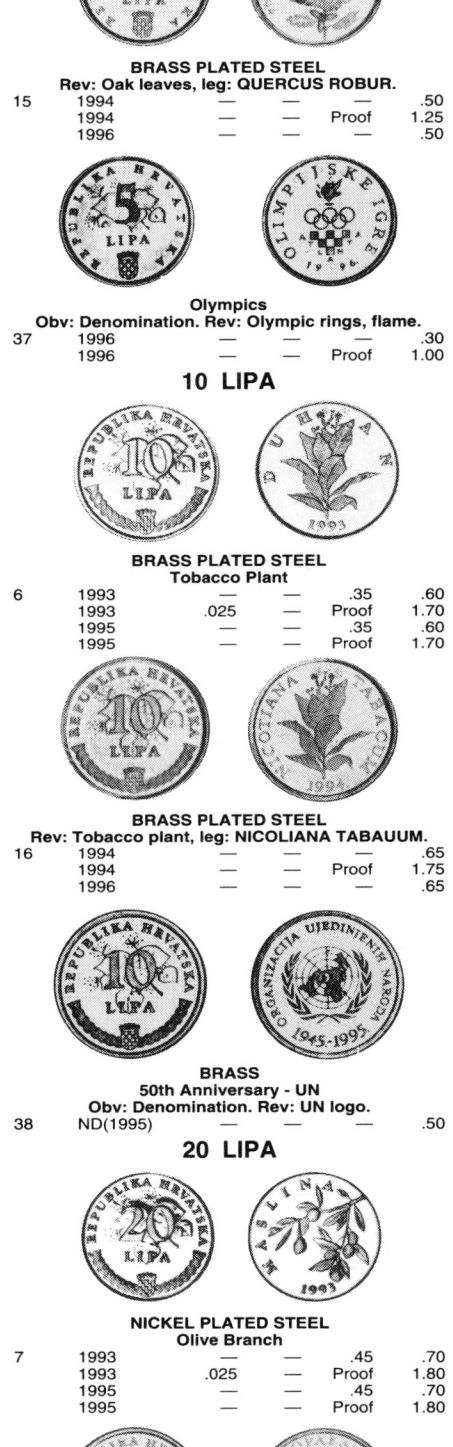

BRASS
50th Anniversary - UN
Obv: Denomination. Rev: UN logo.

38	ND(1995)	—	—	—	.50

20 LIPA

NICKEL PLATED STEEL
Olive Branch

7	1993	—	—	.45	.70
	1993	.025	—	Proof	1.80
	1995	—	—	.45	.70
	1995	—	—	Proof	1.80

NICKEL PLATED STEEL
Rev: Olive branch, leg: OLEA EUROPAEA.

17	1994	—	—	—	.75
	1994	—	—	Proof	1.85

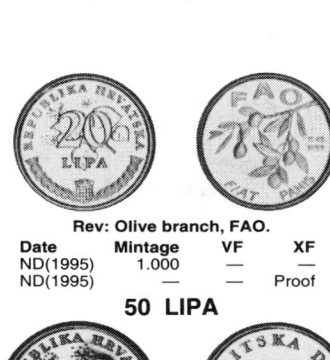

Rev: Olive branch, FAO.

KM#	Date	Mintage	VF	XF	Unc
18	ND(1995)	1.000	—	—	.75
	ND(1995)	—	—	Proof	12.00

50 LIPA

NICKEL PLATED STEEL
Flowers

8	1993	—	—	.55	.80
	1993	.025	—	Proof	2.20
	1995	—	—	.55	.80
	1995	—	—	Proof	2.20

NICKEL PLATED STEEL
Rev: Flowers, leg: DEGENIA VELEBITICA.

19	1994	—	—	—	.85
	1994	—	—	Proof	2.25
	1996	—	—	—	.85

European Soccer
Obv: Denomination.
Rev: Checkered shield, soccer ball.

39	1996	—	—	—	.75

KUNA

COPPER-NICKEL
Nightingale

9	1993	—	—	.75	1.20
	1993	.025	—	Proof	2.75
	1993 w/o dot	—	—	.75	1.20
	1995	—	—	.75	1.20
	1995	—	—	Proof	2.75
	1995 w/dot	—	—	.75	1.20

COPPER-NICKEL
Rev: Nightingale, leg:
LUSCINNIA MEGARHYNCHOS.

20	1994	—	—	—	1.25
	1994	—	—	Proof	3.00
	1996	—	—	—	1.25

Olympics
Obv: Denomination. Rev: Olympic flame, rings.

40	1996	—	—	—	1.00
	1996	—	—	Proof	2.50

---

2 KUNE

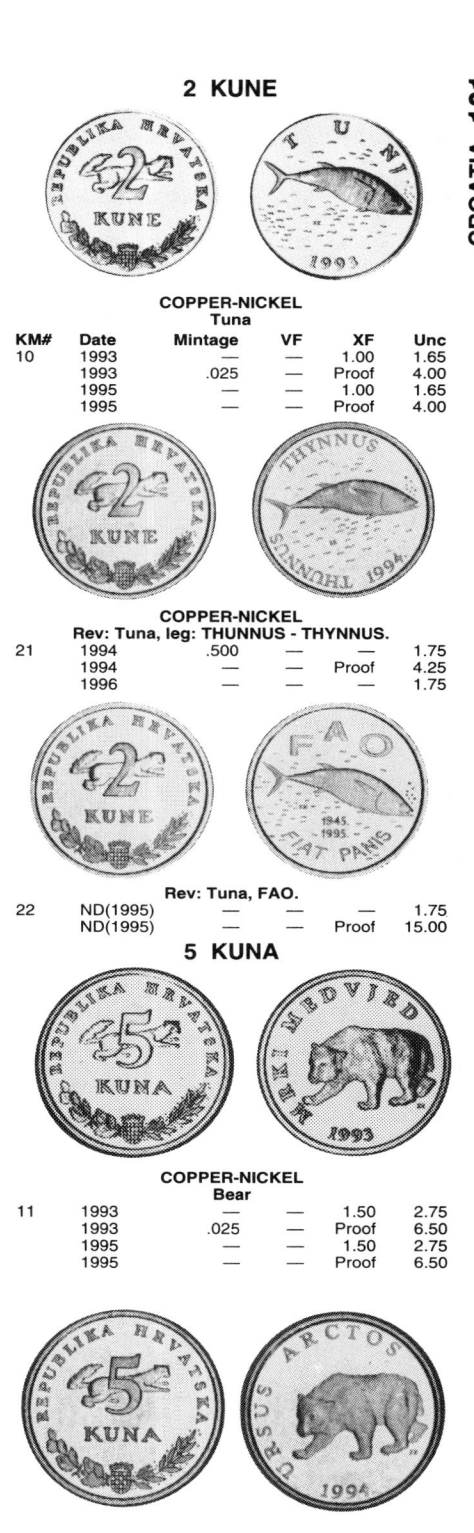

COPPER-NICKEL
Tuna

KM#	Date	Mintage	VF	XF	Unc
10	1993	—	—	1.00	1.65
	1993	.025	—	Proof	4.00
	1995	—	—	1.00	1.65
	1995	—	—	Proof	4.00

COPPER-NICKEL
Rev: Tuna, leg: THYNNUS - THYNNUS.

21	1994	.500	—	—	1.75
	1994	—	—	Proof	4.25
	1996	—	—	—	1.75

Rev: Tuna, FAO.

22	ND(1995)	—	—	—	1.75
	ND(1995)	—	—	Proof	15.00

5 KUNA

COPPER-NICKEL
Bear

11	1993	—	—	1.50	2.75
	1993	.025	—	Proof	6.50
	1995	—	—	1.50	2.75
	1995	—	—	Proof	6.50

COPPER-NICKEL
Rev: Bear, leg: URSUS ARCTOS.

23	1994	—	—	—	3.00
	1994	—	—	Proof	7.00

500th Anniversary - Senj

24	1994	—	—	—	3.00
	1994	—	—	Proof	25.00

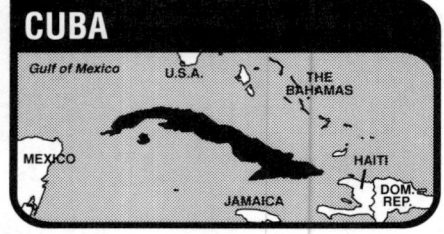

CUBA

The Republic of Cuba, situated at the northern edge of the Caribbean Sea about 90 miles (145 km.) south of Florida, has an area of 42,804 sq. mi. (110,860 sq. km.) and a population of 10.9 million. Capital: Havana. The Cuban economy is based on the cultivation and refining of sugar, which provides 80 percent of export earnings.

Discovered by Columbus in 1492 and settled by Diego Velasquez in the early 1500s, Cuba remained a Spanish possession until 1898, except for a brief British occupancy of Havana in 1762-63. Cuban attempts to gain freedom were crushed, even while Spain was granting independence to its other American possessions. Ten years of warfare, 1868-78, between Spanish troops and Cuban rebels exacted guarantees of rights which were never implemented. The final revolt, begun in 1895, evoked American sympathy, and with the aid of U.S. troops independence was proclaimed on May 20, 1902. Fulgencio Batista seized the government in 1952 and established a dictatorship. Opposition to Batista, led by Fidel Castro, drove him into exile on Jan. 1, 1959. A communist-type, 25-member collective leadership headed by Castro was inaugurated in March, 1962.

RULERS
Spanish, until 1898

MINT MARKS
Key - Havana, 1977-

MONETARY SYSTEM
100 Centavos = 1 Peso

CENTAVO

COPPER-NICKEL

KM#	Date	Mintage	Fine	VF	XF	Unc
9	1915	9.396	.25	1.00	2.00	25.00
	1915	200 pcs.	—	—	Proof	100.00
	1916	9.318	.25	1.00	2.00	25.00
	1916	104 pcs.	—	—	Proof	700.00
	1920	19.378	.25	1.25	2.50	45.00
	1938	2.000	1.00	2.50	6.00	35.00
(9b)	1946	50.000	.10	.20	1.00	7.00
	1961	100.000	.15	.25	.60	1.50

BRASS
| 9a | 1943 | 20.000 | .10 | .40 | 1.25 | 5.00 |

BRASS
Birth of Jose Marti Centennial
| 26 | 1953 | 50.000 | .10 | .15 | .75 | 4.00 |
| | 1953 | 100 pcs. | — | — | Proof | Rare |

COPPER-NICKEL
| 30 | 1958 | 50.000 | — | .15 | .75 | 25.00 |

ALUMINUM
Rev. leg: PATRIA Y LIBERTAD.
33.1	1963	200.020	—	.10	.30	.60
	1966	50.000	—	.10	.40	.80
	1967	—	—	—	—	—
	1969	50.000	—	.10	.40	.80
	1970	50.000	—	.10	.40	.80
	1971	49.960	.20	.40	.80	1.50
	1972	100.000	—	.10	.40	.80
	1978	50.000	—	.10	.40	.80
	1979	100.000	—	.10	.40	.80

KM#	Date	Mintage	Fine	VF	XF	Unc
33.1	1981	—	—	.10	.40	.80
	1982	—	—	.10	.40	.80

Rev. leg: PATRIA O MUERTE.
33.2	1983	—	—	.10	.40	.80
	1984	—	—	.10	.40	.80
	1985	—	—	.10	.40	.80
	1986	—	—	.10	.40	.80
	1987	—	—	.10	.40	.80
	1988	—	—	.10	.40	.80

2 CENTAVOS

COPPER-NICKEL
10	1915	6.090	.25	1.25	3.00	30.00
	1915	150 pcs.	—	—	Proof	125.00
	1916	5.322	.25	1.25	3.50	35.00
	1916	100 pcs.	—	—	Proof	750.00

ALUMINUM
Obv. and rev: Small lettered legends, long edge denticles.
| 104.1 | 1983 | 3.996 | — | .10 | .25 | 1.00 |

Obv. and rev: Large lettered legends, short edge denticles.
104.2	1983	Inc. Ab.	—	.10	.20	.50
	1984	—	—	.10	.25	1.00
	1985	—	—	.10	.20	.50
	1986	—	—	.10	.20	.50

5 CENTAVOS

COPPER-NICKEL
11	1915	5.096	.75	1.50	4.00	45.00
	1915	150 pcs.	—	—	Proof	150.00
	1916	1.714	.75	1.50	5.00	65.00
	1916	100 pcs.	—	—	Proof	800.00
	1920	10.000	.75	1.50	4.50	55.00
(11b)	1946	40.000	.25	.50	.75	8.00
	1960	20.000	.25	.75	1.25	20.00
	1961	70.000	.10	.15	.40	1.00

BRASS
| 11a | 1943 | 6.000 | .50 | 1.00 | 3.50 | 25.00 |

ALUMINUM
34	1963	80.000	—	.10	.25	.75
	1966	50.000	—	.15	.35	1.50
	1968	—	—	.15	.35	1.50
	1969	—	—	.25	.50	2.50
	1971	100.020	—	.10	.25	.75
	1972	100.000	—	.10	.25	.75

10 CENTAVOS

2.5000 g, .900 SILVER, .0723 oz ASW
KM#	Date	Mintage	Fine	VF	XF	Unc
12	1915	5.690	2.00	4.00	12.00	75.00
	1915	125 pcs.	—	—	Proof	750.00
	1916	.560	6.00	20.00	65.00	725.00
	1916	50 pcs.	—	—	Proof	1150.
	1920	3.090	3.50	6.00	20.00	225.00
	1948	5.120	BV	1.25	2.00	6.50
	1949	9.880	BV	1.25	1.75	5.00

50th Year of Republic
| 23 | 1952 | 10.000 | BV | .50 | 1.00 | 3.50 |

20 CENTAVOS

5.0000 g, .900 SILVER, .1446 oz ASW
Rev: High relief star.
13.1	1915 fine reeding					
		.7.915	3.50	8.00	25.00	225.00
	1915	125 pcs.	—	—	Proof	750.00
	1915 coarse reeding					
		Inc. Ab.	125.00	225.00	450.00	—

Rev: Low relief star.
13.2	1915 fine reeding					
		Inc. Ab.	25.00	50.00	150.00	650.00
	1915 coarse reeding					
		Inc. Ab.	2.50	5.00	15.00	65.00
	1916	2.535	3.00	6.00	18.00	225.00
	1916	50 pcs.	—	—	Proof	1200.
	1920	6.130	1.50	3.00	8.00	32.00
	1932	.184	25.00	65.00	275.00	875.00
	1948	6.830	1.20	1.50	3.00	10.00
	1949	13.170	1.20	1.50	3.00	8.00

NOTE: Coins with high relief stars normally exhibit a weak key and palm tree on the reverse. Coins with low relief stars tend to exhibit much more distinct lines running towards the center of the star.

50th Year of Republic
| 24 | 1952 | 8.700 | BV | .75 | 1.50 | 5.00 |

COPPER-NICKEL
Jose Marti
| 31 | 1962 | 83.860 | .35 | 1.00 | 1.50 | 4.00 |
| | 1968 | 25.750 | .45 | 1.25 | 2.00 | 5.00 |

ALUMINUM
| 35 | 1969 | 25.000 | .35 | 1.00 | 1.50 | 3.00 |
| | 1970 | 29.560 | .45 | 1.25 | 1.75 | 4.00 |

KM#	Date	Mintage	Fine	VF	XF	Unc
35	1971	25.000	.35	1.00	1.50	3.00
	1972	—	.35	1.00	1.50	3.00

25 CENTAVOS

6.2500 g, .900 SILVER, .1808 oz ASW
Centennial - Birth of Jose Marti

KM#	Date	Mintage	Fine	VF	XF	Unc
27	1953	19.000	—	BV	2.00	7.50
	1953	—	—	—	Proof	Rare

40 CENTAVOS

10.0000 g, .900 SILVER, .2893 oz ASW
Rev: High relief star.

14.1	1915	2.633	6.00	12.00	25.00	225.00
	1915	100 pcs.	—	—	Proof	750.00
	1920	.540	20.00	35.00	90.00	700.00
	1920	—	—	—	Proof	Rare

Rev: Medium relief star.

14.2	1915	Inc. Ab.	50.00	100.00	200.00	750.00

Rev: Low relief star.

14.3	1915	Inc. Ab.	9.00	15.00	35.00	150.00
	1916	.188	25.00	65.00	350.00	1200.
	1916	50 pcs.	—	—	Proof	1250.
	1920	Inc. Ab.	20.00	50.00	150.00	550.00

NOTE: Coins with high relief stars normally exhibit a weak key and palm tree on the reverse. Coins with low relief stars tend to exhibit much more distinct lines running towards the center of the star.

50th Year of Republic

25	1952	1.250	BV	2.50	5.00	20.00

COPPER-NICKEL
Camilo Cienfuegos Gornaran

32	1962	15.250	2.00	3.00	5.00	8.00

50 CENTAVOS

12.5000 g, .900 SILVER, .3617 oz ASW
Centennial - Birth of Jose Marti

28	ND(1953)	2.000	BV	2.50	5.50	20.00
	ND(1953)	—	—	—	Proof	Rare

PESO

26.7295 g, .900 SILVER, .7735 oz ASW
Rev: High relief star.

KM#	Date	Mintage	Fine	VF	XF	Unc
15.1	1915	1.976	10.00	20.00	60.00	320.00
	1915	100 pcs.	—	—	Proof	850.00

Rev: Low relief star.

15.2	1915	Inc. Ab.	45.00	90.00	300.00	1250.
	1916	.843	10.00	20.00	70.00	950.00
	1916	50 pcs.	—	—	Proof	1650.
	1932	3.550	7.00	9.00	28.00	250.00
	1933	6.000	7.00	9.00	20.00	125.00
	1934	3.000	7.00	9.00	20.00	100.00

NOTE: Coins with high relief stars normally exhibit a weak key and palm tree on the reverse. Coins with low relief stars tend to exhibit much more distinct lines running towards the center of the star.

1.6718 g, .900 GOLD, .0483 oz AGW
Jose Marti

16	1915	6,850	50.00	100.00	175.00	250.00
	1915	140 pcs.	—	—	Proof	1650.
	1916	.011	50.00	100.00	175.00	250.00
	1916	100 pcs.	—	—	Proof	1750.

26.7295 g, .900 SILVER, .7735 oz ASW
'ABC'

22	1934	7.000	12.00	25.00	65.00	250.00
	1935	12.500	12.00	25.00	55.00	200.00
	1936	16.000	12.00	25.00	55.00	200.00
	1937	11.500	150.00	250.00	450.00	1150.
	1938	10.800	12.00	22.50	45.00	125.00
	1939	9.200	12.00	22.50	40.00	100.00

Centennial of Jose Marti

KM#	Date	Mintage	Fine	VF	XF	Unc
29	ND(1953)	1.000	BV	4.50	7.00	25.00
	ND(1953)	—	—	—	Proof	Rare

BRASS

105	1983	10.000	.25	.50	1.00	2.50
	1984	—	.25	.50	1.00	2.50
	1985	—	.25	.50	1.00	2.50
	1986	—	.25	.50	1.00	2.50
	1987	—	.25	.50	1.00	2.50
	1988	—	.25	.50	1.00	2.50
	1989	—	.25	.50	1.00	2.50

BRASS PLATED STEEL
Jose Marti

347	1992	—	—	—	1.00	2.00
	1994	—	—	—	1.00	2.00

2 PESOS

3.3436 g, .900 GOLD, .0967 oz AGW
Jose Marti

17	1915	.010	65.00	85.00	115.00	200.00
	1915	100 pcs.	—	—	Proof	2250.
	1916	.150	60.00	70.00	85.00	120.00
	1916	8 pcs.	—	—	Proof	2500.

3 PESOS

COPPER-NICKEL
Ernesto Che Guevara

346	1990	4.050	—	—	3.00	6.00

NICKEL CLAD STEEL

346a	1992	—	—	—	3.00	6.00
	1992	500 pcs.	—	—	Proof	12.50
	1993	—	—	—	3.00	6.00
	1995	—	—	—	3.00	6.00

4 PESOS

6.6872 g, .900 GOLD, .1935 oz AGW

Jose Marti

KM#	Date	Mintage	Fine	VF	XF	Unc
18	1915	6,300	125.00	175.00	300.00	750.00
	1915	100 pcs.	—		Proof	3250.
	1916	.129	100.00	120.00	150.00	250.00
	1916	90 pcs.	—		Proof	3500.

5 PESOS

8.3592 g, .900 GOLD, .2419 oz AGW
Jose Marti

19	1915			BV	125.00	165.00
	1915	.696	—		Proof	3250.
	1916	1.132	—	BV	125.00	150.00
	1916				Proof	3500.

10 PESOS

16.7185 g, .900 GOLD, .4838 oz AGW
Jose Marti

20	1915	.095	—	BV	250.00	325.00
	1915			—	Proof	7000.
	1916	1.169	—	BV	220.00	275.00
	1916				Proof	14,500.

VISITOR'S COINAGE
CENTAVO

COPPER-NICKEL

KM#	Date	Mintage	VF	XF	Unc
409	1988	—	.50	1.50	3.00

ALUMINUM

410	1988	—	.50	1.50	5.00

5 CENTAVOS

COPPER-NICKEL

411	1981	—	.50	1.50	3.00

Rev: Large 5.

412.1	1981		.50	1.50	3.00

NOTE: Varieties exist.

Rev: Small 5.

412.2	1989		.50	1.50	3.00

STAINLESS STEEL

KM#	Date	Mintage	VF	XF	Unc
412.2a	1989		.50	1.50	3.00

ALUMINUM

413	1988	—	.50	1.50	3.00

STAINLESS STEEL
Peso Convertible Series
Obv: National arms. Rev: Casa Colonial.

575	1994	—	—	—	1.00
	1996				1.00

10 CENTAVOS

COPPER-NICKEL

414	1981	—	.65	2.00	4.00

Small 10.

415.1	1989		.65	2.00	4.00
(415.3)					

STAINLESS STEEL
Small 10.

415.1a	1989		.65	2.00	4.50
(415.1)					

COPPER - NICKEL
Large 10.

415.2	1981	—	.65	2.00	4.50

STAINLESS STEEL

415.2a	1989				4.00

Reduced size.
Obv. and Rev: Same design as KM#415.1

415.3	1989		1.00	2.50	7.50
(415.4)					

ALUMINUM

416	1988	—	.65	2.00	4.00

STAINLESS STEEL
Peso Convertible Series
Obv: National arms. Rev: Castillo de la Fuerza.

576	1994	—	—	—	2.00
	1996				2.00

25 CENTAVOS

COPPER-NICKEL

KM#	Date	Mintage	VF	XF	Unc
417	1981	—	1.00	3.00	7.50

Rev: Large 25.

418.1	1981		1.00	3.00	7.50

Rev: Small 25.

418.2	1989	—	1.00	3.00	7.00

STAINLESS STEEL

418.2a	1989		1.00	3.00	7.00

ALUMINUM

419	1988	—	.75	2.50	5.00

STAINLESS STEEL
Peso Convertible Series
Obv: National arms. Rev: Trinidad.

577	1994	—	—	—	3.00

50 CENTAVOS

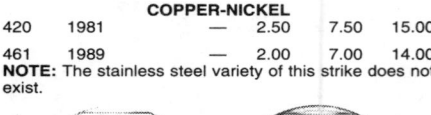

COPPER-NICKEL

420	1981	—	2.50	7.50	15.00
461	1989	—	2.00	7.00	14.00

NOTE: The stainless steel variety of this strike does not exist.

STAINLESS STEEL
Peso Convertible Series
Obv: Cuban arms. Rev: Cathedral of Havana.

KM#	Date	Mintage	VF	XF	Unc
578	1994	—	—	—	5.00

PESO

COPPER-NICKEL

421	1981	—	4.00	12.00	24.00

Obv: Lighthouse. Rev: Denomination and logo.

580	1989	—	4.00	12.00	24.00

NOTE: No variations of the numeral 1 on the reverse is known to exist.

STAINLESS STEEL
Peso Convertible Series
Obv: National arms. Rev: Guama.

579	1994	—	—	—	7.00

CYPRUS

The Republic of Cyprus, a member of the British Commonwealth, lies in the eastern Mediterranean Sea 44 miles (71 km.) south of Turkey and 60 miles (97 km.) west of Syria. It is the third largest island in the Mediterranean Sea, having an area of 3,572 sq. mi. (9,251 sq. km.) and a population of 736,636. Capital: Nicosia. Agriculture, light manufacturing and tourism are the chief industries. Citrus fruit, potatoes, footwear and clothing are exported

The importance of Cyprus dates from the Bronze Age when it was desired as a principal source of copper (from which the island derived its name) and as a strategic trading center. It was during this period that large numbers of Greeks settled on the island and gave it the predominantly Greek character. Its role as an international marketplace made it a prime disseminator of the then prevalent cultures, a role that still influences the civilization of Western man. Because of its fortuitous position and influential role, Cyprus was conquered by a succession of empires: the Assyrian, Egyptian, Persian, Macedonian, Ptolemaic, Roman and Byzantine. It was taken from Isaac Comnenus by Richard the Lion-Heart in 1191, sold to the Templar Knights and for the following 7 centuries was ruled by the Franks, the Venetians and the Ottomans. During the Ottoman period Cyprus acquired its Turkish community (18% of its population). In 1878 the island fell into British hands and was made a crown colony of Britain in 1925. Finally, on Aug. 16, 1960, it became an independent republic.

In 1964, the ethnic Turks withdrew from active participation in the government. Turkish forces invaded Cyprus in 1974, gained control of 40 percent of the island and forcibly separated the Greek and Turkish communities. In 1983, Turkish Cypriots proclaimed their own state in northern Cyprus, which remains without international recognition.

Cyprus is a member of the Commonwealth of Nations. The president is Chief of State and Head of Government.

RULERS
British, until 1960

MINT MARKS
no mint mark - Royal Mint, London, England
H - Birmingham, England

MONETARY SYSTEM
9 Piastres = 1 Shilling
20 Shillings = 1 Pound

1/4 PIASTRE
BRONZE, 21mm

KM#	Date	Mintage	Fine	VF	XF	Unc
1.2	1901	.072	10.00	25.00	60.00	140.00

NOTE: Earlier date (1900) exists for this type.

8	1902	.072	5.00	12.50	30.00	125.00
	1905	.422	4.00	12.50	27.50	100.00
	1908	.036	35.00	100.00	150.00	350.00

16	1922	.072	5.00	15.00	30.00	80.00
	1926	.360	3.50	7.50	15.00	65.00
	1926	—	—	—	Proof	365.00

1/2 PIASTRE

BRONZE

KM#	Date	Mintage	Fine	VF	XF	Unc
11	1908	.036	50.00	150.00	350.00	600.00

17	1922	.036	20.00	50.00	125.00	250.00
	1927	.108	3.50	10.00	35.00	80.00
	1927	—	—	—	Proof	375.00
	1930	.180	3.00	8.00	30.00	75.00
	1930	—	—	—	Proof	365.00
	1931	.090	5.00	15.00	40.00	100.00
	1931	—	—	—	Proof	425.00

COPPER-NICKEL

20	1934	1.440	.75	2.50	6.50	16.50
	1934	—	—	—	Proof	325.00

22	1938	1.080	.35	1.00	4.00	12.50
	1938	—	—	—	Proof	325.00

BRONZE

22a	1942	1.080	.25	1.00	2.50	12.50
	1942	—	—	—	Proof	200.00
	1943	1.620	.25	1.00	2.50	12.50
	1944	2.160	.25	1.00	2.50	12.50
	1945	1.080	.25	1.00	2.50	12.50
	1945	—	—	—	Proof	200.00

29	1949	1.080	.15	.35	1.00	3.50
	1949	—	—	—	Proof	150.00

PIASTRE

BRONZE

12	1908	.027	100.00	200.00	350.00	700.00

KM#	Date	Mintage	Fine	VF	XF	Unc
18	1922	.054	10.00	35.00	125.00	250.00
	1927	.127	5.00	20.00	60.00	150.00
	1927	—	—	—	Proof	400.00
	1930	.096	6.00	22.50	70.00	175.00
	1930	—	—	—	Proof	400.00
	1931	.045	15.00	35.00	75.00	200.00
	1931	—	—	—	Proof	725.00

COPPER-NICKEL

21	1934	1.440	1.00	2.50	6.50	16.50
	1934	—	—	—	Proof	325.00

23	1938	2.700	.60	1.50	3.00	12.50
	1938	—	—	—	Proof	325.00

BRONZE

23a	1942	1.260	.50	1.00	2.50	10.00
	1942	—	—	—	Proof	225.00
	1943	2.520	.50	1.00	2.50	10.00
	1944	3.240	.50	1.00	2.50	10.00
	1945	1.080	.60	1.50	3.00	12.00
	1945	—	—	—	Proof	200.00
	1946	1.080	.60	1.50	3.00	12.00
	1946	—	—	—	Proof	200.00

Obv. leg: DEI GRATIA REX for REX IMPERATOR.

30	1949	1.080	.25	.75	2.00	4.00
	1949	—	—	—	Proof	150.00

3 PIASTRES

1.8851 g, .925 SILVER, .0561 oz ASW

4	1901	.300	8.00	20.00	40.00	100.00
	1901	—	—	—	Proof	800.00

4-1/2 PIASTRES

2.8276 g, .925 SILVER, .0841 oz ASW

5	1901	.400	5.00	15.00	40.00	100.00
	1901	—	—	—	Proof	950.00

KM#	Date	Mintage	Fine	VF	XF	Unc
15	1921	.600	3.50	10.00	30.00	80.00

24	1938	.192	2.00	4.00	12.00	30.00
	1938	—	—	—	Proof	400.00

9 PIASTRES

5.6552 g, .925 SILVER, .1682 oz ASW

6	1901	.600	15.00	40.00	100.00	200.00
	1901	—	—	—	Proof	1250.

9	1907	.060	35.00	100.00	275.00	500.00

13	1913	.050	40.00	125.00	300.00	600.00
	1919	.400	2.50	10.00	30.00	100.00
	1921	.490	2.50	10.00	30.00	100.00

25	1938	.504	2.00	3.50	8.00	30.00
	1938	—	—	—	Proof	400.00
	1940	.800	1.50	3.00	7.00	27.50
	1940	—	—	—	Proof	400.00

SHILLING

COPPER-NICKEL

27	1947	1.440	.50	1.00	5.00	30.00
	1947	—	—	—	Proof	300.00

Obv. leg: ET IND IMP dropped.

31	1949	1.440	.50	1.00	5.00	30.00
	1949	—	—	—	Proof	300.00

18 PIASTRES

11.3104 g, .925 SILVER, .3364 oz ASW

KM#	Date	Mintage	Fine	VF	XF	Unc
7	1901	.200	25.00	100.00	250.00	500.00
	1901	—	—	—	Proof	2500.

10	1907	.020	55.00	225.00	485.00	1250.

14	1913	.025	35.00	140.00	350.00	650.00
	1921	.155	25.00	60.00	150.00	350.00

26	1938	.200	3.50	5.00	10.00	40.00
	1938	—	—	—	Proof	450.00
	1940	.100	4.00	6.50	15.00	50.00
	1940	—	—	—	Proof	450.00

2 SHILLINGS

COPPER-NICKEL

28	1947	.720	1.00	2.50	7.50	35.00
	1947	—	—	—	Proof	400.00

Obv. leg: ET IND. IMP. dropped.

32	1949	.720	1.00	2.50	7.50	35.00
	1949	—	—	—	Proof	400.00

45 PIASTRES

28.2759 g, .925 SILVER, .8409 oz ASW
50th Anniversary of British Rule

KM#	Date	Mintage	Fine	VF	XF	Unc
19	ND(1928)	.080	15.00	25.00	50.00	150.00
	ND(1928)	517 pcs.	—	—	Proof	600.00

DECIMAL COINAGE

50 Mils = 1 Shilling
20 Shillings = 1 Pound
1000 Mils = 1 Pound

3 MILS

BRONZE
Flying Fish

KM#	Date	Mintage	VF	XF	Unc
33	1955	6.250	—	.10	.20
	1955	2,000	—	Proof	2.50

5 MILS

BRONZE

34	1955	10.000	.15	.25	.40
	1955	2,000	—	Proof	3.50
	1956	2.950	.15	.30	.50
	1956	—	—	Proof	300.00

25 MILS

COPPER-NICKEL
Head of Bull

35	1955	2.500	.25	.35	.50
	1955	2,000	—	Proof	3.50

50 MILS

COPPER-NICKEL

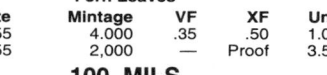

Fern Leaves

KM#	Date	Mintage	VF	XF	Unc
36	1955	4.000	.35	.50	1.00
	1955	2,000	—	Proof	3.50

100 MILS

COPPER-NICKEL

37	1955	2.500	.50	.75	1.50
	1955	2,000	—	Proof	5.00
	1957	*.500	10.00	15.00	50.00
	1957	—	—	Proof	440.00

*NOTE: All but 10,000 of 1957 issue were melted down.

REPUBLIC

1960—

MIL

ALUMINUM

38	1963	5.000	—	—	.15
	1963	.025	—	Proof	1.00
	1971	.500	—	.10	.25
	1972	.500	—	.10	.25
	1972	—	—	Proof	2.00

5 MILS

BRONZE

39	1963	12.000	—	.10	.35
	1963	.025	—	Proof	1.25
	1970	2.500	—	.10	.35
	1971	2.500	—	.10	.35
	1972	2.500	—	.10	.35
	1973	5.000	—	.10	.35
	1974	2.500	—	.10	.35
	1976	2.000	—	.10	.35
	1977	2.000	—	.10	.35
	1978	2.000	—	.10	.35
	1979	2.000	—	.10	.35
	1980	4.000	—	.10	.35
	1980	—	—	Proof	2.50

ALUMINUM
Obv: Small date.

50.1	1981	12.500	—	—	.25

Obv: Large date and legends.

50.2	1982	15.000	—	—	.25
	1982	—	—	Proof	2.00

25 MILS

COPPER-NICKEL
Cedar of Lebanon

KM#	Date	Mintage	VF	XF	Unc
40	1963	2.500	.10	.15	.45
	1963	.025	—	Proof	1.50
	1968	1.500	.10	.15	.45
	1971	1.000	.10	.15	.45
	1972	.500	.10	.15	.50
	1973	1.000	.10	.15	.45
	1974	1.000	.10	.15	.45
	1976	2.000	.10	.15	.45
	1977	.500	.10	.15	.45
	1978	.500	.10	.15	.45
	1979	1.000	.10	.15	.45
	1980	2.000	.10	.15	.45
	1981	3.000	.10	.15	.45
	1982	1.000	.10	.15	.45
	1982	—	—	Proof	3.00

50 MILS

COPPER-NICKEL
Bunch of Grapes

41	1963	2.800	.20	.30	1.00
	1963	.025	—	Proof	1.75
	1970	.500	.20	.35	1.25
	1971	.500	.20	.35	1.25
	1972	.750	.20	.30	1.00
	1973	.750	.20	.30	1.00
	1974	1.500	.20	.30	1.00
	1976	1.500	.20	.30	1.00
	1977	.500	.20	.30	1.00
	1978	.500	.20	.30	1.00
	1979	1.000	.20	.30	1.00
	1980	3.000	.20	.30	1.00
	1981	4.000	.20	.30	1.00
	1982	2.000	.20	.30	1.00
	1982	—	—	Proof	3.50

100 MILS

COPPER-NICKEL
Cyprus Mouflon

42	1963	1.750	.40	.70	2.00
	1963	.025	—	Proof	2.50
	1971	.500	.50	.75	2.00
	1973	.750	.40	.70	2.00
	1974	1.000	.50	.75	2.00
	1976	1.500	.40	.70	2.00
	1977	.500	.50	.75	2.00
	1978	1.000	.50	.75	2.00
	1979	1.000	.40	.70	2.00
	1980	1.000	.40	.70	2.00
	1981	2.000	.40	.70	2.00
	1982	2.000	.40	.70	2.00
	1982	—	—	Proof	5.00

500 MILS

COPPER-NICKEL
Hercules

44	1975	.500	1.25	1.75	3.50
	1977	.300	1.25	1.75	3.50
	1977	—	—	Proof	15.00

MONETARY REFORM

100 Cents = 1 Pound

1/2 CENT

ALUMINUM
Cyclamen

KM#	Date	Mintage	VF	XF	Unc
52	1983	10.000	—	.10	.15
	1983	6,250	—	Proof	1.50

CENT

NICKEL-BRASS
Stylized Bird on a Branch
Rev: Value number surrounded by single line.

53.1	1983	15.000	—	.10	.20
	1983	6,250	—	Proof	1.50

Rev: Value number surrounded by double line.

53.2	1985	5.000	—	.10	.20
	1987	5.000	—	.10	.20
	1988	5.000	—	.10	.20
	1989	—	—	.10	.20
	1990	—	—	.10	.20
	1994	—	—	.10	.20

Obv: Altered wreath around arms.

53.3	1991	—	—	.10	.20
(53.2)	1992	—	—	.10	.20
	1993	—	—	.10	.20
	1994	—	—	.10	.20
	1996	—	—	.10	.20

2 CENTS

NICKEL-BRASS
Stylized Goats
Rev: Value number surrounded by single line.

54.1	1983	12.000	—	.15	.25
	1983	6,250	—	Proof	1.50

Rev: Value number surrounded by double line.

54.2	1985	8.000	—	.15	.25
	1987	—	—	.15	.25
	1988	5.150	—	.15	.25
	1989	—	—	.15	.25
	1990	—	—	.15	.25

Obv: Altered wreath around arms.

54.3	1991	—	—	.15	.25
(54.2)	1992	—	—	.15	.25
	1993	—	—	.15	.25
	1994	—	—	.15	.25
	1996	—	—	.15	.25

5 CENTS

NICKEL-BRASS
Rev: Value number surrounded by single line.

55.1	1983	15.000	—	.20	.50
	1983	6,250	—	Proof	2.00

Rev: Value number surrounded by double line.

55.2	1985	5.000	—	.20	.50
	1987	5.000	—	.20	.50

KM#	Date	Mintage	VF	XF	Unc
55.2	1988	5.060	—	.20	.50
	1989	—	—	.20	.50
	1990	—	—	.20	.50

Obv: Altered wreath around arms.

55.3	1991	—	—	.20	.50
(55.2)	1992	—	—	.20	.50
	1993	—	—	.20	.50
	1994	—	—	.20	.50

10 CENTS

NICKEL-BRASS
Rev: Value number surrounded by single line.

56.1	1983	10.000	—	.35	.75
	1983	6,250	—	Proof	3.00

Rev: Value number surrounded by double line.

56.2	1985	5.000	—	.35	.75
	1987	—	—	.35	.75
	1988	5.035	—	.35	.75
	1989	—	—	.35	.75
	1990	—	—	.35	.75

NOTE: 1994 strike previously listed here has been moved to KM#56.3.

Obv: Altered wreath around arms.

56.3	1991	—	—	.35	.75
(56.2)	1992	—	—	.35	.75
	1993	—	—	.35	.75
	1994	—	—	.35	.75

20 CENTS

NICKEL-BRASS
Pied Wheatear
Rev: Value number framed by single line.

57.1	1983	10.000	—	.50	1.50
	1983	6,200	—	Proof	5.00

Rev: Value number framed by double line.

57.2	1985	5.040	—	.50	1.50
	1987	—	—	.50	1.50
	1988	1.000	—	.50	1.50

BRONZE
Zamon D. Keteus

62.1	1989	—	—	—	1.00
	1989	—	—	Proof	18.00
	1990	—	—	—	1.00

NICKEL-BRASS
Obv: Altered wreath around arms.

62.2	1991	—	—	—	1.00
	1992	—	—	—	1.00

KM#	Date	Mintage	VF	XF	Unc
62.2	1993	—	—	—	1.00
	1994	—	—	—	1.00

50 CENTS

COPPER-NICKEL
Forestry - F.A.O.

58	1985	.033	1.50	3.00	7.50

Abduction of Europa

66	1991	3.005	—	—	2.50
	1993	—	—	—	2.50
	1994	—	—	—	2.50
	1996	—	—	—	2.50

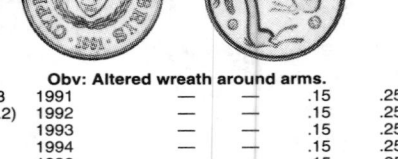

CZECHOSLOVAKIA

The Republic of Czechoslovakia, founded at the end of World War I, was part of the old Austrian-Hungarian Empire. It had an area of 49,371 sq. mi. (127,870 sq. km.) and a population of 15.6 million. Capital: Prague (Praha).

Czechoslovakia proclaimed itself a republic on Oct. 28, 1918, with Tomas G. Masaryk as President. Hitler's rise to power in Germany provoked Czechoslovakia's German minority in the Sudetenland to agitate for autonomy. At Munich (Munchen) in Sept. of 1938, France and Britain, seeking to avoid World War II, forced the cession of the Sudetenland to Germany. In March, 1939, Germany invaded Czechoslovakia and established the "protectorate of Bohemia and Moravia". Bohemia is a historic province in northwest Czechoslovakia that includes the city of Prague, one of the oldest continually occupied sites in Europe. Moravia is an area of considerable mineral wealth in central Czechoslovakia. Slovakia, a province in southeastern Czechoslovakia under Nazi influence was constituted as a republic. The end of World War II saw the re-established independence of Czechoslovakia, while bringing it within the Russian sphere of influence. On Feb. 23-25, 1948, the Communists seized control of the government in a coup d'etat, and adopted a constitution making the country a 'people's republic'. A new constitution adopted June 11, 1960, converted the country into a 'socialist republic' which lasted until 1989. On Nov. 11, 1989, demonstrations against the communist government began and in Dec. of that same year, communism was overthrown, and the Czech and Slovak Federal Republic was formed. In 1993 the CSFR split into the Czech Republic and The Republic of Slovakia.

NOTE: For additional listings see Bohemia and Moravia, Czech Republic and Slovakia.

MONETARY SYSTEM
100 Haleru = 1 Koruna

REPUBLIC
2 HALERE

ZINC

KM#	Date	Mintage	Fine	VF	XF	Unc
5	1923	2.700	3.00	5.00	10.00	15.00
	1924	17.300	2.25	3.50	5.00	9.00
	1925	2.000	3.00	5.00	7.50	15.00

5 HALERU

BRONZE

KM#	Date	Mintage	Fine	VF	XF	Unc
6	1923	37.800	.20	.30	.50	2.00
	1924	10 pcs.	—	—	—	1500.
	1925	12.000	.20	.30	.50	2.50
	1926	1.084	1.50	3.25	6.00	12.00
	1927	8.916	.25	.35	.75	2.50
	1928	5.320	.30	.45	.75	2.50
	1929	12.680	.25	.35	.75	2.50
	1930	5.000	.25	.35	.75	2.50
	1931	7.448	.25	.35	.75	2.50
	1932	3.556	.60	1.00	2.00	5.00
	1938	14.244	.25	.35	.75	2.00

NOTE: There are two varieties of the number 4 in 1924 dated coins: w/ and w/out seraphs.

10 HALERU

BRONZE

KM#	Date	Mintage	Fine	VF	XF	Unc
3	1922	6.000	.30	.45	1.00	2.75
	1923	24.000	.25	.35	.75	2.00
	1924	5.320	.30	.45	1.00	3.00
	1925	24.680	.25	.35	.60	2.25
	1926	10.000	.25	.35	.75	2.25
	1927	10.000	.25	.35	.75	2.25

KM#	Date	Mintage	Fine	VF	XF	Unc
3	1928	14.290	.25	.35	.75	2.25
	1929	5.710	1.25	2.00	3.50	7.00
	1930	6.980	.30	.45	1.00	2.50
	1931	6.740	.30	.45	1.00	2.50
	1932	11.280	.25	.35	.75	2.00
	1933	4.190	.35	.60	1.25	5.00
	1934	13.200	.25	.35	.75	2.00
	1935	3.420	.50	.75	1.50	5.00
	1936	8.560	.25	.35	.75	2.00
	1937	20.200	.25	.35	.75	2.00
	1938	21.400	.25	.35	.75	2.00

20 HALERU

COPPER-NICKEL

KM#	Date	Mintage	Fine	VF	XF	Unc
1	1921	40.000	.25	.35	.60	2.50
	1922	9.100	.25	.35	.60	2.50
	1924	20.931	.25	.35	.60	2.50
	1925	4.244	.60	1.00	2.00	6.00
	1926	14.825	.25	.35	.60	2.50
	1927	11.757	.25	.35	.60	2.50
	1928	14.018	.25	.35	.60	2.50
	1929	4.225	.30	.50	1.25	3.50
	1930	—	.30	.40	.75	3.00
	1931	5.000	.30	.40	.75	3.00
	1933	Inc. Ab.	2.50	3.50	7.00	25.00
	1937	8.208	.25	.35	.60	2.50
	1938	18.787	.25	.35	.60	2.50

25 HALERU

COPPER-NICKEL

KM#	Date	Mintage	Fine	VF	XF	Unc
16	1933	22.711	.50	1.00	2.00	4.00

50 HALERU

COPPER-NICKEL

KM#	Date	Mintage	Fine	VF	XF	Unc
2	1921	3.000	.25	.50	1.00	3.00
	1922	37.000	.20	.40	.60	2.50
	1924	10.000	.20	.40	.60	3.00
	1925	1.415	.50	1.00	2.00	9.00
	1926	1.585	1.25	2.00	4.00	20.00
	1927	2.000	.50	1.00	2.00	9.00
	1931	6.000	.25	.50	1.00	2.50

KORUNA

COPPER-NICKEL

KM#	Date	Mintage	Fine	VF	XF	Unc
4	1922	50.000	.30	.50	.75	2.00
	1923	15.385	.30	.50	.75	2.00
	1924	21.041	.30	.50	.75	2.00
	1925	8.574	.40	.60	1.00	4.00
	1929	5.000	.50	.75	1.25	3.50
	1930	5.000	.40	.60	1.00	4.00
	1937	3.806	.40	.60	1.00	3.00
	1938	8.582	.40	.60	1.00	3.00

5 KORUN

COPPER-NICKEL

KM#	Date	Mintage	Fine	VF	XF	Unc
10	1925	16.475	1.50	2.50	3.50	8.00
	1926	8.912	1.75	2.75	4.00	10.00
	1927	4.614	2.50	4.00	5.75	22.00

7.0000 g, .500 SILVER, .1125 oz ASW

KM#	Date	Mintage	Fine	VF	XF	Unc
11	1928	1.710	2.00	3.00	5.00	10.00
	1929	12.861	1.00	2.00	4.00	8.50
	1930	10.429	1.00	2.00	4.00	8.50
	1931	2.000	2.00	3.00	5.00	12.00
	1932	1.000	5.00	7.50	10.00	35.00

NOTE: Edge varieties exist.

NICKEL

KM#	Date	Mintage	Fine	VF	XF	Unc
11a	1937	.036	100.00	175.00	300.00	500.00
	1938	17.200	1.25	2.50	4.00	6.50

10 KORUN

10.0000 g, .700 SILVER, .2250 oz ASW
10th Anniversary of Independence

KM#	Date	Mintage	Fine	VF	XF	Unc
12	ND(1928)	1.000	2.00	4.00	5.00	9.00

KM#	Date	Mintage	Fine	VF	XF	Unc
15	1930	4.949	2.00	3.50	6.00	10.00
	1931	6.689	2.00	3.00	5.00	9.00
	1932	11.448	1.75	2.50	4.00	8.00
	1933	.915	10.00	20.00	60.00	250.00

20 KORUN

12.0000 g, .700 SILVER, .2700 oz ASW

KM#	Date	Mintage	Fine	VF	XF	Unc
17	1933	2.280	BV	4.00	7.50	14.00
	1934	3.280	BV	4.00	7.50	14.00

Death of President Masaryk

KM#	Date	Mintage	Fine	VF	XF	Unc
18	ND(1937)	1.000	BV	3.00	6.00	9.00

TRADE COINAGE
DUKAT

3.4900 g, .986 GOLD, .1106 oz AGW
5th Anniversary of the Republic
Obv: Coat of arms. Rev: Duke Wenceslas (Vaclav).

KM#	Date	Mintage	VF	XF	Unc
7	1923	1,000	250.00	600.00	1000.

NOTE: The above coins are serially numbered below the duke.

Similar to KM#7 but w/o serial numbers.

KM#	Date	Mintage	VF	XF	Unc
8	1923	.062	55.00	75.00	115.00
	1924	.033	55.00	75.00	115.00
	1925	.066	55.00	75.00	115.00
	1926	.059	55.00	75.00	115.00
	1927	.026	55.00	75.00	115.00
	1928	.019	55.00	75.00	125.00
	1929	.010	60.00	80.00	165.00
	1930	.011	60.00	80.00	165.00
	1931	.043	55.00	75.00	115.00
	1932	.027	55.00	75.00	115.00
	1933	.058	55.00	75.00	115.00
	1934	9,972	80.00	100.00	175.00
	1935	.013	55.00	75.00	125.00
	1936	.015	55.00	75.00	125.00
	1937	324 pcs.	200.00	500.00	1000.
	1938	56 pcs.	600.00	1000.	2000.
	1939	*276 pcs.	200.00	500.00	1000.
	1951	500 pcs.	150.00	450.00	1000.

*NOTE: Czech reports show mintage of 20 for Czechoslovakia and 256 for state of Slovakia.

2 DUKATY

6.9800 g, .986 GOLD, .2212 oz AGW
Duke Wenceslas (Vaclav)

KM#	Date	Mintage	VF	XF	Unc
9	1923	4,000	150.00	225.00	350.00
	1929	3,262	150.00	225.00	350.00
	1930	Inc. Ab.	150.00	250.00	400.00
	1931	2,994	150.00	225.00	350.00
	1932	5,496	150.00	225.00	350.00
	1933	4,671	150.00	225.00	350.00
	1934	2,403	150.00	225.00	350.00
	1935	2,577	150.00	225.00	350.00
	1936	819 pcs.	300.00	400.00	750.00
	1937	8 pcs.	1500.	2000.	5000.
	1938	*186 pcs.	600.00	800.00	1500.
	1951	200 Pcs.	300.00	500.00	1500.

*NOTE: Czech reports show mintage of 14 for Czechoslovakia and 172 for state of Slovakia.

5 DUKATU

17.4500 g, .986 GOLD, .5532 oz AGW
Duke Wenceslas

KM#	Date	Mintage	VF	XF	Unc
13	1929	1,827	350.00	450.00	675.00
	1930	543 Pcs.	500.00	700.00	1250.
	1931	1,528	350.00	450.00	675.00
	1932	1,827	350.00	450.00	675.00
	1933	1,752	350.00	450.00	675.00
	1934	1,101	350.00	450.00	675.00
	1935	1,037	350.00	450.00	675.00
	1936	728 pcs.	500.00	700.00	1000.
	1937	4 pcs.	—	—	7500.
	1938	*56 pcs.	1000.	2000.	3000.
	1951	100 pcs.	400.00	800.00	2800.

*NOTE: Czech reports show mintage of 12 for Czechoslovakia and 44 for state of Slovakia.

10 DUKATU

34.9000 g, .986 GOLD, 1.1064 oz AGW
Duke Wenceslas

KM#	Date	Mintage	VF	XF	Unc
14	1929	1,564	700.00	1100.	1650.
	1930	394 pcs.	1000.	1900.	3000.
	1931	1,239	700.00	1100.	1750.
	1932	1,035	700.00	1100.	1750.
	1933	1,780	700.00	1100.	1750.
	1934	1,298	700.00	1100.	1750.
	1935	600 pcs.	750.00	1350.	2100.
	1936	633 pcs.	750.00	1350.	2100.
	1937	34 pcs.	—	—	12,000.
	1938	*192 pcs.	2000.	2800.	5000.
	1951	100 pcs.	2000.	3500.	7500.

*NOTE: Czech reports show mintage of 20 for Czechoslovakia and 172 for state of Slovakia.

POST WAR COINAGE
20 HALERU

BRONZE

KM#	Date	Mintage	Fine	VF	XF	Unc
20	1947	—	65.00	125.00	200.00	300.00
	1948	24.340	.10	.15	.40	1.00
	1949	25.660	.10	.15	.40	1.00
	1950	11.132	.10	.15	.40	1.00

ALUMINUM

KM#	Date	Mintage	Fine	VF	XF	Unc
31	1951	46.800	.10	.15	.25	1.00
	1952	80.340	.10	.15	.25	1.00

50 HALERU

BRONZE

KM#	Date	Mintage	Fine	VF	XF	Unc
21	1947	50.000	.15	.25	.40	1.00
	1948	20.000	.15	.25	.40	1.00
	1949	12.715	.15	.25	.40	1.00
	1950	17.415	.15	.25	.40	1.00

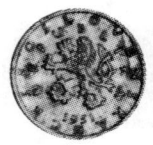 

ALUMINUM

KM#	Date	Mintage	Fine	VF	XF	Unc
32	1951	60.000	.15	.35	.50	.75
	1952	60.000	.25	.45	.60	1.00
	1953	34.920	1.00	2.50	6.00	10.00

KORUNA

COPPER-NICKEL

KM#	Date	Mintage	Fine	VF	XF	Unc
19	1946	88.000	.15	.25	.50	1.00
	1947	12.550	1.50	2.50	3.75	6.50

ALUMINUM

KM#	Date	Mintage	Fine	VF	XF	Unc
22	1947	—	50.00	120.00	200.00	350.00
(32)	1950	62.190	.20	.35	.45	.75
	1951	61.395	.20	.35	.45	1.00
	1952	101.105	.20	.30	.40	.80
	1953	73.905	.40	.75	1.75	4.50

2 KORUNY

COPPER-NICKEL

KM#	Date	Mintage	Fine	VF	XF	Unc
23	1947	20.000	.20	.40	.60	1.25
	1948	20.476	.20	.40	.60	1.50

5 KORUN

ALUMINUM

KM#	Date	Mintage	Fine	VF	XF	Unc
34	1952	40.715	17.50	25.00	40.00	70.00

NOTE: Not released for circulation. Almost the entire mintage was melted.

PEOPLES REPUBLIC
HALER

ALUMINUM

KM#	Date	Mintage	Fine	VF	XF	Unc
35	1953	.030	—	—	.10	.25
	1954	—	—	—	.10	.25
	1955	—	—	—	.10	.25
	1956	—	—	—	.10	.25

KM#	Date	Mintage	Fine	VF	XF	Unc
35	1957	—	—	—	.10	.25
	1958	—	.10	.25	.35	.75
	1959	—	—	—	.10	.25
	1960	—	—	—	.10	.25

3 HALERE

ALUMINUM

KM#	Date	Mintage	Fine	VF	XF	Unc
36	1953	.040	—	.10	.15	.30
	1954	—	—	.10	.15	.30

5 HALERU

ALUMINUM

KM#	Date	Mintage	Fine	VF	XF	Unc
37	1953	.060	.10	.15	.25	.50
	1954	—	.10	.15	.25	.50
	1955	—	.30	.50	.75	2.00

10 HALERU

ALUMINUM

KM#	Date	Mintage	Fine	VF	XF	Unc
38	1953(k)	—	.10	.15	.30	.80
	1953(l)	.160	.10	.15	.30	.80
	1953(u)	—	.25	.50	.75	2.00
	1954	—	.25	.50	.75	2.00
	1955	—	.50	.75	1.25	3.00
	1956	—	.10	.15	.30	.80
	1958	—	.50	.75	1.50	4.00

(k) - Kremnica-130 notches in milled edge.
(l) - Leningrad-133 notches in milled edge.
(u) - Unknown-125 notches in milled edge.

25 HALERU

ALUMINUM

KM#	Date	Mintage	Fine	VF	XF	Unc
39	1953(k)	—	.10	.20	.30	.80
	1953(l)	.160	.30	.50	.60	1.50
	1954	—	.10	.20	.30	.80

(k) - Kremnica-134 notches in milled edge.
(l) - Leningrad-145 notches in milled edge.
(u) - Unknown-135 notches in milled edge.

KORUNA

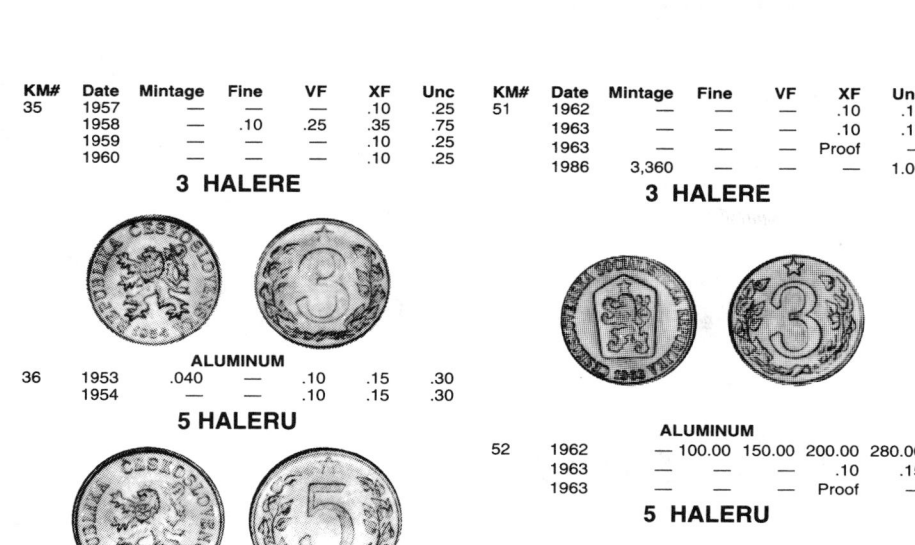

ALUMINUM-BRONZE

KM#	Date	Mintage	Fine	VF	XF	Unc
46	1957	—	.20	.30	.45	2.50
	1958	—	.20	.30	.45	2.50
	1959	—	.15	.25	.35	1.50
	1960	—	.15	.25	.35	1.50

SOCIALIST REPUBLIC
1960 - 1990
HALER

ALUMINUM

KM#	Date	Mintage	Fine	VF	XF	Unc
51	1962	—	—	—	.10	.15
	1963	—	—	—	.10	.15
	1963	—	—	—	Proof	—
	1986	3,360	—	—	—	1.00

3 HALERE

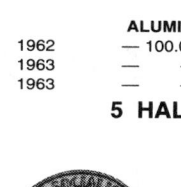

ALUMINUM

KM#	Date	Mintage	Fine	VF	XF	Unc
52	1962	—	100.00	150.00	200.00	280.00
	1963	—	—	—	.10	.15
	1963	—	—	—	Proof	—

5 HALERU

ALUMINUM

KM#	Date	Mintage	Fine	VF	XF	Unc
53	1962	—	—	.10	.15	.25
	1963	—	—	.10	.15	.25
	1966	—	—	.10	.15	.25
	1966	—	—	—	Proof	Rare
	1967	—	—	.10	.15	.25
	1970	—	—	.10	.15	.20
	1972	—	—	.10	.15	.20
	1973	—	—	.10	.15	.20
	1974	—	—	.10	.15	.20
	1975	—	—	.10	.15	.20
	1976	—	—	.10	.15	.20

KM#	Date	Mintage	Fine	VF	XF	Unc
86	1977	—	—	—	.10	.25
	1978	—	—	—	.10	.25
	1979	—	—	—	.10	.25
	1980	—	—	—	.10	.25
	1981	—	—	—	.10	.25
	1981	—	—	—	Proof	—
	1982	—	—	In mint set only		.50
	1983	—	—	—	.10	.25
	1984	—	—	In mint set only		.50
	1985	—	—	In mint set only		.50
	1986	—	—	—	.10	.25
	1986	—	—	—	Proof	—
	1987	—	—	—	.10	.25
	1988	8.000	—	—	.10	.25
	1989	—	—	—	.10	.25
	1990	—	—	—	.10	.25

10 HALERU

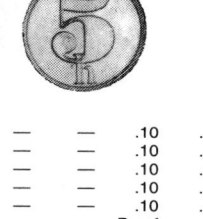

ALUMINUM

KM#	Date	Mintage	Fine	VF	XF	Unc
49.1	1961	—	—	.10	.20	.35
	1962	—	—	.10	.20	.35
	1963	—	—	.10	.20	.35
	1964	—	—	.10	.20	.35
	1965	—	—	.10	.20	.35
	1966	—	—	.10	.20	.35
	1966	—	—	—	Proof	Rare
	1967	—	—	.10	.20	.35
	1968	—	—	.10	.20	.35
	1969	—	—	.10	.15	.35
	1970	—	—	.10	.20	.35
	1971	—	—	.10	.20	.35

 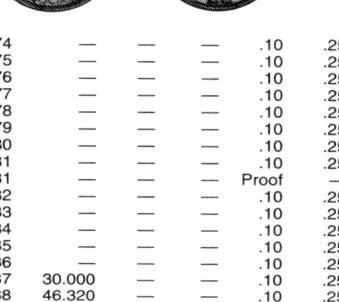

Obv: Flat top 3 in date.

KM#	Date	Mintage	Fine	VF	XF	Unc
49.2	1963	3,600 est.	12.50	25.00	37.50	65.00

KM#	Date	Mintage	Fine	VF	XF	Unc
80	1974	—	—	—	.10	.25
	1975	—	—	—	.10	.25
	1976	—	—	—	.10	.25
	1977	—	—	—	.10	.25
	1978	—	—	—	.10	.25
	1979	—	—	—	.10	.25
	1980	—	—	—	.10	.25
	1981	—	—	—	.10	.25
	1981	—	—	—	Proof	—
	1982	—	—	—	.10	.25
	1983	—	—	—	.10	.25
	1984	—	—	—	.10	.25
	1985	—	—	—	.10	.25
	1986	—	—	—	.10	.25
	1987	30.000	—	—	.10	.25
	1988	46.320	—	—	.10	.25
	1989	—	—	—	.10	.25
	1990	—	—	—	.10	.25

NOTE: Varieties exist.

20 HALERU

BRASS

KM#	Date	Mintage	Fine	VF	XF	Unc
74	1972	—	—	.10	.20	.40
	1973	—	—	.10	.20	.40
	1974	—	—	.10	.20	.40
	1975	—	—	.10	.20	.40
	1976	—	—	.10	.20	.40
	1977	—	—	.10	.20	.40
	1978	—	—	.10	.20	.40
	1979	—	—	.10	.20	.40
	1980	—	—	.10	.15	.30
	1981	—	—	.10	.15	.30
	1981	—	—	—	Proof	—
	1982	—	—	.10	.15	.30
	1983	—	—	.10	.15	.30
	1984	—	—	.10	.15	.30
	1985	—	—	.10	.15	.30
	1986	—	—	.10	.15	.30
	1987	26.945	—	.10	.15	.30
	1988	17.000	—	.10	.15	.30
	1989	—	—	.10	.15	.30
	1990	—	—	.10	.15	.30

NOTE: Varieties exist.

25 HALERU

ALUMINUM

KM#	Date	Mintage	Fine	VF	XF	Unc
54	1962	—	.10	.15	.20	.35
	1963	—	.10	.15	.20	.35
	1964	—	.10	.15	.20	.35
	1964	—	—	—	Proof	—

NOTE: 25 Haleru ceased to be legal tender Dec. 31, 1972.

50 HALERU

BRONZE

KM#	Date	Mintage	Fine	VF	XF	Unc
55.1	1963	—	.10	.20	.30	.45
	1964	—	.10	.20	.30	.45
	1965	—	.10	.20	.30	.45
	1965	—	—	—	Proof	—
	1969	—	.10	.20	.30	.45
	1970	—	.10	.20	.30	.40
	1971	—	.10	.20	.30	.40

Obv: Small date, w/o dots.

55.2	1969	—	12.50	22.50	40.00	75.00

COPPER-NICKEL

KM#	Date	Mintage	Fine	VF	XF	Unc
89	1978	534.500	—	—	.10	.50
	1979	Inc. Ab.	—	—	.10	.50
	1980	Inc. Ab.	—	—	.10	.50
	1981	Inc. Ab.	—	—	.10	.50
	1981	Inc. Ab.	—	—	Proof	—
	1982	Inc. Ab.	—	—	.10	.50
	1983	Inc. Ab.	—	—	.10	.50
	1984	Inc. Ab.	—	—	.10	.50
	1985	Inc. Ab.	—	—	.10	.50
	1986	Inc. Ab.	—	—	.10	.50
	1987	5.108	—	—	.10	.50
	1988	5.012	—	—	.10	.50
	1989	*	—	—	.10	.50
	1990	*	—	—	.10	.50

NOTE: Date varieties exist.

NOTE: Mintage included w/1978's figure.

KORUNA

ALUMINUM-BRONZE

KM#	Date	Mintage	Fine	VF	XF	Unc
50	1961	—	—	.15	.30	.60
	1962	—	—	.15	.30	.60
	1963	—	—	.15	.30	.60
	1964	—	—	.15	.30	.60
	1965	—	—	.15	.30	.60
	1966	—	.40	.65	.90	1.25
	1967	—	—	.15	.30	.60
	1968	—	—	.15	.30	.60
	1969	—	—	.15	.30	.60
	1970	—	—	.15	.30	.60
	1971	—	—	.15	.30	.60
	1975	—	—	.15	.30	.60
	1976	—	—	.15	.30	.60
	1977	—	—	.15	.30	.75
	1979	—	—	.15	.30	.75
	1980	—	—	.15	.30	.75
	1981	—	—	.15	.30	.75
	1981	—	—	—	Proof	—
	1982	—	—	.15	.30	.75
	1983	—	—	.15	.30	.75
	1984	—	—	.15	.30	.75
	1985	—	—	.15	.30	.75
	1986	—	—	.15	.30	.75
	1987	—	—	.15	.30	.75
	1988	—	—	.15	.30	.75
	1989	—	—	.15	.30	.75
	1990	—	—	.15	.30	.75

NOTE: Date varieties exist.

2 KORUNY

COPPER-NICKEL

KM#	Date	Mintage	Fine	VF	XF	Unc
75	1972	—	—	.25	.45	1.00
	1973	—	—	.25	.45	1.00
	1974	—	—	.25	.45	1.00
	1975	—	—	.25	.45	1.00

KM#	Date	Mintage	Fine	VF	XF	Unc
75	1976	—	—	.25	.45	1.00
	1977	—	—	.25	.65	1.50
	1980	—	—	.25	.35	.75
	1981	—	—	.25	.35	.75
	1981	—	—	—	Proof	—
	1982	—	—	.25	.35	.75
	1983	—	—	.25	.35	.75
	1984	—	—	.25	.35	.75
	1985	—	—	.25	.35	.75
	1986	—	—	.25	.35	.75
	1987	—	—	.25	.35	.75
	1988	—	—	.25	.35	.75
	1989	—	—	.25	.35	.75
	1990	—	—	.25	.35	.75

NOTE: Date and edge varieties exist.

3 KORUNY

COPPER-NICKEL

57	1965	—	—	.50	1.00	2.50
	1966	—	—	.50	1.00	2.50
	1966	—	—	—	Proof	Rare
	1968	—	—	.45	.85	2.00
	1969	—	—	.40	.75	1.50

5 KORUN

COPPER-NICKEL

60	1966	—	—	.75	1.00	2.00
	1966	—	—	—	Proof	Rare

1966 Varieties on obverse of coin
Large Date: No space between letter B in REPUBLIC and coat of arms.
Small Date: Space between letter B in REPUBLIC and coat of arms.
Plain Edge: No ornamental inscription on edge (error coin).

NOTE: So far there has been no indication of any of the varieties as being scarce.

	1967	—	—	—	.75	1.50
	1968	—	—	—	.75	1.50
	1969 straight date					
		—	—	—	.75	1.50
	1969 date in semi-circle					
		—	.75	1.25	2.00	3.00
	1970	—	—	—	.75	1.50
	1973 (2 vars.)	—	—	—	.75	1.25
	1974 (3 vars.)	—	—	—	.75	1.25
	1975	—	—	—	.75	1.25
	1978	—	—	—	.75	1.25
	1979	—	—	—	.75	1.25
	1980	—	—	—	.75	1.25
	1981	—	—	—	.75	1.25
	1981	—	—	—	Proof	—
	1982	—	—	—	.75	1.25
	1983	—	—	—	.75	1.25
	1984	—	—	—	.75	1.25
	1985	—	—	—	.75	1.25
	1986	—	—	—	.75	1.25
	1987	—	—	—	.75	1.25
	1988	—	—	—	.75	1.25
	1989	—	—	—	.75	1.25
	1990	—	—	—	.75	1.25

(CSFR)

CZECH SLOVAK
FEDERAL REPUBLIC
1990-1992

MINT MARKS

(k) - Kremnica
(l) - Llantrisant

HALER

ALUMINUM

149	1991	.055	—		In sets only	.10
	1992	.050	—		In sets only	.10

5 HALERU

ALUMINUM

KM#	Date	Mintage	Fine	VF	XF	Unc
150	1991	.010	—	—	.10	.25
	1991	.055	—	In sets only		
	1992	.049	—	—	.10	.25
	1992	.050	—	In sets only		

10 HALERU

ALUMINUM

146	1991	.040	—	—	.20	.50
	1991	.055	—	In sets only		
	1992	.045	—	—	.20	.50
	1992	.050	—	In sets only		

20 HALERU

ALUMINUM-BRONZE

143	1991	.030	—	—	.20	.50
	1991	.055	—	In sets only		—
	1992	.035	—	—	.20	.50
	1992	.050	—	In sets only		—

50 HALERU

COPPER-NICKEL

144	1991	.020	—	—	.35	.75
	1991	.055	—	In sets only		
	1992	.010	—	—	.35	.75
	1992	.050	—	In sets only		

KORUNA

COPPER-ALUMINUM

151	1991	.020	—	—	.50	1.00
	1991	.050	—	In sets only		—
	1992	.020	—	—	.50	1.00
	1992	.050	—	In sets only		—

2 KORUNY

COPPER-NICKEL

148	1991(k)	.021	—	—	.60	1.25
	1991(k)	.055	—	In sets only		
	1991(l)	.020	—	—	.60	1.25
	1992	.010	—	—	—	1.25
	1992	.050	—	In sets only		—

5 KORUN

COPPER-NICKEL

KM#	Date	Mintage	Fine	VF	XF	Unc
152	1991(k)	.021	—	—	.75	2.00
	1991(k)	.055	—	In sets only		
	1991(l)	.020	—	—	—	—
	1992	.010	—	—	.75	2.00
	1992	.050	—	In sets only		

10 KORUN

NICKEL-BRONZE
Thomas G. Masaryk
Designer initials below bust.

139.1	1990	.010	—	—	2.00	5.00
	1992	.025	—	In sets only		—
	1993	2.500	—	—	2.50	7.00

NOTE: Designer initial varieties exist.

Designer name below bust: RONAI.

139.2	1990	Inc. Ab.	—	2.00	5.00	10.00

M.R. Stefanik

153	1991	10.000	—	—	2.00	5.00
	1993	2.526	—	—	2.50	7.00

A. Rasin

159	1992	5.050	—	—	2.00	5.00
	1993	—	—	—	2.00	7.00

CZECH REPUBLIC

The Czech Republic was formerly united with Slovakia as Czechoslovakia. It is bordered in the west by Germany, to the north by Poland, to the east by Slovakia and to the south by Austria. It consists of 3 major regions: Bohemia, Moravia and Silesia and has an area of 30,450 sq. mi. (78,864 sq. km.) and a population of 10.4 million. Capital: Prague (Praha). Agriculture and livestock are chief occupations while coal deposits are the main mineral resources.

The Czech lands were united with the Slovaks to form the Czechoslovak State, which came into existence on Oct. 28, 1918 upon the dissolution of the Austrian-Hungarian Empire. In 1938, this territory was broken up for the benefit of Germany, Poland, and Hungary by the Munich Agreement. In March 1939 the German influenced Slovak government proclaimed Slovakia independent. Germany incorporated the Czech lands into the Third Reich as the "Protectorate of Bohemia and Moravia." A Czech government-in-exile was set up in London in July 1940. The Soviets and USA forces liberated the area by May 1945. Communist influence increased steadily while pressure for liberalization culminated in the overthrow of the Stalinist leader Antonin Novotny and his associates in 1968. The Communist Party then introduced far reaching reforms which resulted in warnings from Moscow (Moskva), followed by occupation and stationing of Soviet forces. Mass demonstrations for reform began again in Nov. 1989 and the Federal Assembly abolished the Communist Party's sole right to govern. The new government formed was the Czech and Slovak Federal Republic. A movement for Democratic Slovakia was apparent in the June 1992 elections and on December 31, 1992, the CSFR was dissolved and the two new republics came into being on Jan. 1, 1993.

NOTE: For earlier issues see Czechoslovakia, Bohemia and Moravia or Slovakia listings.

MINT MARKS

(c) castle = Hamburg

(cr) - cross = British Royal Mint

(l) - leaf = Royal Canadian

(m) - monogram = Jablonec nad Nisau

(mk) - MK in circle = Kremnica

(o) - broken circle = Vienna

MONETARY SYSTEM
1 Czechoslovak Koruna (Kcs) = 1 Czech Koruna (Kc)
1 Koruna = 100 Haleru

10 HALERU

ALUMINUM

KM#	Date	Mintage	VF	XF	Unc
6	1993(c)	100.000	—	—	.20
	1993(m)	94.902	—	—	.20
	1994(c)	—	—	—	.20
	1994(m)	53.127	—	—	.20
	1994(m)	*2,000	—	Proof	—
	1995(m)	—	—	—	.20
	1996(m)	—	—	—	.20
	1997(m)	—	—	—	.20
	1997(m)	—	—	Proof	3.50
	1998(m)	—	—	—	.20
	1998(m)	—	—	Proof	2.00

20 HALERU

ALUMINUM

KM#	Date	Mintage	VF	XF	Unc
2	1993(c)	80.000	—	—	.30
	1993(m)	30.558	—	—	.30
	1994(c)	9.310	—	—	.30
	1994(m)	81.291	—	—	.30
	1994(m)	*2,000	—	Proof	—
	1995(m)	—	—	—	.30
	1996(m)	—	—	—	.30
	1997(m)	—	—	—	.30
	1997(m)	—	—	Proof	5.00
	1998(m)	—	—	—	.30
	1998(m)	—	—	Proof	3.00

50 HALERU

ALUMINUM

3	1993(c)	70.003	—	—	.50
	1993(m)	30.474	—	—	.50
	1994(c)	—	—	—	.50
	1994(m)	21.109	—	—	.50
	1994(m)	*2,000	—	Proof	—
	1995(m)	—	—	—	.50
	1996(m)	—	—	—	.50
	1997(m)	—	—	—	.50
	1997(m)	—	—	Proof	5.00
	1998(m)	—	—	—	.50
	1998(m)	—	—	Proof	3.00

KORUNA

 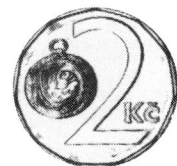

NICKEL CLAD STEEL

7	1993(l)	102.431	—	—	.60
	1994(m)	52.162	—	—	.60
	1994(l)	—	—	—	.60
	1995(m)	—	—	—	.60
	1996(m)	—	—	—	.60
	1997(m)	—	—	—	.60
	1997(m)	—	—	Proof	6.50
	1998(m)	—	—	—	.60
	1998(m)	—	—	Proof	4.00

2 KORUN

NICKEL CLAD STEEL

9	1993(l)	80.001	—	—	.65
	1994(m)	30.310	—	—	.65
	1994(l)	18.360	—	—	.65
	1995(m)	—	—	—	.65
	1996(m)	—	—	—	.65
	1997(m)	—	—	—	.65
	1997(m)	—	—	Proof	8.50
	1998(m)	—	—	—	.65
	1998(m)	—	—	Proof	5.00

5 KORUN

NICKEL PLATED STEEL

8	1993(l)	70.001	—	—	1.00
	1994(m)	30.475	—	—	1.00
	1994(l)	14.400	—	—	1.00
	1995(m)	—	—	—	1.00
	1996(m)	52.162	—	—	1.00
	1997(m)	—	—	—	1.00
	1997(m)	—	—	Proof	10.00

KM#	Date	Mintage	VF	XF	Unc
8	1998(m)	—	—	—	1.00
	1998(m)	—	—	Proof	6.00

10 KORUN

COPPER PLATED STEEL
Brno Cathedral

4	1993(c)	70.001	—	—	2.00
	1994(c)		—	—	2.00
	1994(m)	20.677	—	—	1.50
	1995(m)	—	—	—	1.50
	1996(m)	—	—	—	1.50
	1997(m)	—	—	—	1.50
	1997(m)	—	—	Proof	12.00
	1998(m)	—	—	—	1.50
	1998(m)	—	—	Proof	7.00

NOTE: Position of designer's initials on reverse change with 1996 strike.

20 KORUN

BRASS PLATED STEEL
St. Wenceslas (Duke Vaclav) on Horse

5	1993(c)	55.001	—	1.00	3.00
	1994(c)	.100	in sets only		3.50
	1995(m)	—	in sets only		2.50
	1996(m)	—	in sets only		2.50
	1997(m)	—	—	—	2.50
	1997(m)	—	—	Proof	16.50
	1998(m)	—	—	—	2.50
	1998(m)	—	—	Proof	10.00

50 KORUN

BRASS PLATED STEEL center in
COPPER PLATED STEEL ring
Prague City View

1	1993(c)	35.001	—	2.50	7.50
	1994(c)	.100	in sets only		9.00
	1995(m)	—	in sets only		9.00
	1996(m)	—	in sets only		9.00
	1997(m)	—	in sets only		9.00
	1997(m)	—	—	Proof	35.00
	1998(m)	—	—	—	9.00
	1998(m)	—	—	Proof	20.00

DANISH WEST INDIES

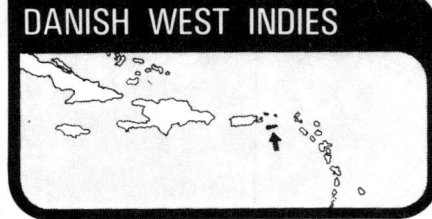

The Danish West Indies (now the U.S. organized unincorporated territory of the Virgin Islands of the United States) consisted of the islands of St. Thomas, St. John, St. Croix, and 62 islets in the Caribbean Sea roughly 40 miles (64 km.) east of Puerto Rico. The islands have a combined area of 133 sq. mi. (352 sq. km.) and a population of *106,000. Capital: Charlotte Amalie. Tourism is the principal industry. Watch movements, costume jewelry, pharmaceuticals, and rum are exported.

The Virgin Islands were discovered by Columbus in 1493, during his second voyage to America. During the 17th century, individual islands, actually the peaks of a submerged mountain range, were held by Spain, Holland, England, France and Denmark. These islands were also the favorite resorts of the buccaneers operating in the Caribbean and the coastal waters of eastern North America. Control of most of the 100-island group finally passed to Denmark, with England securing the easterly remainder. The Danish islands had their own coinage from the early 18th century, based on but unequal to, Denmark's homeland system. In the late 18th and early 19th centuries, Danish minor copper and silver coinage augmented the islands currency. The Danish islands were purchased by the United States in 1917 for $25 million, mainly to forestall their acquisition by Germany and because they command the Anegada Passage into the Caribbean Sea, a strategic point on the defense perimeter of the Panama Canal.

RULERS
Danish, until 1917

MINT MARKS
(h) - Copenhagen - heart
(o) - Altona orb

MINTMASTERS INITIALS
MONEYERS INITIALS

Letter	Date	Name
GJ	1901-1933	Knud Gunnar Jensen
AH	1908-1924	Andreas Frederik Vilhelm Hansen

MONETARY SYSTEM
(From 1904)

5 Bit = 1 Cent
5 Francs = 1 Daler

1/2 CENT - 2 1/2 BIT

BRONZE
Mintmasters initial: P. Moneyers initials: GJ.

KM#	Date	Mintage	VG	Fine	VF	XF
74	1905(h)	.190	2.00	5.00	10.00	20.00
	1905(h)	—	—	—	P/L	Rare

CENT - 5 BIT

BRONZE
Mintmasters initial: P. Moneyers initials: GJ.

75	1905(h)	.500	1.50	3.00	5.50	15.00

Mintmasters initials: VBP. Moneyers initials: AH-GJ.

83	1913(h)	.200	4.00	8.00	22.00	45.00

2 CENTS - 10 BIT

BRONZE
Mintmasters initial: P. Moneyers initials: GJ.

KM#	Date	Mintage	VG	Fine	VF	XF
76	1905(h)	.150	2.25	5.00	10.00	25.00
	1905(h)	20 pcs.	—	—	P/L	Rare

5 CENTS - 25 BIT

NICKEL
Mintmasters initial: P. Moneyers initials: GJ.

77	1905(h)	.199	1.00	2.50	8.00	20.00
	1905(h)	20 pcs.	—	—	P/L	Rare

10 CENTS - 50 BIT

2.5000 g, .800 SILVER, .0643 oz ASW
Mintmasters initial: P. Moneyers initials: GJ.

78	1905(h)	.175	1.75	3.75	10.00	20.00
	1905(h)	20 pcs.	—	—	P/L	Rare

20 CENTS - 1 FRANC

5.0000 g, .800 SILVER, .1286 oz ASW
Mintmasters initial: P. Moneyers initials: GJ.

79	1905(h)	.150	5.00	11.50	36.00	75.00
	1905(h)	20 pcs.	—	—	P/L	Rare

Mintmasters initial: P. Moneyers initials: GJ.

81	1907(h)	.101	8.00	16.50	35.00	70.00
	1907(h)	10 pcs.	—	—	P/L	Rare

40 CENTS - 2 FRANCS

10.0000 g, .800 SILVER, .2572 oz ASW
Mintmasters initial: P. Moneyers initials: GJ.

80	1905(h)	.038	17.50	35.00	75.00	165.00
	1905(h)	20 pcs.	—	—	P/L	Rare

Mintmasters initial: P. Moneyers initials: GJ.

KM#	Date	Mintage	VG	Fine	VF	XF
82	1907(h)	.025	25.00	50.00	120.00	200.00
	1907(h) 10 pcs.	—			P/L	1100.

4 DALER - 20 FRANCS

6.4516 g, .900 GOLD, .1867 oz AGW
Mintmasters initial: P. Moneyers initials: GJ.

KM#	Date	Mintage	Fine	VF	XF	Unc
72	1904(h)	.121	150.00	250.00	350.00	550.00
	1905(h)	I.A.	150.00	275.00	400.00	650.00

10 DALER - 50 FRANCS

16.1290 g, .900 GOLD, .4667 oz AGW
Mintmasters initial: P. Moneyers initials: GJ.

73	1904(h)	2,005	1250.	2000.	4000.	6500.

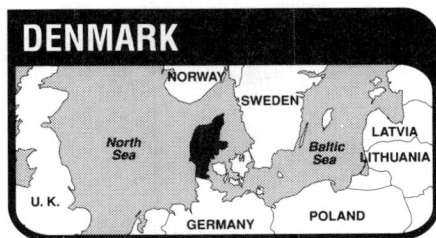

DENMARK

The Kingdom of Denmark, a constitutional monarchy located at the mouth of the Baltic Sea, has an area of 16,639 sq. mi. (43,070 sq. km.) and a population of 5.2 million. Capital: Copenhagen. Most of the country is arable. Agriculture, which employs the majority of the people, is conducted by small farmers served by cooperatives. The largest industries are food processing, iron and metal, and fishing. Machinery, meats (chiefly bacon), dairy products and chemicals are exported.

Denmark, a great power during the Viking period of the 9th-11th centuries, conducted raids on western Europe and England, and in the 11th century united England, Denmark and Norway under the rule of King Canute. Despite a struggle between the crown and the nobility (13th-14th centuries) which forced the King to grant a written constitution, Queen Margaret (1387-1412) succeeded in uniting Denmark, Norway, Sweden, Finland and Greenland under the Danish crown, placing all of Scandinavia under the rule of Denmark. An unwise alliance with Napoleon contributed to the dismembering of the empire and fostered a liberal movement which succeeded in making Denmark a constitutional monarchy in 1849.

The present decimal system of coinage was introduced in 1874.

RULERS

Christian IX, 1863-1906
Frederik VIII, 1906-1912
Christian X, 1912-1947
Frederik IX, 1947-1972
Margrethe II, 1972-

MINT MARKS

(c) - Copenhagen, crown
(h) - Copenhagen, heart
(o) - Altona, orb

MINTMASTERS INITIALS

Copenhagen

Letter	Date	Name
*P,VBP	1893-1918	Vilhelm Buchard Poulsen
HCN	1919-1927	Hans Christian Nielsen
N	1927-1955	Niels Peter Nielsen
C	1956-1971	Alfred Frederik Christiansen
S	1971-1978	Vagn Sorensen
B	1978-1981	Peter M. Bjarno
R, NR	1982-1989	N. Norregaard Rasmussen
LG	1989-	Laust Grove

*NOTE: The letter P was only used on Danish West Indies coins.

MONEYERS INITIALS

Copenhagen

HC	1873-1901	Harald Conradsen
GI, GJ	1901-1933	Knud Gunnar Jensen
AH	1908-1924	Andreas Frederik Vilhelm Hansen
HS, S	1933-1968	Harald Salomon
B	1968-1983	Frode Bahnsen
A	1986-	Johan Alkjaer
HV	1986-	Hanne Varming
JP, JPA	1989-	Jan Petersen

MONETARY SYSTEM

100 Ore = 1 Krone

ORE

BRONZE
Mintmasters initials: VBP.

KM#	Date	Mintage	Fine	VF	XF	Unc
792.2	1902/802(h)					
		2.977	3.00	5.00	11.00	30.00
	1902(h)	I.A.	2.50	3.75	9.00	25.00
	1904/804(h)					
		4.962	1.75	3.50	7.00	20.00
	1904(h)	I.A.	1.25	2.50	5.00	13.50

NOTE: Earlier dates (1894-1899) exist for this type.

Mintmasters initials: VBP. Moneyers initials: GJ.

804	1907(h)	5.975	1.25	3.00	6.00	12.50
	1909(h)	2.985	1.75	4.00	7.50	15.00
	1910(h)	2.994	2.50	5.00	11.00	24.00
	1912(h)	3.006	2.00	5.00	9.00	20.00

KM#	Date	Mintage	Fine	VF	XF	Unc
812.1	1913(h)	5.011	1.25	1.75	2.50	8.50
	1915(h)	4.940	1.75	3.00	5.00	10.00
	1916(h)	2.439	1.75	3.75	6.00	13.50
	1917(h)	4.564	20.00	30.00	50.00	85.00

IRON

812.1a	1918(h)	6.776	2.50	5.00	15.00	40.00

BRONZE
Mintmasters initials: HCN. Moneyers initials: GJ.

812.2	1919(h)	4.586	1.25	1.75	5.00	11.00
	1920(h)	2.367	8.00	12.50	27.50	60.00
	1921(h)	3.121	1.75	3.00	4.25	11.00
	1922(h)	3.267	2.50	3.50	5.50	12.00
	1923(h)	2.938	2.25	3.00	5.00	11.00

IRON

812.2a	1919(h)	.931	6.00	17.50	35.00	75.00

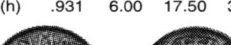

BRONZE

826.1	1926(h)	1.572	3.75	7.50	25.00	60.00
	1927(h) Inc. Ab.	.10	.35	4.25	18.50

Mintmasters initial: N. Moneyers initials: GJ.

826.2	1927(h)	I.A.	5.00	12.25	30.00	90.00
	1928(h)	29.691	.10	.25	3.50	15.00
	1929(h)	5.172	.10	.25	3.50	18.50
	1930(h)	5.306	.10	.20	3.50	22.00
	1932(h)	5.089	.10	.20	3.50	18.50
	1933(h)	2.095	.25	1.25	6.00	30.00
	1934(h)	3.665	—	.10	1.25	9.00
	1935(h)	5.668	—	.10	1.25	7.50
	1936(h)	5.584	—	.10	.50	4.00
	1937(h)	6.877	—	.10	.50	3.75
	1938(h)	3.850	—	.10	.50	3.00
	1939(h)	5.662	—	.10	.35	3.00
	1940(h)	1.965	—	.10	.35	2.50

NOTE: For coins dated 1941 refer to Faeroe Islands listings at the end of Denmark.

ZINC
Mintmasters initial: N. Moneyers initial: S.

832	1941(h)	21.570	.10	.35	6.00	35.00
	1942(h)	6.997	.10	.35	6.00	35.00
	1943(h)	15.082	.10	.35	6.00	35.00
	1944(h)	11.981	.10	.35	6.00	35.00
	1945(h)	.916	1.25	2.50	12.50	45.00
	1946(h)	.712	3.75	8.00	17.50	70.00

839.1	1948(h)	.460	1.50	3.00	9.00	40.00
	1949(h)	2.513	.35	1.00	3.75	40.00
	1950(h)	9.453	.25	.50	3.00	30.00
	1951(h)	2.931	.35	1.25	3.75	40.00
	1952(h)	7.626	.10	.35	2.50	20.00
	1953(h)	11.994	.10	.25	2.50	20.00
	1954(h)	12.642	.10	.25	1.75	17.50
	1955(h)	14.177	.10	.25	1.75	17.50

Mintmasters initial: C. Moneyers initial: S.

839.2	1956(h)	20.211	.10	.25	1.75	6.25
	1957(h)	20.900	.10	.25	1.75	6.25
	1958(h)	16.021	—	.10	.75	5.00
	1959(h)	15.929	—	.10	.75	5.00
	1960(h)	23.982	—	.10	.75	3.75
	1961(h)	18.986	—	.10	.60	3.00
	1962(h)	16.992	—	.10	.50	1.75
	1963(h)	28.986	—	.10	.50	1.75
	1964(h)	21.971	—	.10	.35	1.75
	1965(h)	29.943	—	.10	.25	1.75
	1966(h)	35.907	—	.10	.25	1.75
	1967(h)	32.959	—	.10	.25	1.75
	1968(h)	21.889	—	—	.10	1.00
	1969(h)	29.243	—	—	.10	1.00
	1970(h)	22.970	—	—	.10	.60
	1971(h)	21.983	—	—	.10	.60

Mintmasters initial: S. Moneyers initial: S.

839.3	1972(h)	13.000	—	—	.10	.75

BRONZE
Mintmasters initial: C. Moneyers initial: S.

846	1960(h)	8.990	—	—	1.25	1.75
	1962(h)	I.A.	—	—	1.25	1.75
	1963(h)	9.980	—	—	1.25	1.75
	1964(h)	2.990	—	—	1.25	1.75

NOTE: Only an estimated 100,000 of each date of KM#846 were sold, the balance being remelted.

2 ORE

BRONZE
Mintmasters initials: VBP.

KM#	Date	Mintage	Fine	VF	XF	Unc
793.2	1902/802(h)	3.502	2.00	4.25	8.00	50.00
	1902(h)	I.A.	1.75	3.50	7.00	45.00
	1906(h)	2.498	4.25	9.00	15.00	50.00

NOTE: Earlier dates (1894-1899) exist for this type.

Mintmasters initials: VBP. Moneyers initials: GJ.

KM#	Date	Mintage	Fine	VF	XF	Unc
805	1907(h)	2.502	1.25	3.00	9.75	27.50
	1909(h)	2.485	2.50	5.00	22.50	60.00
	1912(h)	2.480	2.50	5.00	13.50	37.50

KM#	Date	Mintage	Fine	VF	XF	Unc
813.1	1913(h)	.373	30.00	55.00	85.00	175.00
	1914(h)	2.126	3.00	5.50	8.50	35.00
	1915(h)	2.485	2.50	5.50	8.50	30.00
	1916(h)	1.383	3.75	6.25	10.00	35.00
	1917(h)	1.837	17.50	30.00	50.00	100.00

IRON

KM#	Date	Mintage	Fine	VF	XF	Unc
813.1a	1918(h)	4.161	2.50	5.00	17.50	60.00

BRONZE
Mintmasters initials: HCN. Moneyers initials: GJ.

KM#	Date	Mintage	Fine	VF	XF	Unc
813.2	1919(h)	5.503	7.50	13.50	30.00	60.00
	1920(h)	2.528	1.25	1.75	4.25	25.00
	1921(h)	2.158	4.25	6.75	10.00	22.50
	1923(h)	2.625	3.00	6.50	8.00	22.50

IRON

KM#	Date	Mintage	Fine	VF	XF	Unc
813.2a	1919(h)	1.944	22.50	45.00	85.00	200.00

BRONZE

KM#	Date	Mintage	Fine	VF	XF	Unc
827.1	1926(h)	.301	45.00	65.00	200.00	550.00
	1927(h)	15.359	.10	.20	3.75	25.00

Mintmasters initial: N. Moneyers initials: GJ.

KM#	Date	Mintage	Fine	VF	XF	Unc
827.2	1927(h)	I.A.	1.50	2.50	40.00	175.00
	1928(h)	5.758	.10	.20	3.00	20.00
	1929(h)	6.817	.10	.20	3.00	40.00
	1930(h)	2.327	.75	1.50	7.50	75.00
	1931(h)	5.135	.10	.20	3.00	35.00
	1932(h)	I.A.	1.50	2.50	25.00	115.00
	1934(h)	.756	.60	1.25	9.00	50.00
	1935(h)	1.391	.10	.20	1.75	25.00
	1936(h)	2.973	.10	.20	1.25	25.00
	1937(h)	3.437	.10	.20	1.25	12.50
	1938(h)	2.177	—	.10	.60	6.25
	1939(h)	3.165	—	.10	.60	3.75
	1940(h)	1.582	—	.10	.35	2.50

NOTE: For coins dated 1941 refer to Faeroe Islands listings at the end of Denmark.

ALUMINUM
Mintmasters initial: N. Moneyers initial: S.

KM#	Date	Mintage	Fine	VF	XF	Unc
833	1941(h)	26.205	.10	.75	3.00	15.00

ZINC

KM#	Date	Mintage	Fine	VF	XF	Unc
833a	1942(h)	12.934	.10	.50	7.50	45.00
	1943(h)	9.603	.10	.50	7.50	45.00
	1944(h)	6.069	.10	.50	7.50	45.00
833a	1945(h)	.329	4.25	9.00	35.00	100.00
	1947(h)	.589	1.75	3.00	17.50	70.00

KM#	Date	Mintage	Fine	VF	XF	Unc
840.1	1948(h)	1.927	.35	1.25	5.00	30.00
	1949(h)	1.603	5.00	20.00	55.00	175.00
	1950(h)	4.544	1.00	1.75	5.50	35.00
	1951(h)	3.766	1.75	3.00	11.00	55.00
	1952(h)	4.874	.10	.20	2.50	27.50
	1953(h)	8.112	.10	.20	2.50	21.50
	1954(h)	6.497	.10	.20	2.50	18.50
	1955(h)	6.968	—	.10	1.75	11.00

Mintmasters initial: C. Moneyers initial: S.

KM#	Date	Mintage	Fine	VF	XF	Unc
840.2	1956(h)	10.004	—	.10	1.50	6.75
	1957(h)	15.329	—	.10	1.25	6.25
	1958(h)	8.120	—	.10	1.25	5.50
	1959(h)	10.462	—	.10	1.25	5.00
	1960(h)	16.504	—	.10	1.00	3.75
	1961(h)	15.504	—	.10	1.00	3.00
	1962(h)	10.980	—	.10	1.00	3.00
	1963(h)	19.470	—	.10	.35	1.75
	1964(h)	15.411	—	.10	.35	1.50
	1965(h)	20.173	—	.10	.20	1.25
	1966(h)	21.949	—	.10	.20	1.25
	1967(h)	22.439	—	.10	.20	1.25
	1968(h)	17.632	—	—	.10	1.00
	1969(h)	29.276	—	—	.10	1.00
	1970(h)	23.864	—	—	.10	.60
	1971(h)	35.811	—	—	.10	.60

Mintmasters initial: S. Moneyers initial: S.

KM#	Date	Mintage	Fine	VF	XF	Unc
840.3	1972(h)	6.496	—	.15	.35	1.00

BRONZE
Mintmasters initial: C. Moneyers initial: S.

KM#	Date	Mintage	Fine	VF	XF	Unc
847	1960(h)	I.A.	—	—	1.25	1.50
	1962(h)	I.A.	—	—	1.25	1.50
	1963(h)	.990	—	—	1.25	1.50
	1964(h)	3.990	—	—	1.25	1.50
	1965(h)	11.980	—	—	1.25	1.50
	1966(h)	12.000	—	—	1.25	1.50

NOTE: Only an estimated 100,000 of each date of KM#847 were sold, the balance being remelted.

5 ORE

BRONZE
Mintmasters initials: VBP.

KM#	Date	Mintage	Fine	VF	XF	Unc
794.2	1902(h)	.601	12.00	21.50	50.00	160.00
	1904(h)	.397	27.50	50.00	100.00	270.00
	1906(h)	1.000	12.00	21.50	45.00	150.00

NOTE: Earlier dates (1894-1899) exist for this type.

Mintmasters initials: VBP. Moneyers initials: GJ.

KM#	Date	Mintage	Fine	VF	XF	Unc
806	1907(h)	1.000	7.50	13.50	25.00	55.00
	1908(h)	1.198	8.00	15.00	27.50	67.50
	1912(h)	.999	8.50	17.25	30.00	75.00

KM#	Date	Mintage	Fine	VF	XF	Unc
814.1	1913(h)	.216	60.00	125.00	175.00	300.00
	1914(h)	.785	9.00	18.50	25.00	50.00
	1916(h)	.887	11.00	22.50	35.00	65.00
	1917(h)	.494	12.00	25.00	45.00	85.00

IRON

KM#	Date	Mintage	Fine	VF	XF	Unc
814.1a	1918(h)	1.918	7.50	12.00	30.00	90.00

BRONZE

Mintmasters initials: HCN. Moneyers initials: GJ.

KM#	Date	Mintage	Fine	VF	XF	Unc
814.2	1919(h)	.994	4.25	7.50	11.00	25.00
	1920(h)	2.618	7.50	15.00	25.00	50.00
	1921(h)	3.248	6.25	10.00	15.00	30.00
	1923(h)	.369	110.00	220.00	285.00	425.00

IRON

KM#	Date	Mintage	Fine	VF	XF	Unc
814.2a	1919(h)	1.035	17.50	37.50	60.00	185.00

BRONZE

KM#	Date	Mintage	Fine	VF	XF	Unc
828.1	1926(h)	—	—	—*	Unique	—
	1927(h)	7.129	.10	.20	3.25	25.00

NOTE: Bruun Rassmussen Sale 10-86 $12,000. Beware of counterfeits.

Mintmasters initial: N. Moneyers initials: GJ.

KM#	Date	Mintage	Fine	VF	XF	Unc
828.2	1927(h)	I.A.	5.00	9.00	90.00	500.00
	1928(h)	4.685	.10	.50	4.25	30.00
	1929(h)	1.387	.35	.75	6.25	85.00
	1930(h)	1.339	.50	1.00	12.00	90.00
	1932(h)	1.011	.35	.75	11.00	85.00
	1934(h)	.524	.35	.75	9.00	85.00
	1935(h)	1.124	2.50	5.00	25.00	135.00
	1936(h)	1.091	.25	.50	3.75	37.50
	1937(h)	1.209	.25	.50	1.75	37.50
	1938(h)	1.093	.50	1.00	2.50	13.50
	1939(h)	1.402	.50	.25	.60	5.00
	1940(h)	2.735	.50	.25	.60	5.00

NOTE: For coins dated 1941 refer to Faeroe Islands listings at the end of Denmark.

ALUMINUM
Mintmasters initial: N. Moneyers initial: S.

KM#	Date	Mintage	Fine	VF	XF	Unc
834	1941(h)	16.984	.10	1.25	5.00	20.00

ZINC

KM#	Date	Mintage	Fine	VF	XF	Unc
834a	1942(h)	2.963	1.50	3.00	21.00	67.50
	1943(h)	4.522	.60	1.75	13.50	60.00
	1944(h)	3.744	.75	2.25	13.50	60.00
	1945(h)	.864	4.25	11.00	35.00	100.00

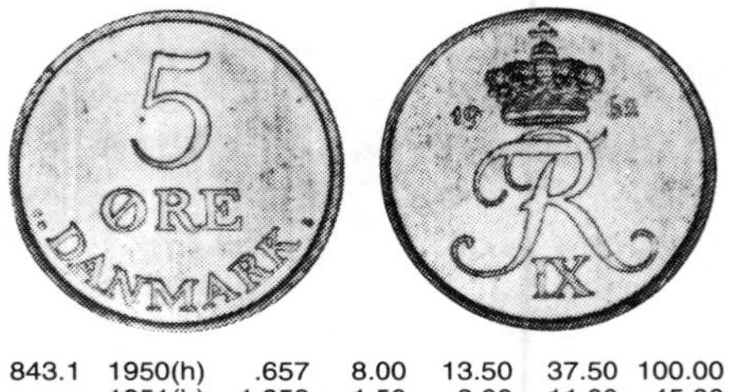

KM#	Date	Mintage	Fine	VF	XF	Unc
843.1	1950(h)	.657	8.00	13.50	37.50	100.00
	1951(h)	1.858	1.50	3.00	11.00	45.00
	1952(h)	3.562	.75	1.50	6.25	30.00
	1953(h)	5.944	.75	1.50	5.00	27.50
	1954(h)	3.060	.50	1.25	3.75	21.00
	1955(h)	2.314	1.50	2.50	5.50	21.00

Mintmasters initial: C. Moneyers initial: S.

KM#	Date	Mintage	Fine	VF	XF	Unc
843.2	1956(h)	5.888	1.50	1.25	3.00	12.00
	1957(h)	8.606	.25	.60	1.75	7.50
	1958(h)	9.598	.25	.60	1.75	6.25
	1959(h)	6.110	.10	.25	1.25	6.25
	1960(h)	11.800	.10	.25	1.25	3.75
	1961(h)	8.995	.25	.50	1.25	3.00
	1962(h)	9.729	.10	.25	1.00	3.00
	1963(h)	8.980	.10	.25	1.00	3.00
	1964(h)	6.738	1.00	1.75	3.75	7.50

BRONZE

KM#	Date	Mintage	Fine	VF	XF	Unc
848.1	1960(h)	3.760	.10	.35	1.25	6.25
	1962(h)	5.873	.35	.75	1.75	11.00
	1963(h)	23.287	—	.10	.60	3.75
	1964(h)	41.521	—	.10	.60	3.75
	1965(h)	14.229	—	.10	.60	3.75

Column 1

KM#	Date	Mintage	Fine	VF	XF	Unc
848.1	1966(h)	23.410	—	.10	.60	3.75
	1967(h)	15.094	—	.10	.60	3.75
	1968(h)	16.105	—	.10	.50	2.50
	1969(h)	23.594	—	.10	.35	1.25
	1970(h)	26.176	—	—	.10	1.25
	1971(h)	10.076	—	—	.10	1.25

Mintmasters initial: S. Moneyers initial: S.

KM#	Date	Mintage	Fine	VF	XF	Unc
848.2	1972(h)	27.938	—	—	.10	1.25

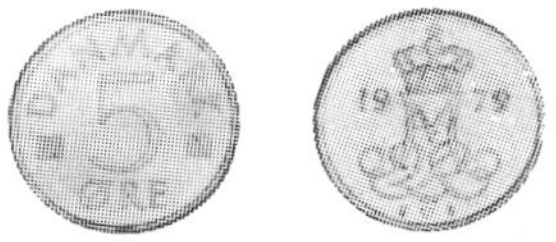

COPPER CLAD IRON
Mintmasters initial: S. Moneyers initial: B.

KM#	Date	Mintage	Fine	VF	XF	Unc
859.1	1973(h)	—	—	—	.10	.75
	1974(h)	71.796	—	—	.10	.75
	1975(h)	45.004	—	—	.10	.75
	1976(h)	73.296	—	—	.10	.75
	1977(h)	74.066	—	—	.10	.75
	1978(h)	52.425	—	—	.10	.75

Mintmasters initial: B. Moneyers initial: B.

859.2	1979(h)	58.953	—	—	.10	.85
	1980(h)	54.362	—	—	.10	.85
	1981(h)	52.201	—	—	.10	.35

Mintmasters initial: R. Moneyers initial: B.

859.3	1982(h)	74.296	—	—	.10	.35
	1983(h)	70.655	—	—	.10	.35
	1984(h)	27.599	—	—	.10	.35
	1985(h)	56.676	—	—	.10	.35
	1986(h)	62.496	—	—	.10	.35
	1987(h)	71.798	—	—	.10	.35
	1988(h)	48.925	—	—	.10	.35

10 ORE

1.4500 g, .400 SILVER, .0186 oz ASW
Mintmasters initials: VBP.

KM#	Date	Mintage	Fine	VF	XF	Unc
795.2	1903/803(h)	3.007	4.50	7.50	15.00	40.00
	1903(h)	I.A.	3.00	6.00	12.50	30.00
	1904(h)	2.449	20.00	32.50	45.00	90.00
	1905(h)	1.571	2.50	5.50	11.50	25.00

NOTE: Earlier dates (1894-1899) exist for this type.

Mintmasters initials: VBP. Moneyers initials: GJ.

807	1907(h)	3.068	3.75	6.25	11.00	22.50
	1910(h)	2.530	4.25	7.50	13.00	25.00
	1911(h)	.579	37.50	55.00	85.00	130.00
	1912(h)	1.951	5.00	8.50	13.00	25.00

818.1	1914(h)	2.128	5.50	8.50	12.50	22.50
	1915(h)	.915	7.50	12.50	17.50	25.00
	1916(h)	2.699	5.50	8.50	13.50	20.00
	1917(h)	6.003	3.00	5.00	7.50	10.00
	1918(h)	5.042	1.75	3.00	5.00	7.50

Mintmasters initials: HCN. Moneyers initials: GJ.

818.2	1919(h)	10.184	1.25	1.75	3.00	4.50

COPPER-NICKEL

818.2a	1920(h)	10.234	3.75	5.50	12.50	45.00
	1921(h)	8.064	3.75	5.00	11.00	37.50
	1922(h)	3.065	25.00	37.50	50.00	85.00
	1923(h)	1.790	350.00	525.00	650.00	875.00

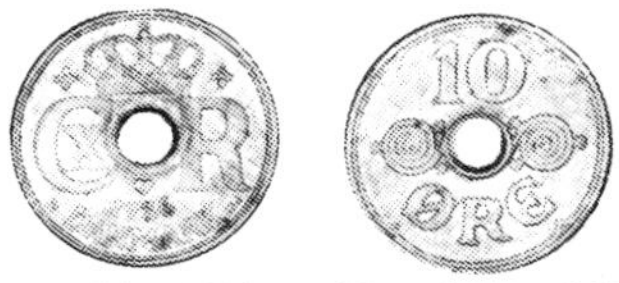

822.1	1924(h)	14.661	.25	1.00	3.00	15.00
	1925(h)	8.678	.35	1.00	6.25	37.50
	1926(h)	4.107	.35	1.00	6.25	45.00

Mintmasters initial: N. Moneyers initials: GJ.

822.2	1929(h)	5.037	1.00	1.50	6.25	50.00
	1931(h)	3.054	1.75	3.00	9.00	60.00
	1933(h)	1.274	8.50	16.00	37.50	100.00

Column 2

KM#	Date	Mintage	Fine	VF	XF	Unc
822.2	1934(h)	2.013	1.50	3.00	6.25	35.00
	1935(h)	2.848	1.75	2.75	5.50	30.00
	1936(h)	3.320	1.75	3.00	6.25	30.00
	1937(h)	2.234	1.25	1.75	5.00	25.00
	1938(h)	2.991	2.25	3.75	5.50	21.00
	1939(h)	2.973	1.25	2.50	4.00	21.00
	1940(h)	2.998	.60	1.25	2.50	12.50
	1941(h)	.748	3.75	6.25	9.00	25.00
	1946(h)	.460	2.75	5.00	6.75	11.00
	1947(h)	1.292	100.00	135.00	200.00	250.00

NOTE: For coins dated 1941 without mint mark or initials refer to Faeroe Islands listings at the end of Denmark.

ZINC

822.2a	1941(h)	7.706	1.25	2.50	12.50	37.50
	1942(h)	8.676	1.25	3.00	12.50	37.50
	1943(h)	2.181	2.50	4.25	15.00	40.00
	1944(h)	7.994	1.75	3.50	9.00	25.00
	1945(h)	1.280	50.00	80.00	115.00	225.00

COPPER-NICKEL
Mintmasters initial: N. Moneyers initial: S.

841.1	1948(h)	5.317	.25	.75	4.25	20.00
	1949(h)	7.595	.10	.25	3.75	17.50
	1950(h)	6.886	.10	.25	3.75	17.50
	1951(h)	8.763	.10	.25	4.25	27.50
	1952(h)	6.810	.10	.25	3.75	17.50
	1953(h)	11.946	.10	.25	3.75	16.00
	1954(h)	19.739	—	.10	1.75	11.00
	1955(h)	17.623	—	.10	1.75	11.00

Mintmasters initial: C. Moneyers initial: S.

841.2	1956(h)	12.323	—	.10	3.00	15.00
	1957(h)	13.227	—	.10	1.25	7.50
	1958(h)	10.870	—	.10	1.25	7.50
	1959(h)	1.255	35.00	50.00	75.00	150.00
	1960(h)	5.107	.10	.35	1.25	4.75

849.1	1960(h)	I.A.	.15	.50	1.00	4.75
	1961(h)	20.258	.10	.50	.50	6.25
	1962(h)	12.785	.10	.50	.50	6.25
	1963(h)	17.171	.10	.50	.50	4.75
	1964(h)	14.282	.10	.50	.50	4.25
	1965(h)	21.857	.10	.50	.50	4.25
	1966(h)	24.160	.10	.50	.25	3.75
	1967(h)	21.544	.10	.50	.25	2.25
	1968(h)	7.586	—	.50	.25	1.75
	1969(h)	31.534	—	—	.10	1.25
	1970(h)	37.813	—	—	.10	.35
	1971(h)	17.719	—	—	.10	.35

Mintmasters initial: S. Moneyers initial: S.

849.2	1972(h)	46.959	—	—	.10	.35

Mintmasters initial: S. Moneyers initial: B.

860.1	1973(h)	37.538	—	—	.10	.35
	1974(h)	38.570	—	—	.10	.35
	1975(h)	62.633	—	—	.10	.35
	1976(h)	64.359	—	—	.10	.35
	1977(h)	61.994	—	—	.10	.35
	1978(h)	30.302	—	—	.10	.35

Mintmasters initial: B. Moneyers initial: B.

860.2	1979(h)	10.224	—	—	.10	.35
	1980(h)	37.233	—	—	.10	.35
	1981(h)	51.565	—	—	.10	.25

Mintmasters initial: R. Moneyers initial: B.

860.3	1982(h)	40.195	—	—	.10	.25
	1983(h)	35.634	—	—	.10	.25
	1984(h)	17.828	—	—	.10	.25
	1985(h)	29.317	—	—	.10	.25
	1986(h)	46.254	—	—	.10	.25
	1987(h)	27.898	—	—	.10	.25
	1988(h)	29.400	—	—	.10	.25

25 ORE

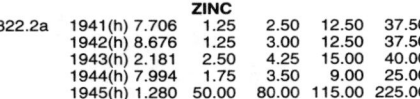

2.4200 g, .600 SILVER, .0467 oz ASW
Mintmasters initials: VBP.

		1.206	20.00	40.00	55.00	115.00

Column 3

KM#	Date	Mintage	Fine	VF	XF	Unc
796.2	1904(h)	1.922	18.50	35.00	50.00	100.00
	1905/805(h)	1.722	8.00	15.00	35.00	70.00
	1905(h)	I.A.	7.50	13.50	30.00	60.00

NOTE: Earlier dates (1894-1900) exist for this type.

Mintmasters initials: VBP. Moneyers initials: GJ.

808	1907(h)	2.009	7.50	13.50	21.50	40.00
	1911(h)	2.015	7.50	13.50	21.50	40.00

815.1	1913(h)	2.016	5.50	9.75	15.00	27.50
	1914(h)	.347	115.00	175.00	225.00	300.00
	1915(h)	2.862	4.25	8.00	12.50	21.00
	1916(h)	.938	13.50	20.00	30.00	45.00
	1917(h)	1.354	55.00	85.00	110.00	160.00
	1918(h)	2.090	8.00	12.50	18.50	27.50

Mintmasters initials: HCN. Moneyers initials: GJ.

815.2	1919(h)	9.295	1.75	2.50	3.75	6.25

COPPER-NICKEL

815.2a	1920(h)	12.288	3.75	6.25	17.50	45.00
	1921(h)	9.444	3.00	5.00	17.50	45.00
	1922(h)	5.701	35.00	45.00	60.00	110.00

823.1	1924(h)	8.035	.35	2.25	5.50	21.50
	1925(h)	1.906	6.25	10.50	25.00	80.00
	1926(h)	2.659	1.75	3.75	7.50	60.00

Mintmasters initial: N. Moneyers initials: GJ.

823.2	1929(h)	.886	2.50	5.00	9.75	60.00
	1930(h)	3.423	3.00	6.25	14.75	75.00
	1932(h)	.846	11.00	17.25	27.50	85.00
	1933(h)	.479	30.00	45.00	60.00	150.00
	1934(h)	1.660	3.00	5.00	11.00	50.00
	1935(h)	1.032	15.00	27.50	42.50	110.00
	1936(h)	1.453	2.50	3.75	8.75	42.50
	1937(h)	1.612	4.25	7.50	12.50	30.00
	1938(h)	1.794	3.75	5.50	11.00	35.00
	1939(h)	1.972	15.00	25.00	40.00	80.00
	1940(h)	1.356	1.75	3.00	5.50	15.00
	1946(h)	2.323	2.25	3.75	5.50	12.00
	1947(h)	1.751	5.50	9.25	12.00	18.50

NOTE: For coins dated 1941 refer to Faeroe Islands listings at the end of Denmark.

ZINC

823.2a	1941(h)	15.332	5.00	9.00	16.00	40.00
	1942(h)	.997	1.75	3.75	7.50	35.00
	1943(h)	5.784	5.00	10.00	18.50	45.00
	1944(h)	10.665	1.75	4.25	7.50	30.00
	1945(h)	4.543	3.00	5.50	8.75	30.00

COPPER-NICKEL
Mintmasters initial: N. Moneyers initial: S.

842.1	1948(h)	1.853	3.00	6.75	13.50	45.00
	1949(h)	15.000	.10	.35	3.00	15.00
	1950(h)	13.771	.10	.35	5.00	27.50
	1951(h)	5.045	.10	.35	6.25	30.00
	1952(h)	2.018	1.00	2.00	15.00	45.00
	1953(h)	9.553	.10	.35	3.00	11.00
	1954(h)	11.337	.10	.35	1.75	7.50
	1955(h)	6.385	.25	.35	1.75	7.50

Mintmasters initial: C. Moneyers initial: S.

842.2	1956(h)	10.228	.10	.25	1.25	6.25
	1957(h)	7.421	.10	.25	1.00	5.00
	1958(h)	3.600	.35	.60	1.50	5.50
	1959(h)	2.211	2.50	5.00	8.00	12.50
	1960(h)	3.453	.35	.60	1.75	6.25

KM#	Date	Mintage	Fine	VF	XF	Unc
850	1960(h)	I.A.	7.50	12.50	17.50	27.50
	1961(h)	20.860	.10	.25	1.00	5.50
	1962(h)	12.563	.10	.25	1.00	4.25
	1964(h)	6.175	.10	.25	1.00	4.25
	1965(h)	13.492	.10	.25	1.00	4.25
	1966(h)	50.220	.10	.25	1.00	4.25
	1967(h)	87.468	6.25	15.00	18.00	27.50

855.1	1966(h)	I.A.	—	.10	.50	3.00
	1967(h)	I.A.	—	.10	.50	2.50
	1968(h)	39.142	—	.10	.50	1.75
	1969(h)	16.974	—	.10	.50	1.25
	1970(h)	5.393	—	—	.35	1.00
	1971(h)	12.725	—	—	.35	.50

Mintmasters initial: S. Moneyers initial: S.

855.2	1972(h)	31.422	—	—	.10	.50

Mintmasters initial: S. Moneyers initial: B.

861.1	1973(h)	30.834	—	—	.10	.50
	1974(h)	22.178	—	—	.10	.50
	1975(h)	28.798	—	—	.10	.50
	1976(h)	48.388	—	—	.10	.50
	1977(h)	32.239	—	—	.10	.50
	1978(h)	17.444	—	—	.10	.35

Mintmasters initial: B. Moneyers initial: B.

861.2	1979(h)	24.261	—	—	.10	.35
	1980(h)	30.448	—	—	.10	.35
	1981(h)	1.427	—	—	.10	.35

Mintmasters initial: R. Moneyers initial: B.

861.3	1982(h)	24.671	—	—	.10	.35
	1983(h)	32.706	—	—	.10	.35
	1984(h)	22.882	—	—	.10	.35
	1985(h)	29.048	—	—	.10	.35
	1986(h)	53.496	—	—	.10	.35
	1987(h)	30.575	—	—	.10	.35
	1988(h)	23.370	—	—	.10	.35

BRONZE
Mintmasters initials: LG. Moneyers initials: JP.
A-Johan Alkjaer

868	1990	109.084	—	—	—	.20
	1991	102.162	—	—	—	.20
	1992	6.293	—	—	—	.20
	1993	14.756	—	—	—	.20
	1994	35.750	—	—	—	.20
	1995	40.000	—	—	—	.20
	1996	46.760	—	—	—	.20
	1997	30.306	—	—	—	.20
	1998	—	—	—	—	.20

NOTE: Beginning with the strikes in 1996, letters and numbers on reverse have raised edges.

50 ORE

BRONZE
Mintmasters initials: NR. Moneyers initials: JP.

866.1	1989	92.236	—	—	—	.25

Mintmasters initials: LG. Moneyers initials: JP.
A-Johan Alkjaer

KM#	Date	Mintage	Fine	VF	XF	Unc
866.2	1990	63.518	—	—	—	.25
	1991	11.115	—	—	—	.25
	1992	14.397	—	—	—	.25
	1993	14.328	—	—	—	.25
	1994	25.055	—	—	—	.25
	1995	15.988	—	—	—	.25
	1996	11.536	—	—	—	.25
	1997	15.574	—	—	—	.25
	1998	—	—	—	—	.25

NOTE: Beginning with the strikes in 1996, letters and numbers on reverse have raised edges.

1/2 KRONE

ALUMINUM-BRONZE
Mintmasters initials: HCN. Moneyers initials: GJ.

831.1	1924(h)	2.150	5.50	10.00	17.50	55.00
	1925(h)	3.432	5.50	10.00	22.50	65.00
	1926(h)	.716	13.50	27.50	42.50	75.00

Mintmasters initial: N. Moneyers initials: GJ.

831.2	1939(h)	.226	80.00	110.00	140.00	185.00
	1940(h)	1.871	5.50	11.00	14.00	22.50

KRONE

7.5000 g, .800 SILVER, .1929 oz ASW
Mintmasters initials: VBP.

819	1915(h)	1.410	3.00	6.25	10.00	25.00
	1916(h)	.992	5.00	10.00	18.50	30.00

ALUMINUM-BRONZE
Mintmasters initials: HCN. Moneyers initials: GJ.

824.1	1924(h)	.999	150.00	375.00	975.00	2350.
	1925(h)	6.314	1.75	9.00	40.00	110.00
	1926(h)	2.706	1.75	9.00	42.50	125.00

Mintmasters initial: N. Moneyers initials: GJ.

824.2	1929(h)	.501	7.50	16.50	80.00	235.00
	1930(h)	.540	22.50	37.50	100.00	375.00
	1931(h)	.540	7.50	16.00	60.00	200.00
	1934(h)	.529	5.00	11.00	45.00	165.00
	1935(h)	.505	35.00	55.00	100.00	250.00
	1936(h)	.558	11.00	20.00	50.00	180.00
	1938(h)	.407	18.50	30.00	50.00	175.00
	1939(h)	1.517	2.50	3.75	11.00	50.00
	1940(h)	1.496	2.50	4.25	11.00	55.00
	1941(h)	.661	9.00	18.50	50.00	250.00

Mintmasters initial: N. Moneyers initial: S.

835	1942(h)	3.952	1.25	3.75	11.00	42.50
	1943(h)	.798	9.00	20.00	110.00	375.00
	1944(h)	1.760	1.75	3.00	17.50	65.00
	1945(h)	2.581	1.75	3.00	9.00	45.00
	1946(h)	4.321	1.25	2.25	6.25	27.50
	1947(h)	5.060	1.25	1.75	3.75	12.50

KM#	Date	Mintage	Fine	VF	XF	Unc
837.1	1947(h)	I.A.	2.75	5.00	8.50	20.00
	1948(h)	4.248	1.25	2.50	5.00	8.75
	1949(h)	1.300	4.25	8.00	16.50	40.00
	1952(h)	2.124	2.50	4.25	8.50	20.00
	1953(h)	.573	3.75	7.50	12.50	25.00
	1954(h)	.584	15.00	26.00	37.50	60.00
	1955(h)	1.359	5.50	9.00	13.50	25.00

Mintmasters initial: C. Moneyers initial: S.

837.2	1956(h)	2.858	2.25	3.75	5.50	8.75
	1957(h)	10.896	.75	1.25	1.75	4.25
	1958(h)	1.507	1.25	2.25	3.00	5.00
	1959(h)	.243	18.50	30.00	35.00	45.00
	1960(h)	100 pcs.	—	—	3000.	3450.

NOTE: 1960 dated coins not released for circulation.

COPPER-NICKEL

851.1	1960(h)	1.000	1.00	1.75	3.75	9.25
	1961(h)	10.348	—	.35	2.50	15.00
	1962(h)	27.068	—	.25	2.50	13.00
	1963(h)	32.083	—	.25	1.75	6.75
	1964(h)	5.984	—	.25	1.75	6.75
	1965(h)	13.799	—	.25	1.25	7.50
	1966(h)	10.890	—	.25	1.25	6.75
	1967(h)	18.304	—	.25	1.25	6.75
	1968(h)	8.213	—	.25	1.00	5.00
	1969(h)	9.597	—	.25	.85	2.50
	1970(h)	9.460	—	—	.60	1.75
	1971(h)	13.985	—	—	.25	1.00

Mintmasters initial: S. Moneyers initial: S.

851.2	1972(h)	21.019	—	—	.25	.60

Mintmasters initial: S. Moneyers initial: B.

862.1	1973(h) narrow rim					
		18.268	—	—	.25	1.00
	1973(h) wide rim					
		Inc. Ab.	—	—	.35	1.00
	1974(h)	17.742	—	—	.35	1.00
	1975(h)	20.136	—	—	.35	1.00
	1976(h)	28.049	—	—	.35	1.00
	1977(h)	25.685	—	—	.35	1.00
	1978(h)	11.286	—	—	.35	1.00

Mintmasters initial: B. Moneyers initial: B.

862.2	1979(h)	25.216	—	—	.25	1.00
	1980(h)	25.825	—	—	.25	1.00
	1981(h)	8.889	—	—	.25	1.00

Mintmasters initial: R. Moneyers initial: B.

862.3	1982(h)	5.011	—	—	.25	.60
	1983(h)	13.946	—	—	.20	.60
	1984(h)	36.439	—	—	.20	.45
	1985(h)	10.843	—	—	.20	.45
	1986(h)	12.556	—	—	.20	.45
	1987(h)	20.120	—	—	.20	.45
	1988(h)	32.074	—	—	.20	.45
	1989(h)	15.704	—	—	.20	.45

MII Monograms
Mintmasters initials: LG. Moneyers initials: JP.
A-Johan Alkjaer

873	1992	81.621	—	—	—	.35
	1993	15.844	—	—	—	.35
	1994	23.658	—	—	—	.35
	1995	34.966	—	—	—	.35
	1996	10.081	—	—	—	.35
	1997	10.121	—	—	—	.35
	1998	—	—	—	—	.35

2 KRONER

15.0000 g, .800 SILVER, .3858 oz ASW
Mintmasters initial: P. Moneyers initials: GJ.
40th Anniversary of Reign

KM#	Date	Mintage	Fine	VF	XF	Unc
802	1903(h)	.103	7.50	18.50	35.00	55.00

Mintmasters initials: VBP. Moneyers initials: GJ.
Death of Christian IX
and Accession of Frederik VIII

803	1906(h)	.151	3.75	9.00	22.50	37.50

Mintmasters initials: VBP.
Death of Frederik VIII
and Accession of Christian X

811	1912(h)	.102	7.50	18.50	35.00	60.00

820	1915(h)	.657	12.50	27.50	45.00	75.00
	1916(h)	.402	7.50	15.00	22.50	45.00

Mintmasters initials: HCN. Moneyers initials: GJ.
Silver Wedding Anniversary

821	1923(h)	.203	—	—	15.00	27.50

ALUMINUM-BRONZE
Mintmasters initials: HCN. Moneyers initials: GJ.

KM#	Date	Mintage	Fine	VF	XF	Unc
825.1	1924(h)	1.138	25.00	125.00	600.00	1975.
	1925(h)	3.248	1.75	12.50	37.50	115.00
	1926(h)	1.126	1.75	12.50	45.00	160.00

Mintmasters initial: N. Moneyers initials: GJ.

825.2	1936(h)	.400	7.50	17.50	80.00	375.00
	1938(h)	.191	18.50	30.00	90.00	260.00
	1939(h)	.723	2.75	5.00	12.50	50.00
	1940(h)	.743	8.00	14.00	27.50	75.00
	1941(h)	.129	40.00	67.50	220.00	500.00

15.0000 g, .800 SILVER, .3858 oz ASW
Mintmasters initials: N. Moneyers initials: HS.
King's 60th Birthday

829	1930(h)	.303	—	—	7.50	12.50

Mintmasters initial: N. Moneyers initial: S.
25th Anniversary of Reign

830	ND(1937)(h)	.209	—	—	8.50	18.50

King's 75th Birthday

836 (Y55)	ND(1945)(h)	.157	—	—	11.00	22.50

ALUMINUM-BRONZE

838.1	1947(h)	1.151	3.00	5.50	13.50	27.50
	1948(h)	.857	2.25	3.75	8.75	20.00
	1949(h)	.272	6.25	12.50	25.00	50.00
	1951(h)	1.576	1.75	3.00	6.25	20.00
	1952(h)	1.958	1.25	2.50	5.50	15.00
	1953(h)	.432	3.00	6.25	12.00	35.00
	1954(h)	.716	3.00	5.50	11.00	22.50
	1955(h)	.457	5.00	8.75	12.50	22.50

Mintmasters initial: C. Moneyers initial: S.

838.2	1956(h)	1.444	2.25	3.75	6.25	11.00
	1957(h)	2.610	1.25	2.25	3.00	6.25
	1958(h)	2.605	1.50	2.50	3.75	7.50
	1959(h)	.192	20.00	30.00	37.50	55.00

15.0000 g, .800 SILVER, .3858 oz ASW
Mintmasters initial: N. Moneyers initial: S.
Greenland Commemorative

KM#	Date	Mintage	Fine	VF	XF	Unc
844	1953(h)	.152	—	6.25	18.50	35.00

Mintmasters initial: C. Moneyers initial: S.
Princess Margrethe's 18th Birthday

845	ND(1958)(h)	.301	—	—	9.00	15.00

COPPER-NICKEL
MII Monogram
Mintmasters initials: LG. Moneyers initials: JP.
A-Johan Alkjaer

874	1992	41.648	—	—	—	.75
	1993	43.864	—	—	—	.75
	1994	27.629	—	—	—	.75
	1995	19.850	—	—	—	.75
	1996	2.884	—	—	—	.75
	1997	25.874	—	—	—	.75
	1998	—	—	—	—	.75

5 KRONER

17.0000 g, .800 SILVER, .4372 oz ASW
Mintmasters initial: C. Moneyers initial: S.
Silver Wedding Anniversary

852	ND(1960)(h)	.410	—	3.50	5.00	12.00

COPPER-NICKEL

KM#	Date	Mintage	Fine	VF	XF	Unc
853.1	1960(h)	6.418	—	1.75	3.00	12.50
	1961(h)	9.744	—	1.75	4.25	20.00
	1962(h)	2.074	—	3.00	5.00	20.00
	1963(h)	.709	—	2.50	3.75	25.00
	1964(h)	1.443	—	1.75	5.00	22.00
	1965(h)	2.574	—	1.75	3.00	18.50
	1966(h)	4.370	—	1.75	2.50	11.00
	1967(h)	1.864	—	1.75	2.50	7.50
	1968(h)	4.132	—	1.75	2.50	6.25
	1969(h)	.072	3.00	6.25	11.00	14.00
	1970(h)	2.246	—	—	1.75	3.00
	1971(h)	4.767	—	—	1.75	2.50

Mintmasters initial: S. Moneyers initial: S.

| 853.2 | 1972(h) | 2.599 | — | — | 1.25 | 1.75 |

17.0000 g, .800 SILVER, .4372 oz ASW
Mintmasters initial: C. Moneyers initial: S.
Wedding of Princess Anne Marie

| 854 | 1964(h) | .359 | — | — | 7.50 | 12.50 |

COPPER-NICKEL
Mintmasters initial: S. Moneyers initial: B.

KM#	Date	Mintage	Fine	VF	XF	Unc
863.1	1973(h) narrow rim	3.774	—	—	1.75	3.00
	1973(h) wide rim	Inc. Ab.	—	—	1.75	3.00
	1974(h)	5.239	—	—	1.75	3.00
	1975(h)	5.810	—	—	3.00	7.50
	1976(h)	7.651	—	—	1.75	3.75
	1977(h)	6.885	—	—	1.75	3.75
	1978(h)	2.984	—	—	1.75	3.75

Mintmasters initial: B. Moneyers initial: B.

863.2	1979(h)	2.861	—	—	1.75	3.00
	1980(h)	3.622	—	—	3.00	5.00
	1981(h)	1.057	—	—	1.75	3.00

Mintmasters initial: R. Moneyers initial: B.

863.3	1982(h)	1.002	—	—	3.00	5.50
	1983(h)	1.044	—	—	1.75	3.00
	1984(h)	.713	—	—	1.75	3.00
	1985(h)	.621	—	—	1.75	3.00
	1986(h)	1.042	—	—	1.75	3.00
	1987(h)	.611	—	—	1.75	3.00
	1988(h)	.648	—	—	1.75	3.00

Mintmasters initials: LG. Moneyers initials: JP.
A-Johan Alkjaer.

869	1990	46.745	—	—	—	1.50
	1991	3.752	—	—	—	1.50
	1992	2.426	—	—	—	1.50
	1993	1.538	—	—	—	1.50

KM#	Date	Mintage	Fine	VF	XF	Unc
869	1994	7.920	—	—	—	1.50
	1995	5.850	—	—	—	1.50
	1997	5.258	—	—	—	1.50
	1998		—	—	—	1.50

10 KRONER

4.4803 g, .900 GOLD, .1296 oz AGW
Mintmasters Initials: VBP.

| 809 | 1908(h) | .308 | BV | BV | 65.00 | 125.00 |
| | 1909(h) | .153 | BV | BV | 75.00 | 125.00 |

| 816 | 1913(h) | .312 | BV | BV | 65.00 | 125.00 |
| | 1917(h) | .132 | BV | BV | 80.00 | 115.00 |

20.4000 g, .800 SILVER, .5247 oz ASW
Mintmasters initial: C. Moneyers initial: S.
Wedding of Princess Margrethe

| 856 | ND(1967)(h) | .419 | — | — | 7.50 | 12.50 |

*****NOTE: 78,383 were melted.**

Wedding of Princess Benedikte

| 857 | ND(1968) C(h)S | .254 | — | — | 7.50 | 15.00 |

*****NOTE: 42,923 were melted.**

Mintmasters initial: S. Moneyers initial: S.
Death of Frederik IX
and Accession of Margrethe II

KM#	Date	Mintage	Fine	VF	XF	Unc
858	1972(h)	.402	—	—	7.50	9.75

COPPER-NICKEL
Mintmasters initial: B. Moneyers initial: B.

| 864.1 | 1979(h) | 76.801 | — | — | 1.75 | 3.75 |
| | 1981(h) | 10.520 | — | 2.50 | 5.00 | 11.00 |

Mintmasters initial: R. Moneyers initial: B.

864.2	1982(h)	1.065	—	2.50	5.00	11.00
	1983(h)	1.123	—	2.50	5.00	11.00
	1984(h)	.748	—	—	3.75	11.00
	1985(h)	.720	—	—	3.75	13.50
	1987(h)	.719	—	—	3.75	11.00
	1988(h)	.718	—	—	3.75	9.25

Mintmasters initial: R. Moneyers initial: A.
Crown Prince's 18th Birthday

| 865 | ND(1986)(h) | 1.090 | — | — | — | 3.75 |
| | ND(1986)(h) | 2,000 | — | — | Proof | 400.00 |

ALUMINUM-BRONZE
Mintmasters initials: NR. Moneyers initials: JP.
A-Johan Alkjaer

| 867.1 | 1989 | 38.346 | — | — | — | 3.00 |

Mintmasters initials: LG. Moneyers initials: JP.
A-Johan Alkjaer

867.2	1990	12.193	—	—	—	3.00
	1991	1.065	—	—	—	3.00
	1992	.484	—	—	—	4.00
	1993	1.069	—	—	—	3.00

COPPER-ALUMINUM-NICKEL
Plain edge.

877	1994	4.058	—	—	—	3.00
	1995	9.461	—	—	—	3.00
	1997	3.725	—	—	—	3.00
	1998		—	—	—	3.00

NOTE: Beginning w/strikes in 1997, letters and numbers on reverse have raised edges.

20 KRONER

8.9606 g, .900 GOLD, .2592 oz AGW
Mintmasters initials: CS.

KM#	Date	Mintage	Fine	VF	XF	Unc
791.1	1873(h)	1.153	BV	105.00	150.00	190.00
	1874(h)	I.A.	750.00	1300.	1850.	2850.
	1876(h)	.351	BV	105.00	160.00	235.00
	1877(h)	I.A.	BV	150.00	250.00	320.00
	1890(h)	.102	BV	135.00	220.00	300.00

Mintmasters initials: VBP.

791.2	1900(h)	.100	BV	125.00	200.00	275.00

810	1908(h)	.243	BV	100.00	135.00	200.00
	1909(h)	.365	BV	105.00	140.00	200.00
	1910(h)	.200	BV	105.00	140.00	200.00
	1911(h)	.183	BV	105.00	140.00	200.00
	1912(h)	.184	BV	105.00	140.00	200.00

817.1	1913(h)	.815	BV	100.00	135.00	175.00
	1914(h)	.920	BV	100.00	135.00	175.00
	1915(h)	.532	BV	100.00	140.00	180.00
	1916(h)	1.401	BV	100.00	140.00	180.00
	1917(h)	I.A.	BV	100.00	135.00	175.00

Mintmasters initials: HCN.

817.2	1926(h)	.358	—	—	3500.	5000.
	1927(h)	I.A.	—	—	3500.	5000.

Mintmasters initial: N.

817.3	1930(h)	1.285	—	—	3500.	5000.
	1931(h)	I.A.	—	—	3500.	5000.

NOTE: The 1926-1931 dated 20 Kroners were not released for circulation.

ALUMINUM-BRONZE
50th Birthday of Queen Margarethe
Mintmasters initials: LG.

870	1990	1.101	—	—	5.00	9.25

Mintmasters initials: LG. Moneyers initials: JP.
A-Johan Alkjaer

871	1990	34.368	—	—	—	50.00
	1991	11.563	—	—	—	50.00
	1993	.674	—	—	—	50.00

NOTE: Date varieties exist.

Silver Wedding Anniversary
Mintmasters initials: LG.

KM#	Date	Mintage	Fine	VF	XF	Unc
875	ND(1992)	.994	—	—	5.00	7.50

COPPER-ALUMINUM-NICKEL
Alternative reeded and plain sections edge.

878.1	1994	2.565	—	—	—	5.00
	1998	8.651	—	—	—	5.00

Rev: Numbers and letters w/raised edges.

878.2	1996	8.651	—	—	—	6.00
	1998		—	—	—	6.00

1000 Years of Danish Coinage

879	ND(1995)	1.000	—	—	5.00	7.50

Wedding of Prince Joachim

881	1995	1.000	—	—	5.00	7.50

25th Anniversary - Queen's Reign
Obv: Full-length portrait. Rev: Crowned arms.

883	ND(1997)		—	—	5.00	7.50

FAEROE ISLANDS

The Faeroe Islands, a self-governing community within the kingdom of Denmark, are situated in the North Atlantic between Iceland and the Shetland Islands. The 17 inhabited islands and numerous islets and reefs have an area of 540 sq. mi. (1,400 sq. km.) and a population of 46,000. Capital: Thorshavn. The principal industries are fishing and livestock. Fish and fish products are exported.

While it is thought that Irish hermits lived on the islands in the 7th and 8th centuries, the present inhabitants are descended from 6th century Norse settlers. The Faeroe Islands became a Norwegian fief in 1035 and became Danish in 1380 when Norway and Denmark were united. They have ever since remained in Danish possession and were granted self-government (except for an appointed governor-general) with their own legislature, executive and flag in 1948.

The islands were occupied by British troops during World War II, after the German occupation of Denmark. The Faeroe Island coinage was struck in London during World War II.

RULERS

Danish

MONETARY SYSTEM

100 Ore = 1 Krone

ORE

BRONZE

1	1941	*.200	27.00	45.00	60.00	85.00

*NOTE: Also struck in 1942 w/1941 dies.

2 ORE

BRONZE

KM#	Date	Mintage	Fine	VF	XF	Unc
2	1941	*.200	6.25	12.50	22.50	50.00

*NOTE: Also struck in 1942 w/1941 dies.

5 ORE

BRONZE

3	1941	*.200	5.00	9.00	18.50	50.00

*NOTE: Also struck in 1942 w/1941 dies.

10 ORE

COPPER-NICKEL

4	1941	*.300	7.50	12.50	27.50	75.00

*NOTE: Also struck in 1942 w/1941 dies.

25 ORE

COPPER-NICKEL

5	1941	*.250	9.00	13.50	30.00	85.00

*NOTE: Also struck in 1942 w/1941 dies.

DJIBOUTI

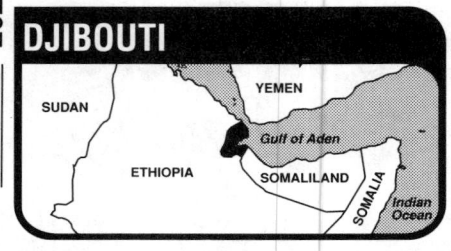

The Republic of Djibouti (formerly French Somaliland and the French Overseas Territory of Afars and Issas), located in northeast Africa at the Bab el Mandeb Strait connecting the Suez Canal and the Red Sea with the Gulf of Aden and the Indian Ocean, has an area of 8,950 sq. mi. (22,000 sq. km.) and a population of 421,320. Capital: Djibouti. The tiny nation has less than one sq. mi. of arable land, and no natural resources except salt, sand, and camels. The commercial activities of the transshipment port of Djibouti and the Addis Abada-Djibouti railroad are the basis of the economy. Salt, fish and hides are exported.

French interest in former French Somaliland began in 1839 with concessions obtained by a French naval lieutenant from the provincial sultans. French Somaliland was made a protectorate in 1884 and its boundaries were delimited by the Franco-British and Ethiopian accords of 1887 and 1897. It became a colony in 1896 and a territory within the French Union in 1946. In 1958 it voted to join the new French Community as an overseas territory, and reaffirmed that choice by a referendum in March, 1967. Its name was changed from French Somaliland to the French Territory of Afars and Issas on July 5, 1967.

The French Tricolor, which had flown over the strategically important territory for 115 years, was lowered for the last time on June 27, 1977, when French Afars and Issas became Africa's 49th independent state, under the name of the Republic of Djibouti.

Djibouti, a seaport and capital city of the Republic of Djibouti (and formerly of French Somaliland and French Afars and Issas) is located on the east coast of Africa at the southernmost entrance to the Red Sea. The capital was moved from Obok to Djibouti in 1892 and established as the transshipment point for Ethiopia's foreign trade via the Franco-Ethiopian railway linking Djibouti and Addis Ababa.

RULERS
French, until 1977

FRENCH SOMALILAND

MINT MARKS
(a) - Paris (privy marks only)

MONETARY SYSTEM
100 Centimes = 1 Franc

FRANC

ALUMINUM

KM#	Date	Mintage	Fine	VF	XF	Unc
4	1948(a)	.200	6.50	12.50	25.00	50.00
	1949(a) Inc. Ab.		8.00	15.00	30.00	60.00

| 8 | 1959(a) | .500 | .25 | .50 | 1.50 | 3.00 |
| | 1965(a) | .200 | .35 | .60 | 2.00 | 4.00 |

2 FRANCS

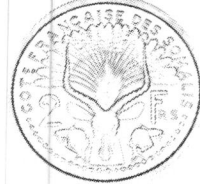

ALUMINUM

| 5 | 1948(a) | .200 | 6.50 | 12.50 | 25.00 | 60.00 |
| | 1949(a) Inc. Ab. | | 8.00 | 15.00 | 30.00 | 70.00 |

KM#	Date	Mintage	Fine	VF	XF	Unc
9	1959(a)	.200	.25	.75	2.50	5.00
	1965(a)	.240	.25	.75	2.50	5.00

5 FRANCS

ALUMINUM

| 6 | 1948(a) | .500 | 5.00 | 10.00 | 25.00 | 40.00 |

| 10 | 1959(a) | .500 | .25 | .75 | 2.50 | 5.50 |
| | 1965(a) | .200 | .25 | .75 | 3.00 | 6.50 |

20 FRANCS

ALUMINUM-BRONZE

| 7 | 1952(a) | .500 | 1.25 | 2.50 | 4.50 | 10.00 |

| 12 | 1965(a) | .200 | 1.00 | 2.00 | 4.00 | 8.00 |

FRENCH AFARS & ISSAS

MINT MARKS
(a) - Paris (privy marks only)

MONETARY SYSTEM
100 Centimes = 1 Franc

FRANC

ALUMINUM

16	1969(a)	.100	1.00	2.00	3.50	6.00
	1971(a)	.100	1.00	2.00	3.50	6.00
	1975(a)	.300	.75	1.25	2.00	3.00

2 FRANCS

ALUMINUM

KM#	Date	Mintage	Fine	VF	XF	Unc
13	1968(a)	.100	1.00	2.00	3.50	6.00
	1975(a)	.180	.75	1.50	2.50	5.00

5 FRANCS

ALUMINUM

| 14 | 1968(a) | .100 | 1.00 | 2.00 | 3.50 | 6.00 |
| | 1975(a) | .300 | .75 | 1.25 | 2.00 | 4.00 |

10 FRANCS

ALUMINUM-BRONZE

17	1969(a)	.100	1.50	3.00	6.00	9.00
	1970(a)	.300	1.00	2.00	4.00	7.00
	1975(a)	.360	.75	1.50	3.00	5.00

20 FRANCS

ALUMINUM-BRONZE

| 15 | 1968(a) | .300 | 1.50 | 2.50 | 4.50 | 8.00 |
| | 1975(a) | .300 | 1.25 | 2.00 | 4.00 | 7.00 |

50 FRANCS

COPPER-NICKEL
Rev: Pair of dromedary camels, denomination.

| 18 | 1970(a) | .300 | 1.50 | 3.00 | 6.00 | 10.00 |
| | 1975(a) | .180 | 1.50 | 3.00 | 6.00 | 10.00 |

100 FRANCS

Rev: Pair of dromedary camels, denomination.
COPPER-NICKEL

| 19 | 1970(a) | .600 | 2.50 | 4.50 | 7.50 | 12.50 |
| | 1975(a) | .400 | 2.50 | 4.50 | 7.50 | 12.50 |

DJIBOUTI

FRANC

ALUMINUM

KM#	Date	Mintage	Fine	VF	XF	Unc
20	1977(a)	.300	.50	.75	1.50	2.50
	1996	—	.50	.75	1.50	2.50

2 FRANCS

ALUMINUM

21	1977(a)	.200	.50	1.00	1.75	3.00

5 FRANCS

ALUMINUM

22	1977(a)	.400	.75	1.25	2.00	3.25
	1986(a)	—	.75	1.00	1.75	3.00
	1989(a)	—	.75	1.00	1.75	3.00
	1991(a)	—	.75	1.00	1.75	3.00

10 FRANCS

ALUMINUM-BRONZE

23	1977(a)	.600	.45	.85	1.50	2.75
	1983(a)	—	.50	1.00	1.75	3.00
	1989(a)	—	.45	.75	1.25	2.25
	1991(a)	—	.45	.75	1.25	2.25
	1996	—	.45	.75	1.25	2.25

NOTE: Varieties exist.

20 FRANCS

ALUMINUM-BRONZE

24	1977(a)	.700	.50	1.00	1.50	3.00
	1982(a)	—	.50	1.00	1.50	3.50
	1983(a)	—	.50	1.00	1.50	3.00
	1986(a)	—	.45	.75	1.25	2.25
	1991(a)	—	.45	.75	1.25	2.25

NOTE: Varieties exist.

50 FRANCS

COPPER-NICKEL
Rev: Pair of dromedary camels, denomination.

25	1977(a)	1.500	.75	1.50	3.00	6.00

KM#	Date	Mintage	Fine	VF	XF	Unc
25	1982(a)	—	.75	1.50	3.00	6.00
	1983(a)	—	.50	1.00	2.25	4.00
	1986(a)	—	.50	1.00	2.25	4.00
	1989(a)	—	.50	1.00	2.25	4.00
	1991(a)	—	.50	1.00	2.25	4.00

100 FRANCS

COPPER-NICKEL
Rev: Pair of dromedary camels, denomination.

26	1977(a)	1.500	1.00	2.00	3.00	6.00
	1983(a)	—	1.00	2.50	3.50	7.00
	1991(a)	—	1.00	1.75	2.75	5.50

500 FRANCS

ALUMINUM-BRONZE

27	1989(a)	—	3.00	4.00	6.00	10.00
	1991(a)	—	3.00	4.00	6.00	10.00

DOMINICAN REPUBLIC

The Dominican Republic, which occupies the eastern two-thirds of the island of Hispaniola, has an area of 18,704 sq. mi. (48,734 sq. km.) and a population of 7.9 million. Capital: Santo Domingo. The largely agricultural economy produces sugar, coffee, tobacco and cocoa. Tourism and casino gaming are also a rising source of revenue.

Columbus discovered Hispaniola in 1492, and named it La Isla Espanola - 'the Spanish Island'. Santo Domingo, the oldest white settlement in the Western Hemisphere, was the base from which Spain conducted its exploration of the New World. Later, French buccaneers settled the western third of Hispaniola, naming the colony St. Dominique, which in 1697, was ceded to France by Spain. In 1804, following a bloody revolt by former slaves, the French colony became the Republic of Haiti - 'mountainous country'. The Spanish called their part of Hispaniola Santo Domingo. In 1822, the Haitians conquered the entire island and held it until 1844, when Juan Pablo Duarte, the national hero of the Dominican Republic, drove them out of Santo Domingo and established an independent Dominican Republic. The republic returned voluntarily to Spanish dominion from 1861 to 1865, after being rejected by France, Britain and the United States. Independence was reclaimed in 1866.

MINT MARKS
(c) - Stylized maple leaf, Royal Canadian Mint
Mo - Mexico
(o) - CHI in oval - Valcambi, Chiasso, Italy
(t) - Tower, Tower Mint, London

MONETARY SYSTEM
100 Centavos = 1 Peso Oro

CENTAVO

BRONZE

KM#	Date	Mintage	Fine	VF	XF	Unc
17	1937	1.000	.50	1.50	7.50	75.00
	1937	—	—	—	Proof	350.00
	1939	2.000	.50	1.25	5.00	40.00
	1941	2.000	.25	.50	3.00	12.00
	1942	2.000	.25	.50	3.00	15.00
	1944	5.000	.20	.50	1.50	10.00
	1947	3.000	.20	.50	1.00	8.00
	1949	3.000	.20	.40	1.00	8.00
	1951	3.000	.20	.35	.75	8.00
	1952	3.000	.20	.35	.75	8.00
	1955	3.000	.15	.35	.75	6.00
	1956	3.000	.15	.35	.75	6.00
	1957	5.000	.10	.25	.75	5.00
	1959	5.000	.10	.25	.75	5.00
	1961	5.000	.10	.20	.50	2.00
	1961	10 pcs.	—	—	Proof	450.00

100th Anniversary - Restoration of the Republic

25	1963	13.000	—	—	.10	.40

31	1968	5.000	—	—	.10	.20
	1971	6.000	—	—	.10	.20
	1972	3.000	—	—	.10	.20
	1972	500 pcs.	—	—	Proof	15.00
	1975	.500	—	—	.10	.20

F.A.O. Issue

KM#	Date	Mintage	Fine	VF	XF	Unc
32	1969	5.000	—	—	.10	.30

Centennial - Death of Juan Pablo Duarte

KM#	Date	Mintage	Fine	VF	XF	Unc
40	1976	3.995	—	—	.10	.20
	1976	5,000	—	—	Proof	1.00
48	1978	2.995	—	—	.10	.15
	1978	5,000	—	—	Proof	2.00
	1979	2.985	—	—	.10	.15
	1979	500 pcs.	—	—	Proof	15.00
	1980	.200	—	—	.10	.15
	1980	3,000	—	—	Proof	1.00
	1981	3,000	—	—	Proof	1.00

COPPER PLATED ZINC
Human Rights - Caonabo

KM#	Date	Mintage	Fine	VF	XF	Unc
64	1984Mo	10.000	—	—	—	.25
	1984Mo	1,600	—	—	Proof	1.50
	1986	18.067	—	—	—	.25
	1986	1,600	—	—	Proof	1.50
	1987	15.000	—	—	—	.25
	1987	1,600	—	—	Proof	1.50

KM#	Date	Mintage	Fine	VF	XF	Unc
72	1989	1,115	—	—	—	1.25

5 CENTAVOS

COPPER-NICKEL

KM#	Date	Mintage	Fine	VF	XF	Unc
18	1937	2.000	1.00	1.75	5.00	50.00
	1937	—	—	—	Proof	450.00
	1939	.200	3.50	8.00	40.00	350.00
	1951	2.000	.75	1.25	2.00	20.00
	1956	1.000	.20	.50	.80	3.50
	1959	1.000	.20	.50	.80	3.50
	1961	4.000	.10	.20	.35	.75
	1961	10 pcs.	—	—	—	Proof 550.00
	1971	.440	.10	.15	.20	.50
	1972	2.000	.10	.15	.20	.40
	1972	500 pcs.	—	—	—	Proof 15.00
	1974	5.000	—	—	.10	.40
	1974	500 pcs.	—	—	—	Proof 15.00

5.0000 g, .350 SILVER, .0563 oz ASW

KM#	Date	Mintage	Fine	VF	XF	Unc
18a	1944	2.000	1.50	3.50	7.50	30.00

COPPER-NICKEL
100th Anniversary - Restoration of the Republic

KM#	Date	Mintage	Fine	VF	XF	Unc
26	1963	4.000	—	.10	.15	.60

Centennial - Death of Juan Pablo Duarte

KM#	Date	Mintage	Fine	VF	XF	Unc
41	1976	5.595	—	—	.10	.50
	1976	5,000	—	—	Proof	2.00
49	1978	1.996	—	—	.10	.35
	1978	5,000	—	—	Proof	1.50
	1979	2.988	—	—	.10	.35
	1979	500 pcs.	—	—	Proof	15.00
	1980	5.300	—	—	.10	.35
	1980	3,000	—	—	Proof	2.00
	1981	4.500	—	—	.10	.35
	1981	3,000	—	—	Proof	2.00

Human Rights - Sanchez and Mello

KM#	Date	Mintage	Fine	VF	XF	Unc
59	1983	3.998	—	—	.10	.30
	1983(t)	1,600	—	—	Proof	2.00
	1984Mo	10.000	—	—	.10	.30
	1984Mo	1,600	—	—	Proof	2.00
	1986	12.898	—	—	.10	.30
	1986	1,600	—	—	Proof	2.00
	1987	10.000	—	—	.10	.30
	1987	1,700	—	—	Proof	2.00

NICKEL CLAD STEEL
Native Culture - Drummer

KM#	Date	Mintage	Fine	VF	XF	Unc
69	1989	50.000	—	—	—	.35

10 CENTAVOS

2.5000 g, .900 SILVER, .0723 oz ASW

KM#	Date	Mintage	Fine	VF	XF	Unc
19	1937	1.000	BV	2.00	5.00	40.00
	1937	—	—	—	Proof	550.00
	1939	.150	3.00	6.00	20.00	300.00
	1942	2.000	1.00	2.00	3.00	30.00
	1944	1.000	1.00	2.00	4.00	50.00
	1951	.500	1.00	2.00	3.00	10.00
	1952	.500	1.00	2.00	3.00	10.00
	1953	.750	1.00	2.00	3.00	8.00
	1956	1.000	.75	1.50	2.50	8.00
	1959	2.000	BV	1.25	2.25	7.00
	1961	2.000	BV	1.00	2.00	6.00

COPPER-NICKEL
Plain edge.

KM#	Date	Mintage	Fine	VF	XF	Unc
19a	1967	10.000	—	—	.15	.50
	1973	8.000	—	—	.15	.50
	1973	500 pcs.	—	—	Proof	20.00
	1975	8.000	—	—	.15	.50

2.5000 g, .650 SILVER, .0522 oz ASW
100th Anniversary - Restoration of the Republic

KM#	Date	Mintage	Fine	VF	XF	Unc
27	1963	4.000	—	BV	1.00	2.00

COPPER-NICKEL
Centennial - Death of Juan Pablo Duarte

KM#	Date	Mintage	Fine	VF	XF	Unc
42	1976	5.595	—	—	.10	.75
	1976	5,000	—	—	Proof	2.00

KM#	Date	Mintage	Fine	VF	XF	Unc
50	1978	3.000	—	—	.10	.50
	1978	5,000	—	—	Proof	2.00
	1979	4.020	—	—	.10	.50
	1979	500 pcs.	—	—	Proof	20.00
	1980	4.400	—	—	.10	.35
	1980	3,000	—	—	Proof	3.00
	1981	6.000	—	—	.10	.35
	1981	3,000	—	—	Proof	3.00

Human Rights - Duarte

KM#	Date	Mintage	Fine	VF	XF	Unc
60	1983	4.998	—	—	.10	.35
	1983(t)	4.000	—	—	.10	.35
	1983(t)	1,600	—	—	Proof	2.50
	1984 Mo	15.000	—	—	.10	.25
	1984 Mo	1,600	—	—	Proof	2.50
	1986	15.515	—	—	.10	.25
	1986	1,600	—	—	Proof	2.50
	1987	20.000	—	—	.10	.25
	1987	1,700	—	—	Proof	2.50

NICKEL CLAD STEEL

KM#	Date	Mintage	Fine	VF	XF	Unc
70	1989	40.000	—	—	—	.40
	1991	3.500	—	—	—	.40

25 CENTAVOS

6.2500 g, .900 SILVER, .1808 oz ASW

KM#	Date	Mintage	Fine	VF	XF	Unc
20	1937	.560	BV	5.00	15.00	65.00
	1937	—	—	—	Proof	650.00
	1939	.160	4.00	8.00	25.00	500.00
	1942	.560	2.00	4.00	10.00	100.00
	1944	.400	2.00	4.00	8.00	80.00
	1947	.400	2.00	4.00	8.00	80.00
	1951	.400	2.00	4.00	8.00	80.00
	1952	.400	2.00	3.00	5.00	12.50
	1956	.400	2.00	2.50	4.00	10.00
	1960	.600	2.00	2.50	4.00	10.00
	1961	.800	2.00	2.50	4.00	10.00

COPPER-NICKEL
Plain edge.

KM#	Date	Mintage	Fine	VF	XF	Unc
20a.1	1967	5.000	—	.10	.20	.75
	1972	.800	—	.10	.40	1.00
	1972	500 pcs.	—	—	Proof	20.00

Reeded edge.

KM#	Date	Mintage	Fine	VF	XF	Unc
20a.2	1974	2.000	—	.10	.40	1.00
	1974	500 pcs.	—	—	Proof	20.00

6.2500 g, .650 SILVER, .1306 oz ASW
100th Anniversary - Restoration of the Republic

KM#	Date	Mintage	Fine	VF	XF	Unc
28	1963	2.400	—	—	BV	1.50	3.00

COPPER-NICKEL
Centennial - Death of Juan Pablo Duarte

KM#	Date	Mintage	Fine	VF	XF	Unc
43	1976	3.195	—	.10	.40	1.00
	1976	5,000	—	—	Proof	2.50

51	1978	.996	—	—	.35	.75
	1978	5,000	—	—	Proof	3.00
	1979	2.089	—	—	.15	.50
	1979	500 pcs.	—	—	Proof	25.00
	1980	2.600	—	—	.15	.50
	1980	3,000	—	—	Proof	3.00
	1981	3.200	—	—	.15	.50
	1981	3,000	—	—	Proof	3.00

Human Rights - Mirabel Sisters

61	1983	.793	—	.10	.20	.50
	1983(t)	5,000	—	—	—	2.50
	1983(t)	1,600	—	—	Proof	8.00
	1984Mo	6.400	—	—	.15	.40
	1984Mo	1,600	—	—	Proof	8.00
	1986	10.132	—	—	.15	.40
	1986	1,600	—	—	Proof	8.00
	1987	6.000	—	—	.15	.40
	1987	1,700	—	—	Proof	8.00

NOTE: Coin and medal rotations and edge reeding varieties exist for the above.

NICKEL CLAD STEEL
Native Culture - Ox Cart

71.1	1989	16.000	—	—	—	.60
	1991	38.000	—	—	—	.60

Obv. and rev: legend and design in beaded circle.

71.2	1989	Inc. Ab.	—	—	—	.60
	1990	20.000	—	—	—	.60

NOTE: Varieties exist.

1/2 PESO

12.5000 g, .900 SILVER, .3617 oz ASW

21	1937	.500	BV	7.50	12.50	70.00
	1937	—	—	—	Proof	750.00
	1944	.100	BV	10.00	25.00	300.00
	1947	.200	BV	7.50	15.00	200.00

KM#	Date	Mintage	Fine	VF	XF	Unc
21	1951	.200	BV	7.50	15.00	150.00
	1952	.140	BV	7.50	12.50	70.00
	1959	.100	BV	6.00	10.00	40.00
	1960	.100	BV	6.00	9.00	30.00
	1961	.400	BV	4.00	6.00	25.00

COPPER-NICKEL
Plain edge.

21a.1	1967	1.500	—	.20	.40	1.50
	1968	.600	—	.30	.50	2.50

Reeded edge.

21a.2	1973	.600	—	.20	.40	1.50
	1973	500 pcs.	—	—	Proof	30.00
	1975	.600	—	.20	.40	1.50

12.5000 g, .650 SILVER, .2612 oz ASW
100th Anniversary - Restoration of the Republic

29	1963	.300	—	BV	4.00	7.50

COPPER-NICKEL
Centennial - Death of Juan Pablo Duarte

44	1976	.195	—	.20	.40	1.50
	1976	5,000	—	—	Proof	3.00

52	1978	.296	—	.20	.40	1.50
	1978	5,000	—	—	Proof	4.00
	1979	.967	—	.20	.40	1.50
	1979	500 pcs.	—	—	Proof	30.00
	1980	1.000	—	.20	.40	1.50
	1980	3,000	—	—	Proof	5.00
	1981	1.300	—	.20	.40	1.50
	1981	3,000	—	—	Proof	5.00

Human Rights - Bono, Espaillat and Rojas

62	1983	.393	—	.20	.40	1.50
	1983(t)	5,000	—	—	—	4.00
	1983(t)	1,600	—	—	Proof	15.00
	1984Mo	3.200	—	.20	.40	1.50
	1984Mo	1,600	—	—	Proof	15.00
	1986	5.225	—	.20	.40	1.50
	1986	1,600	—	—	Proof	15.00
	1987	3.000	—	.20	.40	1.50
	1987	1,700	—	—	Proof	15.00

NOTE: Coin and medal rotations exist for the above.

Beacon at Colon

KM#	Date	Mintage	Fine	VF	XF	Unc
73.1	1989	8.000	—	—	—	2.00

Obv. and rev: Legend and design in inner circle.

73.2	1990	1.500	—	—	—	2.00

PESO

26.7000 g, .900 SILVER, .7725 oz ASW
Rev: HP below bust.

22	1939	.015	15.00	20.00	45.00	750.00
	1939	—	—	—	Proof	2250.
	1952	.020	BV	7.00	10.00	15.00

25th Anniversary of Trujillo Regime

23	1955	.050*	7.50	10.00	15.00	25.00

*30,550 officially melted following Trujillo's assassination in 1961.

COPPER-NICKEL
Centennial - Death of Juan Pablo Duarte

KM#	Date	Mintage	Fine	VF	XF	Unc
53	1978	.035	—	—	1.00	2.00
	1978	5,000	—	—	Proof	7.50
	1979	.045	—	—	1.00	2.00
	1979	500 pcs.	—	—	Proof	35.00
	1980	.020	—	—	1.00	2.00
	1980	3,000	—	—	Proof	6.00
	1981	3,000	—	—	Proof	6.00

Human Rights - Montesinos, Enriquillo and Lemba

63	1983(t)	.093	—	—	1.00	2.50
	1983	5,000	—	—		6.00
	1983(t)	1,600	—	—	Proof	15.00
	1984Mo	.120	—	—	1.00	2.50
	1984Mo	1,600	—	—	Proof	15.00
	1986		—	—	1.00	2.50

NOTE: Coin and medal rotations exist for the above.

NICKEL BONDED STEEL
15th Central American and Caribbean Games

65	1986	.100	—	—	1.00	3.00
	1986	1,700	—	—	Proof	15.00

COPPER-ZINC
Juan Pablo Duarte
Obv: DUARTE on bust.

80.1	1991	40.000	—	—	—	2.00
	1992	35.000	—	—	—	2.00

Obv: DUARTE below bust.

80.2	1992	35.000	—	—	—	2.00

EAST AFRICA

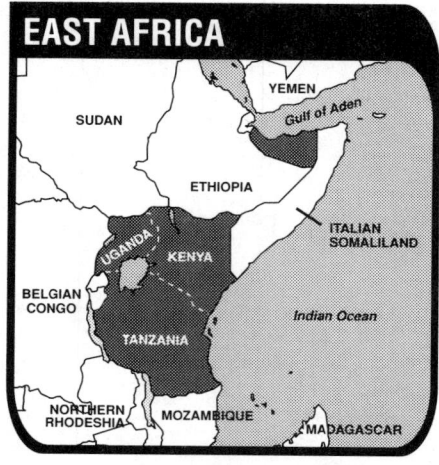

East Africa was an administrative grouping of five separate British territories: Kenya, Tanganyika (now part of Tanzania), the Sultanate of Zanzibar and Pemba (now part of Tanzania), Uganda and British Somaliland (now part of Somalia). See individual entries for specific statistics and history.

The common interest of Kenya, Tanganyika and Uganda invited cooperation in economic matters and consideration of political union. The territorial governors, organized as the East Africa High Commission, met periodically to administer such common activities as taxation, industrial development and education. The authority of the Commission did not infringe upon the constitution and internal autonomy of the individual colonies. A common currency and banknotes, which were also legal tender in Aden, were provided for use of the member colonies by the East Africa Currency Board. The coinage through 1919 had the legend "East Africa and Uganda Protectorate". From 1920 on, the legend has read, "East Africa".

The East African coinage includes two denominations of 1936 which bear the style and titles of Edward VIII.

NOTE: For later coinage see Kenya, Tanzania and Uganda.

RULERS
British

MINT MARKS
A - Ackroyd & Best, Morley
I - Bombay Mint
H - Heaton Mint, Birmingham, England
K,KN - King's Norton Mint, Birmingham, England
SA - Pretoria Mint, South Africa
no mint mark - Royal Mint, London

EAST AFRICA & UGANDA PROTECTORATES

MONETARY SYSTEM
100 Cents = 1 Rupee

1/2 CENT

ALUMINUM

KM#	Date	Mintage	Fine	VF	XF	Unc
6	1907	5 pcs.	400.00	750.00	1500.	3000.
	1908	.900	15.00	25.00	50.00	90.00

COPPER-NICKEL

6a	1909	.900	8.00	15.00	30.00	60.00

CENT

ALUMINUM

KM#	Date	Mintage	Fine	VF	XF	Unc
5	1906	—	500.00	750.00	1500.	2000.
	1907	6.948	5.00	10.00	30.00	50.00
	1907		—	—	Proof	200.00
	1908	2.871	7.00	12.50	30.00	60.00

COPPER-NICKEL

5a	1908		—	—	Unique	—
	1909	25.000	.50	1.25	3.00	7.00
	1910	6.000	.50	1.25	4.00	12.00
7	1911H	25.000	.25	1.00	2.50	15.00
	1912H	20.000	.25	1.00	2.00	8.00
	1913	4.529	.75	1.50	3.75	20.00
	1914	6.000	.75	1.75	5.00	15.00
	1914H	2.500	1.00	3.00	7.50	20.00
	1916H	1.824	.75	2.00	5.00	20.00
	1917H	3.176	.75	2.00	5.00	15.00
	1918H	10.000	.50	1.00	3.25	12.00

5 CENTS

COPPER-NICKEL
Edward VII

A11 (11.1)	1907		—	—	Rare	—

George V

11 (11.2)	1913H	.300	1.50	4.00	15.00	35.00
	1914K	1.240	.75	3.25	6.00	22.50
	1914K*		—	—	Proof	200.00
	1919H	.200	10.00	15.00	40.00	120.00

*NOTE: The 1914K was issued with British West Africa KM#8 in a double (4 pc.) Specimen Set.

10 CENTS

COPPER-NICKEL

2	1906	—	1000.	1500.	2000.	3000.
	1907	1.000	1.50	4.00	10.00	30.00
	1910	.500	3.00	7.00	20.00	55.00

8	1911H	1.250	2.00	5.00	10.00	40.00
	1912H	1.050	2.00	5.00	12.50	55.00
	1913	.050	75.00	150.00	250.00	500.00
	1918H	.400	10.00	20.00	50.00	150.00

25 CENTS

2.9160 g, .800 SILVER, .0750 oz ASW

KM#	Date	Mintage	Fine	VF	XF	Unc
3	1906	.400	3.00	7.00	22.00	60.00
	1910H	.200	4.00	8.00	30.00	90.00

10	1912	.180	4.00	8.00	25.00	80.00
	1913	.300	3.50	7.50	22.50	60.00
	1914H	.080	20.00	35.00	60.00	100.00
	1914H	—	—	—	Proof	400.00
	1918H	.040	150.00	300.00	500.00	900.00

50 CENTS

5.8319 g, .800 SILVER, .1500 oz ASW

4	1906	.200	4.50	12.50	30.00	140.00
	1906	—	—	—	Proof	400.00
	1909	.100	15.00	30.00	85.00	300.00
	1910	.100	10.00	25.00	60.00	225.00

9	1911	.150	7.50	15.00	35.00	140.00
	1911	—	—	—	Proof	250.00
	1912	.100	8.00	20.00	60.00	200.00
	1913	.200	5.00	12.50	30.00	135.00
	1914H	.180	5.00	12.50	30.00	135.00
	1918H	.060	60.00	150.00	250.00	500.00
	1919	.100	250.00	350.00	600.00	1500.

EAST AFRICA

MONETARY SYSTEM

100 Cents = 1 Florin

CENT

COPPER-NICKEL

12	1920H	*2.908	30.00	60.00	100.00	225.00
	1920H					
	*20-30 pcs.	—	—	Proof	300.00
	1920	—	—	—	—	750.00
	1921	**	—	—	—	2000.

*NOTE: Only about 30% of total mintage released to circulation.
**NOTE: Not released for circulation.

5 CENTS

COPPER-NICKEL

13	1920H	*.550	75.00	150.00	200.00	400.00
	1920H					
	*20-30 pcs.	—	—	Proof	450.00

*NOTE: Only about 30% of total mintage released to circulation.

10 CENTS

COPPER-NICKEL

KM#	Date	Mintage	Fine	VF	XF	Unc
14	1920H	*.700	120.00	150.00	225.00	375.00
	1920H					
	*20-30 pcs.	—	—	Proof	600.00

*NOTE: Only about 30% of total mintage released to circulation.

25 CENTS

2.9160 g, .500 SILVER, .0469 oz ASW

15	1920H	.748	25.00	35.00	75.00	150.00
	1920H					
	*20-30 pcs.	—	—	Proof	250.00

50 CENTS

5.8319 g, .500 SILVER, .0937 oz ASW
Fifty Cents-One Shilling

16	1920A	*.012	1500.	2000.	3000.	4000.
	1920H	*.062	500.00	1000.	1500.	2000.
	1920H					
	*20-30 pcs.	—	—	Proof	600.00

*NOTE: Not released for circulation.

FLORIN

11.6638 g, .500 SILVER, .1875 oz ASW

17	1920	1.479	15.00	40.00	100.00	300.00
	1920A	.542	150.00	250.00	500.00	2000.
	1920H	9.689	12.50	30.00	75.00	250.00
	1920H					
	*20-30 pcs.	—	—	Proof	800.00
	1921	2 known	—	—	—	4500.

MONETARY REFORM

(Commencing May, 1921)
100 Cents = 1 Shilling

CENT

BRONZE

22	1922	8.250	.25	.85	4.00	10.00
	1922H	43.750	.25	.50	1.50	6.50
	1923	50.000	.25	.50	1.50	6.50
	1924	Inc. Ab.	.25	.75	3.25	10.00
	1924H	17.500	.25	.75	3.25	8.00
	1924KN	10.720	.25	.75	3.25	8.00
	1924KN	—	—	—	Proof	125.00
	1925	6.000	50.00	100.00	175.00	350.00
	1925KN	6.780	2.00	4.00	15.00	35.00
	1927	10.000	.25	.75	3.00	10.00
	1927	—	—	—	Proof	125.00
	1928H	12.000	.25	.75	3.25	8.00

KM#	Date	Mintage	Fine	VF	XF	Unc
22	1928KN	11.764	.50	2.00	5.00	12.00
	1928KN	—	—	—	Proof	125.00
	1930	15.000	.25	.75	2.00	5.00
	1930	—	—	—	Proof	125.00
	1935	10.000	.25	.50	1.25	3.50

29	1942	25.000	.10	.25	.85	2.50
	1942I	15.000	.15	.30	1.00	3.00

Obv. leg: ET IND.IMP. dropped.

32	1949	4.000	.20	.50	1.00	4.00
	1949	—	.10	—	Proof	125.00
	1950	16.000	.10	.25	.85	2.50
	1950	—	—	—	Proof	150.00
	1951H	9.000	.10	.25	.85	2.50
	1951H	—	—	—	Proof	125.00
	1951KN	11.140	.10	.25	.85	2.50
	1951KN	—	—	—	Proof	125.00
	1952	7.000	.10	.25	.85	2.50
	1952H	13.000	.10	.25	.85	2.50
	1952H	—	—	—	Proof	125.00
	1952KN	5.230	.10	.35	1.25	5.00

35	1954	8.000	.10	.25	.85	2.50
	1954	—	—	—	Proof	150.00
	1955	5.000	.10	.25	.50	1.75
	1955H	6.384	.10	.20	.65	1.75
	1955KN	4.000	.10	.20	.65	1.75
	1956	15.616	.10	.15	.30	1.25
	1956KN	9.680	.10	.20	.40	1.25
	1957	15.000	.10	.20	.65	1.75
	1957H	5.000	1.50	3.00	6.00	15.00
	1957KN	I.A.	.10	.20	.65	1.75
	1959H	10.000	.10	.20	.40	1.25
	1959KN	10.000	.10	.20	.40	1.25
	1961	1.800	.15	.40	2.00	3.50
	1961	—	—	—	Proof	100.00
	1961H	1.800	.15	.40	2.00	3.50
	1962H	10.320	.10	.20	.40	1.25

5 CENTS

BRONZE

18	1921	1.000	2.00	4.00	10.00	35.00
	1922	2.500	.50	1.25	4.50	12.50
	1923	2.400	.50	1.25	4.50	12.50
	1923	—	—	—	Proof	150.00
	1924	4.800	.50	1.00	3.00	15.00
	1925	6.600	.50	1.00	3.00	10.00
	1925	—	—	—	Proof	125.00
	1928	1.200	1.00	2.00	4.00	25.00
	1928	—	—	—	Proof	150.00
	1933	5.000	.50	1.00	2.50	10.00
	1934	3.910	.50	1.00	3.50	15.00
	1934	—	—	—	Proof	150.00
	1935	5.800	.50	1.00	3.00	10.00
	1935	—	—	—	Proof	150.00
	1936	1.000	2.00	6.00	10.00	50.00

KM#	Date	Mintage	Fine	VF	XF	Unc
23	1936H	3.500	.25	.50	1.00	4.50
	1936H	—	—	—	Proof	150.00
	1936KN	2.150	.25	.50	1.00	4.50
	1936KN	—	—	—	Proof	150.00

Thick flan.

25.1	1937H	3.000	.50	1.00	2.00	4.00
	1937KN	3.000	.50	1.00	2.00	6.00
	1939H	2.000	.50	1.00	3.00	13.50
	1939KN	2.000	.50	1.00	3.00	13.50
	1941	—	3.00	7.50	15.00	40.00
	1941I	20.000	.50	1.00	2.00	5.00

Thin flan, reduced weight.

25.2	1941I	Inc. Ab.	.50	1.00	2.00	5.00
	1942	16.000	.50	1.00	2.00	4.00
	1942SA	4.120	1.00	2.00	10.00	30.00
	1943SA					
		17.880	.50	1.00	5.00	10.00

Obv. leg: ET IND.IMP. dropped.

33	1949	4.000	.25	.50	3.00	6.00
	1949	—	—	—	Proof	175.00
	1951H	6.000	.25	.50	2.00	5.00
	1951H	—	—	—	Proof	175.00
	1952	11.200	.20	.40	1.00	3.00
	1952	—	—	—	Proof	150.00

37	1955	2.000	.10	.25	.75	2.00
	1955	—	—	—	Proof	150.00
	1955H	4.000	.20	.50	1.25	3.50
	1955H	—	—	—	Proof	150.00
	1955KN	2.000	.35	.80	2.50	5.00
	1956H	3.000	.15	.35	1.00	3.00
	1956KN	3.000	2.50	4.00	7.50	10.00
	1956KN	—	—	—	Proof	125.00
	1957H	5.000	.10	.25	.75	2.00
	1957KN	5.000	.10	.25	.75	2.00
	1961H	4.000	.15	.35	1.00	3.00
	1963	12.600	—	.10	.30	.75
	1963	—	—	—	Proof	150.00

Post-Independence Issue

39	1964	7.600	—	.10	.20	.50

10 CENTS

BRONZE

19	1921	.130	5.00	10.00	25.00	80.00
	1922	7.120	1.00	3.00	8.00	20.00
	1923	1.200	1.25	4.00	15.00	45.00
	1924	4.900	.65	2.25	6.00	25.00
	1925	4.800	.65	2.25	6.00	25.00

KM#	Date	Mintage	Fine	VF	XF	Unc
19	1927	2.000	.75	2.50	6.50	20.00
	1928	3.800	.75	2.50	6.50	30.00
	1928	—	—	—	Proof	175.00
	1933	6.260	.75	2.50	6.50	17.50
	1934	3.649	.75	2.50	6.50	30.00
	1935	7.300	.65	2.00	5.00	15.00
	1936	.500	1.50	5.00	15.00	50.00

24	1936	2.000	1.00	3.50	8.00	25.00
	1936	—	—	—	Proof	200.00
	1936H	4.330	.25	.50	1.50	5.50
	1936H	—	—	—	Proof	360.00
	1936KN	4.142	.25	.50	1.50	5.50
	1936KN	—	—	—	Proof	145.00

NOTE: For listing of mule dated 1936H w/obv. of KM#24 and rev. of British West Africa KM#16 refer to British West Africa listings.

COPPER-NICKEL

24a	1936KN	—	—	—	—	—

BRONZE
Thick flan.

26.1	1937	2.000	.25	.75	2.50	6.00
	1937	—	—	—	Proof	175.00
	1937H	2.500	.25	.75	2.50	8.00
	1937H	—	—	—	Proof	175.00
	1937KN	2.500	.25	.75	2.50	8.00
	1937KN	—	—	—	Proof	175.00
	1939H	2.000	.25	.70	3.50	15.00
	1939KN	2.030	.25	.70	3.50	12.50
	1939KN	—	—	—	Proof	175.00
	1941I	15.682	.35	1.00	4.00	15.00
	1941I	—	—	—	Proof	175.00
	1941	—	.50	1.50	4.50	16.00
	1941	—	—	—	Proof	175.00

NOTE: Many dates, including 1941I, exist w/o center hole.

Thin flan, reduced weight.

26.2	1942	12.000	.20	.50	1.75	4.00
	1942	—	—	—	Proof	175.00
	1942I	4.317	3.00	5.00	10.00	20.00
	1943SA					
		14.093	.25	.50	4.50	10.00
	1945SA	5.000	.25	.50	3.00	12.50

Obv. leg: ET IND.IMP. dropped.

34	1949	4.000	.25	.50	2.00	5.00
	1949	—	—	—	Proof	175.00
	1950	8.000	.20	.40	1.75	4.00
	1950	—	—	—	Proof	200.00
	1951	14.500	.20	.40	1.25	3.00
	1951	—	—	—	Proof	175.00
	1952	15.800	.20	.40	1.25	3.00
	1952H	2.000	1.00	2.00	5.00	15.00

KM#	Date	Mintage	Fine	VF	XF	Unc
38	1956	6.001	.35	1.00	2.50	10.00
	1956	—	—	—	Proof	175.00
	1964H	1 known	—	—	—	1250.

Post-Independence Issue

40	1964H	10.002	.10	.15	.30	1.00

50 CENTS

3.8879 g, .250 SILVER, .0312 oz ASW
Fifty Cents-Half Shilling

20	1921	6.200	1.00	3.00	7.50	30.00
	1922	Inc. Ab.	1.00	2.00	6.00	27.50
	1923	.396	5.00	8.00	40.00	80.00
	1924	1.000	2.00	4.00	10.00	40.00

27	1937H	4.000	.75	1.25	3.50	12.50
	1937H	—	—	—	Proof	275.00
	1942H	5.000	.75	1.25	4.00	20.00
	1943I	2.000	1.50	3.00	7.50	30.00
	1944SA	1.000	2.00	4.00	9.00	32.50

COPPER-NICKEL
Obv. leg: ET INDIA IMPERATOR dropped.

30	1948	7.290	.20	.40	1.75	6.00
	1948	—	—	—	Proof	250.00
	1949	12.960	.15	.30	1.25	4.00
	1949	—	—	—	Proof	325.00
	1952KN	2.000	.20	.40	1.75	7.50

36	1954	3.700	.15	.35	1.00	3.00
	1954	—	—	—	Proof	225.00
	1955H	1.600	.75	2.00	5.00	12.00
	1955H	—	—	—	Proof	225.00
	1955KHN	—	3.50	6.50	12.50	30.00
	1955KN	—	.15	.35	1.75	4.50
	1956H	2.000	.15	.25	1.25	3.00
	1956H	—	—	—	Proof	225.00
	1956KHN	—	3.50	6.50	12.50	30.00
	1956KN	2.000	.15	.35	1.75	4.00
	1958H	2.600	.15	.40	2.00	5.00
	1960	—	.10	.25	1.25	3.25
	1962KN	4.000	.15	.35	1.75	4.50
	1963	6.000	.10	.25	1.25	3.00

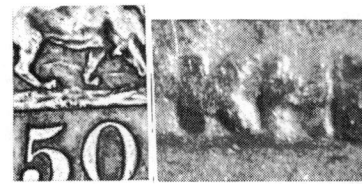

KM#	Date	Mintage	Fine	VF	XF	Unc
31	1950H	12.416	.50	.90	2.25	6.00
	1950KN	10.040	.40	.70	2.00	5.00
	1952	55.605	.35	.60	1.00	3.00
	1952	—	—	—	Proof	175.00
	1952H	8.024	.35	.60	1.25	3.50
	1952KN	9.360	.35	.60	1.25	3.50

EASTERN CARIBBEAN STATES

NOTE: The KHN mint marks above exist because the master dies were produced with both the KN and H mint marks for use at either mint. Each mint was required to remove the others mint mark before striking, but this was not always meticulously done. When one or the other mint mark was not fully removed a weak trace would remain creating the appearance of a wide space K N with a weak H in the middle or an H flanked by a weak K and N, in the field below the lion.

SHILLING

7.7759 g, .250 SILVER, .0625 oz ASW

KM#	Date	Mintage	Fine	VF	XF	Unc
21	1921	6.141	1.50	2.75	8.50	20.00
	1921H	4.240	1.75	3.00	10.00	30.00
	1922	18.858	1.25	2.25	6.50	18.00
	1922H	20.052	1.25	2.25	6.50	18.00
	1923	4.000	5.00	8.00	20.00	35.00
	1924	44.604	1.00	2.00	4.50	12.00
	1925	28.405	1.00	2.00	4.50	15.00
	1925	—	—	—	Proof	250.00

Obv: Bust of King George VI. **Rev:** Type I, thin rim and short milling, EAST AFRICA further from edge than Type II, larger loop on right side of coin below diamond in legend. Edge reeding spaced out.

28.1	1937H	7.672	1.00	2.00	4.00	12.50
	1937H	—	—	—	Proof	300.00
	1941I	7.000	1.25	2.00	6.00	20.00
	1942H	4.430	1.25	2.00	6.00	20.00
	1942H	—	—	—	Proof	300.00
	1944H	10.000	1.25	2.00	7.50	25.00

Rev: Type II, thicker rim and larger milling, EAST AFRICA and leaves very near the edge, small leaf (loop) under diamond on right side.

28.2	1941I	—	—	—	Rare	—

Rev: Type III, retouched central image, especially tuft of grass in front of lion.

28.3	1942I	3.900	1.00	2.00	5.00	20.00
	1943I					
	*25-50 pcs.	400.00	600.00	750.00		1500.

Obv. and rev. as KM#28.1, edge reeding close.

28.4	1944SA	5.820	1.25	2.00	5.00	25.00
	1945SA	10.080	1.25	2.00	5.00	22.50
	1946SA	18.260	1.25	2.00	3.50	17.50

NOTE: For more in-depth comparison of these reverse variety types, see *The Guidebook and Catalogue of British Commonwealth Coins, 1649-1971*, 3rd Ed., Remick, J. Winnipeg, Regency Coin and Stamp, 1971.

COPPER-NICKEL
Obv. leg: ET INDIA IMPERATOR dropped.

31	1948	19.704	.50	.90	1.50	6.50
	1949	38.318	.50	.90	1.50	6.50
	1949	—	—	—	Proof	250.00
	1949H	12.584	.50	.90	1.50	7.50
	1949KN	15.060	.50	.90	1.50	7.50
	1950	56.362	.35	.60	1.00	3.00
	1950	—	—	—	Proof	250.00

The East Caribbean States, formerly the British Caribbean Territories (Eastern group), formed a currency board in 1950 to provide the constituent territories of Trinidad & Tobago, Barbados, British Guiana (now Guyana), British Virgin Islands, Anguilla, St. Kitts, Nevis, Antigua, Dominica, St. Lucia, St. Vincent and Grenada with a common currency, thereby permitting withdrawal of the regular British Pound currency. This was dissolved in 1965 and after the breakup, the East Caribbean Territories, a grouping including Barbados, the Leeward and Windward Islands, came into being. Coinage of the dissolved 'Eastern Group' continues to circulate. Paper currency of the East Caribbean Authority was first issued in 1965 and although Barbados withdrew from the group they continued using them prior to 1973 when Barbados issued a decimal coinage.

A series of 4-dollar coins tied to the FAO coinage program were released in 1970 under the name of the Caribbean Development Bank by eight loosely federated island groupings in the eastern Caribbean. These issues are listed individually in this volume under Antigua, Barbados, Dominica, Grenada, Montserrat, St. Kitts, St. Lucia and St. Vincent.

RULERS

British

BRITISH EAST CARIBBEAN TERRITORIES

MONETARY SYSTEM
100 Cents = 1 Br. W. Indies Dollar

1/2 CENT

BRONZE

KM#	Date	Mintage	Fine	VF	XF	Unc
1	1955	.500	.30	.50	.75	2.00
	1955	2,000	—	—	Proof	3.00
	1958	.200	.50	.75	1.25	2.50
	1958	20 pcs.	—	—	Proof	145.00

CENT

BRONZE

2	1955	8.000	.15	.25	.60	1.00
	1955	2,000	—	—	Proof	3.00
	1957	3.000	.15	.25	1.75	3.00
	1957	—	—	—	Proof	100.00
	1958	1.500	.35	.50	4.50	7.50
	1958	20 pcs.	—	—	Proof	165.00
	1959	.500	.40	.60	6.00	20.00
	1959	—	—	—	Proof	100.00
	1960	2.500	.15	.25	.60	1.25
	1960	—	—	—	Proof	100.00
	1961	2.280	.25	.35	.75	1.25
	1961	—	—	—	Proof	100.00
	1962	2.000	.15	.25	.50	1.25
	1962	—	—	—	Proof	100.00
	1963	.750	.45	.70	1.20	2.50
	1963	—	—	—	Proof	100.00
	1964	2.500	—	—	.20	.35
	1964	—	—	—	Proof	100.00

KM#	Date	Mintage	Fine	VF	XF	Unc
2	1965	4.800	—	—	.20	.35
	1965	—	—	—	P/L	.75
	1965	—	—	—	Proof	5.00

2 CENTS

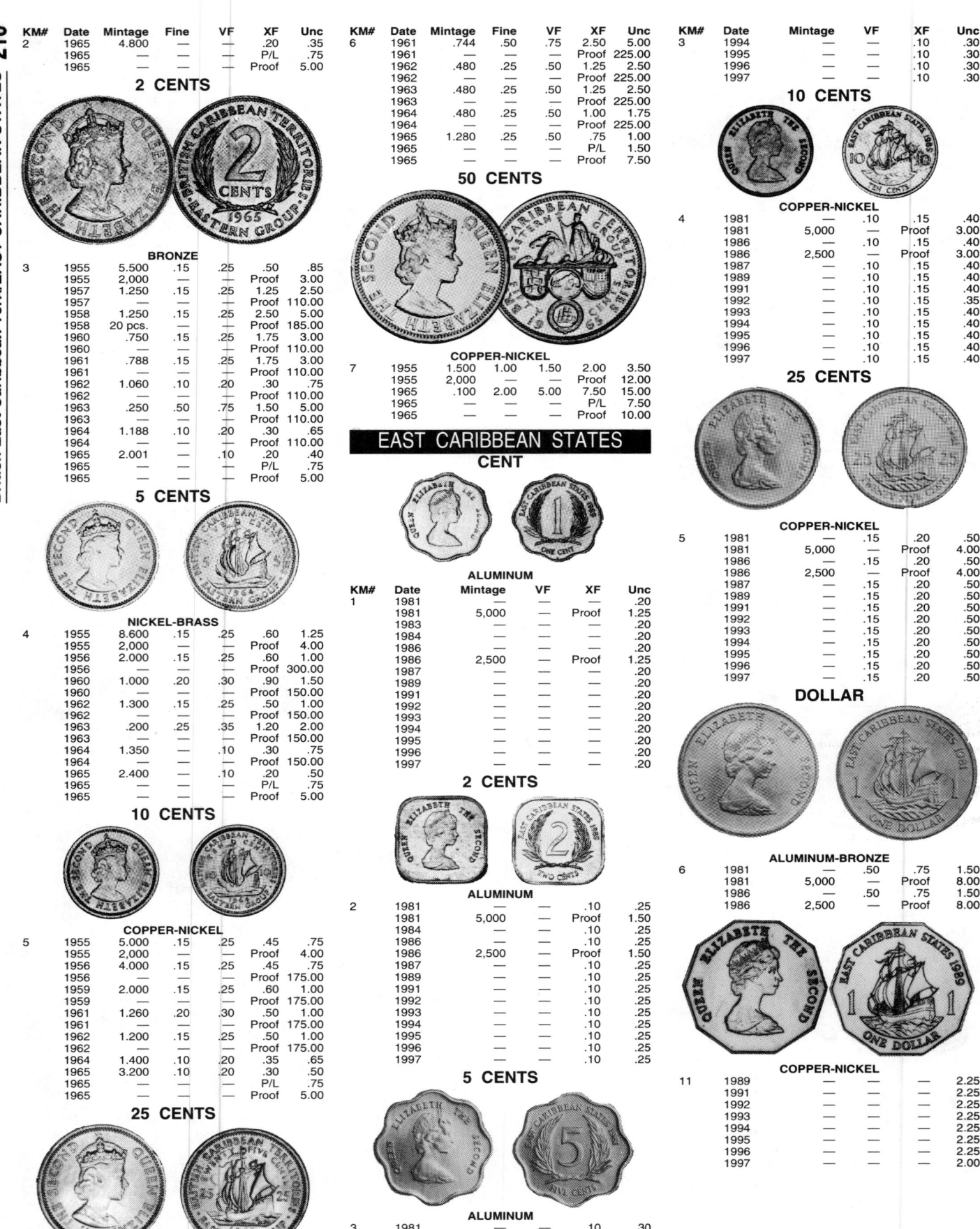

BRONZE

KM#	Date	Mintage	Fine	VF	XF	Unc
3	1955	5.500	.15	.25	.50	.85
	1955	2,000	—	—	Proof	3.00
	1957	1.250	.15	.25	1.25	2.50
	1957	—	—	—	Proof	110.00
	1958	1.250	.15	.25	2.50	5.00
	1958	20 pcs.	—	—	Proof	185.00
	1960	.750	.15	.25	1.75	3.00
	1960	—	—	—	Proof	110.00
	1961	.788	.15	.25	1.75	3.00
	1961	—	—	—	Proof	110.00
	1962	1.060	.10	.20	.30	.75
	1962	—	—	—	Proof	110.00
	1963	.250	.50	.75	1.50	5.00
	1963	—	—	—	Proof	110.00
	1964	1.188	.10	.20	.30	.65
	1964	—	—	—	Proof	110.00
	1965	2.001	—	—	.10	.40
	1965	—	—	—	P/L	.75
	1965	—	—	—	Proof	5.00

5 CENTS

NICKEL-BRASS

KM#	Date	Mintage	Fine	VF	XF	Unc
4	1955	8.600	.15	.25	.60	1.25
	1955	2,000	—	—	Proof	4.00
	1956	2.000	.15	.25	.60	1.00
	1956	—	—	—	Proof	300.00
	1960	1.000	.20	.30	.90	1.50
	1960	—	—	—	Proof	150.00
	1962	1.300	.15	.25	.50	1.00
	1962	—	—	—	Proof	150.00
	1963	.200	.25	.35	1.20	2.00
	1963	—	—	—	Proof	150.00
	1964	1.350	—	—	.10	.75
	1964	—	—	—	Proof	150.00
	1965	2.400	—	—	.20	.50
	1965	—	—	—	P/L	.75
	1965	—	—	—	Proof	5.00

10 CENTS

COPPER-NICKEL

KM#	Date	Mintage	Fine	VF	XF	Unc
5	1955	5.000	.15	.25	.45	.75
	1955	2,000	.15	—	Proof	4.00
	1956	4.000	.15	.25	.45	.75
	1956	—	—	—	Proof	175.00
	1959	2.000	.15	.25	.60	1.00
	1959	—	—	—	Proof	175.00
	1961	1.260	.20	.30	.50	1.00
	1961	—	—	—	Proof	175.00
	1962	1.200	.15	.25	.50	1.00
	1962	—	—	—	Proof	175.00
	1964	1.400	.10	.20	.35	.65
	1965	3.200	.10	.20	.30	.50
	1965	—	—	—	P/L	.75
	1965	—	—	—	Proof	5.00

25 CENTS

COPPER-NICKEL

KM#	Date	Mintage	Fine	VF	XF	Unc
6	1955	7.000	.35	.50	.70	1.00
	1955	2,000	—	—	Proof	6.00
	1957	.800	.75	1.00	2.25	4.50
	1957	—	—	—	Proof	225.00
	1959	1.000	.35	.50	1.25	2.25
	1959	—	—	—	Proof	225.00

KM#	Date	Mintage	Fine	VF	XF	Unc
6	1961	.744	.50	.75	2.50	5.00
	1961	—	—	—	Proof	225.00
	1962	.480	.25	.50	1.25	2.50
	1962	—	—	—	Proof	225.00
	1963	.480	.25	.50	1.25	2.50
	1963	—	—	—	Proof	225.00
	1964	.480	.25	.50	1.00	1.75
	1964	—	—	—	Proof	225.00
	1965	1.280	.25	.50	.75	1.00
	1965	—	—	—	P/L	1.50
	1965	—	—	—	Proof	7.50

50 CENTS

COPPER-NICKEL

KM#	Date	Mintage	Fine	VF	XF	Unc
7	1955	1.500	1.00	1.50	2.00	3.50
	1955	2,000	—	—	Proof	12.00
	1965	.100	2.00	5.00	7.50	15.00
	1965	—	—	—	P/L	7.50
	1965	—	—	—	Proof	10.00

EAST CARIBBEAN STATES

CENT

ALUMINUM

KM#	Date	Mintage	VF	XF	Unc
1	1981	—	—	—	.20
	1981	5,000	—	Proof	1.25
	1983	—	—	—	.20
	1984	—	—	—	.20
	1986	—	—	—	.20
	1986	2,500	—	Proof	1.25
	1987	—	—	—	.20
	1989	—	—	—	.20
	1991	—	—	—	.20
	1992	—	—	—	.20
	1993	—	—	—	.20
	1994	—	—	—	.20
	1995	—	—	—	.20
	1996	—	—	—	.20
	1997	—	—	—	.20

2 CENTS

ALUMINUM

KM#	Date	Mintage	VF	XF	Unc
2	1981	—	—	.10	.25
	1981	5,000	—	Proof	1.50
	1984	—	—	.10	.25
	1986	—	—	.10	.25
	1986	2,500	—	Proof	1.50
	1987	—	—	.10	.25
	1989	—	—	.10	.25
	1991	—	—	.10	.25
	1992	—	—	.10	.25
	1993	—	—	.10	.25
	1994	—	—	.10	.25
	1995	—	—	.10	.25
	1996	—	—	.10	.25
	1997	—	—	.10	.25

5 CENTS

ALUMINUM

KM#	Date	Mintage	VF	XF	Unc
3	1981	—	—	.10	.30
	1981	5,000	—	Proof	2.25
	1984	—	—	.10	.30
	1986	—	—	.10	.30
	1986	2,500	—	Proof	2.25
	1987	—	—	.10	.30
	1989	—	—	.10	.30
	1991	—	—	.10	.30
	1992	—	—	.10	.30
	1993	—	—	.10	.30

KM#	Date	Mintage	VF	XF	Unc
3	1994	—	—	.10	.30
	1995	—	—	.10	.30
	1996	—	—	.10	.30
	1997	—	—	.10	.30

10 CENTS

COPPER-NICKEL

KM#	Date	Mintage	VF	XF	Unc
4	1981	—	—	.15	.40
	1981	5,000	—	Proof	3.00
	1986	—	—	.15	.40
	1986	2,500	—	Proof	3.00
	1987	—	—	.15	.40
	1989	—	—	.15	.40
	1991	—	—	.15	.40
	1992	—	—	.15	.35
	1993	—	—	.15	.40
	1994	—	—	.15	.40
	1995	—	—	.15	.40
	1996	—	—	.15	.40
	1997	—	—	.15	.40

25 CENTS

COPPER-NICKEL

KM#	Date	Mintage	VF	XF	Unc
5	1981	—	.15	.20	.50
	1981	5,000	—	Proof	4.00
	1986	—	.15	.20	.50
	1986	2,500	—	Proof	4.00
	1987	—	.15	.20	.50
	1989	—	.15	.20	.50
	1991	—	.15	.20	.50
	1992	—	.15	.20	.50
	1993	—	.15	.20	.50
	1994	—	.15	.20	.50
	1995	—	.15	.20	.50
	1996	—	.15	.20	.50
	1997	—	.15	.20	.50

DOLLAR

ALUMINUM-BRONZE

KM#	Date	Mintage	VF	XF	Unc
6	1981	—	.50	.75	1.50
	1981	5,000	—	Proof	8.00
	1986	—	.50	.75	1.50
	1986	2,500	—	Proof	8.00

COPPER-NICKEL

KM#	Date	Mintage	VF	XF	Unc
11	1989	—	—	—	2.25
	1991	—	—	—	2.25
	1992	—	—	—	2.25
	1993	—	—	—	2.25
	1994	—	—	—	2.25
	1995	—	—	—	2.25
	1996	—	—	—	2.25
	1997	—	—	—	2.00

ECUADOR

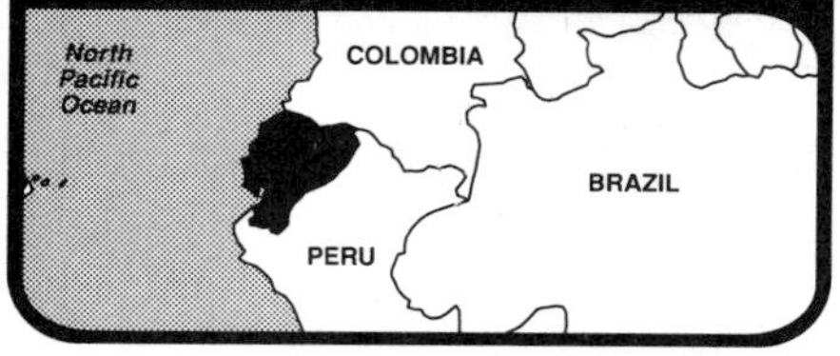

The Republic of Ecuador, located astride the equator on the Pacific Coast of South America, has an area of 105,037 sq. mi. (283,560 sq. km.) and a population of 10.9 million. Capital: Quito. Agriculture is the mainstay of the economy but there are appreciable deposits of minerals and petroleum. It is one of the world's largest exporters of bananas and balsa wood. Coffee, cacao, sugar and petroleum are also valuable exports.

Ecuador was first sighted in 1526 by Francisco Pizarro. Conquest was undertaken by Sebastian de Benalcazar, who founded Quito in 1534. Ecuador was part of the Viceroyalty of New Granada through the 16th and 17th centuries. After previous attempts to attain independence were crushed, Antonio Sucre, the able lieutenant of Bolivar, secured Ecuador's freedom in the Battle of Pinchincha, May 24, 1822. It then joined Venezuela and Colombia in a confederation known as Gran Colombia, and became an independent republic when it left the confederacy in 1830.

MINT MARKS

BIRMm - Birmingham
D - Denver
H - Heaton, Birmingham
HF - LeLocle (Swiss)
LIMA - Lima
Mo - Mexico
PHILA.U.S.A. - Philadelphia
PHILADELPHIA - Philadelphia

ASSAYERS INITIALS

FP - Feliciano Paredes
GJ - Guillermo Jameson
MV - Miguel Vergara
ST - Santiago Taylor

MONETARY SYSTEM

10 Centavos = 1 Decimo
10 Decimos = 1 Sucre
25 Sucres = 1 Condor

MEDIO CENTAVO

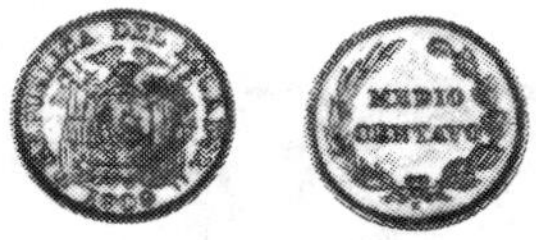

COPPER-NICKEL
Mint mark: HEATON BIRMINGHAM

KM#	Date	Mintage	Fine	VF	XF	Unc
57	1909H	4.000	3.00	7.00	15.00	30.00

UN CENTAVO

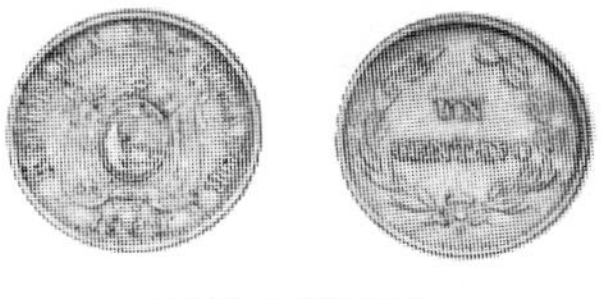

COPPER-NICKEL

KM#	Date	Mintage	Fine	VF	XF	Unc
58	1909H	3.000	3.50	7.50	15.00	30.00

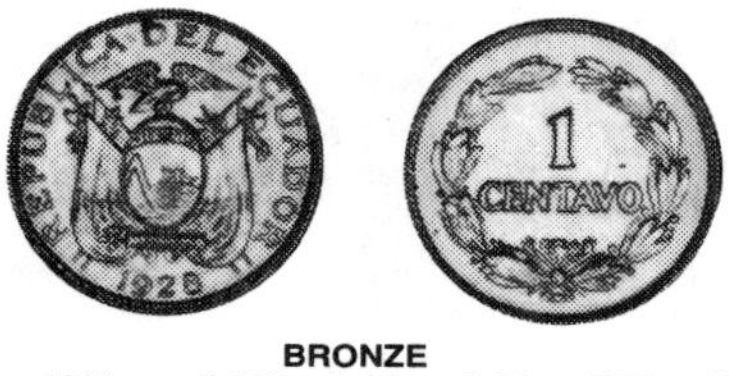

BRONZE

KM#	Date	Mintage	Fine	VF	XF	Unc
67	1928	2.016	1.00	2.00	7.50	15.00

DOS CENTAVOS

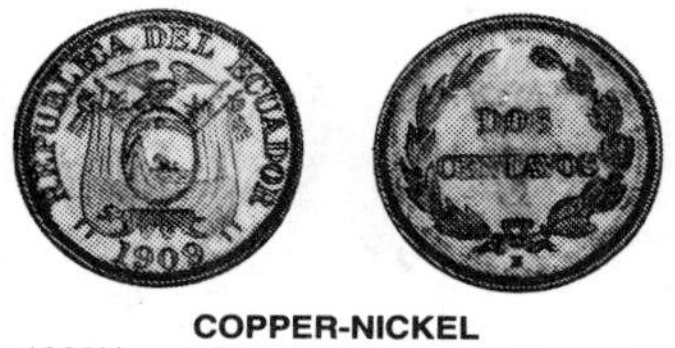

COPPER-NICKEL

KM#	Date	Mintage	Fine	VF	XF	Unc
59	1909H	2.500	2.00	5.00	20.00	50.00
	1909H	—	—	—	Proof	175.00

DOS Y MEDIO CENTAVOS

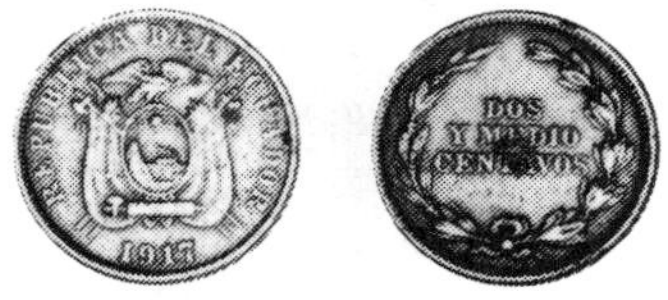

COPPER-NICKEL

KM#	Date	Mintage	Fine	VF	XF	Unc
61	1917	1.600	3.00	10.00	35.00	70.00

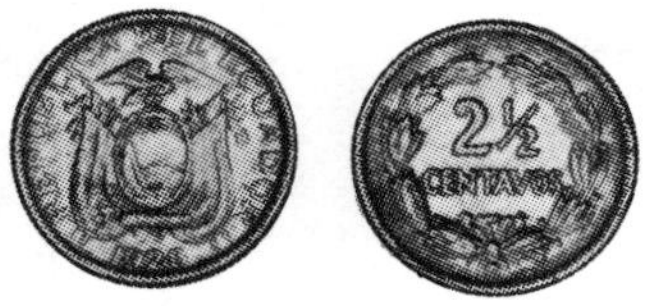

NICKEL

KM#	Date	Mintage	Fine	VF	XF	Unc
68	1928	4.000	2.00	4.00	15.00	30.00

MEDIO DECIMO

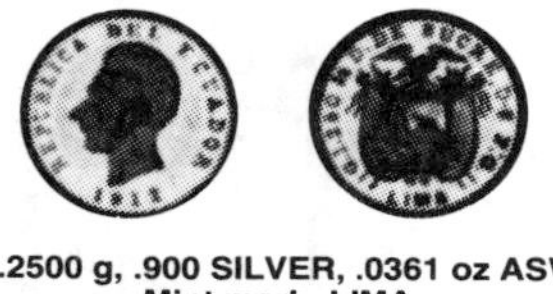

1.2500 g, .900 SILVER, .0361 oz ASW
Mint mark: LIMA

KM#	Date	Mintage	Fine	VF	XF	Unc
55.1	1902/892 JF	1.000	1.00	2.00	7.50	15.00
	1902 JF	I.A.	.75	1.25	5.00	10.00
	1905/805 JF	.500	3.00	5.00	15.00	40.00
	1905/2 JF	I.A.	3.50	6.00	18.00	50.00
	1905 JF	I.A.	.75	1.25	5.00	10.00
	1912/05 FG	.020	3.00	6.00	18.00	50.00
	1912 FG	I.A.	.75	1.25	5.00	10.00
	1912 FG (error) obv: FCUADOR	Inc. Ab.	2.00	3.00	7.50	15.00

NOTE: Earlier dates (1893-1899) exist for this type.

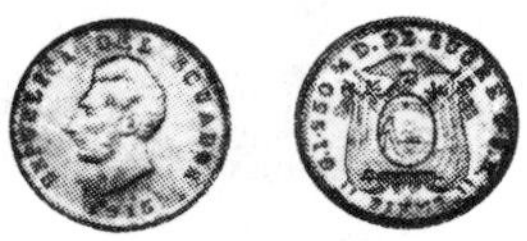

Mint mark: BIRMm
Modified reverse.

KM#	Date	Mintage	Fine	VF	XF	Unc
55.2	1915	2.000	.75	1.25	3.00	8.00
	1915	—	—	—	Proof	150.00

CINCO CENTAVOS

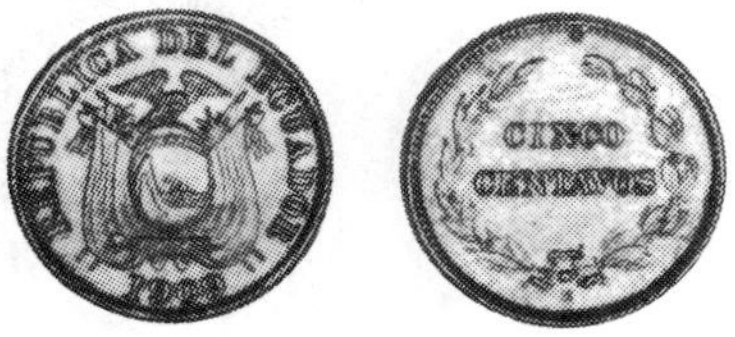

COPPER-NICKEL
Obv: Ribbon tails on flag poles point outward.

KM#	Date	Mintage	Fine	VF	XF	Unc
60.1	1909H	2.000	4.50	10.00	30.00	80.00

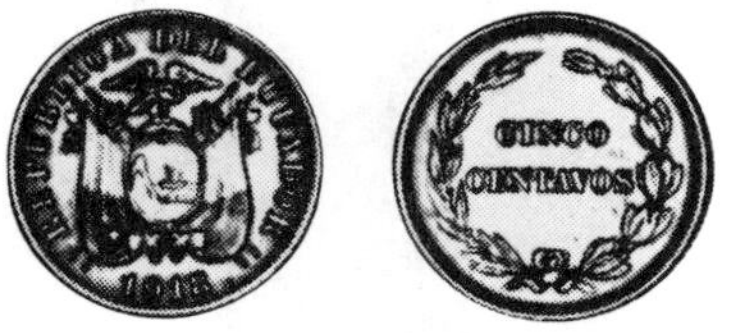

Thin planchet.
Obv: Ribbon tails on flag poles point downward.

KM#	Date	Mintage	Fine	VF	XF	Unc
60.2	1917	1.200	5.50	12.50	35.00	90.00
	1918	7.980	2.00	4.00	10.00	20.00

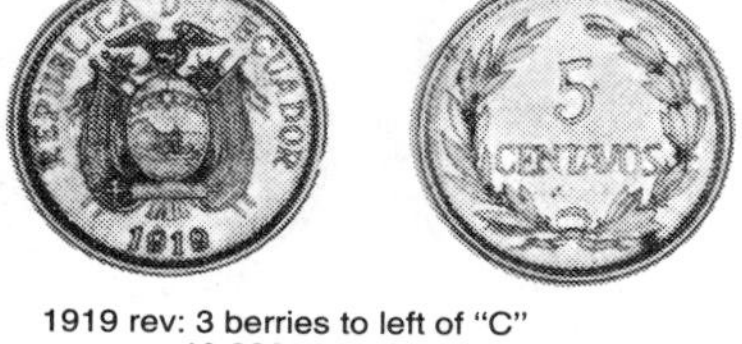

KM#	Date	Mintage	Fine	VF	XF	Unc
63	1919 rev: 3 berries to left of "C"	12.000	.60	1.25	5.00	10.00
	1919 rev: 4 berries loose to left of "C"	Inc. Ab.	1.25	2.50	7.50	15.00
	1919 rev: 4 berries tight to left of "C"	Inc. Ab.	1.25	2.50	7.50	15.00

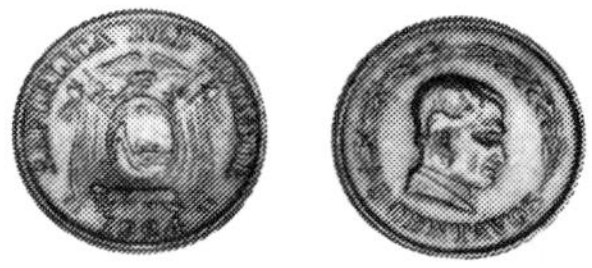

KM#	Date	Mintage	Fine	VF	XF	Unc
65	1924H	10.000	1.00	1.75	5.00	10.00

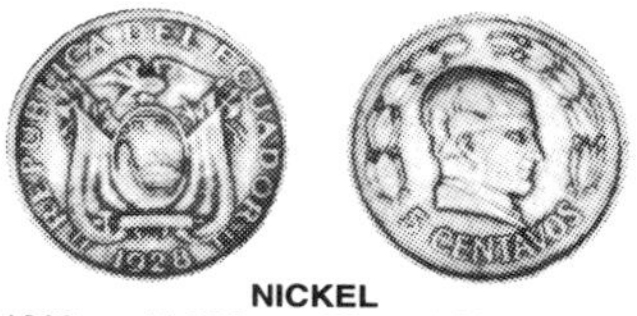

NICKEL

KM#	Date	Mintage	Fine	VF	XF	Unc
69	1928	16.000	.75	1.00	2.00	4.50

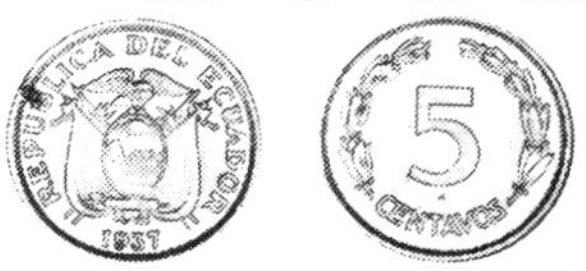

KM#	Date	Mintage	Fine	VF	XF	Unc
75	1937HF	15.000	.10	.20	.75	2.00

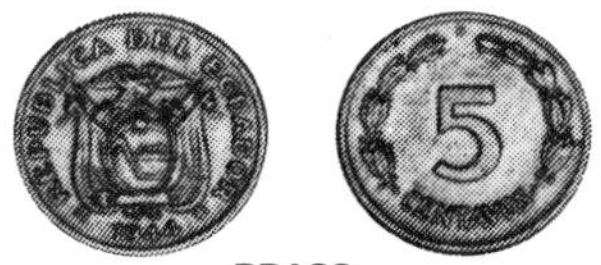

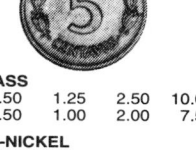

KM#	Date	Mintage	Fine	VF	XF	Unc
			BRASS			
75a	1942	2.000	.50	1.25	2.50	10.00
	1944D	3.000	.50	1.00	2.00	7.50
			COPPER-NICKEL			
75b	1946	40.000	—	—	.40	1.00
			NICKEL CLAD STEEL			
75c	1970	—	—	—	.15	.50
	1970 obv: ECADOR(error)	—	—	—	—	—

UN DECIMO

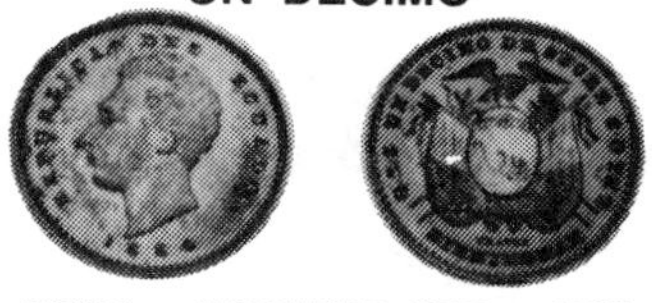

2.5000 g, .900 SILVER, .0723 oz ASW
Mint mark: LIMA
Rev. leg: W/o LEY.

KM#	Date	Mintage	VG	Fine	VF	XF
50.3	1902 JF rev: W/JR below fasces	.519	1.00	2.50	5.00	10.00
	1902 JF rev: w/o JR below fasces	Inc. Ab.	1.00	2.50	5.00	10.00
	1905 JF	.250	1.00	2.50	5.00	10.00
	1912 FG	.030	2.00	3.00	6.00	15.00

NOTE: Earlier dates (1892-1900) exist for this type.

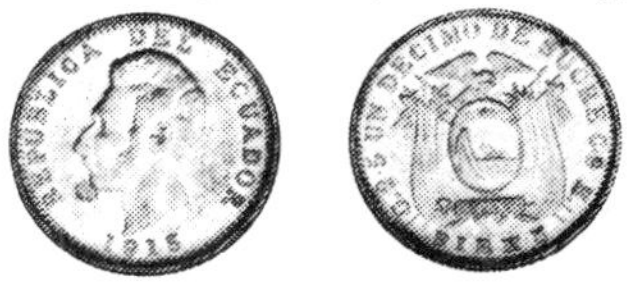

Mint mark: BIRMm
Modified reverse.

KM#	Date	Mintage	VG	Fine	VF	XF
50.4	1915	1.000	BV	1.25	2.00	7.00
	1915	—	—	—	Proof	200.00

Mint mark: PHILA.

KM#	Date	Mintage	VG	Fine	VF	XF
50.5	1916	2.000	BV	1.25	2.00	5.00

DIEZ CENTAVOS

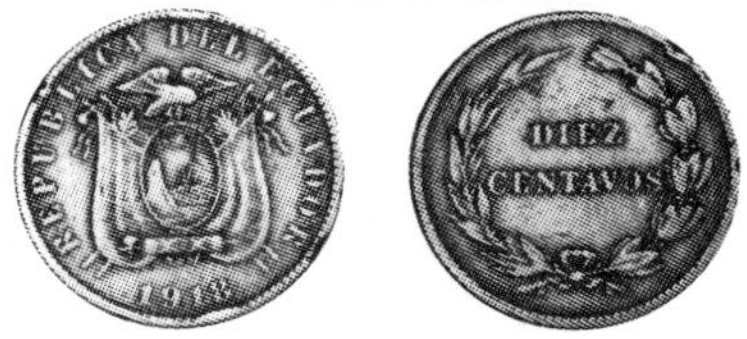

COPPER-NICKEL

KM#	Date	Mintage	Fine	VF	XF	Unc
62	1918	1.000	5.50	11.00	25.00	50.00

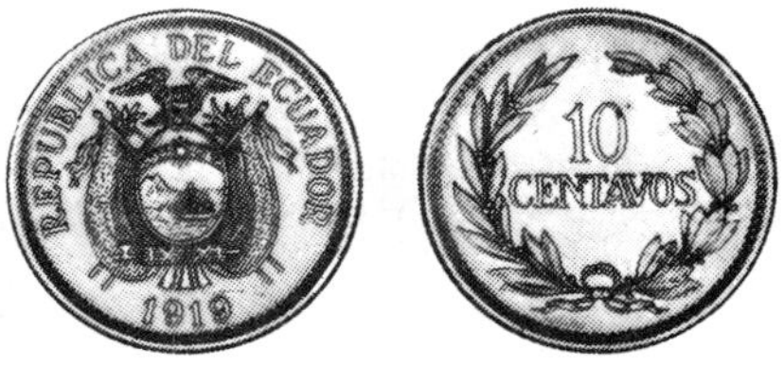

KM#	Date	Mintage	Fine	VF	XF	Unc
64	1919	2.000	1.00	2.00	7.50	15.00
	1919	—	—	—	Proof	200.00

66	1924H	5.000	.75	1.50	3.00	10.00
	1924H	—	—	—	Proof	80.00

NOTE: The H mint mark is very small and is located above the date.

NICKEL

70	1928	16.000	.50	1.00	4.00	9.00

76	1937HF	7.500	.25	.50	1.00	3.50

BRASS

76a	1942	5.000	.60	1.00	3.50	9.00

COPPER-NICKEL

76b	1946	40.000	.10	.15	.25	1.00

NICKEL CLAD STEEL

76c	1964	20.000	—	—	.15	.50
	1968	15.000	—	—	.15	.50
	1972	20.000	—	—	.15	.40

NOTE: Varieties exist.

COPPER-NICKEL CLAD STEEL

76d	1976	10.000	—	—	.15	.40

DOS DECIMOS

Mint mark: LIMA. or LIMA
Rev. leg: W/o LEY.

KM#	Date	Mintage	VG	Fine	VF	XF
51.3	1912/18 FG	.050	5.00	7.50	10.00	25.00
	1912 FG	I.A.	2.00	4.00	7.00	15.00
	1914 FG LIMA	.110	3.00	5.00	10.00	20.00
	1914 FG LIMA	I.A.	2.00	4.00	7.00	15.00
	1915 FG	.157	3.00	5.00	10.00	20.00

NOTE: Small "R" below fasces on rev.
NOTE: Earlier dates (1889-1896) exist for this type.

Mint mark: PHILADELPHIA

51.4	1914 TF	2.500	1.50	3.00	5.00	10.00
	1916 TF	1.000	1.50	3.00	5.00	10.00

NOTE: Earlier date (1895) exists for this type.

20 CENTAVOS

NICKEL

KM#	Date	Mintage	Fine	VF	XF	Unc
77.1	1937HF	7.500	.25	.50	1.00	3.50

BRASS

77.1a	1942	5.000	.60	1.00	6.00	15.00
	1944D	15.000	.40	.75	4.00	10.00

COPPER-NICKEL

KM#	Date	Mintage	Fine	VF	XF	Unc
77.1b	1946	30.000	.10	.20	.35	1.25

NICKEL CLAD STEEL

77.1c	1959	14.400	—	—	.15	.50
	1962	14.400	—	—	.15	.50
	1966	24.000	—	—	.15	.50
	1969	24.000	—	—	.15	.50
	1971	12.000	—	—	.15	.50
	1972	48.432	—	—	.15	.50

COPPER-NICKEL
Obv: Modified coat of arms.

77.2	1974	19.562	—	—	.15	.50

NICKEL COATED STEEL

77.2a	1975	52.437	—	—	—	—
	1978	37.500	—	—	.15	.35
	1980	18.000	—	—	.15	.35
	1981	21.000	—	—	.15	.35

CINQUENTA CENTAVOS

2.5000 g, .720 SILVER, .0579 oz ASW
Mint mark: PHILA • U • S • A

71	1928	1.000	BV	2.00	7.00	15.00
	1930	.155	BV	5.00	15.00	35.00

NICKEL CLAD STEEL

81	1963	20.000	—	.15	.25	.60
	1971	5.000	—	.15	.25	.60
	1974	—	—	.15	.25	.60
	1975	—	—	.15	.25	.60
	1977	40.000	—	.10	.20	.50
	1979	25.000	—	.10	.20	.50
	1982	20.000	—	.10	.20	.50

Obv: Modified coat of arms.

87	1985	30.000	—	.10	.20	.40

90	1988	*	—	—	—	.30
	1988	25 pcs.	—	—	Proof	—

*NOTE: Withdrawn from circulation and remelted, approximately 100,000 pieces released.

UN SUCRE

5.0000 g, .720 SILVER, .1157 oz ASW
Mint mark: PHILA • U • S • A

72	1928	3.000	BV	2.50	10.00	25.00
	1930	.400	2.00	8.00	20.00	50.00
	1934	2.000	BV	2.50	10.00	30.00

NICKEL, 26.5mm

KM#	Date	Mintage	Fine	VF	XF	Unc
78.1	1937 HF	9.000	.50	.75	1.50	5.00

25.9mm

78.2	1946	18.000	.40	.60	.80	2.00

COPPER-NICKEL
Obv: Different ship in coat of arms.

78a	1959	8.400	.25	.50	.65	1.00
	1959	—	—	—	Proof	250.00

NICKEL CLAD STEEL
Obv: Ship in arms similar to KM#78.

78b	1964	20.000	—	.10	.25	.50
	1970	24.000	—	.10	.25	.50
	1971	8.092	—	.10	.25	.50
	1974	40.308	—	.10	.25	.50
	1978	32.000	—	.10	.25	.50
	1979	32.000	—	.10	.25	.50
	1980	110.000	—	.10	.25	.50
	1981	70.000	—	.10	.25	.50

Obv: Modified coat of arms, ship similar to KM#78a.

83	1974	32.000	—	.10	.20	.40
	1975	32.000	—	.10	.20	.40
	1975	—	—	—	Proof	150.00
	1977	32.000	—	.10	.20	.35

Obv: Modified coat of arms.
Rev: Large head.

85.1	1985					.50

Rev: Small head.

85.2	1986					.50

89	1988	*	—	—	—	.40
	1988	25 pcs.	—	—	Proof	—
	1990					.40
	1992					.40

*NOTE: Reportedly withdrawn from circulation and remelted, approximately 100,000 pieces released.

DOS SUCRES

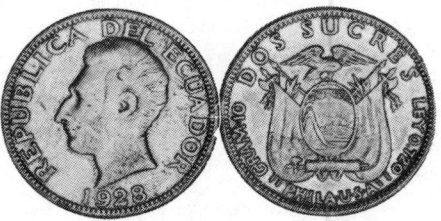

10.0000 g, .720 SILVER, .2315 oz ASW
Mint mark: PHILA • U • S • A

KM#	Date	Mintage	Fine	VF	XF	Unc
73	1928	.500	2.00	7.00	25.00	50.00
	1930	.100	4.00	15.00	40.00	75.00

Mint mark: Mo/MEXICO

80	1944	1.000	2.50	3.50	4.50	7.00

COPPER-NICKEL

82	1973	*2.000	—	—	200.00	300.00

*NOTE: Not released to circulation, all but approximately 35 pieces were remelted.

CINCO SUCRES

25.0000 g, .720 SILVER, .5787 oz ASW
Mint mark: Mo/MEXICO

79	1943	1.000	—	BV	6.00	10.00
	1944	2.600	—	BV	5.00	8.00

COPPER-NICKEL

84	1973	*500 pcs.	—	—	—	1200.

*NOTE: Only 7 pieces were distributed to Ecuadorian government officials, while 8 pieces (5 of these cancelled) reside in the Central Bank Collection. The remaining 485 pieces have been remelted.

NICKEL CLAD STEEL

91	1988	*	—	—	—	.50
	1988	25 pcs.	—	—	Proof	—
	1991		—	—	—	.50

*NOTE: Reportedly withdrawn from circulation and remelted, approximately 100,000 pieces released.

DIEZ SUCRES

NICKEL CLAD STEEL
Similar to KM#92.2 but small arms and letters.

KM#	Date	Mintage	Fine	VF	XF	Unc
92.1	1988	*	—	—	—	1.00
	1988	25 pcs.	—	—	Proof	—

*NOTE: Withdrawn from circulation and remelted, approximately 100,000 pieces released.

Large arms and letters.

92.2	1991		—	—	—	1.00

20 SUCRES

NICKEL CLAD STEEL

94.1	1988		—	—	—	1.75
	1988	25 pcs.	—	—	Proof	—

Obv: Modified coat of arms.

94.2	1991		—	—	—	1.75

50 SUCRES

NICKEL CLAD STEEL

93	1988	*	—	—	—	3.00
	1988	25 pcs.	—	—	Proof	—
	1991 wide date		—	—	—	3.00
	1991 narrow date		—	—	—	3.00

*NOTE: Withdrawn from circulation and remelted, approximately 100,000 pieces released.

100 SUCRES

BRONZE PLATED STEEL center in
NICKEL PLATED STEEL ring
National Bicentennial

96	1995		—	—	—	1.25

BRASS CLAD STEEL center in
STAINLESS STEEL ring
Antonio Jose de Sucre
Obv: Portrait. Rev: Denomination.

101	ND(1997)		—	—	—	1.00

500 SUCRES

BRONZE PLATED STEEL center in
NICKEL PLATED STEEL ring
State Reform
Rev: Isidro Ayora.

97	1995		—	—	—	1.75

ALUMINUM-BRONZE center in
COPPER-NICKEL ring
Isidro Ayora
Obv: Portrait. Rev: Denomination.

KM#	Date	Mintage	Fine	VF	XF	Unc
102	ND(1997)		—	—	—	1.50

1000 SUCRES

BRASS center in STAINLESS STEEL ring
Portrait of Eugenio Espejo

99	1996		—	—	—	2.50

ALUMINUM-BRONZE center in
COPPER-NICKEL ring
Eugenio Espejo
Obv: Portrait. Rev: Denomination.

103	ND(1997)		—	—	—	2.25

UN CONDOR

8.3592 g, .900 GOLD, .2419 oz AGW
Mint mark: BIRMINGHAM

74	1928	.020	100.00	150.00	200.00	350.00

NOTE: 5,000 of these have been released into circulation, the remainder as gold reserve of the Central Bank.

EGYPT

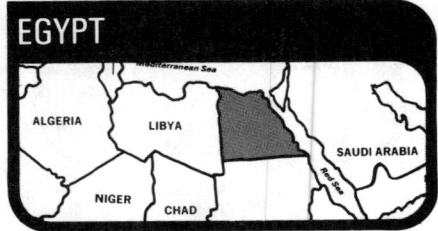

The Arab Republic of Egypt, located on the northeastern corner of Africa, has an area of 385,229 sq. mi. (1,1001,450 sq. km.) and a population of 62.4 million. Capital: Cairo. Although Egypt is an almost rainless expanse of desert, its economy is predominantly agricultural. Cotton, rice and petroleum are exported. Other main sources of income are revenues from the Suez Canal, remittances of Egyptian workers abroad and tourism.

Egyptian history dates back to about 3000 B.C. when the empire was established by uniting the upper and lower kingdoms. Following its 'Golden Age' (16th to 13th centuries B.C.), Egypt was conquered by Persia (525 B.C.) and Alexander the Great (332 B.C.). The Ptolemies, descended from one of Alexander's generals, ruled until the suicide of Cleopatra (30 B.C.) when Egypt became the private domain of the Roman emperor, and subsequently part of the Byzantine world. Various Muslim dynasties ruled Egypt from 641 on, including Ayyubid Sultans to 1250 and Mamluks to 1517, when it was conquered by the Ottoman Turks, interrupted by the occupation of Napoleon (1798-1801). A semi-independent dynasty was founded by Muhammad Ali in 1805 which lasted until 1952. Turkish rule became increasingly casual, permitting Great Britain to inject its influence by purchasing shares in the Suez Canal. British troops occupied Egypt in 1882, becoming the de facto rulers. On Dec. 14, 1914, Egypt was made a protectorate of Britain. British occupation ended on Feb. 28, 1922, when Egypt became a sovereign, independent kingdom. The monarchy was abolished and a republic proclaimed on July 23, 1952.

On Feb. 1, 1958, Egypt and Syria formed the United Arab Republic. Yemen joined on March 8 in an association known as the United Arab States. Syria withdrew from the United Arab Republic on Sept. 29, 1961, and on Dec. 26 Egypt dissolved its ties with Yemen in the United Arab States. On Sept. 2, 1971, Egypt finally shed the name United Arab Republic in favor of the Arab Republic of Egypt.

RULERS
Local Khedives
British, 1882-1922

Local Khedives
Abbas II Hilmi, 1892-1914

Local Sultans
Hussein Kamil, 1914-1917
Ahmed Fuad I, 1917-1922
Kingdom, 1922-1952
  Ahmed Fuad I, 1922-1936
  Farouk, 1936-1952
  Fuad II, 1952-1953
Republic, 1952-

MONETARY SYSTEM
(1885-1916)
10 Ushr-al-Qirsh = 1 Piastre
(Commencing 1916)
10 Milliemes = 1 Piastre (Qirsh)
100 Piastres = 1 Pound (Gunayh)

MINT MARKS
Egyptian coins issued prior to the advent of the British Protectorate series of Sultan Hussein Kamil introduced in 1916 were very similar to Turkish coins of the same period. They can best be distinguished by the presence of the Arabic word *Misr* (Egypt) on the reverse, which generally appears immediately above the Muslim accession date of the ruler, which is presented in Arabic numerals. Each coin is individually dated according to the regnal years.

BP - Budapest, Hungary
H - Birmingham, England
KN - King's Norton, England

ENGRAVER
W - Emil Weigand, Berlin

INITIAL LETTERS, NUMERALS

Alif	ba	ha	ha	dal
١	ب	ح	ح	د
i	ii	iii	iv	v
ra	sin	sad	(?) sm	ta
ر	س	ص	صم	ط
vi	vii	viii	ix	x
tha	'ain	(hamza)	kaf	mim
ظ	ع	ء	ق	م
xi	xii	xiii	xiv	xv
noon	noon w/o dot	ha	(?) ra	ah
ن	ں	هو	مر	اح
xvi	xvii	xviii	xix	xx
es	ba	bkr	ha	raa
اس	با	بكر	حا	را
xxi	xxii	xxiii	xxiv	xxv
ragib	sma	msi	'aa	gha
راغب	سا	صس	عا	غا
xxvi	xxvii	xxviii	xxvix	xxx
'ab	'abd	'ad	'an	md
عب	عبد	عد	عن	مد
xxxi	xxxii	xxxiii	xxxiv	xxxv
mr	mk	mdm	mha	ha
مر	مط	مصر	ملا	ه
xxxvi	xxxvii	xxxviii	xxxix	xl
ya	42a	md6	6md	6mdm
يا	١٢٤	مد٦	أصمد	أصصم
xli	xlii	xliii	xliv	xlv

REGNAL YEAR IDENTIFICATION

4
Duriba fi

Misr   **Accession Date**

DENOMINATIONS

 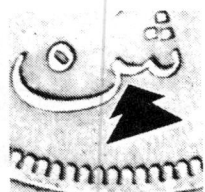

Para   *Qirsh*

NOTE: The unit of value on coins of this period is generally presented on the obverse immediately below the toughra, as shown in the illustrations above.

Piastres 1916-1933

Milliemes   *Piastres 1934 -*

TITLES

المصرية المملكة

al-Mamlaka   *al-Misriya*
(The Kingdom of Egypt)

U.A.R. EGYPT

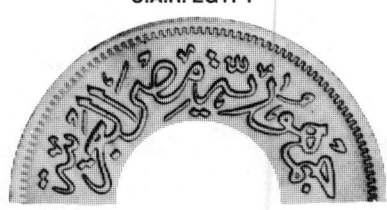

The legend illustrated is *Jumhuriyat Misr al-'Arabiyya* which translates to 'The Arab Republic of Egypt'. Similar legends are found on the modern issues of Syria.

ABDUL HAMID II
AH1293-1327/1876-1909AD

1/40 QIRSH

BRONZE
Accession Date: AH1293

KM#	Year	Mintage	Fine	VF	XF	Unc
287	26	1.999	1.00	2.00	4.00	15.00
	27	1.200	1.50	3.00	7.00	18.00
	29	2.000	1.00	2.00	4.00	15.00
	31H	2.400	1.00	2.00	4.00	15.00
	32H	Inc. Be.	1.00	2.00	4.00	15.00
	33H	1.200	1.00	2.00	4.00	12.00
	35H	1.200	1.00	5.00	7.00	15.00

NOTE: Earlier dates (Yr.10-24) exist for this type.

1/20 QIRSH

BRONZE
Accession Date: AH1293

KM#	Year	Mintage	Fine	VF	XF	Unc
288	26	1.405	1.00	2.00	3.00	12.00
	27	1.402	1.00	2.00	3.00	12.00
	29	3.200	1.00	2.00	3.00	12.00
	31H	3.000	1.00	2.00	3.00	10.00
	32H	Inc. Be.	1.00	2.00	3.00	10.00
	33H	1.400	2.00	3.00	5.00	15.00
	35H	1.400	3.00	6.00	10.00	20.00

NOTE: Earlier dates (Yr.10-24) exist for this type.

1/10 QIRSH

COPPER-NICKEL
Accession Date: AH1293

KM#	Year	Mintage	Fine	VF	XF	Unc
289	27	3.010	1.00	1.50	3.00	10.00
	28	6.000	1.00	1.50	3.00	10.00
	29	1.500	1.00	2.00	4.00	15.00
	30	1.000	1.00	1.50	3.00	12.50
	31H	3.000	1.00	1.50	4.00	15.00
	32H	Inc. Be.	1.00	1.50	3.00	12.50
	33H	2.000	1.00	1.50	2.50	8.50
	35H	2.000	1.25	3.00	6.00	20.00
	Common date	—		—	Proof	100.00

NOTE: Earlier dates (Yr.10-25) exist for this type.

2/10 QIRSH

COPPER-NICKEL
Accession Date: AH1293

KM#	Year	Mintage	Fine	VF	XF	Unc
290	27	1.002	1.00	3.00	6.00	20.00
	28	2.000	1.00	3.00	6.00	20.00
	29	1.500	1.00	3.00	6.00	20.00
	30	—	3.00	6.00	12.00	40.00
	31H	1.000	1.00	3.00	6.00	20.00
	33H	1.500	1.00	3.00	6.00	20.00
	35H	.750	2.00	6.00	10.00	35.00

NOTE: Earlier dates (Yr.10-25) exist for this type.

5/10 QIRSH

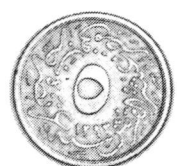

COPPER-NICKEL
Accession Date: AH1293

KM#	Year	Mintage	Fine	VF	XF	Unc
291	27	4.999	.30	1.50	5.00	20.00
	29	12.000	.30	1.50	5.00	20.00
	30	2.000	.50	2.00	6.00	25.00
	33H	1.000	2.00	6.00	12.50	40.00
	Common date	—		—	Proof	145.00

NOTE: Earlier dates (Yr.10-25) exist for this type.

QIRSH

1.4000 g, .833 SILVER, .0375 oz ASW
Accession Date: AH1293

KM#	Year	Mintage	Fine	VF	XF	Unc
292	27 W	.200	1.25	4.00	10.00	27.50
	29 W	.100	1.50	4.00	10.00	30.00
	29H	.100	1.25	3.00	7.50	25.00
	33H	.100	1.25	3.00	7.50	25.00
	33H	—	—	—	Proof	120.00
	Common date	—		—	Proof	135.00

NOTE: Earlier dates (Yr.10-17) exist for this type.

COPPER-NICKEL

KM#	Year	Mintage	Fine	VF	XF	Unc
299	27	.999	2.00	6.00	20.00	50.00
	29	3.500	2.00	5.00	15.00	40.00
	30	.500	2.50	6.00	20.00	55.00
	33H	1.000	2.00	5.00	15.00	40.00

NOTE: Earlier dates (Yr.22-25) exist for this type.

2 QIRSH

2.8000 g, .833 SILVER, .0750 oz ASW
Accession Date: AH1293
Obv: Flower to right of toughra.

293	27 W	1.000	2.00	4.00	10.00	35.00
	29 W	.450	2.00	4.00	10.00	35.00
	29H	1.250	2.00	4.00	10.00	35.00
	30H	.500	3.00	6.00	15.00	40.00
	31H	Inc. Ab.	3.00	6.00	10.00	40.00
	33H	.450	2.00	4.00	10.00	35.00
	Common date	—		—	Proof	145.00

NOTE: Earlier dates (Yr.10-24) exist for this type.

5 QIRSH

7.0000 g, .833 SILVER, .1875 oz ASW
Obv: Flower at right of toughra.

294	27 W	.448	5.00	12.50	20.00	50.00
	29 W	.600	5.00	10.00	20.00	50.00
	29H	3.465	5.00	10.00	20.00	50.00
	30H	1.213	5.00	10.00	22.50	60.00
	31H	1.959	5.00	10.00	22.50	60.00
	32H	Inc.Be.	5.00	10.00	20.00	50.00
	33H	2.800	3.00	7.50	20.00	50.00
	Common date	—		—	Proof	285.00

NOTE: Earlier dates (Yr.10-24) exist for this type.

0.4200 g, .875 GOLD, .0118 oz AGW
Obv: Al-Ghazi at right of toughra.

KM#	Year	Mintage	VG	Fine	VF	XF
298	26	—	25.00	50.00	100.00	150.00
	34	.008	20.00	35.00	65.00	85.00

NOTE: Earlier dates (Yr.7-24) exist for this type.

10 QIRSH

14.0000 g, .833 SILVER, .3749 oz ASW
Accession Date: AH1293
Obv: Flower at right of toughra.

KM#	Year	Mintage	Fine	VF	XF	Unc
295	27 W	.250	15.00	25.00	60.00	150.00

KM#	Year	Mintage	Fine	VF	XF	Unc
295	29 W	*2.450	8.00	15.00	40.00	100.00
	29H	2.950	8.00	15.00	35.00	100.00
	30H	1.000	8.00	15.00	35.00	100.00
	31H	1.250	10.00	20.00	45.00	150.00
	32H	Inc.Be.	8.00	15.00	35.00	100.00
	33H	2.400	8.00	12.50	35.00	100.00
	Common date	—		—	Proof	435.00

*NOTE: Estimated.
NOTE: Earlier dates (Yr.10-24) exist for this type.

0.8544 g, .875 GOLD, .0240 oz AGW
Accession Date: AH1293
Obv: Al-Ghazi at right of toughra.

KM#	Year	Mintage	VG	Fine	VF	XF
282	34	.005	20.00	40.00	80.00	120.00

NOTE: Earlier dates (Yr.5-23) exist for this type.

20 QIRSH

28.0000 g, .833 SILVER, .7499 oz ASW
Accession Date: AH1293

KM#	Year	Mintage	Fine	VF	XF	Unc
296	27 W	.250	15.00	40.00	100.00	425.00
	29 W	.500	12.00	30.00	85.00	400.00
	29H	.425	12.00	30.00	80.00	400.00
	30H	.200	12.00	30.00	80.00	400.00
	31H	.250	12.00	30.00	80.00	400.00
	32H	Inc.Be.	12.00	30.00	85.00	400.00
	33H	.300	12.00	30.00	85.00	400.00
	Common date	—		—	Proof	825.00

NOTE: Earlier dates (Yr.10-24) exist for this type.

MUHAMMAD V
AH1327-1332/1909-1914AD

1/40 QIRSH

BRONZE
Accession Date: AH1327

300	2H	2.000	1.50	3.00	7.50	25.00
	3H	2.000	1.50	3.00	7.50	25.00
	4H	1.200	1.50	3.00	7.50	25.00
	6H	1.200	1.00	2.00	5.00	20.00

1/20 QIRSH

BRONZE
Accession Date: AH1327

301	2H	2.000	1.00	3.00	6.00	18.00
	3H	2.000	1.50	4.00	8.00	25.00
	4H	2.400	1.00	3.00	6.00	18.00
	6H	1.400	.75	2.00	6.00	18.00

1/10 QIRSH

COPPER-NICKEL
Accession Date: AH1327

KM#	Year	Mintage	Fine	VF	XF	Unc
302	2H	3.000	3.00	6.00	10.00	25.00
	3	1.000	5.00	12.00	20.00	50.00
	4H	3.000	1.00	2.00	4.00	12.50
	6H	3.000	.75	1.50	3.00	12.50
	Common date		—	—	Proof	110.00

2/10 QIRSH

COPPER-NICKEL
Accession Date: AH1327

303	2H	1.000	2.00	4.00	7.00	25.00
	3	.500	3.00	10.00	15.00	35.00
	4H	1.000	2.00	4.00	7.00	25.00
	6H	1.000	1.25	3.00	7.00	25.00
	Common date		—	—	Proof	120.00

5/10 QIRSH

COPPER-NICKEL
Accession Date: AH1327

304	2H	2.131	2.50	6.00	15.00	50.00
	3	1.000	5.00	15.00	35.00	75.00
	4H	3.327	1.00	2.50	6.00	25.00
	6H	3.000	1.00	2.50	6.00	25.00

QIRSH

1.4000 g, .833 SILVER, .0375 oz ASW
Accession Date: AH1327

305	2H	.251	2.00	4.00	15.00	28.00
	3H	.171	2.25	4.50	16.00	35.00

COPPER-NICKEL

306	2H	1.000	2.00	5.00	12.00	35.00
	3	.300	20.00	40.00	75.00	150.00
	4H	.500	4.00	8.00	22.50	65.00
	6H	2.500	2.00	4.00	8.00	28.00

2 QIRSH

2.8000 g, .833 SILVER, .0750 oz ASW
Accession Date: AH1327

307	2H	.250	5.00	12.50	28.00	90.00
	3H	.300	5.00	12.50	28.00	90.00

5 QIRSH

7.0000 g, .833 SILVER, .1875 oz ASW
Accession Date: AH1327

KM#	Year	Mintage	Fine	VF	XF	Unc
308	2H	.574	10.00	30.00	60.00	150.00
	3H	2.400	5.00	12.50	30.00	70.00
	4H	1.351	6.00	15.00	35.00	85.00
	6H	7.400	4.00	10.00	20.00	55.00
	Common date		—	—	Proof	350.00

10 QIRSH

14.0000 g, .833 SILVER, .3749 oz ASW
Accession Date: AH1327

309	2H	.300	20.00	30.00	60.00	200.00
	3H	1.300	8.00	15.00	30.00	115.00
	4H	.300	10.00	25.00	40.00	200.00
	6H	4.212	6.00	12.50	25.00	100.00
	Common date		—	—	Proof	475.00

20 QIRSH

28.0000 g, .833 SILVER, .7499 oz ASW
Accession Date: AH1327

310	2H	.075	30.00	50.00	160.00	500.00
	3H	.600	15.00	30.00	80.00	325.00
	4H	.100	25.00	40.00	90.00	425.00
	6H	.875	12.50	25.00	60.00	300.00
	Common date		—	—	Proof	950.00

BRITISH OCCUPATION
1914-1922
HUSSEIN KAMIL
AH1333-1336/1914-1917AD

1/2 MILLIEME

BRONZE
Accession Date: AH1333

KM#	Date	Year	Mintage	VF	XF	Unc
312	AH1335	1916	—Reported, not confirmed			
	1335	1917	4.000	3.50	7.50	25.00

MILLIEME

COPPER-NICKEL
Accession Date: AH1333

313	AH1335	1917	4.002	3.00	6.00	20.00
	1335	1917H	12.000	1.00	3.00	12.00

2 MILLIEMES

COPPER-NICKEL
Accession Date: AH1333

KM#	Date	Year	Mintage	VF	XF	Unc
314	AH1335	1916H	.300	3.00	7.50	30.00
	1335	1917	3.006	2.50	6.50	22.00
	1335	1917H	9.000	1.00	3.00	14.00

5 MILLIEMES

COPPER-NICKEL
Accession Date: AH1333

315	AH1335	1916	3.000	5.00	10.00	25.00
	1335	1916H	3.000	3.50	8.00	20.00
	1335	1917	6.776	2.50	6.00	15.00
	1335	1917H	37.000	1.50	2.50	8.00

10 MILLIEMES

COPPER-NICKEL
Accession Date: AH1333

316	AH1335	1916	1.007	5.00	10.00	35.00
	1335	1916H	1.000	4.00	8.00	25.00
	1335	1917	1.011	5.00	15.00	40.00
	1335	1917H	6.000	2.00	4.00	15.00
	1335	1917KN	4.000	3.00	6.00	20.00

2 PIASTRES

2.8000 g, .833 SILVER, .0749 oz ASW
Accession Date: AH1333

317.1	AH1335	1916	2.505	4.00	10.00	30.00
	1335	1917	4.461	2.50	5.00	20.00

W/o inner circle.

317.2	AH1335	1917H	2.180	2.50	5.00	15.00

5 PIASTRES

7.0000 g, .833 SILVER, .1874 oz ASW
Accession Date: AH1333

318.1	AH1335	1916	6.000	5.00	15.00	35.00
	1335	1917	9.218	4.00	12.50	32.00

W/o inner circle.

318.2	AH1335	1917H	5.036	5.00	15.00	45.00
	1335	1917H	—	—	Proof	325.00

10 PIASTRES

14.0000 g, .833 SILVER, .3749 oz ASW
Accession Date: AH1333

KM#	Date	Year	Mintage	VF	XF	Unc
319	AH1335	1916	2.900	10.00	25.00	95.00
	1335	1917	4.859	10.00	20.00	85.00

W/o inner circle.

320	AH1335	1917H	2.000	10.00	30.00	110.00

20 PIASTRES

28.0000 g, .833 SILVER, .7499 oz ASW
Accession Date: AH1333

321	AH1335	1916	1.500	16.00	35.00	160.00
	1335	1917	.840	16.00	35.00	180.00
	1335	1917	—	—	Proof	750.00

W/o inner circle.

322	AH1335	1917H	.250	40.00	70.00	300.00

100 PIASTRES

8.5000 g, .875 GOLD, .2391 oz AGW
Accession Date: AH1333

324	AH1335	1916	.010	100.00	150.00	300.00
	1335	1916	—	—	Proof	1500.

NOTE: Restrikes may exist.

FUAD I
Sultan, AH1336-1341/1917-1922AD

2 PIASTRES

2.8000 g, .833 SILVER, .0749 oz ASW
Accession Date: AH1335

KM#	Date	Year	Mintage	VF	XF	Unc
325	AH1338	1920H	2.820	75.00	160.00	375.00

5 PIASTRES

7.0000 g, .833 SILVER, .1874 oz ASW
Accession Date: AH1335

326	AH1338	1920H	1.000	35.00	85.00	350.00

10 PIASTRES

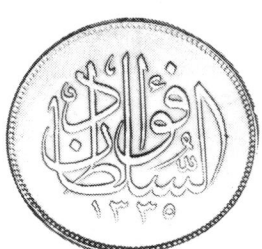

14.0000 g, .833 SILVER, .3749 oz ASW
Accession Date: AH1335

327	AH1338	1920H	.500	35.00	90.00	360.00

20 PIASTRES

28.0000 g, .833 SILVER, .7499 oz ASW
Accession Date: AH1335

328	AH1338	1920H	2 known	—	Rare	—

KINGDOM
1922-1952

FUAD I
King, AH1341-1355/1922-1936AD

1/2 MILLIEME

BRONZE

KM#	Date	Year	Mintage	VF	XF	Unc
330	AH1342	1924H	3.000	5.00	10.00	25.00
	1342	1924H	—	—	Proof	120.00

343	AH1348	1929BP	1.000	15.00	25.00	50.00
	1351	1932H	1.000	7.50	15.00	30.00
	1351	1932H	—	—	Proof	160.00

MILLIEME

BRONZE

331	AH1342	1924H	6.500	3.00	6.00	15.00

344	AH1348	1929BP	4.500	4.00	8.00	20.00
	1351	1932H	2.500	1.25	3.00	15.00
	1351	1932H	—	—	Proof	120.00
	1352	1933H	5.110	3.00	6.00	15.00
	1354	1935H	18.000	.50	2.00	8.00

2 MILLIEMES

COPPER-NICKEL

332	AH1342	1924H	4.500	3.00	8.00	20.00
	1342	1924H	—	—	Proof	120.00

345	AH1348	1929BP	*3.500	1.00	3.00	10.00

2-1/2 MILLIEMES

COPPER-NICKEL

356	AH1352	1933	4.000	3.00	8.00	30.00

5 MILLIEMES

COPPER-NICKEL

333	AH1342	1924	6.000	3.00	7.50	28.00

KM#	Date	Year	Mintage	VF	XF	Unc
346	AH1348	1929BP	4.000	2.00	8.00	25.00
	1352	1933H	3.000	4.00	12.00	35.00
	1354	1935H	8.000	1.00	5.00	12.50
	1354	1935H	—	—	Proof	120.00

10 MILLIEMES

COPPER-NICKEL

334	AH1342	1924	2.000	5.00	15.00	50.00

347	AH1348	1929BP	1.500	3.50	10.00	38.00
	1352	1933H	1.500	3.50	10.00	45.00
	1354	1935H	4.000	2.00	7.50	20.00

2 PIASTRES

2.8000 g, .833 SILVER, .0749 oz ASW

335	AH1342	1923H	2.500	4.50	11.50	35.00

348	AH1348	1929BP	.500	2.00	6.00	20.00

NOTE: Edge varieties exist.

5 PIASTRES

7.0000 g, .833 SILVER, .1874 oz ASW

336	AH1341	1923	.800	10.00	27.00	60.00
	1341	1923H	1.800	6.00	25.00	60.00
	1341	1923H	—	—	Proof	250.00

349	AH1348	1929BP	.800	10.00	35.00	65.00
	1352	1933	1.300	7.50	25.00	55.00
	1352	1933	—	—	Proof	250.00

10 PIASTRES

14.0000 g, .833 SILVER, .3749 oz ASW

KM#	Date	Year	Mintage	VF	XF	Unc
337	AH1341	1923	.400	12.50	40.00	120.00
	1341	1923H	1.000	12.50	40.00	120.00
	1341	1923H	—	—	Proof	450.00

350	AH1348	1929BP	.400	12.50	35.00	95.00
	1352	1933	*.350	12.50	35.00	95.00
	1352	1933	—	—	Proof	475.00

20 PIASTRES

28.0000 g, .833 SILVER, .7499 oz ASW

338	AH1341	1923	.100	40.00	90.00	425.00
	1341	1923H	.050	40.00	90.00	425.00
	1341	1923H	—	—	Proof	875.00

1.7000 g, .875 GOLD, .0478 oz AGW

339	AH1341	1923	.065	40.00	60.00	125.00

Obv: Bust left.

351	AH1348	1929	—	40.00	60.00	120.00
	1348	1929	—	—	Proof	—
	1349	1930	—	40.00	60.00	120.00
	1349	1930	—	—	Proof	—

28.0000 g, .833 SILVER, .7499 oz ASW

KM#	Date	Year	Mintage	VF	XF	Unc
352	AH1348	1929BP	.050	30.00	65.00	375.00
	1352	1933	.025	25.00	50.00	300.00
	1352	1933	—	—	Proof	—

50 PIASTRES

4.2500 g, .875 GOLD, .1195 oz AGW

340	AH1341	1923	.018	70.00	90.00	150.00

353	AH1348	1929	—	80.00	100.00	160.00
	1348	1929	—	—	Proof	—
	1349	1930	—	70.00	80.00	130.00
	1349	1930	—	—	Proof	—

100 PIASTRES

8.5000 g, .875 GOLD, .2391 oz AGW

341	AH1340	1922	.025	120.00	150.00	265.00

Obv: Bust left.

354	AH1348	1929	—	120.00	150.00	265.00
	1349	1930	—	120.00	150.00	265.00
	1349	1930	—	—	Proof	—

500 PIASTRES

42.5000 g, .875 GOLD, 1.1957 oz AGW

KM#	Date	Year	Mintage	VF	XF	Unc
342	AH1340	1922	1,800	—	950.00	1600.
	1340	1922	—	—	Proof	1800.

NOTE: Circulation coins were struck in both red and yellow gold.

355	AH1348	1929	—	—	850.00	1500.
	1349	1930	—	—	850.00	1500.
	1351	1932	—	—	850.00	1500.
	1351	1932	—	—	Proof	1800.

FAROUK
AH1355-1372/1936-1952AD

1/2 MILLIEME

BRONZE

357	AH1357	1938	4.000	4.00	6.00	18.00
	1357	1938	—	—	Proof	100.00

MILLIEME

BRONZE

358	AH1357	1938	26.240	.50	2.00	7.00
	1357	1938	—	—	Proof	120.00
	1364	1945	10.000	3.00	10.00	50.00
	1366	1947	—	3.00	10.00	50.00
	1369	1950	5.000	1.00	3.00	10.00
	1369	1950	—	—	Proof	85.00

COPPER-NICKEL

362	AH1357	1938	3.500	2.50	5.00	15.00

2 MILLIEMES

COPPER-NICKEL

KM#	Date	Year	Mintage	VF	XF	Unc
359	AH1357	1938	2.500	4.00	10.00	25.00
	1357	1938	—	—	Proof	140.00

5 MILLIEMES

BRONZE

360	AH1357	1938	—	1.00	3.00	10.00
	1357	1938	—	—	Proof	65.00
	1362	1943	—	1.00	3.00	10.00

COPPER-NICKEL

363	AH1357	1938	7.000	1.00	3.00	10.00
	1357	1938	—	—	Proof	75.00
	1360	1941	11.500	.50	2.50	8.00

10 MILLIEMES

BRONZE

361	AH1357	1938	—	1.00	3.00	10.00
	1357	1938	—	—	Proof	140.00
	1362	1943	—	.75	3.00	10.00

COPPER-NICKEL

364	AH1357	1938	3.500	1.00	3.00	12.50
	1357	1938	—	—	Proof	85.00
	1360	1941	5.322	1.00	3.00	12.50

2 PIASTRES

2.80000 g, .833 SILVER, .0749 oz ASW

365	AH1356	1937	.500	1.50	3.00	8.00
	1356	1937	—	—	Proof	300.00
	1358	1939	.500	4.00	10.00	75.00
	1358	1939	—	—	Proof	200.00
	1361	1942	10.000	1.50	4.00	10.00
	?	1948		Reported, not confirmed		

NOTE: Normal and flat rim varieties exist for AH1361 dated coins.

2.8000 g, .500 SILVER, .0450 oz ASW

369	AH1363	1944	.032	1.00	2.00	4.00

5 PIASTRES

7.0000 g, .833 SILVER, .1874 oz ASW

KM#	Date	Year	Mintage	VF	XF	Unc
366	AH1356	1937	—	3.00	6.00	15.00
	1356	1937	—	—	Proof	275.00
	1358	1939	8.000	3.00	6.00	15.00
	1358	1939	—	—	Proof	275.00

10 PIASTRES

14.0000 g, .833 SILVER, .3749 oz ASW

367	AH1356	1937	2.800	7.50	10.00	32.00
	1356	1937	—	—	Proof	375.00
	1358	1939	2.850	7.50	10.00	32.00
	1358	1939	—	—	Proof	300.00

20 PIASTRES

28.0000 g, .833 SILVER, .7499 oz ASW

368	AH1356	1937	—	15.00	35.00	95.00
	1356	1937	—	—	Proof	1000.
	1358	1939	—	15.00	35.00	95.00
	1358	1939	—	—	Proof	1200.

1.7000 g, .875 GOLD, .0478 oz AGW
Royal Wedding

370	AH1357	1938	.020	30.00	50.00	90.00
	1357	1938	—	—	Proof	R,NC

50 PIASTRES

4.2500 g, .875 GOLD, .1195 oz AGW
Royal Wedding

371	AH1357	1938	.010	100.00	120.00	225.00
	1357	1938	—	—	Proof	R,NC

100 PIASTRES

8.5000 g, .875 GOLD, .2391 oz AGW

Royal Wedding

KM#	Date	Year	Mintage	VF	XF	Unc
372	AH1357	1938	5,000	150.00	200.00	325.00
	1357	1938	—	Proof		R,NC

NOTE: Circulation coins were struck in both red and yellow gold.

REPUBLIC
1953-1958
MILLIEME

ALUMINUM-BRONZE
Rev: Small sphinx w/outlined base.

				VF	XF	Unc
375	AH1373	1954	—	50.00	100.00	200.00
	1374	1954	—	3.00	6.00	25.00
	1374	1955	—	2.00	5.00	15.00
	1375	1955	—	2.00	5.00	15.00
	1375	1956	—	2.00	5.00	15.00

Rev: Small sphinx w/o base outlined.

376	AH1373	1954	—	—	—	—
	1374	1954	—	2.00	5.00	15.00
	1374	1955	—	1.00	2.00	5.00
	1375	1955	—	1.00	2.00	5.00
	1375	1956	—	1.50	2.50	10.00
	1376	1957	—	—	—	—

Rev: Large sphinx.

377	AH1375	1956	—	.50	1.00	4.00
	1376	1957	—	.75	1.50	5.00
	1377	1958	—	.75	1.50	5.00

5 MILLIEMES

ALUMINUM-BRONZE
Rev: Small sphinx.

378	AH1373	1954	—	5.00	10.00	35.00
	1374	1954	—	4.00	8.00	25.00
	1374	1955	—	10.00	20.00	50.00
	1375	1956	—	3.00	6.00	15.00

Rev: Large sphinx.

379	AH1376	1957	—	2.00	4.00	10.00
	1377	1957	—	2.00	4.00	10.00
	1377	1958	—	2.00	4.00	10.00

10 MILLIEMES

Thin milliemes

Thick milliemes

ALUMINUM-BRONZE
Rev: Small sphinx.

KM#	Date	Year	Mintage	VF	XF	Unc
380	AH1373	1954	thin *milliemes*			
			—	5.00	10.00	25.00
	1374	1954	—	4.00	8.00	20.00
	1374	1955	thick *milliemes*			
			—	3.00	6.00	15.00

Rev: Large sphinx.

381	AH1374	1955	—	50.00	85.00	150.00
	1375	1956	—	3.00	6.00	15.00
	1376	1957	—	2.00	5.00	12.00
	1377	1958	—	2.00	5.00	12.00

5 PIASTRES

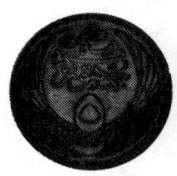 

3.5000 g, .720 SILVER, .0810 oz ASW

382	1375	1956	—	1.50	3.00	8.00
	1376	1956	—	3.00	5.00	10.00
	1376	1957	—	1.50	3.00	8.00

10 PIASTRES

7.0000 g, .625 SILVER, .1406 oz ASW

383	AH1374	1955	1.408	3.50	7.00	18.00

NOTE: Varieties in date sizes exist.

7.0000 g, .720 SILVER, .1620 oz ASW

383a	AH1375	1956	—	3.50	7.00	15.00
	1376	1957	—	3.50	6.00	12.00

20 PIASTRES

14.0000 g, .720 SILVER, .3241 oz ASW

384	AH1375	1956	—	5.00	9.00	18.00

25 PIASTRES

17.5000 g., .720 SILVER, .4051 oz ASW
Suez Canal Nationalization

KM#	Date	Year	Mintage	VF	XF	Unc
385	AH1375	1956	.258	6.00	10.00	20.00

National Assembly Inauguration

389	AH1376	1957	.246	6.00	9.00	17.00

UNITED ARAB REPUBLIC
1958-1971
MILLIEME

ALUMINUM-BRONZE

393	AH1380	1960	—	.10	.15	.30
	1386	1966	—	—	Proof	3.00

2 MILLIEMES

ALUMINUM-BRONZE

403	AH1381	1962	—	.15	.35	.60
	1386	1966	—	—	Proof	3.00

5 MILLIEMES

ALUMINUM-BRONZE

394	AH1380	1960	—	.15	.45	.80
	1386	1966	—	—	Proof	3.00

ALUMINUM

410	AH1386	1967	—	.15	.40	.65

10 MILLIEMES

ALUMINUM-BRONZE
Obv: *Misr* above denomination.

395	AH1377	1958	—	15.00	20.00	40.00
	1380	1960	16.080	.80	1.20	2.25
	1386	1966	—	—	Proof	4.00

Obv: W/o *Misr* above denomination.

KM#	Date	Year	Mintage	VF	XF	Unc
396	AH1377	1958	—	15.00	20.00	40.00

ALUMINUM

| 411 | AH1386 | 1967 | — | .10 | .25 | .65 |

20 MILLIEMES

ALUMINUM-BRONZE
Agriculture and Industrial Fair

| 390 | AH1378 | 1958 | — | .75 | 1.50 | 5.00 |

5 PIASTRES

3.5000 g, .720 SILVER, .0810 oz ASW

| 397 | AH1380 | 1960 | — | 1.75 | 3.00 | 5.00 |
| | 1386 | 1966 | — | — | Proof | 8.00 |

2.5000 g, .720 SILVER, .0578 oz ASW
Diversion of the Nile

| 404 | AH1384 | 1964 | .500 | 1.25 | 2.50 | 4.00 |
| | 1384 | 1964 | 2,000 | — | Proof | 8.00 |

COPPER-NICKEL

| 412 | AH1387 | 1967 | 10.800 | .50 | .75 | 1.50 |

NOTE: Edge varieties exist.

International Industrial Fair

| 414 | AH1388 | 1968 | .500 | .75 | 1.00 | 2.50 |

50th Anniversary - International Labor Organization

KM#	Date	Year	Mintage	VF	XF	Unc
417	AH1389	1969	.500	.75	1.00	2.50

10 PIASTRES

7.0000 g, .720 SILVER, .1620 oz ASW
1st Anniversary of U.A.R. Founding

| 392 | AH1378 | 1959 | — | 3.25 | 6.00 | 17.50 |

| 398 | AH1380 | 1960 | .500 | 3.00 | 4.50 | 7.50 |
| | 1386 | 1966 | — | — | Proof | 15.00 |

5.0000 g, .720 SILVER, .1157 oz ASW
Diversion of the Nile

| 405 | AH1384 | 1964 | .500 | 2.50 | 3.50 | 5.50 |
| | 1384 | 1964 | 2,000 | — | Proof | 15.00 |

COPPER-NICKEL

| 413 | AH1387 | 1967 | 13.200 | .60 | .90 | 2.00 |

Cairo International Agricultural Fair

| 419 | AH1389 | 1969 | 1.000 | .75 | 1.25 | 3.00 |

F.A.O. Issue

| 418 | ND | (1970) | .500 | .75 | 1.25 | 3.50 |

Banque Misr 50 Years

| 420 | AH1390 | 1970 | .500 | .60 | 1.00 | 2.00 |

Cairo International Industrial Fair

KM#	Date	Year	Mintage	VF	XF	Unc
421.1	AH1390	1970	.500	.60	1.00	3.25
(421)						

Obv: New shorter Arabic inscriptions.

| 421.2 | AH1391 | 1971 | .500 | .60 | 1.00 | 2.75 |
| (422) | | | | | | |

20 PIASTRES

14.0000 g, .720 SILVER, .3241 oz ASW

| 399 | AH1380 | 1960 | .400 | 6.00 | 10.00 | 25.00 |
| | 1386 | 1966 | — | — | Proof | 37.50 |

25 PIASTRES

17.5000 g, .720 SILVER, .4051 oz ASW
3rd Year of National Assembly

| 400 | AH1380 | 1960 | .250 | 5.00 | 8.00 | 18.00 |

10.0000 g, .720 SILVER, .2315 oz ASW
Diversion of the Nile

| 406 | AH1384 | 1964 | .250 | 3.00 | 4.50 | 7.00 |
| | 1384 | 1964 | 2,000 | — | Proof | 27.50 |

6.0000 g, .720 SILVER, .1388 oz ASW
President Nasser

KM#	Date	Year	Mintage	VF	XF	Unc
422	AH1390	1970	.700	2.50	4.00	6.50

ARAB REPUBLIC
1971-
MILLIEME

ALUMINUM

KM#	Date	Year	Mintage	VF	XF	Unc
A423	AH1392	1972	—	.10	.30	.50

5 MILLIEMES

ALUMINUM
Mule. Obv: KM#A425. Rev: KM#433.

| A424 | AH1392 | 1972 | — | 10.00 | 20.00 | 45.00 |

| A425 | AH1392 | 1972 | 16.000 | .20 | .50 | 2.50 |

BRASS

| 432 | AH1393 | 1973 | — | .10 | .15 | .30 |

ALUMINUM
Mule. Obv: KM#433. Rev: KM#A425.

| A433 | AH1393 | 1973 | — | 10.00 | 20.00 | 45.00 |

F.A.O. Issue

| 433 | AH1393 | 1973 | 10.000 | .10 | .20 | .35 |

BRASS
Mule. Obv: KM#432. Rev: KM#445.

| 434 | AH1393 | 1973 | — | 5.00 | 10.00 | 20.00 |

International Women's Year

KM#	Date	Year	Mintage	VF	XF	Unc
445	AH1395	1975	10.000	.10	.15	.30

F.A.O. Issue

| 462 | AH1397 | 1977 | 5.000 | .10 | .20 | .50 |

1971 Corrective Revolution

| 463 | AH1397 | 1977 | 2.500 | .10 | .20 | .50 |
| | 1399 | 1979 | 2.500 | .10 | .20 | .50 |

ALUMINUM-BRONZE
Sadat's Corrective Revolution

| 497 | AH1400 | 1980 | 2.500 | Reported, not confirmed |

10 MILLIEMES

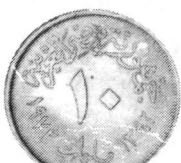

ALUMINUM

| A426 | AH1392 | 1972 | 20.000 | .50 | 2.00 | 6.00 |

NOTE: 2 varieties of edge letterings exist.

BRASS

| 435 | AH1393 | 1973 | — | .10 | .25 | .50 |
| | 1396 | 1976 | — | .75 | 1.50 | 3.00 |

F.A.O. Issue

| 446 | AH1395 | 1975 | 10.000 | .10 | .20 | .35 |

F.A.O. Issue

| 449 | AH1396 | 1976 | 10.000 | .10 | .20 | .30 |

F.A.O. Issue

| 464 | AH1397 | 1977 | 10.000 | .10 | .20 | .85 |

1971 Corrective Revolution

KM#	Date	Year	Mintage	VF	XF	Unc
465	AH1397	1977	2.500	.10	.20	.65
	1399	1979	2.500	.20	.40	1.00

F.A.O. Issue

| 476 | AH1398 | 1978 | 2.000 | .10 | .20 | .80 |

International Year of the Child

| 483 | AH1399 | 1979 | 2.000 | .10 | .20 | .65 |

ALUMINUM-BRONZE
Sadat's Corrective Revolution

| 498 | AH1400 | 1980 | 2.500 | .10 | .25 | 1.00 |

F.A.O. Issue

| 499 | AH1400 | 1980 | 2.000 | .10 | .20 | .60 |

PIASTRE

ALUMINUM-BRONZE
Obv: Christian date left of denomination.

| 553.1 | AH1404 | 1984 | — | — | .15 | .35 |

Obv: Islamic date left of denomination.

| 553.2 | AH1404 | 1984 | — | — | .15 | .35 |

2 PIASTRES

ALUMINUM-BRONZE

| 500 | AH1400 | 1980 | — | .20 | .30 | .60 |

Obv: Christian date left of denomination.

KM#	Date	Year	Mintage	VF	XF	Unc
554.1	AH1404	1984	—	—	.20	.50

Obv: Islamic date left of denomination.

554.2	AH1404	1984	—		.20	.50

5 PIASTRES

COPPER-NICKEL
UNICEF 25th Anniversary

A427	AH1392	1972	.500	.75	1.00	3.00

NOTE: Error in spelling "UNICFE".

Rev: Islamic falcon.

A428	AH1392	1972	—	.50	.75	2.00

Cairo State Fair

436	AH1393	1973	.500	.60	.75	2.25

75th Anniversary - National Bank of Egypt

437	AH1393	1973	1.000	.60	.75	2.00

1st Anniversary October War

A441	AH1394	1974	2.000	.60	.75	2.00

International Women's Year

KM#	Date	Year	Mintage	VF	XF	Unc
447	AH1395	1975	2.000	.50	.65	1.25

Mule. Obv: KM#451. Rev: KM#A428.

450	1396	1976	—	5.00	10.00	20.00

1976 Cairo Trade Fair

451	AH1396	1976	.500	.60	.75	2.00

1971 Corrective Revolution

466	AH1397	1977	1.000	.50	.60	1.50
	1399	1979	—	.50	.60	1.25

50th Anniversary - Textile Industry

467	AH1397	1977	1.000	.50	.75	1.65

F.A.O. Issue

468	AH1397	1977		.50	.75	1.65

NOTE: Edge varieties exist.

Portland Cement

477	AH1398	1978	.500	.50	.75	1.65

F.A.O. Issue

478	AH1398	1978	1.000	.50	.75	1.65

International Year of the Child

484	AH1399	1979	1.000	.50	.75	1.65

Applied Professions

KM#	Date	Year	Mintage	VF	XF	Unc
501	AH1400	1980	.500	.50	.75	1.35

Sadat's Corrective Revolution of May 15, 1971
Similar to 1 Pound, KM#514.

502	AH1400	1980	1.000	.50	.75	1.75

ALUMINUM-BRONZE
Obv: Christian date left of denomination.

555.1	AH1404	1984	—	—	.25	.75

NOTE: Varieties exist w/wide and narrow rims.

Obv: Islamic date left of denomination.

555.2	AH1404	1984	—		.25	.75

Obv: Denomination not shaded.

622.1	AH1404	1984	—		.25	.85

Obv: Denomination shaded.

622.2	AH1404	1984	—		.25	.85

BRASS
Decorated Vase

731	AH1413	1992	—	—	—	.85

10 PIASTRES

COPPER-NICKEL
Cairo International Fair

429	AH1392	1972	.500	.60	1.00	2.50

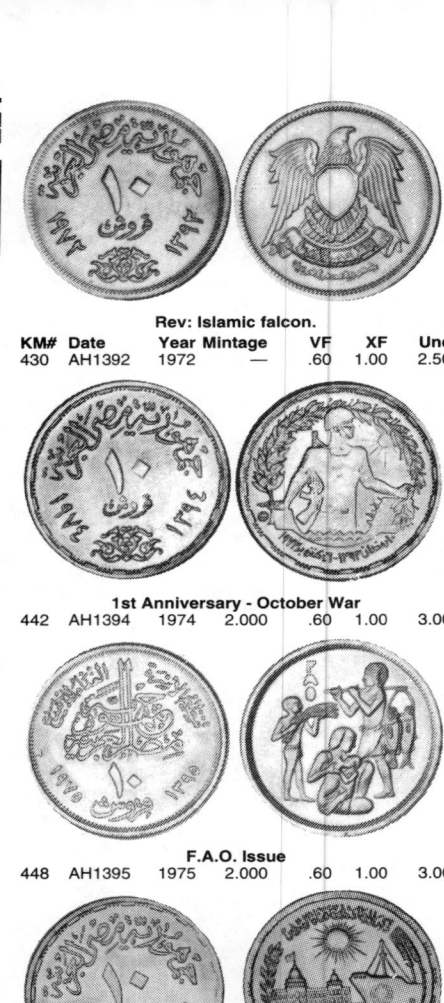

Rev: Islamic falcon.

KM#	Date	Year	Mintage	VF	XF	Unc
430	AH1392	1972	—	.60	1.00	2.50

1st Anniversary - October War

442	AH1394	1974	2.000	.60	1.00	3.00

F.A.O. Issue

448	AH1395	1975	2.000	.60	1.00	3.00

Reopening of the Suez Canal

452	AH1396	1976	5.000	.60	1.00	3.50

Mule. Obv: KM#452. Rev: KM#430.

431	AH1392	1972	—	5.50	12.50	27.50

NOTE: Wide and narrow inscriptions exist for obverse.

F.A.O. Issue

469	AH1397	1977	1.000	.60	1.00	2.25

1971 Corrective Revolution

470	AH1397	1977	1.000	.50	.85	2.50
	1399	1979	1.000	.50	.85	2.50

20th Anniversary - Economic Union

471	AH1397	1977	1.000	.50	.85	2.25

Cairo International Fair

KM#	Date	Year	Mintage	VF	XF	Unc
479	AH1398	1978	—	.50	.85	2.75

25th Anniversary of Abbasia Mint

485	AH1399	1979	1.000	.50	.85	2.25

National Education Day

486	AH1399	1979	1.000		.85	2.25

Doctor's Day

503	AH1400	1980	1.000	.50	.85	2.50

Egyptian-Israeli Peace Treaty

504	AH1400	1980	1.000	1.00	2.00	3.50

F.A.O. Issue

505	AH1400	1980	1.000		.85	2.25

Sadat's Corrective Revolution of May 15, 1971

506	AH1400	1980	1.000	.50	.85	2.25
	1401	1981	—	.60	1.20	3.50

Scientist's Day

KM#	Date	Year	Mintage	VF	XF	Unc
520	AH1401	1981	—	.50	.85	2.25

25th Anniversary - Trade Unions

521	AH1402	1981	—	1.00	2.00	3.50

50th Anniversary of Egyptian Products Co.

599	AH1402	1982	—	.50	.85	2.25

Circulation Coinage

556	AH1404	1984	—		.50	.85

25th Anniversary - National Planning Institute

570	AH1405	1985	.100		—	1.75

60th Anniversary - Egyptian Parliament

573	AH1405	1985	.250		—	1.75

1973 October War

675	AH1410	1989	.250		—	1.75

BRASS
Circulation Coinage

KM#	Date	Year Mintage	VF	XF	Unc
732	AH1413	1992	—	—	1.25

20 PIASTRES

COPPER-NICKEL

507	AH1400	1980	—	.75	1.00	2.35

Circulation Coinage

557	AH1404	1984	—	—	.70	1.65

25th Anniversary - Cairo International Airport

596	AH1405	1985	.050	—	—	2.25

Professions

597	AH1406	1985	.100	—	—	2.50

Soldiers

606	AH1406	1986	.050	—	—	2.50

Census

607	AH1407	1986	.500	—	—	2.25

Investment Bank

652	AH1407	1987	.250	—	—	2.50

Police Day

KM#	Date	Year Mintage	VF	XF	Unc
646	AH1408	1988	.250	—	—	2.75

Dedication of Cairo Opera House

650	AH1409	1988	.250	—	—	2.50

1973 October War

676	AH1410	1989	.250	—	—	2.50

National Health Insurance

685	AH1409	1989	.250	—	—	2.50

Cairo Subway

690	AH1409	1989	.250	—	—	2.75

Mosque

733	AH1413	1992	—	—	—	2.50

25 PIASTRES

6.0000 g, .720 SILVER, .1388 oz ASW
75th Anniversary - National Bank of Egypt

438	AH1393	1973	.100	4.00	6.00	9.00

COPPER-NICKEL

KM#	Date	Year Mintage	VF	XF	Unc
734	AH1413	1993	—	—	—	2.75

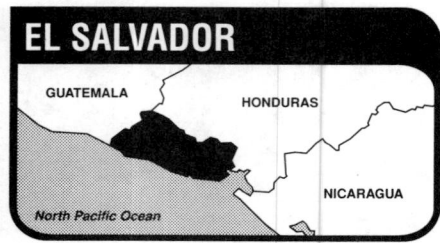

EL SALVADOR

GUATEMALA

HONDURAS

NICARAGUA

North Pacific Ocean

The Republic of El Salvador, a Central American country bordered by Guatemala, Honduras and the Pacific Ocean, has an area of 8,124 sq. mi. (21,040 sq. km.) and a population of 5.9 million. Capital: San Salvador. This most intensely cultivated of Latin America countries produces coffee (the major crop), sugar and balsam for export. Gold, silver and other metals are largely unexploited.

The first Spanish attempt to subjugate the area was undertaken in 1523 by Pedro de Alvarado, Cortes' lieutenant. He was forced to retreat by Indian forces, but returned in 1525 and succeeded in bringing the region under control of the Captaincy General of Guatemala. In 1821, El Salvador and the other Central American provinces jointly declared independence from Spain. In 1823, the Republic of Central America was formed by the five Central American states. When this federation dissolved in 1839, El Salvador became an independent republic.

Clashes with Honduras occurred over a period of several years. A military coup in 1979 overthrew the Romero government but the ruling military-civilian junta failed to quell the civil war. Leftist insurgents, armed by Cuba and Nicaragua, controlled about 25% of the country. The U.S. supported the right wing government with military aid.

In the May 1984 presidential election, voters elected Christian Democrat Jose Napoleon Duarte.

A twelve-year civil war ended in 1992 with the signing of a United Nations-sponsored Peace Accord. Free elections, with full participation of all political parties, were held in 1994 and early 1997. Armando Calderon-Sol was elected president in 1994 for a 5-year term.

MINT MARKS

C.A.M. - Central American Mint, San Salvador
H - Heaton Mint, Birmingham
S - San Francisco
Mo - Mexico

MONETARY SYSTEM

100 Centavos = 1 Peso

CENTAVO

COPPER-NICKEL

KM#	Date	Mintage	Fine	VF	XF	Unc
106	1913H	2.500	1.50	3.50	6.00	35.00

NOTE: Earlier date (1889) exists for this type.

127	1915	5.000	.75	2.50	7.00	20.00
	1919	1.000	1.50	4.00	10.00	35.00
	1920	1.490	1.00	3.00	8.00	25.00
	1925	.200	4.00	8.00	15.00	50.00
	1926	.400	3.00	6.00	12.00	45.00
	1928S	5.000	.75	2.00	6.00	35.00
	1936	2.500	.75	2.00	6.00	22.50

3 CENTAVOS

COPPER-NICKEL

107	1913H	1.000	2.00	6.00	14.00	40.00

NOTE: Earlier date (1889) exists for this type.

128	1915	2.700	2.00	5.00	15.00	40.00

1/4 REAL

BRONZE

KM#	Date	Mintage	Fine	VF	XF	Unc
120	1909	—	20.00	30.00	45.00	60.00

NOTE: The decimal value of the above coin was about 3 Centavos. It was apparently struck in response to the continuing use of the Reales monetary system in local market places and rural areas.

5 CENTAVOS

1.2500 g, .835 SILVER, .0336 oz ASW

121	1911	1.000	2.00	4.00	8.00	30.00

124	1914	2.000	1.50	3.00	6.00	22.50
	1914	20 pcs.	—	—	Proof	200.00

COPPER-NICKEL

129	1915	2.500	.75	2.00	6.00	25.00
	1916	1.500	1.25	3.00	8.00	32.50
	1917	1.000	1.50	4.00	10.00	40.00
	1918/7	1.000	1.25	3.00	8.00	30.00
	1918	Inc. Ab.	1.25	3.00	8.00	32.50
	1919	2.000	1.00	3.00	8.00	25.00
	1920	2.000	.75	2.00	6.00	20.00
	1921	1.780	1.00	2.50	7.00	25.00
	1925	4.000	.50	1.50	5.00	17.50

10 CENTAVOS

SILVER

122	1911	1.000	2.25	4.00	8.00	25.00

125	1914	1.500	2.00	3.50	6.00	22.50
	1914	20 pcs.	—	—	Proof	250.00

25 CENTAVOS

6.2500 g, .835 SILVER, .1678 oz ASW

123	1911	.600	4.75	6.00	8.50	30.00

126	1914	15 DE SEPT DE 1821

KM#	Date	Mintage	Fine	VF	XF	Unc
126		1.400	5.50	6.50	10.00	25.00
	1914 15 SET DE 1821					
	Inc. Ab.	5.50	6.50	10.00	25.00
	1914	20 pcs.	—	—	Proof	500.00

UN PESO

(Un Colon)

115.1	1904CAM	.600	6.50	12.00	20.00	125.00
	1908CAM	1.600	6.50	10.00	18.00	100.00
	1911CAM	.500	6.50	12.00	20.00	100.00
	1914CAM	*.700	—	Reported, not confirmed		

*NOTE: Struck at the Brussels mint, but then remelted for the striking of 1914 minor coinage.
NOTE: Struck in San Salvador and European mints.
NOTE: Earlier dates (1892-1896) exist for this type.

Rev: Heavier portrait (wider right shoulder).

115.2	1904CAM	.400	8.00	15.00	35.00	125.00
	1909CAM	.690	6.50	12.00	20.00	100.00
	1911CAM	1.020	6.50	12.00	20.00	100.00
	1914CAM	2.100	6.50	12.00	20.00	80.00
	1914CAM					
	*20 pcs.	—	—	Proof	1800.

NOTE: Struck at United States mints.

MONETARY REFORM

100 Centavos = 1 Colon

CENTAVO

COPPER-NICKEL

133	1940	1.000	1.25	3.50	7.00	22.00

BRONZE

135.1	1942	5.000	.20	.50	1.00	4.00
(135)	1943	5.000	.20	.50	1.00	4.00
	1945	5.000	.20	.40	.75	2.50
	1947	5.000	.20	.50	1.00	3.00
	1951	10.000	.10	.30	.75	2.00
	1952	10.000	.10	.20	.40	1.25
	1956	10.000	.10	.20	.40	1.00
	1966	5.000	—	—	.10	.50
	1968(f)	5.000	—	—	.10	.50
	1969(b)	5.000	—	—	.10	.50
	1972(f)	20.000	—	—	.10	.30

BRASS CLAD STEEL

135.1a	1989(h)	36.000	—	—	.10	.20
(135d)	1992(h)	—	—	—	.10	.20

BRASS

Obv: Smaller portrait.

KM#	Date	Mintage	Fine	VF	XF	Unc
135.2	1976(g)	20.000	—	—	.10	.20
(135a)	1977(g)	40.000	—	—	.10	.20

COPPER-ZINC
Obv: DH monogram at truncation.
Rev: Denomination in wreath, SM at right base of 1.

135.2a	1981(d)	50.000	—	—	.10	.20
(135c)						

COPPER CLAD STEEL

135.2b	1986(a)	30.000	—	—	.10	.20
(135b)						

BRASS CLAD STEEL

135.2c	1995(a)	—	—	—	.10	.20

2 CENTAVOS

NICKEL-BRASS

147	1974(a)	10.002	—	.10	.15	.20
	1974(a)	2,000	—	Proof sets only		30.00

3 CENTAVOS

NICKEL-BRASS

148	1974(a)	10.002	.10	.15	.20	.40
	1974(a)	2,000	—	Proof sets only		35.00

5 CENTAVOS

COPPER-NICKEL

134	1940	.800	.50	1.00	3.00	8.00
	1951	2.000	.25	.50	1.25	5.00
	1956	8.000	.10	.15	.25	.75
	1959	6.000	.10	.15	.25	.75
	1963	10.000	—	.10	.15	.30
	1966	6.000	.10	.15	.25	.50
	1967(f)	10.000	—	.10	.15	.30
	1972(f)	10.000	—	.10	.15	.30
	1974(g)	10.002	—	.10	.15	.30
	1974(g)	2,000	—	Proof sets only		35.00

COPPER-NICKEL-ZINC

134a	1944	5.000	.25	.50	1.50	5.00
	1948	3.000	.25	.50	1.00	2.50
	1950	2.000	.25	.50	1.50	5.00
	1952	4.000	.20	.35	.75	4.00

COPPER-NICKEL CLAD STEEL

149.1	1975(a)	15.000	—	.10	.15	.30
	1975	2,000	—	Proof sets only		35.00
	1986(h)	30.000	—	.10	.15	.30

NICKEL CLAD STEEL

149.2	1976(g)	15.000	—	.10	.15	.30
	1984(a)	15.000	—	.10	.15	.30

COPPER-NICKEL-ZINC

149a	1977(h)	26.000	—	—	.15	.30

STAINLESS STEEL
Gen. Francisco Morazan

154	1987(h)	30.000	—	—	.10	.15	.30

COPPER-NICKEL CLAD STEEL

KM#	Date	Mintage	Fine	VF	XF	Unc
154a	1991(h)	—	—	.10	.15	.30
	1998(c)	—	—	.10	.15	.30

NICKEL CLAD STEEL

154b	1992(g)	—	—	.10	.15	.30
	1993(g)	—	—	.10	.15	.30
	1994(h)	—	—	.10	.15	.30
	1995(g)	—	—	.10	.15	.30

10 CENTAVOS

COPPER-NICKEL

130	1921	2.000	1.50	5.00	12.00	30.00
	1925	2.000	2.00	6.00	14.00	35.00
	1940	.500	3.50	9.00	20.00	55.00
	1951	1.000	.50	1.50	3.00	8.00
	1967(f)	2.000	—	.10	.50	2.00
	1968(b)	3.000	—	.10	.40	1.00
	1969(b)	3.000	—	.10	.40	1.00
	1972(f)	7.000	—	.10	.25	.75

COPPER-NICKEL-ZINC

130a	1952	2.000	.15	.25	.50	1.50
	1985 Mo	15.000	—	.10	.15	.30

COPPER-NICKEL CLAD STEEL

150	1975(a)	15.000	—	.10	.25	.50
	1975(a)	2,000	—	Proof sets only		35.00

COPPER-NICKEL-ZINC

150a	1977(h)	24.000	—	.10	.20	.45

STAINLESS STEEL
Gen. Francisco Morazan

155	1987(h)	30.000	—	.10	.20	.40

NICKEL CLAD STEEL

155a	1992(a)	—	—	.10	.20	.40
	1993(g)	—	—	.10	.20	.40
	1994(h)	—	—	.10	.20	.40

COPPER-NICKEL CLAD STEEL

155b	1995(c)	—	—	.10	.20	.40
	1998(c)	—	—	.10	.20	.40

25 CENTAVOS

7.5000 g, .900 SILVER, .2170 oz ASW

136	1943	1.000	1.50	2.50	5.00	9.00
	1944	1.000	1.50	2.50	5.00	9.00

2.5000 g, .900 SILVER, .0723 oz ASW

KM#	Date	Mintage	Fine	VF	XF	Unc
137	1953	14.000	.50	1.00	1.50	3.00

NICKEL

139	1970(a)	14.000	—	.10	.20	.60
	1973(g)	28.000	—	.10	.20	.50
	1975(g)	20.000	—	.10	.20	.50
	1977(a)	22.400	—	.10	.20	.50

COPPER-NICKEL

139a	1986 Mo	21.000	—	.10	.20	.50

STAINLESS STEEL

157	1988(h)	20.000	—	.10	.20	.50

COPPER-NICKEL CLAD STEEL

157a	1992(c)	—	—	.10	.20	.50
	1995(c)	—	—	.10	.20	.50

NICKEL CLAD STEEL

157b	1993(a)	—	—	.10	.20	.50
	1994(a)	—	—	.10	.20	.50

50 CENTAVOS

5.0000 g, .900 SILVER, .1446 oz ASW

138	1953	3.000	1.00	2.00	3.00	5.00

NICKEL, 1.65mm thick

140.1	1970(a)	3.000	—	.20	.30	.60

2.00mm thick

140.2	1977(a)	1.500	—	.20	.30	.60

UN COLON

25.0000 g, .900 SILVER, .7234 oz ASW

400th Anniversary - San Salvador

KM#	Date	Mintage	Fine	VF	XF	Unc
131	ND(1925)Mo	2,000	50.00	90.00	125.00	200.00

COPPER-NICKEL
Christopher Columbus

153	1984Mo	10.000	—	.50	1.00	2.50
	1985Mo	20.000	—	.50	1.00	2.50

STAINLESS STEEL
Christopher Columbus

156	1988(h)	30.000	—	.40	.80	2.25

COPPER-NICKEL CLAD STEEL

156a	1991(h)	—	—	.40	.80	2.25

NICKEL CLAD STEEL

156b	1993(a)	—	—	.40	.80	2.25
	1994(g)	—	—	.40	.80	2.25
	1995(h)	—	—	.40	.80	2.25

EQUATORIAL GUINEA

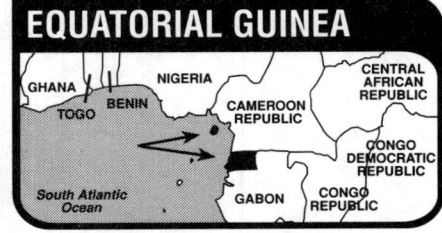

The Republic of Equatorial Guinea (formerly Spanish Guinea) consists of Rio Muni, located on the coast of west Central Africa between Cameroon and Gabon, and the off-shore islands of Fernando Po, Annobon, Corisco, Elobey Grande and Elobey Chico. The equatorial country has an area of 10,831 sq. mi. (28,050 sq. km.) and a population of 420,293. Capital: Malabo. The economy is based on agriculture and forestry. Cacao, wood and coffee are exported.

Fernando Po was discovered between 1474 and 1496 by Portuguese navigators charting a route to the spice islands of the Far East. Portugal retained control of it and the adjacent islands until 1778 when they, together with trading rights to the African coast between the Ogooue and Niger Rivers, were ceded to Spain. Fernando Po was administered, with Spanish consent, by the British from 1827 to 1844 when it was reclaimed by Spain. Mainland Rio Muni was granted to Spain by the Berlin Conference of 1885. The name of the colony was changed from Spanish Guinea to Equatorial Guinea in Dec. of 1963. Independence was attained on Oct. 12, 1968.

Equatorial Guinea converted to the CFA currency system as issued for the Central African States issuing its first 100 Franc denomination in 1985.

NOTE: The 1969 coinage carries the actual minting date in the stars at the sides of the large date.

MINT MARKS
(a) - Paris, privy marks only

PESETA

ALUMINUM-BRONZE

KM#	Date	Mintage	Fine	VF	XF	Unc
1	1969(69)	—	.35	.75	1.25	2.00

5 PESETAS

COPPER-NICKEL

2	1969(69)	—	.75	1.50	2.50	8.00

25 PESETAS

COPPER-NICKEL

3	1969(69)	—	1.50	2.50	6.50	12.00

5.0000 g, .999 SILVER, .1606 oz ASW
World Bank

5	1970	2,475	—	—	Proof	9.00

United Nations

KM#	Date	Mintage	Fine	VF	XF	Unc
6	1970	2,475	—	—	Proof	9.00

50 PESETAS

COPPER-NICKEL

4	1969(69)	—	2.00	3.00	7.50	15.00

MONETARY REFORM
EKUELE

BRASS

32	1975	3.000	1.00	2.00	3.00	5.00

NOTE: Withdrawn from circulation.

5 EKUELE

COPPER-NICKEL

33	1975	2.800	1.00	2.00	3.50	6.00

NOTE: Withdrawn from circulation.

10 EKUELE

COPPER-NICKEL

34	1975	1.300	1.50	2.50	4.50	9.00

NOTE: Withdrawn from circulation.

MONETARY REFORM
EKWELE

ALUMINUM-BRONZE
Obv: T.E. Nkogo.

50	1980	*.200	—	—	—	40.00

25 BIPKWELE

COPPER-NICKEL
T.E. Nkogo

52	1980	*.200	—	12.00	18.00	25.00
	1981	*.800	—	—	—	—

50 BIPKWELE

COPPER-NICKEL
Obv: T.E. Nkogo right. Rev: Value and arms.

53	1980	*.200	—	—	—	30.00
	1981	*.500	—	—	—	—

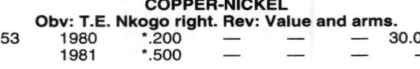

MONETARY REFORM
5 FRANCOS

ALUMINUM-BRONZE

KM#	Date	Mintage	Fine	VF	XF	Unc
62	1985(a)	—		2.50	4.50	8.00

25 FRANCOS

ALUMINUM-BRONZE

60	1985(a)	—		3.50	7.00	15.00

50 FRANCOS

NICKEL

64	1985(a)	—		8.00	16.00	28.00
	1986(a)	—		6.00	12.00	20.00

100 FRANCOS

NICKEL

59	1985(a)	—		10.00	20.00	35.00
	1986(a)	—		7.00	14.00	25.00

ERITREA

The State of Eritrea, a former Ethiopian province fronting on the Red Sea, has an area of 45,300 sq. mi. (117,600 sq. km.) and a population of 3.6 million. It was an Italian colony from 1889 until its incorporation into Italian East Africa in 1936. It was under the British Military Administration from 1941 to Sept. 15, 1952, when the United Nations designated it an autonomous unit within the federation of Ethiopia and Eritrea. On Nov. 14, 1962, it was annexed with Ethiopia. In 1991 the Eritrean Peoples Liberation Front extended its control over the entire territory of Eritrea. Following 2 years of provisional government, Eritrea held a referendum on independence in May 1993. Overwhelming popular approval led to the proclamation of an independent Republic of Eritrea on May 24.

RULERS
Vittorio Emanuele III, 1900-1945

MINT MARKS
R - Rome

MONETARY SYSTEM
100 Centesimi = 1 Lira
5 Lire = 1 Tallero

TALLERO

28.0668 g, .835 SILVER, .7535 oz ASW

KM#	Date	Mintage	Fine	VF	XF	Unc
5	1918R	.510	25.00	50.00	100.00	400.00

REPUBLIC
1 CENT

NICKEL CLAD STEEL
Obv: Antelope. Rev: Soldiers with flag.

KM#	Date	Mintage	VF	XF	Unc
43	1997	—	—	—	.25

5 CENTS

NICKEL CLAD STEEL
Obv: Leopard on log. Rev: Soldiers with flag.

44	1997	—	—	—	.50

10 CENTS

NICKEL CLAD STEEL
Obv: Ostrich. Rev: Soldiers with flag.

KM#	Date	Mintage	VF	XF	Unc
45	1997	—	—	—	.75

25 CENTS

NICKEL CLAD STEEL
Obv: Zebra. Rev: Soldiers with flag.

46	1997	—	—	—	1.00

50 CENTS

NICKEL CLAD STEEL
Obv: Antelope. Rev: Soldiers with flag.

KM#	Date	Mintage	Fine	VF	XF	Unc
47	1997	—		—	—	1.25

100 CENTS

NICKEL CLAD STEEL
Obv: Elephant and calf. Rev: Soldiers with flag.

48	1997	—	—	—	1.50

ESTONIA

FINLAND · SWEDEN · Baltic Sea · RUSSIA · LATVIA · COURLAND

The Republic of Estonia (formerly the Estonian Soviet Socialist Republic of the U.S.S.R.) is the northernmost of the three Baltic States in Eastern Europe. It has an area of 17,462 sq. mi. (45,100 sq. km.) and a population of 1.6 million. Capital: Tallinn. Agriculture and dairy farming are the principal industries. Butter, eggs, bacon, timber and petroleum are exported.

This small and ancient Baltic state had enjoyed but two decades of independence since the 13th century until the present time. After having been conquered by the Danes, the Livonian Knights, the Teutonic Knights of Germany (who reduced the people to serfdom), the Swedes, the Poles and Russia, Estonia declared itself an independent republic on Feb. 24, 1918 but was not freed until Feb. 1919. The peace treaty was signed Feb. 2, 1920. Shortly after the start of World War II, it was again occupied by Russia and incorporated as the 16th state of the U.S.S.R Germany occupied the tiny state from 1941 to 1944, after which it was retaken by Russia. Most of the nations of the world, including the United States and Great Britain, did not recognize Estonia's incorporation into the Soviet Union.

The coinage, issued during the country's brief independence, is obsolete.

On August 20, 1991, the Parliament of the Estonian Soviet Socialist Republic voted to reassert the republic's independence.

REPUBLIC COINAGE

MONETARY SYSTEM
100 Marka = 1 Kroon

MARK

COPPER-NICKEL

KM#	Date	Mintage	Fine	VF	XF	Unc
1	1922	5.025	1.50	2.50	5.50	12.50

NICKEL-BRONZE

1a	1924	1.985	2.00	4.00	7.50	15.00

5	1926	3.979	3.50	6.50	12.00	30.00

3 MARKA

COPPER-NICKEL

2	1922	2.089	2.00	4.00	6.00	12.50

NICKEL-BRONZE

2a	1925	1.134	4.00	7.00	12.50	30.00

6	1926	.903	25.00	50.00	80.00	150.00

5 MARKA

COPPER-NICKEL

KM#	Date	Mintage	Fine	VF	XF	Unc
3	1922	3.983	3.00	5.00	8.00	20.00

NICKEL-BRONZE

3a	1924	1.335	3.50	6.00	9.00	25.00

7	1926	1.038	75.00	150.00	200.00	350.00

10 MARKA

NICKEL-BRONZE

4	1925	2.200	3.50	7.50	12.50	28.00
8	1926	*2.789	650.00	1000.	1500.	2000.

*NOTE: Most of this issue were melted down. Not released to circulation.

MONETARY REFORM
100 Senti = 1 Kroon

SENT

BRONZE

10	1929	23.553	.50	1.00	2.00	4.00

1mm thick planchet

19.1	1939	5.000	4.00	8.00	15.00	30.00

0.9mm thick planchet

19.2	1939	Inc. Ab.	4.00	8.00	15.00	30.00

2 SENTI

BRONZE

15	1934	5.838	1.00	2.00	4.00	8.00

5 SENTI

BRONZE

11	1931	11.000	1.00	2.00	4.00	8.00

10 SENTI

NICKEL-BRONZE

KM#	Date	Mintage	Fine	VF	XF	Unc
12	1931	4.089	1.00	2.00	4.00	8.00

20 SENTI

NICKEL-BRONZE

17	1935	4.250	1.00	2.00	4.00	12.00

25 SENTI

NICKEL-BRONZE

9	1928	2.025	3.00	6.00	10.00	22.00

50 SENTI

NICKEL-BRONZE

18	1936	1.256	3.00	6.00	12.00	25.00

KROON

6.0000 g, .500 SILVER, .0965 oz ASW
10th Singing Festival

14	1933	.350	7.00	14.00	30.00	55.00

ALUMINUM-BRONZE

16	1934	3.304	3.50	6.00	14.00	40.00

NOTE: 1990 restrikes which exist are private issues.

2 KROONI

12.0000 g, .500 SILVER, .1929 oz ASW
Toompea Fortress at Tallinn

20	1930	1.276	3.50	6.00	13.50	38.00

Tercentenary - University of Tartu

KM#	Date	Mintage	Fine	VF	XF	Unc
13	1932	.100	10.00	20.00	30.00	50.00

NEW REPUBLIC

1991-

5 SENTI

BRASS

KM#	Date	Mintage	Fine	VF	XF	Unc
21	1991	—	—	—	—	.25
	1992	—	—	—	—	.25
	1995	—	—	—	—	.25
	1996	—	—	—	—	.25

10 SENTI

BRASS

KM#	Date	Mintage	Fine	VF	XF	Unc
22	1991	—	—	—	—	.50
	1992	—	—	—	—	.50
	1994	—	—	—	—	.50
	1996	—	—	—	—	.50
	1997	—	—	—	—	.50

20 SENTI

BRASS

KM#	Date	Mintage	Fine	VF	XF	Unc
23	1992	—	—	—	—	.75
	1996	—	—	—	—	.75
	1997	—	—	—	—	.75

NICKEL PLATED STEEL

KM#	Date	Mintage	Fine	VF	XF	Unc
23a	1997	—	—	—	—	.75

50 SENTI

BRASS

KM#	Date	Mintage	Fine	VF	XF	Unc
24	1992	—	—	—	—	1.00

KROON

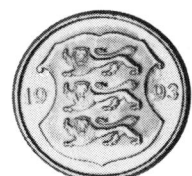 

COPPER-NICKEL

KM#	Date	Mintage	Fine	VF	XF	Unc
28	1992	.020	—	In sets only		—
	1993	—	—	—	—	1.35
	1995	—	—	—	—	1.35
	1998	—	—	—	—	1.35

BRASS

KM#	Date	Mintage	Fine	VF	XF	Unc
35	1998	—	—	—	—	1.00

5 KROONI

BRASS
75th Anniversary - Declaration of Independence

KM#	Date	Mintage	Fine	VF	XF	Unc
29	1993	—	—			2.25
	1993			Proof-like		4.50

75th Anniversary - Estonian National Bank

KM#	Date	Mintage	Fine	VF	XF	Unc
30	1994	—	—	—	—	2.00

ETHIOPIA

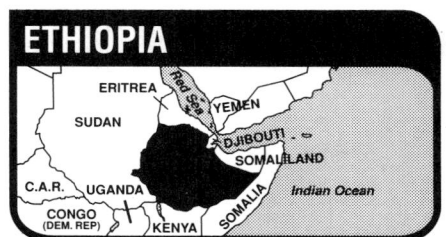

The People's Federal Republic of Ethiopia (formerly the Peoples Democratic Republic and the Empire of Ethiopia), Africa's oldest independent nation, faces the Red Sea in East-Central Africa. The country has an area of 424,214 sq. mi. (1,004,390 sq. km.) and a population of 56 million people who are divided among 40 tribes that speak some 270 languages and dialects. Capital: Addis Ababa. The economy is predominantly agricultural and pastoral. Gold and platinum are mined and petroleum fields are being developed. Coffee, oilseeds, hides and cereals are exported.

Legend claims that Menelik I, the son born to Solomon, King of Israel, by the Queen of Sheba, settled in Axum in North Ethiopia to establish the dynasty which reigned with only brief interruptions until 1974. Modern Ethiopian history began with the reign of Emperor Menelik II (1889-1913) under whose guidance the country emerged from medieval isolation. Progress continued throughout the reigns of Menelik's daughter, Empress Zauditu, and her successor Emperor Haile Selassie I who was coronated in 1930. Ethiopia was invaded by Italy in 1935, and together with Italian Somaliland and Eritrea became part of Italian East Africa. Victor Emmanuel III, as declared by Mussolini, would be Ethiopia's emperor as well as a king of Italy. Liberated by British and Ethiopian troops in 1941, Ethiopia reinstated Haile Selassie I to the throne. The 225th consecutive Solomonic ruler was deposed by a military committee on Sept 12, 1974. In July 1976 Ethiopia's military provisional government referred to the country as Socialist Ethiopia. After establishing a new regime in 1991, Ethiopia became a federated state and is now the Federal Republic of Ethiopia. Following 2 years of provisional government, the province of Eritrea held a referendum on independence in May 1993 leading to the proclamation of its independence on May 24.

No coins, patterns or presentation pieces are known bearing Emperor Lij Yasu's likeness or titles. Coins of Menelik II were struck during this period with dates frozen.

RULERS
Menelik II, 1889-1913
Lij Yasu, 1913-1916
Zauditu, Empress, 1916-1930
Haile Selassie I
  1930-36, 1941-1974
Victor Emmanuel III, of Italy
  1936-1941

MINT MARKS
A - Paris
(a) - Paris, privy marks only

Coinage of Menelik II, 1889-1913
NOTE: The first national issue coinage, dated 1887 and 1888 E.E., carried a cornucopia, A, and fasces on the reverse. Subsequent dates have a torch substituted for the fasces, the A being dropped. All issues bearing these marks were struck at the Paris Mint. Coins without mint marks were struck in Addis Ababa.

MONETARY SYSTEM
(Until about 1903)
40 Besa = 20 Gersh = 1 Birr
(After 1903)
32 Besa = 16 Gersh = 1 Birr

DATING
Ethiopian coinage is dated by the Ethiopian Era calendar (E.E.) which commenced 7 years and 8 months after the advent of A.D. dating.

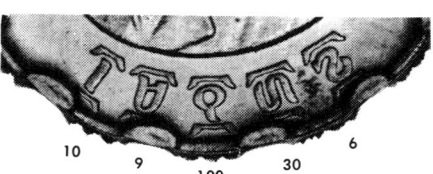

EXAMPLE
1900 (10 and 9 = 19 x 100)
  36 (Add 30 and 6)
1936 E.E.
  8 (Add)
1943/4 AD

GERSH
(1/20 Birr)

1.4038 g, .835 SILVER, .0377 oz ASW
Rev: Lion's left foreleg raised.

KM#	Date	Mintage	Fine	VF	XF	Unc
12	EE1895A (1903)	*44.789	2.00	3.50	6.00	15.00

*NOTE: Struck between 1903-1928.
NOTE: Earlier dates (EE1889-1891) exist for this type.

1/4 BIRR
(Ya Birr Rub/of Birr Fourth)

7.0188 g, .835 SILVER, .1884 oz ASW
Rev: Lion's left foreleg raised.

3	EE1895A (1903)	*.821	4.00	8.00	20.00	90.00

*NOTE: Struck between 1903 and 1925.
NOTE: Earlier dates (EE1887-1889) exist for this type.

BIRR

28.0750 g, .835 SILVER, .7537 oz ASW
Rev: Lion's right foreleg raised.

19	EE1895 (1903)	*.459	12.50	25.00	85.00	250.00
	1895 (1903)	—	—	—	Proof	500.00

*NOTE: Struck in 1901, 1903 and 1904.
NOTE: Earlier date (EE1892) exists for this type.

1/2 WERK
(Ya Werk Alad/of Werk Half)

3.5000 g, .900 GOLD, .1012 oz AGW

20	EE1923 (1931)	—	150.00	275.00	450.00	750.00

WERK

7.0000 g, .900 GOLD, .2025 oz AGW

21	EE1923 (1931)	—	225.00	450.00	700.00	1200.

EMPIRE OF ETHIOPIA
MONETARY SYSTEM
100 Matonas = 100 Santeems
100 Santeems (Cents) = 1 Birr (Dollar)

MATONA

COPPER

KM#	Date	Mintage	Fine	VF	XF	Unc
27	EE1923 (1931)	*1.250	1.50	2.50	5.00	15.00

*NOTE: Struck by ICI in Birmingham, England. Other denominations in the Matona series were struck in Addis Ababa.

CENT
(An de Santeem)

COPPER

32	EE1936 (1944)	20.000	—	.10	.20	.50

NOTE: Coins in the one cent to fifty cent denominations were struck at Philadelphia, Birmingham and the Royal Mint, London between 1944 and 1975 with the date EE1936 frozen.

5 MATONAS

COPPER
Plain edge.

28.1	EE1923 (1931)	1.363	2.00	3.50	6.00	20.00

Reeded edge.

28.2	EE1923 (1931)	Inc. Ab.	2.00	3.50	7.00	25.00

5 CENTS
(Amist Santeem)

COPPER

33	EE1936 (1944)	*219.000	—	.10	.20	.50

*NOTE: Struck between 1944-1962 in Philadelphia and 1964-1966 in Birmingham.

10 MATONAS

NICKEL

29	EE1923 (1931)	.936	1.50	2.50	4.00	10.00

10 CENTS
(Assir Santeem)

COPPER

34	EE1936 (1944)	*348.998	—	.10	.25	.75

*NOTE: Struck between 1945-1963 in Philadelphia, 1964-1966 in Birmingham and 1974-1975 in London.

25 MATONAS

NICKEL

KM#	Date	Mintage	Fine	VF	XF	Unc
30	EE1923 (1931)	2.742	1.25	2.00	3.25	8.00

25 CENTS
(Haya Amist Santeem)

COPPER

35	EE1936 (1944)	*10.000	5.00	10.00	20.00	40.00

*NOTE: 421,500 issued and 1952 withdrawn and replaced by KM#36.

36	EE1936 (1944)	*30.000	.25	.50	1.00	3.00

*NOTE: Issued in 1952 and 1953. Crude and refined edges.

50 MATONAS

NICKEL

31	EE1923 (1931)	1.621	1.50	2.50	4.50	11.50

50 CENTS
(Hamsa Santeem)

7.0307 g, .800 SILVER, .1808 oz ASW

37	EE1936 (1944)	*30.000	2.00	3.50	7.50	15.00

*NOTE: Struck in 1944-1945.

7.0307 g, .700 SILVER, .1582 oz ASW

37a	EE1936 (1944)	*20.434	2.00	3.50	7.50	15.00

*NOTE: Struck in 1947.

PEOPLES DEMOCRATIC REPUBLIC
CENT

ALUMINUM
F.A.O. Issue
Obv: Small lion head.

43.1	EE1969 (1977)	35.034	.20	.30	.50	1.00

5 CENTS

COPPER-ZINC
Obv: Small lion head.

KM#	Date	Mintage	Fine	VF	XF	Unc
44.1	EE1969 (1977)	201.275	.20	.30	.50	1.00

10 CENTS

COPPER-ZINC
Mountain Nyala
Obv: Small lion head.

KM#	Date	Mintage	Fine	VF	XF	Unc
45.1	EE1969 (1977)	202.722	.20	.35	.60	1.50

25 CENTS

COPPER-NICKEL
Obv: Small lion head.

KM#	Date	Mintage	Fine	VF	XF	Unc
46.1	EE1969 (1977)	44.983	.20	.30	.60	1.25

50 CENTS

COPPER-NICKEL
Obv: Small lion head.

KM#	Date	Mintage	Fine	VF	XF	Unc
47.1	EE1969 (1977)	27.772	.40	.75	1.25	2.50

FALKLAND ISLANDS

The Colony of the Falkland Islands and Dependencies, a British colony located in the South Atlantic about 500 miles northeast of Cape Horn, has an area of 4,700 sq. mi. (12,170 sq. km.) and a population of 2,121. East Falkland, West Falkland, South Georgia, and South Sandwich are the largest of the 200 islands. Capital: Stanley. Sheep grazing is the main industry. Wool, whale oil, and seal oil are exported.

The Falklands were discovered by British navigator John Davis (Davys) in 1592, and named by Capt. John Strong - for Viscount Falkland, treasurer of the British navy - in 1690. French navigator Louis De Bougainville established the first settlement, at Port Louis, in 1764. The following year Capt. John Byron claimed the islands for Britain and left a small party at Saunders Island. Spain later forced the French and British to abandon their settlements but did not implement its claim to the islands. In 1829 the Republic of Buenos Aires, which claimed to have inherited the Spanish rights, sent Louis Vernet to develop a colony on the islands. In 1831 he seized three American sealing vessels, whereupon the men of the corvette, the U.S.S. Lexington, destroyed his settlement and proclaimed the Falklands to be 'free of all governance'. Britain, which had never renounced its claim, then re-established its settlement in 1833.

RULERS

British

MONETARY SYSTEM

100 Pence = 1 Pound

1/2 PENNY

BRONZE
Salmon

KM#	Date	Mintage	VF	XF	Unc
1	1974	.140	—	.10	.25
	1974	.023	—	Proof	1.50
	1980	—	—	.10	.15
	1980	.010	—	Proof	1.50
	1982	—	—	.10	.15
	1982	—	—	Proof	1.50
	1983	—	—	.10	.15

PENNY

BRONZE
Gentoo Penguins

KM#	Date	Mintage	VF	XF	Unc
2	1974	.096	.10	.20	.60
	1974	.023	—	Proof	2.00
	1980	—	.10	.20	.60
	1980	.010	—	Proof	2.00
	1982	—	.10	.20	.60
	1982	—	—	Proof	2.00
	1983	—	.10	.20	.60
	1985	—	.10	.20	.45
	1987	.111	—	.20	.45
	1987	—	—	Proof	2.50
	1992	—	.10	.20	.45
	1992	—	—	Proof	2.50

COPPER PLATED STEEL

2a	1998				.40

2 PENCE

BRONZE
Upland Goose

KM#	Date	Mintage	VF	XF	Unc
3	1974	.072	.10	.15	.50
	1974	.023	—	Proof	3.00

KM#	Date	Mintage	VF	XF	Unc
3	1980	—	.10	.15	.40
	1980	.010	—	Proof	3.00
	1982	—	.10	.15	.40
	1982	—	—	Proof	3.00
	1983	—	.10	.15	.40
	1985	—	.10	.15	.40
	1987	.106	—	.15	.40
	1987	—	—	Proof	3.50
	1992	—	.10	.15	.40
	1992	—	—	Proof	3.50

COPPER PLATED STEEL

3a	1998			—	.35

5 PENCE

COPPER-NICKEL
Blackbrowed Albatross

KM#	Date	Mintage	VF	XF	Unc
4.1	1974	.067	.10	.25	.65
	1974	.023	—	Proof	3.50
	1980	—	.10	.25	.65
	1980	.010	—	Proof	4.00
	1982	—	.10	.25	.65
	1982	—	—	Proof	4.00
	1983	—	.10	.25	.65
	1985	—	.10	.20	.65
	1987	5,000	—	.25	.65
	1987	—	—	Proof	4.50
	1992	—	.10	.25	.65
	1992	—	—	Proof	4.50

Reduced size: 18mm.

4.2	1998	—	—	—	.60

10 PENCE

COPPER-NICKEL
Ursine Seal

KM#	Date	Mintage	VF	XF	Unc
5.1	1974	.087	.20	.40	1.50
	1974	.023	—	Proof	4.50
	1980	—	.20	.40	1.50
	1980	.010	—	Proof	5.00
	1982	—	.20	.40	1.50
	1982	—	—	Proof	5.00
	1983	—	.20	.40	1.50
	1985	—	.20	.40	1.50
	1987	4,000	—	.40	1.50
	1987	—	—	Proof	5.50
	1992	—	.20	.40	1.50
	1992	—	—	Proof	5.50

Reduced size: 24.5mm.

5.2	1998	—	—	—	1.00

20 PENCE

COPPER-NICKEL
Romney Marsh Sheep

KM#	Date	Mintage	VF	XF	Unc
17	1982	—	.40	.65	2.00
	1982	—	—	Proof	5.00
	1983	—	.40	.65	2.00

KM#	Date	Mintage	VF	XF	Unc
17	1985	—	.40	.65	2.00
	1987	4,250	—	.60	1.50
	1987			Proof	5.50
	1992	—	.40	.60	1.50
	1992			Proof	5.50

50 PENCE

COPPER-NICKEL
Queen's Silver Jubilee

10	ND(1977)	.100	1.00	1.50	3.00

Falkland Island Fox (extinct)

14	1980	—	1.00	2.00	5.00
	1980	—	—	Proof	6.00
	1982	—	1.00	2.00	5.00
	1982	—	—	Proof	6.00
	1983	—	1.00	2.00	5.00
	1985	—	1.00	2.00	5.00
	1987	4,000	1.00	2.00	5.00
	1987	—	—	Proof	6.50
	1992	—	1.00	2.00	5.00
	1992	—	—	Proof	6.50
	1995	—	—	2.00	5.00

POUND

NICKEL-BRASS

24	1987	—	—	—	3.50
	1987	2,500	—	Proof	12.50
	1992	—	—	—	3.50
	1992	—	—	Proof	12.50

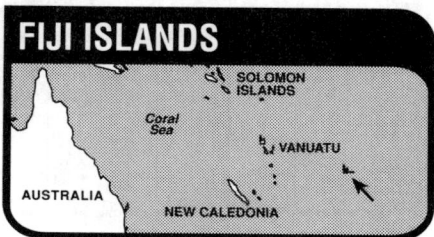

FIJI ISLANDS

The Republic of Fiji, consists of about 320 islands located in the southwestern Pacific 1,100 miles (1,770 km.) north of New Zealand. The islands have a combined area of 7,056 sq. mi. (18,274 sq. km.) and a population of 772,891. Capital: Suva. Fiji's economy is based on agriculture and mining. Sugar, coconut products, manganese, and gold are exported.

The first European to sight Fiji was the Dutch navigator Abel Tasman in 1643 and the islands were visited by British naval captain James Cook in 1774. The first complete survey of the island was conducted by the United States in 1840. Settlement by mercenaries from Tonga, and traders attracted by the sandalwood trade, began in 1801. Following a lengthy period of intertribal warfare, the islands were unconditionally ceded to Great Britain in 1874 by King Cakobau. Fiji became a sovereign and independent nation on Oct. 10, 1970, the 96th anniversary of the cession of the islands to Queen Victoria.

Fiji was declared a Republic in 1987 following two military coups. It left the British Commonwealth and Queen Elizabeth ceased to be the Head of State. A new constitution was introduced in 1991. The country returned to the Commonwealth in 1997 with a revised constitution.

RULERS

British

MINT MARKS
(c) - Royal Australian Mint, Canberra
(o) - Royal Canadian Mint, Ottawa
S - San Francisco, U.S.A.

MONETARY SYSTEM
12 Pence = 1 Shilling
2 Shillings = 1 Florin
20 Shillings = 1 Pound

1/2 PENNY

COPPER-NICKEL

KM#	Date	Mintage	Fine	VF	XF	Unc
1	1934	.096	1.00	3.00	6.00	20.00
	1934	—	—	—	Proof	—

14	1940	.024	6.00	12.50	25.00	55.00
	1940	—	—	—	Proof	350.00
	1941	.096	.75	1.50	4.00	15.00
	1941	—	—	—	Proof	200.00

BRASS

14a	1942S	.250	.25	.50	3.50	17.50
	1943S	.250	.25	.50	3.50	17.50

COPPER-NICKEL
Obv. leg: EMPEROR dropped.

16	1949	.096	.50	1.00	2.00	8.00
	1949	—	—	—	Proof	210.00
	1950	.115	.25	.50	1.50	6.00
	1950	—	—	—	Proof	230.00
	1951	.115	.25	.50	1.50	6.00
	1951	—	—	—	Proof	190.00
	1952	.228	.15	.35	.75	3.00
	1952	—	—	—	Proof	—

KM#	Date	Mintage	Fine	VF	XF	Unc
20	1954	.228	.15	.25	.50	1.25
	1954	—	—	—	Proof	180.00

PENNY

COPPER-NICKEL

2	1934	.480	.50	1.00	5.00	20.00
	1934	—	—	—	Proof	—
	1935	.240	.65	1.25	5.50	22.50
	1935	—	—	—	Proof	—
	1936	.240	.65	1.25	5.50	40.00
	1936	—	—	—	Proof	—

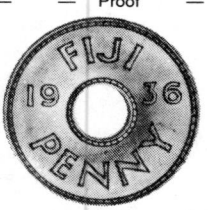

6	1936	.120	.50	1.00	2.00	6.50
	1936	—	—	—	Proof	225.00

7	1937	.360	.50	1.00	3.00	10.00
	1937	—	—	—	Proof	225.00
	1940	.144	2.00	3.00	15.00	40.00
	1940	—	—	—	Proof	225.00
	1941	.228	.50	1.00	2.00	12.50
	1941	—	—	—	Proof	225.00
	1945	.240	2.00	3.00	10.00	35.00
	1945	—	—	—	Proof	225.00

BRASS

7a	1942S	1.000	.50	1.00	3.50	20.00
	1943S	1.000	.50	1.00	3.50	20.00

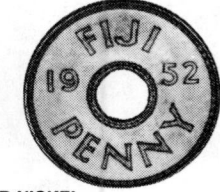

COPPER-NICKEL
Obv. leg: EMPEROR dropped.

17	1949	.120	.25	.50	1.00	7.00
	1949	—	—	—	Proof	325.00
	1950	.058	2.00	5.00	15.00	65.00
	1950	—	—	—	Proof	200.00
	1952	.230	.25	.50	1.00	6.50
	1952	—	—	—	Proof	175.00

21	1954	.511	.20	.50	1.00	4.50
	1954	—	—	—	Proof	175.00
	1955	.230	.25	.50	1.25	7.00
	1955	—	—	—	Proof	175.00
	1956	.230	.25	.50	1.25	7.00
	1956	—	—	—	Proof	175.00
	1957	.360	.10	.25	.75	4.50

KM#	Date	Mintage	Fine	VF	XF	Unc
21	1957	—	—	—	Proof	175.00
	1959	.864	.10	.20	.35	1.25
	1959	—	—	—	Proof	175.00
	1961	.432	.20	.35	.50	1.50
	1961	—	—	—	Proof	175.00
	1963	.432	.20	.35	.50	1.50
	1963	—	—	—	Proof	175.00
	1964	.864	.10	.15	.25	1.00
	1964	—	—	—	Proof	150.00
	1965	1.440	.10	.15	.25	.85
	1966	.720	.10	.15	.25	1.00
	1967	.720	.10	.15	.25	.85
	1968	.720	.10	.15	.25	.85

THREEPENCE

NICKEL-BRASS
Native Dwelling

KM#	Date	Mintage	Fine	VF	XF	Unc
15	1947	.450	1.50	2.50	6.00	25.00
	1947	—	—	—	Proof	190.00

Obv. leg: EMPEROR dropped.

18	1950	.450	.50	1.00	4.00	17.50
	1950	—	—	—	Proof	190.00
	1952	.400	.50	1.00	5.00	22.50
	1952	—	—	—	Proof	190.00

22	1955	.400	.50	1.00	4.00	15.00
	1955	—	—	—	Proof	130.00
	1956	.200	.50	1.00	5.00	35.00
	1956	—	—	—	Proof	155.00
	1958	.200	.50	1.00	4.00	25.00
	1958	—	—	—	Proof	140.00
	1960	.240	.25	.50	3.00	15.00
	1960	—	—	—	Proof	125.00
	1961	.240	.25	.50	1.25	8.00
	1961	—	—	—	Proof	125.00
	1963	.240	.15	.30	.75	5.00
	1963	—	—	—	Proof	115.00
	1964	.240	.15	.30	.50	3.00
	1965	.800	.10	.15	.25	2.00
	1967	.800	.10	.15	.25	2.00

SIXPENCE

2.8276 g, .500 SILVER, .0455 oz ASW
Sea Turtle

3	1934	.160	1.00	2.50	12.50	40.00
	1934	—	—	—	Proof	450.00
	1935	.120	1.50	3.50	15.00	55.00
	1935	—	—	—	Proof	—
	1936	.040	2.00	4.00	18.00	65.00
	1936	—	—	—	Proof	—

8	1937	.040	2.00	4.00	16.00	60.00
	1937	—	—	—	Proof	400.00

Obv: Smaller head.

KM#	Date	Mintage	Fine	VF	XF	Unc
11	1938	.040	2.00	4.00	16.00	60.00
	1938	—	—	—	Proof	—
	1940	.040	2.00	4.00	16.00	60.00
	1940	—	—	—	Proof	—
	1941	.040	3.00	8.00	22.50	85.00
	1941	—	—	—	Proof	—

2.8276 g, .900 SILVER, .0818 oz ASW

11a	1942S	.400	BV	1.00	2.50	7.50
	1943S	.400	BV	1.00	2.50	7.50

COPPER-NICKEL

19	1953	.800	.15	.30	1.00	3.00
	1953	—	—	—	Proof	210.00
	1958	.400	.25	.50	1.50	5.50
	1958	—	—	—	Proof	200.00
	1961	.400	.25	.50	1.00	4.00
	1961	—	—	—	Proof	200.00
	1962	.400	.25	.50	1.00	3.50
	1962	—	—	—	Proof	200.00
	1965	.800	.15	.30	.75	3.00
	1967	.800	.15	.30	.75	3.00

SHILLING

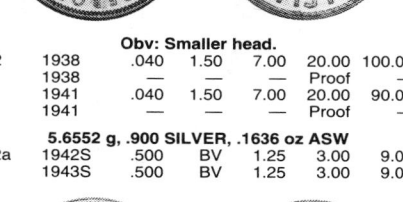

5.6552 g, .500 SILVER, .0909 oz ASW
Outrigger

4	1934	.360	1.50	4.00	16.50	70.00
	1934	—	—	—	Proof	650.00
	1935	.180	1.50	4.00	16.50	90.00
	1935	—	—	—	Proof	—
	1936	.140	1.50	6.00	18.00	90.00
	1936	—	—	—	Proof	—

9	1937	.040	1.50	7.00	20.00	90.00
	1937	—	—	—	Proof	500.00

Obv: Smaller head.

12	1938	.040	1.50	7.00	20.00	100.00
	1938	—	—	—	Proof	—
	1941	.040	1.50	7.00	20.00	90.00
	1941	—	—	—	Proof	—

5.6552 g, .900 SILVER, .1636 oz ASW

12a	1942S	.500	BV	1.25	3.00	9.00
	1943S	.500	BV	1.25	3.00	9.00

COPPER-NICKEL

23	1957	.400	.50	.75	2.00	10.00
	1957	—	—	—	Proof	—
	1958	.400	.50	.75	2.25	12.50
	1958	—	—	—	Proof	—
	1961	.200	.75	1.00	2.25	12.50
	1961	—	—	—	Proof	275.00
	1962	.400	.35	.75	1.25	5.00
	1962	—	—	—	Proof	250.00
	1965	.800	.25	.50	.75	2.50

FLORIN

11.3104 g, .500 SILVER, .1818 oz ASW

KM#	Date	Mintage	Fine	VF	XF	Unc
5	1934	.200	1.50	4.50	20.00	145.00
	1934	—	—	—	Proof	750.00
	1935	.050	2.00	9.00	22.50	220.00
	1935	—	—	—	Proof	—
	1936	.065	2.00	9.00	22.50	220.00
	1936	—	—	—	Proof	—

10	1937	.030	2.50	7.00	20.00	145.00
	1937	—	—	—	Proof	750.00

Obv: Smaller head.

13	1938	.020	4.00	12.00	28.00	180.00
	1938	—	—	—	Proof	—
	1941	.020	4.00	12.00	28.00	180.00
	1941	—	—	—	Proof	—
	1945	.100	9.00	20.00	40.00	220.00
	1945	—	—	—	Proof	—

11.3104 g, .900 SILVER, .3273 oz ASW

13a	1942S	.250	BV	2.50	5.00	17.50
	1943S	.250	BV	2.50	5.00	20.00

COPPER-NICKEL

24	1957	.300	.50	1.00	4.00	12.50
	1957	—	—	—	Proof	375.00
	1958	.220	.50	1.00	4.00	15.00
	1958	—	—	—	Proof	375.00
	1962	.200	.25	.50	2.00	11.50
	1962	—	—	—	Proof	375.00
	1964	.200	.25	.50	1.50	7.50
	1964	—	—	—	Proof	400.00
	1965	.400	.25	.50	1.00	3.50

DECIMAL COINAGE
100 Cents = 1 Dollar

CENT

BRONZE
Tanoa Kava Dish

KM#	Date	Mintage	VF	XF	Unc
27	1969	11.000	—	.10	.20
	1969	.010	—	Proof	.50
	1973	3.000	—	.10	.75
	1975	2.064	—	.10	.35
	1976	2.005	—	.10	.35
	1983	—	—	.10	.35
	1983	3.000	—	Proof	1.00
	1984	2.295	—	.10	.35
	1985	—	—	.10	.35

BRONZE
F.A.O. Issue - Rice

KM#	Date	Mintage	VF	XF	Unc
39	1977	3.000	—	.10	.50
	1978	3.032	—	.10	.35
	1978	2,000	—	Proof	2.50
	1979	2.500	—	.15	1.00
	1980	.314	—	.10	.50
	1980	2,500	—	Proof	1.50
	1981	4.040	—	.10	.50
	1982	5.000	—	.10	.50
	1982	3,000	—	Proof	1.00

49	1986(c)	3.400	—	.10	.50
	1987(c)	3.400	—	.15	1.00

COPPER PLATED ZINC

49a	1990(o)	8.500	—	—	.25
	1992	—	—	—	.25
	1994	—	—	—	.25

2 CENTS

BRONZE
Palm Fan

28	1969	8.000	—	.10	.50
	1969	.010	—	Proof	.75
	1973	2.110	.10	.15	.75
	1975	1.500	.10	.15	.50
	1976	1.005	.10	.10	.40
	1977	1.250	—	.10	.40
	1978	1.502	—	.10	.40
	1978	2,000	—	Proof	3.50
	1979	.500	.10	.20	1.50
	1980	4.020	—	.10	.40
	1980	2,500	—	Proof	2.50
	1981	3.250	—	.10	.40
	1982	4.000	—	.10	.40
	1982	3,000	—	Proof	2.00
	1983	—	—	.10	.40
	1983	3,000	—	Proof	1.50
	1984	1.845	—	.10	.40
	1985	1.700	—	.10	.40

BRONZE

50	1986(c)	1.700	—	.15	.75
	1987(c)	1.700	—	.15	1.00

COPPER PLATED ZINC

50a	1990(o)	5.500	—	—	.35
	1992(o)	—	—	—	.35

5 CENTS

COPPER-NICKEL
Fijian Drum

29	1969	9.200	.10	.20	.75
	1969	.010	—	Proof	.75
	1973	.600	.10	.30	1.50
	1974	.608	.10	.30	1.25
	1975	1.008	.10	.20	.65
	1976	1.205	.10	.20	.50
	1977	.960	.10	.20	.75
	1978	.880	.10	.20	.60
	1978	2,000	—	Proof	5.00
	1979	1.500	.10	.25	1.50
	1980	2.506	.10	.15	.50
	1980	2,500	—	Proof	3.50
	1981	1.980	.10	.15	.35

KM#	Date	Mintage	VF	XF	Unc
29	1982	2.700	.10	.15	.35
	1982	3,000	—	Proof	3.00
	1983	—	.10	.15	.35
	1983	3,000	—	Proof	2.00
	1984	5,000	.10	.20	.60

COPPER-NICKEL

51	1986(c)	1.200	.10	.20	.75
	1987(c)	1.200	.10	.20	.75

NICKEL BONDED STEEL

51a	1990(o)	4.000	—	—	.35
	1992	—	—	—	.35

10 CENTS

COPPER-NICKEL
Throwing Club

30	1969	3.500	.20	.40	1.00
	1969	.010	—	Proof	1.00
	1973	.750	.25	.65	2.00
	1975	.752	.20	.50	1.00
	1976	.805	.20	.50	1.00
	1977	.240	.25	.65	1.25
	1978	.664	.20	.50	1.00
	1978	2,000	—	Proof	6.00
	1979	.702	.25	.65	2.00
	1980	1.000	.15	.30	.75
	1980	2,500	—	Proof	4.50
	1981	1.200	.20	.50	1.00
	1982	1.500	.20	.50	1.00
	1982	3,000	—	Proof	4.00
	1983	3,000	.20	.40	.75
	1983	3,000	—	Proof	3.00
	1984	5,000	.15	.35	.65
	1985	.660	.20	.50	1.00

COPPER-NICKEL

52	1986(c)	.740	.20	.40	1.25
	1987(c)	.740	.20	.40	1.00

NICKEL BONDED STEEL

52a	1990(o)	2.000	—	—	.60
	1992	—	—	—	.60
	1994	—	—	—	.60

20 CENTS

COPPER-NICKEL
Tabua on Braided Sennit Cord

31	1969	2.000	.30	.80	1.50
	1969	.010	—	Proof	1.75
	1973	.250	.35	1.00	2.25
	1974	.252	.35	.75	1.50
	1975	.352	.35	.75	2.00
	1976	.405	.25	.65	1.50
	1977	.200	.35	.75	2.50
	1978	.406	.25	.50	1.00
	1978	2,000	—	Proof	8.00
	1979	.500	.25	.60	1.50
	1980	1.014	.25	.60	1.25
	1980	2,500	—	Proof	6.50
	1981	1.200	.25	.60	1.25
	1982	1.500	.25	.60	1.25
	1982	3,000	—	Proof	6.00
	1983	3,000	.25	.50	1.00
	1983	3,000	—	Proof	5.00
	1984	5,000	.25	.50	1.00
	1985	.240	.20	.35	.70

COPPER-NICKEL

KM#	Date	Mintage	VF	XF	Unc
53	1986(c)	.360	.25	.60	1.50
	1987(c)	.360	.25	.60	1.25

NICKEL BONDED STEEL

53a	1990	1.500	.20	.35	.85
	1992	—	.20	.35	.85
	1995	—	.20	.35	.85

50 CENTS

COPPER-NICKEL
Sailing Canoe - Takia

36	1975	1.000	.75	1.50	5.00
	1976	.805	.75	1.00	3.00
	1978	4,006	1.25	2.50	6.00
	1978	2,000	—	Proof	13.00
	1980	.316	.75	1.00	2.00
	1980	2,500	—	Proof	11.50
	1981	.511	.75	1.25	4.00
	1982	1.000	.75	1.00	3.00
	1982	3,000	—	Proof	10.00
	1983	3,000	.65	1.00	2.50
	1983	3,000	—	Proof	9.00
	1984	5,000	.65	1.00	2.00

COPPER-NICKEL
F. A. O. Issue - First Indians in Fiji Centennial

44	1979	.258	—	—	2.50
	1979	6,004	—	Proof	5.00

10th Anniversary of Independence - Prince Charles

45	1980	.010	—	—	2.50

54	1986(c)	.160	.75	1.00	3.00
	1987(c)	.160	.50	.75	1.75

NICKEL BONDED STEEL

54a	1990(o)	.800	—	.50	1.00
	1992(o)	—	—	.50	1.00
	1994(o)	—	—	.50	1.00

DOLLAR

COPPER-NICKEL

KM#	Date	Mintage	VF	XF	Unc
32	1969	.070	1.00	2.00	4.50
	1969	.010	—	Proof	5.00
	1976	5,007	1.50	3.00	6.50

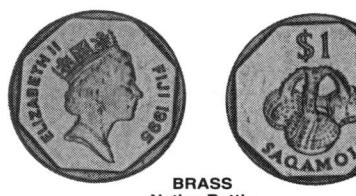

BRASS
Native Rattle

73	1995	—	—	—	3.50

The Republic of Finland, the second most northerly state of the European continent, has an area of 130,559 sq. mi.(338,127 sq. km.) and a population of 5.1 million. Capital: Helsinki. Lumbering, shipbuilding, metal and woodworking are the leading industries. Paper, timber, woodpulp, plywood and metal products are exported.

The Finns, who probably originated in the Volga region of Russia, took Finland from the Lapps late in the 7th century. They were conquered in the 12th century by Eric IX of Sweden, and brought into contact with Western Christendom. In 1809, Sweden was conquered by Alexander I of Russia, and the peace terms gave Finland to Russia which became a grand duchy within the Russian Empire until Dec. 6, 1917, when, shortly after the Bolshevik revolution it declared its independence. After a brief but bitter civil war between the Russian sympathizers and Finnish nationalists in which the Whites (nationalists) were victorious, a new constitution was adopted, and on Dec. 6, 1917 Finland was established as a republic. In 1939 Soviet troops invaded Finland over disputed territorial concessions which were later granted in the peace treaty of 1940. When the Germans invaded Russia, Finland became involved and in the Armistice of 1944 lost the Petsamo area to the Soviets.

RULERS
Nicholas II, 1894-1917

MONETARY SYSTEM
100 Pennia = 1 Markka
Commencing 1963
100 Old Markka = 1 New Markka

MINT MARKS
H - Birmingham 1921
Heart (h) - Copenhagen 1922
No mm - Helsinki

MINTMASTERS INITIALS

Letter	Date	Name
H	1948-1958	Peippo Uolevi Helle
H-M	1990	Raimo Heino & Raimo Makkonen
K	1976-1978	Timo Koivuranta
K-H	1977,1979	Timo Koivuranta & Heikki Haivaoja (Designer)
K-M	1983	Timo Koivuranta & Pertti Makinen
K-N	1978	Timo Koivuranta & Antti Neuvonen
K-T	1982	Timo Koivuranta & Erja Tielinen
L	1885-1912	Johan Conrad Lihr
L	1948	Vesa Uolevi Liuhto
L-M	1991	Arto Lappalainen & Raimo Makkonen
M	1987	Raimo Makkonen
M-G	1998	Raimo Makkonen & Henrick Gummerus
M-L	1997	Raimo Makkonen & Tero Lounas
M-L-L	1995	Raimo Makkonen & Arto Lappalainen & Marita Lappalainen
M-L-M	1989	Marjo Lahtinen & Raimo Makkonen
M-O	1998	Raimo Makkonen & Harri Ojala
M-S	1992,1997	Raimo Makkonen & Erkki Salmela
N	1983-1987	Tapio Nevalainen
P-M	1989-1991, 1994-1995, 1997	Reijo Paavilainen & Raimo Makkonen
P-N	1985	Reijo Paavilainen & Tapio Nevalainen
S	1912-1947	Isak Gustaf Sundell
S	1958-1975	Allan Alarik Soiniemi
S-H	1967-1971	Allen Alarik Soiniemi & Heikki Haivaoja (Designer)
S-J	1960	Allan Alarik Soiniemi & Toivo Jaatinen
S-M	1995	Terho Sakki & Raimo Makkonen
T-M	1996	Arja Tielinen & Raimo Makkonen

GRAND DUCHY
PENNI

COPPER

KM#	Date	Mintage	Fine	VF	XF	Unc
13	1901	1.520	.75	1.25	2.50	5.00
	1902	1.000	.75	1.25	2.50	7.50
	1903 sm.3	1.145	.75	1.25	2.50	7.50
	1903 lg.3	I.A.	1.00	2.00	5.00	12.00
	1904	.500	2.50	5.00	10.00	20.00
	1905	1.390	.50	1.00	2.00	4.00
	1906	1.020	.50	1.00	2.00	4.00
	1907 normal 7					
		2.490	.75	1.25	2.50	7.00
	1907 w/o serif on 7 arm					
		Inc. Ab.	.30	.75	1.75	4.00
	1908	.950	.50	1.00	2.00	5.00
	1909	3.060	.25	.65	1.25	2.50
	1911	2.550	.25	.65	1.25	2.50
	1912	2.450	.25	.65	1.25	2.50
	1913	1.650	.25	.65	1.25	3.00
	1914	1.900	.25	.65	1.25	3.50
	1915	2.250	.25	.65	1.25	2.50
	1916	3.040	.25	.50	1.00	2.00

NOTE: Earlier dates (1895-1900) exist for this type.

5 PENNIA

COPPER

15	1901	.990	1.00	4.00	10.00	50.00
	1905	.620	1.00	4.00	15.00	70.00
	1906	.960	.75	2.50	10.00	50.00
	1907	.770	.75	2.50	10.00	50.00
	1908	1.660	.75	2.50	10.00	30.00
	1910	.060	20.00	35.00	75.00	175.00
	1911	1.050	.75	2.50	6.00	30.00
	1912	.460	1.50	5.00	15.00	50.00
	1913	1.060	.65	1.25	4.00	15.00
	1914	.820	.65	1.25	3.00	15.00
	1915	2.080	.30	.75	3.00	10.00
	1916	4.470	.30	.75	3.00	10.00
	1917	4.070	.30	.75	3.00	10.00

NOTE: Earlier dates (1896-1899) exist for this type.

10 PENNIA

COPPER

14	1905	.500	1.25	5.00	20.00	100.00
	1907	.503	1.25	5.00	20.00	80.00
	1908	.320	1.50	7.50	20.00	80.00
	1909	.180	2.00	10.00	30.00	100.00
	1910	.241	1.50	7.50	20.00	80.00
	1911	.370	1.00	5.00	10.00	50.00
	1912	.191	1.50	7.50	15.00	70.00
	1913	.150	2.50	7.50	30.00	100.00
	1914	.605	.75	1.50	5.00	25.00
	1915	.420	.50	1.00	3.00	10.00
	1916	1.952	.50	1.00	3.00	10.00
	1917	1.600	.75	1.50	4.00	12.00

NOTE: Earlier dates (1895-1900) exist for this type.

25 PENNIA
1.2747 g, .750 SILVER, .0307 oz ASW
Similar to 50 Pennia, KM#2.2.

6.2	1901L	.993	1.00	2.00	5.00	30.00
	1902L	.210	3.00	7.00	15.00	60.00
	1906L	.281	2.00	5.00	10.00	50.00
	1907L	.590	1.00	2.00	5.00	20.00
	1908L	.340	1.00	2.50	5.00	20.00
	1909L	.75	1.00	.75	1.50	3.00
	1910L	.392	2.50	5.00	10.00	50.00
	1913S	.832	.50	1.00	1.50	3.00
	1915S	2.400	.50	.75	1.00	1.50
	1916S	6.392	.50	.75	1.00	1.50
	1917S	5.820	.50	.75	1.00	1.50

NOTE: Earlier dates (1872-1899) exist for this type.

50 PENNIA

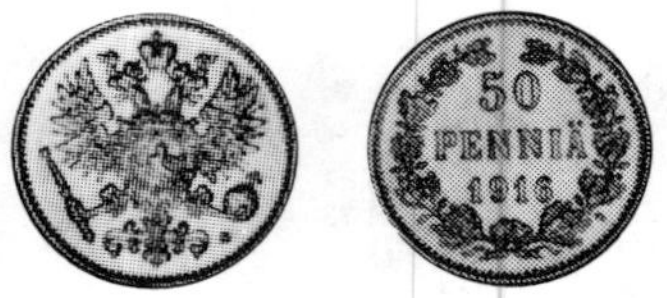

2.5494 g, .750 SILVER, .0615 oz ASW
Dentilated border.

KM#	Date	Mintage	Fine	VF	XF	Unc
2.2	1907L	.260	1.00	3.00	15.00	75.00
	1908L	.353	.75	2.00	10.00	30.00
	1911L	.616	.75	1.25	2.50	5.00
	1914S	.600	.75	1.00	1.50	4.00
	1915S	1.000	.75	1.00	1.50	2.50
	1916S	4.752	.75	1.00	1.50	2.50
	1917S	3.972	.75	1.00	1.50	2.50

***NOTE:** Some specimens may appear as proof-like. Proofs were never made officially by the mint.
NOTE: Earlier dates (1872-1893) exist for this type.

MARKKA

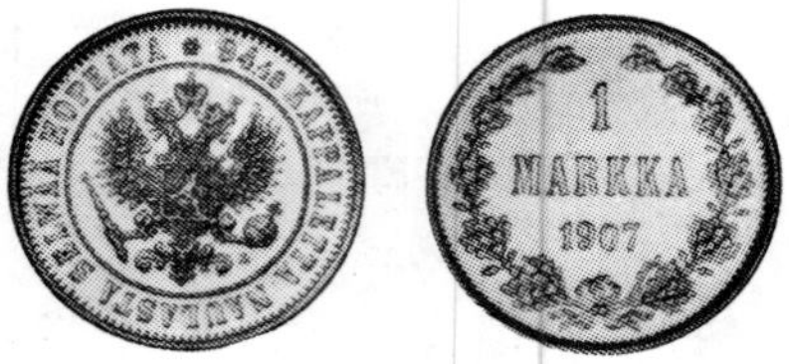

5.1828 g, .868 SILVER, .1446 oz ASW
Dentilated border.

KM#	Date	Mintage	Fine	VF	XF	Unc
3.2	1907L	.350	2.00	3.00	8.00	25.00
	1908L	.153	4.00	10.00	25.00	50.00
	1915S	1.212	2.00	3.00	6.00	10.00

NOTE: Earlier dates (1872-1893) exist for this type.

2 MARKKAA

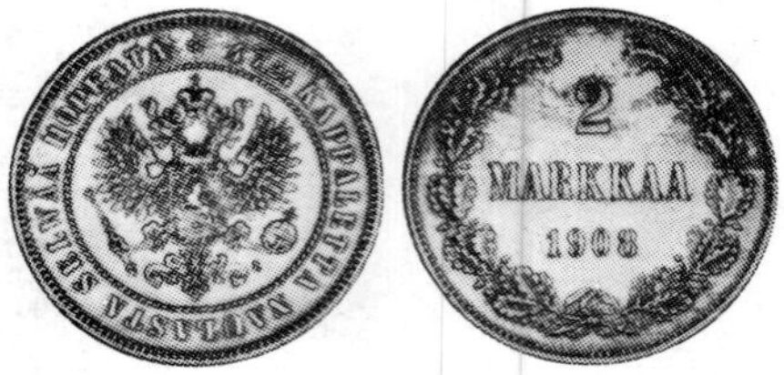

10.3657 g, .868 SILVER, .2893 oz ASW
Dentilated border.

KM#	Date	Mintage	Fine	VF	XF	Unc
7.2	1905L	.024	60.00	100.00	200.00	600.00
	1906L	.225	5.00	8.00	20.00	50.00
	1907L	.125	8.00	15.00	40.00	80.00
	1908L	.124	5.00	10.00	25.00	50.00

NOTE: Earlier dates (1872-1874) exist for this type.

10 MARKKAA

3.2258 g, .900 GOLD, .0933 oz AGW
Regal Issues
Similar to 20 Markkaa, KM#9.2.
Obv: Narrow eagle.

KM#	Date	Mintage	Fine	VF	XF	Unc
8.2	1904L	.102	225.00	275.00	325.00	400.00
	1905L	.043	1000.	1200.	1400.	2000.
	1913S	.396	50.00	60.00	80.00	100.00

NOTE: Earlier dates (1878-1882) exist for this type.

20 MARKKAA

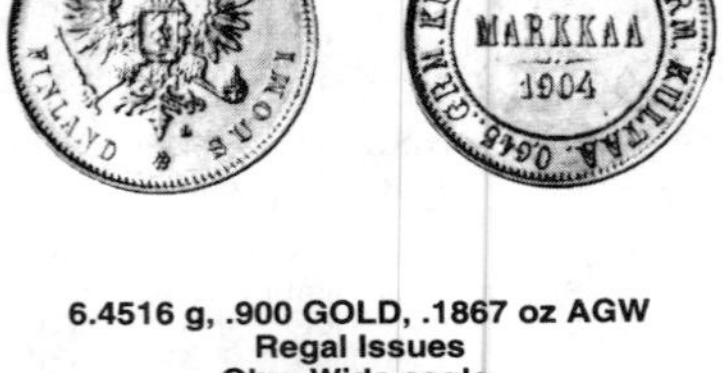

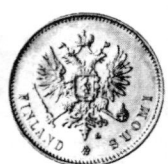

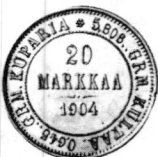

6.4516 g, .900 GOLD, .1867 oz AGW
Regal Issues
Obv: Wide eagle.

KM#	Date	Mintage	Fine	VF	XF	Unc
9.2	1903L	.112	85.00	100.00	125.00	150.00
	1904L	.188	85.00	100.00	120.00	150.00
	1910L	.201	85.00	100.00	120.00	150.00
	1911L	.161	85.00	100.00	125.00	160.00
	1912L	.881	1000.	1500.	2500.	4000.
	1912S	Inc. Ab.	80.00	90.00	100.00	115.00
	1913S	.214	80.00	90.00	100.00	115.00

***NOTE:** Some specimens may appear as proof-like. Proofs were never made officially by the mint.
NOTE: Earlier dates (1878-1891) exist for this type.

CIVIL WAR COINAGE

Kerenski Government Issue

PENNI

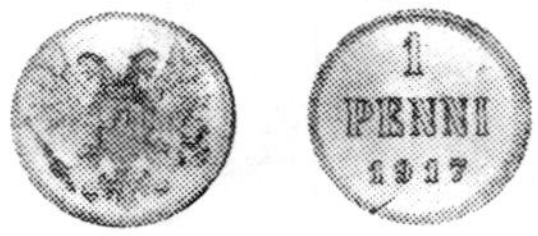

COPPER

KM#	Date	Mintage	Fine	VF	XF	Unc
16	1917	1.650	.25	.75	1.00	1.50

5 PENNIA

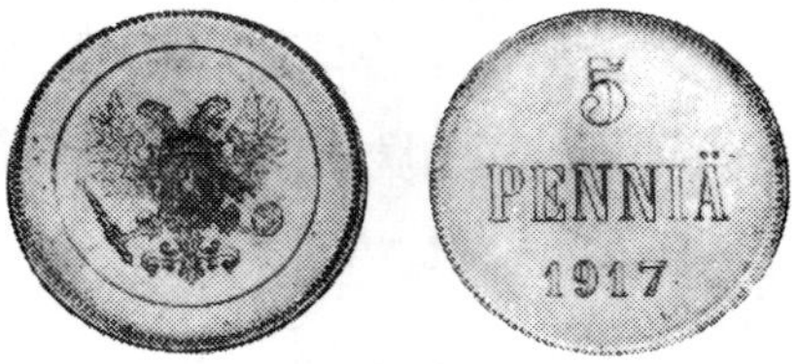

COPPER

KM#	Date	Mintage	Fine	VF	XF	Unc
17	1917	Inc. Ab.	.30	.75	2.50	5.00

10 PENNIA

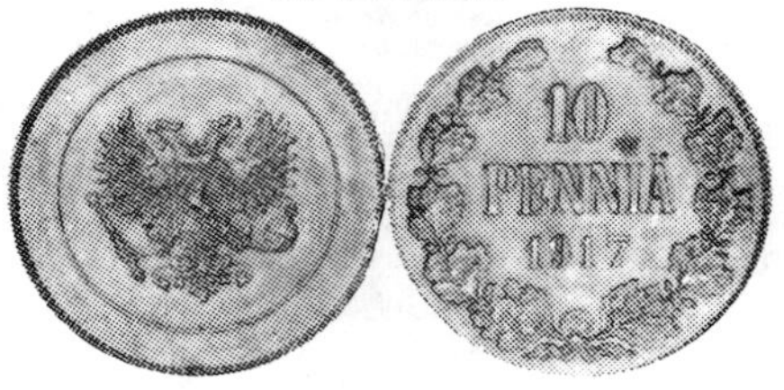

COPPER

KM#	Date	Mintage	Fine	VF	XF	Unc
18	1917	Inc. Ab.	.50	1.00	2.50	7.50

25 PENNIA

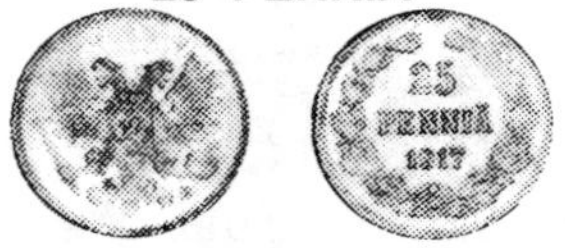

1.2747 g, .750 SILVER, .0307 oz ASW
Obv: Crown above eagle removed.

KM#	Date	Mintage	Fine	VF	XF	Unc
19	1917S	2.310	—	BV	1.00	1.50

50 PENNIA

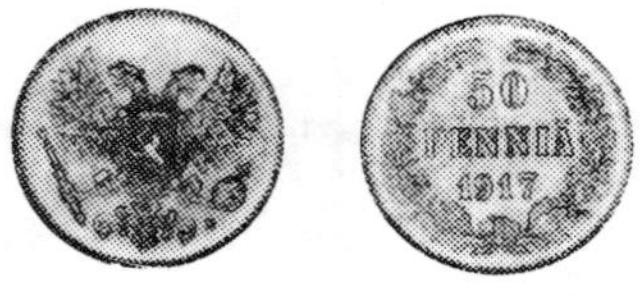

2.5494 g, .750 SILVER, .0615 oz ASW
Obv: Crown above eagle removed.

KM#	Date	Mintage	Fine	VF	XF	Unc
20	1917S	.570	—	BV	1.25	2.00

Liberated Finnish Government Issue

5 PENNIA

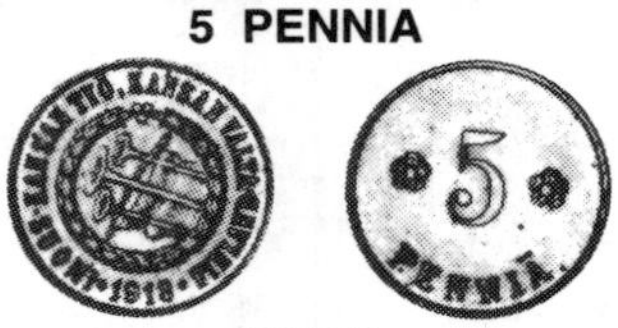

COPPER
Obv: Wreath knot centered between 9 and 1 of date.

KM#	Date	Mintage	Fine	VF	XF	Unc
21.1	1918	.035	20.00	35.00	55.00	90.00

Obv: Wreath knot above second 1 in 1918.

KM#	Date	Mintage	Fine	VF	XF	Unc
21.2	1918	Inc. Ab.	50.00	100.00	200.00	450.00

NOTE: This type was unofficially struck outside of Finland in the early 1920's.

REPUBLIC

PENNI

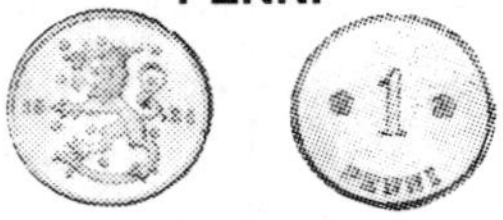

COPPER

KM#	Date	Mintage	Fine	VF	XF	Unc
23	1919	1.200	.25	.65	1.75	3.00
	1920	.720	.25	.65	1.75	3.00
	1921	.510	.35	1.00	2.00	4.00
	1922	1.060	.25	.65	1.75	3.00
	1923	.990	.25	.65	1.75	3.00
	1924	2.180	.25	.65	1.75	3.00

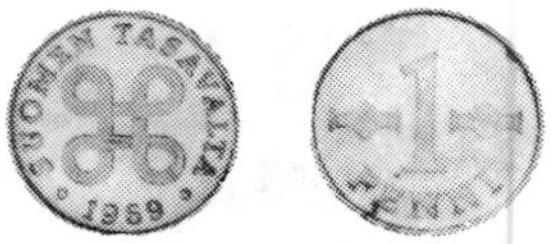

KM#	Date	Mintage	Fine	VF	XF	Unc
44	1963 square edge					
		62.460	—	.10	.40	1.00
	1963 round edge					
		108.870	—	.10	.20	.50
	1964	49.300	—	.10	.40	1.00
	1965	43.112	—	.10	.40	1.00
	1966	36.880	—	.10	.40	1.00
	1967	62.792	—	.10	.40	1.00
	1968	73.416	—	—	.40	1.00
	1969	51.748	—	—	.40	1.00

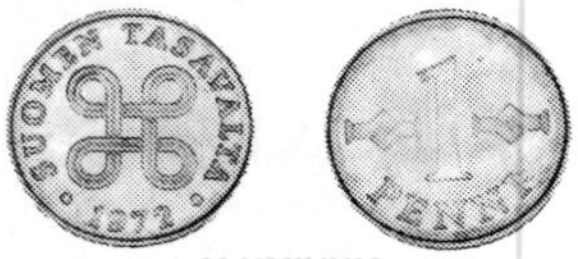

ALUMINUM

KM#	Date	Mintage	Fine	VF	XF	Unc
44a	1969	28.524	—	—	.40	1.00
	1970	85.140	—	—	.10	.50
	1971	70.240	—	—	.10	.50
	1972	95.096	—	—	.10	.50
	1973	115.532	—	—	.10	.25
	1974	100.132	—	—	.10	.25
	1975	111.906	—	—	.10	.25
	1976	34.965	—	—	.10	.50
	1977	61.393	—	—	.10	.25
	1978	90.132	—	—	.10	.25
	1979	33.388	—	—	.10	.25

5 PENNIA

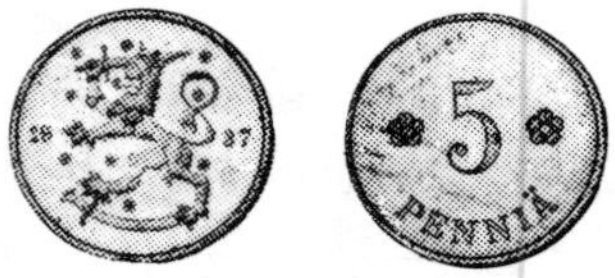

COPPER

KM#	Date	Mintage	Fine	VF	XF	Unc
22	1918	4.270	.10	.25	1.00	4.00
	1919	4.640	.10	.25	1.00	4.00
	1920	7.710	.10	.25	1.00	3.00
	1921	5.910	.10	.25	1.00	3.00
	1922	8.540	.10	.25	1.00	3.00
	1927	1.520	.75	1.50	3.50	15.00
	1928	2.110	.25	.50	1.50	8.00
	1929	1.500	.25	.50	1.50	8.00
	1930	2.140	.75	1.25	3.00	12.00
	1932	2.130	.15	.50	1.00	4.00
	1934	2.180	.15	.50	1.00	4.00
	1935	1.610	.15	.35	1.00	3.00
	1936	2.610	.15	.35	1.00	3.00
	1937	3.830	.10	.25	1.00	3.00
	1938	4.300	.10	.25	1.00	3.00
	1939	2.270	.10	.25	1.00	3.00
	1940	1.610	.25	.50	1.50	5.00

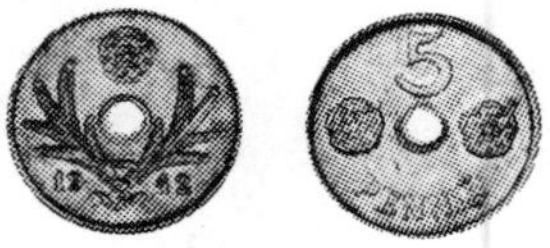

Punched center hole.

KM#	Date	Mintage	Fine	VF	XF	Unc
64.1	1941	5.950	.10	.20	.50	1.25
(32.1)	1942	4.280	.10	.20	.50	1.25
	1943	1.530	.10	.50	1.25	2.50

W/o punched center hole.

KM#	Date	Mintage	Fine	VF	XF	Unc
64.2	1941	Inc. Ab.	25.00	30.00	70.00	100.00
(32.2)	1942	Inc. Ab.	25.00	30.00	70.00	100.00
	1943	Inc. Ab.	50.00	70.00	100.00	125.00

NOTE: The above issues were not authorized by the government and any that exist were illegally removed from the mint.

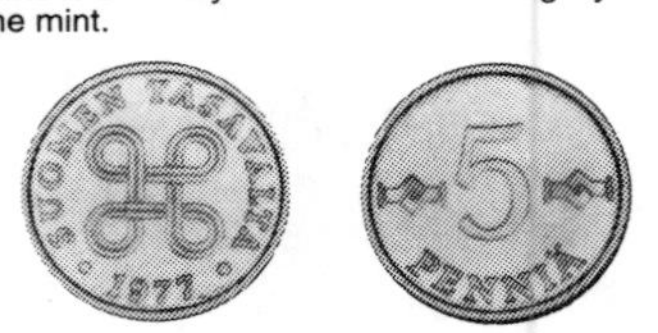

KM#	Date	Mintage	Fine	VF	XF	Unc
45	1963	60.320	—	.10	.50	1.50
	1964	4.634	.50	1.00	2.00	7.50
	1965	10.264	—	.10	.50	1.50
	1966	8.064	—	.10	.50	1.50
	1967	9.968	—	.10	.50	1.50
	1968	6.144	—	.10	.50	1.50
	1969	3.598	—	.15	.50	2.00
	1970	13.772	—	.10	.25	1.00
	1971	20.010	—	—	.25	1.00
	1972	24.122	—	—	.25	1.00
	1973	25.644	—	—	.25	1.00
	1974	21.530	—	—	.25	1.00
	1975	25.010	—	—	.25	1.00
	1976	25.551	—	—	.25	1.00
	1977	1.489	—	.10	.50	1.50

ALUMINUM

KM#	Date	Mintage	Fine	VF	XF	Unc
45a	1977	30.552	—	—	.15	.50
	1978	26.112	—	—	.15	.50
	1979	40.042	—	—	.15	.50
	1980	60.026	—	—	.15	.50
	1981	2.044	—	.20	.40	1.00
	1982	10.012	—	—	.25	.75
	1983	33.885	—	—	—	.25
	1984	25.001	—	—	—	.25
	1985	25.000	—	—	—	.25
	1986	20.000	—	—	—	.25
	1987	2.020	—	—	—	.25
	1988	33.005	—	—	—	.15
	1989	2.200	—	—	—	.25
	1990	2.506	—	—	—	.25

10 PENNIA

COPPER

KM#	Date	Mintage	Fine	VF	XF	Unc
24	1919	3.670	.10	.25	1.00	5.00
	1920	2.380	.10	.25	1.00	5.00
	1921	3.970	.10	.25	1.00	5.00
	1922	2.180	.10	.25	1.00	5.00
	1923	.910	.75	1.50	5.00	15.00
	1924	1.350	.25	.50	2.50	10.00
	1926	1.690	.25	.50	1.00	6.00
	1927	1.330	.50	1.00	2.50	10.00
	1928	1.006	.50	1.00	2.50	10.00
	1929	1.560	.35	.85	2.00	7.00
	1930	.650	.75	1.50	5.00	12.00
	1931	1.040	1.00	2.00	6.00	15.00
	1934	1.680	.35	.85	1.50	6.00
	1935	1.690	.15	.25	1.00	5.00
	1936	2.010	.15	.25	1.00	5.00
	1937	2.420	.10	.25	.50	3.50
	1938	2.940	.10	.25	.50	3.50
	1939	2.100	.10	.25	.50	3.50
	1940	2.010	.25	.50	1.00	5.00

KM#	Date	Mintage	Fine	VF	XF	Unc
33.1	1941	3.610	.10	.25	.50	1.25
	1942	4.970	.10	.25	.50	1.25
	1943	1.860	.25	.75	1.50	2.50

W/o punched center hole.

KM#	Date	Mintage	Fine	VF	XF	Unc
33.2	1941	Inc. Ab.	20.00	30.00	50.00	75.00
	1942	Inc. Ab.	20.00	30.00	50.00	75.00
	1943	Inc. Ab.	30.00	50.00	70.00	100.00

NOTE: The above issues were not authorized by the government and any that exist were illegally removed from the mint.

IRON
Reduced planchet size.

KM#	Date	Mintage	Fine	VF	XF	Unc
34.1	1943	1.430	.10	.25	1.00	3.50
	1944	3.040	.10	.25	1.00	3.00
	1945	1.810	.25	.50	2.00	10.00

W/o punched center hole.

KM#	Date	Mintage	Fine	VF	XF	Unc
34.2	1943	Inc. Ab.	30.00	50.00	70.00	100.00
	1944	Inc. Ab.	30.00	50.00	70.00	100.00
	1945	Inc. Ab.	50.00	70.00	100.00	150.00

NOTE: The above issues were not authorized by the government and any that exist were illegally removed from the mint.

ALUMINUM-BRONZE

KM#	Date	Mintage	Fine	VF	XF	Unc
46	1963S	38.420	—	.10	.25	1.50
	1964S	6.926	—	.10	.50	2.00
	1965S	4.524	—	.10	.25	1.50
	1966S	3.094	—	.10	.25	1.50
	1967S	1.050	.10	.20	1.00	2.50
	1968S	3.004	—	.10	.20	1.50
	1969S	5.046	—	—	.20	1.50
	1970S	3.996	—	—	.20	1.50
	1971S	15.026	—	—	.10	1.00
	1972S	19.900	—	—	.10	1.00
	1973S	9.196	—	—	.10	1.00
	1974S	8.930	—	—	.10	1.00
	1975S	15.064	—	—	.10	.50
	1976K	10.063	—	—	.10	.50
	1977K	10.043	—	—	.10	.50

KM#	Date	Mintage	Fine	VF	XF	Unc
46	1978K	10.062	—	—	.10	.50
	1979K	13.072	—	—	.10	.50
	1980K	23.654	—	—	.10	.50
	1981K	30.036	—	—	.10	.50
	1982K	35.548	—	—	.10	.50

ALUMINUM

KM#	Date	Mintage	Fine	VF	XF	Unc
46a	1983K	6.320	—	—	.25	1.00
	1983N	4.191	—	—	.25	1.00
	1984N	20.061	—	—	.10	.50
	1985N	20.000	—	—	.10	.50
	1986N	15.000	—	—	.10	.50
	1987N	1.400	—	—	.25	1.00
	1987M	8.654	—	—	.25	1.00
	1988M	23.197	—	—	.10	.50
	1989M	2.400	—	—	.25	.50
	1990M	2.254	—	—	.25	.50

COPPER-NICKEL
Flower Pods and Stems

KM#	Date	Mintage	Fine	VF	XF	Unc
65	1990M	338.100	—	—	.10	.15
	1991M	263.899	—	—	.10	.15
	1992M	136.131	—	—	.10	.15
	1993M	56.206	—	—	.10	.15
	1994M	59.946	—	—	.10	.15
	1994M	5,000	—	—	Proof	7.00
	1995M	85.000	—	—	.10	.15
	1995M	3,000	—	—	Proof	7.00
	1996M	123.000	—	—	.10	.15
	1996M	1,200	—	—	Proof	7.00
	1997M	—	—	—	.10	.15
	1997M	2,000	—	—	Proof	7.00
	1998M	—	—	—	.10	15.00
	1998M	2,000	—	—	Proof	7.00

20 PENNIA

ALUMINUM-BRONZE

KM#	Date	Mintage	Fine	VF	XF	Unc
47	1963S	39.970	—	.10	.20	1.50
	1964S	4.248	.10	.25	.50	2.50
	1965S	5.704	—	.10	.20	1.50
	1966S	4.085	—	.10	.20	1.50
	1967S	1.716	—	.10	.20	1.50
	1968S	1.330	—	.10	.20	1.50
	1969S	.201	.50	1.00	1.50	3.50
	1970S	.230	.50	1.00	1.50	3.50
	1971S	5.150	—	.25	.50	1.00
	1972S	10.001	—	.10	.25	.50
	1973S	9.462	—	.10	.25	.50
	1974S	12.705	—	.10	.25	.50
	1975S	12.068	—	—	.10	.50
	1976K	20.058	—	—	.10	.50
	1977K	10.063	—	—	.10	.50
	1978K	10.014	—	—	.10	.50
	1979K	7.513	—	—	.10	.50
	1980K	20.047	—	—	.10	.25
	1981K	30.002	—	—	.10	.25
	1982K	35.050	—	—	.10	.25
	1983K	7.113	—	—	.10	.25
	1983N	12.889	—	—	.10	.25
	1984N	20.029	—	—	.10	.25
	1985N	15.004	—	—	.10	.25
	1986N	20.001	—	—	.10	.25
	1987N	1.200	—	.25	.50	1.00
	1987M	25.670	—	—	.10	.25
	1988M	13.853	—	—	.10	.25
	1989M	40.695	—	—	.10	.25
	1990M	9.168	—	—	.10	.25

NOTE: Some coins dated 1971 are magnetic and command a higher premium.

25 PENNIA

COPPER-NICKEL

KM#	Date	Mintage	Fine	VF	XF	Unc
25	1921H	20.096	.10	.25	1.00	3.00
	1925S	1.250	.50	1.50	5.00	15.00
	1926S	2.820	.40	1.25	3.00	10.00
	1927S	1.120	.50	1.50	5.00	15.00
	1928S	2.920	.40	1.00	3.00	10.00
	1929S	.200	2.00	4.00	10.00	25.00
	1930S	1.090	.50	1.50	5.00	12.00
	1934S	1.260	.40	.75	2.00	7.00
	1935S	2.190	.30	.50	1.50	6.00
	1936S	2.300	.20	.40	1.00	3.00
	1937S	4.020	.20	.40	1.00	3.00
	1938S	4.500	.20	.40	1.00	3.00
	1939S	2.712	.20	.40	1.00	3.00
	1940S	4.840	.15	.30	.75	2.00

COPPER

KM#	Date	Mintage	Fine	VF	XF	Unc
25a	1940S	.072	.50	1.00	3.00	12.00
	1941S	5.980	.10	.35	1.00	3.00
	1942S	6.464	.10	.35	1.00	3.00
	1943S	4.912	.25	.50	1.50	5.00

IRON

KM#	Date	Mintage	Fine	VF	XF	Unc
25b	1943S	2.700	.15	.50	1.50	7.00
	1944S small closed 4's	5.480	.15	.50	1.25	6.00
	1944S large open 4's	Inc. Ab.	.15	.50	1.25	6.00
	1945S	6.810	.25	.75	2.00	8.00

50 PENNIA

COPPER-NICKEL

KM#	Date	Mintage	Fine	VF	XF	Unc
26	1921H	10.072	.15	.30	1.00	3.00
	1923S	6.000	.25	1.00	3.00	12.00
	1929S	.984	.75	1.50	5.00	20.00
	1934S	.612	1.00	2.50	7.50	22.00
	1935S	.610	1.00	2.50	7.50	22.00
	1936S	1.520	.30	.50	1.50	6.00
	1937S	2.350	.15	.25	.75	3.50
	1938S	2.330	.15	.25	.75	3.00
	1939S	1.280	.15	.25	.75	3.00
	1940S	3.152	.15	.25	.75	2.50

COPPER

KM#	Date	Mintage	Fine	VF	XF	Unc
26a	1940S	.480	1.25	2.50	5.00	12.00
	1941S	3.860	.15	.40	1.00	3.00
	1942S	5.900	.15	.40	1.00	3.00
	1943S	3.140	.25	.50	1.50	4.00

IRON

KM#	Date	Mintage	Fine	VF	XF	Unc
26b	1943S	1.580	.25	.50	1.50	15.00
	1944S	7.600	.15	.40	1.00	12.00
	1945S	4.700	.15	.40	1.00	12.00
	1946S	2.632	.30	.50	1.50	12.00
	1947S	1.748	.50	1.50	3.50	15.00
	1948L	1.112	3.00	5.00	10.00	20.00

ALUMINUM-BRONZE

KM#	Date	Mintage	Fine	VF	XF	Unc
48	1963S	17.316	—	.20	.50	2.00
	1964S	3.101	—	.25	1.00	3.00
	1965S	1.667	—	.20	.50	2.50
	1966S	1.051	—	.20	.50	2.00
	1967S	.400	.25	.50	1.50	3.00
	1968S	.816	—	.25	1.00	2.50
	1969S	1.341	—	.20	.50	2.00
	1970S	2.250	—	.20	.30	1.50
	1971S	10.003	—	—	.25	1.00
	1972S	7.892	—	—	.25	1.00
	1973S	5.428	—	—	.25	1.00
	1974S	5.049	—	—	.25	1.00
	1975S	4.305	—	—	.25	1.00
	1976K	7.022	—	—	.25	1.00
	1977K	8.077	—	—	.25	1.00
	1978K	8.048	—	—	.25	1.00
	1979K	8.004	—	—	.25	1.00
	1980K	5.349	—	—	.25	1.00
	1981K	20.031	—	—	.25	.50
	1982K	5.042	—	—	.25	1.00
	1983K	4.044	—	—	.25	1.00
	1983N	1.016	—	.20	.50	1.50
	1984N	3.006	—	—	.25	1.00
	1985N	10.000	—	—	.20	.50
	1986N	9.002	—	—	.20	.50
	1987N	.700	—	.30	.75	1.50
	1987M	4.305	—	—	.20	.50
	1988M	14.735	—	—	.20	.50
	1989M	10.651	—	—	.20	.50
	1990M	5.391	—	—	.20	.50

NOTE: Some 1971 issues are magnetic and command a premium.

COPPER-NICKEL
Polar Bear

KM#	Date	Mintage	Fine	VF	XF	Unc
66	1990M	70.459	—	—	.20	.50
	1991M	90.480	—	—	.20	.50
	1992M	58.996	—	—	.20	.50
	1993M	10.066	—	—	.20	.50
	1994M	3.005	—	—	.20	.50
	1994M	5,000	—	—	Proof	8.00

KM#	Date	Mintage	Fine	VF	XF	Unc
66	1995M	1.048	—	—	.20	.50
	1995M	3,000	—	—	Proof	8.00
	1996M	17.000	—	—	.20	.50
	1996M	1,200	—	—	Proof	8.00
	1997M	—	—	—	.20	.50
	1997M	2,000	—	—	Proof	8.00
	1998M	—	—	—	.20	.50
	1998M	2,000	—	—	Proof	8.00

MARKKA

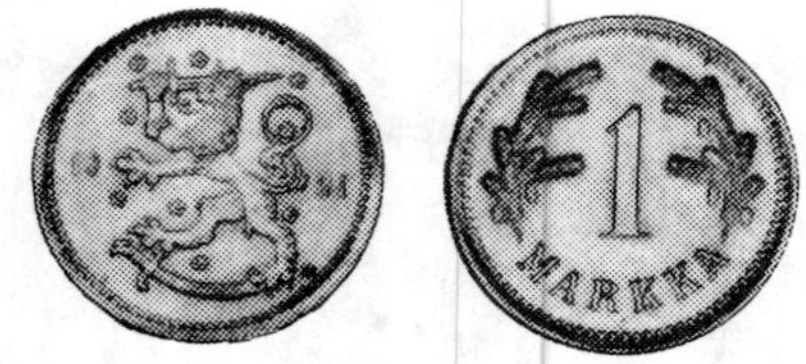

COPPER-NICKEL

KM#	Date	Mintage	Fine	VF	XF	Unc
27	1921H	10.048	.50	1.00	2.50	5.00
	1922 heart	10.000	.75	1.50	3.50	10.00
	1923S	1.780	7.50	15.00	25.00	50.00
	1924S	3.270	3.00	7.00	15.00	30.00

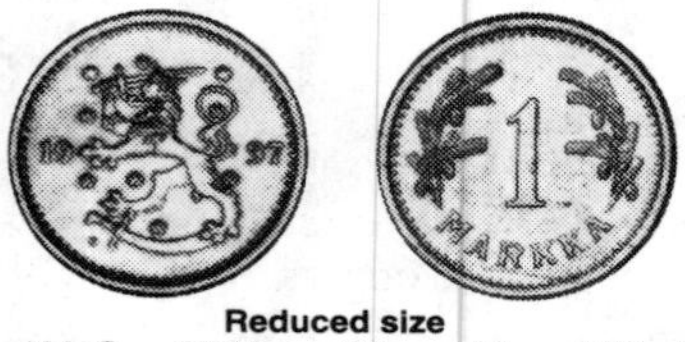

Reduced size

KM#	Date	Mintage	Fine	VF	XF	Unc
30	1928S	3.000	.15	.30	3.00	20.00
	1929S	3.862	.15	.30	3.00	20.00
	1930S	10.284	.15	.30	1.00	12.00
	1931S	2.830	.15	.30	1.00	12.00
	1932S	4.140	.15	.30	1.00	10.00
	1933S	4.032	.15	.30	1.00	10.00
	1936S	.562	.50	1.50	5.00	25.00
	1937S	4.930	.15	.30	1.00	6.00
	1938S	4.410	.15	.25	1.00	6.00
	1939S	3.070	.15	.25	1.00	6.00
	1940S	3.372	.15	.25	1.00	6.00

NOTE: Coins dated 1928S, 1929S and 1930S are known to be restruck on 1921-24, KM#27 coins. (1928S: 2 or 3 known)

COPPER

KM#	Date	Mintage	Fine	VF	XF	Unc
30a	1940S	.084	1.50	3.50	8.00	20.00
	1941S	8.970	.15	.50	1.25	6.00
	1942S	11.200	.15	.50	1.00	4.00
	1943S	7.460	.15	.50	1.25	5.00
	1949H	250 pcs.	1500.	2500.	3500.	5000.
	1950H	.320	.50	1.00	2.00	10.00
	1951H	4.630	.25	.50	1.00	6.00

IRON

KM#	Date	Mintage	Fine	VF	XF	Unc
30b	1943S	7.460	.15	.25	1.00	9.00
	1944S	12.830	.15	.25	1.00	8.00
	1945S	21.950	.15	.25	1.00	8.00
	1946S	2.630	.15	.30	1.25	10.00
	1947S	1.750	.25	.50	1.50	15.00
	1948L	20.500	.15	.25	1.00	8.00
	1949H	17.358	.15	.25	.75	7.00
	1950H	14.654	.15	.25	.75	7.00
	1951H	21.414	.15	.25	.75	7.00
	1952H	5.410	.25	.50	1.50	10.00

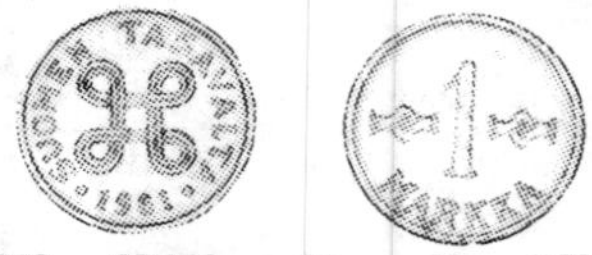

KM#	Date	Mintage	Fine	VF	XF	Unc
36	1952	22.050	.15	.35	1.00	7.00
	1953	28.618	.15	.35	1.00	7.00

NICKEL-PLATED IRON

KM#	Date	Mintage	Fine	VF	XF	Unc
36a	1953	6.000	5.00	8.00	12.50	20.00
	1954	36.400	—	.10	.25	.50
	1955	38.100	—	.10	.25	.50
	1956	35.600	—	.10	.25	.50
	1957	29.100	—	.10	.25	.50
	1958	19.940	.10	.20	.35	.70
	1959 thick letters	23.920	—	.10	.25	.50
	1959 thin letters	Inc. Ab.	—	.10	.25	.50
	1960	22.020	—	.10	.25	.50
	1961	32.220	—	.10	.25	.50
	1962	29.040	—	.10	.25	.50

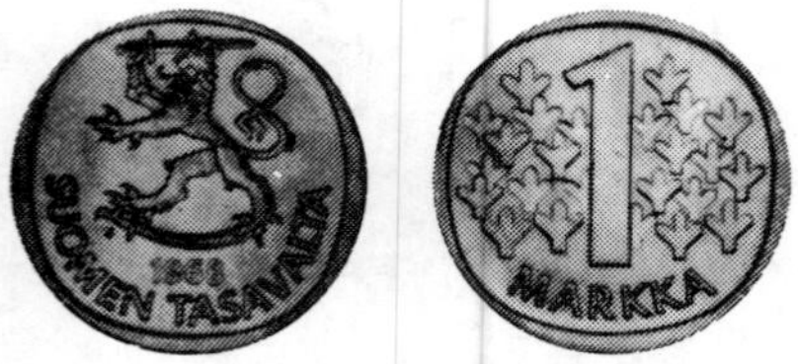

6.4000 g, .350 SILVER, .0720 oz ASW

KM#	Date	Mintage	Fine	VF	XF	Unc
49	1964S	9.999	—	BV	1.50	5.00
	1965S	15.107	—	BV	1.00	3.00
	1966S	15.183	—	BV	.75	2.00
	1967S	6.249	—	BV	.75	2.00
	1968S	3.063	—	BV	.75	2.00

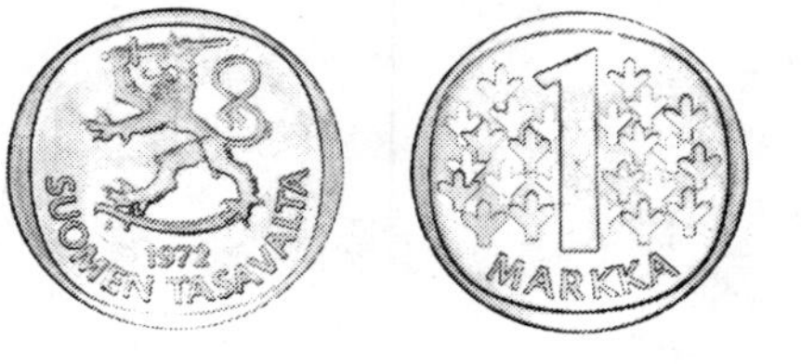

COPPER-NICKEL

KM#	Date	Mintage	Fine	VF	XF	Unc
49a	1969S	1.308	.35	.45	.60	1.00
	1970S	12.255	—	.35	.45	.85
	1971S	19.676	—	.35	.45	.85
	1972S	19.885	—	.35	.45	.85
	1973S	17.060	—	.35	.45	.85
	1974S	18.065	—	.35	.45	.85
	1975S	11.523	—	—	.35	.75
	1976K	12.048	—	—	.35	.75
	1977K	10.077	—	—	.35	.75
	1978K	10.022	—	—	.35	.75
	1979K	11.311	—	—	.35	.75
	1980K	19.306	—	—	.35	.75
	1981K	32.003	—	—	.35	.75
	1982K	30.001	—	—	.35	.75
	1983K	8.075	—	—	.35	.75
	1983N	11.927	—	—	.35	.75
	1984N	15.000	—	—	.35	.75
	1985N	19.001	—	—	.35	.75
	1986N	10.000	—	—	.35	.75
	1987N	.700	—	—	1.00	2.00
	1987M	9.303	—	—	.35	.75
	1988M	27.535	—	—	.35	.75
	1989M	37.520	—	—	.35	.75
	1990M	50.305	—	—	.35	.75
	1991M	15.026	—	—	.35	.75
	1992M	3.628	—	—	.35	.75
	1993M	1.036	—	—	.50	1.00

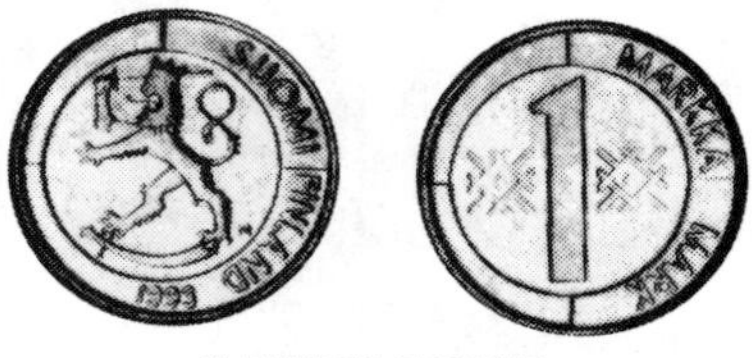

ALUMINUM-BRONZE

KM#	Date	Mintage	Fine	VF	XF	Unc
76	1993M	91.588	—	—	.35	.75
	1994M	152.011	—	—	.35	.75
	1994M	5,000	—	—	Proof	10.00
	1995M	40.008	—	—	.35	.75
	1995M	3,000	—	—	Proof	10.00
	1996M	21.000	—	—	.35	.75
	1996M	1,200	—	—	Proof	10.00
	1997M	—	—	—	.35	.75
	1997M	2,000	—	—	Proof	10.00
	1998M	—	—	—	.35	.75
	1998M	2,000	—	—	Proof	10.00

COPPER-NICKEL

KM#	Date	Mintage	Fine	VF	XF	Unc
76a	1993M	.100	—	In Sets Only		—

5 MARKKAA

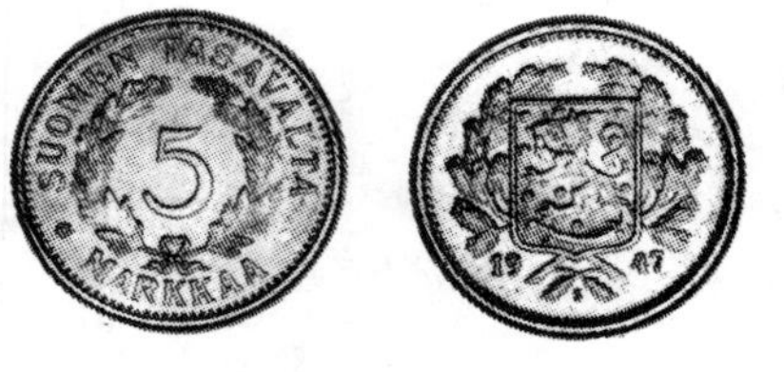

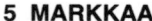

ALUMINUM-BRONZE

KM#	Date	Mintage	Fine	VF	XF	Unc
31	1928S	.580	30.00	50.00	100.00	250.00
	1929S	Inc. Ab.	30.00	50.00	90.00	220.00
	1930S	.592	.75	1.75	7.00	35.00
	1931S	3.090	.50	1.00	6.00	30.00
	1932S	.964	5.00	10.00	40.00	100.00
	1933S	1.050	.50	1.00	6.00	30.00
	1935S	.440	1.50	3.00	12.00	50.00
	1936S	.470	1.50	3.00	12.00	45.00
	1937S	1.032	.50	1.00	6.00	15.00
	1938S	.912	.50	1.00	6.00	15.00
	1939S	.752	.50	1.00	6.00	15.00
	1940S	.820	1.25	2.75	8.00	20.00
	1941S	1.452	.50	1.00	4.00	10.00
	1942S	1.390	.50	1.00	5.00	12.00
	1946S	.618	3.50	7.00	20.00	60.00

BRASS

KM#	Date	Mintage	Fine	VF	XF	Unc
31a	1946S	5.538	.20	.50	1.50	3.50
	1947S	6.550	.25	.75	2.00	6.00
	1948L	8.210	.25	.50	1.50	5.00
	1949H thin H	11.014	.50	1.00	3.00	5.00
	1949H wide H	Inc. Ab.	.20	.50	1.50	3.50
	1950H	4.760	.20	.50	1.50	3.50
	1951H	7.8000	.20	.50	1.50	3.50
	1952H	1.210	2.50	6.00	12.00	25.00

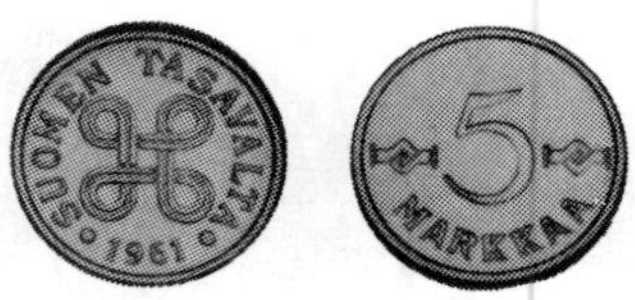

IRON

KM#	Date	Mintage	Fine	VF	XF	Unc
37	1952	10.820	.20	.35	2.00	8.00
	1953	9.772	.20	.35	3.00	10.00

NICKEL-PLATED IRON

KM#	Date	Mintage	Fine	VF	XF	Unc
37a	1953	Inc. Ab.	35.00	60.00	80.00	125.00
	1954	6.696	—	.20	.35	1.50
	1955	9.894	—	.20	.35	1.50
	1956	8.220	—	.20	.35	1.00
	1957	4.276	—	.20	.35	1.00
	1958	3.300	—	.20	.35	1.50
	1959	5.874	—	.20	.35	1.00
	1960	3.066	.10	.25	.35	1.50
	1961	7.254	.10	.25	.35	1.50
	1962	4.542	.50	1.00	3.00	6.00

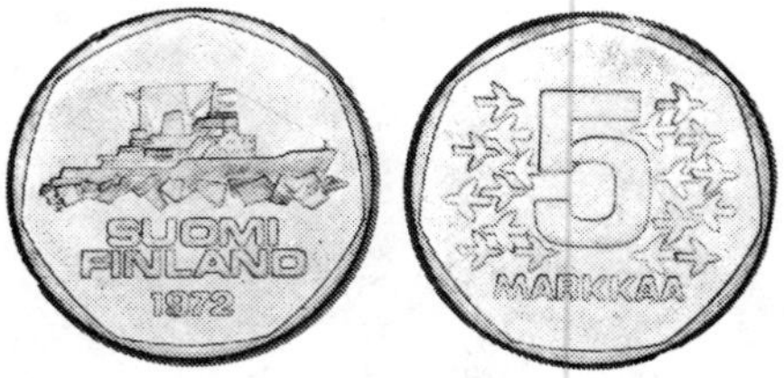

ALUMINUM-BRONZE
Icebreaker - Varma

KM#	Date	Mintage	Fine	VF	XF	Unc
53	1972S	.400	1.50	2.00	2.50	4.00
	1973S	2.188	—	1.25	2.00	3.00
	1974S	.300	—	1.25	2.00	3.00
	1975S	.300	—	1.25	2.00	3.00
	1976K	.400	—	1.25	2.00	3.00
	1977K	.300	—	1.25	2.00	3.00
	1978K	.300	—	1.25	2.00	3.00

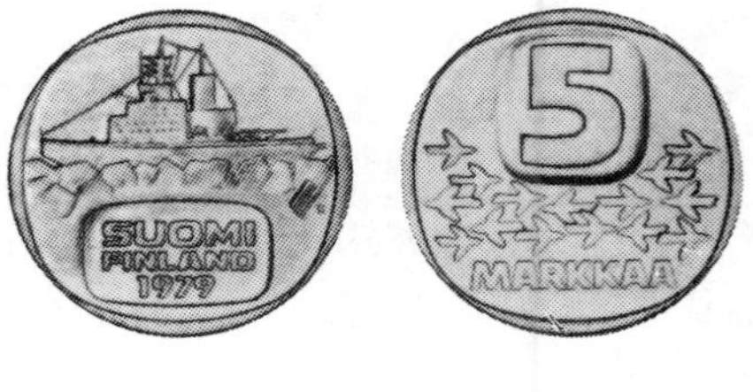

Icebreaker - Urho

KM#	Date	Mintage	Fine	VF	XF	Unc
57	1979K	2.005	—	—	1.50	2.25
	1980K	.501	—	1.50	2.00	3.00
	1981K	1.009	—	—	1.50	2.25
	1982K	3.004	—	—	1.50	2.25
	1983K	8.776	—	—	1.50	2.25
	1983N	11.230	—	—	1.50	2.25
	1984N	15.001	—	—	1.50	2.25
	1985N	8.005	—	—	1.50	2.25
	1986N	5.006	—	—	1.50	2.25
	1987N	.660	—	1.50	2.00	3.00
	1987M	2.348	—	—	1.50	2.25
	1988M	3.042	—	—	1.50	2.25
	1989M	10.175	—	—	1.50	2.25
	1990M	9.925	—	—	1.50	2.25
	1991M	9.910	—	—	2.00	3.00
	1992M	.547	—	—	2.00	3.00
	1993M	.911	—	—	2.00	3.00

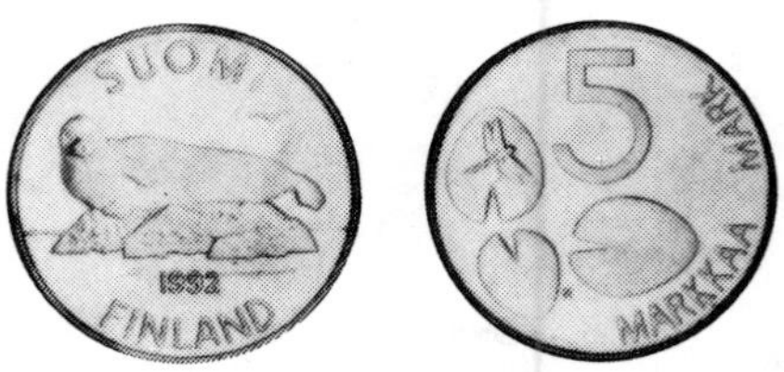

COPPER-ALUMINUM-NICKEL
Lake Saimaa Ringed Seal

KM#	Date	Mintage	Fine	VF	XF	Unc
73	1992M	.800	—	—	—	3.50
	1993M	46.034	—	—	—	2.00
	1994M	19.003	—	—	—	2.00
	1994M	5,000	—	—	Proof	12.00
	1995M	9.016	—	—	—	2.50
	1995M	3,000	—	—	Proof	12.00
	1996M	7.000	—	—	—	2.50
	1996M	1,200	—	—	Proof	12.00
	1997M	—	—	—	—	2.50
	1997M	2,000	—	—	Proof	12.00
	1998M	—	—	—	—	2.50
	1998M	2,000	—	—	Proof	12.00

10 MARKKAA

ALUMINUM-BRONZE

KM#	Date	Mintage	Fine	VF	XF	Unc
63	1928S	.730	2.50	5.00	15.00	75.00
	1929S	Inc. Ab.	2.00	4.00	12.00	70.00
	1930S	.260	1.00	2.50	8.00	65.00
	1931S	1.530	1.00	2.50	8.00	65.00
	1932S	1.010	1.00	2.50	8.00	55.00
	1934S	.154	1.50	3.00	12.00	70.00
	1935S	.081	3.00	5.00	15.00	90.00
	1936S	.304	2.00	4.00	12.00	60.00
	1937S	.181	1.50	2.50	8.00	60.00
	1938S	.631	.75	1.50	5.00	45.00
	1939S	.133	4.00	8.00	15.00	60.00

KM#	Date	Mintage	Fine	VF	XF	Unc
38	1952H	6.390	.20	.50	1.75	5.00
	1953H	22.650	.15	.35	1.00	3.00
	1954H	2.452	.50	1.00	2.00	6.00
	1955H	2.342	.20	.50	1.50	5.00
	1956H	4.240	.20	.40	1.00	4.00
	1958H thin 1	3.292	2.00	5.00	10.00	20.00
	1958H wide 1	Inc. Ab.	.20	.40	1.00	4.00
	1960S	.740	1.00	2.00	5.00	10.00
	1961S thin 1	3.580	.20	.50	1.50	5.00
	1961S wide 1	Inc. Ab.	2.00	4.00	8.00	12.00
	1962S	1.852	.30	.60	1.75	5.00

NOTE: The "1" in the denomination on all 1952 to 1956 issues is the thin variety. 1960 issues are the wide variety, and 1962's are thin. Varieties exist in root length of tree.

BI-METALLIC BRASS center,
COPPER-NICKEL ring
Capercaillie Bird

KM#	Date	Mintage	Fine	VF	XF	Unc
77	1993M	30.002	—	—	—	4.50
	1994M	19.979	—	—	—	4.50
	1994M	5,000	—	—	Proof	18.00
	1995M	4.008	—	—	—	5.00
	1995M	3,000	—	—	Proof	18.00
	1996M	3.300	—	—	—	5.50
	1996M	1,200	—	—	Proof	18.00
	1997M	—	—	—	—	5.50
	1997M	2,000	—	—	Proof	18.00
	1998M	—	—	—	—	5.50
	1998M	2,000	—	—	Proof	18.00

European Unity - Swan in Flight

	Date	Mintage	Fine	VF	XF	Unc
82	1995M	.500	—	—	—	5.00

20 MARKKAA

ALUMINUM-BRONZE

KM#	Date	Mintage	Fine	VF	XF	Unc
32	1931S	.016	30.00	40.00	60.00	100.00
	1932S	.014	30.00	40.00	65.00	110.00
	1934S	.390	2.00	5.00	17.50	70.00
	1935S	.250	2.00	5.00	17.50	70.00
	1936S	.110	3.00	5.00	17.50	90.00
	1937S	.510	1.50	2.00	10.00	50.00
	1938S	.360	1.50	2.00	9.00	40.00
	1939S	.960	1.00	2.00	6.00	15.00

	Date	Mintage	Fine	VF	XF	Unc
39	1952H	.083	7.00	10.00	15.00	30.00
	1953H	2.880	.25	.50	1.50	6.00
	1954H	17.034	.15	.50	1.25	5.00
	1955H	2.800	.25	.50	1.50	6.00
	1956H	2.540	.25	.50	1.50	6.00
	1957H	1.050	.50	1.00	3.00	8.00
	1958H	.515	2.50	5.00	10.00	20.00
	1959S	1.580	.25	.50	1.50	6.00
	1960S	3.850	.15	.50	1.00	5.00
	1961S	4.430	.15	.50	1.00	5.00
	1962S	2.280	.15	.50	1.50	6.00

50 MARKKAA

ALUMINUM-BRONZE

	Date	Mintage	Fine	VF	XF	Unc
40	1952H	.991	1.00	3.00	6.00	15.00
	1953H	10.300	.25	.50	2.00	7.00
	1954H	1.170	1.00	3.00	5.00	10.00
	1955H	.583	2.50	5.00	10.00	20.00
	1956H	.792	1.00	3.00	5.00	10.00
	1958H	.242	20.00	25.00	35.00	50.00
	1960S	.110	20.00	30.00	45.00	70.00
	1961S	1.811	1.00	2.00	3.00	7.00
	1962S	.405	2.00	4.00	7.00	15.00

100 MARKKAA

4.2105 g, .900 GOLD, .1218 oz AGW

	Date	Mintage	Fine	VF	XF	Unc
28	1926S	.050	—	450.00	650.00	850.00

5.2000 g, .500 SILVER, .0836 oz ASW

	Date	Mintage	Fine	VF	XF	Unc
41	1956H	3.012	—	BV	1.50	3.00
	1957H	3.012	—	BV	1.50	3.00
	1958H	1.704	BV	1.50	2.50	4.00
	1959S	1.270	3.00	5.00	7.00	9.00
	1960S	.290	3.50	5.50	7.50	10.00

200 MARKKAA

8.4210 g, .900 GOLD, .2436 oz AGW

KM#	Date	Mintage	Fine	VF	XF	Unc
29	1926S	.050	—	650.00	900.00	1100.

8.3000 g, .500 SILVER, .1334 oz ASW

	Date	Mintage	Fine	VF	XF	Unc
42	1956H	1.552	—	BV	2.50	5.00
	1957H	2.157	—	BV	2.50	5.00
	1958H	1.477	BV	2.50	4.00	7.00
	1958S	.034	300.00	400.00	500.00	600.00
	1959S	.070	25.00	30.00	40.00	60.00

500 MARKKAA

12.0000 g, .500 SILVER, .1929 oz ASW
1952 Olympic Games

	Date	Mintage	Fine	VF	XF	Unc
35	1951H	.019	200.00	250.00	325.00	400.00
	1952H	.586	15.00	18.00	28.00	38.00

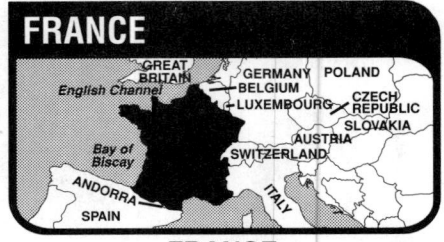

FRANCE

The French Republic, largest of the West European nations, has an area of 210,026 sq. mi. (547,030 sq. km.) and a population of 58.1 million. Capital: Paris. Agriculture, mining and manufacturing are the most important elements of France's diversified economy. Textiles and clothing, iron and steel products, machinery and transportation equipment, agricultural products and wine are exported.

The monarchy under Louis XVIII was again restored in 1815, but the ultrareactionary regime of Charles X (1824-30) was overthrown by a liberal revolution and Louis Philippe of Orleans replaced him as monarch. The monarchy was ousted by the Revolution of 1848 and the Second Republic proclaimed. Louis Napoleon Bonaparte (nephew of Napoleon I) was elected president of the Second Republic. He was proclaimed emperor in 1852. As Napoleon III, he gave France two decades of prosperity under a stable, autocratic regime, but led it to defeat in the Franco-Prussian War of 1870, after which the third Republic was established.

The Third Republic endured until 1940 and the capitulation of France to the swiftly maneuvering German forces. Marshal Henri Petain formed a puppet government that sued for peace and ruled unoccupied France from Vichy. Meanwhile, General Charles de Gaulle escaped to London where he formed a wartime government in exile and the Free French army. De Gaulle's provisional exile government was officially recognized by the Allies after the liberation of Paris in 1944, and De Gaulle, who had been serving as head of the provisional government, was formally elected to that position. In October 1945, the people overwhelmingly rejected a return to the prewar government, thus paving the way for the formation of the Fourth Republic.

De Gaulle was unanimously elected president of the Fourth Republic, but resigned in January 1946 when leftists withdrew their support. In actual operation, the Fourth Republic was remarkably like the Third, with the National Assembly the focus of power. The later years of the Fourth Republic were marked by a burst of industrial expansion unmatched in modern French history. The growth rate, however, was marred by a nagging inflationary trend that weakened the franc and undermined the competitive posture of France's export trade. This and the Algerian conflict led to the recall of De Gaulle to power, the adoption of a new constitution vesting strong powers in the executive, and the establishment in 1958 of the current Fifth Republic.

RULERS

Third Republic, 1871-1940
Vichy State, 1940-1944
De Gaulle's Provisional Govt.,
 1944-1947
Fourth Republic, 1947-1958
Fifth Republic, 1959-

MINT MARKS AND PRIVY MARKS

In addition to the date and mint mark which are customary on western civilization coinage, most coins manufactured by the French Mints contain two small 'Marques et Differents' as the French call them. These privy marks represent the men responsible for the dies which struck the coins. One privy mark is for the Engraver General (since 1880 the title is Chief Engraver). The other privy mark is the signature of the Mint Director of each mint. Since 1880 this privy mark has represented the office rather than the personage of the Mint Director, and a standard privy mark has been used (cornucopia).

For most dates these privy marks are unimportant minor features. During some issue dates, however, the marks changed. To be even more accurate sometimes the marks changed when the date didn't, even though it should have. These coins can be attributed to the proper mintage report only by considering the privy marks. Previous references have by and large ignored these privy marks. It is entirely possible that unattributed varieties may exist for any privy mark transition. All transition years which may have two varieties of privy marks have the known attribution indicated after the date (if it has been confirmed).

ENGRAVER GENERAL'S PRIVY MARKS

Engraver Generals' privy marks may appear on coins of other mints which are dated as follows:

A - PARIS

Mark	Date	Name
	Torch 1896-1926	
	Wing 1927-1958	
🦉	Owl 1958-1974	
➴	Fish 1974-1994	
🐝	Bee 1994-	

MINT DIRECTOR'S PRIVY MARKS

Some modern coins struck from dies produced at the Paris Mint have the 'A' mint mark. In the absence of a mint mark, the cornucopia privy mark serves to attribute a coin to Paris design.

A - PARIS

	None (n) 1897-1920	
🦴	Cornucopia (c) 1901	

B - BEAUMONT - LE-ROGER

🦴	Cornucopia 1943-1958

(b) - BRUSSELS

None
(1939)

BD - PAU

C - CASTELSARRASIN

c 🦴	Cornucopia 1914, 1942-1946

CH - CHALONS

Thunderbolt (tb) - POISSY

🦴	Cornucopia 1922-1924

Star (s) - MADRID

✶	1916

MONETARY SYSTEM
(Commencing 1794)

10 Centimes = 1 Decime
10 Decimes = 1 Franc
  (Commencing 1962)
1 Old Franc = 1 New Centime
100 New Centimes = 1 New Franc

UN (1) CENTIME

BRONZE
Mint: Paris - w/o mint mark.

KM#	Date	Mintage	Fine	VF	XF	Unc
840	1901	1.000	1.00	2.00	5.00	12.00
	1902	1.000	.75	1.50	4.00	10.00
	1903	2.000	.50	1.50	3.00	8.00
	1904	1.000	.75	1.50	4.00	10.00
	1908	4.500	2.00	4.00	10.00	20.00
	1909	1.500	3.00	5.00	12.00	25.00
	1910	1.500	10.00	20.00	40.00	65.00
	1911	5.000	.25	1.00	2.00	5.50
	1912	2.000	.50	1.50	3.00	7.50
	1913	1.500	.50	1.50	3.00	7.50
	1914	1.000	.75	2.00	4.00	10.00
	1916	1.996	.50	1.50	3.00	7.50
	1919	2.407	.25	1.00	2.00	4.50
	1920	2.594	.25	1.00	2.00	4.50

NOTE: No privy marks on KM#840 of any date.
NOTE: Earlier dates (1898-1900) exist for this type.

CHROME-STEEL
1 New Centime = 1 Old Franc
Fifth Republic

KM#	Date	Mintage	Fine	VF	XF	Unc
928	1962	34.200	—	—	.10	.25
	1963	16.811	—	.10	.15	.35
	1964	22.654	—	—	.10	.25
	1965	47.799	—	—	.10	.25
	1966	19.688	—	—	.10	.25
	1967	52.308	—	—	.10	.25
	1968	40.890	—	—	.10	.25
	1969	35.430	—	—	.10	.25
	1970	29.600	—	—	.10	.25
	1971	3.082	—	—	.10	.25
	1972	1.015	—	.10	.15	.35
	1973	1.806	—	.10	.15	.35
	1974	7.949	—	—	.10	.25
	1975	.771	—	.10	.25	1.00
	1976	4.482	—	—	.10	.25
	1977	6.425	—	—	.10	.25
	1978	1.236	—	.10	.15	.35
	1979	2.213	—	—	.10	.25
	1980	.060	—	—	—	1.00
	1981	.050	—	—	—	1.00
	1982	.069	—	—	—	1.00
	1983	.101	—	—	—	1.00
	1984	.050	—	—	—	1.00
	1985	.020	—	—	—	1.00
	1986	.048	—	—	—	1.00
	1987	.100	—	—	—	1.00
	1988	.100	—	—	—	1.00
	1989	.083	—	—	—	1.00
	1990	.015	—	—	—	1.00
	1991	.015	—	—	—	1.00
	1991	—	—	—	Proof	2.00
	1992	.100	—	—	—	1.00
	1992	—	—	—	Proof	2.00
	1993	—	—	—	—	1.00
	1996	—	—	—	—	1.00
	1996	8,000	—	—	Proof	2.00
	1997	—	—	—	—	1.00
	1997	—	—	—	Proof	2.00

NOTE: 1991-1993 dated coins, non-Proof, exist in both coin and medal alignment. Values given here are for medal alignment examples. Pieces struck in coin alignment have been traded for as much as $50.00.

DEUX (2) CENTIMES

BRONZE
Mint: Paris - w/o mint mark.

KM#	Date	Mintage	Fine	VF	XF	Unc
841	1901	1.000	1.00	3.00	5.00	12.50
	1902	.750	1.50	4.00	6.50	17.50
	1903	.750	1.50	4.00	6.50	17.50
	1904	.500	2.00	5.00	9.00	20.00
	1907	.250	10.00	20.00	50.00	100.00
	1908	3.500	.50	1.00	2.00	6.50
	1909	1.750	6.00	12.00	30.00	65.00
	1910	1.750	.50	1.00	2.00	6.50
	1911	5.000	.15	.75	1.50	5.50
	1912	1.500	.25	1.50	2.50	8.00
	1913	1.750	.25	1.50	2.50	8.00
	1914	2.000	.15	.75	1.50	5.50
	1916	.500	.75	2.00	4.00	10.00
	1919	.902	.50	1.50	3.00	7.00
	1920	.598	.75	2.00	4.00	9.00

NOTE: No privy marks appeared on KM#841 of any date.
NOTE: Earlier dates (1898-1900) exist for this type.

CINQ (5) CENTIMES

BRONZE
Mint: Paris - w/o mint mark.

KM#	Date	Mintage	Fine	VF	XF	Unc
842	1901(c)	6.000	2.00	4.00	15.00	60.00
	1902	7.900	2.00	4.00	10.00	50.00
	1903	2.879	5.00	10.00	25.00	80.00
	1904	8.000	1.00	3.00	7.00	25.00
	1905	2.100	6.00	16.00	40.00	100.00
	1906	8.394	1.00	3.00	7.00	25.00
	1907	7.900	1.00	3.00	7.00	25.00
	1908	6.090	3.00	5.00	12.00	32.00
	1909	8.000	1.00	3.00	6.00	25.00
	1910	4.000	2.00	3.00	9.00	50.00
	1911	15.386	.50	1.00	2.00	10.00
	1912	20.000	.25	1.00	2.00	10.00
	1913	12.603	.50	1.00	2.00	10.00
	1914	7.000	.25	1.00	2.00	10.00
	1915	6.032	.50	1.00	2.00	10.00
	1916	41.531	.25	1.00	2.00	8.00
	1916(s)	I.A.	.25	1.00	2.00	8.00
	1917	16.963	.25	1.00	2.00	8.00
	1920	8.152	3.00	5.00	10.00	50.00
	1921	.142	150.00	300.00	500.00	900.00

NOTE: Earlier dates (1898-1900) exist for this type.

COPPER-NICKEL

KM#	Date	Mintage	Fine	VF	XF	Unc
865	1914	—	—	—	Rare	—
	1917	10.458	1.00	2.00	5.00	20.00
	1918	35.592	.25	1.00	2.00	5.00
	1919	43.848	.25	1.00	2.00	4.50
	1920	51.321	.25	.50	2.00	4.00

2.00 g

KM#	Date	Mintage	Fine	VF	XF	Unc
875	1920	Inc. Ab.	10.00	20.00	50.00	100.00
	1921	32.908	.25	.50	2.00	5.00
	1922	31.700	.25	.50	2.00	5.00
	1922(t)	17.717	1.50	3.00	6.00	15.00
	1923	23.322	.50	2.00	2.00	7.00
	1923(t)	45.097	.25	.50	1.00	3.50
	1924	47.018	.25	.50	1.00	3.50
	1924(t)	21.210	.50	2.00	3.00	6.00
	1925	66.838	.25	.50	1.00	2.50
	1926	19.820	.25	2.00	3.00	6.00
	1927	6.066	3.00	10.00	28.00	85.00
	1930	31.902	.20	.50	1.00	2.50
	1931	34.711	.20	.50	1.00	2.50
	1932	31.112	.20	.50	1.00	2.50
	1933	12.970	1.00	2.00	5.00	12.00
	1934	27.144	.30	.65	2.00	5.50
	1935	57.221	.25	.50	1.00	2.50
	1936	64.341	.15	.25	.75	2.50
	1937	26.329	.15	.25	.75	2.50
	1938	21.614	.15	.25	.75	2.50

NICKEL-BRONZE, 1.50 g

KM#	Date	Mintage	Fine	VF	XF	Unc
875a	.1938.	26.330	.15	.50	1.00	3.00
	.1938. star					
		Inc. Ab.	100.00	200.00	300.00	400.00
	.1939.	52.673	.10	.25	.75	2.00

CHROME-STEEL
5 New Centimes = 5 Old Francs
Fifth Republic

KM#	Date	Mintage	Fine	VF	XF	Unc
927	1961	39.000	.10	.20	.50	2.00
	1962	166.360	.10	.15	.20	.75
	1963	71.900	.10	.20	.40	1.00
	1964	126.480	.10	.15	.30	.75

ALUMINUM-BRONZE

KM#	Date	Mintage	Fine	VF	XF	Unc
933	1966	502.512	—	—	—	.10
	1967	11.747	—	—	.10	.25
	1968	110.395	—	—	—	.10
	1969	94.955	—	—	—	.10
	1970	58.900	—	—	—	.10
	1971	93.190	—	—	—	.10
	1972	100.515	—	—	—	.10
	1973	100.344	—	—	—	.10
	1974	103.890	—	—	—	.10
	1975	95.835	—	—	—	.10
	1976	148.395	—	—	—	.10
	1977	115.285	—	—	—	.10
	1978	189.804	—	—	—	.10
	1979	180.000	—	—	—	.10
	1980	180.010	—	—	—	.10
	1981	.050	—	—	—	.50
	1982	138.000	—	—	—	.10
	1983	132.000	—	—	—	.10
	1984	150.000	—	—	—	.10
	1985	170.000	—	—	—	.10
	1986	280.000	—	—	—	.10
	1987	310.000	—	—	—	.10
	1988	200.000	—	—	—	.10
	1989	.072	—	—	—	.20
	1990	79.992	—	—	—	.20
	1991	50.000	—	—	—	.20
	1991	—	—	—	Proof	1.00
	1992	180.000	—	—	—	.20
	1992	—	—	—	Proof	1.00
	1993	—	—	—	—	.20
	1994	—	—	—	—	.20
	1996	—	—	—	—	.20
	1996	—	8,000	—	Proof	1.00
	1997	—	—	—	—	.20
	1997	—	—	—	Proof	1.00

NOTE: 1991-1993 dated coins, non-Proof, exist in both coin and medal alignment.

DIX (10) CENTIMES

BRONZE

KM#	Date	Mintage	Fine	VF	XF	Unc
843	1901(c)	2.700	1.50	3.00	12.00	40.00
	1902	3.800	1.00	2.00	7.00	25.00
	1903	3.650	1.00	2.00	7.00	25.00
	1904	3.800	1.00	2.00	7.00	25.00
	1905	.950	28.00	50.00	125.00	275.00
	1906	3.000	2.00	5.00	12.00	40.00
	1907	4.000	1.00	2.00	5.00	20.00
	1908	3.500	1.00	2.00	5.00	20.00
	1909	2.933	1.00	2.00	5.00	25.00
	1910	3.567	1.00	2.00	5.00	20.00
	1911	7.903	.50	1.50	3.00	12.00
	1912	9.500	.50	1.50	3.00	12.00
	1913	9.000	.50	1.50	3.00	12.00
	1914	6.000	.75	2.00	4.00	14.00
	1915	4.362	.50	1.50	3.00	12.00
	1916	22.477	.25	.75	1.50	7.00
	1916(s)	I.A.	.25	.75	1.50	7.00
	1917	11.914	.25	.75	1.50	7.00
	1920	4.119	1.50	3.50	12.00	40.00
	1921	1.896	10.00	20.00	45.00	125.00

NOTE: Earlier dates (1898-1900) exist for this type.

NICKEL

KM#	Date	Mintage	Fine	VF	XF	Unc
866	1914 dash					

COPPER-NICKEL

KM#	Date	Mintage	Fine	VF	XF	Unc
866a	1917	8.171	1.00	2.00	4.00	25.00
	1918	30.605	.25	.50	1.00	4.00
	1919	33.489	.25	.50	1.00	4.00
	1920	38.845	.25	.50	1.00	4.00
	1921	42.768	.10	.35	.75	3.00
	1922	23.033	.35	.75	1.25	4.50
	1922(t)	12.412	.75	1.50	2.50	7.00
	1923	18.701	.50	1.00	2.00	5.00
	1923(t)	30.016	.25	.50	1.00	3.50
	1924	43.949	.10	.35	.75	2.50
	1924(t)	13.591	2.00	5.00	15.00	40.00
	1925	46.266	.10	.35	.75	2.50
	1926	25.660	.25	.50	1.00	3.50
	1927	16.203	.40	.75	1.25	4.50
	1928	6.967	1.00	3.00	10.00	30.00
	1929	24.531	.10	.35	1.00	2.50
	1930	22.146	.10	.35	1.00	2.50
	1931	49.107	.10	.35	1.00	2.50
	1932	30.317	.10	.35	1.00	2.50
	1933	13.042	.35	.75	1.50	4.50
	1934	24.067	.10	.50	1.00	2.25
	1935	47.487	.10	.50	1.00	2.25
	1936	57.738	.10	.50	1.00	2.25
	1937	25.308	.10	.50	1.00	2.25
	1938	17.063	.25	.75	2.00	5.00

NICKEL-BRONZE

KM#	Date	Mintage	Fine	VF	XF	Unc
889.1	.1938.	24.151	.25	.50	1.00	2.00
	1.938.	Inc. Ab.	—	—	—	—
	.1939.	62.269	.15	.30	.65	1.75

Thin flan.

KM#	Date	Mintage	Fine	VF	XF	Unc
889.2	.1939.	Inc. Ab.	.10	.20	.50	1.25

ZINC
Rev: W/o dash below MES in C MES.

KM#	Date	Mintage	Fine	VF	XF	Unc
895	1941	235.875	1.00	2.00	6.00	15.00

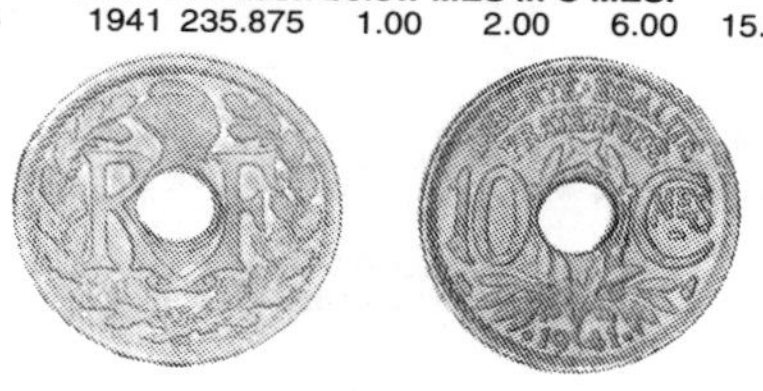

Rev: Dash below MES in C MES.

KM#	Date	Mintage	Fine	VF	XF	Unc
896	1941	Inc. Ab.	.75	1.25	4.00	10.00

Rev: Dot before and after date.

KM#	Date	Mintage	Fine	VF	XF	Unc
897	.1941.	Inc. Ab.	.25	.50	1.00	4.00

Vichy French State Issues, thickness 1.5mm.

KM#	Date	Mintage	Fine	VF	XF	Unc
898.1	1941	70.860	.35	.65	1.50	5.00
	1942	139.598	.30	.60	1.25	2.50
	1943	21.520	1.00	2.00	4.00	12.00

Mint: Paris - w/o mint mark.
Thin flan, 1.3mm.

KM#	Date	Mintage	Fine	VF	XF	Unc
898.2	1941	Inc. Ab.	.25	.50	1.25	3.00
	1942	Inc. Ab.	.20	.40	1.00	2.25
	1943	Inc. Ab.	.75	1.50	3.00	6.00

KM#	Date	Mintage	Fine	VF	XF	Unc
903	1943	22.008	.25	.75	2.50	7.00
	1944	58.463	.25	.50	2.00	5.00

Fourth Republic Issues

KM#	Date	Mintage	Fine	VF	XF	Unc
906.1	1945	38.174	1.00	2.00	3.50	12.00
	1946	—	—	—	Rare	—

Mint mark: B

KM#	Date	Mintage	Fine	VF	XF	Unc
906.2	1945	7.246	1.50	3.00	6.00	16.00
	1946	10.566	2.50	5.00	10.00	25.00

Mint mark: C

KM#	Date	Mintage	Fine	VF	XF	Unc
906.3	1945	8.379	2.00	4.00	8.00	20.00

ALUMINUM-BRONZE
Mint: Paris - w/o mint mark.
10 New Centimes = 10 Old Francs
Fifth Republic

KM#	Date	Mintage	Fine	VF	XF	Unc
929	1962	29.100	—	—	.10	.40
	1963	217.601	—	—	—	.10
	1964	93.409	—	—	.10	.20
	1965	41.220	—	—	.10	.30
	1966	16.429	—	.10	.15	.40
	1967	196.728	—	—	—	.10
	1968	111.700	—	—	—	.10
	1969	129.530	—	—	—	.10
	1970	77.020	—	—	—	.10
	1971	26.280	—	—	—	.10
	1972	45.700	—	—	—	.10
	1973	58.000	—	—	—	.10
	1974	91.990	—	—	—	.10
	1975	74.450	—	—	—	.10
	1976	137.320	—	—	—	.10
	1977	140.110	—	—	—	.10
	1978	154.360	—	—	—	.10
	1979	140.000	—	—	—	.10
	1980	140.010	—	—	—	.10
	1981	135.000	—	—	—	.10
	1982	110.000	—	—	—	.10
	1983	150.000	—	—	—	.10
	1984	200.000	—	—	—	.10
	1985	170.000	—	—	—	.10
	1986	150.000	—	—	—	.10
	1987	150.000	—	—	—	.10
	1988	145.000	—	—	—	.10
	1989	179.984	—	—	—	.10
	1990	179.992	—	—	—	.10
	1991	180.000	—	—	—	.10
	1991	—	—	—	Proof	1.00
	1992	130.000	—	—	—	.10

KM#	Date	Mintage	Fine	VF	XF	Unc
929	1992	—	—	—	Proof	1.00
	1993	—	—	—	—	.10
	1994	—	—	—	—	.10
	1995	—	—	—	—	.10
	1996	—	—	—	—	.10
	1996	8,000	—	—	Proof	1.00
	1997	—	—	—	—	.10
	1997	—	—	—	Proof	1.00

NOTE: 1991-1993 dated coins, non-Proof, exist in both coin and medal alignment.

VINGT (20) CENTIMES

ZINC
Vichy French State Issues

KM#	Date	Mintage	Fine	VF	XF	Unc
899	1941	54.044	1.00	2.00	4.00	12.50

Thick flan, 3.50 g

900.1	1941	31.397	1.00	2.00	4.00	12.50
	1942	112.868	.50	1.00	2.00	7.00
	1943	64.138	.75	1.50	2.50	8.50

Mint: Paris - w/o mint mark.
Thin flan, 3.00 g

900.2	1941	Inc. Ab.	.50	.75	2.00	8.50
	1943	Inc. Ab.	.50	.75	2.00	6.50
	1944	5.250	15.00	30.00	80.00	150.00

IRON

900.2a	1944	.695	25.00	50.00	150.00	200.00

ZINC
Fourth Republic Issues

907.1	1945	6.003	2.00	4.00	9.00	22.00
	1946	2.662	8.00	18.00	35.00	70.00

Mint mark: B

907.2	1945	.100	100.00	200.00	350.00	550.00
	1946	5.525	75.00	150.00	250.00	475.00

Mint mark: C

907.3	1945	.299	20.00	40.00	85.00	150.00

ALUMINUM-BRONZE
Mint: Paris - w/o mint mark.
Fifth Republic

930	1962	48.200	—	—	.10	.40
	1963	190.330	—	—	.10	.30
	1964	127.521	—	—	.10	.30
	1965	27.024	—	—	.10	.40
	1966	21.762	—	.10	.20	.40
	1967	138.780	—	—	.10	.15
	1968	77.408	—	—	.10	.20
	1969	50.570	—	—	.10	.20
	1970	70.040	—	—	.10	.15
	1971	31.080	—	—	.10	.15
	1972	39.740	—	—	.10	.15
	1973	45.240	—	—	.10	.15
	1974	54.250	—	—	.10	.15
	1975	40.570	—	—	.10	.15
	1976	117.610	—	—	—	.10
	1977	100.340	—	—	—	.10
	1978	125.015	—	—	—	.10
	1979	70.000	—	—	—	.10
	1980	20.010	—	—	.10	.15
	1981	125.000	—	—	—	.10
	1982	150.000	—	—	—	.10
	1983	110.000	—	—	—	.10
	1984	200.000	—	—	—	.10

KM#	Date	Mintage	Fine	VF	XF	Unc
930	1985	150.000	—	—	—	.10
	1986	40.000	—	—	—	.10
	1987	60.000	—	—	—	.10
	1988	220.000	—	—	—	.10
	1989	139.985	—	—	—	.10
	1990	49.990	—	—	—	.10
	1991	40.000	—	—	—	.10
	1991	—	—	—	Proof	1.00
	1992	90.000	—	—	—	.10
	1992	—	—	—	Proof	1.00
	1993	—	—	—	—	.10
	1994	—	—	—	—	.10
	1995	—	—	—	—	.10
	1996	—	—	—	—	.10
	1996	8,000	—	—	Proof	1.00
	1997	—	—	—	—	.10
	1997	—	—	—	Proof	1.00

NOTE: 1991-1993 dated coins, non-Proof, exist in both coin and medal alignment.

25 CENTIMES

NICKEL
Mint: Paris - w/o mint mark.
Third Republic

855	1903	16.000	.25	1.00	2.50	12.50

856	1904	16.000	.25	.75	2.50	15.00
	1905	8.000	.50	1.50	4.00	22.00

867	1914(-)	.941	2.00	4.00	8.00	25.00
	1915(-)	.535	3.00	5.00	9.00	35.00
	1916(-)	.100	15.00	30.00	60.00	120.00
	1917(-)	.065	30.00	50.00	85.00	175.00

COPPER-NICKEL

867a	1917	3.085	2.00	5.00	14.00	22.00
	1918	18.330	.25	.50	1.50	4.00
	1919	5.106	1.00	2.50	3.50	8.00
	1920	18.108	.15	.50	1.00	3.50
	1921	18.531	.15	.50	1.00	3.50
	1922	17.766	.15	.50	1.00	3.50
	1923	19.718	.15	.50	1.00	3.50
	1924	24.535	.15	.50	1.00	3.50
	1925	17.807	.15	.50	1.00	3.50
	1926	13.226	.15	.50	1.00	3.50
	1927	13.465	.15	.50	1.00	3.50
	1928	9.960	.25	.50	1.50	4.00
	1929	12.887	.15	.50	1.00	3.00
	1930	28.363	.15	.50	1.00	3.00
	1931	22.121	.15	.50	1.00	3.00
	1932	30.364	.15	.50	1.00	3.00
	1933	28.562	.15	.50	1.00	3.00
	1936	4.657	2.00	4.00	9.00	20.00
	1937	7.780	.25	.50	1.50	4.00

NICKEL-BRONZE

867b	.1938.	5.170	.25	.50	1.00	2.50
	.1939. thick flan (1.55mm)					
		42.964	.15	.35	.75	1.50
	.1939. thin flan (1.35mm)					
		Inc. Ab.	.15	.35	.75	1.50
	.1940.	3.446	6.00	12.00	18.00	35.00

50 CENTIMES

2.5000 g, .835 SILVER, .0671 oz ASW
Mint: Paris - w/o mint mark.

KM#	Date	Mintage	Fine	VF	XF	Unc
854	1901	4.960	2.00	4.00	12.00	40.00
	1902	3.778	2.50	5.00	15.00	45.00
	1903	2.222	12.00	25.00	50.00	150.00
	1904	4.000	1.50	3.50	10.00	30.00
	1905	2.381	5.00	9.00	20.00	80.00
	1906	2.679	2.50	5.00	15.00	45.00
	1907	7.332	1.50	3.50	10.00	30.00
	1908	14.304	.75	1.50	4.00	15.00
	1909	9.900	.75	1.50	4.00	15.00
	1910	15.923	BV	1.00	3.00	10.00
	1911	1.330	20.00	50.00	110.00	225.00
	1912	16.000	BV	.75	1.50	5.00
	1913	14.000	BV	.75	1.50	5.00
	1914	9.657	BV	.75	1.50	6.00
	1915	20.893	BV	.75	1.25	3.00
	1916	52.963	BV	.75	1.25	2.50
	1917	48.629	BV	.75	1.25	2.50
	1918	36.492	BV	.75	1.25	2.50
	1919	24.299	BV	.75	1.50	2.50
	1920	8.509	.75	1.50	3.00	6.00

NOTE: Earlier dates (1897-1900) exist for this type.

ALUMINUM-BRONZE

884	1921	8.692	1.00	3.00	7.00	20.00
	1922	86.226	.15	.25	1.00	4.50
	1923	119.584	.15	.25	.75	3.00
	1924	97.036	.15	.25	1.00	3.50
	1925	48.017	.25	.50	1.25	5.50
	1926	46.447	.25	.50	1.25	5.50
	1927	23.703	.75	1.50	3.00	9.00
	1928	10.329	1.00	2.50	6.00	18.00
	1929	6.669	2.50	6.00	12.50	25.00

894.1	1931	62.775	.15	.25	1.00	3.00
	1932	108.839	.15	.25	.50	2.00
	1932 closed date					
		Inc. Ab.	.15	.25	.50	2.00
	1933	41.937	.15	.25	.75	3.00
	1933 closed date					
		Inc. Ab.	.15	.25	.75	3.00
	1936	16.602	.50	1.00	2.00	5.00
	1937	43.950	.15	.25	.75	3.00
	1938	55.707	.15	.25	.75	3.00
	1939	96.594	.15	.25	.50	2.00
	1940	10.854	.50	1.00	2.00	5.00
	1941	82.958	.15	.25	1.00	3.00
	1947	*2.170	60.00	120.00	200.00	300.00

*NOTE: Struck for colonial use in Africa.

Mint mark: B

894.2	1939	6.200	.50	1.00	2.50	10.00

ALUMINUM
Mint: Paris - w/o mint mark.

894.1a	1941	129.758	.15	.25	.50	2.00
	1944	9.898	.50	1.00	2.50	6.00
	1945	26.224	.15	.25	1.00	3.00
	1946	24.605	.15	.25	1.00	3.00
	1947	51.744	.15	.25	.60	2.00

NOTE: Thick and thin planchets exist.

Mint mark: B

894.2a	1944	.020	— Reported, not confirmed			
	1945	6.357	.50	1.00	3.00	8.00
	1946	29.344	.15	.25	1.00	4.00
	1947	18.504	2.00	5.00	10.00	20.00

Mint mark: C

894.3a	1944	17.220	— Reported, not confirmed			
	1945	2.968	1.00	3.00	6.00	12.00

LB (L. Bazor)

Mint: Paris - w/o mint mark.
Vichy French State Issues

914.1	1942	50.134	.15	.25	.75	2.00
	1943	84.462	.15	.25	.75	1.50
	1944	57.410	1.50	3.00	6.00	12.00

NOTE: Thick and thin planchets exist.

Mint mark: B

KM#	Date	Mintage	Fine	VF	XF	Unc
914.2	1943	21.916	6.00	12.00	30.00	50.00
	1944	27.334	1.50	3.00	7.00	15.00

Mint mark: C

914.3	1944 small C					
		27.213	2.50	5.00	9.00	28.00
	1944 large C					
		Inc. Ab.	—	—	—	—

Mint: Paris - w/o mint mark.
Thin flan.

914.4	1942	—	.15	.25	1.00	2.50
	1943	—	.15	.25	.50	1.25

ALUMINUM-BRONZE
50 New Centimes = 50 Old Francs
Obv: 3 folds in collar.

939.1	1962	37.560	.30	.60	1.50	3.00
	1963	62.482	.20	.40	1.00	2.00
	1964	41.471	.45	.90	2.00	6.00

Obv: 4 folds in collar.

939.2	1962	Inc. Ab.	30.00	70.00	120.00	160.00
	1963	Inc. Ab.	.20	.40	1.00	2.00

1/2 FRANC

NICKEL
Mint: Paris - w/o mint mark.

931.1	1965 small legends					
		184.834	—	—	.15	.30
	1965 large legends					
		Inc. Ab.	—	—	.15	.30
	1966	88.890	—	—	.15	.30
	1967	28.394	—	—	.15	.40
	1968	57.548	—	—	.15	.30
	1969	47.144	—	—	.15	.30
	1970	42.298	—	—	.15	.30
	1971	36.068	—	—	.15	.30
	1972	42.302	—	—	.15	.30
	1972 w/o O.ROTY					
		Inc. Ab.	25.00	50.00	100.00	150.00
	1973	48.372	—	—	.15	.30
	1974	37.072	—	—	.15	.30
	1975	22.803	—	—	.15	.40
	1976	115.314	—	—	.15	.30
	1977	131.644	—	—	.15	.30
	1978	63.360	—	—	.15	.30
	1979	.051	—	—	—	.50
	1980	.060	—	—	—	.50
	1981	.050	—	—	—	.50
	1982	.078	—	—	—	.50
	1983	50.000	—	—	.15	.30
	1984	80.000	—	—	.15	.30
	1985	50.000	—	—	—	1.50
	1986	110.000	—	—	—	1.50
	1987	50.000	—	—	—	.30
	1988	.100	—	—	—	.40
	1989	.083	—	—	—	.40
	1990	.015	—	—	—	.40
	1991	50.000	—	—	—	.40
	1992	30.000	—	—	—	.40
	1993	—	—	—	—	.40
	1994	—	—	—	—	.40
	1995	—	—	—	—	.40
	1996	—	—	—	—	.40
	1997	—	—	—	—	.40

NOTE: 1991-1993 dated coins, non-Proof, exist in both coin and medal alignment.

Plain edge.
Obv: Modified sower.
Rev: Engraver's signature: D'AP.O.ROTY.

931.2	1991	—	—	—	Proof	1.50
	1992	—	—	—	Proof	1.50
	1993	—	—	—	Proof	1.50
	1994	—	—	—	Proof	1.50
	1995	—	—	—	Proof	1.50
	1996	8,000	—	—	Proof	1.50
	1997	—	—	—	Proof	1.50

FRANC

5.0000 g, .835 SILVER, .1342 oz ASW
Mint: Paris - w/o mint mark.

KM#	Date	Mintage	Fine	VF	XF	Unc
844.1	1901	6.200	2.00	4.00	10.00	50.00
	1902	6.000	2.00	4.00	10.00	50.00
	1903	.472	40.00	80.00	200.00	475.00
	1904	7.000	2.00	4.00	10.00	50.00
	1905	6.004	2.00	4.00	10.00	50.00
	1906	1.908	6.00	20.00	40.00	120.00
	1907	2.563	4.00	9.00	25.00	75.00
	1908	3.961	2.50	5.00	12.00	55.00
	1909	10.924	1.25	2.50	5.50	25.00
	1910	7.725	1.25	2.50	5.50	25.00
	1911	5.542	1.75	3.00	12.00	35.00
	1912	10.001	1.25	2.50	5.50	25.00
	1913	13.654	1.25	2.50	5.50	25.00
	1914	14.361	1.25	2.50	5.50	25.00
	1915	47.955	BV	1.25	2.00	6.00
	1916	92.029	BV	1.00	1.50	4.00
	1917	57.153	BV	1.00	1.50	4.00
	1918	50.112	BV	1.00	1.50	4.00
	1919	46.112	BV	1.00	1.50	4.00
	1920	19.322	BV	1.50	3.00	6.00

NOTE: Earlier dates (1898-1900) exist for this type.

Mint mark: C

844.2	1914	.043	150.00	275.00	350.00	475.00

ALUMINUM-BRONZE
Mint: Paris - w/o mint mark.
Chamber of Commerce

876	1920	.590	3.50	6.00	15.00	35.00
	1921	54.572	.25	.50	1.50	6.00
	1922	111.343	.15	.25	1.00	5.00
	1923	140.138	.15	.25	1.00	4.00
	1924 open 4					
		87.715	.15	.25	1.00	5.00
	1924 closed 4					
		Inc. Ab.	.35	.60	2.00	7.00
	1925	36.523	.25	.50	1.50	6.00
	1926	1.580	3.00	8.00	20.00	45.00
	1927	11.330	.50	1.50	3.50	9.00
	1928	.405	—	—	—	—

885	1931	15.504	.25	.50	2.00	6.50
	1932	29.768	.15	.25	1.00	4.00
	1933	15.356	.25	.50	2.00	6.50
	1934	17.286	.25	.50	2.00	5.00
	1935	1.166	6.00	15.00	25.00	70.00
	1936	23.817	.15	.25	1.00	4.00
	1937	30.940	.15	.25	1.00	3.00
	1938	66.165	.15	.25	1.00	2.50
	1939	48.434	.15	.25	1.00	3.00
	1940	25.525	.15	.25	1.00	3.50
	1941	34.705	.15	.25	1.00	3.00

ALUMINUM

885a.1	1941	60.877	.10	.20	1.00	4.00
	1943	4,400	1500.	2000.	—	—
	1944	22.608	.10	.20	1.50	5.00
	1945	61.780	.10	.15	.50	2.00
	1946	52.516	.10	.15	.25	2.00
	1947	110.448	.10	.15	.25	2.00
	1948	96.092	.10	.15	.25	2.00
	1949	41.090	.10	.15	.25	2.00
	1950	27.882	.10	.15	.50	2.50
	1957	16.497	.10	.15	.75	3.00
	1958	21.197	.10	.15	.75	3.00
	1959	41.985	.10	.15	.25	1.25

NOTE: Thick and thin planchets exist.

Mint mark: B

KM#	Date	Mintage	Fine	VF	XF	Unc
885a.2	1944	1.725	— Reported, not confirmed			
	1945	4.251	1.00	3.50	9.00	28.00
	1946	26.493	.10	.20	1.50	5.00
	1947	51.562	.10	.20	1.00	4.00
	1948	45.481	.10	.20	1.00	3.50
	1949	35.840	.10	.20	1.00	4.00
	1950	18.800	1.00	2.00	3.50	15.00
	1957	63.976	.10	.20	1.00	4.00
	1958	13.412	.25	.75	2.00	5.50

Mint mark: C

885a.3	1944	33.600	.50	1.50	3.50	12.00
	1945	5.220	1.50	3.50	9.00	25.00
	1946	9.669	— Reported, not confirmed			

ZINC
Mint mark: A

885b	1943	*.017	175.00	350.00	600.00	1000.

***NOTE:** Struck for Colonial use in Africa.

LB (L. Bazor)

ALUMINUM
Mint: Paris - w/o mint mark.
Vichy French State Issues

902.1	1942	152.144	.25	.50	1.50	4.50
	1942 w/o LB					
		I.A.	—	—	—	—
	1943	205.564	.10	.25	1.00	2.50
	1943 thin flan					
		Inc. Ab.	.10	.25	1.00	2.50
	1944	50.605	.50	1.25	2.00	7.00

Mint mark: B

902.2	1943	68.082	6.00	10.00	30.00	80.00
	1944	13.622	1.50	3.00	12.00	25.00

Mint mark: C

902.3	1944 lg. C					
		74.859	.25	.75	1.50	5.50
	1944 sm. c					
		Inc. Ab.	15.00	30.00	70.00	325.00

NICKEL
Mint: Paris - w/o mint mark.
1 New Franc = 100 Old Francs
Fifth Republic

925.1	1960	406.375	—	—	.20	.40
	1961	119.611	—	—	.20	.40
	1962	14.014	—	—	.20	.50
	1964	77.425	—	—	.20	.40
	1965	44.252	—	—	.20	.40
	1966	38.038	—	—	.20	.40
	1967	11.322	—	—	.20	.50
	1968	51.550	—	—	.20	.40
	1969	70.595	—	—	.20	.40
	1970	42.560	—	—	.20	.40
	1971	42.475	—	—	.20	.40
	1972	48.250	—	—	.20	.40
	1973	70.000	—	—	.20	.40
	1974	82.235	—	—	.20	.40
	1975	101.685	—	—	.20	.40
	1976	192.520	—	—	.20	.40
	1977	230.085	—	—	.20	.40
	1978	136.580	—	—	.20	.40
	1979	.051	—	—	—	.60
	1980	.060	—	—	—	.60
	1981	.050	—	—	—	.60
	1982	.092	—	—	—	.60
	1983	.101	—	—	—	.60
	1984	.050	—	—	—	.60
	1985	7.002	—	—	—	2.00
	1986	.048	—	—	—	2.00
	1987	.100	—	—	—	.40
	1988	.100	—	—	—	.40
	1989	.083	—	—	—	.40
	1990	.015	—	—	—	.40
	1991	55.000	—	—	—	.40
	1992	30.000	—	—	—	.40
	1993	—	—	—	—	.40
	1994 (bee)	—	—	—	—	.40
	1995	—	—	—	—	.40
	1996	—	—	—	—	.40
	1997	—	—	—	—	.40

NOTE: 1991-1993 dated coins, non-Proof, exist in both coin and medal alignment.

Plain edge.
Obv: Modified sower.
Rev: Engraver's signature: D'AP.O.ROTY.

925.2	1991	—	—	—	Proof	2.50
	1992	—	—	—	Proof	2.50
	1993	—	—	—	Proof	2.50
	1994 (fish)	—	—	—	Proof	2.50
	1995	—	—	—	Proof	2.50
	1996	8,000	—	—	Proof	2.50
	1997	—	—	—	Proof	2.50

30th Anniversary of Fifth Republic

KM#	Date	Mintage	Fine	VF	XF	Unc
963	1988	49.921	—	—	—	1.00

200th Anniversary of Estates General

967	1989	5.000	—	—	—	2.50

200th Anniversary of French Republic

1004.1	1992	30.000	—	—	—	1.25

Institut de France

1133	1995	—	—	—	—	1.50

NICKEL CLAD STEEL
100th Anniversary - Birth of Jacques Rueff

1160	1996	—	—	—	—	1.50

2 FRANCS

10,0000 g, .835 SILVER, .2684 oz ASW
Mint: Paris - w/o mint mark.

845.1	1901	1.860	6.50	18.00	50.00	150.00
	1902	2.000	6.50	18.00	50.00	150.00
	1904	1.500	7.50	18.00	40.00	200.00
	1905	2.000	6.50	18.00	50.00	150.00
	1908	2.502	3.50	6.00	20.00	50.00
	1909	1.000	8.00	18.00	40.00	200.00
	1910	2.190	3.50	6.00	20.00	50.00
	1912	1.000	7.00	18.00	50.00	175.00
	1913	.500	15.00	25.00	60.00	200.00
	1914	5.719	1.50	2.50	7.00	25.00
	1915	13.963	BV	1.50	4.00	15.00
	1916	17.887	BV	1.50	4.00	15.00
	1917	16.555	BV	1.50	4.00	15.00
	1918	12.026	BV	1.50	4.00	15.00
	1919	9.261	1.50	2.50	4.50	12.00
	1920	3.014	2.00	4.00	7.00	25.00

NOTE: Earlier dates (1898-1900) exist for this type.

Mint mark: C

845.2	1914	.462	7.50	15.00	30.00	50.00
	1914	—	—	—	Matte Proof	625.00

ALUMINUM-BRONZE
Mint: Paris - w/o mint mark.
French Chamber of Commerce Series

KM#	Date	Mintage	Fine	VF	XF	Unc
877	1920	14.363	6.00	15.00	40.00	90.00
	1921	Inc. Ab.	.75	1.50	3.00	12.50
	1922	29.463	.50	1.00	2.00	7.50
	1923	43.960	.50	1.00	2.00	7.50
	1924 open 4	29.631	.50	1.00	2.00	7.50
	1924 closed 4	Inc. Ab.	.65	1.50	3.00	10.00
	1925/3	31.607	.75	1.75	4.00	12.50
	1925	Inc. Ab.	.50	1.00	2.00	8.00
	1926	2.962	7.00	18.00	50.00	100.00
	1927	1.678	100.00	200.00	400.00	800.00

886	1931	1.717	3.00	6.00	12.00	35.00
	1932	8.943	.75	1.50	3.00	10.00
	1933	8.413	.75	1.50	3.00	10.00
	1934	6.896	1.25	2.50	6.00	12.00
	1935	.298	12.00	20.00	40.00	90.00
	1936	12.394	.25	1.00	2.00	6.00
	1937	11.055	.25	1.00	2.00	6.00
	1938	28.072	.20	.50	1.00	5.00
	1939	25.403	.20	.50	1.00	5.00
	1940	9.716	1.00	2.00	3.50	10.00
	1941	16.684	.25	1.00	2.00	6.00

ALUMINUM

886a.1	1941	Inc. Ab.	.25	.50	1.00	3.00
	1944	7.224	.75	1.50	4.00	12.00
	1945	16.636	.50	1.00	2.50	7.00
	1946	34.930	.20	.50	1.00	3.50
	1947	78.984	.20	.30	1.00	2.50
	1948	32.354	.20	.50	1.00	3.50
	1949	13.683	.25	.50	1.00	2.50
	1950	12.191	.25	.50	1.00	2.50
	1958	9.906	.20	.50	1.00	3.50
	1959	17.774	.20	.50	1.00	3.50

Mint mark: B

886a.2	1944	.170	—	—	—	—
	1945	1.726	3.00	7.00	15.00	40.00
	1946	6.018	2.00	4.00	8.00	25.00
	1947	26.220	.20	.50	1.00	3.50
	1948	39.090	.20	.50	1.00	3.00
	1949	23.955	.20	.50	1.00	3.50
	1950	18.185	.50	1.00	3.00	5.00

Mint mark: C

886a.3	1944	9.828	—	—	—	—
	1945	1.165	5.00	10.00	25.00	65.00
	1946	1.533	—	—	—	—

LB (L. Bazor)

Mint: Paris - w/o mint mark.
Vichy French State Issues

904.1	1943	106.997	.20	.50	1.00	4.00
	1944	25.546	.75	1.50	3.50	6.00

Mint mark: B

904.2	1943	34.131	3.50	7.00	18.00	30.00
	1944	10.298	1.50	3.00	6.00	18.00

Mint mark: C

904.3	1943	7.575	—	Reported, not confirmed		
	1944	19.470	1.25	2.50	5.00	18.00

BRASS
Mint: Philadelphia, U.S.A., w/o mint mark.
Allied Occupation Issue

KM#	Date	Mintage	Fine	VF	XF	Unc
905	1944	50.000	1.00	2.00	5.00	20.00

NICKEL

942.1	1979	130.000	—	—	.40	.65
	1980	100.010	—	—	.40	.65
	1981	120.000	—	—	.40	.65
	1982	90.000	—	—	.40	.65
	1983	90.000	—	—	.40	.65
	1984	.050	—	—	—	.75
	1985	.020	—	—	—	2.00
	1986	.048	—	—	—	2.00
	1987	.100	—	—	—	.75
	1988	.100	—	—	—	.75
	1989	.083	—	—	—	.75
	1990	.015	—	—	—	.75
	1991	.015	—	—	—	.75
	1992	.100	—	—	—	.75
	1993		—	—	—	.75
	1994 (fish)		—	—	—	.75
	1994 (bee)		—	—	—	12.50
	1995		—	—	—	.75
	1996		—	—	—	.75
	1997		—	—	—	.75

Plain edge.
Rev: Engraver's signature: D'AP.O.ROTY.

942.2	1991	—	—	—	Proof	3.50
	1992	—	—	—	Proof	3.50
	1992	—	—	—	—	.75
	1993	—	—	—	Proof	3.50
	1994 (fish)	—	—	—	Proof	3.50
	1995	—	—	—	Proof	3.50
	1996	8,000	—	—	Proof	3.50
	1997	—	—	—	Proof	3.50

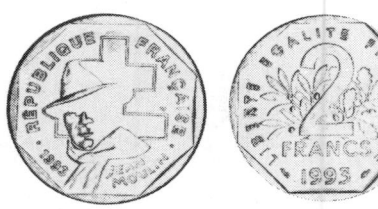

Jean Moulin

1062	1993	—	—	—	—	1.00

Louis Pasteur

1119	1995	—	—	—	—	2.00

Georges Guynemer, WWI Fighter Pilot Ace
Obv: Portrait. Rev: Guynemer's stork emblem.

1187	1997	—	—	—	—	3.00

5 FRANCS

NICKEL
Mint: Paris - w/o mint mark.

KM#	Date	Mintage	Fine	VF	XF	Unc
887	1933	160.078	.75	1.50	3.50	9.00

KM#	Date	Mintage	Fine	VF	XF	Unc
888	1933(a)	56.686	.25	.75	2.50	8.00
	1935(a)	54.164	.25	.75	2.50	8.00
	1936(a)	.117	400.00	700.00	1200.	1850.
	1937(a)	.157	35.00	60.00	120.00	225.00
	1938(a)	4.977	12.00	25.00	50.00	100.00
	1939(a)	—	700.00	1200.	2000.	4000.

ALUMINUM-BRONZE
Struck for colonial use in Algeria.

KM#	Date	Mintage	Fine	VF	XF	Unc
888a.1	1938(a)	10.144	6.00	10.00	18.00	85.00
	1939(a)	I.A.	2.50	5.00	12.00	30.00
	1940(a)	38.758	1.00	2.00	3.50	10.00

Struck for colonial use in Africa.

KM#	Date	Mintage	Fine	VF	XF	Unc
888a.2	1945(a) open 9	13.044	1.00	2.00	4.00	11.00
	1946(a) open 9	21.790	1.00	2.00	4.00	11.00
	1947(a)	2.662	150.00	200.00	300.00	650.00

NOTE: 1974 date exists with both open and closed 9's.

Mint mark: C

KM#	Date	Mintage	Fine	VF	XF	Unc
888a.3	1945 open 9	Inc. Ab.	3.00	7.00	15.00	30.00
	1946 open 9	Inc. Ab.	5.00	15.00	30.00	60.00

ALUMINUM
Mint: Paris - w/o mint mark.

KM#	Date	Mintage	Fine	VF	XF	Unc
888b.1	1945(a) open 9	95.399	.20	.35	1.50	6.00
	1946(a) open 9	61.332	.20	.35	1.50	6.00
	1947(a) open & closed 9	46.576	.20	.35	1.50	6.00
	1948(a) open 9	104.473	1.00	3.00	6.00	12.50
	1949(a) closed 9	203.252	.20	.35	.75	3.00
	1950(a) closed 9	128.372	.20	.35	.75	3.00
	1952(a) closed 9	4.000	20.00	40.00	100.00	225.00

NOTE: 1948 date exists with open and closed 9's.

Mint mark: B

KM#	Date	Mintage	Fine	VF	XF	Unc
888b.2	1945 open 9	6.043	1.50	3.00	5.00	15.00
	1946 open 9	13.360	.75	1.50	3.00	12.00
	1947	30.839	.50	1.00	2.50	8.00
	1948	28.047	20.00	40.00	100.00	175.00
	1949 closed 9	48.414	.50	1.00	2.50	8.00
	1950 closed 9	28.952	.75	1.50	3.50	9.00

NOTE: 1947 and 1948 dates exist with open and closed 9's.

Mint mark: C

KM#	Date	Mintage	Fine	VF	XF	Unc
888b.3	1945 open 9	2.208	7.00	15.00	28.00	60.00
	1946 open 9	1.269	8.00	18.00	38.00	75.00

COPPER-NICKEL
Mint: Paris - w/o mint mark.

KM#	Date	Mintage	Fine	VF	XF	Unc
901	1941(a)	13.782	65.00	100.00	150.00	250.00

NOTE: Never released for circulation.

12.0000 g, .835 SILVER, .3221 oz ASW
5 New Francs = 500 Old Francs
Fifth Republic

KM#	Date	Mintage	Fine	VF	XF	Unc
926	1960	55.182	—	—	BV	4.00
	1961	15.630	—	—	BV	4.00
	1962	42.500	—	—	BV	4.00
	1963	37.936	—	—	BV	4.00
	1964	32.378	—	—	BV	4.00
	1965	5.156	—	—	BV	6.00
	1966	5.017	—	—	BV	6.00
	1967	.502	—	BV	4.00	12.00
	1968	.557	—	BV	3.00	10.00
	1969	.504	—	BV	3.00	10.00

NICKEL CLAD COPPER-NICKEL

KM#	Date	Mintage	Fine	VF	XF	Unc
926a.1	1970	57.890	—	—	1.00	1.25
	1971	142.204	—	—	1.00	1.25
	1972	45.492	—	—	1.00	1.50
	1973	45.079	—	—	1.00	1.25
	1974	26.888	—	—	1.00	1.25
	1975	16.712	—	—	1.00	1.25
	1976	1.662	—	1.00	1.25	2.00
	1977	.485	—	1.00	1.50	2.25
	1978	30.022	—	—	1.00	1.25
	1979	.051	—	—	1.75	3.50
	1980	.060	—	—	—	1.65
	1981	.050	—	—	—	1.65
	1982	.060	—	—	—	1.65
	1983	.101	—	—	—	1.65
	1984	.049	—	—	—	4.50
	1985	.020	—	—	—	6.00
	1986	.048	—	—	—	5.00
	1987	20.000	—	—	—	1.65
	1988	.100	—	—	—	1.65
	1989	.083	—	—	—	1.65
	1990	.015	—	—	—	1.65
	1991	7.500	—	—	—	1.65
	1992	10.000	—	—	—	1.65
	1993	—	—	—	—	1.65
	1994 (bee)	—	—	—	—	1.65
	1994 (fish)	—	—	—	—	1.65
	1995	—	—	—	—	1.65
	1996	—	—	—	—	1.65
	1997	—	—	—	—	1.65

Plain edge.
Obv: Modified sower.
Rev: Engraver's signature: D'AP.O.ROTY.

KM#	Date	Mintage	Fine	VF	XF	Unc
926a.2	1991	—	—	—	Proof	6.50
	1992	—	—	—	Proof	6.50
	1992	—	—	—	—	1.65
	1993	—	—	—	Proof	6.50
	1994 (fish)	—	—	—	Proof	6.50
	1995	—	—	—	Proof	6.50
	1996	8,000	—	—	Proof	6.50
	1997	—	—	—	Proof	6.50

COPPER-NICKEL
Centennial - Erection of Eiffel Tower

KM#	Date	Mintage	Fine	VF	XF	Unc
968	1989	9.910	—	—	—	6.00

Pierre Mendes - France

KM#	Date	Mintage	Fine	VF	XF	Unc
1006	1992	10.000	—	—	—	4.00

NICKEL CLAD COPPER-NICKEL
Voltaire - Poet

KM#	Date	Mintage	Fine	VF	XF	Unc
1063	1994	—	—	—	—	4.00

NICKEL CLAD STEEL
Hercules group design.

KM#	Date	Mintage	Fine	VF	XF	Unc
1155	1996	—	—	—	—	4.50

10 FRANCS

3.2258 g, .900 GOLD, .0933 oz AGW
Mint mark: A

KM#	Date	Mintage	Fine	VF	XF	Unc
846	1901	2.100	BV	45.00	55.00	75.00
	1905	1.426	BV	45.00	55.00	75.00
	1906	3.665	BV	45.00	55.00	75.00
	1907	3.364	BV	45.00	55.00	75.00
	1908	1.650	BV	45.00	55.00	75.00
	1909	.599	BV	45.00	55.00	110.00
	1910	2.110	BV	45.00	55.00	75.00
	1911	1.881	BV	45.00	55.00	75.00
	1912	1.756	BV	45.00	55.00	75.00
	1914	3.041	BV	45.00	55.00	75.00

NOTE: Earlier dates (1899-1900) exist for this type.

10.0000 g, .680 SILVER, .2186 oz ASW
Mint: Paris - w/o mint mark.

KM#	Date	Mintage	Fine	VF	XF	Unc
878	1929	16.292	BV	2.50	6.00	12.00
	1930	36.986	BV	1.75	4.50	9.00
	1931	35.468	BV	1.75	4.50	9.00
	1932	40.288	BV	1.75	3.00	7.00
	1933	31.146	BV	1.75	3.00	7.00
	1934	52.001	BV	1.75	3.00	7.00
	1936	1 known	—	—	—	—
	1937	.052	75.00	125.00	250.00	375.00
	1938	14.090	BV	2.00	6.00	12.50
	1939	8.299	2.50	3.50	8.00	17.50

Long Leaves　　　　Short Leaves

COPPER-NICKEL

KM#	Date	Mintage	Fine	VF	XF	Unc
908.1	1945(ll)	6.557	.25	.75	2.00	6.00
	1945(sl)	I.A.	15.00	30.00	50.00	90.00
	1946(ll)					

KM#	Date	Mintage	Fine	VF	XF	Unc
908.1		24.409	185.00	300.00	400.00	—
	1946(sl)	I.A.	.25	.50	2.00	5.00
	1947	41.627	.25	.50	1.00	3.00

Mint mark: B

KM#	Date	Mintage	Fine	VF	XF	Unc
908.2	1946(II)	8.452	20.00	35.00	50.00	85.00
	1946(sl)	I.A.	.25	.75	2.00	6.00
	1947	17.188	.25	.50	2.00	5.00

Mint: Paris - w/o mint mark.
Obv: Small head.

KM#	Date	Mintage	Fine	VF	XF	Unc
909.1	1947	Inc. Ab.	.30	.75	1.50	3.50
	1948	155.945	.20	.35	.75	2.00
	1949	118.149	.20	.35	.75	2.00

Mint mark: B

KM#	Date	Mintage	Fine	VF	XF	Unc
909.2	1947	Inc. Ab.	1.00	2.50	6.00	17.00
	1948	40.500	.35	.75	2.00	4.00
	1949	29.518	.35	.75	2.00	4.00

ALUMINUM-BRONZE
Mint: Paris w/o mint mark.

KM#	Date	Mintage	Fine	VF	XF	Unc
915.1	1950	13.534	.35	.65	1.50	5.00
	1951	153.689	.20	.35	.75	2.00
	1952	76.810	.20	.35	.75	2.00
	1953	46.272	.25	.50	.75	2.50
	1954	2.207	5.00	15.00	30.00	50.00
	1955	47.466	.20	.35	.75	2.50
	1956	2.570	—	Reported, not confirmed		
	1957	26.351	.50	1.00	2.00	4.50
	1958(w)	27.213	.50	1.00	2.00	4.50
	1959	.125	—	Reported, not confirmed		

Mint mark: B

KM#	Date	Mintage	Fine	VF	XF	Unc
915.2	1950	4.808	1.00	3.00	6.00	17.50
	1951	106.866	.20	.35	.75	2.00
	1952	72.346	.20	.35	.75	2.00
	1953	36.466	.25	.50	1.00	3.00
	1954	21.634	.75	1.50	3.50	7.00
	1958	1.500	—	Reported, not confirmed		

25.0000 g, .900 SILVER, .7234 oz ASW
Mint: Paris - w/o mint mark.
10 New Francs = 1000 Old Francs
Fifth Republic

KM#	Date	Mintage	Fine	VF	XF	Unc
932	1965	8.051	—	BV	6.00	10.00
	1966	9.800	—	BV	6.00	10.00
	1967	10.100	—	BV	6.00	10.00
	1968	3.887	—	BV	8.00	12.00
	1969	.761	—	BV	10.00	15.00
	1970	5.013	—	BV	6.00	10.00
	1971	.513	—	BV	10.00	17.50
	1972	.915	—	BV	8.00	12.00
	1973	.207	—	BV	10.00	20.00

NICKEL-BRASS

KM#	Date	Mintage	Fine	VF	XF	Unc
940	1974	22.447	—	—	2.00	2.50
	1975	59.013	—	—	2.00	2.50
	1976	104.093	—	—	2.00	2.50
	1977	100.028	—	—	2.00	2.50
	1978	97.590	—	—	2.00	2.50
	1979	110.000	—	—	2.00	2.50
	1980	80.010	—	—	2.00	2.50
	1981	.050	—	—	—	2.75
	1982	.074	—	—	—	2.75
	1983	.101	—	—	—	2.75
	1984	39.988	—	—	2.00	2.50
	1985	30.000	—	—	2.00	2.50
	1987	*50.000	—	—	—	2.50

NICKEL-BRONZE
100th Anniversary - Death of Leon Gambetta

KM#	Date	Mintage	Fine	VF	XF	Unc
950	1982	3.045	—	—	2.50	4.00

200th Anniversary - Montgolfier Balloon

	Date	Mintage	Fine	VF	XF	Unc
952	1983	3.001	—	—	2.50	4.00

200th Anniversary - Birth of Stendhal

	Date	Mintage	Fine	VF	XF	Unc
953	1983	2.951	—	—	2.50	4.00

200th Anniversary - Birth of Francois Rude

	Date	Mintage	Fine	VF	XF	Unc
954	1984	10.000	—	—	2.50	3.50

Centennial - Death of Victor Hugo

	Date	Mintage	Fine	VF	XF	Unc
956	1985	10.000	—	—	2.50	3.50

NICKEL

100th Anniversary - Birth of Robert Schuman

KM#	Date	Mintage	Fine	VF	XF	Unc
958	1986	9.961	—	—	3.00	6.50

Madam Republic

	Date	Mintage	Fine	VF	XF	Unc
959	1986	110.015	—	—	3.00	7.50

NOTE: Recalled and melted, no longer legal tender.

ALUMINUM-BRONZE ring & STEEL center
Spirit of Bastille

	Date	Mintage	Fine	VF	XF	Unc
964.1	1988	100.000	—	—	2.50	6.00
	1989	249.980	—	—	2.50	6.00
	1990	250.000	—	—	2.50	6.00
	1991	250.000	—	—	2.50	6.00
	1992	150.000	—	—	2.50	6.00
	1992	—	—	—	Proof	15.00
	1993	—	—	—	2.50	6.00
	1993	—	—	—	Proof	15.00

NOTE: 1991-1992 dated coins, non-Proof, exist in both medal and coin alignment, 1993 in medal alignment only.

Plain edge.

	Date	Mintage	Fine	VF	XF	Unc
964.2	1991	—	—	—	Proof	15.00
	1994	—	—	—	—	6.00
	1994	—	—	—	Proof	15.00
	1995	—	—	—	—	6.00
	1995	—	—	—	Proof	15.00
	1996	—	—	—	—	6.00
	1996	8,000	—	—	Proof	15.00
	1997	—	—	—	—	6.00
	1997	—	—	—	Proof	15.00

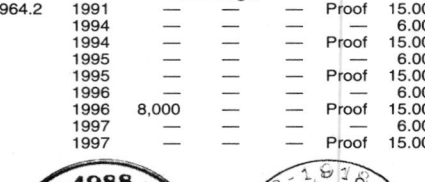

ALUMINUM-BRONZE
100th Anniversary - Birth of Roland Garros

	Date	Mintage	Fine	VF	XF	Unc
965	1988	30.000	—	—	2.50	4.00

ALUMINUM-BRONZE ring & STEEL center
300th Anniversary - Birth of Montesquieu

	Date	Mintage	Fine	VF	XF	Unc
969	1989	.015	—	—	6.50	17.50

20 FRANCS

6.4516 g, .900 GOLD, .1867 oz AGW
Edge inscription: DIEU PROTEGE LA FRANCE.

	Date	Mintage		Fine	VF	XF	Unc
847	1901	2.643	BV	75.00	85.00	110.00	
	1902	2.394	BV	75.00	85.00	110.00	
	1903	4.405	BV	75.00	85.00	110.00	
	1904	7.706	BV	75.00	85.00	110.00	
	1905	9.158	BV	75.00	85.00	110.00	
	1906	14.613	BV	75.00	85.00	110.00	

NOTE: Earlier dates (1899-1900) exist for this type.

Edge inscription: LIBERTE EGALITE FRATERNITE.

	Date	Mintage		Fine	VF	XF	Unc
857	1906	—	BV	70.00	80.00	110.00	
	1907	17.716	BV	70.00	80.00	110.00	
	1908	6.721	BV	70.00	80.00	110.00	
	1909	9.637	BV	70.00	80.00	110.00	
	1910	5.779	BV	70.00	80.00	110.00	
	1911	5.346	BV	70.00	80.00	110.00	
	1912	10.332	BV	70.00	80.00	110.00	
	1913	12.163	BV	70.00	80.00	110.00	
	1914	6.518	BV	70.00	80.00	110.00	

NOTE: Some dates from 1907-1914 have been officially restruck.

KM#	Date Mintage	Fine	VF	XF	Unc
917.2	1951 (4 plumes)				
	46.815	.30	.50	2.00	4.00
	1952 (4 plumes)				
	54.381	.30	.50	2.00	4.00
	1953 (4 plumes)				
	42.410	.30	.50	2.00	4.00
	1954 (4 plumes)				
	1.573	125.00	200.00	350.00	900.00

KM#	Date Mintage	Fine	VF	XF	Unc
918.1	1953 63.172	.50	1.00	2.50	6.00
	1954 .997	15.00	35.00	65.00	110.00
	1958(w) .501	25.00	60.00	100.00	220.00
	Mint mark: B				
918.2	1951 11.829	.75	1.50	3.50	9.00
	1952 13.432	1.50	3.00	6.00	15.00
	1953 23.376	.75	1.50	3.00	8.00
	1954 6.531	3.00	6.00	12.00	30.00

COPPER-ALUMINUM-NICKEL center plug, NICKEL inner ring, COPPER-ALUMINUM-NICKEL outer ring
Mont St. Michel
Obv: 4 bands of stripes in outer ring.

1008.1	1992 60.000	—	—	—	15.00

Obv: 5 bands of stripes in outer ring.

1008.2	1992 Inc. Ab.	—	—	—	6.50
	1992	—	—	—	Proof 25.00
	1993	—	—	—	7.00
	1994	—	—	—	8.00
	1994	—	—	—	Proof 25.00
	1995	—	—	—	9.00
	1995	—	—	—	Proof 25.00
	1996	—	—	—	6.50
	1996 8,000	—	—	—	Proof 25.00
	1997	—	—	—	8.00
	1997	—	—	—	Proof 25.00

NOTE: 1992-1993 dated coins, non-Proof, exist in both coin and medal alignment.

30.0000 g, .900 SILVER, .8682 oz ASW
Mint: Paris - w/o mint mark.
5000 Old Francs = 50 New Francs

941.1	1974 4.299	—	—	—	10.00
	1975 4.551	—	—	—	12.50
	1976 7.739	—	—	—	11.50
	1977 7.884	—	—	—	10.00
	1978 12.028	—	—	—	10.00
	1979 12.041	—	—	—	10.00
	1980 .060	—	—	—	50.00

Rev: Legend begins at the level of the beltline of the goddess to Hercules' left.

941.2	1974	—	15.00	25.00	40.00 65.00

100 FRANCS

ALUMINUM-BRONZE center plug, NICKEL inner ring, COPPER-ALUMINUM-NICKEL outer ring
Mediterranean Games

1016	1993	—	—	—	— 10.00

Pierre De Coubertin
Founder of Modern Day Olympics

1036	1994 15.000	—	—	—	— 10.00

50 FRANCS

16.1290 g, .900 GOLD, .4667 oz AGW
Mint mark: A

831	1904 .020	300.00	600.00	900.00	1900.

ALUMINUM-BRONZE
Mint: Paris - w/o mint mark.

918.1	1950 .600	75.00	150.00	300.00	575.00
	1951 68.630	.50	1.00	2.50	6.00
	1952 74.212	.50	1.00	2.50	6.00

32.2581 g, .900 GOLD, .9335 oz AGW
Mint mark: A
Edge inscription: DIEU PROTEGE LA FRANCE.

832	1901 .010	450.00	475.00	525.00	650.00
	1902 .010	450.00	475.00	525.00	650.00
	1903 .010	450.00	475.00	525.00	650.00
	1904 .020	450.00	475.00	525.00	650.00
	1905 .010	450.00	475.00	525.00	650.00
	1906 .030	450.00	475.00	525.00	650.00

NOTE: Earlier dates (1878-1900) exist for this type.

Edge inscription: LIBERTE EGALITE FRATERNITE.

858	1907 .020	350.00	375.00	400.00	550.00
	1908 .023	350.00	375.00	400.00	550.00
	1909 .020	350.00	375.00	400.00	550.00
	1910 .020	350.00	375.00	400.00	550.00
	1911 .030	350.00	375.00	400.00	550.00
	1912 .020	350.00	375.00	400.00	550.00
	1913 .030	350.00	375.00	400.00	550.00
	1914 1,281	2000.	4500.	7000.	10,000.

Long Leaves   **Short Leaves**
Mint: Paris - w/o mint mark.
20.0000 g, .680 SILVER, .4372 oz ASW

KM#	Date Mintage	Fine	VF	XF	Unc
879	1929(ll) 3.234	BV	6.00	9.00	35.00
	1933(sl)				
	24.447*	BV	4.50	5.50	18.00
	1933(ll) I.A.	BV	4.50	5.50	18.00
	1934(sl)				
	11.785	BV	4.50	10.00	30.00
	1936(sl) .048	300.00	450.00	800.00	—
	1937(sl) 1.189	10.00	15.00	25.00	50.00
	1938(sl)				
	10.910	BV	4.50	7.00	20.00
	1939(sl) 3,918	700.00	1500.	2000.	4500.

***NOTE:** Counterfeits exist in bronze-aluminum with thin silver sheath.

3 Feathers   **4 Feathers**
ALUMINUM-BRONZE
Obv: GEORGES GUIRAUD behind head.

916.1	1950 (3 plumes)				
	5.779	.50	1.00	2.50	7.00
	1950 (4 plumes)				
	—	125.00	200.00	350.00	—
	Mint mark: B				
916.2	1950 (3 plumes)				
	1.50	3.00	7.00	20.00	
	1950 (4 plumes)				
	—	40.00	85.00	150.00	225.00

Mint: Paris - w/o mint mark.
Obv: G. GUIRAUD behind head.

917.1	1950 (3 plumes)				
	120.656	2.00	6.00	12.00	40.00
	1950 (4 plumes)				
	Inc. Ab.	.25	.40	1.50	3.00
	1951 (4 plumes)				
	97.922	.25	.40	1.00	3.00
	1952 (4 plumes)				
	130.281	.25	.40	1.00	3.00
	1953 (4 plumes)				
	60.158	.30	.50	1.00	3.00
	Mint mark: B				
917.2	1950 (3 plumes)				
	43.355	25.00	35.00	50.00	135.00
	1950 (4 plumes)				
	Inc. Ab.	.50	1.00	3.00	7.00

6.5500 g, .900 GOLD, .1895 oz AGW
Mint: Paris - w/o mint mark.

KM#	Date	Mintage	Fine	VF	XF	Unc
880	1929	*15 pcs.	—	—	3000.	7000.
	1932	*50 pcs.	—	—	2500.	5000.
	1933	*300 pcs.	—	—	2000.	3000.
	1934	*10 pcs.	—	—	10,000.	16,000.
	1935	6.102	—	—	350.00	715.00
	1936	7.689	—	—	350.00	715.00

COPPER-NICKEL

KM#	Date	Mintage	Fine	VF	XF	Unc
919.1	1954	97.285	.50	1.25	2.50	6.50
	1955	152.517	.25	.75	1.50	4.50
	1956	7.578	3.50	7.50	15.00	40.00
	1957	11.312	1.50	3.00	6.00	18.00
	1958(w)	3.256	2.50	5.50	12.50	35.00
	1958(o)	I.A.	20.00	45.00	75.00	135.00

Mint mark: B

919.2	1954	86.261	.50	1.25	2.50	5.00
	1955	136.585	.25	.75	1.50	3.50
	1956	19.154	1.00	2.50	5.00	10.00
	1957	25.702	1.00	2.50	5.00	12.50
	1958	54.072	1.00	2.50	5.00	11.50

FRENCH EQUATORIAL AFRICA

French Equatorial Africa, an area consisting of four self governing dependencies (Middle Congo, Ubangi-Shari, Chad and Gabon) in West-Central Africa, had an area of 969,111 sq. mi. (2,509,987 sq. km.). Capital: Brazzaville. The area, rich in natural resources, exported cotton, timber, coffee, cacao, diamonds and gold.

Little is known of the history of these parts of Africa prior to French occupation - which began with no thought of territorial acquisition. France's initial intent was simply to establish a few supply stations along the west coast of Africa to service the warships assigned to combat the slave trade in the early part of the 19th century. French settlement began in 1839. Gabon (then Gabun) and the Middle Congo were secured between 1885 and 1891; Chad and Ubangi-Shari between 1894 and 1897. The four colonies were joined to form French Equatorial Africa in 1910. The dependencies were changed from colonies to territories within the French Union in 1946, and all the inhabitants were made French citizens. In 1958 they voted to become autonomous republics within the new French Community, and attained full independence in 1960.

For later coinage see Central African States, Congo Peoples Republic, Gabon and Chad.

RULERS

French, until 1960

MINT MARKS

(a) - Paris, privy marks only
SA - Pretoria (1942-1943)

ENGRAVERS INITIALS

GLS - Steynberg

MONETARY SYSTEM

100 Centimes = 1 Franc

5 CENTIMES

ALUMINUM-BRONZE
Similar to 10 Centimes, KM#4.

KM#	Date	Mintage	Fine	VF	XF	Unc
3	1943	*44.000	90.00	150.00	275.00	600.00

10 CENTIMES

ALUMINUM-BRONZE

4	1943	*13.000	75.00	100.00	150.00	350.00

25 CENTIMES

ALUMINUM-BRONZE
Similar to 10 Centimes, KM#4.

5	1943	*4.160	175.00	300.00	500.00	800.00

*NOTE: KM#3-5 were not released for circulation.

50 CENTIMES

BRASS
Mint mark: SA

1	1942SA	8.000	1.50	3.00	8.00	18.00

BRONZE

1a	1943SA	16.000	1.25	2.50	7.00	16.00

FRANC

BRASS
Mint mark: SA

2	1942SA	3.000	2.00	3.50	10.00	30.00

BRONZE

KM#	Date	Mintage	Fine	VF	XF	Unc
2a	1943SA	6.000	1.75	2.75	9.00	28.00

ALUMINUM

6	1948(a)	15.000	.15	.25	.50	2.00

2 FRANCS

ALUMINUM

7	1948(a)	5.040	.25	.50	1.50	4.00

NOTE: KM#8-10 previously listed here and under Cameroon are now listed in Equatorial African States, KM#24-26.

FRENCH INDO-CHINA

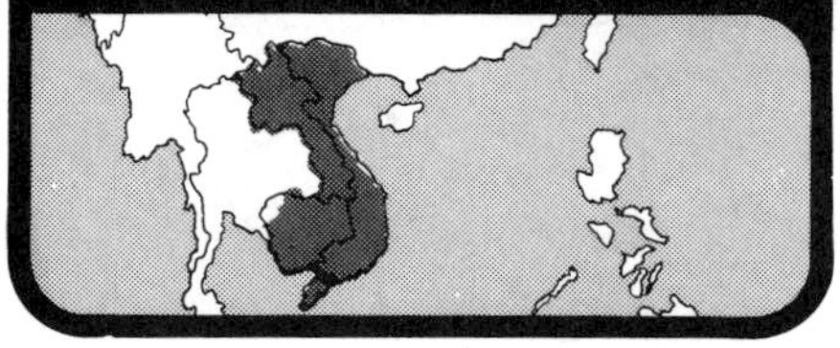

French Indo-China, made up of the protectorates of Annam, Tonkin, Cambodia and Laos and the colony of Cochin-China was located on the Indo-Chinese peninsula of Southeast Asia. The colony had an area of 286,194 sq. mi. (741,242 sq. km.). and a population of 30 million. Principal cities: Saigon, Haiphong, Vientiane, Pnom-Penh and Hanoi.

The forebears of the modern Indo-Chinese peoples originated in the Yellow River Valley of northern China, from whence they were driven into the Indo-Chinese peninsula by the Han Chinese. The Chinese followed southward in the second century B.C., conquering the peninsula and ruling it until 938, leaving a lingering heritage of Chinese learning and culture. Indo-Chinese independence was basically maintained until the arrival of the French in the mid-19th century who established control over all of Vietnam, Laos and Cambodia. Activities directed toward obtaining self-determination accelerated during the Japanese occupation of World War II. The dependencies were changed from colonies to territories within the French Union in 1946, and all the inhabitants were made French citizens.

In Aug. of 1945, an uprising erupted involving the French and Vietnamese Nationalists, culminated in the French military disaster at Dien Bien Phu (May, 1954) and the subsequent Geneva Conference that brought an end to French colonial rule in Indo-China.

For later coinage see Kampuchea, Laos and Vietnam.

RULERS

French, until 1954

MINT MARKS

A - Paris
(a) - Paris, privy marks only
B - Beaumont-le-Roger
C - Castlesarrasin
H - Heaton, Birmingham
(p) - Thunderbolt - Poissy
S - San Francisco, U.S.A.
None - Osaka, Japan
None - Hanoi, Tonkin

MONETARY SYSTEM

5 Sapeques = 1 Cent
100 Cents = 1 Piastre

SAPEQUE

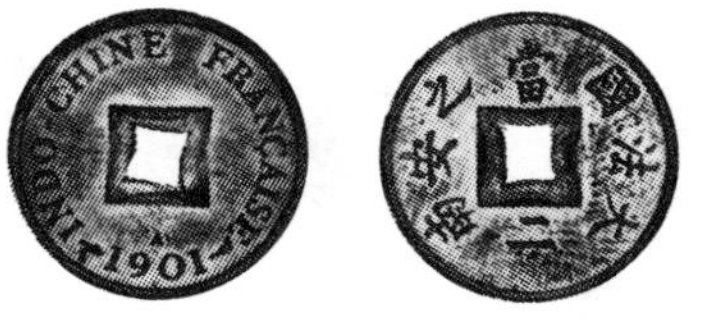

BRONZE
Mint mark: A

KM#	Date	Mintage	Fine	VF	XF	Unc
6	1901	4.843	2.50	7.50	15.00	65.00
	1902	2.500	7.50	20.00	40.00	100.00

NOTE: Earlier dates (1887-1900) exist for this type.

1/4 CENT

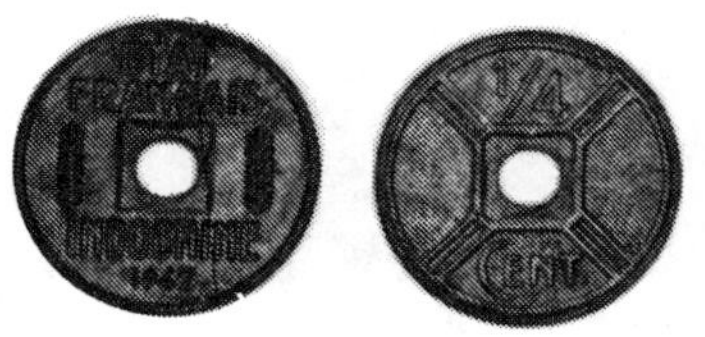

ZINC

25	1942	221.800	10.00	20.00	40.00	90.00
	1943	279.450	18.00	40.00	65.00	150.00
	1944	46.122	150.00	250.00	400.00	1000.

NOTE: Lead counterfeits dated 1941 and 1942 are known.

1/2 CENT

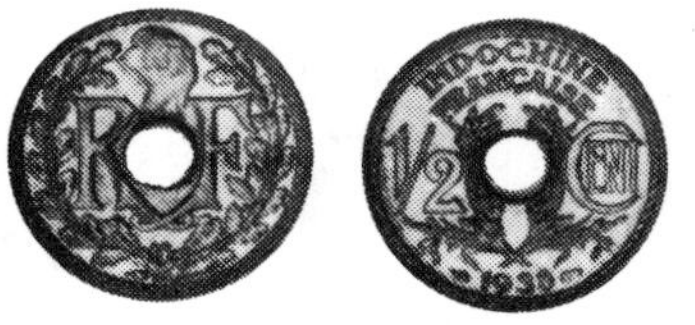

BRONZE

KM#	Date	Mintage	Fine	VF	XF	Unc
20	1935(a)	26.365	.25	.50	2.00	10.00
	1936(a)	23.635	.25	.50	2.00	10.00
	1937(a)	10.244	.50	1.50	5.00	15.00
	1938(a)	16.665	.25	.75	2.50	12.00
	1939(a)	17.305	.25	.75	2.50	12.00
	1940(a)	11.218	4.00	8.00	20.00	40.00

ZINC

20a	1939(a)	.185	100.00	200.00	300.00	600.00
	1940(a)	—	200.00	300.00	400.00	700.00

CENT

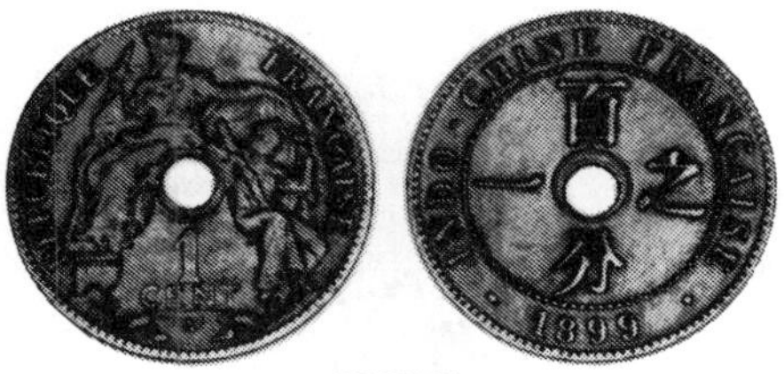

BRONZE
Rev. leg: UN CENTIEME DE PIASTRE.

8	1901	9.750	2.00	3.00	7.50	25.00
	1902	5.050	3.00	5.00	10.00	40.00
	1903	8.000	2.50	4.00	8.00	30.00
	1906	2.000	5.00	8.00	25.00	75.00

NOTE: Earlier dates (1896-1900) exist for this type.

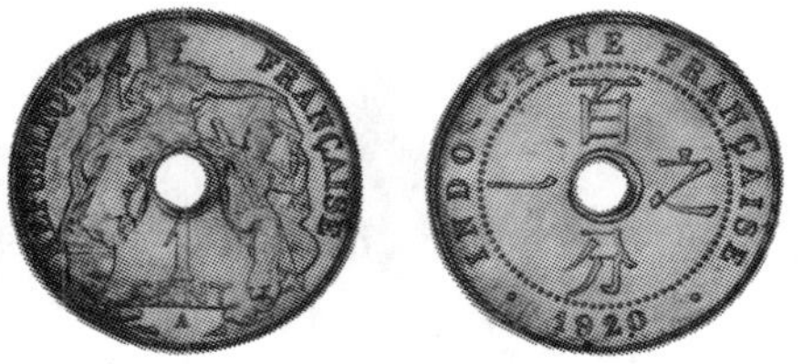

12.1	1908	3.000	10.00	20.00	55.00	225.00
	1909	5.000	20.00	40.00	80.00	275.00
	1910	7.703	1.00	4.00	10.00	25.00
	1911	15.234	.75	3.00	10.00	20.00
	1912	17.027	.75	3.00	10.00	20.00
	1913	3.945	2.00	7.00	18.00	45.00
	1914	11.027	.75	3.00	15.00	30.00
	1916	1.312	8.00	15.00	28.00	50.00
	1917	9.762	1.00	4.00	10.00	20.00
	1918	2.372	6.00	12.50	25.00	50.00
	1919	9.148	1.00	4.00	7.50	20.00
	1920	18.305	.75	3.00	5.00	12.50
	1921	14.722	.75	2.00	3.00	8.00
	1922	8.850	1.00	3.00	5.00	20.00
	1923	1.079	20.00	40.00	65.00	175.00
	1926	11.672	.75	2.00	4.00	10.00
	1927	3.328	5.00	10.00	25.00	50.00
	1930	4.682	1.25	2.75	5.00	10.00
	1931 torch privy mark					
		5.318	20.00	35.00	100.00	350.00
	1931 wing privy mark					
		Inc. Ab.	30.00	60.00	140.00	400.00
	1937	8.902	.25	.50	1.50	6.00
	1938	15.499	.25	.50	1.00	4.00
	1939	15.599	.25	.50	1.00	4.00

Mint: San Francisco - w/o mint mark.

12.2	1920	13.290	1.00	2.50	5.00	17.50
	1921	1.610	35.00	70.00	225.00	450.00

Mint mark: Thunderbolt

12.3	1922	9.476	1.00	1.75	5.00	12.00
	1923	27.891	.50	.75	1.50	5.00

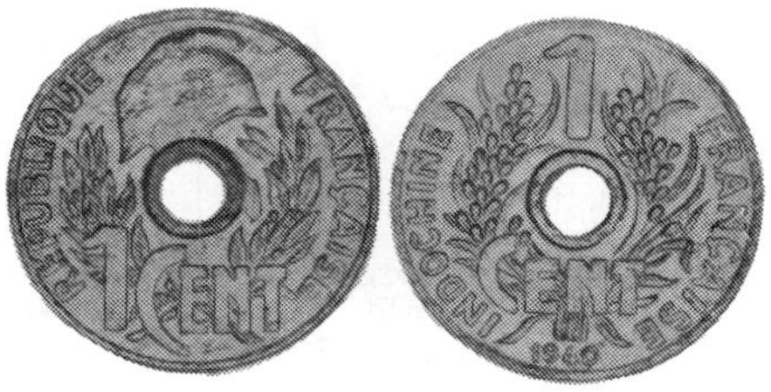

ZINC
Vichy Government Issues

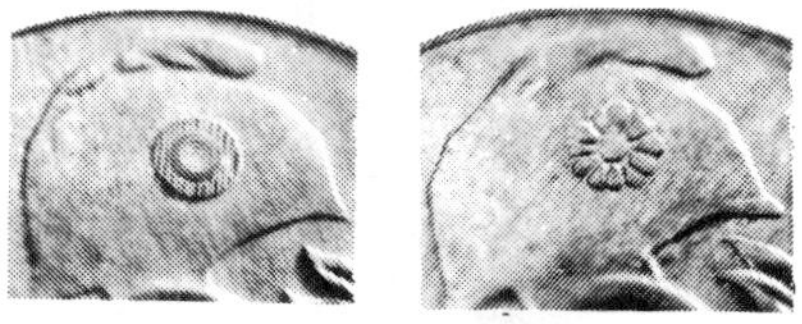

Circles — Rosette

Type 1, circles on Phrygian cap.

24.1	1940 T1	1.990	5.00	10.00	22.50	55.00

Type 2, rosette on Phrygian cap.
Variety 1, 12 petals - Variety 2, 11 petals.

24.2	1940 T2 V1	—	5.00	10.00	25.00	65.00

Type 2, rosette on Phrygian cap.

KM#	Date	Mintage	Fine	VF	XF	Unc
24.3	1940 T2 V2	—	5.00	15.00	30.00	75.00
	1941 T2 V2	—	2.00	5.00	15.00	48.00

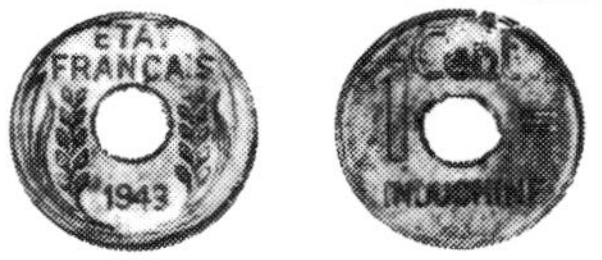

ALUMINUM

26	1943	—	.25	.50	1.00	3.00

NOTE: Edge varieties exist - plain, grooved and partially grooved.

5 CENTS

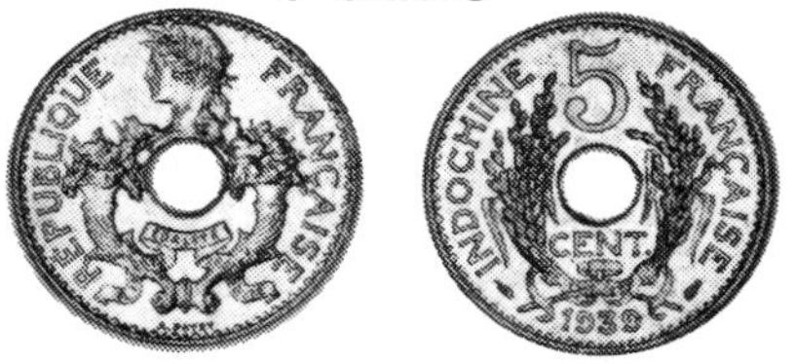

5.0000 g, COPPER-NICKEL, 1.6mm thick

18.1	1923(a)	1.611	3.00	5.00	15.00	40.00
	1924(a)	3.389	1.00	3.00	12.00	35.00
	1925(a)	6.000	1.00	1.75	7.00	20.00
	1930(a)	4.000	1.00	2.00	8.00	25.00
	1937(a)	10.000	.50	1.00	4.00	15.00
	1938(a)	—	10.00	25.00	75.00	175.00
	1938(a)	—	—	—	Proof	250.00

Mint mark: A

18.2	1938	1.480	50.00	85.00	150.00	400.00

4.0000 g, NICKEL-BRASS, 1.3mm thick

18.1a	1938(a)	50.569	.25	.50	1.00	5.00
	1939(a)	38.501	.25	.50	1.00	5.00

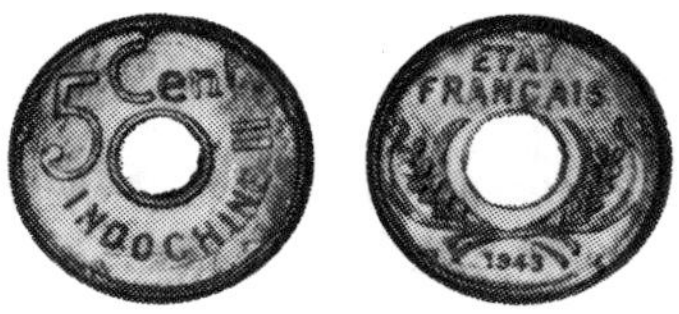

ALUMINUM
Vichy Government Issue

27	1943(a)	—	.25	.50	1.50	4.00

NOTE: Edge varieties exist: reeded - rare, plain, grooved and partially grooved.

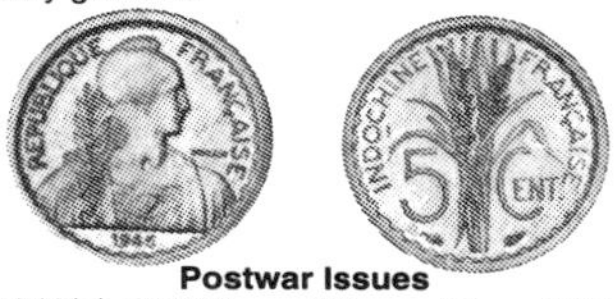

Postwar Issues

30.1	1946(a)	28.000	.25	.60	1.00	4.00

Mint mark: B

30.2	1946	22.000	.25	.60	1.00	4.00

10 CENTS

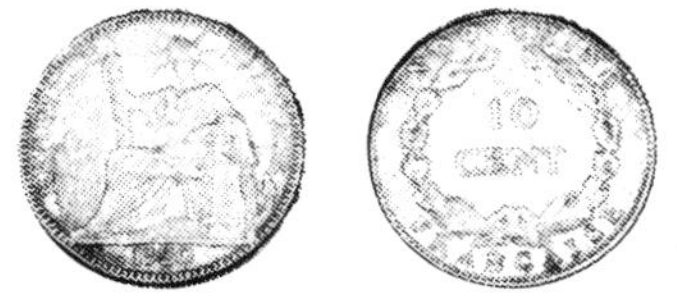

2.7000 g, .835 SILVER, .0725 oz ASW
Rev. leg: TITRE 0,835. POIDS 2 GR. 7

9	1901	2.950	9.00	30.00	75.00	200.00
	1902	7.050	5.00	15.00	35.00	125.00
	1903	1.300	15.00	40.00	100.00	325.00
	1908	1.000	60.00	120.00	250.00	550.00
	1909	1.000	40.00	90.00	175.00	425.00
	1910	2.689	30.00	75.00	125.00	350.00
	1911	2.311	30.00	50.00	100.00	325.00
	1912	2.500	30.00	45.00	90.00	275.00
	1913	4.847	7.50	12.50	35.00	125.00
	1914	2.667	12.00	35.00	75.00	175.00
	1916	2.000	12.00	35.00	75.00	185.00
	1917	1.500	30.00	60.00	115.00	300.00
	1919	1.500	40.00	75.00	150.00	350.00

NOTE: Earlier dates (1898-1900) exist for this type.

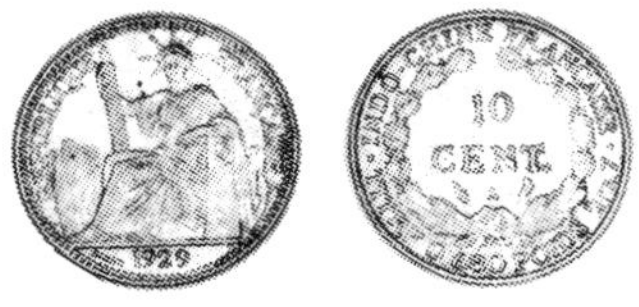

3.0000 g, .400 SILVER, .0386 oz ASW
Mint: San Francisco - w/o mint mark.
Rev: W/o fineness indicated.

14	1920	10.000	10.00	15.00	40.00	100.00

2.7000 g, .680 SILVER, .0590 oz ASW
Mint mark: A
Rev. leg: TITRE 0,680 POIDS 2 GR. 7

KM#	Date	Mintage	Fine	VF	XF	Unc
16.1	1921	12.516	1.50	3.00	9.00	20.00
	1922	22.381	1.50	3.00	9.00	20.00
	1923	21.755	1.50	3.00	9.00	20.00
	1924	2.816	2.00	5.00	16.50	45.00
	1925	4.909	1.75	3.50	15.00	35.00
	1927	6.471	2.50	7.00	17.50	40.00
	1928	1.593	25.00	70.00	150.00	450.00
	1929	5.831	1.50	3.00	10.00	30.00
	1930	6.608	1.50	3.00	10.00	30.00
	1931	100 pcs.	—	—	Proof	300.00
16.2	1937(a)	25.000	1.00	1.50	3.00	8.00

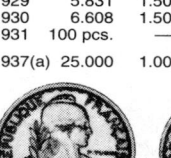 

	1939(a)	16.841	.25	.50	1.00	5.00
21.1	1940(a)	25.505	.25	.50	1.00	5.00

NOTE: The coins above have no dots left and right of date and are magnetic.

COPPER - NICKEL
Obv: Date w/o dots.

21.1a	1941S	50.000	.20	.40	.75	4.00
(21a.2)						

Obv: Date between 2 dots.

21.2	1939.(a)	2.237	8.00	15.00	30.00	75.00
(21a.1)	1941S	50.000	.20	.40	.75	4.00

ALUMINUM

28.1	1945(a)	40.170	.25	.50	1.00	4.50

Mint mark: B

28.2	1945	9.830	.50	1.50	3.00	10.00

20 CENTS

5.4000 g, .835 SILVER, .1450 oz ASW

10	1901	1.375	20.00	50.00	110.00	300.00
	1902	3.525	7.50	15.00	40.00	175.00
	1903	.675	50.00	100.00	200.00	600.00
	1908	.500	100.00	250.00	450.00	850.00
	1909	.200	100.00	200.00	400.00	850.00
	1911	2.340	7.50	15.00	35.00	120.00
	1912	.160	100.00	200.00	450.00	950.00
	1913	1.252	50.00	100.00	200.00	400.00
	1914	2.500	7.50	15.00	25.00	120.00
	1916	1.000	12.50	35.00	100.00	225.00

NOTE: Earlier dates (1898-1900) exist for this type.

.835 SILVER
Mule. Obv: KM#10. Rev: KM#3a.

13	1909 Inc. KM10	100.00	250.00	650.00	1200.

6.0000 g, .400 SILVER, .0772 oz ASW
Mint: San Francisco - w/o mint mark.
Rev: W/o fineness indicated.

15	1920	4.000	12.50	25.00	50.00	125.00

5.4000 g, .680 SILVER, .1181 oz ASW
Mint mark: A
Rev. leg: TITRE 0.680 POIDS 5 GR. 4

17.1	1921	3.663	2.00	4.00	10.00	30.00

KM#	Date	Mintage	Fine	VF	XF	Unc
17.1	1922	5.812	2.00	4.00	8.00	20.00
	1923	7.109	2.00	4.00	8.00	20.00
	1924	1.400	6.00	12.50	30.00	75.00
	1925	2.556	4.00	10.00	22.50	60.00
	1927	3.245	3.00	7.50	15.00	30.00
	1928	.794	10.00	20.00	60.00	200.00
	1929	.644	15.00	30.00	80.00	225.00
	1930	5.576	1.50	3.00	5.00	10.00
17.2	1937(a)	17.500	1.00	1.50	2.50	7.50

NICKEL
Security edge.

23	1939(a)	.318	15.00	30.00	70.00	125.00

COPPER-NICKEL
Reeded edge.

23a.1	.1939.(a)	14.676	.25	.50	1.00	6.00

Mint mark: S

23a.2	.1941.	25.000	.25	.50	1.00	5.00

ALUMINUM

29.1	1945(a)	15.412	.50	1.00	2.50	7.50

Mint mark: B

29.2	1945	6.665	2.00	4.00	8.00	25.00

Mint mark: C

29.3	1945	22.423	1.00	3.00	10.00

50 CENTS

13.5000 g, .900 SILVER, .3906 oz ASW
Rev. leg: TITRE 0.900. POIDS 13 GR. 5

4a.2	1936(a)	4.000	3.00	4.00	6.00	15.00

COPPER-NICKEL
Rev. leg: BRONZE DE NICKEL

31	1946(a)	32.292	2.00	4.00	7.00	20.00

PIASTRE

27.0000 g, .900 SILVER, .7812 oz ASW
Rev. leg: TITRE 0.900. POIDS 27 GR.

KM#	Date	Mintage	Fine	VF	XF	Unc
5a.1	1901	3.150	8.00	12.50	22.50	135.00
	1902	3.327	8.00	12.50	22.50	135.00
	1903	10.077	8.00	10.00	17.50	100.00
	1904	5.751	8.00	10.00	17.50	120.00
	1905	3.561	8.00	10.00	17.50	130.00
	1906	10.194	8.00	10.00	17.50	95.00
	1907	14.062	8.00	10.00	17.50	95.00
	1908	13.986	8.00	10.00	17.50	95.00
	1909	9.201	8.00	10.00	17.50	110.00
	1910	.761	25.00	55.00	120.00	300.00
	1913	3.244	8.00	12.50	22.50	125.00
	1924	2.831	8.00	12.50	22.50	150.00
	1925	2.882	8.00	12.50	22.50	150.00
	1926	6.383	8.00	10.00	17.50	90.00
	1927	8.184	8.00	10.00	17.50	95.00
	1928	5.290	8.00	10.00	17.50	95.00

NOTE: Earlier dates (1895-1900) exist for this type.

Mint: San Francisco - w/o mint mark.

5a.2	1921	4.850	8.00	12.50	25.00	150.00
	1922	1.150	10.00	20.00	40.00	200.00

Mint mark: H

5a.3	1921	8.430	8.00	10.00	17.50	100.00
	1922	8.570	8.00	10.00	17.50	90.00

20.0000 g, .900 SILVER, .5787 oz ASW

19	1931(a)	16.000	5.00	10.00	16.00	45.00

FEDERATED STATES

(French Union)

PIASTRE

COPPER-NICKEL
Security edge.

32.1	1946(a)	2.520	7.50	12.50	20.00	85.00
	1947(a)	.261	10.00	17.50	30.00	125.00

Reeded edge.

32.2	1947(a)	41.958	.50	1.00	2.00	6.00

NOTE: Similar coins dated 1946 w/rev. leg: INDOCHINE - FRANCAISE are Essais.

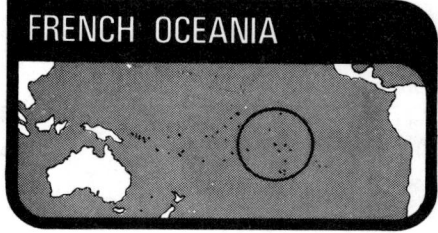

FRENCH OCEANIA

FRENCH POLYNESIA

The Colony of French Oceania (now the Territory of French Polynesia), comprising 130 basalt and coral islands scattered among five archipelagoes in the South Pacific, had an area of 1,544 sq. mi. (3,999 sq. km.). Capital: Papeete. The colony produced phosphates, copra and vanilla.

Tahiti of the Society Islands, the hub of French Oceania, was visited by Capt. Cook in 1769 and by Capt. Bligh in the Bounty 1788-89. The Society Islands were claimed by France in 1768, and in 1903 grouped with the Marquesas Islands, the Tuamotu Archipelago, the Gambier Islands and the Austral Islands under a single administrative head located at Papeete, Tahiti, to form the colony of French Oceania.

RULERS
French

MINT MARKS
(a) - Paris, privy marks only

MONETARY SYSTEM
100 Centimes = 1 Franc

50 CENTIMES

ALUMINUM

KM#	Date	Mintage	Fine	VF	XF	Unc
1	1949(a)	.795	.50	.75	1.50	3.50

FRANC

ALUMINUM

KM#	Date	Mintage	Fine	VF	XF	Unc
2	1949(a)	2.000	.20	.35	1.00	2.50

2 FRANCS

ALUMINUM

KM#	Date	Mintage	Fine	VF	XF	Unc
3	1949(a)	1.000	.40	.60	1.50	3.50

5 FRANCS

ALUMINUM

KM#	Date	Mintage	Fine	VF	XF	Unc
4	1952(a)	2.000	.50	.75	1.50	4.50

The Territory of French Polynesia (formerly French Oceania) has an area of 1,544 sq. mi. (3,941 sq. km.) and a population of 220,000. It is comprised of the same five archipelagoes that were grouped administratively to form French Oceania.

The colony of French Oceania became the Territory of French Polynesia by act of the French National Assembly in March, 1957. In Sept. of 1958 it voted in favor of the new constitution of the Fifth Republic, thereby electing to remain within the new French Community.

Picturesque, mountainous Tahiti, the setting of many tales of adventure and romance, is one of the most inspiringly beautiful islands in the world. Robert Louis Stevenson called it 'God's sweetest works'. It was there that Paul Gaugin, one of the pioneers of the Impressionist movement, painted the brilliant, exotic pictures that later made him famous. The arid coral atolls of Tuamotu comprise the most economically valuable area of French Polynesia. Pearl oysters thrive in the warm, limpid lagoons, and extensive portions of the atolls are valuable phosphate rock.

RULERS
French

MINT MARKS
(a) - Paris, privy marks only

MONETARY SYSTEM
100 Centimes = 1 Franc

50 CENTIMES

ALUMINUM

KM#	Date	Mintage	Fine	VF	XF	Unc
1	1965(a)	.895	.10	.25	.50	1.50

FRANC

ALUMINUM

	Date	Mintage	Fine	VF	XF	Unc
2	1965(a)	5.300	—	.10	.20	.75

Obv. leg: I.E.O.M. added.

	Date	Mintage	Fine	VF	XF	Unc
11	1975(a)	2.000	—	.10	.15	.45
	1977(a)	1.000	—	.10	.15	.45
	1979(a)	1.500	—	.10	.15	.45
	1981(a)	1.000	—	.10	.15	.45
	1982(a)	2.000	—	.10	.15	.45
	1983(a)	2.200	—	.10	.15	.45
	1984(a)	1.500	—	.10	.15	.45
	1985(a)	2.000	—	.10	.15	.45
	1986(a)	2.000	—	.10	.15	.45
	1987(a)	2.000	—	.10	.15	.45
	1989(a)	1.000	—	.10	.15	.45
	1990(a)	—	—	.10	.15	.45
	1991(a)	—	—	.10	.15	.35
	1992(a)	—	—	.10	.15	.35
	1993(a)	—	—	.10	.15	.35
	1994(a)	—	—	.10	.15	.35
	1995(a)	—	—	.10	.15	.35
	1996(a)	—	—	.10	.15	.35

2 FRANCS

ALUMINUM

KM#	Date	Mintage	Fine	VF	XF	Unc
3	1965(a)	2.250	—	.10	.25	1.00

Obv. leg: I.E.O.M. added.

	Date	Mintage	Fine	VF	XF	Unc
10	1973(a)	.400	—	.10	.25	.75
	1975(a)	1.000	—	.10	.25	.75
	1977(a)	1.000	—	.10	.25	.75
	1979(a)	2.000	—	.10	.25	.75
	1982(a)	1.000	—	.10	.25	.75
	1983(a)	1.500	—	.10	.25	.75
	1984(a)	1.200	—	.10	.25	.75
	1985(a)	1.400	—	.10	.25	.75
	1986(a)	1.500	—	.10	.25	.75
	1987(a)	1.000	—	.10	.25	.75
	1988(a)	.500	—	.10	.25	.75
	1989(a)	1.000	—	.10	.25	.75
	1990(a)	—	—	.10	.25	.75
	1991(a)	—	—	.10	.25	.60
	1992(a)	—	—	.10	.25	.60
	1993(a)	—	—	.10	.25	.60
	1995(a)	—	—	.10	.25	.60
	1996(a)	—	—	.10	.25	.60

5 FRANCS

ALUMINUM

	Date	Mintage	Fine	VF	XF	Unc
4	1965(a)	1.520	.10	.25	.50	1.75

Obv. leg: I.E.O.M. added.

	Date	Mintage	Fine	VF	XF	Unc
12	1975(a)	.500	.10	.20	.40	1.25
	1977(a)	.500	.10	.20	.40	1.25
	1979(a)	—	.10	.20	.40	1.25
	1982(a)	.500	.10	.20	.40	1.25
	1983(a)	.800	.10	.20	.40	1.25
	1984(a)	.600	.10	.20	.40	1.25
	1985(a)	—	.10	.20	.40	1.25
	1986(a)	.600	.10	.20	.40	1.25
	1987(a)	.400	.10	.20	.40	1.25
	1988(a)	.400	.10	.20	.40	1.25
	1989(a)	—	.10	.20	.40	1.25
	1990(a)	—	.10	.20	.40	1.25
	1991(a)	—	.10	.20	.40	1.00
	1993(a)	—	.10	.20	.40	1.00
	1994(a)	—	.10	.20	.40	1.00

10 FRANCS

NICKEL

KM#	Date	Mintage	Fine	VF	XF	Unc
5	1967(a)	1.000	.25	.50	.75	1.75

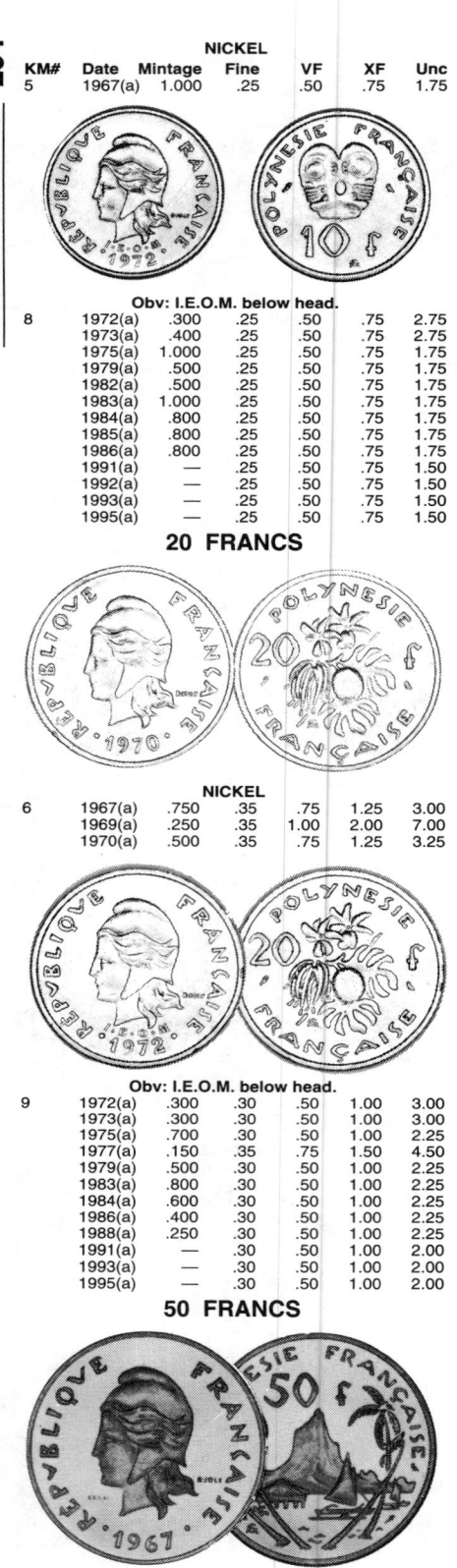

Obv: I.E.O.M. below head.

KM#	Date	Mintage	Fine	VF	XF	Unc
8	1972(a)	.300	.25	.50	.75	2.75
	1973(a)	.400	.25	.50	.75	2.75
	1975(a)	1.000	.25	.50	.75	1.75
	1979(a)	.500	.25	.50	.75	1.75
	1982(a)	.500	.25	.50	.75	1.75
	1983(a)	1.000	.25	.50	.75	1.75
	1984(a)	.800	.25	.50	.75	1.75
	1985(a)	.800	.25	.50	.75	1.75
	1986(a)	.800	.25	.50	.75	1.75
	1991(a)	—	.25	.50	.75	1.50
	1992(a)	—	.25	.50	.75	1.50
	1993(a)	—	.25	.50	.75	1.50
	1995(a)	—	.25	.50	.75	1.50

20 FRANCS

NICKEL

KM#	Date	Mintage	Fine	VF	XF	Unc
6	1967(a)	.750	.35	.75	1.25	3.00
	1969(a)	.250	.35	1.00	2.00	7.00
	1970(a)	.500	.35	.75	1.25	3.25

Obv: I.E.O.M. below head.

KM#	Date	Mintage	Fine	VF	XF	Unc
9	1972(a)	.300	.30	.50	1.00	3.00
	1973(a)	.300	.30	.50	1.00	3.00
	1975(a)	.700	.30	.50	1.00	2.25
	1977(a)	.150	.35	.75	1.50	4.50
	1979(a)	.500	.30	.50	1.00	2.25
	1983(a)	.800	.30	.50	1.00	2.25
	1984(a)	.600	.30	.50	1.00	2.25
	1986(a)	.400	.30	.50	1.00	2.25
	1988(a)	.250	.30	.50	1.00	2.25
	1991(a)	—	.30	.50	1.00	2.00
	1993(a)	—	.30	.50	1.00	2.00
	1995(a)	—	.30	.50	1.00	2.00

50 FRANCS

NICKEL

KM#	Date	Mintage	Fine	VF	XF	Unc
7	1967(a)	.600	.60	1.00	2.00	5.00

Obv: I.E.O.M. below head.

KM#	Date	Mintage	Fine	VF	XF	Unc
13	1975(a)	.500	.60	.80	1.25	4.00
	1979(a)	—	.60	.80	1.25	4.00
	1982(a)	.500	.60	.80	1.25	4.00
	1984(a)	.500	.60	.80	1.25	4.00
	1985(a)	Inc. Ab.	.60	.80	1.25	4.00
	1988(a)	.125	.60	.80	1.25	4.00
	1991(a)	—	.60	.80	1.25	4.00
	1993(a)	—	.60	.80	1.25	4.00
	1995(a)	—	.60	.80	1.25	4.00

100 FRANCS

NICKEL-BRONZE

KM#	Date	Mintage	Fine	VF	XF	Unc
14	1976(a)	2.000	1.20	1.50	2.00	4.00
	1979(a)	—	1.20	1.50	2.25	5.00
	1982(a)	1.000	1.20	1.50	2.25	5.00
	1984(a)	.500	1.20	1.50	2.25	5.00
	1986(a)	.400	1.20	1.50	2.25	5.00
	1987(a)	.500	1.20	1.50	2.25	5.00
	1988(a)	.500	1.20	1.50	2.25	5.00
	1991(a)	—	1.20	1.50	2.25	5.00
	1992(a)	—	1.20	1.50	2.25	5.00
	1995(a)	—	1.20	1.50	2.25	5.00

FRENCH WEST AFRICA

French West Africa (Afrique Occidentale Francaise), a former federation of French colonial territories on the northwest coast of Africa, had an area of 1,831,079 sq. mi. (4,742,495 sq. km.) and a population of about 17.4 million. Capital: Dakar. The constituent territories were Mauritania, Senegal, Dahomey, French Sudan, Ivory Coast, Upper Volta, Niger, French Guinea, and later on the mandated area of Togo. Peanuts, palm kernels, cacao, coffee and bananas were exported.

Prior to the mid-19th century, France, as the other European states, maintained establishments on the west coast of Africa for the purpose of trading in slaves and gum, but made no serious attempt at colonization. From 1854 onward, the coastal settlements were gradually extended into the interior until, by the opening of the 20th century, acquisition ended and organization and development began. French West Africa was formed in 1895 by grouping the several colonies under one administration (at Dakar) while retaining a large measure of autonomy to each of the constituent territories. The inhabitants of French West Africa were made French citizens in 1946. With the exception of French Guinea, all of the colonies voted in 1958 to become autonomous members of the new French Community. French Guinea voted to become the fully independent Republic of Guinea. The present-day independent states are members of the "Union Monetaire Ouest-Africaine".

For later coinage see West African States.

RULERS

French

MINT MARKS

(a) - Paris, privy marks only
(L) - London

MONETARY SYSTEM

100 Centimes = 1 Franc
5 Francs = 1 Unit

COLONIAL COINAGE
50 CENTIMES

ALUMINUM-BRONZE

KM#	Date	Mintage	Fine	VF	XF	Unc
1	1944(L)	10.000	2.00	4.00	10.00	25.00
	1944(L)	—	—	—	Proof	150.00

FRANC

ALUMINUM-BRONZE

KM#	Date	Mintage	Fine	VF	XF	Unc
2	1944(L)	15.000	1.00	2.00	5.00	20.00
	1944(L)	—	—	—	Proof	150.00

ALUMINUM
Rev: Rhim gazelle facing.

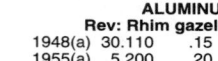

KM#	Date	Mintage	Fine	VF	XF	Unc
3	1948(a)	30.110	.15	.20	.35	1.00
	1955(a)	5.200	.20	.35	.50	1.50

2 FRANCS

ALUMINUM
Rev: Rhim gazelle facing.

KM#	Date	Mintage	Fine	VF	XF	Unc
4	1948(a)	12.665	.20	.30	.50	1.75
	1955(a)	1.400	.25	.40	.75	2.00

5 FRANCS

ALUMINUM-BRONZE
Rev: Rhim gazelle facing.

5	1956(a)	85.000	.35	.50	1.00	2.50

10 FRANCS

ALUMINUM-BRONZE
Rev: Rhim gazelle facing.

6	1956(a)	64.133	.50	1.00	1.50	3.50
8	1957(a)	30.000	.50	1.00	1.50	3.00

NOTE: Issued for circulation in French West Africa, including Togo.

25 FRANCS

ALUMINUM-BRONZE
Rev: Rhim gazelle facing.

7	1956(a)	37.877	.50	1.00	2.00	5.50

9	1957(a)	30.000	.50	1.00	2.00	5.00

NOTE: Issued for circulation in French West Africa, including Togo.

GABON

The Gabonese Republic, a member of the French Community, straddles the equator on the west coast of Africa. The hot and humid rain forest country has an area of 103,347 sq. mi. (267,670 sq. km.) and a population of 1.2 million, almost all of Bantu origin. Capital: Libreville. Extravagantly rich in resources, Gabon exports crude oil, manganese ore, gold and timbers.

Gabon was first visited by Portuguese navigator Diego Cam in the 15th century. Dutch, French and British traders, lured by the rich stands of hard woods and oil palms, quickly followed. The French founded their first settlement on the left bank of the Gabon River in 1839 and established their presence by signing treaties with the tribal chiefs. After gradually extending their influence into the interior during the last half of the 19th century, France occupied Gabon in 1885 and, in 1910, organized it as one of the four territories of French Equatorial Africa. It became an autonomous republic within the French Union in 1946, and on Aug. 17, 1960, became a completely independent republic within the new French Community.

For earlier coinage see French Equatorial Africa, Central African States and the Equatorial African States.

MINT MARKS
(a) - Paris, privy marks only

100 FRANCS

32.0000 g, .900 GOLD, .9260 oz AGW
Independence - President Mba

KM#	Date	Mintage	Fine	VF	XF	Unc
4	1960	500 pcs.	—	—	Proof	450.00

NICKEL

12	1971(a)	1.300	3.50	7.00	15.00	25.00
	1972(a)	2.000	3.50	7.00	15.00	25.00

13	1975(a)	—	2.00	4.00	7.50	15.00
	1977(a)	—	3.00	6.50	12.50	22.50
	1978(a)	—	2.50	4.50	9.00	17.50
	1982(a)	—	1.25	2.50	4.50	9.00

KM#	Date	Mintage	Fine	VF	XF	Unc
13	1983(a)	—	1.25	2.50	4.50	9.00
	1984(a)	—	1.00	2.00	4.00	8.00
	1985(a)	—	1.00	2.00	4.00	8.00

500 FRANCS

COPPER-NICKEL

14	1985(a)	—	3.00	5.00	8.00	16.00

GAMBIA

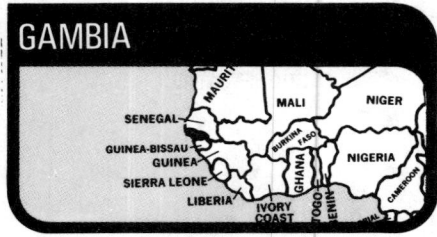

The Republic of The Gambia, an independent member of the British Commonwealth, occupies a strip of land 7 miles (11km.) to 20 miles (32 km.) wide and 200 miles (322 km.) long encompassing both sides of West Africa's Gambia River, and completely surrounded by Senegal. The republic, one of Africa's smallest countries, has an area of 4,127 sq. mi. (11,300 sq. km.) and a population of 989,273. Capital: Banjul. Agriculture and tourism are the principal industries. Peanuts constitute 95 per cent of export earnings.

The Gambia was once part of the great empires of Ghana and Songhay. When Portuguese gold seekers and slave traders visited The Gambia in the 15th century, it was part of the Kingdom of Mali. In 1588 the territory became, through purchase, the first British colony in Africa. English slavers established Fort James, the first settlement, on a small island a dozen miles up the Gambia River in 1664. After alternate periods of union with Sierra Leone and existence as a separate colony The Gambia became a British colony in 1888. On Feb. 18, 1965, The Gambia achieved independence as a constitutional monarchy within the Commonwealth of Nations, with Elizabeth II as Head of State as Queen of The Gambia. It became a republic on April 24, 1970, remaining a member of the Commonwealth, but with the president as Chief of State and Head of Government.

Together with Senegal, The Gambia formed a confederation on February 1, 1982. This confederation was officially dissolved on September 21, 1989. In July, 1994 a military junta took control of The Gambia and disbanded its elected government.

Gambia's 8 Shillings coin is a unique denomination in world coinage.

For earlier coinage see British West Africa.

RULERS
Elizabeth II, 1952-1970

MONETARY SYSTEM
12 Pence = 1 Shilling
4 Shillings = 1 Dirham
20 Shillings = 1 Pound

PENNY

BRONZE
Sailing Vessel

KM#	Date	Mintage	VF	XF	Unc
1	1966	3.600	.20	.40	1.00
	1966	6,600	—	Proof	1.00

3 PENCE

NICKEL-BRASS
Double Spurred Francolin

2	1966	2.000	.30	.50	1.50
	1966	6,600	—	Proof	1.50

6 PENCE

COPPER-NICKEL
Peanuts

3	1966	1.500	.30	.50	1.75
	1966	6,600	—	Proof	1.75

SHILLING

COPPER-NICKEL
Oil Palm

KM#	Date	Mintage	VF	XF	Unc
4	1966	2.500	.50	.80	2.00
	1966	6,600	—	Proof	2.00

2 SHILLINGS

COPPER-NICKEL
African Domestic Ox

5	1966	1.600	.75	1.50	2.50
	1966	6,600	—	Proof	2.50

4 SHILLINGS

COPPER-NICKEL
Slender-snouted Crocodile

6	1966	.800	1.50	2.50	5.50
	1966	6,600	—	Proof	5.50

8 SHILLINGS

COPPER-NICKEL
Hippopotamus

7	1970	.025	2.00	4.00	8.50

DECIMAL COINAGE
100 Bututs = 1 Dalasi

BUTUT

BRONZE
Peanuts

KM#	Date	Mintage	VF	XF	Unc
8	1971	12.449	—	.10	.20
	1971	.032	—	Proof	.50
	1973	3.000	—	.10	.25
	1974	—	—	.10	.25
	1975	—	—	.10	.25

F.A.O. Issue

14	1974	26.062	—	.10	.20
	1985	4.500	—	.15	.25

5 BUTUTS

BRONZE
Sailing Vessel

9	1971	5.400	—	.10	.35
	1971	.032	—	Proof	.50
	1977	1.506	—	.10	.35

10 BUTUTS

NICKEL-BRASS
Double Spurred Francolin

10	1971	3.000	.15	.35	1.25
	1971	.032	—	Proof	1.50
	1977	.750	.15	.35	1.25

25 BUTUTS

COPPER-NICKEL
Oil Palm

11	1971	3.040	.15	.30	.75
	1971	.032	—	Proof	1.25

50 BUTUTS

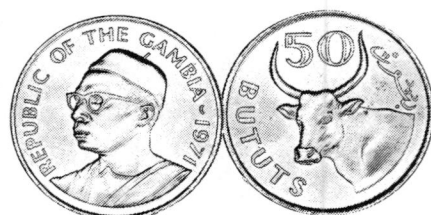

COPPER-NICKEL
African Domestic Ox

12	1971	1.700	.35	.65	1.50
	1971	.032	—	Proof	1.75

DALASI

COPPER-NICKEL
Slender-snouted Crocodile

KM#	Date	Mintage	VF	XF	Unc
13	1971	1.300	2.00	3.50	6.50
	1971	.032	—	Proof	5.00

KM#	Date	Mintage	VF	XF	Unc
29	1987	—	1.75	2.75	4.50

GEORGIA

Georgia (formerly the Georgian Social Democratic Republic under the U.S.S.R.), is bounded by the Black Sea to the west and by Turkey, Armenia and Azerbaijan. It occupies the western part of Transcaucasia covering an area of 26,900 sq. mi. (69,700 sq. km.) and a population of 5.7 million. Capitol: Tbilisi. Hydro-electricity, minerals, forestry and agriculture are the chief industries.

The Georgian dynasty first emerged after the Macedonian victory over the Achaemenid Persian empire in the 4th century B.C. Roman "friendship" was imposed in 65 B.C. after Pompey's victory over Mithradates. The Georgians embraced Christianity in the 4th century A.D. During the next three centuries Georgia was involved in the ongoing conflicts between the Byzantine and Persian empires. The latter developed control until Georgia regained its independence in 450-503 A.D. but then it reverted to a Persian province in 533 A.D., then restored as a kingdom by the Byzantines in 562 A.D. It was established as an Arab emirate in the 8th century. The Seljuk Turks invaded but the crusades thwarted their interests. Over the following centuries, Turkish and Persian rivalries along with civil strife divided the area under the two influences.

Through significant contributions of Georgian kings (King David the Builder 1089-1124 and King Tamara 1136-1224), Georgia reached its peak of political, economic, and military development from the XI - to the XIII century. During these centuries the significant architectural and literary masterpieces that had won international recognition were created. Georgia had also regained territories that had been invaded by Islamic countries.

Czarist Russian interests increased and a treaty of alliance was signed on July 24, 1773 whereby Russia guaranteed Georgian independence and it acknowledged Russian suzerainty. Persia invaded again in 1795 leaving Tiflis in ruins. Russia slowly took over annexing piece by piece and soon developed total domination. After the Russian Revolution the Georgians, Armenians, and Azerbaijanis formed the short-lived Transcaucasian Federal Republic on Sept. 20, 1917 which broke up into three independent republics on May 26, 1918. A Germano-Georgian treaty was signed on May 28, 1918, followed by a Turko-Georgian peace treaty on June 4. The end of WW I and the collapse of the central powers allowed free elections.

On May 20, 1920, Soviet Russia concluded a peace treaty, recognizing its independence, but later invaded on Feb. 11, 1921 and a soviet republic was proclaimed. On March 12, 1922 Stalin included Georgia in a newly formed Transcaucasian Soviet Federated Socialist Republic. On Dec. 5, 1936 the T.S.F.S.R. was dissolved and Georgia became a direct member of the U.S.S.R. The collapse of the U.S.S.R. allowed full transition to independence and on April 9, 1991 a unanimous vote declared the republic an independent state based on its original treaty of independence of May, 1918.

REPUBLIC

MONETARY SYSTEM

100 Thetri = 1 Lari

THETRI

STAINLESS STEEL

KM#	Date	Mintage	VF	XF	Unc
76	1993	—	—	—	.25

2 THETRI

STAINLESS STEEL

77	1993	—	—	—	.35

5 THETRI

STAINLESS STEEL

KM#	Date	Mintage	VF	XF	Unc
78	1993	—	—	—	.80

10 THETRI

STAINLESS STEEL

79	1993	—	—	—	1.25

20 THETRI

STAINLESS STEEL

80	1993	—	—	—	1.50

50 THETRI

BRASS

81	1993	—	—	—	2.00

GERMAN STATES

Although the origin of the German Empire can be traced to the Treaty of Verdun that ceded Charlemagne's lands east of the Rhine to German Prince Louis, it was for centuries little more than a geographic expression, consisting of hundreds of effectively autonomous big and little states. Nominally the states owed their allegiance to the Holy Roman Emperor, who was also a German king, but as the Emperors exhibited less and less concern for Germany the actual power devolved on the lords of the individual states. The fragmentation of the empire climaxed with the tragic denouement of the Thirty Years War, 1618-48, which devastated much of Germany, destroyed its agriculture and medieval commercial eminence and ended the attempt of the Hapsburgs to unify Germany. Deprived of administrative capacity by a lack of resources, the imperial authority became utterly powerless. At this time Germany contained an estimated 1,800 individual states, some with a population of as little as 300. The German Empire of recent history (the creation of Bismarck) was formed on April 14, 1871, when the king of Prussia became German Emperor William I. The new empire comprised 4 kingdoms, 6 grand duchies, 12 duchies and principalities, 3 free cities and the nonautonomous province of Alsace-Lorraine. The states had the right to issue gold and silver coins of higher value than 1 Mark; coins of 1 Mark and under were general issues of the empire.

MINT MARKS

A - Berlin, 1750-date
D - Munich (Germany) 1872-date
E - Muldenhutten (Germany) 1887-1953
F - Stuttgart (Germany) 1872-date
G - Karlsruhe (Germany) 1872-date
J - Hamburg (Germany) 1873-date

MONETARY SYSTEM

After the German unification in 1871 when the old Thaler system was abandoned in favor of the Mark system (100 Pfennig = 1 Mark) the Vereinsthaler continued to circulate as a legal tender 3 Mark coin, and the double Thaler as a 6 Mark coin until 1908. In 1908 the Vereinsthalers were officially demonetized and the Thaler coinage was replaced by the new 3 Mark coin which had the same specifications as the old Vereinsthaler. The double Thaler coinage was not replaced as there was no great demand for a 6 Mark coin. Until the 1930's the German public continued to refer to the 3 Mark piece as a "Thaler".

Commencing 1871
100 Pfennig = 1 Mark

ANHALT-DESSAU

Dessau was part of the 1252 division that included Zerbst and Cothen. In 1396 Zerbst divided into Zerbst and Dessau. In 1508 Zerbst was absorbed into Dessau. Dessau was given to the eldest son of Joachim Ernst in the division of 1603. As other lines became extinct, they fell to Dessau, which united all branches in 1863.

RULERS

Friedrich I, 1871-1904
Friedrich II, 1904-1918

2 MARK

11.1110 g, .900 SILVER, .3215 oz ASW
Friedrich II

KM#	Date	Mintage	Fine	VF	XF	Unc
27	1904A	.050	150.00	300.00	500.00	850.00
	1904A 150 pcs.	—	—	—	Proof	900.00

3 MARK

16.6670 g, .900 SILVER, .4823 oz ASW
Friedrich II

KM#	Date	Mintage	Fine	VF	XF	Unc
29	1909A	.100	50.00	100.00	175.00	275.00
	1911A	.100	50.00	100.00	175.00	275.00
	Common date	—	—		Proof	400.00

Silver Wedding Anniversary

30	1914A	.200	35.00	65.00	100.00	175.00
	1914A	1,000	—	—	Proof	275.00

5 MARK

27.7770 g, .900 SILVER, .8038 oz ASW
Silver Wedding Anniversary

31	1914A	.030	65.00	180.00	285.00	450.00
	1914A	1,000	—	—	Proof	600.00

10 MARK

3.9820 g, .900 GOLD, .1152 oz AGW
Friedrich I

25	1901A	.020	450.00	750.00	1000.	1500.
	1901A 200 pcs.	—	—	Proof	1600.

NOTE: Earlier date (1896) exists for this type.

20 MARK

7.9650 g, .900 GOLD, .2304 oz AGW
Friedrich I

26	1901A	.015	450.00	750.00	1100.	1400.
	1901A 200 pcs.	—	—	Proof	2000.

NOTE: Earlier date (1896) exists for this type.

Friedrich II

28	1904A	.025	450.00	750.00	1000.	1500.
	1904A 200 pcs.	—	—	Proof	2500.

BADEN

Located in southwest Germany. The ruling house of Baden began in 1112. Various branches developed and religious wars between the branches were settled in 1648. The branches unified under Baden-Durlach after the extinction of the Baden-Baden line in 1771. The last ruler abdicated at the end of World War I. The first coins were issued in the late 1300s.

DURLACH LINE

RULERS

Friedrich I as Prince Regent, 1852-1856
  As Grand Duke, 1856-1907
Friedrich II, 1907-1918

UNITED BADEN LINE

2 MARK

11.1110 g, .900 SILVER, .3215 oz ASW

KM#	Date	Mintage	Fine	VF	XF	Unc
269	1901G	.451	25.00	75.00	250.00	500.00
	1902G	5,368	250.00	750.00	1400.	2500.
	1902G	—	—	—	Proof	2250.

NOTE: Earlier dates (1892-1900) exist for this type.

50th Year of Reign

271	1902	.375	15.00	25.00	35.00	60.00

272	1902G	.198	25.00	60.00	120.00	300.00
	1903G	.494	20.00	45.00	110.00	200.00
	1904G	1.122	20.00	40.00	70.00	150.00
	1905G	.610	20.00	45.00	60.00	175.00
	1906G	.108	45.00	90.00	180.00	350.00
	1907G	.913	20.00	40.00	55.00	140.00

Golden Wedding Anniversary

276	1906	.350	15.00	30.00	40.00	65.00
	1906	—	—	—	Matte Proof	—

Death of Friedrich

278	1907	.350	20.00	40.00	50.00	80.00
	1907	—	—	—	Proof	150.00

Friedrich II

KM#	Date	Mintage	Fine	VF	XF	Unc
283	1911G	.080	125.00	300.00	425.00	750.00
	1913G	.140	100.00	225.00	375.00	650.00
	Common date	—	—	—	Proof	1000.

3 MARK

16.6670 g, .900 SILVER, .4823 oz ASW
Friedrich II

280	1908G	.300	10.00	22.00	35.00	65.00
	1909G	.760	10.00	22.00	35.00	65.00
	1910G	.670	10.00	22.00	35.00	65.00
	1911G	.380	10.00	22.00	35.00	65.00
	1912G	.840	10.00	22.00	35.00	60.00
	1914G	.410	10.00	22.00	30.00	55.00
	1915G	.170	20.00	60.00	90.00	140.00
	Common date	—	—	—	Proof	185.00

5 MARK

27.7770 g, .900 SILVER, .8038 oz ASW

268	1901G	.128	25.00	70.00	275.00	900.00
	1902G	.043	35.00	85.00	250.00	900.00
	Common date	—	—	—	Proof	900.00

NOTE: Earlier dates (1891-1900) exist for this type.

50th Year of Reign

273	1902	.050	40.00	90.00	150.00	200.00
	1902	—	—	—	Proof	625.00

KM#	Date	Mintage	Fine	VF	XF	Unc
274	1902G	.128	35.00	65.00	225.00	475.00
	1903G	.439	20.00	45.00	175.00	450.00
	1904G	.238	20.00	45.00	175.00	450.00
	1907G	.244	20.00	45.00	175.00	450.00
	Common date	—	—	—	Proof	400.00

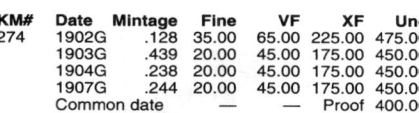

Golden Wedding Anniversary

277	1906	.060	50.00	100.00	150.00	200.00
	1906	—	—	—	Proof	275.00

Death of Friedrich

279	1907	.060	65.00	125.00	160.00	225.00
	1907	—	—	—	Proof	275.00

Friedrich II

281	1908G	.180	40.00	60.00	175.00	600.00
	1913G	.240	35.00	55.00	165.00	425.00
	Common date	—	—	—	Proof	525.00

10 MARK

3.9820 g, .900 GOLD, .1152 oz AGW
Friedrich I
Rev: Type III.

267	1901G	.091	125.00	165.00	225.00	325.00
	Common date	—	—	—	Proof	1300.

NOTE: Earlier dates (1890-1900) exist for this type.

275	1902G	.030	175.00	300.00	450.00	650.00
	1903G	.110	125.00	200.00	250.00	350.00
	1904G	.150	110.00	150.00	225.00	325.00
	1905G	.096	125.00	200.00	250.00	350.00
	1906G	.120	125.00	150.00	225.00	325.00
	1907G	.120	110.00	150.00	225.00	325.00
	Common date	—	—	—	Proof	1000.

Friedrich II

KM#	Date	Mintage	Fine	VF	XF	Unc
282	1909G	.086	225.00	500.00	650.00	850.00
	1910G	.061	225.00	500.00	650.00	850.00
	1911G	.029	2000.	4500.	6500.	8000.
	1912G	.026	700.00	1200.	2200.	3000.
	1913G	.042	500.00	800.00	1100.	1900.
	Common date	—	—	—	Proof	2000.

20 MARK

7.9650 g, .900 GOLD, .2304 oz AGW
Friedrich II

284	1911G	.190	125.00	150.00	200.00	300.00
	1912G	.310	125.00	140.00	200.00	300.00
	1913G	.085	125.00	150.00	225.00	325.00
	1914G	.280	125.00	150.00	200.00	300.00
	Common date	—	—	—	Proof	800.00

BAVARIA
(Bayern)

Located in south Germany. In 1180 the Duchy of Bavaria was given to the Count of Wittelsbach by the emperor. He is the ancestor of all who ruled in Bavaria until 1918. Primogeniture was proclaimed in 1506 and in 1623 the dukes of Bavaria were given the electoral right. Bavaria, which had been divided for the various heirs, was reunited in 1799. The title of king was granted to Bavaria in 1805.

RULERS

Otto, 1886-1913
  Prince Regent Luitpold, 1886-1912
Ludwig III, 1913-1918

MINT MARKS

M-Munich

2 MARK

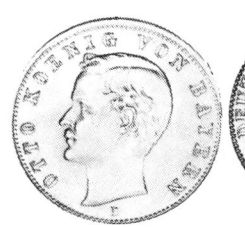 

11.1110 g, .900 SILVER, .3215 oz ASW
Obv: Closed curl.

511.1	1901D	.809	12.00	25.00	55.00	135.00
	1902D	1.321	10.00	22.00	45.00	120.00
	1903D	1.406	10.00	22.00	45.00	110.00
	1904D	2.320	10.00	22.00	45.00	110.00
	1905D	1.406	10.00	22.00	45.00	95.00
	1906D	1.055	10.00	22.00	55.00	120.00
	1907D	2.106	10.00	22.00	45.00	85.00
	1908D	.633	10.00	22.00	45.00	95.00
	1912D	.214	10.00	22.00	45.00	110.00
	1913D	.098	40.00	80.00	160.00	250.00

NOTE: Earlier dates (1891-1900) exist for this type.

90th Birthday of Prince Regent Luitpold

516	1911D	.640	12.00	20.00	30.00	50.00
	1911D	—	—	—	Proof	100.00

Ludwig III

KM#	Date	Mintage	Fine	VF	XF	Unc
519	1914D	.574	40.00	70.00	120.00	185.00

3 MARK

16.6670 g, .900 SILVER, .4823 oz ASW
Otto

515	1908D	.681	12.00	22.00	40.00	75.00
	1909D	1.827	12.00	22.00	40.00	75.00
	1910D	1.496	12.00	22.00	40.00	75.00
	1911D	.843	12.00	22.00	40.00	75.00
	1912D	1.014	12.00	22.00	40.00	75.00
	1913D	.731	12.00	22.00	40.00	75.00
	1913D	—	—	—	Proof	100.00

90th Birthday of Prince Regent Luitpold

517	1911D	.640	15.00	25.00	40.00	75.00
	1911D	—	—	—	Proof	100.00

Ludwig III

520	1914D	.717	17.50	35.00	55.00	100.00
	1914D	—	—	—	Proof	150.00

Golden Wedding Anniversary

523	1918D	130 pcs.	—	15,000.	28,000.	40,000.

5 MARK

27.7770 g, .900 SILVER, .8038 oz ASW
Obv: Closed curl.

KM#	Date	Mintage	Fine	VF	XF	Unc
512.1	1901D	.275	12.00	25.00	80.00	200.00
	1902D	.486	12.00	25.00	65.00	175.00
	1903D	1.012	12.00	25.00	65.00	175.00
	1904D	.548	20.00	40.00	70.00	185.00
	1906D	.070	35.00	75.00	200.00	400.00
	1907D	.753	12.00	20.00	55.00	135.00
	1908D	.537	12.00	20.00	55.00	135.00
	1913D	.420	12.00	20.00	45.00	100.00
	Common date—	—	—	Proof	400.00

NOTE: Earlier dates (1891-1900) exist for this type.

Obv: Open curl.

512.2	1901D	Inc. Ab.	15.00	30.00	70.00	180.00
	1902D	Inc. Ab.	15.00	30.00	70.00	180.00
	1906D	Inc. Ab.	35.00	75.00	200.00	400.00
	1907D	Inc. Ab.	15.00	25.00	55.00	140.00
	1908D	Inc. Ab.	15.00	25.00	55.00	140.00
	1913D	Inc. Ab.	15.00	25.00	50.00	110.00

NOTE: Earlier date (1898) exist for this type.

Obv: Many locks of hair above ear, closed curl.

512.3	1913D	Inc. Ab.	15.00	25.00	50.00	110.00

NOTE: Earlier dates (1891-1899) exist for this type.

Obv: Large lock of hair above ear, closed curl.

512.4	1901D	Inc. Ab.	15.00	30.00	80.00	200.00
	1902D	Inc. Ab.	15.00	30.00	65.00	185.00
	1903D	Inc. Ab.	15.00	30.00	65.00	185.00
	1904D	Inc. Ab.	20.00	40.00	70.00	185.00
	1906D	Inc. Ab.	35.00	75.00	200.00	400.00
	1907D	Inc. Ab.	15.00	25.00	55.00	140.00
	1908D	Inc. Ab.	15.00	25.00	55.00	140.00
	1913D	Inc. Ab.	15.00	25.00	50.00	110.00

NOTE: Earlier dates (1895-1900) exist for this type.

90th Birthday of Prince Regent Luitpold
Rev: Similar to KM#512.

518	1911D	.160	30.00	75.00	120.00	165.00
	1911D	—	—	—	Proof	200.00

Ludwig III
Rev: Similar to KM#512.

KM#	Date	Mintage	Fine	VF	XF	Unc
521	1914D	.142	40.00	85.00	150.00	200.00

10 MARK

3.9820 g, .900 GOLD, .1152 oz AGW
Obv. leg: . . . V. BAYERN

514	1901D	.141	65.00	125.00	200.00	300.00
	1902D	.068	65.00	125.00	200.00	300.00
	1903D	.534	65.00	120.00	180.00	250.00
	1904D	.211	65.00	120.00	180.00	250.00
	1905D	.281	65.00	120.00	180.00	250.00
	1906D	.141	65.00	125.00	190.00	250.00
	1907D	.211	65.00	120.00	190.00	250.00
	1909D	.209	65.00	120.00	190.00	250.00
	1910D	.141	65.00	120.00	190.00	250.00
	1911D	.072	65.00	125.00	200.00	300.00
	1912D	.141	65.00	125.00	190.00	250.00
	Common date	—	—	—	Proof	800.00

NOTE: Earlier date (1900) exists for this type.

20 MARK

Otto
Rev: Type III.

513	1905D	.501	125.00	140.00	160.00	250.00
	1905D	—	—	—	Proof	800.00
	1913D	*.311	—	17,500.	22,500.	25,000.
	1913D	—	—	—	Proof	35,000.

NOTE: Earlier dates (1895-1900) exist for this type.

Ludwig III

522	1914D	*.533	—	2000.	2500.	3000.
	1914D	—	—	—	Proof	3600.

*NOTE: Never officially released.

BREMEN

Located in northwest Germany. The city was founded c. 787 but was nominally under control of the archbishops until 1646 when it became a Free Imperial City. Bremen was granted the mint right in 1369 and there was practically continuous coinage until 1907.

FREE CITY
2 MARK

11.1110 g, .900 SILVER, .3215 oz ASW

250	1904J	.100	20.00	40.00	100.00	200.00
	1904J	200 pcs.	—	—	Proof	400.00

5 MARK

27.7770 g, .900 SILVER, .8038 oz ASW

KM#	Date	Mintage	Fine	VF	XF	Unc
251	1906J	.041	70.00	175.00	300.00	450.00
	1906J	600 pcs.	—	—	Proof	750.00

10 MARK

3.9820 g, .900 GOLD, .1152 oz AGW

253	1907J	.020	400.00	500.00	800.00	1250.
	1907J	—	—	—	Proof	1850.

20 MARK

7.9650 g, .900 GOLD, .2304 oz AGW

252	1906J	.020	400.00	550.00	900.00	1450.
	1906J	—	—	—	Proof	2650.

BRUNSWICK-WOLFENBUTTEL

Located in north-central Germany. Wolfenbuttel was annexed to Brunswick in 1257. The Wolfenbuttel line of the Brunswick house was founded in 1318 and was a fairly constant line until 1884 when Prussia installed a government that lasted until 1913. Brunswick was given to the Kaiser's son-in-law, who was the previous duke's grandson in 1913 and he was forced to abdicate in 1918.

RULERS

Prussian rule, 1884-1913
Ernst August, 1913-1918

3 MARK

16.6670 g, .900 SILVER, .4823 oz ASW
Ernst August Wedding and Accession

1161	1915A	1,700	600.00	1200.	2000.	3000.
	1915A	—	—	—	Proof	3200.

Obv. leg: U.LUNEB added.

1162	1915A	.032	50.00	110.00	175.00	300.00
	1915A	—	—	—	Proof	400.00

5 MARK

27.7770 g, .900 SILVER, .8038 oz ASW
Ernst August Wedding and Accession

KM#	Date	Mintage	Fine	VF	XF	Unc
1163	1915A	1,400	650.00	1250.	2150.	3200.
	1915A	—	—	—	Proof	3400.

Obv. leg: U.LUNEB added.
Rev: Similar to KM#1163.

1164	1915A	8,600	165.00	350.00	600.00	900.00
	1915A	—	—	—	Proof	950.00

HAMBURG

The city of Hamburg is located on the Elbe River about 75 miles from the North Sea. It was founded by Charlemagne in the 9th century. In 1241 it joined Lubeck to form the Hanseatic League. The mint right was leased to the citizens in 1292, however the first local hohlpfennings had been struck almost 50 years earlier. In 1510 Hamburg was formally made a Free City, though in fact it had been free for about 250 years. It was occupied by the French during the Napoleonic period. In 1866 it joined the North German Confederation and became a part of the German Empire in 1871. The Hamburg coinage is almost continuous up to the time of World War I.

2 MARK

11.1110 g, .900 SILVER, .3215 oz ASW

294	1901J	.482	12.50	20.00	50.00	150.00
	1902J	.779	12.50	20.00	50.00	125.00
	1903J	.817	12.50	20.00	40.00	125.00
	1904J	1.248	12.50	20.00	40.00	125.00
	1905J	.204	25.00	40.00	75.00	225.00
	1906J	1.225	12.50	20.00	40.00	125.00
	1907J	1.226	12.50	20.00	40.00	100.00
	1908J	.368	12.50	20.00	25.00	125.00
	1911J	.204	12.50	20.00	45.00	125.00
	1912J	.079	12.50	20.00	95.00	250.00
	1913J	.105	12.50	20.00	55.00	125.00
	1914J	.328	10.00	20.00	40.00	100.00
	Common date	—	—	Proof	275.00	

NOTE: Earlier dates (1892-1900) exist for this type.

3 MARK

16.6670 g, .900 SILVER, .4823 oz ASW

KM#	Date	Mintage	Fine	VF	XF	Unc
296	1908J	.408	15.00	30.00	40.00	65.00
	1909J	1.389	15.00	30.00	40.00	65.00
	1910J	.526	15.00	30.00	40.00	65.00
	1911J	.922	15.00	30.00	40.00	65.00
	1912J	.491	15.00	30.00	40.00	65.00
	1913J	.344	15.00	30.00	40.00	65.00
	1914J	.575	15.00	30.00	40.00	65.00
	Common date	—	—	Proof	200.00	

5 MARK

27.7770 g, .900 SILVER, .8038 oz ASW
Rev: Type II.

293	1901J	.172	17.50	40.00	100.00	300.00
	1902J	.294	17.50	35.00	80.00	250.00
	1903J	.588	17.50	35.00	75.00	160.00
	1904J	.319	15.00	32.00	75.00	175.00
	1907J	.326	15.00	32.00	75.00	175.00
	1908J	.458	15.00	32.00	75.00	160.00
	1913J	.327	15.00	32.00	60.00	140.00
	Common date	—	—	Proof	1500.	

NOTE: Earlier dates (1891-1900) exist for this type.

10 MARK

3.9820 g, .900 GOLD, .1152 oz AGW
Rev: Type II.

292	1901J	.082	70.00	110.00	160.00	300.00
	1902J	.041	150.00	250.00	350.00	450.00
	1903J	.310	65.00	110.00	160.00	250.00
	1905J	.164	65.00	110.00	160.00	250.00
	1906J	.164	65.00	110.00	160.00	250.00
	1907J	.111	65.00	110.00	160.00	250.00
	1908J	.032	150.00	250.00	350.00	450.00
	1909J	.122	65.00	110.00	160.00	250.00
	1909J	—	—	—	Proof	600.00
	1910J	.041	150.00	250.00	350.00	450.00
	1911J	.075	70.00	150.00	200.00	350.00
	1911J	—	—	—	Proof	600.00
	1912J	.048	150.00	250.00	350.00	450.00
	1912J	—	—	—	Proof	600.00
	1913J	.041	150.00	200.00	300.00	400.00
	1913J	—	—	—	Proof	600.00

NOTE: Earlier dates (1890-1900) exist for this type.

20 MARK

7.9650 g, .900 GOLD, .2304 oz AGW
Rev: Type III.

KM#	Date	Mintage	Fine	VF	XF	Unc
295	1908J	14 pcs.	—	—	Rare	—
	1913J	.491	115.00	130.00	150.00	200.00
	1913J	—	—	—	Proof	900.00

NOTE: Earlier dates (1893-1900) exist for this type.

HESSE-DARMSTADT

A state located in southwest Germany founded in 1567. The Landgrave was elevated to the status of Grand Duke in 1806. In 1815 the Congress of Vienna awarded Hesse-Darmstadt the cities of Mainz and Worms which were relinquished along with the newly acquired Hesse-Homburg, to the Prussians in 1866. It became part of the German Empire in 1871.

RULERS

Ernst Ludwig, 1892-1918

2 MARK

11.1110 g, .900 SILVER, .3215 oz ASW
400th Birthday of Philipp The Magnanimous

372	1904	.100	20.00	40.00	65.00	90.00
	1904	2,250	—	—	*Proof	135.00

*NOTE: Obverse matte, reverse polished.

3 MARK

16.6670 g, .900 SILVER, .4823 oz ASW

375	1910A	.200	30.00	60.00	95.00	165.00
	1910A	—	—	—	Proof	325.00

25 Year Jubilee

376	1917A	1,333	—	1750.	2500.	3250.
	1917A	Inc. Ab.	—	—	Proof	6000.

5 MARK

27.7770 g, .900 SILVER, .8038 oz ASW
400th Birthday of Philipp The Magnanimous

KM#	Date	Mintage	Fine	VF	XF	Unc
373	1904	.040	40.00	90.00	145.00	275.00
	1904	700 pcs.	—	—	*Proof	550.00

*NOTE: Obverse Matte, reverse polished.

20 MARK

7.9650 g, .900 GOLD, .2304 oz AGW

371	1901A	.080	125.00	175.00	325.00	500.00
	1901A	600 pcs.	—	—	Proof	1300.
	1903A	.040	125.00	175.00	350.00	750.00
	1903A	100 pcs.	—	—	Proof	1500.

NOTE: Earlier dates (1896-1900) exist for this type.

374	1905A	.045	125.00	200.00	300.00	500.00
	1905A	200 pcs.	—	—	Proof	1500.
	1906A	.085	125.00	175.00	275.00	425.00
	1906A	199 pcs.	—	—	Proof	1500.
	1908A	.040	125.00	175.00	275.00	450.00
	1911A	.150	125.00	175.00	300.00	450.00

LIPPE-DETMOLD

The Counts of Lippe ruled over a small state in northwestern Germany. In 1528/9 they became counts; in 1720 they were raised to the rank of princes, but did not use the title until 1789. Another branch of the family ruled the even smaller Schaumburg-Lippe. Lippe joined North German Confederation in 1866, and became part of the German Empire in 1871. When the insane Prince Alexander succeeded to the throne in 1895, the main branch reached an end, and a ten-year testamentary dispute between the Biesterfeld and the Schaumburg-Lippe lines followed - a Wilhelmine cause celebre. The Biesterfeld line gained the principality in 1905, but abdicated in 1918. In 1947 Lippe was absorbed by the German Land of North Rhine-Westphalia.

RULERS

Alexander, 1895 - 1905
Leopold IV, 1905 - 1918

MINT MARKS

A - Berlin, 1843-1918

2 MARK

11.1110 g, .900 SILVER, .3215 oz ASW

270	1906A	.020	100.00	200.00	300.00	450.00
	1906A	1,100	—	—	Proof	500.00

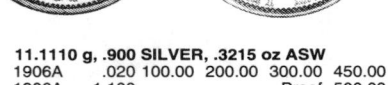

---

3 MARK

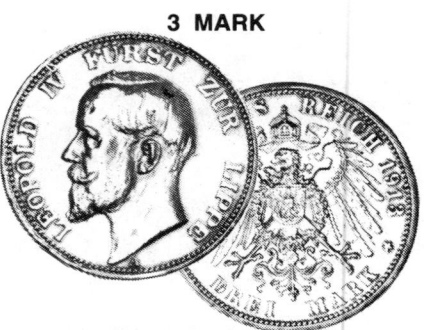

16.6670 g, .900 SILVER, .4823 oz ASW

KM#	Date	Mintage	Fine	VF	XF	Unc
275	1913A	.015	125.00	250.00	325.00	485.00
	1913A	100 pcs.	—	—	Proof	650.00

LUBECK

FREE CITY

Lubeck became a free city of the empire in 1188 and from c. 1190 into the 13th century an imperial mint existed in the town. It was granted the mint right in 1188, 1226 and 1340, but actually began its first civic coinage c. 1350. Occupied by the French during the Napoleonic Wars, it was restored as a free city in 1813 and became part of the German Empire in 1871.

2 MARK

11.1110 g, .900 SILVER, .3215 oz ASW

210	1901A	.025	100.00	175.00	225.00	350.00
	1901A	—	—	—	Proof	450.00

212	1904A	.025	45.00	75.00	130.00	185.00
	1904A	200 pcs.	—	—	Proof	275.00
	1905A	.025	45.00	75.00	130.00	225.00
	1905A	178 pcs.	—	—	Proof	275.00
	1906A	.025	45.00	75.00	130.00	225.00
	1906A	200 pcs.	—	—	Proof	275.00
	1907A	.025	45.00	75.00	130.00	225.00
	1911A	.025	45.00	75.00	130.00	225.00
	1911A	—	—	—	Proof	—
	1912A	.025	45.00	75.00	130.00	225.00
	1912A	—	—	—	Proof	—

3 MARK

16.6670 g, .900 SILVER, .4823 oz ASW

215	1908A	.033	25.00	70.00	125.00	190.00
	1909A	.033	25.00	70.00	125.00	190.00
	1910A	.033	25.00	70.00	125.00	190.00
	1911A	.033	25.00	70.00	125.00	190.00
	1912A	.034	25.00	70.00	125.00	190.00
	1913A	.030	25.00	70.00	125.00	190.00
	1914A	.010	35.00	85.00	150.00	225.00
	Common date					
		—	—	—	Proof	250.00

5 MARK

27.7770 g, .900 SILVER, .8038 oz ASW

KM#	Date	Mintage	Fine	VF	XF	Unc
213	1904A	.010	100.00	250.00	375.00	500.00
	1904A 200 pcs.	—	—	—	Proof	800.00
	1907A	.010	100.00	250.00	375.00	500.00
	1908A	.010	100.00	275.00	400.00	550.00
	1913A	6,000	100.00	275.00	400.00	600.00

10 MARK

3.9820 g, .900 GOLD, .1152 oz AGW

211	1901A	.010	300.00	500.00	800.00	1100.
	1901A 200 pcs.	—	—	—	Proof	1800.
	1904A	.010	300.00	500.00	800.00	1100.
	1904A 130 pcs.	—	—	—	Proof	1800.

214	1905A	.010	300.00	500.00	800.00	1100.
	1905A 247 pcs.	—	—	—	Proof	2250.
	1906A	.010	300.00	500.00	800.00	1100.
	1906A 216 pcs.	—	—	—	Proof	2250.
	1909A	.010	300.00	500.00	800.00	1100.
	1910A	.010	300.00	500.00	800.00	1100.

MECKLENBURG-SCHWERIN

The duchy of Mecklenburg was located along the Baltic coast between Holstein and Pomerania. Schwerin was annexed to Mecklenburg in 1357. During the Thirty Years' War, the dukes of Mecklenburg sided with the Protestant forces against the emperor. Albrecht von Wallenstein, the imperialist general, ousted the Mecklenburg dukes from their territories in 1628. They were restored to their lands in 1632. In 1658 the Mecklenburg dynasty was divided into two lines. No coinage was produced for Mecklenburg-Schwerin from 1708 until 1750. The 1815 Congress of Vienna elevated the duchy to the status of grand duchy and it became a part of the German Empire in 1871 until 1918 when the last grand duke abdicated.

RULERS
Friedrich Franz IV, 1897-1918

MINT MARKS
A - Berlin

2 MARK

11.1110 g, .900 SILVER, .3215 oz ASW
Coming of Age of Grand Duke

330	1901A	.050	125.00	300.00	450.00	1200.
(Y93)	1901A	1,000	—	—	Proof	1200.

Friedrich Franz IV Wedding

KM#	Date	Mintage	Fine	VF	XF	Unc
333	1904A	.100	15.00	35.00	65.00	100.00
(Y96)	1904A	6,000	—	—	Proof	175.00

3 MARK

16.6670 g, .900 SILVER, .4823 oz ASW
100 Years as Grand Duchy

340	1915A	.033	40.00	90.00	160.00	225.00
(Y98)	1915A		—	—	Proof	450.00

5 MARK

27.7770 g, .900 SILVER, .8038 oz ASW
Friedrich Franz IV Wedding

334	1904A	.040	35.00	100.00	175.00	250.00
(Y97)	1904A	2,500	—	—	Proof	500.00

100 Years as Grand Duchy

341	1915A	.010	125.00	250.00	425.00	750.00
(Y99)	1915A		—	—	Proof	900.00

10 MARK

3.9820 g, .900 GOLD, .1152 oz AGW
Coming of Age of Grand Duke
Rev: Type III.

331	1901A	.010	450.00	750.00	1200.	1750.
(Y94)	1901A	200 pcs.	—	—	Proof	1950.

20 MARK

7.9650 g, .900 GOLD, .2304 oz AGW
Coming of Age of Grand Duke
Rev: Type III.

KM#	Date	Mintage	Fine	VF	XF	Unc
332	1901A	5,000	900.00	1750.	2750.	4000.
(Y95)	1901A	200 pcs.	—	—	Proof	3250.

MECKLENBURG-STRELITZ

The duchy of Mecklenburg was located along the Baltic Coast between Holstein and Pomerania. The Strelitz line was founded in 1658 when the Mecklenburg line was divided into two lines. The 1815 Congress of Vienna elevated the duchy to the status of grand duchy. It became a part of the German Empire in 1871 until 1918 when the last grand duke died.

RULERS
Friedrich Wilhelm, 1860-1904
Adolph Friedrich V, 1904-1914
Adolph Friedrich VI, 1914-1918

2 MARK

11.1110 g, .900 SILVER, .3215 oz ASW

115	1905A	.010	135.00	300.00	575.00	750.00
(Y103)	1905A	2,500	—	—	Proof	750.00

3 MARK

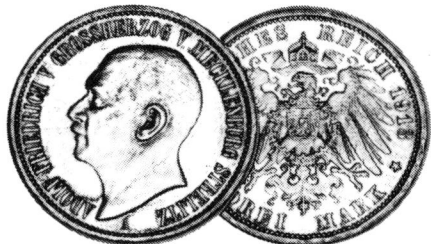

16.6670 g, .900 SILVER, .4823 oz ASW

120	1913A	7,000	200.00	400.00	800.00	1200.
(Y106)	1913A		—	—	Proof	1200.

10 MARK

3.9820 g, .900 GOLD, .1152 oz AGW

116	1905A	1,000	1500.	2250.	3000.	4500.
(Y104)	1905A	150 pcs.	—	—	Proof	3750.

20 MARK

7.9650 g, .900 GOLD, .2304 oz AGW
Rev: Type III.

117	1905A	1,000	2000.	3000.	5000.	6000.
(Y105)	1905A	160 pcs.	—	—	Proof	5500.

OLDENBURG

The county of Oldenburg was situated on the North Sea coast, to the east of the principality of East Friesland. It was originally part of the old duchy of Saxony and the first recorded lord ruled from the beginning of the 11th century. The first count was named in 1091 and had already acquired the county of Delmenhorst prior to that time. The first identifiable Oldenburg coinage was struck in the first half of the 13th century. Oldenburg was divided into Oldenburg and Delmenhorst in 1270, but the two lines were reunited by marriage five generations later. Through another marriage to the heiress of the duchy of Schleswig and county of Holstein, the royal house of Denmark descended through the Oldenburg line beginning in 1448, while a junior branch continued as counts of Oldenburg. The lordship of Jever was added to the county's domains in 1575. In 1667, the last count

died without a direct heir and Oldenburg reverted to Denmark until 1773. In the following year, Oldenburg was given to the bishop of Lubeck, of the Holstein-Gottorp line, and raised to the status of a duchy. Oldenburg was occupied several times during the Napoleonic Wars and became a grand duchy in 1829. In 1817, Oldenburg acquired the principality of Birkenfeld from Prussia and struck coins in denominations used there. World War I spelled the end of temporal power for the grand duke in 1918, but the title has continued up to the present time. Grand Duke Anton Gunther was born in 1923.

RULERS

Friedrich August, 1900-1918

2 MARK

11.1110 g, .900 SILVER, .3215 oz ASW

KM#	Date	Mintage	Fine	VF	XF	Unc
202	1901A	.075	85.00	200.00	450.00	850.00
(Y109)	1901A	260 pcs.	—	—	Proof	950.00

NOTE: Earlier date (1900) exists for this type.

5 MARK

27.7770 g, .900 SILVER, .8038 oz ASW

203	1901A	.010	250.00	700.00	1600.	3250.
(Y110)	1901A	170 pcs.	—	—	Proof	4000.

NOTE: Earlier date (1900) exists for this type.

PRUSSIA

The Kingdom of Prussia, located in north central Germany, came into being in 1701. The ruler received the title of King in Prussia in exchange for his support during the War of the Spanish Succession. During the Napoleonic Wars, Prussia allied itself with Saxony. When they were defeated in 1806 they were forced to cede a large portion of their territory. In 1813 the French were expelled and their territories were returned to them plus additional territories. After defeating Denmark and Austria, in 1864 and 1866 they acquired more territory. Prussia was the pivotal state of unification of Germany in 1871 and their King was proclaimed emperor of all Germany. World War I brought an end to the Empire and the Kingdom of Prussia in 1918.

RULERS

Wilhelm II, 1888-1918

2 MARK

11.1110 g, .900 SILVER, .3215 oz ASW
Mint mark: A

KM#	Date	Mintage	Fine	VF	XF	Unc
522	1901	.398	25.00	50.00	125.00	350.00
	1901	—	—	—	Proof	2500.
	1902	3.948	8.00	14.00	40.00	100.00
	1903	4.079	8.00	14.00	40.00	100.00
	1904A	9.981	8.00	14.00	40.00	100.00
	1905A	6.493	8.00	14.00	35.00	75.00
	1905A	620 pcs.	—	—	Proof	175.00
	1906A	4.019	8.00	14.00	30.00	65.00
	1906A	85 pcs.	—	—	Proof	175.00
	1907A	8.110	8.00	14.00	25.00	55.00
	1908A	2.389	8.00	14.00	30.00	85.00
	1911A	1.181	9.00	17.50	30.00	90.00
	1912A	.733	9.00	17.50	30.00	90.00

NOTE: Earlier dates (1891-1900) exist for this type.

200 Years Kingdom of Prussia

KM#	Date	Mintage	Fine	VF	XF	Unc
525	1901A	2.600	5.00	10.00	15.00	30.00
	1901A	—	—	—	Proof	70.00

100 Years Defeat of Napoleon

532	1913A	1.500	10.00	12.50	20.00	35.00
	1913A	—	—	—	Proof	60.00

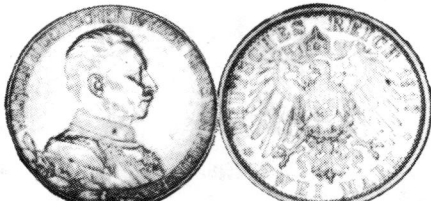

25th Year of Reign

533	1913A	1.500	10.00	12.50	17.50	32.00
	1913A	5,000	—	—	Proof	75.00

3 MARK

16.6670 g, .900 SILVER, .4823 oz ASW

527	1908A	2.859	7.00	12.50	20.00	45.00
	1909A	6.344	7.00	12.50	20.00	45.00
	1910A	5.591	7.00	12.50	20.00	45.00
	1911A	3.242	7.00	12.50	20.00	45.00
	1912A	4.626	7.00	12.50	20.00	45.00
	Common date	—	—	—	Proof	150.00

Berlin University

530	1910A	.200	17.50	35.00	65.00	90.00
	1910A	2,000	—	—	Proof	300.00

Breslau University

531	1911A	.400	12.50	27.50	50.00	75.00
	1911A	—	—	—	Proof	250.00

100 Years Defeat of Napoleon

KM#	Date	Mintage	Fine	VF	XF	Unc
534	1913A	2.000	9.00	14.00	25.00	38.00
	1913A	—	—	—	Proof	100.00

25th Year of Reign

535	1913A	2.000	9.00	14.00	25.00	38.00
	1913A	6,000	—	—	Proof	90.00

538	1914A	2.564	9.00	14.00	22.00	35.00
	1914A	—	—	—	Proof	75.00

Centenary Absorption of Mansfeld

539	1915A	.030	75.00	250.00	400.00	550.00
	1915A	—	—	—	Proof	700.00

5 MARK

27.7770 g, .900 SILVER, .8038 oz ASW
Rev: Type III.

KM#	Date	Mintage	Fine	VF	XF	Unc
523	1901A	.668	15.00	30.00	80.00	325.00
	1902A	1.951	15.00	25.00	70.00	225.00
	1903A	3.856	15.00	22.50	65.00	225.00
	1904A	2.060	15.00	22.50	65.00	225.00
	1906A	.231	20.00	35.00	90.00	300.00
	1907A	2.902	15.00	22.50	50.00	200.00
	1908A	2.231	15.00	22.50	50.00	200.00
	Common date	—	—		Proof	550.00

NOTE: Earlier dates (1891-1900) exist for this type.

200 Years Kingdom of Prussia

526	1901A	.460	22.50	37.50	60.00	95.00
	1901A	—	—		Proof	175.00

536	1913A	1.962	14.00	22.00	32.00	65.00
	1914A	1.587	16.00	24.00	34.00	70.00
	Common date	—	—		Proof	350.00

10 MARK

3.9820 g, .900 GOLD, .1152 oz AGW
Rev: Type III.

520	1901A	.702	55.00	95.00	120.00	200.00
	1901A	—	—		Proof	500.00
	1902A	.271	55.00	95.00	120.00	200.00
	1902A	—	—		Proof	500.00
	1903A	1.685	55.00	95.00	120.00	200.00
	1903A	—	—		Proof	500.00
	1904A	1.178	55.00	95.00	120.00	200.00
	1905A	1.063	55.00	95.00	120.00	200.00
	1905A 117 pcs.	—	—		Proof	500.00
	1906A	.542	55.00	95.00	120.00	175.00
	1906A 150 pcs.	—	—		Proof	500.00
	1907A	.813	55.00	95.00	120.00	175.00
	1907A	—	—		Proof	500.00
	1909A	.532	55.00	95.00	120.00	175.00
	1909A	—	—		Proof	500.00
	1910A	.803	55.00	95.00	120.00	175.00
	1911A	.271	55.00	95.00	120.00	200.00
	1911A	—	—		Proof	500.00
	1912A	.542	55.00	95.00	120.00	175.00
	1912A	—	—		Proof	500.00

NOTE: Earlier dates (1890-1900) exist for this type.

20 MARK

7.9650 g, .900 GOLD, .2304 oz AGW
Rev: Type III.

521	1901A	5.188	BV	115.00	125.00	145.00
	1901A	—	—		Proof	600.00
	1902A	4.138	BV	115.00	125.00	145.00
	1903A	2.870	BV	115.00	125.00	145.00
	1904A	3.453	BV	115.00	125.00	145.00

KM#	Date	Mintage	Fine	VF	XF	Unc
521	1905A	4.176	BV	115.00	125.00	145.00
	1905A 287 pcs.	—	—		Proof	600.00
	1905J	.921	BV	115.00	150.00	200.00
	1906A	7.788	BV	115.00	125.00	145.00
	1906A 124 pcs.	—	—		Proof	600.00
	1906J	.082	125.00	200.00	300.00	450.00
	1907A	2.576	BV	115.00	125.00	145.00
	1908A	3.274	BV	115.00	125.00	145.00
	1909A	5.213	BV	115.00	125.00	145.00
	1909J	.350	115.00	150.00	175.00	200.00
	1909J	—	—		Proof	800.00
	1910A	8.646	BV	115.00	125.00	145.00
	1910J	.753	BV	115.00	150.00	200.00
	1911A	4.746	BV	115.00	125.00	145.00
	1912A	5.569	BV	115.00	125.00	145.00
	1912J	.503	BV	115.00	150.00	200.00
	1913A	6.102	BV	115.00	125.00	145.00
	1913A	—	—		Proof	600.00

NOTE: Earlier dates (1890-1900) exist for this type.

537	1913A	6.102	BV	115.00	135.00	175.00
	1913A	—	—		Proof	1200.
	1914A	2.137	BV	115.00	135.00	175.00
	1914A	—	—		Proof	1200.
	1915A	1.271	750.00	1250.	2500.	3000.

REUSS

The Reuss family, whose lands were located in 1303. Upper and Lower Greiz lines were founded in 1535 and the territories were divided until 1768. In 1778 the ruler was made a prince of the Holy Roman Empire. The principality endured until 1918.

MINT MARKS

A - Berlin
B - Hannover

REUSS-OBERGREIZ

The other branch of the division of 1535, Obergreiz went through a number of consolidations and further divisions. Upon the extinction of the Ruess-Untergreiz line in 1768, the latter passed to Reuss-Obergreiz and this line continued on into the 20th century, obtaining the rank of count back in 1673 and that of prince in 1778.

RULERS

Heinrich XXII, 1859-1902
Heinrich XXIV, 1902-1918

2 MARK

11.1110 g, .900 SILVER, .3215 oz ASW

128	1901A	.010	100.00	200.00	400.00	550.00
	1901A	—	—		Proof	650.00

3 MARK

16.6670 g, .900 SILVER, .4823 oz ASW

130	1909A	.010	120.00	275.00	450.00	650.00
	1909A					
		400 pcs.	—	—	Proof	1150.

SAXE-ALTENBURG

A duchy, located in Thuringia in northwest Germany. It came into being in 1826 when Saxe-Gotha-Altenburg became extinct. The duke of Saxe-Hildburghausen ceded Hildburghausen to Meiningen in exchange for Saxe-Altenburg. The last duke abdicated in 1918.

RULERS

Ernst I, 1853-1908
Ernst II, 1908-1918

2 MARK

11.1110 g, .900 SILVER, .3215 oz ASW
Ernst 75th Birthday

Y#	Date	Mintage	Fine	VF	XF	Unc
144	1901A	.050	100.00	200.00	400.00	600.00
	1901A	500 pcs.	—	—	Proof	700.00

5 MARK

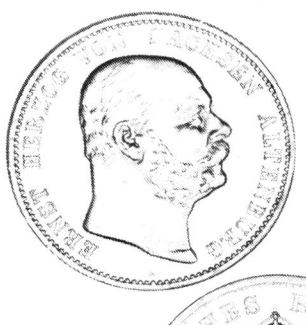

27.7770 g, .900 SILVER, .8038 oz ASW
Ernst 75th Birthday

145	1901A	.020	200.00	425.00	800.00	1200.
	1901A	500 pcs.	—	—	Proof	1250.

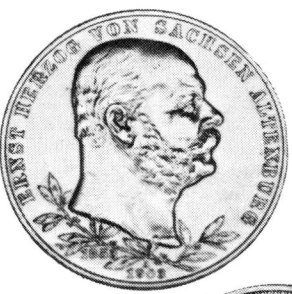

Ernst 50th Year of Reign

147	1903A	.020	100.00	200.00	300.00	425.00
	1903A	300 pcs.	—	—	Proof	500.00

SAXE-COBURG-GOTHA

Located in northwest Germany, Saxe-Coburg-Gotha was created for the duke of Saxe-Coburg-Saalfeld after the dispersal of Saalfeld and the acquisition of Gotha in 1826. The last duke abdicated in 1918.

RULERS

Karl Eduard, 1900-1918

2 MARK

11.1110 g, .900 SILVER, .3215 oz ASW

Y#	Date	Mintage	Fine	VF	XF	Unc
152	1905A	.010	125.00	275.00	600.00	950.00
	1905A	2,000	—	—	Proof	850.00
	1911A	100 pcs.	—	—	Proof	9000.

5 MARK

27.7770 g, .900 SILVER, .8038 oz ASW

153	1907A	.010	300.00	600.00	1000.	1500.
	1907A	—	—	—	Proof	1800.

10 MARK

3.9820 g, .900 GOLD, .1152 oz AGW

154	1905A	9,511	400.00	600.00	1000.	1400.
	1905A	489 pcs.	—	—	Proof	3500.

20 MARK

7.9650 g, .900 GOLD, .2304 oz AGW

155	1905A	.010	400.00	750.00	1200.	1800.
	1905A	484 pcs.	—	—	Proof	3750.

SAXE-MEININGEN

(Sachsen-Meiningen)

The duchy of Saxe-Meiningen was located in Thuringia, sandwiched between Saxe-Weimar-Eisenach on the west and north and the enclave of Schmalkalden belonging to Hesse-Cassel on the east. It was founded upon the division of the Ernestine line in Saxe-Gotha in 1680. In 1735, due to an exchange of some territory, the duchy became known as Saxe-Coburg-Meiningen. In 1826, Saxe-Coburg-Gotha assigned Saalfeld to Saxe-Meiningen. The duchy came under the strong influence of Prussia from 1866, when Bernhard II was forced to abdicate because of his support of Austria. The monarchy ended with the defeat of Germany in 1918.

RULERS
Georg II, 1866-1914
Bernhard III, 1914-1918

2 MARK

11.1110 g, .900 SILVER, .3215 oz ASW

75th Birthday of the Duke

KM#	Date	Mintage	Fine	VF	XF	Unc
196	1901D	.020	100.00	250.00	400.00	650.00

Obv: Long beard.

198	1902D	.020	225.00	750.00	1200.	2000.

Obv: Short beard.

199	1902D	I.A.	100.00	200.00	350.00	700.00
	1913D	5,000	150.00	250.00	450.00	650.00

Death of Georg II

206	1915	.030	35.00	60.00	140.00	200.00

3 MARK

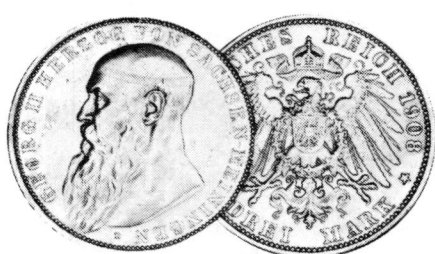

16.6670 g, .900 SILVER, .4823 oz ASW

203	1908D	.035	35.00	100.00	140.00	200.00
	1908D	—	—	—	Proof	200.00
	1913D	.020	35.00	100.00	140.00	200.00

Death of Georg II

207	1915	.030	30.00	75.00	150.00	200.00
	1915	—	—	—	Proof	225.00

5 MARK

27.7770 g, .900 SILVER, .8038 oz ASW
75th Birthday of the Duke

197	1901D	.020	85.00	225.00	425.00	750.00
	1901D	—	—	—	Proof	1200.

Obv: Long beard.

200	1902D	.020	60.00	175.00	325.00	550.00

Obv: Short beard.

KM#	Date	Mintage	Fine	VF	XF	Unc
201	1902D	I.A.	60.00	150.00	325.00	700.00
	1908D	.060	50.00	150.00	275.00	500.00

10 MARK

3.9820 g, .900 GOLD, .1152 oz AGW

202	1902D	2,000	600.00	1400.	2000.	3000.
	1902D	—	—	—	Proof	4250.
	1909D	2,000	600.00	1400.	2000.	3000.
	1909D	—	—	—	Proof	4250.
	1914D	1,002	800.00	1600.	2000.	3000.
	1914D	—	—	—	Proof	4250.

20 MARK

7.9650 g, .900 GOLD, .2304 oz AGW
Rev: Type III.

195	1905D	1,000	1500.	3000.	3500.	5500.
	1905D	—	—	—	Proof	11,000.

NOTE: Earlier date (1900) exists for this type.

205	1910D	1,004	1500.	3000.	3500.	5000.
	1910D	—	—	—	Proof	7000.
	1914D	1,000	1500.	3000.	3500.	5000.
	1914D	—	—	—	Proof	7000.

SAXE-WEIMAR-EISENACH

Saxe-Weimar-Eisenach was founded in 1644. It was raised to the status of a grand duchy in 1814. The last grand duke abdicated in 1918.

RULERS
Karl Alexander, 1853-1901

2 MARK

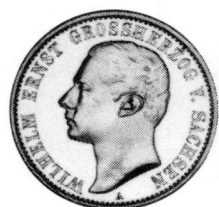 

11.1110 g, .900 SILVER, .3215 oz ASW
80th Birthday of the Grand Duke

Y#	Date	Mintage	Fine	VF	XF	Unc
170	1901A	.100	100.00	300.00	400.00	750.00
	1901A	—	—	—	Proof	800.00

Grand Duke's 1st Marriage

Y#	Date	Mintage	Fine	VF	XF	Unc
172	1903A	.040	35.00	60.00	100.00	140.00
	1903A	*1,000	—	—	Proof	180.00

Jena University 350th Anniversary

174	1908	.050	25.00	50.00	100.00	125.00

3 MARK

16.6670 g, .900 SILVER, .4823 oz ASW
Grand Duke's 2nd Marriage

176	1910A	.133	15.00	35.00	70.00	85.00
	1910A		—	—	Proof	125.00

Centenary of Grand Duchy

177	1915A	.050	25.00	75.00	125.00	175.00
	1915A	200 pcs.	—	—	Proof	400.00

5 MARK

27.7770 g, .900 SILVER, .8038 oz ASW
Grand Duke's 1st Marriage

173	1903A	.024	50.00	100.00	225.00	300.00
	1903A	*1,000	—	—	Proof	425.00

Jena University 350th Anniversary

Y#	Date	Mintage	Fine	VF	XF	Unc
175	1908	.040	60.00	100.00	180.00	220.00
	1908		—	—	Proof	625.00

20 MARK

7.9650 g, .900 GOLD, .2304 oz AGW

171	1901A	5,000	750.00	1500.	2000.	3000.
	1901A		—	—	Proof	4500.

NOTE: Earlier dates (1892-1896) exist for this type.

SAXONY

Saxony, located in southeast Germany was founded in 850. The first coinage was struck c. 990. It was divided into two lines in 1464. The electoral right was obtained by the elder line in 1547. During the time of the Reformation. Saxony was one of the more powerful states in central Europe. It became a kingdom in 1806. At the Congress of Vienna in 1815, they were forced to cede half its territories to Prussia.

RULERS

Albert, 1873-1902
Georg, 1902-1904
Friedrich August III, 1904-1918

MINT MARKS

L - Leipzig

Arms of Electoral Saxony

2-fold arms divided vertically, 2 crossed swords on left, opened crown curving diagonally from upper left to lower right on right side.

2 MARK

11.1110 g, .900 SILVER, .3215 oz ASW
Similar to KM#185.

KM#	Date	Mintage	Fine	VF	XF	Unc
1245	1901E	.440	12.50	55.00	100.00	200.00
(Y180a)	1902E	.543	10.00	55.00	100.00	175.00

NOTE: Earlier dates (1891-1900) exist for this type.

Death of Albert

1255	1902E	.168	15.00	40.00	65.00	90.00
(Y185)	1902E	250 pcs.	—	—	Proof	200.00

KM#	Date	Mintage	Fine	VF	XF	Unc
1257	1903E	.746	30.00	60.00	140.00	275.00
(Y187)	1903E	50 pcs.	—	—	Proof	450.00
	1904E	1.266	17.50	50.00	100.00	200.00

Death of Georg

1261	1904E	.150	15.00	35.00	60.00	90.00
(Y191)	1904E	55 pcs.	—	—	Proof	225.00

1263	1905E	.559	20.00	40.00	80.00	150.00
(Y193)	1905E	100 pcs.	—	—	Proof	200.00
	1906E	.559	20.00	40.00	80.00	150.00
	1907E	1.118	20.00	40.00	80.00	150.00
	1908E	.336	20.00	45.00	75.00	150.00
	1911E	.186	20.00	45.00	75.00	150.00
	1912E	.168	20.00	45.00	75.00	150.00
	1914E	.298	20.00	40.00	70.00	150.00
	Common date		—	—	Proof	225.00

500th Anniversary Leipzig University

1268	1909	.125	15.00	30.00	65.00	90.00
(Y198)	1909	300 pcs.	—	—	Proof	200.00

3 MARK

16.6670 g, .900 SILVER, .4823 oz ASW

1267	1908E	.276	10.00	25.00	40.00	60.00
(Y194)	1909E	1.197	10.00	25.00	30.00	50.00
	1910E	.745	10.00	25.00	30.00	50.00
	1911E	.581	10.00	25.00	30.00	50.00
	1912E	.379	10.00	25.00	30.00	50.00
	1913E	.307	10.00	25.00	30.00	50.00
	Common date		—	—	Proof	150.00

Battle of Leipzig Centennial

KM#	Date	Mintage	Fine	VF	XF	Unc
1275	1913E	1.000	15.00	20.00	35.00	45.00
(Y200)	1913E	.017	—	—	Proof	125.00

Jubilee of Reformation

1276	1917E	100 pcs.	—	Proof 27,500.	40,000.
(Y201)					

5 MARK

27.7770 g, .900 SILVER, .8038 oz ASW
Similar to KM#1256.

1246	1901E	.156	25.00	50.00	300.00	700.00
(Y181a)	1902E	.168	20.00	35.00	250.00	500.00

NOTE: Earlier dates (1891-1900) exist for this type.

Death of Albert

1256	1902E	.100	30.00	60.00	125.00	165.00
(Y186)	1902E	250 pcs.	—	—	Proof	425.00

1258	1903E	.536	20.00	40.00	125.00	450.00
(Y188)	1903E	50 pcs.	—	—	Proof	750.00
	1904E	.291	25.00	50.00	160.00	600.00
	1904E	—	—	—	Proof	850.00

Death of Georg

KM#	Date	Mintage	Fine	VF	XF	Unc
1262	1904E	.037	40.00	125.00	225.00	275.00
(Y192)	1904E	70 pcs.	—	—	Proof	400.00

1266	1907E	.398	20.00	40.00	90.00	150.00
(Y195)	1908E	.317	20.00	40.00	90.00	175.00
	1914E	.298	17.50	35.00	80.00	150.00

500th Anniversary Leipzig University

1269	1909	.050	40.00	90.00	175.00	235.00
(Y199)	1909	300 pcs.	—	—	Proof	525.00

10 MARK

3.9820 g, .900 GOLD, .1152 oz AGW
Rev: Type III.

1247	1901E	.075	80.00	125.00	150.00	275.00
(Y183a)	1902E	.037	80.00	125.00	150.00	325.00

NOTE: Earlier dates (1891-1900) exist for this type.

1259	1903E	.284	80.00	125.00	200.00	300.00
(Y189)	1903E	100 pcs.	—	—	Proof	1100.
	1904E	.149	80.00	125.00	200.00	300.00

KM#	Date	Mintage	Fine	VF	XF	Unc
1264	1905E	.112	70.00	125.00	150.00	275.00
(Y196)	1905E	100 pcs.	—	—	Proof	800.00
	1906E	.075	70.00	125.00	150.00	275.00
	1907E	.112	70.00	125.00	150.00	275.00
	1909E	.112	70.00	125.00	150.00	275.00
	1910E	.075	70.00	125.00	150.00	275.00
	1910E	—	—	—	Proof	850.00
	1911E	.038	70.00	125.00	150.00	325.00
	1912E	.075	70.00	125.00	150.00	300.00

20 MARK

7.9650 g, .900 GOLD, .2304 oz AGW
Rev: Type III.

1260	1903E	.250	120.00	150.00	225.00	350.00
(Y190)	1903E	—	—	—	Proof	1800.

1265	1905E	.500	115.00	125.00	150.00	250.00
(Y197)	1905E	86 pcs.	—	—	Proof	1100.
	1913E	.121	120.00	140.00	200.00	325.00
	1914E	.325	120.00	165.00	225.00	425.00

SCHAUMBURG-LIPPE

Located in northwest Germany, Schaumburg-Lippe was founded in 1640 when Schaumburg-Gehmen was divided between Hesse-Cassel and Lippe-Alverdissen. The two became known as Schaumburg-Hessen and Schaumburg-Lippe. They were elevated into a county independent of Lippe. Schaumburg-Lippe minted currency into the 20th century. The last prince died in 1911.

RULERS
Albrecht Georg, 1893-1911

2 MARK

11.1110 g, .900 SILVER, .3215 oz ASW
Similar to Y#206.

Y#	Date	Mintage	Fine	VF	XF	Unc
203	1904A	5,000	175.00	350.00	600.00	900.00
	1904A	200 pcs.	—	—	—	1100.

NOTE: Earlier date (1898) exists for this type.

3 MARK

16.6670 g, .900 SILVER, .4823 oz ASW
Death of Prince George

206	1911A	.050	30.00	75.00	110.00	175.00
	1911A	—	—	—	Proof	250.00

5 MARK

27.7770 g, .900 SILVER, .8038 oz ASW
Similar to Y#203.

Y#	Date	Mintage	Fine	VF	XF	Unc
204	1904A	3,000	350.00	800.00	1150.	1850.
	1904A	200 pcs.	—	—	Proof	2000.

NOTE: Earlier date (1898) exists for this type.

20 MARK

7.9650 g, .900 GOLD, .2304 oz AGW

205	1904A	5,500	600.00	1000.	1500.	2250.
	1904A	132 pcs.	—	—	Proof	4500.

NOTE: Earlier date (1898) exists for this type.

SCHWARZBURG-SONDERSHAUSEN

The Schwarzburg family held territory in central and northern Thuringia. After many divisions, two lines, Sondershausen and Rudolstadt were founded in 1552. The count of Sondershausen was raised to the rank of prince in 1709. The last prince died in 1909 and the lands passed to Rudolstadt.

RULERS

Karl Gunther, 1880-1909

2 MARK

11.1110 g, .900 SILVER, .3215 oz ASW
25th Anniversary of Reign
Struck w/thick rim.

211	1905	.013	45.00	80.00	175.00	200.00
	1905	5,000	—	—	Proof	250.00

Struck w/thin rim.

211a	1905	.062	25.00	40.00	95.00	125.00
	1905	5,000	—	—	Proof	150.00

3 MARK

16.6670 g, .900 SILVER, .4823 oz ASW
Death of Karl Gunther

212	1909A	.070	35.00	85.00	120.00	225.00
	1909A	—	—	—	Proof	300.00

WALDECK

The county of Waldeck was located on the border of Hesse. Their first coinage appeared ca. 1250. Pyrmont was united with Waldeck in 1625 but was ruled separately for a while in the 19th century. They were reunited in 1812. The rulers gained the status of prince in 1712. The administration was turned over to Prussia in 1867 but the princes retained some sovereignty until 1918.

WALDECK-PYRMONT

RULERS

Friedrich, 1893-1918

MINTMASTERS INITIALS

AW - Albert Welle
FW, F*w, W, .W. - Friedrich Welle

5 MARK

27.7770 g, .900 SILVER, .8038 oz ASW

Y#	Date	Mintage	Fine	VF	XF	Unc
213	1903A	2,000	700.00	1500.	2750.	4200.
	1903A	300 pcs.	—	—	Proof	5000.

20 MARK

7.9650 g, .900 GOLD, .2304 oz AGW

214	1903A	2,000	1000.	2000.	3000.	4500.
	1903A	150 pcs.	—	—	Proof	7000.

WURTTEMBERG

Located in South Germany, between Baden and Bavaria, Wurttemberg obtained the mint right in 1374. In 1495 the rulers became dukes. In 1802 the duke exchanged some of his land on the Rhine with France for territories nearer his capital city. Napoleon elevated the duke to the status of elector in 1803 and made him a king in 1806. The kingdom joined the German Empire in 1871 and endured until the king abdicated in 1918.

RULERS

Wilhelm II, 1891-1918

MINT MARKS

C, CT - Christophstal Mint
F - Freudenstadt Mint
S - Stuttgart Mint
T - Tubingen Mint

2 MARK

11.1110 g, .900 SILVER, .3215 oz ASW

KM#	Date	Mintage	Fine	VF	XF	Unc
631	1901F	.592	9.00	19.00	40.00	100.00
	1902F	.816	8.00	17.00	45.00	100.00
	1903F	.811	9.00	19.00	40.00	100.00
	1904F	1.988	8.00	17.00	35.00	90.00
	1905F	.250	9.00	21.00	35.00	90.00
	1906F	1.505	9.00	21.00	50.00	90.00
	1907F	1.504	8.00	15.00	30.00	90.00
	1908F	.451	8.00	22.00	40.00	100.00
	1912F	.251	8.00	16.00	35.00	90.00
	1913F	.226	8.00	17.00	40.00	100.00
	1914F	.318	8.00	17.00	45.00	100.00
	Common date		—	—	Proof	175.00

NOTE: Earlier dates (1892-1900) exist for this type.

3 MARK

16.6670 g, .900 SILVER, .4823 oz ASW

635	1908F	.300	10.00	20.00	30.00	55.00
	1909F	1.907	10.00	20.00	30.00	50.00
	1910F	.837	10.00	20.00	30.00	50.00
	1911F	.425	10.00	20.00	30.00	50.00
	1912F	.849	10.00	17.50	25.00	40.00
	1913F	.267	10.00	20.00	30.00	65.00
	1914F	.733	10.00	17.50	25.00	40.00
	Common date		—	—	Proof	175.00

Silver Wedding Anniversary
Obv: Normal bar in H of CHARLOTTE.

636	1911F	.493	12.50	20.00	50.00	60.00
	1911F	—	—	—	Proof	125.00

Obv: High bar in H of CHARLOTTE.

637	1911F	7,000	100.00	250.00	450.00	600.00

25th Year of Reign

638	1916F	1,000	—	—	Proof	4500.

NOTE: 650 pieces have been melted.

5 MARK

27.7770 g, .900 SILVER, .8038 oz ASW

KM#	Date	Mintage	Fine	VF	XF	Unc
632	1901F	.211	15.00	30.00	85.00	275.00
	1902F	.361	15.00	30.00	85.00	275.00
	1903F	.722	15.00	30.00	70.00	250.00
	1904F	.391	15.00	30.00	70.00	250.00
	1906F	.064	25.00	60.00	200.00	400.00
	1906F 50 pcs.	—	—	—	Proof	600.00
	1907F	.417	15.00	30.00	70.00	150.00
	1908F	.532	15.00	30.00	60.00	150.00
	1913F	.401	15.00	30.00	55.00	150.00
	Common date	—	—	—	Proof	300.00

NOTE: Earlier dates (1892-1900) exist for this type.

10 MARK

3.9820 g, .900 GOLD, .8038 oz AGW

KM#	Date	Mintage	Fine	VF	XF	Unc
633	1901F	.110	65.00	125.00	175.00	225.00
	1902F	.050	125.00	150.00	200.00	250.00
	1903F	.180	65.00	100.00	165.00	225.00
	1904F	.350	65.00	100.00	150.00	225.00
	1904F	—	—	—	Proof	800.00
	1905F	.200	65.00	100.00	150.00	225.00
	1905F	—	—	—	Proof	800.00
	1906F	.100	65.00	100.00	165.00	225.00
	1906F 50 pcs.	—	—	—	Proof	800.00
	1907F	.150	65.00	100.00	150.00	225.00
	1907F	—	—	—	Proof	800.00
	1909F	.100	65.00	125.00	150.00	225.00
	1909F	—	—	—	Proof	800.00
	1910F	.150	65.00	125.00	175.00	225.00
	1910F	—	—	—	Proof	800.00
	1911F	.050	140.00	275.00	425.00	550.00
	1911F	—	—	—	Proof	800.00
	1912F	.049	140.00	275.00	425.00	650.00
	1912F	—	—	—	Proof	800.00
	1913F	.050	140.00	275.00	425.00	550.00
	1913F	—	—	—	Proof	800.00

NOTE: Earlier dates (1893-1900) exist for this type.

20 MARK

7.9650 g, .900 GOLD, .2304 oz AGW
Rev: Type III.

KM#	Date	Mintage	Fine	VF	XF	Unc
634	1905F	.506	100.00	120.00	145.00	250.00
	1905F	—	—	—	Proof	500.00
	1913F	.043	4000.	8000.	12,500.	20,000.
	1913F	—	—	—	Proof	60,000.
	1914F	.558	3800.	7500.	12,000.	18,000.
	1914F	—	—	—	Proof	60,000.

NOTE: Earlier dates (1894-1900) exist for this type.

GERMANY

(map of Germany and neighboring countries)

1871-1918

Germany, a nation of north-central Europe which from 1871 to 1945 was, successively, an empire, a republic and a totalitarian state, attained its territorial peak as an empire when it comprised a 208,780 sq. mi. (540,740 sq. km.) homeland and an overseas colonial empire.

As the power of the Roman Empire waned, several war-like tribes residing in northern Germany moved south and west, invading France, Belgium, England, Italy and Spain. In 800 A.D. the Frankish king Charlemagne, who ruled most of France and Germany, was crowned Emperor of the Holy Roman Empire, a loose federation of an estimated 1,800 German States that lasted until 1806. Modern Germany was formed from the eastern part of Charlemagne's empire.

After 1812, the German States were reduced to a federation of 32, of which Prussia was the strongest. In 1871, Prussian chancellor Otto von Bismarck united the German states into an empire ruled by William I, the Prussian king. The empire initiated a colonial endeavor and became one of the world's greatest powers. Germany disintegrated as a result of World War I. It was reestablished as the Weimar Republic. The humiliation of defeat, economic depression, poverty and discontent gave rise to Adolf Hitler, 1933, who reconstituted Germany as the Third Reich and after initial diplomatic and military triumphs, expanded his goals beyond Europe into Africa and USSR which let it into final disaster in World War II, ending on VE Day, May 7, 1945.

RULERS
Wilhelm II, 1888-1918

MINT MARKS
A - Berlin
D - Munich
E - Muldenhutten (1887-1953)
F - Stuttgart
G - Karlsruhe
J - Hamburg

MONETARY SYSTEM
(Until 1923)
100 Pfennig = 1 Mark
(Commencing 1945)
100 Pfennig = 1 Mark

PFENNIG

COPPER

KM#	Date	Mintage	Fine	VF	XF	Unc
10	1901A	21.045	.10	.25	1.50	5.50
	1901D	5.337	.25	1.00	3.50	9.00
	1901E	1.397	1.00	6.00	9.00	22.00
	1901F	2.925	.25	2.50	5.00	12.00
	1901G	1.977	2.50	5.00	10.00	32.00
	1901J	2.011	3.00	10.00	15.00	36.00
	1902A	7.474	.50	5.00	10.00	16.00
	1902D	2.811	5.00	10.00	15.00	22.00
	1902E	1.183	5.00	10.00	9.00	22.00
	1902F	1.250	2.50	7.50	12.50	25.00
	1902G	.881	7.50	12.50	17.50	38.00
	1902J	150 pcs.	350.00	1250.	1650.	—
	1903A	12.690	.10	.50	1.50	7.50
	1903D	3.140	2.00	4.00	7.50	15.00
	1903E	1.956	2.00	4.00	7.50	15.00
	1903F	2.945	1.50	3.00	6.00	12.00
	1903G	1.377	2.50	10.00	15.00	28.00
	1903J	2.832	.10	.50	2.00	10.00
	1904A	28.625	.10	.25	1.50	6.00
	1904D	4.118	.10	.50	1.75	6.50
	1904E	2.778	.25	2.50	5.00	20.00
	1904F	4.520	.25	2.00	4.00	12.00
	1904G	3.232	.20	3.00	6.00	15.00
	1904J	4.467	.10	.50	1.75	6.00

KM#	Date	Mintage	Fine	VF	XF	Unc
10	1905A	19.631	.10	.25	1.50	5.00
	1905D	6.084	.10	.25	1.50	5.00
	1905E	3.564	.10	.50	1.50	5.50
	1905F	4.153	.10	.20	1.50	5.00
	1905G	3.051	.20	1.00	3.00	7.00
	1905J	4.085	.10	.20	1.50	5.00
	1906A	46.921	.10	.50	1.50	6.00
	1906D	5.633	.10	.50	1.50	6.00
	1906E	7.278	.10	.50	1.50	6.00
	1906F	7.173	.10	.50	1.50	6.00
	1906G	5.194	.10	.50	1.50	6.00
	1906J	3.622	.10	.50	1.50	6.00
	1907A	33.711	.10	.50	1.50	6.00
	1907D	14.691	.10	.50	1.50	6.00
	1907E	3.719	.10	.50	1.50	6.00
	1907F	7.026	.10	.20	1.50	6.00
	1907G	3.052	.10	.50	1.50	6.00
	1907J	6.722	.10	.50	1.50	6.00
	1908A	21.922	.10	.50	1.50	6.00
	1908D	10.629	.10	.50	1.50	6.00
	1908E	3.400	.10	.50	1.50	6.00
	1908F	6.112	.10	.20	1.50	6.00
	1908G	3.663	.10	.50	1.50	6.00
	1908J	5.581	.10	.50	1.50	6.00
	1909A	21.430	.10	.25	1.00	3.50
	1909D	2.814	.20	1.00	2.50	8.50
	1909E	2.562	1.50	4.00	6.00	12.00
	1909F	2.425	1.50	4.00	6.00	12.00
	1909G	1.220	1.50	4.00	7.50	17.50
	1909J	1.634	1.50	4.00	6.50	15.00
	1910A	10.761	.10	.50	1.50	6.00
	1910D	4.221	.10	.25	1.00	4.00
	1910E	1.600	.25	1.50	5.00	12.00
	1910F	3.009	.20	1.50	5.00	8.50
	1910G	1.834	.25	4.00	6.00	12.00
	1910J	2.450	.25	5.00	7.50	17.50
	1911A	38.172	.10	.50	1.50	5.00
	1911D	8.657	.10	.50	1.50	5.50
	1911E	5.236	.10	.50	1.50	6.00
	1911F	5.780	.10	.50	1.50	6.00
	1911G	2.075	.10	.50	1.50	6.00
	1911J	5.594	.10	.50	1.50	6.00
	1912A	42.693	.10	.50	1.50	5.00
	1912D	10.173	.10	.50	1.50	5.50
	1912E	5.689	.10	.50	1.50	6.00
	1912F	7.441	.10	.50	1.50	6.00
	1912G	5.526	.10	.50	1.50	6.00
	1912J	5.615	.10	.50	1.50	6.00
	1913A	32.671	.10	.50	1.50	5.00
	1913D	8.161	.10	.50	1.50	5.50
	1913E	2.258	1.50	4.00	7.50	17.50
	1913F	6.620	.10	.20	1.00	4.00
	1913G	3.209	.10	.50	1.50	6.00
	1913J	1.456	.50	5.00	10.00	25.00
	1914E	9.976	.10	.50	1.50	5.50
	1914D	1.842	.10	.50	1.50	6.00
	1914E	2.926	.20	1.00	2.00	7.00
	1914F	3.316	.10	.50	1.50	6.00
	1914G	2.100	.20	1.00	2.00	7.00
	1914J	4.368	.10	.50	1.50	5.50
	1915A	14.738	.10	.50	1.50	5.50
	1915D	1.771	.10	.25	2.50	7.00
	1915E	2.779	.20	1.50	3.50	8.50
	1915F	1.411	.20	1.50	3.50	11.50
	1915G	2.041	.20	1.50	4.00	10.00
	1915J	2.981	.20	1.50	3.50	8.50
	1916A	5.960	.10	.50	1.50	5.50
	1916D	5.401	.20	1.00	3.00	8.00
	1916E	.818	1.00	5.00	7.50	12.00
	1916F	1.104	.50	2.00	5.00	10.00
	1916G	.671	1.50	7.50	10.00	18.50
	1916J	.898	1.50	6.00	9.00	15.00
	Common date	—	—	—	Proof	75.00

NOTE: Earlier dates (1890-1900) exist for this type.

ALUMINUM

KM#	Date	Mintage	Fine	VF	XF	Unc
24	1916G	—	125.00	225.00	350.00	550.00
	1917A	27.159	.15	.50	2.00	5.00
	1917A	—	—	—	Proof	40.00
	1917D	6.940	.15	.50	2.00	6.00
	1917E	3.862	.50	2.00	4.50	8.00
	1917E	—	—	—	Proof	40.00
	1917F	5.125	.25	2.00	4.00	7.00
	1917G	3.139	.25	2.00	4.50	8.00
	1917G	—	—	—	Proof	40.00
	1917J	4.182	.25	2.00	4.00	8.00
	1917J	—	—	—	Proof	40.00
	1918A	—	150.00	300.00	500.00	900.00
	1918D	.318	10.00	20.00	27.50	40.00
	Common date	—	—	—	Proof	90.00

2 PFENNIG

COPPER

KM#	Date	Mintage	Fine	VF	XF	Unc
16	1904A	5.414	.10	.25	2.00	15.00
	1904D	1.404	.10	.50	2.50	18.00
	1904E	.744	2.00	6.00	12.50	37.50
	1904F	1.002	.10	1.00	4.50	20.00
	1904G	.495	2.00	6.00	12.50	37.50
	1904J	.044	4.00	10.00	35.00	70.00
	1905A	5.172	.10	.25	2.00	8.00
	1905D	1.570	.10	.50	2.50	9.00
	1905E	.924	.10	1.00	4.00	16.50
	1905F	1.115	.10	1.00	3.00	9.00
	1905G	1.030	.10	1.00	3.50	16.50
	1905J	1.609	.10	1.00	3.50	16.50
	1906A	8.459	.10	.25	2.00	8.00
	1906D	3.539	.10	.25	2.00	8.00
	1906E	2.055	.10	.25	2.00	8.00
	1906F	2.840	.10	.25	2.00	8.00
	1906G	1.527	.10	.25	2.00	8.00
	1906J	1.908	.10	.25	2.00	8.00
	1907A	13.468	.10	.25	2.00	8.00
	1907D	1.921	.10	.25	2.00	8.00
	1907E	.744	.25	2.00	6.00	20.00
	1907F	1.059	.10	.50	2.00	8.00
	1907G	.610	.25	1.00	3.50	8.00
	1907J	.952	.10	.50	2.00	8.00
	1908A	5.421	.10	.25	2.00	8.00
	1908D	1.407	.10	.50	2.00	8.00
	1908E	.745	1.00	5.00	8.00	22.00
	1908F	1.003	.10	.50	2.50	9.00
	1908G	.610	.25	1.00	4.50	9.00
	1908J	.817	.10	.50	3.00	16.50
	1910A	5.421	.10	.25	2.00	8.00
	1910D	1.407	.10	.50	2.00	8.00
	1910E	.745	.25	4.00	7.00	16.50
	1910F	1.003	.25	1.50	4.50	9.00
	1910G	.517	.25	1.50	5.50	16.50
	1910J	.568	.25	1.00	4.00	14.00
	1911A	8.187	.10	1.00	3.00	8.00
	1911D	2.100	.10	.50	3.00	8.00
	1911E	1.133	.10	.50	3.50	8.00
	1911F	1.490	.10	.50	3.50	8.00
	1911G	1.313	.10	.50	3.50	8.00
	1911J	1.883	.10	.50	3.00	8.00
	1912A	13.580	.10	.25	2.00	8.00
	1912D	3.109	.10	.50	2.50	8.00
	1912E	1.808	.10	1.00	3.50	8.00
	1912F	2.366	.10	.50	2.50	8.00
	1912G	1.395	.10	.50	3.00	8.00
	1912J	1.605	.10	.50	3.00	8.00
	1913A	4.212	.10	.25	2.00	8.00
	1913D	2.525	.10	.50	2.00	8.00
	1913E	.413	3.00	15.00	22.00	40.00
	1913F	1.602	.10	.50	2.50	8.00
	1913G	.741	.25	1.00	3.50	8.00
	1913J	1.254	.10	.50	2.00	8.00
	1914A	5.350	.10	.25	2.00	8.00
	1914E	1.201	1.00	3.50	9.00	22.00
	1914F	.158	12.00	45.00	85.00	175.00
	1914G	.610	2.00	6.00	17.50	32.50
	1914J	.817	.10	1.00	3.50	9.00
	1915A	3.897	.10	1.00	3.50	8.00
	1915D	1.407	.10	1.00	2.50	8.00
	1915E	.288	5.00	15.00	28.00	55.00
	1915F	.904	.10	.25	2.00	8.00
	1916A	3.524	.10	1.00	3.50	8.00
	1916D	.915	.25	1.00	2.50	8.00
	1916E	.484	1.00	2.50	6.50	16.50
	1916F	.651	.25	1.00	4.50	9.00
	1916G	.397	.50	2.50	6.50	20.00
	1916J	.531	.50	2.50	6.50	20.00
	Common date		—	—	Proof	85.00

5 PFENNIG

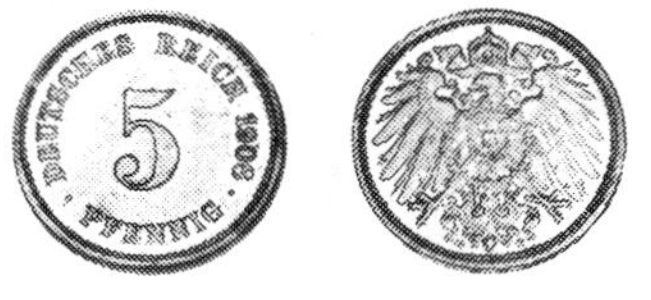

COPPER-NICKEL

KM#	Date	Mintage	Fine	VF	XF	Unc
11	1901A	8.155	.10	.30	2.00	9.00
	1901D	2.779	.10	.30	2.25	11.50
	1901E	1.492	.10	.50	2.25	12.50
	1901F	1.810	.10	.30	2.00	11.50
	1901G	.915	.10	.50	2.25	11.50
	1901J	1.226	.10	.30	2.00	11.50
	1902A	8.949	.10	.30	2.00	9.00
	1902D	2.812	.10	.30	2.00	12.50
	1902E	1.120	.10	.50	2.75	14.50
	1902F	1.800	.10	.50	2.75	14.50
	1902G	1.220	.10	.50	3.50	17.50
	1902J	1.636	.10	.25	2.25	12.50
	1903A	5.932	.10	.30	2.00	9.00
	1903D	1.406	.10	.50	2.75	10.00
	1903E	1.114	.10	1.00	4.00	12.50
	1903F	1.209	.10	.50	4.00	12.50
	1903G	.610	.10	1.50	5.00	15.00
	1903J	.817	.10	1.00	4.00	12.50
	1904A	6.791	.10	.30	2.00	9.00
	1904D	1.408	.10	.50	2.25	12.50
	1904E	.746	.10	1.50	4.00	12.50
	1904F	1.006	.10	.50	2.75	12.50
	1904G	.610	.10	1.00	3.00	14.00
	1904J	.818	.10	.50	2.75	14.00
	1905A	8.129	.10	.20	.75	8.50
	1905D	2.109	.10	.20	.75	8.50
	1905E	1.117	.10	.20	.75	8.50
	1905F	1.505	.10	.20	.75	8.50
	1905G	.915	.10	.50	2.50	10.00
	1905J	1.226	.10	.20	.75	8.50
	1906A	18.970	.10	.20	.50	7.00
	1906D	4.922	.10	.20	.50	7.50
	1906E	2.605	.10	.20	.50	7.50
	1906F	3.512	.10	.20	.50	7.50
	1906G	2.136	.10	.25	1.00	9.00
	1906J	2.859	.10	.20	.50	7.50
	1907A	11.930	.10	.20	.50	7.00
	1907D	2.113	.10	.20	.50	7.50
	1907E	1.517	.10	.25	1.00	9.00
	1907F	1.845	.10	.20	.50	7.50
	1907G	.915	.10	.50	1.00	9.00
	1907J	1.636	.10	.20	.50	7.50
	1908A	22.114	.10	.20	.50	6.50
	1908D	4.991	.10	.20	.50	7.00
	1908E	2.919	.10	.20	.50	8.00
	1908/7F	5.124	30.00	60.00	80.00	150.00
	1908F	Inc. Ab.	.10	.20	.50	7.50
	1908/108G	3.357	—	—	—	—
	1908G	Inc. Ab.	.10	.15	.50	7.00
	1908J	3.264	.10	.20	.50	6.00
	1909A	5.797	.10	.30	2.00	8.00
	1909D	2.753	.10	.50	2.50	9.00
	1909E	.984	.25	2.50	5.00	15.00
	1909F	.252	2.00	5.00	7.50	20.00
	1909/8J	1.632	1.00	5.00	15.00	45.00
	1909J	Inc. Ab.	.10	2.50	5.00	15.00
	1910A	7.344	.10	.20	1.00	6.50
	1910D	2.814	.10	.20	.50	8.50
	1910E	1.290	.10	.50	2.00	12.00
	1910F	1.721	.10	.20	.50	8.50
	1910G	1.222	.10	.20	.50	8.50
	1910J	.152	10.00	42.50	70.00	140.00
	1911A	15.660	.10	.15	.50	6.50
	1911D	2.221	.10	.20	.50	7.00
	1911E	1.770	.10	.20	.50	7.00
	1911F	2.714	.10	.20	.50	7.00
	1911G	1.833	.10	.20	1.00	7.00
	1911J	3.116	.10	.15	.50	7.00
	1912A	19.320	.10	.15	.50	6.50
	1912D	4.015	.10	.20	.50	7.00
	1912E	2.568	.10	.20	.50	7.00
	1912F	3.679	.10	.15	.50	7.00
	1912G	2.440	.10	.20	.50	7.00
	1912J	3.020	.10	.15	.50	7.00
	1913A	15.506	.10	.15	.50	6.50
	1913D	5.519	.10	.20	.50	7.00
	1913E	2.373	.10	.20	.50	9.00
	1913F	2.054	.10	.20	.50	6.00
	1913G	1.221	.10	.20	.50	6.00
	1913J	.253	5.00	12.50	17.50	30.00
	1914A	23.605	.10	.15	.50	6.00
	1914D	3.014	.10	.20	.50	6.00
	1914E	1.710	.10	.20	.50	6.00
	1914F	2.206	.10	.20	.50	6.00
	1914G	1.218	.10	.20	.50	6.00
	1914J	3.235	.10	.15	.50	6.00
	1915D	3.516	.10	.50	2.00	7.00
	1915E	.834	1.00	6.00	8.00	15.00
	1915F	1.894	.10	.50	2.00	6.00
	1915G	.894	.50	5.00	6.50	10.00
	1915J	1.669	.10	.50	3.50	10.00
	1915	—	1.00	5.00	12.50	25.00
	Common date		—	—	Proof	80.00

NOTE: Earlier dates (1890-1900) exist for this type.

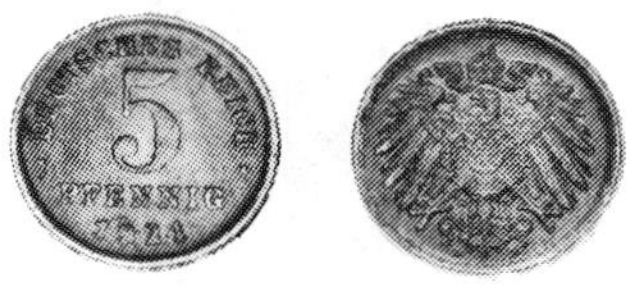

IRON

KM#	Date	Mintage	Fine	VF	XF	Unc
19	1915A	34.631	.10	.25	2.00	9.00
	1915D	2.021	.50	7.50	12.50	22.00
	1915E	4.670	.50	5.00	10.00	22.00
	1915F	3.500	.25	2.50	7.50	17.50
	1915G	3.676	.25	2.00	5.00	15.00
	1915J	2.100	.25	2.00	5.00	15.00
	1916A	51.003	.10	.25	1.50	10.00
	1916D	19.590	.10	.50	1.50	10.00
	1916E	2.271	1.00	10.00	15.00	25.00
	1916F	10.479	.15	1.00	2.00	10.00
	1916G	5.599	.25	1.50	3.50	15.00
	1916J	10.253	.25	3.00	7.50	17.50
	1917A	87.315	.10	.50	1.00	9.00
	1917D	19.581	.10	.50	1.00	9.00
	1917E	11.092	.50	5.00	7.50	12.00
	1917F	10.930	.10	.50	2.00	10.00
	1917F mule w/Polish rev. of Y#5, see Poland					
	1917G	6.720	.25	3.00	6.00	12.00
	1917J	11.686	.25	2.00	5.00	12.00
	1918A	223.516	.10	.50	1.00	8.00
	1918D	29.130	.10	.50	1.00	8.00
	1918E	23.600	.25	1.00	6.00	15.00
	1918F	24.598	.10	.25	1.00	8.00
	1918G	12.697	.10	.50	1.00	8.00
	1918J	20.240	.10	.50	1.00	8.00
	1919A	112.102	.10	.20	.50	7.00
	1919D	41.163	.10	.25	1.00	8.00
	1919E	20.608	.25	3.00	6.00	15.00
	1919F	32.700	.10	.25	1.00	8.00
	1919G	13.925	.10	.50	2.50	12.00
	1919J	16.249	.15	1.00	2.00	9.00
	1920A	80.300	.10	.20	.50	7.00
	1920D	25.502	.10	.50	1.00	8.00
	1920E	11.646	.25	2.50	8.00	25.00
	1920F	24.300	.10	.25	1.00	8.00
	1920G	10.244	.20	2.00	3.50	15.00
	1920J	16.857	.10	.20	1.00	8.00
	1921A	143.418	.10	.20	.50	7.00
	1921D	38.133	.10	.25	1.00	8.00
	1921E	21.104	2.50	5.00	10.00	20.00
	1921F	24.800	.10	.25	1.00	8.00
	1921G	21.289	.10	.25	1.00	8.00
	1921J	28.928	.15	1.00	3.00	12.00
	1922A	89.062	—	—	Rare	—
	1922D	31.240	.10	.25	1.00	8.00
	1922E	19.156	2.50	5.00	10.00	20.00
	1922F	16.436	.10	.25	1.00	8.00
	1922G	19.708	.10	.25	1.00	8.00
	1922J	16.820	.25	2.50	6.00	15.00
	Common date		—	—	Proof	70.00

10 PFENNIG

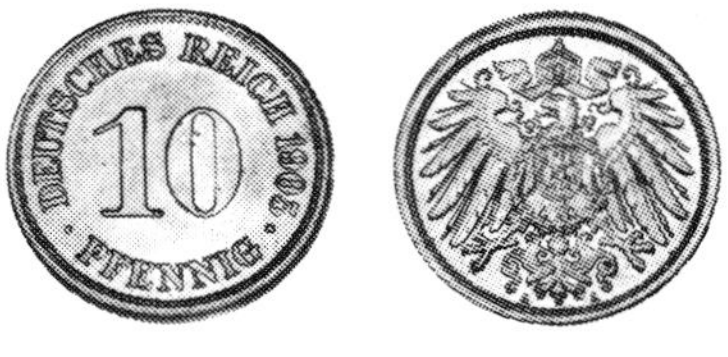

COPPER-NICKEL

KM#	Date	Mintage	Fine	VF	XF	Unc
12	1901A	10.200	.10	.25	1.00	7.00
	1901D	3.259	.10	.25	1.00	12.00
	1901E	1.863	.10	.30	1.00	12.00
	1901F	2.594	.10	.25	1.00	12.00
	1901G	1.527	.10	.25	1.00	12.00
	1901J	1.225	.10	.25	1.00	12.00
	1902A	5.878	.10	.25	1.00	6.00
	1902D	1.406	.10	.25	1.00	12.00
	1902E	.502	.25	3.00	6.00	15.00
	1902F	1.003	.10	.25	1.00	14.00
	1902G	.610	.25	1.50	3.50	14.00
	1902J	.815	.25	1.50	3.00	14.00
	1903A	5.131	.10	.25	1.00	7.00
	1903D	1.406	.10	.30	1.50	12.00
	1903E	.988	.15	.30	1.00	12.00
	1903F	1.003	.10	.25	1.00	12.00
	1903G	.610	.25	.50	1.50	14.00
	1903J	.816	.20	.40	1.50	14.00
	1904A	5.189	.10	.25	1.00	6.00
	1904D	1.056	.10	.30	1.00	12.00
	1904E	.559	.25	1.00	2.50	12.00
	1904F	.753	.10	.25	1.00	12.00
	1904G	.457	1.00	5.00	7.50	16.00
	1904J	.612	.25	1.50	3.50	16.00
	1905A	8.650	.10	.25	1.00	6.00
	1905A	250 pcs.	—	—	Proof	100.00
	1905D	1.846	.10	.25	1.00	7.50
	1905E	.980	.15	.30	1.00	7.50
	1905F	1.310	.10	.25	1.00	7.50
	1905G	.642	.25	1.00	2.00	10.00
	1905J	1.430	.10	.25	1.00	7.50
	1906A	14.470	.10	.25	1.00	7.50
	1906D	4.132	.10	.25	1.00	7.50
	1906E	2.189	.10	.25	1.00	7.50
	1906F	2.953	.10	.25	1.00	7.50
	1906G	1.952	.10	.25	1.00	7.50
	1906J	2.042	.10	.25	1.00	7.50
	1907A	17.971	.10	.25	1.00	6.50
	1907D	2.813	.10	.25	1.00	7.50
	1907E	2.291	.10	.25	1.00	7.50
	1907F	3.206	.10	.25	1.00	7.50
	1907G	1.889	.10	.25	1.00	7.50
	1907J	2.750	.10	.25	1.00	7.50
	1908A	20.410	.10	.25	1.00	6.50
	1908D	6.773	.10	.25	1.00	7.50
	1908E	2.490	.10	.25	1.00	7.50
	1908F	3.535	.10	.25	1.00	7.50
	1908G	1.708	.10	.25	1.00	7.50
	1908J	2.649	.10	.25	1.00	7.50
	1909A	2.270	.25	1.00	2.50	12.00
	1909D	.966	.25	1.50	6.00	18.00
	1909E	.806	.50	3.00	6.00	20.00
	1909F	.780	.50	3.00	8.00	20.00
	1909G	.980	.25	2.50	8.00	20.00
	1909J	.725	.25	2.50	8.00	20.00
	1910A	3.734	.10	.20	.50	6.00
	1910D	1.406	.25	.50	1.00	7.50
	1910E	.300	3.50	7.50	15.00	25.00
	1910F	1.003	.25	.50	1.00	7.50
	1910G	.610	.25	.50	1.00	7.50
	1911A	13.554	.10	.15	.50	6.00
	1911D	2.508	.10	.15	.50	7.00
	1911E	2.246	.10	.15	.50	7.00
	1911F	2.235	.10	.15	.50	7.00
	1911G	1.678	.10	.15	.50	7.00
	1911J	3.062	.10	.15	.50	7.00
	1912A	21.312	.10	.15	.50	6.00
	1912D	6.988	.10	.15	.50	7.00
	1912E	2.649	.10	.15	.50	7.00
	1912F	3.787	.10	.15	.50	7.00
	1912G	2.441	.10	.15	.50	7.00
	1912J	2.730	.10	.15	.50	7.00
	1913A	13.466	.10	.15	.50	6.00
	1913D	3.164	.10	.15	.50	7.00
	1913E	1.478	.10	.15	.50	7.00
	1913F	1.991	.10	.15	.50	7.00
	1913G	1.373	.10	.15	.50	7.00
	1913J	1.550	.10	.15	.50	7.00
	1914A	18.570	.10	.15	.50	6.00
	1914D	2.301	.10	.15	.50	7.00

KM#	Date	Mintage	Fine	VF	XF	Unc
12	1914E	3.478	.10	.15	.50	7.00
	1914F	4.515	.10	.15	.50	7.00
	1914G	2.689	.10	.15	.50	7.00
	1914J	1.589	.10	.15	.50	7.00
	1915A	10.639	.10	.15	.50	7.00
	1915D	2.277	.10	.15	.50	7.00
	1915E	1.027	.25	2.50	5.00	15.00
	1915F	1.508	.10	.15	.50	7.00
	1915G	.363	15.00	50.00	75.00	150.00
	1915J	2.677	.20	1.00	2.50	7.50
	1916D	1.128	.15	1.00	2.50	10.00
	Common date		—	—	Proof	95.00

NOTE: Earlier dates (1890-1900) exist for this type.

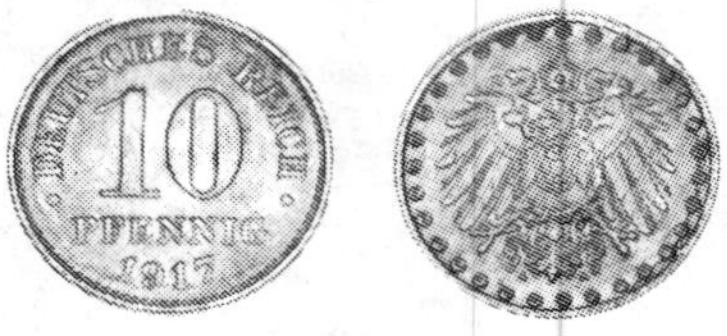

IRON

KM#	Date	Mintage	Fine	VF	XF	Unc
20	1915A	—	125.00	275.00	350.00	475.00
	1916A	69.143	.10	.35	2.00	8.00
	1916D	11.609	.10	.30	2.00	9.00
	1916E	8.280	.15	.50	5.00	10.00
	1916F	7.473	.15	.50	5.00	10.00
	1916G	5.878	.15	.50	5.00	10.00
	1916J	11.683	.15	.50	4.00	9.00
	1916	—	—	—	Rare	—
	1917A	53.198	.10	.20	1.50	4.00
	1917D	16.370	.10	.30	2.00	5.00
	1917E	9.182	.15	.50	3.00	7.00
	1917F	11.341	.15	.50	3.00	7.00
	1917F mule w/Polish rev. of Y#6, see Poland					
	1917G	7.088	.15	.50	4.00	10.00
	1917J	9.205	.15	.50	4.00	10.00
	1918D	.042	300.00	550.00	850.00	1150.
	1921A	16.265	1.00	4.00	7.00	15.00
	1922D	—	2.00	7.50	14.00	25.00
	1922E	2.235	12.50	25.00	45.00	100.00
	1922F	1.928	.50	3.00	6.00	12.00
	1922G	1.358	15.00	30.00	50.00	110.00
	1922J	2.420	1.00	4.00	7.00	15.00
	1922	—	100.00	175.00	250.00	450.00
	Common date		—	—	Proof	95.00

NOTE: The 1915A and 1922 are suspected patterns.

ZINC
Eagle and beaded border similar to KM#20.

KM#	Date	Mintage	Fine	VF	XF	Unc
25	1916F	—	150.00	400.00	600.00	900.00
	1917A	—	85.00	170.00	250.00	375.00
	1917	—	75.00	150.00	225.00	325.00
	1922J	—	—	—	Rare	—

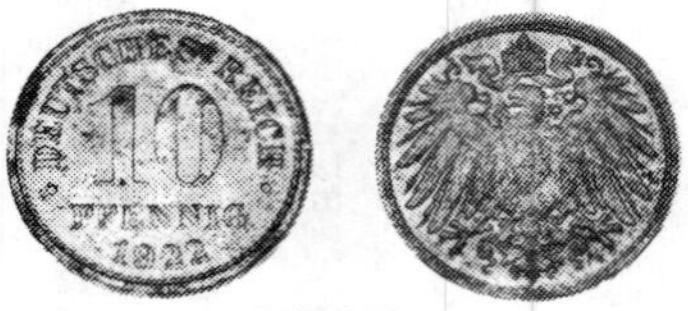

3.10-3.60 g
W/o mint mark.

KM#	Date	Mintage	Fine	VF	XF	Unc
26	1917	75.073	.10	.20	1.00	4.50
	1918	202.008	.10	.20	1.00	4.50
	1918	28 pcs.	—	—	Proof	200.00
	1919	147.800	.10	.20	1.00	4.50
	1919	50 pcs.	—	—	Proof	80.00
	1920	223.019	.10	.20	1.00	4.50
	1920	40 pcs.	—	—	Proof	90.00
	1921	319.334	.10	.20	1.00	4.50
	1921	24 pcs.	—	—	Proof	200.00
	1922	274.499	.10	.20	1.00	4.50
	1922	12 pcs.	—	—	Proof	300.00

25 PFENNIG

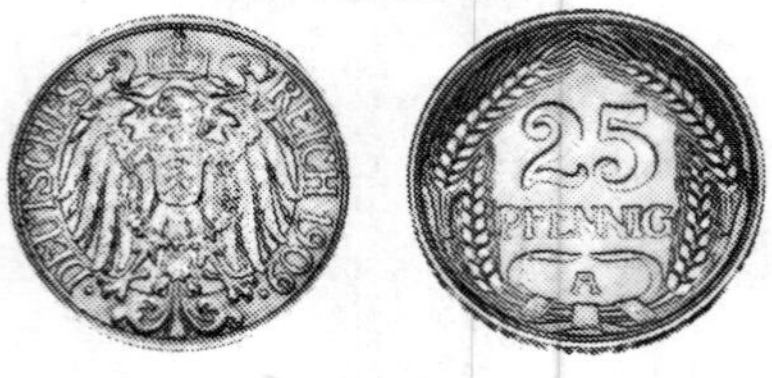

NICKEL

KM#	Date	Mintage	Fine	VF	XF	Unc
18	1909A	.962	2.50	7.00	12.50	22.50
	1909D	1.406	2.50	7.00	12.50	22.50
	1909E	.250	15.00	27.50	40.00	85.00
	1909F	.400	4.00	10.00	20.00	35.00
	1909G	.610	4.00	10.00	20.00	35.00
	1909J	.010	400.00	600.00	900.00	1500.
	1910A	9.522	3.00	8.00	12.50	20.00
	1910D	1.408	3.00	8.00	12.50	20.00
	1910E	1.242	3.00	8.00	12.50	20.00
	1910F	1.605	3.00	8.00	15.00	22.50
	1910G	.330	3.00	8.00	18.50	32.50
	1910J	1.561	3.00	8.00	15.00	20.00
	1911A	3.179	2.50	7.00	12.50	18.00
	1911D	.506	3.00	8.00	18.50	35.00
	1911E	.747	3.00	8.00	18.50	35.00
	1911G	.892	3.00	8.00	18.50	35.00
	1911J	.516	3.00	8.00	18.50	35.00
	1912A	2.590	3.00	8.00	12.50	20.00

KM#	Date	Mintage	Fine	VF	XF	Unc
18	1912D	.900	3.00	8.00	17.50	30.00
	1912F	1.003	3.00	8.00	18.50	32.50
	1912J	.362	12.50	25.00	35.00	70.00
	Common date		—	—	Proof	130.00

50 PFENNIG

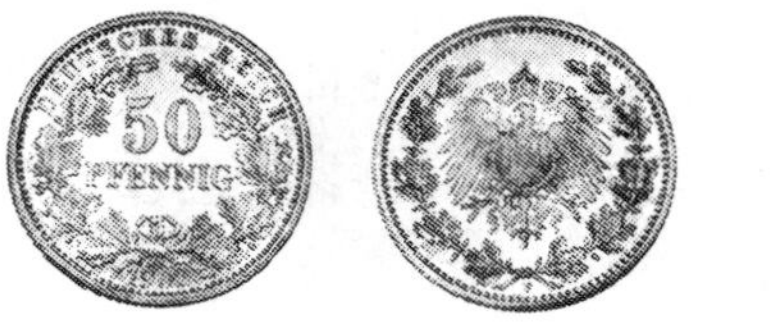

2.7770 g, .900 SILVER, .0803 oz ASW

KM#	Date	Mintage	Fine	VF	XF	Unc
15	1901A	.194	100.00	250.00	400.00	600.00
	1902F	.095	175.00	300.00	475.00	1150.
	1902F	—	—	—	Proof	600.00
	1903A	.384	125.00	220.00	325.00	475.00
	Common date		—	—	Proof	525.00

NOTE: Earlier dates (1896-1900) exist for this type.

1/2 MARK

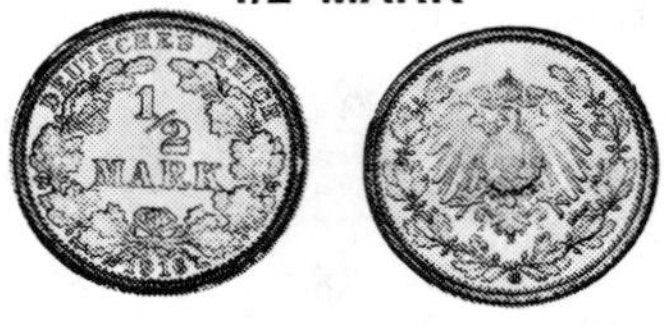

2.7770 g, .900 SILVER, .0803 oz ASW

KM#	Date	Mintage	Fine	VF	XF	Unc
17	1905A	37.766	.75	1.00	4.50	12.00
	1905D	7.636	.75	1.50	4.50	12.00
	1905E	4.908	.75	1.50	4.50	12.00
	1905F	6.310	.75	1.50	4.50	12.00
	1905G	3.886	.75	1.50	4.50	15.00
	1905J	6.316	.75	1.50	4.50	12.00
	1906A	29.754	.75	1.50	4.50	12.00
	1906D	11.977	.75	1.50	4.50	12.00
	1906E	5.821	.75	1.50	4.50	15.00
	1906F	8.036	.75	1.50	4.50	12.00
	1906G	4.273	.75	1.50	4.50	18.00
	1906J	2.179	.75	2.50	7.50	22.50
	1907A	14.168	.75	1.50	4.50	12.00
	1907D	2.884	.75	1.50	4.50	12.00
	1907E	.600	2.50	9.00	20.00	65.00
	1907F	1.202	.75	1.50	4.50	12.00
	1907G	.927	2.50	9.00	20.00	65.00
	1907J	3.268	.75	1.50	4.50	18.00
	1908A	5.018	.75	1.50	4.50	12.00
	1908D	.400	7.50	17.50	25.00	80.00
	1908E	.591	2.50	10.00	25.00	80.00
	1908F	1,000	650.00	1250.	2650.	4000.
	1908G	.675	1.25	5.00	10.00	30.00
	1908/7J	1.309	1.25	5.00	10.00	30.00
	1908J	Inc. Ab.	1.25	5.00	10.00	30.00
	1909A	5.404	.75	1.50	4.50	12.00
	1909/5D	1.001	.75	1.50	4.50	12.00
	1909D	Inc. Ab.	.75	1.50	4.50	12.00
	1909E	.745	1.25	5.00	10.00	28.00
	1909F	.999	.75	2.50	7.50	15.00
	1909G	.607	1.25	5.00	10.00	28.00
	1909J	.816	1.25	5.00	10.00	20.00
	1911A	2.710	1.25	5.00	7.50	22.00
	1911/05D	.703	1.25	5.00	7.50	22.00
	1911D	Inc. Ab.	1.25	5.00	7.50	22.00
	1911E	.376	5.00	17.50	25.00	70.00
	1911F	.502	2.50	7.50	17.50	50.00
	1911G	.610	2.50	7.50	17.50	50.00
	1911J	.418	5.00	17.50	27.50	85.00
	1912A	2.709	1.25	5.00	7.50	25.00
	1912/5D	.703	1.50	10.00	15.00	30.00
	1912D	Inc. Ab.	1.50	10.00	15.00	30.00
	1912E	.369	5.00	17.50	25.00	70.00
	1912F	.501	2.50	7.50	12.50	30.00
	1912J	.399	5.00	17.50	27.50	85.00
	1913A	5.419	.75	1.50	4.50	12.00
	1913/05D	1.406	.75	1.50	4.50	12.00
	1913D	Inc. Ab.	.75	1.50	4.50	12.00
	1913E	.745	2.50	5.00	10.00	22.00
	1913F	1.003	.75	1.50	5.00	12.00
	1913G	.610	1.25	5.00	10.00	22.00
	1913J	.817	1.25	5.00	10.00	28.00
	1914A	13.525	.75	1.50	3.50	10.00
	1914/05D	.328	2.50	10.00	15.00	35.00
	1914D	Inc. Ab.	2.50	10.00	15.00	35.00
	1914J	2.292	.75	3.00	5.00	12.00
	1915A	13.015	.75	1.50	3.50	10.00
	1915/05D	5.117	.75	1.50	3.00	10.00
	1915D	Inc. Ab.	.75	1.50	3.00	10.00
	1915E	3.308	.75	1.50	3.00	10.00
	1915F	5.309	.75	1.50	3.00	10.00
	1915G	2.730	.75	1.50	3.00	10.00
	1915J	2.285	.75	1.50	3.00	10.00
	1916A	9.750	.75	1.50	3.00	10.00
	1916/616D	4.397	.75	1.50	3.00	10.00
	1916/05D	I.A.	.75	1.50	3.00	10.00
	1916/5D	I.A.	.75	1.50	3.00	10.00
	1916D	Inc. Ab.	.75	1.50	3.00	10.00
	1916E	1.640	.75	1.50	3.00	10.00
	1916F	2.410	.75	1.50	3.00	10.00
	1916G	1.779	.75	1.50	3.00	10.00
	1916J	1.464	.75	1.50	3.00	10.00
	1917A	14.692	.75	1.50	3.00	10.00
	1917/05D	.979	.75	1.50	3.00	10.00

KM#	Date	Mintage	Fine	VF	XF	Unc
17	1917D	Inc. Ab.	.75	1.50	3.00	10.00
	1917E	1.561	.75	1.50	3.00	10.00
	1917F	.450	2.50	10.00	15.00	50.00
	1917G	.619	2.50	10.00	15.00	50.00
	1917J	1.039	1.50	4.00	6.00	15.00
	1918A*	14.622	.75	1.50	3.00	10.00
	1918/05D	3.670	.75	1.50	3.00	10.00
	1918D*	Inc. Ab.	.75	1.50	3.00	10.00
	1918E*	2.807	1.50	6.00	10.00	20.00
	1918E	19 pcs.	—	—	Proof	—
	1918F*	4.010	.75	1.50	3.50	10.00
	1918G*	1.032	1.50	6.00	10.00	15.00
	1918J*	3.452	.75	1.50	4.00	12.00
	1919A*	9.124	.75	1.50	4.00	12.00
	1919/1619D	2.195	.75	1.50	5.00	15.00
	1919/05D	I.A.	.75	1.50	5.00	15.00
	1919D*	Inc. Ab.	.75	1.50	5.00	15.00
	1919E*	1.767	2.50	7.50	12.50	20.00
	1919F*	1.559	2.00	6.00	12.00	25.00
	1919J*	1.875	1.00	3.00	5.00	15.00
	Common date		—	—	Proof	115.00

***NOTE:** Some were issued with a black finish to prevent hoarding.

MARK

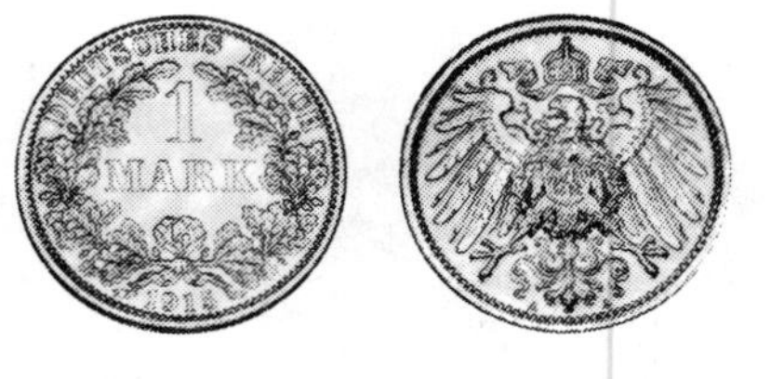

5.5500 g, .900 SILVER, .1606 oz ASW

KM#	Date	Mintage	Fine	VF	XF	Unc
14	1901A	3.821	2.50	5.00	12.00	35.00
	1901/800D	I.A.	2.50	5.00	12.00	35.00
	1901/801D	I.A.	2.50	5.00	12.00	35.00
	1901D	Inc. Ab.	2.50	5.00	15.00	40.00
	1901E	.484	2.50	6.00	20.00	45.00
	1901F	.802	2.50	5.00	12.00	35.00
	1901G	.579	2.50	5.00	25.00	80.00
	1901J	.531	2.50	5.00	25.00	80.00
	1902A	5.222	1.50	4.00	10.00	30.00
	1902D	1.546	1.50	4.00	10.00	30.00
	1902E	.819	1.50	4.00	12.00	55.00
	1902F	.953	1.50	4.00	10.00	55.00
	1902G	.270	6.00	25.00	40.00	135.00
	1902J	.898	2.50	5.00	12.00	75.00
	1903A	3.965	1.25	2.00	5.50	28.00
	1903/803D	.914	1.25	2.50	6.50	30.00
	1903D	Inc. Ab.	1.25	2.50	6.50	30.00
	1903E	.485	5.00	12.00	22.00	75.00
	1903F	.652	5.00	7.50	15.00	65.00
	1903G	.614	2.50	5.00	15.00	65.00
	1903J	.531	5.00	12.00	22.00	75.00
	1904A	3.243	1.25	2.00	5.50	28.00
	1904D	1.761	1.25	2.00	6.50	35.00
	1904E	.931	2.50	4.00	10.00	40.00
	1904F	1.255	2.00	3.50	9.00	35.00
	1904G	.664	2.50	5.00	12.00	45.00
	1904J	1.021	2.50	5.00	12.00	55.00
	1905A	10.303	1.25	2.00	5.00	20.00
	1905D	1.759	1.25	2.00	6.50	28.00
	1905E	.931	2.50	4.00	10.00	40.00
	1905F	Inc.Ab.	2000.	2800.	4500.	6000.
	1905G	.860	2.50	4.00	10.00	40.00
	1905J	1.021	2.50	5.00	6.50	50.00
	1906A	5.414	1.25	2.50	5.50	28.00
	1906D	1.412	1.25	2.50	7.50	28.00
	1906E	.745	1.50	5.00	12.00	40.00
	1906F	2.257	1.25	2.50	5.50	35.00
	1906G	.609	2.50	5.00	12.00	40.00
	1906G	10-30 pcs.	—	—	Proof	—
	1906J	.372	2.50	6.00	15.00	50.00
	1907A	9.201	1.25	2.50	5.00	20.00
	1907D	2.387	1.25	2.50	5.00	20.00
	1907E	1.265	1.25	2.50	6.50	35.00
	1907F	1.704	1.25	2.50	6.50	35.00
	1907G	1.035	1.25	2.50	6.50	35.00
	1907J	1.833	1.25	2.50	6.50	35.00
	1908A	4.338	1.25	2.50	5.00	20.00
	1908D	1.126	1.25	2.50	5.50	30.00
	1908E	.596	2.50	5.00	12.00	50.00
	1908F	.802	1.25	2.50	6.50	45.00
	1908G	.488	2.50	5.00	12.00	35.00
	1908J	.653	2.50	5.00	12.00	35.00
	1909A	4.151	1.25	2.50	5.00	20.00
	1909D	1.968	1.25	2.50	5.50	28.00
	1909E	Inc.Be.	30.00	80.00	140.00	245.00
	1909G	.854	4.00	12.00	22.00	55.00
	1909J	.053	100.00	200.00	285.00	450.00
	1910A	5.870	1.25	1.50	5.00	20.00
	1910D	1.406	1.25	2.50	5.50	28.00
	1910E	1.050	2.50	4.50	7.00	40.00
	1910F	1.631	2.50	4.50	7.00	40.00
	1910G	.610	2.50	5.00	12.00	35.00
	1910J	1.094	2.50	5.00	12.00	40.00
	1911A	5.693	1.25	2.50	5.50	20.00
	1911D	.126	10.00	20.00	40.00	100.00
	1911E	.738	4.00	6.00	15.00	42.00
	1911F	.773	2.50	6.00	15.00	42.00
	1911G	.305	4.00	6.00	15.00	45.00
	1911J	.812	4.00	6.00	15.00	42.00
	1912A	2.439	1.25	2.50	5.50	20.00

KM#	Date	Mintage	Fine	VF	XF	Unc
14	1912D	.632	1.25	2.50	5.50	28.00
	1912E	.708	2.50	5.00	15.00	35.00
	1912F	.502	2.50	5.00	15.00	37.00
	1912J	.409	2.50	6.00	15.00	50.00
	1913F	.450	10.00	27.50	60.00	100.00
	1913G	.275	20.00	40.00	68.00	125.00
	1913J	.368	15.00	30.00	65.00	100.00
	1914A	11.304	1.25	1.50	3.50	12.00
	1914/9D	3.515	1.25	1.50	3.00	10.00
	1914D	Inc. Ab.	1.25	1.50	3.50	12.00
	1914E	2.235	1.25	1.50	3.50	12.00
	1914F	2.300	1.25	1.50	3.50	12.00
	1914G	1.911	1.25	1.50	3.50	12.00
	1914J	2.978	1.25	1.50	3.50	12.00
	1915A	13.817	1.25	1.50	3.50	12.00
	1915D	4.218	1.25	1.50	3.50	12.00
	1915E	2.235	1.25	1.50	3.50	12.00
	1915F	2.911	1.25	1.50	3.50	12.00
	1915G	1.749	1.25	1.50	3.50	12.00
	1915J	1.634	1.25	1.50	3.50	12.00
	1916F	.306	12.00	22.00	35.00	75.00
	Common date		—	—	Proof	150.00

NOTE: Earlier dates (1891-1900) exist for this type.

MILITARY ISSUES - WWI

Issued under the authority of the German Military Commander of the East for use in Estonia, Latvia, Lithuania, Poland, and Northwest Russia.

KOPEK

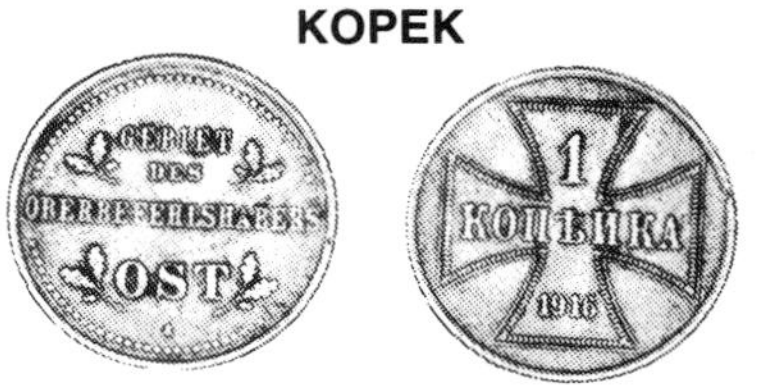

IRON

KM#	Date	Mintage	Fine	VF	XF	Unc
21	1916A	11.942	2.50	5.00	10.00	25.00
	1916A	—	—	—	Proof	75.00
	1916J	8.000	2.50	5.00	10.00	25.00
	1916J	—	—	—	Proof	75.00

2 KOPEKS

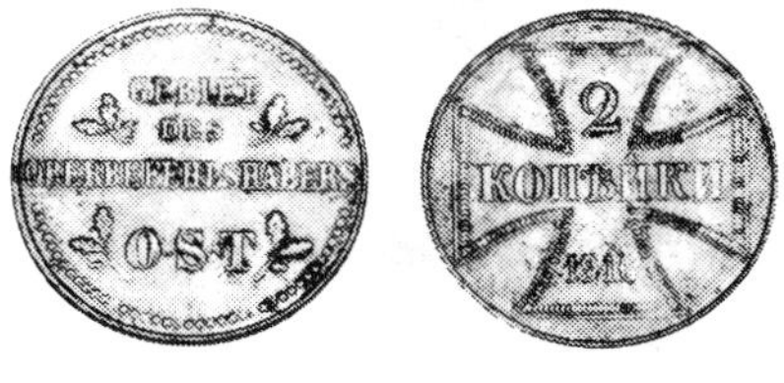

IRON

KM#	Date	Mintage	Fine	VF	XF	Unc
22	1916A	6.973	2.50	5.00	12.50	30.00
	1916A	—	—	—	Proof	75.00
	1916J	8.000	2.50	5.00	12.50	30.00
	1916J	—	—	—	Proof	75.00

3 KOPEKS

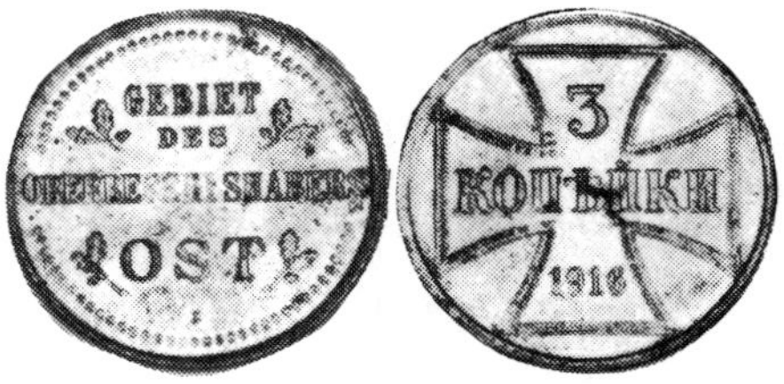

IRON

KM#	Date	Mintage	Fine	VF	XF	Unc
23	1916A	8.670	2.50	5.00	12.50	35.00
	1916A	—	—	—	Proof	75.00
	1916J	8.000	2.50	5.00	12.50	35.00
	1916J	—	—	—	Proof	75.00

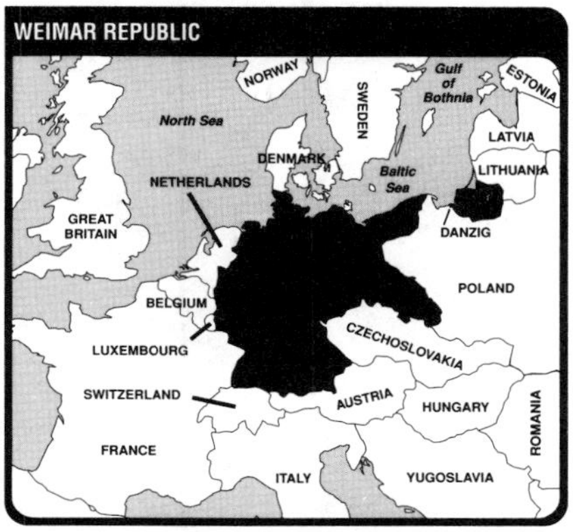

1919-1933

The Imperial German government disintegrated in a flurry of royal abdications as World War I ended. Desperate German parliamentarians, fearful of impending anarchy and civil war, hastily declared a German Republic. The new National Assembly which was convened Feb. 6, 1919 in Weimar had to establish a legal government, draft a constitution, and then conclude a peace treaty with the Allies. Friedrich Ebert was elected as Reichs President. The harsh terms of the peace treaty imposed on Germany were economically and psychologically unacceptable to the German population regardless of political persuasion and the problem of German treaty compliance was to plague the Republic until the worldwide Great Depression of 1929. The new constitution paid less attention to fundamental individual rights and concentrated more power in the President and Central Government to insure a more stable social and economic order. The German bureaucracy survived the transition intact and had a stifling effect on the democratic process. The army started training large numbers of reservists in conjunction with the U.S.S.R. thereby circumventing treaty limitations on the size of the German military.

New anti-democratic ideologies were forming. Communism and Fascism were spreading. The National Socialist German Workers Party, under Hitler's leadership, incorporated the ever present anti-Semitism into a new virulent Nazi Catechism.

In spite of the historic German inflation, the French occupation of the Rhineland, and the loss of vast territories and resources, the republic survived. By 1929 the German economy had been restored to it's pre-war level. Much of the economic gains however were dependent on the extensive assistance provided by the U.S.A. and collapsed along with the world economy in 1929. Even during the good times, the Republic was never able to muster any loyal public support or patriotism. By 1930, Nationalists, Nazis, and Communists held nearly half of the Reichstag seats and the government was forced to rely more and more on presidential decrees as the only means to effectuate policy. In 1932, the Nazis won 230 Reichstag seats. As head of the largest party, Hitler claimed the right to form the next government. President Hindenburg's opposition forced a second election in which the Nazis lost 34 seats. Von Papen, however, convinced Hindenburg to name Hitler Chancellor by arguing that Hitler could be controlled! Hitler formed his cabinet and immediately began consolidating his power and laying the groundwork for the Third Reich.

MONETARY SYSTEM

(During 1923-1924)

100 Rentenpfennig = 1 Rentenmark

(Commencing 1924)

100 Reichspfennig = 1 Reichsmark

RENTENPFENNIG

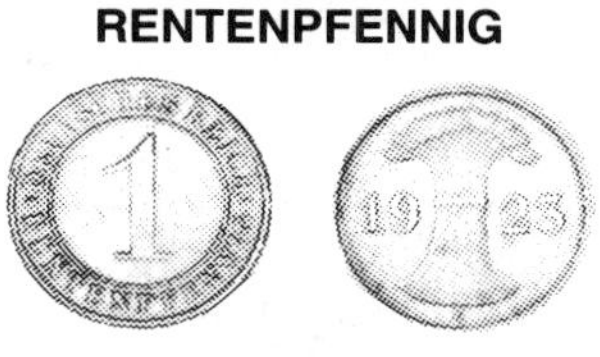

BRONZE

KM#	Date	Mintage	Fine	VF	XF	Unc
30	1923A	12.629	.15	.50	1.50	5.00
	1923D	*2.314	.25	2.00	5.00	22.00
	1923E	2.200	1.50	4.00	12.00	35.00
	1923F	.160	1.50	4.00	12.00	35.00
	1923G	1.004	.25	1.50	8.00	30.00
	1923J	1.470	.25	1.50	6.00	20.00
	1924A	55.273	.15	.50	2.50	7.50
	1924D	17.540	.20	1.50	5.00	10.00
	1924E	6.838	.20	1.50	6.00	12.50
	1924F	10.347	.20	1.50	5.00	10.00
	1924G	7.366	.25	1.50	6.00	12.50
	1924J	11.024	.20	1.50	5.00	10.00
	1925A	—	300.00	500.00	650.00	800.00

KM#	Date	Mintage	Fine	VF	XF	Unc
30	1929F	—	125.00	225.00	350.00	500.00
	Common date		—	—	Proof	120.00

REICHSPFENNIG

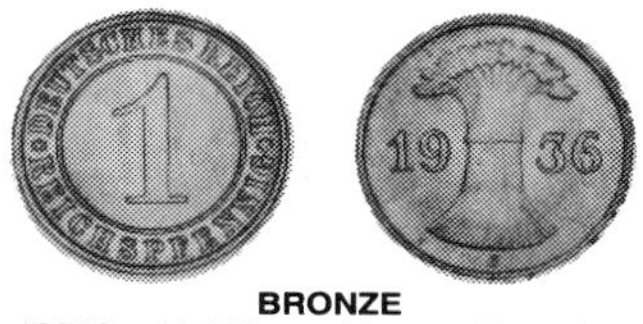

BRONZE

KM#	Date	Mintage	Fine	VF	XF	Unc
37	1924A	13.496	.10	.25	1.00	6.00
	1924D	6.206	.10	.25	1.00	6.00
	1924E	1.100	40.00	175.00	250.00	475.00
	1924F	2.650	.15	.30	1.00	6.00
	1924G	5.100	.15	.50	2.00	8.50
	1924J	24.400	.10	.25	1.00	6.00
	1925A	40.925	.10	.25	1.00	5.00
	1925D	1.558	5.00	12.50	22.50	40.00
	1925E	10.460	.10	.25	1.00	6.00
	1925F	5.673	.10	.25	1.00	6.00
	1925G	13.502	.10	.25	1.00	6.00
	1925J	30.300	.10	.25	1.00	6.00
	1927A	4.671	.10	.25	1.00	6.00
	1927D	4.203	.15	.50	2.00	8.50
	1927E	8.000	.15	.50	3.50	12.00
	1927F	2.350	.25	1.00	2.00	8.50
	1927G	3.236	.15	.50	3.50	12.00
	1928A	19.300	.10	.25	1.00	3.50
	1928D	10.200	.10	.25	1.00	3.50
	1928F	8.672	.10	.25	1.00	3.50
	1928G	3.764	.15	.50	2.00	6.00
	1929A	37.170	.10	.25	1.00	3.50
	1929D	9.337	.10	.25	1.00	3.50
	1929E	6.600	.15	.30	1.00	5.00
	1929F	3.150	.10	.25	1.50	6.00
	1929G	1.986	.15	.50	2.00	6.00
	1930A	40.997	.10	.25	1.00	3.50
	1930D	6.441	.10	.25	1.00	3.50
	1930E	1.412	6.00	12.00	25.00	60.00
	1930F	6.415	.10	.50	1.50	6.00
	1930G	5.017	.10	.25	1.00	3.50
	1931A	38.481	.10	.25	1.00	3.50
	1931D	5.998	.10	.25	1.00	3.50
	1931E	12.800	.15	.50	2.00	6.00
	1931F	12.591	.10	.25	1.00	3.50
	1931G	2.622	.15	.50	2.50	7.50
	1932A	17.096	.10	.25	1.00	3.50
	1933A	37.846	.10	.25	1.00	3.50
	1933E	2.945	.35	2.00	4.50	9.00
	1933F	5.023	.10	.50	1.00	5.00
	1934A	51.214	.10	.25	1.00	5.00
	1934D	7.408	.10	.25	1.00	5.00
	1934E	4.628	.50	3.50	7.50	15.00
	1934F	5.667	.10	.25	1.00	5.00
	1934G	2.450	.15	.30	1.00	5.00
	1934J	4.271	.15	.50	3.00	8.50
	1935A	35.894	.10	.25	1.00	5.00
	1935D	15.489	.10	.25	1.00	5.00
	1935E	8.351	.15	.50	2.50	7.50
	1935F	12.094	.10	.25	1.00	5.00
	1935G	7.454	.10	.25	1.00	5.00
	1935J	8.505	.10	.25	1.00	5.00
	1936A	*50.949	.10	.25	1.00	5.00
	1936D	12.262	.10	.25	1.00	5.00
	1936E	2.576	.50	3.00	10.00	15.00
	1936F	6.915	.10	.25	1.00	5.00
	1936G	*2.940	.15	.30	1.00	5.00
	1936J	*5.421	.15	.50	2.00	7.50
	Common date		—	—	Proof	85.00

2 RENTENPFENNIG

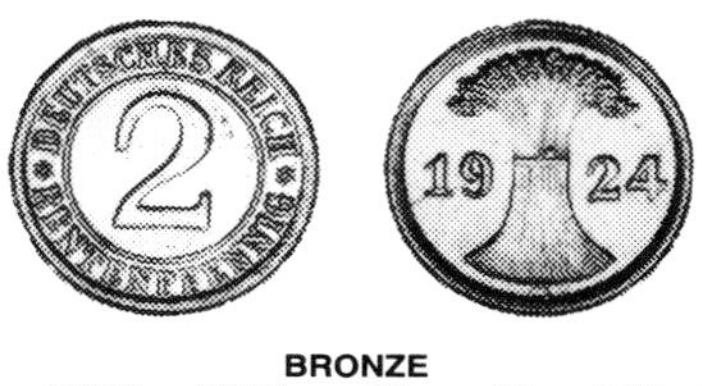

BRONZE

KM#	Date	Mintage	Fine	VF	XF	Unc
31	1923A	8.587	.15	.50	2.50	12.50
	1923D	1.490	.15	.50	3.00	10.00
	1923F	Inc.Ab.	.50	5.00	15.00	35.00
	1923G	Inc.Ab.	.25	1.00	6.50	15.00
	1923J	Inc.Ab.	.50	5.00	12.50	25.00
	1924A	80.864	.10	.25	2.50	10.00
	1924D	19.899	.10	.25	2.50	10.00
	1924E	6.595	.15	.50	3.00	12.00
	1924F	14.969	.15	.50	3.00	10.00
	1924G	10.349	.15	.50	3.00	10.00
	1924J	21.196	.25	1.00	5.00	10.00
	Common date		—	—	Proof	140.00

2 REICHSPFENNIG

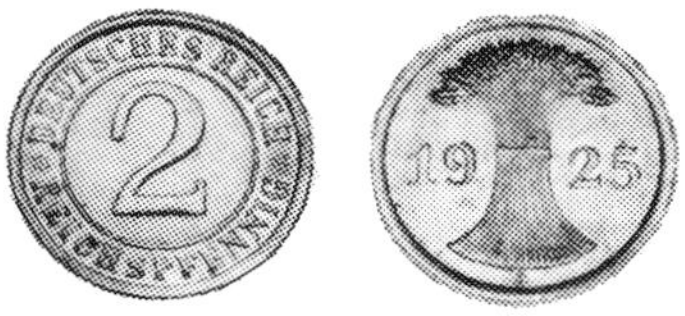

BRONZE

KM#	Date	Mintage	Fine	VF	XF	Unc
38	1923F	—	400.00	600.00	750.00	1000.
	1924A	19.620	.10	.25	1.00	6.00
	1924D	3.482	.10	.30	1.50	12.00
	1924E	4.253	.15	1.50	7.50	20.00
	1924F	4.567	.10	.20	1.00	10.00
	1924G	7.560	.10	.20	1.00	10.00
	1924J	7.489	.10	.25	1.00	10.00
	1925A	22.433	.10	.25	1.00	6.00
	1925D	2.412	.15	.60	2.50	15.00
	1925E	5.414	.10	.30	1.50	10.00
	1925F	4.851	.10	.30	1.50	10.00
	1925G	2.456	.25	1.50	7.50	20.00
	1936A	3.220	.25	2.00	7.50	17.50
	1936D	6.525	.10	.30	1.50	10.00
	1936E	.573	5.00	15.00	22.50	50.00
	1936F	3.100	.15	.50	1.00	6.00
	Common date		—	—	Proof	90.00

4 REICHSPFENNIG

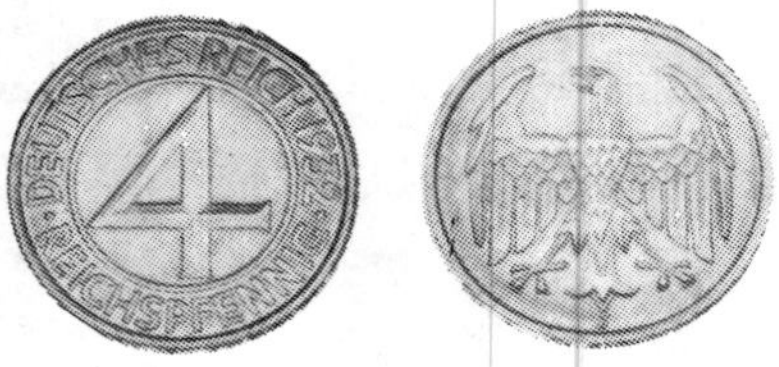

BRONZE

KM#	Date	Mintage	Fine	VF	XF	Unc
75	1932A	27.101	2.50	7.00	12.00	22.00
	1932A	—	—	—	Proof	150.00
	1932D	7.055	2.50	6.00	14.00	25.00
	1932D	—	—	—	Proof	150.00
	1932E	3.729	2.50	9.00	16.50	45.00
	1932E	—	—	—	Proof	150.00
	1932F	5.022	2.50	9.00	16.50	45.00
	1932F	—	—	—	Proof	150.00
	1932G	3.050	3.00	12.00	20.00	55.00
	1932G	—	—	—	Proof	150.00
	1932J	4.094	2.50	9.00	16.50	45.00
	1932J	—	—	—	Proof	150.00

5 RENTENPFENNIG

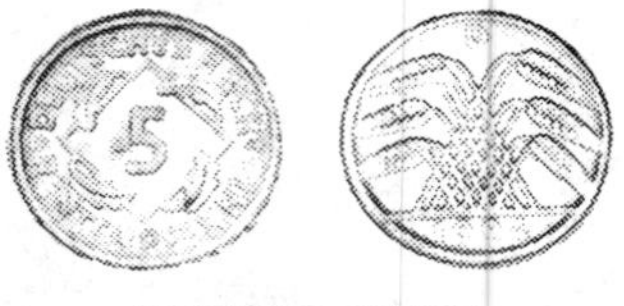

ALUMINUM-BRONZE

KM#	Date	Mintage	Fine	VF	XF	Unc
32	1923A	3.083	.20	1.00	2.50	10.00
	1923D	Inc.Be.	.30	1.50	3.00	17.50
	1923F	Inc.Be.	35.00	75.00	125.00	200.00
	1923G	Inc.Be.	25.00	50.00	100.00	160.00
	1924A	171.966	.10	.50	2.00	7.50
	1924D	31.163	.20	.50	1.00	6.00
	1924E	12.206	.20	.50	1.00	7.50
	1924F	29.032	.20	.50	1.00	7.50
	1924G	19.217	.20	.50	1.00	7.50
	1924J	32.332	.20	.50	1.00	7.50
	1925F	1 known	—	4800.	—	—
	Common date		—	—	Proof	90.00

5 REICHSPFENNIG

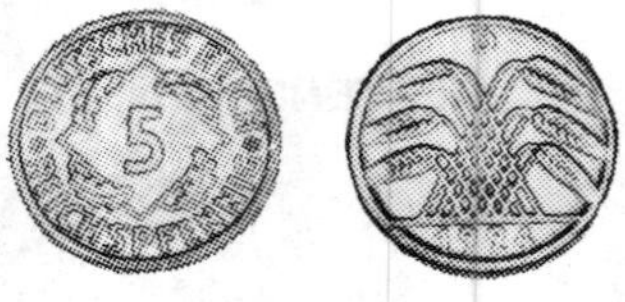

ALUMINUM-BRONZE

KM#	Date	Mintage	Fine	VF	XF	Unc
39	1924A	14.469	.20	.50	2.50	15.00
	1924D	8.139	.20	.50	2.50	8.00
	1924E	5.976	.20	1.00	5.00	15.00
	1924F	3.134	.20	1.00	5.00	15.00
	1924G	4.790	.20	1.00	7.50	17.50
	1924J	2.200	.25	1.00	3.50	12.00
	1925A	85.239	.15	.40	2.00	7.00
	1925D	39.750	.15	.35	2.00	7.00
	1925E	17.554	.20	1.00	5.00	12.00
	1925F large 5	20.990	.15	.35	2.50	6.00
	1925F small 5	Inc. Ab.	.15	.35	2.50	6.00
	1925G	10.232	.20	1.00	5.00	17.50
	1925J	10.950	.20	1.00	5.00	17.50
	1926A	22.377	.15	.40	2.00	12.00
	1926E	5.990	10.00	20.00	35.00	50.00
	1926F	2.871	5.00	12.50	25.00	35.00
	1930A	7.418	.20	.50	3.00	15.00
	1935A	19.178	.15	.25	.50	6.00
	1935D	5.480	.15	.35	1.00	8.00
	1935E	2.384	.20	.50	3.00	12.00
	1935F	4.585	.15	.40	1.50	8.00
	1935G	2.652	.20	.50	3.00	12.00
	1935J	2.614	.20	.50	3.00	12.00
	1936A	36.992	.15	.25	.50	6.00
	1936D	8.108	.15	.35	1.00	8.00
	1936E	2.981	.20	.50	3.00	12.00
	1936F	6.643	.15	.30	1.00	7.00
	1936G	2.274	.20	.35	1.00	8.00

KM#	Date	Mintage	Fine	VF	XF	Unc
39	1936J	4.470	.20	.50	3.00	12.00
	Common date		—	—	Proof	75.00

10 RENTENPFENNIG

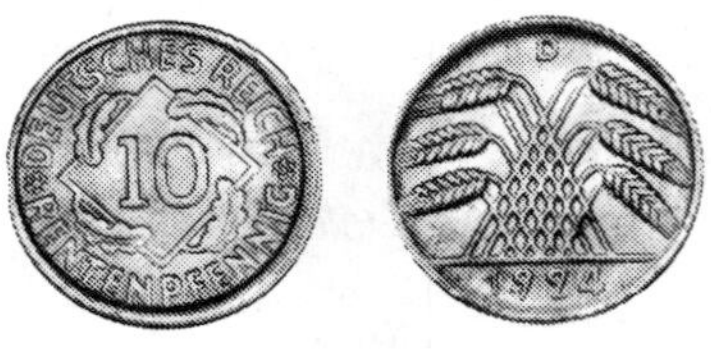

ALUMINUM-BRONZE

KM#	Date	Mintage	Fine	VF	XF	Unc
33	1923A	Inc.Be.	.25	2.50	6.00	17.50
	1923D	Inc.Be.	.50	5.00	10.00	25.00
	1923F	Inc. Be.	45.00	95.00	160.00	275.00
	1923G	Inc. Be.	2.50	12.50	25.00	50.00
	1924A	169.956	.20	.40	2.50	7.50
	1924D	33.894	.15	.50	1.00	10.00
	1924E	18.679	.20	1.00	1.50	15.00
	1924F	42.237	.15	.50	1.00	10.00
	1924F	—	—	—	Proof	95.00
	1924G	18.758	.20	.50	1.00	15.00
	1924J	33.928	.15	.50	1.00	15.00
	1925F	.013	250.00	500.00	750.00	1000.

10 REICHSPFENNIG

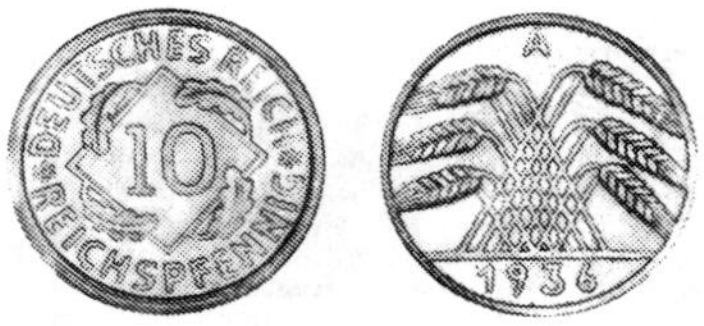

ALUMINUM-BRONZE

KM#	Date	Mintage	Fine	VF	XF	Unc
40	1924A	20.883	.15	.25	1.00	12.50
	1924D	9.639	.15	.50	1.50	15.00
	1924E	5.185	.20	1.00	1.50	17.50
	1924F	2.758	1.00	7.50	15.00	37.50
	1924G	4.363	.20	1.00	1.50	17.50
	1924J	3.993	.15	.50	1.00	15.00
	1925A	102.319	.10	.15	.50	10.00
	1925D	36.853	.10	.15	.50	10.00
	1925E	18.700	.15	.50	1.00	15.00
	1925F	12.516	.10	.15	.50	12.50
	1925G	10.360	.10	.50	1.00	12.50
	1925J	8.755	4.00	12.50	25.00	37.50
	1926A	14.390	.20	2.00	4.00	15.00
	1926G	1.481	2.50	10.00	20.00	37.50
	1928A	2.308	2.00	6.00	9.00	17.50
	1928G	Inc. Be.	40.00	60.00	125.00	180.00
	1929A	25.712	.15	.50	1.50	12.50
	1929D	7.049	.15	.50	1.50	12.50
	1929E	3.138	.20	1.00	2.50	17.50
	1929F	3.740	.20	1.00	2.50	17.50
	1929G	2.729	.30	3.50	6.00	22.00
	1929J	4.086	.20	2.50	5.00	18.50
	1930A	7.540	.20	2.00	2.50	12.50
	1930D	2.148	.25	3.50	5.00	15.00
	1930E	2.090	1.00	5.00	15.00	32.50
	1930F	2.006	1.00	5.00	15.00	32.50
	1930G	1.542	5.00	15.00	30.00	60.00
	1930J	1.637	2.50	5.00	12.50	30.00
	1931A	9.661	.20	2.50	5.00	15.00
	1931D	.664	15.00	35.00	65.00	100.00
	1931F	1.482	2.50	10.00	12.50	32.50
	1931G	.038	200.00	350.00	550.00	800.00
	1932A	4.528	.25	3.50	6.00	17.50
	1932D	2.812	.50	5.00	7.50	17.50
	1932E	1.491	6.00	12.50	17.50	40.00
	1932F	1.806	6.00	12.50	17.50	40.00
	1932G	.137	350.00	750.00	1150.	1500.
	1933A	1.349	15.00	25.00	50.00	100.00
	1933/2G	1.046	6.00	12.50	17.50	40.00
	1933G	Inc. Ab.	5.00	10.00	16.50	40.00
	1933J	1.634	1.00	8.50	15.00	35.00
	1934A	3.200	.20	1.00	6.00	17.50
	1934D	1.252	1.00	7.50	10.00	25.00
	1934E	Inc. Be.	20.00	35.00	50.00	100.00
	1934F	.100	15.00	30.00	50.00	100.00
	1934G	.150	15.00	30.00	50.00	125.00
	1935A	35.890	.10	.15	1.00	8.50
	1935D	8.960	.10	.25	1.50	12.50
	1935E	5.966	.15	.35	2.00	15.00
	1935F	7.944	.10	.30	1.50	12.50
	1935G	4.847	.10	.50	3.00	15.00
	1935J	8.995	.10	.30	1.50	12.50
	1936A	24.527	.10	.15	.50	7.50
	1936D	8.092	.10	.20	1.00	12.50
	1936E	2.441	.20	.50	2.50	15.00
	1936F	4.889	.10	.30	1.50	12.50
	1936G	1.715	.15	.60	2.50	15.00
	1936J	1.632	.25	3.00	8.00	17.50
	Common date		—	—	Proof	85.00

50 PFENNIG

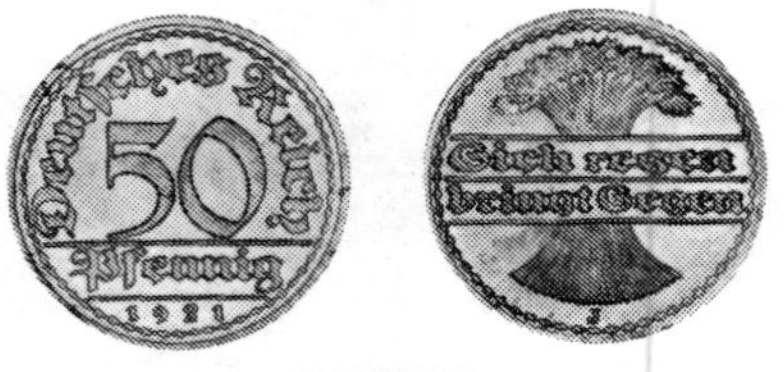

ALUMINUM

KM#	Date	Mintage	Fine	VF	XF	Unc
27	1919A	7.173	.25	1.50	4.00	6.00
	1919D	.791	.50	1.50	3.50	10.00
	1919E	.930	2.00	7.00	15.00	30.00
	1919E	35 pcs.	—	—	Proof	—
	1919F	.160	5.00	10.00	20.00	50.00
	1919G	.660	.75	5.00	7.50	12.50
	1919J	.800	3.00	8.00	17.00	40.00
	1920A	119.793	.10	.15	.25	1.50
	1920D	28.306	.10	.15	.25	1.50
	1920E	14.400	.25	1.50	4.00	10.00
	1920E	226 pcs.	—	—	Proof	65.00
	1920F	10.932	.10	.15	.25	1.50
	1920G	5.040	.20	1.50	2.50	5.00
	1920J	15.423	.10	.25	1.00	4.00
	1921A	184.468	.10	.15	.25	1.50
	1921D	48.729	.10	.15	.25	1.50
	1921E	31.210	.15	1.50	2.50	5.00
	1921E	332 pcs.	—	—	Proof	65.00
	1921F	46.950	.10	.15	.25	1.50
	1921G	19.107	.10	.20	.50	1.50
	1921J	28.013	.10	.25	1.00	4.00
	1922A	145.215	.10	.15	.25	1.50
	1922D	58.019	.10	.15	.25	1.50
	1922E	33.930	.15	1.50	2.50	5.00
	1922E	333 pcs.	—	—	Proof	65.00
	1922F	33.000	.10	.15	.25	1.50
	1922G	36.745	.10	.20	.50	1.50
	1922J	36.202	.25	2.50	4.50	9.00

50 RENTENPFENNIG

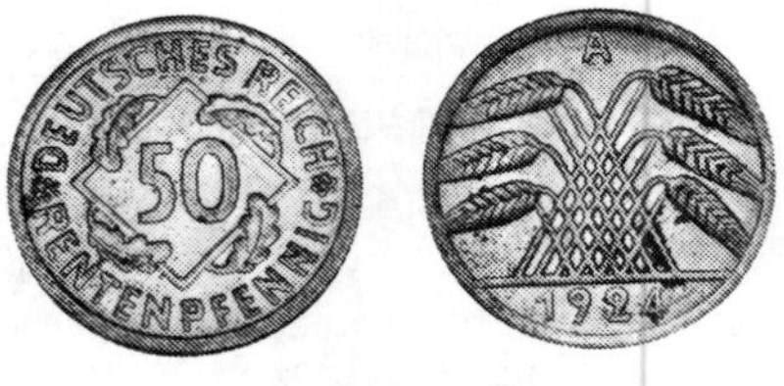

ALUMINUM-BRONZE

KM#	Date	Mintage	Fine	VF	XF	Unc
34	1923A	.451	5.00	15.00	27.50	55.00
	1923D	.192	12.50	17.50	32.50	60.00
	1923F	.120	45.00	90.00	120.00	220.00
	1923G	.120	15.00	25.00	55.00	90.00
	1923J	4,000	600.00	1200.	1600.	2200.
	1924A	117.365	5.00	10.00	17.50	35.00
	1924D	30.971	5.00	10.00	17.50	45.00
	1924E	14.668	5.00	10.00	22.50	50.00
	1924F	21.968	5.00	10.00	17.50	45.00
	1924G	13.349	7.50	15.00	27.50	55.00
	1924J	17.252	5.00	10.00	17.50	45.00
	Common date		—	—	Proof	200.00

50 REICHSPFENNIG

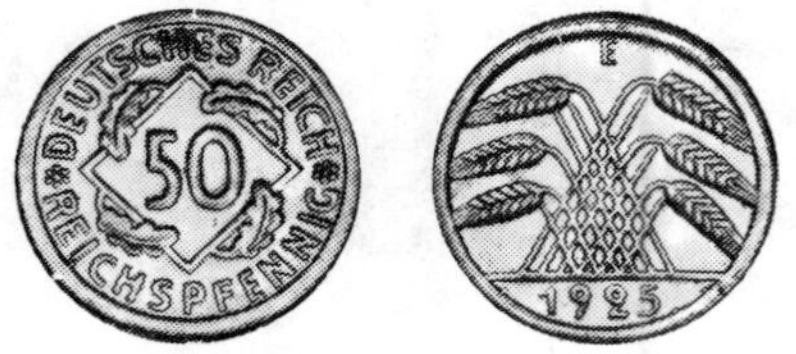

ALUMINUM-BRONZE

KM#	Date	Mintage	Fine	VF	XF	Unc
41	1924A	.801	500.00	1000.	1450.	2000.
	1924A	—	—	—	Proof	2200.
	1924E	Inc.Be.	1000.	2000.	3000.	5000.
	1924F	.055	1250.	2500.	4250.	6750.
	1924F	—	—	—	Proof	10,500.
	1924G	.011	1500.	3250.	5750.	8500.
	1924G	—	—	—	Proof	—
	1925E	1.805	500.00	975.00	1250.	1750.
	1925E	196 pcs.	—	—	Proof	2100.
	1925F	—	—	—	Proof	24,000.

NOTE: Peus Auction #324 4-89 1924F and 1925F proofs realized $10,360 and $23,830 respectively.

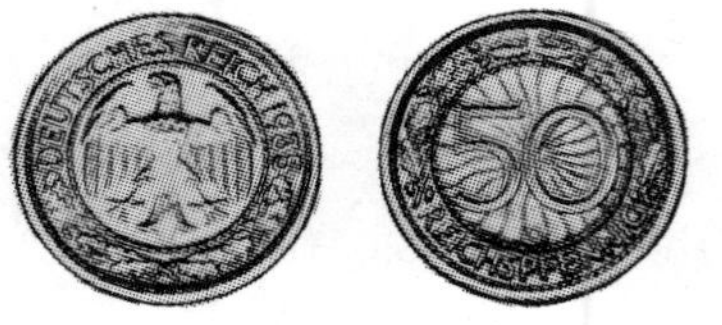

NICKEL

KM#	Date	Mintage	Fine	VF	XF	Unc
49	1927A	16.309	2.00	3.50	5.00	10.00
	1927D	2.228	2.50	5.00	7.50	12.50
	1927E	1.070	5.00	10.00	15.00	20.00
	1927F	1.940	2.50	5.00	7.50	12.50

KM#	Date	Mintage	Fine	VF	XF	Unc
49	1927G	1.756	4.00	7.50	10.00	17.50
	1927J	4.056	2.50	5.00	7.50	12.50
	1928A	43.864	.25	1.50	3.50	7.50
	1928D	14.088	.50	2.50	5.00	10.00
	1928E	8.618	.50	3.50	6.00	12.50
	1928F	9.954	.50	2.50	5.00	10.00
	1928G	6.177	.50	4.50	7.50	15.00
	1928J	6.565	.50	2.50	5.00	10.00
	1929A	10.298	.50	2.00	4.00	7.50
	1929D	1.965	.50	3.50	6.00	12.50
	1929E	—	—	Reported, not confirmed		
	1929F	1.162	5.00	12.50	20.00	32.50
	1930A	4.128	.50	4.50	7.50	12.50
	1930D	1.406	2.00	12.00	17.50	30.00
	1930E	.745	5.00	17.50	25.00	45.00
	1930F	.320	20.00	40.00	65.00	100.00
	1930G	.610	5.00	20.00	40.00	50.00
	1930J	.526	3.00	20.00	35.00	45.00
	1930	—	60.00	125.00	225.00	—
	1931A	5.624	.50	4.00	7.50	10.00
	1931D	1.125	1.50	12.50	17.50	30.00
	1931F	1.484	1.50	12.00	16.00	25.00
	1931G	.060	120.00	250.00	450.00	675.00
	1931J	.291	25.00	50.00	65.00	100.00
	1932E	.598	20.00	50.00	70.00	125.00
	1932G	.096	1000.	1750.	2000.	2800.
	1933G	.333	40.00	85.00	135.00	200.00
	1933J	.654	35.00	75.00	120.00	185.00
	1935A	6.390	.50	4.00	6.00	8.50
	1935D	2.812	2.50	7.50	15.00	20.00
	1935E	.745	7.50	30.00	40.00	50.00
	1935F	2.006	2.50	7.50	10.00	15.00
	1935G	.650	12.50	37.50	50.00	70.00
	1935J	1.635	2.00	15.00	20.00	27.50
	1935	—	1.00	6.00	12.50	25.00
	1936A	7.696	2.50	5.00	7.50	12.50
	1936D	.844	4.00	20.00	35.00	70.00
	1936E	1.190	5.00	15.00	30.00	60.00
	1936F	.602	7.50	17.50	35.00	75.00
	1936G	.936	5.00	15.00	30.00	40.00
	1936J	.490	25.00	75.00	110.00	165.00
	1937A	10.842	.25	2.50	5.00	7.50
	1937D	2.814	.50	4.00	7.50	10.00
	1937F	1.700	.50	2.50	10.00	12.50
	1937J	.300	40.00	80.00	120.00	175.00
	1938E	1.200	7.50	12.50	22.50	30.00
	1938G	1.299	7.50	12.50	25.00	35.00
	1938J	1.333	7.50	15.00	25.00	35.00
	Common date	—	—	Proof	150.00	

MARK

5.0000 g, .500 SILVER, .0803 oz ASW

KM#	Date	Mintage	Fine	VF	XF	Unc
42	1924A	75.536	4.00	9.00	16.50	38.00
	1924D	17.099	5.00	10.00	22.50	45.00
	1924E	12.293	5.00	10.00	22.50	45.00
	1924E	115 pcs.	—	—	Proof	275.00
	1924F	16.550	5.00	10.00	18.00	40.00
	1924G	10.065	6.00	12.00	25.00	65.00
	1924J	13.481	5.00	10.00	20.00	45.00
	1925A	13.878	6.00	12.00	35.00	100.00
	1925D	6.100	8.00	15.00	35.00	80.00
	Common date	—	—	Proof	200.00	

REICHSMARK

5.0000 g, .500 SILVER, .0803 oz ASW

KM#	Date	Mintage	Fine	VF	XF	Unc
44	1925A	34.527	3.00	10.00	20.00	40.00
	1925A	600 pcs.	—	—	Proof	200.00
	1925D	13.854	3.00	12.50	22.50	50.00
	1925E	6.460	7.50	20.00	32.00	60.00
	1925F	8.035	7.50	15.00	27.50	55.00
	1925G	4.520	7.50	15.00	30.00	55.00
	1925J	6.800	7.50	15.00	25.00	55.00
	1926A	35.555	6.50	10.00	22.50	45.00
	1926D	4.424	7.50	15.00	27.50	60.00
	1926E	3.225	7.50	15.00	45.00	90.00
	1926E	31 pcs.	—	—	Proof	200.00
	1926F	3.045	7.50	27.50	40.00	75.00
	1926G	3.410	7.50	27.50	40.00	75.00
	1926J	1.290	25.00	70.00	120.00	225.00
	1927A	.364	120.00	300.00	425.00	750.00
	1927F	1.959	20.00	60.00	100.00	200.00
	1927J	2.451	15.00	45.00	75.00	150.00

2 REICHSMARK

10.0000 g, .500 SILVER, .1608 oz ASW

KM#	Date	Mintage	Fine	VF	XF	Unc
45	1925A	16.145	7.50	12.50	22.00	55.00
	1925D	2.272	10.00	15.00	35.00	65.00
	1925E	1.971	10.00	17.50	40.00	90.00
	1925E	101 pcs.	—	—	Proof	200.00
	1925F	2.414	10.00	17.50	35.00	65.00
	1925G	.929	10.00	20.00	45.00	100.00
	1925J	2.326	10.00	17.50	35.00	65.00
	1926A	31.645	5.00	10.00	20.00	50.00
	1926D	11.322	5.00	10.00	22.00	45.00
	1926E	5.107	7.50	12.50	30.00	65.00
	1926E	30 pcs.	—	—	Proof	—
	1926F	7.115	7.50	12.50	30.00	65.00
	1926G	5.171	7.50	12.50	30.00	65.00
	1926J	5.305	7.50	12.50	30.00	65.00
	1927A	6.399	7.50	12.50	30.00	65.00
	1927D	.466	500.00	1000.	1650.	2500.
	1927E	.373	125.00	325.00	650.00	1200.
	1927E	53 pcs.	—	—	Proof	2150.
	1927F	.502	65.00	125.00	200.00	300.00
	1927J	.540	50.00	100.00	150.00	250.00
	1931A	2.109	20.00	35.00	60.00	115.00
	1931E	1.118	22.50	45.00	75.00	145.00
	1931F	1.505	22.50	45.00	75.00	145.00
	1931G	.915	30.00	70.00	120.00	200.00
	1931J	1.226	22.50	40.00	60.00	125.00
	Common date	—	—	—	Proof	160.00

3 MARK

ALUMINUM
Reeded edge.

	Date	Mintage	Fine	VF	XF	Unc
28	1922A	15.497	.25	2.50	5.00	10.00
	1922A	—	—	—	Proof	75.00
	1922E	2,000	90.00	175.00	300.00	500.00
	1922E	1,000	—	—	Proof	325.00

3rd Anniversary Weimar Constitution

	Date	Mintage	Fine	VF	XF	Unc
29	1922A	32.514	.25	1.00	1.50	2.50
	1922D	8.441	175.00	250.00	350.00	550.00
	1922D	—	—	—	Proof	500.00
	1922E	2.440	.50	5.00	7.50	15.00
	1922E	.022	—	—	Proof	30.00
	1922F	6.023	2.50	12.50	17.50	30.00
	1922G	3.655	.25	2.50	5.00	12.50
	1922J	4.896	.25	1.50	4.00	7.50
	1923E	2.030	17.50	40.00	60.00	85.00
	1923E	2,291	—	—	Proof	75.00

15.0000 g, .500 SILVER, .2411 oz ASW

	Date	Mintage	Fine	VF	XF	Unc
43	1924A	24.386	12.50	32.50	50.00	90.00
	1924D	3.769	12.50	35.00	55.00	120.00
	1924E	3.353	20.00	35.00	55.00	120.00
	1924E	115 pcs.	—	—	Proof	350.00
	1924F	4.518	20.00	35.00	55.00	120.00
	1924G	2.640	20.00	35.00	60.00	130.00
	1924J	3.677	20.00	35.00	55.00	120.00
	1925D	2.558	35.00	75.00	110.00	175.00
	Common date	—	—	—	Proof	280.00

3 REICHSMARK

15.0000 g, .500 SILVER, .2411 oz ASW
1000th Year of the Rhineland

KM#	Date	Mintage	Fine	VF	XF	Unc
46	1925A	3.052	15.00	30.00	45.00	80.00
	1925A	—	—	—	Proof	150.00
	1925D	1.123	17.50	35.00	55.00	95.00
	1925D	—	—	—	Proof	165.00
	1925E	.441	20.00	40.00	60.00	100.00
	1925E	229 pcs.	—	—	Proof	175.00
	1925F	.173	20.00	40.00	60.00	120.00
	1925F	—	—	—	Proof	250.00
	1925G	.300	20.00	40.00	55.00	95.00
	1925G	—	—	—	Proof	150.00
	1925J	.492	20.00	40.00	55.00	90.00
	1925J	—	—	—	Proof	185.00

700 Years of Freedom for Lubeck

	Date	Mintage	Fine	VF	XF	Unc
48	1926A	.200	60.00	95.00	150.00	215.00
	1926A	—	—	—	Proof	265.00

100th Anniversary of Bremerhaven

	Date	Mintage	Fine	VF	XF	Unc
50	1927A	.150	60.00	95.00	160.00	225.00
	1927A	—	—	—	Proof	330.00

1000th Anniversary - Founding of Nordhausen

	Date	Mintage	Fine	VF	XF	Unc
52	1927A	.100	60.00	95.00	165.00	230.00
	1927A	—	—	—	Proof	350.00

400th Anniversary - Philip University in Marburg

	Date	Mintage	Fine	VF	XF	Unc
53	1927A	.130	60.00	90.00	130.00	190.00
	1927A	—	—	—	Proof	250.00

450th Anniversary - Tubingen University

KM#	Date	Mintage	Fine	VF	XF	Unc
54	1927F	.050	150.00	250.00	420.00	575.00
	1927F	—	—	—	Proof	650.00

900th Anniversary - Founding of Naumburg

57	1928A	.100	60.00	90.00	145.00	250.00
	1928A	—	—	Matte Proof		500.00

400th Anniversary - Death of Albrecht Durer

58	1928D	.050	150.00	250.00	420.00	575.00
	1928D	—	—	Matte Proof		1500.

1000th Anniversary - Founding of Dinkelsbuhl

59	1928D	.040	250.00	450.00	675.00	850.00
	1928D	—	—	—	Proof	2000.

200th Anniversary - Birth of Gotthold Lessing

60	1929A	.217	17.50	30.00	60.00	90.00
	1929A	—	—	—	Proof	160.00
	1929D	.056	20.00	35.00	65.00	100.00
	1929D	—	—	—	Proof	250.00
	1929E	.030	20.00	35.00	70.00	110.00
	1929E	—	—	—	Proof	275.00
	1929F	.040	20.00	35.00	65.00	110.00
	1929F	—	—	—	Proof	250.00
	1929G	.024	20.00	35.00	80.00	130.00
	1929G	—	—	—	Proof	300.00
	1929J	.033	20.00	35.00	80.00	120.00
	1929J	—	—	—	Proof	300.00

Waldeck-Prussia Union

KM#	Date	Mintage	Fine	VF	XF	Unc
62	1929A	.170	60.00	95.00	155.00	225.00
	1929A	—	—	—	Proof	250.00

10th Anniversary - Weimar Constitution

63	1929A	1.421	17.50	35.00	50.00	75.00
	1929A	—	—	—	Proof	225.00
	1929A	—	—	Matte Proof		—
	1929D	.499	17.50	35.00	55.00	85.00
	1929D	—	—	—	Proof	225.00
	1929E	.122	22.50	45.00	55.00	90.00
	1929E	—	—	—	Proof	300.00
	1929F	.370	17.50	35.00	55.00	90.00
	1929F	—	—	—	Proof	250.00
	1929G	.256	22.50	45.00	60.00	90.00
	1929G	—	—	—	Proof	250.00
	1929J	.342	17.50	35.00	55.00	90.00
	1929J	—	—	—	Proof	250.00

1000th Anniversary - Meissen

65	1929E	.200	25.00	45.00	65.00	100.00
	1929E	—	—	—	Proof	300.00

Graf Zeppelin Flight

67	1930A	.542	35.00	60.00	85.00	125.00
	1930A	—	—	—	Proof	350.00
	1930D	.141	35.00	60.00	90.00	125.00
	1930D	—	—	—	Proof	250.00
	1930E	.075	35.00	60.00	90.00	150.00
	1930E	—	—	—	Proof	335.00
	1930F	.100	35.00	60.00	90.00	125.00
	1930F	—	—	—	Proof	275.00
	1930G	.061	40.00	65.00	95.00	200.00
	1930G	—	—	—	Proof	335.00
	1930J	.082	40.00	65.00	95.00	190.00
	1930J	—	—	—	Proof	325.00

700th Anniversary - Death of Von Der Vogelweide

69	1930A	.163	35.00	55.00	85.00	125.00
	1930A	—	—	—	Proof	200.00
	1930A	—	—	Matte Proof		—
	1930D	.042	35.00	55.00	85.00	125.00
	1930D	—	—	—	Proof	225.00
	1930E	.022	37.50	75.00	100.00	150.00
	1930E	—	—	—	Proof	225.00
	1930F	.030	37.50	75.00	100.00	150.00
	1930F	—	—	—	Proof	325.00
	1930G	.018	45.00	85.00	120.00	165.00
	1930G	—	—	—	Proof	225.00
	1930J	.025	35.00	55.00	85.00	155.00
	1930J	—	—	—	Proof	225.00

Liberation of Rhineland

KM#	Date	Mintage	Fine	VF	XF	Unc
70	1930A	1.734	22.50	35.00	60.00	85.00
	1930A	—	—	—	Proof	150.00
	1930A	—	—	Matte Proof		—
	1930D	.450	22.50	35.00	60.00	85.00
	1930D	—	—	—	Proof	200.00
	1930E	.038	65.00	125.00	175.00	325.00
	1930E	—	—	—	Proof	200.00
	1930F	.321	22.50	35.00	60.00	85.00
	1930F	—	—	—	Proof	160.00
	1930G	.195	22.50	35.00	65.00	120.00
	1930G	—	—	—	Proof	200.00
	1930J	.261	22.50	35.00	65.00	110.00
	1930J	—	—	—	Proof	200.00

300th Anniversary - Magdeburg Rebuilding

72	1931A	.100	100.00	150.00	220.00	325.00
	1931A	—	—	—	Proof	450.00

Centenary - Death of vom Stein

73	1931A	.150	60.00	90.00	165.00	250.00
	1931A	—	—	—	Proof	300.00

74	1931A	13.324	125.00	200.00	350.00	600.00
	1931D	2.232	145.00	225.00	350.00	600.00
	1931E	2.235	145.00	225.00	350.00	600.00
	1931F	2.357	145.00	225.00	350.00	600.00
	1931G	1.468	145.00	225.00	375.00	700.00
	1931J	1.115	145.00	225.00	375.00	700.00
	1932A	2.933	125.00	200.00	350.00	600.00
	1932D	1.986	145.00	225.00	375.00	700.00
	1932F	.653	250.00	450.00	650.00	1150.
	1932G	.210	325.00	900.00	1500.	2250.
	1932J	1.336	145.00	225.00	375.00	700.00
	1933G	*.152	800.00	1450.	2200.	3250.
	Common date				Proof	1250.

*NOTE: Less than 10 percent of issue was released.

Centenary - Death of Goethe

76	1932A	.217	25.00	50.00	85.00	135.00
	1932A	—	—	—	Proof	250.00
	1932D	.056	25.00	50.00	85.00	135.00
	1932D	—	—	—	Proof	250.00

KM#	Date	Mintage	Fine	VF	XF	Unc
76	1932E	.030	40.00	70.00	100.00	170.00
	1932E	—	—	—	Proof	300.00
	1932F	.040	25.00	50.00	85.00	135.00
	1932F	—	—	—	Proof	250.00
	1932F	—	—	Matte Proof		—
	1932G	.024	45.00	80.00	110.00	180.00
	1932G	—	—	—	Proof	300.00
	1932J	.033	35.00	60.00	100.00	170.00
	1932J	—	—	—	Proof	265.00

5 REICHSMARK

25.0000 g, .500 SILVER, .4019 oz ASW
1000th Year of the Rhineland

	Date	Mintage	Fine	VF	XF	Unc
47	1925A	.684	35.00	60.00	100.00	170.00
	1925A	—	—	—	Proof	325.00
	1925D	.452	35.00	60.00	100.00	180.00
	1925D	—	—	—	Proof	400.00
	1925E	.204	50.00	75.00	120.00	220.00
	1925E	226 pcs.	—	—	Proof	400.00
	1925F	.212	40.00	65.00	110.00	200.00
	1925F	—	—	—	Proof	425.00
	1925G	.089	45.00	70.00	115.00	210.00
	1925G	—	—	—	Proof	475.00
	1925J	.043	70.00	140.00	200.00	375.00
	1925J	—	—	—	Proof	550.00

450th Anniversary - University of Tubingen

KM#	Date	Mintage	Fine	VF	XF	Unc
55	1927F	.040	175.00	275.00	450.00	700.00
	1927F	—	—	—	Proof	750.00

56	1927A	7.926	30.00	75.00	120.00	180.00
	1927D	1.471	35.00	90.00	155.00	255.00
	1927E	1.100	40.00	95.00	170.00	325.00
	1927F	.700	30.00	75.00	150.00	225.00
	1927G	.759	60.00	115.00	220.00	375.00
	1927J	1.006	35.00	90.00	170.00	310.00
	1928A	15.466	30.00	75.00	150.00	200.00
	1928D	4.613	30.00	75.00	150.00	200.00
	1928E	2.310	30.00	90.00	165.00	300.00
	1928F	3.771	30.00	75.00	150.00	200.00
	1928G	1.923	35.00	90.00	165.00	270.00
	1928J	2.450	35.00	90.00	165.00	275.00
	1929A	6.730	30.00	75.00	150.00	200.00
	1929D	2.020	30.00	80.00	160.00	270.00
	1929E	.860	50.00	165.00	255.00	475.00
	1929F	.814	50.00	165.00	255.00	475.00
	1929G	.950	50.00	165.00	255.00	475.00
	1929J	.779	50.00	165.00	255.00	475.00
	1930A	3.790	35.00	90.00	165.00	300.00
	1930D	.606	125.00	275.00	425.00	850.00
	1930E	.354	150.00	400.00	1000.	2200.
	1930F	.630	125.00	325.00	585.00	1000.
	1930G	.367	200.00	500.00	1000.	2000.
	1930J	.740	125.00	325.00	500.00	950.00
	1931A	14.651	30.00	75.00	150.00	200.00
	1931D	3.254	35.00	90.00	160.00	245.00
	1931E	2.245	40.00	90.00	165.00	275.00
	1931F	4.152	35.00	90.00	160.00	270.00
	1931G	1.620	100.00	170.00	245.00	375.00
	1931J	3.092	45.00	125.00	210.00	350.00
	1932A	32.303	35.00	90.00	150.00	200.00
	1932D	8.556	35.00	90.00	150.00	200.00
	1932E	4.013	35.00	95.00	155.00	290.00
	1932F	5.019	35.00	90.00	145.00	250.00
	1932G	3.504	35.00	90.00	145.00	250.00
	1932J	3.752	35.00	95.00	155.00	290.00
	1933J	.423	550.00	1000.	2200.	3250.
	1933J	—	—	—	Proof	4250.
	Common date	—	—	—	Proof	700.00

200th Anniversary - Birth of Gotthold Lessing

KM#	Date	Mintage	Fine	VF	XF	Unc
61	1929A	.087	50.00	100.00	135.00	200.00
	1929A	—	—	—	Proof	350.00
	1929D	.022	50.00	100.00	150.00	225.00
	1929D	—	—	—	Proof	350.00
	1929E	.012	60.00	120.00	165.00	285.00
	1929E	—	—	—	Proof	425.00
	1929F	.016	50.00	100.00	150.00	225.00
	1929F	—	—	—	Proof	375.00
	1929G	9,760	60.00	120.00	165.00	285.00
	1929G	—	—	—	Proof	425.00
	1929J	.013	55.00	110.00	150.00	250.00
	1929J	—	—	—	Proof	400.00

10th Anniversary - Weimar Constitution

64	1929A	.325	45.00	65.00	125.00	200.00
	1929A	—	—	—	Proof	450.00
	1929D	.084	50.00	90.00	135.00	220.00
	1929D	—	—	—	Proof	400.00
	1929E	.045	50.00	90.00	135.00	220.00
	1929E	—	—	—	Proof	625.00
	1929F	.060	60.00	100.00	150.00	230.00
	1929F	—	—	—	Proof	400.00
	1929G	.037	60.00	100.00	160.00	250.00
	1929G	—	—	—	Proof	500.00
	1929J	.049	50.00	90.00	160.00	250.00
	1929J	—	—	—	Proof	650.00

100th Anniversary - Bremerhaven

51	1927A	.050	175.00	275.00	475.00	750.00
	1927A	—	—	—	Proof	900.00

1000th Anniversary - Meissen

66	1929E	.120	150.00	300.00	450.00	650.00
	1929E	—	—	—	Proof	1000.

Graf Zeppelin Flight

KM#	Date	Mintage	Fine	VF	XF	Unc
68	1930A	.217	60.00	100.00	165.00	250.00
	1930A	—	—	—	Proof	425.00
	1930A	—	—	—	Matte Proof	—
	1930D	.056	70.00	110.00	170.00	265.00
	1930D	—	—	—	Proof	600.00
	1930E	.030	70.00	110.00	200.00	350.00
	1930E	—	—	—	Proof	650.00
	1930F	.040	70.00	110.00	170.00	265.00
	1930F	—	—	—	Proof	550.00
	1930G	.024	75.00	115.00	200.00	350.00
	1930G	—	—	—	Proof	650.00
	1930J	.033	70.00	110.00	175.00	300.00
	1930J	—	—	—	Proof	650.00

Liberation of Rhineland

71	1930A	.325	60.00	100.00	160.00	250.00
	1930A	—	—	—	Proof	400.00
	1930D	.084	60.00	100.00	170.00	275.00
	1930D	—	—	—	Proof	550.00
	1930E	.045	70.00	125.00	180.00	300.00
	1930E	—	—	—	Proof	475.00
	1930F	.060	60.00	100.00	165.00	285.00
	1930F	—	—	—	Proof	450.00
	1930G	.037	85.00	165.00	255.00	400.00
	1930G	—	—	—	Proof	550.00
	1930J	.049	75.00	135.00	190.00	325.00
	1930J	—	—	—	Proof	525.00

Centenary - Death of Goethe

KM#	Date	Mintage	Fine	VF	XF	Unc
77	1932A	.011	550.00	1250.	2250.	3350.
	1932A	—	—	—	Proof	4500.
	1932D	2,812	650.00	1350.	2400.	3500.
	1932D	—	—	—	Proof	4000.
	1932E	1,490	700.00	1400.	2500.	3750.
	1932E	—	—	—	Proof	4500.
	1932F	2,006	700.00	1400.	2500.	3750.
	1932F	—	—	—	Proof	5500.
	1932G	1,220	750.00	1500.	2500.	3750.
	1932G	—	—	—	Proof	5000.
	1932J	1,634	750.00	1500.	2500.	3750.
	1932J	—	—	—	Proof	5000.

200 MARK

ALUMINUM

35	1923A	174.900	.15	.50	1.00	1.75
	1923A	—	—	—	Proof	40.00
	1923D	35.189	.20	.60	1.00	1.75
	1923D	—	—	—	Proof	40.00
	1923E	11.250	.20	1.00	2.50	5.00
	1923E	4,095	—	—	Proof	40.00
	1923F	20.090	.25	1.00	2.00	4.00
	1923F	—	—	—	Proof	40.00
	1923G	24.923	.25	1.00	2.00	4.00
	1923G	—	—	—	Proof	40.00
	1923J	16.258	.20	1.00	2.50	5.00
	1923J	—	—	—	Proof	40.00

500 MARK

ALUMINUM

36	1923A	59.278	.20	1.00	1.50	2.50
	1923A	—	—	—	Proof	70.00
	1923D	13.683	.25	1.00	1.50	3.00
	1923D	—	—	—	Proof	70.00
	1923E	2.128	1.00	7.50	12.50	15.00
	1923E	2,053	—	—	Proof	70.00
	1923F	7.963	.25	1.50	2.00	5.00
	1923F	—	—	—	Proof	70.00
	1923G	4.404	.25	2.50	5.00	7.50
	1923G	—	—	—	Proof	70.00
	1923J	1.008	10.00	18.00	35.00	65.00
	1923J	—	—	—	Proof	250.00

1933-1945

A wide range of factors - humiliation of defeat, economic depression, poverty, and a pervasive feeling of discontent - aided Hitler in his climb to power. After the unsuccessful Putsch (uprising against the Bavarian Government) in 1923, Hitler was imprisoned in Landsberg Fortress. While imprisoned Hitler dictated his book ''Mein Kampf'' which became the cornerstone of Nazism espousing Hitler's irrational ideology and the manipulation of power without moral constraint as the basis of strategy.

Master propagandist Josef Goebbels tried to attract the sympathetic attention of the German public. The usual tactic was to have Hitler promise all things to all people provided that they in turn would pledge to him their complete faith and obedience.

Once in power, coercion was used to elicit the appearance of unanimous endorsement. Public works and military rearmament helped overcome the depression. It took the Nazis only about two years to consolidate their system politically. The combined terrorism of the storm troops and the police forces, including the Gestapo, stifled potential opposition. By 1935, Nazi affiliated organizations controlled all German cultural, professional, and economic fields, assuring strict compliance with the party line.

With the passage of the Nurnberg Laws in 1935, the more ominous aspects of Nazi anti-Semitism came to light. Jews were deprived of their citizenship and forbidden to marry non-Jews. This was followed by confiscation of property and the required wearing of the Star of David for identification purposes, eventually culminating in the mass deportation to concentration and death camps.

By 1936, unemployment was virtually eliminated and economic production was up to 1929 levels. All sources of information were under the control of Josef Goebbels, while all police power was in the hands of Heinrich Himmler. Germans who were not convinced by Goebbel's propaganda machine would be silenced by Himmler's Gestapo. Usually the implied threat was enough. The majority of Germans did not suffer any ill effects at first and national pride stirred once again.

Hitler's audacity in foreign affairs met with success due to the trend of appeasement by the western powers. First, Germany withdrew from the League of Nations and the World Disarmament Council. In 1935, the Saar voted to return to Germany and Hitler renounced the reviled 1921 peace treaty and related pacts. In 1936, German forces reoccupied the Rhineland. In 1938, Austria was annexed and at the Munich Conference, which excluded Czechoslovakia, Great Britain and France agreed that the Sudatenland was to become German territory. In 1939, Slovakia became an independent Nazi Puppet State and the "Protectorate" of Bohemia and Moravia was established. Next came the German-Soviet nonaggression pact which secretly divided up Poland between the two totalitarian powers. Great Britain and France finally declared war when Poland was invaded. The years of 1939-1942 were a period of impressive victories for Germany's well trained and equipped forces. However, when Hitler expanded his war beyond western Europe by invading Africa and Russia and declaring war on the U.S.A., it started the chain of events which would culminate in the total and final German defeat on May 7, 1945, VE Day, ending the European theater of the Second World War and The Third Reich.

MINT MARKS

A - Berlin
B - Vienna, 1938-1944
D - Munich
E - Muldenhutten
F - Stuttgart
G - Karlsruhe
J - Hamburg

MONETARY SYSTEMS

100 Reichspfennig = 1 Reichsmark

REICHSPFENNIG

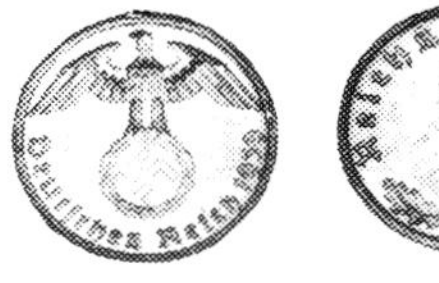

BRONZE

KM#	Date	Mintage	Fine	VF	XF	Unc
89	1936A	Inc.KM37	1.50	4.00	7.50	15.00
	1936E	.150	25.00	50.00	100.00	150.00
	1936F	4.600	22.50	50.00	95.00	145.00
	1936G	Inc.KM37	15.00	30.00	60.00	90.00
	1936J	Inc.KM37	10.00	30.00	50.00	70.00
	1937A	67.180	.10	.25	.50	2.50
	1937D	14.060	.10	.25	.50	2.50
	1937E	10.700	.15	.35	1.00	5.00
	1937F	11.058	.15	.35	1.00	5.00
	1937G	4.250	.15	.35	1.00	5.00
	1937J	6.714	.15	.35	1.00	5.00
	1938A	75.707	.10	.25	.50	5.00
	1938B	2.378	.50	6.00	9.00	12.50
	1938D	13.930	.10	.25	.50	5.00
	1938E	14.503	.10	.25	.50	5.00
	1938F	11.714	.10	.25	.50	5.00
	1938G	8.390	.10	.25	.50	5.00
	1938J	15.458	.10	.25	.50	6.00
	1939A	97.541	.10	.25	.50	5.00
	1939B	22.732	.15	.35	1.00	7.50
	1939D	20.760	.10	.25	.50	5.00
	1939E	12.478	.10	.25	.50	7.50
	1939F	12.482	.10	.25	.50	5.00
	1939G	12.250	.10	.25	.50	5.00
	1939J	8.368	.10	.25	.50	7.50
	1940A	27.094	.10	.25	.50	6.00
	1940F	7.850	.15	.35	1.00	6.00
	1940G	3.875	1.00	5.00	7.50	15.00
	1940J	7.450	.50	4.00	5.00	8.00
	Common date		—	—	Proof	75.00

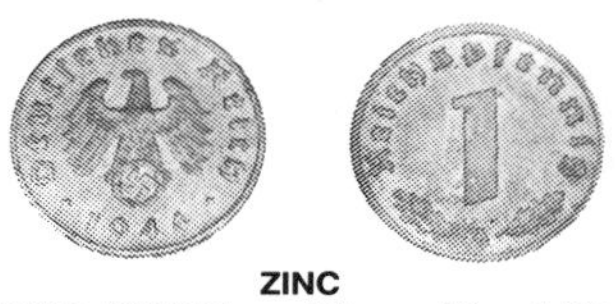

ZINC

KM#	Date	Mintage	Fine	VF	XF	Unc
97	1940A	223.948	.10	.20	1.00	5.00
	1940B	62.198	.10	.20	1.00	2.50
	1940D	43.951	.10	.20	1.00	5.00
	1940E	20.749	.20	1.00	5.00	7.50
	1940F	33.854	.10	.20	1.00	5.00
	1940G	20.165	.10	.20	1.00	5.00
	1940J	24.459	.10	.20	1.00	5.00
	1941A	281.618	.10	.15	.50	4.00
	1941B	62.285	.20	1.00	1.50	7.50
	1941D	73.745	.10	.15	.50	5.00
	1941E	49.041	.10	.50	1.50	7.50
	1941F	51.017	.10	.15	.50	5.00
	1941G	44.810	.10	.50	1.00	7.50
	1941J	57.625	.10	.15	.50	5.00
	1942A	558.877	.10	.15	.50	5.00
	1942B	124.740	.10	.20	1.00	6.00
	1942D	134.145	.10	.15	.50	6.00
	1942E	84.674	.15	1.50	2.50	8.50
	1942F	90.788	.10	.15	.50	6.00
	1942G	59.858	.10	.15	.50	6.00
	1942J	122.934	.10	.50	1.00	6.00
	1943A	372.401	.10	.15	.50	6.00
	1943B	79.315	.10	.50	1.00	6.00
	1943D	91.629	.10	.15	.50	6.00
	1943E	34.191	.50	2.50	7.50	10.00
	1943F	70.269	.10	.50	1.00	6.00
	1943G	24.688	.15	1.50	2.50	7.50
	1943J	37.695	.15	1.50	2.50	7.50
	1944A	124.421	.10	.50	2.00	5.00
	1944B	87.850	.20	1.00	2.00	5.00
	1944D	56.755	.20	1.00	2.50	7.00
	1944E	41.729	.20	2.00	5.00	10.00
	1944F	15.580	.50	4.00	6.00	12.00
	1944G	34.967	.10	.50	1.00	4.00
	1945A	17.145	.25	2.50	7.50	15.00
	1945E	6.800	25.00	45.00	70.00	130.00
	Common date		—	—	Proof	80.00

2 REICHSPFENNIG

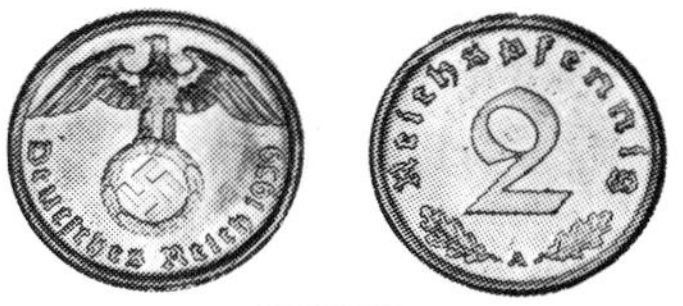

BRONZE

KM#	Date	Mintage	Fine	VF	XF	Unc
90	1936A	Inc.Be.	.50	3.00	8.00	25.00
	1936D	Inc.Be.	.50	3.00	8.00	25.00
	1936F	3.100	5.00	15.00	30.00	50.00
	1937A	34.404	.10	.50	1.50	7.00
	1937D	9.016	.10	.50	1.50	7.00
	1937E	Inc.Be.	6.00	20.00	45.00	80.00
90	1937F	7.487	.10	.50	1.50	7.00
	1937G	.490	2.00	8.50	15.00	35.00
	1937J	.450	2.00	8.50	15.00	30.00
	1938A	27.264	.10	.15	.50	6.00
	1938B	2.714	1.50	4.00	8.00	22.00
	1938D	8.770	.10	.25	1.00	6.00
	1938E	5.450	.25	1.00	2.00	6.00
	1938F	10.090	.10	.25	1.00	6.00
	1938G	3.685	.10	.25	1.00	6.00
	1938J	7.243	.10	.25	1.00	6.00
	1939A	37.348	.10	.25	1.00	6.00
	1939B	9.361	.10	.25	1.00	6.00
	1939D	7.555	.10	.25	1.00	6.00
	1939E	6.650	.25	1.00	4.50	10.00
	1939F	7.019	.10	.25	1.00	6.00
	1939G	4.885	.10	.25	1.00	6.00
	1939J	6.996	.10	.25	1.00	6.00
	1940A	22.681	.10	.25	1.00	6.00
	1940D	3.855	.50	3.00	6.50	12.50
	1940E	3.412	2.50	10.00	15.00	30.00
	1940G	1.161	40.00	70.00	130.00	175.00
	1940J	2.357	1.50	7.50	12.50	25.00
	Common date		—	—	Proof	80.00

5 REICHSPFENNIG

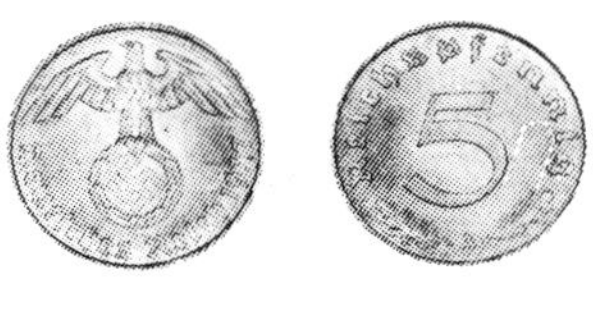

ALUMINUM-BRONZE

KM#	Date	Mintage	Fine	VF	XF	Unc
91	1936A	Inc.Be.	15.00	25.00	55.00	100.00
	1936D	Inc.Be.	10.00	20.00	35.00	60.00
	1936G	Inc.Be.	40.00	80.00	140.00	200.00
	1937A	29.700	.10	.20	1.00	6.00
	1937D	4.992	.10	.20	1.00	7.50
	1937E	4.474	.20	1.00	3.00	10.00
	1937F	2.092	.10	.20	1.00	8.00
	1937G	2.749	2.50	7.50	15.00	20.00
	1937J	6.991	.25	2.50	5.00	12.50
	1938A	54.012	.25	2.50	5.00	7.50
	1938B	3.447	.25	1.50	5.00	10.00
	1938D	17.708	.10	.25	1.50	6.00
	1938E	8.602	.10	.40	4.00	8.00
	1938F	8.147	.10	.25	1.50	7.00
	1938G	7.323	.10	.25	1.50	7.00
	1938J	7.646	.10	.25	1.50	7.00
	1939A	35.337	.10	.25	1.50	7.00
	1939B	8.313	.10	.20	1.00	7.50
	1939D	8.304	.20	1.00	2.00	7.50
	1939E	5.138	.20	1.00	2.00	7.50
	1939F	10.339	.10	.20	1.00	6.00
	1939G	4.266	.25	2.50	7.50	12.50
	1939J	4.177	.20	2.00	7.50	10.00
	Common date		—	—	Proof	95.00

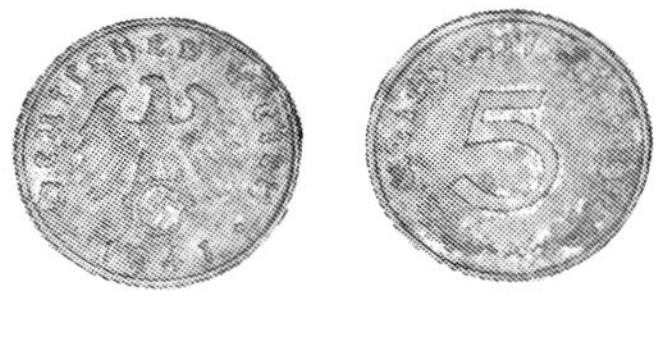

KM#	Date	Mintage	Fine	VF	XF	Unc
100	1940A	174.684	.10	.20	1.00	5.00
	1940B	63.469	.20	1.00	1.50	6.00
	1940D	44.364	.20	1.00	1.50	6.00
	1940E	25.800	.30	2.00	4.00	6.00
	1940F	31.381	.20	1.00	2.00	6.00
	1940G	24.148	.20	1.00	2.50	6.00
	1940J	30.518	.20	1.00	2.00	6.00
	1941A	246.216	.10	.20	1.00	5.00
	1941B	60.297	.10	.30	2.00	7.50
	1941D	51.100	.10	.30	2.00	7.50
	1941E	26.354	.10	.30	2.00	7.50
	1941F	36.725	.10	.30	2.00	7.50
	1941G	21.276	.10	.30	2.00	7.50
	1941J	52.872	.10	.30	2.00	7.50
	1942A	161.042	.10	.20	1.00	5.00
	1942B	12.405	.25	1.50	5.00	7.50
	1942D	15.486	.10	.35	2.50	5.00
	1942E	8.800	7.50	17.50	22.50	35.00
	1942F	24.662	.10	.25	1.50	5.00
	1942G	12.749	.10	.35	2.50	7.50
	1943A	46.830	.15	.50	2.00	7.50
	1943B	.833	10.00	20.00	30.00	80.00
	1943D	13.650	.15	.50	4.00	10.00
	1943E	16.581	2.50	7.50	12.50	17.50
	1943F	9.891	.20	1.00	2.50	6.00
	1943G	7.237	.15	.50	2.00	6.00
	1944A	23.699	3.50	15.00	27.50	37.50
	1944D	26.340	.25	1.50	3.00	5.00
	1944E	19.720	.50	4.00	9.00	15.00
	1944F	6.853	.25	1.50	3.00	7.50
	1944G	3.540	100.00	225.00	350.00	425.00
	Common date		—	—	Proof	75.00

10 REICHSPFENNIG

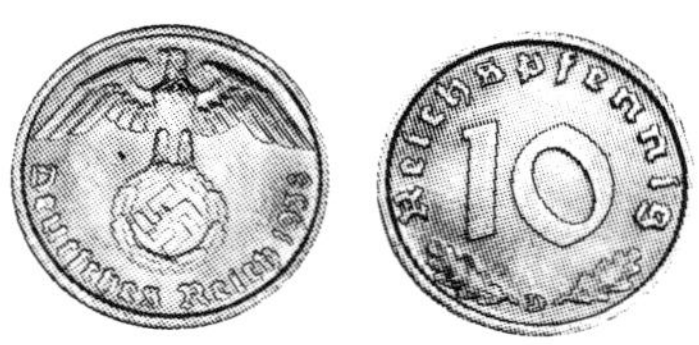

ALUMINUM-BRONZE

KM#	Date	Mintage	Fine	VF	XF	Unc
92	1936A	Inc. Be.	2.50	12.50	20.00	60.00
	1936E	.245	65.00	135.00	175.00	275.00
	1936G	.129	100.00	225.00	350.00	525.00
	1937A	36.830	.10	.50	2.00	7.50
	1937D	6.882	.25	1.50	3.00	10.00
	1937E	3.786	2.00	10.00	18.00	40.00
	1937F	5.934	.50	2.50	5.00	12.50
	1937G	2.131	1.00	5.00	7.50	17.50
	1937J	4.439	.50	2.50	5.00	15.00
	1938A	70.068	.10	.20	1.00	6.00
	1938B	7.852	.50	2.50	5.00	12.50
	1938D	16.990	.10	.50	2.00	8.00
	1938E	10.739	.20	1.00	2.50	9.00
	1938F	12.307	.20	1.00	2.50	9.00
	1938G	8.584	.20	1.00	2.50	9.00
	1938J	10.389	.20	1.00	2.50	9.00
	1939A	40.171	.20	1.00	2.00	8.00
	1939B	7.814	.20	1.00	2.00	9.00
	1939D	11.307	.20	1.00	2.00	9.00
	1939E	5.079	.50	2.50	7.50	15.00
	1939F	6.993	.25	1.50	3.00	10.00
	1939G	5.532	.50	5.00	10.00	20.00
	1939J	5.557	.20	1.00	2.00	6.00
	Common date		—	—	Proof	95.00

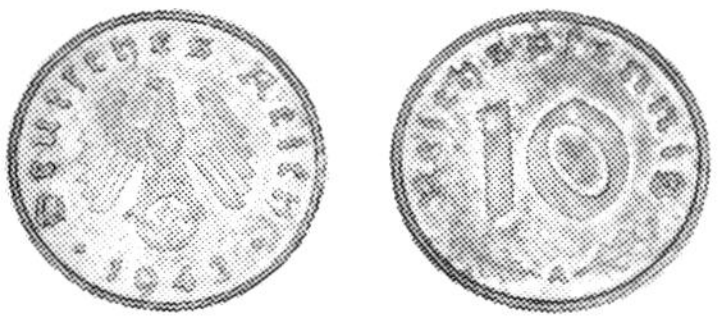

KM#	Date	Mintage	Fine	VF	XF	Unc
101	1940A	212.948	.10	.35	1.50	6.00
	1940B	76.274	.15	.50	2.50	7.50
	1940D	45.434	.15	.50	2.00	6.50
	1940E	34.350	.15	.50	2.00	6.50
	1940F	27.603	.15	.50	2.00	6.50
	1940G	27.308	.15	.50	2.00	6.50
	1940J	41.678	.15	.50	2.00	6.50
	1941A	240.284	.10	.35	1.50	6.00
	1941B	70.747	.15	.50	2.50	7.50
	1941D	77.560	.15	.50	2.00	6.50
	1941E	36.548	.15	.50	2.00	6.50
	1941F	42.834	.15	.50	2.00	6.50
	1941G	28.765	.15	.50	2.00	6.50
	1941J	30.525	.15	.50	2.00	6.50
	1942A	184.545	.10	.20	.50	2.00
	1942B	16.329	.25	2.50	3.50	10.00
	1942D	40.852	.20	1.00	2.50	7.50
	1942E	18.334	.25	1.50	3.00	7.50
	1942F	32.690	.10	.35	1.50	6.00
	1942G	20.295	.25	1.50	2.50	6.00
	1942J	29.957	.25	1.50	2.50	7.50
	1943A	157.357	.15	1.50	2.50	7.50
	1943B	11.940	2.50	7.50	15.00	30.00
	1943D	17.304	.25	2.00	3.00	7.50
	1943E	10.445	2.50	7.50	15.00	30.00
	1943F	24.804	.25	2.50	5.00	7.50
	1943G	3.618	.25	2.50	6.00	12.50
	1943J	1.821	15.00	30.00	50.00	85.00
	1944A	84.164	.15	1.00	2.50	7.50
	1944B	40.781	.50	1.50	3.00	8.00
	1944D	30.369	.35	1.50	3.00	8.00
	1944E	29.963	.50	2.00	4.00	8.00
	1944F	19.639	.50	2.00	4.00	8.00
	1944G	13.023	.50	2.00	4.00	8.00
	1945A	7.112	5.00	12.50	25.00	50.00
	1945E	4.897	10.00	15.00	30.00	65.00
	Common date		—	—	Proof	80.00

50 REICHSPFENNIG

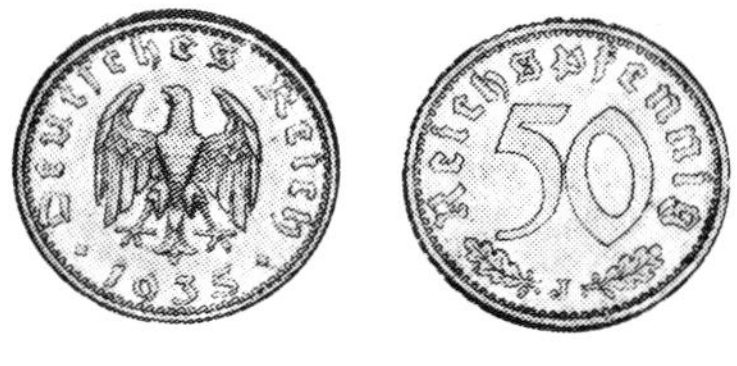

ALUMINUM

KM#	Date	Mintage	Fine	VF	XF	Unc
87	1935A	75.912	.25	2.50	6.00	20.00
	1935A	—	—	—	Proof	75.00
	1935D	19.688	.25	1.00	2.50	17.50
	1935D	—	—	—	Proof	75.00
	1935E	10.418	.50	5.00	7.50	22.50
	1935E	—	—	—	Proof	75.00
	1935F	14.061	.25	1.00	3.00	22.50
	1935F	—	—	—	Proof	75.00
	1935G	8.540	.50	4.00	9.00	32.50
	1935G	—	—	—	Proof	75.00
	1935J	11.438	.35	3.50	7.50	27.50
	1935J	—	—	—	Proof	100.00

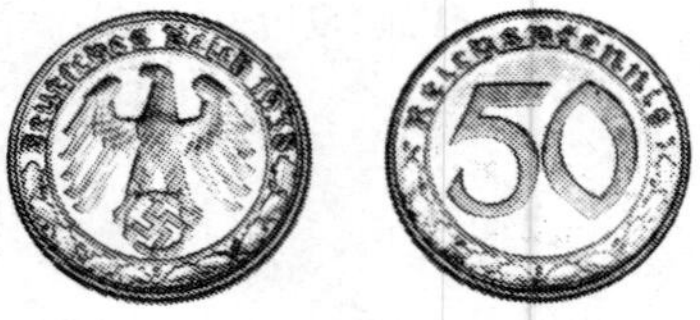

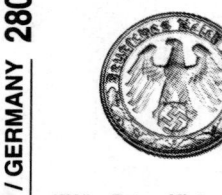

NICKEL

KM#	Date	Mintage	Fine	VF	XF	Unc
95	1938A	5.051	15.00	30.00	50.00	80.00
	1938B	1.124	20.00	40.00	60.00	90.00
	1938D	1.260	20.00	40.00	60.00	90.00
	1938D	1.260	20.00	40.00	60.00	95.00
	1938F	1.210	12.50	28.00	55.00	95.00
	1938G	.460	25.00	50.00	90.00	165.00
	1938J	.730	20.00	38.00	75.00	150.00
	1939A	15.037	17.50	30.00	50.00	70.00
	1939B	2.826	17.50	30.00	55.00	75.00
	1939D	3.648	15.00	30.00	55.00	75.00
	1939E	1.924	15.00	32.00	60.00	85.00
	1939F	2.602	15.00	32.00	60.00	85.00
	1939G	1.565	15.00	32.00	65.00	125.00
	1939J	2.114	15.00	32.00	60.00	90.00
	Common date		—	—	Proof	245.00

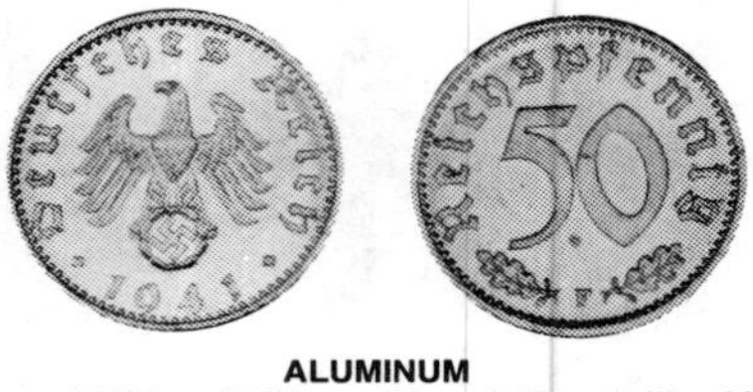

ALUMINUM

KM#	Date	Mintage	Fine	VF	XF	Unc
96	1939A	5.000	.35	2.50	5.00	20.00
	1939B	5.482	.35	2.50	5.00	20.00
	1939D	.600	2.50	12.50	25.00	50.00
	1939E	2.000	.50	5.00	7.50	30.00
	1939F	3.600	.35	3.00	6.00	22.50
	1939G	.560	10.00	20.00	50.00	75.00
	1939J	1.000	2.50	10.00	15.00	40.00
	1940A	56.128	.15	.50	2.50	15.00
	1940B	10.016	.35	3.00	5.00	15.00
	1940D	13.800	.25	1.50	3.00	15.00
	1940E	5.618	1.50	10.00	15.00	40.00
	1940F	6.663	.25	1.50	3.00	15.00
	1940G	5.616	1.50	9.00	12.50	35.00
	1940J	7.335	2.00	12.50	17.50	50.00
	1941A	31.263	.25	1.50	3.00	15.00
	1941B	4.291	2.00	5.00	7.00	15.00
	1941D	7.200	.35	3.00	5.00	15.00
	1941E	3.806	.50	4.00	7.50	20.00
	1941F	5.128	.30	2.00	5.00	15.00
	1941G	3.091	2.50	4.00	7.50	20.00
	1941J	4.165	1.00	6.00	8.00	20.00
	1942A	11.580	.15	.50	2.50	8.50
	1942B	2.876	3.50	15.00	25.00	55.00
	1942D	2.247	.35	3.00	6.00	15.00
	1942E	3.810	2.50	5.00	7.50	22.50
	1942F	5.133	1.00	3.50	5.00	15.00
	1942G	1.400	2.50	5.00	10.00	30.00
	1943A	29.325	.15	.50	2.50	10.00
	1943B	8.229	.50	4.50	7.50	15.00
	1943D	5.315	.20	1.00	3.50	15.00
	1943G	2.892	1.25	7.50	12.50	30.00
	1943J	4.166	5.00	10.00	15.00	35.00
	1944B	5.622	1.00	7.50	10.00	22.50
	1944D	4.886	7.50	15.00	25.00	60.00
	1944F	3.739	1.25	7.50	10.00	30.00
	1944G	1.190	65.00	120.00	185.00	250.00
	Common date		—	—	Proof	125.00

REICHSMARK

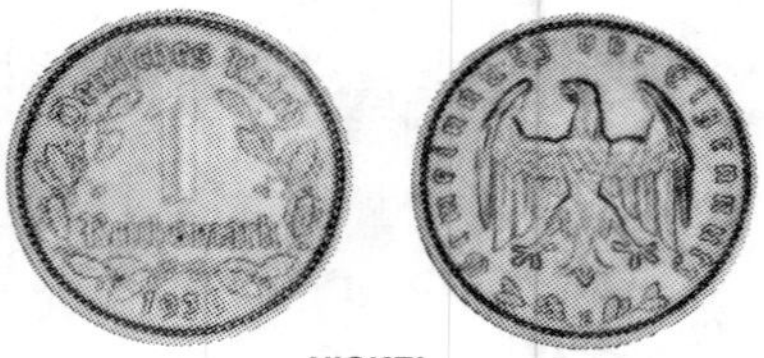

NICKEL

KM#	Date	Mintage	Fine	VF	XF	Unc
78	1933A	6.030	.75	2.50	7.50	15.00
	1933D	4.562	1.00	3.00	9.00	18.00
	1933E	3.500	2.50	7.50	12.50	25.00
	1933F	1.400	4.00	8.50	15.00	27.50
	1933G	2.000	2.50	7.50	15.00	27.50
	1934A	52.345	.50	1.50	2.50	8.00
	1934D	30.597	.50	1.50	2.50	8.00
	1934E	15.135	1.00	3.00	7.00	15.00
	1934F	23.672	.75	2.50	5.00	12.50
	1934G	13.252	1.50	5.00	10.00	18.00
	1934J	16.820	1.00	3.50	7.50	15.00
	1935A	57.896	.75	2.50	5.00	12.50
	1935J	3.621	2.50	7.50	20.00	40.00
	1936A	20.287	1.25	4.00	7.00	12.50
	1936D	4.940	2.50	7.50	15.00	27.50
	1936E	3.200	2.50	10.00	25.00	35.00
	1936F	2.075	2.50	10.00	25.00	45.00
	1936G	.620	35.00	65.00	125.00	200.00
	1936J	2.975	2.50	7.50	12.50	27.50
	1937A	49.976	.50	1.50	2.50	8.00
	1937D	10.529	1.00	3.00	6.00	12.00
	1937E	2.926	3.00	15.00	30.00	50.00

KM#	Date	Mintage	Fine	VF	XF	Unc
78	1937F	6.221	2.50	6.00	12.00	18.00
	1937G	2.143	2.50	10.00	17.50	40.00
	1937J	4.721	2.50	10.00	17.50	40.00
	1938A	9.829	1.25	4.00	6.50	10.00
	1938E	2.073	4.00	17.50	25.00	50.00
	1938F	2.739	5.00	17.50	22.50	40.00
	1938G	4.381	10.00	20.00	35.00	60.00
	1938J	1.269	27.50	70.00	90.00	135.00
	1939A	52.150	5.00	12.50	15.00	35.00
	1939B	9.836	50.00	125.00	190.00	275.00
	1939D	12.522	9.00	22.50	37.50	65.00
	1939E	6.570	20.00	35.00	80.00	120.00
	1939F	10.033	10.00	20.00	40.00	65.00
	1939G	5.475	60.00	130.00	170.00	350.00
	1939J	8.478	15.00	35.00	60.00	100.00
	Common date		—	—	Proof	185.00

2 REICHSMARK

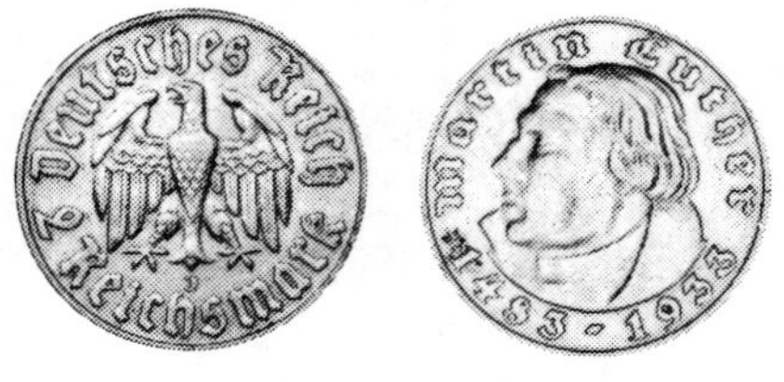

8.0000 g, .625 SILVER, .1607 oz ASW
450th Anniversary - Birth of Martin Luther

KM#	Date	Mintage	Fine	VF	XF	Unc
79	1933A	.542	9.00	18.00	30.00	65.00
	1933A	—	—	—	Proof	135.00
	1933D	.141	10.00	20.00	32.00	70.00
	1933D	—	—	—	Proof	135.00
	1933E	.075	10.00	20.00	38.00	85.00
	1933E	—	—	—	Proof	240.00
	1933F	.100	10.00	20.00	32.00	75.00
	1933F	—	—	—	Proof	240.00
	1933G	.061	12.00	22.50	42.00	90.00
	1933G	—	—	—	Proof	240.00
	1933J	.082	10.00	20.00	38.00	85.00
	1933J	—	—	—	Proof	220.00

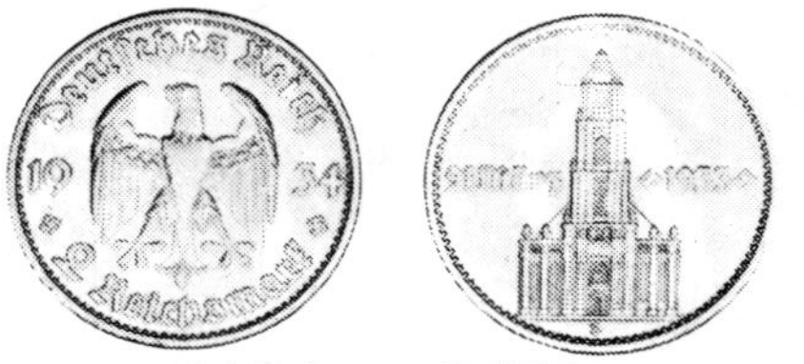

1st Anniversary Nazi Rule
Potsdam Garrison Church

KM#	Date	Mintage	Fine	VF	XF	Unc
81	1934A	2.710	4.50	10.00	27.50	70.00
	1934A	—	—	—	Proof	200.00
	1934D	.703	5.50	12.00	37.50	85.00
	1934D	—	—	—	Proof	200.00
	1934E	.373	7.50	16.50	40.00	110.00
	1934E	—	—	—	Proof	200.00
	1934F	.502	6.00	12.00	32.50	75.00
	1934F	—	—	—	Proof	200.00
	1934G	.305	7.00	15.00	32.50	115.00
	1934G	—	—	—	Proof	200.00
	1934J	.409	7.00	15.00	40.00	110.00
	1934J	—	—	—	Proof	200.00

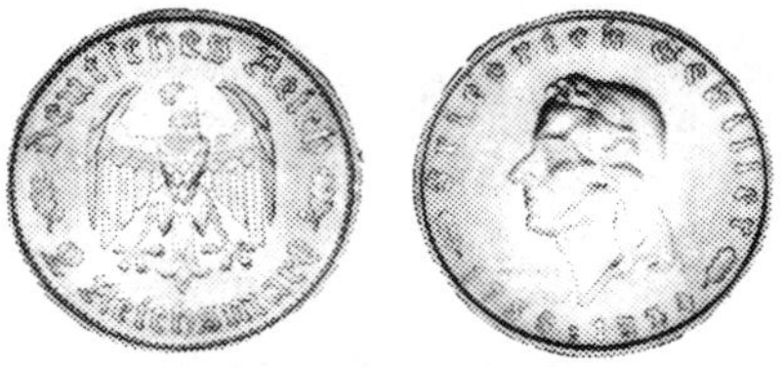

175th Anniversary - Birth of Schiller

KM#	Date	Mintage	Fine	VF	XF	Unc
84	1934F	.300	25.00	55.00	90.00	150.00
	1934F	—	—	—	Proof	225.00

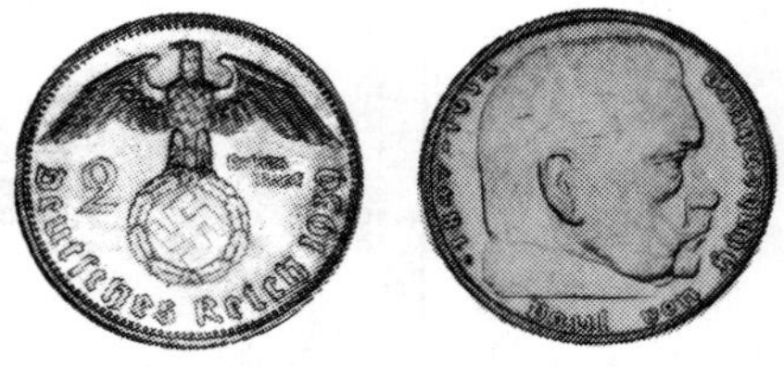

Swastika-Hindenburg Issue

KM#	Date	Mintage	Fine	VF	XF	Unc
93	1936D	.840	3.00	6.00	15.00	20.00
	1936E	Inc.Be.	8.00	30.00	60.00	100.00
	1936G	Inc. Be.	6.00	20.00	35.00	50.00
	1936J	Inc.Be.	20.00	60.00	120.00	200.00
	1937A	23.425	2.50	3.50	5.00	12.00
	1937D	6.190	2.50	3.50	5.00	12.00
	1937E	3.725	2.50	3.50	5.00	12.00
	1937F	5.015	2.50	3.50	5.00	12.00
	1937G	1.913	2.50	3.50	5.00	12.00
	1937J	2.756	2.50	3.50	5.00	12.00
	1938A	13.201	2.50	3.50	5.00	10.00
	1938B	13.163	2.50	3.50	5.00	10.00

KM#	Date	Mintage	Fine	VF	XF	Unc
93	1938D	3.711	2.50	3.50	5.00	10.00
	1938E	4.731	2.50	3.50	5.00	10.00
	1938F	1.882	3.00	4.00	6.00	12.50
	1938G	2.313	2.50	3.50	5.00	10.00
	1938J	2.306	3.00	4.00	5.00	10.00
	1939A	26.855	2.50	3.50	5.00	10.00
	1939B	3.522	2.50	3.50	5.00	10.00
	1939D	5.357	2.50	3.50	5.00	10.00
	1939E	.251	12.50	30.00	40.00	60.00
	1939F	3.180	2.50	3.50	5.00	8.00
	1939G	2.305	2.50	3.50	7.50	12.50
	1939J	3.414	2.50	3.50	7.50	10.00
	Common date		—	—	Proof	185.00

5 REICHSMARK

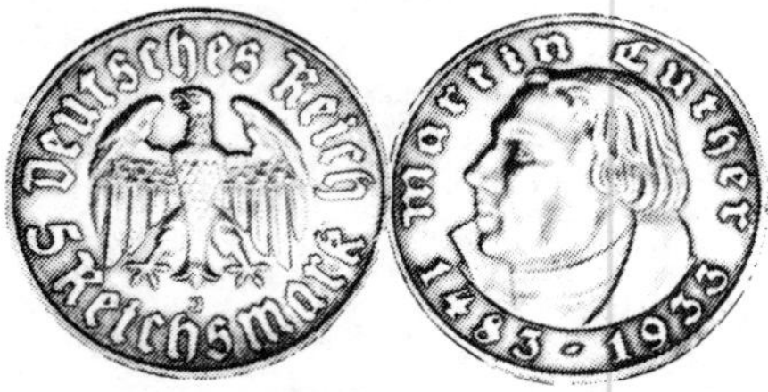

13.8800 g, .900 SILVER, .4016 oz ASW
450th Anniversary - Birth of Martin Luther

KM#	Date	Mintage	Fine	VF	XF	Unc
80	1933A	.108	50.00	100.00	150.00	250.00
	1933A	—	—	—	Proof	330.00
	1933D	.028	60.00	125.00	185.00	300.00
	1933D	—	—	—	Proof	375.00
	1933E	.012	70.00	145.00	200.00	350.00
	1933E	—	—	—	Proof	475.00
	1933F	.020	60.00	125.00	175.00	280.00
	1933F	—	—	—	Proof	375.00
	1933G	.012	100.00	175.00	275.00	375.00
	1933G	—	—	—	Proof	475.00
	1933J	.016	75.00	145.00	200.00	350.00
	1933J	—	—	—	Proof	375.00

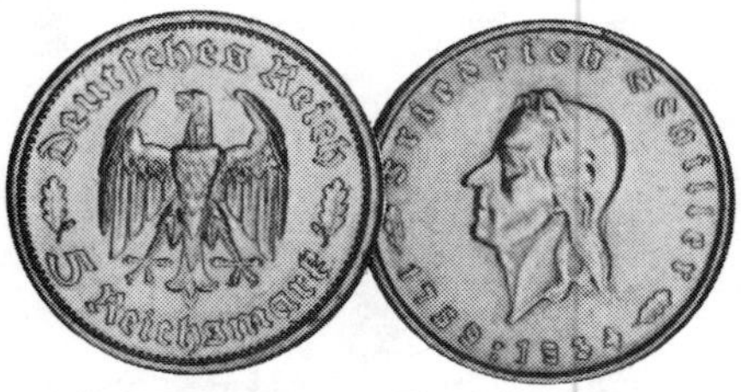

175th Anniversary - Birth of Schiller

KM#	Date	Mintage	Fine	VF	XF	Unc
85	1934F	.100	85.00	195.00	300.00	450.00
	1934F	—	—	—	Proof	700.00

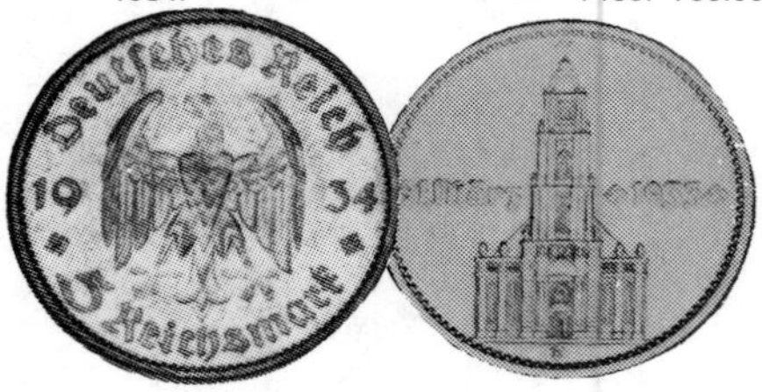

1st Anniversary Nazi Rule
Potsdam Garrison Church

KM#	Date	Mintage	Fine	VF	XF	Unc
82	1934A	2.168	7.50	11.50	32.00	100.00
	1934D	.562	7.50	11.50	32.00	120.00
	1934E	.298	10.00	18.00	50.00	165.00
	1934F	.401	8.00	14.00	45.00	150.00
	1934G	.244	10.00	18.00	50.00	165.00
	1934J	.327	9.00	18.00	45.00	140.00
	Common date		—	—	Proof	300.00

NOTE: Impaired proofs are common and valued around $200.

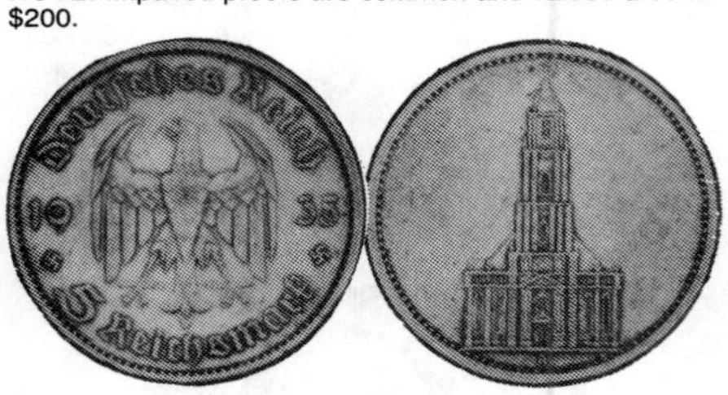

Rev: Date 21 MARZ 1933 dropped.

KM#	Date	Mintage	Fine	VF	XF	Unc
83	1934A	14.526	4.00	6.00	12.00	35.00
	1934D	6.303	4.00	6.00	15.00	50.00
	1934E	2.739	5.00	7.50	17.50	65.00
	1934F	4.844	4.00	6.00	15.00	50.00
	1934G	2.304	5.00	7.50	17.50	65.00
	1934J	4.294	4.00	6.00	15.00	50.00
	1935A	23.407	3.00	5.00	10.00	30.00
	1935D	3.539	4.00	6.00	15.00	50.00
	1935E	2.476	5.00	7.50	17.50	65.00
	1935F	2.177	5.00	7.50	17.50	75.00
	1935G	1.966	5.00	7.50	17.50	75.00
	1935J	1.425	6.00	10.00	25.00	110.00
	Common date		—	—	Proof	250.00

Hindenburg Issue

KM#	Date	Mintage	Fine	VF	XF	Unc
86	1935A	19.325	3.00	6.00	10.00	25.00
	1935D	6.596	3.00	6.00	10.00	25.00
	1935E	3.260	4.00	6.50	12.50	30.00
	1935F	4.372	3.00	6.00	10.00	27.50
	1935G	2.371	3.00	6.00	12.50	32.50
	1935J	2.830	3.00	6.00	12.50	32.50
	1936A	30.611	3.00	6.00	10.00	16.00
	1936D	7.032	3.00	6.00	10.00	18.00
	1936E	3.320	3.00	6.00	12.50	27.50
	1936F	4.926	3.00	6.00	12.50	27.50
	1936G	2.734	3.00	6.00	12.50	30.00
	1936J	3.706	3.00	6.00	12.50	30.00
	Common date	—	—		Proof	200.00

Swastika-Hindenburg Issue

KM#	Date	Mintage	Fine	VF	XF	Unc
94	1936A	8.430	3.00	6.00	10.00	17.50
	1936D	1.872	3.00	7.00	15.00	27.50
	1936E	.870	5.00	8.00	17.50	30.00
	1936F	1.732	3.00	7.00	15.00	27.50
	1936G	.743	5.00	8.50	20.00	35.00
	1936J	.640	8.00	20.00	30.00	75.00
	1937A	6.662	3.00	6.00	10.00	20.00
	1937D	2.173	3.00	6.00	10.00	15.00
	1937E	1.490	5.00	8.00	15.00	27.50
	1937F	1.578	4.00	7.50	15.00	27.50
	1937G	1.472	5.00	8.00	15.00	27.50
	1937J	2.191	3.00	6.00	12.50	25.00
	1938A	6.789	3.00	6.00	10.00	15.00
	1938D	1.304	3.00	6.00	12.50	17.50
	1938E	.425	5.00	8.00	15.00	27.50
	1938F	.740	3.50	6.50	12.50	22.50
	1938G	.861	4.00	7.50	15.00	25.00
	1938J	1.302	3.50	6.50	12.50	20.00
	1939A	3.428	4.00	7.50	12.50	20.00
	1939B	1.942	5.00	8.00	15.00	25.00
	1939D	1.216	7.50	12.50	20.00	30.00
	1939E	1.320	15.00	20.00	40.00	80.00
	1939F	1.060	7.50	12.50	25.00	45.00
	1939G	.567	12.50	18.00	35.00	75.00
	1939J	1.710	5.00	8.00	15.00	25.00
	Common date	—	—		Proof	200.00

MILITARY ISSUES - WWII
5 REICHSPFENNIG

ZINC
Military Issue

KM#	Date	Mintage	Fine	VF	XF	Unc
98	1940A	—	7.00	15.00	30.00	50.00
	1940B	3.020	50.00	100.00	135.00	200.00
	1940D	—	15.00	30.00	60.00	90.00
	1940E	2.445	50.00	100.00	135.00	275.00
	1940F	—	40.00	80.00	165.00	275.00
	1940G	—	40.00	80.00	250.00	325.00
	1940J	—	40.00	80.00	250.00	325.00
	1941A	—	25.00	50.00	100.00	150.00
	1941F	—	40.00	80.00	250.00	325.00
	Common date	—	—		Proof	200.00

NOTE: Circulated only in occupied territories.

10 REICHSPFENNIG

ZINC
Military Issue

KM#	Date	Mintage	Fine	VF	XF	Unc
99	1940A	—	8.00	16.00	32.00	55.00
	1940B	.840	50.00	100.00	200.00	300.00
	1940D	—	40.00	75.00	225.00	300.00
	1940E	5.100	50.00	100.00	200.00	300.00

KM#	Date	Mintage	Fine	VF	XF	Unc
99	1940F	—	50.00	100.00	200.00	300.00
	1940G	.150	40.00	75.00	225.00	300.00
	1940J	—	50.00	100.00	200.00	300.00
	1941A	—	50.00	100.00	175.00	250.00
	1941F	—	50.00	100.00	175.00	250.00

NOTE: Circulated only in occupied territories.

MILITARY ISSUES - WWII
ALLIED OCCUPATION

The western occupation forces restored the civil status of their zones on Sept. 21, 1949, and resumed diplomatic relations with the provinces on July 2, 1951. On May 5, 1955, nine of the ten western provinces, organized as the Federal Republic of Germany, became fully independent. The tenth, Saarland, was restored to the republic on Jan. 1, 1957.

REICHSPFENNIG

ZINC
Modified design, swastika and wreath removed.
Eagle missing tail feathers.

A102	1944D	—	—	2000.	3500.	4500.

A103	1945F	2.984	5.00	10.00	18.00	35.00
	1946F	1.633	15.00	35.00	80.00	130.00
	1946G	1.500	35.00	75.00	125.00	165.00
	Common date	—	—		Proof	185.00

5 REICHSPFENNIG

ZINC

A105	1947A	—	2.50	7.50	15.00	25.00
	1947D	16.528	2.50	4.50	6.50	20.00
	1948A	—	5.00	15.00	25.00	35.00
	1948E	7.666	150.00	300.00	400.00	700.00

10 REICHSPFENNIG

ZINC

A104	1945F	5.942	4.50	7.50	15.00	25.00
	1946F	3.738	10.00	20.00	30.00	100.00
	1946G	1.600	35.00	65.00	100.00	145.00
	1947A	—	4.50	10.00	20.00	30.00
	1947E	2.612	175.00	250.00	400.00	650.00
	1947F	1.269	1.50	3.50	8.00	17.50
	1948A	—	5.00	20.00	25.00	30.00
	1948F	19.579	1.50	3.50	8.00	15.00
	Common date	—	—		Proof	180.00

GERMANY-FEDERAL REPUBLIC

The Federal Republic of Germany, located in northcentral Europe, has an area of 137,744 sq. mi. (356,910 sq. km.) and a population of 81.1 million. Capital: Berlin. The economy centers about one of the world's foremost industrial establishments. Machinery, motor vehicles, iron, steel, yarns and fabrics are exported.

During the post-Normandy phase of World War II, Allied troops occupied the western German provinces of Schleswig-Holstein, Hamburg, Lower Saxony, Bremen, North Rhine-Westphalia, Hesse, Rhineland-Palatinate, Baden-Wurttemberg, Bavaria and Saarland. The conquered provinces were divided into American, British and French occupation zones. Five eastern German provinces were occupied and administered by the forces of the Soviet Union.

The post-World War II division of Germany was ended Oct. 3, 1990, when the German Democratic Republic (East Germany) ceased to exist and its five constituent provinces were formally admitted to the Federal Republic of Germany. An election Dec. 2, 1990, chose representatives to the united federal parliament (Bundestag), which then conducted its opening session in Berlin in the old Reichstag building. Though Berlin technically is the capital of a united Germany, the actual seat of government remains for the time being in Bonn.

MINT MARKS

A - Berlin
D - Munich
F - Stuttgart
G - Karlsruhe
J - Hamburg

MONETARY SYSTEM

100 Pfennig = 1 Deutsche Mark (DM)

PFENNIG

BRONZE-CLAD STEEL
Currency Reform

KM#	Date	Mintage	VF	XF	Unc
A101	1948D	46.325	.50	15.00	40.00
	1948F	68.203	.50	8.00	32.50
	1948F	250 pcs.	—	Proof	150.00
	1948G	45.604	.50	15.00	45.00
	1948J	79.304	.50	15.00	50.00
	1949D	99.863	.50	6.00	27.50
	1949D	—	—	Proof	100.00
	1949F	70.900	.50	6.00	22.50
	1949F	250 pcs.	—	Proof	60.00
	1949G	50.500	.50	10.00	30.00
	1949J	101.932	.50	6.00	27.50
	1949J	—	—	Proof	85.00

COPPER PLATED STEEL
Federal Republic

105	1950D	772.592	—	.10	1.00
	1950F	898.277	—	.10	1.00
	1950F	620 pcs.	—	Proof	27.50
	1950G	515.673	—	.10	1.00
	1950G	1,800	—	Proof	5.00
	1950J	784.424	—	.10	1.00
	1950J	—	—	Proof	12.00
	1966D	65.063	—	.10	2.00
	1966F	75.031	—	.10	2.00
	1966F	100 pcs.	—	Proof	35.00
	1966G	48.261	—	.10	2.00
	1966G	3,070	—	Proof	4.00
	1966J	66.842	—	.10	3.00
	1966J	1,000	—	Proof	8.00

KM#	Date	Mintage	VF	XF	Unc
105	1967D	39.082	—	.10	3.00
	1967F	45.003	—	.10	3.00
	1967F	1,500	—	Proof	6.00
	1967G	20.787	—	.10	3.00
	1967G	4,500	—	Proof	3.50
	1967J	42.583	—	.10	4.00
	1967J	1,500	—	Proof	8.00
	1968D	32.797	—	.10	1.00
	1968F	26.338	—	.10	1.00
	1968F	3,000	—	Proof	5.00
	1968G	20.382	—	.10	1.00
	1968G	6,023	—	Proof	4.00
	1968J	23.414	—	.25	1.00
	1968J	2,000	—	Proof	6.50
	1969D	78.177	—	.10	.50
	1969F	90.172	—	.10	.50
	1969F	5,100	—	Proof	1.50
	1969G	61.836	—	.10	.50
	1969G	8,700	—	Proof	1.25
	1969J	80.221	—	.10	.50
	1969J	5,000	—	Proof	1.50
	1970D	91.151	—	.10	.25
	1970F	105.236	—	.10	.25
	1970F	5,240	—	Proof	1.50
	1970G	82.421	—	.10	.25
	1970G	10,200	—	Proof	1.00
	1970 sm.J	93.455	—	.10	.25
	1970 lg.J	Inc. Ab.	—	.10	.25
	1970J	5,000	—	Proof	1.50
	1971D	116.612	—	.10	.25
	1971D	8,000	—	Proof	1.00
	1971F	157.393	—	.10	.25
	1971F	8,000	—	Proof	1.00
	1971G	77.674	—	.10	.25
	1971G	10,200	—	Proof	1.00
	1971J	120.218	—	.10	.25
	1971J	8,000	—	Proof	1.00
	1972D	90.696	—	.10	.25
	1972D	8,000	—	Proof	1.00
	1972F	105.006	—	.10	.25
	1972F	8,000	—	Proof	1.00
	1972G	60.660	—	.10	.25
	1972G	10,000	—	Proof	1.00
	1972J	93.492	—	.10	.25
	1972J	8,000	—	Proof	1.00
	1973D	38.976	—	.10	.25
	1973D	9,000	—	Proof	1.00
	1973F	45.006	—	.10	.25
	1973F	9,000	—	Proof	1.00
	1973G	25.811	—	.10	.25
	1973G	9,000	—	Proof	1.00
	1973J	40.057	—	.10	.25
	1973J	9,000	—	Proof	1.00
	1974D	90.951	—	.10	.25
	1974D	.035	—	Proof	.40
	1974F	105.091	—	.10	.25
	1974F	.035	—	Proof	.40
	1974G	60.548	—	.10	.25
	1974G	.035	—	Proof	.40
	1974J	93.527	—	.10	.25
	1974J	.035	—	Proof	.40
	1975D	91.053	—	.10	.25
	1975D	.043	—	Proof	.40
	1975F	105.007	—	.10	.25
	1975F	.043	—	Proof	.40
	1975G	60.704	—	.10	.25
	1975G	.043	—	Proof	.40
	1975J	93.495	—	.10	.25
	1975J	.043	—	Proof	.40
	1976D	130.227	—	.10	.25
	1976D	.043	—	Proof	.40
	1976F	150.037	—	.10	.25
	1976F	.043	—	Proof	.40
	1976G	86.586	—	.10	.25
	1976G	.043	—	Proof	.40
	1976J	133.500	—	.10	.25
	1976J	.043	—	Proof	.40
	1977D	143.000	—	.10	.25
	1977D	.052	—	Proof	.40
	1977F	165.000	—	.10	.25
	1977F	.051	—	Proof	.40
	1977G	95.201	—	.10	.25
	1977G	.051	—	Proof	.40
	1977J	146.788	—	.10	.25
	1977J	.051	—	Proof	.40
	1978D	156.000	—	.10	.25
	1978D	.054	—	Proof	.40
	1978F	180.000	—	.10	.25
	1978F	.054	—	Proof	.40
	1978G	103.800	—	.10	.25
	1978G	.054	—	Proof	.40
	1978J	160.200	—	.10	.25
	1978J	.054	—	Proof	.40
	1979D	156.000	—	.10	.25
	1979D	.089	—	Proof	.40
	1979F	180.000	—	.10	.25
	1979F	.089	—	Proof	.40
	1979G	103.800	—	.10	.25
	1979G	.089	—	Proof	.40
	1979J	160.200	—	.10	.25
	1979J	.089	—	Proof	.40
	1980D	200.080	—	.10	.25
	1980D	.110	—	Proof	.40
	1980F	200.620	—	.10	.25
	1980F	.110	—	Proof	.40
	1980G	71.940	—	.10	.25
	1980G	.110	—	Proof	.40
	1980J	143.110	—	.10	.25
	1980J	.110	—	Proof	.40
	1981D	169.550	—	.10	.25
105	1981D	.091	—	Proof	.40
	1981F	274.010	—	.10	.25
	1981F	.091	—	Proof	.40
	1981G	178.010	—	.10	.25
	1981G	.091	—	Proof	.40
	1981J	189.090	—	.10	.25
	1981J	.091	—	Proof	.40
	1982D	130.090	—	.10	.20
	1982D	.078	—	Proof	.40
	1982F	108.390	—	.10	.20
	1982F	.078	—	Proof	.40
	1982G	77.740	—	.10	.20
	1982G	.078	—	Proof	.40
	1982J	124.720	—	.10	.20
	1982J	.078	—	Proof	.40
	1983D	46.800	—	.10	.20
	1983D	.075	—	Proof	.40
	1983F	54.000	—	.10	.20
	1983F	.075	—	Proof	.40
	1983G	31.140	—	.10	.20
	1983G	.075	—	Proof	.40
	1983J	48.060	—	.10	.20
	1983J	.075	—	Proof	.40
	1984D	58.500	—	.10	.20
	1984D	.064	—	Proof	.40
	1984F	67.500	—	.10	.20
	1984F	.064	—	Proof	.40
	1984G	38.900	—	.10	.20
	1984G	.064	—	Proof	.40
	1984J	60.100	—	.10	.20
	1984J	.064	—	Proof	.40
	1985D	19.500	—	.10	.20
	1985D	.056	—	Proof	.40
	1985F	22.500	—	.10	.20
	1985F	.054	—	Proof	.40
	1985G	13.000	—	—	.10
	1985G	.055	—	Proof	.40
	1985J	20.000	—	—	.10
	1985J	.054	—	Proof	.40
	1986D	39.000	—	—	.10
	1986D	.044	—	Proof	.40
	1986F	45.000	—	—	.10
	1986F	.044	—	Proof	.40
	1986G	25.900	—	—	.10
	1986G	.044	—	Proof	.40
	1986J	40.100	—	—	.10
	1986J	.044	—	Proof	.40
	1987D	6.500	—	—	.10
	1987D	.045	—	Proof	.40
	1987F	7.500	—	—	.10
	1987F	.045	—	Proof	.40
	1987G	4.330	—	—	.10
	1987G	.045	—	Proof	.40
	1987J	6.680	—	—	.10
	1987J	.045	—	Proof	.40
	1988D	52.000	—	—	.10
	1988D	.045	—	Proof	.40
	1988F	60.000	—	—	.10
	1988F	.045	—	Proof	.40
	1988G	34.600	—	—	.10
	1988G	.045	—	Proof	.40
	1988J	53.400	—	—	.10
	1988J	.045	—	Proof	.40
	1989D	104.000	—	—	.10
	1989D	.045	—	Proof	.40
	1989F	120.000	—	—	.10
	1989F	.045	—	Proof	.40
	1989G	69.200	—	—	.10
	1989G	.045	—	Proof	.40
	1989J	106.800	—	—	.10
	1989J	.045	—	Proof	.40
	1990D	169.000	—	—	.10
	1990D	.045	—	Proof	.40
	1990F	195.000	—	—	.10
	1990F	.045	—	Proof	.40
	1990G	112.450	—	—	.10
	1990G	.045	—	Proof	.40
	1990J	173.550	—	—	.10
	1990J	.045	—	Proof	.40
	1991A	260.000	—	—	.10
	1991A	.045	—	Proof	.40
	1991D	273.000	—	—	.10
	1991D	.045	—	Proof	.40
	1991F	312.000	—	—	.10
	1991F	.045	—	Proof	.40
	1991G	182.000	—	—	.10
	1991G	.045	—	Proof	.40
	1991J	273.000	—	—	.10
	1991J	.045	—	Proof	.40
	1992A	40.000	—	—	.10
	1992A	.045	—	Proof	.40
	1992D	42.000	—	—	.10
	1992D	.045	—	Proof	.40
	1992F	48.000	—	—	.10
	1992F	.045	—	Proof	.40
	1992G	28.000	—	—	.10
	1992G	.045	—	Proof	.40
	1992J	42.000	—	—	.10
	1992J	.045	—	Proof	.40
	1993A	40.000	—	—	.10
	1993A	.045	—	Proof	.40
	1993D	42.000	—	—	.10
	1993D	.045	—	Proof	.40
	1993F	48.000	—	—	.10
	1993F	.045	—	Proof	.40
	1993G	28.000	—	—	.10
	1993G	.045	—	Proof	.40
	1993J	42.000	—	—	.10
	1993J	.045	—	Proof	.40
	1994A	100.000	—	—	.10
105	1994A	.045	—	Proof	.40
	1994D	105.000	—	—	.10
	1994D	.045	—	Proof	.40
	1994F	120.000	—	—	.10
	1994F	.045	—	Proof	.40
	1994G	70.000	—	—	.10
	1994G	.045	—	Proof	.40
	1994J	105.000	—	—	.10
	1994J	.045	—	Proof	.40
	1995A	100.000	—	—	.15
	1995A	.045	—	Proof	.45
	1995D	105.000	—	—	.15
	1995D	.045	—	Proof	.45
	1995F	120.000	—	—	.15
	1995F	.045	—	Proof	.45
	1995G	70.000	—	—	.15
	1995G	.045	—	Proof	.45
	1995J	105.000	—	—	.15
	1995J	.045	—	Proof	.45
	1996A	80.000	—	—	.20
	1996A	.045	—	Proof	.50
	1996D	84.000	—	—	.20
	1996D	.045	—	Proof	.50
	1996F	96.000	—	—	.20
	1996F	.045	—	Proof	.50
	1996G	56.000	—	—	.20
	1996G	.045	—	Proof	.50
	1996J	84.000	—	—	.20
	1996J	.045	—	Proof	.50
	1997A	.070	In sets only		1.75
	1997A	.045	—	Proof	2.00
	1997D	.070	In sets only		1.75
	1997D	.045	—	Proof	2.00
	1997F	.070	In sets only		1.75
	1997F	.045	—	Proof	2.00
	1997G	.070	In sets only		1.75
	1997G	.045	—	Proof	2.00
	1997J	.070	In sets only		1.75
	1997J	.045	—	Proof	2.00

2 PFENNIG

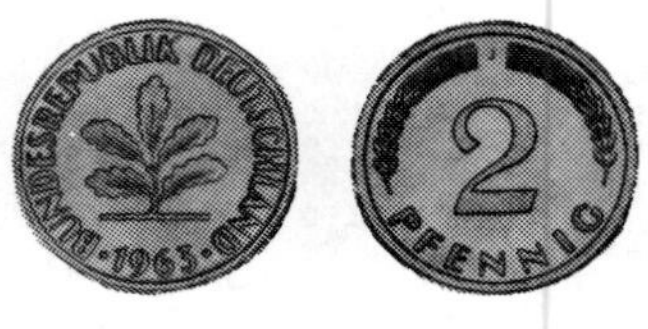

BRONZE
Federal Republic

KM#	Date	Mintage	VF	XF	Unc
106	1950D	26.263	.10	1.00	10.00
	1950D	—	—	Proof	50.00
	1950F	30.278	.10	1.00	10.00
	1950F	200 pcs.	—	Proof	—
	1950G	17.151	.10	50.00	75.00
	1950G	—	—	Proof	90.00
	1950J	27.216	.10	1.00	10.00
	1950J	—	—	Proof	40.00
	1958D	19.440	.10	1.00	10.00
	1958F	24.122	.10	1.00	10.00
	1958F	100 pcs.	—	Proof	—
	1958G	15.255	.10	1.00	10.00
	1958J	21.250	.10	1.00	10.00
	1959D	19.690	—	.25	10.00
	1959F	25.017	—	.25	10.00
	1959F	75 pcs.	—	Proof	—
	1959G	12.899	—	.25	10.00
	1959J	25.482	—	.25	10.00
	1960D	21.979	—	.25	6.00
	1960F	13.060	—	.25	6.00
	1960F	75 pcs.	—	Proof	—
	1960G	5.657	.10	.25	6.00
	1960J	17.799	—	.25	6.00
	1961D	26.662	—	.25	6.00
	1961F	24.990	—	.25	6.00
	1961G	18.060	—	.25	6.00
	1961J	22.147	—	.25	6.00
	1962D	21.297	—	.25	6.00
	1962F	42.189	—	.25	4.00
	1962G	17.297	—	.25	4.00
	1962J	30.706	—	.25	4.00
	1963D	7.648	—	.25	7.00
	1963F	18.299	—	.25	2.00
	1963G	35.838	—	.25	2.00
	1963G	—	—	Proof	—
	1963J	42.884	—	.25	2.00
	1964D	20.336	—	.25	3.00
	1964F	31.400	—	.10	1.00
	1964G	18.431	—	.10	1.00
	1964G	*600 pcs.	—	Proof	12.00
	1964J	13.370	—	.10	1.00
	1965D	48.541	—	.10	1.00
	1965F	27.000	—	.10	1.00
	1965F	*80 pcs.	—	Proof	70.00
	1965G	13.584	—	.10	1.00
	1965G	1,200	—	Proof	5.00
	1965J	33.397	—	.10	1.00
	1966D	65.077	—	.10	.25
	1966F	52.543	—	.10	.25
	1966F	100 pcs.	—	Proof	80.00
	1966G	40.804	—	.10	.25
	1966G	3,070	—	Proof	5.50
	1966J	46.754	—	.10	.25
	1966J	1,000	—	Proof	40.00
	1967D	25.997	—	.10	2.00
	1967F	30.004	—	.10	1.00
	1967F	1,500	—	Proof	7.00
	1967G	6.280	—	1.00	3.00

KM#	Date	Mintage	VF	XF	Unc
106	1967G	4,500	—	Proof	4.50
	1967J	26.725	—	.10	1.00
	1967J	1,500	—	Proof	10.00
	1968D	19.523	—	1.00	3.00
	1968G	15.357	—	.10	1.00
	1968G	3,651	—	Proof	4.00
	1968J	—	150.00	225.00	350.00
	1969J	—	150.00	225.00	350.00

BRONZE CLAD STEEL

KM#	Date	Mintage	VF	XF	Unc
106a	1967G	520 pcs.	—	Proof	720.00
	1968D	19.523	—	.10	.25
	1968F	30.000	—	.10	.25
	1968F	3,000	—	Proof	6.00
	1968G	13.004	—	.10	.25
	1968G	2,372	—	Proof	4.00
	1968J	20.026	—	.10	.25
	1968J	2,000	—	Proof	7.50
	1969D	39.012	—	.10	.25
	1969D	—	—	Proof	1.25
	1969F	45.029	—	.10	.25
	1969F	5,100	—	Proof	1.25
	1969G	32.157	—	.10	.25
	1969G	8,700	—	Proof	1.25
	1969J	40.102	—	.10	.25
	1969J	5,000	—	Proof	2.50
	1970D	45.525	—	.10	.25
	1970F	73.851	—	.10	.25
	1970F	5,140	—	Proof	1.25
	1970G	30.330	—	.10	.25
	1970G	10,200	—	Proof	1.25
	1970 sm.J	46.730	—	.10	.25
	1970 lg.J	Inc. Ab.	—	.10	.25
	1970J	5,000	—	Proof	1.75
	1971D	71.755	—	.10	.25
	1971D	8,000	—	Proof	1.25
	1971F	82.765	—	.10	.25
	1971F	8,000	—	Proof	1.25
	1971G	47.850	—	.10	.25
	1971G	.010	—	Proof	1.25
	1971J	73.641	—	.10	.25
	1971J	8,000	—	Proof	1.25
	1972D	52.403	—	.10	.25
	1972D	8,000	—	Proof	1.00
	1972F	60.272	—	.10	.25
	1972F	8,000	—	Proof	1.00
	1972G	34.864	—	.10	.25
	1972G	.010	—	Proof	1.00
	1972J	53.673	—	.10	.25
	1972J	8,000	—	Proof	1.00
	1973D	26.190	—	.10	.25
	1973D	9,000	—	Proof	1.00
	1973F	30.160	—	.10	.25
	1973F	9,000	—	Proof	1.00
	1973G	17.379	—	.10	.25
	1973G	9,000	—	Proof	1.00
	1973J	26.830	—	.10	.25
	1973J	9,000	—	Proof	1.00
	1974D	58.667	—	.10	.25
	1974D	.035	—	Proof	.50
	1974F	67.596	—	.10	.25
	1974F	.035	—	Proof	.50
	1974G	39.007	—	.10	.25
	1974G	.035	—	Proof	.50
	1974J	60.195	—	.10	.25
	1974J	.035	—	Proof	.50
	1975D	58.634	—	.10	.25
	1975D	.043	—	Proof	.50
	1975F	67.685	—	.10	.25
	1975F	.043	—	Proof	.50
	1975G	39.391	—	.10	.25
	1975G	.043	—	Proof	.50
	1975J	60.207	—	.10	.25
	1975J	.043	—	Proof	.50
	1976D	78.074	—	.10	.25
	1976D	.043	—	Proof	.50
	1976F	90.130	—	.10	.25
	1976F	.043	—	Proof	.50
	1976G	51.988	—	.10	.25
	1976G	.043	—	Proof	.50
	1976J	80.145	—	.10	.25
	1976J	.043	—	Proof	.50
	1977D	84.516	—	.10	.20
	1977D	.051	—	Proof	.40
	1977F	97.504	—	.10	.20
	1977F	.051	—	Proof	.40
	1977G	56.276	—	.10	.20
	1977G	.051	—	Proof	.40
	1977J	86.888	—	.10	.20
	1977J	.051	—	Proof	.40
	1978D	84.500	—	.10	.20
	1978D	.054	—	Proof	.40
	1978F	97.500	—	.10	.20
	1978F	.054	—	Proof	.40
	1978G	56.225	—	.10	.20
	1978G	.054	—	Proof	.40
	1978J	86.775	—	.10	.20
	1978J	.054	—	Proof	.40
	1979D	91.000	—	.10	.20
	1979D	.089	—	Proof	.40
	1979F	105.000	—	.10	.20
	1979F	.089	—	Proof	.40
	1979G	60.550	—	.10	.20
	1979G	.089	—	Proof	.40
	1979J	93.480	—	.10	.20
	1979J	.089	—	Proof	.40
	1980D	93.360	—	.10	.20
	1980D	.110	—	Proof	.40
	1980F	120.360	—	.10	.20
	1980F	.110	—	Proof	.40

KM#	Date	Mintage	VF	XF	Unc
106a	1980G	50.830	—	.10	.20
	1980G	.110	—	Proof	.40
	1980J	102.260	—	.10	.20
	1980J	.110	—	Proof	.40
	1981D	93.910	—	.10	.20
	1981D	.091	—	Proof	.40
	1981F	83.710	—	.10	.20
	1981F	.091	—	Proof	.40
	1981G	89.850	—	.10	.20
	1981G	.091	—	Proof	.40
	1981J	87.250	—	.10	.20
	1981J	.091	—	Proof	.40
	1982D	64.390	—	.10	.20
	1982D	.078	—	Proof	.40
	1982F	36.870	—	.10	.20
	1982F	.078	—	Proof	.40
	1982G	58.590	—	.10	.20
	1982G	.078	—	Proof	.40
	1982J	57.690	—	.10	.20
	1982J	.078	—	Proof	.40
	1983D	71.500	—	.10	.20
	1983D	.075	—	Proof	.40
	1983F	82.500	—	.10	.20
	1983F	.075	—	Proof	.40
	1983G	47.575	—	.10	.20
	1983G	.075	—	Proof	.40
	1983J	73.425	—	.10	.20
	1983J	.075	—	Proof	.40
	1984D	58.500	—	.10	.20
	1984D	.064	—	Proof	.40
	1984F	67.500	—	.10	.20
	1984F	.064	—	Proof	.40
	1984G	38.900	—	.10	.20
	1984G	.064	—	Proof	.40
	1984J	60.100	—	.10	.20
	1984J	.064	—	Proof	.40
	1985D	19.500	—	—	.10
	1985D	.056	—	Proof	.40
	1985F	22.500	—	—	.10
	1985F	.054	—	Proof	.40
	1985G	13.000	—	—	.10
	1985G	.055	—	Proof	.40
	1985J	20.000	—	—	.10
	1985J	.054	—	Proof	.40
	1986D	39.000	—	—	.10
	1986D	.044	—	Proof	.40
	1986F	45.000	—	—	.10
	1986F	.044	—	Proof	.40
	1986G	25.900	—	—	.10
	1986G	.044	—	Proof	.40
	1986J	40.100	—	—	.10
	1986J	.044	—	Proof	.40
	1987D	6.500	1.00	2.50	5.00
	1987D	.045	—	Proof	.40
	1987F	7.500	1.00	2.50	5.00
	1987F	.045	—	Proof	.40
	1987G	4.330	1.00	2.50	5.00
	1987G	.045	—	Proof	.40
	1987J	6.680	1.00	2.50	5.00
	1987J	.045	—	Proof	.40
	1988D	52.000	—	—	.10
	1988D	.045	—	Proof	.40
	1988F	60.000	—	—	.10
	1988F	.045	—	Proof	.40
	1988G	34.600	—	—	.10
	1988G	.045	—	Proof	.40
	1988J	53.400	—	—	.10
	1988J	.045	—	Proof	.40
	1989D	52.000	—	—	.10
	1989D	.045	—	Proof	.40
	1989F	60.000	—	—	.10
	1989F	.045	—	Proof	.40
	1989G	34.600	—	—	.10
	1989G	.045	—	Proof	.40
	1989J	53.400	—	—	.10
	1989J	.045	—	Proof	.40
	1990D	71.500	—	—	.10
	1990D	.045	—	Proof	.40
	1990F	82.500	—	—	.10
	1990F	.045	—	Proof	.40
	1990G	47.570	—	—	.10
	1990G	.045	—	Proof	.40
	1990J	73.420	—	—	.10
	1990J	.045	—	Proof	.40
	1991A	115.000	—	—	.10
	1991A	.045	—	Proof	.40
	1991D	120.750	—	—	.10
	1991D	.045	—	Proof	.40
	1991F	138.000	—	—	.10
	1991F	.045	—	Proof	.40
	1991G	80.500	—	—	.10
	1991G	.045	—	Proof	.40
	1991J	120.750	—	—	.10
	1991J	.045	—	Proof	.40
	1992A	60.000	—	—	.10
	1992A	.045	—	Proof	.40
	1992D	63.000	—	—	.10
	1992D	.045	—	Proof	.40
	1992F	72.000	—	—	.10
	1992F	.045	—	Proof	.40
	1992G	42.000	—	—	.10
	1992G	.045	—	Proof	.40
	1992J	63.000	—	—	.10
	1992J	.045	—	Proof	.40
	1993A	10.000	—	—	.10
	1993A	.045	—	Proof	.40
	1993D	10.500	—	—	.10
	1993D	.045	—	Proof	.40
	1993F	12.000	—	—	.10
	1993F	.045	—	Proof	.40

KM#	Date	Mintage	VF	XF	Unc
106a	1993G	7.000	—	—	.10
	1993G	.045	—	Proof	.40
	1993J	10.000	—	—	.10
	1993J	.045	—	Proof	.40
	1994A	55.000	—	—	.10
	1994A	.045	—	Proof	.40
	1994D	57.750	—	—	.10
	1994D	.045	—	Proof	.40
	1994F	66.000	—	—	.10
	1994F	.045	—	Proof	.40
	1994G	38.500	—	—	.10
	1994G	.045	—	Proof	.40
	1994J	57.750	—	—	.10
	1994J	.045	—	Proof	.40
	1995A	1000.000	—	—	.15
	1995A	.045	—	Proof	.45
	1995D	105.000	—	—	.15
	1995D	.045	—	Proof	.45
	1995F	120.000	—	—	.15
	1995F	.045	—	Proof	.45
	1995G	70.000	—	—	.15
	1995G	.045	—	Proof	.45
	1995J	105.000	—	—	.15
	1995J	.045	—	Proof	.45
	1996A	40.000	—	—	.20
	1996A	.045	—	Proof	.50
	1996D	42.000	—	—	.20
	1996D	.045	—	Proof	.50
	1996F	48.000	—	—	.20
	1996F	.045	—	Proof	.50
	1996G	28.000	—	—	.20
	1996G	.045	—	Proof	.50
	1996J	42.000	—	—	.20
	1996J	.045	—	Proof	.50
	1997A	.070	In sets only		1.75
	1997A	.045	—	Proof	2.00
	1997D	.070	In sets only		1.75
	1997D	.045	—	Proof	2.00
	1997F	.070	In sets only		1.75
	1997F	.045	—	Proof	2.00
	1997G	.070	In sets only		1.75
	1997G	.045	—	Proof	2.00
	1997J	.070	In sets only		1.75
	1997J	.045	—	Proof	2.00

5 PFENNIG

BRASS-CLAD STEEL
Currency Reform

KM#	Date	Mintage	VF	XF	Unc
102	1949D	60.026	.20	7.50	45.00
	1949D	—	.20	Proof	150.00
	1949F	66.082	.20	7.50	30.00
	1949F	250 pcs.	.20	Proof	80.00
	1949G	57.356	.20	7.50	50.00
	1949J	68.977	.20	7.50	40.00
	1949J	—	.20	Proof	80.00

BRASS PLATED STEEL
Federal Republic

KM#	Date	Mintage	VF	XF	Unc
107	1950D	271.962	—	1.50	5.00
	1950F	362.880	—	1.50	5.00
	1950F	500 pcs.	—	1.50	65.00
	1950G	180.492	—	1.50	5.00
	1950G	1,800	—	1.50	4.00
	1950J lg.J	285.283	—	1.50	5.00
	1950J	—	—	1.50	15.00
	1950J sm.J	Inc. Ab.	—	1.50	5.00
	1950J	—	—	1.50	15.00
	1966D	26.036	—	1.50	8.50
	1966F	30.047	—	1.50	8.50
	1966F	100 pcs.	—	1.50	60.00
	1966G	17.333	—	1.50	8.50
	1966G	3,070	—	1.50	7.50
	1966J	26.741	—	1.50	8.50
	1966J	1,000	—	1.50	17.50
	1967D	10.418	—	1.50	8.50
	1967F	12.012	—	1.50	8.50
	1967F	1,500	—	Proof	15.00
	1967G	1.736	2.50	5.00	35.00
	1967G	4,500	—	Proof	7.50
	1967J	10.706	—	1.50	8.50
	1967J	1,500	—	Proof	15.00
	1968D	13.047	—	.25	5.00
	1968F	15.026	—	.25	5.00
	1968F	3,000	—	Proof	9.00
	1968G	13.855	—	.25	5.00
	1968G	6,023	—	Proof	6.00
	1968J	13.362	—	.25	5.00
	1968J	2,000	—	Proof	15.00
	1969D	23.488	—	.10	1.50
	1969F	27.046	—	.10	1.50
	1969F	5,000	—	Proof	3.00
	1969G	15.631	—	.10	1.50
	1969G	8,700	—	Proof	2.50

KM#	Date	Mintage	VF	XF	Unc
107	1969J	24.120	—	.10	1.50
	1969J	5,000	—	Proof	2.00
	1970D	39.940	—	.10	.25
	1970F	45.517	—	.10	.25
	1970F	5,140	—	Proof	2.50
	1970G	27.638	—	.10	.25
	1970G	10,200	—	Proof	1.50
	1970J	40.873	—	.10	.25
	1970J	5,000	—	Proof	2.50
	1971D	57.345	—	.10	.25
	1971D	8,000	—	Proof	1.50
	1971F	66.426	—	.10	.25
	1971F	8,000	—	Proof	1.50
	1971G	38.284	—	.10	.25
	1971G	10,000	—	Proof	1.50
	1971J	58.566	—	.10	.25
	1971J	8,000	—	Proof	1.50
	1972D	52.325	—	.10	.25
	1972D	8,000	—	Proof	1.50
	1972F	60.292	—	.10	.25
	1972F	8,000	—	Proof	1.50
	1972G	34.719	—	.10	.25
	1972G	10,000	—	Proof	1.50
	1972J	54.218	—	.10	.25
	1972J	8,000	—	Proof	1.50
	1973D	15.596	—	.10	.25
	1973D	9,000	—	Proof	1.50
	1973F	18.039	—	.10	.25
	1973F	9,000	—	Proof	1.50
	1973G	10.391	—	.10	.25
	1973G	9,000	—	Proof	1.50
	1973J	16.035	—	.10	.25
	1973J	9,000	—	Proof	1.50
	1974D	15.769	—	.10	.25
	1974D	.035	—	Proof	.50
	1974F	18.143	—	.10	.25
	1974F	.035	—	Proof	.50
	1974G	10.508	—	.10	.25
	1974G	.035	—	Proof	.50
	1974J	16.055	—	.10	.25
	1974J	.035	—	Proof	.50
	1975D	15.715	—	.10	.25
	1975D	.043	—	Proof	.50
	1975F	18.013	—	.10	.25
	1975F	.043	—	Proof	.50
	1975G	10.466	—	.10	.25
	1975G	.043	—	Proof	.50
	1975J	16.201	—	.10	.25
	1975J	.043	—	Proof	.50
	1976D	47.091	—	.10	.25
	1976D	.043	—	Proof	.50
	1976F	54.370	—	.10	.25
	1976F	.043	—	Proof	.50
	1976G	31.367	—	.10	.25
	1976G	.043	—	Proof	.50
	1976J	48.321	—	.10	.25
	1976J	.043	—	Proof	.50
	1977D	52.159	—	.10	.20
	1977D	.051	—	Proof	.40
	1977F	60.124	—	.10	.20
	1977F	.051	—	Proof	.40
	1977G	34.600	—	.10	.20
	1977G	.051	—	Proof	.40
	1977J	53.481	—	.10	.20
	1977J	.051	—	Proof	.40
	1978D	41.600	—	.10	.20
	1978D	.054	—	Proof	.40
	1978F	48.000	—	.10	.20
	1978F	.054	—	Proof	.40
	1978G	27.680	—	.10	.20
	1978G	.054	—	Proof	.40
	1978J	42.720	—	.10	.20
	1978J	.054	—	Proof	.40
	1979D	41.600	—	.10	.20
	1979D	.089	—	Proof	.40
	1979F	48.000	—	.10	.20
	1979F	.089	—	Proof	.40
	1979G	27.680	—	.10	.20
	1979G	.089	—	Proof	.40
	1979J	42.711	—	.10	.20
	1979J	.089	—	Proof	.40
	1980D	39.880	—	.10	.20
	1980D	.110	—	Proof	.40
	1980F	53.270	—	.10	.20
	1980F	.110	—	Proof	.40
	1980G	43.070	—	.10	.20
	1980G	.110	—	Proof	.40
	1980J	59.130	—	.10	.20
	1980J	.110	—	Proof	.40
	1981D	82.250	—	.10	.20
	1981D	.091	—	Proof	.40
	1981F	84.910	—	.10	.20
	1981F	.091	—	Proof	.40
	1981G	41.910	—	.10	.20
	1981G	.091	—	Proof	.40
	1981J	49.290	—	.10	.20
	1981J	.091	—	Proof	.40
	1982D	57.500	—	.10	.20
	1982D	.078	—	Proof	.40
	1982F	53.290	—	.10	.20
	1982F	.078	—	Proof	.40
	1982G	23.750	—	.10	.20
	1982G	.078	—	Proof	.40
	1982J	62.000	—	.10	.20
	1982J	.078	—	Proof	.40
	1983D	46.800	—	.10	.20
	1983D	.075	—	Proof	.40
	1983F	54.000	—	.10	.20
	1983F	.075	—	Proof	.40
	1983G	31.140	—	.10	.20

KM#	Date	Mintage	VF	XF	Unc
107	1983G	.075	—	Proof	.40
	1983J	48.060	—	.10	.20
	1983J	.075	—	Proof	.40
	1984D	36.400	—	.10	.20
	1984D	.064	—	Proof	.40
	1984F	42.000	—	.10	.20
	1984F	.064	—	Proof	.40
	1984G	24.200	—	.10	.20
	1984G	.064	—	Proof	.40
	1984J	37.400	—	.10	.20
	1984J	.064	—	Proof	.40
	1985D	15.600	—	—	.10
	1985D	.056	—	Proof	.40
	1985F	18.000	—	—	.10
	1985F	.054	—	Proof	.40
	1985G	10.400	—	—	.10
	1985G	.055	—	Proof	.40
	1985J	16.000	—	—	.10
	1985J	.054	—	Proof	.40
	1986D	36.400	—	—	.10
	1986D	.044	—	Proof	.40
	1986F	42.000	—	—	.10
	1986F	.044	—	Proof	.40
	1986G	24.200	—	—	.10
	1986G	.044	—	Proof	.40
	1986J	37.400	—	—	.10
	1986J	.044	—	Proof	.40
	1987D	52.000	—	—	.10
	1987D	.045	—	Proof	.40
	1987F	60.000	—	—	.10
	1987F	.045	—	Proof	.40
	1987G	34.600	—	—	.10
	1987G	.045	—	Proof	.40
	1987J	53.400	—	—	.10
	1987J	.045	—	Proof	.40
	1988D	52.400	—	—	.10
	1988D	.045	—	Proof	.40
	1988F	72.000	—	—	.10
	1988F	.045	—	Proof	.40
	1988G	41.500	—	—	.10
	1988G	.045	—	Proof	.40
	1988J	64.100	—	—	.10
	1988J	.045	—	Proof	.40
	1989D	93.600	—	—	.10
	1989D	.045	—	Proof	.40
	1989F	108.000	—	—	.10
	1989F	.045	—	Proof	.40
	1989G	62.280	—	—	.10
	1989G	.045	—	Proof	.40
	1989J	96.120	—	—	.10
	1989J	.045	—	Proof	.40
	1990A	70.000	—	—	.10
	1990D	93.600	—	—	.10
	1990D	.045	—	Proof	.40
	1990F	108.000	—	—	.10
	1990F	.045	—	Proof	.40
	1990G	62.280	—	—	.10
	1990G	.045	—	Proof	.40
	1990J	96.120	—	—	.10
	1990J	.045	—	Proof	.40
	1991A	128.000	—	—	.10
	1991A	.045	—	Proof	.40
	1991D	134.400	—	—	.10
	1991D	.045	—	Proof	.40
	1991F	153.600	—	—	.10
	1991F	.045	—	Proof	.40
	1991G	89.600	—	—	.10
	1991G	.045	—	Proof	.40
	1991J	134.400	—	—	.10
	1991J	.045	—	Proof	.40
	1992A	28.000	—	—	.10
	1992A	.045	—	Proof	.40
	1992D	29.400	—	—	.10
	1992D	.045	—	Proof	.40
	1992F	33.600	—	—	.10
	1992F	.045	—	Proof	.40
	1992G	19.600	—	—	.10
	1992G	.045	—	Proof	.40
	1992J	29.400	—	—	.10
	1992J	.045	—	Proof	.40
	1993A	36.000	—	—	.10
	1993A	.045	—	Proof	.40
	1993D	37.800	—	—	.10
	1993D	.045	—	Proof	.40
	1993F	43.200	—	—	.10
	1993F	.045	—	Proof	.40
	1993G	25.200	—	—	.10
	1993G	.045	—	Proof	.40
	1993J	37.800	—	—	.10
	1993J	.045	—	Proof	.40
	1994A	38.000	—	—	.10
	1994A	.045	—	Proof	.40
	1994D	39.900	—	—	.10
	1994D	.045	—	Proof	.40
	1994F	45.600	—	—	.10
	1994F	.045	—	Proof	.40
	1994G	26.600	—	—	.10
	1994G	.045	—	Proof	.40
	1994J	39.900	—	—	.10
	1994J	.045	—	Proof	.40
	1995A	48.000	—	—	.15
	1995A	.045	—	Proof	.45
	1995D	50.400	—	—	.15
	1995D	.045	—	Proof	.45
	1995F	57.600	—	—	.15
	1995F	.045	—	Proof	.45
	1995G	33.600	—	—	.15
	1995G	.045	—	Proof	.45
	1995J	50.400	—	—	.15
	1995J	.045	—	Proof	.45

KM#	Date	Mintage	VF	XF	Unc
107	1996A	48.000	—	—	.20
	1996A	.045	—	Proof	.50
	1996D	50.400	—	—	.20
	1996D	.045	—	Proof	.50
	1996F	57.600	—	—	.20
	1996F	.045	—	Proof	.50
	1996G	33.600	—	—	.20
	1996G	.045	—	Proof	.50
	1996J	50.400	—	—	.20
	1996J	.045	—	Proof	.50
	1996A	.070	In sets only		1.75
	1997A	.045	—	Proof	2.00
	1997D	.070	In sets only		1.75
	1997D	.045	—	Proof	2.00
	1997F	.070	In sets only		1.75
	1997F	.045	—	Proof	2.00
	1997G	.070	In sets only		1.75
	1997G	.045	—	Proof	2.00
	1997J	.070	In sets only		1.75
	1997J	.045	—	Proof	2.00

10 PFENNIG

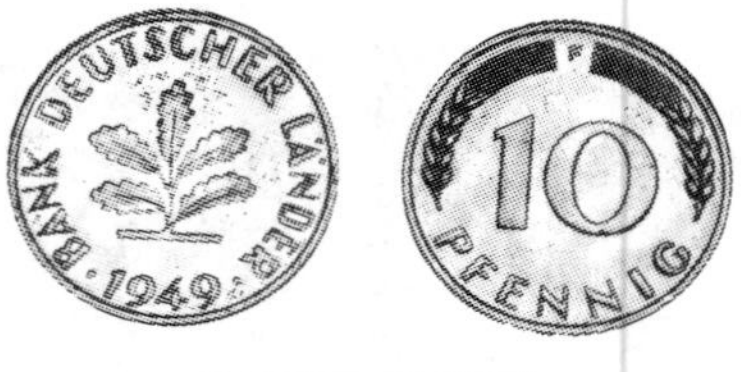

BRASS CLAD STEEL
Currency Reform

KM#	Date	Mintage	VF	XF	Unc
103	1949D	140.558	.50	7.50	25.00
	1949D	—	—	Proof	150.00
	1949F	120.932	.50	7.50	25.00
	1949F	250 pcs.	—	Proof	140.00
	1949G	82.933	1.00	7.50	35.00
	1949 lg.J	154.095	.50	7.50	25.00
	1949J	—	—	Proof	60.00
	1949 sm.J	Inc. Ab.	.50	7.50	25.00
	1949J	—	—	Proof	60.00

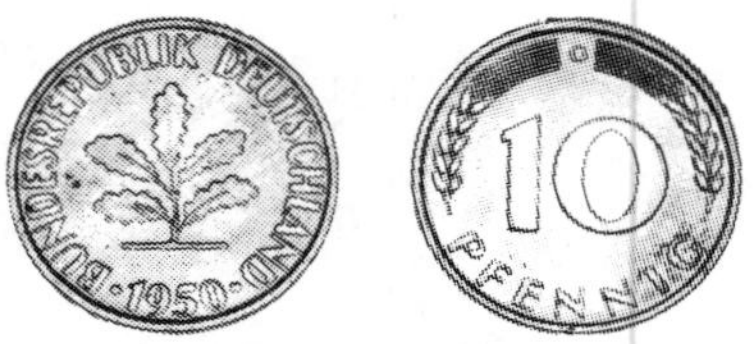

BRASS PLATED STEEL
Federal Republic

KM#	Date	Mintage	VF	XF	Unc
108	1950D	393.209	—	.20	4.00
	1950F	584.340	—	.20	4.00
	1950F	500 pcs.	—	Proof	45.00
	1950G	309.045	—	.20	4.00
	1950G	1,800	—	Proof	5.00
	1950J	402.452	—	.20	4.00
	1950J	—	—	Proof	20.00
	1966D	31.220	—	.20	4.00
	1966F	36.097	—	.20	4.00
	1966F	100 pcs.	—	Proof	75.00
	1966G	25.338	—	.20	4.00
	1966G	3,070	—	Proof	7.50
	1966J	32.116	—	.20	4.00
	1966J	1,000	—	Proof	12.50
	1967D	15.632	—	.20	5.00
	1967F	18.049	—	.20	5.00
	1967F	1,500	—	Proof	15.00
	1967G	1.518	1.00	4.00	15.00
	1967G	4,500	—	Proof	7.50
	1967J	16.051	—	.20	5.00
	1967J	1,500	—	Proof	12.50
	1968D	5.207	—	.20	3.50
	1968F	6.010	—	.20	3.50
	1968F	3,000	—	Proof	10.00
	1968G	12.384	.15	.50	3.50
	1968G	6,023	—	Proof	5.00
	1968J	5.422	—	.20	4.00
	1968J	2,000	—	Proof	10.00
	1969D	41.693	—	.15	2.50
	1969F	48.084	—	.15	.25
	1969F	5,000	—	Proof	3.00
	1969G	48.760	—	.15	.25
	1969G	8,700	—	Proof	2.50
	1969J	42.756	—	.15	.25
	1969J	5,000	—	Proof	2.50
	1970D	54.085	—	.15	.25
	1970F	60.086	—	.15	.25
	1970F	5,140	—	Proof	3.00
	1970G	35.900	—	.15	.25
	1970G	10,200	—	Proof	2.00
	1970J	40.115	—	.15	.25
	1970J	5,000	—	Proof	2.50
	1971D	54.022	—	.15	.25
	1971D	8,000	—	Proof	2.50
	1971F	92.534	—	.15	.25
	1971F	8,000	—	Proof	2.50
	1971G	88.614	—	.15	.25
	1971G	.010	—	Proof	2.00
	1971 sm.J	65.622	—	.15	.25
	1971 lg.J	Inc. Ab.	—	.15	.25
	1971J	8,000	—	Proof	1.50
	1972D	104.345	—	.15	.25
	1972D	8,000	—	Proof	1.50

KM#	Date	Mintage	VF	XF	Unc
108	1972F	110.177	—	.15	.25
	1972F	8,000	—	Proof	1.50
	1972G	71.766	—	.15	.25
	1972G	10,000	—	Proof	1.50
	1972J	96.991	—	.15	.25
	1972J	8,000	—	Proof	1.50
	1973D	26.052	—	.15	.25
	1973D	9,000	—	Proof	1.50
	1973F	30.070	—	.15	.25
	1973F	9,000	—	Proof	1.50
	1973G	17.294	—	.15	.25
	1973G	9,000	—	Proof	1.50
	1973J	26.774	—	.15	.25
	1973J	9,000	—	Proof	1.50
	1974D	15.707	—	.15	.25
	1974D	.035	—	Proof	.75
	1974F	18.135	—	.15	.25
	1974F	.035	—	Proof	.75
	1974G	10.450	—	.15	.25
	1974G	.035	—	Proof	.75
	1974J	16.056	—	.15	.25
	1974J	.035	—	Proof	.75
	1975D	15.654	—	.15	.25
	1975D	.043	—	Proof	.75
	1975F	18.043	—	.15	.25
	1975F	.043	—	Proof	.75
	1975G	10.403	—	.15	.25
	1975G	.043	—	Proof	.75
	1975J	16.111	—	.15	.25
	1975J	.043	—	Proof	.75
	1976D	65.200	—	.15	.25
	1976D	.043	—	Proof	.75
	1976F	75.282	—	.15	.25
	1976F	.043	—	Proof	.75
	1976G	43.372	—	.15	.25
	1976G	.043	—	Proof	.75
	1976J	66.930	—	.15	.25
	1976J	.043	—	Proof	.75
	1977D	64.989	—	.10	.20
	1977D	.051	—	Proof	.50
	1977F	75.052	—	.10	.20
	1977F	.051	—	Proof	.50
	1977G	43.300	—	.10	.20
	1977G	.051	—	Proof	.50
	1977J	66.800	—	.10	.20
	1977J	.051	—	Proof	.50
	1978D	91.000	—	.10	.20
	1978D	.054	—	Proof	.50
	1978F	105.000	—	.10	.20
	1978F	.054	—	Proof	.50
	1978G	60.590	—	.10	.20
	1978G	.054	—	Proof	.50
	1978J	93.490	—	.10	.20
	1978J	.054	—	Proof	.50
	1979D	104.000	—	.10	.20
	1979D	.089	—	Proof	.50
	1979F	120.000	—	.10	.20
	1979F	.089	—	Proof	.50
	1979G	69.200	—	.10	.20
	1979G	.089	—	Proof	.50
	1979J	106.800	—	.10	.20
	1979J	.089	—	Proof	.50
	1980D	65.450	—	.10	.20
	1980D	.110	—	Proof	.50
	1980F	122.780	—	.10	.20
	1980F	.110	—	Proof	.50
	1980G	75.410	—	.10	.20
	1980G	.110	—	Proof	.50
	1980J	70.960	—	.10	.20
	1980J	.110	—	Proof	.50
	1981D	135.200	—	.10	.20
	1981D	.091	—	Proof	.50
	1981F	117.410	—	.10	.20
	1981F	.091	—	Proof	.50
	1981G	69.440	—	.10	.20
	1981G	.091	—	Proof	.50
	1981J	138.360	—	.10	.20
	1981J	.091	—	Proof	.50
	1982D	74.690	—	.10	.20
	1982D	.078	—	Proof	.50
	1982F	85.140	—	.10	.20
	1982F	.078	—	Proof	.50
	1982G	50.840	—	.10	.20
	1982G	.078	—	Proof	.50
	1982J	80.620	—	.10	.20
	1982J	.078	—	Proof	.50
	1983D	33.800	—	.10	.20
	1983D	.075	—	Proof	.50
	1983F	39.000	—	.10	.20
	1983F	.075	—	Proof	.50
	1983G	22.490	—	.10	.20
	1983G	.075	—	Proof	.50
	1983J	34.710	—	.10	.20
	1983J	.075	—	Proof	.50
	1984D	52.000	—	.10	.20
	1984D	.064	—	Proof	.50
	1984F	60.000	—	.10	.20
	1984F	.064	—	Proof	.50
	1984G	34.600	—	.10	.20
	1984G	.064	—	Proof	.50
	1984J	53.400	—	.10	.20
	1984J	.064	—	Proof	.50
	1985D	78.000	—	—	.15
	1985D	.056	—	Proof	.50
	1985F	90.000	—	—	.15
	1985F	.054	—	Proof	.50
	1985G	51.900	—	—	.15
	1985G	.055	—	Proof	.50
	1985J	80.100	—	—	.15
	1985J	.054	—	Proof	.50
108	1986D	41.600	—	—	.15
	1986D	.044	—	Proof	.50
	1986F	48.000	—	—	.15
	1986F	.044	—	Proof	.50
	1986G	27.700	—	—	.15
	1986G	.044	—	Proof	.50
	1986J	42.700	—	—	.15
	1986J	.044	—	Proof	.15
	1987D	58.500	—	—	.10
	1987D	.045	—	Proof	.15
	1987F	67.500	—	—	.10
	1987F	.045	—	Proof	.15
	1987G	38.900	—	—	.10
	1987G	.045	—	Proof	.50
	1987J	60.100	—	—	.15
	1987J	.045	—	Proof	.50
	1988D	109.200	—	—	.15
	1988D	.045	—	Proof	.50
	1988F	126.000	—	—	.15
	1988F	.045	—	Proof	.50
	1988G	72.700	—	—	.15
	1988G	.045	—	Proof	.50
	1988J	112.100	—	—	.15
	1988J	.045	—	Proof	.50
	1989D	119.600	—	—	.15
	1989D	.045	—	Proof	.50
	1989F	138.000	—	—	.15
	1989F	.045	—	Proof	.50
	1989G	79.580	—	—	.15
	1989G	.045	—	Proof	.50
	1989J	122.820	—	—	.15
	1989J	.045	—	Proof	.50
	1990A	100.000	—	—	.15
	1990D	156.000	—	—	.15
	1990D	.045	—	Proof	.50
	1990F	180.000	—	—	.15
	1990F	.045	—	Proof	.50
	1990G	103.800	—	—	.15
	1990G	.045	—	Proof	.50
	1990J	160.200	—	—	.15
	1990J	.045	—	Proof	.50
	1991A	170.000	—	—	.15
	1991A	.045	—	Proof	.40
	1991D	178.550	—	—	.15
	1991D	.045	—	Proof	.40
	1991F	204.000	—	—	.15
	1991F	.045	—	Proof	.40
	1991G	119.000	—	—	.15
	1991G	.045	—	Proof	.40
	1991J	178.500	—	—	.15
	1991J	.045	—	Proof	.40
	1992A	80.000	—	—	.10
	1992A	.045	—	Proof	.40
	1992D	84.000	—	—	.10
	1992D	.045	—	Proof	.40
	1992F	96.000	—	—	.10
	1992F	.045	—	Proof	.40
	1992G	56.000	—	—	.10
	1992G	.045	—	Proof	.40
	1992J	84.000	—	—	.10
	1992J	.045	—	Proof	.40
	1993A	80.000	—	—	.10
	1993A	.045	—	Proof	.40
	1993D	84.000	—	—	.10
	1993D	.045	—	Proof	.40
	1993F	96.000	—	—	.10
	1993F	.045	—	Proof	.40
	1993G	56.000	—	—	.10
	1993G	.045	—	Proof	.40
	1993J	84.000	—	—	.10
	1993J	.045	—	Proof	.40
	1994A	100.000	—	—	.10
	1994A	.045	—	Proof	.40
	1994D	105.000	—	—	.10
	1994D	.045	—	Proof	.40
	1994F	120.000	—	—	.10
	1994F	.045	—	Proof	.40
	1994G	70.000	—	—	.10
	1994G	.045	—	Proof	.40
	1994J	105.000	—	—	.10
	1994J	.045	—	Proof	.40
	1995A	110.000	—	—	.15
	1995A	.045	—	Proof	.45
	1995D	115.000	—	—	.15
	1995D	.045	—	Proof	.45
	1995F	132.000	—	—	.15
	1995F	.045	—	Proof	.45
	1995G	77.000	—	—	.15
	1995G	.045	—	Proof	.45
	1995J	115.500	—	—	.15
	1995J	.045	—	Proof	.45
	1996A	90.000	—	—	.20
	1996A	.045	—	Proof	.50
	1996D	94.500	—	—	.20
	1996D	.045	—	Proof	.50
	1996F	108.000	—	—	.20
	1996F	.045	—	Proof	.50
	1996G	63.000	—	—	.20
	1996G	.045	—	Proof	.50
	1996J	94.500	—	—	.20
	1996J	.045	—	Proof	.50
	1997A	.070	In sets only		1.75
	1997A	.045	—	Proof	2.00
	1997D	.070	In sets only		1.75
	1997D	.045	—	Proof	2.00
	1997F	.070	In sets only		1.75
	1997F	.045	—	Proof	2.00
	1997G	.070	In sets only		1.75
	1997G	.045	—	Proof	2.00
	1997J	.070	In sets only		1.75
	1997J	.045	—	Proof	2.00

50 PFENNIG

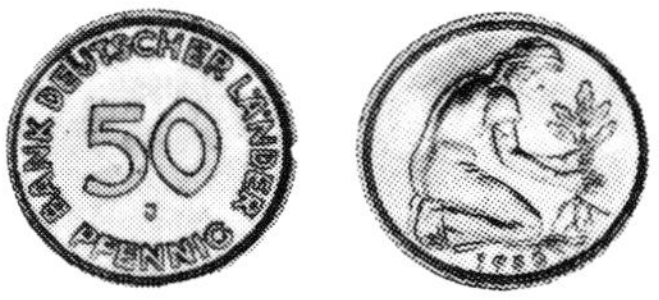

COPPER-NICKEL
Currency Reform

KM#	Date	Mintage	VF	XF	Unc
104	1949D	39.108	.75	4.50	45.00
	1949F	45.118	.75	4.50	45.00
	1949F	200 pcs.	—	Proof	125.00
	1949G	25.924	.75	5.00	55.00
	1949J	42.303	.75	4.50	55.00
	1949J	—	—	Proof	135.00
	1950G	.030	200.00	300.00	500.00

NOTE: The 1950G dated coin was restruck without authorization by a mint official using genuine dies - quantity unknown.

NOTE: Some no-date and half-date specimens of KM#104 have been reported.

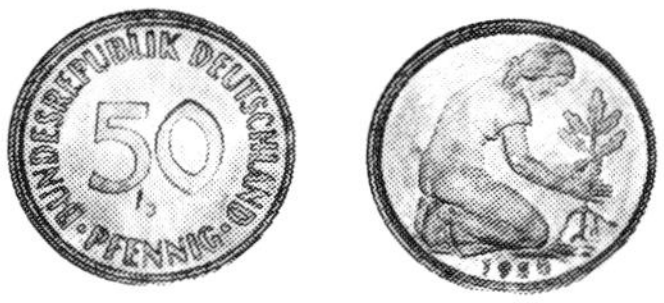

Federal Republic
Reeded edge.

KM#	Date	Mintage	VF	XF	Unc
109.1	1950D	100.735	.50	.75	9.00
	1950F	143.510	.50	.75	9.00
	1950F	450 pcs.	—	Proof	85.00
	1950G	66.421	.50	.75	10.00
	1950G	1,800	—	Proof	5.00
	1950J	102.736	.50	.75	9.00
	1950J	—	—	Proof	25.00
	1966D	8.328	.50	.75	15.00
	1966F	9.605	.50	.75	15.00
	1966F	100 pcs.	—	Proof	125.00
	1966G	5.543	.50	.65	15.00
	1966G	3,070	—	Proof	10.00
	1966J	8.569	.50	.65	15.00
	1966J	1,000	—	Proof	20.00
	1967D	5.207	.50	.65	15.00
	1967F	6.005	.50	.65	15.00
	1967F	1,500	—	Proof	18.00
	1967G	1.843	.50	1.00	18.00
	1967G	4,500	—	Proof	15.00
	1967J	10.684	.50	.65	15.00
	1967J	1,500	—	Proof	18.00
	1968D	7.809	.50	.60	12.00
	1968F	3.000	.50	.60	12.00
	1968F	3,000	—	Proof	15.00
	1968G	6.818	.50	.60	12.00
	1968G	6,023	—	Proof	8.00
	1968J	2.672	.50	.65	17.50
	1968J	2,000	—	Proof	15.00
	1969D	14.561	.45	.55	2.50
	1969F	16.804	.45	.55	2.50
	1969F	5,000	—	Proof	4.00
	1969G	9.704	.45	.55	2.50
	1969G	8,700	—	Proof	3.50
	1969J	14.969	.45	.55	2.50
	1969J	5,000	—	Proof	10.00
	1970D	25.294	.45	.55	1.00
	1970F	26.455	.45	.55	1.00
	1970F	5,140	—	Proof	3.50
	1970G	11.955	.45	.55	1.00
	1970G	10,200	—	Proof	3.00
	1970J	10.683	.45	.55	1.00
	1970J	5,000	—	Proof	3.50
	1971D	23.393	.45	.55	.75
	1971D	8,000	—	Proof	3.00
	1971F	29.746	.45	.55	.75
	1971F	8,000	—	Proof	3.00
	1971G	15.556	.45	.55	.75
	1971G	.010	—	Proof	3.00
	1971 lg.J	24.044	.45	.55	.75
	1971 sm.J	Inc. Ab.	.45	.55	.75
	1971J	8,000	—	Proof	3.00

Plain edge.

KM#	Date	Mintage	VF	XF	Unc
109.2	1972D	26.008	—	.45	.60
	1972D	8,000	—	Proof	2.00
	1972F	30.043	—	.45	.60
	1972F	8,000	—	Proof	2.00
	1972G	17.337	—	.45	.60
	1972G	10,000	—	Proof	2.00
	1972J	26.707	—	.45	.60
	1972J	8,000	—	Proof	2.00
	1973D	7.810	—	.45	1.00
	1973D	9,000	—	Proof	2.00
	1973F	8.994	—	.45	.60
	1973F	9,000	—	Proof	2.00
	1973G	5.201	—	.45	.60
	1973G	9,000	—	Proof	2.00
	1973J	8.011	—	.45	.60
	1973J	9,000	—	Proof	2.00
	1974D	18.264	—	.45	1.00
	1974D	.035	—	Proof	1.00
	1974 lg.F	21.036	—	.45	.60

KM#	Date	Mintage	VF	XF	Unc
109.2	1974 sm.F	Inc. Ab.	—	.45	1.00
	1974F	.035	—	Proof	1.00
	1974G	12.159	—	.45	.60
	1974G	.035	—	Proof	1.00
	1974J	18.752	—	.45	.60
	1974J	.035	—	Proof	1.00
	1975D	13.055	—	.45	1.00
	1975D	.043	—	Proof	1.00
	1975F	15.003	—	.45	.60
	1975F	.043	—	Proof	1.00
	1975G	8.675	—	.45	.60
	1975G	.043	—	Proof	1.00
	1975J	13.379	—	.45	.60
	1975J	.043	—	Proof	1.00
	1976D	10.411	—	.45	1.00
	1976D	.043	—	Proof	1.00
	1976F	12.048	—	.45	.60
	1976F	.043	—	Proof	1.00
	1976G	6.653	—	.45	.60
	1976G	.043	—	Proof	1.00
	1976J	10.716	—	.45	.60
	1976J	.043	—	Proof	1.00
	1977D	10.400	—	.45	1.00
	1977D	.051	—	Proof	.75
	1977F	12.000	—	.45	.60
	1977F	.051	—	Proof	.75
	1977G	6.921	—	.45	.60
	1977G	.051	—	Proof	.75
	1977J	10.708	—	.45	.60
	1977J	.051	—	Proof	.75
	1978D	10.400	—	.45	.60
	1978D	.054	—	Proof	.75
	1978F	12.000	—	.45	.60
	1978F	.054	—	Proof	.75
	1978G	6.640	—	.45	.60
	1978G	.054	—	Proof	.75
	1978J	10.680	—	.45	.60
	1978J	.054	—	Proof	.75
	1979D	10.400	—	.45	.60
	1979D	.089	—	Proof	.75
	1979F	12.000	—	.45	.60
	1979F	.089	—	Proof	.75
	1979G	6.920	—	.45	.60
	1979G	.089	—	Proof	.75
	1979J	10.680	—	.45	.60
	1979J	.089	—	Proof	.75
	1980D	23.250	—	.45	.60
	1980D	.110	—	Proof	.75
	1980F	17.440	—	.45	.60
	1980F	.110	—	Proof	.75
	1980G	22.460	—	.45	.60
	1980G	.110	—	Proof	.75
	1980J	24.030	—	.45	.60
	1980J	.110	—	Proof	.75
	1981D	17.900	—	.45	.60
	1981D	.091	—	Proof	.75
	1981F	29.810	—	.45	.60
	1981F	.091	—	Proof	.75
	1981G	10.880	—	.45	.60
	1981G	.091	—	Proof	.75
	1981J	24.140	—	.45	.60
	1981J	.091	—	Proof	.75
	1982D	21.540	—	.45	.60
	1982D	.078	—	Proof	.75
	1982F	28.900	—	.45	.60
	1982F	.078	—	Proof	.75
	1982G	19.710	—	.45	.60
	1982G	.078	—	Proof	.75
	1982J	17.210	—	.45	.60
	1982J	.078	—	Proof	.75
	1983D	20.800	—	.45	.60
	1983D	.075	—	Proof	.75
	1983F	24.000	—	.45	.60
	1983F	.075	—	Proof	.75
	1983G	13.840	—	.45	.60
	1983G	.075	—	Proof	.75
	1983J	21.360	—	.45	.60
	1983J	.075	—	Proof	.75
	1984D	11.700	—	.45	.60
	1984D	.064	—	Proof	.75
	1984F	13.500	—	.45	.60
	1984F	.064	—	Proof	.75
	1984G	7.800	—	.45	.60
	1984G	.064	—	Proof	.75
	1984J	12.000	—	.45	.60
	1984J	.064	—	Proof	.75
	1985D	15.700	—	—	.50
	1985D	.056	—	Proof	.75
	1985F	18.000	—	—	.50
	1985F	.054	—	Proof	.75
	1985G	10.400	—	—	.50
	1985G	.055	—	Proof	.75
	1985J	16.100	—	—	.50
	1985J	.054	—	Proof	.75
	1986D	2.100	—	—	.50
	1986D	.044	—	Proof	.75
	1986F	2.400	—	—	.50
	1986F	.044	—	Proof	.75
	1986G	1.400	—	—	.50
	1986G	.044	—	Proof	.75
	1986J	2.100	—	—	.50
	1986J	.044	—	Proof	.75
	1987D	.520	2.50	4.50	7.50
	1987D	.045	—	Proof	.75
	1987F	.600	2.50	4.50	7.50
	1987F	.045	—	Proof	.75
	1987G	.350	4.50	9.00	16.00
	1987G	.045	—	Proof	.75
	1987J	.530	2.50	4.50	7.50
	1987J	.045	—	Proof	.75

KM#	Date	Mintage	VF	XF	Unc
109.2	1988D	4.160	—	—	.50
	1988D	.045	—	Proof	.75
	1988F	4.800	—	—	.50
	1988F	.045	—	Proof	.75
	1988G	2.770	—	—	.50
	1988G	.045	—	Proof	.75
	1988J	4.300	—	—	.50
	1988J	.045	—	Proof	.75
	1989D	36.400	—	—	.50
	1989D	.045	—	Proof	.75
	1989F	42.000	—	—	.50
	1989F	.045	—	Proof	.75
	1989G	24.220	—	—	.50
	1989G	.045	—	Proof	.75
	1989J	37.380	—	—	.50
	1989J	.045	—	Proof	.75
	1990A	150.000	—	—	1.00
	1990D	58.500	—	—	.50
	1990D	.045	—	Proof	.75
	1990F	67.500	—	—	.50
	1990F	.045	—	Proof	.75
	1990G	38.920	—	—	.50
	1990G	.045	—	Proof	.75
	1990J	60.070	—	—	.50
	1990J	.045	—	Proof	.75
	1991A	22.000	—	—	.50
	1991A	.045	—	Proof	.75
	1991D	23.100	—	—	.50
	1991D	.045	—	Proof	.75
	1991F	26.400	—	—	.50
	1991F	.045	—	Proof	.75
	1991G	15.400	—	—	.50
	1991G	.045	—	Proof	.75
	1991J	23.100	—	—	.50
	1991J	.045	—	Proof	.75
	1992A	18.000	—	—	.50
	1992A	.045	—	Proof	.75
	1992D	18.900	—	—	.50
	1992D	.045	—	Proof	.75
	1992F	21.600	—	—	.50
	1992F	.045	—	Proof	.75
	1992G	12.600	—	—	.50
	1992G	.045	—	Proof	.75
	1992J	18.900	—	—	.50
	1992J	.045	—	Proof	.75
	1993A	16.000	—	—	.50
	1993A	.045	—	Proof	.75
	1993D	16.800	—	—	.50
	1993D	.045	—	Proof	.75
	1993F	19.200	—	—	.50
	1993F	.045	—	Proof	.75
	1993G	11.200	—	—	.50
	1993G	.045	—	Proof	.75
	1993J	16.800	—	—	.50
	1993J	.045	—	Proof	.75
	1994A	7.500	—	—	.50
	1994A	.045	—	Proof	.75
	1994D	7.875	—	—	.50
	1994D	.045	—	Proof	.75
	1994F	9.000	—	—	.50
	1994F	.045	—	Proof	.75
	1994G	5.250	—	—	.50
	1994G	.045	—	Proof	.75
	1994J	7.875	—	—	.50
	1994J	.045	—	Proof	.75
	1995A	1.300	—	—	2.25
	1995A	.045	—	Proof	6.00
	1995D	1.365	—	—	2.25
	1995D	.045	—	Proof	6.00
	1995F	.020	In sets only		90.00
	1995F	.045	—	Proof	12.00
	1995G	.020	In sets only		100.00
	1995G	.045	—	Proof	12.00
	1995J	.150	—	—	12.00
	1995J	.045	—	Proof	12.00
	1996A	.050	In sets only		12.00
	1996A	.045	—	Proof	13.50
	1996D	.050	In sets only		12.00
	1996D	.045	—	Proof	13.50
	1996F	.050	In sets only		12.00
	1996F	.045	—	Proof	13.50
	1996G	.050	In sets only		12.00
	1996G	.045	—	Proof	13.50
	1996J	.050	In sets only		12.00
	1996J	.045	—	Proof	13.50
	1997A	.070	In sets only		4.75
	1997A	.045	—	Proof	5.00
	1997D	.070	In sets only		4.75
	1997D	.045	—	Proof	5.00
	1997F	.070	In sets only		4.75
	1997F	.045	—	Proof	5.00
	1997G	.070	In sets only		4.75
	1997G	.045	—	Proof	5.00
	1997J	.070	In sets only		4.75
	1997J	.045	—	Proof	5.00

NOTE: Counterfeits of 1972 dated coins w/reeded edges exist.

MARK

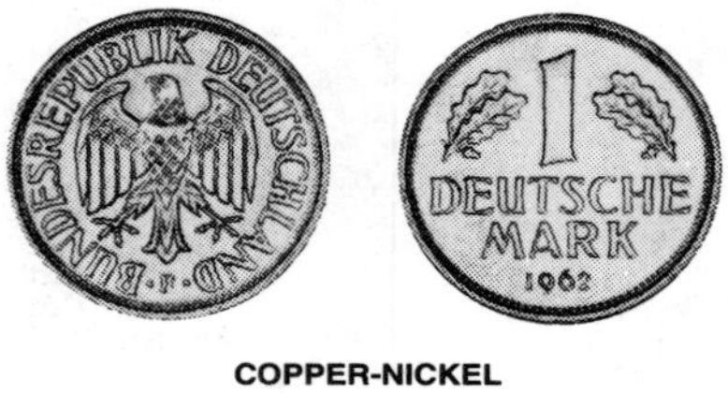

COPPER-NICKEL

Federal Republic

KM#	Date	Mintage	VF	XF	Unc
110	1950D	60.467	.75	4.00	45.00
	1950D	—	—	Proof	200.00
	1950F	69.183	.75	4.00	45.00
	1950F	150 pcs.	—	Proof	450.00
	1950G	39.826	.75	5.00	75.00
	1950G	*200 pcs.	—	Proof	375.00
	1950J	61.483	.75	4.00	50.00
	1950J	—	—	Proof	150.00
	1954D	5.202	1.00	9.00	185.00
	1954D	—	—	Proof	875.00
	1954F	6.000	1.00	9.00	160.00
	1954F	175 pcs.	—	Proof	375.00
	1954G	3.459	1.00	70.00	800.00
	1954G	15 pcs.	—	Proof	1500.
	1954J	5.341	1.00	9.00	185.00
	1954J	—	—	Proof	450.00
	1955D	3.093	1.00	9.00	185.00
	1955F	4.909	1.00	9.00	350.00
	1955F	*20 pcs.	—	Proof	1000.
	1955G	2.500	15.00	90.00	1000.
	1955J	5.294	1.00	9.00	185.00
	1956D	13.231	1.00	6.50	160.00
	1956F	14.700	1.00	6.50	160.00
	1956F	100 pcs.	—	Proof	375.00
	1956G	8.362	1.00	6.50	260.00
	1956J	11.478	1.00	9.00	210.00
	1957D	6.820	1.00	9.00	160.00
	1957D	100 pcs.	—	Proof	350.00
	1957F	6.390	1.00	9.00	160.00
	1957F	100 pcs.	—	Proof	375.00
	1957G	3.841	1.00	9.00	130.00
	1957G	27 pcs.	—	Proof	1500.
	1957J	6.632	1.00	9.00	170.00
	1957J	200 pcs.	—	Proof	325.00
	1958D	4.150	1.00	6.50	160.00
	1958D	200 pcs.	—	Proof	325.00
	1958F	4.109	1.00	6.50	210.00
	1958F	100 pcs.	—	Proof	575.00
	1958G	3.460	1.00	6.50	185.00
	1958G	20 pcs.	—	Proof	2100.
	1958J	4.656	1.00	6.50	185.00
	1958J	37 pcs.	—	Proof	650.00
	1959D	10.409	.85	5.00	120.00
	1959D	40 pcs.	—	Proof	600.00
	1959F	11.972	.85	4.00	65.00
	1959F	100 pcs.	—	Proof	350.00
	1959G	6.921	.85	4.00	75.00
	1959G	20 pcs.	—	Proof	2100.
	1959J	10.691	.85	4.00	65.00
	1959J	25 pcs.	—	Proof	1800.
	1960D	5.453	.85	4.00	65.00
	1960D	100 pcs.	—	Proof	350.00
	1960F	5.709	.85	4.00	65.00
	1960F	100 pcs.	—	Proof	350.00
	1960G	3.632	.85	5.00	125.00
	1960G	100 pcs.	—	Proof	350.00
	1960J	5.612	.85	4.00	55.00
	1960J	36 pcs.	—	Proof	650.00
	1961D	7.536	.85	4.00	55.00
	1961D	60 pcs.	—	Proof	500.00
	1961F	6.029	.85	4.00	55.00
	1961F	50 pcs.	—	Proof	550.00
	1961G	4.843	.85	4.00	60.00
	1961G	70 pcs.	—	Proof	450.00
	1961J	7.483	.85	4.00	55.00
	1961J	28 pcs.	—	Proof	1200.
	1962D	10.327	.85	4.00	35.00
	1962D	40 pcs.	—	4.00	600.00
	1962F	11.122	.85	4.00	35.00
	1962F	45 pcs.	—	Proof	550.00
	1962G	6.054	.85	5.00	55.00
	1962G	100 pcs.	—	Proof	300.00
	1962J	10.822	.85	4.00	30.00
	1962J	28 pcs.	—	Proof	1200.
	1963D	12.624	.85	4.00	30.00
	1963D	40 pcs.	—	Proof	600.00
	1963F	18.292	.85	4.00	30.00
	1963F	45 pcs.	—	Proof	550.00
	1963G	11.253	.85	4.00	30.00
	1963G	200 pcs.	—	Proof	300.00
	1963J	15.906	.85	4.00	30.00
	1963J	28 pcs.	—	Proof	1200.
	1964D	8.048	.85	4.00	30.00
	1964D	30 pcs.	—	Proof	1000.
	1964F	12.796	.85	4.00	30.00
	1964F	25 pcs.	—	Proof	1900.
	1964G	3.465	.85	4.00	30.00
	1964G	368 pcs.	—	Proof	75.00
	1964J	6.958	.85	4.00	30.00
	1964J	33 pcs.	—	Proof	900.00
	1965D	9.388	.75	3.00	22.50
	1965F	9.013	.75	3.00	22.50
	1965F	*80 pcs.	—	Proof	175.00
	1965G	6.232	.75	3.00	30.00
	1965G	1,200	—	Proof	12.50
	1965J	8.024	.75	3.00	22.50
	1966D	11.717	.75	3.00	17.50
	1966F	11.368	.75	3.00	17.50
	1966F	100 pcs.	—	Proof	150.00
	1966G	7.799	.75	3.00	25.00
	1966G	3,070	—	Proof	15.00
	1966J	12.030	.75	3.00	17.50
	1966J	1,000	—	Proof	25.00
	1967D	13.017	.75	3.00	15.00
	1967F	7.500	.75	3.00	15.00
	1967F	1,500	—	Proof	20.00
	1967G	4.324	.75	3.00	15.00
	1967G	4,500	—	Proof	17.50
	1967J	13.357	.75	3.00	15.00

KM#	Date	Mintage	VF	XF	Unc
110	1967J	1,500	—	Proof	20.00
	1968D	1.303	.75	4.00	20.00
	1968F	1.500	.75	4.00	20.00
	1968F	3,000	—	Proof	15.00
	1968G	5.198	.75	3.00	20.00
	1968G	6,023	—	Proof	7.50
	1968J	1.338	.75	5.00	65.00
	1968J	2,000	—	Proof	15.00
	1969D	13.025	.75	1.50	10.00
	1969F	15.021	.75	1.50	10.00
	1969F	5,000	—	Proof	6.00
	1969G	8.665	.75	1.50	10.00
	1969G	8,700	—	Proof	5.00
	1969J	13.370	.75	1.50	10.00
	1969J	5,000	—	Proof	5.00
	1970D	17.928	.75	1.00	8.00
	1970F	19.408	.75	1.00	8.00
	1970F	5,140	—	Proof	6.00
	1970G	20.386	.75	1.00	8.00
	1970G	10,200	—	Proof	5.00
	1970J	10.707	.75	1.00	8.00
	1970J	5,000	—	Proof	5.00
	1971D	24.513	.75	1.00	3.00
	1971D	8,000	—	Proof	5.00
	1971F	28.275	.75	1.00	3.00
	1971F	8,000	—	Proof	5.00
	1971G	16.375	.75	1.00	3.00
	1971G	.010	—	Proof	5.00
	1971J	25.214	.75	1.00	3.00
	1971J	8,000	—	Proof	5.00
	1972D	20.904	.75	1.00	2.00
	1972D	8,000	—	Proof	5.00
	1972F	24.086	.75	1.00	2.00
	1972F	8,000	—	Proof	5.00
	1972G	13.868	.75	1.00	2.00
	1972G	.010	—	Proof	5.00
	1972J	21.360	.75	1.00	2.00
	1972J	8,000	—	Proof	5.00
	1973D	14.327	.75	1.00	2.00
	1973D	9,000	—	Proof	5.00
	1973F	16.592	.75	1.00	2.00
	1973F	9,000	—	Proof	5.00
	1973G	10.409	.75	1.00	2.00
	1973G	9,000	—	Proof	5.00
	1973J	14.704	.75	1.00	2.00
	1973J	9,000	—	Proof	5.00
	1974D	20.876	.75	1.00	2.00
	1974D	.035	—	Proof	2.00
	1974F	24.057	.75	1.00	2.00
	1974F	.035	—	Proof	2.00
	1974G	13.931	.75	1.00	2.00
	1974G	.035	—	Proof	2.00
	1974J	21.440	.75	1.00	2.00
	1974J	.035	—	Proof	2.00
	1975D	18.241	.75	1.00	1.50
	1975D	.043	—	Proof	2.00
	1975F	21.059	.75	1.00	1.50
	1975F	.043	—	Proof	2.00
	1975G	12.142	.75	1.00	1.50
	1975G	.043	—	Proof	2.00
	1975J	18.770	.75	1.00	1.50
	1975J	.043	—	Proof	2.00
	1976D	15.670	.75	1.00	1.50
	1976D	.043	—	Proof	2.00
	1976F	18.105	.75	1.00	1.50
	1976F	.043	—	Proof	2.00
	1976G	10.382	.75	1.00	1.50
	1976G	.043	—	Proof	2.00
	1976J	16.046	.75	1.00	1.50
	1976J	.043	—	Proof	2.00
	1977D	20.801	.75	.85	1.00
	1977D	.051	—	Proof	1.25
	1977F	24.026	.75	.85	1.00
	1977F	.051	—	Proof	1.25
	1977G	13.849	.75	.85	1.00
	1977G	.051	—	Proof	1.25
	1977J	21.416	.75	.85	1.00
	1977J	.051	—	Proof	1.25
	1978D	15.600	.75	.85	1.00
	1978D	.054	—	Proof	1.25
	1978F	18.000	.75	.85	1.00
	1978F	.054	—	Proof	1.25
	1978G	10.380	.75	.85	1.00
	1978G	.054	—	Proof	1.25
	1978J	16.020	.75	.85	1.00
	1978J	.054	—	Proof	1.25
	1979D	18.200	.75	.85	1.00
	1979D	.089	—	Proof	1.25
	1979F	21.000	.75	.85	1.00
	1979F	.089	—	Proof	1.25
	1979G	12.110	.75	.85	1.00
	1979G	.089	—	Proof	1.25
	1979J	18.690	.75	.85	1.00
	1979J	.089	—	Proof	1.25
	1980D	24.330	—	.75	.90
	1980D	.110	—	Proof	1.00
	1980F	9.670	—	.75	.90
	1980F	.110	—	Proof	1.00
	1980G	8.540	—	.75	.90
	1980G	.110	—	Proof	1.00
	1980J	16.010	—	.75	.90
	1980J	.110	—	Proof	1.00
	1981D	21.150	—	.75	.90
	1981D	.091	—	Proof	1.00
	1981F	25.910	—	.75	.90
	1981F	.091	—	Proof	1.00
	1981G	14.090	—	.75	.90
	1981G	.091	—	Proof	1.00
	1981J	18.800	—	.75	.90
	1981J	.091	—	Proof	1.00

KM#	Date	Mintage	VF	XF	Unc
110	1982D	20.590	—	.75	.90
	1982D	.078	—	Proof	1.00
	1982F	22.990	—	.75	.90
	1982F	.078	—	Proof	1.00
	1982G	14.900	—	.75	.90
	1982G	.078	—	Proof	1.00
	1982J	11.520	—	.75	.90
	1982J	.078	—	Proof	1.00
	1983D	18.200	—	.75	.90
	1983D	.075	—	Proof	1.00
	1983F	21.000	—	.75	.90
	1983F	.075	—	Proof	1.00
	1983G	12.100	—	.75	.90
	1983G	.075	—	Proof	1.00
	1983J	18.690	—	.75	.90
	1983J	.075	—	Proof	1.00
	1984D	8.400	—	.75	.90
	1984D	.064	—	Proof	1.50
	1984F	9.700	—	.75	.90
	1984F	.064	—	Proof	1.50
	1984G	5.600	—	.75	.90
	1984G	.064	—	Proof	1.50
	1984J	8.700	—	.75	.90
	1984J	.064	—	Proof	1.50
	1985D	11.700	—	—	.85
	1985D	.056	—	Proof	1.50
	1985F	13.500	—	—	.85
	1985F	.054	—	Proof	1.50
	1985G	7.800	—	—	.85
	1985G	.055	—	Proof	1.50
	1985J	12.000	—	—	.85
	1985J	.054	—	Proof	1.50
	1986D	10.400	—	—	.85
	1986D	.044	—	Proof	1.50
	1986F	12.000	—	—	.85
	1986F	.044	—	Proof	1.50
	1986G	6.900	—	—	.85
	1986G	.044	—	Proof	1.50
	1986J	10.700	—	—	.85
	1986J	.044	—	Proof	1.50
	1987D	3.120	3.50	7.50	15.00
	1987D	.045	—	Proof	1.50
	1987F	3.600	3.50	7.50	15.00
	1987F	.045	—	Proof	1.50
	1987G	2.080	3.50	7.50	15.00
	1987G	.045	—	Proof	1.50
	1987J	3.200	3.50	7.50	15.00
	1987J	.045	—	Proof	1.50
	1988D	20.800	—	—	.85
	1988D	.045	—	Proof	1.50
	1988F	24.000	—	—	.85
	1988F	.045	—	Proof	1.50
	1988G	13.800	—	—	.85
	1988G	.045	—	Proof	1.50
	1988J	21.400	—	—	.85
	1988J	.045	—	Proof	1.50
	1989D	39.000	—	—	.85
	1989D	.045	—	Proof	1.50
	1989F	45.000	—	—	.85
	1989F	.045	—	Proof	1.50
	1989G	25.950	—	—	.85
	1989G	.045	—	Proof	1.50
	1989J	40.050	—	—	.85
	1989J	.045	—	Proof	1.50
	1990A	55.000	—	—	2.00
	1990D	77.740	—	—	.85
	1990D	.045	—	Proof	1.50
	1990F	89.700	—	—	.85
	1990F	.045	—	Proof	1.50
	1990G	51.720	—	—	.85
	1990G	.045	—	Proof	1.50
	1990J	79.830	—	—	.85
	1990J	.045	—	Proof	1.50
	1991A	30.000	—	—	.85
	1991A	.045	—	Proof	1.50
	1991D	31.500	—	—	.85
	1991D	.045	—	Proof	1.50
	1991F	36.000	—	—	.85
	1991F	.045	—	Proof	1.50
	1991G	21.000	—	—	.85
	1991G	.045	—	Proof	1.50
	1991J	31.500	—	—	.85
	1991J	.045	—	Proof	1.50
	1992A	30.000	—	—	.85
	1992A	.045	—	Proof	1.50
	1992D	31.500	—	—	.85
	1992D	.045	—	Proof	1.50
	1992F	36.000	—	—	.85
	1992F	.045	—	Proof	1.50
	1992G	21.000	—	—	.85
	1992G	.045	—	Proof	1.50
	1992J	31.500	—	—	.85
	1992J	.045	—	Proof	1.50
	1993A	8.000	—	—	.85
	1993A	.045	—	Proof	1.50
	1993D	8.400	—	—	.85
	1993D	.045	—	Proof	1.50
	1993F	9.600	—	—	.85
	1993F	.045	—	Proof	1.50
	1993G	5.600	—	—	.85
	1993G	.045	—	Proof	1.50
	1993J	8.400	—	—	.85
	1993J	.045	—	Proof	1.50
	1994A	18.000	—	—	.85
	1994A	.045	—	Proof	1.50
	1994D	18.900	—	—	.85
	1994D	.045	—	Proof	1.50
	1994F	21.800	—	—	.85
	1994F	.045	—	Proof	1.50
	1994G	12.800	—	—	.85

KM#	Date	Mintage	VF	XF	Unc
110	1994G	.045	—	Proof	1.50
	1994J	18.900	—	—	.85
	1994J	.045	—	Proof	1.50
	1995A	.020	In sets only		70.00
	1995A	.045	—	Proof	20.00
	1995D	.020	In sets only		70.00
	1995D	.045	—	Proof	20.00
	1995F	.020	In sets only		70.00
	1995F	.045	—	Proof	20.00
	1995G	.020	In sets only		70.00
	1995G	.045	—	Proof	20.00
	1995J	.100	—	—	18.00
	1995J	.045	—	Proof	20.00
	1996A	.050	In sets only		12.50
	1996A	.045	—	Proof	14.00
	1996D	.050	In sets only		12.50
	1996D	.045	—	Proof	14.00
	1996F	.050	In sets only		12.50
	1996F	.045	—	Proof	14.00
	1996G	.050	In sets only		12.50
	1996G	.045	—	Proof	14.00
	1996J	.050	In sets only		12.50
	1996J	.045	—	Proof	14.00
	1997A	.070	In sets only		4.75
	1997A	.045	—	Proof	5.00
	1997D	.070	In sets only		4.75
	1997D	.045	—	Proof	5.00
	1997F	.070	In sets only		4.75
	1997F	.045	—	Proof	5.00
	1997G	.070	In sets only		4.75
	1997G	.045	—	Proof	5.00
	1997J	.070	In sets only		4.75
	1997J	.045	—	Proof	5.00

2 MARK

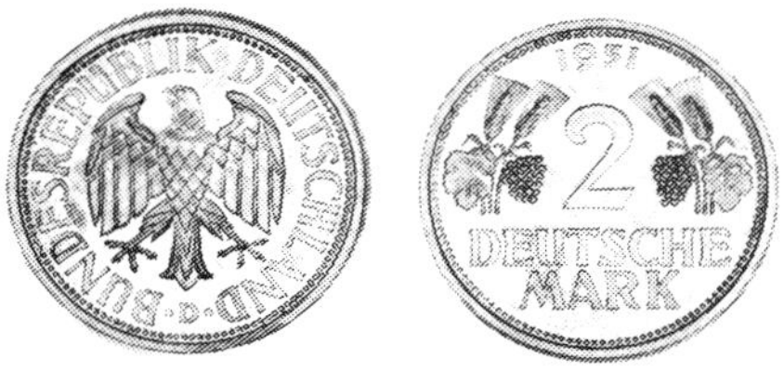

COPPER-NICKEL
Federal Republic

KM#	Date	Mintage	VF	XF	Unc
111	1951D	19.564	32.00	60.00	150.00
	1951D	200 pcs.	—	Proof	450.00
	1951F	22.609	30.00	50.00	110.00
	1951F	150 pcs.	—	Proof	500.00
	1951G	*13.012	40.00	100.00	210.00
	1951G	33 pcs.	—	Proof	1200.
	1951J	20.104	30.00	50.00	110.00
	1951J	180 pcs.	—	Proof	450.00

***NOTE:** The 1951G dated coin was restruck without authorization by a mint official using genuine dies - quantity unknown.

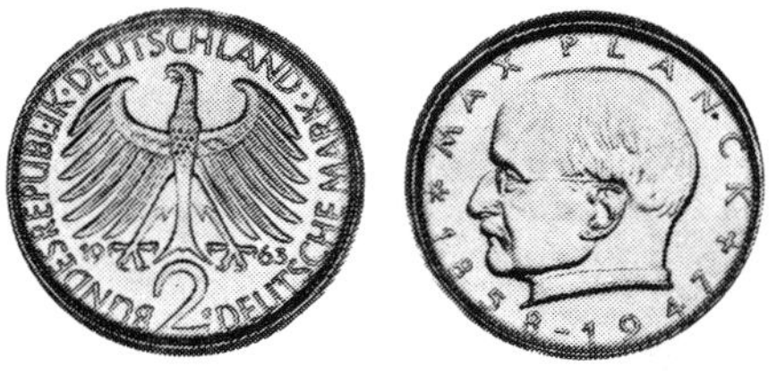

Max Planck

KM#	Date	Mintage	VF	XF	Unc
116	1957D	7.452	2.00	6.00	65.00
	1957D	350 pcs.	—	Proof	235.00
	1957F	6.337	2.00	6.00	65.00
	1957F	100 pcs.	—	Proof	325.00
	1957G	2.598	3.00	7.50	135.00
	1957G	56 pcs.	—	Proof	600.00
	1957J	11.210	2.00	6.00	60.00
	1957J	370 pcs.	—	Proof	175.00
	1958D	12.623	1.50	5.00	50.00
	1958D	1,240	—	Proof	85.00
	1958F	16.825	1.50	4.00	45.00
	1958F	300 pcs.	—	Proof	200.00
	1958G	10.744	1.50	4.00	45.00
	1958G	45 pcs.	—	Proof	700.00
	1958J	9.408	1.50	4.00	45.00
	1958J	100 pcs.	—	Proof	400.00
	1959D	1.020	4.00	10.00	220.00
	1959D	38 pcs.	—	Proof	800.00
	1959F	.203	15.00	60.00	365.00
	1959F	24 pcs.	—	Proof	900.00
	1960D	3.535	1.50	4.00	35.00
	1960D	100 pcs.	—	Proof	325.00
	1960F	3.692	1.50	4.00	35.00
	1960F	50 pcs.	—	Proof	600.00
	1960G	2.695	2.00	4.00	35.00
	1960G	130 pcs.	—	Proof	300.00
	1960J	4.676	1.50	4.00	35.00
	1960J	36 pcs.	—	Proof	800.00
	1961D	3.918	1.50	4.00	35.00
	1961D	50 pcs.	—	Proof	600.00
	1961F	3.872	1.50	4.00	35.00
	1961F	46 pcs.	—	Proof	650.00
	1961G	2.776	2.00	4.00	35.00
	1961G	100 pcs.	—	Proof	325.00
	1961J	2.940	1.50	4.00	35.00
	1961J	28 pcs.	—	Proof	750.00

KM#	Date	Mintage	VF	XF	Unc
116	1962D	4.105	2.00	6.00	35.00
	1962D	50 pcs.	—	Proof	600.00
	1962F	3.344	2.00	6.00	35.00
	1962F	42 pcs.	—	Proof	625.00
	1962G	1.800	2.00	6.00	35.00
	1962G	130 pcs.	—	Proof	300.00
	1962J	3.609	2.00	6.00	25.00
	1962J	28 pcs.	—	Proof	750.00
	1963D	4.411	1.50	4.00	25.00
	1963D	40 pcs.	—	Proof	650.00
	1963F	3.752	1.50	4.00	25.00
	1963F	47 pcs.	—	Proof	600.00
	1963G	3.448	1.50	4.00	25.00
	1963G	200 pcs.	—	Proof	250.00
	1963J	7.348	1.50	4.00	25.00
	1963J	32 pcs.	—	Proof	700.00
	1964D	5.205	1.50	4.00	20.00
	1964D	40 pcs.	—	Proof	650.00
	1964F	4.834	1.50	4.00	20.00
	1964F	36 pcs.	—	Proof	800.00
	1964G	3.044	1.50	4.00	20.00
	1964G	368 pcs.	—	Proof	150.00
	1964J	2.681	1.50	4.00	20.00
	1964J	43 pcs.	—	Proof	600.00
	1965D	3.903	1.50	2.50	15.00
	1965D	35 pcs.	—	Proof	800.00
	1965F	4.045	1.50	2.50	15.00
	1965F	300 pcs.	—	Proof	250.00
	1965G	2.599	1.50	2.50	15.00
	1965G	8,233	—	Proof	5.00
	1965J	4.007	1.50	2.50	15.00
	1965J	36 pcs.	—	Proof	750.00
	1966D	5.855	1.50	2.50	12.00
	1966D	20 pcs.	—	Proof	900.00
	1966F	3.750	1.50	2.50	12.00
	1966F	450 pcs.	—	Proof	250.00
	1966G	3.895	1.50	2.50	12.00
	1966G	3,070	—	Proof	20.00
	1966J	6.014	1.50	2.50	12.00
	1966J	1,000	—	Proof	35.00
	1967D	3.254	1.50	2.50	12.00
	1967D	20 pcs.	—	Proof	900.00
	1967F	3.758	1.50	2.50	12.00
	1967F	1,600	—	Proof	32.00
	1967G	1.878	1.50	4.00	16.50
	1967G	5,363	—	Proof	28.00
	1967J	6.684	1.25	2.50	12.00
	1967J	1,500	—	Proof	32.00
	1968D	4.166	1.50	2.50	15.00
	1968D	30 pcs.	—	Proof	850.00
	1968F	1.050	2.00	5.00	20.00
	1968F	3,100	—	Proof	22.00
	1968G	3.060	2.00	2.50	12.00
	1968G	6,023	—	Proof	15.00
	1968J	.939	2.00	4.00	20.00
	1968J	2,000	—	Proof	28.00
	1969D	2.602	2.00	2.50	15.00
	1969F	3.005	2.00	2.50	15.00
	1969F	5,100	—	Proof	6.00
	1969G	1.754	2.00	2.50	16.50
	1969G	8,700	—	Proof	6.00
	1969J	2.680	2.00	2.50	10.00
	1969J	5,000	—	Proof	6.00
	1970D	5.203	1.50	2.00	4.00
	1970F	6.018	1.50	2.00	4.00
	1970F	5,140	—	Proof	7.50
	1970G	3.461	1.50	2.00	4.00
	1970G	.010	—	Proof	5.00
	1970J	5.691	1.50	2.00	4.00
	1970J	5,000	—	Proof	6.00
	1971D	8.451	1.00	1.25	3.00
	1971D	8,000	—	Proof	5.00
	1971F	10.017	1.00	1.25	3.00
	1971F	8,000	—	Proof	5.00
	1971G	5.631	1.00	1.25	3.00
	1971G	.010	—	Proof	5.00
	1971J	8.786	1.00	1.25	3.00
	1971J	8,000	—	Proof	6.00

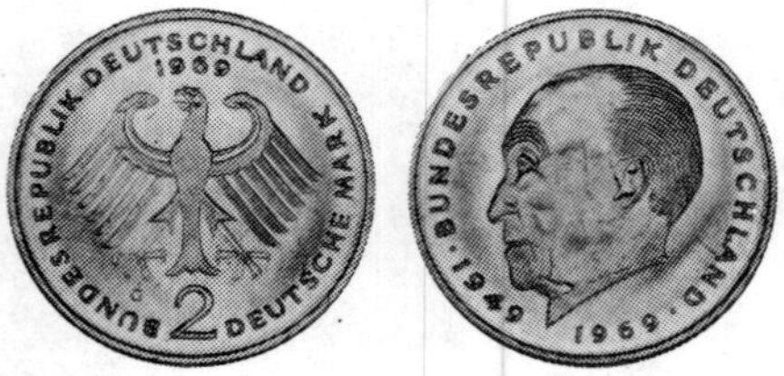

COPPER-NICKEL CLAD NICKEL
Konrad Adenauer

KM#	Date	Mintage	VF	XF	Unc
124	1969D	7.001	—	1.50	3.00
	1969F	7.006	—	1.50	3.00
	1969G	7.010	—	1.50	3.00
	1969J	7.000	—	1.50	3.00
	1970D	7.318	—	1.50	3.00
	1970F	8.422	—	1.50	3.00
	1970G	4.844	—	1.50	3.00
	1970J	7.476	—	1.50	3.00
	1971D	7.287	—	1.50	3.00
	1971F	8.400	—	1.50	3.00
	1971G	4.848	—	1.50	3.00
	1971J	7.476	—	1.50	3.00
	1972D	7.286	—	1.50	3.00
	1972D	8,000	—	Proof	4.50
	1972F	8.392	—	1.50	3.00
	1972F	8,000	—	Proof	4.50
	1972G	4.848	—	1.50	3.00

KM#	Date	Mintage	VF	XF	Unc
124	1972G	.010	—	Proof	4.50
	1972J	7.476	—	1.50	3.00
	1972J	8,000	—	Proof	4.50
	1973D	10.393	—	1.50	3.00
	1973D	9,000	—	Proof	4.50
	1973F	11.015	—	1.50	3.00
	1973F	9,000	—	Proof	4.50
	1973G	9.022	—	1.50	3.00
	1973G	9,000	—	Proof	4.50
	1973J	12.272	—	1.50	3.00
	1973J	9,000	—	Proof	4.50
	1974D	5.151	—	1.50	3.00
	1974D	.035	—	Proof	2.25
	1974F	5.894	—	1.50	3.00
	1974F	.035	—	Proof	2.25
	1974G	3.790	—	1.50	3.00
	1974G	.035	—	Proof	2.25
	1974J	5.282	—	1.50	3.00
	1974J	.035	—	Proof	2.25
	1975D	4.553	—	1.50	2.50
	1975D	.043	—	Proof	2.25
	1975F	5.270	—	1.50	2.50
	1975F	.043	—	Proof	2.25
	1975G	3.035	—	1.50	2.50
	1975G	.043	—	Proof	2.25
	1975J	4.673	—	1.50	2.50
	1975J	.043	—	Proof	2.25
	1976D	4.576	—	1.50	2.50
	1976D	.043	—	Proof	2.25
	1976F	5.257	—	1.50	2.50
	1976F	.043	—	Proof	2.25
	1976G	3.028	—	1.50	2.50
	1976G	.043	—	Proof	2.25
	1976J	4.673	—	1.50	2.50
	1976J	.043	—	Proof	2.25
	1977D	5.906	—	1.50	2.50
	1977D	.051	—	Proof	2.00
	1977F	6.765	—	1.50	2.50
	1977F	.051	—	Proof	2.00
	1977G	3.892	—	1.50	2.50
	1977G	.051	—	Proof	2.00
	1977J	6.007	—	1.50	2.50
	1977J	.051	—	Proof	2.00
	1978D	3.304	—	1.50	2.50
	1978D	.054	—	Proof	2.00
	1978F	3,804	—	1.50	2.50
	1978F	.054	—	Proof	2.00
	1978G	2.217	—	1.50	2.50
	1978G	.054	—	Proof	2.00
	1978J	3.392	—	1.50	2.50
	1978J	.054	—	Proof	2.00
	1979D	3.209	—	1.50	2.50
	1979D	.089	—	Proof	2.00
	1979F	3.689	—	1.50	2.50
	1979F	.089	—	Proof	2.00
	1979G	2.165	—	1.50	2.50
	1979G	.089	—	Proof	2.00
	1979J	3.293	—	1.50	2.50
	1979J	.089	—	Proof	2.00
	1980D	10.810	—	1.50	2.00
	1980D	.110	—	Proof	2.00
	1980F	8.910	—	1.50	2.00
	1980F	.110	—	Proof	2.00
	1980G	1.170	—	1.50	2.00
	1980G	.110	—	Proof	2.00
	1980J	4.670	—	1.50	2.00
	1980J	.110	—	Proof	2.00
	1981D	8.180	—	1.50	2.00
	1981D	.091	—	Proof	2.00
	1981F	7.690	—	1.50	2.00
	1981F	.091	—	Proof	2.00
	1981G	7.070	—	1.50	2.00
	1981G	.091	—	Proof	2.00
	1981J	8.290	—	1.50	2.00
	1981J	.091	—	Proof	2.00
	1982D	9.220	—	1.50	2.00
	1982D	.078	—	Proof	2.00
	1982F	11.260	—	1.50	2.00
	1982F	.078	—	Proof	2.00
	1982G	6.640	—	1.50	2.00
	1982G	.078	—	Proof	2.00
	1982J	9.790	—	1.50	2.00
	1982J	.078	—	Proof	2.00
	1983D	1.560	—	1.50	2.00
	1983D	.075	—	Proof	2.00
	1983F	1.800	—	1.50	2.00
	1983F	.075	—	Proof	2.00
	1983G	1.030	—	1.50	2.00
	1983G	.075	—	Proof	2.00
	1983J	1.600	—	1.50	2.00
	1983J	.075	—	Proof	2.00
	1984D	.052	2.00	4.50	8.50
	1984D	.064	—	Proof	2.00
	1984F	.060	2.00	4.50	8.50
	1984F	.064	—	Proof	2.00
	1984G	.035	3.00	6.00	11.50
	1984G	.064	—	Proof	2.00
	1984J	.053	2.00	4.50	8.50
	1984J	.064	—	Proof	2.00
	1985D	2.600	—	—	2.00
	1985D	.056	—	Proof	2.25
	1985F	3.000	—	—	1.75
	1985F	.054	—	Proof	2.25
	1985G	1.730	—	—	1.75
	1985G	.055	—	Proof	2.25
	1985J	2.670	—	—	1.75
	1985J	.054	—	Proof	2.25
	1986D	2.600	—	—	1.75
	1986D	.044	—	Proof	2.25
	1986F	3.000	—	—	1.75

KM#	Date	Mintage	VF	XF	Unc
124	1986F	.044	—	Proof	2.25
	1986G	1.730	—	—	1.75
	1986G	.044	—	Proof	2.25
	1986J	2.670	—	—	1.75
	1986J	.044	—	Proof	2.25
	1987D	4.420	—	—	1.75
	1987D	.045	—	Proof	2.25
	1987F	5.100	—	—	1.75
	1987F	.045	—	Proof	2.25
	1987G	2.940	—	—	1.75
	1987G	.045	—	Proof	2.25
	1987J	4.540	—	—	1.75
	1987J	.045	—	Proof	2.25

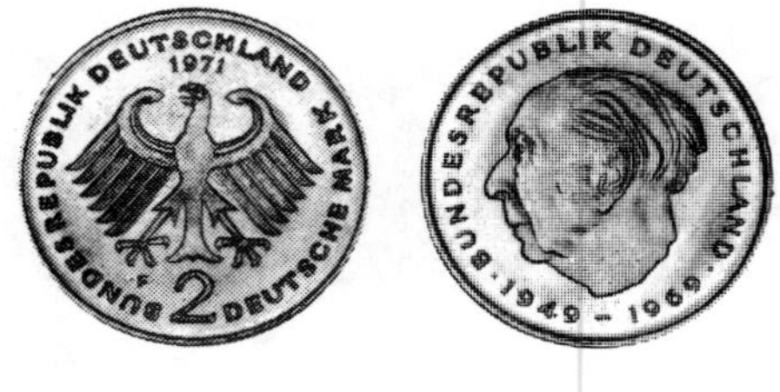

Theodor Heuss

KM#	Date	Mintage	VF	XF	Unc
A127	1970D	7.317	—	1.50	3.00
(127)	1970F	8.426	—	1.50	3.00
	1970G	4.844	—	1.50	3.00
	1970J	7.476	—	1.50	3.00
	1971D	7.280	—	1.50	3.00
	1971F	8.403	—	1.50	3.00
	1971G	4.841	—	1.50	3.00
	1971J	7.476	—	1.50	3.00
	1972D	7.288	—	1.50	3.00
	1972D	8,000	—	Proof	4.50
	1972F	8.401	—	1.50	3.00
	1972F	8,000	—	Proof	4.50
	1972G	4.859	—	1.50	3.00
	1972G	.010	—	Proof	4.50
	1972J	7.476	—	1.50	3.00
	1972J	8,000	—	Proof	4.50
	1973D	10.379	—	1.50	3.00
	1973D	9,000	—	Proof	4.50
	1973F	11.018	—	1.50	3.00
	1973F	9,000	—	Proof	4.50
	1973G	8.975	—	1.50	3.00
	1973G	9,000	—	Proof	4.50
	1973J	12.360	—	1.50	3.00
	1973J	9,000	—	Proof	4.50
	1974D	5.147	—	1.50	3.00
	1974D	.035	—	Proof	2.00
	1974F	5.899	—	1.50	3.00
	1974F	.035	—	Proof	2.00
	1974G	3.820	—	1.50	3.00
	1974G	.035	—	Proof	2.00
	1974J	5.280	—	1.50	3.00
	1974J	.035	—	Proof	2.00
	1975D	4.623	—	1.50	2.00
	1975D	.043	—	Proof	2.00
	1975F	5.251	—	1.50	2.00
	1975F	.043	—	Proof	2.00
	1975G	3.034	—	1.50	2.00
	1975G	.043	—	Proof	2.00
	1975J	4.675	—	1.50	2.00
	1975J	.043	—	Proof	2.00
	1976D	4.546	—	1.50	2.00
	1976D	.043	—	Proof	2.00
	1976F	5.259	—	1.50	2.00
	1976F	.043	—	Proof	2.00
	1976G	3.028	—	1.50	2.00
	1976G	.043	—	Proof	2.00
	1976J	4.681	—	1.50	2.00
	1976J	.043	—	Proof	2.00
	1977D	5.857	—	1.50	2.00
	1977D	.051	—	Proof	1.75
	1977F	6.752	—	1.50	2.00
	1977F	.051	—	Proof	1.75
	1977G	3.892	—	1.50	2.00
	1977G	.051	—	Proof	1.75
	1977J	6.009	—	1.50	2.00
	1977J	.051	—	Proof	1.75
	1978D	3.804	—	1.50	2.00
	1978D	.054	—	Proof	1.75
	1978F	3.804	—	1.50	2.00
	1978F	.054	—	Proof	1.75
	1978G	2.217	—	1.50	2.00
	1978G	.054	—	Proof	1.75
	1978J	3.392	—	1.50	2.00
	1978J	.054	—	Proof	1.75
	1979D	3.209	—	1.50	2.00
	1979D	.089	—	Proof	1.75
	1979F	3.689	—	1.50	2.00
	1979F	.089	—	Proof	1.75
	1979G	2.165	—	1.50	2.00
	1979G	.089	—	Proof	1.75
	1979J	3.293	—	1.50	2.00
	1979J	.089	—	Proof	1.75
	1980D	2.000	—	1.50	1.75
	1980D	.110	—	Proof	1.75
	1980F	2.300	—	1.50	1.75
	1980F	.110	—	Proof	1.75
	1980G	1.300	—	1.50	1.75
	1980G	.110	—	Proof	1.75
	1980J	2.000	—	1.50	1.75
	1980J	.110	—	Proof	1.75
	1981D	2.000	—	1.50	1.75
	1981D	.091	—	Proof	1.75
	1981F	2.300	—	1.50	1.75

KM#	Date	Mintage	VF	XF	Unc
(127)	1981F	.091	—	Proof	1.75
	1981G	1.300	—	1.50	1.75
	1981G	.091	—	Proof	1.75
	1981J	2.000	—	1.50	1.75
	1981J	.091	—	Proof	1.75
	1982D	3.100	—	1.50	1.75
	1982D	.078	—	Proof	1.75
	1982F	3.600	—	1.50	1.75
	1982F	.078	—	Proof	1.75
	1982G	2.100	—	1.50	1.75
	1982G	.078	—	Proof	1.75
	1982J	3.200	—	1.50	1.75
	1982J	.078	—	Proof	1.75
	1983D	1.560	—	1.50	1.75
	1983D	.075	—	Proof	1.75
	1983F	1.800	—	1.50	1.75
	1983F	.075	—	Proof	1.75
	1983G	1.030	—	1.50	1.75
	1983G	.075	—	Proof	1.75
	1983J	1.600	—	1.50	1.75
	1983J	.075	—	Proof	1.75
	1984D	.052	2.00	4.50	8.50
	1984D	.064	—	Proof	2.00
	1984F	.060	2.00	4.50	8.50
	1984F	.064	—	Proof	2.00
	1984G	.035	3.00	6.00	11.50
	1984G	.064	—	Proof	2.00
	1984J	.053	2.00	4.50	8.50
	1984J	.064	—	Proof	2.00
	1985D	2.600	—	—	1.75
	1985D	.056	—	Proof	2.25
	1985F	3.000	—	—	1.75
	1985F	.054	—	Proof	2.25
	1985G	1.730	—	—	1.75
	1985G	.055	—	Proof	2.25
	1985J	2.670	—	—	1.75
	1985J	.054	—	Proof	2.25
	1986D	2.600	—	—	1.75
	1986D	.044	—	Proof	2.25
	1986F	3.000	—	—	1.75
	1986F	.044	—	Proof	2.25
	1986G	1.730	—	—	1.75
	1986G	.044	—	Proof	2.25
	1986J	2.670	—	—	1.75
	1986J	.044	—	Proof	2.25
	1987D	4.420	—	—	1.75
	1987D	.045	—	Proof	2.25
	1987F	5.100	—	—	1.75
	1987F	.045	—	Proof	2.25
	1987G	2.940	—	—	1.75
	1987G	.045	—	Proof	2.25
	1987J	4.540	—	—	1.75
	1987J	.045	—	Proof	2.25

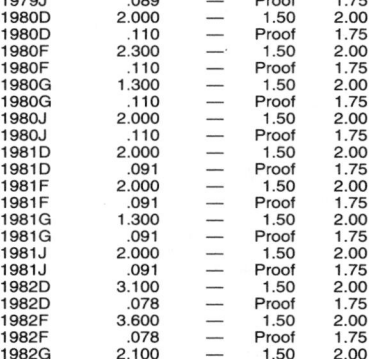

Dr. Kurt Schumacher

KM#	Date	Mintage	VF	XF	Unc
149	1979D	3.209	—	1.50	2.00
	1979D	.089	—	Proof	1.75
	1979F	3.689	—	1.50	2.00
	1979F	.089	—	Proof	1.75
	1979G	2.165	—	1.50	2.00
	1979G	.089	—	Proof	1.75
	1979J	3.293	—	1.50	2.00
	1979J	.089	—	Proof	1.75
	1980D	2.000	—	1.50	2.00
	1980D	.110	—	Proof	1.75
	1980F	2.300	—	1.50	2.00
	1980F	.110	—	Proof	1.75
	1980G	1.300	—	1.50	2.00
	1980G	.110	—	Proof	1.75
	1980J	2.000	—	1.50	2.00
	1980J	.110	—	Proof	1.75
	1981D	2.000	—	1.50	2.00
	1981D	.091	—	Proof	1.75
	1981F	2.000	—	1.50	2.00
	1981F	.091	—	Proof	1.75
	1981G	1.300	—	1.50	2.00
	1981G	.091	—	Proof	1.75
	1981J	2.000	—	1.50	2.00
	1981J	.091	—	Proof	1.75
	1982D	3.100	—	1.50	2.00
	1982D	.078	—	Proof	1.75
	1982F	3.600	—	1.50	2.00
	1982F	.078	—	Proof	1.75
	1982G	2.100	—	1.50	2.00
	1982G	.078	—	Proof	1.75
	1982J	3.200	—	1.50	2.00
	1982J	.078	—	Proof	1.75
	1983D	1.560	—	1.50	2.00
	1983D	.075	—	Proof	1.75
	1983F	1.800	—	1.50	2.00
	1983F	.075	—	Proof	1.75
	1983G	1.030	—	1.50	2.00
	1983G	.075	—	Proof	1.75
	1983J	1.600	—	1.50	2.00
	1983J	.075	—	Proof	1.75
	1984D	.052	2.00	4.50	8.50
	1984D	.064	—	Proof	1.75
	1984F	.060	2.00	4.50	8.50
	1984F	.064	—	Proof	1.75
	1984G	.035	3.00	6.00	11.50
	1984G	.064	—	Proof	1.75
	1984J	.053	2.00	4.50	8.50
	1984J	.064	—	Proof	1.75
	1985D	2.600	—	—	1.75
	1985D	.056	—	Proof	2.25
	1985F	3.000	—	—	1.75
	1985F	.054	—	Proof	2.25
	1985G	1.730	—	—	1.75
	1985G	.055	—	Proof	2.25
	1985J	2.670	—	—	1.75
	1985J	.054	—	Proof	2.25
	1986D	2.600	—	—	1.75
	1986D	.044	—	Proof	2.25
	1986F	3.000	—	—	1.75
	1986F	.044	—	Proof	2.25
	1986G	1.730	—	—	1.75
	1986G	.044	—	Proof	2.25
	1986J	2.670	—	—	1.75
	1986J	.044	—	Proof	2.25
	1987D	4.420	—	—	1.75
	1987D	.045	—	Proof	2.25
	1987F	5.100	—	—	1.75
	1987F	.045	—	Proof	2.25
	1987G	2.940	—	—	1.75
	1987G	.045	—	Proof	2.25
	1987J	4.540	—	—	1.75
	1987J	.045	—	Proof	2.25
	1988D	5.850	—	—	1.75
	1988D	.045	—	Proof	2.25
	1988F	6.750	—	—	1.75
	1988F	.045	—	Proof	2.25
	1988G	3.890	—	—	1.75
	1988G	.045	—	Proof	2.25
	1988J	6.010	—	—	1.75
	1988J	.045	—	Proof	2.25
	1989D	10.400	—	—	1.75
	1989D	.045	—	Proof	2.25
	1989F	12.000	—	—	1.75
	1989F	.045	—	Proof	2.25
	1989G	6.920	—	—	1.75
	1989G	.045	—	Proof	2.25
	1989J	10.680	—	—	1.75
	1989J	.045	—	Proof	2.25
	1990D	18.370	—	—	1.75
	1990D	.045	—	Proof	2.25
	1990F	21.200	—	—	1.75
	1990F	.045	—	Proof	2.25
	1990G	12.220	—	—	1.75
	1990G	.045	—	Proof	2.25
	1990J	18.870	—	—	1.75
	1990J	.045	—	Proof	2.25
	1991A	4.000	—	—	1.75
	1991A	.045	—	Proof	2.25
	1991D	4.200	—	—	1.75
	1991D	.045	—	Proof	2.25
	1991F	4.800	—	—	1.75
	1991F	.045	—	Proof	2.25
	1991G	2.800	—	—	1.75
	1991G	.045	—	Proof	2.25
	1991J	4.200	—	—	1.75
	1991J	.045	—	Proof	2.25
	1992A	7.330	—	—	1.75
	1992A	.045	—	Proof	2.25
	1992D	7.700	—	—	1.75
	1992D	.045	—	Proof	2.25
	1992F	8.800	—	—	1.75
	1992F	.045	—	Proof	2.25
	1992G	5.130	—	—	1.75
	1992G	.045	—	Proof	2.25
	1992J	7.700	—	—	1.75
	1992J	.045	—	Proof	2.25
	1993A	600,000	—	3.00	7.00
	1993A	.045	—	Proof	2.25
	1993D	630,000	—	3.00	7.00
	1993D	.045	—	Proof	2.25
	1993F	720,000	—	3.00	7.00
	1993F	.045	—	Proof	2.25
	1993G	420,000	—	4.00	10.00
	1993G	.045	—	Proof	2.25
	1993J	630,000	—	3.00	7.00
	1993J	.045	—	Proof	2.25

Ludwig Erhard

KM#	Date	Mintage	VF	XF	Unc
170	1988D	5.850	—	—	1.65
	1988D	.045	—	Proof	2.00
	1988F	6.750	—	—	1.65
	1988F	.045	—	Proof	2.00
	1988G	3.890	—	—	1.65
	1988G	.045	—	Proof	2.00
	1988J	6.010	—	—	1.65
	1988J	.045	—	Proof	2.00
	1989D	10.400	—	—	1.65
	1989D	.045	—	Proof	2.00
	1989F	12.000	—	—	1.65
	1989F	.045	—	Proof	2.00
	1989G	6.920	—	—	1.65
	1989G	.045	—	Proof	2.00
	1989J	10.680	—	—	1.65
	1989J	.045	—	Proof	2.00
	1990D	18.370	—	—	1.65
	1990D	.045	—	Proof	2.00
	1990F	21.200	—	—	1.65
	1990F	.045	—	Proof	2.00
	1990G	12.220	—	—	1.65
	1990G	.045	—	Proof	2.00
	1990J	18.870	—	—	1.65
	1990J	.045	—	Proof	2.00
	1991A	4.000	—	—	1.65
	1991A	.045	—	Proof	2.00
	1991D	4.200	—	—	1.65
	1991D	.045	—	Proof	2.00
	1991F	4.800	—	—	1.65
	1991F	.045	—	Proof	2.00
	1991G	2.800	—	—	1.65
	1991G	.045	—	Proof	2.00
	1991J	4.200	—	—	1.65
	1991J	.045	—	Proof	2.00
	1992A	7.330	—	—	1.75
	1992A	.045	—	Proof	2.25
	1992D	7.700	—	—	1.75
	1992D	.045	—	Proof	2.25
	1992F	8.800	—	—	1.75
	1992F	.045	—	Proof	2.25
	1992G	5.130	—	—	1.75
	1992G	.045	—	Proof	2.25
	1992J	7.700	—	—	1.75
	1992J	.045	—	Proof	2.25
	1993A	600,000	—	3.00	7.00
	1993A	.045	—	Proof	2.25
	1993D	630,000	—	3.00	7.00
	1993D	.045	—	Proof	2.25
	1993F	720,000	—	3.00	7.00
	1993F	.045	—	Proof	2.25
	1993G	420,000	—	4.00	10.00
	1993G	.045	—	Proof	2.25
	1993J	630,000	—	3.00	7.00
	1993J	.045	—	Proof	2.25
	1994A	5.000	—	—	1.75
	1994A	.045	—	Proof	2.25
	1994D	5.250	—	—	1.75
	1994D	.045	—	Proof	2.25
	1994F	6.000	—	—	1.75
	1994F	.045	—	Proof	2.25
	1994G	3.500	—	—	1.75
	1994G	.045	—	Proof	2.25
	1994J	5.250	—	—	1.75
	1994J	.045	—	Proof	2.25
	1995A	1.595	—	—	3.50
	1995A	.045	—	Proof	17.50
	1995D	.020	In sets only		60.00
	1995D	.045	—	Proof	17.50
	1995F	.020	In sets only		60.00
	1995F	.045	—	Proof	17.50
	1995G	.920	—	—	6.00
	1995G	.045	—	Proof	17.50
	1995J	.020	In sets only		60.00
	1995J	.045	—	Proof	17.50
	1996A	—	—	—	5.00
	1996A	.045	—	Proof	6.00
	1996D	—	—	—	5.00
	1996D	.045	—	Proof	6.00
	1996F	—	—	—	5.00
	1996F	.045	—	Proof	6.00
	1996G	—	—	—	5.00
	1996G	.045	—	Proof	6.00
	1996J	—	—	—	5.00
	1996J	.045	—	Proof	6.00
	1997A	.070	In sets only		4.25
	1997A	.045	—	Proof	5.00
	1997D	.070	In sets only		4.25
	1997D	.045	—	Proof	5.00
	1997F	.070	In sets only		4.25
	1997F	.045	—	Proof	5.00
	1997G	.070	In sets only		4.25
	1997G	.045	—	Proof	5.00
	1997J	.070	In sets only		4.25
	1997J	.045	—	Proof	5.00

Franz Joseph Strauss

KM#	Date	Mintage	VF	XF	Unc
175	1990D	18.370	—	—	1.75
	1990D	.045	—	Proof	2.25
	1990F	21.200	—	—	1.75
	1990F	.045	—	Proof	2.25
	1990G	12.220	—	—	1.75
	1990G	.045	—	Proof	2.25
	1990J	18.870	—	—	1.75
	1990J	.045	—	Proof	2.25
	1991A	4.000	—	—	1.75
	1991A	.045	—	Proof	2.25
	1991D	4.200	—	—	1.75
	1991D	.045	—	Proof	2.25
	1991F	4.800	—	—	1.75
	1991F	.045	—	Proof	2.25
	1991G	2.800	—	—	1.75

KM# 175

KM#	Date	Mintage	VF	XF	Unc
175	1991G	.045	—	Proof	2.25
	1991J	4.200	—	—	1.75
	1991J	.045	—	Proof	2.25
	1992A	7.330	—	—	1.75
	1992A	.045	—	Proof	2.25
	1992D	7.700	—	—	1.75
	1992D	.045	—	Proof	2.25
	1992F	8.800	—	—	1.75
	1992F	.045	—	Proof	2.25
	1992G	5.130	—	—	1.75
	1992G	.045	—	Proof	2.25
	1992J	7.700	—	—	1.75
	1992J	.045	—	Proof	2.25
	1993A	600,000	—	3.00	7.00
	1993A	.045	—	Proof	2.25
	1993D	630,000	—	3.00	7.00
	1993D	.045	—	Proof	2.25
	1993F	720,000	—	3.00	7.00
	1993F	.045	—	Proof	2.25
	1993G	420,000	—	4.00	10.00
	1993G	.045	—	Proof	2.25
	1993J	630,000	—	3.00	7.00
	1993J	.045	—	Proof	2.25
	1994A	5.000	—	—	1.75
	1994A	.045	—	Proof	2.25
	1994D	5.250	—	—	1.75
	1994D	.045	—	Proof	2.25
	1994F	6.000	—	—	1.75
	1994F	.045	—	Proof	2.25
	1994G	3.500	—	—	1.75
	1994G	.045	—	Proof	2.25
	1994J	5.250	—	—	1.75
	1994J	.045	—	Proof	2.25
	1995A	1.595	—	—	3.50
	1995A	.045	—	Proof	17.50
	1995D	.020	In sets only		60.00
	1995D	.045	—	Proof	17.50
	1995F	.020	In sets only		60.00
	1995F	.045	—	Proof	17.50
	1995G	.620	—	—	7.00
	1995G	.045	—	Proof	17.50
	1995J	.020	In sets only		60.00
	1995J	.045	—	Proof	17.50
	1996A	—	—	—	5.00
	1996A	.045	—	Proof	6.00
	1996D	—	—	—	5.00
	1996D	.045	—	Proof	6.00
	1996F	—	—	—	5.00
	1996F	.045	—	Proof	6.00
	1996G	—	—	—	5.00
	1996G	.045	—	Proof	6.00
	1996J	—	—	—	5.00
	1996J	.045	—	Proof	6.00
	1997A	.070	In sets only		4.25
	1997A	.045	—	Proof	5.00
	1997D	.070	In sets only		4.25
	1997D	.045	—	Proof	5.00
	1997F	.070	In sets only		4.25
	1997F	.045	—	Proof	5.00
	1997G	.070	In sets only		4.25
	1997G	.045	—	Proof	5.00
	1997J	.070	In sets only		4.25
	1997J	.045	—	Proof	5.00

KM# 183

KM#	Date	Mintage	VF	XF	Unc
183	1997D	.045	—	—	5.00
	1997F	.070	In sets only		4.25
	1997F	.045	—	Proof	5.00
	1997G	.070	In sets only		4.25
	1997G	.045	—	Proof	5.00
	1997J	.070	In sets only		4.25
	1997J	.045	—	Proof	5.00

5 MARK

11.2000 g, .625 SILVER, .2250 oz ASW
Federal Republic

KM#	Date	Mintage	VF	XF	Unc
112.1	1951D	20.600	4.00	15.00	65.00
	1951D	—	—	Proof	250.00
	1951F	24.000	4.00	15.00	75.00
	1951F	280 pcs.	—	Proof	250.00
	1951G	13.840	4.00	15.00	75.00
	1951G	—	—	Proof	450.00
	1951J	21.360	4.00	15.00	60.00
	1951J	—	—	Proof	225.00
	1956D	1.092	15.00	60.00	225.00
	1956D	—	—	Proof	450.00
	1956F	1.200	10.00	75.00	375.00
	1956F	23 pcs.	—	Proof	1000.
	1956J	1.068	10.00	60.00	225.00
	1956J	—	—	Proof	450.00
	1957D	.566	10.00	85.00	400.00
	1957D	—	—	Proof	475.00
	1957F	2.100	7.50	50.00	300.00
	1957F	—	—	Proof	500.00
	1957G	.692	10.00	65.00	350.00
	1957G	—	—	Proof	400.00
	1957J	1.630	7.50	30.00	150.00
	1957J	—	—	Proof	250.00
	1958D	1.226	7.50	30.00	150.00
	1958D	—	—	Proof	300.00
	1958F	.600	20.00	125.00	600.00
	1958F	100 pcs.	—	Proof	800.00
	1958G	1.557	7.50	28.00	130.00
	1958G	—	—	Proof	400.00
	1958J	.060	1200.	2750.	3750.
	1958J	—	—	Proof	4000.
	1959D	.496	10.00	45.00	245.00
	1959D	—	—	Proof	400.00
	1959G	.692	15.00	55.00	235.00
	1959G	—	—	Proof	500.00
	1959J	.713	8.00	40.00	225.00
	1959J	—	—	Proof	375.00
	1960D	1.040	7.00	20.00	110.00
	1960D	—	—	Proof	300.00
	1960F	1.576	7.00	20.00	110.00
	1960F	50 pcs.	—	Proof	800.00
	1960G	.692	7.00	22.00	125.00
	1960G	—	—	Proof	250.00
	1960J	1.618	7.00	18.00	90.00
	1960J	—	—	Proof	400.00
	1961D	1.040	4.50	15.00	80.00
	1961D	—	—	Proof	225.00
	1961F	.824	4.50	22.00	125.00
	1961F	—	—	Proof	450.00
	1961J	.518	6.00	28.00	135.00
	1961J	—	—	Proof	550.00
	1963D	2.080	4.50	15.00	60.00
	1963D	—	—	Proof	350.00
	1963F	1.254	4.50	18.00	70.00
	1963F	—	—	Proof	350.00
	1963G	.600	7.50	20.00	100.00
	1963G	*100 pcs.	—	Proof	450.00
	1963J	2.136	4.50	15.00	60.00
	1963J	—	—	Proof	350.00
	1964D	.456	15.00	50.00	175.00
	1964D	—	—	Proof	375.00
	1964F	2.646	4.50	15.00	60.00
	1964F	—	—	Proof	350.00
	1964G	1.649	4.50	15.00	45.00
	1964G	*600 pcs.	—	Proof	80.00
	1964J	1.335	4.00	15.00	45.00
	1964J	—	—	Proof	200.00
	1965D	4.354	4.00	12.50	30.00
	1965D	—	—	Proof	175.00
	1965F	4.050	4.00	8.00	30.00
	1965F	*80 pcs.	—	Proof	425.00
	1965G	2.335	4.00	7.00	25.00
	1965G	8,233	—	Proof	42.00
	1965J	3.605	4.00	7.00	25.00
	1965J	—	—	Proof	250.00
	1966D	5.200	4.00	7.00	25.00
	1966D	—	—	Proof	250.00
	1966F	6.000	4.00	7.00	25.00
	1966F	100 pcs.	—	Proof	425.00
	1966G	3.460	4.00	7.00	25.00
	1966G	3,070	—	Proof	45.00
	1966J	5.340	4.00	7.00	25.00
	1966J	1,000	—	Proof	110.00
	1967D	3.120	4.00	7.00	25.00
	1967D	—	—	Proof	200.00
	1967F	3.598	4.00	7.00	25.00

KM#	Date	Mintage	VF	XF	Unc
112.1	1967F	1,500	—	Proof	75.00
	1967G	1.406	4.00	7.00	25.00
	1967G	4,500	—	Proof	35.00
	1967J	3.204	4.00	7.00	25.00
	1967J	1,500	—	Proof	90.00
	1968D	1.300	4.00	10.00	35.00
	1968D	—	—	Proof	60.00
	1968F	1.497	4.00	10.00	35.00
	1968F	3,000	—	Proof	75.00
	1968G	1.535	4.00	10.00	35.00
	1968G	6,023	—	Proof	35.00
	1968J	1.335	4.00	10.00	35.00
	1968J	2,000	—	Proof	65.00
	1969D	2.080	4.00	7.00	20.00
	1969D	—	—	Proof	25.00
	1969F	2.395	4.00	7.00	20.00
	1969F	5,000	—	Proof	25.00
	1969G	3.484	4.00	7.00	20.00
	1969G	8,700	—	Proof	20.00
	1969J	2.136	4.00	7.00	20.00
	1969J	5,000	—	Proof	25.00
	1970D	2.000	4.00	7.00	20.00
	1970D	—	—	Proof	20.00
	1970F	1.995	4.00	7.00	20.00
	1970F	5,140	—	Proof	25.00
	1970G	6.000	3.50	4.50	8.50
	1970G	10,200	—	Proof	18.00
	1970J	4.000	3.50	4.50	8.50
	1970J	5,000	—	Proof	25.00
	1971D	4.000	3.50	4.50	8.50
	1971D	8,000	—	Proof	20.00
	1971F	3.993	3.50	4.50	8.50
	1971F	8,000	—	Proof	20.00
	1971G	6.010	3.50	4.50	8.50
	1971G	.010	—	Proof	18.00
	1971J	6.000	3.50	4.50	8.50
	1971J	8,000	—	Proof	20.00
	1972D	3.000	3.50	4.50	8.50
	1972D	8,000	—	Proof	20.00
	1972F	8.992	3.50	4.50	8.50
	1972F	8,100	—	Proof	20.00
	1972G	4.999	3.50	4.50	8.50
	1972G	.010	—	Proof	18.00
	1972J	6.000	3.50	4.50	7.50
	1972J	8,000	—	Proof	20.00
	1973D	3.380	3.50	4.50	7.50
	1973D	9,000	—	Proof	18.00
	1973F	3.891	3.50	4.50	7.50
	1973F	9,100	—	Proof	18.00
	1973G	2.240	3.50	4.50	7.50
	1973G	9,000	—	Proof	18.00
	1973J	5.571	3.50	4.50	7.50
	1973J	9,000	—	Proof	18.00
	1974D	4.594	3.50	4.50	7.50
	1974D	.035	—	Proof	15.00
	1974F	6.514	3.50	4.50	7.50
	1974F	.035	—	Proof	15.00
	1974G	3.708	3.50	4.50	7.50
	1974G	.035	—	Proof	15.00
	1974J	2.968	3.50	4.50	7.50
	1974J	.035	—	Proof	15.00

Uninscribed plain edge errors.

KM#	Date	Mintage	VF	XF	Unc
112.2	1959D	Inc. Ab.	60.00	120.00	175.00
	1959J	Inc. Ab.	60.00	120.00	175.00
	1963J	Inc. Ab.	60.00	120.00	175.00
	1964F	Inc. Ab.	60.00	120.00	175.00
	1965F	Inc. Ab.	60.00	120.00	175.00
	1965G	Inc. Ab.	60.00	120.00	175.00
	1966F	Inc. Ab.	125.00	250.00	345.00
	1966G	Inc. Ab.	60.00	120.00	175.00
	1967D	Inc. Ab.	125.00	250.00	345.00
	1967G	Inc. Ab.	60.00	120.00	175.00

Error. W/edge lettering: "GRUSS DICH DEUTSCH LAND AUS HERZENSGRUND"

KM#	Date	Mintage	VF	XF	Unc
112.3	1957J	Inc. Ab.	1250.	1650.	2400.

Error. W/edge lettering: "ALLE MENSCHEN WERDEN BRUDER."

KM#	Date	Mintage	VF	XF	Unc
112.4	1970F	—	1250.	1650.	2400.

COPPER-NICKEL CLAD NICKEL, 10.00 g

KM#	Date	Mintage	VF	XF	Unc
140.1	1975D	65.663	—	3.50	4.50
	1975D	.043	—	Proof	7.00
	1975F	75.002	—	3.50	4.50
	1975F	.043	—	Proof	7.00
	1975G	43.297	—	3.50	4.50
	1975G	.043	—	Proof	7.00
	1975J	67.372	—	3.50	4.50
	1975J	.043	—	Proof	7.00
	1976D	7.821	—	3.50	5.00
	1976D	.043	—	Proof	7.00
	1976F	9.072	—	3.50	5.00
	1976F	.043	—	Proof	7.00
	1976G	5.784	—	3.50	5.00
	1976G	.043	—	Proof	7.00
	1976J	8.068	—	3.50	5.00

Willy Brandt

KM#	Date	Mintage	VF	XF	Unc
183	1994A	5.000	—	—	2.00
	1994A	.045	—	Proof	2.50
	1994D	5.250	—	—	2.00
	1994D	.045	—	Proof	2.50
	1994F	6.000	—	—	2.00
	1994F	.045	—	Proof	2.50
	1994G	3.600	—	—	2.00
	1994G	.045	—	Proof	2.50
	1994J	5.250	—	—	2.00
	1994J	.045	—	Proof	2.50
	1995A	1.595	—	—	3.50
	1995A	.045	—	Proof	17.50
	1995D	.020	In sets only		65.00
	1995D	.045	—	Proof	17.50
	1995F	.020	In sets only		65.00
	1995F	.045	—	Proof	17.50
	1995G	1.220	—	—	4.50
	1995G	.045	—	Proof	17.50
	1995J	.075	—	—	30.00
	1995J	.045	—	Proof	17.50
	1996A	—	—	—	5.50
	1996A	.045	—	Proof	6.50
	1996D	—	—	—	5.50
	1996D	.045	—	Proof	6.50
	1996F	—	—	—	5.50
	1996F	.045	—	Proof	6.50
	1996G	—	—	—	5.50
	1996G	.045	—	Proof	6.50
	1996J	—	—	—	5.50
	1996J	.045	—	Proof	6.50
	1997A	.070	In sets only		4.25
	1997A	.045	—	Proof	5.00
	1997D	.070	In sets only		4.25

KM#	Date	Mintage	VF	XF	Unc
140.1	1976J	.043	—	Proof	7.00
	1977D	8.321	—	3.50	5.00
	1977D	.051	—	Proof	6.00
	1977F	9.612	—	3.50	5.00
	1977F	.051	—	Proof	6.00
	1977G	5.746	—	3.50	5.00
	1977G	.051	—	Proof	6.00
	1977J	8.577	—	3.50	5.00
	1977J	.051	—	Proof	6.00
	1978D	7.854	—	3.50	5.00
	1978D	.054	—	Proof	6.00
	1978F	9.054	—	3.50	5.00
	1978F	.054	—	Proof	6.00
	1978G	5.244	—	3.50	5.00
	1978G	.054	—	Proof	6.00
	1978J	8.064	—	3.50	5.00
	1978J	.054	—	Proof	6.00
	1979D	7.889	—	3.50	5.00
	1979D	.089	—	Proof	6.00
	1979F	9.089	—	3.50	5.00
	1979F	.089	—	Proof	6.00
	1979G	5.279	—	3.50	5.00
	1979G	.089	—	Proof	6.00
	1979J	8.099	—	3.50	5.00
	1979J	.089	—	Proof	6.00
	1980D	8.300	—	3.50	5.00
	1980D	.110	—	Proof	6.00
	1980F	9.640	—	3.50	5.00
	1980F	.110	—	Proof	6.00
	1980G	5.500	—	3.50	5.00
	1980G	.110	—	Proof	6.00
	1980J	8.500	—	3.50	5.00
	1980J	.110	—	Proof	6.00
	1981D	8.300	—	3.50	5.00
	1981D	.091	—	Proof	6.00
	1981F	9.600	—	3.50	5.00
	1981F	.091	—	Proof	6.00
	1981G	5.500	—	3.50	5.00
	1981G	.091	—	Proof	6.00
	1981J	8.500	—	3.50	5.00
	1981J	.091	—	Proof	6.00
	1982D	8.900	—	3.50	5.00
	1982D	.078	—	Proof	6.00
	1982F	10.300	—	3.50	5.00
	1982F	.078	—	Proof	6.00
	1982G	5.990	—	3.50	5.00
	1982G	.078	—	Proof	6.00
	1982J	9.100	—	3.50	5.00
	1982J	.078	—	Proof	6.00
	1983D	6.240	—	3.50	5.00
	1983D	.075	—	Proof	6.00
	1983F	7.200	—	3.50	5.00
	1983F	.075	—	Proof	6.00
	1983G	4.152	—	3.50	5.00
	1983G	.075	—	Proof	6.00
	1983J	6.408	—	3.50	5.00
	1983J	.075	—	Proof	6.00
	1984D	6.000	—	3.50	5.00
	1984D	.064	—	Proof	6.00
	1984F	6.900	—	3.50	5.00
	1984F	.064	—	Proof	6.00
	1984G	4.000	—	3.50	5.00
	1984G	.064	—	Proof	6.00
	1984J	6.100	—	3.50	5.00
	1984J	.064	—	Proof	6.00
	1985D	4.900	—	3.50	5.00
	1985D	.056	—	Proof	6.00
	1985F	5.700	—	3.50	5.00
	1985F	.054	—	Proof	6.00
	1985G	3.300	—	3.50	5.00
	1985G	.055	—	Proof	6.00
	1985J	5.100	—	3.50	5.00
	1985J	.054	—	Proof	6.00
	1986D	4.900	—	3.50	5.00
	1986D	.044	—	Proof	6.00
	1986F	5.700	—	3.50	5.00
	1986F	.044	—	Proof	6.00
	1986G	3.300	—	3.50	5.00
	1986G	.044	—	Proof	6.00
	1986J	5.100	—	3.50	5.00
	1986J	.044	—	Proof	6.00
	1987D	6.760	—	3.50	5.00
	1987D	.045	—	Proof	6.00
	1987F	7.800	—	3.50	5.00
	1987F	.045	—	Proof	6.00
	1987G	4.500	—	3.50	5.00
	1987G	.045	—	Proof	6.00
	1987J	6.940	—	3.50	5.00
	1987J	.045	—	Proof	6.00
	1988D	11.960	—	—	4.00
	1988D	.045	—	Proof	5.00
	1988F	13.800	—	—	4.00
	1988F	.045	—	Proof	5.00
	1988G	7.960	—	—	4.00
	1988G	.045	—	Proof	5.00
	1988J	12.280	—	—	4.00
	1988J	.045	—	Proof	5.00
	1989D	17.160	—	—	4.00
	1989D	.045	—	Proof	5.00
	1989F	19.800	—	—	4.00
	1989F	.045	—	Proof	5.00
	1989G	11.420	—	—	4.00
	1989G	.045	—	Proof	5.00
	1989J	17.620	—	—	4.00
	1989J	.045	—	Proof	5.00
	1990D	20.900	—	—	4.00
	1990D	.045	—	Proof	5.00
	1990F	24.200	—	—	4.00
	1990F	.045	—	Proof	5.00
	1990G	13.910	—	—	4.00

KM#	Date	Mintage	VF	XF	Unc
140.1	1990G	.045	—	Proof	5.00
	1990J	21.470	—	—	4.00
	1990J	.045	—	Proof	5.00
	1991A	18.000	—	—	4.00
	1991A	.045	—	Proof	5.00
	1991D	18.900	—	—	4.00
	1991D	.045	—	Proof	5.00
	1991F	21.600	—	—	4.00
	1991F	.045	—	Proof	5.00
	1991G	12.600	—	—	4.00
	1991G	.045	—	Proof	5.00
	1991J	18.900	—	—	4.00
	1991J	.045	—	Proof	5.00
	1992A	16.000	—	—	4.00
	1992A	.045	—	Proof	5.00
	1992D	16.800	—	—	4.00
	1992D	.045	—	Proof	5.00
	1992F	19.200	—	—	4.00
	1992F	.045	—	Proof	5.00
	1992G	11.200	—	—	4.00
	1992G	.045	—	Proof	5.00
	1992J	16.800	—	—	4.00
	1992J	.045	—	Proof	5.00
	1993A	3.200	—	—	4.00
	1993A	.045	—	Proof	5.00
	1993D	3.380	—	—	4.00
	1993D	.045	—	Proof	5.00
	1993F	3.840	—	—	4.00
	1993F	.045	—	Proof	5.00
	1993G	2.240	—	—	4.00
	1993G	.045	—	Proof	5.00
	1993J	3.360	—	—	4.00
	1993J	.045	—	Proof	5.00
	1994A	4.000	—	—	4.00
	1994A	.045	—	Proof	5.00
	1994D	4.200	—	—	4.00
	1994D	.045	—	Proof	5.00
	1994F	4.800	—	—	4.00
	1994F	.045	—	Proof	5.00
	1994G	2.800	—	—	4.00
	1994G	.045	—	Proof	5.00
	1994J	4.200	—	—	4.00
	1994J	.045	—	Proof	5.00
	1995A	.020	In sets only		80.00
	1995A	.045	—	Proof	30.00
	1995D	.020	In sets only		80.00
	1995D	.045	—	Proof	30.00
	1995F	.020	In sets only		80.00
	1995F	.045	—	Proof	30.00
	1995G	.020	In sets only		80.00
	1995G	.045	—	Proof	30.00
	1995J	.020	In sets only		80.00
	1995J	.045	—	Proof	30.00
	1996A	.050	In sets only		15.00
	1996A	.045	—	Proof	17.50
	1996D	.050	In sets only		15.00
	1996D	.045	—	Proof	17.50
	1996F	.050	In sets only		15.00
	1996F	.045	—	Proof	17.50
	1996G	.050	In sets only		15.00
	1996G	.045	—	Proof	17.50
	1996J	.050	In sets only		15.00
	1996J	.045	—	Proof	17.50
	1997A	.070	In sets only		6.00
	1997A	.045	—	Proof	7.00
	1997D	.070	In sets only		6.00
	1997D	.045	—	Proof	7.00
	1997F	.070	In sets only		6.00
	1997F	.045	—	Proof	7.00
	1997G	.070	In sets only		6.00
	1997G	.045	—	Proof	7.00
	1997J	.070	In sets only		6.00
	1997J	.045	—	Proof	7.00

5.00 g, thin variety

KM#	Date	Mintage	VF	XF	Unc
140.2	1975	—	—	3.50	5.00

NOTE: Illegally produced by a German Mint official.

COMMEMORATIVE 5 MARK

11.2000 g, .625 SILVER, .2250 oz ASW
Centenary - Nurnberg Museum

KM#	Date	Mintage	VF	XF	Unc
113	1952D	.199	600.00	1000.	1850.
	1952D	1,345	—	Proof	4500.

150th Anniversary - Death of Friedrich von Schiller

KM#	Date	Mintage	VF	XF	Unc
114	1955F	.199	275.00	675.00	975.00
	1955F	1,217	—	Proof	2150.

300th Anniversary - Birth of Ludwig von Baden

115	1955G	.198	275.00	600.00	925.00
	1955G	*2,000	—	Proof	2200.

*NOTE: This coin was restruck without authorization by a mint official using genuine dies - quantity unknown.

Centenary - Death of Joseph Freiherr von Eichendorff

117	1957J	.198	275.00	600.00	885.00
	1957J	2,000	—	Proof	2200.

150th Anniversary - Death of Johann Gottlieb Fichte

118.1	1964J	.495	120.00	215.00	275.00
	1964J	5,000	—	Proof	1450.

Error. Plain edge.

118.2	1964J	—	350.00	650.00	1150.

250th Anniversary - Death of Gottfried Wilhelm Leibniz

119.1	1966D	1.940	22.00	40.00	60.00
	1966D	.060	—	Proof	135.00

Error. Plain edge.

119.2	1966D	—	300.00	550.00	875.00

Wilhelm & Alexander von Humboldt

120.1	1967F	2.000	25.00	45.00	70.00
	1967F	.060	—	Proof	225.00

Error. Plain edge.

120.2	1967F	—	300.00	550.00	875.00

150th Anniversary - Birth of Friedrich Raiffeisen

KM#	Date	Mintage	VF	XF	Unc
121	1968J	3.860	3.50	5.00	10.00
	1968J	.140	—	Proof	65.00

500th Anniversary - Death of Johannes Gutenberg

122	1968G	2.900	6.50	13.50	22.50
	1968G	.100	—	Proof	80.00

150th Anniversary - Birth of Max von Pettenkofer
Frosted devices.

123.1	1968D	2.900	5.00	10.00	16.00
	1968D	.100	—	Proof	55.00

Polished devices.

123.2	1968D			Proof	380.00

150th Anniversary - Birth of Theodor Fontane

125.1	1969G	2.830	6.00	12.00	20.00
	1969G	.170	—	Proof	40.00

Error. Incomplete nose and hair.

125.2	1969G			Proof	140.00

375th Anniversary - Death of Gerhard Mercator

126.1	1969F	5.004			5.50
	1969F	.200	—	Proof	22.00

Error. Plain edge.

126.2	1969F		—	300.00	550.00	875.00

Error. W/edge lettering; Einigkeit und Recht und Freiheit.

126.3	1969F		—	600.00	1000.	1600.

Error. W/long R.

126.4	1969F		—	25.00	55.00	100.00

200th Anniversary - Birth of Ludwig van Beethoven

KM#	Date	Mintage	VF	XF	Unc
127	1970F	5.000	—	4.00	7.50
	1970F	.200	—	Proof	22.00

German Unification

128.1	1971G	5.000	4.00	5.50	10.00
	1971G	.200	—	Proof	28.00

Error. W/weak window details.

128.2	1971F			Proof	100.00

500th Anniversary - Birth of Albrecht Durer

129	1971D	8.000			5.00
	1971D	.200	—	Proof	32.00

500th Anniversary - Birth of Nicholas Copernicus

136	1973J	8.000			5.00
	1973J	.250	—	Proof	15.00

125th Anniversary - Frankfurt Parliament

137	1973G	8.000			5.00
	1973G	.250	—	Proof	15.00

25th Anniversary - Constitutional Law

138	1974F	8.000			5.00
	1974F	.250	—	Proof	15.00

250th Anniversary - Birth of Immanuel Kant

KM#	Date	Mintage	VF	XF	Unc
139	1974D	8.000	—		5.00
	1974D	.250	—	Proof	20.00

50th Anniversary - Death of Friedrich Ebert

141	1975J	8.000			5.00
	1975J	.250	—	Proof	20.00

European Monument Protection Year
11.2 g, 2.1mm thick

142.1	1975F	8.000			5.00
	1975F	.250	—	Proof	15.00

5.3 g, 1.4mm thick

142.2	1975F	Inc. Ab.			5.00

Centenary - Birth of Albert Schweitzer

143	1975G	8.000			5.00
	1975G	.250	—	Proof	16.50

300th Anniversary - Death of von Grimmelshausen

144	1976D	8.000			5.00
	1976D	.250	—	Proof	25.00

200th Anniversary - Birth of Carl Friedrich Gauss

145	1977J	8.000			5.00
	1977J	.250	—	Proof	25.00

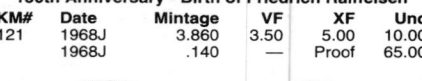

200th Anniversary - Birth of Heinrich von Kleist

KM#	Date	Mintage	VF	XF	Unc
146	1977G	8.000	—	—	5.00
	1977G	.250	—	Proof	20.00

100th Anniversary - Cologne Cathedral

KM#	Date	Mintage	VF	XF	Unc
153	1980F	5.000	—	4.50	8.50
	1980F	.350	—	Proof	13.50

500th Anniversary - Birth of Martin Luther

KM#	Date	Mintage	VF	XF	Unc
159	1983G	8.000	—	—	4.50
	1983G	.350	—	Proof	13.50

100th Anniversary - Birth of Gustav Stresemann

147	1978D	8.000	—	—	5.00
	1978D	.250	—	Proof	16.50

200th Anniversary - Death of Gotthold Ephraim Lessing

154	1981J	6.500	—	—	4.50
	1981J	.350	—	Proof	11.50

150th Anniversary - German Customs Union

160	1984D	8.000	—	—	4.50
	1984D	.350	—	Proof	11.50

225th Anniversary - Death of Balthasar Neumann

148	1978F	8.000	—	—	5.00
	1978F	.259	—	Proof	13.50

150th Anniversary - Death of Carl vom Stein

155	1981G	6.500	—	—	4.50
	1981G	.350	—	Proof	11.50

175th Anniversary - Birth of Felix Bartholdy

161	1984J	8.000	—	—	4.50
	1984J	.350	—	Proof	12.50

150th Anniversary - German Archeological Institute

150	1979J	8.000	—	—	5.00
	1979J	.250	—	Proof	18.50

150th Anniversary - Death of Johann Wolfgang von Goethe

156	1982D	8.000	—	—	4.50
	1982D	.350	—	Proof	11.50

European Year of Music

162	1985F	8.000	—	—	4.50
	1985F	.350	—	Proof	11.50

10.0000 g, COPPER-NICKEL CLAD NICKEL
100th Anniversary - Birth of Otto Hahn

151	1979G	5.000	—	4.00	7.00
	1979G	.350	—	Proof	10.00

10th Anniversary - U.N. Environmental Conference

157	1982F	8.000	—	—	4.50
	1982F	.350	—	Proof	11.50

150th Anniversary - German Railroad

163	1985G	8.000	—	—	4.50
	1985G	.350	—	Proof	10.00

COPPER-NICKEL CLAD NICKEL
750th Anniversary - Death of von der Vogelweide

152	1980D	5.000	—	4.00	7.00
	1980D	.350	—	Proof	10.00

100th Anniversary - Death of Karl Marx

158	1983J	8.000	—	—	4.50
	1983J	.350	—	Proof	11.50

600th Anniversary - Heidelberg University

164	1986D	8.000	—	—	4.50
	1986D	.350	—	Proof	10.00

200th Anniversary - Death of Frederick the Great

KM#	Date	Mintage	VF	XF	Unc
165	1986F	8.000	—	—	4.50
	1986F	.350	—	Proof	12.50

COMMEMORATIVE 10 MARK

15.5000 g, .625 SILVER, .3115 oz ASW
Munich Olympics - 'In Deutschland'

130	1972D	2.500	—	—	9.50
	1972D	.125	—	Proof	35.00
	1972F	2.375	—	—	9.50
	1972F	.125	—	Proof	35.00
	1972G	2.500	—	—	9.50
	1972G	.125	—	Proof	35.00
	1972J	2.500	—	—	9.50
	1972J	.125	—	Proof	35.00

Munich Olympics Symbol: 'Schleife' (knot).

131	1972D	5.000	—	—	9.50
	1972D	.125	—	Proof	25.00
	1972F	4.875	—	—	9.50
	1972F	.125	—	Proof	25.00
	1972G	5.000	—	—	9.50
	1972G	.125	—	Proof	25.00
	1972J	5.000	—	—	9.50
	1972J	.125	—	Proof	25.00

Munich Olympics - 'Athletes'

KM#	Date	Mintage	VF	XF	Unc
132	1972D	5.000	—	—	8.50
	1972D	.150	—	Proof	22.00
	1972F	4.850	—	—	8.50
	1972F	.150	—	Proof	22.00
	1972G	5.000	—	—	8.50
	1972G	.150	—	Proof	22.00
	1972J	5.000	—	—	8.50
	1972J	.150	—	Proof	22.00

Munich Olympics - 'Stadium'

133	1972D	5.000	—	—	8.50
	1972D	.150	—	Proof	22.00
	1972F	4.850	—	—	8.50
	1972F	.150	—	Proof	22.00
	1972G	5.000	—	—	8.50
	1972G	.150	—	Proof	22.00
	1972J	5.000	—	—	8.50
	1972J	.150	—	Proof	22.00

Munich Olympics - 'In Munchen'
Edge lettering separated by periods.

134.1	1972D	2.500	—	—	9.50
	1972D	.150	—	Proof	25.00
	1972F	2.350	—	—	9.50
	1972F	.150	—	Proof	25.00
	1972G	2.500	—	—	9.50
	1972G	.150	—	Proof	25.00
	1972J	2.500	—	—	9.50
	1972J	.150	—	Proof	25.00

Error. W/edge lettering separated by arabesques.

134.2	1972D	2 known	—	—	2760.
	1972F	1 known	—	—	2760.
	1972G	2 known	—	—	2760.
	1972J	600 pcs.	200.00	300.00	550.00

Munich Olympics - 'Olympic Flame'

135	1972D	5.000	—	—	8.50
	1972D	.150	—	Proof	22.00
	1972F	4.850	—	—	8.50
	1972F	.150	—	Proof	22.00
	1972G	5.000	—	—	8.50
	1972G	.150	—	Proof	22.00
	1972J	5.000	—	—	8.50
	1972J	.150	—	Proof	22.00

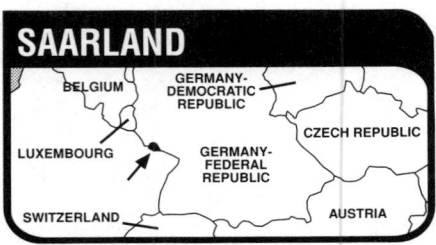

SAARLAND

The Saar, the 10th state of the German Federal Republic, is located in the coal-rich Saar basin on the Franco-German frontier, and has an area of 991 sq. mi. and a population of 1.2 million. Capital: Saarbrucken. It is an important center of mining and heavy industry.

From the late 14th century until the fall of Napoleon, the city of Saarbrucken was ruled by the counts of Nassau-Saarbrucken, but the surrounding territory was subject to the political and cultural domination of France. At the close of the Napoleonic era, the Saarland came under the control of Prussia. France was awarded the Saar coal mines following World War I, and the Saarland was made an autonomous territory of the League of Nations, its future political affiliation to be determined by referendum. The plebiscite, 1935, chose reincorporation into Germany. France reoccupied the Saarland, 1945, establishing strong economic ties and assuming the obligation of defense and foreign affairs. After sustained agitation by West Germany, France agreed, 1955, to the return of the Saar to Germany by Jan. 1957.

MINT MARKS
(a) - Paris - privy marks only

10 FRANKEN

ALUMINUM-BRONZE

KM#	Date	Mintage	Fine	VF	XF	Unc
1	1954(a)	11.000	.75	1.50	2.50	5.00

20 FRANKEN

ALUMINUM-BRONZE

2	1954(a)	12.950	.75	1.50	3.00	7.00

50 FRANKEN

ALUMINUM-BRONZE

3	1954(a)	5.300	3.00	5.00	10.00	20.00

100 FRANKEN

COPPER-NICKEL

4	1955(a)	11.000	2.00	3.00	6.50	15.00

GERMANY-DEMOCRATIC REP.

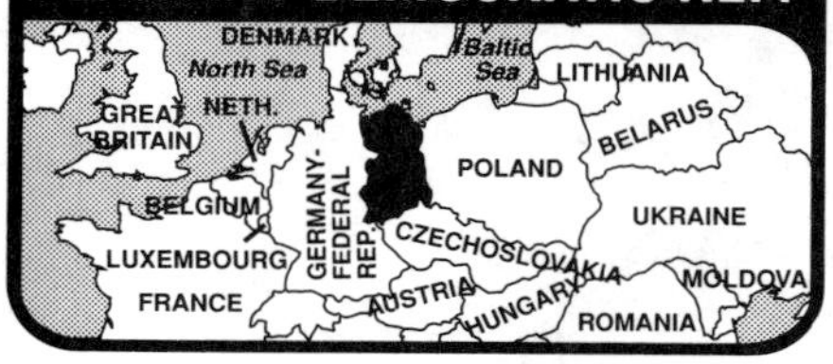

1949-1990

The German Democratic Republic, formerly East Germany, was located on the great north European plain, had an area of 41,768 sq. mi. (108,330 sq. km.) and a population of 16.6 million. The figures included East Berlin which had been incorporated into the G.D.R. Capital: East Berlin. The economy was highly industrialized. Machinery, transport equipment chemicals, and lignite were exported.

During the closing days of World War II in Europe, Soviet troops advancing into Germany from the east occupied the German provinces of Mecklenburg, Brandenburg, Lusatia, Saxony and Thuringia. These five provinces comprised the occupation zone administered by the Soviet Union after the cessation of hostilities. The other three zones were administered by the U.S., Great Britain and France. Under the Potsdam agreement, questions affecting Germany as a whole were to be settled by the commanders of the occupation zones acting jointly and by unanimous decision. When Soviet intransigence rendered the quadripartite commission inoperable, the three western zones were united to form the Federal Republic of Germany, May 23, 1949. Thereupon the Soviet Union dissolved its occupation zone and established it as the Democratic Republic of Germany, Oct. 7, 1949.

The post-WW II division of Germany was ended Oct. 3, 1990, when the German Democratic Republic (East Germany) ceased to exist and its five constituent provinces were formally admitted to the Federal Republic of Germany. An election Dec. 2, 1990, chose representatives to the united federal parliament (Bundestag), which then conducted its opening session in Berlin in the old Reichstag building. Although Berlin technically is the capital of the reunited Germany, the actual seat of government remains for the time being in Bonn.

MINT MARKS

A - Berlin

E - Muldenhutten

MONETARY SYSTEM

100 Pfennig = 1 Mark

PFENNIG

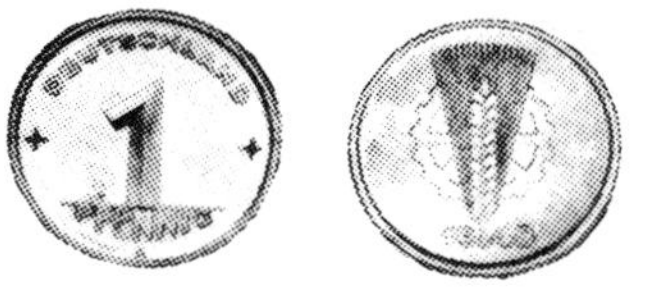

ALUMINUM

KM#	Date	Mintage	VF	XF	Unc
1	1948A	243.000	1.00	8.00	35.00
	1949A	Inc. Ab.	1.00	8.00	35.00
	1949E	55.200	11.50	45.00	300.00
	1950A	Inc. 1948A	1.00	8.00	35.00
	1950E	Inc. 1949E	7.50	20.00	100.00

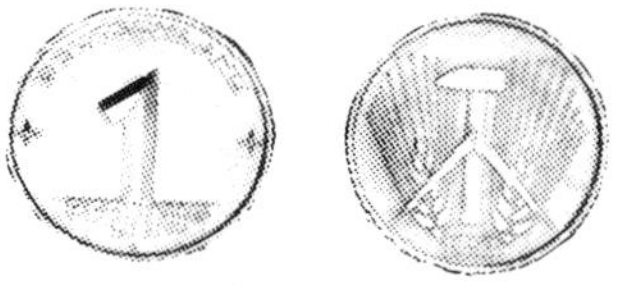

KM#	Date	Mintage	VF	XF	Unc
5	1952A	297.213	.50	1.75	6.00
	1952E	49.296	5.00	12.00	55.00
	1953A	114.002	.50	1.75	6.00
	1953E	50.876	5.00	15.00	60.00

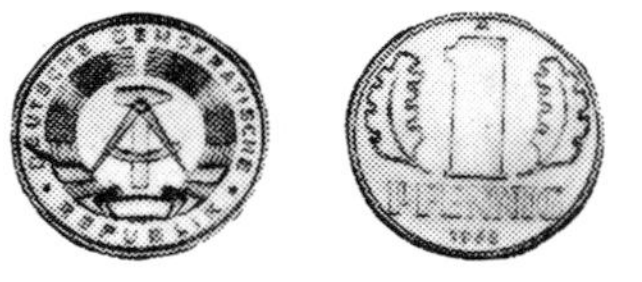

KM#	Date	Mintage	VF	XF	Unc
8.1	1960A	101.808	.25	.75	3.50
	1961A	101.776	.25	.75	3.50
	1962A	81.459	.25	.75	3.50
	1963A	101.402	.25	.75	3.50
	1964A	98.967	.25	.75	3.50
	1965A	38.585	3.00	15.00	35.00
	1968A	813.680	.25	.75	2.50
	1972A	4.801	2.00	10.00	25.00
	1973A	5.518	1.50	8.00	22.50
	1975A	202.752	.25	.75	2.50

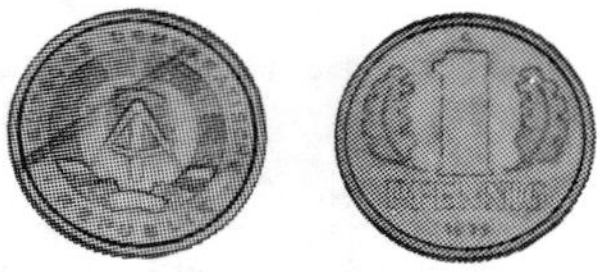

Obv. and rev: Smaller design features.

KM#	Date	Mintage	VF	XF	Unc
8.2	1977A	61.560	.10	.25	2.00
	1978A	200.050	.10	.20	.50
	1979A	100.640	.10	.20	.50
	1979A	—	—	Proof	45.00
	1980A	153.000	.10	.20	.50
	1980A	—	—	Proof	45.00
	1981A	200.436	.10	.20	.50
	1981A	40 pcs.	—	Proof	—
	1982A	99.200	.10	.20	.50
	1982A	2,500	—	Proof	10.00
	1983A	150.000	.10	.20	.50
	1983A	2,550	—	Proof	18.00
	1984A	137.600	.10	.20	.50
	1984A	3,015	—	Proof	4.50
	1985A	125.060	.10	.20	.50
	1985A	2,816	—	Proof	4.50
	1986A	73.900	.10	.20	.50
	1986A	2,800	—	Proof	4.50
	1987A	50.015	.10	.20	.50
	1987A	2,345	—	Proof	4.50
	1988A	75.450	.10	.20	.50
	1988A	2,300	—	Proof	4.50
	1989A	84.410	.10	.20	.50
	1989A	2,300	—	Proof	4.50
	1990A	15.670	.10	.20	2.00

5 PFENNIG

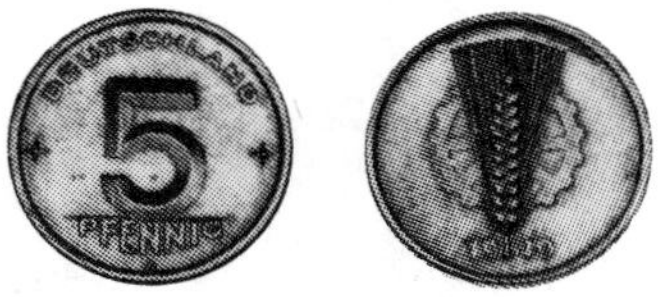

ALUMINUM

KM#	Date	Mintage	VF	XF	Unc
2	1948A	205.072	2.50	5.50	50.00
	1949A	Inc. Ab.	2.50	5.50	45.00
	1950A	Inc. Ab.	2.50	5.50	35.00

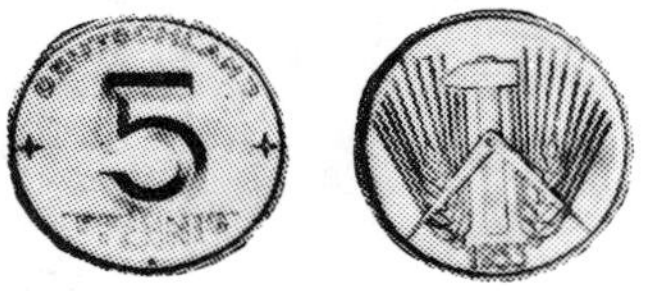

KM#	Date	Mintage	VF	XF	Unc
6	1952A	113.397	2.00	5.00	12.50
	1952E	24.024	3.50	8.00	35.00
	1953A	40.994	2.00	5.00	17.50
	1953E	28.665	5.00	17.50	90.00

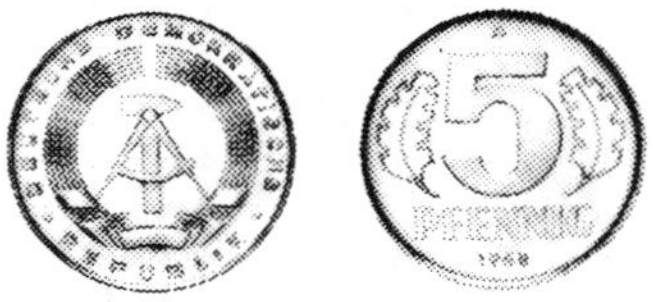

KM#	Date	Mintage	VF	XF	Unc
9.1	1968A	282.303	.50	1.00	2.00
	1972A	51.462	.50	1.00	3.50
	1975A	84.710	.50	1.00	2.00

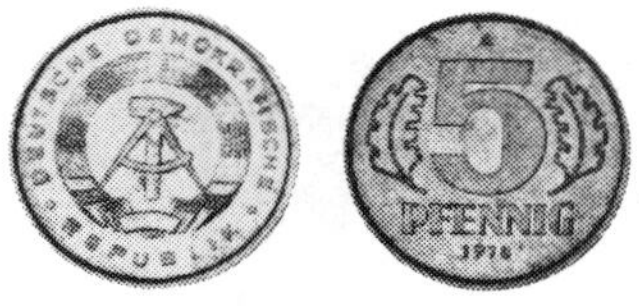

Obv. and rev: Smaller design features.

KM#	Date	Mintage	VF	XF	Unc
9.2	1978A	43.257	.15	.25	.50
	1979A	46.194	.15	.25	.50
	1979A	—	—	Proof	45.00
	1980A	31.977	.15	.25	.50
	1980A	—	—	Proof	45.00
	1981A	33.102	.15	.25	.50
	1981A	40 pcs.	—	Proof	—
	1982A	.916	1.75	7.50	22.50
	1982A	2,500	—	Proof	10.00
	1983A	100.890	.15	.25	.50
	1983A	2,550	—	Proof	18.00
	1984A	*6,000	—	—	30.00
	1984A	3,015	—	Proof	4.50
	1985A	1.000	1.50	6.50	18.50
	1985A	2,816	—	Proof	4.50
	1986A	1.000	1.50	6.50	18.50
	1986A	2,800	—	Proof	4.50
	1987A	*.020	—	—	12.50
	1987A	2,345	—	Proof	4.50
	1988A	35.930	.15	.25	.50
	1988A	2,300	—	Proof	4.50
	1989A	21.550	.15	.25	.50
	1989A	2,300	—	Proof	4.50
	1990A	50.640	.15	.25	.50

NOTE: Varieties exist.

10 PFENNIG

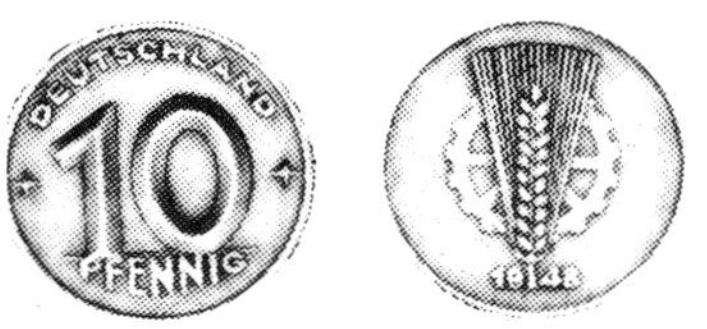

ALUMINUM

KM#	Date	Mintage	VF	XF	Unc
3	1948A	216.537	2.50	17.50	75.00
	1949A	Inc. Ab.	2.50	17.50	70.00
	1950A	Inc. Ab.	2.50	8.50	70.00
	1950E	16.000	17.50	175.00	1000.

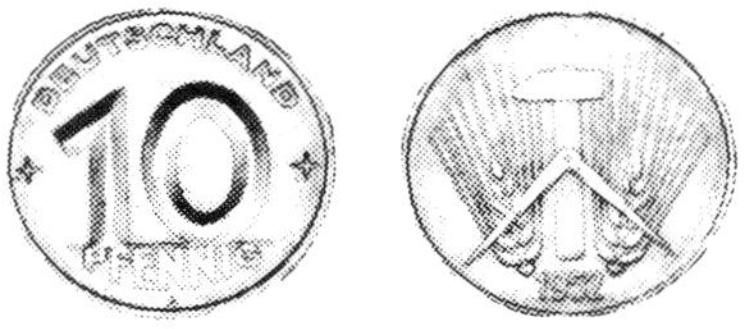

KM#	Date	Mintage	VF	XF	Unc
7	1952A	70.427	1.50	11.50	55.00
	1952E	21.498	15.00	40.00	280.00
	1953A	18.611	3.50	17.50	75.00
	1953E	11.500	15.00	70.00	650.00

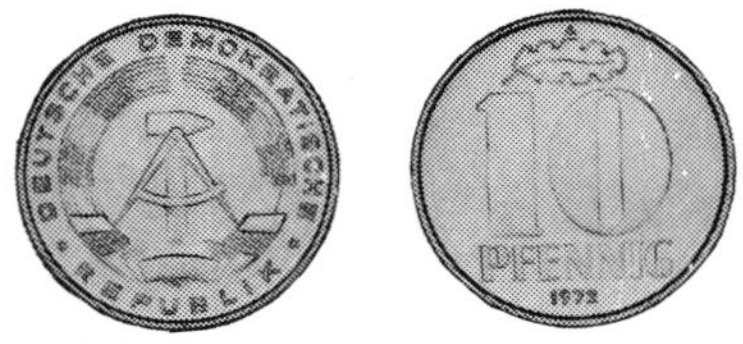

KM#	Date	Mintage	VF	XF	Unc
10	1963A	21.063	6.00	30.00	85.00
	1965A	55.313	.15	.25	2.50
	1967A	96.955	.15	.25	2.50
	1968A	207.461	.15	.25	.75
	1970A	13.387	.15	.25	1.00
	1971A	66.618	.15	.25	.75
	1972A	5.702	.50	3.00	12.00
	1973A	11.257	.15	.25	1.50
	1978A	40.000	.15	.25	1.50
	1979A	54.665	.15	.25	.50
	1979A	—	—	Proof	45.00
	1980A	20.664	.15	.25	.50
	1980A	—	—	Proof	45.00
	1981A	40.704	.15	.25	.50
	1981A	40 pcs.	—	Proof	—
	1982A	40.212	.15	.25	1.50
	1982A	2,500	—	Proof	10.00
	1983A	40.699	.15	.25	.50
	1983A	2,550	—	Proof	20.00
	1984A	*.012	—	—	25.00
	1984A	3,015	—	Proof	4.50
	1985A	1.010	.35	4.50	17.50
	1985A	2,816	—	Proof	4.50
	1986A	1.000	.35	4.50	17.50
	1986A	2,800	—	Proof	4.50
	1987A	*.020	—	—	12.00
	1987A	2,345	—	Proof	4.50
	1988A	10.705	.15	.25	.75
	1988A	2,300	—	Proof	4.50
	1989A	37.640	.15	.25	.50
	1989A	2,300	—	Proof	4.50
	1990A	*.014	—	—	15.00

***NOTE:** Issued in sets only, remainder unaccountable.

NOTE: Inscription and edge varieties exist.

20 PFENNIG

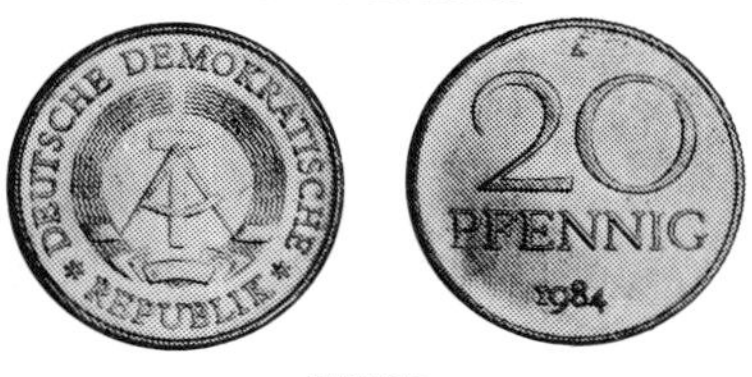

BRASS

KM#	Date	Mintage	VF	XF	Unc
11	1969	167.168	.25	1.50	4.00
	1971	24.563	.25	2.50	6.00
	1972A	5.007	.25	2.50	10.00
	1973A	2.524	.25	4.50	20.00
	1974A	7.458	.25	2.50	10.00
	1979A	.293	.25	1.50	7.50
	1979A	—	—	Proof	50.00
	1980A	2.190	.20	.35	5.00
	1980A	—	—	Proof	50.00
	1981A	.983	.20	.50	7.50
	1981A	40 pcs.	—	Proof	—
	1982A	10.458	.20	2.50	8.50
	1982A	2,500	—	Proof	12.50
	1983A	25.809	.20	.35	3.00
	1983A	2,550	—	Proof	25.00
	1984A	25.009	.20	.35	3.00
	1984A	3,015	—	Proof	5.50
	1985A	1.559	.20	.35	4.00
	1985A	2,816	—	Proof	5.50
	1986A	1.147	.20	.35	4.00
	1986A	2,800	—	Proof	5.50

KM#	Date	Mintage	VF	XF	Unc
11	1987A	*.020	—	—	8.00
	1987A	2,345	—	Proof	5.50
	1988A	*.015	—	—	10.00
	1988A	2,300	—	Proof	5.50
	1989A	14.690	.20	.35	2.00
	1989A	2,300	—	Proof	5.50
	1990A	*.014	—	—	15.00

*NOTE: Issued in sets only, remainder unaccountable.

NOTE: Ribbon width varieties exist.

50 PFENNIG

ALUMINUM-BRONZE

4	1949A	Inc. Be.	—	7500.	—
	1950A	67.703	3.50	8.50	32.50

NOTE: Some authorities believe the 1949 dated piece is a pattern.

ALUMINUM
Obv: Small coat of arms.

12.1	1958A	101.606	.35	2.50	10.00

Obv: Larger coat of arms.

12.2	1968A	19.860	.35	.65	5.00
	1971A	35.829	.35	.65	2.50
	1972A	8.117	.35	.65	4.00
	1973A	6.530	.35	.65	7.50
	1979A	1.027	.35	.65	7.50
	1979A	—	—	Proof	
	1980A	1.118	.35	.65	8.00
	1980A	—	—	Proof	
	1981A	10.546	.35	.65	2.50
	1981A	40 pcs.	—	Proof	
	1982A	79.832	.35	.65	2.50
	1982A	2,500	—	Proof	12.50
	1983A	1.309	.35	.65	7.50
	1983A	2,550	—	Proof	25.00
	1984A	*5,000	—	—	30.00
	1984A	3,015	—	Proof	5.50
	1985A	1.565	.35	.65	7.50
	1985A	2,816	—	Proof	5.50
	1986A	.776	.35	.65	7.50
	1986A	2,800	—	Proof	5.50
	1987A	*.021	—	—	12.00
	1987A	2,345	—	Proof	5.50
	1988A	*.015	—	—	14.00
	1988A	2,300	—	Proof	5.50
	1989A	.031	.35	.65	7.50
	1989A	2,300	—	Proof	5.50
	1990A	*.014	—	—	15.00

*NOTE: Issued in sets only, remainder unaccountable.

NOTE: Inscription varieties exist.

MARK

ALUMINUM

13	1956A	112.108	.50	1.00	9.00
	1962A	45.920	.50	2.00	10.00
	1963A	31.910	.50	2.50	12.00

Rev: Large 1.

35.1	1972A	30.288	.50	2.50	5.00

Rev: Small 1.

35.2	1973A	6.972	.50	2.00	10.00
	1975A	32.094	.50	1.00	6.50
	1977A	119.813	.50	1.00	2.00
	1978A	18.824	.50	1.00	2.00
	1979A	1.003	.50	1.25	7.50

KM#	Date	Mintage	VF	XF	Unc
35.2	1979A	—	—	Proof	—
	1980A	1.069	.50	1.25	7.50
	1980A	—	—	Proof	—
	1981A	1.006	.50	1.25	7.50
	1981A	40 pcs.	—	Proof	—
	1982A	51.619	.50	1.00	2.00
	1982A	2,500	—	Proof	25.00
	1983A	1.065	.50	1.25	7.50
	1983A	2,550	—	Proof	30.00
	1984A	*5,000	—	—	65.00
	1984A	3,015	—	Proof	7.50
	1985A	1.128	—	1.25	7.50
	1985A	2,816	—	Proof	7.50
	1986A	1.000	.50	1.25	7.50
	1986A	2,800	—	Proof	7.50
	1987A	*.021	—	—	5.50
	1987A	2,345	—	Proof	7.50
	1988A	*.015	—	—	7.50
	1988A	2,300	—	Proof	7.50
	1989A	.033	.50	1.00	5.00
	1989A	2,300	—	Proof	7.50
	1990A	*.014	—	—	20.00

*NOTE: Issued in sets only, remainder unaccountable.

2 MARK

ALUMINUM

14	1957A	77.961	1.00	3.00	10.00

48	1974A	5.790	1.00	3.50	12.00
	1975A	32.464	.90	2.00	10.00
	1977A	27.859	.90	2.00	10.00
	1978A	23.415	.90	2.00	10.00
	1979A	.985	.90	1.50	7.50
	1979A	—	—	Proof	—
	1980A	1.019	.90	1.50	7.50
	1980A	—	—	Proof	—
	1981A	.939	.90	1.50	7.50
	1981A	40 pcs.	—	Proof	—
	1982A	60.488	.90	1.00	2.00
	1982A	2,500	—	Proof	55.00
	1983A	1.030	.90	1.00	5.00
	1983A	2,550	—	Proof	75.00
	1984A	*6,000	—	—	30.00
	1984A	3,015	—	Proof	20.00
	1985A	1.310	.90	1.00	5.00
	1985A	2,816	—	Proof	20.00
	1986A	1.000	.90	1.00	6.00
	1986A	2,800	—	Proof	20.00
	1987A	*.030	—	—	6.00
	1987A	2,345	—	Proof	20.00
	1988A	*.015	—	—	6.50
	1988A	2,300	—	Proof	20.00
	1989A	.046	.90	1.00	6.50
	1989A	2,300	—	Proof	20.00
	1990A	*.014	—	—	20.00

*NOTE: Issued in sets only, remainder unaccountable.

5 MARK

COPPER-NICKEL
125th Anniversary of Birth of Robert Koch

KM#	Date	Mintage	XF	Unc	BU
19.1	1968	.100	—	—	23.50

Error: Plain edge.

19.2	1968	—	—	—	—

NICKEL-BRONZE
20th Anniversary D.D.R.

KM#	Date	Mintage	XF	Unc	BU
22.1	1969	50.222	3.00	4.00	5.50

NOTE: 10% nickel and 90% copper.

Error: Plain edge.

22.2	1969	—	—	—	—

Error: Mongolian inscription and dates on edge.

22.3	1969	—	—	—	—

COPPER-NICKEL

22.1a	1969	12,741	40.00	65.00	—

NOTE: 25% nickel and 75% copper.

Brandenburg Gate

29	1971A	4.000	—	—	6.00
	1979A	.032	—	—	40.00
	1979A	2,500	—	Proof	—
	1980A	.030	—	—	32.00
	1980A	2,500	—	Proof	—
	1981A	.030	—	—	28.00
	1981A	2,500	—	Proof	—
	1982A	.028	—	—	26.50
	1982A	2,500	—	Proof	185.00
	1983A	3,000	—	—	1150.
	1984A	.028	—	—	75.00
	1984A	3,015	—	Proof	160.00
	1985A	3,000	—	—	1100.
	1986A	.028	—	—	110.00
	1986A	2,800	—	Proof	165.00
	1987A	.220	—	—	21.50
	1987A	6,424	—	Proof	60.00
	1988A	.028	—	—	38.00
	1988A	2,300	—	Proof	125.00
	1989A	.028	—	—	38.00
	1989A	2,405	—	Proof	125.00
	1990A	.050	—	—	50.00

GHANA

The Republic of Ghana, a member of the British Commonwealth situated on the West Coast of Africa between Ivory Coast and Togo, has an area of 92,100 sq. mi. (238,540 sq. km.) and a population of 14 million, almost entirely African. Capital: Accra. Cocoa (the major crop), coconuts, palm kernels and coffee are exported. Mining, second in importance to agriculture, is concentrated on gold, manganese and industrial diamonds.

The state of Ghana, comprising the Gold Coast and British Togoland, obtained independence on March 6, 1957, becoming the first Negro African colony to do so. On July l, 1960, Ghana adopted a republican constitution, changing from a ministerial to a presidential form of government. The government was overthrown, the constitution suspended and the National Assembly dissolved by the Ghanaian army and police on Feb. 24, 1966. The government was returned to civilian authority in Oct. 1969, but was again seized by military officers in a bloodless coup on Jan. 13, 1972, but 3 further coups occurred in 1978, 1979 and 1981. The latter 2 coups, were followed by suspension of the constitution and banning of political parties. A new constitution, which allowed multiparty politics, was approved in April, 1992.

Ghana's monetary denomination of 'Cedi' is derived from the word 'sedie' meaning cowrie, a shell money commonly employed by coastal tribes.

MONETARY SYSTEM
12 Pence = 1 Shilling

1/2 PENNY

BRONZE
Dr. Kwame Nkrumah

KM#	Date	Mintage	VF	XF	Unc
1	1958	32.200	.10	.25	.50
	1958	.020	—	Proof	.75

PENNY

BRONZE
Dr. Kwame Nkrumah

2	1958	60.000	.15	.35	.75
	1958	.020	—	Proof	1.00

3 PENCE

COPPER-NICKEL
Dr. Kwame Nkrumah

3	1958	25.200	.20	.45	1.00
	1958	.020	—	Proof	1.50

6 PENCE

COPPER-NICKEL
Dr. Kwame Nkrumah

4	1958	15.200	.20	.45	1.00
	1958	—	—	Proof	1.50

SHILLING

COPPER-NICKEL
Dr. Kwame Nkrumah

KM#	Date	Mintage	VF	XF	Unc
5	1958	34.400	.25	.50	1.75
	1958	.020	—	Proof	2.00

2 SHILLINGS

COPPER-NICKEL
Dr. Kwame Nkrumah

6	1958	72.700	.35	.75	2.25
	1958	.020	—	Proof	2.75

DECIMAL COINAGE
100 Pesewas = 1 Cedi

1/2 PESEWA

BRONZE
Bush Drums

12	1967	30.000	.10	.20	.50
	1967	2,000	—	Proof	1.00

PESEWA

BRONZE
Bush Drums

13	1967	30.000	.15	.25	.60
	1967	2,000	—	Proof	1.25
	1975	50.250	.10	.20	.50
	1979	50.000	.10	.20	.50

2-1/2 PESEWAS

COPPER-NICKEL
Cocoa Beans

14	1967	6.000	.10	.20	.75
	1967	2,000	—	Proof	1.50

5 PESEWAS

COPPER-NICKEL
Dr. Kwame Nkrumah

8	1965	30.000	.20	.35	1.25

10 PESEWAS

Cocoa Beans

KM#	Date	Mintage	VF	XF	Unc
15	1967	30.000	.15	.25	.75
	1967	2,000	.15	.25	2.00
	1973	8.000	.15	.25	.75
	1975	20.000	.15	.25	.75

COPPER-NICKEL
Dr. Kwame Nkrumah

9	1965	50.000	.25	.50	1.25

Cocoa Beans

16	1967	13.200	.20	.40	1.50
	1967	2,000	—	Proof	2.50
	1975	20.000	.20	.40	1.25
	1979	5.500	.20	.40	1.25

20 PESEWAS

COPPER-NICKEL
Cocoa Beans

17	1967	25.800	.25	.50	1.75
	1967	2,000	—	Proof	3.00
	1975	—	.25	.50	1.75
	1979	5.000	.25	.50	1.75

25 PESEWAS

COPPER-NICKEL
Dr. Kwame Nkrumah

10	1965	60.100	.35	.75	2.00

50 PESEWAS

COPPER-NICKEL
Dr. Kwame Nkrumah

11	1965	18.200	.75	1.50	3.50

BRASS
F.A.O. Issue - Cocoa Beans

KM#	Date	Mintage	VF	XF	Unc
18	1979	60.000	.45	.75	2.25
24	1984	10.000	.10	.25	.60

CEDI

BRASS
F.A.O. Issue - Cauri

19	1979	160.000	.35	.85	3.00
25	1984	40.000	.10	.25	.75

5 CEDIS

BRASS
Bush Drums

26	1984	88.920	.10	.20	.50
33	1991	—	.10	.20	.50

10 CEDIS

NICKEL CLAD STEEL

29	1991	—		.25	.75

20 CEDIS

NICKEL CLAD STEEL

KM#	Date	Mintage	VF	XF	Unc
30	1991	—		.35	1.00
	1995	—		.35	1.00

50 CEDIS

NICKEL CLAD STEEL

31	1991	—		1.00	2.25

100 CEDIS

BRASS center in COPPER-NICKEL ring
Cocoa Beans

32	1991	—		1.75	3.75
	1997	—		1.75	3.75

200 CEDIS

NICKEL PLATED STEEL
Obv: Cowrie shell.
Rev: National arms, denomination.

35	1996	—			2.75

500 CEDIS

NICKEL BRASS
Obv: Drums. Rev: National arms, denomination.

34	1996	—			4.75

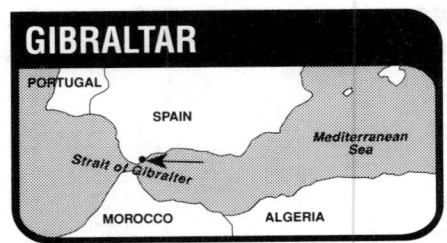

The British Colony of Gibraltar, located at the southern-most point of the Iberian Peninsula, has an area of 2.25 sq. mi. (6.5 sq. km.) and a population of 29,651. Capital (and only town): Gibraltar. Aside from its strategic importance as guardian of the western entrance to the Mediterranean Sea, Gibraltar is also a free port and a British naval base.

Gibraltar, rooted in Greek mythology as one of the Pillars of Hercules, has long been a coveted stronghold. Moslems took it from Spain and fortified it in 711. Spain retook it in 1309, lost it again to the Moors in 1333 and retook it in 1462. After 1540 Spain strengthened its defenses and held it until the War of the Spanish Succession when it was captured by a combined British and Dutch force in 1704. Britain held it against the Franco-Spanish attacks of 1704-05 and through the historic 'Great Siege' of 1779-83. Recently Spain has attempted to discourage British occupancy by harassment and economic devices. In 1967, Gibraltar's inhabitants voted 12,138 to 44 to remain under British rule.

Gibraltar's celebrated Barbary Ape, the last monkey to be found in a wild state in Europe, is featured on the colony's first decimal crown, released in 1972.

RULERS

British

MINT MARKS

PM - Pobjoy Mint

MINT PRIVY MARKS

U - Unc finish

DIE MARKS

1988: AA-AE
1989: AA-AF
1990: AA-AB
1991: AA
1992: AA-BB
1993: AA-BB

MONETARY SYSTEM

4 Farthings = 1 Penny
12 Pence = 1 Shilling
2 Shillings = 1 Florin
5 Shillings = 1 Crown
20 Shillings = 1 Pound

CROWN

COPPER-NICKEL

KM#	Date	Mintage	VF	XF	Unc
4	1967	.125	.50	.85	1.50
	1968	.040	.65	1.00	2.00
	1969	.040	.65	1.00	2.00
	1970	.045	.65	1.00	2.00

DECIMAL COINAGE

5 New Pence = 1 Shilling
25 New Pence = 1 Crown
1 Crown = 1 Royal
100 New Pence = 1 Pound Sterling

PENNY

BRONZE
Barbary Partridge

KM#	Date	Mintage	VF	XF	Unc
20	1988AA	—	—	—	.25
	1988AB	—	—	—	.25
	1989	—	—	—	.25
	1990	—	—	—	.25
	1991	—	—	—	.25
	1992	—	—	—	.25
	1993	—	—	—	.25
	1994AA	—	—	—	.25
	1995	—	—	—	.25
	1996	—	—	—	.25

2 PENCE

BRONZE
Lighthouse on Europa Point

21	1988AA	—	—	—	.50
	1989	—	—	—	.50
	1990	—	—	—	.50
	1991AA	—	—	—	.50
	1992	—	—	—	.50
	1993	—	—	Proof	—
	1994AA	—	—	—	.50
	1995	—	—	—	.50
	1996	—	—	—	.50

5 PENCE

COPPER-NICKEL
Barbary Ape

22	1988	—	—	—	.75
	1989	—	—	—	.75

Reduced size, 18mm

22a	1990	—	—	—	.50
	1991	—	—	—	.50
	1992AB	—	—	—	.50
	1993	—	—	Proof	—
	1994AA	—	—	—	.50
	1995	—	—	—	.50
	1996	—	—	—	.50

10 PENCE

COPPER-NICKEL
Moorish Castle

23	1988AB	—	—	—	1.00
	1989	—	—	—	1.00
	1990AA	—	—	—	1.00
	1991AB	—	—	—	1.00

Reduced size

KM#	Date	Mintage	VF	XF	Unc
23a	1993	—	—	—	1.00
	1994AA	—	—	—	1.00

Euro-Port

112	1992	—	—	—	1.00
	1993AA	—	—	—	1.00
	1995	—	—	—	1.00
	1996	—	—	—	1.00
	1997	—	—	—	1.00

20 PENCE

COPPER-NICKEL
Our Lady of Europe

16	1988AA	—	—	—	1.50
	1988AA	—	—	Proof	—
	1989	—	—	—	1.50
	1990	—	—	—	1.50
	1991	—	—	—	1.50
	1992	—	—	—	1.50
	1993	—	—	Proof	—
	1994AA	—	—	—	1.50
	1995	—	—	—	1.50
	1995	—	—	Proof	—
	1996	—	—	—	1.50

25 NEW PENCE

COPPER-NICKEL
Barbary Ape

5	1971	.075	—	1.75	4.00

COPPER-NICKEL
25th Wedding Anniversary

KM#	Date	Mintage	VF	XF	Unc
6	1972	.070	—	1.00	2.50

COPPER-NICKEL
Queen's Silver Jubilee

10	1977	.065	—	1.00	2.50

50 PENCE

COPPER-NICKEL

17	1988AA	—	—	—	2.00
	1989AB	—	—	—	2.00

Dolphins

39	1990AA	—	—	—	4.00
	1991	—	—	—	4.00
	1992	—	—	—	4.00
	1993AA	—	—	—	4.00
	1994	—	—	—	4.00
	1995	—	—	—	4.00
	1996	—	—	—	4.00

POUND

NICKEL-BRASS

18	1988AA	—	—	—	3.50
	1990	—	—	—	3.50
	1991	—	—	—	3.50
	1992	—	—	—	3.50
	1993	—	—	—	3.50
	1996	—	—	—	3.50

150th Anniversary of Gibraltar Coinage

KM#	Date	Mintage	VF	XF	Unc
32	1989AA	—	—	—	4.00

Referendum of 1967

191	1993	—	—	—	4.50

VIRENIUM
40th Anniversary - Queen Elizabeth II's
1st Royal Visit to Gibraltar

324	1994AA	—	—	—	7.50

National Day - Rock of Gibraltar

340	1995AA	—	—	—	3.50

2 POUNDS

VIRENIUM
Cannon In Tunnel of Fortress

24	1988AA	—	—	—	7.50
	1989	—	—	—	7.50
	1990	—	—	—	7.50
	1993AA	—	—	—	7.50
	1995AC	—	—	—	7.50
	1996	—	—	—	7.50

Columbus and Ship

98	1992AA	—	—	—	6.50

40th Anniversary - Queen Elizabeth II's
1st Royal Visit to Gibraltar

325	1994AA	—	—	—	6.50

GREAT BRITAIN

Great Britain, a member of the United Kingdom of Great Britain and Northern Ireland, located off the northwest coast of the European continent, has an area of 94,227 sq. mi. (244,820 sq. km.) and a population of 56.4 million. Capital: London. The economy is based on industrial activity and trading. Machinery, motor vehicles, chemicals, and textile yarns and fabrics are exported.

After the departure of the Romans, who brought Britain into a more active relationship with Europe, it fell prey to invaders from Scandinavia and the Low Countries who drove the original Britons into Scotland and Wales, and established a profusion of kingdoms that finally united in the 11th century under the Danish King Canute. Norman rule, following the conquest of 1066, stimulated the development of those institutions which have since distinguished British life. Henry VIII (1509-47) turned Britain from continental adventuring and faced it to the sea - a decision that made Britain a world power during the reign of Elizabeth I (1558-1603). Strengthened by the Industrial Revolution and the defeat of Napoleon, 19th century Britain turned to the remote parts of the world and established a colonial empire of such extent and prosperity that the world has never seen its like. World Wars I and II sealed the fate of the Empire and relegated Britain to a lesser role in world affairs by draining her resources and inaugurating a world-wide movement toward national self-determination in her former colonies.

By the mid-20th century, most of the territories formerly comprising the British Empire had gained independence, and the empire had evolved into the Commonwealth of Nations, an association of equal and autonomous states which enjoy special trade interests. The Commonwealth is presently composed of 50 member nations, including the United Kingdom. All recognize the British monarch as head of the Commonwealth. Sixteen continue to recognize the British monarch as Head of State. They are: United Kingdom, Antigua and Barbuda, Australia, Bahamas, Barbados, Canada, Grenada, Jamaica, New Zealand, Papua New Guinea, St. Christopher & Nevis, Saint Lucia, Saint Vincent and the Grenadines, Solomon Islands, and Tuvalu. Elizabeth II is personally, and separately, the Queen of the sovereign, independent countries just mentioned. There is no other British connection between the several individual, national sovereignties.

RULERS

Victoria, 1837-1901
Edward VII, 1901-1910
George V, 1910-1936
Edward VIII, 1936
George VI, 1936-1952
Elizabeth II, 1952-

MINT MARKS

H - Heaton
KN - King's Norton

MONETARY SYSTEM
(Until 1970)

4 Farthings = 1 Penny
12 Pence = 1 Shilling
2 Shillings = 1 Florin
5 Shillings = 1 Crown
20 Shillings = 1 Pound (Sovereign)
21 Shillings = 1 Guinea

1/3 FARTHING

BRONZE
Edward VII

KM#	Date	Mintage	Fine	VF	XF	Unc
791	1902	.288	3.50	6.00	9.00	18.00

George V

823	1913	.288	3.50	5.00	8.00	16.00

*NOTE: Although the designs of the above types are in the homeland style, the issues were struck for Malta.

FARTHING

BRONZE
Blackened finish

KM#	Date	Mintage	Fine	VF	XF	Unc
788.2	1901	8.016	.30	.65	2.00	9.00

NOTE: Earlier dates (1897-1900) exist for this type.

792	1902	5.125	.60	1.50	3.00	10.00
	1903	5.331	.75	1.75	6.50	17.00
1903 shield heraldically colored						
					Proof	675.00
	1904	3.629	1.50	3.00	6.50	18.50
	1905	4.077	.60	1.75	6.50	17.00
	1906	5.340	.50	1.50	6.25	15.00
	1907	4.399	.75	1.50	6.25	16.00
	1908	4.265	.75	1.50	6.25	16.00
	1909	8.852	.50	1.50	6.25	15.00
	1910	2.598	1.75	4.00	8.00	20.00

808.1	1911	5.197	.60	1.00	3.00	8.00
	1912	7.670	.35	.75	2.50	8.00
	1913	4.184	.50	.75	2.50	8.00
	1914	6.127	.35	.75	2.50	8.00
	1915	7.129	.50	.75	5.00	9.00
	1916	10.993	.35	.75	1.75	7.00
	1917	21.435	.15	.35	1.50	5.00
	1918	19.363	.75	1.50	10.00	16.50

Bright finish.

808.2	1918	Inc. Ab.	.20	.40	1.00	5.00
	1919	15.089	.20	.40	1.00	5.00
	1920	11.481	.20	.40	1.00	5.00
	1921	9.469	.20	.40	1.00	6.00
	1922	9.957	.20	.40	1.00	6.00
	1923	8.034	.20	.40	1.00	7.00
	1924	8.733	.20	.40	1.00	7.00
	1925	12.635	.20	.40	1.00	5.00

Obv: Smaller head.

825	1926	9.792	.15	.40	1.00	6.50
	1926	—	—	—	Proof	—
	1927	7.868	.15	.40	1.00	6.00
	1927	—	—	—	Proof	—
	1928	11.626	.15	.35	.85	4.00
	1928	—	—	—	Proof	125.00
	1929	8.419	.15	.35	.85	4.00
	1929	—	—	—	Proof	125.00
	1930	4.195	.25	.50	1.00	6.00
	1930	—	—	—	Proof	—
	1931	6.595	.15	.35	.85	4.00
	1931	—	—	—	Proof	125.00
	1932	9.293	.15	.35	.75	2.50
	1932	—	—	—	Proof	125.00
	1933	4.560	.15	.35	1.00	4.00
	1933	—	—	—	Proof	125.00
	1934	3.053	.35	.75	1.75	7.00
	1934	—	—	—	Proof	125.00
	1935	2.227	1.00	2.00	3.50	10.00
	1935	—	—	—	Proof	150.00
	1936	9.734	.15	.35	.75	3.50
	1936	—	—	—	Proof	150.00

843	1937	8.131	.15	.25	.40	1.75
	1937	.026	—	—	Proof	4.00
	1938	7.450	.15	.30	.60	3.50
	1938	—	—	—	Proof	125.00
	1939	31.440	.10	.25	.40	1.75
	1939	—	—	—	Proof	125.00
	1940	18.360	.10	.25	.50	2.50
	1940	—	—	—	Proof	—
	1941	27.312	.10	.25	.40	1.75
	1941	—	—	—	Proof	—
	1942	28.858	.10	.20	.35	1.75
	1942	—	—	—	Proof	—
	1943	33.346	.10	.15	.30	1.75
	1943	—	—	—	Proof	—
	1944	25.138	.10	.15	.30	1.75
	1944	—	—	—	Proof	—

KM#	Date	Mintage	Fine	VF	XF	Unc
843	1945	23.736	.10	.20	.35	1.75
	1945	—	—	—	Proof	—
	1946	24.365	.10	.20	.35	1.75
	1946	—	—	—	Proof	—
	1947	14.746	.10	.20	.35	1.75
	1947	—	—	—	Proof	—
	1948	16.622	.10	.20	.35	1.75
	1948	—	—	—	Proof	—

Obv. leg: W/o IND IMP.

KM#	Date	Mintage	Fine	VF	XF	Unc
867	1949	8.424	.10	.20	.35	1.75
	1949	—	—	—	Proof	—
	1950	10.325	.10	.20	.35	1.75
	1950	.018	—	—	Proof	3.50
	1951	14.016	.10	.20	.35	2.00
	1951	.020	—	—	Proof	3.50
	1952	5.251	.10	.20	.35	2.00
	1952	—	—	—	Proof	125.00

KM#	Date	Mintage	Fine	VF	XF	Unc
881	1953	6.131	.15	.25	.35	2.00
	1953	.040	—	—	Proof	5.00

Obv. leg: W/o BRITT OMN.

KM#	Date	Mintage	Fine	VF	XF	Unc
895	1954	6.566	.10	.15	.30	2.00
	1954	—	—	—	Proof	125.00
	1955	5.779	.10	.15	.30	2.00
	1955	—	—	—	Proof	—
	1956	1.997	.25	.50	.75	4.00
	1956	—	—	—	Proof	—

1/2 PENNY

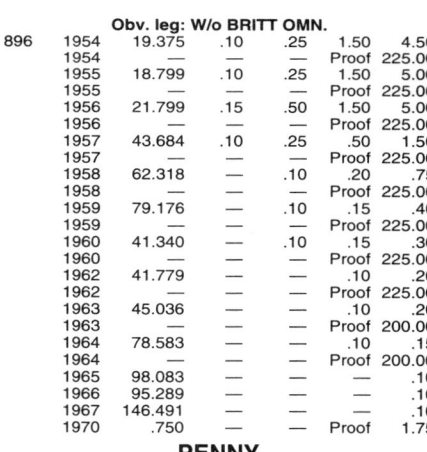

BRONZE

KM#	Date	Mintage	Fine	VF	XF	Unc
789	1901	11.127	.40	.75	2.00	8.00
	1901	—	—	—	Proof	400.00

NOTE: Earlier dates (1895-1900) exist for this type.

Rev: Low horizon.

KM#	Date	Mintage	Fine	VF	XF	Unc
793.1	1902	13.673	8.00	22.50	60.00	120.00

Rev: High horizon.

KM#	Date	Mintage	Fine	VF	XF	Unc
793.2	1902	Inc. Ab.	.50	2.00	5.00	15.00
	1903	11.451	.75	2.50	7.50	30.00
	1904	8.131	1.50	3.50	12.00	40.00
	1905	10.125	1.00	3.00	8.00	25.00
	1906	11.101	.75	2.00	6.00	25.00
	1907	16.849	.75	2.00	6.00	25.00
	1908	16.621	.75	2.00	6.00	25.00
	1909	8.279	1.00	3.00	8.00	30.00
	1910	10.770	1.00	2.50	7.00	25.00

KM#	Date	Mintage	Fine	VF	XF	Unc
809	1911	12.571	.75	1.75	4.50	13.50
	1912	21.186	.50	1.25	4.00	12.50
	1913	17.476	.75	2.25	8.00	25.00
	1914	20.289	.75	1.75	5.00	16.50
	1915	21.563	.75	1.75	5.00	16.50
	1916	39.386	.75	1.50	3.50	12.00
	1917	38.245	.75	1.25	3.50	12.00
	1918	22.321	.75	1.50	3.50	12.00
	1919	28.104	.50	1.50	3.50	12.00
	1920	35.147	.50	1.50	3.50	12.00
	1921	28.027	.75	1.50	3.50	12.00
	1922	10.735	1.00	2.25	6.00	15.00
	1923	12.266	.50	1.50	6.50	14.00
	1924	13.971	.75	2.00	5.00	15.50
	1925	12.216	1.00	2.50	7.00	17.50

Obv: Modified effigy.

KM#	Date	Mintage	Fine	VF	XF	Unc
824	1925	Inc. Ab.	1.50	5.00	10.00	25.00
	1926	6.712	1.50	3.00	6.00	16.50
	1926	—	—	—	Proof	325.00
	1927	15.590	.75	1.25	3.50	11.50
	1927	—	—	—	Proof	275.00

Obv: Smaller head.

KM#	Date	Mintage	Fine	VF	XF	Unc
837	1928	20.935	.25	.75	3.00	11.00
	1928	—	—	—	Proof	250.00
	1929	25.680	.25	.75	3.00	11.00
	1929	—	—	—	Proof	250.00
	1930	12.533	.25	.75	3.00	11.00
	1930	—	—	—	Proof	250.00
	1931	16.138	.25	.75	3.00	11.00
	1931	—	—	—	Proof	250.00
	1932	14.448	.25	.75	3.25	12.00
	1932	—	—	—	Proof	250.00
	1933	10.560	.25	.75	3.25	12.50
	1933	—	—	—	Proof	250.00
	1934	7.704	.50	1.00	3.50	14.00
	1934	—	—	—	Proof	250.00
	1935	12.180	.25	.75	2.50	10.00
	1935	—	—	—	Proof	225.00
	1936	23.009	.25	.65	2.00	5.50
	1936	—	—	—	Proof	225.00

KM#	Date	Mintage	Fine	VF	XF	Unc
844	1937	24.504	.25	.35	.50	1.75
	1937	.026	—	—	Proof	5.00
	1938	40.320	.25	.50	1.25	3.75
	1938	—	—	—	Proof	225.00
	1939	28.925	.25	.50	1.25	3.50
	1939	—	—	—	Proof	225.00
	1940	32.162	.25	.50	2.00	5.50
	1940	—	—	—	Proof	275.00
	1941	45.120	.20	.50	1.50	5.00
	1941	—	—	—	Proof	275.00
	1942	71.909	.10	.20	.60	2.25
	1942	—	—	—	Proof	200.00
	1943	76.200	.10	.25	1.00	2.25
	1943	—	—	—	Proof	200.00
	1944	81.840	.10	.25	1.00	3.00
	1944	—	—	—	Proof	200.00
	1945	57.000	.10	.25	.90	2.75
	1945	—	—	—	Proof	200.00
	1946	22.726	.20	.50	2.75	7.00
	1946	—	—	—	Proof	200.00
	1947	21.266	.10	.25	2.00	5.00
	1947	—	—	—	Proof	200.00
	1948	26.947	.10	.25	.90	2.25
	1948	—	—	—	Proof	200.00

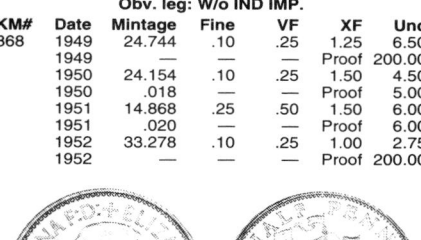

Obv. leg: W/o IND IMP.

KM#	Date	Mintage	Fine	VF	XF	Unc
868	1949	24.744	.10	.25	1.25	6.50
	1949	—	—	—	Proof	200.00
	1950	24.154	.10	.25	1.50	4.50
	1950	.018	—	—	Proof	5.00
	1951	14.868	.25	.50	1.50	6.00
	1951	.020	—	—	Proof	6.00
	1952	33.278	.10	.25	1.00	2.75
	1952	—	—	—	Proof	200.00

KM#	Date	Mintage	Fine	VF	XF	Unc
882	1953	8.926	.20	.40	1.00	2.25
	1953	.040	—	—	Proof	4.50

Obv. leg: W/o BRITT OMN.

KM#	Date	Mintage	Fine	VF	XF	Unc
896	1954	19.375	.10	.25	1.50	4.50
	1954	—	—	—	Proof	225.00
	1955	18.799	.10	.25	1.50	5.00
	1955	—	—	—	Proof	225.00
	1956	21.799	.15	.50	1.50	5.00
	1956	—	—	—	Proof	225.00
	1957	43.684	.10	.25	.50	1.50
	1957	—	—	—	Proof	225.00
	1958	62.318	—	—	.10	.75
	1958	—	—	—	Proof	225.00
	1959	79.176	—	—	.10	.15	.40
	1959	—	—	—	Proof	225.00
	1960	41.340	—	—	.10	.15	.30
	1960	—	—	—	Proof	225.00
	1962	41.779	—	—	.10	.20
	1962	—	—	—	Proof	225.00
	1963	45.036	—	—	.10	.20
	1963	—	—	—	Proof	200.00
	1964	78.583	—	—	.10	.15
	1964	—	—	—	Proof	200.00
	1965	98.083	—	—	—	.10
	1966	95.289	—	—	—	.10
	1967	146.491	—	—	—	.10
	1970	.750	—	—	—	Proof	1.75

PENNY

.4713 g, .925 SILVER, .0140 oz ASW

KM#	Date	Mintage	Fine	VF	XF	Unc
775	1901	.018	—	—	P/L	12.50

NOTE: Earlier dates (1893-1900) exist for this type.

BRONZE

KM#	Date	Mintage	Fine	VF	XF	Unc
790	1901	22.206	.30	.75	2.00	15.00
	1901	—	—	—	Proof	250.00

NOTE: Earlier dates (1895-1900) exist for this type.

Rev: Low sea level.

KM#	Date	Mintage	Fine	VF	XF	Unc
794.1	1902	26.977	4.00	9.00	22.50	65.00

Rev: High sea level.

KM#	Date	Mintage	Fine	VF	XF	Unc
794.2	1902	Inc. Ab.	.60	2.00	4.50	20.00
	1903	21.415	.65	2.50	7.00	30.00
	1904	12.913	1.00	3.00	15.00	50.00
	1905	17.784	.70	2.50	9.00	40.00
	1906	37.990	.60	2.00	7.00	35.00
	1907	47.322	.60	2.00	7.00	35.00
	1908	31.506	.75	2.50	7.50	45.00
	1908	—	—	—	Proof	Rare
	1909	19.617	.65	2.25	7.00	45.00
	1910	29.549	.50	1.75	6.00	30.00

.4713 g, .925 SILVER, .0140 oz ASW

KM#	Date	Mintage	Fine	VF	XF	Unc
795	1902	.021	—	—	P/L	12.50
	1903	.017	—	—	P/L	12.50
	1904	.019	—	—	P/L	12.50
	1905	.018	—	—	P/L	12.50
	1906	.019	—	—	P/L	12.50
	1907	.018	—	—	P/L	12.50
	1908	.018	—	—	P/L	12.50
	1909	2,948	—	—	P/L	15.00
	1910	3,392	—	—	P/L	20.00

BRONZE

KM#	Date	Mintage	Fine	VF	XF	Unc
810	1911	23.079	.50	1.25	5.00	20.00
	1912	48.306	.35	1.00	5.00	20.00
	1912H	16.800	1.00	3.50	18.50	85.00
	1913	65.497	.40	1.25	5.50	26.00
	1914	50.821	.35	1.00	5.00	25.00
	1915	47.311	.50	1.25	6.00	27.50
	1916	86.411	.35	1.00	4.50	22.00
	1917	107.905	.35	1.00	4.50	22.00
	1918	84.227	.35	1.00	4.50	22.00
	1918H	2.573	2.00	20.00	100.00	200.00
	1918KN	I.A.	3.25	30.00	125.00	300.00
	1919	113.761	.35	1.00	4.50	22.00
	1919H	4.526	1.25	6.50	60.00	200.00
	1919KN	I.A.	5.00	35.00	150.00	425.00
	1920	124.693	.35	1.00	4.00	16.50
	1921	129.718	.30	.75	3.00	12.00
	1922	16.347	.75	2.50	10.00	35.00
	1926	4.499	2.50	8.00	20.00	60.00
	1926	—	—	—	Proof	800.00

.4713 g, .925 SILVER, .0140 oz ASW

KM#	Date	Mintage	Fine	VF	XF	Unc
811	1911	1,913	—	—	P/L	15.00
	1912	1,616	—	—	P/L	15.00
	1913	1,590	—	—	P/L	15.00
	1914	1,818	—	—	P/L	15.00
	1915	2,072	—	—	P/L	15.00
	1916	1,647	—	—	P/L	15.00
	1917	1,820	—	—	P/L	15.00
	1918	1,911	—	—	P/L	15.00
	1919	1,699	—	—	P/L	15.00
	1920	1,715	—	—	P/L	15.00

.4713 g, .500 SILVER, .0076 oz ASW

KM#	Date	Mintage	Fine	VF	XF	Unc
811a	1921	1,847	—	—	P/L	15.00
	1922	1,758	—	—	P/L	15.00
	1923	1,840	—	—	P/L	15.00
	1924	1,619	—	—	P/L	15.00
	1925	1,890	—	—	P/L	15.00
	1926	2,180	—	—	P/L	15.00
	1927	1,647	—	—	P/L	15.00

BRONZE
Obv: Modified head.

KM#	Date	Mintage	Fine	VF	XF	Unc
826	1926					
		Inc. KM#810	10.00	35.00	250.00	850.00
	1926	—	—	—	Proof	—
	1927	60.990	.35	1.00	4.50	10.00
	1927	—	—	—	Proof	600.00

Obv: Smaller head.

KM#	Date	Mintage	Fine	VF	XF	Unc
838	1928	50.178	.25	.50	2.75	7.00
	1928	—	—	—	Proof	250.00
	1929	49.133	.25	.50	2.75	8.00
	1929	—	—	—	Proof	250.00
	1930	29.098	.35	1.00	4.50	14.00
	1930	—	—	—	Proof	250.00
	1931	19.843	.35	1.00	4.50	14.00
	1931	—	—	—	Proof	250.00
	1932	8.278	1.50	3.50	15.00	45.00
	1932	—	—	—	Proof	250.00
	1933	—	—	—	Rare	—
	1934	13.966	.50	2.00	9.00	27.50
	1934	—	—	—	Proof	250.00
	1935	56.070	.25	.50	1.75	4.50
	1935	—	—	—	Proof	225.00
	1936	154.296	.20	.35	1.00	4.00
	1936	—	—	—	Proof	225.00

.4713 g, .500 SILVER, .0076 oz ASW
Obv: Modified effigy.

KM#	Date	Mintage	Fine	VF	XF	Unc
839	1928	1,846	—	—	P/L	15.00
	1929	1,837	—	—	P/L	15.00
	1930	1,724	—	—	P/L	15.00
	1931	1,759	—	—	P/L	15.00
	1932	1,835	—	—	P/L	15.00
	1933	1,872	—	—	P/L	15.00
	1934	1,919	—	—	P/L	15.00
	1935	1,975	—	—	P/L	15.00
	1936	1,329	—	—	P/L	15.00

BRONZE

KM#	Date	Mintage	Fine	VF	XF	Unc
845	1937	88.896	.20	.35	1.25	3.50
	1937	.026	—	—	Proof	9.00
	1938	121.560	.20	.35	1.25	3.50
	1938	—	—	—	Proof	225.00
	1939	55.560	.20	.35	1.50	6.50
	1939	—	—	—	Proof	225.00
	1940	42.284	.25	.50	2.25	10.00
	1940	—	—	—	Proof	—
	1944	42.600	.25	.50	2.25	8.00
	1944	—	—	—	Proof	—
	1945	79.531	.20	.35	1.50	6.00
	1945	—	—	—	Proof	—
	1946	66.856	.20	.35	1.00	5.00
	1946	—	—	—	Proof	—
	1947	52.220	.15	.25	.75	3.50
	1947	—	—	—	Proof	—
	1948	63.961	.15	.25	.75	3.50
	1948	—	—	—	Proof	—

.4713 g, .500 SILVER, .0076 oz ASW

KM#	Date	Mintage	Fine	VF	XF	Unc
846	1937	1,329	—	—	P/L	15.00
	1938	1,275	—	—	P/L	15.00
	1939	1,253	—	—	P/L	15.00
	1940	1,375	—	—	P/L	15.00
	1941	1,255	—	—	P/L	15.00
	1942	1,243	—	—	P/L	15.00
	1943	1,347	—	—	P/L	15.00
	1944	1,259	—	—	P/L	15.00
	1945	1,367	—	—	P/L	15.00
	1946	1,479	—	—	P/L	15.00

.4713 g, .925 SILVER, .0140 oz ASW

KM#	Date	Mintage	Fine	VF	XF	Unc
846a	1947	1,387	—	—	P/L	15.00
	1948	1,397	—	—	P/L	15.00

BRONZE
Obv. leg: W/o IND IMP.

KM#	Date	Mintage	Fine	VF	XF	Unc
869	1949	14.324	.20	.35	1.00	4.00
	1949	—	—	—	Proof	—
	1950	.240	2.00	6.00	12.00	22.00
	1950	.018	—	—	Proof	30.00
	1951	.120	3.00	7.00	15.00	25.00
	1951	.020	—	—	Proof	30.00

.4713 g, .925 SILVER, .0140 oz ASW

KM#	Date	Mintage	Fine	VF	XF	Unc
870	1949	1,407	—	—	P/L	15.00
	1950	1,527	—	—	P/L	15.00
	1951	1,480	—	—	P/L	15.00
	1952	1,024	—	—	P/L	15.00

BRONZE

KM#	Date	Mintage	Fine	VF	XF	Unc
883	1953	1.308	.75	1.50	2.50	4.50
	1953	.040	—	—	Proof	9.00

.4713 g, .925 SILVER, .0140 oz ASW

KM#	Date	Mintage	Fine	VF	XF	Unc
884	1953	1,050	—	—	P/L	95.00

BRONZE
Obv. leg. W/o BRITT OMN.

KM#	Date	Mintage	Fine	VF	XF	Unc
897	1954	1 known	—	—	—	—
	1961	48.313	—	.10	.15	.80
	1961	—	—	—	Proof	—
	1962	143.309	—	—	.10	.15
	1962	—	—	—	Proof	—
	1963	125.236	—	—	.10	.15
	1963	—	—	—	Proof	—
	1964	153.294	—	—	—	.10
	1964	—	—	—	Proof	—
	1965	121.310	—	—	—	.10
	1966	165.739	—	—	—	.10
	1967	654.564	—	—	—	.10
	1970	.750	—	—	Proof	2.75

.4713 g, .925 SILVER, .0140 oz ASW

KM#	Date	Mintage	Fine	VF	XF	Unc
898	1954	1,088	—	—	P/L	15.00
	1955	1,036	—	—	P/L	15.00
	1956	1,100	—	—	P/L	15.00
	1957	1,168	—	—	P/L	15.00
	1958	1,112	—	—	P/L	15.00
	1959	1,118	—	—	P/L	15.00
	1960	1,124	—	—	P/L	15.00
	1961	1,200	—	—	P/L	15.00
	1962	1,127	—	—	P/L	15.00
	1963	1,133	—	—	P/L	15.00
	1964	1,215	—	—	P/L	15.00
	1965	1,143	—	—	P/L	15.00
	1966	1,206	—	—	P/L	15.00
	1967	1,068	—	—	P/L	15.00
	1968	964 pcs.	—	—	P/L	15.00
	1969	1,002	—	—	P/L	15.00
	1970	980 pcs.	—	—	P/L	15.00
	1971	1,108	—	—	P/L	15.00
	1972	1,026	—	—	P/L	15.00
	1973	1,004	—	—	P/L	15.00
	1974	1,138	—	—	P/L	15.00
	1975	1,050	—	—	P/L	15.00
	1976	1,158	—	—	P/L	15.00
	1977	1,240	—	—	P/L	17.50
	1978	1,178	—	—	P/L	17.50
	1979	1,188	—	—	P/L	17.50
	1980	1,198	—	—	P/L	17.50
	1981	1,288	—	—	P/L	17.50
	1982	1,218	—	—	P/L	17.50
	1983	1,228	—	—	P/L	17.50
	1984	1,354	—	—	P/L	17.50
	1985	1,248	—	—	P/L	17.50
	1986	1,378	—	—	P/L	17.50
	1987	1,512	—	—	P/L	17.50
	1988	1,402	—	—	P/L	17.50
	1989	1,353	—	—	P/L	17.50
	1990	1,523	—	—	P/L	17.50
	1991	1,514	—	—	P/L	17.50
	1992	1,556	—	—	P/L	17.50
	1993	1,440	—	—	P/L	17.50
	1994	1,443	—	—	P/L	17.50
	1995	1,466	—	—	P/L	17.50
	1996	1,629	—	—	P/L	17.50
	1997	1,786	—	—	P/L	17.50
	1998	—	—	—	P/L	17.50

2 PENCE

.9426 g, .925 SILVER, .0280 oz ASW

776	1901	.014	—	—	P/L	12.50

NOTE: Earlier dates (1893-1900) exist for this type.

796	1902	.014	—	—	P/L	12.50
	1903	.013	—	—	P/L	12.50
	1904	.014	—	—	P/L	12.50
	1905	.011	—	—	P/L	12.50
	1906	.011	—	—	P/L	12.50
	1907	8,760	—	—	P/L	12.50
	1908	.015	—	—	P/L	12.50
	1909	2,695	—	—	P/L	15.00
	1910	2,998	—	—	P/L	20.00
812	1911	1,635	—	—	P/L	17.50
	1912	1,678	—	—	P/L	17.50
	1913	1,880	—	—	P/L	17.50
	1914	1,659	—	—	P/L	17.50
	1915	1,465	—	—	P/L	17.50
	1916	1,509	—	—	P/L	17.50
	1917	1,506	—	—	P/L	17.50
	1918	1,547	—	—	P/L	17.50
	1919	1,567	—	—	P/L	17.50
	1920	1,630	—	—	P/L	17.50

.9426 g, .500 SILVER, .0152 oz ASW

812a	1921	1,794	—	—	P/L	20.00
	1922	3,074	—	—	P/L	20.00
	1923	1,527	—	—	P/L	20.00
	1924	1,602	—	—	P/L	20.00
	1925	1,670	—	—	P/L	20.00
	1926	1,902	—	—	P/L	20.00
	1927	1,766	—	—	P/L	20.00

Obv: Modified effigy.

840	1928	1,706	—	—	P/L	17.50
	1929	1,862	—	—	P/L	17.50
	1930	1,901	—	—	P/L	17.50
	1931	1,897	—	—	P/L	17.50
	1932	1,960	—	—	P/L	17.50
	1933	2,066	—	—	P/L	17.50
	1934	1,927	—	—	P/L	17.50

KM#	Date	Mintage	Fine	VF	XF	Unc
840	1935	1,928	—	—	P/L	17.50
	1936	1,365	—	—	P/L	20.00

847	1937	1,472	—	—	P/L	17.50
	1938	1,374	—	—	P/L	17.50
	1939	1,436	—	—	P/L	17.50
	1940	1,277	—	—	P/L	17.50
	1941	1,345	—	—	P/L	17.50
	1942	1,231	—	—	P/L	17.50
	1943	1,239	—	—	P/L	17.50
	1944	1,345	—	—	P/L	17.50
	1945	1,355	—	—	P/L	17.50
	1946	1,365	—	—	P/L	17.50

.9426 g, .925 SILVER, .0280 oz ASW

847a	1947	1,479	—	—	P/L	17.50
	1948	1,385	—	—	P/L	17.50

Obv. leg: W/o IND IMP.

871	1949	1,395	—	—	P/L	17.50
	1950	1,405	—	—	P/L	17.50
	1951	1,580	—	—	P/L	17.50
	1952	1,064	—	—	P/L	17.50
885	1953	1,025	—	—	P/L	85.00

Obv. leg: W/o BRITT OMN.

899	1954	1,020	—	—	P/L	20.00
	1955	1,082	—	—	P/L	20.00
	1956	1,088	—	—	P/L	20.00
	1957	1,094	—	—	P/L	20.00
	1958	1,164	—	—	P/L	20.00
	1959	1,106	—	—	P/L	20.00
	1960	1,112	—	—	P/L	20.00
	1961	1,118	—	—	P/L	20.00
	1962	1,197	—	—	P/L	20.00
	1963	1,131	—	—	P/L	20.00
	1964	1,137	—	—	P/L	20.00
	1965	1,221	—	—	P/L	20.00
	1966	1,206	—	—	P/L	20.00
	1967	986 pcs.	—	—	P/L	20.00
	1968	1,048	—	—	P/L	20.00
	1969	1,002	—	—	P/L	20.00
	1970	980 pcs.	—	—	P/L	20.00
	1971	1,018	—	—	P/L	20.00
	1972	1,026	—	—	P/L	20.00
	1973	1,004	—	—	P/L	20.00
	1974	1,042	—	—	P/L	20.00
	1975	1,148	—	—	P/L	20.00
	1976	1,158	—	—	P/L	20.00
	1977	1,138	—	—	P/L	22.00
	1978	1,282	—	—	P/L	22.00
	1979	1,188	—	—	P/L	22.00
	1980	1,198	—	—	P/L	22.00
	1981	1,178	—	—	P/L	22.00
	1982	1,330	—	—	P/L	22.00
	1983	1,228	—	—	P/L	22.00
	1984	1,238	—	—	P/L	22.00
	1985	1,366	—	—	P/L	22.00
	1986	1,378	—	—	P/L	22.00
	1987	1,390	—	—	P/L	22.00
	1988	1,526	—	—	P/L	22.00
	1989	1,353	—	—	P/L	22.00
	1990	1,523	—	—	P/L	22.00
	1991	1,384	—	—	P/L	22.00
	1992	1,424	—	—	P/L	22.00
	1993	1,440	—	—	P/L	22.00
	1994	1,443	—	—	P/L	22.00
	1995	1,466	—	—	P/L	22.00
	1996	1,629	—	—	P/L	22.00
	1997	1,786	—	—	P/L	22.00
	1998	—	—	—	P/L	22.00

3 PENCE

1.4138 g, .925 SILVER, .0420 oz ASW

777	1901	6.100	1.25	2.00	5.00	20.00
	1901	8,976	—	—	P/L	30.00

NOTE: Earlier dates (1893-1900) exist for this type.

797.1	1902	8.287	.75	1.50	4.00	12.50
	1902	8,976	—	—	P/L	25.00
	1902	.015	—	—	Proof	25.00
	1903	5.235	1.00	3.00	10.00	35.00
	1903	8,976	—	—	P/L	25.00
	1904	3.630	6.00	12.50	35.00	70.00
	1904	8,876	—	—	P/L	22.50

KM#	Date	Mintage	Fine	VF	XF	Unc
797.2	1904	Inc. Ab.	4.50	10.00	30.00	60.00
	1905	3.563	4.50	9.00	25.00	50.00
	1905	8,976	—	—	P/L	22.50
	1906	3.174	4.00	8.00	20.00	40.00
	1906	8,800	—	—	P/L	22.50
	1907	4.841	1.50	3.00	9.00	25.00
	1907	.011	—	—	P/L	22.50
	1908	8.176	1.50	3.00	9.00	30.00
	1908	8,760	—	—	P/L	22.50
	1909	4.055	2.00	5.00	10.00	30.00
	1909	1,983	—	—	P/L	22.50
	1910	4.565	.75	2.00	7.50	25.00
	1910	1,140	—	—	P/L	25.00

813	1911	5.843	.60	1.00	3.00	12.75
	1911	1,991	—	—	P/L	27.50
	1911	6,007	—	—	Proof	35.00
	1912	8.934	.60	1.00	3.00	12.75
	1912	1,246	—	—	P/L	27.50
	1913	7.144	.60	1.00	4.00	15.00
	1913	1,228	—	—	P/L	27.50
	1914	6.735	.50	.85	3.50	15.00
	1914	982 pcs.	—	—	P/L	27.50
	1915	5.452	.60	1.00	3.00	12.75
	1915	1,293	—	—	P/L	27.50
	1916	18.556	.50	.75	3.00	12.50
	1916	1,128	—	—	P/L	27.50
	1917	21.664	.50	.75	3.00	12.50
	1917	1,237	—	—	P/L	27.50
	1918	20.632	.50	.75	3.00	12.50
	1918	1,375	—	—	P/L	27.50
	1919	16.846	.50	.75	3.00	12.50
	1919	1,258	—	—	P/L	27.50
	1920	16.705	.50	.75	3.50	12.50
	1920	1,399	—	—	P/L	27.50

1.4138 g, .500 SILVER, .0227 oz ASW

813a	1920	Inc. Ab.	BV	.65	3.00	12.00
	1921	8.751	BV	1.50	3.00	15.00
	1921	1,386	—	—	P/L	25.00
	1922	7.981	BV	1.50	3.50	16.00
	1922	1,373	—	—	P/L	25.00
	1923	1,430	—	—	P/L	25.00
	1924	1,515	—	—	P/L	25.00
	1925	3.733	1.25	2.50	9.00	22.00
	1925	1,438	—	—	P/L	25.00
	1926	4.109	2.50	6.00	16.50	35.00
	1926	1,504	—	—	P/L	25.00
	1927	1,690	—	—	P/L	25.00

Obv: Modified effigy.

827	1926	Inc. Ab.	1.00	2.00	8.00	16.00
	1928	1,835	—	—	P/L	22.50
	1929	1,761	—	—	P/L	22.50
	1930	1,948	—	—	P/L	22.50
	1931	1,818	—	—	P/L	22.50
	1932	2,042	—	—	P/L	22.50
	1933	1,920	—	—	P/L	22.50
	1934	1,887	—	—	P/L	22.50
	1935	2,007	—	—	P/L	22.50
	1936	1,307	—	—	P/L	25.00

Rev: Oak sprigs w/acorns.

831	1927	.015	—	—	Proof	60.00
	1927	*—	—	—	Matte Proof	—
	1928	1.302	2.50	5.00	10.00	30.00
	1928	—	—	—	Proof	250.00
	1930	1.319	1.50	3.00	7.50	25.00
	1930	—	—	—	Proof	200.00
	1931	6.252	BV	.50	1.50	5.25
	1931	—	—	—	Proof	200.00
	1932	5.887	BV	.50	1.50	5.25
	1932	—	—	—	Proof	200.00
	1933	5.579	BV	.50	1.50	5.25
	1933	—	—	—	Proof	200.00
	1934	7.406	BV	.50	1.50	5.25
	1934	—	—	—	Proof	200.00
	1935	7.028	BV	.50	1.50	5.25
	1935	—	—	—	Proof	175.00
	1936	3.239	BV	.50	1.50	5.25
	1936	—	—	—	Proof	175.00

*NOTE: There are reportedly 3-4 known of this variety, struck specifically for use in photographs.

KM#	Date	Mintage	Fine	VF	XF	Unc
848	1937	8.148	BV	.50	1.50	5.50
	1937	.026	—	—	Proof	10.00
	1938	6.402	BV	.50	2.50	5.25
	1938	—	—	—	Proof	175.00
	1939	1.356	.75	1.25	2.75	12.00
	1939	—	—	—	Proof	175.00
	1940	7.914	BV	.50	1.00	5.50
	1940	—	—	—	Proof	—
	1941	7.979	BV	.50	1.00	5.50
	1941	—	—	—	Proof	—
	1942	4.144	1.50	3.00	6.50	20.00
	1943	1.379	2.00	4.50	8.00	25.00
	1944	2.006	3.25	8.50	17.50	50.00
	1945	.320*	—	—	2000.	—

***NOTE:** Issue melted, one known.

NICKEL-BRASS

KM#	Date	Mintage	Fine	VF	XF	Unc
849	1937	45.708	.25	.40	1.00	6.50
	1937	.026	—	—	Proof	8.50
	1938	14.532	.40	.80	4.00	20.00
	1938	—	—	—	Proof	—
	1939	5.603	.70	2.00	6.00	30.00
	1939	—	—	—	Proof	—
	1940	12.636	.25	.80	2.50	10.00
	1940	—	—	—	Proof	—
	1941	60.239	.25	.40	1.00	7.00
	1941	—	—	—	Proof	—
	1942	103.214	.20	.30	1.00	4.50
	1942	—	—	—	Proof	—
	1943	101.702	.20	.30	1.00	4.50
	1943	—	—	—	Proof	—
	1944	69.760	.25	.40	1.00	6.00
	1944	—	—	—	Proof	—
	1945	33.942	.25	.50	1.50	8.00
	1945	—	—	—	Proof	—
	1946	.621	2.50	7.50	40.00	225.00
	1946	—	—	—	Proof	350.00
	1948	4.230	.60	1.50	5.50	30.00
	1948	—	—	—	Proof	—

1.4138 g, .500 SILVER, .0227 oz ASW

KM#	Date	Mintage	Fine	VF	XF	Unc
850	1937	1,351	—	—	P/L	20.00
	1938	1,350	—	—	P/L	20.00
	1939	1,234	—	—	P/L	20.00
	1940	1,290	—	—	P/L	20.00
	1941	1,253	—	—	P/L	20.00
	1942	1,325	—	—	P/L	20.00
	1943	1,335	—	—	P/L	20.00
	1944	1,345	—	—	P/L	20.00
	1945	1,355	—	—	P/L	20.00
	1946	1,365	—	—	P/L	20.00

1.4138 g, .925 SILVER, .0420 oz ASW

KM#	Date	Mintage	Fine	VF	XF	Unc
850a	1947	1,375	—	—	P/L	20.00
	1948	1,491	—	—	P/L	20.00

Obv. leg: W/o IND IMP.

KM#	Date	Mintage	Fine	VF	XF	Unc
872	1949	1,395	—	—	P/L	20.00
	1950	1,405	—	—	P/L	20.00
	1951	1,468	—	—	P/L	20.00
	1952	1,012	—	—	P/L	22.50

NICKEL-BRASS
Obv. leg: W/o IND IMP.

KM#	Date	Mintage	Fine	VF	XF	Unc
873	1949	.464	5.00	11.00	60.00	165.00
	1949	—	—	—	Proof	175.00
	1950	1.600	1.00	3.00	12.50	50.00
	1950	.018	—	—	Proof	22.50
	1951	1.184	1.50	3.50	12.50	30.00
	1951	.020	—	—	Proof	22.00
	1952	25.494	.25	.75	1.25	6.00
	1952	—	—	—	Proof	175.00

KM#	Date	Mintage	Fine	VF	XF	Unc
886	1953	30.618	.15	.25	.50	2.50
	1953	.040	—	—	Proof	4.50

1.4138 g, .925 SILVER, .0420 oz ASW

KM#	Date	Mintage	Fine	VF	XF	Unc
887	1953	1,078	—	—	P/L	85.00

NICKEL-BRASS
Obv. leg: W/o BRITT OMN.

KM#	Date	Mintage	Fine	VF	XF	Unc
900	1954	41.720	—	.15	.50	4.00
	1954	—	—	—	Proof	175.00
	1955	41.075	—	.15	1.00	6.00
	1955	—	—	—	Proof	—
	1956	36.902	—	.15	1.00	6.00
	1956	—	—	—	Proof	—
	1957	24.294	—	.15	.50	4.00
	1957	—	—	—	Proof	—
	1958	20.504	—	.25	1.00	6.00
	1958	—	—	—	Proof	300.00
	1959	28.499	—	.15	.50	3.50
	1959	—	—	—	Proof	—
	1960	83.078	—	.15	.40	2.75
	1960	—	—	—	Proof	150.00
	1961	41.102	—	.15	.30	1.00
	1961	—	—	—	Proof	—
	1962	47.242	—	.15	.30	1.00
	1962	—	—	—	Proof	—
	1963	35.280	—	.15	.25	.55
	1963	—	—	—	Proof	—
	1964	47.440	—	.15	.25	.55
	1964	—	—	—	Proof	—
	1965	23.907	—	.15	.25	.55
	1966	55.320	—	.15	.25	.55
	1967	49.000	—	.15	.25	.55
	1970	.750	—	—	Proof	2.50

1.4138 g, .925 SILVER, .0420 oz ASW
Obv. leg: W/o BRITT OMN.

KM#	Date	Mintage	Fine	VF	XF	Unc
901	1954	1,076	—	—	P/L	20.00
	1955	1,082	—	—	P/L	20.00
	1956	1,088	—	—	P/L	20.00
	1957	1,094	—	—	P/L	20.00
	1958	1,100	—	—	P/L	20.00
	1959	1,172	—	—	P/L	20.00
	1960	1,112	—	—	P/L	20.00
	1961	1,118	—	—	P/L	20.00
	1962	1,125	—	—	P/L	20.00
	1963	1,205	—	—	P/L	20.00
	1964	1,213	—	—	P/L	20.00
	1965	1,221	—	—	P/L	20.00
	1966	1,206	—	—	P/L	20.00
	1967	986 pcs.	—	—	P/L	20.00
	1968	964 pcs.	—	—	P/L	20.00
	1969	1,088	—	—	P/L	20.00
	1970	980 pcs.	—	—	P/L	20.00
	1971	1,018	—	—	P/L	20.00
	1972	1,026	—	—	P/L	20.00
	1973	1,098	—	—	P/L	20.00
	1974	1,138	—	—	P/L	20.00
	1975	1,148	—	—	P/L	20.00
	1976	1,158	—	—	P/L	20.00
	1977	1,138	—	—	P/L	22.00
	1978	1,178	—	—	P/L	22.00
	1979	1,294	—	—	P/L	22.00
	1980	1,198	—	—	P/L	22.00
	1981	1,178	—	—	P/L	22.00
	1982	1,218	—	—	P/L	22.00
	1983	1,342	—	—	P/L	22.00
	1984	1,354	—	—	P/L	22.00
	1985	1,366	—	—	P/L	22.00
	1986	1,378	—	—	P/L	22.00
	1987	1,390	—	—	P/L	22.00
	1988	1,528	—	—	P/L	22.00
	1989	1,353	—	—	P/L	22.00
	1990	1,523	—	—	P/L	22.00
	1991	1,384	—	—	P/L	22.00
	1992	1,424	—	—	P/L	22.00
	1993	1,440	—	—	P/L	22.00
	1994	1,433	—	—	P/L	22.00
	1995	1,466	—	—	P/L	22.00
	1996	1,629	—	—	P/L	22.00
	1997	1,786	—	—	P/L	22.00
	1998	—	—	—	P/L	22.00

4 PENCE (GROAT)

1.8851 g, .925 SILVER, .0561 oz ASW

KM#	Date	Mintage	Fine	VF	XF	Unc
778	1901	.012	—	—	P/L	15.00

NOTE: Earlier dates (1893-1900) exist for this type.

KM#	Date	Mintage	Fine	VF	XF	Unc
798	1902	.010	—	—	P/L	15.00
	1903	9,729	—	—	P/L	15.00
	1904	.012	—	—	P/L	15.00
	1905	.011	—	—	P/L	15.00
	1906	.011	—	—	P/L	15.00
	1907	.011	—	—	P/L	15.00
	1908	9,929	—	—	P/L	15.00
	1909	2,428	—	—	P/L	20.00
	1910	2,755	—	—	P/L	22.50

KM#	Date	Mintage	Fine	VF	XF	Unc
814	1911	1,768	—	—	P/L	17.50
	1912	1,700	—	—	P/L	17.50
	1913	1,798	—	—	P/L	17.50
	1914	1,651	—	—	P/L	17.50
	1915	1,441	—	—	P/L	17.50
	1916	1,499	—	—	P/L	17.50
	1917	1,478	—	—	P/L	17.50
	1918	1,479	—	—	P/L	17.50
	1919	1,524	—	—	P/L	17.50
	1920	1,460	—	—	P/L	17.50

1.8851 g, .500 SILVER, .0303 oz ASW

KM#	Date	Mintage	Fine	VF	XF	Unc
814a	1921	1,542	—	—	P/L	17.50
	1922	1,609	—	—	P/L	17.50
	1923	1,635	—	—	P/L	17.50
	1924	1,665	—	—	P/L	17.50
	1925	1,786	—	—	P/L	17.50
	1926	1,762	—	—	P/L	17.50
	1927	1,681	—	—	P/L	17.50

Obv: Modified effigy.

KM#	Date	Mintage	Fine	VF	XF	Unc
841	1928	1,642	—	—	P/L	20.00
	1929	1,969	—	—	P/L	20.00
	1930	1,744	—	—	P/L	20.00
	1931	1,915	—	—	P/L	20.00
	1932	1,937	—	—	P/L	20.00
	1933	1,931	—	—	P/L	20.00
	1934	1,893	—	—	P/L	20.00
	1935	1,995	—	—	P/L	20.00
	1936	1,323	—	—	P/L	22.50

KM#	Date	Mintage	Fine	VF	XF	Unc
851	1937	1,325	—	—	P/L	20.00
	1938	1,424	—	—	P/L	20.00
	1939	1,332	—	—	P/L	20.00
	1940	1,367	—	—	P/L	20.00
	1941	1,345	—	—	P/L	20.00
	1942	1,325	—	—	P/L	20.00
	1943	1,335	—	—	P/L	20.00
	1944	1,345	—	—	P/L	20.00
	1945	1,355	—	—	P/L	20.00
	1946	1,365	—	—	P/L	20.00

1.8851 g, .925 SILVER, .0561 oz ASW

KM#	Date	Mintage	Fine	VF	XF	Unc
851a	1947	1,375	—	—	P/L	20.00
	1948	1,385	—	—	P/L	20.00

Obv. leg: W/o IND IMP.

KM#	Date	Mintage	Fine	VF	XF	Unc
874	1949	1,503	—	—	P/L	20.00
	1950	1,515	—	—	P/L	20.00
	1951	1,580	—	—	P/L	20.00
	1952	1,064	—	—	P/L	22.50
888	1953	1,078	—	—	P/L	85.00

Obv. leg: W/o BRITT OMN.

KM#	Date	Mintage	Fine	VF	XF	Unc
902	1954	1,076	—	—	P/L	20.00
	1955	1,082	—	—	P/L	20.00
	1956	1,088	—	—	P/L	20.00
	1957	1,094	—	—	P/L	20.00
	1958	1,100	—	—	P/L	20.00
	1959	1,106	—	—	P/L	20.00
	1960	1,180	—	—	P/L	20.00
	1961	1,118	—	—	P/L	20.00
	1962	1,197	—	—	P/L	20.00
	1963	1,205	—	—	P/L	20.00
	1964	1,213	—	—	P/L	20.00
	1965	1,221	—	—	P/L	20.00
	1966	1,206	—	—	P/L	20.00
	1967	986 pcs.	—	—	P/L	20.00
	1968	964 pcs.	—	—	P/L	20.00
	1969	1,002	—	—	P/L	20.00
	1970	1,068	—	—	P/L	20.00
	1971	1,108	—	—	P/L	20.00
	1972	1,118	—	—	P/L	20.00
	1973	1,098	—	—	P/L	20.00
	1974	1,138	—	—	P/L	20.00
	1975	1,148	—	—	P/L	20.00
	1976	1,158	—	—	P/L	20.00
	1977	1,138	—	—	P/L	22.00
	1978	1,178	—	—	P/L	22.00
	1979	1,188	—	—	P/L	22.00
	1980	1,306	—	—	P/L	22.00
	1981	1,288	—	—	P/L	22.00
	1982	1,330	—	—	P/L	22.00
	1983	1,342	—	—	P/L	22.00
	1984	1,354	—	—	P/L	22.00
	1985	1,366	—	—	P/L	22.00
	1986	1,378	—	—	P/L	22.00
	1987	1,390	—	—	P/L	22.00
	1988	1,402	—	—	P/L	22.00
	1989	1,353	—	—	P/L	22.00
	1990	1,523	—	—	P/L	22.00
	1991	1,514	—	—	P/L	22.00
	1992	1,556	—	—	P/L	22.00
	1993	1,440	—	—	P/L	20.00
	1994	1,433	—	—	P/L	22.00
	1995	1,466	—	—	P/L	22.00
	1996	1,629	—	—	P/L	22.00
	1997	1,786	—	—	P/L	22.00
	1998	—	—	—	P/L	22.00

6 PENCE

3.0100 g, .925 SILVER, .0895 oz ASW

779	1901	5.109	2.50	5.00	10.00	20.00

NOTE: Earlier dates (1893-1900) exist for this type.

799	1902	6.356	2.00	4.00	15.00	38.00
	1902	.015	—		Matte Proof	30.00
	1903	5.411	2.75	9.00	30.00	60.00
	1904	4.487	3.50	10.00	32.50	80.00
	1905	4.236	3.50	10.00	32.50	75.00
	1906	7.641	2.50	5.50	20.00	60.00
	1907	8.734	2.50	8.00	22.00	60.00
	1908	6.739	3.50	12.00	30.00	75.00
	1909	6.584	3.00	10.00	30.00	65.00
	1910	12.491	2.25	7.00	16.00	40.00

815	1911	9.165	1.00	2.00	8.50	30.00
	1911	6,007	—	—	Proof	45.00
	1912	10.984	1.00	3.00	15.00	50.00
	1913	7.500	1.50	4.50	20.00	60.00
	1914	22.715	1.00	2.00	7.00	25.00
	1915	15.695	1.00	2.00	7.00	25.00
	1916	22.207	1.00	2.00	7.00	25.00
	1917	7.725	1.50	3.50	12.50	40.00
	1918	27.559	1.00	1.75	7.00	25.00
	1919	13.375	1.00	3.00	12.00	35.00
	1920	14.136	1.00	3.00	12.00	35.00

2.8276 g, .500 SILVER, .0455 oz ASW
Narrow rim.

KM#	Date	Mintage	Fine	VF	XF	Unc
815a.1	1920	Inc. Ab.	.75	2.00	12.50	37.50
	1921	30.340	.75	2.00	10.00	32.00
	1922	16.879	.75	2.00	10.00	32.00
	1923	6.383	1.25	3.00	15.00	38.00
	1924	17.444	.75	2.00	10.00	32.00
	1925	12.721	.75	2.50	12.00	32.00

Wide rim.

815a.2	1925	Inc. Ab.	.75	1.50	9.00	25.00
	1926	21.810	1.00	3.50	15.00	35.00

Obv: Modified effigy, slightly smaller bust.

828	1926	Inc. Ab.	BV	1.50	8.00	22.50
	1927	8.925	BV	1.50	12.50	25.00
	1927	—	—	—	Proof	250.00

NICKEL, 2.9 g

828a	1927	—	—	—	Proof	—

2.8276 g, .500 SILVER, .0455 oz ASW
Rev: Oak sprigs w/acorns.

832	1927	.015	—	—	Proof	25.00
	1927	*—	—		Matte Proof	—
	1928	23.123	BV	1.00	3.00	15.00
	1928	—	—	—	Proof	—
	1929	28.319	BV	1.00	3.00	15.00
	1929	—	—	—	Proof	—
	1930	16.990	BV	1.00	3.50	16.50
	1930	—	—	—	Proof	250.00
	1931	16.873	BV	1.00	8.50	17.50
	1931	—	—	—	Proof	250.00
	1932	9.406	.75	1.50	15.00	27.50
	1932	—	—	—	Proof	250.00
	1933	22.185	BV	1.00	7.00	14.00
	1933	—	—	—	Proof	250.00
	1934	9.304	.75	1.50	9.50	15.00
	1934	—	—	—	Proof	225.00
	1935	13.996	BV	.75	6.25	14.00
	1935	—	—	—	Proof	225.00
	1936	24.380	BV	.75	2.75	12.50
	1936	—	—	—	Proof	250.00

NOTE: Varieties in edge milling exist.
***NOTE:** There are reportedly 3-4 known of this variety, struck specifically for use in photographs.

852	1937	22.303	—	BV	1.00	4.00
	1937	.026	—	—	Proof	9.00
	1938	13.403	.75	1.50	3.50	12.00
	1938	—	—	—	Proof	225.00
	1939	28.670	BV	.75	1.50	6.50
	1939	—	—	—	Proof	225.00
	1940	20.875	BV	.75	1.50	6.50
	1940	—	—	—	Proof	275.00
	1941	23.087	BV	.75	1.50	6.50
	1941	—	—	—	Proof	275.00
	1942	44.943	BV	.75	1.50	5.00
	1943	46.927	—	BV	1.00	5.00
	1943	—	—	—	Proof	200.00
	1944	36.953	—	BV	1.00	4.00
	1944	—	—	—	Proof	200.00
	1945	39.939	—	BV	1.00	4.00
	1945	—	—	—	Proof	200.00
	1946	43.466	—	BV	1.00	4.00
	1946	—	—	—	Proof	200.00

COPPER-NICKEL

862	1947	29.993	—	.20	.75	5.00
	1947	—	—	—	Proof	250.00
	1948	88.324	—	.20	.75	5.00
	1948	—	—	—	Proof	250.00

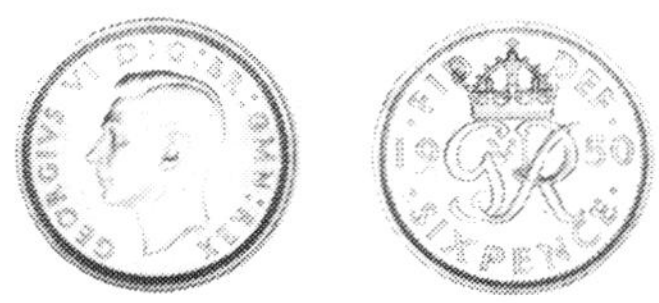

Rev. leg: W/o IND IMP.

KM#	Date	Mintage	Fine	VF	XF	Unc
875	1949	41.336	—	.20	.75	6.00
	1949	—	—	—	Proof	225.00
	1950	32.742	—	.20	.75	6.00
	1950	.018	—	—	Proof	7.00
	1951	40.399	—	.20	.75	6.00
	1951	.020	—	—	Proof	7.00
	1952	1.013	1.25	2.75	12.50	45.00
	1952	—	—	—	Proof	225.00

889	1953	70.324	—	.15	.50	1.50
	1953	.040	—	—	Proof	3.50

Obv. leg: W/o BRITT OMN.

903	1954	105.241	—	.15	.60	4.00
	1954	—	—	—	Proof	150.00
	1955	109.930	—	.15	.30	2.00
	1955	—	—	—	Proof	150.00
	1956	109.842	—	.15	.30	2.00
	1956	—	—	—	Proof	—
	1957	105.654	—	.15	.30	1.50
	1957	—	—	—	Proof	150.00
	1958	123.519	—	.15	.60	4.00
	1958	—	—	—	Proof	150.00
	1959	93.089	—	.15	.30	1.00
	1959	—	—	—	Proof	150.00
	1960	103.283	—	.15	.35	3.50
	1960	—	—	—	Proof	150.00
	1961	115.052	—	.15	.35	2.75
	1961	—	—	—	Proof	150.00
	1962	166.484	—	.15	.25	1.00
	1962	—	—	—	Proof	150.00
	1963	120.056	—	.15	.25	.60
	1963	—	—	—	Proof	150.00
	1964	152.336	—	.15	.25	.50
	1964	—	—	—	Proof	150.00
	1965	129.644	—	.10	.20	.40
	1966	175.676	—	.10	.20	.40
	1967	240.788	—	.10	.20	.40
	1970	.750	—	—	Proof	2.00

SHILLING

5.6552 g, .925 SILVER, .1682 oz ASW

780	1901	3.426	3.00	7.00	20.00	55.00

NOTE: Earlier dates (1893-1900) exist for this type.

800	1902	7.890	2.50	7.00	20.00	55.00
	1902	.015	—		Matte Proof	60.00
	1903	2.062	5.50	15.00	60.00	110.00
	1904	2.040	5.50	15.00	60.00	115.00
	1905	.488	32.50	80.00	350.00	900.00
	1906	10.791	2.75	8.00	25.00	60.00
	1907	14.083	3.00	10.00	30.00	70.00
	1908	3.807	9.00	20.00	65.00	150.00
	1909	5.665	5.50	15.00	65.00	130.00
	1910	26.547	2.25	7.00	20.00	55.00

KM#	Date	Mintage	Fine	VF	XF	Unc
816	1911	20.066	2.00	3.00	12.50	35.00
	1911	6,007	—	—	Proof	65.00
	1912	15.594	2.00	3.50	16.50	55.00
	1913	9.002	3.00	6.00	30.00	75.00
	1914	23.416	2.00	2.50	7.00	30.00
	1915	39.279	2.00	2.50	7.00	30.00
	1916	35.862	2.00	2.50	7.00	30.00
	1917	22.203	2.00	2.50	12.50	35.00
	1918	34.916	2.00	2.50	7.00	30.00
	1919	10.824	2.25	3.50	15.00	37.50

5.6552 g, .500 SILVER, .0909 oz ASW

KM#	Date	Mintage	Fine	VF	XF	Unc
816a	1920	22.825	BV	2.50	14.00	35.00
	1921	22.649	BV	2.50	26.00	50.00
	1922	27.216	BV	3.00	15.00	42.50
	1923	14.575	BV	2.50	12.00	42.50
	1924	9.250	BV	2.50	26.00	50.00
	1925	5.419	2.50	7.50	30.00	70.00
	1926	22.516	BV	5.00	12.00	45.00

Obv: Modified effigy, slightly smaller bust.

KM#	Date	Mintage	Fine	VF	XF	Unc
829	1926	Inc. Ab.	BV	2.00	15.00	40.00
	1927	9.262	BV	2.00	22.50	45.00

Rev: Larger lion and crown.

KM#	Date	Mintage	Fine	VF	XF	Unc
833	1927	Inc. Ab.	BV	2.00	15.00	40.00
	1927	*—	—	Matte	Proof	—
	1927	.015	—	—	Proof	45.00
	1928	18.137	—	BV	8.00	18.00
	1928	—	—	—	Proof	425.00
	1929	19.343	—	BV	6.00	18.00
	1929	—	—	—	Proof	—
	1930	3.137	1.50	3.50	23.00	50.00
	1930	—	—	—	Proof	500.00
	1931	6.994	BV	2.00	7.00	18.00
	1931	—	—	—	Proof	425.00
	1932	12.168	BV	2.00	7.00	18.00
	1932	—	—	—	Proof	425.00
	1933	11.512	BV	2.00	6.00	18.00
	1933	—	—	—	Proof	425.00
	1934	6.138	BV	3.00	12.00	40.00
	1934	—	—	—	Proof	425.00
	1935	9.183	—	BV	8.00	18.00
	1935	—	—	—	Proof	400.00
	1936	11.911	—	BV	7.25	15.00
	1936	—	—	—	Proof	400.00

***NOTE:** There are reportedly 1-2 of this variety, struck specifically for use in photographs.

Rev: English crest.

KM#	Date	Mintage	Fine	VF	XF	Unc
853	1937	8.359	—	BV	2.00	7.50
	1937	.026	—	—	Proof	11.00
	1938	4.833	—	BV	3.00	20.00
	1938	—	—	—	Proof	400.00
	1939	11.053	—	BV	2.00	7.00
	1939	—	—	—	Proof	400.00
	1940	11.099	—	BV	2.00	7.00
	1940	—	—	—	Proof	—
	1941	11.392	—	BV	2.00	7.00
	1941	—	—	—	Proof	—
	1942	17.454	—	BV	2.00	5.00
	1943	11.404	—	BV	2.00	5.00
	1944	11.587	—	BV	2.00	5.00
	1945	15.143	—	BV	2.00	5.00
	1945	—	—	—	Proof	—
	1946	18.664	—	BV	1.50	4.00
	1946	—	—	—	Proof	—

Rev: Scottish crest.

KM#	Date	Mintage	Fine	VF	XF	Unc
854	1937	6.749	—	BV	2.00	7.50
	1937	.026	—	—	Proof	9.00
	1938	4.798	—	BV	4.00	18.00
	1938	—	—	—	Proof	400.00
	1939	10.264	—	BV	2.50	7.00
	1939	—	—	—	Proof	400.00
	1940	9.913	—	BV	2.50	7.00
	1940	—	—	—	Proof	—
	1941	8.086	—	BV	3.00	15.00
	1941	—	—	—	Proof	—
	1942	13.677	—	BV	2.50	7.00
	1943	9.824	—	BV	2.50	7.00
	1944	10.990	—	BV	2.50	9.00
	1945	15.106	—	BV	2.00	5.00
	1945	—	—	—	Proof	—
	1946	16.382	—	BV	2.00	5.00
	1946	—	—	—	Proof	—

COPPER-NICKEL
Rev: English crest.

KM#	Date	Mintage	Fine	VF	XF	Unc
863	1947	12.121	.10	.25	1.00	7.00
	1947	—	—	—	Proof	400.00
	1948	45.577	.10	.20	.50	5.00
	1948	—	—	—	Proof	200.00

Rev: Scottish crest.

KM#	Date	Mintage	Fine	VF	XF	Unc
864	1947	12.283	.10	.25	1.00	7.00
	1947	—	—	—	Proof	—
	1948	45.352	.10	.20	.50	5.00
	1948	—	—	—	Proof	200.00

Rev: English crest, leg: W/o IND IMP.

KM#	Date	Mintage	Fine	VF	XF	Unc
876	1949	19.328	.10	.25	1.25	7.50
	1949	—	—	—	Proof	—
	1950	19.244	.10	.25	1.50	8.50
	1950	.018	—	—	Proof	10.00
	1951	9.957	.10	.25	1.50	8.50
	1951	.020	—	—	Proof	10.00

Rev: Scottish crest.

KM#	Date	Mintage	Fine	VF	XF	Unc
877	1949	21.243	.10	.25	1.25	7.50
	1949	—	—	—	Proof	—
	1950	14.300	.10	.25	1.50	9.00
	1950	.018	—	—	Proof	10.00
	1951	10.961	.10	.25	1.50	9.00
	1951	.020	—	—	Proof	10.00

Rev: English arms.

KM#	Date	Mintage	Fine	VF	XF	Unc
890	1953	41.943	—	.15	.35	2.25
	1953	.040	—	—	Proof	7.50

Rev: Scottish arms.

KM#	Date	Mintage	Fine	VF	XF	Unc
891	1953	20.664	—	.15	.35	2.25
	1953	.040	—	—	Proof	7.50

Obv. leg: W/o BRITT OMN. Rev: English arms.

KM#	Date	Mintage	Fine	VF	XF	Unc
904	1954	30.162	—	.15	.35	2.25
	1954	—	—	—	Proof	200.00
	1955	45.260	—	.15	.35	2.25
	1955	—	—	—	Proof	—
	1956	44.970	—	.15	.50	6.00
	1956	—	—	—	Proof	—
	1957	42.774	—	.15	.35	2.00
	1957	—	—	—	Proof	—
	1958	14.392	.25	.75	2.50	18.50
	1958	—	—	—	Proof	—
	1959	19.443	—	.15	.35	2.00
	1959	—	—	—	Proof	—
	1960	27.028	—	.15	.35	2.00
	1960	—	—	—	Proof	—
	1961	39.817	—	.15	.35	2.00
	1961	—	—	—	Proof	—
	1962	36.704	—	.15	.25	1.50
	1962	—	—	—	Proof	—
	1963	49.434	—	—	.25	.60
	1963	—	—	—	Proof	—
	1964	8.591	—	—	.25	.85
	1964	—	—	—	Proof	—
	1965	9.216	—	—	.25	.85
	1966	15.002	—	—	.25	.85
	1970	.750	—	—	Proof	4.00

Rev: Scottish arms.

KM#	Date	Mintage	Fine	VF	XF	Unc
905	1954	26.772	—	.15	.35	2.25
	1954	—	—	—	Proof	150.00
	1955	27.951	—	.15	.35	2.75
	1955	—	—	—	Proof	—
	1956	42.854	—	.15	1.00	12.00
	1956	—	—	—	Proof	—
	1957	17.960	—	.15	1.75	18.50
	1957	—	—	—	Proof	—
	1958	40.823	—	.15	.35	2.25
	1958	—	—	—	Proof	—
	1959	1.013	1.00	3.00	6.00	25.00
	1959	—	—	—	Proof	—
	1960	14.376	—	.15	.50	2.50
	1960	—	—	—	Proof	—
	1961	2.763	.25	.50	1.25	7.00
	1961	—	—	—	Proof	—
	1962	17.475	—	.15	.25	1.50
	1962	—	—	—	Proof	—
	1963	32.300	—	.15	.25	.75
	1963	—	—	—	Proof	—
	1964	5.239	—	.15	.25	1.50
	1965	2.774	—	.15	.25	1.50
	1966	15.604	—	.15	.25	.85
	1970	.750	—	—	Proof	2.75

FLORIN - TWO SHILLINGS

11.3104 g, .925 SILVER, .3364 oz ASW

KM#	Date	Mintage	Fine	VF	XF	Unc
781	1901	2.649	6.50	12.50	25.00	70.00

NOTE: Earlier dates (1893-1900) exist for this type.

KM#	Date	Mintage	Fine	VF	XF	Unc
801	1902	2.190	7.50	15.00	30.00	70.00
	1902	.015	—	Matte Proof		75.00
	1903	.995	10.00	30.00	65.00	140.00
	1904	2.770	10.00	40.00	100.00	200.00
	1905	1.188	25.00	75.00	175.00	475.00
	1906	6.910	8.00	25.00	55.00	130.00
	1907	5.948	8.00	25.00	70.00	175.00
	1908	3.280	9.00	27.50	110.00	240.00
	1909	3.483	10.00	37.50	125.00	275.00
	1910	5.651	6.00	14.00	40.00	90.00

KM#	Date	Mintage	Fine	VF	XF	Unc
817	1911	5.951	4.00	7.50	30.00	65.00
	1911	6.007	—	—	Proof	85.00
	1912	8.572	4.50	9.00	45.00	95.00
	1913	4.545	6.00	12.00	50.00	110.00
	1914	21.253	3.00	5.00	15.00	45.00
	1915	12.358	3.00	4.00	15.00	45.00
	1916	21.064	3.00	4.00	15.00	45.00
	1917	11.182	3.00	6.00	15.50	65.00
	1918	29.212	3.00	4.00	15.00	45.00
	1919	9.469	3.50	5.00	22.50	50.00

11.3104 g, .500 SILVER, .1818 oz ASW

KM#	Date	Mintage	Fine	VF	XF	Unc
817a	1920	15.388	1.75	4.50	22.50	50.00
	1921	34.864	1.75	3.00	16.50	40.00
	1922	23.861	1.75	3.00	14.00	50.00
	1923	21.547	1.75	3.00	13.50	40.00
	1924	4.582	2.50	6.00	26.00	65.00
	1925	1.404	10.00	21.50	95.00	185.00
	1926	5.125	3.50	8.00	30.00	80.00

KM#	Date	Mintage	Fine	VF	XF	Unc
834	1927	.015	—	—	Proof	60.00
	1927	*—	—	Matte Proof		—
	1928	11.088	1.50	2.50	6.00	25.00
	1928	—	—	—	Proof	—
	1929	16.397	1.50	2.50	6.00	25.00
	1929	—	—	—	Proof	—
	1930	5.734	1.75	3.00	14.00	37.50
	1930	—	—	—	Proof	—
	1931	6.556	1.75	3.00	8.00	35.00
	1931	—	—	—	Proof	300.00
	1932	.717	12.50	25.00	85.00	225.00
	1932	—	—	—	Proof	1750.
	1933	8.685	1.50	2.50	8.00	25.00
	1933	—	—	—	Proof	300.00
	1935	7.541	1.50	2.50	6.00	22.50
	1935	—	—	—	Proof	300.00
	1936	9.897	1.50	2.25	7.75	22.50
	1936	—	—	—	Proof	300.00

*NOTE: There are reportedly 1-2 known of this variety, struck specifically for use in photographs.

KM#	Date	Mintage	Fine	VF	XF	Unc
855	1937	13.007	—	BV	2.50	7.50
	1937	.026	—	—	Proof	15.00
	1938	7.909	BV	2.25	5.00	16.50
	1938	—	—	—	Proof	200.00
	1939	20.851	—	BV	2.50	6.50
	1939	—	—	—	Proof	200.00

KM#	Date	Mintage	Fine	VF	XF	Unc
855	1940	18.700	—	BV	2.50	6.50
	1940	—	—	—	Proof	—
	1941	24.451	—	BV	2.50	6.50
	1941	—	—	—	Proof	—
	1942	39.895	—	BV	2.50	6.50
	1942	—	—	—	Proof	250.00
	1943	26.712	—	BV	2.25	6.00
	1944	27.560	—	BV	2.25	6.00
	1944	—	—	—	Proof	—
	1945	25.858	—	BV	2.25	6.00
	1945	—	—	—	Proof	—
	1946	22.300	—	BV	2.25	6.00
	1946	—	—	—	Proof	—

COPPER-NICKEL

KM#	Date	Mintage	Fine	VF	XF	Unc
865	1947	22.910	.20	.35	1.00	4.00
	1947	—	—	—	Proof	—
	1948	67.554	.20	.35	.65	3.00
	1948	—	—	—	Proof	175.00

Rev. leg: W/o IND IMP.

KM#	Date	Mintage	Fine	VF	XF	Unc
878	1949	28.615	.20	.35	1.50	9.00
	1949	—	—	—	Proof	—
	1950	24.357	.20	.35	1.50	9.00
	1950	.018	—	—	Proof	12.00
	1951	27.412	.20	.35	1.50	6.00
	1951	.020	—	—	Proof	14.00

KM#	Date	Mintage	Fine	VF	XF	Unc
892	1953	11.959	.20	.30	.60	4.00
	1953	.040	—	—	Proof	8.00

Obv. leg: W/o BRITT OMN.

KM#	Date	Mintage	Fine	VF	XF	Unc
906	1954	13.085	.20	.50	3.50	27.50
	1954	—	—	—	Proof	250.00
	1955	25.887	.20	.30	.50	3.75
	1955	—	—	—	Proof	—
	1956	47.824	.20	.30	.50	3.50
	1956	—	—	—	Proof	200.00
	1957	33.071	.20	.40	2.50	25.00
	1957	—	—	—	Proof	—
	1958	9.565	.25	.50	1.50	9.00
	1958	—	—	—	Proof	325.00
	1959	14.080	.25	.50	3.50	30.00
	1959	—	—	—	Proof	—
	1960	13.832	—	—	.20	3.00
	1960	—	—	—	Proof	—
	1961	37.735	—	—	.20	.45	4.00
	1961	—	—	—	Proof	—
	1962	35.148	—	—	.20	.35	2.50
	1962	—	—	—	Proof	—
	1963	26.471	—	—	.20	.30	2.00
	1963	—	—	—	Proof	—
	1964	16.539	—	—	.20	.30	2.00
	1965	48.163	—	—	.20	.30	1.50
	1966	83.999	—	—	.20	.30	1.50
	1967	39.718	—	—	.20	.30	1.50
	1970	.750	—	—	—	Proof	4.00

1/2 CROWN

14.1380 g, .925 SILVER, .4205 oz ASW

KM#	Date	Mintage	Fine	VF	XF	Unc
782	1901	1.577	5.25	13.00	35.00	85.00

NOTE: Earlier dates (1893-1900) exist for this type.

KM#	Date	Mintage	Fine	VF	XF	Unc
802	1902	1.316	10.00	20.00	40.00	90.00
	1902	.015	—	Matte Proof		100.00
	1903	.275	30.00	80.00	300.00	850.00
	1904	.710	22.00	60.00	215.00	460.00
	1905	.166	100.00	300.00	1000.	1750.
	1906	2.886	9.00	25.00	90.00	185.00
	1907	3.694	10.00	30.00	70.00	200.00
	1908	1.759	12.00	30.00	125.00	225.00
	1909	3.052	10.00	22.50	100.00	185.00
	1910	2.558	8.50	20.00	70.00	145.00

KM#	Date	Mintage	Fine	VF	XF	Unc
818.1	1911	2.915	5.00	12.00	40.00	120.00
	1911	6.007	—	—	Proof	130.00
	1912	4.701	5.00	12.00	40.00	100.00
	1913	4.090	6.50	15.00	50.00	140.00
	1914	18.333	4.00	7.00	12.50	50.00
	1915	32.433	4.00	6.00	12.50	45.00
	1916	29.530	4.00	6.00	12.50	45.00
	1917	11.172	4.50	7.00	20.00	60.00
	1918	29.080	4.00	6.00	12.50	45.00
	1919	10.267	4.50	8.00	22.50	65.00

14.1380 g, .500 SILVER, .2273 oz ASW
Rev: Crown touches shield.

KM#	Date	Mintage	Fine	VF	XF	Unc
818.1a	1920	17.983	2.25	5.00	17.50	75.00
	1921	23.678	2.25	5.00	22.50	85.00
	1922	16.397	2.25	5.00	22.50	85.00

Rev: Groove between crown and shield.

KM#	Date	Mintage	Fine	VF	XF	Unc
818.2	1922	Inc. Ab.	2.50	5.00	17.50	65.00
	1923	26.309	2.00	4.50	12.50	40.00
	1924	5.866	3.00	7.50	37.50	70.00
	1925	1.413	12.50	30.00	150.00	400.00
	1926	4.474	3.00	10.00	40.00	95.00

Obv: Modified effigy; larger beads.

KM#	Date	Mintage	Fine	VF	XF	Unc
830	1926	Inc. Ab.	3.00	10.00	50.00	135.00
	1927	6.838	2.50	6.00	15.50	55.00

KM#	Date	Mintage	Fine	VF	XF	Unc
835	1927	.015	—	—	Proof	45.00
	1927	*—	—	Matte Proof		—
	1928	18.763	2.00	3.00	7.50	30.00
	1928	—	—	—	Proof	—
	1929	17.633	2.00	3.00	7.50	30.00
	1929	—	—	—	Proof	—
	1930	.810	10.00	25.00	130.00	275.00
	1930	—	—	—	Proof	1000.
	1931	11.264	2.00	4.00	8.00	30.00

KM#	Date	Mintage	Fine	VF	XF	Unc
835	1931	—	—	—	Proof	600.00
	1932	4.794	3.50	8.00	17.50	50.00
	1932	—	—	—	Proof	600.00
	1933	10.311	2.00	4.00	8.00	30.00
	1933	—	—	—	Proof	600.00
	1934	2.422	3.25	7.00	25.00	85.00
	1934	—	—	—	Proof	600.00
	1935	7.022	2.00	3.00	6.50	28.00
	1935	—	—	—	Proof	600.00
	1936	7.039	2.00	3.00	6.00	25.00
	1936	—	—	—	Proof	600.00

*NOTE: There are reportedly 1-2 known of this variety, struck specifically for use in photographs.

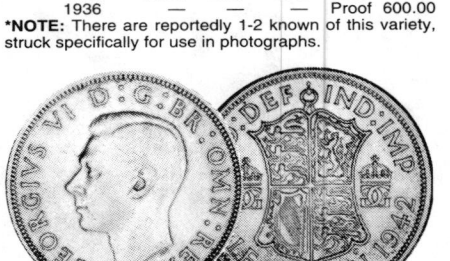

KM#	Date	Mintage	Fine	VF	XF	Unc
856	1937	9.106	BV	2.00	3.50	12.00
	1937	.026	—	—	Proof	16.00
	1938	6.426	BV	2.50	7.50	30.00
	1938	—	—	—	Proof	400.00
	1939	15.479	BV	2.00	3.50	12.00
	1939	—	—	—	Proof	400.00
	1940	17.948	BV	2.00	3.00	10.00
	1940	—	—	—	Proof	—
	1941	15.774	BV	1.75	2.75	8.00
	1941	—	—	—	Proof	—
	1942	31.220	BV	1.75	2.75	8.00
	1943	15.463	BV	1.75	2.75	8.00
	1943	—	—	—	Proof	—
	1944	15.255	BV	1.75	2.75	8.00
	1945	19.849	BV	1.50	2.50	6.50
	1945	—	—	—	Proof	—
	1946	22.725	BV	1.50	2.50	6.50
	1946	—	—	—	Proof	—

COPPER-NICKEL

KM#	Date	Mintage	Fine	VF	XF	Unc
866	1947	21.910	.25	.50	1.25	5.00
	1947	—	—	—	Proof	400.00
	1948	71.165	.25	.50	1.25	5.00
	1948	—	—	—	Proof	350.00

Rev. leg: W/o IND IMP.

KM#	Date	Mintage	Fine	VF	XF	Unc
879	1949	28.273	.25	.50	1.25	8.00
	1949	—	—	—	Proof	—
	1950	28.336	.25	.50	1.50	8.00
	1950	.018	—	—	Proof	12.00
	1951	9.004	.50	.75	1.50	8.00
	1951	.020	—	—	Proof	12.00
	1952	1 known	—	11,000.	—	—

KM#	Date	Mintage	Fine	VF	XF	Unc
893	1953	4.333	.50	.75	1.50	4.50
	1953	.040	—	—	Proof	12.00

Obv. leg: W/o BRITT OMN.

KM#	Date	Mintage	Fine	VF	XF	Unc
907	1954	11.615	.50	1.00	5.00	25.00
	1954	—	—	—	Proof	400.00
	1955	23.629	.25	.50	1.00	6.00
	1955	—	—	—	Proof	—
	1956	33.935	.25	.50	1.00	6.00
	1956	—	—	—	Proof	—
	1957	34.201	.25	.50	.75	4.50
	1957	—	—	—	Proof	—
	1958	15.746	.25	.75	4.00	15.00
	1958	—	—	—	Proof	—
	1959	9.029	1.00	1.50	6.50	30.00
	1959	—	—	—	Proof	—
	1960	19.929	.25	.50	.75	6.00
	1960	—	—	—	Proof	—
	1961	25.888	.25	.50	.75	2.50
	1961	—	—	—	P/L	10.00
	1961	—	—	—	Proof	—
	1962	24.013	.25	.50	.75	2.50
	1962	—	—	—	Proof	—
	1963	17.625	.25	.50	.75	2.50
	1963	—	—	—	Proof	—
	1964	5.974	.25	.50	.75	3.50
	1965	9.778	.20	.30	.50	2.00
	1966	13.375	.20	.30	.50	1.50
	1967	33.058	.20	.30	.50	1.50
	1970	.750	—	—	Proof	4.00

CROWN

28.2759 g, .925 SILVER, .8409 oz ASW

KM#	Date	Mintage	Fine	VF	XF	Unc
803	1902	.256	25.00	45.00	85.00	180.00
	1902	.015	—	Matte Proof		200.00

28.2759 g, .500 SILVER, .4546 oz ASW

KM#	Date	Mintage	Fine	VF	XF	Unc
836	1927	.015	—	—	Proof	150.00
	1927	*—	—	Matte Proof		—
	1928	9.034	60.00	95.00	135.00	260.00
	1928	—	—	—	Proof	1200.
	1929	4.994	65.00	100.00	145.00	285.00
	1929	—	—	—	Proof	1500.
	1930	4.847	65.00	100.00	145.00	285.00
	1930	—	—	—	Proof	1500.

KM#	Date	Mintage	Fine	VF	XF	Unc
836	1931	4,056	70.00	110.00	155.00	325.00
	1931	—	—	—	Proof	—
	1932	2,395	85.00	175.00	250.00	550.00
	1932	—	—	—	Proof	2500.
	1933	7,132	65.00	100.00	145.00	285.00
	1933	—	—	—	Proof	—
	1934	932 pcs.	450.00	750.00	1500.	2500.
	1934	—	—	—	Proof	3200.
	1936	2,473	90.00	180.00	250.00	500.00
	1936	—	—	—	Proof	1500.

*NOTE: There are reportedly 1-2 known of this variety, struck specifically for use in photographs.

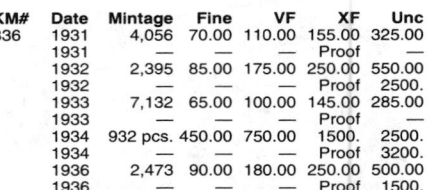

George V Silver Jubilee

KM#	Date	Mintage	Fine	VF	XF	Unc
842	1935 incused edge lettering	.715	6.00	8.00	12.50	30.00
	1935 specimen in box of issue	—	—	—	—	75.00
	1935 (error) edge lettering: MEN.ANNO-REGNI XXV. Inc. Ab.	—	—	Proof		900.00

.925 SILVER

KM#	Date	Mintage	Fine	VF	XF	Unc
842a	1935 raised edge lettering	2,500	—	—	Proof	450.00

47.8300 g, .917 GOLD, 1.4096 oz AGW

KM#	Date	Mintage	Fine	VF	XF	Unc
842b	1935	28 pcs.	—	—	Proof	—

.925 SILVER

KM#	Date	Mintage	Fine	VF	XF	Unc
857	1937	.419	8.00	12.00	18.50	35.00
	1937	.026	—	—	Proof	65.00
	1937	—	—	—	V.I.P. Proof	350.00

COPPER-NICKEL
Festival of Britain

KM#	Date	Mintage	Fine	VF	XF	Unc
880	1951	2.004	—	—	P/L	10.00
	1951		—	—	Proof	25.00
	1951	30-50 pcs.	—	V.I.P. Proof		300.00

Coronation of Queen Elizabeth II

894	1953	5.963	—	—		6.00	9.00
	1953	.040	—	—	Proof		25.00
	1953	20-30 pcs.	—	V.I.P. Proof			300.00

British Exhibition in New York

909	1960	1.024	—	—		6.50	9.50
	1960	.070	—	—	P/L		22.00
	1960	30-50 pcs.	—	V.I.P. Proof			300.00

Winston Churchill

910	1965	9.640	—	—	.65	1.00
	1965	—	—	Specimen		325.00

NOTE: The Specimen is struck with satin-finish.

GOLD SERIES
1/2 SOVEREIGN
MINT MARKS

C - Ottawa, Canada
I - Bombay, India
M - Melbourne, Australia
P - Perth, Australia
S - Sydney, Australia

SA - Pretoria, South Africa

NOTE: 1/2 Sovereigns were struck at various foreign mints. The mint mark on the St. George/dragon type is usually found on the base below the right rear hoof of the horse. On shield type reverse the mint mark is found below the shield. Refer to appropriate country listings elsewhere in this catalog for coins having mint marks.

3.9940 g, .917 GOLD, .1177 oz AGW

KM#	Date	Mintage	Fine	VF	XF	Unc
784	1901	2.038	BV	60.00	75.00	125.00

NOTE: Earlier dates (1893-1900) exist for this type.

804	1902	4.244	BV	60.00	75.00	100.00
	1902	.015	—	—	Proof	225.00
	1903	2.522	BV	60.00	70.00	100.00
	1904	1.717	BV	60.00	70.00	100.00
	1905	3.024	BV	60.00	70.00	100.00
	1906	4.245	BV	60.00	70.00	100.00
	1907	4.233	BV	60.00	70.00	100.00
	1908	3.997	BV	60.00	70.00	100.00
	1909	4.011	BV	60.00	70.00	100.00
	1910	5.024	BV	60.00	70.00	100.00

819	1911	6.104	BV	60.00	70.00	100.00
	1911	3,764	—	—	Proof	325.00
	1912	6.224	BV	60.00	70.00	100.00
	1913	6.094	BV	60.00	70.00	100.00
	1914	7.251	BV	60.00	70.00	100.00
	1915	2.043	BV	60.00	70.00	100.00

SOVEREIGN
MINT MARKS

C - Ottawa, Canada
I - Bombay, India
M - Melbourne, Australia
P - Perth, Australia
S - Sydney, Australia
SA - Pretoria, South Africa

NOTE: Sovereigns were struck at various colonial mints. The mint mark on the St. George/dragon type is usually found on the base below the right rear hoof of the horse. On shield type reverse the mint mark is found below the shield or on the obverse below the truncation. Refer to appropriate country listings elsewhere in this catalog for coins having these mint marks.

7.9881 g, .917 GOLD, .2354 oz AGW

785	1901	1.579	—	—	BV	130.00

NOTE: Earlier dates (1893-1900) exist for this type.

805	1902	4.738	—	—	BV	120.00
	1902	.015	—	—	Proof	275.00
	1903	8.889	—	—	BV	120.00
	1904	10.041	—	—	BV	120.00
	1905	5.910	—	—	BV	120.00
	1906	10.467	—	—	BV	120.00
	1907	18.459	—	—	BV	120.00
	1908	11.729	—	—	BV	120.00
	1909	12.157	—	—	BV	120.00
	1910	22.380	—	—	BV	120.00

KM#	Date	Mintage	Fine	VF	XF	Unc
820	1911	30.044	—	—	BV	120.00
	1911	3,764	—	—	Proof	500.00
	1912	30.318	—	—	BV	120.00
	1913	24.540	—	—	BV	120.00
	1914	11.501	—	—	BV	120.00
	1915	20.295	—	—	BV	120.00
	1916	1.554	—	—	BV	115.00	135.00
	1917	1.015	2850.	3175.	6375.	12,500.
	1925	4.406	—	—	BV	120.00

859	1937	5,500	—	—	Proof	650.00
	1937	1 pc.	—	Matte Proof		Unique

908	1957	2.072	—	—	BV	120.00
	1957	—	—	—	Proof	—
	1958	8.700	—	—	BV	115.00
	1958	—	—	—	Proof	
	1959	1.358	—	—	BV	115.00
	1959	—	—	—	Proof	
	1962	3.000	—	—	BV	115.00
	1962	—	—	—	Proof	
	1963	7.400	—	—	BV	115.00
	1963	—	—	—	Proof	
	1964	3.000	—	—	BV	115.00
	1965	3.800	—	—	BV	115.00
	1966	7.050	—	—	BV	115.00
	1967	5.000	—	—	BV	115.00
	1968	4.203	—	—	BV	115.00

919	1974	5.003	—	—	BV	115.00
	1976	4.150	—	—	BV	115.00
	1978	6.350	—	—	BV	115.00
	1979	9.100	—	—	BV	115.00
	1979	.050	—	—	Proof	120.00
	1980	5.100	—	—	BV	115.00
	1980	.091	—	—	Proof	120.00
	1981	5.000	—	—	BV	115.00
	1981	.033	—	—	Proof	120.00
	1982	2.950	—	—	BV	115.00
	1982	.023	—	—	Proof	125.00
	1983	.021	—	—	Proof	125.00
	1984	.020	—	—	Proof	125.00

2 POUNDS

15.9761 g, .917 GOLD, .4708 oz AGW

806	1902	.046	250.00	300.00	475.00	575.00
	1902	8,066	—	—	Proof	650.00

NOTE: Proof issues with mint mark S below right rear hoof of horse were struck at Sydney, refer to Australia listings.

5 POUNDS

39.9403 g, .917 GOLD, 1.1773 oz AGW

KM#	Date	Mintage	Fine	VF	XF	Unc
807	1902	*.035	625.00	700.00	850.00	1100.
	1902	8,066	—	—	Proof	1250.

NOTE: Proof issues with mint mark S below right rear hoof of horse were struck at Sydney, refer to Australia listings.

*NOTE: 27,000 pieces were remelted.

DECIMAL COINAGE

1971-1981
100 New Pence = 1 Pound
1982—
100 Pence = 1 Pound

1/2 NEW PENNY

BRONZE

KM#	Date	Mintage	Fine	VF	XF	Unc
914	1971	1,394.188	—	—	.10	.20
	1971	.350	—	—	Proof	1.00
	1972	.150	—	—	Proof	3.00
	1973	365.680	—	—	.15	.40
	1973	.100	—	—	Proof	1.00
	1974	365.448	—	—	.15	.35
	1974	.100	—	—	Proof	1.00
	1975	197.600	—	—	.15	.45
	1975	.100	—	—	Proof	1.00
	1976	412.172	—	—	.15	.35
	1976	.100	—	—	Proof	1.00
	1977	66.368	—	—	.15	.25
	1977	.194	—	—	Proof	1.00
	1978	59.532	—	—	.15	.25
	1978	.088	—	—	Proof	1.00
	1979	219.132	—	—	.15	.25
	1979	.081	—	—	Proof	1.00
	1980	202.788	—	—	.15	.25
	1980	.143	—	—	Proof	1.00
	1981	32.484	—	—	.15	.45
	1981	.100	—	—	Proof	1.00

1/2 PENNY

BRONZE
Rev: HALF PENNY above crown and fraction.

KM#	Date	Mintage	Fine	VF	XF	Unc
926	1982	190.752	—	—	.15	.25
	1982	.107	—	—	Proof	1.00
	1983	7.600	—	—	.25	.60
	1983	.108	—	—	Proof	1.50
	1984	*.159	—	—	—	2.00
	1984	.107	—	—	Proof	2.50

*NOTE: Issued in sets only.
NOTE: Above denomination now demonetized.

NEW PENNY

BRONZE

KM#	Date	Mintage	Fine	VF	XF	Unc
915	1971	1,521.666	—	—	.15	.25
	1971	.350	—	—	Proof	1.25
	1972	.150	—	—	Proof	3.00
	1973	280.196	—	—	.15	.60
	1973	.100	—	—	Proof	1.25
	1974	330.892	—	—	.15	.60
	1974	.100	—	—	Proof	1.25
	1975	221.604	—	—	.15	.60
	1975	.100	—	—	Proof	1.25
	1976	241.800	—	—	.15	.30

KM#	Date	Mintage	Fine	VF	XF	Unc
915	1976	.100	—	—	Proof	1.25
	1977	285.430	—	—	.15	.30
	1977	.194	—	—	Proof	1.25
	1978	292.770	—	—	.15	.65
	1978	.088	—	—	Proof	1.25
	1979	459.000	—	—	.15	.25
	1979	.081	—	—	Proof	1.25
	1980	416.304	—	—	.15	.25
	1980	.143	—	—	Proof	1.25
	1981	301.800	—	—	.15	.25
	1981	.100	—	—	Proof	1.25

PENNY

BRONZE

KM#	Date	Mintage	Fine	VF	XF	Unc
927	1982	121.429	—	—	.15	.25
	1982	.107	—	—	Proof	1.25
	1983	243.002	—	—	.15	.40
	1983	.108	—	—	Proof	1.25
	1984	154.760	—	—	.15	.75
	1984	.107	—	—	Proof	1.25

KM#	Date	Mintage	Fine	VF	XF	Unc
935	1985	200.605	—	—	.15	.35
	1985	.102	—	—	Proof	1.25
	1986	369.989	—	—	.15	.35
	1986	.125	—	—	Proof	1.25
	1987	499.946	—	—	.15	.25
	1987	.089	—	—	Proof	1.25
	1988	793.492	—	—	.15	.25
	1988	.125	—	—	Proof	1.25
	1989	658.142	—	—	.15	.25
	1989	.100	—	—	Proof	1.25
	1990	529.048	—	—	.15	.25
	1990	.100	—	—	Proof	1.25
	1991	206.458	—	—	.15	.25
	1991	—	—	—	Proof	1.25
	1992	—	—	—	—	.50
	1992	—	—	—	—	1.75

*NOTE: Issued in sets only.

COPPER PLATED STEEL

KM#	Date	Mintage	Fine	VF	XF	Unc
935a	1992	253.867	—	—	.15	.25
	1993	602.590	—	—	.15	.25
	1993	—	—	—	Proof	1.25
	1994	843.834	—	—	.15	.25
	1994	—	—	—	Proof	1.25
	1995	303.314	—	—	.15	.25
	1995	—	—	—	Proof	1.25
	1996	—	—	—	—	.25
	1996	723.840	—	—	Proof	1.25
	1997	—	—	—	—	.25
	1997	372.174	—	—	Proof	1.25

Obv: Rank-Bradley effigy of Queen Elizabeth II.
Rev: Crowned portcullis.

KM#	Date	Mintage	Fine	VF	XF	Unc
986	1998	—	—	—	—	.20
	1998	*.100	—	—	Proof	1.25

2 NEW PENCE

BRONZE

KM#	Date	Mintage	Fine	VF	XF	Unc
916	1971	1,454.856	—	—	.10	.20
	1971	.350	—	—	Proof	1.50
	1972	.150	—	—	Proof	3.50
	1973	.100	—	—	Proof	3.50
	1974	.100	—	—	Proof	3.50
	1975	145.545	—	—	.15	.40
	1975	.100	—	—	Proof	1.50
	1976	181.379	—	—	.15	.30
	1976	.100	—	—	Proof	1.50
	1977	109.281	—	—	.15	.30
	1977	.194	—	—	Proof	1.50
	1978	189.658	—	—	.15	.40
	1978	.088	—	—	Proof	1.50
	1979	268.300	—	—	.15	.25
	1979	.081	—	—	Proof	1.50
	1980	408.527	—	—	.15	.25
	1980	.143	—	—	Proof	1.50
	1981	353.191	—	—	.15	.25
	1981	.100	—	—	Proof	1.50

2 PENCE

BRONZE

KM#	Date	Mintage	Fine	VF	XF	Unc
928	1982	*.205	—	—	—	1.00
	1982	.107	—	—	Proof	1.50
	1983	*.631	—	—	—	1.00
	1983	.108	—	—	Proof	1.50
	1984	*.159	—	—	—	1.50
	1984	.107	—	—	Proof	1.50

KM#	Date	Mintage	Fine	VF	XF	Unc
936	1985	107.113	—	—	.15	.25
	1985	.102	—	—	Proof	1.50
	1986	168.968	—	—	.15	.50
	1986	.125	—	—	Proof	1.50
	1987	218.101	—	—	.15	.25
	1987	.089	—	—	Proof	1.50
	1988	419.889	—	—	.15	.25
	1988	.125	—	—	Proof	1.50
	1989	359.226	—	—	.15	.25
	1989	.100	—	—	Proof	1.50
	1990	204.500	—	—	.15	.25
	1990	.100	—	—	Proof	1.50
	1991	86.625	—	—	.15	.25
	1991	—	—	—	Proof	1.50
	1992	96.000	—	—	—	.50
	1992	—	—	—	—	2.00

COPPER PLATED STEEL

KM#	Date	Mintage	Fine	VF	XF	Unc
936a	1992	102.247	—	—	.15	.25
	1993	235.674	—	—	.15	.25
	1993	—	—	—	Proof	1.50
	1994	531.628	—	—	.10	.25
	1994	—	—	—	Proof	1.50
	1995	124.482	—	—	.10	.25
	1995	—	—	—	Proof	1.50
	1996	296.278	—	—	.10	.25
	1996	—	—	—	Proof	1.50
	1997	267.290	—	—	.10	.25
	1997	—	—	—	Proof	1.50
	1998	—	—	—	.10	.25

Obv: Rank-Bradley effigy of Queen Elizabeth II.
Rev: Prince of Wales badge.

KM#	Date	Mintage	Fine	VF	XF	Unc
987	1998	—	—	—	—	.25
	1998	*.100	—	—	Proof	1.50

5 NEW PENCE

COPPER-NICKEL

KM#	Date	Mintage	Fine	VF	XF	Unc
911	1968	98.868	—	—	.15	.30
	1969	119.270	—	—	.15	.40
	1970	225.948	—	—	.15	.40
	1971	81.783	—	—	.15	.50
	1971	.350	—	—	Proof	1.75
	1972	.150	—	—	Proof	3.50
	1973	.100	—	—	Proof	3.50
	1974	.100	—	—	Proof	3.50
	1975	116.906	—	—	.15	.30
	1975	.100	—	—	Proof	1.50
	1976	.100	—	—	Proof	3.50
	1977	24.308	—	—	.15	.35
	1977	.194	—	—	Proof	1.50
	1978	61.094	—	—	.15	.55
	1978	.088	—	—	Proof	1.50
	1979	155.456	—	—	.15	.30
	1979	.081	—	—	Proof	1.50
	1980	203.020	—	—	.15	.30
	1980	.143	—	—	Proof	1.50
	1981	.100	—	—	Proof	1.75

5 PENCE

COPPER-NICKEL

KM#	Date	Mintage	Fine	VF	XF	Unc
929	1982	*.205	—	—	—	2.25
	1982	.107	—	—	Proof	1.75
	1983	*.637	—	—	—	1.75
	1983	.108	—	—	Proof	1.75
	1984	*.159	—	—	—	1.75
	1984	.107	—	—	Proof	1.50

*NOTE: Issued in sets only.

	Date	Mintage	Fine	VF	XF	Unc
937	1985	*178	—	—	—	2.00
	1985	.102	—	—	Proof	1.50
	1986	*.167	—	—	—	1.00
	1986	.125	—	—	Proof	1.50
	1987	48.220	—	—	.15	.30
	1987	.089	—	—	Proof	1.75
	1988	120.775	—	—	.15	.30
	1988	.125	—	—	Proof	1.75
	1989	101.406	—	—	.15	.30
	1989	.100	—	—	Proof	1.75
	1990	*—	—	—	—	2.50
	1990	—	—	—	Proof	2.75

*NOTE: Issued in sets only.

Reduced size.

	Date	Mintage	Fine	VF	XF	Unc
937b	1990	1,634.840	—	—	—	.35
	1990		—	—	Proof	1.75
	1991	724.979	—	—	—	.35
	1991		—	—	Proof	1.75
	1992	453.174	—	—	—	.35
	1992		—	—	Proof	1.75
	1993		—	—	—	.35
	1993		—	—	Proof	1.75
	1994	93.602	—	—	—	.35
	1994		—	—	Proof	1.75
	1995	183.384	—	—	—	.35
	1995		—	—	Proof	1.75
	1996	302.902	—	—	—	.35
	1996		—	—	Proof	1.75
	1997	178.014	—	—	—	.35
	1997		—	—	Proof	1.50

NOTE: Varieties in thickness and edge milling exist.

Obv: Rank-Bradley effigy of Queen Elizabeth II.
Rev: Crowned Scottish thistle.

	Date	Mintage	Fine	VF	XF	Unc
988	1998	—	—	—	—	.30
	1998	*.100	—	—	Proof	1.50

10 NEW PENCE

COPPER-NICKEL

	Date	Mintage	Fine	VF	XF	Unc
912	1968	336.143	—	—	.25	.50
	1969	314.008	—	—	.25	.60
	1970	133.571	—	—	.25	1.00
	1971	63.205	—	—	.25	1.00
	1971	.350	—	—	Proof	1.75
	1972	.150	—	—	Proof	3.75
	1973	152.174	—	—	.25	.50
	1973	.100	—	—	Proof	1.75
	1974	92.741	—	—	.25	.50
	1974	.100	—	—	Proof	1.75
	1975	181.559	—	—	.25	.50
	1975	.100	—	—	Proof	1.75
	1976	228.220	—	—	.25	.50
	1976	.100	—	—	Proof	1.75
	1977	59.323	—	—	.25	.60
	1977	.194	—	—	Proof	1.75
	1978	.088	—	—	Proof	5.25

KM#	Date	Mintage	Fine	VF	XF	Unc
912	1979	115.457	—	—	.25	.60
	1979	.081	—	—	Proof	1.75
	1980	88.650	—	—	.25	.65
	1980	.143	—	—	Proof	1.75
	1981	3.433	—	.25	.50	2.00
	1981	.100	—	—	Proof	1.75

10 PENCE

COPPER-NICKEL

	Date	Mintage	Fine	VF	XF	Unc
930	1982	*.205	—	—	—	2.75
	1982	.107	—	—	Proof	1.75
	1983	*.637	—	—	—	2.75
	1983	.108	—	—	Proof	1.75
	1984	*.159	—	—	—	2.00
	1984	.107	—	—	Proof	1.75

*NOTE: Issued in sets only.

	Date	Mintage	Fine	VF	XF	Unc
938	1985	*.178	—	—	—	2.75
	1985	.102	—	—	Proof	1.75
	1986	*.167	—	—	—	1.75
	1986	.125	—	—	Proof	1.75
	1987	*.172	—	—	—	2.75
	1987	.089	—	—	Proof	2.75
	1988	*.134	—	—	—	2.75
	1988	.125	—	—	Proof	2.75
	1989	*.078	—	—	—	3.50
	1989	.100	—	—	Proof	2.75
	1990	*	—	—	—	3.50
	1990	.100	—	—	Proof	2.75
	1991	*	—	—	—	3.50
	1991	—	—	—	Proof	2.75
	1992	*	—	—	—	3.50
	1992		—	—	Proof	3.50

*NOTE: Issued in sets only.

Reduced size.

	Date	Mintage	Fine	VF	XF	Unc
938b	1992	1,395.497	—	—	.25	.50
	1992		—	—	Proof	2.75
	1993	*	—	—	—	1.00
	1993	—	—	—	Proof	1.75
	1994	*	—	—	—	1.00
	1994	—	—	—	Proof	1.75
	1995	43.259	—	—	—	1.00
	1995	—	—	—	Proof	1.75
	1996	118.738	—	—	—	1.00
	1996	—	—	—	Proof	1.75
	1997	1.966	—	—	—	1.00
	1997	—	—	—	Proof	1.75

NOTE: Varieties in thickness and edge milling exist.
*NOTE: Issued in sets only.

Obv: Rank-Bradley effigy of Queen Elizabeth II.
Rev: Crowned lion.

	Date	Mintage	Fine	VF	XF	Unc
989	1998	—	—	—	—	.40
	1998		—	—	Proof	1.75

20 PENCE

COPPER-NICKEL

	Date	Mintage	Fine	VF	XF	Unc
931	1982	740.815	—	—	.45	.65
	1982	.107	—	—	Proof	5.00
	1983	158.463	—	—	.45	.65
	1983	.108	—	—	Proof	2.50
	1984	65.351	—	—	.45	.65
	1984	.107	—	—	Proof	2.50

KM#	Date	Mintage	Fine	VF	XF	Unc
939	1985	74.274	—	—	.45	.75
	1985	.102	—	—	Proof	5.00
	1986	*.167	—	—	—	1.00
	1986	.125	—	—	Proof	5.00
	1987	137.450	—	—	.45	.75
	1987	.089	—	—	Proof	5.00
	1988	38.038	—	—	.45	.75
	1988	.125	—	—	Proof	5.00
	1989	132.014	—	—	.45	.75
	1989	.100	—	—	Proof	5.00
	1990	88.098	—	—	.45	.75
	1990	.100	—	—	Proof	5.00
	1991	35.901	—	—	.45	1.00
	1991		—	—	Proof	5.00
	1992	31.205	—	—	.45	1.00
	1992		—	—	Proof	5.00
	1993	123.124	—	—	.45	.75
	1993	—	—	—	Proof	5.00
	1994	67.131	—	—	.45	1.00
	1994		—	—	Proof	5.00
	1995	102.005	—	—	.45	.75
	1995		—	—	Proof	5.00
	1996	83.164	—	—	.45	.75
	1996		—	—	Proof	5.00
	1997	74.939	—	—	.45	.75
	1997		—	—	Proof	5.00

*NOTE: Issued in sets only.

Obv: Rank-Bradley effigy of Queen Elizabeth II.

	Date	Mintage	Fine	VF	XF	Unc
990	1998	—	—	—	—	.60
	1998	*.100	—	—	Proof	2.00

50 NEW PENCE

COPPER-NICKEL

	Date	Mintage	Fine	VF	XF	Unc
913	1969	188.400	—	—	1.25	2.50
	1970	19.461	—	—	1.25	3.50
	1971	.350	—	—	Proof	3.50
	1972	.150	—	—	Proof	6.50
	1974	.100	—	—	Proof	3.00
	1975	.100	—	—	Proof	3.00
	1976	43.747	—	—	1.75	3.50
	1976	.100	—	—	Proof	2.50
	1977	49.536	—	—	1.75	3.50
	1977	.194	—	—	Proof	2.50
	1978	72.005	—	—	1.75	3.50
	1978	.088	—	—	Proof	2.75
	1979	58.680	—	—	1.75	2.25
	1979	.081	—	—	Proof	2.75
	1980	89.086	—	—	1.75	2.25
	1980	.143	—	—	Proof	2.50
	1981	74.003	—	—	1.75	2.25
	1981	.100	—	—	Proof	2.50

50 PENCE

COPPER-NICKEL
Entry Into E.E.C.

	Date	Mintage	Fine	VF	XF	Unc
918	1973	89.775	—	—	1.25	2.00
	1973	.357	—	—	Proof	6.00

KM#	Date	Mintage	Fine	VF	XF	Unc
932	1982	51.312	—	—	1.25	1.75
	1982	.107	—	—	Proof	2.50
	1983	23.436	—	—	1.25	2.00
	1983	.125	—	—	Proof	2.50
	1984	*.107	—	—	—	2.75
	1984	.125	—	—	Proof	2.50

*NOTE: Issued in sets only.

940.1	1985	.680	—	—	1.25	2.75
(940)	1985	.102	—	—	Proof	2.75
	1986	*.167	—	—	—	2.75
	1986	.125	—	—	Proof	2.75
	1987	*.172	—	—	—	2.75
	1987	.089	—	—	Proof	2.75
	1988	*.134	—	—	—	2.75
	1988	.125	—	—	Proof	3.50
	1989	*.078	—	—	—	3.50
	1989	.100	—	—	Proof	2.75
	1990	*	—	—	—	3.50
	1990	.100	—	—	Proof	6.00
	1991	*	—	—	—	3.50
	1991	—	—	—	Proof	6.50
	1992	*	—	—	—	3.50
	1992	—	—	—	Proof	6.50
	1993	*	—	—	—	3.50
	1993	—	—	—	Proof	3.50
	1995	—	—	—	—	2.75
	1995	*	—	—	Proof	3.50
	1996	—	—	—	—	2.75
	1996	—	—	—	Proof	3.50
	1997	*—	—	—	—	2.75
	1997	*—	—	—	Proof	3.50

*NOTE: Issued in sets only.

Reduced size.

940.2	1997	383.254	—	—	—	2.75
(940a)	1997	—	—	—	Proof	3.50

British Presidency of European Council of Ministers

963	ND(1992)	.109	—	—	—	2.75
	ND(1992)	*.100	—	—	Proof	13.50

50th Anniversary of Normandy Invasion

966	1994	6.673	—	—	—	2.50
	1994	—	—	—	Proof	13.50

**Obv: Rank-Bradley effigy of Queen Elizabeth II.
Rev: Seated Brittania.**

KM#	Date	Mintage	Fine	VF	XF	Unc
991	1998	—	—	—	—	1.75
	1998	*.100	—	—	Proof	2.50

**25th Anniversary - Britain in the Common Market
Obv: Rank-Bradley effigy of Queen Elizabeth II.
Rev: Bouquet of stars.**

992	1998	—	—	—	—	2.75
	1998	*.100	—	—	Proof	10.00

**National Health Service
Obv: Rank-Bradley effigy of Queen Elizabeth II.
Rev: Radiant hands.**

996	1998	—	—	—	—	3.50
	1998	—	—	BU w/folder		15.00
	1998	—	—	—	Proof	17.50

POUND

NICKEL-BRASS

933	1983	443.054	—	—	2.25	3.50
	1983	.108	—	—	Proof	6.00

Rev: Scottish thistle.

934	1984	146.257	—	—	2.25	3.50
	1984	.107	—	—	Proof	6.00

Rev: Welsh leek.

941	1985	228.431	—	—	2.00	3.50
	1985	.102	—	—	Proof	6.00
	1990	97.269	—	—	2.00	3.50
	1990	.100	—	—	Proof	6.00

Northern Ireland - Blooming Flax

KM#	Date	Mintage	Fine	VF	XF	Unc
946	1986	10.410	—	—	2.00	3.50
	1986	.125	—	—	Proof	6.00
	1991	38.444	—	—	2.00	3.50
	1991	—	—	—	Proof	6.00

Oak Tree

948	1987	39.299	—	—	—	3.50
	1987	.125	—	—	Proof	6.00
	1992	36.320	—	—	—	3.50
	1992	—	—	—	Proof	6.00

COPPER-ZINC-NICKEL

954	1988	7.119	—	—	—	3.50
	1988	*.125	—	—	Proof	7.00

**NICKEL-BRASS
Scottish Flora
Obv: Queen's portrait. Rev: Scottish thistle.**

959	1989	70.581	—	—	—	3.50
	1989	.100	—	—	Proof	6.00

Royal Coat of Arms

964	1993	114.745	—	—	—	3.50
	1993	—	—	—	Proof	6.00

Scotland

967	1994	29.753	—	—	—	3.50
	1994	—	—	—	Proof	6.00

Wales - Welsh Dragon

969	1995	34.504	—	—	—	3.50
	1995	.100	—	—	Proof	6.00

Northern Ireland Celtic Collar on Cross

972	1996	89.886	—	—	—	3.50
	1996	*.100	—	—	Proof	6.00

Obv: Queen's portrait. Rev: Plantagenet lions.

KM#	Date	Mintage	VF	XF	Unc
975	1997	35.001	—	—	3.00
	1997	*.100	—	Proof	6.00

Obv: Rank-Bradley effigy of Queen Elizabeth II.
Rev: British Royal Arms.

KM#	Date	Mintage	Fine	VF	XF	Unc
993	1998	—	—	—	—	3.50
	1998	*.100	—	—	Proof	6.00

TRADE COINAGE
Britannia Series

Issued to facilitate British trade in the Orient, the reverse design incorporates the denomination in Chinese characters and Malay script.

This issue was struck at the Bombay (B) and Calcutta (C) Mints in India, except for 1925 and 1930 issues which were struck at London. Through error the mint marks did not appear on some early (1895-1900) issues as indicated.

DOLLAR

26.9568 g, .900 SILVER, .7800 oz ASW

	Date	Mintage	Fine	VF	XF	Unc
T5 (T2)	1901/0B	25.680	40.00	60.00	100.00	200.00
	1901B	Inc. Ab.	15.00	20.00	25.00	60.00
	1901B	Inc. Ab.	—	—	Proof	800.00
	1901C	1.514	25.00	45.00	100.00	200.00
	1902B	30.404	15.00	20.00	25.00	60.00
	1902B	Inc. Ab.	—	—	Proof	800.00
	1902C	1.267	25.00	45.00	80.00	175.00
	1902C	Inc. Ab.	—	—	Proof	800.00
	1903/2B	3.956	15.00	25.00	40.00	75.00
	1903B	Inc. Ab.	15.00	20.00	25.00	60.00
	1903B	Inc. Ab.	—	—	Proof	800.00
	1904/898B	.649	50.00	80.00	125.00	200.00
	1904/3B	I.A.	30.00	50.00	100.00	225.00
	1904/0B	I.A.	80.00	125.00	175.00	300.00
	1904B	Inc. Ab.	40.00	60.00	100.00	250.00
	1904B	Inc. Ab.	—	—	Proof	700.00
	1907B	1.946	15.00	20.00	25.00	60.00
	1908/3B	6.871	40.00	60.00	100.00	175.00
	1908/7B	I.A.	35.00	50.00	90.00	125.00
	1908B	Inc. Ab.	15.00	20.00	25.00	60.00
	1908B	Inc. Ab.	—	—	Proof	700.00
	1909/8B	5.954	30.00	45.00	80.00	125.00
	1909B	Inc. Ab.	15.00	20.00	25.00	60.00
	1910/00B	5.553	40.00	60.00	100.00	175.00
	1910B	Inc. Ab.	15.00	20.00	25.00	60.00
	1911/00 B	—	30.00	50.00	100.00	150.00
	1911B	37.471	15.00	20.00	25.00	50.00
	1912B	5.672	15.00	20.00	25.00	50.00
	1912B	Inc. Ab.	—	—	Proof	800.00
	1913/2 B	—	100.00	150.00	250.00	700.00
	1913B	1.567	30.00	60.00	125.00	300.00
	1913B	Inc. Ab.	—	—	Proof	800.00
	1921B *5 known	—	—	—	—	15,000.
	1921B (restrike)	—	—	—	Proof	4500.
	1925	6.870	15.00	20.00	25.00	70.00
	1929/1B	5.100	30.00	50.00	80.00	200.00
	1929B	Inc. Ab.	15.00	20.00	25.00	60.00
	1929B	Inc. Ab.	—	—	Proof	800.00
	1930B	10.400	15.00	20.00	25.00	50.00
	1930B	Inc. Ab.	—	—	Proof	800.00

KM# (T2)	Date	Mintage	Fine	VF	XF	Unc
	1930	6.660	15.00	20.00	25.00	50.00
	1934B	17.335	75.00	150.00	200.00	500.00
	1934B	Inc. Ab.	—	—	Proof	3500.
	1934B (restrike) 20 known	—	—	Proof	3000.
	1935B **15 known	1000.	1500.	2500.	5000.
	1935B	—	—	—	Proof	7500.
	1935B (restrike) 20 known	—	—	Proof	4000.

NOTE: Earlier dates (1895-1900) exist for this type.
*NOTE: Original mintage 50,211.
**NOTE: Original mintage 6,811,995.

GREECE

The Hellenic (Greek) Republic is situated in southeastern Europe on the southern tip of the Balkan Peninsula. The republic includes many islands, the most important of which are Crete and the Ionian Islands. Greece (including islands) has an area of 50,944 sq. mi. (131,940 sq. km.) and a population of 10.3 million. Capital: Athens. Greece is still largely agricultural. Tobacco, cotton, fruit and wool are exported.

Greece, the Mother of Western civilization, attained the peak of its culture in the 5th century B.C., when it contributed more to government, drama, art and architecture than any other people to this time. Greece fell under Roman domination in the 2nd and 1st centuries B.C., becoming part of the Byzantine Empire until Constantinople fell to the Crusaders in 1202. With the fall of Constantinople to the Turks in 1453, Greece became part of the Ottoman Empire. Independence from Turkey was won with the revolution of 1821-27. In 1833, Greece was established as a monarchy, with sovereignty guaranteed by Britain, France and Russia. After a lengthy power struggle between the monarchist forces and democratic factions, Greece was proclaimed a republic in 1925. The monarchy was restored in 1935 and reconfirmed by a plebiscite in 1946. The Italians invaded Greece via Albania on Oct. 28, 1940 but were driven back well within the Albanian border. Germany began their invasion in April 1941 and quickly overran the entire country and drove off a British Expeditionary force by the end of April. King George II and his new government went into exile. The German-Italian occupation of Greece lasted until Oct. 1944 after which only German troops remained until the end of the occupation. On April 21, 1967, a military junta took control of the government and suspended the constitution. King Constantine II made an unsuccessful attempt against the junta in the fall of 1968 and consequently fled to Italy. The monarchy was formally abolished by plebiscite, Dec. 8, 1974, and Greece was established as the 'Hellenic Republic,' the third republic in Greek history.

RULERS

George I, 1863-1913
Constantine I, 1913-1917, 1920-1922
Alexander I, 1917-1920
George II, 1922-1923, 1935-1947
Paul I, 1947-1964
Constantine II, 1964-1973

MINT MARKS

(a) - Paris, privy marks only
A - Paris
B - Vienna
H - Heaton, Birmingham
K - Bordeaux
KN - King's Norton
(p) - Poissy - Thunderbolt

MONETARY SYSTEM
Commencing 1831
100 Lepta = 1 Drachma

KINGDOM
1828-1925

5 LEPTA

NICKEL
Rev: Owl on amphora.

KM#	Date	Mintage	Fine	VF	XF	Unc
62	1912(a)	25.053	.75	1.50	4.50	20.00

10 LEPTA

NICKEL

Rev: Owl on amphora.

KM#	Date	Mintage	Fine	VF	XF	Unc
63	1912(a)	28.973	.75	1.50	4.50	20.00

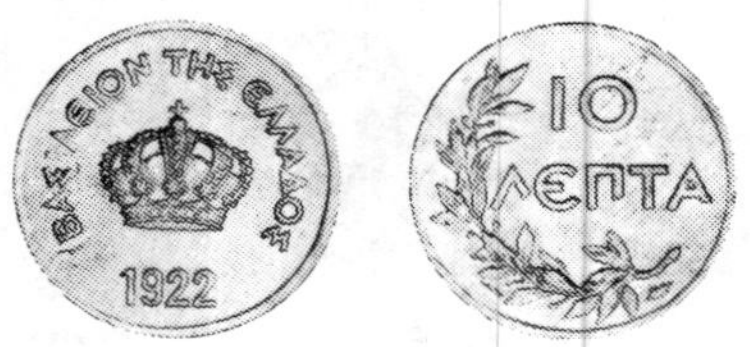

1.5200 g, ALUMINUM
1.7mm thick

66.1	1922(p)	120.00	1.00	2.50	7.50	25.00

1.6500 g, 2.2mm thick

66.2	1922(p)	—	—	—	—	—

20 LEPTA

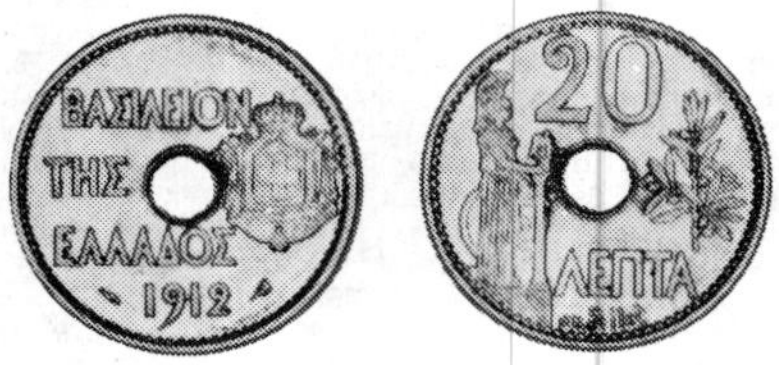

NICKEL
Rev: Goddess Athena.

64	1912(a)	10.145	.75	1.50	6.00	30.00

50 LEPTA

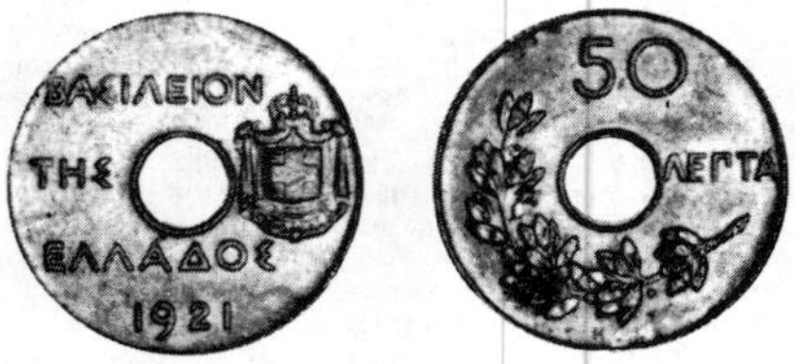

COPPER-NICKEL

65	1921H	1.000	300.00	600.00	1200.	2500.
	1921KN	1.524	500.00	1000.	2000.	3750.

DRACHMA

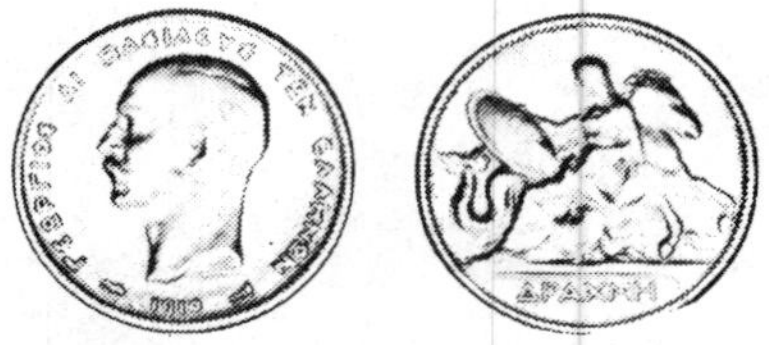

5.0000 g, .835 SILVER, .1342 oz ASW
Obv: George I. Rev: Mythological figure Thetis with shield of Achilles, seated on sea-horse.

60	1910(a)	4.570	5.00	10.00	20.00	60.00
	1911(a)	1.881	6.00	12.00	28.00	70.00

2 DRACHMAI

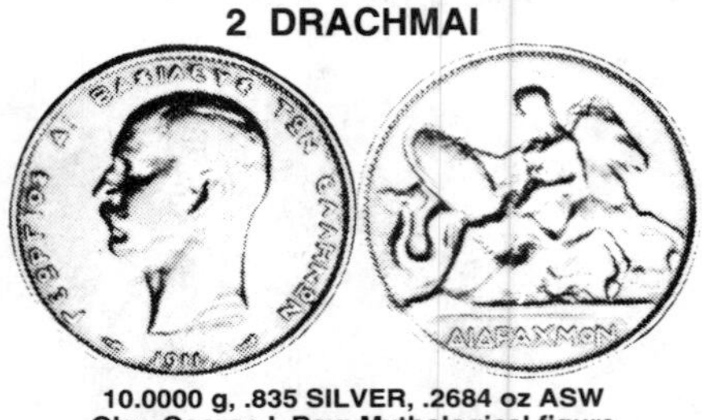

10.0000 g, .835 SILVER, .2684 oz ASW
Obv: George I. Rev: Mythological figure Thetis with shield of Achilles seated on sea-horse.

61	1911(a)	1.500	6.50	22.50	55.00	120.00

REPUBLIC

1925-1935

20 LEPTA

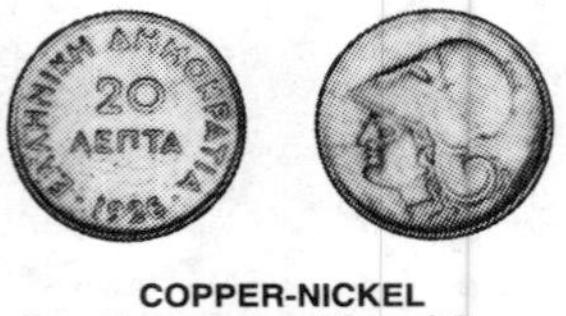

COPPER-NICKEL
Rev: Helmeted goddess Athena.

67	1926	20.000	.65	1.25	3.50	7.00

50 LEPTA

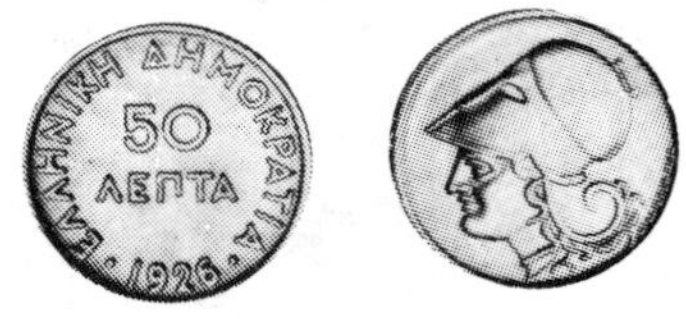

COPPER-NICKEL

KM#	Date	Mintage	Fine	VF	XF	Unc
68	1926	20.000	.25	.75	2.50	6.00
	1926B (1930)	20.000	.25	.75	2.50	6.00

DRACHMA

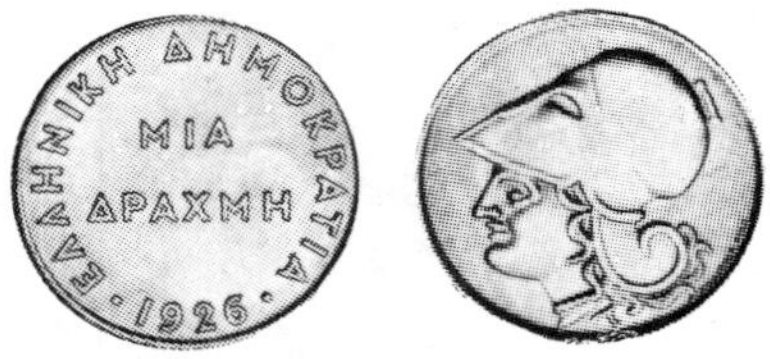

COPPER-NICKEL

69	1926	15.000	.25	.75	2.50	6.00
	1926B (1930)	20.000	.25	.75	2.50	6.00

2 DRACHMAI

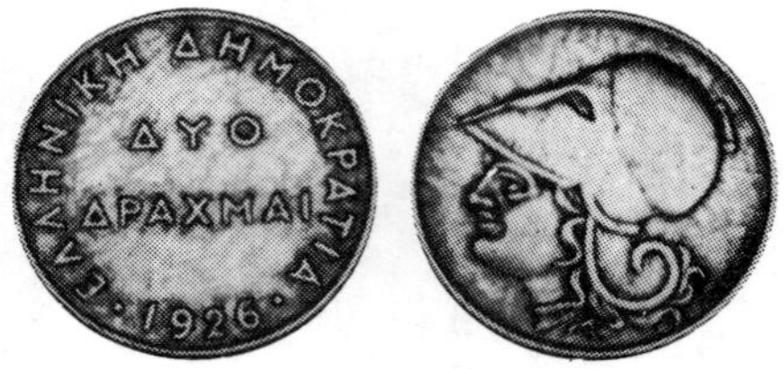

COPPER-NICKEL

70	1926	22.000	.65	1.25	3.50	10.00

5 DRACHMAI

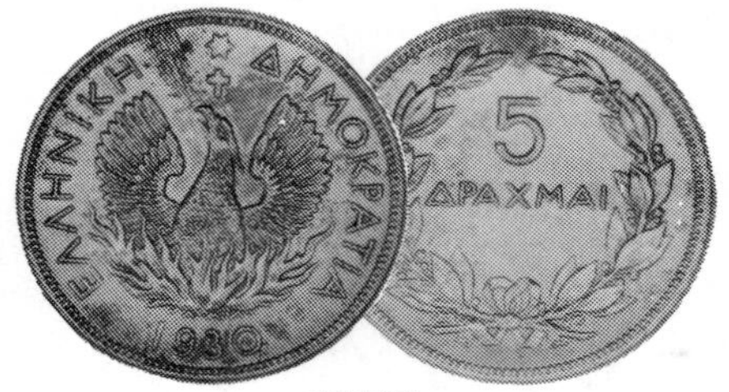

NICKEL
LONDON MINT: In second set of berries on left only 1 berry will have a dot on it.
Obv: Phoenix.

71.1	1930	23.500	.65	1.25	4.00	22.00
	1930	—	—	—	Proof	400.00

BRUSSELS MINT: 2 berries will have dots.

71.2	1930	1.500	1.50	3.50	10.00	50.00

10 DRACHMAI

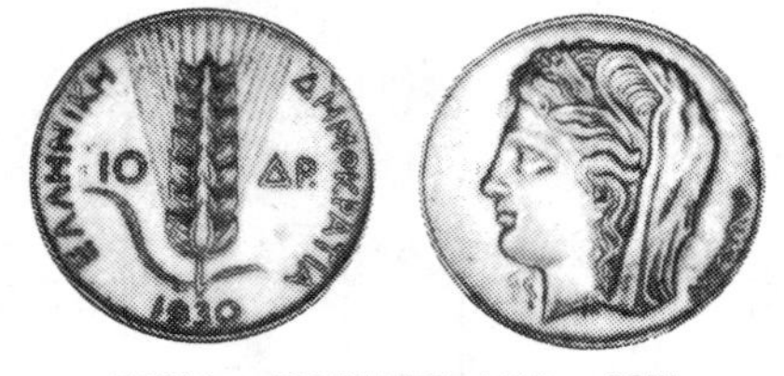

7.0000 g, .500 SILVER, .1125 oz ASW

72	1930	7.500	3.50	7.00	18.00	60.00
	1930	—	—	—	Proof	500.00

20 DRACHMAI

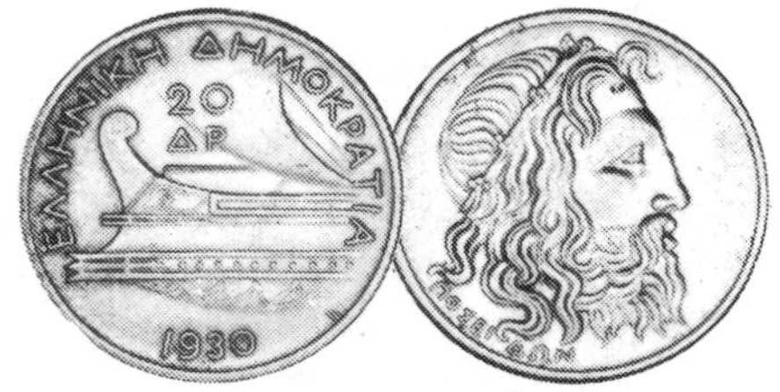

11.3100 g, .500 SILVER, .1818 oz ASW
Obv: Prow of ancient ship. Rev: Neptune.

73	1930	11.500	4.50	7.50	18.00	85.00
	1930	—	—	—	Proof	600.00

KINGDOM

1935-1973

5 LEPTA

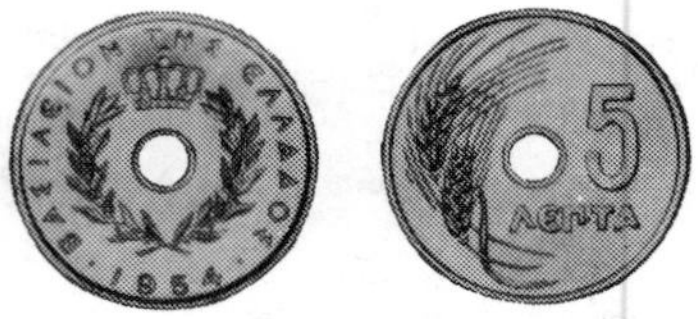

ALUMINUM

KM#	Date	Mintage	Fine	VF	XF	Unc
77	1954	15.000	—	.10	.50	1.00
	1971	1.002	.20	.50	1.00	4.00

NOTE: 1971 dated coins have smaller hole at center.

10 LEPTA

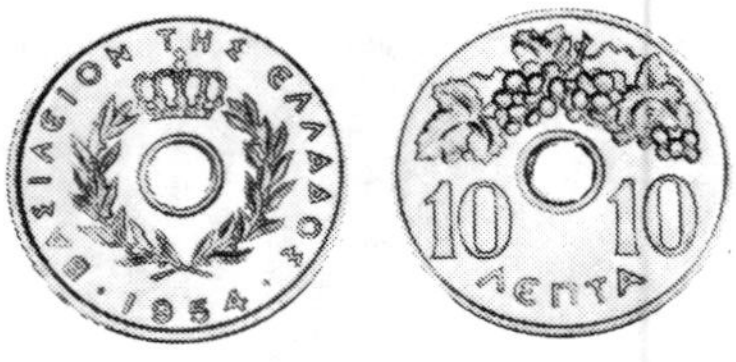

ALUMINUM

78	1954	48.000	—	.10	.35	1.75
	1959	20.000	—	.10	.35	1.75
	1964	12.000	—	.10	.35	1.75
	1965*	—	—	—	—	3.00
	1965*	4,987	—	—	Proof	5.00
	1966	20.000	—	.10	.35	1.75
	1969	20.000	—	.10	.35	1.75
	1971	5.922	—	.25	1.00	4.50

***NOTE:** Only sold in sets.
NOTE: 1971 dated coins have smaller hole at center.

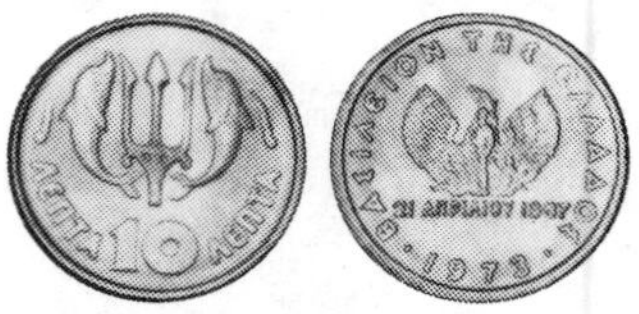

Obv: Soldier and Phoenix.

102	1973	2.742	—	.10	1.00	4.00

20 LEPTA

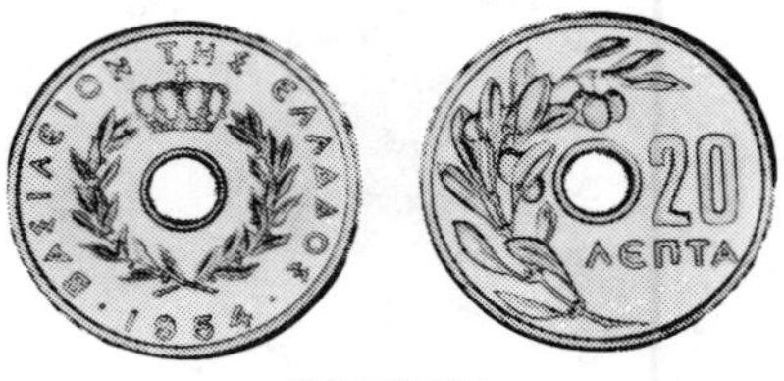

ALUMINUM

79	1954	24.000	—	.10	.50	2.00
	1959	20.000	—	.10	.50	2.00
	1964	8.000	—	.10	.50	2.00
	1966	15.000	—	.10	.50	2.00
	1969	20.000	—	.10	.50	2.00
	1971	4.108	—	.20	1.00	2.50

NOTE: 1971 dated coins have smaller hole at center.

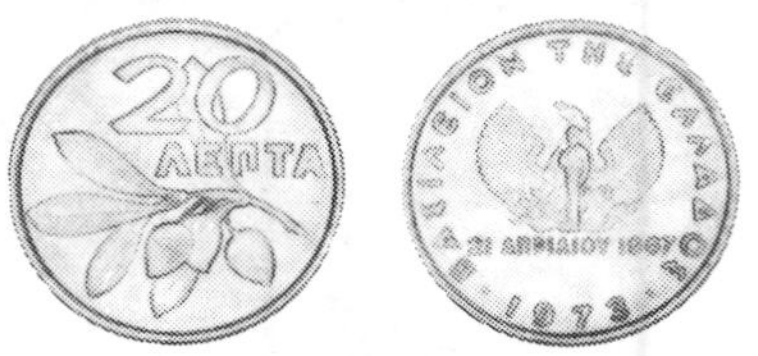

Obv: Soldier in front of phoenix, anniversary date below.
Rev: Olive branch, denomination.

104	1973	2.718	—	.20	.60	4.00

50 LEPTA

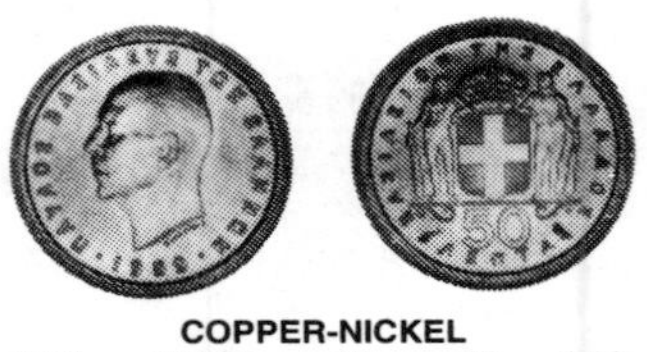

COPPER-NICKEL

80	1954	37.228	.15	.25	1.00	2.50
	1957	5.108	.25	1.00	10.00	30.00
	1957	—	—	—	Proof	150.00
	1959	10.160	.15	.25	1.00	2.50
	1962 plain edge 20.500		.15	.25	.75	1.50

KM#	Date	Mintage	Fine	VF	XF	Unc
80	1962 serrated edge					
		Inc. Ab.	.15	.25	.75	1.50
	1964	20.000	.15	.25	.75	1.50
	1965*	—	—	—		3.00
	1965*	4,987	—	—	Proof	4.50

*NOTE: Only sold in sets.

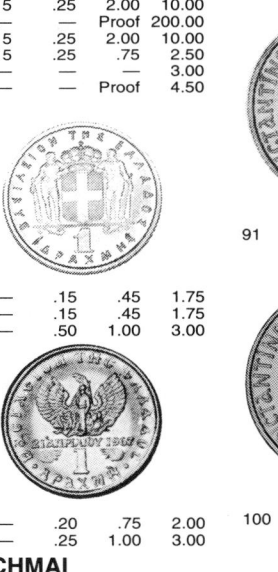

88	1966	30.000	.20	.50	1.00	3.50
	1970	10.160	.30	.60	1.50	4.50

	Obv: Small head.					
97.1	1971	10.999	—	.10	.15	1.00
	1973	9.342	—	.20	.50	2.00

	Obv: Large head.					
97.2	1973	Inc. Ab.	—	.20	.50	2.00

DRACHMA

COPPER-NICKEL

81	1954	24.091	.15	.25	.75	2.50
	1957	8.151	.15	.25		10.00
	1957	—	—		Proof	200.00
	1959	10.180	.15	.25	2.00	10.00
	1962	20.060	.15	.25	.75	2.50
	1965*	—	—	—		3.00
	1965*	4,987	—	—	Proof	4.50

*NOTE: Only sold in sets.

89	1966	20.000	—	.15	.45	1.75
	1967	20.000	—	.15	.45	1.75
	1970	7.001	—	.50	1.00	3.00

98	1971	11.985	—	.20	.75	2.00
	1973	8.196	—	.25	1.00	3.00

2 DRACHMAI

COPPER-NICKEL

82	1954	12.609	.50	.75	1.50	5.00
	1957	10.171	.50	.75	2.50	10.00
	1957	—	—		Proof	300.00
	1959	5.000	.50	.75	2.50	10.00
	1962	10.096	.50	.75	1.50	5.00
	1965*	—	—	—		3.00
	1965*	4,987	—	VF	Proof	5.00

*NOTE: Only sold in sets.

KM#	Date	Mintage	Fine	VF	XF	Unc
90	1966	10.000	.15	.25	.50	1.75
	1967	10.000	.15	.25	.50	1.75
	1970	7.000	.50	1.00	2.00	4.00

99	1971	9.998	.15	.25	.75	2.00
	1973	7.972	.20	.50	1.50	3.50

5 DRACHMAI

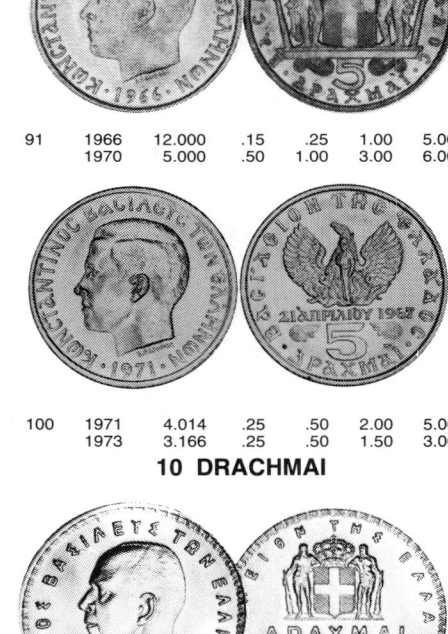

COPPER-NICKEL

83	1954	21.000	.25	.50	1.00	5.00
	1965*	—	—	—		4.00
	1965*	4,987	—	—	Proof	6.00

*NOTE: Only sold in sets.

91	1966	12.000	.15	.25	1.00	5.00
	1970	5.000	.50	1.00	3.00	6.00

100	1971	4.014	.25	.50	2.00	5.00
	1973	3.166	.25	.50	1.50	3.00

10 DRACHMAI

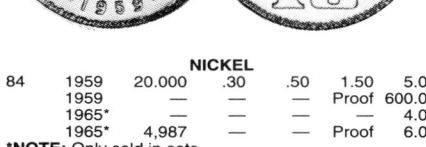

NICKEL

84	1959	20.000	.30	.50	1.50	5.00
	1959	—	—	—	Proof	600.00
	1965*	—	—	—		4.00
	1965*	4,987	—	—	Proof	6.00

*NOTE: Only sold in sets.

COPPER-NICKEL

KM#	Date	Mintage	Fine	VF	XF	Unc
96	1968	40.000	.25	.50	.75	3.50

	Rev: Phoenix					
101	1971	.502	.25	.50	1.00	5.00
	1973	.541	.50	1.00	2.50	5.00

20 DRACHMAI

7.5000 g, .835 SILVER, .2013 oz ASW

85	1960	20.000	—	BV	2.50	4.00
	1960	—	—	—	Proof	350.00
	1965*	—	—	—		5.00
	1965*	4,987	—	—	Proof	7.00

*NOTE: Only sold in sets.

COPPER-NICKEL
Rev: Narrow rim w/faint veil or no veil.

111.1	1973	3.092	.25	.50	1.50	6.00

Rev: Wide rim w/heavy veil and broken wave design at rear hoof.

111.2	1973	Inc. Ab.	1.00	2.00	4.00	12.00

Rev: Wide rim w/continuous wave design at rear hoof.

111.3	1973	Inc. Ab.	.25	.50	1.00	5.00

30 DRACHMAI

18.0000 g, .835 SILVER, .4832 oz ASW
Centennial - Royal Greek Dynasty

KM#	Date	Mintage	Fine	VF	XF	Unc
86	ND(1963)	3.000	—	BV	4.00	7.00

12.0000 g, .835 SILVER, .3221 oz ASW
Constantine and Anne-Marie Wedding

87	1964 Berne: small edge lettering					
		1.000	—	BV	3.50	5.00
	1964 Kongsberg: large edge lettering					
		1.000	—	BV	3.50	5.00

50 DRACHMAI

12.5000 g, .835 SILVER, .3355 oz ASW
1967 Revolution

93	1967(1970)	.100	—	—	25.00	30.00

REPUBLIC

1973 —

10 LEPTA

ALUMINUM
Obv: Modified design; soldier replaced w/phoenix.
Rev: Pair of dolphins flank trident.

103	1973	4.110	—	.10	.50	1.75

Obv: Shield in wreath.
Rev: Charging bull, right.

113	1976	2.043	—	.10	.30	1.50
	1978	.797	.50	1.00	2.50	5.00
	1978	.020	—	—	Proof	5.00

20 LEPTA

ALUMINUM
Obv: Similar to 10 Lepta, KM#103.

KM#	Date	Mintage	Fine	VF	XF	Unc
105	1973	5.246	—	.20	.50	2.50

Rev: Similar to 10 Lepta, KM#113.
Obv: Bust of stallion, left.

114	1976	2.506	—	.20	.40	2.50
	1978	.803	.50	1.00	2.50	5.00
	1978	.020	—	—	Proof	5.00

50 LEPTA

NICKEL-BRASS

106	1973	19.512	—	.10	.15	1.00

Markos Botsaris

115	1976	55.646	—	.10	.15	1.00
	1978	12.010	—	.10	.15	1.00
	1978	.020	—	—	Proof	3.00
	1980	6.682	—	.10	.15	1.25
	1982	3.365	—	.10	.15	1.25
	1984	1.208	—	.10	.15	1.25
	1986	—	—	.10	.15	1.25

DRACHMA

NICKEL-BRASS

107	1973	12.842	—	.10	.35	1.50

Konstantinos Kanaris

116	1976	133.560	—	.10	.15	1.00
	1978	21.200	—	.10	.15	1.00
	1978	.020	—	—	Proof	2.50
	1980	52.503	—	.10	.15	1.00
	1982	54.186	—	.10	.15	1.00
	1984	33.665	—	.10	.15	1.00
	1986	17.901	—	.10	.15	1.00

NOTE: Varieties exist for the 1976 dated coins.

COPPER
Bouboulina - Heroine
Obv: Sailing ship.

150	1988	36.707	—	—	—	.20
	1990	—	—	—	—	.20
	1992	—	—	—	—	.20
	1993	—	—	—	—	.20
	1993	—	—	—	Proof	3.50

2 DRACHMAI

NICKEL-BRASS

KM#	Date	Mintage	Fine	VF	XF	Unc
108	1973	10.935	.10	.20	.50	2.00

Georgios Karaiskakis

117	1976	115.801	—	.15	.25	1.00
	1978	16.772	—	.15	.25	1.00
	1978	.020	—	—	Proof	2.50
	1980	45.955	—	.15	.25	1.00

2 DRACHMES

NICKEL-BRASS
Georgios Karaiskakis

130	1982	64.414	—	.10	.20	1.00
	1984	31.861	—	.10	.20	1.00
	1986	21.019	—	.10	.20	1.00

COPPER
Manto Mavrogenous

151	1988	30.273	—	—	—	.30
	1990	—	—	—	—	.30
	1992	—	—	—	—	.30
	1993	—	—	—	—	.30
	1993	—	—	—	Proof	4.50

5 DRACHMAI

COPPER-NICKEL
Denomination spelling ends with I.

109.1	1973	13.931	.25	.50	1.00	1.75

Denomination spelling ends with A.

109.2	1973	Inc. Ab.	1.00	2.00	4.00	10.00

Aristotle

118	1976	104.133	.10	.20	.35	1.00
	1978	17.404	.10	.20	.35	1.00
	1978	.020	—	—	Proof	2.00
	1980	33.701	.10	.20	.35	1.00

5 DRACHMES

COPPER-NICKEL

KM#	Date	Mintage	Fine	VF	XF	Unc
131	1982	42.647	.10	.20	.35	1.00
	1984	29.778	.10	.20	.35	1.00
	1986	16.730	.10	.20	.35	1.00
	1988	19.671	—	—	.30	.65
	1990	—	—	—	.30	.65
	1992	—	—	—	.30	.65
	1993	—	—	—	.30	.65
	1993	—	—	—	Proof	4.50
	1998	—	—	—	.30	.65

10 DRACHMAI

COPPER-NICKEL

KM#	Date	Mintage	Fine	VF	XF	Unc
110	1973	8.456	.25	.50	1.25	3.00

Democritus

119	1976	83.445	.15	.25	.50	1.00
	1978	14.637	.15	.25	.50	1.00
	1978	.020	—	—	Proof	2.50
	1980	28.733	.15	.25	.50	1.00

10 DRACHMES

COPPER-NICKEL

132	1982	33.539	.15	.25	.50	1.00
	1984	23.802	.15	.25	.50	1.00
	1986	24.441	.15	.25	.50	1.00
	1988	16.869	—	—	.20	.40	.85
	1990	—	—	.20	.40	.85
	1992	—	—	.20	.40	.85
	1993	—	—	.20	.40	.85
	1993	—	—	—	Proof	5.00
	1998	—	—	.20	.40	.85

20 DRACHMAI

COPPER-NICKEL

112	1973	10.079	.20	.30	.50	1.50

Pericles

KM#	Date	Mintage	Fine	VF	XF	Unc
120	1976	65.353	.20	.30	.50	1.25
	1978	8.808	.20	.30	.50	1.50
	1978	.020	—	—	Proof	3.00
	1980	17.562	.20	.30	.50	1.25

20 DRACHMES

COPPER-NICKEL

133	1982	24.299	.20	.30	.50	1.00
	1984	13.412	.20	.30	.50	1.25
	1986	10.553	.20	.30	.50	1.00
	1988	16.196	—	—	.50	1.00

NICKEL-BRONZE
Dionysus Solomos - Composer of National Anthem

154	1990	—	—	—	—	1.25
	1992	—	—	—	—	1.25
	1993	—	—	—	—	1.25
	1993	—	—	—	Proof	6.50
	1998	—	—	—	—	1.25

50 DRACHMAI

COPPER-NICKEL
Solon the Archon of Athens

124	1980	32.251	.40	.60	1.00	2.50

50 DRACHMES

COPPER-NICKEL
Obv: Denomination in modern Greek.

134	1982	18.899	.40	.60	1.00	1.50
	1984	11.411	.40	.60	1.00	1.50

NICKEL-BRASS

Homer
Obv: Ancient sailing boat.

KM#	Date	Mintage	Fine	VF	XF	Unc
147	1986	12.078	—	.50	1.00	2.50
	1988	23.589	—	—	.75	1.50
	1990	—	—	—	.75	1.75
	1992	—	—	—	.75	1.75
	1993	—	—	—	.75	1.75
	1993	—	—	—	Proof	7.50
	1994	—	—	—	.75	1.75

BRASS
150th Anniversary of the Constitution
Obv: Portrait of Dimitrios Kallergis.

164	ND(1994)	—	—	—	—	2.50

150th Anniversary of the Constitution
Obv: Portrait of Makrygiannis.
Rev: Center of Parliament Building.

168	ND(1994)	—	—	—	—	2.50

100 DRACHMES

BRASS
Macedonia - Alexander the Great

159	1990	—	—	—	—	2.35
	1992	—	—	—	—	2.35
	1993	—	—	—	—	2.35
	1993	—	—	—	Proof	8.50
	1994	—	—	—	—	2.35

CRETE

The island of Crete (Kriti), located 60 miles southeast of the Peloponnesus, was the center of a brilliant civilization that flourished before the advent of Greek culture. After being conquered by the Romans, Byzantines, Moslems and Venetians, Crete became part of the Turkish Empire in 1669. As a consequence of the Greek Revolution of the 1820s, it was ceded to Egypt. Egypt returned the island to the Turks in 1840, and they ceded it to Greece in 1913, after the Second Balkan War.

RULERS
Prince George, 1898-1906

MINT MARKS
A - Paris
(a) - Paris (privy marks only)

LEPTON

BRONZE, 15mm

1.1	1901A	1.711	2.50	6.00	14.00	40.00

NOTE: Earlier date (1900) exists for this type.

16mm

1.2	1901A	Inc. Ab.	3.50	6.50	15.00	42.00

2 LEPTA

BRONZE

KM#	Date	Mintage	Fine	VF	XF	Unc
2	1901A	.707	4.50	8.50	17.50	50.00

NOTE: Earlier date (1900) exists for this type.

50 LEPTA

2.5000 g, .835 SILVER, .0671 oz ASW

6	1901(a)	.600	15.00	50.00	100.00	265.00

DRACHMA

5.0000 g, .835 SILVER, .1342 oz ASW

7	1901(a)	.500	25.00	50.00	150.00	500.00

2 DRACHMAI

10.0000 g, .835 SILVER, .2685 oz ASW

8	1901(a)	.175	40.00	100.00	300.00	900.00

5 DRACHMAI

25.0000 g, .900 SILVER, .7234 oz ASW

9	1901(a)	.150	50.00	150.00	465.00	2000.

GREENLAND

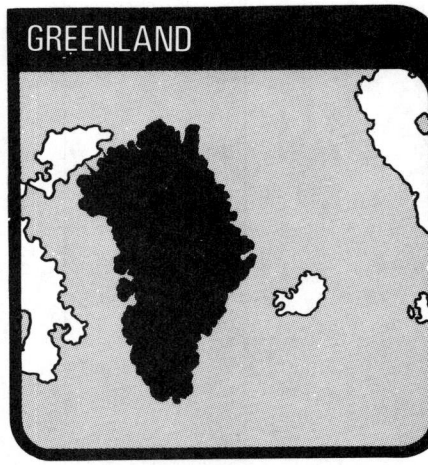

Greenland, an integral part of the Danish realm and the largest island in the world, is situated between the North Atlantic Ocean and the Polar Sea, almost entirely within the Arctic Circle. It has an area of 840,000 sq. mi. (2,175,600 sq. km.) and a population of 57,000. Capital: Nuuk (formerly Godthaab). Greenland is the world's only source of natural cryolite, a fluoride of sodium and aluminum important in making aluminum. Fish products and minerals are exported.

Eric the Red discovered Greenland in 982 and established the first settlement in 986. Greenland was a republic until 1261, when the sovereignty of Norway was extended to the island. The original colony was abandoned about 1400 when increasing cold interfered with the breeding of cattle. Successful recolonization was undertaken by Denmark in 1721. In 1921 Denmark extended its claim to include the entire island, and made it a colony of the crown in 1924. The island's colonial status was abolished by amendment to the Danish constitution on June 5, 1953, and Greenland became an integral part of the Kingdom of Denmark. It has been an autonomous state since May 1, 1979.

RULERS

Danish

MINT MARKS

Heart (h) Copenhagen

MINTMASTERS INITIALS

HCN - Hans Christian Nielsen,
1919-1927
C - Alfred Kristian Frederik Christiansen,
1956-1971

MONEYERS INITIALS

GJ - Knud Gunnar Jensen,
1901-1933
S - Harald Salomon, 1933-1968

MONETARY SYSTEM

100 Ore = 1 Krone

25 ORE

COPPER-NICKEL

KM#	Date	Mintage	Fine	VF	XF	Unc
5	1926HCN(h)GJ	.310	2.75	5.00	8.50	18.50

Center hole added to KM#5.

6	1926HCN(h)GJ	.060	15.00	35.00	—	—

NOTE: KM#5 was withdrawn from circulation and hole added in the USA.

50 ORE

ALUMINUM-BRONZE

KM#	Date	Mintage	Fine	VF	XF	Unc
7	1926HCN(h)GJ	.196	5.00	8.00	12.00	25.00

KRONE

ALUMINUM-BRONZE

8	1926HCN(h)GJ	.287	3.75	7.50	13.50	40.00

10	1957C(h)S	.100	6.00	10.00	16.50	40.00

COPPER-NICKEL

10a	1960C(h)S	.109	3.00	6.00	10.00	18.50
	1964C(h)S	.110	4.00	8.00	12.50	20.00

5 KRONER

BRASS

9	1944	.100	32.00	55.00	85.00	120.00

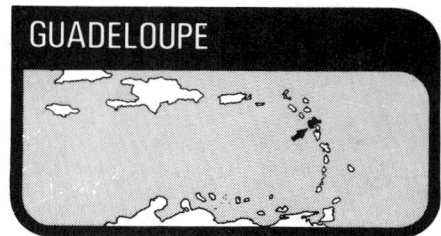

GUADELOUPE

The French Overseas Department of Guadeloupe, located in the Leeward Islands of the West Indies about 300 miles (493 km.) southeast of Puerto Rico, has an area of 687 sq. mi. (1,780 sq. km.) and a population of 306,000. Actually it is two islands separated by a narrow salt water stream: volcanic Basse-Terre to the west and the flatter limestone formation of Grande-Terre to the east. Capital: Basse-Terre, on the island of that name. The principal industries are agriculture, the distillation of liquors, and tourism. Sugar, bananas, and rum are exported.

Guadeloupe was discovered by Columbus in 1493 and settled in 1635 by two Frenchmen, L'Olive and Duplessis, who took possession in the name of the French Company of the Islands of America. When repeated efforts by private companies to colonize the island failed, it was relinquished to the French crown in 1674, and established as a dependency of Martinique. The British occupied the island on two occasions, 1759-63 and 1810-16, before it passed permanently to France. A colony until 1946 Guadeloupe was then made an overseas territory of the French Union. In 1958 it voted to become an Overseas Department within the new French Community.

The well-known R.F. in garland oval countermark of the French Government is only legitimate if on a French Colonies 12 deniers 1767 C#4. Two other similar but incuse RF countermarks are on cut pieces in the values of 1 and 4 escalins. Contemporary and modern counterfeits are known of both these types.

MONETARY SYSTEM
100 Centimes = 1 Franc

50 CENTIMES

COPPER-NICKEL

KM#	Date	Mintage	Fine	VF	XF	Unc
45	1903	.600	12.00	30.00	70.00	165.00
(35)	1921	.600	9.00	22.00	55.00	135.00

FRANC

COPPER-NICKEL

KM#	Date	Mintage	Fine	VF	XF	Unc
46	1903	.700	17.50	40.00	80.00	200.00
(36)	1921	.700	10.00	25.00	60.00	160.00

GUATEMALA

The Republic of Guatemala, the northernmost of the five Central American republics, has an area of 42,042 sq. mi. (108,890 sq. km.) and a population of 10.7 million. Capital: Guatemala City. The economy of Guatemala is heavily dependent on agriculture, however, the country is rich in nickel resources which are being developed. Coffee, cotton and bananas are exported.

Guatemala, once the site of an ancient Mayan civilization, was conquered by Pedro de Alvarado, the resourceful lieutenant of Cortes who undertook the conquest from Mexico. Cruel but strategically skillful, he progressed rapidly along the Pacific coastal lowlands to the highland plain of Quetzaltenango where the decisive battle for Guatemala was fought. After routing the Indian forces, he established the city of Guatemala, 1524. The Spanish Captaincy-General of Guatemala included all Central America but Panama. Guatemala declared its independence of Spain in 1821 and was absorbed into the Mexican empire of Augustin Iturbide, 1822-23. From 1823 to 1839 Guatemala was a constituent state of the Central American Republic. Upon dissolution of that confederation, Guatemala became an independent republic. Like El Salvador, Guatemala suffered from internal strife between right-wing military government and leftist indigenous peoples from ca. 1954 to ca. 1997.

MINT MARK
H - Heaton, Birmingham
MONETARY SYSTEM
8 Reales = 1 Peso
100 Centavos = 1 Peso, 1859-1924
100 Centavos = 1 Quetzal, 1925-

1/4 REAL

COPPER-NICKEL

KM#	Date	Mintage	Fine	VF	XF	Unc
175	1901H	5.056	.15	.35	.75	2.00

NOTE: Earlier date (1900) exists for this type.

MEDIO (1/2) REAL

COPPER-NICKEL

KM#	Date	Mintage	Fine	VF	XF	Unc
176	1901	6.652	.35	.65	1.00	2.50

NOTE: Earlier date (1900) exists for this type.

UN (1) REAL

COPPER-NICKEL

KM#	Date	Mintage	Fine	VF	XF	Unc
177	1901	7.388	—	.30	.85	1.50
	1910	4.000	—	.35	.85	1.75
	1911	2.000	—	.40	1.25	2.50
	1912	8.000	—	.30	.85	1.50

NOTE: Earlier date (1900) exists for this type.

PROVISIONAL COINAGE
12-1/2 CENTAVOS

BRONZE

KM#	Date	Mintage	Fine	VF	XF	Unc
230	1915	6.000	.75	1.25	3.00	8.00

25 CENTAVOS

BRONZE

KM#	Date	Mintage	Fine	VF	XF	Unc
231	1915	4.000	.75	1.25	2.50	7.00

50 CENTAVOS

ALUMINUM-BRONZE
Thin numerals in denomination.

232.1	1922	3.803	.65	1.00	3.00	10.00

Thick numerals in denomination.

232.2	1922	Inc. Ab.	.65	1.00	3.00	10.00

PESO

ALUMINUM-BRONZE

233	1923	1.477	1.00	1.50	3.50	15.00

5 PESOS

ALUMINUM-BRONZE

234	1923	.440	1.50	2.75	6.50	25.00

MONETARY REFORM
100 Centavos = 1 Quetzal
MEDIO (1/2) CENTAVO

BRASS

248	1932	6.000	.15	.50	1.00	4.00
	1932	—	—	—	Proof	—
	1946	.640	.50	1.00	2.50	10.00

UN (1) CENTAVO

COPPER
Obv: Incuse legend on scroll.

237	1925	.357	3.50	6.50	13.50	30.00

BRONZE

237a	1925	Inc. Ab.	5.00	8.00	15.00	40.00

COPPER

KM#	Date	Mintage	Fine	VF	XF	Unc
247	1929	.500	2.00	3.00	6.00	22.50
	1929	—			Proof	—

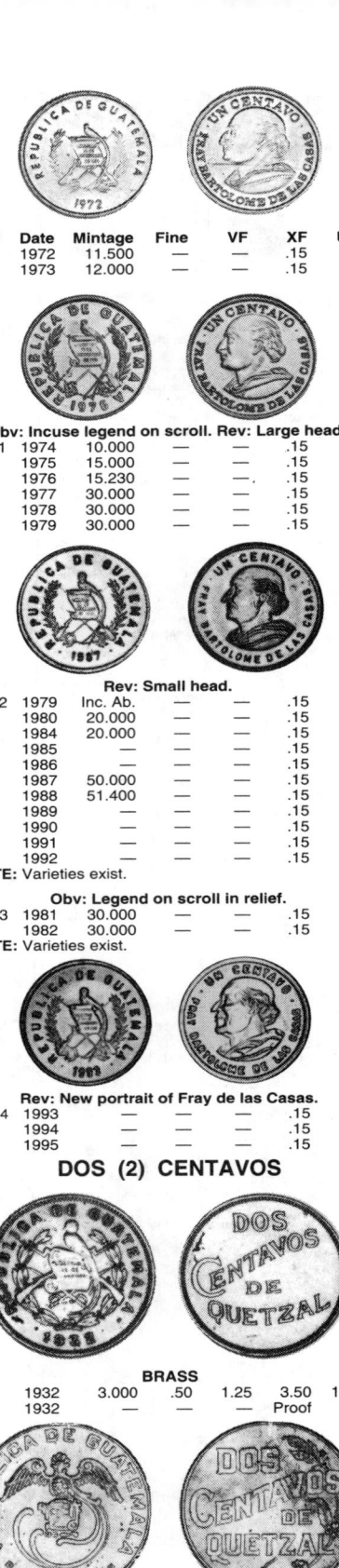

BRASS

KM#	Date	Mintage	Fine	VF	XF	Unc
249	1932	3.000	.40	1.00	3.00	10.00
	1932	—			Proof	—
	1933	1.500	.60	1.50	4.50	12.00
	1933	—			Proof	—
	1934	1.000	.50	1.25	4.50	12.00
	1934	—			Proof	—
	1936	1.500	.40	1.00	4.50	12.00
	1936	—			Proof	—
	1938/7	1.000	.40	1.00	5.00	12.50
	1938	Inc. Ab.	.40	1.00	4.50	12.00
	1938	—			Proof	—
	1939	1.500	.50	1.25	4.50	9.50
	1939	—			Proof	—
	1946	.539	—	.15	.65	4.50
	1947	1.121	—	.15	.35	2.50
	1948	1.651	—	.15	.35	3.50
	1949	1.022	—	.15	.45	3.50

KM#	Date	Mintage	Fine	VF	XF	Unc
251	1943	.450	3.00	6.00	10.00	22.00
	1944	2.050	.50	1.25	2.50	8.00

Fray Bartolome de las Casas

KM#	Date	Mintage	Fine	VF	XF	Unc
254	1949	1.091	—	.15	.35	3.50
	1950	3.663	—	.15	.25	1.75
	1951	3.586	—	.15	.40	1.00
	1952	1.445	—	.15	.25	1.00
	1953	2.214	—	.15	.25	1.00
	1954	1.455	—	.15	.30	2.25

NICKEL-BRASS
Obv: Larger bust.

KM#	Date	Mintage	Fine	VF	XF	Unc
259	1954	10.000	—		.15	.50
	1957	1.600	—	.15	.25	.75
	1958	2.000	—	.15	.25	.60

BRASS
Obv: Larger legend.

KM#	Date	Mintage	Fine	VF	XF	Unc
260	1958	10.001	—		.15	.35
	1961	1.826	—		.15	.30
	1963	4.926	—		.15	.30
	1964	4.280	—		.15	.30

Size reduced, 19mm.

KM#	Date	Mintage	Fine	VF	XF	Unc
265	1965	3.845	—		.15	.25
	1966	6.100	—		.15	.25
	1967	6.400	—		.15	.25
	1968	2.590	—		.15	.25
	1969	13.780	—		.15	.25
	1970	10.511	—		.15	.25

NOTE: Varieties in size and style of date exist.

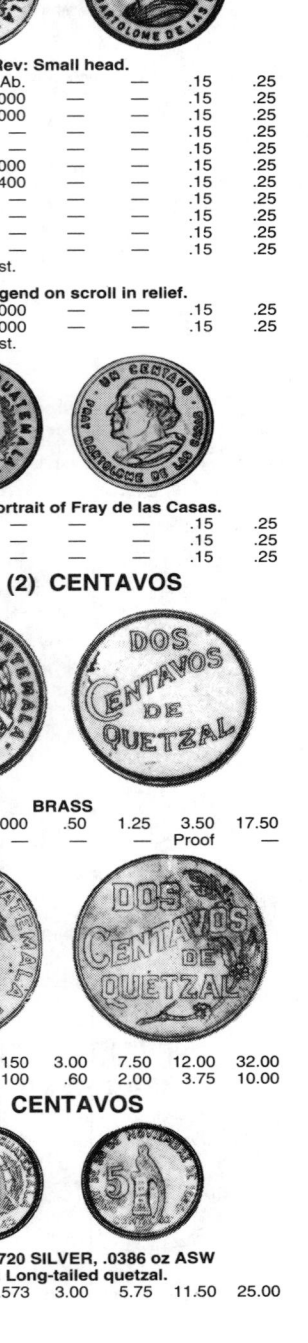

KM#	Date	Mintage	Fine	VF	XF	Unc
273	1972	11.500	—		.15	.25
	1973	12.000	—		.15	.25

Obv: Incuse legend on scroll. Rev: Large head.

KM#	Date	Mintage	Fine	VF	XF	Unc
275.1	1974	10.000	—		.15	.25
	1975	15.000	—		.15	.25
	1976	15.230	—	—.	.15	.25
	1977	30.000	—		.15	.25
	1978	30.000	—		.15	.25
	1979	30.000	—		.15	.25

Rev: Small head.

KM#	Date	Mintage	Fine	VF	XF	Unc
275.2	1979	Inc. Ab.	—		.15	.25
	1980	20.000	—		.15	.25
	1984	20.000	—		.15	.25
	1985	—	—		.15	.25
	1986	—	—		.15	.25
	1987	50.000	—		.15	.25
	1988	51.400	—		.15	.25
	1989	—	—		.15	.25
	1990	—	—		.15	.25
	1991	—	—		.15	.25
	1992	—	—		.15	.25

NOTE: Varieties exist.

Obv: Legend on scroll in relief.

KM#	Date	Mintage	Fine	VF	XF	Unc
275.3	1981	30.000	—		.15	.25
	1982	30.000	—		.15	.25

NOTE: Varieties exist.

Rev: New portrait of Fray de las Casas.

KM#	Date	Mintage	Fine	VF	XF	Unc
275.4	1993	—	—		.15	.25
	1994	—	—		.15	.25
	1995	—	—		.15	.25

DOS (2) CENTAVOS

BRASS

KM#	Date	Mintage	Fine	VF	XF	Unc
250	1932	3.000	.50	1.25	3.50	17.50
	1932	—			Proof	—

KM#	Date	Mintage	Fine	VF	XF	Unc
252	1943	.150	3.00	7.50	12.00	32.00
	1944	1.100	.60	2.00	3.75	10.00

5 CENTAVOS

1.6667 g, .720 SILVER, .0386 oz ASW
Obv: Long-tailed quetzal.

KM#	Date	Mintage	Fine	VF	XF	Unc
238.1	1925	.573	3.00	5.75	11.50	25.00

KM#	Date	Mintage	Fine	VF	XF	Unc
238.1	1944	1.026	BV	1.25	2.50	12.00
	1945	4.026	BV	.75	1.50	7.50
	1947	1.834	BV	1.00	1.50	5.00
	1948	1.103	BV	1.00	1.50	9.00
	1949	.551	.50	1.50	3.00	15.00

1.6667 g, .720 SILVER, .0386 oz ASW
Obv: Short-tailed quetzal.

KM#	Date	Mintage	Fine	VF	XF	Unc
238.2	1928	1.000	BV	1.00	2.00	7.50
	1928	—			Proof	—
	1929	1.000	BV	1.00	2.00	7.50
	1929	—			Proof	—
	1932	2.000	BV	1.00	1.50	6.50
	1932	—			Proof	—
	1933	.600	BV	1.00	2.50	9.00
	1933	—			Proof	—
	1934	1.200	BV	1.00	2.00	7.50
	1934	—			Proof	—
	1937	.400	BV	1.00	1.50	7.50
	1937	—			Proof	—
	1938	.300	.50	1.50	2.50	9.00
	1938	—			Proof	—
	1943	.900	BV	.75	1.50	5.00

KM#	Date	Mintage	Fine	VF	XF	Unc
255	1949	.305	.50	1.50	3.50	12.50

NOTE: Varieties exist.

KM#	Date	Mintage	Fine	VF	XF	Unc
257.1	1950	.453	BV	1.00	2.00	9.00
	1951	1.032	BV	1.00	1.50	5.00
	1952	.913	BV	1.00	1.50	4.00
	1953	.447	BV	1.00	2.50	4.00
	1954	.520	BV	1.00	1.50	8.00
	1955	2.062	BV	1.00	1.50	3.00
	1956	1.301	BV	1.00	1.50	3.00
	1957	2.941	BV	1.00	1.50	2.50

Small crude date	Large crude date

1.6667 g, .720 SILVER, .0386 oz ASW
Obv: Long-tailed quetzal.

KM#	Date	Mintage	Fine	VF	XF	Unc
257.2	1958 small date					
		3.025	BV	.75	1.00	1.50
	1958 large date					
		Inc. Ab.	BV	1.00	1.50	3.00
	1959	.232	BV	1.00	1.50	2.00

Obv: Short-tailed quetzal.

KM#	Date	Mintage	Fine	VF	XF	Unc
257.3	1958 small date					
		Inc. Ab.	BV	1.00	1.50	3.00

Rev: Level ground at tree.

KM#	Date	Mintage	Fine	VF	XF	Unc
261	1960	4.770	—	BV	.50	1.00
	1961	6.756	—	BV	.50	1.00
	1964	1.529	—	BV	.50	1.00

COPPER-NICKEL

KM#	Date	Mintage	Fine	VF	XF	Unc
266	1965	1.642	—	.15	.50	2.00
	1966	3.600	—		.15	.35
	1967	2.800	—		.15	.35
	1968	4.030	—		.15	.35
	1969	7.210	—		.15	.35
	1970	8.121	—		.15	.35

NOTE: Date size varieties exist.

Obv: Leg. on scroll incuse. Sm. shield and quetzal.

KM#	Date	Mintage	Fine	VF	XF	Unc
270	1971	8.270	—		.15	.35

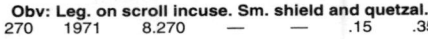

KM#	Date	Mintage	Fine	VF	XF	Unc
270	1974	10.575	—	—	.15	.35
	1975	10.000	—	—	.15	.35
	1976	6.000	—	—	.15	.35
	1977	20.000	—	—	.15	.35

Obv: Lg. shield and quetzal.

276.1	1977	Inc. Ab.	—	—	.15	.35
	1978	15.000	—	—	.15	.30
	1979	12.000	—	—	.15	.30

Obv: Legend on scroll in relief.

276.2	1980	8.000	—	—	.15	.30

Rev: Different tree.

276.3	1981	8.000	—	—	.15	.30
	1985	—	—	—	.15	.30

Obv: Legend on scroll incuse.
Rev: Smaller tree, less ground below.

276.4	1985	—	—	—	.15	.30
	1986 lg. date	—	—	—	.15	.30
	1986 sm. date	—	—	—	—	—
	1987	25.000	—	—	.15	.30
	1988	21.800	—	—	.15	.30
	1989	—	—	—	.15	.30
	1990	—	—	—	.15	.30
	1991	—	—	—	.15	.30
	1992	—	—	—	.15	.30
	1993	—	—	—	.15	.30
	1994	—	—	—	.15	.30
	1995	—	—	—	.15	.30
	1996	—	—	—	.15	.30

NOTE: Varieties exist.

Obv: Smaller letters
REPUBLICA DE GUATEMALA.

276.5	1995	—	—	—	.15	.30

Obv: Smaller sized emblem.

276.6	1997	—	—	—	.15	.30

10 CENTAVOS

3.3333 g, .720 SILVER, .0772 oz ASW
Obv: Long-tailed quetzal.

239.1	1925	.573	3.50	6.50	13.50	30.00
	1944	.155	1.00	2.75	5.75	15.00
	1945	1.499	BV	1.25	2.00	4.00
	1947	.471	BV	1.50	2.50	7.50
	1948	.324	BV	1.50	2.50	4.50
	1949	.145	BV	2.00	3.50	10.00

NOTE: Varieties exist.

3.3333 g, .720 SILVER, .0772 oz ASW
Obv: Short-tailed quetzal.

239.2	1928	.500	BV	2.50	5.00	10.00
	1928	—	—	—	Proof	—
	1929	.500	BV	2.00	3.50	12.50
	1929	—	—	—	Proof	—
	1932	.500	BV	2.00	3.50	10.00
	1932	—	—	—	Proof	—
	1933	.650	BV	1.75	3.00	10.00
	1933	—	—	—	Proof	—
	1934	.300	BV	1.75	3.00	15.00
	1934	—	—	—	Proof	—
	1936	.200	BV	2.50	4.50	17.50
	1936	—	—	—	Proof	—
	1938	.150	1.00	3.00	5.00	12.50

KM#	Date	Mintage	Fine	VF	XF	Unc
239.2	1938	—	—	—	Proof	—
	1943	.600	BV	1.25	2.50	7.50
	1947					
	Inc.KM239.1		BV	2.50	3.00	7.50

NOTE: Varieties exist.

Rev: Small monolith.

256.1	1949	.281	BV	2.50	3.50	10.00
	1950	.550	BV	1.50	2.50	5.00
	1951	.263	BV	2.50	4.50	12.00
	1952	.307	BV	1.50	2.50	5.00
	1953	.388	BV	1.50	2.50	5.00
	1955	.896	BV	1.50	2.50	5.00
	1956	.501	BV	1.50	2.50	7.50
	1958	1.528	BV	1.50	2.50	6.00

Rev: Larger monolith.

256.2	1957	1.123	BV	1.25	2.00	3.00
	1958	Inc. Ab.	BV	1.50	2.50	5.00
	1958 medal rotation					
		Inc. Ab.	6.00	12.00	22.50	40.00

Obv: Long-tailed quetzal. Rev: Small monolith.

256.3	1958	Inc. Ab.	BV	1.25	2.00	3.00
	1959	.461	BV	1.25	2.00	3.00
	1959 medal rotation					
		Inc. Ab.	6.00	12.00	22.50	37.50

262	1960	1.743	BV	1.50	2.00	2.50
	1961	2.647	BV	1.50	2.00	2.50
	1964	.965	BV	1.50	2.00	2.50

COPPER-NICKEL

267	1965	2.227	—	.15	.25	.75
	1966	1.550	—	.15	.35	.85
	1967	3.120	—	.15	.25	.75
	1968	3.220	—	.15	.25	.75
	1969	3.530	—	.15	.25	.75
	1970	4.153	—	.15	.25	.75

NOTE: Varieties exist.

Obv: Small wreath.

271.1	1971	4.580	—	.15	.25	.75

Obv: Large wreath.

271.2	1971	Inc. Ab.	—	.15	.25	.75
	1973	—	—	.15	.25	.75

KM#	Date	Mintage	Fine	VF	XF	Unc
274	1974	3.500	—	—	.15	.25 .75
	1975 dots flank date					
		6.000	—	.15	.25	.75

Wide rim toothed border.

277.1	1976	2.000	—	.15	.25	.75

Obv: Legend on scroll incuse.

277.2	1977	5.000	—	.15	.25	.75

Round beads instead of toothed border.

277.3	1978	8.500	—	.15	.25	.75
	1979	11.000	—	.15	.25	.75

Rev: Larger 10.

277.6	1986	—	—	.15	.25	.75
	1987	17.000	—	.15	.25	.75
	1988	13.250	—	.15	.25	.75
	1989	—	—	.15	.25	.75
	1990	—	—	.15	.25	.75
	1991	—	—	.15	.25	.75
	1992	—	—	.15	.25	.75
	1993	—	—	.15	.25	.75
	1994	—	—	.15	.25	.75

NOTE: Varieties exist.

Obv: Legend on scroll in relief, quetzal in silhouette.
Rev: Different design.

277.4	1980	5.000	—	.15	.25	.75
	1981	4.000	—	.15	.25	.75

Obv: Quetzal is solid, larger monolith.

277.5	1983	20.000	—	.15	.25	.75
	1986	—	—	.15	.25	.75

Obv: Smaller letters in
REPUBLICA DE GUATEMALA.

277.7	1995	—	—	.15	.25	.75
	1996	—	—	.15	.25	.75

1/4 QUETZAL

8.3333 g, .720 SILVER, .1929 oz ASW
Lettered edge

240.1	1925	1.160	3.75	8.00	25.00	50.00

Obv: W/o NOBLES below scroll.

KM#	Date	Mintage	Fine	VF	XF	Unc
240.2	1925	Inc. Ab.	37.50	75.00	175.00	400.00

8.3333 g, .720 SILVER, .1929 oz ASW
Rev: Larger design.

KM#	Date	Mintage	Fine	VF	XF	Unc
243.1	1926	2.000	2.00	4.00	10.00	30.00
	1926	—	—	—	Proof	—
	1928	.400	2.50	4.50	10.00	32.50
	1928	—	—	—	Proof	—
	1929	.400	2.50	5.00	12.50	35.00
	1929	—	—	—	Proof	—

Reeded edge.

KM#	Date	Mintage	Fine	VF	XF	Unc
243.2	1946	.203	3.00	6.50	13.50	22.00
	1947	.134	3.75	8.00	12.50	18.50
	1948	.129	3.75	7.50	12.00	18.50
	1949/8	.025	5.25	10.00	16.50	27.50
	1949	Inc. Ab.	15.00	38.50	80.00	145.00

25 CENTAVOS

8.3333 g, .720 SILVER, .1929 oz ASW

KM#	Date	Mintage	Fine	VF	XF	Unc
253	1943	.900	2.50	5.50	10.00	40.00

KM#	Date	Mintage	Fine	VF	XF	Unc
258	1950	.081	2.25	4.00	8.00	17.50
	1951	.011	7.50	16.50	27.50	75.00
	1952	.112	BV	2.75	6.00	10.00
	1954	.246	BV	2.75	5.00	9.00
	1955	.409	BV	2.75	5.00	9.00
	1956	.342	BV	2.75	5.00	9.00
	1957	.257	BV	2.75	5.00	9.00
	1958	.394	BV	2.75	5.00	9.00
	1959/8	.277	BV	2.75	5.00	9.00
	1959	Inc. Ab.	BV	2.75	6.00	12.50

KM#	Date	Mintage	Fine	VF	XF	Unc
263	1960	.560	BV	2.25	3.25	6.00
	1960 medal rotation					
		Inc. Ab.	20.00	50.00	100.00	175.00
	1961	.750	BV	2.25	3.25	6.00
	1963	1.100	BV	2.00	3.00	5.50
	1964	.299	BV	2.25	3.25	6.00

NOTE: Planchet size and weight vary in 1960 type as well as density of reeding.

COPPER-NICKEL

KM#	Date	Mintage	Fine	VF	XF	Unc
268	1965	1.178	.15	.25	.60	1.75
	1966	.910	.15	.25	.60	1.75

Rev: Modified design.

KM#	Date	Mintage	Fine	VF	XF	Unc
269	1967	1.140	.15	.25	.60	1.75
	1968	1.540	.15	.25	.60	1.50
	1969	2.070	.15	.25	.60	1.50
	1970	2.501	.15	.25	.60	1.50

KM#	Date	Mintage	Fine	VF	XF	Unc
272	1971	2.850	.15	.25	.50	1.00
	1975	1.592	.15	.25	.50	1.00
	1976	2.000	.15	.25	.50	1.00

Obv: Legend on scroll incuse. Rev: Large head.

KM#	Date	Mintage	Fine	VF	XF	Unc
278.1	1977	2.000	.15	.25	.50	1.00
	1978	4.400	.15	.25	.35	.85
	1979	5.400	.15	.25	.35	.85

Obv: Legend on scroll in relief. Rev: Small head.
Wide rim.

KM#	Date	Mintage	Fine	VF	XF	Unc
278.2	1981	1.600	.15	.25	.50	1.00

Obv: Quetzal is solid. Narrow rim.

KM#	Date	Mintage	Fine	VF	XF	Unc
278.4	1982	2.000	.15	.25	.50	1.00

Obv: Legend on scroll incuse.
Rev: Small head and denomination.

KM#	Date	Mintage	Fine	VF	XF	Unc
278.3	1984	2.000	.15	.25	.50	1.00

Rev: Large head and denomination.

KM#	Date	Mintage	Fine	VF	XF	Unc
278.5	1985	—	.15	.25	.35	.85
	1986	—	.15	.25	.35	.85
	1987	13.316	.15	.25	.35	.85
	1988	6.600	.15	.25	.35	.85
	1989	—	.15	.25	.35	.85
	1990	—	.15	.25	.35	.85
	1991	—	.15	.25	.35	.85

KM#	Date	Mintage	Fine	VF	XF	Unc
278.5	1992	—	.15	.25	.35	.85
	1993	—	.15	.25	.35	.85
	1994	—	.15	.25	.35	.85
	1995	—	.15	.25	.35	.85

NOTE: Varieties exist in number of wing feathers and details on head.

Edge: REPUBLICA DE GUATEMALA CA
Obv. and rev: Smaller design w/wider rims.

KM#	Date	Mintage	Fine	VF	XF	Unc
278.6	1996	—	.15	.25	.35	.85

1/2 QUETZAL

16.6667 g, .720 SILVER, .3858 oz ASW

KM#	Date	Mintage	Fine	VF	XF	Unc
241.1	1925	.400	16.50	27.50	58.00	220.00

Obv: W/o NOBLES below scroll.

KM#	Date	Mintage	Fine	VF	XF	Unc
241.2	1925	Inc. Ab.	70.00	100.00	200.00	600.00

50 CENTAVOS

12.0000 g, .720 SILVER, .2777 oz ASW

KM#	Date	Mintage	Fine	VF	XF	Unc
264	1962	1.983	—	BV	2.50	5.00
	1963/2	.350	3.50	7.50	12.50	20.00
	1963	Inc. Ab.	—	BV	2.50	5.00

QUETZAL

33.3333 g, .720 SILVER, .7716 oz ASW

KM#	Date	Mintage	Fine	VF	XF	Unc
242	1925	*.010	475.00	650.00	950.00	2000.

*NOTE: 7,000 pcs. were withdrawn and remelted soon after issue and more met with the same fate in 1932.

5 QUETZALES

8.3592 g, .900 GOLD, .2419 oz AGW

244	1926	.048	125.00	185.00	250.00	325.00

10 QUETZALES

16.7185 g, .900 GOLD, .4838 oz AGW

245	1926	.018	250.00	325.00	425.00	700.00

20 QUETZALES

33.4370 g, .900 GOLD, .9676 oz AGW

246	1926	.049	425.00	525.00	725.00	950.00

GUERNSEY

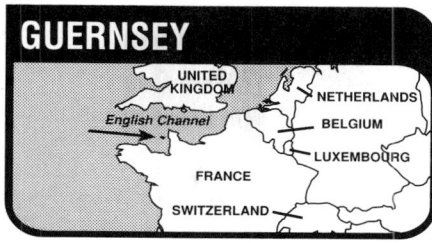

The Bailiwick of Guernsey, a British crown dependency located in the English Channel 30 miles (48 km.) west of Normandy, France, has an area of 30 sq. mi. (194 sq. km.) (including the isles of Alderney, Jethou, Herm, Brechou, and Sark), and a population of 54,000. Capital: St. Peter Port. Agriculture and cattle breeding are the main occupations.

Militant monks from the duchy of Normandy established the first permanent settlements on Guernsey prior to the Norman invasion of England, but the prevalence of prehistoric monuments suggests an earlier occupancy. The island, the only part of the duchy of Normandy belonging to the British crown, has been a possession of Britain since the Norman Conquest of 1066. During the Anglo-French wars, the harbors of Guernsey were employed in the building and outfitting of ships for the English privateers preying on French shipping. Guernsey is administered by its own laws and customs. Acts passed by the British Parliament are not applicable to Guernsey unless the island is specifically mentioned. During World War II, German troops occupied the island from June 30, 1940 till May 9, 1945.

RULERS

British

MINT MARKS

H - Heaton, Birmingham

MONETARY SYSTEM

8 Doubles = 1 Penny
12 Pence = 1 Shilling
5 Shillings = 1 Crown
20 Shillings = 1 Pound

DOUBLE

BRONZE

KM#	Date	Mintage	Fine	VF	XF	Unc
10	1902H	.084	.20	.60	2.25	4.00
	1902H	—	—	—	Proof	250.00
	1903H	.112	.15	.30	1.25	2.50
	1911H	.045	.50	1.50	4.00	12.00

NOTE: Earlier dates (1885-1899) exist for this type.

11	1911H	.090	.30	1.20	3.00	6.00
	1914H	.045	1.50	3.00	6.00	12.00
	1929H	.079	.30	.85	2.50	5.50
	1933H	.096	.30	.85	2.50	5.50
	1938H	.096	.30	.85	2.50	5.50

2 DOUBLES

BRONZE
Obv: Leaves w/1 stem.

8	1902H	.018	4.50	9.00	21.00	32.50
	1902H	—	—	—	Proof	250.00
	1903H	.018	6.00	12.50	25.00	37.50
	1906H	.018	6.00	12.50	25.00	37.50
	1908H	.018	6.00	12.50	25.00	37.50
	1911H	.029	4.50	9.00	15.00	27.50

NOTE: Earlier dates (1868-1899) exist for this type.

KM#	Date	Mintage	Fine	VF	XF	Unc
12	1914H	.029	4.50	9.00	18.50	27.50
	1914H	—	—	—	Proof	125.00
	1917H	.015	20.00	40.00	80.00	175.00
	1918H	.057	1.25	2.50	9.00	15.00
	1920H	.057	1.25	2.50	9.00	15.00
	1929H	.079	.35	1.25	6.00	10.00

4 DOUBLES

BRONZE
Obv: Leaves w/3 stems.

5	1902H	.105	.85	1.75	3.00	7.50
	1902H	—	—	—	Proof	250.00
	1903H	.052	1.50	3.00	9.00	25.00
	1906H	.052	1.50	3.00	9.00	25.00
	1908H	.026	3.00	7.50	15.00	30.00
	1910H	.052	1.50	3.00	9.00	25.00
	1910H	—	—	—	Proof	250.00
	1911H	.052	2.25	4.50	13.50	27.50

NOTE: Varieties exist.
NOTE: Earlier dates (1864-1893) exist for this type.

13	1914H	.209	.75	1.50	4.50	12.50
	1918H	.157	.75	1.50	6.00	17.50
	1920H	.157	.45	1.25	4.50	10.00
	1945H	.096	.45	1.25	4.50	10.00
	1949H	.019	1.50	3.00	12.00	20.00

Guernsey Lily

15	1956	.240	.25	.45	.75	2.00
	1956	2,100	—	—	Proof	4.00
	1966	.010	—	—	Proof	1.75

8 DOUBLES

BRONZE

7	1902H	.235	1.25	2.25	6.00	12.50
	1902H	—	—	—	Proof	250.00
	1903H	.118	.50	1.75	4.50	10.00
	1910H	.091	1.25	2.50	12.50	25.00
	1910H	—	—	—	Proof	250.00
	1911H	.078	3.00	8.50	15.00	30.00

NOTE: Earlier dates (1864-1893) exist for this type.

KM#	Date	Mintage	Fine	VF	XF	Unc
14	1914H	.157	.65	1.75	4.50	10.00
	1914H	—	—	—	Proof	150.00
	1918H	.157	.65	1.75	4.50	10.00
	1920H	.157	.50	1.50	4.00	9.00
	1920H	—	—	—	Proof	150.00
	1934H	.124	.50	1.50	4.00	9.00
	1934H	500 pcs.	—	—	Proof	175.00
	1938H	.120	.50	1.50	4.00	9.00
	1938H	—	—	—	Proof	250.00
	1945H	.192	.40	.85	2.00	5.50
	1947H	.240	.30	.60	2.25	5.00
	1949H	.230	.30	.60	2.25	5.00

3 Flowered Lily

KM#	Date	Mintage	Fine	VF	XF	Unc
16	1956	.500	.10	.20	.50	1.25
	1956	2,100	—	—	Proof	4.00
	1959	.500	.10	.20	.50	1.25
	1959	—	—	—	Proof	—
	1966	.010	—	—	Proof	1.75

3 PENCE

COPPER-NICKEL
Guernsey Cow
Thin flan.

KM#	Date	Mintage	Fine	VF	XF	Unc
17	1956	.500	.10	.20	.50	1.25
	1956	2,100	—	—	Proof	4.00

Thick flan.

KM#	Date	Mintage	Fine	VF	XF	Unc
18	1959	.500	.10	.20	.50	1.00
	1959	—	—	—	Proof	150.00
	1966	.010	—	—	Proof	1.75

10 SHILLINGS

COPPER-NICKEL
900th Anniversary - Norman Conquest

KM#	Date	Mintage	Fine	VF	XF	Unc
19	1966	.300	—	1.00	1.25	1.75
	1966	.010	—	—	Proof	3.00

DECIMAL COINAGE
100 Pence = 1 Pound

1/2 NEW PENNY

BRONZE

KM#	Date	Mintage	Fine	VF	XF	Unc
20	1971	2.066	—	—	.15	.30
	1971	.010	—	—	Proof	1.00

NEW PENNY

BRONZE
Gannet

KM#	Date	Mintage	Fine	VF	XF	Unc
21	1971	1.922	—	—	.15	.25
	1971	.010	—	—	Proof	1.00

PENNY

BRONZE
Gannet

KM#	Date	Mintage	Fine	VF	XF	Unc
27	1977	.640	—	—	.15	.25
	1979	2.400	—	—	.15	.25
	1979	.020	—	—	Proof	1.00
	1981	.010	—	—	Proof	2.00

Rev: Chancre crab.

KM#	Date	Mintage	Fine	VF	XF	Unc
40	1985	.060	—	—	.15	.30
	1985	2,500	—	—	Proof	2.00
	1986	1.010	—	—	.15	.30
	1986	2,500	—	—	Proof	2.00
	1987	5,000	—	—	.15	.30
	1987	*2,500	—	—	Proof	2.00
	1988	.500	—	—	.15	.30
	1988	2,500	—	—	Proof	2.00
	1989	1.000	—	—	.15	.30
	1989	*2,500	—	—	Proof	2.00
	1990	5,000	—	—	.15	.30
	1990	700 pcs.	—	—	Proof	4.00

COPPER PLATED STEEL

KM#	Date	Mintage	Fine	VF	XF	Unc
40a	1992	*	—	—	—	.30
	1992	*	—	—	Proof	5.00
	1994	.750	—	—	—	.30
	1997	2.000	—	—	—	.30

*NOTE: Only sold in sets.

2 NEW PENCE

BRONZE
Windmill From Sark

KM#	Date	Mintage	Fine	VF	XF	Unc
22	1971	1.680	—	—	.15	.35
	1971	.010	—	—	Proof	1.00

2 PENCE

BRONZE

Windmill From Sark

KM#	Date	Mintage	Fine	VF	XF	Unc
28	1977	.700	—	—	.15	.25
	1979	2.400	—	—	.15	.25
	1979	.020	—	—	Proof	1.00
	1981	.010	—	—	Proof	2.00

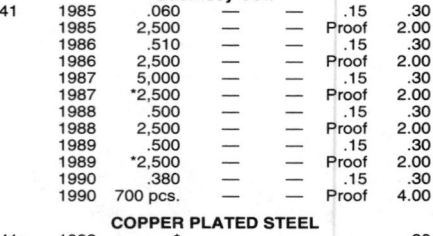

Guernsey Cow

KM#	Date	Mintage	Fine	VF	XF	Unc
41	1985	.060	—	—	.15	.30
	1985	2,500	—	—	Proof	2.00
	1986	.510	—	—	.15	.30
	1986	2,500	—	—	Proof	2.00
	1987	5,000	—	—	.15	.30
	1987	*2,500	—	—	Proof	2.00
	1988	.500	—	—	.15	.30
	1988	2,500	—	—	Proof	2.00
	1989	.500	—	—	.15	.30
	1989	*2,500	—	—	Proof	2.00
	1990	.380	—	—	.15	.30
	1990	700 pcs.	—	—	Proof	4.00

COPPER PLATED STEEL

KM#	Date	Mintage	Fine	VF	XF	Unc
41a	1992	*	—	—	—	.30
	1992	*	—	—	Proof	5.00
	1996	.500	—	—	—	.30

*NOTE: Only sold in sets.

5 NEW PENCE

COPPER-NICKEL
Guernsey Lily

KM#	Date	Mintage	Fine	VF	XF	Unc
23	1968	.800	—	.15	.25	.40
	1971	.010	—	—	Proof	1.50

5 PENCE

COPPER-NICKEL
Guernsey Lily

KM#	Date	Mintage	Fine	VF	XF	Unc
29	1977	.250	—	—	.20	.45
	1979	.200	—	—	.20	.45
	1979	.020	—	—	Proof	2.00
	1981	.010	—	—	Proof	3.00
	1982	.200	—	—	.20	.45

KM#	Date	Mintage	Fine	VF	XF	Unc
42.1	1985	.035	—	—	.20	.45
	1985	2,500	—	—	Proof	2.50
	1986	.100	—	—	.20	.45
	1986	2,500	—	—	Proof	2.50
	1987	.300	—	—	.20	.45
	1987	*2,500	—	—	Proof	2.50
	1988	.405	—	—	.20	.45
	1988	2,500	—	—	Proof	2.50
	1989	5,000	—	—	.20	.50
	1989	*2,500	—	—	Proof	2.50
	1990	*2,520	—	—	.20	.60
	1990	700 pcs.	—	—	Proof	5.00

Reduced size.

KM#	Date	Mintage	Fine	VF	XF	Unc
42.2	1990	2.400	—	—	.20	.45
	1990	700 pcs.	—	—	Proof	5.00
	1992	1.300	—	—	—	.50
	1992	*	—	—	Proof	6.00
	1997	*	—	—	—	.50

*NOTE: Only sold in sets.

10 NEW PENCE

COPPER-NICKEL
Guernsey Cow

KM#	Date	Mintage	Fine	VF	XF	Unc
24	1968	.600	—	.20	.40	1.00
	1970	.300	—	.20	.40	1.00
	1971	.010	—	—	Proof	2.00

10 PENCE

COPPER-NICKEL
Guernsey Cow

KM#	Date	Mintage	Fine	VF	XF	Unc
30	1977	.480	—	—	.25	.85
	1979	.659	—	—	.25	.85
	1979	.020	—	—	Proof	2.00
	1981	.010	—	—	Proof	3.00
	1982	.200	—	—	.25	1.00
	1984	.400	—	—	.25	.85

Tomato Plant

43.1	1985	.110	—	—	.25	.60
	1985	2,500	—	—	Proof	2.50
	1986	.300	—	—	.25	.60
	1986	2,500	—	—	Proof	6.00
	1987	.250	—	—	.25	.60
	1987	*2,500	—	—	Proof	2.50
	1988	.300	—	—	.25	.60
	1988	2,500	—	—	Proof	2.50
	1989	.200	—	—	.25	.60
	1989	*2,500	—	—	Proof	2.50
	1990	3,500	—	—	.25	.60
	1990	700 pcs.	—	—	Proof	5.00

Reduced size, 24.5mm.

43.2	1992	3.500	—	—	—	.60
	1992	*	—	—	Proof	6.00

*NOTE: Only sold in sets.

20 PENCE

COPPER-NICKEL
Guernsey Milk Can

38	1982	.500	—	—	.45	.90
	1983	.500	—	—	.45	.90

44	1985	.035	—	—	.45	.85
	1985	2,500	—	—	Proof	3.00
	1986	.010	—	—	.45	.85
	1986	2,500	—	—	Proof	3.00
	1987	5,000	—	—	.45	.85
	1987	*2,500	—	—	Proof	3.00
	1988	5,000	—	—	.45	.85
	1988	2,500	—	—	Proof	3.00
	1989	.093	—	—	.45	.85
	1989	*2,500	—	—	Proof	3.00

KM#	Date	Mintage	Fine	VF	XF	Unc
44	1990	.113	—	—	.45	.85
	1990	700 pcs.	—	—	Proof	6.00
	1992	.800	—	—	—	1.00
	1992	*	—	—	Proof	7.00
	1997	*	—	—	—	1.00

*NOTE: Only sold in sets.

50 NEW PENCE

COPPER-NICKEL
Ducal Cap of Duke of Normandy

25	1969	.200	—	1.00	1.50	2.50
	1970	.200	—	1.00	1.50	2.50
	1971	.010	—	—	Proof	3.00

50 PENCE

COPPER-NICKEL
Ducal Cap of Duke of Normandy

34	1979	.020	—	—	Proof	4.50
	1981	.200	—	—	.90	1.45
	1981	.010	—	—	Proof	5.50
	1982	.150	—	—	.90	1.45
	1983	.200	—	—	.90	1.45
	1984	.200	—	—	.90	1.45

45.1	1985	.035	—	—	.90	1.45
	1985	2,500	—	—	Proof	4.00
	1986	.010	—	—	.90	1.45
	1986	2,500	—	—	Proof	4.00
	1987	5,000	—	—	.90	1.45
	1987	*2,500	—	—	Proof	4.50
	1988	6,000	—	—	.90	1.45
	1988	2,500	—	—	Proof	4.00
	1989	.055	—	—	.90	1.45
	1989	*2,500	—	—	Proof	4.50
	1990	.080	—	—	.90	1.45
	1990	700 pcs.	—	—	Proof	7.50
	1992	.065	—	—	—	2.00
	1992	*	—	—	Proof	10.00

*NOTE: Only sold in sets.

Smaller size: 27.3mm.
Obv: Queen's portrait. Rev: Crossed flowers.

45.2	1997	1.000	—	—	—	1.75

POUND

COPPER-NICKEL-ZINC

Guernsey Lily

KM#	Date	Mintage	Fine	VF	XF	Unc
37	1981	.200	—	1.80	2.00	3.50
	1981	.010	—	—	Proof	4.50

ALUMINUM-BRONZE
H.M.S. Crescent

39	1983	.269	—	1.80	2.00	3.50

COPPER-NICKEL-ZINC

46	1985	.035	—	—	1.75	2.50
	1985	2,500	—	—	Proof	6.50
	1986	.010	—	—	1.75	2.50
	1986	2,500	—	—	Proof	6.50
	1987	5,000	—	—	1.75	2.50
	1987	*2,500	—	—	Proof	6.50
	1988	5,000	—	—	1.75	2.50
	1988	2,500	—	—	Proof	6.50
	1989	5,000	—	—	1.75	2.50
	1989	*2,500	—	—	Proof	6.50
	1990	3,500	—	—	1.75	2.50
	1990	700 pcs.	—	—	Proof	10.00
	1992	*	—	—	—	3.50
	1992	*	—	—	Proof	12.50
	1997	*	—	—	Proof	3.50

*NOTE: Only sold in sets.

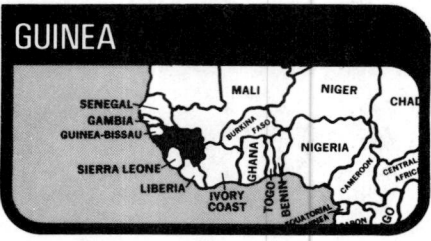

GUINEA

The Republic of Guinea, situated on the Atlantic Coast of Africa between Sierra Leone and Guinea-Bissau, has an area of 94,964 sq. mi. (245,860 sq. km.) and a population of 6.4 million. Capital: Conakry. Although Guinea contains one-third of the world's reserves of bauxite and significant deposits of iron ore, gold and diamonds, the economy is still dependent on argiculture. Aluminum, bananas, copra and coffee are exported.

The coast of Guinea was known to Portuguese navigators of the 15th century but was seldom visited by European traders of the 16th-18th centuries because of its dangerous coastal waters. French penetration of the area began in the mid-19th century with the entering into of protectorate treaties with several of the coastal chiefs. After a long struggle with Guinea's native leader Samory Toure, France secured the area and until 1890 administered it as a part of Senegal. In 1895 the colony (Guinee Francais) became an autonomous part of the federation of French West Africa. The inhabitants were extended French citizenship in 1946 when the colony became an overseas territory of the French Union. Guinea became an independent republic on Oct. 2, 1958, when it declined to enter the new French Community.

MONETARY SYSTEM
100 Centimes = 1 Franc
FRANC

COPPER-NICKEL
Ahmed Sekou Toure

KM#	Date	Mintage	Fine	VF	XF	Unc
4	1962	—	1.25	2.00	3.50	7.00
	1962	—			Proof	50.00

5 FRANCS

ALUMINUM-BRONZE
Ahmed Sekou Toure
1	1959	—	2.75	4.75	9.00	22.50

COPPER-NICKEL
| 5 | 1962 | — | 1.25 | 2.00 | 3.00 | 6.50 |
| | 1962 | — | — | | Proof | 70.00 |

*NOTE: Mule of two obverses of KM5 exists.

10 FRANCS

ALUMINUM-BRONZE
Ahmed Sekou Toure
| 2 | 1959 | — | 5.00 | 10.00 | 20.00 | 45.00 |

COPPER-NICKEL
KM#	Date	Mintage	Fine	VF	XF	Unc
6	1962	—	1.75	2.75	6.00	11.50
	1962				Proof	85.00

25 FRANCS

ALUMINUM-BRONZE
Ahmed Sekou Toure
| 3 | 1959 | — | 9.00 | 16.00 | 30.00 | 90.00 |

COPPER-NICKEL
| 7 | 1962 | — | 2.50 | 4.00 | 7.50 | 14.00 |
| | 1962 | — | — | | Proof | 120.00 |

50 FRANCS

COPPER-NICKEL
Ahmed Sekou Toure
| 8 | 1969 | 4.000 | — | | 35.00 | 55.00 |

NOTE: Not released into circulation.

DECIMAL COINAGE
100 Cauris = 1 Syli
50 CAURIS

ALUMINUM
Nkrumah
| 42 | 1971 | — | 1.00 | 2.00 | 3.50 | 6.00 |

SYLI

ALUMINUM
| 43 | 1971 | — | 2.00 | 3.00 | 5.50 | 12.50 |

2 SYLIS

ALUMINUM
KM#	Date	Mintage	Fine	VF	XF	Unc
44	1971	—	1.00	2.00	4.00	8.00

5 SYLIS

ALUMINUM
| 45 | 1971 | — | 1.25 | 2.25 | 4.50 | 9.00 |

MONETARY REFORM
FRANC

BRASS CLAD STEEL
| 56 | 1985 | — | .10 | .20 | .40 | 1.00 |

5 FRANCS

BRASS CLAD STEEL
| 53 | 1985 | — | .10 | .20 | .40 | 1.00 |

10 FRANCS

BRASS CLAD STEEL
| 52 | 1985 | — | .20 | .40 | .80 | 1.25 |

25 FRANCS

BRASS
| 60 | 1987 | — | .20 | .40 | .85 | 1.75 |

50 FRANCS

COPPER-NICKEL
| 63 | 1994 | — | .30 | .60 | 1.25 | 2.75 |

GUINEA-BISSAU

The Republic of Guinea-Bissau, formerly Portuguese Guinea, an overseas province on the west coast of Africa between Senegal and Guinea, has an area of 13,948 sq. mi. (36,120 sq. km.) and a population of 1.1 million. Capital: Bissau. The country has undeveloped deposits of oil and bauxite. Peanuts, oil-palm kernels and hides are exported.

Portuguese Guinea was discovered by Portuguese navigator Nuno Tristao in 1446. Trading rights in the area were granted to Cape Verde islanders but few prominent posts were established before 1851, and they were principally coastal installations. The chief export of this colony's early period was slaves for South America, a practice that adversely affected trade with the native people and retarded subjection of the interior. Territorial disputes with France delayed final demarcation of the colony's frontiers until 1905.

The African Party for the Independence of Guinea-Bissau was founded in 1956, and several years later began a guerrilla warfare that grew in effectiveness until 1974, when the rebels controlled most of the colony. Portugal's costly overseas wars in her African territories resulted in a military coup in Portugal in April 1974, that appreciably brightened the prospects for freedom for Guinea-Bissau. In August, 1974, the Lisbon government signed an agreement granting independence to Portuguese Guinea effective Sept. 10, 1974. The new republic took the name of Guinea-Bissau.

RULERS
Portuguese until 1974

PORTUGUESE GUINEA

MONETARY SYSTEM
100 Centavos = 1 Escudo

5 CENTAVOS

BRONZE

KM#	Date	Mintage	Fine	VF	XF	Unc
1	1933	.100	3.50	7.00	20.00	60.00

10 CENTAVOS

BRONZE

2	1933	.250	12.50	25.00	75.00	280.00

ALUMINUM

12	1973	.100	2.00	4.00	10.00	20.00

20 CENTAVOS

BRONZE

3	1933	.350	4.50	9.00	25.00	50.00

KM#	Date	Mintage	Fine	VF	XF	Unc
13	1973	.100	2.00	4.00	10.00	20.00

50 CENTAVOS

NICKEL-BRONZE

4	1933	.600	7.00	15.00	45.00	200.00

BRONZE
500th Anniversary of Discovery

6	ND(1946)	2.000	1.00	2.00	5.00	18.00

8	1952	10.000	.50	1.00	2.00	5.00

ESCUDO

NICKEL-BRONZE

5	1933	.800	10.00	22.00	60.00	250.00

BRONZE
500th Anniversary of Discovery

7	ND(1946)	2.000	1.50	3.50	7.50	20.00

14	1973	.250	1.75	4.00	10.00	28.00

2-1/2 ESCUDOS

COPPER-NICKEL

9	1952	3.010	1.00	2.00	4.00	10.00

5 ESCUDOS

COPPER-NICKEL

KM#	Date	Mintage	Fine	VF	XF	Unc
15	1973	.800	1.50	3.00	6.50	15.00

10 ESCUDOS

5.0000 g, .720 SILVER, .1157 oz ASW

10	1952	1.200	3.50	7.00	20.00	60.00

COPPER-NICKEL

16	1973	1.700	2.00	4.00	12.00	30.00

20 ESCUDOS

 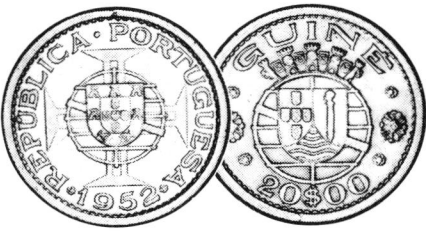

10.0000 g, .720 SILVER, .2315 oz ASW

11	1952	.750	5.00	10.00	25.00	60.00

GUINEA-BISSAU

MONETARY SYSTEM
100 Centavos = 1 Peso

50 CENTAVOS

ALUMINUM
F.A.O. Issue

17	1977	6.000	2.00	3.00	5.00	9.00

PESO

ALUMINUM-BRONZE
F.A.O. Issue

18	1977	7.000	2.25	3.50	6.50	10.00

2-1/2 PESOS

ALUMINUM-BRONZE
F.A.O. Issue

KM#	Date	Mintage	Fine	VF	XF	Unc
19	1977	4.000	2.25	4.50	7.00	12.00

ALUMINUM

19a	1977	—	—	—	—	—

5 PESOS

COPPER-NICKEL
F.A.O. Issue

20	1977	6.000	2.50	5.00	7.50	13.50

20 PESOS

COPPER-NICKEL
F.A.O. Issue

21	1977	2.500	4.00	7.50	12.50	20.00

GUYANA (British Guiana)

 (map region)

The Cooperative Republic of Guyana, an independent member of the British Commonwealth situated on the northeast coast of South America, has an area of 83,000 sq. mi. (214,970 sq. km.) and a population of 729,000. Capital: Georgetown. The economy is basically agrarian. Sugar, rice and bauxite are exported.

The original area of Essequibo and Demerary, which included present-day Suriname, French Guiana, and parts of Brazil and Venezuela was sighted by Columbus in 1498. The first European settlement was made late in the 16th century by the Dutch, however, the region was claimed for the British by Sir Walter Raleigh during the reign of Elizabeth I. For the next 150 years, possession alternated between the Dutch and the British, with a short interval of French control. The British exercised de facto control after 1796, although the area, which included the Dutch colonies of Essequibo, Demerary and Berbice, was not ceded to them by the Dutch until 1814. From 1803 to 1831, Essequibo and Demerary were administered separately from Berbice. The three colonies were united in the British Crown Colony of British Guiana in 1831. British Guiana won internal self-government in 1952 and full independence, under the traditional name of Guyana, on May 26, 1966. Guyana became a republic on Feb. 23, 1970. It is a member of the Commonwealth of Nations. The president is the Chief of State. The prime minister is the Head of Government.

RULERS

British, until 1966

BRITISH GUIANA AND WEST INDIES

MONETARY SYSTEM

12 Pence = 1 Shilling
4 Shillings 2 Pence = 1 Dollar

4 PENCE

1.8851 g, .925 SILVER, .0560 oz ASW

KM#	Date	Mintage	Fine	VF	XF	Unc
26	1901	.060	3.00	7.50	17.50	55.00

NOTE: Earlier dates (1891-1900) exist for this type.

27	1903	.060	3.00	7.50	17.50	55.00
	1903	—	—	Matte Proof		450.00
	1908	.030	5.00	12.50	25.00	90.00
	1909	.036	5.00	12.50	25.00	90.00
	1910	.066	3.00	10.00	22.50	85.00

28	1911	.030	6.00	14.50	35.00	115.00
	1913	.030	6.00	14.50	35.00	115.00
	1916	.030	6.00	14.50	35.00	115.00

BRITISH GUIANA

4 PENCE

1.8851 g, .925 SILVER, .0560 oz ASW

29	1917	.072	3.00	7.50	22.50	90.00
	1917	—	—	Matte Proof		450.00
	1918	.210	1.25	3.50	15.00	55.00
	1921	.090	3.00	7.50	17.50	70.00
	1923	.012	20.00	45.00	85.00	160.00

KM#	Date	Mintage	Fine	VF	XF	Unc
29	1925	.030	3.50	8.50	32.50	100.00
	1926	.030	3.50	8.50	25.00	65.00
	1931	.015	10.00	25.00	60.00	120.00
	1931	—	—	—	Proof	175.00
	1935	.036	3.00	—	7.50	20.00	55.00
	1935	—	—	—	Proof	175.00
	1936	.063	1.75	—	2.50	10.00	30.00
	1936	—	—	—	Proof	225.00

30	1938	.030	1.75	2.50	10.00	25.00
	1938	—	—	—	Proof	175.00
	1939	.048	1.75	2.50	7.50	20.00
	1939	—	—	—	Proof	175.00
	1940	.090	1.25	2.00	3.50	18.50
	1940	—	—	—	Proof	175.00
	1941	.120	1.25	1.75	3.00	12.50
	1941	—	—	—	Proof	175.00
	1942	.180	1.25	1.75	3.00	12.50
	1942	—	—	—	Proof	175.00
	1943	.240	1.25	1.75	2.50	8.00
	1943	—	—	—	Proof	400.00

1.8851 g, .500 SILVER, .0303 oz ASW

30a	1944	.090	.75	1.25	2.50	8.00
	1945	.120	.50	1.00	2.00	7.00
	1945	—	—	—	Proof	200.00

GUYANA

MONETARY SYSTEM

100 Cents = 1 Dollar

MINT MARKS

FM - Franklin Mint, U.S.A.*

NOTE: From 1975-1985 the Franklin Mint produced coinage in up to 3 different qualities. Qualities of issue are designated in ( ) after each date and are defined as follows:

(M) MATTE - Normal circulation strike or a dull finish produced by sandblasting special uncirculated (polish finish) or proof quality dies.

(U) SPECIAL UNCIRCULATED - Polished or proof-like in appearance without any frosted features.

(P) PROOF - The highest quality obtainable having mirror-like fields and frosted features.

CENT

 (coin obverse)

NICKEL-BRASS
Stylized Lotus Flower

KM#	Date	Mintage	VF	XF	Unc
31	1967	6.000	—	.10	.25
	1967	5,100	—	Proof	2.00
	1969	4.000	—	.10	.25
	1970	6.000	—	.10	.25
	1971	4.000	—	.10	.25
	1972	4.000	—	.10	.25
	1973	4.000	—	.10	.25
	1974	11.000	—	.10	.20
	1975	—	—	.10	.25
	1976	—	—	.10	.25
	1977	16.000	—	.10	.20
	1978	10.450	—	.10	.20
	1979	—	—	.10	.20
	1980	12.000	—	.10	.20
	1981	10.000	—	.10	.20
	1982	8.000	—	.10	.20
	1983	12.000	—	.10	.20
	1985	8.000	—	.10	.20
	1987	6.000	—	.10	.20
	1988	.080	—	.10	.20
	1989	—	—	.10	.20
	1991	—	—	.10	.20
	1992	—	—	.10	.20

 (coin)

BRONZE
10th Anniversary of Independence - Manatee

37	1976FM(M)	.015	—	.15	1.00
	1976FM(U)	50 pcs.	—	—	—
	1976FM(P)	.028	—	Proof	1.25
	1977FM(M)	—	—	—	3.00
	1977FM(U)	.015	—	.20	1.00
	1977FM(P)	7,215	—	Proof	1.25
	1978FM(M)	—	—	—	3.00
	1978FM(U)	.015	—	.20	1.00
	1978FM(P)	5,044	—	Proof	1.25
	1979FM(U)	.015	—	.20	1.00

KM#	Date	Mintage	VF	XF	Unc
37	1979FM(P)	3,547	—	Proof	1.25
	1980FM(U)	.030	—	.20	1.00
	1980FM(P)	2,763	—	Proof	1.50

5 CENTS

NICKEL-BRASS
Stylized Lotus Flower

32	1967	4.600	—	.10	.25
	1967	5,100	—	Proof	2.25
	1972	1.200	—	.10	.30
	1974	3.000	—	.10	.30
	1975	—	—	.10	.30
	1976	—	—	.10	.30
	1977	1.500	—	.10	.30
	1978	*2,000	—	.50	4.00
	1979	—	—	—	—
	1980	1.000	—	.10	.30
	1981	1.000	—	.10	.30
	1982	2.000	—	.10	.30
	1985	3.000	—	.10	.30
	1986	4.000	—	.10	.30
	1987	3.000	—	.10	.30
	1988	2.000	—	.10	.30
	1989	—	—	.10	.30
	1990	—	—	.10	.30
	1991	—	—	.10	.30
	1992	—	—	.10	.30

NOTE: Varieties exist.

BRASS
10th Anniversary of Independence - Jaguar

38	1976FM(M)	.015	—	.20	1.50
	1976FM(U)	50 pcs.	—	—	—
	1976FM(P)	.028	—	Proof	1.50
	1977FM(M)	—	—	—	5.00
	1977FM(U)	.015	—	.20	1.50
	1977FM(P)	7,215	—	Proof	1.75
	1978FM(M)	—	—	—	5.00
	1978FM(U)	.015	—	.20	1.50
	1978FM(P)	5,044	—	Proof	1.75
	1979FM(U)	.015	—	.20	1.50
	1979FM(P)	3,547	—	Proof	1.75
	1980FM(U)	.030	—	.20	1.50
	1980FM(P)	2,763	—	Proof	2.00

10 CENTS

COPPER-NICKEL

33	1967	4.000	.10	.20	.35
	1967	5,100	—	Proof	2.50
	1973	1.500	.10	.20	.35
	1974	1.700	.10	.20	.35
	1976	—	.10	.20	.35
	1977	4.000	.10	.20	.35
	1978	2.010	.10	.20	.35
	1979	—	.10	.20	.35
	1980	1.000	.10	.20	.35
	1981	1.000	.10	.20	.35
	1982	2.000	.10	.20	.35
	1985	3.000	.10	.20	.35
	1986	4.000	.10	.20	.35
	1987	3.000	.10	.20	.35
	1988	2.000	.10	.20	.35
	1989	—	.10	.20	.35
	1990	—	.10	.20	.35
	1991	—	.10	.20	.35
	1992	—	.10	.20	.35

10th Anniversary of Independence - Squirrel Monkey

39	1976	2.006	—	.20	1.00
	1976FM(M)	.010	—	.20	1.00
	1976FM(U)	50 pcs.	—	—	—
	1976FM(P)	.028	—	Proof	2.00
	1977	1.500	—	.20	1.00
	1977FM(M)	—	—	—	8.00
	1977FM(U)	.010	—	.20	1.00
	1977FM(P)	7,215	—	Proof	2.00

KM#	Date	Mintage	VF	XF	Unc
39	1978FM(M)	—	—	—	8.00
	1978FM(U)	.010	—	.20	1.00
	1978FM(P)	5,044	—	Proof	2.00
	1979FM(U)	.010	—	.20	1.00
	1979FM(P)	3,547	—	Proof	2.00
	1980FM(U)	.020	—	.20	1.00
	1980FM(P)	2,763	—	Proof	2.50

25 CENTS

COPPER-NICKEL

34	1967	3.500	.15	.25	.65
	1967	5,100	—	Proof	3.00
	1972	1.000	.15	.25	.65
	1974	4.000	.15	.25	.65
	1975	—	.15	.25	.65
	1976	—	.15	.25	.65
	1977	4.000	.15	.25	.65
	1978	2.006	.15	.25	.65
	1981	1.000	.15	.25	.65
	1982	1.500	.15	.25	.65
	1984	1.000	.15	.25	.65
	1985	2.000	.15	.25	.65
	1986	4.000	.15	.25	.65
	1987	3.000	.15	.25	.65
	1988	4.000	.15	.25	.65
	1989	—	.15	.25	.65
	1990	—	.15	.25	.65
	1991	—	.15	.25	.65
	1992	—	.15	.25	.65

10th Anniversary of Independence - Harpy Eagle

40	1976FM(M)	4,000	—	.30	1.75
	1976FM(U)	50 pcs.	—	—	—
	1976FM(P)	.028	—	Proof	2.00
	1977	2.000	.15	.25	1.00
	1977FM(M)	—	—	—	10.00
	1977FM(U)	4,000	—	.30	4.00
	1977FM(P)	7,215	—	Proof	2.00
	1978FM(M)	—	—	—	10.00
	1978FM(U)	4,000	—	.30	4.00
	1978FM(P)	5,044	—	Proof	2.00
	1979FM(U)	4,000	—	.30	4.00
	1979FM(P)	3,547	—	Proof	2.00
	1980FM(U)	8,437	—	.30	4.00
	1980FM(P)	2,763	—	Proof	2.50

50 CENTS

COPPER-NICKEL

35	1967	1.000	.25	.35	.75
	1967	5,100	—	Proof	3.50

10th Anniversary of Independence - Hoatzin

41	1976FM(M)	2,000	—	.40	5.00
	1976FM(U)	50 pcs.	—	—	—
	1976FM(P)	.028	—	Proof	3.50
	1977FM(M)	—	—	—	20.00
	1977FM(U)	2,000	—	.40	5.00
	1977FM(P)	7,215	—	Proof	3.00
	1978FM(M)	—	—	—	20.00
	1978FM(U)	2,000	—	.40	5.00
	1978FM(P)	5,044	—	Proof	3.00
	1979FM(U)	2,000	—	.40	5.00
	1979FM(P)	3,547	—	Proof	3.00
	1980FM(U)	4,437	—	.40	3.50
	1980FM(P)	2,763	—	Proof	4.00

DOLLAR

COPPER-NICKEL
F.A.O. Issue

KM#	Date	Mintage	VF	XF	Unc
36	1970	.500	.50	1.50	3.50
	1970	5,000	—	Proof	5.00

10th Anniversary of Independence - Common Caiman

42	1976FM(M)	600 pcs.	—	.50	5.00
	1976FM(U)	50 pcs.	—	—	—
	1976FM(P)	.028	—	Proof	5.50
	1977FM(M)	—	—	—	30.00
	1977FM(U)	500 pcs.	—	.50	5.00
	1977FM(P)	7,215	—	Proof	7.00
	1978FM(M)	—	—	—	30.00
	1978FM(U)	500 pcs.	—	.50	5.00
	1978FM(P)	5,044	—	Proof	7.00
	1979FM(U)	500 pcs.	—	.50	5.00
	1979FM(P)	3,547	—	Proof	7.00
	1980FM(U)	1,437	—	.50	5.00
	1980FM(P)	2,763	—	Proof	8.00

COPPER PLATED STEEL
Hand Gathering Rice

50	1996	—	—	—	.50

5 DOLLARS

COPPER PLATED STEEL
Sugar Cane

51	1996	—	—	—	.75

10 DOLLARS

NICKEL PLATED STEEL
Seven Sided Gold Mining Scene

52	1996	—	—	—	1.25

HAITI

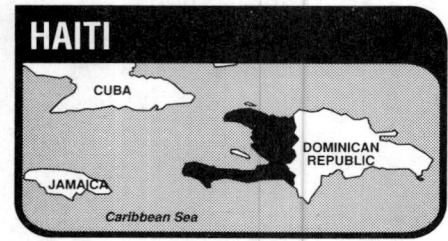

CUBA

JAMAICA

DOMINICAN REPUBLIC

Caribbean Sea

The Republic of Haiti, which occupies the western one-third of the island of Hispaniola in the Caribbean Sea between Puerto Rico and Cuba, has an area of 10,714 sq. mi.(27,750 sq. km.) and a population of 6.5 million. Capital: Port-au-Prince. The economy is based on agriculture; but light manufacturing and tourism are increasingly important. Coffee, bauxite, sugar, essential oils and handicrafts are exported.

Columbus discovered Hispaniola in 1492. Spain colonized the island, making Santo Domingo the base for exploration of the Western Hemisphere. The area that is now Haiti was ceded to France by Spain in 1697. Slaves brought from Africa to work the coffee and sugar cane plantations made it one of the richest colonies of the French Empire. A slave revolt in the 1790's led to the establishment of the Republic of Haiti in 1804, making it the oldest Black republic in the world and the second oldest republic (after the United States) in the Western Hemisphere.

The French language is used on Haitian coins although it is spoken by only about 10% of the populace. A form of Creole is the language of the Haitians.

Two dating systems are used on Haiti's 19th century coins. One is Christian, the other Revolutionary - beginning in 1803 when the French were permanently ousted by a native revolt. Thus, a date of AN30, (i.e., year 30) is equivalent to 1833 A.D. Some coins carry both date forms. In the listings which follow coins dated only in the Revolutionary system are listed by AN years in the date column.

MINT MARKS

A - Paris
(a) - Paris, privy marks only
HEATON - Birmingham
R - Rome
(w) = Waterbury (Connecticut, USA) (Scoville Mfg. Co.)

MONETARY SYSTEM
100 Centimes = 1 Gourde

5 CENTIMES

COPPER-NICKEL

KM#	Date	Mintage	Fine	VF	XF	Unc
52	1904 (a)	—	2.50	5.50	12.50	35.00
	1904 (a)	—	—	—	Proof	120.00

NOTE: Struck at Waterbury, Connecticut by the Scovill Mfg. Co. Design incorporates Paris privy and mint director's marks.

President Nord Alexis

53	1904(w)	2.000	.50	2.00	4.00	15.00
	1904(w)	—	—	—	Proof	90.00
	1905(w)	20.000	.30	1.00	2.50	10.00
	1905(w)	—	—	—	Proof	100.00
	1906(w)	10.000	—	Reported, not confirmed		

President Dumarsais Estime

57	1949	10.000	.10	.20	.40	1.25

NICKEL-SILVER
President Paul E. Magloire

KM#	Date	Mintage	Fine	VF	XF	Unc
59	1953	3.000	.15	.25	.50	1.50

COPPER-NICKEL
President Francois Duvalier

62	1958	15.000	—	—	.10	.25
	1970	5.000	—	—	.10	.20

F.A.O. Issue - President Jean-Claude Duvalier

119	1975	16.000	—	—	.10	.20

F.A.O. Issue

145	1981R	.015	—	.10	.25	.65

STEEL
Obv: Portrait of national hero, Charlemagne Peralte. Rev: National emblem.

154	1995	—	—	—	—	.25

NICKEL PLATED STEEL

154a	1995	—	—	—	—	.35

10 CENTIMES
(0.10 GOURDES)

COPPER-NICKEL
President Nord Alexis

54	1906(w)	10.000	.50	1.50	5.00	15.00
	1906(w)	—	—	—	Proof	100.00

President Dumarsais Estime

58	1949	5.000	.15	.25	.50	1.50

NICKEL-SILVER
President Paul E. Magloire

60	1953	1.500	—	.10	.25	1.25

COPPER-NICKEL
President Francois Duvalier

KM#	Date	Mintage	Fine	VF	XF	Unc
63	1958	7.500	—	.10	.15	.35
	1970	2.500	—	.10	.10	.20

F.A.O. Issue - President Jean-Claude Duvalier

120	1975	12.000	—	—	.10	.20
	1983	2.000	—	—	.10	.30

F.A.O. Issue

146	1981R	.015	—	.10	.25	.85

Obv: Portrait. Rev: National emblem.

157	1995	—	—	—	—	.45

20 CENTIMES
(0.20 Gourdes)

COPPER-NICKEL
President Nord Alexis

55	1907(w)	5.000	1.00	2.00	4.50	15.00
	1907(w)	—	—	—	Proof	125.00
	1908(w)	—	—	Reported, not confirmed		

NICKEL-SILVER
President Paul E. Magloire

61	1956	2.500	.20	.35	.75	2.50

President Francois Duvalier

77	1970	1.000	—	.10	.20	.80

COPPER-NICKEL

F.A.O. Issue - President Jean-Claude Duvalier

KM#	Date	Mintage	Fine	VF	XF	Unc
100	1972	1.500	—	.10	.25	1.00
	1975	4.000	—	.10	.20	.80
	1983	1.500	—	.10	.20	.80

F.A.O. Issue

147	1981R	.015	—	.10	.25	1.00

Obv: Portrait of national hero, Charlemagne Peralte.
Rev: National emblem.

152	1986	2.500	—	.10	.20	.60
	1989		—	.10	.20	.60
	1991		—	.10	.20	.60

NICKEL PLATED STEEL

152a	1995	—	—	—	.75

50 CENTIMES
(0.50 Gourdes)

COPPER-NICKEL
President Nord Alexis

56	1907(w)	2.000	.90	1.75	5.50	15.00
	1907(w)	—			Proof	175.00
	1908(w)	.800	1.00	2.50	8.50	20.00
	1908(w)				Proof	200.00

F.A.O. Issue - President Jean-Claude Duvalier

101	1972	.600	—	.10	.25	1.50

COPPER-NICKEL-ZINC

101a	1975	1.200	—	.10	.20	1.00
	1979	2.000	—	.10	.20	1.00
	1983	1.000	—	.10	.20	1.00
	1985		—	—	—	.75

NOTE: Varieties exist.

COPPER-NICKEL

F.A.O. Issue

KM#	Date	Mintage	Fine	VF	XF	Unc
148	1981R	.015	—	.10	.50	1.50

Obv: Portrait of national hero, Charlemagne Peralte.
Rev: National emblem.

153	1986	2.000	—	.10	.25	1.00
	1989		—	.10	.25	1.00
	1991		—	.10	.25	1.00

NICKEL PLATED STEEL

153a	1995	—	—	—	1.25

1 GOURDE

ALUMINUM-BRONZE
Obv: Hilltop edifice. Rev: National emblem.

KM#	Date	Mintage	VF	XF	Unc
155	1995	—	—	—	1.75

BRASS PLATED STEEL

155a	1995	—	—	—	2.00

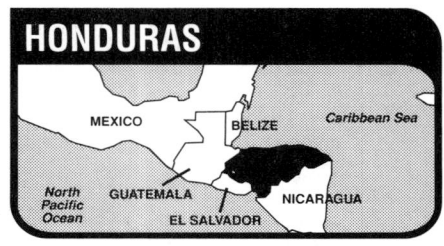

HONDURAS

The Republic of Honduras, situated in Central America alongside El Salvador, between Nicaragua and Guatemala, has an area of 43,277 sq. mi. (112,090 sq. km.) and a population of 5.6 million. Capital: Tegucigalpa. Agriculture, mining (gold and silver), and logging are the major economic activities, with increasing tourism. Precious metals, bananas, timber and coffee are exported.

The eastern part of Honduras was part of the ancient Mayan Empire; however, the largest Indian community in Honduras was the not too well known Lencas. Honduras was claimed for Spain by Columbus in 1502, during his last voyage to the Americas. The first settlement was made by Cristobal de Olid under orders from Hernando Cortes, then in Mexico. The area, regarded as one of the most promising sources of gold and silver in the New World, was a part of the Captaincy General of Guatemala throughout the colonial period. After declaring its independence from Spain in 1821, Honduras fell under the Mexican empire of Augustin de Iturbide, and then joined the Central American Republic (1823-39). Upon dissolution of that federation, Honduras became an independent republic. 1876 to 1933 saw a period of instability and for a time U.S. military occupation. From 1933 to 1940 General Andino was dictator. Since 1990 democratic practices have become more consistent.

MONETARY SYSTEM
100 Centavos = 1 Peso

UN (1) CENTAVO

BRONZE
Plain, reeded, and plain and reeded edges.

KM#	Date	Mintage	VG	Fine	VF	XF
46	1901/0	.098	5.25	12.50	22.00	37.50
	1901	Inc. Ab.	5.25	12.50	22.00	37.50
	1902 lg. 0	—	3.50	8.00	15.00	32.50
	1902 sm. 0	—	3.50	8.00	15.00	32.50
	1903/2/0	—	5.50	15.00	25.00	45.00
	1903/2/1	—	5.50	15.00	25.00	45.00
	1904	—	4.50	12.50	22.00	42.50
	1907/4	.234	6.50	16.50	25.00	45.00
	1907	Inc. Ab.	6.50	16.50	25.00	45.00

NOTE: Earlier dates (1881-1900) exist for this type.
NOTE: Varieties exist.

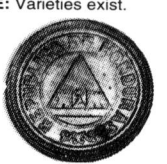 

Obv: KM#46. Rev: Altered KM#49.

59	1907 large UN					
		Inc. KM46	.50	1.50	3.25	6.00
	1907 small UN					
		Inc. KM46	.50	1.50	3.25	6.00
	1908	.263	8.50	17.50	35.00	55.00

NOTE: Earlier dates (1890-1900) exist for this type.
NOTE: Varieties exist.

Obv: KM#49. Rev: Altered KM#49.

61	1908 Inc. KM59	6.00	15.00	28.00	42.50

NOTE: Earlier dates (1890-1895) exist for this type.
NOTE: This date found with die-cutting error or broken die that reads REPLBLICA.
NOTE: Varieties exist.

Obv: KM#45. Rev: Altered KM#45.

KM#	Date	Mintage	VG	Fine	VF	XF
65	1910/5	.410	10.00	22.00	35.00	60.00
	1910 lg. 0	.410	8.50	20.00	32.50	50.00
	1911/811	.062	10.00	22.00	35.00	60.00
	1911/885	I.A.	10.00	22.00	35.00	60.00
	1911/886	I.A.	10.00	22.00	35.00	60.00
	1911	Inc. Ab.	6.00	15.00	25.00	40.00
	1911 CENTAVOS	Inc. Ab.	—	—	Rare	—

NOTE: Varieties exist.

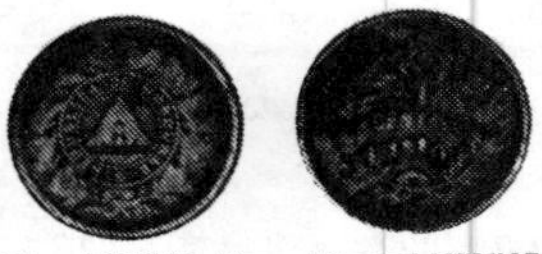

Obv: KM#48. Rev: Altered KM#45.

66	1910	Inc. Ab.	8.00	22.50	37.50	60.00
	1610 (error) inverted 9	Inc. Ab.	50.00	100.00	175.00	350.00
	1910 (error) second 1 inverted	Inc. Ab.	15.00	30.00	55.00	100.00

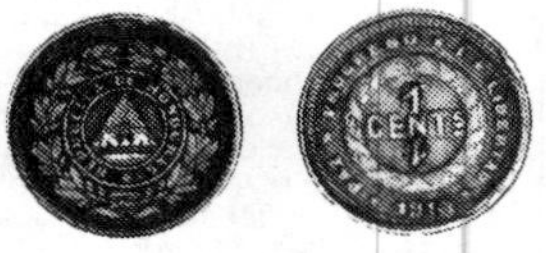

Obv: KM#48. Rev: Altered KM#48.

67	1910	Inc. Ab.	3.75	8.00	15.00	25.00
	1911	Inc. Ab.	— Reported, not confirmed			

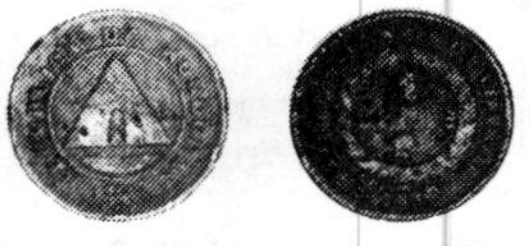

Obv: KM#45. Rev: Altered KM#48.

68	1910	Inc. Ab.	17.50	40.00	65.00	125.00

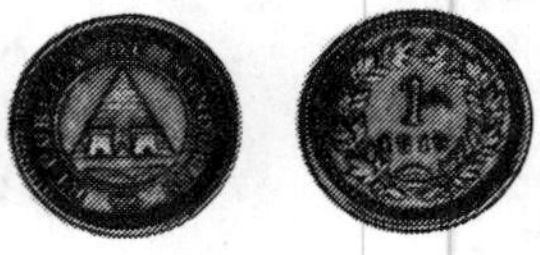

Similar to KM#65, CENTAVO omitted.

70	1919	.168	1.75	3.50	6.00	20.00
	1920	.030	3.00	5.50	10.00	25.00

2 CENTAVOS

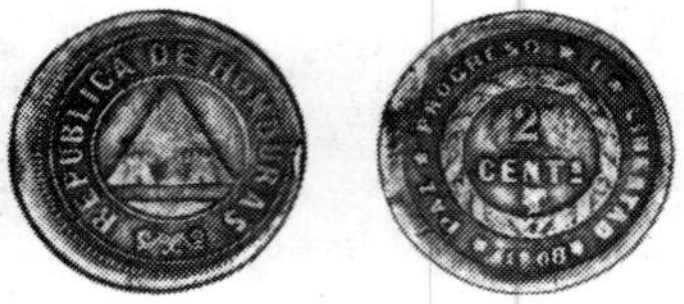

BRONZE

Obv: KM#46. Rev: Altered KM#49.

64	1907	Inc. Be.	—	—	Rare	—
	1908	Inc. Be.	40.00	75.00	150.00	300.00

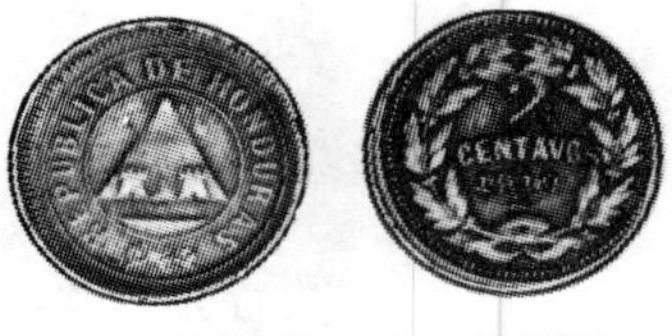

Obv: KM#46. Rev: Altered KM#46.

69	1910	.435	1.25	3.50	6.00	16.00
	1911	.068	3.25	8.00	13.50	28.50
	1912 CENTAVOS	.088	1.00	2.50	4.50	14.00
	1912 CENTAVO	Inc. Ab.	1.75	3.75	7.00	18.50
	1913	.258	1.00	2.50	5.00	15.00

NOTE: Reverse dies often very crudely recut, especially 1910 and 1911. Some coins of 1910 appear to be struck over earlier 1 or 2 Centavos, probably 1907 or 1908.

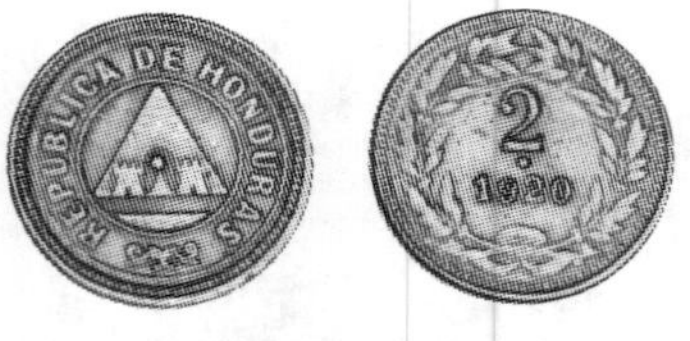

Rev: CENTAVOS omitted.

71	1919	.117	1.50	3.00	5.00	16.00
	1920	.283	.65	1.25	2.75	10.00
	1920 dot	I.A.	.85	1.50	3.00	10.00

NOTE: Varieties exist.

5 CENTAVOS

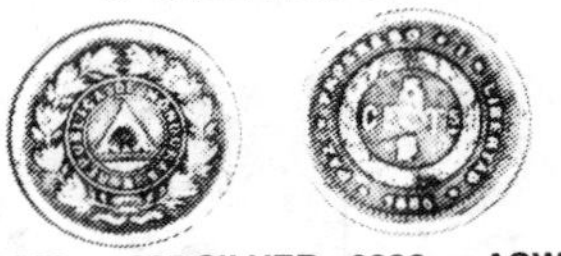

1.2500 g, .835 SILVER, .0336 oz ASW

KM#	Date	Mintage	VG	Fine	VF	XF
48	1902	—	25.00	52.50	110.00	165.00

NOTE: Earlier dates (1884-1895) exist for this type.

25 CENTAVOS

6.2500 g, .835 SILVER, .1678 oz ASW

50a	1901/801	—	4.00	6.50	15.00	28.00
	1901/11	—	4.00	6.50	15.00	28.00
	1901 lg. first 1	.054	4.00	6.00	10.00	20.00
	1902/802	—	10.00	18.00	27.50	45.00
	1902/812	—	10.00	18.00	27.50	45.00
	1902/891	—	10.00	18.00	27.50	45.00
	1902/1F	—	4.00	6.00	10.00	20.00
	1902F	—	4.00	7.50	15.00	27.50
	1904	—	12.50	27.50	47.50	75.00
	1907/4	.014	6.00	10.00	17.50	30.00
	1907	Inc. Ab.	6.50	11.50	20.00	32.00
	1910	745 pcs.	— Reported, not confirmed			
	1912 .835/.900	7,168	10.00	17.50	35.00	60.00
	1913/0	.052	—	—	—	—
	1913/2	I.A.	—	—	—	—
	1913	Inc. Ab.	7.50	13.50	22.50	37.50

NOTE: Varieties exist.
NOTE: Earlier dates (1899-1900) exist for this type.

50 CENTAVOS

12.5000 g, .900 SILVER, .3617 oz ASW

51	1910	602 pcs.	500.00	900.00	—	—

NOTE: Earlier dates (1883-1897) exist for this type.

12.5000 g, .835/.900 SILVER, .3355 oz ASW

51a	1908/897	447 pcs.	40.00	90.00	150.00	225.00
	1908	Inc. Ab.	25.00	55.00	85.00	135.00
	1911	90 pcs.	— Reported, not confirmed			

PESO

25.0000 g, .900 SILVER, .7234 oz ASW
Rev: Large CENTRO-AMERICA.

52	1902	—	27.50	50.00	80.00	130.00
	1903 flat top 3	—	27.50	45.00	70.00	120.00
	1903 round top 3	—	30.00	55.00	90.00	160.00
	1904	.020	30.00	55.00	90.00	160.00
	1914	—	200.00	500.00	900.00	1500.

NOTE: Earlier dates (1883-1899) exist for this type.
NOTE: Overdates and recut dies are prevalent.

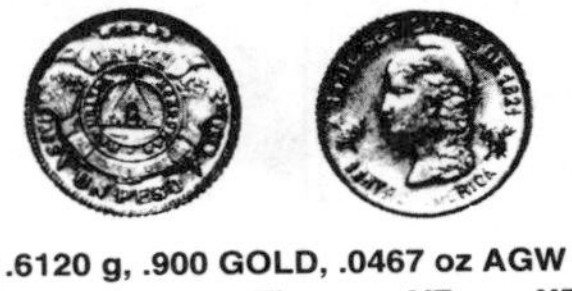

1.6120 g, .900 GOLD, .0467 oz AGW

KM#	Date	Mintage	Fine	VF	XF	Unc
56	1901	—	150.00	300.00	600.00	900.00
	1902	—	140.00	300.00	500.00	800.00
	1907	—	140.00	250.00	450.00	700.00
	1912	350 pcs.	— Reported, not confirmed			
	1913	6,000	— Reported, not confirmed			
	1914/882	—	275.00	450.00	600.00	900.00
	1914/03	—	275.00	450.00	600.00	900.00
	1919	—	150.00	300.00	550.00	800.00
	1920	—	150.00	300.00	550.00	800.00
	1922	—	140.00	250.00	450.00	650.00
	ND	—	—	—	—	—

NOTE: Earlier dates (1887-1899) exist for this type.

5 PESOS

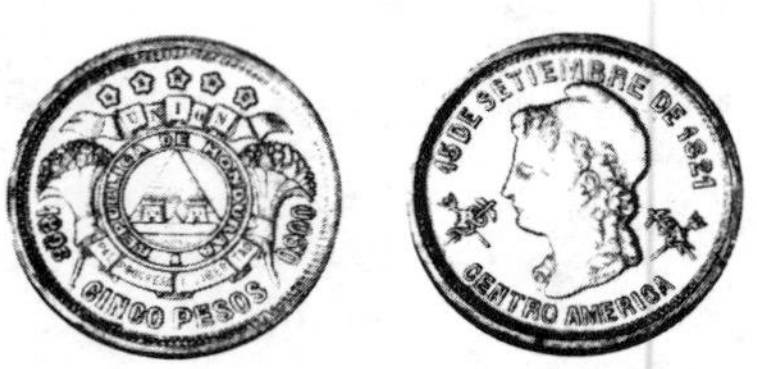

8.0645 g, .900 GOLD, .2333 oz AGW

KM#	Date	Mintage	Fine	VF	XF	Unc
53	1902	—	450.00	650.00	1000.	1500.
	1908/888	—	450.00	650.00	1000.	1500.
	1913	1,200	450.00	650.00	1000.	1500.

NOTE: Earlier dates (1883-1900) exist for this type.

MONETARY REFORM

100 Centavos = 1 Lempira

CENTAVO

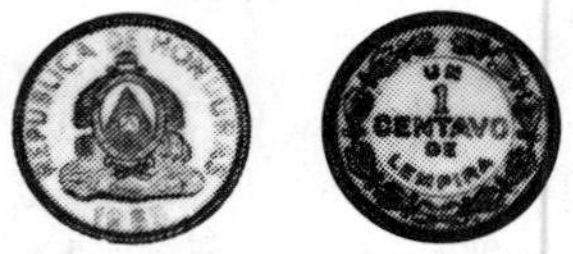

BRONZE, thick planchet, 2.00 g, 15mm

77.1	1935	2.000	.25	.75	2.00	7.50
	1939	2.000	.25	.50	1.50	6.00
	1949	4.000	.10	.30	.75	2.50

Thin planchet, 1.50 g, 16mm

77.2	1954	3.500	.10	.15	.25	1.00
	1956	2.000	.10	.15	.25	.50
	1957/6	28.000	—	—	—	—
	1957	Inc. Ab.	—	.10	.15	.30

COPPER-CLAD STEEL
Obv: W/o clouds behind pyramids.

77a	1974	—	—	.10	.15	.25
	1985	—	—	.10	.15	.25
	1992	—	—	.10	.15	.25

COPPER PLATED STEEL
Obv: Clouds behind pyramids.

77b	1988	50.000	—	.10	.15	.25

2 CENTAVOS

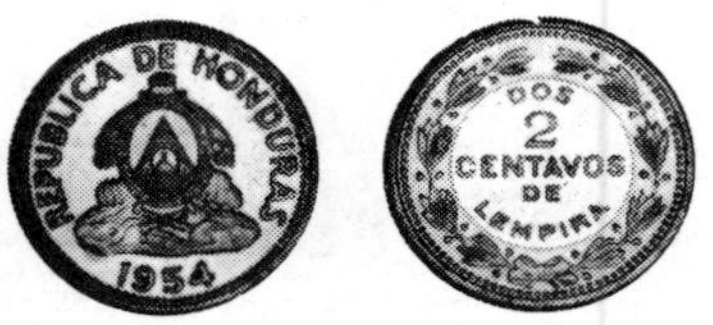

BRONZE

78	1939	2.000	.25	.50	1.50	6.00
	1949	3.000	.10	.25	1.00	4.00
	1954	2.000	.10	.25	1.00	3.00
	1956	20.000	—	.10	.15	.40

BRONZE-CLAD STEEL

78a	1974	—	—	.10	.15	.25

5 CENTAVOS

COPPER-NICKEL
Dentilated border.

72.1	1931	2.000	.50	1.50	2.50	15.00
	1932	1.000	.35	.75	1.50	10.00
	1949	2.000	.20	.50	1.00	4.00
	1956	10.070	—	.15	.25	.60
	1972	5.000	—	.10	.15	.35

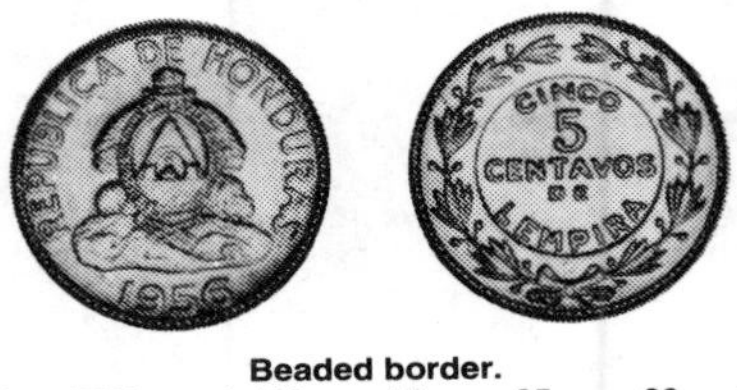

Beaded border.

72.2	1954	1.400	.15	.25	.60	2.50
	1980	20.000	—	.10	.15	.35

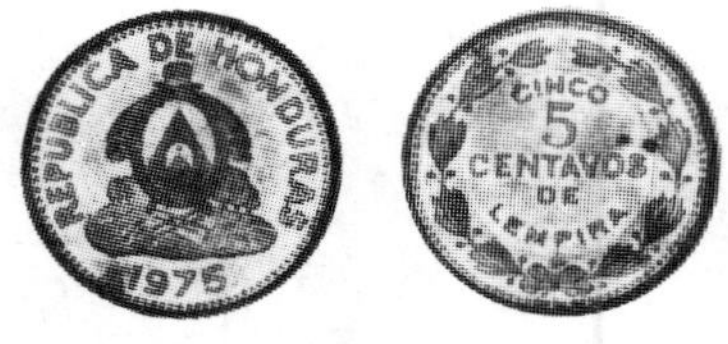

BRASS
Obv: Lg. letters and coat of arms, clouds behind pyramids.

72.2a	1975	20.000	—	.10	.15	.35
	1989	—	—	.10	.15	.35

Obv: Sm. letters and coat of arms.

KM#	Date	Mintage	Fine	VF	XF	Unc
72.3	1993	—		.10	.15	.35
	1994	—		.10	.15	.35

10 CENTAVOS

COPPER-NICKEL
Dentilated border.

76.1	1932	1.500	.75	1.50	4.00	25.00
	1951	1.000	.25	.75	1.50	4.00
	1956	7.560	.10	.15	.25	.75

BRASS
Obv: Lg. letters and coat of arms.

76.1a	1976	—	.10	.15	.25	.60
	1989	—	.10	.15	.25	.60

COPPER-NICKEL
Beaded border.

76.2	1954	1.200	.10	.20	.35	1.00
	1967	—	.10	.25	.50	2.00
	1980	15.000	.10	.25	.50	2.00
	1993	—	.10	.25	.50	2.00

BRASS
Obv: Sm. letters and coat of arms, clouds behind pyramids.

76.2a	1993	—	—	.10	.20	.45
	1994	—	—	.10	.20	.45
	1995	—	—	.10	.20	.45

Obv: Sm. letters and coat of arms, no clouds.

76.3	1995	—	—	.10	.20	.45

20 CENTAVOS

2.5000 g, .900 SILVER, .0723 oz ASW
Chief Lempira

73	1931	1.000	1.00	3.00	6.00	17.50
	1932	.750	1.25	3.25	7.00	17.50
	1951	1.500	BV	1.25	2.50	7.00
	1952	2.500	BV	1.25	2.00	6.00
	1958	2.000	BV	1.25	2.00	5.00

COPPER-NICKEL

79	1967	12.000	—	.10	.20	.60

Different style lettering.

KM#	Date	Mintage	Fine	VF	XF	Unc
81	1973	15.000	—	.10	.20	.60

83.1	1978	30.000	—	.10	.20	.60
	1990	—	—	.10	.20	.60

NICKEL PLATED STEEL
Obv: Sm. arms and legend, no clouds.

83.1a	1991	—	—	.10	.20	.60
	1993	—	—	.10	.20	.60
	1994	—	—	.10	.20	.60

50 CENTAVOS

6.2500 g, .900 SILVER, .1808 oz ASW
Chief Lempira

74	1931	.500	1.00	3.00	6.00	30.00
	1932	1.100	1.00	2.00	5.00	25.00
	1937	1.000	1.00	2.00	5.00	25.00
	1951	.500	1.00	2.00	4.00	20.00

COPPER-NICKEL

80	1967	4.800	—	.25	.35	1.25

F.A.O. Issue

82	1973	4.400	—	.25	.35	1.25

84	1978	12.000		.25	.35	1.00
	1990	—		.25	.35	1.00

NICKEL PLATED STEEL

84.1a	1991	—	—	.25	.35	1.00
	1994	—	—	.25	.35	1.00

Obv: No clouds behind pyramid in arms.

84a.2	1995	—	—	.25	.35	1.00

NICKEL-STEEL
50th Anniversary - FAO

KM#	Date	Mintage	Fine	VF	XF	Unc
88	1994	2.000	—	—	—	1.50

LEMPIRA

12.5000 g, .900 SILVER, .3617 oz ASW
Chief Lempira

75	1931	.550	BV	3.50	7.00	30.00
	1932	1.000	—	BV	6.00	25.00
	1933	.400	BV	3.50	7.00	30.00
	1934	.600	BV	3.50	7.00	25.00
	1935	1.000	—	BV	6.00	25.00
	1937	4.000	—	BV	5.00	17.50

HONG KONG

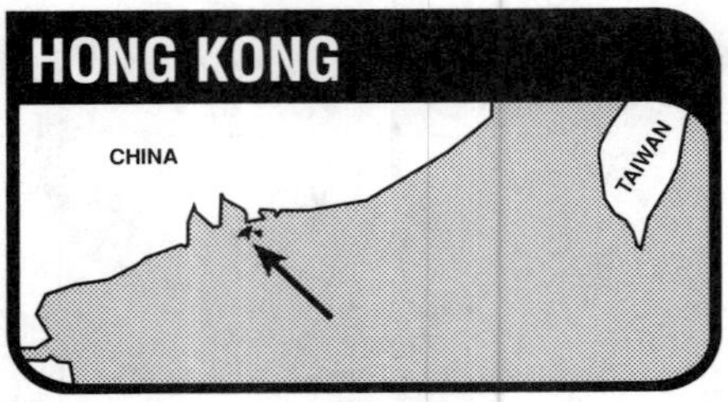

Hong Kong, a former British colony reverted to control of the People's Republic of China on July 1, 1997 as a Special Administrative Region. It is situated at the mouth of the Canton or Pearl River 90 miles (145 km.) southeast of Canton, has an area of 403 sq. mi. (1,040 sq. km.) and an estimated population of 6.3 million. Capital: Victoria. The free port of Hong Kong, the commercial center of the Far East, is a trans-shipment point for goods destined for China and the countries of the Pacific Rim. Light manufacturing and tourism are important components of the economy.

Long a haven for fishermen-pirates and opium smugglers, the island of Hong Kong was ceded to Britain at the conclusion of the first Opium War, 1839-1842. At the time, the acquisition of a 'barren rock' was ridiculed by both London and English merchants operating in the Far East. The Kowloon Peninsula and Stonecutter's Island were ceded in 1860, and the so-called New Territories, comprising most of the mainland of the colony, were leased to Britain for 99 years in 1898.

The legends on Hong Kong coinage are bilingual: English and Chinese. The rare 1941 cent was dispatched to Hong Kong in several shipments. One fell into Japanese hands while another was melted down by the British and a third was sunk during enemy action.

RULERS

British 1842-1997

MINT MARKS

H - Heaton
KN - King's Norton

MONETARY SYSTEM

10 Mils (Wen, Ch'ien) = 1 Cent (Hsien)
10 Cents = 1 Chiao
100 Cents = 10 Chiao = 1 Dollar (Yuan)

CENT

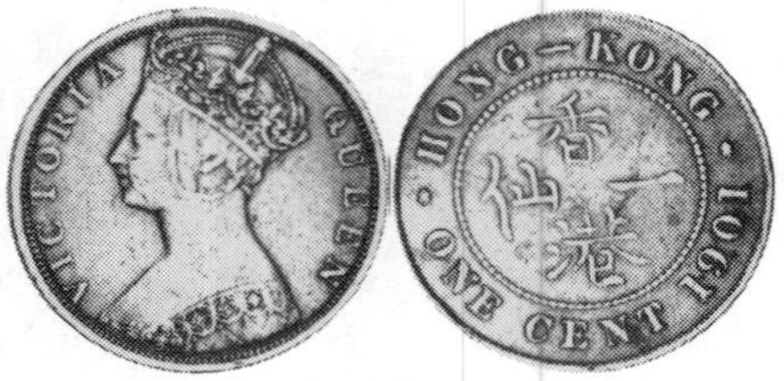

BRONZE
Obv: 5 pearls in center of crown.

KM#	Date	Mintage	Fine	VF	XF	Unc
4.3	1901	5.000	2.50	5.50	16.00	70.00
	1901H	10.000	2.50	5.50	16.00	60.00

NOTE: Earlier dates (1879-1900) exist for this type.

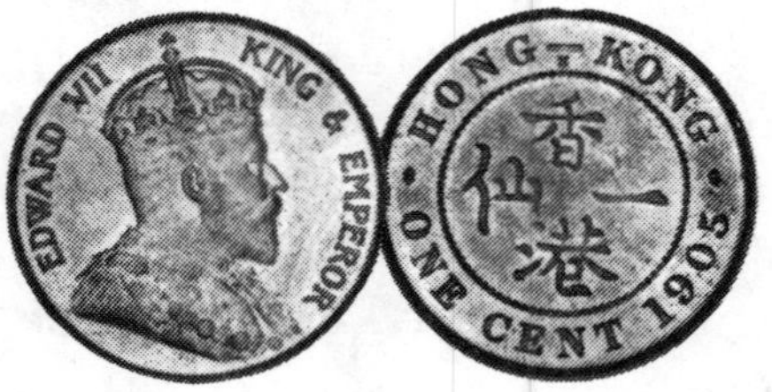

KM#	Date	Mintage	Fine	VF	XF	Unc
11	1902	5.000	2.50	4.50	15.00	40.00
	1903	5.000	2.50	4.50	15.00	40.00
	1904H	10.000	1.75	3.50	12.00	32.00
	1905	2.500	3.75	7.50	20.00	55.00
	1905H	12.500	2.50	4.50	15.00	40.00

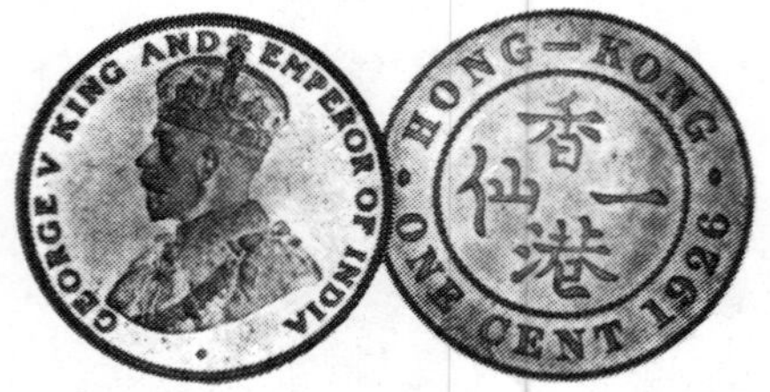

KM#	Date	Mintage	Fine	VF	XF	Unc
16	1919H	2.500	2.00	4.00	14.00	40.00
	1923	2.500	1.50	3.00	10.00	28.00
	1924	5.000	1.25	2.50	5.50	20.00
	1925	2.500	1.25	2.50	5.50	20.00
	1926	2.500	1.25	2.50	5.50	20.00
	1926	—	—	—	Proof	350.00

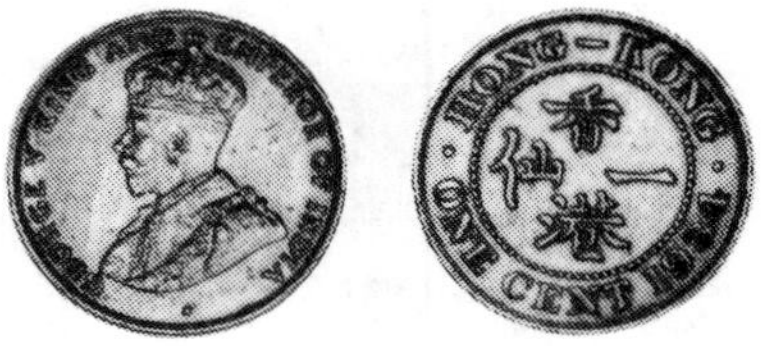

KM#	Date	Mintage	Fine	VF	XF	Unc
17	1931	5.000	.75	1.00	2.00	5.50
	1931	—	—	—	Proof	250.00
	1933	6.500	.75	1.00	2.00	5.50
	1933	—	—	—	Proof	250.00
	1934	5.000	.75	1.00	2.00	5.50
	1934	—	—	—	Proof	250.00

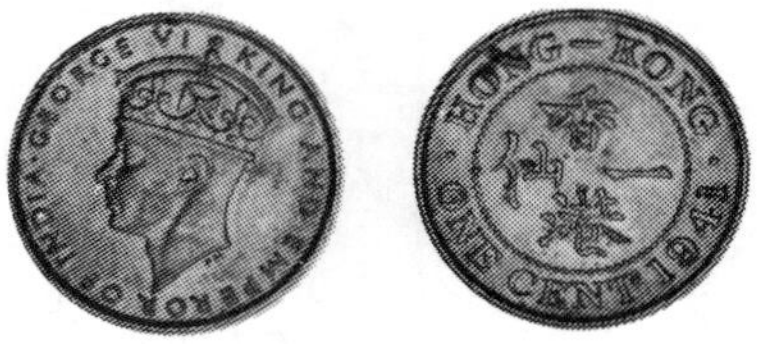

KM#	Date	Mintage	Fine	VF	XF	Unc
24	1941	5.000	650.00	1350.	2800.	4500.
	1941	—	—	—	Proof	8500.

5 CENTS

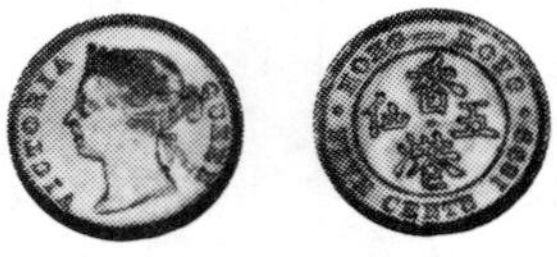

1.3577 g, .800 SILVER, .0349 oz ASW

KM#	Date	Mintage	Fine	VF	XF	Unc
5	1901	10.000	1.00	2.00	4.00	15.00

NOTE: Coins dated 1866-68 struck at Hong Kong Mint; 1872-1901 at the Royal Mint.
NOTE: Earlier dates (1866-1900) exist for this type.

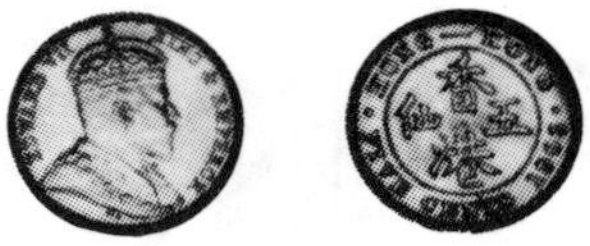

KM#	Date	Mintage	Fine	VF	XF	Unc
12	1903	6.000	1.00	2.00	4.00	12.50
	1903	—	—	—	Proof	225.00
	1904	8.000	1.00	2.00	4.00	12.50
	1904	—	—	—	Proof	200.00
	1905	1.000	1.25	3.00	6.50	17.50
	1905H	7.000	1.00	2.00	4.00	12.50

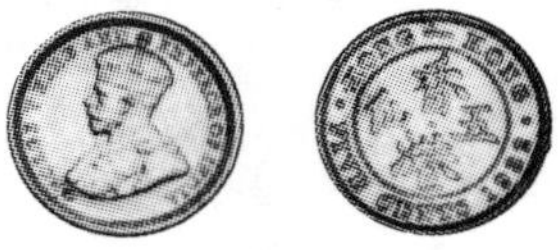

KM#	Date	Mintage	Fine	VF	XF	Unc
18	1932	3.000	1.00	1.50	2.50	6.50
	1932	—	—	—	Proof	165.00
	1933	2.000	1.00	1.50	2.75	7.50
	1933	—	—	—	Proof	165.00

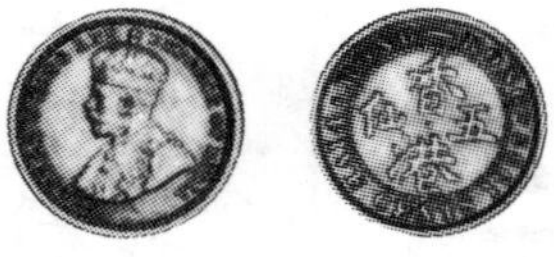

COPPER-NICKEL

KM#	Date	Mintage	Fine	VF	XF	Unc
18a	1935	1.000	1.00	2.00	4.50	16.50
	1935	—	—	—	Proof	115.00

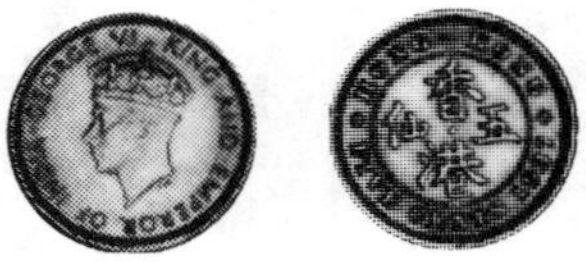

NICKEL

KM#	Date	Mintage	Fine	VF	XF	Unc
20	1937	3.000	.75	1.25	2.25	7.50
	1937	—	—	—	Proof	85.00

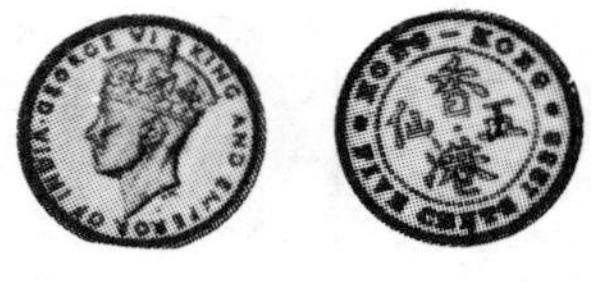

KM#	Date	Mintage	Fine	VF	XF	Unc
22	1938	3.000	.50	1.00	2.00	6.50
	1938	—	—	—	Proof	125.00
	1939H	3.090	.50	1.00	2.00	6.50
	1939H	—	—	—	Proof	125.00
	1939KN	4.710	.50	1.00	2.00	6.50
	1941H	.777	275.00	425.00	700.00	1150.
	1941KN	1.075	100.00	175.00	350.00	700.00

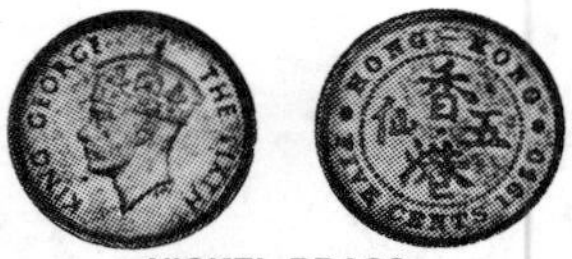

NICKEL-BRASS

KM#	Date	Mintage	Fine	VF	XF	Unc
26	1949	15.000	.25	.50	1.25	7.50
	1949	—	—	—	Proof	125.00
	1950	20.400	.25	.50	1.25	7.50
	1950	—	—	—	Proof	125.00

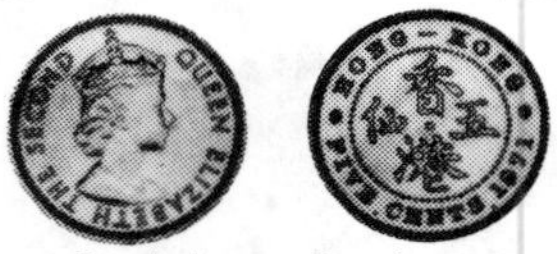

Reeded, security edges.

KM#	Date	Mintage	Fine	VF	XF	Unc
29.1	1958H	5.000	—	.25	.75	4.50
	1960	5.000	—	.15	.50	3.50
	1960	—	—	—	Proof	65.00
	1963	7.000	—	.15	.50	3.50
	1963	—	—	—	Proof	65.00
	1964H	—	16.00	35.00	90.00	225.00
	1965	18.000	—	.10	.40	2.00
	1965H	6.000	—	.10	.40	2.00
	1967	10.000	—	.10	.40	2.00

Error: Reeded, w/o security edge.

KM#	Date	Mintage	Fine	VF	XF	Unc
29.2	1958H	Inc. Ab.	2.50	5.00	9.00	20.00
	1960	Inc. Ab.	2.50	5.00	9.00	20.00

Reeded edges.

KM#	Date	Mintage	Fine	VF	XF	Unc
29.3	1971KN	14.000	—	—	.25	.50
(32)	1971H	6.000	—	—	.25	.50
	1972H	14.000	—	—	.25	.50
	1977	6.000	—	—	.25	.50
	1978	10.000	—	—	.25	.50
	1979	4.000	—	—	.25	.50

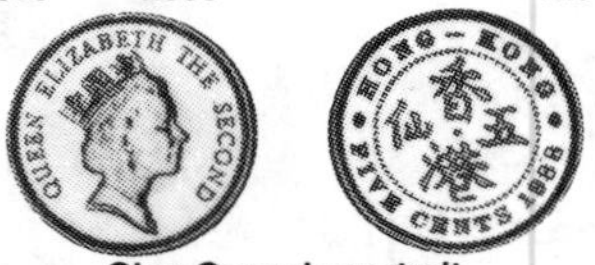

Obv: Queen's portrait.
Rev: Legend around inscription.

KM#	Date	Mintage	Fine	VF	XF	Unc
61	1988	.040	—	—	.25	.50
	1988	.020	—	—	Proof	2.00

10 CENTS

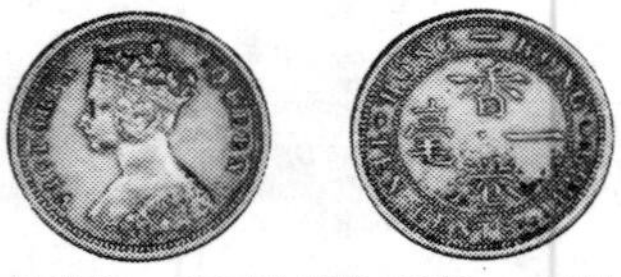

2.7154 g, .800 SILVER, .0698 oz ASW
Obv: 11 pearls on right arch of crown.

KM#	Date	Mintage	Fine	VF	XF	Unc
6.3	1901	25.000	1.00	2.00	3.50	18.50

NOTE: Coins dated 1866-68 struck at the Hong Kong Mint; 1869-1901 at the Royal Mint.
NOTE: Earlier dates (1866-1900) exist for this type.

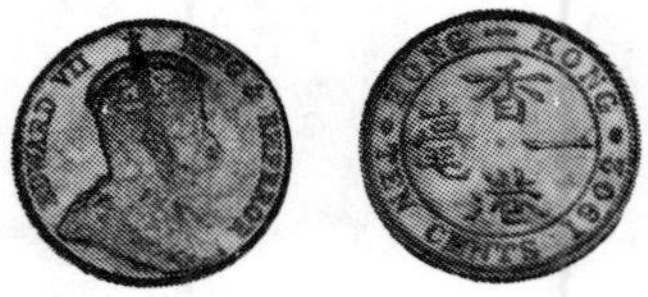

KM#	Date	Mintage	Fine	VF	XF	Unc
13	1902	18.000	1.00	2.00	3.50	16.50
	1902	—	—	—	Proof	200.00
	1903	25.000	1.00	2.00	3.50	16.50
	1903	—	—	—	Proof	200.00
	1904	30.000	1.00	2.00	3.50	16.50
	1904	—	—	—	Proof	165.00
	1905	33.487	225.00	400.00	650.00	1500.
	1905	—	—	—	Proof	1750.

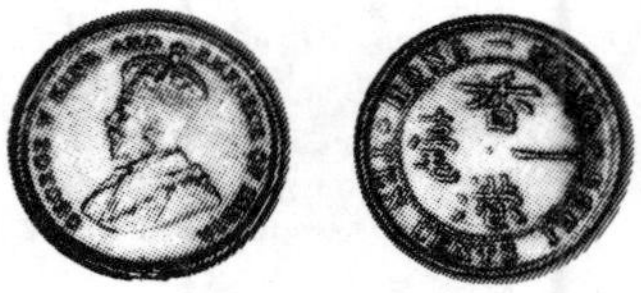

COPPER-NICKEL

KM#	Date	Mintage	Fine	VF	XF	Unc
19	1935	10.000	.50	1.00	3.00	15.00
	1935	—	—	—	Proof	75.00
	1936	5.000	.50	1.00	3.00	15.00
	1936	—	—	—	Proof	75.00

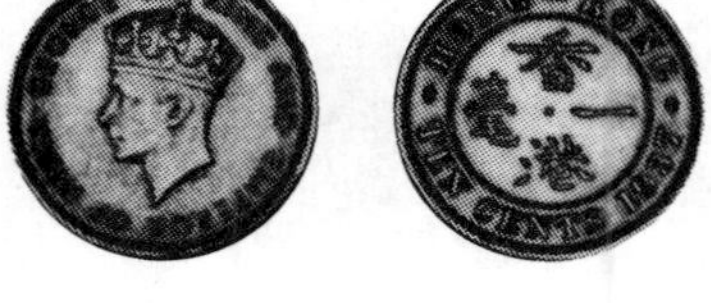

NICKEL

KM#	Date	Mintage	Fine	VF	XF	Unc
21	1937	17.500	.50	.80	1.50	6.50
	1937	—	—	—	Proof	85.00

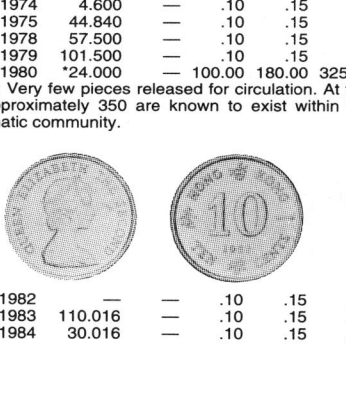

23	1938	7.500	.65	1.00	2.25	7.50
	1938	—	—	—	Proof	85.00
	1939H	5.000	.65	1.00	2.25	7.50
	1939KN	5.000	.65	1.00	2.25	7.50
	1939KN	—	—	—	Proof	85.00

NICKEL-BRASS
Reeded, security edge.

25	1948	30.000	.25	.50	1.25	6.50
	1948	—	—	—	Proof	65.00
	1949	35.000	.25	.50	1.25	6.50
	1949	—	—	—	Proof	65.00
	1950	20.000	.25	.50	1.25	6.50
	1950	—	—	—	Proof	65.00
	1951	5.000	.50	1.00	3.00	22.50
	1951	—	—	—	Proof	85.00

Error: Reeded, w/o security edge.

25a	1950	Inc. Ab.	3.50	6.50	12.50	25.00

Reeded, w/security edge.

28.1	1955	10.000	.15	.25	.50	5.50
	1955	—	—	—	Proof	50.00
	1956	3.110	.25	.50	1.25	15.00
	1956	—	—	—	Proof	50.00
	1956H	4.488	.15	.25	1.00	10.00
	1956KN	2.500	.25	.50	2.00	16.50
	1957H	5.250	.15	.25	.50	10.00
	1957KN	2.800	.15	.25	1.00	15.00
	1958KN	10.000	.15	.25	.50	10.00
	1959	20.000	.10	.15	.25	6.00
	1960	12.500	.10	.15	.25	6.00
	1960	—	—	—	Proof	50.00
	1960H	10.000	.10	.15	.25	6.00
	1961	20.000	.10	.15	.25	4.00
	1961	—	—	—	Proof	50.00
	1961H	5.000	.15	.25	.50	5.00
	1961KN	5.000	.15	.25	.50	5.00
	1963	27.000	.10	.15	.25	4.00
	1963	—	—	—	Proof	50.00
	1963H	3.000	.20	.30	.50	4.00
	1963KN	I.A.	.10	.15	.25	3.50
	1964	9.000	.10	.15	.25	2.00
	1964H	21.000	.10	.15	.25	2.00
	1965	40.000	.10	.15	.25	2.00
	1965H	8.000	.10	.15	.25	2.50
	1965KN	I.A.	.10	.15	.25	2.50
	1967	10.000	.10	.15	.25	2.00
	1968H	15.000	.10	.15	.25	2.00

Error: Reeded, w/o security edge.

28.2	1956H	Inc. Ab.	2.25	4.50	8.50	25.00
	1963	—	2.25	4.50	8.50	25.00

Reeded edge.

28.3	1971H	22.000	—	.10	.15	.65
(33)	1972KN	20.000	—	.10	.15	.65
	1973	2.250	.15	.25	.65	3.50
	1974	4.600	—	.10	.15	.65
	1975	44.840	—	.10	.15	.65
	1978	57.500	—	.10	.15	.65
	1979	101.500	—	.10	.15	.65
	1980	*24.000	—	100.00	180.00	325.00

*NOTE: Very few pieces released for circulation. At this time approximately 350 are known to exist within the numismatic community.

49	1982	—	—	.10	.15	.25
	1983	110.016	—	.10	.15	.25
	1984	30.016	—	.10	.15	.25

KM#	Date	Mintage	Fine	VF	XF	Unc
55	1985	34.016	—	.10	.15	.25
	1986	40.000	—	.10	.15	.25
	1987	—	—	.10	.15	.25
	1988	30.000	—	.10	.15	.25
	1988	.020	—	—	Proof	2.00
	1989	40.000	—	.10	.15	.25
	1990	—	—	.10	.15	.25
	1991	—	—	.10	.15	.25
	1992	24.000	—	.10	.15	.25

BRASS PLATED STEEL
Bauhinia Flower

66	1993	—	—	.10	.15	.30
	1993	—	—	—	Proof	2.00
	1994	—	—	.10	.15	.30
	1995	—	—	.10	.15	.30
	1996	—	—	.10	.15	.30
	1997	—	—	.10	.15	.30

Obv: Bauhinia flower. Rev: Sailing junk.

72	1997	—	—	.15	.20	.40
	1997	*.097	—	—	Proof	2.00

20 CENTS

5.4308 g, .800 SILVER, .1397 oz ASW

14	1902	.250	20.00	40.00	90.00	250.00
	1902	—	—	—	Proof	1200.
	1904	.250	20.00	40.00	90.00	250.00
	1905	.750	285.00	525.00	1100.	1750.
	1905	—	—	—	Proof	3000.

NICKEL-BRASS

36	1975	71.000	—	.10	.20	.35
	1976	42.000	—	.10	.20	.35
	1977	Inc. Ab.	—	.10	.20	.35
	1978	86.000	—	.10	.20	.35
	1979	94.500	—	.10	.20	.35
	1980	65.000	—	.10	.20	.35
	1982	30.000	—	.10	.20	.35
	1983	15.000	—	.10	.20	.35

BRASS
Obv: Mature Queen's portrait.

59	1985	10.000	—	.10	.20	.35
	1988	*.040	—	.10	.20	.35
	1988	*.020	—	—	Proof	2.00
	1989	17.000	—	.10	.20	.35
	1990	—	—	.10	.20	.35
	1991	—	—	.10	.20	.35
	1992	131.000	—	.10	.20	.35

NICKEL-BRASS

Bauhinia Flower

KM#	Date	Mintage	Fine	VF	XF	Unc
67	1993	—	—	.10	.20	.40
	1993	—	—	—	Proof	2.00
	1994	—	—	.10	.20	.40
	1995	—	—	.10	.20	.40
	1997	—	—	.10	.20	.40

Obv: Bauhinia flower. Rev: Butterfly kites.

73	1997	—	—	.15	.25	.50
	1997	—	—	—	Proof	2.00

50 CENTS

13.5769 g, .800 SILVER, .3492 oz ASW, 31mm

15	1902	.100	25.00	35.00	50.00	125.00
	1902	—	—	—	Proof	650.00
	1904	.100	25.00	35.00	50.00	100.00
	1904	—	—	—	Proof	650.00
	1905	.300	20.00	25.00	40.00	90.00
	1905	—	—	—	Proof	650.00

COPPER-NICKEL
Reeded, security edge.

27.1	1951	15.000	1.00	2.00	3.50	12.00
	1951	—	—	—	Proof	250.00

Error: Reeded, w/o security edge.

27.2	1951	Inc. Ab.	3.00	5.00	10.00	22.00

Reeded, security edge.

30.1	1958H	4.000	—	.50	1.25	4.50
	1960	4.000	—	.40	1.00	4.00
	1960	—	—	—	Proof	100.00
	1961	6.000	—	.40	1.00	3.50
	1961	—	—	—	Proof	100.00
	1963H	10.000	—	.40	1.00	3.50
	1964	5.000	—	.40	1.00	3.50
	1965KN	8.000	—	.40	1.00	3.00
	1966	5.000	—	.40	1.00	3.50
	1967	12.000	—	.40	1.00	3.00
	1968	12.000	—	.40	1.00	3.00
	1970H	4.600	—	.40	1.00	3.00

Error: Reeded, w/o security edge.

30.2	1958H	Inc. Ab.	2.00	4.00	8.00	20.00

Reeded edge.

34	1971KN	—	—	.20	.40	1.50
	1972	30.000	—	.20	.40	1.50
	1973	36.800	—	.20	.40	1.50

10 CENTS (column 2 top)

KM#	Date	Mintage	Fine	VF	XF	Unc
34	1974	6.000	—	.20	.40	1.50
	1975	8.000	—	.20	.40	1.50

NICKEL-BRASS

KM#	Date	Mintage	Fine	VF	XF	Unc
41	1977	60.001	—	.20	.30	.80
	1978	70.000	—	.20	.30	.80
	1979	60.640	—	.20	.30	.80
	1980	120.000	—	.20	.30	.80

Obv: Mature Queen's portrait.

KM#	Date	Mintage	Fine	VF	XF	Unc
62	1988	*.040	—	.20	.30	.80
	1988	*.020	—	—	Proof	4.00
	1990	27,000	—	.20	.30	.80

BRASS PLATED STEEL
Bauhinia Flower

KM#	Date	Mintage	Fine	VF	XF	Unc
68	1993	—	—	.20	.30	.80
	1993	—	—	—	Proof	4.00
	1994	—	—	.20	.30	.80
	1995	—	—	.20	.30	.80
	1997	—	—	.20	.30	.80

Obv: Bauhinia flower. Rev: Ox.

KM#	Date	Mintage	Fine	VF	XF	Unc
74	1997	—	—	—	.40	1.00
	1997	*.097	—	—	Proof	4.00

DOLLAR

COPPER-NICKEL
Reeded, security edge.

KM#	Date	Mintage	Fine	VF	XF	Unc
31.1	1960H	40.000	—	—	.60	1.75	5.50
	1960H	—	—	—	Proof	3350.
	1960KN	40.000	—	—	.60	1.75	5.50
	1970H	15.000	—	—	.60	1.25	4.50

NOTE: Mint mark is below "LL" of "DOLLAR".

Error: Reeded, w/o security edge.

KM#	Date	Mintage	Fine	VF	XF	Unc
31.2	1960H	Inc. Ab.	4.00	7.00	15.00	30.00

Reeded edge.

KM#	Date	Mintage	Fine	VF	XF	Unc
35	1971H	8.000	—	.60	1.25	4.50
	1972	20.000	—	.60	1.25	3.50
	1973	8.125	—	.60	1.25	4.50
	1974	26.000	—	.60	1.25	3.50
	1975	22.500	—	.60	1.25	3.50

KM#	Date	Mintage	Fine	VF	XF	Unc
43	1978	120.000	—	.40	.70	1.50
	1979	104.908	—	.40	.70	1.50
	1980	100.000	—	.40	.70	1.50

Obv: Mature Queen's portrait.
Rev: Lion within legend.

KM#	Date	Mintage	Fine	VF	XF	Unc
63	1987	—	—	.30	.50	1.00
	1988	20.000	—	.30	.50	1.00
	1988	.020	—	—	Proof	7.50
	1989	20.000	—	.30	.50	1.00
	1990	—	—	.30	.50	1.00
	1991	—	—	.30	.50	1.00
	1992	25.000	—	.30	.50	1.00

NICKEL PLATED STEEL
Bauhinia Flower

KM#	Date	Mintage	Fine	VF	XF	Unc
69	1993	—	—	.30	.50	1.00
	1993	—	—	—	Proof	7.50

COPPER-NICKEL

KM#	Date	Mintage	Fine	VF	XF	Unc
69a	1994	—	—	.30	.50	1.00
	1995	—	—	.30	.50	1.00
	1996	—	—	.30	.50	1.00
	1997	—	—	.30	.50	1.00

Obv: Bauhinia flower. Rev: Chinese unicorn.

KM#	Date	Mintage	Fine	VF	XF	Unc
75	1997	—	—	.35	.65	1.50
	1997	—	—	—	Proof	7.50

2 DOLLARS

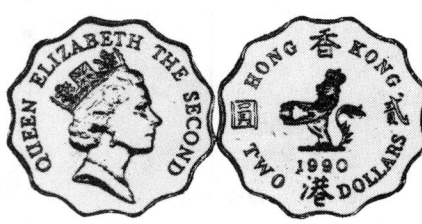

COPPER-NICKEL

KM#	Date	Mintage	Fine	VF	XF	Unc
37	1975	60.000	—	.45	.85	1.75
	1978	.504	—	.45	1.00	10.00
	1979	9.032	—	.45	.85	1.75
	1980	30.000	—	.45	.85	1.75
	1981	30.000	—	.45	.85	1.75
	1982	30.000	—	.45	.85	1.75
	1983	7.002	—	.45	.85	1.75
	1984	22.002	—	.45	.85	1.75

Obv: Mature Queen's portrait.

KM#	Date	Mintage	Fine	VF	XF	Unc
60	1985	10.002	—	.45	.65	1.25
	1986	15.000	—	.45	.65	1.25
	1987	—	—	.45	.65	1.25
	1988	5.000	—	.45	.65	1.25
	1988	.020	—	—	Proof	10.00
	1989	33.000	—	.45	.65	1.25
	1990	—	—	.45	.65	1.25
	1991	—	—	.45	.65	1.25
	1992	4.370	—	.45	.65	1.25

Bauhinia Flower

KM#	Date	Mintage	Fine	VF	XF	Unc
64	1993	—	—	.45	.65	1.25
	1993	—	—	—	Proof	10.00
	1994	—	—	.45	.65	1.25
	1995	—	—	.45	.65	1.25
	1997	—	—	.45	.65	1.25

Obv: Bauhinia flower. Rev: Ho Ho Brothers.

KM#	Date	Mintage	Fine	VF	XF	Unc
76	1997	—	—	.50	.85	1.75
	1997	*.097	—	—	Proof	10.00

5 DOLLARS

COPPER-NICKEL

KM#	Date	Mintage	Fine	VF	XF	Unc
39	1976	30.000	—	1.00	1.50	2.50
	1978	10.000	—	1.00	1.50	3.00
	1979	12.000	—	1.00	1.50	2.50

KM#	Date	Mintage	Fine	VF	XF	Unc
46	1980	40.000	—	1.00	1.50	2.50
	1981	20.000	—	1.00	1.50	2.50
	1982	10.000	—	1.00	1.50	2.50
	1983	4.000	—	1.00	1.50	2.50
	1984	4.500	—	1.00	1.50	2.50

KM#	Date	Mintage	Fine	VF	XF	Unc
56	1985	6.000	—	.75	1.25	2.25
	1986	8.000	—	.75	1.25	2.25
	1987		—	.75	1.25	2.25
	1988	16.000	—	.75	1.25	2.25
	1988	.020	—	—	Proof	15.00
	1989	37.000	—	.75	1.25	2.25
	1991		—	.75	1.25	2.25

Bauhinia Flower

65	1993		—	—	.75	1.25	2.25
	1993		—	—	—	Proof	15.00
	1994		—	—	.75	1.25	2.25
	1995		—	—	.75	1.25	2.25
	1997		—	—	.75	1.25	2.25

Obv: Bauhinia flower. Rev: Shou character.

77	1997		—	—	1.00	1.65	3.25
	1997	*.097	—	—	—	Proof	15.00

10 DOLLARS

NICKEL-BRASS center COPPER-NICKEL ring
Bauhinia Flower

70	1993		—	—	2.00	4.00	8.50
	1993	*.030	—	—	—	Proof	15.00
	1994		—	—	1.50	2.50	4.50
	1995		—	—	1.50	2.50	4.50

NICKEL-BRASS center, COPPER-NICKEL ring
Obv: Bauhinia flower. Rev: Suspension bridge.

78	1997		—	—	1.75	3.25	6.50
	1997	*.097	—	—	—	Proof	15.00

HUNGARY

The Republic of Hungary, located in central Europe, has an area of 35,929 sq. mi. (93,030 sq. km.) and a population of 10.7 million. Capital: Budapest. The economy is based on agriculture, bauxite and a rapidly expanding industrial sector. Machinery, chemicals, iron and steel, and fruits and vegetables are exported.

The ancient kingdom of Hungary, founded by the Magyars in the 9th century, achieved its greatest extension in the mid-14th century when its dominions touched the Baltic, Black and Mediterranean Seas. After suffering repeated Turkish invasions, Hungary accepted Habsburg rule to escape Turkish occupation, regaining independence in 1867 with the Emperor of Austria as king of a dual Austro-Hungarian monarchy. After World War I, Hungary lost 2/3 of its territory and 1/2 of its population and underwent a period of drastic political revision. The short-lived republic of 1918 was followed by a chaotic interval of communist rule, 1919, and the restoration of the monarchy in 1920 with Admiral Horthy as regent of the kingdom. Although a German ally in World War II, Hungary was occupied by German troops who imposed a pro-Nazi dictatorship, 1944. Soviet armies drove out the Germans in 1945 and assisted the communist minority in seizing power. A revised constitution published on Aug. 20, 1949, established Hungary as a 'People's Republic' of the Soviet type. On October 23, 1989, Hungary was proclaimed the Republic of Hungary.

RULERS
Austrian until 1918

MONETARY SYSTEM
1892-1925
100 Filler = 1 Korona
1926-1945
100 Filler = 1 Pengo
Commencing 1946
100 Filler = 1 Forint

NOTE: Many coins of Hungary through 1948, especially 1925-1945, have been restruck in recent times. These may be identified by a rosette in the vicinity of the mint mark. Restrike mintages for KM#440-449, 451-458, 468-469, 475-477, 480-483, 494, 496-498 are usually about 1000 pieces, later date mintages are not known.

FILLER

BRONZE
Mint mark: KB

KM#	Date	Mintage	Fine	VF	XF	Unc
480	1901	5.994	4.00	8.00	17.00	32.50
	1902	16.299	.20	.50	1.25	4.00
	1903	2.291	12.00	25.00	65.00	110.00
	1906	.061	65.00	120.00	180.00	275.00
	1914	—	65.00	90.00	135.00	210.00
	1914	—	—	—	Proof	350.00

NOTE: Earlier dates (1892-1900) exist for this type.

2 FILLER

BRONZE
Mint mark: KB

481	1901	25.805	.50	1.00	2.50	5.00
	1902	6.937	5.50	8.50	13.50	20.00
	1903	4.052	12.00	20.00	35.00	50.00
	1904	4.203	6.00	12.00	25.00	40.00
	1905	9.335	.70	1.75	3.00	6.00
	1906	3.140	1.75	2.50	5.00	7.50
	1907	9.943	5.50	9.00	12.00	17.50
	1908	16.486	.50	1.00	2.50	5.00
	1909	19.075	.50	1.00	2.50	5.00
	1910	5.338	4.50	7.50	10.00	15.00
	1910	(restrike w/rosette)				
		—	—	—	Proof	10.00
	1914	4.106	.50	1.00	2.50	5.00
	1915	1.294	1.50	2.00	4.00	7.00

NOTE: Earlier dates (1892-1900) exist for this type.

IRON

KM#	Date	Mintage	Fine	VF	XF	Unc
497	1916	—	6.00	10.00	15.00	25.00
	1917	—	1.00	2.50	6.00	12.00
	1918	—	2.00	4.50	9.00	15.00

NOTE: Varieties in planchet thickness exist for 1917.

10 FILLER

NICKEL
Mint mark: KB

482	1906	.056	75.00	175.00	250.00	325.00
	1908	6.819	.25	.50	1.50	4.00
	1909	17.204	.30	.60	2.00	4.00
	1914	—	175.00	275.00	550.00	900.00

NOTE: Earlier dates (1892-1896) exist for this type.
NOTE: Edge varieties exist.

COPPER-NICKEL-ZINC

494	1914	4.400	200.00	300.00	500.00	900.00
	1915	Inc. Ab.	.30	.60	1.50	4.00
	1915	(restrike w/rosette)				
		Inc. Ab.	—	—	Proof	4.00
	1916	Inc. Ab.	.50	1.25	2.50	5.00

IRON

496	1915	11.500	9.00	20.00	32.50	55.00
	1916	Inc. Ab.				
	1918	Inc. Ab.	15.00	30.00	55.00	85.00
	1918	(restrike)	—	—	Proof	18.00
	1920	3.275	4.50	9.00	15.00	25.00
	1920	(restrike)	—	—	Proof	18.00

NOTE: Varieties exist.

20 FILLER

NICKEL
Mint mark: KB

483	1906	.067	275.00	400.00	600.00	1250.00
	1907	1.248	3.00	6.00	12.00	24.00
	1908	10.770	.75	1.75	3.75	7.50
	1914	5.387	3.75	6.50	10.00	15.00
	1914	(restrike)	—	—	Proof	12.50

NOTE: Earlier dates (1892-1894) exist for this type.
NOTE: Edge varieties exist.

IRON

498	1914	18.826	18.00	32.50	45.00	70.00
	1916	Inc. Ab.	.50	1.25	2.50	7.00
	1917	Inc. Ab.	.75	1.75	3.50	8.00
	1918	Inc. Ab.	.75	1.75	3.50	8.00
	1918	(restrike)	—	—	Proof	6.00
	1920	12.000	2.50	5.00	9.00	18.00
	1921	Inc. Ab.	18.00	32.50	45.00	70.00
	1921	(restrike)	—	—	Proof	12.00
	1922		—	—	Rare	—

NOTE: Edge varieties exist.

BRASS

498a	1922	400 pcs.	—	—	P/L	175.00
	1922	(restrike)	—	—	Proof	50.00

KORONA

5.0000 g, .835 SILVER, .1342 oz ASW
Mint mark: KB

KM#	Date	Mintage	Fine	VF	XF	Unc
484	1906	.024	150.00	200.00	300.00	425.00

NOTE: Obverse varieties exist.
NOTE: Earlier dates (1892-1896) exist for this type.

492	1912	4.004	2.50	5.00	10.00	15.00
	1913	5,214	50.00	80.00	140.00	200.00
	1914	5.886	BV	3.75	6.50	10.00
	1915	3.934	BV	3.00	4.50	6.00
	1916	—	BV	3.50	6.00	8.00

2 KORONA

10.0000 g, .835 SILVER, .2685 oz ASW
Mint mark: KB

493	1912	4.000	BV	4.50	6.50	13.50
	1913	3.000	BV	4.50	6.50	13.50
	1914	.500	20.00	30.00	50.00	80.00

5 KORONA

24.0000 g, .900 SILVER, .6944 oz ASW
Mint mark: KB

488	1906	1,263	1000.	1500.	2000.	2500.
	1907	.500	12.00	20.00	40.00	85.00
	1908	1.742	10.00	18.00	40.00	75.00
	1909	1.299	10.00	18.00	40.00	90.00
	1909 U.P.	(restrike)	—	—	Proof	30.00

NOTE: Earlier date (1900) exists for this type.

40th Anniversary - Coronation of Franz Josef

KM#	Date	Mintage	Fine	VF	XF	Unc
489	1907	.300	15.00	22.00	35.00	55.00
	1907	(restrike)	—	Proof		30.00
	1907 U.P.	(restrike)	—	Proof		30.00

10 KORONA

3.3875 g, .900 GOLD, .0980 oz AGW
Mint mark: KB

485	1901	.230	BV	45.00	55.00	65.00
	1902	.243	BV	45.00	55.00	65.00
	1903	.228	BV	45.00	55.00	65.00
	1904	1.531	BV	45.00	55.00	65.00
	1905	.869	BV	45.00	55.00	65.00
	1906	.748	BV	45.00	55.00	65.00
	1907	.752	BV	45.00	55.00	65.00
	1908	.509	BV	45.00	55.00	65.00
	1909	.574	BV	45.00	55.00	65.00
	1910	1.362	BV	45.00	55.00	65.00
	1911	1.828	BV	45.00	55.00	65.00
	1912	.739	50.00	60.00	70.00	85.00
	1913	.137	50.00	75.00	100.00	125.00
	1914	.115	50.00	80.00	135.00	160.00
	1915	.054	1000.	2000.	3000.	4000.

NOTE: Earlier dates (1892-1900) exist for this type.

20 KORONA

6.7750 g, .900 GOLD, .1960 oz AGW
Mint mark: KB

486	1901	.510	BV	80.00	90.00	115.00
	1902	.523	BV	80.00	90.00	115.00
	1903	.505	BV	80.00	90.00	115.00
	1904	.572	BV	80.00	90.00	115.00
	1905	.526	BV	80.00	90.00	115.00
	1906	.353	BV	80.00	90.00	115.00
	1907	.194	100.00	150.00	175.00	200.00
	1908	.138	BV	80.00	90.00	115.00
	1909	.459	BV	80.00	90.00	115.00
	1910	.085	125.00	175.00	250.00	300.00
	1911	.063	BV	80.00	90.00	115.00
	1912	.211	BV	80.00	90.00	115.00
	1913	.320	110.00	140.00	165.00	200.00
	1914	.176	BV	80.00	90.00	115.00
	1915	.690	110.00	140.00	165.00	200.00

NOTE: Earlier dates (1892-1900) exist for this type.

Rev: Bosnian arms added.

495	1914	—	BV	90.00	100.00	135.00
	1915	—	—	—	—	—
	1916	—	125.00	175.00	275.00	400.00

KM#	Date	Mintage	Fine	VF	XF	Unc
500	1918	—	—	—	Rare	—

100 KORONA

33.8753 g, .900 GOLD, .9802 oz AGW
Mint mark: KB
40th Anniversary - Coronation of Franz Josef

490	1907	.011	500.00	650.00	900.00	1200.
	1907 U.P.	(restrike)	—	—	—	800.00

REGENCY

1926-1945

MONETARY SYSTEM
100 Filler = 1 Pengo

FILLER

BRONZE
Mint mark: BP

505	1926	6.471	.50	1.00	2.00	4.00
	1927	16.529	.10	.20	.50	3.00
	1928	7.000	.25	.50	1.00	3.75
	1929	.418	5.00	10.00	20.00	35.00
	1930	3.734	.30	.60	1.50	5.00
	1931	10.849	.10	.20	.60	3.00
	1932	5.000	.25	.50	1.00	4.00
	1932	(restrike)	—	—	Proof	3.75
	1933	5.000	.25	.50	1.00	4.00
	1934	3.111	.30	.60	1.20	4.50
	1935	6.889	.25	.50	1.00	4.00
	1936	10.000	.10	.20	.60	2.50
	1938	10.575	.10	.20	.60	2.50
	1939	10.425	.10	.20	.60	2.50

2 FILLER

BRONZE
Mint mark: BP

506	1926	17.777	.10	.20	.40	2.00
	1927	44.836	.10	.20	.40	2.00
	1928	11.448	.10	.20	.40	2.00
	1929	8.995	.10	.25	.50	2.50
	1930	6.943	.10	.25	.50	2.50
	1931	.826	.40	.90	2.50	6.50
	1932	4.174	4.00	8.00	15.00	25.00
	1933	.501	3.00	6.00	10.00	18.00
	1934	9.499	.10	.20	.40	2.00
	1935	10.000	.10	.20	.40	2.00
	1936	2.049	.15	.30	.75	4.00
	1937	7.951	.10	.25	.50	2.00
	1938	14.125	.10	.20	.40	1.50
	1939	16.875	.10	.20	.40	1.50
	1940	7.000	.10	.25	.50	1.50

STEEL

KM#	Date	Mintage	Fine	VF	XF	Unc
518.1	1940	64.500	1.00	2.00	5.00	10.00

518.2	1940	78.000	.50	1.00	2.00	4.50
	1941	12.000	30.00	65.00	125.00	200.00
	1942	13.000	.50	1.00	2.00	4.50
	1942	(restrike)	—	—	Proof	6.50

ZINC

519	1943	37.000	.10	.20	.70	3.00
	1943	(restrike)	—	—	Proof	6.50
	1944	55.159	.10	.20	.70	2.50

NOTE: Variations in planchets exist.

10 FILLER

COPPER-NICKEL
Mint mark: BP

507	1926	20.001	.50	1.50	3.00	10.00
	1927	12.255	.50	1.50	3.00	7.00
	1935	4.740	.50	1.50	3.00	4.50
	1936	3.005	.50	1.50	3.00	4.50
	1938	6.700	.50	1.50	3.00	4.50
	1939	4.460	3.00	5.00	10.00	20.00
	1940	.960	15.00	30.00	50.00	75.00

STEEL

507a	1940	45.927	.10	.20	.80	3.50
	1941	24.963	.10	.20	.80	3.50
	1942	44.110	.10	.20	.80	3.50

20 FILLER

COPPER-NICKEL
Mint mark: BP

508	1926	25.000	1.50	3.50	10.00	15.00
	1927	.830	10.00	30.00	60.00	100.00
	1938	20.150	.10	.25	1.00	2.50
	1939	2.020	6.50	10.00	20.00	35.00
	1940	2.470	4.00	7.50	18.00	30.00

STEEL

520	1941	75.007	.10	.20	.90	4.00
	1943	7.500	.10	.20	.90	4.00
	1944	25.000	.10	.20	.90	4.00
	1944	(restrike)	—	—	Proof	7.00

50 FILLER

COPPER-NICKEL
Mint mark: BP

KM#	Date	Mintage	Fine	VF	XF	Unc
509	1926	14.921	.75	2.00	3.50	6.00
	1938	20.079	.20	.40	1.00	3.00
	1939	2.770	6.50	15.00	30.00	50.00
	1939	(restrike)	—	—	Proof	20.00
	1940	6.230	4.00	7.50	18.00	30.00

PENGO

5.0000 g, .640 SILVER, .1029 oz ASW
Mint mark: BP

510	1926	15.000	BV	2.50	6.50	20.00
	1927	18.000	BV	1.50	4.50	12.00
	1937	4.000	BV	1.50	2.50	6.00
	1938	5.000	BV	1.50	2.50	6.00
	1939	13.000	BV	1.00	2.00	5.00

ALUMINUM

521	1941	80.000	.10	.20	.50	1.00
	1942	19.000	.10	.20	.50	1.00
	1943	2.000	1.00	4.00	8.00	15.00
	1944	16.000	.10	.20	.50	1.00

2 PENGO

10.0000 g, .640 SILVER, .2058 oz ASW
Mint mark: BP

511	1929	5.000	1.25	3.00	6.50	12.50
	1931	.110	10.00	25.00	45.00	90.00
	1932	.602	1.50	4.00	8.00	15.00
	1933	1.051	1.25	3.00	6.00	12.50
	1935	.050	25.00	65.00	120.00	250.00
	1936	.711	2.00	5.00	10.00	20.00
	1937	1.500	1.25	3.00	4.75	8.50
	1938	6.417	1.25	3.00	4.75	8.50
	1939	2.103	1.25	3.00	4.75	8.50

Tercentenary - Founding of Pazmany University

513	1935	.050	3.00	6.00	10.00	20.00
	1935	(restrike not marked)		Proof		22.50

Death of Rakoczi Bicentennial

KM#	Date	Mintage	Fine	VF	XF	Unc
514	1935	.100	2.00	4.00	6.00	10.00
	1935	(restrike not marked)		Proof		22.50

50th Anniversary - Death of Liszt

515	1936	.200	1.50	2.50	4.50	8.00
	1936	(restrike not marked)		Proof		18.00

ALUMINUM

522.1	1941	24.000	.15	.30	.50	.80
	1942	8.000	.15	.30	.50	.80
	1943	10.000	.15	.30	.50	.80

Rev: Base of 2 is wavy.

522.2	1941	.040	10.00	20.00	35.00	65.00
	1941 rose	restrike	—	—	—	—

5 PENGO

25.0000 g, .640 SILVER, .5145 oz ASW
Mint mark: BP
10th Anniversary - Regency of Admiral Horthy
Raised, sharp edge reeding.

512.1	1930	3.650	4.50	9.00	12.00	17.50

25.3300 g, .640 SILVER, .5213 oz ASW, 36.1mm

512.2	1930	(restrike)	—	—	Proof	18.50

25.0000 g, .640 SILVER, .5145 oz ASW, 36.1mm
900th Anniversary - Death of St. Stephan

KM#	Date	Mintage	Fine	VF	XF	Unc
516	1938	.600	4.50	9.00	14.00	25.00
	1938	(restrike not marked)			Proof	27.50

Admiral Miklos Horthy
Smooth, ornamented edge.

517	1938	60 pcs.	—	—	—	800.00
	1939	.408	4.50	9.00	14.00	25.00

ALUMINUM
75th Birthday of Admiral Horthy

523	1943	2.000	.50	1.00	2.00	4.00
	1943	(restrike)			Proof	6.00

PROVISIONAL GOVERNMENT
1944-1946
5 PENGO

ALUMINUM
Mint mark: BP

525	1945	5.002	.50	1.00	3.00	6.50
	1945	PROBAVERET (restrike)	—	—	Proof	17.50

REPUBLIC
1946-1949

MONETARY SYSTEM
100 Filler = 1 Forint

2 FILLER

BRONZE
Mint mark: BP

529	1946	13.665	.15	.25	.50	1.00
	1947	23.865	.15	.25	.50	1.00
	1947	(restrike)			Proof	5.00

---

5 FILLER

ALUMINUM
Mint mark: BP

KM#	Date	Mintage	Fine	VF	XF	Unc
535	1948	24.000	.25	.50	1.00	3.00
	1951	15.000	.20	.40	.80	2.00

10 FILLER

ALUMINUM-BRONZE
Mint mark: BP

530	1946	23.565	.15	.30	.70	2.00
	1947	29.580	.15	.30	.70	2.00
	1947	(restrike)	—	—	Proof	4.50
	1948	4.885	1.00	2.00	3.00	6.50
	1950	8.000	.50	1.00	2.50	5.00

ALUMINUM

530a	1950		1.00	2.00	3.00	6.50

20 FILLER

ALUMINUM-BRONZE
Mint mark: BP

531	1946	16.560	.25	.50	1.00	2.00
	1946	(restrike)	—	—	Proof	4.50
	1947	18.260	.25	.50	1.25	2.50
	1948	5.180	1.00	2.00	3.00	8.00
	1950	6.000	.75	1.50	2.50	7.00

50 FILLER

ALUMINUM
Mint mark: BP

536	1948	15.000	1.00	2.00	3.00	8.00
	1948	(restrike)	—	—	Proof	10.00

FORINT

ALUMINUM
Mint mark: BP

532	1946	38.500	1.00	2.00	3.00	8.00
	1947	2.600	3.00	6.00	10.00	20.00
	1949	17.000	1.50	2.50	5.00	10.00

2 FORINT

ALUMINUM
Mint mark: BP

533	1946	10.000	1.50	2.50	5.00	12.00
	1947	3.500	3.00	5.00	10.00	20.00

5 FORINT

20.0000 g, .835 SILVER, .5369 oz ASW
Mint mark: BP

Lajos Kossuth
Thick planchet.

KM#	Date	Mintage	Fine	VF	XF	Unc
534	1946	.040	5.00	10.00	15.00	30.00

12.0000 g, .500 SILVER, .1929 oz ASW
1.7mm thin planchet.

534a	1946		—	—	—	—
	1947	10.000	BV	1.75	3.00	5.00
	1947	(restrike)	—	—	Proof	8.00

13.0000 g, .835 SILVER, .3490 oz ASW

534b	1966	5.000	(restrike)		Proof	15.00
	1967	5.000	(restrike)		Proof	15.00

12.0000 g, .500 SILVER, .1929 oz ASW
Centenary of 1848 Revolution - Petofi

537	1948	.100	BV	2.00	4.00	8.00
	1948	(restrike)	—	—	Proof	15.00

10 FORINT

20.0000 g, .500 SILVER, .3215 oz ASW
Mint mark: BP
Centenary of 1848 Revolution - Szechenyi

538	1948	.100	2.50	3.50	6.50	12.00
	1948	(restrike)	—	—	Proof	20.00

20 FORINT

28.0000 g, .500 SILVER, .4501 oz ASW
Mint mark: BP
Centenary of 1848 Revolution - Tancsics

KM#	Date	Mintage	Fine	VF	XF	Unc
539	1948	.050	5.00	9.00	15.00	20.00
	1948	(restrike)	—	—	Proof	35.00

PEOPLES REPUBLIC

1949-1989

MONETARY SYSTEM
100 Filler = 1 Forint

2 FILLER

ALUMINUM
Mint mark: BP

KM#	Date	Mintage	Fine	VF	XF	Unc
546	1950	24.990	—	.10	.20	.50
	1952	5.600	—	.10	.30	1.00
	1953	9.400	—	.10	.20	.50
	1954	10.000	—	.10	.20	.50
	1955	6.029	—	.10	.25	.75
	1956	4.000	—	.15	.30	1.00
	1957	5.000	—	.10	.25	.50
	1960	3.000	.10	.15	.30	.60
	1961	2.000	.20	.40	.60	1.00
	1962	3.000	.10	.15	.30	.60
	1963	2.082	.10	.20	.35	.70
	1965	.540	—	4.00	8.00	16.00
	1971	1.041	.10	.15	.30	.60
	1972	1.000	.10	.15	.30	.60
	1973	2.820	.10	.15	.30	.60
	1974	.050	—	.40	.80	1.50
	1975	.050	—	.40	.80	1.50
	1976	.050	—	.40	.80	1.50
	1977	.060	—	.40	.80	1.50
	1978	.050	—	.40	.80	1.50
	1979	.030	—	.75	1.25	2.50
	1980	.030	—	.75	1.25	2.50
	1981	.030	—	.75	1.25	2.50
	1982	.030	—	.75	1.25	2.50
	1983	.030	—	.75	1.25	2.50
	1984	.030	—	.75	1.25	2.50
	1985	.030	—	.75	1.25	2.50
	1986	.030	—	.75	1.25	2.50
	1987	.030	—	.75	1.25	2.50
	1988	.030	—	.75	1.25	2.50
	1989	.030	—	.75	1.25	2.50

COPPER-NICKEL

KM#	Date	Mintage	Fine	VF	XF	Unc
546a	1966	5,000		—	Proof	4.00
	1967	5,000		—	Proof	4.00

5 FILLER

ALUMINUM
Mint mark: BP

KM#	Date	Mintage	Fine	VF	XF	Unc
549	1953	10.000	.10	.15	.30	.50
	1955	6.005	.15	.20	.50	1.00
	1956	6.012	.15	.20	.50	1.00
	1957	5.000	.20	.30	.60	1.20
	1959	8.000	.15	.20	.50	1.00
	1960	7.000	.15	.20	.50	1.00
	1961	4.410	.20	.30	.60	1.20
	1962	5.590	.20	.30	.60	1.20
	1963	4.020	.20	.30	.60	1.20
549	1964	3.600	.20	.30	.60	1.20
	1965	6.000	.20	.30	.60	1.20
	1970	3.900	—	2.50	5.00	10.00
	1971	.100	—	.25	.50	1.00
	1972	.050	—	.25	.50	1.00
	1973	.105	—	.25	.50	1.00
	1974	.060	—	.25	.50	1.00
	1975	.060	—	.25	.50	1.00
	1976	.050	—	.25	.50	1.00
	1977	.060	—	.25	.50	1.00
	1978	.050	—	.25	.50	1.00
	1979	.030	—	.50	1.00	2.00
	1980	.030	—	.50	1.00	2.00
	1981	.030	—	.50	1.00	2.00
	1982	.030	—	.50	1.00	2.00
	1983	.030	—	.50	1.00	2.00
	1984	.030	—	.50	1.00	2.00
	1985	.030	—	.50	1.00	2.00
	1986	.030	—	.50	1.00	2.00
	1987	.030	—	.50	1.00	2.00
	1988	.030	—	.50	1.00	2.00
	1989	.030	—	.50	1.00	2.00

COPPER-NICKEL

KM#	Date	Mintage	Fine	VF	XF	Unc
549a	1966	5,000	—	—	Proof	5.00
	1967	5,000	—	—	Proof	5.00

10 FILLER

ALUMINUM
Mint mark: BP

KM#	Date	Mintage	Fine	VF	XF	Unc
547	1950	5.040	10.00	20.00	30.00	50.00
	1951	80.950	1.50	3.00	5.00	10.00
	1955	10.019	2.00	4.00	7.00	15.00
	1957	13.000	2.00	4.00	7.00	15.00
	1958	12.015	2.00	4.00	7.00	15.00
	1959	15.000	2.00	4.00	7.00	15.00
	1960	5.000	2.50	5.00	8.00	17.00
	1961	13.000	2.00	4.00	7.00	15.00
	1962	4.000	2.50	5.00	9.00	18.00
	1963	8.000	2.50	5.00	8.00	17.00
	1964	17.008	2.00	4.00	7.00	15.00
	1965	21.880	2.00	4.00	7.00	15.00
	1966	8.120	2.50	5.00	8.00	17.00

COPPER-NICKEL

KM#	Date	Mintage	Fine	VF	XF	Unc
547a	1966	5,000	—	—	Proof	6.00
	1967	5,000	—	—	Proof	6.00

ALUMINUM, reduced size

KM#	Date	Mintage	Fine	VF	XF	Unc
572	1967	5,000	5.00	10.00	20.00	45.00
	1968	16.000	.50	1.00	2.50	5.00
	1969	50.760	.50	1.00	2.50	5.00
	1970	28.470	.50	1.00	2.50	5.00
	1971	28.800	—	.50	1.25	2.50
	1972	17.220	—	.50	1.25	2.50
	1973	33.720	—	.50	1.25	2.50
	1974	24.930	—	.50	1.25	2.50
	1975	30.000	—	.50	1.25	2.50
	1976	20.025	—	.50	1.25	2.50
	1977	30.075	—	.50	1.25	2.50
	1978	36.005	—	.40	1.00	2.00
	1979	36.060	—	.40	1.00	2.00
	1980	36.010	—	.40	1.00	2.00
	1981	36.000	—	.40	1.00	2.00
	1982	45.015	—	.30	.75	1.50
	1983	45.030	—	.30	.75	1.50
	1984	42.075	—	.30	.75	1.50
	1985	40.035	—	.30	.75	1.50
	1986	48.075	—	.30	.75	1.50
	1987	45.000	—	.30	.75	1.50
	1988	48.015	—	.30	.75	1.50
	1989	55.515	—	—	.10	.50

20 FILLER

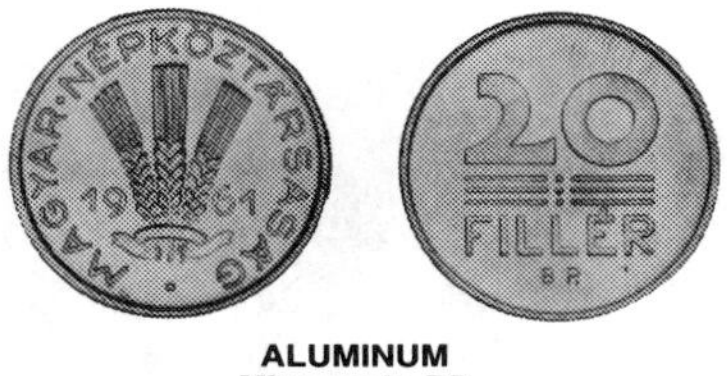

ALUMINUM
Mint mark: BP

KM#	Date	Mintage	Fine	VF	XF	Unc
550	1953	45.000	1.00	2.00	4.00	8.00
	1955	10.023	1.25	2.50	5.00	10.00
	1957	5.000	1.75	3.50	7.00	15.00
	1958	10.000	1.25	2.50	5.00	10.00
	1959	13.000	1.25	2.50	5.00	10.00
	1961	9.000	1.25	2.50	5.00	10.00
	1963	7.000	1.50	3.00	6.00	12.00
	1964	10.400	1.25	2.50	5.00	10.00
550	1965	15.000	1.25	2.50	5.00	10.00
	1966	5.000	1.50	3.00	6.50	12.50

COPPER-NICKEL

KM#	Date	Mintage	Fine	VF	XF	Unc
550a	1966	5,000	—	—	Proof	8.00
	1967	5,000	—	—	Proof	8.00

ALUMINUM
Reduced size.

KM#	Date	Mintage	Fine	VF	XF	Unc
573	1967	10.000	.25	.75	2.50	6.00
	1968	56.500	.10	.40	1.25	3.00
	1969	28.550	.15	.45	1.50	4.00
	1970	19.960	.20	.60	2.00	5.00
	1971	31.090	.10	.20	.75	2.00
	7971(error)	.011	3.50	7.50	15.00	30.00
	1972	21.070	.15	.30	.75	1.50
	1973	22.970	.15	.30	.75	1.50
	1974	35.010	.15	.30	.75	1.50
	1975	30.010	.15	.30	.75	1.50
	1976	30.010	.15	.30	.75	1.50
	1977	30.050	.15	.30	.75	1.50
	1978	30.140	.15	.30	.75	1.50
	1979	32.010	.15	.30	.75	1.50
	1980	45.010	.10	.20	.50	1.00
	1981	34.030	.10	.20	.50	1.00
	1982	35.010	.10	.20	.50	1.00
	1983	43.210	.10	.20	.50	1.00
	1984	42.270	.10	.20	.50	1.00
	1985	40.440	.10	.20	.50	1.00
	1986	48.000	.10	.20	.50	1.00
	1987	55.000	.10	.20	.50	1.00
	1988	48.010	.10	.20	.50	1.00
	1989	64.660		—	.10	.50

F.A.O. Issue

KM#	Date	Mintage	Fine	VF	XF	Unc
627	1983	.050	—	.50	1.00	2.50

50 FILLER

ALUMINUM
Mint mark: BP

KM#	Date	Mintage	Fine	VF	XF	Unc
551	1953	10.017	1.50	3.00	6.00	12.00
	1965	3.005	1.25	2.50	5.00	10.00
	1966	1.500	1.75	3.50	7.00	15.00

COPPER-NICKEL

KM#	Date	Mintage	Fine	VF	XF	Unc
551a	1966	5,000	—	—	Proof	10.00
	1967	5,000	—	—	Proof	10.00

ALUMINUM

KM#	Date	Mintage	Fine	VF	XF	Unc
574	1967	20.000	.50	1.00	2.00	4.00
	1968	13.861	.60	1.25	2.50	5.00
	1969	10.085	.60	1.25	2.50	5.00
	1971	.050	.30	.60	1.25	2.50
	1972	.470	.20	.50	1.00	2.00
	1973	7.600	.20	.50	1.00	2.00
	1974	5.000	.20	.50	1.00	2.00
	1975	10.160	.10	.30	.75	1.50
	1976	15.130	.10	.30	.75	1.50
	1977	10.050	.10	.30	.75	1.50
	1978	10.110	.10	.30	.75	1.50
	1979	10.070	.10	.30	.75	1.50
	1980	15.000	.10	.30	.75	1.50
	1981	10.030	.10	.30	.75	1.50
	1982	10.000	.10	.30	.75	1.50
	1983	10.070	.10	.30	.75	1.50
	1984	14.060	.10	.30	.75	1.50
	1985	12.020	.10	.30	.75	1.50
	1986	17.140	.10	.30	.75	1.50
	1987	23.000	—	.10	.50	1.00
	1988	18.050	—	.10	.50	1.00
	1989	18.200	—	.10	.50	1.00

FORINT

ALUMINUM
Mint mark: BP

KM#	Date	Mintage	Fine	VF	XF	Unc
545	1949	19.440	1.50	3.00	6.00	12.00
	1950	39.060	2.25	4.50	9.00	18.00
	1952	63.018	2.00	4.00	8.00	16.00

555	1957	7.500	2.00	4.00	8.00	16.00
	1958	5.070	1.50	3.00	6.00	12.00
	1960	5.000	1.25	2.50	5.00	10.00
	1961	5.000	1.25	2.50	5.00	10.00
	1963	3.000	1.50	3.00	6.50	12.50
	1964	6.080	1.00	2.00	4.00	8.00
	1965	9.810	1.00	2.00	4.00	8.00
	1966	5.680	1.75	3.50	7.50	15.00

Reduced size, 22.8mm

575	1967	60.000	.65	1.25	2.50	5.00
	1968	53.230	.65	1.25	2.50	6.00
	1969	27.664	1.00	2.00	4.00	8.00
	1970	11.290	1.00	2.00	4.00	10.00
	1971	.100	.10	.20	.50	1.00
	1972	.110	.25	.50	1.00	2.00
	1973	1.990	.10	.20	.50	1.00
	1974	4.990	.10	.20	.50	1.00
	1975	10.000	.10	.20	.40	.80
	1976	15.000	.10	.20	.40	.80
	1977	10.050	.10	.20	.40	.80
	1978	.050	.20	.40	.85	1.75
	1979	10.070	.10	.20	.35	.70
	1980	20.040	.10	.20	.35	.70
	1981	25.040	.10	.20	.35	.70
	1982	10.000	.10	.20	.35	.70
	1983	20.140	.10	.20	.35	.70
	1984	6.010	.15	.30	.60	1.20
	1985	.030	.25	.50	1.00	2.00
	1986	.030	.25	.50	1.00	2.00
	1987	13.000	.10	.20	.50	1.00
	1988	20.080	.10	.20	.35	.75
	1989	115.920	—	.15	.30	.60

2 FORINT

COPPER-NICKEL
Mint mark: BP

548	1950	18.500	1.75	3.50	7.00	15.00
	1951	4.000	2.00	4.00	8.00	16.00
	1952	4.530	2.00	4.00	8.00	16.00

556	1957	5.000	1.50	3.00	6.00	12.50
	1958	1.033	1.75	3.50	7.00	15.00
	1960	4.000	1.50	3.00	6.00	12.50
	1961	.690	2.00	4.00	8.00	16.00
	1962	1.190	1.50	3.00	6.00	12.50

COPPER-NICKEL-ZINC

556a	1962	1.210	1.25	2.50	5.00	10.00
	1963	3.100	1.25	2.50	5.00	10.00
	1964	3.250	1.25	2.50	5.00	10.00
	1965	4.395	1.25	2.50	5.00	10.00
	1966	6.630	1.25	2.50	5.00	10.00

BRASS

KM#	Date	Mintage	Fine	VF	XF	Unc
591	1970	49.195	.50	1.00	2.00	4.00
	1971	10.830	.10	.50	1.00	2.00
	1972	10.015	.10	.50	1.00	2.00
	1973	.820	1.00	2.00	4.00	8.00
	1974	10.000	.25	.75	1.50	3.00
	1975	20.030	.25	.75	1.50	3.00
	1976	15.000	.25	.75	1.50	3.00
	1977	10.115	.25	.75	1.50	3.00
	1978	12.000	.25	.75	1.50	3.00
	1979	10.127	.25	.75	1.50	3.00
	1980	12.005	.25	.75	1.50	3.00
	1981	10.010	.25	.75	1.50	3.00
	1982	10.005	.25	.75	1.50	3.00
	1983	20.160	.25	.75	1.50	3.00
	1984	5.000	.75	1.50	3.00	6.00
	1985	10.675	.25	.75	1.50	3.00
	1986	.030	1.50	3.00	6.00	12.00
	1987	5.030	.50	1.00	2.00	4.00
	1988	5.035	.50	1.00	2.00	4.00
	1989	79.223	.10	.25	.50	1.00

5 FORINT

COPPER-NICKEL
Mint mark: BP
Lajos Kossuth

576	1967	20.000	.50	1.00	2.50	5.00
	1968	.029	5.00	10.00	20.00	35.00

NICKEL

594	1971	20.004	.20	.35	.75	1.50
	1972	5.000	.25	.50	1.00	2.00
	1973	.100	.35	.75	1.50	3.00
	1974	.050	.35	.75	1.50	3.00
	1975	.050	.35	.75	1.50	3.00
	1976	5.090	.25	.50	1.00	2.00
	1977	.050	.35	.75	1.50	3.00
	1978	6.000	.25	.50	1.00	2.00
	1979	10.000	.25	.50	1.00	2.00
	1980	6.002	.25	.50	1.00	2.00
	1981	5.002	.25	.50	1.00	2.00
	1982	.936	.30	.60	1.25	2.50

F.A.O. Issue

628	1983	.050	—	1.00	2.00	3.50

COPPER-NICKEL
Lajos Kossuth

635	1983	15.240	.15	.25	.50	1.00
	1984	25.018	.15	.25	.50	1.00
	1985	25.286	.15	.25	.50	1.00
	1986	1.030	.20	.35	.75	1.50
	1987	.030	.30	.60	1.25	2.50
	1988	4.050	.20	.35	.75	1.50
	1989	39.014	.15	.25	.50	1.00

10 FORINT

12.5000 g, .800 SILVER, .3215 oz ASW
Mint mark: BP
10th Anniversary of Forint

KM#	Date	Mintage	Fine	VF	XF	Unc
552	1956	.022	3.00	5.00	8.00	16.00

NICKEL

595	1971	24.998	.35	.75	1.50	3.00
	1972	25.078	.35	.75	1.50	3.00
	1973	.078	.60	1.25	2.50	5.00
	1974	.050	.60	1.25	2.50	5.00
	1975	.050	.60	1.25	2.50	5.00
	1976	3.568	.50	1.00	2.00	4.00
	1977	4.618	.50	1.00	2.00	4.00
	1978	.050	.60	1.25	2.50	5.00
	1979	5.000	.50	1.00	2.00	4.00
	1980	2.550	.50	1.00	2.00	4.00
	1982	.030	.60	1.25	2.50	5.00

F.A.O. Issue

620	1981	.060	—	—	2.50	5.00

F.A.O. Issue

629	1983	.050	—	—	2.50	5.00

ALUMINUM-BRONZE
Circulation Coinage

636	1983	11.004	.25	.50	1.00	2.00
	1984	7.578	.25	.50	1.00	2.00
	1985	27.648	.25	.50	1.00	2.00
	1986	15.006	.25	.50	1.00	2.00
	1987	10.000	.25	.50	1.00	2.00
	1988	5.000	.25	.50	1.00	2.00
	1989	37.094	.25	.50	1.00	2.00

20 FORINT

17.5000 g, .800 SILVER, .4501 oz ASW
Mint mark: BP
10th Anniversary of Forint

KM#	Date	Mintage	Fine	VF	XF	Unc
553	1956	.022	4.50	8.00	12.00	20.00

COPPER-NICKEL
Dozsa - Circulation Coinage

KM#	Date	Mintage	Fine	VF	XF	Unc
630	1982	13.404	.25	.50	.80	1.60
	1983	18.006	.25	.50	.80	1.60
	1984	31.016	.25	.50	.80	1.60
	1985	20.122	.25	.50	.80	1.60
	1986	6.000	.35	.65	1.25	2.25
	1987	.030	.40	.75	1.50	3.00
	1988	.030	.40	.75	1.50	3.00
	1989	31.890	.25	.50	.80	1.60

Forestry For Development

KM#	Date	Mintage	Fine	VF	XF	Unc
637	1984	.015	—	—	—	3.00
	1984	5,000	—	—	Proof	7.00

F.A.O. Issue

KM#	Date	Mintage	Fine	VF	XF	Unc
653	1985	.025	—	—	—	3.00
	1985	—	—	—	Proof	6.50

REPUBLIC

1989—

MONETARY SYSTEM
100 Filler = 1 Forint

2 FILLER

ALUMINUM
Mint mark: BP

KM#	Date	Mintage	Fine	VF	XF	Unc
673	1990	.010	—	—	—	2.00
	1991	.010	—	—	—	3.00
	1992	.030	—	—	—	4.00

5 FILLER

ALUMINUM
Mint mark: BP

KM#	Date	Mintage	Fine	VF	XF	Unc
674	1990	.010	—	—	—	2.00
	1991	.010	—	—	—	3.00
	1992	.030	—	—	—	4.00

10 FILLER

ALUMINUM
Mint mark: BP

KM#	Date	Mintage	Fine	VF	XF	Unc
675	1990	46.515	—	—	—	.25
	1991	2.370	—	—	—	.25
	1992	15.825	—	—	—	.25
	1993	.030	—	—	—	.25
	1993	—	—	—	Proof	1.00
	1994	.030	—	—	—	.25
	1994	—	—	—	Proof	1.00
	1995	—	—	—	—	.25
	1995	—	—	—	Proof	1.00
	1996	—	—	—	Proof	.25

20 FILLER

ALUMINUM
Mint mark: BP

KM#	Date	Mintage	Fine	VF	XF	Unc
676	1990	59.360	—	—	—	.25
	1991	20.210	—	—	—	.25
	1992	.030	—	—	—	.25
	1993	.030	—	—	—	.25
	1993	—	—	—	Proof	1.80
	1994	.030	—	—	—	.25
	1994	—	—	—	Proof	1.80
	1995	—	—	—	—	.25
	1995	—	—	—	Proof	1.80
	1996	—	—	—	—	.25

50 FILLER

ALUMINUM
Mint mark: BP

KM#	Date	Mintage	Fine	VF	XF	Unc
677	1990	20.550	—	—	—	.25
	1991	31.250	—	—	—	.25
	1992	.440	—	—	—	.25
	1993	.030	—	—	—	.25
	1993	—	—	—	Proof	2.00
	1994	.030	—	—	—	.25
	1994	—	—	—	Proof	2.00
	1995	—	—	—	—	.25
	1995	—	—	—	Proof	2.00
	1996	—	—	—	—	.25
	1997	—	—	—	—	.25
	1997	—	—	—	Proof	2.00

FORINT

BRASS

KM#	Date	Mintage	Fine	VF	XF	Unc
692	1992	23.890	—	—	—	.25
	1992	1,000	—	—	Proof	4.00
	1993	75.100	—	—	—	.25
	1993	.030	—	—	Proof	1.00
	1994	66.605	—	—	—	.25
	1994	.015	—	—	Proof	1.00
	1995	—	—	—	—	.25
	1995	—	—	—	Proof	1.00
	1996	—	—	—	—	.25
	1996	—	—	—	Proof	1.00
	1997	—	—	—	—	.25
	1997	—	—	—	Proof	1.00

2 FORINT

COPPER-NICKEL

KM#	Date	Mintage	Fine	VF	XF	Unc
693	1992	10.380	—	—	—	.35
	1992	1,000	—	—	Proof	5.00
	1993	82.915	—	—	—	.35
	1993	.030	—	—	Proof	1.50
	1994	68.370	—	—	—	.35

KM#	Date	Mintage	Fine	VF	XF	Unc
693	1994	.015	—	—	Proof	1.50
	1995	—	—	—	—	.35
	1995	—	—	—	Proof	1.50
	1996	—	—	—	—	.35
	1997	—	—	—	—	.35
	1997	—	—	—	Proof	1.50

5 FORINT

BRASS
Great White Egret

KM#	Date	Mintage	Fine	VF	XF	Unc
694	1992	1.145	—	—	—	.75
	1992	1,000	—	—	Proof	6.00
	1993	—	—	—	—	.75
	1993	—	—	—	Proof	2.00
	1994	—	—	—	—	.75
	1994	—	—	—	Proof	2.00
	1995	—	—	—	—	.75
	1995	—	—	—	Proof	2.00
	1996	—	—	—	—	.75
	1997	—	—	—	—	.75
	1997	—	—	—	Proof	2.00

10 FORINT

COPPER-NICKEL CLAD BRASS

KM#	Date	Mintage	Fine	VF	XF	Unc
695	1992	2,000	—	—	—	6.00
	1992	1,000	—	—	Proof	8.00
	1993	35.565	—	—	—	1.00
	1993	.030	—	—	Proof	3.00
	1994	69.078	—	—	—	1.00
	1994	.015	—	—	Proof	3.00
	1995	—	—	—	—	1.00
	1995	—	—	—	Proof	3.00
	1996	—	—	—	—	1.00
	1997	—	—	—	—	1.00
	1997	—	—	—	Proof	3.00

20 FORINT

NICKEL-BRASS

KM#	Date	Mintage	Fine	VF	XF	Unc
696	1992	2,000	—	—	—	8.00
	1992	1,000	—	—	Proof	10.00
	1993	42.965	—	—	—	1.50
	1993	.030	—	—	Proof	4.00
	1994	68.965	—	—	—	1.50
	1994	.015	—	—	Proof	4.00
	1995	—	—	—	—	1.50
	1995	—	—	—	Proof	4.00
	1996	—	—	—	—	1.50
	1997	—	—	—	—	1.50
	1997	—	—	—	Proof	4.00

50 FORINT

COPPER-NICKEL CLAD BRASS
Obv: Saker falcon.

KM#	Date	Mintage	Fine	VF	XF	Unc
697	1992	2,000	—	—	—	10.00
	1992	1,000	—	—	Proof	12.00
	1993	.861	—	—	—	3.00
	1993	.030	—	—	Proof	5.00
	1994	8.397	—	—	—	3.00
	1994	.015	—	—	Proof	5.00
	1995	—	—	—	—	3.00
	1995	—	—	—	Proof	5.00
	1996	—	—	—	—	3.00
	1997	—	—	—	—	3.00
	1997	—	—	—	Proof	5.00

100 (SZAZ) FORINT

BRASS

KM#	Date	Mintage	Fine	VF	XF	Unc
698	1992	2,000	—	—	—	12.00
	1992	1,000	—	—	Proof	15.00
	1993	.925	—	—	—	2.50
	1993	.030	—	—	Proof	6.00
	1994	7.861	—	—	—	2.50
	1994	.015	—	—	Proof	6.00
	1995	—	—	—	—	2.50
	1995	—	—	—	Proof	6.00
	1996	—	—	—	—	2.50

BRASS PLATED STEEL center in
STAINLESS STEEL ring
Obv: Crowned arms.
Rev: Denomination in inner circle.

721	1996	—	—	—	—	4.00
	1996	—	—	—	Proof	12.50
	1997	—	—	—	—	4.00
	1997	—	—	—	Proof	12.50
	1998	—	—	—	—	4.00

ICELAND

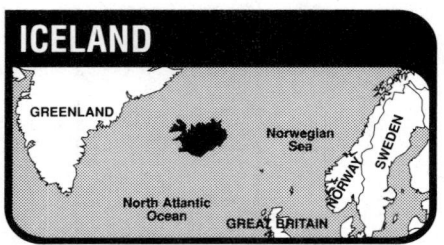

The Republic of Iceland, an island of recent volcanic origin in the North Atlantic east of Greenland and immediately south of the Arctic Circle, has an area of 39,768 sq. mi. (103,000 sq. km.) and a population of 275,277. Capital: Reykjavik. Fishing is the chief industry and accounts for more than 70 percent of the exports.

Iceland was settled by Norwegians in the 9th century and established as an independent republic in 930. The Icelandic assembly called the 'Althing', also established in 930, is the oldest parliament in the world. Iceland came under Norwegian sovereignty in 1262, and passed to Denmark when Norway and Denmark were united under the Danish crown in 1380. In 1918 it was established as a virtually independent kingdom in union with Denmark. On June 17, 1944, while Denmark was still under occupation by troops of the Third Reich, Iceland was established by plebiscite as an independent republic.

RULERS
Christian X, 1912-1944

MINT MARKS
Heart (h) - Copenhagen

MINTMASTERS INITIALS
HCN - Hans Christian Nielsen,
1919-1927
N - Niels Peter Nielsen, 1927-1955

MONEYERS INITIALS
GJ - Knud Gunnar Jensen,
1901-1933

MONETARY SYSTEM
100 Aurar = 1 Krona

KINGDOM
EYRIR

BRONZE
Mint mark: Heart

KM#	Date	Mintage	Fine	VF	XF	Unc
5.1	1926 HCN-GJ					
		.405	1.50	3.00	7.50	27.50
	1931 N-GJ	.462	1.00	2.50	6.00	25.00
	1937 N-GJ wide date					
		.211	2.00	4.00	8.00	30.00
	1937 N-GJ narrow date					
		Inc. Ab.	2.00	4.00	8.00	30.00
	1938 N-GJ	.279	1.00	2.00	4.00	13.50
	1939 N-GJ large 3					
		.305	1.00	2.00	3.50	12.00
	1939 N-GJ small 3					
		Inc. Ab.	1.00	2.00	3.50	12.00

Mint: London

5.2	1940	1.000	.25	.50	1.00	2.50
	1940	—	—	—	Proof	225.00
	1942	2.000	.25	.40	.75	2.00

2 AURAR

BRONZE
Mint mark: Heart

6.1	1926 HCN-GJ					
		.498	1.50	3.00	8.00	30.00
	1931 N-GJ	.446	1.00	2.50	7.00	25.00
	1938 N-GJ	.206	6.00	12.00	17.50	40.00
	1940 N-GJ	.257	5.00	10.00	15.00	32.50

NOTE: Varieties exist in the appearance of the numeral 8 in 1938 dated coins. As the die slowly deteriorated 'globs' were added into the upper loop and later in the lower loop.

Mint: London

KM#	Date	Mintage	Fine	VF	XF	Unc
6.2	1940	1.000	.40	.75	1.50	3.00
	1940	—	—	—	Proof	265.00
	1942	2.000	.20	.50	1.00	2.00

5 AURAR

BRONZE
Mint mark: Heart

7.1	1926 HCN-GJ					
		.355	5.00	10.00	25.00	70.00
	1931 N-GJ	.311	5.00	10.00	25.00	70.00

Mint: London

7.2	1940	1.000	.60	1.25	2.50	5.00
	1940	—	—	—	Proof	285.00
	1942	2.000	.35	.85	1.50	3.00

10 AURAR

COPPER-NICKEL
Mint mark: Heart

1.1	1922HCN GJ					
		.300	2.00	3.50	7.00	35.00
	1923HCN GJ					
		.302	3.00	4.50	9.00	37.50
	1925HCN GJ					
		.321	15.00	25.00	40.00	85.00
	1929 N-GJ	.176	15.00	25.00	45.00	90.00
	1933 N-GJ	.157	10.00	20.00	30.00	70.00
	1936 N-GJ	.213	3.00	6.00	10.00	32.50
	1939/6 N-GJ					
		.208	5.00	10.00	15.00	40.00
	1939 N-GJ I.A.	4.00	8.00	12.00	30.00	

Mint: London

1.2	1940	1.500	.35	.75	1.50	4.50
	1940	—	—	—	Proof	225.00

ZINC

1a	1942	2.000	1.50	3.00	6.00	24.00

25 AURAR

COPPER-NICKEL
Mint mark: Heart

2.1	1922HCN GJ					
		.300	1.00	2.50	4.00	30.00
	1923HCN GJ					
		.304	1.00	2.50	4.00	30.00
	1925HCN GJ					
		.207	2.50	4.50	10.00	40.00
	1933 N-GJ	.104	10.00	15.00	25.00	80.00
	1937 N-GJ near 7					
		.201	3.00	5.00	9.00	38.00
	1937 N-GJ far 7					
		I.A.	3.00	5.00	9.00	38.00

Mint: London

2.2	1940	1.500	.25	.50	1.00	2.50
	1940	—	—	—	Proof	245.00

ZINC

KM#	Date	Mintage	Fine	VF	XF	Unc
2a	1942	2.000	1.00	2.50	5.00	20.00

KRONA

ALUMINUM-BRONZE
Mint mark: Heart

KM#	Date	Mintage	Fine	VF	XF	Unc
3.1	1925HCN GJ	.252	3.00	6.00	25.00	125.00
	1929 N-GJ	.154	5.00	10.00	32.00	160.00
	1940 N-GJ	.209	1.50	2.50	5.00	15.00

Mint: London

KM#	Date	Mintage	Fine	VF	XF	Unc
3.2	1940	.715	1.00	2.00	4.00	10.00
	1940	—	—	—	Proof	Rare

2 KRONUR

ALUMINUM-BRONZE
Mint mark: Heart

KM#	Date	Mintage	Fine	VF	XF	Unc
4.1	1925HCN GJ	.126	7.50	12.50	40.00	160.00
	1929 N-GJ	.077	10.00	20.00	65.00	265.00

Mint: London

KM#	Date	Mintage	Fine	VF	XF	Unc
4.2	1940	.546	.75	1.50	3.50	10.00
	1940	—	—	—	Proof	Rare

REPUBLIC

EYRIR

BRONZE

KM#	Date	Mintage	Fine	VF	XF	Unc
8	1946	4.000	.10	.15	.50	1.00
	1946	—	—	—	Proof	250.00
	1953	4.000	.10	.15	.40	.75
	1953	—	—	—	Proof	65.00
	1956	2.000	.10	.15	.40	.75
	1956	—	—	—	Proof	65.00
	1957	2.000	.10	.15	.40	.75
	1957	—	—	—	Proof	65.00
	1958	2.000	.10	.15	.40	.75
	1958	—	—	—	Proof	65.00
	1959	1.600	.10	.15	.40	.75
	1959	—	—	—	Proof	65.00
	1966	1.000	.10	.15	.40	.75
	1966	.015	—	—	Proof	3.25

NOTE: Values for the 1953-59 proof issues are for impaired proofs. Brilliant proofs may bring 3 to 4 times these figures.

5 AURAR

BRONZE

KM#	Date	Mintage	Fine	VF	XF	Unc
9	1946	4.000	.10	.25	.50	1.25
	1946	—	—	—	Proof	400.00
	1958	.400	.50	2.00	3.50	5.00
	1958	—	—	—	Proof	100.00
	1959	.600	.50	2.00	3.00	4.50
	1959	—	—	—	Proof	100.00
	1960	1.200	.15	.40	1.00	1.75
	1960	—	—	—	Proof	100.00
	1961	1.200	.15	.40	1.00	1.75
	1961	—	—	—	Proof	100.00
9	1963	1.200	.10	.30	.75	1.50
	1963	—	—	—	Proof	100.00
	1965	.800	.10	.20	.50	1.00
	1966	1.000	.10	.20	.50	1.00
	1966	.015	—	—	Proof	3.25

NOTE: Values for the 1958-63 proof issues are for impaired proofs. Brilliant proofs may bring 3 to 4 times these figures.

10 AURAR

COPPER-NICKEL

KM#	Date	Mintage	Fine	VF	XF	Unc
10	1946	4.000	—	.10	.20	.60
	1946	—	—	—	Proof	400.00
	1953	4.000	—	.10	.20	.50
	1953	—	—	—	Proof	65.00
	1957	1.200	.25	.75	2.00	5.00
	1957	—	—	—	Proof	65.00
	1958	.500	.20	.50	1.00	2.00
	1958	—	—	—	Proof	65.00
	1959	3.000	.20	.50	1.50	4.00
	1959	—	—	—	Proof	65.00
	1960	1.000	.10	.20	.40	1.00
	1960	—	—	—	Proof	65.00
	1961	2.000	—	—	.10	.30
	1961	—	—	—	Proof	65.00
	1962	3.000	—	—	.10	.20
	1962	—	—	—	Proof	65.00
	1963	4.000	—	—	.10	.20
	1963	—	—	—	Proof	65.00
	1965	2.000	—	—	.10	.20
	1966	4.000	—	—	.10	.20
	1967	2.000	—	—	.10	.20
	1969 coarse edge reeding	3.200	—	—	.10	.20
	1969 fine edge reeding	Inc. Ab.	—	—	.10	.20

NOTE: Values for the 1953-63 proof issues are for impaired proofs. Brilliant proofs may bring 3 to 4 times these figures.

ALUMINUM

KM#	Date	Mintage	Fine	VF	XF	Unc
10a	1970	4.800	—		.10	.20
	1971	11.200	—	—	.10	.20
	1973	4.800	—	—	.10	.20
	1974	4.800	—	—	.10	.20
	1974	.015	—	—	Proof	3.25

25 AURAR

COPPER-NICKEL

KM#	Date	Mintage	Fine	VF	XF	Unc
11	1946	2.000	.10	.15	.35	1.25
	1946	—	—	—	Proof	400.00
	1951	2.000	.10	.15	.35	.75
	1951	—	—	—	Proof	75.00
	1954	2.000	.10	.15	.35	.75
	1954	—	—	—	Proof	75.00
	1957	1.000	.20	.50	1.50	3.50
	1957	—	—	—	Proof	75.00
	1958	.500	.20	.40	.60	1.00
	1958	—	—	—	Proof	75.00
	1959	2.000	.20	.50	1.50	3.00
	1959	—	—	—	Proof	75.00
	1960	1.000	—	—	.10	.30
	1960	—	—	—	Proof	75.00
	1961	1.200	—	—	.10	.30
	1961	—	—	—	Proof	75.00
	1962	2.000	—	—	.10	.25
	1962	—	—	—	Proof	75.00
	1963	3.000	—	—	.10	.25
	1963	—	—	—	Proof	75.00
	1965	4.000	—	—	.10	.25
	1966	2.000	—	—	.10	.25
	1967	3.000	—	—	.10	.25
	1967	.015	—	—	Proof	3.25

NOTE: Values for the 1951-63 proof issues are for impaired proofs. Brilliant proofs may bring 3 to 4 times these figures.

50 AURAR

NICKEL-BRASS

KM#	Date	Mintage	Fine	VF	XF	Unc
17	1969	1.000	—	—	.10	.30
	1970	2.000	—	—	.10	.30
	1971	2.000	—	—	.10	.30
	1973	1.000	—	—	.10	.30
	1974	2.000	—	—	.10	.30
	1974	.015	—	—	Proof	3.25

KRONA

ALUMINUM-BRONZE

KM#	Date	Mintage	Fine	VF	XF	Unc
12	1946	2.175	—	.10	.40	1.50
	1946	—	—	—	Proof	400.00

NICKEL-BRASS

KM#	Date	Mintage	Fine	VF	XF	Unc
12a	1957	1.000	.10	.15	.40	1.50
	1957	—	—	—	Proof	85.00
	1959	.500	.10	.20	.75	2.00
	1959	—	—	—	Proof	85.00
	1961	.500	.10	.20	.75	2.00
	1961	—	—	—	Proof	85.00
	1962	1.000	.10	.15	.20	.60
	1962	—	—	—	Proof	85.00
	1963	1.500	—	.10	.15	.50
	1963	—	—	—	Proof	85.00
	1965	2.000	—	—	.10	.50
	1966	2.000	—	—	.10	.50
	1969	2.000	—	—	.10	.25
	1970	3.000	—	—	.10	.25
	1971	2.500	—	—	.10	.25

Large Date, Royal Mint **Thin Date, Ottawa Mint**

KM#	Date	Mintage	Fine	VF	XF	Unc
	1973 large round knob 3	2.500	—	—	.10	.50
	1973 thin, sharp end 3	3.500	—	—	.10	.25
	1974	5.000	—	—	.10	.25
	1975	10.500	—	—	.10	.25
	1975	.015	—	—	Proof	3.25

NOTE: Values for the 1957-1963 proof issues are for impaired proofs. Brilliant proofs may bring 3 to 4 times these figures.

ALUMINUM

KM#	Date	Mintage	Fine	VF	XF	Unc
23	1976	10.000	—	—	.10	.20
	1977	10.000	—	—	.10	.20
	1978	13.000	—	—	.10	.20
	1980	7.225	—	—	.10	.20
	1980	.015	—	—	Proof	3.25

2 KRONUR

ALUMINUM-BRONZE
Republic

KM#	Date	Mintage	Fine	VF	XF	Unc
13	1946	1.086	.20	.40	.80	3.50
	1946	—	—	—	Proof	450.00

NICKEL-BRASS

KM#	Date	Mintage	Fine	VF	XF	Unc
13a.1	1958	.500	.20	.50	1.00	3.00
	1958	—	—	—	Proof	115.00
	1962	.500	.20	.50	1.00	3.00
	1962	—	—	—	Proof	115.00
	1963	.750	.15	.30	.60	2.00
	1963	—	—	—	Proof	115.00
	1966	1.000	.10	.20	.40	1.50
	1966	.015	—	—	Proof	3.25

NOTE: Values for the 1958-63 proof issues are for impaired proofs. Brilliant proofs may bring 3 to 4 times these figures.

Thick planchet, 11.50 g.

KM#	Date	Mintage	Fine	VF	XF	Unc
13a.2	1966	300 pcs.	—	—	325.00	400.00

5 KRONUR

COPPER-NICKEL

KM#	Date	Mintage	Fine	VF	XF	Unc
18	1969	1.000	—	.15	.25	.50
	1970	1.000	—	.15	.25	.50
	1971	.500	.10	.20	.50	1.00
	1973	1.100	—	.10	.20	.40
	1974	1.200	—	.10	.15	.25
	1975	1.500	—	.10	.15	.25
	1976	.500	—	.10	.20	.40
	1977	1.000	—	.10	.15	.25
	1978	4.672	—	.10	.15	.25
	1980	2.400	—	.10	.15	.25
	1980	.015	—	—	Proof	3.25

10 KRONUR

COPPER-NICKEL

15	1967	1.000	.15	.25	.50	1.50
	1969	.500	.15	.30	.75	2.00
	1970	1.000	—	.15	.30	.75
	1971	1.500	—	.15	.30	.75
	1973	1.500	—	.15	.30	.75
	1974	2.000	—	.10	.25	.60
	1975	2.500	—	.10	.25	.60
	1976	2.500	—	.10	.25	.60
	1977	2.000	—	.10	.25	.60
	1978	10.500	—	.10	.25	.60
	1980	4.600	—	.10	.25	.60
	1980	.015	—	—	Proof	3.25

50 KRONUR

NICKEL
50th Anniversary of Sovereignty

16	1968	.100	1.50	2.50	4.00	7.00

COPPER-NICKEL
Parliament Building

19	1970	.800	.25	.50	1.00	2.00
	1971	.500	.25	.50	1.00	2.50
	1973	.050	1.00	1.50	2.50	4.00
	1974	.200	.25	.50	1.00	2.00
	1975	.500	.20	.35	.75	1.50
	1976	.500	.20	.35	.75	1.50
	1977	.200	.20	.35	.75	1.50
	1978	2.040	.20	.35	.50	1.00
	1980	1.500	.20	.35	.50	1.00
	1980	.015	—	—	Proof	3.25

MONETARY REFORM

100 Old Kronur = 1 New Krona

5 AURAR

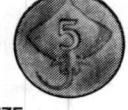

BRONZE

KM#	Date	Mintage	Skate Fine	VF	XF	Unc
24	1981	15.000	—	—	—	.25
	1981	.015	—	—	Proof	3.50

10 AURAR

BRONZE
Cuttle-fish

25	1981	50.000	—	—	—	.25
	1981	.015	—	—	Proof	5.00

50 AURAR

BRONZE
Shrimp

26	1981	10.000	—	—	.10	.35
	1981	.015	—	—	Proof	6.00

BRONZE COATED STEEL

26a	1986	2.000	—	—	—	.30

KRONA

COPPER-NICKEL
Cod

27	1981	18.000	—	—	.15	.50
	1981	.015	—	—	Proof	8.00
	1984	7.000	—	—	.15	.50
	1987	7.500	—	—	.15	.50

NICKEL COATED STEEL

27a	1989	5.000	—	—	—	.50
	1991	5.180	—	—	—	.50
	1992	5.000	—	—	—	.50
	1994	5.000	—	—	—	.50
	1996	6.000	—	—	—	.50

5 KRONUR

COPPER-NICKEL
Obv: Four national icons.
Rev: Two dolphins, denomination.

28	1981	4.350	—	—	.25	1.25
	1981	.015	—	—	Proof	10.00
	1984	1.000	—	—	.25	1.25
	1987	3.000	—	—	.25	1.25
	1992	2.000	—	—	.25	1.25

NICKEL CLAD STEEL

28a	1996	1.500	—	—	—	1.25

10 KRONUR

COPPER-NICKEL
Obv: Four national icons.
Rev: 4 Capelins, denomination.
Reeded edge.

29.1	1984	10.000	—	—	.35	1.50
	1987	7.500	—	—	.35	1.50
	1994	2.500	—	—	.35	1.50

NICKEL CLAD STEEL

29.1a	1996	4.000	—	—	—	1.50

Security edge (error).

29.2	1984	Inc. Ab.	—	—	.35	1.50

---

50 KRONUR

COPPER-ZINC-NICKEL
Crab

KM#	Date	Mintage	Fine	VF	XF	Unc
31	1987	4.000	—	—	—	3.25
	1992	2.000	—	—	—	3.25
	1994	—	—	—	—	3.25
	1996	—	—	—	—	3.25

100 KRONUR

NICKEL-BRASS
Lumpfish

35	1995	—	—	—	—	4.50

European Colonies In India

(map showing: Bombay Presidency, Farrukhabad, Banaras, Patna, Murshidabad, Calcutta, Bengal Presidency, Surat, Diu, Damao, Bacaim, Bombay, Chaul, Goa, Madras Presidency, Yanaon, Machhiipattan, Pulicat, Arcot, Madras, Tellicherry, Mahe, Pondichery, Calicut, Malabar Coast, Tranquebar, Karikal, Negapatam, Cochin, Madras, Tuticorin)

INDIA - PORTUGUESE

Vasco da Gama, the Portuguese explorer, first visited India in 1498. Portugal seized control of a number of islands and small enclaves on the west coast of India, and for the next hundred years enjoyed a monopoly on trade. With the arrival of powerful Dutch and English fleets in the first half of the 17th century, Portuguese power in the area declined until virtually all of India that remained under Portuguese control were the west coast enclaves of Goa, Damao and Diu. They were forcibly annexed by India in 1962.

RULERS
Portuguese, until 1961

MONETARY SYSTEM
960 Reis = 16 Tanga = 1 Rupia

1/12 TANGA

BRONZE
Carlos I
Roman numeral dating.

KM#	Date	Mintage	Fine	VF	XF	Unc
13	1901	.960	2.00	4.00	8.00	28.00
	1901	—	—	—	P/L	125.00
	1903	.960	2.00	4.00	8.00	28.00

OITAVO (1/8) TANGA

BRONZE
Carlos I
Roman numeral dating.

KM#	Date	Mintage	Fine	VF	XF	Unc
14	1901	.960	2.50	5.00	10.00	37.50
	1901	—	—	—	P/L	150.00
	1903	.960	2.50	5.00	10.00	37.50

QUARTO (1/4) TANGA
(15 Reis)

BRONZE
Carlos I
Roman numeral dating.

KM#	Date	Mintage	Fine	VF	XF	Unc
15	1901	.800	3.50	6.50	12.50	42.00
	1901	—	—	—	P/L	175.00
	1903	.800	3.50	6.50	12.50	42.00

1/2 TANGA
(30 Reis)

BRONZE
Carlos I
Roman numeral dating.

16	1901	.800	4.50	9.00	17.50	55.00
	1901	—	—	—	P/L	200.00
	1903	.800	4.50	9.00	17.50	55.00

TANGA
(60 Reis)

BRONZE

19	1934	.100	3.50	8.00	25.00	100.00

KM#	Date	Mintage	Fine	VF	XF	Unc
24	1947	1.000	1.00	2.00	4.50	13.50

28	1952	9.600	.35	.75	2.50	7.00

2 TANGAS

COPPER-NICKEL

20	1934	.150	3.50	8.00	25.00	100.00

4 TANGAS

COPPER-NICKEL

21	1934	.100	4.50	10.00	30.00	120.00

QUARTO DE (1/4) RUPIA

COPPER-NICKEL

25	1947	.800	2.00	4.00	9.00	22.50
	1952	4.000	1.00	2.00	4.00	18.00

MEIA (1/2) RUPIA

6.0000 g, .835 SILVER, .1610 oz ASW

23	1936	.100	4.00	9.00	18.00	65.00

COPPER-NICKEL

26	1947	.600	3.00	6.00	12.50	32.50
	1952	2.000	1.25	2.50	5.00	20.00

UMA (1) RUPIA

11.6600 g, .917 SILVER, .3438 oz ASW

Carlos I

KM#	Date	Mintage	Fine	VF	XF	Unc
17	1903	.200	4.50	9.00	20.00	50.00
	1904	.100	6.50	12.50	32.00	70.00

| 18 | 1912/1 | .300 | — | — | — | — |
| | 1912 | Inc. Ab. | 15.00 | 35.00 | 70.00 | 145.00 |

12.0000 g, .917 SILVER, .3536 oz ASW

| 22 | 1935 | .300 | 6.00 | 10.00 | 20.00 | 50.00 |

12.0000 g, .500 SILVER, .1929 oz ASW

| 27 | 1947 | .900 | 3.50 | 7.50 | 18.00 | 45.00 |

COPPER-NICKEL

| 29 | 1952 | 1.000 | 2.00 | 5.00 | 12.00 | 32.00 |
| | 1954 | — | 25.00 | 50.00 | 100.00 | 200.00 |

DECIMAL COINAGE
100 Centavos = 1 Escudo

10 CENTAVOS

BRONZE

30	1958	5.000	.25	.45	1.00	2.00
	1959	Inc. Ab.	.25	.45	1.00	2.00
	1961	1.000	.25	.40	.85	1.75

30 CENTAVOS

BRONZE

KM#	Date	Mintage	Fine	VF	XF	Unc
31	1958	5.000	.60	1.25	2.50	8.00
	1959	Inc. Ab.	1.25	.50	6.00	12.50

60 CENTAVOS

COPPER-NICKEL

| 32 | 1958 | 5.000 | 1.25 | 2.50 | 5.00 | 10.00 |
| | 1959 | Inc. Ab. | 1.00 | 2.00 | 4.00 | 10.00 |

ESCUDO

COPPER-NICKEL

| 33 | 1958 | 6.000 | 1.00 | 2.00 | 4.00 | 9.00 |
| | 1959 | Inc. Ab. | 1.00 | 2.00 | 4.00 | 9.00 |

3 ESCUDOS

COPPER-NICKEL

| 34 | 1958 | 5.000 | 1.50 | 3.25 | 6.50 | 12.50 |
| | 1959 | Inc. Ab. | 1.50 | 3.25 | 7.00 | 13.50 |

6 ESCUDOS

COPPER-NICKEL

| 35 | 1959 | 4.000 | 2.50 | 4.50 | 8.50 | 22.50 |

INDIA-BRITISH

The civilization of India, which began about 2500 B.C., flourished under a succession of empires - notably those of the Mauryas, the Kushans, the Guptas, the Delhi Sultans and the Mughals - until undermined in the 18th and 19th centuries by European colonial powers.

The Portuguese were the first to arrive, off Calicut in May 1498. It wasn't until 1612, after the Portuguese and Spanish power had begun to wane, that the British East India Company established its initial settlement at Surat. Britain could not have chosen a more propitious time as the central girdle of petty states, and the southern Vijayanagar Empire were crumbling and ripe for foreign exploitation. By the end of the century, English traders were firmly established in Bombay, Madras, Calcutta and lesser places elsewhere, and Britain was implementing its announced policy to create such civil and military institutions 'as may be the foundation of secure English domination for all time'. By 1757, following the successful conclusion of a war of colonial rivalry with France during which the military victories of Robert Clive, a young officer with the British East India Company, made him a powerful man in India, the British were firmly settled in India as not only traders but as conquerors. During the next 60 years, the British East India Company acquired dominion over most of India by bribery and force, and governed it directly or through puppet princelings.

As a result of the Sepoy Mutiny of 1857-58, a large scale mutiny among Indian soldiers of the Bengal army, control of the government of India was transferred from the East India Company to the British Crown. At this point in world history, India was the brightest jewel in the British imperial diadem, but even then a movement for greater Indian representation in government presaged the Indian Empire's twilight hour less than a century later - it would pass into history on Aug. 15, 1947.

1/12 ANNA

COPPER

KM#	Date	Mintage	Fine	VF	XF	Unc
483	1901(c)	21.345	.35	.75	1.75	4.00
	1901(c)	—	—	—	Proof	50.00
	1901(c) (restrike)	—	—	—	P/L	20.00

NOTE: Earlier dates (1877-1899) exist for this type.

Thick planchets.

497	1903(c)	7.883	.35	1.25	6.00	15.00
	1903(c)	—	—	—	Proof	60.00
	1903(c) (restrike)	—	—	—	P/L	20.00
	1904(c)	16.506	.25	1.00	4.00	12.00
	1904(c)	—	—	—	Proof	60.00
	1904(c) (restrike)	—	—	—	P/L	20.00
	1905(c)	13.060	.25	1.00	4.00	12.00
	1905(c) (restrike)	—	—	—	P/L	20.00
	1906(c)	9.072	.25	1.00	4.00	12.00
	1906(c)	—	—	—	Proof	60.00
	1906(c) (restrike)	—	—	—	P/L	20.00

BRONZE
Thin planchets.

498	1906(c)	2.184	.35	.75	5.00	15.00
	1906(c)	—	—	—	Proof	50.00
	1907(c)	20.985	.25	.50	3.00	9.00
	1907(c)	—	—	—	Proof	50.00
	1907(c) (restrike)	—	—	—	P/L	20.00
	1908(c)	22.036	.25	.50	3.00	9.00
	1908(c)	—	—	—	Proof	50.00
	1908(c) (restrike)	—	—	—	P/L	20.00
	1909(c)	12.316	.25	.50	3.00	9.00
	1909(c) (restrike)	—	—	—	P/L	20.00
	1910(c)	23.520	.25	.50	3.00	9.00
	1910(c) (restrike)	—	—	—	P/L	20.00

BRONZE

NOTE: Calcutta Mint issues have no mint mark. Bombay Mint issues have a small raised bead or dot below the center of the date.

509	1912(c)	25.938	.50	.75	1.50	4.50
	1912(c)	—	—	—	Proof	50.00
	1912(c) (restrike)	—	—	—	P/L	20.00
	1913(c)	16.149	.25	.50	1.00	3.00
	1913(c)	—	—	—	Proof	40.00
	1913(c) (restrike)	—	—	—	P/L	20.00
	1914(c)	19.814	.25	.50	.75	2.00
	1914(c)	—	—	—	Proof	40.00
	1914(c) (restrike)	—	—	—	P/L	20.00

KM#	Date	Mintage	Fine	VF	XF	Unc
509	1915(c)	20.563	.25	.50	.75	2.00
	1915(c)	—	—	—	Proof	40.00
	1915(c)	(restrike)	—	—	P/L	20.00
	1916(c)	14.438	.25	.50	.75	2.00
	1916(c)	—	—	—	Proof	40.00
	1916(c)	(restrike)	—	—	P/L	20.00
	1917(c)	35.174	.25	.50	.75	2.00
	1917(c)	—	—	—	Proof	40.00
	1917(c)	(restrike)	—	—	P/L	20.00
	1918(c)	24.192	.25	.50	.75	2.00
	1918(c)	—	—	—	Proof	40.00
	1918(c)	(restrike)	—	—	P/L	20.00
	1919(c)	17.472	.25	.50	.75	2.00
	1919(c)	—	—	—	Proof	40.00
	1919(c)	(restrike)	—	—	P/L	20.00
	1920(c)	39.878	.25	.50	.75	2.00
	1920(c)	—	—	—	Proof	40.00
	1920(c)	(restrike)	—	—	P/L	20.00
	1921(c)	19.334	.25	.50	.75	2.00
	1921(c)	—	—	—	Proof	40.00
	1921(c)	(restrike)	—	—	P/L	20.00
	1923(c)	8.429	.25	.50	.75	2.00
	1923(c)	—	—	—	Proof	40.00
	1923(b)	8.717	.25	.50	.75	2.00
	1923(b)	—	—	—	Proof	40.00
	1923(b)	(restrike)	—	—	P/L	20.00
	1924(c)	7.200	.25	.50	.75	2.00
	1924(c)	—	—	—	Proof	40.00
	1924(b)	9.869	.25	.50	.75	2.00
	1924(b)	—	—	—	Proof	40.00
	1924(b)	(restrike)	—	—	P/L	20.00
	1925(c)	5.818	.25	.50	.75	2.00
	1925(c)	—	—	—	Proof	40.00
	1925(b)	6.415	.25	.50	.75	2.00
	1925(b)	—	—	—	Proof	40.00
	1925(b)	(restrike)	—	—	P/L	20.00
	1926(c)	4.147	.25	.50	.75	2.00
	1926(c)	—	—	—	Proof	40.00
	1926(b)	15.464	.25	.50	.75	2.00
	1926(b)	—	—	—	Proof	40.00
	1926(b)	(restrike)	—	—	P/L	20.00
	1927(c)	6.662	.25	.50	.75	2.00
	1927(c)	—	—	—	Proof	40.00
	1927(b)	6.788	.25	.50	.75	2.00
	1927(b)	—	—	—	Proof	40.00
	1927(b)	(restrike)	—	—	P/L	20.00
	1928(c)	8.064	.25	.50	.75	2.00
	1928(c)	—	—	—	Proof	40.00
	1928(b)	6.135	.25	.50	.75	2.00
	1928(b)	—	—	—	Proof	40.00
	1928	(restrike)	—	—	P/L	20.00
	1929(c)	15.130	.25	.50	.75	2.00
	1929(c)	—	—	—	Proof	40.00
	1929(c)	(restrike)	—	—	P/L	20.00
	1930(c)	13.498	.25	.50	.75	2.00
	1930(c)	—	—	—	Proof	40.00
	1930(c)	(restrike)	—	—	P/L	20.00
	1931(c)	18.278	.25	.50	.75	2.00
	1931(c)	—	—	—	Proof	40.00
	1931(c)	(restrike)	—	—	P/L	20.00
	1932(c)	23.213	.25	.50	.75	2.00
	1932(c)	—	—	—	Proof	40.00
	1932(c)	(restrike)	—	—	P/L	20.00
	1933(c)	16.896	.25	.50	.75	2.00
	1933(c)	—	—	—	Proof	40.00
	1933(c)	(restrike)	—	—	P/L	20.00
	1934(c)	17.146	.25	.50	.75	2.00
	1934(c)	—	—	—	Proof	40.00
	1934(c)	(restrike)	—	—	P/L	20.00
	1935(c)	19.142	.25	.50	.75	2.00
	1935(c)	—	—	—	Proof	40.00
	1935(c)	(restrike)	—	—	P/L	20.00
	1936(c)	23.213	.25	.50	.75	2.00
	1936(b)	12.887	.25	.50	.75	2.00
	1936(b)	(restrike)	—	—	P/L	20.00

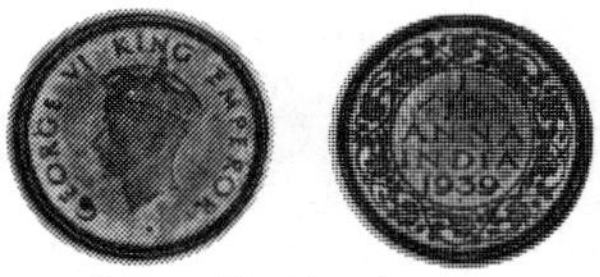

First head

NOTE: Calcutta Mint issues have no mint mark. Bombay Mint issues have a small dot below the date except for those dated 1942 which have a dot on either side of ANNA and the date, and one dot after "INDIA".

KM#	Date	Mintage	Fine	VF	XF	Unc
526	1938(c)	—	—	—	Proof	35.00
	1939(c)	3.571	.50	1.00	2.00	3.50
	1939(b)	17.407	.25	.50	1.00	2.50

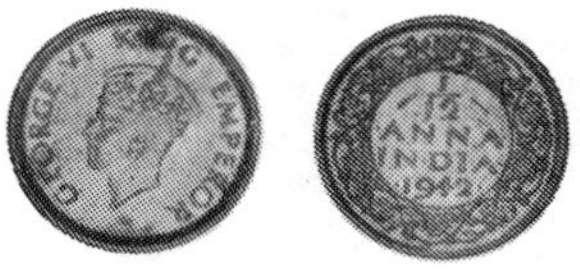

Second head.

KM#	Date	Mintage	Fine	VF	XF	Unc
527	1938(c)	(restrike)	—	—	P/L	20.00
	1939(c)	5.245	.25	.50	1.00	2.50
	1939(c)	—	—	—	Proof	35.00
	1939(b)	31.306	.25	.50	.75	2.00
	1939(b)	—	—	—	Proof	35.00
	1939(b)	(restrike)	—	—	P/L	20.00
	1941(b)	6.137	.25	.50	.75	2.00
	1942(b)	6.124	1.00	2.25	3.50	7.00
	1942(b)	—	—	—	Proof	35.00
	1942(b)	(restrike)	—	—	P/L	20.00

1/2 PICE

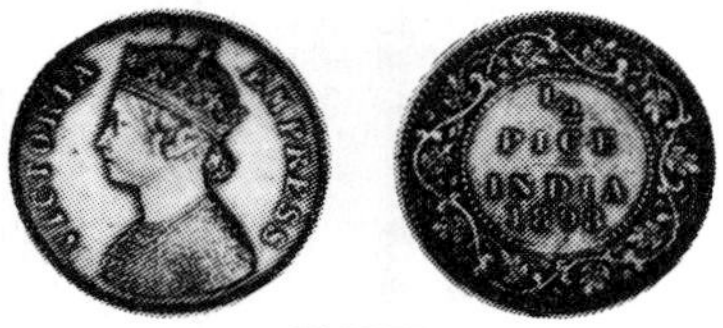

COPPER

KM#	Date	Mintage	Fine	VF	XF	Unc
484	1901(c)	16.057	1.00	1.75	3.50	8.50
	1901(c)	—	—	—	Proof	50.00
	1901(c)	(restrike)	—	—	P/L	20.00

NOTE: Earlier dates (1877-1900) exist for this type.

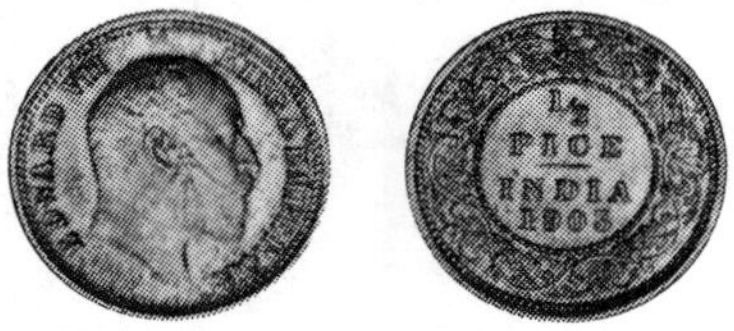

KM#	Date	Mintage	Fine	VF	XF	Unc
499	1903(c)	5.376	.75	1.50	5.00	15.00
	1903(c)	—	—	—	Proof	45.00
	1903(c)	(restrike)	—	—	P/L	20.00
	1904(c)	8.464	.75	1.50	5.00	15.00
	1904(c)	—	—	—	Proof	45.00
	1904(c)	(restrike)	—	—	P/L	20.00
	1905(c)	8.922	.75	1.50	5.00	15.00
	1905(c)	(restrike)	—	—	P/L	20.00
	1906(c)	6.346	.75	1.50	5.00	15.00
	1906(c)	—	—	—	Proof	45.00
	1906(c)	(restrike)	—	—	P/L	20.00

BRONZE
Thinner planchets.

KM#	Date	Mintage	Fine	VF	XF	Unc
500	1904(c)	—	—	—	Proof	45.00
	1906(c)	5.860	.75	1.50	4.50	12.50
	1906(c)	—	—	—	Proof	45.00
	1907(c)	8.060	.75	1.50	4.50	12.50
	1907(c)	—	—	—	Proof	45.00
	1907(c)	(restrike)	—	—	P/L	20.00
	1908(c)	10.035	.75	1.50	4.50	12.50
	1908(c)	—	—	—	Proof	45.00
	1908(c)	(restrike)	—	—	P/L	20.00
	1909(c)	8.493	.50	1.00	4.00	10.00
	1909(c)	(restrike)	—	—	P/L	20.00
	1910(c)	17.408	.75	1.50	4.50	12.50

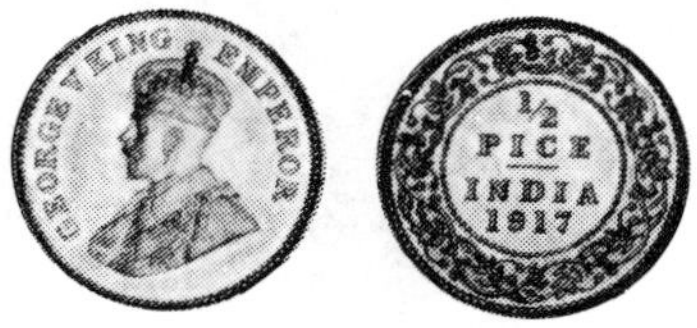

KM#	Date	Mintage	Fine	VF	XF	Unc
510	1912(c)	12.911	.25	.50	.75	3.00
	1912(c)	—	—	—	Proof	40.00
	1912(c)	(restrike)	—	—	P/L	20.00
	1913(c)	10.897	.25	.50	.75	3.00
	1913(c)	—	—	—	Proof	40.00
	1913(c)	(restrike)	—	—	P/L	20.00
	1914(c)	4.877	.15	.30	.50	2.50
	1914(c)	—	—	—	Proof	40.00
	1914(c)	(restrike)	—	—	P/L	20.00
	1915(c)	9.830	.15	.30	.50	2.50
	1915(c)	—	—	—	Proof	40.00
	1915(c)	(restrike)	—	—	P/L	20.00
	1916(c)	5.734	.15	.30	.50	2.50
	1916(c)	—	—	—	Proof	40.00
	1916(c)	(restrike)	—	—	P/L	20.00
	1917(c)	15.296	.15	.30	.50	2.50
	1917(c)	—	—	—	Proof	40.00
	1917(c)	(restrike)	—	—	P/L	20.00
	1918(c)	6.244	.15	.30	.50	2.50
	1918(c)	—	—	—	Proof	40.00
	1918(c)	(restrike)	—	—	P/L	20.00
	1919(c)	11.162	.15	.30	.50	2.50
	1919(c)	—	—	—	Proof	40.00
	1919(c)	(restrike)	—	—	P/L	20.00
	1920(c)	4.493	.15	.30	.50	2.50
	1920(c)	—	—	—	Proof	40.00
	1920(c)	(restrike)	—	—	P/L	20.00
	1921(c)	6.234	.15	.30	.50	2.50
	1921(c)	—	—	—	Proof	40.00
	1921(c)	(restrike)	—	—	P/L	20.00
	1922(c)	6.336	.15	.30	.50	2.50
	1922(c)	—	—	—	Proof	40.00
	1922(c)	(restrike)	—	—	P/L	20.00
	1923(c)	7.411	.15	.30	.50	2.50
	1923(c)	—	—	—	Proof	40.00
	1923(c)	(restrike)	—	—	P/L	20.00
	1924(c)	9.523	.15	.30	.50	2.50
	1924(c)	—	—	—	Proof	40.00
	1924(c)	(restrike)	—	—	P/L	20.00
	1925(c)	3.981	.15	.30	.50	2.50
	1925(c)	—	—	—	Proof	40.00
	1925(c)	(restrike)	—	—	P/L	20.00
	1926(c)	7.885	.15	.30	.50	2.50
	1926(c)	—	—	—	Proof	40.00
	1926(c)	(restrike)	—	—	P/L	20.00
	1927(c)	5.888	.15	.30	.50	2.50
	1927(c)	—	—	—	Proof	40.00
	1927(c)	(restrike)	—	—	P/L	20.00
	1928(c)	5.453	.15	.30	.50	2.50

KM#	Date	Mintage	Fine	VF	XF	Unc
510	1928(c)	—	—	—	Proof	40.00
	1928(c)	(restrike)	—	—	P/L	20.00
	1929(c)	7.654	.15	.30	.50	2.50
	1929(c)	—	—	—	Proof	40.00
	1929(c)	(restrike)	—	—	P/L	20.00
	1930(c)	7.181	.15	.30	.50	2.50
	1930(c)	—	—	—	Proof	40.00
	1930(c)	(restrike)	—	—	P/L	20.00
	1931(c)	8.794	.15	.30	.50	2.50
	1931(c)	—	—	—	Proof	40.00
	1931(c)	(restrike)	—	—	P/L	20.00
	1932(c)	5.440	.15	.30	.50	2.50
	1932(c)	—	—	—	Proof	40.00
	1932(c)	(restrike)	—	—	P/L	20.00
	1933(c)	9.242	.15	.30	.50	2.50
	1933(c)	—	—	—	Proof	40.00
	1933(c)	(restrike)	—	—	P/L	20.00
	1934(c)	8.947	.15	.30	.50	2.50
	1934(c)	—	—	—	Proof	40.00
	1934(c)	(restrike)	—	—	P/L	20.00
	1935(c)	15.501	.15	.30	.50	2.00
	1935(c)	—	—	—	Proof	40.00
	1935(c)	(restrike)	—	—	P/L	20.00
	1936(c)	26.726	.10	.25	.40	1.25
	1936(c)	(restrike)	—	—	P/L	20.00

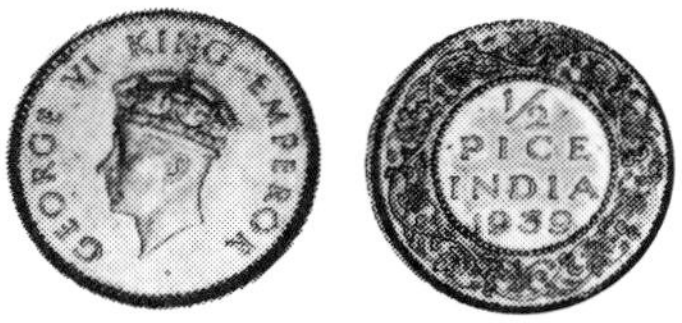

Obv: First head, high relief.

NOTE: Calcutta Mint issues have no mint mark. Bombay Mint issues have a small dot below the date.

KM#	Date	Mintage	Fine	VF	XF	Unc
528	1938(c)	—	—	—	Proof	30.00
	1938(c)	(restrike)	—	—	P/L	25.00
	1939(c)	17.357	.15	.40	.65	1.75
	1939(c)	—	—	—	Proof	30.00
	1939(b)	9.343	.15	.40	.65	1.75
	1939(b)	—	—	—	Proof	30.00
	1939(b)	(restrike)	—	—	P/L	25.00
	1940(c)	23.770	.15	.40	.65	1.75
	1940(c)	—	—	—	Proof	30.00
	1940(c)	(restrike)	—	—	P/L	25.00

NOTE: Calcutta Mint reported 11,161,600 mintage for 1938 but only proof and modern P/L restrikes are known.

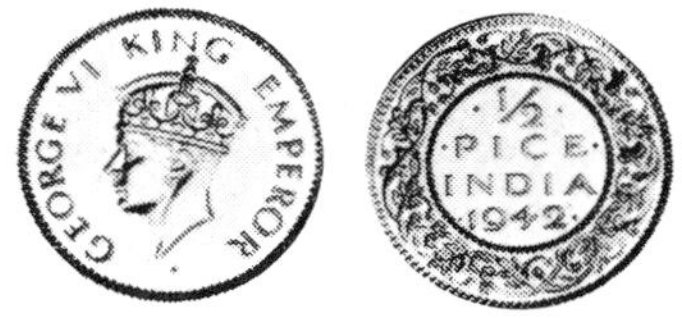

Obv: Second head, low relief.

KM#	Date	Mintage	Fine	VF	XF	Unc
529	1942(b)	—	—	—	Proof	50.00
	1942(b)	(restrike)	—	—	P/L	35.00

1/4 ANNA

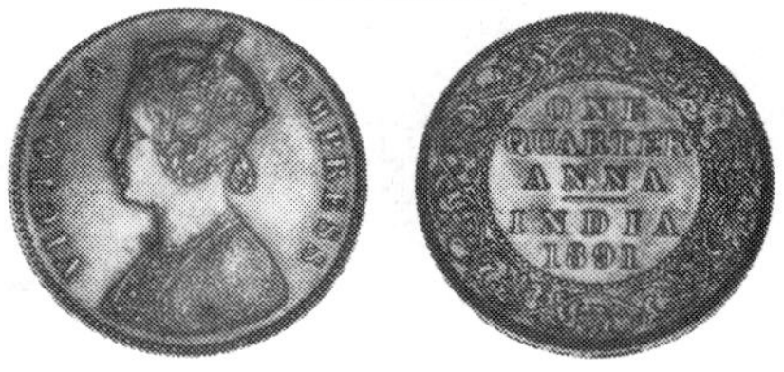

COPPER

KM#	Date	Mintage	Fine	VF	XF	Unc
486	1901(c)	136.091	.35	.75	1.50	4.50
	1901(c)	—	—	—	Proof	65.00
	1901(c)	(restrike)	—	—	P/L	25.00

NOTE: Earlier dates (1877-1900) exist for this type.

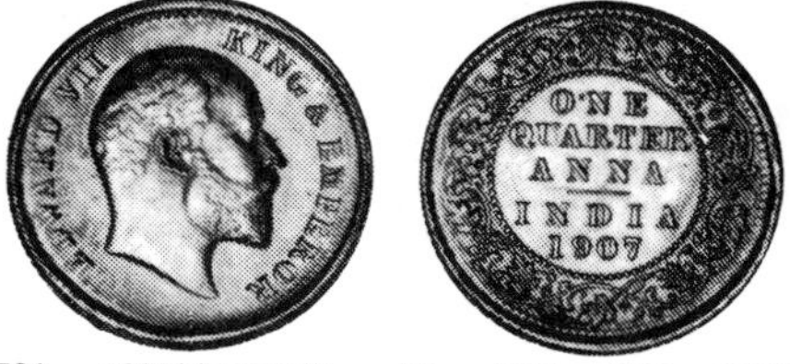

KM#	Date	Mintage	Fine	VF	XF	Unc
501	1903(c)	105.974	.35	1.75	7.50	35.00
	1903(c)	—	—	—	Proof	50.00
	1903(c)	(restrike)	—	—	P/L	25.00
	1904(c)	104.595	.35	1.75	7.50	35.00
	1904(c)	—	—	—	Proof	50.00
	1904(c)	(restrike)	—	—	P/L	25.00
	1905(c)	130.058	.35	1.75	7.50	35.00
	1905(c)	—	—	—	Proof	50.00
	1905(c)	(restrike)	—	—	P/L	25.00
	1906(c)	47.229	.35	1.75	7.50	35.00
	1906(c)	—	—	—	Proof	50.00

BRONZE
Thinner planchet.

KM#	Date	Mintage	Fine	VF	XF	Unc
502	1906(c)	115.786	.35	1.25	6.50	30.00
	1906(c)	—	—	—	Proof	40.00
	1907(c)	234.682	.35	1.25	6.50	30.00

KM#	Date	Mintage	Fine	VF	XF	Unc
502	1907(c)	—	—	—	Proof	40.00
	1907(c) (restrike)		—	—	P/L	20.00
	1908(c)	58.066	.35	1.25	6.50	30.00
	1908(c)	—	—	—	Proof	40.00
	1908(c) (restrike)		—	—	P/L	20.00
	1909(c)	29.966	.35	1.25	6.50	30.00
	1909(c)	—	—	—	Proof	40.00
	1909(c) (restrike)		—	—	P/L	20.00
	1910(c)	47.265	.35	1.25	6.50	30.00
	1910(c) (restrike)		—	—	P/L	20.00

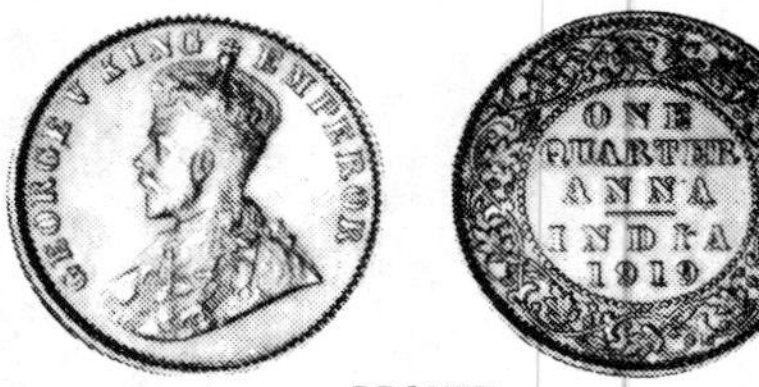

BRONZE

NOTE: Calcutta Mint issues have no mint mark. Bombay Mint issues have a small dot below the date. The pieces dated 1911, like the other coins with that date, show the "Pig" elephant.

KM#	Date	Mintage	Fine	VF	XF	Unc
511	1911(c)	55.918	.75	2.00	5.00	20.00
	1911(c)	—	—	—	Proof	55.00
	1911(c) (restrike)		—	—	P/L	20.00
512	1912(c)	107.456	.20	.40	1.00	4.00
	1912(c)	—	—	—	Proof	35.00
	1912(c) (restrike)		—	—	P/L	20.00
	1913(c)	82.061	.25	.50	1.25	4.50
	1913(c)	—	—	—	Proof	35.00
	1913(c) (restrike)		—	—	P/L	20.00
	1914(c)	40.576	.20	.40	.80	3.50
	1914(c)	—	—	—	Proof	35.00
	1914(c) (restrike)		—	—	P/L	20.00
	1915(c)	—	— Reported, not confirmed			
	1916(c)	1.632	3.50	7.00	12.00	25.00
	1916(c)	—	—	—	Proof	50.00
	1917(c)	69.370	.20	.40	.80	3.50
	1917(c)	—	—	—	Proof	35.00
	1917(c) (restrike)		—	—	P/L	20.00
	1918(c)	84.045	.20	.40	.80	3.50
	1918(c)	—	—	—	Proof	35.00
	1918(c) (restrike)		—	—	P/L	20.00
	1919(c)	212.467	.20	.40	.80	3.50
	1919(c)	—	—	—	Proof	35.00
	1919(c) (restrike)		—	—	P/L	20.00
	1920(c)	96.019	.20	.40	.80	3.50
	1920(c)	—	—	—	Proof	35.00
	1920(c) (restrike)		—	—	P/L	20.00
	1921(c)	—	—	—	Proof	35.00
	1924(b)	16.322	.20	.40	.80	3.50
	1924(b)	—	—	—	Proof	35.00
	1925(c)	14.598	.20	.40	.80	3.50
	1925(b)	14.588	.20	.40	.80	3.50
	1925(b)	—	—	—	Proof	35.00
	1926(c)	17.389	.20	.40	.80	3.50
	1926(c)	—	—	—	Proof	35.00
	1926(b)	16.073	.20	.40	.80	3.50
	1926(b)	—	—	—	Proof	35.00
	1926(b) (restrike)		—	—	P/L	20.00
	1927(c)	6.925	.20	.40	.80	3.50
	1927(c)	—	—	—	Proof	35.00
	1927(b)	12.440	.20	.40	.80	3.50
	1927(b)	—	—	—	Proof	35.00
	1927(b) (restrike)		—	—	P/L	20.00
	1928(c)	25.779	.20	.40	.80	3.50
	1928(c)	—	—	—	Proof	35.00
	1928(b)	10.057	.20	.40	.80	3.50
	1928(b)	—	—	—	Proof	35.00
	1928(b) (restrike)		—	—	P/L	20.00
	1929(c)	61.542	.20	.40	.80	3.50
	1929(c)	—	—	—	Proof	35.00
	1929(c) (restrike)		—	—	P/L	20.00
	1930(c)	40.698	.20	.40	.80	3.50
	1930(c)	—	—	—	Proof	35.00
	1930(b)	9.646	.20	.40	.80	3.50
	1930(b)	—	—	—	Proof	35.00
	1930(b) (restrike)		—	—	P/L	20.00
	1931(c)	6.835	.20	.40	.80	3.50
	1931(c)	—	—	—	Proof	35.00
	1931(c) (restrike)		—	—	P/L	20.00
	1933(c)	40.230	.20	.40	.80	3.50
	1933(c)	—	—	—	Proof	35.00
	1933(c) (restrike)		—	—	P/L	20.00
	1934(c)	80.506	.20	.40	.80	3.50
	1934(c)	—	—	—	Proof	35.00
	1934(c) (restrike)		—	—	P/L	20.00
	1935(c)	92.595	.20	.40	.80	3.50
	1935(c)	—	—	—	Proof	35.00
	1935(c) (restrike)		—	—	P/L	20.00
	1936(c)	227.501	.20	.40	.80	3.50
	1936(b)	61.926	.20	.40	.80	3.50
	1936(b)	—	—	—	Proof	35.00
	1936(b) (restrike)		—	—	P/L	20.00

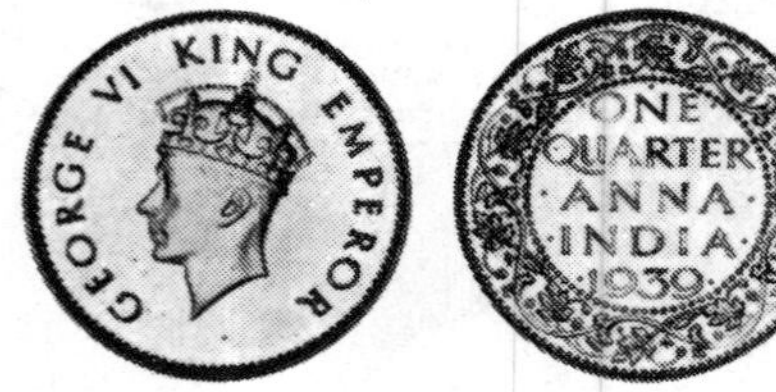

Obv: First head, high relief.

NOTE: Calcutta Mint issues have no mint mark. Bombay Mint issues have a small dot above N of "ONE".

KM#	Date	Mintage	Fine	VF	XF	Unc
530	1938(c)	33.792	.25	.40	.75	2.00
	1938(c)	—	—	—	Proof	35.00
	1938(b)	16.796	.25	.40	.75	2.00
	1938(b) (restrike)		—	—	P/L	30.00
	1939(c)	78.279	.30	.50	1.00	2.50
	1939(c)	—	—	—	Proof	35.00
	1939(b)	60.171	.30	.50	1.00	3.50
	1939(b)	—	—	—	Proof	35.00
	1939(b) (restrike)		—	—	P/L	30.00
	1940(b)	116.721	.35	.75	1.50	3.50

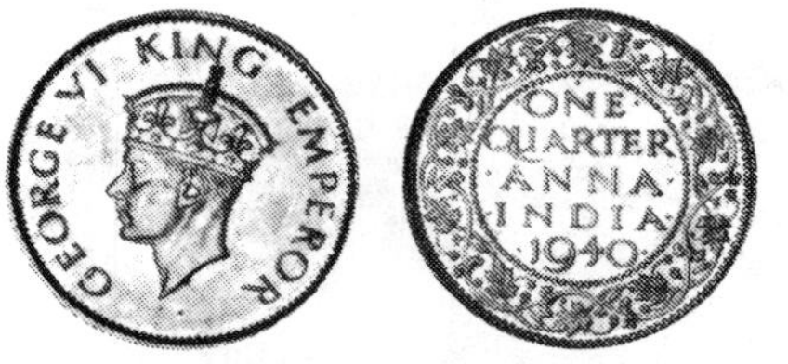

Obv: Second head, low relief.

KM#	Date	Mintage	Fine	VF	XF	Unc
531	1940(c)	140.410	.15	.35	.65	1.25
	1940(c)	—	—	—	Proof	35.00
	1940(b) Inc. KM530		.15	.35	.65	1.25
	1940(b) (restrike)		—	—	P/L	25.00
	1941(c)	121.107	.15	.35	.65	1.25
	1941(c) (restrike)		—	—	P/L	25.00
	1941(b)	1.446	—	.60	1.50	5.00
	1942(c)	34.298	.15	.35	.65	1.25
	1942(b)	8.768	.15	.35	.65	1.25
	1942(b) (restrike)		—	—	P/L	25.00

PICE

NOTE: There are three types of the crown, which is on the obverse at the top. These are shown below and are designated as (RC) Round Crown, (HC) High Crown, and (FC) Flat Crown. Calcutta Mint issues have no mint mark. The issues from the other mints have the mint mark below the date as following: Lahore, raised "L"; Pretoria, small round dot; Bombay, diamond dot or "large" round dot. On the Bombay issues dated 1944 the mint mark appears to be a large dot over a diamond.

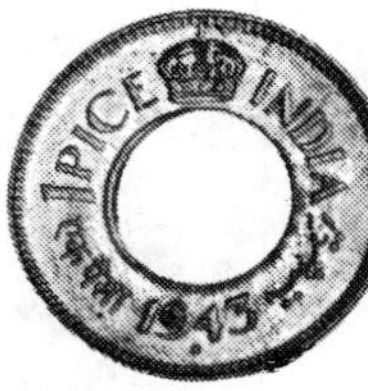

Round Crown (RC)

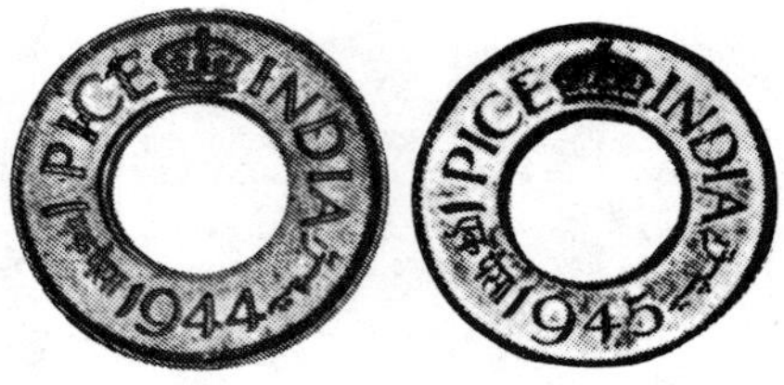

High Crown (HC) **Flat Crown (FC)**

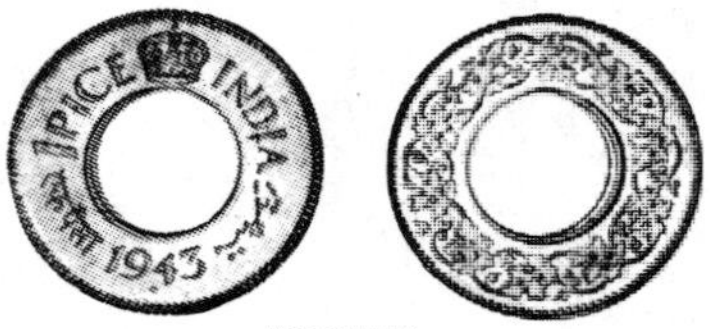

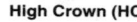

BRONZE

Obv: Small date, small legends.

KM#	Date	Mintage	Fine	VF	XF	Unc
532	1943(b) (RC) diamond	164.659	.25	.40	.85	2.75

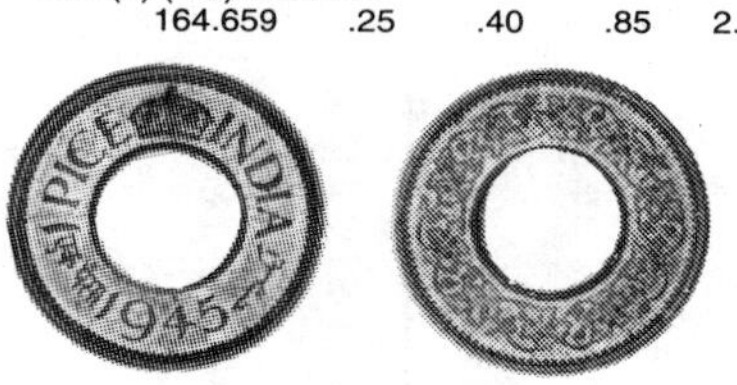

Obv: Large date, large legends.

KM#	Date	Mintage	Fine	VF	XF	Unc
533	1943(b) (HC) large dot	—	.15	.35	.65	1.25
	1943(p) (HC) small dot	98.997	.15	.35	.65	1.25
	1944(c) (HC)	—	.15	.35	.65	1.25
	1944(c) (HC)	—	—	—	Proof	25.00
	1944(b) (HC) large dot	195.354	.15	.35	.65	1.25
	1944(b) (HC) diamond	—	.20	.40	.75	2.00
	1944(b) (FC) large dot	—	.20	.40	.75	2.00
	1944(b) (restrike)		—	—	P/L	20.00
	1944(p) (HC) small dot	141.003	.20	.40	.75	2.00
	1944L (HC)	29.802	.15	.35	.65	1.25
	1945(c) (FC)	156.322	.15	.35	.65	1.25
	1945(b) (FC) diamond	237.197	.15	.35	.65	1.25
	1945(b) (FC) large dot	Inc. Ab.	.15	.35	.65	1.25
	1945(b) (restrike)		—	—	P/L	20.00
	1945L (FC)	238.825	.15	.35	.65	1.25
	1947(c) (HC)	153.702	.15	.35	.65	1.25
	1947(b) (HC) diamond	43.654	.15	.35	.65	1.25
	1947(b)	—	—	—	Proof	25.00
	1947 (restrike)		—	—	P/L	20.00

1/2 ANNA

NOTE: Calcutta Mint struck this denomination each year 1942-1945, denoted by a dot before and after the word INDIA on the reverse. Bombay Mint struck only with the dates 1942 and 1945, denoted by INDIA without dots before and after. Calcutta also issued proof coins each year while Bombay issued none. However, Bombay later produced proof-like restrikes using old dies from both Bombay and Calcutta indiscriminately; they are all attributed here to Bombay. Source: Pridmore.

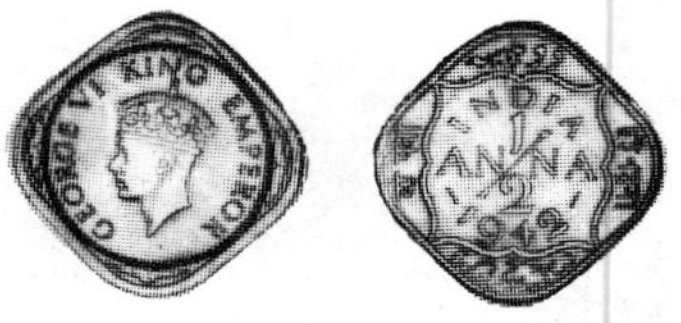

NICKEL-BRASS

Obv: Second head.

Rev. leg: INDIA (w/o dots).

NOTE: Bombay Mint issues dated 1942-1945 are without a dot before and after India.

KM#	Date	Mintage	Fine	VF	XF	Unc
534b.1	1942(b)	7.945	.15	.35	.65	1.25
	1942(b) (restrike)		—	—	P/L	40.00
	1943(b) (restrike)		—	—	P/L	40.00
	1944(b) (restrike)		—	—	P/L	40.00
	1945(b)	6.264	— Reported, not confirmed			
	1945(b) (restrike)		—	—	P/L	25.00

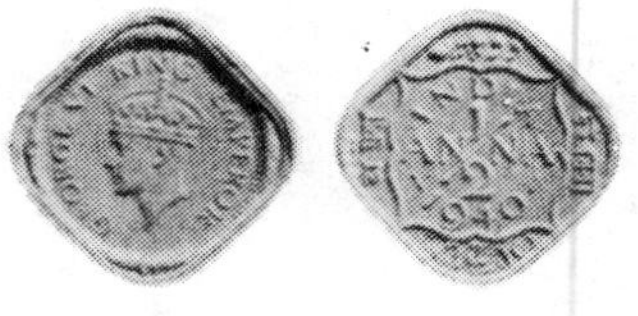

Rev. leg: • INDIA •

KM#	Date	Mintage	Fine	VF	XF	Unc
534b.2	1942(c)	159.000	.10	.20	.45	1.25
	1942(c)	—	—	—	Proof	30.00
	1943(c)	437.760	.10	.20	.45	1.25
	1943(c)	—	—	—	Proof	40.00
	1944(c)	514.800	.10	.20	.45	1.25
	1944(c)	—	—	—	Proof	40.00
	1945(c)	215.732	.10	.20	.45	1.25
	1945(c)	—	—	—	Proof	40.00

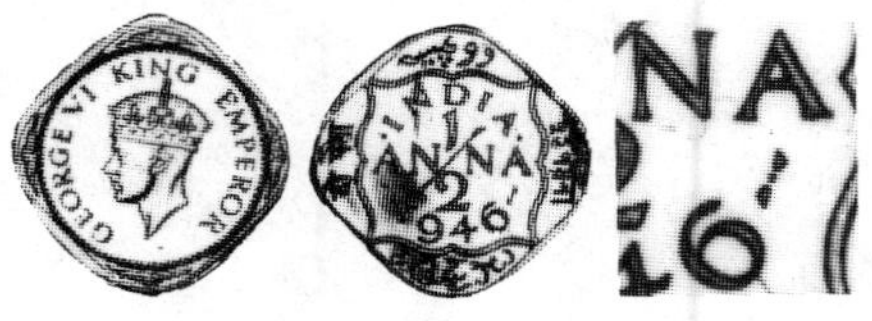

COPPER-NICKEL

NOTE: Calcutta Mint continued to issue this denomination with the dot before and after INDIA in 1946 and 1947. Bombay also struck in 1946 and 1947, the 1946 issue denoted by a small dot in the center of the dashes before and after the date on the reverse (as well as a dot before and after INDIA, like Calcutta); the characteristics of the 1947 Bombay issue have not been determined but are thought also to resemble the 1946 issue. This denomination is also reported to have been struck in a quantity of 50,829,000 pieces in 1946 at the new Lahore Mint but no way of distinguishing this issue has been found. The proof issue in 1946 was struck by Bombay, not Calcutta. Source: Pridmore.

KM#	Date	Mintage	Fine	VF	XF	Unc
535.1	1946(b)	48.744	.10	.20	.45	1.25
	1946(b)	—	—	—	Proof	30.00
	1946(b) (restrike)		—	—	P/L	25.00
	1947(b)	24.144	— Reported, not confirmed			
	1947(b) (restrike)		—	—	P/L	50.00

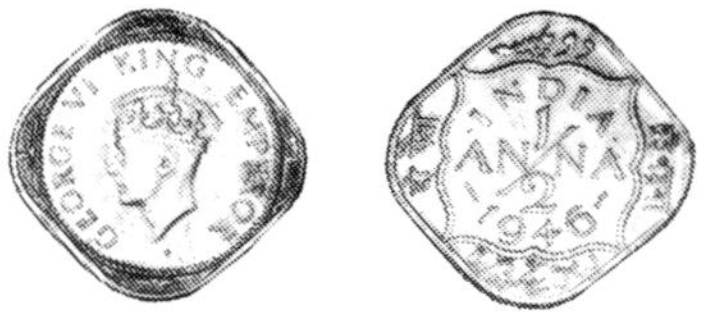

KM#	Date	Mintage	Fine	VF	XF	Unc
535.2	1946(c)	75.159	.10	.20	.45	1.25
	1947(c)	126.392	.10	.20	.45	1.25
	1947(c)	—	—	—	Proof	40.00
	1947(c) (restrike)		—	—	P/L	25.00

ANNA

NOTE: Struck only at the Bombay Mint, the pieces have as mint mark a small incuse "B" in the space below the cross pattee of the crown on the obverse.

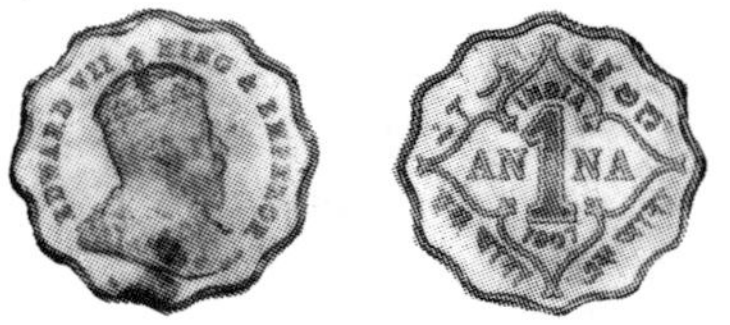

COPPER-NICKEL

KM#	Date	Mintage	Fine	VF	XF	Unc
504	1906B	.200	20.00	50.00	125.00	300.00
	1907B	37.256	.50	1.25	2.00	5.00
	1907B	—	—	—	Proof	60.00
	1908B	22.536	.50	1.25	2.00	5.00
	1908B	—	—	—	Proof	60.00
	1909B	24.800	.50	1.25	2.00	5.00
	1909B	—	—	—	Proof	60.00
	1910B	40.200	.50	1.25	2.00	5.00
	1910B	—	—	—	Proof	60.00

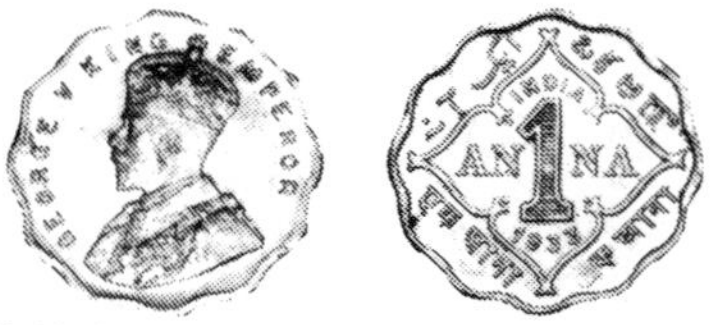

NOTE: Until 1920 all were struck at the Bombay Mint without mint mark. From 1923 on the Bombay Mint issues have a small raised bead or dot below the date. Calcutta Mint issues have no mint mark.

KM#	Date	Mintage	Fine	VF	XF	Unc
513	1912(b)	39.400	.40	1.00	2.50	6.00
	1912	—	—	—	Proof	50.00
	1913(b)	39.776	.40	1.00	2.50	6.00
	1913	—	—	—	Proof	50.00
	1914(b)	48.000	.25	.50	1.75	4.00
	1914	—	—	—	Proof	50.00
	1915(b)	7.670	.25	.50	1.75	4.00
	1915	—	—	—	Proof	50.00
	1916(b)	39.087	.25	.50	1.75	4.00
	1917(b)	58.067	.25	.50	1.75	4.00
	1917	—	—	—	Proof	50.00
	1918(b)	80.692	.25	.50	1.75	4.00
	1918(b)	—	—	—	Proof	50.00
	1919(b)	122.795	.25	.50	1.75	4.00
	1919(b)	—	—	—	Proof	50.00
	1919(c)	—	—	—	Proof	50.00
	1920(b)	9.264	.25	.50	1.75	4.50
	1920(b)	—	—	—	Proof	50.00
	1923(b)	7.125	.25	.50	1.75	4.50
	1923(b)	—	—	—	Proof	50.00
	1924(c)	16.640	.25	.50	1.75	4.00
	1924(c)	—	—	—	Proof	50.00
	1924(b)	17.285	.25	.50	2.00	5.00
	1924(b)	—	—	—	Proof	50.00
	1924(b) (restrike)		—	—	P/L	20.00
	1925(c)	22.388	.25	.50	2.00	5.00
	1925(c)	—	—	—	Proof	50.00
	1925(b)	11.763	.25	.50	2.00	5.00
	1925(b)	—	—	—	Proof	50.00
	1925(b) (restrike)		—	—	P/L	20.00
	1926(c)	13.440	.25	.50	2.00	5.00
	1926(c)	—	—	—	Proof	50.00
	1926(b)	8.088	.25	.50	2.00	5.00
	1926(b)	—	—	—	Proof	50.00
	1926(b) (restrike)		—	—	P/L	20.00
	1927(c)	6.296	.25	.50	2.00	5.00
	1927(c)	—	—	—	Proof	50.00
	1927(b)	12.953	.25	.50	2.00	5.00
	1927(b)	—	—	—	Proof	50.00
	1927(b) (restrike)		—	—	P/L	20.00
	1928(c)	29.568	.25	.50	2.00	5.00
	1928(c)	—	—	—	Proof	50.00
	1928(b)	4.832	.25	.50	2.00	5.00
	1928(b)	—	—	—	Proof	50.00
	1928(b) (restrike)		—	—	P/L	20.00
	1929(c)	42.200	.25	.50	2.00	5.00
	1929(c)	—	—	—	Proof	50.00
	1929(c) (restrike)		—	—	P/L	20.00
	1930(c)	22.816	.25	.50	2.00	5.00
	1930(c)	—	—	—	Proof	50.00
	1930(c) (restrike)		—	—	P/L	20.00
	1933(c)	17.432	.25	.50	2.00	5.00
	1933(c)	—	—	—	Proof	50.00
	1933(c) (restrike)		—	—	P/L	20.00
	1934(c)	34.216	.25	.40	1.50	4.00
	1934(c)	—	—	—	Proof	50.00
	1934(c) (restrike)		—	—	P/L	20.00
	1935(c)	12.952	.25	.40	1.50	4.00

KM#	Date	Mintage	Fine	VF	XF	Unc
513	1935(c)	—	—	—	Proof	50.00
	1935(b)	41.112	.25	.40	1.50	4.00
	1935(b)	—	—	—	Proof	50.00
	1935(b) (restrike)		—	—	P/L	20.00
	1936(c)	21.592	.25	.40	1.50	4.00
	1936(b)	107.136	.20	.35	1.25	3.00
	1936(b)	—	—	—	Proof	50.00

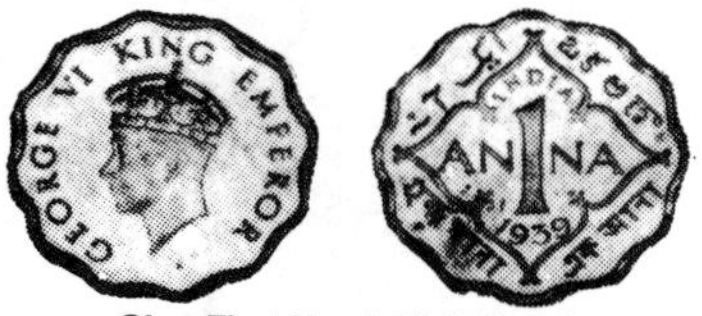

Obv: First Head, High Relief.

NOTE: Calcutta Mint issues have no mint mark. Bombay Mint issues have a small dot below the date.

KM#	Date	Mintage	Fine	VF	XF	Unc
536	1938(c)	7.128	.30	.75	1.50	5.00
	1938(c)	—	—	—	Proof	40.00
	1938(b)	3.126	.50	1.00	2.00	3.50
	1938(b) (restrike)		—	—	P/L	20.00
	1939(c)	18.192	.15	.40	1.00	2.50
	1939(b)	36.157	.15	.40	1.00	2.50
	1939(b) (restrike)		—	—	P/L	20.00
	1940(c)	60.945	.30	.75	1.50	3.00
	1940(c) (restrike)		—	—	P/L	20.00

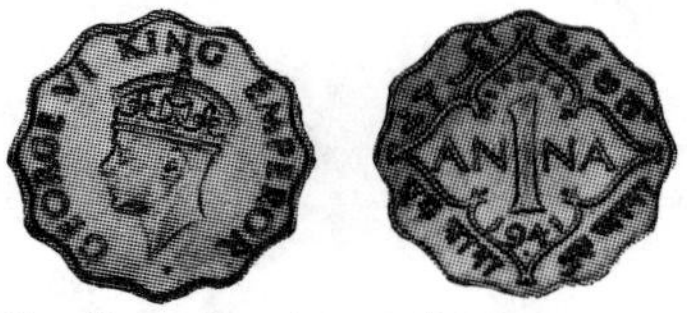

Obv: Second head, low relief, large crown.
Rev: Large "I".

KM#	Date	Mintage	Fine	VF	XF	Unc
537	1940(c)	76.392	.10	.25	.50	2.00
	1940(b)	144.712	.10	.25	.50	2.00
	1940(b) (restrike)		—	—	P/L	20.00
	1941(c)	62.480	.10	.15	.25	1.50
	1941(b)	40.170	.10	.15	.25	1.50
	1941(b) (restrike)		—	—	P/L	25.00

NICKEL-BRASS

KM#	Date	Mintage	Fine	VF	XF	Unc
537a	1942(c)	194.056	.10	.25	.50	2.00
	1942(c)	—	—	—	Proof	35.00
	1942(b)	103.240	.10	.25	.50	2.00
	1942(b) (restrike)		—	—	P/L	20.00
	1943(c)	352.256	.10	.25	.50	2.00
	1943(c)	—	—	—	Proof	35.00
	1943(b)	134.500	.10	.25	.50	2.00
	1943(b) (restrike)		—	—	P/L	20.00
	1944(c)	457.608	.10	.25	.50	2.00
	1944(c)	—	—	—	Proof	35.00
	1944(b)	175.208	.10	.25	.50	2.00
	1944(b) (restrike)		—	—	P/L	20.00

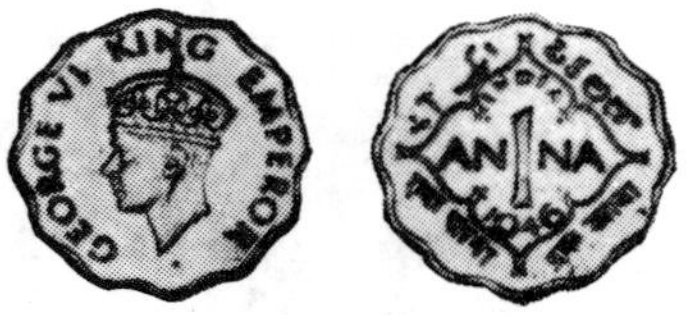

COPPER-NICKEL
Obv: Second head, low relief, small crown.
Rev: Small "I".

KM#	Date	Mintage	Fine	VF	XF	Unc
538	1945(c)	278.360	.10	.25	.50	2.00
	1945(b)	61.228	.10	.25	.50	2.00
	1946(c)	100.820	.10	.15	.35	1.50
	1946(b)	82.052	.10	.15	.35	1.50
	1946(b)	—	—	—	Proof	40.00
	1946(b) (restrike)		—	—	P/L	25.00
	1947(c)	148.656	.10	.25	.35	1.50
	1947(c)	—	—	—	Proof	40.00
	1947(b)	50.096	.10	.15	.35	1.50
	1947(b)	—	—	—	Proof	40.00

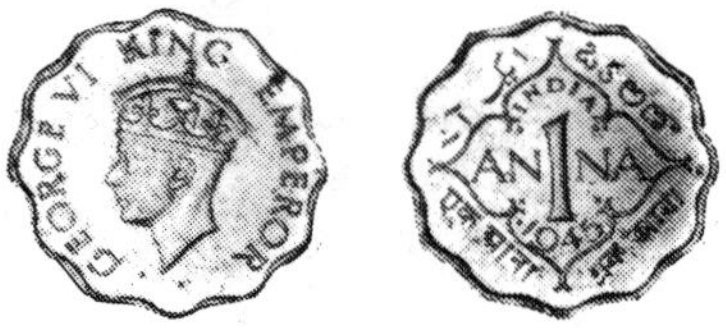

NICKEL-BRASS
Obv: Second head, low relief, large crown.
Rev: Small "I".

KM#	Date	Mintage	Fine	VF	XF	Unc
539	1945(c)	278.360	.10	.25	.75	2.00
	1945(c)	—	—	—	Proof	35.00
	1945(b)	61.228	.10	.25	.75	2.00
	1945(b) (restrike)		—	—	P/L	25.00

2 ANNAS

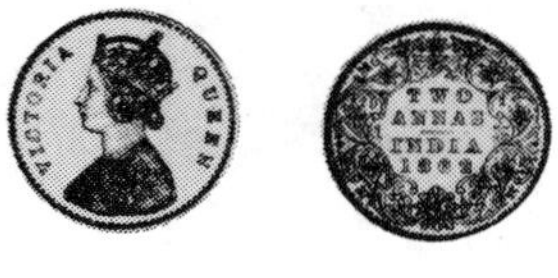

1.4600 g, .917 SILVER, .0430 oz ASW

KM#	Date	Mintage	Fine	VF	XF	Unc
488	1901C B/II, "C" incuse	8.944	1.25	2.50	5.00	10.00
	1901C	Inc. Ab.	—	—	Proof	35.00
	1901B B/I "B" incuse	—	2.50	5.00	10.00	20.00
	1901B B/II, "B" incuse	1.706	1.25	2.50	5.00	10.00
	1901B	—	—	—	Proof	100.00
	1901B (restrike)		—	—	P/L	30.00
	1901B B/I "B" raised	—	2.50	5.00	10.00	20.00
	1901B B/II, "B" raised	Inc. Ab.	1.25	2.50	5.00	10.00

NOTE: Earlier dates (1877-1900) exist for this type.

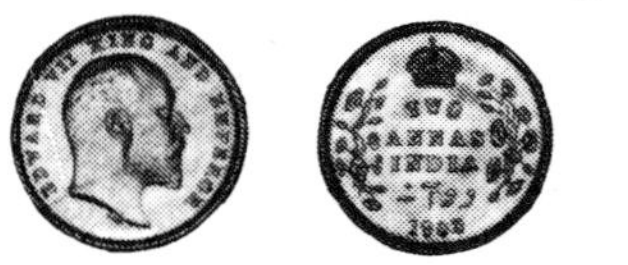

KM#	Date	Mintage	Fine	VF	XF	Unc
505	1903(c)	4.434	1.75	3.50	7.00	14.00
	1903(c)	—	—	—	Proof	65.00
	1903(c) (restrike)		—	—	P/L	25.00
	1904(c)	14.632	1.50	3.00	6.00	12.00
	1904(c)	—	—	—	Proof	65.00
	1904(c) (restrike)		—	—	P/L	25.00
	1905(c)	19.303	1.50	3.00	6.00	12.00
	1905(c) (restrike)		—	—	P/L	25.00
	1906(c)	13.031	1.50	3.00	6.00	12.00
	1906(c) (restrike)		—	—	P/L	25.00
	1907(c)	22.145	1.50	3.00	6.00	12.00
	1907(c)	—	—	—	Proof	65.00
	1908(c)	21.600	1.50	3.00	6.00	12.00
	1908(c)	—	—	—	Proof	65.00
	1908(c) (restrike)		—	—	P/L	25.00
	1909(c)	6.769	1.75	3.50	7.00	14.00
	1909(c)	—	—	—	Proof	65.00
	1909(c) (restrike)		—	—	P/L	25.00
	1910(c)	1.604	1.25	2.50	5.00	10.00
	1910(c)	—	—	—	Proof	65.00
	1910(c) (restrike)		—	—	P/L	25.00

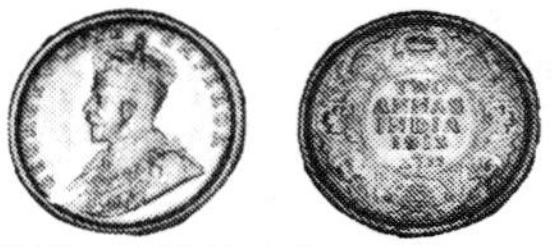

1.4600 g, .917 SILVER, .0430 oz ASW

NOTE: Calcutta Mint issues have no mint mark. Bombay Mint issues have a small raised bead or dot below the lotus flower at the bottom of the reverse. The 2 Annas dated 1911, like the other coins with the same date, has the "Pig" elephant. On these pieces like on the 1/4 Rupee, the King's bust is slightly smaller and has a higher relief than the later issues with the redesigned elephant.

KM#	Date	Mintage	Fine	VF	XF	Unc
514	1911(c)	16.760	1.50	3.00	6.00	12.00
	1911(c)	—	—	—	Proof	75.00
	1911(c) (restrike)		—	—	P/L	50.00
515	1912(c)	7.724	1.25	2.50	5.00	10.00
	1912(c)	—	—	—	Proof	50.00
	1912(b)	2.462	1.50	3.00	6.00	12.00
	1912(b)	—	—	—	Proof	50.00
	1912(b) (restrike)		—	—	P/L	25.00
	1913(c)	13.959	1.25	2.50	5.00	10.00
	1913(c)	—	—	—	Proof	50.00
	1913(b)	5.461	1.25	2.50	5.00	10.00
	1913(b)	—	—	—	Proof	50.00
	1913(b) (restrike)		—	—	P/L	25.00
	1914(c)	13.622	1.25	2.50	5.00	10.00
	1914(c)	—	—	—	Proof	50.00
	1914(b)	8.579	1.25	2.50	5.00	10.00
	1914(b) (restrike)		—	—	P/L	25.00
	1915(c)	5.892	1.25	2.50	5.00	10.00
	1915(c)	—	—	—	Proof	50.00
	1915(b)	5.943	1.25	2.50	5.00	10.00
	1915(b) (restrike)		—	—	P/L	25.00
	1916(c)	19.787	1.25	2.00	4.00	8.00
	1916(c)	—	—	—	Proof	50.00
	1916(c) (restrike)		—	—	P/L	25.00
	1917(c)	25.560	1.25	2.00	4.00	8.00
	1917(c)	—	—	—	Proof	50.00
	1917(c) (restrike)		—	—	P/L	25.00

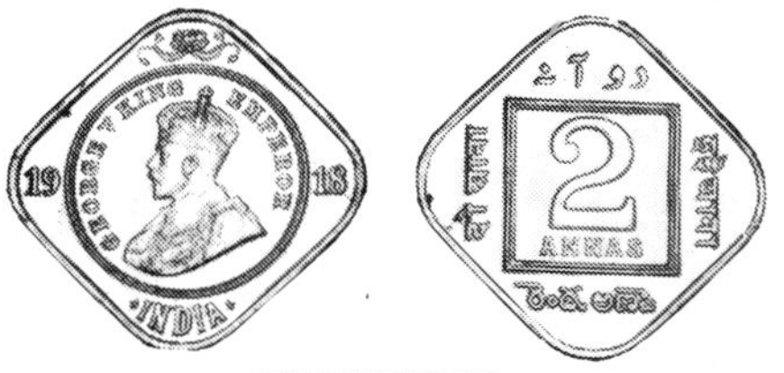

COPPER-NICKEL

NOTE: Calcutta Mint issues have no mint mark. Bombay Mint issues have a small raised dot on the reverse at the bottom near the rim.

KM#	Date	Mintage	Fine	VF	XF	Unc
516	1918(c)	53.412	1.25	1.75	4.00	10.00
	1918(c)	—	—	—	Proof	50.00
	1918(b)	9.191	1.25	1.75	4.00	10.00
	1918(b)	—	—	—	Proof	50.00
	1918(b) (restrike)		—	—	P/L	20.00
	1919(c)	89.040	1.25	1.75	4.00	10.00

KM#	Date	Mintage	Fine	VF	XF	Unc
516	1919(c)	—	—	—	Proof	50.00
	1919(c) (restrike)		—	—	P/L	20.00
	1920(b)	—	—	—	Proof	125.00
	1920(c)	13.520	1.25	1.75	4.00	10.00
	1920(c)	—	—	—	Proof	50.00
	1923(c)	7.656	1.25	1.75	4.00	10.00
	1923(c)	—	—	—	Proof	50.00
	1923(b)	6.431	1.25	1.75	4.00	10.00
	1923(b)	—	—	—	Proof	50.00
	1923(b) (restrike)		—	—	P/L	20.00
	1924(c)	8.384	1.25	1.75	4.00	10.00
	1924(c)	—	—	—	Proof	50.00
	1924(b)	4.818	1.25	1.75	4.00	10.00
	1924(b)	—	—	—	Proof	50.00
	1924(b) (restrike)		—	—	P/L	20.00
	1925(c)	10.848	1.25	1.75	4.00	10.00
	1925(c)	—	—	—	Proof	50.00
	1925(b)	8.348	1.25	1.75	4.00	10.00
	1925(b)	—	—	—	Proof	50.00
	1925(b) (restrike)		—	—	P/L	20.00
	1926(c)	8.352	1.25	1.75	4.00	10.00
	1926(c)	—	—	—	Proof	50.00
	1926(b)	2.927	1.50	3.00	6.00	12.00
	1926(b)	—	—	—	Proof	50.00
	1926(b) (restrike)		—	—	P/L	20.00
	1927(c)	6.424	1.25	1.75	4.00	10.00
	1927(c)	—	—	—	Proof	50.00
	1927(b)	4.835	1.25	1.75	4.00	10.00
	1927(b)	—	—	—	Proof	50.00
	1927(b) (restrike)		—	—	P/L	20.00
	1928(c)	7.352	1.25	1.75	4.00	10.00
	1928(c)	—	—	—	Proof	50.00
	1928(b)	4.876	1.25	1.75	4.00	10.00
	1928(b)	—	—	—	Proof	50.00
	1928(b) (restrike)		—	—	P/L	20.00
	1929(c)	13.408	1.25	1.75	4.00	10.00
	1929(c)	—	—	—	Proof	50.00
	1929(c) (restrike)		—	—	P/L	20.00
	1930(c)	8.888	1.25	1.75	4.00	10.00
	1930(c)	—	—	—	Proof	50.00
	1930(c) (restrike)		—	—	P/L	20.00
	1930(b)	—	1.25	1.75	4.00	10.00
	1933(c)	4.300	1.50	3.00	6.00	12.00
	1933(c)	—	—	—	Proof	50.00
	1933(c) (restrike)		—	—	P/L	20.00
	1934(c)	7.016	1.25	1.75	4.00	10.00
	1934(c)	—	—	—	Proof	50.00
	1934(c) (restrike)		—	—	P/L	20.00
	1935(c)	12.344	1.25	1.75	4.00	10.00
	1935(b)	21.017	1.00	1.50	3.00	8.00
	1935(b)	—	—	—	Proof	50.00
	1935(b) (restrike)		—	—	P/L	20.00
	1936(b)	36.295	1.00	1.50	3.00	8.00
	1936(b)	—	—	—	Proof	50.00

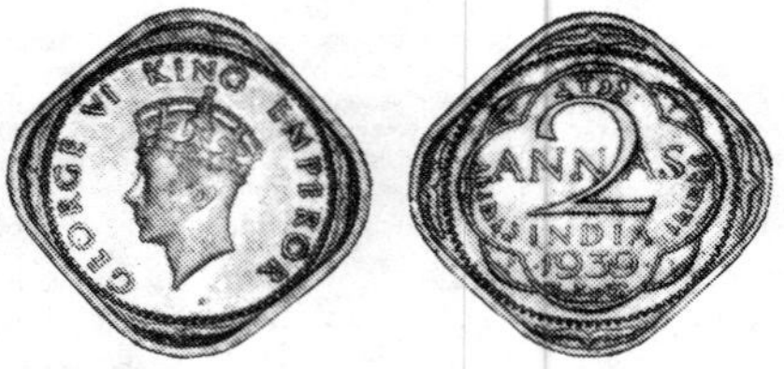

Obv: First head, high relief.

NOTE: Calcutta Mint issues have no mint mark. Bombay Mint issues have a small dot before and after the date.

KM#	Date	Mintage	Fine	VF	XF	Unc
540	1939(c)	4.148	1.25	3.00	6.00	15.00
	1939(b)	3.392	2.00	5.00	10.00	25.00

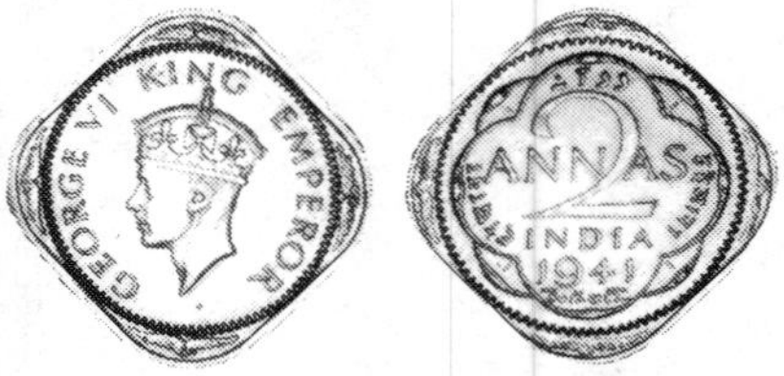

Obv: Second head, low relief, large crown.
Rev: Large "2".

KM#	Date	Mintage	Fine	VF	XF	Unc
541	1939(c)	Inc. Ab.	1.25	2.00	2.50	4.00
	1939(c)	—	—	—	Proof	40.00
	1939(b)	Inc. Ab.	.20	.30	.50	1.50
	1939(b)	—	—	—	Proof	40.00
	1939(b) (restrike)		—	—	P/L	25.00
	1940(c)	37.636	.20	.30	.50	2.00
	1940(c)	—	—	—	Proof	40.00
	1940(b)	50.599	.20	.30	.50	2.00
	1940(b) (restrike)		—	—	P/L	25.00
	1941(c)	63.456	.20	.30	.50	1.50
	1941(b)	10.760	.20	.30	.75	2.50
	1941(b)	—	—	—	Proof	40.00
	1941(b) (restrike)		—	—	P/L	25.00

NICKEL-BRASS

KM#	Date	Mintage	Fine	VF	XF	Unc
541a	1942(b) small 4	133.000	.25	.35	.50	2.25
	1942(b) large 4	Inc. Ab.	.20	.35	.50	2.25
	1943(b)	343.680	.25	.35	.50	2.25
	1944L	6.352	.50	1.25	2.00	5.00
	1944(b) small 4	219.700	.25	.35	.50	2.25
	1944(b) large 4	Inc. Ab.	.25	.35	.50	2.25

NOTE: On 1944 Lahore issues a tiny L replaces the decorative stroke in the 4 quatrefoil angles.

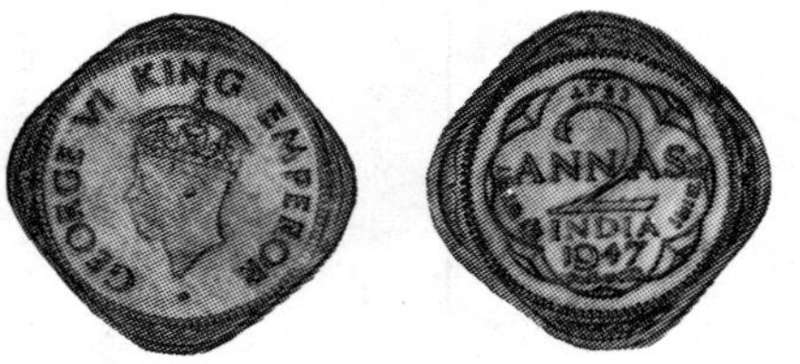

COPPER-NICKEL
Obv: Second head, low relief, small crown.
Rev: Small "2".

KM#	Date	Mintage	Fine	VF	XF	Unc
542	1946(c)	67.276	.20	.30	.50	2.25
	1946(b)	52.500	.20	.30	.50	2.25
	1946(b)	—	—	—	Proof	40.00
	1946(b) (restrike)		—	—	P/L	25.00
	1946(l)	*25.480	.20	.30	.50	2.25
	1947(c)	57.428	.20	.30	.50	2.25
	1947(b)	38.908	.20	.30	.50	2.25
	1947(b)	—	—	—	Proof	40.00
	1947(b) (restrike)		—	—	P/L	25.00

NOTE: W/o L mint mark but w/small diamond-shaped mark left of "1" on rev.

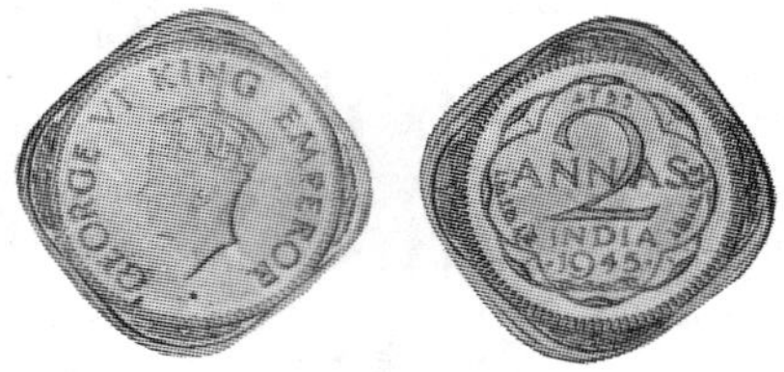

NICKEL-BRASS
Obv: Second head, low relief, large crown.
Rev: Small "2".

KM#	Date	Mintage	Fine	VF	XF	Unc
543	1945(c)	24.260	.25	.75	1.25	2.75
	1945(c)	—	—	—	Proof	40.00
	1945(b)	136.688	.25	.35	.50	1.50
	1945(b) (restrike)		—	—	P/L	25.00

1/4 RUPEE

NOTE: The distinguishing features of the 3 busts and 2 reverses are as following:
BUST A - The front of dress has 4 panels w/flower at right on bottom panel.
BUST B - Front of dress has 3-3/4 panels w/flower at center on incomplete bottom panel.
BUST C - Front of dress has 3 panels w/flower at left on bottom panel.

REVERSE I - The 2 large petals above the base of the top flower are long and curved downward; long stroke between "1/4".
REVERSE II - The 2 large petals above the base of the top flower are short and horizontal; short stroke between "1/4".

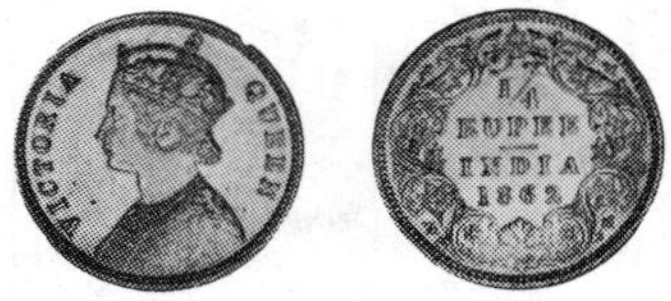

2.9200 g, .917 SILVER, .0860 oz ASW.

KM#	Date	Mintage	Fine	VF	XF	Unc
490	1901C C/II, "C" incuse	4.476	2.00	3.00	6.00	15.00
	1901C	—	—	—	Proof	125.00
	1901C (restrike)		—	—	P/L	30.00

NOTE: Earlier dates (1877-1900) exist for this type.

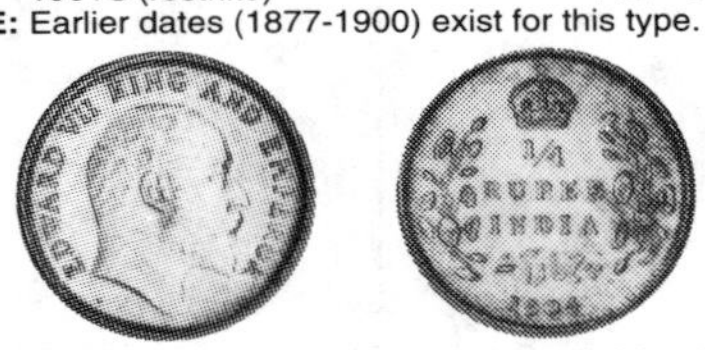

KM#	Date	Mintage	Fine	VF	XF	Unc
506	1903(c)	7.060	1.50	3.00	8.00	20.00
	1903(c)	—	—	—	Proof	100.00
	1903(c) (restrike)		—	—	P/L	30.00
	1904(c)	10.026	1.50	3.00	8.00	20.00
	1904(c)	—	—	—	Proof	100.00
	1904(c) (restrike)		—	—	P/L	30.00
	1905(c)	6.300	1.50	3.00	8.00	20.00
	1905(c)	—	—	—	Proof	100.00
	1905(c) (restrike)		—	—	P/L	30.00
	1906(c)	10.672	1.50	3.00	8.00	20.00
	1906(c) (restrike)		—	—	P/L	30.00
	1907(c)	11.464	1.50	3.00	8.00	20.00
	1907(c)	—	—	—	Proof	100.00
	1907(c) (restrike)		—	—	P/L	30.00
	1908(c)	7.084	1.50	3.00	8.00	20.00
	1908(c)	—	—	—	Proof	100.00
	1908(c) (restrike)		—	—	P/L	30.00
	1909(c)	—	—	—	Proof	125.00
	1909(c) (restrike)		—	—	P/L	30.00
	1910(c)	8.024	1.50	3.00	8.00	20.00
	1910(c)	—	—	—	Proof	100.00
	1910(c) (restrike)		—	—	P/L	30.00

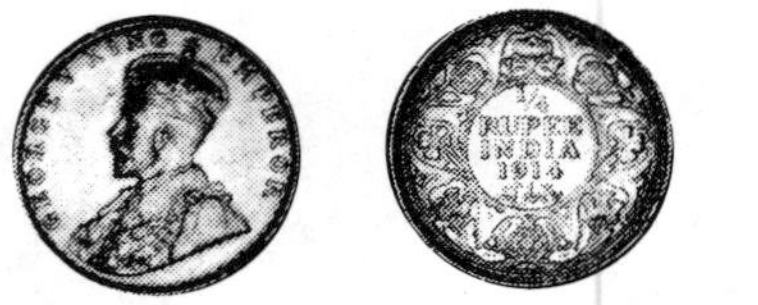

NOTE: Calcutta Mint issues have no mint mark. Bombay Mint issues have a small raised bead or dot in the space below the lotus flower at the bottom of the reverse. The 1/4 Rupee dated 1911, like the other coins with the same date, has the "Pig" elephant. On these pieces the King's bust is slightly smaller and has a higher relief than later issues with the re-designed elephant.

KM#	Date	Mintage	Fine	VF	XF	Unc
517	1911(c)	2.245	2.00	4.00	8.00	20.00
	1911(c)	—	—	—	Proof	90.00
	1911(c) (restrike)		—	—	P/L	60.00
518	1912(c)	9.587	2.00	2.75	5.00	12.00
	1912(c)	—	—	—	Proof	65.00
	1912(b)	2.200	2.00	2.75	5.00	12.00
	1912(b)	—	—	—	Proof	65.00
	1912(b) (restrike)		—	—	P/L	22.00
	1913(c)	12.686	2.00	2.75	5.00	12.00
	1913(c)	—	—	—	Proof	65.00
	1913(b)	2.276	2.00	2.75	5.00	12.00
	1913(b)	—	—	—	Proof	65.00
	1913(b) (restrike)		—	—	P/L	22.00
	1914(c)	1.423	2.00	2.75	5.00	12.00
	1914(c)	—	—	—	Proof	65.00
	1914(b)	7.949	2.00	2.75	5.00	10.00
	1914(b) (restrike)		—	—	P/L	22.00
	1915(c)	.851	2.25	4.00	10.00	35.00
	1915(c)	—	—	—	Proof	65.00
	1915(b)	2.096	2.00	2.75	5.00	12.00
	1915(b) (restrike)		—	—	P/L	22.00
	1916(c)	13.178	2.00	2.75	5.00	12.00
	1916(c)	—	—	—	Proof	65.00
	1916(c) (restrike)		—	—	P/L	22.00
	1917(c)	21.072	2.00	2.75	5.00	12.00
	1917(c)	—	—	—	Proof	65.00
	1917(c) (restrike)		—	—	P/L	22.00
	1918(c)	50.575	2.00	2.75	5.00	12.00
	1918(c)	—	—	—	Proof	65.00
	1919(b)	—	3.50	7.50	15.00	30.00
	1919(c)	26.135	2.00	2.75	5.00	12.00
	1919(c)	—	—	—	Proof	65.00
	1920(b)	—	3.25	6.50	12.50	25.00
	1925(b)	4.007	2.00	2.75	5.00	12.00
	1925(b)	—	—	—	Proof	65.00
	1925(b) (restrike)		—	—	P/L	22.00
	1926(c)	8.169	2.00	2.75	5.00	12.00
	1926(c)	—	—	—	Proof	65.00
	1926(c) (restrike)		—	—	P/L	22.00
	1928(b)	4.023	2.00	2.75	5.00	12.00
	1928(b)	—	—	—	Proof	65.00
	1929(c)	4.013	2.00	2.75	5.00	12.00
	1929(c)	—	—	—	Proof	65.00
	1929(c) (restrike)		—	—	P/L	22.00
	1930(c)	3.222	2.00	2.75	5.00	12.00
	1930(c)	—	—	—	Proof	65.00
	1930(c) (restrike)		—	—	P/L	22.00
	1934(c)	3.946	2.00	2.75	5.00	10.00
	1936(c)	25.744	1.25	2.25	4.00	8.00
	1936(b)	9.864	1.25	2.25	4.00	8.00
	1936(b) (restrike)		—	—	P/L	22.00

NOTE: The silver coinage of George VI is a very complex series with numerous obverse and reverse die varieties. Two different designs of the head appear on the obverse of most denominations struck for George VI. The "First Head" shows the King's effigy in high relief; the "Second Head" in low relief. In 1941-42 the "Second Head" was slightly reduced in size and the rim decoration enlarged. This type continued to be used on the silver coins and on some of the smaller denominations.

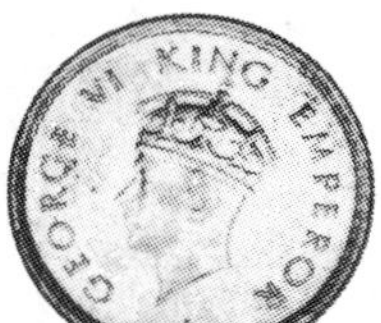

First Head

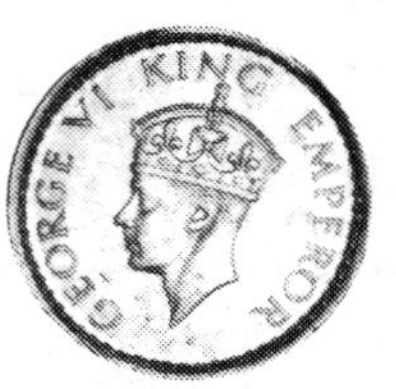

Second Head (small)

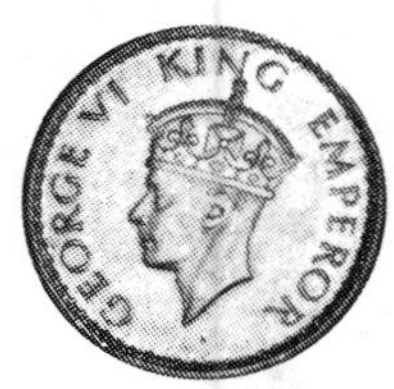

Second Head (large)

From 1942 to 1945 the reverse designs of the silver coins change slightly every year. However, a distinct reverse variety occurs on Rupees and 1/4 Rupees dated 1943-44 and on the half Rupee dated 1944, all struck at Bombay. This variety may be distinguished from the other coins by the design of the center bottom flower as illustrated, and is designated as Reverse B.

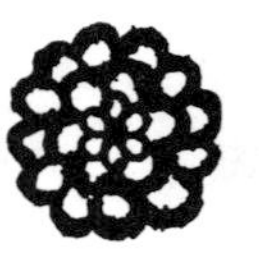

On the normal common varieties dated 1943-44 the three "scalloped circles" are not connected to each other and the bead in the center is not attached to the nearest circle.

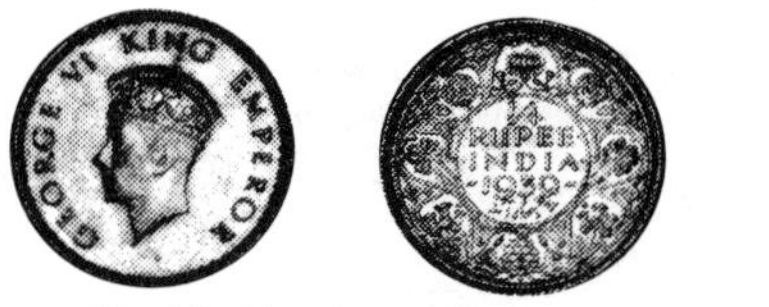

Obv: First head, reeded edge.

NOTE: Calcutta Mint issues have no mint mark. Bombay coins have a small bead below the lotus flower at the bottom on the reverse, except those dated 1943-1944 with reverse B which have a diamond. Lahore Mint issues have a small "L" in the same position. The nickel coins have a diamond below the date on the reverse.

KM#	Date	Mintage	Fine	VF	XF	Unc
544	1938(c)	—	—	—	Proof	65.00
	1938(c) (restrike)		—	—	P/L	25.00
	1939(c)	3.072	2.00	3.50	6.00	12.00
	1939(c)	—	—	—	Proof	65.00
	1939(b)	6.770	2.00	3.50	5.00	10.00
	1939(b) (restrike)		—	—	P/L	25.00

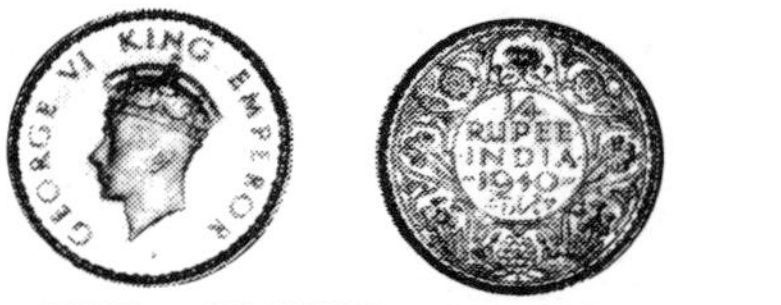

2.9200 g, .500 SILVER, .0469 oz ASW

544a	1940(b)	24.635	2.00	3.50	5.00	10.00

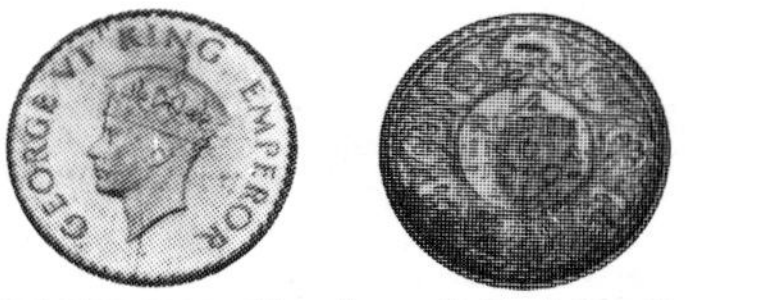

Obv: Large second head, small rim decoration.
Rev: Reeded edge.

545	1940(c)	68.675	BV	1.50	2.50	6.00
	1940(c)	—	—	—	Proof	65.00
	1940(b)	28.947	BV	1.50	2.50	6.00

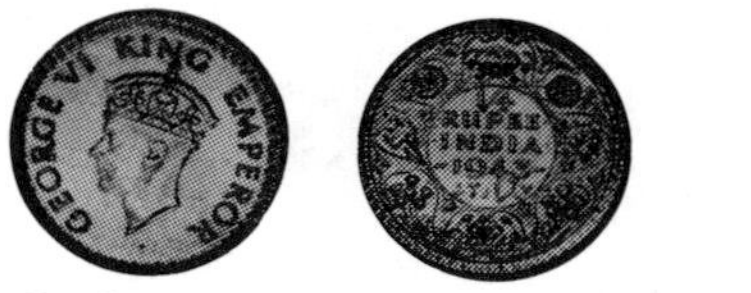

Obv: Small second head, large rim decoration.
Reeded edge.

546	1942(c)	88.096	BV	1.50	2.25	4.50
	1943(c)	90.994	BV	1.50	2.25	4.50

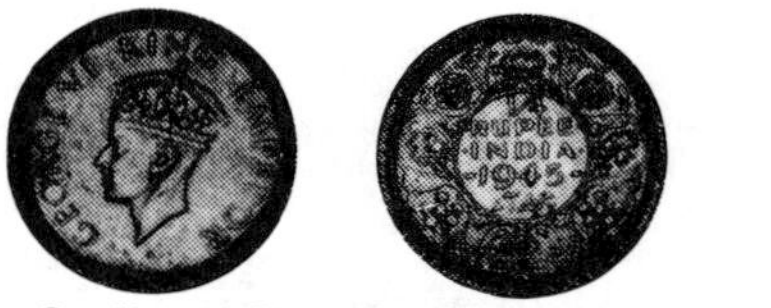

Obv: Small second head, large rim decoration.
Security edge.

547	1943B	95.200	BV	1.50	2.25	4.50
	1943B	—	—	—	Proof	60.00
	1943B reverse B	Inc. Ab.	BV	1.50	2.25	4.50
	1943L	23.700	BV	1.50	2.25	4.50
	1944B	170.504	BV	1.50	2.25	4.50
	1944B reverse B	Inc. Ab.	BV	1.50	2.25	4.50
	1944L	86.400	BV	1.50	2.25	4.50
	1945(b) small 5	181.648	BV	1.50	2.25	4.50
	1945(b) large 5	Inc. Ab.	BV	.85	1.75	4.00
	1945L small 5	29.751	BV	1.50	2.25	4.50
	1945L large 5	Inc. Ab.	BV	1.00	2.00	5.00

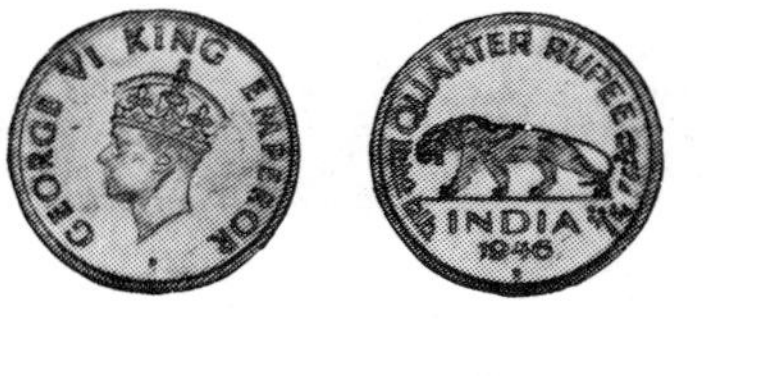

NICKEL
Reeded edge.
Rev: Indian tiger.

KM#	Date	Mintage	Fine	VF	XF	Unc
548	1946(b)	83.600	.40	.75	1.50	3.50
	1947(b)	109.948	.40	.75	1.50	3.50
	1947(b)	—	—	—	Proof	50.00

4 ANNAS

NOTE: Calcutta Mint issues have no mint mark. Bombay Mint issues have a small raised dot on the reverse at the bottom near the rim.

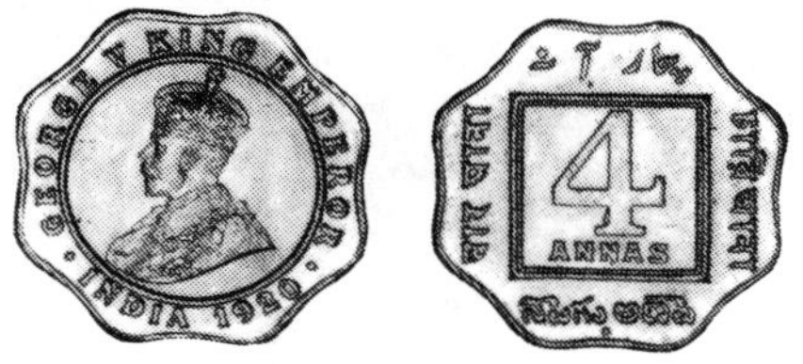

COPPER-NICKEL

519	1919(c)	18.632	2.50	5.00	10.00	20.00
	1919(c)	—	—	—	Proof	150.00
	1919(b)	7.672	3.25	6.50	12.50	25.00
	1919 (restrike)		—	—	P/L	25.00
	1920(c)	18.191	2.50	5.00	10.00	20.00
	1920(c)	—	—	—	Proof	150.00
	1920(b)	1.666	2.50	5.00	10.00	20.00
	1920(b)	—	—	—	Proof	150.00
	1920(b) (restrike)		—	—	P/L	25.00
	1921(c)	—	—	—	Proof	150.00
	1921(c) (restrike)		—	—	P/L	75.00
	1921(b)	1.219	3.00	6.50	12.50	25.00
	1921(b)	—	—	—	Proof	150.00
	1921 (restrike)		—	—	P/L	25.00

8 ANNAS

NOTE: Calcutta Mint issues have no mint mark. Bombay Mint issues have a small raised dot on the reverse at the bottom near the rim.

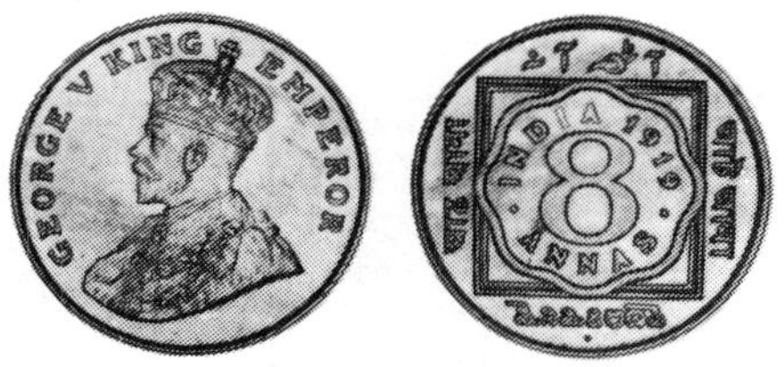

COPPER-NICKEL

520	1919(c)	2.980	3.75	7.50	15.00	30.00
	1919(c)	—	—	—	Proof	150.00
	1919(b)	1.400	4.00	8.50	17.50	35.00
	1919(b) (restrike)		—	—	P/L	30.00
	1920(c)	—	—	—	Proof	150.00
	1920(c) (restrike)		—	—	P/L	75.00
	1920(b)	1.000	12.50	25.00	50.00	100.00
	1920(b)	—	—	—	Proof	150.00
	1920(b) (restrike)		—	—	P/L	30.00

1/2 RUPEE

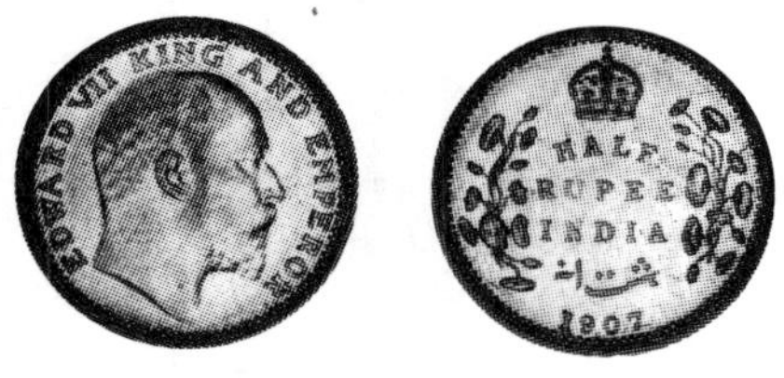

5.8300 g, .917 SILVER, .1719 oz ASW

NOTE: Calcutta Mint issues have no mint mark. Bombay Mint issues have a small incuse "B" in the space below the cross pattee of the crown on the reverse.

507	1904(c)	—	—	—	Proof	175.00
	1904(c) (restrike)		—	—	P/L	40.00
	1905(c)	.823	3.50	10.00	25.00	50.00
	1905(c) (restrike)		—	—	P/L	40.00
	1906(c)	3.036	3.50	10.00	25.00	50.00
	1906B	.400	3.75	12.50	30.00	60.00
	1906B (restrike)		—	—	P/L	40.00
	1907(c)	2.786	3.50	10.00	25.00	50.00
	1907(c)	—	—	—	Proof	150.00
	1907B	1.856	3.50	10.00	25.00	50.00
	1907B	—	—	—	Proof	150.00
	1907B (restrike)		—	—	P/L	40.00
	1908(c)	1.577	3.50	10.00	25.00	50.00
	1908(c)	—	—	—	Proof	150.00
	1908(c) (restrike)		—	—	P/L	40.00
	1909(c)	1.569	3.50	10.00	25.00	50.00
	1909(c)	—	—	—	Proof	150.00
	1909(c) (restrike)		—	—	P/L	40.00
	1909B	—	—	—	Proof	450.00
	1909B (restrike)		—	—	P/L	90.00
	1910(c)	3.413	3.50	10.00	25.00	50.00
	1910(c)	—	—	—	Proof	150.00
	1910B	.809	3.50	10.00	25.00	50.00
	1910B "B" raised		10.00	15.00	30.00	55.00
	1910B	—	—	—	Proof	150.00
	1910B (restrike)		—	—	P/L	40.00

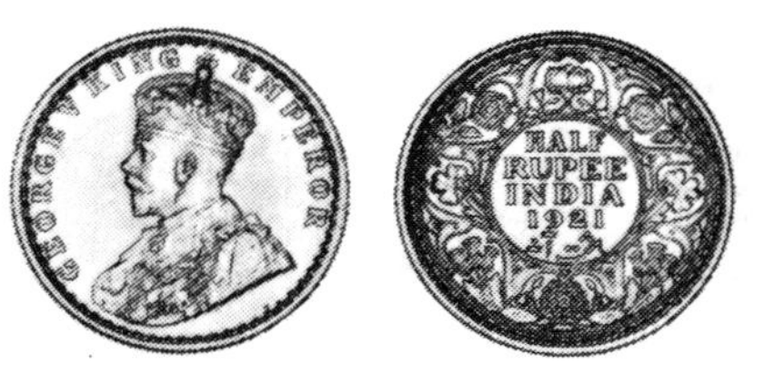

NOTE: Calcutta Mint issues have no mint marks. Bombay Mint issues have a small raised bead or dot in the space below the lotus flower at the bottom of the reverse. The half Rupee dated 1911 like the Rupee and all other issues of that year has the "Pig" elephant. It was struck only at the Calcutta Mint.

KM#	Date	Mintage	Fine	VF	XF	Unc
521	1911(c)	2.293	2.00	6.00	12.50	30.00
	1911(c)	—	—	—	Proof	175.00
	1911(c) (restrike)		—	—	P/L	75.00
522	1912(c)	3.390	2.00	6.00	12.00	28.00
	1912(c)	—	—	—	Proof	125.00
	1912(b)	1.505	2.00	6.00	12.00	28.00
	1912(b)	—	—	—	Proof	125.00
	1912(b) (restrike)		—	—	P/L	22.00
	1913(c)	2.723	2.00	6.00	12.00	28.00
	1913(c)	—	—	—	Proof	125.00
	1913(b)	1.825	2.00	6.00	12.00	28.00
	1913(b)	—	—	—	Proof	125.00
	1913(b) (restrike)		—	—	P/L	22.00
	1914(c)	1.400	2.00	6.00	12.00	28.00
	1914(c)	—	—	—	Proof	125.00
	1914(b)	.903	2.00	6.00	12.50	30.00
	1914(b) (restrike)		—	—	P/L	22.00
	1915(c)	2.804	2.00	6.00	12.00	28.00
	1915(c)	—	—	—	Proof	125.00
	1916(c)	3.644	2.00	6.00	12.00	28.00
	1916(c)	—	—	—	Proof	125.00
	1916(b)	5.880	2.00	6.00	12.00	28.00
	1917(c)	—	—	—	Proof	125.00
	1917(b)	8.822	2.00	6.00	12.00	28.00
	1917(b)	—	—	—	Proof	125.00
	1918(c) (restrike)		—	—	P/L	22.00
	1918(b)	10.325	2.00	6.00	12.00	28.00
	1918(b) (restrike)		—	—	P/L	22.00
	1919(b)	8.958	2.00	6.00	12.00	28.00
	1919(b)	—	—	—	Proof	125.00
	1919(b) (restrike)		—	—	P/L	22.00
	1919(c) (restrike)		—	—	P/L	22.00
	1921(c)	5.804	2.00	6.00	12.00	28.00
	1921(c)	—	—	—	Proof	125.00
	1921(c) (restrike)		—	—	P/L	22.00
	1922(c)	5.551	2.00	6.00	12.00	28.00
	1922(c)	—	—	—	Proof	125.00
	1922(b)	1.037	2.00	6.00	12.00	28.00
	1922(b)	—	—	—	Proof	125.00
	1922(b) (restrike)		—	—	P/L	22.00
	1923(c)	3.925	2.00	6.00	12.00	28.00
	1923(c) (restrike)		—	—	P/L	22.00
	1923(b)	2.076	2.00	6.00	12.00	28.00
	1923(b)	—	—	—	Proof	125.00
	1923(b) (restrike)		—	—	P/L	22.00
	1924(c)	4.007	2.00	6.00	12.00	28.00
	1924(c)	—	—	—	Proof	125.00
	1924(b)	2.664	2.00	6.00	12.00	28.00
	1924(b)	—	—	—	Proof	125.00
	1924(b) (restrike)		—	—	P/L	22.00
	1925(c)	4.119	2.00	6.00	12.00	28.00
	1925(c)	—	—	—	Proof	125.00
	1925(b)	1.627	2.00	6.00	12.00	28.00
	1925(b)	—	—	—	Proof	125.00
	1925(b) (restrike)		—	—	P/L	22.00
	1926(c)	4.027	2.00	6.00	12.00	28.00
	1926(c)	—	—	—	Proof	125.00
	1926(b)	2.011	2.00	6.00	12.00	28.00
	1926(b)	—	—	—	Proof	125.00
	1926(b) (restrike)		—	—	P/L	22.00
	1927(c)	2.032	2.00	6.00	12.00	28.00
	1927(c)	—	—	—	Proof	125.00
	1927(c) (restrike)		—	—	P/L	22.00
	1928(b)	2.466	2.00	6.00	12.00	28.00
	1928(b)	—	—	—	Proof	125.00
	1929(c)	4.050	2.00	6.00	12.00	28.00
	1929(c)	—	—	—	Proof	125.00
	1929(c) (restrike)		—	—	P/L	22.00
	1930(c)	2.036	2.00	6.00	12.00	28.00
	1930(c)	—	—	—	Proof	125.00
	1930(c) (restrike)		—	—	P/L	22.00
	1933/2(c)	4.056	5.00	10.00	25.00	50.00
	1933(c)	Inc. Ab.	2.00	6.00	12.00	28.00
	1933(c)	—	—	—	Proof	75.00
	1933(c) (restrike)		—	—	P/L	22.00
	1934(c)	4.056	2.00	6.00	12.00	28.00
	1934(c)	—	—	—	Proof	125.00
	1934(c) (restrike)		—	—	P/L	22.00
	1936(c)	16.919	2.00	6.00	12.00	28.00
	1936(b)	6.693	2.00	6.00	12.00	28.00
	1936(b) (restrike)		—	—	P/L	22.00

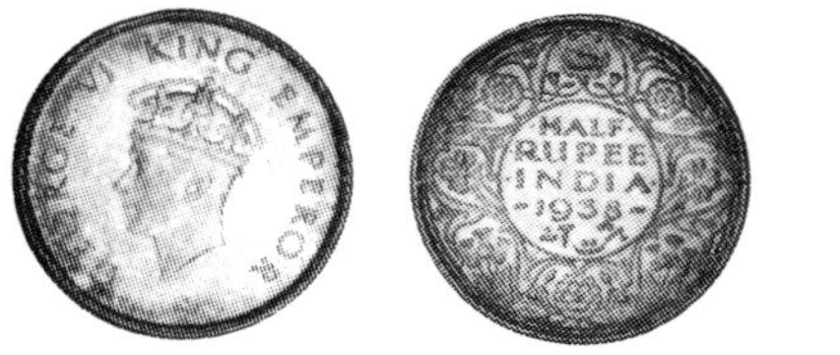

Obv: First head, reeded edge.

NOTE: Calcutta Mint issues have no mint mark. Bombay coins dated 1938-43 and 1945 have a bead below the lotus flower at the bottom of the reverse. Specimens dated 1944 with Reverse B have a diamond in the same position. Those dated 1944 with the normal common reverse have either a bead or a diamond. Lahore Mint issues have a small raised "L" in the same position as the Bombay coins. Bombay Mint 1943 coins have either large or small denticles on obverse. The nickel pieces of the last issue have a diamond below the date on the reverse.

KM#	Date	Mintage	Fine	VF	XF	Unc
549	1938(c)	—	—	—	Proof	100.00
	1938(b)	2.200	BV	3.00	7.50	15.00
	1938(b) (restrike)		—	—	P/L	25.00
	1939(c)	3.300	BV	3.00	7.50	15.00
	1939(c)	—	—	—	Proof	75.00
	1939(b)	10.096	BV	3.00	7.50	15.00
	1939(b)	—	—	—	Proof	75.00
	1939(b) (restrike)		—	—	P/L	25.00

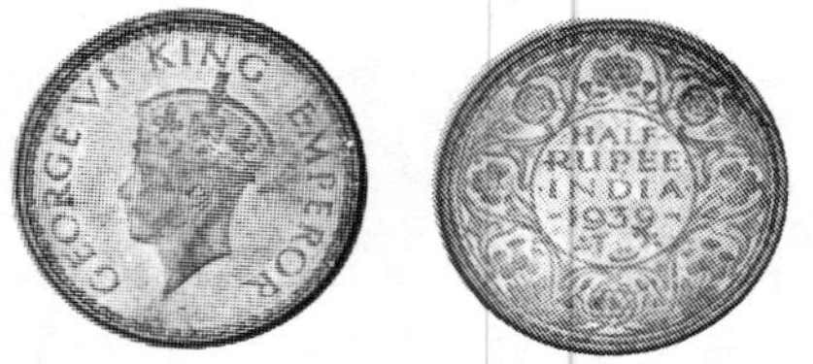

Obv: Large second head, small rim decoration, reeded edge.

KM#	Date	Mintage	Fine	VF	XF	Unc
550	1939(c)	Inc. Ab.	BV	3.00	6.50	15.00
	1939(b)	Inc. Ab.	BV	3.00	6.50	13.50

5.8300 g, .500 SILVER, .0937 oz ASW

KM#	Date	Mintage	Fine	VF	XF	Unc
550a	1940(c)	32.898	BV	3.00	6.00	12.00
	1940(c)	—	—	—	Proof	75.00
	1940(b)	17.811	BV	3.00	6.50	13.50
	1940(b) (restrike)		—	—	P/L	25.00

Obv: Large second head, small rim decoration, security edge.

KM#	Date	Mintage	Fine	VF	XF	Unc
551	1941(b)	26.100	BV	2.00	5.00	12.50
	1942(b)	61.600	BV	2.00	5.00	12.50

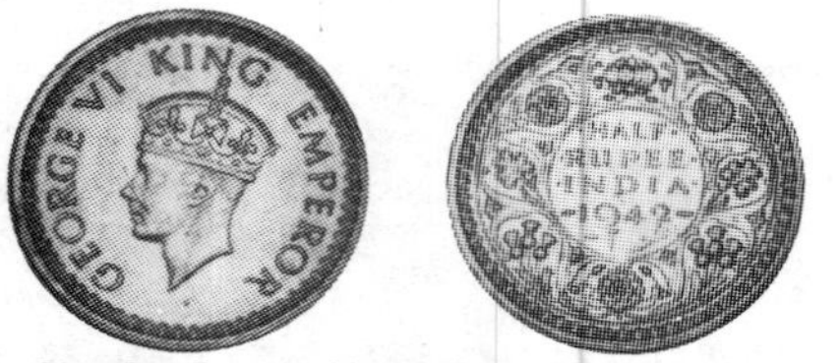

Obv: Small second head, large rim decoration.
Rev: Denomination and inner circle smaller.
Security edge.

KM#	Date	Mintage	Fine	VF	XF	Unc
552	1942(b)	Inc. Ab.	BV	2.00	4.50	9.00
	1943(b) dot	90.400	BV	2.00	4.50	9.00
	1943(b)	—	—	—	Proof	75.00
	1943(b) Diamond	—	BV	2.00	4.50	9.00
	1943L	9.000	BV	2.00	4.50	9.00
	1943L	—	—	—	Proof	75.00
	1944(b) dot	46.200	BV	2.00	4.50	9.00
	1944(b) Diamond	Inc. Ab.	BV	2.00	4.50	9.00
	1944L	79.100	BV	2.00	4.50	9.00
	1944L	—	—	—	Proof	75.00
	1945(b)	32.722	BV	2.00	4.50	9.00
	1945L small dot	79.192	BV	2.00	4.50	9.00
	1945L	—	—	—	Proof	75.00
	1945L large dot	Inc. Ab.	2.50	5.00	10.00	20.00

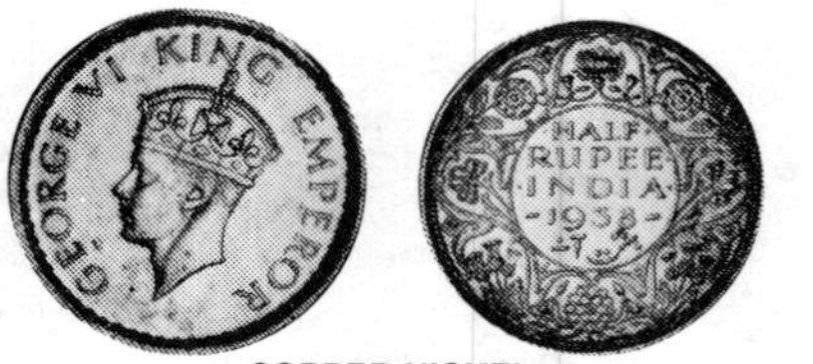

COPPER-NICKEL
Mule. Obv: KM#552. Rev: KM#549.

KM#	Date	Mintage	Fine	VF	XF	Unc
A553	1938(c) (restrike)		—	—	P/L	—

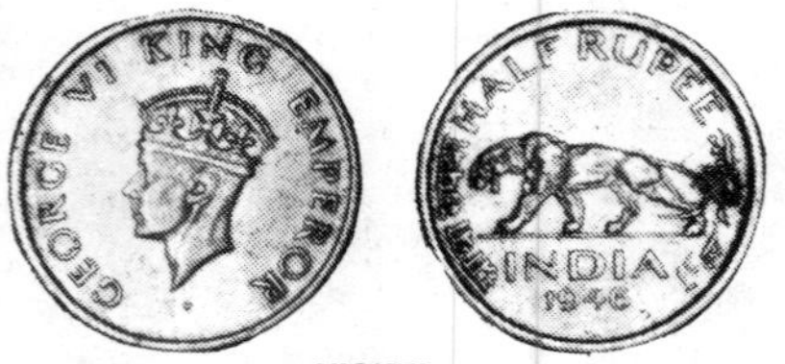

NICKEL
Reeded edge.
Rev: Indian tiger.

KM#	Date	Mintage	Fine	VF	XF	Unc
553	1946(b)	47.500	.50	1.00	2.25	4.50
	1947(b)	62.724	.50	1.00	2.00	4.00
	1947(b)	—	—	—	Proof	65.00

RUPEE

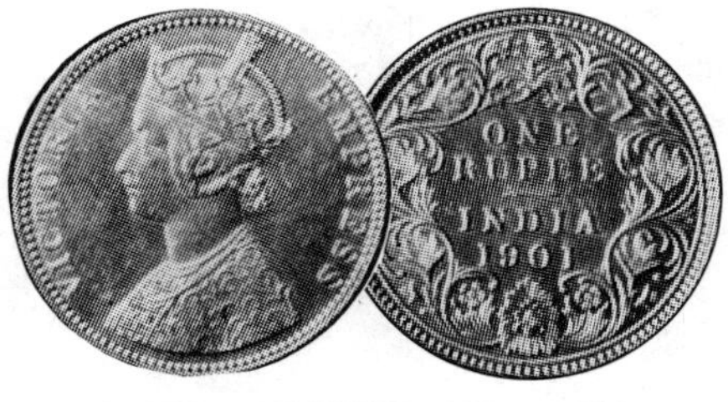

11.6600 g, .917 SILVER, .3438 oz ASW

KM#	Date	Mintage	Fine	VF	XF	Unc
492	1901C C/I, "C" incuse	72.017	5.00	8.00	12.00	25.00
	1901C	Inc. Ab.	—	—	Proof	175.00
	1901B A/I, "B" incuse	130.258	5.00	8.00	12.00	25.00
	1901B	—	—	—	Proof	175.00
	1901B (restrike)		—	—	P/L	35.00
	1901B C/I, "B" incuse	Inc. Ab.	5.00	8.00	12.00	25.00

NOTE: Earlier dates (1877-1900) exist for this type.

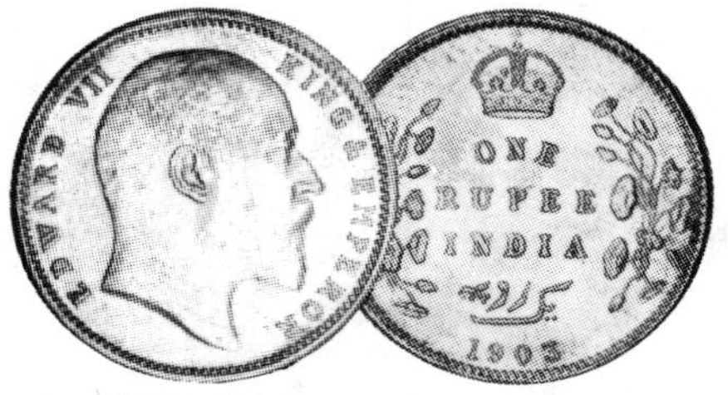

NOTE: Calcutta Mint issues have no mint mark. Bombay Mint issues have a small incuse "B" in the space below the cross pattee of the crown on the reverse.

KM#	Date	Mintage	Fine	VF	XF	Unc
508	1903(c)	49.403	5.00	8.00	12.00	25.00
	1903(c)	—	—	—	Proof	350.00
	1903B (in relief)	52.969	5.00	8.00	12.00	25.00
	1903B	—	—	—	Proof	350.00
	1903B (incuse)	Inc. Ab.	5.00	8.00	12.00	25.00
	1903B (restrike)		—	—	P/L	30.00
	1904(c)	58.339	5.00	8.00	12.00	25.00
	1904(c)	—	—	—	Proof	350.00
	1904B	101.949	5.00	8.00	12.00	25.00
	1904B	—	—	—	Proof	350.00
	1904B (restrike)		—	—	P/L	30.00
	1905(c)	51.258	5.00	8.00	12.00	25.00
	1905(c)	—	—	—	Proof	350.00
	1905B	76.202	5.00	8.00	12.00	25.00
	1905B	—	—	—	Proof	350.00
	1905B (restrike)		—	—	P/L	30.00
	1906(c)	104.797	5.00	8.00	15.00	30.00
	1906B	158.953	5.00	8.00	15.00	30.00
	1906B	—	—	—	Proof	350.00
	1906B (restrike)		—	—	P/L	30.00
	1907(c)	81.338	5.00	8.00	15.00	30.00
	1907(c)	—	—	—	Proof	350.00
	1907B	170.912	5.00	8.00	15.00	30.00
	1907B	—	—	—	Proof	350.00
	1907B (restrike)		—	—	P/L	30.00
	1908(c)	20.218	5.00	8.00	15.00	30.00
	1908(c)	—	—	—	Proof	350.00
	1908B	10.715	8.50	15.00	30.00	60.00
	1908B	—	—	—	Proof	350.00
	1908B (restrike)		—	—	P/L	30.00
	1909(c)	12.759	5.00	8.00	15.00	30.00
	1909(c)	—	—	—	Proof	350.00
	1909B	9.539	8.50	15.00	30.00	60.00
	1909B	—	—	—	Proof	350.00
	1909B (restrike)		—	—	P/L	30.00
	1910(c)	12.627	5.00	8.00	12.00	25.00
	1910(c)	—	—	—	Proof	350.00
	1910B	10.885	5.00	8.00	12.00	25.00
	1910B	—	—	—	Proof	350.00
	1910B (restrike)		—	—	P/L	30.00

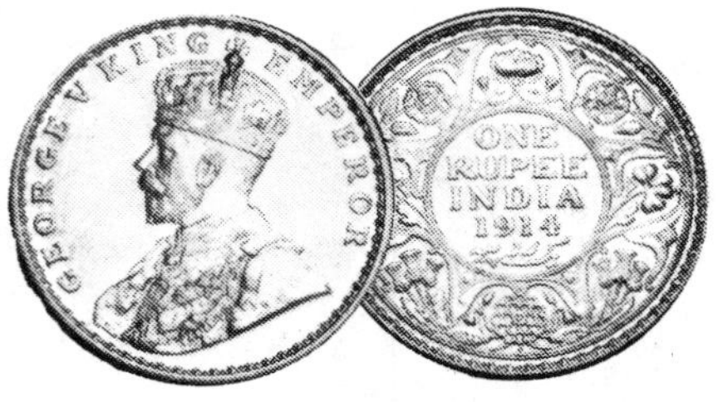

NOTE: Calcutta Mint issues have no mint mark. Bombay Mint issues have a small raised bead or dot in the space below the lotus flower at the bottom of the reverse.

Obverse Dies

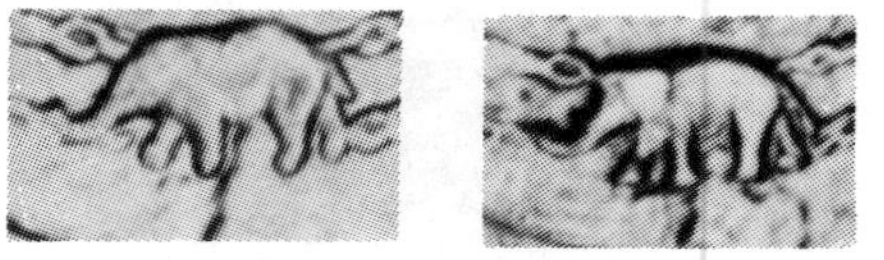

Type I **Type II**

Type I - Obv. die w/elephant with pig-like feet and short tail. Nicknamed "pig rupee".

Type II - Obv. die w/redesigned elephant with outlined ear, heavy feet and long tail.

The Rupees dated 1911 were rejected by the public because the elephant, on the Order of the Indian Empire shown on the King's robe, was thought to resemble a pig, an animal considered unclean by most Indians. Out of a total of 9.4 million pieces struck at both mints, only 700,000 were issued, and many of these were withdrawn and melted with unissued pieces. The issues dated 1912 and later have a re-designed elephant.

Type I

KM#	Date	Mintage	Fine	VF	XF	Unc
523	1911(c)	4.300	10.00	20.00	40.00	100.00
	1911(c)	—	—	—	Proof	600.00
	1911(b)	5.143	10.00	20.00	40.00	100.00
	1911(b) (restrike)		—	—	P/L	75.00

Type II

KM#	Date	Mintage	Fine	VF	XF	Unc
524	1912(c)	45.122	5.00	9.50	15.00	35.00
	1912(c)	—	—	—	Proof	500.00
	1912(b)	79.067	5.00	8.00	12.50	25.00
	1912(b)	—	—	—	Proof	500.00
	1912B (restrike)		—	—	P/L	30.00
	1913(c)	75.800	5.00	8.00	12.50	25.00
	1913(c)	—	—	—	Proof	500.00
	1913(b)	87.466	5.00	8.00	12.50	25.00
	1913(b)	—	—	—	Proof	500.00
	1913(b) (restrike)		—	—	P/L	30.00
	1914(c)	33.100	5.00	8.00	12.50	25.00
	1914(c)	—	—	—	Proof	500.00
	1914(b)	15.270	5.00	8.00	12.50	25.00
	1914(b)	—	—	—	Proof	500.00
	1914(b) (restrike)		—	—	P/L	30.00
	1915(c)	9.900	8.50	15.00	30.00	60.00
	1915(c)	—	—	—	Proof	500.00
	1915(b)	5.372	10.00	20.00	40.00	80.00
	1915(b)	—	—	—	Proof	500.00
	1915(b) (restrike)		—	—	P/L	30.00
	1916(c)	115.000	5.00	8.00	12.50	20.00
	1916(c)	—	—	—	Proof	500.00
	1916(b)	97.900	5.00	8.00	12.50	20.00
	1916(b)	—	—	—	Proof	500.00
	1916(b) (restrike)		—	—	P/L	30.00
	1917(c)	114.974	5.00	8.00	12.50	20.00
	1917(c)	—	—	—	Proof	500.00
	1917(b)	151.583	5.00	8.00	12.50	20.00
	1917(b)	—	—	—	Proof	500.00
	1917(b) (restrike)		—	—	P/L	30.00
	1918(c)	205.420	5.00	8.00	12.50	20.00
	1918(c)	—	—	—	Proof	500.00
	1918(b)	210.550	5.00	8.00	12.50	20.00
	1918(b)	—	—	—	Proof	500.00
	1918(b) (restrike)		—	—	P/L	30.00
	1919(c)	211.206	5.00	8.00	12.50	20.00
	1919(c)	—	—	—	Proof	500.00
	1919(b)	226.706	5.00	8.00	12.50	20.00
	1919(b)	—	—	—	Proof	500.00
	1919(b) (restrike)		—	—	P/L	30.00
	1920(c)	50.500	5.00	8.00	12.50	20.00
	1920(c)	—	—	—	Proof	500.00
	1920(b)	55.937	5.00	8.00	12.50	20.00
	1920(b)	—	—	—	Proof	500.00
	1920B (restrike)		—	—	P/L	30.00
	1921(b)	5.115	12.00	22.00	45.00	125.00
	1921(b)	—	—	—	Proof	500.00
	1922(b)	2.051	12.00	22.00	45.00	125.00
	1922(b)	—	—	—	Proof	500.00
	1935(c)	—	—	—	Proof	500.00
	1935(c) (restrike)		—	—	P/L	125.00
	1936(c)	—	—	—	Proof	500.00

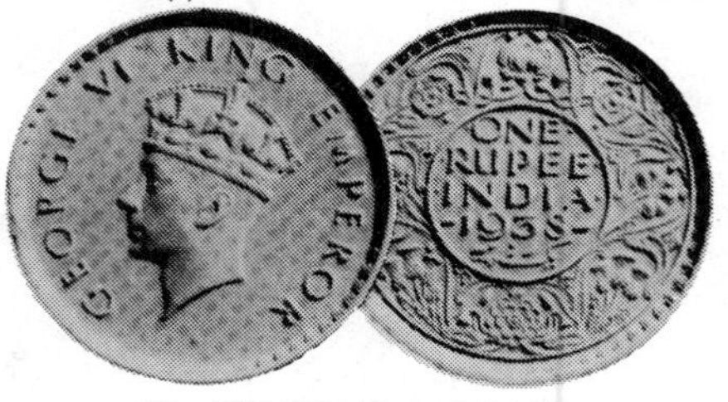

Obv: "First Head", reeded edge.

KM#	Date	Mintage	Fine	VF	XF	Unc
554	1938(c)	—	—	—	Proof	275.00
	1939(c)	—	—	—	Proof	350.00

NOTE: No rupees with the "First Head" were struck for circulation. Those dated 1938-39 were struck in 1940 before the fineness of the silver coins was reduced to .500.

The pieces struck at Calcutta have no mint mark. Bombay issues dated 1938-41 and 1944-45 have a bead below the lotus flower at the bottom of the reverse while those dated 1942-44 have a small diamond mark in the same position. On the specimens dated 1944 with Reverse B the mint mark appears to be a "bead over a diamond". Lahore Mint issues have a small raised "L" in the same position as the Bombay coins. The last issue nickel rupees struck at Bombay have a small diamond below the date on the reverse. The rupees dated 1943 occur with large and small "Second Head" and with

large and small date figure "3".

Obv: Large "Second Head", small rim decoration, reeded edge.

KM#	Date	Mintage	Fine	VF	XF	Unc
555	1938(b) w/o dot					
		7.352	7.50	11.50	16.50	27.50
	1938(b) dot I.A.		7.50	11.50	16.50	27.50
	1938(b) (restrike)	—			P/L	50.00
	1939(b) dot					
		2.450	150.00	300.00	600.00	1200.

11.6600 g, .500 SILVER, .1874 oz ASW
Security edge

556	1939(b)	— 200.00	400.00	800.00	1500.
	1940(b)153.120	BV	4.00	10.00	20.00
	1941(b)111.480	BV	4.00	10.00	20.00
	1943(b) Inc. Be.	BV	4.00	10.00	20.00

Obv: Small "Second Head", large rim decoration, security edge.

557	1942(b)244.500	BV	4.00	10.00	20.00
	1943(b) 65.995	BV	4.00	10.00	20.00
	1943(b) Rev. B				
	Inc. Ab.	BV	4.00	10.00	20.00
	1944(b) Rev. B				
	146.206	BV	4.00	10.00	20.00
	1944(b) Inc. Ab.	BV	4.00	10.00	20.00
	1944L small L				
	91.400	BV	4.00	10.00	20.00
	1944L large L				
	Inc. Ab.	BV	4.00	10.00	20.00
	1945(b) small date				
	142.666	BV	3.00	6.00	12.50
	1945(b) large date				
	Inc. Ab.	BV	3.00	7.50	15.00
	1945(b)	—	—	Proof	—
	1945L 118.126	BV	3.00	6.00	12.50

Reeded edge (error).

557.2	1944(b)	—	—	—	—	—
(558)	1945(b)	—	—	—	—	—

COPPER-NICKEL

557a	1943(b) (restrike)	—	—	P/L	125.00

Mule. Obv: KM#557. Rev: KM#555.

A559	1938(c) (restrike)	—	—	P/L	150.00

NICKEL
Security edge.
Rev: Indian tiger.

559	1947(b)118.128	1.50	2.50	5.00	10.00
	1947B	—	—	Proof	75.00
	1947(l) 41.911	1.50	3.00	6.00	12.00

NOTE: Bombay issue has diamond mark below date, Lahore w/o privy mark.

---

15 RUPEES

7.9881 g, .917 GOLD, .2354 oz AGW

KM#	Date	Mintage	Fine	VF	XF	Unc
525	1918(b)	2.110	120.00	165.00	225.00	325.00
	1918(b) 12 pcs.	—			Proof	1250.
	1918(b) (restrike)	—			P/L	300.00

NOTE: The above issue was equal in weight and fineness to the British sovereign.

TRADE COINAGE
SOVEREIGN

7.9881 g, .917 GOLD, .2354 oz AGW

525A	1918l	1.295	120.00	135.00	165.00	200.00
	1918l	—			Proof	—
	1918l (restrike)	—			P/L	175.00

NOTE: The fifth branch of the Royal Mint was established in a section of the Bombay Mint as of December 21, 1917. This was a war-time measure, its purpose being to strike into sovereigns the gold blanks supplied by the Bombay and other Indian mints. The Bombay sovereigns bear the mint mark I and were struck from August 15, 1918 to April 22, 1919. The branch-mint was closed in May, 1919.

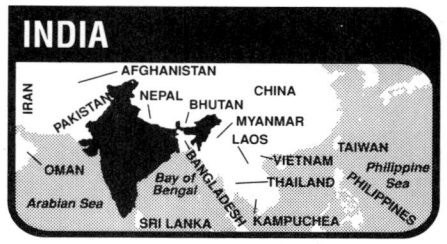

INDIA

The Republic of India, a subcontinent jutting southward from the mainland of Asia, has an area of 1,269,346 sq. mi. (3,287,590 sq. km.) and a population of over 900 million, second only to that of the People's Republic of China. Capital: New Delhi. India's economy is based on agriculture and industrial activity. Engineering goods, cotton apparel and fabrics, handicrafts, tea, iron and steel are exported.

The people of India have had a continuous civilization since about 2,500 B.C., when an urban culture based on commerce and trade, and to a lesser extent, agriculture, was developed by the inhabitants of the Indus River Valley. The origins of this civilization are uncertain, but it declined about 1,500 B.C., when the region was conquered by the Aryans. Over the following 2,000 years, the Aryans developed a Brahmanic civilization and introduced the caste system. Several successive empires flourished in India over the following centuries, notably those of the Mauryans, Guptas, and Mughals. In the 8th century A.D., the Arabs expanded into western India, bringing with them the Islamic faith. A Muslim dynasty (the Mughal Empire) controlled virtually the entire subcontinent during the period preceding the arrival of the Europeans; an Indo-Islamic style of art and architecture evolved, of which the Taj Mahal is a splendid example.

The Portuguese were the first Europeans to arrive, off Calicut in May 1498. It wasn't until 1612, after Portuguese and Spanish power began to wane, that the British East India Company established its initial settlement at Surat. By the end of the century, English traders were firmly established in Bombay, Madras, and Calcutta, as well as in some parts of the interior, and Britain was implementing a policy to create the civil and military institutions that would insure British dominion over the country. By 1757, following the successful conclusion of a war of colonial rivalry with France, the British were firmly established in India as not only traders, but as conquerors. During the next 60 years, the British East India Company acquired dominion over most of India by intrigue and force, and ruled directly, or through puppet princelings.

The Indian Mutiny (called the first War of Independence by Indian Nationalists) of 1857-58, begun by Indian troops in the service of the British East India Company, revealed the intensity of the growing resentment against British domination. The widespread rebellion against British rule was unsuccessful, but resulted in the transfer of government from the company to the British crown, and was a source of inspiration, to later Indian nationalists. Agitation for representation in the government continued.

Following World War I, in which India sent six million troops to fight at the side of the Allies, Indian nationalism intensified under the banner of the Indian National Congress and the leadership of Mohandas Karamchand Gandhi, who called for non-violent revolt against British authority. The Government of India Act of 1935 proposed a federal status linking the British Indian provinces with the many princely states; in addition, provincial legislatures were to be created. The federal status was never implemented, but the legislatures were created after the election of 1937, with the National Congress winning majorities in most of the provinces.

When Britain declared war on Germany in Sept. 1939, the Viceroy declared India also to be at war with a common enemy. The Congress, however, demanded independence as a condition for cooperation; Britain refused. But as the Japanese advanced into Asia, Britain offered to transfer to Indians power over all but military affairs during the war, and set forth a plan for postwar independence. Congress was willing to accept the wartime transfer of power, but both Congress and the Muslim League rejected Britain's plan for independence; Congress because it did not sufficiently safeguard Indian unity, the Muslims (who wanted a separate Muslim state) because of fears of what would happen to Muslims within a united India.

Early in 1947, Prime Minister Clement Attlee announced that Britain would leave India "by a date not later than June 1948," even though the Hindus and Muslims could not agree among themselves on a plan for selfgovernment. The National Congress, aware that the Muslim League would revolt rather than accept an all-India government, reluctantly agreed to the formation of a separate Muslim state. The Muslim-majority provinces of the North West Frontier. Sindh and West Punjab in the west, and East Bengal in the east were separated from India to form the Muslim state of Pakistan, which became independent on Aug. 14, 1947. India became independent on the following day. Because British India coins dated 1947 were struck until 1950, they can be considered the first coins of Independent India. India became a republic on Jan. 26, 1950.

The Republic of India is a member of the Commonwealth of Nations. The president is the Chief of State. The prime minister is the Head of Government.

MINT MARKS
(Mint marks usually appear directly below the date.)

B -Mumbai (Bombay), proof issues only
(B) - Bombay, diamond
C - Ottawa
   (1985 25 Paise; 1988 10, 25 & 50 Paise)
(C) - Calcutta, no mint mark
H - Birmingham (1985 Rupee only)
(H) - Hyderabad, star (1963-)
(Hd) - Hyderabad, diamond split vertically
   (1953-1960)
(Hy) - Hyderabad, incuse dot in diamond
   (1960-1968)
(L) - London, diamond below first date digit
M - Mumbai (Bombay), proof only after 1996
(M) - Mexico City, M beneath O
(N) - Noida, dot
(S) - Seoul, star below first date digit

From 1950 through 1964 the Republic of India proof coins carry the regular diamond mint mark and can be distinguished from circulation issues only by their proof-like finish. From 1969 proofs carry the capital "B" mint mark. Some Bombay issues after 1969 have a "proof-like" appearance although bearing the diamond mint mark of circulation issues. Beginning in 1972 proofs of the larger denominations - 10, 20 and 100 rupees - were partly frosted on their main features, including numerals. From 1975 all proofs were similarly frosted, from the 1 paisa to 100 rupees. Proof-like issues are often erroneously offered as proofs.

MONETARY SYSTEM
(Until 1957)

4 Pice = 1 Anna
16 Annas = 1 Rupee

PICE

BRONZE
Var. 1: 1.6mm thick, 0.3mm edge rim.

KM#	Date	Mintage	VF	XF	Unc
1.1 (565.1)	1950(B)	32.080	1.00	2.00	3.00

Var. 2: 1.6mm thick, 1.0mm edge rim.

1.2 (565.2)	1950(B)	Inc. Ab.	.40	.80	1.50
	1950(B)	—	—	Proof	2.50
	1950(C)	14.000	.50	1.00	1.75

Var. 3: 1.2mm thick, 0.8mm edge rim.

1.3 (566)	1951(B)	104.626	.20	.40	.75
	1951(C)	127.300	.20	.40	.75
	1952(B)	213.830	.25	.40	.80
	1953(B)	242.358	.25	.50	1.00
	1953(C)	111.000	.25	.50	1.00
	1953(Hd)	Inc. Ab.	15.00	20.00	30.00
	1954(B)	136.758	.25	.50	1.00
	1954(B)	—	—	Proof	5.00
	1954(C)	52.600	.35	.70	1.25
	1954(Hd)	Inc. Ab.	10.00	15.00	24.00
	1955(B)	24.423	.50	1.25	2.00
	1955(Hd)	Inc. Ab.	15.00	20.00	30.00

1/2 ANNA

COPPER-NICKEL

2.1 (567)	1950(B)	26.076	.20	.40	1.00
	1950(B)	—	—	Proof	3.00
	1950(C)	3.100	1.25	2.00	3.25

Rev: Larger date.

2.2 (567)	1954(B)	14.000	.40	.65	1.25
	1954(B)	—	—	Proof	5.00
	1954(C)	20.800	.30	.50	1.00
	1955(B)	22.488	.40	.65	1.25

ANNA

COPPER-NICKEL

KM#	Date	Mintage	VF	XF	Unc
3.1 (568)	1950(B)	9.944	.45	.75	1.50
	1950(B)	—	—	Proof	4.00

Rev: Larger date, first Hindi letter varieties.

3.2 (568)	1954(B)	20.388	.35	.60	1.25
	1954(B)	—	—	Proof	6.50
	1955(B)	—	15.00	20.00	30.00

2 ANNAS

COPPER-NICKEL

4 (569)	1950(B)	7.536	.75	1.50	2.50
	1950(B)	—	—	Proof	5.00
	1954(B)	10.548	.75	1.50	2.50
	1954(B)	—	—	Proof	8.00
	1955(B)	—	15.00	20.00	30.00

1/4 RUPEE

NICKEL
Var. 1: Large lion.

5.1 (570)	1950(B)	7.650	.60	1.50	2.50
	1950(B)	—	—	Proof	5.00
	1950(C)	7.800	.60	1.50	2.50
	1951(B)	41.439	.45	1.00	2.00
	1951(C)	13.500	.55	1.00	2.00
	1954(B)	—	—	Proof	6.00
	1954(C)	58.300	.65	1.50	2.50
	1955(B)	57.936	2.00	4.00	6.00

Var. 2: Small lion.

5.2 (571)	1954(C)	Inc. Ab.	.40	1.00	1.75
	1955(C)	28.900	.40	1.00	1.75
	1956(C)	22.000	.70	1.25	2.00

1/2 RUPEE

NICKEL
Var. 1: Large lion.

6.1 (572)	1950(B)	12.352	.75	1.25	2.50
	1950(B)	—	—	Proof	5.50
	1950(C)	1.100	1.25	2.00	5.00
	1951(B)	9.239	1.00	1.50	3.50
	1954(B)	—	—	Proof	8.00
	1954(C)	36.300	.50	1.00	2.50
	1955(B)	18.977	.75	1.50	4.50

Var. 2: Small lion.
Obv: Dots missing between words.

6.2 (573)	1956(C)	24.900	.50	1.00	2.50

RUPEE

NICKEL

KM#	Date	Mintage	VF	XF	Unc
7.1 (574)	1950(B)	19.412	1.50	2.50	4.50
	1950(B)	—	—	Proof	7.00

Rev: First Hindi letter varieties.

7.2 (574)	1954(B)	Inc. Ab.	2.00	3.00	5.50
	1954(B)	—	—	Proof	10.00

DECIMAL COINAGE

100 Naye Paise = 1 Rupee (1957-63)
100 Paise = 1 Rupee (1964)

NOTE: The Paisa was at first called "Naya Paisa" (= New Paisa), so that people would distinguish from the old non-decimal Paisa (or Pice, equal to 1/64 Rupee). After 7 years, the word 'new' was dropped, and the coin was simply called a "Paisa".

NOTE: Many of the Paisa standard types come with three obverse varieties.

1957-1989
OBV. I: Side lions toothless with 2 to 3 fur rows, dot in wheel center, short squat ID in 'INDIA'.

1967-1994
OBV. II: Asoka lion pedestal more imposing. Side lions with 3 to 4 fur rows, more elegant "D" in "INDIA". The shape of the "D" in INDIA is the easiest way to distinguish this obverse.

1979-
OBV: III: Similar to obverse I but 2 teeth, 4 to 5 fur rows, bull fatter, w/o central wheel dot.

NOTE: Paisa standard pieces with mint mark B, 1969 to date, were struck only in proof.

NOTE: Indian mintage figures are not divided by mint, and often include dates other than the year in which struck. They should be regarded with reserve.

NAYA PAISA

BRONZE

KM#	Date	Mintage	VF	XF	Unc
8	1957(B)	618.630	.30	.50	.85
(575)	1957(C)	Inc. Ab.	.30	.50	.85
	1957(Hd)	Inc. Ab.	.30	.50	.85
	1958(B)	468.630	.45	.75	1.50
	1958(Hd)	Inc. Ab.	.45	.75	1.50
	1959(B)	351.120	.30	.50	.85
	1959(C)	Inc. Ab.	.30	.50	.85
	1959(Hd)	Inc. Ab.	.30	.50	.85
	1960(B)	357.940	.30	.50	.85
	1960(B)	—	—	Proof	2.00
	1960(C)	Inc. Ab.	2.25	3.50	5.00
	1960(Hd)	Inc. Ab.	3.25	4.00	5.00
	1961(B)	573.170	.30	.50	.85
	1961(B)	—	—	Proof	2.00
	1961(C)	Inc. Ab.	.30	.50	.85
	1961(Hy)	Inc. Ab.	.50	.75	1.25
	1962(B)	—	—	—	—

NOTE: 1962(B) has only been found in some of the 1962 uncirculated mint sets.

NOTE: Varieties of the split diamond have been reported.

NICKEL-BRASS

KM#	Date	Mintage	VF	XF	Unc
8a	1962(B)	235.103	.20	.35	.70
(575a)	1962(B)	—	—	Proof	1.50
	1962(C)	Inc. Ab.	.20	.35	.70
	1962(Hy)	Inc. Ab.	.50	.75	1.25
	1963(B)	343.313	.20	.35	.70
	1963(B)	—	—	Proof	1.50
	1963(C)	Inc. Ab.	.25	.50	1.00
	1963(H)	Inc. Ab.	.25	.40	.80

PAISA

NICKEL-BRASS
Obverse 1

KM#	Date	Mintage	VF	XF	Unc
9	1964(B)	539.068	.20	.35	.60
(582)	1964(C)	Inc. Ab.	.20	.35	.60
	1964(H)	Inc. Ab.	.20	.35	.60

BRONZE

KM#	Date	Mintage	VF	XF	Unc
9a (582a)	1964(H)	Inc. Ab.	—	—	—

ALUMINUM
Obverse 1

KM#	Date	Mintage	VF	XF	Unc
10.1	1965(B)	223.480	.40	.65	1.00
(592)	1965(Hy)	Inc. Ab.	.40	.65	1.00
	1966(B)	404.200	.20	.30	.50
	1966(C)	Inc. Ab.	.20	.30	.50
	1966(Hy)	Inc. Ab.	.20	.30	.50
	1967(B)	450.433	.20	.30	.50
	1967(C)	Inc. Ab.	.20	.30	.50
	1967(Hy)	Inc. Ab.	.20	.30	.50
	1968(B)	302.720	.20	.30	.50
	1968(C)	Inc. Ab.	.20	.30	.50
	1968(Hy)	Inc. Ab.	.20	.30	.50
	1969(B)	125.930	.65	1.00	1.50
	1969B	9,147	—	Proof	1.50
	1969(H)	Inc. Ab.	.65	1.00	1.50
	1970(B)	15.800	2.00	2.50	5.00
	1970B	3,046	—	Proof	1.00
	1971B	4,375	—	Proof	1.00
	1971(H)	112.100	.20	.30	.50
	1972(B)	62.090	.20	.30	.50
	1972B	7,895	—	Proof	1.00
	1972(H)	Inc. Ab.	.20	.30	.50
	1973B	7,562	—	Proof	1.00
	1974B	—	—	Proof	1.00
	1975B	—	—	Proof	1.00
	1976B	—	—	Proof	1.00
	1977B	—	—	Proof	1.00
	1978B	—	—	Proof	1.00
	1979B	—	—	Proof	1.00
	1980B	—	—	Proof	1.00
	1981B	—	—	Proof	1.00

NOTE: 1970(B) is found only in the uncirculated sets of that year. It has a mirrorlike surface.

Obverse 2

KM#	Date	Mintage	VF	XF	Unc
10.2	1969(C)	Inc. Ab.	1.00	1.50	2.50
(606)	1970(C)	Inc. Ab.	.40	.65	1.00

2 NAYE PAISE

COPPER-NICKEL

KM#	Date	Mintage	VF	XF	Unc
11	1957(B)	406.230	.15	.40	.80
(576)	1957(C)	Inc. Ab.	.15	.40	.80
	1958(B)	245.660	.15	.40	.80
(576)	1958(C)	Inc. Ab.	.15	.40	.80
	1959(B)	171.445	.15	.40	.80
	1959(C)	Inc. Ab.	.15	.40	.80
	1960(B)	121.820	.15	.40	.80
	1960(B)	—	—	Proof	2.00
	1960(C)	Inc. Ab.	.20	.40	.80
	1961(B)	190.610	.20	.40	.80
	1961(B)	—	—	Proof	2.00
	1961(C)	Inc. Ab.	.20	.40	.80
	1962(B)	318.181	.20	.40	.80
	1962(B)	—	—	Proof	1.50
	1962(C)	Inc. Ab.	.20	.40	.80
	1963(B)	372.380	.20	.40	.80
	1963(B)	—	—	Proof	1.50
	1963(C)	Inc. Ab.	.20	.40	.80

2 PAISE

COPPER-NICKEL
Obverse 1

KM#	Date	Mintage	VF	XF	Unc
12	1964(B)	323.504	.20	.40	.80
(583)	1964(C)	Inc. Ab.	.20	.40	.80

ALUMINUM
Obverse 1. Rev: 10mm '2'.

KM#	Date	Mintage	VF	XF	Unc
13.1	1965(B)	175.770	.20	.40	.80
(593)	1965(C)	Inc. Ab.	.40	.65	1.00
	1966(B)	386.795	.20	.30	.50
	1966(C)	Inc. Ab.	.20	.30	.50
	1967(B)	454.593	.20	.30	.50

NOTE: Obv. 1 INDIA starts farther from right lion.

Obverse 1. Rev: 10-1/2mm '2'.

KM#	Date	Mintage	VF	XF	Unc
13.2 (595)	1967(C)	Inc. Ab.	.40	.65	1.25

Obverse 2. Rev: 10mm '2'.

KM#	Date	Mintage	VF	XF	Unc
13.3 (596)	1967(B)	—	3.00	5.00	8.00

Obverse 1. Rev: 11mm '2'.

KM#	Date	Mintage	VF	XF	Unc
13.4	1968(B)	—	Reported, not confirmed		
(602)	1968(C)	—	6.00	8.00	10.00
	1977(B)	—	.60	1.00	1.50
	1978(B)	—	.40	.65	1.00

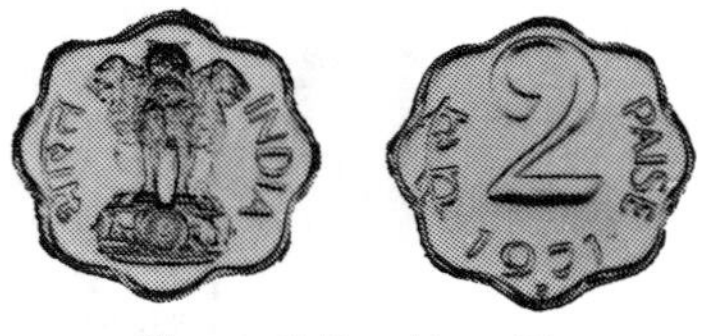

Obverse 2. Rev: 11mm '2'.

KM#	Date	Mintage	VF	XF	Unc
13.5	1968(B)	305.205	.10	.25	.50
(603)	1968(C)	Inc. Ab.	.20	.30	.50
	1969(B)	5.335	2.00	3.00	5.00
	1969B	9,147	—	Proof	1.00
	1970(B)	—	—	—	5.00
	1970B	3,046	—	Proof	1.00
	1970(C)	79.100	.20	.30	.50
	1971B	4,375	—	Proof	1.00
	1971(C)	207.900	.20	.30	.50

Rev: Smaller date.

KM#	Date	Mintage	VF	XF	Unc
13.6	1972B	7,895	—	Proof	1.00
(603)	1972(C)	261.270	.20	.30	.50
	1972(H)	Inc. Ab.	.20	.30	.50
	1973B	7,562	—	Proof	1.00
	1973(C)	—	.15	.25	.50
	1973(H)	—	.15	.25	.50
	1974B	—	—	Proof	1.00
	1974(C)	—	.15	.25	.50
	1974(H)	—	.15	.25	.50
	1975B	—	—	Proof	1.00
	1975(C)	184.500	.40	.65	1.00
	1975(H)	Inc. Ab.	.15	.25	.50
	1976(B)	68.140	.15	.25	.50
	1976B	—	—	Proof	1.00
	1976(H)	—	1.50	2.25	3.00
	1977(B)	251.955	.25	.40	.70
	1977B	—	—	Proof	1.00
	1977(H)	Inc. Ab.	.15	.25	.50
	1978B	—	—	Proof	1.00
	1978(H)	144.010	.15	.25	.50
	1979B	—	—	Proof	1.00
	1979(H)	—	.65	1.00	1.50
	1980B	—	—	Proof	1.00
	1981B	—	—	Proof	1.00

NOTE: Varieties of date size exist.

NOTE: 1970(B) is found only in the uncirculated sets of that year. It has a mirrorlike surface.

3 PAISE

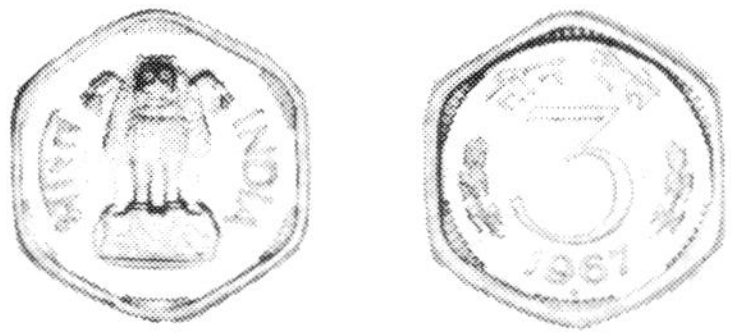

ALUMINUM
Obverse 1

KM#	Date	Mintage	VF	XF	Unc
14.1	1964(B)	138.890	.20	.40	.70
(584)	1964(C)	Inc. Ab.	.20	.40	.70
	1965(B)	459.825	.20	.30	.60
	1965(C)	Inc. Ab.	.20	.30	.60
	1966(B)	390.440	.20	.30	.60
	1966(C)	Inc. Ab.	.20	.30	.60
	1966(Hy)	Inc. Ab.	.20	.30	.60
	1967(B)	167.018	.20	.30	.60
	1967(C)	Inc. Ab.	.20	.30	.60
	1967(H)	Inc. Ab.	.75	1.25	2.00
	1968(B)	—	3.00	4.00	6.00
	1968(H)	—	—	—	—

Obverse 2

KM#	Date	Mintage	VF	XF	Unc
14.2	1967(C)	—	4.00	6.00	8.00
(597)	1967(H)	Inc. Ab.	4.00	6.00	8.00
	1968(B)	246.390	—	.25	.50
	1968(C)	Inc. Ab.	.10	.25	.50
	1968(H)	Inc. Ab.	.20	.35	.60
	1969(B)	—	.10	.25	.50
	1969B	9,147	—	Proof	1.00
	1969(C)	7.025	.20	.30	.50
	1969(H)	Inc. Ab.	1.75	2.50	4.00
	1970(B)	—	—	—	5.00
	1970B	3,046	—	Proof	1.00
	1970(C)	15.300	.10	.25	.50
	1971B	4,375	—	Proof	1.00
	1971(C)	203.100	—	.25	.50
	1971(H)	Inc. Ab.	—	.25	.50

NOTE: 1970(B) is found only in the uncirculated sets of that year. It has a mirrorlike surface.

Obverse 2

KM#	Date	Mintage	VF	XF	Unc
15	1972B	7,895	—	Proof	1.00
(617)	1973B	7,562	—	Proof	1.00
	1974B	—	—	Proof	1.00
	1975B	—	—	Proof	1.00
	1976B	—	—	Proof	1.00
	1977B	—	—	Proof	1.00
	1978B	—	—	Proof	1.00
	1979B	—	—	Proof	1.00
	1980B	—	—	Proof	1.00
	1981B	—	—	Proof	1.00

5 NAYE PAISE

COPPER-NICKEL

KM#	Date	Mintage	VF	XF	Unc
16	1957(B)	227.210	.25	.45	1.00
(577)	1957(C)	Inc. Ab.	.25	.45	1.00
	1958(B)	214.320	.25	.45	1.00
	1958(C)	Inc. Ab.	.25	.45	1.00
	1959(B)	137.105	.25	.45	1.00
	1959(C)	Inc. Ab.	2.50	4.00	7.00
	1960(B)	93.345	.25	.45	1.00
	1960(B)	—	—	Proof	2.00
	1960(C)	Inc. Ab.	.25	.45	1.00
	1960(Hy)	Inc. Ab.	4.00	6.50	11.50
	1961(B)	197.620	.25	.45	1.00
	1961(B)	—	—	Proof	2.00
	1961(C)	Inc. Ab.	.35	.60	1.00
	1961(Hy)	Inc. Ab.	4.00	6.50	11.50
	1962(B)	224.277	.25	.45	1.00
	1962(B)	—	—	Proof	1.50
	1962(C)	Inc. Ab.	.25	.45	1.00
	1962(Hy)	Inc. Ab.	1.50	2.50	5.00

KM#	Date	Mintage	VF	XF	Unc
(577)	1963(B)	332.600	.20	.35	.80
	1963(B)	—	—	Proof	1.50
	1963(C)	Inc. Ab.	2.00	3.00	6.00
	1963(H)	Inc. Ab.	1.50	2.50	5.00

5 PAISE

COPPER-NICKEL
Obverse 1

KM#	Date	Mintage	VF	XF	Unc
17 (585)	1964(B)	156.000	.40	.60	1.00
	1964(C)	Inc. Ab.	.40	.60	1.00
	1964(H)	Inc. Ab.	4.50	7.50	11.50
	1965(B)	203.855	.25	.45	.75
	1965(C)	Inc. Ab.	.40	.60	1.00
	1965(H)	Inc. Ab.	4.50	7.50	11.50
	1966(B)	101.395	.75	1.25	2.00
	1966(C)	Inc. Ab.	.40	.60	1.00

6mm Short 5 — 7mm Tall 5

ALUMINUM
Obverse 1
Rev: 6mm, short 5.

KM#	Date	Mintage	VF	XF	Unc
18.1 (598.1)	1967(B)	608.533	.35	.60	1.00

Rev: 7mm, tall 5.

KM#	Date	Mintage	VF	XF	Unc
18.2 (598.2)	1967(B)	Inc.Ab.	.15	.25	.50
	1967(C)	Inc.Ab.	.15	.25	.50
	1967(H)	Inc.Ab.	.15	.25	.50
	1968(B)	—	3.50	5.00	8.50
	1968(C)	—	3.50	5.00	8.50
	1968(H)	666.750	.75	1.25	2.00
	1971(H)	499.200	.10	.25	.50

Obverse 2

KM#	Date	Mintage	VF	XF	Unc
18.3 (599)	1967(H)	—	4.50	7.00	10.00
	1968(B)	Inc. KM18.2	.15	.25	.50
	1968(C)	Inc. KM18.2	.15	.25	.50
	1968(H)	Inc. KM18.2	.40	.60	1.00
	1969(B)	3.740	2.00	3.50	5.00
	1969B	9,147	—	Proof	1.00
	1970(B)	39.900	1.25	2.00	3.50
	1970B	3,046	—	Proof	1.00
	1970(C)	Inc. Ab.	.25	.35	.60
	1970(H)	Inc. Ab.	.25	.40	.75
	1971(B) Inc. w/1971(H) of KM598	—	.10	.15	.50
	1971B	4,375	—	Proof	1.00
	1971(C)	Inc. Ab.	.10	.15	.50
	1971(H)	—	.25	.45	.75

Obverse 1, new reverse.

KM#	Date	Mintage	VF	XF	Unc
18.4 (618)	1972(H)	512.430	.35	.60	1.00

Rev: Larger 5.

KM#	Date	Mintage	VF	XF	Unc
18.5 (626)	1973(H)	—	2.50	3.50	5.50
	1977(B)	—	2.00	3.00	5.00
	1978(B)	—	.75	1.25	2.00

Obverse 2

KM#	Date	Mintage	VF	XF	Unc
18.6 (619)	1972(B)	Inc. KM18.4	.10	.15	.50
	1972B	7,895	—	Proof	1.00
	1972(C)	Inc. KM18.4	.10	.15	.50
	1972(H)	—	3.50	5.00	7.00
	1973(B)	—	.10	.15	.50

KM#	Date	Mintage	VF	XF	Unc
(619)	1973B	7,562	—	Proof	1.00
	1973(C)	—	.20	.30	.60
	1973(H)	—	.10	.15	.50
	1974B	—	—	Proof	1.00
	1974(B)	—	.10	.15	.50
	1974(C)	—	.10	.15	.50
	1974(H)	—	.10	.15	.50
	1975(B)	—	.10	.15	.50
	1975B	—	—	Proof	1.00
	1975(C)	289.080	.20	.30	.60
	1975(H)	Inc. Ab.	.10	.15	.50
	1976(B)	53.205	.10	.15	.50
	1976(C)	—	—	.10	.20
	1976(H)	—	.10	.15	.50
	1977(B)	257.900	.10	.15	.50
	1977(C)	Inc. Ab.	.10	.15	.50
	1977(H)	Inc. Ab.	.10	.15	.50
	1978(B)	—	Reported, not confirmed		
	1978(C)	—	.10	.15	.50
	1978(H)	—	.10	.15	.50
	1979(B)	—	.10	.15	.50
	1979(C)	—	.20	.35	.80
	1979(H)	—	.10	.15	.50
(598.1)					
	1980(B)	21.440	.10	.15	.50
	1980B	—	—	Proof	1.00
	1980(C)	Inc. Ab.	.20	.30	.60
	1980(H)	Inc. Ab.	.10	.15	.50
	1981B	—	—	Proof	1.00
	1981(C)	4.365	.10	.15	.50
	1981(H)	Inc. Ab.	.10	.15	.50
	1982B	3.499	—	Proof	1.00
	1982(C)	Inc. Ab.	.10	.15	.50
	1982(H)	Inc. Ab.	.10	.15	.50
	1983(C)	3.110	.25	.50	1.00
	1983(H)	Inc. Ab.	.10	.15	.50
	1984(B)	—	Reported, not confirmed		
	1984(C)	—	.25	.50	1.00
	1984(H)	Inc. Ab.	.10	.15	.50

NOTE: Due to faulty dies, 1981(H) often resembles the non-existant 1981(B).

F.A.O. Issue - FOOD & WORK FOR ALL

KM#	Date	Mintage	VF	XF	Unc
19 (640)	1976(B)	34.680	.20	.50	1.00
	1976B	—	—	Proof	1.00
	1976(C)	60.040	.35	.50	1.00
	1976(H)	60.290	.35	.75	1.50

F.A.O. Issue - SAVE FOR DEVELOPMENT

KM#	Date	Mintage	VF	XF	Unc
20 (644)	1977(B)	20.100	.30	.50	1.00
	1977B	2,224	—	Proof	1.25
	1977(C)	40.470	.30	.50	1.00
	1977(H)	20.380	.50	1.00	2.00

F.A.O. Issue - FOOD & SHELTER FOR ALL

KM#	Date	Mintage	VF	XF	Unc
21 (648)	1978(B)	28.440	.35	.50	1.00
	1978B	—	—	Proof	1.25
	1978(C)	30.870	.35	.50	1.00
	1978(H)	21.100	.45	.80	1.50

International Year of the Child

KM#	Date	Mintage	VF	XF	Unc
22 (652)	1979(B)	39.860	.35	.50	1.00
	1979B	—	—	Proof	1.25
	1979(C)	80.370	.35	.50	1.00
	1979(H)	1.100	1.50	2.00	2.50

Weight reduced.

KM#	Date	Mintage	VF	XF	Unc
23 (691)	1984(C)	—	6.00	8.00	10.00
	1985(B)	54.860	.40	.60	1.00
	1985(C)	Inc. Ab.	5.00	7.00	8.50
	1985(H)	Inc. Ab.	.10	.15	.50
	1986(B)	—	Reported, not confirmed		
	1986(C)	—	.10	.15	.50
	1986(H)	—	.10	.15	.50
	1987(B)	—	Reported, not confirmed		
	1987(C)	—	.25	.50	1.00
	1987(H)	—	.15	.20	.50
	1988(C)	—	.10	.15	.50
	1988(H)	—	.10	.15	.50
	1989(C)	—	.10	.15	.45
	1989(H)	—	.10	.15	.45
	1990(C)	—	.10	.15	.45
	1990(H)	—	.10	.15	.45
	1991(C)	—	.10	.15	.45
	1991(H)	—	.10	.15	.45
	1992(B)	—	.30	.50	.80
	1992(C)	—	1.00	1.50	2.00
	1992(H)	—	.10	.25	.35
	1993(C)	—	1.00	1.50	2.00
	1993(H)	—	.15	.35	.50
	1994(H)	—	.10	.15	.35

10 NAYE PAISE

COPPER-NICKEL
Rev: 6.5mm "10".

KM#	Date	Mintage	VF	XF	Unc
24.1 (578.1)	1957(B)	139.655	.25	.50	1.00
	1957(C)	Inc. Ab.	.25	.50	1.00

Rev: 7mm "10".

KM#	Date	Mintage	VF	XF	Unc
24.2 (578.2)	1958(B)	123.160	.25	.50	1.00
	1958(C)	Inc. Ab.	.25	.50	1.00
	1959(B)	148.570	.25	.50	1.00
	1959(C)	Inc. Ab.	.25	.50	1.00
	1960(B)	52.335	.35	.75	2.00
	1960(B)	—	—	Proof	2.00
	1961(B)	172.545	.25	.50	1.00
	1961(B)	—	—	Proof	2.00
	1961(C)	Inc. Ab.	.25	.50	1.00
	1961(Hy)	Inc. Ab.	3.50	6.50	11.50
	1962(B)	172.777	.25	.50	1.00
	1962(B)	—	—	Proof	1.50
	1962(C)	Inc. Ab.	.25	.50	1.00
	1962(Hy)	Inc. Ab.	3.25	5.00	9.00
	1963(B)	182.834	.25	.50	1.00
	1963(B)	—	—	Proof	1.50
	1963(C)	Inc. Ab.	.25	.50	1.00
	1963(H)	Inc. Ab.	1.00	2.50	5.00

10 PAISE

COPPER-NICKEL
Obverse 1. Rev: 6.5mm '10'.

KM#	Date	Mintage	VF	XF	Unc
25 (586)	1964(B) open 4	84.112	.20	.50	1.00
	1964(B) closed 4	Inc. Ab.	5.00	7.00	10.00
	1964(C)	Inc. Ab.	.20	.50	1.00
	1964(H)	Inc. Ab.	3.00	5.00	7.00
	1965(B)	253.430	.20	.40	.75
	1965(C)	Inc. Ab.	.20	.40	.75
	1965(Hy)	Inc. Ab.	4.00	6.00	8.00
	1965(H)	Inc. Ab.	3.00	5.00	7.00
	1966(B)	326.990	.20	.40	.75
	1966(C)	Inc. Ab.	.20	.40	.75
	1966(Hy)	Inc. Ab.	.40	.75	1.25
	1967(B)	59.443	.40	.75	1.25
	1967(C)	Inc. Ab.	.40	.75	1.25
	1967(H)	Inc. Ab.	3.00	5.00	7.00

NICKEL-BRASS
Obverse 1

KM#	Date	Mintage	VF	XF	Unc
26.1 (604)	1968(H)	55.940	—	—	—

Obverse 2. Rev: 6.5mm '10'.

KM#	Date	Mintage	VF	XF	Unc
26.2 (605)	1968(B)	Inc. KM26.1	.20	.50	1.00
	1968(C)	Inc. KM26.1	.20	.50	1.00
	1968(H)	Inc. KM26.1	.20	.50	1.00

Obverse 2. Rev: 7mm '10'.

KM#	Date	Mintage	VF	XF	Unc
26.3 (607)	1969(B)	65.405	.20	.50	1.00
	1969B	9,147	—	Proof	1.50
	1969(C)	Inc. Ab.	.20	.50	1.00
	1969(H)	Inc. Ab.	.20	.50	1.00
	1970(B)	48.400	.20	.50	1.00
	1970B	3,046	—	Proof	1.50
	1970(C)	Inc. Ab.	.20	.50	1.00
	1971(B)	88.800	.20	.50	1.00
	1971B	4,375	—	Proof	1.30

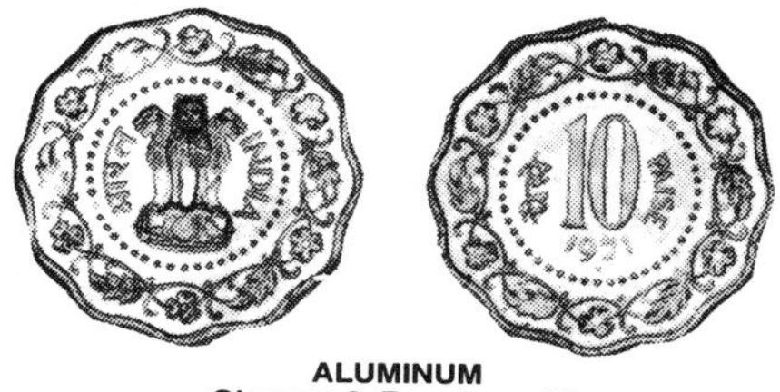

ALUMINUM
Obverse 2. Rev: 9mm 10.

KM#	Date	Mintage	VF	XF	Unc
27.1 (615.1)	1971(B)	146.100	.20	.35	.70
	1971(C)	Inc. Ab.	.20	.35	.70
	1971(H)	Inc. Ab.	.25	.50	1.00
	1972(B)	735.090	.20	.35	.70
	1972B	7,895	—	Proof	1.30
	1972(C)	Inc. Ab.	.20	.35	.70
	1973(B)	—	.20	.30	.70
	1973B	7,567	—	Proof	1.30
	1973(C)	—	.20	.30	.70
	1973(H)	—	.20	.50	1.00
	1974(B)	—	.20	.30	.70
	1974(C)	—	.20	.30	.70
	1974(H)	—	.30	.60	1.25
	1975(B)	—	.20	.30	.70
	1975(C)	298.830	.20	.30	.70
	1976(C)	Inc. Ab.	.25	.60	1.25
	1977(B)	25.288	.25	.50	1.00
	1977(C)	Inc. Ab.	.25	.50	1.00
	1978(B)	48.215	.15	.30	.70
	1978(C)	Inc. Ab.	.15	.30	.70
	1978(H)	Inc. Ab.	.15	.30	.70

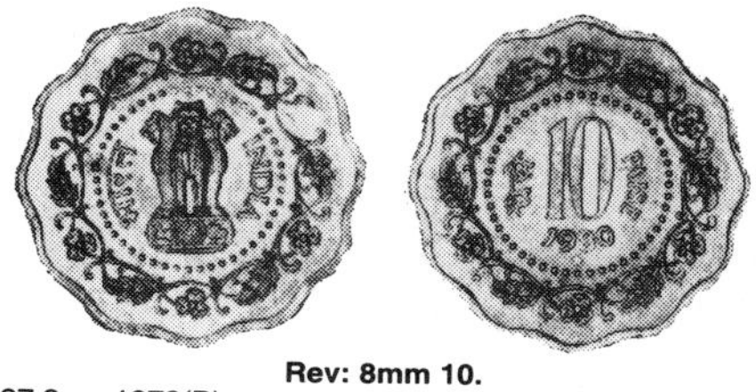

Rev: 8mm 10.

KM#	Date	Mintage	VF	XF	Unc
27.2 (615.2)	1979(B)	—	.40	.60	1.00
	1979(C)	—	.40	.60	1.00
	1979(H)	—	.40	.60	1.00
	1980(C)	—	10.00	12.00	15.00

Obverse 3

KM#	Date	Mintage	VF	XF	Unc
27.3 (615.3)	1980(B)	—	.20	.30	.70
	1980(C)	—	.20	.30	.70
	1980(H)	—	.20	.30	.70
	1981(B)	—	.20	.30	.70
	1981(C)	—	.20	.30	.70
	1982(C)	—	.20	.30	.70
	1982(H)	—	.20	.30	.70

F.A.O. Issue

KM#	Date	Mintage	VF	XF	Unc
28 (631)	1974(B)	146.070	.30	.50	.75
	1974B	—	—	Proof	1.00
	1974(C)	168.500	.30	.50	.75
	1974(H)	10.010	.80	1.50	2.00

F.A.O. Issue - Women's Year

KM#	Date	Mintage	VF	XF	Unc
29 (635)	1975(B)	69.160	.30	.50	.75
	1975B	—	—	Proof	1.00
	1975(C)	84.820	.30	.50	.75

NOTE: Mint mark is below wheat stalk.

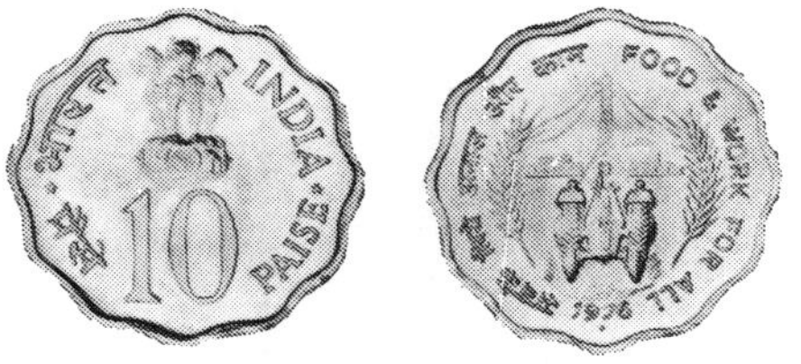

F.A.O. Issue - FOOD & WORK FOR ALL

KM#	Date	Mintage	VF	XF	Unc
30 (641)	1976(B)	36.040	.40	.60	1.00
	1976B	—	—	Proof	1.00
	1976(C)	26.180	.40	.60	1.00

F.A.O. Issue - SAVE FOR DEVELOPMENT

KM#	Date	Mintage	VF	XF	Unc
31 (645)	1977(B)	17.040	.25	.40	.75
	1977B	2,224	—	Proof	1.00
	1977(C)	8.020	.30	.50	1.00

F.A.O. Issue - FOOD & SHELTER FOR ALL

KM#	Date	Mintage	VF	XF	Unc
32 (649)	1978(B)	24.470	.25	.40	.75
	1978B	—	—	Proof	1.00
	1978(C)	26.160	.25	.40	.75
	1978(H)	12.100	.30	.50	1.00

International Year of the Child

KM#	Date	Mintage	VF	XF	Unc
33 (653)	1979(B)	39.270	.25	.40	.75
	1979B	—	—	Proof	1.00
	1979(C)	61.700	.25	.40	.75
	1979(H)	2.250	.60	1.00	2.50

Mule. Obv: KM#32. Rev: KM#33.

KM#	Date	Mintage	VF	XF	Unc
34 (654)	1979(B)	—	5.00	7.50	10.00

Rural Women's Advancement

KM#	Date	Mintage	VF	XF	Unc
35 (658)	1980(B)	38.080	.25	.40	.75
	1980B	—	—	Proof	1.00
	1980(C)	42.830	.25	.40	.75
	1980(H)	11.070	.40	.75	1.25

World Food Day

KM#	Date	Mintage	VF	XF	Unc
36 (662)	1981(B)	83.280	.25	.40	.75
	1981B	—	—	Proof	1.00
	1981(C)	33.930	.25	.50	1.00

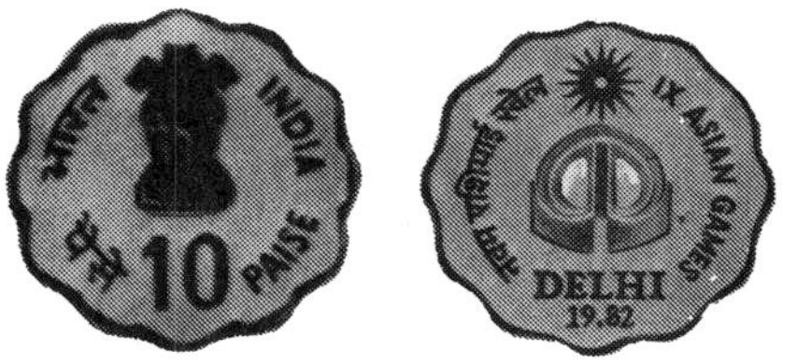

IX Asian Games

KM#	Date	Mintage	VF	XF	Unc
37 (667)	1982(B)	—	.25	.45	.75
	1982B	—	—	Proof	1.00
	1982(C)	30.560	.25	.45	.75
	1982(H)	17.080	.25	.45	.75

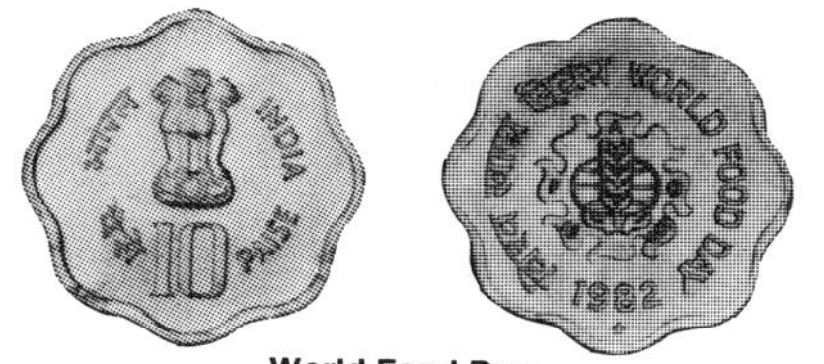

World Food Day

KM#	Date	Mintage	VF	XF	Unc
38 (668)	1982(C)	2.970	.40	.60	1.00
	1982(H)	11.690	.40	.60	1.00

KM#	Date	Mintage	VF	XF	Unc
39 (677)	1983(B)	—	.10	.25	.50
	1983(C)	—	.10	.25	.50
	1983(H)	—	.10	.25	.50
	1984(B)	112.050	.10	.25	.50
	1984(C)	Inc. Ab.	.10	.25	.50
	1984(H)	Inc. Ab.	.10	.25	.50
	1985(B)	184.655	.20	.30	.50
	1985(C)	Inc. Ab.	.20	.30	.50
	1985(H)	Inc. Ab.	.20	.30	.50
	1986(B)	298.525	.10	.15	.30
	1986(C)	Inc. Ab.	.20	.30	.50
	1986(H)	Inc. Ab.	.20	.30	.50
	1987(C)	299.460	.15	.25	.45
	1987(H)	Inc. Ab.	.15	.25	.45
	1988(B)	264.510	.10	.15	.30
	1988(C)	Inc. Ab.	.10	.15	.30
	1988(H)	Inc. Ab.	1.00	1.50	2.00
	1989(B)	—	.15	.25	.45
	1989(C)	—	.15	.25	.45
	1989(H)	—	.15	.25	.45
	1990(B)	—	.25	.40	.75
	1991(B)	—	.15	.25	.45
	1991(C)	—	.15	.25	.45
	1991(H)	—	.15	.25	.45
	1993(C)	—	.15	.30	.60
	1993(H)	—	.30	.50	.75

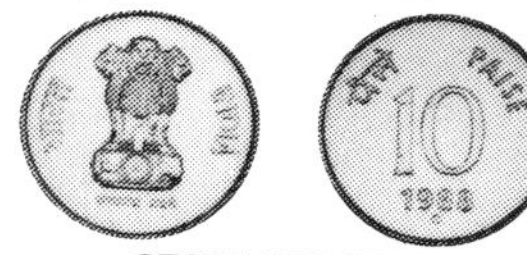

STAINLESS STEEL

KM#	Date	Mintage	VF	XF	Unc
40.1 (702)	1988C	183.040	.10	.15	.25
	1988(B)	4.040	.25	.40	.75
	1988(C) BHARAT	—	3.00	4.00	6.00

MARAT BHARAT

Date	Mintage	VF	XF	Unc
1988(H)	Inc. Ab.	3.00	5.00	8.00

KM#	Date	Mintage	VF	XF	Unc
(702)	1988(N)	—	.15	.25	.40
	1989(B)	—	.60	1.00	1.50
	1989(C) BHARAT	—	.40	.70	1.00
	1989(H)	—	.20	.30	.50
	1989(N)	—	.25	.40	.75
	1990(B)	—	.15	.25	.40
	1990(C)	—	.40	.70	1.00
	1990(H)	—	.20	.30	.50
	1990(N) small mm		.15	.25	.40
	1990(N) large mm		1.25	1.75	2.50
	1991(B)	—	1.00	1.50	2.00
	1991(C)	—	.15	.30	.50
	1991(H)	—	.15	.25	.40
	1991(N)	—	.15	.25	.40
	1992(N)	—	.65	1.00	1.50
	1993(H)	—	.15	.20	.35
	1996(C)	—	.15	.20	.35
	1996(N)	—	.15	.20	.35
	1997(C)	—	.15	.20	.35
	1997(H)	—	.20	.30	.50

NOTE: Two varieties of mintmark size exist.

Error: MARAT for BHARAT.

KM#	Date	Mintage	VF	XF	Unc
40.2 (702)	1988(C) MARAT	—	1.25	2.00	3.00
	1989(C) MARAT	—	5.00	7.00	10.00

20 PAISE

NICKEL-BRASS
Lotus Blossom

KM#	Date	Mintage	VF	XF	Unc
41 (564)	1968(B)	10.585	.50	1.00	1.50
	1968(C)	Inc. Ab.	.50	1.00	1.50
	1969(B)	197.940	.40	.85	1.50
	1969(C)	—	.40	.85	1.50
	1970(B)	Inc. Ab.	.30	.60	1.00
	1970(C)	Inc. Ab.	.30	.60	1.00
	1970(H)	Inc. Ab.	.30	.60	1.00
	1971(B)	124.200	.30	.60	1.00

NOTE: Varieties of high and low date exist.

ALUMINUM-BRONZE
Centennial - Birth of Mahatma Gandhi
Obv. legend: .7-.9mm from rims.

KM#	Date	Mintage	VF	XF	Unc
42.1 (608.1)	ND(1969)(B)	45,010	.40	.65	1.00
	ND(1969)B	9,147	—	Proof	2.00
	ND(1969)(C)	45.070	.50	.80	1.50
	ND(1969)(H)	3.000	.75	1.50	2.50

Obv. legend: 1.2mm from rim.

KM#	Date	Mintage	VF	XF	Unc
42.2 (608.2)	ND(1969)(B)	—	2.00	3.00	5.00
	ND(1969)(C)	—	3.00	5.00	8.00

NOTE: Struck during 1969 and 1970.

Eyes, mustache recut, legends 1.2mm from rim.

KM#	Date	Mintage	VF	XF	Unc
42.3	ND(1969)B	—	.60	1.00	1.50

F.A.O. Issue - FOOD FOR ALL
Wide rims.

KM#	Date	Mintage	VF	XF	Unc
43.1 (612)	1970(B)	5.160	.75	1.25	2.00
	1970B	3,046	—	Proof	2.00
	1970(C)	5.010	.75	1.25	2.00

Narrow rims, lions' fur recut.

KM#	Date	Mintage	VF	XF	Unc
43.2 (616)	1971(B)	.060	.70	.90	1.25
	1971B	4,375	—	Proof	2.00

ALUMINUM

KM#	Date	Mintage	VF	XF	Unc
44 (669)	1982(B)	—	.25	.40	.75
	1982(H)	—	.25	.40	.75
	1982(H w/o mm)	—	.25	.40	.75
	1983(C)	28.505	.25	.40	.75
	1983(H)	Inc. Ab.	.25	.40	.75
	1984(C)	Inc. Ab.	.25	.40	.75
	1984(H)	Inc. Ab.	.25	.40	.75
	1985(B)	84.495	.25	.40	.75
	1985(C)	Inc. Ab.	.25	.40	.75
	1985(H)	Inc. Ab.	.25	.40	.75
	1986(B)	155.610	.25	.40	.75
	1986(C)	Inc. Ab.	.15	.30	.50
	1986(H)	Inc. Ab.	.15	.30	.50
	1987(C)	—	.15	.30	.50
	1987(H)	153.073	.15	.30	.50
	1988(B)	125.048	.15	.30	.50
	1988(C)	Inc. Ab.	.15	.30	.50
	1988(H)	Inc. Ab.	.35	.60	1.00
	1989(C)	—	.35	.60	1.00
	1989(H)	—	.15	.25	.40
	1990(C)	—	.35	.60	1.00
	1990(H)	—	.15	.25	.40
	1991(C)	—	.15	.25	.40
	1991(H)	—	.15	.25	.40
	1992(H)	—	.15	.25	.40
	1994(H)	—	.15	.25	.40

F.A.O. Issue
Similar to 10 Paise, KM#38.

KM#	Date	Mintage	VF	XF	Unc
45 (685)	1982(C)	—	1.25	2.00	3.00
	1982(H)	—	1.00	1.50	2.00

F.A.O. - Fisheries

KM#	Date	Mintage	VF	XF	Unc
46 (678)	1983(C)	Inc. KM44	1.00	1.50	2.00
	1983(H)	Inc. KM44	1.00	1.50	2.00

25 NAYE PAISE

NICKEL
Rev: Small 25.

KM#	Date	Mintage	VF	XF	Unc
47.1 (579.1)	1957(B)	5.640	.75	1.25	2.00
	1957(C)	Inc. Ab.	.75	1.25	2.00
	1959(B)	43.080	.45	.75	1.25
	1959(C)	Inc. Ab.	.45	.75	1.25
	1960(B)	115.320	.30	.60	1.00
	1960(B)	—	—	Proof	2.00
	1960(C)	Inc. Ab.	.30	.60	1.00

Rev: Large 25.

KM#	Date	Mintage	VF	XF	Unc
47.2 (579.2)	1961(B)	109.008	.30	.60	1.00
	1961(B)	—	.30	Proof	2.00
	1961(C)	Inc. Ab.	.30	.60	1.00
	1962(B)	79.242	.30	.60	1.00
	1962(B)	—	.30	Proof	2.00
	1962(C)	Inc. Ab.	.30	.60	1.00
	1963(B)	101.565	.30	.60	1.00
	1963(B)	—	.30	Proof	2.00
	1963(C)	Inc. Ab.	.30	.60	1.00

25 PAISE

NICKEL
Obverse 1, Reverse 1 (lg. 25)

KM#	Date	Mintage	VF	XF	Unc
48.1 (587)	1964(B)	85.321	.30	.60	1.25
	1964(C)	Inc. Ab.	.30	.60	1.25

Obverse 1, Reverse 2 (sm. 25)

KM#	Date	Mintage	VF	XF	Unc
48.2 (594)	1965(B)	143.662	.30	.60	1.00
	1965(C)	Inc. Ab.	.30	.60	1.00
	1966(B)	59.040	.30	.60	1.00
	1966(C)	Inc. Ab.	.30	.60	1.00
	1967(B)	30.027	4.50	6.00	8.00

Obverse 2, Reverse 2

KM#	Date	Mintage	VF	XF	Unc
48.3 (600)	1967(C)	Inc. KM48.2	.30	.70	1.50
	1968(C)	Inc. KM48.2	1.50	2.25	3.50

Obverse 1, lion w/o whiskers.

KM#	Date	Mintage	VF	XF	Unc
48.4 (A620)	1972(B)	—	3.25	4.00	5.00

COPPER-NICKEL
Obverse 1a, lion w/whiskers, faces and wheel redesigned.

KM#	Date	Mintage	VF	XF	Unc
49.1 (620)	1972(B)	367.640	.20	.40	.70
	1972B	7,895	—	Proof	1.00
	1972(H)	Inc. Ab.	.45	.75	1.25
	1973(B)	—	.20	.40	.70
	1973B	7,567	—	Proof	1.00
	1973(H)	—	.35	.60	1.00
	1974(B)	—	.20	.40	.70
	1974B	—	—	Proof	1.00
	1974(H)	—	.45	.75	1.25
	1975(B)	559.980	.20	.40	.70
	1975B	—	—	Proof	1.00
	1975(H)	Inc. Ab.	3.00	4.00	5.00
	1976(B)	30.016	.60	1.00	1.50
	1976B	Inc. Ab.	—	Proof	1.00
	1976(H)	Inc. Ab.	.60	1.00	1.50
	1977(B)	270.520	.20	.40	.70
	1977(C)	Inc. Ab.	.35	.60	1.00
	1977(H)	Inc. Ab.	.35	.60	1.00
	1978B	—	—	Proof	1.00
	1978(C)	131.632	.25	.40	.70
	1978(H)	—	.25	.40	.70
	1979(C)	—	.50	1.00	1.50
	1979(H)	—	.50	1.00	1.50
	1980(C)	6.175	.25	.40	.70
	1980(H)	Inc. Ab.	.25	.40	.70
	1981(B)	11.048	.25	.40	.70
	1981(C)	Inc. Ab.	1.50	2.00	2.50
	1981(H)	Inc. Ab.	.45	.75	1.25
	1982(C)	38.288	.45	.75	1.25
	1983(C)	137.488	.45	.75	1.25
	1984(B)	98.740	.45	.75	1.25
	1984(C)	Inc. Ab.	.45	.75	1.25
	1985(B)	113.872	.45	.75	1.25
	1985C	Inc. Ab.	.15	.25	.50
	1985(C)	Inc. Ab.	.45	.75	1.25
	1985(H)	Inc. Ab.	.45	.75	1.25
	1986(B)	362.624	.60	.90	1.50
	1986(C)	Inc. Ab.	.60	.90	1.50
	1986(H)	Inc. Ab.	.60	.90	1.50
	1987(C)	341.160	.60	.90	1.50
	1987(H)	Inc. Ab.	.60	.90	1.50
	1988(B)	—	—	—	—
	1988(H)	303.252	.60	.90	1.50

Obverse 2
9mm between lion nosetips, 15mm across field.

KM#	Date	Mintage	VF	XF	Unc
49.2 (621)	1972(C)	—	.35	.60	1.00
	1977(B)	Inc. KM49.1	.35	.60	1.00
	1977B	Inc. KM49.1	—	Proof	1.50
	1978(B)	Inc. KM49.1	2.50	3.50	5.00
	1979B	—	—	Proof	1.50

NOTE: Flat edges on 1984(B), (C) and 1985(C) indicate Korean-made blanks.

Obverse 2
10mm between lion nosetips, 16-16.3mm across field. Bull has three legs.

KM#	Date	Mintage	VF	XF	Unc
49.3 (622)	1972(C)	Inc. KM49.1	1.00	1.50	2.50
	1973(C)	—	.60	1.00	1.50
	1974(C)	—	.60	1.00	1.50

Obverse 1b, central lion, bull & horse re-engraved.

KM#	Date	Mintage	VF	XF	Unc
49.4 (A623)	1974(B)	—	3.50	5.00	6.50
	1975(B)	—	4.00	6.00	8.00
	1975(H)	—	1.00	2.00	3.00
	1976(H)	—	6.00	8.00	10.00
	1978(B)	—	2.00	3.00	4.00

KM#	Date	Mintage	VF	XF	Unc
(A623)	1979(B)	—	2.50	3.75	5.00
	1980(B)	—	Reported, not confirmed		
	1981(B)	—	4.00	6.00	8.00

Obverse 3

49.5	1986(B)	—	.15	.30	.50
(B623)	1986(C)	—	.45	.75	1.25
	1986(H)	—	.45	.75	1.25
	1987(B)	—	.15	.30	.50
	1987(C)	—	.25	.40	.70
	1987(C) long 7				
		—	.25	.40	.70
	1988(B)	—	.20	.35	.60
	1988(C) 8's 1.3mm tall				
		—	.45	.75	1.25
	1988(C) 8's 1.8 mm tall				
		—	.45	.75	1.25
	1988(H)	—	.45	.75	1.25
	1989(B)	—	.45	.75	1.25
	1989(C)	—	2.00	2.50	3.00
	1990(B)	—	2.00	2.50	3.00

9 1/2mm between lion nosetips. Bull has four legs.

49.6	1974(C)	—	.30	.50	1.00
	1975(C)	—	.30	.50	1.00
	1976(C)	—	1.00	1.50	2.50

Rural Women's Advancement

50	1980(B)	15.050	.30	.50	1.00
(659)	1980B	—	—	Proof	1.00
	1980(C)	8.520	.50	1.00	1.50
	1980(H)	10.380	1.00	1.50	2.00

World Food Day

51	1981(B)	2.170	1.00	1.50	2.00
(663)	1981B	—	—	Proof	2.00
	1981(C)	4.500	1.00	1.50	2.00
	1981(H)	9.340	1.00	1.50	2.50

IX Asian Games

52	1982(B)	12.000	.30	.50	1.00
(670)	1982B	—	—	Proof	1.00
	1982(C)	12.000	.30	.50	1.00
	1982(H)	.330	2.50	3.50	5.00

Forestry

53	1985(B)	Inc.KM49.1	1.50	2.00	2.75
(692)	1985(C)	—	2.50	3.50	5.00
	1985(H)	Inc.KM49.1	5.00	7.00	10.00

STAINLESS STEEL
Rhinoceros

54	1988C	305.280	.10	.20	.40
(703)	1988(B)	—	.45	.75	1.25
	1988(C)	18.920	.45	.75	1.25
	1988(H)	—	6.00	8.00	10.00
	1988(N)	Inc. Ab.	.45	.75	1.25
	1989(B)	—	.65	1.00	1.50
	1989(C)	—	.65	1.00	1.50
	1989(H)	—	.65	1.00	1.50
	1989(N)	—	.15	.30	.50

KM#	Date	Mintage	VF	XF	Unc
(703)	1990(B)	—	.25	.40	.70
	1990(C)	—	.25	.40	.70
	1990(H)	—	.25	.40	.70
	1990(N) small mm				
		—	.40	.65	1.00
	1991(B)	—	.25	.40	.70
	1991(C)	—	.25	.40	.70
	1991(H)	—	.25	.40	.70
	1991(N)	—	.25	.40	.70
	1992(B)	—	.25	.40	.70
	1992(C)	—	.65	1.00	1.50
	1992(H)	—	.65	1.00	1.50
	1992(N)	—	.15	.30	.50
	1993(B)	—	.50	.70	1.00
	1993(C)	—	.50	.70	1.00
	1993(H)	—	.50	.70	1.00
	1993(N)	—	.50	.70	1.00
	1994(B)	—	.15	.30	.50
	1994(C)	—	.10	.20	.40
	1994(H)	—	.10	.20	.40
	1994(N)	—	.10	.20	.40
	1995(B)	—	.10	.20	.40
	1995(C)	—	.10	.20	.40
	1995(H)	—	.10	.20	.40
	1995(N)	—	.10	.20	.40
	1996(B)	—	.10	.20	.40
	1996(C)	—	.10	.20	.40
	1996(H)	—	.10	.20	.40
	1996(N)	—	.10	.20	.35
	1997(C)	—	.10	.20	.40
	1998(C)	—	.10	.20	.40

NOTE: Varieties of date size exist.

50 NAYE PAISE

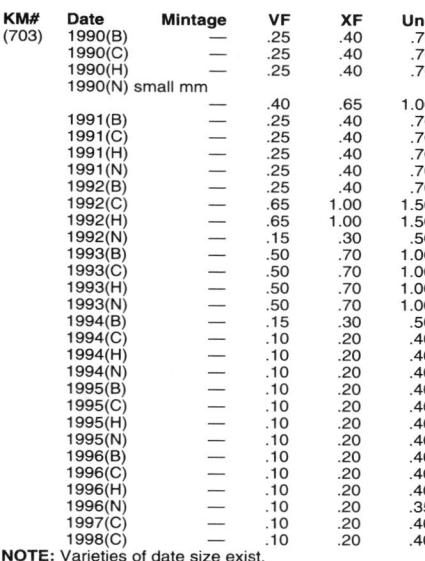

NICKEL

55	1960(B)	11.224	1.00	1.50	2.50
(580)	1960(B)	—	—	Proof	3.00
	1960(C)	Inc. Ab.	.50	1.25	2.00
	1961(B)	45.992	.25	.60	1.25
	1961(B)	—	—	Proof	3.00
	1961(C)	Inc. Ab.	.25	.60	1.25
	1962(B)	64.228	.25	.60	1.25
	1962(B)	—	—	Proof	3.00
	1962(C)	Inc. Ab.	.25	.60	1.25
	1963(B)	58.168	.25	.60	1.25
	1963(B)	—	—	Proof	3.00
	1963(C)	Inc. Ab.	1.00	1.50	2.50

50 PAISE

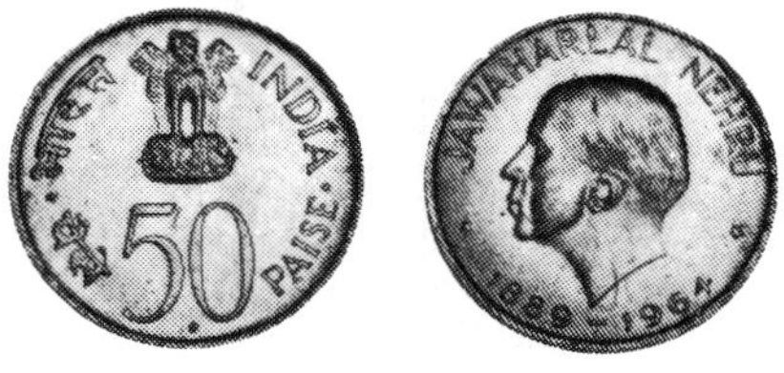

NICKEL
Death of Jawaharlal Nehru
Rev. leg: English.

56	ND(1964)(B)	21.900	.40	.65	1.00
(588)	ND(1964)B	—	—	Proof	2.50
	ND(1964)(C)	7.160	.50	1.00	1.50

Rev. leg: Hindi.

57	ND(1964)(B)	36.190	.40	.65	1.00
(589)	ND(1964)(C)	28.350	.40	.65	1.00

NOTE: Nehru commemorative issues were struck from 1964 until 1967.

Obverse 1, Reverse 1

58.1	1964(C)	23.361	.50	1.00	1.75
(590)	1967(B)	19.267	.50	1.00	1.75

NOTE: Varieties of 1967(B) reverse edges exist, half teeth and the scarce full teeth.

Obverse 2, Reverse 2

KM#	Date	Mintage	VF	XF	Unc
58.2	1967(C)	—	.60	1.00	1.50
(601)	1968(B)	28.076	.25	.60	1.00
	1968(C)	Inc. Ab.	.25	.60	1.00
	1969(B)	59.388	.25	.60	1.00
	1969(C)	Inc. Ab.	.35	.75	1.25
	1970(B)	Inc. Ab.	.35	.75	1.25
	1970(C)	Inc. Ab.	.25	.60	1.00
	1971(C)	57.900	.25	.50	.85

NOTE: A scarce 1968(B) variety exists w/crude obverse, no whiskers, thick horsetail.

Obverse 1, Reverse 2

58.3	1970(B)	Inc. 1969	1.00	2.00	3.00
(613)	1970B	3,046	—	Proof	2.00
	1971B	4,375	—	Proof	2.00

Centennial - Birth of Mahatma Gandhi

59	ND(1969)(B)	10.260	.25	.50	1.00
(609)	ND(1969)B	9,147	—	Proof	2.00
	ND(1969)(C)	12.100	.25	.50	1.00

NOTE: Struck during 1969 and 1970.

COPPER-NICKEL
25th Anniversary of Independence

60	ND(1972)(B)	43.800	.30	.50	1.00
(623)	ND(1972)B	7,895	—	Proof	2.00
	ND(1972)(C)	40.080	.30	.50	1.00

Obverse 2. Rev: Lettering spaced out.

61	1972(B)	—	.35	.60	1.00
(624)	1972(C)	—	.35	.60	1.00
	1973(B)	—	.35	.60	1.00
	1973(C)	—	1.00	1.50	2.50

F.A.O. Issue - Grow More Food

62	1973(B)	28.720	.30	.50	1.00
(628)	1973B	.011	—	Proof	2.00
	1973(C)	40.100	.30	.50	1.00

Obverse 2, Rev. Lettering close.

KM#	Date	Mintage	VF	XF	Unc
63	1974(B)	—	.25	.50	1.00
(632)	1974B	—	—	Proof	2.00
	1974(C)	—	.35	.75	1.50
	1975(B)	225.880	.25	.50	1.00
	1975B	—	—	Proof	2.00
	1975(C)	Inc. Ab.	.25	.50	1.00
	1975(H)	—	—	.75	1.25	2.00
	1976(B)	99.564	.25	.50	1.00
	1976B	Inc. Ab.	—	Proof	2.00
	1976(C)	Inc. Ab.	.35	.75	1.50
	1976(H)	Inc. Ab.	.75	1.25	2.00
	1977(B)	97.272	.25	.50	1.00
	1977B	Inc. Ab.	—	Proof	2.00
	1977(C)	Inc. Ab.	.40	.75	1.50
	1977(H)	Inc. Ab.	.40	.75	1.50
	1978B	25.648	—	Proof	2.00
	1978(C)	—	.25	.50	1.00
	1979B	—	—	Proof	2.00
	1980(B)	—	.25	.50	1.00
	1980B	—	—	Proof	2.00
	1980(C)	—	5.00	8.00	10.00
	1981B	—	—	Proof	2.00
	1983(C)	62.634	4.00	6.50	8.00

National Integration

KM#	Date	Mintage	VF	XF	Unc
64	1982(B)	9.804	.40	.75	1.25
(671)	1982B	—	—	Proof	3.00
	1982(C)	Inc. Ab.	5.00	8.00	10.00

Obverse 3

KM#	Date	Mintage	VF	XF	Unc
65	1984(B)	61.548	.25	.50	.85
(680)	1984(C)	Inc. Ab.	.40	.70	1.50
	1984(H)	—	.75	1.25	2.00
	1985(B)	210.964	.25	.50	.85
	1985(C)	Inc. Ab.	.25	.50	.85
	1985(H)	Inc. Ab.	.40	.70	1.25
	1985(S)	Inc. Ab.	.20	.30	.65
	1986(C)	117.576	.25	.50	.85
	1987(B)	—	.25	.50	.85
	1987(C)	145.140	.25	.50	.85
	1987(H)	Inc. Ab.	.40	.75	1.50
	1988(B)	149.092	.25	.50	.85
	1988(C)	Inc. Ab.	.40	.75	1.50
	1988(H)	Inc. Ab.	.40	.70	1.25
	1989(B)	—	.25	.50	1.00
	1989(C)	—	.40	.75	1.50
	1990(B)	—	.40	.75	1.50

Golden Jubilee of Reserve Bank of India

KM#	Date	Mintage	VF	XF	Unc
66	ND(1985)(B)				
(681)		Inc.KM65	.50	.85	1.75
	ND(1985)B				
		Inc.KM680	—	Proof	15.00
	ND(1985)(C)	—	.65	1.00	2.00
	ND(1985)(H)				
		Inc.KM65	.75	1.25	2.50

Death of Indira Gandhi

KM#	Date	Mintage	VF	XF	Unc
67.1	ND(1985)(B)				
(686)		Inc.KM65	.20	.40	1.00
	ND(1985)B				
		Inc.KM65	—	Proof	17.50
	ND(1985)(C)				
		Inc.KM65	.20	.40	1.00
	ND(1985)(H)				
		Inc.KM65	.65	1.00	1.50

Mule. Obv: KM#68. Rev: KM#67.

KM#	Date	Mintage	VF	XF	Unc
67.2	ND(1985)(C)	—	—	—	—

F.A.O. Fisheries

KM#	Date	Mintage	VF	XF	Unc
68.1	1986(B)	Inc.KM65	.30	.50	1.00
(696)	1986B	Inc.KM65	—	Proof	15.00
	1986(C)	—	.50	1.00	1.75
	1986(H)	Inc.KM65	.40	.75	1.25

Mule. Obv: KM#67. Rev: KM#68.

KM#	Date	Mintage	VF	XF	Unc
68.2	1986(C)	—	—	—	—

STAINLESS STEEL
Parliament Building in New Delhi

KM#	Date	Mintage	VF	XF	Unc
69	1988C	272.160	.20	.30	.50
(704)	1988(B)	—	.20	.40	.75
	1988(C)	2.195	4.00	6.50	8.00
	1988(N)	Inc. Ab.	4.00	6.50	8.00
	1988(N)	—	.20	.40	.75
	1989(B)	—	.20	.40	.75
	1989(C)	—	1.50	2.00	3.00
	1989(H)	—	.50	1.00	2.00
	1989(N)	—	.15	.50	1.00
	1990(B)	—	.15	.50	1.00
	1990(C)	—	.15	.50	1.00
	1990(H)	—	.15	.50	1.00
	1990(N)	—	.15	.50	1.00
	1991(B)	—	.15	.50	1.00
	1991(C)	—	.15	.50	1.00
	1991(H) small mm				
		—	.35	.75	1.50
	1991(H) large mm				
		—	.15	.25	.50
	1991(N)	—	.10	.35	.60
	1992(B)	—	.10	.35	.60
	1992(C)	—	.10	.35	.60
	1992(H)	—	.10	.35	.60
	1992(N)	—	.10	.35	.60
	1993(C)	—	.10	.35	.60
	1993(N)	—	.10	.35	.60
	1994(B)	—	.10	.35	.60
	1994(C)	—	.10	.35	.60
	1994(N)	—	.10	.35	.60
	1995(C)	—	.10	.20	.35
	1995(B)	—	.10	.20	.35
	1995(H)	—	.20	.30	.50
	1995(N)	—	.10	.20	.35
	1996(B)	—	.10	.20	.35
	1996(C)	—	.10	.20	.35
	1996(H)	—	.10	.20	.35
	1996(N)	—	.10	.20	.35
	1997(B)	—	.10	.20	.35
	1997(C)	—	.10	.20	.35
	1997(H)	—	.10	.20	.35
	1997(N)	—	.10	.20	.35
	1998(C)	—	.10	.20	.35

NOTE: Varieties of date size exist.

50th Anniversary of Independence

KM#	Date	Mintage	VF	XF	Unc
70	1997(B)	—	.25	.40	.75
	1997(C)	—	.25	.40	.75
	1997(H)	—	.25	.40	.75
	1997(N)	—	.25	.40	.75

RUPEE

NICKEL, 10.00 g
Obverse 1

KM#	Date	Mintage	VF	XF	Unc
75.1	1962(B)	—	—	Proof	4.00
(581)	1962(C)	3.689	1.00	2.00	3.00

Rev: Smaller date and denomination.

KM#	Date	Mintage	VF	XF	Unc
75.2	1970(B)	Inc. Ab.	3.50	5.00	7.00
(581)	1970B	3,046	—	Proof	3.00
	1971B	4,375	—	Proof	3.00
	1972B	7,895	—	Proof	2.50
	1973B	7,567	—	Proof	2.50
	1974B	—	—	Proof	2.50

Death of Jawaharlal Nehru

KM#	Date	Mintage	VF	XF	Unc
76	ND(1964)(B)	10.010	.65	1.00	2.00
(591)	ND(1964)B	—	—	Proof	5.00
	ND(1964)(C)	10.020	.65	1.00	2.00

NOTE: Nehru commemorative issues were struck until 1967.

Centennial - Birth of Mahatma Gandhi

KM#	Date	Mintage	VF	XF	Unc
77	ND(1969)(B)	5.180	.70	1.25	2.00
(610)	ND(1969)B	9,147	—	Proof	3.00
	ND(1969)(C)	6.690	1.00	1.50	2.50

NOTE: Struck during 1969 and 1970.

COPPER-NICKEL, 8.00 g

KM#	Date	Mintage	VF	XF	Unc
78.1	1975(B)	98.850	.40	.85	1.50
(636)	1975B	—	—	Proof	2.50
	1975(C)	—	6.50	8.00	10.00
	1976(B)	161.895	.35	.75	1.50
	1976B	Inc. Ab.	—	Proof	2.50
	1977(B)	177.105	.35	.75	1.50
	1977B	Inc. Ab.	—	Proof	2.50
	1978(B)	127.348	.40	.80	1.50
	1978B	Inc. Ab.	—	Proof	2.50
	1978(C)	Inc. Ab.	.50	1.00	1.75
	1979(C)	—	8.00	11.00	15.00

Obverse 2

KM#	Date	Mintage	VF	XF	Unc
78.2	1975(C)	Inc. 78.1	.40	.85	1.50
(637)	1976(C)	Inc. 78.1	.50	1.25	2.25
	1997(B)	—	Reported, not confirmed		

Obverse 3

KM#	Date	Mintage	VF	XF	Unc
78.3	1979(B)	—	.35	.60	1.00
(655)	1979B	—	—	Proof	2.50
	1979(C)	—	.40	.75	1.50
	1980(B)	84.768	.35	.60	1.00
	1980B	—	—	Proof	2.50
	1980(C)	Inc. Ab.	.40	.75	1.25
	1981(B)	82.458	.35	.60	1.00
	1981B	—	—	Proof	2.50
	1981(C)	Inc. Ab.	.40	.75	1.25
	1982(B)	116.811	.40	.75	1.25

NOTE: Border varieties of long vs. short teeth on 1981 reverse and 1982 obverse.

15th Anniversary of I.C.D.S.
Milled edge.

KM#	Date	Mintage	VF	XF	Unc
86	ND(1990)(B)	—	.20	.40	1.00
(712)	ND(1990)(H)	—	.40	1.25	2.50

Security Edge.

KM#	Date	Mintage	VF	XF	Unc
79.1	1982(B)	—	2.50	3.50	5.00
(679.1)	1983(B)	32.490	.30	.50	1.00
	1983(C)	Inc. Ab.	.30	.50	1.00
	1984(B)	152.378	.25	.40	.75
	1984(C)	Inc. Ab.	.25	.40	.75
	1984(H)	Inc. Ab.	1.50	2.25	3.00
	1985(B)	444.516	.25	.40	.75
	1985(C)	Inc. Ab.	.25	.40	.75
	1985H	Inc. Ab.	.25	.40	.75
	1985(L)	Inc. Ab.	.25	.40	.75
	1986(B)	1,396.074	.25	.40	.75
	1986(C)	Inc. Ab.	.25	.40	.75
	1986(H)	Inc. Ab.	1.50	2.25	3.00
	1987(B)	685.502	.25	.40	.75
	1987(C)	Inc. Ab.	.25	.40	.75
	1987(H)	Inc. Ab.	.25	.40	.75
	1988(B)	240.447	.75	1.25	2.00
	1988(C)	Inc. Ab.	.25	.40	.75
	1988(H)	Inc. Ab.	.40	.75	1.25
	1989(B)	—	1.50	2.25	3.00
	1989(C)	—	.25	.45	.75
	1989(H)	—	.25	.45	.75
	1990(C)	—	1.50	2.25	3.00
	1990(H)	—	.25	.45	.75

NOTE: Lions' hair and ears on 1984(B)-1989(B) issues vary from others.

Youth Year
Security edge.

KM#	Date	Mintage	VF	XF	Unc
80	1985(B)	Inc.KM79.1	.35	.60	1.25
(693)	1985(C)	Inc.KM79.1	.35	.60	1.25
	1985(C)	Inc.KM79.1	—	Proof	5.00
	1985(H)	—	1.00	1.50	2.50

SAARC Year - Care for the Girl Child

87.1	1990(B)	—	.40	.80	2.00
(713.1)	1990(H)	—	.50	1.00	2.50

Milled Edge.

87.2	1990(B)	—	.65	1.50	3.00
(713.2)					

NOTE: Edge varieties exist.

F.A.O. - Small Farmers

81	1987(B)	234.223	.35	.60	1.25
(699)	1987B	—		Proof	5.00
	1987(C)	Inc. Ab.	.35	.60	1.25
	1987(H)	191.120	.35	.60	1.25

F.A.O. - Farming Scene

88	1990(C)	—	3.00	5.00	8.00
(714)	1990(H)	—	5.00	7.00	10.00

Obv: Horse in pedestal shorter, more detailed.

79.2	1988(B)	—	1.00	1.50	2.50
	1989(N)	—	1.00	1.50	2.50
	1990(N)	—	1.00	1.50	2.50

F.A.O. - Rainfed Farming

82	1988(B)	Inc.KM79.1	1.00	1.50	3.00
(710)	1988(C)	—	1.00	1.50	3.00
	1988(H)	—	1.50	2.50	5.00

Rajiv Gandhi

89	ND(1991)(B)	—	.20	.40	1.00
(715)	ND(1991)(H)	—	.40	.75	2.00

NOTE: Edge varieties exist.
NOTE: The Bombay mm occasionally resembles the Noida mm.

100th Anniversary of Nehru's Birth

83	1989(B)	—	.25	.50	1.00
(705)	1989B	—		Proof	5.00
	1989(H)	—	.50	1.00	2.00
	1989(N)	—	Reported, not confirmed		

Obv: Lions' chest hairs restyled.

79.3	1988(B)	—	.25	.50	1.00
	1989(B)	—	.25	.50	1.00
	1990(B)	—	.25	.50	1.00

Obv: Similar to 79.1.
Milled edge.

79.4	1989(C)	—	5.00	7.00	11.00
	1989(H)	—	—	—	—
	1990(C)	—	.35	.50	1.00
	1990(H)	—	.50	.75	1.50
	1991(C)	—	.35	.50	1.00

NOTE: Traces of security edge are occasionally encountered.

Commonwealth Parliamentary Conference

90	1991(B)	—	.20	.40	1.00
(716)	1991(B)	—	—	P/L	3.00
	1991B	—	—	Proof	5.00

F.A.O. - Food & Environment

84	1989(B)	—	.50	1.25	3.00
(709)	1989(H)	—	4.00	6.00	8.00

Tourism Year

91	1991(B)	—	.20	.40	1.00
(717)	1991(H)	—	.60	1.25	2.50
	1991(B)	—	—	P/L	3.00
	1991B	—	—	Proof	5.00

Dr. Ambedkar
Milled edge.

85	1990(B)	—	.20	.40	1.00
(711)	1990(H)	—	.40	1.25	2.50

STAINLESS STEEL
Milled edge, sometimes faint.

92.1	1992(B)	—	.15	.25	.40
(718)	1992(H)	—	.20	.30	.55
	1993(B)	—	.15	.30	.50
	1993(C)	—	.20	.30	.50
	1993(H)	—	.20	.30	.50
	1993(N)	—	.15	.30	.50

Obv: Lions similar to KM#79.3.

79.5	1990(C)	—	.50	1.00	2.00
	1990(B)	—	.35	.60	1.00
	1991(B)	—	.20	.35	.85
	1991(H)	—	.35	.60	1.00

NOTE: A scarce variety exists for the calcutta (C) mint issues 1989-1991 with side lions having bulging eyes.

KM#	Date	Mintage	VF	XF	Unc
(718)	1994(B)	—	.15	.20	.40
	1994(C)	—	.15	.25	.50
	1994(H)	—	.15	.25	.50
	1994(N)	—	.15	.25	.50
	1995(B)	—	.15	.25	.50
	1995(C)	—	.15	.25	.50
	1995(H)	—	.15	.25	.50
	1995(N)	—	.15	.25	.50
	1996(B)	—	.25	.25	.50
	1996(C)	—	.20	.30	.55
	1996(H)	—	.20	.30	.55
	1996(N)	—	.20	.30	.55

Plain edge.

KM#	Date	Mintage	VF	XF	Unc
92.2	1996(B)	—	.15	.20	.30
	1996(C)	—	.15	.20	.30
	1996(H)	—	.15	.20	.30
	1996(N)	—	.15	.20	.30
	1997(B)	—	.15	.20	.30
	1997(C)	—	.15	.20	.30
	1997(M)	—	.15	.20	.30
	1997(N)	—	.15	.20	.30
	1998(C)	—	.15	.20	.30

COPPER-NICKEL
Milled edge.
Quit India

KM#	Date	Mintage	VF	XF	Unc
93	ND(1992)(B)	—	.35	.85	2.00
(719)	ND(1992)(C)	—	1.00	2.00	5.00
	ND(1992)(H)	—	2.00	3.50	8.00

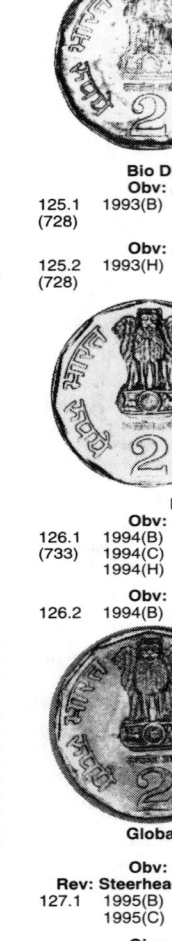

World Food Day

KM#	Date	Mintage	VF	XF	Unc
94 (720)	1992(C)	—	.70	1.50	3.00

Inter Parliamentary Union Conference

KM#	Date	Mintage	VF	XF	Unc
95 (722)	1993(B)	—	.40	1.00	2.50

STAINLESS STEEL
International Year of the Family

KM#	Date	Mintage	VF	XF	Unc
96	1994(B)	—	.40	.75	2.00
(729)	1994(C)	—	1.00	3.00	8.00

Eighth World Tamil Conference
Milled edge.
Obv: Asoka column. Rev: St. Thiruvalluvar.
Similar to 2 Rupees, KM#129.

KM#	Date	Mintage	VF	XF	Unc
97.1	1995(B)	—	.40	.80	1.25
	1995(C)	—	.50	1.00	1.75
	1995(H)	—	.70	1.25	2.00
	1995(N)	—	.50	1.00	1.50

Plain edge.

KM#	Date	Mintage	VF	XF	Unc
97.2	1995(H)	—	4.00	7.00	10.00
	1995(N)	—	4.00	7.00	10.00

2 RUPEES

COPPER-NICKEL
IX Asian Games

KM#	Date	Mintage	VF	XF	Unc
120	1982(B)	12.720	.35	.50	1.25
(672)	1982B	Inc. Ab.	—	Proof	2.50
	1982(C)	Inc. Ab.	.35	.50	1.25

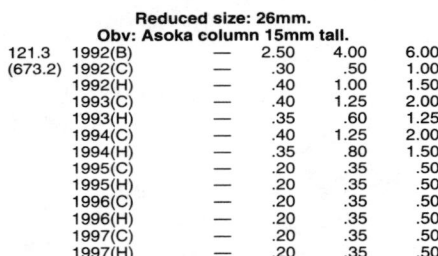

National Integration
Obv: Asoka column 14mm tall. Rev: Small date.

KM#	Date	Mintage	VF	XF	Unc
121.1	1982(B)	Inc. KM120	.30	1.00	1.75
(673.1)	1982B	—	—	Proof	3.50
	1982(C)	Inc. KM120	.30	1.00	2.25

Obv: Asoka column 15mm tall. Rev: Large date.

KM#	Date	Mintage	VF	XF	Unc
121.2	1990(B)	—	.40	1.00	2.25
(673.1)	1990(C)	—	.40	1.00	2.25
	1990(H)	—	.80	3.00	5.00

Reduced size: 26mm.
Obv: Asoka column 15mm tall.

KM#	Date	Mintage	VF	XF	Unc
121.3	1992(B)	—	2.50	4.00	6.00
(673.2)	1992(C)	—	.30	.50	1.00
	1992(H)	—	.40	1.00	1.50
	1993(C)	—	.40	1.25	2.00
	1993(H)	—	.35	.60	1.25
	1994(C)	—	.40	1.25	2.00
	1994(H)	—	.35	.80	1.50
	1995(C)	—	.20	.35	.50
	1995(H)	—	.20	.35	.50
	1996(C)	—	.20	.35	.50
	1996(H)	—	.20	.35	.50
	1997(C)	—	.20	.35	.50
	1997(H)	—	.20	.35	.50

Obv: Asoka column 14mm tall.

KM#	Date	Mintage	VF	XF	Unc
121.4	1992(B)	—	.25	.40	.75
	1992(H)	—	3.25	5.50	7.00
	1993(B)	—	.25	.50	1.00
	1994(B)	—	.20	.35	.75
	1994(H)	—	2.75	5.00	6.50
	1994(N)	—	2.75	5.00	6.50
	1995(B)	—	.20	.30	.40
	1995(H)	—	3.00	5.50	8.00
	1995(N)	—	.20	.35	.50
	1996(B)	—	2.50	4.00	6.00
	1996(B/H)	—	5.00	10.00	15.00
	1996(H)	—	Reported, not confirmed		

Obv: Asoka column 13mm tall.

KM#	Date	Mintage	VF	XF	Unc
121.5	1995(B)	—	2.50	4.00	6.00
	1996(B)	—	.15	.25	.40
	1996(H)	—	.20	.30	.50
	1997(H)	—	.20	.30	.50
	1998(M)	—	.20	.30	.50

Small Family Happy Family
Obv: Asoka column 14mm tall.

KM#	Date	Mintage	VF	XF	Unc
124.1 (723)	1993(B)	—	.50	.90	1.50

Obv: Asoka column 15mm tall.

KM#	Date	Mintage	VF	XF	Unc
124.2 (723)	1993(H)	—	2.00	3.00	5.00

Bio Diversity - World Food Day
Obv: Asoka column 14mm tall.

KM#	Date	Mintage	VF	XF	Unc
125.1 (728)	1993(B)	—	.50	.90	1.50

Obv: Asoka column 15mm tall.

KM#	Date	Mintage	VF	XF	Unc
125.2 (728)	1993(H)	—	2.00	3.00	5.00

FAO - Water For Life
Obv: Asoka column 15mm tall.

KM#	Date	Mintage	VF	XF	Unc
126.1	1994(B)	—	.60	1.10	2.00
(733)	1994(C)	—	1.00	2.00	4.00
	1994(H)	—	2.00	4.50	11.00

Obv: Asoka column 14mm tall.

KM#	Date	Mintage	VF	XF	Unc
126.2	1994(B)	—	2.00	4.50	8.00

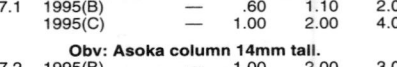

Globalizing Indian Agriculture -
Agriexpo 95
Obv: Asoka column 15mm tall.
Rev: Steerhead in wreath of two stalks of wheat.

KM#	Date	Mintage	VF	XF	Unc
127.1	1995(B)	—	.60	1.10	2.00
	1995(C)	—	1.00	2.00	4.00

Obv: Asoka column 14mm tall.

KM#	Date	Mintage	VF	XF	Unc
127.2	1995(B)	—	1.00	2.00	3.00

Eighth World Tamil Conference
Obv: Asoka column 13mm tall.
Rev: St. Thiruvalluvar.

KM#	Date	Mintage	VF	XF	Unc
128	1995(B)	—	.60	.90	1.25

100th Anniversary - Birth of Patel

KM#	Date	Mintage	VF	XF	Unc
129	1996(B)	—	.60	.90	1.25

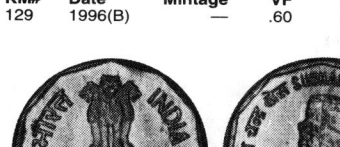

Subhas Chandra Bose

130	1996(C)	—	10.00	12.00	15.00
	1997(B)	—	.60	.90	1.25
	1997(B)	—	—	Proof	3.25
	1997(C)	—	.60	.90	1.25
	1997(H)	—	.60	.90	1.25

50th Anniversary of Independence

131	1997(H)	—	.60	.90	1.25

5 RUPEES

COPPER-NICKEL
Death of Indira Gandhi

150	ND(1985)(B)	59.288	.75	1.50	3.00
(687)	ND(1985)B	Inc. Ab.	—	Proof	27.50
	ND(1985)(H)	Inc. Ab.	3.50	6.00	15.00

Centennial - Nehru's Birth

151	1989(B) short rim teeth				
		—	1.00	2.00	3.00
	1989(B) long rim teeth, tiny mm				
		—	2.00	3.00	4.50
(706)	1989B	—	—	Proof	25.00
	1989(H)	—	3.50	6.00	15.00

Circulation Coinage

154	1992(B)	—	.20	.40	.75
(721)	1992(C)	—	.20	.50	1.00
	1992(H)	—	.20	.40	.75
	1993(B)	—	.20	.40	.75
	1993(C)	—	.20	.40	.75
	1994(B)	—	.20	.40	.75
	1994(C)	—	.20	.40	.75
	1994(H)	—	.20	.40	.75
	1995(B)	—	.20	.40	.75
	1995(C)	—	.20	.40	.75
	1995(H)	—	.20	.40	.75
	1995(N)	—	.20	.40	.75
	1996(B)	—	.20	.40	.75
	1996(C)	—	.20	.40	.75
	1996(H)	—	.20	.40	.75
	1996(N)	—	.20	.40	.75
	1997(C)	—	.20	.40	.75
	1997(H)	—	.20	.40	.75
	1998(C)	—	.20	.40	.75

World of Work

KM#	Date	Mintage	VF	XF	Unc
155	ND(1994)(B)	—	.75	1.00	1.50
(730)	ND(1994)B	—	—	Proof	5.00
	ND(1994)(H)	—	2.50	4.00	8.00
	ND(1994)(N)	—	Reported, not confirmed		

50 Years - United Nations

156	1995(B)	—	.75	1.00	1.50
	1995(H)	—	Reported, not confirmed		
	1995(N)	—	1.00	1.50	2.50

50th Anniversary - FAO
Obv: Asoka column.
Rev: Hand clutching stalks of wheat.

157	1995(B)	—	.75	1.00	1.50
	1995(H)	—	2.50	4.00	8.00
	1995(N)	—	1.00	1.50	2.50

Eighth World Tamil Conference
Obv: Asoka column. Rev: St. Thiruvalluvar.

158	1995(B)	—	.75	1.00	1.50

Mother's Health is Child's Health

159	1996(B)	—	.75	1.00	1.50
	1996(H)	—	.75	1.00	1.50

2nd International Crop Science Conference

160	1996(C)	*.011	5.00	7.00	10.00

NOTE: This conference was never held.

10 RUPEES

15.0000 g, .800 SILVER, .3858 oz ASW
Centennial - Mahatma Gandhi's Birth

185	ND(1969)(B)	3.160	—	4.00	6.00
(611)	ND(1969)B	9,147	—	Proof	8.50
	ND(1969)(C)	.100	—	7.00	10.00

NOTE: Struck during 1969 and 1970.

F.A.O. Issue

KM#	Date	Mintage	VF	XF	Unc
186	1970(B)	.300	—	4.00	7.50
(614)	1970B	3,046	—	Proof	9.00
	1970(C)	.100	—	6.00	10.00
	1971(B)	—	—	6.00	10.00
	1971B	1,594	—	Proof	10.00

INDONESIA

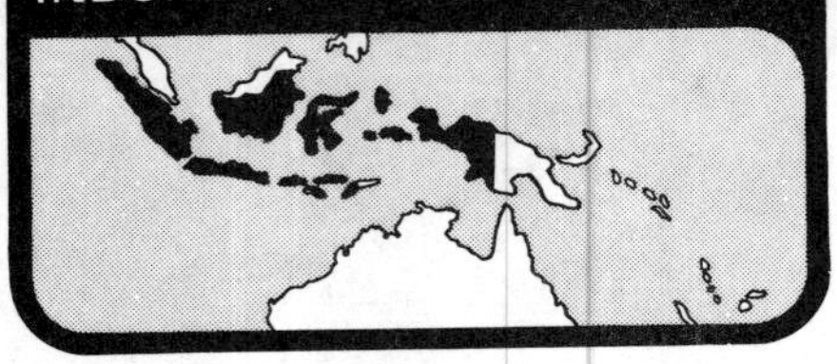

The Republic of Indonesia, the world's largest archipelago, extends for more than 3,000 miles (4,827 km.) along the equator from the mainland of southeast Asia to Australia. The 17,508 islands comprising the archipelago have a combined area of 788,425 sq. mi. (1,919,440 sq. km.) and a population of 202 million, including East Timor. Capital: Jakarta. Petroleum, timber, rubber, and coffee are exported.

Had Columbus succeeded in reaching the fabled Spice Islands, he would have found advanced civilizations a millennium old, and temples still ranked among the finest examples of ancient art. During the opening centuries of the Christian era, the islands were influenced by Hindu priests and traders who spread their culture and religion. Moslem invasions began in the 13th century, fragmenting the island kingdoms into small states which were unable to resist Western colonial infiltration. Portuguese traders established posts in the 16th century, but they were soon outnumbered by the Dutch who arrived in 1596 and gradually asserted control over the islands comprising present-day Indonesia. Dutch dominance, interrupted by British incursions during the Napoleonic Wars, established the Netherlands East Indies as one of the richest colonial possessions in the world.

The Indonesian independence movement, which began between the two world wars, was encouraged by the Japanese during their 3 1/2-year occupation during World War II. Indonesia proclaimed its independence on Aug. 17, 1945, three days after the surrender of Japan and full sovereignty. On Dec. 27, 1949, after four years of guerilla warfare including two large scale campaigns by the Dutch in an effort to reassert control, complete independence was established. Rebellions in Bandung and on the Molluccan Islands occurred in 1950. Through the efforts of President Mohammad Achmad Sukarno (1950-67) the new Republic not only held together but developed within intellectually. West Irian, formerly Netherlands New Guinea, came under the administration of Indonesia on May 1, 1963. In 1965, the army staged an anti-communist coup in which thousands perished.

On November 28, 1975 the Portuguese Province of Timor, an overseas province occupying the eastern half of the East Indian island of Timor, attained independence as the People's Democratic Republic of East Timor. On December 5, 1975 the government of the People's Democratic Republic was seized by a guerrilla faction sympathetic to the Indonesian territorial claim to East Timor which ousted the constitutional government and replaced it with the Provisional Government of East Timor. On July 17, 1976, the Provisional Government enacted a law that dissolved the free republic and made East Timor the 27th province of Indonesia.

Coinage for the Indonesian Archipelago is varied and extensive. The Dutch struck coins for the islands at various mints in the Netherlands and the islands under the auspices of the VOC (United East India Company), the Batavian Republic and the Kingdom of the Netherlands. The British issued a coinage during the various occupations by the British East Indian Company, 1811-24. Modern coinage issued by the Republic of Indonesia includes separate series for West Irian and for the Riau Archipelago, an area of small islands between Singapore and Sumatra.

NETHERLANDS EAST INDIES

RULERS

Dutch, 1816-1942

MINT MARKS

D - Denver, U.S.A.
P - Philadelphia, U.S.A.
S - San Francisco, U.S.A.
(U) - Caduceus, Utrecht

MONETARY SYSTEM

100 Cents = 1 Gulden

1/2 CENT

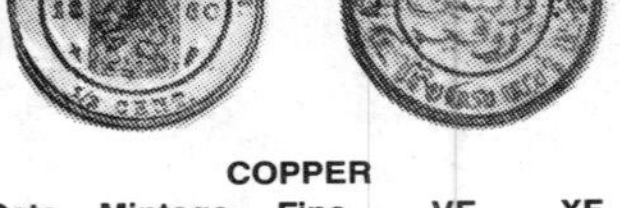

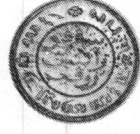

COPPER

KM#	Date	Mintage	Fine	VF	XF	Unc
306	1902(u)	20.000	3.50	6.00	12.50	25.00
	1902(u)	—	—	—	Proof	—
	1908(u)	10.600	3.50	6.00	12.50	25.00
306	1908(u)	—	—	—	Proof	50.00
	1909(u)	4.400	12.50	20.00	35.00	60.00

NOTE: Earlier dates (1855-1860) exist for this type.

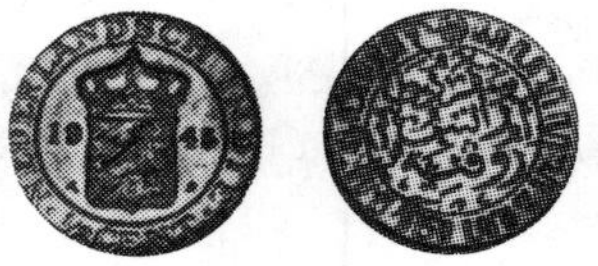

BRONZE
Mintmasters mark: Sea horse

KM#	Date	Mintage	Fine	VF	XF	Unc
314.1	1914(u)	50.000	1.00	2.00	3.25	5.00
	1916(u)	10.000	2.00	6.00	10.00	15.00
	1921(u)	4.000	6.00	12.50	25.00	40.00
	1932(u)	10.000	2.00	6.00	10.00	15.00
	1933(u)	15.000	2.00	3.25	5.00	8.50

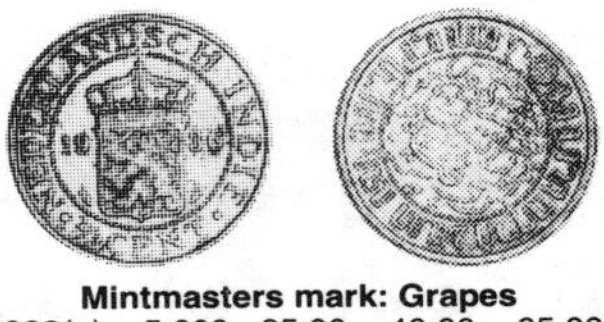

Mintmasters mark: Grapes

KM#	Date	Mintage	Fine	VF	XF	Unc
314.2	1933(u)	5.000	25.00	40.00	65.00	100.00
	1934(u)	30.000	1.25	2.50	5.00	7.00
	1935(u)	14.000	1.75	3.50	7.00	12.50
	1936(u)	12.000	1.75	3.50	7.00	12.50
	1936(u)	—	—	—	Proof	35.00
	1937(u)	8.400	1.25	2.50	5.00	10.00
	1937(u)	—	—	—	Proof	40.00
	1938(u)	3.600	4.00	8.00	15.00	25.00
	1939(u)	2.000	7.50	15.00	50.00	55.00
	1945P	400.000	.10	.25	.50	1.00

CENT

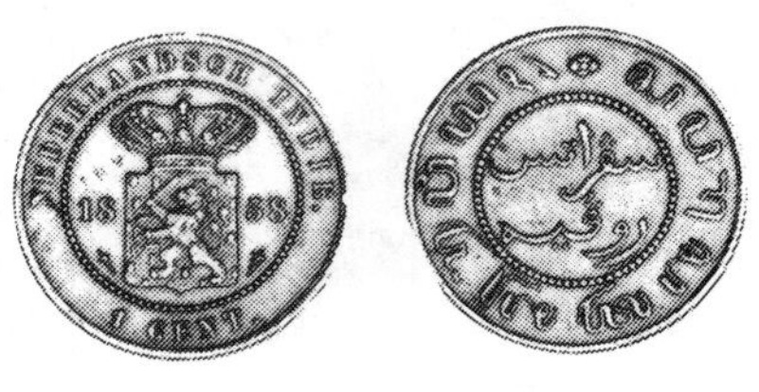

COPPER
Obv: Legend begins and ends beside date.

KM#	Date	Mintage	Fine	VF	XF	Unc
307.2	1901(u)	15.000	6.00	12.50	25.00	50.00
	1901(u)	—	—	—	Proof	60.00
	1902(u)	10.000	3.00	6.00	12.50	25.00
	1907(u)	7.500	5.00	10.00	20.00	35.00
	1907(u)	—	—	—	Proof	100.00
	1908(u)	12.500	3.00	6.00	12.50	25.00
	1908(u)	—	—	—	Proof	60.00
	1909(u)	7.500	3.00	6.00	12.50	25.00
	1912(u)	25.000	3.00	6.00	12.50	25.00

NOTE: Earlier dates (1856-1899) exist for this type.

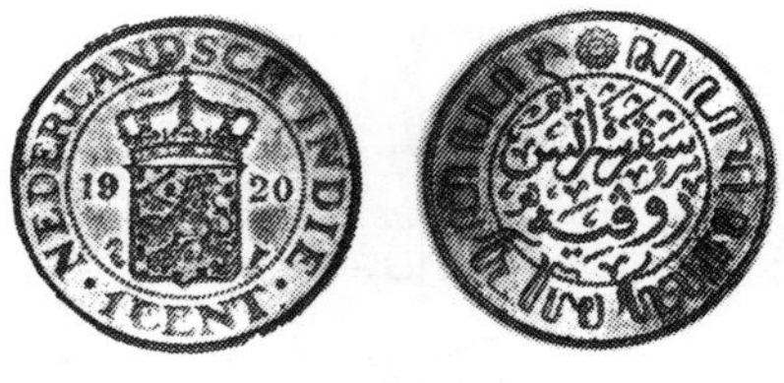

BRONZE

KM#	Date	Mintage	Fine	VF	XF	Unc
315	1914(u)	85.000	1.25	2.50	5.00	10.00
	1914(u)	—	—	—	Proof	40.00
	1916(u)	16.440	2.50	5.00	12.50	25.00
	1919(u)	20.000	2.50	5.00	12.50	25.00
	1919(u)	—	—	—	Proof	65.00
	1920(u)	120.000	1.25	2.50	5.00	10.00
	1926(u)	10.000	5.00	10.00	20.00	35.00
	1929(u)	50.000	1.25	2.50	5.00	10.00
	1929(u)	—	—	—	Proof	100.00

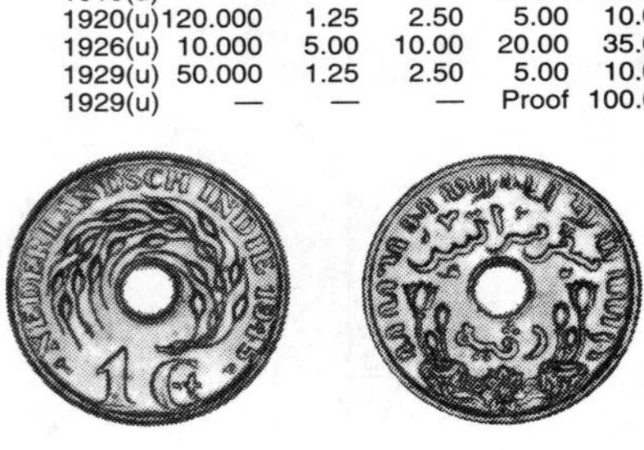

KM#	Date	Mintage	Fine	VF	XF	Unc
317	1936(u)	52.000	.50	1.00	2.00	4.00
	1937(u)	120.400	.50	1.00	2.00	4.00
	1937(u)	—	—	—	Proof	50.00
	1938(u)	150.000	.25	1.25	2.50	5.00
	1939(u)	81.400	.25	1.25	2.50	5.00
	1942P	100.000	.25	.50	1.00	2.00
	1945P	335.000	—	.10	.25	.50
	1945D	133.800	.10	.25	.50	1.00
	1945S	102.568	.10	.25	.50	1.00

2-1/2 CENTS

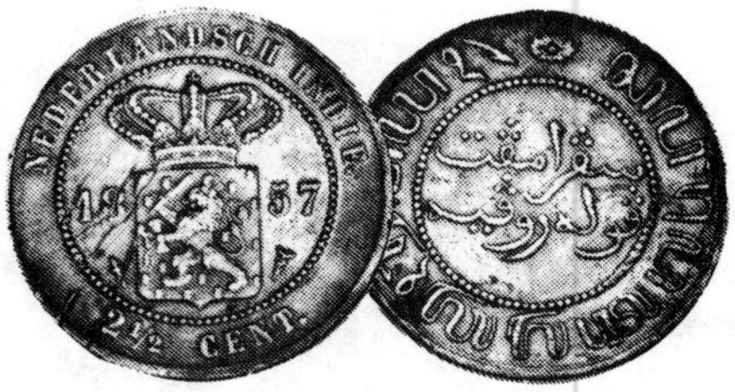

COPPER

KM#	Date	Mintage	Fine	VF	XF	Unc
308	1902(u)	6.000	8.00	12.50	20.00	40.00
	1907(u)	3.000	15.00	25.00	40.00	75.00
	1908(u)	5.940	6.00	10.00	17.50	35.00
	1908(u)	—	—	—	Proof	135.00
	1909(u)	3.060	8.00	12.50	20.00	40.00
	1913(u)	4.000	8.00	12.50	20.00	40.00
	1913(u)	—	—	—	Proof	135.00

NOTE: Earlier dates (1856-1899) exist for this type.

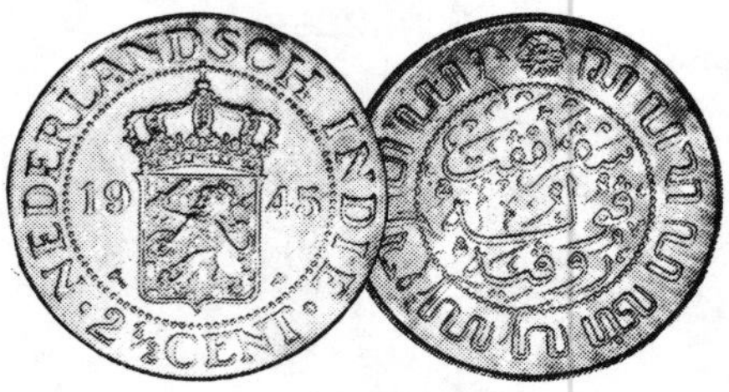

BRONZE

KM#	Date	Mintage	Fine	VF	XF	Unc
316	1914(u)	22.000	2.00	5.00	10.00	17.50
	1914(u)	—	—	—	Proof	165.00
	1915(u)	6.000	5.00	10.00	20.00	45.00
	1920(u)	48.000	2.00	5.00	10.00	17.50
	1920(u)	—	—	—	Proof	165.00
	1945P	200.000	.25	.50	1.00	2.50

5 CENTS

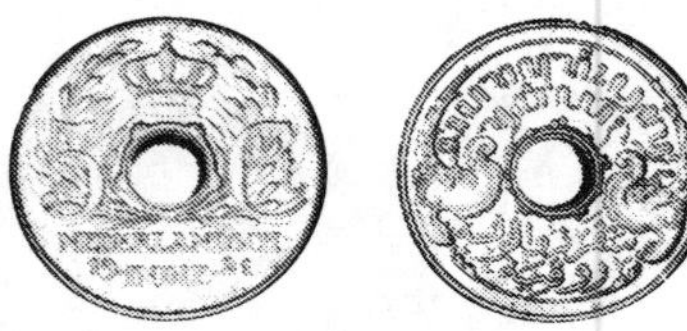

COPPER-NICKEL

KM#	Date	Mintage	Fine	VF	XF	Unc
313	1913(u)	60.000	.75	1.25	2.50	6.00
	1913(u)	—	—	—	Proof	100.00
	1921(u)	40.000	1.25	2.50	6.00	13.50
	1921(u)	—	—	—	Proof	220.00
	1922(u)	20.000	2.00	4.00	8.00	17.50

1/10 GULDEN

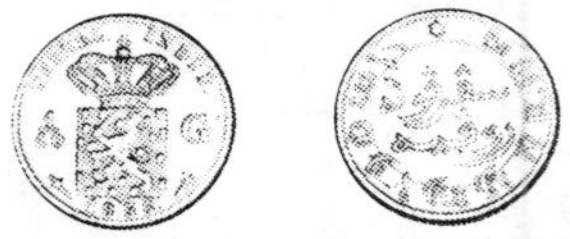

1.2500 g, .720 SILVER, .0289 oz ASW

KM#	Date	Mintage	Fine	VF	XF	Unc
304	1901(u)	5.000	2.00	4.00	7.50	15.00
	1901(u)	—	—	—	Proof	120.00

NOTE: Earlier dates (1854-1900) exist for this type.

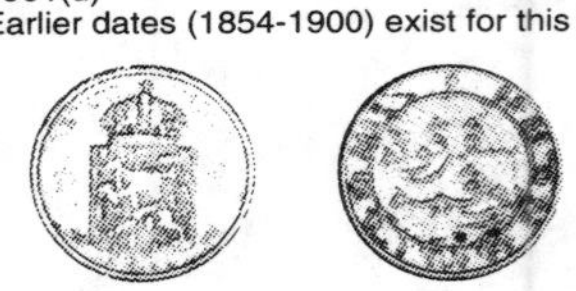

KM#	Date	Mintage	Fine	VF	XF	Unc
309	1903(u)	5.000	2.50	5.00	10.00	20.00
	1903(u)	—	—	—	Proof	110.00
	1904(u)	5.000	2.50	5.00	10.00	20.00
	1905(u)	5.000	2.50	5.00	10.00	20.00
	1906(u)	7.500	1.00	2.50	5.00	10.00
	1907(u)	14.000	1.00	2.50	5.00	10.00
	1907(u)	—	—	—	Proof	55.00
	1908(u)	3.000	2.50	5.00	10.00	20.00
	1909(u)	10.000	1.00	2.50	5.00	10.00
	1909(u)	—	—	—	Proof	110.00

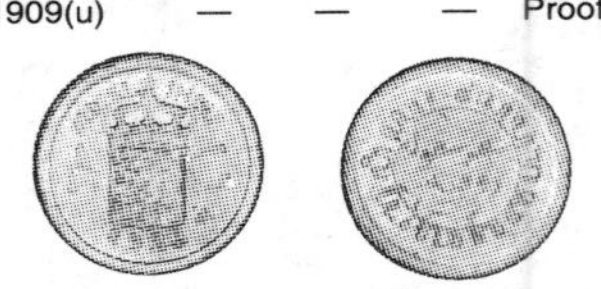

Obv. & rev: Wide rims and small leg.

KM#	Date	Mintage	Fine	VF	XF	Unc
311	1910(u)	15.000	1.50	3.00	5.00	10.00
	1910(u)	—	—	—	Proof	140.00
	1911(u)	10.000	1.50	3.00	5.00	10.00
	1912(u)	25.000	1.00	2.00	5.00	10.00
	1913(u)	15.000	1.00	2.00	5.00	10.00
	1914(u)	25.000	1.00	2.00	5.00	10.00
	1915(u)	15.000	1.00	2.00	5.00	10.00

KM#	Date	Mintage	Fine	VF	XF	Unc
311	1918(u)	30.000	1.00	2.00	5.00	10.00
	1919(u)	20.000	1.00	2.00	5.00	10.00
	1920(u)	8.500	1.50	3.00	6.00	12.50
	1928(u)	30.000	.50	1.00	2.00	4.00
	1930(u)	15.000	.50	1.00	2.00	4.00

Obv. & rev: Narrow rims and large leg.

KM#	Date	Mintage	Fine	VF	XF	Unc
318	1937(u)	20.000	.25	.50	1.00	2.00
	1937(u)	—			Proof	130.00
	1938(u)	30.000	.50	1.00	2.00	4.00
	1939(u)	5.400	1.00	2.00	4.00	8.00
	1939(u)	—			Proof	130.00
	1940(u)	10.000	.50	1.00	2.00	4.00
	1941P	41.850	.15	.35	.65	1.25
	1941S	58.150	.20	.40	.75	1.50
	1942S	75.000	.10	.25	.50	1.00
	1945P	100.720	.10	.25	.50	1.00
	1945S	19.280	.25	.50	1.00	2.00

1/4 GULDEN

3.1800 g, .720 SILVER, .0736 oz ASW

KM#	Date	Mintage	Fine	VF	XF	Unc
305	1901(u)	2.000	10.00	15.00	27.50	45.00
	1901(u)	—			Proof	100.00

NOTE: Earlier dates (1854-1900) exist for this type.

KM#	Date	Mintage	Fine	VF	XF	Unc
310	1903(u)	2.000	4.50	10.00	17.50	35.00
	1903(u)	—			Proof	100.00
	1904(u)	2.000	4.50	10.00	17.50	35.00
	1904(u)	—			Proof	100.00
	1905(u)	2.000	4.50	10.00	17.50	35.00
	1905(u)	—			Proof	170.00
	1906(u)	4.000	4.00	7.50	15.00	30.00
	1907(u)	4.400	4.00	7.50	15.00	30.00
	1907(u)	—			Proof	100.00
	1908(u)	2.000	4.50	10.00	17.50	35.00
	1909(u)	4.000	4.00	7.50	15.00	30.00
	1909(u)	—			Proof	100.00

Obv. & rev: Wide rims and small leg.

KM#	Date	Mintage	Fine	VF	XF	Unc
312	1910(u)	6.000	7.50	15.00	30.00	60.00
	1911(u)	4.000	7.50	15.00	30.00	60.00
	1911(u)	—			Proof	100.00
	1912(u)	10.000	4.00	7.50	15.00	30.00
	1913(u)	6.000	4.00	7.50	15.00	30.00
	1914(u)	10.000	4.00	7.50	15.00	30.00
	1915(u)	6.000	4.00	7.50	15.00	30.00
	1917(u)	12.000	2.00	4.00	8.00	16.00
	1919(u)	6.000	4.00	7.50	15.00	30.00
	1920(u)	20.000	1.25	2.50	5.00	10.00
	1921(u)	24.000	1.25	2.50	5.00	10.00
	1929(u)	5.000	2.00	4.00	8.00	16.00
	1930(u)	7.000	2.00	4.00	8.00	16.00
	1930(u)	—			Proof	160.00

Obv. & rev: Narrow rims and large leg.

KM#	Date	Mintage	Fine	VF	XF	Unc
319	1937(u)	8.000	1.25	2.50	3.75	5.00
	1938(u)	12.000	1.25	2.50	3.75	5.00
	1939(u)	10.400	.75	1.50	3.00	4.00
	1941P	34.947	.25	.50	1.00	2.00
	1941S	5.053	1.25	2.50	3.75	5.00
	1942S	32.000	.25	.50	1.00	2.00
	1945S	56.000	.25	.50	1.00	2.00

TRADE COINAGE
DUCAT

.986 GOLD

These gold coins, intended primarily for circulation in the Netherlands East Indies will be found listed as KM#83 in the Netherlands section.

WORLD WAR II COINAGE

Netherlands and Netherlands East Indies coins of the 1941-45 period were struck at U.S. Mints (P-Philadelphia, D-Denver, S-San Francisco) and bear the mint mark and a palm tree (acorn on Homeland issues) flanking the date. The following issues, KM330 and KM331, are of the usual Netherlands types, being distinguished from similar 1944-45 issues produced in the name of the Homeland by the presence of the palm tree, but were produced for release in the colony. See other related issues under Curacao and Surinam.

HOMELAND COINAGE
GULDEN

10.0000 g, .720 SILVER, .2315 oz ASW

KM#	Date	Mintage	Fine	VF	XF	Unc
330	1943D	20.000	2.75	4.50	7.50	10.00

2 1/2 GULDEN

25.0000 g, .720 SILVER, .5787 oz ASW

331	1943D	2.000	5.00	10.00	15.00	20.00

INDONESIA

MONETARY SYSTEM
100 Sen = 1 Rupiah

SEN

ALUMINUM

KM#	Date	Mintage	VF	XF	Unc
7	1952(u)	100.000	.25	.50	1.00

5 SEN

 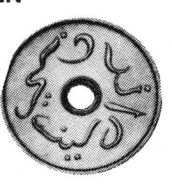

ALUMINUM

KM#	Date	Mintage	VF	XF	Unc
5	1951(u)	—	.10	.25	.50
	1954		.10	.25	.50

10 SEN

ALUMINUM

6	1951(u)	—	.15	.25	.45
	1954	50.000	.15	.25	.45

12	1957	50.224	.25	.50	1.00

25 SEN

ALUMINUM

8	1952(u)	200.00	.10	.20	.40

11	1955	25.767	.10	.20	.40
	1957	99.752	.10	.20	.40

50 SEN

COPPER-NICKEL

9	1952(u)	100.000	.15	.25	.45

	Date	Mintage	VF	XF	Unc
10.1	1954	1.290	1.75	3.00	5.00
	1955	15.000	.15	.25	.45

Rev: Different head, larger lettering.

10.2	1957	24.977	.15	.25	.45

ALUMINUM

KM#	Date	Mintage	VF	XF	Unc
13	1958	100.000	.15	.25	.50

Rev: Modified eagle.

	1959	100.000	.15	.25	.50
14	1961	128.528	.15	.25	.50

RUPIAH

ALUMINUM
Rev: Fantail flycatcher, denomination.

20	1970	136.010	—	.15	.25

2 RUPIAH

ALUMINUM

21	1970	139.230	—	.15	.25

5 RUPIAH

ALUMINUM
Rev: Black drongo, denomination.

22	1970	448.000	.15	.30	.75

Family Planning Program

37	1974	447.910	.10	.15	.30

Family Planning Program

KM#	Date	Mintage	VF	XF	Unc
43	1979	413.200	.10	.15	.30
	1995	6.420	.20	.30	.60
	1996	—	.20	.30	.60

10 RUPIAH

COPPER-NICKEL
F.A.O. Issue

33	1971	286.360	.10	.20	.45

BRASS-CLAD STEEL
National Saving Program

38	1974	222.910	.10	.20	.45

ALUMINUM
F.A.O. Issue

44	1979	285.670	.10	.20	.45

25 RUPIAH

COPPER-NICKEL
Rev: Victoria crowned pigeon, denomination.

34	1971	1221.610	.10	.20	.40

 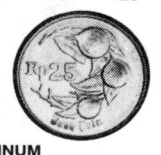

ALUMINUM
Nutmeg Plant

55	1991	30.000	—	—	.75
	1992	64.000	—	—	.75
	1993	20.000	—	—	.75
	1994	250.000	—	—	.75
	1995	184.48	—	—	.75
	1996	—	—	—	.75

50 RUPIAH

COPPER-NICKEL
Rev: Greater bird of paradise, denomination.

35	1971	1035.435	.10	.20	.40

ALUMINUM-BRONZE
Komodo Dragon Lizard

52	1991	67.000	.10	.20	.50
	1992	70.000	.10	.20	.50
	1993	120.000	.10	.20	.50
	1994	300.000	.10	.20	.40
	1995	591.880	.10	.20	.40

KM#	Date	Mintage	VF	XF	Unc
52	1996	—	.10	.20	.40
	1997	.150	.10	.20	.40
	1998	.150	.10	.20	.40

100 RUPIAH

COPPER-NICKEL

36	1973	252.868	.25	.50	1.25

Forestry For Prosperity

42	1978	907.773	.25	.50	1.35

ALUMUNIM-BRONZE
Cow Racing

53	1991	94.000	—	—	.75
	1992	120.000	—	—	.75
	1993	300.000	—	—	.75
	1994	550.000	—	—	.75
	1995	798.100	—	—	.75
	1996	41.000	—	—	.75
	1997	150.000	—	—	.75
	1998	59.000	—	—	.75

500 RUPIAH

ALUMINUM-BRONZE
Stick of Jasmine

54	1991	71.000	—	—	2.50
	1992	100.000	—	—	2.50
	1993	—	—	—	2.50
	1994	—	—	—	2.50

Obv: National emblem. Rev: Denomination.

59	1997	—	—	—	2.50

RIAU ARCHIPELAGO

A group of 3,214 islands off the tip of the Malay Peninsula. Coins were issued near the end of 1963 (although dated 1962) and recalled as worthless on Sept. 30, 1964. They were legal tender from Oct. 15, 1963 to July 1, 1964.

INSCRIPTION ON EDGE
KEPULAUAN RIAU

SEN

ALUMINUM

KM#	Date	Mintage	Fine	VF	XF	Unc
5	1962	—	.35	.75	1.25	2.25

5 SEN

ALUMINUM

6	1962	—	.25	.50	1.00	1.75

10 SEN

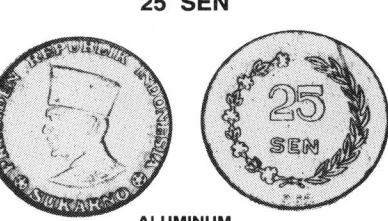

ALUMINUM

7	1962	—	.25	.50	1.00	2.00

25 SEN

ALUMINUM
Rev: "25" style similar to Irian Barat, KM#8.1.

8.1	1962					

Rev: Different style "5".

8.2	1962	—	.75	1.25	2.25	4.50

50 SEN

ALUMINUM
Rev: 17 laurel leaves.

9 (9.1)	1962	—	.75	1.50	2.50	5.00

NOTE: KM#9.2, previously listed here, has been determined to be a contemporary counterfeit. A dropped S in the word SEN is the counterfeits most noticeable feature.

IRIAN BARAT

(West Irian, Irian Jaya, Netherlands New Guinea)

A province of Indonesia comprising the western half of the island of New Guinea. A special set of coins dated 1962 were issued in 1964 and were recalled December 31, 1971 and are no longer legal tender.

NO INSCRIPTION ON EDGE

SEN

ALUMINUM
Plain edge.

KM#	Date	Mintage	Fine	VF	XF	Unc
5	1962		.25	.50	1.00	2.00

5 SEN

ALUMINUM
Plain edge.

6	1962	—	.25	.50	1.00	2.25

10 SEN

ALUMINUM
Plain edge.

7	1962	—	.25	.50	1.25	2.50

25 SEN

ALUMINUM
Reeded edge.

8.1	1962	—	—	—	—	—

Rev: Different style "5".

8.2	1962	—	.75	1.50	2.50	4.75

50 SEN

ALUMINUM
Reeded edge.

9	1962	—	.75	1.50	2.50	5.00

TIMOR

(East Timor)

An island in the Lesser Sunda group, presently part of Indonesia but a treaty of 1859 fixed the division between Portugal and the Netherlands. Portugal discovered and owned the eastern half of the island including the Island of Atauro, located to its north, and the enclave of Ocussi situated on the northeastern portion of the island since 1524 and made coins for this colony. From 1865-1896, Timor was under the jurisdiction of Macao but was made a province in 1896 and became a colony in 1926. All of Timor fell under Japanese occupation from 1942-1945.

In 1951 they became an overseas province.

MONETARY SYSTEM
100 Avos = 1 Pataca

COLONIAL COINAGE

10 AVOS

BRONZE

KM#	Date	Mintage	Fine	VF	XF	Unc
5	1945	.050	20.00	50.00	110.00	250.00
	1948	.500	.65	1.25	3.50	10.00
	1951	6.250	.50	1.00	2.50	8.00

20 AVOS

NICKEL-BRONZE

6	1945	.050	10.00	20.00	45.00	120.00

50 AVOS

3.5000 g, .650 SILVER, .0731 oz ASW

7	1945	.100	20.00	40.00	60.00	125.00
	1948	.500	3.50	6.00	14.00	32.00
	1951	6.250	2.50	3.50	10.00	22.00

MONETARY REFORM

100 Centavos = 1 Escudo

10 CENTAVOS

BRONZE

10	1958	1.000	.65	1.25	3.50	9.00

20 CENTAVOS

BRONZE

17	1970	1.000	.35	.75	1.50	3.50

30 CENTAVOS

BRONZE

11	1958	2.000	.75	1.50	3.00	8.00

50 CENTAVOS

BRONZE

KM#	Date	Mintage	Fine	VF	XF	Unc
18	1970	1.000	.35	.75	1.75	4.50

60 CENTAVOS

COPPER-ZINC-NICKEL

12	1958	1.000	1.00	2.00	5.00	12.00

ESCUDO

COPPER-ZINC-NICKEL

13	1958	1.200	1.25	2.50	6.50	17.50

BRONZE

19	1970	1.200	.50	1.00	2.50	6.00

2-1/2 ESCUDOS

COPPER-NICKEL

20	1970	1.000	.50	1.00	2.00	5.00

3 ESCUDOS

3.5000 g, .650 SILVER, .0731 oz ASW

14	1958	1.000	3.00	5.00	12.00	25.00

5 ESCUDOS

COPPER-NICKEL

21	1970	1.200	.75	1.25	3.00	7.00

6 ESCUDOS

7.0000 g, .650 SILVER, .1463 oz ASW

15	1958	1.000	4.00	6.00	12.00	25.00

10 ESCUDOS

7.0000 g, .650 SILVER, .1463 oz ASW

KM#	Date	Mintage	Fine	VF	XF	Unc
16	1964	.600	4.00	6.00	10.00	22.00

COPPER-NICKEL

22	1970	.700	1.25	2.00	4.00	10.00

IRAN

The Islamic Republic of Iran, located between the Caspian Sea and the Persian Gulf in southwestern Asia, has an area of 636,296 sq. mi. (1,648,000 sq. km.) and a population of 40 million. Capital: Tehran. Although predominantly an agricultural state, Iran depends heavily on oil for foreign exchange. Crude oil, carpets and agricultural products are exported.

Iran (historically known as Persia until 1931AD) is one of the world's most ancient and resilient nations. Strategically astride the lower land gate to Asia, it has been conqueror and conquered, sovereign nation and vassal state, ever emerging from its periods of glory or travail with its culture and political individuality intact. Iran (Persia) was a powerful empire under Cyrus the Great (600-529 B.C.), its borders extending from the Indus to the Nile. It has also been conquered by the predatory empires of antique and recent times - Assyrian, Medean, Macedonian, Seljuq, Turk, Mongol - and more recently been coveted by Russia, the Third Reich and Great Britain. Revolts against the absolute power of the Persian shahs resulted in the establishment of a constitutional monarchy in 1906.

With 4,000 troops, Reza Khan marched on the capital arriving in Tehran in the early morning of Feb. 22, 1921. The government was taken over with hardly a shot and Zia ad-Din was set up as premier, but the real power was with Reza Khan, although he was officially only the minister of war. In 1923, Reza Khan appointed himself prime minister and summoned the "majlis." Who eventually gave him military powers and he became independent of the shah's authority. In 1925 Reza Khan Pahlavi was elected Shah of Persia. A few weeks later his eldest son, Shahpur Mohammed Reza was appointed Crown Prince and was crowned on April 25, 1926.

In 1931 the Kingdom of Persia became known as the Kingdom of Iran. In 1979 the monarchy was toppled and an Islamic Republic proclaimed.

TITLES

دار الخلافة

Dar al-Khilafat

RULERS

Qajar Dynasty

Muzaffar al-Din Shah,
AH1313-1324/1896-1907AD

Muhammad Ali Shah,
AH1324-1327/1907-1909AD

Sultan Ahmad Shah,
AH1327-1344/1909-1925AD

Pahlavi Dynasty

Reza Shah, as prime minister,
SH1302-1304/1923-1925AD
as Shah,
SH1304-1320/1925-1941AD

Mohammad Reza Pahlavi, Shah
SH1320-1358/1941-1979AD

Islamic Republic, SH1358-/1979-AD

MINTNAME

طهران

Tehran

COIN DATING

Iranian coins were dated according to the Moslem lunar calendar until March 21, 1925 (AD), when dating was switched to a new calendar based on the solar year, indicated by the notation SH. The monarchial calender system was adopted in 1976 = MS2535 and was abandoned in 1978 = MS2537. The previously used solar year calendar was restored at that time.

MONETARY SYSTEM

1825-1931
(AH1241-1344, SH1304-09)
50 Dinars = 1 Shahi
20 Shahis = 1 Kran (Qiran)
10 Krans = 1 Toman
1932-Date (SH1310-Date)
5 Dinars = 1 Shahi
20 Shahis = 1 Rial (100 Dinars)
10 Rials = 1 Toman

NOTE: The Toman ceased to be an official unit in 1932, but continues to be applied in popular usage. Thus, '135 Rials' is always expressed as '13 Toman, 5 Rials'. The term 'Rial' is often used in conversation, as well as either 'Kran' or 'Ezar' (short for Hazar = 1000) is used.

NOTE: The Law of 18 March 1930 fixed the gold Pahlavi at 20 Rials. No gold coins were struck. The Law of 13 March 1932 divided the Pahlavi into 100 Rials, instead of 20. The Rial's weight was reduced from 0.3661 grams of pure gold to 0.0732. Since 1937 gold has been allowed to float and the Pahlavi is quoted daily in Rials in the marketplaces.

50 DINARS

COPPER-NICKEL

KM#	Date	Mintage	Fine	VF	XF	Unc
961 (Y23)	AH1318	10.000	.75	1.50	4.00	8.00
	1319	12.000	.75	1.50	4.00	8.00
	1321	10.000	.75	1.50	4.00	8.00
	1326	8.000	1.25	2.50	10.00	20.00
	1332	6.000	1.00	2.00	5.00	12.50
	1337	7.000	.75	1.50	3.50	7.50

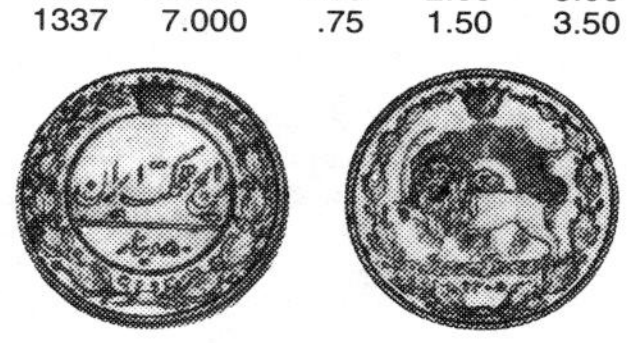

KM#	Date	Mintage	Fine	VF	XF	Unc
1091 (Y95)	SH1305	11.000	.80	2.00	5.00	12.50
	1307	2.500	.80	2.00	5.00	12.50

100 DINARS

COPPER-NICKEL

KM#	Date	Mintage	Fine	VF	XF	Unc
962 (Y24)	AH1318	10.000	1.00	1.50	4.00	10.00
	1319	9.000	.75	1.50	4.00	8.00
	1321/19	5.000	4.00	6.00	11.50	30.00
	1321	Inc. Ab.	.75	1.50	4.00	8.00
	1326	6.000	1.50	2.50	6.00	15.00
	1332	5.000	1.00	2.00	5.00	12.50
	1337	6.500	.75	1.50	3.00	6.50

KM#	Date	Mintage	Fine	VF	XF	Unc
1092 (Y96)	SH1305	4.500	1.00	1.50	3.50	10.00
	1307	3.750	1.00	1.50	3.50	10.00

SHAHI SEFID

(White Shahi)

Called the White (i.e., silver) Shahi to distinguish it from the Black or Copper Shahi, the Shahi Sefid was actually worth 3 Shahis (150 Dinars) or 3-1/8 Shahis (156-1/4 Dinars). It was used primarily for distribution on New Year's day (Now-Ruz) as good-luck gifts. Since 1926 special privately struck tokens, having no monetary value, have been used instead of coins.

The Shahi Sefid, worth 150 or 156-1/4 Dinars, was broader, but much thinner, than the 1/4 Kran (Rob'i), worth 250 Dinars.

0.6908 g, .900 SILVER, .0200 oz ASW

Obv. leg: *Muzaffar al-din Shah.*

KM#	Date	Mintage	VG	Fine	VF	XF
965 (Y25)	AH1319	—	8.00	15.00	30.00	60.00
	1320	.150	8.00	15.00	30.00	60.00
	8310 (error)		8.00	15.00	30.00	60.00
	1039 (error)		15.00	25.00	50.00	100.00
	ND	—	4.00	8.00	20.00	40.00

NOTE: Earlier dates (AH1313-1318) exist for this type.

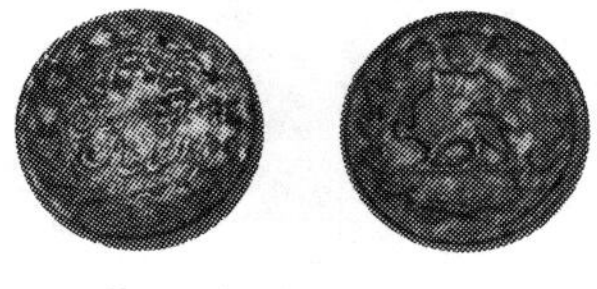

Denomination omitted.

KM#	Date	Mintage	VG	Fine	VF	XF
966 (Y25a)	AH1319	—	—	—	Rare	—
	ND	—	25.00	50.00	80.00	165.00

NOTE: A number of varieties and mulings of KM#965 and KM#966 with other denominations, esp. 1/4 Krans and 500 Dinar pieces, are reported. These command a premium over others of the same types.

NOTE: A total of 58,000 pieces were reported struck in AH1322, 1323 and 1324, but none are known with those dates. The specimens were either struck from old dies or were undated types.

Obv. leg: *Muzaffar al-din Shah.*
Rev. leg: *Sahib al-Zaman.*

KM#	Date	Mintage	VG	Fine	VF	XF
967 (Y-A25)	ND	—	25.00	50.00	85.00	165.00

NOTE: Thick and thin lettering varieties exist.

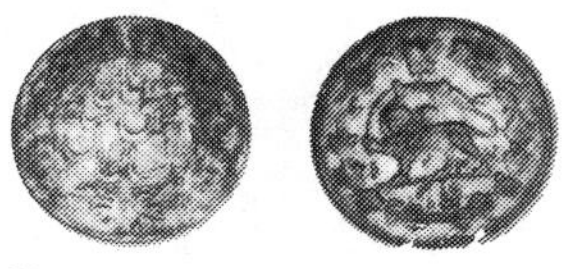

Obv. leg: *Muhammad Ali Shah.*

KM#	Date	Mintage	VG	Fine	VF	XF
1006 (Y44)	AH1325	—	15.00	30.00	60.00	110.00
	1326	—	10.00	16.00	32.00	65.00
	1327	—	8.00	12.00	25.00	52.00

Obv. leg: *Sahib al-Zaman.*

KM#	Date	Mintage	VG	Fine	VF	XF
1007 (Y-B44)	AH1326	—	40.00	60.00	125.00	175.00

Obv. KM#1006. Rev: Obv. of KM#1007.

KM#	Date	Mintage	VG	Fine	VF	XF
1008 (Y-A44)	ND	—	30.00	50.00	80.00	150.00

Obv. leg: *Ahmad Shah.*
Rev: Date below wreath.

KM#	Date	Mintage	VG	Fine	VF	XF
1031 (Y64)	AH1328	—	3.00	5.00	10.00	20.00
	1329	—	3.00	6.00	12.00	25.00
	1330	.189	2.00	4.00	10.00	20.00

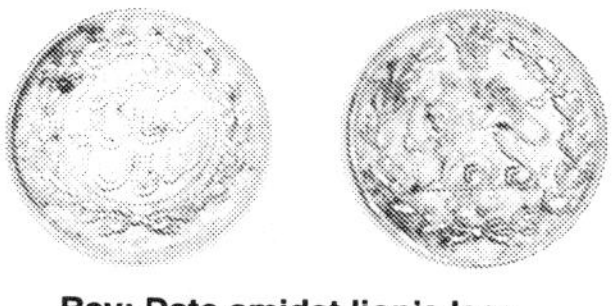

Rev: Date amidst lion's legs.

KM#	Date	Mintage	VG	Fine	VF	XF
1032 (Y-A64)	AH1332	.010	20.00	30.00	50.00	85.00

Obv. leg: *Ahmad Shah.*
Rev. leg: *Sahib-al-Zaman.*

KM#	Date	Mintage	VG	Fine	VF	XF
1033 (Y-B64)	ND	—	40.00	60.00	125.00	200.00

KM#	Date	Mintage	VG	Fine	VF	XF
1047 (Y-A70)	AH1333	.078	2.00	5.00	10.00	20.00
	1334	.006	4.00	12.00	20.00	40.00
	1335	.073	3.00	8.00	15.00	30.00
	1335 dated 1337 on rev. amid legs	Inc. Ab.	20.00	40.00	80.00	165.00
	1337	.076	3.00	8.00	15.00	30.00
	1337 also dated on rev.	—	20.00	40.00	75.00	150.00
	1339	.010	4.00	12.00	20.00	40.00
	1342	.020	4.00	12.00	20.00	40.00

NOTE: Varieties exist.

Obv: KM#1047. Rev. leg: *Sahib-al-Zaman.*

KM#	Date	Mintage	VG	Fine	VF	XF
1048 (Y-A70a)	AH1335	—	30.00	50.00	80.00	150.00

NOTE: Mintage included in KM#1047 of AH1335.

Obv. leg: *Sahib al-Zaman.*

KM#	Date	Mintage	VG	Fine	VF	XF
1049 (Y-B70)	AH1332	Inc. KM#1032	5.00	10.00	18.00	35.00
	1333	Inc. KM#1047	5.00	10.00	20.00	40.00
	1337	Inc. KM#1047	5.00	10.00	20.00	40.00
	1341	.003	10.00	15.00	25.00	50.00
	1342	Inc. KM#1047	10.00	15.00	25.00	50.00
	ND	—	5.00	10.00	20.00	40.00

Obv: KM#1047 dated AH1339. Rev: Similar to KM#1049 w/AH1341 between lions legs, AH1327 below wreath.

KM#	Date	Mintage	VG	Fine	VF	XF
1050 (Y-D70)	AH1339//1341-1327	—	30.00	50.00	80.00	150.00

NOTE: Numerous silver Nouruz tokens, some with dates SH1328-1346, are available in Tehran for a fraction of the price of true Shahis. A selection of these will be listed in a future edition of *Unusual World Coins.*

1/4 KRAN

(Rob'i = 5 Shahis)

1.1513 g, .900 SILVER, 15mm, .0333 oz ASW
Obv. leg: *Muzaffar al-din Shah.*

KM#	Date	Mintage	VG	Fine	VF	XF
968 (Y26)	AH1319	—	12.50	20.00	35.00	65.00
	ND	—	3.00	8.00	15.00	28.00

NOTE: Earlier dates (AH1314-1318) exist for this type.
NOTE: 300 specimens reportedly struck in AH1322, but none known to exist.

Obv. leg: *Muhammad Ali Shah.*

KM#	Date	Mintage	VG	Fine	VF	XF
1009 (Y45)	AH1325	—	20.00	30.00	50.00	100.00
	1326	—	7.50	15.00	27.50	40.00
	1327	—	5.00	10.00	20.00	35.00

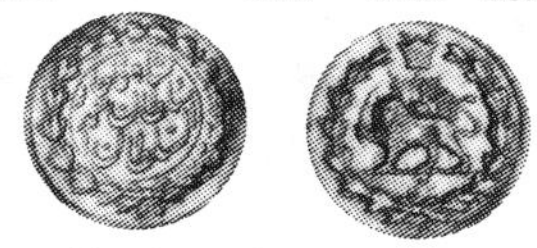

Obv. leg: *Ahmad Shah.*

KM#	Date	Mintage	VG	Fine	VF	XF
1035 (Y65)	AH1327	—	3.00	5.00	10.00	20.00
	1328	—	2.00	4.00	7.50	15.00
	1329	.130	7.50	12.50	20.00	40.00
	1330	.156	2.00	4.00	7.50	15.00
	1331	.030	— Reported, not confirmed			
	1313 (error for 1331)	Inc. Ab.	— Reported, not confirmed			

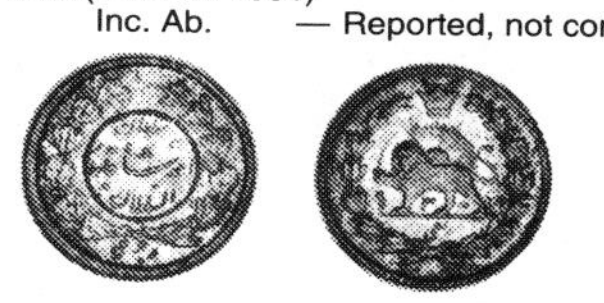

Rev: Date amidst legs.

KM#	Date	Mintage	VG	Fine	VF	XF
1051 (Y-C70.1)	AH1332	.252	2.00	5.00	10.00	20.00
	1333	Inc. Ab.	3.00	6.00	12.00	25.00
	1334	.070	5.00	10.00	20.00	50.00
	1335	.260	2.00	4.00	8.00	15.00
	1336	.160	2.00	4.00	8.00	15.00
	1337	.080	3.00	6.00	12.00	25.00
	1339	.028	4.00	9.00	15.00	30.00
	1341	.022	5.00	12.00	20.00	40.00
	1342	.110	3.00	6.00	12.00	25.00
	1343	.186	2.00	4.00	8.00	15.00

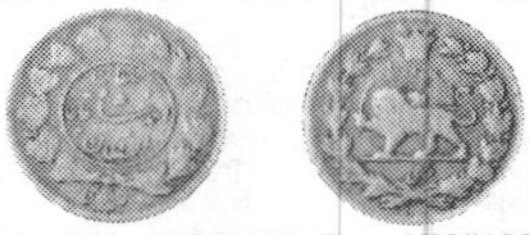

Mule. Obv: KM#1051. Rev: KM#1009.

1052 (Y-C70.2)	AH1327	—	30.00	60.00	125.00	175.00
	ND	—	20.00	40.00	60.00	115.00

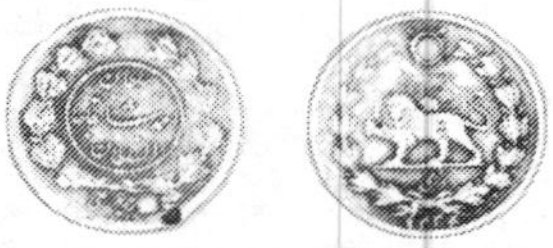

Obv: KM#1051, date below wreath.

1053 (Y-C70.3)	AH1334	Inc. KM#1051	40.00	75.00	150.00	250.00

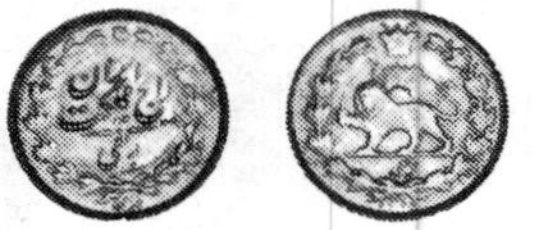

1093 (Y100)	SH1304	*.024	7.50	20.00	50.00	85.00

NOTE: 8,000 reported struck in SH1305, but that year not yet found and presumed not to exist.

500 DINARS

(10 Shahis = 1/2 Kran)

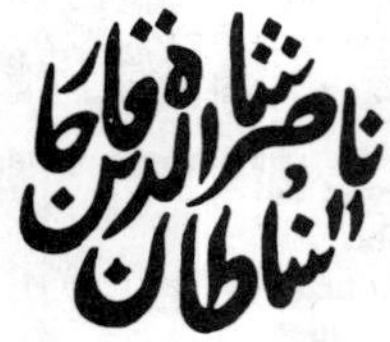

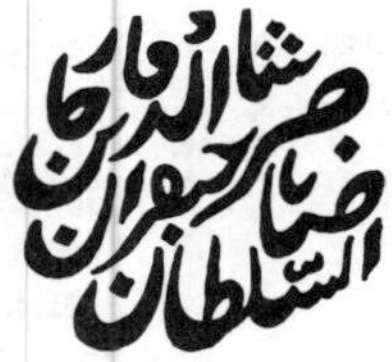

First Nasir al-din legend Second Nasir al-din legend with *Sahibqiran* added

Forms of the denomination:

500 DINARS: ۵۰۰ دینار

or

پانصد دینار

10 SHAHIS: ده شاهی

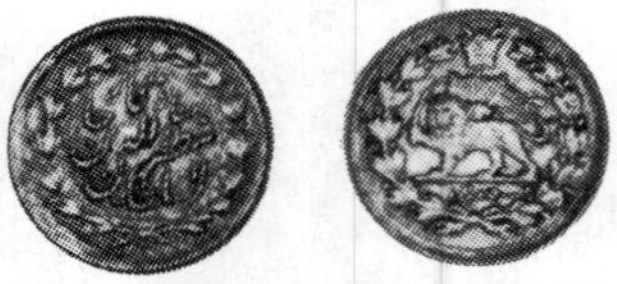

2.3025 g, .900 SILVER, .0666 oz ASW
Obv. leg: *Muzaffar al-din, 500 Dinars*
Rev: Date amidst legs, arranged variously.

969 (Y27.1)	AH1319	—	12.50	20.00	40.00	100.00
	1322	—	10.00	20.00	30.00	50.00
	ND	—	5.00	10.00	20.00	35.00

NOTE: Earlier dates (AH1313-1318) exist for this type.

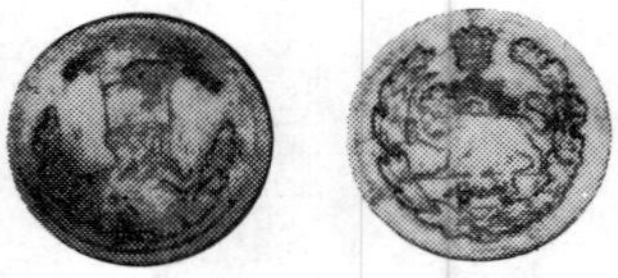

977 (Y30)	AH1323	.130	15.00	20.00	35.00	80.00

NOTE: AH1319 is a pattern.

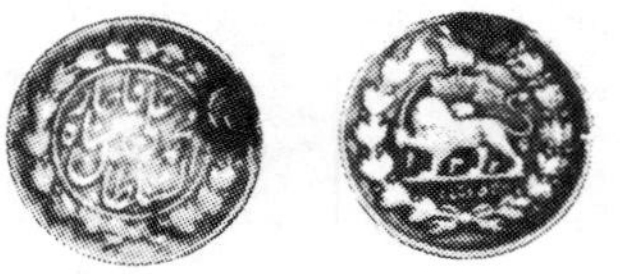

Obv. leg: *Muhammad Ali Shah.*

KM#	Date	Mintage	VG	Fine	VF	XF
1010 (Y46)	AH1325	.218	20.00	40.00	75.00	160.00
	1326	.218	15.00	25.00	50.00	110.00
	1336 (error for 1326)	Inc. Ab.	20.00	35.00	60.00	125.00

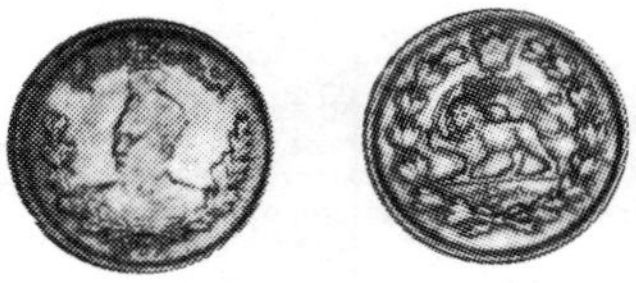

Obv: Date.

1013 (Y48)	AH1326	Inc. KM1010	20.00	40.00	85.00	150.00
	1327	—	20.00	40.00	85.00	150.00

Obv: KM#1013. Rev: KM#1010.
Obv. and rev: Date.

1014 (Y48a)	AH1325	—	75.00	125.00	175.00	320.00
	1326	—	60.00	100.00	150.00	240.00

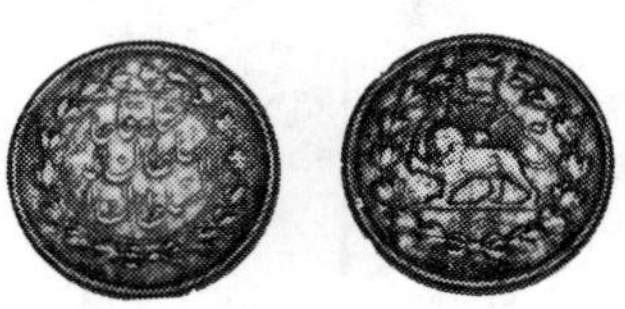

Obv. leg: *Ahmad Shah.*

1036 (Y66)	AH1327	—	3.00	5.00	12.50	20.00
	1328	—	3.00	5.00	12.50	20.00
	1329	.044	6.00	10.00	20.00	40.00
	1330	.627	3.00	5.00	12.50	20.00

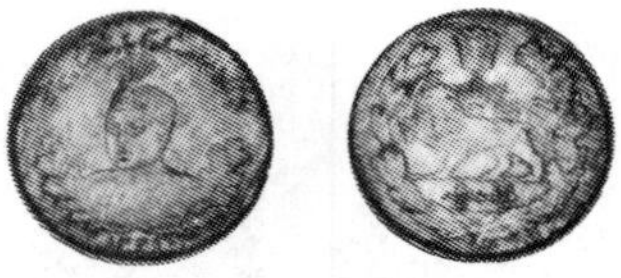

Obv: Date.

1054 (Y70)	AH1331	Inc. 1330	1.50	3.00	6.00	15.00
	1332	.560	1.00	2.00	5.00	10.00
	1333	.292	1.00	2.00	5.00	10.00
	1334	.065	1.50	3.00	6.00	12.00
	1335	.150	4.00	8.00	15.00	30.00
	1336	.240	2.50	4.00	8.00	20.00
	1339	—	10.00	17.50	25.00	40.00
	1343	.160	3.00	6.00	10.00	25.00

NOTE: 10,000 reported struck in AH1337 probably dated AH1336.

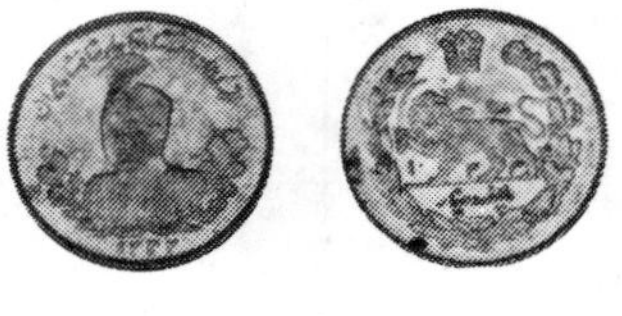

Obv. and rev: Date.

1055 (Y70a)	AH1332	Inc. KM1054	15.00	30.00	50.00	90.00

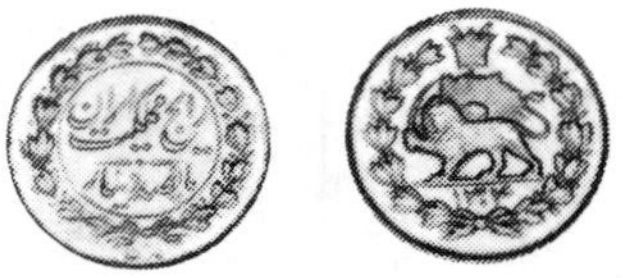

KM#	Date	Mintage	Fine	VF	XF	Unc
1094 (Y-A101)	SH1304	—	450.00	525.00	700.00	1000.

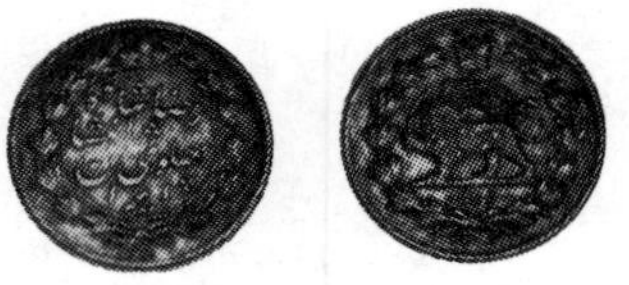

Obv. leg: *Reza Shah.*

1098 (Y105)	SH1305	.010	75.00	125.00	200.00	400.00

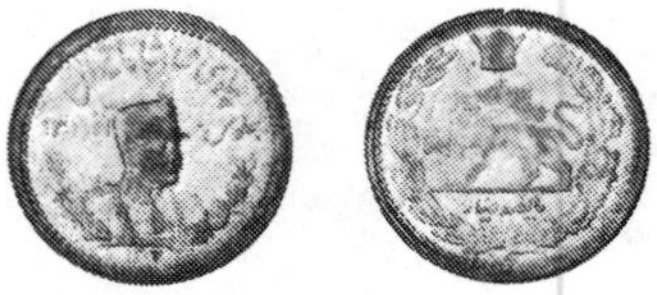

KM#	Date	Mintage	Fine	VF	XF	Unc
1102 (Y-A109)	SH1306	.005	40.00	60.00	85.00	120.00
	1307	.046	4.50	7.50	15.00	30.00
	1308	.464	4.50	7.50	15.00	30.00

NOTE: Some of the coins reported in SH1308 were dated 1307.

1000 DINARS

(Kran, Qiran)

Forms of the denomination:

1000 DINARS: یکهزار دینار

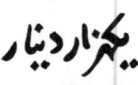

1 KRAN: یکقران

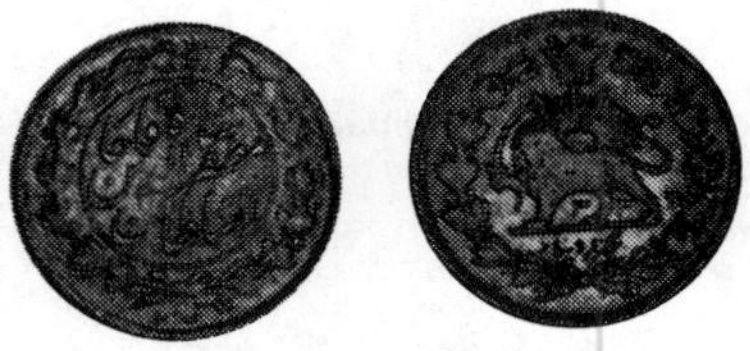

Obv: Crown added above leg.
Rev: Date amidst lion's legs.

972 (Y-A27a)	AH1319	—	150.00	225.00	350.00	—
	1322	—	75.00	150.00	225.00	—

NOTE: Earlier dates (AH1317-1318) exist for this type.

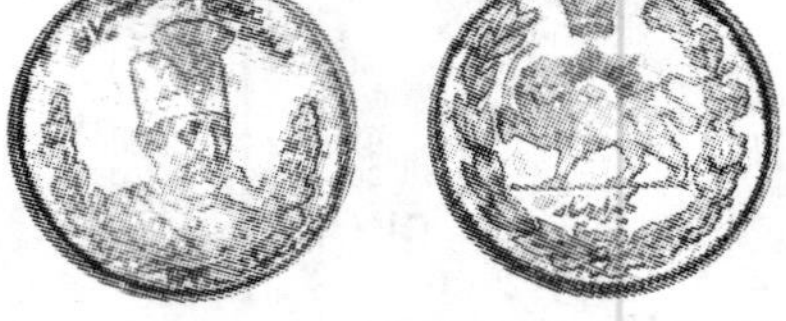

978 (Y31)	AH1323	.125	20.00	30.00	65.00	125.00

NOTE: AH1319 is a pattern.

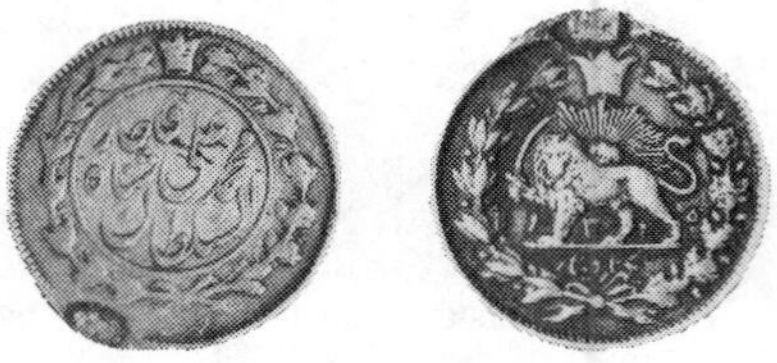

Obv. leg: *Muhammad Ali Shah.*

1011 (Y-A47)	AH1325	.289	150.00	300.00	600.00	—
	1326	.289	150.00	300.00	600.00	—

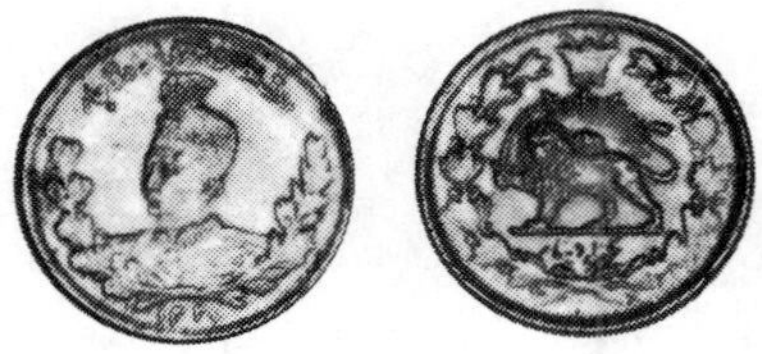

Obv: Date.

1015 (Y49)	AH1326	Inc. KM#1011	45.00	70.00	150.00	375.00
	1327/6	—	—	—	—	—
	1327	—	40.00	60.00	125.00	350.00

Obv: KM#1015. Rev: KM#1011.
Obv. and rev: Date.

1016 (Y49a)	AH1326	Inc. KM#1011	125.00	200.00	350.00	—

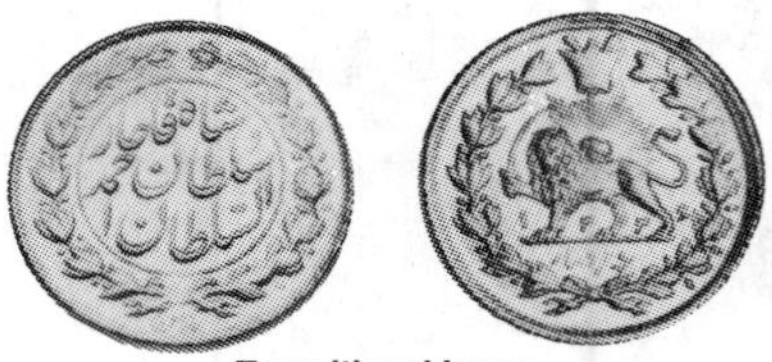

Transitional Issue
Obv: KM#1038. Rev: KM#1011.

1037 (Y-A71)	AH1326	—	—	—	Rare	—

Obv. leg: *Ahmad Shah.*

KM#	Date	Mintage	Fine	VF	XF	Unc
1038	AH1327	—	15.00	25.00	40.00	70.00
(Y67)	1328	—	4.00	8.00	15.00	40.00
	1329	3.000	4.00	8.00	15.00	40.00
	1330	—	4.00	8.00	15.00	40.00

24mm

1039	AH1330	—	3.50	7.00	18.00	30.00
(Y67a)	1330	—	—	Proof	Rare	

NOTE: KM#1039 differs from KM#1038 in that it is about 1mm broader and has a much thicker rim and more clearly defined denticles. Struck in Germany, without Iranian authorization, for circulation in western Iran during World War I. Also, the lion lacks the triangular face & fierce expression of KM#1038 and the point of the Talwar (scimitar) does not touch the sunburst as it does on Tehran issues.

23mm

1056	AH1330 (error) for 1340					
(Y71)		—	30.00	65.00	125.00	175.00
	1331	1.310	5.00	8.00	25.00	40.00
	1332	1.891	3.00	5.00	12.50	30.00
	1333	2.179	7.50	12.00	25.00	40.00
	1334	1.273	3.00	5.00	12.50	25.00
	1335	2.162	3.00	5.00	12.50	25.00
	1336	1.412	3.50	6.00	15.00	30.00
	1337	3.330	3.00	5.00	12.50	25.00
	1339	.035	12.50	25.00	55.00	90.00
	1340	.028	15.00	30.00	60.00	100.00
	1341	.170	8.00	15.00	35.00	60.00
	1342	.255	3.00	6.00	20.00	30.00
	1343	1.345	3.00	6.00	20.00	30.00
	1344	2.978	4.00	6.00	20.00	35.00

10th Year of Reign

1059	AH1337	.975	25.00	40.00	75.00	150.00
(Y73)						

1095	SH1304	2.573	3.00	5.00	10.00	20.00
(Y101)	1305	2.265	4.00	7.00	12.50	25.00

Obv. leg: *Reza Shah.*

1099	SH1305	Inc. KM#1095				
(Y106)			3.00	5.00	10.00	20.00
	1306/5	3.130	5.00	8.00	15.00	25.00
	1306	Inc. Ab.	3.00	5.00	10.00	20.00

KM#	Date	Mintage	Fine	VF	XF	Unc
1103	SH1306	Inc. KM#1099				
(Y109)			4.00	8.00	15.00	30.00
	1307	4.300	4.00	6.00	10.00	20.00
	1308	.603	4.00	6.00	10.00	20.00

2000 DINARS

(2 Krans)

Forms of the denomination:

2 KRANS: دو قران

2000 DINARS: دو هزار دینار

9.2100 g, .900 SILVER, .2665 oz ASW
Obv: Crown added. **Rev. leg:** *2000 Dinars,*
position of date amidst legs varies.

974	AH1319	—	10.00	20.00	35.00	90.00
(Y28a)	1320	13.959	10.00	20.00	35.00	75.00

NOTE: Earlier dates (AH1314-1318) exist for this type.
NOTE: Blundered dates exist.

Rev. leg: *2 Krans.*

975	AH1320	Inc. Ab.	12.50	20.00	40.00	100.00
(Y28b)	1321 (always '13201')					
	18.108	15.00	22.50	45.00	100.00	
	1322	8.640	8.00	15.00	30.00	80.00

NOTE: Position of digits varies between lion's legs.

979	AH1323					
(Y32)	Inc. 1322	15.00	30.00	60.00	120.00	
	'13'*	60.00	100.00	200.00	—	
	13233 (error)	—	—	—	—	

*23 of 1323 filled in or never punched
NOTE: AH1319 is a pattern.

Obv. leg: *Muhammad Ali Shah.*
Rev: *2 Krans.*

1012	AH1325	3.076	15.00	25.00	50.00	100.00
(Y47)	1326	3.069	7.50	11.50	20.00	50.00
	1327	—	7.50	11.50	20.00	50.00

Portrait of Shah.

KM#	Date	Mintage	Fine	VF	XF	Unc
1017	AH1326					
(Y50)	Inc. KM1012	1500.	2000.	2500.	—	

Obv. leg: *Ahmad Shah.*
Rev: Date below wreath, *2 Krans.*

1040	AH1327					
(Y68)	Inc. 1328	4.50	7.00	12.00	30.00	
	1328	30.000	4.50	7.00	12.00	20.00
	1329	29.250	4.50	7.00	12.00	20.00

Obv: Date below wreath, *2000 Dinars,*
Tehran Mint. **Rev:** Fierce, triangular face on lion.

1041	AH1330	2.901	5.00	8.00	15.00	35.00
(Y68a.1)						

Berlin Mint. Rev: Lion's face has
friendly expression.

1042	AH1330	—	4.00	7.00	10.00	27.00
(Y68a.2)						

NOTE: See paragraph after 1000 Dinars, KM#1039.

Rev: Date amid legs, *2000 Dinars.*

1043	AH1330	Inc. KM#1041				
(Y68b)			4.00	7.00	10.00	30.00
	1331	13.412	5.00	10.00	17.00	40.00

1057	AH1330 (error) for 1340					
(Y72)	Inc. KM1340	50.00	100.00	150.00	250.00	
	1331	Inc. KM#1043				
			6.00	12.50	25.00	50.00
	1332	12.926	5.00	7.50	15.00	30.00
	1333	Inc. Ab.	5.00	7.50	15.00	30.00
	1334	4.299	5.00	7.50	15.00	30.00
	1335	9.777	5.00	7.50	15.00	30.00
	1336	5.401	5.00	7.50	15.00	30.00
	1337	2.951	5.00	7.50	15.00	30.00
	1339	1.085	6.00	12.50	25.00	50.00
	1340	.254	9.00	15.00	30.00	65.00
	1341	4.460	5.00	7.50	15.00	30.00
	1342	2.245	5.00	8.00	20.00	35.00
	1343	5.205	5.00	8.00	20.00	35.00
	1344/34					
		12.354	7.00	12.00	25.00	55.00
	1344	Inc. Ab.	6.00	10.00	20.00	40.00

9.2100 g, .900 SILVER, .2665 oz ASW
10th Anniversary of Reign

KM#	Date	Mintage	Fine	VF	XF	Unc
1060 (Y74)	AH1337	3.503	25.00	40.00	100.00	225.00

1096 (Y102)	SH1304	11.920	6.00	10.00	15.00	35.00
	1305	9.785	5.00	8.00	12.00	25.00

Rev: Date below bow.

1100 (Y107)	SH1305	Inc.KM1096	5.00	10.00	20.00	30.00
	1306	9.380	4.00	7.00	12.50	25.00

Mule. Obv: KM#1104. Rev: KM#1057.

1105 (Y-A110)	SH1306	—	—	Reported, not confirmed		

1104 (Y110)	SH1306	Inc.KM1100	4.00	6.00	12.50	25.00
	1306	—	—	—	Proof	375.00
	1306H	11.714	3.00	5.00	10.00	20.00
	1306L	7.500	3.00	5.00	8.00	18.00
	1307	11.146	3.00	6.00	15.00	25.00
	1308	1.611	4.00	10.00	20.00	30.00

5000 DINARS

(5 Krans)

23.0251 g, .900 SILVER, .6662 oz ASW
Muzaffar al-din Shah

Dav.#288

976 (Y29)	AH1320	.250	8.00	11.50	18.50	30.00

NOTE: Actual mintage must be considerably greater. Struck in St. Petersburg.

Royal Birthday

Dav.#287

KM#	Date	Mintage	Fine	VF	XF	Unc
980 (Y-A40)	AH1322	—	400.00	550.00	800.00	1200.00

Obv: W/o additional inscriptions flanking head.

Dav.#289

981 (Y33)	AH1324	3,000	700.00	1000.	1750.	—

Muhammad Ali Shah

Dav.#290

1018 (Y-A50)	AH1327	—	575.00	850.00	1750.	—

NOTE: Obverse always weakly struck with little detail in head and face.

Ahmad Shah

Dav.#291

1058 (Y69)	AH1331	—	60.00	150.00	250.00	500.00
	1332	3.000	8.00	12.00	30.00	85.00
	1333	.667	10.00	15.00	35.00	90.00
	1334	.443	10.00	15.00	35.00	90.00
	1335	1.884	10.00	15.00	35.00	90.00
	1337	.165	12.00	25.00	55.00	110.00
	1339	.090	20.00	30.00	60.00	125.00
	1340	.303	12.00	25.00	55.00	110.00
	1341	.757	10.00	15.00	35.00	90.00
	1342/32	.546	10.00	15.00	35.00	90.00
	1342	Inc. Ab.	10.00	15.00	35.00	90.00
	1343	.935	10.00	15.00	35.00	90.00
	1344/34					
		2.284	10.00	15.00	30.00	85.00
	1344	Inc. Ab.	15.00	20.00	40.00	95.00

NOTE: Beware of altered date AH1331 specimens. 9,000 reported minted in AH1336, probably dated earlier.

Reza Shah Pahlavi

Dav.#292

KM#	Date	Mintage	Fine	VF	XF	Unc
1097 (Y103)	SH1304	.500	10.00	15.00	30.00	80.00
	1305	1.363	12.00	20.00	37.50	90.00

Dav.#293

1101 (Y108)	SH1305	Inc. KM#1097	10.00	15.00	35.00	100.00
	1306	3.186	10.00	15.00	30.00	85.00

Mule. Obv: KM#1106. Rev: KM#1058.

Dav.#-

1107 (Y-A111)	SH1306	—	—	Reported, not confirmed		

Dav.#294

1106 (Y111)	SH1306	Inc. KM#1101	9.00	12.50	20.00	37.50
	1306	—	—	—	Proof	400.00
	1306H	4.711	6.00	10.00	17.50	32.50
	1306L	3.000	6.00	7.50	30.00	45.00
	1307	3.928	6.00	7.50	15.00	30.00
	1308	.584	12.50	25.00	50.00	100.00

NOTE: Mint marks located as on 2000 Dinars, KM#1104.

GOLD COINAGE

NOTE: Modern imitations exist of many types, particularly the small 1/5, 1/2 and 1 Toman coins. These are usually underweight (or rarely overweight), and are sold in the bazaars at a small premium over bullion. They are usually crude and probably not intended to deceive collectors, but some are sold for jewelry and some are dated outside the reign of the ruler whose name or portrait they bear.

A few deceptive counterfeits are known of the large 10 Toman pieces.

2000 DINARS

(1/5 Toman)

.5749 g, .900 GOLD, .0166 oz AGW
Obv: Bust of Muzaffar al-Din Shah.

991	ND	—	75.00	135.00	200.00	300.00

Obv: Date and denomination added.

992 (Y-A34)	AH1319	—	50.00	100.00	150.00	250.00
	1322	—	50.00	100.00	150.00	250.00
	1323	—	50.00	100.00	150.00	250.00
	1324	—	50.00	100.00	150.00	250.00

Obv: Bust of Muhammad Ali-Shah.
turned half-left, divided date.
Rev: Leg. in closed wreath.

1024 (Y52)	AH1326	—	100.00	190.00	270.00	475.00
	1327	—	100.00	190.00	270.00	475.00

Obv. leg: *Ahmad Shah*.
Rev: Lion and sun.

1066 (Y75)	AH1328	—	100.00	175.00	250.00	500.00
	1329	—	70.00	125.00	200.00	325.00
	1330					

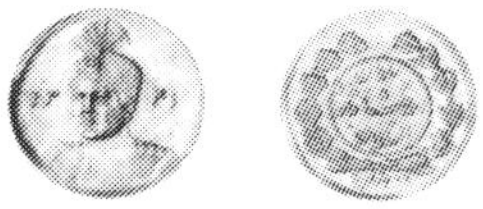

Obv: Portrait type of Ahmad Shah.
Rev: Legend.

KM#	Date	Mintage	Fine	VF	XF	Unc
1070	AH1332	—	20.00	35.00	60.00	130.00
(Y79)	1333	—	15.00	30.00	55.00	115.00
	1334	—	15.00	30.00	40.00	75.00
	1335	—	12.50	25.00	35.00	50.00
	1337	—	12.50	25.00	35.00	50.00
	1339	—	15.00	30.00	40.00	75.00
	1340	—	17.00	35.00	50.00	90.00
	1341	—	15.00	30.00	40.00	75.00
	1342	—	15.00	30.00	40.00	75.00
	1343	—	15.00	30.00	40.00	60.00

5000 DINARS

(1/2 Toman)

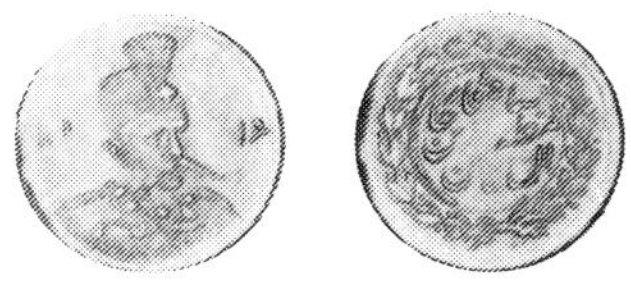

1.4372 g, .900 GOLD, .0416 oz AGW
Obv: Portrait right.

KM#	Date	Mintage	Fine	VF	XF	Unc
994	AH1319	—	30.00	60.00	100.00	200.00
(Y35)	1320	—	30.00	60.00	100.00	200.00
	1321	—	30.00	60.00	100.00	200.00
	1322	—	30.00	60.00	100.00	200.00
	1323	—	25.00	50.00	75.00	150.00
	1324	—	25.00	50.00	75.00	150.00

NOTE: Earlier dates (AH1316-1318) exist for this type.

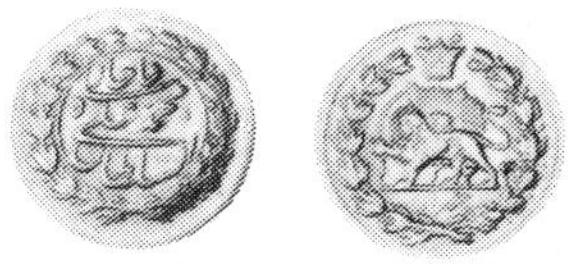

Obv. leg: *Muhammad Ali Shah.*
Rev: Lion and sun.

KM#	Date	Mintage	Fine	VF	XF	Unc
1021	AH1324	—	125.00	175.00	275.00	400.00
(Y56)	1325	—	150.00	225.00	350.00	450.00

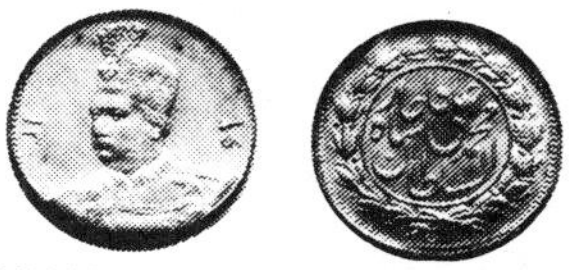

KM#	Date	Mintage	Fine	VF	XF	Unc
1025	AH1326	—	125.00	200.00	300.00	450.00
(Y53)	1362 (error)		150.00	250.00	350.00	525.00
	1327	—	125.00	200.00	300.00	450.00

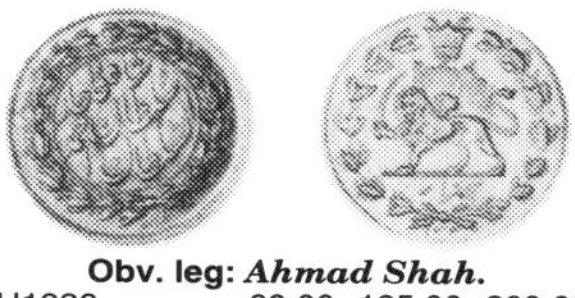

Obv. leg: *Ahmad Shah.*

KM#	Date	Mintage	Fine	VF	XF	Unc
1067	AH1328	—	60.00	125.00	200.00	275.00
(Y76)	1329	—	60.00	100.00	150.00	200.00
	1330	—	60.00	100.00	175.00	225.00

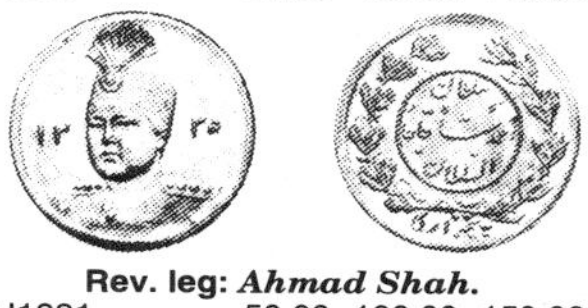

Rev. leg: *Ahmad Shah.*

KM#	Date	Mintage	Fine	VF	XF	Unc
1071	AH1331	—	50.00	100.00	150.00	300.00
(Y80)	1332	—	40.00	60.00	100.00	150.00
	1333	—	25.00	40.00	75.00	125.00
	1334	—	25.00	30.00	40.00	70.00
	1335	—	25.00	30.00	40.00	70.00
	1336	—	25.00	35.00	50.00	90.00
	1337	—	25.00	30.00	40.00	70.00
	1339	—	25.00	35.00	60.00	110.00
	1340	—	25.00	35.00	60.00	110.00
	1341	—	25.00	30.00	45.00	90.00
	1342	—	25.00	30.00	45.00	90.00
	1343	—	25.00	30.00	45.00	90.00

Mule. Obv: Ahmed portrait.
Rev. leg: *Sahib al-Zaman.*

KM#	Date	Mintage	Fine	VF	XF	Unc
1072	AH1340	—	100.00	150.00	250.00	400.00
(Y80a)						

TOMAN

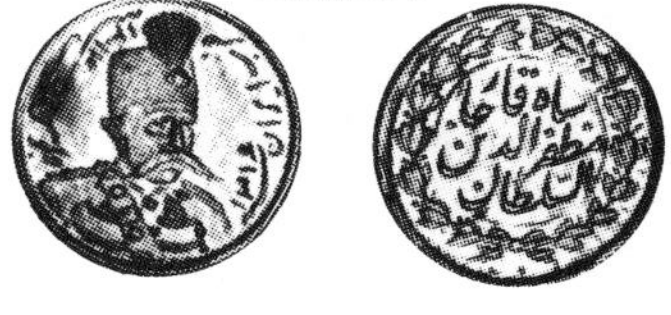

2.8744 g, .900 GOLD, .0943 oz AGW
Obv: Muzaffar bust 1/2 right, accession date, AH1314, above left, AH1316-1324.

KM#	Date	Mintage	Fine	VF	XF	Unc
995	AH1319	—	60.00	100.00	160.00	250.00
(Y36)	1321	—	60.00	100.00	160.00	250.00

NOTE: Earlier dates (AH1316-1318) exist for this type.

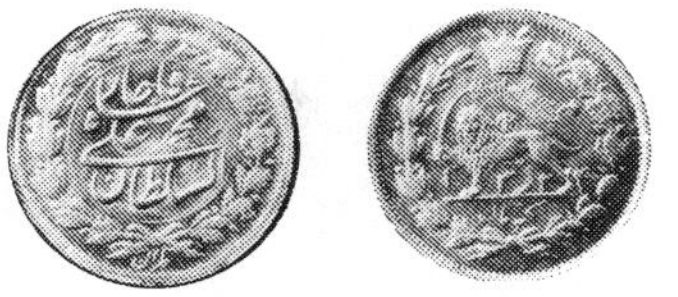

Obv. leg: *Muhammad Ali Shah,* AH1324.
Rev: Lion and sun.

KM#	Date	Mintage	Fine	VF	XF	Unc
1022	AH1324	—	250.00	450.00	675.00	900.00
(Y-A56)						

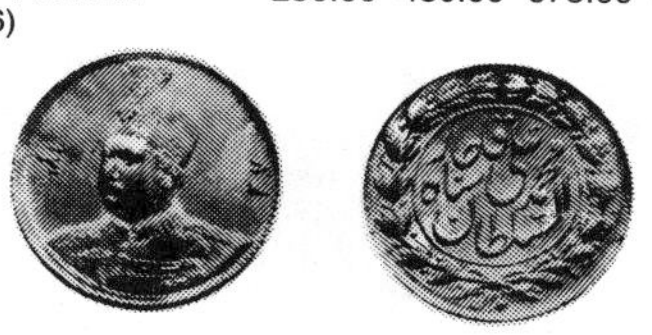

Obv: Mohammad Ali portrait half-left, AH1326.
Rev: Leg. in closed wreath.

KM#	Date	Mintage	Fine	VF	XF	Unc
1026	AH1327	—	200.00	350.00	500.00	750.00
(Y54)						

Obv. leg: *Ahmad Shah,* AH1328-1332.
Rev: Lion and sun.

KM#	Date	Mintage	Fine	VF	XF	Unc
1068	AH1329	—	200.00	300.00	500.00	750.00
(Y77)						

Mule. Obv: KM#1074.
Rev: Ahmad Shah Pattern 2 Toman.

KM#	Date	Mintage	Fine	VF	XF	Unc
1073	AH1332	—	300.00	600.00	900.00	1500.
(Y-A81)	1333	—	300.00	600.00	900.00	1500.

NOTE: The reverse die used was of an unadopted pattern.

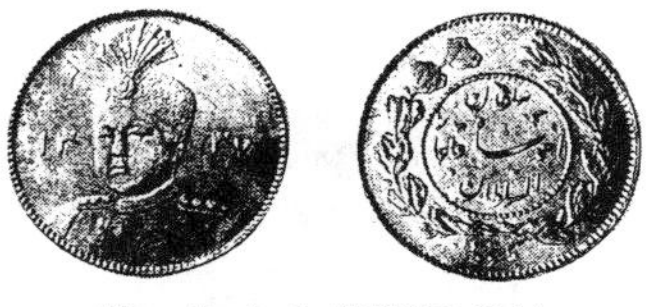

Obv: Portrait, AH1332-1344
Rev. leg: Ahmad Shah type.

KM#	Date	Mintage	Fine	VF	XF	Unc
1074	AH1334	—	45.00	60.00	100.00	175.00
(Y81)	1335	—	45.00	70.00	100.00	175.00
	1337	—	45.00	60.00	100.00	175.00
	1339	—	45.00	70.00	100.00	175.00
	1340	—	45.00	70.00	100.00	175.00
	1341	—	40.00	50.00	90.00	150.00
	1342	—	40.00	50.00	90.00	150.00
	1343	—	40.00	50.00	90.00	150.00

MONETARY REFORM

5 Dinars = 1 Shahi
100 Dinars = 1 Rial
100 Rials = 1 Pahlavi

The pahlavi was made equal in weight to the British sovereign. It was originally valued at 100 Rials, but has always fluctuated with market prices of gold and silver.

DINAR

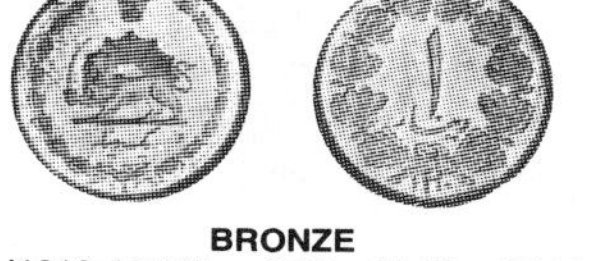

BRONZE

KM#	Date	Mintage	Fine	VF	XF	Unc
1121	SH1310	10.000	8.00	15.00	30.00	60.00
(Y93)						

2 DINARS

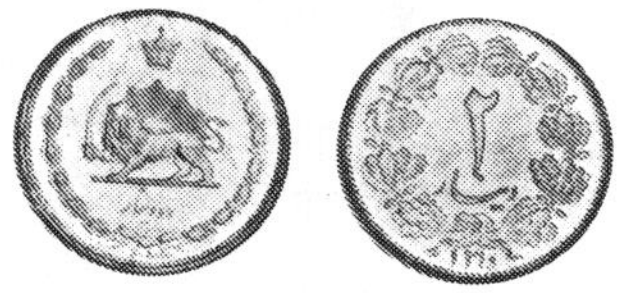

BRONZE

KM#	Date	Mintage	Fine	VF	XF	Unc
1122	SH1310	5.000	7.00	15.00	35.00	70.00
(Y94)						

5 DINARS

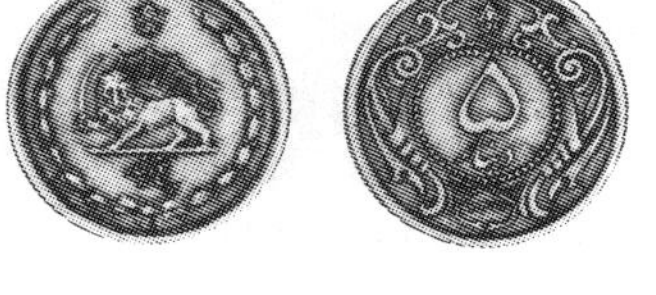

COPPER-NICKEL

KM#	Date	Mintage	Fine	VF	XF	Unc
1123	SH1310	3.750	8.00	15.00	40.00	125.00
(Y97)						

COPPER

KM#	Date	Mintage	Fine	VF	XF	Unc
1123a	SH1314	.480	75.00	100.00	175.00	300.00
(Y97a)						

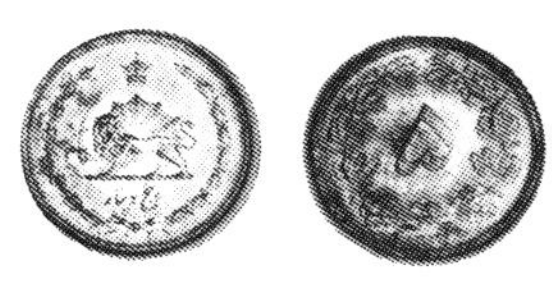

ALUMINUM-BRONZE

KM#	Date	Mintage	Fine	VF	XF	Unc
1138	SH1315	5.665	2.50	4.00	10.00	20.00
(Y125)	1316	Inc. Ab.	.40	.75	1.50	5.00
	1317	13.025	.40	.75	1.50	5.00
	1318	—	.40	.75	1.50	5.00
	1319	—	.40	.75	1.50	5.00
	1320	—	.40	.75	1.50	4.00
	1321	—	.40	.75	1.50	5.00

10 DINARS

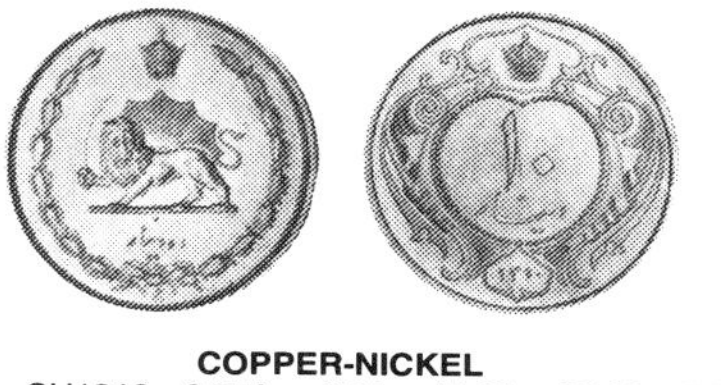

COPPER-NICKEL

KM#	Date	Mintage	Fine	VF	XF	Unc
1124	SH1310	3.750	9.00	15.00	30.00	75.00
(Y98)						

COPPER

KM#	Date	Mintage	Fine	VF	XF	Unc
1124a	SH1314	11.350	11.50	20.00	45.00	125.00
(Y98a)						

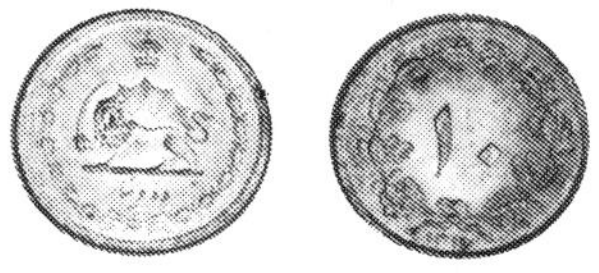

ALUMINUM-BRONZE

KM#	Date	Mintage	Fine	VF	XF	Unc
1139	SH1315	6.195	2.00	5.00	15.00	25.00
(Y126)	1316	Inc. Ab.	.80	1.50	4.00	10.00
	1317	17.120	.40	.80	2.00	6.00
	1318	—	.40	.80	2.00	6.00
	1319	—	.40	.80	2.00	6.00
	1320	—	.40	.80	2.00	6.00
	1321	—	.45	1.00	2.50	6.00

25 DINARS

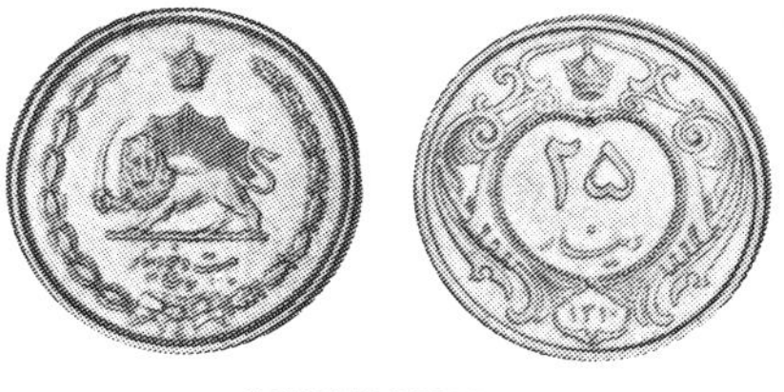

COPPER-NICKEL

KM#	Date	Mintage	Fine	VF	XF	Unc
1125	SH1310	.750	15.00	30.00	60.00	175.00
(Y99)						

COPPER

KM#	Date	Mintage	Fine	VF	XF	Unc
1125a	SH1314	1.152	30.00	60.00	85.00	250.00
(Y99a)						

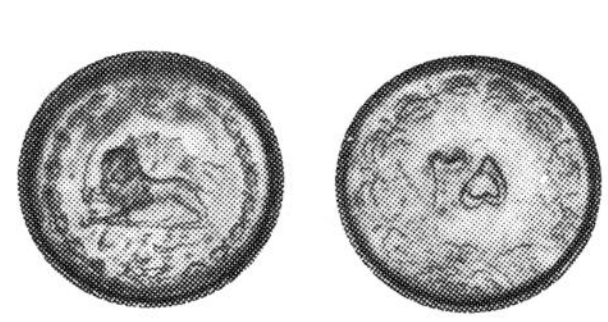

ALUMINUM-BRONZE

KM#	Date	Mintage	Fine	VF	XF	Unc
1140	SH1326	—	3.00	6.00	15.00	30.00
(Y127)	1327	—	10.00	15.00	30.00	60.00
	1329	—	4.00	7.00	20.00	40.00

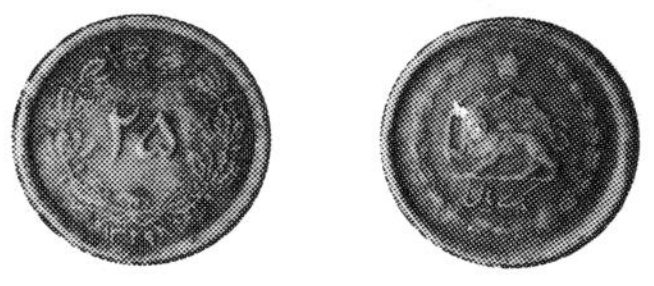

Mule. Obv: 25 Dinars, KM#1140.
Rev: 1 Rial, KM#1143.

KM#	Date	Mintage	Fine	VF	XF	Unc
1141	1329	—	100.00	150.00	250.00	400.00
(Y127a)						

1/4 RIAL

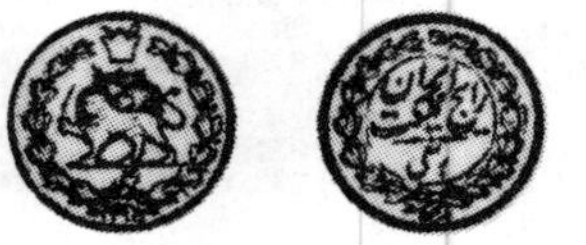

1.2500 g, .828 SILVER, .0332 oz ASW

KM#	Date	Mintage	Fine	VF	XF	Unc
1127 (Y104)	SH1315	.600	1.00	1.25	1.75	4.00

NOTE: The second '1' is often short, so that the date looks like 1305.

1/2 RIAL

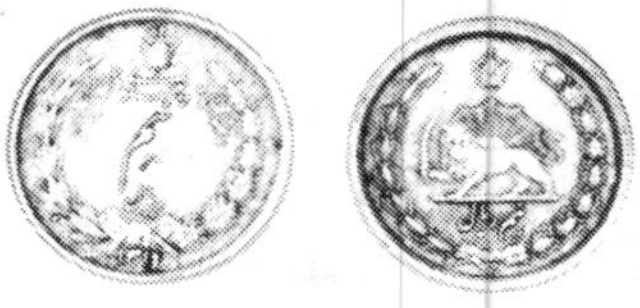

2.5000 g, .828 SILVER, .0665 oz ASW

KM#	Date	Mintage	Fine	VF	XF	Unc
1128	SH1310	2.000	1.00	3.00	6.00	15.00
(Y112)	1311	—	30.00	40.00	50.00	90.00
	1312	—	1.00	3.00	5.00	14.00
	1313	1.945	1.50	3.00	6.00	15.00
	1314	.100	3.00	9.00	20.00	40.00
	1315	.800	2.00	4.00	9.00	20.00

NOTE: All 1/2 Rials dated SH1311-1315 are recut dies, usually from SH1310.

10 SHAHIS

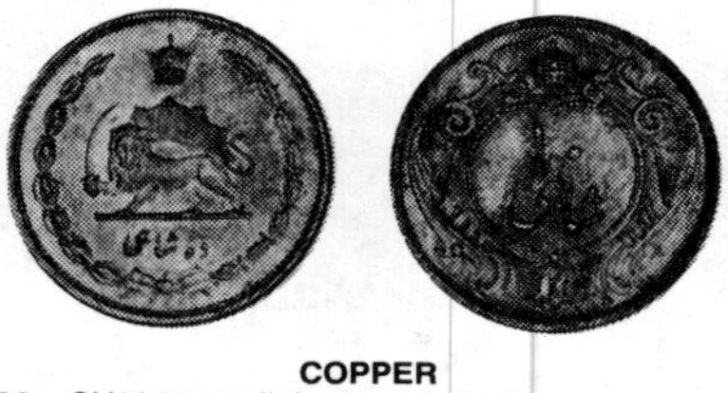

COPPER

KM#	Date	Mintage	Fine	VF	XF	Unc
1126 (Y92)	SH1314 small date, reeded edge	15.714	3.00	4.00	12.50	30.00
	1314 lg. dt.	Inc. Ab.	3.00	4.00	12.50	30.00
	1314 plain edge	Inc. Ab.	5.00	7.00	15.00	40.00

50 DINARS

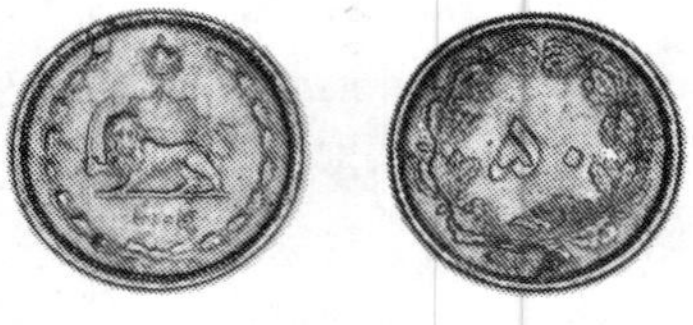

ALUMINUM-BRONZE

KM#	Date	Mintage	Fine	VF	XF	Unc
1142	SH1315	15.968	3.00	4.50	10.00	35.00
(Y128)	1316	34.200	1.25	2.50	6.00	20.00
	1317	17.314	.60	1.50	4.00	15.00
	1318	—	.60	1.50	4.00	15.00
	1319	—	1.50	2.50	6.00	20.00
	1320	—	.75	1.50	3.00	10.00
	1321/0	—	.75	1.50	3.00	15.00
	1322/10	—	.75	1.50	3.00	15.00
	1322/12	—	.75	1.50	3.00	10.00
	1322/0	—	.75	1.50	3.00	10.00
	1322/1	—	.75	1.50	3.00	10.00
	1331	8.162	3.50	4.50	10.00	25.00
	1332	22.892	2.00	3.00	5.00	10.00

COPPER

KM#	Date	Mintage	Fine	VF	XF	Unc
1142a	SH1322	—	2.00	4.00	7.00	12.00
(Y128a)	1322/0	—	2.00	6.00	9.00	15.00

ALUMINUM-BRONZE
Reduced thickness

KM#	Date	Mintage	Fine	VF	XF	Unc
1156	SH1332	—	25.00	30.00	40.00	50.00
(Y137)	1333	4.036	.75	1.50	2.50	8.00
	1334	1.370	.75	1.50	4.00	10.00
	1335	.926	.75	1.50	2.50	8.00
	1336	-*	1.00	1.25	2.00	8.00
	1342	.800	.60	1.00	1.75	6.00
	1343	1.400	.60	1.00	1.75	6.00
	1344	1.600	.35	.65	1.25	5.00
	1345	1.690	.35	.65	1.25	5.00
	1346	153.648**	.20	.25	.50	2.00
	1347	2.000	.20	.25	.50	2.00
	1348	1.500	.20	.25	.50	2.00
	1349	.360	2.00	3.00	4.50	12.50
	1350	—	.30	.50	.75	2.00
	1351	—	.30	.50	.75	2.00
	1353	.060	.30	.50	.75	2.00
	1354	.016	.75	1.25	2.00	5.00

***NOTE:** Mint reports record 126,500 in SH1337 & 20,000 in SH1338; these were probably dated SH1336.

****NOTE:** Mintage report seems excessive for this and all SH1346 coinage.

BRASS-COATED STEEL

KM#	Date	Mintage	Fine	VF	XF	Unc
1156a	MS2535	.027	.80	1.00	2.00	3.00
(Y137a)	2536	—	1.00	1.50	2.50	4.00
	2537	—	1.00	1.50	2.50	4.00
	SH1357	—	1.00	2.00	3.50	6.00
	1358	—	3.00	4.00	6.00	10.00

RIAL

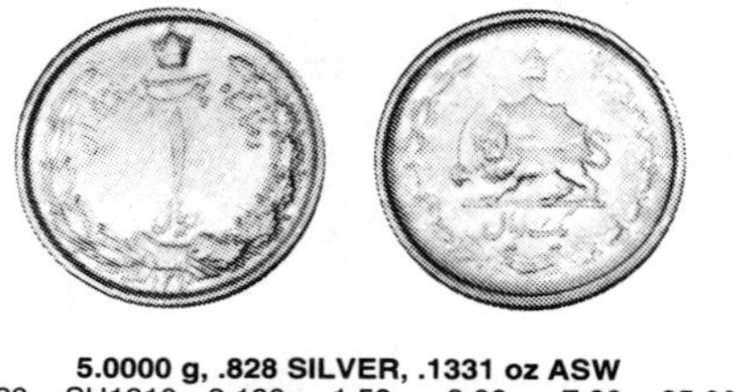

5.0000 g, .828 SILVER, .1331 oz ASW

KM#	Date	Mintage	Fine	VF	XF	Unc
1129	SH1310	2.190	1.50	3.00	7.00	25.00
(Y113)	1311	10.256	1.50	2.00	5.00	20.00
	1312	25.768	1.50	2.00	5.00	15.00
	1313	6.670	1.50	3.00	6.00	20.00

NOTE: All coins dated SH1311-13 cut or punched over SH1310.

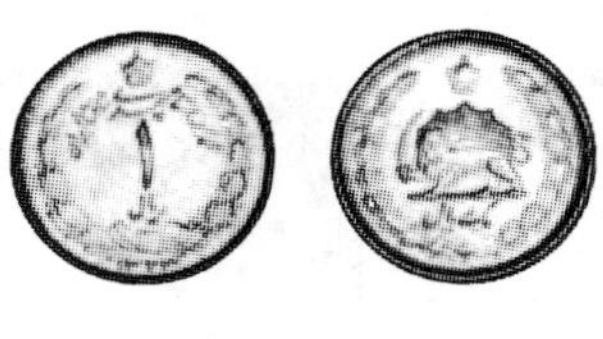

1.6000 g, .600 SILVER, .0308 oz ASW

KM#	Date	Mintage	Fine	VF	XF	Unc
1143	SH1322	—	.50	1.00	2.00	5.00
(Y129)	1323/3	—	—	—	—	—
	1323	—	.50	1.00	2.00	5.00
	1324/3	—	—	—	—	—
	1324	—	.50	1.00	2.00	5.00
	1325	—	.75	1.50	2.00	5.00
	1326	.567	35.00	40.00	50.00	100.00
	1327	5.795	1.50	2.50	4.00	8.00
	1328	1.565	1.50	2.50	4.00	8.00
	1329	.144	35.00	40.00	50.00	100.00
	1330	—	2.00	3.00	5.00	15.00
	1424 (error for 1324)	—	—	—	—	—

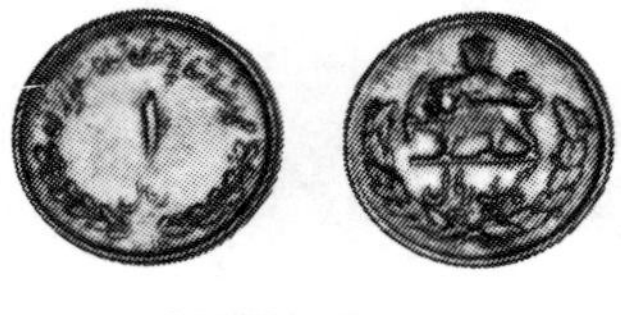

COPPER-NICKEL

KM#	Date	Mintage	Fine	VF	XF	Unc
1157	SH(13)31	4.735	1.00	2.00	5.00	15.00
(Y138)	(13)32	*3.320	4.00	8.00	15.00	30.00
	(13)33	16.405	.60	1.00	2.00	5.00
	(13)33	—	.60	1.00	2.00	5.00
	(13)34	8.980	.60	1.00	2.00	5.00
	(13)35	8.910	.50	1.00	1.00	5.00
	(13)36	4.450	1.00	2.00	8.00	20.00

***NOTE:** Much rarer than mintage would indicate.

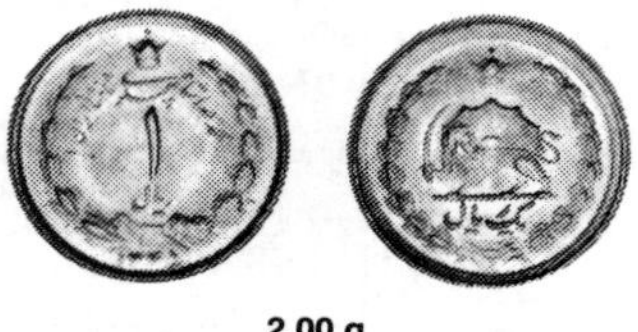

2.00 g

KM#	Date	Mintage	Fine	VF	XF	Unc
1171 (Y-A140)	SH1337	8.005	.50	1.00	2.00	5.00

1.75 g

KM#	Date	Mintage	Fine	VF	XF	Unc
1171a (Y-A140a)	SH1338	14.940	.10	.20	.40	3.00
	1339	8.400	.25	.50	1.00	4.00
	1340	8.490	.25	.50	1.00	4.00
	1341	8.680	.25	.50	1.00	4.00
	1342	13.332	.10	.20	.40	3.00
	1343	14.746	.10	.15	.25	2.00
	1344	12.050	.10	.20	.50	3.50
	1345	13.786	.10	.15	.20	2.00
	1346	155.321	.10	.15	.20	2.00
	1347	20.664	.10	.15	.25	3.00
	1348	22.960	.10	.15	.20	2.00
	1349	19.918	.10	.15	.20	2.00
	1350	24.248	.10	.20	.65	2.00
	1351/0	21.825	.10	.25	.40	3.00
	1351	Inc. Ab.	.10	.15	.20	2.00
	1352	31.449	.10	.15	.20	2.00
	1353 large date	33.700	.10	.20	.25	3.00
	1353 sm.dt.	Inc. Ab.	.10	.15	.20	2.00
	1354	—	.10	.15	.20	2.00
	MS2536	—	.10	.15	.25	3.00

NOTE: Date varieties exist.

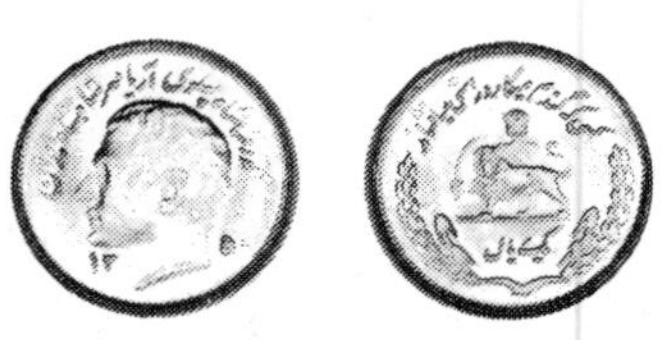

F.A.O. Issue

KM#	Date	Mintage	Fine	VF	XF	Unc
1183	SH1350	2.770	.10	.15	.25	1.00
(Y152)	1351	8.605	.10	.15	.25	1.00
	1353	2.000	.50	.80	1.25	2.00
	1354	1.000	.50	.80	1.25	2.00

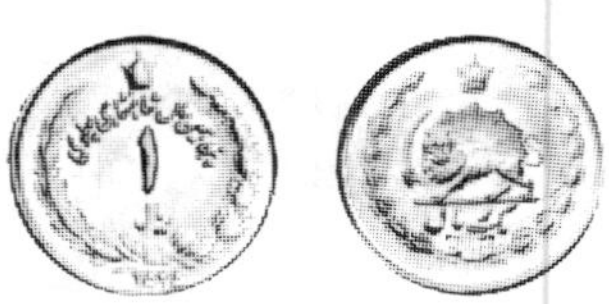

50th Anniversary of Pahlavi Rule

KM#	Date	Mintage	Fine	VF	XF	Unc
1205 (Y154)	MS2535	61.945	.50	1.00	1.50	2.50

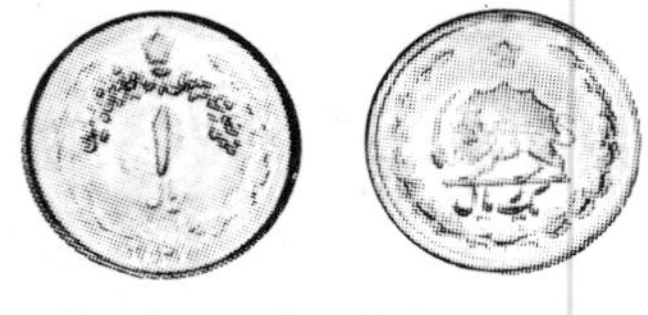

Obv: *Aryamehr* added to legend.

KM#	Date	Mintage	Fine	VF	XF	Unc
1172	MS2536	71.150	.10	.15	.25	2.00
(Y154a)	2537	—	.10	.15	.25	2.00
	2537/6537 (error 2/6)	—	—	—	—	6.00
	SH1357/6	—	.25	.50	.75	5.00
	1357	—	.25	.50	.75	3.00

2 RIALS

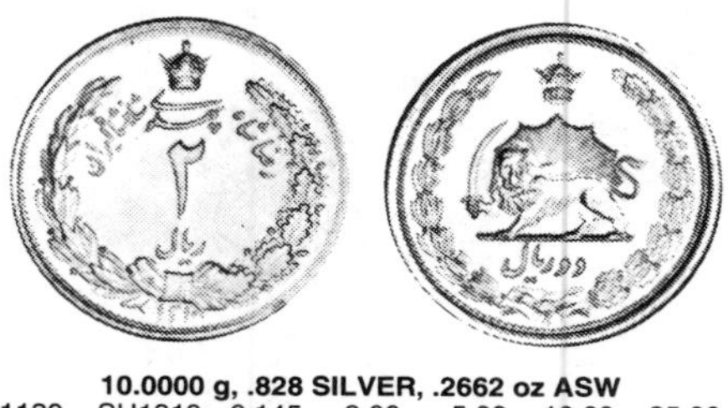

10.0000 g, .828 SILVER, .2662 oz ASW

KM#	Date	Mintage	Fine	VF	XF	Unc
1130	SH1310	6.145	2.00	5.00	10.00	25.00
(Y114)	1311	8.838	2.00	5.00	10.00	22.00
	1312	19.175	2.00	5.00	10.00	20.00
	1313	4.015	2.00	7.00	15.00	32.00

NOTE: All coins dated SH1311-13 cut or punched over SH1310.

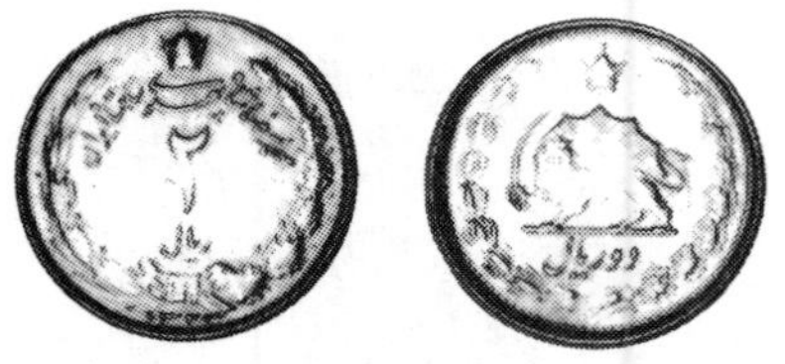

3.2000 g, .600 SILVER, .0617 oz ASW

KM#	Date	Mintage	Fine	VF	XF	Unc
1144	SH1322	—	.50	1.00	3.50	7.00
(Y130)	1323/2	—	10.00	20.00	30.00	50.00
	1323	—	.50	1.00	3.00	6.00
	1324	—	.50	1.00	3.00	6.00
	1325	—	1.25	3.00	5.00	11.00
	1326	.187	50.00	60.00	75.00	125.00
	1327	3.140	1.50	3.00	5.00	12.50
	1328	1.198	2.50	4.50	7.50	16.00
	1329	—	65.00	80.00	100.00	150.00
	1330	—	5.00	8.00	12.50	30.00

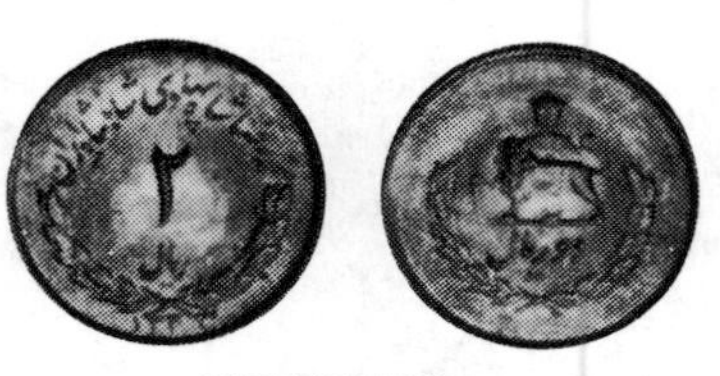

COPPER-NICKEL

KM#	Date	Mintage	Fine	VF	XF	Unc
1158	SH1331	5.335	1.25	3.00	7.00	20.00
(Y139)	1332	6.870	1.00	2.00	4.00	8.00
	1333	13.668	.15	.75	2.00	7.00
	1334	7.185	.15	.75	2.00	7.00
	1335	2.400	.15	.75	3.00	12.50
	1336	.325	15.00	25.00	40.00	75.00

KM#	Date	Mintage	Fine	VF	XF	Unc
1173	SH1338	17.610	.10	.25	.75	4.00
(Y-B140)	1339	8.575	.10	.25	.50	4.00
	1340	5.668	.10	.25	.50	4.00
	1341	5.820	.10	.25	.75	4.00
	1342	8.570	.10	.25	.50	4.00
	1343	11.250	.10	.25	.50	3.00
	1344	5.155	.10	.25	.50	4.00
	1345	2.267	.15	.30	1.00	5.00
	1346	92.792	—	.10	.20	4.00
	1347	10.300	—	.10	1.00	6.00
	1348	9.319	.20	.45	1.10	4.00
	1349	9.895	.20	.40	1.00	4.00
	1350	9.545	.15	.35	1.00	4.00
	1351	13.305	.15	.35	1.00	3.00
	1352	15.910	—	.10	.20	3.00
	1353	28.477	—	.10	.20	3.00
	1354/3	—	.20	.40	1.00	5.00
	1354	41.700	—	.10	.20	3.00
	MS2536	54.725	—	.10	.20	3.00

Obv: *Aryamehr* added to legend.

1174	MS2536					
(Y-B140a)	Inc. Ab.		.25	.50	1.00	4.00
	2537		.25	.50	1.00	4.00
	SH1357	—	.25	.50	1.00	4.00

50th Anniversary of Pahlavi Rule

1206	MS2535	59.568	.25	.50	1.00	2.50
(Y155)						

5 RIALS

25.0000 g, .828 SILVER, .6655 oz ASW

Dav.#295

1131	SH1310	5.471	7.50	8.00	12.00	20.00
(Y115)	1311	4.527	7.50	8.00	12.00	20.00
	1312/0	5.502	7.50	10.00	15.00	25.00
	1312	Inc. Ab.	7.50	8.00	12.00	20.00
	1313	1.208	7.50	10.00	15.00	25.00

NOTE: Most coins dated SH1311-13 are cut or punched over SH1310.

8.0000 g, .600 SILVER, .1543 oz ASW

KM#	Date	Mintage	Fine	VF	XF	Unc
1145	SH1322	—	1.00	2.00	3.50	6.00
(Y131)	1323	—	1.00	2.50	3.50	6.00
	1324	—	1.00	2.00	4.50	10.00
	1325	—	1.00	2.00	3.50	6.00
	1326	.061	60.00	70.00	85.00	140.00
	1327	.836	2.00	5.00	7.50	20.00
	1328	.282	2.50	10.00	20.00	40.00
	1329	—	75.00	85.00	100.00	175.00

COPPER-NICKEL

1159	SH1331	3.660	.50		5.00	20.00
(Y140)	1332	16.350	.25	1.00	3.00	10.00
	1333	6.582	.25	1.00	3.00	10.00
	1334	.300	10.00	15.00	25.00	50.00
	1336	1.410	.50	2.00	5.00	20.00

7.00 g, 26mm

1175	SH1337	3.660	1.00	2.50	7.50	22.50
(Y-C140)	1338	10.467	.50	2.50	8.00	20.00

5.00 g

1175a	SH1338					
(Y-C140a)		I.A.	.25	.40	2.00	6.00
	1339	3.980	.25	.40	2.00	6.00
	1340	3.814	.25	.40	2.00	6.00
	1341	2.332	.25	.40	2.00	6.00
	1342	7.838	.25	.40	1.00	4.00
	1343	9.484	.25	.40	1.00	4.00
	1344	3.468	.25	.40	1.00	4.00
	1345	6.092	.25	.40	1.00	4.00
	1346/36	74.781	.25	.40	1.50	5.00
	1346	Inc. Ab.	.25	.40	1.00	4.00

4.60 g, 24.5mm
Obv. leg: *Aryamehr* added.

1176	SH1347					
(Y-C140b)		7.745	.50	.85	1.50	4.00
	1348	9.193	.50	.75	1.00	4.00
	1349	7.300	.50	.75	1.00	4.00
	1350	10.160	.35	.75	1.00	3.00
	1351	20.582	.25	.75	1.00	3.00
	1352	23.590	.25	.75	1.00	3.00
	1353	28.367	.25	.75	1.00	3.00
	1353 large date	Inc. Ab.	.25	.75	1.00	3.00
	1354	27.294	.25	.75	1.00	3.00
	MS2536	47.906	.20	.50	1.00	3.00
	2537	—	.35	.65	1.00	3.00
	SH1357	—	.50	.75	1.00	3.00

50th Anniversary of Pahlavi Rule

KM#	Date	Mintage	Fine	VF	XF	Unc
1207	MS2535	37.144	.25	.50	1.00	3.00
(Y156)						

10 RIALS

16.0000 g, .600 SILVER, .3086 oz ASW

1146	SH1323/2	—	2.00	3.50	7.00	20.00
(Y132)	1323	—	2.00	3.00	5.00	12.00
	1324	—	2.00	3.00	5.00	15.00
	1325	—	2.00	3.00	6.00	17.50
	1326	—	100.00	125.00	150.00	225.00

NOTE: Counterfeits are known dated SH1322.

COPPER-NICKEL, 12.00 g

1177	SH1333		—	—	—	—
(Y-D140)	1335	6.225	.50	2.00	4.00	10.00
	1336	4.415	1.00	3.00	7.50	15.00
	1337	.715	3.00	6.00	9.00	20.00
	1338	1.210	.50	2.00	6.00	14.00
	1339	2.775	.50	2.00	4.00	10.00
	1340	3.660	.50	2.00	4.00	10.00
	1341	.744	20.00	35.00	50.00	75.00
	1343	6.874	.50	2.00	4.00	10.00

Thin flan, 9.00 g

1177a	SH1341					
(Y-D140a)	Inc. KM1177		.35	1.00	2.50	5.00
	1342	3.763	.35	1.00	2.00	4.00
	1343					
	Inc. KM1177		.35	.75	1.50	2.50
	1344	1.627	.35	.75	1.50	2.50

Rev: Value in words.

1178	SH1345	1.699	.50	.60	2.00	5.00
(Y149)	1346	38.897	.40	.50	1.00	4.00
	1347	8.220	.40	.65	1.50	8.00
	1348	7.156	.40	.50	1.00	4.00
	1349	7.397	.40	.50	1.00	4.00
	1350	8.972	.40	.50	1.00	4.00
	1351	9.912	.40	.50	1.00	4.00
	1352	28.776	.50	2.00	4.50	7.00

Rev: Value in numerals.

1179	SH1352	I.A.	.30	.60	1.00	4.00
(Y149a)	1353	22.234	.30	.60	1.00	3.00
	1354	23.482	.30	.60	1.00	4.00
	MS2536	24.324	.30	.60	1.00	3.00
	2537	—	.30	.60	1.00	4.00
	SH1357	—	.30	1.00	1.50	4.00

F.A.O. Issue

KM#	Date	Mintage	Fine	VF	XF	Unc
1182 (Y150)	SH1348	.150	.25	.50	1.00	3.50

50th Anniversary of Pahlavi Rule

KM#	Date	Mintage	Fine	VF	XF	Unc
1208 (Y157)	MS2535	29.859	.25	.50	.75	3.00

20 RIALS

COPPER-NICKEL
Rev: Value in words.

KM#	Date	Mintage	Fine	VF	XF	Unc
1180 (Y151)	SH1350	2.349	.25	1.00	3.00	6.00
	1351	11.416	.25	.85	1.00	3.00
	1352	7.172	.25	.85	1.25	5.00

Rev: Value in numerals.

KM#	Date	Mintage	Fine	VF	XF	Unc
1181 (Y151a)	SH1352	Inc.KM1180	.25	.75	1.00	3.50
	1353	12.601	.25	.75	1.00	3.75
	1354	16.246	.25	.75	1.00	4.00
	MS2536	—	.40	.75	1.00	4.00
	2537	—	.50	.75	1.00	4.00
	SH1357	—	.50	1.00	1.50	5.00

NOTE: Varieties exist in date size.

7th Asian Games

KM#	Date	Mintage	Fine	VF	XF	Unc
1196 (Y153)	SH1353	I.A.	1.00	2.00	3.00	5.00

50th Anniversary of Pahlavi Rule

KM#	Date	Mintage	Fine	VF	XF	Unc
1209 (Y158)	MS2535	—	.50	1.00	2.00	4.00

F.A.O. Issue

KM#	Date	Mintage	Fine	VF	XF	Unc
1211 (Y160)	MS2535	10.000	.50	1.00	2.00	4.00
	2536	23.370	.50	1.00	3.00	5.00

50th Anniversary of Bank Melli

KM#	Date	Mintage	Fine	VF	XF	Unc
1214 (Y162)	SH1357	—	4.00	5.00	6.50	12.50

F.A.O. Issue

KM#	Date	Mintage	Fine	VF	XF	Unc
1215 (Y163)	SH1357	5.000	.50	.75	2.00	6.00

1/4 PAHLAVI

2.0340 g, .900 GOLD, 14mm, .0589 oz AGW

KM#	Date	Mintage	Fine	VF	XF	Unc
1160 (Y141)	SH1332	.041	BV	35.00	45.00	60.00
	1333	.007	35.00	45.00	100.00	150.00
	1334	—	BV	35.00	60.00	100.00
	1335	.041	BV	35.00	45.00	60.00
	1336	—	—	—	Rare	—

Thinner & broader, 16mm

KM#	Date	Mintage	Fine	VF	XF	Unc
1160a (Y141a)	SH1336	.007	150.00	350.00	750.00	1250.
	1337	.033	—	BV	22.00	30.00
	1338	.136	—	BV	22.00	30.00
	1339	.156	—	BV	22.00	30.00
	1340	.060	—	BV	22.00	30.00
	1342	.080	—	BV	22.00	30.00
	1343	.040	—	Reported, not confirmed		
	1344	.030	—	30.00	35.00	55.00
	1345	.040	—	BV	22.00	30.00
	1346	.030	—	BV	22.00	30.00
	1347	.060	—	BV	22.00	30.00
	1348	.060	—	BV	22.00	30.00
	1349	.080	—	BV	22.00	30.00
	1350	.080	—	BV	22.00	30.00
	1351	.103	—	BV	22.00	30.00
	1352	.050	—	BV	22.00	30.00
	1353	—	—	BV	22.00	30.00

Obv. leg: *Aryamehr* added.

KM#	Date	Mintage	Fine	VF	XF	Unc
1198 (Y141b)	SH1354	.106	—	BV	22.00	30.00
	1355	.186	—	BV	22.00	30.00
	MS2536	—	—	BV	22.00	30.00
	2537	—	—	BV	22.00	30.00
	SH1358	—	BV	35.00	75.00	115.00

1/2 PAHLAVI

4.0680 g, .900 GOLD, .1177 oz AGW

KM#	Date	Mintage	Fine	VF	XF	Unc
1132 (Y123)	SH1310	696 pcs.	75.00	150.00	275.00	375.00
	1311	286 pcs.	75.00	175.00	300.00	400.00
	1312	892 pcs.	75.00	150.00	250.00	350.00
	1313	531 pcs.	75.00	175.00	300.00	400.00
	1314	—	75.00	175.00	300.00	400.00
	1315	1,042	75.00	175.00	275.00	375.00

KM#	Date	Mintage	Fine	VF	XF	Unc
1147 (Y133)	SH1320	—	150.00	350.00	750.00	1250.
	1321	—	BV	100.00	200.00	300.00
	1322	—	—	BV	40.00	50.00
	1323	.076	—	BV	40.00	50.00
	1324	—	—	Reported, not confirmed		

Obv: High relief head.

KM#	Date	Mintage	Fine	VF	XF	Unc
1149 (Y135)	SH1324	—	BV	40.00	50.00	60.00
	1325	—	BV	40.00	50.00	60.00
	1326	.036	BV	50.00	65.00	110.00
	1327	.036	BV	50.00	65.00	110.00
	1328	—	BV	60.00	75.00	130.00
	1329	75 pcs.	—	250.00	400.00	750.00
	1330	.098	—	—	—	1350.

Obv: Low relief head.

KM#	Date	Mintage	Fine	VF	XF	Unc
1161 (Y142)	SH1330	Inc.KM1149	BV	40.00	50.00	55.00
	1332	—	—	300.00	450.00	750.00
	1333	—	BV	55.00	70.00	100.00
	1334	—	—	55.00	70.00	100.00
	1335	—	—	BV	45.00	55.00
	1336	.132	—	BV	45.00	55.00
	1337	.102	—	BV	40.00	50.00
	1338	.140	—	BV	40.00	50.00
	1339	.142	—	BV	40.00	50.00
	1340	.439	—	BV	40.00	50.00
	1342	.040	—	BV	40.00	50.00
	1343	—	—	Reported, not confirmed		
	1344	.030	BV	65.00	75.00	110.00
	1345	.040	—	BV	45.00	50.00
	1346	.040	—	BV	45.00	50.00
	1347	.050	—	BV	45.00	50.00
	1348	.040	—	BV	45.00	50.00
	1349	.080	—	BV	45.00	50.00
	1350	.080	—	BV	45.00	50.00
	1351	.103	—	BV	45.00	50.00
	1352	.067	—	BV	45.00	50.00
	1353	—	—	BV	45.00	50.00

Obv. leg: *Aryamehr* added.

KM#	Date	Mintage	Fine	VF	XF	Unc
1199 (Y142a)	SH1354	.037	—	BV	45.00	50.00
	1355	.153	—	BV	45.00	50.00
	MS2536	—	—	BV	45.00	50.00
	2537	—	—	BV	45.00	50.00
	SH1358	—	—	—	275.00	375.00

PAHLAVI

8.1360 g, .900 GOLD, .2354 oz AGW

KM#	Date	Mintage	Fine	VF	XF	Unc
1133	SH1310					
(Y124)		304 pcs.	300.00	500.00	850.00	1200.

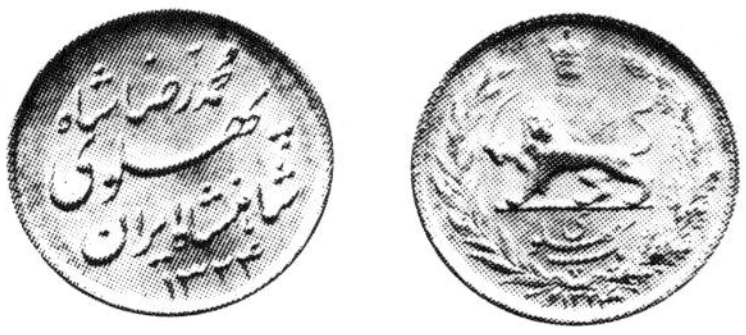

KM#	Date	Mintage	Fine	VF	XF	Unc
1148	SH1320*	—	250.00	600.00	1250.	1750.
(Y134)	1321*	—	—	—	1750.	2500.
	1322	—	—	BV	80.00	100.00
	1323	.311	—	BV	80.00	100.00
	1324	—	—	BV	80.00	100.00

***NOTE:** Possibly a pattern.

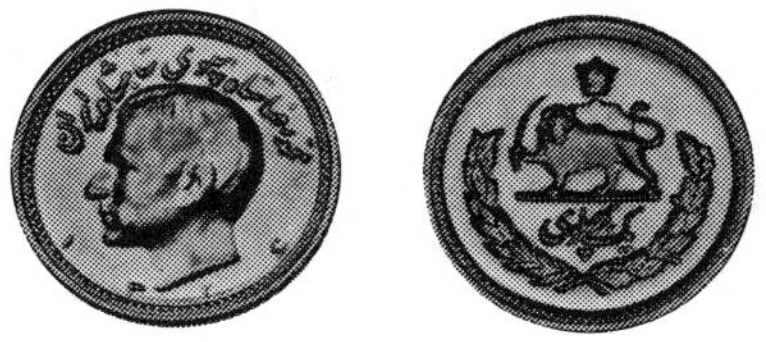

Obv: High relief head.

KM#	Date	Mintage	Fine	VF	XF	Unc
1150	SH1324	—	BV	90.00	100.00	110.00
(Y136)	1325	—	BV	90.00	100.00	110.00
	1326	.151	BV	90.00	100.00	110.00
	1327	.020	BV	90.00	100.00	110.00
	1328	4,000	BV	125.00	185.00	260.00
	1329	4,000	BV	125.00	185.00	260.00
	1330	.048	BV	125.00	185.00	260.00

Obv: Low relief head.

KM#	Date	Mintage	Fine	VF	XF	Unc
1162	SH1330	—	—	BV	80.00	100.00
(Y143)	1331	—	—	500.00	800.00	1200.
	1332	—	—	500.00	800.00	1200.
	1333	—	BV	100.00	120.00	160.00
	1334	—	BV	100.00	120.00	160.00
	1335	—	—	BV	80.00	100.00
	1336	.453	—	BV	80.00	100.00
	1337	.665	—	BV	80.00	100.00
	1338	.776	—	BV	80.00	100.00
	1339	.847	—	BV	80.00	100.00
	1340	.528	—	BV	80.00	100.00
	1342	.020	—	BV	80.00	100.00
	1343	.010	— Reported, not confirmed			
	1344	—	BV	110.00	110.00	160.00
	1345	.020	—	BV	80.00	100.00
	1346	.030	—	BV	80.00	100.00
	1347	.040	—	BV	80.00	100.00
	1348	.070	—	BV	80.00	100.00
	1349	.070	—	BV	80.00	100.00
	1350	.060	—	BV	80.00	100.00
	1351	.100	—	BV	80.00	100.00
	1352	.320	—	BV	80.00	100.00
	1353	—	—	BV	80.00	100.00

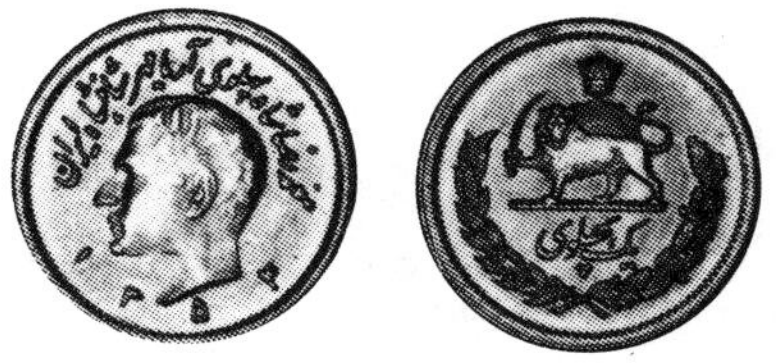

Obv. leg: *Aryamehr* added.

KM#	Date	Mintage	Fine	VF	XF	Unc
1200	SH1354	.021	—	BV	80.00	100.00
(1162a)	1355	.203	—	BV	80.00	100.00
(Y143a)						
	MS2536	—	—	BV	80.00	100.00
	2537	—	—	BV	80.00	100.00
	SH1358	—	—	125.00	200.00	300.00

2-1/2 PAHLAVI

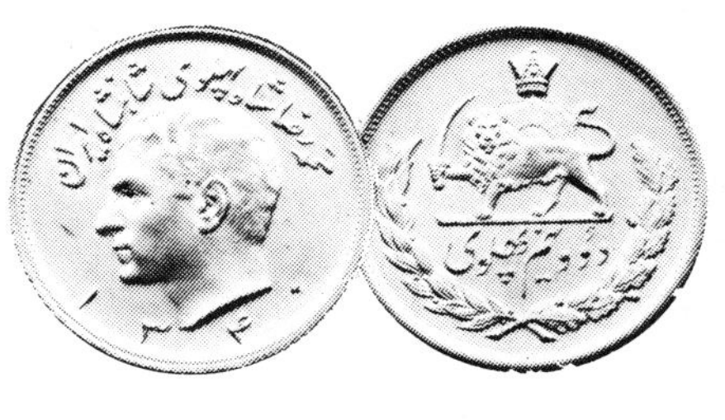

20.3400 g, .900 GOLD, .5885 oz AGW

KM#	Date	Mintage	Fine	VF	XF	Unc
A1163	SH1338	—	—	—	—	—

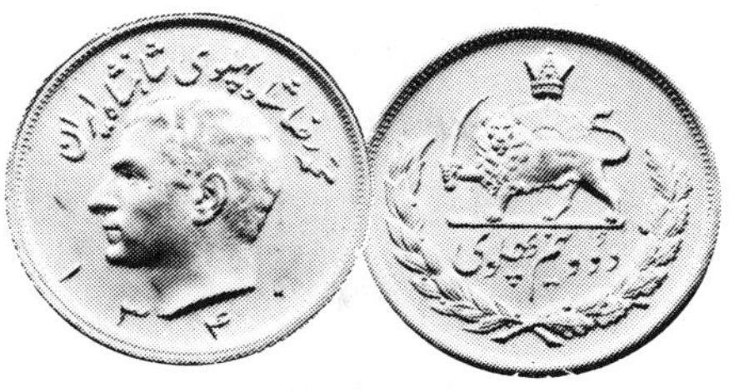

KM#	Date	Mintage	Fine	VF	XF	Unc
1163	SH1339	1,682	BV	200.00	225.00	250.00
(Y144)	1340	2,788	BV	200.00	225.00	250.00
	1342	30 pcs.	—	—	Rare	—
	1347	2,000	— Reported, not confirmed			
	1348	3,000	BV	200.00	225.00	250.00
	1349	3,000	— Reported, not confirmed			
	1350	2,000	BV	200.00	225.00	250.00
	1351	2,500	BV	200.00	225.00	250.00
	1352	3,000	BV	200.00	225.00	250.00
	1353	—	BV	200.00	225.00	250.00

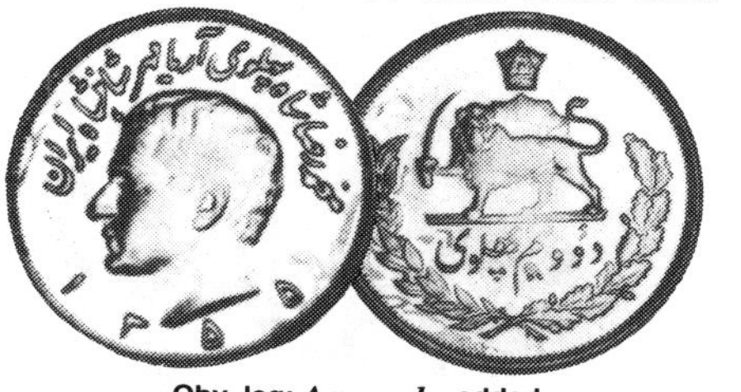

Obv. leg: *Aryamehr* added.

KM#	Date	Mintage	Fine	VF	XF	Unc
1201	SH1354	.018	—	BV	200.00	225.00
(Y144a)	1355	.016	—	BV	200.00	225.00
	MS2536	—	—	BV	200.00	225.00
	2537	—	—	BV	200.00	225.00
	SH1358	—	—	—	Rare	—

5 PAHLAVI

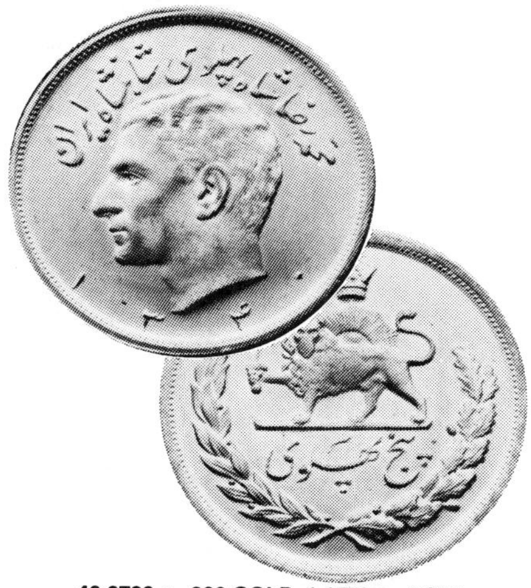

40.6799 g, .900 GOLD, 1.1772 oz AGW

KM#	Date	Mintage	Fine	VF	XF	Unc
1164	SH1339	2,225	BV	400.00	450.00	500.00
(Y145)	1340	2,430	BV	400.00	450.00	500.00
	1342	20 pcs.	—	—	Rare	—
	1347	500 pcs.	— Reported, not confirmed			
	1348	2,000	BV	400.00	450.00	500.00
	1349	700 pcs.	— Reported, not confirmed			
	1350	2,000	BV	400.00	450.00	500.00
	1351	2,500	BV	400.00	450.00	500.00
	1352	2,100	BV	400.00	450.00	500.00
	1353	—	BV	400.00	450.00	500.00

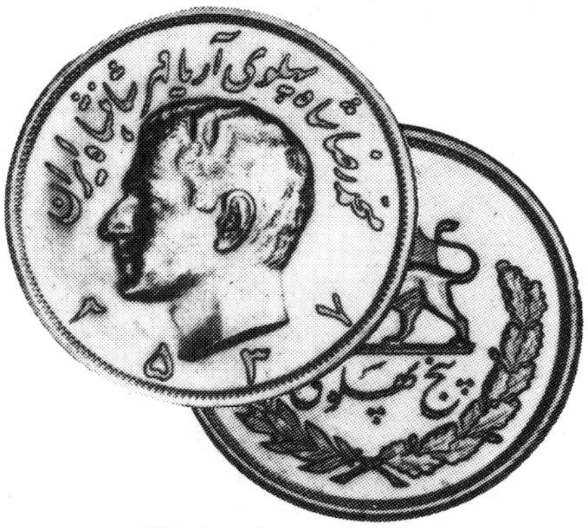

Obv. leg: *Aryamehr* added.

KM#	Date	Mintage	Fine	VF	XF	Unc
1202	SH1354	.010	—	BV	425.00	475.00
(Y145a)	1355	.017	—	BV	425.00	475.00
(Y145a)	MS2536	—	—	BV	425.00	475.00
	2537	—	—	BV	425.00	475.00
	SH1358	—	—	550.00	700.00	900.00

ISLAMIC REPUBLIC

50 DINARS

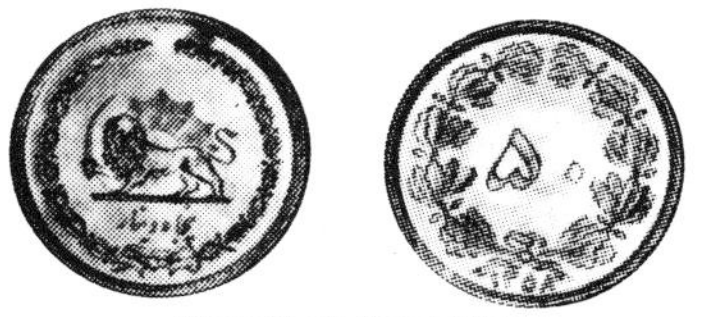

BRASS CLAD STEEL
Obv: W/o crown.

KM#	Date	Mintage	Fine	VF	XF	Unc
1231	SH1358	—	—	6.50	8.00	12.00
(Y176)						

RIAL

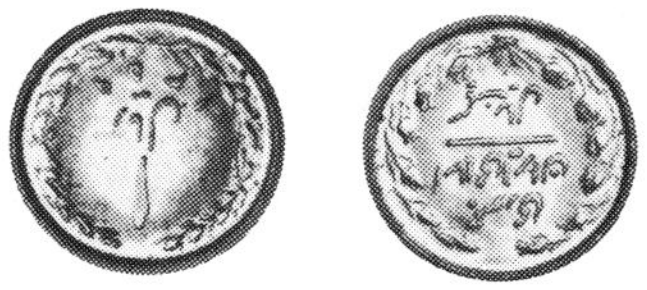

COPPER-NICKEL

KM#	Date	Mintage	Fine	VF	XF	Unc
1232	SH1358	—	—	.25	.75	1.75
(Y164)	1359	—	—	.25	.75	1.75
	1360	—	—	.25	.75	1.75
	1361	—	—	.25	.75	1.75
	1362	—	—	.25	.75	1.75
	1363	—	— Reported, not confirmed			
	1364	—	—	.25	.75	1.75
	1365	—	—	.15	.65	1.25
	1366	—	—	.15	.65	1.25
	1367	—	—	.15	.65	1.25

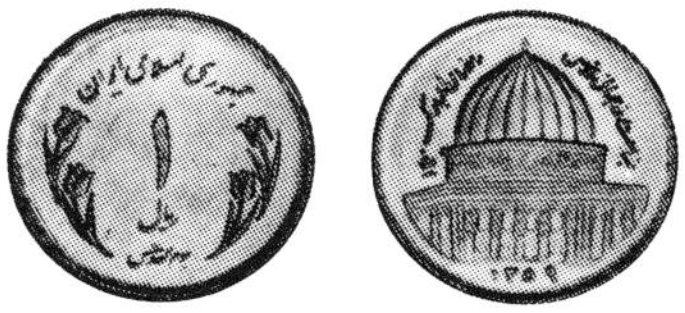

BRONZE CLAD STEEL
Mosque of Omar, World Jerusalem Day

KM#	Date	Mintage	Fine	VF	XF	Unc
1245	SH1359	—	—	.50	1.75	2.50
(Y171)						

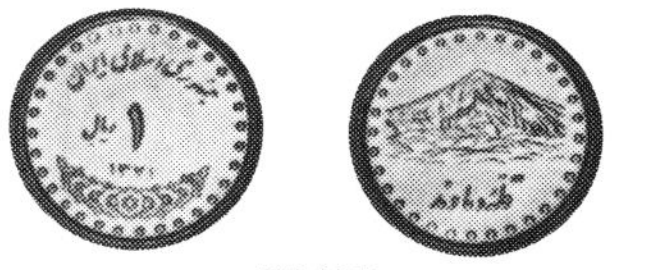

BRASS
Mount Damavand

KM#	Date	Mintage	Fine	VF	XF	Unc
1263	SH1371	—	—	2.50	5.00	10.00
(Y185)						

2 RIALS

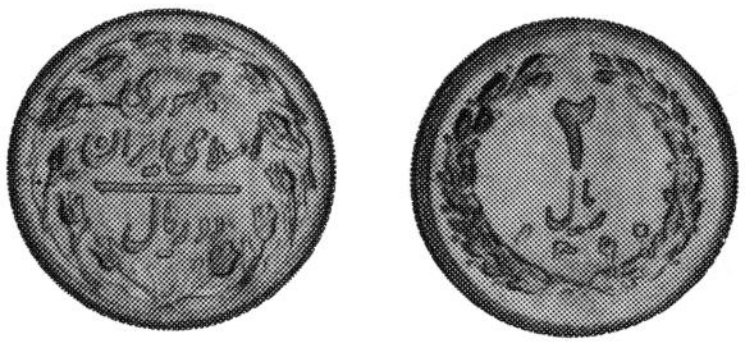

COPPER-NICKEL

KM#	Date	Mintage	Fine	VF	XF	Unc
1233	SH1358	—	—	.60	1.00	3.00
(Y165)	1359	—	—	.50	1.00	3.00
	1360	—	—	.50	1.00	3.00
	1361	—	—	.50	.75	2.75
	1362	—	—	.35	.50	2.50
	1363	—	—	.50	.75	2.75
	1364	—	—	.35	.50	2.50
	1365	—	—	.25	.50	2.00
	1366	—	—	.25	.50	2.00
	1367	—	—	.25	.50	2.00

5 RIALS

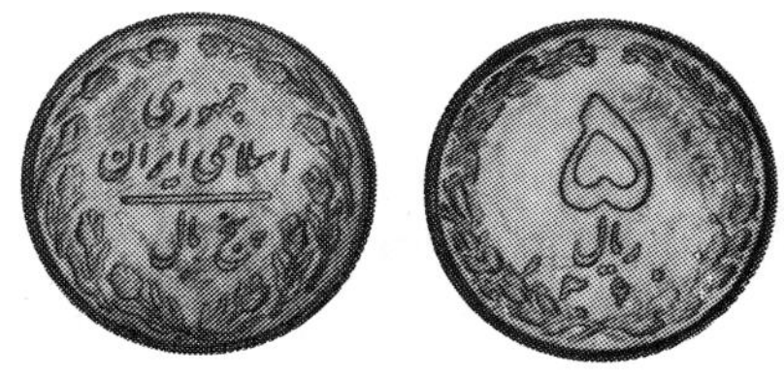

COPPER-NICKEL

KM#	Date	Mintage	Fine	VF	XF	Unc
1234	SH1358	—	—	.75	1.00	3.00
(Y166)	1359	—	—	.75	1.00	3.00
	1360	—	—	.75	1.00	3.00
	1361	—	—	.75	1.00	3.00

KM#	Date	Mintage	Fine	VF	XF	Unc
(Y166)	1362	—	—	.75	1.00	3.00
	1363	—	—	.75	1.00	3.00
	1364	—	—	.75	1.00	3.00
	1365	—	—	.75	1.00	3.00
	1366	—	—	.75	1.00	3.00
	1367	—	—	.75	1.00	3.00
	1368	—	—	.75	1.00	3.00

NOTE: Date varieties exist.

BRASS
Tomb of Hafez

1258	SH1371	—	—	—	—	2.75
(Y182)	1372	—	—	—	—	2.75
	1373	—	—	—	—	2.75
	1375	—	—	—	—	2.75

10 RIALS

 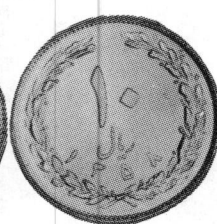

COPPER-NICKEL

1235.1	SH1358	—	—	1.00	2.50	4.50
(Y167.1)	1358 lg. dt.	—	—	1.00	2.50	4.50
	1359	—	—	1.00	2.50	4.50
	1360	—	—	1.00	2.50	4.50
	1361	—	—	1.00	2.00	4.00

Rev: Redesigned wreath.

1235.2	SH1361	—	—	1.00	2.00	4.00
(Y167.2)	1362	—	—	1.00	2.00	4.00
	1363	—	—	1.00	2.00	4.00
	1364	—	—	.90	1.50	4.00
	1365	—	—	.90	1.50	4.00
	1366	—	—	.90	1.50	4.00
	1366 sm. dt.	—	—	.90	1.50	4.00
	1367	—	—	.65	1.50	3.00

NOTE: Date varieties exist.

1st Anniversary of Revolution

1243	SH1358	—	—	1.50	2.50	4.50
(Y169)						

Moslem Unity
Reeded edge, 6.97 g.

1249	SH1361	—	—	1.50	2.50	4.50
(Y175.1)						

World Jerusalem Day
Plain edge, 3.02 g.
Obv: Small denomination numerals.

1253.1	SH1368	—	—	1.00	2.00	4.00
(Y175.2)						

Obv: Large denomination numerals.

KM#	Date	Mintage	Fine	VF	XF	Unc
1253.2	SH1368	—	—	1.00	2.00	4.00
(Y175.3)						

ALUMINUM-BRONZE
Tomb of Ferdousi

1259	SH1371	—	—	1.00	2.00	4.00
(Y180)	1372	—	—	1.00	2.00	4.00
	1373	—	—	1.00	2.00	4.00
	1374	—	—	1.00	2.00	4.00

20 RIALS

COPPER-NICKEL

1236	SH1358	—	—	1.00	1.65	4.50
(Y168)	1359	—	—	1.00	1.65	4.50
	1360	—	—	1.00	1.65	4.50
	1361	—	—	1.00	1.65	4.50
	1362	—	—	1.00	1.65	4.50
	1363	—	—	1.00	1.65	4.50
	1364	—	—	1.00	1.65	4.50
	1365	—	—	1.00	1.65	4.50
	1366	—	—	1.00	1.65	4.50
	1367	—	—	1.00	1.65	4.50

NOTE: Date varieties exist.

1400th Anniversary of Mohammed's Flight

1244	SH1358	—	—	2.50	3.50	5.00
(Y170)						

2nd Anniversary of Islamic Revolution

1246	SH1359	—	—	2.50	3.50	5.00
(Y174)						

3rd Anniversary of Islamic Revolution

1247	SH1360	—	—	2.50	3.50	5.00
(Y173)						

Islamic Banking Week

KM#	Date	Mintage	Fine	VF	XF	Unc
1251	SH1367	—	—	2.50	3.50	5.00
(Y177)						

8 Years of Sacred Defense
Obv: 22 dots around rim. 2.00mm thick.

1254.1	SH1368	—	—	2.50	3.50	5.00
(Y178.1)						

1.70mm thick.
Rev: Redesigned thick wreath.

1254.2	SH1368	—	—	2.50	3.50	5.00
(Y178.2)						

Obv: 20 dots around rim.

1254.3	SH1368	—	—	2.50	3.50	5.00

50 RIALS

ALUMINUM-BRONZE
Oil and Agriculture
Lettered edge.
Rev: Map in relief.

1237.1	SH1359	—	—	2.00	3.50	8.00
(Y172.1)	1360	—	—	2.00	3.50	8.00
	1361	—	—	2.00	3.50	8.00
	1362	—	—	2.00	3.50	8.00
	1364	—	—	2.00	3.50	8.00
	1365	—	—	2.00	3.50	8.00

NOTE: 2 varieties of edge lettering exist.

Rev: Map incuse.

1237.2	SH1366	—	—	4.00	6.00	9.00
(Y172.2)	1367	—	—	—	4.50	7.00
	1368	—	—	—	4.50	7.00

COPPER-NICKEL
Lettered edge

1237.1a	SH1368	—	—	2.00	3.50	8.00
(Y172a)	1369	—	—	2.00	3.50	8.00
	1370	—	—	2.00	3.50	8.00

10th Anniversary of Revolution

1252	SH1367	—	—	3.00	5.00	7.50
(Y179)						

Shrine of Hazrat Masumah

KM#	Date	Mintage	Fine	VF	XF	Unc
1260	SH1371	—	—	2.50	4.00	6.00
(Y181)	1372	—	—	2.50	4.00	6.00
	1373	—	—	2.50	4.00	6.00
	1374	—	—	2.50	4.00	6.00
	1375	—	—	2.50	4.00	6.00

100 RIALS

COPPER-NICKEL
Shrine of Imam Reza
Obv: Thin denomination, numerals.

1261.1	SH1371	—	—	—	—	6.00
(Y183)						

Obv: Thick denomination, numerals.

1261.2	1372	—	—	—	—	6.00
(Y183)	1373	—	—	—	—	6.00
	1375	—	—	—	—	6.00

250 RIALS

COPPER-NICKEL center in BRASS ring
Stylized Flower

1262	SH1372	—	—	—	—	7.50
(Y184)	1373	—	—	—	—	7.50
	1374	—	—	—	—	7.50
	1375	—	—	—	—	7.50

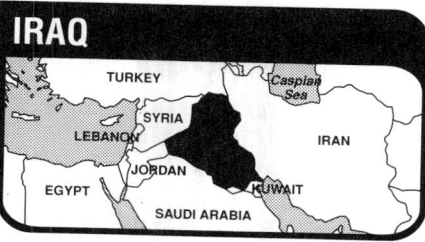

IRAQ

The Republic of Iraq, historically known as Mesopotamia, is located in the Near East and is bordered by Kuwait, Iran, Turkey, Syria, Jordan and Saudi Arabia. It has an area of 167,925 sq. mi. (434,920 sq. km.) and a population of 14 million. Capital: Baghdad. The economy of Iraq is based on agriculture and petroleum. Crude oil accounted for 94 percent of the exports before the war with Iran began in 1980.

Mesopotamia was the site of a number of flourishing civilizations of antiquity - Sumeria, Assyria, Babylonia, Parthia, Persia - and of the Biblical cities of Ur, Nineveh and Babylon. Desired because of its favored location which embraced the fertile alluvial plains of the Tigris and Euphrates Rivers, Mesopotamia - 'land between the rivers' - was conquered by Cyrus the Great of Persia, Alexander of Macedonia and by Arabs who made the legendary city of Baghdad the capital of the ruling caliphate. Suleiman the Magnificent conquered Mesopotamia for Turkey in 1534, and it formed part of the Ottoman Empire until 1623, and from 1638 to 1917. Great Britain, given a League of Nations mandate over the territory in 1920, recognized Iraq as a kingdom in 1922. Iraq became an independent constitutional monarchy presided over by the Hashemite family, direct descendants of the prophet Mohammed, in 1932. In 1958, the army-led revolution of July 14 overthrew the monarchy and proclaimed a republic.

NOTE: The 'I' mint mark on 1938 and 1943 issues appears on the obverse near the point of the bust. Some of the issues of 1938 have a dot to denote a composition change from nickel to copper-nickel.

RULERS

Ottoman, until 1917
British, 1921-1922
Faisal I, 1921-1933
Ghazi I, 1933-1939
Faisal II,
  Regency, 1939-1953
  King, 1953-1958

MINT MARKS

I - Bombay

MONETARY SYSTEM

Falus, Fulus   *Fals, Fils*   *Falsan*

50 Fils = 1 Dirham
200 Fils = 1 Riyal
1000 Fils = 1 Dinar (Pound)

TITLES

al-Iraq   العراق

المملكة العراقية
al-Mamlaka(t) al-Iraqiya(t)

الجمهورية العرقية
al-Jumhuriya(t) al-Iraqiya(t)

KINGDOM
FILS

BRONZE
Faisal I

KM#	Date	Mintage	Fine	VF	XF	Unc
95	1931	4.000	1.00	3.00	10.00	25.00
	1931	—	—	—	Proof	—
	1933	6.000	1.00	3.00	10.00	25.00
	1933	—	—	—	Proof	—

Ghazi I

KM#	Date	Mintage	Fine	VF	XF	Unc
102	1936	3.000	1.25	4.00	10.00	25.00
	1936	—	—	—	Proof	—
	1938	36.000	.25	.50	1.00	2.50
	1938	—	—	—	Proof	—
	1938-I	3.000	.50	2.00	5.00	15.00

Faisal II

109	1953	41.000	.25	.40	.60	1.00
	1953	200 pcs.	—	—	Proof	75.00

2 FILS

BRONZE
Faisal I

96	1931	2.500	1.25	4.00	10.00	25.00
	1931	—	—	—	Proof	—
	1933	1.000	1.50	5.00	15.00	35.00
	1933	—	—	—	Proof	—

Faisal II

110	1953	.500	.50	1.00	3.00	12.50
	1953	200 pcs.	—	—	Proof	100.00

4 FILS

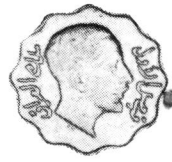 

NICKEL
Faisal I

97	1931	4.500	1.50	5.00	15.00	50.00
	1931	—	—	—	Proof	—
	1933	6.500	1.50	5.00	15.00	50.00
	1933	—	—	—	Proof	—

Ghazi I

105	1938	1.000	1.00	2.00	6.00	15.00
	1938	—	—	—	Proof	—
	1939	1.000	1.25	2.50	10.00	30.00
	1939	—	—	—	Proof	—

COPPER-NICKEL

105a	1938.	2.750	.75	1.00	2.00	6.00
	1938.	—	—	—	Proof	—
	1938-I	2.500	1.00	2.00	7.50	15.00

BRONZE

105b	1938.	8.000	.50	1.00	2.00	6.00
	1938.	—	—	—	Proof	—

Faisal II

KM#	Date	Mintage	Fine	VF	XF	Unc
107	1943-I	1.500	2.00	3.00	7.00	15.00

COPPER-NICKEL

| 111 | 1953 | 20.750 | .60 | .75 | 1.00 | 2.00 |
| | 1953 | 200 pcs. | — | — | Proof | 75.00 |

10 FILS

NICKEL
Faisal I

98	1931	2.400	2.00	6.00	16.50	50.00
	1931		—	—	Proof	—
	1933	2.200	2.00	6.00	16.50	50.00
	1933		—	—	Proof	—

Ghazi I

103	1937	.400	3.00	5.00	16.50	50.00
	1937		—	—	Proof	—
	1938	.600	2.50	4.00	10.00	35.00
	1938		—	—	Proof	—

COPPER-NICKEL

103a	1938.	1.100	1.00	2.00	4.00	10.00
	1938.		—	—	Proof	—
	1938-I	1.500	1.50	2.50	6.00	15.00

BRONZE

| 103b | 1938. | 8.250 | .50 | 1.00 | 3.00 | 7.00 |
| | 1938. | | — | — | Proof | — |

Faisal II

| 108 | 1943-I | 1.500 | 3.00 | 7.00 | 20.00 | 50.00 |

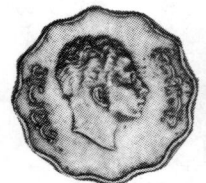 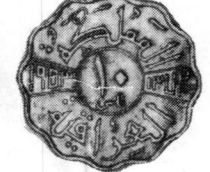

COPPER-NICKEL

| 112 | 1953 | 11.400 | .50 | .75 | 1.00 | 2.00 |
| | 1953 | 200 pcs. | — | — | Proof | 75.00 |

20 FILS

3.6000 g, .500 SILVER, .0579 oz ASW
Faisal I

KM#	Date	Mintage	Fine	VF	XF	Unc
99	1931	1.500	2.50	9.00	25.00	75.00
	1931		—	—	Proof	—
	1933	1.100	2.50	9.00	25.00	75.00
	1933		—	—	Proof	—
	1933 (error) 1252					
	Inc. Ab.	20.00	60.00	100.00	200.00

Ghazi I

| 106 | 1938 | 1.200 | 1.50 | 3.00 | 7.00 | 20.00 |
| | 1938-I | 1.350 | 1.50 | 3.50 | 8.00 | 25.00 |

Faisal II

| 113 | 1953 | .250 | 25.00 | 50.00 | 75.00 | 145.00 |
| | 1953 | 200 pcs. | — | — | Proof | 300.00 |

2.8000 g, .500 SILVER, .0450 oz ASW

| 116 | 1955 | 4.000 | 1.50 | 3.00 | 5.00 | 10.00 |
| | 1955 | | — | — | Proof | 80.00 |

50 FILS

9.0000 g, .500 SILVER, .1447 oz ASW
Faisal I

100	1931	8.800	2.50	9.00	25.00	75.00
	1931		—	—	Proof	—
	1933	.800	6.00	15.00	35.00	100.00
	1933		—	—	Proof	—

Ghazi I

104	1937	1.200	2.50	7.00	10.00	30.00
	1937		—	—	Proof	—
	1938	5.300	1.75	3.75	6.00	25.00
	1938		—	—	Proof	—
	1938-I	7.500	1.75	3.75	6.00	25.00

Faisal II

| 114 | 1953 | .560 | 50.00 | 100.00 | 150.00 | 250.00 |
| | 1953 | 200 pcs. | — | — | Proof | 450.00 |

7.0000 g, .500 SILVER, .1126 oz ASW

KM#	Date	Mintage	Fine	VF	XF	Unc
117	1955	12.000	2.50	4.00	6.00	12.50
	1955				Proof	80.00

100 FILS

10.0000 g, .900 SILVER, .2893 oz ASW
Faisal II

| 115 | 1953 | 1.200 | 5.00 | 7.50 | 20.00 | 50.00 |
| | 1953 | 200 pcs. | — | — | Proof | 250.00 |

10.0000 g, .500 SILVER, .1607 oz ASW

| 118 | 1955 | 1.000 | — | 700.00 | 1000. | 1500. |
| | 1955 | | — | — | Proof | 300.00 |

RIYAL
(200 Fils)

20.0000 g, .500 SILVER, .3215 oz ASW
Faisal I

Dav.#255

| 101 | 1932 | .500 | 7.50 | 15.00 | 35.00 | 225.00 |
| | 1932 | | — | — | Proof | 1000. |

REPUBLIC
FILS

BRONZE

| 119 | 1959 | 72.000 | .15 | .25 | .40 | .75 |
| | 1959 | 400 pcs. | — | — | Proof | 30.00 |

5 FILS

 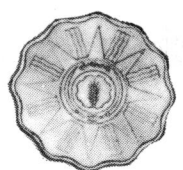

COPPER-NICKEL

KM#	Date	Mintage	Fine	VF	XF	Unc
120	1959	30.000	.15	.25	.50	1.00
	1959	400 pcs.	—	—	Proof	30.00

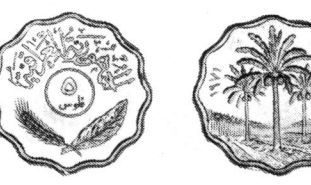

| 125 | 1967 | 17.000 | .15 | .25 | .35 | .50 |
| | 1971 | 15.000 | .15 | .25 | .35 | .50 |

STAINLESS STEEL

125a	1971	2.000	.20	.30	.50	.75
	1974	15.000	.10	.15	.25	.35
	1975	94.800	.10	.15	.25	.35
	1980	20.160	.10	.15	.25	.35
	1981	29.840	.10	.15	.25	.35

F.A.O. Issue

| 141 | 1975 | 2.000 | .10 | .15 | .25 | .50 |

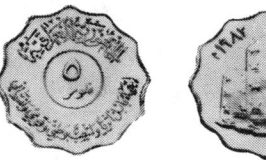

Babylon - Ruins

| 159 | 1982 | — | .10 | .15 | .25 | .50 |

COPPER-NICKEL

| 159a | 1982 | — | — | — | Proof | 3.00 |

10 FILS

COPPER-NICKEL

| 121 | 1959 | 24.000 | .25 | .35 | .65 | 1.50 |
| | 1959 | 400 pcs. | — | — | Proof | 30.00 |

| 126 | 1967 | 13.400 | .20 | .30 | .60 | 1.25 |
| | 1971 | 12.000 | .20 | .30 | .60 | 1.25 |

STAINLESS STEEL

126a	1971	1.550	.25	.35	.65	1.50
	1974	12.000	.20	.30	.50	1.00
	1975	52.456	.20	.30	.50	1.00
	1979	13.800	.20	.30	.50	1.00
	1980	11.264	.20	.30	.50	1.00
	1981	63.736	.20	.30	.50	1.00

F.A.O. Issue

KM#	Date	Mintage	Fine	VF	XF	Unc
142	1975	1.000	.15	.25	.50	.75

Babylon - Ishtar Gate

| 160 | 1982 | — | — | — | — | .75 |

COPPER-NICKEL

| 160a | 1982 | — | — | — | Proof | 3.00 |

25 FILS

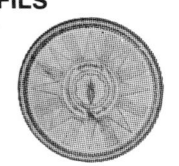

2.5000 g, .500 SILVER, .0401 oz ASW

| 122 | 1959 | 12.000 | .50 | .75 | 1.50 | 3.00 |
| | 1959 | 400 pcs. | — | — | Proof | 40.00 |

COPPER-NICKEL

127	1969	6.000	.20	.30	.50	1.00
	1970	6.000	.20	.30	.50	1.00
	1972	12.000	.20	.30	.50	1.00
	1975	48.000	.20	.30	.50	1.00
	1981	60.000	.20	.30	.50	1.00

Babylon - Lion

| 161 | 1982 | — | — | — | — | 1.25 |
| | 1982 | — | — | — | Proof | 4.00 |

50 FILS

5.0000 g, .500 SILVER, .0803 oz ASW

| 123 | 1959 | 24.000 | .75 | 1.25 | 2.00 | 4.50 |
| | 1959 | 400 pcs. | — | — | Proof | 80.00 |

COPPER-NICKEL

128	1969	12.000	.25	.35	.65	1.25
	1970	12.000	.25	.35	.65	1.25
	1972	12.000	.25	.35	.65	1.25
	1975	36.000	.25	.35	.65	1.25
	1979	1.500	.25	.35	.65	1.75
	1980	23.520	.25	.35	.65	1.25
	1981	138.995	.25	.35	.65	1.00
	1990	—	.25	.35	.65	1.00

Babylon - Bull

KM#	Date	Mintage	Fine	VF	XF	Unc
162	1982	—	.25	.50	.75	2.50
	1982	—	—	—	Proof	6.00

100 FILS

10.0000 g, .500 SILVER, .1607 oz ASW

| 124 | 1959 | 6.000 | 2.00 | 3.00 | 4.50 | 9.00 |
| | 1959 | 400 pcs. | — | — | Proof | 150.00 |

COPPER-NICKEL

129	1970	6.000	.35	.50	.75	1.50
	1972	6.000	.35	.50	.75	1.50
	1975	12.000	.35	.50	.75	1.50
	1979	1.000	.35	.75	1.50	3.00

250 FILS

NICKEL
F.A.O. Issue - Agrarian Reform Day

| 130 | 1970 | .500 | — | 1.50 | 3.00 | |
| | 1970 | 1,000 | — | — | Proof | |

NOTE: Edge inscription w/FAO-250-repeated times, relief and incuse varieties reported.

1st Anniversary Peac 5.00

| 131 | 1971 | .500 | — | 3.50 | | |
| | 1971 | 1,000 | — | | | |

6.50

Silv

| 135 | 1972 | | | | | |

25th Anniversary of Central Bank

KM#	Date	Mintage	Fine	VF	XF	Unc
136	1972	.250	—	1.50	3.00	6.50

Oil Nationalization

	138	1973	.260	—	1.50	3.00	7.00
		1973	5,000	—	—	Proof	12.00

International Year of the Child

144	1979	.010	—	—	Proof	8.00

COPPER-NICKEL
1st Anniversary of Hussein as President

	1980	—	—	1.00	2.00	5.00

	—	—	1.00	2.00	5.00
	25.568	—	1.00	2.00	5.00
	—	—	1.00	2.00	5.00

Food Day

		1.00	2.00	4.50

Nonaligned Nations Baghdad Conference

KM#	Date	Mintage	Fine	VF	XF	Unc
155	1982	—	—	1.00	2.00	5.50

Babylon - Top of Hammurabi Stele

163	1982	—	—	1.00	2.00	4.50
	1982	—	—	—	Proof	8.00

500 FILS

NICKEL
50th Anniversary of Iraqi Army

132	1971	.100	—	2.50	4.50	11.50
	1971	5,000	—	—	Proof	15.00

Oil Nationalization

139	1973	.260	—	2.50	4.50	10.00
	1973	5,000	—	—	Proof	15.00

9.08 g
Obv. denomination: *500 Fals*

165	1982	—	—	—	2.50	4.00	7.50

Reduced weight, 8.98 g
Obv. denomination: *500 Falsan*

165a	1982	—	—	20.00	35.00	85.00

9.08 g
Babylon - Lion of Babylon
Obv. denomination: *500 Fals*

KM#	Date	Mintage	Fine	VF	XF	Unc
168	1982	—	—	2.00	3.50	8.50
	1982	—	—	—	Proof	12.50

Obv. denomination: *500 Falsan*

168a	1982	—	—	18.00	30.00	75.00

DINAR

31.0000 g, .900 SILVER, .8971 oz ASW
50th Anniversary of Iraqi Army
Obv: Similar to 500 Fils, KM#132.

133	1971	.020	—	—	—	22.00
	1971	—	—	—	Proof	37.50

31.0000 g, .500 SILVER, .4983 oz ASW
25th Anniversary of Central Bank
Obv: Similar to 250 Fils, KM#136.

137	1972	.050	—	—	—	20.00
	1972	—	—	—	Proof	32.50

Oil Nationalization

KM#	Date	Mintage	Fine	VF	XF	Unc
140	1973	.060	—	—	—	20.00
	1973	5,000	—	—	Proof	35.00

NICKEL
Battle of Qadissyiat - Saddam Hussein

149	1980	—	—	—	3.50	9.00
	1980	—	—	—	Proof	12.50

50th Anniversary of Iraq Air Force -
Saddam Hussein

153	1981	—	—	—	3.50	9.00

Circulation Coinage

170	1981	—	—	—	—	3.50

Nonaligned Nations Baghdad Conference

156	1982	—	—	—	3.50	9.00

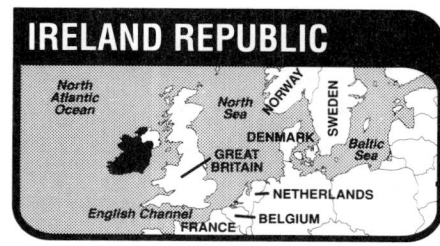

Tower of Babylon

KM#	Date	Mintage	Fine	VF	XF	Unc
164	1982	—	—	—	3.50	9.00
	1982	—	—	—	Proof	12.50

The Republic of Ireland, which occupies five-sixths of the island of Ireland located in the Atlantic Ocean west of Great Britain, has an area of 27,136 sq. mi. (70,280 sq. km.) and a population of 4.3 million. Capital: Dublin. Agriculture and dairy farming are the principal industries. Meat, livestock, dairy products and textiles are exported.

A race of tall, red-haired Celts from Gaul arrived in Ireland about 400 B.C., assimilated the native Erainn and Picts, and established a Gaelic civilization. After the arrival of St. Patrick in 432AD, Ireland evolved into a center of Latin learning which sent missionaries to Europe and possibly North America. In 1154, Pope Adrian IV gave all of Ireland to English King Henry II to administer as a Papal fief. Because of the enactment of anti-Catholic laws and the awarding of vast tracts of Irish land to Protestant absentee landowners, English control did not become reasonably absolute until 1800 when England and Ireland became the 'United Kingdom of Great Britain and Ireland'. Religious freedom was restored to the Irish in 1829, but agitation for political autonomy continued until the Irish Free State was established as a dominion on Dec. 6, 1921. Ireland proclaimed itself a republic on April 18, 1949. The government, however, does not use the term "Republic of Ireland", which tacitly acknowledges the partitioning of the island into Ireland and Northern Ireland, but refers to the country simply as "Ireland".

RULERS

British, until 1921

MONETARY SYSTEM

4 Farthings = 1 Penny
12 Pence = 1 Shilling
2 Shillings = 1 Florin
20 Shillings = 1 Pound

FARTHING

BRONZE
European Woodcock
Obv. leg: EIREANN = Irish Free State.

KM#	Date	Mintage	Fine	VF	XF	Unc
1	1928	.300	.50	1.50	4.50	10.00
	1928	6,001	—	—	Proof	15.00
	1930	.288	.75	1.50	4.50	17.50
	1931	.192	4.50	8.00	15.00	35.00
	1931	—	—	—	Proof	—
	1932	.192	5.00	10.00	18.00	45.00
	1933	.480	.75	1.50	4.00	16.50
	1935	.192	5.00	8.00	15.00	35.00
	1936	.192	5.00	8.00	16.50	37.50
	1937	.480	.50	1.50	3.00	14.50

Obv. leg: EIRE = Ireland.

9	1939	.786	.50	1.00	2.00	7.50
	1939	—	—	—	Proof	815.00
	1940	.192	2.00	4.00	8.00	20.00
	1941	.480	.50	.75	2.00	6.50
	1943	.480	.50	.75	2.00	6.50
	1944	.480	.75	1.25	3.00	10.00
	1946	.480	.50	.75	2.00	6.00
	1946	—	—	—	Proof	—
	1949	.192	.75	3.00	6.00	18.00
	1949	—	—	—	Proof	300.00
	1953	.192	.25	.50	1.25	3.00
	1953	—	—	—	Proof	300.00
	1959	.192	.25	.50	1.25	3.00
	1966	.096	.35	.75	1.50	3.50

1/2 PENNY

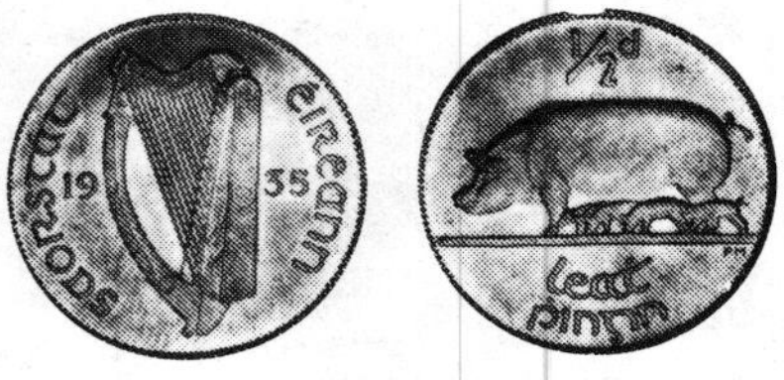

BRONZE
Sow with Piglets
Obv. leg: EIREANN = Irish Free State.

KM#	Date	Mintage	Fine	VF	XF	Unc
2	1928	2.880	.75	2.00	5.00	14.00
	1928	6,001	—	—	Proof	15.00
	1933	.720	5.00	15.00	80.00	750.00
	1935	.960	2.00	6.00	50.00	275.00
	1937	.960	1.00	3.00	15.00	35.00

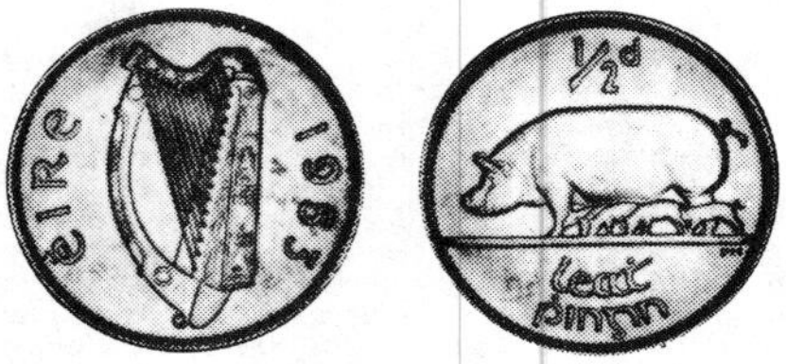

Obv. leg: EIRE = Ireland.

10	1939	.240	10.00	17.50	60.00	200.00
	1939	—	—	—	Proof	1000.
	1940	1.680	1.00	4.50	40.00	150.00
	1941	2.400	.20	.50	2.50	20.00
	1942	6.931	.10	.25	1.50	8.00
	1943	2.669	.20	.50	3.00	22.00
	1946	.720	1.00	2.50	15.00	60.00
	1949	1.344	.10	.25	1.50	12.50
	1949	—	—	—	Proof	—
	1953	2.400	.10	.15	.25	1.00
	1953				Proof	400.00
	1964	2.160	.10	.15	.25	1.00
	1965	1.440	.10	.15	.75	2.00
	1966	1.680	.10	.15	.25	1.00
	1967	1.200	.10	.15	.25	1.00

PENNY

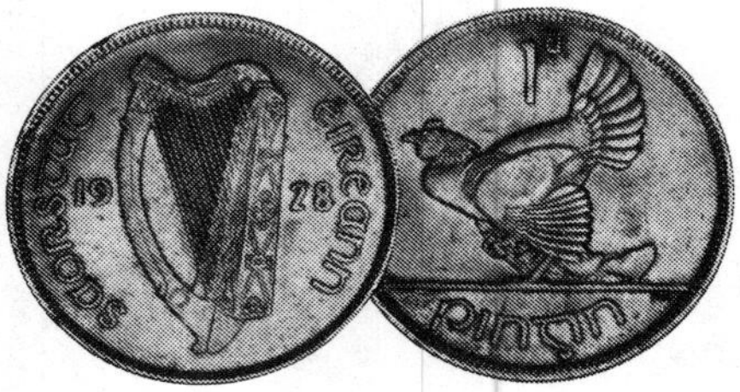

BRONZE
Hen with Chicks
Obv. leg: EIREANN = Irish Free State.

3	1928	9.000	.50	1.00	4.00	20.00
	1928	6,001	—	—	Proof	18.50
	1931	2.400	1.00	2.00	12.00	60.00
	1931				Proof	1500.
	1933	1.680	1.00	2.50	25.00	125.00
	1935	5.472	.50	1.00	8.00	32.00
	1937	5.400	.50	1.00	15.00	70.00
	1937				Proof	1500.

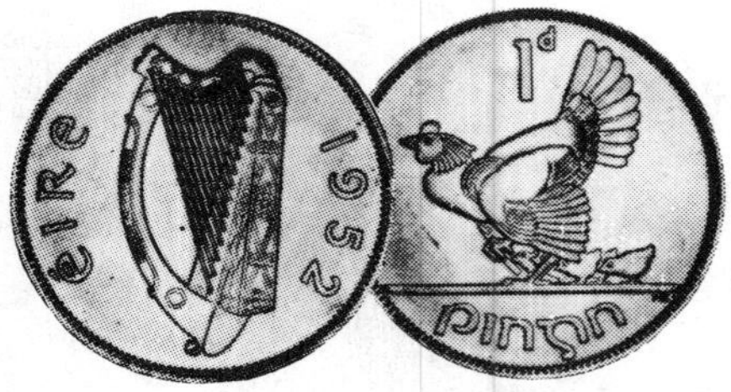

Obv. leg: EIRE = Ireland.

KM#	Date	Mintage	Fine	VF	XF	Unc
11	1938	—	—	—	Unique	15,000.
	1940	.312	3.00	10.00	75.00	225.00
	1941	4.680	.25	.50	8.00	50.00
	1942	17.520	.25	.50	2.00	11.50
	1943	3.360	.75	1.50	7.50	45.00
	1946	4.800	.25	.50	3.00	20.00
	1948	4.800	.25	.50	3.00	8.00
	1949	4.080	.25	.50	3.00	8.00
	1949	—	—	—	Proof	600.00
	1950	2.400	.25	.50	3.50	12.50
	1950	—	—	—	Proof	600.00
	1952	2.400	.25	.50	2.00	6.00
	1962	1.200	.75	2.50	3.50	12.50
	1962	—	—	—	Proof	175.00
	1963	9.600	.20	.40	.75	2.00
	1963	—	—	—	Proof	175.00
11	1964	6.000	.20	.40	.75	1.50
	1964	—	—	—	Proof	—
	1965	11.160	.20	.40	.75	1.50
	1966	6.000	.20	.40	.75	1.50
	1967	2.400	.20	.40	.75	1.50
	1968	21.000	.20	.40	.75	1.50
	1968	—	—	—	Proof	350.00

NOTE: Varieties exist.

3 PENCE

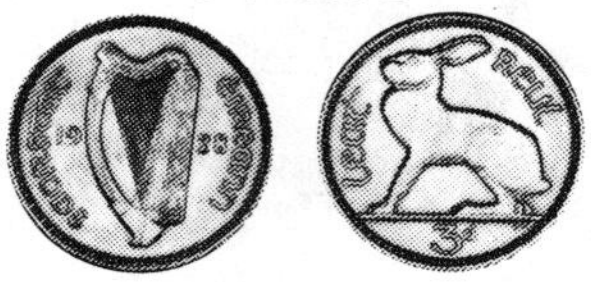

NICKEL
Blue Hare
Obv. leg: EIREANN = Irish Free State.

4	1928	1.500	.50	1.00	3.50	10.00
	1928	6,001	—	—	Proof	20.00
	1933	.320	3.00	10.00	75.00	400.00
	1934	.800	1.00	2.00	12.50	70.00
	1935	.240	3.00	8.00	35.00	225.00

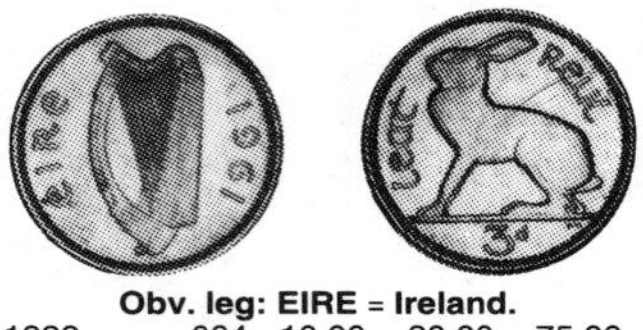

Obv. leg: EIRE = Ireland.

12	1939	.064	10.00	20.00	75.00	525.00
	1939	—	—	—	Proof	1500.
	1940	.720	1.50	3.00	12.50	50.00

COPPER-NICKEL

12a	1942	4.000	.25	.75	6.00	30.00
	1942				Proof	500.00
	1943	1.360	.50	2.00	15.00	80.00
	1943	—	—	—	Proof	—
	1946	.800	1.00	2.00	10.00	45.00
	1946	—	—	—	Proof	200.00
	1948	1.600	1.00	2.00	35.00	125.00
	1949	1.200	.25	.50	3.00	25.00
	1949	—	—	—	Proof	200.00
	1950	1.600	.25	.50	3.00	20.00
	1950	—	—	—	Proof	500.00
	1953	1.600	.25	.50	2.00	10.00
	1956	1.200	.25	.50	2.00	8.00
	1961	2.400	.15	.25	.50	6.00
	1962	3.200	.15	.25	.50	8.00
	1963	4.000	.15	.25	.50	2.50
	1964	4.000	.10	.15	.25	1.50
	1965	3.600	.10	.15	.25	1.50
	1966	4.000	.10	.15	.25	1.00
	1967	2.400	.10	.15	.25	1.00
	1968	4.000	.10	.15	.25	1.00
	1968	—	—	—	Proof	—

6 PENCE

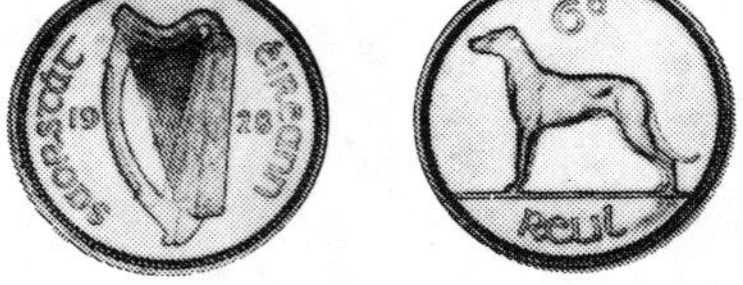

NICKEL
Irish Wolfhound
Obv. leg: EIREANN = Irish Free State.

5	1928	3.201	.50	1.00	5.00	17.50
	1928	6,001	—	—	Proof	25.00
	1934	.600	1.00	2.00	17.50	125.00
	1935	.520	1.00	3.00	30.00	320.00

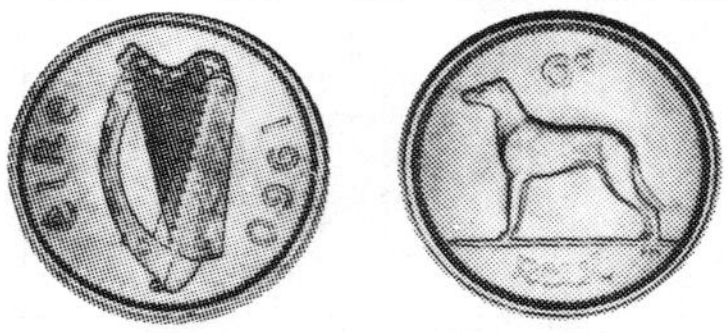

Obv. leg: EIRE = Ireland.

13	1939	.876	.75	2.00	7.00	55.00
	1939	—	—	—	Proof	1150.
	1940	1.120	.75	2.00	6.00	45.00

COPPER-NICKEL

KM#	Date	Mintage	Fine	VF	XF	Unc
13a	1942	1.320	.50	1.00	5.00	40.00
	1945	.400	2.00	8.00	50.00	165.00
	1946	.720	2.00	10.00	100.00	450.00
	1947	.800	1.00	12.00	30.00	70.00
	1948	.800	1.00	1.50	10.00	45.00
	1949	.600	1.50	3.50	10.00	50.00
	1950	.800	1.00	5.00	25.00	70.00
	1952	.800	.50	1.00	5.00	16.00
	1952	—	—	—	Proof	175.00
	1953	.800	.50	1.00	5.00	16.00
	1955	.600	1.00	2.50	8.00	20.00
	1956	.600	.75	2.00	4.00	14.00
	1958	.600	1.00	2.50	6.00	65.00
	1958	—	—	—	Proof	350.00
13a	1959	2.000	.25	.50	3.00	14.00
	1960	2.020	.25	.50	2.00	10.00
	1961	3.000	.25	.25	1.00	6.50
	1962	4.000	.25	.75	4.00	60.00
	1963	4.000	.15	.25	.50	3.00
	1964	6.000	.15	.25	.50	3.00
	1966	2.000	.15	.25	.50	1.50
	1967	4.000	.15	.25	.50	1.50
	1968	8.000	.15	.25	.50	1.50
	1969	2.000	.15	.25	.50	1.50

SHILLING

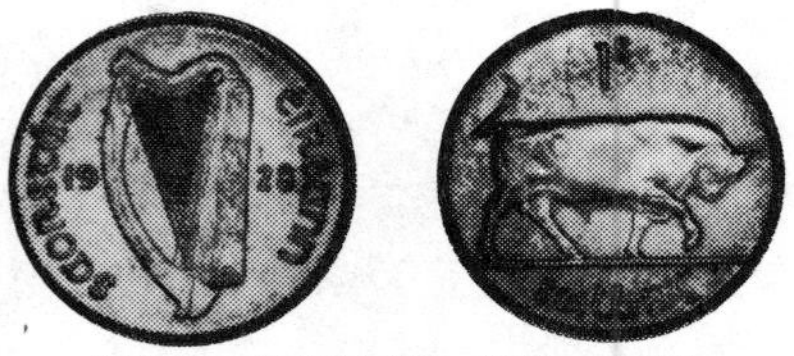

5.6552 g, .750 SILVER, .1364 oz ASW
Bull
Obv: EIREANN = Irish Free State.

6	1928	2.700	1.50	5.00	10.00	22.50
	1928	6,001	—	—	Proof	27.50
	1930	.460	5.00	25.00	150.00	550.00
	1930	—	—	—	Proof	1200.
	1931	.400	4.50	18.00	90.00	250.00
	1933	.300	5.00	20.00	100.00	350.00
	1935	.400	2.00	7.00	25.00	80.00
	1937	.100	12.00	65.00	500.00	2000.

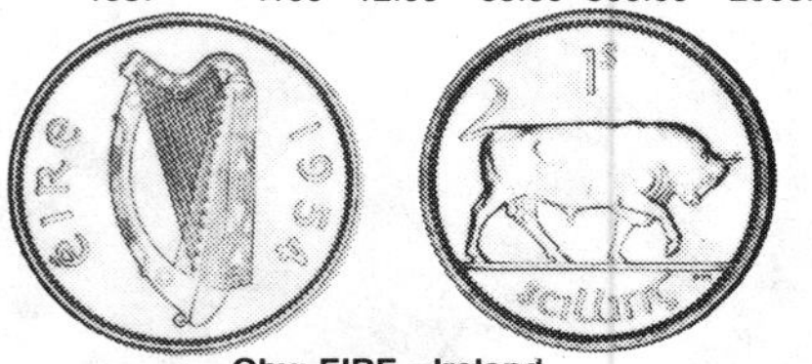

Obv: EIRE = Ireland.

14	1939	1.140	2.50	4.50	12.50	32.50
	1939	—	—	—	Proof	775.00
	1940	.580	3.00	5.00	15.00	40.00
	1941	.300	4.00	12.00	22.50	45.00
	1942	.286	4.00	7.50	15.00	40.00

COPPER-NICKEL

14a	1951	2.000	.25	.50	2.50	15.00
	1951	—	—	—	Proof	500.00
	1954	3.000	.25	.50	2.50	11.50
	1954	—	—	—	Proof	—
	1955	1.000	1.00	2.00	5.00	15.00
	1955	—	—	—	Proof	—
	1959	2.000	.25	.50	4.00	35.00
	1962	4.000	.25	.50	1.00	7.00
	1963	4.000	.25	.50	1.00	3.00
	1964	4.000	.25	.50	1.00	2.00
	1966	3.000	.25	.50	1.00	2.00
	1968	4.000	.25	.50	1.00	3.00

FLORIN

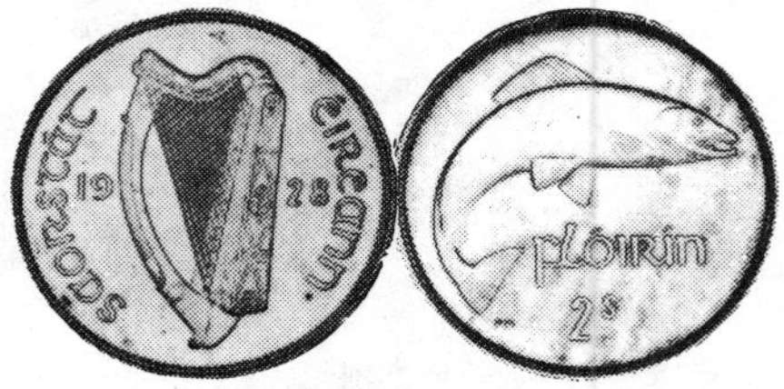

11.3104 g, .750 SILVER, .2727 oz ASW
Atlantic Salmon
Obv: EIREANN = Irish Free State.

7	1928	2.025	3.00	7.00	15.00	40.00
	1928	6,001	—	—	Proof	42.50
	1930	.330	6.50	25.00	150.00	500.00
	1931	.200	8.00	35.00	225.00	600.00
	1933	.300	5.00	25.00	195.00	575.00
	1934	.150	10.00	60.00	325.00	750.00
	1934	—	—	—	Proof	2750.
	1935	.390	5.00	17.50	85.00	200.00
	1937	.150	10.00	35.00	225.00	750.00

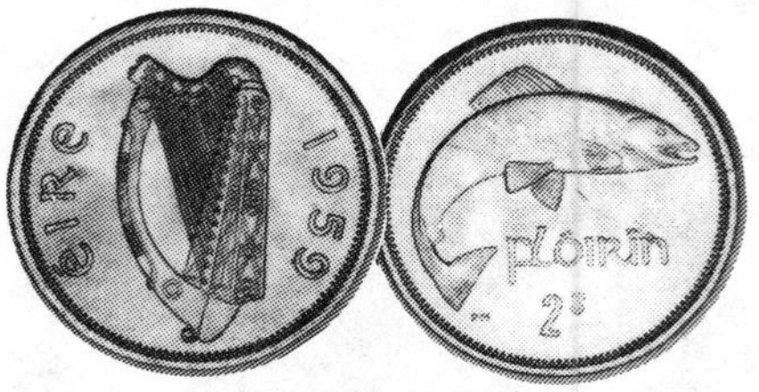

Obv: EIRE = Ireland.

15	1939	1.080	2.00	5.00	18.00	45.00
	1939	—	—	—	Proof	800.00
	1940	.670	3.00	6.00	20.00	50.00
	1941	.400	3.00	8.00	22.50	60.00
	1941	—	—	—	Proof	800.00
	1942	.109	5.00	15.00	25.00	55.00
	1943	*	1200.	2000.	4000.	8000.

*NOTE: Approximately 35 known.

COPPER-NICKEL

KM#	Date	Mintage	Fine	VF	XF	Unc
15a	1951	1.000	1.00	2.00	6.00	15.00
	1951	—	—	—	Proof	600.00
	1954	1.000	1.00	2.00	6.00	18.00
	1954	—	—	—	Proof	450.00
	1955	1.000	1.00	2.00	5.00	15.00
	1955	—	—	—	Proof	450.00
	1959	2.000	.50	1.00	2.50	10.00
	1961	2.000	.50	1.00	7.00	28.00
	1962	2.400	.50	1.00	2.00	10.00
	1963	3.000	.25	.50	.75	4.00
	1964	4.000	.25	.50	.75	2.00
	1965	2.000	.25	.50	.75	2.00
	1966	3.625	.25	.50	.75	2.00
	1968	1.000	.25	.35	1.00	4.50

1/2 CROWN

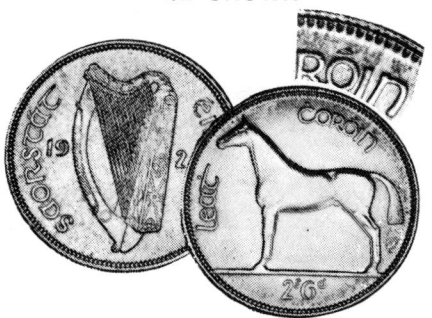

14.1380 g, .750 SILVER, .3409 oz ASW
Irish Hunter
Obv: EIREANN = Irish Free State.
Rev: Close O and I in COROIN, 8 tufts in
horse's tail, w/156 beads in border.

KM#	Date	Mintage	Fine	VF	XF	Unc
8	1928	2.160	3.50	10.00	20.00	50.00
	1928	6.001	—	—	Proof	45.00
	1930	.352	4.50	20.00	125.00	450.00
	1931	.160	8.50	30.00	250.00	700.00
	1933	.336	4.50	20.00	125.00	450.00
	1934	.480	4.00	15.00	40.00	150.00
	1937	.040	65.00	150.00	750.00	1750.

Obv: EIRE = Ireland.
Rev: Normal spacing between O and I in COROIN,
7 tufts in horse's tail, w/151 beads in border.

KM#	Date	Mintage	Fine	VF	XF	Unc
16	1939	.888	3.00	8.00	17.50	55.00
	1939	—	—	—	Proof	800.00
	1940	.752	3.00	8.00	15.00	50.00
	1941	.320	4.00	12.50	30.00	75.00
	1942	.286	4.00	12.50	25.00	50.00
	1943	*	100.00	400.00	1250.	2250.

*NOTE : Approximately 500 known.

COPPER-NICKEL

KM#	Date	Mintage	Fine	VF	XF	Unc
16a	1951	.800	1.50	3.00	10.00	40.00
	1951	—	—	—	Proof	600.00
	1954	.400	2.00	4.00	15.00	50.00
	1954	—	—	—	Proof	500.00
	1955	1.080	1.00	2.00	6.00	30.00
	1955	—	—	—	Proof	200.00
	1959	1.600	1.00	1.75	3.00	12.50
	1961	1.600	1.00	1.75	3.50	25.00
	1961	—	—	—	Proof	—
	1962	3.200	.50	1.00	2.50	12.50
	1962	—	—	—	Proof	—
	1963	2.400	.50	1.00	2.00	7.50
	1964	3.200	.50	1.00	2.00	6.00
	1966	.700	.75	1.50	3.00	6.00
	1967	2.000	.50	1.00	2.00	6.00

NOTE: 1967 exists struck with a polished reverse die.
Estimated value is $15.00 in uncirculated.

KM#8 long base 2			KM#16-16a short base 2	
		Mule. Obv: KM#16a. Rev: KM#8.		

KM#	Date	Mintage	VG	Fine	VF	XF
17	1961	Inc. Ab.	—	8.00	25.00	200.00

10 SHILLINGS

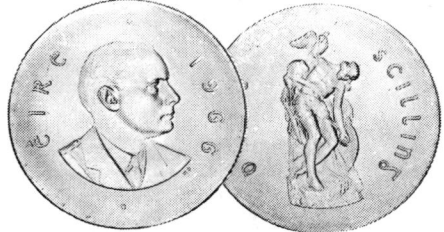

18.1400 g, .833 SILVER, .4858 oz ASW
50th Anniversary of Easter Uprising

KM#	Date	Mintage	Fine	VF	XF	Unc
18	1966	*2.000	BV	BV	4.50	9.00
	1966	.020	—	—	Proof	15.00

NOTE: *Approximately 1.270 melted down.

DECIMAL COINAGE
100 Pence = 1 Pound (Punt)

1/2 PENNY

BRONZE

KM#	Date	Mintage	Fine	VF	XF	Unc
19	1971	100.500	—	—	.10	.30
	1971	.050	—	—	Proof	1.00
	1975	10.500	—	—	.10	.30
	1976	5.464	—	—	.10	.30
	1978	20.302	—	—	—	.25
	1980	20.616	—	—	—	.25
	1982	9.660	—	—	—	.30
	1985	2.784	—	—	—	—
	1986	*12,250	—	—	—	—
	1986	6,750	—	—	Proof	1.25

*NOTE: This mintage figure represents a surplus of coins
minted for Polished Standard Select Sets (Proof Sets)
later released into circulation. The entire surplus was
presumably remelted due to demonitization of this
denomination Jan. 1, 1987.

PENNY

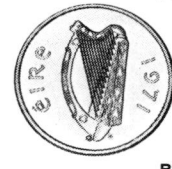 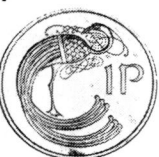

BRONZE

KM#	Date	Mintage	Fine	VF	XF	Unc
20	1971	100.500	—	—	.10	.20
	1971	.050	—	—	Proof	1.25
	1974	10.000	—	—	.10	.25
	1975	10.000	—	—	.10	.25
	1976	38.164	—	—	.10	.20
	1978	25.746	—	—	.10	.20
	1979	21.766	—	—	.10	.20
	1980	86.712	—	—	.10	.20
	1982	54.189	—	—	.10	.20
	1985	19.242	—	—	.10	.20
	1986	36.584	—	—	.10	.20
	1986	6,750	—	—	Proof	1.25
	1988	56.772	—	—	.10	.20

COPPER PLATED STEEL

	Date	Mintage	Fine	VF	XF	Unc
20a	1990	65.099	—	—	.10	.15
	1992	25.643	—	—	.10	.15
	1993	10.000	—	—	.10	.15
	1994	45.800	—	—	.10	.15
	1995	70.836	—	—	.10	.15
	1996	—	—	—	.10	.15

2 PENCE

BRONZE

KM#	Date	Mintage	Fine	VF	XF	Unc
21	1971	75.500	—	—	.10	1.00
	1971	.050	—	—	Proof	1.50
	1975	20.010	—	—	.10	.30
	1976	5.414	—	—	.10	.50
	1978	12.000	—	—	.10	.30
	1979	32.373	—	—	.10	.30
	1980	59.828	—	—	.10	.30
	1982	30.435	—	—	.10	.30
	1985	14.469	—	—	.10	.30
	1986	23.865	—	—	.10	.30

KM#	Date	Mintage	Fine	VF	XF	Unc
21	1986	6,750	—	—	Proof	1.50
	1988	35.868	—	—	.10	.30

COPPER PLATED STEEL

	Date	Mintage	Fine	VF	XF	Unc
21a	1990	34.284	—	—	.10	.25
	1992	10.215	—	—	.10	.25
	1995	55.459	—	—	.10	.25
	1996	—	—	—	.10	.25

5 PENCE

COPPER-NICKEL

KM#	Date	Mintage	Fine	VF	XF	Unc
22	1969	5.000	—	.10	.15	1.00
	1970	10.000	—	—	.10	.50
	1971	8.000	—	—	.10	.50
	1971	.050	—	—	Proof	2.00
	1974	7.000	—	—	.10	.50
	1975	10.000	—	—	.10	.50
	1976	20.616	—	—	.10	.50
	1978	28.536	—	—	.10	.50
	1980	22.190	—	—	.10	.50
	1982	24.404	—	—	.10	.50
	1985	4.202	—	—	.10	.50
	1986	15.298	—	.10	.15	1.00
	1986	6,750	—	—	Proof	2.00
	1990	7.547	—	—	.10	.50

Reduced size: 18.5mm.

KM#	Date	Mintage	Fine	VF	XF	Unc
28	1992	74.526	—	—	.10	.40
	1993	89.109	—	—	.10	.40
	1994	31.058	—	—	.10	.40
	1995	14.667	—	—	.10	.40
	1996	—	—	—	.10	.40

10 PENCE

COPPER-NICKEL

KM#	Date	Mintage	Fine	VF	XF	Unc
23	1969	27.000	—	—	.40	1.25
	1971	4.000	—	—	.40	1.25
	1971	.050	—	—	Proof	2.50
	1973	2.500	—	—	.40	1.50
	1974	7.500	—	—	.35	1.25
	1975	15.000	—	—	.35	1.25
	1976	9.433	—	—	.35	1.25
	1978	30.905	—	—	.25	1.00
	1980	44.605	—	—	.25	1.00
	1982	7.374	—	—	.25	1.00
	1985	4.100	—	—	.25	1.25
	1986	*4,250	—	.20	.50	2.25
	1986	6,750	—	—	Proof	2.50

*NOTE: This mintage figure represents a surplus of coins
minted for Polished Standard Select Sets (Proof Sets),
later released into circulation.

Reduced size: 20.0mm.

KM#	Date	Mintage	Fine	VF	XF	Unc
29	1993	80.061	—	—	—	.75
	1994	58.510	—	—	—	.75
	1995	16.115	—	—	—	.75
	1996	—	—	—	—	.75

20 PENCE

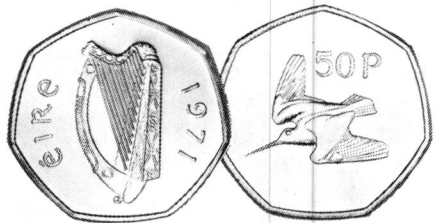

NICKEL-BRONZE

KM#	Date	Mintage	Fine	VF	XF	Unc
25	1986	50.430	—	—	.50	1.50
	1986	6.750	—	—	Proof	3.50
	1988	20.661	—	—	.50	1.50
	1990	—	—	—	.50	1.50
	1992	—	—	—	.50	1.50
	1994	11.086	—	—	.50	1.50
	1995	18.160	—	—	.50	1.50
	1996	—	—	—	.50	1.50

50 PENCE

COPPER-NICKEL

KM#	Date	Mintage	Fine	VF	XF	Unc
24	1970	9.000	—	—	1.50	4.00
	1971	.600	—	1.00	2.00	6.50
	1971	.050	—	—	Proof	3.50
	1974	1.000	—	1.00	2.00	7.50
	1975	2.000	—	—	1.50	4.00
	1976	3.000	—	—	1.25	3.00
	1977	4.800	—	—	1.25	3.00
	1978	4.500	—	—	1.25	3.00
	1979	4.000	—	—	1.25	3.00
	1981	6.000	—	—	1.00	2.00
	1982	2.000	—	—	1.25	3.00
	1983	7.000	—	—	1.00	1.75
	1986	3,250	—	1.00	2.00	6.00
	1986	6.750	—	—	Proof	7.50
	1988	*12.000	—	—	1.00	1.75
	1996	—	—	—	1.00	1.75
	1997	—	—	—	1.00	1.75

NOTE: The 1986, circulation, mintage figure represents a surplus of coins minted for Polished Standard Select Set (Proof Sets), later released into circulation.

Dublin Millennium

KM#	Date	Mintage	Fine	VF	XF	Unc
26	1988	5.000	—	—	—	2.50
	1988	.050	—	—	Proof	15.00

POUND

(Punt)

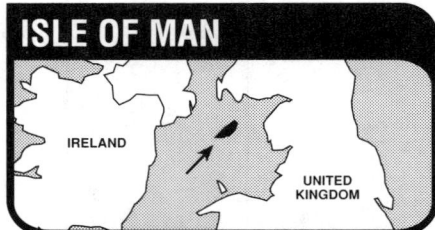

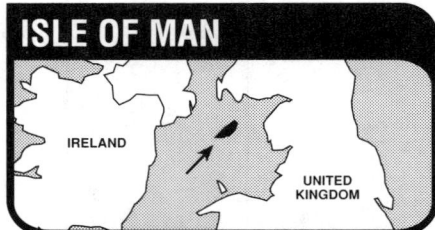

COPPER-NICKEL

KM#	Date	Mintage	Fine	VF	XF	Unc
27	1990	62.292	—	—	—	5.00
	1990	.050	—	—	Proof	27.50
	1994	14.925	—	—	—	5.00
	1995	9.242	—	—	—	5.00
	1996	—	—	—	—	5.00

ISLE OF MAN

The Isle of Man, a dependency of the British Crown located in the Irish Sea equidistant from Ireland, Scotland and England, has an area of 227 sq. mi. (588 sq. km.) and a population of 68,000. Capital: Douglas. Agriculture, dairy farming, fishing and tourism are the chief industries.

The prevalence of prehistoric artifacts and monuments on the island give evidence that its mild, almost subtropical climate was enjoyed by mankind before the dawn of history. Vikings came to the Isle of Man during the 9th century and remained until ejected by Scotland in 1266. The island came under the protection of the British Crown in 1288, and in 1406 was granted, in perpetuity, to the earls of Derby, from whom it was inherited, 1736, by the Duke of Atholl. Rights and title were purchased from the Duke of Atholl in 1765 by the British Crown; the remaining privileges of the Atholl family were transferred to the crown in 1829. The Isle of Man is ruled by its own legislative council and the House of Keys, one of the oldest legislative assemblies in the world. Acts of Parliament passed in London do not affect the island unless it is specifically mentioned.

RULERS
(Commencing 1765)

British

MINT MARKS

PM - Pobjoy Mint

PRIVY MARKS

(b) - Baby Crib

(a) - Big Apple - 1988
(at) - Angel Blowing Trumpet - 1997
(b) - Baby Crib - 1982
(ba) - Basel Bugle - 1990
(bb) - Big Ben - 1987-1988
(br) - Brooklyn Bridge - 1989
(bs) - Teddy Bear in Stocking - 1996
(c) - Chicago Water Tower CICF - 1990-1991
(cc) - Christmas cracker - 1991
(d) - Dome - 1989
(f) - FUN logo - 1988
(fl) - Fleur de Lis - 1990
(fr) - Frauenkirche - Munich Numismata - 1990-1991
(h) - Horse - Hong Kong Int. - 1990
(l) - Statue of Liberty - 1987
(lc) - Lion crowned - 1989
(m) - Queen mother's portrait - 1980
(ma) - Maple leaf - CNA - 1990
(mt) - Mistletoe - Christmas - 1987, 1989
(ns) - North Star - 1995
(p) - Carrier Pigeon - Basel - 1988-1989
(pi) - Pine tree - 1986
(pt) - Partridge in a pear tree - 1988
(py) - Poppy - 1995
(s) - Bridge - SINPEX - 1987
(sb) - Soccer ball - 1982
(sc) - Santa Claus - 1995
(sg) - Sleigh - Christmas - 1990
(SL) - St. Louis Arch - 1987
(ss) - Sailing Ship - Sydney - 1988
(t) - Stylized triskelion - 1979
(tb) - Tower Bridge - 1990
(ti) - TICC logo - Tokyo - 1990
(v) - Viking ship - 1990
(vw) - Viking ship in wreath - 1986
(w) - Stylized triskelion - 1985
(x) - Snowman - 1998

PRIVY LETTERS

A - ANA - 1985-1992
C - Coinex, London - 1985-1989
F - FUN - 1987
H - Hong Kong Expo - 1985
L - Long Beach - 1985-1987
T - Torex, Toronto - 1986
U - Uncirculated - 1988, 1990, 1994, 1995
X - Ameripex - 1986

DECIMAL COINAGE

5 New Pence = 1 Shilling
25 New Pence = 1 Crown
100 New Pence = 1 Pound

1/2 NEW PENNY

BRONZE
St. James's Weed

KM#	Date	Mintage	VF	XF	Unc
19	1971	.495	—	.10	.25
	1971	.010	—	Proof	1.50
	1972	1.000	—	—	20.00
	1973	1.000	—	—	20.00
	1974	1.000	—	—	20.00
	1975	.825	—	.10	.15

1/2 PENNY

BRONZE
Atlantic Herring

KM#	Date	Mintage	VF	XF	Unc
32	1976	.600	—	.10	.25
	1978	—	—	.10	.25
	1978	—	—	Proof	1.00
	1979(t) AA	—	—	.10	.25
	1979(t) AB	—	—	.10	.25

F.A.O. Issue

KM#	Date	Mintage	VF	XF	Unc
40	1977 PM on rev.	.700	—	.10	.25
	1977 w/o PM on rev.	Inc. Ab.	—	—	5.00

Atlantic Herring

KM#	Date	Mintage	VF	XF	Unc
58	1980 AA	—	—	.10	.25
	1980 AB	—	—	.10	.25
	1980	—	—	Proof	1.00
	1981 AA	—	—	.10	.25
	1982 AA	—	—	.10	.25
	1982(b)	—	—	.10	.25
	1982(b)	.025	—	Proof	1.00
	1983 AA	—	—	.10	.25

F.A.O. Issue

KM#	Date	Mintage	VF	XF	Unc
72.1	1981	—	—	—	.10

Rev: World Food Day, 16-10-81.

KM#	Date	Mintage	VF	XF	Unc
72.2	1981	10.000	—	—	.10

Quincentenary of the College of Arms
Fuchsia Blossom

KM#	Date	Mintage	VF	XF	Unc
111	1984 AA	—	—	—	.10

KM#	Date	Mintage	VF	XF	Unc
142	1985(w) AA	—	—	—	.10
	1985	.050	—	Proof	2.00

NEW PENNY

BRONZE
Celtic Cross

KM#	Date	Mintage	VF	XF	Unc
20	1971	.100	—	.10	.35
	1971	.010	—	Proof	2.00
	1972	1,000	—	—	20.00
	1973	1,000	—	—	20.00
	1974	1,000	—	—	20.00
	1975	.855	—	.10	.20

PENNY

BRONZE
Loaghtyn Sheep

KM#	Date	Mintage	VF	XF	Unc
33	1976	.900	—	.20	.75
	1977	1.000	—	.20	.75
	1978	—	—	.20	.75
	1978	—	—	Proof	1.25
	1979 AA(t)	—	—	.20	.75
	1979 AB(t)	—	—	.20	.75
	1979 AC(t)	—	—	.20	.75
	1979 AD	—	—	.20	.75
	1979 AE	—	—	.20	.75

Manx Cat

KM#	Date	Mintage	VF	XF	Unc
59	1980 AA	—	—	.20	.75
	1980 AB	—	—	.20	.75
	1980 AC	—	—	.20	.75
	1980	—	—	Proof	1.50
	1981 AA	—	—	.20	.75
	1982 AA	—	—	.20	.75
	1982(b)	—	—	.20	.75
	1982(b)	.025	—	Proof	1.50
	1983 AA	—	—	.20	.75
	1983 AB	—	—	.20	.75

Obv: Effigy of adolescent Queen Elizabeth II.
Rev: Shag bird.

KM#	Date	Mintage	VF	XF	Unc
112	1984 AA	—	—	.10	.25

KM#	Date	Mintage	VF	XF	Unc
143	1985(t) AA	—	—	.10	.25
	1985	.050	—	Proof	2.00
	1986 AA	—	—	.10	.25
	1987 AA	—	—	.10	.25
	1987 AB	—	—	.10	.30
	1987 AC	—	—	.10	.30

Precision Tools

KM#	Date	Mintage	VF	XF	Unc
207	1988 AA	—	—	—	.20
	1988 AB	—	—	.10	.30
	1988 AC	—	—	.10	.30
	1988 AD	—	—	.10	.30
	1989 AA	—	—	—	.20
	1989 AB	—	—	.10	.30
	1989 AC	—	—	.10	.30
	1989 AD	—	—	.10	.30

KM#	Date	Mintage	VF	XF	Unc
207	1989 AE	—	—	.10	.30
	1990 AA	—	—	—	.20
	1991 AA	—	—	—	.20
	1991 AE	—	—	—	.20
	1992	—	—	—	.20
	1993 AA	—	—	—	.20
	1994 AA	—	—	—	.20
	1995 AA	—	—	—	.20

BRONZE PLATED STEEL
Sports - Rugby Ball

KM#	Date	Mintage	VF	XF	Unc
588	1996 AA	—	—	—	.20

COPPER PLATED STEEL
Obv: Rank-Bradley portrait of Queen Elizabeth.
Rev: Rugby ball, denomination.

KM#	Date	Mintage	VF	XF	Unc
823	1998 AA	—	—	—	.20

2 NEW PENCE

BRONZE
Falcons

KM#	Date	Mintage	VF	XF	Unc
21	1971	.100	—	.20	.75
	1971	.010	—	Proof	2.50
	1972	1,000	—	—	20.00
	1973	1,000	—	—	20.00
	1974	1,000	—	—	20.00
	1975	.725	—	.20	.75

2 PENCE

BRONZE
Manx Shearwater

KM#	Date	Mintage	VF	XF	Unc
34	1976	.800	—	.20	.55
	1977	1.000	—	.20	.55
	1978	—	—	—	.55
	1978	—	—	Proof	1.25
	1979 AA(t)	.010	—	.20	.55
	1979 AB(t)	—	—	.20	.55
	1979 AC(t)	—	—	.20	.55
	1979 AD(t)	—	—	.20	.55
	1979 AE(t)	—	—	.20	.55
	1979 AF(t)	—	—	.20	.55
	1979 AG(t)	—	—	.20	.55
	1979 AH(t)	—	—	.20	.55

Obv: Effigy of adolescent Queen Elizabeth.
Rev: Red-billed chough.

KM#	Date	Mintage	VF	XF	Unc
60	1980 AA	—	—	.20	.50
	1980 AB	—	—	.20	.50
	1980 AC	—	—	.20	.50
	1980 AD	—	—	.20	.50
	1980	—	—	Proof	1.25
	1981 AA	—	—	.20	.50
	1981 AB	—	—	.20	.50
	1982 AA	—	—	.20	.50
	1982(b)	—	—	.20	.50
	1982(b)	.025	—	Proof	1.25

KM#	Date	Mintage	VF	XF	Unc
60	1983 AA	—	—	.20	.50
	1983 AB	—	—	.20	.50
	1983 AC	—	—	.20	.50
	1983 AD	—	—	.20	.50
	1983 AE	—	—	.20	.50

Quincentenary - The College of Arms
Peregrine Falcon

KM#	Date	Mintage	VF	XF	Unc
113	1984 AA	—	—	.20	.50

KM#	Date	Mintage	VF	XF	Unc
144	1985(t) AA	—	—	.20	.50
	1985 AB	—	—	.20	.50
	1985	.050	—	Proof	3.00
	1986 AA	—	—	.20	.50
	1986 AB	—	—	.20	.50
	1986 AD	—	—	.20	.50
	1987 AA	—	—	.20	.50
	1987 AB	—	—	.20	.50
	1987 AC	—	—	.20	.50
	1987 AD	—	—	.20	.50

Stone Cross With Handworking Tools

KM#	Date	Mintage	VF	XF	Unc
208	1988 AA	—	—	—	.30
	1988 AB	—	—	.10	.30
	1988 AC	—	—	.10	.30
	1988 AD	—	—	.10	.30
	1989 AA	—	—	—	.30
	1989 AB	—	—	.10	.30
	1989 AC	—	—	.10	.30
	1990 AA	—	—	—	.30
	1991 AA	—	—	—	.30
	1992 AA	—	—	—	.30
	1993 AA	—	—	—	.30
	1994 AA	—	—	—	.30
	1995 AA	—	—	—	.30

BRONZE CLAD STEEL
Sports - Bicyclists

KM#	Date	Mintage	VF	XF	Unc
589	1996 AA	—	—	—	.20

BRONZE PLATED STEEL
Obv: Rank-Bradley portrait of Queen Elizabeth.
Rev: Two bicyclists.

KM#	Date	Mintage	VF	XF	Unc
901	1998 AA	—	—	—	.20

5 NEW PENCE

COPPER-NICKEL
Tower of Refuge

KM#	Date	Mintage	VF	XF	Unc
22	1971	.100	—	.10	.50
	1971	.010	—	Proof	2.50
	1972	1,000	—	—	25.00
	1973	1,000	—	—	25.00
	1974	1,000	—	—	25.00
	1975	1.400	—	.10	.25

5 PENCE

COPPER-NICKEL
The Laxey Wheel, Lady Isabella
Mint mark: PM on obverse and reverse.

35.1	1976	.800	—	.10	.60
	1977	—	—	.10	.60
	1978	—	—	.10	.60
	1978	—	—	Proof	1.50
	1979(t) AA	—	—	.10	.60

Mint mark: PM on obverse only.

35.2	1976PM	Inc. Ab.	—	.15	.75

Loagthyn Sheep

61	1979 AA	—	—	.15	.75
	1980 AA	—	—	.15	.75
	1980 AB	—	—	.15	.75
	1980 AC	—	—	.15	.75
	1980	—	—	Proof	1.50
	1981 AA	—	—	.15	.75
	1982 AA	—	—	.15	.75
	1982(b)	—	—	.15	.75
	1982(b)	.025	—	Proof	1.50
	1983 AA	—	—	.15	.75

Quincentenary - The College of Arms
Cushag

114	1984 AA	—	—	.10	.50

145	1985(w) AA	—	—	.10	.50
	1985	.050	—	Proof	3.00
	1986 AA	—	—	.10	.50
	1986 AB	—	—	.10	.50
	1986 AC	—	—	.10	.50
	1986 AD	—	—	.10	.50
	1987 AA	—	—	.10	.50

Windsurfing

KM#	Date	Mintage	VF	XF	Unc
209.1	1988 AA	—	—	—	.50
	1989 AA	—	—	—	.50
	1990	—	—	—	.50

Reduced size: 18mm.

209.2	1990 AA	—	—	—	.50
	1991 AA	—	—	—	.50
	1991 AB	—	—	—	.50
	1992 AA	—	—	—	.50
	1993 AA	—	—	—	.50

Golf Clubs and Ball

392	1994 AA	—	—	—	.50
	1995	—	—	—	.50

Sports - Golfer

590	1996 AA	—	—	—	.50

Obv: Rank-Broadley portrait of Queen Elizabeth.
Rev: Golfer in action.

902	1998 AA	—	—	—	.50

10 NEW PENCE

COPPER-NICKEL
Triskelion

23	1971	.100	—	.20	.50
	1971	.010	—	Proof	3.50
	1972	1,000	—	—	25.00
	1973	1,000	—	—	25.00
	1974	1,000	—	—	25.00
	1975	1.500	—	.20	.40

10 PENCE

COPPER-NICKEL
Triskelion
Mint mark: PM on obverse and reverse.

36.1	1976	2.800	—	.20	.80
	1977	—	—	.20	.80
	1978	—	—	.20	.80
	1978	—	—	Proof	2.00
	1979(t) AA	—	—	.20	.80
	1979(t) AB	—	—	.20	.80

Mint mark: PM on obverse only.

36.2	1976	Inc. Ab.	—	.20	1.00

Gyrfalcon

KM#	Date	Mintage	VF	XF	Unc
62	1980 AA	—	—	.25	1.00
	1980 AB	—	—	.25	1.00
	1980	—	—	Proof	2.00
	1981 AA	—	—	.25	1.00
	1982 AA	—	—	.25	1.00
	1982 AB	—	—	.25	1.00
	1982 AB(b)	—	—	.25	1.00
	1982 AC	—	—	.25	1.00
	1982 AD	—	—	.25	1.00
	1982(b)	.025	—	Proof	2.00
	1983 AA	—	—	.25	1.00
	1983 AB	—	—	.25	1.00
	1983 AC	—	—	.25	1.00
	1983 AD	—	—	.25	1.00

Quincentenary - The College of Arms
Loagthyn Ram

115	1984 AA	—	—	.20	.80
	1984 AB	—	—	.20	.80
	1984 AC	—	—	.20	.80
	1984 AD	—	—	.20	.80
	1984 AE	—	—	.20	.80
	1984 AF	—	—	.20	.80
	1984 AG	—	—	.20	.80

146	1985(w) AA	—	—	.20	.80
	1985(w) AB	—	—	.20	.80
	1985	.050	—	Proof	3.00
	1986 AA	—	—	.20	.80
	1987 AA	—	—	.20	.80

Island and Portcullis on Globe

210	1988 AA	—	—	—	.75
	1989 AA	—	—	—	.75
	1990	—	—	—	.75
	1991	—	—	—	.75
	1992	—	—	—	.75

Triskeles Symbol

337	1992 AA	—	—	—	.75
	1992 AB	—	—	—	.75
	1992 AC	—	—	—	.75
	1993 AA	—	—	—	.75
	1994 AA	—	—	—	.75
	1995 AA	—	—	—	.75

NOTE: Varieties exist.

Sports - Sailboat

KM#	Date	Mintage	VF	XF	Unc
591	1996 AA	—			1.00

Obv: Rank-Broadley portrait of Queen Elizabeth.
Rev: Sailboat.

903	1998 AA	—	—	—	1.00

20 PENCE

**COPPER-NICKEL
Medieval Norse History**

90	1982 AA	.030	—	.35	1.00
	1982 AB	—	—	.35	1.00
	1982 AB(b)	—	.50	1.00	5.00
	1982 AC	—	—	.35	1.00
	1982 AD	—	—	.35	1.00
	1982(b)	.025	—	Proof	6.00
	1982 BB	—	—	Proof	1.00
	1983 AA	—	—	.35	1.00

**Atlantic Herring
Quincentenary of the College of Arms**

116	1984 AA	—	—	.35	1.00

147	1985(w) AA	—	—	.35	1.00
	1985	.050	—	Proof	3.00
	1986 AA	—	—	.35	1.00
	1986 AB	—	—	.35	1.00
	1986 AC	—	—	.35	1.00
	1987 AA	—	—	.35	1.00

Farm Combine Harvester

211	1988 AA	—	—	—	1.00
	1989	—	—	—	1.00
	1990	—	—	—	1.00
	1991	—	—	—	1.00
	1992 AA	—	—	—	1.00
	1993 AA	—	—	—	1.00

Farm Combine Harvester

391	1993 AA	—	—	—	1.00
	1994 AA	—	—	—	1.00
	1995 AA	—	—	—	1.00

Sports - Rallying Cars

KM#	Date	Mintage	VF	XF	Unc
592	1996 AA	—			1.25

Obv: Rank-Broadley portrait of Queen Elizabeth.
Rev: Race cars.

904	1998 AA	—	—	—	1.25

50 NEW PENCE

**COPPER-NICKEL
Viking Ship Sailing Right**

24	1971	.100	—	.75	1.50
	1971	.010	—	Proof	7.50
	1972	1,000	—	—	30.00
	1973	1,000	—	—	30.00
	1974	1,000	—	—	30.00
	1975	.227	—	.75	1.50

50 PENCE

**COPPER-NICKEL
Viking Ship Sailing Left**

39	1976	.250	—	.75	2.00
	1977	.050	—	.75	2.50
	1978	.025	—	.75	2.50
	1978	—	—	Proof	3.50
	1979 AA(t)	—	—	.75	3.00

**Manx Day of Tynwald, July 8
Edge inscription: H.M.Q.E.II ROYAL VISIT I.O.M.;
upright w/obv. on top.
JULY 1979**

51.1	1979 AA	.050	—	—	5.00
	1979 AB	—	—	—	5.00

Edge inscription upright w/rev. on top.

51.2	1979	—	—	—	5.00
	1979	—	—	—	5.00

Inscription not centered in flat sections.

51.3	1979	—	—	—	5.00
	1979	—	—	—	5.00

No edge inscription.

51.4	1979	—	—	—	5.00
	1979	—	—	—	5.00

**Odin's Raven, Point of Ayre Lighthouse
Plain edge.**

53	1979 AA	—	—	—	3.00
	1979 AB	—	—	—	3.00

**Edge inscription: ODINS RAVEN VIKING
EXHIBN NEW YORK 1980**

KM#	Date	Mintage	VF	XF	Unc
69	1980 AA	.020	—	—	4.00

Viking Longship

70	1980 AA	.010	—	.75	2.00
	1980 AB	—	—	.75	2.00
	1980	—	—	Proof	2.50
	1981 AA	—	—	.75	2.00
	1982 AC	—	—	.75	2.00
	1982(b)	—	—	.75	2.00
	1982(b)	.025	—	Proof	2.50
	1983 AA	—	—	.75	2.00
	1984 AA	—	—	.75	2.00

**Quincentenary - The College of Arms
Viking Longship**

125	1984 AA	—	—	—	2.00

148	1985(w) AA	—	—	—	2.00
	1985(w) AB	—	—	—	2.00
	1985(w)	*.050	—	Proof	4.00
	1986 AA	—	—	—	2.00
	1986 AB	—	—	—	2.00
	1987 AA	—	—	—	2.00

Computer

212	1988 AA	—	—	—	2.50
	1989 AA	—	—	—	2.50
	1990 AA	—	—	—	2.50
	1991	—	—	—	2.50
	1992	—	—	—	2.50
	1993 AA	—	—	—	2.50
	1994 AA	—	—	—	2.50
	1995 AA	—	—	—	2.50

SOVEREIGN (POUND)

VIRENIUM

KM#	Date	Mintage	VF	XF	Unc
44	1978 AA	—	—	—	3.00
	1978 AB	—	—	—	3.00
	1978 AC	—	—	—	2.50
	1978 AD	3,780	—	—	7.50
	1978 BB	—	—	—	—
	1978 BC	.150	—	Proof	3.50
	1979 AA	—	—	—	2.50
	1979 AA(t)	—	—	—	2.50
	1979 AB	—	—	—	2.50
	1979 AB(t)	—	—	—	2.50
	1979 AC	—	—	—	2.50
	1979 AC(t)	—	—	—	2.50
	1979 BB	—	—	Proof	3.50
	1979 crossed oars (t)	—	—	—	2.50
	1980 AA DMIHE	—	—	—	2.50
		*.030	—	—	2.50
	1980 AA DMIHEN	—	—	—	2.50
	1980 AA TT	—	—	—	2.50
	1980 AB DMIHE	—	—	—	2.50
	1980 AB DMIHEN	—	—	—	2.50
	1980 AB TT	—	—	—	2.50
	1980 AC DMIHE	.100	—	—	2.50
	1980	5,000	—	Proof	10.00
	1981 AA	—	—	—	2.50

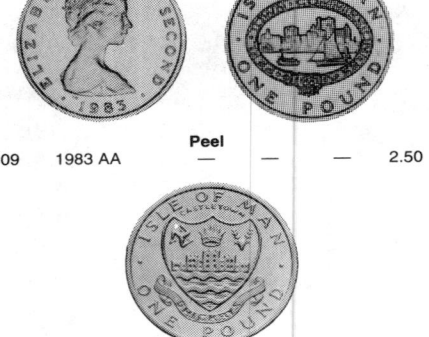

Peel

109	1983 AA	—	—	—	2.50

Castletown

128	1984 D	—	—	—	3.00
	1984 AA	—	—	—	3.00

Ramsey

151	1985 AA(w)	—	—	—	2.50
	1985	*.025	—	Proof	5.00

Douglas

175	1986	—	—	—	2.50
	1986	*.025	—	Proof	5.00

182	1987 AA	—	—	—	3.50

Telecommunicator

KM#	Date	Mintage	VF	XF	Unc
213	1988 AA	—	—	—	3.50
	1988 BB	—	—	—	3.50
	1988 D	—	—	—	3.50
	1989 AA	—	—	—	3.50
	1990 AA	—	—	—	3.50
	1991 AA	—	—	—	3.50
	1992 AB	—	—	—	3.50
	1993 AA	—	—	—	3.50
	1994 AA	—	—	—	3.50
	1995 AA	—	—	—	3.50

NICKEL-BRASS
Sports - Cricket Equipment

594	1996 AA	—	—	—	3.75

VIRENIUM
Douglas Centenary - City Arms

655	1996	—	—	—	3.75

Obv: Rank-Broadley portrait of Queen Elizabeth II.
Rev: Cricket equipment.

906	1998 AA	—	—	—	3.75

2 POUNDS

VIRENIUM
Tower of Refuge

167	1986 (VW)	—	—	—	6.50
	1986	—	—	Proof	8.50
	1987 AA	—	—	—	6.50

Manx Airlines

214	1988 AA	—	—	—	6.50
	1988 D	—	—	—	6.50
	1989	—	—	—	6.50
	1990 AA	—	—	—	6.50
	1991 AA	—	—	—	6.50
	1992 AA	—	—	—	6.50

ISRAEL

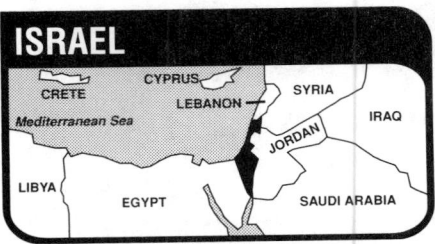

The state of Israel, a Middle Eastern republic at the eastern end of the Mediterranean Sea, bounded by Lebanon on the north, Syria on the northeast, Jordan on the east, and Egypt on the southwest, has an area of 9,000 sq. mi. (20,770 sq. km.) and a population of 4.9 million. Capital: Jerusalem. Finished diamonds, chemicals, citrus, textiles, and minerals are exported.

Palestine, which corresponds to Canaan of the Bible, was settled by the Philistines about the 12th century B.C. and shortly thereafter was invaded by the Jews who established the kingdoms of Israel and Judah. Because of its position as part of the land bridge connecting Asia and Africa, Palestine was invaded and conquered by nearly all of the historic empires of ancient Europe and Asia. In the 16th century it became a part of the Ottoman Empire. After falling to the British in World War I, it, together with Transjordan, was mandated to Great Britain by the League of Nations, 1922.

For more than half a century prior to the termination of the British mandate over Palestine, 1948, Zionist leaders had sought to create a Jewish homeland for Jews who were dispersed throughout the world. For almost as long, Jews fleeing persecution had immigrated to Palestine. The Nazi persecutions of the 1930s and 1940s increased the Jewish movement to Palestine and generated international support for the creation of a Jewish state, first promulgated by the Balfour Declaration of 1917 which asserted British support for the endeavor. The dream of a Jewish homeland was realized on May 14, 1948 when Palestine was proclaimed the State of Israel.

TITLES

Filastin   فلسطين

Paleshtina (E.I.)

MONETARY SYSTEM
1000 Mils = 1 Pound

PALESTINE

MIL

BRONZE

KM#	Date	Mintage	Fine	VF	XF	Unc
1	1927	10.000	.50	2.00	3.00	10.00
	1927	66 pcs.	—	—	Proof	550.00
	1935	.704	2.00	3.00	5.00	25.00
	1937	1.200	1.50	2.00	10.00	100.00
	1939	3.700	1.00	2.00	10.00	30.00
	1939	—	—	—	Proof	400.00
	1940	.396	6.50	12.50	50.00	120.00
	1941	1.920	1.00	2.00	5.00	20.00
	1942	4.480	1.00	2.00	5.00	25.00
	1943	2.800	.75	2.00	5.00	25.00
	1944	1.400	.75	2.00	5.00	15.00
	1946	1.632	2.00	4.00	8.00	30.00
	1946	—	—	—	Proof	450.00
	1947	*2.880	—	—	—	10,000.

*NOTE: Only 5 known. The entire issue was to be melted down.

2 MILS

BRONZE

	Date	Mintage	Fine	VF	XF	Unc
2	1927	5.000	2.00	3.00	5.00	20.00
	1927	66 pcs.	—	—	Proof	575.00
	1941	1.600	1.00	2.00	6.00	30.00
	1941	—	—	—	Proof	400.00
	1942	2.400	1.00	2.50	5.00	25.00

KM#	Date	Mintage	Fine	VF	XF	Unc
2	1945	.960	2.00	5.00	15.00	125.00
	1946	.960	4.00	10.00	30.00	175.00
	1947	*.480	—	—	—	—

*NOTE: The entire issue was melted down.

5 MILS

COPPER-NICKEL

KM#	Date	Mintage	Fine	VF	XF	Unc
3	1927	10.000	.75	2.00	5.00	25.00
	1927	66 pcs.	—	—	Proof	475.00
	1934	.500	6.50	12.50	50.00	175.00
	1935	2.700	.75	2.00	7.00	50.00
	1939	2.000	.75	2.00	5.00	30.00
	1939	—	—	—	Proof	425.00
	1941	.400	10.00	20.00	35.00	175.00
	1941	—	—	—	Proof	375.00
	1946	1.000	2.00	4.00	8.00	30.00
	1946	—	—	—	Proof	450.00
	1947	*1.000	—	—	—	—

*NOTE: The entire issue was melted down.

BRONZE

3a	1942	2.700	1.50	2.00	8.00	50.00
	1944	1.000	2.00	5.00	10.00	40.00

10 MILS

COPPER-NICKEL

KM#	Date	Mintage	Fine	VF	XF	Unc
4	1927	5.000	2.00	6.00	10.00	45.00
	1927	66 pcs.	—	—	Proof	475.00
	1933	.500	4.00	8.00	65.00	250.00
	1933	—	—	—	Proof	350.00
	1934	.500	5.00	12.00	85.00	500.00
	1934	—	—	—	Proof	375.00
	1935	1.150	1.00	10.00	35.00	300.00
	1935	—	—	—	Proof	425.00
	1937	.750	2.00	5.00	15.00	200.00
	1937	—	—	—	Proof	425.00
	1939	1.000	1.00	5.00	15.00	100.00
	1939	—	—	—	Proof	350.00
	1940	1.500	1.00	5.00	15.00	100.00
	1940	—	—	—	Proof	350.00
	1941	.400	6.00	15.00	50.00	200.00
	1941	—	—	—	Proof	350.00
	1942	.600	4.00	10.00	30.00	175.00
	1946	1.000	2.00	15.00	25.00	60.00
	1946	—	—	—	Proof	300.00
	1947	*1.000	—	—	—	—

*NOTE: The entire issue was melted down.

BRONZE

4a	1942	1.000	4.00	5.00	15.00	100.00
	1943	1.000	7.00	10.00	20.00	150.00

20 MILS

COPPER-NICKEL

KM#	Date	Mintage	Fine	VF	XF	Unc
5	1927	1.500	7.00	12.00	35.00	100.00
	1927	66 pcs.	—	—	Proof	625.00
	1933	.250	10.00	20.00	50.00	350.00
	1934	.125	40.00	70.00	175.00	500.00
	1934	—	—	—	Proof	—
	1935	.575	5.00	15.00	50.00	225.00
	1940	.200	10.00	15.00	50.00	350.00
	1940	—	—	—	Proof	500.00
	1941	.100	50.00	75.00	150.00	600.00
	1941	—	—	—	Proof	1200.

BRONZE

5a	1942	1.100	6.00	12.00	25.00	175.00
	1944	1.000	20.00	50.00	80.00	200.00

50 MILS

5.8319 g, .720 SILVER, .1350 oz ASW

KM#	Date	Mintage	Fine	VF	XF	Unc
6	1927	8.000	3.50	10.00	15.00	75.00
	1927	66 pcs.	—	—	Proof	650.00
	1931	.500	12.00	30.00	75.00	400.00
	1933	1.000	5.00	10.00	25.00	125.00
	1934	.399	10.00	25.00	50.00	125.00
	1935	5.600	4.00	5.00	10.00	30.00
	1939	3.000	4.00	6.00	12.00	20.00
	1939	—	—	—	Proof	275.00
	1940	2.000	5.00	20.00	30.00	60.00
	1940	—	—	—	Proof	150.00
	1942	5.000	4.00	6.00	12.00	30.00

100 MILS

11.6638 g, .720 SILVER, .2700 oz ASW

7	1927	2.000	5.00	10.00	25.00	125.00
	1927	66 pcs.	—	—	Proof	800.00
	1931	.250	40.00	75.00	175.00	1000.
	1931	—	—	—	Proof	1400.
	1933	.500	15.00	30.00	100.00	600.00
	1934	.200	60.00	85.00	175.00	700.00
	1935	2.850	10.00	14.00	20.00	75.00
	1939	1.500	6.00	12.00	25.00	80.00
	1939	—	—	—	Proof	250.00
	1940	1.000	8.50	15.00	25.00	80.00
	1942	2.500	8.50	15.00	25.00	75.00

ISRAEL

HEBREW COIN DATING

Modern Israel's coins carry Hebrew dating formed from a combination of the 22 consonant letters of the Hebrew alphabet and read from right to left. The Jewish calendar dates back more than 5700 years, but only five milleniums are assumed in the dating of coins. Thus, the year 5735 (1975AD) appears as 735, with the first two characters from the right indicating the number of years in hundreds; tav (400), plus shin (300). The next is lamedh (30), followed by a separation mark which has the appearance of double quotation marks, then heh (5).

The separation mark - generally similar to a single quotation mark through 5718 (1958 AD), and like a double quotation mark thereafter - serves the purpose of indicating that the letters form a number, not a word, and on some issues can be confused with the character yodh (10), which in a stylized rendering can appear similar, although slightly larger and thicker. The separation mark does not appear in either form on a few commemorative issues.

The Jewish New Year falls in September or October by Christian calendar reckoning. Where dual dating is encountered, with but a few exceptions the Hebrew dating on the coins of modern Israel is 3760 years greater than the Christian dating; 5735 is equivalent to 1975AD, with the 5000 assumed until 1981, when full dates appear on the coins. These exceptions are most of the Hanukka coins, (Feast of Lights), the Bank of Israel gold 50 Pound commemorative of 5725 (1964AD) and others. In such special instances the differential from Christian dating is 3761 years, except in the instance of the 5720 Chanuka Pound, which is dated 1960AD, as is the issue of 5721 a Chanuka Pound, an arrangement which reflects the fact that the events fall early in the Jewish year and late in the Christian.

The Star of David is not a mint mark. It appears only on some coins sold by Israel Government Coins and Medals Corporation Ltd. owned by Israel government, a division of the Prime Minister's office and sole distributor of the Bank of Israel for collectors. It was first used in 1971 on the science coin to signify that it was minted in Jerusalem, but was later used by different mint facilities.

1948	תש״ח	(5)708
1949	תשט	(5)709
1952	תש״ב	(5)712
1954	תש״ד	(5)714
1955	תשט״ו	(5)715
1957	תש״ז	(5)717
1958	תשי״ח	(5)718
1958	תשי״ח	(5)718
1959	תשיט	(5)719
1959	תשי״ט	(5)719
1960	תש״ך	(5)720
1960	תשך	(5)720
1961	תשכ״א	(5)721
1962	תשכ״ב	(5)722
1963	תשכ״ג	(5)723
1964	תשכ״ד	(5)724
1965	תשכ״ה	(5)725
1966	תשכ״ו	(5)726
1967	תשכ״ז	(5)727
1968	תשכ״ח	(5)728
1969	תשכ״ט	(5)729
1970	תש״ל	(5)730
1971	תשל״א	(5)731
1972	תשל״ב	(5)732
1973	תשל״ג	(5)733
1974	תשל״ד	(5)734
1975	תשל״ה	(5)735
1976	תשל״ו	(5)736
1977	תשל״ז	(5)737
1978	תשל״ח	(5)738
1979	תשל״ט	(5)739
1980	תש״ם	(5)740
1981	תשמ״א	(5)741
1981	ה תשמ״א	(5)741
1982	ה תשמ״ב	(5)742
1983	ה תשמ״ג	(5)743
1984	ה תשמ״ד	(5)744
1985	ה תשמ״ה	(5)745
1986	ה תשמ״ו	(5)746
1987	ה תשמ״ז	(5)747
1988	ה תשמ״ח	(5)748
1989	ה תשמ״ט	(5)749
1990	ה תש״ד	(5)750
1991	ה תשנ״א	(5)751
1992	ה תשנ״ב	(5)752
1993	ה תשנ״ג	(5)753
1994	ה תשנ״ד	(5)754
1995	ה תשנ״ה	(5)755
1996	ה תשנ״ו	(5)756
1997	ה תשנ״ז	(5)757
1998	ה תשנ״ח	(5)758
1999	ה תשנ״ט	(5)759

MINT MARKS

(o) - Ottawa
(s) - San Francisco
None - Jerusalem

(M) MATTE - Normal circulation strike or a dull finish produced by sandblasting special uncirculated (polish finish) or proof quality dies.

(U) SPECIAL UNCIRCULATED - Polished or proof-like in appearance without any frosted features.

(P) PROOF - The highest quality obtainable having mirror-like fields and frosted features.

MONETARY SYSTEM
1000 Mils = 1 Pound

25 MILS

ALUMINUM

KM#	Date	Year	Mintage	VF	XF	Unc
8	5708	(1948)	.043	75.00	200.00	850.00
	5709 open link					
		(1949)	.650	25.00	75.00	150.00
	5709 closed link					
		(1949)	—	10.00	15.00	25.00

NOTE: KM#8 was released April 6, 1949.

MONETARY REFORM
1000 Prutah = 1 Lirah

NOTE: The 1949 Prutah coins, except for the 100 and 500 Prutah values, occur with and without a small pearl under the bar connecting the wreath on the reverse. Only the 50 and 100 Prutah coins were issued in 5709. All later coins were struck with frozen dates.

PRUTA

ALUMINUM Anchor

9	5709 w/pearl					
		(1949)	2.685	.50	1.00	2.00
	5709 w/o pearl					
		(1949)	2.500	1.00	2.50	10.00
	5709	(1949)	.020	— Proof		500.00

5 PRUTAH

BRONZE 4-Stringed Lyre

10	5709 w/pearl					
		(1949)	5.045	.50	1.00	2.50
	5709	(1949)	.025	— Proof		500.00
	5709 w/o pearl					
		(1949)	5.000	.50	2.00	10.00

10 PRUTAH

BRONZE Amphora

11	5709 w/pearl					
		(1949)	7.448	.75	2.50	30.00

KM#	Date	Year	Mintage	VF	XF	Unc
11	5709 w/o pearl					
		(1949)	7.500	.50	1.00	4.00
	5709	(1949)	.020	— Proof		500.00

ALUMINUM Ceremonial Jug

17	5712	(1952)	26.042	.35	.75	2.50

20	5717	(1957)	1.000	.35	.75	2.50

COPPER ELECTROPLATED ALUMINUM

20a	5717	(1957)	1.088	.35	.75	2.50

25 PRUTAH

COPPER-NICKEL Grapes

12	5709 w/pearl					
		(1949)	10.520	.50	.75	2.00
	5709	(1949)	.020	— Proof		500.00
	5709 w/o pearl					
		(1949)	2.500	10.00	20.00	50.00

NICKEL-CLAD STEEL

12a	5714	(1954)	3.697	.50	1.00	3.00

50 PRUTAH

COPPER-NICKEL Grape Leaves Reeded edge.

13.1	5709 w/pearl					
		(1949)	12.040	5.00	10.00	25.00
	5709 w/o pearl					
		(1949)	Inc. Ab.	1.00	2.00	4.50
	5709	(1949)	.020	— Proof		500.00
	5714	(1954)	.250	10.00	17.50	35.00

Plain edge.

13.2	5714	(1954)	4.500	.50	1.00	3.00

NICKEL-CLAD STEEL

13.2a	5714	(1954)	17.774	.50	1.00	3.00

100 PRUTAH

COPPER-NICKEL Date Palm

14	5709	(1949)	6.062	.75	1.25	3.50
	5709	(1949)	.020	— Proof		500.00
	5715	(1955)	5.868	1.00	1.50	4.00

NICKEL-CLAD STEEL
Reduced size, 25.6mm, Bern die.
Rev: Large wreath, close to edge.

KM#	Date	Year	Mintage	VF	XF	Unc
18	5714	(1954)	.700	1.00	1.50	3.00

Utrecht die. Rev: Small wreath, away from edge.

19	5714	(1954)	.020	300.00	450.00	1000.

250 PRUTAH

COPPER-NICKEL Barley Spears

15	5709 w/pearl					
		(1949)	1.496	2.50	10.00	20.00
	5709 w/o pearl					
		(1949)	.524	1.00	2.00	5.00

500 PRUTAH

25.5000 g, .500 SILVER, .4099 oz ASW
Pomegranates

Dav.#257

16	5709	(1949)	.034	8.50	12.50	25.00

NOTE: Not placed into circulation.

NOTE: 1 Lirah, KM#22 and 5 Lirot, KM#21 and 23 have been moved to be included with coinage reflecting the Monetary Reform of 1958.

MONETARY REFORM
Commencing January 1, 1958-1980
100 Agorot = 1 Lirah

AGORAH

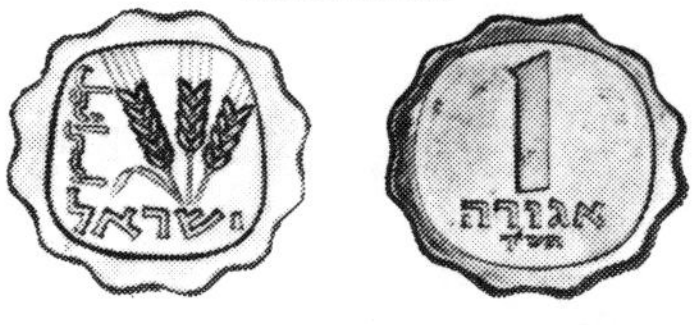

1960 normal date

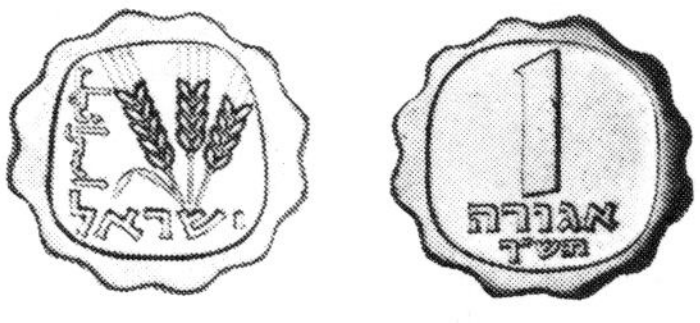

1960 large date

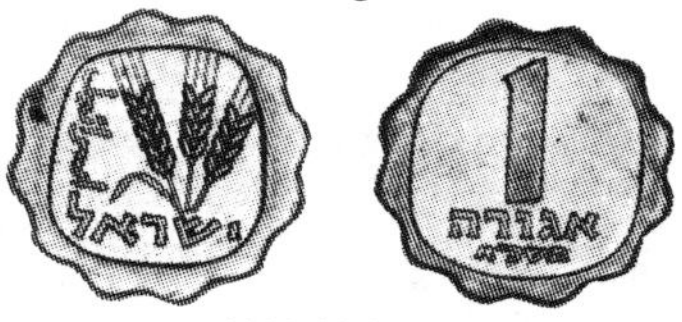

1961 thick date

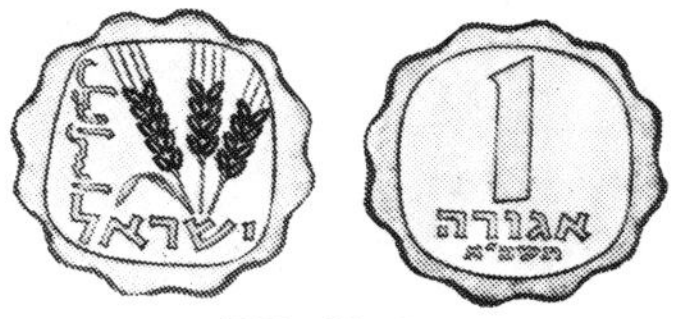

1961 wide date

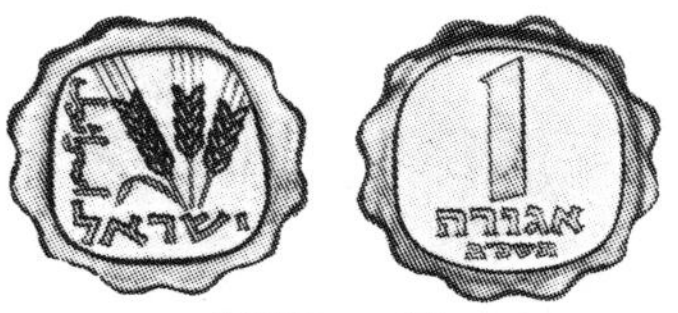

1962 large date

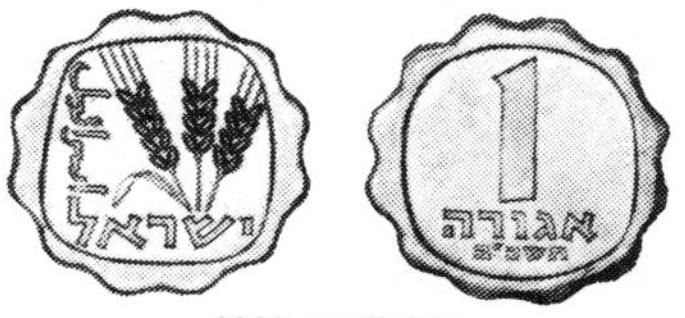

1962 small date

ALUMINUM

KM#	Date	Year	Mintage	VF	XF	Unc
24.1	5720 "Lamed" w/serif	(1960)	12.768	5.00	10.00	20.00
	5720 "Lamed" w/o lower serif	(1960)	Inc. Ab.	10.00	20.00	100.00
	5720 large date	(1960)	300 pcs.	150.00	300.00	750.00
	5721	(1961)	19.262	.50	2.00	5.00
	5721 thick date	(1961)	Inc. Ab.	5.00	15.00	100.00
	5721 wide date	(1961)	Inc. Ab.	5.00	15.00	100.00
	5722 large date	(1962)	14.500	.10	.40	.75
	5722 small date, small serifs	(1962)	Inc. Ab.	5.00	10.00	20.00
	5723	(1963)	14.804	.10	.40	.75
	5723 inverted reverse	(1963)	.010	4.00	9.00	20.00
	5724	(1964)	27.552	—	—	.75
	5725	(1965)	20.708	—	—	.25
	5726	(1966)	10.165	—	—	.25
	5727	(1967)	6.781	—	—	.25
	5728	(1968)	20.899	—	—	.25
	5729	(1969)	22.120	—	—	.25
	5730	(1970)	17.748	—	—	.25
	5731	(1971)	10.290	—	—	.25
	5732	(1972)	24.512	—	—	.25
	5733	(1973)	20.496	—	—	.25
	5734	(1974)	42.080	—	—	.25
	5735	(1975)	1.574	—	—	.25
	5736	(1976)	4.512	—	—	.25
	5737	(1977)	9.680	—	—	.25
	5738	(1978)	8.864	—	—	.25
	5739	(1979)	4.048	—	—	.25
	5740	(1980)	2.600	—	—	1.00

Obv: Star of David in field.

KM#	Date	Year	Mintage	VF	XF	Unc
24.2	5731	(1971)	.175	—	—	1.00
	5732	(1972)	.100	—	—	1.00
	5734	(1974)	.100	—	—	1.00
	5735	(1975)	.100	—	—	1.00
	5736	(1976)	.070	—	—	1.00
	5737	(1977)	.060	—	—	1.00
	5738	(1978)	.057	—	—	1.00
	5739	(1979)	.050	—	—	1.00

5 AGOROT

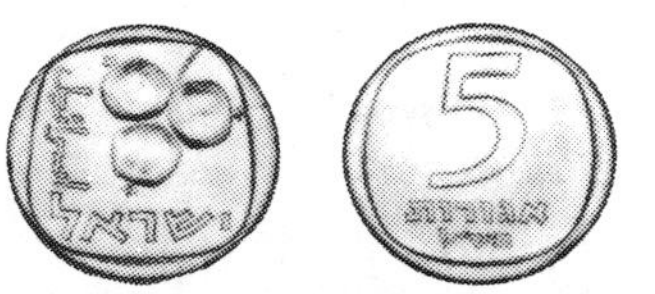

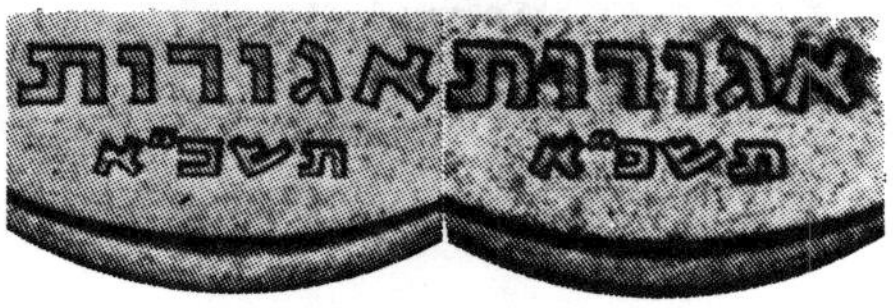

1961 normal — 1961 I.C.I.

ALUMINUM-BRONZE

KM#	Date	Year	Mintage	VF	XF	Unc
25	5720	(1960)	8.019	5.00	10.00	25.00
	5721 sharp, flat date	(1961)	15.090	.25	.50	1.50
	5721 I.C.I. issue w/high date w/serifs	(1961)	5.000	10.00	20.00	75.00
	5722 large date	(1962)	11.198	.25	.50	1.00
	5722 small date	(1962)	Inc. Ab.	5.00	10.00	25.00
	5723	(1963)	1.429	.25	.50	1.25
	5724	(1964)	.021	12.00	145.00	450.00
	5725	(1965)	.201	—	.10	.25
	5726	(1966)	.291	—	.10	.25
	5727	(1967)	2.195	—	.10	.25
	5728	(1968)	4.020	—	.10	.25
	5729	(1969)	2.200	—	.10	.25
	5730	(1970)	4.004	—	.10	.25
	5731	(1971)	14.010	—	.10	.25
	5732	(1972)	9.005	—	.10	.25
	5733	(1973)	25.720	—	.10	.25
	5734	(1974)	10.470	—	.10	.25
	5735	(1975)	10.232	—	.10	.25

Obv: Star of David in field.

KM#	Date	Year	Mintage	VF	XF	Unc
25a	5731	(1971)	.126	—	—	1.00
	5732	(1972)	.069	—	—	1.00

COPPER-NICKEL

KM#	Date	Year	Mintage	VF	XF	Unc
25c	5734	(1974)	.093	In sets only		1.00
	5735	(1975)	.062	In sets only		1.00
	5736	(1976)	—	In sets only		1.00
	5737	(1977)	.060	In sets only		1.00
	5738	(1978)	128 pcs.	—	—	1.00
	5739	(1979)	.018	—	—	1.00

ALUMINUM

KM#	Date	Year	Mintage	VF	XF	Unc
25b	5736(M)	(1976)	13.156	—	.10	.50
	5737(M)	(1977)	16.800	—	.10	.50
	5737(o)	(1977)	15.000	—	.10	.50
	5738(M)	(1978)	21.480	—	.10	.50
	5738(o)(U)					.50
		(1978)	38.760	—	.10	.50
	5739(M)	(1979)	12.836	—	.10	.50

10 AGOROT

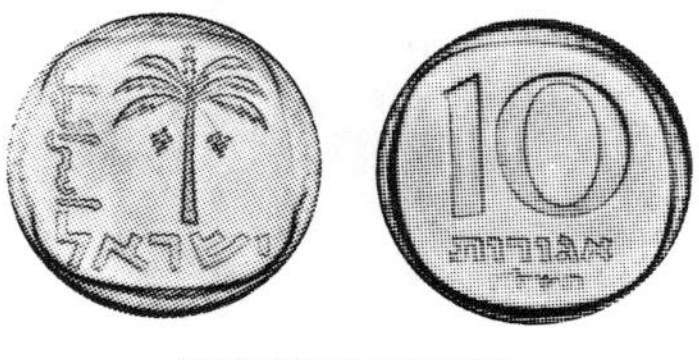

ALUMINUM-BRONZE

KM#	Date	Year	Mintage	VF	XF	Unc
26	5720	(1960)	14.397	.50	1.00	10.00
	5721	(1961)	12.821	.50	1.00	6.00
	5721	(1961)	*"Fatha"* in Arabic, leg: "Israel" Inc. Ab.	25.00	80.00	325.00

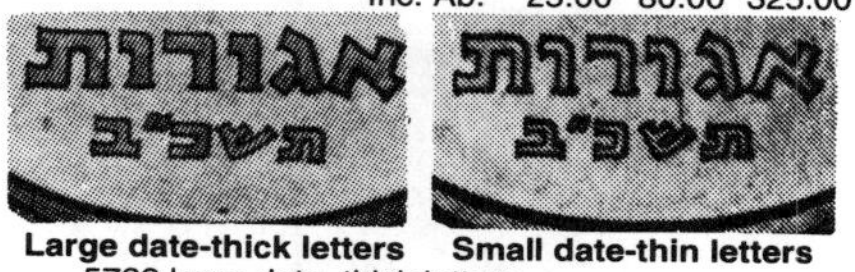

Large date-thick letters — Small date-thin letters

KM#	Date	Year	Mintage	VF	XF	Unc
	5722 large date, thick letters	(1962)	8.845	.25	.50	1.00
	5722 small date, thin letters	(1962)	Inc. Ab.	5.00	10.00	20.00
	5723	(1963)	3.931	.25	.50	1.00
	5724 large date	(1964)	3.612	.25	.50	1.00
	5724 small date	(1964)	Inc. Ab.	10.00	20.00	50.00
	5725	(1965)	.201	—	.20	.25
	5726	(1966)	7.276	—	.10	.25
	5727	(1967)	6.426	—	.10	.25
	5728	(1968)	4.825	—	.10	.25
	5729	(1969)	6.810	—	.10	.25
	5730	(1970)	6.131	—	.10	.25
	5731	(1971)	6.810	—	.10	.25
	5732	(1972)	19.653	—	.10	.25
	5733	(1973)	16.205	—	.10	.25
	5734	(1974)	22.040	—	.10	.25
	5735	(1975)	25.135	—	.10	.25
	5736	(1976)	54.870	—	.10	.25
	5737	(1977)	27.886	—	.10	.25

Obv: Star of David in field.

KM#	Date	Year	Mintage	VF	XF	Unc
26a	5731	(1971)	.175	—	—	.25
	5732	(1972)	.100	—	—	.25

COPPER-NICKEL

KM#	Date	Year	Mintage	VF	XF	Unc
26c	5734	(1974)	.100	In sets only		1.00
	5735	(1975)	.100	In sets only		1.00
	5736	(1976)	.070	In sets only		1.00
	5737	(1977)	.060	In sets only		1.00
	5738	(1978)	.057	In sets only		1.00
	5739	(1979)	—	In sets only		1.00

ALUMINUM

KM#	Date	Year	Mintage	VF	XF	Unc
26b	5737(o)(U)	(1977)	30.100	—	.10	.25
	5738(M)	(1978)	24.050	—	.10	.25
	5738(o)(U)	(1978)	104.336	—	.10	.25
	5739	(1979)	22.201	—	.10	.25
	5740	(1980)	4.752	—	.10	.25

NOTE: Most of the 5740 dated coins were melted down before being issued.

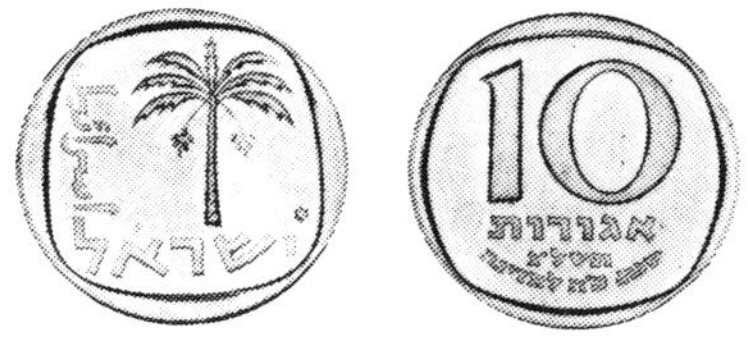

COPPER-NICKEL
25th Anniversary of Independence

KM#	Date	Year	Mintage	VF	XF	Unc
65	5733	(1973)	.100	In sets only		1.00

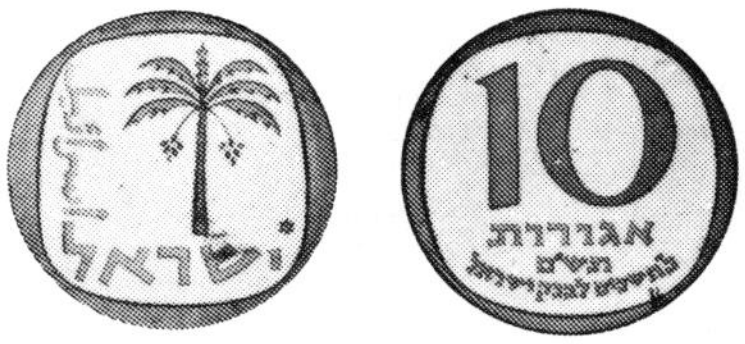

NICKEL
25th Anniversary - Bank of Israel

KM#	Date	Year	Mintage	VF	XF	Unc
98	5740	(1980)	.035	In sets only		2.00

25 AGOROT

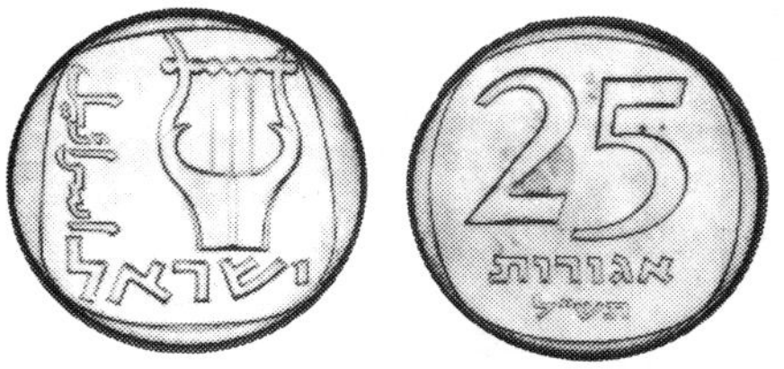

ALUMINUM-BRONZE

KM#	Date	Year	Mintage	VF	XF	Unc
27	5720	(1960)	4.391	.25	.50	3.00
	5721	(1961)	5.009	.10	.20	1.00
	5722	(1962)	.882	.15	.30	1.00
	5723	(1963)	.194	.50	1.00	5.00
	5724	(1964)	Five trial pieces only			
	5725	(1965)	.187	.10	.20	.50
	5726	(1966)	.320	—	.10	.40
	5727	(1967)	.325	—	.10	.40
	5728	(1968)	.445	—	.10	.40
	5729	(1969)	.432	—	.10	.40
	5730	(1970)	.417	—	.10	.40
	5731	(1971)	.500	—	.10	.40
	5732	(1972)	1.883	—	.10	.40
	5733	(1973)	3.370	—	.10	.40
	5734	(1974)	2.320	—	.10	.40
	5735	(1975)	3.968	—	.10	.40
	5736	(1976)	3.901	—	.10	.40
	5737	(1977)	1.832	—	.10	.40
	5738	(1978)	12.200	—	.10	.40
	5739	(1979)	10.842	—	.10	.40

Obv: Star of David in field.

KM#	Date	Year	Mintage	VF	XF	Unc
27a	5731	(1971)	.126	—	—	.40
	5732	(1972)	.069	—	—	.40

COPPER-NICKEL

KM#	Date	Year	Mintage	VF	XF	Unc
27b	5734	(1974)	.093	In sets only		1.00
	5735	(1975)	.062	In sets only		1.00
	5736	(1976)	—	In sets only		1.00
	5737	(1977)	.060	In sets only		1.00
	5738	(1978)	.057	In sets only		1.00
	5739	(1979)	.032	In sets only		1.00

1/2 LIRAH

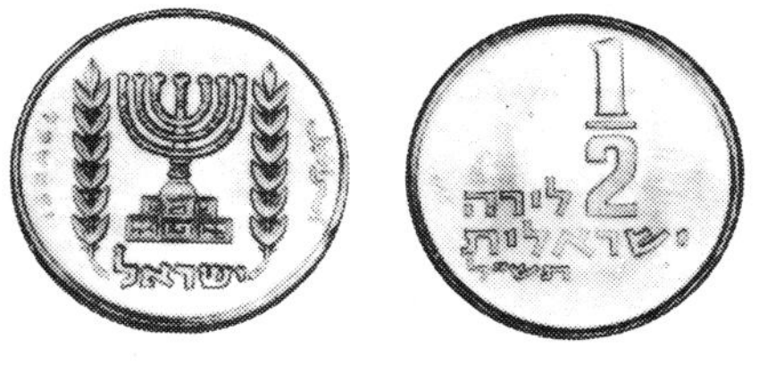

COPPER-NICKEL

KM#	Date	Year Mintage	VF	XF	Unc
36.1	5723	large animals			
	(1963)	5.607	.50	2.00	5.00
	5723	small animals			
	(1963)	Inc. Ab.	3.00	15.00	30.00
	5724	(1964) 3.762	.10	.75	2.00
	5725	(1965) 1.551	.10	.15	1.00
	5726	(1966) 2.139	.10	.15	.50
	5727	(1967) 1.942	.10	.15	.50
	5728	(1968) 1.183	.10	.15	.50
	5729	(1969) .450	.10	.20	.60
	5730	(1970) 1.001	.10	.20	.60
	5731	(1971) .500	.10	.20	.60
	5732	(1972) .421	.10	.20	.60
	5733	(1973) 3.225	.10	.15	.50
	5734	(1974) 4.275	.10	.15	.50
	5735	(1975) 11.066	.10	.15	.50
	5736	(1976) 4.959	.10	.15	.50
	5737	(1977) 4.983	.10	.15	.50
	5738	(1978) 14.325	.10	.15	.50
	5739	(1979) 21.391	.10	.15	.50

Obv: Star of David in field.

36.2	5731	(1971) .175	In sets only		1.00
	5732	(1972) .100	In sets only		1.00
	5734	(1974) .100	In sets only		1.00
	5735	(1975) .100	In sets only		1.00
	5736	(1976) .070	In sets only		1.00
	5737	(1977) .060	In sets only		1.00
	5738	(1978) .057	In sets only		1.00
	5739	(1979) .050	In sets only		1.00

LIRAH

COPPER-NICKEL
Hanukkah - Law Is Light

22	5719	1958 .150	—	—	2.00
	5719	1958 5,000	—	Proof	30.00

37	5723	large animals			
	(1963)	4.212	.50	1.50	3.00
	5723	small animals			
	(1963)	Inc. Ab.	1.00	10.00	20.00
	5724	(1964)	Only ten trial pieces struck		
	5725	(1965) .166	.25	.50	1.25
	5726	(1966) .290	.25	.50	1.25
	5727	(1967) .180	.25	.50	1.25

47.1	5727	(1967) 3.830	.10	.25	1.00
	5728	(1968) 3.932	.10	.25	1.00
	5729	(1969) 12.484	.10	.25	.75
	5730	(1970) 4.794	.10	.25	.75
	5731	(1971) 2.993	.10	.25	.75
	5732	(1972) 2.489	.10	.25	.75
	5733	(1973) 10.265	.10	.25	.75
	5734	(1974) 6.287	.10	.25	.75
	5735	(1975) 13.225	.10	.25	.75
	5736	(1976) 4.268	.10	.25	.75
	5737	(1977) 11.129	.10	.25	.75
	5738	(1978) 61.752	.10	.25	.75
	5739	(1979) 34.815	.10	.25	.75
	5740	(1980) 10.840	.10	.25	.75

NOTE: Most of the 5740 dated coins were melted down before being issued.

Obv: Star of David in field.

47.2	5731	(1971) .126	In sets only		1.50
	5732	(1972) .069	In sets only		1.50
	5734	(1974) .093	In sets only		1.50
	5735	(1975) .062	In sets only		1.50
	5736	(1976) —	In sets only		1.50
	5737	(1977) Inc. Ab.	In sets only		1.50

KM#	Date	Year Mintage	VF	XF	Unc
47.2	5738	(1978) Inc. Ab.	In sets only		1.50
	5739	(1979) —	In sets only		1.50

5 LIROT

COPPER-NICKEL

90	5738	(1978) 8.350	.35	.70	1.75
	5739	(1979) 37.646	.35	.60	1.50

MONETARY REFORM
Commencing February 24, 1980-1985

10 Old Agorot = 1 New Agorah
100 New Agorot = 1 Sheqel

NEW AGORAH

ALUMINUM
Date Palm

106	5740	(1980) *200.000	—	—	.10
	5741	(1981) 1.000	—	.10	.20
	5742	(1982) 1.000	—	.10	.20

*NOTE: 110 million coins were reportedly melted down.

5 NEW AGOROT

ALUMINUM
Menorah

107	5740	(1980) 69.532	—	—	.10
	5741	(1981) 1.000	—	.10	.20
	5742	(1982) 5.000	—	—	.10

10 NEW AGOROT

BRONZE
Pomegranate

108	5740	(1980) *167.932	—	—	.10
	5741	(1981) 241.160	—	—	.10
	5742	(1982) 23.000	—	—	.10
	5743	(1983) 2.500	—	.10	.15
	5744	(1984) .500	—	.10	.20

*NOTE: 70.200 million coins were reportedly melted down.

1/2 SHEQEL

COPPER-NICKEL

109	5740	(1980) 52.308	—	.25	.50
	5741	(1981) 53.272	—	.25	.50
	5742	(1982) 18.808	—	.25	.50
	5743	(1983) .250	—	.35	.70
	5744	(1984) .250	—	.35	.70

SHEQEL

COPPER-NICKEL
Chalice

111	5741	(1981) 154.540	—	.65	.85

KM#	Date	Year Mintage	VF	XF	Unc
111	5742	(1982) 15.850	—	.65	.85
	5743	(1983) 26.360	—	.65	.85
	5744	(1984) 32.205	—	.65	.85
	5745	(1985) .500	—	.65	1.00

5 SHEQALIM

ALUMINUM-BRONZE

118	5742	(1982) 30.000	—	.75	1.25
	5743	(1983) .994	—	1.00	2.00
	5744	(1984) 17.389	—	.75	1.25
	5745	(1985) .250	—	1.00	2.50

10 SHEQALIM

COPPER-NICKEL
Ancient Galley

119	5742	(1982) 36.084	—	.75	1.25
	5743	(1983) 17.851	—	.75	1.25
	5744	(1984) 31.950	—	.75	1.25
	5745	(1985) 25.864	—	.50	.75

Hanukkah - Trade Coin

134	5743	(1983) 2.000	—	1.00	1.50

Theodor Herzl

137	5744	(1984) 2.003	—	1.00	1.50

50 SHEQALIM

ALUMINUM-BRONZE
Circulation Coins

139	5744	(1984) 13.994	—	.50	1.00
	5745	(1985) 1.000	—	.75	1.50

David Ben Gurion

147	5745	(1985) 1.000	—	1.00	1.50

100 SHEQALIM

COPPER-NICKEL
Circulation Coins

KM#	Date	Year	Mintage	VF	XF	Unc
143	5744	(1984)	30.028	—	1.00	2.00
	5745	(1985)	19.638	—	1.00	2.00

Hanukkah

146	5744	(1984)	2.000	—	1.25	2.25

Zeev Jabotinsky

151	5745	(1985)	2.000	—	1.25	2.25

MONETARY REFORM
September 4, 1985 -
10 Sheqalim = 1 Agora
1000 Sheqalim = 1 New Sheqel

AGORAH

ALUMINUM-BRONZE

156	5745	(1985)	58.144	—	—	.50
	5746	(1986)	95.272	—	—	.50
	5747	(1987)	1.080	—	—	.50
	5748	(1988)	15.768	—	—	.50
	5749	(1989)	10.801	—	—	.50
	5750	(1990)	4.968	—	—	.50
	5751	(1991)	.010	In sets only		1.00
	5754	(1994)	8.000	—	—	.50
	5755	(1995)	.010	—	—	.50

Hanukkah

171	5747	(1986)	1.004	—	.15	.75
	5748	(1987)	.540	—	.15	.75
	5748	(1988)	.504	—	.15	.75
	5749	(1988)	Inc. Ab	—	.15	.75
	5750	(1989)	2.160	—	.15	.75
	5751	(1990)	4.968	—	.15	.75

NICKEL
40th Anniversary of Israel

193	5748	(1988)	.504	—	—	.25

5 AGOROT

ALUMINUM-BRONZE

KM#	Date	Year	Mintage	VF	XF	Unc
157	5745	(1985)	34.504	—	.10	.15
	5746	(1986)	12.384	—	.10	.15
	5747	(1987)	14.257	—	.10	.15
	5748	(1988)	9.360	—	.10	.15
	5749	(1989)	4.896	—	.10	.15
	5750	(1990)	.576	—	.10	.15
	5751	(1991)	4.464	—	.10	.15
	5752	(1992)	—	—	.10	.15
	5753	(1993)	8.000	—	.10	.15
	5754	(1994)	8.000	—	.10	.15
	5755	(1995)	7.500	—	.10	.15

Hanukkah

172	5746	(1986)	1.004	—	.10	.30
	5747	(1987)	.536	—	.10	.30
	5748	(1988)	.504	—	.10	.30
	5749	(1989)	2.016	—	.10	.30
	5750	(1990)	1.488	—	.10	.30
	5751	(1991)	—	—	.10	.30
	5752	(1992)	.960	—	.10	.30
	5753	(1993)	.012	—	.10	.30
	5754	(1994)	.012	—	.10	.30
	5755	(1995)	—	—	.10	.30
	5756	(1996)	—	—	.10	.30
	5757	(1997)	—	—	.10	.30

NICKEL
40th Anniversary of Israel

194	5748	(1988)	.504	—	—	.30

10 AGOROT

ALUMINUM-BRONZE

158	5745	(1985)	45.000	—	.10	.20
	5746	(1986)	92.754	—	.10	.20
	5747	(1987)	19.351	—	.10	.20
	5748	(1988)	8.640	—	.10	.20
	5749	(1989)	.420	—	.10	.20
	5750	(1990)	2.376	—	.10	.20
	5751	(1991)	59.425	—	.10	.20
	5752	(1992)	—	—	.10	.20
	5753	(1993)	25.920	—	.10	.20
	5754	(1994)	—	—	.10	.20
	5756	(1996)	—	—	.10	.20

NOTE: Coins dated 5751 (1991) exist with 6mm and 7mm long date and thick and thin letters and 7mm and 7.5mm 10.

Hanukkah

173	5746	(1986)	1.004	—	.10	.40
	5747	(1987)	.834	—	.10	.40
	5748	(1988)	.798	—	.10	.40
	5749	(1989)	2.052	—	.10	.40
	5750	(1990)	1.488	—	.10	.40
	5751	(1991)	—	—	.10	.40
	5752	(1992)	1.404	—	.10	.40
	5753	(1993)	.012	—	.10	.40
	5754	(1994)	.012	—	.10	.40
	5755	(1995)	—	—	.10	.40
	5756	(1996)	—	—	.10	.40
	5757	(1997)	—	—	.10	.40

NICKEL
40th Anniversary of Israel

KM#	Date	Year	Mintage	VF	XF	Unc
195	5748	(1988)	.504	—	—	.40

1/2 NEW SHEQEL

ALUMINUM-BRONZE

159	5745	(1985)	20.328	—	.35	.75
	5746	(1986)	4.392	—	.35	.75
	5747	(1987)	.144	—	.35	2.00
	5748	(1988)	.020	In sets only		3.00
	5749	(1989)	.756	—	.35	.75
	5750	(1990)	.648	—	.35	.75
	5751	(1991)	.288	—	.35	.75
	5752	(1992)	—	—	.35	.75
	5753	(1992)	5.184	—	.35	.75
	5754	(1993)	8.000	—	.35	.75
	5755	(1994)	8.000	—	.35	.75
	5755	(1995)	.010	—	.35	.75

Baron Edmund de Rothschild

167	5746	(1986)	2.000	—	.50	1.50

Hanukkah

174	5746	(1986)	1.004	—	.35	.85
	5747	(1987)	.532	—	.35	.85
	5748	(1988)	.504	—	.35	.85
	5749	(1989)	2.016	—	.35	.85
	5750	(1990)	.960	—	.35	.85
	5751	(1991)	—	—	.35	.85
	5752	(1992)	.304	—	.35	.85
	5753	(1993)	.012	—	.35	.85
	5754	(1994)	.012	—	.35	.85
	5755	(1995)	—	—	.35	.85
	5756	(1996)	—	—	.35	.85
	5757	(1997)	—	—	.35	.85

NICKEL
40th Anniversary of Israel

196	5748	(1988)	.500	—	—	.50

NEW SHEQEL

COPPER-NICKEL

160	5745	(1985)	29.088	—	.65	1.50
	5746	(1986)	20.960	—	.65	1.50
	5747	(1987)	.216	—	.65	3.00
	5748	(1988)	20.376	—	.65	1.50
	5749	(1989)	8.706	—	.65	1.50

KM#	Date	Year	Mintage	VF	XF	Unc
160	5750	(1990)	.756	—	.65	1.50
	5751	(1991)	1.152	—	.65	1.50
	5752	(1992)	—	—	.65	1.50
	5753	(1993)	8.640	—	.65	1.50
	5754	(1994)	8,000	—	.65	1.50
	5755	(1995)	.010	—	.65	1.50

NICKEL CLAD STEEL

160a	5754	(1994)	—	—	—	1.00
	5754o	(1994)	—	—	—	1.00
	5755	(1995)	—	—	—	1.00

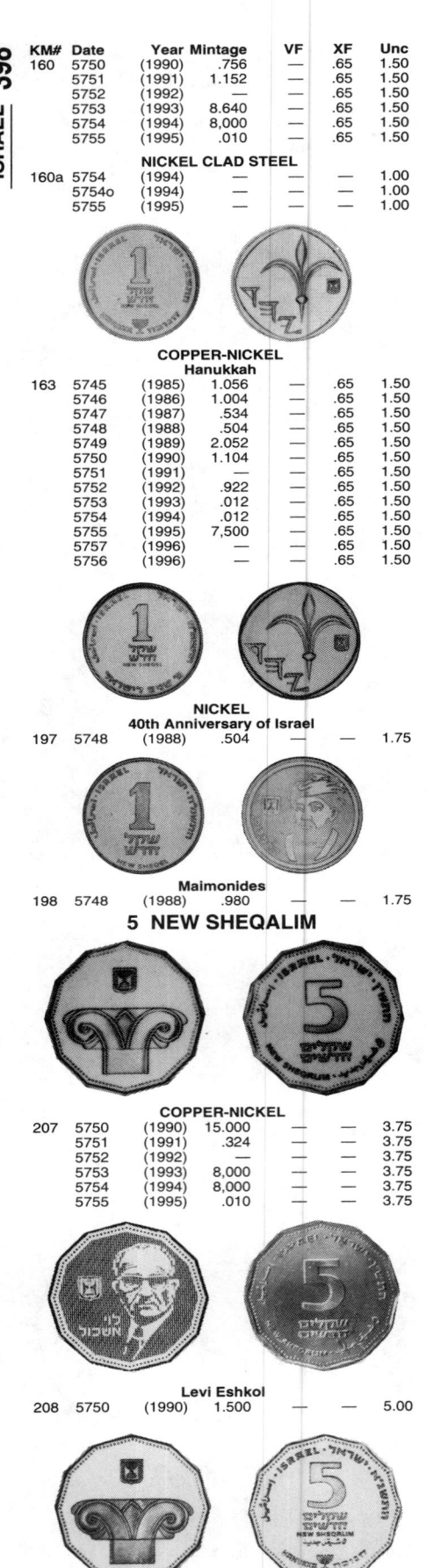

COPPER-NICKEL
Hanukkah

163	5745	(1985)	1.056	—	.65	1.50
	5746	(1986)	1.004	—	.65	1.50
	5747	(1987)	.534	—	.65	1.50
	5748	(1988)	.504	—	.65	1.50
	5749	(1989)	2.052	—	.65	1.50
	5750	(1990)	1.104	—	.65	1.50
	5751	(1991)	—	—	.65	1.50
	5752	(1992)	.922	—	.65	1.50
	5753	(1993)	.012	—	.65	1.50
	5754	(1994)	.012	—	.65	1.50
	5755	(1995)	7,500	—	.65	1.50
	5757	(1996)	—	—	.65	1.50
	5756	(1996)	—	—	.65	1.50

NICKEL
40th Anniversary of Israel

197	5748	(1988)	.504	—	—	1.75

Maimonides

198	5748	(1988)	.980	—	—	1.75

5 NEW SHEQALIM

COPPER-NICKEL

207	5750	(1990)	15.000	—	—	3.75
	5751	(1991)	.324	—	—	3.75
	5752	(1992)	—	—	—	3.75
	5753	(1993)	8,000	—	—	3.75
	5754	(1994)	8,000	—	—	3.75
	5755	(1995)	.010	—	—	3.75

Levi Eshkol

208	5750	(1990)	1.500	—	—	5.00

Hanukka - Ancient Column

217	5750	(1990)	.500	—	—	3.75
	5751	(1991)	—	—	—	3.75
	5752	(1992)	.501	—	—	3.75
	5753	(1993)	.012	—	—	3.75
	5754	(1994)	.012	—	—	3.75
	5755	(1995)	7,500	—	—	3.75

Chaim Weizmann

KM#	Date	Year	Mintage	VF	XF	Unc
237	5752	1992	1.501	—	—	5.00

10 NEW SHEQALIM

AUREATE BONDED BRONZE center
in NICKEL BONDED STEEL ring

270	5755	(1995)	*.018	—	—	6.00

Golda Meir

273	5755	(1995)	1.500	—	—	8.00

Hannukah
Obv: Denomination.
Rev: Palm tree and baskets.

315	5757	(1997)	.010	—	—	6.00

ITALY

The Italian Republic, a 700-mile-long peninsula extending into the heart of the Mediterranean Sea, has an area of 116,304 sq. mi. (301,230 sq. km.) and a population of 60 million. Capital: Rome. The economy centers around agriculture, manufacturing, forestry and fishing. Machinery, textiles, clothing and motor vehicles are exported.

From the fall of Rome until modern times, 'Italy' was little more than a geographical expression. Although nominally included in the Empire of Charlemagne and the Holy Roman Empire, it was in reality divided into a number of independent states and kingdoms presided over by wealthy families, soldiers of fortune or hereditary rulers. The 19th century unification movement fostered by Mazzini, Garibaldi and Cavour attained fruition in 1860-70 with the creation of the Kingdom of Italy and the installation of Victor Emmanuel, king of Sardinia, as king of Italy. Benito Mussolini came to power during the post-World War I period of economic and political unrest, and installed a Fascist dictatorship with a figurehead king as titular Head of State. Mussolini entered Italy into the German-Japanese anti comitern pact (Tri-Partite Pact) and withdrew from the League of Nations. The war did not go well for Italy and Germany was forced to assist Italy in its failed invasion of Greece. The Allied invasion of Sicily on July 10, 1943 and bombings of Rome brought the Fascist council to a no vote of confidence on July 23, 1943. Mussolini was arrested but soon escaped and set up a government in Salo. Rome fell to the Allied forces in June, 1944 and the country was allowed the status of cobelligerent against Germany. The Germans held northern Italy for another year. Mussolini was eventually captured and executed by partisans.

Following the defeat of the Axis powers, the Italian monarchy was dissolved by plebiscite, and the Italian Republic proclaimed.

KINGDOM

RULERS
Vittorio Emanuele III, 1900-1946
Umberto II, 1946
Republic, 1946-

MINT MARKS
R - Rome, Italy

MONETARY SYSTEM
100 Centesimi = 1 Lira

CENTESIMO

COPPER
Mint mark: R

KM#	Date	Mintage	Fine	VF	XF	Unc
35	1902	.026	165.00	450.00	850.00	1500.
	1903	5.655	1.00	2.00	4.00	15.00
	1904/0	14.626	2.00	3.00	7.50	20.00
	1904	Inc. Ab.	1.00	2.00	4.00	9.00
	1905/0	8.531	2.00	3.00	7.50	20.00
	1905	Inc. Ab.	1.00	2.00	4.00	9.00
	1908	3.859	1.00	2.00	4.00	9.00

40	1908	.057	150.00	225.00	450.00	800.00
	1909	3.539	1.00	2.00	4.00	9.00
	1910	3.599	1.00	2.00	4.00	9.00
	1911	.700	5.00	10.00	15.00	25.00
	1912	3.995	1.00	2.00	4.00	9.00
	1913	3.200	1.00	2.00	4.00	9.00

KM#	Date	Mintage	Fine	VF	XF	Unc
40	1914	11.585	1.00	2.00	4.00	9.00
	1915	9.757	1.00	2.00	4.00	9.00
	1916	9.845	1.00	2.00	4.00	9.00
	1917	2.400	1.00	2.00	4.00	9.00
	1918	2.710	5.00	10.00	15.00	25.00

2 CENTESIMI

COPPER
Mint mark: R

KM#	Date	Mintage	Fine	VF	XF	Unc
38	1903	5.000		.60	4.00	12.50
	1905	1.260	4.00	8.50	18.00	30.00
	1906	3.145	.60	1.50	3.50	7.50
	1907	.230	25.00	50.00	75.00	150.00
	1908	1.518	1.00	2.50	5.00	15.00

KM#	Date	Mintage	Fine	VF	XF	Unc
41	1908	.298	9.00	15.00	25.00	80.00
	1909	2.419	.60	1.50	3.00	15.00
	1910	.590	2.00	4.00	9.00	30.00
	1911	2.777	.60	1.50	3.00	15.00
	1912	.840	.60	2.00	5.00	16.00
	1914	1.648	.50	1.30	2.00	15.00
	1915	4.860	.50	1.30	2.50	15.00
	1916	1.540	.50	1.30	2.00	15.00
	1917	3.638	.50	1.30	2.00	15.00

5 CENTESIMI

COPPER
Mint mark: R

KM#	Date	Mintage	Fine	VF	XF	Unc
42	1908	.824	10.00	25.00	50.00	130.00
	1909	1.734	.75	1.75	3.50	15.00
	1912	.743	1.75	3.00	6.00	30.00
	1913 dot after D					
		1.964	4.00	10.00	15.00	50.00
	1913 w/o dot after D					
		Inc. Ab.	40.00	75.00	150.00	250.00
	1915	1.038	3.50	7.50	12.50	30.00
	1918	4.242	.75	1.75	3.50	15.00

KM#	Date	Mintage	Fine	VF	XF	Unc
59	1919	13.208	.75	2.00	3.00	10.00
	1920	33.372	.30	.75	2.00	5.00
	1921	80.111	.30	.75	2.00	5.00
	1922	42.914	.30	.75	2.00	5.00
	1923	29.614	.30	.75	2.00	5.00
	1924	20.352	.30	.75	2.00	5.00
	1925	40.460	.30	.75	2.00	5.00
	1926	21.158	.30	.75	2.00	5.00
	1927	15.800	.30	.75	2.00	5.00
	1928	16.090	.30	.75	2.00	5.00
	1929	29.000	.30	.75	2.00	5.00
	1930	22.694	.30	.75	2.00	5.00
	1931	20.000	.30	.75	2.00	5.00
	1932	11.456	.30	.75	2.00	5.00
	1933	20.720	.30	.75	2.00	5.00
	1934	16.000	.30	.75	2.00	5.00
	1935	11.000	.30	.75	2.00	5.00
	1936	9.462	.30	.75	2.00	5.00
	1937	.972	4.00	8.00	12.50	25.00

KM#	Date	Mintage	Fine	VF	XF	Unc
73	1936, yr. XIV					
		Inc. Ab.	2.00	4.00	9.00	18.00
	1937, yr. XV					
		7.207	.30	.75	1.00	3.00
	1938, yr. XVI					
		24.000	.20	.65	1.00	3.00

KM#	Date	Mintage	Fine	VF	XF	Unc
73	1939, yr. XVII					
		22.000	.20	.65	1.00	3.00

ALUMINUM-BRONZE

KM#	Date	Mintage	Fine	VF	XF	Unc
73a	1939, yr. XVII					
		1.000	.30	.75	1.25	3.00
	1940, yr. XVIII					
		9.630	.30	.75	1.00	3.00
	1941, yr. XIX					
		16.340	.30	.75	1.00	3.00
	1942, yr. XX					
		25.200	.30	.75	1.25	3.00
	1943, yr. XXI					
		13.922	2.00	5.00	10.00	20.00

10 CENTESIMI

COPPER
Mint mark: R
Similar to 5 Centesimi, KM#42.

KM#	Date	Mintage	Fine	VF	XF	Unc
43	1908	—	—	—	Rare	—

50th Anniversary of Kingdom

KM#	Date	Mintage	Fine	VF	XF	Unc
51	1911	2.000	3.50	6.50	12.50	35.00

KM#	Date	Mintage	Fine	VF	XF	Unc
60	1919	.986	20.00	35.00	50.00	100.00
	1920	37.995	.50	1.25	4.00	10.00
	1921	66.510	.50	1.25	4.00	10.00
	1922	45.217	.50	1.25	4.00	10.00
	1923	31.529	.50	1.25	4.00	10.00
	1924	35.312	.50	1.25	4.00	10.00
	1925	22.370	.50	1.25	4.00	10.00
	1926	25.190	.50	1.25	4.00	10.00
	1927	22.673	.50	1.25	4.00	10.00
	1928	15.680	.50	2.00	7.50	20.00
	1929	15.593	.50	1.25	4.00	10.00
	1930	17.115	.50	1.25	4.00	10.00
	1931	10.750	.50	1.25	4.00	10.00
	1932	5.678	1.25	2.50	7.50	20.00
	1933	10.250	.50	1.25	4.00	10.00
	1934	18.300	.50	1.25	4.00	10.00
	1935	10.500	.50	1.25	4.00	10.00
	1936	8.770	.50	1.50	4.50	12.50
	1937	5.500	.50	1.50	4.50	12.50

KM#	Date	Mintage	Fine	VF	XF	Unc
74	1936, yr. XIV					
		Inc. Ab.	.75	1.50	3.00	12.50
	1937, yr. XV					
		7.212	.25	.75	1.50	4.00
	1938, yr. XVI					
		18.750	.25	.75	1.50	4.00
	1939, yr. XVII					
		24.750	.25	.75	1.50	4.00

ALUMINUM-BRONZE

KM#	Date	Mintage	Fine	VF	XF	Unc
74a	1939, yr. XVII					
		.750	.50	1.50	2.00	4.00
	1940, yr. XVIII					
		23.355	.20	.60	1.00	4.00
	1941, yr. XIX					
		27.050	.20	.60	1.00	4.00
	1942, yr. XX					
		18.100	.20	.60	1.00	4.00
	1943, yr. XXI					
		25.400	.25	.60	2.00	5.00

20 CENTESIMI

NiCKEL

Mint mark: R

KM#	Date	Mintage	Fine	VF	XF	Unc
44	1908	14.315	.50	1.00	3.00	10.00
	1909	19.280	.50	1.00	3.00	10.00
	1910	21.887	.50	1.00	3.00	10.00
	1911	13.671	.50	1.00	3.00	10.00
	1912	21.040	.50	1.00	3.00	10.00
	1913	20.729	.50	1.00	3.00	10.00
	1914	14.308	.50	1.00	3.00	10.00
	1919	3.475	1.00	3.50	10.00	25.00
	1920	27.284	.50	1.00	3.00	10.00
	1921	50.372	.50	1.00	3.00	10.00
	1922	17.134	.50	1.00	3.00	10.00
	1926	500 pcs.	—	—	—	165.00
	1927	100 pcs.	—	—	—	225.00
	1928	50 pcs.	—	—	—	275.00
	1929	50 pcs.	—	—	—	275.00
	1930	50 pcs.	—	—	—	275.00
	1931	50 pcs.	—	—	—	275.00
	1932	50 pcs.	—	—	—	275.00
	1933	50 pcs.	—	—	—	275.00
	1934	50 pcs.	—	—	—	275.00
	1935	50 pcs.	—	—	—	275.00

COPPER-NICKEL
Plain and reeded edges, overstruck on KM#28.

KM#	Date	Mintage	Fine	VF	XF	Unc
58	1918	43.097	.50	1.00	4.00	9.00
	1919	33.432	.50	1.00	4.00	9.00
	1920	.923	3.00	5.00	10.00	30.00

NICKEL, 21.5mm

KM#	Date	Mintage	Fine	VF	XF	Unc
75	1936, yr. XIV					
		.117	17.50	40.00	85.00	175.00
	1937, yr. XV					
		50 pcs.	—	—	—	350.00
	1938, yr. XVII					
		20 pcs.	—	—	—	475.00

STAINLESS STEEL (magnetic)
Plain edge, 22.5mm.

KM#	Date	Mintage	Fine	VF	XF	Unc
75a	1939, yr. XVII					
		10.462	2.00	6.00	14.00	35.00
	1940, yr. XVIII					
		35.350	1.40	3.50	10.00	25.00
	1942, yr. XX					
		48.500	1.40	3.50	10.00	28.00

Reeded edge, 21.8mm.

KM#	Date	Mintage	Fine	VF	XF	Unc
75b	1939, yr. XVII					
		Inc. Ab.	—	—	—	—
	1939, yr. XVIII					
		Inc. Ab.	.35	.70	2.00	7.00
	1940, yr. XVIII					
		Inc. Ab.	.20	.40	1.40	4.00
	1941, yr. XIX					
		97.300	.20	.40	1.40	4.00
	1942, yr. XX					
		Inc. Ab.	.25	.50	1.00	3.50
	1943, yr. XXI					
		18.453	.35	.70	1.75	5.00

STAINLESS STEEL (non-magnetic)
Plain edge, 22.5mm.

KM#	Date	Mintage	Fine	VF	XF	Unc
75c	1939, yr. XVII					
		Inc. Ab.	2.00	6.00	14.00	35.00

Reeded edge, 21.8mm.

KM#	Date	Mintage	Fine	VF	XF	Unc
75d	1939, yr. XVII					
		Inc. Ab.	.35	.70	2.00	7.00
	1939, yr. XVIII					
		25.300	.35	1.00	2.75	7.00
	1940, yr. XVIII					
		Inc. Ab.	.20	.40	1.40	4.00

25 CENTESIMI

NICKEL
Mint mark: R

KM#	Date	Mintage	Fine	VF	XF	Unc
36	1902	7.773	15.00	35.00	65.00	135.00
	1903	5.895	12.50	25.00	50.00	110.00

50 CENTESIMI

NICKEL
Mint mark: R
Plain edge

KM#	Date	Mintage	Fine	VF	XF	Unc
61.1	1919	3.700	2.50	5.00	20.00	50.00
	1920	29.450	.75	1.50	3.00	15.00
	1921	16.849	.75	1.50	3.00	15.00
	1924	.599	60.00	120.00	300.00	600.00
	1925	24.884	1.50	2.50	8.00	20.00
	1926	500 pcs.	—	—	—	285.00
	1927	100 pcs.	—	—	—	375.00
	1928	50 pcs.	—	—	—	450.00

Reeded edge.

KM#	Date	Mintage	Fine	VF	XF	Unc
61.2	1919	Inc. Ab.	2.50	6.25	12.50	100.00
	1920	Inc. Ab.	2.50	6.25	12.50	100.00
	1921	Inc. Ab.	2.50	6.25	12.50	100.00
	1924	Inc. Ab.	25.00	50.00	85.00	275.00
	1925	Inc. Ab.	2.00	4.00	10.00	50.00
	1929	50 pcs.	—	—	—	365.00
	1930	50 pcs.	—	—	—	365.00
	1931	50 pcs.	—	—	—	365.00
	1932	50 pcs.	—	—	—	365.00
	1933	50 pcs.	—	—	—	365.00
	1934	50 pcs.	—	—	—	365.00
	1935	50 pcs.	—	—	—	365.00

KM#	Date	Mintage	Fine	VF	XF	Unc
76	1936, yr. XIV	.118	15.00	35.00	80.00	160.00
	1937, yr. XV	50 pcs.	—	—	—	365.00
	1938, yr. XVII	20 pcs.	—	—	—	500.00

STAINLESS STEEL (non-magnetic)

KM#	Date	Mintage	Fine	VF	XF	Unc
76a	1939, yr. XVII	9.373	.35	.75	2.00	7.00
	1939, yr. XVIII	10.005	.35	.75	2.00	7.00
	1940, yr. XVIII	19.005	.25	.60	1.50	4.50

STAINLESS STEEL (magnetic)

KM#	Date	Mintage	Fine	VF	XF	Unc
76b	1939, yr. XVII	Inc. Ab.	.35	.75	2.00	7.00
	1940, yr. XVIII	Inc. Ab.	.25	.60	1.50	4.50
	1941, yr. XIX	58.100	.25	.60	1.50	4.50
	1942, yr. XX	26.450	.25	.60	1.50	4.50
	1943, yr. XXI	.361	25.00	45.00	75.00	150.00

LIRA

5.0000 g, .835 SILVER, .1342 oz ASW
Mint mark: R

KM#	Date	Mintage	Fine	VF	XF	Unc
32	1901	2.590	5.00	12.50	25.00	100.00
	1902	4.084	3.50	7.50	20.00	90.00
	1905	.700	30.00	60.00	150.00	400.00
	1906	4.665	3.50	5.00	12.50	50.00
	1907	8.472	2.50	5.00	12.50	50.00

KM#	Date	Mintage	Fine	VF	XF	Unc
45	1908	2.212	20.00	40.00	80.00	200.00
	1909	3.475	3.50	7.50	20.00	100.00
	1910	5.525	2.50	5.00	15.00	70.00
	1912	5.865	2.50	4.00	9.00	35.00
	1913	16.177	2.00	3.50	6.00	25.00

KM#	Date	Mintage	Fine	VF	XF	Unc
57	1915	5.229	2.75	4.00	12.50	35.00
	1916	1.835	5.00	10.00	20.00	60.00
	1917	9.744	2.75	4.00	10.00	25.00

NICKEL

KM#	Date	Mintage	Fine	VF	XF	Unc
62	1922	82.267	.60	1.00	7.00	20.00
	1923	20.175	.60	1.00	7.00	20.00
	1924 closed 2	29.288	.60	1.00	7.00	20.00
	1926	500 pcs.	—	—	—	225.00
	1927	100 pcs.	—	—	—	325.00
	1928	19.996	1.00	2.00	15.00	40.00
	1929	50 pcs.	—	—	—	350.00
	1930	50 pcs.	—	—	—	350.00
	1931	50 pcs.	—	—	—	350.00
	1932	50 pcs.	—	—	—	350.00
	1933	50 pcs.	—	—	—	350.00
	1934	50 pcs.	—	—	—	350.00
	1935	50 pcs.	—	—	—	350.00

KM#	Date	Mintage	Fine	VF	XF	Unc
77	1936, yr. XIV	.119	15.00	30.00	60.00	125.00
	1937, yr. XV	50 pcs.	—	—	—	365.00
	1938, yr. XVII	20 pcs.	—	—	—	500.00

STAINLESS STEEL (non-magnetic)

KM#	Date	Mintage	Fine	VF	XF	Unc
77a	1939, yr. XVII	10.034	.40	1.50	4.00	14.00
	1939, yr. XVIII	15.977	.35	.75	1.50	6.00
	1940, yr. XVIII	25.997	.30	.60	1.25	5.00

STAINLESS STEEL (magnetic)

KM#	Date	Mintage	Fine	VF	XF	Unc
77b	1939, yr. XVII	Inc. Ab.	.40	1.50	4.00	14.00
	1939, yr. XVIII	Inc. Ab.	.35	.75	1.50	6.00
	1940, yr. XVIII	Inc. Ab.	.30	.60	1.25	5.00
	1941, yr. XIX	8.550	.50	1.75	5.00	16.00
	1942, yr. XX	5.700	.35	.75	1.50	6.00
	1943, yr. XXI	11.500	10.00	20.00	35.00	75.00

2 LIRE

10.0000 g, .835 SILVER, .2684 oz ASW
Mint mark: R

KM#	Date	Mintage	Fine	VF	XF	Unc
33	1901	.072	200.00	400.00	800.00	1500.
	1902	.549	50.00	100.00	180.00	450.00
	1903	.054	300.00	500.00	1000.	3000.
	1904	.157	125.00	250.00	450.00	700.00
	1905	1.643	10.00	20.00	50.00	200.00
	1906	.970	12.50	25.00	75.00	200.00
	1907	1.245	10.00	20.00	50.00	200.00

KM#	Date	Mintage	Fine	VF	XF	Unc
46	1908	2.283	6.00	15.00	50.00	150.00
	1910	.719	25.00	50.00	125.00	300.00
	1911	.535	30.00	60.00	150.00	400.00
	1912	2.166	6.00	15.00	50.00	150.00

50th Anniversary of Kingdom

KM#	Date	Mintage	Fine	VF	XF	Unc
52	1911	1.000	12.50	25.00	50.00	125.00

KM#	Date	Mintage	Fine	VF	XF	Unc
55	1914	10.390	4.00	6.00	12.00	30.00
	1915	7.948	4.00	6.00	12.00	30.00
	1916	10.923	4.00	6.00	12.00	30.00
	1917	6.123	6.00	12.50	25.00	60.00

NICKEL

KM#	Date	Mintage	Fine	VF	XF	Unc
63	1923	32.260	1.00	2.50	6.00	20.00
	1924	45.051	1.00	2.50	6.00	20.00
	1925	14.628	1.00	2.50	6.00	30.00
	1926	5.101	5.00	10.00	50.00	150.00
	1927	1.632	25.00	50.00	100.00	300.00
	1928	50 pcs.	—	—	—	400.00
	1929	50 pcs.	—	—	—	400.00
	1930	50 pcs.	—	—	—	400.00
	1931	50 pcs.	—	—	—	400.00
	1932	50 pcs.	—	—	—	400.00
	1933	50 pcs.	—	—	—	400.00
	1934	50 pcs.	—	—	—	400.00
	1935	50 pcs.	—	—	—	400.00

KM#	Date	Mintage	Fine	VF	XF	Unc
78	1936, yr. XIV	.120	20.00	45.00	90.00	200.00
	1937, yr. XV	50 pcs.	—	—	—	400.00
	1938, yr. XVII	20 pcs.	—	—	—	550.00

STAINLESS STEEL (non-magnetic)

KM#	Date	Mintage	Fine	VF	XF	Unc
78a	1939, yr. XVII	2.900	.60	1.75	5.00	16.00
	1939, yr. XVIII	4.873	.40	.90	2.50	9.00
	1940, yr. XVIII	5.742	.40	.90	2.00	5.00

STAINLESS STEEL (magnetic)

KM#	Date	Mintage	Fine	VF	XF	Unc
78b	1939, yr. XVII	Inc. Ab.	.60	1.75	5.00	16.00
	1939, yr. XVIII	Inc. Ab.	.40	.90	2.50	9.00

KM#	Date	Mintage	Fine	VF	XF	Unc
78b	1940, yr. XVIII					
		Inc. Ab.	.40	.90	2.00	5.00
	1941, yr. XIX					
		1.865	.50	1.50	3.00	10.00
	1942, yr. XX					
		2.450	40.00	80.00	160.00	325.00
	1943, yr. XXI					
		.600	20.00	40.00	100.00	200.00

5 LIRE

25.0000 g, .900 SILVER, .7234 oz ASW
Mint mark: R

KM#	Date	Mintage	Fine	VF	XF	Unc
34	1901	114 pcs.	—	—	15,000.	20,000.

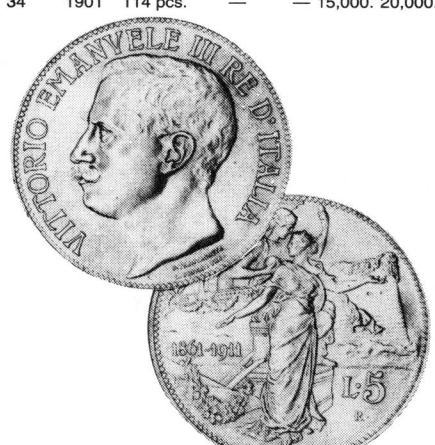

50th Anniversary of Kingdom

| 53 | 1911 | .060 | 150.00 | 300.00 | 500.00 | 950.00 |

| 56 | 1914 | .273 | 500.00 | 850.00 | 2500. | 4000. |

5.0000 g, .835 SILVER, .1342 oz ASW

Edge inscription: *FERT*.

KM#	Date	Mintage	Fine	VF	XF	Unc
67.1	1926	5.405	5.00	15.00	30.00	120.00
	1927	92.887	1.50	3.00	7.00	22.50
	1928	9.908	6.00	15.00	40.00	160.00
	1929	33.803	2.00	4.00	8.00	25.00
	1930	19.525	2.00	4.00	10.00	27.50
	1931	50 pcs.	—	—	—	400.00
	1932	50 pcs.	—	—	—	400.00
	1933	50 pcs.	—	—	—	400.00
	1934	50 pcs.	—	—	—	400.00
	1935	50 pcs.	—	—	—	400.00

Edge inscription: **FERT**

67.2	1927	Inc. Ab.	2.00	4.00	8.00	35.00
	1928	Inc. Ab.	10.00	20.00	50.00	200.00
	1929	Inc. Ab.	3.00	6.00	12.00	40.00

79	1936, yr. XIV					
		1.016	10.00	20.00	40.00	100.00
	1937, yr. XV					
		.100	15.00	30.00	60.00	135.00
	1938, yr. XVIII					
		20 pcs.	—	—	—	550.00
	1939, yr. XVIII					
		20 pcs.	—	—	—	550.00
	1940, yr. XIX					
		20 pcs.	—	—	—	550.00
	1941, yr. XX					
		20 pcs.	—	—	—	550.00

10 LIRE

3.2258 g, .900 GOLD, 18mm, .0933 oz AGW
Mint mark: R

47	1910	5,202*	—	—	Rare	—
	1912	6,796	700.00	1250.	2000.	3500.
	1926	40 pcs.	—	—	6000.	9000.
	1927	30 pcs.	—	—	5000.	7000.

*NOTE: All but one piece melted.

10.0000 g, .835 SILVER, .2684 oz ASW
Edge inscription: *FERT*.

68.1	1926	1.748	65.00	135.00	275.00	600.00
	1927	44.801	7.00	15.00	35.00	75.00
	1928	6.652	25.00	65.00	150.00	300.00
	1929	6.800	35.00	75.00	175.00	350.00
	1930	3.668	60.00	125.00	250.00	500.00
	1931	50 pcs.	—	—	—	750.00
	1932	50 pcs.	—	—	—	750.00
	1933	50 pcs.	—	—	—	750.00
	1934	50 pcs.	—	—	—	750.00

Edge inscription: **FERT**

68.2	1927	Inc. Ab.	10.00	20.00	50.00	100.00
	1928	Inc. Ab.	75.00	150.00	300.00	600.00
	1929	Inc. Ab.	25.00	65.00	140.00	280.00

80	1936, yr. XIV					
		.619	15.00	30.00	60.00	135.00
	1937, yr. XV					
		50 pcs.	—	—	—	685.00
	1938, yr. XVII					
		20 pcs.	—	—	—	850.00
	1939, yr. XVIII					
		20 pcs.	—	—	—	850.00
	1940, yr. XIX					
		20 pcs.	—	—	—	850.00
	1941, yr. XX					
		20 pcs.	—	—	—	850.00

---

20 LIRE

6.4516 g, .900 GOLD, .1867 oz AGW
Mint mark: R

KM#	Date	Mintage	Fine	VF	XF	Unc
37.1	1902	181 pcs.	—	6000.	12,000.	15,000.
	1903	1,800	450.00	800.00	1300.	1800.
	1905	8,715	250.00	400.00	650.00	900.00
	1908		—	—	Rare	

Obv: Small anchor at bottom indicates gold in coin is from Eritrea.

| 37.2 | 1902 | 115 pcs. | 4000. | 9000. | 18,000. | 25,000. |

Obv: Uniformed bust.

48	1910	*.033	—	—	—	30,000.
	1912	.059	275.00	400.00	750.00	1100.
	1926	40 pcs.	—	—	5000.	8000.
	1927	30 pcs.	—	—	—	10,000.

*NOTE: Six pieces currently known to exist.

1st Anniversary of Fascist Government

| 64 | 1923 | .020 | 200.00 | 350.00 | 650.00 | 850.00 |

15.0000 g, .800 SILVER, .3858 oz ASW

69	1927, yr. V					
		100 pcs.	—	—	4000.	5500.
	1927, yr. VI					
		3.518	50.00	90.00	225.00	500.00
	1928, yr. VI					
		2.487	70.00	110.00	325.00	625.00
	1929, yr. VII					
		50 pcs.	—	—	—	1800.
	1930, yr. VIII					
		50 pcs.	—	—	—	1800.
	1931, yr. IX					
		50 pcs.	—	—	—	1800.
	1932, yr. X					
		50 pcs.	—	—	—	1800.
	1933, yr. XI					
		50 pcs.	—	—	—	1800.
	1934, yr. XII					
		50 pcs.	—	—	—	1800.

20.0000 g, .600 SILVER, .3858 oz ASW
10th Anniversary - End of World War I

KM#	Date	Mintage	Fine	VF	XF	Unc
70	1928, yr. VI	—	75.00	160.00	300.00	700.00

NOTE: Similar 20 and 100 Lire pieces struck in gold, silver and silvered brass are modern fantasies. Refer to *UNUSUAL WORLD COINS*, 3rd edition, Krause Publications, 1992.

20.0000 g, .800 SILVER, .5145 oz ASW

81	1936, yr. XIV					
		.010	250.00	500.00	1000.	2000.
	1937, yr. XV					
		50 pcs.	—	—	—	2750.
	1938, yr. XVII					
		20 pcs.	—	—	—	3000.
	1939, yr. XVIII					
		20 pcs.	—	—	—	3000.
	1940, yr. XIX					
		20 pcs.	—	—	—	3250.
	1941, yr. XX					
		20 pcs.	—	—	—	3250.

50 LIRE

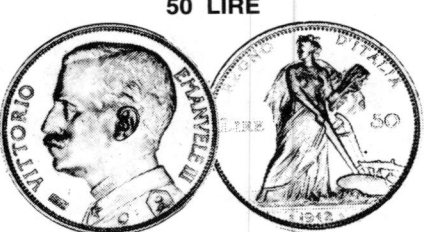

16.1290 g, .900 GOLD, .4667 oz AGW
Mint mark: R

49	1910	2,096			Rare	—
	1912	.011	450.00	750.00	1250.	1750.
	1926	40 pcs.	—	—	—	15,000.
	1927	30 pcs.	—	—	—	18,000.

50th Anniversary of Kingdom

54	1911	.020	300.00	500.00	750.00	1450.

4.3995 g, .900 GOLD, .1273 oz AGW

KM#	Date	Mintage	Fine	VF	XF	Unc
71	1931, yr. IX					
		.032	90.00	125.00	155.00	250.00
	1931, yr. X					
		Inc. Ab.	200.00	300.00	400.00	600.00
	1932, yr. X					
		.012	200.00	300.00	400.00	600.00
	1933, yr. XI					
		6,463	300.00	400.00	600.00	800.00

82	1936, yr. XIV					
		790 pcs.	1000.	1800.	3500.	5500.

REPUBLIC
1946-
LIRA

ALUMINUM
Mint mark: R

87	1946	.104	10.00	30.00	85.00	150.00
	1947	.012	60.00	140.00	250.00	450.00
	1948	9.000	.40	1.00	3.00	12.00
	1949	13.200	.40	1.00	2.50	10.00
	1950	1.942	1.00	2.00	6.00	17.50

91	1951	3.680	.20	.50	1.00	8.00
	1952	2.720	.20	.50	1.00	5.00
	1953	2.800	.20	.50	1.00	3.00
	1954	41.040	.10	.25	.50	1.85
	1955	32.640	.10	.25	.50	1.85
	1956	1.840	.20	.50	4.00	15.00
	1957	7.440	.10	.25	.50	2.00
	1958	5.280	.10	.25	.50	2.00
	1959	1.680	.10	.25	.50	2.00
	1968	.100	—	In sets only		17.00
	1969	.310	—	In sets only		5.00
	1970	1.011	—	—	—	2.50
	1980	1.500	—	—	—	1.50
	1981	.500	—	—	—	1.50
	1982	.085	—	In sets only		2.50
	1983	.076	—	In sets only		6.00
	1984	.077	—	In sets only		4.00
	1985	.073	—	In sets only		2.00
	1985	.020	In Proof sets only			4.00
	1986	—	—	In sets only		2.00
	1986	—	In Proof sets only			4.00
	1987	.177	—	In sets only		2.50
	1987	—	In Proof sets only			4.50
	1988	.077	—	In sets only		2.00
	1988	—	In Proof sets only			4.50
	1989	—	—	In sets only		2.00
	1989	—	In Proof sets only			4.50
	1990	—	—	In sets only		2.00
	1990	—	In Proof sets only			4.50
	1991	—	—	In sets only		2.00
	1991	—	In Proof sets only			4.50
	1992	—	—	In sets only		2.00
	1992	—	In Proof sets only			4.50
	1993	—	—	In sets only		2.00
	1993	—	In Proof sets only			4.50
	1994	—	—	In sets only		2.00
	1995	—	—	In sets only		2.00

2 LIRE

ALUMINUM
Mint mark: R

88	1946	.123	7.50	20.00	60.00	120.00
	1947	.012	65.00	150.00	275.00	475.00
	1948	7.200	.50	1.50	3.00	9.00
	1949	1.350	5.00	12.00	25.00	50.00
	1950	2.640	.60	1.75	4.00	13.50

KM#	Date	Mintage	Fine	VF	XF	Unc
94	1953	4.125	.25	.50	.75	4.00
	1954	22.500	.25	.50	.75	2.00
	1955	2.750	.25	.50	.75	3.50
	1956	1.500	1.00	3.00	5.00	15.00
	1957	6.313	.25	.50	.75	2.50
	1958	.125	20.00	60.00	140.00	200.00
	1959	2.000	.25	.50	.75	2.50
	1968	.100	—	In sets only		15.00
	1969	.310	—	In sets only		4.00
	1970	1.140	—	—	—	2.50
	1980	.500	—	—	—	1.00
	1981	.500	—	—	—	1.00
	1982	.085	—	In sets only		2.50
	1983	.076	—	In sets only		6.00
	1984	.077	—	In sets only		4.00
	1985	.073	—	In sets only		1.00
	1985	.020	In Proof sets only			3.50
	1986	—	—	In sets only		1.00
	1986	—	In Proof sets only			3.50
	1987	.177	—	In sets only		1.50
	1987	—	In Proof sets only			4.00
	1988	.077	—	In sets only		1.00
	1988	—	In Proof sets only			4.50
	1989	—	—	In sets only		1.00
	1989	—	In Proof sets only			4.50
	1990	—	—	In sets only		1.00
	1990	—	In Proof sets only			4.50
	1991	—	—	In sets only		1.00
	1991	—	In Proof sets only			4.50
	1992	—	—	In sets only		1.00
	1992	—	In Proof sets only			4.50
	1993	—	—	In sets only		1.00
	1993	—	In Proof sets only			4.50
	1994	—	—	In sets only		1.00
	1995	—	—	In sets only		1.00

5 LIRE

ALUMINUM
Mint mark: R

89	1946	.081	100.00	250.00	350.00	650.00
	1947	.017	125.00	275.00	425.00	750.00
	1948	25.125	.50	1.50	5.00	15.00
	1949	71.100	.30	.75	2.00	10.00
	1950	114.790	.30	.75	2.00	10.00

92	1951	40.260	.10	.25	.50	3.00
	1952	57.400	.10	.25	.50	4.00
	1953	196.200	.10	.25	.50	2.00
	1954	436.400	.10	.25	.50	1.50
	1955	159.000	.10	.25	.50	2.00
	1956	.400	15.00	50.00	250.00	800.00
	1966	1.200	.25	.50	1.00	1.50
	1967	10.600	.10	.25	.50	1.00
	1968	7.500	—	—	.10	.75
	1969	7.910	—	—	.10	.75
	1969 inverted I					
		.969	1.00	2.00	4.00	22.50
	1970	3.200	—	—	.10	.75
	1971	8.600	—	—	.10	.75
	1972	16.400	—	—	.10	.50
	1973	28.800	—	—	.10	.50
	1974	6.600	—	—	.10	.50
	1975	7.000	—	—	.10	.50
	1976	8.800	—	—	.10	.50
	1977	6.700	—	—	.10	.50
	1978	3.600	—	—	.10	.50
	1979	4.200	—	—	.10	.50
	1980	3.663	—	—	.10	.50
	1981	7.788	—	—	.10	.50
	1982	.855	—	—	.10	.50
	1983	14.020	—	—	.10	.50
	1984	.122	—	—	.10	.50
	1985	3.000	—	—	.10	.50
	1985	.020	—	—	Proof	2.50
	1986	5.000	—	—	.10	.50
	1986	—	—	—	Proof	2.50
	1987	7.000	—	—	.10	.50
	1987	—	—	—	Proof	2.50
	1988	5.000	—	—	.10	.50
	1988	—	—	—	Proof	2.50

KM#	Date	Mintage	Fine	VF	XF	Unc
92	1989 coin rotation	—	—	—	.10	.50
	1989 medal rotation					
		—	—	—	—	10.00
	1989	—	—	—	Proof	2.50
	1990	—	—	—	.10	.50
	1990	—	—	—	Proof	2.50
	1991	—	—	—	.10	.50
	1991	—	—	—	Proof	2.50
	1992	—	—	—	.10	.50
	1992	—	—	—	Proof	2.50
	1993	—	—	—	.10	.50
	1993	—	—	—	Proof	2.50
	1994	—	—	—	.10	.50
	1995	—	—	—	.10	.50

10 LIRE

ALUMINUM
Mint mark: R

KM#	Date	Mintage	Fine	VF	XF	Unc
90	1946	.101	50.00	120.00	200.00	300.00
	1947	.012	200.00	600.00	1200.	1850.
	1948	14.400	1.00	4.00	25.00	65.00
	1949	49.500	.50	1.00	3.00	15.00
	1950	53.311	.50	1.00	3.00	15.00

KM#	Date	Mintage	Fine	VF	XF	Unc
93	1951	96.600	.10	.25	2.00	10.00
	1952	105.150	.10	.25	1.50	8.00
	1953	151.500	.10	.25	1.00	6.00
	1954	95.250	.50	1.00	5.00	40.00
	1955	274.950	.10	.15	1.00	3.00
	1956	76.650	.10	.25	1.25	6.00
	1965	1.050	.25	.50	1.50	8.00
	1966	16.500	.10	.25	1.00	3.00
	1967	29.450	.10	.25	1.00	2.00
	1968	32.200	—	—	.10	.75
	1969	23.710	—	—	.10	.75
	1970	14.100	—	—	.10	.75
	1971	23.550	—	—	.10	.75
	1972	61.300	—	—	.10	.50
	1973	145.800	—	—	.10	.50
	1974	85.000	—	—	.10	.50
	1975	76.800	—	—	.10	.50
	1976	82.000	—	—	.10	.50
	1977	80.750	—	—	.10	.50
	1978	43.800	—	—	.10	.50
	1979	98.000	—	—	.10	.50
	1980	81.109	—	—	.10	.50
	1981	46.967	—	—	.10	.50
	1982	45.986	—	—	.10	.50
	1983	15.110	—	—	.10	.50
	1984	11.122	—	—	.10	.50
	1985	15.000	—	—	.10	.50
	1985	.020	—	—	Proof	3.50
	1986	16.000	—	—	.10	.50
	1986	—	—	—	Proof	3.50
	1987	13.000	—	—	.10	.50
	1987	—	—	—	Proof	3.50
	1988	13.000	—	—	.10	.50
	1988	—	—	—	Proof	3.50
	1989	—	—	—	.10	.50
	1989	—	—	—	Proof	3.50
	1990	—	—	—	.10	.50
	1990	—	—	—	Proof	3.50
	1991	—	—	—	.10	.50
	1991	—	—	—	Proof	3.50
	1992	—	—	—	.10	.50
	1992	—	—	—	Proof	3.50
	1993	—	—	—	.10	.50
	1993	—	—	—	Proof	3.50
	1994	—	—	—	.10	.50
	1995	—	—	—	.10	.50

20 LIRE

ALUMINUM-BRONZE
Mint mark: R

KM#	Date	Mintage	Fine	VF	XF	Unc
97.1	1957 serif 7					

KM#	Date	Mintage	Fine	VF	XF	Unc
97.1		*60.075	.20	.40	2.00	10.00
	1957 pln. 7					
		Inc. Ab.	.20	.40	2.00	10.00
	1958	80.550	.20	.40	2.00	10.00
	1959	4.005	.50	1.25	5.00	50.00

Plain edge

97.2	1968	.100	—	2.50	5.00	35.00
	1969	16.735	.10	.15	.25	1.00
	1970	31.500	.10	.15	.25	.65
	1971	12.375	.10	.15	.25	1.00
	1972	34.400	.10	.15	.25	.65
	1973	20.000	.10	.15	.25	.65
	1974	17.000	.10	.15	.20	.65
	1975	25.000	.10	.15	.20	.65
	1976	15.000	.10	.15	.20	.65
	1977	10.000	.10	.15	.20	.65
	1978	8.415	.10	.15	.20	.65
	1979	32.000	.10	.15	.20	.50
	1980	61.795	.10	.15	.20	.50
	1981	68.557	.10	.15	.20	.50
	1982	44.774	.10	.15	.20	.50
	1983	15.110	.10	.15	.20	.50
	1984	5.122	.10	.15	.20	.50
	1985	15.000	.10	.15	.20	.50
	1985	.020	—	—	Proof	3.50
	1986	13.000	.10	.15	.20	.50
	1986	—	—	—	Proof	3.50
	1987	8.234	.10	.15	.20	.50
	1987	—	—	—	Proof	3.50
	1988	13.000	.10	.15	.20	.50
	1988	—	—	—	Proof	3.50
	1989	—	.10	.15	.20	.50
	1989	—	—	—	Proof	3.50
	1990	—	.10	.15	.20	.50
	1990	—	—	—	Proof	3.50
	1991	—	.10	.15	.20	.50
	1991	—	—	—	Proof	3.50
	1992	—	.10	.15	.20	.50
	1992	—	—	—	Proof	3.50
	1993	—	.10	.15	.20	.50
	1993	—	—	—	Proof	3.50
	1994	—	.10	.15	.20	.50
	1995	—	.10	.15	.20	3.50

50 LIRE

STAINLESS STEEL
Mint mark: R

KM#	Date	Mintage	Fine	VF	XF	Unc
95	1954	17.600	1.00	3.00	20.00	75.00
	1955	70.500	.50	1.50	10.00	40.00
	1956	69.400	.50	1.50	10.00	40.00
	1957	8.925	2.00	4.00	25.00	120.00
	1958	.825	4.00	10.00	50.00	200.00
	1959	8.800	.50	1.50	15.00	80.00
	1960	2.025	2.00	4.00	20.00	100.00
	1961	11.100	.50	1.50	10.00	40.00
	1962	17.700	.50	1.50	10.00	40.00
	1963	31.600	.20	.75	2.50	20.00
	1964	37.900	.20	.75	2.50	18.00
	1965	25.300	.20	.50	1.50	12.00
	1966	27.400	.20	.40	.80	8.00
	1967	28.000	.20	.40	.80	6.00
	1968	17.800	.20	.30	.50	1.50
	1969	23.010	.20	.30	.50	1.50
	1970	21.411	.10	.20	.50	1.50
	1971	33.410	.10	.20	.50	1.50
	1972	39.000	.10	.20	.50	1.50
	1973	48.700	.10	.20	.50	1.50
	1974	64.100	.10	.20	.35	1.00
	1975	87.000	.10	.15	.25	.75
	1976	180.600	.10	.15	.25	.75
	1977	293.800	.10	.15	.25	.75
	1978	416.808	.10	.15	.25	.75
	1979	256.630	.10	.15	.25	.75
	1980	—	.10	.15	.25	.75
	1981	—	.10	.15	.25	.75
	1982	—	.10	.15	.25	.75
	1983	—	.10	.15	.25	.75
	1984	—	.10	.15	.25	.75
	1985	—	.10	.15	.25	.75
	1985	.020	—	—	Proof	3.50
	1986	—	.10	.15	.25	.75
	1986	—	—	—	Proof	3.50
	1987	14.682	.10	.15	.25	.75
	1987	—	—	—	Proof	3.50
	1988	20.000	.10	.15	.25	.75
	1988	—	—	—	Proof	3.50
	1989	—	.10	.15	.25	.75
	1989	—	—	—	Proof	3.50

Reduced size.

95a	1990	3600.000	—	—	—	.35

KM#	Date	Mintage	Fine	VF	XF	Unc
95a	1990	—	—	—	Proof	4.00
	1991	—	—	—	—	.35
	1991	—	—	—	Proof	4.00
	1992	—	—	—	—	.35
	1992	—	—	—	Proof	4.00
	1993	—	—	—	—	.35
	1993	—	—	—	Proof	4.00
	1994	—	—	—	—	.35
	1995	—	—	—	—	.35

COPPER-NICKEL
Mintmark: R

183	1996	—	—	—	—	.35
	1996	—	—	—	Proof	4.00

100 LIRE

STAINLESS STEEL
Mint mark: R

KM#	Date	Mintage	Fine	VF	XF	Unc
96	1955	8.600	1.00	3.00	20.00	185.00
	1956	99.800	.25	1.00	4.00	50.00
	1957	90.600	.25	1.50	15.00	150.00
	1958	25.640	.25	1.50	15.00	150.00
	1959	19.500	.25	1.50	12.00	120.00
	1960	20.700	.25	1.50	10.00	100.00
	1961	11.860	.25	1.50	10.00	100.00
	1962	21.700	.20	.50	3.00	40.00
	1963	33.100	.20	.50	2.00	30.00
	1964	31.300	.20	.50	1.50	20.00
	1965	37.000	.20	.50	1.50	20.00
	1966	52.500	.15	.25	1.00	15.00
	1967	23.700	.15	.25	1.00	15.00
	1968	34.200	.15	.25	.50	3.00
	1969	27.710	.15	.25	.50	3.00
	1970	25.011	.15	.25	.50	3.00
	1971	25.910	.15	.25	.50	3.00
	1972	31.170	.15	.25	.50	3.00
	1973	30.780	.15	.25	.50	5.00
	1974	83.880	.15	.25	.35	.85
	1975	106.650	.15	.25	.35	.85
	1976	160.020	.15	.25	.35	.85
	1977	253.980	.15	.25	.35	.85
	1978	343.626	.15	.25	.35	.85
	1979	187.913	.15	.25	.35	.85
	1980	—	.15	.25	.35	.85
	1981	—	.15	.25	.35	.85
	1982	—	.15	.25	.35	.85
	1983	—	.15	.25	.35	.85
	1984	—	.15	.25	.35	.85
	1985	—	.15	.25	.35	.85
	1985	.020	—	—	Proof	4.50
	1986	—	.15	.25	.35	.85
	1986	—	—	—	Proof	4.50
	1987	25.000	.15	.25	.35	.85
	1987	—	—	—	Proof	4.50
	1988	23.000	.15	.25	.85	1.00
	1988	—	—	—	Proof	4.50
	1989	—	.15	.25	.85	1.00
	1989	—	—	—	Proof	4.50

Reduced size.

96a	1990	3560.000	—	—	—	.50
	1990	—	—	—	Proof	4.50
	1991	—	—	—	—	.50
	1991	—	—	—	Proof	4.50
	1992	—	—	—	—	.50
	1992	—	—	—	Proof	4.50

100th Anniversary - Birth of Guglielmo Marconi

102	ND(1974)					
		50.000	.15	.25	.50	1.75

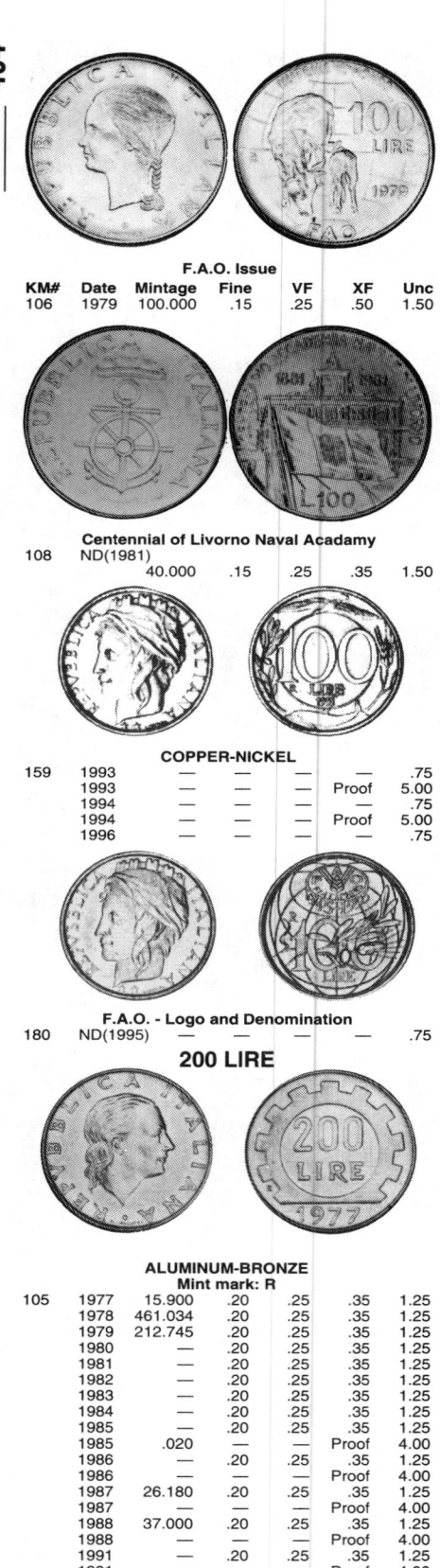
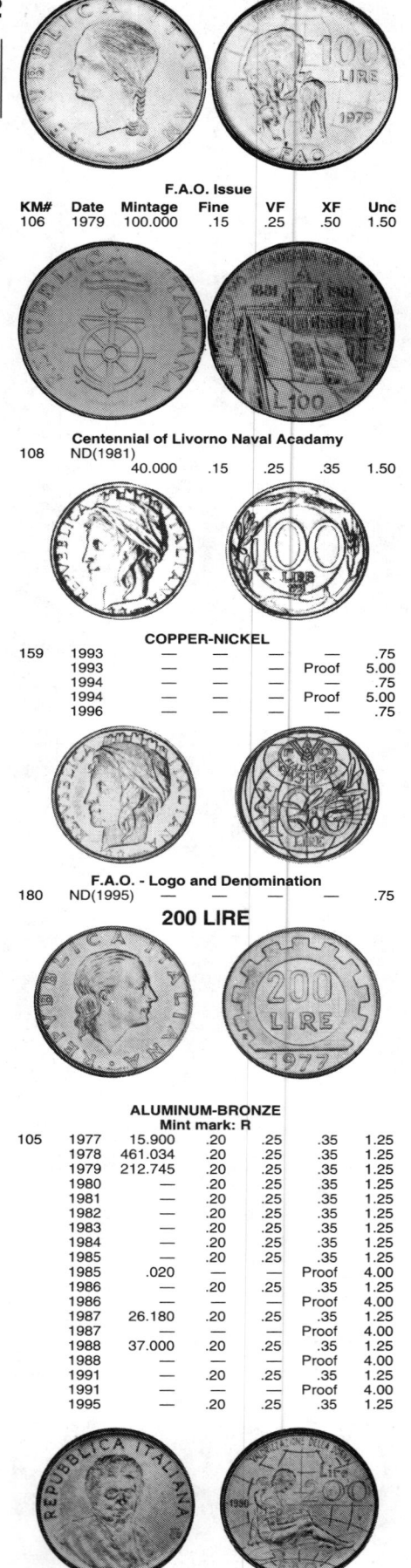

F.A.O. Issue

KM#	Date	Mintage	Fine	VF	XF	Unc
106	1979	100.000	.15	.25	.50	1.50

Centennial of Livorno Naval Acadamy

108	ND(1981)					
		40.000	.15	.25	.35	1.50

COPPER-NICKEL

159	1993	—	—	—		.75
	1993	—	—	—	Proof	5.00
	1994	—	—	—		.75
	1994	—	—	—	Proof	5.00
	1996	—	—	—		.75

F.A.O. - Logo and Denomination

180	ND(1995)	—	—	—		.75

200 LIRE

ALUMINUM-BRONZE
Mint mark: R

105	1977	15.900	.20	.25	.35	1.25
	1978	461.034	.20	.25	.35	1.25
	1979	212.745	.20	.25	.35	1.25
	1980	—	.20	.25	.35	1.25
	1981	—	.20	.25	.35	1.25
	1982	—	.20	.25	.35	1.25
	1983	—	.20	.25	.35	1.25
	1984	—	.20	.25	.35	1.25
	1985	—	.20	.25	.35	1.25
	1985	.020	—	—	Proof	4.00
	1986	—	.20	.25	.35	1.25
	1986	—	—	—	Proof	4.00
	1987	26.180	.20	.25	.35	1.25
	1987	—	—	—	Proof	4.00
	1988	37.000	.20	.25	.35	1.25
	1988	—	—	—	Proof	4.00
	1991	—	.20	.25	.35	1.25
	1991	—	—	—	Proof	4.00
	1995	—	.20	.25	.35	1.25

F.A.O. - International Women's Year

107	1980	50.000	.20	.25	.35	1.25

World Food Day

KM#	Date	Mintage	Fine	VF	XF	Unc
109	1981	50.000	.20	.25	.35	1.25

BRONZITAL
Taranto Naval Yards

130	ND(1989)					
		50.000	—	—	—	1.25
	ND(1989)	—	—	—	Proof	4.00

State Council Building

135	ND(1990)	—	—	—	—	1.25
	ND(1990)	—	—	—	Proof	4.00

ALUMINUM-BRONZE
Genoa Stamp Exposition

151	1992	110.000	—	—	—	1.35
	1992	—	—	—	Proof	4.00

70th Anniversary of Military Aviation

155	1993	—	—	—	—	1.35

180th Anniversary - Carabinieri

164	ND(1994)	—	—	—	—	1.35

BRASS
Centennial - Customs Service Academy
Obv: 2 large buildings. Rev: Shield above denomination, hat and sword.

184	ND(1996)	—	—	—	—	1.00

Centennial - Italian Naval League
Rev: League seal.

KM#	Date	Mintage	Fine	VF	XF	Unc
188	ND(1997)	—	—	—	—	1.00

500 LIRE

11.0000 g, .835 SILVER, .2953 oz ASW
Mint mark: R
(Dates appear on edge of coin in raised lettering.)

98	1958	24.240	—	BV	4.00	7.00
	1958	Inc. Ab.	—	—	P/L	30.00
	1959	19.360	—	BV	4.00	7.00
	1959	Inc. Ab.	—	—	P/L	30.00
	1960	24.080	—	BV	4.00	7.00
	1960	Inc. Ab.	—	—	P/L	30.00
	1961	6.560	—	BV	10.00	25.00
	1961	Inc. Ab.	—	—	P/L	50.00
	1964	4.880	—	BV	4.50	10.00
	1964	Inc. Ab.	—	—	P/L	30.00
	1965	3.120	—	BV	4.50	10.00
	1965	Inc. Ab.	—	—	—	30.00
	1966	13.120	—	BV	3.25	5.00
	1966	Inc. Ab.	—	—	P/L	25.00
	1967	2.480	—	BV	3.25	5.00
	1967	Inc. Ab.	—	—	P/L	25.00
	1968	.100	—	—	—	110.00
	1968	Inc. Ab.	—	—	P/L	120.00
	1969	.310	—	—	—	15.00
	1969	Inc. Ab.	—	—	P/L	30.00
	1970	1.140	—	—	—	12.50
	1970	Inc. Ab.	—	—	P/L	25.00
	1980	.500	—	—	—	15.00
	1980	Inc. Ab.	—	—	P/L	25.00
	1981	.500	—	—	—	16.50
	1981	Inc. Ab.	—	—	P/L	30.00
	1982	.115	—	—	—	16.50
	1982	Inc. Ab.	—	—	P/L	30.00
	1983	.076	—	—	—	165.00
	1984	.077	—	—	—	60.00
	1985	.073	—	—	—	30.00
	1985	.015	—	—	Proof	60.00
	1986	.095	—	—	—	35.00
	1986	Inc. Ab.	—	—	Proof	60.00
	1987	.060	—	—	—	40.00
	1987	.015	—	—	Proof	65.00
	1988	.055	—	—	—	165.00
	1988	.010	—	—	Proof	185.00
	1989	.060	—	—	—	65.00
	1989	.010	—	—	Proof	85.00
	1990	.060	—	—	—	75.00
	1990	.010	—	—	Proof	85.00
	1991	—	—	—	—	65.00
	1991	—	—	—	Proof	85.00
	1992	—	—	—	—	35.00
	1992	—	—	—	Proof	60.00
	1993	—	—	—	—	35.00
	1993	—	—	—	Proof	60.00
	1994	—	—	—	—	35.00
	1995	—	—	—	—	35.00

*NOTE: Varieties exist in the 1966 issue.

Italian Unification Centennial

99	ND(1961)					
		27.120	—	BV	3.00	6.50
	ND(1961)					
		Inc. Ab.	—	—	Proof	25.00

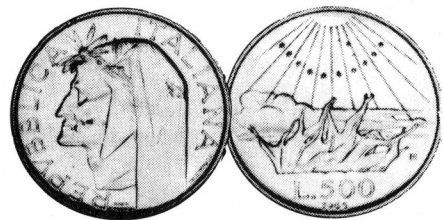

700th Anniversary - Birth of Dante Alighieri

KM#	Date	Mintage	Fine	VF	XF	Unc
100	1965	4.272	—	BV	4.00	8.50
	1965	Inc. Ab.	—	—	Proof	15.00

ACMONITAL ring, BRONZITAL center

KM#	Date	Mintage	Fine	VF	XF	Unc
111	1982	200.000	—	.40	.60	2.00
	1983	230.000	—	.40	.60	1.25
	1984	—	—	.40	.60	1.25
	1985	—	—	.40	.60	1.25
	1985	.020	—	—	Proof	15.00
	1986	—	—	.40	.60	1.25
	1986	—	—	—	Proof	12.50
	1987	200.000	—	.40	.60	1.25
	1987	—	—	—	Proof	20.00
	1988	142.000	—	.40	.60	1.25
	1988	—	—	—	Proof	25.00
	1989	—	—	.40	.60	1.25
	1989	—	—	—	Proof	20.00
	1990	—	—	.40	.60	1.25
	1990	—	—	—	Proof	20.00
	1991	—	—	.40	.60	1.25
	1991	—	—	—	Proof	20.00
	1992	—	—	.40	.60	1.25
	1992	—	—	—	Proof	20.00
	1995	—	—	—	.60	1.25

NOTE: Varieties exist on 1982 and 1995 obverse portraits.

Centennial - Bank of Italy

160	1993	.050	—	—	—	3.00
	1993	.010	—	—	Proof	10.00

NOTE: Large and small designer's name, GROSSI, exist.

500th Anniversary - Publication of Mathematical Work by Luca Pacioli

167	1994	—	—	—	—	1.50

**BRASS CENTER in STAINLESS STEEL ring
Istituto Nazionale di Statistica - Building**

181	ND(1996)	—	—	—	—	1.50

[coin image]

50th Anniversary - National Police Code

**Obv: Allegorical portrait.
Rev: Mythological figure above coat of arms.**

KM#	Date	Mintage	Fine	VF	XF	Unc
187	ND(1997)	—	—	—	—	2.00

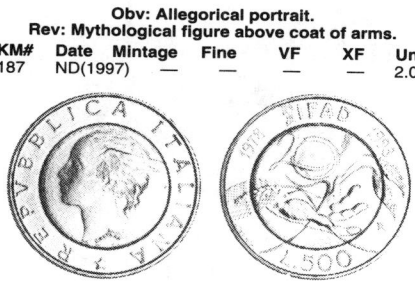

**ALUMINUM BRONZE center in
STAINLESS STEEL ring
F.A.O - 20 Years
Obv: Allegorical portrait.
Rev: Hand and grains.**

193	ND(1998)	—	—	—	—	1.50

1000 LIRE

**COPPER-NICKEL center in
ALUMINUM-BRONZE ring
European Union
Obv: Allegorical portrait.
Rev: Error map of European Union
showing the old West Germany.**

190	1997	—	—	—	—	3.50

 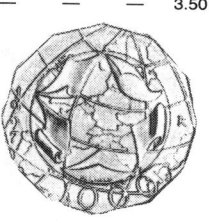

**COPPER-NICKEL center in BRASS ring
European Union
Obv: Allegorical portrait.
Rev: Correct map of Europe.**

194	1997	—	—	—	—	3.50

JAMAICA

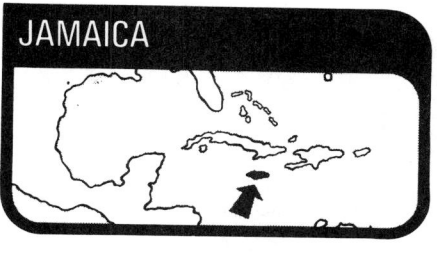

Jamaica, a member of the British Commonwealth situated in the Caribbean Sea 90 miles south of Cuba, has an area of 4,244 sq. mi. (10,990 sq. km.) and a population of 2.1 million. Capital: Kingston. The economy is founded chiefly on mining, tourism and agriculture. Alumina, bauxite, sugar, rum and molasses are exported.

Jamaica was discovered by Columbus on May 3, 1494, and settled by Spain in 1509. The island was captured in 1655 by a British naval force under the command of Admiral William Penn, sent by Oliver Cromwell and ceded to Britain by the Treaty of Madrid, 1670. For more than 150 years, the Jamaican economy of sugar, slaves and piracy was one of the most prosperous in the new world. Dissension between the property-oriented island legislature and the home government prompted parliament to establish a crown colony government for Jamaica in 1866. From 1958 to 1961 Jamaica was a member of the West Indies Federation, withdrawing when Jamaican voters rejected the association. The colony attained independence on Aug. 6, 1962. Jamaica is a member of the Commonwealth of Nations. Elizabeth II is the Head of State, as Queen of Jamaica.

In 1758, the Jamaican Assembly authorized stamping a certain amount of Spanish milled coinage. Token coinage by merchants aided the island's monetary supply in the early 19th century. Sterling coinage was introduced in Jamaica in 1825, with the additional silver three halfpence under William IV and Victoria. Certain issues of three pence of William IV and Victoria were intended for colonial use, including Jamaica, as were the last dates of three pence for George VI.

There was an extensive token and work tally coinage for Jamaica in the late 19th and early 20th centuries.

A decimal standard currency system was adopted on Sept. 8, 1969.

RULERS

British, until 1962

MINT MARKS

C - Royal Canadian Mint, Ottawa
H - Heaton
FM - Franklin Mint, U.S.A.**
(fm) - Franklin Mint, U.S.A.*
no mint mark - Royal Mint, London

*NOTE: During 1970 the Franklin Mint produced matte and proof coins (1 cent-1 dollar) using dies similar to/or Royal Mint without the FM mint mark.

**NOTE: From 1975-1985 the Franklin Mint produced coinage in up to 3 different qualities. Qualities of issue are designated in ( ) after each date and are defined as follows:

(M) MATTE - Normal circulation strike or a dull finish produced by sandblasting special uncirculated (polish finish) or proof quality dies.

(U) SPECIAL UNCIRCULATED - Polished or proof-like in appearance without any frosted features.

(P) PROOF - The highest quality obtainable having mirror-like fields and frosted features.

MONETARY SYSTEM

4 Farthings = 1 Penny
12 Pence = 1 Shilling
8 Reales = 6 Shillings, 8 Pence
(Commencing 1969)
100 Cents = 1 Dollar

FARTHING

**COPPER-NICKEL
Rev: Horizontal shading in arms.**

KM#	Date	Mintage	Fine	VF	XF	Unc
18	1902	.144	2.00	4.00	15.00	40.00
	1903	.144	2.00	4.00	15.00	40.00

Rev: Vertical shading in arms.

KM#	Date	Mintage	Fine	VF	XF	Unc
21	1904	.192	1.00	2.50	12.00	30.00
	1904	—	—	—	Proof	250.00
	1905	.192	1.00	2.50	12.00	30.00
	1906	.528	1.00	2.00	8.00	25.00
	1907	.192	1.00	2.50	12.00	30.00
	1909	.144	2.00	4.00	15.00	40.00
	1910	.048	2.00	4.00	20.00	45.00

KM#	Date	Mintage	Fine	VF	XF	Unc
24	1914	.192	2.00	4.00	12.00	35.00
	1916H	.480	.75	2.00	6.00	20.00
	1916H	—	—	—	Proof	250.00
	1918C	.208	1.00	2.00	8.00	25.00
	1918C	—	—	—	Proof	225.00
	1919C	.401	.75	2.00	6.00	20.00
	1926	.240	1.00	2.00	8.00	25.00
	1928	.480	.75	2.00	6.00	20.00
	1928	—	—	—	Proof	225.00
	1932	.480	.75	2.00	6.00	20.00
	1932	—	—	—	Proof	—
	1934	.480	.75	2.00	6.00	20.00
	1934	—	—	—	Proof	—

NICKEL-BRASS

KM#	Date	Mintage	Fine	VF	XF	Unc
27	1937	.480	.50	1.50	5.00	15.00
	1937	—	—	—	Proof	175.00

Obv: Larger head.

KM#	Date	Mintage	Fine	VF	XF	Unc
30	1938	.480	.20	.40	1.50	7.00
	1938	—	—	—	Proof	—
	1942	.480	.20	.40	1.50	7.00
	1945	.480	.20	.40	1.50	7.00
	1945	—	—	—	Proof	120.00
	1947	.192	.35	1.50	4.00	12.00
	1947	—	—	—	Proof	120.00

Obv. leg: W/o AND EMPEROR OF INDIA.

KM#	Date	Mintage	Fine	VF	XF	Unc
33	1950	.288	.10	.25	.80	3.25
	1950	—	—	—	Proof	175.00
	1952	.288	.10	.25	.80	3.25
	1952	—	—	—	Proof	175.00

1/2 PENNY

COPPER-NICKEL
Rev: Horizontal shading in arms.

KM#	Date	Mintage	Fine	VF	XF	Unc
19	1902	.048	1.25	4.00	15.00	50.00
	1903	.048	1.25	4.00	15.00	50.00

Rev: Vertical shading in arms.

KM#	Date	Mintage	Fine	VF	XF	Unc
22	1904	.048	1.50	5.00	25.00	70.00
	1905	.048	1.50	5.00	25.00	70.00
	1906	.432	.65	1.50	7.50	25.00
	1907	.504	.65	1.50	7.50	25.00
	1909	.144	.75	2.00	10.00	40.00
	1910	.144	.75	2.00	10.00	40.00

KM#	Date	Mintage	Fine	VF	XF	Unc
25	1914	.096	2.00	5.00	25.00	75.00
	1916H	.192	.35	1.50	6.00	20.00
	1918C	.251	.35	1.50	6.00	20.00
	1918C	—	—	—	Proof	200.00
	1919C	.312	.35	1.00	5.00	20.00
	1920	.480	.35	1.00	5.00	20.00
	1926	.240	.35	1.00	5.00	30.00
	1928	.120	.35	1.00	5.00	20.00
	1928	—	—	—	Proof	200.00

NICKEL-BRASS

KM#	Date	Mintage	Fine	VF	XF	Unc
28	1937	.960	.50	1.00	3.50	12.00
	1937	—	—	—	Proof	175.00

Obv: Larger head.

KM#	Date	Mintage	Fine	VF	XF	Unc
31	1938	.960	.25	.75	3.50	12.00
	1938	—	—	—	Proof	175.00
	1940	.960	.25	.75	3.50	12.00
	1940	—	—	—	Proof	175.00
	1942	.960	.25	.75	3.50	12.00
	1945	.960	.25	.75	3.50	12.00
	1945	—	—	—	Proof	175.00
	1947	.960	.25	.75	3.50	12.00
	1947	—	—	—	Proof	200.00

Obv. leg: W/o AND EMPEROR OF INDIA.

KM#	Date	Mintage	Fine	VF	XF	Unc
34	1950	1.440	.10	.20	.30	3.25
	1950	—	—	—	Proof	175.00
	1952	1.200	.10	.20	.30	3.25
	1952	—	—	—	Proof	175.00

KM#	Date	Mintage	Fine	VF	XF	Unc
36	1955	1.440	.10	.15	.40	2.00
	1955	—	—	—	Proof	150.00
	1957	.600	.20	.40	1.00	3.00
	1957	—	—	—	Proof	—
	1958	.960	.10	.20	.50	2.00
	1958	—	—	—	Proof	150.00

KM#	Date	Mintage	Fine	VF	XF	Unc
36	1959	.960	.10	.20	.50	2.00
	1959	—	—	—	Proof	—
	1961	.480	.20	.40	1.00	4.00
	1961	—	—	—	Proof	—
	1962	.960	.10	.15	.30	1.75
	1962	—	—	—	Proof	150.00
	1963	.960	.10	.15	.30	1.75
	1963	—	—	—	Proof	150.00

Rev: New arms.

KM#	Date	Mintage	Fine	VF	XF	Unc
38	1964	1.440	.10	.15	.20	.80
	1965	1.200	.10	.15	.20	.80
	1966	1.680	.10	.15	.20	.80

COPPER-NICKEL-ZINC
Jamaican Coinage Centennial

KM#	Date	Mintage	Fine	VF	XF	Unc
41	1969	.030	.10	—	.25	.75
	1969	5,000	—	—	Proof	2.50

PENNY

COPPER-NICKEL
Rev: Horizontal shading in arms.

KM#	Date	Mintage	Fine	VF	XF	Unc
20	1902	.060	2.25	6.00	25.00	60.00
	1903	.060	2.25	6.00	25.00	60.00

Rev: Vertical shading in arms.

KM#	Date	Mintage	Fine	VF	XF	Unc
23	1904	.024	2.50	7.50	30.00	80.00
	1904	—	—	—	Proof	250.00
	1905	.048	2.00	4.75	22.50	60.00
	1906	.156	1.25	2.50	12.00	40.00
	1907	.108	1.25	2.50	12.00	40.00
	1909	.144	1.25	2.50	12.00	40.00
	1910	.144	1.25	2.50	12.00	40.00

KM#	Date	Mintage	Fine	VF	XF	Unc
26	1914	.024	10.00	20.00	65.00	175.00
	1916H	.024	10.00	20.00	65.00	160.00
	1918C	.187	2.00	5.00	15.00	60.00
	1918C	—	—	—	Proof	200.00
	1919C	.251	1.25	4.75	12.00	50.00
	1920	.360	.75	2.50	9.50	32.50
	1926	.240	.75	2.50	9.50	30.00
	1928	.360	.75	2.50	9.50	30.00
	1928	—	—	—	Proof	200.00

NICKEL-BRASS

KM#	Date	Mintage	Fine	VF	XF	Unc
29	1937	1.200	1.00	1.75	3.25	12.00
	1937	—	—	—	Proof	200.00

Obv: Larger head.

KM#	Date	Mintage	Fine	VF	XF	Unc
32	1938	1.200	.35	.65	3.25	12.00
	1938	—	—	—	Proof	200.00
	1940	1.200	.35	.65	3.25	12.00
	1940	—	—	—	Proof	200.00
	1942	1.200	.35	.65	3.25	12.00
	1942	—	—	—	Proof	200.00
	1945	1.200	.35	.65	3.25	12.00
	1945	—	—	—	Proof	200.00
	1947	.480	.35	.65	3.25	12.00
	1947	—	—	—	Proof	200.00

Obv. leg: W/o AND EMPEROR OF INDIA.

KM#	Date	Mintage	Fine	VF	XF	Unc
35	1950	.600	.20	.35	2.00	10.00
	1950	—	—	—	Proof	200.00
	1952	.725	.20	.35	2.00	10.00
	1952	—	—	—	Proof	200.00

KM#	Date	Mintage	Fine	VF	XF	Unc
37	1953	1.200	.10	.20	.50	1.50
	1953	—	—	—	Proof	115.00
	1955	.960	.10	.25	1.00	4.00
	1955	—	—	—	Proof	115.00
	1957	.600	.10	.25	1.00	4.00
	1957	—	—	—	Proof	—
	1958	1.080	.10	.20	.30	3.00
	1958	—	—	—	Proof	100.00
	1959	1.368	.10	.20	.30	2.50
	1959	—	—	—	Proof	—
	1960	1.368	.10	.20	.30	2.50
	1960	—	—	—	Proof	—
	1961	1.368	.10	.20	.30	2.50
	1961	—	—	—	Proof	—
	1962	1.920	.10	.20	.30	2.50
	1962	—	—	—	Proof	100.00
	1963	.720	1.00	2.00	8.00	50.00
	1963	—	—	—	Proof	100.00

KM#	Date	Mintage	Fine	VF	XF	Unc
39	1964	.480	.10	.15	.25	.75
	1965	1.200	.10	.15	.20	.35
	1966	1.200	.10	.15	.20	.35
	1967	2.760	.10	.15	.20	.35

COPPER-NICKEL-ZINC
Jamaican Coinage Centennial

KM#	Date	Mintage	Fine	VF	XF	Unc
42	1969	.030	.10	.15	.30	.75
	1969	5,000	—	—	Proof	2.50

DECIMAL COINAGE

The Franklin Mint and Royal Mint have both been striking the 1 cent through 1 dollar coinage. The 1970 issues were all struck with dies similar to/or Royal Mint without the FM mint mark. The Royal Mint issues have the name JAMAICA extending beyond the native head dress feathers. Those struck after 1970 by the Franklin Mint have the name JAMAICA within the head dress feathers.

CENT

BRONZE
Ackee Fruit

KM#	Date	Mintage	VF	XF	Unc
45	1969	30.200	—	.10	.25
	1969	.019	—	Proof	.50
	1970(RM) small date	10.000	—	.10	.25
	1970FM(M) large date	5,000	—	.10	.25
	1970FM(P)	.012	—	Proof	.50
	1971(RM)	5.625	—	.10	.25

KM#	Date	Mintage	VF	XF	Unc
51	1971FM(M)	4,834	—	.10	.25
	1971FM(P)	.014	—	Proof	.50
	1972FM(M)	7,982	—	.10	.25
	1972FM(P)	.017	—	Proof	.50
	1973FM(M)	.029	—	.10	.25
	1973FM(P)	.028	—	Proof	.50
	1974FM(M)	.028	—	.10	.25
	1974FM(P)	.022	—	Proof	.50
	1975FM(M)	.036	—	.10	.25
	1975FM(U)	4,683	—	—	.25
	1975FM(P)	.016	—	Proof	.50

F.A.O. Issue

KM#	Date	Mintage	VF	XF	Unc
52	1971	.020	—	.10	.30
	1972	5.000	—	.10	.30
	1973	5.500	—	.10	.30
	1974	3.000	—	.10	.30

ALUMINUM
F.A.O. Issue

KM#	Date	Mintage	VF	XF	Unc
64	1975	15.000	—	.10	.20
	1976	16.000	—	.10	.20
	1977	—	—	.10	.20
	1978	8.400	—	.10	.20
	1980	10.000	—	.10	.20

KM#	Date	Mintage	VF	XF	Unc
64	1981	8.000	—	.10	.20
	1982	10.000	—	.10	.20
	1983	1.342	—	—	.15
	1984	8.704	—	—	.15
	1985	5.112	—	—	.15
	1985	—	—	Proof	.50
	1986	17.534	—	—	.15
	1987	9.968	—	—	.15
	1987	—	—	Proof	.50
	1988	—	—	Proof	.50
	1989	—	—	Proof	.50
	1990	—	—	—	.15
	1990	—	—	Proof	.50
	1991	—	—	—	.15
	1991	—	—	Proof	.50
	1992	—	—	Proof	.50
	1993	—	—	Proof	.50

KM#	Date	Mintage	VF	XF	Unc
68	1976FM(M)	.028	—	—	.15
	1976FM(U)	1,802	—	—	.25
	1976FM(P)	.024	—	Proof	.50
	1977FM(M)	.028	—	—	.15
	1977FM(U)	597 pcs.	—	—	1.50
	1977FM(P)	.010	—	Proof	.50
	1978FM(M)	.028	—	—	.15
	1978FM(U)	1,282	—	—	.40
	1978FM(P)	6,058	—	Proof	.60
	1979FM(M)	.028	—	—	.15
	1979FM(U)	2,608	—	—	.40
	1979FM(P)	4,049	—	Proof	.60
	1980FM(M)	.028	—	—	.15
	1980FM(U)	3,668	—	—	.35
	1980FM(P)	2,688	—	Proof	.75
	1981FM(U)	482 pcs.	—	—	1.50
	1981FM(P)	1,577	—	Proof	.75
	1982FM(U)	—	—	—	.35
	1982FM(P)	—	—	Proof	.75
	1984FM(U)	—	—	—	.35
	1984FM(P)	—	—	Proof	.75

Mule. 2 obverses of KM#64.

KM#	Date	Mintage	VF	XF	Unc
136	1982 FM	—	—	220.00	250.00

Mule. 2 reverses of KM#64.

KM#	Date	Mintage	VF	XF	Unc
137	1982FM	—	—	250.00	300.00

21st Anniversary of Independence

KM#	Date	Mintage	VF	XF	Unc
101	ND(1983)M(U)	—	—	—	.35
	ND(1983)FM(P)	—	—	Proof	.75

5 CENTS

COPPER-NICKEL
American Crocodile

KM#	Date	Mintage	VF	XF	Unc
46	1969	12.008	—	.10	.50
	1969	.030	—	Proof	.65
	1970FM(M)	5,000	—	.10	.50
	1970FM(P)	.012	—	Proof	.65
	1972	6.000	—	.10	.50
	1975	6.010	—	.10	.50
	1977	2.400	—	.10	.50
	1978	2.000	—	.10	.50
	1980	2.272	—	.10	.50
	1981	2.001	—	.10	.50
	1982	2.000	—	.10	.50
	1983	.992	—	.10	.50
	1984	3.508	—	.10	.50
	1985	4.760	—	.10	.50
	1985	—	—	Proof	.65
	1986	14.504	—	.10	.50
	1987	13.166	—	.10	.50
	1987	—	—	Proof	.65
	1988	9.780	—	.10	.50
	1988	—	—	Proof	.65
	1989	—	—	.10	.50
	1989	—	—	Proof	.65

NICKEL PLATED STEEL

KM#	Date	Mintage	VF	XF	Unc
46a	1990	—	—	.10	.50
	1990	—	—	Proof	.65
	1991	—	—	.10	.50
	1991	—	—	Proof	.65
	1992	—	—	.10	.50
	1992	—	—	Proof	.65
	1993	—	—	.10	.50
	1993	—	—	Proof	.65

COPPER-NICKEL

KM#	Date	Mintage	VF	XF	Unc
53	1971FM(M)	4,834	—	.10	.35
	1971FM(P)	.014	—	Proof	.50
	1972FM(M)	7,982	—	.10	.35
	1972FM(P)	.017	—	Proof	.50
	1973FM(M)	.017	—	.10	.35
	1973FM(P)	.028	—	Proof	.50
	1974FM(M)	.016	—	.10	.35
	1974FM(P)	.022	—	Proof	.50
	1975FM(M)	6,240	—	.10	.35
	1975FM(U)	4,683	—	—	.35
	1975FM(P)	.016	—	Proof	.50
	1976FM(M)	5,560	—	.10	.35
	1976FM(U)	1,802	—	—	.35
	1976FM(P)	.024	—	Proof	.50
	1977FM(M)	5,560	—	.10	.40
	1977FM(U)	597 pcs.	—	—	1.50
	1977FM(P)	.010	—	Proof	.50
	1978FM(M)	5,560	—	.10	.40
	1978FM(U)	1,282	—	—	.60
	1978FM(P)	6,058	—	Proof	.75
	1979FM(M)	5,560	—	.10	.40
	1979FM(U)	2,608	—	—	.50
	1979FM(P)	4,049	—	Proof	.75
	1980FM(M)	5,560	—	.10	.40
	1980FM(U)	3,668	—	—	.50
	1980FM(P)	2,688	—	Proof	1.00
	1981FM(U)	482 pcs.	—	—	1.50
	1981FM(P)	1,577	—	Proof	1.00
	1982FM(U)	—	—	—	.50
	1982FM(P)	—	—	Proof	1.00
	1984FM(U)	—	—	—	.50
	1984FM(P)	—	—	Proof	1.00

21st Anniversary of Independence

102	ND(1983)FM(U)	—	—	—	.50
	ND(1983)FM(P)	—	—	Proof	1.00

10 CENTS

COPPER-NICKEL
Lignum Vitae

47	1969	19.508	—	.10	.50
	1969	.030	—	Proof	.75
	1970FM(M)	5,000	—	.10	.50
	1970FM(P)	.012	—	Proof	.75
	1972	6.000	—	.10	.50
	1975	10.010	—	.10	.40
	1977	8.000	—	.10	.40
	1981	8.000	—	.10	.30
	1982	8.000	—	.10	.30
	1983	2.000	—	.10	.30
	1984	5.000	—	.10	.30
	1985	8.310	—	.10	.30
	1985	—	—	Proof	.75
	1986	21.677	—	.10	.30
	1987	29.089	—	.10	.30
	1987	—	—	Proof	.75
	1988	15.660	—	.10	.30
	1988	—	—	Proof	.75
	1989	—	—	.10	.30
	1989	—	—	Proof	.75

NICKEL PLATED STEEL

47a	1990		—	.10	.30
	1990		—	Proof	.75

COPPER-NICKEL

54	1971FM(M)	4,834	—	.10	.35
	1971FM(P)	.014	—	Proof	.75
	1972FM(M)	7,982	—	.10	.35
	1972FM(P)	.017	—	Proof	.75
	1973FM(M)	.015	—	.10	.35

KM#	Date	Mintage	VF	XF	Unc
54	1973FM(P)	.028	—	Proof	.75
	1974FM(M)	.014	—	.10	.35
	1974FM(P)	.022	—	Proof	.75
	1975FM(M)	3,120	—	.10	.35
	1975FM(P)	4,683	—	—	.35
	1975FM(P)	.016	—	Proof	.75
	1976FM(M)	2,780	—	.10	.35
	1976FM(U)	1,802	—	—	.35
	1976FM(P)	.024	—	Proof	.75
	1977FM(M)	2,780	—	.10	.50
	1977FM(U)	597 pcs.	—	—	1.50
	1977FM(P)	.010	—	Proof	.75
	1978FM(M)	2,780	—	.10	.50
	1978FM(U)	4,062	—	—	.60
	1978FM(P)	6,058	—	Proof	1.00
	1979FM(M)	2,780	—	.10	.50
	1979FM(U)	2,608	—	—	.60
	1979FM(P)	4,049	—	Proof	1.00
	1980FM(M)	2,780	—	.10	.50
	1980FM(U)	3,668	—	—	.50
	1980FM(P)	2,688	—	Proof	1.50
	1981FM(U)	482 pcs.	—	—	1.50
	1981FM(P)	1,577	—	Proof	1.50
	1982FM(U)	—	—	—	.50
	1982FM(P)	—	—	Proof	1.50
	1984FM(U)	—	—	—	.50
	1984FM(P)	—	—	Proof	1.50

21st Anniversary of Independence

103	ND(1983)FM(U)	—	—	—	.50
	ND(1983)FM(P)	—	—	Proof	1.50

NICKEL PLATED STEEL
Paul Bogle

146.1	1991	—	—	—	.50
	1991	—	—	Proof	1.50
	1992	—	—	—	.50
	1992	—	—	Proof	1.50
	1993	—	—	—	.50
	1993	—	—	Proof	1.50
	1994	—	—	—	.50
	1994	—	—	Proof	1.50

COPPER PLATED STEEL
Reduced size.

146.2	1995	—	—	—	.25

20 CENTS

COPPER-NICKEL
Mahoe Tree

48	1969	3.758	—	.20	.75
	1969	.030	—	Proof	1.00
	1970FM(M)	5,000	—	.20	.75
	1970FM(P)	.012	—	Proof	1.00
	1975	.010	—	.20	.85
	1982	1.000	—	.20	.65
	1984	2.000	—	.20	.65
	1986	2.530	—	.20	.65
	1987	5.545	—	.20	.65
	1987	—	—	Proof	1.00
	1988	5.016	—	.20	.65
	1988	—	—	Proof	1.00
	1989	—	—	.20	.65
	1989	—	—	Proof	1.00
	1990	—	—	Proof	1.00

KM#	Date	Mintage	VF	XF	Unc
55	1971FM(M)	4,834	—	.20	.50
	1971FM(P)	.014	—	Proof	1.00
	1972FM(M)	7,982	—	.20	.50
	1972FM(P)	.017	—	Proof	1.00
	1973FM(M)	.013	—	.20	.50
	1973FM(P)	.028	—	Proof	1.00
	1974FM(M)	.012	—	.20	.50
	1974FM(P)	.022	—	Proof	1.00
	1975FM(M)	1,560	—	.20	.50
	1975FM(U)	4,683	—	—	.50
	1975FM(P)	.016	—	Proof	1.00
	1976FM(M)	1,390	—	.20	.50
	1976FM(U)	1,802	—	—	.50
	1976FM(P)	.024	—	Proof	1.00

F.A.O. Issue

69	1976	3.000	—	.20	1.00
	1981	—	—	.20	1.00
	1982	Inc. KM48	—	.20	1.00
	1984	—	—	.20	1.00
	1987	—	—	.20	1.00

73	1977FM(M)	1,390	—	.20	.75
	1977FM(U)	597 pcs.	—	—	2.00
	1977FM(P)	.010	—	Proof	1.00
	1978FM(M)	1,390	—	.20	.75
	1978FM(U)	1,282	—	—	.75
	1978FM(P)	6,058	—	Proof	1.50
	1979FM(M)	1,390	—	.20	.75
	1979FM(U)	2,608	—	—	.75
	1979FM(P)	4,049	—	Proof	1.50
	1980FM(M)	1,390	—	.20	.60
	1980FM(U)	3,668	—	—	.60
	1980FM(P)	2,688	—	Proof	2.00
	1981FM(U)	482 pcs.	—	—	2.00
	1981FM(P)	1,577	—	Proof	2.00
	1982FM(U)	—	—	—	.60
	1982FM(P)	—	—	Proof	2.00
	1984FM(U)	—	—	—	.60
	1984FM(P)	—	—	Proof	2.00

World Food Day
Obv: JAMAICA more compact.

90	1981FM(M)	—	—	—	1.50

21st Anniversary of Independence

104	ND(1983)FM(U)	—	—	—	.60
	ND(1983)FM(P)	—	—	Proof	2.00

KM#	Date	Mintage	VF	XF	Unc
120	1981	—	—	—	.60
	1984	2.000	—	—	.60
	1985	2.988	—	—	.60
	1986	2.530	—	—	.60
	1988	—	—	—	.60

25 CENTS

COPPER-NICKEL
Streamer-tail Hummingbird

KM#	Date	Mintage	VF	XF	Unc
49	1969	.758	—	.40	1.00
	1969	.030	—	Proof	1.50
	1970FM(M)	5,000	—	.40	1.00
	1970FM(P)	.012	—	Proof	1.50
	1973	.160	—	.40	1.00
	1975	3.110	—	.40	1.00
	1982	1.000	—	.40	1.00
	1984	2.002	—	.40	1.00
	1985	1.999	—	.40	1.00
	1985	—	—	Proof	1.50
	1986	2.635	—	.40	1.00
	1987	6.006	—	.40	1.00
	1987	—	—	Proof	1.50
	1988	3.034	—	.40	1.00
	1988	—	—	Proof	1.50
	1989	—	—	.40	1.00
	1989	—	—	Proof	1.50
	1990	—	—	Proof	1.50

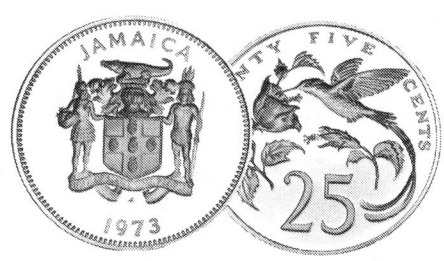

KM#	Date	Mintage	VF	XF	Unc
56	1971FM(M)	4,834	—	.25	1.00
	1971FM(P)	.014	—	Proof	1.25
	1972FM(M)	8,382	—	.25	1.00
	1972FM(P)	.017	—	Proof	1.25
	1973FM(M)	.013	—	.25	1.00
	1973FM(P)	.028	—	Proof	1.25
	1974FM(M)	.012	—	.25	1.00
	1974FM(P)	.022	—	Proof	1.25
	1975FM(M)	1,503	—	.25	1.00
	1975FM(U)	4,683	—	—	1.00
	1975FM(P)	.016	—	Proof	1.25
	1976FM(M)	1,112	—	.25	1.00
	1976FM(U)	1,802	—	—	1.00
	1976FM(P)	.024	—	Proof	1.25
	1977FM(M)	1,112	—	.25	1.25
	1977FM(U)	597 pcs.	—	—	3.00
	1977FM(P)	.010	—	Proof	1.25
	1978FM(M)	1,112	—	.25	1.25
	1978FM(U)	1,282	—	—	1.25
	1978FM(P)	6,058	—	Proof	2.00
	1979FM(M)	1,112	—	.25	1.25
	1979FM(U)	2,608	—	—	1.25
	1979FM(P)	4,049	—	Proof	2.00
	1980FM(M)	1,112	—	.25	1.00
	1980FM(U)	3,668	—	—	1.00
	1980FM(P)	2,688	—	Proof	3.00
	1981FM(U)	482 pcs.	—	—	3.00
	1981FM(P)	1,577	—	Proof	3.00
	1982FM(U)	—	—	—	1.00
	1982FM(P)	—	—	Proof	3.00
	1984FM(U)	—	—	—	1.00
	1984FM(P)	—	—	Proof	3.00

21st Anniversary of Independence

KM#	Date	Mintage	VF	XF	Unc
105	ND(1983)FM(U)	—	—	—	1.50
	ND(1983)FM(P)	—	—	Proof	3.00

25th Anniversary - Bank of Jamaica

154	1985	—	—	.75	3.50

NICKEL PLATED STEEL
Marcus Garvey

147	1991	—	—	—	1.00
	1991	—	—	Proof	3.00
	1992	—	—	—	1.00
	1992	—	—	Proof	3.00
	1993	—	—	—	1.00
	1993	—	—	Proof	3.00
	1994	—	—	—	1.00

COPPER PLATED STEEL

167	1995	—	—	—	.50

50 CENTS

COPPER-NICKEL
Marcus Garvey

65	1975	12.010	.15	.50	1.50
	1984	2.000	.15	.50	1.50
	1985	2.119	.15	.50	1.50
	1985	—	—	Proof	3.00
	1986	3.404	.15	.50	1.50
	1987	5.545	.15	.50	1.50
	1988	10.505	.15	.50	1.50
	1988	—	—	Proof	3.00
	1989	—	.15	.50	1.50
	1989	—	—	Proof	3.00
	1990	—	—	Proof	3.00

KM#	Date	Mintage	VF	XF	Unc
70	1976FM(M)	1,112	—	.25	1.50
	1976FM(U)	1,802	—	—	1.50
	1976FM(P)	.024	—	Proof	1.50
	1977FM(M)	556 pcs.	—	.50	3.50
	1977FM(U)	597 pcs.	—	—	3.50
	1977FM(P)	.010	—	Proof	1.50
	1978FM(M)	556 pcs.	—	.50	3.50
	1978FM(U)	1,838	—	—	2.00
	1978FM(P)	6,058	—	Proof	2.50
	1979FM(M)	556 pcs.	—	.50	3.50
	1979FM(U)	1,282	—	—	2.00
	1979FM(P)	4,049	—	Proof	3.00
	1980FM(M)	556 pcs.	—	.50	3.50
	1980FM(U)	3,668	—	—	2.00
	1980FM(P)	2,688	—	Proof	3.00
	1981FM(U)	482 pcs.	—	—	3.50
	1981FM(P)	1,577	—	Proof	3.00
	1982FM(U)	—	—	—	2.00
	1982FM(P)	—	—	Proof	3.00
	1984FM(U)	—	—	—	2.00
	1984FM(P)	—	—	Proof	3.00

21st Anniversary of Independence

106	ND(1983)FM(U)	—	—	—	2.00
	ND(1983)FM(P)	—	—	Proof	4.00

DOLLAR

COPPER-NICKEL
Sir Alexander Bustamante

50	1969	.047	—	1.00	2.00
	1969	.030	—	Proof	3.00
	1970FM(M)	5,000	—	.30	2.50
	1970FM(P)	.014	—	Proof	3.00

57	1971FM	5,024	—	.30	2.50
	1971FM(P)	.015	—	Proof	2.75
	1972F(M)	7,982	—	.30	2.00
	1972FM(P)	.017	—	Proof	2.50
	1973FM	.010	—	.30	2.00
	1973FM(P)	.028	—	Proof	2.50
	1974FM(M)	8,961	—	.30	2.00
	1974FM(P)	.022	—	Proof	2.50
	1975FM(M)	5,312	—	.30	2.50

KM#	Date	Mintage	VF	XF	Unc
57	1975FM(U)	4,683	—	—	2.50
	1975FM(P)	.016	—	Proof	2.75
	1976FM(M)	284 pcs.	—	.50	17.50
	1976FM(U)	1,802	—	—	4.00
	1976FM(P)	.024	—	Proof	2.50
	1977FM(M)	287 pcs.	—	.50	17.50
	1977FM(U)	597 pcs.	—	—	8.00
	1977FM(P)	.010	—	Proof	3.00
	1978FM(U)	1,566	—	—	4.00
	1978FM(P)	6,058	—	Proof	4.00
	1979FM(M)	284 pcs.	—	.50	17.50
	1979FM(U)	2,608	—	—	4.00
	1979FM(P)	4,049	—	Proof	5.00

Reduced size, 34mm.
Similar to KM#57.

KM#	Date	Mintage	VF	XF	Unc
84.1	1980FM(M)	284 pcs.	—	.50	15.00
	1980FM(U)	3,668	—	—	3.00
	1980FM(P)	2,688	—	Proof	12.00
	1981FM(U)	482 pcs.	—	—	8.00
	1981FM(P)	1,577	—	Proof	15.00
	1982FM(U)	—	—	—	4.00
	1982FM(P)	—	—	Proof	15.00

Reeded edge.

KM#	Date	Mintage	VF	XF	Unc
84.2	1985	—	—	—	3.00
	1987	—	—	Proof	5.00
	1988	—	—	Proof	5.00
	1989	—	—	Proof	5.00
	1990	—	—	—	3.00

NICKEL-BRASS
Sir Alexander Bustamante
Edge: Reeded over "Bank of Jamaica".

KM#	Date	Mintage	VF	XF	Unc
145	1990	—	—	—	2.25
	1990	—	—	Proof	5.00
	1991	—	—	—	2.25
	1991	—	—	Proof	5.00
	1992	—	—	—	2.25
	1992	—	—	Proof	10.00
	1993	—	—	—	2.25
	1993	—	—	Proof	2.25
	1994	—	—	—	2.25

BRASS PLATED STEEL
Edge: Reeded, no inscription.

KM#	Date	Mintage	VF	XF	Unc
145a	1993	—	—	—	2.25
	1993	500 pcs.	—	Proof	12.00
	1993	—	—	—	2.25
	1994	—	—	—	2.25

NICKEL CLAD STEEL

KM#	Date	Mintage	VF	XF	Unc
164	1994	—	—	—	.75
	1995	—	—	—	.75
	1996	—	—	—	.75

5 DOLLARS

STEEL
National Hero - Norman Manley

KM#	Date	Mintage	VF	XF	Unc
163	1994	—	—	—	.75
	1995	—	—	—	.75

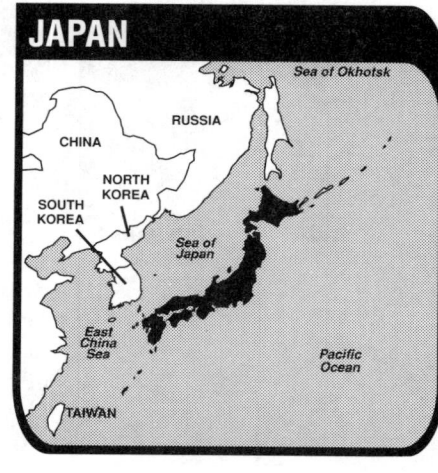

JAPAN

Japan, a constitutional monarchy situated off the east coast of Asia, has an area of 145,809 sq. mi. (377,835 sq. km.) and a population of 123.2 million. Capital: Tokyo. Japan, one of the major industrial nations of the world, exports machinery, motor vehicles, electronics and chemicals.

Japan, founded (so legend holds) in 660 B.C. by a direct descendant of the Sun Goddess, was first brought into contact with the west by a storm-blown Portuguese ship in 1542. European traders and missionaries proceeded to enlarge the contact until the Shogunate, sensing a military threat in the foreign presence, expelled all foreigners and restricted relations with the outside world in the 17th century. After Commodore Perry's U.S. flotilla visited in 1854, Japan rapidly industrialized, abolished the Shogunate and established a parliamentary form of government, and by the end of the 19th century achieved the status of a modern economic and military power. A series of wars with China and Russia, and participation with the Allies in World War I, enlarged Japan territorially but brought its interests into conflict with the Far Eastern interests of the United States, Britain and the Netherlands, causing it to align with the Axis Powers for the pursuit of World War II. After its defeat in World War II, General Douglas MacArthur forced Japan to renounce military aggression as a political instrument, and he instituted constitutional democratic self-government. Japan quickly gained a position as an economic world power.

Japanese coinage of concern to this catalog includes those issued for the Ryukyu Islands (also called Liuchu), a chain of islands extending southwest from Japan toward Taiwan (Formosa), before the Japanese government converted the islands into a prefecture under the name Okinawa. Many of the provinces of Japan issued their own definitive coinage under the Shogunate.

RULERS

Emperors
Mutsuhito (Meiji), 1867-1912

Years 1-45   明治   or   治明
Yoshihito (Taisho), 1912-1926

Years 1-15   大正   or   正大
Hirohito (Showa), 1926-1989

Years 1-64   昭和   or   和昭
Akihito (Heisei), 1989-

Years 1 -   平成

NOTE: The personal name of the emperor is followed by the name that he chose for his regnal era.

MONETARY SYSTEM

10 Rin = 1 Sen
100 Sen = 1 Yen

DATING

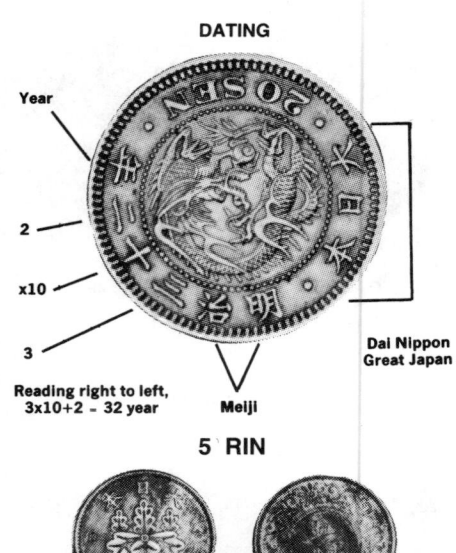

Reading right to left,
3x10+2 – 32 year

Year
2
x10
3
Meiji
Dai Nippon
Great Japan

5 RIN

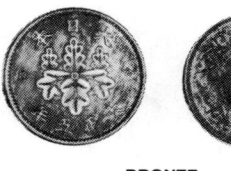

BRONZE

Y#	Date	Mintage	Fine	VF	XF	Unc
41	Taisho					
	Yr.5(1916)	8.000	.50	2.00	3.50	10.00
	Yr.6(1917)	5.287	.50	2.00	4.00	12.50
	Yr.7(1918)	11.661	.25	1.00	2.50	7.50
	Yr.8(1919)	17.130	.25	1.00	2.50	7.50

SEN

BRONZE

Y#	Date	Mintage	Fine	VF	XF	Unc
20	Meiji					
	Yr.34(1901)	5.555	2.00	4.50	16.00	55.00
	Yr.35(1902)	4.444	5.00	10.00	25.00	145.00
	Yr.39(1906)	—	(none struck for circulation)			
	Yr.42(1909)	—	(none struck for circulation)			

NOTE: Earlier dates (Yr.31-33) exist for this type.

Y#	Date	Mintage	Fine	VF	XF	Unc
35	Taisho					
	Yr.2(1913)	15.000	2.00	3.00	5.00	30.00
	Yr.3(1914)	10.000	2.00	3.00	5.00	30.00
	Yr.4(1915)	13.000	2.00	3.00	5.00	30.00

Y#	Date	Mintage	Fine	VF	XF	Unc
42	Yr.5(1916)	19.193	.50	1.00	1.50	25.00
	Yr.6(1917)	27.183	.25	.50	1.00	20.00
	Yr.7(1918)	121.794	.25	.50	1.00	7.50
	Yr.8(1919)	209.959	.15	.25	.50	3.50
	Yr.9(1920)	118.829	.15	.25	.50	3.50
	Yr.10(1921)					

Y#	Date	Mintage	Fine	VF	XF	Unc
42		252.440	.15	.25	.50	3.50
	Yr.11(1922)	253.210	.15	.25	.50	3.50
	Yr.12(1923)	155.500	.15	.25	.50	3.50
	Yr.13(1924)	106.250	.15	.25	.50	3.50

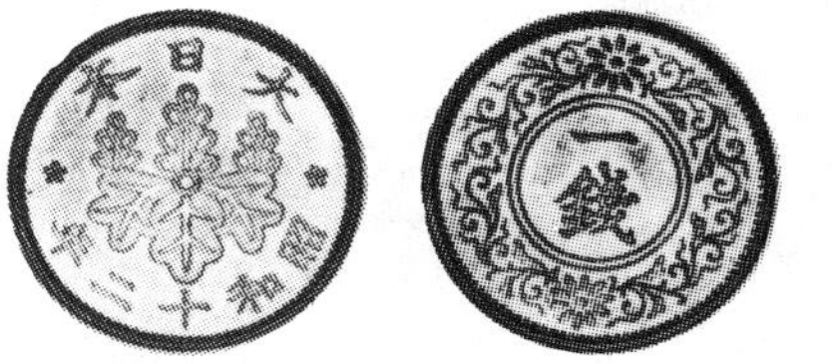

Y#	Date	Mintage	Fine	VF	XF	Unc
	Showa					
47	Yr.2(1927)	26.500	1.50	2.50	3.50	30.00
	Yr.4(1929)	3.000	3.50	7.50	15.00	40.00
	Yr.5(1930)	5.000	2.50	4.50	7.50	60.00
	Yr.6(1931)	25.001	.25	.50	1.50	10.00
	Yr.7(1932)	35.066	.25	.50	1.50	7.50
	Yr.8(1933)	38.936	.15	.25	.50	1.50
	Yr.9(1934)	100.004	.15	.25	.50	1.50
	Yr.10(1935)	200.009	.15	.25	.50	1.50
	Yr.11(1936)	109.170	.15	.25	.50	1.50
	Yr.12(1937)	133.196	.15	.25	.50	1.50
	Yr.13(1938)	87.649	.15	.25	.50	1.50

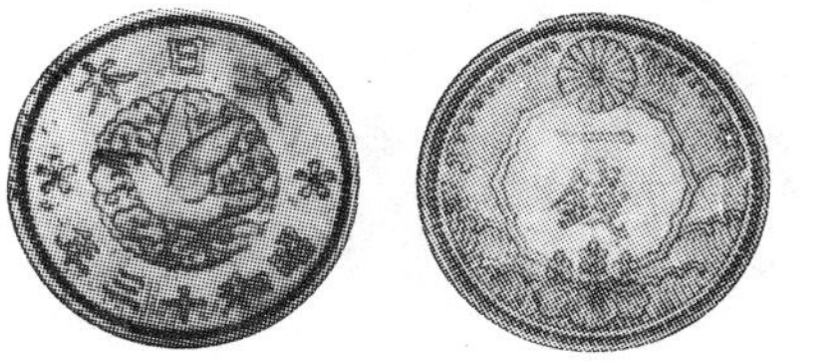

Y#	Date	Mintage	Fine	VF	XF	Unc
55	Yr.13(1938)	113.605	.15	.25	.50	1.50

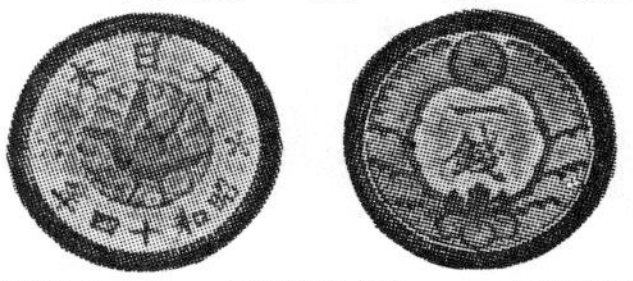

四 TYPE A **ALUMINUM** 四 TYPE B

Y#	Date	Mintage	Fine	VF	XF	Unc
56	Yr.13(1938)	45.502	—	.25	.50	8.50
	Yr.14(1939) Type A	444.602	—	.50	.75	12.00
	Yr.14(1939) Type B	Inc. Ab.	—	.25	.50	1.50
	Yr.15(1940)	602.110	—	.25	.50	1.50

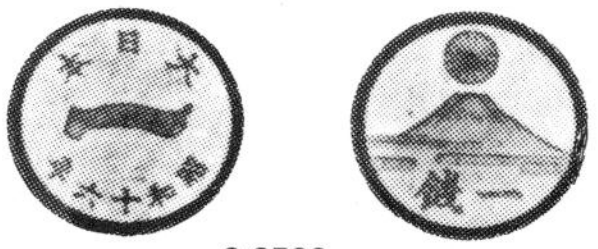

0.6500 g

Y#	Date	Mintage	Fine	VF	XF	Unc
59	Yr.16(1941)	1016.620	—	.15	.25	.50
	Yr.17(1942)	119.709	—	.15	.25	.75
	Yr.18(1943)	1,163.949	—	.15	.25	.50

Thinner, 0.5500 g

Y#	Date	Mintage	Fine	VF	XF	Unc
59a	Yr.18(1943)	627.191	—	.15	.50	1.00

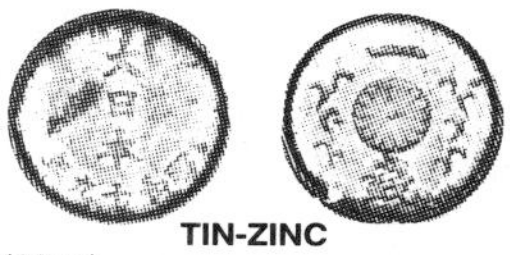

TIN-ZINC

Y#	Date	Mintage	Fine	VF	XF	Unc
62	Yr.19(1944)	1,641.661	—	.15	.25	.50
	Yr.20(1945)	I.A.	—	.15	.25	.75

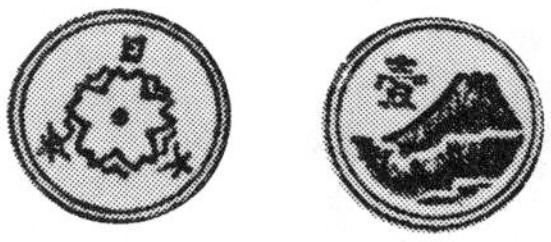

REDDISH BROWN BAKED CLAY

KM#	Date	Mintage	Fine	VF	XF	Unc
110	ND(1945)	—	4.00	6.00	15.00	20.00

NOTE: Circulated unofficially for a few days before the end of WWII in Central Japan. Varieties of color exist.

5 SEN

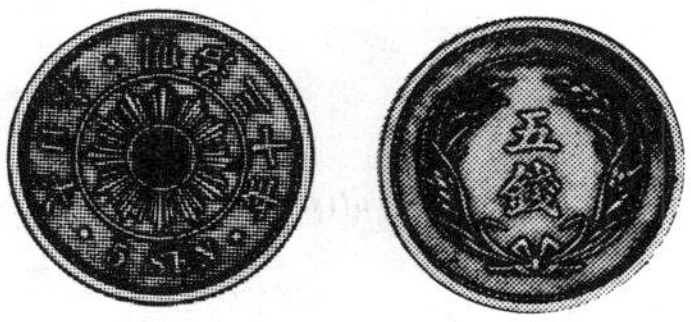

COPPER-NICKEL

Y#	Date	Mintage	Fine	VF	XF	Unc
	Meiji					
21	Yr.34(1901)	7.124	7.50	15.00	25.00	115.00
	Yr.35(1902)	2.448	12.00	25.00	40.00	285.00
	Yr.36(1903)	.372	150.00	250.00	400.00	2500.
	Yr.37(1904)	1.628	20.00	35.00	75.00	390.00
	Yr.38(1905)	6.000	5.00	10.00	17.50	115.00
	Yr.39(1906)	—	*(none struck for circulation)			

***NOTE:** Spink-Taisei Hong Kong sale 9-91 BU realized $10,000.

NOTE: Earlier dates (Yr.30-33) exist for this type.

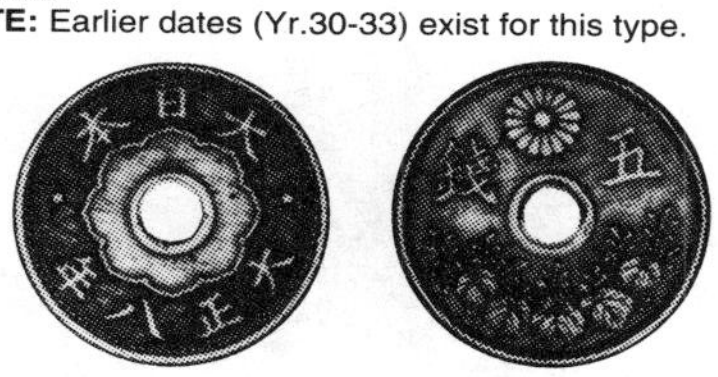

Y#	Date	Mintage	Fine	VF	XF	Unc
	Taisho					
43	Yr.6(1917)	6.781	7.50	15.00	25.00	50.00
	Yr.7(1918)	9.131	5.00	10.00	20.00	32.50
	Yr.8(1919)	44.980	3.00	6.00	12.00	20.00
	Yr.9(1920)	21.906	3.00	6.00	12.00	20.00

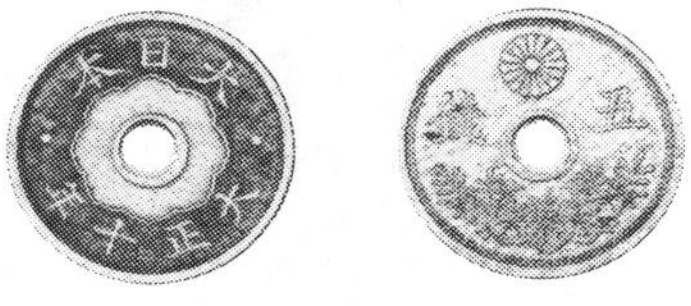

19.1mm

Y#	Date	Mintage	Fine	VF	XF	Unc
44	Yr.9(1920)	100.455	.35	.75	2.00	12.50
	Yr.10(1921)	133.020	.25	.50	1.50	4.00
	Yr.11(1922)	163.908	.25	.50	1.50	4.00
	Yr.12(1923)	80.000	.25	.50	1.50	4.00

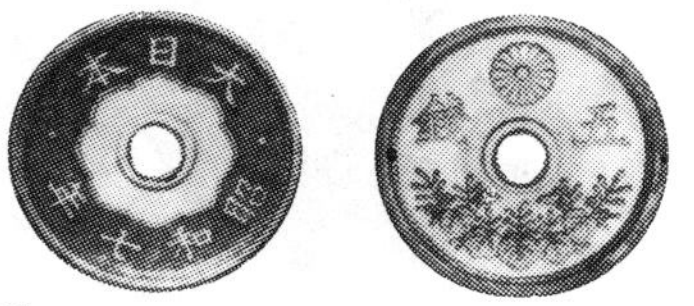

Y#	Date	Mintage	Fine	VF	XF	Unc
	Showa					
48	Yr.7(1932)	8.000	.25	.50	1.75	5.00

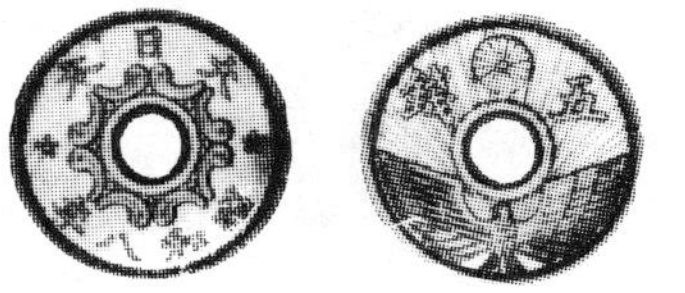

NICKEL

Y#	Date	Mintage	Fine	VF	XF	Unc
53	Yr.8(1933)	16.150	.50	1.50	3.00	5.50
	Yr.9(1934)	33.851	.50	1.00	2.00	4.50
	Yr.10(1935)	13.680	1.00	2.00	3.50	7.50
	Yr.11(1936)	36.321	.50	1.00	2.00	4.50
	Yr.12(1937)	44.402	.50	1.00	2.00	4.50
	Yr.13(1938)	*10.000	4 known	Rare	—	

***NOTE:** Almost entire mintage remelted.

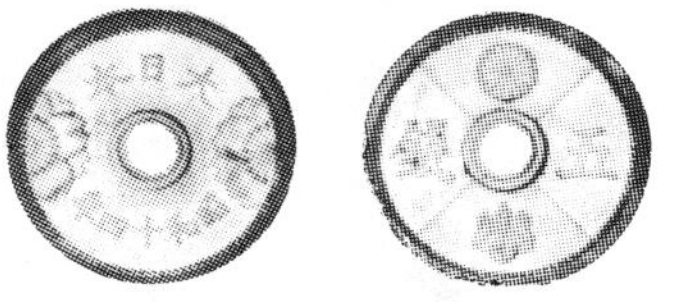

ALUMINUM-BRONZE

Y#	Date	Mintage	Fine	VF	XF	Unc
57	Yr.13(1938)	40.001	.50	1.00	1.50	4.00
57	Yr.14(1939)	97.903	.50	1.00	1.50	4.00
	Yr.15(1940)	34.501	.50	1.00	1.50	4.00

ALUMINUM
Variety 1 - 1.2000 g

Y#	Date	Mintage	Fine	VF	XF	Unc
60	Yr.15(1940)	167.638	—	.25	1.00	3.00
	Yr.16(1941)	242.361	—	.25	.75	2.50

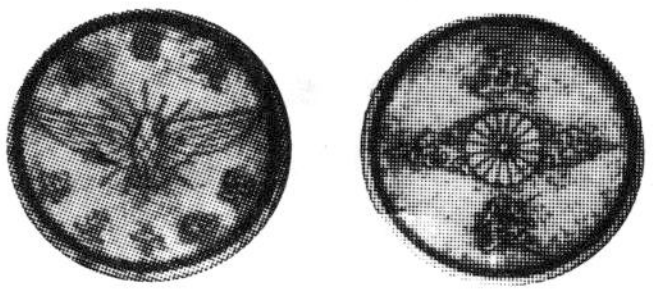

Variety 2 - 1.0000 g

Y#	Date	Mintage	Fine	VF	XF	Unc
60a	Yr.16(1941)	478.023	1.50	3.50	7.50	35.00
	Yr.17(1942)	I.A.	—	.25	.75	2.00

Variety 3 - 0.8000 g

Y#	Date	Mintage	Fine	VF	XF	Unc
60b	Yr.18(1943)	276.493	—	.25	.75	2.00

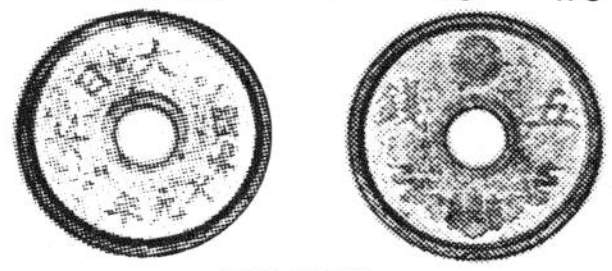

TIN-ZINC

Y#	Date	Mintage	Fine	VF	XF	Unc
63	Yr.19(1944)	70.003	—	.25	.75	2.50

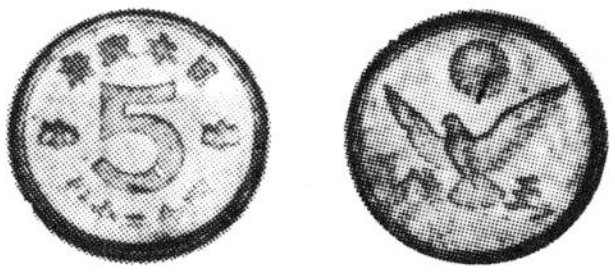

Y#	Date	Mintage	Fine	VF	XF	Unc
65	Yr.20(1945)	180.008	—	.50	1.25	3.50
	Yr.21(1946)	I.A.	—	.50	1.25	3.50

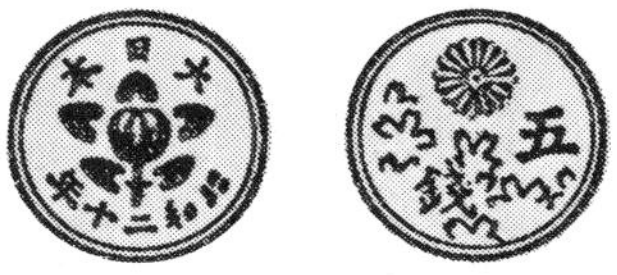

REDDISH BROWN BAKED CLAY

KM#	Date	Mintage	Fine	VF	XF	Unc
111	Yr.20(1945)	—	50.00	75.00	100.00	175.00

NOTE: Not issued for circulation. Varieties of color exist.

10 SEN

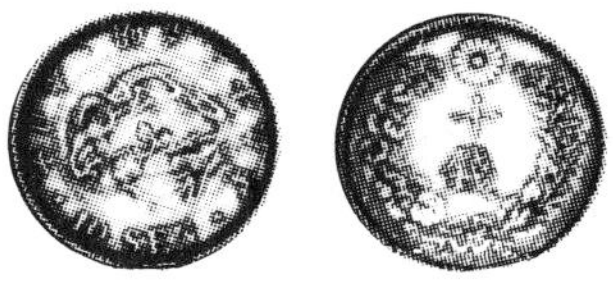

2.6957 g, .800 SILVER, .0693 oz ASW

Y#	Date	Mintage	Fine	VF	XF	Unc
	Meiji					
23	Yr.34(1901)	.797	125.00	175.00	250.00	750.00
	Yr.35(1902)	1.204	100.00	150.00	200.00	750.00
	Yr.37(1904)	11.106	4.50	7.50	10.00	35.00
	Yr.38(1905)	34.182	4.50	7.50	10.00	35.00
	Yr.39(1906)	4.710	4.50	7.50	10.00	35.00

NOTE: Earlier dates (Yr.6-33) exist for this type.

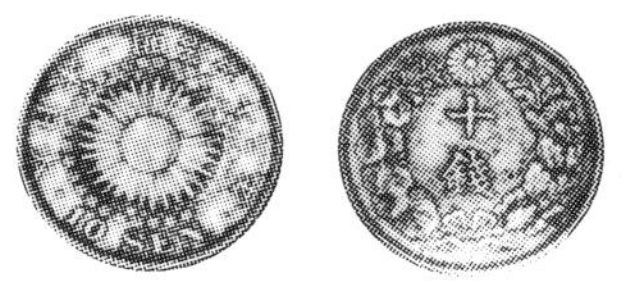

2.2500 g, .720 SILVER, .0521 oz ASW

Y#	Date	Mintage	Fine	VF	XF	Unc
29	Yr.40(1907)	12.000	2.50	5.00	10.00	50.00
	Yr.41(1908)	12.273	2.50	5.00	10.00	50.00
	Yr.42(1909)	20.279	1.00	3.50	5.00	25.00
	Yr.43(1910)	20.339	1.00	3.50	5.00	25.00
	Yr.44(1911)	38.729	1.00	3.50	5.00	25.00
	Yr.45(1912)	10.755	1.00	3.50	5.00	25.00

Obv: Japanese character *first*.

Y#	Date	Mintage	Fine	VF	XF	Unc
	Taisho					
36.1	Yr.1(1912)					
		10.344	2.50	5.00	10.00	55.00

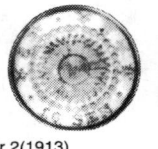 

36.2	Yr.2(1913)					
		13.321	1.00	2.50	5.00	12.00
	Yr.3(1914)					
		10.325	1.00	2.50	5.00	12.00
	Yr.4(1915)					
		16.836	1.50	3.00	5.00	12.00
	Yr.5(1916)					
		10.324	1.00	2.50	4.00	12.00
	Yr.6(1917)					
		35.170	.75	2.00	3.00	10.00

COPPER-NICKEL

45	Yr.9(1920)	4.894	.50	1.00	3.00	25.00
	Yr.10(1921)					
		61.870	.25	.50	1.50	5.00
	Yr.11(1922)					
		159.770	.25	.50	1.50	5.00
	Yr.12(1923)					
		190.010	.25	.50	1.50	4.50
	Yr.14(1925)					
		54.475	.25	.50	1.50	5.00
	Yr.15(1926)					
		58.675	.25	.50	1.50	5.00

	Showa					
49	Yr.2(1927)					
		36.050	.25	.50	1.50	5.00
	Yr.3(1928)					
		41.450	.25	.50	1.50	5.00
	Yr.4(1929)					
		10.000	.50	1.00	2.00	20.00
	Yr.6(1931)	1.850	.75	1.50	2.50	7.50
	Yr.7(1932)					
		23.151	.25	.50	1.50	5.00

NICKEL

54	Yr.8(1933)					
		14.570	.50	1.00	2.00	5.50
	Yr.9(1934)					
		37.351	.25	.75	1.50	4.75
	Yr.10(1935)					
		35.586	.30	1.00	1.75	5.25
	Yr.11(1936)					
		77.948	.25	.75	1.50	4.75
	Yr.12(1937)					
		40.001	.30	1.00	1.75	5.25

ALUMINUM-BRONZE

Y#	Date	Mintage	Fine	VF	XF	Unc
58	Yr.13(1938)					
		47.077	.35	.75	1.50	4.75
	Yr.14(1939)					
		121.796	.25	.50	1.00	4.50
	Yr.15(1940)					
		16.135	.75	1.50	3.00	12.00

ALUMINUM, 1.5000 g

61	Yr.15(1940)					
		575.628	—	.20	.35	1.50
	Yr.16(1941) I.A.		—	.20	.35	1.50

1.2000 g

61a	Yr.16(1941)					
		944.947	.10	.35	.50	2.00
	Yr.17(1942) I.A.		—	.20	.35	1.50
	Yr.18(1943) I.B.		.20	.50	2.00	5.00

1.0000 g

61b	Yr.18(1943)					
		756.037		.20	.35	1.50

TIN-ZINC

64	Yr.19(1944)					
		450.022	—	.20	.35	1.50

REDDISH BROWN BAKED CLAY

KM#	Date	Mintage	Fine	VF	XF	Unc
112	Yr.20(1945)	—	50.00	80.00	125.00	175.00

NOTE: Not issued for circulation. Varieties of color exist.

ALUMINUM

Y#	Date	Mintage	Fine	VF	XF	Unc
68	Yr.20(1945)					
		237.590	—	.20	.35	1.00
	Yr.21(1946) I.A.		—	.20	.35	1.00

20 SEN

明	明
Type I	Type II
Character	Character
Closed	Open

5.3800 g, .800 SILVER, .1383 oz ASW

	Meiji					
24	Yr.34(1901)	.500	150.00	225.00	350.00	2250.
	Yr.37(1904)					
		5.250	5.00	10.00	20.00	70.00
	Yr.38(1905)					
		8.444	5.00	10.00	20.00	70.00

NOTE: Earlier dates (Yr.6-33) exist for this type.

4.0500 g, .800 SILVER, .1042 oz ASW

30	Yr.39(1906)					
		6.555	7.50	15.00	25.00	200.00

Y#	Date	Mintage	Fine	VF	XF	Unc
30	Yr.40(1907)					
		20.000	2.50	5.50	15.00	75.00
	Yr.41(1908)					
		15.000	2.50	5.50	15.00	75.00
	Yr.42(1909)					
		8.824	2.50	5.50	15.00	75.00
	Yr.43(1910)					
		21.175	2.50	5.50	15.00	75.00
	Yr.44(1911)	.500	60.00	120.00	250.00	1000.

50 SEN

13.5000 g, .800 SILVER, .3472 oz ASW

	Meiji					
25	Yr.34(1901)					
		1.790	25.00	45.00	80.00	375.00
	Yr.35(1902)					
		1.023	50.00	85.00	150.00	625.00
	Yr.36(1903)					
		1.503	30.00	50.00	90.00	425.00
	Yr.37(1904)					
		5.373	7.50	12.50	25.00	125.00
	Yr.38(1905)					
		9.566	7.50	12.50	25.00	125.00

NOTE: Earlier dates (Yr.6-33) exist for this type.

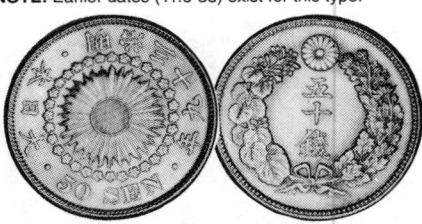

10.1000 g, .800 SILVER, .2597 oz ASW

31	Yr.39(1906)					
		12.478	4.00	8.00	25.00	225.00
	Yr.40(1907)					
		24.062	3.50	7.50	18.00	65.00
	Yr.41(1908)					
		25.470	3.50	7.50	18.00	65.00
	Yr.42(1909)					
		21.998	3.50	7.50	18.00	65.00
	Yr.43(1910)					
		15.323	3.50	7.50	18.00	65.00
	Yr.44(1911)					
		9.900	3.50	7.50	18.00	65.00
	Yr.45(1912)					
		3.677	9.00	15.00	25.00	85.00

Obv: Japanese character *first*.

	Taisho					
37.1	Yr.1(1912)	1.928	15.00	25.00	45.00	160.00

37.2	Yr.2(1913)	5.910	5.00	10.00	22.00	60.00
	Yr.3(1914)	1.872	20.00	35.00	55.00	175.00
	Yr.4(1915)	2.011	17.50	30.00	50.00	160.00
	Yr.5(1916)	8.736	4.00	8.00	16.00	35.00
	Yr.6(1917)	9.963	4.00	8.00	16.00	35.00

4.9600 g, .720 SILVER, .1148 oz ASW

46	Yr.11(1922)					

Y#	Date	Mintage	Fine	VF	XF	Unc
46		76.320	BV	1.50	5.00	25.00
	Yr.12(1923)					
		185.180	BV	1.50	3.00	18.00
	Yr.13(1924)					
		78.520	BV	1.50	3.00	18.00
	Yr.14(1925)					
		47.808	BV	1.50	3.00	20.00
	Yr.15(1926)					
		32.572	BV	1.50	3.00	20.00

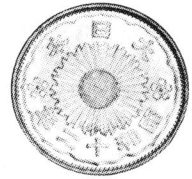 

Y#	Date	Mintage	Fine	VF	XF	Unc
	Showa					
50	Yr.3(1928)					
		38.592	BV	1.00	2.50	9.00
	Yr.4(1929)					
		12.568	BV	1.50	5.00	25.00
	Yr.5(1930)					
		10.200	BV	2.00	5.50	15.00
	Yr.6(1931)					
		27.677	BV	1.00	2.50	9.00
	Yr.7(1932)					
		24.132	BV	1.00	2.50	9.00
	Yr.8(1933)					
		10.001	BV	2.00	7.00	20.00
	Yr.9(1934)					
		20.003	BV	1.50	2.50	9.00
	Yr.10(1935)					
		11.738	BV	1.50	2.50	9.00
	Yr.11(1936)					
		44.272	BV	1.50	2.50	7.00
	Yr.12(1937)					
		48.000	BV	1.50	2.50	7.00
	Yr.13(1938)					
		3.600	50.00	75.00	125.00	250.00

BRASS

Y#	Date	Mintage	Fine	VF	XF	Unc
67	Yr.21(1946)					
		268.187	.25	.50	1.00	2.50
	Yr.22(1947) I.A.	—	650.00	1000.	1700.	

NOTE: Coins dated Showa 22 (1947) were not released to circulation.
NOTE: Varieties exist.

Y#	Date	Mintage	Fine	VF	XF	Unc
69	Yr.22(1947)					
		849.234	.10	.20	.40	1.00
	Yr.23(1948) I.A.	.10	.20	.40	1.00	

YEN

26.9568 g, .900 SILVER, .7800 oz ASW

Type II: Reduced size, 38.1mm.

Y#	Date	Mintage	Fine	VF	XF	Unc
	Meiji					
A25.3	Yr.34(1901)					
		1.256	15.00	30.00	50.00	160.00
	Yr.35(1902)	.668	25.00	50.00	75.00	225.00
	Yr.36(1903)					
		5.131	15.00	27.50	42.50	140.00
	Yr.37(1904)					
		6.970	15.00	27.50	42.50	140.00
	Yr.38(1905)					
		5.031	15.00	27.50	42.50	140.00
	Yr.39(1906)					
		3.471	25.00	50.00	85.00	245.00
	Yr.41(1908)	.334	50.00	100.00	150.00	450.00
	Yr.45(1912)					
		5.000	12.50	25.00	42.50	120.00

Y#	Date	Mintage	Fine	VF	XF	Unc
	Taisho					
38	Yr.3(1914)					
		11.500	12.50	22.50	35.00	110.00

REGULAR COINAGE
YEN

 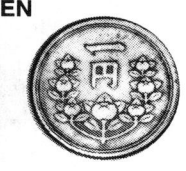

BRASS

Y#	Year	Date	Mintage	VF	XF	Unc
	Showa					
70	23	(1948)	451.209	.25	.50	2.00
	24	(1949)	Inc. Ab.	.15	.35	1.25
	25	(1950)	Inc. Ab.	.15	.35	1.25

ALUMINUM

Y#	Year	Date	Mintage	VF	XF	Unc
74	30	(1955)	381.700	—	—	.10
	31	(1956)	500.900	—	—	.10
	32	(1957)	492.000	—	—	.10
	33	(1958)	374.900	—	—	.10
	34	(1959)	208.600	—	—	.10
	35	(1960)	300.000	—	—	.10
	36	(1961)	432.400	—	—	.10
	37	(1962)	572.000	—	—	.10
	38	(1963)	788.700	—	—	.10
	39	(1964)				
			1665.100	—	—	.10
	40	(1965)				
			1743.256	—	—	.10
	41	(1966)	807.344	—	—	.10
	42	(1967)	220.600	—	—	.10
	44	(1969)	184.700	—	—	.10
	45	(1970)	556.400	—	—	.10
	46	(1971)	904.950	—	—	.10
	47	(1972)				
			1274.950	—	—	.10
	48	(1973)				
			1470.000	—	—	.10
	49	(1974)				
			1750.000	—	—	.10
	50	(1975)				
			1656.150	—	—	.10
	51	(1976)	928.800	—	—	.10
	52	(1977)	895.000	—	—	.10
	53	(1978)	864.000	—	—	.10
	54	(1979)				
			1015.000	—	—	.10
	55	(1980)				

Y#	Year	Date	Mintage	VF	XF	Unc
74			1145.000	—	—	.10
	56	(1981)	1206.000	—	—	.10
	57	(1982)				
			1017.000	—	—	.10
	58	(1983)	1086.000	—	—	.10
	59	(1984)	981.850	—	—	.10
	60	(1985)	837.150	—	—	.10
	61	(1986)	417.960	—	—	.10
	62	(1987)	955.520	—	—	.10
	62	(1987)	.230	—	Proof	1.50
	63	(1988)	1268.842	—	—	.10
	63	(1988)	.200	—	Proof	1.50
	64	(1989)	116.100	—	—	.50

Obv: Small tree.
Rev: Large 1 on wide ring in center, date below, w/Japanese *first* as third character.

Y#	Year	Date	Mintage	VF	XF	Unc
	Heisei					
95.1	1	(1989)	2366.770	—	—	.15
	1	(1989)	.200	—	Proof	1.50

Y#	Year	Date	Mintage	VF	XF	Unc
95.2	2	(1990)	2768.753	—	—	.15
	2	(1990)	.200	—	Proof	1.50
	3	(1991)	2300.900	—	—	.15
	3	(1991)	.220	—	Proof	1.50
	4	(1992)	1298.880	—	—	.15
	4	(1992)	.250	—	Proof	1.50
	5	(1993)	1260.990	—	—	.15
	5	(1993)	.250	—	Proof	1.50
	6	(1994)	1040.540	—	—	.15
	6	(1994)	.227	—	Proof	1.50
	7	(1995)	1041.674	—	—	.15
	7	(1995)	.200	—	Proof	1.50
	8	(1996)	942.024	—	—	.15
	8	(1996)	.189	—	Proof	1.50
	9	(1997)	782.874	—	—	.15
	9	(1997)	.212	—	Proof	1.50
	10	(1998)		—	—	.15
	10	(1998)		—	Proof	1.50

5 YEN

4.1666 g, .900 GOLD, .1205 oz AGW

Y#	Date	Mintage	Fine	VF	XF	Unc
	Meiji					
32	Yr.36(1903)	.021	900.00	1000.	1300.	2250.
	Yr.44(1911)	.059	900.00	1000.	1300.	2150.
	Yr.45(1912)	.059	850.00	1000.	1300.	2150.

NOTE: Earlier dates (Yr.30-31) exist for this type.

Y#	Date	Mintage	Fine	VF	XF	Unc
	Taisho					
39	Yr.2(1913)	.040	750.00	1000.	1250.	1850.
	Yr.13(1924)	.076	650.00	850.00	1000.	1550.
	Showa					
51	Yr.5(1930)	.852				
		20,000.	35,000.	50,000.	65,000.	

BRASS

Y#	Year	Date	Mintage	VF	XF	Unc
71	23	(1948)	74.520	.50	.75	12.50
	24	(1949)	179.692	.15	.40	8.00
			Old script.			
72	24	(1949)	111.896	.15	.25	9.00
	25	(1950)	181.824	.15	.25	6.50
	26	(1951)	197.980	.15	.25	6.50
	27	(1952)	55.000	.30	.60	15.00
	28	(1953)	45.000	.30	.60	6.50
	32	(1957)	10.000	4.00	8.00	15.00
	33	(1958)	50.000	.25	.50	3.50

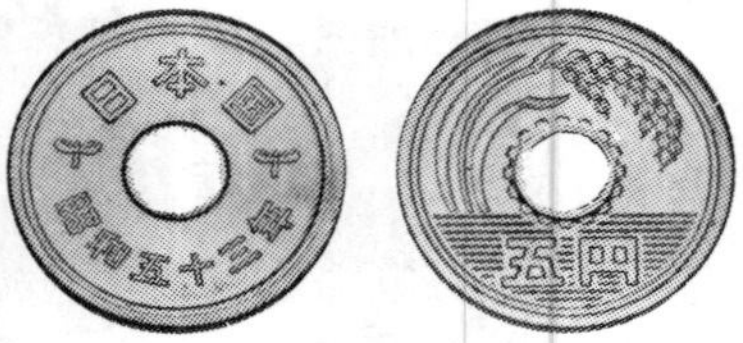

New script.

Y#	Year	Date	Mintage	VF	XF	Unc
72a	34	(1959)	33.000	.25	.50	3.00
	35	(1960)	34.800	.20	.40	3.00
	36	(1961)	61.000	.15	.35	2.50
	37	(1962)	126.700	.10	.30	1.50
	38	(1963)	171.800	.10	.30	1.50
	39	(1964)	379.700	.10	.30	1.50
	40	(1965)	384.200	.10	.30	1.50
	41	(1966)	163.100	.10	.30	1.50
	42	(1967)	26.000	.25	.50	1.50
	43	(1968)	114.000	—	.10	.15
	44	(1969)	240.000	—	.10	.15
	45	(1970)	340.000	—	.10	.15
	46	(1971)	362.050	—	.10	.15
	47	(1972)	562.950	—	.10	.15
	48	(1973)	745.000	—	.10	.15
	49	(1974)	950.000	—	.10	.15
	50	(1975)	970.000	—	.10	.15
	51	(1976)	200.000	—	.10	.15
	52	(1977)	340.000	—	.10	.15
	53	(1978)	318.000	—	.10	.15
	54	(1979)	317.000	—	.10	.15
	55	(1980)	385.000	—	.10	.15
	56	(1981)	95.000	—	.10	.15
	57	(1982)	455.000	—	.10	.15
	58	(1983)	410.000	—	.10	.15
	59	(1984)	202.850	—	.10	.15
	60	(1985)	153.150	—	.10	.15
	61	(1986)	113.960	—	.10	.15
	62	(1987)	631.545	—	.10	.15
	62	(1987)	.230	—	Proof	1.75
	63	(1988)	368.920	—	—	.15
	63	(1988)	.200	—	Proof	1.75
	64	(1989)	67.332	—	—	.65

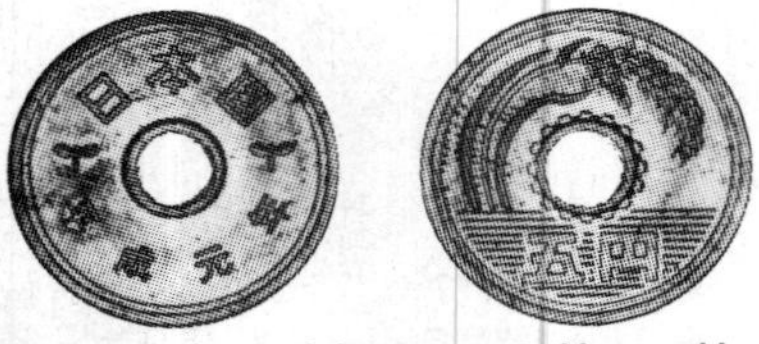

Obv: Inscription and date separated by seed leaf. Japanese character *first* in date. Rev: Gear around hole, rice stalk above denomination.

Y#	Year	Date	Mintage	VF	XF	Unc
	Heisei					
96.1	1	(1989)	960.460	—	—	.35
	1	(1989)	.200	—	Proof	1.75

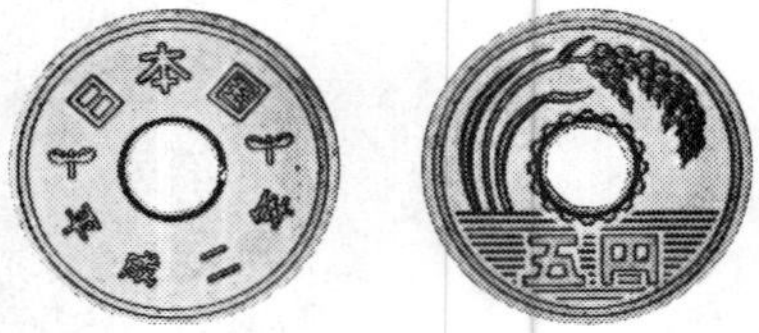

Y#	Year	Date	Mintage	VF	XF	Unc
96.2	2	(1990)	520.753	—	—	.35
	2	(1990)	.200	—	Proof	1.75
	3	(1991)	516.900	—	—	.35
	3	(1991)	.220	—	Proof	1.75
	4	(1992)	300.880	—	—	.35
	4	(1992)	.250	—	Proof	1.75
	5	(1993)	412.990	—	—	.35
	5	(1993)	.250	—	Proof	1.75
	6	(1994)	197.540	—	—	.35
	6	(1994)	.227	—	Proof	1.75
	7	(1995)	351.674	—	—	.35
	7	(1995)	.200	—	Proof	1.75
	8	(1996)	207.024	—	—	.35
	8	(1996)	.189	—	Proof	1.75
	9	(1997)	238.874	—	—	.35
	9	(1997)	.212	—	Proof	1.75
	10	(1998)	—	—	—	.35
	10	(1998)	—	—	Proof	1.75

10 YEN

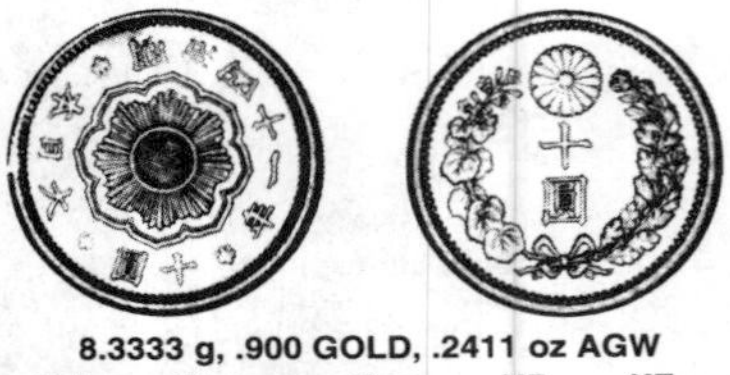

8.3333 g, .900 GOLD, .2411 oz AGW

Y#	Date	Mintage	Fine	VF	XF	Unc
	Meiji					
33	Yr.34(1901)	1.654	450.00	600.00	725.00	1100.
	Yr.35(1902)	3.023	450.00	600.00	725.00	1150.
	Yr.36(1903)	2.902	450.00	600.00	725.00	1150.
33	Yr.37(1904)	.724	500.00	800.00	1250.	2100.
	Yr.40(1907)	.157	500.00	800.00	1250.	2100.
	Yr.41(1908)	1.160	450.00	600.00	725.00	1150.
	Yr.42(1909)	2.165	400.00	600.00	725.00	1100.
	Yr.43(1910)	8,982	7500.	10,000.	15,000.	25,000.

NOTE: Earlier dates (Yr.30-33) exist for this type.

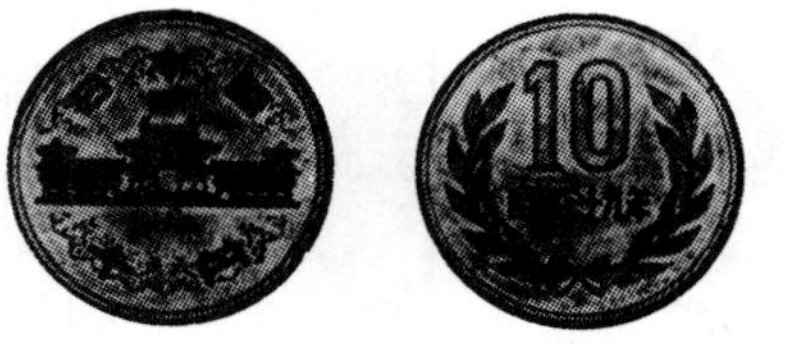

BRONZE
Obv: Ancient phoenix temple Hoo-do surrounded by arabesque pattern.
Reeded edge.

Y#	Year	Date	Mintage	VF	XF	Unc
	Showa					
73	26	(1951)	101.068	.20	.35	45.00
	27	(1952)	486.632	.20	.35	35.00
	28	(1953)	466.300	.20	.35	35.00
	29	(1954)	520.900	.20	.35	45.00
	30	(1955)	123.100	.20	.35	20.00
	32	(1957)	50.000	.25	.65	35.00
	33	(1958)	25.000	.40	1.00	45.00

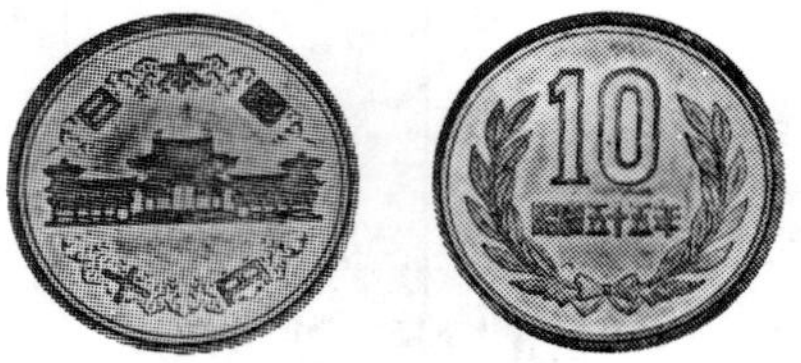

Plain edge.

Y#	Year	Date	Mintage	VF	XF	Unc
73a	34	(1959)	62.400	—	.20	9.00
	35	(1960)	225.900	—	.20	1.25
	36	(1961)	229.900	—	.20	1.25
	37	(1962)	284.200	—	.20	1.25
	38	(1963)	411.300	—	.20	.60
	39	(1964)	479.200	—	.20	.60
	40	(1965)	387.600	—	.20	.60
	41	(1966)	395.900	—	.20	.60
	42	(1967)	158.900	—	.20	.60
	43	(1968)	363.600	—	.20	.40
	44	(1969)	414.800	—	.20	.40
	45	(1970)	382.700	—	.20	.40
	46	(1971)	610.050	—	.20	.40
	47	(1972)	634.950	—	.20	.40
	48	(1973)	1345.000	—	.20	.35
	49	(1974)	1780.000	—	.20	.35
	50	(1975)	1280.260	—	.20	.35
	51	(1976)	1369.740	—	.20	.35
	52	(1977)	1467.000	—	.20	.35
	53	(1978)	1435.000	—	.20	.35
	54	(1979)	1207.000	—	.20	.35
	55	(1980)	1127.000	—	.20	.35
	56	(1981)	1369.000	—	.20	.35
	57	(1982)	890.000	—	.20	.35
	58	(1983)	870.000	—	.20	.35
	59	(1984)	533.850	—	.20	.35
	60	(1985)	335.150	—	.20	.35
	61	(1986)	68.960	—	.25	.75
	62	(1987)	165.545	—	.20	.35
	62	(1987)	.230	—	Proof	1.75
	63	(1988)	617.912	—	—	.35
	63	(1988)	.200	—	Proof	1.75
	64	(1989)	74.692	—	.25	.75

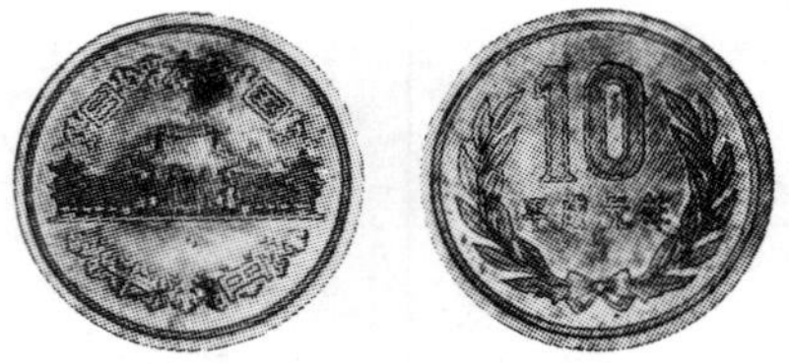

Rev: Japanese character *first* in date.

Y#	Year	Date	Mintage	VF	XF	Unc
	Heisei					
97.1	1	(1989)	666.108	—	—	.45
	1	(1989)	.200	—	Proof	1.75

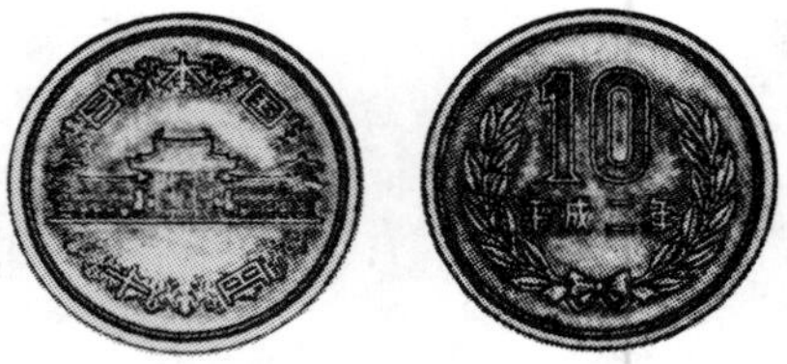

Y#	Year	Date	Mintage	VF	XF	Unc
97.2	2	(1990)	754.753	—	—	.45
	2	(1990)	.200	—	Proof	1.75
	3	(1991)	631.900	—	—	.45
	3	(1991)	.220	—	Proof	1.75
	4	(1992)	537.880	—	—	.45
	4	(1992)	.250	—	Proof	1.75
	5	(1993)	248.990	—	—	.45
	5	(1993)	.250	—	Proof	1.75
	6	(1994)	190.540	—	—	.45
	6	(1994)	.227	—	Proof	1.75
	7	(1995)	248.674	—	—	.45
	7	(1995)	.200	—	Proof	1.75
	8	(1996)	546.024	—	—	.45
	8	(1996)	.189	—	Proof	1.75
	9	(1997)	490.874	—	—	.45
	9	(1997)	.212	—	Proof	1.75
	10	(1998)	—	—	—	.45
	10	(1998)	—	—	Proof	1.75

50 YEN

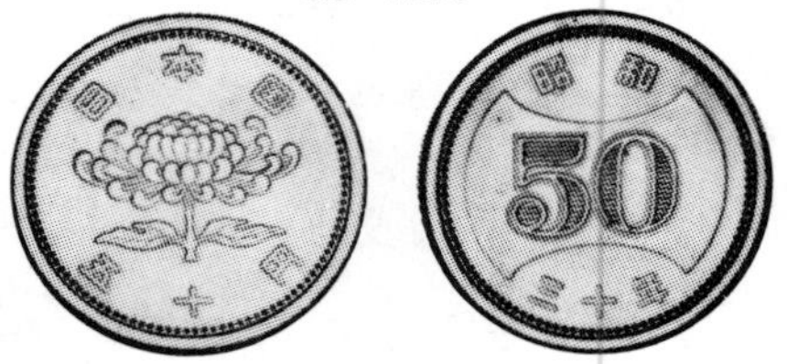

NICKEL

Y#	Year	Date	Mintage	VF	XF	Unc
	Showa					
75	30	(1955)	63.700	.75	1.50	17.50
	31	(1956)	91.300	.75	1.00	17.50
	32	(1957)	39.000	.75	1.50	17.50
	33	(1958)	18.000	1.00	2.50	30.00

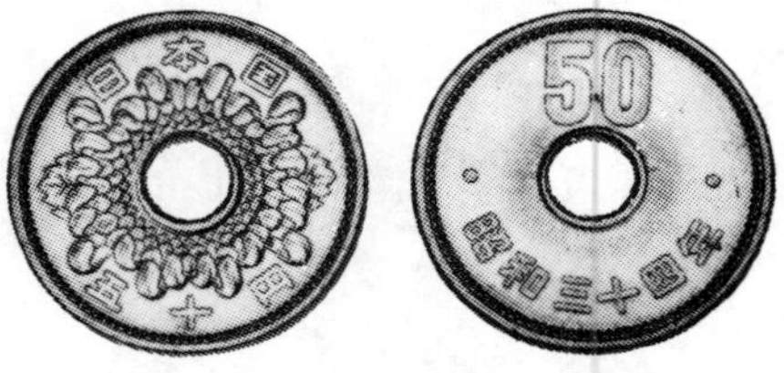

Y#	Year	Date	Mintage	VF	XF	Unc
76	34	(1959)	23.900	1.00	2.50	17.50
	35	(1960)	6.000	12.50	22.50	40.00
	36	(1961)	16.000	2.00	4.00	20.00
	37	(1962)	50.300	.75	1.25	5.00
	38	(1963)	55.000	.75	1.25	5.00
	39	(1964)	69.200	.75	1.25	4.00
	40	(1965)	189.300	.75	1.25	3.00
	41	(1966)	171.500	.75	1.25	2.50

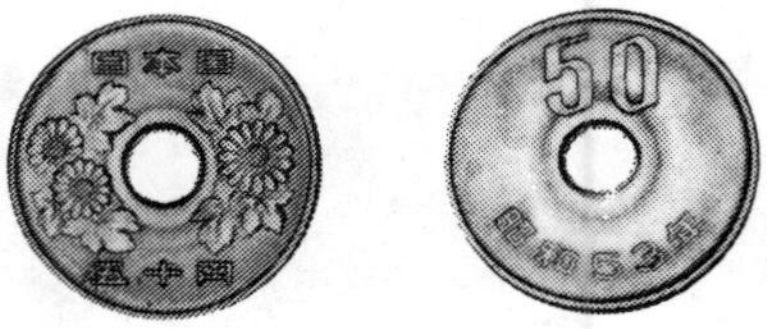

COPPER-NICKEL

Y#	Year	Date	Mintage	VF	XF	Unc
81	42	(1967)	238.400	—	.75	1.00
	43	(1968)	200.000	—	.75	1.00
	44	(1969)	210.900	—	.75	1.00
	45	(1970)	269.800	—	.75	1.00
	46	(1971)	80.950	—	.75	1.00
	47	(1972)	138.980	—	.75	1.00
	48	(1973)	200.970	—	.75	1.00
	49	(1974)	470.000	—	.75	1.00
	50	(1975)	238.120	—	.75	1.00
	51	(1976)	241.880	—	.75	1.00
	52	(1977)	176.000	—	.75	1.00
	53	(1978)	234.000	—	.75	1.00
	54	(1979)	110.000	—	.75	1.00
	55	(1980)	51.000	—	.75	1.00
	56	(1981)	179.000	—	.75	1.00
	57	(1982)	30.000	—	.75	1.00
	58	(1983)	30.000	—	.75	1.00
	59	(1984)	29.850	—	.75	1.00
	60	(1985)	10.150	—	.75	1.00
	61	(1986)	9.960	—	.75	1.00
	62	(1987)	.545	—	—	70.00
	62	(1987)	.230	—	Proof	75.00
	63	(1988)	108.912	—	—	1.00
	63	(1988)	.200	—	Proof	2.00

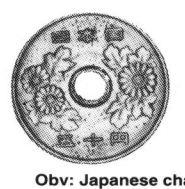 

Obv: Japanese character *first* in date.

Y#	Year	Date	Mintage	VF	XF	Unc
	Heisei					
101.1	1	(1989)	244.800	—	—	1.00
	1	(1989)	.200	—	Proof	2.00

Y#	Year	Date	Mintage	VF	XF	Unc
101.2	2	(1990)	274.753	—	—	1.00
	2	(1990)	.200	—	Proof	2.00
	3	(1991)	208.900	—	—	1.00
	3	(1991)	.220	—	Proof	2.00
	4	(1992)	48.880	—	—	1.00
	4	(1992)	.250	—	Proof	2.00
	5	(1993)	50.990	—	—	1.00
	5	(1993)	.250	—	Proof	2.00
	6	(1994)	65.540	—	—	1.00
	6	(1994)	.227	—	Proof	2.00
	7	(1995)	111.674	—	—	1.00
	7	(1995)	.200	—	Proof	2.00
	8	(1996)	82.024	—	—	1.00
	8	(1996)	.189	—	Proof	2.00
	9	(1997)	149.876	—	—	1.00
	9	(1997)	.212	—	Proof	2.00
	10	(1998)	—	—	—	1.00
	10	(1998)	—	—	Proof	2.00

100 YEN

4.8000 g, .600 SILVER .0926 oz ASW

Y#	Year	Date	Mintage	VF	XF	Unc
	Showa					
77	32	(1957)	30.000	1.50	2.50	9.00
	33	(1958)	70.000	1.50	2.50	6.00

Y#	Year	Date	Mintage	VF	XF	Unc
78	34	(1959)	110.000	1.50	2.50	9.00
	35	(1960)	50.000	1.50	2.50	9.00
	36	(1961)	15.000	1.50	2.50	9.00
	38	(1963)	45.000	1.50	2.50	6.00
	39	(1964)	10.000	1.75	3.50	7.50
	40	(1965)	62.500	1.50	2.50	4.00
	41	(1966)	97.500	1.50	2.50	4.00

1964 Olympic Games

Y#	Year	Date	Mintage	VF	XF	Unc
79	39	1964	80.000	1.00	2.50	4.00

COPPER-NICKEL

Y#	Year	Date	Mintage	VF	XF	Unc
82	42	(1967)	432.200	—	1.50	2.50
	43	(1968)	471.000	—	1.50	2.50
	44	(1969)	323.700	—	1.50	2.50
	45	(1970)	237.100	—	1.50	2.50
	46	(1971)	481.050	—	1.50	2.50
	47	(1972)	468.950	—	1.50	2.50
	48	(1973)	680.000	—	1.50	2.50
	49	(1974)	660.000	—	1.50	2.50
	50	(1975)	437.160	—	1.50	2.50

Y#	Year	Date	Mintage	VF	XF	Unc
82	51	(1976)	322.840	—	1.50	2.50
	52	(1977)	440.000	—	1.50	2.50
	53	(1978)	292.000	—	1.50	2.50
	54	(1979)	382.000	—	1.50	2.50
	55	(1980)	588.000	—	1.50	2.50
	56	(1981)	348.000	—	1.50	2.50
	57	(1982)	110.000	—	1.50	2.50
	58	(1983)	50.000	—	1.50	2.50
	59	(1984)	41.850	—	1.50	2.50
	60	(1985)	58.150	—	1.50	2.50
	61	(1986)	99.960	—	1.50	2.50
	62	(1987)	193.545	—	1.50	2.50
	62	(1987)	.230	—	Proof	5.00
	63	(1988)	362.912	—	1.50	2.50
	63	(1988)	.200	—	Proof	5.00

NOTE: Varieties exist for Yr.42.

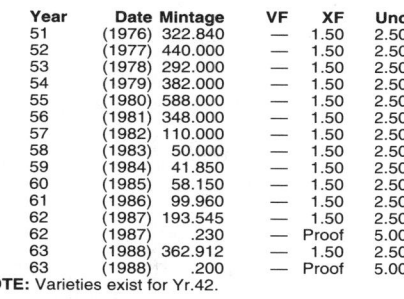

Osaka Expo '70

Y#	Year	Date	Mintage	VF	XF	Unc
83	45	(1970)	40.000	2.00	3.00	5.50

Winter Olympic Games - Sapporo

Y#	Year	Date	Mintage	VF	XF	Unc
84	47	1972	30.000	3.00	5.00	7.50

Okinawa Expo '75

Y#	Year	Date	Mintage	VF	XF	Unc
85	50	(1975)	120.000	1.50	2.50	3.00

50th Anniversary of Reign

Y#	Year	Date	Mintage	VF	XF	Unc
86	51	(1976)	70.000	2.00	3.00	5.50

Rev: Japanese character *first* in date.

Y#	Year	Date	Mintage	VF	XF	Unc
	Heisei					
98.1	1	(1989)	368.800	—	—	2.00
	1	(1989)	.200	—	Proof	5.00

Y#	Year	Date	Mintage	VF	XF	Unc
98.2	2	(1990)	444.753	—	—	2.00
	2	(1990)	.200	—	Proof	5.00
	3	(1991)	374.900	—	—	2.00
	3	(1991)	.220	—	Proof	5.00
	4	(1992)	211.050	—	—	2.00
	4	(1992)	.250	—	Proof	5.00
	5	(1993)	81.990	—	—	2.00
	5	(1993)	.250	—	Proof	5.00

Y#	Year	Date	Mintage	VF	XF	Unc
98.2	6	(1994)	81.540	—	—	2.00
	6	(1994)	.227	—	Proof	5.00
	7	(1995)	92.674	—	—	2.00
	7	(1995)	.200	—	Proof	5.00
	8	(1996)	37.024	—	—	2.00
	8	(1996)	.189	—	Proof	5.00
	9	(1997)	271.876	—	—	2.00
	9	(1997)	.212	—	Proof	5.00
	10	(1998)	—	—	—	2.00
	10	(1998)	—	—	Proof	5.00

500 YEN

COPPER-NICKEL
Obv: Pawlownia flower.

Y#	Year	Date	Mintage	VF	XF	Unc
	Showa					
87	57	(1982)	300.000	—	7.00	10.00
	58	(1983)	240.000	—	7.00	10.00
	59	(1984)	342.850	—	7.00	10.00
	60	(1985)	97.150	—	7.00	10.00
	61	(1986)	49.960	—	7.00	10.00
	62	(1987)	2.545	7.00	9.00	15.00
	62	(1987)	.230	—	Proof	25.00
	63	(1988)	148.018	—	7.00	10.00
	63	(1988)	.200	—	Proof	15.00
	64	(1989)	16.042	—	7.00	12.00

1985 Tsukuba Expo

Y#	Year	Date	Mintage	VF	XF	Unc
88	60	(1985)	70.000	—	7.00	10.00

100th Anniversary - Governmental Cabinet System

Y#	Year	Date	Mintage	VF	XF	Unc
89	60	(1985)	70.000	—	7.00	10.00

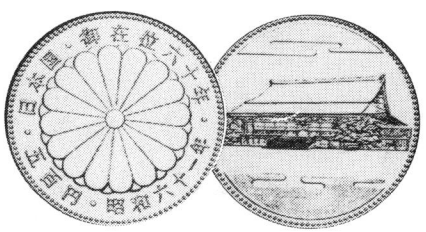

60 Years of Reign of Hirohito

Y#	Year	Date	Mintage	VF	XF	Unc
90	61	(1986)	50.000	—	7.00	10.00

Opening of Seikan Tunnel

Y#	Year	Date	Mintage	VF	XF	Unc
93	63	(1988)	20.000	—	8.00	12.50

Opening of Seto Bridge

Y#	Year	Date	Mintage	VF	XF	Unc
94	63	(1988)	20.000	—	8.00	12.50

Rev: Japanese character *first* in date.
Heisei

Y#	Year	Date	Mintage	VF	XF	Unc
99.1	1	(1989)	192.652	—	7.00	10.00
	1	(1989)	.200	—	Proof	15.00
99.2	2	(1990)	159.753	—	7.00	10.00
	2	(1990)	.200	—	Proof	15.00
	3	(1991)	169.900	—	7.00	10.00
	3	(1991)	.220	—	Proof	15.00
	4	(1992)	87.880	—	7.00	10.00
	4	(1992)	.250	—	Proof	15.00
	5	(1993)	131.990	—	7.00	10.00
	5	(1993)	.250	—	Proof	15.00
	6	(1994)	105.545	—	7.00	10.00
	6	(1994)	.227	—	Proof	15.00
	7	(1995)	182.665	—	—	10.00
	7	(1995)	.200	—	Proof	15.00
	8	(1996)	99.024	—	—	10.00
	8	(1996)	.189	—	Proof	15.00
	9	(1997)	271.876	—	—	10.00
	9	(1997)	.212	—	Proof	15.00
	10	(1998)	—	—	—	15.00
	10	(1998)	—	—	Proof	15.00

Enthronement of Emperor Akihito

Y#	Year	Date	Mintage	VF	XF	Unc
102	2	(1990)	30.000	—	—	15.00

20th Anniversary - Reversion of Okinawa

Y#	Year	Date	Mintage	VF	XF	Unc
106	4	(1992)	19.953	—	—	17.50
	4	(1992)	.047	—	Proof	25.00

Royal Wedding of Crown Prince

Y#	Year	Date	Mintage	VF	XF	Unc
107	5	(1993)	29.800	—	—	15.00
	5	(1993)	.200	—	Proof	20.00

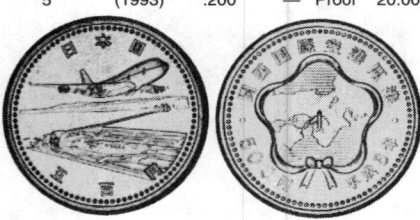

Opening of Kansai International Airport

Y#	Year	Date	Mintage	VF	XF	Unc
110	6	(1994)	19.900	—	—	17.50
	6	(1994)	.100	—	Proof	40.00

12th Asian Games - Runners

Y#	Year	Date	Mintage	VF	XF	Unc
111	6	(1994)	9.900	—	—	15.00
	6	(1994)	.100	—	Proof	30.00

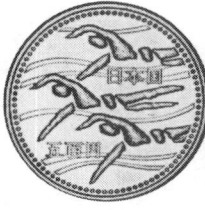 

12th Asian Games - Swimmers

Y#	Year	Date	Mintage	VF	XF	Unc
112	6	(1994)	9.900	—	—	15.00
	6	(1994)	.100	—	Proof	30.00

12th Asian Games - Jumper

Y#	Year	Date	Mintage	VF	XF	Unc
113	6	(1994)	9.900	—	—	15.00
	6	(1994)	.100	—	Proof	30.00

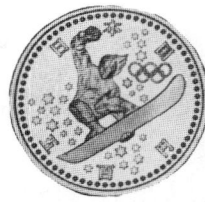 

1998 Nagano Winter Olympics - Snowboarder
Rev: Ptarmigan, denomination, dates.

Y#	Year	Date	Mintage	VF	XF	Unc
114	9	(1997)	19.867	—	—	12.00
	9	(1997)	0.133	—	Proof	25.00

1998 Nagano Winter Olympics - Bobsledding
Rev: Ptarmigan, denomination, dates.

Y#	Year	Date	Mintage	VF	XF	Unc
117	9	(1997)	19.867	—	—	12.00
	9	(1997)	.133	—	Proof	25.00

1998 Nagano Winter Olympics - Acrobatic Skier
Rev: Ptarmigan, denomination, dates.

Y#	Year	Date	Mintage	VF	XF	Unc
118	10	(1998)	19.867	—	—	12.00
	10	(1998)	.133	—	Proof	25.00

1000 YEN

20.0000 g, .925 SILVER, .5948 oz ASW
1964 Olympic Games
Dav.#276

Y#	Year Showa	Date	Mintage	VF	XF	Unc
80	39	1964	15.000	20.00	30.00	45.00

OCCUPATION COINAGE

The following issues were struck at the Osaka Mint for use in the Netherlands East Indies. The only inscription found on them is *Dai Nippon:* (Great Japan). The war situation had worsened to the point that shipping the coins became virtually impossible. Consequently, none of these coins were issued in the East Indies and almost the entire issue was lost or were remelted at the mint. Y#'s are for the Netherlands Indies and dates are from the Japanese Shinto dynastic calendar.

SEN

ALUMINUM

Y#	Date	Year	Mintage	VF	XF	Unc
22	2603	1943	233.190	75.00	100.00	150.00
	2604	1944	66.810	65.00	90.00	125.00

NOTE: 5 Sen listed as Pn48.

10 SEN

TIN ALLOY

	Date	Year	Mintage	VF	XF	Unc
24	2603	1943	69.490	35.00	60.00	120.00
	2604	1944	110.510	25.00	50.00	100.00

NOTE: Yeoman #22 and #24 as assigned to Netherlands Indies listings.

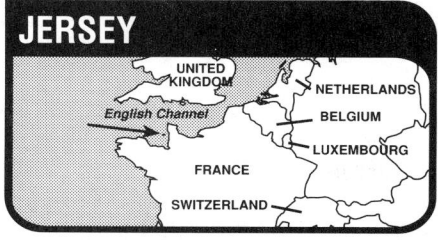

JERSEY

The Bailiwick of Jersey, a British Crown dependency located in the English Channel 12 miles (19 km.) west of Normandy, France, has an area of 45 sq. mi. (117 sq. km.) and a population of 74,000. Capital: St. Helier. The economy is based on agriculture and cattle breeding - the importation of cattle is prohibited to protect the purity of the island's world-famous strain of milch cows.

Jersey was occupied by Neanderthal man 100,000 B.C., and by Iberians of 2000 B.C. who left their chamber tombs in the island's granite cliffs. Roman legions almost certainly visited the island although they left no evidence of settlement. The country folk of Jersey still speak an archaic form of Norman-French, lingering evidence of the Norman annexation of the island in 933 A.D. Jersey was annexed to England in 1206, 140 years after the Norman Conquest. The dependency is administered by its own laws and customs; laws enacted by the British Parliament do not apply to Jersey unless it is specifically mentioned. During World War II, German troops occupied the island from July 1, 1940 until May 9, 1945.

Coins of pre-Roman Gaul and of Rome have been found in abundance on Jersey.

RULERS
British

MINT MARKS
H - Heaton, Birmingham

MONETARY SYSTEM
12 Pence = 1 Shilling
5 Shillings = 1 Crown
20 Shillings = 1 Pound
100 New Pence = 1 Pound

1/24 SHILLING

BRONZE

KM#	Date	Mintage	Fine	VF	XF	Unc
9	1909	.120	1.00	2.50	11.50	25.00

11	1911	.072	1.00	2.50	11.50	25.00
	1913	.072	1.00	2.50	11.50	25.00
	1923	.072	1.00	2.50	11.50	25.00

13	1923	.072	.75	3.00	5.50	22.50
	1923	—	—	—	Proof	550.00
	1926	.120	.75	2.50	4.50	20.00
	1926	—	—	—	Proof	550.00

15	1931	.072	.50	1.00	3.00	15.00
	1931	—	—	—	Proof	165.00

KM#	Date	Mintage	Fine	VF	XF	Unc
15	1933	.072	.50	1.00	3.00	15.00
	1933	—	—	—	Proof	165.00
	1935	.072	.50	1.00	3.00	15.00
	1935	—	—	—	Proof	165.00

17	1937	.072	.50	1.00	3.00	15.00
	1937	—	—	—	Proof	125.00
	1946	.072	.50	1.00	3.00	15.00
	1946	—	—	—	Proof	125.00
	1947	.072	.50	1.00	3.00	15.00
	1947	—	—	—	Proof	125.00

1/12 SHILLING

BRONZE

KM#	Date	Mintage	Fine	VF	XF	Unc
10	1909	.180	.50	3.00	12.50	60.00

12	1911	.204	.25	1.25	5.00	35.00
	1913	.204	.25	1.25	5.00	35.00
	1923	.204	.25	1.25	5.00	35.00

14	1923	.301	.25	1.25	5.00	30.00
	1926	.083	.50	1.50	10.00	40.00

16	1931	.204	.25	1.00	3.00	12.00
	1931	—	—	—	Proof	125.00
	1933	.204	.25	1.00	3.00	12.00
	1933	—	—	—	Proof	125.00
	1935	.204	.25	1.00	3.00	12.00
	1935	—	—	—	Proof	125.00

KM#	Date	Mintage	Fine	VF	XF	Unc
18	1937	.204	.25	.50	2.50	10.00
	1937	—	—	—	Proof	125.00
	1946	.204	.25	.50	2.50	10.00
	1946	—	—	—	Proof	125.00
	1947	.444	.15	.25	1.50	7.50
	1947	—	—	—	Proof	125.00

Liberation Commemorative

19	1945	1.000	.15	.35	.75	5.00
	1945	—	—	—	Proof	100.00

NOTE: Struck between 1949-52.

20	ND(1954)	.720	.15	.25	.60	3.00
	ND(1954)	—	—	—	Proof	100.00

21	1957	.720	.10	.15	.25	2.00
	1957	2,100	—	—	Proof	7.50
	1964	1.200	.10	.15	.25	1.00
	1964	.020	—	—	Proof	2.00

300th Anniversary - Accession of King Charles II

23	ND(1960)	1.200	.10	.15	.25	1.50
	ND(1960)	4,200	—	—	Proof	4.00

Mule. Obv: KM#20. Rev: KM#23.

24	ND(1960)	—	—	—	Proof	65.00

Norman Conquest

KM#	Date	Mintage	Fine	VF	XF	Unc
26	ND(1966)	1.200	.10	.15	.25	1.00
	ND(1966)	.030	—	—	Proof	2.00

1/4 SHILLING
(3 Pence)

NICKEL-BRASS

22	1957	2.000	.10	.15	.50	3.00
	1957	6,300	—	—	Proof	7.50
	1960	4,200	—	—	Proof	8.50

25	1964	1.200	.10	.15	.20	.75
	1964	.020	—	—	Proof	2.00

Norman Conquest

27	ND(1966)	1.200	.10	.15	.35	1.25
	ND(1966)	.030	—	—	Proof	2.00

5 SHILLINGS

COPPER-NICKEL
Norman Conquest
Obv: Similar to 1/4 Shilling, KM#27.

28	ND(1966)	.300	—	1.00	2.00	3.50
	ND(1966)	.030	—	—	Proof	6.00

DECIMAL COINAGE
100 New Pence = 1 Pound
Many of the following coins are also struck in silver, gold and platinum for collectors.

1/2 NEW PENNY

BRONZE

KM#	Date	Mintage	VF	XF	Unc
29	1971	3.000	—	.10	.20
	1980	.200	—	.10	.20
	1980	.010	—	Proof	1.35

1/2 PENNY

BRONZE

45	1981	.050	—	—	.10
	1981	.015	—	Proof	.90

NEW PENNY

BRONZE

KM#	Date	Mintage	VF	XF	Unc
30	1971	4.500	—	.10	.20
	1980	3.000	—	.10	.20
	1980	.010	—	Proof	1.80

PENNY

BRONZE

46	1981	.050	—	.10	.15
	1981	.015	—	Proof	1.10

Le Hocq Watch Tower, St. Clement

54	1983	.500	—	.10	.25
	1984	1.000	—	.10	.25
	1985	1.000	—	.10	.25
	1986	2.000	—	.10	.25
	1987	1.500	—	.10	.25
	1988	1.000	—	.10	.25
	1989	1.500	—	.10	.25
	1990	2.000	—	.10	.25
	1992	—	In sets only		.50

COPPER PLATED STEEL

54b	1994	2,000	—	.10	.50
	1997	.320	—	.10	.50

2 NEW PENCE

BRONZE

31	1971	2.225	—	.10	.30
	1975	.750	—	.10	.40
	1980	2.000	—	.10	.30
	1980	.010	—	Proof	2.25

2 PENCE

BRONZE

47	1981	.050	—	.10	.20
	1981	.015	—	Proof	1.35

L'Hermitage, St. Helier

55	1983	.800	—	.10	.25
	1984	.750	—	.10	.25
	1985	.250	—	.10	.25
	1986	1.000	—	.10	.25
	1987	2.000	—	.10	.25
	1988	.750	—	.10	.25

KM#	Date	Mintage	VF	XF	Unc
55	1989	1.000	—	.10	.25
	1990	2.600	—	.10	.25
	1997	5,500	In sets only		.50

BRONZE CLAD STEEL

55b	1992			.10	.50

NOTE: Released into circulation in 1998.

5 NEW PENCE

COPPER-NICKEL

32	1968	3.600	.15	.25	1.00
	1980	.800	.15	.25	1.00
	1980	.010	—	Proof	2.75

5 PENCE

COPPER-NICKEL

48	1981	.050	.15	.25	1.00
	1981	.015	—	Proof	1.80

Seymour Tower, Grouville, L'Avathison

56.1	1983	.400	.10	.20	1.00
	1984	.300	.10	.20	1.00
	1985	.600	.10	.20	1.00
	1986	.200	.10	.20	1.00
	1987	—	In sets only		.50
	1988	.400	.10	.20	1.00
	1989	—	.10	.20	1.00

COPPER-NICKEL, Reduced size

56.2	1990	4.000	—	—	.35
	1991	2.000	—	—	.35
	1992	1.000	—	—	.50
	1993	—	—	—	.50
	1997	5,500	In sets only		1.00

10 NEW PENCE

COPPER-NICKEL

33	1968	1.500	.20	.35	1.00
	1975	1.022	.20	.30	.90
	1980	1.000	.20	.30	.75
	1980	.010	—	Proof	5.50

10 PENCE

COPPER-NICKEL

KM#	Date	Mintage	VF	XF	Unc
49	1981	.050	—	.30	1.00
	1981	.015	—	Proof	2.25

La Houque Bie, Faldouet, St. Martin

57.1	1983	.030	—	.30	1.00
	1984	.100	—	.30	1.00
	1985	.100	—	.30	1.00
	1986	.400	—	.30	.75
	1987	.800	—	.30	.75
	1988	.650	—	.30	.75
	1989	.700	—	.30	.75
	1990	.850	—	.30	.75

COPPER-NICKEL, Reduced size

57.2	1992	7.000	—	.30	.50
	1997	5,500	In sets only		1.00

20 PENCE

COPPER-NICKEL
100th Anniversary of Lighthouse at Corbiere
Rev: Date below lighthouse.

53	1982	.200	—	.50	1.50

COPPER-NICKEL
Obv: Date below bust.

66	1983	.400	—	.50	1.00
	1984	.250	—	.50	1.00
	1986	.100	—	.50	1.00
	1987	.100	—	.50	1.00
	1989	.100	—	.50	1.00
	1990	.150	—	.50	1.00
	1992	—	In sets only		2.00
	1994	.200	—	.50	1.00
	1998	—	—	.50	1.00

25 PENCE

COPPER-NICKEL
Queen's Silver Jubilee

KM#	Date	Mintage	VF	XF	Unc
44	ND(1977)	.262	.75	1.00	3.00

50 NEW PENCE

COPPER-NICKEL

34	1969	.480	—	.90	1.50
	1980	.100	—	.90	1.50
	1980	.010	—	Proof	9.00

50 PENCE

COPPER-NICKEL

50	1981	.050	—	1.00	1.75
	1981	.015	—	Proof	3.00

Grosnez Castle

58.1	1983	.050	—	1.00	1.75
	1984	.050	—	1.00	1.75
	1986	.030	—	1.00	1.75
	1987	.150	—	1.00	1.75
	1988	.130	—	1.00	1.75
	1989	.180	—	1.00	1.75
	1990	.370	—	1.00	1.75
	1992	—	In sets only		2.50
	1994	.200	—	1.00	1.75
	1997	5,500	In sets only		2.50

COPPER-NICKEL
Smaller size, 27.3mm.

58.2	1997	1.500	—	—	2.50

40th Anniversary - Liberation of 1945

63	1985	.065	—	1.25	2.00

POUND

COPPER-NICKEL
Bicentennial - Battle of Jersey

KM#	Date	Mintage	VF	XF	Unc
51	ND(1981)	.200	—	2.00	3.25
	ND(1981)	.015	—	Proof	10.00

NICKEL-BRASS
Parish of St. Helier

59	1983	.100	—	2.00	3.25

Parish of St. Saviour

60	1984	.020	—	2.00	3.25

Parish of St. Brelade

61	1984	.020	—	2.00	3.25

Parish of St. Clement

62	1985	.025	—	2.00	3.25

Parish of St. Lawrence

65	1985	.010	—	2.00	3.50

Parish of St. Peter

68	1986	.010	—	2.00	3.25

Parish of Grouville

69	1986	.010	—	2.00	3.25

Parish of St. Martin
Obv: Similar to KM#69. Rev: Arms.

KM#	Date	Mintage	VF	XF	Unc
71	1987	.010	—	2.00	3.50

Parish of St. Ouen

72	1987	.010	—	2.00	3.25

Parish of Trinity

73	1988	.010	—	2.00	4.00

Parish of St. John

74	1988	.010	—	2.00	3.25

Parish of St. Mary's

75	1989	.025	—	2.00	3.25

Schooner - *The Tickler*

84	1991	.015	—	—	3.25

Sailing Ship - *Percy Douglas*

85	1991	.020	—	—	3.25

Sailing Ship - *Hebe*

86	1992	2,000	—	—	3.25

Ornamented Coat of Arms

87	1992	.020	—	—	3.50

Sailing Ship - *Gemini*

KM#	Date	Mintage	VF	XF	Unc
88	1993		—	—	3.25

Sailing Ship - *Century*

90	1993		—	—	3.25

COPPER-NICKEL
Schooner - *Resolute*

91	1994	.060	—	—	3.25
	1997	.101	—	—	3.25

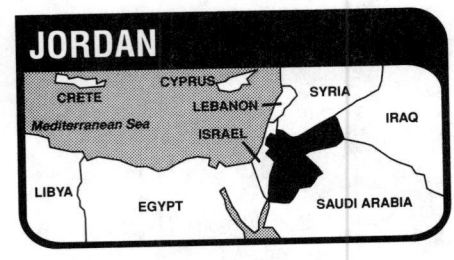

JORDAN

The Hashemite Kingdom of Jordan, a constitutional monarchy in southwest Asia, has an area of 37,738 sq. mi. (91,880 sq. km.) and a population of 3.5 million. Capital: Amman. Agriculture and tourism comprise Jordan's economic base. Chief exports are phosphates, tomatoes and oranges.

Jordan is the Edom and Moab of the time of Moses. It became part of the Roman province of Arabia in 106 A.D., was conquered by the Arabs in 633-36, and was part of the Ottoman Empire from the 16th century until World War I. At that time, the regions presently known as Jordan and Israel were mandated to Great Britain by the League of Nations as Transjordan and Palestine. In 1922 Transjordan was established as the semi-autonomous Emirate of Transjordan, ruled by the Hashemite Prince Abdullah but still nominally a part of the British mandate. The mandate over Transjordan was terminated in 1946, The country becoming the independent Hashemite Kingdom of Transjordan. The kingdom was renamed the Hashemite Kingdom of Jordan in 1950.

NOTE: Several 1964 and 1965 issues were limited to respective quantities of 3,000 and 5,000 examples struck to make up sets for sale to collectors.

TITLES

المملكة الاردنية الهاشمية

el-Mamlaka(t)   el-Urduniya(t)   el-Hashemiya(t)

RULERS

Abdullah Ibn al-Hussein, 1946-1951
Talal Ibn Abdullah, 1951-1952
Hussein Ibn Talal, 1952-1999

MONETARY SYSTEM

100 Fils = 1 Dirham
1000 Fils = 10 Dirhams = 1 Dinar

Commencing 1992
100 Piastres = 1 Dinar

FIL

BRONZE

KM#	Date	Year	Mintage	VF	XF	Unc
1	AH1368	1949	.350	1.00	1.50	3.50
	1368	1949	—	—	Proof	—

NOTE: *FIL* is an error for *FILS*, the correct Arabic singular.

FILS

BRONZE

2	AH1368	1949	Inc. Ab.	.50	.90	2.25
	1368	1949	25 pcs.	—	Proof	50.00

8	AH1374	1955	.200	.35	.50	1.00
	1374	1955	—	—	Proof	
	1379	1960	.150	.40	.60	1.25
	1379	1960	—	—	Proof	
	1382	1963	.200	.25	.50	1.00
	1382	1963	—	—	Proof	
	1383	1964	3,000	1.50	3.00	5.00
	1385	1965	5,000	1.00	2.00	4.00
	1385	1965	.010	—	Proof	3.00

KM#	Date	Year	Mintage	VF	XF	Unc
			Hussein			
14	AH1387	1968	.060	.15	.25	.75

KM#	Date	Year	Mintage	VF	XF	Unc
35	AH1398	1978	—	.15	.25	.60
	1398	1978	.020	—	Proof	.75
	1401	1981	.100	.10	.20	.50
	1404	1984	.100	.10	.20	.50
	1406	1985	—	.10	.20	.50
	1406	1985	5,000	—	Proof	.75

5 FILS (1/2 QIRSH)

BRONZE

KM#	Date	Year	Mintage	VF	XF	Unc
3	AH1368	1949	3.300	.40	.75	1.50
	1368	1949	25 pcs.	—	Proof	60.00

KM#	Date	Year	Mintage	VF	XF	Unc
9	AH1374	1955	3.500	.35	.50	.75
	1374	1955	—	—	Proof	—
	1380	1960	.540	.50	.70	1.25
	1380	1960	—	—	Proof	—
	1382	1962	.250	.45	.70	1.25
	1382	1962	—	—	Proof	—
	1383	1964	3,000	—	4.50	7.50
	1384	1964	2.500	.30	.50	1.00
	1385	1965	5,000	1.25	2.50	4.00
	1385	1965	.010	—	Proof	5.00
	1387	1967	2.000	.10	.20	.40

KM#	Date	Year	Mintage	VF	XF	Unc
			Hussein			
15	AH1387	1968	.800	.10	.25	.50
	1390	1970	1.400	—	.20	.40
	1392	1972	.400	.10	.25	.65
	1394	1974	2.000	.10	.20	.40
	1395	1975	9.000	.10	.15	.30

KM#	Date	Year	Mintage	VF	XF	Unc
36	AH1398	1978	60.200	.10	.15	.30
	1398	1978	.020	—	Proof	1.25
	1406	1985	—	.10	.15	.30
	1406	1985	5,000	—	Proof	1.25

10 FILS (QIRSH, PIASTRE)

BRONZE

KM#	Date	Year	Mintage	VF	XF	Unc
4	AH1368	1949	2.700	.75	1.25	2.00
	1368	1949	25 pcs.	—	Proof	80.00

KM#	Date	Year	Mintage	VF	XF	Unc
10	AH1374	1955	1.500	.60	1.00	2.00
	1374	1955	—	—	Proof	—
	1380	1960	.060	1.25	2.00	3.50
	1380	1960	—	—	Proof	—
	1382	1962	2.300	.30	.50	1.00
	1382	1962	—	—	Proof	50.00
	1383	1964	1.253	.30	.50	1.00
	1385	1965	1.003	.20	.40	1.00
	1385	1965	.010	—	Proof	2.00
	1387	1967	1.000	.20	.35	1.00

KM#	Date	Year	Mintage	VF	XF	Unc
			Hussein			
16	AH1387	1968	.500	.20	.40	.75
	1390	1970	1.000	.20	.35	.60
	1392	1972	.600	.20	.40	.75
	1394	1974	1.000	.20	.40	.65
	1395	1975	5.000	.20	.35	.50

KM#	Date	Year	Mintage	VF	XF	Unc
37	AH1398	1978	30.000	.10	.15	.40
	1398	1978	.020	—	Proof	1.50
	1404	1984	10.000	.10	.15	.40
	1406	1985	—	.10	.15	.40
	1406	1985	5,000	—	Proof	1.50
	1409	1989	8,000	.10	.15	.40

20 FILS

COPPER-NICKEL

KM#	Date	Year	Mintage	VF	XF	Unc
5	AH1368	1949	1.570	.50	1.00	1.75
	1368	1949	25 pcs.	—	Proof	90.00

KM#	Date	Year	Mintage	VF	XF	Unc
13	AH1383	1964	3,000	1.50	3.00	5.00
	1385	1965	5,000	1.50	3.00	5.00
	1385	1965	.010	—	Proof	5.00

25 FILS (1/4 DIRHAM)

COPPER-NICKEL

KM#	Date	Year	Mintage	VF	XF	Unc
			Hussein			
17	AH1387	1968	.200	.15	.35	.75
	1390	1970	.240	.15	.35	.75
	1394	1974	.800	.15	.35	.75
	1395	1975	2.000	.15	.35	.75
	1397	1977	1.600	.15	.35	.75

KM#	Date	Year	Mintage	VF	XF	Unc
38	AH1398	1978	—	.20	.30	.75
	1398	1978	.020	—	Proof	2.00
	1401	1981	2.000	.20	.30	.75
	1404	1984	4.000	.20	.30	.75
	1406	1985	—	.20	.30	.75
	1406	1985	5,000	—	Proof	2.00
	1411	1991	5.000	.20	.30	.75

50 FILS (1/2 DIRHAM)

COPPER-NICKEL

KM#	Date	Year	Mintage	VF	XF	Unc
6	AH1368	1949	2.500	.75	2.00	3.50
	1368	1949	25 Pcs.	—	Proof	100.00

KM#	Date	Year	Mintage	VF	XF	Unc
11	AH1374	1955	2.500	.75	1.50	3.50
	1374	1955	—	—	Proof	—
	1382	1962	.750	.85	1.00	1.50
	1382	1962	—	—	Proof	—
	1383	1964	1.003	.40	.60	1.00
	1385	1965	1.505	.40	.60	1.00
	1385	1965	.010	—	Proof	3.50

KM#	Date	Year	Mintage	VF	XF	Unc
			Hussein			
18	AH1387	1968	.400	.40	.75	1.75
	1390	1970	1.000	.40	.60	1.25
	1393	1973	—	.40	.60	1.25
	1394	1974	1.000	.40	.60	1.25
	1395	1975	2.000	.40	.60	1.25
	1397	1977	6.000	.40	.60	1.25

KM#	Date	Year	Mintage	VF	XF	Unc
39	AH1398	1978	6.168	.25	.50	1.25
	1398	1978	.020	—	Proof	2.50

KM#	Date	Year	Mintage	VF	XF	Unc
39	1400	1979	—	.25	.50	1.25
	1401	1981	5.000	.25	.50	1.25
	1404	1984	10.000	.25	.50	1.25
	1406	1985	—	.25	.50	1.25
	1406	1985	5,000	—	Proof	2.50
	1409	1989	6.000	.25	.50	1.25
	1411	1991	10.000	.25	.50	1.25

100 FILS (DIRHAM)

COPPER-NICKEL

KM#	Date	Year	Mintage	VF	XF	Unc
7	AH1368	1949	2.000	2.00	3.00	5.00
	1368	1949	25 pcs.	—	Proof	120.00

12	AH1374	1955	.500	2.00	2.50	4.00
	1374	1955	—	—	Proof	
	1382	1962	.600	1.00	1.50	3.00
	1382	1962	—	—	Proof	
	1383	1964	3,000	1.50	3.00	5.00
	1385	1965	.405	1.00	1.25	2.25
	1385	1965	.010	—	Proof	4.00

Hussein

19	AH1387	1968	.175	.75	1.50	2.50
	1395	1975	2.500	.40	1.00	2.00
	1397	1977	2.000	.40	1.00	2.00

40	AH1398	1978	3.000	.40	1.00	2.00
	1398	1978	.020	—	Proof	3.00
	1400	1979	—	.40	1.00	2.00
	1401	1981	4.000	.40	1.00	2.00
	1404	1984	5.000	.40	1.00	1.50
	1406	1985	—	.40	1.00	1.50
	1406	1985	5,000	—	Proof	3.00
	1409	1989	4.000	.40	1.00	1.50
	1411	1991	6.000	.40	1.00	1.50

1/4 DINAR

COPPER-NICKEL
F.A.O. Issue

20	AH1389	1969	.060	2.00	3.00	5.50

KM#	Date	Year	Mintage	VF	XF	Unc
28	AH1390	1970	.500	1.00	1.50	4.00
	1394	1974	.400	1.00	1.50	4.00
	1395	1975	.100	1.00	1.50	4.00
	1396	1976	—	1.00	1.50	4.00

25th Anniversary of Reign

30	AH1397	1977	.200	1.00	2.00	4.50

41	AH1398	1978	.200	1.00	2.00	4.50
	1398	1978	.020	—	Proof	5.00
	1401	1981	.800	.75	1.50	3.50
	1406	1985	—	.75	1.50	3.50
	1406	1985	5,000	—	Proof	5.00

1/2 DINAR

COPPER-NICKEL
1400th Anniversary of Islam

42	AH1400	1980	2.006	1.50	2.50	5.00

DINAR

NICKEL-BRONZE
King Hussein's 50th Birthday

KM#	Date	Year	Mintage	VF	XF	Unc
47	AH1406	1985	—	—	—	7.50
	1406	1985	5,000	—	Proof	10.00

MONETARY REFORM

100 Piastres = 1 Dinar

1/2 QIRSH (Piastre)

COPPER PLATED STEEL
Obv: King Hussein facing left.
Rev: Denomination.

60	AH1416	1996	—	—	.35	.65

QIRSH (PIASTRE)

BRONZE PLATED STEEL

56	AH1414	1994	—	—	.65	1.25
	1416	1996	—	—	.65	1.25

2-1/2 PIASTRES

STAINLESS STEEL

53	AH1412	1992	—	—	.75	1.50
	1413	1993	—	—	.75	1.50

5 PIASTRES

NICKEL PLATED STEEL

54	AH1412	1992	—	—	1.00	2.00
	1413	1993	—	—	1.00	2.00
	1416	1996	—	—	1.00	2.00

1/4 DINAR

NICKEL-BRASS
Obv: King Hussein facing left.
Rev: Denomination.

61	AH1416	1996	—	—	—	3.00
	1417	1997	—	—	—	3.00

1/2 DINAR

BRASS
Obv: King Hussein facing left.

KM#	Date	Year	Mintage	VF	XF	Unc
58	AH1416	1996	—	—	—	4.00
	1417	1997	—	—	—	4.00

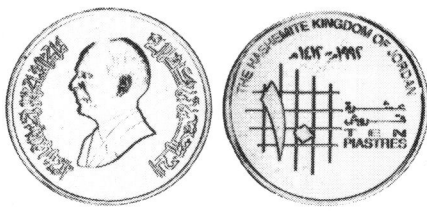

COPPER-NICKEL center in ALUMINUM-BRONZE ring
Obv: King Hussein. Rev: Denomination.

63	AH1417	1997	—	—	—	5.00

10 PIASTRES

NICKEL PLATED STEEL

55	AH1412	1992	—	—	1.25	2.25
	1413	1993	—	—	1.25	2.25
	1416	1996	—	—	1.25	2.25
	1417	1997	—	—	1.25	2.25

DINAR

BRASS
50th Anniversary - F.A.O.
Obv: King Hussein facing left.
Rev: F.A.O. logo.

62	AH1415	1995	—	—	—	10.00

Obv: King Hussein facing left.

59	AH1416	1996	—	—	—	7.50
	1417	1997	—	—	—	7.50

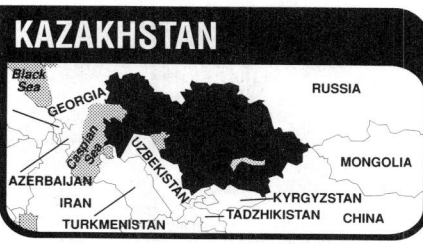

KAZAKHSTAN

The Republic of Kazakhstan (formerly Kazakhstan S.S.R.) is bordered to the west by the Caspian Sea and Russia, to the north by Russia, in the east by the Peoples Republic of China and in the south by Uzbekistan and Kirghizia and has an area of 1,049,155 sq. mi. (2,717,300 sq. km.) and a population of 16.7 million. Capital: Alma-Ata (formerly Vemy). Rich in mineral resources including coal, tungsten, copper, lead, zinc and manganese with huge oil and natural gas reserves. Agriculture is very important, (it previously represented 20 percent of the total arable acreage of the combined U.S.S.R.) Non-ferrous metallurgy, heavy engineering and chemical industries are leaders in its economy.

The Kazakhs are a branch of the Turkic peoples which led the nomadic life of herdsmen until WW I. In the 13th century they came under Genghis Khan's eldest son Juji and later became a part of the Golden Horde, a western Mongol empire. Around the beginning of the 16th century they were divided into 3 confederacies, known as "zhuz" or hordes, in the steppes of Turkistan. At the end of the 17th century an incursion by the Kalmucks, a remnant of the Oirat Mongol confederacy, resulted in heavy losses on both sides which facilitated Russian penetration. Resistance to Russian settlements varied throughout the 1800's, but by 1900 over 100 million acres were declared Czarist state property and used for a planned peasant colonization. After a revolution in 1905 Kazakh deputies were elected. In 1916 the tsarist government ordered mobilization of all males, between 19 and 43, for auxiliary service. The Kazakhs rose in defiance which led the governor general of Turkistan to send troops against the rebels. Shortly after the Russian revolution, Kazakh Nationalists asked for full autonomy. The Communist coup d'etat of Nov. 1917 led to civil war. In 1919-20 the Red army defeated the "White" Russian forces and occupied Kazakhstan and fought against the Nationalist government formed on Nov. 17, 1917 by Ali Khan Bukey Khan. The Kazakh Autonomous Soviet Socialist Republic was proclaimed on Aug. 26, 1920 within the R.S.F.S.R. Russian and Ukrainian colonization continued while 2 purges in 1927 and 1935 quelled any Kazakh feelings of priority in the matters of their country. On Dec. 5, 1936 Kazakhstan qualified for full status as an S.S.R. and held its first congress in 1937. Independence was declared on Dec. 16, 1991 and Kazakhstan joined the C.I.S.

MONETARY SYSTEM
100 Tyin = 1 Tenge

2 TYIN

YELLOW BRASS

KM#	Date	Mintage	VF	XF	Unc
1	1993	—	—	—	.45

COPPER CLAD BRASS

1a	1993	—	—	—	.45

5 TYIN

YELLOW BRASS

2	1993	—	—	—	.60

COPPER CLAD BRASS

2a	1993	—	—	—	.60

10 TYIN

YELLOW BRASS

3	1993	—	—	—	.80

COPPER CLAD BRASS

3a	1993	—	—	—	.80

---

20 TYIN

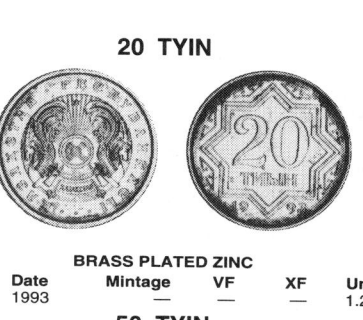

BRASS PLATED ZINC

KM#	Date	Mintage	VF	XF	Unc
4	1993	—	—	—	1.25

50 TYIN

BRASS PLATED ZINC

5	1993	—	—	—	1.50

TENGE

COPPER-NICKEL

6	1992	—	—	—	1.00
	1993	—	—	—	.50

3 TENGE

COPPER-NICKEL

8	1993	—	—	—	.75

5 TENGE

COPPER-NICKEL

9	1993	—	—	—	1.25

10 TENGE

COPPER-NICKEL

10	1993	—	—	—	2.00

20 TENGE

COPPER-NICKEL

11	1993	—	—	—	3.00

50th Anniversary - United Nations

KM#	Date	Mintage	VF	XF	Unc
12	1995	—			3.50

150th Anniversary - Jambyl
Obv: National emblem.
Rev: Man w/stringed instrument.

| 18 | 1996 | — | | | 4.00 |

5th Anniversary - Independence
Obv: National emblem.
Rev: Monument and buildings.

| 19 | 1996 | — | | | 3.50 |

Centennial - Birth of Muchtar Euesow
Obv: National emblem.

| 20 | ND(1997) | — | | | 3.50 |

Year of Peace and Harmony - Stylized Dove
Obv: National emblem.

| 21 | 1997 | — | | | 3.50 |

New Capitol City - Astana
Obv: National emblem.
Rev: Flower-like design.

| 22 | 1998 | — | | | 3.50 |

KENYA

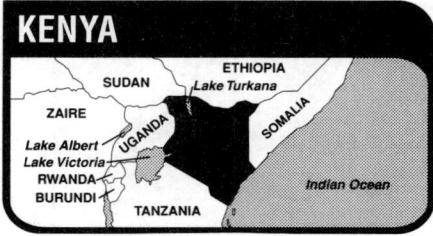

The Republic of Kenya, located on the east coast of Central Africa, has an area of 224,961 sq. mi (582,650 sq. km.) and a population of 20.1 million. Capital: Nairobi. The predominantly agricultural country exports coffee, tea and petroleum products.

The Arabs came to the coast of Kenya in the 8th century and established posts to conduct an ivory and slave trade. The Portuguese, the inveterate wanderers of the Age of Exploration, followed in the 16th century. After a lengthy and bitter struggle with the sultans of Zanzibar who controlled much of the southeastern coast of Africa, the Portuguese were driven away (late 17th century) and for many years Kenya was simply a port of call on the route to India. German and British interests in the 19th century produced agreements defining their respective spheres of influence. The British sphere was administrated by the Imperial East Africa Co. until 1895, when the British government purchased the company's rights in the East Africa Protectorate which, in 1920, was designated as Kenya Colony and protectorate - the latter being a 10-mile wide coastal strip together with Mombasa, Lamu and other small islands nominally retained by the Sultan of Zanzibar. Kenya achieved self-government in June of 1963 as a consequence of the 1952-60 Mau Mau terrorist campaign to secure land reforms and political rights for Africans. Independence was attained on Dec. 12, 1963. Kenya became a republic in 1964. It is a member of the Commonwealth of Nations. The president is Chief of State and Head of Government.

Mombasa was a thriving Arabic commercial center when first visited by Portuguese navigator Vasco da Gama in 1498. During the following two centuries Portugal made repeated efforts to capture the island stronghold but was unable to hold it against the assaults of the Muscat Arabs. In 1823 the ruling Mazuri family placed the city under British protection. Britain repudiated the protectorate and it was then seized by Seyyid Said of Oman, 1837, and annexed to Zanzibar. In 1887 the sultan of Zanzibar relinquished the port of Mombasa to British administration. It was occupied by the Imperial British East Africa Company and for the following two decades was the capital of British East Africa.

RULERS

British, until 1964

MONETARY SYSTEM

100 Cents = 1 Shilling

5 CENTS

NICKEL-BRASS
President Jomo Kenyatta

KM#	Date	Mintage	Fine	VF	XF	Unc
1	1966	28.000	—	.25	.50	1.00
	1966	27 pcs.	—	—	Proof	65.00
	1967	9.600	—	.25	.50	1.00
	1968	12.000	—	.25	.50	1.00

10	1969	.800	—	.50	1.00	2.25
	1969	15 pcs.	—	—	Proof	100.00
	1970	10.000	—	.15	.25	.50
	1971	29.680	—	.15	.25	.40
	1973	500 pcs.	—	—	Proof	15.00
	1974	5.599	—	.15	.25	.40
	1975	28.000	—	.15	.25	.40
	1978	23.168	—	.15	.25	.40

President Arap Moi

KM#	Date	Mintage	Fine	VF	XF	Unc
17	1980	—	—	.15	.25	.50
	1984	—	—	.15	.25	.75
	1986	—	—	.15	.25	.75
	1987	—	—	.15	.25	.75
	1989	—	—	.15	.25	.50
	1990	—	—	.15	.25	.40
	1991	—	—	.15	.25	.40

10 CENTS

NICKEL-BRASS
President Jomo Kenyatta

2	1966	26.000	.20	.65	1.25	2.50
	1966	27 pcs.	—	—	Proof	65.00
	1967	7.300	.20	.65	1.25	2.50
	1968	12.000	.20	.65	1.25	2.50

11	1969	3.900	—	.15	.25	.65
	1969	15 pcs.	—	—	Proof	100.00
	1970	7.200	—	.15	.25	.65
	1971	32.400	—	.15	.25	.50
	1973	3.000	—	.15	.25	.75
	1973	500 pcs.	—	—	Proof	20.00
	1974	3.000	—	.15	.25	.75
	1975	3.000	—	.15	.25	.75
	1977	45.600	—	.15	.25	.50
	1978	22.600	—	.15	.25	.50

President Arap Moi

18	1980	—		.15	.25	1.00
	1984	—		.15	.25	1.25
	1986	—		.15	.25	1.25
	1987	—		.15	.25	1.25
	1989	—		.15	.25	1.00
	1990	—		.15	.25	1.00
	1991	—		.15	.25	.75

BRASS PLATED STEEL

| 18a | 1994 | — | | .20 | .30 | 1.00 |

COPPER PLATED STEEL
Obv: Denomination and arms.
Rev: Bust of President Arap Moi.

| 31 | 1995 | — | | .10 | .20 | .40 |

25 CENTS

COPPER-NICKEL
President Jomo Kenyatta

KM#	Date	Mintage	Fine	VF	XF	Unc
3	1966	4.000	.30	1.00	2.00	3.50
	1966	27 pcs.	—	Proof		75.00
	1967	4.000	.30	1.00	2.00	3.50

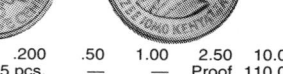

12	1969	.200	.50	—	2.50	10.00
	1969	15 pcs.	—	—	Proof	110.00
	1973	500 pcs.	—	—	Proof	18.00

50 CENTS

COPPER-NICKEL
President Jomo Kenyatta

4	1966	4.000	.20	.40	1.00	2.75
	1966	27 pcs.	—	—	Proof	75.00
	1967	5.120	.20	.40	.85	2.25
	1968	6.000	.20	.40	.85	2.00

13	1969	.400	.40	.80	1.50	3.00
	1969	15 pcs.	—	—	Proof	110.00
	1971	9.600	—	.20	.40	.75
	1973	3.360	.20	.40	.80	1.75
	1973	500 pcs.	—	—	Proof	18.00
	1974	12.640	—	.20	.40	.75
	1975	8.000	—	.20	.40	.75
	1977	16.000	—	.20	.40	.75
	1978	20.480	—	.20	.40	.75

President Arap Moi

19	1980	—	—	.15	.25	.75
	1989	—	—	.15	.25	.75
	1990	—	—	.15	.25	.75

NICKEL PLATED STEEL

19a	1994	—	—	.25	.35	1.00

BRASS PLATED STEEL

28	1995	—	—	.15	.25	.50

SHILLING

COPPER-NICKEL
President Jomo Kenyatta

5	1966	20.000	.25	.50	1.00	3.00
	1966	27 pcs.	—	—	Proof	75.00
	1967	4.000	.25	.50	1.00	2.50
	1968	8.000	.20	.40	.80	2.00

KM#	Date	Mintage	Fine	VF	XF	Unc
14	1969	4.000	.15	.30	.75	1.75
	1969	15 pcs.	—	—	Proof	110.00
	1971	24.000	.10	.30	.65	1.50
	1973	2.480	.20	.40	.80	2.50
	1973	500 pcs.	—	—	Proof	20.00
	1974	13.520	.10	.30	.65	1.50
	1975	40.856	.10	.30	.65	1.50
	1978	20.000	.10	.30	.65	1.50

President Arap Moi

20	1980	—	.15	.25	.50	1.00
	1989	—	.15	.25	.50	1.00

NICKEL PLATED STEEL

20a	1994	—	—	.25	.35	.65	1.50

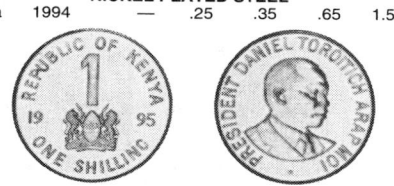

BRASS PLATED STEEL

29	1995	—	.10	.20	.40	.70
	1997	—	.10	.20	.40	.70

2 SHILLINGS

COPPER-NICKEL
President Jomo Kenyatta

6	1966	3.000	1.00	2.00	3.00	6.00
	1966	27 pcs.	—	—	Proof	95.00
	1968	1.100	1.00	2.75	4.50	9.00

15	1969	.100	2.00	4.00	8.00	12.50
	1969	15 pcs.	—	—	Proof	120.00
	1971	1.920	.60	1.25	3.50	7.50
	1973	500 pcs.	—	—	Proof	25.00

5 SHILLINGS

BRASS
10th Anniversary of Independence

KM#	Date	Mintage	Fine	VF	XF	Unc
16	1973	.100	4.50	10.00	17.50	30.00
	1973	1,500	—	—	Proof	45.00

COPPER-NICKEL
President Arap Moi

23	1985	—	.35	.75	1.50	3.00

NICKEL PLATED STEEL

23a	1994	—	.50	1.00	2.25	4.50

BRASS center in COPPER-NICKEL ring
President Arap Moi

30	1995	—	—	—	—	2.25

10 SHILLINGS

COPPER-NICKEL center, BRASS ring

27	1994	—	—	—	—	2.75
	1995	—	—	—	—	2.75

KIRIBATI

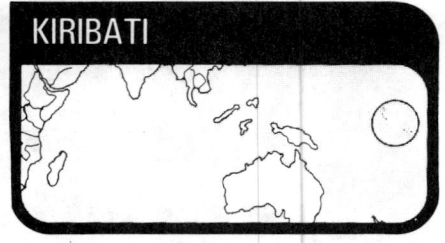

The Republic of Kiribati (formerly the Gilbert Islands), 30 coral atolls and islands spread over more than 1,000,000 sq. mi. (2,590,000 sq. km.) of the southwest Pacific Ocean, has an area of 332 sq. mi. (717 sq. km.) and a population of 64,200. Capital: Bairiki, on Tarawa. In addition to the Gilbert Islands proper, Kiribati includes Ocean Island, the Central and Southern Line Islands, and the Phoenix Islands, though possession of Canton and Enderbury of the Phoenix Islands is disputed with the United States. Most families engage in subsistence fishing. Copra and phosphates are exported, mostly to Australia and New Zealand.

The Gilbert Islands and the group formerly called the Ellice Islands (now Tuvalu) comprised a single British crown colony, the Gilbert and Ellice Islands.

The Islands were first sighted by Spanish mutineers in 1537. Succeeding visits were made by the English navigators John Byron (1764), James Cook (1777), and Thomas Gilbert and John Marshall (1788). An American, Edward Fanning, arrived in 1798. Britain declared a protectorate over the Gilbert and Ellice Islands, and in 1915 began the formation of a colony which was completed with the addition of the Phoenix Islands in 1937. The Central and Southern Line Islands were administratively attached to the Gilbert and Ellice Islands colony in 1972, and remained attached to the Gilberts when Tuvalu was created in 1975. The colony became self-governing in 1971. Kiribati attained independence on July 12, 1979.

RULERS

British, until 1979

MONETARY SYSTEM

100 Cents = 1 Dollar

CENT

BRONZE
Frigate Bird

KM#	Date	Mintage	VF	XF	Unc
1	1979	.090	—	.15	.45
	1979	.010	—	Proof	1.00
	1992	—	—	.15	.45

2 CENTS

BRONZE
B'abai Plant

2	1979	.025	—	.15	.35
	1979	.010	—	Proof	1.25
	1992	—	—	.15	.35

5 CENTS

COPPER-NICKEL
Tokai Lizard

3	1979	.020	.15	.30	1.50
	1979	.010	—	Proof	2.50

10 CENTS

COPPER-NICKEL
Bread Fruit

KM#	Date	Mintage	VF	XF	Unc
4	1979	.020	.15	.25	1.25
	1979	.010	—	Proof	3.00

20 CENTS

COPPER-NICKEL
Dolphins

5	1979	.020	.35	1.00	3.50
	1979	.010	—	Proof	5.00

50 CENTS

COPPER-NICKEL
Panda Nut

6	1979	.020	.50	.85	2.75
	1979	.010	—	Proof	6.00

DOLLAR

COPPER-NICKEL
Outrigger Sailboat

7	1979	.020	.85	1.25	4.00
	1979	.010	—	Proof	8.00

2 DOLLARS

NICKEL-BRASS
10th Anniversary of Independence

14	1989	—	—	—	5.00

KOREA

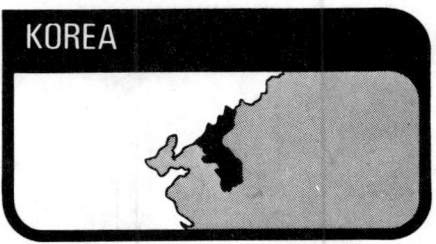

Korea, 'Land of the Morning Calm', occupies a mountainous peninsula in northeast Asia bounded by Manchuria, the Yellow Sea and the Sea of Japan.

According to legend, the first Korean dynasty, that of the House of Tangun, ruled from 2333 B.C. to 1122 B.C. It was followed by the dynasty of Kija, a Chinese scholar, which continued until 193 B.C. and brought a high civilization to Korea. The first recorded period in the history of Korea, the period of the Three Kingdoms, lasted from 57 B.C. to 935 A.D. and achieved the first political unification of the peninsula. The Kingdom of Koryo, from which Korea derived its name, was founded in 935 and continued until 1392, when it was superseded by the Yi Dynasty of King Yi. Sung Kye was to last until the Japanese annexation in 1910.

At the end of the 16th century Korea was invaded and occupied for 7 years by Japan, and from 1627 until the late 19th century it was a semi-independent tributary of China. Japan replaced China as the predominant foreign influence at the end of the Sino-Japanese War (1894-95), only to find her position threatened by Russian influence from 1896 to 1904. The Russian threat was eliminated by the Russo-Japanese War (1904-05) and in 1905 Japan established a direct protectorate over Korea. On Aug. 22, 1910, the last Korean ruler signed the treaty that annexed Korea to Japan as a government generalcy in the Japanese Empire. Japanese suzerainty was maintained until the end of World War II.

From 1633 to 1891 the monetary system of Korea employed cast coins with a square center hole. Fifty-two agencies were authorized to procure these coins from a lesser number of coin foundries. They exist in thousands of varieties. Seed, or mother coins, were used to make the impressions in the molds in which the regular cash coins were cast. Czarist-Russian Korea experimented with Korean coins when Alexiev of Russia, Korea's Financial Advisor, founded the First Asian Branch of the Russo-Korean Bank on March 1, 1898, and authorized the issuing of a set of new Korean coins with a crowned Russian-style quasi-eagle. British-Japanese opposition and the Russo-Japanese War operated to end the Russian coinage experiment in 1904.

RULERS

Yi Hyong (Kojong), 1864-1897
  as Emperor Kwang Mu, 1897-1907
    Japanese Puppet
Yung Hi (Sunjong), 1907-1910

KINGDOM
MONETARY SYSTEM
1892-1902

100 Fun = 1 Yang
5 Yang = 1 Whan

5 FUN

COPPER, 17.20 g

KM#	Year	Date	Fine	VF	XF	Unc
	Kuang Mu					
1116	6	(1902)	4.00	7.50	17.50	100.00

NOTE: Earlier dates (Yr.2-3) exist for this type.

1/4 YANG

COPPER-NICKEL
Obv: Dragon crowded by small tight circle, 11.25mm.

	Kuang Mu					
1117	5	(1901)	115.00	250.00	500.00	1000.

NOTE: Earlier dates (Yr.1-4) exist for this type.

MONETARY REFORM
RULERS

Kuang Mu, Years 5-11 (1901-1907AD)
Yung Hi, Years 1-4 (1907-1910AD)
MONETARY SYSTEM
100 Chon = 1 Won

RUSSIAN DOMINATION
1896-1904
CHON

BRONZE, 6.80 g

KM#	Year	Mintage	Fine	VF	XF	Unc
	Kuang Mu					
1121	6(1902)	3.001	1000.	2000.	4250.	6000.

5 CHON

COPPER-NICKEL, 4.30 g

	Kuang Mu					
1122	6(1902)	2.800	1150.	1650.	2500.	5000.

1/2 WON

13.5000 g, .800 SILVER, .3473 oz ASW

	Kuang Mu					
1123	5(1901)	1.831	2000.	5000.	7500.	12,000.

NOTE: Ponterio & Assoc. Witte Museum sale 8-89 choice BU realized $12,500.

JAPANESE PROTECTION
1905-1910
1/2 CHON

BRONZE, 3.56 g

	Kuang Mu					
1124	10(1906)					
		24.000	2.75	7.00	12.50	90.00
		2.10 g				
1145	11(1907)	*.800	—	—	Rare	—

2.10 g

	Yung Hi					
1136	1(1907)	*I.A.	85.00	200.00	400.00	750.00
	2(1908)	21.000	5.00	12.00	22.50	140.00
	3(1909)	8.200	5.00	12.00	22.50	140.00
	4(1910)	5.070	85.00	200.00	400.00	750.00

*NOTE: Mintage for year 1 is included in the mintage for year 11 of KM#1124.

CHON

BRONZE, 7.13 g

KM#	Year	Mintage	Fine	VF	XF	Unc
	Kuang Mu					
1125	9(1905)	11.800	9.00	15.00	30.00	100.00
	10(1906)	I.A.	6.50	12.00	25.00	100.00

4.20 g

1132	11(1907)					
		11.200	3.50	7.50	15.00	80.00

	Yung Hi					
1137	1(1907)	I.A.	4.50	12.00	27.50	100.00
	2(1908)	6.800	3.00	7.00	13.00	80.00
	3(1909)	9.200	3.00	7.00	13.00	80.00
	4(1910)	3.500	4.00	11.00	23.00	90.00

5 CHON

COPPER-NICKEL, 4.50 g

	Kuang Mu					
1126	9(1905)	20.000	7.00	14.00	24.00	80.00
	11(1907)					
		160.0000	9.00	17.00	27.00	90.00
	Yung Hi					
1138	3(1909)	—	900.00	1750.	3000.	4000.

10 CHON

2.7000 g, .800 SILVER, .0695 oz ASW, 17.5mm, 1.5mm thick

	Kuang Mu					
1127	10(1906)	2.000	15.00	25.00	50.00	100.00

2.25 g, 1.0mm thick

1133	11(1907)	2.400	12.00	20.00	40.00	100.00

2.2500 g, .800 SILVER, .0578 oz ASW

	Yung Hi					
1139	2(1908)	6.300	12.00	20.00	35.00	75.00
	3(1909)	—	—	—	Rare	—
	4(1910)	9.500	10.00	18.00	32.00	65.00

20 CHON

5.3900 g, .800 SILVER, .1386 oz ASW, 22.5mm

KM#	Year	Mintage	Fine	VF	XF	Unc
	Kuang Mu					
1128	9(1905)	1.000	30.00	70.00	120.00	225.00
	10(1906)	2.500	25.00	50.00	100.00	150.00

4.0500 g, .800 SILVER, .1042 oz ASW

1134	11(1907)	1.500	16.50	30.00	55.00	110.00

4.5000 g, .800 SILVER, .1157 oz ASW

	Yung Hi					
1140	2(1908)	3.000	16.50	30.00	55.00	110.00
	3(1909)	2.000	16.50	30.00	55.00	110.00
	4(1910)	2.000	16.50	30.00	55.00	110.00

1/2 WON

13.4800 g, .800 SILVER, .3467 oz ASW

	Kuang Mu					
1129	9(1905)	.600	55.00	100.00	185.00	375.00
	10(1906)	1.200	60.00	110.00	175.00	350.00

10.1300 g, .800 SILVER, .2606 oz ASW

1135	11(1907)	1.000	60.00	110.00	200.00	350.00

	Yung Hi					
1141	2(1908)	1.400	70.00	135.00	210.00	400.00

The Democratic Peoples Republic of Korea, situated in northeastern Asia on the northern half of the Korean peninsula between the Peoples Republic of China and the Republic of Korea, has an area of 46,540 sq. mi. (120,540 sq. km.) and a population of 20 million. Capital: Pyongyang. The economy is based on heavy industry and agriculture. Metals, minerals and farm produce are exported.

Japan replaced China as the predominant foreign influence in Korea in 1895 and annexed the peninsular country in 1910. Defeat in World War II brought an end to Japanese rule. U.S. troops entered Korea from the south and Soviet forces entered from the north. The Cairo conference (1943) had established that Korea should be 'free and independent'. The Potsdam conference (1945) set the 38th parallel as the line dividing the occupation forces of the United States and Russia. When Russia refused to permit a U.N. commission designated to supervise reunification elections to enter North Korea, an election was held in South Korea which established the Republic of Korea on Aug. 15, 1948. North Korea held an unsupervised election on Aug. 25, 1948, and on Sept. 9, 1948, proclaimed the establishment of the Democratic Peoples Republic of Korea.

NOTE: For earlier coinage see Korea.

MONETARY SYSTEM
100 Chon = 1 Won

CIRCULATION RESTRICTIONS
W/o star: KM#1-4 - General circulation
1 star: KM#5-8 - Issued to visitors from Communist countries.
2 stars: KM#9-12 - Issued to visitors from hard currency countries.

CHON

ALUMINUM

KM#	Date	Mintage	Fine	VF	XF	Unc
1	1959	—	.15	.25	.50	1.00
	1970	—	.20	.35	.75	1.50

Rev: Stars in field.

| 5 | 1959 | — | | | .50 | 1.00 |

Rev: Star left of 1.

| 9 | 1959 | — | | | .50 | 1.00 |

5 CHON

ALUMINUM

| 2 | 1959 | — | .50 | .75 | 1.00 | 2.00 |
| | 1974 | — | .25 | .50 | 1.00 | 2.00 |

Rev: Stars in field.

| 6 | 1974 | — | | | 1.00 | 2.00 |

Rev: Star left of 5.

KM#	Date	Mintage	Fine	VF	XF	Unc
10	1974	—			1.00	2.00

10 CHON

ALUMINUM

| 3 | 1959 | — | | .50 | .75 | 1.00 | 2.00 |

Rev: Stars in field.

| 7 | 1959 | — | | | 1.00 | 2.00 |

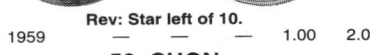

Rev: Star left of 10.

| 11 | 1959 | — | | | 1.00 | 2.00 |

50 CHON

ALUMINUM

| 4 | 1978 | — | .75 | 1.00 | 1.75 | 3.00 |

Rev: Stars in field.

| 8 | 1978 | — | | | 1.75 | 3.00 |

Rev: Star behind rider.

| 12 | 1978 | — | | | 1.75 | 3.00 |

WON

COPPER-NICKEL
Kim Il Sung's Birth Place

| 13 | 1987 | — | | | — | 4.00 |
| | 1987 | — | | | Proof | 5.00 |

Kim Il Sung's Arch of Triumph

KM#	Date	Mintage	Fine	VF	XF	Unc
14	1987	—			—	4.00
	1987	—			Proof	5.00

Kim Il Sung's Tower of Juche

| 15 | 1987 | — | | | — | 4.00 |
| | 1987 | — | | | Proof | 5.00 |

ALUMINUM

| 18 | 1987 | — | | | — | 3.50 |

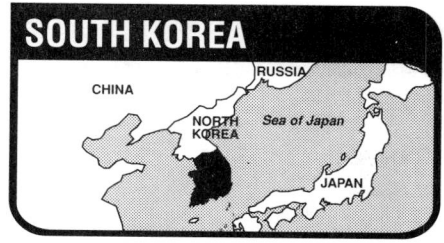

SOUTH KOREA

The Republic of Korea, situated in northeastern Asia on the southern half of the Korean peninsula between North Korea and the Korean Strait, has an area of 38,025 sq. mi. (98,480 sq. km.) and a population of 42.5 million. Capital: Seoul. The economy is based on agriculture and light and medium industry. Some of the world's largest oil tankers are built here. Automobiles, plywood, electronics, and textile products are exported.

Japan replaced China as the predominant foreign influence in Korea in 1895 and annexed the peninsular country in 1910. Defeat in World War II brought an end to Japanese rule. U.S. troops entered Korea from the south and Soviet forces entered from the north. The Cairo conference (1943) had established that Korea should be 'free and independent'. The Potsdam conference (1945) set the 38th parallel as the line dividing the occupation forces of the United States and Russia. When Russia refused to permit a U.N. commission designated to supervise reunification elections to enter North Korea, an election was held in South Korea on May 10, 1948. By its determination, the Republic of Korea was inaugurated on Aug. 15, 1948.

NOTE: For earlier coinage see Korea.

MINT MARKS
(a) - Paris, privy marks only

MONETARY SYSTEM
100 Chon = 1 Hwan

10 HWAN

BRONZE
Rose of Sharon

KM#	Date	Mintage	Fine	VF	XF	Unc
1	4292 (1959)					
		100.000	1.00	2.00	6.00	11.50
	4294 (1961)					
		100.000	.20	.35	.75	3.00

50 HWAN

NICKEL-BRASS
Iron Clad Turtle Boat

2	4292 (1959)					
		24.640	.30	.50	1.00	3.00
	4294 (1961)					
		20.000	.30	.50	1.00	2.50

100 HWAN

COPPER-NICKEL
Rhee Syngman

3	4292 (1959)					
		49.640	1.25	1.75	2.75	6.00

NOTE: Quantities of KM#1-3 dated 4292 in uncirculated condition were countermarked 'SAMPLE' in Korean for distribution to government and banking agencies. KM#3 was withdrawn from circulation June 10, 1962 and melted; KM#1 and KM#2 continued to circulate as 1 Won and 5 Won coins for 13 years respectively until demonetized and withdrawn from circulation March 22, 1975.

MONETARY REFORM

10 Hwan = 1 Won

Prior to the following issue, the Bank of Korea, on its authority, created a number of patterns in 1, 5 and 10 Won denominations, for example with the Kyongju Observatory design.

WON
BRASS
Rose of Sharon

KM#	Date	Mintage	Fine	VF	XF	Unc
4	1966	7.000	.20	.40	1.00	9.00
	1967	48.500	—	.15	.25	1.25

ALUMINUM

4a	1968	66.500	—	.10	.20	.85
	1969	85.000	—	—	—	.25
	1970	45.000	—	—	—	.25
	1974	12.000	—	.15	.25	1.75
	1975	10.000	—	.10	.20	.50
	1976	20.000	—	—	—	.30
	1977	30.000	—	—	—	.30
	1978	30.000	—	—	—	.15
	1979	30.000	—	—	—	.15
	1980	20.000	—	—	—	.15
	1981	20.000	—	—	—	.15
	1982	30.000	—	—	—	.15
	1982	2,000	—	—	Proof	—

31	1983	40.000	—	—	—	.15
	1984	20.000	—	—	—	.15
	1985	10.000	—	—	—	.15
	1987	10.000	—	—	—	.15
	1988	6.500	—	—	—	.15
	1989	10.000	—	—	—	.15
	1990	6.000	—	—	—	.15
	1991	5.000	—	—	—	.15
	1995	.015	—	—	—	.15
	1996	.015	—	—	—	.15
	1997	.015	—	—	—	.15

5 WON

BRONZE
Iron Clad Turtle Boat

5	1966	4.500	.15	.25	1.50	20.00
	1967	18.000	.15	.25	1.00	16.50
	1968	20.000	.15	.25	1.00	16.50
	1969	25.000	—	.10	.25	3.25
	1970	50.000	—	.10	.25	3.00

BRASS

5a	1970	Inc. Ab.	—	—	.10	1.25
	1971	64.038	—	—	—	.10
	1972	60.084	—	—	—	.10
	1977	1.000	—	—	.10	.85
	1978	1.000	—	—	.10	.85
	1979	1.000	—	—	.10	.75
	1980	.200	—	.25	.50	3.00
	1981	.200	—	.25	.50	1.75
	1982	.200	—	.25	.50	1.75
	1982	2,000	—	—	Proof	—

32	1983	6.000	—	—	.10	.25
	1987	1.000	—	—	.10	.25
	1988	.500	—	—	.10	.25
	1989	.500	—	—	.10	.25
	1990	.600	—	—	.10	.25
	1991	.500	—	—	.10	.25
	1995	.015	—	—	.10	.25
	1996	.015	—	—	.10	.25
	1997	.015	—	—	.10	.25

10 WON

BRONZE
Pagoda at Pul Guk Temple

KM#	Date	Mintage	Fine	VF	XF	Unc
6	1966	10.600	.15	.25	1.50	22.50
	1967	22.500	.15	.25	1.50	22.50
	1968	35.000	.15	.25	1.50	17.50
	1969	46.500	.15	.25	1.50	17.50
	1970	157.000	.15	.25	1.50	15.00

BRASS

6a	1970	Inc. Ab.	—	.35	1.25	12.50
	1971	220.000	—	—	.15	1.75
	1972	270.000	—	—	.15	1.75
	1973	30.000	—	.10	.35	5.25
	1974	15.000	—	.10	.35	5.25
	1975	20.000	—	.10	.50	10.00
	1977	1.000	—	.10	.35	3.50
	1978	80.000	—	.10	.15	1.25
	1979	200.000	—	—	.10	.55
	1980	150.000	—	—	.10	.55
	1981	.100	—	.25	.75	5.00
	1982	20.000	—	—	.10	.60
	1982	2,000	—	—	Proof	—

33.1	1983	25.000	—	—	.10	.35
(33)	1985	35.000	—	—	.10	.35
	1986	195.000	—	—	.10	.35
	1987	155.000	—	—	.10	.35
	1988	189.000	—	—	.10	.35
	1989	310.000	—	—	.10	.35
	1990	395.000	—	—	.10	.35
	1991	300.000	—	—	.10	.35
	1992	150.000	—	—	.10	.35
	1993	110.000	—	—	.10	.35
	1994	300.000	—	—	.10	.35
	1995	380.000	—	—	.10	.35
	1996	290.000	—	—	.10	.35
	1997	177.000	—	—	.10	.35

Rev: Wider numbers in denomination.

33.2	1997	—	—	—	—	.35

50 WON

COPPER-NICKEL
F.A.O. Issue

20	1972	6.000	.20	.40	1.00	14.50
	1973	40.000	—	.15	.25	3.50
	1974	25.000	—	.15	.25	1.50
	1977	1.000	—	.15	.25	2.00
	1978	1.500	—	.15	.25	1.40
	1979	20.000	—	.10	.20	1.25
	1980	10.000	—	.10	.20	1.25
	1981	25.000	—	.10	.20	1.25
	1982	40.000	—	.10	.20	.75
	1982	2,000	—	—	Proof	—

F.A.O. Issue

34	1983	50.000	—	—	.10	.45
	1984	40.000	—	—	.10	.45

KM#	Date	Mintage	Fine	VF	XF	Unc
34	1985	4.000	—	—	.10	.45
	1987	32.000	—	—	.10	.45
	1988	53.000	—	—	.10	.45
	1989	70.000	—	—	.10	.45
	1990	85.000	—	—	.10	.35
	1991	80.000	—	—	.10	.35
	1992	50.000	—	—	.10	.35
	1993	5.000	—	—	.10	.35
	1994	102.000	—	—	.10	.35
	1995	98.000	—	—	.10	.35
	1996	52.000	—	—	.10	.35
	1997	129.000	—	—	.10	.35

100 WON

COPPER-NICKEL

9	1970	1.500	.50	.75	1.50	17.50
	1971	13.000	.15	.25	.50	12.50
	1972	20.000	—	.20	.40	10.00
	1973*	80.000	—	.15	.30	2.00
	1974*	50.000	—	.15	.35	4.50
	1975	75.000	—	.15	.35	5.00
	1977	30.000	—	.15	.35	2.25
	1978	40.000	—	.15	.25	1.50
	1979	130.000	—	.15	.25	1.50
	1980	60.000	—	.15	.25	1.50
	1981	.100	—	.25	.50	4.00
	1982	50.000	—	.15	.25	1.25
	1982	2,000	—	—	Proof	—

*NOTE: Die varieties exist.

30th Anniversary of Liberation - Yu Kwan Soon

21	ND(1975)	4.998	.20	.50	.75	2.25
	ND(1975)	2,000	—	—	Proof	125.00

1st Anniversary of the 5th Republic

24	1981	4.980	.20	.35	.65	2.00
	1981 unfrosted	.018	—	—	Proof	30.00
	1981	2,000	—	—	Proof	175.00

Admiral Lee Soon-shin

35.1 (35)	1983	8.000	—	.15	.25	.60

Rev: Modified design.

35.2 (35)	1984	40.000	—	.15	.25	.60
	1985	16.000	—	.15	.30	1.25
	1986	131.000	—	.15	.25	.60
	1987	170.000	—	.15	.25	.60
	1988	298.000	—	.15	.25	.60
	1989	250.000	—	.15	.25	.60
	1990	185.000	—	.15	.25	.60
	1991	400.000	—	.15	.25	.60
	1992	425.000	—	.15	.25	.60
	1993	185.000	—	.15	.25	.60
	1994	401.000	—	.15	.25	.60
	1995	228.000	—	.15	.25	.60
	1996	447.000	—	.15	.25	.60
	1997	147.000	—	.15	.25	.60

500 WON

COPPER-NICKEL
Manchurian Crane

KM#	Date	Mintage	Fine	VF	XF	Unc
27	1982	15.000	—	—	1.00	3.75
	1982	2,000	—	—	Proof	—
	1983	64.000	—	—	1.00	2.50
	1984	70.000	—	—	1.00	2.50
	1987	1.000	—	—	1.00	2.50
	1988	27.000	—	—	1.00	2.50
	1989	25.000	—	—	1.00	2.50
	1990	60.000	—	—	1.00	2.50
	1991	90.000	—	—	1.00	2.00
	1992	105.000	—	—	1.00	2.00
	1993	32.000	—	—	1.00	2.00
	1994	50.600	—	—	1.00	2.00
	1995	87.000	—	—	1.00	2.00
	1996	122.000	—	—	1.00	2.00
	1997	62.000	—	—	1.00	2.00

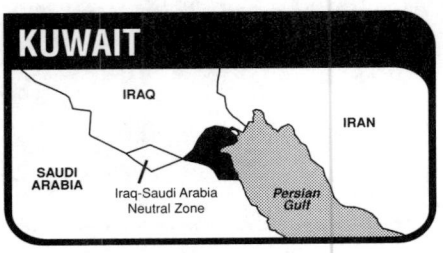

KUWAIT

The State of Kuwait, a constitutional monarchy located on the Arabian Peninsula at the northwestern corner of the Persian Gulf, has an area of 6,880 sq. mi. (17,820 sq. km.) and a population of 1.7 million. Capital: Kuwait. Petroleum, the basis of the economy, provides 95 per cent of the exports.

The modern history of Kuwait began with the founding of the city of Kuwait, 1740, by tribesmen who wandered northward from the region of the Qatar Peninsula of eastern Arabia. Fearing that the Turks would take over the sheikhdom, Sheikh Mubarak entered into an agreement with Great Britain, 1899, placing Kuwait under the protection of Britain and empowering Britain to conduct its foreign affairs. Britain terminated the protectorate on June 19, 1961, giving Kuwait its independence (by a simple exchange of notes) but agreeing to furnish military aid on request.

Kuwait was invaded and occupied by an army from neighboring Iraq Aug. 2, 1990. Soon thereafter Iraq declared that the country would become a province of Iraq. An international coalition of military forces primarily based in Saudi Arabia led by the United States under terms set by the United Nations, attacked Iraqi military installations to liberate Kuwait. This occurred Jan. 17 1991. Kuwait City was liberated Feb. 27, and a cease-fire was declared Feb. 28. New paper currency was introduced March 24, 1991 to replace earlier notes.

TITLES

الكويت

al-Kuwait

RULERS
British Protectorate, until 1961
LOCAL
Al Sabah Dynasty

Mubarak Ibn Sabah,
 1896-1915
Jabir Ibn Mubarak,
 1915-1917
Salim Ibn Mubarak,
 1917-1921
Ahmad Ibn Jabir,
 1921-1950
Abdullah Ibn Salim,
 1950-1965
Sabah Ibn Salim,
 1965-1977
Jabir Ibn Ahmad,
 1977-

MONETARY SYSTEM
1000 Fils = 1 Dinar

FILS

NICKEL-BRASS

KM#	Date	Year	Mintage	VF	XF	Unc
2	AH1380	1961	2.000	.50	1.00	1.50
	1380	1961	60 pcs.	—	Proof	30.00

9	AH1382	1962	.500	.10	.15	.35
	1382	1962	60 pcs.	—	Proof	30.00
	1384	1964	.600	.25	.75	1.50
	1385	1966	.500	.25	.75	1.50
	1386	1967	1.875	.25	.75	1.50
	1389	1970	.375	.35	1.00	2.50
	1390	1971	.500	.25	.75	1.50
	1391	1971	.500	.25	.75	1.50
	1392	1972	.500	.25	.75	1.50
	1393	1973	.375	.35	1.00	2.50
	1395	1975	.500	.25	.75	1.50
	1396	1976	2.500	.15	.25	.50
	1397	1977	2.500	.15	.25	.50
	1399	1979	1.500	.15	.25	.50
	1400	1980	—	.15	.25	.50

KM#	Date	Year	Mintage	VF	XF	Unc
9	1403	1983	—	.15	.25	.50
	1407	1987	—	.15	.25	.50
	1408	1988	.500	.15	.25	.50

5 FILS

NICKEL-BRASS

KM#	Date	Year	Mintage	VF	XF	Unc
3	AH1380	1961	2.400	.60	1.25	2.00
	1380	1961	60 pcs.	—	Proof	35.00

KM#	Date	Year	Mintage	VF	XF	Unc
10	AH1382	1962	1.800	.10	.20	.45
	1382	1962	60 pcs.	—	Proof	35.00
	1384	1964	.600	.30	.75	2.00
	1386	1967	1.600	.20	.35	1.00
	1388	1968	.800	.30	.75	2.25
	1389	1969	—	.30	.75	2.25
	1389	1970	.600	.30	.75	2.25
	1390	1971	.600	.30	.75	2.25
	1391	1971	.600	.30	.75	2.25
	1392	1972	.800	.25	.65	1.75
	1393	1973	.800	.25	.65	1.75
	1394	1974	1.200	.10	.20	1.00
	1395	1975	5.020	.10	.20	.50
	1396	1976	.180	.35	1.00	3.00
	1397	1977	4.000	.10	.20	.40
	1399	1979	6.700	.10	.20	.40
	1400	1980	—	.10	.20	.40
	1401	1981	7.000	.10	.20	.40
	1403	1983	—	.10	.20	.40
	1405	1985	—	.10	.20	.40
	1407	1987	—	.10	.20	.40
	1408	1988	3.000	.10	.20	.40
	1410	1990	—	.10	.20	.40
	1415	1995	—	.10	.20	.40

NOTE: Varieties exist.

10 FILS

NICKEL-BRASS

KM#	Date	Year	Mintage	VF	XF	Unc
4	AH1380	1961	2.600	.65	1.25	2.00
	1380	1961	60 pcs.	—	Proof	40.00

KM#	Date	Year	Mintage	VF	XF	Unc
11	AH1382	1962	1.360	.15	.25	.65
	1382	1962	60 pcs.	—	Proof	40.00
	1384	1964	.800	.35	.85	2.50
	1386	1967	1.360	.30	.75	1.75
	1388	1968	.672	.35	.85	2.50
	1389	1969	.480	.50	1.00	2.75
	1389	1970	.640	.35	.85	2.50
	1390	1971	.480	.50	1.00	2.75
	1391	1971	.800	.35	.85	2.50
	1392	1972	1.120	.15	.40	2.00
	1393	1973	1.440	.15	.40	2.00
	1394	1974	1.280	.15	.40	2.00
	1395	1975	5.280	.15	.25	.75
	1396	1976	2.400	.15	.25	.75
	1397	1977	—	.15	.25	.75
	1399	1979	6.160	.15	.25	.75
	1400	1980	—	.15	.25	.75
	1401	1981	8.320	.15	.25	.75
	1403	1983	—	.15	.25	.75
	1405	1985	—	.15	.25	.75
	1407	1987	—	.15	.25	.75
	1408	1988	5.000	.15	.25	.75
	1410	1990	—	.15	.25	.75

NOTE: Varieties exist.

20 FILS

COPPER-NICKEL

KM#	Date	Year	Mintage	VF	XF	Unc
5	AH1380	1961	2.000	.75	1.50	2.50
	1380	1961	60 pcs.	—	Proof	45.00

KM#	Date	Year	Mintage	VF	XF	Unc
12	AH1382	1962	1.200	.25	.35	.75
	1382	1962	60 pcs.	—	Proof	45.00
	1384	1964	.480	.50	1.00	3.00
	1386	1967	1.280	.35	.85	2.00
	1388	1968	.672	.35	.85	2.50
	1389	1969	.800	.35	.85	2.50
	1389	1970	.480	.50	1.00	3.00
	1390	1971	.480	.50	1.00	3.00
	1391	1971	.960	.35	.85	2.00
	1392	1972	1.440	.20	.45	2.00
	1393	1973	1.280	.20	.45	2.00
	1394	1974	1.600	.20	.45	1.50
	1395	1975	2.400	.20	.30	1.25
	1396	1976	3.200	.20	.30	1.25
	1397	1977	3.400	.20	.30	1.25
	1399	1979	5.520	.20	.30	1.25
	1400	1980	—	.20	.30	1.00
	1401	1981	8.960	.20	.30	1.00
	1403	1983	—	.20	.30	1.00
	1405	1985	—	.20	.30	1.00
	1407	1987	—	.20	.30	1.00
	1408	1988	5.000	.20	.30	1.00
	1410	1990	—	.20	.30	1.00
	1415	1995	—	.20	.30	1.00

NOTE: Varieties exist.

50 FILS

COPPER-NICKEL

KM#	Date	Year	Mintage	VF	XF	Unc
6	AH1380	1961	1.720	.85	1.75	2.75
	1380	1961	60 pcs.	—	Proof	60.00

KM#	Date	Year	Mintage	VF	XF	Unc
13	AH1382	1962	.900	.50	.75	1.25
	1382	1962	60 pcs.	—	Proof	60.00
	1384	1964	.300	.75	1.50	4.00
	1386	1967	.800	.40	.85	2.50
	1388	1968	.200	1.00	2.00	6.00
	1389	1969	.400	.50	1.00	3.00
	1389	1970	.500	.50	1.00	3.00
	1390	1971	.300	.75	1.50	4.00
	1391	1971	.500	.50	1.00	3.00
	1392	1972	.900	.50	.85	2.50
	1393	1973	.800	.50	.85	2.50
	1394	1974	1.000	.35	.50	2.00
	1395	1975	1.950	.35	.50	2.00
	1396	1976	2.250	.25	.35	2.00
	1397	1977	6.000	.25	.35	1.35
	1399	1979	6.050	.25	.35	1.35
	1400	1980	—	.25	.35	1.35
	1401	1981	3.000	.25	.35	1.35
	1403	1983	—	.25	.35	1.35
	1405	1985	—	.25	.35	1.35
	1407	1987	2.000	.25	.35	1.35
	1408	1988	3.000	.25	.35	1.35
	1410	1990	—	.25	.35	1.35
	1413	1993	—	.25	.35	1.35
	1415	1995	—	.25	.35	1.35

NOTE: Varieties exist.

100 FILS

COPPER-NICKEL

KM#	Date	Year	Mintage	VF	XF	Unc
7	AH1380	1961	1.260	1.00	2.00	3.25
	1380	1961	60 pcs.	—	Proof	90.00

KM#	Date	Year	Mintage	VF	XF	Unc
14	AH1382	1962	.640	.50	.65	1.50
	1382	1962	60 pcs.	—	Proof	90.00
	1384	1964	.160	1.75	3.00	6.00
	1386	1967	.640	1.00	1.50	3.00
	1388	1968	.160	1.75	3.00	6.00
	1389	1969	.320	1.00	2.00	4.00
	1391	1971	.240	1.25	2.00	4.00
	1392	1972	.400	1.00	1.50	3.00
	1393	1973	.480	1.00	1.50	3.00
	1394	1974	.480	1.00	1.50	3.00
	1395	1975	3.040	.50	.75	1.75
	1396	1976	—	.50	.75	1.75
	1397	1977	1.600	.50	.75	1.75
	1399	1979	3.040	.50	.75	1.75
	1400	1980	—	.50	.75	1.75
	1401	1981	2.960	.50	.75	1.75
	1403	1983	—	.50	.75	1.75
	1405	1985	—	.50	.75	1.75
	1407	1987	2.000	.50	.75	1.75
	1408	1988	2.000	.50	.75	1.75
	1410	1990	—	.50	.75	1.75

NOTE: Varieties exist.

LAOS

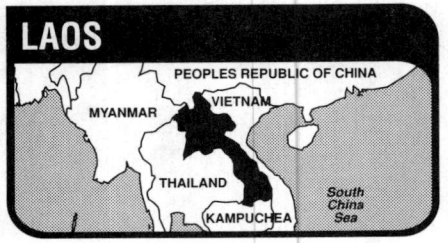

The Lao Peoples Democratic Republic, located on the Indo-Chinese Peninsula between the Socialist Republic of Vietnam and the Kingdom of Thailand, has an area of 91,429 sq. mi. (236,800 km.) and a population of 3.6 million. Capital Vientiane. Agriculture employs 95 per cent of the people. Tin, lumber and coffee are exported.

The first United Kingdom of Lan Xang (Million Elephants) was established in the mid-14th century by King Fa Ngum who ruled an area including present Laos, northeastern Thailand, and the southern part of China's Yunnan province from his capital at Luang Prabang. Thailand and Vietnam obtained control over much of the present Lao territory in the 18th century and remained dominant until France established a protectorate over the area in 1893 and incorporated it into the Union of Indo-China. The Independence of Laos was proclaimed in March of 1945, during the last days of the Japanese occupation of World War II. France reoccupied Laos in 1946, and established it as a constitutional monarchy within the French Union in 1949. In 1953 war erupted between the government and the Pathet Lao, a Communist movement supported by the Vietnamese Communist forces. Peace was declared in 1954 with Laos becoming fully independent in 1955 and the Pathet Lao being permitted to occupy two northern provinces. Civil war broke out again in 1960 with the United States supporting the government of the Kingdom of Laos and the North Vietnamese helping the Communist Pathet Lao, and continued, with intervals of truce and political compromise, until the formation of the Lao Peoples Democratic Republic on Dec. 2, 1975.

NOTE: For earlier coinage see French Indo-China.

RULERS
Sisavang Vong, 1904-1959
Savang Vatthana, 1959-1975

MONETARY SYSTEM
100 Cents = 1 Piastre
Commencing 1955
100 Att = 1 Kip

MINT MARKS
(a) - Paris, privy marks only
Key - Havana
None - Berlin

NOTE: Private bullion issues previously listed here are now listed in *Unusual World Coins,* 3rd Edition, Krause Publications, Inc., 1992.

KINGDOM
1893-1975
10 CENTS

ALUMINUM

KM#	Date	Mintage	Fine	VF	XF	Unc
4	1952(a)	2.000	—	.25	.60	1.25

20 CENTS

ALUMINUM

5	1952(a)	3.000	—	.35	.75	1.50

50 CENTS

ALUMINUM

KM#	Date	Mintage	Fine	VF	XF	Unc
6	1952(a)	1.400	—	.75	1.25	2.50

PEOPLES DEMOCRATIC REPUBLIC
1975-

MINT MARKS
None - Leningrad (50 Kip)

MONETARY SYSTEM
100 Att = 1 Kip

10 ATT

ALUMINUM

22	1980	—	—	.20	.40	.85

20 ATT

ALUMINUM

23	1980	—	—	.20	.40	.85

50 ATT

ALUMINUM

24	1980	—	—	.45	.90	1.50

KIP

COPPER-NICKEL
10th Anniversary of Peoples Democratic Republic

37	1985	—	—	.50	1.00	2.00

5 KIP

COPPER-NICKEL
10th Anniversary of Peoples Democratic Republic

38	1985	—	—	.75	1.50	3.00

10 KIP

COPPER-NICKEL
10th Anniversary of Peoples Democratic Republic

KM#	Date	Mintage	Fine	VF	XF	Unc
39	1985	—	—	1.25	2.50	5.00

LATVIA

The Republic of Latvia, the central Baltic state in east Europe, has an area of 24,595 sq. mi. (43,601 sq. km.) and a population of *2.6 million. Capital: Riga. Livestock raising and manufacturing are the chief industries. Butter, bacon, fertilizers and telephone equipment are exported.

The Latvians, of Aryan descent, were nomadic tribesmen who settled along the Baltic prior to the 13th century. Lacking a central government, they were easily conquered by the German Teutonic Knights, Russia, Sweden and Poland. Following the third partition of Poland by Austria, Prussia and Russia in 1795, Latvia came under Russian domination and did not experience autonomy until the Russian Revolution of 1917 provided an opportunity for freedom. The Latvian Republic was established on Nov. 18, 1918. The republic was occupied by Soviet troops and annexed to the Soviet Union in 1940. Following the German occupation of 1941-44, it was retaken by Russia and reestablished as a member republic of the Soviet Union. Western countries, including the United States, did not recognize Latvia's incorporation into the Soviet Union.

The coinage issued during the early 20th Century Republic is now obsolete.

Latvia declared their independence from the USSR on August 22, 1991.

REPUBLIC COINAGE

MONETARY SYSTEM
100 Santimu = 1 Lats

SANTIMS

BRONZE

KM#	Date	Mintage	Fine	VF	XF	Unc
1	1922	5.000	.65	1.40	2.75	8.00
	1923	10 pcs.	—	—	—	1500.
	1924	4.990	.65	1.40	2.75	8.00
	1926	5.000	.65	1.40	2.75	8.00
	1928 designer's name below ribbon					
		5.000	.65	1.40	2.75	8.00
	1928 w/o designer's name below ribbon					
		Inc. Ab.	2.00	5.00	10.00	32.50
	1932	5.000	.65	1.40	2.75	8.00
	1932	—	—	—	Proof	—
	1935	5.000	.65	1.40	2.75	8.00

10	1937	2.700	.65	1.40	2.75	8.00
	1938	1.900	.65	1.40	2.75	10.00
	1939	*3.400	.50	1.00	2.00	3.00

*NOTE: Most were never placed into circulation.

2 SANTIMI

BRONZE

2	1922 designer's name below ribbon					
		10.000	1.00	2.00	5.00	10.00
	1922 w/o designer's name					
		Inc. Ab.	5.00	10.00	17.50	35.00
	1923	2 pcs.	—	—	—	2000.
	1926	5.000	.75	1.50	4.00	9.00
	1928	5.000	.75	1.50	4.00	9.00
	1932	5.000	.75	1.50	4.00	9.00
	1932	—	—	—	—	Proof	—

19mm

KM#	Date	Mintage	Fine	VF	XF	Unc
11.1	1937	.045	10.00	20.00	30.00	60.00

19.5mm

11.2	1939	*5.000	1.00	2.50	4.00	9.00

*NOTE: Most were never placed into circulation.

5 SANTIMI

BRONZE

3	1922 designer's name below ribbon					
		15.000	.50	1.00	3.00	8.00
	1922 w/o designer's name					
		Inc. Ab.	3.00	6.00	10.00	20.00
	1923	2 pcs.	—	—	—	2250.

10 SANTIMU

NICKEL

4	1922	15.000	.50	1.00	3.00	6.00

20 SANTIMU

NICKEL

5	1922	15.000	.50	1.00	3.00	8.00

50 SANTIMU

NICKEL

6	1922	9.000	1.00	3.00	5.00	10.00

LATS

5.0000 g, .835 SILVER, .1342 oz ASW

7	1923	—	—	—	900.00	—
	1924	10.000	2.00	3.50	7.00	25.00

---

2 LATI

10.0000 g, .835 SILVER, .2684 oz ASW

KM#	Date	Mintage	Fine	VF	XF	Unc
8	1925	6.386	2.50	3.00	6.00	30.00
	1926	1.114	2.50	3.50	7.00	32.50

5 LATI

25.0000 g, .835 SILVER, .6712 oz ASW

9	1929	1.000	9.00	12.00	20.00	42.50
	1929	—	—	—	Proof	—
	1931	2.000	8.00	11.50	18.00	37.50
	1931	—	—	—	Proof	—
	1932	.600	9.00	12.00	20.00	42.50
	1932	—	—	—	Proof	—

NEW REPUBLIC

1991-

SANTIMS

COPPER PLATED IRON

15	1992	—	—	—	—	.25

2 SANTIMI

BRONZE PLATED STEEL

21	1992	—	—	—	—	.50

5 SANTIMI

BRASS

16	1992	—	—	—	—	.75

10 SANTIMU

BRASS

17	1992	—	—	—	—	1.25

20 SANTIMU

BRASS

22	1992	—	—	—	—	1.50

50 SANTIMU

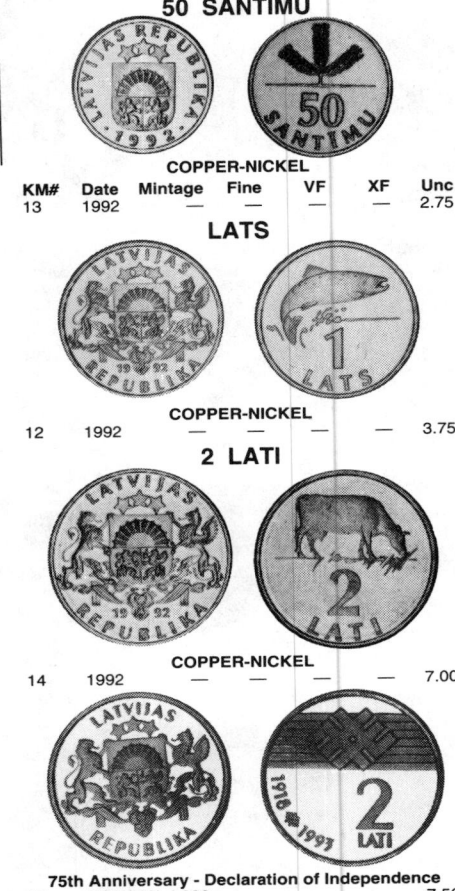

COPPER-NICKEL

KM#	Date	Mintage	Fine	VF	XF	Unc
13	1992	—	—	—	—	2.75

LATS

COPPER-NICKEL

| 12 | 1992 | — | — | — | — | 3.75 |

2 LATI

COPPER-NICKEL

| 14 | 1992 | — | — | — | — | 7.00 |

75th Anniversary - Declaration of Independence

| 18 | ND(1993) | 4.000 | — | — | — | 7.50 |
| | ND(1993) *.200 | — | — | Proof | 11.50 |

LEBANON

The Republic of Lebanon, situated on the eastern shore of the Mediterranean Sea between Syria and Israel, has an area of 4,015 sq. mi. (10,400 sq. km.) and a population of 3.5 million. Capital: Beirut. The economy is based on agriculture, trade and tourism. Fruit, other foodstuffs and textiles are exported.

Almost at the beginning of recorded history, Lebanon appeared as the well-wooded hinterland of the Phoenicians who exploited its famous forests of cedar. The mountains were a Christian refuge and a Crusader stronghold. Lebanon, the history of which is essentially the same as that of Syria, came under control of the Ottoman Turks early in the 16th century. Following the collapse of the Ottoman Empire after World War I, Lebanon, along with Syria, became a French mandate. The French drew a border around the predominantly Christian Lebanon Sanjak or administrative subdivision and on Sept. 1, 1920 proclaimed the area the State of Grand Lebanon (Etat du Grand Liban) a republic under French control. France announced the independence of Lebanon on Nov. 26, 1941, but the last British and French troops didn't leave until the end of August 1946.

TITLES

الجمهورية اللبنانية

al-Jomhuriya(t) al-Lubnaniya(t)

MINT MARKS

(a) - Paris, privy marks only
(u) - Utrecht, privy marks only

MONETARY SYSTEM

100 Piastres = 1 Livre (Pound)

FRENCH PROTECTORATE

1/2 PIASTRE

COPPER-NICKEL

KM#	Date	Mintage	Fine	VF	XF	Unc
9	1934(a)	.200	2.00	5.00	12.50	40.00
	1936(a)	1.200	1.25	3.00	7.50	25.00

ZINC

| 9a | 1941(a) | 1.000 | .50 | 1.00 | 4.00 | 10.00 |

PIASTRE

COPPER-NICKEL

3	1925(a)	1.500	.50	2.00	7.50	25.00
	1931(a)	.300	1.00	4.00	12.50	45.00
	1933(a)	.500	1.00	4.00	10.00	45.00
	1936(a)	2.200	.50	1.00	6.50	20.00

ZINC

| 3a | 1940(a) | 2.000 | .50 | .75 | 4.00 | 10.00 |

2 PIASTRES

ALUMINUM-BRONZE

KM#	Date	Mintage	Fine	VF	XF	Unc
1	1924(a)	1.800	1.25	3.00	12.50	50.00

| 4 | 1925(a) | 1.000 | 3.00 | 8.00 | 20.00 | 75.00 |

2-1/2 PIASTRES

ALUMINUM-BRONZE

| 10 | 1940(a) | 1.000 | 1.00 | 2.00 | 3.50 | 12.00 |

5 PIASTRES

ALUMINUM-BRONZE

| 2 | 1924(a) | 1.000 | 1.25 | 3.00 | 10.00 | 45.00 |

Rev: Both privy marks to left of '5'.

| 5.1 | 1925(a) | 1.500 | .75 | 1.50 | 8.00 | 30.00 |

Rev: Privy marks to left and right of 5 Piastres.

5.2	1925(a) Inc. Ab.	1.00	2.00	7.50	30.00
	1931(a)	.400	1.50	4.00	12.50	40.00
	1933(a)	.500	1.50	4.00	12.50	40.00
	1936(a)	.900	1.00	2.00	7.50	25.00
	1940(a)	1.000	.75	1.50	5.00	15.00

10 PIASTRES

2.0000 g, .680 SILVER, .0437 oz ASW

| 6 | 1929 | .880 | 3.00 | 7.00 | 25.00 | 70.00 |

25 PIASTRES

5.0000 g, .680 SILVER, .1093 oz ASW

7	1929	.600	3.00	7.00	25.00	75.00
	1933(a)	.200	4.50	15.00	40.00	125.00
	1936(a)	.400	3.50	10.00	27.50	85.00

50 PIASTRES

10.0000 g, .680 SILVER, .2186 oz ASW

KM#	Date	Mintage	Fine	VF	XF	Unc
8	1929	.500	5.00	10.00	40.00	125.00
	1933(a)	.100	7.00	20.00	65.00	185.00
	1936(a)	.100	7.00	17.50	50.00	150.00

WORLD WAR II COINAGE

1/2 PIASTRE

BRASS

11	ND	—	1.00	2.50	5.00	12.00

NOTE: Three varieties known. Usually crudely struck, off center, etc. Perfectly struck, centered unc. specimens command a considerable premium. Size of letters also vary.

PIASTRE

BRASS

12	ND	—	1.00	3.00	7.50	16.50

NOTE: Two varieties known. Usually crudely struck, off center, etc. Perfectly struck, centered unc. specimens command a considerable premium.

ALUMINUM

12a	ND	—	—	—	—	—

2-1/2 PIASTRES

ALUMINUM

13	ND	—	1.50	3.50	8.00	17.50

NOTE: Seven varieties known. Usually crudely struck, off center, etc. Perfectly struck, centered unc. specimens command a considerable premium.

ALUMINUM-BRONZE

13a	ND	—	—	650.00	850.00	—

5 PIASTRES

ALUMINUM

A14	ND	—	—	—	2000.	3000.

NOTE: Did not enter circulation in significant numbers.

REPUBLIC

PIASTRE

ALUMINUM-BRONZE

19	1955(a)	4.000	—	.10	.20	.35

2-1/2 PIASTRES

ALUMINUM-BRONZE

KM#	Date	Mintage	Fine	VF	XF	Unc
20	1955(a)	5.000	—	.10	.25	.50

5 PIASTRES

ALUMINUM

14	1952(a)	3.600	.50	1.00	1.50	4.00

18	1954	4.440	.10	.30	.50	1.25

ALUMINUM-BRONZE

21	1955(a)	3.000	.10	.20	.30	.50
	1961(a)	—	.10	.15	.20	.40

NICKEL-BRASS

25.1	1968	2.000	—	.10	.15	.20
	1969	4.000	—	.10	.15	.20
	1970	—	—	.10	.15	.25

25.2	1972(a)	12.000	—	—	.10	.15
	1975(a)	—	—	—	.10	.15
	1980	—	—	—	.10	.15

10 PIASTRES

ALUMINUM

15	1952(a)	3.600	.50	1.00	5.00	15.00

ALUMINUM-BRONZE

22	1955	2.175	.20	.40	.60	1.00

KM#	Date	Mintage	Fine	VF	XF	Unc
23	1955(a)	6.000	.10	.25	.50	.75

COPPER-NICKEL

24	1961	7.000	—	.10	.25	.50
	1961	—	—	—	Proof	—

NICKEL-BRASS

26	1968(a)	2.000	—	.10	.15	.25
	1969(a)	5.000	—	—	.10	.20
	1970(a)	8.000	—	—	.10	.20
	1972(a)	12.000	—	—	.10	.20
	1975(a)	—	—	—	.10	.20

25 PIASTRES

ALUMINUM-BRONZE

16.1	1952(u)	7.200	.10	.40	.60	1.00

Different style of inscription and larger date.

16.2	1961(u)	5.000	.10	.40	.50	.75

NICKEL-BRASS

27.1	1968	1.500	.10	.15	.25	.50
	1969	2.500	.10	.15	.20	.40
	1970	—	.10	.15	.20	.40
	1972	8.000	.10	.15	.20	.30
	1975	—	.10	.15	.20	.30

Rev: Different, wider, bold 25.

27.2	1980	—	.10	.15	.20	.30

50 PIASTRES

4.9710 g, .600 SILVER, .0959 oz ASW

17	1952(u)	7.200	BV	1.00	1.50	3.50

NICKEL

28.1	1968	2.000	.20	.40	.60	1.00
	1969	3.488	.10	.25	.40	.75

KM#	Date	Mintage	Fine	VF	XF	Unc
28.1	1970	2.000	.10	.25	.40	.50
	1971	2.000	.10	.25	.40	.50
	1975	—	.10	.25	.40	.50
	1978	22.400	.10	.25	.40	.50

Rev: Different 50.

28.2	1980	—	.10	.25	.40	.50

LIVRE

NICKEL
F.A.O. Issue

29	1968	.300	.25	.50	1.00	3.00

30	1975	—	.20	.40	.60	1.00
	1975	—	—	—	Proof	—
	1977	8.000	.20	.40	.60	1.00
	1980	12.000	.20	.40	.60	1.00
	1981	—	.20	.40	.60	1.00
	1986	—	.20	.40	.60	1.00

NOTE: Varieties exist.

50 LIVRES

STAINLESS STEEL
Obv: Arabic legend and denomination.
Rev: French legend and denomination.

37	1996	—	—	—	.45	1.00

100 LIVRES

COPPER-ZINC
Obv: Arabic legend and denomination.
Rev: French legend and denomination.

38	1995	—	—	—	.50	1.25
	1996	—	—	—	.50	1.25

250 LIVRES

BRASS
Obv: Arabic legend and denomination.
Rev: French legend and denomination.

36	1995	—	—	—	.65	1.75
	1996	—	—	—	.65	1.75

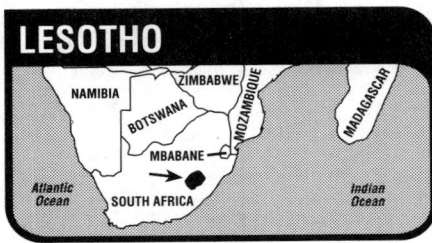

LESOTHO

The Kingdom of Lesotho, a constitutional monarchy located within the east-central part of the Republic of South Africa, has an area of 11,720 sq. mi. (30,350 sq. km.) and a population of 1.5 million. Capital: Maseru. The economy is based on subsistence agriculture and livestock raising. Wool, mohair, and cattle are exported.

Lesotho (formerly Basutoland) was sparsely populated until the end of the 16th century. Between the 16th and 19th centuries an influx of refugees from tribal wars led to the development of a distinct Basotho group. During the reign of tribal chief Moshesh I (1823-70), a series of wars with the Orange Free State resulted in the loss of large areas of territory to South Africa. Moshesh appealed to the British for help, and Basutoland was constituted a native state under British protection. In 1871 it was annexed to Cape Colony, but was restored to direct control by the Crown in 1884. From 1884 to 1959 legislative and executive authority was vested in a British High Commissioner. The constitution of 1959 recognized the expressed wish of the people for independence, which was attained on Oct. 4, 1966.

Lesotho is a member of the Commonwealth of Nations. King Latsie III is Head of State.

RULERS
Moshoeshoe II, 1966-1990
Letsie III, 1990-1995
Moshoeshoe II, 1995-

MONETARY SYSTEM
100 Licente/Lisente = 1 Maloti/Loti

SENTE

NICKEL-BRASS
Traditional House

KM#	Date	Mintage	VF	XF	Unc
16	1979	4.500	—	.15	.40
	1979	.010	—	Proof	.65
	1980	—	—	.15	.40
	1980	.010	—	Proof	.65
	1981	2,500	—	Proof	.65
	1983	—	—	.15	.40
	1985	—	—	.15	.40
	1989	—	—	.15	.40

BRASS

54	1992	—	—	.15	.75

2 LISENTE

NICKEL-BRASS
Steer

17	1979	3.000	—	.20	.50
	1979	.010	—	Proof	1.00
	1980	—	—	.20	.50
	1980	.010	—	Proof	1.00
	1981	2,500	—	Proof	2.00
	1985	—	—	.20	.50
	1989	—	—	.20	.50

BRASS

55	1992	—	—	.20	1.00

---

5 LICENTE/LISENTE

NICKEL-BRASS
Aloe Plant

KM#	Date	Mintage	VF	XF	Unc
18	1979	2.700	—	.25	.60
	1979	.010	—	Proof	1.25
	1980	—	—	.25	.60
	1980	.010	—	Proof	1.25
	1981	2,500	—	Proof	2.50
	1989	—	—	.25	.60

BRASS

56	1994	—	—	.25	.75

10 LICENTE/LISENTE

COPPER-NICKEL
Angora Goat

19	1979	2.000	.15	.30	.75
	1979	.010	—	Proof	1.75
	1980	—	.15	.30	.75
	1980	.010	—	Proof	1.75
	1981	2,500	—	Proof	3.00
	1983	—	.15	.30	.75
	1989	—	.15	.30	.75

Obv: National arms.
Rev: Angora goat.

61	1992	—	—	—	.75

25 LISENTE

COPPER-NICKEL
Woman in Native Costume Weaving Baskets

20	1979	1.200	.10	.20	1.00
	1979	.010	—	Proof	2.00
	1980	—	.10	.20	1.00
	1980	.010	—	Proof	2.00
	1981	2,500	—	Proof	3.50
	1985	—	.10	.20	1.00
	1989	—	.10	.20	1.00

50 LICENTE/LISENTE

28.1000 g, .900 SILVER, .8131 oz ASW
Independence Attained
Rev: Small 900/1000 at right of date.

KM#	Date	Mintage	VF	XF	Unc
4.1	1966	—	—	—	10.00
	1966	—	—	Proof	17.50

Rev: Large 900/1000 at right of date.

4.2	1966	—	—	—	10.00
	1966	5,000	—	Proof	17.50

Rev: Mint mark and fineness below date.

4.3	1966	—	—	—	10.00
	1966	—	—	Proof	17.50

COPPER-NICKEL
Horse and Rider

21	1979	.480	.35	.50	1.25
	1979	.010	—	Proof	2.50
	1980	—	.35	.50	1.25
	1980	.010	—	Proof	2.50
	1981	2,500	—	Proof	4.00
	1983	—	.35	.50	1.25
	1989	—	.35	.50	1.25

LOTI

COPPER-NICKEL

22	1979	1.275	.65	1.25	3.00
	1979	.010	—	Proof	5.00
	1980	—	.75	1.50	4.00
	1980	.010	—	Proof	5.00
	1981	2,500	—	Proof	7.00
	1989	—	.75	1.50	4.00

50th Anniversary - UN

60	1995	—	—	—	8.00

2 MALOTI

NICKEL CLAD STEEL
Obv: National arms. Rev: Maize plants.

58	1996				2.50

5 MALOTI

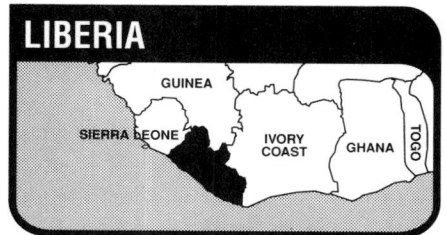

NICKEL CLAD STEEL
Obv: National arms. Rev: 5 wheat ears.

KM#	Date	Mintage	VF	XF	Unc
59	1996	—	—	—	5.50

LIBERIA

The Republic of Liberia, located on the southern side of the west African bulge between Sierra Leone and Ivory Coast, has an area of 43,000 sq. mi. (111,370 sq. km) and a population of 2.2 million. Capital: Monrovia. The major industries are agriculture, mining and lumbering. Iron ore, diamonds, rubber, coffee and coca are exported.

The Liberian coast was explored and charted by Portuguese navigator Pedro de Cintra in 1461. For the following three centuries Portuguese traders visited the area regularly to trade for gold, slaves and pepper. The modern country of Liberia, Africa's first republic, was settled in 1822 by the American Colonization Society as a homeland for American freed slaves, with the U.S. government furnishing funds and assisting in negotiations for procurement of land from the native chiefs. The various settlements united in 1839 to form the Commonwealth of Liberia, and in 1847 established the country as a republic with a constitution modeled after that of the United States.

U.S. money was declared legal tender in Liberia in 1943, replacing British West African currency.

Most of the Liberian pattern series, particularly of the 1888-90 period are acknowledged to have been 'unofficial' privately sponsored issues, but they are without exception avidly collected by most collectors of Liberian coins. The 'K' number designations on these pieces refer to a listing of Liberian patterns compiled and published by Ernst Kraus.

MINT MARKS

B - Bern, Switzerland
H - Heaton, Birmingham
(l) - London
(s) - San Francisco, U.S.
FM - Franklin Mint, U.S.A.*
PM - Pobjoy Mint

*NOTE: From 1975-1985 the Franklin Mint produced coinage in up to 3 different qualities. Qualities of issue are designated in ( ) after each date and are defined as follows:

(M) MATTE - Normal circulation strike or a dull finish produced by sandblasting special uncirculated (polish finish) or proof quality dies.

(U) SPECIAL UNCIRCULATED - Polished or prooflike in appearance without any frosted features.

(P) PROOF - The highest quality obtainable having mirror-like fields and frosted features.

MONETARY SYSTEM
100 Cents = 1 Dollar

1/2 CENT

BRASS

KM#	Date	Mintage	Fine	VF	XF	Unc
10	1937	1.000	.10	.25	.40	.85

COPPER-NICKEL

10a	1941	.250	.15	.35	.50	1.00

CENT

BRONZE

5	1906H	.180	4.50	10.00	22.00	50.00
	1906H	—	—	—	Proof	135.00

NOTE: Earlier date (1896) exists for this type.

BRASS

KM#	Date	Mintage	Fine	VF	XF	Unc
11	1937	1.000	.20	.50	1.50	6.00

COPPER-NICKEL

11a	1941	.250	.50	2.50	7.50	40.00

BRONZE

KM#	Date	Mintage	Fine	VF	XF	Unc
13	1960	.500	—	—	.10	.35
	1961	7.000	—	—	.10	.35
	1968(l)	3.000	—	—	.10	.35
	1968(s)	.014	—	—	Proof	1.00
	1969	5,056	—	—	Proof	1.00
	1970	3,464	—	—	Proof	1.00
	1971	3,032	—	—	Proof	1.00
	1972(d)	10.000	—	—	.10	.35
	1972(s)	4,866	—	—	Proof	1.00
	1973	.011	—	—	Proof	1.00
	1974	9,362	—	—	Proof	1.00
	1975	5.000	—	—	.10	.35
	1975	4,056	—	—	Proof	1.00
	1976	2,131	—	—	Proof	1.00
	1977	2.500	—	—	.10	.35
	1977	920 pcs.	—	—	Proof	1.00
	1978FM	7,311	—	—	Proof	1.00
	1983FM	2.500	—	—	.10	.35
	1984	2.500	—	—	.10	.35

Edge inscription: O.A.U. July 1979.

13a	1979FM	1,857	—	—	Proof	1.00

2 CENTS

BRONZE

6	1906H	.108	5.00	12.00	30.00	75.00
	1906H	—	—	—	Proof	165.00

NOTE: Earlier date (1896) exists for this type.

BRASS

12	1937	1.000	.15	.35	1.00	6.00

COPPER-NICKEL

12a	1941	.810	.10	.25	.50	2.50
	1978FM	7,311	—	—	Proof	2.00

Edge inscription: O.A.U. July 1979.

12b	1979FM	1,857	—	—	Proof	2.00

5 CENTS

COPPER-NICKEL

14	1960	1.000	—	.10	.15	.50
	1961	3.200	—	.10	.15	.50
	1968	.015	—	—	Proof	.75
	1969	5,056	—	—	Proof	.75
	1970	3,464	—	—	Proof	1.25
	1971	3,032	—	—	Proof	1.25
	1972(d)	3.000	—	.10	.15	.35
	1972(s)	4,866	—	—	Proof	.75
	1973	.011	—	—	Proof	.75

KM#	Date	Mintage	Fine	VF	XF	Unc
14	1974	9,362	—	—	Proof	.75
	1975	3.000	—	.10	.15	.35
	1975	4,056	—	—	Proof	.75
	1976	2,131	—	—	Proof	.75
	1977	—	—	.10	.15	.50
	1977	920 pcs.	—	—	Proof	.75
	1978FM	7,311	—	—	Proof	.75
	1983FM	1.000	—	.10	.15	.35
	1984	1.000	—	.10	.15	.35

Edge inscription: O.A.U. July 1979.

14a	1979FM	1,857	—	—	Proof	2.00

10 CENTS

2.3200 g, .925 SILVER, .0690 oz ASW

7	1906H	.035	5.00	12.50	32.50	100.00
	1906H	—	—	—	Proof	250.00

NOTE: Earlier date (1896) exists for this type.

2.0700 g, .900 SILVER, .0599 oz ASW

15	1960	1.000	BV	.75	1.25	3.00
	1961	1.200	BV	.75	1.25	3.00

COPPER-NICKEL, 2.10 g

15a.1	1966	2.000	—	.15	.25	.50

1.80 g

15a.2	1968	.014	—	—	Proof	1.25
	1969	5,056	—	—	Proof	1.25
	1970(d)	2.500	—	.15	.25	.50
	1970(s)	3,464	—	—	Proof	1.50
	1971	3,032	—	—	Proof	1.50
	1972	4,866	—	—	Proof	1.25
	1973	.011	—	—	Proof	1.00
	1974	9,362	—	—	Proof	1.00
	1975	4,500	—	.15	.20	.35
	1975	4,056	—	—	Proof	1.00
	1976	2,131	—	—	Proof	1.00
	1977	—	—	.15	.25	.75
	1977	920 pcs.	—	—	Proof	1.00
	1978FM	7,311	—	—	Proof	1.00
	1983FM	.500	—	.15	.25	.75
	1984FM	.500	—	.15	.25	.75
	1987	10.000	—	.15	.25	.75

Edge inscription: O.A.U. July 1979.

15b	1979FM	1,857	—	—	Proof	2.00

25 CENTS

5.8000 g, .925 SILVER, .1725 oz ASW

8	1906H	.034	6.00	12.50	35.00	120.00
	1906H	—	—	—	Proof	275.00

NOTE: Earlier date (1896) exists for this type.

5.1800 g, .900 SILVER, .1499 oz ASW

16	1960	.900	BV	1.50	2.00	4.50
	1961	1.200	BV	1.50	2.00	4.50

COPPER-NICKEL, 5.20 g

16a.1	1966	.800	—	.25	.65	1.25

4.80 g

16a.2	1968(d)	1.600	—	.25	.50	1.00
	1968(s)	.014	—	—	Proof	1.50
	1969	5,056	—	—	Proof	1.50
	1970	3,464	—	—	Proof	1.75
	1971	3,032	—	—	Proof	1.75
	1972	4,866	—	—	Proof	1.50
	1973	2.000	—	.25	.50	1.00
	1973	.011	—	—	Proof	1.25
	1974	9,362	—	—	Proof	1.00
	1975	1.600	—	.25	.50	1.00
	1975	4,056	—	—	Proof	1.25

NOTE: 1 and 1.5mm rim varieties exist.

Rev: Larger letters, higher inscription.

KM#	Date	Mintage	Fine	VF	XF	Unc
16a.3	1968	2.400				
		(restrike)	—	.25	.50	1.00

NOTE: Struck in 1988.

F.A.O. Issue

30	1976	.800	—	.25	.75	1.75
	1976	2,131	—	—	Proof	3.50
	1977	920 pcs.	—	—	Proof	3.50
	1978FM	7,311	—	—	Proof	2.25

Edge inscription: O.A.U. July 1979.

30a	1979FM	1,857	—	—	Proof	3.50

50 CENTS

11.6000 g, .925 SILVER, .3450 oz ASW

9	1906H	.024	10.00	20.00	50.00	265.00
	1906H	—	—	—	Proof	425.00

NOTE: Earlier date (1896) exists for this type.

10.3700 g, .900 SILVER, .3001 oz ASW

17	1960	1.100	BV	3.00	4.00	8.00
	1961	.800	BV	3.00	4.00	8.00

COPPER-NICKEL, 10.40 g

17a.1	1966	.200	—	.75	1.00	1.50

COPPER-NICKEL, 8.90 g

17a.2	1968(l)	1.000	—	.60	.80	1.50
	1968(s)	.014	—	—	Proof	1.50
	1969	5,056	—	—	Proof	1.50
	1970	3,464	—	—	Proof	2.50
	1971	3,032	—	—	Proof	2.50
	1972	4,866	—	—	Proof	1.50
	1973	1.000	—	.60	.75	1.25
	1973	.011	—	—	Proof	1.50
	1974	9,362	—	—	Proof	1.50
	1975	.800	—	.60	.75	1.25
	1975	4,056	—	—	Proof	1.50

31	1976	1.000	—	.60	1.00	2.50
	1976	2,131	—	—	Proof	5.00
	1977	920 pcs.	—	—	Proof	5.00
	1978FM	7,311	—	—	Proof	3.50
	1987	1.800	—	.60	1.00	2.50

Edge inscription: O.A.U. July 1979.

31a	1979FM	1,857	—	—	Proof	5.00

DOLLAR

20.7400 g, .900 SILVER, .6001 oz ASW

KM#	Date	Mintage	Fine	VF	XF	Unc
18	1961	.200	BV	5.00	6.50	13.00
	1962	1.000	BV	5.00	6.50	12.00

COPPER-NICKEL, 20.70 g

18a.1	1966	1.000	—	1.00	1.50	2.25

COPPER-NICKEL, 18.00 g

18a.2	1968(l)	1.000	—	1.00	1.50	2.25
	1968(s)	.014	—	—	Proof	2.00
	1969	5,056	—	—	Proof	2.00
	1970(d)	2.000	—	1.00	1.50	3.00
	1970(s)	3,464	—	—	Proof	6.00
	1971	3,032	—	—	Proof	4.50
	1972	4,866	—	—	Proof	4.50
	1973	.011	—	—	Proof	3.00
	1974	9,362	—	—	Proof	3.00
	1975	.400	—	1.25	1.75	3.00
	1975	4,056	—	—	Proof	3.00

32	1976	2.000	—	2.50	4.50	8.00
	1976	2,131	—	—	Proof	10.00
	1977	920 pcs.	—	—	Proof	11.50
	1978FM	7,311	—	—	Proof	12.50
	1987	1.500	—	1.50	3.00	6.00

LIBYA

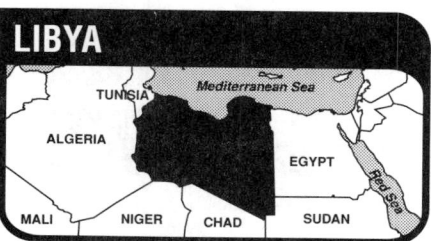

The Socialist People's Libyan Arab Jamahariya, located on the north-central coast of Africa between Tunisia and Egypt, has an area of 679,362 sq. mi. (1,759,540 sq. km.) and a population of 3.9 million. Capital: Tripoli. Crude oil, which accounts for 90 per cent of the export earnings, is the mainstay of the economy.

Libya has been subjected to foreign rule throughout most of its history, various parts of it having been ruled by the Phoenicians, Carthaginians, Vandals, Byzantines, Greeks, Romans, Egyptians, and in the following centuries the Arabs' language, culture and religion were adopted by the indigenous population. Libya was conquered by the Ottoman Turks in 1553, and remained under Turkish domination, becoming a Turkish vilayet in 1835, until it was conquered by Italy and made into a colony in 1911. The name 'Libya', the ancient Greek name for North Africa exclusive of Egypt, was given to the colony by Italy in 1934. Libya came under Allied administration after the fall of Tripoli on Jan. 23, 1943, divided into zones of British and French control. On Dec. 24, 1951, in accordance with a United Nations resolution, Libya proclaimed its independence as a constitutional monarchy, thereby becoming the first country to achieve independence through the United Nations. The monarchy was overthrown by a coup d'etat on Sept. 1, 1969, and Libya was established as a republic.

TITLES

المملكة الليبية

al-Mamlaka(t) al-Libiya(t)

الجمهورية الليبية

al-Jomhuriya(t) al-Arabiya(t) al-Libiya(t)

RULERS

Idris I, 1951-1969

MONETARY SYSTEM

10 Milliemes = 1 Piastre
100 Piastres = 1 Pound

MILLIEME

BRONZE

KM#	Date	Year	Mintage	VF	XF	Unc
1	—	1952	7.750	.10	.15	.50
	—	1952	32 pcs.	—	Proof	75.00

NICKEL-BRASS

6	AH1385	1965	11.000	.10	.15	.25

2 MILLIEMES

BRONZE

2	—	1952	6.650	.10	.25	.75
	—	1952	32 pcs.	—	Proof	75.00

5 MILLIEMES

BRONZE

KM#	Date	Year	Mintage	VF	XF	Unc
3	—	1952	7.680	.15	.35	1.00
	—	1952	32 pcs.	—	Proof	75.00

NICKEL-BRASS

7	AH1385	1965	8.500	.10	.15	.30

PIASTRE

COPPER-NICKEL

4	—	1952	10.200	.35	.60	1.25
	—	1952	32 pcs.	—	Proof	100.00

10 MILLIEMES

COPPER-NICKEL

8	AH1385	1965	17.000	.10	.20	.40

2 PIASTRES

COPPER-NICKEL

5	—	1952	6.075	.35	.75	1.50
	—	1952	32 pcs.	—	Proof	125.00

20 MILLIEMES

COPPER-NICKEL

9	AH1385	1965	8.750	.15	.35	2.00

50 MILLIEMES

COPPER-NICKEL

10	AH1385	1965	8.000	.25	.50	3.00

100 MILLIEMES

COPPER-NICKEL

KM#	Date	Year	Mintage	VF	XF	Unc
11	AH1385	1965	8.000	.50	1.00	3.50

SOCIALIST PEOPLES REPUBLIC

MONETARY SYSTEM
1000 Dirhams = 1 Dinar

1000 Dirhams = 1 Dinar

DIRHAM

BRASS CLAD STEEL

12	AH1395	1975	20.000	.25	.50	2.00

18	AH1399	1979	1.000	2.00	4.00	7.00

5 DIRHAMS

BRASS CLAD STEEL

13	AH1395	1975	23.000	.25	.60	2.50

19	AH1399	1979	2.000	2.00	4.00	7.00

10 DIRHAMS

COPPER-NICKEL CLAD STEEL

14	AH1395	1975	52.750	.25	.65	2.75

20	AH1399	1979	4.000	2.00	4.00	8.00

20 DIRHAMS

COPPER-NICKEL CLAD STEEL

15	AH1395	1975	25.500	.50	1.75	5.00

KM#	Date	Year	Mintage	VF	XF	Unc
21	AH1399	1979	6.000	2.50	5.00	10.00

50 DIRHAMS

COPPER-NICKEL

16	AH1395	1975	25.640	1.00	2.50	7.00

22	AH1399	1979	9.120	3.00	6.00	12.00

100 DIRHAMS

COPPER-NICKEL

17	AH1395	1975	15.433	1.50	3.50	9.00

23	AH1399	1979	15.000	4.00	8.00	16.00

LIECHTENSTEIN

The Principality of Liechtenstein, located in central Europe on the east bank of the Rhine between Austria and Switzerland, has an area of 61 sq. mi. (160 sq. km.) and a population of 27,200. Capital: Vaduz. The economy is based on agriculture and light manufacturing. Canned goods, textiles, ceramics and precision instruments are exported.

The lordships of Schellenburg and Vaduz were merged into the principality of Liechtenstein. It was a member of the Rhine Confederation from 1806 to 1815, and of the German Confederation from 1815 to 1866 when it became independent. Liechtenstein's long and close association with Austria was terminated by World War I. In 1921 it adopted the coinage of Switzerland, and two years later entered into a customs union with the Swiss, who also operated its postal and telegraph systems and represent it in international affairs. The tiny principality abolished its army in 1868 and has avoided involvement in all European wars since that time.

RULERS
Prince John II, 1858-1929
Prince Franz I, 1929-1938
Prince Franz Josef II, 1938-1990
Prince Hans Adam II, 1990-

MONETARY SYSTEM
100 Heller = 1 Krone

KRONE

5.0000 g, .835 SILVER, .1342 oz ASW

Y#	Date	Mintage	Fine	VF	XF	Unc
2	1904	.075	10.00	18.00	28.00	45.00
	1910	.045	10.00	18.00	28.00	45.00
	1915	.075	10.00	18.00	28.00	45.00

NOTE: Earlier date (1900) exists for this type.

2 KRONEN

10.0000 g, .835 SILVER, .2684 oz ASW

3	1912	.050	12.00	20.00	35.00	60.00
	1915	.038	15.00	25.00	40.00	75.00

5 KRONEN

24.0000 g, .900 SILVER, .6944 oz ASW

4	1904	.015	80.00	130.00	165.00	285.00
	1910	.010	80.00	160.00	220.00	320.00
	1915	.010	80.00	160.00	220.00	320.00

NOTE: Earlier date (1900) exists for this type.

MONETARY REFORM
100 Rappen = 1 Frank

1/2 FRANK

2.5000 g, .835 SILVER, .0751 oz ASW

Y#	Date	Mintage	Fine	VF	XF	Unc
7	1924	*.030	65.00	125.00	165.00	225.00

*NOTE: 15,745 pieces were remelted.

FRANK

5.0000 g, .835 SILVER, .1342 oz ASW

8	1924	*.060	25.00	50.00	90.00	175.00

*NOTE: 45,355 pieces were remelted.

2 FRANKEN

10.0000 g, .835 SILVER, .2684 oz ASW

9	1924	*.050	40.00	90.00	150.00	215.00

*NOTE: 41,707 pieces were remelted.

5 FRANKEN

25.0000 g, .900 SILVER, .7234 oz ASW

10	1924	*.015	250.00	350.00	500.00	900.00

*NOTE: 11,260 pieces were remelted.

LITHUANIA

The Republic of Lithuania, southernmost of the Baltic states in east Europe, has an area of 25,174 sq. mi. (65,201 sq. km.) and a population of *3.6 million. Capital: Vilnius. The economy is based on livestock raising and manufacturing. Hogs, cattle, hides and electric motors are exported.

Lithuania emerged as a grand duchy in the 14th century. In the 15th century it was a major power of central Europe, stretching from the Baltic to the Black Sea. It was joined with Poland in 1569. Following the third partition of Poland by Austria, Prussia and Russia, 1795, Lithuania came under Russian domination and did not regain its independence until shortly before the end of World War I when it declared itself a sovereign republic. The republic was occupied by Soviet troops and annexed to the U.S.S.R. in 1940. Following the German occupation of 1941-44, it was retaken by Russia and reestablished as a member republic of the Soviet Union. Western countries, including the United States, did not recognize Lithuania's incorporation into the Soviet Union.

Lithuania declared its independence March 11, 1990 and it was recognized by the United States on Sept. 2, 1991, followed by the Soviet government in Moscow on Sept. 6. They were seated in the UN General Assembly on Sept. 17, 1991.

REPUBLIC COINAGE
MONETARY SYSTEM
100 Centas = 1 Litas

CENTAS

ALUMINUM-BRONZE

KM#	Date	Mintage	Fine	VF	XF	Unc
71	1925	5.000	3.00	6.00	12.00	32.00

BRONZE

79	1936	9.995	2.00	4.00	8.00	26.00

2 CENTAI

BRONZE

80	1936	4.951	4.00	8.00	15.00	40.00

5 CENTAI

ALUMINUM-BRONZE

72	1925	12.000	2.00	4.00	10.00	25.00

BRONZE

81	1936	4.800	2.50	4.50	14.00	40.00

ALUMINUM-BRONZE

KM#	Date	Mintage	Fine	VF	XF	Unc
73	1925	12.000	1.75	3.00	9.00	25.00

20 CENTU

ALUMINUM-BRONZE

74	1925	8.000	2.00	3.00	10.00	35.00

50 CENTU

ALUMINUM-BRONZE

75	1925	5.000	5.00	7.00	20.00	50.00

LITAS

2.7000 g, .500 SILVER, .0434 oz ASW

76	1925	5.985	1.75	3.00	8.00	30.00
	1925	10-12 pcs.	—	—	Proof	650.00

2 LITU

5.4000 g, .500 SILVER, .0868 oz ASW

77	1925	3.000	3.50	5.50	12.00	35.00
	1925	10-12 pcs.	—	—	Proof	650.00

5 LITAI

13.5000 g, .500 SILVER, .2170 oz ASW

78	1925	1.000	4.00	8.00	18.00	55.00
	1925	10-12 pcs.	—	—	Proof	650.00

NOTE: The 1925 Litas, 2 Litu and 5 Litai, KM#76-78 respectively, were each struck as proof record specimens by The Royal Mint. Less than 12 pieces of each type are estimated to exist.

9.0000 g, .750 SILVER, .2170 oz ASW

Dr. Jonas Basanavicius
Edge: TAUTOS GEROVE TAVO GEROVE.
Obv: Designer's initials below bust, lettered edge.

KM#	Date	Mintage	Fine	VF	XF	Unc
82	1936	2.612	3.00	4.50	12.00	20.00

10 LITU

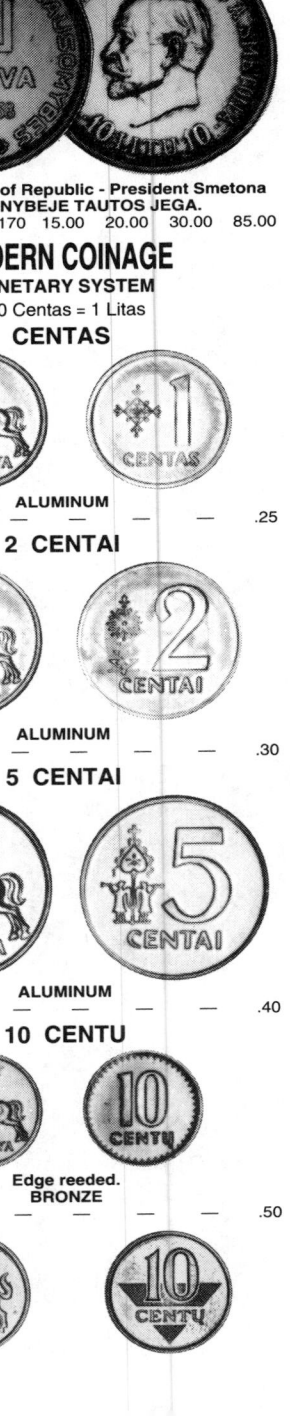

18.0000 g, .750 SILVER, .4340 oz ASW
Grand Duke Vytautas Didysis (Vytautas the Great)
Edge: VIENYBEJE TAUTOS JEGA.

83	1936	.720	7.00	12.50	20.00	55.00

20th Anniversary of Republic - President Smetona
Edge: VIENYBEJE TAUTOS JEGA.

84	ND(1938)	.170	15.00	20.00	30.00	85.00

MODERN COINAGE
MONETARY SYSTEM
100 Centas = 1 Litas

CENTAS

ALUMINUM

85	1991	—	—	—	—	.25

2 CENTAI

ALUMINUM

86	1991	—	—	—	—	.30

5 CENTAI

ALUMINUM

87	1991	—	—	—	—	.40

10 CENTU

Edge reeded.
BRONZE

88	1991	—	—	—	—	.50

BRASS
Obv: Lithuanian knight. Rev: Denomination.

KM#	Date	Mintage	Fine	VF	XF	Unc
106	1997	—	—	—	—	.40

20 CENTU

Edge reeded.
BRONZE

89	1991	—	—	—	—	.70

BRASS
Obv: Lithuanian knight. Rev: Denomination.

107	1997	—	—	—	—	.70

50 CENTU

Edge reeded.
BRONZE

90	1991	—	—	—	—	.85

BRASS
Similar to 20 Centu, KM#107.
Obv: Lithuanian knight. Rev: Denomination.

108	1997	—	—	—	—	.85

LITAS

COPPER-NICKEL

91	1991	—	—	—	—	2.00

75th Anniversary - Central Bank
Obv: Knight and denomination. Rev: Portrait.

109	1997	.200	—	—	—	7.00

2 LITAI

COPPER-NICKEL

92	1991	—	—	—	—	2.75

5 LITAI

COPPER-NICKEL

93	1991	—	—	—	—	4.00

LUXEMBOURG

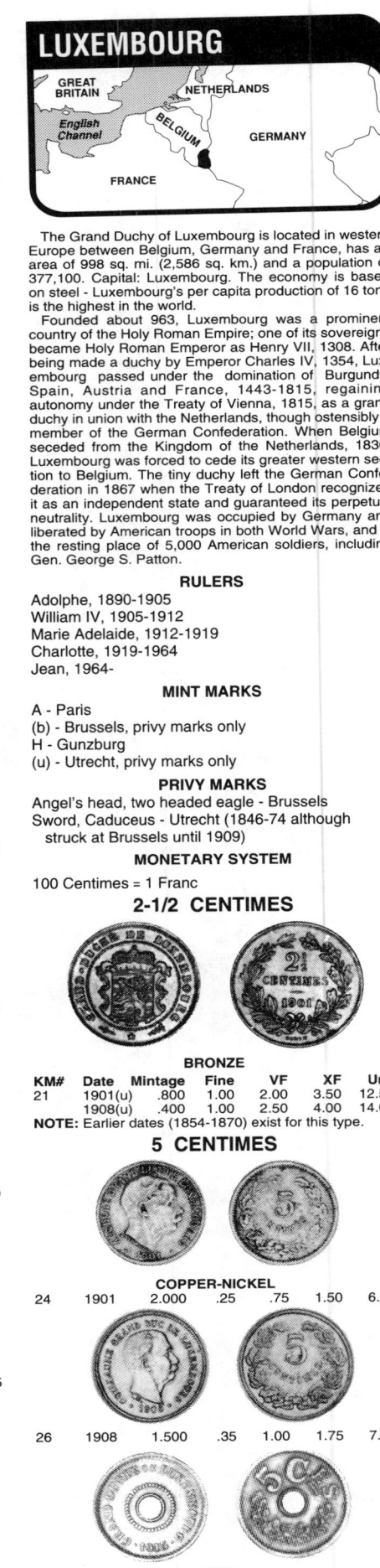

The Grand Duchy of Luxembourg is located in western Europe between Belgium, Germany and France, has an area of 998 sq. mi. (2,586 sq. km.) and a population of 377,100. Capital: Luxembourg. The economy is based on steel - Luxembourg's per capita production of 16 tons is the highest in the world.

Founded about 963, Luxembourg was a prominent country of the Holy Roman Empire; one of its sovereigns became Holy Roman Emperor as Henry VII, 1308. After being made a duchy by Emperor Charles IV, 1354, Luxembourg passed under the domination of Burgundy, Spain, Austria and France, 1443-1815, regaining autonomy under the Treaty of Vienna, 1815, as a grand duchy in union with the Netherlands, though ostensibly a member of the German Confederation. When Belgium seceded from the Kingdom of the Netherlands, 1830, Luxembourg was forced to cede its greater western section to Belgium. The tiny duchy left the German Confederation in 1867 when the Treaty of London recognized it as an independent state and guaranteed its perpetual neutrality. Luxembourg was occupied by Germany and liberated by American troops in both World Wars, and is the resting place of 5,000 American soldiers, including Gen. George S. Patton.

RULERS

Adolphe, 1890-1905
William IV, 1905-1912
Marie Adelaide, 1912-1919
Charlotte, 1919-1964
Jean, 1964-

MINT MARKS

A - Paris
(b) - Brussels, privy marks only
H - Gunzburg
(u) - Utrecht, privy marks only

PRIVY MARKS

Angel's head, two headed eagle - Brussels
Sword, Caduceus - Utrecht (1846-74 although struck at Brussels until 1909)

MONETARY SYSTEM

100 Centimes = 1 Franc

2-1/2 CENTIMES

BRONZE

KM#	Date	Mintage	Fine	VF	XF	Unc
21	1901(u)	.800	1.00	2.00	3.50	12.50
	1908(u)	.400	1.00	2.50	4.00	14.00

NOTE: Earlier dates (1854-1870) exist for this type.

5 CENTIMES

COPPER-NICKEL

24	1901	2.000	.25	.75	1.50	6.00

26	1908	1.500	.35	1.00	1.75	7.50

ZINC

27	1915	1.200	1.00	2.50	5.50	15.00

IRON

KM#	Date	Mintage	Fine	VF	XF	Unc
30	1918	1.200	1.00	2.50	5.00	15.00
	1921	.600	1.75	3.50	7.50	22.50
	1922	.400	12.00	20.00	40.00	80.00

COPPER-NICKEL

33	1924	3.000	.20	.40	.80	4.50

BRONZE

40	1930	5.000	.10		.25	.60	2.50

10 CENTIMES

COPPER-NICKEL

25	1901	4.000	.25	.75	1.50	7.50

ZINC

28	1915	1.400	1.25	3.00	5.00	15.00

IRON

31	1918	1.603	1.50	3.50	7.50	20.00
	1921	.626	2.00	4.50	9.00	22.50
	1923	.350	12.00	20.00	40.00	85.00

COPPER-NICKEL

34	1924	3.500	.25	.50	1.00	4.50

BRONZE

41	1930	5.000	.10	.25	.75	3.00

25 CENTIMES

ZINC

KM#	Date	Mintage	Fine	VF	XF	Unc
29	1916	.800	1.50	3.50	7.50	15.00
	1920	—	200.00	400.00	600.00	1000.

IRON

32	1919	.804	2.75	5.50	11.00	30.00
	1920	.800	2.25	4.00	8.50	25.00
	1922	.600	2.25	4.00	8.50	25.00

COPPER-NICKEL

37	1927	2.500	.35	.65	1.25	5.00

BRONZE

42	1930	1.000	.35	.85	1.75	6.50

COPPER-NICKEL

42a	1938 coin	2.000	1.00	2.00	4.00	7.00
	1938 medal	—	100.00	200.00	400.00	700.00

BRONZE

45	1946	4.000	—	.15	.25	.75
	1947	4.000	—	.15	.25	.75

ALUMINUM

45a	1954	7.000	—	—	—	.10
	1957	3.020	—	—	—	.10
	1960	3.020	—	—	—	.10
	1963	4.000	—	—	—	.10
	1965	2.000	—	—	—	.10
	1967	3.000	—	—	—	.10
	1968	.600	.10	.25	.50	1.00
	1970	4.000	—	—	—	.10
	1972	4.000	—	—	—	.10

50 CENTIMES

NICKEL

43	1930	2.000	.25	.50	1.00	5.00

FRANC

NICKEL

KM#	Date	Mintage	Fine	VF	XF	Unc
35	1924	1.000	.25	.75	1.25	8.00
	1928	2.000	.20	.50	1.00	7.00
	1935	1.000	.25	.75	1.25	6.00

COPPER-NICKEL

44	1939	5.000	.25	.75	1.50	5.00

46.1	1946	4.000	.15	.35	.50	1.00
	1947	2.000	.20	.40	.75	1.00

46.2	1952	5.000	.10	.25	.50	1.00

46.3	1953	2.000	—	.10	.15	.40
	1955	1.000	—	.10	.15	.40
	1957	2.000	—	.10	.15	.40
	1960	2.000	—	.10	.15	.40
	1962	2.000	—	.10	.15	.40
	1964	2.000	—	.10	.15	.40

55	1965	3.000	—	—	.10	.20
	1966	1.000	—	—	.10	.20
	1968	3.000	—	—	.10	.20
	1970	3.000	—	—	.10	.20
	1972	3.000	—	—	.10	.20
	1973	3.000	—	—	.10	.20
	1976	3.000	—	—	.10	.20
	1977	1.000	—	—	.10	.20
	1978	3.000	—	—	.10	.20
	1979	2.775	—	—	.10	.20
	1980	4.000	—	—	.10	.20
	1981	5.000	—	—	.10	.20
	1982	3.000	—	—	.10	.20
	1983	3.000	—	—	.10	.20
	1984	3.000	—	—	.10	.20

Rev: IML added.

KM#	Date	Mintage	Fine	VF	XF	Unc
59	1986	3.000	—	—	.10	.20
	1987	3.000	—	—	.10	.20

NICKEL-STEEL

63	1988	3.000	—	—	—	.40
	1989	3.000	—	—	—	.40
	1990	25.000	—	—	—	.40
	1991	10.000	—	—	—	.40
	1992	.010	—	In sets only		.50
	1993	.010	—	In sets only		.50
	1994	.010	—	In sets only		.50
	1995	.010	—	In sets only		.50

2 FRANCS

NICKEL

36	1924	1.000	1.00	2.25	4.00	15.00

5 FRANCS

8.0000 g, .625 SILVER, .1608 oz ASW

38	1929	2.000	BV	3.00	7.00	20.00

COPPER-NICKEL

50	1949	2.000	.30	.60	1.00	2.50

51	1962	2.000	.10	.25	.40	.75

56	1971	1.000	—	—	.15	.50
	1976	1.000	—	—	.15	.50
	1979	1.000	—	—	.15	.50
	1981	1.000	—	—	.15	.50

BRASS

KM#	Date	Mintage	Fine	VF	XF	Unc
60.1	1986	9.000	—	—	.15	.40
	1987	7.000	—	—	.15	.40
	1988	2.000	—	—	.15	.40

Rev: Larger crown w/cross touching rim.

60.2	1986	Inc. Ab.	—	—	.15	.40

65	1989	2.000	—	—	—	.60
	1990	4.010	—	—	—	.60
	1991	.010	—	In sets only		.75
	1992	.020	—	In sets only		.75
	1993	.010	—	In sets only		.75
	1994	.010	—	In sets only		.75
	1995	.010	—	In sets only		.75

10 FRANCS

13.5000 g, .750 SILVER, .3255 oz ASW

39	1929	1.000	BV	5.00	10.00	30.00

NICKEL

57	1971	3.000	—	—	.30	.60
	1972	3.000	—	—	.30	.60
	1974	3.000	—	—	.30	.60
	1976	3.000	—	—	.30	.60
	1977	3.000	—	—	.30	.60
	1978	3.000	—	—	.30	.60
	1979	1.000	—	—	.30	.60
	1980	1.000	—	—	.30	.60

20 FRANCS

8.5000 g, .835 SILVER, .2282 oz ASW
600th Anniversary - John the Blind

47	ND(1946)	.100	—	—	7.00	15.00

BRONZE

KM#	Date	Mintage	Fine	VF	XF	Unc
58	1980	3.000	—	—	.60	1.00
	1981	3.000	—	—	.60	1.00
	1982	3.000	—	—	.60	1.00
	1983	2.000	—	—	.60	1.00

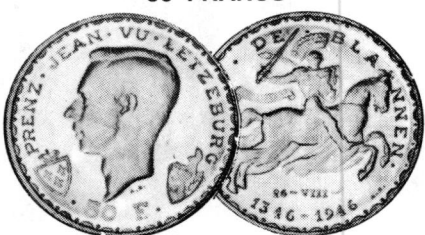

BRONZE

67	1990	1.110	—	—	—	2.00
	1991	.010	—	In sets only		2.50
	1992	.010	—	In sets only		2.50
	1993	.010	—	In sets only		2.50
	1994	.010	—	In sets only		2.50
	1995	.010	—	In sets only		2.50

50 FRANCS

12.5000 g, .835 SILVER, .3356 oz ASW
600th Anniversary - John the Blind

48	ND(1946)	.100	—	—	12.50	18.00

NICKEL

62	1987	3.000	—	—	1.50	3.50
	1988	1.000	—	—	1.50	3.50
	1989	1.200	—	—	1.50	3.50

Similar to 5 Francs, KM#65.

66	1989	2.000	—	—	—	3.50
	1990	2.010	—	—	—	3.50
	1991	1.000	—	—	—	3.50
	1992	.010	—	In sets only		4.00
	1993	.010	—	In sets only		4.00
	1994	.010	—	In sets only		4.00
	1995	.010	—	In sets only		4.00

100 FRANCS

25.0000 g, .835 SILVER, .6711 oz ASW
600th Anniversary - John the Blind

49	ND(1946)	.098	—	—	22.50	40.00
	ND(1946) w/o designer's name					
	(restrike)	2.000	—	—	—	120.00

18.0000 g, .835 SILVER .4832 oz ASW

KM#	Date	Mintage	Fine	VF	XF	Unc
52	1963	.050	—	—	10.00	15.00

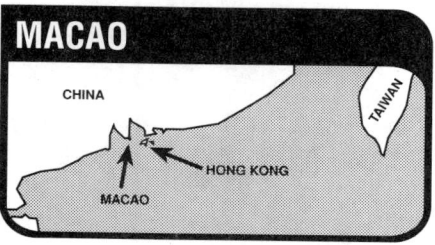

54	1964	.050	—	—	7.50	12.50

MACAO

The Province of Macao, a Portuguese overseas province located in the South China Sea 40 miles southwest of Hong Kong, consists of the peninsula of Macao and the islands of Taipa and Coloane. It has an area of 6.2 sq. mi. (16 sq. km.) and a population of 500,000. Capital: Macao. Macao's economy is based on light industry, commerce, tourism, fishing, and gold trading -Macao is one of the entirely free markets for gold in the world. Cement, textiles, fireworks, vegetable oils, and metal products are exported.

Established by the Portuguese in 1557, Macao is the oldest European settlement in the Far East. The Chinese, while agreeing to Portuguese settlement, did not recognize Portuguese sovereign rights and the Portuguese remained largely under control of the Chinese until 1849, when the Portuguese abolished the Chinese custom house and declared the independence of the port. The Manchu government formally recognized the Portuguese right to 'perpetual occupation' of Macao in 1887.

In 1987, Portugal and China agreed that Macao will become a Chinese Territory in 1999.

RULERS
Portuguese

MINT MARKS
(p) - Pobjoy Mint
(s) - Singapore Mint

MONETARY SYSTEM
100 Avos = 1 Pataca

5 AVOS

BRONZE

KM#	Date	Mintage	VF	XF	Unc
1	1952	.500	1.00	2.00	6.50

NICKEL-BRASS

1a	1967	5.000	—	.15	.45

10 AVOS

BRONZE

2	1952	12.500	.30	.60	2.25

NICKEL-BRASS

2a	1967	5.525	.15	.25	.60
	1968	6.975	.15	.25	.60
	1975	20.000	.10	.20	.50
	1976	Inc. Ab.	.10	.20	.50

BRASS

20	1982	24.580	—	.10	.30
	1983	—	—	.10	.30
	1984	—	—	.10	.30
	1985	—	—	.10	.30
	1988	—	—	.10	.30

70	1993	—	—	—	.45

20 AVOS

BRASS

KM#	Date	Mintage	VF	XF	Unc
21	1982	9.960	—	.15	.35
	1983	—	—	.15	.35
	1984	—	—	.15	.35
	1985	—	—	.15	.35

71	1993	—	—	—	.60

50 AVOS

COPPER-NICKEL

3	1952	2.560	.50	1.00	4.50

7	1972	1.600	.25	.35	.85
	1973	4.840	.25	.35	.85

9	1978	3.000	.10	.30	.75

BRASS

22	1982	16.952	—	.15	.50
	1983	—	—	.15	.50
	1984	—	—	.15	.50
	1985	—	—	.15	.50

72	1993	—	—	—	.85

PATACA

3.0000 g, .720 SILVER, .0694 oz ASW

4	1952	4.500	1.00	2.00	6.00

NICKEL

KM#	Date	Mintage	VF	XF	Unc
6	1968	5.000	.35	.50	1.75
	1975	6.000	.20	.35	1.50

COPPER-NICKEL

KM#	Date	Mintage	VF	XF	Unc
6a	1980	—	.20	.35	1.50

Obv: High stars.

23.1	1982(s)	6.427	.20	.40	1.25
	1983(s)	—	.20	.40	1.25
	1984(s)	—	.20	.40	1.25
	1985(s)	—	.20	.40	1.25

Obv: Low stars.

23.2	1982(p)	—	.20	.40	1.00
	1983(p)	—	.20	.40	1.00

57	1992	—	—		1.75

5 PATACAS

15.0000 g, .720 SILVER, .3472 oz ASW

5	1952	.900	4.00	6.50	18.00

10.0000 g, .650 SILVER, .2089 oz ASW

5a	1971	.500	3.00	5.00	10.00

COPPER-NICKEL
Obv: High stars. Rev: Large dragon.

24.1	1982(s)	1.102	.75	1.25	2.75
	1983(s)	—	.75	1.25	2.75
	1984(s)	—	.75	1.25	2.75
	1985(s)	—	.75	1.25	2.75
	1988(s)	—	.75	1.25	2.75

Obv: Low stars. Rev: Small dragon.

24.2	1982(p)	—	.75	1.25	2.75

56	1992	—	—	—	4.50

10 PATACAS

COPPER-NICKEL center in BRASS ring
Obv: "MACAU" and date.
Rev: Cathedral and denomination.

KM#	Date	Mintage	VF	XF	Unc
83	1997	—	—	—	6.50

The Republic of Macedonia is land-locked, and is bordered in the north by Yugoslavia, to the east by Bulgaria, in the south by Greece and to the west by Albania and has an area of 9,923 sq. mi. (25,713 sq. km.) and a population at the 1991 census was 2,038,847, of which the predominating ethnic groups were Macedonians. The capital is Skopje.

The Slavs settled in Macedonia since the 6th century, who had been Christianized by Byzantium, were conquered by the non-Slav Bulgars in the 7th century and in the 9th century formed a Macedo-Bulgarian empire, the western part of which survived until Byzantine conquest in 1014. In the 14th century, it fell to Serbia, and in 1355 to the Ottomans. After the Balkan Wars of 1912-13 Turkey was ousted, and Serbia received the greater part of the territory, the balance going to Bulgaria and Greece. In 1918, Yugoslav Macedonia was incorporated into Serbia as 'South Serbia', becoming a republic in the S.F.R. of Yugoslavia. Claims to the historical Macedonian territory have long been a source of contention between Bulgaria and Greece.

On Nov. 20, 1991 parliament promulgated a new constitution, and declared its independence on Nov. 20, 1992, but failed to secure EC and US recognition owing to Greek objections to use of the name "Macedonia".

On Dec. 11, 1992, the UN Security Council authorized the expedition of a small peacekeeping force to prevent hostilities spreading to Macedonia.

There is a 120-member single-chamber National Assembly.

50 DENI

BRASS
Seagull Flying Off Shore

KM#	Date	Mintage	Fine	VF	XF	Unc
1	1993	—	—	.10	.20	.50

DENAR

BRASS
Yugoslavian Sheep Dog Standing Left

2	1993	—	—	.15	.30	.75

F.A.O. - Yugoslavian Sheep Dog

5	1995	.070	—	—		.50

COPPER-NICKEL-ZINC

5a	1995	—	—	—		.50

2 DENARI

BRASS
Fish Above Water

3	1993	—	—	.25	.50	1.25

F.A.O. - Fish

KM#	Date	Mintage	Fine	VF	XF	Unc
6	1995	.070	—	—	—	.85

COPPER-NICKEL-ZINC

| 6a | 1995 | — | — | — | — | .85 |

5 DENARI

BRASS
European Lynx

| 4 | 1993 | — | — | .35 | .75 | 1.75 |

F.A.O. - European Lynx

| 7 | 1995 | .070 | — | — | — | 1.25 |

COPPER-NICKEL-ZINC

| 7a | 1995 | — | — | — | — | 1.25 |

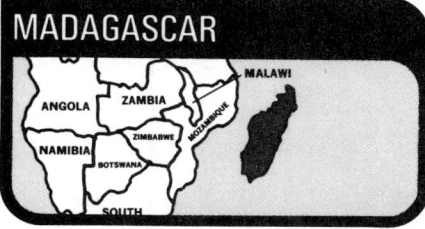

The Democratic Republic of Madagascar, an independent member of the French Community located in the Indian Ocean 250 miles (402 km.) off the southeast coast of Africa, has an area of 226,658 sq. mi. (587,040 sq. km.) and a population of 10 million. Capital: Antananarivo. The economy is primarily agricultural; large bauxite deposits are presently being developed. Coffee, vanilla, graphite, and rice are exported.

Successive waves of immigrants from south-east Asia, Africa, Arabia and India populated Madagascar beginning about 2,000 years ago. Diago Diaz, a Portuguese navigator, sighted the island of Madagascar on Aug. 10, 1500, when his ship became separated from an India-bound fleet. Attempts at settlement by the British during the reign of Charles I and by the French during the 17th and 18th centuries were of no avail, and the island became a refuge and supply base for Indian Ocean pirates. Despite considerable influence on the island, the British accepted the imposition of a French protectorate in 1886 in return for French recognition of Britain's sphere of influence in Zanzibar. Madagascar was made a French colony in 1896 after absolute control had been established by military force. Britain occupied the island after the fall of France, 1942, to prevent its seizure by the Japanese, returning it to the Free French in 1943. On Oct. 14, 1958, following a decade of intermittent but bitter warfare, Madagascar, as the Malagasy Republic, became an autonomous state within the French Community. On June 27, 1960, it became a sovereign, independent nation, though remaining nominally within the French Community. The Malagasy republic was renamed the Democratic Republic of Madagascar in 1975.

MONETARY SYSTEM
100 Centimes = 1 Franc

MINT MARKS
(a) - Paris, privy marks only
SA - Pretoria

50 CENTIMES

BRONZE
Mint: Pretoria

KM#	Date	Mintage	Fine	VF	XF	Unc
1	1943SA	2.000	1.50	2.50	10.00	32.50

FRANC

BRONZE
Mint: Pretoria

| 2 | 1943SA | 5.000 | 3.00 | 6.00 | 20.00 | 60.00 |

ALUMINUM

| 3 | 1948(a) | 7.400 | .15 | .30 | .50 | 2.00 |
| | 1958(a) | 2.600 | .15 | .30 | .50 | 2.25 |

2 FRANCS

ALUMINUM

KM#	Date	Mintage	Fine	VF	XF	Unc
4	1948(a)	10.000	.15	.35	.65	1.75

5 FRANCS

ALUMINUM

| 5 | 1953(a) | 30.012 | .25 | .55 | .85 | 2.00 |

10 FRANCS

ALUMINUM-BRONZE

| 6 | 1953(a) | 25.000 | .35 | .65 | 1.25 | 3.50 |

20 FRANCS

ALUMINUM-BRONZE

| 7 | 1953(a) | 15.000 | .75 | 1.50 | 3.00 | 6.50 |

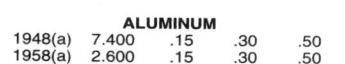
MALAGASY REPUBLIC

MINT MARKS
(a) - Paris, privy marks only

MONETARY SYSTEM
5 Francs = 1 Ariary

FRANC

STAINLESS STEEL

8	1965(a)	1.170	.10	.15	.30	1.00
	1966(a)	—	.10	.15	.30	1.00
	1970(a)	—	.10	.15	.30	1.00
	1974(a)	1.250	.10	.15	.30	1.00
	1975(a)	7.355	.10	.15	.30	1.00
	1976(a)	—	.10	.15	.30	1.00
	1977(a)	—	.10	.15	.30	1.00
	1979(a)	—	.10	.15	.30	1.00
	1980(a)	—	.15	.20	.40	1.20
	1981(a)	—	.15	.20	.40	1.20
	1982(a)	—	.15	.20	.40	1.20
	1983(a)	—	.15	.20	.40	1.20
	1986(a)	—	.15	.20	.40	1.20
	1987(a)	—	.15	.20	.40	1.20
	1988(a)	—	.15	.20	.40	1.20
	1989(a)	—	.15	.20	.40	1.20
	1991(a)	—	.15	.20	.40	1.20
	1993(a)	—	.15	.20	.40	1.20

2 FRANCS

STAINLESS STEEL

KM#	Date	Mintage	Fine	VF	XF	Unc
9	1965(a)	.760	.15	.25	.50	1.20
	1970(a)	—	.15	.25	.45	1.00
	1974(a)	1.250	.15	.25	.45	1.00
	1975(a)	8.250	.15	.25	.45	1.00
	1976(a)	—	.15	.25	.45	1.00
	1977(a)	—	.15	.25	.45	1.00
	1979(a)	—	.15	.25	.45	1.00
	1980(a)	—	.15	.25	.45	1.00
	1981(a)	—	.15	.25	.45	1.00
	1982(a)	—	.15	.25	.45	1.00
	1983(a)	—	.15	.25	.45	1.00
	1984(a)	—	.15	.25	.45	1.00
	1986(a)	—	.15	.25	.45	1.00
	1987(a)	—	.15	.25	.45	1.00
	1988(a)	—	.15	.25	.45	1.00
	1989(a)	—	.15	.25	.45	1.00

5 FRANCS - ARIARY

STAINLESS STEEL

KM#	Date	Mintage	Fine	VF	XF	Unc
10	1966(a)	—	.15	.25	.60	1.50
	1967(a)	—	.15	.25	.60	1.50
	1968(a)	7.500	.15	.25	.60	1.50
	1970(a)	—	.15	.25	.60	1.50
	1972(a)	19.100	.15	.25	.60	1.50
	1976(a)	—	.15	.25	.60	1.50
	1977(a)	—	.15	.25	.60	1.50
	1979(a)	—	.15	.25	.60	1.50
	1980(a)	—	.20	.30	.65	1.60
	1981(a)	—	.20	.30	.65	1.60
	1983(a)	—	.20	.30	.65	1.60
	1984(a)	—	.20	.30	.65	1.60
	1986(a)	—	.20	.30	.65	1.60
	1987(a)	—	.20	.30	.65	1.60
	1988(a)	—	.20	.30	.65	1.60
	1989(a)	—	.20	.30	.65	1.60

10 FRANCS - ROA (2) ARIARY

ALUMINUM-BRONZE
F.A.O. Issue

KM#	Date	Mintage	Fine	VF	XF	Unc
11	1970(a)	7.000	.20	.30	.70	1.75
	1971(a)	10.000	.20	.30	.70	1.75
	1972(a)	5.050	.20	.30	.70	1.75
	1973(a)	3.000	.20	.30	.70	1.75
	1974(a)	—	.20	.30	.70	1.75
	1975(a)	—	.20	.30	.70	1.75
	1976(a)	9.500	.20	.30	.70	1.75
	1977(a)	—	.20	.30	.70	1.75
	1978(a)	—	.20	.30	.70	1.75
	1980(a)	—	.25	.35	.80	2.00
	1981(a)	—	.25	.35	.80	2.00
	1982(a)	—	.25	.35	.80	2.00
	1983(a)	—	.25	.35	.80	2.00
	1984(a)	—	.25	.35	.80	2.00
	1986(a)	—	.25	.35	.80	2.00
	1987(a)	3.200	.25	.35	.80	2.00
	1988(a)	—	.25	.35	.80	2.00
	1989(a)	—	.25	.35	.80	2.00

COPPER-PLATED STEEL

KM#	Date	Mintage	Fine	VF	XF	Unc
11a	1991		.25	.45	.1.50	3.50

20 FRANCS - EFATRA (4) ARIARY

ALUMINUM-BRONZE

F.A.O. Issue

KM#	Date	Mintage	Fine	VF	XF	Unc
12	1970(a)	4.000	.25	.35	.75	2.25
	1971(a)	2.000	.25	.35	.75	2.25
	1972(a)	2.000	.30	.40	.80	2.50
	1973(a)	3.000	.30	.40	.80	2.50
	1974(a)	—	.30	.40	.80	2.50
	1975(a)	—	.30	.40	.80	2.50
	1976(a)	2.700	.30	.40	.80	2.50
	1977(a)	—	.30	.40	.80	2.50
	1978(a)	—	.30	.40	.80	2.50
	1979(a)	—	.30	.40	.80	2.50
	1981(a)	—	.35	.45	.85	2.75
	1982(a)	—	.35	.45	.85	2.75
	1983(a)	—	.35	.45	.85	2.75
	1984(a)	—	.35	.45	.85	2.75
	1986(a)	—	.35	.45	.85	2.75
	1987(a)	5.200	.35	.45	.85	2.75
	1988(a)	—	.35	.45	.85	2.75
	1989(a)	—	.35	.45	.85	2.75

DEMOCRATIC REPUBLIC

MONETARY SYSTEM

5 Francs = 1 Ariary

5 FRANCS / 1 ARIARY

STAINLESS STEEL
Obv: Flower and bank name.
Rev: Denomination and bovine head.

KM#	Date	Mintage	Fine	VF	XF	Unc
21	1996	—	—	—	—	2.50

10 FRANCS / 2 ARIARY

COPPER PLATED STEEL
Obv: Bank name and plant.
Rev: Value, bovine head.

KM#	Date	Mintage	Fine	VF	XF	Unc
22	1996	—	—	—	—	3.00

5 ARIARY

COPPER PLATED STEEL
Rice Plant

KM#	Date	Mintage	Fine	VF	XF	Unc
17	1992	—	.65	1.25	2.25	4.00

Obv: Denomination and bankname. Rev: Rice plant.

KM#	Date	Mintage	Fine	VF	XF	Unc
23	1996	—	—	—	—	2.50

10 ARIARY

NICKEL
F.A.O. Issue

KM#	Date	Mintage	Fine	VF	XF	Unc
13	1978	8.001	1.50	3.00	6.00	12.00

COPPER-NICKEL

KM#	Date	Mintage	Fine	VF	XF	Unc
13b	1983	—	2.00	4.00	8.00	15.00

STAINLESS STEEL
Cutting Peat

KM#	Date	Mintage	Fine	VF	XF	Unc
18	1992	—	.75	1.50	3.00	5.50

20 ARIARY

NICKEL
F.A.O. Issue

14	1978	8.001	2.00	4.00	8.00	16.50

COPPER-NICKEL

14b	1983	—	2.50	4.50	9.00	17.50

STAINLESS STEEL
Farmer on Tractor Discing Field

19	1992	—	1.25	2.50	4.50	10.00

NICKEL CLAD STEEL
Farmer on Tractor Discing Field
Obv: Denomination and new country name.

KM#	Date	Mintage	Fine	VF	XF	Unc
24	1994	—	—	—	—	6.50

50 ARIARY

STAINLESS STEEL

KM#	Date	Mintage	Fine	VF	XF	Unc
20	1992	—	2.00	3.50	6.00	12.50

NICKEL CLAD STEEL
Obv: Denomination and new country name.
Rev: Two towering trees.

KM#	Date	Mintage	Fine	VF	XF	Unc
25	1996	—	—	—	—	8.00

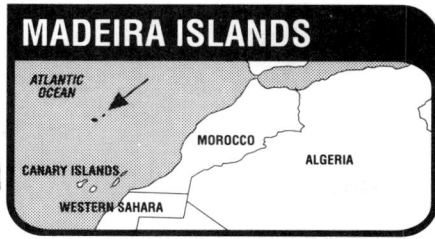

MADEIRA ISLANDS

MALAWI

FLORIN

The Madeira Islands, which belong to Portugal, are located 360 miles (492 km.) off the northwest coast of Africa. They have an area of 307 sq. mi. (795 sq. km.) and a population of 270,976. The group consists of two inhabited islands named Madeira and Porto Santo and two groups of uninhabited rocks named Desertas and Selvagens. Capital: Funchal. The two staple products are wine and sugar. Bananas and pineapples are also produced for export.

Although the evidence is insufficient, it is thought that the Phoenicians visited Madeira at an early period. It is also probable that the entire archipelago was explored in early times by Genoese adventurers; an Italian map dated 1351 shows the Madeira Islands quite clearly. The Portuguese navigator Goncalvez Zarco first sighted Porto Santo in 1418, having been driven there by a storm while he was exploring the coast of West Africa. Madeira itself was discovered in 1420. The islands were uninhabited when visited by Zarco, but their colonization was immediately begun by Prince Henry the Navigator, aided by the knights of the Order of Christ. British troops occupied the islands in 1801, and again in 1807-14.

RULERS
Portuguese

25 ESCUDOS

COPPER-NICKEL
Autonomy of Madeira - Zarco

KM#	Date	Mintage	Fine	VF	XF	Unc
4	1981	.750	—	—	—	5.00

100 ESCUDOS

COPPER-NICKEL
Autonomy of Madeira - Zarco

5	1981	.250	—	—	—	10.00

The Republic of Malawi (formerly Nyasaland), located in southeastern Africa to the west of Lake Malawi (Nyasa), has an area of 45,747 sq. mi. (118,480 sq. km.) and a population of 7 million. Capital: Lilongwe. The economy is predominantly agricultural. Tobacco, tea, peanuts and cotton are exported.

Although the Portuguese, heirs to the restless spirit of Prince Henry, were the first Europeans to reach the Malawi area, the first meaningful contact was made by missionary-explorer Dr. David Livingstone who arrived at Lake Malawi on Sept. 16, 1859, and remained to make extensive explorations in the 1860's. Subsequent clashes between settlements of Scottish missionaries and Arab slave traders, and the procurement of development rights by Cecil Rhodes, 1884, stimulated British interest and brought about the establishment of the Nyasaland protectorate in 1891. In 1953 Nyasaland reluctantly joined the Federation of Rhodesia and Nyasaland and, after prolonged protest, was granted self-government within the federation. Nyasaland became the independent nation of Malawi on July 6, 1964, and became a republic two years later. Malawi is a member of the Commonwealth of Nations. The president is the Chief of State and Head of Government.

NOTE: For earlier coinage see Rhodesia and Nyasaland.

MONETARY SYSTEM
12 Pence = 1 Shilling
2 Shillings = 1 Florin
5 Shillings = 1 Crown
20 Shillings = 1 Pound

PENNY

BRONZE

KM#	Date	Mintage	Fine	VF	XF	Unc
6	1967	6.000	.35	.65	1.25	2.50
	1968	3.600	3.00	6.00	12.00	25.00

6 PENCE

COPPER-NICKEL-ZINC
Obv: Dr. Hastings Kamuzu Banda.
Rev: Rooster.

1	1964	14.800	.25	.50	1.00	2.50
	1964	.010	—	—	Proof	1.50
	1967	6.000	.50	1.00	2.50	5.00

SHILLING

COPPER-NICKEL-ZINC
Obv: Dr. Hastings Kamuzu Banda.
Rev: Bundled cobs of corn.

2	1964	11.900	.35	.65	1.25	2.50
	1964	.010	—	—	Proof	1.50
	1968	3.000	.75	1.50	3.00	5.50

COPPER-NICKEL-ZINC
Obv: Dr. Hastings Kamuzu Banda.
Rev: African Elephants.

KM#	Date	Mintage	Fine	VF	XF	Unc
3	1964	6.500	.75	1.50	3.00	5.00
	1964	.010	—	—	Proof	3.50

1/2 CROWN

COPPER-NICKEL-ZINC
Obv: Dr. Hastings Kamuzu Banda.
Rev: Arms.

4	1964	6.400	1.00	2.00	4.00	6.00
	1964	.010	—	—	Proof	4.00

DECIMAL COINAGE
100 Tambala = 1 Kwacha

TAMBALA

BRONZE
Obv: Dr. Hastings Kamuzu Banda.
Rev: Rooster.

7.1	1971	15.000	.15	.20	.40	.75
	1971	4,000	—	—	Proof	1.00
	1973	5.000	.15	.20	.40	.75
	1974	12.500	.15	.20	.40	.75

Obv: Accent mark above W in MALAWI.

7.2	1975	—	.15	.20	.40	.75
	1976	10.000	.15	.20	.40	.75
	1977	10.000	.15	.20	.40	.75
	1979	15.000	.15	.20	.40	.75
	1982	15.000	.15	.20	.40	.75

COPPER PLATED STEEL

7.2a	1984	.201	.20	.30	.50	.80
	1985	—	.20	.30	.50	.80
	1985	.010	—	—	Proof	3.00
	1987	—	.20	.30	.50	.80
	1989	—	.20	.30	.50	.80
	1991	—	.20	.30	.50	.80
	1994	—	.20	.30	.50	.80

Obv: Portrait of President Bakili Muluzi.
Rev: 2 fish.

24	1995	—	—	—	—	.65

2 TAMBALA

BRONZE
Obv: Dr. Hastings Kamuzu Banda.
Rev: Paradise Wydah.

8.1	1971	10.000	.25	.40	.75	1.50
	1971	4,000	—	—	Proof	1.75

KM#	Date	Mintage	Fine	VF	XF	Unc
8.1	1973	5.000	.25	.40	.75	1.50
	1974	5.000	.25	.40	.75	1.50

Obv: Accent mark above W in MALAWI.

KM#	Date	Mintage	Fine	VF	XF	Unc
8.2	1975		.25	.40	.75	1.50
	1976	5.000	.25	.40	.75	1.50
	1977	5.000	.25	.40	.75	1.50
	1979	7.637	.25	.40	.75	1.50
	1982	15.000	.25	.40	.75	1.50

COPPER PLATED STEEL

KM#	Date	Mintage	Fine	VF	XF	Unc
8.2a	1984	.150	.30	.50	.85	2.00
	1985		.30	.50	.85	2.00
	1985	.010	—	—	Proof	4.00
	1987	—	.30	.50	.85	2.00
	1989	—	.30	.50	.85	2.00
	1991	—	.30	.50	.85	1.75
	1994	—	.30	.50	.85	1.75

Obv: Portrait of President Bakili Muluzi.
Rev: Bird on branch.

25	1995		—	—	—	1.00

5 TAMBALA

COPPER-NICKEL
Obv: Dr. Hastings Kamuzu Banda.
Rev: Purple Heron.

9.1	1971	7.000	.25	.45	.85	1.75
	1971	4,000	—	—	Proof	2.00

Obv: Accent mark above W in MALAWI.

9.2	1985	.010	—	—	Proof	5.00

NICKEL CLAD STEEL

9.2a	1989	—	.30	.50	.85	2.00
	1994	—	.30	.50	.85	2.00

STEEL
Obv: Portrait of President Bakili Muluzi.
Rev: Purple Heron.

26	1995		—	—	—	1.50

10 TAMBALA

COPPER-NICKEL
Obv: Dr. Hastings Kamuzu Banda.
Rev: Bundled cobs of corn.

10.1	1971	4.000	.30	.50	1.00	2.25
	1971	4,000	—	—	Proof	2.50

Obv: Accent mark above W in MALAWI.

10.2	1985	.010	—	—	Proof	6.00

NICKEL CLAD STEEL

10.2a	1989	—	.40	.80	1.50	2.75

STEEL
Obv: Portrait of President Bakili Muluzi.
Rev: Bundled corn.

27	1995		—	—	—	2.00

20 TAMBALA

COPPER-NICKEL
Obv: Dr. Hastings Kamuzu Banda.
Rev: Elephant cow and calf.

KM#	Date	Mintage	Fine	VF	XF	Unc
11.1	1971	3.000	.75	1.50	2.50	4.00
	1971	4,000	—	—	Proof	4.50

Obv: Accent mark above W in MALAWI.

11.2	1985	.010	—	—	Proof	7.00

NICKEL CLAD STEEL

11.2a	1989	—	.60	1.20	2.25	3.75
	1994	—	.60	1.20	2.25	3.75

Obv: Portrait of President Bakili Muluzi.
Rev: Female elephant and calf.

29	1996		—	—	—	3.50

50 TAMBALA

COPPER-NICKEL-ZINC
Obv: Dr. Hastings Kamuzu Banda.
Rev: Arms.

19	1986	—	2.00	3.00	5.00	10.00
	1994	—	2.00	3.00	5.00	10.00

NOTE: The 1989 date for this coin does not exist.

BRASS PLATED STEEL
Obv: Portrait of President Bakili Muluzi.
Rev: Lions supporting national arms.

30	1996		—	—	—	5.00

KWACHA

COPPER-NICKEL
Decimalization of Coinage
Obv: Similar to 5 Kwacha, KM#15.

12	1971	.020	1.00	2.00	3.50	6.00
	1971	4,000	—	—	Proof	6.50

COPPER-NICKEL-ZINC
Obv: Dr. Hastings Kamuzu Banda.
Rev: Rooster.

KM#	Date	Mintage	Fine	VF	XF	Unc
20	1992	—	1.00	2.00	3.00	5.50
	1993	—	2.00	4.00	6.00	10.00

BRASS
Obv: Portrait of President Bakili Muluzi.
Rev: Eagle w/extended talons.

28	1996		—	—	—	7.50

MALAYSIA

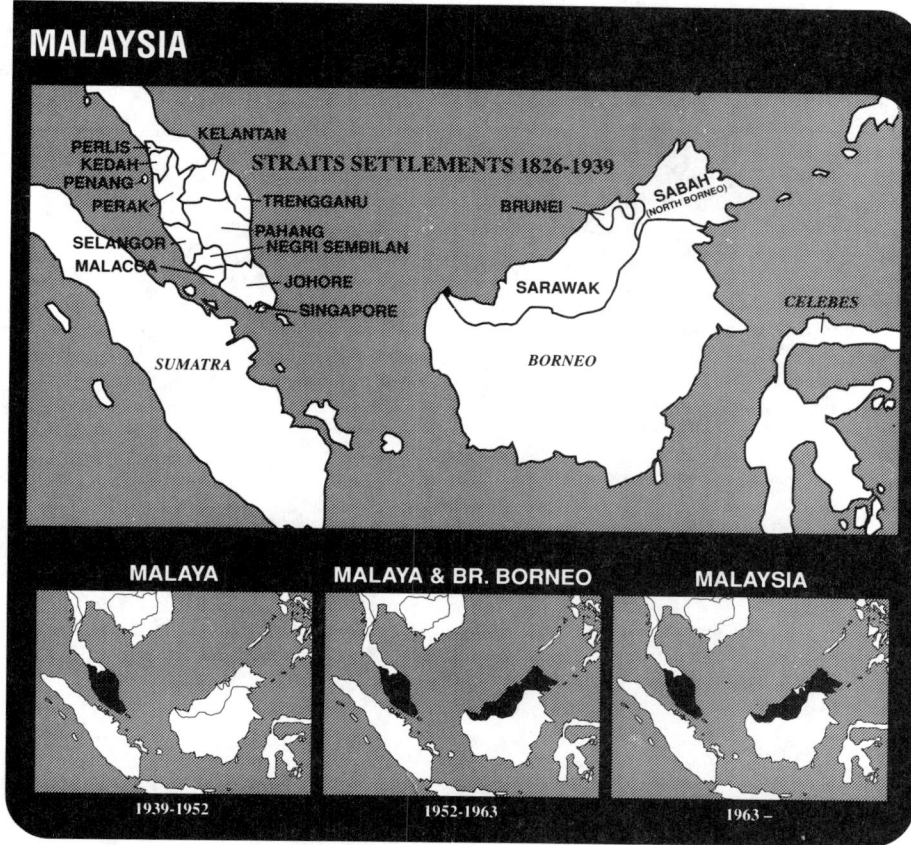

STRAITS SETTLEMENTS 1826-1939

MALAYA	MALAYA & BR. BORNEO	MALAYSIA
  **1939-1952**	  **1952-1963**	**1963 –**

BRONZE

KM#	Date	Mintage	Fine	VF	XF	Unc
16	1901	15.230	1.25	4.00	13.50	42.00

NOTE: Earlier dates (1887-1900) exist for this type.

19	1903	7.053	1.50	4.50	13.50	37.50
	1903	—	—	—	Proof	200.00
	1904	6.647	1.50	4.50	13.50	37.50
	1904	—	—	—	Proof	200.00
	1906	7.504	3.50	8.00	22.50	60.00
	1907	5.015	1.00	4.00	15.00	40.00
	1908	Inc. Ab.	1.00	2.50	10.00	30.00
	1908	—	—	—	Proof	200.00

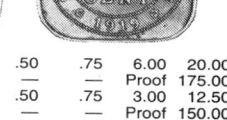

32	1919	20.165	.50	.75	6.00	20.00
	1919	—	—	—	Proof	175.00
	1920	55.000	.50	.75	3.00	12.50
	1920	—	—	—	Proof	150.00
	1926/0	5.000	2.00	5.00	10.00	25.00
	1926	Inc. Ab.	.50	.75	7.50	25.00

5 CENTS

1.3600 g, .800 SILVER, .0349 oz ASW

10	1901	3.000	1.50	2.50	12.50	45.00

NOTE: Earlier dates (1871-1900) exist for this type.

20	1902	1.920	5.00	12.00	50.00	90.00
	1902	—	—	—	Proof	350.00
	1903	2.270	5.00	12.00	50.00	90.00
	1903	—	—	—	Proof	350.00

1.3600 g, .600 SILVER, .0262 oz ASW

20a	1910B	13.012	1.25	2.25	5.50	12.00
	1910B	—	—	—	Proof	350.00

1.3600 g, .400 SILVER, .0174 oz ASW

31	1918	3.100	.50	1.00	5.00	12.00
	1919	6.900	.50	1.25	5.00	12.00
	1920	4.000	120.00	250.00	600.00	1200.

COPPER-NICKEL

34	1920	20.000	1.00	12.00	50.00	100.00
	1920	—	—	—	Proof	525.00

STRAITS SETTLEMENTS

Straits Settlements, a former British crown colony situated on the Malay Peninsula of Asia, was formed in 1826 by combining the territories of Singapore, Penang and Malacca. The colony was administered by the East India Company until its abolition in 1853. Straits Settlements was a part of British India from 1858 to 1867 at which time it became a Crown Colony. This name was changed to Malaya in 1939.

RULERS
British

MINT MARKS
H - Heaton, Birmingham
B - Bombay

MONETARY SYSTEM
100 Cents = 1 Dollar

COLONIAL ISSUES
1867-1939
1/4 CENT

BRONZE
Reeded edge

KM#	Date	Mintage	Fine	VF	XF	Unc
14	1901	2.000	2.00	4.00	20.00	50.00

NOTE: Earlier dates (1889-1899) exist for this type.

17	1904 plain edge					
		—	—	—	Proof	500.00
	1904 milled edge					
		—	—	—	Proof	500.00
	1905	2.008	1.25	6.00	15.00	40.00
	1905	—	—	—	Proof	250.00
	1908	1.200	1.25	6.00	17.50	45.00

KM#	Date	Mintage	Fine	VF	XF	Unc
27	1916	4.000	1.00	2.00	4.50	12.00
	1916	—	—	—	Proof	220.00

1/2 CENT
BRONZE

18	1904	—	—	—	Proof	350.00
	1908	2.000	2.50	5.00	15.00	45.00

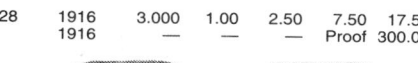

28	1916	3.000	1.00	2.50	7.50	17.50
	1916	—	—	—	Proof	300.00

37	1932	5.000	.75	1.00	3.00	12.50
	1932	—	—	—	Proof	240.00

1.3600 g, .600 SILVER, .0262 oz ASW
Similar to KM#31, smaller bust, broader rim.

KM#	Date	Mintage	Fine	VF	XF	Unc
36	1926	10.000	.50	.75	4.00	12.00
	1926	—	—	—	Proof	240.00
	1935	3.000	.50	.75	4.00	9.00
	1935	—	—	—	Proof	240.00

10 CENTS

2.7100 g, .800 SILVER, .0697 oz ASW

| 11 | 1901 | 2.700 | 1.75 | 2.75 | 7.00 | 25.00 |

NOTE: Earlier dates (1871-1900) exist for this type.

21	1902	6.118	2.50	10.00	25.00	60.00
	1902	—	—	—	Proof	250.00
	1903	1.401	3.00	12.00	32.50	80.00
	1903	—	—	—	Proof	250.00

2.7100 g, .600 SILVER, .0522 oz ASW

21a	1909B	11.088	5.00	20.00	40.00	90.00
	1910B	1.657	1.00	2.00	3.00	10.00
	1910B	—	—	—	Proof	250.00

Obv: Dot below bust.

| 29 | 1916 | .600 | 3.00 | 7.00 | 20.00 | 35.00 |
| | 1917 | 5.600 | 1.00 | 2.00 | 7.00 | 22.00 |

2.7100 g, .400 SILVER, .0348 oz ASW
Obv: Cross below bust.

29a	1918	7.500	1.00	2.50	8.00	22.00
	1919	11.500	1.00	2.50	8.00	22.00
	1920	4.000	5.00	15.00	40.00	115.00

2.7100 g, .600 SILVER, .0522 oz ASW
Obv: Plain field below bust.

29b	1926	20.000	1.00	1.50	5.00	15.00
	1926	—	—	—	Proof	225.00
	1927	23.000	.50	.75	1.00	3.25
	1927	—	—	—	Proof	225.00

20 CENTS

5.4300 g, .800 SILVER, .1396 oz ASW

| 12 | 1901 | .600 | 3.00 | 4.50 | 12.50 | 40.00 |

NOTE: Earlier dates (1871-1900) exist for this type.

22	1902	1.105	6.00	15.00	50.00	120.00
	1902	—	—	—	Proof	300.00
	1903	1.150	6.00	15.00	50.00	120.00
	1903	—	—	—	Proof	300.00

5.4300 g, .600 SILVER, .1047 oz ASW

KM#	Date	Mintage	Fine	VF	XF	Unc
22a	1910B	3.276	2.00	3.50	10.00	25.00
	1910B	—	—	—	Proof	300.00

Obv: Dot below bust.

30	1916B	.545	4.00	10.00	30.00	70.00
	1916B	—	—	—	Proof	250.00
	1917B	.652	2.50	4.50	25.00	55.00

5.4300 g, .400 SILVER, .0698 oz ASW
Obv: Cross below bust.

| 30a | 1919B | 2.500 | 2.50 | 4.50 | 12.00 | 35.00 |
| | 1919B | — | — | — | Proof | 250.00 |

5.4300 g, .600 SILVER, .1047 oz ASW
Obv: Plain field below bust.

30b	1926	2.500	1.50	3.00	12.00	35.00
	1926	—	—	—	Proof	250.00
	1927	3.000	1.50	2.50	6.00	12.00
	1927	—	—	—	Proof	250.00
	1935 round top 3					
		1.000	1.50	2.50	3.50	7.00
	1935 flat top 3					
	Inc. Ab.		1.50	2.50	3.50	7.00

50 CENTS

13.5769 g, .800 SILVER, .3492 oz ASW

| 13 | 1901 | .120 | 25.00 | 50.00 | 120.00 | 280.00 |

NOTE: Earlier dates (1886-1900) exist for this type.

23	1902	.148	50.00	80.00	175.00	280.00
	1902	—	—	—	Proof	900.00
	1903	.193	50.00	80.00	175.00	280.00
	1903	—	—	—	Proof	900.00
	1904	—	—	—	Proof	1000.
	1905B raised					
		.498	35.00	65.00	135.00	260.00
	1905B raised	—	—	—	Proof	950.00
	1905B incuse	—	—	—	Proof	950.00

10.1000 g, .900 SILVER, .2922 oz ASW

24	1907	.464	5.50	10.00	22.00	60.00
	1907H	2.667	5.50	10.00	22.00	60.00
	1907H	—	—	—	Proof	200.00
	1908	2.869	7.00	12.50	27.50	80.00
	1908H					
	Inc. 1907H		7.00	10.00	22.00	60.00

8.4200 g, .500 SILVER, .1353 oz ASW

Obv: Cross below bust.

KM#	Date	Mintage	Fine	VF	XF	Unc
35.1	1920	3.900	1.50	2.50	4.00	8.00
	1920	—	—	—	Proof	250.00
	1921	2.579	2.00	3.00	5.00	10.00
	1921	—	—	—	Proof	250.00

Obv: Dot below bust.

| 35.2 | 1920 | Inc. Ab. | 120.00 | 185.00 | 300.00 | 550.00 |

DOLLAR

26.9500 g, .900 SILVER, .7799 oz ASW

25	1903	—	—	—	Proof	1000.
	1903B incuse					
		15.010	15.00	25.00	50.00	100.00
	1903B raised					
		Inc. Ab.	70.00	120.00	250.00	600.00
	1903B raised	—	—	—	Proof	1100.
	1904B	20.365	12.50	20.00	35.00	85.00
	1904B	—	—	—	Proof	1000.

20.2100 g, .900 SILVER, .5848 oz ASW
Reduced size, 34.5mm.

26	1907	6.842	7.50	—	20.00	60.00
	1907H	4.000	7.50	10.00	20.00	60.00
	1907H	—	—	—	Proof	550.00
	1908	4.152	7.50	10.00	20.00	60.00
	1908	—	—	—	Proof	550.00
	1909	1.014	10.00	15.00	25.00	80.00
	1909	—	—	—	Proof	550.00

16.8500 g, .500 SILVER, .2709 oz ASW

33	1919	6.000	15.00	30.00	90.00	140.00
	1919(restrike)	—	—	—	Proof	80.00
	1920	8.164	10.00	20.00	30.00	70.00
	1920(restrike)	—	—	—	Proof	80.00
	1925	—	450.00	850.00	1250.	—
	1925	—	—	—	Proof	3500.
	1925(restrike)	—	—	—	Proof	600.00
	1926	—	450.00	850.00	1250.	—
	1926	—	—	—	Proof	3500.
	1926(restrike)	—	—	—	Proof	600.00

SARAWAK

Sarawak is a former British colony located on the northwest coast of Borneo. The Japanese occupation during World War II so thoroughly devastated the economy that Rajah Sir Charles Vyner Brooke ceded it to Great Britain on July 1, 1946. In September, 1963 the colony joined the Federation of Malaysia.

RULERS
Charles J. Brooke, Rajah, 1868-1917
Charles V. Brooke, Rajah, 1917-1946

MINT MARKS
H - Heaton, Birmingham

MONETARY SYSTEM
100 Cents = 1 Dollar

453

British North Borneo / MALAYSIA

1/2 CENT

BRONZE

KM#	Date	Mintage	Fine	VF	XF	Unc
20	1933H	2.000	1.00	2.00	4.00	9.00
	1933H	—			Proof	240.00

CENT

COPPER-NICKEL

| 12 | 1920H | 5.000 | 3.00 | 7.50 | 18.00 | 60.00 |

BRONZE

18	1927H	5.000	1.25	2.25	4.50	9.00
	1927H	—			Proof	210.00
	1929H	2.000	1.25	2.50	5.00	10.00
	1930H	3.000	1.25	2.50	5.00	10.00
	1930H	—			Proof	210.00
	1937H	3.000	1.25	2.25	4.50	9.00
	1941H*	3.000	250.00	350.00	525.00	900.00
	1942	—	Reported, not confirmed			

*NOTE: Estimate 50 pcs. exist.

5 CENTS

1.3500 g, .800 SILVER, .0347 oz ASW

8	1908H	.040	30.00	50.00	90.00	140.00
	1908H	—			Proof	350.00
	1911H	.040	30.00	50.00	90.00	140.00
	1913H	.100	25.00	50.00	80.00	120.00
	1913H	—			Proof	350.00
	1915H	.100	25.00	50.00	90.00	130.00
	1915H	—			Proof	350.00

NOTE: Earlier date (1900) exists for this type.

1.3500 g, .400 SILVER, .0174 oz ASW

| 13 | 1920H | .100 | 40.00 | 60.00 | 100.00 | 180.00 |
| | 1920H | — | | | Proof | 400.00 |

COPPER-NICKEL

14	1920H	.400	2.00	4.00	8.00	20.00
	1927H	.600	2.00	4.00	8.00	20.00
	1927H	—			Proof	275.00

10 CENTS

2.7100 g, .800 SILVER, .0697 oz ASW

9	1906H	.050	20.00	30.00	55.00	100.00
	1906H	—			Proof	350.00
	1910H	.050	20.00	30.00	55.00	100.00
	1910H	—			Proof	350.00
	1911/10H	.100	20.00	30.00	60.00	120.00
	1911H	Inc. Ab.	15.00	20.00	40.00	90.00
	1913H	.100	15.00	20.00	40.00	90.00

KM#	Date	Mintage	Fine	VF	XF	Unc
9	1913H				Proof	350.00
	1915H	.100	30.00	45.00	75.00	185.00
	1915H	—			Proof	350.00

NOTE: Earlier date (1900) exists for this type.

2.7100 g, .400 SILVER, .0349 oz ASW

| 15 | 1920H | .150 | 18.00 | 27.50 | 50.00 | 90.00 |
| | 1920H | — | | | Proof | 350.00 |

COPPER-NICKEL

16	1920H	.800	2.00	4.00	8.00	17.50
	1927H	1.000	2.00	3.00	6.00	17.50
	1927H	—			Proof	300.00
	1934H	2.000	2.00	3.00	6.00	17.50
	1934H	—			Proof	300.00

20 CENTS

5.4300 g, .800 SILVER, .1396 oz ASW

10	1906H	.025	30.00	62.50	110.00	220.00
	1906H	—			Proof	550.00
	1910H	.025	30.00	62.50	110.00	220.00
	1910H	—			Proof	550.00
	1911H	.015	30.00	62.50	110.00	220.00
	1913H	.025	30.00	62.50	110.00	220.00
	1913H	—			Proof	550.00
	1915H	.025	125.00	175.00	300.00	500.00
	1915H	—			Proof	725.00

NOTE: Earlier date (1900) exists for this type.

5.4300 g, .400 SILVER, .0699 oz ASW

| 17 | 1920H | .025 | 65.00 | 120.00 | 220.00 | 400.00 |
| | 1920H | — | | | Proof | 600.00 |

5.0800 g, .400 SILVER, .0653 oz ASW

| 17a | 1927H | .250 | 5.00 | 10.00 | 22.50 | 50.00 |
| | 1927H | — | | | Proof | 400.00 |

50 CENTS

13.5700 g, .800 SILVER, .3490 oz ASW

| 11 | 1906H | .010 | 225.00 | 325.00 | 500.00 | 950.00 |
| | 1906H | — | | | Proof | 1350. |

NOTE: Earlier date (1900) exists for this type.

10.3000 g, .500 SILVER, .1656 oz ASW

KM#	Date	Mintage	Fine	VF	XF	Unc
19	1927H	.200	12.00	20.00	38.00	90.00
	1927H	—			Proof	400.00

BRITISH NORTH BORNEO

British North Borneo (now known as Sabah), a former British protectorate and crown colony, occupies the northern tip of the island of Borneo. The island of Labuan, which lies 6 miles off the northwest coast of the island of Borneo, was attached to Singapore settlement in 1907. It became an independent settlement of the Straits Colony in 1912 and was incorporated with British North Borneo in 1946. In 1963 it became part of Malaysia.

RULERS

British

MINT MARKS

H - Heaton, Birmingham

MONETARY SYSTEM

100 Cents = 1 Straits Dollar

1/2 CENT

BRONZE

| 1 | 1907H | 1.000 | 15.00 | 30.00 | 45.00 | 130.00 |

NOTE: Earlier dates (1885-1891) exist for this type.

CENT

BRONZE

| 2 | 1907H | 1.000 | 20.00 | 50.00 | 75.00 | 125.00 |
| | 1907H | — | | | Proof | 400.00 |

NOTE: Earlier dates (1892-1896) exist for this type.

COPPER-NICKEL

3	1904H	2.000	2.00	3.50	8.50	22.50
	1921H	1.000	2.00	3.50	12.50	27.50
	1935H	1.000	1.25	2.50	6.50	22.50
	1938H	1.000	1.25	2.50	6.50	22.50
	1941H	1.000	1.25	2.50	6.50	22.50

2-1/2 CENTS

COPPER-NICKEL

4	1903H	2.000	2.50	5.00	20.00	50.00
	1903H	—			Proof	300.00
	1920H	.280	5.00	15.00	35.00	75.00

5 CENTS

COPPER-NICKEL

KM#	Date	Mintage	Fine	VF	XF	Unc
5	1903H	1.000	2.50	5.00	15.00	40.00
	1920H	.100	5.00	10.00	32.00	60.00
	1921H	.500	2.50	5.00	15.00	40.00
	1927H	.150	3.00	5.00	15.00	40.00
	1928H	.150	2.00	4.00	12.00	35.00
	1938H	.500	1.50	3.00	7.50	20.00
	1940H	.500	1.50	3.00	7.50	20.00
	1941H	1.000	1.50	3.00	7.50	20.00

25 CENTS

2.8300 g, .500 SILVER, .0454 oz ASW

KM#	Date	Mintage	Fine	VF	XF	Unc
6	1929H	.400	10.00	18.00	30.00	60.00
	1929H	—	—	—	Proof	175.00

MALAYA

Malaya, a former member of the British Commonwealth located in the southern part of the Malay peninsula, consisted of 11 states: the unfederated Malay states of Johore, Kelantan, Kedah, Perlis and Trengganu; the federated Malay states of Negri-Sembilan, Pahang, Perak and Selangor; former members of the Straits Settlements Penang and Malacca. Malaya was occupied by the Japanese during the years 1942-1945. The only local opposition to the Japanese had come mainly from the Chinese Communists who then continued their guerilla operations after the Japanese had surrendered. They were finally defeated in 1956. Malaya was granted full independence on Aug. 31, 1957, and became part of Malaysia in 1963.

RULERS

British

MINT MARKS

I - Calcutta Mint(1941)
I - Bombay Mint(1945)
No Mint mark - Royal Mint

MONETARY SYSTEM

100 Cents = 1 Dollar

1/2 CENT

BRONZE

KM#	Date	Mintage	Fine	VF	XF	Unc
1	1940	6.000	.50	1.25	2.00	4.00
	1940	—	—	—	Proof	150.00

CENT

BRONZE

KM#	Date	Mintage	Fine	VF	XF	Unc
2	1939	20.000	.25	.40	.60	1.50
	1939	—	—	—	Proof	150.00
	1940	23.600	.25	.40	.60	1.50
	1940	—	—	—	Proof	—
	1941-I	33.620	.75	1.25	5.00	10.00

Reduced size.

KM#	Date	Mintage	Fine	VF	XF	Unc
6	1943	50.000	.10	.20	.35	.80
	1943	—	—	—	Proof	150.00
	1945	40.033	.10	.20	.35	.80
	1945	—	—	—	Proof	150.00

5 CENTS

1.3600 g, .750 SILVER, .0327 oz ASW

KM#	Date	Mintage	Fine	VF	XF	Unc
3	1939	2.000	.50	1.00	1.50	2.50
	1939	—	—	—	Proof	250.00
	1941	4.000	.40	.50	1.20	2.00
	1941	—	—	—	Proof	250.00
	1941-I	Inc. Ab.	.40	.50	1.20	2.00

1.3600 g, .500 SILVER, .0218 oz ASW

KM#	Date	Mintage	Fine	VF	XF	Unc
3a	1943	10.000	.30	.40	.65	1.50
	1943	—	—	—	Proof	250.00
	1945	8.800	.30	.40	.65	1.50
	1945	—	—	—	Proof	250.00
	1945-I	4.600	.50	.75	1.00	2.00

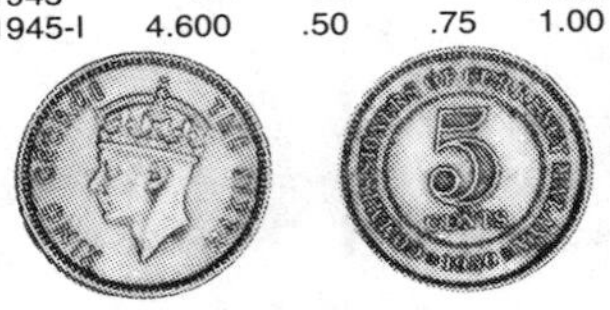

COPPER-NICKEL

KM#	Date	Mintage	Fine	VF	XF	Unc
7	1948	30.000	.10	.25	.75	2.00
	1948	—	—	—	Proof	220.00
	1950	40.000	.10	.25	.75	2.00
	1950	—	—	—	Proof	220.00

10 CENTS

2.7100 g, .750 SILVER, .0653 oz ASW

KM#	Date	Mintage	Fine	VF	XF	Unc
4	1939	10.000	.75	1.00	1.25	2.50
	1939	—	—	—	Proof	280.00
	1941	17.000	.75	1.00	1.25	2.50
	1941	—	—	—	Proof	280.00
	1941-I	—	—	—	Proof	Rare

2.7100 g, .500 SILVER, .0435 oz ASW

KM#	Date	Mintage	Fine	VF	XF	Unc
4a	1943	5.000	.75	1.00	1.50	2.50
	1943	—	—	—	Proof	280.00
	1945	3.152	.75	1.00	1.50	3.00
	1945-I	—	—	—	Proof	Rare

COPPER-NICKEL

KM#	Date	Mintage	Fine	VF	XF	Unc
8	1948	23.885	.15	.30	.75	2.25
	1948	—	—	—	Proof	280.00
	1949	26.115	.25	.50	1.20	3.00
	1949	—	—	—	Proof	280.00
	1950	65.000	.15	.30	.75	2.25
	1950	—	—	—	Proof	280.00

20 CENTS

5.4300 g, .750 SILVER, .1309 oz ASW

KM#	Date	Mintage	Fine	VF	XF	Unc
5	1939	8.000	1.25	1.75	2.25	4.50
	1939	—	—	—	Proof	280.00

5.4300 g, .500 SILVER, .0872 oz ASW

KM#	Date	Mintage	Fine	VF	XF	Unc
5a	1943	5.000	1.25	1.75	2.25	4.50
	1943	—	—	—	Proof	260.00
	1945	10.000	2.00	4.00	8.00	10.00
	1945-I	—	—	—	Proof	Rare

COPPER-NICKEL

KM#	Date	Mintage	Fine	VF	XF	Unc
9	1948	40.000	.30	.50	1.50	4.50
	1948	—	—	—	Proof	280.00
9	1950	20.000	.30	.50	1.50	4.50
	1950	—	—	—	Proof	280.00

MALAYA & BRITISH BORNEO

Malaya & British Borneo, a Currency Commission named the Board of Commissioners of Currency, Malaya and British Borneo, was initiated on Jan. 1, 1952, for the purpose of providing a common currency for use in Johore, Kelantan, Kedah, Perlis, Trengganu, Negri Sembilan, Pahang, Perak, Selangor, Penang, Malacca, Singapore, North Borneo, Sarawak and Brunei.

RULERS

British

MINT MARKS

KN - King's Norton, Birmingham
H - Heaton, Birmingham
No Mint mark - Royal Mint

MONETARY SYSTEM

100 Cents = 1 Dollar

CENT

BRONZE

KM#	Date	Mintage	VF	XF	Unc
5	1956	6.250	.10	.25	.50
	1956	—	—	Proof	125.00
	1957	12.500	.10	.25	.50
	1957	—	—	Proof	—
	1958	5.000	.10	.25	.50
	1958	—	—	Proof	125.00
	1961	10.000	.10	.20	.50
	1961	—	—	Proof	125.00

KM#	Date	Mintage	VF	XF	Unc
6	1962	45.000	—	.10	.35
	1962	*25 pcs.	—	Proof	125.00

5 CENTS

COPPER-NICKEL

KM#	Date	Mintage	VF	XF	Unc
1	1953	20.000	.25	.50	1.50
	1953	—	—	Proof	200.00
	1957	10.000	.50	.75	2.00
	1957	—	—	Proof	—
	1957H	10.000	.50	.75	2.00
	1957KN	Inc. Ab.	1.25	1.75	3.00
	1958	10.000	.25	.50	1.50
	1958	—	—	Proof	200.00
	1958H	10.000	.50	.75	2.00
	1961	90.000	.15	.50	1.25
	1961	—	—	Proof	—
	1961H	5.000	2.00	4.00	9.00
	1961KN	Inc. Ab.	.50	1.00	2.50

10 CENTS

COPPER-NICKEL

KM#	Date	Mintage	VF	XF	Unc
2	1953	20.000	.40	.80	2.00
	1953	—	—	Proof	200.00
	1956	10.000	.40	1.00	2.50
	1956	—	—	Proof	200.00
	1957H	10.000	.40	1.20	3.00
	1957H	—	—	Proof	200.00
	1957KN	10.000	.40	1.20	3.00
	1958	10.000	.40	.80	2.00
	1958	—	—	Proof	200.00
	1960	10.000	.40	.80	2.00
	1960	—	—	Proof	200.00
	1961	60.784	.20	.50	1.00
	1961	—	—	Proof	200.00
	1961H	69.220	.20	.50	1.00
	1961KN	Inc. Ab.	.50	.80	2.75

20 CENTS

COPPER-NICKEL

KM#	Date	Mintage	VF	XF	Unc
3	1954	10.000	.80	1.50	2.50
	1954	—	—	Proof	220.00
	1956	5.000	.75	1.25	2.00
	1956	—	—	Proof	220.00
	1957H	2.500	1.20	1.80	3.00
	1957KN	2.500	1.20	1.80	4.00
	1961	32.000	.50	.75	2.00
	1961	—	—	Proof	200.00
	1961H	23.000	.75	1.25	2.00

50 CENTS

COPPER-NICKEL, security edge

KM#	Date	Mintage	VF	XF	Unc
4.1	1954	8.000	1.00	2.00	4.50
	1954	—	—	Proof	280.00
	1955H	4.000	1.50	2.50	5.00
	1956	3.440	1.50	2.25	5.00
	1956	—	—	Proof	280.00
	1957H	2.000	1.50	2.50	5.00
	1957KN	2.000	2.00	2.75	6.00
	1958H	4.000	1.00	1.50	5.00
	1961	17.000	1.00	1.50	3.50
	1961	—	—	Proof	280.00
	1961H	4.000	1.50	2.50	5.00

Error, w/o security edge.

KM#	Date	Mintage	VF	XF	Unc
4.2	1954	Inc. Ab.	90.00	120.00	300.00
	1957KN	Inc. Ab.	90.00	120.00	300.00
	1958H	Inc. Ab.	90.00	120.00	300.00
	1961	Inc. Ab.	90.00	120.00	300.00
	1961H	Inc. Ab.	90.00	120.00	300.00

MALAYSIA

The independent limited constitutional monarchy of Malaysia, which occupies the southern part of the Malay Peninsula in southeast Asia and the northern part of the island of Borneo, has an area of 127,317 sq. mi. (329,750 sq. km.) and a population of 15.4 million. Capital: Kuala Lumpur. The economy is based on agriculture, mining and forestry. Rubber, tin, timber and palm oil are exported.

Malaysia came into being on Sept. 16, 1963, as a federation of Malaya (Johore, Kelantan, Kedah, Perlis, Trengganu, Negri-Sembilan, Pahang, Perak, Selangor, Penang, Malacca), Singapore, Sabah (British North Borneo) and Sarawak. Following two serious racial riots involving Malayans and Chinese, Singapore withdrew from the federation on Aug. 9, 1965, to become an independent republic within the British Commonwealth.

MINT MARKS

FM Franklin Mint, U.S.A.*

*NOTE: From 1975-1985 the Franklin Mint produced coinage in up to 3 different qualities. Qualities of issue are designated in ( ) after each date and are defined as follows:

(M) MATTE - Normal circulation strike or a dull finish produced by sandblasting special uncirculated (polish finish) or proof quality dies.

(U) SPECIAL UNCIRCULATED - Polished or proof-like in appearance without any frosted features.

(P) PROOF - The highest quality obtainable having mirror-like fields and frosted features.

MONETARY SYSTEM

100 Sen = 1 Ringgit (Dollar)

SEN

BRONZE
Parliament Building

KM#	Date	Mintage	VF	XF	Unc
1	1967	45.000	—	.10	.15
	1967	500 pcs.	—	Proof	5.00
	1968	10.500	—	.10	.15

KM#	Date	Mintage	VF	XF	Unc
1	1970	2.535	.15	.50	1.50
	1971	47.862	—	.10	.15
	1973	21.400	—	.10	.15
	1980FM(P)	5,000	—	Proof	1.00
	1981FM(P)	6,628	—	Proof	1.00

NOTE: Varieties exist.

COPPER-CLAD STEEL

KM#	Date	Mintage	VF	XF	Unc
1a	1973	Inc. Ab.	.15	.45	.65
	1976	27.406	—	.10	.15
	1977	21.751	—	.10	.15
	1978	30.844	—	.10	.15
	1979	15.714	—	.10	.15
	1980	16.152	—	.10	.15
	1981	24.633	—	.10	.15
	1982	37.295	—	.10	.15
	1983	19.333	—	.10	.15
	1984	26.267	—	.10	.15
	1985	52.402	—	.10	.15
	1986	48.920	—	.10	.15
	1987	35.284	—	.10	.15
	1988	56.749	—	.10	.15

BRONZE

KM#	Date	Mintage	VF	XF	Unc
1c	1976	100 pcs.	25.00	65.00	125.00

 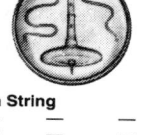

BRONZE CLAD STEEL
Drum

KM#	Date	Mintage	VF	XF	Unc
49	1989	28.429	—	—	.15
	1990	102.539	—	—	.15
	1991	100.315	—	—	.15
	1992	122.824	—	—	.15
	1993	153.806	—	—	.15
	1994	185.085	—	—	.15
	1995	208.611	—	—	.15

5 SEN

COPPER-NICKEL

KM#	Date	Mintage	VF	XF	Unc
2	1967	75.464	—	.10	.20
	1967	500 pcs.	—	Proof	20.00
	1968	74.536	—	.10	.20
	1971	16.658	—	.30	.50
	1973	102.942	—	.10	.15
	1976	65.659	—	.10	.15
	1977	10.609	—	.30	.50
	1978	50.044	—	.10	.15
	1979	38.824	—	.10	.15
	1980	33.893	—	.10	.15
	1980FM(P)	6,628	—	Proof	2.00
	1981	51.490	—	.10	.15
	1981FM(P)	—	—	Proof	3.00
	1982	118.594	—	.10	.15
	1985	15.553	—	.10	.15
	1987	17.723	—	.10	.15
	1988	26.788	—	.10	.15

NOTE: Varieties exist.

Top With String

KM#	Date	Mintage	VF	XF	Unc
50	1989	20.484	—	—	.15
	1990	58.909	—	—	.15
	1991	46.092	—	—	.15
	1992	67.844	—	—	.15
	1993	70.703	—	—	.15
	1994	83.026	—	—	.15
	1995	53.069	—	—	.15

10 SEN

COPPER-NICKEL

KM#	Date	Mintage	VF	XF	Unc
3	1967	106.708	.10	.15	.30
	1967	500 pcs.	—	Proof	25.00
	1968	128.292	.10	.15	.30
	1971	.042	35.00	45.00	65.00
	1973	214.832	.10	.15	.30
	1976	148.841	.10	.15	.30
	1977	52.720	.10	.15	.30
	1978	21.162	.10	.15	.30
	1979	50.633	.10	.15	.30
	1980	51.797	.10	.15	.30
	1980FM(P)	6,628	—	Proof	3.00
	1981	236.639	.10	.15	.30
	1981FM(P)	—	—	Proof	5.00

KM#	Date	Mintage	VF	XF	Unc
3	1982	145.639	—	.10	.25
	1983	30.832	—	.10	.25
	1988	17.852	—	.10	.25

NOTE: Varieties exist.

Ceremonial Table

KM#	Date	Mintage	VF	XF	Unc
51	1989	32.392	—	—	.25
	1990	132.982	—	—	.25
	1991	133.293	—	—	.25
	1992	89.919	—	—	.25
	1993	44.224	—	—	.25
	1994	7.122	—	—	.25
	1995	82.217	—	—	.25
	1996	—	—	—	.25

20 SEN

COPPER-NICKEL

KM#	Date	Mintage	VF	XF	Unc
4	1967	49.560	.10	.30	.45
	1967	500 pcs.	—	Proof	35.00
	1968	40.440	.10	.30	.45
	1969	15.000	.15	.35	.50
	1970	1.054	.50	.75	1.00
	1971	9.958	.15	.35	.50
	1973	116.075	.10	.20	.35
	1976	47.396	.10	.20	.35
	1977	66.139	.10	.20	.35
	1978	6.847	.15	.30	.45
	1979	17.346	.10	.20	.35
	1980	32.837	.10	.20	.35
	1980FM(P)	6,628	—	Proof	4.00
	1981	144.128	.10	.20	.35
	1981FM(P)	—	—	Proof	6.00
	1982	97.905	—	.10	.25
	1983	8.105	—	.10	.25
	1987	26.225	—	.10	.25
	1988	67.218	—	.10	.25

NOTE: Varieties exist.

Basket Containing Food and Utensils

KM#	Date	Mintage	VF	XF	Unc
52	1989	28.945	—	—	.35
	1990	56.249	—	—	.35
	1991	82.774	—	—	.35
	1992	48.975	—	—	.35
	1993	55.753	—	—	.35
	1994	2.680	—	—	.35

50 SEN

COPPER-NICKEL

KM#	Date	Mintage	VF	XF	Unc
5.1 (5)	1967	15.000	.25	.50	1.00
	1967	500 pcs.	—	Proof	45.00
	1968	12.000	.25	.50	1.00
	1969	2.000	.50	.75	1.50

Error, w/o security edge.

KM#	Date	Mintage	VF	XF	Unc
5.2 (6)	1967	Inc. Ab.	75.00	140.00	240.00
	1968	Inc. Ab.	75.00	140.00	240.00
	1969	Inc. Ab.	250.00	350.00	550.00

Lettered edge.

KM#	Date	Mintage	VF	XF	Unc
5.3 (8)	1971	8.404	.30	.60	1.00
	1973	50.135	.25	.50	.75
	1976	—	.25	.40	.60
	1977	17.720	.25	.40	.60
	1978	11.033	.25	.40	.60
	1979	5.361	.25	.40	.60
	1980	15.911	.25	.40	.60
	1980FM(P)	6,628	—	Proof	4.50
	1981	22.969	—	.25	.50
	1982	20.585	—	.25	.50

KM#	Date	Mintage	VF	XF	Unc
5.3	1983	11.560	—	.25	.50
(8)	1984	10.139	—	.25	.50
	1985	7.115	—	.25	.50
	1986	8.193	—	.25	.50
	1987	7.696	—	.25	.50
	1988	26.788	—	.25	.50

Plain edge.

5.4	1981FM(P)	—	—	Proof	10.00

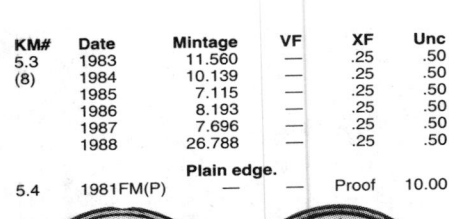

53	1989	6.639	—	—	.65
	1990	26.276	—	—	.65
	1991	20.721	—	—	.65
	1992	15.135	—	—	.65
	1993	7.656	—	—	.65
	1994	6.566	—	—	.65
	1995	1.650	—	—	.65
	1997	—	—	—	.65

Ceremonial Kite

RINGGIT

NICKEL
10th Anniversary - Bank Negara

7	ND(1969)	1.000	1.00	1.50	2.75

COPPER-NICKEL

9.1	1971	2.000	.50	.75	1.50
	1971	500 pcs.	—	Proof	800.00
	1980	.472	.60	.85	1.65
	1980FM(P)	6,628	—	Proof	8.00
	1981	.765	.60	.85	1.65
	1982	.202	.60	.85	1.65
	1984	.355	.60	.85	1.65
	1985	.302	.60	.85	1.65
	1986	.253	.60	.85	1.65
	1987	.177	.60	.85	1.65

Kuala Lumpur Anniversary

12	1972	.500	.60	.85	2.50
	1972	500 pcs.	—	Proof	350.00

COPPER-ZINC
30th Anniversary of Independence

43	ND(1987)	1.000	—	.60	1.75
	ND(1987)	.020	—	Proof	10.00

ALUMINUM-BRONZE
Native Dagger and Scabbard

KM#	Date	Mintage	VF	XF	Unc
54	1989	20.410	—	—	1.75
	1990	80.102	—	—	1.75
	1991	169.001	—	—	1.75
	1992	139.042	—	—	1.75
	1993	178.894	—	—	1.75

COPPER-ZINC
Obv: Denomination spelled out.

64	1993	Inc. Ab.	—	—	2.00
	1994	36.899	—	—	1.75
	1995	132.173	—	—	1.75
	1996	—	—	—	1.75

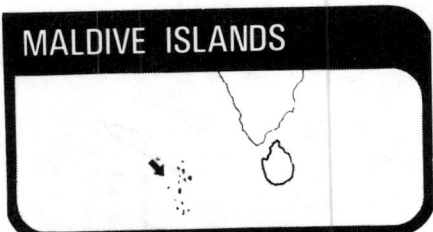

MALDIVE ISLANDS

The Republic of Maldives, an archipelago of 2,000 coral islets in the northern Indian Ocean 417 miles (671 km.) west of Ceylon, has an area of 115 sq. mi. (298 sq. km.) and a population of 189,000. Capital: Male. Fishing employs 95 percent of the male work force. Dried fish, copra and coir yarn are exported.

The Maldive Islands were visited by Arab traders and converted to Islam in 1153. After being harassed in the 16th and 17th centuries by Mopla pirates of the Malabar coast and Portuguese raiders, the Maldivians voluntarily placed themselves under the suzerainty of Ceylon. In 1887 the islands became an internally self-governing British protectorate and a nominal dependency of Ceylon. Traditionally a sultanate, the Maldives became a republic in 1953 but restored the sultanate in 1954. The Sultanate of the Maldive Islands attained complete internal and external autonomy on July 26, 1965, and on Nov. 11, 1968, again became a republic.

RULERS
Muhammad Imad al-Din V,
  AH1318-1322/1900-1904AD
Muhammad Shams al-Din III,
  AH1322-1353/1904-1935AD
Hasan Nur al-Din II,
  AH1353-1364/1935-1945AD
Abdul-Majid Didi,
  AH1364-1371/1945-1953AD
First Republic,
  AH1371-1372/1953-1954AD
Muhammad Farid Didi,
  AH1372-1388/1954-1968AD
Second Republic, AH1388 to
  date/1968AD to date

MINTNAME

Mahle (Male)

MONETARY SYSTEM
100 Lari = 1 Rupee (Rufiyaa)

MUHAMMAD IMAD AL-DIN V ISKANDAR

AH1318-1322/1900-1904AD

2 LARIAT

COPPER/BRASS, 1.40-2.20 g

KM#	Date	Fine	VF	XF	Unc
39	AH1319	1.50	3.50	5.00	7.50

NOTE: Previously listed date AH1311 is merely poor die cutting of AH1319. Many die varieties exist. Earlier date (AH1318) exists for this type.

4 LARIAT

COPPER/BRASS, 2.50-4.50 g
Plain or reeded edge.

40.1	AH1320	1.50	2.50	4.50	8.00

NOTE: Many die varieties exist.

Rev: Arabic *Sana(t)* below date.

40.2	AH1320	3.50	8.00	12.00	16.00

NOTE: Silver strikes are most likely presentation pieces.

MUHAMMAD SHAMS AL-DIN III ISKANDAR
AH1322-1353/1904-1935AD
LARIN

BRONZE, 0.90 g

KM#	Date	Fine	VF	XF	Unc
41	AH1331	1.00	1.25	1.75	3.00

Struck at Birmingham, England, Mint. Rare mint proof strikes in silver and gold exist.

4 LARIAT

BRONZE, 3.30 g

42	AH1331	1.00	1.50	2.75	6.00

Struck at Birmingham, England, Mint. Rare mint proof strikes in silver and gold exist.

REPUBLIC
MONETARY SYSTEM
100 Laari = 1 Rufiyaa
LAARI
BRONZE

KM#	Date	Year	Mintage	VF	XF	Unc
43	AH1379	1960	.300	.15	.25	.50
	1379	1960	1,270	—	Proof	2.25

ALUMINUM

49	AH1389	1970	.500	.10	.20	.40
	1399	1979	—	.10	.20	.40
	1399	1979	.100	—	Proof	1.00

Palm Tree

68	AH1404	1984	—	—	.10	.15
	1404	1984	2,500	—	Proof	2.00

2 LAARI

BRONZE

44	AH1379	1960	.600	.20	.35	.75
	1379	1960	1,270	—	Proof	2.75
50	AH1389	1970	.500	.15	.25	.50

ALUMINUM

	1399	1979	—	.15	.25	.50
	1399	1979	.100	—	Proof	1.00

5 LAARI

NICKEL-BRASS

45	AH1379	1960	.300	.25	.40	.75
	1379	1960	1,270	—	Proof	3.50
	1389	1970	.300	.20	.30	.40

BRONZE

45b	AH1379	1960	—	.25	.40	.75

ALUMINUM

45a	AH1389	1970	—	—	Proof	3.50
	1399	1979	—	—	.10	.20
	1399	1979	—	—	Proof	2.00

Bonito Fish

KM#	Date	Year	Mintage	VF	XF	Unc
69	AH1404	1984	—	—	.10	.25
	1404	1984	2,500	—	Proof	2.00
	1411	1990	—	—	.10	.25

10 LAARI

NICKEL-BRASS

46	AH1379	1960	.600	.50	.75	1.50
	1379	1960	1,270	—	Proof	4.00

ALUMINUM

46a	AH1399	1979	—	—	.10	.25
	1399	1979	—	—	Proof	2.00

Maldivian Sailing Ship - Dhivehi Odi

70	AH1404	1984	—	—	.10	.20
	1404	1984	2,500	—	Proof	2.50

25 LAARI

NICKEL-BRASS
Security edge.

47.1	AH1379	1960	.300	.60	1.00	1.50
	1379	1960	1,270	—	Proof	5.00

Reeded edge.

47.2	AH1379	1960	—	2.00	3.50	6.00
	1399	1979	—	—	.10	.25
	1399	1979	.100	—	Proof	3.00

Mosque

71	AH1404	1984	—	—	.15	.45
	1404	1984	—	—	Proof	3.50
	1411	1990	—	—	.15	.45
	1416	1996	—	—	.15	.45

50 LAARI

NICKEL-BRASS
Security edge.

48.1	AH1379	1960	.300	1.00	1.75	2.50
	1379	1960	1,270	—	Proof	7.00

Reeded edge.

48.2	AH1379	1960	—	3.00	5.00	8.00
	1399	1979	—	.10	.20	.40
	1399	1979	.100	—	Proof	6.00

Loggerhead Sea Turtle

KM#	Date	Year	Mintage	VF	XF	Unc
72	AH1404	1984	—	.15	.35	1.25
	1404	1984	—	—	Proof	5.00
	1411	1990	—	.15	.35	1.25
	1415	1995	—	.15	.35	1.25

RUFIYAA

COPPER-NICKEL CLAD STEEL

73	AH1402	1982	—	.20	.50	2.00

COPPER-NICKEL

73a	AH1404	1984	—	.20	.50	2.00
	1404	1984	—	—	Proof	10.00
	1411	1990	—	.20	.50	2.00
	1416	1996	—	.20	.50	2.00

2 RUFIYAA

BRASS
Edge: Lettering over reeding
"REPUBLIC OF MALDIVES".
Rev: Pacific Triton sea shell.

88	AH1415	1995	—	—	—	5.00

MALI

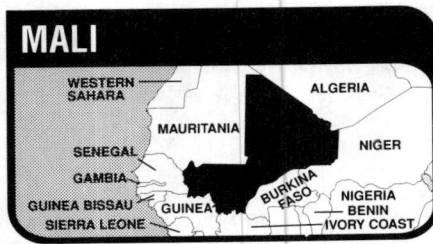

The Republic of Mali, a landlocked country in the interior of West Africa southwest of Algeria, has an area of 478,767 sq. mi. (1,240,000 sq. km.) and a population of 8.1 million. Capital: Bamako. Livestock, fish, cotton and peanuts are exported.

Malians are descendants of the ancient Malinke Kingdom of Mali that controlled the middle Niger from the 11th to the 17th centuries. The French penetrated the Sudan (now Mali) about 1880, and established their rule in 1898 after subduing fierce native resistance. In 1904 the area became the colony of Upper Senegal-Niger (changed to French Sudan in 1920), and became part of the French Union in 1946. In 1958 French Sudan became the Sudanese Republic with complete internal autonomy. Senegal joined with the Sudanese Republic in 1959 to form the Mali Federation which, in 1960, became a fully independent member of the French Community. Upon Senegal's subsequent withdrawal from the Federation, the Sudanese, on Sept. 22, 1960, proclaimed their nation the fully independent Republic of Mali and severed all ties with France.

MINT MARKS
(a) - Paris, privy marks only

5 FRANCS

ALUMINUM

KM#	Date	Mintage	Fine	VF	XF	Unc
2	1961	—	.15	.25	.50	1.25

10 FRANCS

ALUMINUM

3	1961	—	.50	1.00	2.00	5.00

11	1976(a)	5.000	1.25	2.50	4.50	12.50

25 FRANCS

ALUMINUM

4	1961	—	.35	.65	1.50	3.50

KM#	Date	Mintage	Fine	VF	XF	Unc
12	1976(a)	5.000	2.50	4.00	8.00	18.00

50 FRANCS

NICKEL-BRASS
F.A.O. Issue

9	1975(a)	10.000	.25	.50	1.00	2.50
	1977(a)	—	.25	.50	1.00	2.50

100 FRANCS

NICKEL-BRASS
F.A.O. Issue

10	1975(a)	23.000	.65	1.25	2.50	5.00

MALTA

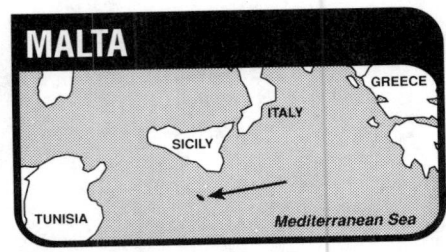

Mediterranean Sea

The Republic of Malta, an independent parliamentary democracy within the British Commonwealth, is situated in the Mediterranean Sea between Sicily and North Africa. With the islands of Gozo and Comino, Malta has an area of 122 sq. mi. (320 sq. km.) and a population of 386,000. Capital: Valletta. Malta has no proven mineral resources, an agriculture insufficient to its needs, and a small, but expanding, manufacturing facility. Clothing, textile yarns and fabrics, and knitted wear are exported.

For more than 3,500 years Malta was ruled, in succession by Phoenicians, Carthaginians, Romans, Arabs, Normans, the Knights of Malta, France and Britain. Napoleon seized Malta by treachery in 1798. The French were ousted by a Maltese insurrection assisted by Britain, and in 1814 Malta, of its own free will, became a part of the British Empire. Malta obtained full independence in Sept., 1964; electing to remain within the Commonwealth with the British monarch as the nominal head of state.

Malta became a republic on Dec. 13, 1974, but remained a member of the Commonwealth of Nations. The president is Chief of State. The prime minister is the Head of Government.

RULERS
British, until 1964

BRITISH COINAGE
MONETARY SYSTEM
4 Farthings = 1 Penny

1/3 FARTHING

COPPER
NOTE: From 1827 through 1913 homeland type 1/3 Farthings along with other coinage of Great Britain circulated in Malta. The 1/3 Farthing corresponded to the copper Grano or 1/12 Penny. These are found listed under Great Britain.

DECIMAL COINAGE

10 Mils = 1 Cent
100 Cents = 1 Pound
MINT MARKS
FM - Franklin Mint, U.S.A.*

*NOTE: From 1975-1985 the Franklin Mint produced coinage in up to 3 different qualities. Qualities of issue are designated in ( ) after each date and are defined as follows:

(M) MATTE - Normal circulation strike or a dull finish produced by sandblasting special uncirculated (polish finish) or proof quality dies.

(U) SPECIAL UNCIRCULATED - Polished or prooflike in appearance without any frosted features.

(P) PROOF - The highest quality obtainable having mirror-like fields and frosted features.

2 MILS

ALUMINUM
Maltese Cross

KM#	Date	Mintage	VF	XF	Unc
5	1972	.030	.10	.15	.30
	1972	.013	—	Proof	.50
	1976FM(M)	5,000	—	—	2.00
	1976FM(P)	.026	—	Proof	.50
	1977FM(U)	5,252	—	—	1.00
	1977FM(P)	6,884	—	Proof	1.00
	1978FM(U)	5,252	—	—	1.00
	1978FM(P)	3,244	—	Proof	1.00
	1979FM(U)	537 pcs.	—	—	3.00
	1979FM(P)	6,577	—	Proof	1.00
	1980FM(U)	385 pcs.	—	—	3.00
	1980FM(P)	3,451	—	Proof	1.00
	1981FM(U)	444 pcs.	—	—	3.00
	1981FM(P)	1,453	—	Proof	1.00

10th Anniversary of Decimalization

KM#	Date	Mintage	VF	XF	Unc
54	1982FM(U)	850 pcs.	—	—	3.00
	1982FM(P)	1,793	—	Proof	1.00

3 MILS

ALUMINUM
Bee and Honeycomb

KM#	Date	Mintage	VF	XF	Unc
6	1972	—	.10	.15	.40
	1972	8,000	—	Proof	.75
	1976FM(M)	5,000	—	—	2.50
	1976FM(P)	.026	—	Proof	.75
	1977FM(U)	5,252	—	—	1.50
	1977FM(P)	6,884	—	Proof	1.25
	1978FM(U)	5,252	—	—	2.50
	1978FM(P)	3,244	—	Proof	1.25
	1979FM(U)	537 pcs.	—	—	5.00
	1979FM(P)	6,577	—	Proof	1.25
	1980FM(U)	385 pcs.	—	—	5.00
	1980FM(P)	3,451	—	Proof	1.25
	1981FM(U)	449 pcs.	—	—	5.00
	1981FM(P)	1,453	—	Proof	1.25

10th Anniversary of Decimalization

KM#	Date	Mintage	VF	XF	Unc
55	1982FM(U)	850 pcs.	—	—	4.00
	1982FM(P)	1,793	—	Proof	1.25

5 MILS

ALUMINUM
Earthen Lampstand

KM#	Date	Mintage	VF	XF	Unc
7	1972	4.320	.10	.15	.40
	1972	.013	—	Proof	1.00
	1976FM(M)	5,000	—	—	3.00
	1976FM(P)	.026	—	Proof	1.00
	1977FM(U)	5,252	—	—	2.00
	1977FM(P)	6,884	—	Proof	1.50
	1978FM(U)	5,252	—	—	2.00
	1978FM(P)	3,244	—	Proof	1.50
	1979FM(U)	537 pcs.	—	—	7.00
	1979FM(P)	6,577	—	Proof	1.50
	1980FM(U)	385 pcs.	—	—	7.00
	1980FM(P)	3,451	—	Proof	1.50
	1981FM(U)	449 pcs.	—	—	7.00
	1981FM(P)	1,453	—	Proof	1.50

10th Anniversary of Decimalization

KM#	Date	Mintage	VF	XF	Unc
56	1982FM(U)	850 pcs.	—	—	5.00
	1982FM(P)	1,793	—	Proof	1.50

CENT

BRONZE
George Cross

KM#	Date	Mintage	VF	XF	Unc
8	1972	5.650	.10	.15	.40
	1972	.013	—	Proof	1.25
	1975	1.500	.10	.20	.50
	1976FM(M)	5,000	—	—	3.50
	1976FM(P)	.026	—	Proof	1.25
	1977	2.793	.10	.15	.40
	1977FM(U)	5,252	—	—	2.50
	1977FM(P)	6,884	—	Proof	1.75
	1978FM(U)	5,252	—	—	2.50
	1978FM(P)	3,244	—	Proof	1.75
	1979FM(U)	537 pcs.	—	—	9.00
	1979FM(P)	6,577	—	Proof	1.75
	1980FM(U)	385 pcs.	—	—	9.00
	1980FM(P)	3,451	—	Proof	1.75
	1981FM(U)	449 pcs.	—	—	9.00
	1981FM(P)	1,453	—	Proof	1.75
	1982	—	.10	.15	.25

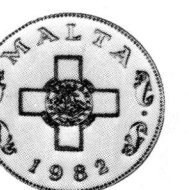

10th Anniversary of Decimalization

KM#	Date	Mintage	VF	XF	Unc
57	1982FM(U)	850 pcs.	—	—	7.50
	1982FM(P)	1.793	—	Proof	1.75

COPPER-ZINC
Common Weasel
Obv: Similar to 1 Pound, KM#82.

KM#	Date	Mintage	VF	XF	Unc
78	1986	21.526	.15	.25	.50
	1986	.010	—	Proof	2.00

KM#	Date	Mintage	VF	XF	Unc
93	1991	—	.15	.25	.50
	1995	—	.15	.25	.50

2 CENTS

COPPER-NICKEL
Penthesilea, Queen of the Amazons

KM#	Date	Mintage	VF	XF	Unc
9	1972	5.640	.10	.15	.40
	1972	.013	—	Proof	1.50
	1976	1.000	.15	.20	.60
	1976FM(M)	2,500	—	—	4.50
	1976FM(P)	.026	—	Proof	1.50
	1977	6.105	.10	.15	.40
	1977FM(U)	2,752	—	—	4.50
	1977FM(P)	6,884	—	Proof	2.50
	1978FM(U)	2,752	—	—	4.50
	1978FM(P)	3,244	—	Proof	2.50
	1979FM(U)	537 pcs.	—	—	12.00
	1979FM(P)	6,577	—	Proof	2.50
	1980FM(U)	385 pcs.	—	—	12.00
	1980FM(P)	3,451	—	Proof	2.50
	1981FM(U)	449 pcs.	—	—	12.00
	1981FM(P)	1,453	—	Proof	2.50
	1982	—	.10	.15	.30

10th Anniversary of Decimalization

KM#	Date	Mintage	VF	XF	Unc
58	1982FM(U)	850 pcs.	—	—	10.00
	1982FM(P)	1,793	—	Proof	2.50

Olive Branch
Obv: Similar to 1 Pound, KM#82.

KM#	Date	Mintage	VF	XF	Unc
79	1986	.280	.15	.25	.45
	1986	.010	—	Proof	3.00

KM#	Date	Mintage	VF	XF	Unc
94	1991	—	.15	.25	.45
	1992	—	.15	.25	.45
	1993	—	.15	.25	.45

5 CENTS

COPPER-NICKEL
Floral Altar in the Temple of Hagar Qim

KM#	Date	Mintage	VF	XF	Unc
10	1972	4.180	.20	.30	.50
	1972	.013	—	Proof	1.75
	1976	1.009	.20	.30	.60
	1976FM(M)	2,500	—	—	5.00
	1976FM(P)	.026	—	Proof	2.00
	1977	—	.20	.30	.50
	1977FM(U)	2,752	—	—	5.00
	1977FM(P)	6,884	—	Proof	3.00
	1978FM(U)	2,752	—	—	5.00
	1978FM(P)	3,244	—	Proof	3.00
	1979FM(U)	537 pcs.	—	—	15.00
	1979FM(P)	6,577	—	Proof	3.00
	1980FM(U)	385 pcs.	—	—	15.00
	1980FM(P)	3,451	—	Proof	3.00
	1981FM(U)	449 pcs.	—	—	15.00
	1981FM(P)	1,453	—	Proof	3.00

10th Anniversary of Decimalization

KM#	Date	Mintage	VF	XF	Unc
59	1982FM(U)	850 pcs.	—	—	12.50
	1982FM(P)	1,793	—	Proof	3.00

Fresh Water Crab

KM#	Date	Mintage	VF	XF	Unc
77	1986	.150	.25	.45	1.00
	1986	.010	—	Proof	3.50

KM#	Date	Mintage	VF	XF	Unc
95	1991	—	.25	.45	1.00
	1995	—	.25	.45	1.00

10 CENTS

COPPER-NICKEL

Barge of the Grand Master

KM#	Date	Mintage	VF	XF	Unc
11	1972	10.680	.40	.60	1.00
	1972	.013	—	Proof	2.25
	1976FM(M)	1,000	—	—	6.00
	1976FM(P)	.026	—	Proof	2.50
	1977FM(U)	1,252	—	—	6.00
	1977FM(P)	6,884	—	Proof	3.50
	1978FM(U)	1,252	—	—	6.00
	1978FM(P)	3,244	—	Proof	3.50
	1979FM(U)	537 pcs.	—	—	17.50
	1979FM(P)	6,577	—	Proof	3.50
	1980FM(U)	385 pcs.	—	—	15.00
	1980FM(P)	3,451	—	Proof	3.50
	1981FM(U)	449 pcs.	—	—	15.00
	1981FM(P)	1,453	—	Proof	3.50

10th Anniversary of Decimalization

KM#	Date	Mintage	VF	XF	Unc
60	1982FM(U)	850 pcs.	—	—	14.00
	1982FM(P)	1,793	—	Proof	3.50

KM#	Date	Mintage	VF	XF	Unc
76	1986	4.188	.40	.70	1.50
	1986	.010	—	Proof	4.00

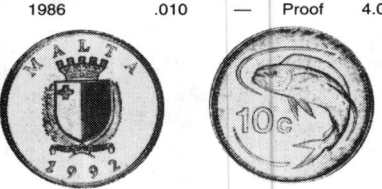

Obv: Crowned shield. Rev: Dolphinfish.

KM#	Date	Mintage	VF	XF	Unc
96	1991	—	.40	.70	1.50
	1992	—	.40	.70	1.50

25 CENTS

BRASS
1st Anniversary - Republic of Malta

KM#	Date	Mintage	VF	XF	Unc
29	1975	4.750	1.00	1.50	2.50
	1975	—		Matte Proof	150.00

BRONZE

29a	1975	6,000	—	Proof	12.50

COPPER-NICKEL

29b	1976FM(M)	300 pcs.	—	—	40.00
	1976FM(P)	.026	—	Proof	3.00
	1977FM(U)	552 pcs.	—	—	20.00
	1977FM(P)	6,884	—	Proof	4.50
	1978FM(U)	552 pcs.	—	—	20.00
	1978FM(P)	3,244	—	Proof	4.50
	1979FM(U)	537 pcs.	—	—	20.00
	1979FM(P)	6,577	—	Proof	4.50
	1980FM(U)	385 pcs.	—	—	20.00
	1980FM(P)	3,451	—	Proof	4.50
	1981FM(U)	449 pcs.	—	—	20.00
	1981FM(P)	1,453	—	Proof	4.50

10th Anniversary of Decimalization

KM#	Date	Mintage	VF	XF	Unc
61	1982FM(U)	850 pcs.	—	—	15.00
	1982FM(P)	1,793	—	Proof	4.50

Ghirlanda Flower
Obv: Similar to 1 Pound, KM#82.

KM#	Date	Mintage	VF	XF	Unc
80	1986	3.090	1.00	1.80	2.50
	1986	.010	—	Proof	5.00

Obv: Crowned shield. Rev: Ghirlanda flower.

KM#	Date	Mintage	VF	XF	Unc
97	1991	—	1.00	1.50	2.50
	1993	—	1.00	1.50	2.50
	1995	—	1.00	1.50	2.50

50 CENTS

COPPER-NICKEL
Great Siege Monument

KM#	Date	Mintage	VF	XF	Unc
12	1972	5.500	1.75	2.00	3.50
	1972	.013	—	Proof	4.50
	1976FM(M)	150 pcs.	—	—	90.00
	1976FM(P)	.026	—	Proof	5.00
	1977FM(U)	402 pcs.	—	—	25.00
	1977FM(P)	6,884	—	Proof	6.00
	1978FM(U)	402 pcs.	—	—	25.00
	1978FM(P)	3,244	—	Proof	6.00
	1979FM(U)	537 pcs.	—	—	25.00
	1979FM(P)	6,577	—	Proof	6.00
	1980FM(U)	385 pcs.	—	—	25.00
	1980FM(P)	3,451	—	Proof	6.00
	1981FM(U)	449 pcs.	—	—	25.00
	1981FM(P)	1,453	—	Proof	6.00

10th Anniversary of Decimalization

KM#	Date	Mintage	VF	XF	Unc
62	1982FM(U)	850 pcs.	—	—	20.00
	1982FM(P)	1,793	—	Proof	6.00

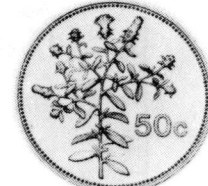

Tulliera Plant
Obv: Similar to 1 Pound, KM#82.

KM#	Date	Mintage	VF	XF	Unc
81	1986	2.086	1.75	2.25	4.50
	1986	.010	—	Proof	7.00

Obv: Similar to 5 Cents, KM#95.

KM#	Date	Mintage	VF	XF	Unc
98	1991	—	1.75	2.25	4.50
	1992	—	1.75	2.25	4.50

POUND

10.0000 g, .987 SILVER, .3173 oz ASW
Manwel Dimech

13	1972	.055	—	4.50	8.00

Sir Temi Zammit

19	1973	.030	—	4.50	8.00

5.6600 g, .925 SILVER, .1683 oz ASW
Kelb tal-Fenek, an ancient Maltese dog.

45	1977	.066	—	6.00	15.00
	1977	2,500	—	Proof	30.00

Departure of Foreign Forces

51	1979FM(U)	.050	—	4.00	7.00
	1979FM(P)	7,871	—	Proof	17.50

NICKEL
Merill Bird

82	1986	2.272	—	4.00	7.50
	1986	.010	—	Proof	10.00

Obv: Similar to 2 Cents, KM#94.

99	1991	—	—	3.50	6.00

MARTINIQUE

The French Overseas Department of Martinique, located in the Lesser Antilles of the West Indies between Dominica and Saint Lucia, has an area of 425 sq. mi. (1,100 sq. km.) and a population of 290,000. Capital: Fort-de-France. Agriculture and tourism are the major sources of income. Bananas, sugar, and rum are exported.

Christopher Columbus discovered Martinique, probably on June 15, 1502. France took possession on June 25, 1635, and has maintained possession since that time except for three short periods of British occupation during the Napoleonic Wars. A French department since 1946, Martinique voted a reaffirmation of that status in 1958, remaining within the new French Community. Martinique was the birthplace of Napoleon's Empress Josephine, and the site of the eruption of Mt. Pelee in 1902 that claimed 40,000 lives.

The official currency of Martinique is the French franc. The 1897-1922 coinage of the Colony of Martinique is now obsolete.

MONETARY SYSTEM
100 Centimes = 1 Franc

50 CENTIMES

COPPER-NICKEL

KM#	Date	Mintage	VG	Fine	VF	XF
40	1922	.500	7.50	15.00	35.00	80.00

NOTE: Earlier date (1897) exists for this type.

FRANC

COPPER-NICKEL

KM#	Date	Mintage				
41	1922	.350	10.00	20.00	35.00	90.00

NOTE: Earlier date (1897) exists for this type.

MAURITANIA

The Islamic Republic of Mauritania, located in northwest Africa bounded by Spanish Sahara, Mali, Algeria, Senegal and the Atlantic Ocean, has an area of 397,955 sq. mi. (1,030,700 sq. km.) and a population of 1.9 million. Capital: Nouakchott. The economy centers about herding, agriculture, fishing and mining. Iron ore, copper concentrates and fish products are exported.

The indigenous Negroid inhabitants were driven out of Mauritania by Berber invaders of the Islamic faith in the 11th century. The Berbers in turn were conquered by Arab invaders, the Beni Hassan, in the 16th century. Arab traders carried on a gainful trade in gum arabic, gold and slaves with Portuguese, Dutch, English and French traders until late in the 19th century when France took control of the area and made it a part of French West Africa, in 1920. Mauritania became a part of the French Union in 1946 and was made an autonomous republic within the new French Community in 1958, when the Islamic Republic of Mauritania was proclaimed. The republic became independent on November 28, 1960, and withdrew from the French Community in 1966.

On June 28, 1973, in a move designed to emphasize its non-alignment with France, Mauritania converted its currency from the old French-supported C.F.A. franc unit to a new unit called the Ouguiya.

MONETARY SYSTEM
5 Khoums = 1 Ouguiya
100 Ouguiya = 500 CFA Francs

1/5 OUGUIYA
(Khoums)

ALUMINUM

KM#	Date	Year	Mintage	Fine	VF	XF	Unc
1	AH1393	1973	1.000	.35	.75	1.50	2.75

OUGUIYA

COPPER-NICKEL-ALUMINUM
Rev: Arabic leg. in one line.

2	AH1393	1973	—	5.00	10.00	17.50	30.00

Rev: Arabic leg. in two lines.

6	AH1394	1974	—	2.50	5.50	10.00	18.50
	1401	1981	—	1.50	3.00	4.50	7.50
	1403	1983	—	1.00	2.00	3.50	6.50
	1406	1986	—	.75	1.50	2.50	4.00
	1407	1987	—	.50	1.00	2.00	3.50
	1410	1990	—	.50	1.00	2.00	3.50
	1414	1993	—	.50	1.00	2.00	3.50
	1416	1995	—	.50	1.00	2.00	3.50

5 OUGUIYA

COPPER-NICKEL-ALUMINUM

3	AH1393	1973	—	2.50	5.50	10.00	15.00
	1394	1974	—	2.50	5.50	10.00	17.50

KM#	Date	Year	Mintage	Fine	VF	XF	Unc
3	1401	1981	—	2.00	4.00	6.00	12.50
	1404	1984	—	1.50	2.50	4.50	10.00
	1407	1987	—	.75	1.50	2.50	4.00
	1410	1990	—	.50	1.00	2.00	3.50
	1414	1993	—	.50	1.00	2.00	3.50
	1416	1995	—	.50	1.00	2.00	3.50

10 OUGUIYA

COPPER-NICKEL

4	AH1393	1973	—	2.50	5.50	10.00	17.50
	1394	1974	—	2.50	5.50	10.00	17.50
	1401	1981	—	2.00	5.00	7.50	15.00
	1403	1983	—	1.25	2.50	4.00	8.00
	1407	1987	—	1.25	2.50	4.00	8.00
	1410	1990	—	.75	1.50	2.50	4.50
	1411	1991	—	.75	1.50	2.50	4.50
	1414	1993	—	.75	1.50	2.50	4.50
	1416	1995	—	.75	1.50	2.50	4.50

20 OUGUIYA

COPPER-NICKEL

5	AH1393	1973	—	2.00	5.00	10.00	18.00
	1394	1974	—	2.00	5.00	10.00	18.00
	1403	1983	—	1.25	2.50	4.00	8.00
	1407	1987	—	1.25	2.50	4.00	8.00
	1410	1990	—	1.25	2.50	4.00	8.00
	1414	1993	—	1.25	2.50	4.00	8.00
	1416	1995	—	1.25	2.50	4.00	8.00

MAURITIUS

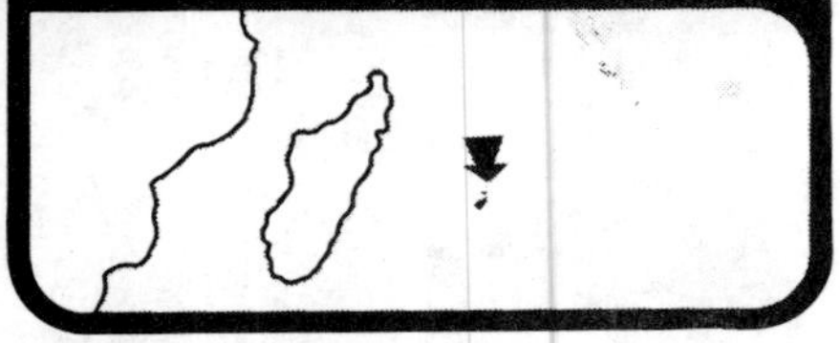

The Republic of Mauritius, a member nation of the British Commonwealth located in the Indian Ocean 500 miles (805 km.) east of Madagascar, has an area of 790 sq. mi. (1,860 sq. km.) and a population of 1 million. Capital: Port Louis. Sugar provides 90 percent of the export revenue.

Cartographic evidence indicates that Arabs and Malays arrived at Mauritius during the Middle Ages. Domingo Fernandez, a Portuguese navigator, visited the island in the early 16th century, but Portugal made no attempt at settlement. The Dutch took possession, and named the island, in 1598. Their colony failed to prosper and was abandoned in 1710. France claimed Mauritius in 1715 and developed a strong and prosperous colony that endured until the island was captured by the British, 1810, during the Napoleonic Wars. British possession was confirmed by the Treaty of Paris, 1814. Mauritius became independent on March 12, 1968. It is a member of the Commonwealth of Nations.

The first coins struck under British auspices for Mauritius were undated (1822) and bore French legends.

RULERS

British, until 1968

MINT MARKS

SA - Pretoria Mint

MONETARY SYSTEM

100 Cents = 1 Rupee

CENT

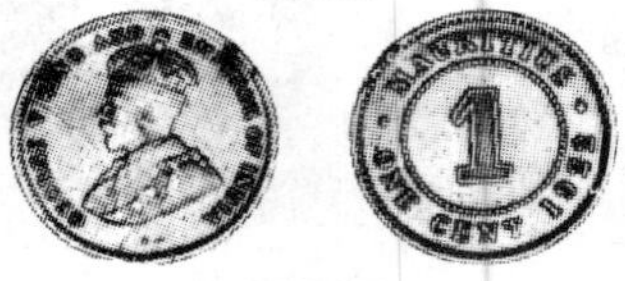

BRONZE

KM#	Date	Mintage	Fine	VF	XF	Unc
12	1911	1.000	1.00	2.00	12.00	40.00
	1912	.500	1.25	2.50	18.50	55.00
	1917	.500	1.00	2.00	12.00	35.00
	1920	.500	1.50	3.00	22.50	60.00
	1921	.500	2.00	4.00	22.50	60.00
	1922	1.800	.75	1.50	9.00	25.00
	1923	.200	3.00	7.00	35.00	75.00
	1924	.200	3.00	7.00	35.00	75.00

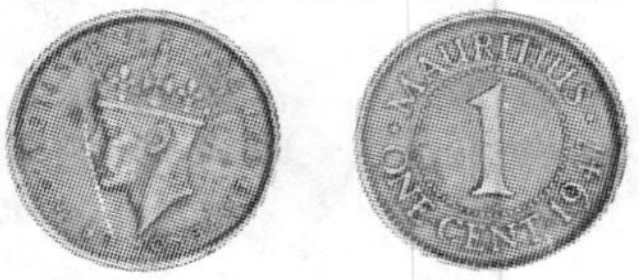

KM#	Date	Mintage	Fine	VF	XF	Unc
21	1943SA	.520	.50	1.25	4.00	10.00
	1944SA	.500	.50	1.25	4.00	10.00
	1945SA	.500	.50	1.25	4.00	10.00
	1946SA	.500	.50	1.25	4.00	10.00
	1947SA	.500	.50	1.25	4.00	10.00

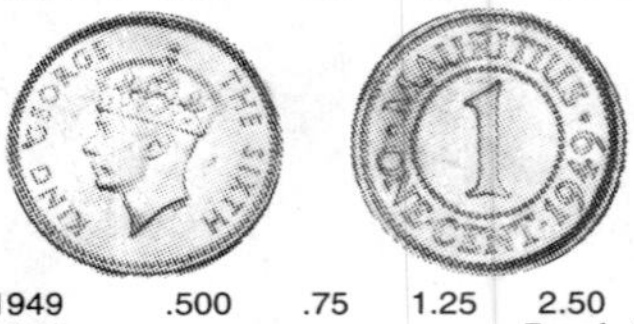

KM#	Date	Mintage	Fine	VF	XF	Unc
25	1949	.500	.75	1.25	2.50	7.50
	1949	—	—	—	Proof	100.00
	1952	.500	.75	1.25	2.50	7.50
	1952	—	—	—	Proof	100.00

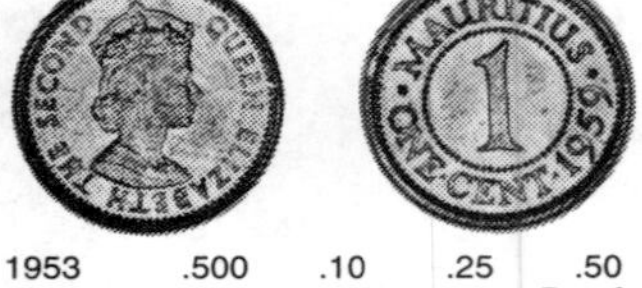

KM#	Date	Mintage	Fine	VF	XF	Unc
31	1953	.500	.10	.25	.50	1.50
	1953	—	—	—	Proof	75.00
	1955	.501	.10	.25	.50	2.50
	1955	—	—	—	Proof	75.00
	1956	.500	.10	.20	.50	2.50
	1956	—	—	—	Proof	75.00
	1957	.501	.10	.20	.50	2.50
	1959	.501	.10	.20	.50	2.50
	1959	—	—	—	Proof	75.00
	1960	.500	.10	.20	.50	2.50
	1960	—	—	—	Proof	75.00
	1961	.500	.10	.20	.50	2.50
31	1961	—	—	—	Proof	75.00
	1962	.500	.10	.20	.50	1.50
	1962	—	—	—	Proof	50.00
	1963	.500	.10	.20	.50	1.50
	1963	—	—	—	Proof	50.00
	1964	1.500	—	.10	.20	.50
	1964	—	—	—	Proof	50.00
	1965	1.500	—	.10	.20	.50
	1969	.500	—	.10	.15	.30
	1970	1.500	—	—	.10	.20
	1971	1.000	—	—	.10	.20
	1971	750 pcs.	—	—	Proof	20.00
	1975	.400	—	—	.10	.20
	1978	9,268	—	—	Proof	1.00

2 CENTS

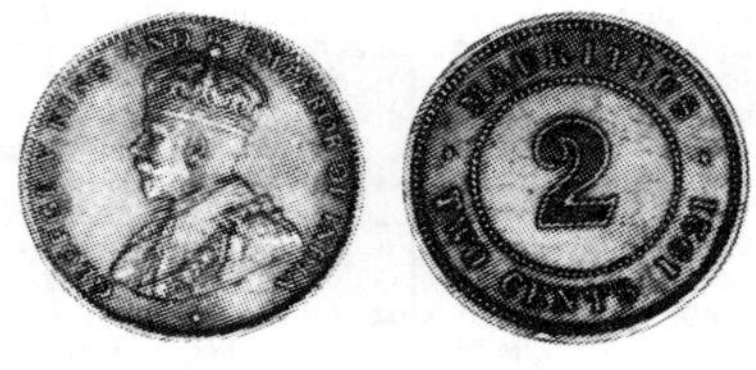

BRONZE

KM#	Date	Mintage	Fine	VF	XF	Unc
13	1911	.500	2.00	4.00	15.00	40.00
	1911	—	—	—	Proof	300.00
	1912	.250	3.00	5.00	30.00	70.00
	1917	.250	1.25	2.50	12.00	35.00
	1920	.250	1.50	3.00	20.00	45.00
	1921	.250	1.50	3.00	20.00	45.00
	1922	.900	.50	1.00	8.00	30.00
	1923	.400	1.25	2.50	18.50	45.00
	1924	.400	1.25	2.50	18.50	45.00

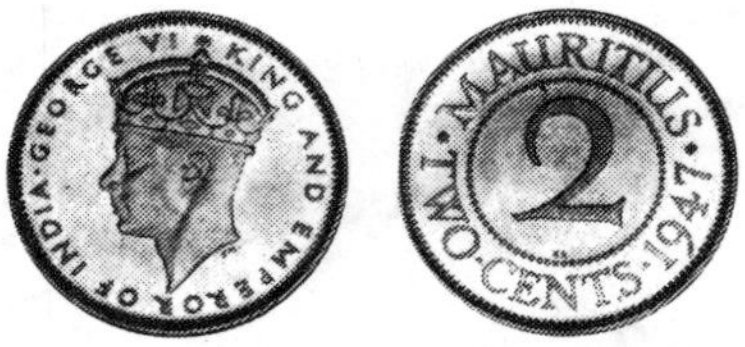

KM#	Date	Mintage	Fine	VF	XF	Unc
22	1943SA	.290	.75	2.00	4.00	10.00
	1944SA	.500	.75	2.00	4.00	10.00
	1945SA	.250	.75	2.00	4.00	10.00
	1946SA	.400	.75	2.00	4.00	10.00
	1947SA	.250	.75	2.00	4.00	10.00

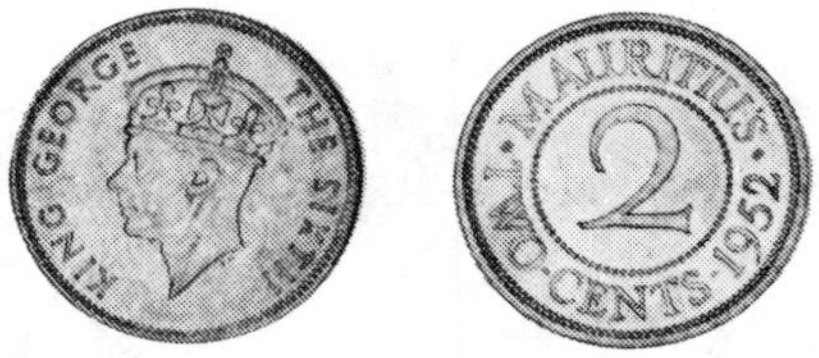

KM#	Date	Mintage	Fine	VF	XF	Unc
26	1949	.250	.75	1.25	2.50	6.50
	1949	—	—	—	Proof	120.00
	1952	.250	.75	1.25	2.50	6.50
	1952	—	—	—	Proof	120.00

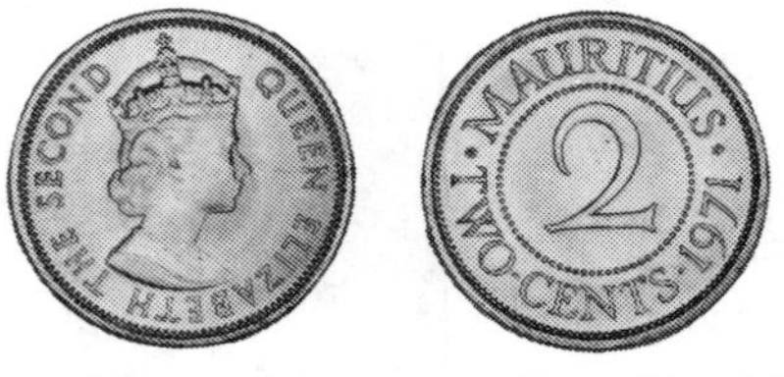

KM#	Date	Mintage	Fine	VF	XF	Unc
32	1953	.250	.10	.25	.50	2.50
	1953	—	—	—	Proof	100.00
	1954	—	—	—	Proof	300.00
	1955	.501	.10	.25	.50	2.50
	1955	—	—	—	Proof	100.00
	1956	.250	.10	.25	.50	3.50
	1956	—	—	—	Proof	100.00
	1957	.501	.10	.25	.50	3.50
	1959	.503	.10	.25	.50	3.50
	1959	—	—	—	Proof	100.00
	1960	.250	.10	.25	.50	3.50
	1960	—	—	—	Proof	100.00
	1961	.500	.10	.25	.50	3.50
	1961	—	—	—	Proof	100.00
	1962	.500	.10	.25	.50	1.50
	1962	—	—	—	Proof	75.00
	1963	.500	.10	.25	.50	1.50
	1963	—	—	—	Proof	75.00
	1964	1.00	—	.10	.25	.50
	1964	—	—	—	Proof	50.00
	1965	.750	.10	.20	.40	.60
	1966	.500	.10	.20	.40	.50
	1967	.250	.10	.20	.40	.50
	1969	.500	.10	.20	.40	.50
	1971	1.000	—	.10	.20	.40
	1971	750 pcs.	—	—	Proof	20.00
	1975	5.200	—	—	.10	.35
	1978	—	—	—	.10	.35
	1978	9,268	—	—	Proof	1.50

5 CENTS

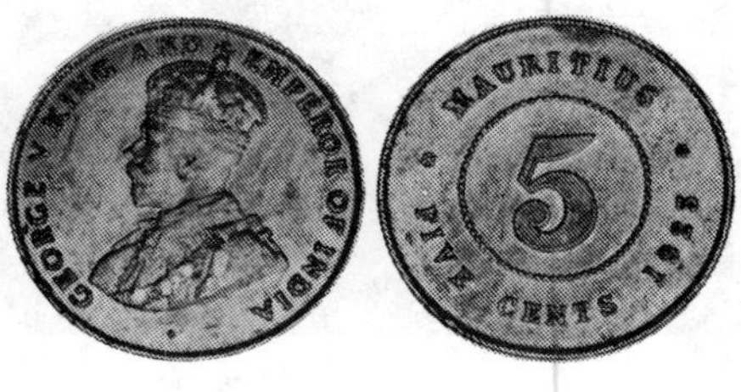

BRONZE

KM#	Date	Mintage	Fine	VF	XF	Unc
14	1917	.600	2.00	4.50	27.50	80.00
	1920	.200	2.00	4.50	32.50	100.00
	1921	.100	3.00	6.50	35.00	120.00
	1922	.360	2.00	4.50	32.50	100.00
	1923	.400	3.00	6.50	35.00	120.00
	1924	.400	2.00	4.50	32.50	100.00

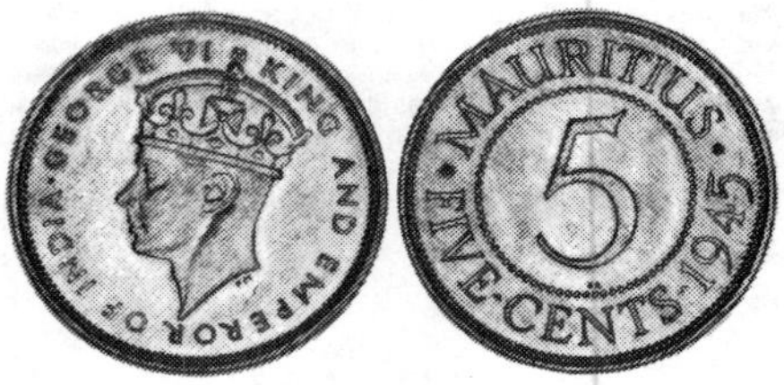

KM#	Date	Mintage	Fine	VF	XF	Unc
20	1942SA	.940	1.50	2.50	6.50	15.00
	1944SA	1.000	1.25	1.75	4.00	10.00
	1945SA	.500	1.25	1.75	4.00	12.00

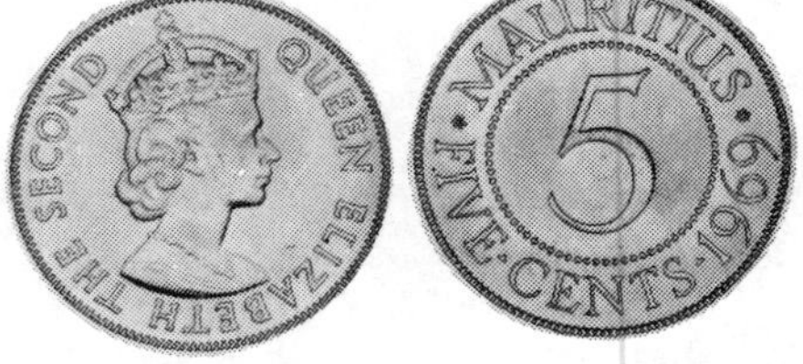

KM#	Date	Mintage	Fine	VF	XF	Unc
34	1956	.201	.25	.50	.75	5.00
	1956	—	—	—	Proof	100.00
	1957	.203	.25	.50	2.00	8.00
	1957	—	—	—	Proof	100.00
	1959	.801	.25	.50	1.00	4.00
	1959	—	—	—	Proof	75.00
	1960	.400	.25	.50	1.00	4.00
	1960	—	—	—	Proof	75.00
	1963	.200	.25	.50	1.00	2.00
	1963	—	—	—	Proof	70.00
	1964	.600	.25	.50	1.00	2.00
	1964	—	—	—	Proof	70.00
	1965	.200	.25	.50	.75	2.00
	1966	.200	.25	.50	.75	1.50
	1967	.200	.25	.50	.75	2.00
	1969	.500	.10	.15	.25	.50
	1970	.800	.10	.15	.25	.50
	1971	.500	.10	.15	.25	.50
	1971	750 pcs.	—	—	Proof	20.00
	1975	3.700	.10	.15	.25	.50
	1978	8.000	—	.10	.20	.50
	1978	9,268	—	—	Proof	2.00

10 CENTS

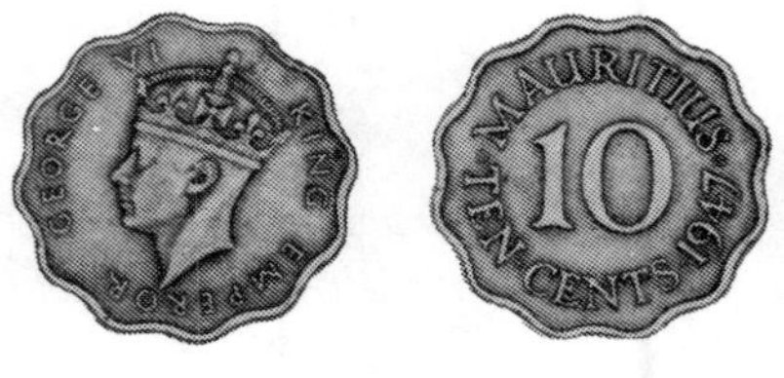

COPPER-NICKEL

KM#	Date	Mintage	Fine	VF	XF	Unc
24	1947	.500	.75	1.50	8.00	35.00
	1947	—	—	—	Proof	200.00

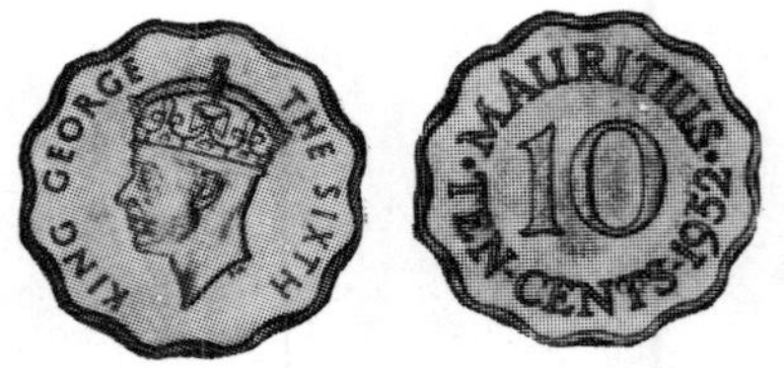

KM#	Date	Mintage	Fine	VF	XF	Unc
30	1952	.250	.50	.75	1.50	6.50
	1952	—	—	—	Proof	150.00

KM#	Date	Mintage	Fine	VF	XF	Unc
33	1954	.252	.20	.35	.75	2.50
	1954	—	—	—	Proof	150.00
	1957	.250	.20	.35	.75	2.50
	1959	.253	.20	.35	.75	2.50
	1959	—	—	—	Proof	175.00
	1960	.050	.20	.35	.75	2.00
	1960	—	—	—	Proof	175.00
	1963	.200	.15	.30	.60	1.50
	1963	—	—	—	Proof	175.00
	1964	.200	.15	.30	.60	1.00
	1965	.200	.15	.30	.60	1.00
	1966	.200	.10	.25	.50	.75
	1969	.200	.10	.25	.50	.75
	1970	.500	.10	.25	.50	.75
	1971	.300	.10	.25	.50	.75
	1971	750 pcs.	—	—	Proof	20.00
	1975	6.675	.10	.25	.50	.75
	1978	13.000	.10	.25	.50	.75
	1978	9,268	—	—	Proof	2.50

1/4 RUPEE

2.9200 g, .916 SILVER, .0816 oz ASW

15	1934	.400	2.00	7.00	20.00	60.00
	1934	—	—	—	Proof	600.00
	1935	.400	2.00	7.00	20.00	60.00
	1935	—	—	—	Proof	750.00
	1936	.400	2.00	6.00	18.00	50.00
	1936	—	—	—	Proof	650.00

18	1938	2.000	3.00	10.00	30.00	80.00
	1938	—	—	—	Proof	375.00

2.9200 g, .500 SILVER, .0470 oz ASW

18a	1946	2.000	7.50	20.00	40.00	100.00
	1946	—	—	—	Proof	400.00

COPPER-NICKEL

27	1950	2.000	.50	1.00	2.00	9.50
	1950	—	—	—	Proof	175.00
	1951	1.000	.50	1.00	2.00	9.50
	1951	—	—	—	Proof	175.00

36	1960	1.000	.35	.75	1.00	2.00
	1960	—	—	—	Proof	100.00
	1964	.400	.25	.50	.75	1.50
	1964	—	—	—	Proof	100.00
	1965	.400	.25	.50	.75	1.25
	1970	.400	.20	.35	.65	1.25
	1971	.540	.25	.50	.75	1.25
	1971	750 pcs.	—	—	Proof	20.00
	1975	8.940	.15	.30	.60	1.00
	1978	*8.800	.15	.30	.60	1.00
	1978	9,268	—	—	Proof	3.50

*NOTE: Variety exists with lower hole in 8 filled.

1/2 RUPEE

5.8300 g, .916 SILVER, .1717 oz ASW

KM#	Date	Mintage	Fine	VF	XF	Unc
16	1934	1.000	2.50	5.00	15.00	50.00
	1934	—	—	—	Proof	450.00

5.8300 g, .500 SILVER, .0937 oz ASW

23	1946	1.000	10.00	25.00	125.00	200.00
	1946	—	—	—	Proof	700.00

COPPER-NICKEL

28	1950	1.000	.50	1.00	1.75	7.00
	1950	—	—	—	Proof	175.00
	1951	.570	.75	1.25	2.00	8.00
	1951	—	—	—	Proof	225.00

37.1	1965	.200	.50	1.00	2.00	6.00
	1971	.400	.25	.50	.75	1.50
	1971	750 pcs.	—	—	Proof	25.00
	1975	4.160	.25	.50	.75	1.50
	1978	.400	.25	.50	.75	1.50
	1978	9,268	—	—	Proof	4.00

Error. W/o security edge.

| 37.2 | 1971 | Inc. Ab. | | | | |

RUPEE

11.6600 g, .916 SILVER, .3434 oz ASW

17	1934	1.500	4.00	8.00	20.00	50.00
	1934	—	—	—	Proof	600.00

19	1938	.200	10.00	20.00	60.00	175.00
	1938	—	—	—	Proof	550.00

COPPER-NICKEL

29.1	1950	1.500	.75	1.50	3.00	16.00
	1950	—	—	—	Proof	200.00
	1951	1.000	.50	1.25	2.00	12.00
	1951	—	—	—	Proof	300.00

Error. W/o security edge.

| 29.2 | 1951 | Inc. Ab. | — | — | — | — |

KM#	Date	Mintage	Fine	VF	XF	Unc
35.1	1956	1.000	.25	.75	1.50	7.50
	1956	—	—	—	Proof	200.00
	1964	.200	.50	1.00	3.00	5.00
	1971	.600	.25	.60	1.00	2.00
	1971	750 pcs.	—	—	Proof	50.00
	1975	4.525	.25	.60	1.00	2.00
	1978	2.000	.25	.60	1.00	2.00
	1978	9,268	—	—	Proof	5.00

Error. W/o security edge.

| 35.2 | 1971 | Inc. Ab. | .25 | .75 | 1.25 | 2.50 |

10 RUPEES

COPPER-NICKEL
Independence Commemorative
Obv: Young Queen Elizabeth. Rev: Dodo bird.

38	1971	.050	—	1.50	3.00	7.50

MONETARY REFORM
CENT

COPPER PLATED STEEL

51	1987	*5,000	—	—	—	.20
	1987	*2,500	—	—	Proof	1.00

5 CENTS

COPPER PLATED STEEL

52	1987	*5,000	—	—	—	.30
	1987	*2,500	—	—	Proof	2.00
	1990	—	—	—	—	.30
	1991	—	—	—	—	.30
	1993	—	—	—	—	.30
	1994	—	—	—	—	.30

20 CENTS

NICKEL PLATED STEEL

53	1987	*5,000	—	—	—	.50
	1987	*2,500	—	—	Proof	3.00
	1990	—	—	—	—	.50
	1991	—	—	—	—	.50
	1993	—	—	—	—	.50
	1994	—	—	—	—	.50

1/2 RUPEE

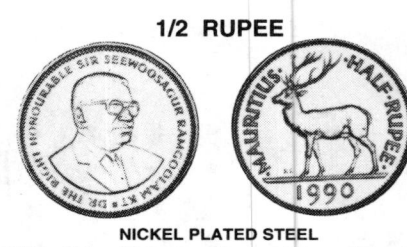

NICKEL PLATED STEEL

KM#	Date	Mintage	Fine	VF	XF	Unc
54	1987	*5,000	—	—	—	1.00
	1987	*2,500	—	—	Proof	5.00
	1990	—	—	—	—	1.00

RUPEE

COPPER-NICKEL

KM#	Date	Mintage	Fine	VF	XF	Unc
55	1987	*5,000	—	—	—	1.50
	1987	*2,500	—	—	Proof	10.00
	1990	—	—	—	—	1.50
	1991	—	—	—	—	1.50

5 RUPEES

COPPER-NICKEL

KM#	Date	Mintage	Fine	VF	XF	Unc
56	1987	*5,000	—	—	—	3.00
	1987	*2,500	—	—	Proof	16.00
	1991	—	—	—	—	3.00
	1992	—	—	—	—	3.00

10 RUPEES

COPPER-NICKEL
Obv: Portrait. Rev: Sugar cane harvesting.

KM#	Date	Mintage	Fine	VF	XF	Unc
61	1997	—	—	—	—	4.00

MEXICO

MINTS OF MEXICO

Locations of the various mints where coins were produced in Mexico.

Casas De Moneda De Mexico
Ubicacion de las diferentes cecas donde se troquelo moneda en Mexico.

The United States of Mexico, located immediately south of the United States has an area of 759,529 sq. mi. (1,967,183 sq. km.) and an estimated population of 88 million. Capital: Mexico City. The economy is based on agriculture, manufacturing and mining. Oil, cotton, silver, coffee, and shrimp are exported.

Mexico was the site of highly advanced Indian civilizations 1,500 years before conquistador Hernando Cortes conquered the wealthy Aztec empire of Montezuma, 1519-21, and founded a Spanish colony which lasted for nearly 300 years. During the Spanish period, Mexico, then called New Spain, stretched from Guatemala to the present states of Wyoming and California, its present northern boundary having been established by the secession of Texas during 1836 and the war of 1846-48 with the United States.

Independence from Spain was declared by Father Miguel Hidalgo on Sept. 16, 1810, (Mexican Independence Day) and was achieved by General Agustin de Iturbide in 1821. Iturbide became emperor in 1822 but was deposed when a republic was established a year later. For more than half a century following the birth of the republic, the political scene of Mexico was characterized by turmoil which saw two emperors (including the unfortunate Maximilian), several dictators and an average of one new government every nine months passing swiftly from obscurity to oblivion. The land, social, economic and labor reforms promulgated by the Reform Constitution of Feb. 5, 1917 established the basis for sustained economic development and participative democracy that have made Mexico one of the most politically stable countries of modern Latin America.

REPUBLIC

MINT MARKS

M, Mo - Mexico City

Z, Zs - Zacatecas

ASSAYERS INITIALS

CULIACAN MINT

Initials	Years	Mintmaster
JQ, Q	1899-1903	Jesus S. Quiroz
FV, V	1903	Francisco Valdez
MH, H	1904	Merced Hernandez
RP, P	1904-1905	Ramon Ponce de Leon

MEXICO CITY MINT

Because of the great number of assayers for this mint (Mexico City is a much larger mint than any of the others) there is much confusion as to which initial stands for which assayer at any one time. Therefore we feel that it would be of no value to list the assayers.

ZACATECAS MINT

| FZ | 1886-1905 | Francisco de P. Zarate |
| FM | 1904-1905 | Francisco Mateos |

DECIMAL COINAGE

MONETARY SYSTEM

100 Centavos = 1 Peso

UN (1) CENTAVO

COPPER
Mint mark: C
Reduced size.

KM#	Date	Mintage	Fine	VF	XF	Unc
394	1901	.220	15.00	22.50	35.00	65.00
	1902	.320	15.00	22.50	45.00	90.00
	1903	.536	7.50	12.50	20.00	45.00
	1904/3	.148	35.00	50.00	75.00	125.00
	1905	.110	100.00	150.00	300.00	550.00

NOTE: Varieties exist.

Mint mark: M,Mo

KM#	Date	Mintage	Fine	VF	XF	Unc
394.1	1901	1.494	3.00	8.00	17.50	50.00
	1902/899					
		2.090	30.00	60.00	100.00	175.00
	1902	Inc. Ab.	2.25	4.00	10.00	35.00
	1903	8.400	1.50	2.25	4.00	20.00
	1904	10.250	1.50	2.00	4.00	20.00
	1905	3.643	2.25	4.00	10.00	40.00

NOTE: Varieties exist.
NOTE: Earlier dates (1899-1900) exist for this type.

5 CENTAVOS

.903 SILVER
Mint mark: Cn
Obv: Restyled eagle.

KM#	Date	Mintage	Fine	VF	XF	Unc
400	1901 Q	.148	1.75	2.25	4.50	12.50
	1902 Q narrow C, heavy serifs					
		.262	1.75	2.50	6.00	15.00
	1902 Q wide C, light serifs					
		Inc. Ab.	1.75	2.50	6.00	15.00
	1903/1 Q	.331	2.00	2.50	6.00	15.00
	1903 Q	Inc. Ab.	1.75	2.25	4.50	12.50
	1903/1898 V					
		Inc. Ab.	3.50	4.50	9.00	22.50
	1903 V	Inc. Ab.	1.75	2.25	4.50	12.50
	1904 H	.352	1.75	2.25	5.00	15.00

NOTE: Varieties exist.

NOTE: Earlier dates (1898-1900) exist for this type.

Mint mark: Mo

KM#	Date	Mintage	Fine	VF	XF	Unc
400.2	1901 M	.100	1.75	2.25	4.50	12.50
	1902 M	.144	1.25	2.00	3.75	10.00
	1903 M	.500	1.25	2.00	3.75	10.00
	1904/804 M	1.090	1.75	2.50	6.00	15.00
	1904/94 M	I.A.	1.75	2.50	6.00	15.00
	1904 M	Inc. Ab.	1.25	2.00	6.00	12.50
	1905 M	.344	1.75	3.75	7.50	17.50

NOTE: Earlier dates (1898-1900) exist for this type.

Mint mark: Zs

400.3	1901 Z	.040	1.75	2.50	5.00	15.00
	1902/1 Z	.034	2.00	4.50	9.00	22.50
	1902 Z	Inc. Ab.	1.75	3.75	7.50	17.50
	1903 Z	.217	1.25	2.00	5.00	12.50
	1904 Z	.191	1.75	2.50	5.00	12.50
	1904 M	Inc. Ab.	1.75	2.50	6.00	15.00
	1905 M	.046	2.00	4.50	9.00	22.50

NOTE: Earlier dates (1898-1900) exist for this type.

10 CENTAVOS

2.7070 g, .903 SILVER, .0785 oz ASW
Mint mark: Cn
Obv: Restyled eagle.

404	1901 Q	.235	1.50	2.50	5.00	20.00
	1902 Q	.186	1.50	2.50	5.00	20.00
	1903 Q	.256	1.50	2.50	6.00	20.00
	1903 V	Inc. Ab.	1.50	2.50	5.00	15.00
	1904 H	.307	1.50	2.50	5.00	15.00

NOTE: Varieties exist.
NOTE: Earlier dates (1898-1900) exist for this type.

Mint mark: Mo

404.2	1901 M	.080	2.50	3.50	7.00	20.00
	1902 M	.181	1.50	2.50	5.00	17.50
	1903 M	.581	1.50	2.50	5.00	17.50
	1904 M	1.266	1.25	2.00	4.50	15.00
	1904 MM (error)	Inc. Ab.	2.50	5.00	10.00	25.00
	1905 M	.266	2.00	3.75	7.50	20.00

NOTE: Earlier dates (1898-1900) exist for this type.

Mint mark: Zs

404.3	1901 Z	.070	2.50	5.00	10.00	25.00
	1902 Z	.120	2.50	5.00	10.00	25.00
	1903 Z	.228	1.50	3.00	10.00	20.00
	1904 Z	.368	1.50	3.00	10.00	20.00
	1904 M	Inc. Ab.	1.50	3.00	10.00	25.00
	1905 M	.066	7.50	15.00	30.00	60.00

NOTE: Earlier dates (1898-1900) exist for this type.

20 CENTAVOS

5.4150 g, .903 SILVER, .1572 oz ASW
Mint mark: Cn
Obv: Restyled eagle.

405	1901 Q	.185	5.00	10.00	30.00	120.00
	1902/802 Q	.098	6.00	10.00	30.00	120.00
	1902 Q	Inc. Ab.	4.00	9.00	30.00	120.00
	1903 Q	.093	4.00	9.00	30.00	120.00
	1904/3 H	.258	—	—	—	—
	1904 H	Inc. Ab.	5.00	10.00	30.00	120.00

NOTE: Earlier dates (1898-1900) exist for this type.

Mint mark: Mo

405.2	1901 M	.110	4.00	8.00	20.00	85.00
	1902 M	.120	4.00	8.00	20.00	85.00
	1903 M	.213	4.00	8.00	20.00	85.00
	1904 M	.276	4.00	8.00	20.00	85.00
	1905 M	.117	6.50	20.00	50.00	150.00

NOTE: Varieties exist.
NOTE: Earlier dates (1898-1900) exist for this type.

Mint mark: Zs

405.3	1901/0 Z	.130	25.00	50.00	100.00	250.00
	1901 Z	Inc. Ab.	5.00	10.00	20.00	100.00
	1902 Z	.105	5.00	10.00	20.00	100.00
	1903 Z	.143	5.00	10.00	20.00	100.00
	1904 Z	.246	5.00	10.00	20.00	100.00
	1904 M	Inc. Ab.	5.00	10.00	20.00	100.00
	1905 M	.059	10.00	20.00	50.00	150.00

NOTE: Earlier dates (1898-1900) exist for this type.

PESO

27.0730 g, .903 SILVER, .7860 oz ASW
Mint mark: Cn
Liberty cap

KM#	Date	Mintage	Fine	VF	XF	Unc
409	1901 JQ	1.473	10.00	15.00	30.00	80.00
	1902 JQ	1.194	10.00	15.00	45.00	125.00
	1903 JQ	1.514	10.00	15.00	30.00	80.00
	1903 FV	I.A.	25.00	50.00	100.00	225.00
	1904 MH	1.554	10.00	15.00	30.00	80.00
	1904 RP	I.A.	45.00	85.00	125.00	300.00
	1905 RP	.598	20.00	40.00	75.00	225.00

NOTE: Earlier dates (1898-1900) exist for this type.

Mint mark: Mo

409.2	1901 AM	14.505	7.50	10.00	20.00	70.00
	1902/1 AM	16.224	150.00	300.00	500.00	950.00
	1902 AM	I.A.	7.50	10.00	20.00	70.00
	1903 AM	22.396	7.50	10.00	20.00	70.00
	1903 MA (error)	Inc. Ab.	1500.	2500.	3500.	7500.
	1904 AM	14.935	7.50	10.00	20.00	70.00
	1905 AM	3.557	15.00	25.00	55.00	125.00
	1908 AM	7.575	10.00	12.50	20.00	60.00
	1908 GV	I.A.	10.00	12.50	17.50	40.00
	1909 GV	2.924	10.00	12.50	17.50	45.00

NOTE: Varieties exist.
NOTE: Earlier dates (1898-1900) exist for this type.

Mint mark: Zs

409.3	1901 AZ	5.706	4000.	6500.	10,000.	—
	1901 FZ	I.A.	10.00	12.50	20.00	60.00
	1902 FZ	7.134	10.00	12.50	20.00	60.00
	1903/2 FZ	3.080	12.50	15.00	50.00	125.00
	1903 FZ	I.A.	10.00	12.50	20.00	65.00
	1904 FZ	2.423	10.00	15.00	25.00	70.00
	1904 FM	I.A.	10.00	15.00	25.00	85.00
	1905 FM	.995	20.00	40.00	60.00	150.00

NOTE: Varieties exist.
NOTE: Earlier dates (1898-1900) exist for this type.

1.6920 g, .875 GOLD, .0476 oz AGW
Mint mark: Cn

410.2	1901/0 Q	2,350	65.00	100.00	150.00	225.00
	1902 Q	2,480	65.00	100.00	150.00	225.00
	1902 Cn/MoQ/C	Inc. Ab.	65.00	100.00	150.00	225.00
	1904 H	3,614	65.00	100.00	150.00	225.00
	1904 Cn/Mo/ H	Inc. Ab.	65.00	100.00	150.00	250.00
	1905 P	1,000	— Reported, not confirmed			

NOTE: Earlier dates (1873-1899) exist for this type.

Mint mark: Mo

410.5	1901/801 M large date	8,293	40.00	60.00	80.00	175.00
	1901 M small date	Inc. Ab.	40.00	60.00	80.00	175.00
	1902 M large date	.011	40.00	60.00	80.00	175.00
	1902 M small date	Inc. Ab.	40.00	60.00	80.00	175.00
	1903 M large date	.010	40.00	60.00	80.00	175.00
	1903 M small date	Inc. Ab.	50.00	80.00	120.00	180.00
	1904 M	9,845	40.00	60.00	80.00	175.00
	1905 M	3,429	40.00	60.00	80.00	175.00

NOTE: Earlier dates (1870-1900) exist for this type.

CINCO (5) PESOS

8.4600 g, .875 GOLD, .2380 oz AGW
Mint mark: Cn

KM#	Date	Mintage	Fine	VF	XF	Unc
412.2	1903 Q	1,000	200.00	300.00	400.00	800.00

NOTE: Earlier dates (1873-1900) exist for this type.

Mint mark: Mo

412.6	1901 M	1,071	175.00	350.00	450.00	750.00
	1902 M	1,478	175.00	350.00	450.00	750.00
	1903 M	1,162	175.00	350.00	450.00	750.00
	1904 M	1,415	175.00	350.00	450.00	750.00
	1905 M	563 pcs.	200.00	400.00	550.00	1500.

NOTE: Earlier dates (1870-1900) exist for this type.

DIEZ (10) PESOS

16.9200 g, .875 GOLD, .4760 oz AGW
Mint mark: Cn

413.2	1903 Q	774 pcs.	400.00	600.00	1000.	1750.

NOTE: Earlier dates (1881-1895) exist for this type.

Mint mark: Mo

413.7	1901 M	562 pcs.	350.00	500.00	800.00	1400.
	1902 M	719 pcs.	350.00	500.00	800.00	1400.
	1903 M	713 pcs.	350.00	500.00	800.00	1400.
	1904 M	694 pcs.	350.00	500.00	800.00	1400.
	1905 M	401 pcs.	400.00	600.00	950.00	1500.

NOTE: Earlier dates (1870-1900) exist for this type.

VEINTE (20) PESOS

33.8400 g, .875 GOLD, .9520 oz AGW
Mint mark: Cn

414.2	1901/0 Q	1,496	—	—	—	—
	1901 Q	Inc. Ab.	500.00	650.00	950.00	2000.
	1902 Q	1,059	500.00	650.00	950.00	2000.
	1903 Q	1,121	500.00	650.00	950.00	2000.
	1904 H	4,646	500.00	650.00	950.00	2000.
	1905 P	1,738	500.00	900.00	1200.	2250.

NOTE: Earlier dates (1870-1900) exist for this type.

Mint mark: Mo

414.6	1901 M	.029	500.00	600.00	800.00	1300.
	1902 M	.038	500.00	600.00	800.00	1300.
	1903/2 M	.031	500.00	600.00	800.00	1300.
	1903 M	I.A.	500.00	600.00	800.00	1300.
	1904 M	.052	500.00	600.00	800.00	1300.
	1905 M	9,757	500.00	600.00	800.00	1300.

NOTE: Earlier dates (1870-1900) exist for this type.

UNITED STATES

MINT MARK

o
M - Mexico City

CENTAVO

BRONZE, 20mm

KM#	Date	Mintage	Fine	VF	XF	Unc
415	1905	6.040	3.25	5.75	12.50	95.00
	1906 narrow date					
		*67.505	.50	.75	1.25	14.00
	1906 wide date					
		Inc. Ab.	.65	1.25	2.25	22.00
	1910	8.700	1.50	2.50	6.50	90.00
	1911	16.450	.60	1.00	2.75	22.50
	1912	12.650	.75	1.25	3.00	32.00
	1913	12.850	.65	1.00	2.75	33.00
	1914	17.350	.60	.85	2.50	14.50
	1915	2.277	9.00	21.50	65.00	300.00
	1916	.500	40.00	72.00	160.00	1200.
	1920	1.433	20.00	45.00	100.00	400.00
	1921	3.470	4.25	13.50	42.50	275.00
	1922	1.880	8.00	15.00	45.00	300.00
	1923	4.800	.50	.75	1.75	13.50
	1924/3	2.000	50.00	140.00	250.00	500.00
	1924	Inc. Ab.	4.00	10.00	20.00	275.00
	1925	1.550	3.75	9.25	22.00	225.00
	1926	5.000	.90	1.75	3.50	26.00
	1927/6	6.000	25.00	40.00	60.00	140.00
	1927	Inc. Ab.	.60	1.25	4.50	36.00
	1928	5.000	.60	.80	3.25	16.50
	1929	4.500	.60	.80	1.75	18.00
	1930	7.000	.75	1.00	2.25	19.00
	1933	10.000	.25	.35	1.75	16.50
	1934	7.500	.40	.95	3.25	35.00
	1935	12.400	.15	.25	.40	11.50
	1936	20.100	.15	.20	.30	8.00
	1937	20.000	.15	.25	.35	3.50
	1938	10.000	.10	.15	.30	2.25
	1939	30.000	.10	.20	.30	1.25
	1940	10.000	.20	.30	.60	6.50
	1941	15.800	.15	.25	.35	2.25
	1942	30.400	.15	.20	.30	1.25
	1943	4.310	.30	.50	.75	9.00
	1944	5.645	.15	.25	.50	7.00
	1945	26.375	.10	.15	.25	1.00
	1946	42.135	—	.15	.20	.60
	1947	13.445	—	.10	.15	.80
	1948	20.040	—	.15	.30	1.10
	1949	6.235	.10	.15	.30	1.75

***NOTE:** 50,000,000 pcs. were struck at the Birmingham Mint.

NOTE: Varieties exist. Wide and narrow dates exist for 1911 and 1914.

Zapata Issue
Reduced size, 16mm.

KM#	Date	Mintage	Fine	VF	XF	Unc
416	1915	.179	16.00	27.50	50.00	75.50

BRASS, 16mm

KM#	Date	Mintage	VF	XF	Unc	BU
417	1950	12.815	.15	.30	1.75	2.00
	1951	25.740	.15	.25	.65	1.10
	1952	24.610	.10	.25	.40	.75
	1953	21.160	.10	.25	.40	.85
	1954	25.675	.10	.15	.85	1.20
	1955	9.820	.15	.25	.85	1.50
	1956	11.285	.15	.25	.80	1.45
	1957	9.805	.15	.25	.85	1.35
	1958	12.155	.10	.25	.45	.80
	1959	11.875	.10	.25	.75	1.25
	1960	10.360	.10	.15	.40	.65
	1961	6.385	.10	.15	.45	.85
	1962	4.850	.10	.15	.55	.90
	1963	7.775	.10	.15	.25	.45
	1964	4.280	.10	.15	.20	.35
	1965	2.255	.10	.15	.25	.40
	1966	1.760	.10	.25	.60	.75
	1967	1.290	.10	.15	.40	.70
	1968	1.000	.10	.20	.85	1.25
	1969	1.000	.10	.15	.75	1.25

Reduced size, 13mm.

KM#	Date	Mintage	VF	XF	Unc	BU
418	1970	1.000	.20	.40	1.30	1.80
	1972	1.000	.20	.45	2.50	3.25
	1972/2	—	.50	1.25	3.25	5.00
	1973	1.000	1.65	2.75	8.00	9.75

2 CENTAVOS

BRONZE, 25mm

KM#	Date	Mintage	Fine	VF	XF	Unc
419	1905	.050	125.00	275.00	425.00	1200.
	1906/inverted 6					
		9.998	25.00	50.00	110.00	375.00
	1906 wide date					
		I.A.	4.00	10.00	21.50	80.00
	1906 narrow date					
		*I.A.	6.50	12.50	25.00	85.00
	1920	1.325	6.50	21.50	60.00	350.00
	1921	4.275	2.50	4.75	10.00	90.00
	1922	—	275.00	600.00	1500.	4000.
	1924	.750	8.50	20.00	55.00	450.00
	1925	3.650	2.50	3.50	9.00	40.00
	1926	4.750	1.00	2.25	5.50	35.00
	1927	7.250	.60	1.00	4.50	22.75
	1928	3.250	.75	1.50	3.75	25.00
	1929	.250	55.00	150.00	550.00	1000.
	1935	1.250	4.25	9.25	22.50	200.00
	1939	5.000	.60	.90	2.25	20.00
	1941	3.550	.45	.60	1.25	18.00

***NOTE:** 5,000,000 pcs. were struck at the Birmingham Mint.

Zapata Issue
Reduced size, 20mm.

KM#	Date	Mintage	Fine	VF	XF	Unc
420	1915	.487	6.50	9.00	13.50	65.00

5 CENTAVOS

NICKEL

KM#	Date	Mintage	Fine	VF	XF	Unc
421	1905	1.420	6.00	9.50	22.50	290.00
	1906/5	10.615	12.00	23.50	60.00	375.00
	1906	*Inc. Ab.	.75	1.20	3.25	50.00
	1907	4.000	1.25	3.50	10.00	350.00
	1909	2.052	3.25	9.50	42.50	360.00
	1910	6.181	1.15	3.20	5.50	77.00
	1911 narrow date					
		4.487	.75	3.00	5.00	85.00
	1911 wide date					
		Inc. Ab.	2.50	4.25	9.00	110.00
	1912 small mint mark					
		.420	97.50	120.00	210.00	725.00
	1912 large mint mark					
		Inc. Ab.	60.00	85.00	160.00	575.00
	1913	2.035	1.65	3.75	9.00	100.00
	1914	2.000	.75	1.75	3.50	65.00

NOTE: 5,000,000 pcs. appear to have been struck at the Birmingham Mint in 1914 and all of 1909-1911. The Mexican Mint report does not mention receiving the 1914 dated coins.

NOTE: Varieties exist. Wide and narrow dates exist for 1913.

BRONZE

KM#	Date	Mintage	Fine	VF	XF	Unc
422	1914	2.500	10.00	21.50	45.00	250.00
	1915	11.424	2.50	4.50	14.50	145.00
	1916	2.860	13.50	32.00	170.00	690.00
	1917	.800	60.00	150.00	320.00	820.00
	1918	1.332	32.00	80.00	200.00	625.00
	1919	.400	100.00	190.00	335.00	925.00
	1920	5.920	3.00	7.50	40.00	285.00
	1921	2.080	9.00	21.50	70.00	275.00
	1924	.780	35.00	80.00	235.00	625.00
	1925	4.040	4.75	10.00	42.50	225.00
	1926	3.160	5.50	11.00	43.50	300.00
	1927	3.600	3.25	6.75	27.50	220.00
	1928 large date					
		1.740	10.00	17.50	68.00	250.00
	1928 small date					
		Inc. Ab.	25.00	45.00	90.00	385.00
	1929	2.400	4.75	10.00	40.00	180.00
	1930 large oval 0 in date					
		2.600	4.00	7.50	27.50	210.00
	1930 small square 0 in date					
		Inc. Ab.	50.00	115.00	220.00	565.00
	1931	—	525.00	725.00	1150.	3250.
	1933	8.000	1.25	2.00	3.25	25.00
	1934	10.000	1.00	1.50	2.50	22.50
	1935	21.980	.75	1.20	2.25	22.50

COPPER-NICKEL

KM#	Date	Mintage	VF	XF	Unc	BU
423	1936	46.700	.65	1.25	6.50	9.00
	1937	49.060	.50	1.00	6.00	9.00
	1938	3.340	5.00	12.50	65.00	250.00
	1940	22.800	.75	1.50	8.00	12.00
	1942	7.100	1.50	3.20	35.00	45.00

BRONZE
'Josefa' Ortiz de Dominguez

KM#	Date	Mintage	VF	XF	Unc	BU
424	1942	.900	20.00	60.00	375.00	525.00
	1943	54.660	.40	.65	3.00	4.00
	1944	53.463	.25	.35	.75	1.00
	1945	44.262	.25	.35	.90	1.65
	1946	49.054	.50	.75	2.00	2.75
	1951	50.758	.60	.85	3.00	4.75
	1952	17.674	1.25	2.25	9.25	11.50
	1953	31.568	1.10	1.75	7.00	10.00
	1954	58.680	.40	.75	2.75	4.00
	1955	31.114	1.85	2.50	11.00	15.00

COPPER-NICKEL
'White Josefa'

KM#	Date	Mintage	VF	XF	Unc	BU
425	1950	5.700	.75	1.50	6.25	8.00

NOTE: 5,600,000 pieces struck at Connecticut melted.

BRASS

KM#	Date	Mintage	VF	XF	Unc	BU
426	1954 dot	—	9.00	32.00	325.00	375.00
	1954 w/o dot	—	12.00	25.00	250.00	290.00
	1955	12.136	.75	1.50	9.00	12.50
	1956	60.216	.20	.30	.90	1.50
	1957	55.288	.15	.20	.90	1.50
	1958	104.624	.15	.20	.60	1.00
	1959	106.000	.15	.25	.90	1.50
	1960	99.144	.10	.15	.50	.75
	1961	61.136	.10	.15	.40	.70
	1962	47.232	.10	.15	.30	.55
	1963	156.680	—	.15	.20	.35
	1964	71.168	—	.15	.20	.40
	1965	155.720	—	.15	.25	.35
	1966	124.944	—	.15	.40	.65
	1967	118.816	—	.15	.25	.40
	1968	189.588	—	.15	.50	.75
	1969	210.492	—	.15	.55	.80

COPPER-NICKEL

KM#	Date	Mintage	VF	XF	Unc	BU
426a	1960	—	300.00	—	—	—
	1962	19 pcs.	300.00	—	—	—

BRASS
Reduced size, 18mm.

KM#	Date	Mintage	VF	XF	Unc	BU
427	1970	163.368	.10	.15	.35	.45
	1971	198.844	.10	.15	.25	.30
	1972	225.000	.10	.15	.25	.30
	1973 flat top 3					
		595.070	.10	.15	.25	.40
	1973 round top 3					
		Inc. Ab.	.10	.15	.20	.30
	1974	401.584	.10	.15	.30	.40
	1975	342.308	.10	.15	.25	.35
	1976	367.524	.10	.15	.40	.60

NOTE: Due to some minor alloy variations this type is often encountered with a bronze color toning.

10 CENTAVOS

2.5000 g, .800 SILVER, .0643 oz ASW

KM#	Date	Mintage	VF	XF	Unc	BU
428	1905	3.920	5.25	7.00	35.00	50.00
	1906	8.410	4.75	6.25	25.00	35.00
	1907/6	5.950	45.00	115.00	275.00	350.00
	1907	Inc. Ab.	5.50	7.75	35.00	42.50
	1909	2.620	8.00	12.50	70.00	90.00
	1910/00	3.450	12.00	35.00	75.00	100.00
	1910	8.00	12.50	25.00	30.00	
	1911 narrow date					
		2.550	10.00	15.00	88.00	125.00
	1911 wide date					
		Inc. Ab.	6.00	8.50	42.50	60.00
	1912	1.350	10.00	16.00	135.00	155.00
	1912 low 2 I.A.	8.00	16.00	125.00	150.00	
	1913/2	1.990	7.75	15.00	35.00	65.00
	1913	Inc. Ab.	6.00	8.50	33.50	45.00
	1914	3.110	4.50	5.75	13.50	18.50

NOTE: Wide and narrow dates exist for 1914.

1.8125 g, .800 SILVER, .0466 oz ASW
Reduced size, 15mm.

KM#	Date	Mintage	VF	XF	Unc	BU
429	1919	8.360	8.00	15.00	95.00	115.00

BRONZE

KM#	Date	Mintage	VF	XF	Unc	BU
430	1919	1.232	20.00	47.50	440.00	525.00
	1920	6.612	12.50	38.50	400.00	475.00
	1921	2.255	30.00	65.00	625.00	875.00
	1935	5.970	12.00	23.50	125.00	175.00

1.6600 g, .720 SILVER, .0384 oz ASW

KM#	Date	Mintage	VF	XF	Unc	BU
431	1925/15	5.350	18.00	35.00	110.00	125.00
	1925/3	Inc. Ab.	18.00	35.00	115.00	130.00
	1925	Inc. Ab.	2.00	4.00	35.00	47.50
	1926/16	2.650	25.00	55.00	160.00	175.00
	1926	Inc. Ab.	3.50	6.00	62.50	80.00
	1927	2.810	2.25	3.00	17.50	21.50
	1928	5.270	1.75	2.25	12.00	14.25
	1930	2.000	3.75	5.00	18.75	22.50
	1933	Inc. Ab.	1.50	3.00	10.00	12.50
	1934	8.000	1.75	2.25	8.00	9.50
	1935	3.500	2.75	4.00	11.50	14.00

COPPER-NICKEL

KM#	Date	Mintage	VF	XF	Unc	BU
432	1936	33.030	.65	2.25	8.25	10.00
	1937	3.000	2.75	42.50	225.00	250.00
	1938	3.650	1.75	5.50	60.00	75.00
	1939	6.920	1.00	3.50	30.00	40.00
	1940	12.300	.40	1.00	5.00	6.50
	1942	14.380	.60	1.50	7.00	8.50
	1945	9.558	.40	.70	3.50	4.00
	1946	46.230	.25	.45	2.25	3.10

BRONZE
Benito Juarez

KM#	Date	Mintage	VF	XF	Unc	BU
433	1955	1.818	.60	3.00	22.00	30.00
	1956	5.255	.50	3.00	22.00	35.00
	1957	11.925	.20	.40	5.50	8.00
	1959	26.140	.20	.35	.65	1.25
	1966	5.873	.15	.25	.65	1.50
	1967	32.318	.10	.15	.30	.40

COPPER-NICKEL
Variety I
Rev: 5 full rows of kernels, sharp stem, wide date.

KM#	Date	Mintage	VF	XF	Unc	BU
434.1	1974	6.000	—	.35	.85	1.00
	1975	5.550	.10	.35	.85	1.75
	1976	7.680	.10	.20	.30	.40
	1977	144.650	1.25	2.25	3.50	4.50
	1978	271.870	—	1.00	1.50	2.25
	1979	375.660	—	.50	1.00	1.75
	1980/79	21.290	2.45	3.75	6.00	7.00
	1980	I.A.	1.50	2.00	4.50	5.00

Variety II
Rev: 5 full, plus 1 partial row at left, blunt stem, narrow date.

KM#	Date	Mintage	VF	XF	Unc	BU
434.2	1974	Inc. Ab.	—	.10	.25	.35
	1977	Inc. Ab.	—	.10	.30	.35
	1978	Inc. Ab.	—	.10	.30	.40
	1979	Inc. Ab.	.15	.50	1.00	2.00
	1980	Inc. Ab.	—	.10	.30	.35

Variety III
Rev: 5 full, plus 1 partial row, blunt stem and wide date.

KM#	Date	Mintage	VF	XF	Unc	BU
434.3	1980/79	—	—	—	—	—

Variety III
Rev: 5 full, plus 1 partial row, sharp stem and narrow date.

KM#	Date	Mintage	VF	XF	Unc	BU
434.4	1979	—	—	—	—	—

20 CENTAVOS

5.0000 g, .800 SILVER, .1286 oz ASW

KM#	Date	Mintage	VF	XF	Unc	BU
435	1905	2.565	9.00	15.00	150.00	175.00
	1906	6.860	7.25	14.50	60.00	80.00
	1907 straight 7					
		4.000	8.50	17.50	70.00	100.00
	1907 curved 7					
		5.435	7.50	13.50	75.00	95.00
	1908	.350	85.00	200.00	1500.	—
	1910	1.135	9.50	15.00	80.00	95.00
	1911	1.150	14.00	32.00	125.00	150.00
	1912	.625	35.00	70.00	335.00	375.00
	1913	1.000	14.50	30.00	95.00	115.00
	1914	1.500	10.00	21.50	72.50	85.00

3.6250 g, .800 SILVER, .0932 oz ASW
Reduced size, 19mm.

KM#	Date	Mintage	VF	XF	Unc	BU
436	1919	4.155	25.00	50.00	195.00	245.00

BRONZE

KM#	Date	Mintage	VF	XF	Unc	BU
437	1920	4.835	40.00	110.00	650.00	725.00
	1935	20.000	5.50	8.50	95.00	135.00

3.3333 g, .720 SILVER, .0772 oz ASW

KM#	Date	Mintage	VF	XF	Unc	BU
438	1920	3.710	4.75	10.00	165.00	215.00
	1921	6.160	4.50	10.00	100.00	145.00
	1925	1.450	8.00	17.00	125.00	150.00
	1926/5	1.465	18.00	45.00	325.00	375.00
	1926	Inc. Ab.	4.50	6.25	80.00	110.00
	1927	1.405	3.75	6.25	80.00	115.00
	1928	3.630	2.50	4.50	14.50	19.50
	1930	1.000	3.50	6.25	25.00	32.00
	1933	2.500	2.25	2.75	10.00	12.50
	1934	2.500	2.25	3.00	12.00	14.00
	1935	2.460	2.25	2.75	10.00	12.50
	1937	10.000	2.25	2.50	4.75	5.50
	1939	8.800	1.75	2.00	4.00	4.50
	1940	3.000	1.75	2.00	3.50	5.00
	1941	5.740	1.50	2.00	3.00	3.50
	1942	12.460	1.50	2.00	3.25	3.80
	1943	3.955	2.00	2.50	3.50	4.25

BRONZE

KM#	Date	Mintage	VF	XF	Unc	BU
439	1943	46.350	.75	2.75	18.00	25.00
	1944	83.650	.40	.65	9.00	11.00
	1945	26.801	1.10	3.50	10.50	13.00
	1946	25.695	.90	2.00	6.00	8.25
	1951	11.385	2.50	5.50	80.00	100.00
	1952	6.560	2.50	4.50	25.00	32.50
	1953	26.948	.35	.75	8.25	12.00
	1954	40.108	.35	.80	9.00	12.50
	1955	16.950	2.50	6.00	65.00	80.00

KM#	Date	Mintage	VF	XF	Unc	BU
440	1955					
		Inc. KM439	.65	1.50	15.00	20.00
	1956	22.431	.30	.35	3.00	5.00
	1957	13.455	.45	1.25	9.00	12.00
	1959	6.017	4.00	7.50	65.00	95.00
	1960	39.756	.15	.25	.85	1.25
	1963	14.869	.25	.35	.90	1.25
	1964	28.654	.25	.40	.90	1.25
	1965	74.162	.20	.40	.85	1.20
	1966	43.745	.15	.25	.90	1.30
	1967	46.487	.20	.55	1.20	1.50
	1968	15.477	.30	.55	1.35	1.65
	1969	63.647	.20	.40	1.00	1.50
	1970	76.287	.15	.20	.90	1.30
	1971	49.892	.30	.50	1.40	1.75

KM#	Date	Mintage	VF	XF	Unc	BU
441	1971		.20	.35	1.75	2.35
		Inc. KM440	.20	.35	1.75	2.35
	1973	78.398	.25	.35	.95	1.50
	1974	34.200	.20	.35	1.25	1.75

COPPER-NICKEL
Francisco Madero

KM#	Date	Mintage	VF	XF	Unc	BU
442	1974	112.000	.10	.15	.25	.30
	1975	611.000	.10	.15	.30	.35
	1976	394.000	.10	.15	.35	.45
	1977	394.350	.10	.15	.40	.45
	1978	527.950	.10	.15	.25	.30
	1979	524.615	.10	.15	.30	.40
	1979 Doubled die obv. large/small letters					
		—	1.25	2.00	4.00	8.00
	1980	326.500	.15	.25	.40	.60
	1981 open 8					
		106.205	.30	.50	1.00	2.00
	1981 closed 8, high date					
		248.500	.30	.50	1.00	2.00
	1981 closed 8, low date					
		—	1.50	3.50	4.25	
	1981/1982	—	30.00	75.00	160.00	190.00
	1982	286.855	.40	.60	.90	1.10
	1983 round top 3					
		100.930	.25	.40	1.75	2.25
	1983 flat top 3					
		Inc. Ab.	.25	.50	1.25	1.75
	1983	998 pcs.	—	—	Proof	15.00

NOTE: The 1981/1982 overdate is often mistaken as 1982/1981.

BRONZE
Olmec Culture

KM#	Date	Mintage	VF	XF	Unc	BU
491	1983	260.000	.20	.25	.90	1.10
	1983	53 pcs.	—	—	Proof	165.00
	1984	180.320	.20	.25	1.50	1.70

25 CENTAVOS

3.3330 g, .300 SILVER, .0321 oz ASW

KM#	Date	Mintage	VF	XF	Unc	BU
443	1950	77.060	.50	.75	1.75	2.25
	1951	41.172	.50	.75	1.60	2.00
	1952	29.264	.75	1.10	1.80	2.50
	1953	38.144	.60	.70	1.50	2.00

COPPER-NICKEL
Francisco Madero

KM#	Date	Mintage	VF	XF	Unc	BU
444	1964	20.686	—	.15	.25	.40
	1966 closed beak					
		.180	.65	1.00	2.50	3.00
	1966 open beak					
		Inc. Ab.	1.75	3.50	10.00	14.00

50 CENTAVOS

12.5000 g, .800 SILVER, .3215 oz ASW

KM#	Date	Mintage	VF	XF	Unc	BU
445	1905	2.446	14.00	21.50	150.00	225.00
	1906	16.966	4.50	8.50	27.50	40.00
	1907 straight 7					
		18.920	4.50	7.25	25.00	28.50
	1907 curved 7					
		14.841	5.25	8.00	25.00	28.50

KM#	Date	Mintage	VF	XF	Unc	BU
445	1908	.488	65.00	150.00	525.00	625.00
	1912	3.736	10.00	12.50	45.00	60.00
	1913/07	10.510	30.00	70.00	225.00	275.00
	1913/2	Inc. Ab.	18.00	22.50	65.00	85.00
	1913	Inc. Ab.	5.50	8.50	25.00	30.00
	1914	7.710	6.75	13.50	35.00	45.00
	1916	.480	50.00	75.00	200.00	290.00
	1917	37.112	5.50	8.50	20.00	22.50
	1918	1.320	60.00	110.00	250.00	335.00

9.0625 g, .800 SILVER, .2331 oz ASW
Reduced size, 27mm.

KM#	Date	Mintage	VF	XF	Unc	BU
446	1918/7	2.760	525.00	625.00	1250.	—
	1918	Inc. Ab.	16.00	50.00	325.00	400.00
	1919	29.670	8.00	17.50	100.00	125.00

8.3333 g, .720 SILVER, .1929 oz ASW

KM#	Date	Mintage	VF	XF	Unc	BU
447	1919	10.200	8.00	18.50	87.50	110.00
	1920	27.166	6.00	8.50	75.00	85.00
	1921	21.864	6.50	9.00	85.00	100.00
	1925	3.280	14.00	30.00	130.00	160.00
	1937	20.000	3.75	5.00	7.50	8.50
	1938	.100	40.00	75.00	275.00	350.00
	1939	10.440	5.25	7.25	14.00	16.50
	1942	.800	5.50	7.50	15.00	17.00
	1943	41.512	2.75	4.00	5.50	6.50
	1944	55.806	3.00	3.75	5.50	6.50
	1945	56.766	3.00	3.75	6.00	6.50

7.9730 g, .420 SILVER, .1076 oz ASW

KM#	Date	Mintage	VF	XF	Unc	BU
448	1935	70.800	2.20	2.75	5.00	6.00

6.6600 g, .300 SILVER, .0642 oz ASW
Cuauhtemoc

KM#	Date	Mintage	VF	XF	Unc	BU
449	1950	13.570	1.50	1.80	3.00	4.00
	1951	3.650	2.00	2.50	3.75	5.00

BRONZE

KM#	Date	Mintage	VF	XF	Unc	BU
450	1955	3.502	1.20	2.20	27.50	35.00
	1956	34.643	.65	1.00	3.25	4.50
	1957	9.675	1.00	2.00	6.50	7.50
	1959	4.540	.35	.50	1.50	2.00

COPPER-NICKEL

KM#	Date	Mintage	VF	XF	Unc	BU
451	1964	43.806	.15	.20	.45	.65
	1965	14.326	.20	.25	.45	.65
	1966	1.726	.20	.40	1.30	1.75
	1967	55.144	.20	.30	.65	1.00
	1968	80.438	.15	.30	.65	.80
	1969	87.640	.20	.35	.80	1.15

Obv: Stylized eagle.

KM#	Date	Mintage	VF	XF	Unc	BU
452	1970	76.236	.15	.20	.90	1.25
	1971	125.288	.15	.20	.90	1.30
	1972	16.000	1.25	2.00	3.00	4.75
	1975 Dots					
		177.958	.60	1.25	3.50	6.00
	1975 No dots					
		Inc. Ab.	.15	.20	.50	.75
	1976 Dots					
		37,480	.75	1.25	5.00	6.00
	1976 No dots					
		Inc. Ab.	.15	.20	.50	.75
	1977	12.410	6.50	10.00	32.50	42.50
	1978	85.400	.15	.25	.50	.75
	1979 round 2nd 9 in date					
		229.000	.15	.25	.50	.65
	1979 square 9's in date					
		Inc. Ab.	.20	.40	1.60	2.10
	1980 narrow date, square 9					
		89.978	.45	.75	1.00	2.00
	1980 wide date, round 9					
		178.188	.20	.25	1.00	1.15
	1981 rectangular 9, narrow date					
		142.212	.50	.75	1.75	2.50
	1981 round 9, wide date					
		Inc. Ab.	.30	.50	1.25	1.75
	1982	45.474	.20	.40	1.50	2.40
	1983	90.318	.50	.75	2.25	2.85
	1983	998 pcs.	—	—	Proof	15.00

NOTE: Coins dated 1975 and 1976 exist with and without dots in centers of three circles on plumage on reverse. Edge varieties exist.

STAINLESS STEEL
Palenque Culture

KM#	Date	Mintage	VF	XF	Unc	BU
492	1983	99.540	—	.30	1.50	2.50
	1983	53 pcs.	—	—	Proof	165.00

UN (1) PESO

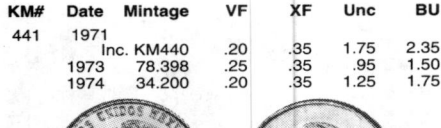 

27.0700 g, .903 SILVER, .7859 oz ASW
'Caballito'

KM#	Date	Mintage	VF	XF	Unc	BU
453	1910	3.814	35.00	55.00	160.00	215.00
	1911 long lower left ray on rev.					
		1.227	40.00	65.00	200.00	235.00
	1911 short lower left ray on rev.					
		Inc. Ab.	125.00	200.00	600.00	725.00
	1912	.322	95.00	200.00	350.00	400.00
	1913/2	2.880	35.00	65.00	275.00	350.00
	1913	Inc. Ab.	35.00	60.00	180.00	220.00
	1914	.120	600.00	950.00	2750.	—

NOTE: 1913 coins exist with even and unevenly spaced date.

18.1300 g, .800 SILVER, .4663 oz ASW

454	1918	3.050	32.00	120.00	1400.	2150.
	1919	6.151	18.50	45.00	900.00	1600.

16.6600 g, .720 SILVER, .3856 oz ASW

455	1920/10	8.830	40.00	80.00	300.00	—
	1920	Inc. Ab.	6.50	21.50	160.00	200.00
	1921	5.480	8.00	21.50	160.00	200.00
	1922	33.620	3.50	5.00	22.00	28.00
	1923	35.280	3.50	5.00	22.00	28.00
	1924	33.060	3.50	5.00	22.00	28.00
	1925	9.160	4.50	9.50	60.00	80.00
	1926	28.840	3.50	5.00	20.00	25.00
	1927	5.060	6.50	9.50	72.50	90.00
	1932	50.770	3.00	4.00	5.00	6.50
	1933/2	43.920	15.00	25.00	80.00	—
	1933	Inc. Ab.	3.00	4.00	5.25	6.75
	1934	22.070	3.75	4.50	9.50	10.50
	1935	8.050	4.50	6.00	11.50	13.50
	1938	30.000	3.00	4.00	6.00	7.25
	1940	20.000	3.00	3.50	5.00	6.00
	1943	47.662	3.00	3.25	4.50	5.00
	1944	39.522	3.00	3.50	4.50	5.00
	1945	37.300	3.00	3.50	4.50	5.00

14.0000 g, .500 SILVER, .2250 oz ASW
Jose Morelos y Pavon

456	1947	61.460	2.00	2.75	5.00	6.00
	1948	22.915	2.50	4.00	6.00	7.00
	1949	*4.000	—	1200.	1600.	2500.
	1949		—	—	Proof	5000.

*NOTE: Not released for circulation.

13.3300 g, .300 SILVER, .1285 oz ASW
Jose Morelos y Pavon

KM#	Date	Mintage	VF	XF	Unc	BU
457	1950	3.287	3.00	4.25	8.00	9.50

16.0000 g, .100 SILVER, .0514 oz ASW
100th Anniversary of Constitution

458	1957	.500	4.00	5.50	14.00	18.00

Jose Morelos y Pavon

459	1957	28.273	.75	1.00	2.25	3.00
	1958	41.899	.75	.85	1.85	2.60
	1959	27.369	1.60	2.00	5.50	7.00
	1960	26.259	.75	1.10	3.25	3.50
	1961	52.601	.60	.90	2.25	3.00
	1962	61.094	.60	.90	2.25	3.00
	1963	26.394	BV	.80	2.00	2.40
	1964	15.615	BV	.75	2.00	2.40
	1965	5.004	BV	.65	1.85	2.10
	1966	30.998	BV	.65	1.85	2.25
	1967	9.308	BV	.65	2.75	3.50

COPPER-NICKEL
Jose Morelos y Pavon

460	1970 narrow date					
		102.715	.25	.35	.75	.90
	1970 wide date					
		Inc. Ab.	1.25	2.50	8.00	10.00
	1971	426.222	.20	.25	.50	.65
	1972	120.000	.20	.25	.40	.65
	1974	63.700	.20	.25	.65	.90

	1975 tall narrow date					
		205.979	.25	.45	1.00	1.35

	1975 short wide date					
		Inc. Ab.	.30	.40	.75	1.00
	1976	94.489	.15	.20	.50	.75
	1977 thick date					
		94.364	.25	.45	1.00	1.25
	1977 thin date					

KM#	Date	Mintage	VF	XF	Unc	BU
460		Inc. Ab.	1.00	1.75	4.50	12.00
	1978 closed 8					
		208.300	.20	.30	1.00	1.15
	1978 open 8					
		55.140	.75	1.25	9.00	15.00
	1979 thin date					
		117.884	.20	.30	1.25	1.75
	1979 thick date					
		Inc. Ab.	.40	.60	1.45	1.90
	1980 closed 8					
		318.800	.25	.35	.80	1.00
	1980 open 8					
		23.865	.75	1.50	9.00	12.75
	1981 closed 8					
		413.349	.20	.30	.85	1.00
	1981 open 8					
		58.616	.50	1.25	7.00	8.50
	1982	235.000	.25	.75	2.25	2.50
	1983 wide date					
		100.000	.50	1.10	3.00	3.50
	1983 narrow date					
		Inc. Ab.	.30	.45	3.25	3.75
	1983	1,051	—	—	Proof	15.00

STAINLESS STEEL
Jose Morelos y Pavon

496	1984	722.802	.10	.25	.80	1.00
	1985	985.000	.10	.25	.50	.75
	1986	740.000	.10	.25	.50	.75
	1987	250.000	—	.25	.50	.80
	1987	2 known	—	—	Proof	1250.

DOS (2) PESOS

1.6666 g, .900 GOLD, .0482 oz AGW

KM#	Date	Mintage	Fine	VF	XF	Unc
461	1919	1.670	—	BV	25.00	32.00
	1920	4.282	—	BV	25.00	32.00
	1944	.010	27.50	35.00	50.00	80.00
	1945	*.140	—	—	BV + 20%	
	1946	.168	30.00	45.00	55.00	80.00
	1947	.025	27.50	35.00	50.00	65.00
	1948	.045	—	no specimens known		

*NOTE: During 1951-1972 a total of 4,590,493 pieces were restruck, most likely dated 1945. In 1996 matte restrikes were produced.

26.6667 g, .900 SILVER, .7717 oz ASW
Centennial of Independence

KM#	Date	Mintage	VF	XF	Unc	BU
462	1921	1.278	30.00	55.00	300.00	400.00

DOS Y MEDIO (2-1/2) PESOS

2.0833 g, .900 GOLD, .0602 oz AGW

KM#	Date	Mintage	Fine	VF	XF	Unc
463	1918	1.704	—	BV	28.00	45.00
	1919	.984	—	BV	28.00	45.00
	1920/10	.607	—	BV	55.00	100.00
	1920	Inc. Ab.	—	BV	28.00	45.00
	1944	.020	—	BV	28.00	45.00
	1945	*.180	—	—		BV + 18%
	1946	.163	—	BV	28.00	45.00
	1947	.024	200.00	265.00	325.00	500.00
	1948	.063	BV	35.00	40.00	65.00

*NOTE: During 1951-1972 a total of 5,025,087 pieces were restruck, most likely dated 1945. In 1996 matte restrikes were produced.

CINCO (5) PESOS

4.1666 g, .900 GOLD, .1205 oz AGW

464	1905	.018	100.00	150.00	200.00	500.00
	1906	4.638	—	BV	50.00	70.00
	1907	1.088	—	BV	50.00	70.00
	1910	.100	BV	55.00	70.00	120.00
	1918/7	.609	BV	55.00	70.00	120.00
	1918	Inc. Ab.	—	BV	50.00	70.00
	1919	.506	—	BV	50.00	70.00
	1920	2.385	—	BV	50.00	70.00
	1955	*.048	—	—		BV + 11%

*NOTE: During 1955-1972 a total of 1,767,645 pieces were restruck, most likely dated 1955. In 1996 matte restrikes were produced.

30.0000 g, .900 SILVER, .8681 oz ASW
Cuauhtemoc

KM#	Date	Mintage	VF	XF	Unc	BU
465	1947	5.110	BV	6.25	8.75	9.75
	1948	26.740	BV	6.00	8.00	8.75

27.7800 g, .720 SILVER, .6431 oz ASW
Opening of Southern Railroad

KM#	Date	Mintage	VF	XF	Unc	BU
466	1950	.200	25.00	30.00	40.00	50.00

NOTE: It is recorded that 100,000 pieces were melted to be used for the 1968 Mexican Olympic 25 Pesos.

Miguel Hidalgo y Costilla

467	1951	4.958	BV	5.75	7.50	10.00
	1952	9.595	BV	5.50	7.00	9.50
	1953	20.376	BV	5.25	7.00	9.50
	1954	.030	27.50	45.00	70.00	85.00

Bicentennial of Hidalgo's Birth

468	1953	1.000	BV	5.50	7.50	10.00

18.0500 g, .720 SILVER, .4178 oz ASW
Reduced size, 36mm.

469	1955	4.271	3.75	4.25	4.75	7.00
	1956	4.596	3.75	4.25	4.75	7.00
	1957	3.464	3.75	4.25	4.75	7.00

100th Anniversary of Constitution

470	1957	.200	6.00	8.00	14.00	16.00

Centennial of Carranza's Birth

KM#	Date	Mintage	VF	XF	Unc	BU
471	1959	1.000	BV	5.00	7.00	9.50

Small date		Large date			

COPPER-NICKEL
Vicente Guerrero

472	1971	28.457	.50	.95	2.50	3.25
	1972	75.000	.60	1.25	2.00	2.50
	1973	19.405	1.25	2.10	5.00	7.50
	1974	34.500	.50	.80	1.75	2.25
1976 small date						
		26.121	.75	1.45	3.50	4.25
1976 large date						
		121.550	.35	.50	1.50	1.75
	1977	102.000	.50	.75	1.50	2.00
	1978	25.700	1.00	1.50	5.25	6.75

Quetzalcoatl

485	1980	266.900	.25	.50	1.75	2.25
	1981	30.500	.45	.65	2.75	3.25
	1982	20.000	1.50	2.35	4.25	5.25
	1982	1,051	—	—	Proof	18.00
	1983	7 known	—	—	Proof	1150.
	1984	16.300	1.25	2.00	4.75	6.00
	1985	76.900	2.25	4.00	4.50	5.25

BRASS
Circulation Coinage

502	1985	30.000	—	.15	.35	.50
	1987	81.900	8.00	9.50	12.50	15.00
	1988	76.600	—	.10	.25	.35
	1988	2 known	—	—	Proof	600.00

DIEZ (10) PESOS

8.3333 g, .900 GOLD, .2411 oz AGW
Miguel Hidalgo

KM#	Date	Mintage	Fine	VF	XF	Unc
473	1905	.039	110.00	125.00	155.00	200.00
	1906	2.949	—	BV	100.00	150.00
	1907	1.589	—	BV	100.00	150.00
	1908	.890	—	BV	100.00	150.00
	1910	.451	—	BV	100.00	150.00
	1916	.026	110.00	120.00	150.00	275.00
	1917	1.967	—	BV	100.00	150.00
	1919	.266	—	BV	100.00	150.00

KM#	Date	Mintage	Fine	VF	XF	Unc
473	1920	.012	150.00	250.00	400.00	650.00
	1959	*.050	—			BV + 7%

*NOTE: During 1961-1972 a total of 954,983 pieces were restruck, most likely dated 1959. In 1996 matte restrikes were produced.

28.8800 g, .900 SILVER, .8357 oz ASW
Miguel Hidalgo

KM#	Date	Mintage	VF	XF	Unc	BU
474	1955	.585	BV	6.00	8.75	10.75
	1956	3.535	BV	5.50	8.50	11.00

100th Anniversary of Constitution

475	1957	.100	12.50	25.00	42.00	48.00

150th Anniversary - War of Independence

476	1960	1.000	BV	6.00	9.00	12.00

COPPER-NICKEL

Miguel Hidalgo
Thin flan, 1.6mm.

KM#	Date	Mintage	VF	XF	Unc	BU
477.1	1974	3.900	.50	1.00	3.50	4.25
	1974	—			Proof	625.00
	1975	1.000	2.25	3.25	7.75	15.00
	1976	74.500	.25	.75	1.75	2.25
	1977	79.620	.50	1.00	2.00	3.00

Thick flan, 2.3mm.

477.2	1978	124.850	.50	.75	2.50	2.75
	1979	57.200	.50	.75	2.25	2.50
	1980	55.200	.50	.75	2.50	3.75
	1981	222.768	.40	.60	2.25	2.60
	1982	151.770	.50	.80	2.50	3.50
	1982	1,051	—	—	Proof	18.00
	1983	3 known	—	—	Proof	1600.
	1985	58.000	1.25		5.75	7.50

STAINLESS STEEL
Miguel Hidalgo

512	1985	257.000	—	.15	.50	.75
	1986	392.000	—	.15	.50	1.50
	1987	305.000	—	.15	.35	.50
	1988	500.300	—	.15	.25	.35
	1989	—	.20	.25	.75	1.50
	1990	—		.25	.75	1.25
	1990	2 known			Proof	500.00

NOTE: Date varieties exist.

VEINTE (20) PESOS

16.6666 g, .900 GOLD, .4823 oz AGW

KM#	Date	Mintage	Fine	VF	XF	Unc
478	1917	.852	—	BV	170.00	200.00
	1918	2.831	—	BV	170.00	200.00
	1919	1.094	—	BV	170.00	200.00
	1920/10	.462	—	BV	175.00	210.00
	1920	Inc. Ab.	—	BV	170.00	200.00
	1921/11	.922	—	BV	175.00	210.00
	1921	Inc. Ab.	—	BV	170.00	200.00
	1959	*.013	—			BV + 4%

*NOTE: During 1960-1971 a total of 1,158,414 pieces were restruck, most likely dated 1959. In 1996 matte restrikes were produced.

COPPER-NICKEL

KM#	Date	Mintage	VF	XF	Unc	BU
486	1980	84.900	.50	.85	2.50	3.40
	1981	250.573	.60	.80	2.50	3.50
	1982	236.892	1.00	1.75	2.75	3.85
	1982	1,051	—	—	Proof	18.00
	1983	3 known	—	—	Proof	
	1984	55.000	1.00	1.50	3.75	7.50

BRASS
Guadalupe Victoria, First President

508	1985 wide date					
		25.000	.10	.20	1.00	1.25
	1985 narrow date					
		Inc. Ab.	.10	.25	1.50	2.00
	1986	10.000	1.00	1.75	5.00	6.00
	1988	355.200	.10	.20	.50	1.00
	1989	—		.15	.30	1.50
	1990	—		.15	.30	2.50
	1990	3 known	—	—	Proof	475.00

VEINTICINCO (25) PESOS

22.5000 g, .720 SILVER, .5209 oz ASW
Summer Olympics - Mexico City
Type I, rings aligned.

KM#	Date	Mintage	VF	XF	Unc	BU
479.1	1968	27.182	BV	4.00	4.75	6.00

Type II, center ring low.

479.2	1968	Inc. Ab.	4.00	5.00	9.00	10.50

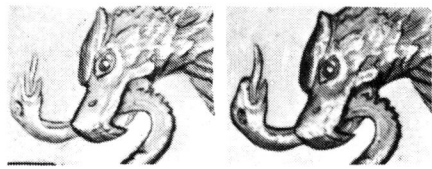

Normal tongue   Long curved tongue
Type III, center rings low.
Snake with long curved tongue.

479.3	1968	Inc. Ab.	4.25	5.25	9.50	11.00

Benito Juarez

480	1972	2.000	BV	4.00	5.50	6.50

50 PESOS

41.6666 g, .900 GOLD, 1.2057 oz AGW
Centennial of Independence

KM#	Date	Mintage	Fine	VF	XF	Unc
481	1921	.180	—	—	BV	650.00
	1922	.463	—	—	BV	510.00
	1923	.432	—	—	BV	510.00
	1924	.439	—	—	BV	510.00
	1925	.716	—	—	BV	510.00
	1926	.600	—	—	BV	510.00
	1927	.606	—	—	BV	510.00
	1928	.538	—	—	BV	510.00
	1929	.458	—	—	BV	510.00
	1930	.372	—	—	BV	510.00
	1931	.137	—	—	BV	565.00
	1944	.593	—	—	BV	510.00
	1945	1.012	—	—	BV	510.00
	1946	1.588	—	—	BV	510.00
	1947	.309	—	—		BV + 3%
	1947	—	—	—	Specimen	6500.

NOTE: During 1949-1972 a total of 3,975,654 pieces were restruck, most likely dated 1947. In 1996 matte restrikes were produced.

COPPER-NICKEL
Coyolxauhqui

KM#	Date	Mintage	VF	XF	Unc	BU
490	1982	222.890	1.00	2.50	5.00	6.25
	1983	45.000	1.50	3.00	6.00	6.50
	1983	1,051	—	—	Proof	22.00
	1984	73.537	1.00	1.35	3.50	4.00
	1984	4 known	—	—	Proof	750.00

NOTE: Doubled die examples of 1982 and 1983 dates exist.

Benito Juarez

495	1984	94.216	.65	1.25	2.75	3.50
	1985	296.000	.25	.45	1.50	2.25
	1986	50.000	5.00	7.00	11.00	12.50
	1987	210.000	.25	.45	1.00	1.25
	1988	80.200	6.25	9.00	12.50	14.50

STAINLESS STEEL

495a	1988	353.300	—	.20	.75	1.50
	1990	—	—	.30	1.00	2.00
	1992	—	—	.25	1.00	2.75

CIEN (100) PESOS

Low 7's **High 7's**
27.7700 g, .720 SILVER, .6429 oz ASW
Jose Morelos y Pavon

KM#	Date	Mintage	VF	XF	Unc	BU
483.1	1977 low 7's, sloping shoulder					
		5.225	BV	4.25	6.00	10.00
	1977 high 7's, sloping shoulder					
		Inc. Ab.	BV	4.25	6.00	10.50

483.2	1977 date in line, higher right shoulder					
(484)		Inc. KM483	BV	4.25	5.00	6.50
	1978	9.879	BV	4.25	6.50	8.50
	1979	.784	BV	4.25	6.50	8.50
	1979	—	—	—	Proof	550.00

ALUMINUM-BRONZE
Venustiano Carranza

493	1984	227.809	.45	.60	2.75	4.00
	1985	377.423	.30	.50	2.00	3.00
	1986	43.000	1.00	2.50	4.75	7.50
	1987	165.000	.60	1.25	2.50	3.50
	1988	433.100	.30	.50	2.00	2.75
	1989	—	.35	.65	2.00	2.75
	1990	—	.15	.40	1.50	2.50
	1990	1 known	—	—	Proof	650.00
	1991	—	.15	.25	1.00	2.50
	1992	—	.30	.75	1.75	3.00

500 PESOS

COPPER-NICKEL

Francisco Madero

KM#	Date	Mintage	VF	XF	Unc	BU
529	1986	20.000	—	1.00	2.50	3.00
	1987	180.000	—	.75	2.00	2.50
	1988	230.000	—	.50	2.00	2.50
	1988	2 known	—	—	Proof	650.00
	1989	—	—	.75	2.00	3.00
	1990	—	—	.75	2.00	3.50
	1992	—	—	1.00	2.25	3.50

1000 PESOS

ALUMINUM-BRONZE
Juana de Asbaje

536	1988	229.300	.85	1.25	3.75	4.25
	1989	—	.85	1.25	3.45	4.25
	1990	—	.85	1.25	2.25	4.25
	1990	2 known	—	—	Proof	550.00
	1991	—	1.00	1.50	2.50	4.25
	1992	—	1.00	1.50	2.25	3.50

MONETARY REFORM

1 New Peso = 1000 Old Pesos

5 CENTAVOS

STAINLESS STEEL

KM#	Date	Mintage	VF	XF	Unc
546	1992	—	—	.15	.25
	1993	—	—	.15	.25
	1994	—	—	.15	.25
	1995	—	—	.15	.25
	1996	—	—	.15	.25
	1997	—	—	.15	.25

10 CENTAVOS

STAINLESS STEEL

547	1992	—	—	.20	.30
	1993	—	—	.20	.30
	1994	—	—	.20	.30
	1995	—	—	.20	.30
	1996	—	—	.20	.30
	1997	—	—	.20	.30

20 CENTAVOS

ALUMINUM-BRONZE

548	1992	—	—	.25	.35
	1993	—	—	.25	.35
	1994	—	—	.25	.35
	1995	—	—	.25	.35
	1996	—	—	.25	.35

50 CENTAVOS

ALUMINUM-BRONZE

549	1992	—	—	.45	.85
	1993	—	—	.45	.75
	1994	—	—	.45	.75
	1995	—	—	.45	.75
	1996	—	—	.45	.75
	1997	—	—	.45	.75

NEW PESO

STAINLESS STEEL ring,
ALUMINUM-BRONZE center

KM#	Date	Mintage	VF	XF	Unc
550	1992	—	—	.60	1.25
	1993	—	—	.60	1.25
	1994	—	—	.60	1.25
	1995	—	—	.60	1.25
	1996	—	—	.60	1.25

PESO

STAINLESS STEEL ring,
ALUMINUM-BRONZE center
Similar to KM#550, but denom. w/o N.

603	1996	—	—	—	1.35
	1997	—	—	—	1.35

2 NEW PESOS

STAINLESS STEEL ring,
ALUMINUM-BRONZE center

551	1992	—	—	1.50	2.50
	1993	—	—	1.00	2.25
	1994	—	—	1.00	2.25
	1995	—	—	1.00	2.25

2 PESOS

STAINLESS STEEL ring,
ALUMINUM-BRONZE center
Similar to KM#551, but denom. w/o N.

604	1996	—	—	—	2.35
	1997	—	—	—	2.35

5 NEW PESOS

STAINLESS STEEL ring,
ALUMINUM-BRONZE center

552	1992	—	—	2.00	4.00
	1993	—	—	2.00	4.00
	1994	—	—	2.00	4.00
	1995	—	—	Proof	25.00

5 PESOS

STAINLESS STEEL ring,
w/ALUMINUM BRONZE center
Similar to KM#552, but denom. w/o N.

605	1996	—	—	—	4.00
	1997	—	—	—	4.00

10 NEW PESOS

ALUMINUM-BRONZE ring w/
11.1400 g, .925 SILVER, .1666 oz ASW center

KM#	Date	Mintage	VF	XF	Unc
553	1992	—	—	—	8.50
	1993	—	—	—	8.50
	1994	—	—	—	8.50
	1995	—	—	—	8.50

10 PESOS

COPPER-NICKEL ZINC center in BRASS ring
Obv: National emblem. Rev: Aztec design.

616	1997	—	—	—	6.00
	1998	—	—	—	6.00

20 NEW PESOS

ALUMINUM-BRONZE ring w/
16.9000 g, .925 SILVER, .2499 oz ASW center

561	1993	—	—	—	13.50
	1994	—	—	—	13.50
	1995	—	—	—	13.50

20 PESOS

ALUMINUM-BRONZE ring w/
16.9000 g, .925 SILVER, .2499 oz ASW center
Similar to KM#561, but denom. w/o N.

607	1996	—	—	—	13.50

The Republic of Moldova (formerly the Moldavian S.S.R.) is bordered in the north, east and south by the Ukraine and on the west by Romania. It has an area of 13,000 sq.mi. (33,700 sq.km.) and a population of 4.4 milion. The capital is Chisinau. Agricultural products are mainly cereals, grapes, tobacco, sugar beets and fruits. Industry is dominated by food processing, clothing, building materials and agricultural machinery manufacturing.

The historical Romanian principality of Moldova was established in the 14th century. It fell under Turkish suzerainty in the 16th century. From 1812 to 1918 Russians occupied the eastern portion of Moldova, which they named Bessarabia. In March 1918 the Bessarabian legislature voted in favor of reunification with Romania. At the Paris Peace Conference in 1920 the union was officially recognized by United States, France, U.K., and Italy a.s.o. The new Soviet government did not accept the union. In 1924, due to Soviet pressure against Romania a Moldavian Autonomous Soviet Socialist Republic (A.S.S.R.) was established within the USSR on border strip that extends east of Nistru River (today it is Transdniestria or Transdniester).

Following the Molotov-Ribbentrop Pact (1939), the Soviet - German agreement which divided Eastern Europe, the Soviet forces reoccupied the region in June 1940 and the Moldavian S.S.R. was proclaimed. The Transdniestria region was transferred to the new republic, while Ukrainian S.S.R. obtained possession of southern part of Bessarabia. The region was liberated by Romanian forces in 1941. The Soviets reconquered the territory in (1944).

A declaration of republican sovereignty was adopted in June 1990 and in Aug. 1991 the area was renamed Moldova, an independent republic. In Dec. 1991 Moldova became a member of the C.I.S. In 1992, as a result of Russian involvement, Transdniestria seceded from Moldova. In May 1992 fighting began between Moldavian separatists (Romanians) and rebels aided by contingents of Cossacks and the Russian 14th Army. The Moldavian government made several futile requests for United Nations intervention. On July 3, 1992, Russian and Moldavian presidents agreed upon a neutral demarcation line with the withdrawl of Russian forces from Transdniestria. This status will remain until a more feasible constitution is proclaimed.

RULERS
Romanian, until 1940

MONETARY SYSTEM
100 Bani = 1 Leu

BAN

ALUMINUM

KM#	Date	Mintage	VF	XF	Unc
1	1993	—	—	—	.20
	1995	—	—	—	.20

5 BANI

ALUMINUM

2	1993	—	—	—	.30
	1995	—	—	—	.30
	1996	—	—	—	.30

10 BANI

ALUMINUM

7	1995	—	—	—	.40
	1997	—	—	—	.40

25 BANI

ALUMINUM

KM#	Date	Mintage	VF	XF	Unc
3	1993	—			.50

50 BANI

ALUMINUM

4	1993	—			.75

BRASS CLAD STEEL
Obv: Heraldic eagle.
Rev: Denomination and grape vine.

10	1997	—			1.50

LEU

NICKEL CLAD STEEL

5	1992	—			1.50

5 LEI

NICKEL CLAD STEEL

6	1993	—			3.50

MONACO

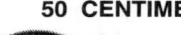

The Principality of Monaco, located on the Mediterranean coast nine miles from Nice, has an area of 0.58 sq. mi. (1.9 sq. km.) and a population of 26,000. Capital: MonacoVille. The economy is based on tourism and the manufacture of cosmetics, gourmet foods and highly specialized electronics. Monaco also derives its revenue from a tobacco monopoly and the sale of postage stamps for philatelic purpose. Gambling in Monte Carlo accounts for only a small fraction of the country's revenue.

Monaco derives its name from 'Monoikos', the Greek surname for Hercules, the mythological strong man who, according to legend, formed the Monacan headland during one of his twelve labors. Monaco has been ruled by the Grimaldi dynasty since 1297 - Prince Rainier III, the present and 31st monarch of Monaco, is still of that line - except for a period during the French Revolution until Napoleon's downfall when the Principality was annexed to France. Since 1865, Monaco has maintained a customs union with France which guarantees its privileged position as long as the royal line remains intact. Under the new constitution proclaimed on December 17, 1962, the Prince shares his power with an 18-member unicameral National Council.

RULERS

Albert I, 1889-1922
Louis II, 1922-1949
Rainier III, 1949-

MINT MARKS

M - Monaco
A - Paris

PRIVY MARKS

(a) - Paris (privy marks only)
(p) - Thunderbolt - Poissy

MONETARY SYSTEM

10 Centimes = 1 Decime
10 Decimes = 1 Franc

50 CENTIMES

ALUMINUM-BRONZE

KM#	Date	Mintage	Fine	VF	XF	Unc
110	1924(p)	.150	3.50	8.00	18.00	40.00

113	1926(p)	.100	4.00	9.00	20.00	45.00

FRANC

ALUMINUM-BRONZE

111	1924(p)	.150	3.00	7.00	14.00	30.00

114	1926(p)	.100	4.00	9.00	16.00	35.00

ALUMINUM

KM#	Date	Mintage	Fine	VF	XF	Unc
120	ND(1943a)	2.500	.50	1.00	2.00	4.50

ALUMINUM-BRONZE

120a	ND(1945a)	1.509	.50	1.00	2.00	5.00

2 FRANCS

ALUMINUM-BRONZE

112	1924(p)	.075	8.00	14.00	30.00	70.00

115	1926(p)	.075	7.00	12.00	25.00	60.00

ALUMINUM

121	ND(1943a)	1.250	.75	1.50	5.00	10.00

ALUMINUM-BRONZE

121a	ND(1945a)	1.080	.50	1.00	2.50	6.00

5 FRANCS

ALUMINUM

122	1945(a)	1.000	1.50	3.00	7.00	15.00

10 FRANCS

COPPER-NICKEL

123	1946(a)	1.000	1.50	3.00	6.00	12.50

ALUMINUM-BRONZE

KM#	Date	Mintage	Fine	VF	XF	Unc
130	1950(a)	.500	.50	1.00	2.00	4.00
	1951(a)	.500	.50	1.00	2.00	4.00

VINGT (20) FRANCS

COPPER-NICKEL

KM#	Date	Mintage	Fine	VF	XF	Unc
124	1947(a)	1.000	2.00	4.00	8.00	20.00

ALUMINUM-BRONZE

KM#	Date	Mintage	Fine	VF	XF	Unc
131	1950(a)	.500	.65	1.25	2.50	6.00
	1951(a)	.500	.65	1.25	2.50	6.00

CINQUANTE (50) FRANCS

ALUMINUM-BRONZE

KM#	Date	Mintage	Fine	VF	XF	Unc
132	1950(a)	.500	1.50	3.00	5.00	12.00

CENT (100) FRANCS

32.2580 g, .900 GOLD, .9335 oz AGW

KM#	Date	Mintage		Fine	VF	XF
105	1901A	.015	BV	420.00	500.00	750.00
	1904A	.010	BV	420.00	500.00	750.00

NOTE: Earlier dates (1891-1896) exist for this type.

COPPER-NICKEL

KM#	Date	Mintage	Fine	VF	XF	Unc
133	1950(a)	.500	2.00	4.00	8.00	18.00

NICKEL

KM#	Date	Mintage	Fine	VF	XF	Unc
134	1956(a)	.500	1.50	2.50	5.50	15.00

MONETARY REFORM

100 Old Francs = 1 New Franc

CENTIME

STAINLESS STEEL

KM#	Date	Mintage	Fine	VF	XF	Unc
155	1976(a)	.025	—	.10	.25	3.50
	1977(a)	.025	—	.10	.25	3.50
	1978(a)	.075	—	.10	.25	3.50
	1979(a)	.075	—	.10	.25	3.50
	1982(a)	.010	—	.10	.25	3.50

5 CENTIMES

COPPER-ALUMINUM-NICKEL

KM#	Date	Mintage	Fine	VF	XF	Unc
156	1976(a)	.025	—	.15	.30	4.00
	1977(a)	.025	—	.15	.30	4.00
	1978(a)	.075	—	.15	.30	4.00
	1979(a)	.075	—	.15	.30	4.00
	1982(a)	.010	—	.15	.30	4.00

10 CENTIMES

ALUMINUM-BRONZE

KM#	Date	Mintage	Fine	VF	XF	Unc
142	1962(a)	.750	—	.10	.20	1.00
	1974(a)	.179	—	.10	.20	1.75
	1975(a)	.172	—	.10	.20	1.75
	1976(a)	.178	—	.10	.20	1.75
	1977(a)	.172	—	.10	.20	1.75
	1978(a)	.112	—	.10	.20	2.00
	1979(a)	.112	—	.10	.20	2.00
	1982(a)	.100	—	.10	.20	2.00

20 CENTIMES

ALUMINUM-BRONZE

KM#	Date	Mintage	Fine	VF	XF	Unc
143	1962(a)	.750	—	.15	.25	1.25
	1974(a)	.104	—	.15	.25	2.25
	1975(a)	.097	—	.15	.25	2.25
	1976(a)	.103	—	.15	.25	2.25
	1977(a)	.097	—	.15	.25	2.25
	1978(a)	.081	—	.15	.25	2.25
	1979(a)	.081	—	.15	.25	2.25
	1982(a)	.100	—	.15	.25	2.25

50 CENTIMES

ALUMINUM-BRONZE

KM#	Date	Mintage	Fine	VF	XF	Unc
144	1962(a)	.375	—	1.00	2.00	4.00

1/2 FRANC

NICKEL

KM#	Date	Mintage	Fine	VF	XF	Unc
145	1965(a)	.375	.25	.50	1.00	2.00
	1968(a)	.250	.25	.50	1.00	2.00
	1974(a)	.069	.30	.60	1.25	3.00
	1975(a)	.070	.30	.60	1.25	3.00
	1976(a)	.068	.30	.60	1.25	3.00
	1977(a)	.062	.30	.60	1.25	3.00
	1978(a)	.414	.25	.50	1.00	2.25
	1979(a)	.414	.25	.50	1.00	2.25
	1982(a)	.457	.25	.50	1.00	2.25
	1989(a)	—	.25	.50	1.00	2.25

FRANC

NICKEL

KM#	Date	Mintage	Fine	VF	XF	Unc
140	1960(a)	.500	.30	.65	1.25	2.75
	1966(a)	.175	.35	.75	1.50	3.50
	1968(a)	.250	.35	.75	1.50	3.50
	1974(a)	.194	.35	.75	1.50	3.50
	1975(a)	.195	.35	.75	1.50	3.50
	1976(a)	.193	.35	.75	1.50	3.50
	1977(a)	.188	.35	.75	1.50	3.50
	1978(a)	.783	.35	.75	1.50	3.00
	1979(a)	.783	.35	.75	1.50	3.00
	1982(a)	.525	.35	.75	1.50	3.00
	1986(a)	—	.30	.60	1.25	2.50
	1989(a)	—	.30	.60	1.25	2.25

2 FRANCS

NICKEL

KM#	Date	Mintage	Fine	VF	XF	Unc
157	1979(a)	.162	.55	.75	1.50	3.50
	1981(a)	.275	.55	.75	1.50	3.50
	1982(a)	.446	.55	.75	1.50	3.50

5 FRANCS

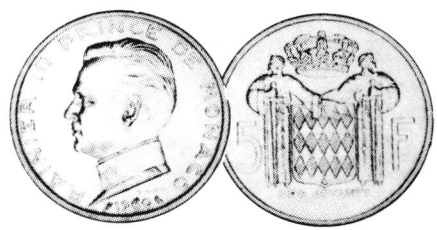

12.0000 g, .835 SILVER, .3221 oz ASW

KM#	Date	Mintage	Fine	VF	XF	Unc
141	1960(a)	.125	—	—	7.50	10.00
	1966(a)	.125	—	—	7.50	10.00

NICKEL-CLAD COPPER-NICKEL

KM#	Date	Mintage	Fine	VF	XF	Unc
150	1971(a)	.250	—	1.50	2.25	4.00
	1974(a)	.152	—	1.50	2.25	4.00
	1975(a)	8,000	—	2.50	6.00	12.50
	1976(a)	8,000	—	2.50	6.00	12.50
	1977(a)	.042	—	2.00	5.00	10.00
	1978(a)	.022	—	2.00	5.00	10.00
	1979(a)	.022	—	2.00	5.00	10.00
	1982(a)	.152	—	2.00	5.00	10.00
	1989(a)	—	—	2.00	5.00	10.00

10 FRANCS

25.0000 g, .900 SILVER, .7234 oz ASW
10th Wedding Anniversary of Prince and Princess

KM#	Date	Mintage	Fine	VF	XF	Unc
146	1966(a)	.038	—	—	—	20.00

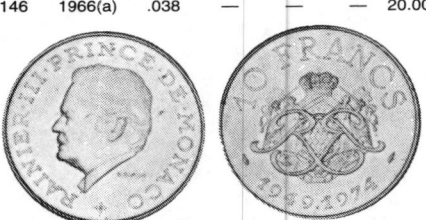

COPPER-NICKEL-ALUMINUM
25th Anniversary of Reign

151	ND(1974)(a)					
		.025	—	2.50	3.50	7.50

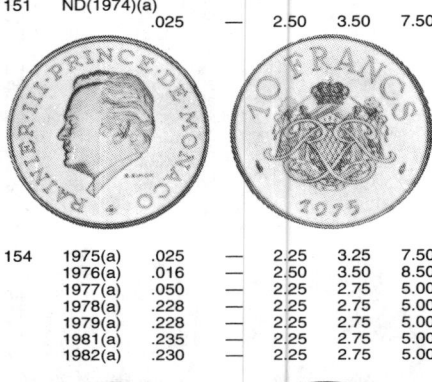

154	1975(a)	.025	—	2.25	3.25	7.50
	1976(a)	.016	—	2.50	3.50	8.50
	1977(a)	.050	—	2.25	2.75	5.00
	1978(a)	.228	—	2.25	2.75	5.00
	1979(a)	.228	—	2.25	2.75	5.00
	1981(a)	.235	—	2.25	2.75	5.00
	1982(a)	.230	—	2.25	2.75	5.00

Princess Grace

160	1982(a)	.030	—	—	—	12.50

NICKEL-ALUMINUM-BRONZE
Prince Pierre Foundation

162	1989(a)	—	—	—	—	6.50

ALUMINUM-BRONZE ring, STEEL center

163	1989(a)	—	—	—	—	9.00
	1991(a)	—	—	—	—	14.00
	1992(a)	—	—	—	—	12.50
	1993(a)	—	—	—	—	14.00
	1994(a)	—	—	—	—	14.00
	1995(a)	—	—	—	—	8.00
	1996(a)	—	—	—	—	8.00
	1997(a)	—	—	—	—	8.00
	1998(a)	—	—	—	—	8.00

20 FRANCS

COPPER-ALUMINUM-NICKEL center within
PURE NICKEL inner ring, within
COPPER-ALUMINUM-NICKEL outer ring
Prince's Palace

KM#	Date	Mintage	Fine	VF	XF	Unc
165	1992(a)	—	—	—	—	17.50
	1997(a)	—	—	—	—	15.50

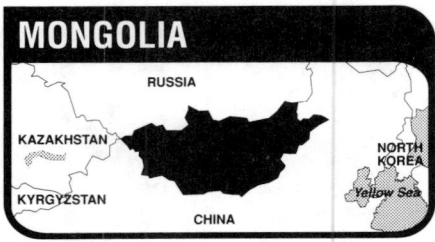

MONGOLIA

The State of Mongolia, (formerly the Mongolian Peoples Republic) a landlocked country in central Asia between Russia and the People's Republic of China, has an area of 604,250 sq. mi. (1,565,000 sq. km.) and a population of 2.26 million. Capital: Ulan Bator. Animal herds and flocks are the chief economic asset. Wool, cattle, butter, meat and hides are exported.

Mongolia (often referred to as Outer Mongolia), one of the world's oldest countries, attained its greatest power in the 13th century when Genghis Khan and his successors conquered all of China and extended their influence westward as far as Hungary and Poland. The empire dissolved in later centuries and in 1691 was brought under suzerainty of the Manchus, who had conquered China in 1644. After the Chinese republican movement led by Sun Yat-sen overthrew the Manchus and set up the Chinese Republic in 1911. Mongolia, with the support of Russia, proclaimed their independence from China and, on March 13, 1921 a Provisional Peoples Government was established and later, on Nov. 26, 1924 the government proclaimed the Mongolian Peoples Republic.

Although nominally a dependency of China, Outer Mongolia voted at a plebiscite Oct. 20, 1945 to sever all ties with China and become an independent nation. Opposition to the communist party developed in late 1989 and after demonstrations and hunger strikes, the Politburo resigned on March 12, 1990 and the new State of Mongolia was organized.

On Feb. 12, 1992 it became the first to discard communism as the national political system by adopting a new constitution.

For earlier issues see Russia - Tannu Tuva.

MONETARY SYSTEM
100 Mongo = 1 Tugrik

PEOPLES REPUBLIC
MONGO

COPPER

KM#	Year	Date	Fine	VF	XF	Unc
1	15	(1925/1926)	5.00	8.00	12.00	20.00

ALUMINUM-BRONZE

9	27	(1937/1938)	2.50	3.50	7.00	15.00

15	35	(1945/1946)	2.00	3.00	5.50	11.50

ALUMINUM

KM#	Date	Mintage	Fine	VF	XF	Unc
21	1959	9.000	.25	.60	1.00	1.75

27	1970	—	.25	.60	.85	1.25

KM#	Date	Mintage	Fine	VF	XF	Unc
27	1977	—	.25	.60	.85	1.25
	1980	—	.25	.60	.85	1.25
	1981	—	.25	.60	.85	1.25

2 MONGO

COPPER

KM#	Year	Date	Fine	VF	XF	Unc
2	15	(1925/1926)	3.50	6.50	12.00	20.00

ALUMINUM-BRONZE

| 10 | 27 | (1937/1938) | 2.50 | 3.50 | 6.00 | 12.00 |

| 16 | 35 | (1945/1946) | 1.00 | 2.00 | 4.00 | 7.00 |

ALUMINUM

KM#	Date	Mintage	Fine	VF	XF	Unc
22	1959	4.000	.25	.65	1.50	3.00

28	1970	—	.25	.65	1.20	2.25
	1977	—	.25	.65	1.20	2.25
	1980	—	.25	.65	1.20	2.25
	1981	—	.25	.65	1.20	2.25

5 MONGO

COPPER

KM#	Year	Date	Fine	VF	XF	Unc
3	15	(1925/1926)	5.00	10.00	20.00	35.00

NOTE: Variety in obverse legend exists.

ALUMINUM-BRONZE

| 11 | 27 | (1937/1938) | 2.75 | 3.50 | 6.00 | 12.00 |

KM#	Year	Date	Fine	VF	XF	Unc
17	35	(1945/1946)	1.75	2.50	5.00	10.00

ALUMINUM

KM#	Date	Mintage	Fine	VF	XF	Unc
23	1959	2.400	.25	1.00	2.00	3.00

29	1970	—	.25	.85	1.75	2.75
	1977	—	.25	.85	1.75	2.75
	1980	—	.25	.85	1.75	2.75
	1981	—	.25	.85	1.75	2.75

10 MONGO

1.7996 g, .500 SILVER, .0289 oz ASW

| 4 | Yr.15(1925/1926) | 1.500 | 3.00 | 5.00 | 9.00 | 17.50 |

COPPER-NICKEL

KM#	Year	Date	Fine	VF	XF	Unc
12	27	(1937/1938)	2.00	3.50	7.00	14.00

| 18 | 35 | (1945/1946) | 1.50 | 3.00 | 5.00 | 9.00 |

ALUMINUM

KM#	Date	Mintage	Fine	VF	XF	Unc
24	1959	3.000	.75	1.50	3.00	5.00

COPPER-NICKEL

30	1970	—	.35	.85	1.75	2.75
	1977	—	.35	.85	1.75	2.75
	1980	—	.35	.85	1.75	2.75
	1981	—	.35	.85	1.75	2.75

15 MONGO

2.6994 g, .500 SILVER, .0433 oz ASW

KM#	Date	Mintage	Fine	VF	XF	Unc
5	Yr.15(1925/1926)	.417	3.50	6.00	12.00	20.00

COPPER-NICKEL

KM#	Year	Date	Fine	VF	XF	Unc
13	27	(1937/1938)	2.00	3.00	6.00	12.00

| 19 | 35 | (1945) | 1.50 | 2.25 | 4.00 | 8.00 |

ALUMINUM

KM#	Date	Mintage	Fine	VF	XF	Unc
25	1959	4.600	.35	.85	1.75	3.50

COPPER-NICKEL

31	1970	—	.25	.65	1.25	2.50
	1977	—	.25	.65	1.25	2.50
	1980	—	.25	.65	1.25	2.50
	1981	—	.25	.65	1.25	2.50

20 MONGO

3.5992 g, .500 SILVER, .0578 oz ASW

| 6 | Yr.15(1925/1926) | 1.625 | 4.00 | 7.50 | 14.00 | 25.00 |

COPPER-NICKEL

KM#	Year	Date	Fine	VF	XF	Unc
14	27	(1937/1938)	2.50	4.50	10.00	18.00

| 20 | 35 | (1945) | 1.50 | 2.50 | 5.00 | 10.00 |

ALUMINUM

KM#	Date	Mintage	Fine	VF	XF	Unc
26	1959	3.600	.60	1.25	2.25	3.50

COPPER-NICKEL

			Fine	VF	XF	Unc
32	1970	—	.40	.80	1.50	2.50
	1977	—	.40	.80	1.50	2.50
	1980	—	.40	.80	1.50	2.50
	1981	—	.40	.80	1.50	2.50

50 MONGO

9.9979 g, .900 SILVER, .2893 oz ASW

	Yr.15(1925/1926)					
7	.920	7.50	12.00	18.50	30.00

COPPER-NICKEL

				VF	XF	Unc
33	1970	—	.50	1.00	1.75	3.00
	1977	—	.50	1.00	1.75	3.00
	1980	—	.50	1.00	1.75	3.00
	1981	—	.50	1.00	1.75	3.00

TUGRIK

19.9957 g, .900 SILVER, .5786 oz ASW

	Yr.15(1925/1926)					
8	.400	12.00	16.50	22.50	40.00

STATE OF MONGOLIA
20 TUGRIK

ALUMINUM
Obv: National emblem. Rev: Denomination.

KM#	Date	Mintage	VF	XF	Unc
122	1994				1.50

50 TUGRIK

ALUMINUM
Obv: National emblem. Rev: Denomination.

KM#	Date	Mintage	VF	XF	Unc
123	1994				1.75

100 TUGRIK

COPPER-NICKEL
Obv: National emblem. Rev: Denomination.

124	1994	—			3.50

200 TUGRIK

COPPER-NICKEL
Obv: Similar to 100 Tugrik, KM#124.

125	1994	—			3.50

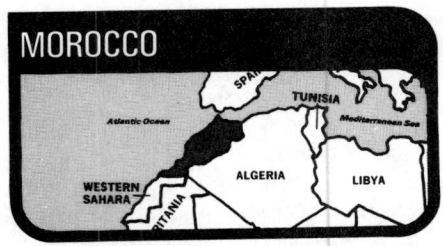

MOROCCO

The Kingdom of Morocco, situated on the northwest corner of Africa, has an area of 275,117 sq. mi. (446,550 sq. km.) and a population of 22.5 million. Capital: Rabat. The economy is essentially agricultural. Phosphates, fresh and preserved vegetables, canned fish, and raw materials are exported.

Morocco's strategic position at the gateway to western Europe has been the principal determinant of its violent, frequently unfortunate history. Time and again the fertile plain between the rugged Atlas Mountains and the sea has echoed the battle's trumpet as Phoenicians, Romans, Vandals, Visigoths, Byzantine Greeks and Islamic Arabs successively conquered and occupied the land. Modern Morocco is a remnant of an early empire formed by the Arabs at the close of the 7th century which encompassed all of northwest Africa and most of the Iberian Peninsula. During the 17th and 18th centuries, while under the control of native dynasties, it was the headquarters of the famous Sale pirates. Morocco's strategic position involved it in the competition of 19th century European powers for political influence in Africa, and resulted in the division of Morocco into French and Spanish spheres of interest which were established as protectorates in 1912. Morocco became independent on March 2, 1956, after France agreed to end its protectorate. Spain signed similar agreements on April 7 of the same year.

TITLES

المغربية

Al-Maghribiya(t)

المملكة المغربية

Al-Mamlaka(t) al-Maghribiya(t)

المحمدية الشريفة

Al-Mohammediya(t) esh-Sherifiya(t)

RULERS
Filali Sharifs

'Abd al-Aziz,
  AH1311-1326/1894-1908AD
Al-Hafiz,
  AH1326-1330/1908-1912AD

French Protectorate
  AH1330/1912AD

Yusuf,
  AH1330-1346/1912-1927AD
Mohammed V,
  AH1346-1375/1927-1955AD

Kingdom

Mohammed V,
  AH1376-1381/1956-1962AD
Al-Hasan II,
  AH1381/1962AD

MINTS

(a) - Paris privy marks only

Bi - England (Birmingham) بانكلند

Ln = bi-England (London) بانكلند

Pa = bi-Bariz (Paris) بباريز

Be = Berlin برلين

Fs = Fes (Fas, Fez) فاس

Py - Poissy Inscribed "Paris" but with thunderbolt privy mark.

NOTE: Some of the above forms of the mintnames are shown as they appear on the coins, not in regular Arabic script.

MONETARY SYSTEM
Until 1921

50 Mazunas = 1 Dirham
10 Dirhams = 1 Rial

NOTES

On the silver coins the denominations are written in words and each series has its own characteristic names:

Y#4-8 (1299-1314) Denomination in Shar'i Dirhams.
Y#9-13 (1313-1319) Denomination in 'Preferred' Dirhams.
Y#18-22 (1320-1323) Denomination in fractions of a Rial, but on the 3 larger sizes, the equivalent is given in "Urti parts", 1 Rial 20 = Urti parts.
Y#23-25 (1329) Denomination in Dirhams and in fraction of a Rial.
Y#30-33 (1331-1336) Denomination in Yusuti or "Treasury" Dirhams.

On most of the larger denominations, the denomination is given in the form of a rhymed couplet.

'Abd al-Aziz
AH1311-1326/1894-1908AD
MAZUNA

BRONZE

Y#	Date	Mintage	Fine	VF	XF	Unc
14	AH1320Be	5 pcs.	—	—	Proof	1000.
	1320Bi	3.000	2.00	5.00	9.00	20.00
	1320Fs	—	20.00	35.00	50.00	120.00
	1321Bi	.900	2.50	6.00	12.00	35.00

NOTE: 5 million examples of 1320 Pa were struck and melted, but at least one specimen is known to exist.

2 MAZUNAS

BRONZE

Y#	Date	Mintage	Fine	VF	XF	Unc
15.1	AH1320Be	5 pcs.	—	—	Proof	850.00
	1320Bi	1.500	2.00	5.00	10.00	25.00
	1320Bi	—	—	—	Proof	250.00
	1320Fs	—	2.00	5.00	10.00	25.00
	1320Pa	—	—	—	Proof	
	1321Bi	.450	2.00	5.00	10.00	25.00
	1321Pa	6.500	2.00	5.00	10.00	25.00
	1322Fs	—	2.00	5.00	10.00	25.00
	1323Fs	—	2.00	5.00	10.00	25.00

NOTE: Varieties exist.

Rev: Rim design reversed.

15.2	AH1320Fs	—	10.00	25.00	35.00	60.00

5 MAZUNAS

BRONZE

16	AH1320Be					
	*5 pcs.	—	—	Proof	700.00	
	1320Bi	2.400	1.00	3.00	7.00	25.00
	1320Bi	—	—	—	Proof	325.00
	1320Fs	—	10.00	25.00	50.00	100.00
	1320Pa	—	—	—	Proof	375.00
	1321Bi	.720	2.00	4.00	8.00	32.00
	1321Fs	—	Reported, not confirmed			
	1321Pa	7.950	5.00	10.00	20.00	37.50
	1322Fs	—	25.00	60.00	100.00	150.00

*NOTE: An additional 799,764 pieces are reported struck, but very few are known.
NOTE: Varieties exist.

---

10 MAZUNAS

BRONZE

Y#	Date	Mintage	Fine	VF	XF	Unc
17	AH1320Be	2.400	1.25	2.50	6.00	25.00
	1320Bi	1.200	1.50	4.00	6.50	25.00
	1320Fs	—	8.00	20.00	50.00	110.00
	1321Be	2.600	1.25	3.00	6.00	25.00
	1321Bi	.360	1.00	2.00	3.25	25.00
	1321Fs	—	8.00	20.00	45.00	100.00
	1323Fs lg.10	—	35.00	60.00	75.00	150.00
	1323Fs sm.10	—	35.00	60.00	75.00	150.00

1/2 DIRHAM

1.4558 g, .835 SILVER, .0391 oz ASW
Rev: Arrow heads point inward.

9.2	AH1319Pa	—	2.50	5.00	10.00	28.00

NOTE: Earlier dates (AH1314-1318) exist for this type.

1.2500 g, .835 SILVER, .0336 oz ASW

18	AH1320Ln	3.920	1.25	4.00	10.00	20.00
	1320Pa	2.400	1.50	4.00	10.00	20.00
	1321Ln	2.105	Inc. 1320Ln			
			3.00	5.00	10.00	20.00

DIRHAM

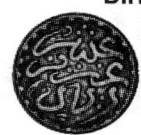 

2.5000 g, .835 SILVER, .0671 oz ASW

19	AH1320Ln	2.940	3.00	8.00	15.00	40.00
	1321Ln	.770	3.00	8.00	15.00	40.00

2-1/2 DIRHAMS

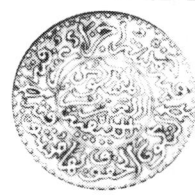 

6.2500 g, .835 SILVER, .1678 oz ASW

20	AH1320Be	.380	4.00	12.50	20.00	50.00
	1320Ln	3.056	4.00	10.00	12.50	40.00
	1320Pa	.640	4.00	11.00	17.50	45.00
	1321Be	4.450	4.00	7.00	10.00	32.50
	1321Ln	1.889	4.00	7.00	10.00	32.50
	1321Ln	—	—	—	Proof	375.00
	1321Pa	—	40.00	60.00	125.00	275.00

5 DIRHAMS

12.5000 g, .835 SILVER, .3356 oz ASW

21	AH1320Be	2.510	7.00	15.00	30.00	75.00
	1320Ln	.900	7.00	15.00	30.00	75.00
	1321Be	—	—	—	Rare	
	1321Ln	1.041	7.00	15.00	30.00	75.00
	1321Ln	—	—	—	Proof	450.00
	1321Pa	1.800	7.00	17.50	35.00	85.00
	1322Pa	.540	7.00	20.00	40.00	100.00
	1323Pa	1.090	7.00	20.00	40.00	100.00

---

10 DIRHAMS

25.0000 g, .900 SILVER, .7234 oz ASW

Y#	Date	Mintage	Fine	VF	XF	Unc
22	AH1320Ln	.330	17.50	25.00	40.00	120.00
	1320Ln	—	—	—	Proof	Rare
	1321Pa	.300	20.00	27.50	40.00	120.00

Al-Hafiz
AH1326-1330/1908-1912AD
2-1/2 DIRHAMS

6.2500 g, .835 SILVER, .1678 oz ASW

23	AH1329Pa	3.130	4.00	8.50	18.00	40.00

5 DIRHAMS

12.5000 g, .835 SILVER, .3356 oz ASW

24	AH1329Pa	4.660	7.00	10.00	25.00	90.00

10 DIRHAMS

25.0000 g, .900 SILVER, .7234 oz ASW

Y#	Date	Mintage	Fine	VF	XF	Unc
25	AH1329Pa	7.040	10.00	20.00	40.00	100.00

Yusuf
AH1330-1346/1912-1927AD

MAZUNA

BRONZE

| 26 | AH1330Pa | 1.850 | 2.00 | 5.00 | 15.00 | 30.00 |

2 MAZUNAS

 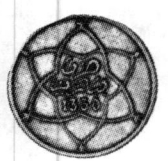

BRONZE

| 27 | AH1330Pa | 2.790 | 2.00 | 4.00 | 12.00 | 30.00 |

NOTE: Coins reportedly dated 1331Pa probably bore date 1330.

5 MAZUNAS

BRONZE

| 28.1 | AH1330Pa | 3.180 | 2.00 | 5.00 | 11.00 | 25.00 |
| | 1340Pa | — | 2.00 | 4.00 | 10.00 | 22.50 |

Rev: Privy marks.

| 28.2 | 1340Pa | 2.000 | 1.00 | 2.00 | 5.00 | 25.00 |
| | 1340Py | 2.010 | 2.00 | 5.00 | 8.00 | 27.50 |

10 MAZUNAS

BRONZE

| 29.1 | AH1330Pa | 1.500 | .75 | 2.50 | 10.00 | 30.00 |
| | 1340Pa | 1.000 | .75 | 1.50 | 7.50 | 25.00 |

Rev: Privy marks.

Y#	Date	Mintage	Fine	VF	XF	Unc
29.2	AH1340Py	1.000		3.00	12.00	30.00

DIRHAM

2.5000 g, .835 SILVER, .0671 oz ASW

| 30 | AH1331Pa | .500 | 30.00 | 45.00 | 75.00 | 200.00 |
| | 1331Pa | — | — | — | Proof | 800.00 |

2-1/2 DIRHAMS

6.2500 g, .835 SILVER, .1678 oz ASW

| 31 | AH1331Pa | 2.500 | 30.00 | 45.00 | 90.00 | 225.00 |

5 DIRHAMS

.835 SILVER

| 32 | AH1331Pa | 1.500 | 7.00 | 16.00 | 25.00 | 60.00 |
| | 1336Pa | 11.500 | 6.00 | 11.00 | 20.00 | 50.00 |

10 DIRHAMS

25.0000 g, .900 SILVER, .7234 oz ASW

| 33 | AH1331Pa | 7.000 | 9.00 | 20.00 | 35.00 | 70.00 |
| | 1336Pa | 2.600 | 9.00 | 17.50 | 20.00 | 55.00 |

FRENCH PROTECTORATE
MONETARY SYSTEM
100 Centimes = 1 Franc
100 Francs = 1 Dirham
NOTE: Y46-51 were struck for more than 20 years without change of date, until a new currency was intro-

duced in 1974. Final mintage statistics are not yet available.

25 CENTIMES

COPPER-NICKEL
Obv. and rev: W/o privy marks.

Y#	Date	Mintage	Fine	VF	XF	Unc
34.1	ND (1921)Pa	13.000	1.00	3.00	8.00	40.00

Rev: Thunderbolt above CENTIMES.

| 34.2 | ND (1924)Py | 6.020 | 1.00 | 3.00 | 8.00 | 40.00 |

Rev: Thunderbolt and torch at left and right of CENTIMES.

| 34.3 | ND(1924)Py | Inc. Ab. | 1.00 | 3.00 | 8.00 | 40.00 |

50 CENTIMES

NICKEL
Obv. and rev: W/o privy marks.

| 35.1 | ND(1921)Pa | 11.000 | .50 | 1.00 | 6.50 | 45.00 |

Rev: Thunderbolt at bottom.

| 35.2 | ND(1924)Py | 3.000 | 1.00 | 2.00 | 8.00 | 45.00 |

FRANC

NICKEL
Obv. and rev: W/o privy marks.

| 36.1 | ND(1921)Pa | 13.510 | .50 | 1.00 | 6.50 | 37.50 |

Rev: Thunderbolt below 1.

| 36.2 | ND(1924)Py | 3.000 | 1.25 | 2.50 | 10.00 | 55.00 |

Mohammed V
AH1346-1375/1927-1955AD

50 CENTIMES

ALUMINUM-BRONZE

Y#	Date	Year	Mintage	VF	XF	Unc
40	AH1364(a)	1945	—	.20	1.50	2.50

FRANC

ALUMINUM-BRONZE

41	AH1364(a)	1945	12.000	.25	1.00	2.50

ALUMINUM

46	AH1370(a)	1951	—	.10	.25	1.00

2 FRANCS

ALUMINUM-BRONZE

42	AH1364(a)	1945	12.000	.50	2.50	6.00

ALUMINUM

47	AH1370(a)	1951	—	.10	.50	2.00

5 FRANCS

5.0000 g, .680 SILVER, .1093 oz ASW

37	AH1347(a)	—	4.000	2.50	7.00	32.00
	1352(a)	—	5.000	1.50	4.00	18.00

ALUMINUM-BRONZE

Y#	Date	Mintage	Fine	VF	XF	Unc
43	AH1365(a)					
		20.000	.15	.35	.60	1.50

ALUMINUM

Y#	Date	Mintage	Fine	VF	XF	Unc
48	AH1370(a)		.10	.15	.30	1.00

10 FRANCS

10.0000 g, .680 SILVER, .2186 oz ASW

38	AH1347(a)	1.600	4.00	10.00	22.00	80.00
	1352(a)	2.900	2.25	3.00	8.00	27.50

COPPER-NICKEL

44	AH1366(a)					
		20.000	.35	.75	1.00	1.50

ALUMINUM-BRONZE

49	AH1371(a)	—	.10	.35	.75	1.50

20 FRANCS

20.0000 g, .680 SILVER, .4372 oz ASW

39	AH1347(a)	—	5.00	12.00	32.50	80.00
	1352(a)	2.000	5.00	8.00	25.00	50.00

COPPER-NICKEL

45	AH1366(a)	6.000	.25	.50	1.00	2.00
	1366	—	—		Proof	50.00

ALUMINUM-BRONZE

Y#	Date	Mintage	Fine	VF	XF	Unc
50	AH1371(a)		.10	.25	.75	1.50

50 FRANCS

ALUMINUM-BRONZE

51	AH1371(a)	—	.25	.50	.65	1.00

GOLD

51a	AH1371(a)	—	—	—	Rare	—

100 FRANCS

2.5000 g, .720 SILVER, .0579 oz ASW

Y#	Date	Year	Mintage	VF	XF	Unc
A54	AH1370(a)	1951	10.000	—	—	250.00

NOTE: Most were remelted.

52	AH1372(a)	1953	5.000	2.50	3.50	5.00

200 FRANCS

8.0000 g, .720 SILVER, .1851 oz ASW

53	AH1372(a)	1953	9.200	2.00	4.00	8.00

KINGDOM

1956-

Mohammed V

AH1376-1381/1956-1962AD

500 FRANCS

22.5000 g, .900 SILVER, .6511 oz ASW

54	AH1376(a)	1956	2.000	8.00	10.00	20.00

MONETARY REFORM
100 Francs = 1 Dirham
DIRHAM

6.0000 g, .600 SILVER, .1157 oz ASW

Y#	Date	Year	Mintage	VF	XF	Unc
55	AH1380(a)	1960	18.830	1.00	2.50	5.00

Al-Hasan II
AH1381/1962AD
DIRHAM

NICKEL

56	AH1384(a)	1965	22.190	.50	.75	1.00
	1388(a)	1968	5.000	.50	.75	1.00
	1389(a)	1969	10.000	.50	.75	1.00

5 DIRHAM

11.7500 g, .720 SILVER, .2720 oz ASW

57	AH1384(a)	1965	1,800	5.00	7.50	14.50
	1384(a)	1965	200 pcs.	—	Proof	50.00

MONETARY REFORM
1974-
100 Santimat = 1 Dirham
SANTIM

ALUMINUM

58	AH1394	1974	10.240	—	.50	1.25
	1394	1974	.020	—	Proof	1.00
	1395	1975	1.700	—	.10	1.00
	1395	1975	.014	—	Proof	2.50

Obv: Royal arms.
Rev: Fish and denomination.

93	AH1407	1987	—	—	—	.25

5 SANTIMAT

BRASS
F.A.O. Issue

59	AH1394	1974	54.820	—	.15	.30
	1394	1974	.020	—	Proof	1.25
	1395	1975	11.000	—	.10	.25
	1398	1978	12.600	—	.10	.25

BRASS
F.A.O. Issue

Y#	Date	Year	Mintage	VF	XF	Unc
83	AH1407	1987	—	—	—	.30

10 SANTIMAT

BRASS
F.A.O. Issue

60	AH1394	1974	67.950	—	.15	.30
	1394	1974	.020	—	Proof	1.75
	1395	1975	10.900	—	.10	.20
	1398	1978	1.000	—	.10	.30

F.A.O. Issue

84	AH1407	1987	—	—	—	.40

20 SANTIMAT

BRASS

61	AH1394	1974	59.840	.30	.40	.50
	1394	1974	—	—	Proof	2.50
	1395	1975	10.700	.10	.15	.35
	1397	1977	22.800	.10	.15	.35
	1398	1978	2.200	.10	.15	.35

F.A.O. Issue

85	AH1407	1987	—	—	—	.50

50 SANTIMAT

COPPER-NICKEL

62	AH1394	1974	40.380	.20	.40	.60
	1394	1974	.020	—	Proof	3.00
	1398	1978	1.100	.25	.50	.75

1/2 DIRHAM

COPPER-NICKEL
Obv: Portrait of King.
Rev: Arms above denomination.

87	AH1407	1987	—	—	—	1.25

DIRHAM

COPPER-NICKEL

Y#	Date	Year	Mintage	VF	XF	Unc
63	AH1394	1974	37.850	.30	.50	.75
	1394	1974	37.850	—	Proof	4.50
	1398	1978	18.100	.15	.35	.75

88	AH1407	1987	—	—	—	2.75

5 DIRHAMS

COPPER-NICKEL
World Food Conference

64	AH1395	1975	.500	—	1.00	3.50
	1395	1975	500 pcs.	—	Proof	8.00

72	AH1400	1980	10.000	1.50	4.00	6.50
(A63)						

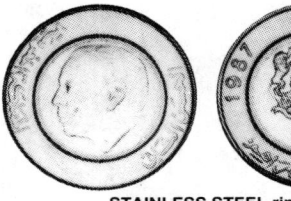

STAINLESS STEEL ring,
ALUMINUM-BRONZE center

82	AH1407	1987	—	2.00	4.50	8.50

10 DIRHAMS

COPPER-NICKEL center in BRASS ring
Obv: King. Rev: National arms.

92	AH1415	1995	—	—	—	6.50

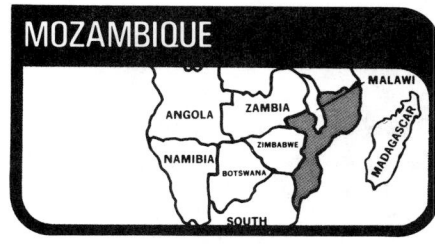

MOZAMBIQUE

The Republic of Mozambique, a former overseas province of Portugal stretching for 1,430 miles (2,301 km.) along the southeast coast of Africa, has an area of 302,330 sq. mi. (801,590 sq. km.) and a population of 14.1 million, 99 percent of whom are native Africans of the Bantu tribes. Capital: Maputo. Agriculture is the chief industry. Cashew nuts, cotton, sugar, copra and tea are exported.

Vasco de Gama explored all the coast of Mozambique in 1498 and found Arab trading posts already established along the coast. Portuguese settlement dates from the establishment of the trading post of Mozambique in 1505. Within five years Portugal absorbed all the former Arab sultanates along the east African coast. The area was organized as a colony in 1907 and became an overseas province in 1952. In Sept. of 1974, after more than a decade of guerrilla warfare with the forces of the Mozambique Liberation Front, Portugal agreed to the independence of Mozambique, effective June 25, 1975. The Socialist party, led by President Joaquim Chissano was in power until the 2nd of November, 1990 when they became a republic.

Mozambique became a member of the Commonwealth of Nations in November 1995. The President is Head of State; the Prime Minister is Head of Government.

RULERS
Portuguese, until 1975

MONETARY SYSTEM
100 Centavos = 1 Escudo

10 CENTAVOS

BRONZE

KM#	Date	Mintage	Fine	VF	XF	Unc
63	1936	2.000	1.50	3.00	14.00	32.00

| 72 | 1942 | 2.000 | .75 | 1.50 | 6.00 | 15.00 |

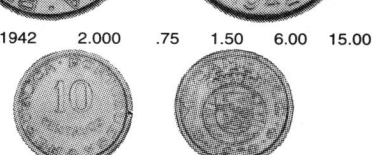

| 83 | 1960 | 3.750 | — | .25 | .50 | 1.50 |
| | 1961 | 10.300 | — | .15 | .25 | 1.00 |

20 CENTAVOS

BRONZE

| 64 | 1936 | 2.500 | 1.75 | 3.50 | 20.00 | 45.00 |

| 71 | 1941 | 2.000 | 1.00 | 2.50 | 15.00 | 35.00 |

KM#	Date	Mintage	Fine	VF	XF	Unc
75	1949	8.000	.25	.75	2.00	6.00
	1950	12.500	.25	.75	1.25	4.00

| 85 | 1961 | 12.500 | — | .15 | .50 | 1.75 |

Reduced size, 16mm

| 88 | 1973 | 1.798 | 4.00 | 10.00 | 18.00 | 35.00 |
| | 1974 | 13.044 | 4.00 | 9.00 | 15.00 | 30.00 |

50 CENTAVOS

COPPER-NICKEL

| 65 | 1936 | 2.500 | 1.50 | 4.00 | 18.00 | 50.00 |

BRONZE

| 73 | 1945 | 2.500 | .75 | 2.50 | 12.50 | 25.00 |

NICKEL-BRONZE

| 76 | 1950 | 20.000 | .30 | 1.00 | 3.50 | 10.00 |
| | 1951 | 16.000 | .30 | 1.00 | 3.50 | 10.00 |

BRONZE

| 81 | 1953 | 5.010 | .25 | .75 | 3.00 | 10.00 |
| | 1957 | 24.990 | — | .25 | 1.00 | 5.00 |

| 89 | 1973 | 6.841 | — | .15 | .75 | 3.00 |
| | 1974 | 23.810 | — | .15 | .75 | 3.00 |

ESCUDO

COPPER-NICKEL

KM#	Date	Mintage	Fine	VF	XF	Unc
66	1936	2.000	3.50	14.00	40.00	85.00

BRONZE

| 74 | 1945 | 2.000 | 2.00 | 5.00 | 15.00 | 35.00 |

| 1 | | | | | 1950 | |

NICKEL-BRONZE

| 77 | 1950 | 10.000 | .75 | 2.00 | 3.50 | 12.50 |
| | 1951 | 10.000 | .50 | 1.50 | 2.50 | 10.00 |

BRONZE

82	1953	2.013	.30	1.00	3.50	12.50
	1957	2.987	.20	.75	3.00	12.50
	1962	.600	.35	1.25	6.00	14.50
	1963	3.258	—	.25	2.00	6.00
	1965	5.000	—	.10	1.00	3.50
	1968	4.500	—	.10	1.00	3.50
	1969	1.642	—	.15	1.00	4.00
	1973	.501	.20	.50	2.00	6.50
	1974	25.281	—	.10	.75	2.50

2-1/2 ESCUDOS

3.5000 g, .650 SILVER, .0731 oz ASW

| 61 | 1935 | 1.200 | 6.50 | 15.00 | 40.00 | 100.00 |

68	1938	1.000	3.00	8.00	15.00	35.00
	1942	1.200	2.00	6.00	12.50	28.00
	1950	4.000	1.25	2.50	9.00	14.00
	1951	4.000	1.50	3.00	6.00	17.50

COPPER-NICKEL

| 78 | 1952 | 4.000 | .30 | 1.00 | 4.00 | 9.00 |

KM#	Date	Mintage	Fine	VF	XF	Unc
78	1953	4.000	.30	.75	3.00	7.00
	1954	4.000	.25	.60	2.00	6.00
	1955	4.000	.30	.75	3.50	7.50
	1965	8.000	.10	.25	.50	2.00
	1973	1.767	.25	.65	2.50	6.50

5 ESCUDOS

7.0000 g, .650 SILVER, .1463 oz ASW

62	1935	1.000	6.50	15.00	42.00	110.00

69	1938	.800	7.50	20.00	55.00	120.00
	1949	8.000	2.00	5.50	12.50	28.00

4.0000 g, .650 SILVER, .0835 oz ASW

84	1960	8.000	1.00	2.00	3.00	6.00

COPPER-NICKEL

86	1971	8.000	.20	.50	1.00	3.00
	1973	3.352	.20	.50	1.75	4.50

10 ESCUDOS

12.5000 g, .835 SILVER, .3356 oz ASW

67	1936	.497	12.00	30.00	60.00	125.00

70	1938	.530	10.00	20.00	45.00	100.00

5.0000 g, .720 SILVER, .1157 oz ASW

79	1952	1.503	2.00	4.00	10.00	25.00

KM#	Date	Mintage	Fine	VF	XF	Unc
79	1954	1.335	2.00	4.00	10.00	25.00
	1955	1.162	2.50	5.00	12.00	27.50
	1960	2.000	1.00	2.00	3.50	7.00

5.0000 g, .680 SILVER, .1093 oz ASW

79a	1966	.500	1.00	2.00	5.00	12.50

COPPER-NICKEL

79b	1968	5.000	.30	.60	1.75	6.00
	1970	4.000	.30	.60	1.50	5.00
	1974	3.366	.30	.60	1.50	7.00

20 ESCUDOS

10.0000 g, .720 SILVER, .2315 oz ASW

80	1952	1.004	1.50	3.00	5.00	12.50
	1955	.996	1.75	3.50	5.50	13.50
	1960	2.000	1.25	2.50	4.50	11.50

10.0000 g, .680 SILVER, .2186 oz ASW

80a	1966	.250	—	3.50	6.50	15.00

NICKEL

87	1971	2.000	.35	.75	1.75	5.00
	1972	1.158	.35	.75	2.00	6.00

PEOPLES REPUBLIC
100 Centimos = 1 Metica
CENTIMO

ALUMINUM

90	1975	15.050	—	—	125.00	225.00

2 CENTIMOS

COPPER-ZINC

91	1975	8.242	—	—	80.00	130.00

5 CENTIMOS

COPPER-ZINC

92	1975	14.898	—	—	65.00	115.00

10 CENTIMOS

COPPER-ZINC

KM#	Date	Mintage	Fine	VF	XF	Unc
93	1975	18.000	—	—	70.00	125.00

20 CENTIMOS

COPPER-NICKEL

94	1975	8.050	—	—	150.00	250.00

50 CENTIMOS

COPPER-NICKEL

95	1975	3.050	—	—	175.00	275.00

METICA

COPPER-NICKEL

96	1975	2.550	—	—	55.00	85.00

2-1/2 METICAS

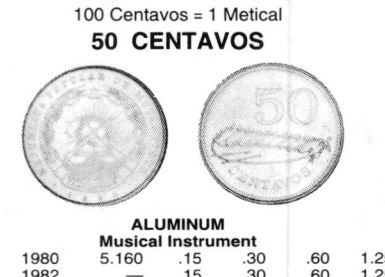

COPPER-NICKEL

97	1975	1.500	—	—	125.00	200.00

MONETARY REFORM
100 Centavos = 1 Metical
50 CENTAVOS

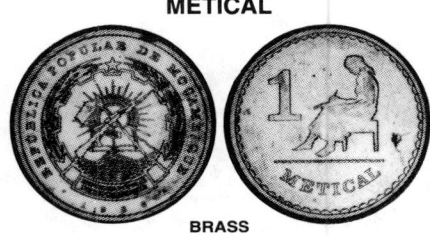

ALUMINUM
Musical Instrument

98	1980	5.160	.15	.30	.60	1.25
	1982		.15	.30	.60	1.25

METICAL

BRASS

Female Student

KM#	Date	Mintage	Fine	VF	XF	Unc
99	1980	.032	1.50	3.00	5.00	10.00
	1982	—	1.50	3.00	5.00	10.00

ALUMINUM

99a	1986	—	.20	.40	.60	1.00

BRASS CLAD STEEL

115	1994	—	—	—	—	.50

2-1/2 METICAIS

ALUMINUM, 1.80-2.00 g
Ship and Crane in Harbor

100	1980	1.088	.25	.50	1.00	1.75
	1982	—	.25	.50	1.00	1.75
	1986	—	.25	.50	1.00	1.75

NOTE: Edge varieties exist.

5 METICAIS

ALUMINUM
Tractor

101	1980	7.736	.35	.75	1.25	2.00
	1982	—	.35	.75	1.25	2.00
	1986	—	.35	.75	1.25	2.00

BRASS CLAD STEEL

116	1994	—	—	—	—	1.00

10 METICAIS

COPPER-NICKEL
Industrial Skyline

102	1980	.152	.75	1.50	2.50	6.00
	1981	—	.75	1.50	2.50	6.00

ALUMINUM

102a	1986	—	.25	.45	1.00	2.00

BRASS CLAD STEEL
Cotton Plant

117	1994	—	—	—	—	1.25

20 METICAIS

COPPER-NICKEL
Panzer Tank

KM#	Date	Mintage	Fine	VF	XF	Unc
103	1980	.078	1.00	2.00	4.00	9.00

ALUMINUM

103a	1986	—	.40	.80	1.50	3.00

BRASS CLAD STEEL
Pepper Plant

118	1994	—	—	—	—	1.50

50 METICAIS

NICKEL CLAD STEEL
Leopard's Head

119	1994	—	—	—	—	2.00

100 METICAIS

NICKEL CLAD STEEL
Lobster

120	1994	—	—	—	—	2.25

500 METICAIS

NICKEL CLAD STEEL

121	1994	—	—	—	—	3.50

MYANMAR (Burma)

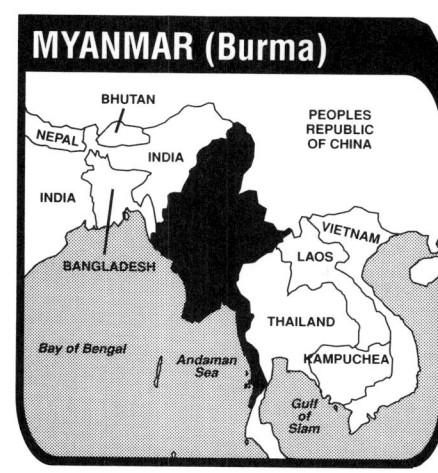

The Union of Myanmar, formerly Burma, a country of Southeast Asia fronting on the Bay of Bengal and the Andaman Sea, has an area of 261,218 sq. mi. (678,500 sq. km.) and a population of 38.8 million. Capital: Yangon (Rangoon). Myanmar is an agricultural country heavily dependent on its leading product (rice) which occupies two-thirds of the cultivated area and accounts for 40 per cent of the value of exports. Mineral resources are extensive, but production is low. Petroleum, lead, tin, silver, zinc, nickel cobalt, and precious stones are exported.

The first European to reach Burma, about 1435, was Nicolo Di Conti, a merchant of Venice. During the beginning of the reign of Bodawpaya (1781-1819AD) the kingdom comprised most of the same area as it does today including Arakan which was taken over in 1784-85. The British East India Company, while unsuccessful in its 1612 effort to establish posts along the Bay of Bengal, was enabled by the Anglo-Burmese Wars of 1824-86 to expand to the whole of Burma and to secure its annexation to British India. In 1937, Burma was separated from India, becoming a separate British colony with limited self-government. Burma became an independent nation outside the British Commonwealth on Jan. 4, 1948, the constitution of 1948 providing for a parliamentary democracy and the nationalization of certain industries. However, political and economic problems persisted, and on March 2, 1962, Gen. Ne Win took over the government, suspended the constitution, installed himself as chief of state, and pursued a socialistic program with nationalization of nearly all industry and trade. On Jan. 4, 1974, a new constitution adopted by referendum established Burma as a 'socialist republic' under one-party rule. The country name was changed to Myanmar in 1989.

The coins issued by kings Mindon and Thibaw between 1852 and 1885 circulated in Upper Burma. Indian coins were current in Lower Burma, which was annexed in 1852. Burmese coins are frequently known by the equivalent Indian denominations, although their values are inscribed in Burmese units. Upper Burma was annexed in 1885 and the Burmese coinage remained in circulation until 1889, when Indian coins became current throughout Burma. Coins were again issued in the old Burmese denominations after independence in 1948, but these were replaced by decimal issues in 1952. The Chula-Sakarat (CS) dating is sometimes referred to as BE-Burmese Era and began in 638AD.

RULERS

British, 1886-1948

MONETARY SYSTEM
(Until 1952)

4 Pyas = 1 Pe
2 Pe = 1 Mu
2 Mu = 1 Mat
5 Mat = 1 Kyat

NOTE: Originally 10 light Mu = 1 Kyat, eventually 8 heavy Mu = 1 Kyat.

Indian Equivalents
1 Silver Kyat = 1 Rupee = 16 Annas
1 Gold Kyat = 1 Mohur = 16 Rupees

2 PYAS

COPPER-NICKEL
Obv: Chinze.

KM#	Date	Mintage	Fine	VF	XF	Unc
27	1949	7.000	.25	.50	1.00	3.00
	1949	100 pcs.	—	—	Proof	100.00

PE

 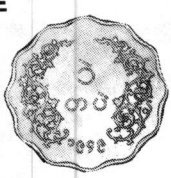

COPPER-NICKEL
Obv: Chinze.

KM#	Date	Mintage	Fine	VF	XF	Unc
28	1949	8.000	.35	.75	1.50	4.00
	1949	100 pcs.	—	—	Proof	100.00
	1950	9.500	.35	.75	1.50	4.00
	1950	—	—	—	Proof	—
	1951	6.500	.50	1.00	2.00	5.00
	1951	—	—	—	Proof	—

2 PE

 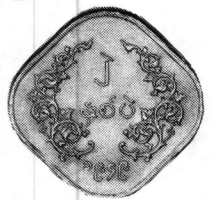

COPPER-NICKEL
Obv: Chinze.

29	1949	7.100	.50	1.00	2.00	5.00
	1949	100 pcs.	—	—	Proof	100.00
	1950	8.500	.50	1.00	2.00	5.00
	1950	—	—	—	Proof	—
	1951	7.480	.50	1.00	2.00	5.00
	1951	—	—	—	Proof	—

4 PE

NICKEL
Obv: Chinze.

30	1949	6.500	1.25	2.50	5.00	15.00
	1949	100 pcs.	—	—	Proof	100.00
	1950	6.120	1.00	2.00	4.00	12.00

8 PE

 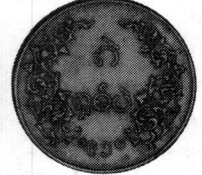

NICKEL
Obv: Chinze.

31	1949	3.270	1.50	3.00	6.00	25.00
	1949	100 pcs.	—	—	Proof	100.00
	1950	3.900	1.25	2.50	5.00	20.00
	1950	—	—	—	Proof	—

COPPER-NICKEL
Obv: Chinze.

KM#	Date	Year	Mintage	Fine	VF	XF	Unc
31a	CS1314	1952	1.642	50.00	100.00	150.00	200.00
	1314	1952	—	—	—	Proof	400.00

DECIMAL COINAGE
100 Pyas = 1 Kyat

PYA

BRONZE

Obv: Chinze.

KM#	Date	Year	Mintage	Fine	VF	XF	Unc
32	CS1314	1952	.500	.10	.15	.20	.35
	1314	1952	100 pcs.	—	—	Proof	60.00
	1315	1953	14.000	.10	.15	.20	.35
	1315	1953	—	—	—	Proof	—
	1317	1955	30.000	.10	.15	.20	.35
	1317	1955	—	—	—	Proof	—
	1318	1956	100 pcs.	—	—	Proof	60.00
	1324	1962	100 pcs.	—	—	Proof	60.00
	1327	1965	15.000	.10	.15	.20	.35
	1327	1965	—	—	—	Proof	—

ALUMINUM
Aung San

38	CS1328	1966	8.000	.10	.15	.25	.50

5 PYAS

COPPER-NICKEL
Obv: Chinze.

33	CS1314	1952	20.000	.10	.15	.35	.75
	1314	1952	100 pcs.	—	—	Proof	65.00
	1315	1953	59.700	.10	.15	.35	.75
	1315	1953	—	—	—	Proof	—
	1317	1955	40.272	.10	.15	.35	.75
	1317	1955	—	—	—	Proof	—
	1318	1956	20.000	.10	.15	.35	.75
	1318	1956	100 pcs.	—	—	Proof	65.00
	1323	1961	12.000	.10	.15	.35	.75
	1323	1961	—	—	—	Proof	—
	1324	1962	10.000	.10	.15	.35	.75
	1324	1962	100 pcs.	—	—	Proof	65.00
	1325	1963	40.400	.10	.15	.25	.60
	1325	1963	—	—	—	Proof	—
	1327	1965	43.600	.10	.15	.20	.40
	1327	1965	—	—	—	Proof	—
	1328	1966	20.000	.10	.15	.20	.40
	1328	1966	—	—	—	Proof	—

 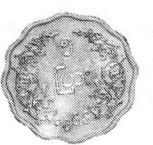

ALUMINUM
Aung San

39	CS1328	1966	—	.10	.20	.35	.60

ALUMINUM-BRONZE
F.A.O. Issue - Rice Plant

51	1987	—	.10	.20	.40	.70

10 PYAS

COPPER-NICKEL
Obv: Chinze.

34	CS1314	1952	20.000	.10	.20	.40	1.00
	1314	1952	100 pcs.	—	—	Proof	70.00
	1315	1953	37.250	.10	.20	.40	1.00
	1315	1953	—	—	—	Proof	—
	1317	1955	22.750	.10	.20	.40	1.00
	1317	1955	—	—	—	Proof	—
	1318	1956	35.000	.10	.15	.40	1.00
	1318	1956	100 pcs.	—	—	Proof	70.00
	1324	1962	6.000	.10	.20	.40	1.00
	1324	1962	100 pcs.	—	—	Proof	70.00
	1325	1963	10.750	.10	.20	.40	1.00
	1325	1963	10.750	—	—	Proof	—
	1327	1965	32.620	.10	.20	.40	1.00
	1327	1965	—	—	—	Proof	—

 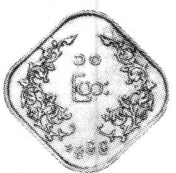

ALUMINUM
Aung San

KM#	Date	Year	Mintage	Fine	VF	XF	Unc
40	CS1328	1966	—	.15	.30	.60	1.00

BRASS
F.A.O. Issue - Rice Plant

49	1983	—	.10	.20	.40	.80

25 PYAS

COPPER-NICKEL
Obv: Chinze.

35	CS1314	1952	13.540	.10	.20	.50	1.25
	1314	1952	100 pcs.	—	—	Proof	75.00
	1316	1954	18.000	.10	.20	.50	1.25
	1316	1954	—	—	—	Proof	—
	1317	1955	—	—	—	Proof	75.00
	1318	1956	14.000	.10	.20	.50	1.25
	1318	1956	100 pcs.	—	—	Proof	75.00
	1321	1959	6.000	.10	.20	.50	1.25
	1321	1959	—	—	—	Proof	—
	1323	1961	4.000	.10	.20	.50	1.25
	1323	1961	—	—	—	Proof	—
	1324	1962	3.200	.10	.20	.50	1.25
	1324	1962	100 pcs.	—	—	Proof	75.00
	1325	1963	16.000	.10	.15	.30	.75
	1325	1963	—	—	—	Proof	—
	1327	1965	26.000	.10	.15	.30	.75
	1327	1965	—	—	—	Proof	—

ALUMINUM
Aung San

41	CS1328	1966	—	.15	.30	.60	1.00

BRONZE
F.A.O. Issue - Rice Plant

48	1980	—	.15	.30	.60	1.00

F.A.O. Issue - Rice Plant

50	1986	—	.10	.20	.35	.60

COPPER PLATED STEEL

50a	1991	—	.15	.50	.60	1.00

50 PYAS

COPPER-NICKEL
Obv: Chinze.

KM#	Date	Year	Mintage	Fine	VF	XF	Unc
36	CS1314	1952	2.500	.20	.50	.75	1.75
	1314	1952	100 pcs.	—	—	Proof	80.00
	1316	1954	12.000	.20	.50	.75	1.75
	1316	1954	—	—	—	Proof	—
	1318	1956	8.000	.20	.50	.75	1.75
	1318	1956	100 pcs.	—	—	Proof	80.00
	1323	1961	2.000	.15	.40	.75	1.75
	1323	1961	—	—	—	Proof	—
	1324	1962	.600	.25	.75	1.25	2.25
	1324	1962	100 pcs.	—	—	Proof	80.00
	1325	1963	4.800	.15	.25	.65	1.25
	1325	1963	—	—	—	Proof	—
	1327	1965	2.800	.15	.40	.75	1.75
	1327	1965	—	—	—	Proof	—
	1328	1966	3.400	.10	.30	.75	1.75
	1328	1966	—	—	—	Proof	—

ALUMINUM
Aung San

42	CS1328	1966	—	.15	.40	1.00	2.00

BRASS
F.A.O. Issue - Rice Plant

KM#	Date	Mintage	Fine	VF	XF	Unc
46	1975	—	.15	.25	.65	1.25
	1976	—	.15	.25	.65	1.25

KYAT

COPPER-NICKEL

KM#	Date	Year	Mintage	Fine	VF	XF	Unc
37	CS1314	1952	2.500	.35	.75	1.50	3.00
	1314	1952	100 pcs.	—	—	Proof	85.00
	1315	1953	7.500	.25	.50	1.00	2.00
	1315	1953	—	—	—	Proof	—
	1318	1956	3.500	.35	.75	1.50	3.00
	1318	1956	100 pcs.	—	—	Proof	85.00
	1324	1962	100 pcs.	—	—	Proof	85.00
	1327	1965	1.000	.35	.75	1.50	3.00
	1327	1965	—	—	—	Proof	—

F.A.O. Issue - Rice Plant

KM#	Date	Mintage	Fine	VF	XF	Unc
47	1975	20.000	.25	.50	1.00	2.00

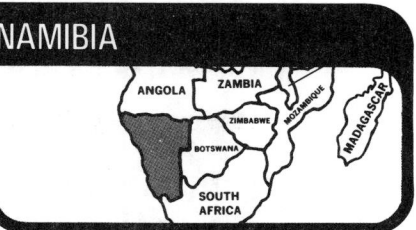

NAMIBIA

The Republic of Namibia, once the German colonial territory of German South West Africa, and later South West Africa, is situated on the Atlantic coast of southern Africa, bounded on the north by Angola, on the east by Botswana, and on the south by South Africa. It has an area of 318,261 sq. mi. (824,290 sq. km.) and a population of *1.4 million. Capital: Windhoek. Diamonds, copper, lead, zinc, and cattle are exported.

South Africa undertook the administration of South West Africa under the terms of a League of Nations mandate on Dec. 17, 1920. When the League of Nations was dissolved in 1946, its supervisory authority for South West Africa was inherited by the United Nations. In 1946 the UN denied South Africa's request to annex South West Africa. South Africa responded by refusing to place the territory under a UN trusteeship. In 1950 the International Court of Justice ruled that South Africa could not unilaterally modify the international status of South West Africa. A 1966 UN resolution declaring the mandate terminated was rejected by South Africa, and the status of the area remains in dispute. In June 1968 the UN General Assembly voted to rename the territory Namibia. In 1971 the International Court of Justice ruled that South Africa's presence in Namibia was illegal. In Dec. 1973 the UN appointed a UN Commissioner and a multi-racial Advisory Council was appointed. An interim government was formed in 1977 and independence was to be declared by Dec. 31, 1978. This resolution was rejected by major UN powers. In April 1978 South Africa accepted a plan for UN-supervised elections which led to a political abstention by the South West Africa People's Organization (SWAPO) party leading to dissolvement of the Minister's Council and National Assembly in Jan. 1983. A Multi-Party Conference (MPC) was formed in May 1984 which held talks with SWAPO. The MPC petitioned South Africa for self-government and on June 17, 1985 the Transitional Government of National Unity was installed. Negotiations were held in 1988 between Angola, Cuba, and South Africa reaching a peaceful settlement on Aug. 5, 1988. By April 1989 Cuban troops were to withdraw from Angola and South African troops from Namibia. The Transitional Government resigned on Feb. 28, 1988 for the upcoming elections of the constituent assembly in Nov. 1989. Independence was finally achieved on March 12, 1990 within the Commonwealth of Nations. The President is the Head of State; the Prime Minister is Head of Government.

MONETARY SYSTEM
100 Cents = 1 Namibia Dollar
1 Namibia Dollar = 1 South African Rand

5 CENTS

NICKEL PLATED STEEL

KM#	Date	Mintage	VF	XF	Unc
1	1993	—	—	.20	.50

10 CENTS

NICKEL PLATED STEEL

2	1993	—	—	.35	1.00

50 CENTS

NICKEL PLATED STEEL

3	1993	—	—	.75	1.75

DOLLAR

BRASS

KM#	Date	Mintage	VF	XF	Unc
4	1993	—	—	1.25	3.00
	1996	—	—	1.25	3.00

5 DOLLARS

BRASS

5	1993	—	—	2.75	5.50

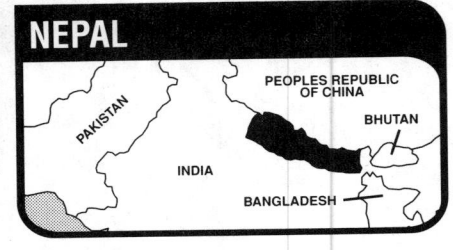

NEPAL

(map showing PAKISTAN, PEOPLES REPUBLIC OF CHINA, INDIA, BHUTAN, BANGLADESH)

The Kingdom of Nepal, the world's only surviving Hindu kingdom, is a landlocked country occupying the southern slopes of the Himalayas. It has an area of 56,136 sq. mi. (140,800 sq. km.) and a population of 18 million. Capital: Kathmandu. Nepal has deposits of coal, copper, iron and cobalt, but they are largely unexploited. Agriculture is the principal economic activity. Rice, timber and jute are exported, with tourism being the other major foreign exchange earner.

Apart from a brief Muslim invasion in the 14th century, Nepal was able to avoid the mainstream of Northern Indian politics, due to its impregnable position in the mountains. It is therefore a unique survivor of the medieval Hindu and Buddhist culture of Northern India which was largely destroyed by the successive waves of Muslim invasions.

Prior to the late 18th century, Nepal, as we know it today, was divided among a number of small states. Unless otherwise stated, the term "Nepal" applies to the small fertile valley, about 4,500 ft. above sea level, in which the three main cities of Kathmandu, Patan and Bhatgaon are situated.

During the reign of King Yaksha Malla (1428-1482AD), the Nepalese kingdom, with capital at Bhatgaon, was extended northwards into Tibet, and also controlled a considerable area to the south of the hills. After Yaksha Malla's death, the Kingdom was divided among his sons, so four kingdoms were established with capitals at Bhatgaon, Patan, Kathmandu and Banepa, all situated within the small valley, less than 20 miles square. Banepa was quickly absorbed within the territory of Bhatgaon, but the other 3 kingdoms remained until 1769. The internecine strife between the 3 kings effectively stopped Nepal from becoming a major military force during this period, although with its fertile land and strategic position, it was by far the wealthiest and most powerful of the Himalayan states.

Apart from agriculture, Nepal owed its prosperity to its position on one of the easiest trade routes between the great monasteries of central Tibet, and India. Nepal made full use of this, and a trading community was set up in Lhasa during the 16th century, and Nepalese coins became the accepted currency medium in Tibet.

The seeds of discord between Nepal and Tibet were sown during the first half of the 18th century, when the Nepalese debased the coinage, and the fate of the Malla kings of Nepal was sealed when Prithvi Narayan Shah, King of the small state of Gorkha, to the west of Kathmandu, was able to gain control of the transhimalayan trade routes during the years after 1750.

Prithvi Narayan spent several years consolidating his position in hill areas before he finally succeeded in conquering the Kathmandu Valley in 1768, where he established the Shah dynasty, and moved his capital to Kathmandu.

After Prithvi Narayan's death a period of political instability ensued which lasted until the 1840's when the Rana family reduced the monarch to a figurehead and established the post of hereditary Prime Minister. A popular revolution in 1950 toppled the Rana family and reconstituted power in the throne. In 1959 King Mahendra declared Nepal a constitutional monarchy, and in 1962 a new constitution set up a system of panchayat (village council) democracy. In 1990, following political unrest, the king's powers were reduced. The country then adopted a system of parliamentary democracy.

DATING
Saka Era (SE)
Up until 1888AD all coins of the Gorkha Dynasty were dated in the Saka era (SE). To convert from Saka to AD take Saka date + 78 = AD date. Coins dated with this era have SE before the date in the following listing.

Vikrama Samvat Era (VS)
From 1888AD most copper coins were dated in the Vikrama Samvat (VS) era. To convert take VS date - 57 = AD date. Coins with this era have VS before the year in the listing. With the exception of a few gold coins struck in 1890 & 1892, silver and gold coins only changed to the VS era in 1911AD, but now this era is used for all coins struck in Nepal.

RULERS
SHAH DYNASTY
Prithvi Vira Vikrama

पृथ्वी वीर विक्रम

SE1803-1833/1881-1911AD
VS1938-1968/
Queen of Prithvi Vira Vikrama:
Lakshmi Divyeswari

लद्मी दिन्ये्श्वरी

Tribhuvana Vira Vikrama

त्रिभुवनवीर विक्रम

VS1968-2007, 2007-2011/
1911-1950, 1951-1955AD
Jnanendra Vira Vikrama

ज्ञानेन्दवीर विक्रम

VS2007/1950-1951AD
Mahendra Vira Vikrama

महेन्द्रवीर विक्रम

VS2012-2028/1955-1971AD
Queen of Mahendra Vira Vikrama:
Ratna Rajya Lakshmi

रन्न राज लद्मी

Virendra Vir Vikram

वीरेन्द्र वीर विक्रम

VS2028/1971-AD
Queen of Virendra Vir Vikram
Aishvarya Rajya Lakshmi

ऐश्वर्य रान्य लद्ग्ये द्वी

VS2028-/1971-AD
MONETARY SYSTEM
Many of the mohars circulated in Tibet as well as in Nepal, and on a number of occasions coins were struck from bullion supplied by the Tibetan authorities. The smaller denominations never circulated in Tibet, but some of the mohars were cut for use as small change in Tibet.

In these listings only major changes in design have been noted. There are numerous minor varieties of ornamentation or spelling.

COPPER
Initially the copper paisa was not fixed in value relative to the silver coins, and generally fluctuated in value from 1/32 mohar in 1865AD to around 1/50 mohar after c1880AD, and was fixed at that value in 1903AD.
4 Dam = 1 Paisa
2 Paisa = 1 Dyak, Adhani
COPPER and SILVER
Decimal Series
100 Paisa = 1 Rupee
Although the value of the copper paisa was fixed at 100 paisa to the rupee in 1903, it was not until 1932 that silver coins were struck in the decimal system.

GOLD COINAGE
Nepalese gold coinage until recently did not carry any denominations and was traded for silver, etc. at the local bullion exchange rate. The three basic weight standards used in the following listing are distinguished for convenience, although all were known as Asarphi (gold coin) locally as follows:

GOLD MOHAR
5.60 g multiples and fractions
TOLA
12.48 g multiples and fractions
GOLD RUPEE or ASARPHI
11.66 g multiples and fractions
(Reduced to 10.00 g in 1966)
NOTE: In some instances the gold and silver issues were struck from the same dies.

NUMERALS
Nepal has used more variations of numerals on their coins than any other nation. The most common are illustrated in the numeral chart in the introduction. The chart below illustrates some variations encompassing the last four centuries.

1	2	3	4	5	6	7	8	9	0
१	२	३	४	५	६	७	८	९	०
१	२	७	५	६	७	८	९		
१		७	५	५	७	८		९	

NUMERICS

Half	आधा
One	एक
Two	दुइ
Four	चार
Five	पाँच
Ten	दस
Twenty	विस
Twenty-five	पचीस
Fifty	पचास
Hundred	सय

DENOMINATIONS

Paisa	पैसा
Dam	दाम
Mohar	मोर
Rupee	रुपैयाँ
Ashrapi	अश्रफी
Asarfi	असर्फी

SHAH DYNASTY
PRITHVI VIRA VIKRAMA
SE1803-1833/VS1938-1968
1881-1911AD

Copper Coinage
DAM

KM#	Date	Year	Fine	VF	XF	Unc
620.2	VS(19)64	(1907)	7.50	12.00	15.00	20.00

KM#	Date	Year	Fine	VF	XF	Unc
621	VS(19)68	(1911)	4.50	7.50	10.00	17.50

1/2 PAISA

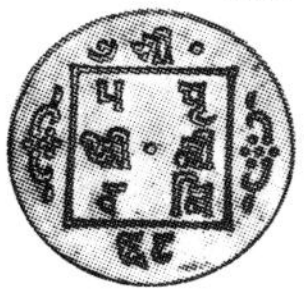

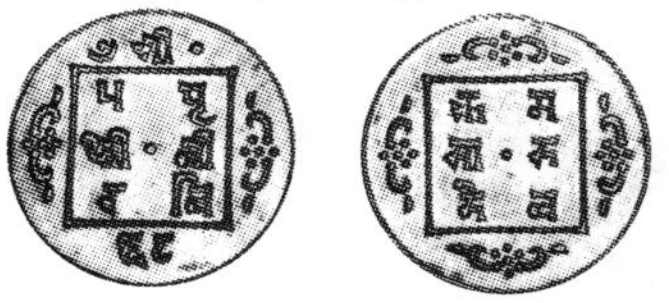

COPPER

KM#	Date	Year	Fine	VF	XF	Unc
622	VS(19)64	(1907)	4.50	7.50	10.00	17.50
	(19)68	(1911)	4.50	7.50	10.00	17.50

PAISA

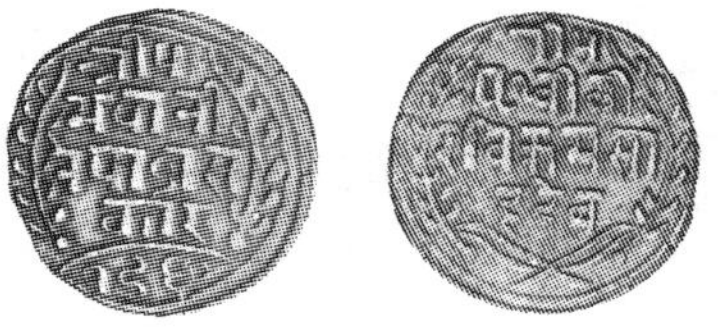

COPPER
Obv. and rev: Leg. within wreaths.

KM#	Date	Year	Good	VG	Fine	VF
628	VS1959	(1902)	1.00	1.50	3.00	5.00
	1960	(1903)	1.00	1.50	3.00	5.00
	1961	(1904)	1.00	1.50	3.00	5.00
	1962	(1905)	1.00	1.50	3.00	5.00
	1963	(1906)	1.00	1.50	3.00	5.00
	1964	(1907)	1.00	1.50	3.00	5.00

NOTE: Varieties in wreaths exist.
NOTE: Earlier dates (VS1949-1957) exist for this type.

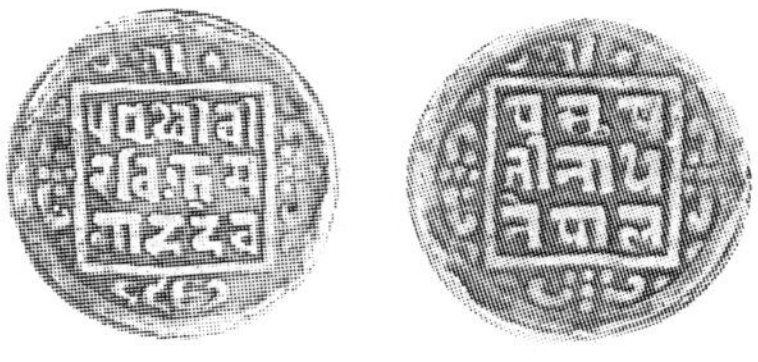

Obv. and rev: Leg. within squares.

629	VS1959	(1902)	1.00	1.50	2.50	4.00
	1962	(1905)	1.00	1.50	2.50	4.00
	1963	(1906)	1.00	1.50	2.50	4.00
	1964	(1907)	1.00	1.50	2.50	4.00
	1965	(1908)	1.00	1.50	2.50	4.00
	1966	(1909)	1.00	1.50	2.50	4.00
	1967	(1910)	1.00	1.50	2.50	4.00
	1968	(1911)	1.00	1.50	2.50	4.00

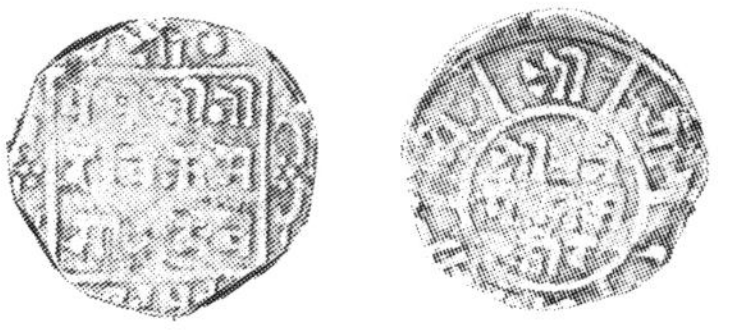

Obv: Leg. within square. Rev: Leg. within circle.

630	VS1959	(1902)	7.50	12.50	20.00	33.50

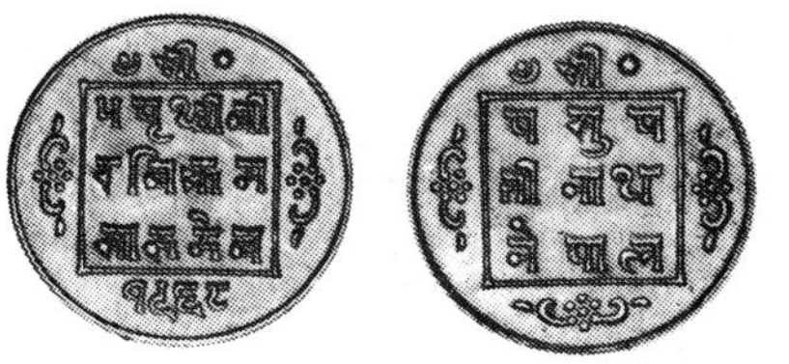

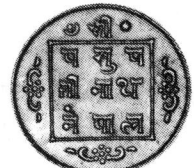

KM#	Date	Year	Fine	VF	XF	Unc
631	VS1964	(1907)	5.50	9.00	15.00	22.50
	1968	(1911)	8.50	13.50	20.00	30.00

2 PAISA

COPPER
Obv: Leg. within square. Rev: Leg. within circle.

KM#	Date	Year	Good	VG	Fine	VF
633	VS1959	(1902)	12.50	17.50	25.00	50.00

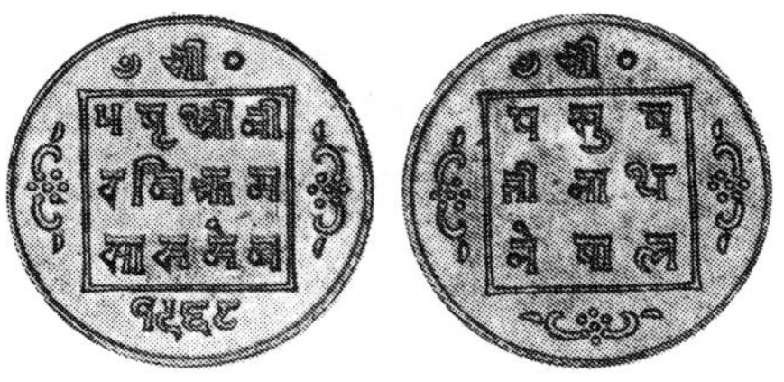

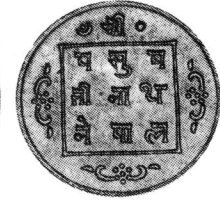

KM#	Date	Year	Fine	VF	XF	Unc
634	VS1964	(1907)	8.50	13.50	20.00	30.00
	1968	(1911)	9.00	15.00	22.50	35.00

Silver Coinage

DAM

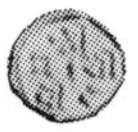

SILVER, uniface, 0.04 g
5 characters around sword.

KM#	Date	Year	Fine	VF	XF	Unc
635	ND	(1881-1911)	8.00	10.00	15.00	25.00

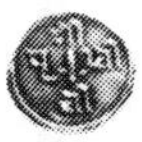

4 characters around sword.

636	ND	(1881-1911)	15.00	25.00	30.00	40.00

1/32 MOHAR

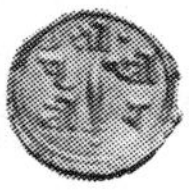

SILVER, uniface, 0.18 g
Sun and moon.

KM#	Date	Year	VG	Fine	VF	XF
637	ND	(1881-1911)	5.00	8.50	12.50	16.50

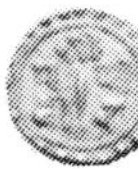

W/o sun and moon.

638	ND	(1881-1911)	5.00	8.50	12.50	16.50

1/16 MOHAR

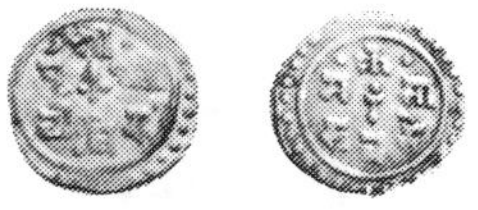

SILVER, 0.35 g

KM#	Date	Year	Fine	VF	XF	Unc
639	ND	(1881-1911)	6.00	10.00	13.50	20.00

NOTE: Varieties exist.

1/8 MOHAR

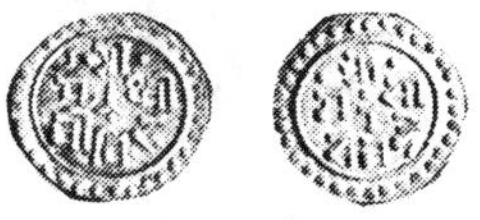

SILVER, 0.70 g

640	ND	(1881-1911)	7.50	12.50	18.50	27.50

NOTE: Varieties exist.

1/4 MOHAR

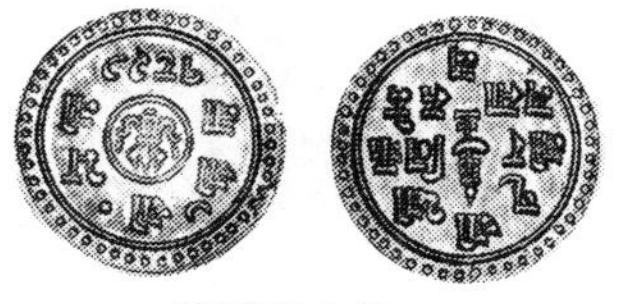

SILVER, 1.40 g
Rev: Moon and dot for sun.

KM#	Date	Year	VG	Fine	VF	XF
643	SE1827	(1905)	1.75	3.00	5.00	7.00

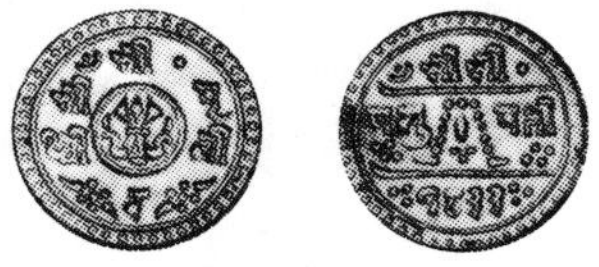

Machine struck

644	SE1833	(1911)	1.75	3.00	5.00	7.00
	1833	(1911)	—	—	Proof	25.00

1/2 MOHAR

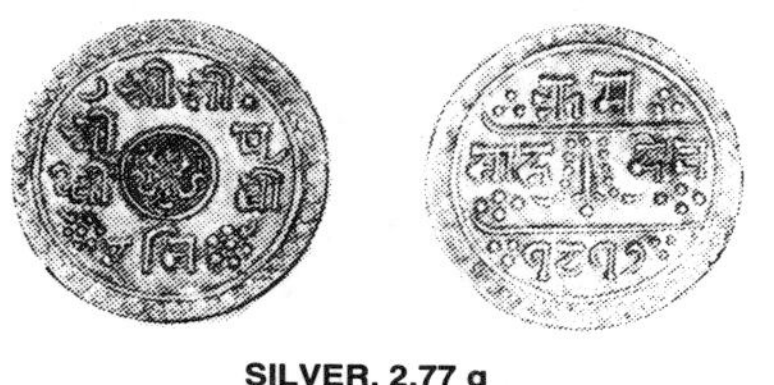

SILVER, 2.77 g
Machine struck, plain edge.

KM#	Date	Year	Fine	VF	XF	Unc
647	SE1824	(1902)	20.00	25.00	30.00	35.00

NOTE: Varieties exist.
NOTE: Earlier dates (SE1816-1817) exist for this type.

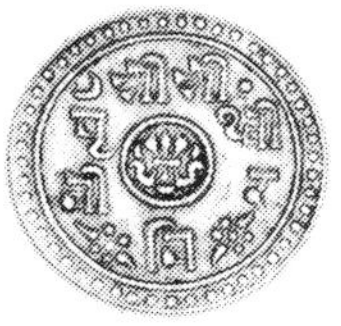

KM#	Date	Year	Fine	VF	XF	Unc
648	SE1826	(1904)	3.00	5.00	7.00	10.00
	1827	(1905)	3.00	5.00	7.00	10.00
	1829	(1907)	3.50	5.50	8.50	11.50

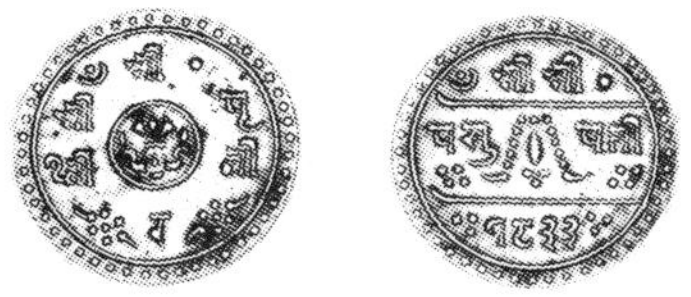

Machine struck, milled edge.

649	SE1832	(1910)	20.00	25.00	30.00	35.00
	1833	(1911)	2.25	3.50	5.00	7.00
	1833	(1911)	—	—	Proof	35.00

MOHAR

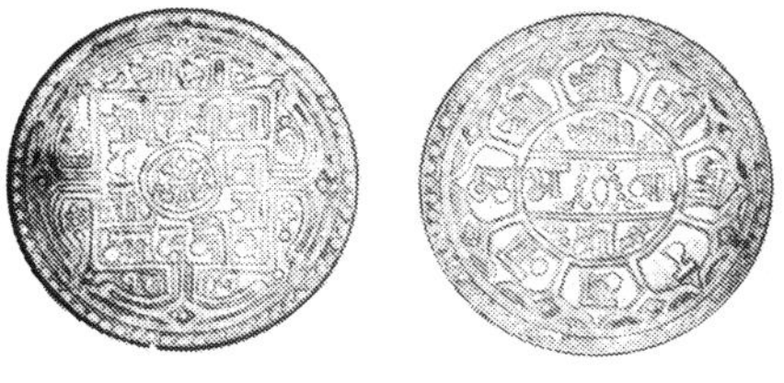

SILVER, 5.60 g
Machine struck, plain edge.

651.1	SE1823	(1901)	4.50	6.50	8.00	10.00
	1824	(1902)	4.50	6.50	8.00	10.00
	1825	(1903)	4.50	6.50	8.00	10.00
	1826	(1904)	4.50	6.50	8.00	10.00
	1827	(1905)	4.50	6.50	8.00	10.00

NOTE: Earlier dates (SE1803-1822) exist for this type.

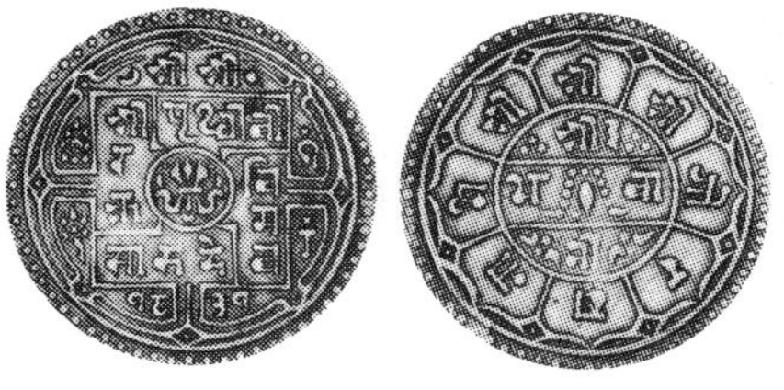

Machine struck, milled edge.

651.2	SE1826	(1904)	4.50	6.50	8.00	10.00
	1827	(1905)	4.50	6.50	8.00	10.00
	1828	(1906)	4.50	6.50	8.00	10.00
	1829	(1907)	4.50	6.50	8.00	10.00
	1830	(1908)	4.50	6.50	8.00	10.00
	1831	(1909)	4.50	6.50	8.00	10.00
	1832	(1910)	4.50	6.50	8.00	10.00
	1833	(1911)	—	25.00	35.00	50.00

NOTE: The date 1833 was only issued in presentation sets.

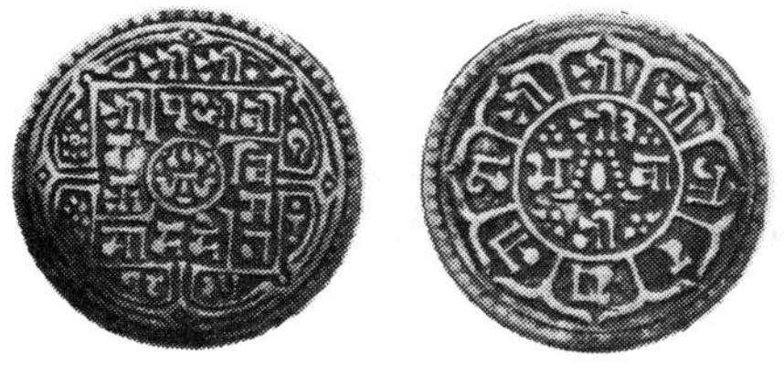

Rev: Gold die, in error.

652	SE1825	(1903)	10.00	15.00	25.00	32.50

2 MOHARS

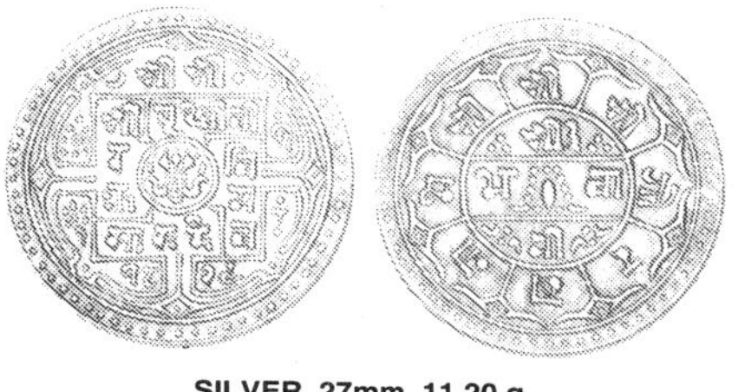

SILVER, 27mm, 11.20 g
Machine struck, milled edge, 27mm.

655	SE1829	(1907)	15.00	27.50	40.00	60.00
	1831	(1909)	6.00	9.00	12.50	20.00

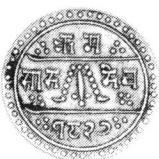

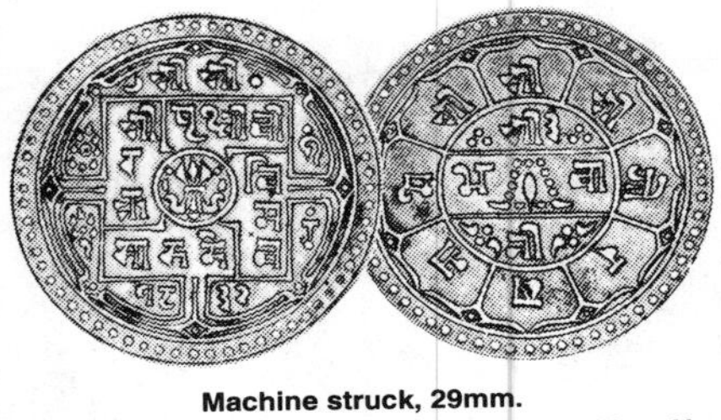

Machine struck, 29mm.

KM#	Date	Year	Fine	VF	XF	Unc
656	SE1832	(1910)	7.00	9.00	11.50	18.50
	1833	(1911)	6.00	8.00	10.00	16.50

4 MOHARS

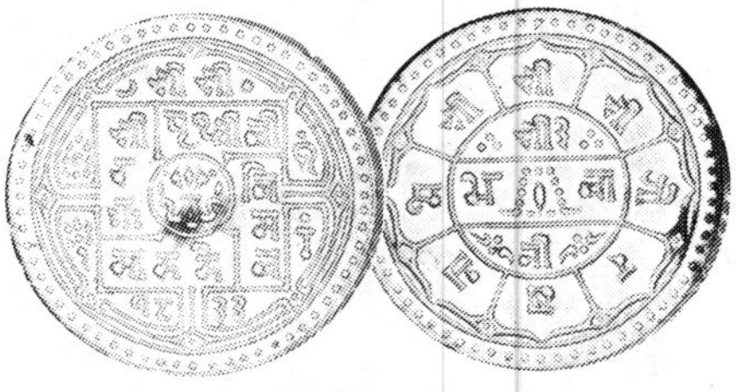

SILVER, 22.40 g
Milled edge.

658	SE1833	(1911)	60.00	100.00	140.00	200.00

Gold Coinage

DAM

GOLD, uniface, 0.04 g
5 characters around sword.
Similar to 1/64 Mohar, KM#664.

659	ND	(1881-1911)	10.00	14.00	20.00	27.50

4 characters around sword.
Similar to 1/64 Mohar, KM#663.

660	ND	(1881-1911)	10.00	14.00	20.00	27.50

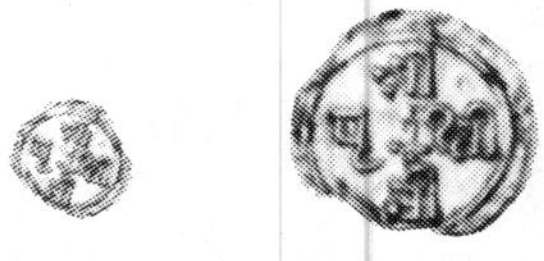

Actual Size 2 x Actual Size
Circle around characters.

661	ND	(1881-1911)	10.00	14.00	20.00	27.50

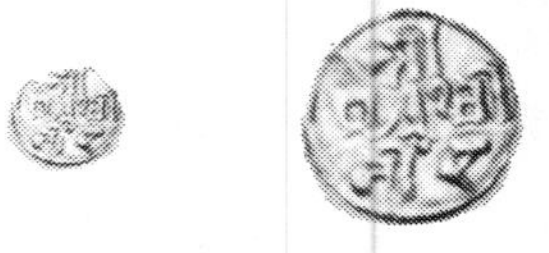

Actual Size 2 x Actual Size
2 characters below sword.

662	ND	(1881-1911)	10.00	14.00	20.00	27.50

1/64 MOHAR

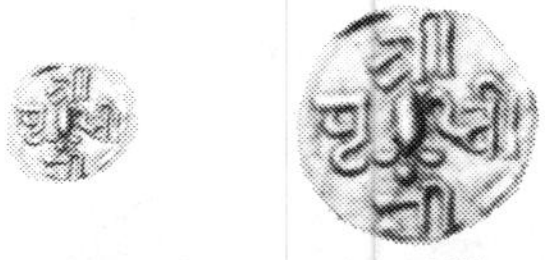

Actual Size 2 x Actual Size
GOLD, uniface, 0.09 g
Obv: 4 characters around sword.

663	ND	(1881-1911)	12.50	17.50	22.50	30.00

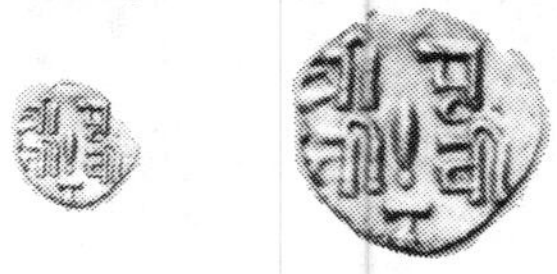

Actual Size 2 x Actual Size
Obv: 5 characters around sword.

664	ND	(1881-1911)	12.50	17.50	22.50	30.00

1/32 MOHAR

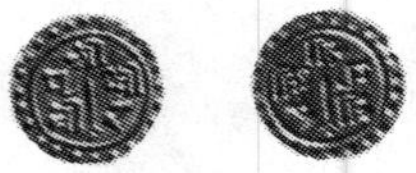

GOLD, uniface, 0.18 g
5 characters around sword.

665	ND	(1881-1911)	20.00	40.00	75.00	100.00

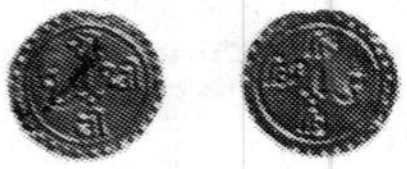

4 characters around sword.

KM#	Date	Year	Fine	VF	XF	Unc
666	ND	(1881-1911)	15.00	30.00	75.00	100.00

1/16 MOHAR

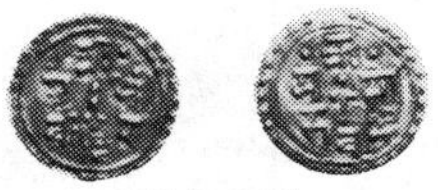

GOLD, 0.35 g

667	ND	(1881-1911)	15.00	40.00	75.00	100.00

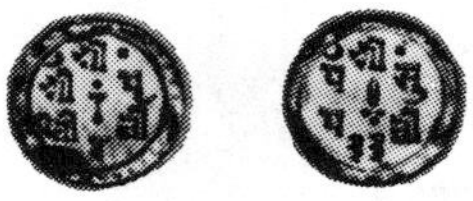

668	SE(18)33	(1911)	15.00	30.00	75.00	100.00

1/8 MOHAR

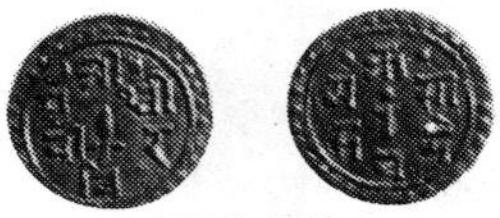

GOLD, 0.70 g
Obv: 6 characters.

669.1	ND	(1881-1911)	22.50	40.00	75.00	100.00

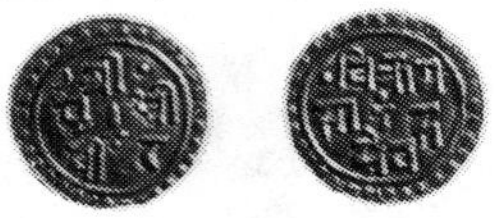

Obv: 5 characters.

669.2	ND	(1881-1911)	22.50	40.00	75.00	100.00

NOTE: Varieties exist.

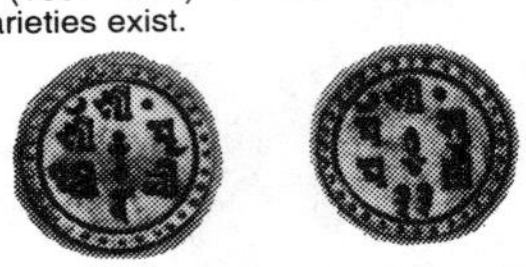

670	SE(18)33	(1911)	22.50	40.00	75.00	100.00

1/4 MOHAR

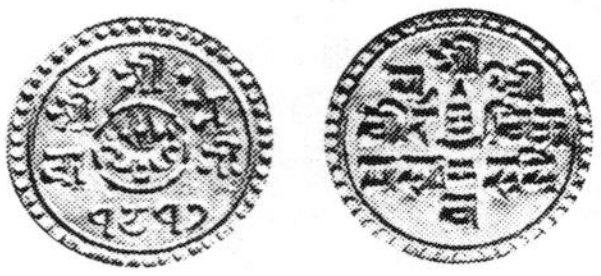

GOLD, 1.40 g

671.1	SE1823	(1901)	45.00	60.00	80.00	100.00
	1829	(1907)	40.00	50.00	60.00	75.00

NOTE: Earlier date (SE1823) exists for this type.

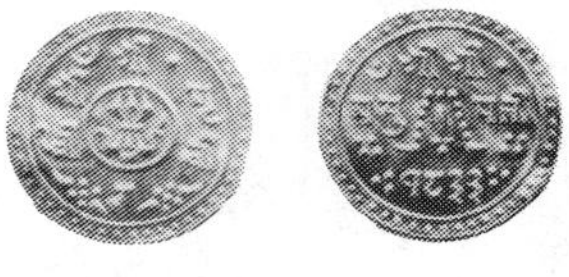

671.2	SE1833	(1911)	40.00	50.00	60.00	75.00

1/2 MOHAR

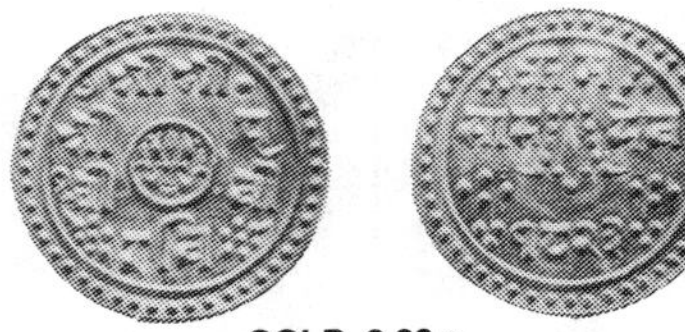

GOLD, 2.80 g

672.3	SE1823	(1901)	70.00	80.00	100.00	125.00

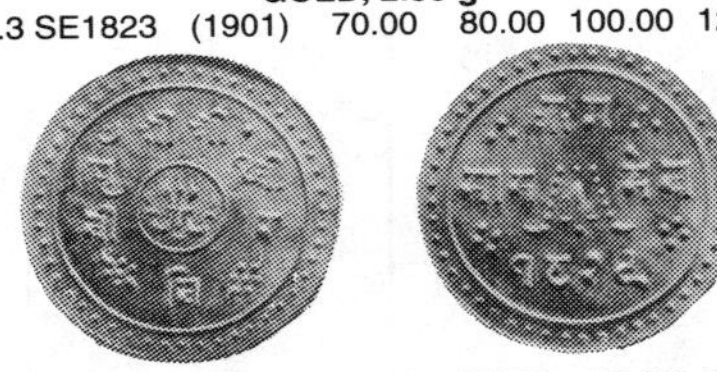

672.4	SE1829	(1907)	65.00	75.00	85.00	100.00

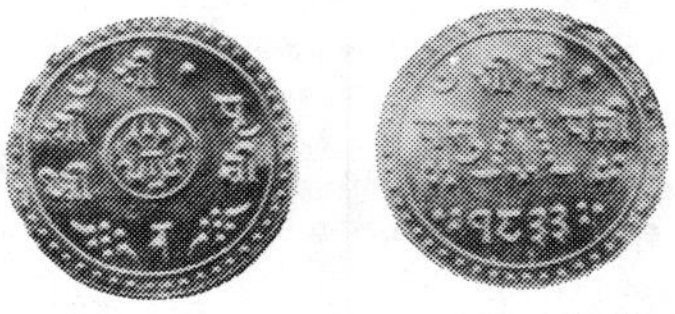

672.5	SE1833	(1911)	65.00	75.00	85.00	100.00

MOHAR

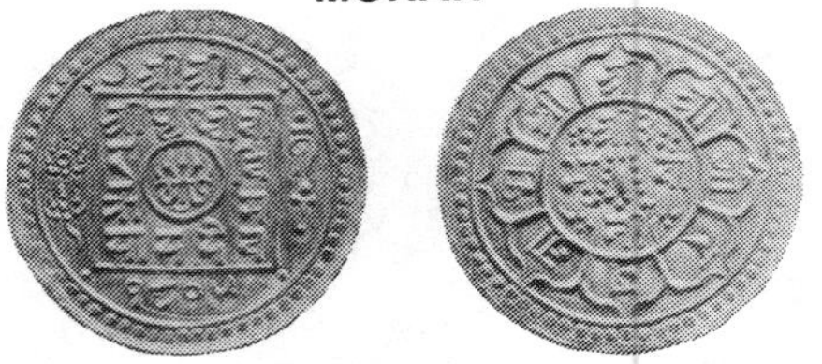

GOLD, 5.60 g

KM#	Date	Year	Fine	VF	XF	Unc
673.1	SE1823	(1901)	115.00	125.00	140.00	165.00
	1825	(1903)	115.00	125.00	140.00	165.00
	1826	(1904)	115.00	125.00	140.00	165.00
	1827	(1905)	115.00	125.00	140.00	165.00

NOTE: Earlier dates (SE1804-1820) exist for this type.

Milled edge.

673.2	SE1828	(1906)	115.00	125.00	140.00	165.00
	1829	(1907)	115.00	125.00	140.00	165.00
	1831	(1909)	115.00	125.00	140.00	165.00
	1833	(1911)	115.00	125.00	140.00	165.00

TOLA

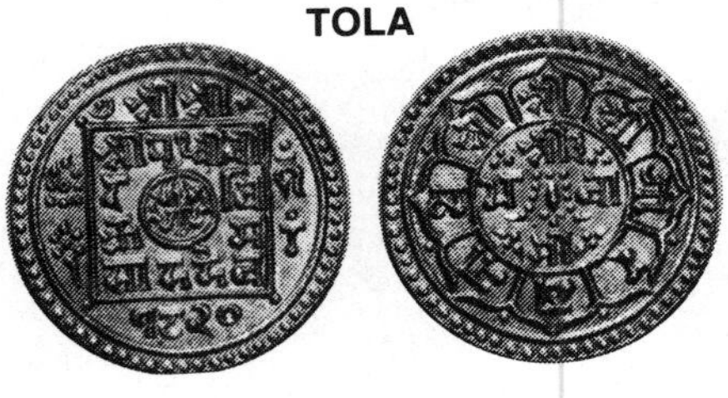

GOLD, 12.48 g
Plain edge.

674.3	SE1823	(1901)	235.00	255.00	275.00	300.00
	1824	(1902)	235.00	255.00	275.00	300.00
	1825	(1903)	235.00	255.00	275.00	300.00
	1826	(1904)	235.00	255.00	275.00	300.00

NOTE: Earlier dates (SE1807-1820) exist for this type.

Vertical edge milling.

675.1	SE1828	(1906)	235.00	255.00	275.00	300.00
	1829	(1907)	235.00	255.00	275.00	300.00
	1831	(1909)	235.00	255.00	275.00	300.00
	1832	(1910)	235.00	255.00	275.00	300.00
	1833	(1911)	235.00	255.00	275.00	300.00

DUITOLA ASARPHI

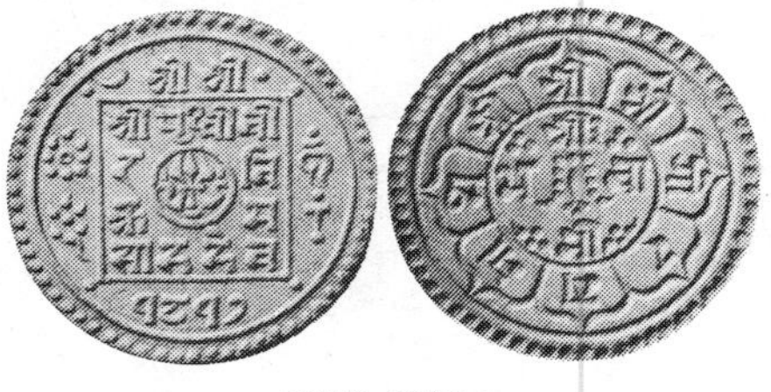

GOLD, 23.32 g
Plain edge.

678	SE1825	(1902)	600.00	700.00	800.00	1000.

NOTE: Earlier date (SE1817) exists for this type.

Milled edge, 27mm.

679	SE1829	(1907)	600.00	650.00	750.00	800.00

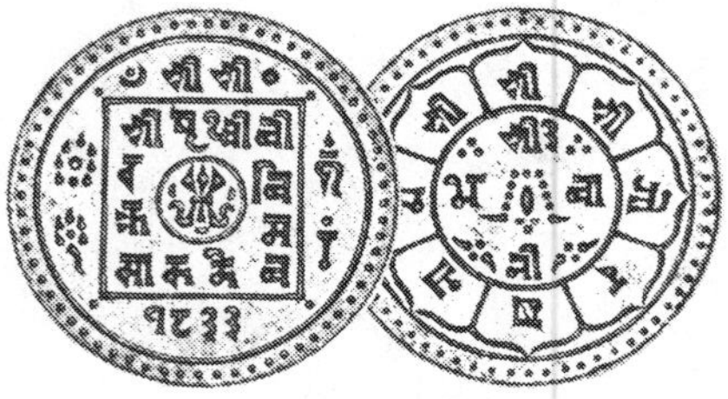

Milled edge, 29mm.

680	SE1833	(1911)	600.00	650.00	750.00	800.00

QUEEN LAKSHMI DIVYESWARI

(Regent for Tribhuvana Vira Vikrama)

Silver Coinage

1/2 MOHAR

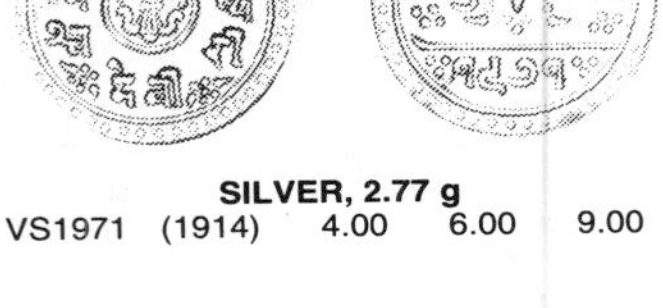

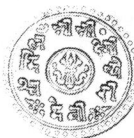

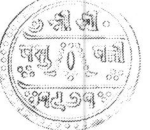

SILVER, 2.77 g

681	VS1971	(1914)	4.00	6.00	9.00	11.50

MOHAR

SILVER, 5.60 g

KM#	Date	Year	Fine	VF	XF	Unc
682	VS1971	(1914)	4.50	6.50	9.00	11.50

Gold Coinage
MOHAR

GOLD, 5.60 g

KM#	Date	Year				
683	VS1971	(1914)	100.00	125.00	145.00	175.00

TRIBHUVANA VIRA VIKRAMA
VS1968-2007/1911-1950AD

Copper Coinage
1/2 PAISA

COPPER

KM#	Date	Year			Fine	VF
684	VS1978	(1921)	—	—	50.00	75.00
	1985	(1928)	—	—	50.00	75.00

NOTE: Struck only for presentation sets.

PAISA

COPPER
Machine struck

KM#	Date	Year	Good	VG	Fine	VF
685.1	VS1968	(1911)	10.00	20.00	50.00	75.00

Hand struck

KM#	Date	Year	Good	VG	Fine	VF
685.2	VS1969	(1912)	1.00	1.50	2.25	3.50
	1970	(1913)	1.00	1.50	2.25	3.50
	1971	(1914)	1.00	1.50	2.25	3.50
	1972	(1915)	1.00	1.50	2.25	3.50
	1973	(1916)	1.00	1.50	2.25	3.50
	1974	(1917)	1.00	1.50	2.25	3.50
	1975	(1918)	1.00	1.50	2.25	3.50
	1976	(1919)	1.00	1.50	2.25	3.50
	1977	(1920)	1.00	1.50	2.25	3.50

13.5 mm

KM#	Date	Year	Fine	VF	XF	Unc
686.1	VS1975	(1918)	—		37.50	50.00

11.5 mm

KM#	Date	Year	Good	VG	Fine	VF
686.2	VS1975	(1918)	—	—	60.00	90.00

NOTE: The above issues are believed to be patterns.

Machine struck, 3.75 g

KM#	Date	Year	Fine	VF	XF	Unc
687.1	VS1975	(1918)	1.25	1.75	3.00	6.00
(687.2)	1976	(1919)	1.25	1.75	3.00	6.00
	1977	(1920)	1.25	1.75	3.00	6.00
	1977 inverted date					
		(1920)	3.00	4.50	7.50	15.00

NOTE: Varieties of the Khukris exist.

Crude, hand struck.

KM#	Date	Year	Good	VG	Fine	VF
687.2	VS1978	(1921)	2.00	3.00	4.50	7.50
(687.1)	1979	(1922)	2.00	3.00	4.50	7.50
	1980	(1923)	4.00	5.00	7.50	12.50
	1981	(1924)	4.00	5.00	7.50	12.50
	1982	(1925)	4.00	5.00	7.50	12.50
	1983	(1926)	4.00	5.00	7.50	12.50

NOTE: Varieties of the Khukris exist.

Machine struck, reduced weight, 2.80 g.

KM#	Date	Year	Fine	VF	XF	Unc
688	VS1978	(1921)	1.25	1.75	3.00	6.00
	1979	(1922)	1.25	1.75	3.00	6.00
	1980	(1923)	1.50	3.00	5.00	10.00
	1981	(1924)	1.50	3.00	5.00	10.00
	1982	(1925)	1.25	1.75	3.00	6.00
	1984	(1927)	1.25	1.75	3.00	6.00
	1985	(1928)	1.25	1.75	3.00	6.00
	1986	(1929)	1.25	1.75	3.00	6.00
	1987	(1930)	1.25	1.75	3.00	6.00

2 PAISA

COPPER
Machine struck, 7.50 g.

KM#	Date	Year	VG	Fine	VF	XF
689.1	VS1976	(1919)	1.00	2.00	3.00	5.00
(689.2)	1977	(1920)	1.00	2.00	3.00	5.00
	1977 inverted date					
		(1920)	3.50	5.00	8.50	13.50

NOTE: Varieties of the Khukris exist.

Crude struck.

KM#	Date	Year	Good	VG	Fine	VF
689.2	VS1978	(1921)	1.00	2.00	3.50	6.50
(689.1)	1979	(1922)	1.00	2.00	3.50	6.50
	1980	(1923)	1.00	2.00	3.50	6.50
	1981	(1924)	1.00	2.00	3.50	6.50
	1982	(1925)	1.00	2.00	3.50	6.50
	1983	(1926)	1.00	2.00	3.50	6.50
	1984	(1927)	1.00	2.00	3.50	6.50
	1985	(1928)	1.00	2.00	3.50	6.50
	1986	(1929)	1.00	2.50	4.00	7.50
	1987	(1930)	1.50	2.50	4.00	7.50
	1988	(1931)	2.00	3.00	5.00	9.00

NOTE: Varieties of the Khukris exist.

Machine struck, reduced weight, 5.00 g.

KM#	Date	Year	VG	Fine	VF	XF
689.3	VS1978	(1921)	1.00	2.00	3.00	4.50
	1979	(1922)	1.00	2.00	3.00	4.50
	1980	(1923)	1.00	2.00	3.00	4.50
	1981	(1924)	1.00	2.00	3.00	4.50
	1982	(1925)	1.00	2.00	3.00	4.50
	1983	(1926)	1.00	2.00	3.00	4.50
	1984	(1927)	1.00	2.00	3.00	4.50
	1991	(1934)	1.50	2.50	4.00	6.00

5 PAISA

COPPER
Machine struck, 18.00 g.

KM#	Date	Year	Fine	VF	XF	Unc
690.1	VS1976	(1919)	6.00	10.00	14.00	20.00
(690.2)	1977	(1920)	1.25	2.25	3.50	6.00
	1977 inverted date					
		(1920)	3.00	5.00	8.50	12.50

NOTE: Varieties of the Khukris exist.
*NOTE: Previously listed date VS1975 (1918) is considered a pattern.

Crude struck

KM#	Date	Year	Fine	VF	XF	Unc
690.2	VS1978	(1921)	1.75	3.00	5.00	8.00
(690.1)	1979	(1922)	1.75	3.00	5.00	8.00
	1980	(1923)	1.75	3.00	5.00	8.00
	1981	(1924)	1.75	3.00	5.00	8.00
	1982	(1925)	1.75	3.00	5.00	8.00
	1983	(1926)	1.75	3.00	5.00	8.00
	1984	(1927)	1.75	3.00	5.00	8.00
	1985	(1928)	1.75	3.00	5.00	8.00
	1986	(1929)	1.75	3.00	5.00	8.00
	1987	(1930)	1.75	3.00	5.00	8.00
	1988	(1931)	6.00	10.00	14.00	20.00

NOTE: Varieties of the Khukris exist.

Machine struck, reduced weight, 14.00 g

KM#	Date	Year	Fine	VF	XF	Unc
690.3	VS1978	(1921)	1.25	2.25	3.50	5.00
	1979	(1922)	1.25	2.25	3.50	5.00
	1980	(1923)	1.25	2.25	3.50	5.00
	1981	(1924)	1.25	2.25	3.50	5.00
	1982	(1925)	1.25	2.25	3.50	5.00
	1983	(1926)	1.25	2.25	3.50	5.00
	1984	(1927)	1.25	2.25	3.50	5.00
	1991	(1934)	15.00	20.00	25.00	30.00

NOTE: Varieties exist with both open and closed handles on Khukris.

Silver Coinage
DAM

SILVER, uniface, 0.04 g

KM#	Date					
691	ND (1911-1950)	15.00	25.00	30.00	50.00	

1/4 MOHAR

SILVER, 1.40 g

KM#	Date	Year	VG	Fine	VF	XF
692	VS1969	(1912)	1.75	3.00	5.00	7.00
	1970	(1913)	1.75	3.00	5.00	7.00

1/2 MOHAR

SILVER, 2.80 g

KM#	Date	Year	Fine	VF	XF	Unc
693	VS1968	(1911)	2.25	3.50	5.00	7.00
	1970	(1913)	2.25	3.50	5.00	7.00
	1971	(1914)	2.25	3.50	5.00	7.00

MOHAR

SILVER, 5.60 g

KM#	Date	Year	Fine	VF	XF	Unc
694	VS1968	(1911)	4.50	6.50	8.00	10.00
	1969	(1912)	4.50	6.50	8.00	10.00
	1971	(1914)	4.50	6.50	8.00	10.00

2 MOHARS

SILVER, 11.20 g

KM#	Date	Year	Fine	VF	XF	Unc
695	VS1968	(1911)	BV	7.50	10.00	16.50
	1969	(1912)	BV	7.50	10.00	16.50
	1970	(1913)	BV	7.50	10.00	16.50
	1971	(1914)	BV	7.50	10.00	16.50
	1972	(1915)	BV	7.50	10.00	16.50
	1973	(1916)	BV	7.50	10.00	16.50
	1974	(1917)	BV	7.50	10.00	16.50
	1975	(1918)	BV	7.50	10.00	16.50
	1976	(1919)	BV	7.50	10.00	16.50
	1977	(1920)	BV	7.50	10.00	16.50
	1978	(1921)	BV	7.50	10.00	16.50
	1979	(1922)	BV	7.50	10.00	16.50
	1980	(1923)	BV	7.50	10.00	16.50
	1982	(1925)	BV	7.50	10.00	16.50
	1983	(1926)	BV	7.50	10.00	16.50
	1984	(1927)	BV	7.50	10.00	16.50
	1985	(1928)	BV	7.50	10.00	16.50
	1986	(1929)	BV	7.50	10.00	16.50
	1987	(1930)	BV	7.50	10.00	16.50
	1988	(1931)	BV	7.50	10.00	16.50
	1989	(1932)	BV	7.50	10.00	16.50

4 MOHARS

SILVER, 22.40 g

KM#	Date	Year	Fine	VF	XF	Unc
696	VS1971	(1914)	40.00	75.00	125.00	175.00

Gold Coinage

DAM

GOLD, uniface, 0.04 g

KM#		Date	Fine	VF	XF	Unc
697	ND	(1911-50)	25.00	40.00	75.00	100.00

1/32 MOHAR

GOLD, uniface, 0.18 g

KM#		Date	Fine	VF	XF	Unc
698	ND	(1911-50)	35.00	60.00	90.00	125.00

1/16 MOHAR

GOLD, 0.35 g

KM#	Date		Fine	VF	XF	Unc
699	VS(19)77	(1920)	50.00	90.00	120.00	150.00

1/8 MOHAR

GOLD, 0.70 g

KM#	Date		Fine	VF	XF	Unc
700	VS(19)76	(1919)	75.00	120.00	150.00	200.00

1/2 MOHAR

GOLD, 2.80 g

KM#	Date	Year		
701	VS1969	(1912)	—	Reported, not confirmed
717	VS1995	(1938)	—	Reported, not confirmed

MOHAR

GOLD, 5.60 g

KM#	Date	Year	Fine	VF	XF	Unc
702	VS1969	(1912)	100.00	125.00	140.00	175.00
	1975	(1918)	100.00	125.00	140.00	175.00
	1978	(1921)	100.00	125.00	140.00	175.00
	1979	(1922)	100.00	125.00	140.00	175.00
	1981	(1924)	100.00	125.00	140.00	175.00
	1983	(1926)	100.00	125.00	140.00	175.00
	1985	(1928)	100.00	125.00	140.00	175.00
	1986	(1929)	100.00	125.00	140.00	175.00
	1987	(1930)	100.00	125.00	140.00	175.00
	1989	(1932)	100.00	125.00	140.00	175.00
	1990	(1933)	100.00	125.00	140.00	175.00
	1991	(1934)	100.00	125.00	140.00	175.00
	1998	(1941)	100.00	125.00	140.00	175.00
	1999	(1942)	100.00	125.00	140.00	175.00
	2000	(1943)	100.00	125.00	140.00	175.00
	2003	(1946)	100.00	125.00	140.00	175.00
	2005	(1948)	100.00	125.00	140.00	175.00

KM#	Date	Mintage	Fine	VF	XF	Unc
722	VS1993(1936)					
		.376	—	Reported, not confirmed		
	1994(1937)					
		.283	—	Reported, not confirmed		

(TOLA) ASHRAPHI

GOLD, 12.48 g, 26.5 g

KM#	Date	Year	Fine	VF	XF	Unc
703.1	VS1969	(1912)	225.00	245.00	275.00	300.00
	1974	(1917)	225.00	245.00	275.00	300.00
	1975	(1918)	225.00	245.00	275.00	300.00
	1976	(1919)	225.00	245.00	275.00	300.00
	1977	(1920)	225.00	245.00	275.00	300.00
	1978	(1921)	225.00	245.00	275.00	300.00
	1979	(1922)	225.00	245.00	275.00	300.00
	1980	(1923)	225.00	245.00	275.00	300.00
	1981	(1924)	225.00	245.00	275.00	300.00
	1982	(1925)	225.00	245.00	275.00	300.00
	1983	(1926)	225.00	245.00	275.00	300.00
	1984	(1927)	225.00	245.00	275.00	300.00
	1985	(1928)	225.00	245.00	275.00	300.00
	1986	(1929)	225.00	245.00	275.00	300.00
	1987	(1930)	225.00	245.00	275.00	300.00
	1988	(1931)	225.00	245.00	275.00	300.00
	1989	(1932)	225.00	245.00	275.00	300.00
	1990	(1933)	225.00	245.00	275.00	300.00
	1991	(1934)	225.00	245.00	275.00	300.00
	1998	(1941)	225.00	245.00	275.00	300.00
	1999	(1942)	225.00	245.00	275.00	300.00
	2000	(1943)	225.00	245.00	275.00	300.00
	2003	(1946)	225.00	245.00	275.00	300.00

29.5mm

KM#	Date	Year	Fine	VF	XF	Unc
703.2	VS2005	(1948)	225.00	245.00	275.00	300.00

Obv: Trident in center.

KM#	Date	Year	Fine	VF	XF	Unc
727	VS1992	(1935)	235.00	250.00	285.00	325.00

DUITOLA ASARPHI

GOLD
Similar to 1 Tola, KM#703.

KM#	Date	Year	Fine	VF	XF	Unc
728	VS2005	(1948)	450.00	500.00	550.00	650.00

DECIMAL COINAGE

100 Paisa = 1 Rupee

1/4 PAISA

COPPER

KM#	Date	Year	Fine	VF	XF	Unc
704	VS2000	(1943)	15.00	25.00	30.00	40.00
	2004	(1947)	15.00	25.00	30.00	40.00

1/2 PAISA

COPPER

KM#	Date	Year	Mintage	VF	XF	Unc
705	VS2004	(1947)	—	25.00	30.00	40.00

PAISA

COPPER

KM#	Date	Mintage	Fine	VF	XF	Unc
706	VS1990(1933)	—	.75	1.50	3.00	5.00
	1991(1934)	—	.75	1.50	3.00	5.00
	1992(1935)	—	.75	1.50	3.00	5.00
	1993(1936)	—	.75	1.50	3.00	5.00
	1994(1937)	.456	.75	1.50	3.00	5.00
	1995(1938)	—	.75	1.50	3.00	5.00
	1996(1939)	—	.75	1.50	3.00	5.00
	1997(1940)	—	.75	1.50	3.00	5.00

KM#	Date	Year	Fine	VF	XF	Unc
707	VS2005	(1948)	.75	1.25	1.75	2.50

BRASS

KM#	Date	Year	Fine	VF	XF	Unc
707a	VS2001	(1944)	.30	.50	.75	1.00
	2003	(1946)	.30	.50	.75	1.00
	2004	(1947)	3.00	5.00	7.00	10.00
	2005	(1948)	.30	.50	.75	1.00
	2006	(1949)	.60	1.00	1.25	1.75

2 PAISA

COPPER

KM#	Date	Year	VG	Fine	VF	XF
708	VS1992	(1935)	3.00	5.00	8.50	13.50

KM#	Date	Mintage	Fine	VF	XF	Unc
709.1	VS1992(1935)	—	2.00	4.00	6.50	10.00
	1993(1936)	.473	1.00	2.00	3.00	5.00
	1994(1937)	1.133	1.00	2.00	3.00	5.00
	1995(1938)	—	1.00	2.00	3.00	5.00
	1996(1939)	—	1.00	2.00	3.00	5.00
	1997(1940)	—	2.00	4.00	6.50	10.00

KM#	Date	Year	Fine	VF	XF	Unc
709.2	VS1992	(1935)	.60	1.00	1.75	3.00
	1994	(1937)	.50	.75	1.50	2.50
	1995	(1938)	2.00	3.50	5.00	7.50
	1996	(1939)	.30	.50	1.00	1.50
	1997	(1940)	.50	.75	1.50	2.50
	1998	(1941)	.50	.75	1.50	2.50
	1999	(1942)	.50	.75	1.50	2.50

710	VS1999	(1942)	.30	.50	1.00	2.00
	2000	(1943)	.30	.50	1.00	2.00
	2003	(1945)	.30	.50	1.00	2.00
	2005	(1948)	3.00	5.00	7.00	10.00

BRASS

710a	VS1999	(1942)	.30	.50	1.00	2.00
	2000	(1943)	.30	.50	1.00	2.00
	2001	(1944)	.30	.50	1.00	2.00
	2005	(1948)	1.75	3.00	5.00	7.50
	2008	(1951)	.30	.50	1.00	2.00
	2009	(1952)	.30	.50	1.00	2.00
	2010	(1953)	.30	.50	1.00	2.00

5 PAISA

COPPER

KM#	Date	Mintage	Fine	VF	XF	Unc
711	VS1992(1935)	—	1.50	3.00	4.50	6.50
	1993(1936)	.878	1.50	3.00	4.50	6.50
	1994(1937)	.403	1.50	3.00	4.50	6.50
	1995(1938)	—	1.00	2.00	3.00	5.00
	1996(1939)	—	1.50	3.00	4.50	6.50
	1997(1940)	—	1.50	3.00	4.50	6.50
	1998(1941)	—	—	Reported, not confirmed		

COPPER-NICKEL-ZINC

KM#	Date	Year	Fine	VF	XF	Unc
712	VS2000	(1943)	.65	1.00	1.50	2.50
	2009	(1952)	1.75	3.00	5.00	8.50
	2010	(1953)	1.25	2.00	3.00	5.00

COPPER-NICKEL

712a	VS2010	(1953)	(restrike)			
			.65	1.00	1.50	2.50

1/16 RUPEE

SILVER

713	VS(19)96	(1939)	12.50	20.00	32.50	50.00

20 PAISA

2.2161 g, .333 SILVER, .0237 oz ASW

714	VS1989	(1932)	2.25	4.00	5.00	6.50
	1991	(1934)	1.75	3.50	4.50	6.00
	1992	(1935)	1.75	3.50	4.50	6.00
	1993	(1936)	1.75	3.50	4.50	6.00
	1994	(1937)	3.75	6.50	10.00	15.00
	1995	(1938)	1.75	3.50	4.50	6.00
	1996	(1939)	1.75	3.50	4.50	6.00
	1997	(1940)	1.75	3.50	4.50	6.00
	1998	(1941)	1.75	3.50	4.50	6.00
	1999	(1942)	1.75	3.50	4.50	6.00
	2000	(1943)	1.75	3.50	4.50	6.00
	2001	(1944)	1.75	3.50	4.50	6.00
	2003	(1945)	1.75	3.50	4.50	6.00
	2004	(1947)	1.75	3.50	4.50	6.00
715	VS1989	(1932)	2.25	4.00	6.00	8.50

NOTE: The date VS1989 is given in different style characters. Refer to 50 Paisa KM#719 and 1 Rupee, KM#724 for style.

716	VS2006	(1949)	.75	1.00	1.25	1.75
	2007	(1950)	—	Reported, not confirmed		
	2009	(1952)	.75	1.00	1.50	2.50
	2010	(1953)	.75	1.00	1.50	2.50

50 PAISA

5.5403 g, .800 SILVER, .1425 oz ASW

718	VS1989	(1932)	5.50	6.50	8.00	10.00
	1991	(1934)	2.50	4.50	7.00	10.00
	1992	(1935)	2.50	4.50	7.00	10.00
	1993	(1936)	2.50	4.50	7.00	10.00
	1994	(1937)	2.50	4.50	7.00	10.00
	1995	(1938)	2.50	4.50	7.00	10.00
	1996	(1939)	2.50	4.50	7.00	10.00
	1997	(1940)	2.50	4.50	7.00	10.00
	1998	(1941)	2.50	4.50	7.00	10.00
	1999	(1942)	2.50	4.50	7.00	10.00
	2000	(1943)	2.50	4.50	7.00	10.00
	2001	(1944)	2.50	4.50	7.00	10.00
	2003	(1946)	2.50	4.50	7.00	10.00
	2004	(1947)	2.50	4.50	7.00	10.00
	2005	(1948)	2.50	4.50	7.00	10.00

719	VS1989	(1932)	2.50	4.50	7.00	9.00

NOTE: The date is given in different characters.

5.5403 g, .333 SILVER, .0593 oz ASW
Obv: 4 dots around trident.

KM#	Date	Year	Fine	VF	XF	Unc
720	VS2005	(1948)	45.00	65.00	90.00	125.00

Obv: W/o dots around trident.

721	VS2006	(1949)	1.50	2.00	2.75	4.50
	2007	(1950)	1.50	2.00	2.75	4.50
	2009/7	(1952/0)	1.50	2.25	3.00	5.00
	2009	(1952)	1.50	2.00	2.75	4.50
	2010	(1953)	1.50	2.00	2.75	4.50

RUPEE

11.0806 g, .800 SILVER, .2850 oz ASW

KM#	Date	Mintage	Fine	VF	XF	Unc
723	VS1989(1932)	—	2.50	5.00	8.00	20.00
	1991(1934)	—	2.50	5.00	8.00	16.50
	1992(1935)	—	2.50	5.00	8.00	16.50
	1993(1936)	—	2.50	5.00	8.00	16.50
	1994(1937)	1.717	2.50	5.00	8.00	16.50
	1995(1938)	2.097	2.50	5.00	8.00	16.50
	1996(1939)	—	2.50	5.00	8.00	16.50
	1997(1940)	—	2.50	5.00	8.00	16.50
	1998(1941)	—	2.50	5.00	8.00	16.50
	1999(1942)	—	2.50	5.00	8.00	16.50
	2000(1943)	—	2.50	5.00	8.00	16.50
	2001(1944)	—	2.50	5.00	8.00	16.50
	2003(1946)	—	2.50	5.00	8.00	16.50
	2005(1948)	—	2.50	5.00	8.00	16.50

KM#	Date	Year	Fine	VF	XF	Unc
724	VS1989	(1932)	7.50	10.00	12.50	15.00

NOTE: The date is given in different characters.

11.0806 g, .333 SILVER, .1186 oz ASW
Obv: 4 dots around trident.

KM#	Date	Year	Fine	VF	XF	Unc
725	VS2005	(1948)	5.00	7.50	10.00	13.50

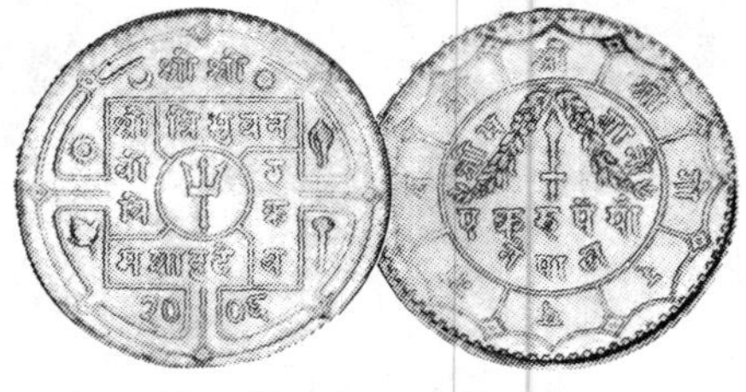

Obv: W/o dots around trident.

726	VS2006	(1949)	2.50	3.50	5.00	7.50
	2007	(1950)	2.50	3.50	5.00	7.50
	2008	(1951)	2.50	3.50	5.00	7.50
	2009	(1951)	2.50	3.50	5.00	7.50
	2010	(1952)	2.50	3.50	5.00	7.50

JNANENDRA VIRA VIKRAMA

VS2007/1950-1951AD

50 PAISA

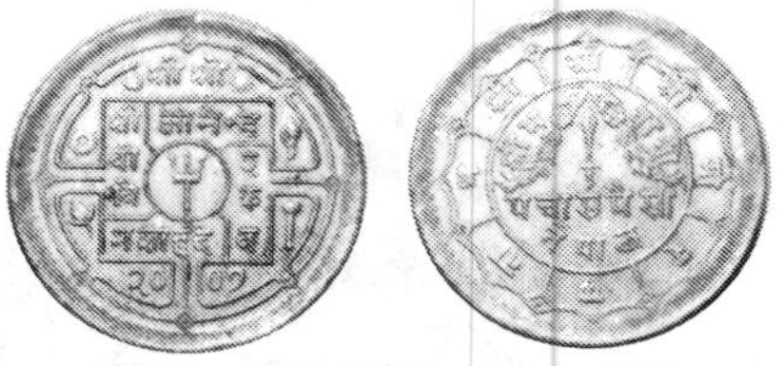

5.5403 g, .333 SILVER, .0593 oz ASW

KM#	Date	Year	Mintage	VF	XF	Unc
729	VS2007	(1950)	26 pcs.	175.00	275.00	350.00

RUPEE

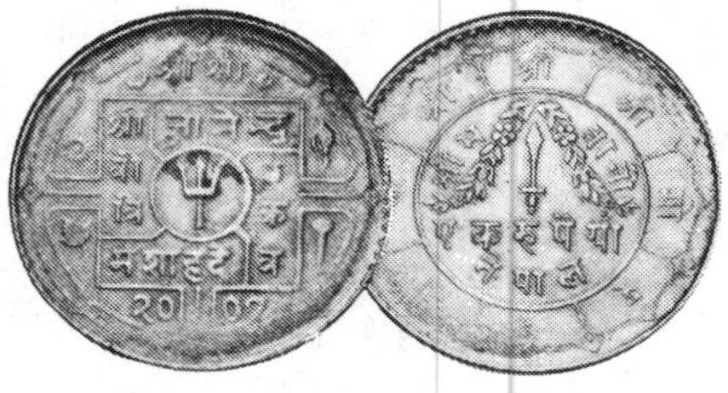

11.0806 g, .333 SILVER, .1186 oz ASW

KM#	Date	Year	Fine	VF	XF	Unc
730	VS2007	(1950)	4.50	6.50	9.00	12.50

MOHAR

GOLD

731	VS2007	(1950)	—	—	Rare	—

TOLA

GOLD

732	VS2007	(1950)	—	—	Rare	—

TRIVHUVANA VIRA VIKRAMA

VS2007-2011/1951-1955AD

50 PAISA

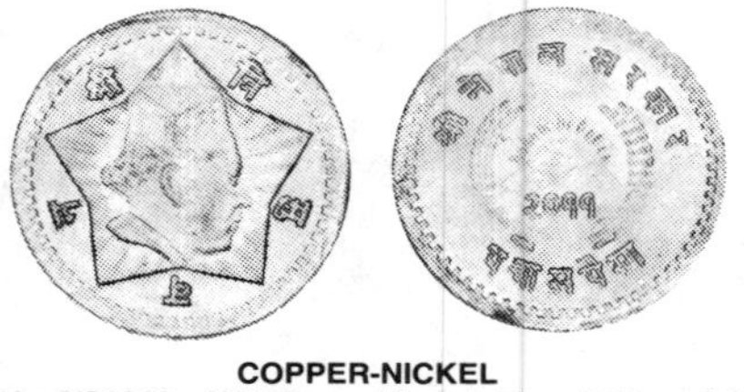

COPPER-NICKEL

740	VS2010	(1953)	.50	1.00	2.00	3.00
	2011	(1954)	.35	.75	1.50	2.00

RUPEE

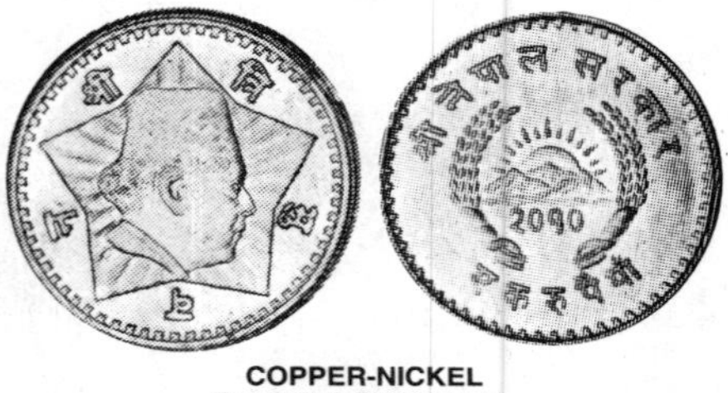

COPPER-NICKEL
Equal denticles at rim.

742	VS2010	(1953)	.75	1.25	2.00	3.50
	2011	(1954)	.75	1.25	2.00	3.50

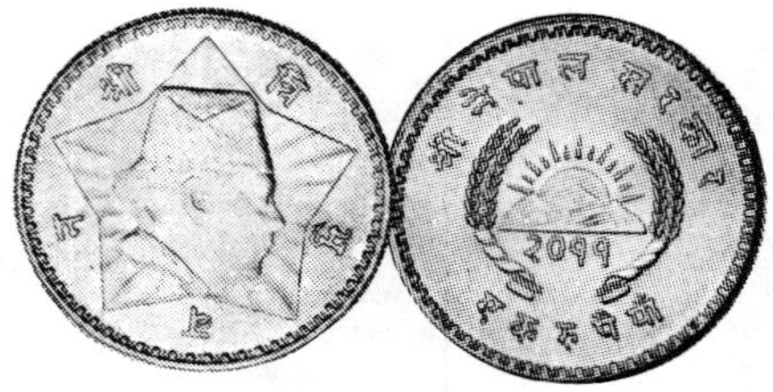

Unequal denticles at rim.

KM#	Date	Year	Fine	VF	XF	Unc
743	VS2011	(1954)	.75	1.25	2.00	3.50

ANONYMOUS COINAGE

PAISA

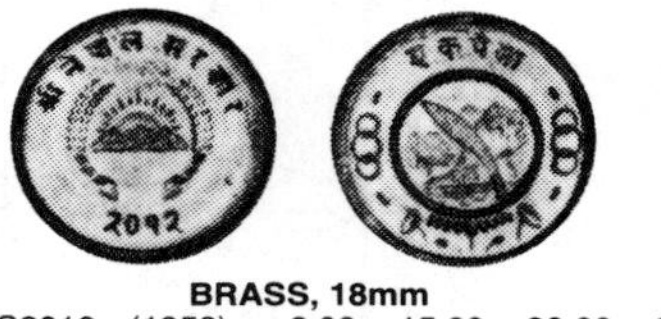

BRASS, 18mm

733	VS2010	(1953)	8.00	15.00	20.00	25.00
	2011	(1954)	17.50	25.00	35.00	40.00
	2012	(1955)				
			(restrike)	1.00	1.50	2.00

17.5mm

734	VS2012	(1955)	1.25	2.00	2.50	3.50

2 PAISA

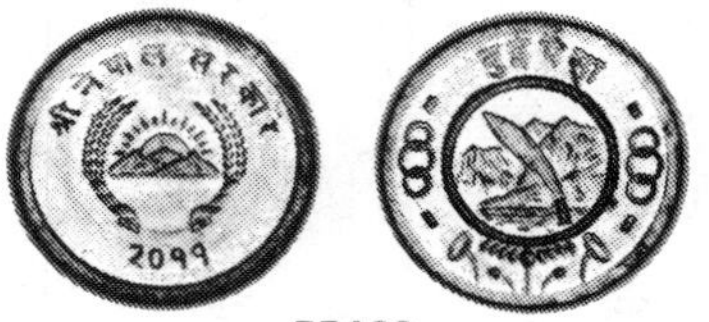

BRASS

735	VS2010	(1953)	12.50	20.00	37.50	60.00
	2011	(1954)	30.00	40.00	50.00	75.00
	2011	(1954)		(restrike)	1.50	2.50

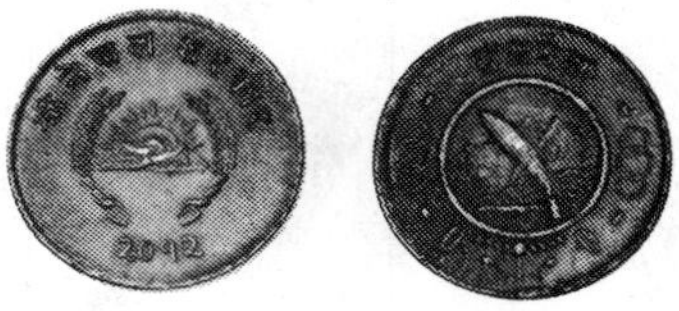

749	VS2012	(1955)	.30	.50	.75	1.50
	2013	(1956)	.30	.50	.75	1.50
	2014	(1957)	.30	.50	.75	1.50

4 PAISA

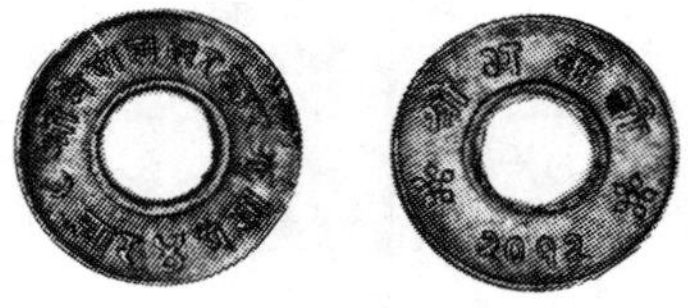

BRASS

754	VS2012	(1955)	1.00	1.75	3.00	5.00

5 PAISA

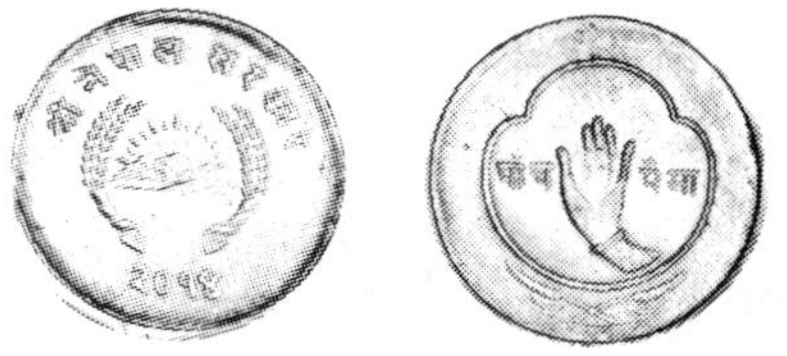

BRONZE, 3.89 g

736	VS2010	(1953)	2.75	4.50	7.00	10.00
	2011	(1954)	.65	1.00	2.75	5.00
	2012	(1955)	.30	.50	.75	1.00
	2013	(1956)	.30	.50	.75	1.00
	2014	(1957)	.30	.50	.75	1.00

COPPER-NICKEL, 4.04 g (OMS?)

736a	VS2014	(1957)	— Reported, not confirmed

10 PAISA

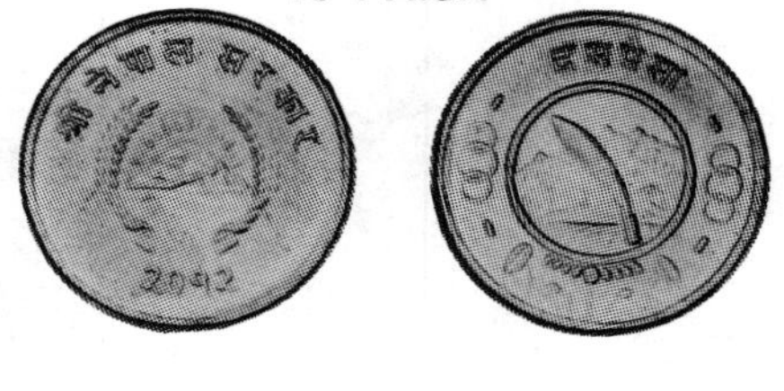

BRONZE

KM#	Date	Year	Fine	VF	XF	Unc
737	VS2010	(1953)	2.75	4.50	7.00	10.00
	2011	(1954)	.15	.25	.50	1.00
	2011	(1954)		(restrike)	.15	.25
	2012	(1955)	.15	.25	.50	1.00

20 PAISA

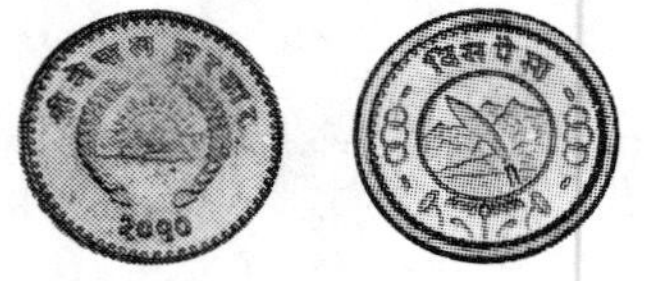

COPPER-NICKEL

738	VS2010	(1953)	12.50	20.00	30.00	40.00
	2010	(1953)		(restrike)	2.50	3.00
	2011	(1954)	32.50	40.00	50.00	60.00

25 PAISA

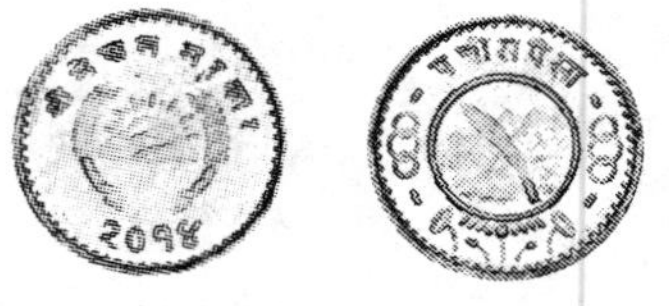

COPPER-NICKEL

739	VS2010	(1953)	2.00	3.50	4.50	6.00
	2011	(1954)	2.00	3.50	4.50	6.00
	2012	(1955)	1.25	2.00	2.50	3.50
	2014	(1957)	1.25	2.00	2.50	3.50

1/2 ASARPHI

GOLD, 5.80 g
Portrait type.

KM#	Date	Year	Mintage	VF	XF	Unc
741	VS2010	(1953)	—	120.00	140.00	160.00

NOTE: KM#741 is believed to be a restrike.

ASARPHI

GOLD, 11.66 g

744	VS2010	(1953)	—	175.00	200.00	250.00

MAHENDRA VIRA VIKRAMA

VS2012-2028/1955-1971AD

PAISA

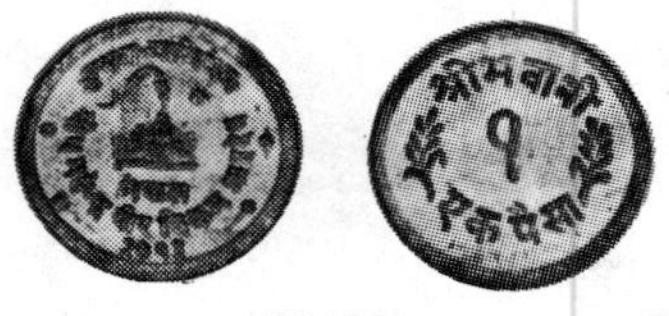

BRASS
Mahendra Coronation

KM#	Date	Year	Fine	VF	XF	Unc
745	VS2013	(1956)	.30	.50	.75	1.00

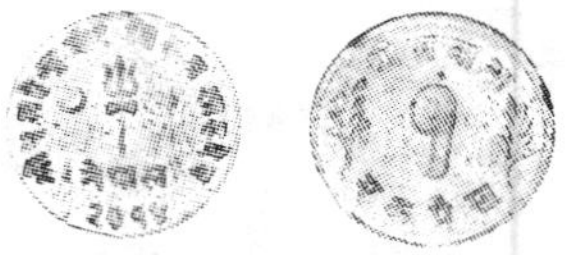

Rev: Numerals w/shading.

746	VS2014	(1957)	.10	.15	.25	.40
	2015	(1958)	.10	.15	.25	.40
	2018	(1961)	.10	.15	.25	.40
	2019	(1962)	.10	.15	.25	.40
	2020	(1963)	.10	.15	.25	.40

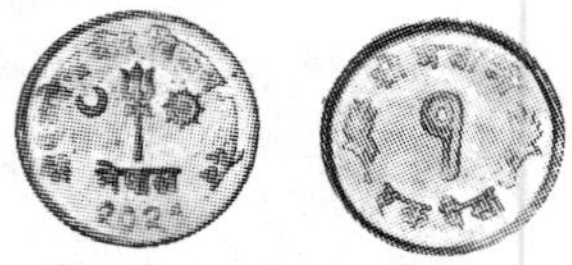

Rev: Numerals w/o shading.

747	VS2021	(1964)	.10	.15	.20	.30
	2022	(1965)	.10	.15	.25	.40

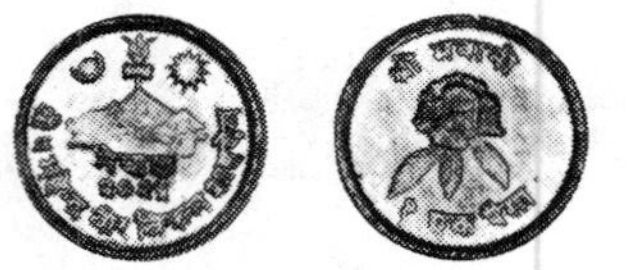

ALUMINUM
National Flower

KM#	Date	Year	Mintage	VF	XF	Unc
748	VS2023	(1966)	—	.10	.15	.25
	2025	(1968)	—	.10	.15	.25
	2026	(1969)	—	.10	.15	.25
	2027	(1970)	2,187	—	Proof	1.25
	2028	(1971)	—	.10	.15	.25
	2028	(1971)	2,380	—	Proof	1.25

2 PAISA

BRASS
Mahendra Coronation
Narrow rim.

KM#	Date	Year	Fine	VF	XF	Unc
750.1	VS2013	(1956)	.30	.50	.75	1.00

Wide rim.

750.2	VS2013	(1956)	.30	.50	.75	1.00

Rev: Numerals w/shading.

751	VS2014	(1957)	.10	.15	.25	.40
	2015	(1958)	.10	.15	.25	.40
	2016	(1959)	.10	.15	.25	.40
	2018	(1961)	.10	.15	.25	.40
	2019	(1962)	.10	.15	.25	.40
	2020	(1963)	.10	.15	.25	.40

Rev: Numerals w/o shading.

752	VS2021	(1964)	.10	.15	.20	.35
	2022	(1965)	.10	.15	.25	.50
	2023	(1966)	.10	.15	.25	.50

ALUMINUM
Himalayan Monal

KM#	Date	Year	Mintage	VF	XF	Unc
753	VS2023	(1966)	—	.10	.15	.25
	2024	(1967)	—	.10	.15	.25
	2025	(1968)	—	.10	.15	.25
	2026	(1969)	—	.10	.15	.25
	2027	(1970)	—	.10	.15	.25
	2027	(1970)	2,187	—	Proof	1.50
	2028	(1971)	—	.10	.15	.25
	2028	(1971)	2,380	—	Proof	1.50

5 PAISA

BRONZE
Mahendra Coronation
Wide rim w/accent mark.

KM#	Date	Year	Fine	VF	XF	Unc
756.1	VS2013	(1956)	10.00	20.00	30.00	40.00

W/o accent mark.

756.3	VS2013	(1956)	1.00	2.00	3.00	5.00

Narrow rim
(restrike)

756.2	VS2013	(1956)	.35	.60	1.00	1.50

Rev: Numerals w/shading.

KM#	Date	Year	Fine	VF	XF	Unc
757	VS2014	(1957)	.10	.20	.30	.75
	2015	(1958)	.10	.30	.30	.75
	2016	(1959)	.10	.30	.50	1.00
	2017	(1960)	.10	.20	.30	.75
	2018	(1961)	.10	.20	.30	.75
	2019	(1962)	.10	.20	.30	.75
	2020	(1963)	.10	.20	.30	.75

ALUMINUM-BRONZE
Rev: Numerals w/o shading.

758	VS2021	(1964)	.50	1.00	1.50	2.50

BRONZE

758a	VS2021	(1964)	.10	.15	.25	.50
	2022	(1965)	.10	.15	.30	.60
	2023	(1966)	.10	.15	.30	.60

ALUMINUM

KM#	Date	Year	Mintage	VF	XF	Unc
759	VS2023	(1966)	—	.15	.25	.50
	2024	(1967)	—	.10	.20	.35
	2025	(1968)	—	.10	.20	.35
	2026	(1969)	—	.10	.20	.25
	2027	(1970)	—	.10	.20	.35
	2027	(1970)	2,187	—	Proof	1.75
	2028	(1971)	—	.10	.20	.35
	2028	(1971)	2,038	—	Proof	1.75

10 PAISA

BRONZE
Mahendra Coronation

KM#	Date	Year	Fine	VF	XF	Unc
761	VS2013	(1956)	.25	.50	.75	1.50

Rev: Numerals w/shading.

762	VS2014	(1957)	2.75	4.50	7.00	10.00
	2015	(1958)	.15	.25	.50	.75
	2016	(1959)	3.00	5.00	7.00	10.00
	2018	(1961)	.15	.25	.50	.75
	2019	(1962)	.15	.25	.50	.75
	2020	(1963)	.15	.25	.50	.75

ALUMINUM-BRONZE
Rev: Numerals w/o shading.

KM#	Date	Year	Fine	VF	XF	Unc
763	VS2021	(1964)	.75	1.25	2.00	3.00

BRONZE, 25mm
Modified design

764	VS2021	(1964)	.10	.15	.25	.50
	2022	(1965)	.10	.15	.25	.50
	2023	(1966)	.10	.15	.25	.50

BRASS

KM#	Date	Year	Mintage	VF	XF	Unc
765	VS2023	(1966)	—	.15	.25	.50
	2024	(1967)	—	.15	.25	.50
	2025	(1968)	—	15.00	17.50	20.00
	2026	(1969)	—	.10	.20	.35
	2027	(1970)	—	.10	.20	.35
	2027	(1970)	2,187	—	Proof	2.00
	2028	(1971)	—	.10	.20	.35
	2028	(1971)	2,380	—	Proof	2.00

F.A.O. Issue

766	VS2028	(1971)	1.500	.10	.15	.20

25 PAISA

COPPER-NICKEL
Mahendra Coronation

KM#	Date	Year	Fine	VF	XF	Unc
770	VS2013	(1956)	.30	.50	.70	1.00

 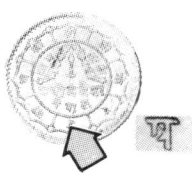

Obv: 4 characters in line above trident.
Rev: Small character at bottom (outer circle).

771	VS2015	(1958)	1.50	2.50	4.00	6.00
	2018	(1961)	.25	.40	.60	.80
	2020	(1963)	.25	.40	.60	.80
	2022	(1965)	2.00	3.50	6.00	9.00

2.9900 g, .950 SILVER, .0913 oz ASW

771a	VS2017/615	(1960)	—	—	—	100.00

COPPER-NICKEL
Rev: Large different character at bottom.

772	VS2021	(1964)	.30	.50	.70	1.00
	2022	(1965)	.30	.50	.70	1.00
	2023	(1966)	.30	.50	.70	1.00

Obv: 5 characters in line above trident.

KM#	Date	Year	Mintage	VF	XF	Unc
773	VS2024	(1967)	—	.35	.50	.75
	2025	(1968)	—	15.00	20.00	25.00
	2026	(1969)	—	.35	.50	.75
	2027	(1970)	—	.35	.50	.75
	2027	(1970)	2,187	—	Proof	2.50
	2028	(1971)	—	.35	.50	.75
	2028	(1971)	2,380	—	Proof	2.50

50 PAISA

COPPER-NICKEL
Mahendra Coronation

KM#	Date	Year	Fine	VF	XF	Unc
776	VS2013	(1956)	.35	.75	1.00	1.50

 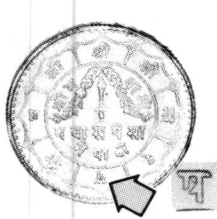

Rev: Small character at bottom (outer circle).

KM#	Date	Year	Fine	VF	XF	Unc
777	VS2011	(1954)	.50	1.00	1.50	3.00
	2012	(1955)	.25	.50	.75	1.00
	2013	(1956)	.25	.50	1.00	2.00
	2014	(1957)	.25	.50	1.00	2.00
	2015	(1958)	.25	.50	1.00	2.00
	2016	(1959)	.25	.50	1.00	2.00
	2017	(1960)	.25	.30	.75	1.25
	2018	(1961)	.25	.50	1.00	2.00
	2020	(1963)	.25	.30	.75	1.50

Rev: Large different character at bottom.

KM#	Date	Year	Fine	VF	XF	Unc
778	VS2021	(1964)	.25	.35	.50	.75
	2022	(1965)	.25	.50	.75	1.50
	2023	(1966)	.25	.50	.75	1.00

Reduced size, 23.5mm.
Obv: 4 characters in line above trident.

KM#	Date	Year	Fine	VF	XF	Unc
779	VS2023	(1966)	.25	.50	.75	1.50

Obv: 5 characters in line above trident.

KM#	Date	Year	Mintage	VF	XF	Unc
780	VS2025	(1968)	—	.30	.50	1.00
	2026	(1969)	—	.30	.50	.85
	2027	(1970)	2,187	—	Proof	3.00
	2028	(1971)	2,380	—	Proof	3.00

RUPEE

COPPER-NICKEL, 29.6mm

KM#	Date	Year	Fine	VF	XF	Unc
784	VS2011	(1954)	1.25	2.25	3.50	5.00
	2012	(1955)	1.00	1.75	2.50	4.00

Reduced size, 28.8mm.
Rev: Small character at bottom (outer circle).

KM#	Date	Year	Fine	VF	XF	Unc
785	VS2012	(1955)	.50	.85	1.25	1.75
	2013	(1956)	.50	.85	1.25	1.75
	2014	(1957)	.50	.85	1.25	1.75
	2015	(1958)	.50	.85	1.25	1.75
	2016	(1959)	.50	.85	1.25	1.75
	2018	(1961)	.50	.85	1.25	1.75
	2020	(1963)	.50	.85	1.25	1.75

Rev: Large character at bottom.

KM#	Date	Year	Fine	VF	XF	Unc
786	VS2021	(1964)	.50	.75	1.00	1.50
	2022	(1965)	.50	1.00	1.50	2.50
	2023	(1966)	4.50	7.50	10.00	15.00

Reduced size, 27mm.
Obv: 4 characters in line above trident.

KM#	Date	Year	Fine	VF	XF	Unc
787	VS2023	(1966)	.75	1.00	1.35	2.00

Obv: 5 characters in line above trident.

KM#	Date	Year	Mintage	VF	XF	Unc
788	VS2025	(1968)	—	1.00	1.50	2.00
	2026	(1969)	—	1.00	1.40	2.00
	2027	(1970)	2,187	—	Proof	4.50
	2028	(1971)	2,380	—	Proof	4.50

Mahendra Coronation

KM#	Date	Year		Fine	VF	XF	Unc
790	VS2013	(1956)	—	1.25	1.75	2.50

10 RUPEES

15.6000 g, .600 SILVER, .3009 oz ASW
F.A.O. Issue

KM#	Date	Year	Mintage	VF	XF	Unc
794	VS2025	(1968)	1.000	3.00	4.00	6.50

1/6 ASARFI

GOLD, 1.90 g
Mahendra Coronation

KM#	Date	Year	Fine	VF	XF	Unc
767	VS2013	(1956)	—	50.00	60.00	100.00

1/5 ASARFI

GOLD, 2.33 g

KM#	Date	Year			
768	VS2010	(1953)	—	50.00	60.00	100.00
	2012	(1955)	—	Reported, not confirmed		

1/4 ASARFI

GOLD, 2.90 g

KM#	Date	Year	Fine	VF	XF	Unc
774	VS2010	(1953)	60.00	70.00	80.00	100.00
	2012	(1955)	—	Reported, not confirmed		

NOTE: Coins dated VS2010 are believed to be restrikes.

Reduced weight, 2.50 g.

KM#	Date	Year			XF	Unc
775	VS2026	(1969)	—		75.00	100.00

1/2 ASARFI

GOLD, 5.80 g
Mahendra Coronation

KM#	Date	Year		Fine	VF	XF	Unc
781	VS2013	(1956)	—	120.00	135.00	160.00

KM#	Date	Year			VF	XF	Unc
782	VS2012	(1955)	—	120.00	135.00	160.00
	2019	(1962)	—	120.00	135.00	160.00

5.00 g
Virendra Marriage

KM#	Date	Year			VF	XF	Unc
783	VS2026	(1969)	—		150.00	175.00

ASARFI

GOLD

KM#	Date	Year	Mintage	VF	XF	Unc
789	VS2012	(1955)	—	225.00	250.00	300.00
	2019	(1962)	—	225.00	250.00	300.00

Mahendra Coronation

KM#	Date	Year	Mintage	VF	XF	Unc
791	VS2013	(1956)	—	225.00	250.00	300.00

10.00 g

KM#	Date	Year	Mintage	VF	XF	Unc
792	VS2026	(1969)	—	225.00	250.00	300.00

2 ASARFI

GOLD

KM#	Date	Year	Fine	VF	XF	Unc
793	VS2012	(1955)	—	500.00	550.00	625.00

In the name of Queen Ratna Rajya Lakshmi

50 PAISA

COPPER-NICKEL

795	VS2012	(1955)	3,000	100.00	125.00	150.00

RUPEE

COPPER-NICKEL

KM#	Date	Year	Mintage	VF	XF	Unc
797	VS2012	(1955)	2,000	100.00	150.00	175.00

1/2 ASARFI

GOLD

796 VS2012 (1955) Reported, not confirmed

ASARFI

GOLD, 11.66 g

798 VS2012 (1955) Reported, not confirmed

VIRENDRA VIR VIKRAMA

VS2028-/1971-AD

PAISA

ALUMINUM
National Flower

799	VS2028	(1971)	.010	.20	.30	.40
	2029	(1972)	3.036	.10	.15	.25
	2029	(1972)	3,943	—	Proof	.60
	2030	(1973)	1.279	.10	.15	.25
	2030	(1973)	8,891	—	Proof	.40
	2031	(1974)	.430	.10	.15	.25
	2031	(1974)	.011	—	Proof	.40
	2032	(1975)	.324	.10	.15	.25
	2033	(1976)	.217	—	.10	.25
	2034	(1977)	1.040	.10	.15	.25
	2035	(1978)	.394	.10	.15	.25
	2036	(1979)	—	.10	.15	.25

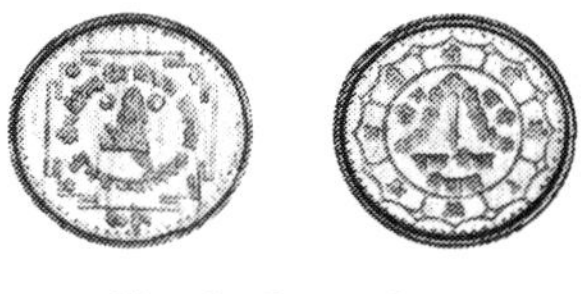

Virendra Coronation

800	VS2031	(1974)	.075	.10	.15	.25

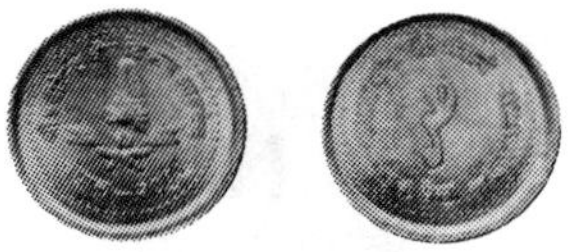

KM#	Date	Year	Mintage	VF	XF	Unc
1012	VS2039	(1982)	—	4.00	6.00	8.00
	2040	(1983)	.042	Reported, not confirmed		

2 PAISA

ALUMINUM
Himalayan Monal

801	VS2028	(1971)	8,319	.20	.30	.50
	2029	(1972)	5.206	.10	.15	.25
	2029	(1972)	3,943	—	Proof	.70
	2030	(1973)	2.563	.10	.15	.25
	2030	(1973)	8,891	—	Proof	.50
	2031	(1974)	.011	—	Proof	.50
	2033	(1976)	.072	.10	.15	.30
	2035	(1978)	.026	.10	.15	.30

5 PAISA

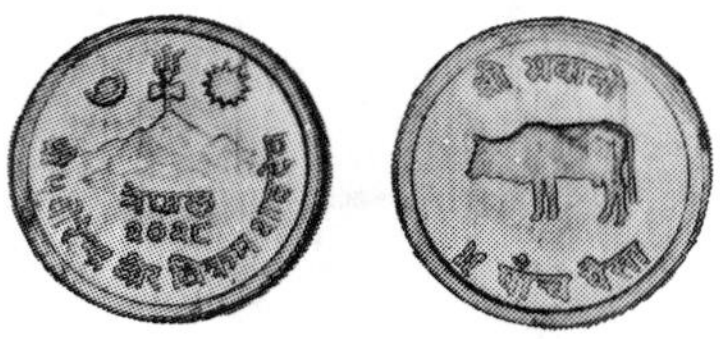

ALUMINUM

802	VS2028	(1971)	3.700	.10	.20	.50
	2029	(1972)	23.578	.10	.20	.50
	2029	(1972)	3,943	—	Proof	.85
	2030	(1973)	12.320	.10	.20	.50
	2030	(1973)	8,891	—	Proof	.60
	2031	(1974)	15.730	.10	.20	.50
	2031	(1974)	.011	—	Proof	.60
	2032	(1975)	19.747	.10	.20	.50
	2033	(1976)	29.619	.10	.20	.50
	2034	(1977)	27.222	.10	.20	.50
	2035	(1978)	27.613	.10	.20	.50
	2036	(1979)	—	.10	.20	.50
	2037	(1980)	13.235	.10	.20	.50
	2038	(1981)	15.137	.10	.20	.50
	2039	(1982)	8.971	.10	.20	.50

F.A.O. Issue

803	VS2031	(1974)	4.584	—	.10	.15

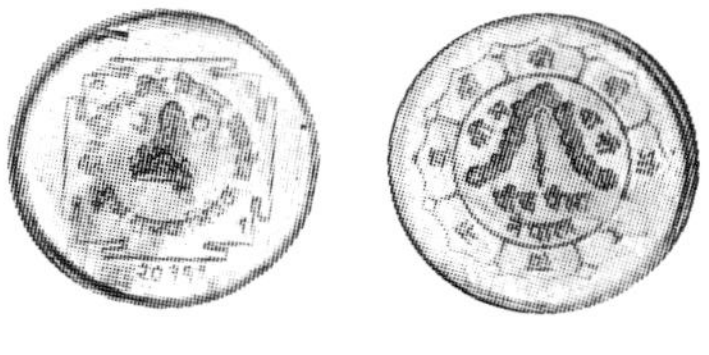

Virendra Coronation

804	VS2031	(1974)	2.869	.10	.25	.50

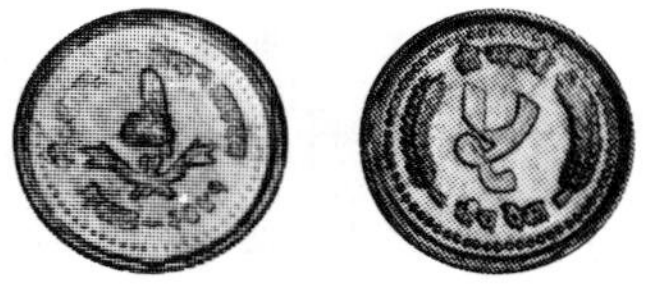

1013	VS2039	(1982)	8.971	7.00	10.00	15.00
	2040	(1983)	6.430	—	.10	.25
	2041	(1984)	9.634	—	.10	.25
	2042	(1985)	.058	—	.10	.25
	2043	(1986)	2.937	—	.10	.25
	2044	(1987)	3.126	—	.10	.25
	2045	(1988)	1.030	—	.10	.25
	2046	(1989)	—	—	.10	.25
	2047	(1990)	—	—	.10	.25

10 PAISA

BRASS

KM#	Date	Year	Mintage	VF	XF	Unc
806	VS2028	(1971)	5.035	.25	.40	.70

807	VS2029	(1972)	3.297	.15	.25	.40
	2029	(1972)	3,943	—	Proof	1.00
	2030	(1973)	5.670	.15	.25	.40
	2030	(1973)	8,891	—	Proof	.70
	2031	(1974)	.011	—	Proof	.70

ALUMINUM
Virendra Coronation

808	VS2031	(1974)	.192	.10	.20	.35

BRASS
F.A.O. Issue and International Women's Year

809	VS2032	(1975)	2.500	.10	.15	.25

Agricultural Development

810	VS2033	(1976)	10.000	.10	.15	.25

ALUMINUM
International Year of the Child

811	VS2036	(1979)	.213	.10	.15	.25

Education for Village Women

812	VS2036	(1979)	Inc. Ab.	.10	.15	.50

1014.1	VS2039	(1982)	796 pcs.	7.00	10.00	15.00
	2040	(1983)	—	—	.10	.30
	2041	(1984)	7.834	—	.10	.30
	2042	(1985)	.099	—	.10	.30

Rev: Smaller corn ears.

KM#	Date	Year	Mintage	VF	XF	Unc
1014.2	VS2043	(1986)	.010	—	.10	.30
	2044	(1987)	30.172	—	.10	.30
	2045	(1988)	4.140	—	.10	.30
	2046	(1989)	—	—	.10	.30
	2047	(1990)	—	—	.10	.30
	2048	(1991)	—	—	.10	.30

Reduced size.

1014.3	VS2051	(1994)	—	—	.10	.30

1087	VS2051	(1994)	—	—	.10	.30
	2053	(1996)	—	—	.10	.30

20 PAISA

BRASS
F.A.O. Issue

813	VS2035	(1978)	.234	.35	.75	1.00

International Year of the Child

814	VS2036	(1979)	.030	.35	.75	1.00

25 PAISA

COPPER-NICKEL

815	VS2028	(1971)	5,691	.40	.60	.80
	2029	(1972)	3,943	—	Proof	1.25
	2030	(1973)	8,676	.30	.40	.50
	2030	(1973)	8,891	—	Proof	.80
	2031	(1974)	1.172	.35	.50	.75
	2031	(1974)	.011	—	Proof	.80
	2032	(1975)	4.584	.30	.40	.50
	2033	(1976)	1.837	.30	.40	.50
	2034	(1977)	3.808	.30	.40	.50
	2035	(1978)	5.964	.30	.40	.50
	2036	(1979)	—	.30	.40	.50
	2037	(1980)	2.047	.30	.40	.50
	2038	(1981)	1.580	.30	.40	.50
	2039	(1982)	7.185	.30	.40	.50

NOTE: Varieties exist.

BRASS
World Food Day

817	VS2038	(1981)	2.000	—	.10	.30

International Year of Disabled Persons

KM#	Date	Year	Mintage	VF	XF	Unc
818	VS2038	(1981)	Inc. Ab.	.10	.25	.50

ALUMINUM

1015.1	VS2039	(1982)				
			Inc. KM815	4.00	6.00	8.00
	2040	(1983)	7.603	.10	.25	.50
	2041	(1984)	15.534	.10	.25	.50
	2042	(1985)	12.586	.10	.25	.50
	2043	(1986)	.054	.10	.25	.50
	2044	(1987)	13.633	.10	.25	.50
	2045	(1988)	13.046	.10	.25	.50
	2046	(1989)	—	.10	.25	.50
	2047	(1990)	—	.10	.25	.50
	2048	(1991)	—	.10	.25	.50
	2049	(1992)	—	.10	.25	.50
	2050	(1993)	—	.10	.25	.50

Reduced size: 24mm

1015.2	VS2051	(1994)		.10	.25	.50

1088	VS2051	(1994)	—	.10	.25	.50
	2053	(1996)	—	.10	.25	.50

50 PAISA

COPPER-NICKEL

821	VS2028	(1971)	5,343	.35	.50	1.00
	2029	(1972)	.347	.35	.50	.90
	2029	(1972)	3,943	—	Proof	1.50
	2030	(1973)	.998	.35	.50	.90
	2030	(1973)	8,891	—	Proof	1.00
	2031	(1974)	.016	.35	.50	1.00
	2031	(1974)	.011	—	Proof	1.00
	2032	(1975)	.227	.35	.50	.90
	2033	(1976)	3.446	.35	.50	.75
	2034	(1977)	6.016	.35	.50	.75
	2035	(1978)	2.355	.35	.50	.75
	2036	(1979)	—	.35	.50	.75
	2037	(1980)	4.861	.35	.50	.75
	2038	(1981)	.929	.35	.50	.75
	2039	(1982)	2.954	.35	.50	.75

NOTE: Milled edge for VS2030 dated coins is known to exist.
NOTE: Obverse die varieties are known to exist.

19mm

821a	VS2039	(1982)	Inc. Ab.	.10	.25	.50
	2040	(1983)	.072	.10	.25	.50
	2041	(1984)	5.917	.10	.25	.50

COPPER-NICKEL, 1mm thick
Virendra Coronation

822.1	VS2031	(1974)	.136	.50	.75	1.25

KM#	Date	Year	Mintage	VF	XF	Unc
846	VS2031	(1974)	—	—	—	100.00

World Food Day

823	VS2038	(1981)	2.000	.10	.30	.60

International Year of Disabled Persons

824	VS2038	(1981)	Inc. Ab.	.50	.75	1.25

Family Planning

1016	VS2041	(1984)	—	.10	.25	.50

STAINLESS STEEL, 23.5mm
Obv: Smaller trident in center.

1018.1						
	VS2044	(1987)	6.341	.10	.25	.50
	2045	(1988)	7.350	.10	.25	.50
	2046	(1989)	—	.10	.25	.50
	2047	(1990)	—	.10	.25	.50
	2048	(1991)	—	.10	.25	.50
	2049	(1992)	—	.10	.25	.50

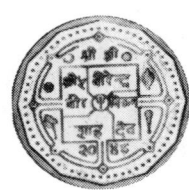 

Obv: Larger trident in center.

1018.2						
	VS2048	(1981)	—	.10	.25	.50

ALUMINUM

1072	VS2051	(1994)	—	—	.15	.30
	2053	(1996)	—	—	.15	.30

Virendra Coronation

816.1	VS2031	(1974)	.431	.35	.50	.75

RUPEE

COPPER-NICKEL, 10.2 g

KM#	Date	Year	Mintage	VF	XF	Unc
828	VS2028	(1971)	5,030	.50	1.00	2.00
	2029	(1972)	.022	.50	1.00	1.50
	2029	(1972)	3,943	—	Proof	2.50
	2030	(1973)	5,667	.50	1.00	2.00
	2030	(1973)	8,891	—	Proof	2.00
	2031	(1974)	.011	—	Proof	1.50

COPPER-NICKEL, 7.5 g

KM#	Date	Year	Mintage	VF	XF	Unc
828a	VS2033	(1976)	.058	.50	1.00	1.50
	2034*	(1977)	30.000	.25	.50	1.00
	2035	(1978)	—	.25	.50	1.00
	2036	(1979)	—	.25	.50	1.00
	2036*	(1980)	30.000	.25	.50	1.00

*NOTE: These 2 dates were struck at the Canberra Mint.

COPPER-NICKEL, 2mm thick
Virendra Coronation

KM#	Date	Year	Mintage	VF	XF	Unc
829.1	VS2031	(1974)	—	.75	1.25	1.75

KM#	Date	Year	Mintage	VF	XF	Unc
848	VS2031	(1974)	—	—	—	150.00

F.A.O. Issue and International Women's Year

KM#	Date	Year	Mintage	VF	XF	Unc
831	VS2032	(1975)	1.500	.25	.50	1.25

Family Planning

KM#	Date	Year	Mintage	VF	XF	Unc
1019	VS2041	(1984)	.021	—	—	.75

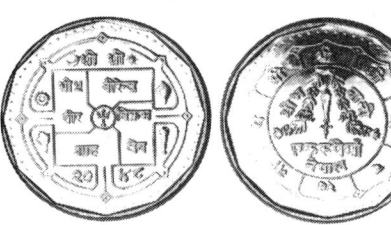

STAINLESS STEEL
Obv: Smaller trident in center.

KM#	Date	Year	Mintage	VF	XF	Unc
1061	VS2045	(1988)	—	.25	.50	1.00
	2048	(1991)	—	.25	.50	1.00
	2048	(1991)	—	—	Proof	2.00
	2049	(1992)	—	.25	.50	1.25

BRASS PLATED STEEL

KM#	Date	Year	Mintage	VF	XF	Unc
1073	VS2051	(1994)	—	.25	.50	1.00

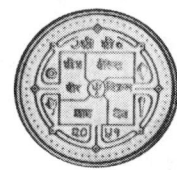 

BRASS
Obv: Traditional design. Rev: Small building.

1073a	VS2053	(1996)	—	—	—	2.50

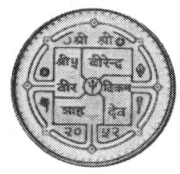 

U.N. 50th Anniversary

1092	VS2052	(1995)	—	—	—	1.75

2 RUPEES

COPPER-NICKEL
World Food Day

832	VS2038	(1981)	1.000	.50	.75	1.50

F.A.O. Issue

1025	VS2039	(1982)	.366	.50	.75	1.50

NOTE: Size of obverse square varies.
NOTE: Reverse varieties exist.

Family Planning

1020	VS2041	(1984)	.011	.50	.75	1.50

BRASS PLATED STEEL

1074	VS2051	(1994)	—	.35	.60	1.25

5 RUPEES

COPPER-NICKEL
Rural Women's Advancement

KM#	Date	Year	Mintage	VF	XF	Unc
833	VS2037	(1980)	.050	.75	1.50	3.00

National Bank Silver Jubilee

834	VS2038	(1981)	.064	.75	1.50	3.00

NOTE: Flan size varieties have been reported.

Circulation Coinage

1009	VS2039	(1982)	Inc. Ab.	.50	1.00	2.00
	2040	(1983)	.478	.30	.50	1.00

Family Planning

1017	VS2041	(1984)	.458	.50	1.00	2.00

Year of Youth

1023	VS2042	(1985)	1.124	—	—	2.50

Social Services

1047	VS2042	(1985)	Inc. Ab.	—	—	3.50

World Food Day

KM#	Date	Year Mintage	VF	XF	Unc
1028	VS2043	(1986) .099	—	—	3.50

15th World Buddhist Conference

| 1042 | VS2043 | (1986) .135 | — | — | 3.50 |

NOTE: Varieties exist.

10th Year of National Social Security Administration

| 1030 | VS2044 | (1987) .104 | — | — | 3.50 |

World Food Day

| 1053 | VS2047 | (1990) | — | — | 4.00 |

New Constitution

| 1063 | VS2047 | (1990) | — | — | 3.25 |

Parliament Session

| 1062 | VS2048 | (1991) | — | — | 3.00 |

BRASS PLATED STEEL

| 1075 | VS2051 | (1994) | — | — | 1.50 |

10 RUPEES

BRASS PLATED STEEL

KM#	Date	Year Mintage	VF	XF	Unc
1076	VS2051	(1994)	—	—	3.00

COPPER-NICKEL
75th Anniversary - International Labor Org.

| 1083 | VS2051 | (1994) | — | — | 5.00 |

50th Anniversary - F.A.O. Logo

| 1089 | VS2052 | (1995) | — | — | 4.00 |

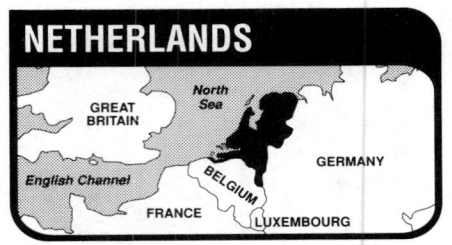

NETHERLANDS

The Kingdom of the Netherlands, a country of western Europe fronting on the North Sea and bordered by Belgium and Germany, has an area of 15,770 sq. mi. (41,500 sq. km.) and a population of 15.7 million. Capital: Amsterdam, but the seat of government is at The Hague. The economy is based on dairy farming and a variety of industrial activities. Chemicals, yarns and fabrics, and meat products are exported.

After being a part of Charlemagne's empire in the 8th and 9th centuries, the Netherlands came under control of Burgundy and the Austrian Hapsburgs, and finally was subjected to Spanish dominion in the 16th century. Led by William of Orange, the Dutch revolted against Spain in 1568. The seven northern provinces formed the Union of Utrecht and declared their independence in 1581, becoming the Republic of the United Netherlands. In the following century, the 'Golden Age' of Dutch history, the Netherlands became a great sea and colonial power, a patron of the arts and a refuge for the persecuted. The United Dutch Republic ended in 1795 when the French formed the Batavian Republic. Napoleon made his brother Louis, the King of Holland in 1806, however he abdicated in 1810 when Napoleon annexed Holland. The French were expelled in 1813, and all the provinces of Holland and Belgium were merged into the Kingdom of the United Netherlands under William I, in 1814. The Belgians withdrew in 1830 to form their own kingdom, the last substantial change in the configuration of European Netherlands. German forces invaded in 1940 as the royal family fled with cargos of wealth to England where a government-in-exile was formed. A German High Commissioner, Arthur Seyss-Inquart, was placed in command until 1945 when the arrival of Allied military forces ended the occupation.

WORLD WAR II COINAGE

Coinage of the Netherlands Homeland Types - KM#152, 153, 163, 164, 161.1 and 161.2 - were minted by U.S. mints in the name of the government in exile and its remaining Curacao and Surinam Colonies during the years 1941-45. The Curacao and Surinam strikings, distinguished by the presence of a palm tree in combination with a mint mark (P-Philadelphia; D-Denver; S-San Francisco) flanking the date, are incorporated under those titles in this volume. Pieces of this period struck in the name of the homeland bear an acorn and mint mark and are incorporated in the following tabulation.

NOTE: Excepting the World War II issues struck at U.S. mints, all of the modern coins were struck at the Utrecht Mint and bear the caduceus mint mark of that facility. They also bear the mintmasters marks.

RULERS
KINGDOM OF THE NETHERLANDS
Wilhelmina I, 1890-1948
Juliana, 1948-1980
Beatrix, 1980-

MINT MARKS
D - Denver, 1943-1945
P - Philadelphia, 1941-1945
S - San Francisco, 1944-1945

MINT PRIVY MARKS
Utrecht

Date	Privy Mark
1806-present	Caduceus

MINTMASTERS PRIVY MARKS
U. S. Mints

1941-1945	Palm tree
	Utrecht Mint
1888-1909	Halberd
1909	Halberd and star
1909-1933	Seahorse
1933-1942	Grapes
1943-1945	No privy mark
1945-1969	Fish
1969-1979	Cock
1980	Cock and star (temporal)
1980-1988	Anvil with hammer
1989-	Bow and arrow

NOTE: A star adjoining the privy mark indicates that the piece was struck at the beginning of the term of office of a successor. (The star was used only if the successor had not chosen his own mark yet.)

MONETARY SYSTEM
100 Cents = 1 Gulden
2-1/2 Gulden = 1 Rijksdaalder

1/2 CENT

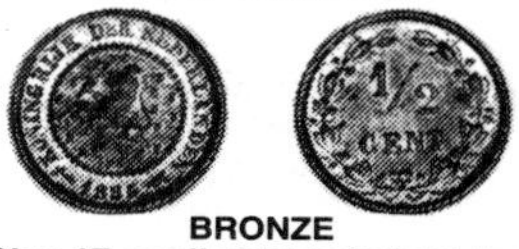

BRONZE
Obv: 17 small shields in field, leg: KONINGRIJK. . .

KM#	Date	Mintage	Fine	VF	XF	Unc
109	1901	6.000	1.50	4.00	7.00	17.50

NOTE: Earlier dates (1878-1900) exist for this type.

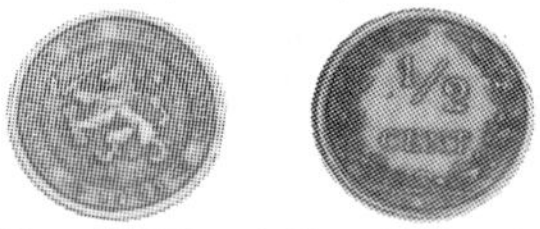

KM#	Date	Mintage	Fine	VF	XF	Unc
133	1903	10.000	1.00	2.00	4.00	15.00
	1906	10.000	1.00	2.00	4.00	15.00

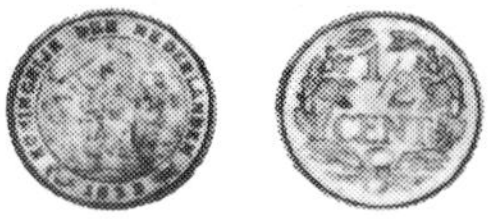

Obv: 15 large shields in field around larger lion, smaller date and leg. Rev: CENT in larger letters.

KM#	Date	Mintage	Fine	VF	XF	Unc
138	1909	5.000	1.00	2.00	4.00	12.50
	1911	5.000	1.00	2.00	4.00	12.50
	1912	5.000	1.00	2.00	4.00	12.50
	1914	5.000	1.00	2.00	4.00	12.50
	1915	2.500	8.00	12.00	20.00	40.00
	1916	4.000	2.00	4.00	8.00	16.50
	1917	5.000	1.00	2.00	4.00	12.50
	1921	1.500	7.00	15.00	25.00	50.00
	1922/1	—	25.00	50.00	100.00	250.00
	1922	2.500	5.00	10.00	17.50	35.00
	1928	4.000	1.00	2.00	4.00	12.50
	1930	6.000	1.00	2.00	4.00	12.50
	1934	5.000	.75	1.75	3.50	8.00
	1936	5.000	.75	1.75	3.50	8.00
	1937	1.600	1.00	2.50	5.50	14.00
	1938	8.400	.70	1.50	3.00	8.00
	1940	6.000	.70	1.50	3.00	8.00

CENT

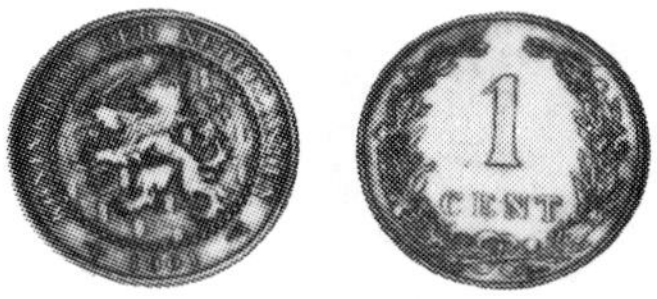

BRONZE
Obv: 15 large shields in field, leg: KONINKRIJK.

KM#	Date	Mintage	Fine	VF	XF	Unc
130	1901	10.000	1.00	3.00	8.00	30.00

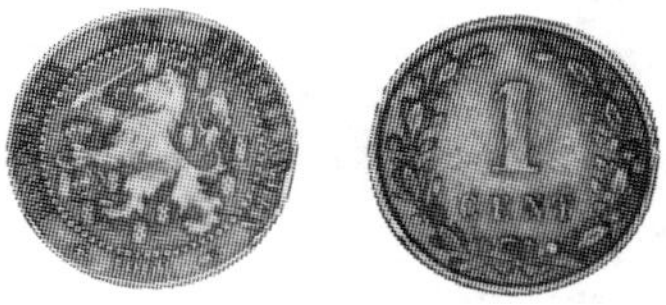

Obv: 10 large shields in field, leg: KONINGRIJK.

KM#	Date	Mintage	Fine	VF	XF	Unc
131	1901	10.000	1.00	3.00	8.00	30.00

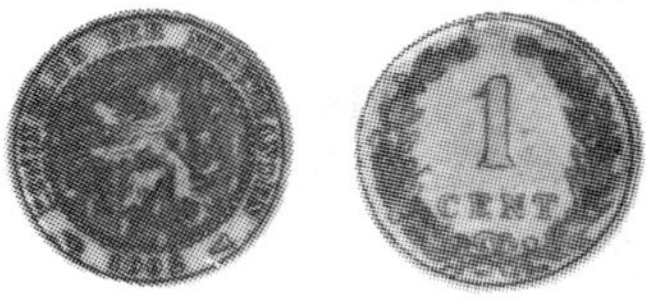

Obv: 15 medium shields in field, leg: KONINGRIJK.

KM#	Date	Mintage	Fine	VF	XF	Unc
132.1	1902	10.000	1.00	2.00	3.00	20.00
	1904	15.000	1.00	2.00	3.00	20.00
	1905	10.000	1.00	2.00	3.00	20.00
	1906	9.000	1.00	2.00	3.00	20.00
	1907	6.000	6.00	12.00	22.50	50.00

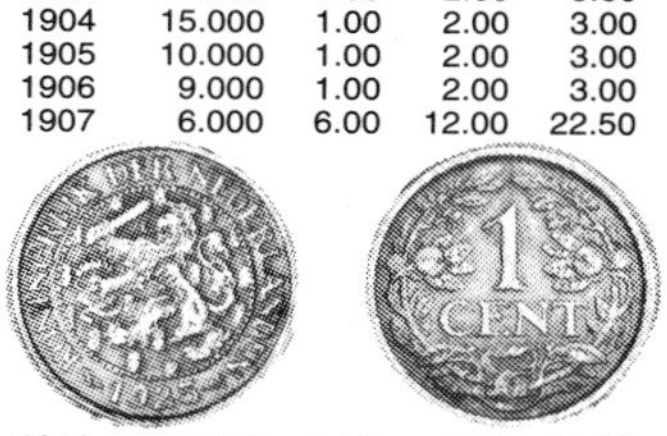

KM#	Date	Mintage	Fine	VF	XF	Unc
152	1913	5.000	1.50	4.00	10.00	40.00
	1914	9.000	1.00	2.00	4.00	18.00
	1915	10.800	1.00	2.00	4.00	18.00
	1916	21.700	.75	1.00	2.00	12.00
	1916	—	—	—	Proof	110.00
	1917	20.000	.75	1.00	4.00	12.00
	1918	10.000	1.00	2.00	6.00	15.00
	1919	6.000	1.75	2.50	6.00	20.00
	1920	11.400	.75	1.50	2.00	12.00
	1921	12.600	.75	1.50	2.00	12.00
	1922	20.000	.75	1.50	2.00	12.00
	1924	1.400	15.00	25.00	40.00	90.00
	1925	18.600	.75	1.50	2.00	12.00
152	1926	10.000	.75	1.50	2.00	12.00
	1927	10.000	.75	1.50	2.00	12.00
	1928	10.000	.75	1.50	2.00	12.00
	1929	20.000	.75	1.50	2.00	12.00
	1930	10.000	.75	1.50	2.00	12.00
	1931	3.400	3.00	6.00	12.00	40.00
	1937	10.000	.75	1.50	2.00	7.50
	1938	16.600	.50	1.00	1.50	6.00
	1939	22.000	.50	1.00	1.50	6.00
	1940	24.600	.50	1.00	1.50	6.00
	1941	66.600	.25	.60	1.00	3.00

NOTE: For similar coins dated 1942P see Netherlands Antilles (Curacao); 1943P, 1957-1960 see Surinam.

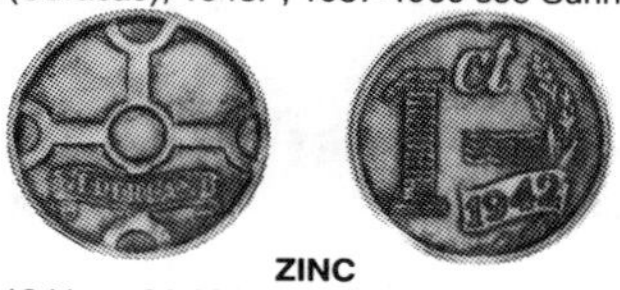

ZINC

KM#	Date	Mintage	Fine	VF	XF	Unc
170	1941	31.800	1.00	2.00	6.00	22.00
	1942	241.000	.25	.50	1.50	5.00
	1943	71.000	.75	1.50	4.00	10.00
	1944	29.600	1.00	2.00	6.00	22.00

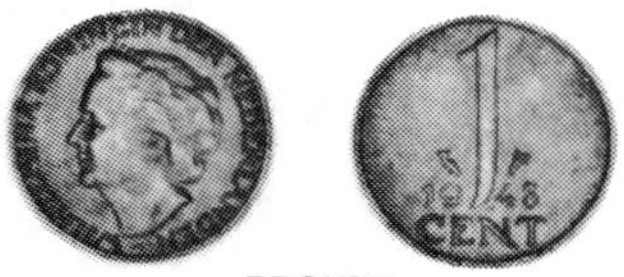

BRONZE

KM#	Date	Mintage	VF	XF	Unc	BU
175	1948	130.400	.25	.50	1.50	10.00
	1948	—	—	—	Proof	40.00

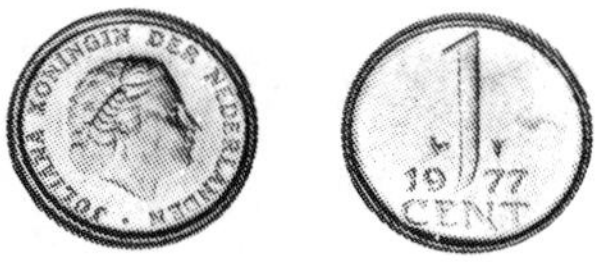

large date small date

KM#	Date	Mintage	VF	XF	Unc	BU
180	1950	91.000	.10	.25	.75	5.00
	1950	—	—	—	Proof	45.00
	1951	45.800	.10	.25	.75	5.00
	1951	—	—	—	Proof	45.00
	1952	68.000	.10	.25	.75	5.00
	1952	—	—	—	Proof	45.00
	1953	54.000	.10	.25	.75	5.00
	1953	—	—	—	Proof	45.00
	1954	54.000	.10	.25	.75	5.00
	1954	—	—	—	Proof	45.00
	1955	52.000	.10	.25	.75	5.00
	1955	—	—	—	Proof	45.00
	1956	34.800	.10	.25	.75	5.00
	1956	—	—	—	Proof	45.00
	1957	48.000	.10	.25	.75	5.00
	1957	—	—	—	Proof	45.00
	1958	34.000	.10	.25	.75	5.00
	1958	—	—	—	Proof	40.00
	1959	36.000	.10	.25	.75	5.00
	1959	—	—	—	Proof	35.00
	1960	40.000	.10	.25	.75	5.00
	1960	—	—	—	Proof	35.00
	1961	52.000	—	.10	.35	3.00
	1961	—	—	—	Proof	35.00
	1962	57.000	—	.10	.35	3.00
	1962	—	—	—	Proof	35.00
	1963	70.000	—	.10	.35	3.00
	1963	—	—	—	Proof	35.00
	1964	73.000	—	.10	.35	3.00
	1964	—	—	—	Proof	35.00
	1965	91.000	—	.10	.35	2.00
	1965	—	—	—	Proof	35.00
	1966 large date	104.000	—	.10	.25	2.00
	1966 large date	—	—	—	Proof	35.00
	1966 small date	Inc. Ab.	—	.10	.25	2.00
	1966 small date	—	—	—	Proof	20.00
	1967	140.000	—	.10	.25	2.00
	1967	—	—	—	Proof	25.00
	1968	28.000	—	.10	.25	2.00
	1968	—	—	—	Proof	20.00
	1969 fish privy mark	50.000	—	.10	.25	2.00
	1969 fish privy mark	—	—	—	Proof	20.00
	1969 cock privy mark	50.000	—	.10	.25	2.00
	1969 cock privy mark	—	—	—	Proof	20.00
	1970	100.000	—	.10	.15	1.50
	1970	—	—	—	Proof	20.00
	1971	70.000	—	.10	.15	1.50
	1972	40.000	—	—	.10	1.00
	1973	34.000	—	—	.10	1.00
	1974	46.000	—	—	.10	1.00
	1975	25.000	—	—	.10	1.00
	1976	15.000	—	—	.10	1.00
	1977	15.000	—	—	.10	1.00
	1978	15.000	—	—	.10	1.00
	1979	15.000	—	—	.10	1.00
	1980 cock & star privy mark	15.300	—	—	.10	.30

2-1/2 CENTS

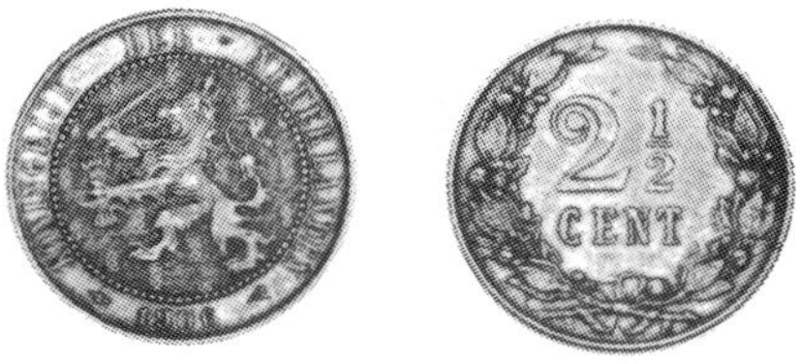

BRONZE
Obv: 15 large shields in field.

KM#	Date	Mintage	Fine	VF	XF	Unc
134	1903	4.000	2.00	4.00	8.00	30.00
	1904	4.000	2.00	4.00	8.00	30.00
	1905	4.000	2.00	4.00	8.00	30.00
	1906	8.000	2.00	4.00	8.00	30.00

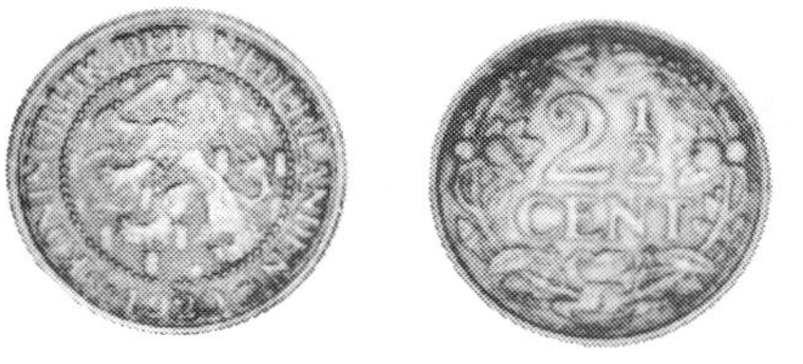

KM#	Date	Mintage	Fine	VF	XF	Unc
150	1912	2.000	5.00	15.00	25.00	60.00
	1913	4.000	3.00	5.00	8.00	28.00
	1914	2.000	5.00	15.00	25.00	60.00
	1915	3.000	4.00	10.00	20.00	55.00
	1916	8.000	2.00	4.00	8.00	22.50
	1918	4.000	3.00	5.00	10.00	28.00
	1919	2.000	4.00	8.00	20.00	45.00
	1929	8.000	2.00	4.00	6.00	15.00
	1941	19.800	1.25	2.00	3.00	6.00

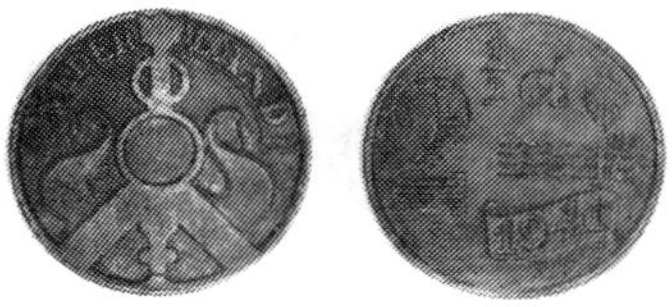

ZINC

KM#	Date	Mintage	Fine	VF	XF	Unc
171	1941	27.600	1.00	3.50	8.00	25.00
	1942	*.200	500.00	2000.	4000.	8000.

***NOTE:** Almost entire issue melted, about 30 pcs. known.

5 CENTS

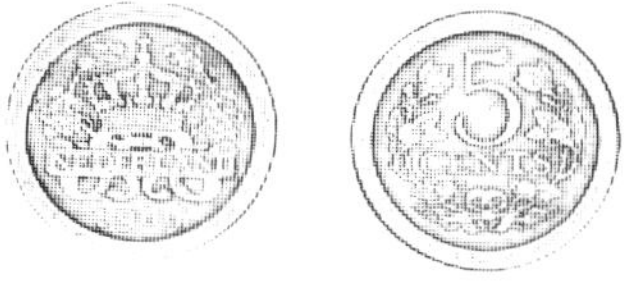

COPPER-NICKEL

KM#	Date	Mintage	Fine	VF	XF	Unc
137	1907	6.000	3.00	8.00	12.00	40.00
	1908	5.430	4.00	10.00	15.00	45.00
	1909	2.570	20.00	40.00	60.00	120.00

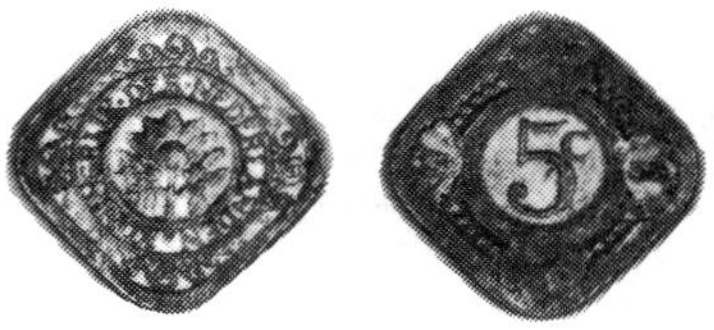

KM#	Date	Mintage	Fine	VF	XF	Unc
153	1913	6.000	1.50	3.00	8.00	30.00
	1914	7.400	1.50	3.00	8.00	30.00
	1923	10.000	1.50	3.00	8.00	30.00
	1929	8.000	1.50	3.00	8.00	30.00
	1932	2.000	6.00	15.00	25.00	50.00
	1933	1.400	20.00	40.00	60.00	100.00
	1934	2.600	4.00	8.00	15.00	35.00
	1936	2.600	4.00	8.00	15.00	35.00
	1938	4.200	2.00	4.00	6.00	15.00
	1939	4.600	2.00	4.00	6.00	15.00
	1940	7.200	2.00	4.00	6.00	15.00

NOTE: For a similar coin dated 1943, see Netherlands Antilles (Curacao).

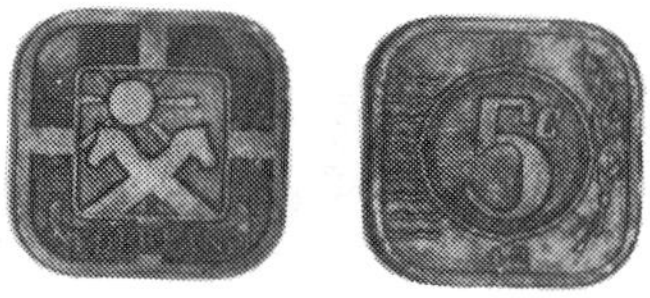

ZINC

KM#	Date	Mintage	Fine	VF	XF	Unc
172	1941	32.200	1.00	2.50	6.00	20.00
	1942	11.800	2.50	4.00	8.00	30.00
	1943	7.000	6.00	12.00	20.00	60.00

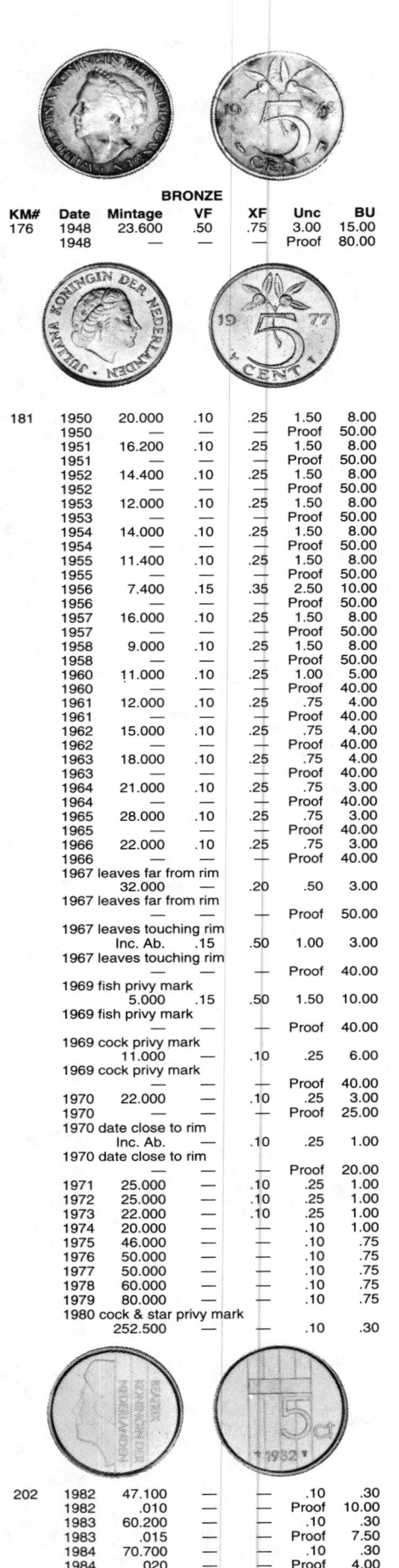

BRONZE

KM#	Date	Mintage	VF	XF	Unc	BU
176	1948	23.600	.50	.75	3.00	15.00
	1948	—	—	—	Proof	80.00
181	1950	20.000	.10	.25	1.50	8.00
	1950	—	—	—	Proof	50.00
	1951	16.200	.10	.25	1.50	8.00
	1951	—	—	—	Proof	50.00
	1952	14.400	.10	.25	1.50	8.00
	1952	—	—	—	Proof	50.00
	1953	12.000	.10	.25	1.50	8.00
	1953	—	—	—	Proof	50.00
	1954	14.000	.10	.25	1.50	8.00
	1954	—	—	—	Proof	50.00
	1955	11.400	.10	.25	1.50	8.00
	1955	—	—	—	Proof	50.00
	1956	7.400	.15	.35	2.50	10.00
	1956	—	—	—	Proof	50.00
	1957	16.000	.10	.25	1.50	8.00
	1957	—	—	—	Proof	50.00
	1958	9.000	.10	.25	1.50	8.00
	1958	—	—	—	Proof	50.00
	1960	11.000	.10	.25	1.00	5.00
	1960	—	—	—	Proof	40.00
	1961	12.000	.10	.25	.75	4.00
	1961	—	—	—	Proof	40.00
	1962	15.000	.10	.25	.75	4.00
	1962	—	—	—	Proof	40.00
	1963	18.000	.10	.25	.75	4.00
	1963	—	—	—	Proof	40.00
	1964	21.000	.10	.25	.75	3.00
	1964	—	—	—	Proof	40.00
	1965	28.000	.10	.25	.75	3.00
	1965	—	—	—	Proof	40.00
	1966	22.000	.10	.25	.75	3.00
	1966	—	—	—	Proof	40.00
	1967 leaves far from rim					
		32.000	—	.20	.50	3.00
	1967 leaves far from rim					
		—	—	—	Proof	50.00
	1967 leaves touching rim					
		Inc. Ab.	.15	.50	1.00	3.00
	1967 leaves touching rim					
		—	—	—	Proof	40.00
	1969 fish privy mark					
		5.000	.15	.50	1.50	10.00
	1969 fish privy mark					
		—	—	—	Proof	40.00
	1969 cock privy mark					
		11.000	—	.10	.25	6.00
	1969 cock privy mark					
		—	—	—	Proof	40.00
	1970	22.000	—	.10	.25	3.00
	1970	—	—	—	Proof	25.00
	1970 date close to rim					
		Inc. Ab.	—	.10	.25	1.00
	1970 date close to rim					
		—	—	—	Proof	20.00
	1971	25.000	—	.10	.25	1.00
	1972	25.000	—	.10	.25	1.00
	1973	22.000	—	.10	.25	1.00
	1974	20.000	—	—	.10	1.00
	1975	46.000	—	—	.10	.75
	1976	50.000	—	—	.10	.75
	1977	50.000	—	—	.10	.75
	1978	60.000	—	—	.10	.75
	1979	80.000	—	—	.10	.75
	1980 cock & star privy mark					
		252.500	—	—	.10	.30
202	1982	47.100	—	—	.10	.30
	1982	.010	—	—	Proof	10.00
	1983	60.200	—	—	.10	.30
	1983	.015	—	—	Proof	7.50
	1984	70.700	—	—	.10	.30
	1984	—	—	—	Proof	4.00
	1985	36.100	—	—	.10	.30
	1985	.017	—	—	Proof	4.00
	1986	7.700	—	—	.10	.80
	1986	.020	—	—	Proof	4.00
	1987	33.300	—	—	.10	.30

KM#	Date	Mintage	VF	XF	Unc	BU
202	1987	.018	—	—	Proof	4.00
	1988	22.600	—	—	—	.30
	1988	.020	—	—	Proof	4.00
	1989	27.100	—	—	—	.30
	1989	.015	—	—	Proof	4.00
	1990	39.300	—	—	—	.30
	1990	.015	—	—	Proof	4.00
	1991	73.100	—	—	—	.30
	1991	.014	—	—	Proof	4.00
	1992	52.700	—	—	—	.30
	1992	.013	—	—	Proof	4.00
	1993	40.000	—	—	—	.30
	1993	.012	—	—	Proof	4.00
	1994	14.000	—	—	—	.50
	1994	.013	—	—	Proof	4.00
	1995	6.000	—	—	—	.30
	1995	.012	—	—	Proof	4.00
	1996	40.000	—	—	—	.30
	1996	.014	—	—	Proof	4.00
	1997	36.000	—	—	—	.30
	1997	.012	—	—	Proof	4.00
	1998	—	—	—	—	.30
	1998	—	—	—	Proof	4.00
	1999	—	—	—	—	.30
	1999	—	—	—	Proof	4.00

10 CENTS

1.4000 g, .640 SILVER, .0288 oz ASW
Obv: Small head, divided legend.

KM#	Date	Mintage	Fine	VF	XF	Unc
119	1901	2.000	10.00	25.00	60.00	150.00

NOTE: Earlier date (1898) exists for this type.

Obv: Large head.

135	1903	6.000	3.00	10.00	22.50	50.00

Obv: Small head, continuous legend.

136	1904	3.000	5.00	15.00	30.00	75.00
	1905	2.000	7.00	20.00	40.00	100.00
	1906	4.000	3.00	10.00	22.50	60.00
145	1910	2.250	10.00	25.00	50.00	125.00
	1911	4.000	4.00	10.00	25.00	60.00
	1912	4.000	4.00	10.00	25.00	60.00
	1913	5.000	4.00	10.00	25.00	60.00
	1914	9.000	1.50	4.00	10.00	25.00
	1915	5.000	1.50	4.00	10.00	25.00
	1916	5.000	1.50	4.00	10.00	25.00
	1917	10.000	1.00	3.00	8.00	20.00
	1918	20.000	.75	2.00	6.00	18.00
	1919	10.000	1.00	3.00	8.00	20.00
	1921	5.000	1.50	5.00	8.00	25.00
	1925	5.000	1.50	5.00	8.00	25.00
163	1926	2.700	2.00	6.00	12.00	50.00
	1927	2.300	2.00	6.00	12.00	50.00
	1928	10.000	.50	1.50	4.00	20.00
	1930	5.000	.75	2.50	5.00	22.00
	1934	2.000	2.00	6.00	12.00	50.00
	1935	8.000	.50	1.00	2.00	12.00
	1936	15.000	.25	.50	1.50	5.00
	1937	18.600	.25	.50	1.50	5.00
	1938	21.400	.25	.50	1.50	4.00
	1939	20.000	.25	.50	1.50	4.00
	1941	43.000	.25	.40	1.00	3.00
	1943P acorn privy mark					
		Inc. Be.	.50	1.00	2.00	8.00
	1944P	120.000	.25	.40	.75	2.00
	1944D	25.400	1000.	2000.	2800.	4500.
	1944S	64.040	.50	1.25	2.50	12.00
	1945P	90.560	150.00	300.00	600.00	800.00

NOTE: For similar coins dated 1941P-1943P with palm tree privy mark, see Netherlands Antilles (Curacao) and Surinam.

ZINC

KM#	Date	Mintage	Fine	VF	XF	Unc
173	1941	29.800	.75	1.50	4.00	20.00
	1942	95.600	.25	.50	1.50	15.00
	1943	29.000	.75	1.50	4.00	20.00

NICKEL

KM#	Date	Mintage	VF	XF	Unc	BU
177	1948	69.200	.25	.50	1.00	6.00
	1948	—	—	—	Proof	90.00
182	1950	56.600	.10	.35	.75	4.00
	1950	—	—	—	Proof	60.00
	1951	54.200	.10	.35	.75	4.00
	1951	—	—	—	Proof	60.00
	1954	8.200	.20	.50	1.00	8.00
	1954	—	—	—	Proof	60.00
	1955	18.200	.10	.35	.75	4.00
	1955	—	—	—	Proof	60.00
	1956	12.000	.10	.35	.75	4.00
	1956	—	—	—	Proof	60.00
	1957	18.600	.10	.35	.75	4.00
	1957	—	—	—	Proof	60.00
	1958	34.000	.10	.35	.75	3.00
	1958	—	—	—	Proof	60.00
	1959	44.000	.10	.35	.75	3.00
	1959	—	—	—	Proof	50.00
	1960	12.000	.10	.35	.75	3.50
	1960	—	—	—	Proof	50.00
	1961	25.000	—	.10	.25	2.50
	1961	—	—	—	Proof	50.00
	1962	30.000	—	.10	.25	2.50
	1962	—	—	—	Proof	50.00
	1963	35.000	—	.10	.25	2.50
	1963	—	—	—	Proof	60.00
	1964	41.000	—	.10	.25	2.50
	1964	—	—	—	Proof	60.00
	1965	59.000	—	.10	.25	2.50
	1965	—	—	—	Proof	60.00
	1966	44.000	—	—	.10	2.00
	1966	—	—	—	Proof	50.00
	1967	39.000	—	—	.10	2.00
	1967	—	—	—	Proof	50.00
	1968	42.000	—	—	.10	2.00
	1968	—	—	—	Proof	40.00
	1969 fish privy mark					
		29.100	—	—	.10	1.50
	1969 fish privy mark					
		—	—	—	Proof	40.00
	1969 cock privy mark					
		24.000	—	—	.10	1.50
	1969 cock privy mark					
		—	—	—	Proof	40.00
	1970	50.000	—	—	.10	1.00
	1970	—	—	—	Proof	40.00
	1971	55.000	—	—	.10	1.00
	1972	60.000	—	—	.10	1.00
	1973	90.000	—	—	.10	1.00
	1974	75.000	—	—	.10	2.00
	1975	110.000	—	—	.10	1.00
	1976	85.000	—	—	.10	1.00
	1977	100.000	—	—	.10	1.00
	1978	110.000	—	—	.10	1.00
	1979	120.000	—	—	.10	1.00
	1980 cock & star privy mark					
		195.300	—	—	.10	.50

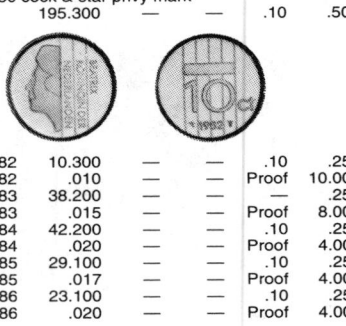

KM#	Date	Mintage	VF	XF	Unc	BU
203	1982	10.300	—	—	.10	.25
	1982	.010	—	—	Proof	10.00
	1983	38.200	—	—	—	.25
	1983	.015	—	—	Proof	8.00
	1984	42.200	—	—	.10	.25
	1984	.020	—	—	Proof	4.00
	1985	29.100	—	—	.10	.25
	1985	.017	—	—	Proof	4.00
	1986	23.100	—	—	.10	.25
	1986	.020	—	—	Proof	4.00

KM#	Date	Mintage	VF	XF	Unc	BU
203	1987	21.700	—	—	.10	.25
	1987	.018	—	—	Proof	4.00
	1988	2.200	—	.10	.20	.75
	1988	.020	—	—	Proof	4.00
	1989	5.300	—	—	—	.25
	1989	.015	—	—	Proof	4.00
	1990	13.300	—	—	—	.25
	1990	.015	—	—	Proof	4.00
	1991	41.100	—	—	—	.25
	1991	.014	—	—	Proof	4.00
	1992	41.300	—	—	—	.25
	1992	.013	—	—	Proof	4.00
	1993	30.100	—	—	—	.25
	1993	.012	—	—	Proof	4.00
	1994	25.685	—	—	—	.25
	1994	.013	—	—	Proof	4.00
	1995	35.100	—	—	—	.25
	1995	.012	—	—	Proof	4.00
	1996	34.900	—	—	—	.25
	1996	.014	—	—	Proof	4.00
	1997	20.100	—	—	—	.25
	1997	.012	—	—	Proof	4.00
	1998	—	—	—	—	.25
	1998	—	—	—	Proof	4.00
	1999	—	—	—	—	.25
	1999	—	—	—	Proof	4.00

25 CENTS

3.5750 g, .640 SILVER, .0736 oz ASW
Obv: Bust w/wide truncation.

KM#	Date	Mintage	Fine	VF	XF	Unc
120.1	1901	1.600	35.00	80.00	175.00	400.00

NOTE: Earlier date (1898) exists for this type.

Obv: Bust w/narrow truncation.

120.2	1901	Inc. Ab.	7.00	25.00	50.00	125.00
	1901	3 pcs.	—	—	Proof	1400.
	1902	1.200	7.00	25.00	50.00	125.00
	1903	1.200	7.00	25.00	50.00	125.00
	1904	1.600	6.00	22.50	45.00	110.00
	1905	1.200	7.00	25.00	50.00	125.00
	1906	2.000	5.00	20.00	40.00	90.00

146	1910	.880	15.00	40.00	80.00	200.00
	1910	—	—	—	Proof	350.00
	1911	1.600	6.00	20.00	40.00	100.00
	1912	1.600	6.00	20.00	40.00	100.00
	1913	1.200	8.00	25.00	50.00	150.00
	1914	5.600	2.50	10.00	20.00	60.00
	1915	2.000	3.00	10.00	20.00	80.00
	1916	2.000	2.50	10.00	20.00	80.00
	1917	4.000	2.50	8.00	15.00	60.00
	1918	6.000	2.00	6.00	12.00	40.00
	1919	4.000	2.50	8.00	15.00	60.00
	1925	2.000	2.50	10.00	20.00	80.00

164	1926	2.000	5.00	15.00	25.00	80.00
	1928	8.000	.75	1.50	5.00	20.00
	1939	4.000	.75	2.00	4.00	8.00
	1940	9.000	.50	1.00	3.00	6.00
	1941	40.000	.35	.60	1.50	2.50
1943P acorn privy mark		Inc. Be.	.50	1.25	3.50	12.00
1944P acorn privy mark		40.000	.35	.60	1.50	2.50
1945P acorn privy mark		92.000	40.00	110.00	250.00	450.00

NOTE: For similar coins dated 1941P and 1943P with palm tree privy mark, see Netherlands Antilles (Curacao).

ZINC

174	1941	34.600	.50	1.00	3.00	30.00

KM#	Date	Mintage	Fine	VF	XF	Unc	BU
174	1942	27.800	.50	1.00	3.00	30.00	
	1943	13.600	2.00	5.00	10.00	60.00	

NICKEL

KM#	Date	Mintage	VF	XF	Unc	BU
178	1948	27.400	.25	.50	1.50	8.00
	1948	—	—	—	Proof	90.00

183	1950	43.000	.20	.30	1.50	4.00
	1950	—	—	—	Proof	65.00
	1951	33.200	.20	.30	1.50	5.00
	1951	—	—	—	Proof	65.00
	1954	6.400	.50	1.50	2.00	10.00
	1954	—	—	—	Proof	65.00
	1955	10.000	.20	.30	1.50	5.00
	1955	—	—	—	Proof	65.00
	1956	8.000	.20	.30	1.50	7.00
	1956	—	—	—	Proof	65.00
	1957	8.000	.20	.30	1.50	7.00
	1957	—	—	—	Proof	65.00
	1958	15.000	.20	.30	1.00	3.00
	1958	—	—	—	Proof	65.00
	1960	9.000	.20	.30	1.50	8.00
	1960	—	—	—	Proof	60.00
	1961	6.000	.40	1.25	1.50	6.00
	1961	—	—	—	Proof	50.00
	1962	12.000	.20	.30	1.00	2.00
	1962	—	—	—	Proof	50.00
	1963	18.000	.20	.30	1.00	2.00
	1963	—	—	—	Proof	50.00
	1964	25.000	.20	.30	1.00	2.00
	1964	—	—	—	Proof	50.00
	1965	18.000	.20	.30	1.00	2.00
	1965	—	—	—	Proof	50.00
	1966	25.000	—	.20	.75	1.50
	1966	—	—	—	Proof	50.00
	1967	18.000	—	.20	.75	1.50
	1967	—	—	—	Proof	60.00
	1968	26.000	—	.20	.75	1.50
	1968	—	—	—	Proof	60.00
1969 fish privy mark		14.000	—	.20	.30	1.00
1969 fish privy mark		—	—	—	Proof	60.00
1969 cock privy mark		21.000	—	.20	.75	1.50
1969 cock privy mark		—	—	—	Proof	60.00
	1970	39.000	—	.20	.30	1.00
	1970	—	—	—	Proof	60.00
	1971	40.000	—	.20	.30	1.00
	1972	50.000	—	.20	.30	1.00
	1973	45.000	—	.20	.30	1.00
	1974	10.000	—	.20	.50	1.50
	1975	25.000	—	.20	.30	1.00
	1976	64.000	—	.20	.30	1.00
	1977	55.000	—	.20	.30	1.00
	1978	35.000	—	.20	.30	1.00
	1979	45.000	—	.20	.30	1.00
1980 cock & star privy mark		159.300	—	.20	—	.50

ALUMINUM

183a	1980	15 pcs.	—	—	—	400.00

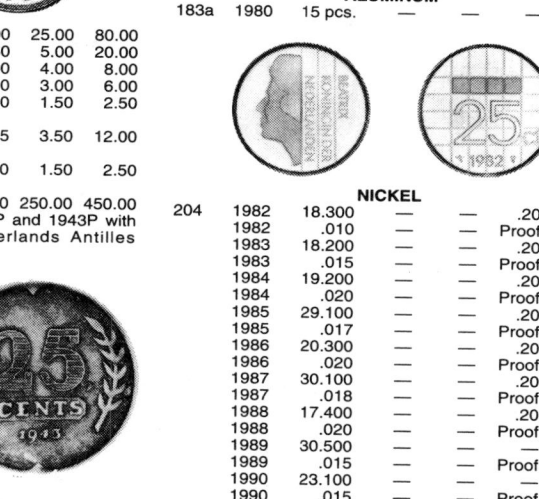

NICKEL

204	1982	18.300	—	—	.20	.25
	1982	.010	—	—	Proof	15.00
	1983	18.200	—	—	.20	.25
	1983	.015	—	—	Proof	12.00
	1984	19.200	—	—	.20	.25
	1984	.020	—	—	Proof	6.00
	1985	29.100	—	—	.20	.25
	1985	.017	—	—	Proof	6.00
	1986	20.300	—	—	.20	.25
	1986	.020	—	—	Proof	6.00
	1987	30.100	—	—	.20	.25
	1987	.018	—	—	Proof	6.00
	1988	17.400	—	—	.20	.25
	1988	.020	—	—	Proof	6.00
	1989	30.500	—	—	—	.25
	1989	.015	—	—	Proof	6.00
	1990	23.100	—	—	—	.25
	1990	.015	—	—	Proof	6.00
	1991	25.100	—	—	—	.25

KM#	Date	Mintage	VF	XF	Unc	BU
204	1991	.014	—	—	Proof	6.00
	1992	41.600	—	—	—	.25
	1992	.013	—	—	Proof	6.00
	1993	15.100	—	—	—	.50
	1993	.012	—	—	Proof	6.00
	1994	1.700	—	—	—	1.25
	1994	.013	—	—	Proof	6.00
	1995	30.300	—	—	—	1.00
	1995	.012	—	—	Proof	6.00
	1996	24.900	—	—	—	.25
	1996	.014	—	—	Proof	6.00
	1997	29.900	—	—	—	.25
	1997	.012	—	—	Proof	6.00
	1998	—	—	—	—	.25
	1998	—	—	—	Proof	6.00
	1999	—	—	—	—	.25
	1999	—	—	—	Proof	6.00

1/2 GULDEN
(50 Cents)

5.0000 g, .945 SILVER, .1519 oz ASW
Rev: W/o 50 C. below shield.

KM#	Date	Mintage	Fine	VF	XF	Unc
121.2	1904	1.000	20.00	50.00	100.00	250.00
	1905	4.000	6.00	15.00	35.00	80.00
	1906	1.000	20.00	50.00	100.00	250.00
	1907	3.300	6.00	15.00	35.00	80.00
	1907	—	—	—	Proof	300.00
	1908	4.000	6.00	15.00	35.00	80.00
	1909	3.000	6.00	15.00	35.00	80.00

147	1910	4.000	6.00	15.00	40.00	100.00
	1912	4.000	6.00	15.00	40.00	100.00
	1913	8.000	5.00	12.00	30.00	80.00
	1919	8.000	5.00	12.00	30.00	80.00

5.0000 g, .720 SILVER, .1157 oz ASW

160	1921	5.000	1.00	2.00	4.00	22.50
	1921	—	—	—	Proof	200.00
	1922	11.240	.75	1.50	3.00	15.00
	1928	5.000	.75	2.00	4.00	22.50
	1929	9.500	.75	1.50	3.00	12.50
	1930	18.500	.75	1.50	2.50	10.00

GULDEN
(100 Cents)

10.0000 g, .945 SILVER, .3038 oz ASW

122.1	1901	2.000	20.00	40.00	90.00	250.00
	1901	—	—	—	Proof	400.00

NOTE: Earlier date (1898) exists for this type.

Rev: W/o 100 C. below shield.

KM#	Date	Mintage	Fine	VF	XF	Unc
122.2	1904	2.000	12.00	20.00	40.00	120.00
	1905	1.000	20.00	40.00	90.00	200.00
	1905	—	—	—	Proof	650.00
	1906	.500	100.00	200.00	350.00	500.00
	1906	—	—	—	Proof	1000.
	1907	5.100	8.00	20.00	50.00	110.00
	1908	4.700	8.00	20.00	50.00	110.00
	1908	—	—	—	Proof	350.00
	1909	2.000	12.00	30.00	60.00	140.00

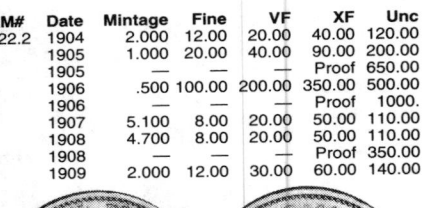

KM#	Date	Mintage	Fine	VF	XF	Unc
148	1910	1.000	30.00	60.00	200.00	400.00
	1910	—	—	—	Proof	600.00
	1911	2.000	25.00	50.00	150.00	350.00
	1912	3.000	8.00	20.00	45.00	110.00
	1913	8.000	6.00	18.00	40.00	100.00
	1914	15.785	5.00	15.00	30.00	80.00
	1915	14.215	5.00	15.00	30.00	80.00
	1916	5.000	15.00	30.00	60.00	175.00
	1917	2.300	20.00	35.00	70.00	185.00

10.0000 g, .720 SILVER, .2315 oz ASW
Obv. leg. ends below truncation.

KM#	Date	Mintage	Fine	VF	XF	Unc
161.1	1922	9.550	2.00	3.00	8.00	40.00
	1922	—	—	—	Proof	350.00
	1923	8.050	2.00	3.00	8.00	35.00
	1924	8.000	2.00	4.00	8.00	50.00
	1928	6.150	BV	2.00	6.00	25.00
	1929	32.350	BV	2.00	4.00	12.00
	1930	13.500	BV	2.00	4.00	15.00
	1931	38.100	BV	2.00	4.00	12.00
	1938	5.000	2.00	4.00	8.00	30.00
	1939	14.200	BV	BV	2.50	6.00
	1940	21.300	BV	BV	2.50	6.00
	1940	—	—	—	Proof	175.00
	1944P acorn privy mark					
	I.A.	50.00	125.00	200.00	375.00	

Obv. leg. ends at right of truncation.

KM#	Date	Mintage	Fine	VF	XF	Unc
161.2	1944P acorn privy mark					
	105.125	7.00	15.00	25.00	60.00	
	1945P acorn privy mark					
	25.375	200.00	400.00	500.00	1200.	

NOTE: For similar coins dated 1943D with palm tree privy mark, see Netherlands East Indies.

6.5000 g, .720 SILVER, .1504 oz ASW

KM#	Date	Mintage	VF	XF	Unc	BU
184	1954	6.600	—	BV	3.00	
	1954	—	—	—	Proof	65.00
	1955	37.500	—	BV	2.00	5.00
	1955	—	—	—	Proof	65.00
	1956	38.900	—	BV	2.00	5.00
	1956	—	—	—	Proof	65.00
	1957	27.000	—	BV	2.00	5.00
	1957	—	—	—	Proof	65.00
	1958	30.000	—	BV	2.00	5.00
	1958	—	—	—	Proof	65.00
	1963	5.000	—	BV	3.00	6.00
	1963	—	—	—	Proof	80.00
	1964	9.000	—	BV	2.00	4.00
	1964	—	—	—	Proof	80.00

KM#	Date	Mintage	VF	XF	Unc	BU
184	1965	21.000	—	BV	1.50	3.00
	1965	—	—	—	Proof	80.00
	1966	5.000	—	BV	2.00	4.00
	1966	—	—	—	Proof	80.00
	1967	7.000	—	BV	2.00	4.00
	1967	—	—	—	Proof	110.00

NICKEL

KM#	Date	Mintage	VF	XF	Unc	BU
184a	1967	31.000	—	.75	2.00	8.00
	1967	—	—	—	Proof	55.00
	1968	61.000	—	.75	2.00	8.00
	1969 fish	27.500	—	—	1.00	2.50
	1969 fish	—	—	—	Proof	50.00
	1969 cock					
		15.500	—	—	1.00	2.50
	1969 cock	—	—	—	Proof	50.00
	1970	18.000	—	.75	2.00	8.00
	1970	—	—	—	Proof	50.00
	1971	50.000	—	—	.75	3.00
	1972	60.000	—	—	.75	2.00
	1973	27.000	—	—	.75	3.00
	1975	9.000	—	—	.75	2.00
	1976	32.000	—	—	.75	2.00
	1977	38.000	—	—	.75	2.00
	1978	30.000	—	—	.75	2.00
	1979	25.000	—	—	.75	2.00
	1980 cock & star privy mark					
		118.300	—	—	.65	1.00

Investiture of New Queen

	Date	Mintage	VF	XF	Unc	BU
200	1980	30.500	—	—	.65	1.00

SILVER

	Date	Mintage	VF	XF	Unc	BU
200a	1980	157 pcs.	—	—	—	500.00

GOLD

	Date	Mintage	VF	XF	Unc	BU
200b	1980	7 pcs.	—	—	Rare	—

 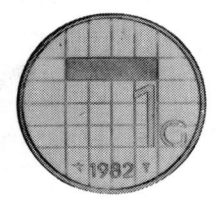

NICKEL

	Date	Mintage	VF	XF	Unc	BU
205	1982	31.300	—	—	—	1.00
	1982	.010	—	—	Proof	20.00
	1983	5.200	—	—	—	1.00
	1983	.015	—	—	Proof	15.00
	1984	4.200	—	—	—	1.00
	1984	.020	—	—	Proof	7.50
	1985	3.100	—	—	—	1.00
	1985	.017	—	—	Proof	7.50
	1986	12.100	—	—	—	1.00
	1986	.018	—	—	Proof	7.50
	1987	20.100	—	—	—	1.00
	1987	.020	—	—	Proof	7.50
	1988	13.600	—	—	—	1.00
	1988	.020	—	—	Proof	7.50
	1989	1.100	—	—	—	2.00
	1989	.015	—	—	Proof	7.50
	1990	1.100	—	—	—	2.00
	1990	.015	—	—	Proof	7.50
	1991	.500	—	—	—	2.00
	1991	.014	—	—	Proof	7.50
	1992	10.100	—	—	—	1.00
	1992	.013	—	—	Proof	7.50
	1993	15.100	—	—	—	1.00
	1993	.012	—	—	Proof	7.50
	1994	16.600	—	—	—	1.00
	1994	.013	—	—	Proof	7.50
	1995	12.600	—	—	—	1.00
	1995	.012	—	—	Proof	7.50
	1996	6.660	—	—	—	1.00
	1996	.014	—	—	Proof	7.50
	1997	12.800	—	—	—	1.00
	1997	.012	—	—	Proof	7.50
	1998	—	—	—	—	1.00
	1998	—	—	—	Proof	7.50
	1999	—	—	—	—	1.00
	1999	—	—	—	Proof	7.50

2-1/2 GULDEN

25.0000 g, .720 SILVER, .5787 oz ASW

KM#	Date	Mintage	Fine	VF	XF	Unc
165	1929	4.400	5.00	8.00	12.00	30.00
	1930	11.600	4.00	6.00	9.00	18.00
	1931	4.400	4.00	6.00	9.00	18.00
	1932	6.320	4.00	7.00	10.00	20.00
	1932 deep hair lines					
	Inc. Ab.	40.00	100.00	150.00	250.00	
	1933	3.560	6.00	10.00	15.00	30.00
	1937	4.000	5.00	7.00	10.00	20.00
	1938	2.000	6.00	10.00	15.00	30.00
	1938 deep hair lines					
	Inc. Ab.	25.00	50.00	100.00	200.00	
	1939	3.760	4.00	6.00	9.00	20.00
	1940	4.640	12.00	18.00	30.00	50.00

NOTE: For similar coins dated 1943D with palm tree privy mark, see Netherlands East Indies.

15.0000 g, .720 SILVER, .3472 oz ASW

KM#	Date	Mintage	VF	XF	Unc	BU
185	1959	7.200	—	BV	3.00	8.00
	1959	—	—	—	Proof	175.00
	1960	12.800	—	BV	3.00	8.00
	1960	—	—	—	Proof	175.00
	1961	10.000	—	BV	3.00	8.00
	1961	—	—	—	Proof	175.00
	1962	5.000	—	BV	4.00	10.00
	1962	—	—	—	Proof	175.00
	1963	4.000	BV	4.00	8.00	15.00
	1963	—	—	—	Proof	175.00
	1964	2.800	BV	4.00	8.00	15.00
	1964	—	—	—	Proof	175.00
	1966	5.000	—	BV	4.00	9.00
	1966	—	—	—	Proof	175.00

NICKEL

	Date	Mintage	VF	XF	Unc	BU
191	1969 fish privy mark					
		1.200	1.50	2.50	4.00	8.00
	1969 fish privy mark w/front hair lock					
		—	—	—	Proof	70.00
	1969 fish privy mark w/o front hair lock					
		—	—	—	Proof	Rare
	1969 cock privy mark					
		15.600	—	—	2.00	5.00
	1969 cock privy mark					
		—	—	—	Proof	70.00
	1970	22.000	—	—	1.50	3.00
	1970	—	—	—	Proof	70.00
	1971	8.000	—	—	1.50	3.00
	1972	20.000	—	—	1.50	3.00
	1978	5.000	—	—	1.50	3.00
	1980 cock & star privy mark					
		37.300	—	—	1.50	2.00

400th Anniversary - The Union of Utrecht

KM#	Date	Mintage	VF	XF	Unc	BU
197	1979	25.000	—	—	1.50	2.00

Investiture of New Queen

201	1980	30.500	—	—	—	2.00
			SILVER			
201a	1980	157 pcs.	—	—	—	500.00
			GOLD			
201b	1980	7 pcs.	—	—	Rare	—

NICKEL

206	1982	14.300	—	—	—	2.00
	1982	.010	—	—	Proof	35.00
	1983	3.800	—	—	—	2.00
	1983	.015	—	—	Proof	27.50
	1984	5.200	—	—	—	2.00
	1984	.020	—	—	Proof	16.00
	1985	3.100	—	—	—	2.00
	1985	.017	—	—	Proof	16.00
	1986	5.800	—	—	—	2.00
	1986	.020	—	—	Proof	16.00
	1987	2.500	—	—	—	2.00
	1987	.018	—	—	Proof	16.00
	1988	6.200	—	—	—	2.00
	1988	.020	—	—	Proof	16.00
	1989	4.100	—	—	—	2.00
	1989	.015	—	—	Proof	16.00
	1990	1.100	—	—	—	2.00
	1990	.015	—	—	Proof	16.00
	1991	.500	—	—	—	3.00
	1991	.014	—	—	Proof	16.00
	1992	.500	—	—	—	3.00
	1992	.013	—	—	Proof	16.00
	1993	.500	—	—	—	3.00
	1993	.012	—	—	Proof	16.00
	1994	.500	—	—	—	3.00
	1994	.013	—	—	Proof	16.00
	1995	.200	—	—	—	4.00
	1995	.012	—	—	Proof	16.00
	1996	.200	—	—	—	2.00
	1996	.014	—	—	Proof	16.00
	1997	.300	—	—	—	2.00
	1997	.012	—	—	Proof	16.00
	1998	—	—	—	—	2.00
	1998	—	—	—	Proof	16.00
	1999	—	—	—	—	2.00
	1999	—	—	—	Proof	16.00

5 GULDEN

3.3645 g, .900 GOLD, .0973 oz AGW

KM#	Date	Mintage	Fine	VF	XF	Unc
151	1912	1.000	40.00	60.00	100.00	150.00
	1912	120 pcs.	—	Matte Proof		700.00

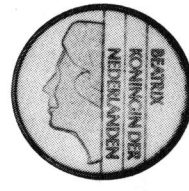 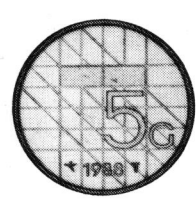

BRONZE CLAD NICKEL

KM#	Date	Mintage	VF	XF	Unc	BU
210	1987	2 pcs.	—	—	Proof	—
	1988	73.700	—	—	—	3.50
	1988	.020	—	—	Proof	5.00
	1989	69.100	—	—	—	3.50
	1989	.015	—	—	Proof	5.00
	1990	47.300	—	—	—	3.50
	1990	.015	—	—	Proof	5.00
	1991	17.100	—	—	—	3.50
	1991	.014	—	—	Proof	5.00
	1992	.500	—	—	—	4.50
	1992	.013	—	—	Proof	5.00
	1993	5.500	—	—	—	3.50
	1993	.012	—	—	Proof	5.00
	1994	.500	—	—	—	4.50
	1994	.013	—	—	Proof	5.00
	1995	.500	—	—	—	4.50
	1995	.012	—	—	Proof	5.00
	1996	.200	—	—	—	4.50
	1996	.014	—	—	Proof	5.00
	1997	.300	—	—	—	4.50
	1997	.012	—	—	Proof	5.00
	1998	—	—	—	—	4.50
	1998	—	—	—	Proof	5.00
	1999	—	—	—	—	4.50
	1999	—	—	—	Proof	5.00

10 GULDEN

6.7290 g, .900 GOLD, .1947 oz AGW

KM#	Date	Mintage	Fine	VF	XF	Unc
149	1911	.775	—	BV	75.00	100.00
	1911	8 pcs.	—	—	Proof	1750.
	1912	3.000	—	BV	75.00	100.00
	1912	20 pcs.	—	—	Proof	1500.
	1913	1.133	—	BV	75.00	100.00
	1917	4.000	—	BV	75.00	100.00

162	1925	2.000	—	BV	75.00	100.00
	1925	12 pcs.	—	—	Proof	1500.
	1926	2.500	—	BV	75.00	100.00
	1926	—	—	—	Proof	1300.
	1927	1.000	—	BV	75.00	100.00
	1932	4.324	—	BV	75.00	100.00
	1933	2.462	—	BV	75.00	100.00

TRADE COINAGE
DUCAT

3.5000 g, .983 GOLD, .1106 oz AGW
Mint: Utrecht

KM#	Date	Mintage	Fine	VF	XF	Unc
83.1	1901	.029	100.00	200.00	275.00	550.00
	1903/1	.091	250.00	500.00	1000.	1500.
	1903	Inc. Ab.	90.00	150.00	250.00	385.00
	1905	.088	90.00	150.00	250.00	385.00
	1906	.029	100.00	200.00	275.00	500.00
	1908	.091	90.00	150.00	250.00	385.00
	1909 halberd w/star privy mark					
		.106	80.00	140.00	225.00	385.00
	1909 sea horse privy mark					
		.030	125.00	225.00	300.00	500.00
	1910	.421	80.00	150.00	225.00	385.00
	1910	—	—	—	Proof	750.00
	1912	.148	80.00	150.00	225.00	385.00
	1912	—	—	—	Proof	650.00
	1913	.205	80.00	150.00	225.00	385.00
	1914	.247	80.00	150.00	225.00	385.00
	1916	.117	80.00	150.00	225.00	385.00
	1916	—	—	—	Proof	500.00

KM#	Date	Mintage	Fine	VF	XF	Unc
83.1	1917	.217	BV	65.00	80.00	120.00
	1920	.293	BV	65.00	80.00	120.00
	1920	—	—	—	Proof	650.00
	1921	.409	BV	60.00	70.00	100.00
	1922	.050	80.00	150.00	225.00	450.00
	1923	.107	BV	75.00	150.00	250.00
	1924	.084	BV	75.00	150.00	250.00
	1925	.573	BV	60.00	70.00	100.00
	1925	Inc. Ab.	—	—	Proof	275.00
	1926	.191	BV	60.00	80.00	120.00
	1927	.654	—	BV	45.00	55.00
	1928	.572	—	BV	45.00	55.00
	1932	.088	150.00	300.00	500.00	850.00
	1937	.117	BV	70.00	90.00	120.00

NOTE: Earlier dates (1849-1899) exist for this type.

NETHERLANDS ANTILLES

Caribbean Sea

COLOMBIA

VENEZUELA

The Netherlands Antilles, comprises two groups of islands in the West Indies: Aruba (until 1986), Bonaire and Curacao and their dependencies near the Venezuelan coast and St. Eustatius, Saba, and the southern part of St. Martin (St. Maarten) southeast of Puerto Rico. The island group has an area of 371 sq. mi. (960 sq. km.) and a population of 225,000. Capital: Willemstad. Chief industries are the refining of crude oil and tourism. Petroleum products and phosphates are exported.

On Dec. 15, 1954, the Netherlands Antilles were given complete domestic autonomy and granted equality within the Kingdom with Surinam and the Netherlands. On Jan. I, 1986, Aruba achieved "status aparte" as the fourth part of the Dutch realm which was a step towards total independence.

CURACAO

The island of Curacao, the largest of the Netherlands Antilles, which is an autonomous part of the Kingdom of the Netherlands located in the Caribbean Sea 40 miles off the coast of Venezuela, has an area of 173 sq. mi. (472 sq. km.) and a population of 127,900. Capital: Willemstad. The chief industries are banking and tourism. Salt, phosphates and cattle are exported.

Curacao was discovered by Spanish navigator Alonso de Ojeda in 1499 and was settled by Spain in 1527. The Dutch West India Company took the island from Spain in 1634 and administered it until 1787, when it was surrendered to the United Netherlands. The Dutch held it thereafter except for two periods during the Napoleonic Wars, 1800-1803 and 1807-16, when it was occupied by the British. During World War II, Curacao refined 60 percent of the oil used by the Allies; the refineries were protected by U.S. troops after Germany invaded the Netherlands in 1940.

MINT MARKS

D - Denver
P - Philadelphia
(u) - Utrecht

MONETARY SYSTEM
100 Cents = 1 Gulden

CENT

BRONZE

KM#	Date	Mintage	Fine	VF	XF	Unc
39	1942P	2.500	1.00	2.00	3.50	10.00

NOTE: This coin was also circulated in Surinam. For similar coins dated 1943P & 1957-1960, see Surinam.

41	1944D	3.000	.50	1.00	2.00	4.50
	1947(u)	1.500	.50	1.00	3.00	8.00
	1947(u)	80 pcs.	—	—	Proof	20.00

2-1/2 CENTS

BRONZE

42	1944D	1.000	.50	1.00	2.00	6.00
	1947(u)	.500	.50	1.00	2.50	7.00
	1947(u)	80 pcs.	—	—	Proof	20.00
	1948(u)	1.000	.25	.75	1.25	3.50
	1948(u)	75 pcs.	—	—	Proof	20.00

5 CENTS

COPPER-NICKEL

KM#	Date	Mintage	Fine	VF	XF	Unc
40	1943	8.595	1.25	2.50	4.00	7.00

NOTE: The above piece does not bear either a palm tree privy mark or a mint mark, but it was struck expressly for use in Curacao and Surinam. This homeland type of KM#153 was last issued in the Netherlands in 1940.

47	1948	1.000	.35	1.00	2.00	5.00
	1948	75 pcs.	—	—	Proof	40.00

1/10 GULDEN

1.4000 g, .640 SILVER, .0288 oz ASW

36	1901(u)	.300	8.00	16.00	35.00	90.00
	1901(u)	40 pcs.	—	—	Proof	250.00

43	1944D	1.500	.50	1.25	2.50	6.50
	1947(u)	1.000	.50	1.25	2.50	6.50
	1947(u)	80 pcs.	—	—	Proof	60.00

48	1948(u)	1.000	.50	1.25	2.50	6.50
	1948(u)	75 pcs.	—	—	Proof	60.00

10 CENTS

1.4000 g, .640 SILVER, .0288 oz ASW

37	1941P	.800	2.50	4.50	12.00	25.00
	1943P	4.500	1.50	3.00	7.50	18.00

NOTE: Both these coins were also circulated in Surinam. For coins dated 1942P, see Surinam.

1/4 GULDEN

3.5800 g, .640 SILVER, .0736 oz ASW

44	1944D	1.500	.65	1.50	3.00	7.00
	1947(u)	1.000	.65	1.50	3.00	7.00
	1947(u)	80 pcs.	—	—	Proof	80.00

25 CENTS

3.5800 g, .640 SILVER, .0736 oz ASW

38	1941P	1.100	1.50	3.50	6.00	12.50
	1943/1P	2.500	2.00	4.00	7.00	16.00
	1943P	Inc.Ab.	1.25	2.50	4.00	8.00

NOTE: Both coins were also circulated in Surinam. For similar coins dated 1943, 1944 & 1945-P with acorn mint mark see Netherlands.

GULDEN

10.0000 g, .720 SILVER, .2315 oz ASW

KM#	Date	Mintage	Fine	VF	XF	Unc
45	1944D	.500	2.50	4.50	9.00	18.00

2-1/2 GULDEN

25.0000 g, .720 SILVER, .5787 oz ASW

46	1944D	.200	—	BV	5.00	9.00

NETHERLANDS ANTILLES

RULERS
Juliana, 1948-1980
Beatrix, 1980

MINT MARKS
Utrecht - privy marks only
FM - Franklin Mint, U.S.A.
NOTE: See Kingdom of the Netherlands for more details.

NOTE: From 1975-1985 the Franklin Mint produced coinage in up to 3 different qualities. Qualities of issue are designated in ( ) after each date and are defined as follows:

(M) MATTE - Normal circulation strike or a dull finish produced by sandblasting special uncirculated (polish finish) or proof quality dies.

(U) SPECIAL UNCIRCULATED - Polished or proof-like in appearance without any frosted features.

(P) PROOF - The highest quality obtainable having mirror-like fields and frosted features.

MONETARY SYSTEM
100 Cents = 1 Gulden

CENT

BRONZE

1	1952	1.000	.50	1.50	3.00	9.00
	1952	100 pcs.	—	—	Proof	40.00
	1954	1.000	.35	.65	1.25	5.00
	1954	200 pcs.	—	—	Proof	20.00
	1957	1.000	.35	.65	1.25	3.00
	1957	250 pcs.	—	—	Proof	20.00
	1959	1.000	.35	.65	1.25	3.00
	1959	250 pcs.	—	—	Proof	20.00
	1960	300 pcs.	—	—	Proof	20.00
	1961	1.000	.25	.50	1.00	1.75
	1961	—	—	—	Proof	20.00
	1963	1.000	.25	.50	1.00	1.75
	1963	—	—	—	Proof	20.00
	1964	—	—	—	Proof	25.00
	1965	1.200	.25	.50	1.00	2.00

mark see Netherlands.

KM#	Date	Mintage	Fine	VF	XF	Unc
1	1965	—	—	—	Proof	20.00
	1967	.850	.25	.50	1.00	2.00
	1967	—	—	—	Proof	20.00
	1968 fish	.900	.25	.50	1.00	2.00
	1968 star & fish					
		.700	1.00	1.50	3.00	6.00
	1970	.200	.50	1.00	2.00	4.00
	1970	—	—	—	Proof	20.00

KM#	Date	Mintage	Fine	VF	XF	Unc
8	1970	1.200	.10	.25	.50	.85
	1970	—	—	—	Proof	17.50
	1971	3.000	.10	.15	.25	.75
	1971	—	—	—	Proof	17.50
	1972	1.000	.10	.15	.25	.75
	1973	3.000	.10	.15	.25	.50
	1973	—	—	—	Proof	17.50
	1974	3.000	.10	.15	.25	.50
	1974	—	—	—	Proof	17.50
	1975	2.000	.10	.15	.25	.50
	1975	—	—	—	Proof	17.50
	1976	3.000	—	—	.10	.25
	1977	4.000	—	—	.10	.15	.25
	1978	2.000	—	—	.10	.15	.25

ALUMINUM

KM#	Date	Mintage	Fine	VF	XF	Unc
8a	1979	7.500	—	—	.10	.15	.25
	1979	—	—	—	Proof	7.50
	1980	2.500	—	—	.10	.15	.25
	1981	2.400	—	—	.10	.15	.25
	1982	2.400	—	—	.10	.15	.25
	1983	2.900	—	—	.10	.15	.25
	1984	3.600	—	—	.10	.15	.25
	1985	3.000	—	—	.10	.15	.25

KM#	Date	Mintage	Fine	VF	XF	Unc
32	1989	1.350	—	—	—	.20
	1990	2.700	—	—	—	.20
	1991	4.000	—	—	—	.20
	1992	3.038	—	—	—	.20
	1993	3.988	—	—	—	.20
	1994	—	—	—	—	.20
	1995	—	—	—	—	.20
	1996	—	—	—	—	.20
	1997	—	—	—	—	.20
	1998	—	—	—	—	.20

2-1/2 CENTS

BRONZE

KM#	Date	Mintage	Fine	VF	XF	Unc
5	1956	.400	.50	1.00	2.50	5.50
	1956	500 pcs.	—	—	Proof	30.00
	1959	1.000	.25	.50	1.00	2.00
	1959	250 pcs.	—	—	Proof	30.00
	1965 fish	.500	.25	.50	1.25	3.00
	1965	—	—	—	Proof	25.00
	1965 fish & star					
		.150	.75	1.00	4.00	12.00

KM#	Date	Mintage	Fine	VF	XF	Unc
9	1970	.500	.15	.35	.75	1.50
	1970	—	—	—	Proof	20.00
	1971	3.000	.10	.20	.40	.60
	1971	—	—	—	Proof	20.00
	1973	1.000	.10	.20	.40	.60
	1973	—	—	—	Proof	20.00
	1974	1.000	.10	.20	.40	.60
	1974	—	—	—	Proof	20.00
	1975	1.000	.10	.20	.40	.60
	1976	1.000	.10	.20	.40	.60
	1977	1.000	.10	.20	.40	.60
	1978	1.500	.10	.20	.40	.60

ALUMINUM

KM#	Date	Mintage	Fine	VF	XF	Unc
9a	1979	2.000	—	.10	.20	.45
	1979	—	—	—	Proof	10.00
	1980	2.000	—	.10	.20	.45
	1981	1.000	—	.10	.20	.45
	1982	1.000	—	.10	.20	.45
	1983	1.000	—	.10	.20	.45
	1984	1.000	—	.10	.20	.45
	1985	1.000	—	.10	.20	.45

5 CENTS

COPPER-NICKEL

KM#	Date	Mintage	Fine	VF	XF	Unc
6	1957	.500	.25	.75	1.25	2.50
	1957	250 pcs.	—	—	Proof	40.00
	1962	.250	.50	1.00	2.00	5.00
	1962	200 pcs.	—	—	Proof	30.00
	1963	.400	.25	.50	1.00	2.00
	1963	—	—	—	Proof	30.00
	1965	.500	.25	.50	1.00	2.00
	1965	—	—	—	Proof	30.00
	1967	.600	.25	.50	1.00	2.00
	1967	—	—	—	Proof	30.00
	1970	.450	.25	.50	1.00	2.00
	1970	—	—	—	Proof	30.00

KM#	Date	Mintage	Fine	VF	XF	Unc
13	1971	2.000	.10	.20	.40	.75
	1971	—	—	—	Proof	22.50
	1974	.500	.25	.50	1.00	2.00
	1974	—	—	—	Proof	22.50
	1975	2.000	.10	.20	.40	.75
	1975	—	—	—	Proof	22.50
	1976	1.500	.10	.20	.40	.75
	1977	1.000	.10	.20	.40	.75
	1978	1.500	.10	.20	.40	.75
	1979	1.500	.10	.20	.40	.75
	1980	1.500	—	.10	.20	.50
	1981	1.000	—	.10	.20	.50
	1982	1.000	—	.10	.20	.50
	1983	1.000	—	.10	.20	.50
	1984	1.500	—	.10	.20	.50
	1985	1.500	—	.10	.20	.50

ALUMINUM

KM#	Date	Mintage	Fine	VF	XF	Unc
33	1989	.900	—	—	—	.50
	1990	1.800	—	—	—	.50
	1991	2.500	—	—	—	.50
	1992	1.588	—	—	—	.50
	1993	2.488	—	—	—	.50
	1994	1.488	—	—	—	.50
	1995	.988	—	—	—	.50
	1996	.788	—	—	—	.50
	1997	—	—	—	—	.50
	1998	—	—	—	—	.50

1/10 GULDEN

1.4000 g, .640 SILVER, .0288 oz ASW

KM#	Date	Mintage	Fine	VF	XF	Unc
3	1954	.200	2.00	4.00	8.00	20.00
	1954	200 pcs.	—	—	Proof	40.00
	1956	.250	1.00	2.00	3.50	7.50
	1956	500 pcs.	—	—	Proof	30.00
	1957	.250	1.00	2.00	3.50	7.50
	1957	250 pcs.	—	—	Proof	40.00
	1959	.250	1.00	2.00	3.50	7.50
	1959	250 pcs.	—	—	Proof	40.00
	1960	.400	BV	.50	1.00	2.50
	1960	300 pcs.	—	—	Proof	30.00
	1962	.400	BV	.50	1.00	2.50
	1962	200 pcs.	—	—	Proof	35.00
	1963	.900	BV	.50	1.00	2.00
	1963	—	—	—	Proof	35.00
	1966 fish	1.000	BV	.50	1.00	2.00
	1966 fish & star					
		.200	BV	.50	1.00	2.00
	1970	.300	BV	.50	1.00	2.00
	1970	—	—	—	Proof	35.00

10 CENTS

NICKEL

KM#	Date	Mintage	Fine	VF	XF	Unc
10	1970	1.000	—	.30	.75	1.25

KM#	Date	Mintage	Fine	VF	XF	Unc
10	1970	—	—	—	Proof	25.00
	1971	3.000	—	.15	.30	.50
	1971	—	—	—	Proof	25.00
	1974	1.000	—	.30	.75	1.75
	1974	—	—	—	Proof	25.00
	1975	1.500	—	.25	.50	1.00
	1975	—	—	—	Proof	25.00
	1976	2.000	—	.15	.30	.50
	1977	1.000	—	.15	.30	.50
	1978	1.500	—	.15	.30	.50
	1979	1.500	—	.15	.30	.50
	1979	—	—	—	Proof	12.50
	1980	1.500	—	.10	.20	.45
	1981	1.000	—	.10	.20	.45
	1982	1.000	—	.10	.20	.45
	1983	1.000	—	.10	.20	.45
	1984	1.000	—	.10	.20	.45
	1985	1.000	—	.10	.20	.45

NICKEL BONDED STEEL

KM#	Date	Mintage	Fine	VF	XF	Unc
34	1989	.900	—	—	—	.60
	1990	1.800	—	—	—	.45
	1991	2.500	—	—	—	.45
	1992	.888	—	—	—	.45
	1993	1.988	—	—	—	.45
	1994	.988	—	—	—	.45
	1995	.088	—	—	—	.45
	1996	.888	—	—	—	.45
	1997	—	—	—	—	.45
	1998	—	—	—	—	.45

1/4 GULDEN

3.5800 g, .640 SILVER, .0736 oz ASW

KM#	Date	Mintage	Fine	VF	XF	Unc
4	1954	.200	2.00	4.00	9.00	28.00
	1954	200 pcs.	—	—	Proof	45.00
	1956	.200	.75	1.50	3.00	12.00
	1956	500 pcs.	—	—	Proof	40.00
	1957	.200	.75	1.50	3.00	12.00
	1957	250 pcs.	—	—	Proof	45.00
	1960	.240	BV	.65	1.50	3.50
	1960	300 pcs.	—	—	Proof	40.00
	1962	.240	BV	.65	1.50	3.50
	1962	200 pcs.	—	—	Proof	40.00
	1963	.300	BV	.65	1.50	3.50
	1963	—	—	—	Proof	40.00
	1965	.500	BV	.65	1.50	3.50
	1965	—	—	—	Proof	40.00
	1967 fish	.310	BV	.65	1.50	3.50
	1967 fish	—	—	—	Proof	40.00
	1967 fish & star					
		.200	BV	.65	1.50	3.50
	1970	.150	BV	.65	1.50	3.50
	1970	—	—	—	Proof	35.00

25 CENTS

NICKEL

KM#	Date	Mintage	Fine	VF	XF	Unc
11	1970	.750	.30	.60	1.25	2.50
	1970	—	—	—	Proof	30.00
	1971	3.000	—	.30	.50	1.00
	1971	—	—	—	Proof	30.00
	1975	1.000	—	.30	.50	1.00
	1975	—	—	—	Proof	30.00
	1976	1.000	—	.30	.50	1.00
	1977	1.000	—	.30	.50	1.00
	1978	1.000	—	.25	.40	.75
	1979	1.000	—	.25	.40	.75
	1979	—	—	—	Proof	17.50
	1980 cock & star					
		1.000	—	.25	.40	.75
	1981	1.000	—	.25	.35	.60
	1982	1.000	—	.25	.35	.60
	1983	1.000	—	.25	.35	.60
	1984	1.000	—	.25	.35	.60
	1985	.750	—	.25	.35	.60

NICKEL BONDED STEEL

Obv: Orange blossom.

KM#	Date	Mintage	Fine	VF	XF	Unc
35	1989	.900	—	—	—	.60
	1990	1.800	—	—	—	.60
	1991	2.000	—	—	—	.60
	1992	.888	—	—	—	.60
	1993	.988	—	—	—	.60
	1994	.988	—	—	—	.60
	1995	.288	—	—	—	.60
	1996	.413	—	—	—	.60
	1997	—	—	—	—	.60
	1998	—	—	—	—	.60

50 CENTS

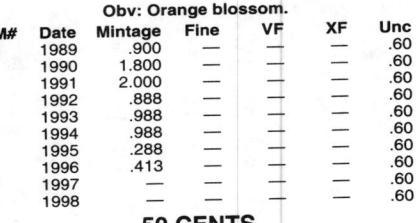

AUREATE STEEL

KM#	Date	Mintage	Fine	VF	XF	Unc
37	1989	.700	—	—	.60	1.25
	1990	1.400	—	—	.60	1.25
	1991	2.000	—	—	.60	1.25
	1992	1.188	—	—	.60	1.25
	1993	1.988	—	—	.60	1.25
	1994	.988	—	—	.60	1.25
	1995	9,000	—	In sets only		1.75
	1996	7,500	—	In sets only		1.75
	1997	—	—	—	.60	1.25
	1998	—	—	—	.60	1.25

2-1/2 GULDEN

AUREATE STEEL

KM#	Date	Mintage	Fine	VF	XF	Unc
38	1989	.020	—	—	—	3.50
	1990	.050	—	—	—	3.00
	1991	.050	—	—	—	3.00
	1992	.013	—	—	—	3.50
	1993	8,560	—	In sets only		4.25
	1994	9,000	—	In sets only		3.50
	1995	9,000	—	In sets only		3.50
	1996	7,500	—	In sets only		3.50
	1997	—	—	In sets only		3.50
	1998	—	—	—		3.50

AUREATE STEEL
Obv: Orange blossom.

KM#	Date	Mintage	Fine	VF	XF	Unc
36	1989	.300	—	—	—	.85
	1990	.600	—	—	—	.85
	1991	.500	—	—	—	.85
	1992	.038	—	—	—	1.00
	1993	8,560	—	In sets only		2.00
	1994	9,000	—	In sets only		1.50
	1995	9,000	—	In sets only		1.50
	1996	7,500	—	In sets only		1.50
	1997	—	—	—	—	.85
	1998	—	—	—	—	.85

GULDEN

10.0000 g, .720 SILVER, .2315 oz ASW

KM#	Date	Mintage	Fine	VF	XF	Unc
2	1952	1.000	BV	2.00	3.50	8.00
	1952	100 pcs.	—	—	Proof	125.00
	1963	.100	BV	2.50	4.00	10.00
	1963	—	—	—	Proof	100.00
	1964 fish	.300	BV	2.00	3.00	6.50
	1964	—	—	—	Proof	100.00
	1964 fish & star					
		.200	BV	2.50	4.00	10.00
	1970	.050	BV	2.50	5.00	12.50
	1970	—	—	—	Proof	100.00

25.0000 g, .720 SILVER, .5787 oz ASW

KM#	Date	Mintage	Fine	VF	XF	Unc
7	1964	—	—	—	BV	4.50	8.00
	1964	—	—	—	Proof	200.00

NICKEL
Obv: Bust of Queen Juliana.

KM#	Date	Mintage	Fine	VF	XF	Unc
12	1970	.500	.65	1.00	2.00	4.00
	1970	—	—	—	Proof	50.00
	1971	3.000	—	.75	1.50	3.00
	1971	—	—	—	Proof	50.00
	1978	.500	—	—	.75	1.50
	1979	.500	—	—	.75	1.50
	1979	—	—	—	Proof	25.00
	1980 cock & star					
		.500	—	—	.75	1.50

NICKEL
Obv: Bust of Queen Juliana.

KM#	Date	Mintage	Fine	VF	XF	Unc
19	1978	.100	—	—	2.00	4.00
	1979	.200	—	—	2.00	4.00
	1979	—	—	—	Proof	35.00
	1980 cock & star					
		.200	—	1.50	2.00	3.50

Obv: Bust of Queen Beatrix.

KM#	Date	Mintage	Fine	VF	XF	Unc
24	1980 cock & star					
		.200	—	.65	1.00	2.00
	1981	.200	—	.65	1.00	2.00
	1982	.500	—	—	.65	1.45
	1983	.500	—	—	.65	1.45
	1984	.500	—	—	.65	1.45
	1985	.400	—	—	.65	1.45

Obv: Bust of Queen Beatrix.

KM#	Date	Mintage	Fine	VF	XF	Unc
25	1980 cock & star					
		.100	—	—	2.00	4.00
	1981	.100	—	—	2.00	4.00
	1982	.100	—	—	2.00	4.00
	1984	.013	—	—	2.00	4.00
	1985	.013	—	—	2.00	4.00

NEW CALEDONIA

The French Overseas Territory of New Caledonia, a group of about 25 islands in the South Pacific, is situated about 750 miles (1,207 km.) east of Australia. The territory, which includes the dependencies of Ile des Pins, Loyalty Islands, Ile Huon, Isles Belep, Isles Chesterfield, and Ile Walpole, has a total land area of 7,358 sq. mi. (19,060 sq. km.) and a population of *156,000. Capital: Noumea. The islands are rich in minerals; New Caledonia has the world's largest known deposit of nickel. Nickel, nickel castings, coffee and copra are exported.

The first European to sight New Caledonia was the British navigator Capt. James Cook in 1774. The French took possession in 1853, and established a penal colony on the island in 1854. The European population of the colony remained disproportionately convict until 1894. New Caledonia became an overseas territory within the French Community in 1946, and in 1958 and 1972 chose to remain affiliated with France.

MINT MARKS
(a) - Paris, privy marks only

MONETARY SYSTEM
100 Centimes = 1 Franc

50 CENTIMES

ALUMINUM
Rev: Kagu bird.

KM#	Date	Mintage	VF	XF	Unc
1	1949(a)	1.000	.50	1.00	3.50

FRANC

ALUMINUM
Rev: Kagu bird.

2	1949(a)	4.000	.25	.75	2.50

8	1971(a)	1.000	.25	.75	2.00

Obv. leg: I.E.O.M. added.

10	1972(a)	.600	.25	.75	2.50
	1973(a)	1.000	.15	.25	.75
	1977(a)	1.500	.15	.25	.75
	1979(a)	—	.10	.20	.50
	1981(a)	1.000	.10	.20	.50
	1982(a)	1.000	.10	.20	.50
	1983(a)	2.000	.10	.20	.50
	1984(a)	—	.10	.20	.50
	1985(a)	2.000	.10	.20	.50
	1988(a)	2.000	.10	.20	.50
	1989(a)	1.000	.10	.20	.50
	1990(a)	—	.10	.20	.50
	1991(a)	—	.10	.20	.50
	1994(a)	—	.10	.20	.50

2 FRANCS

ALUMINUM
Rev: Kagu bird.

KM#	Date	Mintage	VF	XF	Unc
3	1949(a)	3.000	.50	1.50	4.50

9	1971(a)	1.000	.25	1.00	2.00

Obv. leg: I.E.O.M. added.

14	1973(a)	.400	.20	.75	2.50
	1977(a)	1.500	.20	.50	1.00
	1979(a)	—	.20	.40	.65
	1982(a)	1.000	.20	.35	.65
	1983(a)	2.000	.20	.35	.65
	1987(a)	2.000	.20	.35	.65
	1989(a)	1.200	.20	.35	.65
	1990(a)	—	.20	.35	.65
	1991(a)	—	.20	.35	.65
	1995(a)	—	.20	.35	.65

5 FRANCS

ALUMINUM
Rev: Kagu bird.

4	1952(a)	4.000	.50	1.00	3.50

Obv. leg: I.E.O.M. added.

16	1983(a)	.500	.50	1.00	2.50
	1986(a)	1.000	.50	1.00	2.50
	1989(a)	.500	.50	1.00	2.50
	1990(a)	—	.50	1.00	2.50
	1991(a)	—	.50	1.00	2.50
	1992(a)	—	.50	1.00	2.50
	1994(a)	—	.50	1.00	2.50

10 FRANCS

NICKEL

5	1967(a)	.400	1.00	2.00	4.50
	1970(a)	1.000	.50	.75	2.50

Obv. leg: I.E.O.M. added.

KM#	Date	Mintage	VF	XF	Unc
11	1972(a)	.600	.50	.75	2.00
	1973(a)	.400	.50	.75	2.00
	1977(a)	1.000	.50	.75	1.00
	1979(a)	—	.35	.50	1.00
	1983(a)	.800	.35	.50	1.00
	1986(a)	1.000	.35	.50	1.00
	1989(a)	.500	.35	.50	1.00
	1990(a)	—	.35	.50	1.00
	1991(a)	—	.35	.50	1.00
	1995(a)	—	.35	.50	1.00

20 FRANCS

NICKEL

6	1967(a)	.300	1.25	2.50	5.00
	1970(a)	1.200	.60	1.00	2.00

Obv. leg: I.E.O.M. added.

12	1972(a)	.700	.75	1.00	2.00
	1977(a)	.350	.75	1.00	3.00
	1979(a)	—	.50	.85	1.50
	1983(a)	.600	.50	.85	1.50
	1986(a)	.800	.50	.85	1.50
	1990(a)	—	.50	.85	1.50
	1991(a)	—	.50	.85	1.50
	1992(a)	—	.50	.85	1.50

50 FRANCS

NICKEL

7	1967(a)	.700	1.50	3.00	7.00

Obv. leg: I.E.O.M. added.

13	1972(a)	.300	1.50	2.00	5.00
	1979(a)	—	1.50	2.00	5.00
	1983(a)	.300	1.50	2.00	5.00
	1987(a)	.300	1.50	2.00	5.00
	1991(a)	—	1.50	2.00	5.00
	1992(a)	—	1.50	2.00	5.00

100 FRANCS

NICKEL-BRONZE

KM#	Date	Mintage	VF	XF	Unc
15	1976(a)	2.000	1.50	2.50	6.00
	1979(a)	—	1.50	2.50	6.00
	1984(a)	.600	1.50	2.50	6.00
	1987(a)	.800	1.50	2.50	6.00
	1988(a)	—	1.50	2.50	6.00
	1991(a)	—	1.50	2.50	6.00
	1994	—	1.50	2.50	6.00
	1995(a)	—	1.50	2.50	6.00

NEW ZEALAND

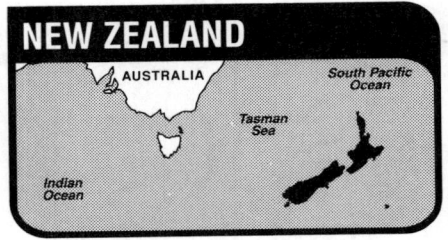

New Zealand, a parliamentary state located in the Southwest Pacific 1,250 miles (2,011 km.) east of Australia, has an area of 103,883 sq. mi. (268,680 sq. km.) and a population of *3.4 million. Capital: Wellington. Wool, meat, dairy products and some manufactured items are exported.

The first European to sight New Zealand was the Dutch navigator Abel Tasman in 1642. The islands were explored by British navigator Capt. James Cook who surveyed it in 1769 and annexed the land to Great Britain. The British government disavowed the annexation and for the next 70 years the only white settlers to arrive were adventurers attracted by the prospects of lumbering, sealing and whaling. Great Britain annexed the land in 1840 by treaty with the native chiefs and made it a dependency of New South Wales. The colony was granted self-government in 1852, a ministerial form of government in 1856, and full dominion status on Sept. 26, 1907. Full internal and external autonomy, which New Zealand had in effect possessed for many years, was formally extended in 1947. New Zealand is a member of the Commonwealth of Nations. The Queen of England is Chief of State.

Prior to 1933 English coins were the official legal tender but Australian coins were accepted in small transactions. Currency fluctuations caused a distintive New Zealand coinage to be introduced in 1933. The 1935 Waitangi crown and proof set were originally intended to mark the introduction but delays caused their date to be changed to 1935. The 1940 halfcrown marked the centennial of British rule, the 1949 and 1953 crowns commemorated Royal visits and the 1953 proof set marked the coronation of Queen Elizabeth.

Decimal Currency was introduced in 1967 with special sets commemorating the last issued of pound sterling (1965) and the first of the decimal issues. Since then dollars and set of coins have been issued nearly every year.

RULERS

British

MONETARY SYSTEM

12 Pence = 1 Shilling
2 Shillings = 1 Florin
2 Shillings & 6 Pence = Half Crown
5 Shillings = 1 Crown
20 Shillings = 1 Pound
2 Dollars = 1 Pound

1/2 PENNY

BRONZE
Hei Tiki

KM#	Date	Mintage	Fine	VF	XF	Unc
12	1940	3.432	.25	.65	2.50	18.00
	1940	—	—	—	Proof	200.00
	1941	.960	.25	.65	2.50	18.00
	1941	—	—	—	Proof	250.00
	1942	1.960	.35	.75	8.00	35.00
	1944	2.035	.50	1.00	6.00	20.00
	1945	1.516	.50	1.00	4.00	20.00
	1945	—	—	—	Proof	200.00
	1946	3.120	.50	1.00	4.00	20.00
	1946	—	—	—	Proof	200.00
	1947	2.726	.25	—	.50	2.00	15.00
	1947	—	—	—	Proof	175.00

20	1949	1.766	.10	.25	4.00	20.00
	1949	—	—	—	Proof	175.00
	1950	1.426	.10	.25	3.00	15.00
	1950	—	—	—	Proof	200.00
	1951	2.342	.10	.25	2.00	9.00

KM#	Date	Mintage	Fine	VF	XF	Unc
20	1951	—	—	—	Proof	175.00
	1952	2.400	.10	.20	1.50	8.00
	1952	—	—	—	Proof	175.00

Obv: W/o shoulder strap.

23.1	1953	.720	.10	.25	2.00	10.00
	1953	7,000	—	—	Proof	6.00
	1953	—	—	—	Matte Proof	125.00
	1954	.240	.75	1.25	8.50	35.00
	1954	—	—	—	Proof	150.00
	1955	.240	.75	1.25	8.50	35.00
	1955	—	—	—	Proof	150.00

Obv: W/shoulder strap.

23.2	1956	1.200	.10	.35	1.00	9.00
	1956	—	—	—	Proof	150.00
	1957	1.440	.10	.35	1.00	9.00
	1957	—	—	—	Proof	150.00
	1958	1.920	.10	.30	.75	6.00
	1958	—	—	—	Proof	150.00
	1959	1.920	.10	.20	.50	6.00
	1959	—	—	—	Proof	150.00
	1960	2.400	.10	.20	.50	6.00
	1960	—	—	—	Proof	150.00
	1961	2.880	.10	.15	.40	4.00
	1961	—	—	—	Proof	150.00
	1962	2.880	.10	.15	.40	4.00
	1962	—	—	—	Proof	150.00
	1963	1.680	.10	.15	.30	3.00
	1963	—	—	—	Proof	150.00
	1964	2.885	.10	.15	.20	2.00
	1964	—	—	—	Proof	150.00
	1965	.175	.10	.15	.20	1.00
	1965	.025	—	—	P/L	1.50
	1965	*10 pcs.	—	—	Proof	—

PENNY

BRONZE
Tui Bird

13	1940	5.424	.25	1.00	4.00	25.00
	1940	—	—	—	Proof	250.00
	1941	1.200	.25	1.00	7.00	35.00
	1942	3.120	.25	1.00	8.00	55.00
	1942	—	—	—	Proof	300.00
	1943	8.400	.25	.50	4.00	20.00
	1943	—	—	—	Proof	250.00
	1944	3.696	.50	1.00	4.00	20.00
	1944	—	—	—	Proof	250.00
	1945	4.764	.25	.50	4.00	25.00
	1945	—	—	—	Proof	250.00
	1946	6.720	.25	.50	3.50	20.00
	1946	—	—	—	Proof	250.00
	1947	5.880	.25	.50	3.50	20.00
	1947	—	—	—	Proof	250.00

BRONZE, burnished

13a	1945	—	—	—	100.00	275.00

NOTE: Struck in error by the Royal Mint on Great Britain blanks.

BRONZE

21	1949	2.016	.20	.60	4.00	25.00
	1949	—	—	—	Proof	250.00
	1950	5.784	.15	.50	3.00	20.00
	1950	—	—	—	Proof	200.00
	1951	6.888	.15	.50	2.00	15.00
	1951	—	—	—	Proof	200.00
	1952	10.800	.15	.50	1.25	12.00
	1952	—	—	—	Proof	175.00

Obv: W/o shoulder strap.

KM#	Date	Mintage	Fine	VF	XF	Unc
24.1	1953	2.400	.10	.25	3.00	12.00
	1953	7,000	—	—	Proof	12.00
	1953	—	—	Matte	Proof	125.00
	1954	1.080	.25	1.00	9.00	35.00
	1954	—	—	—	Proof	200.00
	1955	3.720	.10	.25	3.00	15.00
	1955	—	—	—	Proof	175.00
	1956	Inc. Be.	30.00	50.00	150.00	500.00

Obv: W/shoulder strap.

24.2	1956	3.600	.10	.20	2.50	12.00
	1956	—	—	—	Proof	175.00
	1957	2.400	.20	.50	2.00	10.00
	1957	—	—	—	Proof	175.00
	1958	10.800	.10	.20	1.50	9.00
	1958	—	—	—	Proof	175.00
	1959	8.400	.10	.20	1.50	9.00
	1959	—	—	—	Proof	175.00
	1960	7.200	.10	.20	.50	5.00
	1960	—	—	—	Proof	150.00
	1961	7.200	.10	.20	.50	4.00
	1961	—	—	—	Proof	150.00
	1962	6.000	—	.10	.45	3.00
	1962	—	—	—	Proof	150.00
	1963	2.400	—	.10	.20	2.00
	1963	—	—	—	Proof	150.00
	1964	18.000	—	.10	.15	1.00
	1964	—	—	—	Proof	150.00
	1965	.175	—	.50	1.00	3.00
	1965	.025	—	—	P/L	2.50
	1965	*10 pcs.	—	—	Proof	—

3 PENCE

COPPER, 34mm
Crossed Patu

1	1933	6.000	.35	.75	4.00	20.00
	1933	*20 pcs.	—	—	Proof	500.00
	1934	6.000	.35	.75	4.00	20.00
	1934	*20 pcs.	—	—	Proof	1650.
	1935	.040	50.00	125.00	210.00	700.00
	1935	364 pcs.	—	—	Proof	600.00
	1936	2.760	.35	.75	4.00	25.00
	1936	—	—	—	Proof	500.00

7	1937	2.880	.35	.75	3.00	20.00
	1937	*200 pcs.	—	—	Proof	450.00
	1939	3.000	.35	.60	2.75	20.00
	1939	—	—	—	Proof	450.00
	1940	2.000	.35	1.00	4.00	30.00
	1940	—	—	—	Proof	450.00
	1941	1.760	.40	1.50	15.00	100.00
	1941	—	—	—	Proof	400.00
	1942	3.120	.30	.60	2.50	18.00
	1942 w/1 dot	Inc. Ab.	4.00	8.00	120.00	350.00
	1943	4.400	.30	.50	1.50	12.50
	1944	2.840	.30	.50	1.50	15.00
	1944	—	—	—	Proof	400.00
	1945	2.520	.30	.50	1.50	10.00
	1945	—	—	—	Proof	400.00
	1946	6.080	.30	.50	1.50	10.00
	1946	—	—	—	Proof	400.00

COPPER-NICKEL

7a	1947	6.400	.15	.35	3.00	18.50
	1947	*20 pcs.	—	—	Proof	350.00

KM#	Date	Mintage	Fine	VF	XF	Unc
15	1948	4.000	.30	.70	4.00	20.00
	1948	—	—	—	Proof	200.00
	1950	.800	.50	2.00	15.00	100.00
	1950	—	—	—	Proof	250.00
	1951	3.600	.30	.70	3.00	12.00
	1951	—	—	—	Proof	200.00
	1952	8.000	.30	.70	2.50	10.00
	1952	—	—	—	Proof	200.00

Obv: W/o shoulder strap.

25.1	1953	4.000	.15	.35	.75	7.50
	1953	7,000	—	—	Proof	8.00
	1953	—	—	Matte	Proof	150.00
	1954	4.000	.15	.35	1.00	10.00
	1954	—	—	—	Proof	200.00
	1955	4.000	.15	.35	1.00	10.00
	1955	—	—	—	Proof	200.00
	1956	Inc. Be.	2.50	4.00	40.00	180.00
	1956	—	—	—	Proof	300.00

Obv: W/shoulder strap.

25.2	1956	4.800	.10	.20	.50	5.00
	1956	—	—	—	Proof	200.00
	1957	8.000	.10	.20	.30	4.00
	1957	—	—	—	Proof	200.00
	1958	4.800	.10	.20	.30	3.00
	1958	—	—	—	Proof	200.00
	1959	4.000	.10	.20	.30	3.00
	1959	—	—	—	Proof	200.00
	1960	4.000	.10	.20	.30	3.00
	1960	—	—	—	Proof	200.00
	1961	4.800	.10	.15	.30	2.00
	1961	—	—	—	Proof	200.00
	1962	6.000	.10	.15	.30	2.00
	1962	—	—	—	Proof	200.00
	1963	4.000	.10	.15	.25	.50
	1963	—	—	—	Proof	200.00
	1964	6.400	.10	.15	.25	.50
	1964	—	—	—	Proof	200.00
	1965	.175	—	.10	.15	.50
	1965	.025	—	—	P/L	1.00
	1965	*10 pcs.	—	—	Proof	—

6 PENCE

2.8300 g, .500 SILVER, .0454 oz ASW
Huia Bird

2	1933	3.000	.60	1.50	12.50	50.00
	1933	*20 pcs.	—	—	Proof	500.00
	1934	3.600	.60	1.50	12.50	50.00
	1934	*20 pcs.	—	—	Proof	1650.
	1935	.560	2.00	6.00	50.00	250.00
	1935	364 pcs.	—	—	Proof	300.00
	1936	1.480	.75	2.25	12.50	50.00
	1936	—	—	—	Proof	—

8	1937	1.280	.50	1.50	8.50	60.00
	1937	*200 pcs.	—	—	Proof	400.00
	1939	.700	.50	1.50	10.00	60.00
	1939	—	—	—	Proof	400.00
	1940	.800	.50	2.25	15.00	75.00
	1940	—	—	—	Proof	400.00
	1941	.440	2.00	4.00	50.00	300.00
	1941	—	—	—	Proof	600.00
	1942	.360	2.00	4.00	50.00	300.00
	1943	1.800	.50	1.00	8.00	35.00
	1944	1.160	1.00	2.00	9.00	35.00
	1944	—	—	—	Proof	350.00
	1945	.940	2.00	4.00	12.00	35.00
	1945	—	—	—	Proof	350.00
	1946	2.120	1.00	2.00	5.00	20.00
	1946	—	—	—	Proof	350.00

COPPER-NICKEL

8a	1947	3.200	1.00	2.00	9.00	50.00
	1947	*20 pcs.	—	—	Proof	350.00

KM#	Date	Mintage	Fine	VF	XF	Unc
16	1948	2.000	1.00	2.00	5.00	45.00
	1948	—	—	—	Proof	300.00
	1950	.800	1.00	4.00	20.00	125.00
	1950	—	—	—	Proof	300.00
	1951	1.800	.50	1.00	2.00	5.00
	1951	—	—	—	Proof	300.00
	1952	3.200	.50	1.00	2.50	20.00
	1952	—	—	—	Proof	250.00

Obv: W/o shoulder strap.

26.1	1953	1.200	.15	.30	3.00	10.00
	1953	.014	—	—	Proof	8.00
	1953	—	—	Matte	Proof	150.00
	1954	1.200	.15	.30	3.00	18.00
	1954	—	—	—	Proof	200.00
	1955	1.600	.15	.30	3.00	20.00
	1957	Inc. Be.	1.50	3.50	75.00	200.00
	1957	—	—	—	Proof	650.00

Obv: W/shoulder strap.

26.2	1955	—	—	—	Proof	2800.
	1956	2.000	.20	.50	1.50	5.00
	1956	—	—	—	Proof	200.00
	1957	2.400	.20	.50	.75	5.00
	1957	—	—	—	Proof	200.00
	1958	3.000	.15	.50	.75	5.00
	1958	—	—	—	Proof	200.00
	1959	2.000	.15	.50	.75	3.00
	1959	—	—	—	Proof	200.00
	1960	1.600	.15	.25	.40	2.00
	1960	—	—	—	Proof	200.00
	1961	.800	.10	.15	.25	3.00
	1961	—	—	—	Proof	200.00
	1962	1.200	.10	.15	.25	3.00
	1962	—	—	—	Proof	200.00
	1963	.800	.10	.15	.25	2.50
	1963	—	—	—	Proof	200.00
	1964	7.800	—	.10	.15	2.50
	1964	—	—	—	Proof	200.00
	1965	.175	—	—	.10	1.00
	1965 brkn. wing	Inc. Ab.	—	20.00	30.00	65.00
	1965	.025	—	—	P/L	1.00
	1965	*10 pcs.	—	—	Proof	—

SHILLING

5.6500 g, .500 SILVER, .0908 oz ASW
Maori Warrior

3	1933	3.000	1.50	3.00	25.00	120.00
	1933	*20 pcs.	—	—	Proof	650.00
	1934	3.600	1.50	3.50	20.00	100.00
	1934	*20 pcs.	—	—	Proof	2100.
	1935	.560	2.50	4.00	35.00	180.00
	1935	364 pcs.	—	—	Proof	300.00

9	1937	.890	1.25	3.00	15.00	90.00
	1937	*200 pcs.	—	—	Proof	600.00
	1940	.500	1.25	2.00	12.50	110.00
	1940	—	—	—	Proof	600.00
	1941	.360	1.75	4.00	45.00	280.00
	1941	—	—	—	Proof	600.00
	1942	.240	1.75	4.00	45.00	280.00
	1943	.900	2.00	4.00	15.00	65.00
	1944	.480	2.00	4.00	15.00	65.00
	1944	—	—	—	Proof	600.00
	1945	1.030	1.00	3.00	10.00	50.00
	1945	—	—	—	Proof	600.00
	1946	1.060	1.00	3.00	10.00	50.00
	1946	—	—	—	Proof	600.00

COPPER-NICKEL

KM#	Date	Mintage	Fine	VF	XF	Unc
9a	1947	2.800	1.50	3.00	30.00	100.00
	1947	*20 pcs.	—	—	Proof	400.00

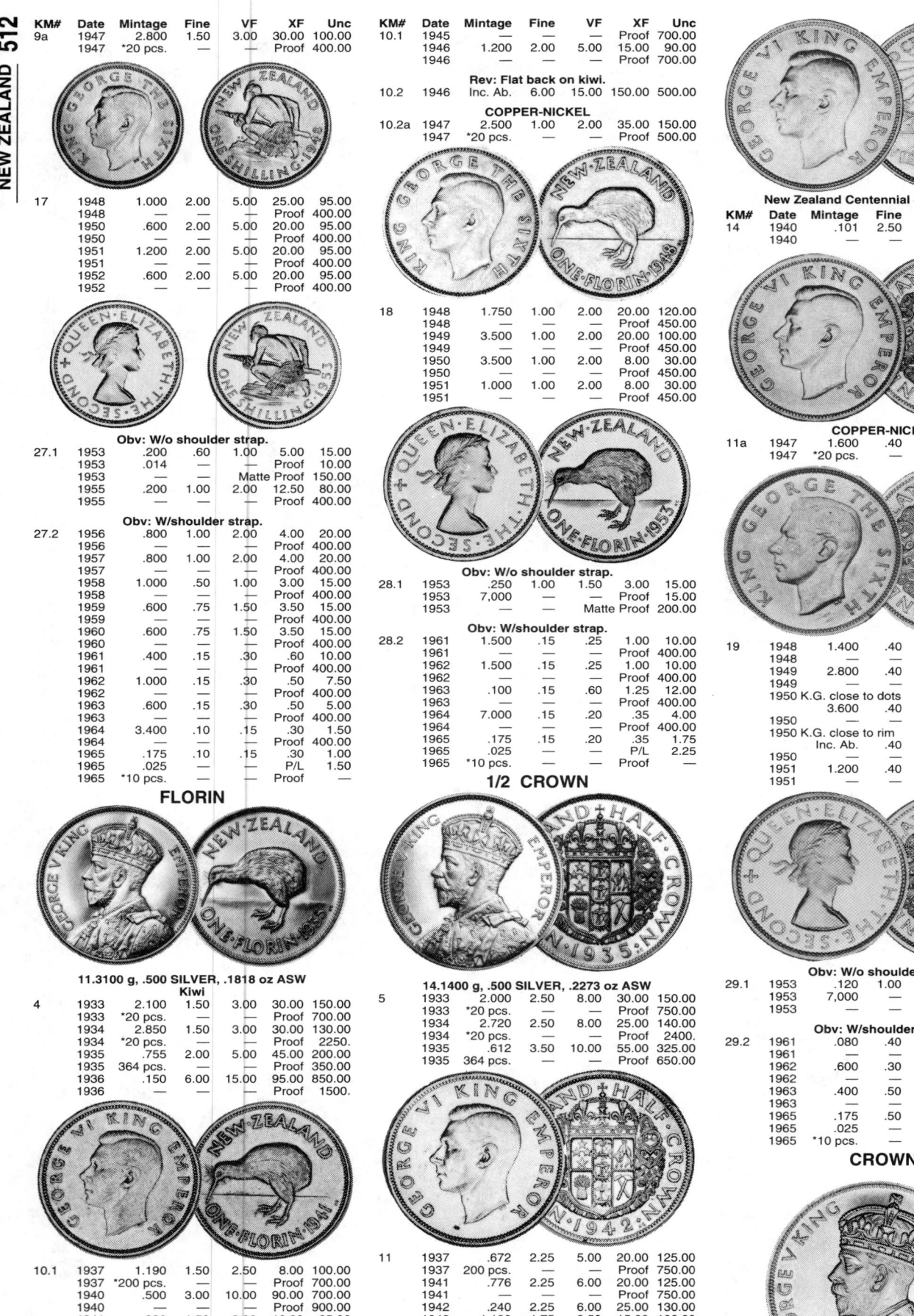

KM#	Date	Mintage	Fine	VF	XF	Unc
17	1948	1.000	2.00	5.00	25.00	95.00
	1948	—	—	—	Proof	400.00
	1950	.600	2.00	5.00	20.00	95.00
	1950	—	—	—	Proof	400.00
	1951	1.200	2.00	5.00	20.00	95.00
	1951	—	—	—	Proof	400.00
	1952	.600	2.00	5.00	20.00	95.00
	1952	—	—	—	Proof	400.00

Obv: W/o shoulder strap.

KM#	Date	Mintage	Fine	VF	XF	Unc
27.1	1953	.200	.60	1.00	5.00	15.00
	1953	.014	—	—	Proof	10.00
	1953	—	—	Matte	Proof	150.00
	1955	.200	1.00	2.00	12.50	80.00
	1955	—	—	—	Proof	400.00

Obv: W/shoulder strap.

KM#	Date	Mintage	Fine	VF	XF	Unc
27.2	1956	.800	1.00	2.00	4.00	20.00
	1956	—	—	—	Proof	400.00
	1957	.800	1.00	2.00	4.00	20.00
	1957	—	—	—	Proof	400.00
	1958	1.000	.50	1.00	3.00	15.00
	1958	—	—	—	Proof	400.00
	1959	.600	.75	1.50	3.50	15.00
	1959	—	—	—	Proof	400.00
	1960	.600	.75	1.50	3.50	15.00
	1960	—	—	—	Proof	400.00
	1961	.400	.15	.30	.60	10.00
	1961	—	—	—	Proof	400.00
	1962	1.000	.15	.30	.50	7.50
	1962	—	—	—	Proof	400.00
	1963	.600	.15	.30	.50	5.00
	1963	—	—	—	Proof	400.00
	1964	3.400	.10	.15	.30	1.50
	1964	—	—	—	Proof	400.00
	1965	.175	.10	.15	.30	1.00
	1965	.025	—	—	P/L	1.50
	1965	*10 pcs.	—	—	Proof	—

FLORIN

11.3100 g, .500 SILVER, .1818 oz ASW
Kiwi

KM#	Date	Mintage	Fine	VF	XF	Unc
4	1933	2.100	1.50	3.00	30.00	150.00
	1933	*20 pcs.	—	—	Proof	700.00
	1934	2.850	1.50	3.00	30.00	130.00
	1934	*20 pcs.	—	—	Proof	2250.
	1935	.755	2.00	5.00	45.00	200.00
	1935	364 pcs.	—	—	Proof	350.00
	1936	.150	6.00	15.00	95.00	850.00
	1936	—	—	—	Proof	1500.

KM#	Date	Mintage	Fine	VF	XF	Unc
10.1	1937	1.190	1.50	2.50	8.00	100.00
	1937	*200 pcs.	—	—	Proof	700.00
	1940	.500	3.00	10.00	90.00	700.00
	1940	—	—	—	Proof	900.00
	1941	.820	1.50	3.00	10.00	85.00
	1941	—	—	—	Proof	700.00
	1942	.150	1.50	4.00	30.00	100.00
	1943	1.400	1.25	3.00	10.00	70.00
	1944	.140	3.00	10.00	40.00	190.00
	1944	—	—	—	Proof	900.00
	1945	.515	2.00	4.00	10.00	70.00

KM#	Date	Mintage	Fine	VF	XF	Unc
10.1	1945	—	—	—	Proof	700.00
	1946	1.200	2.00	5.00	15.00	90.00
	1946	—	—	—	Proof	700.00

Rev: Flat back on kiwi.

KM#	Date	Mintage	Fine	VF	XF	Unc
10.2	1946	Inc. Ab.	6.00	15.00	150.00	500.00

COPPER-NICKEL

KM#	Date	Mintage	Fine	VF	XF	Unc
10.2a	1947	2.500	1.00	2.00	35.00	150.00
	1947	*20 pcs.	—	—	Proof	500.00

KM#	Date	Mintage	Fine	VF	XF	Unc
18	1948	1.750	1.00	2.00	20.00	120.00
	1948	—	—	—	Proof	450.00
	1949	3.500	1.00	2.00	20.00	100.00
	1949	—	—	—	Proof	450.00
	1950	3.500	1.00	2.00	8.00	30.00
	1950	—	—	—	Proof	450.00
	1951	1.000	1.00	2.00	8.00	30.00
	1951	—	—	—	Proof	450.00

Obv: W/o shoulder strap.

KM#	Date	Mintage	Fine	VF	XF	Unc
28.1	1953	.250	1.00	1.50	3.00	15.00
	1953	7,000	—	—	Proof	15.00
	1953	—	—	Matte	Proof	200.00

Obv: W/shoulder strap.

KM#	Date	Mintage	Fine	VF	XF	Unc
28.2	1961	1.500	.15	.25	1.00	10.00
	1961	—	—	—	Proof	400.00
	1962	1.500	.15	.25	1.00	10.00
	1962	—	—	—	Proof	400.00
	1963	.100	.15	.60	1.25	12.00
	1963	—	—	—	Proof	400.00
	1964	7.000	.15	.20	.35	4.00
	1964	—	—	—	Proof	400.00
	1965	.175	.15	.20	.35	1.75
	1965	.025	—	—	P/L	2.25
	1965	*10 pcs.	—	—	Proof	—

1/2 CROWN

14.1400 g, .500 SILVER, .2273 oz ASW

KM#	Date	Mintage	Fine	VF	XF	Unc
5	1933	2.000	2.50	8.00	30.00	150.00
	1933	*20 pcs.	—	—	Proof	750.00
	1934	2.720	2.50	8.00	25.00	140.00
	1934	*20 pcs.	—	—	Proof	2400.
	1935	.612	3.50	10.00	55.00	325.00
	1935	364 pcs.	—	—	Proof	650.00

KM#	Date	Mintage	Fine	VF	XF	Unc
11	1937	.672	2.25	5.00	20.00	125.00
	1937	200 pcs.	—	—	Proof	750.00
	1941	.776	2.25	6.00	20.00	125.00
	1941	—	—	—	Proof	750.00
	1942	.240	2.25	6.00	25.00	130.00
	1943	1.120	1.75	3.50	15.00	100.00
	1944	.180	5.00	10.00	75.00	400.00
	1944	—	—	—	Proof	750.00
	1945	.420	3.00	6.00	20.00	140.00
	1945	—	—	—	Proof	750.00
	1946	.960	3.00	6.00	20.00	140.00
	1946	—	—	—	Proof	750.00

New Zealand Centennial - Maori Wahine

KM#	Date	Mintage	Fine	VF	XF	Unc
14	1940	.101	2.50	4.00	12.00	40.00
	1940	—	—	—	Proof	5500.

COPPER-NICKEL

KM#	Date	Mintage	Fine	VF	XF	Unc
11a	1947	1.600	.40	2.00	7.00	135.00
	1947	*20 pcs.	—	—	Proof	600.00

KM#	Date	Mintage	Fine	VF	XF	Unc
19	1948	1.400	.40	1.50	7.00	125.00
	1948	—	—	—	Proof	550.00
	1949	2.800	.40	1.50	7.00	115.00
	1949	—	—	—	Proof	550.00
	1950 K.G. close to dots					
		3.600	.40	1.00	2.00	25.00
	1950	—	—	—	Proof	550.00
	1950 K.G. close to rim					
		Inc. Ab.	.40	1.00	2.00	25.00
	1950	—	—	—	Proof	550.00
	1951	1.200	.40	1.00	2.00	25.00
	1951	—	—	—	Proof	550.00

Obv: W/o shoulder strap.

KM#	Date	Mintage	Fine	VF	XF	Unc
29.1	1953	.120	1.00	2.50	4.00	20.00
	1953	7,000	—	—	Proof	12.00
	1953	—	—	Matte	Proof	250.00

Obv: W/shoulder strap.

KM#	Date	Mintage	Fine	VF	XF	Unc
29.2	1961	.080	.40	.80	2.00	10.00
	1961	—	—	—	Proof	500.00
	1962	.600	.30	.70	1.50	7.50
	1962	—	—	—	Proof	500.00
	1963	.400	.50	.70	1.50	6.00
	1963	—	—	—	Proof	500.00
	1965	.175	.50	.70	1.00	2.50
	1965	.025	—	—	P/L	3.00
	1965	*10 pcs.	—	—	Proof	—

CROWN

28.2800 g, .500 SILVER, .4546 oz ASW
Treaty of Waitangi in 1840
Woka Nene and Governor Hobson

KM#	Date	Mintage	Fine	VF	XF	Unc
6	1935	764 pcs.	1200.	1500.	2500.	3000.
	1935	364 pcs.	—	—	Proof	2900.

Proposed Royal Visit
Silver Fern Leaf

22	1949	.200	—	2.50	3.50	12.00
	1949	*3 pcs.	—	—	Proof	4500.

COPPER-NICKEL
Queen Elizabeth II Coronation

30	1953	.250	—	—	2.00	5.00
	1953	7,000	—	—	Proof	25.00
	1953	4-10 pcs.	—	Matte Proof		350.00

DECIMAL COINAGE
MINTS
(c) Royal Australian Mint, Canberra
(l) Royal Mint, Llantrisant
(o) Royal Canadian Mint, Ottawa
MONETARY SYSTEM
100 Cents = 1 Dollar

CENT

BRONZE
Silver Fern Leaf

KM#	Date	Mintage	VF	XF	Unc
31	1967	.250	—	.10	.15
	1967	.050	—	P/L	1.00
	1967	10 pcs.	—	Proof	—
	1968	.035	—	.15	1.25
	1968	.040	—	P/L	1.50
	1969	.050	—	.15	1.25
	1969	.050	—	P/L	1.50
	1970	.030	—	.15	.75
	1970	20,010	—	P/L	1.25
	1971(c) serifs on date numerals				
		10.000	—	.20	5.00
	1971(l) w/o serifs				
		.015	—	.15	3.25
	1971(l)	5,000	—	Proof	15.00
	1972	10.055	—	.15	3.25
	1972	8,045	—	Proof	6.00
	1973	15.055	—	.10	2.75
	1973	8,000	—	Proof	6.00
	1974	35.035	—	.10	2.50
	1974	8,000	—	Proof	5.00
	1975	60.015	—	.10	1.25
	1975	.010	—	Proof	5.00
	1976	20.016	—	.10	.75
	1976	.011	—	Proof	5.00
	1977	.020	—	.20	7.00
	1977	.012	—	Proof	5.50
	1978(o)	15.023	—	.10	1.50
	1978(o)	.015	—	Proof	4.00
	1979(o)	35.025	—	.10	.75
	1979(o)	.016	—	Proof	4.00
	1980(l) smooth shoulder folds in gown				
		.027	—	.10	1.50
	1980(l)	.017	—	Proof	4.00
	1980(o) incised shoulder folds in gown				
		40.000	—	.10	1.00
	1981(o) incised shoulder folds in gown				
		10.000	—	.10	.50
	1981(l) smooth shoulder folds in gown				
		.025	—	.10	1.25
	1981(l) smooth shoulder folds in gown				
		.018	—	Proof	4.00
	1982(o) blunt tipped 2				
		10.000	—	.10	.50
	1982(l) round tipped 2				
		.025	—	.10	1.00
	1982(l) round tipped 2				
		.018	—	Proof	3.00
	1983(o) round top 3				
		40.000	—	.10	.50
	1983(l) flat top 3				
		.025	—	.10	1.00
	1983(l) flat top 3				
		.018	—	Proof	3.00
	1984(o) wiry hair, bushy eyebrow				
		30.000	—	.10	.25
	1984(l) smooth shoulder folds				
		.025	—	—	1.00
	1984(l) smooth shoulder folds				
		.015	—	Proof	1.75
	1985(o) wiry hair, bushy eyebrow				
		40.000	—	—	.25
	1985(c) smooth shoulder folds				
		.020	—	—	1.50
	1985(c)	.012	—	Proof	1.25

Obv: Similar to 1 Dollar, KM#57.

58	1986(o)	25.000	—	—	.25
	1986(l)	.018	—	—	1.50
	1986(l)	.010	—	Proof	1.25
	1987(o)	27.500	—	—	.25
	1987(l)	.018	—	—	1.50
	1987(l)	.010	—	Proof	1.25
	1988(l)	.015	—	—	8.00
	1988(l)	9,000	—	Proof	2.50

NOTE: The 1988 one cent was only struck for sets, no circulated strikes are available.

2 CENTS

BRONZE
Kowhai Leaves

KM#	Date	Mintage	VF	XF	Unc
32	1967	.250	—	.10	.15
	1967	.050	—	P/L	1.00
	1967	10 pcs.	—	Proof	—
	1968	.035	—	.15	.75
	1968	.040	—	P/L	1.50
	1969	.050	—	.15	.50
	1969	.050	—	P/L	1.50
	1970	.030	—	.15	3.25
	1970	20,010	—	P/L	1.50
	1971(c) serifs on date numerals				
		15.050	—	.20	4.50
	1971(l) w/o serifs				
		.015	—	.20	4.50
	1971(l)	5,000	—	Proof	17.00
	1972	17.525	—	.15	3.25
	1972	8,045	—	Proof	6.50
	1973	38.565	—	.10	2.75
	1973	8,000	—	Proof	6.25
	1974	50.015	—	.10	2.75
	1974	8,000	—	Proof	4.00
	1975	20.015	—	.10	1.25
	1975	.010	—	Proof	4.00
	1976	15.016	—	.10	.75
	1976	.011	—	Proof	4.00
	1977	20.000	—	.10	.75
	1977	.012	—	Proof	4.00
	1978	.023	—	.10	7.75
	1978	.015	—	Proof	4.00
	1979	.025	—	.10	5.00
	1979	.015	—	Proof	4.00
	1980(l) smooth shoulder folds on gown				
		.027	—	.10	1.25
	1980(l)	.017	—	Proof	3.50
	1980(o) incised shoulder folds on gown				
		10.000	—	.10	1.25
	1981(o) incised shoulder folds on gown				
		25.000	—	.10	1.25
	1981(l) smooth shoulder folds on gown				
		.025	—	.10	1.25
	1981(l)	.018	—	Proof	3.50
	1982(o) blunt open 2				
		50.000	—	.10	1.00
	1982(l) pointed tight 2				
		.025	—	.10	.75
	1982(l)	.018	—	Proof	3.50
	1983(o) round topped 3				
		15.000	—	.10	1.00
	1983(l) flat topped 3				
		.025	—	.10	.75
	1983(l)	.018	—	Proof	3.50
	1984(o) wiry hair, bushy eyebrow				
		10.000	—	.10	.75
	1984(l) smooth shoulder folds				
		.025	—	.10	2.50
	1984(l)	.015	—	—	2.00
	1985(o) wiry hair, bushy eyebrow				
		22.500	—	.10	.75
	1985(c) smooth shoulder folds				
		.020	—	.10	2.50
	1985(c)	.012	—	Proof	1.50

Mule. Obv: Bahamas 5 Cent, KM#3. Rev: KM#32.

33	ND(1967)	*.050	10.00	15.00	25.00

Obv: Similar to 1 Dollar, KM#57.

59	1986(l)	.018	—	—	6.50
	1986(l)	.010	—	Proof	1.50
	1987(o)	36.250	—	—	.35
	1987(l)	.018	—	—	2.00
	1987(l)	.010	—	Proof	1.50
	1988(l)	.015	—	—	6.50
	1988(l)	9,000	—	Proof	1.50

5 CENTS

COPPER-NICKEL
Tuatara

34	1967	.250	—	.10	.25
	1967 w/o sea line				
	Inc. Ab.	4.00	10.00	35.00	
	1967	.050	—	P/L	1.25
	1967	10 pcs.	—	Proof	—
	1968	.035	—	.15	1.50
	1968	.040	—	P/L	2.00
	1969	.050	—	.15	.50
	1969	.050	—	P/L	1.60
	1970	.030	—	.15	.50
	1970	20,010	—	P/L	2.00
	1971(c) serifs on date numerals				
		11.520	—	.15	4.50
	1971(l) w/o serifs				
		.015	—	.15	4.50

KM#	Date	Mintage	VF	XF	Unc
34	1971(l)	5,000	—	Proof	20.00
	1972	20.015	—	.10	3.25
	1972	8,045	—	Proof	7.00
	1973	4.039	—	.10	2.50
	1973	8,000	—	Proof	6.50
	1974	18.015	—	.10	3.25
	1974	8,000	—	Proof	5.00
	1975	32.015	—	.10	2.00
	1975	.010	—	Proof	5.50
	1976	.016	—	.20	9.75
	1976	.011	—	Proof	5.00
	1977	.020	—	.15	6.50
	1977	.012	—	Proof	5.00
	1978	20.023	—	.10	.50
	1978	.015	—	Proof	5.00
	1979	.025	—	.15	7.00
	1979	.016	—	Proof	5.00
	1980(l) smooth shoulder folds on gown				
		.027	—	.10	1.25
	1980(l)	.017	—	Proof	5.00
	1980(o) incised shoulder folds on gown				
		12.000	—	.10	1.00
	1981(o) incised shoulder folds on gown				
		20.000	—	.10	1.00
	1981(l) smooth shoulder folds on gown				
		.025	—	.10	1.25
	1981(l)	.018	—	Proof	4.00
	1982(o) blunt 2				
		50.000	—	.10	1.00
	1982(l) pointed 2				
		.025	—	.10	1.25
	1982(l)	.018	—	Proof	4.00
	1983(l)	.025	—	.10	3.25
	1983(l)	.018	—	Proof	4.00
	1984(l)	.025	—	.10	5.00
	1984(l)	.015	—	Proof	4.00
	1985(o) wiry hair, bushy eyebrow				
		14.000	—	.10	1.00
	1985(c)	.020	—	.10	2.50
	1985(c)	.012	—	Proof	4.00

Mule. Obv: KM#34. Rev: Canada 10 Cent, KM#77.

KM#	Date	Mintage	VF	XF	Unc
64	1981(o) serif on 1				
		—	—	Rare	—

60	1986(o)	18.000	—	.10	.25
	1986(l)	.018	—	—	2.00
	1986(l)	.010	—	Proof	4.00
	1987(o)	60.000	—	.10	.25
	1987(l)	.018	—	—	2.00
	1987(l)	.010	—	Proof	4.00
	1988(c) round topped numerals				
		8.000	—	.10	.50
	1988(l) flat topped numerals				
		.015	—	—	2.00
	1988(l)	9,000	—	Proof	4.00
	1989(o)	36.000	—	—	.25
	1989(c)	.015	—	—	2.00
	1989(c)	8.500	—	Proof	4.00
	1990(l)	.018	—	—	1.00
	1990(l)	.010	—	Proof	4.00
	1991(c)	.020	—	—	2.00
	1991(c)	9,000	—	Proof	4.00
	1992(l)	.015	—	—	3.50
	1992(l)	9,000	—	Proof	4.00
	1993(l)	.015	—	—	2.00
	1993(l)	.010	—	Proof	4.00
	1994(l)	20.000	—	—	.25
	1994(l)	.010	—	Proof	4.00
	1995(l)	—	—	—	.25
	1995(l)	*4,000	—	Proof	4.00
	1996(l)	—	—	—	.25
	1997(l)	—	—	—	.25

1990 Anniversary Celebrations

72	1990	.010	—	—	1.00

10 CENTS

COPPER-NICKEL
Maori Mask

35	1967	.250	—	.10	.25
	1967	.050	—	P/L	1.50

KM#	Date	Mintage	VF	XF	Unc
35	1967	10 pcs.	—	Proof	—
	1968	.035	—	.15	2.00
	1968	.040	—	P/L	2.50
	1969	3.050	—	.15	1.00
	1969	.050	—	Proof	2.00

41	1970	.030	—	.15	1.00
	1970	20.010	—	P/L	2.00
	1971(c) serifs on date numerals				
		2.800	1.00	3.50	30.00
	1971(l) w/o serifs				
		.015	—	.15	5.00
	1971(l)	5,000	—	Proof	30.00
	1972	2.039	—	.15	2.50
	1972	8,000	—	Proof	10.00
	1973	3.525	—	.10	2.50
	1973	8,000	—	Proof	7.50
	1974	4.619	—	.10	2.50
	1974	8,000	—	Proof	7.50
	1975	7.015	—	.10	2.50
	1975	.010	—	Proof	6.00
	1976	5.016	—	.10	2.00
	1976	.011	—	Proof	6.00
	1977	5.000	—	.10	1.25
	1977	.012	—	Proof	6.00
	1978	16.023	—	.10	2.50
	1978	.015	—	Proof	5.00
	1979	6.000	—	.10	.75
	1979	.016	—	Proof	5.00
	1980(l) smooth shoulder folds on gown				
		.027	—	.10	1.00
	1980(l)	.017	—	Proof	5.00
	1980(o) incised shoulder folds on gown				
		28.000	—	.10	3.00
	1981(o) oval holes in 8				
		5.000	—	.10	3.00
	1981(l) round holes in 8				
		.025	—	.10	1.50
	1981(l)	.018	—	Proof	5.00
	1982(o) blunt open 2				
		18.000	—	.10	3.00
	1982(l) point tipped 2				
		.025	—	.10	2.00
	1982(l)	.018	—	Proof	5.00
	1983(l)	.025	—	.10	3.25
	1983(l)	.018	—	Proof	4.50
	1984(l)	.025	—	.10	3.25
	1984(l)	.015	—	Proof	4.50
	1985(o) wiry hair, bushy eyebrow				
		8.000	—	.10	4.00
	1985(c) smooth shoulder folds on gown				
		.020	—	.10	3.25
	1985(c)	.012	—	Proof	4.50

61	1986(l)	.018	—	.15	6.00
	1986(l)	.010	—	Proof	4.50
	1987(o)	21.000	—	.10	2.00
	1987(l)	.018	—	.10	2.00
	1987(l)	.010	—	Proof	4.50
	1988(c)	12.000	—	.10	.25
	1988(l)	.015	—	.10	2.00
	1988(l)	9,000	—	Proof	4.50
	1989(c)	9.000	—	—	.25
	1989(c)	8,500	—	Proof	4.50
	1989(o)	.015	—	—	2.00
	1990(c)	.018	—	—	1.50
	1990(c)	.010	—	Proof	4.50
	1991(c)	.020	—	—	2.00
	1991(c)	.015	—	Proof	4.50
	1992	.015	—	—	2.00
	1992	9,000	—	Proof	4.50
	1993	.015	—	—	1.00
	1993	.010	—	Proof	4.50
	1994	—	—	—	1.00
	1994	.010	—	Proof	4.50
	1995	—	—	—	1.00
	1995	*4,000	—	Proof	4.50
	1996	—	—	—	1.00
	1997	—	—	—	1.00

1990 Anniversary Celebrations
Obv: Similar to 1 Dollar, KM#76.

KM#	Date	Mintage	VF	XF	Unc
73	1990	.010	—	—	2.00

20 CENTS

COPPER-NICKEL
Kiwi

36	1967	.250	—	.20	.50
	1967	.050	—	P/L	1.75
	1967	10 pcs.	—	Proof	—
	1968	.035	—	.20	2.00
	1968	.040	—	P/L	3.00
	1969	.050	—	.20	.75
	1969	.050	—	P/L	2.50
	1970	.030	—	.25	1.00
	1970	20.010	—	P/L	3.00
	1971(c) serifs on date numerals				
		1.600	1.00	4.50	25.00
	1971(l) w/o serifs				
		.015	—	.25	5.00
	1971(l)	5,000	—	Proof	50.00
	1972	1.531	—	.15	2.50
	1972	8,000	—	Proof	15.00
	1973	3.043	—	.15	2.50
	1973	8,000	—	Proof	8.00
	1974	4.527	—	.15	5.00
	1974	8,000	—	Proof	9.00
	1975	5.015	—	.15	2.50
	1975	.012	—	Proof	7.50
	1976	7.516	—	.15	2.50
	1976	.011	—	Proof	7.00
	1977	7.500	—	.15	2.50
	1977	.012	—	Proof	7.50
	1978	2.523	—	.15	2.50
	1978	.015	—	Proof	6.00
	1979	8.000	—	.15	1.25
	1979	.016	—	Proof	6.00
	1980(l) smooth shoulder folds on gown				
		.027	—	.15	1.25
	1980(l)	.017	—	Proof	6.00
	1980(o) incised shoulder folds on gown				
		9.000	—	.15	6.00
	1981(o) incised shoulder folds on gown				
		7.500	—	.15	6.00
	1981(l) smooth shoulder folds on gown				
		.025	—	.15	1.25
	1981(l)	.018	—	Proof	5.00
	1982(o) blunt 2				
		17.500	—	.15	6.00
	1982(l) pointed 2				
		.025	—	.15	1.25
	1982(l)	.018	—	Proof	5.00
	1983(o) round topped 3				
		2.500	—	.15	6.00
	1983(l) flat topped 3				
		.025	—	.15	1.25
	1983(l)	.018	—	Proof	5.00
	1984(o) wiry hair, bushy eyebrows				
		1.500	—	.15	6.00
	1984(l) smooth shoulder folds on gown				
		.025	—	.15	.75
	1984(l)	.018	—	Proof	5.00
	1985(o) pointed tip 5				
		6.000	—	.15	8.00
	1985(c) round tip 5				
		.020	—	.15	2.00
	1985(c)	.012	—	Proof	5.00

Obv: Similar to 1 Dollar, KM#57.

62	1986(o)	12.500	—	.15	.50
	1986(l)	.018	—	.25	2.00
	1986(l)	.010	—	Proof	5.00
	1987(o)	14.000	—	.15	.50
	1987(l)	.018	—	.25	2.00
	1987(l)	.010	—	Proof	5.00
	1988(c)	6.500	—	.15	.50
	1988(l)	.015	—	.25	2.00
	1988(l)	9,000	—	Proof	5.00
	1989(o)	2.000	—	—	.50
	1989(o)	8,500	—	Proof	5.00
	1989(c)	.015	—	—	2.00

1990 Anniversary Celebrations

74	1990(c)	.010	—	—	2.50

DOLLAR

KM#	Date	Mintage	VF	XF	Unc
81	1990(l)	5.000	—	—	.50
	1990(c)	.018	—	—	2.00
	1990(c)	.010	—	Proof	5.00
	1991(c)	.020	—	—	2.00
	1991(c)	.015	—	Proof	5.00
	1992(l)	.015	—	—	2.00
	1992(l)	9,000	—	Proof	5.00
	1993(l)	.015	—	—	2.00
	1993(l)	.010	—	Proof	5.00
	1994(l)	—	—	—	2.00
	1994(l)	.010	—	Proof	5.00
	1995(l)	—	—	—	2.00
	1995(l)	*4,000	—	Proof	5.00
	1996(l)	—	—	—	2.00
	1997(l)	—	—	—	2.00

50 CENTS

NICKEL
Mule. Obv: KM#37.
Rev: Canada 1 Dollar. Rev: KM#120.

KM#	Date	Mintage	VF	XF	Unc
95	1985	6 known	1200.	1900.	

200th Anniversary - Captain Cook's Voyage
Similar to KM#37.
Edge inscribed COOK BI-CENTENARY 1769-1969

39	1969	.050	—	.75	3.25
	1969	.050	—	P/L	4.00

COPPER-NICKEL
Decimalization Commemorative, lettered edge

KM#	Date	Mintage	VF	XF	Unc
38.1	1967	.250	—	.75	1.50
	1967	.050	—	P/L	3.00
	1967	10 pcs.	—	Proof	—

Regular Issue, reeded edge

38.2	1971	.045	—	2.00	4.00
	1971	5,000	—	Proof	27.50
	1972	.042	—	2.00	4.00
	1972	8,045	—	Proof	15.00
	1972 RAM case				
		3,000	—	Proof	40.00
	1973	.037	—	2.00	4.00
	1973	.016	—	Proof	6.00
	1975	.030	—	2.00	4.00
	1975	.020	—	Proof	6.00
	1976	.036	—	2.00	4.00
	1976	.022	—	Proof	6.00

63	1986(o)	5.200	—	.35	1.00
	1986(l)	.018	—	.50	1.50
	1986(l)	.010	—	Proof	6.00
	1987(o)	3.600	—	.35	1.00
	1987(l)	.018	—	.50	1.50
	1987(l)	.010	—	Proof	6.00
	1988(c)	4.400	—	.35	1.00
	1988(l)	.015	—	.50	.75
	1988(l)	9,000	—	Proof	6.00
	1989(c)	.015	—	—	1.50
	1989(c)	8,500	—	Proof	6.00
	1990(l)	.018	—	—	1.50
	1990(l)	.010	—	Proof	6.00
	1991(c)	.200	—	—	1.50
	1991(c)	.015	—	Proof	6.00
	1992(l)	.015	—	—	1.50
	1992(l)	9,000	—	Proof	6.00
	1993(l)	.015	—	—	1.50
	1993(l)	.010	—	Proof	6.00
	1995(l)	—	—	—	1.50
	1995(l)	*4,000	—	Proof	6.00
	1996(l)	—	—	—	1.50
	1997(l)	—	—	—	1.50

200th Anniversary - Captain Cook's Voyage

40.1	1969	.400	—	.75	1.50
	1969	.050	—	P/L	4.00

No hyphen in edge inscription.

40.2	1969	—	—	—	10.00

ALUMINUM-BRONZE
Kiwi Bird

78	1990(l)	40.000	—	—	1.25
	1990(l)	.018	—	Proof	2.50
	1990(l)	.010	—	—	5.00
	1991(l)	10.000	—	—	1.25
	1991(c)	.020	—	—	2.50
	1991(c)	.015	—	Proof	5.00
	1992(l)	.015	—	—	2.50
	1992(l)	9,000	—	Proof	5.00
	1993(l)	.015	—	—	2.50
	1993(l)	.010	—	Proof	5.00
	1994(l)	.016	—	—	3.00
	1994(l)	.010	—	Proof	5.00
	1995(l)	.010	—	—	3.00
	1995(l)	*4,000	—	Proof	5.00
	1996(l)	—	—	—	2.00
	1997(l)	—	—	—	2.00

COPPER-NICKEL
H.M.B. Endeavour

37	1967	.250	—	.45	.75
	1967 dot above 1				
	Inc. Ab.	3.00	6.00	30.00	
	1967	.050	—	P/L	2.00
	1967	10 pcs.	—	Proof	—
	1968	.035	—	.45	2.50
	1968	.040	—	P/L	3.50
	1970	.030	—	.45	4.00
	1970	20,010	—	P/L	3.50
	1971(c) serifs on date numerals				
		1.123	1.00	5.00	35.00
	1971(l) w/o serifs				
		.015	—	.35	4.00
	1971(l)	5,000	—	Proof	50.00
	1972	1.423	—	.35	5.00
	1972	8,045	—	Proof	20.00
	1973	2.523	—	.35	4.00
	1973	8,000	—	Proof	12.50
	1974	1.215	—	.35	4.00
	1974	8,000	—	Proof	12.50
	1975	3.815	—	.35	4.00
	1975	.010	—	Proof	9.00
	1976	2.016	—	.35	4.00
	1976	.011	—	Proof	9.00
	1977	2.000	—	.35	2.50
	1977	.012	—	Proof	9.00
	1978	2.023	—	.35	2.50
	1978	.015	—	Proof	7.00
	1979	2.400	—	.35	2.50
	1979	.016	—	Proof	7.00
	1980(l) smooth back line to hair				
		.027	—	.35	2.50
	1980(l)	.017	—	Proof	7.00
	1980(o) strong back line to hair				
		8.000	—	.50	12.00
	1981(o) blunt end on 9				
		4.000	—	.50	12.00
	1981(l) pointed end on 9				
		.025	—	.35	1.50
	1981(l)	.018	—	Proof	7.00
	1982(o) blunt end on 2				
		6.000	—	.50	12.00
	1982(l) pointed end on 2				
		.025	—	.35	3.25
	1982(l)	.018	—	Proof	7.00
	1983(l)	.025	—	.35	3.25
	1983(l)	.018	—	Proof	7.00
	1984(o) wiry hair, bushy eyebrows				
		2.000	—	.50	12.00
	1984(l) incised shoulder folds on gown				
		.025	—	.35	3.25
	1984(l)	.015	—	Proof	6.00
	1985(o) wiry hair, bushy eyebrows				
		2.000	—	.50	12.00
	1985(c)	.020	—	.35	3.25
	1985(c)	.012	—	Proof	6.00

1990 Anniversary Celebrations

75	1990(c)	.010	—	—	6.00

ALUMINUM-BRONZE center, COPPER-NICKEL ring
H.M.B. Endeavour

90	1994	.053	—	—	20.00

2 DOLLARS

ALUMINUM-BRONZE
Great Egret

KM#	Date	Mintage	VF	XF	Unc
79	1990(I)	30.000	—	—	2.25
	1990(I)	.018	—	—	3.00
	1990(I)	.010	—	Proof	5.00
	1991(I)	10.000	—	—	2.25
	1991(c)	.020	—	—	3.00
	1991(c)	.015	—	Proof	7.00
	1992(I)	.015	—	—	3.00
	1992(I)	9.000	—	Proof	8.00
	1994(I)	.016	—	—	3.00
	1994(I)	.010	—	Proof	8.00
	1995(I)	.010	—	—	3.50
	1995(I)	*4,000	—	Proof	8.00
	1996(I)	—	—	—	3.00
	1997(I)	—	—	—	3.00

COPPER-ALUMINUM-NICKEL
Sacred Kingfisher

87	1993	.040	—	—	7.50

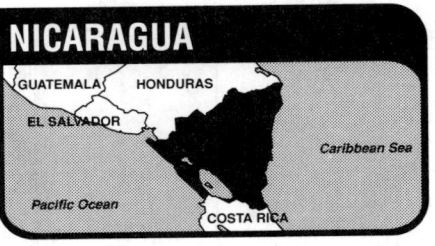

The Republic of Nicaragua, situated in Central America between Honduras and Costa Rica, has an area of 50,193 sq. mi. (129,494 sq. km.) and a population of *3.7 million. Capital: Managua. Agriculture, mining (gold and silver) and hardwood logging are the principal industries. Cotton, meat, coffee and sugar are exported.

Columbus sighted the coast of Nicaragua on Sept. 12, 1502 during the course of his last voyage of discovery. It was first visited in 1522 by conquistadores from Panama, under the command of Gil Gonzalez. The first settlements were established in 1524 at Granada and Leon by Francisco Hernandez de Cordoba. Nicaragua was incorporated, for administrative purpose, in the Captaincy General of Guatemala, which included every Central American state but Panama. On September 15, 1821 the Captaincy General of Guatemala declared itself and all the Central American provinces independent of Spain. The next year Nicaragua united with the Mexican Empire of Augustin de Iturbide, only to join in 1823 the federation of the Central American Republic. Within Nicaragua rival cities or juntas such as Leon, Granada and El Viejo vied for power, wealth and influence, often attacking each other at will. To further prove their legitimacy as well as provide an acceptable circulating coinage in those turbulent times (1821-1825), provisional mints functioned intermittantly at Granada, Leon and El Viejo. The early coinage reflected traditional but crude Spanish colonial cob-style designs. Nicaragua's first governor was Pedro Arias Davila, appointed on June 1, 1827. When the federation was dissolved, Nicaragua declared itself an independent republic on April 30, 1838.

Dissension between the Liberals and Conservatives of the contending cities kept Nicaragua in turmoil, which made it possible for William Walker to make himself President in 1855. The two major political parties finally united to drive him out and in 1857 he was expelled. A relative peace followed, but by 1912, Nicaragua had requested the U.S. Marines to restore order which began a U.S. involvement which lasted until the Good Neighbor Policy was adopted in 1933. Anastasio Somoza Garcia assumed the Presidency in 1936. This family dynasty dominated Nicaragua until its overthrow in 1979. Formal elections in 1990 renewed a democratic government in power.

MINT MARKS
H - Heaton, Birmingham
HF - Huguenin Freres, Le Locle
Mo - Mexico City
  - Philadelphia, Pa.
  - Sherritt
  - Waterbury, Ct.

MONETARY SYSTEM
100 Centavos = 1 Cordoba
12-1/2 Pesos = 1 Cordoba

1/2 CENTAVO

BRONZE

KM#	Date	Mintage	Fine	VF	XF	Unc
10	1912H	.900	1.00	2.50	15.00	40.00
	1912H	—	—	—	Proof	275.00
	1915H	.320	1.50	4.00	30.00	100.00
	1916H	.720	1.50	4.00	30.00	100.00
	1917	.720	1.50	4.00	12.00	65.00
	1922	.400	2.00	5.00	20.00	80.00
	1924	.400	1.00	3.00	12.00	70.00
	1934	.500	1.00	3.00	10.00	45.00
	1936	.600	.50	.75	5.00	20.00
	1937	1.000	.40	.60	4.00	15.00

CENTAVO

BRONZE

11	1912H	.450	1.00	3.00	10.00	45.00
	1912H	—	—	—	Proof	275.00
	1914H	.300	3.00	6.00	18.00	85.00
	1915H	.500	2.00	5.00	15.00	100.00

KM#	Date	Mintage	Fine	VF	XF	Unc
11	1916H	.450	2.00	5.00	15.00	100.00
	1917	.450	2.00	5.00	15.00	65.00
	1919	.750	1.00	4.00	12.50	45.00
	1920	.700	1.00	4.00	12.50	40.00
	1922	.500	1.00	4.00	12.50	45.00
	1924	.300	1.00	5.00	15.00	50.00
	1927	.250	1.50	7.50	18.00	65.00
	1928	.500	1.00	4.00	12.00	35.00
	1929	.500	1.00	4.00	12.00	30.00
	1930	.250	1.50	7.50	18.00	60.00
	1934	.500	1.00	3.00	6.00	25.00
	1935	.500	.50	2.00	4.00	15.00
	1936	.500	.50	2.00	4.00	15.00
	1937	1.000	.10	.50	3.00	12.50
	1938	2.000	.10	.50	3.00	10.00
	1940	2.000	.10	.50	3.00	10.00

BRASS

20	1943	1.000	.50	1.50	4.50	18.00

5 CENTAVOS

COPPER-NICKEL

12	1912H	.460	1.00	3.00	12.50	50.00
	1912H	—	—	—	Proof	300.00
	1914H	.300	1.00	4.00	18.00	85.00
	1915H	.160	2.00	5.00	50.00	225.00
	1919	.100	1.00	4.00	30.00	110.00
	1920	.150	1.00	3.00	25.00	90.00
	1927	.100	2.00	5.00	25.00	80.00
	1928	.100	1.00	3.00	18.00	50.00
	1929	.100	1.00	3.00	15.00	45.00
	1930	.100	1.00	3.00	15.00	45.00
	1934	.200	1.00	3.00	12.50	40.00
	1935	.200	1.00	3.00	12.50	35.00
	1936	.300	.50	1.00	5.00	18.00
	1937	.300	.50	1.00	8.00	25.00
	1938	.800	.50	1.00	5.00	15.00
	1940	.800	.50	1.00	5.00	12.50

BRASS
Plain edge.

21	1943	2.000	.75	2.50	10.00	60.00

COPPER-NICKEL
B.N.N. on edge.

24.1	1946	4.000	.10	.25	2.50	18.00
	1946	—	—	—	Proof	200.00
	1950	—	.10	.25	2.50	18.00
	1952	4.000	.10	.25	3.50	25.00
	1952	—	—	—	Proof	250.00
	1954	4.000	.10	.15	.25	5.00
	1954	—	—	—	Proof	250.00
	1956	5.000	.10	.15	.50	5.00
	1956	—	—	—	Proof	250.00

B.C.N. on edge.

24.2	1962	3.000	—	—	.10	2.00
	1962	—	—	—	Proof	150.00
	1964	4.000	—	—	.10	2.00
	1965	10.000	—	—	.10	2.00

NICKEL CLAD STEEL

24.3a	1972	10.000	—	—	.10	.50

ALUMINUM
F.A.O. Issue

27	1974	2.000	—	—	.40	2.00

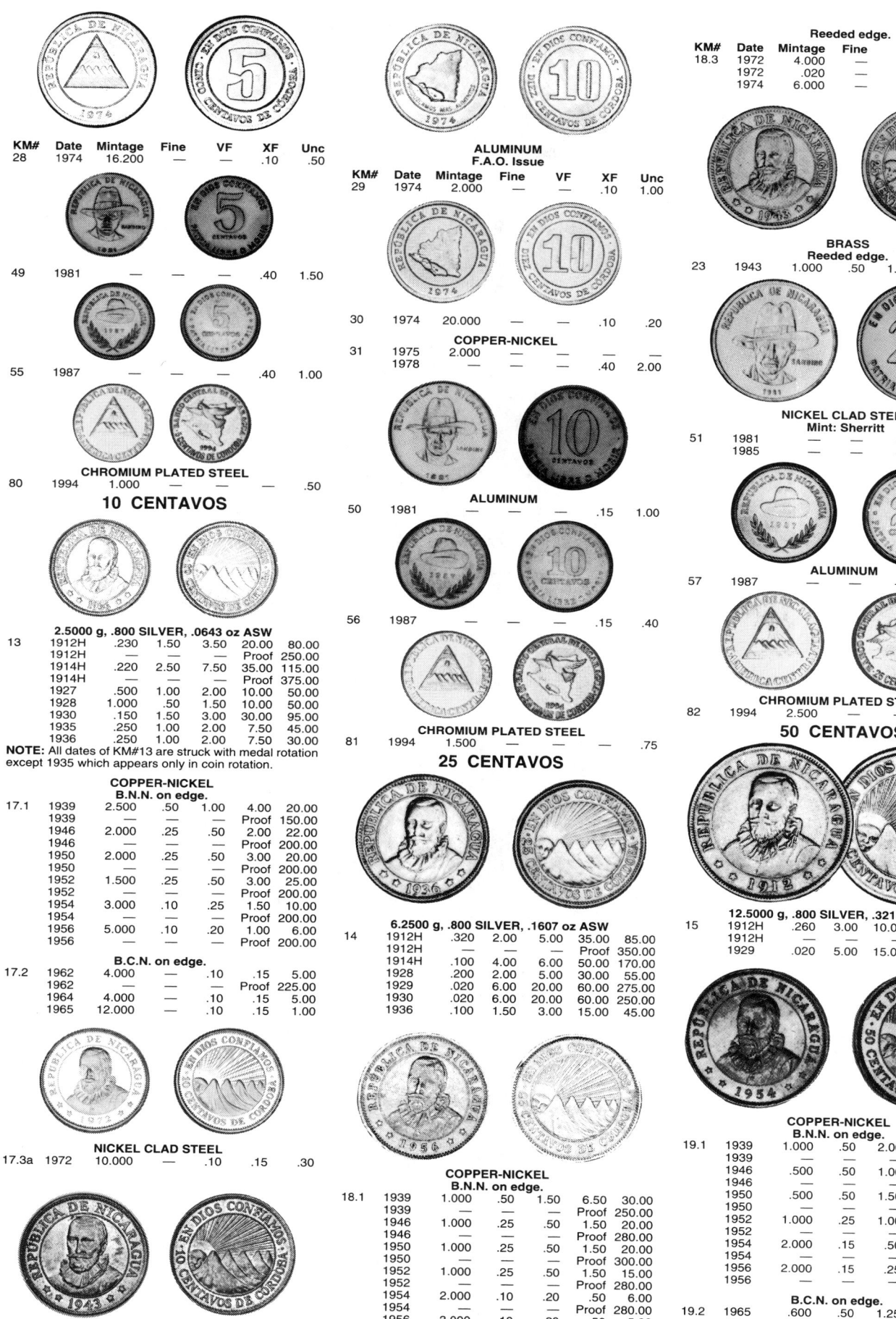

KM#	Date	Mintage	Fine	VF	XF	Unc
28	1974	16.200	—	—	.10	.50

KM#	Date	Mintage	Fine	VF	XF	Unc
49	1981				.40	1.50
55	1987				.40	1.00

CHROMIUM PLATED STEEL

KM#	Date	Mintage	Fine	VF	XF	Unc
80	1994	1.000				.50

10 CENTAVOS

2.5000 g, .800 SILVER, .0643 oz ASW

KM#	Date	Mintage	Fine	VF	XF	Unc
13	1912H	.230	1.50	3.50	20.00	80.00
	1912H	—	—	—	Proof	250.00
	1914H	.220	2.50	7.50	35.00	115.00
	1914H	—	—	—	Proof	375.00
	1927	.500	1.00	2.00	10.00	50.00
	1928	1.000	.50	1.50	10.00	50.00
	1930	.150	1.50	3.00	30.00	95.00
	1935	.250	1.00	2.00	7.50	45.00
	1936	.250	1.00	2.00	7.50	30.00

NOTE: All dates of KM#13 are struck with medal rotation except 1935 which appears only in coin rotation.

COPPER-NICKEL
B.N.N. on edge.

KM#	Date	Mintage	Fine	VF	XF	Unc
17.1	1939	2.500	.50	1.00	4.00	20.00
	1939	—	—	—	Proof	150.00
	1946	2.000	.25	.50	2.00	22.00
	1946	—	—	—	Proof	200.00
	1950	2.000	.25	.50	3.00	20.00
	1950	—	—	—	Proof	200.00
	1952	1.500	.25	.50	3.00	25.00
	1952	—	—	—	Proof	200.00
	1954	3.000	.10	.25	1.50	10.00
	1954	—	—	—	Proof	200.00
	1956	5.000	.10	.20	1.00	6.00
	1956	—	—	—	Proof	200.00

B.C.N. on edge.

KM#	Date	Mintage	Fine	VF	XF	Unc
17.2	1962	4.000	—	.10	.15	5.00
	1962	—	—	—	Proof	225.00
	1964	4.000	—	.10	.15	5.00
	1965	12.000	—	.10	.15	1.00

NICKEL CLAD STEEL

KM#	Date	Mintage	Fine	VF	XF	Unc
17.3a	1972	10.000	—	.10	.15	.30

BRASS
Reeded edge.

KM#	Date	Mintage	Fine	VF	XF	Unc
22	1943	2.000	.50	1.00	5.00	40.00

ALUMINUM
F.A.O. Issue

KM#	Date	Mintage	Fine	VF	XF	Unc
29	1974	2.000	—	—	.10	1.00
30	1974	20.000	—	—	.10	.20

COPPER-NICKEL

KM#	Date	Mintage	Fine	VF	XF	Unc
31	1975	2.000	—	—	—	—
	1978				.40	2.00

ALUMINUM

KM#	Date	Mintage	Fine	VF	XF	Unc
50	1981				.15	1.00
56	1987				.15	.40

CHROMIUM PLATED STEEL

KM#	Date	Mintage	Fine	VF	XF	Unc
81	1994	1.500	—	—	—	.75

25 CENTAVOS

6.2500 g, .800 SILVER, .1607 oz ASW

KM#	Date	Mintage	Fine	VF	XF	Unc
14	1912H	.320	2.00	5.00	35.00	85.00
	1912H	—	—	—	Proof	350.00
	1914H	.100	4.00	6.00	50.00	170.00
	1928	.200	2.00	5.00	30.00	55.00
	1929	.020	6.00	20.00	60.00	275.00
	1930	.020	6.00	20.00	60.00	250.00
	1936	.100	1.50	3.00	15.00	45.00

COPPER-NICKEL
B.N.N. on edge.

KM#	Date	Mintage	Fine	VF	XF	Unc
18.1	1939	1.000	.50	1.50	6.50	30.00
	1939	—	—	—	Proof	250.00
	1946	1.000	.25	.50	1.50	20.00
	1946	—	—	—	Proof	280.00
	1950	1.000	.25	.50	1.50	20.00
	1950	—	—	—	Proof	300.00
	1952	1.000	.25	.50	1.50	15.00
	1952	—	—	—	Proof	280.00
	1954	2.000	.10	.20	.50	6.00
	1954	—	—	—	Proof	280.00
	1956	3.000	.10	.20	.50	5.00
	1956	—	—	—	Proof	280.00

B.C.N. on edge.

KM#	Date	Mintage	Fine	VF	XF	Unc
18.2	1964	3.000	.10	.20	.40	4.00
	1965	4.400	.10	.20	.30	4.00

Reeded edge.

KM#	Date	Mintage	Fine	VF	XF	Unc
18.3	1972	4.000	—	.10	.15	2.00
	1972	.020	—	—	Proof	2.50
	1974	6.000	—	.10	.15	2.00

BRASS
Reeded edge.

KM#	Date	Mintage	Fine	VF	XF	Unc
23	1943	1.000	.50	1.50	8.50	50.00

NICKEL CLAD STEEL
Mint: Sherritt

KM#	Date	Mintage	Fine	VF	XF	Unc
51	1981				.25	1.50
	1985				.25	1.50

ALUMINUM

KM#	Date	Mintage	Fine	VF	XF	Unc
57	1987				.25	2.00

CHROMIUM PLATED STEEL

KM#	Date	Mintage	Fine	VF	XF	Unc
82	1994	2.500				1.00

50 CENTAVOS

12.5000 g, .800 SILVER, .3215 oz ASW

KM#	Date	Mintage	Fine	VF	XF	Unc
15	1912H	.260	3.00	10.00	40.00	165.00
	1912H	—	—	—	Proof	500.00
	1929	.020	5.00	15.00	50.00	260.00

COPPER-NICKEL
B.N.N. on edge.

KM#	Date	Mintage	Fine	VF	XF	Unc
19.1	1939	1.000	.50	2.00	10.00	50.00
	1939	—	—	—	Proof	250.00
	1946	.500	.50	1.00	8.00	45.00
	1946	—	—	—	Proof	300.00
	1950	.500	.50	1.50	10.00	50.00
	1950	—	—	—	Proof	300.00
	1952	1.000	.25	1.00	5.00	30.00
	1952	—	—	—	Proof	300.00
	1954	2.000	.15	.50	2.00	5.00
	1954	—	—	—	Proof	300.00
	1956	2.000	.15	.25	1.00	8.00
	1956	—	—	—	Proof	300.00

B.C.N. on edge.

KM#	Date	Mintage	Fine	VF	XF	Unc
19.2	1965	.600	.50	1.25	3.50	8.00
	1965	—	—	—	Proof	150.00

Reeded edge.

KM#	Date	Mintage	Fine	VF	XF	Unc
19.3	1972	—	—	—	—	—
	1972	.020	—	—	Proof	2.50
	1974	2.000	.10	.25	.50	3.50

KM#	Date	Mintage	Fine	VF	XF	Unc
42	1980 Mo	5.000	.10	.25	.50	1.75
	1981 Mo	—	.10	.25	.50	1.75

NICKEL CLAD STEEL

| 42a | 1983 | — | — | — | .40 | 2.50 |
| | 1985 | — | — | — | — | — |

ALUMINUM-BRONZE

| 58 | 1987 | — | — | — | .40 | 2.50 |

CHROMIUM PLATED STEEL

| 83 | 1994 | 6.000 | — | — | — | 1.25 |

UN (1) CORDOBA

25.0000 g, .900 SILVER, .7234 oz ASW

| 16 | 1912H | .035 | 30.00 | 75.00 | 275.00 | 1850. |
| | 1912H | — | — | — | Proof | 2850. |

COPPER-NICKEL
Reeded edge.

| 26 | 1972 | 20.000 | .10 | .20 | 2.00 | 4.00 |
| | 1972 | — | — | — | Proof | 5.00 |

43	1980 Mo	10.000	.10	.20	.50	2.00
	1981 Mo	—	.10	.20	.50	2.00
	1983 Mo	—	.10	.20	.50	2.00

NICKEL CLAD STEEL

KM#	Date	Mintage	Fine	VF	XF	Unc
43a	1984	—	—	.10	.50	2.00
	1985	—	—	.10	.50	2.00

ALUMINUM-BRONZE

| 59 | 1987 | — | — | .75 | 1.00 | 3.75 |

NICKEL CLAD STEEL
Obv: National emblem. Rev: Denomination.

| 89 | 1997 | 32.000 | — | — | — | 2.50 |

5 CORDOBAS

COPPER-NICKEL

| 44 | 1980 | 10.000 | .15 | .25 | 1.00 | 3.00 |

NICKEL CLAD STEEL

| 44a | 1984 | — | — | .25 | 1.00 | 3.50 |

ALUMINUM-BRONZE

| 60 | 1987 | — | — | 1.00 | 2.50 | 4.00 |

NICKEL CLAD STEEL
Obv: National emblem. Rev: Denomination.

| 90 | 1997 | 50.000 | — | — | — | 4.00 |

500 CORDOBAS

ALUMINUM

KM#	Date	Mintage	VF	XF	Unc
63	1987	—	—	2.50	6.50

NIGERIA

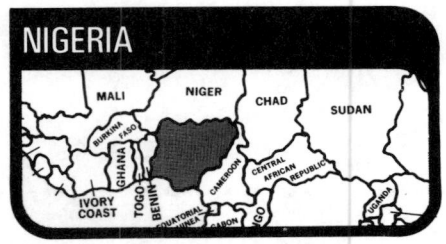

The Federal Republic of Nigeria, situated on the Atlantic coast of West Africa has an area of 356,669 sq. mi. (923,770 sq. km.) and a population of *115.2 million. Capital: Lagos. The economy is based on petroleum and agriculture. Crude oil, cocoa, tobacco and tin are exported.

Following the Napoleonic Wars, the British expanded their trade with the interior of Nigeria. British claims to a sphere of influence in that area were recognized by the Berlin Conference of 1885, and in the following year the Royal Niger Company was chartered. Direct British control of the territory was initiated in 1900, and in 1914 the amalgamation of Northern and Southern Nigeria into the Colony and Protectorate of Nigeria was effected. In 1960, following a number of territorial and constitutional changes, Nigeria was granted independence within the British Commonwealth as a federation of the Northern, Western and Eastern regions. Nigeria altered its political relationship with Great Britain on Oct. 1, 1963, by proclaiming itself a republic. It did, however, elect to remain a member of the Commonwealth of Nations. The Supreme Commander of Armed Forces is the Head of the Federal Military Government. Nigeria was suspended from the Commonwealth in Nov. 1995.

On May 30, 1967, the Eastern Region of the republic - an area occupied principally by the proud and resourceful Ibo tribe - seceded from Nigeria and proclaimed itself the independent Republic of Biafra with Odumegwu Ojukwu as Chief of State. Civil war erupted and raged for 31 months. Casualties, including civilian, were about two million, the majority succumbing to malnutrition and disease. Biafra surrendered to the federal government on January 15, 1970.

For earlier coinage refer to British West Africa.

RULERS
Elizabeth II, 1952-1963

MONETARY SYSTEM
12 Pence = 1 Shilling
20 Shillings = 1 Pound

1/2 PENNY

BRONZE

KM#	Date	Mintage	VF	XF	Unc
1	1959	52.800	.15	.25	.75
	1959	6,031	—	Proof	2.50

PENNY

BRONZE

| 2 | 1959 | 93.368 | .15 | .25 | 1.25 |
| | 1959 | 6,031 | — | Proof | 2.50 |

3 PENCE

NICKEL-BRASS

| 3 | 1959 | 52.000 | .20 | .40 | 1.50 |
| | 1959 | 6,031 | — | Proof | 3.50 |

6 PENCE

COPPER-NICKEL

KM#	Date	Mintage	VF	XF	Unc
4	1959	35.000	.40	.80	2.50
	1959	6,031	—	Proof	5.00

SHILLING

COPPER-NICKEL

5	1959	18.000	.65	1.45	3.50
	1959	6,031	—	Proof	6.50
	1961	48.584	.65	1.45	3.50
	1961	—	Reported, not confirmed		
	1962	39.416	.65	1.45	3.50

2 SHILLINGS

COPPER-NICKEL
Security edge

6.1	1959	15.000	1.25	2.50	6.00
	1959	6,031	—	Proof	9.00

Reeded edge

6.2	1959	Inc. Ab.	1.25	2.50	6.00

REPUBLIC
100 Kobo = 1 Naira (10 Shillings)

1/2 KOBO

BRONZE

7	1973	166.618	.45	1.00	3.50
	1973	.010	—	Proof	3.50

KOBO

BRONZE

8	1973	586.944	.25	.50	2.00
	1973	.010	—	Proof	3.50
	1974	14.500	.25	.50	3.00
	1987	—	.25	.50	3.00
	1988	—	.25	.50	3.00

COPPER PLATED STEEL

8a	1991	—	—	—	.25

5 KOBO

COPPER-NICKEL

KM#	Date	Mintage	VF	XF	Unc
9	1973	96.920	.35	.75	2.75
	1973	.010	—	Proof	4.00
	1974	—	.45	.85	3.00
	1976	9.800	.45	.85	3.00
	1986	—	.45	.85	3.00
	1987	—	.45	.85	3.00
	1988	—	.45	.85	3.00
	1989	—	.45	.85	3.00

10 KOBO

COPPER-NICKEL

10	1973	340.870	.50	1.00	3.50
	1973	.010	—	Proof	5.00
	1974	—	.60	1.20	3.75
	1976	7.000	.60	1.20	3.75
	1987	—	.60	1.20	3.75
	1988	—	.60	1.20	3.75
	1989	—	.60	1.20	3.75
	1990	—	.60	1.20	3.75

COPPER PLATED STEEL

12	1991	—	—	—	.45

25 KOBO

COPPER-NICKEL

11	1973	4.616	1.00	2.50	7.50
	1973	.010	—	Proof	8.50
	1975	—	1.00	2.50	7.50

COPPER PLATED STEEL

11a	1991	—	—	—	.65

50 KOBO

NICKEL PLATED STEEL

13	1991	—	—	—	1.25
	1993	—	—	—	1.25

NAIRA

NICKEL PLATED STEEL

KM#	Date	Mintage	VF	XF	Unc
14	1991	—	—	—	1.75
	1993	—	—	—	1.75

BIAFRA

MONETARY SYSTEM
12 Pence = 1 Shilling

3 PENCE

ALUMINUM

1	1969	—	15.00	20.00	30.00

6 PENCE

ALUMINUM
Obv. value: 6 PENCE.

12	1969	2 pcs. known	—	—	—

SHILLING

ALUMINUM

2	1969	—	10.00	15.00	22.50

Obv. value: ONE SHILLING

3	1969	—	—	250.00	350.00

2-1/2 SHILLINGS

ALUMINUM

4	1969	—	11.50	17.50	30.00

NORWAY

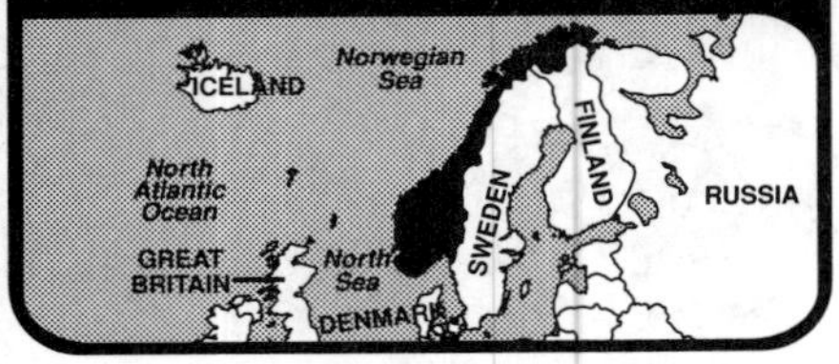

The Kingdom of Norway, a constitutional monarchy located in northwestern Europe, has an area of 150,000 sq. mi. (324,220 sq. km.), including the island territories of Spitzbergen (Svalbard) and Jan Mayen, and a population of *4.2 million. Capital: Oslo. The diversified economic base of Norway includes shipping, fishing, forestry, agriculture, and manufacturing. Nonferrous metals, paper and paperboard, paper pulp, iron, steel and oil are exported.

A united Norwegian kingdom was established in the 9th century, the era of the indomitable Norse Vikings who ranged far and wide, visiting the coasts of northwestern Europe, the Mediterranean, Greenland and North America. In the 13th century the Norse kingdom was united briefly with Sweden, then passed through inheritance in 1380 to the rule of Denmark which was maintained until 1814. In 1814 Norway fell again under the rule of Sweden. The union lasted until 1905 when the Norwegian Parliament arranged a peaceful separation and invited a Danish prince (King Haakon VII) to ascend the throne of an independent Kingdom of Norway. His son Olav V became King in 1957. Just prior to his death on Jan. 17, 1991, King Olav committed 10,000 troops to the Persian Gulf.

RULERS

Swedish, until 1905
Haakon VII, 1905-1957
Olav V, 1957-1991
Harald V, 1991-

MINT MARKS

(h) - Crossed hammers - Kongsberg

MINTMASTERS INITIALS

Letter	Date	Name
AB,B	1961-1980	Arne Jon Bakken
AB*	1980	Ole R. Kolberg
I,IT	1880-1918	Ivar Trondsen, engraver
IAR	—	Angrid Austlid Rise, engraver
K	1981	Ole R. Kolberg
OH	1959	Oivind Hansen, engraver

MONETARY SYSTEM

100 Ore = 1 Krone (30 Skilling)

ORE

BRONZE

KM#	Date	Mintage	Fine	VF	XF	BU
352	1902	4.500	2.00	4.00	10.00	35.00

NOTE: Earlier dates (1876-1899) exist for this type.
NOTE: Varieties exist.

KM#	Date	Mintage	Fine	VF	XF	BU
361	1906	3.000	2.00	4.00	9.00	20.00
	1907	2.550	2.00	4.00	10.00	25.00

KM#	Date	Mintage	Fine	VF	XF	BU
367	1908	1.450	10.00	15.00	40.00	140.00
	1910	2.480	1.00	2.50	7.00	27.50
	1911	3.270	1.00	2.50	7.00	40.00
	1912	2.850	3.00	7.00	30.00	140.00
	1913	2.840	1.00	2.50	5.00	25.00
	1914	5.020	1.00	2.50	5.00	30.00
	1915	1.540	8.00	20.00	40.00	175.00
	1921	3.805	17.50	35.00	70.00	200.00
	1922	Inc. Ab.	.50	2.00	12.00	50.00
	1923	.770	6.00	12.00	25.00	125.00
	1925	3.000	.50	1.50	10.00	45.00
	1926	2.200	.50	1.50	10.00	45.00
	1927	.800	4.00	10.00	25.00	125.00
	1928	3.000	.25	.75	4.00	20.00
	1929	4.990	.25	.75	4.00	16.50
	1930 lg.dt.	2.010	.50	1.00	5.00	22.00
	1930 sm.dt.	I.A.	.50	1.00	5.00	22.00
367	1931	2.000	.50	1.00	5.00	22.00
	1932	2.500	.50	1.00	5.00	22.00
	1933	2.000	.50	1.00	5.00	16.50
	1934	2.000	.50	1.00	5.00	16.50
	1935	5.495	.25	.75	2.00	10.00
	1936	6.855	.25	.75	2.00	10.00
	1937	6.020	.20	.50	1.25	6.00
	1938	4.920	.20	.50	1.25	6.00
	1939	2.500	.20	.50	1.25	10.00
	1940	5.010	.20	.50	1.25	6.00
	1941	12.260	.10	.25	1.25	6.00
	1946	2.200	.10	.25	1.25	10.00
	1947	4.870	.10	.25	.75	5.00
	1948	9.405	.10	.25	.75	4.00
	1949	2.785	.10	.25	.75	6.00
	1950	5.730	.10	.25	.75	4.00
	1951	16.670	.10	.25	.75	4.00
	1952	Inc. Ab.	.10	.25	.75	3.00

IRON

KM#	Date	Mintage	Fine	VF	XF	BU
367a	1918	6.000	5.00	8.00	15.00	50.00
	1919	12.930	1.50	3.50	10.00	22.50
	1920	4.445	6.00	10.00	20.00	75.00
	1921	2.270	30.00	35.00	55.00	150.00

World War II German Occupation

KM#	Date	Mintage	Fine	VF	XF	BU
387	1941	13.410	.15	.50	1.50	10.00
	1942	37.710	.15	.50	1.50	4.50
	1943	33.030	.15	.50	1.50	4.50
	1944	8.820	.25	.75	2.00	8.00
	1945	1.740	4.00	8.00	12.50	28.00

BRONZE

KM#	Date	Mintage	Fine	VF	XF	BU
398	1952	Inc. KM367	—	.10	.80	5.00
	1953	7.440	—	.10	.80	3.50
	1954	7.650	—	.10	.80	3.50
	1955	8.635	—	.10	.80	3.50
	1956	11.705	—	.10	.80	3.50
	1957	15.750	—	.10	.60	2.50

KM#	Date	Mintage	Fine	VF	XF	BU
403	1958	2.820	.25	.50	2.00	7.00
	1959	9.120	.10	.20	.75	6.00
	1960	7.890	—	.10	.25	2.50
	1961	5.671	—	.10	.25	2.50
	1962	12.180	—	.10	.20	1.25
	1963	8.010	—	.10	.25	2.50
	1964	11.020	—	—	.10	.75
	1965	8.081	—	—	.10	1.50
	1966	12.431	—	—	.10	1.00
	1967	13.026	—	—	.10	.75
	1968	.126	.50	1.00	2.00	7.00
	1969	6.291	—	—	.10	.50
	1970	6.608	—	—	.10	.50
	1971	18.966	—	—	.10	.40
	1972	21.103	—	—	.10	.40

NOTE: Varieties exist.

2 ORE

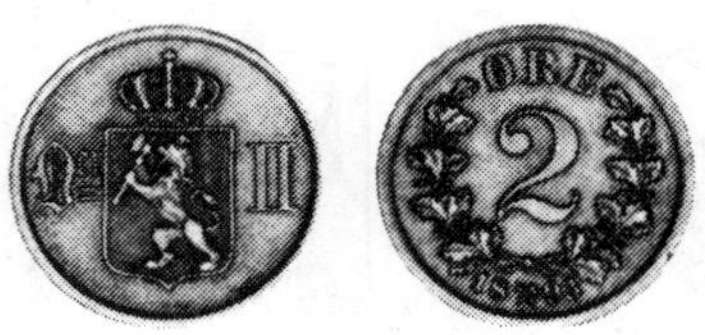

BRONZE

KM#	Date	Mintage	Fine	VF	XF	BU
353	1902	1.005	1.50	4.00	10.00	60.00

NOTE: Earlier dates (1876-1899) exist for this type.

KM#	Date	Mintage	Fine	VF	XF	BU
362	1906	.500	5.00	10.00	35.00	200.00
	1907	.980	3.00	4.00	15.00	90.00

KM#	Date	Mintage	Fine	VF	XF	BU
371	1909	.520	6.00	10.00	38.00	175.00
	1910	.500	6.00	10.00	38.00	300.00
	1911	.195	6.00	10.00	38.00	200.00
	1912	.805	6.00	10.00	38.00	200.00
	1913	2.010	.75	2.00	10.00	75.00
	1914	2.990	.75	2.00	10.00	75.00
	1915	Inc. Ab.	4.00	9.00	50.00	300.00
	1921	2.028	.50	1.00	10.00	50.00
	1922	2.288	.50	1.00	10.00	50.00
	1923	.745	1.00	2.00	20.00	100.00
	1928	2.250	.50	1.00	5.00	40.00
	1929	.750	1.00	2.00	12.00	75.00
	1931	1.570	.50	1.00	5.00	30.00
	1932	.630	3.50	6.00	25.00	150.00
	1933	.750	.50	1.50	6.00	50.00
	1934	.500	.50	1.50	6.00	50.00
	1935	2.223	.25	1.00	4.00	30.00
	1936	4.533	.25	1.00	4.00	30.00
	1937	3.790	.20	.50	2.25	15.00
	1938	3.765	.20	.50	2.25	15.00
	1939	4.420	.20	.50	2.25	15.00
	1940	2.655	.20	.50	2.25	15.00
	1946	1.575	.20	.50	3.00	15.00
	1947	4.679	.10	.25	1.00	10.00
	1948	1.003	1.00	3.00	4.00	16.00
	1949	1.455	.10	.25	1.00	7.00
	1950	5.790	.10	.25	1.00	6.00
	1951	10.540	.10	.25	1.00	6.00
	1952	Inc. Ab.	.10	.25	1.00	6.00

IRON

KM#	Date	Mintage	Fine	VF	XF	BU
371a	1917	.720	75.00	115.00	225.00	425.00
	1918	1.280	35.00	50.00	90.00	220.00
	1919	3.365	10.00	15.00	35.00	125.00
	1920	2.635	10.00	15.00	45.00	200.00

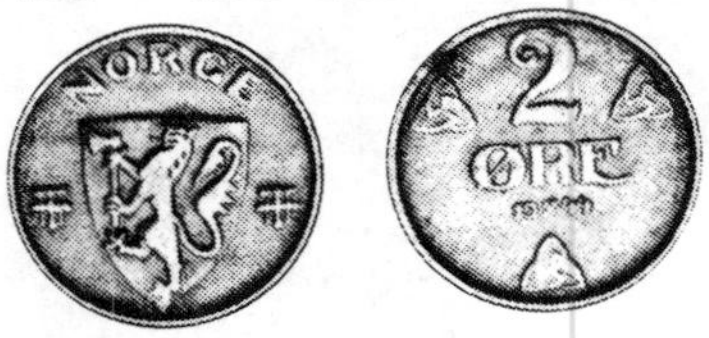

World War II German Occupation

KM#	Date	Mintage	Fine	VF	XF	BU
394	1943	6.575	.50	.75	1.50	7.00
	1944	9.805	.50	.75	1.50	7.00
	1945	2.520	1.50	3.00	5.00	15.00

BRONZE

KM#	Date	Mintage	Fine	VF	XF	BU
399	1952	Inc. Ab.	—	.10	.80	6.50
	1953	6.705	—	.10	.80	5.50
	1954	2.805	—	.10	.80	5.50
	1955	3.600	—	.10	.80	5.50
	1956	6.780	—	.10	.80	5.50
	1957	6.090	—	.10	.80	5.50

Rev: Small lettering.

KM#	Date	Mintage	Fine	VF	XF	BU
404	1958	2.700	.20	.50	1.50	6.50

Rev: Large lettering.

KM#	Date	Mintage	Fine	VF	XF	BU
410	1959	4.125	.10	.20	1.00	6.00
	1960	3.735	—	.10	.75	10.00
	1961	4.477	—	.10	.30	2.00
	1962	6.205	—	.10	.30	2.00
	1963	4.840	—	.10	.30	2.00
	1964	7.250	—	.10	.15	1.25
	1965	6.241	—	.10	.25	2.50
	1966	10.485	—	—	.10	2.00
	1967	11.993	—	—	.10	1.25
	1968	3,467	— In mint sets only			700.00
	1969	.316	.50	1.00	1.50	4.50

KM#	Date	Mintage	Fine	VF	XF	BU
410	1970	6.794	—	—	.10	.80
	1971	15.462	—	—	.10	.60
	1972	15.898	—	—	.10	.50

5 ORE

BRONZE

KM#	Date	Mintage	Fine	VF	XF	BU
349	1902	.705	2.50	6.00	35.00	200.00

NOTE: Earlier dates (1875-1899) exist for this type.

KM#	Date	Mintage	Fine	VF	XF	BU
364	1907	.200	3.50	9.00	40.00	200.00

KM#	Date	Mintage	Fine	VF	XF	BU
368	1908	.600	20.00	35.00	75.00	350.00
	1911	.480	2.00	10.00	40.00	200.00
	1912	.520	4.00	75.00	50.00	400.00
	1913	1.000	1.25	2.50	17.50	110.00
	1914	1.000	1.25	2.50	17.50	110.00
	1915	Inc. Ab.	8.00	25.00	75.00	500.00
	1916	.300	6.00	12.50	30.00	200.00
	1921	.683	1.50	6.00	40.00	200.00
	1922	2.296	1.25	5.00	25.00	125.00
	1923	.456	2.50	7.50	40.00	200.00
	1928	.848	.60	3.00	15.00	85.00
	1929	.452	3.00	9.00	40.00	200.00
	1930	1.292	.60	2.50	20.00	100.00
	1931	.808	.60	2.50	20.00	100.00
	1932	.500	3.00	10.00	30.00	150.00
	1933	.300	3.00	10.00	40.00	250.00
	1935	.496	1.50	5.00	15.00	100.00
	1936	.760	1.00	2.50	12.50	75.00
	1937	1.552	.50	1.50	10.00	35.00
	1938	1.332	.50	1.50	10.00	35.00
	1939	1.370	.50	1.50	8.00	35.00
	1940	2.554	.30	1.00	6.00	25.00
	1941	3.576	.30	1.00	5.00	18.00
	1951	8.128	.25	.50	2.00	15.00
	1952	Inc. Ab.	1.50	3.50	8.00	50.00

IRON

KM#	Date	Mintage	Fine	VF	XF	BU
368a	1917	1.700	20.00	35.00	60.00	125.00
	1918/7	.432	120.00	175.00	325.00	800.00
	1918	Inc. Ab.	110.00	165.00	300.00	800.00
	1919	3.464	8.00	25.00	50.00	150.00
	1920	1.629	25.00	50.00	90.00	250.00

World War II German Occupation

KM#	Date	Mintage	Fine	VF	XF	BU
388	1941	6.608	.50	1.50	4.50	30.00
	1942	10.312	.50	1.50	4.00	15.00
	1943	6.184	.75	2.00	6.00	25.00
	1944	4.256	1.25	3.00	8.00	25.00
	1945	.408	125.00	185.00	300.00	475.00

BRONZE

KM#	Date	Mintage	Fine	VF	XF	BU
400	1952	Inc. KM368	.10	1.00	2.00	30.00
	1953	6.216	.10	1.00	2.00	15.00
	1954	4.536	.10	1.00	2.00	15.00
	1955	6.570	.10	1.00	2.00	15.00
	1956	2.959	.10	1.00	2.00	25.00
	1957	5.624	.10	1.00	2.00	10.00

KM#	Date	Mintage	Fine	VF	XF	BU
405	1958	2.205	1.00	2.00	5.00	30.00
	1959	3.208	.10	.50	2.00	15.00
	1960	5.519	.10	.20	1.00	10.00
	1961	4.554	.10	.20	1.00	10.00
	1962	7.764	.10	.15	.75	5.00
	1963	3.204	.10	.15	.75	5.00
	1964	6.108	—	.10	.50	2.50
	1965	6.841	—	.10	.50	2.50
	1966	8.415	—	.10	.50	2.50
	1967	9.071	—	.10	.50	2.50
	1968	4.286	—	.10	.80	3.50
	1969	4.328	—	.10	.30	1.50
	1970	7.351	—	.10	.30	1.25
	1971	13.450	—	.10	.30	1.50
	1972	19.002	—	—	.10	.75
	1973	9.584	—	—	.10	.75

KM#	Date	Mintage	Fine	VF	XF	BU
415	1973	52.886	—	—	.10	.35
	1974	37.150	—	—	.10	.35
	1975	32.479	—	—	.10	.35
	1976	24.233	—	—	.10	.25
	1977	29.646	—	—	.10	.25
	1978	13.838	—	—	.10	.25
	1979	25.255	—	—	.10	.25
	1980	12.315	—	—	.10	.25
	1980 w/o star					
		27.515	—	—	.10	.25
	1981	24.529	—	—	.10	.25
	1982	16.849	—	—	.10	.25

NOTE: Varieties exist.

10 ORE

1.5000 g, .400 SILVER, .0192 oz ASW

KM#	Date	Mintage	Fine	VF	XF	BU
350	1901	2.021	5.00	7.50	22.50	50.00
	1903	1.501	5.00	7.50	22.50	50.00

NOTE: Earlier dates (1875-1899) exist for this type.

KM#	Date	Mintage	Fine	VF	XF	BU
372	1909	2.000	4.00	7.50	17.50	60.00
	1911	1.650	5.00	8.50	25.00	125.00
	1912	2.350	4.00	7.50	17.50	50.00
	1913	2.000	4.00	6.00	12.50	40.00
	1914	1.180	7.00	11.00	25.00	75.00
	1915	2.820	1.50	3.00	6.00	30.00
	1916	1.500	6.00	9.00	25.00	75.00
	1917	5.950	1.00	2.00	4.00	8.00
	1918/7	1.650	—	—	—	—
	1918	Inc. Ab.	1.50	2.50	7.50	20.00
	1919	7.800	1.00	2.00	4.00	8.00

COPPER-NICKEL

KM#	Date	Mintage	Fine	VF	XF	BU
378	1920	2.535	10.00	15.00	20.00	50.00
	1921	6.465	5.00	10.00	15.00	40.00
	1922	3.965	5.00	10.00	15.00	40.00
	1923	7.135	10.00	15.00	20.00	50.00

KM#	Date	Mintage	Fine	VF	XF	BU
383	1924	12.079	.30	.75	7.50	30.00
	1925	7.051	.30	.75	7.50	45.00
	1926	11.764	.30	.75	7.50	30.00
	1927	.527	5.00	15.00	100.00	525.00
	1937	5.000	.30	.75	4.00	22.00
	1938	3.413	.30	.75	4.00	30.00
	1939	1.538	1.00	2.50	8.00	40.00
	1940	4.800	.30	.75	1.50	10.00
	1941	10.150	.30	.75	1.50	8.00
	1945	1.719	.10	.25	1.50	16.50

KM#	Date	Mintage	Fine	VF	XF	BU
383	1946	3.723	.10	.25	1.50	7.00
	1947	7.257	.10	.25	1.50	5.00
	1948	3.105	.10	.25	2.00	5.50
	1949	11.546	.10	.25	1.50	5.50
	1951	5.150	.10	.25	1.50	5.50

ZINC
World War II German Occupation

KM#	Date	Mintage	Fine	VF	XF	BU
389	1941	15.310	.75	2.00	5.00	25.00
	1942	50.388	.35	1.00	3.00	10.00
	1943	13.378	.75	2.00	4.50	20.00
	1944	3.549	7.50	12.50	25.00	125.00
	1945	5.646	4.00	8.00	15.00	50.00

NICKEL-BRASS
World War II Government in Exile

KM#	Date	Mintage	Fine	VF	XF	BU
391	1942	*6.000	—	—	100.00	200.00

NOTE: All melted down except for 9,667.

COPPER-NICKEL

KM#	Date	Mintage	Fine	VF	XF	BU
396	1951	17.400	.10	.30	2.00	25.00
	1952	Inc. Ab.	.10	.20	1.25	15.00
	1953	7.700	.10	.20	1.25	15.00
	1954	10.105	.10	.20	1.25	15.00
	1955	9.830	.10	.20	1.25	25.00
	1956	10.066	.10	.20	1.25	15.00
	1957	22.900	.10	.20	1.25	10.00

Rev: Small lettering.

KM#	Date	Mintage	Fine	VF	XF	BU
406	1958	1.425	.50	1.50	2.50	12.50

Rev: Large lettering.

KM#	Date	Mintage	Fine	VF	XF	BU
411	1959	2.500	—	.75	2.50	10.00
	1960	12.490	—	.10	.50	6.00
	1961	10.386	—	.10	.50	15.00
	1962	16.210	—	.10	.50	3.00
	1963	17.560	—	.10	.50	3.00
	1964	9.781	—	.10	.25	1.25
	1965	10.561	—	.10	.50	4.50
	1966	16.610	—	.10	.50	2.25
	1967	18.243	—	.10	.30	2.25
	1968	24.698	—	.10	.30	2.25
	1969	27.157	—	.10	.20	2.00
	1970	.639	.50	1.00	2.00	5.00
	1971	8.904	—	.10	.15	1.25
	1972	24.834	—	—	.10	.75
	1973	22.301	—	—	.10	.75

KM#	Date	Mintage	Fine	VF	XF	BU
416	1974	30.995	—	—	.10	.50
	1975	21.845	—	—	.10	.50
	1976	42.403	—	—	.10	.35
	1977	43.304	—	—	.10	.35
	1978	37.395	—	—	.10	.35
	1979	25.808	—	—	.10	.35
	1980	28.620	—	—	.10	.35
	1980 w/o star					
		14.050	—	—	.10	.35
	1981	43.083	—	—	.10	.35
	1982	40.974	—	—	.10	.35
	1983	45.637	—	—	.10	.35
	1984	100.066	—	—	.10	.30
	1985	103.108	—	—	.10	.30
	1986	146.392	—	—	.10	.30
	1987	166.040	—	—	.10	.30
	1988	94.677	—	—	.10	.30
	1989	97.274	—	—	.10	.30
	1990	150.290	—	—	.10	.30
	1991	—	—	—	.10	.30
	1992	—	—	—	.10	.30

NOTE: Varieties exist in monogram.

25 ORE

2.4000 g, .600 SILVER, .0463 oz ASW

KM#	Date	Mintage	Fine	VF	XF	BU
360	1901	.607	10.00	16.00	45.00	125.00
	1902	.612	10.00	16.00	45.00	125.00
	1904	.600	10.00	16.00	45.00	125.00

NOTE: Earlier dates (1896-1900) exist for this type.

373	1909	.600	10.00	20.00	40.00	95.00
	1911	.400	20.00	30.00	60.00	150.00
	1912	.200	65.00	100.00	200.00	450.00
	1913	.400	15.00	25.00	60.00	140.00
	1914	.400	15.00	25.00	60.00	140.00
	1915	1.032	6.00	10.00	20.00	50.00
	1916	.368	20.00	40.00	65.00	200.00
	1917	.400	20.00	40.00	60.00	165.00
	1918/6	.800	10.00	17.50	32.50	50.00
	1918	Inc. Ab.	7.00	10.00	20.00	50.00
	1919	1.600	5.00	8.00	15.00	35.00

COPPER-NICKEL

381	1921	4.800	7.50	10.00	15.00	32.50
	1922	14.200	7.50	10.00	15.00	32.50
	1923	5.200	15.00	20.00	27.50	55.00

382	1921	Inc. KM381	3.00	5.00	25.00	400.00
	1922	Inc. KM381	3.00	4.00	18.00	250.00
	1923	Inc. KM381	1.50	3.00	15.00	150.00

384	1924	4.000	.50	2.00	6.00	50.00
	1927	6.200	.50	1.50	6.00	50.00
	1929	.800	1.50	6.00	32.00	200.00
	1939	1.220	.25	.75	3.00	40.00
	1940	1.160	.25	.75	3.00	40.00
	1946	1.850	.20	.50	1.50	10.00
	1947	2.592	.20	.50	1.50	6.00
	1949	2.602	.20	.50	1.50	10.00
	1950	2.800	.20	.50	1.50	10.00

NICKEL-BRASS
World War II Government in Exile

392	1942	*2.400	—	—	100.00	200.00

***NOTE:** All melted down except for 10,300 pieces.

ZINC
World War II German Occupation

395	1943	14.105	1.00	1.50	3.50	25.00
	1944	3.031	4.00	7.50	17.50	50.00
	1945	3.010	6.00	10.00	20.00	60.00

COPPER-NICKEL

KM#	Date	Mintage	Fine	VF	XF	BU
401	1952	4.060	.10	.25	1.00	20.00
	1953	3.320	.10	.25	1.00	25.00
401	1954	3.140	.10	.25	1.00	20.00
	1955	2.000	.10	.25	1.00	50.00
	1956	3.980	.10	.25	1.00	15.00
	1957	7.660	.10	.25	1.00	15.00

NOTE: Varieties exist w/mint mark on square or w/o square.

407	1958	1.316	.50	1.00	2.50	20.00
	1959	1.184	.50	1.00	2.50	20.00
	1960	3.964	—	.10	1.00	10.00
	1961	4.656	—	.10	.90	5.50
	1962	6.304	—	.10	.90	5.50
	1963	3.640	—	.10	.90	5.50
	1964	4.953	—	.10	.40	2.00
	1965	2.798	—	.10	.60	10.00
	1966	6.075	—	.10	.60	2.50
	1967	6.641	—	.10	.60	2.50
	1968	4.963	—	.10	.40	2.00
	1969	12.427	—	.10	.15	1.50
	1970	1.545	—	.10	.60	5.00
	1971	5.247	—	—	.10	1.00
	1972	7.929	—	—	.10	1.00
	1973	8.516	—	—	.10	1.00

417	1974	8.048	—	—	.10	.50
	1975	15.595	—	—	.10	.50
	1976	24.721	—	—	.10	.40
	1977	20.150	—	—	.10	.40
	1978	11.259	—	—	.10	.40
	1979	16.666	—	—	.10	.40
	1980	6.289	—	—	.10	.40
	1980 w/o star	8.176	—	—	.10	.40
	1981	17.971	—	—	.10	.40
	1982	16.863	—	—	.10	.40

50 ORE

5.0000 g, .600 SILVER, .0964 oz ASW
Rev: W/o 15 SK.

356	1901	.404	7.50	22.00	55.00	165.00
	1902	.301	7.50	22.00	55.00	165.00
	1904	.101	60.00	100.00	200.00	500.00

NOTE: Earlier dates (1895-1900) exist for this type.

374	1909	.200	20.00	35.00	65.00	135.00
	1911	.200	30.00	45.00	80.00	200.00
	1912	.200	40.00	60.00	100.00	250.00
	1913	.200	30.00	45.00	80.00	200.00
	1914	.800	5.00	9.00	17.50	75.00
	1915	.300	17.50	25.00	50.00	150.00
	1916	.700	6.00	9.00	17.50	60.00
	1918	3.090	2.00	4.00	10.00	30.00
	1919	1.219	2.50	4.50	10.00	30.00

COPPER-NICKEL

379	1920	1.236	25.00	35.00	50.00	100.00
	1921	7.345	8.00	12.50	20.00	45.00
	1922	3.000	8.00	12.50	20.00	45.00
	1923	4.540	45.00	65.00	85.00	160.00

KM#	Date	Mintage	Fine	VF	XF	BU
380	1920	Inc. KM379	30.00	50.00	150.00	850.00
	1921	Inc. KM379	3.00	8.00	50.00	450.00
	1922	Inc. KM379	2.50	6.00	40.00	300.00
	1923	Inc. KM379	2.50	6.00	35.00	250.00

386	1926	2.000	.35	1.50	12.50	75.00
	1927	2.502	.35	1.50	10.00	60.00
	1928/7	1.458	.50	2.50	12.00	60.00
	1928	Inc. Ab.	.35	1.50	12.50	75.00
	1929	.600	1.50	6.00	55.00	450.00
	1939	.900	.25	.60	4.00	75.00
	1940	2.193	.20	.50	3.00	20.00
	1941	2.373	.20	.50	3.00	15.00
	1945	1.354	.20	.50	2.00	25.00
	1946	1.533	.20	.50	3.00	15.00
	1947	2.465	.20	.50	3.00	12.50
	1948	5.911	.20	.40	1.50	12.00
	1949	1.030	.25	1.00	4.00	20.00

NICKEL-BRASS
World War II Government in Exile

393	1942	*1.600	—	—	110.00	170.00

***NOTE:** All melted down except for 9,238.

ZINC
World War II German Occupation

390	1941	7.761	1.25	3.00	7.50	75.00
	1942	7.606	1.00	2.50	6.00	30.00
	1943	3.349	15.00	20.00	50.00	135.00
	1944	1.542	10.00	15.00	30.00	85.00
	1945	.226	175.00	275.00	425.00	650.00

COPPER-NICKEL

402	1953	2.370	.20	.60	1.50	25.00
	1954	.230	3.50	9.00	60.00	350.00
	1955	1.930	.10	.40	2.00	50.00
	1956	1.630	.10	.40	2.00	50.00
	1957	1.800	.10	.40	2.00	25.00

408	1958	1.560	.25	.75	2.50	45.00
	1959	.340	1.00	2.00	10.00	60.00
	1960	1.584	—	.10	1.50	15.00
	1961	2.425	—	.10	.75	10.00
	1962	3.064	—	.10	.75	10.00
	1963	2.168	—	.10	.75	10.00
	1964	2.692	—	.10	.50	5.00
	1965	1.248	.25	.75	2.50	30.00

KM#	Date	Mintage	Fine	VF	XF	BU
408	1966	4.262	—	.10	.25	5.00
	1967	4.001	—	.10	.25	5.00
	1968	5.431	—	.10	.25	3.50
	1969	7.591	—	.10	.25	1.50
	1970	.481	.25	.75	2.00	7.00
	1971	2.489	—	.10	.15	1.25
	1972	4.453	—	.10	.15	1.00
	1973	3.317	—	.10	.15	1.00

KM#	Date	Mintage	Fine	VF	XF	BU
418	1974	8.494	—	.10	.15	.60
	1975	10.123	—	.10	.15	.60
	1976	15.177	—	.10	.15	.50
	1977	19.412	—	.10	.15	.40
	1978	15.305	—	.10	.15	.40
	1979	10.152	—	.10	.15	.40
	1980	7.082	—	.10	.15	.40
	1980 w/o star					
		7.066	—	.10	.15	.40
	1981	3.402	—	.10	.15	.40
	1982	11.157	—	.10	.15	.40
	1983	15.762	—	.10	.15	.40
	1984	8.615	—	.10	.15	.40
	1985	4.444	—	.10	.15	.40
	1986	4.178	—	.10	.15	.40
	1987	5.167	—	.10	.15	.40
	1988	9.610	—	.10	.15	.40
	1989	5.785	—	.10	.15	.40
	1990	1.729	—	.10	.15	.40
	1991	2.924	—	.10	.15	.40
	1992	—	—	.10	.15	.40
	1992	.020	—	—	Proof	10.00
	1993	—	—	.10	.15	.40
	1994	—	—	.10	.15	.40
	1994	.012	—	—	Proof	10.00
	1995	—	—	—	—	.40
	1996	—	—	—	—	.40

NOTE: Varieties exist in shield.

BRONZE
Obv: Crown. Rev: Stylized animal, denomination.

460	1996	—	—	—	—	.50

KRONE

7.5000 g, .800 SILVER, .1929 oz ASW

357	1901	.152	20.00	45.00	100.00	300.00
	1904	.100	55.00	100.00	185.00	450.00

NOTE: Earlier dates (1877-1900) exist for this type.

369	1908 crossed hammers on shield					
		.180	35.00	50.00	100.00	200.00
	1908 crossed hammers w/o shield					
		.170	20.00	40.00	75.00	150.00
	1910	.100	55.00	100.00	200.00	450.00
	1912	.200	35.00	60.00	100.00	250.00
	1913	.230	25.00	50.00	100.00	225.00
	1914	.602	10.00	20.00	40.00	90.00
	1915	.498	12.50	22.50	45.00	100.00
	1916	.400	15.00	25.00	50.00	250.00
	1917	.600	10.00	17.50	25.00	75.00

COPPER-NICKEL

KM#	Date	Mintage	Fine	VF	XF	BU
385	1925	8.686	.30	3.00	15.00	120.00
	1926	1.984	.50	4.00	20.00	200.00
	1927	1.000	1.00	5.00	45.00	400.00
	1936	.700	1.25	5.50	50.00	400.00
	1937	1.000	1.00	4.00	25.00	225.00
	1938	.926	.60	2.50	15.00	120.00
	1939	2.253	.60	1.50	7.50	75.00
	1940	3.890	.30	1.00	5.00	40.00
	1946	5.499	.25	.50	2.50	16.00
	1947	.802	1.00	2.00	10.00	60.00
	1949	7.846	.20	.50	2.50	12.00
	1950	9.942	.20	.50	2.50	12.00
	1951	4.761	.20	.50	2.50	12.00

397	1951	3.819	.20	.50	2.00	25.00
	1953	1.465	.20	.50	2.00	50.00
	1954	3.045	.20	.50	2.00	50.00
	1955	1.970	.20	.50	2.00	65.00
	1956	4.300	.20	.50	2.00	45.00
	1957	7.630	.20	.50	2.00	25.00

409	1958	.540	3.00	7.00	30.00	300.00
	1959	4.450	—	.20	2.00	30.00
	1960	1.790	—	.20	2.00	25.00
	1961	3.934	—	.20	.75	12.00
	1962	6.015	—	.20	.75	12.00
	1963	4.677	—	.20	.75	12.00
	1964	3.469	—	.20	.50	6.00
	1965	3.222	—	.20	1.00	40.00
	1966	3.084	—	.20	.75	15.00
	1967	6.680	—	.20	.75	15.00
	1968	6.149	—	.20	.75	15.00
	1969	5.186	—	.20	.35	3.00
	1970	8.637	—	.20	.40	10.00
	1971	10.258	—	.20	.35	2.00
	1972	13.179	—	.20	.35	1.50
	1973	9.140	—	.20	.35	1.50

419	1974	16.537	—	.20	.35	1.00
	1975	26.044	—	.20	.35	1.00
	1976	35.927	—	.20	.35	.75
	1977	26.264	—	.20	.35	.75
	1978	23.360	—	.20	.35	.75
	1979	15.897	—	.20	.35	.75
	1980	5.918	—	.20	.35	2.25
	1981	16.308	—	.20	.35	.75
	1982	29.187	—	.20	.35	.75
	1983	34.293	—	.20	.35	.75
	1984	3.677	—	.20	.35	1.25
	1985	10.985	—	.20	.35	.75
	1986	5.612	—	.20	.35	.75
	1987	11.015	—	.20	.35	.75
	1988	14.880	—	.20	.35	.75
	1989	5.605	—	.20	.35	.75
	1990	8.804	—	.20	.35	.75
	1990	.015	—	—	Proof	85.00
	1991	15.080	—	.20	.35	.75

NOTE: Varieties exist w/and w/o star mint mark.

KM#	Date	Mintage	Fine	VF	XF	BU
436	1992	—	—	.20	.35	.75
	1992	.020	—	—	Proof	10.00
	1993	—	—	.20	.35	.75
	1994	—	—	.20	.35	.75
	1994	.012	—	—	Proof	10.00
	1995	—	—	.20	.35	.75
	1996	—	—	.20	.35	.75

Obv: Monogram cross. Rev: Bird on vine above date and denomination.

462	1997	—	—	—	—	.75
	1997	—	—	—	Proof	10.00
	1998	—	—	—	—	.75
	1998	—	—	—	Proof	10.00

2 KRONER

15.0000 g, .800 SILVER, .3858 oz ASW

359	1902	.153	30.00	55.00	120.00	375.00
	1904	.076	45.00	80.00	150.00	400.00

NOTE: Earlier dates (1878-1900) exist for this type.
NOTE: Restrikes are made by the Royal Mint, Norway in gold, silver and bronze.

Norway Independence
Obv: Large shield.

363	1906	.100	10.00	15.00	25.00	70.00

Obv: Smaller shield.

365	1907	.055	20.00	30.00	50.00	125.00

Border Watch

366	1907	.028	60.00	125.00	225.00	500.00

KM#	Date	Mintage	Fine	VF	XF	BU
370	1908	.200	20.00	30.00	60.00	150.00
	1910	.150	35.00	55.00	100.00	300.00
	1912	.150	30.00	50.00	100.00	300.00
	1913	.270	15.00	25.00	50.00	125.00
	1914	.255	17.50	30.00	60.00	150.00
	1915	.225	17.50	30.00	60.00	150.00
	1916	.250	35.00	50.00	90.00	200.00
	1917	.378	10.00	17.50	30.00	100.00

Constitution Centennial

377	1914	.226	6.00	10.00	17.50	75.00

5 KRONER

COPPER-NICKEL

412	1963	7.074	—	1.00	3.00	15.00
	1964	7.346	—	1.00	2.00	8.00
	1965	2.233	—	1.00	2.50	70.00
	1966	2.502	—	1.00	2.50	30.00
	1967	.583	1.00	1.75	5.00	30.00
	1968	1.813	—	1.00	2.00	20.00
	1969	2.404	—	1.00	2.00	10.00
	1970	.202	1.50	2.50	5.00	15.00
	1971	.178	1.50	2.50	6.00	20.00
	1972	2.281	—	—	1.00	2.75
	1973	2.778	—	—	1.00	4.00

420	1974	1.983	—	—	1.00	4.00
	1975	2.946	—	—	1.00	2.25
	1976	9.056	—	—	1.00	1.75
	1977	4.630	—	—	1.00	1.50
	1978	5.853	—	—	1.00	1.50
	1979	6.818	—	—	1.00	1.50
	1980	1.578	—	—	1.00	2.25
	1981	1.105	—	—	1.00	1.75
	1982	3.920	—	—	1.00	1.50
	1983	2.932	—	—	1.00	1.50
	1984	1.233	—	—	1.00	1.75
	1985	1.441	—	—	1.00	1.50
	1987	.900	—	—	1.00	2.25
	1988	.865	—	—	1.00	2.25

NOTE: Varieties exist w/large and small shields.

100th Anniversary of Krone System

KM#	Date	Mintage	Fine	VF	XF	BU
421	ND(1975)	1.192	—	1.00	1.50	3.00

150th Anniversary - Immigration to America

422	ND(1975)	1.223	—	1.00	1.50	3.00

350th Anniversary of Norwegian Army

423	ND(1978)	2.990	—	1.00	1.50	2.50

300th Anniversary of the Mint

428	1986	2.345	—	1.00	1.50	2.50
	1986	5,000	—	—	P/L	35.00

175th Anniversary of the National Bank

430	1991	.544	—	—	—	7.00

Harald V

437	1992	*.500	—	—	—	2.00
	1992	.020	—	—	Proof	10.00
	1993	—	—	—	—	2.50
	1994	—	—	—	—	2.00
	1994	.012	—	—	Proof	10.00

*NOTE: 100,000 of the 1992 dated coins are in mint sets.

1000 Years of Norwegian Coinage

456	1995	.511	—	—	—	3.00

50th Anniversary - United Nations

KM#	Date	Mintage	Fine	VF	XF	BU
458	ND(1995)	.498	—	—	—	3.00

Centennial - Nasen's Return From the Arctic
Rev: Ship on ice.

459	1996	—	—	—	—	3.00
	1996	.012	—	—	Proof	20.00

350th Anniversary - Norwegian Postal Service
Obv: Arms.

461	ND(1997)	—	—	—	—	3.00

Obv: Order of St. Olaf.
Rev: Denomination and date.

463	1998	—	—	—	—	2.00
	1998	—	—	—	Proof	10.00

10 KRONER

4.4803 g, .900 GOLD, .1296 oz AGW

KM#	Date	Mintage	Fine	VF	XF	Unc
358	1902	.025	175.00	350.00	500.00	750.00

NOTE: Earlier date (1877) exists for this type.

375	1910	.053	100.00	165.00	300.00	450.00

20.0000 g, .900 SILVER, .5787 oz ASW
Constitution Sesquicentennial

KM#	Date	Mintage	Fine	VF	XF	BU
413	ND(1964)	1.408	—	—	3.00	5.00

NOTE: Edge lettering varieties exist.

COPPER-ZINC-NICKEL

KM#	Date	Mintage	Fine	VF	XF	BU
427	1983	20.193	—	—	2.00	5.00
	1984	26.169	—	—	1.75	3.00
	1985	22.458	—	—	1.75	3.00
	1986	29.060	—	—	1.75	3.00
	1987	8.809	—	—	1.75	3.00
	1988	2.630	—	—	1.75	3.00
	1989	3.259	—	—	1.75	3.00
	1990	3.004	—	—	1.75	3.00
	1991	—	—	—	1.75	3.00

Church Roof Top

457	1995	—	—	—	—	4.00

20 KRONER
(5 Speciedaler)

8.9606 g, .900 GOLD, .2593 oz AGW

KM#	Date	Mintage	Fine	VF	XF	Unc
355	1902	.050	150.00	200.00	300.00	450.00

NOTE: Earlier dates (1876-86) exist for this type.

376	1910	.250	165.00	225.00	325.00	450.00

NICKEL-BRONZE

453	1994	—	—	—	—	6.50
	1994	.012	—	—	Proof	25.00
	1995	—	—	—	—	6.50

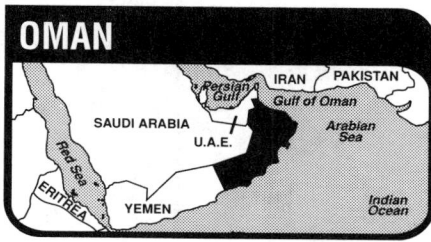

The Sultanate of Oman (formerly Muscat and Oman), an independent monarchy located in the southeastern part of the Arabian Peninsula, has an area of 82,030 sq. mi. (212,460 sq. km.) and a population of *1.3 million. Capital: Muscat. The economy is based on agriculture, herding and petroleum. Petroleum products, dates, fish and hides are exported.

The first European contact with Muscat and Oman was made by the Portuguese who captured Muscat, the capital and chief port, in 1508. They occupied the city, utilizing it as a naval base and factory and holding it against land and sea attacks by Arabs and Persians until finally ejected by local Arabs in 1650. It was next occupied by the Persians who maintained control until 1741, when it was taken by Ahmed ibn Sa'id of the present ruling family. Muscat and Oman was the most powerful state in Arabia during the first half of the 19th century, until weakened by the persistent attack of interior nomadic tribes. British influence, initiated by the signing of a treaty of friendship with the Sultanate in 1798, remains a dominant fact of the civil and military phases of the government, although Britain recognizes the Sultanate as a sovereign state.

Sultan Sa'id bin Taimur was overthrown by his son, Qabus bin Sa'id, on July 23, 1970. The new sultan changed the nation's name to Sultanate of Oman.

TITLES

Muscat مسقط

Oman عُمان

MUSCAT & OMAN

RULERS
Faisal bin Turkee,
 AH1306-1332/1888-1913AD
Taimur bin Faisal,
 AH1332-1351/1913-1932AD
Sa'id bin Taimur,
 AH1351-1390/1932-1970AD
Qabus bin Sa'id, AH1390-/1970-AD

MONETARY SYSTEM
Until 1972

4 Baisa = 1 Anna
64 Baisa = 1 Rupee
200 Baisa = 1 Saidi/Dasin Dog Dhofari Rial
 Commencing 1972
1000 Baisa = 1 Omani Rial

2 BAISA

COPPER-NICKEL

KM#	Date	Mintage	Fine	VF	XF	Unc
25	AH1365	1.500	.50	.75	1.00	2.00
	1365	—	—	—	Proof	4.00

NOTE: Coins of AH1365 have the monetary unit spelled Baiza; on all other coins it is spelled Baisa.

NOTE: Most of the proof issues of the AH1359 and 1365 dated coins of Muscat & Oman now on the market are probably later restrikes produced by the Bombay Mint.

BRONZE

36	AH1390	4.000	.10	—	.15	.25	.45
	1390	—	—	—	—	Proof	1.50

---

3 BAISA

BRONZE

KM#	Date	Mintage	Fine	VF	XF	Unc
30	AH1378	8.000	.75	1.00	1.50	2.00
	1378	—	—	—	Proof	—

NOTE: Struck for use in Dhofar province.

32	AH1380	10.000	.35	.50	.60	1.25
	1380 Inc. Ab.	—	—	—	Proof	—

5 BAISA

COPPER-NICKEL

26	AH1365	3.849	1.00	1.25	1.50	2.00
	1365	—	—	—	Proof	5.00

33	AH1381	5.000	.40	.60	1.00	1.50
	1381 Inc. Ab.	—	—	—	Proof	—

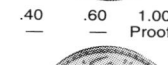

BRONZE

37	AH1390	3.400	.10	.15	.25	.45
	1390	—	—	—	Proof	2.00

10 BAISA

COPPER-NICKEL

22	AH1359	.532	2.50	3.25	4.00	5.00
	1359	—	—	—	Proof	7.50

NOTE: Struck for use in Dhofar province.

BRONZE

38	AH1390	4.500	.10	.15	.25	.45
	1390	—	—	—	Proof	2.50

20 BAISA

COPPER-NICKEL

23	AH1359	.035	3.00	5.00	7.50	10.50
	1359	—	—	—	Proof	13.50

NOTE: Struck for use in Dhofar province.

KM#	Date	Mintage	Fine	VF	XF	Unc
27	AH1365	1.135	1.00	2.00	2.75	4.00
	1365	—	—	—	Proof	6.50

Mule. Obv: KM#23. Rev: KM#27.

| 28 | AH1359/1365 (restrike) | — | — | — | 17.50 |

25 BAISA

COPPER-NICKEL

39	AH1390	2.000	.15	.20	.35	.65
	1390	—	—	—	Proof	2.75

50 BAISA

COPPER-NICKEL

24	AH1359	.065	.20	6.50	8.50	12.50
	1359	—	—	—	Proof	16.50

NOTE: Struck for use in Dhofar province.

40	AH1390	1.600	.20	.35	.60	1.00
	1390	—	—	—	Proof	3.50

100 BAISA

COPPER-NICKEL

41	AH1390	1.000	.30	.45	.70	1.25
	1390	—	—	—	Proof	5.00

1/2 DHOFARI RIAL

14.0300 g, .500 SILVER, .2256 oz ASW

29	AH1367	.200	12.00	14.00	18.00	25.00
	1367	—	—	—	Proof	40.00

NOTE: Struck for use in Dhofar province.

1/2 SAIDI RIAL

14.0300 g, .500 SILVER, .2256 oz ASW

KM#	Date	Mintage	Fine	VF	XF	Unc
34	AH1380	.300	3.00	3.50	4.75	7.50
	1380	—	—	—	Proof	75.00
	1381	.850	3.00	3.50	4.75	7.50

SAIDI RIAL

28.0700 g, .833 SILVER, .7518 oz ASW

31	AH1378	1.000	—	12.00	15.00	20.00
	1378					
		100 pcs.	—	—	Proof	650.00

SULTANATE OF OMAN

1972-

MONETARY SYSTEM

1000 Baiza = 1 Omani Rial

5 BAIZA

BRONZE

KM#	Date	Year	Mintage	VF	XF	Unc
50	AH1395	(1975)	6.000	.10	.20	.45
	1400	(1980)	3.000	.10	.20	.45
	1406	(1986)	2.000	.10	.20	.45
	1410	(1990)	5.000	.10	.20	.45

10 BAIZA

BRONZE
F.A.O. Issue

51	AH1395	(1975)	1.000	.15	.30	.65

52	AH1395	(1975)	6.000	.15	.30	.65
	1400	(1980)	5.250	.15	.30	.65
	1406	(1986)	3.000	.15	.30	.65
	1410	(1990)	6.000	.15	.30	.65

F.A.O. - 50 Years

94	ND(1995)	—	—	—	1.25

---

25 BAIZA

COPPER-NICKEL

KM#	Date	Year	Mintage	VF	XF	Unc
45a	AH1395	(1975)	4.500	.20	.40	.85
	1400	(1980)	5.250	.20	.40	.85
	1406	(1986)	4.000	.20	.40	.85
	1410	(1990)	7.000	.20	.40	.85

50 BAIZA

COPPER-NICKEL

46a	AH1395	(1975)	2.500	.30	.60	1.50
	1400	(1980)	2.750	.30	.60	1.50
	1406	(1986)	3.000	.30	.60	1.50
	1410	(1990)	4.000	.30	.60	1.50

U.N. - 50 Years

95	ND	(1995)	—	—	—	3.00

100 BAIZA

COPPER-NICKEL

68	AH1404	1984	4.000	.40	.80	2.25

ALUMINUM-BRONZE Center,
COPPER-NICKEL Ring
100 Years of Coinage

82	AH1411	1991	—	—	—	4.50
	1411	1991	1,000	—	Proof	8.50

1/4 OMANI RIAL

ALUMINUM-BRONZE

66	AH1400	1980	4.000	.75	1.00	2.00

1/2 OMANI RIAL

COPPER-NICKEL

F.A.O. Issue

KM#	Date	Year Mintage	VF	XF	Unc
64	AH1398	1978 .015	2.75	3.50	5.00

ALUMINUM-BRONZE

67	AH1400	1980	2.000	2.75	3.50	5.00

PAKISTAN

The Islamic Republic of Pakistan, located on the Indian sub-continent between India and Afghanistan, has an area of 310,404 sq. mi. (803,940 sq. km.) and a population of 130 million. Capital: Islamabad. Pakistan is mainly an agricultural land although the industrial base is expanding rapidly. Yarn, textiles, cotton, rice, medical instruments, sports equipment and leather are exported.

Afghan and Turkish intrusions into northern India between the 11th and 18th centuries resulted in large numbers of Indians being converted to Islam. The idea of a separate Moslem state independent of Hindu India developed in the 1930's and was agreed to by Britain in 1946. The Islamic majority areas of India, consisting of the separate geographic entities known as East and West Pakistan, achieved self-government as Pakistan, with dominion status in the British Commonwealth, when the British withdrew from India on Aug. 14, 1947. Pakistan became a republic in 1956. When a basic constitutional crisis initiated by the election of Dec. 1, 1970 - the first direct general election in Pakistani history - could not be resolved by the leaders of East and West Pakistan, the East Pakistanis seceded from the Islamic Republic of Pakistan (March 26, 1971) and formed the independent People's Republic of Bangladesh. After many years of vacillation between civilian and military regimes, the people of Pakistan held a free national election in November, 1988 and installed the first of a series of democratic governments under a parliamentary system.

Undivided Pakistan was the fifth most populous country in the world. It remains one of the largest in population.

TITLE

باكستان

Pakistan

MONETARY SYSTEM

3 Pies = 1 Pice
4 Pice = 1 Anna
16 Annas = 1 Rupee

PIE

BRONZE

KM#	Date	Mintage	Fine	VF	XF	Unc
11	1951	2.950	.25	.50	1.00	2.50
	1951	—	—	—	Proof	4.00
	1953	.110	.25	.75	1.50	3.00
	1953	—	—	—	Proof	5.00
	1955	.211	.25	.75	1.50	3.00
	1956	3.390	.25	.50	1.00	2.50
	1957	—	.25	.50	1.00	2.50

PICE

BRONZE

1	1948	101.070	.20	.40	.75	1.50
	1948	—	—	—	Proof	2.00
	1949	25.740	.20	.40	.75	1.50
	1951	14.050	.20	.45	.85	1.75
	1952	41.680	.20	.40	.75	1.50

NOTE: Varieties exist.

NICKEL-BRASS

12	1953	47.540	.15	.30	.50	1.00
	1953	—	—	—	Proof	1.50
	1955	31.280	.15	.30	.50	1.00
	1956	9.710	.20	.35	.60	1.15
	1957	57.790	.15	.30	.50	1.00

KM#	Date	Mintage	Fine	VF	XF	Unc
12	1958	52.470	.15	.30	.50	1.00
	1959	41.620	.15	.30	.50	1.00

1/2 ANNA

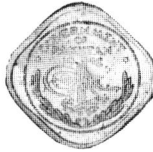

COPPER-NICKEL

2	1948	73.920	.15	.30	.50	1.00
	1948	—	—	—	Proof	1.50
	1949 dot after date					
		16.940	.20	.35	.60	1.15
	1951	75.360	.15	.30	.50	1.00

NICKEL-BRASS

13	1953	8.350	.20	.35	.60	1.15
	1953	—	—	—	Proof	1.50
	1955	17.310	.15	.30	.50	1.00
	1958	38.250	.15	.30	.50	1.00

ANNA

COPPER-NICKEL

3	1948	73.460	.15	.30	.50	1.00
	1948	—	—	—	Proof	1.50
	1949	11.140	.20	.35	.60	1.15
	1949 dot after date					
	Inc. KM8		.15	.30	.50	1.00
	1951	40.800	.15	.30	.50	1.00
	1952	15.430	.20	.35	.60	1.15

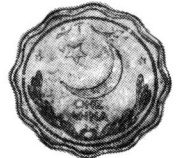

8	1950	94.830	3.00	4.50	6.50	10.00
	1950	—	—	—	Proof	15.00

14	1953	9.350	.15	.30	.50	1.00
	1953	—	—	—	Proof	1.50
	1954	35.360	.15	.30	.50	1.00
	1955	6.230	.20	.35	.60	1.15
	1956	4.580	.20	.35	.60	1.15
	1957	12.500	.15	.30	.50	1.00
	1958	44.320	.15	.30	.50	1.00

2 ANNAS

COPPER-NICKEL

4	1948	55.930	.15	.30	.50	1.00
	1948	—	—	—	Proof	1.50
	1949	19.720	.15	.30	.50	1.00
	1949 dot after date					
	Inc. KM9	.20	.35	.60	1.15	
	1951	33.130	.15	.30	.50	1.00

KM#	Date	Mintage	Fine	VF	XF	Unc
9	1950	21.190	3.50	5.00	7.50	12.50
	1950	—			Proof	20.00

15	1953	7.910	.15	.30	.50	1.00
	1953	—			Proof	1.50
	1954	5.740	.15	.30	.50	1.00
	1955	6.230	.15	.30	.50	1.00
	1956	1.370	.20	.35	.60	1.15
	1957	2.570	.20	.35	.60	1.15
	1958	6.200	.15	.30	.50	1.00
	1959	8.010	.15	.30	.50	1.00

1/4 RUPEE

NICKEL

5	1948	52.680	.20	.30	.50	1.00
	1948	—			Proof	2.25
	1949	46.000	.20	.30	.50	1.00
	1951	19.120	.20	.35	.60	1.15

10	1950	19.400	5.00	7.50	12.00	20.00
	1950	—			Proof	25.00

1/2 RUPEE

NICKEL

6	1948	33.260	.40	.60	.75	1.50
	1948	—			Proof	2.00
	1949	20.300	.40	.60	.75	1.50
	1951	11.430	.40	.65	.90	1.75

RUPEE

NICKEL

7	1948	46.200	.75	1.25	2.00	3.50
	1948	—			Proof	5.00
	1949	37.100	.75	1.25	2.00	3.50

NOTE: Varieties exist.

DECIMAL COINAGE

100 Paisa (Pice) = 1 Rupee

PICE

BRONZE

KM#	Date	Mintage	Fine	VF	XF	Unc
16	1961	74.910	.15	.30	.50	1.00

PAISA

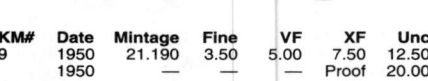

BRONZE

17	1961	134.650	.15	.25	.40	.80
	1961	—			Proof	1.50
	1962	149.380	.15	.25	.40	.80
	1963	127.810	.15	.25	.40	.80

24	1964	39.890	.20	.35	.50	1.00
	1964	—			Proof	1.50
	1965	69.660	.20	.35	.50	1.00

NICKEL-BRASS

24a	1965	32.950	.20	.35	.50	1.00
	1966	179.370	.15	.25	.40	.80

ALUMINUM

29	1967	170.070	—	.10	.15	.30
	1968	—	—	.10	.15	.30
	1969	—	—	.10	.15	.30
	1970	204.606	—	.10	.15	.30
	1971	191.880	—	.10	.15	.30
	1972	108.510	—	.10	.15	.30
	1973	Inc. Ab.	—	.10	.15	.30

F.A.O. Issue - Cotton

33	1974	14.230	—	.10	.15	.30
	1975	43.000	—	.10	.15	.30
	1976	49.180	—	.10	.15	.30
	1977	62.750	—	.10	.15	.30
	1978	20.380	—	.10	.15	.30
	1979	5.630	—	.10	.15	.30

2 PAISA

BRONZE

25	1964	67.660	.15	.25	.35	.70
	1964	—			Proof	1.50
	1965	27.880	.15	.25	.35	.70
	1966	50.590	.15	.25	.35	.70

ALUMINUM

28	1966	11.940	—	.10	.15	.30
	1967	73.970	—	.10	.15	.30
	1968	—	—	.10	.15	.30

KM#	Date	Mintage	Fine	VF	XF	Unc
25a	1968	—		.10	.15	.30
	1969	—		.10	.15	.30
	1970	24.401		.10	.15	.30
	1971	10.140	—	.10	.15	.30
	1972	4.040	.10	.15	.20	.40
	1974	3.600	.10	.15	.20	.40

F.A.O. Issue - Rice Plant

34	1974	3.600	.10	.15	.20	.40
	1975	4.020	.10	.15	.20	.40
	1976	5.750	.10	.15	.20	.40

5 PICE

NICKEL-BRASS

18	1961	40.050	.20	.30	.40	.80

5 PAISA

 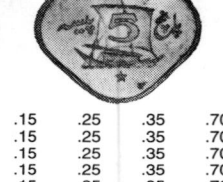

NICKEL-BRASS

19	1961	40.790	.15	.25	.35	.70
	1961	—			Proof	1.50
	1962	48.200	.15	.25	.35	.70
	1963	45.020	.15	.25	.35	.70

26	1964	82.730	.15	.25	.35	.70
	1965	72.570	.15	.25	.35	.70
	1966	32.900	.15	.25	.35	.70
	1967	24.470	.15	.25	.35	.70
	1968	—	.15	.25	.35	.70
	1969	5.690	.20	.30	.40	.80
	1970	24.655	.15	.25	.35	.70
	1971	23.860	.15	.25	.35	.70
	1972	40.345	.15	.25	.35	.70
	1973	Inc. Ab.	.15	.25	.35	.70
	1974	7.695	.20	.30	.40	.80

ALUMINUM
F.A.O. Issue - Sugar Cane

35	1974	23.395	—	.10	.15	.30
	1975	50.030	—	.10	.15	.30
	1976	58.255	—	.10	.15	.30
	1977	32.840	—	.10	.15	.30
	1978	61.940	—	.10	.15	.30
	1979	65.485	—	.10	.15	.30
	1980	55.940	—	.10	.15	.30
	1981	18.290	—	.10	.15	.30

52	1981	16.730	—	.10	.15	.30
	1982	51.210	—	.10	.15	.30
	1983	42.915	—	.10	.15	.30
	1984	45.105	—	.10	.15	.30
	1985	46.555	—	.10	.15	.30
	1986	20.065	—	—	.10	.20
	1987	37.710	—	—	.10	.20

KM#	Date	Mintage	Fine	VF	XF	Unc
52	1988	40.150	—	—	.10	.20
	1989	—	—	—	.10	.20
	1990	—	—	—	.10	.20
	1991	—	—	—	.10	.20
	1992	—	—	—	.10	.20
	1993	—	—	—	.10	.20
	1994	—	—	—	.10	.20

10 PICE

COPPER-NICKEL

KM#	Date	Mintage	Fine	VF	XF	Unc
20	1961	22.230	.20	.30	.50	1.00

10 PAISA

COPPER-NICKEL

KM#	Date	Mintage	Fine	VF	XF	Unc
21	1961	31.090	.15	.25	.35	.70
	1961	—	—	—	Proof	2.00
	1962	29.440	.15	.25	.35	.70
	1963	19.760	.15	.25	.35	.70
27	1964	52.580	.15	.25	.35	.70
	1965	51.540	.15	.25	.35	.70
	1966	—	.15	.25	.35	.70
	1967	16.430	.15	.25	.35	.70
	1968	—	.15	.25	.35	.70

Reduced size

KM#	Date	Mintage	Fine	VF	XF	Unc
31	1969	—	.15	.25	.35	.70
	1970	30.250	.15	.25	.35	.70
	1971	26.270	.15	.25	.35	.70
	1972	24.845	.15	.25	.35	.70
	1973	Inc. Ab.	.15	.25	.35	.70
	1974	4.780	.20	.30	.40	.80

ALUMINUM
F.A.O. Issue - Wheat Ears

KM#	Date	Mintage	Fine	VF	XF	Unc
36	1974	18.640	—	.10	.15	.30
	1975	28.875	—	.10	.15	.30
	1976	43.755	—	.10	.15	.30
	1977	29.045	—	.10	.15	.30
	1978	55.185	—	.10	.15	.30
	1979	56.100	—	.10	.15	.30
	1980	40.985	—	.10	.15	.30
	1981	15.500	—	.10	.15	.30
53	1981	7.995	.10	.15	.20	.40
	1982	39.770	—	.10	.15	.30
	1983	44.705	—	.10	.15	.30
53	1984	35.255	—	.10	.15	.30
	1985	41.545	—	.10	.15	.30
	1986	43.280	—	—	.10	.20
	1987	39.090	—	—	.10	.20
	1988	42.510	—	—	.10	.20
	1989	—	—	—	.10	.20
	1990	—	—	—	.10	.20
	1991	—	—	—	.10	.20
	1992	—	—	—	.10	.20
	1993	—	—	—	.10	.20
	1994	—	—	—	.10	.20

25 PAISA

NICKEL

KM#	Date	Mintage	Fine	VF	XF	Unc
22	1963	16.900	.15	.25	.35	.70
	1964	7.990	.15	.25	.35	.70
	1965	9.290	.15	.25	.35	.70
	1966	6.650	.15	.25	.35	.70
	1967	3.740	.20	.30	.40	.80

COPPER-NICKEL

KM#	Date	Mintage	Fine	VF	XF	Unc
30	1967	(?)5.500	.10	.15	.25	.50
	1968	(?)5.500	.10	.15	.25	.50
	1969	—	.10	.15	.25	.50
	1970	30.392	.10	.15	.25	.50
	1971	12.664	.10	.15	.25	.50
	1972	10.824	.10	.15	.25	.50
	1973	—	.10	.15	.25	.50
	1974	9.756	.10	.20	.30	.55
37	1975	14.264	.10	.15	.20	.40
	1976	20.440	.10	.15	.20	.40
	1977	22.092	.10	.15	.20	.40
	1978	33.544	.10	.15	.20	.40
	1979	29.648	.10	.15	.20	.40
	1980	49.556	.10	.15	.20	.40
	1981	33.952	.10	.15	.20	.40
58	1981	5.648	—	.10	.15	.35
	1982	28.940	—	.10	.15	.35
	1983	40.844	—	.10	.15	.35
	1984	50.988	—	.10	.15	.35
	1985	53.748	—	.10	.15	.35
	1986	75.764	—	.10	.15	.35
	1987	53.560	—	.10	.15	.35
	1988	58.900	—	.10	.15	.35
	1989	—	—	.10	.15	.35
	1990	—	—	.10	.15	.35
	1991	—	—	.10	.15	.35
	1992	—	—	.10	.15	.35
	1993	—	—	.10	.15	.35
	1994	—	—	.10	.15	.35

NOTE: Varieties exist in date and crescent size.

50 PAISA

NICKEL

KM#	Date	Mintage	Fine	VF	XF	Unc
23	1963	8.110	.15	.25	.40	.80
	1964	4.580	.20	.30	.50	1.00
	1965	8.980	.15	.25	.40	.80
	1966	2.860	.20	.30	.50	1.00
	1967	—	Reported, not confirmed			
	1968	—	.15	.25	.40	.80
	1969	—	.15	.25	.40	.80

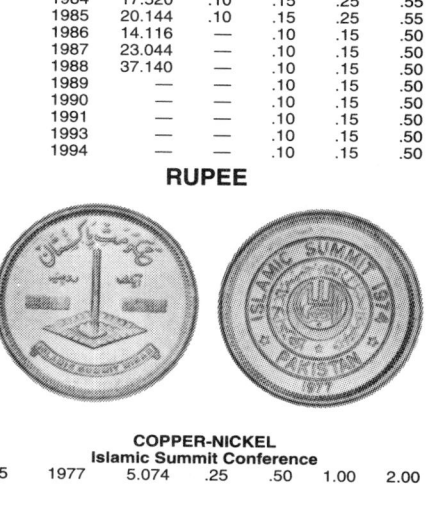

COPPER-NICKEL

KM#	Date	Mintage	Fine	VF	XF	Unc
32	1969	—	.15	.25	.35	.70
	1970	—	.15	.25	.35	.70
	1971	4.670	.15	.25	.35	.70
	1972	4.900	.15	.25	.35	.70
	1974	1.128	.20	.30	.40	.80
38	1975	9.180	.15	.20	.30	.60
	1976	—	.15	.20	.30	.60
	1977	5.548	.15	.20	.30	.60
	1978	18.252	.15	.20	.30	.60
	1979	14.596	.15	.20	.30	.60
	1980	22.332	.15	.20	.30	.60
	1981	13.552	.15	.20	.30	.60

NOTE: Varieties in date size exist.

100th Anniversary - Birth of Mohammad Ali Jinnah

KM#	Date	Mintage	Fine	VF	XF	Unc
39	1976	5.600	.15	—	.50	1.00

1400th Hejira Anniversary

KM#	Date	Year	Mintage	VF	XF	Unc
51	AH1401	(1981)	—	.25	.50	1.00

KM#	Date	Mintage	Fine	VF	XF	Unc
54	1981	4.612	.10	.15	.25	.55
	1982	15.844	.10	.15	.25	.55
	1983	9.608	.10	.15	.25	.55
	1984	17.520	.10	.15	.25	.55
	1985	20.144	.10	.15	.25	.55
	1986	14.116	—	.10	.15	.50
	1987	23.044	—	.10	.15	.50
	1988	37.140	—	.10	.15	.50
	1989	—	—	.10	.15	.50
	1990	—	—	.10	.15	.50
	1991	—	—	.10	.15	.50
	1993	—	—	.10	.15	.50
	1994	—	—	.10	.15	.50

RUPEE

COPPER-NICKEL
Islamic Summit Conference

KM#	Date	Mintage	Fine	VF	XF	Unc
45	1977	5.074	.25	.50	1.00	2.00

**100th Anniversary - Birth of
Allama Mohammad Iqbal**

KM#	Date	Mintage	Fine	VF	XF	Unc
46	1977	5.000	.25	.50	1.00	2.00

1400th Hejira Anniversary

KM#	Date	Year	Mintage	VF	XF	Unc
55	AH1401	(1981)	.045	.60	1.25	2.50

World Food Day

KM#	Date	Mintage	Fine	VF	XF	Unc
56	1981	.045	.35	.75	1.50	3.00

			26.5mm			
57.1	1979	—	.30	.40	.55	1.15
	1980	14.522	.30	.40	.55	1.15
	1981	12.038	.30	.40	.55	1.15
			25mm			
57.2	1981	4.084	.25	.40	.55	1.00
	1982	27.878	.20	.35	.50	1.00
	1983	18.746	.20	.35	.50	1.00
	1984	14.562	.20	.35	.50	1.00
	1985	4.934	.25	.40	.55	1.00
	1986	11.840	.15	.25	.40	.80
	1987	50.416	.15	.25	.40	.80
	1988	10.644	.15	.25	.40	.80
	1989	—		— Reported, not confirmed		
	1990	—	.15	.25	.40	.80

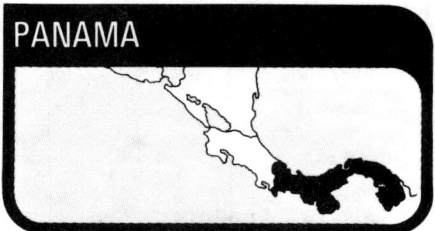

PANAMA

The Republic of Panama, a Central American country situated between Costa Rica and Colombia, has an area of 29,762 sq. mi. (78,200 sq. km.) and a population of *2.4 million. Capital: Panama City. The Panama Canal is the country's biggest asset; servicing world related transit trade and international commerce. Bananas, refined petroleum, sugar and shrimp are exported.

Panama was visited by Christopher Columbus in 1502 during his fourth voyage to America, and explored by Vasco Nunez de Balboa in 1513. Panama City, founded in 1519, was a primary transshipment center for treasure and supplies to and from Spain's American colonies. Panama declared its independence in 1821 and joined the Confederation of Greater Colombia. In 1903, after Colombia rejected a treaty enabling the United States to build a canal across the Isthmus, Panama with the support of the United States proclaimed its independence from Colombia and became a sovereign republic.

The 1904 2-1/2 centesimos known as the 'Panama Pill' or 'Panama Pearl' is one of the world's smaller silver coins and a favorite with collectors.

MINT MARKS
FM - Franklin Mint, U.S.A.*
CHI in circle - Valcambi Mint, Balerna, Switzerland

***NOTE:** From 1975-1985 the Franklin Mint produced coinage in up to 3 different qualities. Qualities of issue are designated in ( ) after each date and are defined as follows:

(M) MATTE - Normal circulation strike or a dull finish produced by sandblasting special uncirculated (polish finish) or proof quality dies.

(U) SPECIAL UNCIRCULATED - Polished or proof-like in appearance without any frosted features.

(P) PROOF - The highest quality obtainable having mirror-like fields and frosted features.

MONETARY SYSTEM
100 Centesimos = 1 Balboa

1/2 CENTESIMO

COPPER-NICKEL

KM#	Date	Mintage	Fine	VF	XF	Unc
6	1907	1.000	.50	1.00	2.00	6.00
	1907	—	Reported, not confirmed			

NOTE: Previously listed re-engraved overdates were struck from very common doubled dies. The plain date in unc. is scarcer.

CENTESIMO

BRONZE
Urraca

14	1935	.200	2.00	5.00	12.00	55.00
	1937	.200	1.00	2.50	7.00	35.00

50th Anniversary of the Republic

17	1953	1.500	.10	.20	.50	3.00

KM#	Date	Mintage	VF	XF	Unc
22	1961	2.500	.15	.25	2.00
	1962	2.000	.15	.25	1.00

KM#	Date	Mintage	VF	XF	Unc
22	1962	*50 pcs.	—	Proof	160.00
	1966	3.000	.10	.15	.75
	1966	.013	—	Proof	1.00
	1967	7.600	.10	.15	.75
	1967	.020	—	Proof	1.00
	1968	25.000	.10	.15	.75
	1968	.023	—	Proof	1.00
	1969	.014	—	Proof	1.00
	1970	9,528	—	Proof	1.00
	1971	.011	—	Proof	1.00
	1972	.013	—	Proof	1.00
	1973	.017	—	Proof	1.00
	1974	*10.000	.10	.15	.35
	1974	*.018	—	Proof	1.00
	1975	10.000	.10	.15	.35
	1977	10.000	.10	.15	.35
	1978	10.000	.10	.15	.35
	1979	10.000	.10	.15	.35
	1980	20.500	.10	.15	.35
	1982	20.000	.10	.15	.35
	1983FM(P)	—	—	Proof	1.50
	1983	5.000	.10	.15	.35
	1984FM(P)	—	—	Proof	1.50
	1985FM(P)	**	—	Proof	1.50
	1986	20.000	.10	.15	.35
	1987	20.000	—	—	.25

NOTE: Varieties exist.
***NOTE:** 1974 circulation coins were struck at West Point and New York, the proof coins at San Francisco.
****NOTE:** Unauthorized striking.

COPPER COATED ZINC

22a	1983	45.000	.10	.15	.25

33.1	1975(RCM)	.500	.10	.20	.50
	1975FM(M)	.125	.10	.25	1.00
	1975FM(U)	1,410	—	—	3.00
	1975FM(P)	.041	—	Proof	.50
	1976(RCM)	.050	.10	.20	1.00
	1976FM(M)	.063	.10	.20	1.00
	1976FM(P)	.012	—	Proof	.50
	1977FM(U)	.063	.10	.20	1.00
	1977FM(P)	9,548	—	Proof	.50
	1979FM(U)	.020	.10	.20	1.00
	1979FM(P)	5,949	—	Proof	.50
	1980FM(U)	.040	.10	.20	1.00
	1981FM(P)	1,973	—	Proof	1.00
	1982FM(U)	5,000	.15	.30	2.00
	1982FM(P)	1,480	—	Proof	1.00

75th Anniversary of Independence

45	1978FM(U)	.050	.10	.20	1.00
	1978FM(P)	.011	—	Proof	1.25

COPPER PLATED ZINC

124	1991	—	—	—	.10
	1993	30.000	—	—	.10

125	1996	180.000	—	—	.10

1-1/4 CENTESIMOS

BRONZE

KM#	Date	Mintage	Fine	VF	XF	Unc
15	1940	1.600	.50	1.00	2.50	10.00

2-1/2 CENTESIMOS

1.2500 g, .900 SILVER, .0362 oz ASW

KM#	Date	Mintage	Fine	VF	XF	Unc
1	1904	.400	4.00	6.00	10.00	25.00

NOTE: The above piece is popularly referred to as the "Panama Pill".

COPPER-NICKEL
Rev. leg: DOS Y MEDIOS

KM#	Date	Mintage	Fine	VF	XF	Unc
7.1	1907	.800	1.00	3.00	12.50	50.00

Rev. leg: DOS Y MEDIO

KM#	Date	Mintage	Fine	VF	XF	Unc
7.2	1916	.800	1.00	3.50	20.00	125.00
	1918*	7 known	—	1600.	2400.	—

***NOTE:** Unauthorized issue, 1 million pieces melted June 1918.

KM#	Date	Mintage	Fine	VF	XF	Unc
8	1929	1.000	1.00	3.50	17.50	120.00
	1929	—	—	—	Proof	R,NC

KM#	Date	Mintage	Fine	VF	XF	Unc
16	1940	1.200	.50	1.00	3.50	10.00

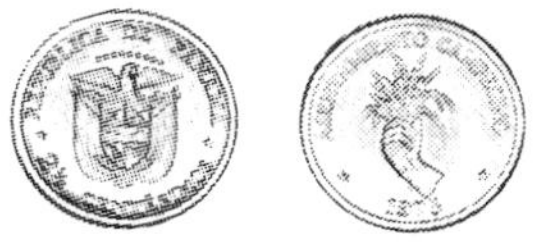

COPPER-NICKEL CLAD COPPER
F.A.O. Issue

KM#	Date	Mintage	VF	XF	Unc
32	1973	2.000	—	.10	.35
	1975	1.000	—	.10	.50

Victoriano Lorenzo

KM#	Date	Mintage	VF	XF	Unc
34.1	1975(RCM)	.040	.35	.65	1.10
	1975FM(M)	.050	.35	.60	1.00
	1975FM(U)	1,410	1.00	1.75	2.50
	1975FM(P)	.041	—	Proof	1.00
	1976(RCM)	.020	.35	.60	1.35
	1976FM(M)	.025	.35	.60	1.25
	1976FM(P)	.024	—	Proof	1.00
	1977FM(U)	.025	.35	.60	1.25
	1977FM(P)	9,548	—	Proof	1.00
	1979FM(U)	.012	.35	.60	1.50
	1979FM(P)	5,949	—	Proof	1.00
	1980FM(U)	.040	.35	.60	1.25
	1981FM(P)	1,973	—	Proof	2.00
	1982FM(U)	2,000	.75	1.50	2.25
	1982FM(P)	1,480	—	Proof	2.50

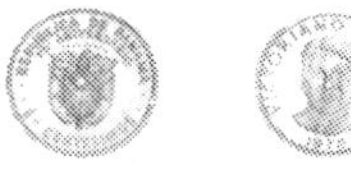

75th Anniversary of Independence

KM#	Date	Mintage	VF	XF	Unc
46	1978FM(U)	.040	.25	.50	1.25
	1978FM(P)	.011	—	Proof	1.00

5 CENTESIMOS

2.5000 g, .900 SILVER, .0723 oz ASW

KM#	Date	Mintage	Fine	VF	XF	Unc
2	1904	1.500	2.50	5.00	12.50	50.00
	1904	12 pcs.	—	—	Proof	1000.
	1916	.100	40.00	70.00	130.00	300.00

COPPER-NICKEL

KM#	Date	Mintage	Fine	VF	XF	Unc
9	1929	.500	2.50	4.50	12.00	75.00
	1932	.332	2.50	4.50	13.50	80.00

KM#	Date	Mintage	VF	XF	Unc
23.1	1961	1.000	.50	1.00	2.00

KM#	Date	Mintage	VF	XF	Unc
23.2	1962	2.600	.10	.25	1.50
	1962	*25 pcs.	—	Proof	350.00
	1966	4.900	.10	.20	.50
	1966	.013	—	Proof	1.00
	1967	2.600	.10	.20	.50
	1967	.020	—	Proof	1.00
	1968	6.000	.10	.20	.50
	1968	.023	—	Proof	1.00
	1969	.014	—	Proof	1.00
	1970	5.000	.10	.20	.50
	1970	9,528	—	Proof	1.00
	1971	.011	—	Proof	1.00
	1972	.013	—	Proof	1.00
	1973	5.000	.10	.20	.50
	1973	.017	—	Proof	1.00
	1974	.019	—	Proof	1.00
	1975	5.000	.10	.15	.50
	1982	8.000	.10	.15	.50
	1983	7.500	.10	.15	.50
	1993	6.000	.10	.15	.40
	1993	—	—	Proof	250.00

NOTE: The 1962 & 1966 Royal Mint strikes are normally sharper in detail. The stars on the reverse above the eagle are flat while previous dates are raised.
NOTE: Varieties exist.
NOTE: The 1993 Proof strike was not authorized by the Panamanian government.

COPPER - NICKEL CLAD COPPER
Carlos J. Finlay

KM#	Date	Mintage	VF	XF	Unc
35.1	1975(RCM)	.080	.25	.50	1.00
	1975FM(M)	.015	.25	.50	1.00
	1975FM(U)	1,410	—	—	2.50
	1975FM(P)	.041	—	Proof	1.00
	1976(RCM)	.020	.25	.50	1.25
	1976FM(M)	.013	.25	.50	1.50
	1976FM(P)	.012	—	Proof	1.00
	1977FM(U)	.013	.25	.50	1.50
	1977FM(P)	9,548	—	Proof	1.00
	1979FM(U)	.012	.25	.50	1.50
	1979FM(P)	5,949	—	Proof	1.00
	1980FM(U)	.043	.25	.50	1.00
	1981FM(P)	1,973	—	Proof	1.50
	1982FM(U)	3,000	.75	2.50	8.00
	1982FM(P)	1,480	—	Proof	1.50

COPPER-NICKEL CLAD COPPER
75th Anniversary of Independence

KM#	Date	Mintage	VF	XF	Unc
47	1978FM(U)	.030	—	—	1.00
	1978FM(P)	.011	—	Proof	1.00

COPPER-NICKEL
Obv: National arms. Rev: Denomination.

KM#	Date	Mintage	VF	XF	Unc
126	1996	4.000	—	—	.40

10 CENTESIMOS

5.0000 g, .900 SILVER, .1447 oz ASW

KM#	Date	Mintage	Fine	VF	XF	Unc
3	1904	1.100	3.50	8.00	22.00	150.00
	1904	12 pcs.	—	—	Proof	1000.

1/10 BALBOA

2.5000 g, .900 SILVER, .0723 oz ASW
High relief.

KM#	Date	Mintage	Fine	VF	XF	Unc
10.1	1930	.500	1.75	3.00	10.00	35.00
	1930	20 pcs.	—		Matte Proof	1000.
	1931	.200	2.50	5.00	16.50	100.00
	1932	.150	3.00	6.00	18.00	120.00
	1933	.100	6.50	12.50	35.00	175.00
	1934	.075	8.00	16.00	40.00	200.00
	1947	1.000	.75	1.50	3.50	12.50

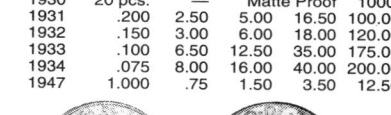

Low relief.

KM#	Date	Mintage	Fine	VF	XF	Unc
10.2	1962	5.000	—	BV	1.00	2.50
	1962	*25 pcs.	—	—	Proof	500.00

COPPER-NICKEL CLAD COPPER

KM#	Date	Mintage	VF	XF	Unc
10a	1966TI	6.955	.25	.35	1.00
	1966TII	1.000	.50	2.00	10.00
	1966	.013	—	Proof	1.00
	1967	.020	—	Proof	1.00
	1968	5.000	.20	.30	1.00
	1968	.023	—	Proof	1.00
	1969	.014	—	Proof	1.00
	1970	7.500	.15	.25	.75
	1970	9,528	—	Proof	1.00
	1971	.011	—	Proof	1.00
	1972	.013	—	Proof	1.00
	1973	10.000	.15	.20	.60
	1973	.017	—	Proof	1.00
	1974	.018	—	Proof	1.00
	1975	.500	.25	.50	1.50
	1980	5.000	.20	.30	.75
	1982	7.740	.15	.25	.50
	1983(RCM)	7.750	.15	.25	.50
	1986(RCM)	1.000	.15	.25	1.50
	1993	7.000	.15	.25	.40
	1993	—	—	Proof	300.00

NOTE: Two varieties exist, Type I is similar to the 1962 strike on a thick flan (London) with diamonds on both

sides of DE and Type II is similar to the 1947 strikes on a thin flan (U.S.) with elongated diamonds on both sides of DE.
NOTE: The 1993 Proof strike was not authorized by the Panamanian government.

2.5000 g, .900 SILVER, .0723 oz ASW
50th Anniversary of the Republic

KM#	Date	Mintage	Fine	VF	XF	Unc
18	1953	3.300	BV	.75	1.50	3.50

24	1961	2.500	BV	.75	1.25	2.50

COPPER-NICKEL CLAD COPPER
Obv: National arms. Rev: Balboa's portrait.

127	1996	21.000				.50

10 CENTESIMOS

COPPER-NICKEL CLAD COPPER
Manuel E. Amador

KM#	Date	Mintage	VF	XF	Unc
36.1	1975(RCM)	.050	.20	.50	1.00
	1975FM(M)	.013	.20	.50	1.50
	1975FM(U)	1,410	—	—	2.50
	1975FM(P)	.041	—	Proof	1.00
	1976(RCM)	.020	.20	1.00	1.50
	1976FM(M)	6,250	.50	1.25	2.25
	1976FM(P)	.012	—	Proof	1.00
	1977FM(U)	6,250	.50	1.25	2.25
	1977FM(P)	9,548	—	Proof	1.00
	1979FM(U)	.010	.20	.50	1.50
	1979FM(P)	5,949	—	Proof	1.50
	1980FM(U)	.040	.20	.50	1.00
	1981FM(P)	1,973	—	Proof	1.50
	1982FM(U)	2,500	.75	1.50	2.50
	1982FM(P)	1,480	—	Proof	1.50

75th Anniversary of Independence

48	1978FM(U)	.020	.20	.50	1.25
	1978FM(P)	.011	—	Proof	1.25

25 CENTESIMOS

12.5000 g, .900 SILVER, .3617 oz ASW

KM#	Date	Mintage	Fine	VF	XF	Unc
4	1904	1.600	5.00	12.00	35.00	125.00
	1904	12 pcs.	—	—	Proof	1500.

1/4 BALBOA

6.2500 g, .900 SILVER, .1809 oz ASW
High relief.

KM#	Date	Mintage	Fine	VF	XF	Unc
11.1	1930	.400	2.00	3.00	20.00	65.00
	1930	20 pcs.	—	Matte Proof		2000.
	1931	.048	15.00	30.00	220.00	1500.
	1932	.126	2.50	5.00	60.00	400.00
	1933	.120	2.50	5.00	25.00	185.00
	1934	.090	2.50	5.00	20.00	150.00
	1947	.700	1.00	2.00	4.00	25.00

Low relief.

11.2	1962	4.000	BV	1.00	2.00	3.50
	1962	25 pcs.	—	—	Proof	500.00

COPPER-NICKEL CLAD COPPER

KM#	Date	Mintage	VF	XF	Unc
11a	1966(RCM)	7.400	.35	.50	1.00
	1966(RCM)	.013	—	Proof	2.00
	1967	.020	—	Proof	1.50
	1968	1.200	.35	.60	1.25
	1968	.023	—	Proof	1.50
	1969	.014	—	Proof	1.50
	1970	2.000	.35	.60	1.25
	1970	9,528	—	Proof	2.00
	1971	.011	—	Proof	1.50
	1972	.013	—	Proof	1.50
	1973	.800	.40	1.00	1.50
	1973	.017	—	Proof	1.50
	1974	.018	—	Proof	1.50
	1975	1.500	.35	.50	1.50
	1979	2.000	.25	.45	1.00
	1980	2.000	.25	.45	1.00
	1982	3.000	.25	.45	1.00
	1983(RCM)	6.000	.25	.45	1.00
	1986(RCM)	3.000	.25	.50	1.50
	1993	4.000	.25	.45	1.00
	1993	—	—	Proof	350.00

NOTE: Varieties exist.
NOTE: The 1993 Proof strikes were not authorized by the Panamanian government.

6.2500 g, .900 SILVER, .1809 oz ASW
50th Anniversary of the Republic

KM#	Date	Mintage	Fine	VF	XF	Unc
19	1953	1.200	BV	1.50	3.00	18.50

25	1961	2.000	BV	1.25	1.75	3.75

COPPER-NICKEL CLAD COPPER
Obv: National arms. Rev: Balboa's portrait.

KM#	Date	Mintage	VF	XF	Unc
128	1996	7.200	—	—	.75

25 CENTESIMOS

COPPER-NICKEL CLAD COPPER
Justo Arosemena

37.1	1975(RCM)	.040	.25	.50	1.00
	1975FM(M)	5,000	1.00	1.75	3.00
	1975FM(U)	1,410	—	—	4.00
	1975FM(P)	.041	—	Proof	1.00
	1976(RCM)	.012	.35	.50	1.25
	1976FM(M)	2,500	.75	1.50	3.00
	1976FM(P)	.012	—	Proof	1.00
	1977FM(U)	2,500	.75	1.50	2.50
	1977FM(P)	9,548	—	Proof	1.00
	1979FM(U)	4,000	.50	1.00	1.75
	1979FM(P)	5,949	—	Proof	1.00
	1980FM(U)	4,000	.50	1.00	1.75
	1981FM(P)	1,973	—	Proof	2.00
	1982FM(U)	2,000	.75	1.50	2.75
	1982FM(P)	1,480	—	Proof	2.00

75th Anniversary of Independence

49	1978FM(U)	8,000	.35	.75	1.50
	1978FM(P)	.011	—	Proof	1.50

50 CENTESIMOS

25.0000 g, .900 SILVER, .7235 oz ASW

KM#	Date	Mintage	Fine	VF	XF	Unc
5	1904	1.800*	12.00	25.00	60.00	225.00
	1904	12 pcs.	—	—	Proof	1500.
	1905	1.000*	20.00	40.00	120.00	375.00

***NOTE:** 1,000,000 melted in 1931 to issue 1 Balboa coin at San Francisco Mint.

1/2 BALBOA

12.5000 g, .900 SILVER, .3617 oz ASW
High relief.

KM#	Date	Mintage	Fine	VF	XF	Unc
12.1	1930	.300	3.50	8.00	25.00	95.00
	1930	20 pcs.	—	Matte Proof		2200.
	1932	.063	5.00	10.00	125.00	650.00
	1933	.120	4.00	6.00	35.00	325.00
	1934	.090	4.00	6.00	35.00	275.00
	1947	.450	BV		3.50	10.00	30.00

Low relief.

12.2	1962	.700	BV	2.00	3.00	6.50
	1962	25 pcs.	—	—	Proof	750.00

12.5000 g, .400 CLAD SILVER, .1608 oz ASW
Obv: Normal helmet.

KM#	Date	Mintage	VF	XF	Unc
12a.1	1966(RCM)	1.000	1.50	2.00	4.50
	1966(RCM)	.013	—	Proof	3.00
	1967	.300	1.50	2.00	5.00
	1967	.020	—	Proof	3.00
	1968	1.000	1.50	2.00	4.50
	1968	.023	—	Proof	3.00
	1969	.014	—	Proof	3.00
	1970	.610	1.50	2.00	5.00
	1970	9,528	—	Proof	4.00
	1971	.011	—	Proof	3.00
	1972	.013	—	Proof	3.00
	1993	—	—	Proof	450.00

NOTE: Varieties exist.
NOTE: The 1993 Proof strike was not authorized by the Panamanian government.

Error: Type II helmet rim incomplete

12a.2	1966	Inc. Ab.	3.50	7.50	20.00

COPPER-NICKEL CLAD COPPER

12b	1973	1.000	1.00	1.25	1.75
	1973	.017	—	Proof	2.00
	1974	.018	—	Proof	2.00
	1975	1.200	.75	1.25	1.75
	1979	1.000			.75	1.00
	1980	.400	—		.75	1.50
	1982	.400	—		.75	1.50
	1983(RCM)	1.850	—		.75	1.00
	1986(RCM)	.200	.75	1.50	5.00
	1993	.600	.75	1.25	2.00

NOTE: Varieties exist.

12.5000 g, .900 SILVER, .3617 oz ASW
50th Anniversary of the Republic

KM#	Date	Mintage	Fine	VF	XF	Unc
20	1953	.600	—	BV	3.50	6.50
	1953	*5 pcs.	—	—	Proof	1850.

26	1961	.350	—	BV	4.00	10.00

COPPER-NICKEL CLAD COPPER
Obv: National arms. Rev: Balboa's portrait.

KM#	Date	Mintage	VF	XF	Unc
129	1996	.200	—	—	2.50

50 CENTESIMOS

COPPER-NICKEL CLAD COPPER
Fernando de Lesseps

38.1	1975(RCM)	.020	1.00	1.50	2.00
	1975FM(M)	2,000	1.50	3.00	5.00
	1975FM(U)	1,410			6.50
	1975FM(P)	.041	—	Proof	2.00
	1976(RCM)	.012	1.00	1.50	2.50
	1976FM(M)	1,250	1.00	2.25	5.00
	1976FM(P)	.012	—	Proof	2.00
	1977FM(U)	1,250	1.00	2.25	5.00
	1977FM(P)	9,548	—	Proof	2.00
	1979FM(U)	2,000	1.00	2.00	3.50
	1979FM(P)	5,949	—	Proof	2.00
	1980FM(U)	2,000	1.00	2.00	3.00
	1981FM(P)	1,973	—	Proof	3.00
	1982FM(U)	1,000	1.00	2.50	6.00
	1982FM(P)	1,480	—	Proof	3.00

75th Anniversary of Independence

50	1978FM(U)	8,000	1.00	2.00	3.50
	1978FM(P)	.011	—	Proof	5.00

BALBOA

26.7300 g, .900 SILVER, .7735 oz ASW
Vasco Nunez de Balboa

KM#	Date	Mintage	Fine	VF	XF	Unc
13	1931	.200	6.00	8.00	17.50	65.00
	1931	20 pcs.	—	Matte Proof		3000.
	1934	.225	6.00	7.50	16.00	65.00
	1947	.500	BV	4.00	6.00	12.50

50th Anniversary of the Republic
Obv: Similar to KM#13.

21	1953	.050	5.50	7.00	12.00	25.00

KM#	Date	Mintage	VF	XF	Unc
27	1966(RCM)	.300	—	—	10.00
	1966(RCM)	.013	—	Proof	15.00
	1967	.020	—	Proof	12.00
	1968	.023	—	Proof	12.00
	1969	.014	—	Proof	12.00
	1970	.013	—	Proof	15.00
	1971	.018	—	Proof	13.50
	1972	.023	—	Proof	12.00
	1973	.030	—	Proof	12.00
	1974	.030	—	Proof	12.00

NOTE: More than 200,000 of 1966 dates were melted down in 1971 for silver for the 20 Balboas.
NOTE: Varieties exist.

PAPUA NEW GUINEA

Papua New Guinea, an independent member of the British Commonwealth, occupies the eastern half of the island of New Guinea. It lies north of Australia near the equator and borders on West Irian. The country, which includes nearby Bismark archipelago, Buka and Bougainville, has an area of 178,260 sq. mi. (461,690 sq. km.) and a population of *3.7 million who are divided into more than 1,000 seperate tribes speaking more than 700 mutually unintelligible languages. Capital: Port Moresby. The economy is agricultural, and exports copra, rubber, cocoa, coffee, tea, gold and copper.

In 1884 Germany annexed the area known as German New Guinea (also Neu Guinea or Kaiser Wilhelmsland) comprising the northern section of eastern New Guinea, and granted its administration and development to the Neu-Guinea Compagnie. Administration reverted to Germany in 1889 following the failure of the company to exercise adequate administration. While a German protectorate, German New Guinea had an area of 92,159 sq. mi. (238,692 sq. km.) and a population of about 250,000. Capital: Herbertshohe, 1 of 4 capitals of German New Guinea. The seat of government was transferred to Rabaul in 1910. Copra was the chief crop. Australian troops occupied German New Guinea in Aug. 1914, shortly after Great Britain declared war on Germany. It was mandated to Australia by the Leage of Nations in 1920, known as the Territory of New Guinea. The territory was invaded and most of it was occupied by Japan in 1942. Following the Japanese surrender, it came under U.N. trusteeship, Dec. 13, 1946, with Australia as the administering power.

The Papua and New Guinea act, 1949, provided for the government of Papua and New Guinea as one administrative unit. On Dec. 1, 1973, Papua New Guinea became selfgoverning with Australia retaining responsibility for defense and foreign affairs. Full independence was achieved on Sept. 16, 1975. Papua New Guinea is a member of the Commonwealth of Nations. Elizabeth II is Head of State, as Queen of Papua New Guinea.

NEW GUINEA

New Guinea, the world's largest island after Greenland, was discovered by Spanish navigator Jorge de Menezes, who landed on the northwest shore in 1527. European interests, attracted by exaggerated estimates of the resources of the area, resulted in the island being claimed in part by Spain, the Netherlands, Great Britain and Germany.

RULERS
British, 1910-1952

MONETARY SYSTEM
12 Pence = 1 Shilling
20 Shillings = 1 Pound

1/2 PENNY

COPPER-NICKEL

KM#	Date	Mintage	Fine	VF	XF	Unc
1	1929	.025	—	—	350.00	500.00
	1929	—	—	—	Proof	750.00

NOTE: Entire mintage returned to Melbourne Mint which later sold 400 pcs. in sets with KM#2. Balance of mintage was destroyed.

PENNY

COPPER-NICKEL

KM#	Date	Mintage	Fine	VF	XF	Unc
2	1929	.063	—	—	350.00	500.00
	1929	—	—	—	Proof	750.00

NOTE: Entire mintage returned to Melbourne Mint which later sold 400 pcs. in sets with KM#1. Balance of mintage was destroyed.

BRONZE

KM#	Date	Mintage	Fine	VF	XF	Unc
6	1936	.360	.75	1.00	2.00	6.00
	1936	—	—	—	Proof	300.00

KM#	Date	Mintage	Fine	VF	XF	Unc
7	1938	.360	1.75	4.00	8.00	18.00
	1944	.240	1.00	2.00	5.00	10.00

3 PENCE

COPPER-NICKEL

KM#	Date	Mintage	Fine	VF	XF	Unc
3	1935	1.200	3.00	6.00	10.00	35.00
	1935	—	—	—	Proof	250.00

KM#	Date	Mintage	Fine	VF	XF	Unc
10	1944	.500	2.00	4.00	8.50	30.00

6 PENCE

COPPER-NICKEL

KM#	Date	Mintage	Fine	VF	XF	Unc
4	1935	2.000	2.50	4.00	8.00	35.00
	1935	—	—	—	Proof	250.00

KM#	Date	Mintage	Fine	VF	XF	Unc
9	1943	.130	3.00	6.00	15.00	45.00

SHILLING

5.3800 g, .925 SILVER, .1600 oz ASW

KM#	Date	Mintage	Fine	VF	XF	Unc
5	1935	2.100	BV	2.00	3.00	7.50
	1936	1.360	BV	2.00	3.00	7.50

KM#	Date	Mintage	Fine	VF	XF	Unc
8	1938	3.400	BV	2.00	3.00	7.50
	1945	2.000	BV	2.00	3.00	7.50

PAPUA NEW GUINEA

MINT MARKS
FM - Franklin Mint, U.S.A.*

*NOTE: From 1975-1985 the Franklin Mint produced coinage in up to 3 different qualities. Qualities of issue are designated in ( ) after each date and are defined as follows:

(M) MATTE - Normal circulation strike or a dull finish produced by sandblasting special uncirculated (polish finish) or proof quality dies.

(U) SPECIAL UNCIRCULATED - Polished or proof-like in appearance without any frosted features.

(P) PROOF - The highest quality obtainable having mirror-like fields and frosted features.

MONETARY SYSTEM
100 Toea = 1 Kina

TOEA

BRONZE
Paradise Bird - Wing Butterfly

KM#	Date	Mintage	VF	XF	Unc
1	1975	14.400	—	.15	.25
	1975FM(M)	.083	—	—	.30
	1975FM(U)	4,134	—	—	1.00
	1975FM(P)	.067	—	Proof	1.00
	1976	25.175	—	—	.20
	1976FM(M)	.084	—	—	.20
	1976FM(U)	976 pcs.	—	—	1.00
	1976FM(P)	.016	—	Proof	1.00
	1977FM(M)	.084	—	—	.20
	1977FM(U)	603 pcs.	—	—	1.50
	1977FM(P)	7,721	—	Proof	1.50
	1978	—	—	—	.25
	1978FM(M)	.083	—	—	.20
	1978FM(U)	777 pcs.	—	—	1.00
	1978FM(P)	5,540	—	Proof	1.50
	1979FM(M)	.084	—	—	.20
	1979FM(U)	1,366	—	—	1.00
	1979FM(P)	2,728	—	Proof	1.50
	1980FM(U)	1,160	—	—	1.00
	1980FM(P)	2,125	—	Proof	1.50
	1981	—	—	—	1.00
	1981FM(M)	—	—	—	.20
	1981FM(P)	.010	—	Proof	2.50
	1982FM(M)	—	—	—	1.00
	1982FM(P)	—	—	Proof	2.50
	1983	—	—	—	.25
	1983FM(U)	360 pcs.	—	—	.30
	1983FM(P)	—	—	Proof	2.50
	1984	—	—	—	.25
	1984FM(P)	—	—	Proof	2.50
	1987	—	—	—	.25
	1990	—	—	—	.25
	1995	—	—	—	.25

2 TOEA

BRONZE
Ornate Butterfly Cod

KM#	Date	Mintage	VF	XF	Unc
2	1975	11.400	—	.10	.30
	1975FM(M)	.042	—	—	.35
	1975FM(U)	4,134	—	—	1.25
	1975FM(P)	.067	—	Proof	1.25
	1976	15.175	—	.10	.25
	1976FM(M)	.042	—	—	.25
	1976FM(U)	976 pcs.	—	—	1.25
	1976FM(P)	.016	—	Proof	1.25
	1977FM(M)	.042	—	—	.25
	1977FM(U)	603 pcs.	—	—	1.75
	1977FM(P)	7,721	—	Proof	2.00
	1978	—	—	—	.30
	1978FM(M)	.042	—	—	.25
	1978FM(U)	777 pcs.	—	—	1.25
	1978FM(P)	5,540	—	Proof	2.00
	1979FM(M)	.042	—	—	.25
	1979FM(U)	1,366	—	—	1.25
	1979FM(P)	2,728	—	Proof	2.00
	1980FM(U)	1,160	—	—	1.25
	1980FM(P)	2,125	—	Proof	2.00
	1981	—	—	—	.25
	1981FM(P)	.010	—	Proof	3.00
	1982FM(M)	—	—	—	1.25
	1982FM(P)	—	—	Proof	3.00
	1983	—	—	—	.25
	1983FM(U)	360 pcs.	—	—	2.00
	1983FM(P)	—	—	Proof	3.00
	1984	—	—	—	.25
	1984	—	—	Proof	3.00
	1987	—	—	—	.25
	1990	—	—	—	.25
	1995	—	—	—	.25

5 TOEA

COPPER-NICKEL
Plateless Turtle

KM#	Date	Mintage	VF	XF	Unc
3	1975	11.000	.15	.25	.75
	1975FM(M)	.017	—	—	.75
	1975FM(U)	4,134	—	—	1.50
	1975FM(P)	.067	—	Proof	2.00
	1976	24.000	.15	.25	.75
	1976FM(M)	.017	—	—	.75
	1976FM(U)	976 pcs.	—	—	1.50
	1976FM(P)	.016	—	Proof	2.00
	1977FM(M)	.017	—	—	.75
	1977FM(U)	603 pcs.	—	—	2.00
	1977FM(P)	7,721	—	Proof	2.50
	1978	2,000	—	—	3.00
	1978FM(M)	.017	—	—	.75
	1978FM(U)	777 pcs.	—	—	1.50
	1978FM(P)	5,540	—	Proof	2.50
	1979	—	—	—	.75
	1979FM(M)	.017	—	—	.75
	1979FM(U)	1,366	—	—	1.50
	1979FM(P)	2,728	—	Proof	2.50
	1980FM(U)	1,160	—	—	1.50
	1980FM(P)	2,125	—	Proof	2.50
	1981FM(P)	.010	—	Proof	4.00
	1982	—	—	—	.75
	1982FM(M)	—	—	—	1.50
	1982FM(P)	—	—	Proof	4.00
	1983FM(U)	360 pcs.	—	—	2.50
	1983FM(P)	—	—	Proof	4.00
	1984	—	—	—	.75
	1984FM(P)	—	—	Proof	4.00
	1987	—	—	—	.75
	1990	—	—	—	.75
	1995	—	—	—	.75

10 TOEA

COPPER-NICKEL
Cuscus

KM#	Date	Mintage	VF	XF	Unc
4	1975	8.600	.20	.35	.65
	1975FM(M)	8,300	—	—	1.00
	1975FM(U)	4,134	—	—	1.75
	1975FM(P)	.067	—	Proof	2.00
	1976	—	.20	.35	.65
	1976FM(M)	8,300	—	—	1.00
	1976FM(U)	976 pcs.	—	—	1.75
	1976FM(P)	.016	—	Proof	2.00
	1977FM(M)	8,300	—	—	1.00
	1977FM(U)	603 pcs.	—	—	2.25
	1977FM(P)	7,721	—	Proof	3.00
	1978FM(M)	8,300	—	—	1.00
	1978FM(U)	777 pcs.	—	—	1.75
	1978FM(P)	5,540	—	Proof	3.00
	1979FM(M)	8,300	—	—	1.00
	1979FM(U)	1,366	—	—	1.75
	1979FM(P)	2,728	—	Proof	3.00
	1980FM(U)	1,160	—	—	1.75
	1980FM(P)	2,125	—	Proof	3.00
	1981FM(P)	.010	—	Proof	5.00
	1982FM(M)	—	—	—	1.75
	1982FM(P)	—	—	Proof	5.00
	1983FM(U)	360 pcs.	—	—	2.75
	1983FM(P)	—	—	Proof	5.00
	1984FM(P)	—	—	Proof	5.00

20 TOEA

COPPER-NICKEL
Bennett's Cassowary

KM#	Date	Mintage	VF	XF	Unc
5	1975	15.500	.30	.65	1.25
	1975FM(M)	4,150	—	—	2.35
	1975FM(U)	4,134	—	—	2.35
	1975FM(P)	.067	—	Proof	3.00
	1976FM(M)	4,150	—	—	2.25
	1976FM(U)	976 pcs.	—	—	2.25
	1976FM(P)	.016	—	Proof	3.00

KM#	Date	Mintage	VF	XF	Unc
5	1977FM(M)	4,150	—	—	2.25
	1977FM(U)	603 pcs.	—	—	2.75
	1977FM(P)	7,721	—	Proof	4.00
	1978	2.500	.45	1.00	1.50
	1978FM(M)	4,150	—	—	2.25
	1978FM(U)	777 pcs.	—	—	2.25
	1978FM(P)	5,540	—	Proof	4.00
	1979FM(M)	4,150	—	—	2.25
	1979FM(U)	1,366	—	—	2.25
	1979FM(P)	2,728	—	Proof	4.00
	1980FM(U)	1,160	—	—	2.25
	1980FM(P)	2,125	—	Proof	4.00
	1981	—	.25	.50	1.00
	1981FM(P)	.010	—	Proof	6.00
	1982FM(M)	—	—	—	2.25
	1982FM(P)	—	—	Proof	6.00
	1983FM(U)	360 pcs.	—	—	3.25
	1983FM(P)	—	—	Proof	6.00
	1984	—	.25	.50	1.00
	1984FM(P)	—	—	Proof	6.00
	1987	—	.25	.50	1.00
	1990	—	.25	.50	1.00
	1995	—	.25	.50	1.00

50 TOEA

COPPER-NICKEL
South Pacific Festival of Arts

KM#	Date	Mintage	VF	XF	Unc
15	1980	—	.75	1.25	2.75
	1980FM(U)	1,160	—	—	15.00
	1980FM(P)	2,125	—	Proof	10.00

9th South Pacific Games

KM#	Date	Mintage	VF	XF	Unc
31	1991	.025	—	—	6.50

KINA

COPPER-NICKEL
Sea and River Crocodiles

KM#	Date	Mintage	VF	XF	Unc
6	1975	2.000	1.35	2.00	3.25
	1975FM(M)	829 pcs.	—	—	10.00
	1975FM(U)	4,134	—	—	3.50
	1975FM(P)	.067	—	Proof	3.50
	1976FM(M)	829 pcs.	—	—	10.00
	1976FM(U)	976 pcs.	—	—	3.50
	1976FM(P)	.016	—	Proof	4.00
	1977FM(M)	829 pcs.	—	—	10.00
	1977FM(U)	603 pcs.	—	—	15.00
	1977FM(P)	7,721	—	Proof	5.00
	1978FM(M)	829 pcs.	—	—	10.00
	1978FM(U)	777 pcs.	—	—	3.50
	1978FM(P)	5,540	—	Proof	5.00
	1979FM(M)	829 pcs.	—	—	10.00
	1979FM(U)	1,366	—	—	3.50
	1979FM(P)	2,728	—	Proof	6.50
	1980FM(U)	1,160	—	—	3.50
	1980FM(P)	2,125	—	Proof	6.50
	1981FM(P)	.010	—	Proof	3.50
	1982FM(M)	—	—	—	3.50
	1982FM(P)	—	—	Proof	8.00
	1983FM(U)	360 pcs.	—	—	16.50
	1983FM(P)	—	—	Proof	8.00
	1984FM(P)	—	—	Proof	8.00

The Republic of Paraguay, a landlocked country in the heart of South America surrounded by Argentina, Bolivia and Brazil, has an area of 157,048 sq. mi. (406,750 sq. km.) and a population of *4.5 million, 95 percent of whom are of mixed Spanish and Indian descent. Capital: Asuncion. The country is predominantly agrarian, with no important mineral deposits or oil reserves. Meat, timber, hides, oilseeds, tobacco and cotton account for 70 percent of Paraguay's export revenue.

Paraguay was first visited by Alejo Garcia, a shipwrecked Spaniard, in 1524. The interior was explored by Sebastian Cabot in 1527 and 1528, when he sailed up the Parana and Paraguay rivers. Asuncion, which would become the center of a Spanish colonial province embracing much of southern South America, was established by the Spanish explorer Juan de Salazar on Aug. 15, 1537. For a century and a half the history of Paraguay was largely the history of the agricultural colonies established by the Jesuits in the south and east to Christianize the Indians. In 1811, following the outbreak of the South American wars of independence, Paraguayan patriots overthrew the local Spanish authorities and proclaimed their country's independence.

MONETARY SYSTEM
100 Centavos (Centesimos) = 1 Peso

5 CENTAVOS

COPPER-NICKEL

KM#	Date	Mintage	Fine	VF	XF	Unc
6	1903	.600	1.00	2.00	6.50	15.00

NOTE: Earlier date (1900) exists for this type.

KM#	Date	Mintage	Fine	VF	XF	Unc
9	1908	.400	1.50	5.00	30.00	75.00

10 CENTAVOS

COPPER-NICKEL

KM#	Date	Mintage	Fine	VF	XF	Unc
7	1903	1.200	1.00	2.00	6.50	15.00

NOTE: Earlier date (1900) exists for this type.

KM#	Date	Mintage	Fine	VF	XF	Unc
10	1908	.800	2.50	5.00	25.00	70.00

20 CENTAVOS

COPPER-NICKEL

KM#	Date	Mintage	Fine	VF	XF	Unc
8	1903	.750	1.00	2.00	7.50	17.50

NOTE: Earlier date (1900) exists for this type.

KM#	Date	Mintage	Fine	VF	XF	Unc
11	1908	1.000	2.50	5.00	25.00	70.00

50 CENTAVOS

COPPER-NICKEL

12	1925	4.000	.50	1.50	5.00	10.00

ALUMINUM

15	1938	.400	1.00		3.50	7.50

PESO

COPPER-NICKEL

13	1925	3.500	.50	1.00	5.00	8.00

ALUMINUM

16	1938	—	.50	1.50	3.00	6.50

2 PESOS

COPPER-NICKEL

14	1925	2.500	.50	1.00	6.00	9.00

ALUMINUM

17	1938	—	.50	1.50	3.00	6.50

5 PESOS

COPPER-NICKEL

18	1939	4.000	1.00	2.50	7.50	15.00

10 PESOS

COPPER-NICKEL

KM#	Date	Mintage	Fine	VF	XF	Unc
19	1939	4.000	1.00	2.00	7.00	14.00

MONETARY REFORM

100 Centimos = 1 Guarani

CENTIMO

ALUMINUM-BRONZE
Flower

20	1944	3.500	.10	.50	1.00	2.00
	1948HF	2.000	.10	.50	1.00	2.00
	1950HF	1.096	.10	.25	.75	1.50

5 CENTIMOS

ALUMINUM-BRONZE
Passion Flower

21	1944	2.195	.10	.50	1.00	2.50
	1947HF	13.111	.10	.20	.50	1.00

10 CENTIMOS

ALUMINUM-BRONZE
Orchid

22	1944	.975	.25	.75	2.50	5.00
	1947	6.656	.10	.25	.50	1.00
	1947HF	—	.10	.25	.50	1.00

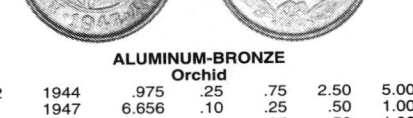

25	1953	5.000	.10	.15	.30	.60

NOTE: Medal rotation dies.

15 CENTIMOS

ALUMINUM-BRONZE

26	1953	5.000	.10	.20	.35	.75

NOTE: Medal rotation dies.

25 CENTIMOS

ALUMINUM-BRONZE
Orchid

23	1944	.700	.25	1.00	3.00	10.00

KM#	Date	Mintage	Fine	VF	XF	Unc
23	1948HF	.600	.25	.75	2.50	7.00
	1951HF	1.000	.25	.75	1.25	2.50

27	1953	2.000	.10	.15	.30	.75

NOTE: Medal rotation dies.

50 CENTIMOS

ALUMINUM-BRONZE

24	1944	2.485	.25	1.00	2.00	5.00
	1951	2.893	.25	.50	1.25	2.00

28	1953	2.000	.10	.15	.30	.75

NOTE: Medal rotation dies.

GUARANI

STAINLESS STEEL

151	1975	10.000	—	—	.15	.50
	1975	1,000	—	—	Proof	6.00
	1976	12.000	—	—	.10	.40
	1976	1,000	—	—	Proof	8.00

F.A.O. Issue

165	1978	15.000	—	—	.15	.50
	1980	13.000	—	—	.15	.50
	1980	1,000	—	—	Proof	5.00
	1984	15.000	—	—	.10	.30
	1986	15.000	—	—	.10	.30
	1988	15.000	—	—	.10	.30

NOTE: Varieties exist.

BRASS PLATED STEEL
F.A.O. Issue

180	1993	—	—	—	.15	.50

5 GUARANIES

STAINLESS STEEL

152	1975	7.500	—	—	.15	.50
	1975	1,000	—	—	Proof	6.00

F.A.O. Issue

KM#	Date	Mintage	Fine	VF	XF	Unc
166	1978	10.000	—	—	.15	.60
	1980	12.000	—	—	.15	.60
	1980	1,000	—	—	Proof	5.00
	1985	15.000	—	—	.10	.40
	1986	15.000	—	—	.10	.40

NOTE: Varieties exist.

NICKEL-BRONZE

| 166a | 1992 | 15.000 | — | — | .10 | .30 |

10 GUARANIES

STAINLESS STEEL

153	1975	10.000	—	—	.20	.75
	1975	1,000	—	—	Proof	8.00
	1976	10.000	—	—	.20	.75
	1976	1,000	—	—	Proof	10.00

F.A.O. Issue

167	1978	15.000	—	.10	.20	.75
	1980	15.000	—	.10	.20	.75
	1980	1,000	—	—	Proof	7.00
	1984	20.000	—	.10	.15	.50
	1986	35.000	—	.10	.15	.50
	1988	40.000	—	.10	.15	.50

NOTE: Varieties exist.

NICKEL-BRONZE
F.A.O. Issue - Cow

| 178 | 1990 | 40.000 | — | — | .10 | .40 |

50 GUARANIES

STAINLESS STEEL

154	1975	9.500	.20	.40	.60	1.25
	1975	1,000	—	—	Proof	10.00

General Estigarribia

169	1980	10.700	.20	.40	.60	1.25
	1980	1,000	—	—	Proof	9.00
	1986	15.000	.20	.40	.60	1.25
	1988	25.000	.20	.30	.50	1.00

NOTE: Varieties exist.

COPPER-ZINC-NICKEL
Acaray River Dam

KM#	Date	Mintage	Fine	VF	XF	Unc
179	1992	35.000	—	—	—	.75
	1995	35.000	—	—	—	.75

100 GUARANIES

COPPER-ZINC-NICKEL

| 177 | 1990 | 35.000 | — | — | — | 2.25 |

BRASS PLATED STEEL

177a	1993	35.000	—	—	—	1.50
	1995	35.000	—	—	—	1.50
	1996	—	—	—	—	1.50

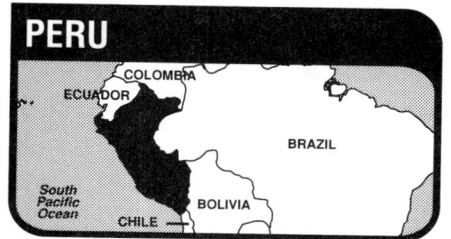

PERU

The Republic of Peru, located on the Pacific coast of South America, has an area of 496,225 sq. mi. (1,285,220 sq. km.) and a population of *21.4 million. Capital: Lima. The diversified economy includes mining, fishing and agriculture. Fish meal, copper, sugar, zinc and iron ore are exported.

Once part of the great Inca Empire that reached from northern Ecuador to central Chile, the conquest of Peru by Francisco Pizarro began in 1531. Desirable as the richest of the Spanish viceroyalties, it was torn by warfare between avaricious Spaniards until the arrival in 1569 of Francisco de Toledo, who initiated 2-1/2 centuries of efficient colonial rule which made Lima the most aristocratic colonial capital and the stronghold of Spain's American possessions. Jose de San Martin of Argentina proclaimed Peru's independence on July 28, 1821; Simon Bolivar of Venezuela secured it in December, 1824 when he defeated the last Spanish army in South America. After several futile attempts to re-establish its South American empire, Spain recognized Peru's independence in 1879.

Andres de Santa Cruz, whose mother was a high-ranking Inca, was the best of Bolivia's early presidents, and temporarily united Peru and Bolivia 1836-39, thus realizing his dream of a Peruvian/Bolivian confederation. This prompted the separate coinages of North and South Peru. Peruvian resistance and Chilean intervention finally broke up the confederation, sending Santa Cruz into exile. A succession of military strongman presidents ruled Peru until Marshall Castilla revitalized Peruvian politics in the mid-19th century and repulsed Spain's attempt to reclaim its one-time colony. Subsequent loss of southern territory to Chile in the War of the Pacific, 1879-81, and gradually increasing rejection of foreign economic domination, combined with recent serious inflation, affected the country numismatically.

As a result of the discovery of silver at Potosi in 1545, a mint was eventually authorized in 1565 with the first coinage taking place in 1568. The mint had an uneven life span during the Spanish Colonial period from 1568-1572. It was closed from 1573-1576, reopened from 1577-1588. It remained closed until 1659-1660 when an unauthorized coinage in both silver and gold were struck. After being closed in 1660, it remained closed until 1684 when it struck cob style coins until 1752.

MINT MARKS

L, LIMAE (monogram), Lima
   (monogram), LIMA = Lima
P,(P) = Philadelphia
S = San Francisco
(W) = Waterbury, CT, USA

NOTE: The LIMAE monogram appears in three forms. The early LM monogram form looks like a dotted L with M. The later LIMAE monogram has all the letters of LIMAE more readily distinguishable. The third form appears as an M monogram during early Republican issues.

MINT ASSAYERS INITIALS

The letter(s) following the dates of Peruvian coins are the assayer's initials appearing on the coins. They generally appear at the 11 o'clock position on the Colonial coinage and at the 5 o'clock position along the rim on the obverse or reverse on the Republican coinage.

DATING

Peruvian 5, 10 and 20 centavos, issued from 1918-1944, bear the dates written in Spanish. The following table translates those written dates into numerals:

1918 - UN MIL NOVECIENTOS DIECIOCHO
1919 - UN MIL NOVECIENTOS DIECINUEVE
1920 - UN MIL NOVECIENTOS VEINTE
1921 - UN MIL NOVECIENTOS VEINTIUNO
1923 - UN MIL NOVECIENTOS VEINTITRES
1926 - UN MIL NOVECIENTOS VEINTISEIS
1934 - UN MIL NOVECIENTOS TREINTICUATRO
1935 - UN MIL NOVECIENTOS TREINTICINCO
1937 - UN MIL NOVECIENTOS TREINTISIETE
1939 - UN MIL NOVECIENTOS TREINTINUEVE
1940 - UN MIL NOVECIENTOS CUARENTA
1941 - UN MIL NOVECIENTOS CUARENTIUNO
U. S. Mints
1942 - MIL NOVECIENTOS CUARENTA Y DOS
Lima Mint

1942 - UN MIL NOVECIENTOS CUARENTIDOS

U. S. Mints

1943 - MIL NOVECIENTOS CUARENTA Y TRES

1944 - MIL NOVECIENTOS CUARENTA Y CUATRO

Lima Mint

1944 - MIL NOVECIENTOS CUARENTICUATRO

MONETARY SYSTEM

100 Centavos (10 Dineros) = 1 Sol

10 Soles = 1 Libra

CENTAVO

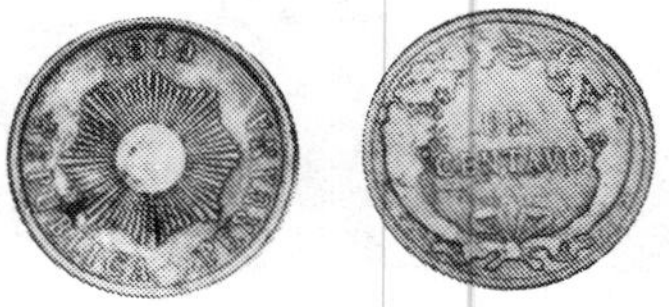

BRONZE
Sharper diework

KM#	Date	Mintage	Fine	VF	XF	Unc
187.2	1919 (P)	4.000	.50	1.00	2.50	8.50

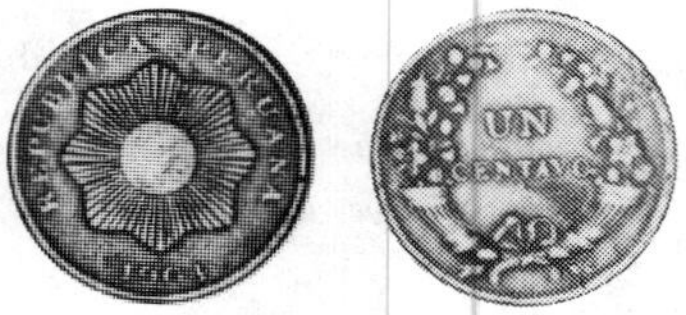

Thick planchet
Obv: Small date at bottom and legend.

KM#	Date	Mintage	Fine	VF	XF	Unc
208.1	1901	.600	1.00	2.50	4.00	14.00
	1904	1.000	4.50	8.00	14.00	45.00

Obv: Large date and legend.

KM#	Date	Mintage	Fine	VF	XF	Unc
208.2	1933	.275	1.50	3.00	5.50	16.00
	1934	1.185	.75	1.50	2.50	7.50
	1935	1.105	.75	1.50	2.50	7.50
	1936	.565	1.50	3.00	5.50	16.00
	1937/6	.735	1.00	2.00	4.00	12.00
	1937	Inc. Ab.	.75	1.50	2.50	7.50
	1938	.340	.75	1.50	2.50	7.50
	1939	1.225	1.50	3.00	5.50	15.00
	1940	1.250	1.50	3.00	5.50	15.00
	1941	2.593	.40	.75	1.50	6.00

NOTE: Varieties exist.

Thin planchet

KM#	Date	Mintage	Fine	VF	XF	Unc
208a	1941	Inc.KM208	.40	.75	1.50	6.00
	1942	2.865	.50	1.00	1.75	7.50
	1943	—		Reported, not confirmed		
	1944	—	4.00	9.00	16.00	40.00

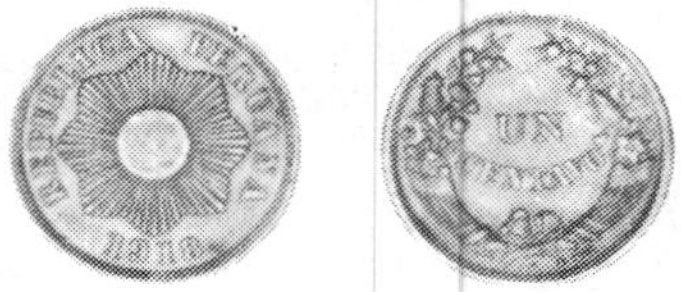

Thick planchet
Rev: Curved CENTAVO.

KM#	Date	Mintage	Fine	VF	XF	Unc
211	1909	.252	7.50	15.00	20.00	50.00
	1909/999 R	I.A.	7.50	15.00	20.00	50.00
	1909 R	Inc. Ab.	7.50	15.00	20.00	50.00
	1915	.250	3.00	6.00	10.00	25.00
	1916	.360	1.00	2.00	4.50	14.00
	1916 R	Inc. Ab.	1.00	2.00	4.50	14.00
	1917	.830	1.00	2.00	4.00	14.00
	1917 R	Inc. Ab.	1.00	2.00	4.00	14.00
	1918	1.060	1.00	2.00	4.00	12.00
	1918 R	Inc. Ab.	1.00	2.00	4.00	12.00
	1920	.360	1.00	2.50	4.50	15.00
	1920 R	Inc. Ab.	1.00	2.50	4.50	15.00
	1933 R	Inc. KM208	1.00	2.50	4.50	15.00
	1934	Inc.KM208	4.50	8.00	14.00	45.00
	1935 R	Inc. KM208	4.00	7.00	12.00	40.00
	1936 R	Inc. KM208	1.50	3.50	6.00	15.00
	1937	—	—	—	—	—
	1937 R	Inc. KM208	1.50	3.50	6.00	15.00
	1939 R	Inc. KM208	4.50	8.00	14.00	45.00

NOTE: Engravers initial R appeared below ribbon on most or all new dies, but often became weak or filled. Most coins show at least a faint trace of R. Date varieties also exist.

Thin planchet

KM#	Date	Mintage	Fine	VF	XF	Unc
211a	1941	Inc.KM208	1.00	2.00	3.50	12.50
	1942	Inc. KM208a	.50	1.00	1.75	7.50
	1943	—	2.50	5.00	12.50	30.00
	1944	2.490	.15	.40	.75	2.50
	1945	2.157	.15	.40	.75	2.50
	1946	3.198	.15	.40	.75	2.00
	1947	2.976	.15	.40	.75	2.50
	1948	3.195	.15	.40	.75	2.00
	1949	1.104	.25	.65	1.25	3.50

NOTE: Many varieties exist.

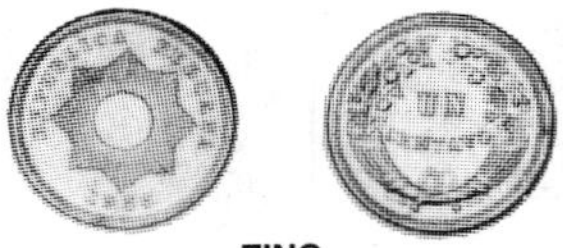

ZINC

KM#	Date	Mintage	Fine	VF	XF	Unc
227	1950	3.196	.35	.75	1.25	4.00
	1951	3.289	.25	.40	.65	2.00
	1952	3.050	.25	.40	.65	2.00
	1953	3.260	.35	.60	1.00	3.00
	1954	3.215	.75	1.50	2.50	8.00
	1955	3.400	.25	.40	.65	2.00
	1956 pointed 6	2.500	.25	.40	.65	2.00
	1956 knobbed 6	Inc. Ab.	.25	.40	.65	2.00
	1957	4.400	.40	.85	1.50	5.00
	1958/7	—	.35	.60	1.00	3.00
	1958	2.600	.35	.60	1.00	3.00
	1959	3.200	.25	.40	.65	2.00
	1960/50	3.060	.35	.60	1.00	3.00
	1960	Inc. Ab.	.75	1.50	3.00	6.00
	1961/51	2.600	.25	.40	.65	2.00
	1961	Inc. Ab.	.25	.40	.65	2.00
	1962/52	2.600	.25	.40	.65	2.00
	1962	Inc. Ab.	.25	.40	.65	2.00
	1963/53	2.400	.25	.40	.65	2.00
	1963	Inc. Ab.	.25	.40	.65	2.00
	1965	.360	.75	1.50	2.50	8.00

NOTE: Varieties exist. Copper plated examples of type dated 1951 are known.

2 CENTAVOS

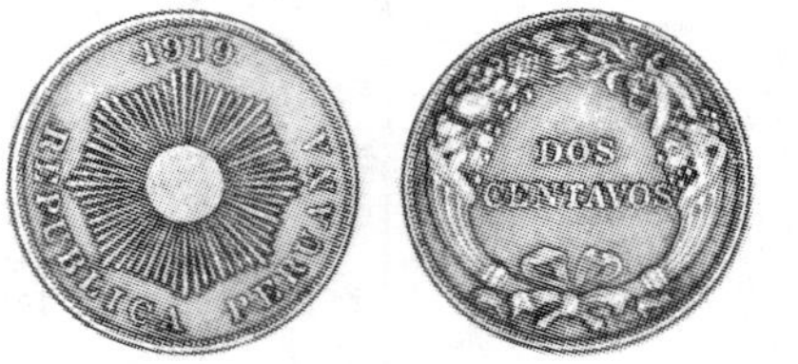

COPPER or BRONZE
Sharper diework.

KM#	Date	Mintage	Fine	VF	XF	Unc
A212 (188.3)	1919(P)	3.000	.35	.75	2.00	6.50

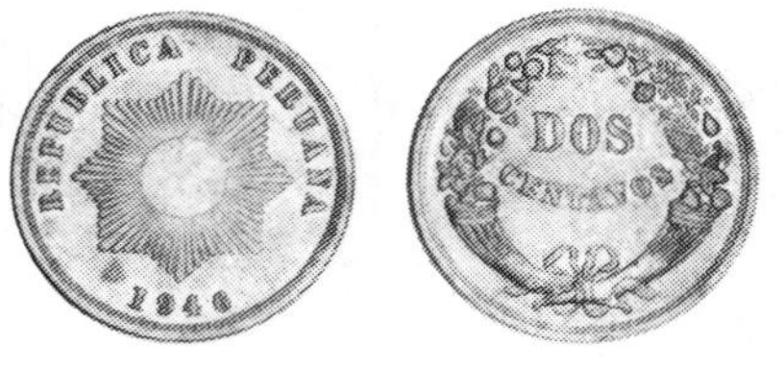

Thick planchet
Obv: Date at bottom.

KM#	Date	Mintage	Fine	VF	XF	Unc
212.1	1917 C	.073	4.00	6.50	10.00	25.00
	1918/17	.580	3.50	6.00	9.00	22.50
	1918/17 C	I.A.	3.50	6.00	9.00	22.50
	1918	Inc. Ab.	3.50	6.00	12.00	30.00
	1918 C	Inc. Ab.	3.50	6.00	12.00	30.00
	1920/7 C	.328	2.00	4.00	8.00	20.00
	1920	Inc. Ab.	1.00	1.75	3.00	10.00
	1920 C	Inc. Ab.	1.00	1.75	3.00	10.00
	1933	.285	1.00	1.75	3.00	10.00
	1933 C	Inc. Ab.	1.00	1.75	3.00	10.00
	1934	.973	.75	1.50	2.50	9.00
	1934 C	Inc. Ab.	.75	1.50	2.50	9.00
	1935	.950	.75	1.50	2.50	9.00
	1935 C	Inc. Ab.	.75	1.50	2.50	9.00
	1936	.763	.75	1.50	2.50	9.00
	1936/5 C	I.A.	1.50	2.50	5.00	15.00
	1936 C	Inc. Ab.	.75	1.25	2.25	7.50
	1937	.963	.75	1.50	2.50	9.00
	1937 C	Inc. Ab.	.75	1.50	2.50	9.00
	1938 C	.428	1.00	1.75	3.00	10.00
	1939/8 C	—		Reported, not confirmed		
	1939/8	—	1.50	2.50	5.00	15.00
	1939 C inverted A for V in CENTAVOS	.783	.75	1.50	2.50	9.00
	1940	—	—	—	—	—
	1940 C	.565	1.00	1.75	3.00	10.00
	1941/0	I.A.	—	—	—	—
	1941/0 C	I.A.	—	—	—	—
	1941/22	I.A.	—	—	—	—
	1941	Inc. Ab.	—	—	—	—
	1941 C	Inc. Ab.	2.00	5.00	10.00	15.00

NOTE: Engravers initial C appeared below ribbon on most or all new dies, but often became weak or filled. Most coins show at least a faint trace of C. Other varieties also exist.

Thin planchet

KM#	Date	Mintage	Fine	VF	XF	Unc
212.2	1941/32	.870	—	—	—	—
	1941/33 C	I.A.	1.00	2.00	3.50	10.00
	1941/33	I.A.	—	—	—	—
	1941/38	I.A.	—	—	—	—
	1941/38 C	I.A.	1.00	2.00	3.50	10.00
	1941/39 C	I.A.	1.00	2.00	3.50	10.00
	1941/0	I.A.	1.00	2.00	3.50	10.00
	1941	Inc. Ab.	.35	.75	1.25	4.00
	1942/22	4.418	—	—	—	—

KM#	Date	Mintage	Fine	VF	XF	Unc
212.2	1942/32	4.418	—	—	—	—
	1942	Inc. Ab.	.25	.50	1.00	3.00
	1943/2	1.829	.50	1.00	2.00	7.00
	1943	Inc. Ab.	.50	1.00	2.00	7.00
	1944	2.068	.75	1.50	3.00	9.00
	1945	2.288	.75	1.50	3.00	9.00
	1946	2.121	.25	.50	.75	2.50
	1947	1.280	.25	.50	.75	2.50
	1948	1.518	.25	.50	.75	3.00
	1949/8	.938	.25	.60	3.50	5.00
	1949	Inc. Ab.	—	—	—	—

NOTE: Varieties exist.

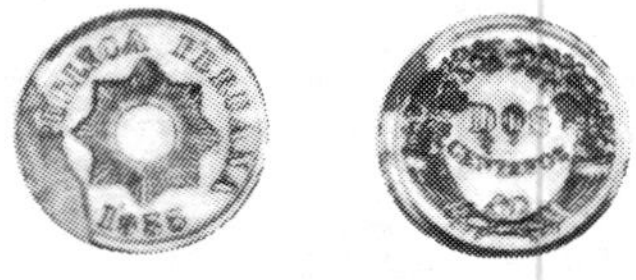

ZINC

KM#	Date	Mintage	Fine	VF	XF	Unc
228	1950	1.702	.35	.75	1.25	3.00
	1951	3.289	.35	.75	1.25	3.00
	1952	1.155	.35	.75	1.25	3.00
	1953	1.150	.40	.85	1.50	4.00
	1954	—	2.00	4.00	8.00	22.00
	1955	1.185	.35	.75	1.25	3.00
	1956	.400	.50	1.00	2.00	5.00
	1957	.520	1.50	3.00	6.00	15.00
	1958	.200	1.25	2.50	4.50	13.50

NOTE: Copper plated examples of type dated 1951 exist.

1/2 DINERO

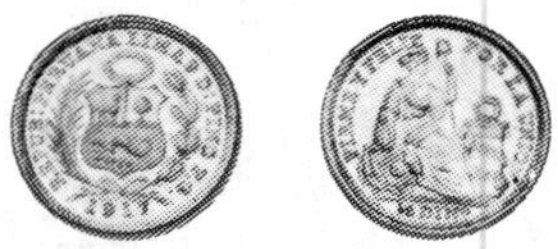

1.2500 g, .900 SILVER, .0362 oz ASW
Mint: Lima
Obv: W/o JR on stems.

KM#	Date	Mintage	Fine	VF	XF	Unc
206.2	1901/801 JF	.500	.60	1.25	2.50	6.00
	1901/801/701 JF	Inc. Ab.	.60	1.25	2.50	6.00
	1901/891/791	Inc. Ab.	.60	1.25	2.00	5.00
	1901/891 JF	Inc. Ab.	.60	1.25	2.00	5.00
	1901 JF	I.A.	.75	1.50	3.50	8.00
	1902/802 JF	.616	.60	1.25	2.00	5.00
	1902/892 JF	Inc. Ab.	.60	1.25	2.00	5.00
	1902/92	I.A.	.60	1.25	2.00	5.00
	1902 JF	I.A.	.75	1.50	3.50	8.00
	1903/803 JF	1.798	.50	1.00	1.75	3.50
	1903/893 JF	Inc. Ab.	.50	1.00	1.75	3.50
	1903/897 JF	Inc. Ab.	1.00	1.75	4.00	10.00
	1903 JF	I.A.	.75	1.50	3.00	7.00
	1904/804 JF	.723	.60	1.25	2.00	5.00
	1904/804 JF (error FFLIZ)	Inc. Ab.	3.00	6.00	12.00	25.00
	1904/884 JF	Inc. Ab.	.60	1.25	2.00	6.00
	1904/891 JF	Inc. Ab.	.60	1.25	2.00	6.00
	1904/893 JF	Inc. Ab.	.60	1.25	2.00	5.00
	1904/894 JF	Inc. Ab.	.60	1.25	2.00	5.00
	1904/894 JF (error FFLIZ)	Inc. Ab.	2.00	4.50	8.00	12.00
	1904 JF	I.A.	.75	1.50	3.00	7.00
	1904 JF (error FFLIZ)	Inc. Ab.	2.00	4.50	8.00	12.00
	1905/805 JF	1.400	.75	1.50	3.50	8.00
	1905/891 JF	Inc. Ab.	1.00	2.00	4.50	12.00
	1905/893 JF	Inc. Ab.	1.00	2.00	4.50	12.00
	1905/894	Inc. Ab.	1.00	2.00	4.50	12.00
	1905/895 JF	Inc. Ab.	.50	1.25	2.00	5.00
	1905/3 JF	I.A.	1.00	2.00	4.50	12.00
	1905 JF	I.A.	.75	1.50	3.00	7.00
	1906/806 JF	.900	.75	1.50	3.50	8.00
	1906/886 JF	Inc. Ab.	.75	1.50	3.50	8.00
	1906/895 JF	Inc. Ab.	.75	1.50	3.50	8.00
	1906/896 JF	Inc. Ab.	.50	1.25	2.00	5.00
	1906 JF	I.A.	.75	1.50	3.00	8.00
	1907 FG	.600	.60	1.25	2.00	5.00
	1908/7 FG	.200	1.50	3.00	6.00	15.00
	1908 FG	I.A.	.75	1.50	3.50	8.00
	1909/7 FG	—	3.00	6.00	12.50	27.50
	1909 FG	—	.75	1.50	3.50	8.00

KM#	Date	Mintage	Fine	VF	XF	Unc
206.2	1910 FG	.640	.50	1.00	1.75	3.50
	1911 FG	.460	.50	1.25	2.00	5.00
	1912 FG	.120	.60	1.25	2.50	6.00
	1913 FG	.480	.50	1.00	1.75	3.50
	1914/04 FG	—	1.00	2.50	5.50	15.00
	1914/03 FG	—	1.00	2.50	5.50	15.00
	1914/3 FG	—	.75	1.50	3.50	8.00
	1914 FG	—	.50	1.00	1.75	3.50
	1916/3 FG	.860	.50	1.00	1.75	3.50
	1916/3 FG (error) FERUANA					
		—	1.00	2.00	4.50	12.00
	1916 FG	I.A.	.35	.75	1.25	2.50
	1916/5 FG (error) PERUANA					
		Inc. Ab.	1.00	2.00	4.50	12.00
	1916/5 FG (error) FERUANA					
		Inc. Ab.	1.00	2.00	4.50	12.00
	1916 FG (error) FERUANA					
		Inc. Ab.	1.00	2.00	4.50	12.00
	1916	—	—	—	Matte	—
	1917/87 FG	.140	.50	1.00	1.75	3.50
	1917 FG	I.A.	.50	1.00	1.75	3.50

NOTE: Most coins 1900-06 show faint to strong traces of 9/8 or 90/89 in date. Non-overdates without such traces are scarce. Most coins of 1907-17 have engravers initial R at left of shield tip on reverse. Many other varieties exist.

NOTE: Earlier dates (1893-1900) exist for this type.

5 CENTAVOS

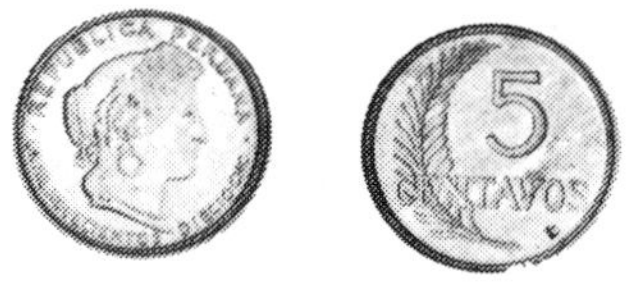

COPPER-NICKEL
Mint: Philadelphia
Obv. date: UN MIL NOVECIENTOS DIECIOCHO.

KM#	Date	Mintage	Fine	VF	XF	Unc
213.1	1918	4.000	.50	1.25	2.50	10.00
	1919	10.000	.40	1.00	2.00	7.00
	1923	2.000	1.00	2.00	3.50	12.50
	1926	4.000	1.50	3.00	6.00	20.00

Mint: London

KM#	Date	Mintage	Fine	VF	XF	Unc
213.2	1934	4.000	.75	2.00	3.00	8.50
	1934	—	—	—	Proof	—
	1935	4.000	.50	1.25	2.00	6.00
	1935	—	—	—	Proof	—
	1937	2.000	.75	2.00	3.00	8.50
	1937	—	—	—	Proof	—
	1939	2.000	.50	1.25	2.00	6.00
	1939	—	—	—	Proof	—
	1940	2.000	.50	1.25	2.00	6.00
	1940	—	—	—	Proof	—
	1941	2.000	.50	1.25	2.00	6.00
	1941	—	—	—	Proof	—

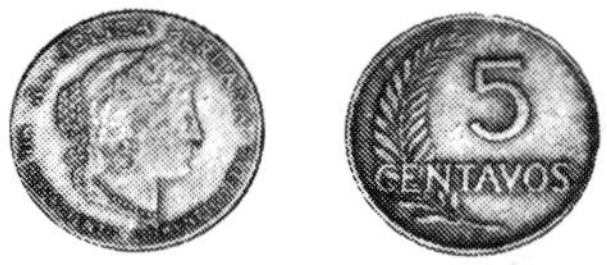

BRASS
Mint: Philadelphia
Obv. date: MIL NOVECIENTOS CUARENTA Y DOS.

KM#	Date	Mintage	Fine	VF	XF	Unc
213.2a.1	1942	4.000	1.00	3.00	5.00	12.00
	1943	4.000	1.00	3.00	5.00	12.00
	1944	4.000	1.00	2.75	4.50	10.00

Mint mark: S

KM#	Date	Mintage	Fine	VF	XF	Unc
213.2a.2	1942	4.000	1.00	3.00	5.00	12.00
	1943	4.000	2.50	4.50	8.00	20.00

Mint: Lima
Obv. date: MIL NOVECIENTOS CUARENTICUATRO.

KM#	Date	Mintage	Fine	VF	XF	Unc
213.2a.3	1944	1.106	1.50	3.50	6.00	15.00

Thick planchet
Obv: Short legend.

KM#	Date	Mintage	Fine	VF	XF	Unc
223.1	1945	2.768	.35	.75	1.50	4.00
	1946/5	4.270	1.00	2.50	5.00	14.00
	1946	Inc. Ab.	.25	.50	1.00	3.50

Obv: Long legend.

KM#	Date	Mintage	Fine	VF	XF	Unc
223.3	1947	7.683	.25	.50	1.00	3.00
	1948	6.711	.25	.50	1.00	3.00
	1949/8	5.550	1.00	2.00	4.00	10.00

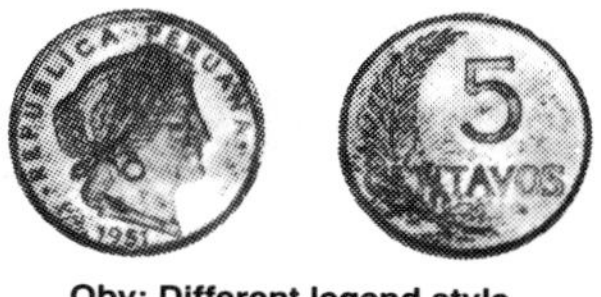

Obv: Different legend style.

KM#	Date	Mintage	Fine	VF	XF	Unc
223.4	1949	Inc. Ab.	1.00	2.00	4.00	10.00
	1950	7.933	.25	.50	1.00	3.00
	195.1	8.064	.25	.50	1.00	3.00
	1951	Inc. Ab.	1.00	2.00	4.00	20.00

Thin planchet

KM#	Date	Mintage	Fine	VF	XF	Unc
223.2	1951	Inc. Ab.	.10	.25	.50	2.50
	1952	7.840	.10	.25	.50	2.50
	1953	6.976	.10	.25	.50	2.50
	1953 AFP	—	—	—	—	—
	1954	6.244	.10	.20	.40	1.00

KM#	Date	Mintage	Fine	VF	XF	Unc
223.2	1955	8.064	.10	.20	.40	2.00
	1956	16.200	—	.10	.35	1.50
	1957 sm. dt.					
		16.000	—	.10	.25	.75
	1957 lg.dt.	I.A.	—	.10	.25	.75
	1958	4.600	—	.10	.25	1.00
	1959	8.300	—	.10	.25	1.00
	1960/50	9.900	—	—	Rare	—
	1960 lg. dt.	I.A.	—	.10	.25	.75
	1960 sm. dt.	I.A.	—	.10	.25	.75
	1961	10.200	—	.10	.20	.75
	1962 curved 9					
		11.064	—	.10	.20	.75
	1962 straight 9					
		Inc. Ab.	—	.10	.20	.75
	1963	12.012	—	.10	.20	.75
	1964/3	12.304	—	.10	.35	1.50
	1964	Inc. Ab.	—	—	.10	.75
	1965 small date					
		12.500	—	—	.10	.50
	1965 lg. dt.	I.A.	—	.10	.20	1.00
	1965	—	—	—	Proof	20.00

NOTE: Varieties exist.

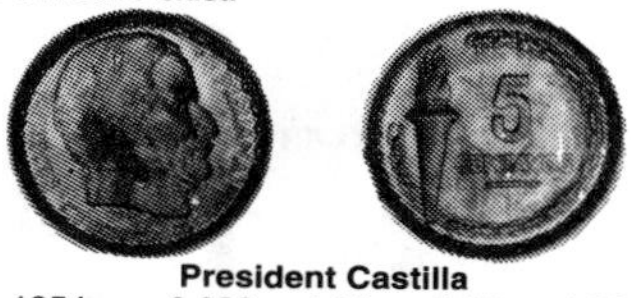

President Castilla

KM#	Date	Mintage	Fine	VF	XF	Unc
232	1954	2.080	1.00	2.00	4.00	8.00

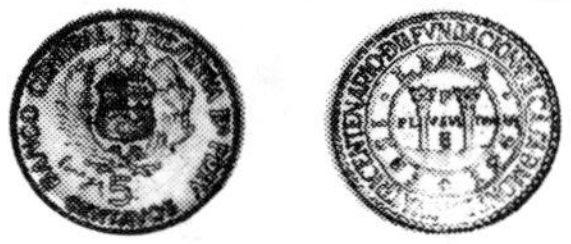

400th Anniversary of Lima Mint

KM#	Date	Mintage	Fine	VF	XF	Unc
290	1965	.712	—	—	.25	.50
	1965	—	—	—	Proof	100.00

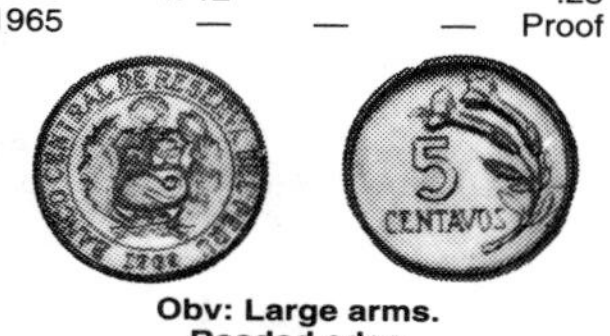

Obv: Large arms.
Reeded edge

KM#	Date	Mintage	Fine	VF	XF	Unc
244.1	1966*	14.620	—	—	.10	.20
	1966	1,000	—	—	Proof	2.50
	1967	14.088	—	—	.10	.20
	1968	17.880	—	—	.10	.20

***NOTE:** PAREJA in field at lower left of arms.

Plain edge

KM#	Date	Mintage	Fine	VF	XF	Unc
244.2	1969	17.880	—	—	—	.10
	1970	—	—	—	—	.10
	1971	24.320	—	—	—	.10
	1972	24.342	—	—	—	.10
	1973	25.074	—	—	—	.10

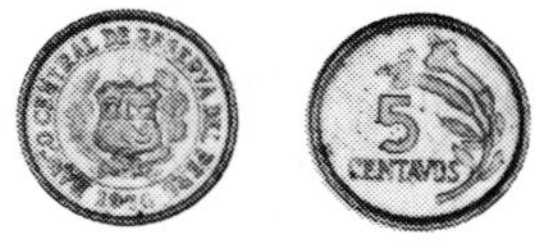

Obv: Small arms.

KM#	Date	Mintage	Fine	VF	XF	Unc
244.3	1973	Inc. Ab.	—	—	—	.10
	1974	—	—	—	—	.10
	1975	—	—	—	—	.10

DINERO

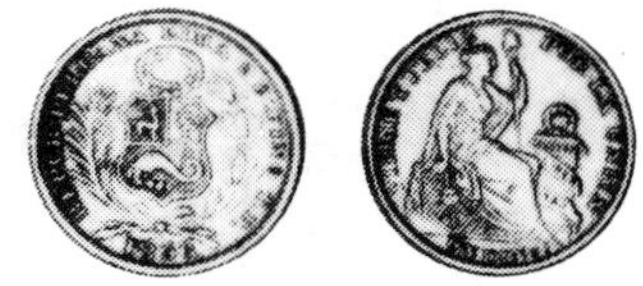

2.5000 g, .900 SILVER, .0723 oz ASW
Mint: Lima
Obv: Large wreath.
Rev: Denomination in curved line.

KM#	Date	Mintage	Fine	VF	XF	Unc
204.2	1902/1 JF	.375	1.00	2.00	3.50	10.00
	1902/891 JF					
		Inc. Ab.	1.00	2.00	3.50	10.00
	1902/892 JF					
		Inc. Ab.	1.00	2.00	3.50	10.00
	1902/897 JF					
		Inc. Ab.	1.00	2.00	3.50	10.00
	1902 JF	I.A.	1.00	2.00	3.50	10.00
	1903/803 JF					
		.887	1.00	2.00	3.50	10.00
	1903/807 JF					
		Inc. Ab.	1.00	2.00	3.50	10.00
	1903/892 JF					
		Inc. Ab.	.75	2.00	3.50	8.00
	1903/893 JF					
		Inc. Ab.	.75	2.00	3.50	8.00
	1903/92 JF	I.A.	.75	2.00	3.50	8.00
	1903 JF	I.A.	.75	1.75	2.50	6.00
	1904 JF	.380	1.00	2.50	4.00	12.50
	1905/1 JF	.700	1.00	2.50	4.00	10.00

KM#	Date	Mintage	Fine	VF	XF	Unc
204.2	1905/3 JF	I.A.	1.00	2.50	4.00	10.00
	1905 JF	I.A.	.75	2.00	3.50	8.00
	1906 JF	.826	.75	2.00	3.50	8.00
	1907 JF	.500	—	—	Rare	—
	1907 FG/JF					
		Inc. Ab.	1.25	2.50	4.50	10.00
	1907 FG	I.A.	1.00	1.75	3.00	8.00
	1908/6 FG/JF					
		Inc. Ab.	1.00	2.25	4.00	10.00
	1908 FG/JF					
		.200	1.00	2.25	4.00	10.00
	1908 FG/GF					
		Inc. Ab.	1.00	2.25	4.00	10.00
	1908 FG	I.A.	1.00	1.75	3.00	8.00
	1909 FG	—	2.00	4.00	8.00	15.00
	1909 FG/FO	—	2.00	4.00	8.00	15.00
	1909 FG/FF	—	2.00	4.00	8.00	15.00
	1910 FG	.210	.60	1.25	2.50	8.00
	1910 FG/JF	I.A.	1.00	2.25	4.00	12.50
	1910 FG/JG	I.A.	1.00	2.25	4.00	12.50
	1911 FG	.200	.75	1.50	3.00	8.00
	1911 FG/JF					
		Inc. Ab.	1.00	2.25	4.00	12.50
	1911 FG/JG					
		Inc. Ab.	1.00	2.25	4.00	12.50
	1912 FG	.400	.60	1.25	2.50	8.00
	1912/02 FG/JF					
		Inc. Ab.	1.00	2.25	4.00	12.50
	1912 FG/JF	I.A.	1.00	2.25	4.00	12.50
	1912 FG/JG	I.A.	1.00	2.25	4.00	12.50
	1913/1 FG/JF					
		Inc. Ab.	1.00	2.25	4.00	12.50
	1913/2 FG	.360	1.00	2.25	4.00	12.50
	1913/7 FG/G					
		Inc. Ab.	1.00	2.25	4.00	12.50
	1913 FG	I.A.	.60	1.25	2.50	8.00
	1913 FG/G	I.A.	.60	1.25	2.50	8.00
	1913 FG/JB	I.A.	.60	1.25	2.50	8.00
	1916 FG large date					
		.430	1.25	2.50	4.50	10.00
	1916 FG small date					
		Inc. Ab.	.60	1.25	2.00	6.00
	1916 FG/JG	I.A.	2.00	5.00	7.50	15.00
	1916 FG/FF	I.A.	2.00	5.00	7.50	15.00

NOTE: Earlier dates (1893-1900) exist for this type.
NOTE: Varieties exist.

10 CENTAVOS

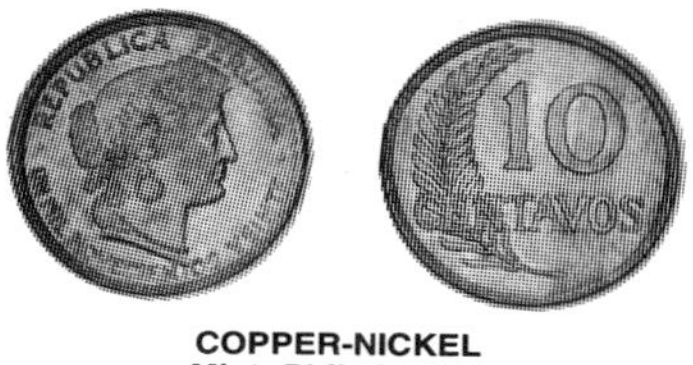

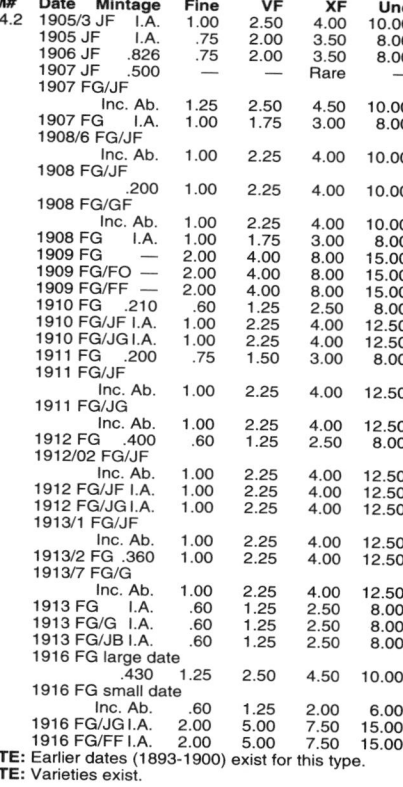

COPPER-NICKEL
Mint: Philadelphia
Obv. date: UN MIL NOVECIENTOS DIECIOCHO.

KM#	Date	Mintage	Fine	VF	XF	Unc
214.1	1918	3.000	.40	1.00	2.00	7.00
	1919	2.500	.40	1.00	2.00	7.00
	1920	3.080	.35	.75	1.50	6.00
	1921	6.920	.35	.75	1.50	6.00
	1926	3.000	2.50	5.00	8.50	22.50

Mint: London

KM#	Date	Mintage	Fine	VF	XF	Unc
214.2	1935	1.000	.75	1.50	3.00	12.00
	1935	—	—	—	Proof	—
	1937	1.000	.40	1.00	2.00	7.00
	1937	—	—	—	Proof	—
	1939	2.000	.35	.75	1.25	5.00
	1939	—	—	—	Proof	—
	1940	2.000	.35	.75	1.25	5.00
	1940	—	—	—	Proof	100.00
	1941	2.000	.35	.75	1.25	5.00
	1941	—	—	—	Proof	—

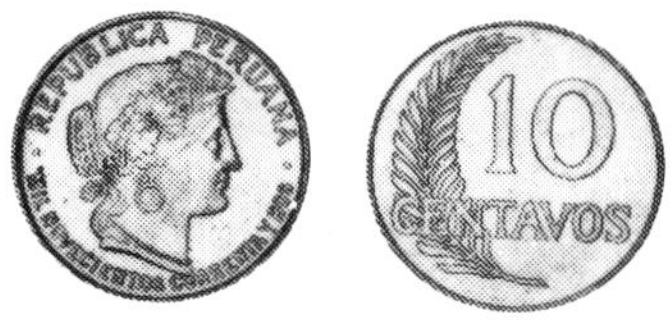

BRASS
Mint: Philadelphia
Obv: Date begins MIL. . ., spelled out w/a "Y".

KM#	Date	Mintage	Fine	VF	XF	Unc
214a.1	1942	2.000	1.50	3.00	6.00	16.00
	1943	2.000	1.50	3.00	6.00	16.00
	1944	2.000	1.50	3.50	7.00	20.00

Mint mark: S

KM#	Date	Mintage	Fine	VF	XF	Unc
214a.2	1942	2.000	6.00	12.00	20.00	45.00
	1943	2.000	1.50	3.00	6.00	16.00

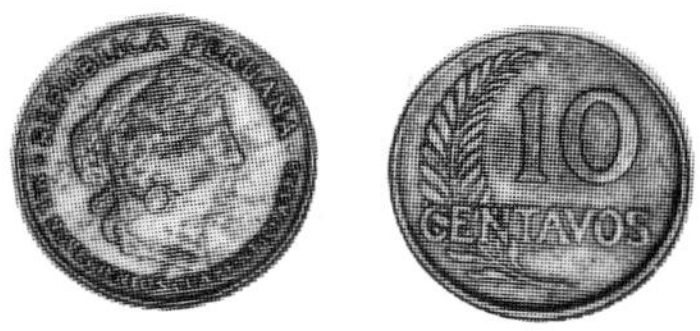

Mint: Lima
Obv: Date begins UN MIL. . ., spelled out w/an "I."

KM#	Date	Mintage	Fine	VF	XF	Unc
214a.3	1942	—	5.00	9.00	15.00	35.00

Obv: Date begins MIL . . ., spelled out w/an "I."

KM#	Date	Mintage	Fine	VF	XF	Unc
214a.4	1944	—	3.50	7.00	12.00	30.00

NOTE: Varieties exist.

Thick planchet
Obv: Short legend.

224.1	1945	2.810	.25	—	1.50	4.00
	1946/5	4.863	.50	1.00	2.50	8.00
	1946	Inc. Ab.	.35	.75	2.00	7.00

Thin planchet, 1.3mm
Obv: Long legend.

224.2	1951	Inc. Ab.	.10	.20	.40	2.00
	1951 AFP	—	.10	.20	.40	2.00
	1952	6.694	.10	.20	.40	3.00
	1952 AFP	—	.10	.20	.40	3.00
	1953	5.668	.10	.20	.40	2.00
	1953 AFP	—	.10	.20	.40	2.00
	1954	7.786	—	.10	.35	1.50
	1954 AFP	—	—	.10	.35	1.50
	1955	6.690	—	.10	.35	1.50
	1955 AFP	—	—	.10	.35	1.50
	1956/5	8.410	.10	—	.75	3.50
	1956	Inc. Ab.	—	.10	.25	1.00
	1956 AFP	—	—	.20	.40	2.00
	1957	8.420	—	.10	.25	.75
	1957 AFP	—	—	.10	.25	1.00
	1958	10.380	—	.10	.25	1.00
	1958 AFP	—	—	—	—	—
	1959	8.300	—	—	.10	.75
	1959 AFP	—	—	—	—	—
	1960	12.600	—	—	.10	.50
	1961	12.700	—	—	.10	.60
	1962	14.598	—	—	.10	.50
	1963	16.100	—	—	.10	.50
	1964	16.504	—	—	.10	.60
	1965	17.808	—	—	.10	.50
	1965	—	—	—	Proof	25.00

NOTE: Date varieties exist.

Thick planchet.
Obv: Long legend.

226.1	1947	6.806	.25	.50	1.00	3.00
	1948	5.771	.25	.50	1.25	4.00
	1949/8	4.730	.50	1.00	1.50	7.50

Obv: Different legend style.

226.2	1949	Inc. Ab.	.25	.50	1.25	4.00
	1950	5.298	.25	.50	1.00	3.00
	1950 AFP					
		Inc. Ab.	.20	.40	.80	2.00
	1951	7.324	6.00	10.00	15.00	35.00
	1951/0 AFP	—	.25	.50	1.00	3.00
	1951 AFP	—	.20	.40	.80	2.00

President Castilla

233	1954	1.818	1.00	2.00	4.50	10.00

400th Anniversary of Lima Mint

237	1965	.572	—	—	.35	.75
	1965	—	—	—	Proof	150.00

Obv: Large arms.
Reeded edge

245.1	1966*	14.930	—	—	.10	.25
	1966	1,000	—	—	Proof	2.50
	1967	19.330	—	—	.10	.25
	1968	24.390	—	—	.10	.25

NOTE: Date varieties exist.
*NOTE: PAREJA in field at lower left of arms.

Obv: Vicuna arms.
Plain edge

245.2	1967	—	—	—	.10	.25
	1969	24.390	—	—	.10	.25
	1970	29.110	—	—	.10	.20

KM#	Date	Mintage	Fine	VF	XF	Unc
245.2	1971	30.590	—	—	.10	.20
	1972	34.442	—	—	.10	.20
	1973	33.864	—	—	.10	.20

NOTE: Date varieties exist.

Obv: Small arms.

245.3	1973	Inc. Ab.	—	—	.10	.15
	1974	—	—	—	.10	.15
	1975	10.430	—	—	.10	.15

263	1975	—	—	—	.10	.15

1/5 SOL

5.0000 g, .900 SILVER, .1447 oz ASW
Mint: Lima
Rev: Libertad incuse.

205.2	1901 JF	.638	1.50	3.00	5.50	12.00
	1903/1 JF	.702	2.00	4.00	7.00	17.50
	1903/13 JF	I.A.	1.75	3.50	6.00	15.00
	1903 JF	I.A.	1.50	3.00	5.50	12.00
	1906 JF	.660	1.50	3.00	5.50	12.00
	1907 JF	1.370	1.25	2.00	4.00	6.00
	1907 FG	I.A.	1.50	3.00	5.50	12.00
	1908/7 FG	.560	1.75	3.50	6.00	15.00
	1908 FG	I.A.	1.50	3.00	5.50	12.00
	1909 FG	.042	2.00	4.00	9.00	27.50
	1910/00 FG					
		.165	3.00	7.00	12.00	25.00
	1910 FG	I.A.	3.00	7.00	12.00	25.00
	1911 FG	.250	1.50	3.00	5.50	9.00
	1911 FG-R	I.A.	1.50	3.00	5.50	9.00
	1912 FG	.300	1.25	2.00	4.00	6.00
	1912 FG-R	I.A.	1.50	3.00	5.50	9.00
	1913 FG	.223	1.75	3.50	6.00	15.00
	1913 FG-R	I.A.	1.75	3.50	6.00	15.00
	1914 FG	.010	5.00	10.00	20.00	40.00
	1915 FG	—	25.00	35.00	60.00	100.00
	1916 FG	.425	2.00	5.00	10.00	25.00
	1916 FG-R	I.A.	1.50	3.00	5.00	9.00
	1917 FG-R	.020	8.00	15.00	30.00	60.00

NOTE: Earlier dates (1895-1900) exist for this type.
NOTE: Some coins 1893-1900 have engravers initials JR left of shield tip on reverse and some 1911-17 have R in same location. Die varieties exist.

20 CENTAVOS

COPPER-NICKEL
Mint: Philadelphia
Obv. date: UN MIL NOVECIENTOS DIECIOCHO.

215.1	1918	2.500	.40	1.00	2.50	8.00
	1919	1.250	.50	1.25	3.00	10.00
	1920	1.464	.50	1.25	3.00	10.00
	1921	8.536	.35	.85	2.00	7.00
	1926	2.500	.75	2.50	6.00	20.00

Mint: London

215.2	1940	1.000	.25	.75	1.75	5.50
	1940	—	—	—	Proof	125.00
	1941	1.000	.35	1.00	2.50	7.50
	1941	—	—	—	Proof	125.00

BRASS
Mint: Philadelphia

Obv. date: MIL NOVECIENTOS CUARENTA Y TRES.

KM#	Date	Mintage	Fine	VF	XF	Unc
215a.1	1942	.500	3.00	6.00	12.50	50.00
	1943	.500	3.00	6.00	12.50	50.00
	1944	.500	4.00	7.50	15.00	55.00

Mint mark: S

215a.2	1942	.500	6.00	12.00	25.00	90.00
	1943	.500	3.00	6.00	12.50	60.00

Mint: Lima
Thick planchet
Obv: Large head, divided leg.

221.1	1942	.300	1.00	2.50	5.00	12.50
	1943	1.900	.75	1.50	2.50	7.50
	1944	2.963	.60	1.25	2.00	6.00

Obv: Large head w/AFP on truncation,
continuous leg.

221.2	1946	3.410	.25	.50	.85	3.00
	1947	4.307	.25	.50	.85	3.00
	1948	3.578	.25	.50	.85	3.00
	1949/8	2.709	.75	1.50	2.50	6.50

Obv: Different legend style.

221.4	1949	Inc. Ab.	.50	1.00	1.75	4.50
	1950	2.427	1.00	1.75	3.00	8.00
	1951	2.941	3.00	7.50	12.50	30.00

COPPER

221.2a	1947	300 pcs.	—	—	—	75.00

BRASS
Thin planchet, 1.3mm, AFP

221.2b	1951	Inc. Ab.	.20	.40	.75	2.00
	1951 w/o AFP					
		—	—	—	—	—
	1952	4.410	.20	.40	.75	2.50
	1952 w/o AFP					
		Inc. Ab.	—	—	—	—
	1953	2.615	.20	.40	.75	2.00
	1954	1.816	1.50	2.50	4.00	9.00
	1955 large date					
		4.050	—	.10	.15	.30	1.50
	1955 small date					
		I.A.	.15	.25	.50	2.00
	1956	3.760	.10	.15	.30	1.50
	1957	3.680	.10	.15	.30	1.00
	1958	3.100	.10	.15	.30	1.00
	1959	5.450	—	.10	.20	.75
	1959 w/o AFP					
		—	—	—	—	—
	1960/90 w/o AFP					
		—	—	—	—	—
	1960	6.750	—	.10	.20	.75
	1960 w/o AFP					
		—	.25	.75	1.50	4.00
	1961	6.800	—	.10	.20	.75
	1961 w/o AFP					
		—	—	—	—	—
	1962	7.357	—	.10	.20	.75
	1963/2	8.843	.15	.25	.50	2.00
	1963	Inc. Ab.	—	.10	.20	1.00
	1964	9.550	—	.10	.20	.75
	1965	—	—	.10	.20	.75
	1965 w/o AFP					
		—	—	—	—	—

NOTE: Date varieties exist.

COPPER-NICKEL
Reeded edge.

221.2c	1958	—	—	—	—	150.00
	1965	—	—	—	Proof	30.00

Obv: Small head, continuous leg.

KM#	Date	Mintage	Fine	VF	XF	Unc
221.3	1945	3.043	.25	.50	.75	1.50
	1946/5	Inc. Ab.	.25	.65	1.00	2.00
	1946	Inc. Ab.	.25	.50	.75	1.50

President Castilla

| 234 | 1954 | .799 | 2.00 | 4.00 | 8.00 | 15.00 |

| 264 | 1975 | — | .10 | .20 | .50 | 1.00 |

25 CENTAVOS

BRASS
400th Anniversary of Lima Mint

| 238 | 1965 | 1.113 | — | .25 | .35 | .75 |
| | 1965 | — | — | Proof | | 200.00 |

Reeded edge. Obv: Large arms.

246.1	1966*	9.300	—	.15	.25	.50
	1966	1,000	—	—	Proof	2.50
	1967	8.150	—	.15	.25	.50
	1968	7.440	—	.15	.25	.50

*NOTE: PAREJA in field at lower left of arms.

Plain edge.

246.2	1968 AP	I.A.	—	.15	.25	.50
	1969 AP on rev.					
		7.440	—	.20	.40	1.00
	1969 w/o AP					
		Inc. Ab.	—	.15	.25	.50
	1970	6.341	—	.20	.40	1.00
	1971	3.196	—	.20	.40	1.00
	1972	5.523	—	.20	.40	1.00
	1973	7.492	—	.15	.25	.50

Obv: Small arms.

259	1973	Inc. Ab.	—	.10	.15	.25
	1974	—	—	.10	.15	.25
	1975	—	—	.10	.15	.25

1/2 SOL

12.5000 g, .900 SILVER, .3617 oz ASW
Obv: Large wreath.
Rev: Denomination in straight line.

KM#	Date	Mintage	Fine	VF	XF	Unc
203	1907 FG-JR					
		1.000	BV	4.00	10.00	20.00
	1908/7 FG-JR					
		.030	8.00	15.00	40.00	100.00
	1908 FG-JR					
		I.A.	12.00	25.00	50.00	125.00
	1914 FG-JR					
		.173	BV	4.50	15.00	35.00
	1915 FG-JR					
		.570	BV	3.50	6.50	15.00
	1916 FG	.384	BV	3.50	6.50	15.00
	1916 FG-JR					
		—	BV	3.50	6.50	15.00
	1917 FG-JR					
		.178	BV	4.00	10.00	20.00

NOTE: Most coins 1907-17 have engravers initials JR left of shield tip on reverse. Date varieties exist.

12.5000 g, .500 SILVER, .2009 oz ASW

216	1922 LIBERTAD incuse, J.R. on rev.					
		.465	BV	4.50	18.00	48.00
	1922 LIBERTAD in relief					
		Inc. Ab.	BV	4.50	18.00	48.00
	1923 LIBER/TAD GM round top 3					
		2.520	BV	2.50	6.00	20.00
	1923/2 flat top 3					
		Inc. Ab.	BV	2.50	5.50	17.50
	1923 flat top 3					
		Inc. Ab.	BV	2.50	5.50	17.50
	1924 GM	.238	3.00	6.00	20.00	50.00
	1926 GM	.694	BV	3.50	7.00	20.00
	1927 GM	2.640	BV	2.50	5.50	15.00
	1928/7 GM					
		3.028	—	—	—	—
	1928 GM	I.A.	BV	2.50	5.50	15.00
	1929 GM	3.068	BV	2.50	5.50	15.00
	1935 AP	2.653	BV	2.50	5.00	14.00
	1935		—	—	—	—

NOTE: Engravers initials appear on stems of obverse wreath. Date varieties exist.

BRASS
Mint: London
Obv: 5 palm leaves point to llama on shield.

220.1	1935	10.000	.50	1.25	2.25	7.00
	1941	4.000	.50	1.25	2.25	7.00

Mint: Philadelphia

220.2	1942	4.000	1.50	3.00	5.00	15.00
	1943	4.000	3.00	6.50	12.50	35.00
	1944	Inc. Ab.	1.50	3.00	5.00	15.00

Mint mark: S

220.3	1942	1.668	1.50	3.00	5.00	15.00
	1943	6.332	1.50	3.00	5.00	15.00

NOTE: The coins struck in Philadelphia and San Francisco have a serif on the "4" of the date; the Lima and London coins do not.

Mint: Lima
Obv: 3 palm leaf points to llama on shield.

220.4	1941	2.000	3.00	6.50	12.50	35.00
	1942	Inc. Ab.	1.50	3.00	5.00	15.00
	1942 AP					
	1943	2.000	.50	1.00	2.00	8.00
	1944/2	4.000				
	1944	Inc. Ab.	.40	.85	1.75	7.00

KM#	Date	Mintage	Fine	VF	XF	Unc
220.4	1944 AP	I.A.	—	—	—	—
	1945	4.000	.75	1.50	3.00	10.00

NOTE: Dates 1941-44 have thick flat-top 4 w/o serifs. 1945 has narrow 4 like KM#220.5.

Obv: 3 palm leaves point to llama on shield.

220.5	1942 long-top 2					
		Inc. Ab.	1.50	3.00	5.00	15.00
	1944	Inc. Ab.	.75	1.50	3.00	10.00
	1944 AP	I.A.	.50	1.00	2.00	7.00
	1945	Inc. Ab.	.75	1.50	3.00	10.00
	1945 AP	I.A.	.75	1.50	3.00	10.00
	1946/5 AP					
		3.744	2.00	3.50	6.50	17.50
	1946 AP	I.A.	.40	.75	1.25	4.00
	1947 AP	6.066	.40	.75	1.25	5.00
	1947	Inc. Ab.	.40	.75	1.25	5.00
	1948	3.324	.40	.75	1.25	4.00
	1949/8	.420	1.00	2.00	4.00	12.00
	1949	Inc. Ab.	1.50	3.00	6.00	18.00
	1950	.091	1.25	2.25	4.50	15.00
	1951/8	.930	.50	1.00	2.00	7.00
	1951	Inc. Ab.	.50	1.00	2.00	7.00
	1952	.935	.75	1.50	3.00	10.00
	1953	.817	.50	1.00	2.00	7.00
	1954	.637	.75	1.50	3.00	10.00
	1955	1.383	.15	.35	.75	4.00
	1956	2.309	.10	.25	.40	1.50
	1957	2.700	.10	.25	.50	2.00
	1958	2.691	.10	.25	.40	1.50
	1959	3.609	.10	.25	.40	1.50
	1960	5.600	.10	.20	.35	.75
	1961	4.400	.10	.20	.35	.75
	1962	3.540	.10	.20	.35	1.00
	1963	4.345	.10	.20	.35	.75
	1964	5.315	.10	.20	.35	1.50
	1965	7.090	.10	.20	.35	1.75
	1965	—	—	—	Proof	50.00

NOTE: 1942, 1944 AP and all 1945-49 have narrow 4 w/o serif on crossbar. 1944 w/o AP has flat-top 4 like KM#220.4. Engravers initials AP appear on wreath stems of some 1944-45, all 1946 and some 1947 coins. Varieties exist, including narrow and wide dates for 1956 and 1961 issues.

400th Anniversary of Lima Mint

239	ND(1965)	10.971	—	.10	.15	.35
	ND(1965)	—	—	—	Proof	400.00

Obv: Large arms. Rev: Vicuna.

247	1966	13.720	—	.10	.20	.50
	1966	1,000	—	—	Proof	4.00
	1967	15.500	—	.10	.20	.50
	1968	13.890	—	.10	.20	.50
	1968 JAS	—	—	.10	.20	.50
	1969	13.890	—	.10	.20	.50
	1970	11.901	—	.10	.20	.50
	1971	7.524	—	.15	.20	.50
	1972	19.441	—	.10	.20	.50
	1973	14.951	—	.10	.20	.50

NOTE: Date varieties exist for 1970.

Obv: Small arms.

260	1973	Inc. Ab.	—	.10	.20	.50
	1974/1	—	—	.10	.20	.50
	1974	14.518	—	.10	.20	.50
	1975	14.039	—	.10	.20	.50

265	1975	62.682	—	.10	.20	.30
	1976	369.828	—	.10	.20	.30
	1977	18.943	—	.10	.20	.30

SOL

25.0000 g, .900 SILVER, .7234 oz ASW
Type XII
Legends have smaller lettering, 37mm.
Rev: Libertad incuse.

KM#	Date	Mintage	Fine	VF	XF	Unc
196.26	1914 FG	.620	6.00	7.00	9.00	22.00
	1915/4 FG					
		1.736	6.00	8.00	16.00	50.00
	1915 FG	I.A.	6.00	7.00	9.00	20.00

NOTE: Earlier dates (1893-1897) exist for this type.
NOTE: Varieties exist.

Rev: LIBERTAD incuse, 36.5mm.

196.27	1916 FG	1.927	6.00	7.00	8.00	20.00

Type XIII
Rev: LIBERTAD in relief.

196.28	1916 FG	I.A.		7.00	8.00	20.00

25.0000 g, .500 SILVER, .4019 oz ASW
Obv: Fineness omitted. Rev: LIBERTAD in relief.

217.1	1922	—	—	—	Rare	—
	1923	3,600	15.00	30.00	70.00	275.00

Rev: LIBERTAD incuse.

217.2	1923	1,400	35.00	75.00	165.00	475.00

Mint: Philadelphia
Small letters.

218.1	1923	*2.369	BV	5.50	8.50	15.00
	1924/824					
		*3.113	5.50	10.00	20.00	40.00

KM#	Date	Mintage	Fine	VF	XF	Unc
218.1	1924/3	*I.A.	5.50	10.00	20.00	40.00
	1924	Inc. Ab.	BV	5.50	8.50	15.00
	1925	*1.291	BV	5.50	10.00	20.00
	1926	*2.157	BV	5.50	8.50	15.00

*NOTE: The Philadelphia and Lima strikings may be distinguished by the fact that the letters in the legends are smaller on those pieces produced at Philadelphia. All bear the name of the Lima Mint.

Mint: Lima
Large letters.
Obv: Engraver's initials GM on stems flanking date.

218.2	1924	.096	5.50	9.00	20.00	65.00
	1925	1.005	BV	5.50	8.50	15.00
	1930	.076	BV	5.50	10.00	20.00
	1931	.024	BV	5.50	10.00	22.00
	1933	5,000	6.00	12.00	20.00	40.00
	1934/3	2.855	BV	5.50	10.00	20.00
	1934	Inc. Ab.	BV	5.50	7.00	12.50
	1935	.695	BV	5.50	10.00	20.00

BRASS

222	1943	10.000	.35	1.25	3.00	8.00
	1944	Inc. Ab.	.35	1.25	3.00	7.00
	1945	—	.50	1.50	3.50	9.00
	1946	1.752	.50	1.50	3.00	8.00
	1947	3.302	.35	1.00	2.00	6.00
	1948	1.992	.35	1.00	2.00	6.00
	1949/8	.751	2.00	4.00	7.00	20.00
	1949	Inc. Ab.	3.50	7.50	12.00	25.00
	1950	1.249	7.00	10.00	15.00	25.00
	1951/0	2.094	.25	.50	1.50	6.00
	1951	Inc. Ab.	.25	.50	1.50	6.00
	1952	2.037	.25	.50	1.50	6.00
	1953	1.243	3.00	6.00	10.00	25.00
	1954	1.220	.35	.75	1.75	6.00
	1955	1.323	.35	.75	1.75	6.00
	1956	3.450	.15	.35	.75	3.00
	1957	3.086	.15	.35	1.00	5.00
	1958	3.390	.15	.35	.75	3.00
	1959	4.975	.15	.35	1.00	5.00
	1960	5.800	.15	.35	.75	1.50
	1961	5.200	.15	.35	.75	2.00
	1962	5.102	.15	.35	.75	1.50
	1963	5.499	.15	.35	.75	2.00
	1964	5.888	.15	.35	.75	2.00
	1965	5.504	.15	.35	.75	2.00
	1965	—	—	—	Proof	75.00

NOTE: Date varieties exist.

400th Anniversary of Lima Mint

240	ND(1965)	3.103	—	.35	.75	1.50
	ND(1965)	-I.A.	—	—	Proof	500.00

KM#	Date	Mintage	Fine	VF	XF	Unc
248	1966	16.410	—	.10	.25	.60
	1966	1,000	—	—	Proof	5.00
	1967	13.920	—	.10	.25	.60
	1968	12.260	—	.10	.25	.60
	1969	12.260	—	.10	.25	.60
	1970	12.336	—	.10	.25	.60
	1971	11.927	—	.10	.25	.60
	1972	3.945	—	.10	.25	.60
	1973	12.856	—	.10	.25	.60
	1974	14.966	—	.10	.25	.60
	1975	—	—	.10	.25	.60

BRASS, 21mm

266.1	1975	354.485	—	—	.10	.25
	1976	114.660	—	—	.10	.25

17mm
Mint mark: LIMA (monogram)

266.2	1978	9.000	—	—	.15	.35
	1979	4.842	—	—	.15	.35
	1980	28.826	—	—	.15	.35
	1981	51.630	—	—	.15	.35
	1982	4.155	—	—	.15	.35

5 SOLES

2.3404 g, .900 GOLD, .0677 oz AGW
Mint: Lima

235	1956	4,510	—	—	—	50.00
	1957	2,146	—	—	—	50.00
	1958	3,325		Reported, not confirmed		
	1959	1,536	—	—	—	50.00
	1960	8,133	—	—	—	50.00
	1961	1,154	—	—	—	50.00
	1962	1,550	—	—	—	50.00
	1963	3,945	—	—	—	50.00
	1964	2,063	—	—	—	50.00
	1965	.014	—	—	—	50.00
	1966	4,738	—	—	—	50.00
	1967	3,651	—	—	—	50.00
	1968	129 pcs.		Reported, not confirmed		
	1969	127 pcs.	—	—	—	175.00

COPPER-NICKEL
Mint: Paris

252	1969	10.000	.20	.40	.60	1.50

150th Anniversary of Independence
Mint mark: LIMA (monogram)

254	1971	3.480	.20	.40	.80	2.00

Regular Issue

KM#	Date	Mintage	Fine	VF	XF	Unc
257	1972	2.068	—	.10	.35	1.00
	1973	.475	—	.10	.35	1.00
	1974	—	—	.10	.35	1.50
	1975	—	—	.10	.35	1.50

267	1975	—	—	.10	.35	1.00
	1976	17.016	—	.10	.35	1.00
	1977	94.272	—	.10	.35	1.00

BRASS

271	1978	38.016	—	.10	.20	.60
	1979	64.524	—	.10	.20	.60
	1980	76.964	—	.10	.20	.60
	1981	31.632	—	.10	.20	.60
	1982	23.262	—	.10	.20	.60
	1983	650 pcs.	20.00	30.00	40.00	60.00

10 SOLES

4.6807 g, .900 GOLD, .1354 oz AGW
Mint: Lima

236	1956	5,410	—	—	BV	75.00
	1957	1,300	—	—	BV	75.00
	1958	3,325	Reported, not confirmed			
	1959	1,103	—	—	BV	75.00
	1960	7,178	—	—	BV	75.00
	1961	1,634	—	—	BV	75.00
	1962	1,676	—	—	BV	75.00
	1963	3,372	—	—	BV	75.00
	1964	1,554	—	—	BV	75.00
	1965	.014	—	—	BV	75.00
	1966	2,601	—	—	BV	75.00
	1967	3,002	—	—	BV	75.00
	1968	100 pcs.	—	BV	100.00	200.00
	1969	100 pcs.	—	BV	100.00	200.00

COPPER-NICKEL
Mint: Paris

253	1969	15.000	—	.25	.50	.75	1.75

150th Anniversary of Independence
Mint mark: LIMA (monogram)

255	1971	2.460	.25	.50	1.00	2.50

KM#	Date	Mintage	Fine	VF	XF	Unc
258	1972	2.235	—	.10	.40	1.25
	1973	1.765	—	.10	.40	1.25
	1974	—	—	.10	.40	1.25
	1975	—	—	.10	.40	1.25

BRASS
Obv: Large arms, small letters.
Inner circle 19.1mm.

272.1	1978	46.970	—	.10	.40	.85

Obv: Small arms, large letters.
Inner circle 17.2mm.

272.2	1978		—	.10	.40	.85
	1979	82.220	—	.10	.40	.85
	1980	99.595	—	.10	.40	.85
	1981	25.660	—	.10	.40	.85
	1982	61.035	—	.10	.40	.85
	1983	15.820	—	.10	.40	.85

150th Anniversary - Birth of Admiral Grau

287	1984	30.000	—	—	.20	.50

20 SOLES

9.3614 g, .900 GOLD, .2709 oz AGW
Mint: Lima

229	1950	1,800	—	—	BV	150.00
	1951	9,264	—	—	BV	150.00
	1952	424 pcs.	—	—	BV	200.00
	1953	1,435	—	—	BV	150.00
	1954	1,732	—	—	BV	150.00
	1955	1,971	—	—	BV	150.00
	1956	1,201	—	—	BV	150.00
	1957	.011	—	—	BV	150.00
	1958	.011	—	—	BV	150.00
	1959	.012	—	—	BV	150.00
	1960	7,753	—	—	BV	150.00
	1961	1,825	—	—	BV	150.00
	1962	2,282	—	—	BV	150.00
	1963	3,892	—	—	BV	150.00
	1964	1,302	—	—	BV	150.00
	1965	.012	—	—	BV	150.00
	1966	4,001	—	—	BV	150.00
	1967	5,003	—	—	BV	150.00
	1968	640 pcs.	—	—	BV	200.00
	1969	640 pcs.	—	—	BV	200.00

50 SOLES

23.4056 g, .900 GOLD, .6772 oz AGW
Mint: Lima

230	1950	1,927	—	—	BV	350.00
	1951	5,292	—	—	BV	350.00
	1952	1,201	—	—	BV	450.00
	1953	1,464	—	—	BV	350.00
	1954	1,839	—	—	BV	350.00
	1955	1,898	—	—	BV	350.00

KM#	Date	Mintage	Fine	VF	XF	Unc
230	1956	.011	—	—	BV	350.00
	1957	.011	—	—	BV	350.00
	1958	.011	—	—	BV	350.00
	1959	5,734	—	—	BV	350.00
	1960	2,139	—	—	BV	350.00
	1961	1,110	—	—	BV	350.00
	1962	3,319	—	—	BV	350.00
	1963	3,089	—	—	BV	350.00
	1964/3	2,425	—	—	BV	350.00
	1964	Inc. Ab.	—	—	BV	350.00
	1965	.023	—	—	BV	350.00
	1966	3,409	—	—	BV	350.00
	1967	5,805	—	—	BV	350.00
	1968	443 pcs.	—	—	BV	450.00
	1969	443 pcs.	—	—	BV	450.00
	1970	553 pcs.	—	—	BV	450.00

ALUMINUM-BRONZE

273	1979	1.323	—	.15	.35	1.00
	1980	42.573	—	.10	.20	.50
	1981	19.923	—	.10	.20	.50
	1982 LIMA	18.471	—	.10	.20	.50
	1982 w/o LIMA	Inc. Ab.	—	.15	.35	1.00
	1983	8.175	—	.10	.20	.50

BRASS
150th Anniversary - Birth of Admiral Grau

297	1984	11.475	—	—	.20	.50
	1985	8.525	—	—	.20	.50

100 SOLES

COPPER-NICKEL

283	1980	100.000	—	—	.20	.40	1.50
	1982		—	—	.20	.40	1.50

BRASS
150th Anniversary - Birth of Admiral Grau
Mint mark: LIMA (monogram)

288	1984	20.000	—	—	.15	.35	1.00

500 SOLES

BRASS
150th Anniversary - Birth of Admiral Grau
Mint mark: LIMA (monogram)

289	1984	16.962	—	—	.20	.50	2.00

KM#	Date	Mintage	Fine	VF	XF	Unc
		Admiral Grau W/o Date				
310	1985	13.038	—	.20	.50	2.50

MONETARY REFORM

1986 - 1990
1000 Soles de Oro = 1 Inti

CENTIMO

BRASS
Mint mark: LIMA (monogram)

KM#	Date	Mintage	Fine	VF	XF	Unc
291	1985	4.180	—	—	—	.25
	1986	.020	—	—	—	.35
	1987	—	—	—	—	.35
	1988	—	—	—	—	.35

5 CENTIMOS

BRASS
Mint mark: LIMA (monogram)

292	1985	20.000	—	—	—	.35
	1986	—	—	—	—	.45
	1987	—	—	—	—	.45
	1988	—	—	—	—	.45

10 CENTIMOS

BRASS
Mint mark: LIMA (monogram)

293	1985	143.900	—	—	—	1.00
	1986	48.730	—	—	—	.65
	1987	42.370	—	—	—	.65
	1988	—	—	—	—	.65

20 CENTIMOS

BRASS
Mint mark: LIMA (monogram)

294	1985	4.739	—	—	—	1.25
	1986	96.699	—	—	—	1.00
	1987	59.668	—	—	—	1.00
	1988	—	—	—	—	1.00

50 CENTIMOS

BRASS
Mint mark: LIMA (monogram)

295	1985	43.320	—	—	—	1.25
	1986	72.802	—	—	—	1.25
	1987	63.878	—	—	—	1.25
	1988	80.000	—	—	—	1.25

INTI

COPPER-NICKEL
Mint mark: LIMA (monogram)

296	1985	15.760	—	—	—	1.50
	1986	87.240	—	—	—	1.00
	1987	120.000	—	—	—	.75
	1988	17.304	—	—	—	1.50

5 INTIS

COPPER-NICKEL
Mint mark: LIMA (monogram)
Admiral Grau

KM#	Date	Mintage	Fine	VF	XF	Unc
300	1985	3,972	—	—	—	1.75
	1986	.028	—	—	—	1.75
	1987	20.106	—	—	—	1.75
	1988	34.084	—	—	—	1.75

MONETARY REFORM

1991 -

1/M Intis = 1 Nuevo Sol
100 (New) Centimos = 1 Nuevo Sol

CENTIMO

BRASS
Mint mark: LIMA (monogram)

303	1991 CHAVEZ	—	—	—	—	.35
	1992 CHAVEZ	—	—	—	—	.45
	1993	—	—	—	—	.35

NOTE: Varieties exist.

5 CENTIMOS

BRASS
Mint mark: LIMA (monogram)

304	1991 CHAVEZ	—	—	—	—	.45
	1992 CHAVEZ	—	—	—	—	.50
	1993	—	—	—	—	.45
	1993 CHAVEZ	—	—	—	—	.45
	1994	—	—	—	—	.45
	1996	—	—	—	—	.45

NOTE: Varieties exist.

10 CENTIMOS

BRASS
Mint mark: LIMA (monogram)

305	1991	—	—	—	—	.65
	1992	—	—	—	—	.70
	1993	—	—	—	—	.65
	1993 CHAVEZ	—	—	—	—	.65
	1994	—	—	—	—	.65
	1995	—	—	—	—	.65

NOTE: Varieties exist.

20 CENTIMOS

BRASS
Mint mark: LIMA (monogram)

306	1991 CHAVEZ	—	—	—	—	.85
	1992	—	—	—	—	.85
	1993	—	—	—	—	.85
	1994	—	—	—	—	.85

50 CENTIMOS

COPPER-NICKEL
Mint mark: LIMA (monogram)

KM#	Date	Mintage	Fine	VF	XF	Unc
307	1991	—	—	—	—	1.50
	1992	—	—	—	—	1.75
	1993	—	—	—	—	1.50
	1994	—	—	—	—	1.50

NOTE: Varieties exist.

NUEVO SOL

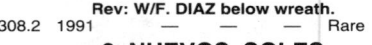

COPPER-NICKEL
Mint mark: LIMA (monogram)

308.1	1991	—	—	—	—	4.50
	1992	—	—	—	—	4.50
	1993	—	—	—	—	4.50
	1994	—	—	—	—	3.50

Rev: W/F. DIAZ below wreath.

308.2	1991	—	—	—	—	Rare

2 NUEVOS SOLES

BRASS center in STEEL ring

313	1994	—	—	—	—	4.50
	1995	—	—	—	—	2.50

5 NUEVOS SOLES

BRASS center in STEEL ring

316	1994	—	—	—	—	6.50
	1995	—	—	—	—	4.50

PHILIPPINES

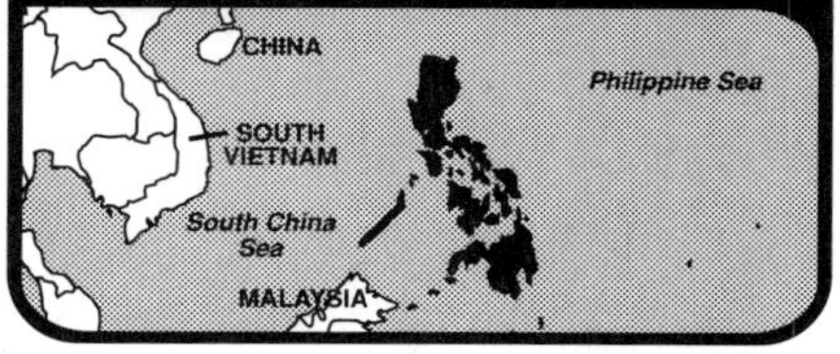

The Republic of the Philippines, an archipelago in the western Pacific 500 miles (805 km.) from the southeast coast of Asia, has an area of 115,830 sq. mi. (300,000 sq. km.) and a population of *64.9 million. Capital: Manila. The economy of the 7,000-island group is based on agriculture, forestry and fishing. Timber, coconut products, sugar and hemp are exported.

Migration to the Philippines began about 30,000 years ago when land bridges connected the islands with Borneo and Sumatra. Ferdinand Magellan claimed the islands for Spain in 1521. The first permanent settlement was established by Miguel de Legazpi at Cebu in April of 1565; Manila was established in 1572. A British expedition captured Manila and occupied the Spanish colony in October 1762, but returned it to Spain by the treaty of Paris, 1763. Spain held the Philippines despite growing Filipino nationalism until 1898 when they were ceded to the United States at the end of the Spanish-American War. The Philippines became a self-governing commonwealth under the United States in 1935, and attained independence as the Republic of the Philippines on July 4, 1946.

MINT MARKS

(b) Brussels, privy marks only
BSP - Bangko Sentral Pilipinas
D - Denver, 1944-1945
(Lt) - Llantrisant
M, MA - Manila
PM - Pobjoy Mint
S - San Francisco, 1903-1947
SGV - Madrid
(Sh) - Sherritt
(US) - United States
FM - Franklin Mint, U.S.A.*
(VDM) - Vereinigte Deutsche Metall Werks; Altona, Germany
Star - Manila (Spanish)

***NOTE:** From 1975-1977 the Franklin Mint produced coinage in up to 3 different qualities. Beginning in 1978 only (U) and (P) were struck. Qualities of issue are designated in ( ) after each date and are defined as follows:

(M) MATTE - Normal circulation strike or a dull finish produced by sandblasting special uncirculated (polish finish) or proof quality dies.

(U) SPECIAL UNCIRCULATED - Polished or proof-like in appearance without any frosted features.

(P) PROOF - The highest quality obtainable having mirror-like fields and frosted features.

UNITED STATES ADMINISTRATION

1903-1935
100 Centavos = 1 Peso

1/2 CENTAVO

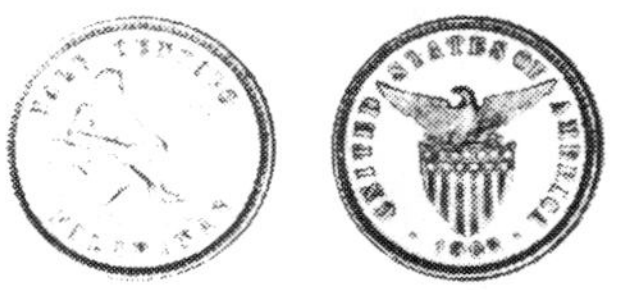

BRONZE

KM#	Date	Mintage	Fine	VF	XF	Unc
162	1903	12.084	.50	1.00	2.00	15.00
	1903	2,558	—	—	Proof	40.00
	1904	5.654	.50	1.00	2.50	20.00
	1904	1,355	—	—	Proof	50.00
	1905	471 pcs.	—	—	Proof	100.00
	1906	500 pcs.	—	—	Proof	80.00
	1908	500 pcs.	—	—	Proof	80.00

CENTAVO

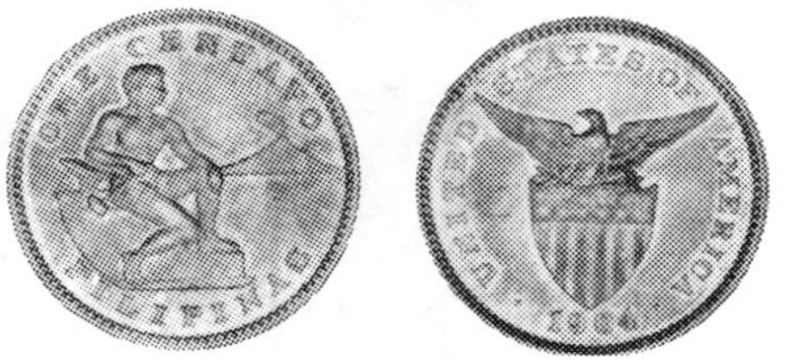

BRONZE

KM#	Date	Mintage	Fine	VF	XF	Unc
163	1903	10.790	.50	1.00	2.00	20.00
	1903	2,558	—	—	Proof	45.00
	1904	17.040	.50	1.00	2.00	18.00
	1904	1,355	—	—	Proof	50.00
	1905	10.000	.50	1.00	2.00	30.00
	1905	471 pcs.	—	—	Proof	100.00
	1906	500 pcs.	—	—	Proof	80.00
	1908	500 pcs.	—	—	Proof	80.00
	1908S	2.187	1.00	2.00	6.00	38.00
	1909S	1.738	4.00	10.00	20.00	100.00
	1910S	2.700	1.00	2.00	6.00	35.00
	1911S	4.803	.50	2.00	6.00	30.00
	1912S	3.000	1.00	2.00	6.00	35.00
	1913S	5.000	.75	2.00	6.00	32.00
	1914S	5.000	.50	2.00	6.00	32.00
	1915S	2.500	12.50	25.00	60.00	250.00
	1916S	4.330	5.00	10.00	25.00	115.00
	1917/6S	7.070	2.50	5.00	10.00	75.00
	1917S	Inc. Ab.	.75	2.00	6.00	32.00
	1918S	11.660	.75	2.00	3.00	25.00
	1918S large S					
		Inc. Ab.	25.00	50.00	100.00	500.00
	1919S	4.540	.75	2.00	5.00	28.00
	1920S	2.500	6.00	12.00	25.00	120.00
	1920	3.552	1.00	2.00	3.00	28.00
	1921	7.283	.50	1.00	3.00	28.00
	1922	3.519	.50	1.00	3.00	28.00
	1925M	9.332	.25	1.00	3.00	28.00
	1926M	9.000	.25	1.00	3.00	28.00
	1927M	9.270	.25	1.00	3.00	28.00
	1928M	9.150	.25	1.00	3.00	28.00
	1929M	5.657	.75	1.50	3.00	25.00
	1930M	5.577	.75	1.50	3.00	25.00
	1931M	5.659	.75	1.50	3.00	25.00
	1932M	4.000	.75	2.00	3.00	28.00
	1933M	8.393	.50	.75	3.00	22.00
	1934M	3.179	1.00	2.00	3.00	28.00
	1936M	17.455	.50	1.00	3.00	12.00

5 CENTAVOS

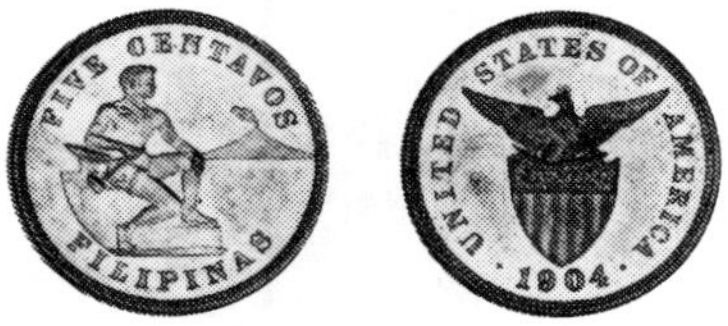

COPPER-NICKEL

KM#	Date	Mintage	Fine	VF	XF	Unc
164	1903	8.910	.50	1.00	2.50	22.00
	1903	2,558	—	—	Proof	65.00
	1904	1.075	.60	1.50	3.50	27.00
	1904	1,355	—	—	Proof	70.00
	1905	471 pcs.	—	—	Proof	135.00
	1906	500 pcs.	—	—	Proof	120.00
	1908	500 pcs.	—	—	Proof	120.00
	1916S	.300	10.00	20.00	60.00	300.00
	1917S	2.300	1.00	2.00	5.00	60.00
	1918S	2.780	1.00	2.00	5.00	60.00
	1919S	1.220	1.00	3.00	6.00	75.00
	1920	1.421	2.00	4.00	8.00	115.00
	1921	2.132	2.00	4.00	8.00	100.00
	1925M	1.000	2.00	4.00	8.00	100.00
	1926M	1.200	2.00	4.50	10.00	75.00
	1927M	1.000	2.00	4.00	8.00	85.00
	1928M	1.000	2.00	4.50	10.00	100.00

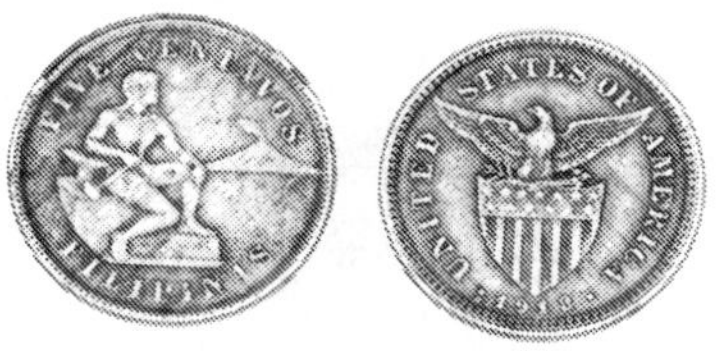

Mule. Obv: KM#164. Rev: 20 Centavos, KM#170.

KM#	Date	Mintage	Fine	VF	XF	Unc
173	1918S	—	100.00	200.00	450.00	1850.

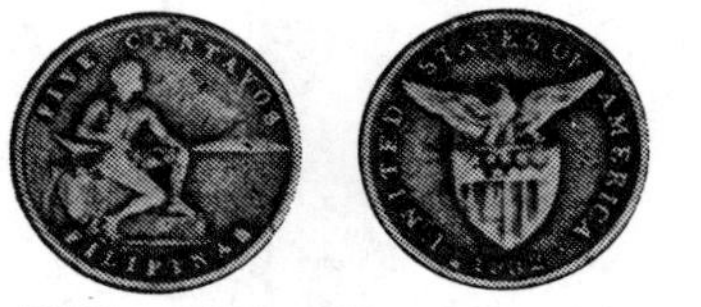

KM#	Date	Mintage	Fine	VF	XF	Unc
175	1930M	2.905	1.00	2.00	3.00	65.00
	1931M	3.477	1.00	2.00	3.00	65.00
	1932M	3.956	1.00	2.00	3.00	65.00
	1934M	2.154	1.00	3.00	5.00	75.00
	1935M	2.754	1.00	2.00	4.00	70.00

10 CENTAVOS

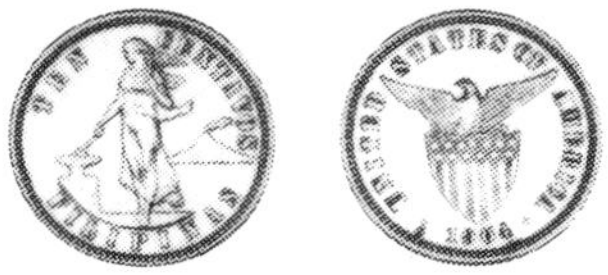

2.6924 g, .900 SILVER, .0779 oz ASW

KM#	Date	Mintage	Fine	VF	XF	Unc
165	1903	5.103	1.50	2.00	3.00	30.00
	1903	2,558	—	—	Proof	90.00
	1903S	1.200	6.00	10.00	30.00	200.00
	1904	.011	7.50	12.50	25.00	100.00
	1904	1,355	—	—	Proof	90.00
	1904S	5.040	1.50	2.00	3.00	40.00
	1905	471 pcs.	—	—	Proof	135.00
	1906	500 pcs.	—	—	Proof	125.00

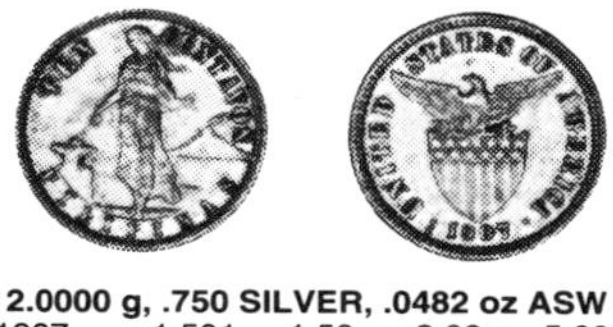

2.0000 g, .750 SILVER, .0482 oz ASW

KM#	Date	Mintage	Fine	VF	XF	Unc
169	1907	1.501	1.50	3.00	5.00	45.00
	1907S	4.930	1.00	2.50	3.50	42.00
	1908	500 pcs.	—	—	Proof	160.00
	1908S	3.364	1.00	1.75	3.50	42.00
	1909S	.312	8.00	20.00	40.00	275.00
	1910S	5-10 pcs.	Unknown in any collection			
	1911S	1.101	1.50	3.50	8.00	60.00
	1912S	1.010	1.50	4.00	8.00	65.00
	1913S	1.361	1.50	4.50	8.50	65.00
	1914S	1.180	2.50	5.00	12.50	180.00
	1915S	.450	7.00	15.00	30.00	250.00
	1917S	5.991	.75	1.75	2.75	27.50
	1918S	8.420	.75	1.75	2.75	27.50
	1919S	1.630	1.00	1.75	3.50	35.00
	1920	.520	4.00	5.00	10.00	75.00
	1921	3.863	.75	1.50	2.50	22.50
	1929M	1.000	.75	1.50	2.50	25.00
	1935M	1.280	.75	1.50	2.50	22.50

20 CENTAVOS

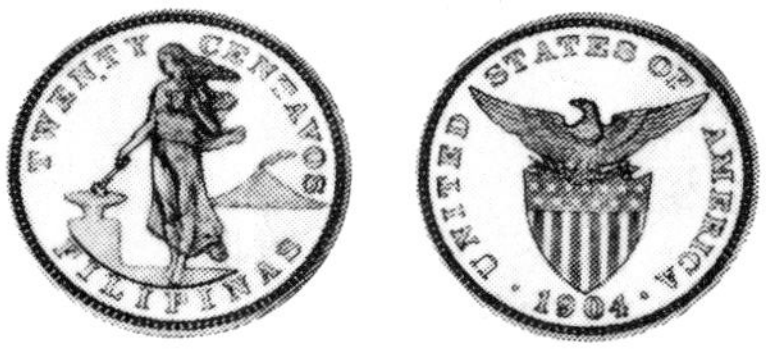

5.3849 g, .900 SILVER, .1558 oz ASW

KM#	Date	Mintage	Fine	VF	XF	Unc
166	1903	5.353	2.00	3.00	5.00	30.00
	1903	2,558	—	—	Proof	85.00
	1903S	.150	10.00	20.00	50.00	190.00
	1904	.011	12.00	22.00	35.00	120.00
	1904	1,355	—	—	Proof	100.00
	1904S	2.060	2.00	3.00	5.00	38.00
	1905	471 pcs.	—	—	Proof	185.00
	1905S	.420	6.00	8.00	17.50	85.00
	1906	500 pcs.	—	—	Proof	190.00

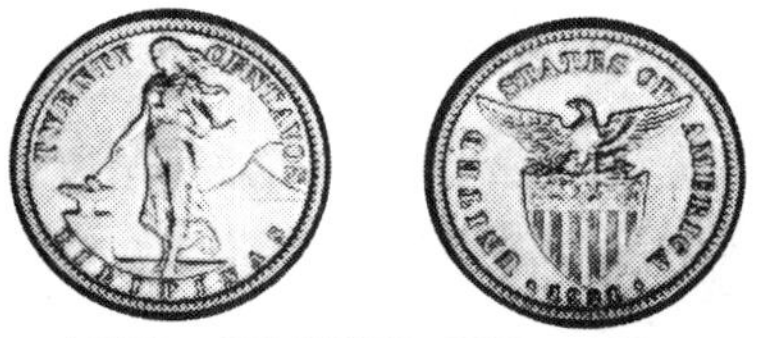

4.0000 g, .750 SILVER, .0965 oz ASW

KM#	Date	Mintage	Fine	VF	XF	Unc
170	1907	1.251	2.00	4.00	6.00	50.00
	1907S	3.165	2.00	3.00	5.00	35.00
	1908	500 pcs.	—	—	Proof	145.00
	1908S	1.535	2.00	3.00	5.00	35.00
	1909S	.450	3.00	8.00	20.00	200.00
	1910S	.500	3.00	8.00	20.00	220.00
	1911S	.505	3.00	8.00	20.00	165.00
	1912S	.750	2.00	5.00	10.00	110.00
	1913S/S	.949	7.00	15.00	25.00	170.00
	1913S	Inc. Ab.	2.00	5.00	8.00	80.00
	1914S	.795	1.50	3.00	8.00	80.00
	1915S	.655	1.50	3.00	15.00	130.00
	1916S	1.435	1.00	3.00	10.00	110.00
	1917S	3.151	.80	2.00	4.00	30.00
	1918S	5.560	.80	2.00	4.00	30.00
	1919S	.850	.80	2.00	6.00	40.00
	1920	1.046	1.00	3.00	10.00	110.00
	1921	1.843	.80	2.00	3.00	30.00
	1929M	1.970	.80	2.00	3.00	30.00

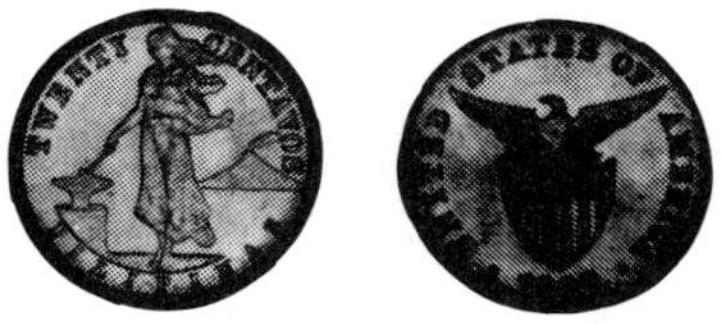

Mule. Obv: KM#170. Rev: 5 Centavos, KM#164.

KM#	Date	Mintage	Fine	VF	XF	Unc
174	1928/7M	.100	5.00	12.00	50.00	300.00

50 CENTAVOS

13.4784 g, .900 SILVER, .3900 oz ASW

KM#	Date	Mintage	Fine	VF	XF	Unc
167	1903	3.102	3.00	6.00	12.50	80.00
	1903	2,558	—	—	Proof	135.00
	1903S	—	2000.	3500.	5000.	—
	1904	.011	15.00	25.00	42.50	145.00
	1904	1,355	—	—	Proof	165.00
	1904S	2.160	3.00	6.50	12.50	130.00
	1905	471 pcs.	—	—	Proof	350.00
	1905S	.852	3.00	8.00	21.50	200.00
	1906	500 pcs.	—	—	Proof	300.00

10.0000 g, .750 SILVER, .2411 oz ASW

KM#	Date	Mintage	Fine	VF	XF	Unc
171	1907	1.201	2.00	5.00	11.00	90.00
	1907S	2.112	2.00	4.00	9.00	80.00
	1908	500 pcs.	—	—	Proof	275.00
	1908S	1.601	2.00	4.00	9.00	70.00
	1909S	.528	3.00	6.00	13.50	165.00
	1917S	.674	3.00	6.00	11.50	150.00
	1918S	2.202	2.00	4.00	6.50	65.00
	1919S	1.200	2.00	4.50	7.00	90.00
	1920	.420	2.00	4.00	6.50	55.00
	1921	2.317	2.00	4.00	6.50	25.00

PESO

26.9568 g, .900 SILVER, .7800 oz ASW

KM#	Date	Mintage	Fine	VF	XF	Unc
168	1903	2.791	9.00	15.00	42.00	190.00
	1903	2,558	—	—	Proof	250.00
	1903S	11.361	7.00	12.00	28.00	130.00
	1904	.011	35.00	65.00	120.00	300.00
	1904	1,355	—	—	Proof	260.00
	1904S	6.600	7.00	14.00	30.00	135.00
	1905	471 pcs.	—	—	Proof	850.00
	1905S	6.056	12.00	18.00	45.00	175.00
	1906	500 pcs.	—	—	Proof	500.00
	1906S	.201	700.00	1200.	2700.	8500.00

NOTE: Counterfeits of the 1906S exist.

20.0000 g, .800 SILVER, .5144 oz ASW

KM#	Date	Mintage	Fine	VF	XF	Unc
172	1907					
		2 pcs. known	—	—	Proof	Rare
	1907S	10.276	BV	4.50	7.00	65.00
	1908	500 pcs.	—	—	Proof	500.00
	1908S	20.955	BV	4.50	7.00	60.00
	1909S	7.578	BV	4.50	8.00	70.00
	1910S	3.154	BV	5.50	10.00	90.00
	1911S	.463	9.00	15.00	45.00	500.00
	1912S	.680	9.00	15.00	45.00	550.00

COMMONWEALTH

CENTAVO

BRONZE

KM#	Date	Mintage	VF	XF	Unc	BU
179	1937M	15.790	1.00	1.75	12.00	15.00
	1938M	10.000	.75	1.50	10.00	12.00
	1939M	6.500	1.00	1.75	12.00	15.00
	1940M	4.000	.75	1.25	8.00	10.00
	1941M	5.000	1.00	2.00	15.00	20.00
	1944S	58.000	.15	.20	.50	1.50

5 CENTAVOS

COPPER-NICKEL

KM#	Date	Mintage	VF	XF	Unc	BU
180	1937M	2.494	1.50	3.00	17.50	35.00
	1938M	4.000	1.25	2.00	10.00	20.00
	1941M	2.750	1.50	2.50	15.00	30.00

COPPER-NICKEL-ZINC

KM#	Date	Mintage	VF	XF	Unc	BU
180a	1944	21.198	.15	.50	1.25	2.00
	1944S	14.040	.15	.25	.75	1.25
	1945S	72.796	.15	.20	.50	1.00

10 CENTAVOS

2.0000 g, .750 SILVER, .0482 oz ASW

KM#	Date	Mintage	VF	XF	Unc	BU
181	1937M	3.500	1.00	2.50	15.00	20.00
	1938M	M inverted W				
		3.750	.75	1.75	10.00	15.00
	1941M	2.500	1.00	2.00	12.50	18.00
	1944D	31.592	BV	.75	1.50	2.50
	1945D	137.208	BV	.50	1.00	2.00

20 CENTAVOS

4.0000 g, .750 SILVER, .0965 oz ASW

KM#	Date	Mintage	VF	XF	Unc	BU
182	1937M	2.665	1.00	4.00	15.00	30.00
	1938M	3.000	1.00	2.00	5.00	10.00
	1941M	1.500	1.00	2.00	8.00	17.50
	1944D	28.596	BV	1.00	2.00	3.00
	1944D/S	—	—	40.00	150.00	200.00
	1945D	82.804	BV	.75	1.50	2.50

50 CENTAVOS

10.0000 g, .750 SILVER, .2411 oz ASW
Establishment of the Commonwealth

KM#	Date	Mintage	VF	XF	Unc	BU
176	1936	.020	25.00	35.00	65.00	85.00

KM#	Date	Mintage	VF	XF	Unc	BU
183	1944S	19.187	BV	2.50	4.50	6.50
	1945S	18.120	BV	2.50	4.50	6.50

PESO

20.0000 g, .900 SILVER, .5787 oz ASW
Establishment of the Commonwealth -
Presidents Roosevelt and Quezon

KM#	Date	Mintage	VF	XF	Unc	BU
177	1936	.010	40.00	55.00	110.00	125.00

Establishment of the Commonwealth -
Governor General Murphy and President Quezon
Rev: Similar to KM#177.

KM#	Date	Mintage	VF	XF	Unc	BU
178	1936	.010	40.00	55.00	110.00	125.00

REPUBLIC

CENTAVO

BRONZE

KM#	Date	Mintage		VF	XF	Unc
186	1958	20.000	—	.10	.25	.60
	1960	40.000	—	.10	.15	.50
	1962	30.000	—	.10	.15	.50
	1963	130.000	—	.10	.15	.50

5 CENTAVOS

BRASS

KM#	Date	Mintage		VF	XF	Unc
187	1958	10.000	—	.10	.20	.60

KM#	Date	Mintage	VF	XF	Unc	BU
187	1959	10.000	—	.10	.20	.60
	1960	40.000	—	.10	.15	.50
	1962	40.000	—	.10	.20	.60
	1963	50.000	—	.10	.15	.50
	1964	100.000	—	—	.10	.50
	1966	10.000	—	.10	.20	.60

10 CENTAVOS

NICKEL-BRASS

188	1958	10.000	.10	.15	.25	.65
	1960	70.000	.10	.15	.20	.60
	1962	50.000	.10	.15	.20	.60
	1963	50.000	.10	.15	.20	.60
	1964	100.000	—	.10	.20	.60
	1966	110.000	—	.10	.20	.60

25 CENTAVOS

NICKEL-BRASS
Obv: 8 smoke rings from volcano.

189.1	1958	10.000	.20	.25	.50	.75
	1960	10.000	.20	.30	.50	.75
	1962	40.000	.10	.25	.50	.75
	1964	49.800	.10	.20	.35	.65
	1966	50.000	.10	.20	.40	.70

Obv: 6 smoke rings from volcano.

189.2	1966	40.000	.10	.20	.40	.70

50 CENTAVOS

10.0000 g, .750 SILVER, .2411 oz ASW
General Douglas MacArthur

184	1947S	.200	BV	2.50	4.00	7.00

NICKEL-BRASS

190	1958	5.000	.30	.45	1.00	1.50
	1964	25.000	.20	.30	.60	1.00

1/2 PESO

12.5000 g, .900 SILVER, .3617 oz ASW

100th Anniversary - Birth of Dr. Jose Rizal

KM#	Date	Mintage	VF	XF	Unc	BU
191	1961	.100	—	3.00	4.00	5.00

PESO

20.0000 g, .900 SILVER, .5787 oz ASW
General Douglas MacArthur

185	1947S	.100	BV	6.00	10.00	15.00

26.6000 g, .900 SILVER, .7697 oz ASW
100th Anniversary - Birth of Dr. Jose Rizal

192	1961	.100	—	4.50	7.50	10.00

100th Anniversary - Birth of Andres Bonifacio

193	1963	.100	—	4.50	7.50	10.00

100th Anniversary - Birth of Apolinario Mabini

194	1964	.100	—	4.50	7.50	10.00

25th Anniversary of Bataan Day

195	1967	.100	—	4.50	7.50	10.00

NOTE: KM#195 is a proof-like issue.

MONETARY REFORM
100 Sentimos = 1 Piso

SENTIMO

ALUMINUM
Lapu-Lapu

KM#	Date	Mintage	VF	XF	Unc
196	1967	10.000	—	—	.10
	1968	27.940	—	—	.10
	1969/6	12.060	—	—	.10
	1970	130.000	—	—	.10
	1974	165.000	—	—	.10
	1974	.010	—	Proof	3.50

205	1975FM(M)	.108	—	—	.10
	1975FM(U)	5,875	—	—	2.00
	1975FM(P)	.037	—	Proof	1.50
	1975 Lt	10.000	—	—	.10
	1975(US)	60.190	—	—	.10
	1976FM(M)	.010	—	—	.10
	1976FM(U)	1,826	—	1.00	2.50
	1976FM(P)	9,901	—	Proof	2.00
	1976(US)	60.000	—	—	.10
	1977	4.808	—	—	.10
	1977FM(M)	.010	—	—	1.00
	1977FM(U)	354 pcs.	—	—	4.00
	1977FM(P)	4,822	—	Proof	2.00
	1978	24.813	—	—	.10
	1978FM(M)	.010	—	—	1.00
	1978FM(P)	4,792	—	Proof	2.00

Rev: Redesigned seal.

224	1979BSP	—	—	—	.10
	1979FM(U)	.010	—	—	1.00
	1979FM(P)	3,645	—	Proof	2.00
	1980BSP	12.601	—	—	.10
	1980FM(U)	.010	—	—	1.00
	1980FM(P)	3,133	—	Proof	2.00
	1981BSP	33.391	—	—	.10
	1981FM(U)	—	—	—	1.00
	1981FM(P)	1,795	—	Proof	2.00
	1982BSP	51.730	—	—	.10
	1982FM(P)	—	—	Proof	2.00

NOTE: Varieties in date exist.

King Lapu-Lapu - Sea Shell

238	1983	62.090	—	—	.15
	1983	—	—	Proof	2.00
	1984	.320	—	—	.15
	1985	.016	—	—	.15
	1986	.080	—	—	.15
	1987	13.570	—	—	.15
	1988	26.861	—	—	.15
	1989	—	—	—	.15
	1990	—	—	—	.15
	1991	—	—	—	.15
	1992	—	—	—	.15
	1993	—	—	—	.15

COPPER PLATED STEEL
Obv: Denomination. Rev: Central bank seal.

273	1995	—	—	—	.15
	1996	—	—	—	.15

5 SENTIMOS

BRASS

Melchora Aquino

KM#	Date	Mintage	VF	XF	Unc
197	1967	40.000	—	—	.10
	1968	50.000	—	—	.10
	1970	5.000	—	.10	.20
	1972	71.744	—	—	.10
	1974	90.025	—	—	.10
	1974	.010	—	Proof	4.50

206	1975FM(M)	.104	—	—	.10
	1975FM(U)	5,875	—	—	2.50
	1975FM(P)	.037	—	Proof	2.00
	1975(US)	98.928	—	—	.10
	1975 Lt	10.000	—	—	.10
	1976FM(M)	.010	—	—	1.50
	1976FM(U)	1,826	—	—	5.00
	1976FM(P)	9,901	—	Proof	2.50
	1976(US)	98.000	—	—	.10
	1977	19.367	—	—	.10
	1977FM(M)	.010	—	—	1.50
	1977FM(U)	354 pcs.	—	—	4.00
	1977FM(P)	4,822	—	Proof	2.50
	1978	61.838	—	—	.10
	1978FM(U)	.010	—	—	1.50
	1978FM(P)	4,792	—	Proof	2.50

Rev: Redesigned seal.

225	1979BSP	12.805	—	—	.10
	1979FM(U)	.010	—	—	1.00
	1979FM(P)	3,645	—	Proof	2.50
	1980BSP	111.339	—	—	.10
	1980FM(U)	.010	—	—	1.00
	1980FM(P)	3,133	—	Proof	2.50
	1981BSP	—	—	—	.10
	1981FM(U)	—	—	—	1.00
	1981FM(P)	1,795	—	Proof	3.00
	1982BSP	—	—	—	.10
	1982FM(P)	—	—	Proof	3.00

ALUMINUM
Waling-Waling Orchid

239	1983	100.016	—	—	.10
	1983	—	—	Proof	2.00
	1984	141.744	—	—	.10
	1985	50.416	—	—	.10
	1986	11.664	—	—	.10
	1987	79.008	—	—	.10
	1988	90.487	—	—	.10
	1989	—	—	—	.10
	1990	—	—	—	.10
	1991	—	—	—	.10
	1992	—	—	—	.10

COPPER plated STEEL
Hole punched out of center.
Rev. leg: 1993 BANGKO CENTRAL NG PILIPINAS.

268	1995	—	—	—	.20
	1996	—	—	—	.20

10 SENTIMOS

COPPER-NICKEL
Francisco Baltasar

198	1967	50.000	—	—	.10
	1968	60.000	—	—	.10
	1969	40.000	—	—	.10
	1970	50.000	—	—	.10
	1971	80.000	—	—	.10
	1972	121.390	—	—	.10
	1974	60.208	—	—	.10
	1974	.010	—	Proof	5.00

KM#	Date	Mintage	VF	XF	Unc
207	1975FM(M)	.104	—	—	.10
	1975FM(U)	5,875	—	—	2.50
	1975FM(P)	.037	—	Proof	2.00
	1975(VDM)	10.000	—	—	.10
	1975(US)	50.000	—	—	.10
	1976FM(M)	.010	—	—	.15
	1976FM(U)	1,826	—	—	6.00
	1976FM(P)	9,901	—	Proof	3.00
	1976(US)	50.000	—	—	.10
	1977	29.314	—	—	.10
	1977FM(M)	.010	—	—	1.50
	1977FM(U)	354 pcs.	—	—	6.50
	1977FM(P)	4,822	—	Proof	3.00
	1978	60.042	—	—	.10
	1978FM(U)	.010	—	—	2.00
	1978FM(P)	4,792	—	Proof	3.00

Rev: Redesigned seal.

226	1979BSP	6.446	—	—	.10
	1979FM(U)	.010	—	—	1.00
	1979FM(P)	3,645	—	Proof	3.00
	1980BSP	—	—	—	.10
	1980FM(U)	.010	—	—	1.00
	1980FM(P)	3,133	—	Proof	3.25
	1981BSP	—	—	—	.10
	1981FM(U)	—	—	—	1.00
	1981FM(P)	1,795	—	Proof	3.50
	1982BSP	—	—	—	.10
	1982FM(P)	—	—	Proof	3.50

NOTE: Varieties with thick and thin legends exist for coins with BSP mint mark.

ALUMINUM
World Conference on Fisheries - F.A.O.
Rev: Fish's name in error: PANDAKA PYGMEA

240.1	1983	95.640	—	—	.25
	1983	—	—	Proof	3.00
	1987	Inc. Be.	—	—	.25

Rev: Fish's name: PANDAKA PYGMAEA

240.2	1983	—	—	—	.15
	1984	235.900	—	—	.15
	1985	90.169	—	—	.15
	1986	4.270	—	—	.15
	1987	99.520	—	—	.15
	1988	117.166	—	—	.15
	1989	—	—	—	.15
	1990	—	—	—	.15
	1991	—	—	—	.15
	1992	—	—	—	.15
	1993	—	—	—	.15
	1994	—	—	—	.15

BRONZE PLATED STEEL
Central Bank Seal

270	1995	—	—	—	.20
	1996	—	—	—	.20
	1997	—	—	—	.20

25 SENTIMOS

COPPER-NICKEL

Juan Luna

KM#	Date	Mintage	VF	XF	Unc
199	1967	40.000	—	.10	.10
	1968	10.000	—	.10	.25
	1969	10.000	—	.10	.25
	1970	40.000	—	.10	.25
	1971	60.000	—	.10	.25
	1972	90.000	—	.10	.25
	1974	10.000	—	.10	.25
	1974	.010	—	Proof	10.00

208	1975FM(M)	.104	—	—	.40
	1975FM(U)	5,875	—	—	3.50
	1975FM(P)	.037	—	Proof	3.00
	1975(US)	10.000	—	.10	.25
	1975(VDM)	10.000	—	.10	.25
	1976FM(M)	.010	—	.10	.25
	1976FM(U)	1,826	—	—	8.00
	1976FM(P)	9,901	—	Proof	3.50
	1976(US)	10.000	—	.10	.25
	1977	24.654	—	.10	.25
	1977FM(M)	.010	—	—	1.50
	1977FM(U)	354 pcs.	—	—	8.00
	1977FM(P)	4,822	—	Proof	4.50
	1978	40.466	—	.10	.25
	1978FM(U)	.010	—	—	2.50
	1978FM(P)	4,792	—	Proof	4.00

Rev: Redesigned seal.

227	1979BSP	20.725	—	.10	.25
	1979FM(U)	.010	—	—	1.50
	1979FM(P)	3,645	—	Proof	4.50
	1980BSP	—	—	.10	.25
	1980FM(U)	.010	—	—	1.50
	1980FM(P)	3,133	—	Proof	4.50
	1981BSP	—	—	.10	.25
	1981FM(U)	—	—	—	1.50
	1981FM(P)	1,795	—	Proof	5.00
	1982BSP	—	—	.10	.25
	1982FM(P)	—	—	Proof	5.00

BRASS
Butterfly

241.1	1983	92.944	—	.10	.35
	1983	—	—	Proof	3.00
	1984	254.324	—	.10	.35
	1985	84.922	—	.10	.35
	1986	65.284	—	.10	.35
	1987	1.680	—	.10	.35
	1988	51.062	—	—	.35
	1989	—	—	—	.35
	1990	—	—	—	.35

Reduced size.

241.2	1991	—	—	—	.30
	1992	—	—	—	.30
	1993	—	—	—	.30
	1994	—	—	—	.30

Central Bank Seal

271	1995	—	—	—	.25
	1996	—	—	—	.25
	1997	—	—	—	.25

50 SENTIMOS

COPPER-NICKEL-ZINC
Marcelo H. del Pilar

KM#	Date	Mintage	VF	XF	Unc
200	1967	20.000	.10	.20	.50
	1971	10.000	.10	.20	.60
	1972 serif on 2				
		30.000	.10	.20	.50
	1972 plain 2	20.517	.10	.20	.50
	1974	5.004	.10	.20	.60
	1974	.010	—	Proof	16.50
	1975	5.714	.10	.20	.60

COPPER-NICKEL
Monkey-eating Eagle
Eagle's name - PITHECOPHAGA

KM#	Date	Mintage	VF	XF	Unc
242.1	1983	27.644	.10	.20	.50
	1983			Proof	5.00
	1984	121.408	.10	.20	.50
	1985	107.048	.10	.20	.50
	1986	120.000	.10	.20	.50
	1987	1.078	.10	.20	.50
	1988	24.008	.10	.20	.50
	1989	—	.10	.20	.50
	1990		.10	.20	.50

Error. Eagle's name PITHECOBHAGA

242.2	1983	Inc. Ab.	.10	.20	.50

BRASS
Reduced size.

242.3	1991	—	—	.10	.30
	1992	—	—	.10	.30
	1993	—	—	.10	.30
	1994	—	—	.10	.30

PISO

26.4500 g, .900 SILVER, .7653 oz ASW
Centennial - Birth of Aguinaldo

KM#	Date	Mintage	XF	Unc	BU
201	1969	.100	5.00	8.00	12.00

NOTE: These coins are 'proof-like' issues.

NICKEL
Pope Paul VI Visit

KM#	Date	Mintage	XF	Unc	BU
202	1970	.070	1.00	2.50	4.00

COPPER-NICKEL
Jose Rizal

KM#	Date	Mintage	VF	XF	Unc
203	1972	121.821	.15	.25	.75
	1974	45.631	.15	.25	.75
	1974	.010	—	Proof	25.00

209.1	1975FM(M)	.104	—	—	1.00
	1975FM(U)	5,877	—	—	3.50
	1975FM(P)	.037	—	Proof	3.00
	1975(VDM)	10.000	.15	.25	.75
	1975(US)	30.000	.15	.25	.75
	1976FM(M)	.010	—	—	1.00
	1976FM(U)	1,826	—	—	10.00
	1976FM(P)	9,901	—	Proof	5.00
	1976(US)	30.000	.15	.25	.75
	1977	14.771	.15	.25	.75
	1977FM(M)	.012	—	—	4.00
	1977FM(U)	354 pcs.	—	—	10.00
	1977FM(P)	4,822	—	Proof	5.50
	1978	19.408	.15	.25	.75
	1978FM(U)	.010	—	—	4.00
	1978FM(P)	4,792	—	Proof	5.50

Rev. leg: ISANG BANSA ISANG DIWA below shield.

209.2	1979BSP	.321	.15	.25	1.00
	1979FM(U)	.010	—	—	2.50
	1979FM(P)	3,645	—	Proof	6.00
	1980BSP	19.693	.15	.25	.75
	1980FM(U)	.010	—	—	2.50
	1980FM(P)	3,133	—	Proof	12.50
	1981BSP	7.944	.15	.25	.75
	1981FM(U)	—	—	—	3.00
	1981FM(P)	1,795	—	Proof	6.00
	1982FM(P)	—	—	Proof	6.00
	1982BSP large date				
		52.110	.15	.25	.75
	1982BSP small date				
	Inc. Ab.		.15	.25	.75

Tamaraw Bull
Large legends and design elements.

KM#	Date	Mintage	VF	XF	Unc
243.1	1983	55.869	.10	.25	1.00
	1983	—	—	Proof	7.00
	1984	4.997	.10	.25	1.00
	1985	182.592	.10	.25	1.00
	1986	19.072	.10	.25	1.00
	1987	1.391	.10	.25	1.00
	1988	54.636	.10	.25	1.00

Smaller legends and design elements.

243.3	1989	—	.10	.25	1.00
	1990	—	.10	.25	1.00

STAINLESS STEEL
Reduced size.

243.2	1991	—	—	—	.50
	1992	—	—	—	.50
	1993	—	—	—	.50
	1994	—	—	—	.50

COPPER-NICKEL
Philippine Cultures Decade

251	1989	—	—	—	1.00

Waterfall, Ship and Flower

257	1991	—	—	—	1.00

NICKEL CLAD STEEL
50th Anniversary - Battle of Kagitingan

260	1992	—	—	—	.50
	1996	—	—	—	.50

COPPER-NICKEL
Obv: Date 1995.
Rev: Bank seal, date 1993.

269	1995	—	—	—	.50
	1996	—	—	—	.50
	1997	—	—	—	.50

2 PISO

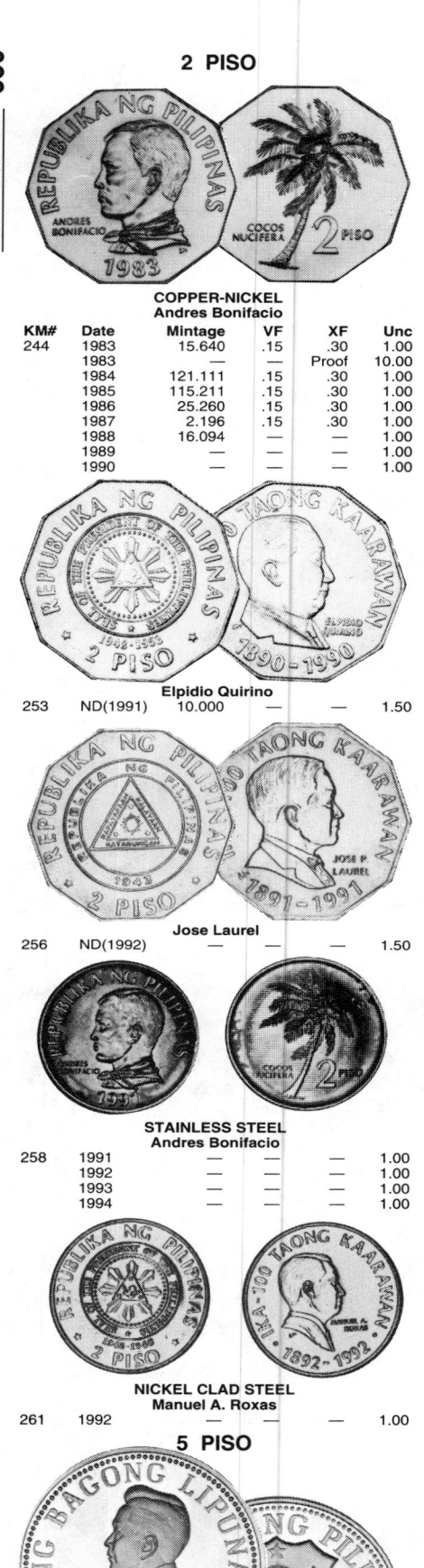

COPPER-NICKEL
Andres Bonifacio

KM#	Date	Mintage	VF	XF	Unc
244	1983	15.640	.15	.30	1.00
	1983	—		Proof	10.00
	1984	121.111	.15	.30	1.00
	1985	115.211	.15	.30	1.00
	1986	25.260	.15	.30	1.00
	1987	2.196	.15	.30	1.00
	1988	16.094	—	—	1.00
	1989	—	—	—	1.00
	1990	—	—	—	1.00

Elpidio Quirino

253	ND(1991)	10.000	—	—	1.50

Jose Laurel

256	ND(1992)	—	—	—	1.50

STAINLESS STEEL
Andres Bonifacio

258	1991	—	—	—	1.00
	1992	—	—	—	1.00
	1993	—	—	—	1.00
	1994	—	—	—	1.00

NICKEL CLAD STEEL
Manuel A. Roxas

261	1992	—	—	—	1.00

5 PISO

Ferdinand E. Marcos

KM#	Date	Mintage	VF	XF	Unc
210.1	1975FM(M)	3,850	—	—	15.00
	1975FM(U)	7,875	—	—	10.00
	1975FM(P)	.039	—	Proof	7.50
	1975(Sh)	20.000	.50	.75	1.50
	1976FM(U)	.010	—	—	5.00
	1976FM(U)	1,826	—	—	17.50
	1976FM(P)	9,901	—	Proof	7.50
	1977FM(M)	.010	—	—	5.00
	1977FM(U)	354 pcs.	—	—	15.00
	1977FM(P)	4,822	—	Proof	7.50
	1978FM(U)	.010	—	—	5.00
	1978FM(P)	4,792	—	Proof	7.50
	1982	—	.50	.75	1.50

Obv. leg: ISANG BANSA ISANG DIWA below shield.

210.2	1979FM(U)	.010	—	—	3.00
	1979FM(P)	3,645	—	Proof	8.00
	1980FM(U)	.010	—	—	3.00
	1980FM(P)	3,133	—	Proof	8.00
	1981FM(U)	.011	—	—	3.00
	1981FM(P)	1,795	—	Proof	10.00
	1982FM(P)	—	—	Proof	10.00

NICKEL-BRASS
Emilio Aguinaldo - Pterocarpus Indicus Flower

259	1991	—	—	—	3.50
	1992	—	—	—	3.50
	1993	—	—	—	3.50
	1994	—	—	—	3.50

30th Chess Olympiad

262	1992	—	—	—	4.50

NOTE: Varieties exist.

Leyte Gulf Landings

263	1994	7,800	—	—	4.00

Obv: Aguinaldo. Rev: Central Bank Seal.

272	1995	—	—	—	1.00
	1996	—	—	—	1.00
	1997	—	—	—	1.00
	1997 BSP	—	—	—	1.00

POLAND

The Republic of Poland, located in central Europe, has an area of 120,725 sq. mi. (312,680 sq. km.) and a population of *38.2 million. Capital: Warsaw. The economy is essentially agricultural, but industrial activity provides the products for foreign trade. Machinery, coal, coke, iron, steel and transport equipment are exported.

Poland, which began as a Slavic duchy in the 10th century and reached its peak of power between the 14th and 16th centuries, has had a turbulent history of invasion, occupation or partition by Mongols, Turkey, Hungary, Sweden, Austria, Prussia and Russia.

The first partition took place in 1772. Prussia took Polish Pomerania. Russia took part of the eastern provinces. Austria took Galicia, in which lay the fortress city of Kracow (Crakow). The second partition occurred in 1793 when Russia took another slice of the eastern provinces and Prussia took what remained of western Poland. The third partition, 1795, literally removed Poland from the map. Russia took what was left of the eastern provinces. Prussia seized most of central Poland, including Warsaw. Austria took what was left of the south. Napoleon restored to Poland much of the territory lost to Prussia and Austria, but after his defeat another partition returned the Duchy of Warsaw to Prussia, made Kracow into a tiny republic, and declared what remained to be the Kingdom of Poland under the czar and in permanent union with Russia.

Poland re-emerged as an independent state recognized by the Treaty of Versailles on June 28, 1919, and maintained its independence until 1939 when it was invaded by, and partitioned between, Germany and Russia. Poland's present boundaries were determined by the U.S.-British-Russian agreement of Aug. 16, 1945. The Government of National Unity was replaced when the Polish Comunist-Socialist faction won a decisive victory at the polls in 1947 and established a 'Peoples Democratic Republic' of the Soviet type in 1952. On December 29, 1989 Poland was proclaimed as the Republic of Poland.

MINT MARKS
MV, MW, MW-monogram - Warsaw Mint, 1965
FF - Stuttgart Germany 1916-1917
(w) - Warsaw 1923-39
CHI - Valcambi, Switzerland
Other letters appearing with date denote the Mint Master at the time the coin was struck.

WWI OCCUPATION COINAGE

Germany released a 1, 2 and 3 Kopek coinage series in 1916 which circulated during their occupation of Poland. They will be found listed as Germany KM#21, 22 and 23.

GERMAN-AUSTRIAN REGENCY
100 Fenigow = 1 Marka

FENIG

IRON

Y#	Date	Mintage	Fine	VF	XF	Unc
4	1918 FF	51.484	.35	.85	2.00	4.00
	1918 FF	—	—	—	Proof	200.00

5 FENIGOW

IRON

5	1917 FF	18.700	.25	—	.75	1.50	3.00
	1917 FF	—	—	—	Proof	100.00
	1918 FF	22.690	.25	—	.75	1.50	3.00
	1918 FF	—	—	—	Proof	200.00

Mule. Obv: Poland Y#5. Rev: German KM#15.

5.1	1917 FF	—	50.00	100.00	150.00	200.00

10 FENIGOW

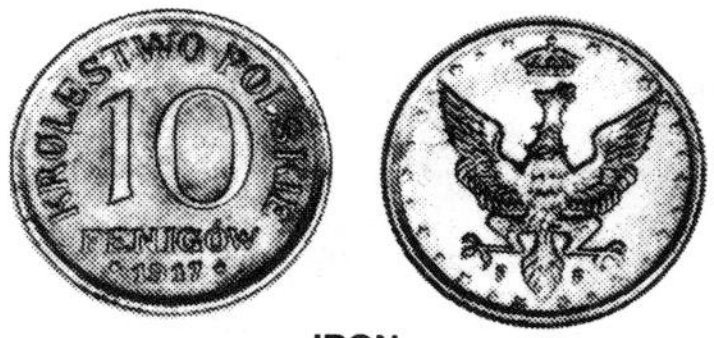

IRON

Y#	Date	Mintage	Fine	VF	XF	Unc
6	1917 FF obv. leg. touches edge	33.000	7.50	15.00	20.00	25.00
	1917 FF	—	—	—	Proof	100.00
	1917 FF obv. leg. away from edge	Inc. Ab.	.25	.75	1.25	3.00
	1918 FF obv. leg. touches edge	14.990	.50	1.00	2.50	7.50
	1918 FF obv. leg. away from edge	Inc. Ab.	.50	1.00	1.75	4.50
	1918 FF obv. leg. away from edge	—	—	—	Proof	200.00

ZINC

Y#	Date	Mintage	Fine	VF	XF	Unc
6a	1917 FF	—	25.00	45.00	85.00	150.00

NOTE: Error planchet.

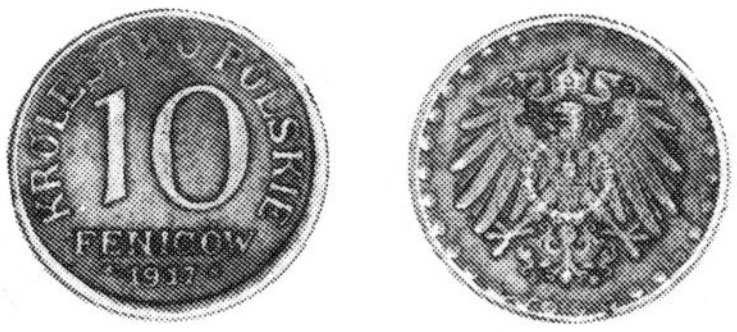

Mule. Obv: Y#6.
Rev: German 10 Pfennig, KM#20.

Y#	Date	Mintage	Fine	VF	XF	Unc
6.1	1917 FF	—	50.00	100.00	150.00	200.00

20 FENIGOW

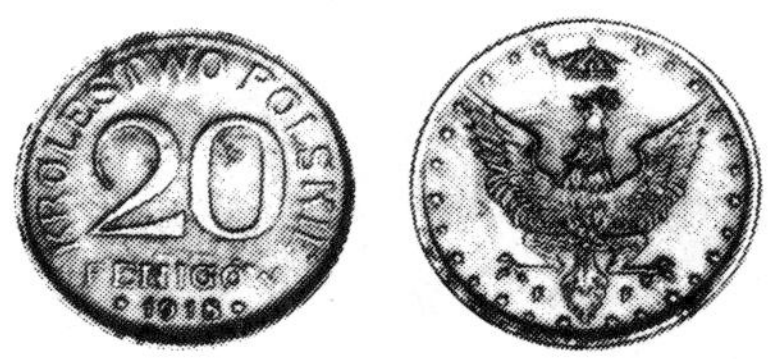

IRON

Y#	Date	Mintage	Fine	VF	XF	Unc
7	1917 FF	1.900	2.00	4.00	6.00	10.00
	1918 FF	19.260	.75	1.25	2.50	5.00

ZINC

Y#	Date	Mintage	Fine	VF	XF	Unc
7a	1917FF	—	35.00	60.00	100.00	200.00

NOTE: Error planchet.

REPUBLIC COINAGE

100 Groszy = 1 Zloty

GROSZ

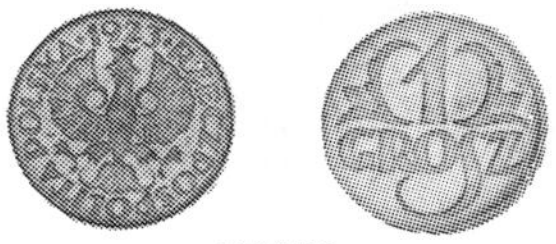

BRASS

Y#	Date	Mintage	Fine	VF	XF	Unc
8	1923	—	18.00	25.00	75.00	200.00

NOTE: Some authorities consider this strike a pattern.

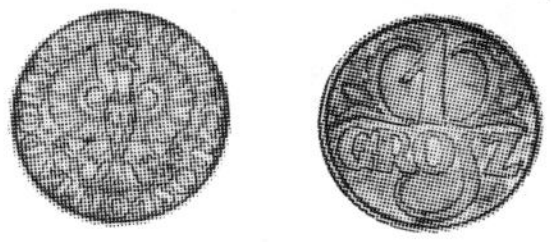

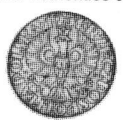

BRONZE

Y#	Date	Mintage	Fine	VF	XF	Unc
8a	1923	30.000	.25	.50	1.75	10.00
	1925(w)	40.000	.25	.50	1.75	9.00
	1927(w)	17.000	.25	.50	1.75	10.00
	1928(w)	13.600	.25	.50	1.75	9.00
	1930(w)	22.500	4.00	10.00	25.00	40.00
	1931(w)	9.000	.50	1.00	2.00	10.00
	1932(w)	12.000	.50	1.00	2.00	10.00
	1933(w)	7.000	.50	1.00	2.00	10.00
	1934(w)	5.900	.75	1.25	2.50	12.00
	1935(w)	7.300	.75	1.00	2.00	5.00
	1936(w)	12.600	.75	1.00	2.00	5.00
	1937(w)	17.370	.25	.50	.75	2.00
	1938(w)	20.530	.25	.50	.75	2.00
	1939(w)	12.000	.25	.50	.75	2.00

2 GROSZE

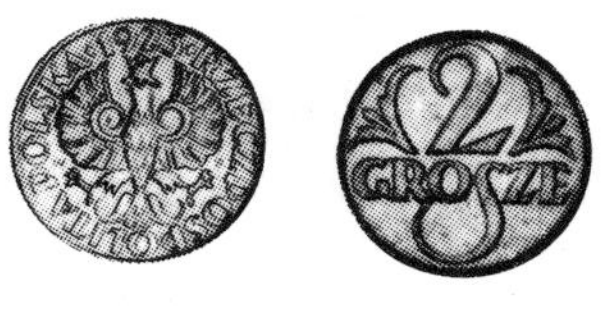

BRASS

Y#	Date	Mintage	Fine	VF	XF	Unc
9	1923	20.500	3.50	15.00	35.00	50.00

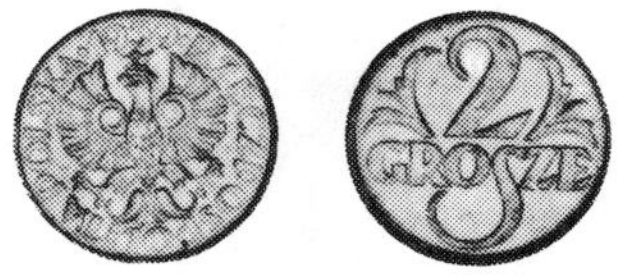

BRONZE

Y#	Date	Mintage	Fine	VF	XF	Unc
9a	1925(w)	39.000	.50	2.00	4.50	10.00
	1927(w)	15.300	.50	2.00	4.50	10.00
	1928(w)	13.400	.50	2.00	4.50	10.00
	1930(w)	20.000	.50	2.00	4.50	10.00
	1931(w)	9.500	1.75	2.50	5.50	12.75
	1932(w)	6.500	2.00	4.00	6.00	15.00
	1933(w)	7.000	2.00	4.00	6.00	15.00
	1934(w)	9.350	1.75	3.00	7.50	17.50
	1935(w)	5.800	.20	.75	2.00	5.00
	1936(w)	5.800	.20	.75	2.00	5.00
	1937(w)	17.360	.20	.40	.60	2.50
	1938(w)	20.530	.20	.40	.60	2.50
	1939(w)	12.000	.20	.40	.60	2.50

5 GROSZY

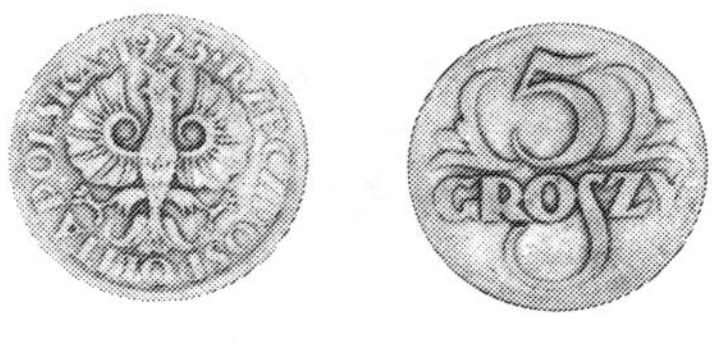

BRASS

Y#	Date	Mintage	Fine	VF	XF	Unc
10	1923	32.000	.50	2.00	5.00	10.00

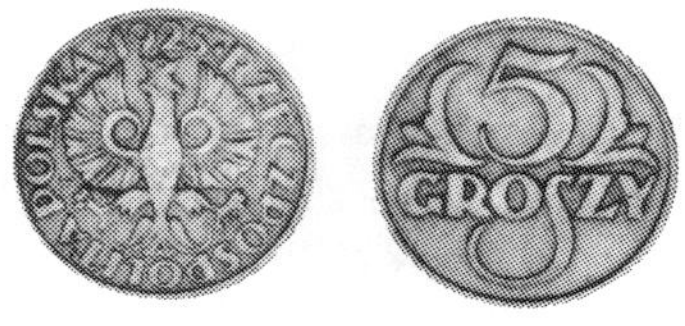

BRONZE

Y#	Date	Mintage	Fine	VF	XF	Unc
10a	1923	350 pcs.	—	—	Proof	150.00
	1925(w)	45.500	.20	.40	4.00	8.00
	1928(w)	8.900	.20	.40	5.00	10.00
	1930(w)	14.200	.20	.40	5.00	12.00
	1931(w)	1.500	.50	1.00	10.00	20.00
	1934(w)	.420	5.00	7.50	35.00	75.00
	1935(w)	4.660	.20	.40	.60	5.00
	1936(w)	4.660	.20	.40	.60	3.00
	1937(w)	9.050	.20	.40	.60	2.25
	1938(w)	17.300	.20	.40	.60	2.25
	1939(w)	10.000	.20	.40	.60	2.25

10 GROSZY

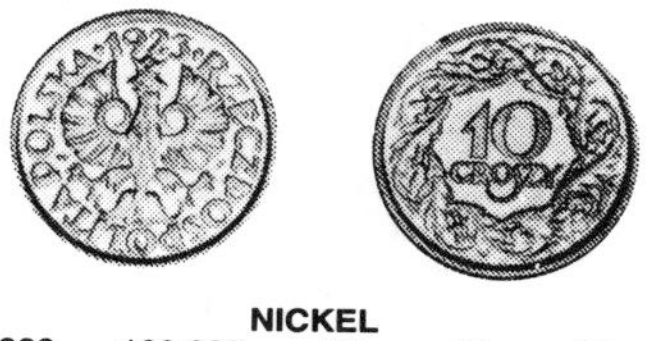

NICKEL

Y#	Date	Mintage	Fine	VF	XF	Unc
11	1923	100.000	.20	.45	.80	1.25

20 GROSZY

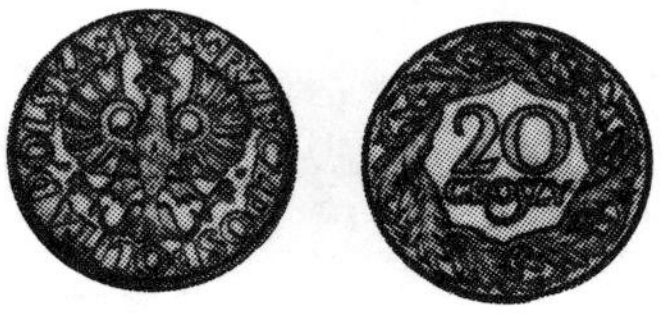

NICKEL

Y#	Date	Mintage	Fine	VF	XF	Unc
12	1923	150.000	.35	.75	1.25	2.00
	1923	10 pcs.	—	—	Proof	300.00

50 GROSZY

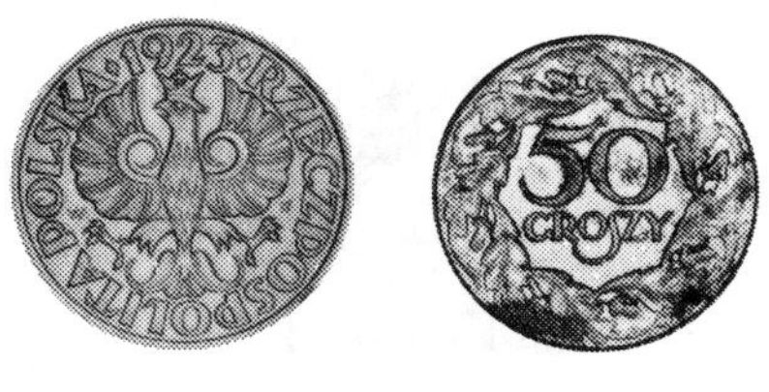

NICKEL

Y#	Date	Mintage	Fine	VF	XF	Unc
13	1923	100.000	.40	.80	1.50	3.50
	1923	10 pcs.	—	—	Proof	350.00

ZLOTY

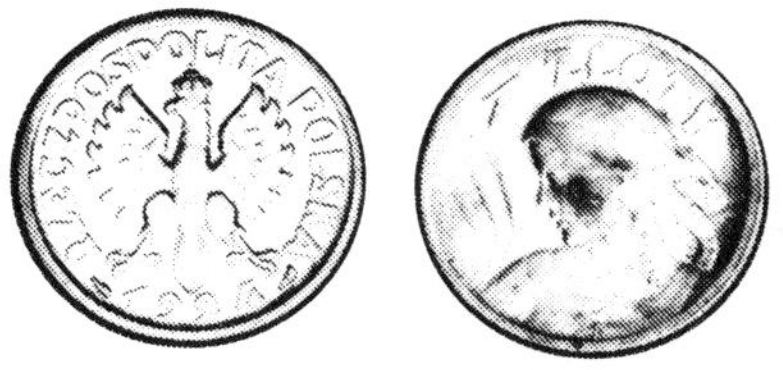

5.0000 g, .750 SILVER, .1206 oz ASW

Y#	Date	Mintage	Fine	VF	XF	Unc
15	1924 (Paris) torches at sides of date	16.000	2.50	6.00	20.00	55.00
	1925 (London) dot after date	24.000	2.50	5.00	12.00	30.00
	1924 (Birmingham)	8 pcs.	—	—	Proof	600.00

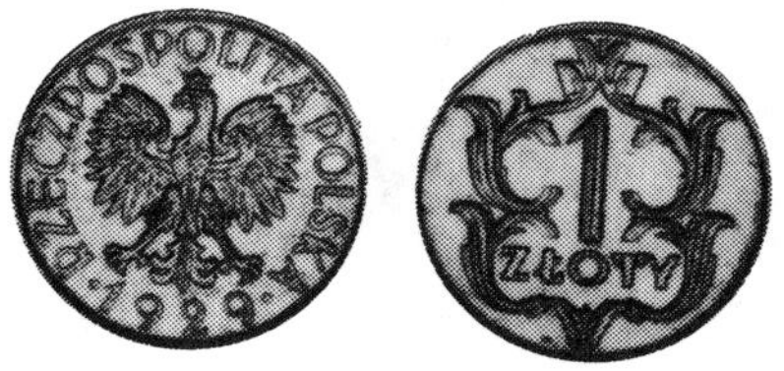

NICKEL

Y#	Date	Mintage	Fine	VF	XF	Unc
14	1929(w)	32.000	.75	1.50	2.50	6.50

2 ZLOTE

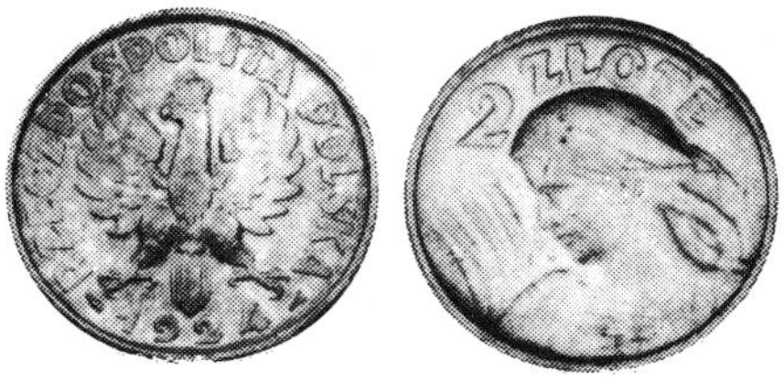

10.0000 g, .750 SILVER, .2411 oz ASW

Y#	Date	Mintage	Fine	VF	XF	Unc
16	1924 (Paris) torches at sides of date	8.200	5.00	10.00	20.00	85.00
	1924H (Birmingham)	1.200	17.50	35.00	175.00	450.00
	1924 (Birmingham)	60 pcs.	—	—	Proof	600.00
	1924 (Philadelphia) w/o torches	.800	10.00	20.00	60.00	125.00
	1925 (London) dot after date	11.000	4.00	8.00	17.50	47.50
	1925 (Philadelphia)	5.200	6.00	12.00	40.00	75.00

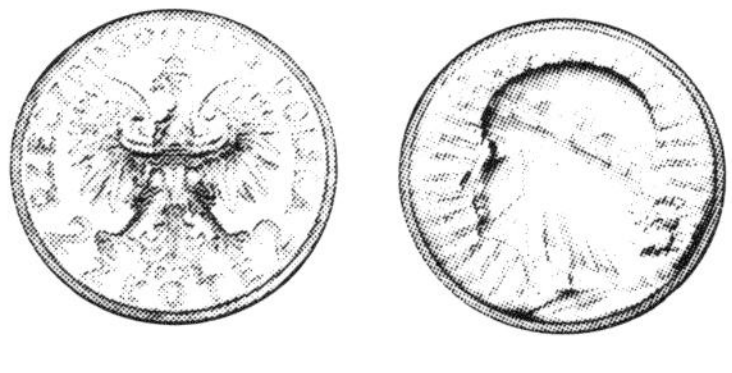

4.4000 g, .750 SILVER, .1061 oz ASW

Y#	Date	Mintage	Fine	VF	XF	Unc
20	1932(w)	15.700	2.00	4.00	7.00	14.00
	1933(w)	9.250	2.00	4.00	7.00	14.00
	1934(w)	.250	4.00	7.00	12.00	25.00

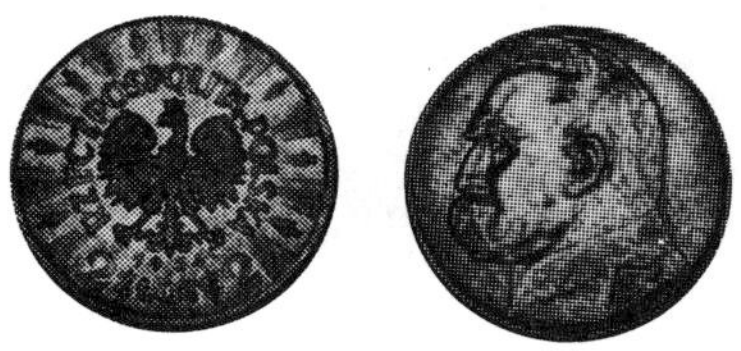

Y#	Date	Mintage	Fine	VF	XF	Unc
27	1934(w)	10.425	3.00	6.00	10.00	25.00
	1936(w)	.075	20.00	75.00	125.00	250.00

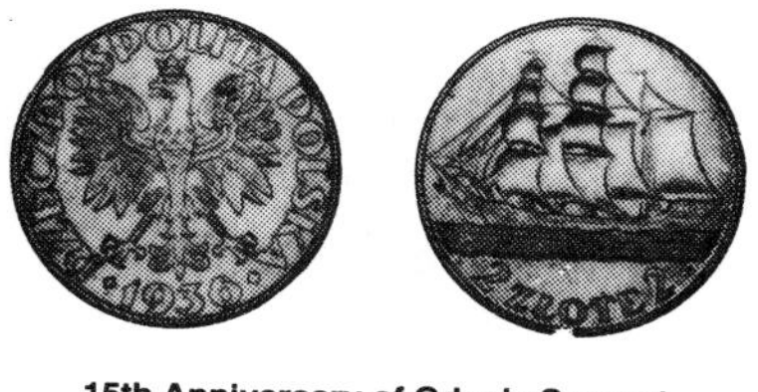

15th Anniversary of Gdynia Seaport

Y#	Date	Mintage	Fine	VF	XF	Unc
30	1936(w)	3.918	3.00	6.00	12.00	30.00

5 ZLOTYCH

18.0000 g, .750 SILVER, .4340 oz ASW

Y#	Date	Mintage	Fine	VF	XF	Unc
18	1928(w) conjoined arrow and 'K' mint mark					
		7.500	15.00	30.00	55.00	120.00
	1928 error 'SUPRMA' edge inscription					
		Inc. Ab.	40.00	75.00	100.00	225.00
	1928 w/o mint mark					
		*10.000	12.50	22.50	55.00	120.00
	1930(w)	5.900	60.00	120.00	275.00	450.00
	1931(w)	2.200	75.00	150.00	500.00	500.00
	1932(w)	3.100	90.00	175.00	350.00	—

*NOTE: 4,300,000 struck in London and 5,700,000 in Belgium.

Centennial of 1830 Revolution

19.1	1930(w)	1.000	7.00	16.50	35.00	90.00

High relief.

19.2	1930(w)	200 pcs.	70.00	175.00	375.00	750.00

11.0000 g, .750 SILVER, .2652 oz ASW

Y#	Date	Mintage	Fine	VF	XF	Unc
21	1932 (Warsaw)					
		1.000	15.00	50.00	200.00	475.00
	1932 (London) w/o mint mark					
		3.000	1.20	2.50	6.00	15.00
	1933(w)	11.000	1.20	2.00	5.00	12.50
	1933(w)	100 pcs.	—	—	Proof	—
	1934(w)	.250	1.20	2.50	7.00	20.00

Rifle Corps Aug. 6, 1914

25	1934(w)	.300	5.00	8.00	16.50	40.00

Jozef Piesudski

28	1934(w)	6.510	2.50	4.00	9.00	22.00
	1935(w)	1.800	3.00	4.50	10.00	25.00
	1936(w)	1.000	3.00	4.50	10.00	25.00
	1938(w)	.289	5.00	7.50	15.00	30.00

15th Anniversary of Gdynia Seaport

Y#	Date	Mintage	Fine	VF	XF	Unc
31	1936(w)	1.000	7.00	12.00	25.00	50.00

10 ZLOTYCH

3.2258 g, .900 GOLD, .0933 oz AGW
Boleslaus I

Y#	Date	Mintage		VF	XF	Unc
32	ND(1925)(w)	.050		55.00	75.00	100.00

22.0000 g, .750 SILVER, .5305 oz ASW

Y#	Date	Mintage	Fine	VF	XF	Unc
22	1932 (Warsaw)					
		3.100	4.00	6.00	12.50	30.00
	1932 (London) w/o mint mark					
		6.000	4.00	6.00	12.50	30.00
	1932(w)	100 pcs.	—	—	Proof	—
	1933(w)	2.800	4.00	6.00	12.50	30.00
	1933(w)	100 pcs.	—	—	Proof	—

Jan III Sobieski's Victory Over the Turks
Obv: Similar to Y#22.

23	ND(1933)(w)	.300	8.00	16.00	25.00	55.00
	ND(1933)(w)					
		100 pcs.	—	—	Proof	—

70th Anniversary of 1863 Insurrection
Obv: Similar to Y#23.

Y#	Date	Mintage	Fine	VF	XF	Unc
24	ND(1933)(w)	.300	10.00	20.00	35.00	60.00
	ND(1933)(w)					
		100 pcs.	—	—	Proof	—

Rifle Corps Aug. 6, 1914

26	1934(w)	.300	9.00	17.50	25.00	50.00

Jozef Piesudski

29	1934(w)	.200	12.00	18.00	28.00	55.00
	1935(w)	1.670	4.00	10.00	18.00	35.00
	1936(w)	2.130	4.00	10.00	18.00	35.00
	1937(w)	.908	4.00	10.00	20.00	40.00
	1938(w)	.234	6.00	15.00	25.00	50.00
	1939(w)	—	4.00	10.00	20.00	40.00

20 ZLOTYCH

6.4516 g, .900 GOLD, .1867 oz AGW
Boleslaus I

Y#	Date	Mintage		VF	XF	Unc
33	ND(1925)(w)	.027		100.00	110.00	150.00

WWII GERMAN OCCUPATION
GROSZ

ZINC

Y#	Date	Mintage	Fine	VF	XF	Unc
34	1939(w)	33.909	.50	1.00	1.75	3.00

5 GROSZY

Y#	Date	Mintage	Fine	VF	XF	Unc
ZINC						
35	1939(w)	15.324	.50	1.50	2.00	4.50

10 GROSZY

Y#	Date	Mintage	Fine	VF	XF	Unc
ZINC						
36	1923(w)	42.175	.20	.30		1.50

NOTE: Actually struck in 1941-44.

20 GROSZY

Y#	Date	Mintage	Fine	VF	XF	Unc
ZINC						
37	1923(w)	40.025	.15	.25	.50	1.50

NOTE: Actually struck in 1941-44.

50 GROSZY

Y#	Date	Mintage	Fine	VF	XF	Unc
NICKEL PLATED IRON						
38	1938(w)	32.000	1.00	2.00	4.00	7.50
IRON						
38a	1938	—	1.25	2.50	5.00	8.50

NOTE: Varieties exist.

POST WAR COINAGE
GROSZ

Y#	Date	Mintage	Fine	VF	XF	Unc
ALUMINUM						
39	1949	400.116	.10	.20	.30	.75

2 GROSZE

Y#	Date	Mintage	Fine	VF	XF	Unc
ALUMINUM						
40	1949	300.106	.10	.25	.50	1.00

5 GROSZY

Y#	Date	Mintage	Fine	VF	XF	Unc
BRONZE						
41	1949	300.000	.10	.25	.50	1.00
ALUMINUM						
41a	1949	200.000	.10	.25	.75	1.50

10 GROSZY

Y#	Date	Mintage	Fine	VF	XF	Unc
COPPER-NICKEL						
42	1949	200.000	.20	.40	.60	1.50
ALUMINUM						
42a	1949	31.047	.10	.25	.75	2.50

20 GROSZY

Y#	Date	Mintage	Fine	VF	XF	Unc
COPPER-NICKEL						
43	1949	133.383	.25	.45	.75	2.00
ALUMINUM						
43a	1949	197.472	.10	.25	.75	2.50

50 GROSZY

Y#	Date	Mintage	Fine	VF	XF	Unc
COPPER-NICKEL						
44	1949	109.000	.35	.65	1.00	2.50
ALUMINUM						
44a	1949	59.393		.25	1.50	5.00

ZLOTY

Y#	Date	Mintage	Fine	VF	XF	Unc
COPPER-NICKEL						
45	1949	87.053	1.00	1.50	2.25	4.00
ALUMINUM						
45a	1949	43.000	.10	.25	2.50	7.50

PEOPLES REPUBLIC
5 GROSZY

Y#	Date	Mintage	VF	XF	Unc
ALUMINUM					
A46	1958	53.521	—	.10	.20
	1959	28.564	—	.10	.15
	1960	12.246	.50	1.50	2.75
	1961	29.502	—	.10	.20
	1962	90.257	—	.10	.15
	1963	20.878	—	.10	.15
	1965MW	5.050	.75	2.00	4.00
	1967MW	10.056	.75	2.00	4.00
	1968MW	10.196	.75	2.00	4.00
	1970MW	20.095	—	.10	.20
	1971MW	20.000	—	.10	.20
	1972MW	10.000	—	.10	.20

10 GROSZY

Y#	Date	Mintage	VF	XF	Unc
ALUMINUM					
AA47	1961	73.400	.75	2.50	4.00
	1962	25.362	1.75	5.00	20.00
	1963	40.434	—	.50	1.50
	1965MW	50.521	.25	1.00	2.00
	1966MW	70.749	—	.50	1.50
	1967MW	62.059	—	.50	1.50
	1968MW	62.204	—	.50	1.50
	1969MW	71.566	—	.50	1.00
	1970MW	38.844	—	.10	.50
	1971MW	50.000	—	.10	.50
	1972MW	60.000	—	.10	.50
	1973	—		Rare	
	1973MW	80.000	—	.10	.25
	1974	50.000	—	—	—
	1975MW	50.000	—	.10	.15
	1976MW	100.000	—	—	.10
	1977MW	100.000	—	—	.10
	1978MW	71.204	—	—	.10
	1979MW	73.191	—	—	.10
	1980MW	60.623	—	—	.10
	1981MW	70.000	—	—	.10

Y#	Date	Mintage	VF	XF	Unc
AA47	1983MW	9.600	—	—	.10
	1985MW	9.957	—	—	.10

NOTE: Varieties in date size exist.

20 GROSZY

Y#	Date	Mintage	VF	XF	Unc
ALUMINUM					
A47	1957	3.940	5.00	17.00	40.00
	1961	53.108	1.75	3.75	8.00
	1962	19.140	2.00	5.00	12.50
	1963	41.217	—	.50	2.00
	1965MW	32.022	—	.50	2.00
	1966MW	23.860	—	.50	2.00
	1967MW	29.099	—	1.00	5.00
	1968MW	29.191	—	1.00	5.00
	1969MW	40.227	—	.50	1.50
	1970MW	20.028	—	.10	1.00
	1971MW	20.000	—	.10	1.00
	1972MW	60.000	—	.10	1.00
	1973	50.000	—	.10	.50
	1973MW	65.000	—	.10	.50
	1975MW	50.000	—	.10	.50
	1976MW large date	100.000	—	.10	.50
	1976MW small date	Inc. Ab.	—	.10	.50
	1977MW	80.730	—	.10	.20
	1978MW	50.730	—	.10	.20
	1979MW	45.252	—	.10	.20
	1980MW	30.020	—	.10	.20
	1981MW	60.082	—	.10	.20
	1985MW	16.227	—	.10	.20

NOTE: Date varieties exist.

50 GROSZY

Y#	Date	Mintage	VF	XF	Unc
ALUMINUM					
48.1	1957	91.316	.75	2.00	5.00
	1965MW	22.090	.25	1.50	4.00
	1967MW	2.027	1.25	4.00	15.00
	1968MW	2.065	1.25	4.00	15.00
	1970MW	3.273	.15	.30	2.00
	1971MW	7.000	.10	.25	1.00
	1972MW	10.000	.10	.25	.50
	1973MW	39.000	.10	.20	.50
	1974MW	33.000	.10	.20	.50
	1975	25.000	.10	.20	.50
	1976	25.000	.10	.20	.40
	1977MW	50.000	.10	.20	.40
	1978	18.600	.10	.20	.40
	1978MW	50.020	.10	.20	.40
	1982MW	16.067	.10	.20	.40
	1983MW	39.667	.10	.20	.40
	1984MW	44.217	.10	.20	.40
	1985MW	49.052	.10	.20	.40

Obv: Redesigned eagle.

Y#	Date	Mintage	VF	XF	Unc
48.2	1986MW	45.796	.10	.20	.40
	1986MW	5,000	—	Proof	3.50
	1987MW	21.257	.10	.20	.40
	1987MW	5,000	—	Proof	3.50

ZLOTY

Y#	Date	Mintage	VF	XF	Unc
ALUMINUM					
49.1	1957	58.631	1.00	3.50	20.00
	1965MW	15.015	.50	1.00	3.00
	1966MW	18.185	.75	2.00	4.00
	1967MW	1.002	2.25	6.00	15.00
	1968MW	1.176	2.25	6.00	15.00
	1969MW	3.024	1.25	3.00	6.00

Y#	Date	Mintage	VF	XF	Unc
49.1	1970MW	6.016	.15	.50	1.50
	1971MW	6.000	.15	.50	1.00
	1972MW	7.000	.15	.50	1.00
	1973MW	15.000	.10	.50	1.00
	1974MW	42.000	.10	.15	.50
	1975	22.000	.10	.15	.50
	1975MW	33.000	.10	.15	.50
	1976	22.000	.10	.50	1.00
	1977MW	65.000	.10	.50	1.00
	1978	16.400	.10	.50	1.00
	1978MW	80.000	.10	.50	1.00
	1980MW	100.002	.10	.15	.50
	1981MW	4.082	.10	.15	1.00
	1982MW	59.643	.10	.15	.30
	1983MW	49.636	.10	.15	.25
	1984MW	61.036	.10	.15	.25
	1985MW	167.939	.10	.15	.25

Obv: Redesigned eagle.

49.2	1986MW	130.697	.10	.15	.25
	1986MW	5,000	—	Proof	3.50
	1987MW	100.081	.10	.15	.25
	1987MW	5,000	—	Proof	3.50
	1988MW	96.400	.10	.15	.25
	1988MW	5,000	—	Proof	3.50

49.3	1989MW	49.410	.10	.15	.25
	1989MW	5,000	—	Proof	3.50
	1990MW	30.667	.10	.15	.25
	1990MW	5,000	—	Proof	3.50

2 ZLOTE

ALUMINUM

46	1958	82.640	.20	1.50	6.00
	1959	7.170	.50	4.00	20.00
	1960	36.131	.20	.50	3.00
	1970MW	2.014	.30	1.00	4.00
	1971MW	3.000	.20	1.00	4.00
	1972MW	3.000	.20	1.00	4.00
	1973MW	10.000	.15	.50	1.50
	1974MW	46.000	.15	.30	1.00

BRASS

80.1	1975	25.000	.15	.25	.50
	1976	60.000	.15	.25	.50
	1977	50.000	.15	.25	.50
	1978	2.600	.15	.25	1.75
	1978MW	2.382	.15	.25	1.75
	1979MW	85.752	.15	.25	.50
	1980MW	66.610	.15	.25	.50
	1981MW	40.306	.15	.25	.50
	1982MW	45.318	.15	.25	.50
	1983MW	35.244	.15	.25	.50
	1984MW	59.999	.15	.25	.50
	1985MW	100.300	.15	.25	.50

Obv: Redesigned eagle.

80.2	1986MW	60.718	.15	.25	.50
	1986MW	5,000	—	Proof	3.50
	1987MW	44.673	.15	.25	.50
	1987MW	5,000	—	Proof	3.50
	1988MW	94.651	.15	.25	.50
	1988MW	5,000	—	Proof	3.50

ALUMINUM, 17.9mm

Y#	Date	Mintage	VF	XF	Unc
80.3	1989MW	91.494	.10	.20	.40
	1989MW	5,000	—	Proof	3.50
	1990MW	40.723	.10	.20	.40
	1990MW	5,000	—	Proof	3.50

5 ZLOTYCH

ALUMINUM

47	1958	1.328	7.50	12.50	20.00
	1959	56.811	.75	2.50	7.00
	1960	16.301	.25	1.50	5.00
	1971MW	1.000	7.50	12.50	20.00
	1973MW	5.000	.20	1.00	4.00
	1974MW	46.000	.20	.50	2.50

BRASS

81.1	1975	25.000	.20	.40	.80
	1976	60.000	.20	.40	.80
	1977	50.000	.20	.40	.80
	1978MW	—	—	Rare	
	1979MW	5.098	.20	.40	1.50
	1980MW	10.100	.20	.40	.80
	1981MW	4.008	.20	.40	1.75
	1982MW	25.379	.20	.40	.80
	1983MW	30.531	.20	.40	.80
	1984MW	85.598	.20	.40	.80
	1985MW	20.501	.20	.40	.80

NOTE: Varieties of size of letters exist.

24mm
Obv: Redesigned eagle.

81.2	1986MW	57.108	.20	.40	.80
	1986MW	5,000	—	Proof	3.50
	1987MW	58.843	.20	.40	.80
	1987MW	5,000	—	Proof	3.50
	1988MW	18.668	.20	.40	.80
	1988MW	5,000	—	Proof	3.50

ALUMINUM, 20mm

81.3	1989MW	30.253	.15	.30	.60
	1989MW	5,000	—	Proof	3.50
	1990MW	38.248	.15	.30	.60
	1990MW	5,000	—	Proof	3.50

10 ZLOTYCH

COPPER-NICKEL, 31mm

Tadeusz Kosciuszko

Y#	Date	Mintage	VF	XF	Unc
50	1959	13.107	.50	1.75	6.00
	1960	27.551	.50	1.75	6.00
	1966MW	4.157	1.00	8.00	18.00

Reduced size, 28mm.

50a	1969MW	5.428	.50	1.50	5.00
	1970MW	13.783	.50	1.00	1.75
	1971MW	12.000	.50	1.00	1.75
	1972MW	10.000	.50	1.00	1.75
	1973MW	3.900	.50	2.00	8.00

Mikolaj Kopernik

51	1959	12.559	.75	1.25	2.50
	1965MW	3.000	1.00	5.00	15.00

Reduced size.

51a	1967MW	2.128	.75	2.00	7.50
	1968MW	9.389	.75	1.25	2.00
	1969MW	8.612	.75	1.25	2.75

600th Anniversary of Jagiello University
Legends raised.

52	ND(1964)	2.610	.50	1.25	2.50

Legends incuse.

52a	ND(1964)	2.612	.50	1.25	2.50

700th Anniversary of Warsaw

54	1965MW	3.492	.50	1.25	2.75

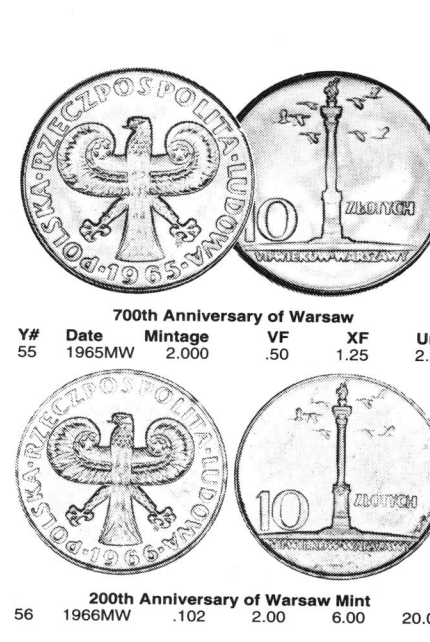

700th Anniversary of Warsaw

Y#	Date	Mintage	VF	XF	Unc
55	1965MW	2.000	.50	1.25	2.50

200th Anniversary of Warsaw Mint

56	1966MW	.102	2.00	6.00	20.00

20th Anniversary - Death of General Swierczewski

58	1967MW	2.000	.50	1.00	2.00

Centennial - Birth of Marie Curie

59	1967MW	2.000	.50	1.00	2.25

25th Anniversary - Peoples Army

60	1968MW	2.000	.50	1.00	2.00

25th Anniversary - Peoples Republic

61	1969MW	2.000	.50	1.00	2.00

25th Anniversary - Provincial Annexations

62	1970MW	2.000	.50	1.00	2.00

F.A.O. Issue

Y#	Date	Mintage	VF	XF	Unc
63	1971MW	2.000	.50	1.00	2.50

50th Anniversary - Battle of Upper Silesia

64	1971MW	2.000	.50	1.00	2.00

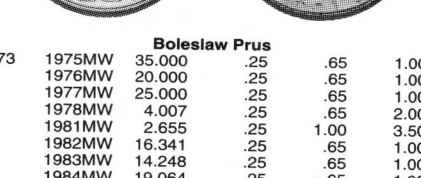

50th Anniversary - Gdynia Seaport

65	1972MW	2.000	.50	1.00	2.00

Boleslaw Prus

73	1975MW	35.000	.25	.65	1.00
	1976MW	20.000	.25	.65	1.00
	1977MW	25.000	.25	.65	1.00
	1978MW	4.007	.25	.65	2.00
	1981MW	2.655	.25	1.00	3.50
	1982MW	16.341	.25	.65	1.00
	1983MW	14.248	.25	.65	1.00
	1984MW	19.064	.25	.65	1.00

Adam Mickiewicz

74	1975MW	35.000	.25	.65	1.00
	1976MW	20.000	.25	.65	1.00

25mm

152.1	1984MW	15.756	.20	.50	1.00
	1985MW	5.282	.20	.50	1.00
	1986MW	31.043	.20	.50	1.00
	1986MW	5,000	—	Proof	4.00
	1987MW	69.636	.20	.50	1.00
	1987MW	5,000	—	Proof	4.00
	1988MW	102.493	.20	.50	1.00
	1988MW	5,000	—	Proof	4.00

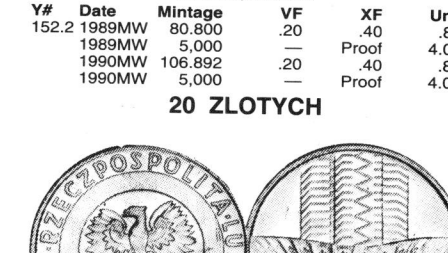

BRASS, 21.8mm

Y#	Date	Mintage	VF	XF	Unc
152.2	1989MW	80.800	.20	.40	.80
	1989MW	5,000	—	Proof	4.00
	1990MW	106.892	.20	.40	.80
	1990MW	5,000	—	Proof	4.00

20 ZLOTYCH

COPPER-NICKEL

67	1973	25.000	.25	1.00	2.50
	1974	12.000	.25	.75	1.50
	1976	20.000	.25	.75	1.50

Marceli Nowotko

69	1974MW	10.000	.25	1.00	2.50
	1975	10.000	.25	1.00	2.00
	1976	20.000	.25	.75	1.50
	1976MW	30.000	.25	.75	1.50
	1977MW	16.000	.25	1.00	2.00
	1983MW	.152	.25	5.00	12.50

25th Anniversary of the Comcon

70	1974MW	2.000	.75	1.25	2.25

International Women's Year

75	1975MW	2.000	.75	1.25	2.25

Maria Konopnicka

95	1978MW	2.010	.75	1.25	2.25

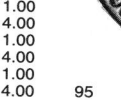

50 ZLOTYCH

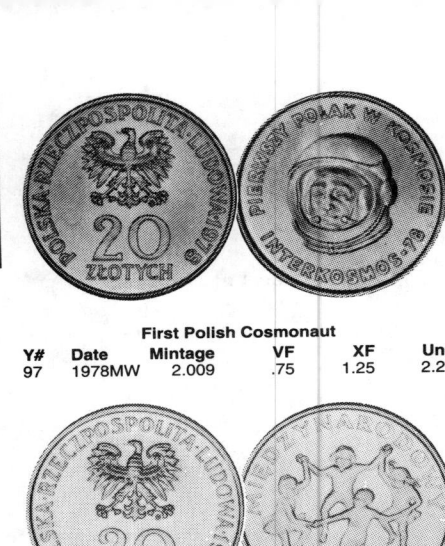

First Polish Cosmonaut

Y#	Date	Mintage	VF	XF	Unc
97	1978MW	2.009	.75	1.25	2.25

International Year of the Child

99	1979MW	2.007	1.00	1.50	3.00

1980 Olympics - Runner

108	1980MW	2.012	1.00	1.75	5.00
	1980MW	100 pcs.	—	Proof	40.00

50th Anniversary - Training Ship *Dar Pomorza*

112	1980MW	2.007	1.00	1.75	3.50

Circulation Coinage

153.1	1984MW	12.703	.25	.60	1.25
	1985MW	15.514	.25	.60	1.25
	1986MW	37.959	.25	.60	1.25
	1986MW	5,000	—	Proof	4.00
	1987MW	22.213	.25	.60	1.25
	1987MW	5,000	—	Proof	4.00
	1988MW	14.994	.25	.60	1.25
	1988MW	5,000	—	Proof	4.00

Reduced size, 23.9mm

153.2	1989MW	95.974	.25	.35	.75
	1989MW	5,000	—	Proof	4.00
	1990MW	104.712	.25	.35	.75
	1990MW	5,000	—	Proof	4.00

12.6400 g, .750 SILVER, .3048 OZ ASW
Fryderyk Chopin

Y#	Date	Mintage	VF	XF	Unc
66	1972MW	.050	—	Proof	15.00
	1974MW	.010	—	Proof	22.50

COPPER-NICKEL
Duke Mieszko I

100	1979MW	2.640	1.00	2.00	5.00

King Boleslaw I Chrobry

114	1980MW	2.564	1.00	2.00	5.00

Duke Kazimierz I Odnowiciel

117	1980MW	2.504	1.00	2.00	5.00

General Broni Wladyslaw Sikorski

122	1981MW	2.505	1.00	2.00	5.00

King Boleslaw II Smialy

124	1981MW	2.538	1.00	2.00	4.50

World Food Day

Y#	Date	Mintage	VF	XF	Unc
127	1981MW	2.524	1.00	2.00	4.50

King Wladyslaw I Herman

128	1981MW	2.500	1.00	2.00	4.50

King Boleslaw III Krzywousty

133	1982MW	2.616	1.00	2.00	4.50

150th Anniversary of Great Theater

142	1983MW	.615	1.00	4.00	8.00

King Jan III Sobieski

145	1983MW	2.576	1.00	2.00	4.50

Ignacy Lukasiewicz

146	1983MW	.612	1.00	4.00	8.00

Y#	Date	Mintage	VF	XF	Unc
216	1990MW	28.707	—	—	1.00
	1990MW	5,000		Proof	12.00

REPUBLIC
MONETARY REFORM
January 1, 1995

100 Old Zlotych = 1 Grosz
1000 Old Zlotych = 10 Groszy
10,000 Old Zlotych = 1 Zloty
50,000 Old Zlotych = 5 Zlotych

As far back as 1990 production was initiated for the new 1 Grosz - 1 Zlotych coins for a forthcoming monetary reform. It wasn't announced until the Act of July 7, 1994 and was enacted on January 1, 1995.

GROSZ

BRASS

276	1990	—	—	—	.10
	1991	—	—	—	.10
	1992	—	—	—	.10
	1993	—	—	—	.10
	1995	—	—	—	.10

2 GROSZE

BRASS

277	1990	—	—	—	.15
	1991	—	—	—	.15
	1992	—	—	—	.15
	1997	—	—	—	.15

5 GROSZY

BRASS

278	1990	—	—	—	.25
	1991	—	—	—	.25
	1992	—	—	—	.25
	1993	—	—	—	.25

10 GROSZY

COPPER-NICKEL

279	1990	—	—	—	.40
	1991	—	—	—	.40
	1992	—	—	—	.40
	1993	—	—	—	.40

20 GROSZY

COPPER-NICKEL

280	1990	—	—	—	.65
	1991	—	—	—	.65
	1992	—	—	—	.65

50 GROSZY

COPPER-NICKEL

Y#	Date	Mintage	VF	XF	Unc
281	1990	—	—	—	1.00
	1991	—	—	—	1.00
	1992	—	—	—	1.00
	1995	—	—	—	1.00

ZLOTY

COPPER-NICKEL

282	1990	—	—	—	1.75
	1991	—	—	—	1.75
	1992	—	—	—	1.75
	1993	—	—	—	1.75
	1994	—	—	—	1.75

2 ZLOTE

COPPER-NICKEL center, BRASS ring

283	1994	—	—	—	3.50
	1995	—	—	—	3.50

5 ZLOTYCH

BRASS center, COPPER-NICKEL ring

284	1994	—	—	—	6.50
	1996	—	—	—	6.50

DANZIG

A seaport on the northern coast of Poland giving access to the Baltic Sea. An important port from early times. Has at different times belonged to the Teutonic Knights, Pomerania, Russia, and Prussia. Danzig was a free city from 1919 to 1939 during which most of its modern coinage was made.

FREE CITY
MONETARY SYSTEM
100 Pfennig = 1 Gulden

PFENNIG

BRONZE

KM#	Date	Mintage	Fine	VF	XF	Unc
140	1923	4.000	1.00	3.00	5.00	10.00
	1923	—	—	—	Proof	50.00
	1926	1.500	1.50	4.00	8.00	16.00
	1929	1.000	2.50	7.50	12.00	20.00
	1930	2.000	1.25	3.50	6.50	12.00
	1937	3.000	1.25	3.50	6.50	12.00

2 PFENNIG

BRONZE

KM#	Date	Mintage	Fine	VF	XF	Unc
141	1923	1.000	1.75	4.50	7.50	15.00
	1923	—	—	—	Proof	65.00
	1926	1.750	1.75	4.50	7.50	15.00
	1937	.500	2.75	6.50	11.00	18.50

5 PFENNIG

COPPER-NICKEL

142	1923	3.000	1.25	2.75	6.00	12.00
	1923	—	—	—	Proof	100.00
	1928	1.000	3.50	8.25	14.00	27.50
	1928	—	—	—	Proof	175.00

ALUMINUM-BRONZE

151	1932	4.000	1.25	2.25	6.00	16.00

10 PFENNIG

COPPER-NICKEL

143	1923	5.000	2.00	3.00	8.00	18.00
	1923	—	—	—	Proof	115.00

ALUMINUM-BRONZE

152	1932	5.000	1.50	2.50	7.00	17.00

1/2 GULDEN

2.5000 g, .750 SILVER, .0603 oz ASW

144	1923	1.000	7.50	20.00	35.00	65.00
	1923	—	—	—	Proof	150.00
	1927	.400	17.50	35.00	70.00	125.00
	1927	—	—	—	Proof	250.00

NICKEL

153	1932	1.400	8.00	25.00	37.50	65.00

GULDEN

5.0000 g, .750 SILVER, .1206 oz ASW

145	1923	2.500	11.00	22.50	37.50	75.00
	1923	—	—	—	Proof	200.00

NICKEL

KM#	Date	Mintage	Fine	VF	XF	Unc
154	1932	2.500	8.00	25.00	35.00	55.00

2 GULDEN

10.0000 g, .750 SILVER, .2411 oz ASW

KM#	Date	Mintage	Fine	VF	XF	Unc
146	1923	1.250	25.00	50.00	90.00	175.00
	1923	—	—	—	Proof	250.00

10.0000 g, .500 SILVER, .1608 oz ASW

155	1932	1.250	—	150.00	200.00	370.00

5 GULDEN

25.0000 g, .750 SILVER, .6028 oz ASW

147	1923	.700	65.00	135.00	220.00	400.00
	1923	—	—	—	Proof	550.00
	1927	.160	150.00	250.00	375.00	600.00
	1927	—	—	—	Proof	1000.

14.8200 g, .500 SILVER, .2382 oz ASW

156	1932	.430	125.00	225.00	350.00	950.00

157	1932	.430	150.00	350.00	850.00	1500.

NICKEL

KM#	Date	Mintage	Fine	VF	XF	Unc
158	1935	.800	100.00	160.00	235.00	450.00

10 GULDEN

NICKEL

159	1935	.380	300.00	500.00	700.00	1350.

PORTUGAL

The Portuguese Republic, located in the western part of the Iberian Peninsula in southwestern Europe, has an area of 35,553 sq. mi. (92,080 sq. km.) and a population of *10.5 million. Capital: Lisbon. Portugal's economy is based on agriculture, tourism, minerals, fisheries and a rapidly expanding industrial sector. Textiles account for 33% of the exports and Portuguese wine has become world famous. Portugal has become Europe's number one producer of copper and the world's largest producer of cork.

After centuries of domination by Romans, Visigoths and Moors, Portugal emerged in the 12th century as an independent kingdom financially and philosophically prepared for the great period of exploration that would follow. Attuned to the inspiration of Prince Henry the Navigator (1394-1460), Portugal's daring explorers of the 15th and 16th centuries roamed the world's oceans from Brazil to Japan in an unprecedented burst of energy and endeavor that culminated in 1494 with Portugal laying claim to half the transoceanic world. Unfortunately for the fortunes of the tiny kingdom, the Portuguese population was too small to colonize this vast territory. Less than a century after Portugal laid claim to half the world, English, French and Dutch trading companies had seized the lion's share of the world's colonies and commerce, and Portugal's place as an imperial power was lost forever. The monarchy was overthrown in 1910 and a republic established.

On April 25, 1974, the government of Portugal was seized by a military junta which reached agreements providing for independence for the Portuguese overseas provinces of Portuguese Guinea (Guinea-Bissau), Mozambique, Cape Verde Islands, Angola, and St. Thomas and Prince Islands (Sao Tome and Principe).

On January 1, 1986, Portugal became the eleventh member of the European Economic Community and in the first half of 1992 held its first EEC Presidency.

RULERS

Carlos I, 1889-1908
Manuel II, 1908-1910
Republic, 1910 to date

MINT MARKS

No Mint mark - Lisbon

MONETARY SYSTEM

1600 Reis = 1 Escudo
6400 Reis = 4 Escudos = 1 Peca
              Commencing 1910
100 Centavos = 1 Escudo

5 REIS

BRONZE

KM#	Date	Mintage	Fine	VF	XF	Unc
530	1901	1.070	1.00	3.00	5.00	12.00
	1904	.720	.50	1.00	2.50	7.00
	1905	1.340	.25	.75	1.50	5.00
	1906/0	1,260	.30	1.00	2.50	7.00
	1906/9	Inc. Ab.	.30	1.00	2.50	7.00
	1906	Inc. Ab.	.25	.75	1.50	5.00

NOTE: Earlier dates (1890-1900) exist for this type.

555	1910	1.000	.25	.75	1.25	3.50

100 REIS

2.5000 g, .835 SILVER, .0671 oz ASW

KM#	Date	Mintage	Fine	VF	XF	Unc
548	1909	6.363	1.00	2.00	4.00	9.00
	1910	Inc. Ab.	1.00	2.00	3.00	7.00

200 REIS

5.0000 g, .917 SILVER, .1474 oz ASW

KM#	Date	Mintage	VG	Fine	VF	XF
534	1901	.205	15.00	30.00	60.00	150.00
	1903	.200	4.00	7.50	15.00	35.00

NOTE: Earlier dates (1891-1893) exist for this type.

5.0000 g, .835 SILVER, .1342 oz ASW

KM#	Date	Mintage				
549	1909	7.656	1.50	3.00	5.00	10.00

500 REIS

12.5000 g, .917 SILVER, .3684 oz ASW

KM#	Date	Mintage	Fine	VF	XF	Unc
535	1901	1.050	5.00	10.00	20.00	45.00
	1903	.680	4.00	6.00	10.00	25.00
	1904	—		Reported, not confirmed		
	1906/3	.240	10.00	20.00	45.00	75.00
	1906	Inc. Ab.	7.00	16.00	35.00	65.00
	1907	.384	4.00	6.00	10.00	22.00
	1908	1.840	4.00	6.00	10.00	22.00

NOTE: Earlier dates (1891-1900) exist for this type.

KM#	Date	Mintage	Fine	VF	XF	Unc
547	1908	2.500	3.50	4.50	6.00	15.00
	1909/8	1.513	6.00	12.50	17.50	37.50
	1909	Inc. Ab.	4.00	6.00	12.00	27.50

Peninsular War Centennial

556	1910	.200	10.00	20.00	40.00	75.00

Marquis De Pombal

557	1910	.400	6.50	12.50	22.50	50.00
	1910	—			Proof	600.00

1000 REIS

25.0000 g, .917 SILVER, .7368 oz ASW
Peninsular War Centennial

KM#	Date	Mintage	VG	Fine	VF	XF
558	1910	.200	15.00	25.00	45.00	100.00
	1910				Proof	900.00

REPUBLIC

100 Centavos = 1 Escudo

CENTAVO

BRONZE

KM#	Date	Mintage	Fine	VF	XF	Unc
565	1917	2.250	.20	.40	.75	3.50
	1918	22.996	.20	.40	.75	3.50
	1920	12.535	.25	.50	1.00	5.00
	1921	4.492	1.00	2.00	3.50	12.00
	1922	Inc. Ab.	—	—	Rare	—

2 CENTAVOS

IRON

567	1918	.170	15.00	30.00	55.00	120.00

BRONZE

568	1918	4.295	.20	.40	.75	3.50
	1920	10.109	.20	.40	.75	4.00
	1921	.679	2.00	4.00	10.00	20.00

4 CENTAVOS

COPPER NICKEL

566	1917	4.961	.25	.50	1.00	4.00
	1919	10.067	.25	.50	1.00	3.50

5 CENTAVOS

BRONZE

569	1920	.114	2.50	5.00	10.00	25.00
	1921	5.916	.50	.75	1.00	5.00
	1922	Inc. Ab.	20.00	50.00	85.00	165.00

KM#	Date	Mintage	Fine	VF	XF	Unc
572	1924	6.480	.30	.60	1.50	5.00
	1925	7.260	.50	1.25	3.50	10.00
	1927	26.320	.20	.50	1.00	4.00

10 CENTAVOS

2.5000 g, .835 SILVER, .0671 oz ASW

563	1915	3.418	1.00	2.00	3.00	6.00

COPPER-NICKEL

570	1920	1.120	.35	.75	2.00	8.00
	1921	1.285	.35	.75	2.00	8.00

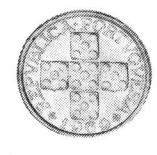 

BRONZE

573	1924	1.210	1.00	2.00	5.00	20.00
	1925	9.090	.25	.65	2.00	9.00
	1926	26.250	.25	.65	2.50	10.00
	1930	1.730	7.00	18.00	40.00	120.00
	1938	2.000	2.50	4.50	12.00	35.00
	1940	3.384	.75	1.50	2.25	7.50

583	1942	1.035	.25	1.00	2.00	12.00
	1943	18.765	.15	.50	1.00	9.00
	1944	5.090	.20	1.00	1.50	9.00
	1945	6.090	.20	1.00	1.50	10.00
	1946	7.740	.20	.50	1.00	9.00
	1947	9.283	.20	.50	1.00	6.50
	1948	5.900	.50	4.00	10.00	30.00
	1949	15.240	.10	.15	.50	3.50
	1950	8.860	.15	.50	1.00	15.00
	1951	5.040	.15	.50	1.50	15.00
	1952	4.960	.25	2.00	4.00	25.00
	1953	7.548	.15	.50	1.00	9.00
	1954	2.452	.20	1.00	2.00	8.00
	1955	10.000	—	.10	.25	3.25
	1956	3.336	—	.10	.25	3.25
	1957	6.654	—	.10	.25	2.25
	1958	7.320	—	.10	.25	2.25
	1959	7.140	—	.10	.25	2.25
	1960	15.055	—	.10	.25	1.25
	1961	5.020	—	.10	.25	1.25
	1962	14.980	—	.10	.15	.50
	1963	5.393	—	.10	.15	1.50
	1964	10.257	—	.10	.15	.50
	1965	15.550	—	.10	.15	1.00
	1966	10.200	—	.10	.15	.45
	1967	18.592	—	.10	.15	.45
	1968	22.515	—	.10	.15	.45
	1969	3.871	—	.10	.15	1.00

ALUMINUM

KM#	Date	Mintage	VF	XF	Unc
594	1969	—	50.00	100.00	275.00
	1970	—		Rare	—
	1971	25.673	—	—	.10
	1972	10.558	—	—	.10
	1973	3.149	—	—	1.00
	1974	17.043	—	—	.10
	1975	22.410	—	—	.10
	1976	19.907	—	—	.10
	1977	8.431	—	—	.10

KM#	Date	Mintage	VF	XF	Unc
594	1978	2.205	—	—	.10
	1979	9.083	—	—	.75

20 CENTAVOS

  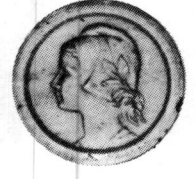

5.0000 g, .835 SILVER, .1342 oz ASW

KM#	Date	Mintage	Fine	VF	XF	Unc
562	1913	.540	3.00	10.00	20.00	55.00
	1916	.706	2.25	5.00	10.00	27.50

COPPER-NICKEL

571	1920	1.568	.35	.75	2.00	10.00
	1921	3.030	.35	.75	2.00	10.00
	1922	.580	85.00	175.00	375.00	650.00

BRONZE

574	1924	6.220	.50	1.25	3.50	12.00
	1925	10.580	.50	1.25	3.50	12.00

584	1942	10.170	.15	.50	3.00	20.00
	1943	Inc. Ab.	.15	.50	2.00	20.00
	1944	7.290	.15	.50	2.00	20.00
	1945	7.552	.15	.50	2.00	20.00
	1948	2.750	.20	.75	5.00	25.00
	1949	12.250	.10	.15	.50	6.00
	1951	3.185	.20	.75	4.00	25.00
	1952	1.815	.50	1.50	6.00	35.00
	1953	9.426	—	.10	.50	6.00
	1955	5.574	—	.10	.50	4.00
	1956	5.000	—	.10	.50	4.00
	1957	1.450	—	Reported, not confirmed		
	1958	7.470	—	.10	.50	4.00
	1959	4.780	—	.10	.50	2.00
	1960	4.790	—	.10	.50	2.00
	1961	5.180	—	.10	.50	2.00
	1962	2.500	—	.10	1.00	5.00
	1963	7.990	—	.10	.50	1.25
	1964	7.010	—	.10	.50	1.00
	1965	7.365	—	.10	.50	1.00
	1966	8.075	—	.10	.25	.65
	1967	9.220	—	.10	.25	.65
	1968	10.372	—	.10	.25	.65
	1969	8.657	—	.10	.50	1.00

KM#	Date	Mintage	VF	XF	Unc
595	1969	10.891	—	.10	.15
	1970	16.120	—	.10	.15
	1971	1.933	—	.15	1.50
	1972	16.354	—	.10	.15
	1973	4.900	—	.10	.15
	1974	26.975	—	.10	.15

50 CENTAVOS

12.5000 g, .835 SILVER, .3356 oz ASW

KM#	Date	Mintage	Fine	VF	XF	Unc
561	1912	1.695	3.25	5.00	10.00	20.00
	1913	4.443	3.25	5.00	7.50	15.00
	1914	4.992	3.25	5.00	10.00	20.00
	1916	5.080	3.25	5.00	7.50	15.00

ALUMINUM-BRONZE

575	1924	.810	10.00	25.00	60.00	120.00
	1925	—	250.00	450.00	850.00	1600.
	1926	4.340	.50	2.00	5.00	15.00

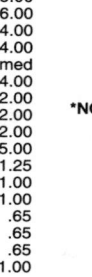

COPPER-NICKEL

577	1927	2.330	.50	2.00	7.00	35.00
	1928	6.823	.50	2.00	7.00	40.00
	1929	9.779	.50	2.00	7.00	35.00
	1930	1.116	.50	3.00	12.00	70.00
	1931	7.127	.50	2.00	10.00	70.00
	1935*	.902	1.50	6.00	15.00	120.00
	1938	.923	1.00	5.00	12.00	120.00
	1940	2.000	—	.10	1.50	25.00
	1944	2.974	—	.10	.50	10.00
	1945	5.700	—	.10	.50	10.00
	1946	4.334	—	.10	1.00	20.00
	1947	6.998	—	.10	.50	11.50
	1951	4.610	—	.10	.25	6.00
	1952	2.421	.10	.25	.50	12.50
	1953	2.369	.10	.25	.50	13.00
	1955	3.057	—	.10	.25	6.00
	1956	3.003	—	.10	.25	6.00
	1957	3.940	—	.10	.25	4.00
	1958	2.687	—	.10	.25	2.50
	1959	4.027	—	.10	.25	2.50
	1960	2.592	—	.10	.20	2.00
	1961	3.324	—	.10	.15	.75
	1962	6.678	—	.10	.15	.75
	1963	2.346	—	.10	.20	1.00
	1964	7.654	—	—	.10	.75
	1965	3.366	—	—	.10	.75
	1966	6.085	—	—	.10	.75
	1967	19.391	—	—	.10	.50
	1968	11.448	—	—	.10	.50

*NOTE: For exclusive use in Azores.

BRONZE

KM#	Date	Mintage	VF	XF	Unc
596	1969	3.481	—	.10	1.00
	1970	17.280	—	.10	1.00
	1971	9.139	—	.10	1.00
	1972	24.729	—	.10	.75
	1973	35.588	—	.10	.75
	1974	28.719	—	.10	.50
	1975	17.793	—	.10	.50
	1976	23.734	—	.10	.50
	1977	16.340	—	.10	.50
	1978	48.348	—	.10	.50
	1979	61.652	—	.10	.50

ESCUDO

25.0000 g, .835 SILVER, .6711 oz ASW
October 5, 1910, Birth of the Republic

KM#	Date	Mintage	Fine	VF	XF	Unc
560	1910	*1.000	12.50	20.00	40.00	75.00

*NOTE: Struck in 1914.

564	1915	1.818	8.00	12.00	20.00	35.00
	1916	1.405	8.00	12.00	20.00	40.00

ALUMINUM-BRONZE

576	1924	2.709	1.50	4.00	9.00	20.00
	1926	2.346	10.00	25.00	60.00	120.00

COPPER-NICKEL

578	1927	1.917	.50	1.00	6.50	35.00
	1928	7.462	.50	1.00	6.50	40.00
	1929	1.617	.50	1.00	6.50	40.00
	1930	1.911	2.00	4.00	18.00	120.00
	1931	2.039	2.00	4.00	18.00	145.00
	1935*	—	20.00	50.00	150.00	850.00
	1939	.304	3.50	8.50	25.00	155.00
	1940	1.259	.50	1.00	3.50	28.00
	1944	.993	2.50	6.00	20.00	110.00
	1945	Inc. Ab.	.25	.50	2.00	12.00
	1946	2.507	.25	.50	2.00	12.00
	1951	2.500	.25	.50	1.50	6.00
	1952	2.500	.50	1.00	3.50	18.00
	1957	1.656	.10	.25	1.00	5.00
	1958	1.447	.10	.25	1.00	5.00
	1959	1.908	.10	.25	.75	3.00
	1961	2.505	.10	.25	.50	2.00
	1962	2.757	.10	.25	.50	2.00
	1964	1.611	.10	.25	.50	2.00

KM#	Date	Mintage	Fine	VF	XF	Unc
578	1965	1.683	.10	.25	.50	2.00
	1966	2.607	.10	.20	.40	1.25
	1968	4.099	.10	.20	.40	1.25

***NOTE:** For exclusive use in Azores.

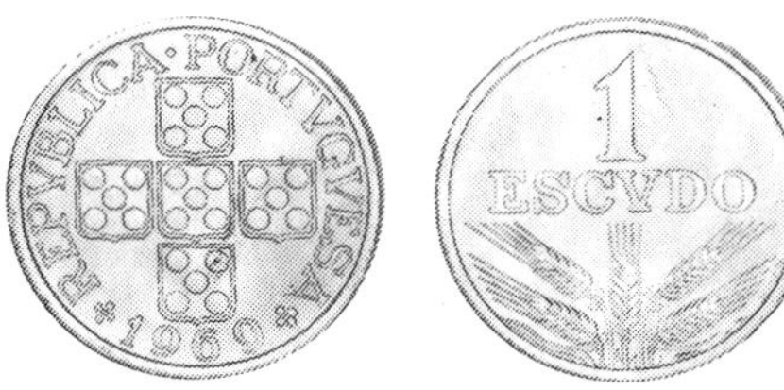

BRONZE

KM#	Date	Mintage	VF	XF	Unc
597	1969	3.020	.10	.15	1.00
	1970	6.009	.10	.15	1.00
	1971	7.860	.10	.15	1.00
	1972	3.815	.10	.15	1.00
	1973	20.467	.10	.15	.50
	1974	11.444	.10	.15	.50
	1975	8.473	.10	.15	.75
	1976	7.353	.10	.15	.75
	1977	6.218	.10	.15	.50
	1978	7.061	.10	.15	.50
	1979	14.241	.10	.15	.50
	1980	16.780	.10	.15	.50

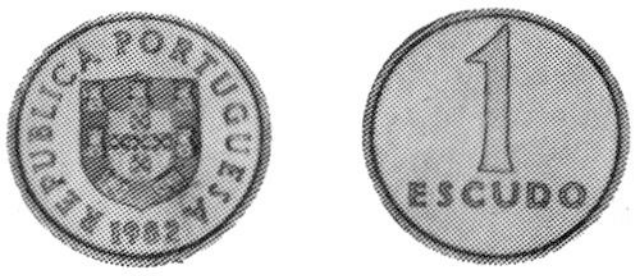

NICKEL-BRASS

614	1981	30.165	—	.10	.20
(611)	1982	53.018	—	.10	.20
	1983	53.165	—	.10	.20
	1984	59.463	—	.10	.20
	1985	46.832	—	.10	.20
	1986	8.030	—	.10	.50

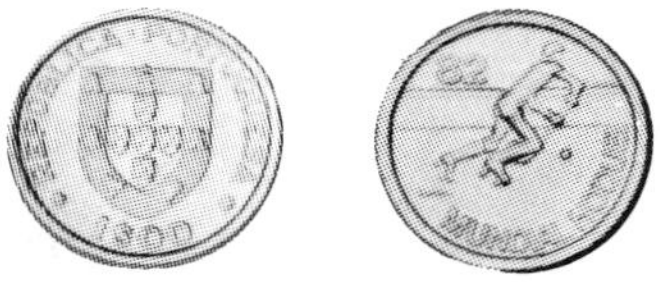

World Roller Hockey Championship Games

612	ND(1983)	1.990	—	.10	.20

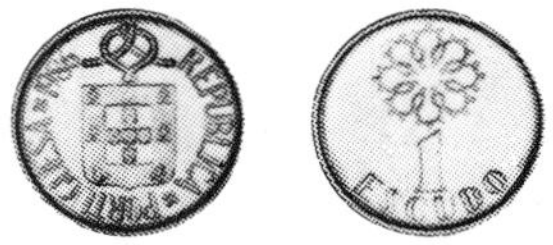

631	1986	14.882	—	.10	.20
	1987	21.922	—	.10	.20
	1988	17.168	—	.10	.20
	1989	17.194	—	.10	.20
	1990	19.008	—	.10	.20
	1991	21.500	—	—	.20
	1992	22.000	—	—	.20
	1993	10.505	—	—	.20
	1994	—	—	—	.20
	1996	—	—	—	.20
	1996	—	—	Proof	.50
	1997	—	—	—	.20
	1997	—	—	Proof	.50
	1998	—	—	—	1.00
	1998	—	—	Proof	2.00

2-1/2 ESCUDOS

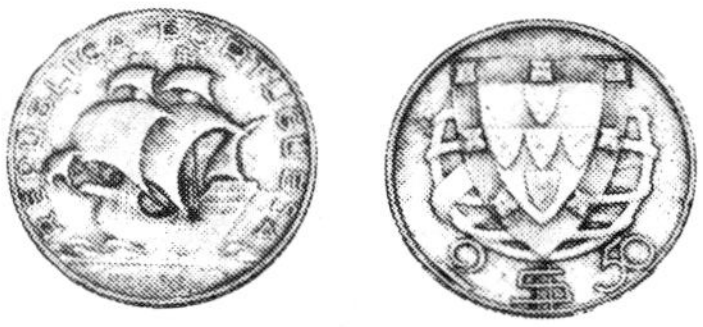

3.5000 g, .650 SILVER, .0731 oz ASW

KM#	Date	Mintage	Fine	VF	XF	Unc
580	1932	2.592	1.25	3.00	12.00	30.00
	1933	2.457	2.00	7.50	18.00	50.00
	1937	1.000	30.00	60.00	165.00	300.00
	1940	2.763	BV	2.50	6.00	16.50
	1942	3.847	BV	1.00	2.00	6.50
	1943	8.302	BV	1.00	1.50	4.00
	1944	9.134	BV	1.00	1.50	4.00
	1945	6.316	BV	1.00	2.00	7.00
	1946	3.208	BV	1.00	2.00	6.00
	1947	2.610	BV	1.00	2.00	6.00
	1948	1.814	2.00	5.00	10.00	25.00
	1951	4.000	BV	1.00	1.50	3.00

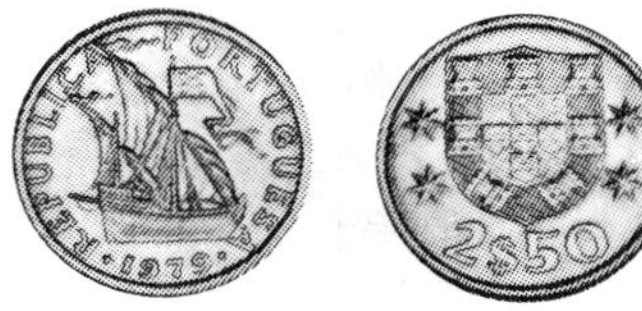

COPPER-NICKEL

KM#	Date	Mintage	VF	XF	Unc
590	1963	12.711	.10	.50	8.00
	1964	17.948	.10	.50	8.00
	1965	19.512	.10	.50	6.00
	1966	3.828	.50	1.50	20.00
	1967	5.545	.10	.50	5.00
	1968	6.087	.10	.20	2.00
	1969	9.969	.10	.20	1.50
	1970	2.400	.10	.20	1.50
	1971	6.791	.10	.20	1.50
	1972	6.713	.10	.20	1.50
	1973	9.104	.10	.20	.50
	1974	22.743	.10	.20	.50
	1975	16.624	.10	.20	.50
	1976	21.516	.10	.20	.40
	1977	45.726	.10	.20	.40
	1978	27.375	.10	.20	.40
	1979	44.804	.10	.20	.40
	1980	22.319	.10	.20	.40
	1981	25.420	.10	.20	.40
	1982	45.910	.10	.20	.40
	1983	62.946	.10	.20	.40
	1984	58.210	.10	.20	.40
	1985	60.142	.10	.20	.40

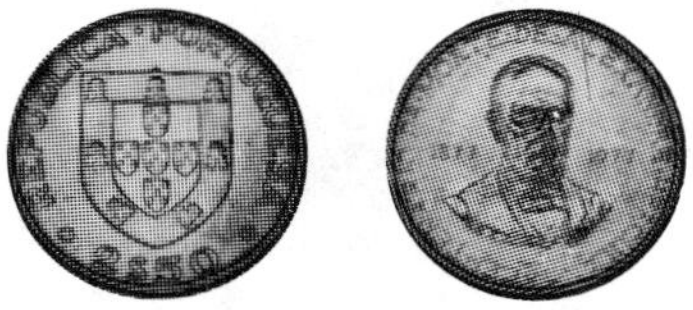

100th Anniversary - Death of Alexandre Herculano

605	ND(1977)	5.990	.15	.35	1.00
	ND(1977)	.013	—	Proof	2.00

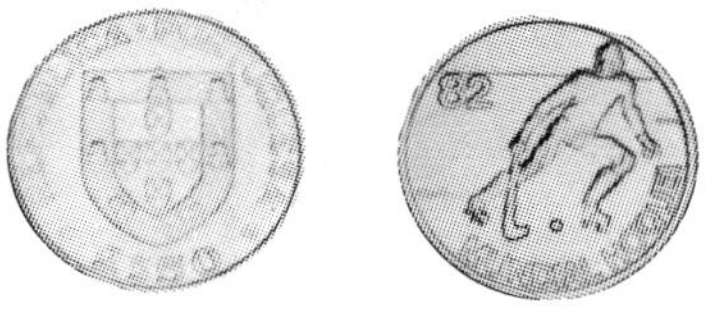

World Roller Hockey Championship Games

613	ND(1983)	1.990	—	.10	.50

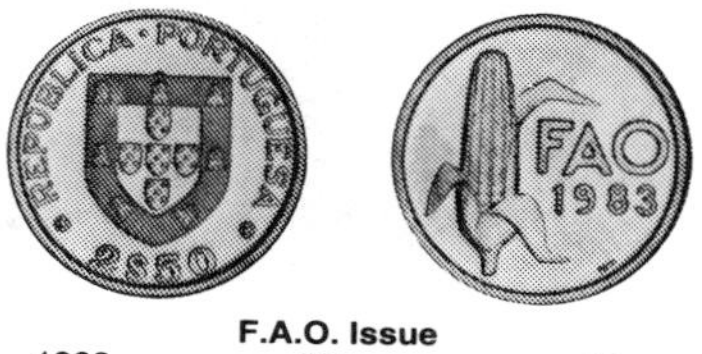

F.A.O. Issue

617	1983	.995	—	.10	.50

5 ESCUDOS

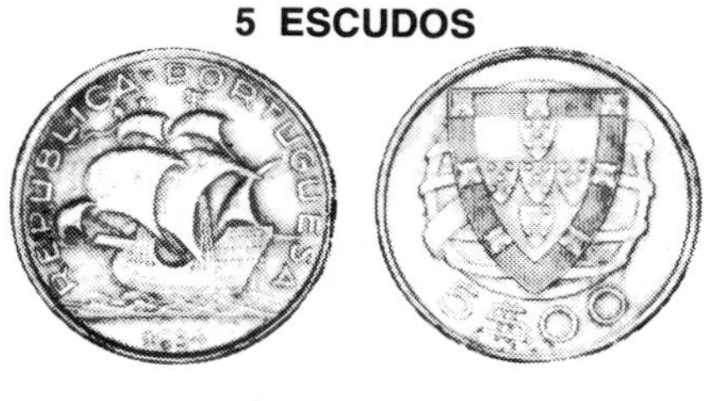

7.0000 g, .650 SILVER, .1463 oz ASW

KM#	Date	Mintage	Fine	VF	XF	Unc
581	1932	.800	3.50	9.00	30.00	115.00
	1933	6.717	BV	1.50	5.00	20.00
	1934	1.012	BV	2.75	10.00	27.50
	1937	1.500	7.00	18.00	50.00	135.00
	1940	1.500	BV	2.75	10.00	27.50
	1942	2.051	BV	2.00	3.00	8.00
	1943	1.354	BV	2.75	10.00	30.00
	1946	.404	2.50	3.50	6.50	20.00
	1947	2.420	BV	2.00	2.50	6.00
	1948	2.018	BV	2.00	2.50	6.00
	1951	.966	BV	2.00	2.50	5.00

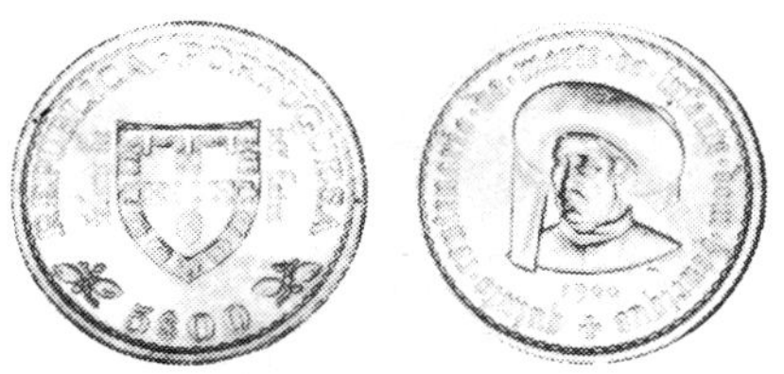

500th Anniversary - Death of

Prince Henry the Navigator

KM#	Date	Mintage	Fine	VF	XF	Unc
587	1960	.800	—	2.00	3.00	5.00
	1960	—	—	—	Matte	20.00

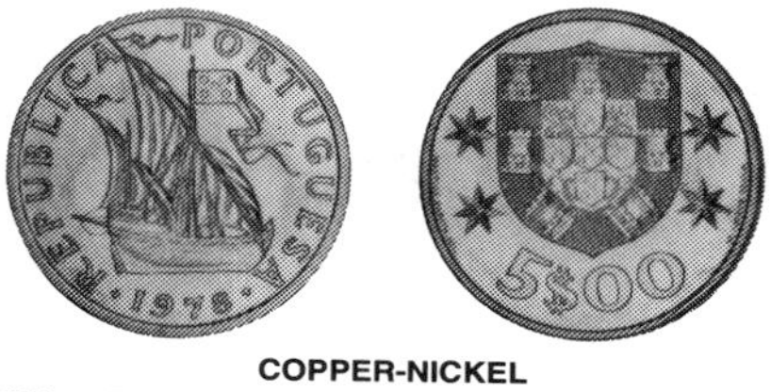

COPPER-NICKEL

KM#	Date	Mintage	VF	XF	Unc
591	1963	2.200	.10	2.00	10.00
	1964	4.268	.10	2.00	10.00
	1965	7.294	.10	2.00	10.00
	1966	8.120	.10	1.50	8.00
	1967	8.128	.10	1.00	4.00
	1968	5.023	.10	.50	2.00
	1969	3.571	.10	.50	2.00
	1970	1.200	.10	.50	2.00
	1971	2.721	.10	.50	1.00
	1972	1.880	.10	.50	2.00
	1973	2.836	.10	.50	1.00
	1974	3.984	.10	.25	.75
	1975	7.496	.10	.25	.75
	1976	11.379	.10	.25	.75
	1977	29.058	.10	.25	.75
	1978	.672	.50	1.00	3.00
	1979	19.546	.10	.25	.65
	1980	46.244	.10	.25	.65
	1981	15.267	.10	.25	.65
	1982	31.318	.10	.25	.65
	1983	51.056	.10	.25	.65
	1984	46.794	.10	.25	.65
	1985	45.441	.10	.25	.60
	1986	18.753	.10	.25	.60

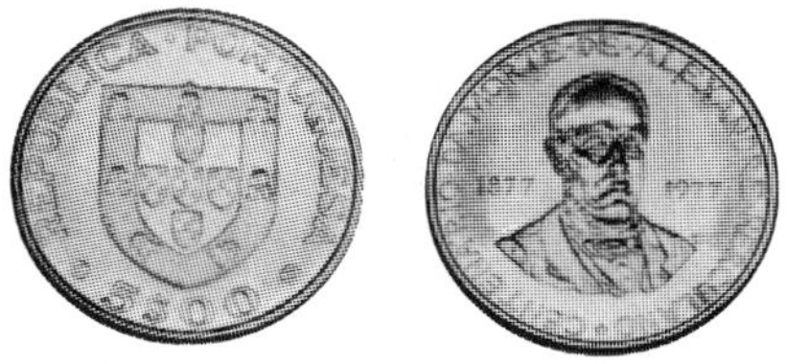

100th Anniversary - Death of Alexandre Herculano

606	ND(1977)	9.176	.35	.75	2.00
	ND(1977)	.010	—	Proof	4.00

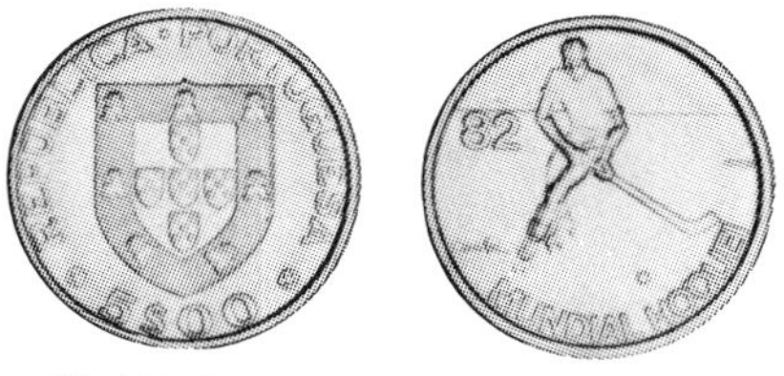

World Roller Hockey Championship Games

615	ND(1983)	1.990	.25	.50	1.00

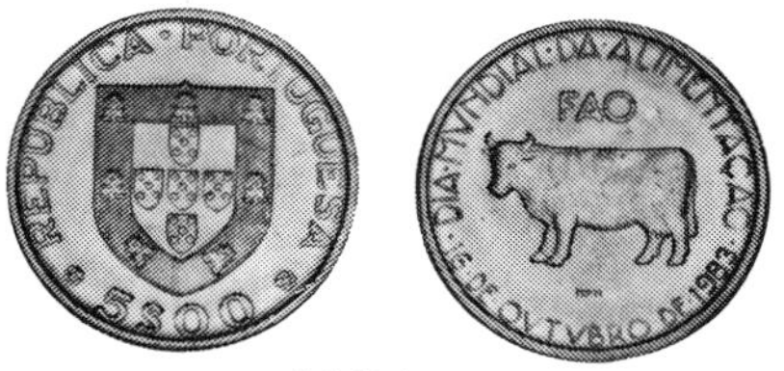

F.A.O. Issue

618	ND(1983)	.995	.30	.60	1.25

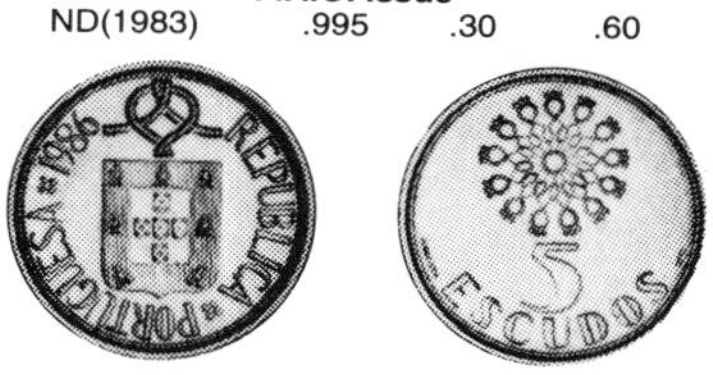

NICKEL-BRASS

632	1986	21.426	.10	.25	.50
	1987	40.548	.10	.25	.50
	1988	19.382	.10	.25	.50
	1989	27.641	.10	.25	.50
	1990	77.977	.10	.25	.50
	1991	32.000	—	—	.50
	1992	16.000	—	—	.50
	1993	8.300	—	—	.50
	1994	—	—	—	.50
	1996	—	—	—	.50
	1996	—	—	Proof	.75
	1997	—	—	—	.50
	1997	—	—	Proof	.75
	1998	—	—	—	1.00
	1998	—	—	Proof	2.00

10 ESCUDOS

12.5000 g, .835 SILVER, .3356 oz ASW
Battle of Ourique

KM#	Date	Mintage	Fine	VF	XF	Unc
579	1928	.200	6.00	12.00	18.00	40.00

KM#	Date	Mintage	Fine	VF	XF	Unc
582	1932	3.220	3.00	6.00	10.00	30.00
	1933	1.780	7.00	20.00	35.00	150.00
	1934	.400	5.00	7.50	20.00	60.00
	1937	.500	15.00	40.00	75.00	175.00
	1940	1.200	3.00	6.00	10.00	35.00
	1942	.186	45.00	100.00	200.00	350.00
	1948	.507	10.00	15.00	30.00	55.00

12.5000 g, .680 SILVER, .2732 oz ASW

KM#	Date	Mintage	Fine	VF	XF	Unc
586	1954	5.764	2.00	3.00	5.00	7.50
	1955	4.056	2.00	3.00	5.00	7.50

500th Anniversary - Death of
Prince Henry the Navigator

KM#	Date	Mintage	Fine	VF	XF	Unc
588	1960	.200	—	4.00	7.00	12.50
	1960	—	—	—	Matte	30.00

COPPER-NICKEL CLAD NICKEL

KM#	Date	Mintage	VF	XF	Unc
600	1971	3.876	.20	.40	2.00
	1972	2.694	.20	.40	2.00
	1973	5.418	.20	.40	2.00
	1974	4.043	.20	.40	2.00

NICKEL-BRASS

KM#	Date	Mintage	VF	XF	Unc
633	1986	12.818	.20	.40	1.00

KM#	Date	Mintage	VF	XF	Unc
633	1987	32.815	.20	.40	1.00
	1988	32.579	.20	.40	1.00
	1989	12.788	.20	.40	1.00
	1990	26.560	.20	.40	1.00
	1991	9.500	—	—	1.00
	1992	5.600	—	—	1.00
	1993	.020	In mint sets only		10.00
	1994	.020	In mint sets only		10.00
	1996	—	—	—	2.00
	1996	—	—	Proof	2.50
	1997	—	—	—	2.00
	1997	—	—	Proof	2.50
	1998	—	—	—	2.50
	1998	—	—	Proof	3.00

Rural World

638	1987	2.000	.40	.60	1.50

20 ESCUDOS

21.0000 g, .800 SILVER, .5401 oz ASW
25th Anniversary of Financial Reform

585	1953	1.000	4.00	6.00	8.00
	1953	—		Matte	—

NOTE: A small quantity of KM#585, 587, 588, 589 & 592 were later given a matte finish by the Lisbon Mint on private contract.

500th Anniversary - Death of
Prince Henry the Navigator

589	1960	.200	8.00	16.00	28.00
	1960	—	—	Matte	60.00

10.0000 g, .650 SILVER, .2090 oz ASW
Opening of Salazar Bridge

592	1966	2.000	2.00	3.00	4.50
	1966	200 pcs.	—	Matte	35.00

COPPER-NICKEL

KM#	Date	Mintage	VF	XF	Unc
634	1986	45.361	.15	.25	1.00
	1987	68.216	.15	.25	1.00
	1988	57.482	.15	.25	1.00
	1989	25.060	.15	.25	1.00
	1990	.050	In mint sets only		10.00
	1991	.050	In mint sets only		10.00
	1992	.020	In mint sets only		10.00
	1993	.020	In mint sets only		10.00
	1994	.020	In mint sets only		10.00
	1996	—	In mint sets only		10.00
	1996	—	—	Proof	2.50
	1997	—	In mint sets only		10.00
	1997	—	—	Proof	2.50
	1998	—	—	—	3.00
	1998	—	—	Proof	4.00

25 ESCUDOS

COPPER-NICKEL

607	1977	7.657	.40	.80	1.75
	1978	12.277	.40	.80	1.75

100th Anniversary - Death of Alexandre Herculano

608	ND(1977)	5.990	.50	1.00	2.50
	ND(1977)	.013	—	Proof	8.00

International Year of the Child

609	1979	.990	.50	1.00	2.50
	1979	.010	—	P/L	8.00

Increased size, 28.5mm.

610	1980	.750	.40	.80	1.75
	1981	19.924	.40	.80	1.75
	1982	12.158	.40	.80	1.75
	1983	5.622	.40	.80	1.75
	1984	3.453	.40	.80	1.75
	1985	25.027	.40	.80	1.75
	1986	—	.40	.80	1.75

World Roller Hockey Championship Games

KM#	Date	Mintage	VF	XF	Unc
616	ND(1983)	1.990	.50	1.00	2.50

F.A.O. Issue

619	1983	.995	.60	1.25	3.00

10th Anniversary of Revolution
Obv: Waves breaking over arms. Rev: Stylized 25.

623	1984	1.980	.40	.75	1.75

International Year of Disabled Persons

624	ND(1984)	1.990	.40	.75	1.75

600th Anniversary - Battle of Aljubarrota

627	ND(1985)	.500	.50	1.00	2.75

COPPER-NICKEL
Admission to European Common Market

635	1986	4.990	.40	.75	2.00

50 ESCUDOS

18.0000 g, .650 SILVER, .3761 oz ASW
500th Anniversary - Birth of Pedro Alvares Cabral

KM#	Date	Mintage	VF	XF	Unc
593	1968	1.000	—	—	6.00
	1968	400 pcs.	—	Matte	28.00

NOTE: A small quantity of KM593, 598, 599, 601 & 602 were later given a matte finish by the Lisbon Mint on private contract.

500th Anniversary - Birth of Vasco Da Gama

598	ND(1969)	1.000	—	—	6.00
	ND(1969)	400 pcs.	—	Matte	28.00

Centennial - Birth of Marshal Carmona

599	ND(1969)	.500	—	—	6.00
	ND(1969)	400 pcs.	—	Matte	28.00

125th Anniversary - Bank of Portugal

601	ND(1971)	.500	—	—	6.00
	ND(1971)	—	—	Matte	28.00

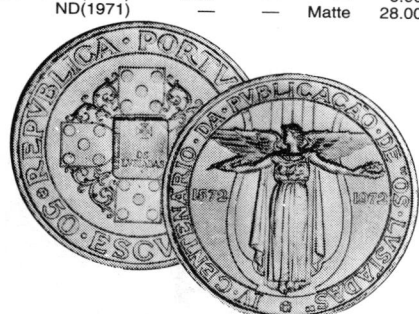

400th Anniversary of Heroic Epic 'Os Lusiadas'

602	ND(1972)	1.000	—	—	6.00
	ND(1972)	—	—	Matte	28.00

COPPER-NICKEL

KM#	Date	Mintage	VF	XF	Unc
636	1986	51.110	—	—	3.00
	1987	28.248	—	—	3.00
	1988	41.905	—	—	3.00
	1989	18.327	—	—	3.00
	1990	.050	In mint sets only		15.00
	1991	2.000	—	—	3.00
	1992	.020	In mint sets only		15.00
	1993	.020	In mint sets only		15.00
	1994	.020	In mint sets only		15.00
	1995	.020	In mint sets only		15.00
	1996	—	In mint sets only		8.00
	1996	—		Proof	5.00
	1997	—	In mint sets only		8.00
	1997	—	—	Proof	5.00
	1997	—	—		5.00
	1997	—	—	Proof	6.00

100 ESCUDOS

18.0000 g, .650 SILVER, .3762 oz ASW
1974 Revolution

603	ND(1976)	.950	—	—	5.00
	ND(1976)	.010	—	Proof	15.00

COPPER-NICKEL
International Year of Disabled Persons

625	ND(1984)	.990	.75	1.00	3.50

50th Anniversary - Death of Fernando Pessoa - Poet

628	1985	.480	.75	1.00	4.00

800th Anniversary - Death of
King Alfonso Henriques

629	1985	.500	.75	1.00	3.00

600th Anniversary - Battle of Aljubarrota

KM#	Date	Mintage	VF	XF	Unc
630	ND(1985)	.500	.75	1.00	3.50

World Cup Soccer - Mexico

637	1986	.500	.75	1.00	3.50

Golden Age of Portuguese Discoveries - Gil Eanes

639	1987	1.000	.75	1.00	3.50

Golden Age of Portuguese Discoveries - Nuno Tristao

640	1987	1.000	.75	1.00	3.50

Golden Age of Portuguese Discoveries - Diogo Cao

641	1987	1.000	.75	1.00	3.50

Amadeo De Souza Cardoso

644	1987	.800	.75	1.00	3.50

Golden Age of Portuguese Discoveries - Bartolomeu Dias

KM#	Date	Mintage	VF	XF	Unc
642	ND(1988)	1.000	.75	1.00	3.50

**ALUMINUM-BRONZE center,
COPPER-NICKEL ring
Pedro Nunes
Edge: 5 reeded and 5 plain sections.**

645.1	1989	20.000	—	1.00	2.25
	1990	52.000	—	1.00	2.25
	1991	45.500	—	1.00	2.25
	1992	14.500	—	1.00	2.25
	1993	.020	In mint sets only		15.00
	1994	.020	In mint sets only		15.00
	1996	—	In mint sets only		15.00
	1996	—	—	Proof	10.00
	1997	—	—		7.00
	1997	—	—	Proof	10.00
	1998	—	—		7.00
	1998	—	—	Proof	10.00

Edge: 6 reeded and 6 plain sections.

645.2	1989	—	—	1.00	2.25
	1990	—	—	1.50	3.75
	1991	—	—	1.00	2.25

**COPPER-NICKEL
Discovery of the Canary Islands**

646	1989	2.000	—	—	4.50

Discovery of Madeira

647	1989	2.000	—	—	4.50

Discovery of the Azores

648	ND(1989)	2.000	—	—	4.50

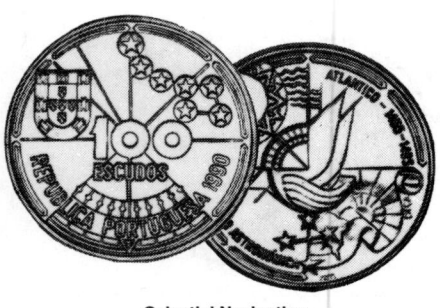

Celestial Navigation

KM#	Date	Mintage	VF	XF	Unc
649	1990	2.000	—	—	4.50

350th Anniversary - Restoration of Portuguese Independence

651	ND(1990)	1.000	—	—	4.50

Camilo Castelo Branco

656	1990	1.000	—	—	3.50

**COPPER-NICKEL ring,
ALUMINUM-BRONZE center
50th Anniversary - F.A.O.**

678	1995	.500	—	—	4.00
	1995	.017	In Proof sets only		15.00

**COPPER-NICKEL
400th Anniversary - Antonio Prior de Crato**

680	ND(1995)	—	—	—	3.50

**ALUMINUM-BRONZE center in
COPPER-NICKEL ring**

Lisbon World Expo '98 - Sea Lion
Obv: National arms and denomination.

KM#	Date	Mintage	VF	XF	Unc
693	1997	—	—	—	3.50
	1997	7,000	In mint sets only		15.00

200 ESCUDOS

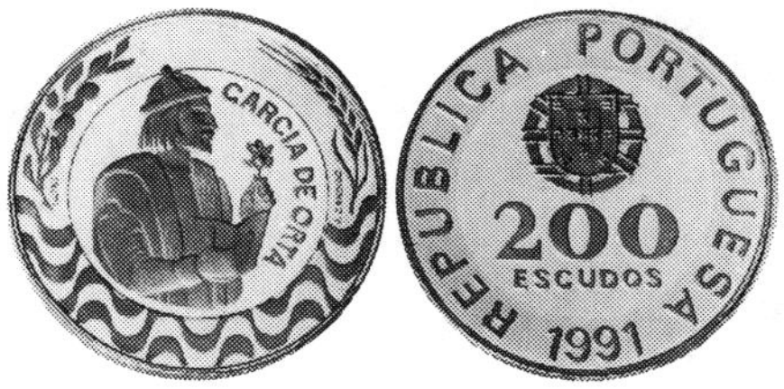

COPPER-NICKEL center, ALUMINUM-BRONZE ring
Garcia De Orta

655	1991	33.000	—	—	4.50
	1992	11.000	—	—	4.50
	1993	.020	In mint sets only		18.00
	1996	—	In mint sets only		18.00
	1996	—	—	Proof	20.00
	1997	—	—	—	12.50
	1997	—	—	Proof	20.00
	1998	—	—	—	12.50
	1998	—	—	Proof	20.00

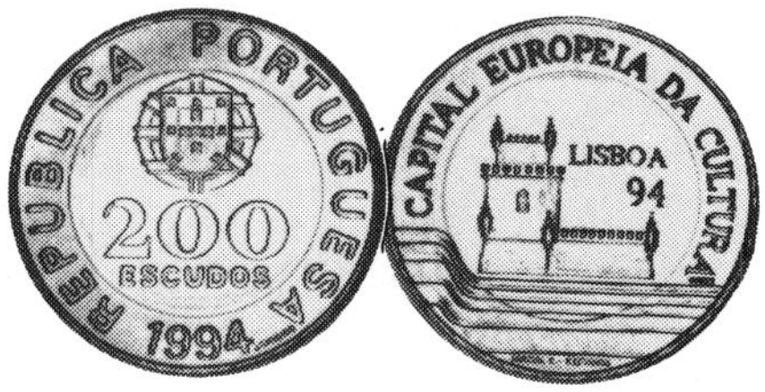

ALUMINUM-BRONZE ring, COPPER-NICKEL center
Lisbon - European Cultural Capital

669	1994	1.000	—	—	5.50
	1994	7,000		Proof sets	20.00

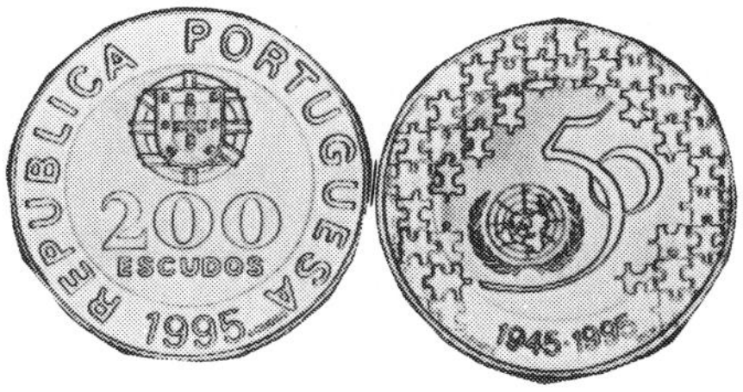

50th Anniversary - United Nations

679	1995	.500	—	—	5.50
	1995	.017		Proof sets	20.00

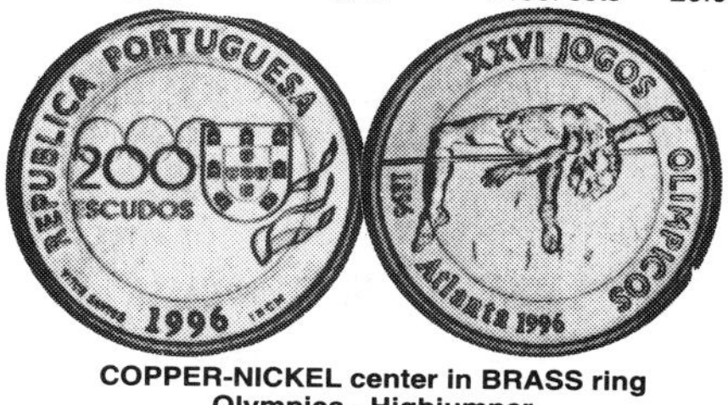

COPPER-NICKEL center in BRASS ring
Olympics - Highjumper

687	1996	—	—	—	4.50
	1996	—	—	Proof	20.00

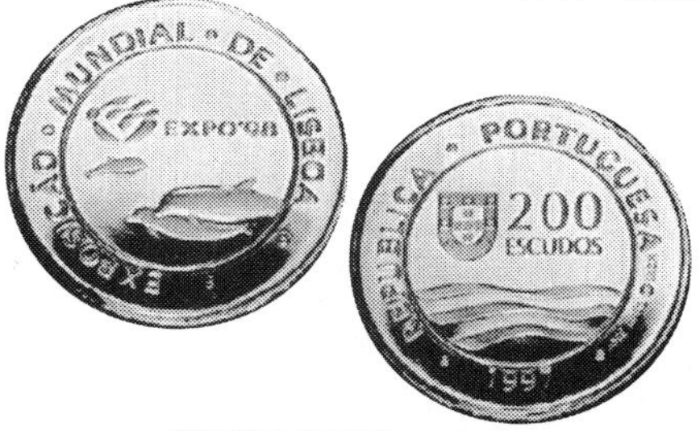

COPPER-NICKEL center in COPPER-ALUMINUM ring
Lisbon World Expo '98 - Dolphins
Obv: National arms and denomination.

694	1997	—	—	—	4.50
	1997	7,000	In Proof sets only		20.00

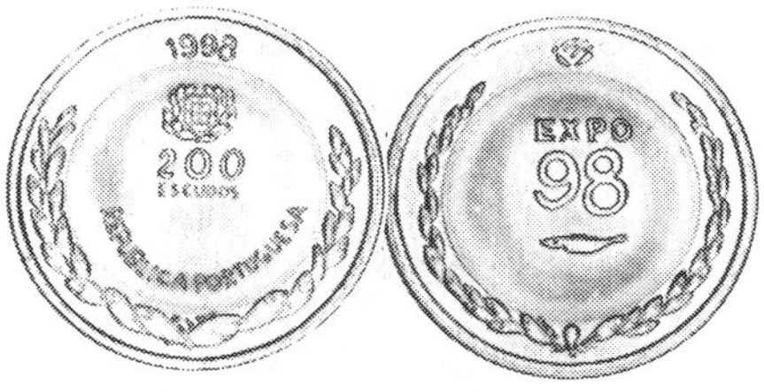

COPPER-NICKEL center in ALUMINUM-BRONZE ring
International Year of the Oceans Expo
Obv: Arms above denominations.

KM#	Date	Mintage	VF	XF	Unc
706	1998				
		*.050 (in sets only)	—	—	8.00
	1998	*.020	In Proof sets only		12.00

QATAR

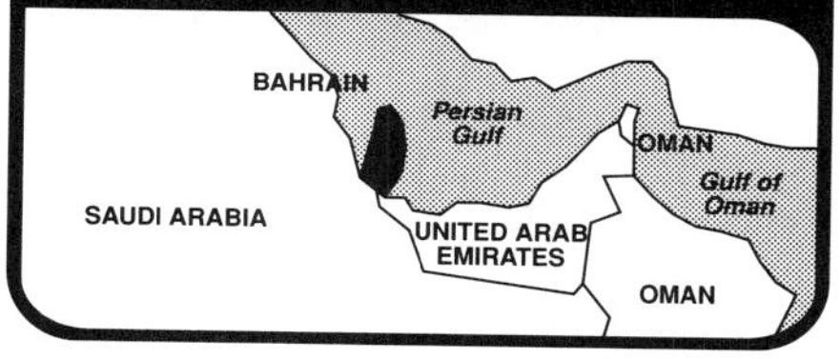

The State of Qatar, an emirate in the Persian Gulf between Bahrain and Trucial Oman, has an area of 4,247 sq. mi. (11,000 sq. km.) and a population of *469,000. Capital: Doha. Oil is the chief industry and export.

Qatar was under Turkish control from 1872 until the beginning of World War I when the Ottoman Turks evacuated the Qatar Peninsula. In 1916 Sheikh Abdullah placed Qatar under the protection of Great Britain and gave Britain responsibility for its defense and foreign relations. Qatar joined with Dubai in a Monetary Union and issued coins and paper money in 1966 and 1969. When Britain announced in 1968 that it would end treaty relationships with the Persian Gulf sheikhdoms in 1971, this union was dissolved, Qatar joined Bahrain and the seven trucial sheikhdoms (the latter now called the United Arab Emirates) in an effort to form a union of Arab Emirates. However the nine sheikhdoms were unable to agree on terms of union, and Qatar declared its independence as the State of Qatar on Sept. 3, 1971.

TITLES

دولة قطر

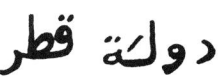

Daulat Qatar

RULERS

Al-Thani Dynasty

Qasim Bin Muhammad, 1876-1913
Abdullah Bin Qasim, 1913-1948
Ali Bin Abdullah, 1948-1960
Ahmad Bin Ali, 1960-1972
Khalifah bin Hamad, 1972-1995
Hamad bin Khalifah, 1995-

MONETARY SYSTEM

100 Dirhem = 1 Riyal

DIRHEM

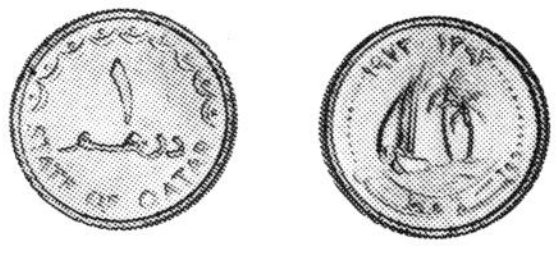

BRONZE

KM#	Date	Year	Mintage	VF	XF	Unc
2	AH1393	1973	.500	.10	.20	.50

5 DIRHEMS

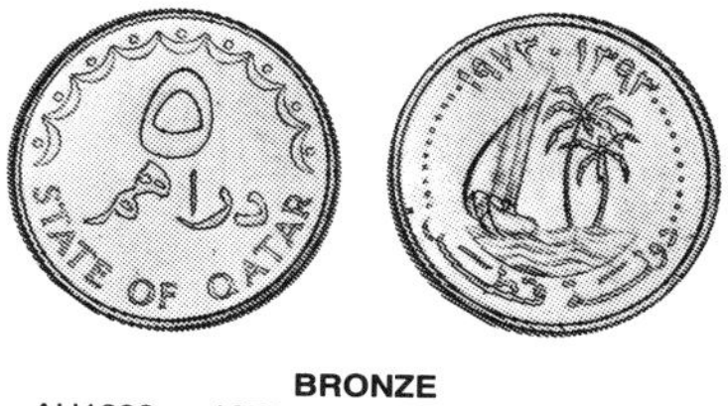

BRONZE

3	AH1393	1973	1.000	.10	.20	.65
	1398	1978	1.000	.10	.20	.65

10 DIRHEMS

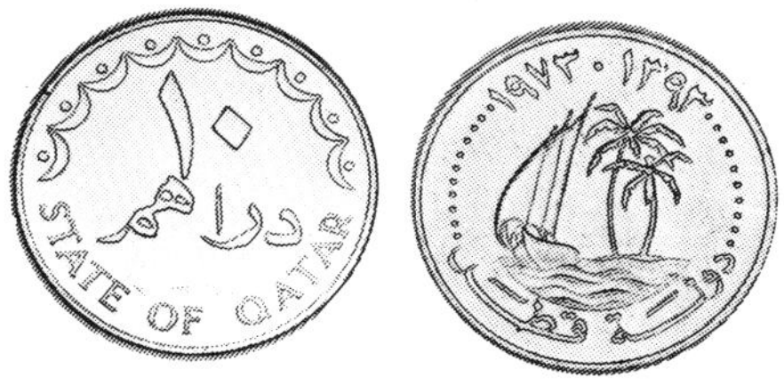

BRONZE

1	AH1392	1972	1.500	.20	.40	1.00
	1393	1973	1.500	.20	.40	1.00

25 DIRHEMS

COPPER-NICKEL

KM#	Date	Year	Mintage	VF	XF	Unc
4	AH1393	1973	1.500	.25	.50	1.25
	1396	1976	2.000	.25	.50	1.50
	1398	1978	—	.25	.50	1.50
	1401	1981	—	.25	.50	1.50
	1407	1987	—	.25	.50	1.50
	1410	1990	—	.25	.50	1.50
	1414	1993	—	.25	.50	1.50

50 DIRHEMS

COPPER-NICKEL

KM#	Date	Year	Mintage	VF	XF	Unc
5	AH1393	1973	1.500	.40	.80	1.75
	1398	1978	2.000	.40	.80	2.00
	1401	1981	—	.40	.80	2.00
	1407	1987	—	.40	.80	2.00
	1410	1990	—	.40	.80	2.00
	1414	1993	—	.40	.80	2.00

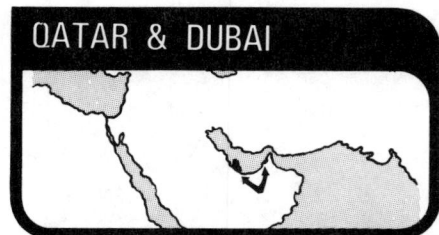

QATAR & DUBAI

The State of Qatar, which occupies the Qatar Peninsula jutting into the Persian Gulf from eastern Saudi Arabia, has an area of 4,247 sq. mi. (11,000 sq. km.) and a population of *469,000. Capital: Doha. The traditional occupations of pearling, fishing, and herding have been replaced in economics by petroleum-related industries. Crude oil, petroleum products, and tomatoes are exported.

Dubai is one of the seven sheikhdoms comprising the United Arab Emirates (formerly Trucial States) located along the southern shore of the Persian Gulf. It has a population of about 60,000. Capital (of the United Arab Emirates): Abu Dhabi.

Qatar, which initiated protective treaty relations with Great Britain in 1916, achieved independence on Sept. 3, 1971, upon withdrawal of the British military presence from the Persian Gulf, and replaced its special treaty arrangement with Britain with a treaty of general friendship. Dubai attained independence on Dec. 1, 1971, upon termination of Britain's protective treaty with the trucial Sheikhdoms, and on Dec. 2, 1971, entered into the union of the United Arab Emirates.

Despite the fact that the Emirate of Qatar and the Sheikhdom of Dubai were merged under a monetary union, the two territories were governed independently from each other. Qatar now uses its own currency while Dubai uses the United Arab Emirates currency and coins.

TITLES

Qatar Wa Dubai   قطر ودبي

RULERS

Ahmad II, 1960-1972

MONETARY SYSTEM

100 Dirhem = 1 Riyal

DIRHEM

BRONZE
Obv: Denomination. Rev: Goitered gazelle.

KM#	Date	Year	Mintage	VF	XF	Unc
1	AH1386	1966	1.000	.10	.20	.50

5 DIRHEMS

BRONZE
Obv: Denomination. Rev: Goitered gazelle.

2	AH1386	1966	2.000	.10	.20	.65
	1389	1969	2.000	.10	.20	.65

10 DIRHEMS

BRONZE
Obv: Denomination. Rev: Goitered gazelle.

3	AH1386	1966	2.000	.20	.40	1.00

25 DIRHEMS

COPPER-NICKEL

Obv: Denomination. Rev: Goitered gazelle.

KM#	Date	Year	Mintage	VF	XF	Unc
4	AH1386	1966	2.000	.25	.50	1.50
	1389	1969	2.000	.25	.50	1.50

50 DIRHEMS

COPPER-NICKEL
Obv: Denomination. Rev: Goitered gazelle.

5	AH1386	1966	2.000	.40	.80	2.00

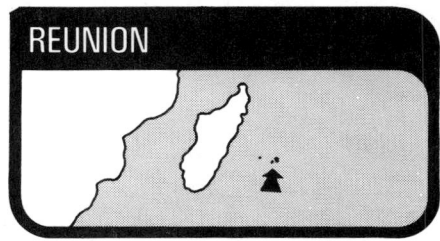

REUNION

The Department of Reunion, an overseas department of France located in the Indian Ocean 400 miles (640 km.) east of Madagascar, has an area of 969 sq. mi. (2,510 sq. km.) and a population of *566,000. Capital: Saint-Denis. The island's volcanic soil is extremely fertile. Sugar, vanilla, coffee and rum are exported.

Although first visited by Portuguese navigators in the 16th century, Reunion was uninhabited when claimed for France by Capt. Goubert in 1638. It was first colonized as Isle de Bourbon by the French in 1662 as a layover station for ships rounding the Cape of Good Hope to India. It was renamed Reunion in 1793. The island remained in French possession except for the period of 1810-15, when it was occupied by the British. Reunion became an overseas department of France in 1946, and in 1958 voted to continue that status within the new French Union.

During the first half of the 19th century, Reunion was officially known as Isle de Bonaparte (1801-14) and Isle de Bourbon (1814-48). Reunion coinage of those periods is so designated.

MINT MARKS
(a) - Paris, privy marks only

MONETARY SYSTEM
100 Centimes = 1 Franc

FRANC

ALUMINUM
KM#	Date	Mintage	VF	XF	Unc
6.1	1948(a)	3.000	.35	.60	2.00
	1964(a)	1.000	.35	.60	2.50
	1968(a)	.450	.60	1.25	4.00
	1969(a)	.500	.60	.85	3.00
	1971(a)	.800	.60	.85	2.50
	1973(a)	.500	.60	.85	3.00

Thinner Planchet
| 6.2 | 1969(a) | Inc. Ab. | .75 | 1.50 | 4.50 |

Mule. Obv: French Colonial. Rev: KM#6.1.
| 7 | 1948(a) | Inc. Ab. | — | — | — |

2 FRANCS

ALUMINUM
8	1948(a)	2.000	.35	.85	3.00
	1968(a)	.100	3.00	5.00	10.00
	1969(a)	.150	1.75	3.50	6.50
	1970(a)	.300	.85	1.75	3.50
	1971(a)	.300	.85	1.75	3.50
	1973(a)	.500	.85	1.75	3.50

5 FRANCS

ALUMINUM
KM#	Date	Mintage	VF	XF	Unc
9	1955(a)	3.000	.60	1.00	2.50
	1969(a)	.100	2.50	5.00	9.00
	1970(a)	.200	1.75	3.50	6.50
	1971(a)	.100	1.75	3.50	6.50
	1972(a)	.300	.85	1.75	3.00
	1973(a)	.250	.85	1.75	3.00

10 FRANCS

ALUMINUM-BRONZE
10	1955(a)	1.500	.45	.75	2.50
	1962(a)	.700	1.75	3.50	6.50
	1964(a)	1.000	.45	.75	2.50

ALUMINUM-NICKEL-BRONZE
10a	1964(a)	Inc. Ab.	.45	.75	2.50
	1969(a)	.300	1.25	2.50	5.50
	1970(a)	.300	1.25	2.50	4.50
	1971(a)	.200	1.75	3.75	7.50
	1972(a)	.400	1.25	2.50	5.50
	1973(a)	.700	.85	1.75	3.00

20 FRANCS

ALUMINUM-BRONZE
11	1955(a)	1.250	.75	1.50	3.50
	1960(a)	.100	3.00	6.00	12.00
	1961(a)	.300	2.50	4.75	8.00
	1962(a)	.190	2.75	5.50	9.00
	1964(a)	.750	.75	1.50	3.00

ALUMINUM-NICKEL-BRONZE
11a	1969(a)	.200	2.75	5.50	9.00
	1970(a)	.200	2.75	5.50	9.00
	1971(a)	.200	2.75	5.50	9.00
	1972(a)	.300	2.00	3.50	6.50
	1973(a)	.550	.75	1.50	3.00

50 FRANCS

NICKEL
12	1962(a)	1.000	1.50	2.50	4.50
	1964(a)	.500	2.00	3.00	5.50
	1969(a)	.100	2.75	5.00	8.50
	1970(a)	.100	2.75	5.00	8.50
	1973(a)	.350	2.00	3.50	6.00

100 FRANCS

NICKEL
13	1964(a)	2.000	1.00	2.00	3.50
	1969(a)	.200	2.25	4.50	7.00
	1970(a)	.150	2.25	5.00	8.50
	1971(a)	.100	2.75	6.00	12.50
	1972(a)	.400	2.00	3.50	5.50
	1973(a)	.200	2.25	4.50	7.00

RHODESIA

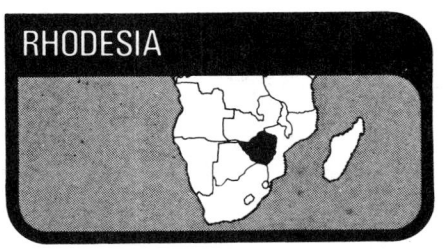

Rhodesia (never recognized by the British government and was referred to as Southern Rhodesia, now Zimbabwe) located in the east-central part of southern Africa, has an area of 150,804 sq. mi. (390,580 sq. km.) and a population of 9.9 million. Capital: Harare. The economy is based on agriculture and mining. Tobacco, sugar, asbestos, copper and chrome ore and coal are exported.

The Rhodesian area, the habitat of paleolithic man, contains extensive evidence of earlier civilizations, notably the world-famous ruins of Zimbabwe, a gold-trading center that flourished about the 14th or 15th century AD. The Portuguese of the 16th century were the first Europeans to attempt to develop south-central Africa, but it remained for Cecil Rhodes and the British South Africa Co. to open the hinterlands. Rhodes obtained a concession for mineral rights from local chiefs in 1888 and administered his African empire (named Southern Rhodesia in 1895) through the British South Africa Co. until 1923, when the British government annexed the area after the white settlers voted for existence as a separate colony, rather than for incorporation into the Union of South Africa.

RULERS
British, until 1966

MONETARY SYSTEM
12 Pence = 1 Shilling = 10 Cents
10 Shillings = 1 Dollar
20 Shillings = 1 Pound

3 PENCE = 2-1/2 CENTS

COPPER-NICKEL
KM#	Date	Mintage	Fine	VF	XF	Unc
8	1968	2.400	.25	.50	.75	2.00
	1968	10 pcs.	—	—	Proof	1000.

6 PENCE = 5 CENTS

COPPER-NICKEL
Flame Lily
1	1964	13.500	.15	.25	.40	1.25
	1964	2,060	—	—	Proof	10.00

SHILLING = 10 CENTS

COPPER-NICKEL
2	1964	15.500	.15	.25	.65	1.50
	1964	2,060	—	—	Proof	10.00

2 SHILLINGS = 20 CENTS

COPPER-NICKEL
Bird Sculpture

KM#	Date	Mintage	Fine	VF	XF	Unc
3	1964	10.500	.25	.50	1.25	3.00
	1964	2,060	—	—	Proof	12.50

REPUBLIC
MONETARY SYSTEM
100 Cents = 1 Dollar

1/2 CENT

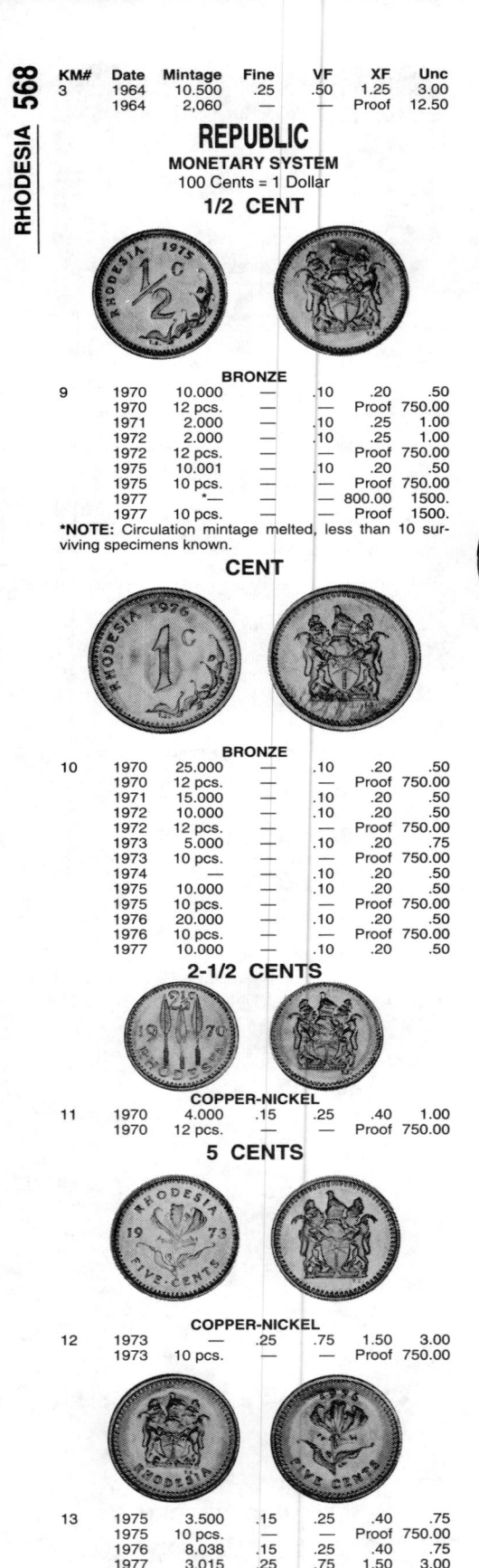

BRONZE

KM#	Date	Mintage	Fine	VF	XF	Unc
9	1970	10.000	—	.10	.20	.50
	1970	12 pcs.	—	—	Proof	750.00
	1971	2.000	—	.10	.25	1.00
	1972	2.000	—	.10	.25	1.00
	1972	12 pcs.	—	—	Proof	750.00
	1975	10.001	—	.10	.20	.50
	1975	10 pcs.	—	—	Proof	750.00
	1977	*—	—	—	800.00	1500.
	1977	10 pcs.	—	—	Proof	1500.

*NOTE: Circulation mintage melted, less than 10 surviving specimens known.

CENT

BRONZE

KM#	Date	Mintage	Fine	VF	XF	Unc
10	1970	25.000	—	.10	.20	.50
	1970	12 pcs.	—	—	Proof	750.00
	1971	15.000	—	.10	.20	.50
	1972	10.000	—	.10	.20	.50
	1972	12 pcs.	—	—	Proof	750.00
	1973	5.000	—	.10	.20	.75
	1973	10 pcs.	—	—	Proof	750.00
	1974	—	—	.10	.20	.50
	1975	10.000	—	.10	.20	.50
	1975	10 pcs.	—	—	Proof	750.00
	1976	20.000	—	.10	.20	.50
	1976	10 pcs.	—	—	Proof	750.00
	1977	10.000	—	.10	.20	.50

2-1/2 CENTS

COPPER-NICKEL

KM#	Date	Mintage	Fine	VF	XF	Unc
11	1970	4.000	.15	.25	.40	1.00
	1970	12 pcs.	—	—	Proof	750.00

5 CENTS

COPPER-NICKEL

KM#	Date	Mintage	Fine	VF	XF	Unc
12	1973	—	.25	.75	1.50	3.00
	1973	10 pcs.	—	—	Proof	750.00

KM#	Date	Mintage	Fine	VF	XF	Unc
13	1975	3.500	.15	.25	.40	.75
	1975	10 pcs.	—	—	Proof	750.00
	1976	8.038	.15	.25	.40	.75
	1977	3.015	.25	.75	1.50	3.00

10 CENTS

KM#	Date	Mintage	Fine	VF	XF	Unc
	COPPER-NICKEL					
14	1975	2.003	.15	.30	.60	1.50
	1975	10 pcs.	—	—	Proof	750.00

20 CENTS

COPPER-NICKEL

KM#	Date	Mintage	Fine	VF	XF	Unc
15	1975	1.937	.50	.75	1.00	3.00
	1975	10 pcs.	—	—	Proof	750.00
	1977	—	.50	.75	1.50	3.50

25 CENTS

COPPER-NICKEL

KM#	Date	Mintage	Fine	VF	XF	Unc
16	1975	1.011	.50	1.00	2.00	4.00
	1975	10 pcs.	—	—	Proof	750.00

RHODESIA & NYASALAND

The Federation of Rhodesia and Nyasaland was located in the east-central part of southern Africa. The multiracial federation has an area of about 487,000 sq. mi. (1,261,330 sq. km.) and a population of 6.8 million. Capital: Salisbury, in Southern Rhodesia.

The geographical unity of the three British possessions suggested the desirability of political and economic union as early as 1924. Despite objections by the African constituency of Northern Rhodesia and Nyasaland, who feared that African self-determination would be retarded by the dominant influence of prosperous and self-governing Southern Rhodesia. The Central African Federation was established in Sept. of 1953. As feared, the Federation was effectively and profitably dominated by the European constituency of Southern Rhodesia despite the fact that the three component countries largely retained their prefederation political structure. It was dissolved at the end of 1963, largely because of the effective opposition of the Nyasaland African Congress. Northern Rhodesia and Nyasaland became the independent states of Zambia and Malawi in 1964. Southern Rhodesia unilaterally declared its independence the following year which was not recognized by the British Government.

The coinage is obsolete.

For earlier coinage refer to Southern Rhodesia. For later coinage refer to Malawi, Zambia, Rhodesia and Zimbabwe.

RULERS
Elizabeth II, 1952-1964

MONETARY SYSTEM
12 Pence = 1 Shilling
5 Shillings = 1 Crown
20 Shillings = 1 Pound

1/2 PENNY

BRONZE
Giraffes

KM#	Date	Mintage	Fine	VF	XF	Unc
1	1955	.720	.15	.25	.50	2.50
	1955	2,010	—	—	Proof	5.00
	1956	.480	.20	.50	1.00	3.00
	1956	—	—	—	Proof	400.00
	1957	1.920	.10	.15	.25	2.00
	1957	—	—	—	Proof	400.00
	1958	2.400	.10	.15	.25	2.00
	1958	—	—	—	Proof	400.00
	1964	1.440	.10	.15	.25	2.00

PENNY

BRONZE
Elephants

KM#	Date	Mintage	Fine	VF	XF	Unc
2	1955	2.040	.15	.25	.75	3.00
	1955	2,010	—	—	Proof	5.00
	1956	4.800	.15	.25	.50	2.50
	1956	—	—	—	Proof	400.00
	1957	7.200	.10	.15	.25	2.00
	1957	—	—	—	Proof	—
	1958	2.880	.10	.15	.25	2.00
	1958	—	—	—	Proof	400.00
	1961	4.800	.10	.15	.25	1.50
	1961	—	—	—	Proof	—
	1962	6.000	.10	.15	.25	1.50
	1963	6.000	.10	.15	.25	1.50
	1963	—	—	—	Proof	400.00

3 PENCE

COPPER-NICKEL
Flame Lily

3	1955	1.200	.20	.50	1.00	4.00
	1955	10 pcs.	—	—	Proof	400.00
	1956	3.200	.50	1.00	2.50	20.00
	1956	—	—	—	Proof	600.00
	1957	6.000	.20	.50	.75	3.00
	1957	—	—	—	Proof	600.00
	1962	4.000	.20	.50	.75	3.00
	1962	—	—	—	Proof	—
	1963	2.000	.20	.50	.75	3.00
	1963	—	—	—	Proof	—
	1964	3.600	.15	.25	.50	1.50

6 PENCE

COPPER-NICKEL
Lion

4	1955	.400	.50	1.00	2.50	7.50
	1955	10 pcs.	—	—	Proof	400.00
	1956	.800	.75	2.00	7.00	40.00
	1956	—	—	—	Proof	—
	1957	4.000	.20	.50	1.00	4.00
	1957	—	—	—	Proof	—
	1962	2.800	.20	.50	1.00	4.00
	1962	—	—	—	Proof	—
	1963	.800	5.00	10.00	20.00	45.00
	1963	—	—	—	Proof	—

SHILLING

COPPER-NICKEL
Antelope

5	1955	.200	1.50	2.50	7.00	18.00
	1955	10 pcs.	—	—	Proof	400.00
	1956	1.700	.75	1.50	3.50	30.00
	1956	—	—	—	Proof	—
	1957	3.500	.50	1.00	2.50	8.00
	1957	—	—	—	Proof	—

2 SHILLINGS

COPPER-NICKEL
African Fish Eagle

6	1955	1.750	1.25	2.50	5.00	12.50
	1955	10 pcs.	—	—	Proof	400.00
	1956	1.850	1.25	2.50	4.50	12.00
	1956	—	—	—	Proof	—
	1957	1.500	1.25	2.50	4.50	12.00
	1957	—	—	—	Proof	—

1/2 CROWN

COPPER-NICKEL

KM#	Date	Mintage	Fine	VF	XF	Unc
7	1955	1.600	1.50	3.00	6.00	15.00
	1955	10 pcs.	—	—	Proof	550.00
	1956	.160	7.50	15.00	35.00	250.00
	1956	—	—	—	Proof	—
	1957	2.400	7.50	15.00	35.00	75.00
	1957	—	—	—	Proof	—

ROMANIA

Romania (formerly the Socialist Republic of Romania), a country in southeast Europe, has an area of 91,699 sq. mi. (237,500 sq. km.) and a population of 23.2 million. Capital: Bucharest. Machinery, foodstuffs, raw minerals and petroleum products are exported. Heavy industry and oil have become increasingly important to the economy since 1959.

The area of Romania, generally referred to as Dacia, inhabited by Dacians or Getae, a people of Thracian stock. The kingdom of Dacia existed as early as 200 BC.

In 1526, Hungary came under Turkish rule. Transylvania became a separate principality under the protection of the Sultan (1541).

At the close of the sixteenth century, the three principalities were united (Transylvania in 1599 and Moldavia in 1600) by Prince Mihai Viteazul of Wallachia, who made continual war on the Turks in an attempt to gain and maintain independence. The Ottomans restored, at great pain, their control of the principalities after Michael's death, imposing political restrictions.

The last Turkish vassal was eliminated in 1699 and Austria obtained the possession of Transylvania by the Treaty of Karlowitz. Under Hapsburg's administration, the region was made into a grand principality in 1765.

Because of the decline of Turkish power during the eighteenth century, the Austrian and later Russian influence became preeminent in the area.

The European insurrectionist movements reached the region in 1848, in Moldova and Wallachia the provisional revolutionary governments were put down by a Russo-Turkish military intervention. In Transylvania the Romanians, as native and majority of the population, continued to native and majority of the population, continued to fight for social and national emancipation, which went unrecognized by the Hungarian revolutionary government. In 1867, Transylvania was incorporated under Hungarian administration during establishment of the dual Austro-Hungarian Empire. Romania, successfully involved in war against Turkey (1877-78), proclaimed itself to be completely independent. The historical region of Dobruja, including the Delta of Danube, was returned, but Romania was forced to cede its southern area of Bessarabia to Russia.

In 1881, Carol I became king. In 1888, Romania became a constitutional monarchy with a bicameral legislature.

Neutral during the First Balkan War (1912), Romania joined Serbia and Greece in the Second Balkan War (1913) against Bulgaria.

When WW I began, the kingdom was neutral until 1916, when the Romanian army invaded Transylvania, but Austro-German, Turkish and Bulgarian forces occupied the south of the country. The Romanians persisted in keeping Moldavia. With the triumph of the Allies, the Romanian army liberated their southern region and reoccupied Transylvania. Bukovina (Oct. 28, 1918) and Transylvania (Dec. 1) proclaimed their reunification with Romania. In 1919, the Romanian army shattered the Bolshevik forces, which were installed in Hungary.

A new constitution was adopted in 1923. The Romanian government struggled with domestic problems, agrarian reform and economic reconstruction.

In the background of WW II, in 1940, after the defeat of France, following the Soviet-Nazi agreement of August 1939, the Red army occupied Bessarabia and northern Bukovina (June). Later, nothern Transylvania was annexed by Hungary (August) and southern Dobruja was returned to Bulgaria (September). In this context, King Carol II abdicated in favor of his son Mihai.

The government was reorganized along Fascist lines between September 14, 1940 - January 23, 1941. A military dictatorship followed. When the Germans invaded the Soviet Union, Romania also became involved in recovering the regions of Bessarabia and northern Bukovina annexed by Stalin in 1940.

On August 23, 1944, King Mihai I proclaimed an armistice with the Allied Forces. The Romanian army drove out the Germans and Hungarians in northern Transylvania, but the country was subsequently occupied by the Soviet army. That monarchy was abolished on December 30, 1947, and Romania became a "People's Republic" based on the Soviet regime. The anti-Communist combative resistance movement developed in spite of the Soviet army presence until 1956. The partisans remained in the mountains until 1964. With the accession of N. Ceausescu to power, Romania began to exercise a considerable degree of independence, In 1965, it was proclaimed a "Socialist Republic". After 1977, an oppressed and impoverished domestic scene worsened.

On December 17, 1989, an anti-Communist revolt in Timisoara. On December 22, 1989 the Communist government was overthrown. Ceausescu and his wife were arrested and later executed. The new government established a republic, the constitutional name being Romania.

RULERS

Carol I (as Prince), 1866-81 (as King),
1881-1914
Ferdinand I, 1914-1927
Mihai I, 1927-1930
Carol II, 1930-1940
Mihai I, 1940-1947

MINT MARKS

(a) - Paris, privy marks only
(b) - Brussels, privy marks only
angel head (1872-1876),
no marks (1894-1924)
B - Hamburg
FM - Franklin Mint
H - Heaton
HF - Huguenin, Le Locle
J - Hamburg
KN - Kings Norton
(p) - Thunderbolt - Poissy
zig zag (1924)
V - Vienna
Huguenin - Le Locle
( ) - no marks, 1930 (10, 20 Lei),
1932 (100 Lei), Royal Mint - London

MONETARY SYSTEM

100 Bani = 1 Leu

5 BANI

COPPER-NICKEL

KM#	Date	Mintage	Fine	VF	XF	Unc
31	1905	2.000	.50	1.00	3.00	9.00
	1905	—	—	—	Proof	40.00
	1906	48.000	.25	.50	2.00	8.00
	1906J	24.000	.25	.50	1.50	6.00

10 BANI

COPPER-NICKEL

32	1905	10.820	.50	1.00	3.50	15.00
	1906	24.180	.25	.75	2.50	10.00
	1906J	17.000	.25	.75	1.50	6.00

20 BANI

COPPER-NICKEL

33	1905	2.500	1.00	4.00	14.00	40.00
	1906	3.000	1.00	3.00	11.00	30.00
	1906J	2.500	1.00	3.50	11.00	26.00

25 BANI

ALUMINUM

44	1921HF	20.000	.50	1.00	2.50	7.50

NOTE: Sizes of center hole vary from 4.0-4.5mm.

50 BANI

2.5000 g, .835 SILVER, .0671 oz ASW

Rev: Small letters.

KM#	Date	Mintage	Fine	VF	XF	Unc
23	1901	.205	6.00	15.00	45.00	200.00

NOTE: Earlier dates (1894-1900) exist for this type.

41	1910	3.600	1.50	3.00	8.00	16.50
	1910	—	—	—	Proof	150.00
	1911	3.000	2.00	4.00	10.00	20.00
	1912	1.800	1.50	3.00	8.00	16.50
	1914	1.600	1.25	2.00	4.00	10.00
	1914	—	—	—	Proof	90.00

NOTE: Edge varieties exist.

ALUMINUM

45	1921HF	30.000	.50	1.00	3.50	9.00

NOTE: Sizes of center hole vary from 4.0-4.5mm.

LEU

5.0000 g, .835 SILVER, .1342 oz ASW

24	1901	.370	4.00	10.00	30.00	125.00
	1901	—	—	—	Proof	250.00

NOTE: Earlier dates (1894-1900) exist for this type.

40th Anniversary - Reign of Carol I
Rev: A MICHAUX below truncation.

34.1	ND(1906)	2.500	4.00	9.00	24.00	55.00
	ND(1906)	—	—	—	Proof	200.00

Rev: A. MICHAUX below truncation.

34.2	ND(1906)	—	—	—	—	—

42	1910	4.600	3.00	6.00	9.00	24.00
	1910	—	—	—	Proof	350.00
	1911	2.573	4.00	8.00	12.00	30.00
	1912	3.540	3.00	5.00	8.00	18.00
	1914	4.283	2.00	3.00	6.00	14.00
	1914	—	—	—	Proof	100.00

NOTE: Edge varieties exist.

COPPER-NICKEL

46	1924(b) thin					
		100.000	.50	1.50	3.50	9.00
	1924(p) thick					
		100.006	.50	1.50	4.00	10.00

NICKEL-BRASS

KM#	Date	Mintage	Fine	VF	XF	Unc
56.1	1938	27.900	.10	.60	1.60	4.00
	1939	72.200	.10	.50	1.50	3.00
	1940	Inc. Ab.	.10	.50	1.00	2.50
	1941	Inc. Ab.	.10	.50	1.50	3.50

W/o mint mark.

56.2	1940	—	—	—	—	—

2 LEI

10.0000 g, .835 SILVER, .2684 oz ASW

25	1901	.012	350.00	500.00	850.00	1850.

NOTE: Earlier dates (1894-1900) exist for this type.

43	1910	1.800	4.00	8.00	15.00	35.00
	1910	—	—	—	Proof	200.00
	1911	1.000	6.00	12.00	25.00	50.00
	1912	1.500	4.00	7.00	12.00	30.00
	1914	2.452	3.00	5.00	9.00	20.00
	1914	—	—	—	Proof	120.00

NOTE: Edge varieties exist.

COPPER-NICKEL

47	1924(b)	50.000	.60	1.75	4.00	10.00
	1924(p)	50.008	.60	1.75	4.50	12.00

ZINC

58	1941	101.778	.50	1.50	3.00	9.00

5 LEI

25.0000 g, .900 SILVER, .7234 oz ASW
Reeded edge.

17.2	1901B	.460	40.00	65.00	150.00	340.00
	1901B	—	—	—	Proof	950.00

40th Anniversary - Reign of Carol I

KM#	Date	Mintage	Fine	VF	XF	Unc
39	1906(b)	.028	235.00	350.00	500.00	900.00

NICKEL

KM#						
55	1937	*12.000	1.25	2.50	4.50	10.00
	1938	*8.000	3.00	6.00	14.00	30.00

*NOTE: 16.731 melted.

100 LEI

32.2580 g, .900 GOLD, .9335 oz AGW
40th Anniversary - Reign of Carol I

40	ND(1906)(b)	.003	500.00	900.00	1450.	2200.

14.0000 g, .500 SILVER, .1929 oz ASW

52	1932(a)	2.000	10.00	20.00	45.00	135.00
	1932( )	16.400	5.00	10.00	20.00	90.00
	1932	—	—	—	Proof	250.00

NICKEL

54	1936	20.230	2.00	4.00	8.00	14.00
	1938	*3.250	3.00	7.00	12.50	38.00

*NOTE: 17.030 melted.

NICKEL-CLAD STEEL

64	1943	40.590	.25	.50	1.20	4.00
	1944	21.289	.25	.50	1.40	5.00

200 LEI

6.0000 g, .835 SILVER, .1611 oz ASW

63	1942	30.025	1.50	2.50	6.00	15.00

40th Anniversary - Reign of Carol I

KM#	Date	Mintage	Fine	VF	XF	Unc
35	ND(1906)	.200	40.00	70.00	160.00	320.00
	ND(1906)	—	—	—	Proof	950.00

NICKEL-BRASS
King Mihai I

48	1930H	15.000	1.00	2.50	6.00	18.00
	1930KN	15.000	1.00	3.50	8.00	22.00
	1930(a)	30.000	.50	2.50	5.00	15.00

ZINC

61	1942	140.000	.50	1.25	2.75	7.00

10 LEI

NICKEL-BRASS
King Carol II

49	1930( )	15.000	1.00	3.00	7.50	22.00
	1930	—	—	—	Proof	—
	1930(a)	30.000	1.00	3.00	7.00	20.00
	1930H	7.500	2.50	4.50	10.00	27.50
	1930KN	7.500	3.00	7.00	15.00	35.00
	1930(a)	—	—	—	Proof	175.00

12-1/2 LEI

4.0323 g, .900 GOLD, .1167 oz AGW
40th Anniversary - Reign of Carol I

36	1906	.032	65.00	90.00	120.00	250.00

20 LEI

6.4516 g, .900 GOLD, .1867 oz AGW
40th Anniversary - Reign of Carol I

37	1906(b)	.015	115.00	145.00	190.00	320.00

NICKEL-BRASS
King Mihai I

KM#	Date	Mintage	Fine	VF	XF	Unc
50	1930 London	40.000	2.00	6.50	17.50	35.00
	1930	—	—	—	Proof	—
	1930H	5.000	3.00	8.00	25.00	50.00
	1930KN	5.000	3.00	10.00	30.00	70.00

King Carol II

51	1930	6.750	1.50	3.00	12.00	22.00
	1930	—	—	—	Proof	—
	1930(a)	17.500	1.00	2.00	10.00	20.00
	1930H	7.750	2.00	4.00	16.00	37.50
	1930KN	7.750	2.50	6.00	25.00	55.00
	1930(a)	—	—	—	Proof	185.00

ZINC

62	1942	44.000	.75	1.50	3.00	8.00
	1943	25.783	1.00	2.25	4.00	9.00
	1944	5.034	1.50	3.00	5.00	12.00

25 LEI

8.0645 g, .900 GOLD, .2333 oz AGW
40th Anniversary - Reign of Carol I

38	1906(b)	.024	140.00	180.00	300.00	450.00

50 LEI

16.1290 g, .900 GOLD, .4667 oz AGW

BRASS

KM#	Date	Mintage	Fine	VF	XF	Unc
66	1945	1.399	.50	1.00	4.00	10.00

NOTE: Many of these coins were privately silver plated.

250 LEI

13.5000 g, .750 SILVER, .3255 oz ASW

53	1935	4.500	9.00	18.00	45.00	135.00

12.0000 g, .835 SILVER, .3222 oz ASW
Lettered edge: NUNCA CREDINTA REGE NATIUNE.

57	1939	10.000	6.00	12.00	30.00	75.00
	1940	8.000	9.00	17.00	40.00	120.00

NOTE: Line on edge interrupted by two rhombs.

Rev: Date divided by portcullis.
Lettered edge: TOTUL PENTRU TARA.

59.1	1940	—	—	—	—	4500.

NOTE: Mintage unissued and reportedly remelted.

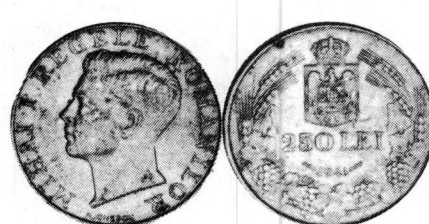

Rev: Date not divided.
Lettered edge: TOTUL PENTRU TARA

59.2	1941	2.250	8.00	14.00	30.00	65.00

Lettered edge: NIHIL SINE DEO

59.3	1941(B)	13.750	6.00	9.00	15.00	28.00

500 LEI

25.0000 g, .835 SILVER, .6711 oz ASW
Basarabia Reunion
Rev: On bended knee, King Stephen presents
Putna Monastery to the Lord.

KM#	Date	Mintage	Fine	VF	XF	Unc
60	1941	.775	8.00	12.00	18.00	34.00

12.0000 g, .700 SILVER, .2701 oz ASW

65	1944	9.731	2.50	3.50	5.00	10.00

BRASS

67	1945	3.422	1.00	2.00	4.00	8.00

NOTE: Many of these coins were privately silver plated.

ALUMINUM

68	1946	5.823	.50	1.00	3.00	8.00

NOTE: W/o designers name result of filled die.

2000 LEI

BRASS

69	1946	24.619	.50	1.00	3.00	7.00

NOTE: Many of these coins were privately silver plated.

10000 LEI

BRASS

76	1947	11.850	1.00	2.00	4.00	8.00

NOTE: Many of these coins were privately silver plated.

25000 LEI

12.0000 g, .700 SILVER, .2701 oz ASW

KM#	Date	Mintage	Fine	VF	XF	Unc
70	1946	2.372	2.00	3.00	6.00	12.00

100000 LEI

25.0000 g, .700 SILVER, .5626 oz ASW

71	1946	2.002	5.00	7.00	10.00	18.00

MONETARY REFORM

(August 15, 1947)

100 Bani = 1 Leu

50 BANI

BRASS

72	1947	13.266	1.00	2.00	3.00	8.00

LEU

BRASS

73	1947	88.341	1.00	2.25	3.50	8.50

2 LEI

BRONZE

74	1947	40.000	1.00	2.50	4.00	12.00

5 LEI

ALUMINUM

75	1947	56.026	1.50	2.50	6.00	16.00

PEOPLES REPUBLIC

1947-1965

LEU

COPPER-NICKEL-ZINC

KM#	Date	Mintage	Fine	VF	XF	Unc
78	1949	—	.75	1.50	3.00	7.00
	1950	—	.75	1.50	3.25	7.00
	1951	—	1.00	2.00	4.00	9.00
		ALUMINUM				
78a	1951	—	1.00	2.00	5.00	11.50
	1952	—	6.00	12.00	22.00	50.00

2 LEI

COPPER-NICKEL-ZINC

79	1950	—	1.00	2.50	5.00	10.00
	1951	—	2.00	5.00	10.00	20.00
		ALUMINUM				
79a	1951	—	.75	2.00	4.00	9.50
	1952	—	6.00	12.50	26.00	60.00

5 LEI

ALUMINUM

77	1948	—	1.50	2.50	4.50	18.00
	1949	—	1.25	2.00	3.50	10.00
	1950	—	1.25	2.00	3.50	10.00
	1951	—	1.25	2.00	4.00	12.00

20 LEI

ALUMINUM

80	1951	—	2.00	6.00	15.00	42.00

MONETARY REFORM

(January 26, 1952)

100 Bani = 1 Leu

BAN

COPPER-NICKEL-ZINC
Obv: W/o star at top of arms.

81.1	1952	—	.20	.50	1.00	2.00

Obv: Star at top of arms.

81.2	1953	—	1.00	2.00	5.00	12.00
	1954	—	2.00	4.00	6.50	20.00

3 BANI

COPPER-NICKEL-ZINC

Obv: W/o star at top of arms.

KM#	Date	Mintage	Fine	VF	XF	Unc
82.1	1952	—	1.00	2.00	4.00	10.00

Obv: Star at top of arms.

82.2	1953	—	.50	1.00	2.00	5.00
	1954	—	2.50	6.00	16.00	40.00

5 BANI

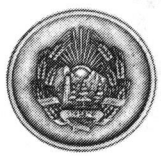 

COPPER-NICKEL-ZINC
Obv: W/o star at top of arms.

83.1	1952	—	.50	1.00	2.50	6.00

Obv: Star at top of arms.

83.2	1953	—	.25	.50	1.50	4.00
	1954	—	.25	.50	1.50	4.00
	1955	—	.25	.50	1.50	4.00
	1956	—	.25	.50	1.25	3.50
	1957	—	.25	.50	1.75	5.00

NICKEL CLAD STEEL
Obv: RPR on ribbon in arms.

89	1963	—	.20	.50	1.00	2.00

10 BANI

COPPER-NICKEL
Obv: W/o star at top of arms.

84.1	1952	—	1.00	2.00	7.00	15.00

Obv: Star at top of arms, leg: ROMANA.

84.2	1954	—	.30	1.50	3.00	7.00

Obv. leg: ROMINA.

84.3	1955	—	.10	.20	.75	3.00
	1956	—	.10	.20	.75	3.00

15 BANI

NICKEL CLAD STEEL

87	1960	—	.10	.20	.50	1.50

---

25 BANI

COPPER-NICKEL
Obv: W/o star at top of arms.

KM#	Date	Mintage	Fine	VF	XF	Unc
85.1	1952	—	1.00	2.50	8.00	18.00

Obv: Star at top of arms, leg: ROMANA.

85.2	1953	—	.20	.75	2.00	5.00
	1954	—	.20	.60	1.50	4.00

Obv. leg: ROMINA.

85.3	1955	—	.15	.35	.80	3.00

NICKEL CLAD STEEL

88	1960	—	.15	.30	.50	1.50

50 BANI

COPPER-NICKEL

86	1955	—	1.00	2.00	3.50	12.00
	1956	—	.50	1.00	2.00	8.00

LEU

NICKEL CLAD STEEL

90	1963	—	.25	.50	.75	2.00

3 LEI

NICKEL CLAD STEEL

91	1963	—	.25	.50	1.20	3.00

SOCIALIST REPUBLIC

1965-1989

5 BANI

NICKEL CLAD STEEL
Obv: ROMANIA on ribbon in arms.

KM#	Date	Mintage	Fine	VF	XF	Unc
92	1966	—	.10	.20	.60	1.50

ALUMINUM

| 92a | 1975 | — | — | .10 | .20 | .50 |

15 BANI

NICKEL CLAD STEEL

| 93 | 1966 | — | — | .15 | .35 | 1.00 |

ALUMINUM

| 93a | 1975 | — | — | .10 | .25 | .75 |

25 BANI

NICKEL CLAD STEEL

| 94 | 1966 | — | — | .20 | .50 | 1.50 |

ALUMINUM

| 94a | 1982 | — | — | .50 | 1.00 | 3.00 |

LEU

NICKEL CLAD STEEL

| 95 | 1966 | — | .10 | .25 | .60 | 2.00 |

3 LEI

NICKEL CLAD STEEL

| 96 | 1966 | — | .25 | .50 | 1.00 | 2.50 |

5 LEI

ALUMINUM

| 97 | 1978 | — | — | .50 | 1.00 | 3.50 |

*NOTE: Large and small dot varieties on reverse exist for this coin.

REPUBLIC

1989-

LEU

COPPER CLAD STEEL
National Bank of Romania

KM#	Date	Mintage	Fine	VF	XF	Unc
113	1992	*60.000	—	.20	.50	1.50

Coat of Arms

115	1993	*61.000	—	.10	.25	1.00
	1994	*10.000	—	—	.20	.75
	1995	—	—	—	.10	.65
	1996	—	—	.50	1.00	2.50

5 LEI

NICKEL PLATED STEEL

114	1992 CD VG					
		*30.000	—	.25	.60	2.00
	1993 CD					
		*70.000	—	—	.30	1.00
	1994	*10.000	—	—	.20	.70
	1995	—	—	—	.20	.65
	1996	—	—	Reported, not confirmed		

10 LEI

NICKEL CLAD STEEL
Anniversary of Revolution

108	1990	*30.000	—	.50	1.00	2.00
	1991	* 31.303	—	.25	.60	1.25
	1992	*60.000	—	.25	.50	.75

*NOTE: Rotated die varieties exist.

116	1993	*6.000	—	—	.50	1.00
	1994	*7.000	—	—	.40	1.00
	1995	—	—	—	.30	.75

NICKEL PLATED STEEL
50 Years - F.A.O.

| 117.1 | 1995 | .200 | — | — | 2.00 | 4.00 |

Obv: N in diamond at right for Numismatists.

| 117.2 | 1995 | .030 | — | — | 3.00 | 5.50 |

1996 Olympic Games - U.S.A.
Rev: Swimmer.

KM#	Date	Mintage	Fine	VF	XF	Unc
120	1996	.010	—	—	—	4.50

1996 Olympic Games - U.S.A. -
4 Olympic Scenes

| 121 | 1996 | .010 | — | — | — | 4.50 |

1996 Olympic Games - U.S.A. -
Windsurfer

| 122 | 1996 | .010 | — | — | — | 4.50 |

1996 Olympic Games - U.S.A. -
Sailboat w/2 Racers

| 123 | 1996 | .010 | — | — | — | 4.50 |

1996 Olympic Games - U.S.A. -
Canoe w/2 Racers

| 124 | 1996 | .010 | — | — | — | 4.50 |

1996 Olympic Games - U.S.A. -
Scullcraft w/Racers

| 125 | 1996 | .010 | — | — | — | 4.50 |

World Food Summit - Rome

| 126 | 1996 | .050 | — | — | — | 3.00 |

Euro Soccer - Players

| 134 | 1996 | .050 | — | — | — | 4.50 |

20 LEI

BRASS CLAD STEEL

King Stefan Cel Mare

KM#	Date	Mintage	Fine	VF	XF	Unc
109	1991	*43.200	—	—	1.00	2.50
	1992	*48.000	—	—	.60	1.50
	1993	*33.800	—	—	.50	1.25
	1994	*5.000	—	—	1.25	3.00
	1995	—	—	—	.75	2.00
	1996	—	—	.75	1.50	4.00

NOTE: Date varieties exist.

50 LEI

BRASS CLAD STEEL
Prince Alexandru Ioan Cuza

110	1991	*29.600	—	—	1.50	3.00
	1992	*70.800	—	—	1.00	1.85
	1993	*34.600	—	—	1.00	1.85
	1994	*30.000	—	—	1.00	2.00
	1995	—	—	—	1.00	2.00
	1996	—	—	—	1.00	2.50

NOTE: 1992 date varieties exist.

100 LEI

NICKEL PLATED STEEL
Prince Mihai Viteazul

111	1991	*12.600	—	—	2.50	6.00
	1992	*70.500	—	—	1.50	3.00
	1993	*78.000	—	—	1.50	3.00
	1994	*125.000	—	—	1.50	2.50
	1995	—	—	—	1.50	3.00
	1996	—	—	—	2.50	5.00

NOTE: 1992 date varieties exist. Edge variety with TOTUL PENTRU TARA; w/o ROMANIA has been determined to a false coin by prominent authorities.

RUSSIA

Russia, formerly the central power of the Union of Soviet Socialist Republics and now of the Commonwealth of Independent States occupies the northern part of Asia and the eastern part of Europe, in 1991 had an area of 8,649,538 sq. mi. (22,402,200 sq. km.) and a population of *288.7 million. Capital: Moscow. Exports include iron and steel, crude oil, timber, and nonferrous metals.

The first Russian dynasty was founded in Novgorod by the Viking Rurik in 862 A.D. Under Yaroslav the Wise (1019-54) the subsequent Kievan state became one of the great commercial and cultural centers of Europe before falling to the Mongols of the Batu Khan, 13th century, who were suzerains of Russia until late in the 15th century when Ivan III threw off the Mongol yoke. The Russian Empire was enlarged, solidified and Westernized during the reigns of Ivan the Terrible, Peter the Great and Catherine the Great, and by 1881 extended to the Pacific and into Central Asia. Contemporary Russian history began in March of 1917 when Tsar Nicholas II abdicated under pressure and was replaced by a provisional government composed of both radical and conservative elements. This government rapidly lost ground to the Bolshevik wing of the Socialist Democratic Labor Party which attained power following the Bolshevik Revolution which began on Nov. 7, 1917. After the Russian Civil War, the regional governments, national states and armies became federal republics of the Russian Socialist Federal Soviet Republic. These autonomous republics united to form the Union of Soviet Socialist Republics that was established as a federation under the premiership of Lenin on Dec. 30, 1922.

In the fall of 1991, events moved swiftly in the Soviet Union. Estonia, Latvia and Lithuania won their independence and were recognized by Moscow, Sept. 6. The Commonwealth of Independent States was formed Dec. 8, 1991 in Mensk by Belarus, Russia and Ukraine. It was expanded at a summit Dec. 21, 1991 to include 11 of the 12 remaining republics (excluding Georgia) of the old USSR.

EMPIRE

RULERS
Nicholas II, 1894-1917

MINT MARKS
Л - Leningrad, 1991
М - Moscow, 1990
СПБ - St. Petersburg, 1724-1914

(l) - LM monogram in oval - Leningrad, 1977-

(m) - MM monogram in oval - Moscow, 1977-

(sp) - SP monogram - St. Petersburg, 1997-

MINTMASTERS INITIALS

LENINGRAD MINT

Initials	Years	Mintmaster
АГ	1921-1922	A.F. Hartman
ПЛ	1922-1927	P.V. Latishev

LONDON MINT

Т.Р.	1924	Thomas Ross
ФР	1924	Thomas Ross

ST. PETERSBURG MINT

ЭБ	1899-1913	Elikum Babayantz
ФЗ	1899-1901	Felix Zaleman
АР	1901-05	Alexander Redko
ЭБ	1906-1913	Elikum Babayantz
ВС	1913-17	Victor Smirnov

NOTE: St. Petersburg Mint became Petrograd in 1914 and Leningrad in 1924. It was renamed St. Petersburg in 1991.

MONETARY SYSTEM

1/4 Kopek = Polushka ПОЛУШКА
1/2 Kopek = Denga, Denezhka
   ДЕНГА, ДЕНЕЖКА
Kopek КОП°ИКА
(2, 3 & 4) Kopeks КОП°ИКИ
(5 and up) Kopeks КОП°ЕКЪ
(1924 - 5 and up) Kopeks КОПЕЕК
3 Kopeks = Altyn, Altynnik
   АЛТЫНЪ, АЛТЫННИКЪ
10 Kopeks = Grivna, Grivennik
   ГРИВНА, ГРИВЕННИКЪ
25 Kopeks = Polupoltina, Polupoltinnik
   ПОЛУПОЛТИНА
   ПОЛУПОЛТИННИКЪ
50 Kopeks = Poltina, Poltinnik
   ПОЛТИНА, ПОЛТИННИКЪ
100 Kopeks = Rouble, Ruble РУБЛЪ
10 Roubles = Imperial ИМПЕРІАЛЪ
10 Roubles = Chervonetz ЧЕРВОНЕЦ

NOTE: Mintage figures for years after 1885 are for fiscal years and may or may not reflect actual rarity, the commemorative and 1917 silver figures being exceptions.

POLUSHKA
(1/4 Kopek)

COPPER, 3.00 g
Mint mark: СПБ

Y#	Date	Mintage	Fine	VF	XF	Unc
47.1	1909	2.000	1.00	2.00	4.00	12.00
	1910	8.000	4.00	8.00	15.00	30.00
	Common date	—	—	—	Proof	35.00

NOTE: Earlier dates (1894-1900) exist for this type.

Mint: Petrograd - w/o mint mark

Y#	Date	Mintage	Fine	VF	XF	Unc
47.2	1915	.500	2.00	5.00	10.00	20.00
	1916	1.200	40.00	80.00	150.00	300.00

DENGA

(1/2 Kopek)

COPPER, 4.00 g
Mint mark: СПБ

Y#	Date	Mintage	Fine	VF	XF	Unc
48.1	1908	8.000	.25	.50	1.00	5.00
	1909	49.500	.25	.50	1.00	4.00
	1910	24.000	.25	.50	1.00	5.00
	1911	35.800	.25	.50	1.00	5.00
	1912	28.000	.25	.50	1.00	5.00
	1913	50.000	.25	.50	1.00	5.00
	1914	14.000	.25	.50	1.00	5.00
	Common date	—	—	—	Proof	35.00

Mint: Petrograd - w/o mint mark

Y#	Date	Mintage	Fine	VF	XF	Unc
48.2	1915	12.000	.25	.50	1.00	5.00
	1916	9.400	.25	.50	1.00	5.00

KOPEK

COPPER, 4.00 g
Mint mark: СПБ

Y#	Date	Mintage	Fine	VF	XF	Unc
9.2	1901	30.000	.25	.50	1.50	8.00
	1902	20.000	2.50	5.00	10.00	20.00
	1903	74.400	.25	.50	1.50	8.00
	1904	30.600	.25	.50	1.50	8.00
	1905	23.000	.25	.50	1.50	8.00
	1906	20.000	.25	.50	1.50	8.00
	1907	20.000	.25	.50	1.50	8.00
	1908	40.000	.25	.50	1.50	8.00
	1909	27.500	.25	.50	1.50	8.00
	1910	36.500	.25	.50	1.50	8.00
	1911	38.150	.25	.50	1.50	8.00
	1912	31.850	.25	.50	1.50	8.00
	1913	61.500	.25	.50	1.50	8.00
	1914	32.500	.25	.50	1.50	8.00
	Common date	—	—	—	Proof	35.00

NOTE: Earlier dates (1867-1900) exist for this type.

Mint: Petrograd - w/o mint mark

Y#	Date	Mintage	Fine	VF	XF	Unc
9.3	1915	58.000	.25	.50	1.50	8.00
	1916	46.500	.25	.50	1.50	8.00
	1917	—	—	—	Unique	—

2 KOPEKS

COPPER
Mint mark: СПБ

Y#	Date	Mintage	Fine	VF	XF	Unc
10.2	1901	20.000	.50	1.00	2.00	8.00
	1902	10.000	.50	1.00	2.00	8.00
	1903	29.200	.50	1.00	2.00	8.00
	1904	13.300	.50	1.00	2.00	8.00
	1905	15.000	.50	1.00	2.00	8.00
	1906	6.250	.50	1.00	2.00	8.00
	1907	7.500	.50	1.00	2.00	8.00
	1908	19.000	.50	1.00	2.00	8.00
	1909	16.250	.50	1.00	2.00	8.00
	1910	12.000	.50	1.00	2.00	8.00
	1911	17.200	.50	1.00	2.00	8.00
	1912	17.050	.50	1.00	2.00	8.00
	1913	26.000	.50	1.00	2.00	8.00
	1914	20.000	.50	1.00	2.00	8.00
	Common date	—	—	—	Proof	35.00

NOTE: Earlier dates (1867-1900) exist for this type.

Mint: Petrograd - w/o mint mark

Y#	Date	Mintage	Fine	VF	XF	Unc
10.3	1915	33.750	.50	1.00	2.00	5.00
	1916	31.500	.50	1.00	2.00	5.00

3 KOPEKS

(Altyn)

COPPER
Mint mark: СПБ

Y#	Date	Mintage	Fine	VF	XF	Unc
11.2	1901	10.000	.75	1.50	3.00	15.00
	1902	3.333	.75	1.50	3.00	15.00
	1903	11.400	.75	1.50	3.00	15.00
	1904	6.934	.75	1.50	3.00	15.00
	1905	3.333	.75	1.50	3.00	15.00
	1906	5.667	.75	1.50	3.00	15.00
	1907	2.500	.75	1.50	3.00	15.00
	1908	12.667	.75	1.50	3.00	15.00
	1909	6.733	.75	1.50	3.00	15.00
	1910	6.667	.75	1.50	3.00	15.00
	1911	9.467	.75	1.50	3.00	15.00
	1912	8.533	.75	1.50	3.00	15.00
	1913	15.333	.75	1.50	3.00	15.00
	1914	8.167	.75	1.50	3.00	15.00
	Common date	—	—	—	Proof	35.00

NOTE: Earlier dates (1867-1900) exist for this type.

Mint: Petrograd - w/o mint mark

Y#	Date	Mintage	Fine	VF	XF	Unc
11.3	1915	19.833	.75	1.50	3.00	16.00
	1916	25.667	.75	1.50	3.00	16.00
	1917	—	—	—	Rare	—

5 KOPEKS

.8998 g, .500 SILVER, .0144 oz ASW
Mint mark: СПБ
Obv: Eagle.
Reeded edge.

Y#	Date	Mintage	Fine	VF	XF	Unc
19a.1	1901 ФЗ	5.790	1.00	2.00	4.00	15.00
	1901 АР	I.A.	1.00	2.00	4.00	15.00
	1902 АР	6.000	1.00	2.00	4.00	15.00
	1903 АР	9.000	1.00	2.00	4.00	15.00
	1904 АР	9 pcs.	—	—	Rare	—
	1905 АР	10.000	1.00	2.00	4.00	15.00
	1906 ЭБ	4.000	1.00	2.00	4.00	15.00
	1908 ЭБ	.400	1.00	2.00	4.00	15.00
	1909 ЭБ	3.100	1.00	2.00	4.00	15.00
	1910 ЭБ	2.500	1.00	2.00	4.00	15.00
	1911 ЭБ	2.700	1.00	2.00	4.00	15.00
	1912 ЭБ	3.000	1.00	2.00	4.00	15.00
	1913 ЭБ	I.B.	—	—	Proof	120.00
	1913 ВС	1.300	1.00	2.00	4.00	15.00
	1914 ВС	4.200	1.00	2.00	4.00	15.00
	Common date	—	—	—	Proof	120.00

NOTE: Earlier dates (1867-1900) exist for this type.

Mint: Petrograd - w/o mint mark

Y#	Date	Mintage	Fine	VF	XF	Unc
19a.2	1915 ВС	3.000	1.00	2.00	4.00	15.00

COPPER
Mint mark: СПБ

Y#	Date	Mintage	Fine	VF	XF	Unc
12.2	1911	3.800	6.00	12.50	25.00	50.00
	1912	2.700	10.00	17.50	35.00	70.00

NOTE: Earlier dates (1867-1881) exist for this type.

Mint: Petrograd - w/o mint mark

Y#	Date	Mintage	Fine	VF	XF	Unc
12.3	1916	8.000	40.00	80.00	150.00	250.00
	1917	—		—	Rare	—

10 KOPEKS

1.7996 g, .500 SILVER, .0289 oz ASW
Mint mark: СПБ
Reeded edge.

Y#	Date	Mintage	Fine	VF	XF	Unc
20a.2	1901 ФЗ	15.000	.50	1.00	2.00	15.00
	1901 АР	I.A.	.50	1.00	2.00	15.00
	1902 АР	17.000	.50	1.00	2.00	15.00
	1903 АР	28.500	.50	1.00	2.00	15.00
	1904 АР	20.000	.50	1.00	2.00	15.00
	1905 АР	25.000	.50	1.00	2.00	15.00
	1906 ЭБ	17.500	.50	1.00	2.00	15.00
	1907 ЭБ	20.000	.50	1.00	2.00	15.00
	1908 ЭБ	8.210	.50	1.00	2.00	15.00
	1909 ЭБ	25.290	.50	1.00	2.00	15.00
	1910 ЭБ	20.000	.50	1.00	2.00	15.00
	1911 ЭБ	19.180	.50	1.00	2.00	15.00
	1912 ЭБ	20.000	.50	1.00	2.00	15.00
	1913 ЭБ	I.B.	—	—	Proof	135.00
	1913 ВС	7.250	.50	1.00	2.00	15.00
	1914 ВС	51.250	.50	1.00	2.00	15.00
	Common date	—	—	—	Proof	135.00

NOTE: Earlier dates (1867-1900) exist for this type.

Mint: Petrograd - w/o mint mark

Y#	Date	Mintage	Fine	VF	XF	Unc
20a.3	1915 ВС	82.500	.50	.75	1.00	6.00
	1916 ВС	121.500	.50	.75	1.00	6.00
	1917 ВС	17.600	—	20.00	30.00	80.00

Mint: Osaka, Japan - w/o mint mark

Y#	Date	Mintage	Fine	VF	XF	Unc
20a.1	1916	70.001	1.00	2.00	4.00	20.00

15 KOPEKS

2.6994 g, .500 SILVER, .0434 oz ASW
Mint mark: СПБ
Reticulated edge.

Y#	Date	Mintage	Fine	VF	XF	Unc
21a.2	1901 ФЗ	6.670	.75	1.00	2.00	10.00
	1901 АР	I.A.	.75	1.00	2.00	10.00
	1902 АР	28.667	.75	1.00	2.00	10.00
	1903 АР	16.667	.75	1.00	2.00	10.00
	1904 АР	15.600	.75	1.00	2.00	10.00
	1905 АР	24.000	.75	1.00	2.00	10.00
	1906 ЭБ	23.333	.75	1.00	2.00	10.00
	1907 ЭБ	30.000	.75	1.00	2.00	10.00
	1908 ЭБ	29.000	.75	1.00	2.00	10.00
	1909 ЭБ	21.667	.75	1.00	2.00	10.00
	1911 ЭБ	6.313	.75	1.00	2.00	10.00
	1912 ЭБ	13.333	.75	1.00	2.00	10.00
	1912 ВС	Inc. Ab.	2.00	5.00	12.50	40.00
	1913 ЭБ	I.B.	—	—	Proof	135.00
	1913 ВС	5.300	.75	1.00	2.00	10.00
	1914 ВС	43.367	.75	1.00	2.00	10.00
	Common date	—	—	—	Proof	135.00

NOTE: Earlier dates (1867-1900) exist for this type.

Mint: Petrograd - w/o mint mark

Y#	Date	Mintage	Fine	VF	XF	Unc
21a.3	1915 ВС	59.333	.75	1.50	2.00	10.00
	1916 ВС	96.773	.75	1.50	2.00	10.00
	1917 ВС	14.320	—	20.00	30.00	80.00

Mint: Osaka, Japan - w/o mint mark
Reeded edge

Y#	Date	Mintage	Fine	VF	XF	Unc
21a.1	1916	96.666	BV	1.00	2.00	10.00

20 KOPEKS

3.5992 g, .500 SILVER, .0579 oz ASW
Mint mark: СПБ
Reeded edge

Y#	Date	Mintage	Fine	VF	XF	Unc
22a.1	1901 ФЗ	7.750	.75	1.00	2.00	12.50
	1901 АР	I.A.	—	—	Proof	200.00
	1902 АР	10.000	.75	1.00	2.00	12.50
	1903 АР	I.A.	.75	1.00	2.00	12.50
	1904 АР	13.000	.75	1.00	2.00	12.50
	1905 АР	11.000	.75	1.00	2.00	12.50
	1906 ЭБ	15.000	.75	1.00	2.00	12.50
	1907 ЭБ	20.000	.75	1.00	2.00	12.50
	1908 ЭБ	5.000	.75	1.00	2.00	12.50
	1909 ЭБ	18.875	.75	1.00	2.00	12.50
	1910 ЭБ	11.000	.75	1.00	2.00	12.50
	1911 ЭБ	7.100	.75	1.00	2.00	12.50
	1912 ЭБ	15.000	.75	1.00	2.00	12.50
	1912 ВС	I.A.	5.00	10.00	20.00	60.00
	1913 ЭБ	I.B.	—	—	Proof	135.00

Y#	Date	Mintage	Fine	VF	XF	Unc
22a.1	1913 BC	4.250	.75	1.00	2.00	12.50
	1914 BC	52.750	.75	1.00	2.00	12.50
	Common date	—			Proof	135.00

NOTE: Earlier dates (1867-1893) exist for this type.

Mint: Petrograd - w/o mint mark

22a.2	1915 BC	105.500	BV	1.00	2.00	10.00
	1916 BC	131.670	BV	1.00	2.00	10.00
	1917 BC	3.500	—	25.00	35.00	100.00
	Common date	—			Proof	135.00

25 KOPEKS

4.9990 g, .900 SILVER, .1446 oz ASW
Mint: St. Petersburg - w/o mint mark

57	1901	*150 pcs.	—	—	Proof	750.00

NOTE: Earlier dates (1895-1900) exist for this type.

50 KOPEKS

9.9980 g, .900 SILVER, .2893 oz ASW
Mint: St. Petersburg - w/o mint mark

58.2	1901 АР	.412	5.00	12.50	35.00	80.00
	1901 ФЗ	I.A.	5.00	12.50	35.00	80.00
	1902 АР	.036	10.00	20.00	40.00	175.00
	1903 АР	—	—	—	Proof	2000.
	1904 АР	4,010	100.00	200.00	400.00	1200.
	1906 ЭБ	.010	25.00	50.00	100.00	300.00
	1907 ЭБ	.200	10.00	20.00	40.00	175.00
	1908 ЭБ	.040	10.00	20.00	40.00	175.00
	1909 ЭБ	.050	10.00	20.00	40.00	175.00
	1910 ЭБ	.150	10.00	20.00	40.00	175.00
	1911 ЭБ	.800	10.00	20.00	40.00	80.00
	1912 ЭБ	7.085	5.00	8.00	15.00	45.00
	1913 ЭБ	6.420	7.50	15.00	35.00	70.00
	1913 BC	I.A.	5.00	10.00	20.00	45.00
	1914 BC	1.200	5.00	10.00	20.00	45.00
	Common date	—			Proof	475.00

NOTE: Earlier dates (1895-1900) exist for this type.

ROUBLE

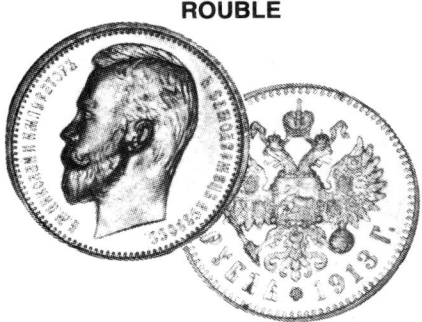

19.9960 g, .900 SILVER, .5786 oz ASW
Mint: St. Petersburg - w/o mint mark
Mintmasters initials and stars found on edge.

59.3	1901 ФЗ	2.608	10.00	17.50	35.00	200.00
	1901 АР	I.A.	40.00	80.00	125.00	450.00
	1902 АН	.140	20.00	30.00	50.00	400.00
	1903 АР	.056	40.00	80.00	180.00	750.00
	1904 АР	.012	75.00	150.00	300.00	900.00
	1905 АР	.021	40.00	80.00	180.00	750.00
	1906 ЭБ	.046	40.00	80.00	180.00	750.00
	1907 ЭБ	.400	20.00	30.00	50.00	400.00
	1908 ЭБ	.130	75.00	150.00	300.00	900.00
	1909 ЭБ	.051	40.00	80.00	180.00	600.00
	1910 ЭБ	.075	25.00	40.00	80.00	450.00
	1911 ЭБ	.129	40.00	80.00	180.00	400.00
	1912 ЭБ	2.111	15.00	25.00	50.00	200.00
	1913 ЭБ	.022	50.00	100.00	200.00	700.00
	1913 BC	I.A.	50.00	100.00	200.00	700.00
	1914 BC	.536	25.00	35.00	90.00	550.00
	1915 BC	*5,000	30.00	60.00	125.00	350.00
	Common date	—			Proof	900.00

NOTE: Earlier dates (1895-1900) exist for this type.
NOTE: Varieties exist with plain edge. These are mint errors and rare.

Centennial - Napoleon's Defeat

Y#	Date	Mintage	Fine	VF	XF	Unc
68	1912 ЭБ	.046	60.00	110.00	225.00	400.00
	1912 ЭБ	—	—	—	Proof	2000.

Alexander III Memorial

69	1912 ЭБ	2,100	200.00	400.00	1000.	1600.
	1912 ЭБ	—	—	—	Proof	2250.

Mint: St. Petersburg - w/o mint mark
300th Anniversary - Romanov Dynasty

70	1913 BC	1.472	15.00	25.00	40.00	135.00

5 ROUBLES

4.3013 g, .900 GOLD, .1244 oz AGW
Mint: St. Petersburg - w/o mint mark

62	1901 ФЗ	7.500	—	BV	65.00	80.00
	1901 АР	I.A.	—	BV	65.00	80.00
	1902 АР	6.240	—	BV	65.00	80.00
	1903 АР	5.148	—	BV	65.00	80.00
	1904 АР	2.016	—	BV	65.00	80.00
	1906 ЭБ	10 pcs.	—	—	7000.	10,000.
	1907 ЭБ	109 pcs.	—	—	4000.	7500.
	1909 ЭБ	—	BV	60.00	75.00	90.00
	1910 ЭБ	.200	BV	60.00	75.00	100.00
	1911 ЭБ	.100	BV	60.00	150.00	250.00
	Common date	—			Proof	1500.

NOTE: Earlier dates (1897-1900) exist for this type.

10 ROUBLES

8.6026 g, .900 GOLD, .2489 oz AGW

64	1901 ФЗ	2.377	—	BV	120.00	170.00
	1901 АР	I.A.	—	BV	120.00	170.00
	1902 АР	2.019	—	BV	120.00	170.00
	1903 АР	2.817	—	BV	120.00	160.00
	1904 АР	1.025	—	BV	120.00	160.00
	1906 ЭБ	10 pcs.	—	—	Proof	8500.
	1909 ЭБ	.050	BV	110.00	125.00	200.00
	1910 ЭБ	.100	BV	110.00	125.00	200.00
	1911 ЭБ	.050	BV	110.00	125.00	200.00
	Common date	—			Proof	2500.

NOTE: Earlier dates (1898-1900) exist for this type.

P.C.O.C.P. (R.S.F.S.R.)

РСФСР (Российской Социалистической Федера-

тивнои Советских Республик) R.S.F.S.R. (Russian Soviet Federated Socialist Republic)

MONETARY SYSTEM
100 Kopeks = 1 Rouble

10 KOPEKS

1.8000 g, .500 SILVER, .0289 oz ASW

Y#	Date	Mintage	Fine	VF	XF	Unc
80	1921	.950	5.00	10.00	25.00	50.00
	1921	—	—	—	Proof	250.00
	1922	18.640	1.00	2.00	4.50	12.00
	1922	—	—	—	Proof	115.00
	1923	33.424	1.00	2.00	4.00	10.00
	1923	—	—	—	Proof	60.00

15 KOPEKS

2.7000 g, .500 SILVER, .0434 oz ASW

81	1921	.933	6.00	12.00	30.00	60.00
	1921	—	—	—	Proof	275.00
	1922	13.633	2.00	3.00	6.00	16.00
	1922	—	—	—	Proof	140.00
	1923	28.504	1.50	2.50	4.50	12.00
	1923	—	—	—	Proof	80.00

20 KOPEKS

3.6000 g, .500 SILVER, .0578 oz ASW

82	1921	.825	6.00	12.00	30.00	60.00
	1921	—	—	—	Proof	300.00
	1922	14.220	2.00	4.00	8.00	20.00
	1922	—	—	—	Proof	165.00
	1923	27.580	2.00	3.50	7.00	15.00
	1923	—	—	—	Proof	100.00

NOTE: Varieties exist.

50 KOPEKS

9.9980 g, .900 SILVER, .2893 oz ASW
Mintmasters initials on edge.

83	1921 АГ	1.400	5.00	7.00	10.00	25.00
	1921 АГ	—	—	—	Proof	325.00
	1922 АГ	8.224	5.00	7.00	10.00	25.00
	1922 АГ	—	—	—	Proof	350.00
	1922 ПЛ	I.A.	5.00	7.00	10.00	25.00
	1922 ПЛ	—	—	—	Proof	250.00

ROUBLE

19.9960 g, .900 SILVER, .5786 oz ASW
Mintmasters initials on edge.

84	1921 АГ	1.000	8.50	15.00	30.00	85.00
	1921 АГ	—	—	—	Proof	425.00
	1922 АГ	2.050	10.00	20.00	40.00	100.00

Y#	Date	Mintage	Fine	VF	XF	Unc
84	1922 АГ	—	—	—	Proof	600.00
	1922 ПЛ	I.A.	10.00	20.00	40.00	100.00
	1922 ПЛ	—	—	—	Proof	450.00

NOTE: Varieties exist.

CHERVONETS

See CCCP - Trade Coinage

C.C.C.P. (U.S.S.R.)

СССР (Союз Советских Социалистических Республик) U.S.S.R. (Union of Soviet Socialist Republics).

MONETARY SYSTEM

100 Kopecks = 1 Rouble

1/2 KOPEK

COPPER

Y#	Date	Mintage	Fine	VF	XF	Unc
75	1925	45.380	3.50	7.50	14.50	30.00
	1927	—	3.50	7.50	14.50	30.00
	1927	—	—	—	Proof	100.00
	1928	—	4.50	8.00	16.50	35.00

KOPEK

BRONZE

Y#	Date	Mintage	Fine	VF	XF	Unc
76	1924 reeded edge	34.705	5.00	10.00	20.00	45.00
	1924 reeded edge	—	—	—	Proof	125.00
	1924 plain edge	Inc. Ab.	30.00	60.00	120.00	250.00
	1925	141.806	45.00	90.00	160.00	275.00

ALUMINUM-BRONZE

Y#	Date	Mintage	Fine	VF	XF	Unc
91	1926	87.915	.50	1.00	1.50	5.50
	1926	—	—	—	Proof	60.00
	1927	—	.50	1.00	1.50	5.00
	1928	—	.50	1.00	1.50	5.00
	1929	95.950	.50	1.00	1.50	5.00
	1930	85.351	.50	1.00	1.50	5.00
	1931	106.100	.50	1.00	1.50	5.00
	1932	56.900	.50	1.00	1.50	5.00
	1933	111.257	.50	1.00	1.50	5.00
	1934	100.245	.50	1.00	1.50	5.00
	1935	66.405	.50	1.00	2.00	6.00

NOTE: Varieties exist.

Y#	Date	Mintage	Fine	VF	XF	Unc
98	1935	Inc.Y91	.50	1.00	2.50	9.00
	1936	132.204	.50	1.00	2.00	7.50

Y#	Date	Mintage	Fine	VF	XF	Unc
105	1937	—	.25	.65	1.00	4.00
	1938	—	.25	.65	1.00	4.00
	1939	—	.25	.65	1.00	4.00
	1940	—	.25	.65	1.00	4.00
	1941	—	.50	1.00	2.00	6.00
	1945	—	.50	1.00	2.00	6.00
	1946	—	.50	1.00	2.00	6.00

NOTE: Varieties exist.

Obv: 8 and 7 ribbons on wreath.

Y#	Date	Mintage	Fine	VF	XF	Unc
112	1948	—	.50	1.00	2.00	5.00
	1949	—	.50	1.00	2.00	5.00
	1950	—	.50	1.00	2.50	8.00
	1951	—	.50	1.00	2.50	8.00
	1952	—	.30	.75	1.50	3.00
	1953	—	.30	.75	1.50	3.00
	1954	—	.30	.75	1.50	3.00
	1955	—	.30	.75	1.50	3.00
	1956	—	.30	.75	1.50	3.00

NOTE: Varieties exist.

Obv: 7 and 7 ribbons on wreath.

Y#	Date	Mintage	Fine	VF	XF	Unc
119	1957	—	1.00	2.00	4.00	12.00

COPPER-NICKEL

Y#	Date	Mintage	Fine	VF	XF	Unc
126	1958	30.265	—	—	—	250.00

NOTE: Never officially released for circulation. Majority of mintage remelted.

BRASS

Y#	Date	Mintage	Fine	VF	XF	Unc
126a	1961	—	.10	.15	.25	1.00
	1962	—	.10	.15	.25	.50
	1963	—	.10	.15	.25	.50
	1964	—	.20	.30	.50	2.00
	1965	—	.10	.15	.25	.50
	1966	—	.10	.15	.25	.50
	1967	—	.10	.15	.25	.50
	1968	—	.10	.15	.25	.50
	1969	—	.10	.15	.25	.50
	1970	—	.10	.15	.25	.50
	1971	—	.10	.15	.25	.50
	1972	—	.10	.15	.25	.50
	1973	—	.10	.15	.25	.50
	1974	—	.10	.15	.25	.50
	1975	—	.10	.15	.25	.50
	1976	—	.10	.15	.25	.50
	1977	—	.10	.15	.25	.50
	1978	—	.10	.15	.25	.50
	1979	—	.10	.15	.25	.50
	1980	—	.10	.15	.25	.50
	1981	—	.10	.15	.25	.50
	1982	—	.10	.15	.25	.50
	1983	—	.10	.15	.25	.50
	1984	—	.10	.15	.25	.50
	1985	—	.10	.15	.25	.50
	1986	—	.10	.15	.25	.50
	1987	—	.10	.15	.25	.50
	1988	—	.10	.15	.25	.50
	1989	—	.10	.15	.20	.35
	1990	—	.10	.15	.20	.35
	1991(m)	—	.10	.15	.20	.35
	1991(l)	—	.10	.15	.20	.35

NOTE: Varieties exist.

2 KOPEKS

BRONZE

Y#	Date	Mintage	Fine	VF	XF	Unc
77	1924 reeded edge	119.996	5.00	12.00	22.00	50.00
	1924 plain edge	30.00	60.00	120.00	250.00	
	1925	Inc. Ab.	—	—	Rare	—

NOTE: Varieties exist.

ALUMINUM-BRONZE

Y#	Date	Mintage	Fine	VF	XF	Unc
92	1926	105.053	.25	.50	1.00	4.00
	1926	—	—	—	Proof	65.00
	1927	—	—	—	Rare	—
	1928	—	.25	.50	1.00	4.00
	1929	80.000	.25	.50	1.00	5.00
	1930	134.186	.25	.50	1.00	4.00
	1931	99.523	.25	.50	1.00	4.00
	1932	39.573	.35	.65	1.25	4.50
	1933	54.874	.50	1.00	2.00	7.00
	1934	61.574	.35	.65	1.25	4.50
	1935	81.121	.35	.65	1.50	5.00

NOTE: Varieties exist.

Y#	Date	Mintage	Fine	VF	XF	Unc
99	1935	—	.50	1.00	2.50	9.00
	1936	94.354	.25	.50	2.00	7.00

NOTE: Varieties exist.

Y#	Date	Mintage	Fine	VF	XF	Unc
106	1937	—	.25	.65	1.00	3.00
	1938	—	.25	.65	1.00	3.00
	1939	—	.25	.65	1.00	3.00
	1940	—	.25	.65	1.00	3.00
	1941	—	.25	.65	1.00	3.00
	1945	—	.50	1.00	2.00	5.00
	1946	—	.25	.65	1.00	4.00
	1948	—	40.00	70.00	130.00	225.00

Obv: 8 and 7 ribbons on wreath.

Y#	Date	Mintage	Fine	VF	XF	Unc
113	1948	—	.25	.50	1.00	2.50
	1949	—	.25	.50	1.00	2.50
	1950	—	.25	.50	1.00	2.50
	1951	—	.50	1.00	2.00	6.00
	1952	—	.25	.50	1.00	3.00
	1953	—	.20	.50	1.00	2.00
	1954	—	.20	.50	1.00	2.00
	1955	—	.20	.50	1.00	2.00
	1956	—	.20	.50	1.00	2.00

NOTE: Varieties exist.

Obv: 7 and 7 ribbons on wreath.

Y#	Date	Mintage	Fine	VF	XF	Unc
120	1957	—	.50	1.00	2.50	9.00

COPPER-NICKEL

Y#	Date	Mintage	Fine	VF	XF	Unc
127	1958	39.591	—	—	—	250.00

NOTE: Never officially released for circulation. Majority of mintage remelted.

BRASS

Y#	Date	Mintage	Fine	VF	XF	Unc
127a	1961	—	.10	.15	.25	.50
	1962	—	.10	.15	.25	.50
	1963	—	.10	.15	.25	.50
	1964	—	.15	.25	.50	1.00
	1965	—	.10	.15	.25	.50
	1966	—	.10	.15	.25	.50
	1967	—	.10	.15	.25	.50
	1968	—	.10	.15	.25	.50
	1969	—	.10	.15	.25	.50
	1970	—	.10	.15	.25	.50
	1971	—	.10	.15	.25	.50
	1972	—	.10	.15	.25	.50
	1973	—	.10	.15	.25	.50
	1974	—	.10	.15	.25	.50
	1975	—	.10	.15	.25	.50
	1976	—	.10	.15	.25	.50
	1977	—	.10	.15	.25	.50
	1978	—	.10	.15	.25	.50
	1979	—	.10	.15	.25	.50
	1980	—	.10	.15	.25	.50
	1981	—	.10	.15	.25	.50
	1982	—	.10	.15	.25	.50
	1983	—	.10	.15	.25	.50
	1984	—	.10	.15	.25	.50
	1985	—	.10	.15	.25	.50
	1986	—	.10	.15	.25	.50
	1987	—	.10	.15	.25	.50
	1988	—	.10	.15	.25	.50
	1989	—	.10	.15	.20	.35
	1990	—	.10	.15	.20	.35
	1991(m)	—	.10	.15	.20	.35
	1991(l)	—	.10	.15	.20	.35

3 KOPEKS

BRONZE

Y#	Date	Mintage	Fine	VF	XF	Unc
78	1924 reeded edge	101.283	50.00	100.00	175.00	275.00
	1924 plain edge	Inc. Ab.	6.00	12.50	25.00	65.00

NOTE: Varieties exist.

ALUMINUM-BRONZE

Y#	Date	Mintage	Fine	VF	XF	Unc
93	1926	19.940	1.25	2.00	4.00	7.00
	1926				Proof	75.00
	1926 obv. of Y#100	—	—		Rare	—
	1927	—	5.00	10.00	20.00	40.00
	1928	—	1.00	2.00	4.00	7.00
	1929	50.150	1.00	2.00	4.00	8.00
	1930	74.159	.50	.75	1.50	5.00
	1931	121.168	.50	.75	1.50	5.00
	1931 w/o CCCP obv.	—	—		Rare	—
	1932	37.718	.50	.75	1.50	5.00
	1933	44.764	.50	.75	2.00	6.00
	1934	44.529	.50	.75	2.00	6.00
	1935	58.303	.50	.75	2.50	7.00

NOTE: Varieties exist.

Y#	Date	Mintage	Fine	VF	XF	Unc
100	1935	—	.50	2.00	5.00	14.00
	1936	62.757	.25	1.00	4.00	10.00

NOTE: Varieties exist.

Y#	Date	Mintage	Fine	VF	XF	Unc
107	1937	—	.25	.50	1.00	4.00
	1938	—	.25	.50	1.00	4.00
	1939	—	.25	.50	1.00	4.00
	1940	—	.25	.50	1.00	3.00
	1941	—	.25	.50	1.00	4.00
	1943	—	.25	.50	1.00	5.00
	1945	—	.50	1.00	3.00	9.00
	1946	—	.25	.50	1.00	5.00
	1948	—	40.00	70.00	130.00	225.00

NOTE: Varieties exist.

Obv: 8 and 7 ribbons on wreath.

Y#	Date	Mintage	Fine	VF	XF	Unc
114	1948	—	.25	.50	1.00	5.00
	1949	—	.25	.50	1.00	4.00
	1950	—	.25	.50	1.00	4.00
	1951	—	.50	1.00	2.00	7.00
	1952	—	.25	.50	1.00	4.00
	1953	—	.25	.50	1.00	3.00
	1954	—	.25	.50	1.00	3.00
	1955	—	.25	.50	1.00	3.00
	1956	—	.25	.50	1.00	3.00
	1957	—	2.50	5.00	10.00	30.00

NOTE: Varieties exist.

Obv: 7 and 7 ribbons on wreath.

Y#	Date	Mintage	Fine	VF	XF	Unc
121	1957	—	.50	1.00	2.50	9.00

COPPER-ZINC

Y#	Date	Mintage	Fine	VF	XF	Unc
128	1958	26.676	—	—	—	250.00

NOTE: Never officially released for circulation. Majority of mintage remelted.

ALUMINUM-BRONZE

Y#	Date	Mintage	Fine	VF	XF	Unc
128a	1961	—	.10	.15	.25	.60
	1962	—	.10	.15	.25	.60
	1965	—	.10	.15	.25	.60
	1966	—	.10	.15	.25	.60
	1967	—	.10	.15	.25	.60
	1968	—	.10	.15	.25	.60
	1969	—	.10	.15	.25	.60
	1970	—	.10	.15	.25	.60
	1971	—	.10	.15	.25	.60
	1972	—	.10	.15	.25	.60
	1973	—	.10	.15	.25	.60
	1974	—	.10	.15	.25	.60
	1975	—	.10	.15	.25	.60
	1976	—	.10	.15	.25	.60
	1977	—	.10	.15	.25	.60
	1978	—	.10	.15	.25	.60
	1979	—	.10	.15	.25	.60
	1980	—	.10	.15	.25	.60
	1981	—	.10	.15	.25	.60
	1982	—	.10	.15	.25	.60
	1983	—	.10	.15	.25	.60
	1984	—	.10	.15	.25	.60
	1985	—	.10	.15	.25	.60
	1986	—	.10	.15	.25	.60
	1987	—	.10	.15	.25	.60
	1988	—	.10	.15	.25	.60
	1989	—	.10	.15	.25	.60
	1990	—	.10	.15	.20	.40
	1991(m)	—	.10	.15	.20	.40
	1991(l)	—	.10	.15	.20	.40

NOTE: Varieties exist.

5 KOPEKS

BRONZE

Y#	Date	Mintage	Fine	VF	XF	Unc
79	1924 reeded edge	88.510	50.00	100.00	175.00	275.00
	1924 plain edge	Inc. Ab.	7.00	15.00	30.00	75.00

NOTE: Varieties exist.

ALUMINUM-BRONZE

Y#	Date	Mintage	Fine	VF	XF	Unc
94	1926	14.697	1.00	2.00	6.00	10.00
	1926				Proof	85.00
	1927	—	2.00	4.00	12.00	30.00
	1928	—	.75	1.25	3.00	7.00
	1929	20.220	.75	1.25	3.00	7.00
	1930	44.490	.75	1.25	2.00	6.00
	1931	89.540	.75	1.25	2.00	6.00
	1932	65.100	.75	1.25	2.00	6.00
	1933	18.135	3.00	6.00	15.00	50.00
	1934	5.354	2.00	4.00	12.00	30.00
	1935	11.735	3.00	6.00	15.00	50.00

NOTE: Varieties exist.

Y#	Date	Mintage	Fine	VF	XF	Unc
101	1935	—	2.00	4.00	9.00	26.00
	1936	5.242	2.00	4.00	9.00	28.00

NOTE: Varieties exist.

Y#	Date	Mintage	Fine	VF	XF	Unc
108	1937	—	2.00	4.00	9.00	28.00
	1938	—	.25	.50	1.00	4.50
	1939	—	.25	.50	1.00	4.50
	1940	—	.25	.50	1.00	4.00
	1941	—	.25	.50	1.00	4.50
	1943	—	.25	.50	1.00	4.50
	1945	—	1.00	2.00	5.00	12.00
	1946	—	.25	.50	1.00	6.00

NOTE: Varieties exist.

Obv: 8 and 7 ribbons on wreath.

Y#	Date	Mintage	Fine	VF	XF	Unc
115	1948	—	.25	.50	1.50	5.00
	1949	—	.25	.50	1.00	4.00
	1950	—	.25	.50	1.00	4.00
	1951	—	.50	1.00	2.00	5.00
	1952	—	.25	.50	1.00	4.00
	1953	—	.25	.50	1.00	4.00
	1954	—	.25	.50	1.00	4.00
	1955	—	.25	.50	1.00	4.00
	1956	—	.25	.50	1.00	4.00

NOTE: Varieties exist.

Obv: 7 and 7 ribbons on wreath.

Y#	Date	Mintage	Fine	VF	XF	Unc
122	1957	—	1.00	2.00	3.00	9.00

NOTE: Varieties exist.

COPPER-ZINC

Y#	Date	Mintage	Fine	VF	XF	Unc
129	1958	61.119	—	—	—	375.00

NOTE: Never officially released for circulation. Majority of mintage remelted.

ALUMINUM-BRONZE

Y#	Date	Mintage	Fine	VF	XF	Unc
129a	1961	—	.10	.15	.30	.75
	1962	—	.10	.15	.30	.75
	1965	—	.25	.50	1.00	3.00
	1966	—	.20	.30	.75	2.00
	1967	—	.15	.25	.50	1.50
	1968	—	.15	.25	.50	1.50
	1969	—	.20	.30	.75	2.00
	1970	—	.50	1.00	2.00	5.00
	1971	—	.15	.25	.50	1.50
	1972	—	.15	.25	.50	1.50
	1973	—	.10	.15	.30	.75
	1974	—	.10	.15	.30	.75
	1975	—	.10	.15	.30	.75
	1976	—	.10	.15	.30	.75
	1977	—	.10	.15	.30	.75
	1978	—	.10	.15	.30	.75
	1979	—	.10	.15	.30	.75
	1980	—	.10	.15	.30	.75
	1981	—	.10	.15	.30	.75
	1982	—	.10	.15	.30	.75
	1983	—	.10	.15	.30	.75
	1984	—	.10	.15	.30	.75
	1985	—	.10	.15	.30	.75
	1986	—	.10	.15	.30	.75
	1987	—	.10	.15	.30	.75
	1988	—	.10	.15	.30	.75
	1989	—	.10	.15	.25	.50
	1990	—	.15	.25	.45	1.25
	1991(m)	—	.10	.15	.25	.50
	1991(l)	—	.10	.15	.25	.50
	1991Л	—	.10	.15	.25	.50

NOTE: Varieties exist.

10 KOPEKS

1.8000 g, .500 SILVER, .0289 oz ASW

Y#	Date	Mintage	Fine	VF	XF	Unc
86	1924	67.351	.50	1.00	3.00	9.00
	1924	—	—	—	Proof	200.00
	1925	101.013	.50	1.00	2.50	8.00
	1925	—	—	—	Proof	75.00
	1927	—	.50	1.00	3.00	9.00
	1927	—	—	—	Proof	75.00
	1928	—	.50	1.00	2.50	8.00
	1929	64.900	.50	1.00	3.00	9.00
	1930	163.424	.50	1.00	2.50	8.00
	1931	8.791	—	—	Rare	—

NOTE: Varieties exist.

COPPER-NICKEL

Y#	Date	Mintage	Fine	VF	XF	Unc
95	1931	122.511	1.00	2.00	4.00	8.00
	1932	171.641	.25	.50	1.00	4.00
	1933	163.125	.25	.50	1.00	4.00
	1934	104.059	.25	.50	1.00	5.00

NOTE: Varieties exist.

Y#	Date	Mintage	Fine	VF	XF	Unc
102	1935	79.628	.25	.50	1.00	5.00
	1936	122.260	.25	.50	1.00	4.00

Y#	Date	Mintage	Fine	VF	XF	Unc
109	1937	—	.50	1.00	2.50	6.00
	1938	—	.30	.75	1.25	2.50
	1939	—	.30	.60	1.00	2.00
	1940	—	.30	.60	1.00	2.00
	1941	—	.30	.60	1.00	3.00
	1942	—	7.50	15.00	40.00	75.00
	1943	—	.30	.60	1.00	2.00
	1944	—	.50	1.00	2.00	5.00
	1945	—	.30	.75	1.25	3.00
	1946	—	.30	.75	1.25	3.00
	1946 obv. of Y#102	—	—	—	Rare	—

NOTE: Varieties exist.

Obv: 8 and 7 ribbons on wreath.

Y#	Date	Mintage	Fine	VF	XF	Unc
116	1948	—	.25	.50	2.00	5.00
	1949	—	.25	.50	1.00	3.00
	1950	—	.25	.50	1.00	5.00
	1951	—	.25	.50	1.00	5.00
	1952	—	.25	.50	1.00	4.00
	1953	—	.25	.50	1.00	2.00
	1954	—	.25	.50	1.00	2.00
	1955	—	.25	.50	1.00	2.00
	1956	—	.25	.50	1.00	2.00
	1956 rev. of Y#123					
		—	50.00	75.00	150.00	250.00

NOTE: Varieties exist.

Obv: 7 and 7 ribbons on wreath.

Y#	Date	Mintage	Fine	VF	XF	Unc
123	1957 rev. of Y#116					
		—	50.00	75.00	150.00	250.00
	1957	—	.25	.50	2.00	6.00

Y#	Date	Mintage	Fine	VF	XF	Unc
A130	1958	108.023	—	—	—	350.00

NOTE: Never officially released for circulation. Majority of mintage remelted.

COPPER-NICKEL-ZINC

Y#	Date	Mintage	Fine	VF	XF	Unc
130	1961	—	.10	.20	.35	.75
	1962	—	.10	.20	.35	.75
	1965	—	.10	.20	.35	.75
	1966	—	.10	.20	.35	.75
	1967	—	.10	.20	.35	.75
	1968	—	.10	.20	.35	.75
	1969	—	.10	.20	.35	.75
	1970	—	.10	.20	.35	.75
	1971	—	.10	.20	.35	.75
	1972	—	.10	.20	.35	.75
	1973	—	.10	.20	.35	.75
	1974	—	.10	.20	.35	.75
	1975	—	.10	.20	.35	.75
	1976	—	.10	.20	.35	.75
	1977	—	.10	.20	.35	.75
	1978	—	.10	.20	.35	.75
	1979	—	.10	.20	.35	.75
	1980	—	.10	.20	.35	.75
	1981	—	.10	.20	.35	.75
	1982	—	.10	.20	.35	.75
	1983	—	.10	.20	.35	.75
	1984	—	.10	.20	.35	.75
	1985	—	.10	.20	.35	.75
	1986	—	.10	.20	.35	.75
	1987	—	.10	.20	.35	.75
	1988	—	.10	.20	.35	.75
	1989	—	.10	.20	.30	.50
	1990	—	.25	.50	1.00	2.50
	1990 Л	—	.10	.20	.30	.50
	1991	—	.15	.25	.50	1.25
	1991 Л	—	.10	.20	.30	.50
	1991 М	—	.10	.20	.30	.50
	1991(l)	—	.10	.20	.30	.50
	1991(m)	—	.10	.20	.30	.50

50th Anniversary of Revolution

Y#	Date	Mintage	Fine	VF	XF	Unc
136	1967	49.789	—	.20	.30	1.00
	1967	.211	—	—	BU	—

COPPER CLAD STEEL
Kremlin Tower and Dome

Y#	Date	Mintage	Fine	VF	XF	Unc
296	1991 M	—	.10	.15	.25	.35

15 KOPEKS

2.7000 g, .500 SILVER, .0434 oz ASW

Y#	Date	Mintage	Fine	VF	XF	Unc
87	1924	72.426	.75	1.25	3.50	10.00
	1924	—	—	—	Proof	200.00
	1925	112.709	.75	1.25	2.50	8.00
	1925	—	—	—	Proof	75.00
	1927	—	.75	1.25	2.50	8.00
	1927	—	—	—	Proof	75.00
	1928	—	.75	1.25	2.50	8.00
	1929	46.400	.75	1.25	2.50	8.00
	1930	79.868	.75	1.25	2.50	8.00
	1931	5.099	—	—	Rare	

NOTE: Varieties exist.

COPPER-NICKEL

Y#	Date	Mintage	Fine	VF	XF	Unc
96	1931	75.859	.50	1.00	1.75	4.50
	1932	136.046	.50	1.00	1.75	4.00
	1933	127.591	.50	1.00	1.75	4.00
	1934	58.367	.50	1.00	2.50	5.50

NOTE: Varieties exist.

Y#	Date	Mintage	Fine	VF	XF	Unc
103	1935	51.308	.50	1.00	1.75	4.50
	1936	52.183	.35	.75	1.50	4.00

Y#	Date	Mintage	Fine	VF	XF	Unc
110	1937	—	.35	.75	1.50	3.00
	1938	—	.30	.50	1.00	2.00
	1939	—	.30	.50	1.00	2.00
	1940	—	.30	.50	1.00	2.00
	1941	—	.30	.50	1.00	2.00
	1942	—	7.50	15.00	40.00	75.00
	1943	—	.35	.75	1.25	2.50
	1944	—	1.00	2.00	5.00	10.00
	1945	—	.50	1.25	2.50	5.00
	1946	—	.35	.75	2.00	4.00

NOTE: Varieties exist.

Obv: 8 and 7 ribbons on wreath.

Y#	Date	Mintage	Fine	VF	XF	Unc
117	1948	—	.35	.75	2.00	4.00
	1949	—	.35	.75	1.50	3.50
	1950	—	.30	.50	1.00	2.00
	1951	—	.50	1.00	2.50	8.00
	1952	—	.30	.50	1.00	2.00
	1953	—	.30	.50	1.00	2.00
	1954	—	.30	.50	1.00	2.00
	1955	—	.30	.50	1.00	2.00
	1956	—	.30	.50	1.00	2.00

NOTE: Varieties exist.

Obv: 7 and 7 ribbons on wreath.

Y#	Date	Mintage	Fine	VF	XF	Unc
124	1957	—	.30	.50	1.00	5.00

Y#	Date	Mintage	Fine	VF	XF	Unc
A131	1958	80.052	—	—	—	450.00

NOTE: Never officially released for circulation. Majority of mintage remelted.

COPPER-NICKEL-ZINC

Y#	Date	Mintage	Fine	VF	XF	Unc
131	1961	—	.10	.20	.40	.75
	1962	—	.10	.20	.40	1.00
	1965	—	.10	.20	.40	.75
	1966	—	.10	.20	.40	.75
	1967	—	.10	.20	.40	.75
	1968	—	.10	.20	.40	.75
	1969	—	.10	.20	.40	.75
	1970	—	.10	.20	.40	.75
	1971	—	.10	.20	.40	.75
	1972	—	.10	.20	.40	.75
	1973	—	.10	.20	.40	.75
	1974	—	.10	.20	.40	.75
	1975	—	.10	.20	.40	.75
	1976	—	.10	.20	.40	.75
	1977	—	.10	.20	.40	.75
	1978	—	.10	.20	.40	.75
	1979	—	.10	.20	.40	.75
	1980	—	.10	.20	.40	.75
	1981	—	.10	.20	.40	.75
	1982	—	.10	.20	.40	.75
	1983	—	.10	.20	.40	.75
	1984	—	.10	.20	.40	.75
	1985	—	.10	.20	.40	.75
	1986	—	.10	.20	.40	.75
	1987	—	.10	.20	.40	.75
	1988	—	.10	.20	.40	.75
	1989	—	.10	.20	.30	.50
	1990	—	.10	.20	.30	.50
	1991(l)	—	.10	.20	.30	.50
	1991(m)	—	.10	.20	.30	.50

50th Anniversary of Revolution

Y#	Date	Mintage	Fine	VF	XF	Unc
137	1967	49.789	.15	.30	.50	1.50
	1967	.211	—	—	BU	—

20 KOPEKS

3.6000 g, .500 SILVER, .0578 oz ASW

Y#	Date	Mintage	Fine	VF	XF	Unc
88	1924	93.810	1.00	1.75	3.50	10.00
	1924	—	—	—	Proof	225.00
	1925	135.188	1.00	1.75	3.00	9.00
	1925	—	—	—	Proof	75.00
	1927	—	1.00	2.00	4.00	12.00
	1928	—	1.00	1.75	3.00	9.00
	1929	67.250	1.00	1.75	3.00	9.00
	1930	125.658	1.00	1.75	3.00	9.00
	1931	9.530	—	—	Rare	—

COPPER-NICKEL

Y#	Date	Mintage	Fine	VF	XF	Unc
97	1931	82.200	.50	1.00	2.00	5.00
	1932	175.350	.50	1.00	2.00	5.00
	1933	143.927	.50	1.00	2.00	5.00
	1934	70.425	—	—	Rare	—

NOTE: Varieties exist.

Y#	Date	Mintage	Fine	VF	XF	Unc
104	1935	125.165	.50	1.00	2.00	4.50
	1936	52.968	.50	1.00	2.00	5.00

NOTE: Varieties exist.

Y#	Date	Mintage	Fine	VF	XF	Unc
111	1937	—	.40	.60	1.00	3.00
	1938	—	.40	.60	1.00	3.00
	1939	—	.40	.60	1.00	3.00
	1940	—	.40	.60	1.00	3.00
	1941	—	.40	.60	1.00	3.00
	1942	—	.50	.75	1.50	4.00
	1943	—	.40	.60	1.00	3.00
	1944	—	.60	1.25	2.50	6.00
	1945	—	.40	.60	1.50	4.00
	1946	—	.45	.75	2.00	5.00

NOTE: Varieties exist.

Obv: 8 and 7 ribbons on wreath.

Y#	Date	Mintage	Fine	VF	XF	Unc
118	1948	—	.45	.75	1.50	4.00
	1949	—	.45	.75	1.50	4.00
	1950	—	1.00	2.00	5.00	10.00
	1951	—	.50	1.00	2.50	7.00
	1952	—	.40	.60	1.00	2.00
	1953	—	.40	.60	1.00	2.00
	1954	—	.40	.60	1.00	2.00
	1955	—	.40	.60	1.00	2.00
	1956	—	.40	.60	1.00	2.00

NOTE: Varieties exist.

Obv: 7 and 7 ribbons on wreath.

Y#	Date	Mintage	Fine	VF	XF	Unc
125	1957	—	.40	.60	1.00	4.00

Y#	Date	Mintage	Fine	VF	XF	Unc
A132	1958	175.355	—	—	—	450.00

NOTE: Never officially released for circulation. Majority of mintage remelted.

COPPER-NICKEL-ZINC

Y#	Date	Mintage	Fine	VF	XF	Unc
132	1961	—	.15	.30	.50	1.00
	1962	—	.15	.35	.75	1.50
	1965	—	.15	.30	.50	1.00
	1966	—	.15	.30	.50	1.00
	1967	—	.15	.30	.50	1.00
	1968	—	.15	.30	.50	1.00
	1969	—	.15	.30	.50	1.00
	1970	—	.15	.30	.50	1.00
	1971	—	.15	.30	.50	1.00
	1972	—	.15	.30	.50	1.00
	1973	—	.15	.30	.50	1.00
	1974	—	.15	.30	.50	1.00
	1975	—	.15	.30	.50	1.00
132	1976	—	1.00	2.00	4.00	7.50
	1977	—	.15	.30	.50	1.00
	1978	—	.15	.30	.50	1.00
	1979	—	.15	.30	.50	1.00
	1980	—	.15	.30	.50	1.00
	1981	—	.15	.30	.50	1.00
	1982	—	.15	.30	.50	1.00
	1983	—	.15	.30	.50	1.00
	1984	—	.15	.30	.50	1.00
	1985	—	.15	.30	.50	1.00
	1986	—	.15	.30	.50	1.00
	1987	—	.15	.30	.50	1.00
	1988	—	.15	.30	.50	1.00
	1989	—	.10	.20	.30	.75
	1990	—	.10	.20	.30	.75
	1991	—	.20	.40	.65	1.50
	1991 Л	—	.10	.20	.30	.50
	1991 M	—	.10	.20	.30	.50
	1991(l)	—	.10	.20	.30	.75
	1991(m)	—	.10	.20	.30	.75

NOTE: Varieties exist.

50th Anniversary of Revolution

Y#	Date	Mintage	Fine	VF	XF	Unc
138	1967	49.789	.40	.60	.75	2.00
	1967	.211	—	Proof-like		—

50 KOPEKS

9.9980 g, .900 SILVER, .2893 oz ASW
Edge: Weight shown in old Russian units.

Y#	Date	Mintage	Fine	VF	XF	Unc
89.1	1924 ПЛ	26.559	5.00	7.00	11.50	25.00
	1924 ПЛ	—	—	—	Proof	250.00
	1924 ТР	40.000	5.00	7.00	11.50	25.00

Edge: Weight shown in grams only.

Y#	Date	Mintage	Fine	VF	XF	Unc
89.2	1925 ПЛ	43.558	5.00	7.00	11.50	25.00
	1925 ПЛ	—	—	—	Proof	125.00
	1926 ПЛ	24.374	5.00	7.00	11.50	25.00
	1926 ПЛ	—	—	—	Proof	125.00
	1927 ПЛ	—	5.00	8.00	15.00	35.00
	1927 ПЛ	—	—	—	Proof	165.00

NOTE: Varieties exist.

COPPER-NICKEL

Y#	Date	Mintage	Fine	VF	XF	Unc
133	1958	40.600	—	—	—	—

NOTE: Never officially released for circulation. Majority of mintage remelted.

COPPER-NICKEL-ZINC
Plain edge.

Y#	Date	Mintage	Fine	VF	XF	Unc
133a.1	1961	—	1.00	2.00	5.00	12.00

NOTE: Varieties exist.

Lettered edge with date.

Y#	Date	Mintage	Fine	VF	XF	Unc
133a.2	1964	—	.20	.40	.75	1.50

Y#	Date	Mintage	Fine	VF	XF	Unc
133a.2						
	1965	—	.20	.40	.75	1.50
	1966	—	.20	.40	.75	1.50
	1967	—	.20	.40	.75	1.50
	1968	—	.20	.40	.75	1.50
	1969	—	.20	.40	.75	1.50
	1970	—	.20	.40	.75	1.50
	1971	—	.20	.40	.75	1.50
	1972	—	.20	.40	.75	1.50
	1973	—	.20	.40	.75	1.50
	1974	—	.20	.40	.75	1.50
	1975	—	.20	.40	.75	1.50
	1976	—	.20	.40	.75	1.50
	1977	—	.20	.40	.75	1.50
	1978	—	.20	.40	.75	1.50
	1979	—	.20	.40	.75	1.50
	1980	—	.20	.40	.75	1.50
	1981	—	.20	.40	.75	1.50
	1982	—	.20	.40	.75	1.50
	1983	—	.20	.40	.75	1.50
	1984	—	.20	.40	.75	1.50
	1985	—	.20	.40	.75	1.50
	1986 w/1985 edge					
		—	1.00	2.00	4.00	10.00
	1986	—	.20	.40	.75	1.50
	1987	—	.20	.40	.75	1.50
	1988 w/1987 edge					
		—	1.00	2.00	4.00	10.00
	1988	—	.20	.40	.75	1.50
	1989	—	.15	.25	.50	1.00
	1990 w/1989 edge					
		—	2.50	5.00	10.00	25.00
	1990	—	.15	.25	.50	1.00
	1991 M	—	.15	.25	.50	1.00
	1991 L	—	.15	.25	.50	1.00

50th Anniversary of Revolution

139	ND(1967)	49.789	—	1.00	1.50	2.50
	ND(1967)	.211	—	—	BU	—

COPPER-NICKEL
Government Bank Issue
Mint mark: Л

292	1991		.15	.25	.35	.50

ROUBLE

19.9960 g, .900 SILVER, .5786 oz ASW
Edge: 18 grams (43.21d).

90.1	1924 ПЛ	12.998	7.50	12.50	25.00	70.00
	1924 ПЛ	—	—	—	Proof	750.00

NOTE: Varieties exist.

Edge: 4 Zolotniks 21 Dolyas.

90.2	1924		—	—	Rare	—

COPPER-NICKEL

134	1958	30.700	—	—	—	—

NOTE: Never officially released for circulation. Majority of mintage remelted.

COPPER-NICKEL-ZINC
Plain edge.

Y#	Date	Mintage	Fine	VF	XF	Unc
134a.1						
	1961	—	2.00	3.50	6.00	15.00

Lettered edge with date.

134a.2						
	1964	—	.40	.75	1.50	2.50
	1965	—	.40	.75	1.50	2.50
	1966	—	.40	.75	1.50	2.50
	1967 w/1966 edge					
		—	3.00	6.00	12.00	30.00
	1967	—	.40	.75	1.50	2.50
	1968	—	.40	.75	1.50	2.50
	1969	—	.40	.75	1.50	2.50
	1970	—	.40	.75	1.50	2.50
	1971	—	.40	.75	1.50	2.50
	1972	—	.40	.75	1.50	2.50
	1973	—	.40	.75	1.50	2.50
	1974	—	.40	.75	1.50	2.50
	1975	—	.40	.75	1.50	2.50
	1976	—	.40	.75	1.50	2.50
	1977	—	.40	.75	1.50	2.50
	1978	—	.40	.75	1.50	2.50
	1979	—	.40	.75	1.50	2.50
	1980	—	.40	.75	1.50	2.50
	1981	—	.40	.75	1.50	2.50
	1982	—	.40	.75	1.50	2.50
	1983	—	.40	.75	1.50	2.50
	1984	—	.40	.75	1.50	2.50
	1985	—	.40	.75	1.50	2.50
	1986	—	.40	.75	1.50	2.50
	1987	—	.40	.75	1.50	2.50
	1988	—	.40	.75	1.50	2.50
	1990 w/1989 edge					
		—	1.50	3.00	6.00	15.00
	1989	—	.25	.50	1.00	2.50
	1990	—	.25	.50	1.00	2.50
	1991(m)	—	.25	.50	1.00	2.50
	1991(l)	—	.25	.50	1.00	2.50

NOTE: Values listed below for 1965-1980 Commemorative Roubles in Proof are for true Proof coins. Prooflike examples are known to exist and are valued at a moderate premium over the uncirculated values listed here.

20th Anniversary of World War II Victory

135.1	1965	59.989	—	.50	1.00	2.50
	1965	—	—	—	Proof	10.00

Lettered edge with date.

140.1	1967	52.289	—	.50	1.00	2.50
	1967	—	—	—	Proof	10.00

Centennial of Lenin's Birth

Y#	Date	Mintage	Fine	VF	XF	Unc
141	1970	99.889	—	.50	1.00	2.50
	1970	—	—	—	Proof	25.00

30th Anniversary of World War II Victory
Date on edge.

142.1	1975	14.989	—	.50	1.00	2.50
	1975	—	—	—	Proof	10.00

NOTE: Varieties exist.

60th Anniversary of Bolshevik Revolution

143.1	1977	4.987	—	.50	1.00	2.50
	1977	—	—	—	Proof	10.00

Mule. Obv: KM#143.1. Rev: KM#144.

A144	1977	Inc. Be.	—	—	Rare	—

1980 Olympics - Emblem

144	1977	8.665	—	.50	1.00	2.50
	1977	—	—	—	Proof	7.50

1980 Olympics - Moscow Kremlin

153.1	1978	6.490	—	.50	1.00	2.50
	1978	—	—	—	Proof	7.50

Rev: Clock on tower shows Roman 6 instead of 4.

153.2	1978	Inc. Ab.	—	8.00	16.00	25.00

1980 Olympics - Moscow University

164	1979	4.665	—	.50	1.00	2.50
	1979	—	—	—	Proof	7.50

NOTE: Varieties in window arrangements exist.

1980 Olympics - Monument, Sputnik and Sojuz

Y#	Date	Mintage	Fine	VF	XF	Unc
165	1979	4.665	—	.50	1.00	2.50
	1979		—	—	Proof	7.50

COPPER-NICKEL
1980 Olympics - Dolgorukij Monument

177	1980	4.490	—	.50	1.00	2.50
	1980		—	—	Proof	7.50

1980 Olympics - Torch

178	1980	4.490	—	.50	1.00	2.50
	1980		—	—	Proof	7.50

20th Anniversary of Manned
Space Flights - Yuri Gagarin

188.1	1981	3.962	—	.50	1.00	3.00
	1981	.038	—	—	Proof	7.50

Russian-Bulgarian Friendship

189.1	1981	1.984	—	.50	1.00	3.00
	1981	.016	—	—	Proof	15.00

60th Anniversary of the Soviet Union

190.1	ND(1982)	1.921	—	.50	1.50	3.50
	ND(1982)	.079	—	—	Proof	6.00

Centennial - Death of Karl Marx

Y#	Date	Mintage	Fine	VF	XF	Unc
191.1	1983	1.921	—	.50	1.50	3.50
	1983	.079	—	—	Proof	6.00

20th Anniversary of First Woman in Space -
Valentina Tereshkova

192.1	1983	1.945	—	.50	1.00	3.00
	1983	.055	—	—	Proof	5.00

Ivan Fedorov - First Russian Printer

193.1	1983	1.965	—	.50	1.00	3.00
	1983	.035	—	—	Proof	5.00

150th Anniversary - Birth of
Dmitri Ivanovich Mendeleyev

194.1	1984	1.965	—	.50	1.00	3.00
	1984	.035	—	—	Proof	5.00

125th Anniversary - Birth of Alexander Popov

195.1	1984	1.965	—	.50	1.00	3.00
	1984	.035	—	—	Proof	5.00

185th Anniversary - Birth of
Alexander Sergeevich Pushkin

196.1	1984	1.965	—	.50	1.00	3.00
	1984	.035	—	—	Proof	5.00

115th Anniv. - Birth of Vladimir Lenin

Y#	Date	Mintage	Fine	VF	XF	Unc
197.1	1985	1.960	—	.50	1.50	3.50
	1985	.040	—	—	Proof	6.00

40th Anniversary of World War II Victory

198.1	1985	5.960	—	.50	1.00	3.00
	1985	.040	—	—	Proof	6.00

12th World Youth Festival in Moscow

199.1	1985	5.960	—	.50	1.00	3.00
	1985	.040	—	—	Proof	6.00

165th Anniversary - Birth of Friedrich Engels

200.1	1985	1.960	—	.50	1.50	3.50
	1985	.040	—	—	Proof	6.00

International Year of Peace
Rouble written with inverted "V" for Л.

201.1	1986	3.955	—	.50	1.00	3.00
	1986	.045	—	—	Proof	5.00

Rouble written РУБЛЬ

201.3	1986	3.955	—	.50	1.00	3.00
	1986	.045	—	—	Proof	5.00

Rouble written *****

201.4	1986		—	—	—	—

275th Anniversary - Birth of Mikhail Lomonosov

Y#	Date	Mintage	Fine	VF	XF	Unc
202.1	1986	1.965	—	.50	1.00	3.00
	1986	.035	—	—	Proof	5.00

175th Anniversary - Battle of Borodino - Soldiers

203	1987	3.780	—	.50	1.00	3.00
	1987	.220	—	—	Proof	5.00

NOTE: Varieties exist w/wheat in coat of arms.

175th Anniversary - Battle of Borodino - Kutzov Monument

204	1987	3.780	—	.50	1.00	3.00
	1987	.220	—	—	Proof	5.00

NOTE: Varieties exist w/wheat in coat of arms.

130th Anniversary - Birth of Constantin Tsiolkovsy

205	1987	3.830	—	.50	1.00	3.00
	1987	.170	—	—	Proof	5.00

70th Anniversary of Bolshevik Revolution

206	1987	3.800	—	.50	1.00	3.00
	1987	.200	—	—	Proof	6.00

NOTE: Varieties exist w/wheat in coat of arms.

120th Anniversary - Birth of Maxim Gorki

209	1988	3.775	—	.50	1.00	3.00
	1988	.225	—	—	Proof	6.00

160th Anniversary - Birth of Leo Tolstoi

Y#	Date	Mintage	Fine	VF	XF	Unc
216	1987 (error)					
	1988	3.775	—	.50	1.00	3.00
	1988	.225	—	—	Proof	5.00

150th Anniversary - Birth of Musorgsky

220	1989	2.700	—	.50	1.00	3.00
	1989	.300	—	—	Proof	5.50

175th Anniversary - Birth of M.Y. Lermontov

228	1989	2.700	—	.50	1.00	3.00
	1989	.300	—	—	Proof	6.00

100th Anniversary - Birth of Hamza Hakim-zade Niyazi

232	1989	1.800	—	.50	1.00	3.00
	1989	.200	—	—	Proof	6.00

100th Anniversary - Death of Mihai Eminescu

233	1989	1.800	—	.50	1.00	3.00
	1989	.200	—	—	Proof	6.00

175th Anniversary - Birth of T.G. Shevchenko

235	1989	2.700	—	.50	1.00	3.00
	1989	.300	—	—	Proof	5.50

100th Anniversary - Birth of Tschaikovsky - Composer

Y#	Date	Mintage	Fine	VF	XF	Unc
236	1990	2.600	—	—	—	3.00
	1990	.400	—	—	Proof	6.50

Anniversary - Birth of Marshal Zhukov

237	1990	1.600	—	—	—	3.00
	1990	.400	—	—	Proof	6.50

130th Anniversary - Birth of Anton Chekhov

240	1990	2.600	—	—	—	3.00
	1990	.400	—	—	Proof	6.50

125th Anniversary - Birth of Janis Rainis

257	1990	2.600	—	—	—	3.00
	1990	.400	—	—	Proof	6.50

500th Anniversary - Birth of Francisk Scorina

258	1990	2.600	—	—	—	3.00
	1990	.400	—	—	Proof	6.50

550th Anniversary - Birth of Alisher Navoi

260	1990 (error)	—	—	—	—	
	1991	2.150	—	—	—	3.00
	1991	.350	—	—	Proof	5.50

125th Anniversary - Birth of P. N. Lebedev

Y#	Date	Mintage	Fine	VF	XF	Unc
261	1991	2.150	—	—	—	3.00
	1991	.350	—	—	Proof	5.50

100th Birthday of Sergey Prokofiev

263	1991	2.150	—	—	—	3.00
	1991	.350	—	—	Proof	5.50

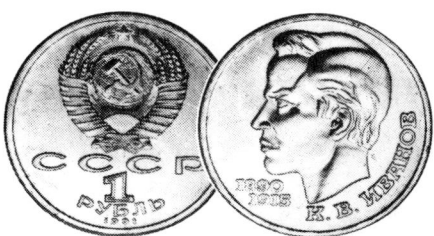

K. T. Ivanov

282	1991	3.150	—	—	—	3.00
	1991	.350	—	—	Proof	5.50

Turkman Poet Makhtumkuli

283	1991	2.150	—	—	—	3.00
	1991	.350	—	—	Proof	5.50

850th Anniversary - Birth of Nizami Gyanzhevi - Poet

284	1991	2.200	—	—	—	3.00
	1991	.300	—	—	Proof	5.50

Government Bank Issue

293	1991(l)	—	—	—	—	.75
	1991(m)	—	—	—	—	1.25

---

2 ROUBLES

COPPER-NICKEL

Y#	Date	Mintage	Fine	VF	XF	Unc
A134	1958	20.976	—	—	—	250.00

NOTE: Never officially released for circulation. Majority of mintage remelted.

3 ROUBLES

COPPER-NICKEL

B134	1958	4.050	—	—	—	—

NOTE: Never officially released for circulation. Majority of mintage remelted.

5 ROUBLES

COPPER-NICKEL

C134	1958	5.150	—	—	—	300.00

NOTE: Never officially released for circulation. Majority of mintage remelted.

Government Bank Issue

BRASS center, COPPER-NICKEL ring
Wildlife - Owl

280	1991(l)	.500	—	—	—	1.50
	1991(l)	.050	—	—	BU	6.50

Wildlife - Mountain Goat

281	1991(l)	.500	—	—	—	1.50
	1991(l)	.050	—	—	BU	6.50

COPPER-NICKEL

294	1991(l)	—	—	—	—	2.50
	1991(m)	—	—	—	—	5.00

10 ROUBLES

Government Bank Issue

ALUMINUM-BRONZE center, COPPER-NICKEL ring

Y#	Date	Mintage	Fine	VF	XF	Unc
295	1991(l)	—	.25	.50	1.00	3.00
	1991(m)	—	1.50	3.00	5.00	10.00
	1992(l)(error)	—	—	30.00	50.00	80.00

COMMONWEALTH OF INDEPENDENT STATES
MONETARY REFORM
1992
1,000 "old" Roubles = 1 New Rouble

1 KOPEK

NICKEL CLAD STEEL
Obv: St. George. Rev: Denomination.

600	1997 M	—	—	—	—	.25
	1997 SP	—	—	—	—	.25
	1998 M	—	—	—	—	.25

5 KOPEKS

NICKEL CLAD STEEL
Obv: St. George. Rev: Denomination.

601	1997 M	—	—	—	—	.50
	1997 SP	—	—	—	—	.50
	1998 M	—	—	—	—	.50

10 KOPEKS

BRASS
Obv: St. George. Rev: Denomination.

602	1997 M	—	—	—	—	.75
	1997 SP	—	—	—	—	.75
	1998 M	—	—	—	—	.75

50 KOPEKS

BRASS
Obv: St. George. Rev: Denomination.

603	1997 M	—	—	—	—	1.00
	1997 SP	—	—	—	—	1.00

ROUBLE

BRASS CLAD STEEL
Double-headed Eagle

311	1992	—	2.00	5.00	10.00	20.00
	1992 Л	—	—	—	—	1.25
	1992 М	—	—	—	—	1.00
	1992(m)	—	—	—	—	2.00

COPPER-NICKEL-ZINC
Rev: Denomination.

Y#	Date	Mintage	Fine	VF	XF	Unc
604	1997(m)	—	—	—	—	1.25
	1997(sp)	—	—	—	—	1.25
	1998 M	—	—	—	—	1.25

2 ROUBLES

COPPER-NICKEL-ZINC
Rev: Denomination.

605	1997(m)	—	—	—	—	1.65
	1997(sp)	—	—	—	—	1.65

5 ROUBLES

BRASS CLAD STEEL
Double-headed Eagle

312	1992 Л	—	—	—	—	1.75
	1992 M	—	—	—	—	1.50
	1992(m)	—	—	—	—	2.00
	1992(l)	—	—	—	—	2.50

COPPER-NICKEL CLAD COPPER
Rev: Denomination.

606	1997(m)	—	—	—	—	2.00
	1997(sp)	—	—	—	—	2.00

10 ROUBLES

**ALUMINUM-BRONZE center,
COPPER-NICKEL ring**
Wildlife - Red-breasted Kazarka

307	1992(l)	.300	—	—	—	1.50

Wildlife - Tiger

308	1992(l)	.300	—	—	—	1.50

Wildlife - Cobra

309	1992(l)	.300	—	—	—	1.50

COPPER-NICKEL
Double-headed Eagle

Y#	Date	Mintage	Fine	VF	XF	Unc
313	1992(l)	—	—	—	—	1.50
	1992(m)	—	—	—	—	2.00
	1993(l)	—	—	—	—	1.50
	1993(m)	—	—	—	—	10.00
313a	1992(m)	—	—	—	—	10.00
	1993(l)	—	—	—	—	1.50
	1993(m)	—	—	—	—	1.50

COPPER-NICKEL CLAD STEEL

20 ROUBLES

COPPER-NICKEL
Double-headed Eagle

314	1992(l)	—	—	—	—	2.00
	1992(m)	—	—	—	—	2.50
	1993(m)	—	—	—	—	20.00

COPPER-NICKEL CLAD STEEL

314a	1993(l)	—	—	—	—	2.50
	1993(m)	—	—	—	—	2.50

50 ROUBLES

**ALUMINUM-BRONZE center,
COPPER-NICKEL ring**
Double-headed Eagle

315	1992(l)	—	.50	.75	1.00	2.50
	1992(m)	—	.75	1.00	1.50	3.50

ALUMINUM-BRONZE

329	1993(l)	—	—	—	—	2.50
	1993(m)	—	—	—	—	2.50

**ALUMINUM-BRONZE center,
COPPER-NICKEL ring**
Wildlife - Bear

330	1993(l)	.300	—	—	—	1.50

Wildlife - Gecko

331	1993(l)	.300	—	—	—	1.50

Wildlife - Caucasian Grouse

Y#	Date	Mintage	Fine	VF	XF	Unc
332	1993(l)	.300	—	—	—	1.50

Wildlife - Far Eastern Stork

333	1993(l)	.300	—	—	—	1.50

Wildlife - Black Sea Porpoise

334	1993(l)	.300	—	—	—	1.50

Wildlife - Spalax

367	1994(l)	.300	—	—	—	1.50

Wildlife - Bison

368	1994(l)	.300	—	—	—	1.50

Wildlife - Gazelle

369	1994(l)	.300	—	—	—	1.50

Wildlife - Peregrine Falcon

370	1994(l)	.300	—	—	—	1.50

Wildlife - 2 Flamingos

371	1994(l)	.300	—	—	—	1.50

100 ROUBLES

**COPPER-NICKEL center,
ALUMINUM-BRONZE ring
Double-headed Eagle**

Y#	Date	Mintage	Fine	VF	XF	Unc
316	1992(l)	—	.50	.75	1.00	3.00
	1992(m)	—	.75	1.00	1.50	4.50

COPPER-NICKEL-ZINC

338	1993(l)	—	.25	.50	1.00	3.00
	1993(m)	—	.25	.50	1.00	3.00

TANNU TUVA

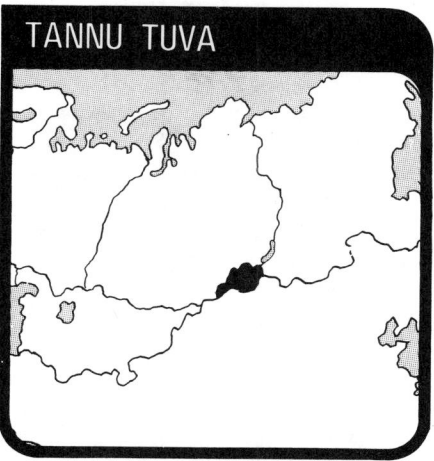

The Tannu-Tuva Peoples Republic (Tuva), an autonomous part of Russia located in central Asia on the northwest border of Outer Mongolia, has an area of 64,000 sq. mi. (165,760 sq. km.) and a population of about 175,000. Capital: Kyzyl. The economy is based on herding, forestry and mining.

As Urianghi, Tuva was part of Outer Mongolia of the Chinese Empire when tsarist Russia, after fomenting a separatist movement, extended its protection to the mountainous country in 1914. Tuva declared its independence as the Tannu-Tuva Peoples Republic in 1921 under the auspices of the Tuva Peoples Revolutionary Party. In 1926, following Russia's successful mediation of the resultant Tuvinian-Mongolian territorial dispute, Tannu-Tuva and Outer Mongolia formally recognized each other's independence. The Tannu-Tuva Peoples Republic became an autonomous region of the U.S.S.R. on Oct. 13, 1944.

MONETARY SYSTEM
100 Kopejek (Kopeks) = 1 Aksha

KOPEJEK

ALUMINUM-BRONZE

KM#	Date	Mintage	VG	Fine	VF	XF
1	1934	—	20.00	30.00	45.00	75.00

2 KOPEJEK

ALUMINUM-BRONZE

2	1933	—	—	—	—	—
	1934	—	22.50	32.50	55.00	85.00

3 KOPEJEK

ALUMINUM-BRONZE

3	1933	—	—	—	—	—
	1934	—	20.00	30.00	45.00	75.00

5 KOPEJEK

ALUMINUM-BRONZE

4	1934	—	22.50	32.50	55.00	85.00

10 KOPEJEK

COPPER-NICKEL

KM#	Date	Mintage	VG	Fine	VF	XF
5	1934	—	22.50	32.50	55.00	85.00

15 KOPEJEK

COPPER-NICKEL

6	1934	—	22.50	32.50	55.00	85.00

20 KOPEJEK

COPPER-NICKEL

7	1934	—	22.50	32.50	55.00	85.00

RWANDA

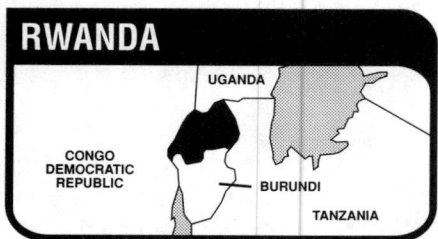

The Republic of Rwanda, located in central Africa between the Republic of the Congo and Tanzania, has an area of 10,169 sq. mi. (26,340 sq. km.) and a population of 7.3 million. Capital: Kigali. The economy is based on agriculture and mining. Coffee and tin are exported.

German Lieutenant Count von Goetzen was the first European to visit Rwanda, 1894. Four years later the court of the Mwami (the Tutsi king of Rwanda) willingly permitted the kingdom to become a protectorate of Germany. In 1916, during the African campaigns of World War I, Belgian troops from Congo occupied Rwanda. After the war it, together with Burundi, became a Belgian League of Nations mandate under the name of the Territory of Ruanda-Urundi. Following World War II, Ruanda-Urundi became a Belgian administered U.N. trust territory. The Tutsi monarchy was deposed by the U.N. supervised election of 1961, after which Belgium granted Rwanda internal autonomy. On July 1, 1962, the U.N. terminated the Belgian trusteeship and granted full independence to both Rwanda and Burundi.

For earlier coinage see Belgian Congo, and Rwanda and Burundi.

MINT MARKS
(a) - Paris, privy marks only
(b) - Brussels, privy marks only

MONETARY SYSTEM
100 Centimes = 1 Franc

1/2 FRANC

ALUMINUM

KM#	Date	Mintage	VF	XF	Unc
9	1970	5.000	.50	.85	1.75

FRANC

COPPER-NICKEL

KM#	Date	Mintage	VF	XF	Unc
5	1964(b)	3.000	5.00	10.00	20.00
	1965(b)	4.500	.50	.85	1.75

ALUMINUM

KM#	Date	Mintage	VF	XF	Unc
8	1969	5.000	.50	1.50	3.50

KM#	Date	Mintage	VF	XF	Unc
12	1974	13.000	.20	.50	1.00
	1977	15.000	.15	.25	.75
	1985	—	.10	.15	.65

2 FRANCS

ALUMINUM

F.A.O. Issue

KM#	Date	Mintage	VF	XF	Unc
10	1970	5.000	.10	.20	.50

5 FRANCS

BRONZE

KM#	Date	Mintage	VF	XF	Unc
6	1964(b)	4.000	.25	.50	1.75
	1965(b)	3.000	5.00	10.00	20.00

KM#	Date	Mintage	VF	XF	Unc
13	1974	7.000	1.00	3.00	6.00
	1977	7.002	1.00	2.00	4.00
	1987	—	.25	.50	1.85

10 FRANCS

COPPER-NICKEL

KM#	Date	Mintage	VF	XF	Unc
7	1964(b)	6.000	1.00	2.00	4.50

KM#	Date	Mintage	VF	XF	Unc
14.1	1974	6.000	3.00	5.00	10.00

Reduced size.

KM#	Date	Mintage	VF	XF	Unc
14.2	1985	—	.50	.85	1.85

20 FRANCS

BRASS

KM#	Date	Mintage	VF	XF	Unc
15	1977(a)	22.000	1.00	2.00	4.00

50 FRANCS

BRASS

KM#	Date	Mintage	VF	XF	Unc
16	1977(a)	9.000	2.50	3.50	7.00

RWANDA-BURUNDI

Ruanda-Urundi, a Belgian League of Nations mandate and United Nations trust territory comprising the provinces of Ruanda-Urundi of the former colony of German East Africa, was located in central Africa between the present Democratic Republic of the Congo, Uganda and mainland Tanzania. The mandate-trust territory had an area of 20,916 sq. mi. (54,272 sq. km.) and a population of 4.3 million.

For specific statistics and history of Ruanda and of Urundi see individual entries.

When Rwanda and Burundi were formed into a mandate for administration by Belgium, their names were combined as Ruanda-Urundi and they were organized as an integral part of the Belgian Congo. During the mandate-trust territory period, they utilized the coinage of the Belgian Congo, which from 1954 through 1960 carried the appropriate dual identification. After the Belgian Congo acquired independence as the Democratic Republic of the Congo, the provinces of Ruanda and Urundi reverted to their former names of Rwanda and Burundi and utilized a common currency issued by a Central Bank (B.E.R.B.) established for that purpose until the time when, as independent republics, each issued its own national coinage.

For earlier coinage see Belgian Congo.

MONETARY SYSTEM
100 Centimes = 1 Franc

FRANC

BRASS

KM#	Date	Mintage	VF	XF	Unc
1	1960	2.000	3.50	7.50	17.50
	1961	16.000	.50	1.00	2.50
	1964	3.000	3.00	6.50	15.00

NOTE: For later coinage see individual listings under Rwanda and Burundi.

SAHARAWI ARAB D.R.

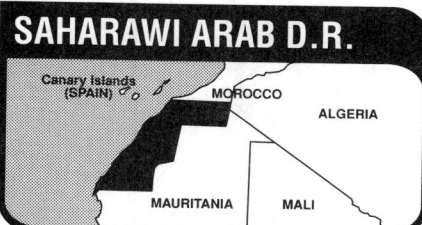 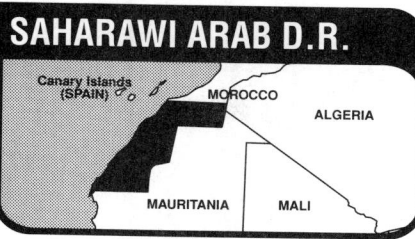

The Saharawi Arab Democratic Republic, located in northwest Africa has an area of 102,703 sq. mi. and a population (census taken 1974) of 76,425. Formerly known as Spanish Sahara, the area is bounded on the north by Morocco, on the east and southeast by Mauritania, on the northeast by Algeria, and on the west by the Atlantic Ocean. Capital: El Aaium. Agriculture, fishing and mining are the two main industries. Exports are barley, livestock and phosphates.

A Spanish trading post was established in 1476 but was abandoned in 1524. A Spanish protectorate for the region was proclaimed in 1884. The status of the Spanish Sahara changed from a colony to an overseas province in 1958. Spain relinquished its holdings in 1975 and it was divided between Mauritania, which gave up its claim in August, 1979 and Morocco, which subsequently occupied the entire territory. The official languages are Spanish and an Arab dialect: The Hassaniya.

1 PESETA

COPPER-NICKEL
Arab and Camel

KM#	Date	Mintage	VF	XF	Unc
14	1992	—	—		.75

2 PESETAS

COPPER-NICKEL
Arab and Camel

KM#	Date	Mintage	VF	XF	Unc
15	1992	—	—	—	1.25

5 PESETAS

COPPER-NICKEL
Arab and Camel

KM#	Date	Mintage	VF	XF	Unc
16	1992	—	—	—	2.00

50 PESETAS

COPPER-NICKEL
Arab and Camel

KM#	Date	Mintage	VF	XF	Unc
1	1990	—	—	—	6.00

100 PESETAS
COPPER-NICKEL
Arab and Sailing Ship

KM#	Date	Mintage	VF	XF	Unc
18	1990	—	—	—	10.00

SAINT HELENA

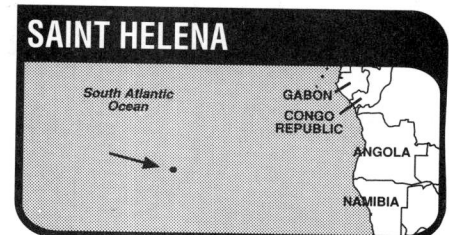

Saint Helena, a British colony located about 1,150 miles (1,850 km.) from the west coast of Africa, has an area of 47 sq. mi. (410 sq. km.) and a population of *7,000. Capital: Jamestown. Flax, lace, and rope are produced for export. Ascension and Tristan da Cunha are dependencies of Saint Helena.

The island was discovered and named by the Portuguese navigator Joao de Nova Castella in 1502. The Portuguese imported livestock, fruit trees, and vegetables but established no permanent settlement. The Dutch occupied the island temporarily, 1645-51. The original European settlement was founded by representatives of the British East India Company sent to annex the island after the departure of the Dutch. The Dutch returned and captured Saint Helena from the British on New Year's Day, 1673, but were in turn ejected by a British force under Sir Richard Munden. Thereafter Saint Helena was the undisputed possession of Great Britain. The island served as the place of exile for Napoleon, several Zulu chiefs, and an ex-sultan of Zanzibar.

RULERS
British

PENNY

BRONZE
Tuna

KM#	Date	Mintage	Fine	VF	XF	Unc
1	1984	—	—	—	.15	.35
	1984	*.010	—	—	Proof	1.25

Obv: Similar to 2 Pence, KM#12.

KM#	Date	Mintage	Fine	VF	XF	Unc
13	1991	—	—	—	.15	.35

COPPER PLATED STEEL

KM#	Date	Mintage	Fine	VF	XF	Unc
13a	1997	—	—	—	.15	.35

2 PENCE

BRONZE
Donkey with Fire Wood

KM#	Date	Mintage	Fine	VF	XF	Unc
2	1984	—	—	—	.20	.50
	1984	*.010	—	—	Proof	1.50

KM#	Date	Mintage	Fine	VF	XF	Unc
12	1991	—	—	—	.20	.50

5 PENCE

COPPER-NICKEL
Rain Piper

KM#	Date	Mintage	Fine	VF	XF	Unc
3	1984	—	—	—	.20	.50
	1984	—	—	—	Proof	1.75

| 14 | 1991 | — | — | — | .20 | .50 |

10 PENCE

COPPER-NICKEL
Arum Lily

4	1984	—	—	—	.30	1.00
	1984	—	—	—	Proof	2.00

Obv: Similar to 2 Pence, KM#12.

| 15 | 1991 | — | — | — | .30 | 1.00 |

20 PENCE

COPPER-NICKEL
Obv: Quee's portrait. Rev: Flower.

| 21 | 1998 | — | — | — | — | 1.25 |

50 PENCE

COPPER-NICKEL
Sea Turtle

5	1984	—	—	—	1.50	3.50
	1984	—	—	—	Proof	4.00

POUND

NICKEL-BRASS
Sooty Terns

6	1984	—	—	—	2.25	5.00
	1984	—	—	—	Proof	5.00

Obv: Similar to 2 Pence, KM#12.

KM#	Date	Mintage	Fine	VF	XF	Unc
17	1991	—	—	—	2.25	5.00

SAINT PIERRE & MIQUELON

The Territorial Collectivity of Saint Pierre and Miquelon, a French overseas territory located 10 miles (16 km.) off the south coast of Newfoundland, has an area of 93 sq. mi. (242 sq. km.) and a population of *6,000. Capital: Saint Pierre. The economy of the barren archipelago is based on cod fishing and fur farming. Fish and fish products, and mink and silver fox pelts are exported.

The islands, occupied by the French in 1604, were captured by the British in 1702 and held until 1763 when they were returned to the possession of France and employed as a fishing station. They passed between France and England on six more occasions between 1778 and 1814 when they were awarded permanently to France by the Treaty of Paris. The rugged, soil-poor granite islands, which will support only evergreen shrubs, are all that remain to France of her extensive colonies in North America. In 1958 Saint Pierre and Miquelon voted in favor of the new constitution of the Fifth Republic of France, thereby choosing to remain within the new French Community.

RULERS

French

MINT MARKS

(a) - Paris, privy marks only

MONETARY SYSTEM

100 Centimes = 1 Franc

FRANC

ALUMINUM

KM#	Date	Mintage	Fine	VF	XF	Unc
1	1948(a)	.600	.50	.75	1.50	5.00

2 FRANCS

ALUMINUM

| 2 | 1948(a) | .300 | .75 | 1.00 | 2.00 | 6.00 |

 SAINT THOMAS & PRINCE

SAINT THOMAS & PRINCE

The Democratic Republic of Sao Tome and Principe (formerly the Portuguese overseas province of Saint Thomas and Prince Islands) is located in the Gulf of Guinea 150 miles (241 km.) off the west African coast. It has an area of 372 sq. mi. (960 sq. km.) and a population of *121,000. Capital: Sao Tome. The economy of the islands is based on cocoa, copra and coffee.

Saint Thomas and Saint Prince were uninhabited when discovered by Portuguese navigators Joao de Santarem and Pedro de Escobar in 1470. After the failure of their initial settlement, 1485, the Portuguese successfully colonized St. Thomas with a colony of prisoners and exiled Jews, 1493. An initial prosperity based on the sugar trade gave way to a time of misfortune, 1567-1709, that saw the colony attacked and occupied or plundered by the French and Dutch, ravaged by the slave revolt of 1595; and finally rendered destitute by the transfer of the world sugar trade to Brazil. In the late 1800s, the colony turned from the production of sugar to cocoa, the basis of its present economy

The islands were designated a Portuguese overseas province in 1951. On April 25, 1974, the government of Portugal was seized by a military junta which reached agreements providing for independence for the Portuguese overseas provinces of Portuguese Guinea (Guinea-Bissau), Mozambique, Cape Verde Islands, Angola, and Saint Thomas and Prince Islands. The Democratic Republic of Sao Tome and Principe was declared on July 12, 1975.

RULERS
Portuguese, until 1975

MINT MARKS
R = Rio

MONETARY SYSTEM
100 Centavos = 1 Escudo

10 CENTAVOS

KM# 2	Date 1929	Mintage .500	Fine 1.00	VF 2.00	XF 5.00	Unc 17.50

NICKEL-BRONZE

		BRONZE				
15	1962	.500	.15	.25	.75	2.50
		ALUMINUM				
15a	1971	1.000	—	.15	.35	1.25

20 CENTAVOS

NICKEL-BRONZE

3	1929	.250	1.25	2.50	6.00	18.00

BRONZE
18mm

16.1	1962	.250	.15	.30	.85	4.00

16mm

KM# 16.2	Date 1971	Mintage .750	Fine —	VF .15	XF .35	Unc 1.75

50 CENTAVOS

NICKEL-BRONZE

1	1928	—	10.00	20.00	90.00	500.00
	1929	.400	2.50	5.00	30.00	300.00

8	1948	.080	1.00	2.00	12.50	48.00

COPPER-NICKEL

10	1951	.048	1.00	2.00	12.50	48.00

BRONZE
20mm

17.1	1962	.480	.20	.40	1.00	3.00

22mm

17.2	1971	.600	.15	.25	.75	2.00

ESCUDO

COPPER-NICKEL

4	1939	.100	5.00	10.00	75.00	300.00

NICKEL-BRONZE

9	1948	.060	2.50	5.00	15.00	75.00

COPPER-NICKEL

KM# 11	Date 1951	Mintage .018	Fine 3.50	VF 8.50	XF 27.50	Unc 100.00

BRONZE

18	1962	.160	.25	.60	1.75	6.00
	1971	.350	.15	.30	1.00	2.50

2-1/2 ESCUDOS

3.5000 g, .650 SILVER, .0732 oz ASW

5	1939	.080	5.00	12.00	50.00	250.00
	1948	.120	3.00	6.00	18.00	110.00

12	1951	.064	3.00	6.00	12.00	45.00

COPPER-NICKEL

19	1962	.140	.25	.60	1.75	5.00
	1971	.250	.15	.30	.75	2.00

5 ESCUDOS

7.0000 g, .650 SILVER, .1462 oz ASW

6	1939	.060	7.50	15.00	75.00	300.00
	1948	.100	5.00	10.00	25.00	120.00

25mm

13	1951	.072	3.00	6.00	20.00	50.00

4.0000 g, .600 SILVER, .0771 oz ASW
22mm

KM#	Date	Mintage	Fine	VF	XF	Unc
20	1962	.088	.75	1.50	3.00	8.00

COPPER-NICKEL

| 22 | 1971 | .100 | .50 | 1.00 | 2.00 | 5.00 |

10 ESCUDOS

12.5000 g, .835 SILVER, .3356 oz ASW

| 7 | 1939 | .040 | 10.00 | 20.00 | 75.00 | 350.00 |

12.5000 g, .720 SILVER, .2894 oz ASW

| 14 | 1951 | .040 | 3.00 | 10.00 | 30.00 | 55.00 |

COPPER-NICKEL

| 23 | 1971 | .100 | .50 | 1.00 | 2.00 | 7.00 |

20 ESCUDOS

NICKEL

| 24 | 1971 | .075 | .70 | 1.50 | 3.50 | 9.00 |

50 ESCUDOS

18.0000 g, .650 SILVER, .3762 oz ASW
500th Anniversary of Discovery

KM#	Date	Mintage	Fine	VF	XF	Unc
21	1970	.150				6.50
	1970	*200 pcs.			Matte	—

NOTE: The "Matte" or "Matte-proof" versions were produced at the Lisbon Mint on private contract.

REPUBLIC

MONETARY SYSTEM
100 Centimos = 1 Dobra

50 CENTIMOS

BRASS
F.A.O. Issue

KM#	Date	Mintage	VF	XF	Unc
25	1977	2.000	.10	.20	.75
	1977	2,500		Proof	3.00

DOBRA

BRASS
F.A.O. Issue

| 26 | 1977 | 1.500 | .15 | .25 | 1.00 |
| | 1977 | 2,500 | — | Proof | 3.00 |

2 DOBRAS

COPPER-NICKEL
F.A.O. Issue

| 27 | 1977 | 1.000 | .25 | .40 | 1.50 |
| | 1977 | 2,500 | — | Proof | 3.50 |

5 DOBRAS

COPPER-NICKEL
F.A.O. Issue

| 28 | 1977 | .750 | .35 | .65 | 2.00 |
| | 1977 | 2,500 | — | Proof | 5.00 |

10 DOBRAS

COPPER-NICKEL
F.A.O. Issue

| 29 | 1977 | .300 | .60 | 1.25 | 4.00 |
| | 1977 | 2,500 | — | Proof | 7.00 |

COPPER-NICKEL CLAD STEEL

KM#	Date	Mintage	VF	XF	Unc
29a	1990	—	.60	1.25	4.00

20 DOBRAS

COPPER-NICKEL
F.A.O. Issue

| 30 | 1977 | .500 | 1.00 | 2.00 | 6.00 |
| | 1977 | 2,500 | | Proof | 10.00 |

50 DOBRAS

COPPER-NICKEL CLAD STEEL
F.A.O. Issue

| 52 | 1990 | — | — | — | 6.00 |

100 DOBRAS

CHROME CLAD STEEL
Obv: National arms.
Rev: Denomination above bird.

| 87 | 1997 | — | — | — | 1.25 |

250 DOBRAS

CHROME CLAD STEEL
Obv: National arms.
Rev: Denomination above bird.

| 88 | 1997 | — | — | — | 1.50 |

500 DOBRAS

CHROME CLAD STEEL
Monkey

| 89 | 1997 | — | — | — | 2.00 |

1000 DOBRAS

CHROME CLAD STEEL
Flowers and Denomination

| 90 | 1997 | — | — | — | 2.75 |

2000 DOBRAS

CHROME CLAD STEEL
Tropical Food Plants

KM#	Date	Mintage	VF	XF	Unc
91	1997	—	—	—	3.75

SAN MARINO

The Republic of San Marino, the oldest and smallest republic in the world is located in north central Italy entirely surrounded by the Province of Emilia-Romagna. It has an area of 24 sq. mi. (60 sq. km.) and a population of *23,000. Capital: San Marino. The principal economic activities are farming, livestock raising, cheesemaking, tourism and light manufacturing. Building stone, lime, wheat, hides and baked goods are exported. The government derives most of its revenue from the sale of postage stamps for philatelic purposes.

According to tradition, San Marino was founded about 350AD by a Christian stonecutter as a refuge against religious persecution. While gradually acquiring the institutions of an independent state, it avoided the factional fights of the Middle Ages and, except for a brief period in fief to Cesare Borgia, retained its freedom despite attacks on its sovereignty by the Papacy, the Lords of Rimini, Napoleon and Mussolini. In 1862 San Marino established a customs union with, and put itself under the protection of, Italy. A Communist-Socialist coalition controlled the Government for 12 years after World War II. The Christian Democratic Party has been the core of government since 1957. In 1978 a Communist-Socialist coalition again came into power and remained in control until 1991.

San Marino has its own coinage, but Italian and Vatican City coins and currency are also in circulation.

MINT MARKS

M - Milan
R - Rome

MONETARY SYSTEM
100 Centesimi = 1 Lira

5 CENTESIMI

BRONZE

KM#	Date	Mintage	Fine	VF	XF	Unc
12	1935R	.400	1.25	2.00	3.00	5.50
	1936R	.400	1.25	2.00	3.00	5.50
	1937R	.400	1.25	2.00	3.00	5.50
	1938R	.200	1.50	2.25	3.50	6.50

10 CENTESIMI

BRONZE

KM#	Date	Mintage	Fine	VF	XF	Unc
13	1935R	.300	1.50	2.25	3.50	7.00
	1936R	.300	1.50	2.25	3.50	7.00
	1937R	.300	1.50	2.25	3.50	7.00
	1938R	.400	1.50	2.25	3.50	7.00

LIRA

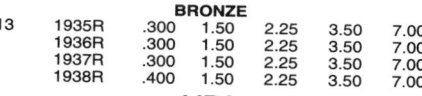

5.0000 g, .835 SILVER, .1342 oz ASW

KM#	Date	Mintage	Fine	VF	XF	Unc
4	1906R	.030	15.00	22.50	40.00	75.00

NOTE: Earlier date (1898) exists for this type.

ALUMINUM

KM#	Date	Mintage	VF	XF	Unc
14	1972	.291	—	.10	.20

KM#	Date	Mintage	VF	XF	Unc
22	1973	.291	—	.10	.20
30	1974	.276	—	.20	.75
40	1975	.291	—	.20	.75
51	1976	.195	—	.10	.20

F.A.O. Issue

63	1977	1.180	—	.10	.20
76	1978	.130	—	.15	.30
89	1979	.125	—	.15	.30

1980 Olympics

102	1980	.125	—	.15	.30
116	1981	.100	—	.15	.30

Social Conquest

131	1982R	.078	—	.15	.30

Nuclear War Threat - Beast of War

145	1983R	.072	—	.20	.40

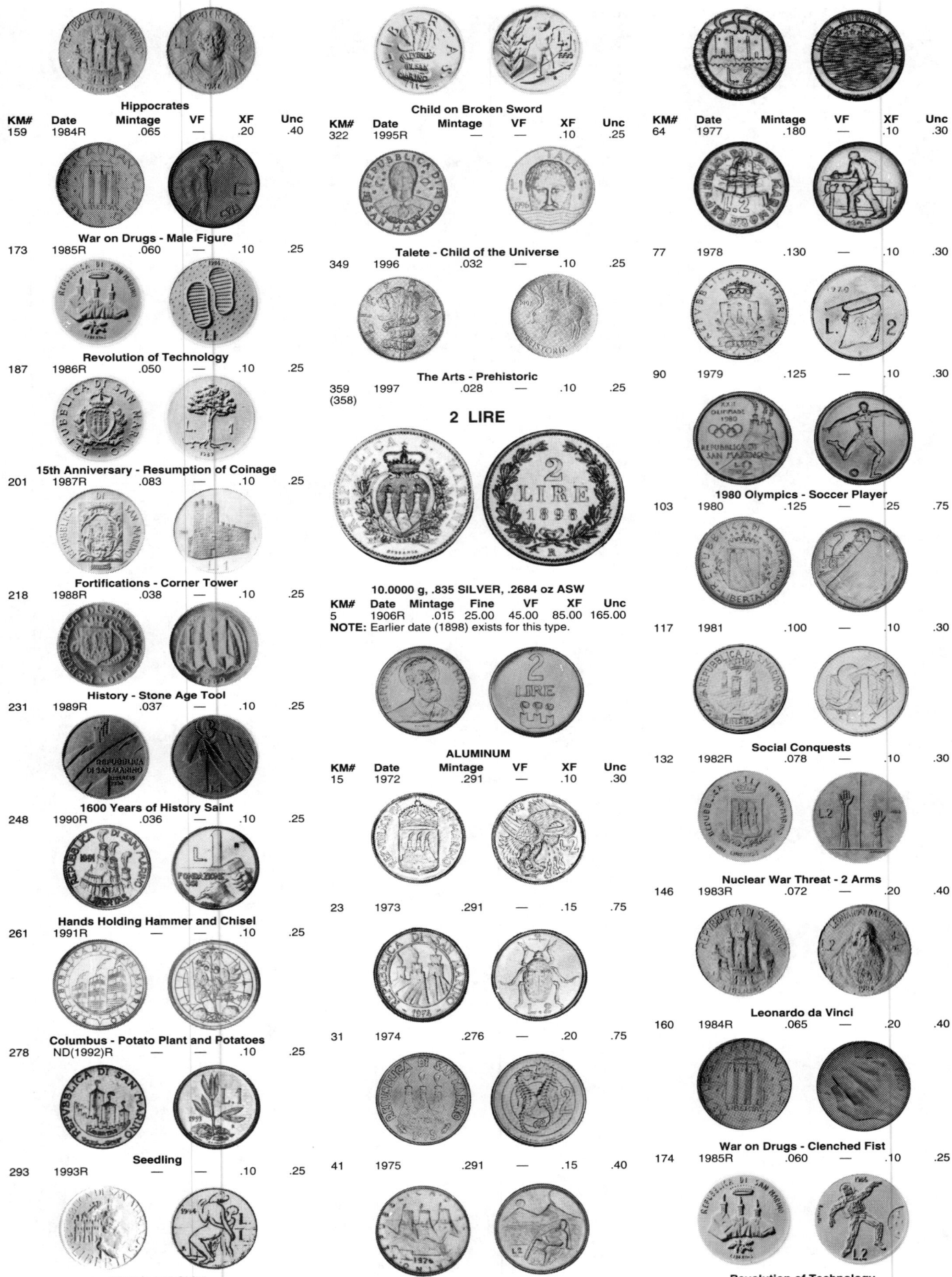

Hippocrates

KM#	Date	Mintage	VF	XF	Unc
159	1984R	.065	—	.20	.40

War on Drugs - Male Figure

| 173 | 1985R | .060 | — | .10 | .25 |

Revolution of Technology

| 187 | 1986R | .050 | — | .10 | .25 |

15th Anniversary - Resumption of Coinage

| 201 | 1987R | .083 | | .10 | .25 |

Fortifications - Corner Tower

| 218 | 1988R | .038 | | .10 | .25 |

History - Stone Age Tool

| 231 | 1989R | .037 | | .10 | .25 |

1600 Years of History Saint

| 248 | 1990R | .036 | | .10 | .25 |

Hands Holding Hammer and Chisel

| 261 | 1991R | | | .10 | .25 |

Columbus - Potato Plant and Potatoes

| 278 | ND(1992)R | | | .10 | .25 |

Seedling

| 293 | 1993R | | | .10 | .25 |

Mother and Child

| 306 | 1994R | .040 | | .10 | .25 |

Child on Broken Sword

KM#	Date	Mintage	VF	XF	Unc
322	1995R	—	—	.10	.25

Talete - Child of the Universe

| 349 | 1996 | .032 | | .10 | .25 |

The Arts - Prehistoric

| 359 (358) | 1997 | .028 | — | .10 | .25 |

2 LIRE

10.0000 g, .835 SILVER, .2684 oz ASW

KM#	Date	Mintage	Fine	VF	XF	Unc
5	1906R	.015	25.00	45.00	85.00	165.00

NOTE: Earlier date (1898) exists for this type.

ALUMINUM

KM#	Date	Mintage	VF	XF	Unc
15	1972	.291		.10	.30
23	1973	.291	—	.15	.75
31	1974	.276	—	.20	.75
41	1975	.291	—	.15	.40
52	1976	.195		.10	.30

KM#	Date	Mintage	VF	XF	Unc
64	1977	.180	—	.10	.30
77	1978	.130		.10	.30
90	1979	.125	—	.10	.30

1980 Olympics - Soccer Player

| 103 | 1980 | .125 | — | .25 | .75 |

| 117 | 1981 | .100 | — | .10 | .30 |

Social Conquests

| 132 | 1982R | .078 | | .10 | .30 |

Nuclear War Threat - 2 Arms

| 146 | 1983R | .072 | — | .20 | .40 |

Leonardo da Vinci

| 160 | 1984R | .065 | — | .20 | .40 |

War on Drugs - Clenched Fist

| 174 | 1985R | .060 | — | .10 | .25 |

Revolution of Technology

| 188 | 1986R | .050 | | .10 | .25 |

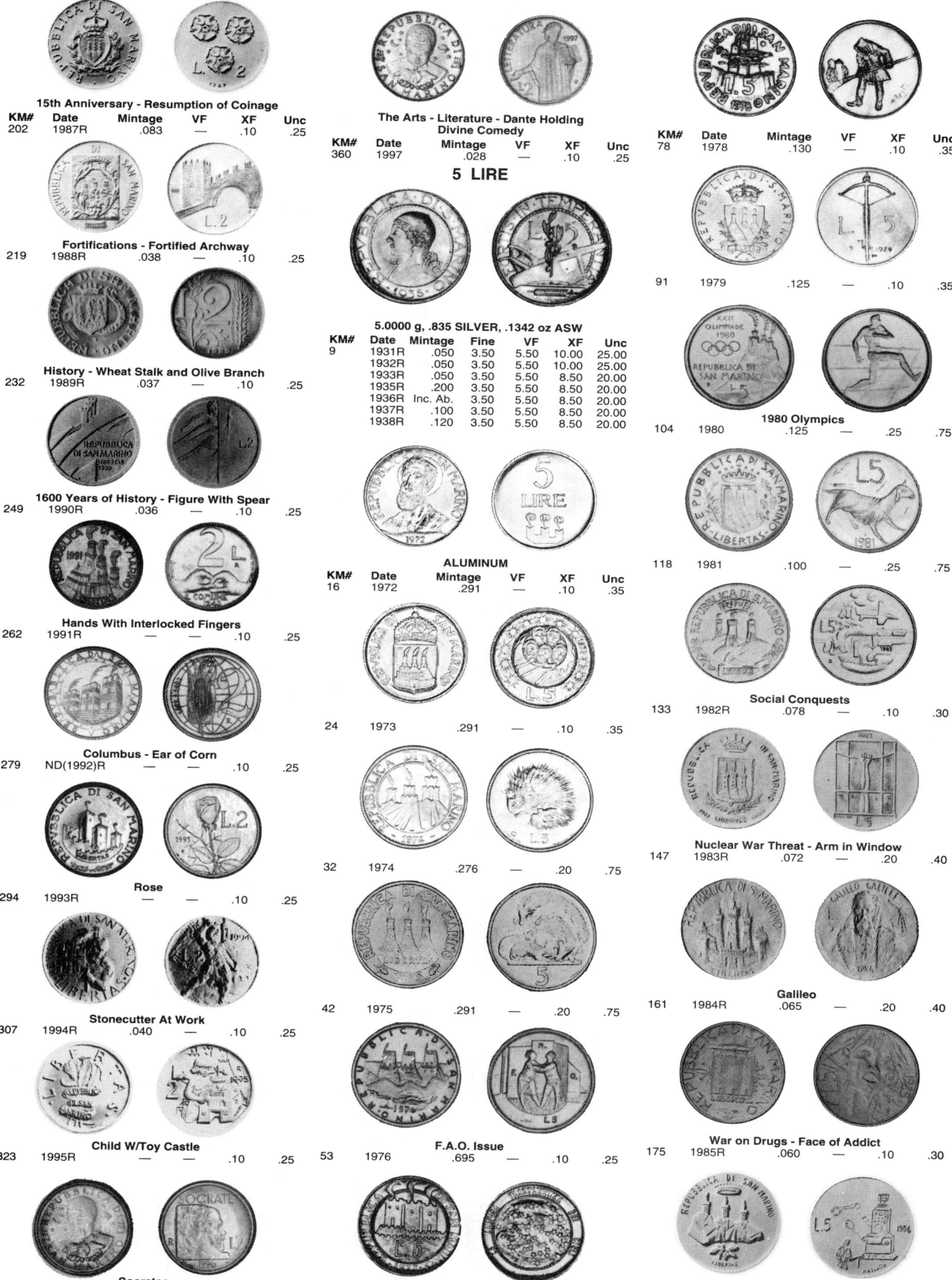

15th Anniversary - Resumption of Coinage

KM#	Date	Mintage	VF	XF	Unc
202	1987R	.083	—	.10	.25

Fortifications - Fortified Archway

219	1988R	.038	—	.10	.25

History - Wheat Stalk and Olive Branch

232	1989R	.037	—	.10	.25

1600 Years of History - Figure With Spear

249	1990R	.036	—	.10	.25

Hands With Interlocked Fingers

262	1991R	—	—	.10	.25

Columbus - Ear of Corn

279	ND(1992)R	—	—	.10	.25

Rose

294	1993R	—	—	.10	.25

Stonecutter At Work

307	1994R	.040	—	.10	.25

Child W/Toy Castle

323	1995R	—	—	.10	.25

Socrates

350	1996	.032	—	.10	.25

The Arts - Literature - Dante Holding Divine Comedy

KM#	Date	Mintage	VF	XF	Unc
360	1997	.028	—	.10	.25

5 LIRE

5.0000 g, .835 SILVER, .1342 oz ASW

KM#	Date	Mintage	Fine	VF	XF	Unc
9	1931R	.050	3.50	5.50	10.00	25.00
	1932R	.050	3.50	5.50	10.00	25.00
	1933R	.050	3.50	5.50	8.50	20.00
	1935R	.200	3.50	5.50	8.50	20.00
	1936R	Inc. Ab.	3.50	5.50	8.50	20.00
	1937R	.100	3.50	5.50	8.50	20.00
	1938R	.120	3.50	5.50	8.50	20.00

ALUMINUM

KM#	Date	Mintage	VF	XF	Unc
16	1972	.291	—	.10	.35

24	1973	.291	—	.10	.35

32	1974	.276	—	.20	.75

42	1975	.291	—	.20	.75

F.A.O. Issue

53	1976	.695	—	.10	.25

65	1977	.180	—	.10	.35

KM#	Date	Mintage	VF	XF	Unc
78	1978	.130	—	.10	.35

91	1979	.125	—	.10	.35

1980 Olympics

104	1980	.125	—	.25	.75

118	1981	.100	—	.25	.75

Social Conquests

133	1982R	.078	—	.10	.30

Nuclear War Threat - Arm in Window

147	1983R	.072	—	.20	.40

Galileo

161	1984R	.065	—	.20	.40

War on Drugs - Face of Addict

175	1985R	.060	—	.10	.30

Revolution of Technology

189	1986R	.050	—	—	.30

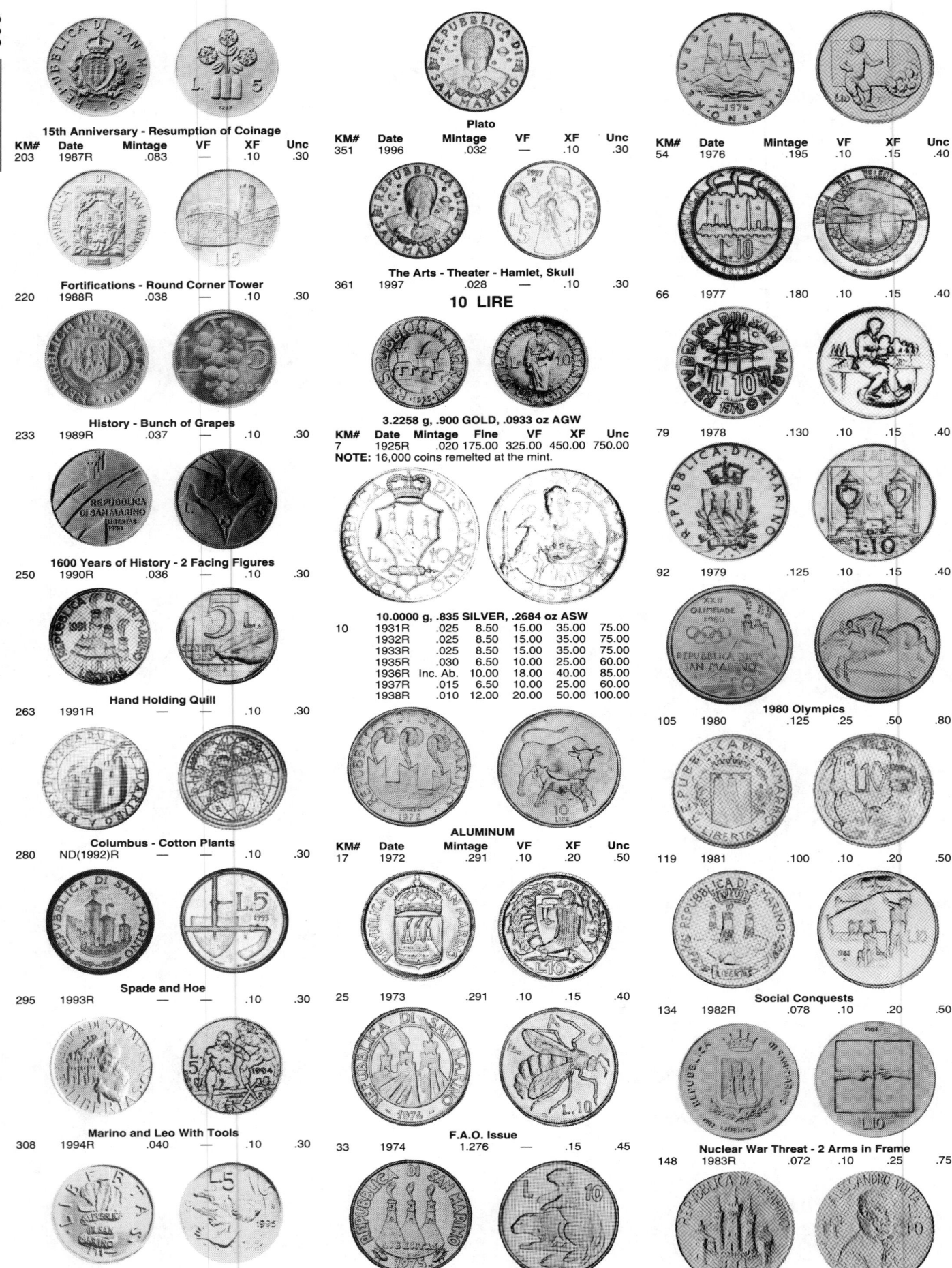

15th Anniversary - Resumption of Coinage

KM#	Date	Mintage	VF	XF	Unc
203	1987R	.083	—	.10	.30

Fortifications - Round Corner Tower

220	1988R	.038	—	.10	.30

History - Bunch of Grapes

233	1989R	.037	—	.10	.30

1600 Years of History - 2 Facing Figures

250	1990R	.036	—	.10	.30

Hand Holding Quill

263	1991R	—	—	.10	.30

Columbus - Cotton Plants

280	ND(1992)R	—	—	.10	.30

Spade and Hoe

295	1993R	—	—	.10	.30

Marino and Leo With Tools

308	1994R	.040	—	.10	.30

Child W/2 Deer

324	1995R	—	—	.10	.30

Plato

KM#	Date	Mintage	VF	XF	Unc
351	1996	.032	—	.10	.30

The Arts - Theater - Hamlet, Skull

361	1997	.028	—	.10	.30

10 LIRE

3.2258 g, .900 GOLD, .0933 oz AGW

KM#	Date	Mintage	Fine	VF	XF	Unc
7	1925R	.020	175.00	325.00	450.00	750.00

NOTE: 16,000 coins remelted at the mint.

10.0000 g, .835 SILVER, .2684 oz ASW

10	1931R	.025	8.50	15.00	35.00	75.00
	1932R	.025	8.50	15.00	35.00	75.00
	1933R	.025	8.50	15.00	35.00	75.00
	1935R	.030	6.50	10.00	25.00	60.00
	1936R	Inc. Ab.	10.00	18.00	40.00	85.00
	1937R	.015	6.50	10.00	25.00	60.00
	1938R	.010	12.00	20.00	50.00	100.00

ALUMINUM

KM#	Date	Mintage	VF	XF	Unc
17	1972	.291	.10	.20	.50
25	1973	.291	.10	.15	.40

F.A.O. Issue

33	1974	1.276	—	.15	.45
43	1975	.291	.10	.25	.75

KM#	Date	Mintage	VF	XF	Unc
54	1976	.195	.10	.15	.40
66	1977	.180	—	.15	.40
79	1978	.130	.10	.15	.40
92	1979	.125	.10	.15	.40

1980 Olympics

105	1980	.125	.25	.50	.80
119	1981	.100	.10	.20	.50

Social Conquests

134	1982R	.078	.10	.20	.50

Nuclear War Threat - 2 Arms in Frame

148	1983R	.072	.10	.25	.75

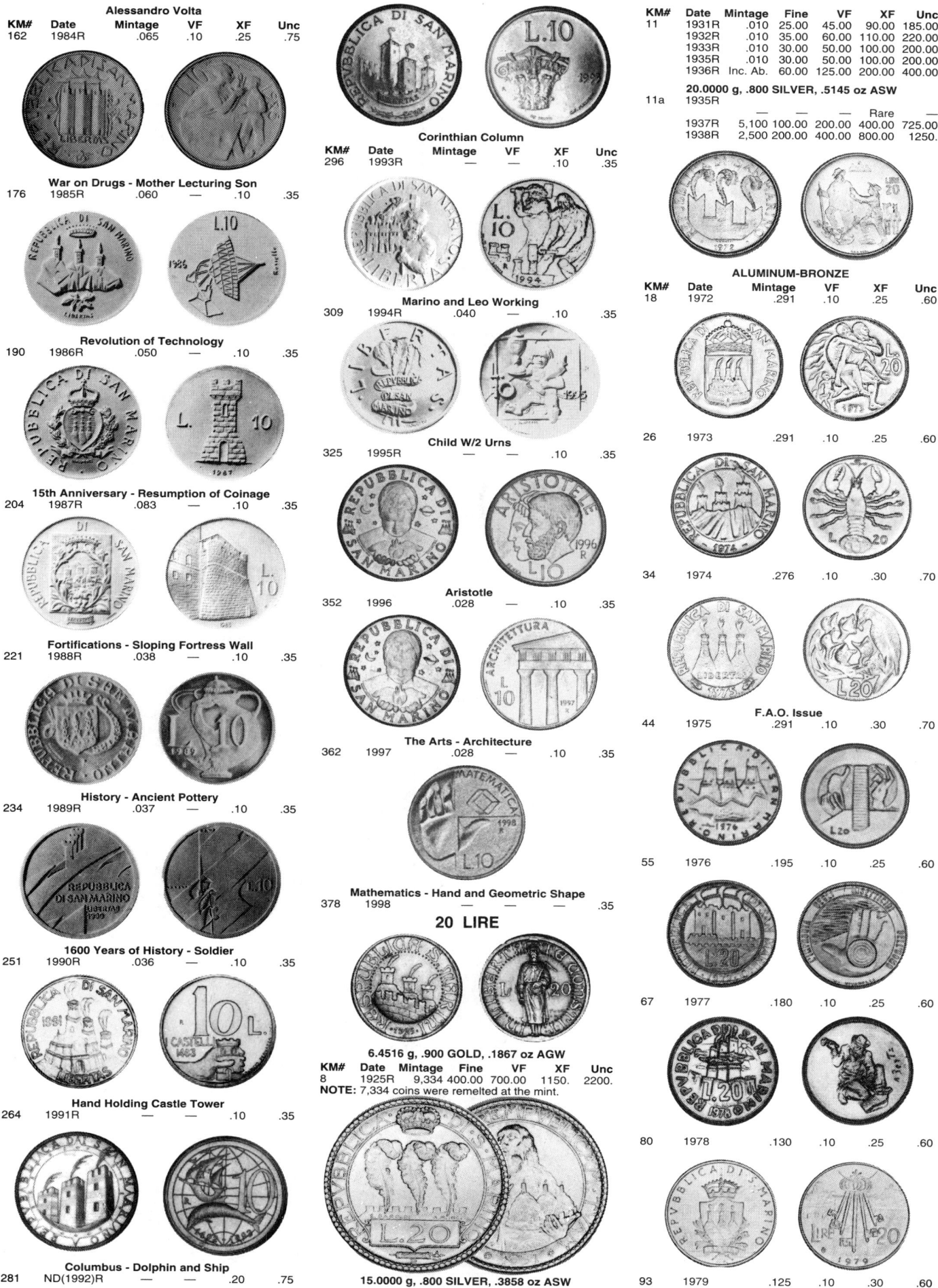

Alessandro Volta

KM#	Date	Mintage	VF	XF	Unc
162	1984R	.065	.10	.25	.75

War on Drugs - Mother Lecturing Son

176	1985R	.060	—	.10	.35

Revolution of Technology

190	1986R	.050	—	.10	.35

15th Anniversary - Resumption of Coinage

204	1987R	.083		.10	.35

Fortifications - Sloping Fortress Wall

221	1988R	.038	—	.10	.35

History - Ancient Pottery

234	1989R	.037	—	.10	.35

1600 Years of History - Soldier

251	1990R	.036	—	.10	.35

Hand Holding Castle Tower

264	1991R	—	—	.10	.35

Columbus - Dolphin and Ship

281	ND(1992)R	—	—	.20	.75

Corinthian Column

KM#	Date	Mintage	VF	XF	Unc
296	1993R	—		.10	.35

Marino and Leo Working

309	1994R	.040	—	.10	.35

Child W/2 Urns

325	1995R		—	.10	.35

Aristotle

352	1996	.028		.10	.35

The Arts - Architecture

362	1997	.028	—	.10	.35

Mathematics - Hand and Geometric Shape

378	1998	—	—	—	.35

20 LIRE

6.4516 g, .900 GOLD, .1867 oz AGW

KM#	Date	Mintage	Fine	VF	XF	Unc
8	1925R	9,334	400.00	700.00	1150.	2200.

NOTE: 7,334 coins were remelted at the mint.

15.0000 g, .800 SILVER, .3858 oz ASW

KM#	Date	Mintage	Fine	VF	XF	Unc
11	1931R	.010	25.00	45.00	90.00	185.00
	1932R	.010	35.00	60.00	110.00	220.00
	1933R	.010	30.00	50.00	100.00	200.00
	1935R	.010	30.00	50.00	100.00	200.00
	1936R	Inc. Ab.	60.00	125.00	200.00	400.00

20.0000 g, .800 SILVER, .5145 oz ASW

11a	1935R	—	—	—	Rare	
	1937R	5,100	100.00	200.00	400.00	725.00
	1938R	2,500	200.00	400.00	800.00	1250.

ALUMINUM-BRONZE

KM#	Date	Mintage	VF	XF	Unc
18	1972	.291	.10	.25	.60
26	1973	.291	.10	.25	.60
34	1974	.276	.10	.30	.70

F.A.O. Issue

44	1975	.291	.10	.30	.70
55	1976	.195	.10	.25	.60
67	1977	.180	.10	.25	.60
80	1978	.130	.10	.25	.60
93	1979	.125	.10	.30	.60

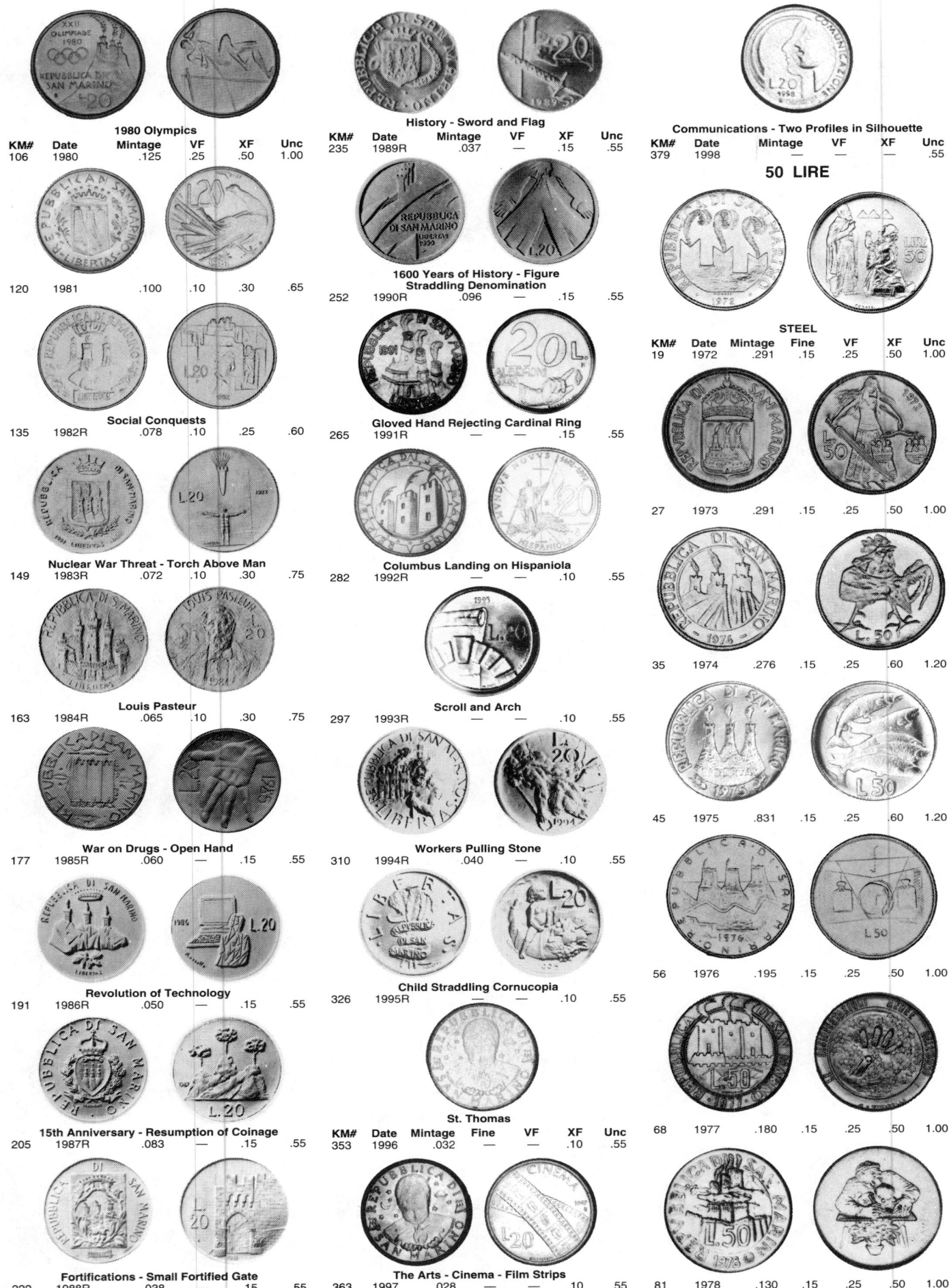

1980 Olympics

KM#	Date	Mintage	VF	XF	Unc
106	1980	.125	.25	.50	1.00

| 120 | 1981 | .100 | .10 | .30 | .65 |

Social Conquests

| 135 | 1982R | .078 | .10 | .25 | .60 |

Nuclear War Threat - Torch Above Man

| 149 | 1983R | .072 | .10 | .30 | .75 |

Louis Pasteur

| 163 | 1984R | .065 | .10 | .30 | .75 |

War on Drugs - Open Hand

| 177 | 1985R | .060 | — | .15 | .55 |

Revolution of Technology

| 191 | 1986R | .050 | — | .15 | .55 |

15th Anniversary - Resumption of Coinage

| 205 | 1987R | .083 | — | .15 | .55 |

Fortifications - Small Fortified Gate

| 222 | 1988R | .038 | — | .15 | .55 |

History - Sword and Flag

KM#	Date	Mintage	VF	XF	Unc
235	1989R	.037	—	.15	.55

1600 Years of History - Figure Straddling Denomination

| 252 | 1990R | .096 | — | .15 | .55 |

Gloved Hand Rejecting Cardinal Ring

| 265 | 1991R | — | — | .15 | .55 |

Columbus Landing on Hispaniola

| 282 | 1992R | — | — | .10 | .55 |

Scroll and Arch

| 297 | 1993R | — | — | .10 | .55 |

Workers Pulling Stone

| 310 | 1994R | .040 | — | .10 | .55 |

Child Straddling Cornucopia

| 326 | 1995R | — | — | .10 | .55 |

St. Thomas

KM#	Date	Mintage	Fine	VF	XF	Unc
353	1996	.032	—	—	.10	.55

The Arts - Cinema - Film Strips

| 363 | 1997 | .028 | | | .10 | .55 |

Communications - Two Profiles in Silhouette

KM#	Date	Mintage	VF	XF	Unc
379	1998	—	—	—	.55

50 LIRE

STEEL

KM#	Date	Mintage	Fine	VF	XF	Unc
19	1972	.291	.15	.25	.50	1.00
27	1973	.291	.15	.25	.50	1.00
35	1974	.276	.15	.25	.60	1.20
45	1975	.831	.15	.25	.60	1.20
56	1976	.195	.15	.25	.50	1.00
68	1977	.180	.15	.25	.50	1.00
81	1978	.130	.15	.25	.50	1.00

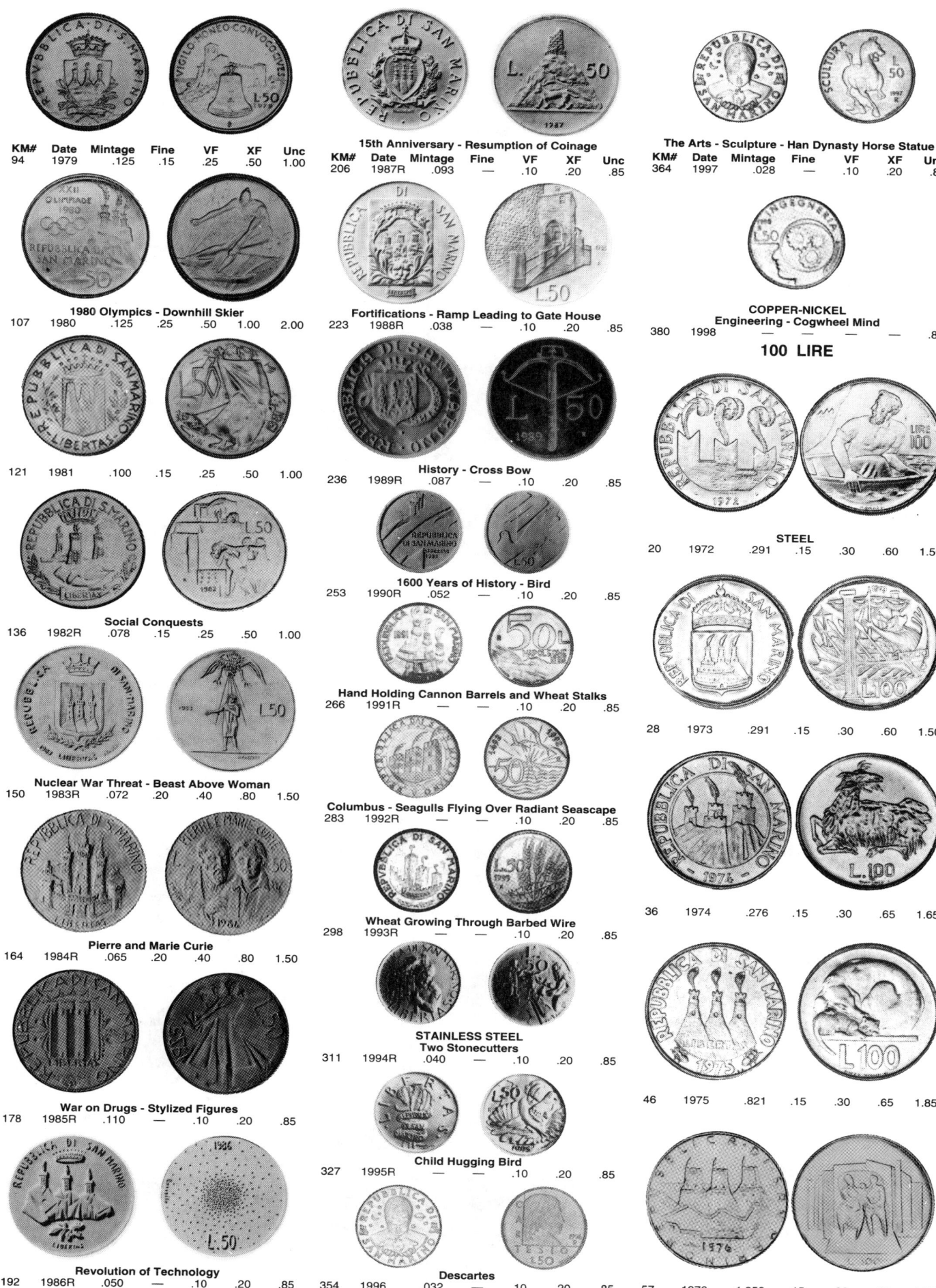

KM#	Date	Mintage	Fine	VF	XF	Unc
94	1979	.125	.15	.25	.50	1.00

1980 Olympics - Downhill Skier

| 107 | 1980 | .125 | .25 | .50 | 1.00 | 2.00 |

| 121 | 1981 | .100 | .15 | .25 | .50 | 1.00 |

Social Conquests

| 136 | 1982R | .078 | .15 | .25 | .50 | 1.00 |

Nuclear War Threat - Beast Above Woman

| 150 | 1983R | .072 | .20 | .40 | .80 | 1.50 |

Pierre and Marie Curie

| 164 | 1984R | .065 | .20 | .40 | .80 | 1.50 |

War on Drugs - Stylized Figures

| 178 | 1985R | .110 | — | .10 | .20 | .85 |

Revolution of Technology

| 192 | 1986R | .050 | — | .10 | .20 | .85 |

15th Anniversary - Resumption of Coinage

KM#	Date	Mintage	Fine	VF	XF	Unc
206	1987R	.093	—	.10	.20	.85

Fortifications - Ramp Leading to Gate House

| 223 | 1988R | .038 | — | .10 | .20 | .85 |

History - Cross Bow

| 236 | 1989R | .087 | — | .10 | .20 | .85 |

1600 Years of History - Bird

| 253 | 1990R | .052 | — | .10 | .20 | .85 |

Hand Holding Cannon Barrels and Wheat Stalks

| 266 | 1991R | — | — | .10 | .20 | .85 |

Columbus - Seagulls Flying Over Radiant Seascape

| 283 | 1992R | — | — | .10 | .20 | .85 |

Wheat Growing Through Barbed Wire

| 298 | 1993R | — | — | .10 | .20 | .85 |

STAINLESS STEEL
Two Stonecutters

| 311 | 1994R | .040 | — | .10 | .20 | .85 |

Child Hugging Bird

| 327 | 1995R | — | — | .10 | .20 | .85 |

Descartes

| 354 | 1996 | .032 | — | .10 | .20 | .85 |

The Arts - Sculpture - Han Dynasty Horse Statue

KM#	Date	Mintage	Fine	VF	XF	Unc
364	1997	.028	—	.10	.20	.85

COPPER-NICKEL
Engineering - Cogwheel Mind

| 380 | 1998 | | | | | .85 |

100 LIRE

STEEL

| 20 | 1972 | .291 | .15 | .30 | .60 | 1.50 |

| 28 | 1973 | .291 | .15 | .30 | .60 | 1.50 |

| 36 | 1974 | .276 | .15 | .30 | .65 | 1.65 |

| 46 | 1975 | .821 | .15 | .30 | .65 | 1.85 |

| 57 | 1976 | 1.853 | .15 | .30 | .60 | 1.50 |

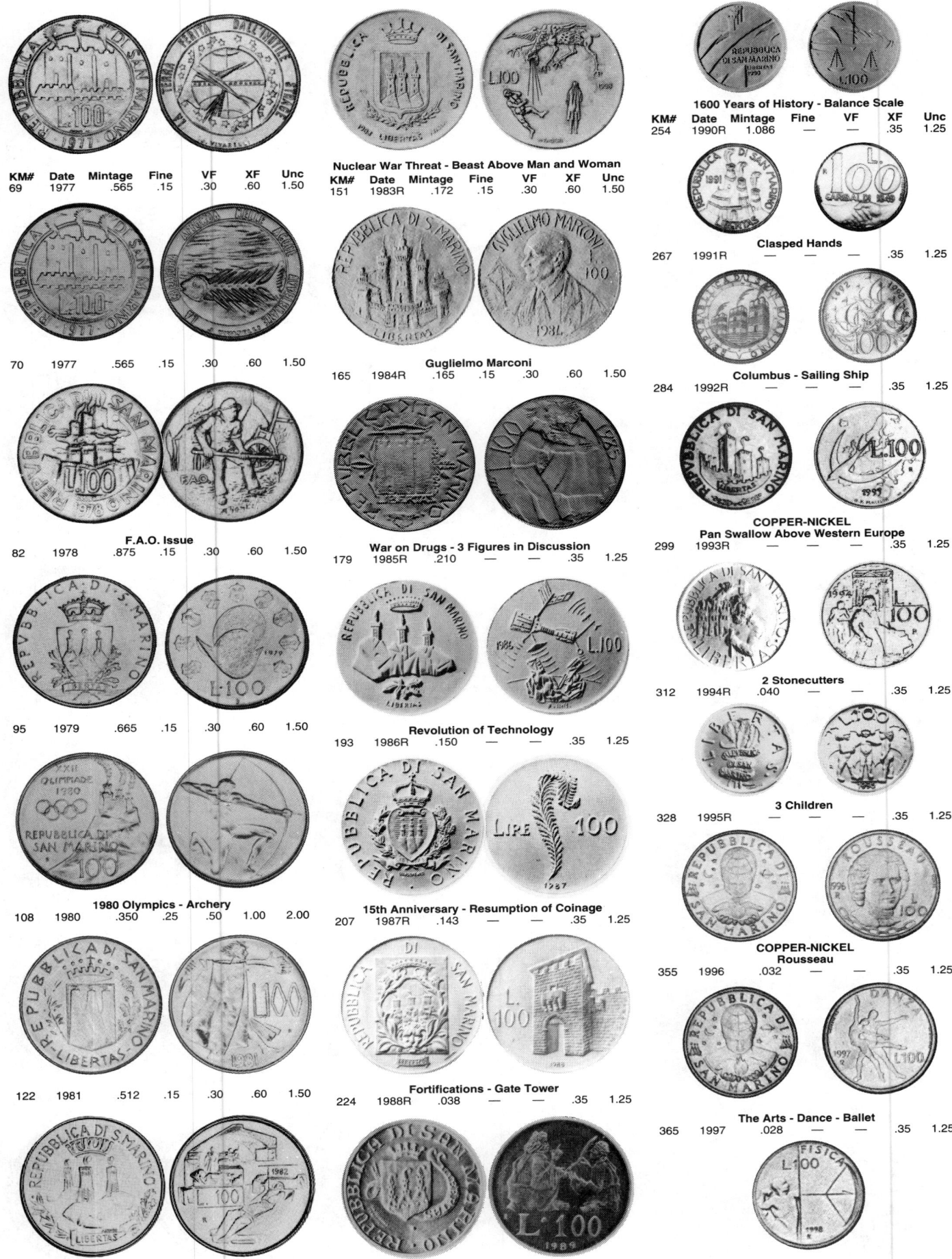

KM#	Date	Mintage	Fine	VF	XF	Unc
69	1977	.565	.15	.30	.60	1.50

F.A.O. Issue

| 70 | 1977 | .565 | .15 | .30 | .60 | 1.50 |

| 82 | 1978 | .875 | .15 | .30 | .60 | 1.50 |

F.A.O. Issue

| 95 | 1979 | .665 | .15 | .30 | .60 | 1.50 |

1980 Olympics - Archery

| 108 | 1980 | .350 | .25 | .50 | 1.00 | 2.00 |

| 122 | 1981 | .512 | .15 | .30 | .60 | 1.50 |

Social Conquests

| 137 | 1982R | .178 | .15 | .30 | .60 | 1.50 |

Nuclear War Threat - Beast Above Man and Woman

KM#	Date	Mintage	Fine	VF	XF	Unc
151	1983R	.172	.15	.30	.60	1.50

Guglielmo Marconi

| 165 | 1984R | .165 | .15 | .30 | .60 | 1.50 |

War on Drugs - 3 Figures in Discussion

| 179 | 1985R | .210 | — | — | .35 | 1.25 |

Revolution of Technology

| 193 | 1986R | .150 | | | .35 | 1.25 |

15th Anniversary - Resumption of Coinage

| 207 | 1987R | .143 | — | — | .35 | 1.25 |

Fortifications - Gate Tower

| 224 | 1988R | .038 | | | .35 | 1.25 |

History - Teacher and Student

| 237 | 1989R | .037 | — | — | .35 | 1.25 |

1600 Years of History - Balance Scale

KM#	Date	Mintage	Fine	VF	XF	Unc
254	1990R	1.086	—	—	.35	1.25

Clasped Hands

| 267 | 1991R | | | | .35 | 1.25 |

Columbus - Sailing Ship

| 284 | 1992R | | | | .35 | 1.25 |

COPPER-NICKEL
Pan Swallow Above Western Europe

| 299 | 1993R | | | | .35 | 1.25 |

2 Stonecutters

| 312 | 1994R | .040 | | | .35 | 1.25 |

3 Children

| 328 | 1995R | | | | .35 | 1.25 |

COPPER-NICKEL
Rousseau

| 355 | 1996 | .032 | | | .35 | 1.25 |

The Arts - Dance - Ballet

| 365 | 1997 | .028 | | | .35 | 1.25 |

Physics - Human, Crossbow

| 381 | 1998 | | | | | 1.25 |

200 LIRE

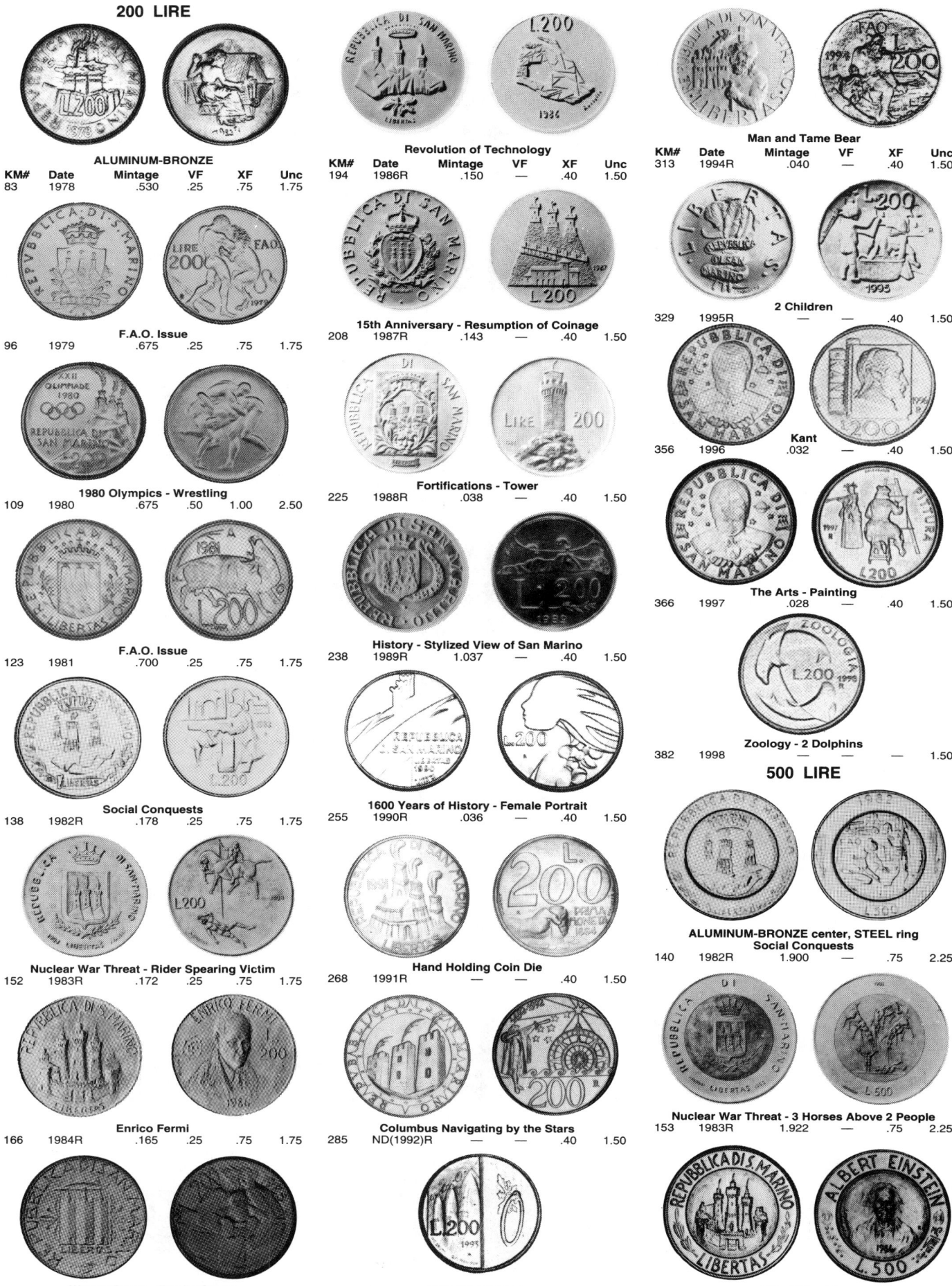

ALUMINUM-BRONZE

KM#	Date	Mintage	VF	XF	Unc
83	1978	.530	.25	.75	1.75

F.A.O. Issue

96	1979	.675	.25	.75	1.75

1980 Olympics - Wrestling

109	1980	.675	.50	1.00	2.50

F.A.O. Issue

123	1981	.700	.25	.75	1.75

Social Conquests

138	1982R	.178	.25	.75	1.75

Nuclear War Threat - Rider Spearing Victim

152	1983R	.172	.25	.75	1.75

Enrico Fermi

166	1984R	.165	.25	.75	1.75

War on Drugs - Family Group

180	1985R	.210	—	.40	1.50

Revolution of Technology

KM#	Date	Mintage	VF	XF	Unc
194	1986R	.150	—	.40	1.50

15th Anniversary - Resumption of Coinage

208	1987R	.143	—	.40	1.50

Fortifications - Tower

225	1988R	.038	—	.40	1.50

History - Stylized View of San Marino

238	1989R	1.037	—	.40	1.50

1600 Years of History - Female Portrait

255	1990R	.036	—	.40	1.50

Hand Holding Coin Die

268	1991R	—	—	.40	1.50

Columbus Navigating by the Stars

285	ND(1992)R	—	—	.40	1.50

Door and Arches

300	1993R	—	—	.40	1.50

Man and Tame Bear

KM#	Date	Mintage	VF	XF	Unc
313	1994R	.040	—	.40	1.50

2 Children

329	1995R	—	—	.40	1.50

Kant

356	1996	.032	—	.40	1.50

The Arts - Painting

366	1997	.028	—	.40	1.50

Zoology - 2 Dolphins

382	1998	—	—	—	1.50

500 LIRE

ALUMINUM-BRONZE center, STEEL ring
Social Conquests

140	1982R	1.900	—	.75	2.25

Nuclear War Threat - 3 Horses Above 2 People

153	1983R	1.922	—	.75	2.25

Albert Einstein

167	1984R	2.633	—	.65	2.00

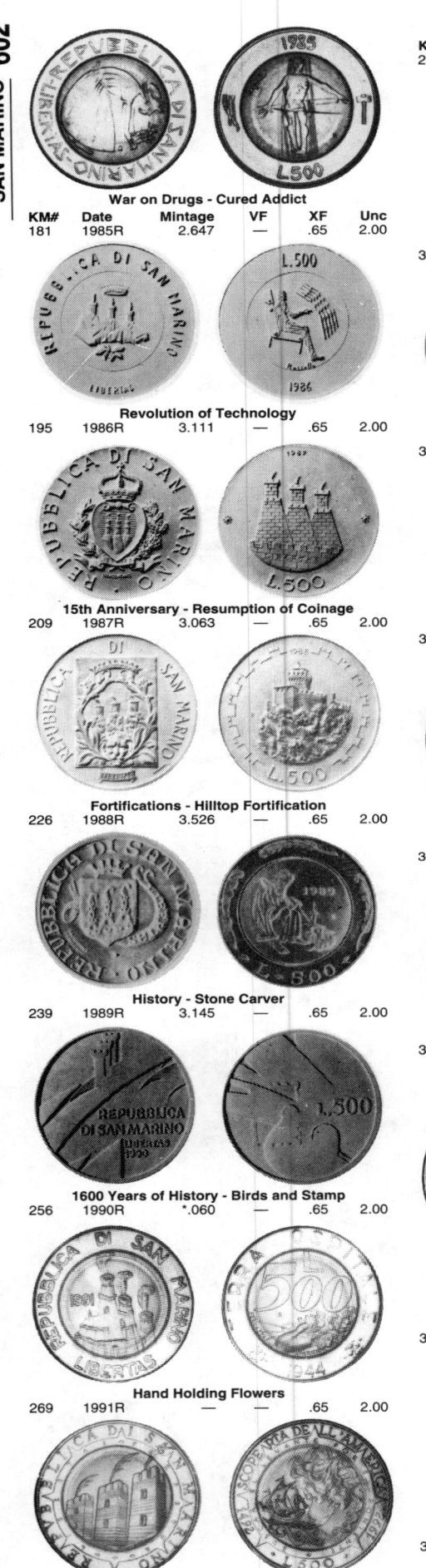

War on Drugs - Cured Addict

KM#	Date	Mintage	VF	XF	Unc
181	1985R	2.647	—	.65	2.00

Revolution of Technology

| 195 | 1986R | 3.111 | — | .65 | 2.00 |

15th Anniversary - Resumption of Coinage

| 209 | 1987R | 3.063 | — | .65 | 2.00 |

Fortifications - Hilltop Fortification

| 226 | 1988R | 3.526 | — | .65 | 2.00 |

History - Stone Carver

| 239 | 1989R | 3.145 | — | .65 | 2.00 |

1600 Years of History - Birds and Stamp

| 256 | 1990R | *.060 | — | .65 | 2.00 |

Hand Holding Flowers

| 269 | 1991R | — | — | .65 | 2.00 |

Columbus - Winds Blowing Ship

KM#	Date	Mintage	VF	XF	Unc
286	1992R	—	—	—	2.00

Growth from a Tree Stump

| 301 | 1993R | — | — | — | 2.00 |

Saint Marino Receiving Mt. Titano

| 314 | 1994R | .040 | — | — | 2.00 |

Hegel

| 357 | 1996 | — | — | — | 2.00 |

The Arts - Music - Woman Playing Pipes

| 367 | 1997 | .028 | — | — | 2.00 |

Chemistry - Laboratory

| 383 | 1998 | — | — | — | 2.00 |

1000 LIRE

**COPPER-NICKEL center in
ALUMINUM-BRONZE ring
Obv: Heraldic lion.
Rev: Statue, building and denomination.**

| 368 | 1997 | — | — | — | 7.50 |

Geology - Family Standing on Earth

| 384 | 1998 | — | — | — | 7.50 |

SAUDI ARABIA

The Kingdom of Saudi Arabia, an independent and absolute hereditary monarchy comprising the former sultanate of Nejd, the old kingdom of Hejaz, Asir and Al Hasa, occupies four-fifths of the Arabian peninsula. The kingdom has an area of 830,000 sq. mi. (2,149,690 sq. km.) and a population of *16.1 million. Capital: Riyadh. The economy is based on oil, which provides 85 percent of Saudi Arabia's revenue.

Mohammed united the Arabs in the 7th century and his followers founded a great empire with its capital at Medina. The Turks established nominal rule over much of Arabia in the 16th and 17th centuries, and in the 18th century divided it into principalities.

The Kingdom of Saudi Arabia was created by King Abd Al-Aziz Bin Saud (1882-1953), a descendant of earlier Wahhabi rulers of the Arabian peninsula. In 1901 he seized Riyadh, capital of the Sultanate of Nejd, and in 1905 established himself as Sultan. In 1913 he captured the Turkish province of Al Hasa; took the Hejaz in 1925 and by 1926 most of Asir. In 1932 he combined Nejd and Hejaz into the single kingdom of Saudi Arabia. Asir was incorporated into the kingdom a year later.

TITLES

العربية السعودية

Al-Arabiya(t) as-Sa'udiya(t)

المملكة العربية السعودية

Al-Mamlaka(t) al-'Arabiya(t) as-Sa'udiya(t)

HEJAZ

Hejaz, a province of Saudi Arabia and a former vilayet of the Ottoman empire, occupies an 800-mile long (1,287 km.) coastal strip between Nejd and the Red Sea. The province was a Turkish dependency until freed in World War I. Husain Ibn Ali, Amir of Mecca, opposed the Turkish control and, with the aid of Lawrence of Arabia, wrested much of Hejaz from the Turks and in 1916 assumed the title of King of Hejaz. Abd Al-Aziz Bin Sa'ud, of Nejd conquered Hejaz in 1925, and in 1926 combined it and Nejd into a single kingdom.

TITLES

al-Hejaz الحجاز

RULERS

al Husain Ibn Ali,
AH1334-42/1916-24AD
Abd Al-Aziz Bin Sa'ud,
AH1343-1373/1925-1953AD

MONETARY SYSTEM

40 Para = 1 Piastre (Ghirsh)
20 Piastres = 1 Riyal
100 Piastres = 1 Dinar

COUNTERMARKED MINOR COINAGE

Following the defeat of the Ottomans in 1916, Turkish 20 and 40 Para coins of Mohamed V and Mohamed VI were countermarked "al-Hejaz" in arabic. The countermark was applied to the obverse side effacing the Ottoman Sultan's toughra, and thus refuting Turkish rule in Hejaz.

Countermarks on the reverse are rare errors. The 10 Paras of Mohamed V and 10 and 20 Paras (billon) of Mahmud II and Abdul Mejid I exist with a smaller, 6 mm unofficial countermark. These may not be contemporary. Other host coins are either local or spurious.

10 PARA

**NICKEL
Accession Date: AH1327
c/m: Large Hejaz on Turkey 10 Para, KM#760.**

Obv: El Ghazi.

KM#	Date	Year	Good	VG	Fine	VF
2	7	—	—	—	—	Rare
	8	—	—	—	—	Rare

20 PARA

NICKEL
Accession Date: AH1327
c/m: *Hejaz* on Turkey 20 Para, KM#761.

KM#	Date	Year	Good	VG	Fine	VF
3	ND	2	5.00	7.00	15.00	30.00
		3	4.00	6.00	12.00	25.00
		4	2.00	4.00	10.00	20.00
		5	2.00	4.00	10.00	20.00
		Effaced	2.00	4.00	7.00	15.00

40 PARA

NICKEL
Accession Date: AH1327
c/m: *Hejaz* on Turkey 40 Para, KM#766.

KM#	Date	Year	Good	VG	Fine	VF
4	ND	3	4.00	6.00	15.00	30.00
		4	2.00	5.00	10.00	20.00
		5	2.00	5.00	10.00	20.00
		Effaced	2.00	5.00	7.00	15.00

COPPER-NICKEL
c/m: *Hejaz* on Turkey 40 Para, KM#779.

KM#	Date	Year	Good	VG	Fine	VF
5	ND	8	4.00	6.00	10.00	20.00
		9	6.00	10.00	25.00	60.00
		Effaced	3.00	5.00	8.00	15.00

Accession Date: AH1336
c/m: *Hejaz* on Turkey 40 Para, KM#828.

KM#	Date	Year	Good	VG	Fine	VF
6	ND	4	10.00	20.00	40.00	75.00

COUNTERMARKED SILVER COINAGE

Silver coins of various sizes were also countermarked "al-Hejaz". The most common host coins include the Maria Theresa Thaler of Austria, British India rupees and 5, 10 and 20 Piastres of Turkey and Egypt. The countermark occurs in various sizes and styles of script. These countermarks may have been applied by local silversmiths to discourage re-exportation of the badly needed hard currency and silver of known fineness.

Some crown sized examples exist with both the "al-Hejaz" and "Nejd" countermarks. The authenticity of the silver countermarked coins has long been discussed, and it is likely that most were privately produced.

2 PIASTRES

NOTE: KM#7-9 formerly listed as "controversial" have been deleted.

5 PIASTRES

SILVER
Accession Date: AH1327
c/m: *Hejaz* on Turkey 5 Kurush, KM#750.

KM#	Date	Year	Good	VG	Fine	VF
10	ND	(1-7)	12.50	20.00	40.00	75.00

c/m: *Hejaz* on Turkey 5 Kurush, KM#771.

11	ND	(7-9)	12.50	20.00	40.00	75.00

c/m: *Hejaz* on Egypt 5 Qirsh, KM#308.

12	ND(2H-4H,6H)		12.50	20.00	40.00	75.00

10 PIASTRES

SILVER
Accession Date: AH1327
c/m: *Hejaz* on Turkey 10 Kurush, KM#751.

KM#	Date	Year	Good	VG	Fine	VF
13	ND	(1-7)	20.00	30.00	60.00	100.00

c/m: *Hejaz* on Turkey 10 Kurush, KM#772.

14	ND	(7-10)	20.00	30.00	60.00	100.00

---

c/m: *Hejaz* on Egypt 10 Qirsh, KM#309.

KM#	Date	Year	Good	VG	Fine	VF
15	ND(2H-4H,6H)		20.00	30.00	60.00	100.00

20 PIASTRES

SILVER
Accession Date: AH1327
c/m: *Hejaz* on Egypt 20 Qirsh, KM#310.

KM#	Date	Year	Good	VG	Fine	VF
16	ND(2H-4H,6H)		35.00	60.00	100.00	150.00

c/m: *Hejaz* on Turkey 20 Kurush, KM#780.

17	ND	(8-10)	35.00	60.00	100.00	150.00

c/m: *Hejaz* on Austria M.T. Thaler, KM#T1.

KM#	Date	Year	Good	VG	Fine	VF
18	ND (1780) (restrike)		15.00	30.00	60.00	125.00

REGULAR COINAGE

NOTE: All the regular coins of Hejaz bear the accessional date AH1334 of Al-Husain Ibn Ali, plus the regnal year. Many of the bronze coins occur with a light silver wash mostly on thicker specimens. A variety of planchet thicknesses exist.

1/8 PIASTRE

BRONZE

KM#	Date	Year	VG	Fine	VF	XF
21	AH1334	5	15.00	25.00	50.00	75.00

NOTE: Reeded and plain edge varieties exist.

1/4 PIASTRE

BRONZE, 1.14 g

KM#	Date	Year	VG	Fine	VF	XF
22	AH1334	5	4.00	10.00	20.00	35.00
	1334	6/5	75.00	300.00	600.00	1200.
	1334	6	100.00	250.00	500.00	700.00

NOTE: Reeded and plain edge varieties exist.

25	AH1334	8	5.00	10.00	20.00	35.00

1/2 PIASTRE

BRONZE

KM#	Date	Year	VG	Fine	VF	XF
23	AH1334	5	3.00	10.00	20.00	35.00

NOTE: Reeded and plain edge varieties exist.

Similar to 1/4 Piastre, KM#25.

KM#	Date	Year	VG	Fine	VF	XF
26	AH1334	8	—	—	Rare	

NOTE: All known specimens were overstruck as Nejd KM#1.

PIASTRE

BRONZE

KM#	Date	Year	VG	Fine	VF	XF
24	AH1334	5	6.00	10.00	20.00	35.00
		6/5	100.00	200.00	400.00	600.00

27	AH1334	8	10.00	20.00	35.00	60.00

5 PIASTRES

6.1000 g, .917 SILVER, .1798 oz ASW

KM#	Date	Year	VG	Fine	VF	XF
28	AH1334	8	15.00	40.00	75.00	150.00

10 PIASTRES

12.0500 g, .917 SILVER, .3552 oz ASW

KM#	Date	Year	VG	Fine	VF	XF
29	AH1334	8	100.00	200.00	400.00	800.00

20 PIASTRES
(1 Ryal)

24.1000 g, .917 SILVER, .7105 oz ASW

KM#	Date	Year	VG	Fine	VF	XF
30	AH1334	8	20.00	45.00	90.00	120.00
		9	30.00	62.50	125.00	200.00

DINAR HASHIMI

GOLD

KM#	Date	Year	Fine	VF	XF	Unc
31	AH1334	8	125.00	250.00	350.00	450.00

NEJD

Nejd, a province of Saudi Arabia which may be described as an open steppe, occupies the core of the Arabian peninsula. The province became a nominal dependency of the Turkish empire in 1871 and a sultanate of King Abd Al-Aziz Bin Sa'ud in 1906.

TITLES

نجد

Nejd

RULERS

Abd Al-Aziz Bin Sa'ud,
AH1322-1373/1905-1953AD
(Over all of Hejaz after 1925, and then in all Saudi Arabia after 1932).

MONETARY SYSTEM

40 Para = 1 Piastre (Ghirsh)
20 Piastres = 1 Riyal
100 Piastres = 1 Dinar

COUNTERMARKED SILVER COINAGE

Following the defeat of the Ottomans in 1916, silver coins of various sizes were also countermarked "Nejd". The most common host coins include the Maria Theresa thalers of Austria, and 5, 10, and 20 Kurush or Qirsh of Turkey and Egypt. The countermark occurs in various other sizes and styles of script. These countermarks may have been applied by local silversmiths to discourage re-exportation of the badly needed hard currency and silver of known fineness.

Some crown sized examples exist with both the "al-Hejaz" and "Nejd" countermarks. The authenticity of the silver countermarked coins has long been discussed, and it is likely that most were privately produced. Other host coins are either local or spurious.

5 PIASTRES
SILVER
Accession Date: AH1327
c/m: *Nejd* on Egypt 5 Qirsh, KM#308.

KM#	Date	Year	Good	VG	Fine	VF
1	ND(2H-4H,6H)		25.00	50.00	100.00	150.00

c/m: *Nejd* on Egypt 5 Qirsh, KM#318.

2	ND (AH1335/ 1916-17H)		25.00	50.00	100.00	150.00

c/m: *Nejd* on Turkey 5 Kurush, KM#750.

| 3 | ND | (1-7) | 25.00 | 50.00 | 100.00 | 150.00 |

c/m: *Nejd* on Turkey 5 Kurush, KM#771.

| 4 | ND | (7-9) | 25.00 | 50.00 | 100.00 | 150.00 |

RUPEE
SILVER
c/m: *Nejd* on India Rupee, KM#450.

| 5 | ND | (1835) | 25.00 | 50.00 | 100.00 | 150.00 |

c/m: *Nejd* on India Rupee, KM#457.

| 6 | ND | (1840) | 25.00 | 50.00 | 125.00 | 275.00 |

c/m: *Nejd* on India Rupee, KM#458.

| 7 | ND | (1840) | 25.00 | 50.00 | 125.00 | 225.00 |

c/m: *Nejd* on India Rupee, KM#473.

| 8 | ND | (1862-76) | 25.00 | 50.00 | 100.00 | 150.00 |

c/m: *Nejd* on Indian Rupee, KM#492.

| A9 | ND | (1877-1901) | 25.00 | 50.00 | 100.00 | 150.00 |

10 PIASTRES

SILVER
Accession Date: AH1293
c/m: *Nejd* on Egypt 10 Qirsh, KM#295.

KM#	Date	Year	Good	VG	Fine	VF
9	ND(10W-29W)		50.00	70.00	125.00	200.00
	(29H-33H)		50.00	70.00	125.00	200.00

Accession Date: AH1327
c/m: *Nejd* on Turkey 10 Kurush, KM#751.

| 10 | ND | (1-7) | 50.00 | 70.00 | 125.00 | 200.00 |

c/m: *Nejd* on Turkey 10 Kurush, KM#772.

| 11 | ND | (7-10) | 50.00 | 70.00 | 125.00 | 200.00 |

20 PIASTRES
SILVER
Accession Date: AH1255
c/m: *Nejd* on Turkey 20 Kurush, KM#675.

| B12 | ND | (6-23) | 75.00 | 125.00 | 200.00 | 350.00 |

Accession Date: AH1277
c/m: *Nejd* on Turkey 20 Kurush, KM#693.

| C12 | ND | (1-15) | 75.00 | 125.00 | 200.00 | 350.00 |

Accession Date: AH1293
c/m: *Nejd* on Turkey 20 Kurush, KM#722.

| A12 | ND | (1-3) | 75.00 | 125.00 | 200.00 | 350.00 |

Accession Date: AH1327
c/m: *Nejd* on Egypt 20 Qirsh, KM#310.

| 12 | ND | (2H-6H) | 75.00 | 125.00 | 200.00 | 350.00 |

c/m: *Nejd* on Egypt 20 Qirsh, KM#321.

| A13 | ND(1916-17H) | | 75.00 | 125.00 | 200.00 | 350.00 |

c/m: *Nejd* on Turkey 20 Kurush, KM#780.

| 13 | ND | (8-10) | 75.00 | 125.00 | 200.00 | 350.00 |

c/m: *Nejd* on Austria M.T. Thaler, KM#T1.

| 14 | ND | (1780)
(restrike) | 40.00 | 80.00 | 200.00 | 425.00 |

HEJAZ and NEJD
TRANSITIONAL COINAGE

Struck at occupied Mecca, Hejaz Mint by Abd Al-Aziz Bin Sa'ud while establishing his kingdom.

1/4 GHIRSH

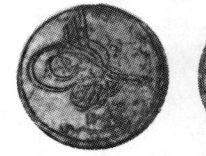

COPPER

KM#	Date	Mintage	VG	Fine	VF	XF
1	AH1343	—	15.00	25.00	50.00	75.00

NOTE: Several varieties exist as well as reeded and plain edges. Some specimens struck over Bronze Hejaz KM#23 and KM#26 and some occur with a light silver wash.

1/2 GHIRSH

COPPER
Obv. leg. right of toughra: *Al-Faisal al Saud.*

KM#	Date	Mintage	VG	Fine	VF	XF
2.1	AH1343	—	6.00	15.00	30.00	50.00

Obv. leg. right of toughra: *al-Faisal.*

| 2.2 | AH1343 | — | 15.00 | 30.00 | 50.00 | 100.00 |

NOTE: Varieties exist. Some specimens struck over Bronze Hejaz KM#24 and KM#27 and some occur with a light silver wash.

| 3 | AH1344, yr. 2 | — | 4.00 | 10.00 | 25.00 | 45.00 |

REGULAR COINAGE
ROYAL TITLES
Appearing on Coins

AH1344 (1926AD)
King of Hejaz and Sultan of Nejd

1/4 GHIRSH

COPPER-NICKEL

| 4 | AH1344 | — | 1.25 | 2.00 | 6.00 | 15.00 |
| | 1344 | — | | Proof | — | — |

1/2 GHIRSH

COPPER-NICKEL

| 5 | AH1344 | — | 2.50 | 4.00 | 12.00 | 18.00 |
| | 1344 | — | | Proof | — | — |

GHIRSH

COPPER-NICKEL

| 6 | AH1344 | — | 2.00 | 3.00 | 7.00 | 15.00 |
| | 1344 | — | | Proof | — | — |

HEJAZ and NEJD and DEPENDENCIES
ROYAL TITLES
Appearing on Coins

AH1346-1348 (1928-1930AD)
King of Hejaz and Nejd and Dependencies

1/4 GHIRSH

COPPER-NICKEL

KM#	Date	Mintage	VG	Fine	VF	XF
7	AH1346	3.000	3.00	5.00	8.00	20.00

13	AH1348	—	3.00	5.00	8.00	20.00
	1348	—			Proof	—

1/2 GHIRSH

 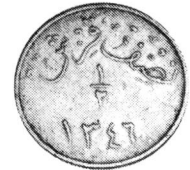

COPPER-NICKEL

8	AH1346	3.000	3.00	5.00	8.00	20.00

14	AH1348	—	3.00	5.00	8.00	25.00
	1348	—			Proof	—

GHIRSH

COPPER-NICKEL

9	AH1346	3.000	3.00	5.00	10.00	35.00

15	AH1348	—	3.00	5.00	8.50	25.00
	1348	—			Proof	—

1/4 RIYAL

6.0500 g, .917 SILVER, .1783 oz ASW

10	AH1346	.400	12.50	20.00	45.00	75.00
	1346	—			Proof	—
	1348	.200	17.50	30.00	60.00	100.00
	1348	—			Proof	—

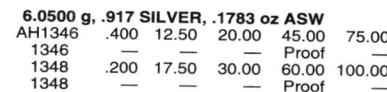

1/2 RIYAL

12.1000 g, .917 SILVER, .3567 oz ASW

KM#	Date	Mintage	VG	Fine	VF	XF
11	AH1346	.200	55.00	100.00	165.00	300.00
	1346	—			Proof	200.00
	1348	.100	55.00	100.00	165.00	300.00
	1348	—			Proof	—

RIYAL

24.1000 g, .917 SILVER, .7105 oz ASW

12	AH1346	.800	15.00	25.00	50.00	80.00
	1346	—			Proof	350.00
	1348	.400	20.00	30.00	85.00	120.00
	1348	—			Proof	—

SAUDI ARABIA

RULERS

Abd Al-Aziz Bin Sa'ud,
  AH1344-1373/1926-1953AD
Sa'ud Bin Abd Al-Aziz (Ibn Sa'ud),
  AH1373-1383/1953-1964AD
Faisal Bin Abd Al-Aziz,
  AH1383-1395/1964-1975AD
Khalid Bin Abd Al-Aziz,
  AH1395-1403/1975-1982AD
Fahad Bin Abd Al-Aziz, AH1403-/1982-AD

MONETARY SYSTEM
Until 1960

22 Ghirsh = 1 Riyal
40 Riyals = 1 Guinea
20 Ghirsh = 1 Riyal

NOTE: Copper-nickel, reeded-edge coins dated AH1356 and silver coins dated AH1354 were struck at Philadelphia between 1944-1949.

ROYAL TITLES
Appearing on coins

**AH1356 (1937AD) and later
King of the Kingdom of Saudi Arabia**

1/4 GHIRSH

COPPER-NICKEL
Plain edge.

19.1	AH1356	1.000		.25	2.00	6.00	15.00

Reeded edge.

19.2	AH1356	21.500		.25	.50	1.00	2.50

NOTE: Struck in 1947 (AH1366-67) at Philadelphia.

1/2 GHIRSH

COPPER-NICKEL
Plain edge.

KM#	Date	Mintage	VG	Fine	VF	XF
20.1	AH1356	1.000	1.25	3.00	8.00	20.00

Reeded edge.

20.2	AH1356	10.850	.20	.50	1.50	3.00

NOTE: Struck in 1947 (AH1366-67) at Philadelphia.

GHIRSH

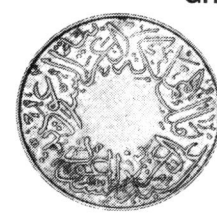 

COPPER-NICKEL
Plain edge.

21.1	AH1356	4.000	1.00	2.00	6.00	15.00

Reeded edge.

21.2	AH1356	7.150	.50	1.00	2.50	5.00

NOTE: Struck in 1947 (AH1366-67) at Philadelphia.

KM#	Date	Mintage	Fine	VF	XF	Unc
40	AH1376	10.000	.15	.25	.50	3.00
	1378	50.000	.15	.25	.50	2.00

2 GHIRSH

COPPER-NICKEL

41	AH1376	50.000	.10	.35	.75	5.00
	1379	28.110	.10	.35	.70	3.50

4 GHIRSH

COPPER-NICKEL

42	AH1376	49.100	.25	.50	1.00	6.00
	1378	10.000	.25	.50	1.00	5.00

1/4 RIYAL

3.1000 g, .917 SILVER, .0913 oz ASW

16	AH1354	.900	1.75	2.50	3.00	5.00
	1354	—			Proof	150.00

2.9500 g, .917 SILVER, .0869 oz ASW

KM#	Date	Mintage	Fine	VF	XF	Unc
37	AH1374	4.000	BV	1.00	3.00	5.00

1/2 RIYAL

5.8500 g, .917 SILVER, .1724 oz ASW

KM#	Date	Mintage	Fine	VF	XF	Unc
17	AH1354	.950	1.50	4.00	6.00	12.00

5.9500 g, .917 SILVER, .1754 oz ASW

KM#	Date	Mintage	Fine	VF	XF	Unc
38	AH1374	2.000	1.50	3.00	4.50	10.00

RIYAL

11.6000 g, .917 SILVER, .3419 oz ASW

KM#	Date	Mintage	Fine	VF	XF	Unc
18	AH1354	60.000	BV	2.50	5.00	12.00
	1354	20.000	—		Proof	—
	1367	Inc. Ab.	BV	2.50	5.00	15.00
	1370	—	BV	2.50	5.00	17.50

39	AH1374	48.000	BV	2.50	6.00	17.50

COUNTERMARKED COINAGE
70 = '65'/COUNTERMARK

The following pieces are countermarked examples of earlier types bearing the Arabic numerals "65". They were countermarked in a move to break money changers' monopoly on small coins in AH1365 (1946AD). These countermarks vary in size and are found with the Arabic numbers raised in a circle. Incuse countermarks are considered a recent fabrication.

1/4 GHIRSH

c/m: '65' on 1/4 Ghirsh, KM#4.

KM#	Date	Mintage	Good	VG	Fine	VF
22	AH1344	—	2.50	4.00	10.00	20.00

c/m: '65' on 1/4 Ghirsh, KM#7.

23	AH1346	—	2.50	4.00	10.00	20.00

c/m: '65' on 1/4 Ghirsh, KM#13.

24	AH1348	—	2.50	4.00	10.00	20.00

Plain edge.
c/m: '65' on 1/4 Ghirsh, KM#19.

KM#	Date	Mintage	Good	VG	Fine	VF
25	AH1356	—	2.50	4.00	8.00	15.00

1/2 GHIRSH

c/m: '65' on 1/2 Ghirsh, KM#5.

26	AH1344	—	2.50	4.00	7.50	25.00

 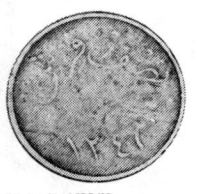

c/m: '65' on 1/2 Ghirsh, KM#8.

27	AH1346	—	2.50	4.00	7.50	25.00

c/m: '65' on 1/2 Ghirsh, KM#14.

28	AH1348	—	2.50	4.00	7.50	25.00

Plain edge
c/m: '65' on 1/2 Ghirsh, KM#20.1.

29	AH1356	—	1.25	2.25	5.00	12.00

GHIRSH

c/m: '65' on 1 Ghirsh, KM#6.

30	AH1344	—	2.50	4.00	20.00	38.00

c/m: '65' on 1 Ghirsh, KM#9.

31	AH1346	—	2.50	4.00	10.00	25.00

c/m: '65' on 1 Ghirsh, KM#15.

32	AH1348	—	5.00	10.00	30.00	40.00

Plain edge.
c/m: '65' on 1 Ghirsh, KM#21.

33	AH1356	—	2.00	3.00	8.00	20.00

MONETARY REFORM

5 Halala = 1 Ghirsh
100 Halala = 1 Riyal

HALALA

BRONZE

KM#	Date	Mintage	Fine	VF	XF	Unc
44	AH1383	5.000	.50	.60	.85	3.00

Obv: Different inscription.
Rev: Arabic H for Hegira left of curved year.

60	AH1397	—			Rare	—

NOTE: Not released for circulation.

5 HALALA
(1 Ghirsh)

COPPER-NICKEL

45	AH1392	130.000	.10	.15	.30	.50

53	AH1397	20.000	.15	.25	.60	2.00
	1400	—	.15	.25	.60	2.00

F.A.O. Issue

KM#	Date	Year	Mintage	VF	XF	Unc
57	AH1398	1978	1.500	.30	.50	1.00

KM#	Date	Mintage	Fine	VF	XF	Unc
61	AH1408	80.000	—	.30	.50	1.00
	1408	5,000	—		Proof	5.00

10 HALALA
(2 Ghirsh)

COPPER-NICKEL

46	AH1392	55.000	.10	.20	.35	.50

54	AH1397	50.000	.15	.25	1.00	2.50
	1400	29.500	.25	.75	1.00	3.00

F.A.O. Issue

KM#	Date	Year	Mintage	VF	XF	Unc
58	AH1398	1978	1.000	.25	.50	1.00

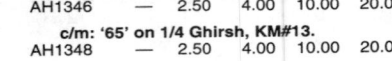

KM#	Date	Mintage	Fine	VF	XF	Unc
62	AH1408	100.000	—	.30	.60	1.25
	1408	5,000	—	Proof		6.00

25 HALALA
(1/4 Riyal)

COPPER-NICKEL
Error. Denomination in masculine gender.

KM#	Date	Mintage	Fine	VF	XF	Unc
47	AH1392	48.465	1.00	2.00	6.00	15.00

Denomination in feminine gender.

KM#	Date	Mintage	Fine	VF	XF	Unc
48	AH1392	Inc. Ab.	.25	.50	1.00	2.00

F.A.O. Issue

KM#	Date	Year	Mintage	VF	XF	Unc
49	AH1392	1973	.200	.20	.50	1.00

KM#	Date	Mintage	Fine	VF	XF	Unc
55	AH1397	20.000	.35	.50	1.00	3.00
	1400	57.000	.35	.50	.85	2.50

KM#	Date	Mintage	Fine	VF	XF	Unc
63	AH1408	100.000	—	.40	.70	1.50
	1408	5,000	—	Proof		7.50

50 HALALA
(1/2 Riyal)

COPPER-NICKEL
F.A.O. Issue

KM#	Date	Year	Mintage	VF	XF	Unc
50	AH1392	1972	.500	.30	.60	2.50

KM#	Date	Mintage	Fine	VF	XF	Unc
51	AH1392	16.000	.20	.35	.60	2.00

KM#	Date	Mintage	Fine	VF	XF	Unc
56	AH1397	20.000	.50	.75	1.00	3.00
	1400	21.600	.75	1.00	1.50	3.50

KM#	Date	Mintage	Fine	VF	XF	Unc
64	AH1408	70.000	.20	.50	2.25	3.50
	1408	5,000	—		Proof	15.00

100 HALALA
(1 Riyal)

COPPER-NICKEL

KM#	Date	Year	Mintage	VF	XF	Unc
52	AH1396	(1976)	.250	.65	1.00	3.00
	1400	(1980)	30.000	.65	1.00	3.00

F.A.O. Issue

KM#	Date	Year	Mintage	VF	XF	Unc
59	AH1397	1977	—	—	125.00	225.00
	1398	1978	10.000	.75	1.50	2.50

NOTE: AH1397 date struck as samples for the Saudi-Arabia government by the British Royal Mint.

KM#	Date	Mintage	Fine	VF	XF	Unc
65	AH1408	40.000	—	1.00	2.00	3.00
	1408	5,000	—		Proof	22.00
	1414	5,000	—	1.00	2.00	3.00

TRADE COINAGE
GUINEA

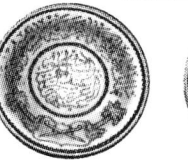 

7.9881 g, .917 GOLD, .2354 oz AGW

KM#	Date	Mintage	Fine	VF	XF	Unc
36	AH1370	2.000	—	BV	100.00	125.00

KM#	Date	Mintage	Fine	VF	XF	Unc
43	AH1377	1.579	—	BV	110.00	140.00

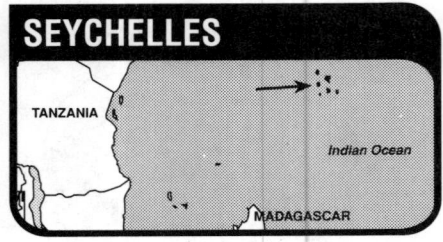

SEYCHELLES

The Republic of Seychelles, an archipelago of 85 granite and coral islands situated in the Indian Ocean 600 miles (965 km.) northeast of Madagascar, has an area of 156 sq. mi. (455 sq. km.) and a population of *70,000. Among these islands are the Aldabra Islands, the Farquhar Group, and Ile Desroches, which the United Kingdom ceded to the Seychelles upon its independence. Capital: Victoria, on Mahe. The economy is based on fishing, a plantation system of agriculture, and tourism. Copra, cinnamon and vanilla are exported.

Although the Seychelles are marked on Portuguese charts of the early 16th century, the first recorded visit to the islands, by an English ship, occurred in 1609. The Seychelles were annexed to France by Captain Lazare Picault in 1743 and permanently settled in 1768, with the intention of establishing spice plantations to compete with the Dutch monopoly of the spice trade. British troops seized the islands in 1810, during the Napoleonic Wars; they were formally ceded to Britain by the Treaty of Paris, 1814. The Seychelles were a dependency of Mauritius until Aug. 31, 1903, when they became a separate British Crown Colony. The colony was granted limited internal self-government in 1970, and attained independence on June 28, 1976, becoming Britain's last African possession to do so. Seychelles is a member of the Commonwealth of Nations. The president is the Head of State and of Government.

RULERS
British, until 1976

MINT MARKS
PM - Pobjoy Mint
None - British Royal Mint

MONETARY SYSTEM
100 Cents = 1 Rupee

CENT

BRONZE

KM#	Date	Mintage	VF	XF	Unc
5	1948	.300	.25	.50	1.25
	1948	—	—	Proof	50.00

14	1959	.030	.75	1.50	3.00
	1959	—	—	Proof	—
	1961	.030	.50	1.00	2.25
	1961	—	—	Proof	—
	1963	.040	.50	1.00	1.50
	1963	—	—	Proof	—
	1965	.020	2.00	3.00	5.00
	1969	*5,000	15.00	25.00	60.00
	1969	—	—	Proof	5.00

*Latest reports indicate only 5,000 circulation strikes have been released to date in addition to proof issues.

ALUMINUM
F.A.O. Issue - Cow

| 17 | 1972 | 2.350 | — | .10 | .25 |

2 CENTS

BRONZE

KM#	Date	Mintage	VF	XF	Unc
6	1948	.350	.35	.60	1.50
	1948	—	—	Proof	75.00

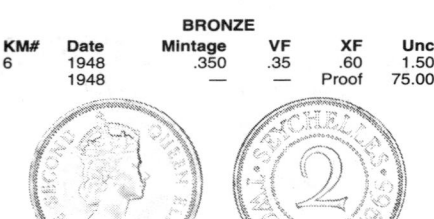

15	1959	.030	.50	1.00	2.50
	1959	—	—	Proof	—
	1961	.030	.50	1.00	2.75
	1961	—	—	Proof	—
	1963	.040	.75	1.25	2.50
	1963	—	—	Proof	—
	1965	.020	2.00	3.00	4.00
	1968	.020	2.00	3.00	5.50
	1969	5,000	—	Proof	4.00

5 CENTS

BRONZE

| 7 | 1948 | .300 | .40 | .80 | 2.00 |
| | 1948 | — | — | Proof | 100.00 |

16	1964	.020	1.00	2.00	4.50
	1964	—	—	Proof	—
	1965	.040	1.50	2.50	5.50
	1967	.020	1.50	3.00	8.00
	1968	.040	1.00	2.00	7.00
	1969	.100	.50	1.00	5.00
	1969	—	—	Proof	4.00
	1971	.025	.50	1.50	2.50

ALUMINUM
F.A.O. Issue - Cabbage

| 18 | 1972 | 2.200 | — | .10 | .25 |
| | 1975 | 1.200 | — | .10 | .25 |

10 CENTS

COPPER-NICKEL

1	1939	.036	8.00	20.00	70.00
	1939	—	—	Proof	150.00
	1943	.036	6.00	12.00	40.00
	1944	.036	6.00	12.00	40.00
	1944	—	—	Proof	175.00

| 8 | 1951 | .036 | 2.00 | 5.00 | 9.00 |
| | 1951 | — | — | Proof | 135.00 |

	1953	.130	.50	1.00	3.00
	1953	—	—	Proof	100.00
	1965	.040	1.00	1.50	5.00
	1967	.020	4.00	7.50	15.00
	1968	.050	1.00	4.00	12.50
	1969	.060	1.00	2.00	7.00
	1969	—	—	Proof	2.00
	1970	.075	.50	1.00	4.50
	1971	.100	.50	1.00	1.75
	1972	.120	.30	.50	1.00
	1973	.100	.15	.25	1.00
	1974	.100	.15	.25	.75

NICKEL-BRASS

KM#	Date	Mintage	VF	XF	Unc
10	1953	.130	.50	1.00	3.00

25 CENTS

2.9200 g, .500 SILVER .0469 oz ASW

2	1939	.036	7.50	35.00	125.00
	1939	—	—	Proof	200.00
	1943	.036	5.00	25.00	100.00
	1944	.036	3.50	20.00	85.00
	1944	—	—	Proof	300.00

COPPER-NICKEL

| 9 | 1951 | .036 | 2.00 | 7.50 | 35.00 |
| | 1951 | — | — | Proof | 160.00 |

11	1954	.124	.75	1.25	4.00
	1954	—	—	Proof	120.00
	1960	.040	.75	1.25	2.00
	1960	—	—	Proof	—
	1964	.040	1.00	2.00	5.00
	1965	.040	1.00	2.00	5.00
	1966	.010	3.50	10.00	22.50
	1967	.020	2.50	4.00	15.00
	1968	.020	2.50	4.00	15.00
	1969	.100	1.00	2.00	4.00
	1969	—	—	Proof	3.00
	1970	.040	1.50	3.00	10.00
	1972	.120	.50	.75	1.50
	1973	.100	.50	.75	1.50
	1974	.100	.50	.75	1.50

1/2 RUPEE

5.8300 g, .500 SILVER, .0937 oz ASW

| 3 | 1939 | .036 | 12.00 | 50.00 | 150.00 |
| | 1939 | — | — | Proof | 250.00 |

COPPER-NICKEL

12	1954	.072	.50	1.25	3.75
	1954	—	—	Proof	150.00
	1960	.060	.50	1.00	3.00
	1960	—	—	Proof	150.00
	1966	.015	1.50	5.00	20.00

KM#	Date	Mintage	VF	XF	Unc
12	1967	.020	3.00	8.00	25.00
	1968	.020	3.00	8.00	30.00
	1969	.060	.75		12.00
	1969	—		Proof	3.00
	1970	.050	.75	1.00	8.00
	1971	.100	.75	1.00	3.00
	1972	.120	.50	.75	1.00
	1974	.100	.50	.75	1.00

RUPEE

11.6600 g, .500 SILVER, .1874 oz ASW

4	1939	.090	15.00	60.00	165.00
	1939	—		Proof	400.00

COPPER-NICKEL

13	1954	.150	.50	1.00	3.00
	1954	—		Proof	200.00
	1960	.060	.75	1.25	3.50
	1960	—		Proof	—
	1966	.045	1.25	2.25	8.50
	1967	.010	3.50	7.50	27.50
	1968	.040	2.50	5.00	20.00
	1969	.050	1.50	3.00	12.50
	1969	—		Proof	5.00
	1970	.050	1.50	2.50	10.00
	1971	.100	.75	1.50	5.00
	1972	.120	.75	1.50	2.00
	1974	.100	—		1.50

5 RUPEES

COPPER-NICKEL

19	1972	.220	1.50	2.50	5.00

10 RUPEES

COPPER-NICKEL

20	1974	—	2.00	3.50	7.00

REPUBLIC
CENT

ALUMINUM
Declaration of Independence

KM#	Date	Mintage	VF	XF	Unc
21	1976	.109	.10	.20	.50
	1976	8,500	—	Proof	1.50

Boueteur Fish

30	1977	—		.15	.50
	1978	—		.15	.50

BRASS

46.1	1982	.500	—	.15	.50
	1982			Proof	2.25

Obv: Altered coat of arms.

46.2	1990 PM	—		.15	.45
	1992 PM	—		.15	.45

5 CENTS

ALUMINUM
Declaration of Independence

22	1976	.209	.10	.20	.50
	1976	8,500	—	Proof	1.50

NOTE: Varieties exist.

F.A.O. Issue - Bourgeois Fish

31	1977	.300		.15	.50
	1978	—		.15	.50

BRASS
World Food Day

43	1981	.720	—	.15	.45

47.1	1982	1.500		.10	.30
	1982	Inc. Ab.	—	Proof	2.50

Obv: Altered coat of arms.

47.2	1990 PM	—		.10	.30
	1992 PM	—		.10	.30
	1995 PM	—		.10	.30
	1997 PM	—		.10	.30

10 CENTS

NICKEL-BRASS

Declaration of Independence

KM#	Date	Mintage	VF	XF	Unc
23	1976	.209	.20	.50	1.50
	1976	8,500	—	Proof	2.50

F.A.O. Issue - Sailfish

32	1977	.125	.10	.35	1.50
	1978	—	.10	.35	1.50

BRASS
World Food Day

44	1981	.145	.10	.25	1.00

48.1	1982	1.000	.10	.25	1.00
	1982	Inc. Ab.	—	Proof	2.75

Obv: Altered coat of arms.

48.2	1990 PM	—	.10	.25	1.00
	1992 PM	—	.10	.25	1.00
	1994 PM	—	.10	.25	1.00
	1997 PM	—	.10	.25	1.00

25 CENTS

COPPER-NICKEL
Declaration of Independence

24	1976	.209	.50	1.00	3.00
	1976	8,500	—	Proof	3.50

Black Parrot

33	1977	—	.25	.75	2.50
	1978	—	.25	.75	2.50

49.1	1982	.375	.25	.75	2.50
	1982	Inc. Ab.	—	Proof	3.00

Obv: Altered coat of arms.

49.2	1989 PM	1.500	.25	.75	2.50
	1992 PM	—	.25	.75	2.50
	1997 PM	—	.25	.75	2.50

NICKEL CLAD STEEL

49.3	1993 PM	—	.25	.75	2.50

50 CENTS

COPPER-NICKEL
Declaration of Independence

KM#	Date	Mintage	VF	XF	Unc
25	1976	.209	.50	1.00	2.50
	1976	8,500	—	Proof	3.50

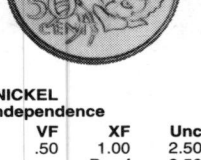

Vanilla Orchid

34	1977	—	.20	.45	1.00
	1978	—	.20	.45	1.00

RUPEE

COPPER-NICKEL
Declaration of Independence

26	1976	.259	.75	1.00	1.75
	1976	8,500	—	Proof	2.50

Triton Conch Shell

35	1977	—	.50	.75	1.50
	1978	—	.50	.75	1.50

50.1	1982	2.000	.25	.50	1.25
	1982	Inc. Ab.	—	Proof	5.00
	1983	—	.25	.50	1.25

Obv: Altered coat of arms.

50.2	1992 PM	—	.25	.50	1.25

5 RUPEES

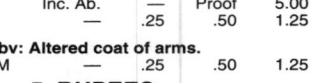

COPPER-NICKEL
Declaration of Independence

27	1976	.050	1.25	1.75	3.00

COPPER-NICKEL
Coco-de-mer Palm Tree

KM#	Date	Mintage	VF	XF	Unc
36	1977	—	1.00	1.50	2.25
	1978	—	1.00	1.50	2.25

51.1	1982	.300	1.00	1.50	2.00
	1982	Inc. Ab.	—	Proof	5.00

Obv: Altered coat of arms.

51.2	1992 PM	—	1.00	1.50	2.00

10 RUPEES

COPPER-NICKEL
Declaration of Independence

28	1976	.050	2.00	2.75	5.00

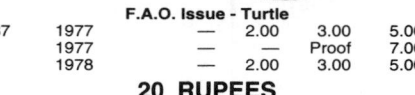

F.A.O. Issue - Turtle

37	1977	—	2.00	3.00	5.00
	1977	—	—	Proof	7.00
	1978	—	2.00	3.00	5.00

20 RUPEES

COPPER-NICKEL
5th Anniversary of Central Bank

52	1983	—	4.00	5.00	6.00

SIERRA LEONE

The Republic of Sierra Leone, a British Commonwealth nation located in western Africa between Guinea and Liberia, has an area of 27,699 sq. mi. (71,740 sq. km.) and a population of *4.1 million. Capital: Freetown. The economy is predominantly agricultural but mining contributes significantly to export revenues. Diamonds, iron ore, palm kernels, cocoa, and coffee are exported.

The coast of Sierra Leone was first visited by Portuguese and British slavers in the 15th and 16th centuries. The first settlement, at Freetown, 1787, was established as a refuge for freed slaves within the British Empire, runaway slaves from the United States and Negroes discharged from the British armed forces. The first settlers were virtually wiped out by tribal attacks and disease. The colony was re-established under the auspices of the Sierra Leone Company and transferred to the British Crown in 1807. The interior region was secured and established as a protectorate in 1896. Sierra Leone became independent within the Commonwealth on April 27, 1961, and adopted a republican constitution ten years later. It is a member of the Commonwealth of Nations. The president is Chief of State and Head of Government.

For similar coinage refer to British West Africa.

RULERS

British, until 1971

MONETARY SYSTEM
Until 1906
100 Cents = 50 Pence = 1 Dollar
Until 1964
12 Pence = 1 Shilling
Commencing 1964
100 Cents = 1 Leone

NOTE: "$" indicates the claim that the coins struck by the Pobjoy Mint are backed by U.S. Dollars. See 1 Leone, KM#71.

1/2 CENT

BRONZE
Bonga Fish

KM#	Date	Mintage	VF	XF	Unc
16	1964	.600	—	.15	.25
	1964	.010	—	Proof	1.00

31	1980	—	.15	.30	1.00
	1980	.010	—	Proof	1.50

CENT

BRONZE
Palm Branches and Fruit Stalks

17	1964	35.000	—	.15	.25
	1964	.010	—	Proof	1.25

KM#	Date	Mintage	VF	XF	Unc
32	1980	—	.15	.30	1.00
	1980	.010	—	Proof	1.50

5 CENTS

COPPER-NICKEL
Kapok Tree

18	1964	.900	.15	.25	.50
	1964	.010	—	Proof	1.50

33	1980	—	.15	.30	.75
	1980	.010	—	Proof	2.50
	1984	—	.15	.30	.75

10 CENTS

COPPER-NICKEL
Cocoa Beans

19	1964	24.000	.25	.40	.65
	1964	.010	—	Proof	1.25

34	1978	.200	.25	.50	1.00
	1980	—	.20	.40	.75
	1980	.010	—	Proof	5.00
	1984	—	.20	.40	.75

20 CENTS

COPPER-NICKEL

20	1964	11.000	.35	.60	1.25
	1964	.010	—	Proof	2.00

30	1978	2.375	.35	.65	1.50
	1980	—	.35	.60	1.25
	1980	.010	—	Proof	7.00
	1984	—	.35	.60	1.25

50 CENTS

KM#	Date	Mintage	VF	XF	Unc
25	1972	1.000	1.00	1.75	3.00
	1972	2,000	—	Proof	5.00
	1980	—	1.00	1.50	2.75
	1980	.010	—	Proof	10.00
	1984	—	1.00	1.50	2.75

LEONE

COPPER-NICKEL
10th Anniversary of Bank

26	ND(1974)	.103	1.50	2.50	5.50

O.A.U. Summit Conference

36	1980	.075	1.75	2.75	6.00

NICKEL-BRONZE

KM#	Date	Mintage	VF	XF	Unc
43	1987	—	.50	.75	1.50
	1988	—	.50	.75	1.50

2 LEONES

COPPER-NICKEL
F.A.O. Regional Conference for Africa

29	1976	.020	1.00	2.00	4.50

10 LEONES

NICKEL CLAD STEEL
Obv: Denomination. Rev: Mammy Yoko portrait.

44	1996	—	—	—	.75

50 LEONES

NICKEL CLAD STEEL
Obv: Building above denomination.
Rev: Sir Henry Lightfoot bust.

45	1996	—	—	—	1.25

100 LEONES

NICKEL CLAD STEEL
Obv: Cocoa pods.
Rev: Naimbana bust.

46	1996	—	—	—	1.75

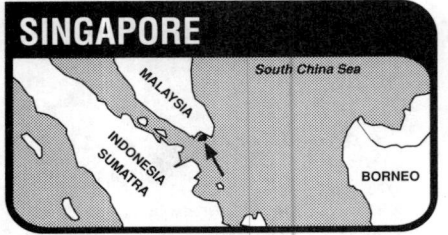

SINGAPORE

The Republic of Singapore, a British Commonwealth nation situated off the southern tip of the Malay peninsula, has an area of 224 sq. mi. (633 sq. km.) and a population of *2.7 million. Capital: Singapore. The economy is based on entrepot trade, manufacturing and oil. Rubber, petroleum products, machinery and spices are exported.

Singapore's modern history - it was an important shipping center in the 14th century before the rise of Malacca and Penang - began in 1819 when Sir Thomas Stamford Raffles, an agent for the British East India Company, founded the town of Singapore. By 1825 its trade exceeded that of Malacca and Penang combined. The opening of the Suez Canal (1869) and the demand for rubber and tin created by the automobile and packaging industries combined to make Singapore one of the major ports of the world. In 1826 Singapore, Penang and Malacca were combined to form the Straits Settlements, which was made a Crown Colony in 1867. Singapore became a separate Crown Colony in 1946 when the Straits Settlements was dissolved. It joined in the formation of Malaysia in 1963, but broke away on Aug. 9, 1965, to become an independent republic. The President is Chief of State. The prime minister is Head of Government.

For earlier coinage see Straits Settlements, Malaya, Malaya and British Borneo.

MINT MARKS

sm Singapore Mint monogram

MONETARY SYSTEM
100 Cents = 1 Dollar

CENT

BRONZE
Apartment Building

KM#	Date	Mintage	VF	XF	Unc
1	1967	7.500	—	.20	.40
	1967	2,000	—	Proof	2.25
	1968	2.969	—	.25	.50
	1968	5,000	—	Proof	2.00
	1969	7.220	—	.20	.30
	1969	3,000	—	Proof	10.00
	1970	1.402	—	.40	.80
	1971	9.731	—	.20	.25
	1972	1.665	—	.20	.70
	1972	749 pcs.	—	Proof	40.00
	1973	6.377	—	.10	.20
	1973	1,000	—	Proof	5.00
	1974	9.421	—	—	.20
	1974	1,500	—	Proof	4.00
	1975	24.226	—	—	.20
	1975	3,000	—	Proof	1.50
	1976	2.500	—	.10	.60
	1976 sm	3,500	—	Proof	1.25
	1977 sm	3,500	—	Proof	1.25
	1978 sm	4,000	—	Proof	1.25
	1979 sm	3,500	—	Proof	1.25
	1980 sm	.014	—	Proof	1.00
	1982 sm	.020	—	Proof	1.00
	1983 sm	.015	—	Proof	1.00
	1984 sm	.015	—	Proof	1.00

COPPER-CLAD STEEL

1a	1976	13.665	—	—	.25
	1977	13.940	—	—	.25
	1978	5.931	—	—	.25
	1979	11.986	—	—	.15
	1980	19.922	—	—	.15
	1981	38.084	—	—	.10
	1982	24.105	—	—	.10
	1983	2.204	—	—	.10
	1984	5.695	—	—	.10
	1985	.148	—	.15	.35

BRONZE
Vanda Miss Joaquim Plants

49	1986	20.000	—	—	.10
	1987		—	—	.10
	1988		—	—	.10

KM#	Date	Mintage	VF	XF	Unc
49	1989	20.080	—	—	.10
	1990	10.000	—	—	.10

NOTE: For previously listed dates 1992-1995 refer to KM#98.

COPPER PLATED ZINC
49b	1991				.10

Similar to KM#49 but motto ribbon on arms curves down at center.

98	1992	20.000	—	—	.10
	1993	39.920	—	—	.10
	1994	130.810	—	—	.10
	1995	220.000	—	—	.10
	1996		—	—	.10
	1997		—	—	.10

5 CENTS

COPPER-NICKEL
Great White Egret

2	1967	28.000	—	.15	.30
	1967	2,000	—	Proof	3.25
	1968	4.217	—	.20	.40
	1968	5,000	—	Proof	3.00
	1969	14.778	—	.10	.30
	1969	3,000	—	Proof	15.00
	1970	4.065	—	.20	.40
	1971	13.202	—	.10	.20
	1972	9.817	—	.10	.20
	1972	749 pcs.	—	Proof	50.00
	1973	2.980	—	.30	.50
	1973	1,000	—	Proof	7.50
	1974	10.868	—	.10	.20
	1974	1,500	—	Proof	6.50
	1975	1.729	—	.40	1.00
	1975	3,000	—	Proof	2.50
	1976	15.541	—	.10	.15
	1976 sm	3,500	—	Proof	2.25
	1977	9.956	—	.10	.15
	1977 sm	3,500	—	Proof	2.25
	1978	5.956	—	.10	.20
	1978 sm	4,000	—	Proof	2.25
	1979	9.974	—	—	.10
	1979 sm	3,500	—	Proof	2.25
	1980	20.534	—	—	.15
	1980 sm	.014	—	Proof	2.00
	1981	.110	—	—	.10
	1982	.160	—	—	.10
	1982 sm	.020	—	Proof	2.00
	1983	.040	—	—	.10
	1983 sm	.015	—	Proof	2.00
	1984	18.880	—	—	.10
	1984 sm	.015	—	Proof	2.00
	1985	.148	—	—	.10

ALUMINUM
F.A.O. Issue
8	1971	3.049	—	.10	.35

COPPER-NICKEL CLAD STEEL
2a	1980	12.001	—	—	.10
	1981	23.866	—	—	.10
	1982	24.413	—	—	.10
	1983	4.016	—	—	.10
	1984	18.880	—	—	.10

ALUMINUM-BRONZE
Fruit Salad Plant

50	1985	14.840	—	—	.10
	1986	15.480	—	—	.10
	1987	31.040	—	—	.10
	1988	45.180	—	—	.10
	1989	69.988	—	—	.10
	1990	26.052	—	—	.10
	1991		—	—	.10

Similar to KM#50 but motto ribbon on arms curves down at center.

99	1992		—	—	.10
	1993	7.296	—	—	.10

KM#	Date	Mintage	VF	XF	Unc
99	1994		—	—	.10
	1995	90.000	—	—	.10
	1996		—	—	.10
	1997		—	—	.10

10 CENTS

COPPER-NICKEL
Stylized Great Crowned Seahorse

3	1967	40.000	—	.15	.30
	1967	2,000	—	Proof	4.50
	1968	36.261	—	.20	.40
	1968	5,000	—	Proof	4.25
	1969	25.000	—	.10	.50
	1969	3,000	—	Proof	20.00
	1970	21.304	—	.20	.50
	1971	33.041	—	.10	.30
	1972	2.675	—	.10	.35
	1972	749 pcs.	—	Proof	60.00
	1973	14.290	—	.10	.25
	1973	1,000	—	Proof	10.00
	1974	13.450	—	.10	.25
	1974	1,500	—	Proof	7.50
	1975	.828	.10	.60	1.25
	1975	3,000	—	Proof	4.00
	1976	29.718	—	.10	.25
	1976 sm	3,500	—	Proof	3.50
	1977	11.776	—	.10	.20
	1977 sm	3,500	—	Proof	3.50
	1978	5.936	—	.10	.30
	1978 sm	4,000	—	Proof	3.50
	1979	12.001	—	.10	.20
	1979 sm	3,500	—	Proof	3.50
	1980	40.299	—	.10	.20
	1980 sm	.014	—	Proof	3.00
	1981	58.600	—	.10	.20
	1982	48.514	—	.10	.20
	1982 sm	.020	—	Proof	3.00
	1983	10.415	—	.10	.20
	1983 sm	.015	—	Proof	3.00
	1984	29.700	—	.10	.20
	1984 sm	.015	—	Proof	3.00
	1985	.148	—	.10	.20

Star Jasmine Plant

51	1985	45.040	—	—	.20
	1986	113.000	—	—	.20
	1987	90.000	—	—	.20
	1988	54.455	—	—	.20
	1989	134.190	—	—	.20
	1990	51.720	—	—	.20
	1991	159.770	—	—	.20

Similar to KM#51 but motto ribbon on arms curves down at center.

100	1992		—	—	.20
	1993	89.855	—	—	.20
	1994		—	—	.20
	1995		—	—	.20
	1996		—	—	.20
	1997		—	—	.20

20 CENTS

 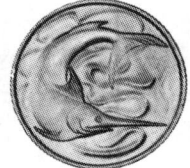

COPPER-NICKEL
Swordfish

4	1967	36.500	.15	.30	.60
	1967	2,000	—	Proof	7.00
	1968	10.934	.15	.30	.60
	1968	5,000	—	Proof	6.00
	1969	8.460	.15	.30	.60
	1969	3,000	—	Proof	30.00
	1970	3.250	.15	.30	.60
	1971	1.732	.15	.70	2.00
	1972	9.107	.15	.30	.60
	1972	749 pcs.	—	Proof	70.00
	1973	8.838	.15	.30	.60
	1973	1,000	—	Proof	17.50
	1974	4.567	.15	.30	.60
	1974	1,500	—	Proof	12.50
	1975	1.546	.15	.50	1.00
	1975	3,000	—	Proof	6.50
	1976	19.760	.15	.25	.50
	1976 sm	3,500	—	Proof	6.00

KM#	Date	Mintage	VF	XF	Unc
4	1977	7.074	.15	.30	.60
	1977 sm	3,500	—	Proof	6.00
	1978	4.450	.15	.30	.60
	1978 sm	4,000	—	Proof	6.00
	1979	14.865	—	.15	.30
	1979 sm	3,500	—	Proof	6.00
	1980	27.903	—	.15	.30
	1980 sm	.014	—	Proof	5.00
	1981	46.997	—	.15	.30
	1982	25.234	—	.15	.30
	1982 sm	.020	—	Proof	4.00
	1983	6.424	—	.15	.30
	1983 sm	.015	—	Proof	4.00
	1984	9.290	—	.15	.30
	1984 sm	.015	—	Proof	4.00
	1985	.148	—	.15	.30

Powder-puff Plant

52	1985	25.980	—	.15	.30
	1986	47.560	—	.15	.30
	1987	80.010	—	.15	.30
	1988	35.783	—	.15	.30
	1989	51.890	—	.15	.30
	1990	49.958	—	.15	.30
	1991	60.000	—	.15	.30

Similar to KM#52 but motto ribbon on arms curves down at center.

101	1992	—	—	—	.30
	1993	24.998	—	—	.30
	1994	—	—	—	.30
	1995	—	—	—	.30
	1996	—	—	—	.30
	1997	—	—	—	.30

50 CENTS

COPPER-NICKEL
Zebra Fish

5	1967	11.000	.30	.40	.80
	1967	2,000	—	Proof	10.00
	1968	3.189	.30	.60	1.50
	1968	5,000	—	Proof	8.50
	1969	2.008	.30	.60	1.50
	1969	3,000	—	Proof	35.00
	1970	3.102	.30	.60	1.50
	1971	3.933	.30	.60	1.50
	1972	5.427	.30	.50	.90
	1972	749 pcs.	—	Proof	90.00
	1973	4.474	.30	.50	.90
	1973	1,000	—	Proof	30.00
	1974	11.550	—	.40	.75
	1974	1,500	—	Proof	22.50
	1975	1.432	.35	.75	2.00
	1975	3,000	—	Proof	10.00
	1976	5.728	.30	.50	.90
	1976 sm	3,500	—	Proof	8.50
	1977	6.953	—	.40	.75
	1977 sm	3,500	—	Proof	8.50
	1978	3.934	—	.40	.75
	1978 sm	4,000	—	Proof	8.50
	1979	8.461	—	.40	.75
	1979 sm	3,500	—	Proof	8.50
	1980	14.717	—	.35	.60
	1980 sm	.014	—	Proof	7.00
	1981	29.542	—	.35	.60
	1982	13.756	—	.35	.60
	1982 sm	.020	—	Proof	5.00
	1983	4.482	—	.35	.60
	1983 sm	.015	—	Proof	5.00
	1984	3.658	—	.35	.60
	1984 sm	.015	—	Proof	5.00
	1985	.148	—	.35	.60

Yellow Allamanda Plant
Reeded edge.

53.1	1985	14.960	—	.35	.60
	1986	15.022	—	.35	.60
	1987	30.000	—	.35	.60
	1988	25.000	—	.35	.60

Lettered edge.

KM#	Date	Mintage	VF	XF	Unc
53.2	1989	20.046	—	.35	.60
	1990	472.000	—	.35	.60
	1991	508.000	—	.35	.60

Similar to KM#53 but motto ribbon on arms curves down at center.

102	1992	—	—	—	.60
	1993	4.878	—	—	.60
	1994	—	—	—	.60
	1995	49.440	—	—	.60
	1996	—	—	—	.60
	1997	—	—	—	.60

DOLLAR

COPPER-NICKEL

6	1967	3.000	.65	1.00	2.00
	1967	2,000	—	Proof	22.50
	1968	2.194	.65	1.00	2.00
	1968	5,000	—	Proof	20.00
	1969	1.871	.65	1.00	2.00
	1969	3,000	—	Proof	75.00
	1970	.560	.65	1.25	2.50
	1971	.900	.65	1.00	2.00
	1972	.458	.75	2.00	4.00
	1972	749 pcs.	—	Proof	150.00
	1973	.341	.75	1.50	3.00
	1973	1,000	—	Proof	50.00
	1974	.352	.75	1.50	3.00
	1974	1,500	—	Proof	40.00
	1975	.430	.75	1.50	3.00
	1975	3,000	—	Proof	20.00
	1976	.165	.75	2.00	4.00
	1976 sm	3,500	—	Proof	13.50
	1977	.132	.75	3.00	6.00
	1977 sm	3,500	—	Proof	13.50
	1978	.037	1.00	6.00	12.00
	1978 sm	4,000	—	Proof	13.50
	1979	.100	—	2.00	4.00
	1979 sm	3,500	—	Proof	13.50
	1980	.166	—	2.00	4.00
	1980 sm	.014	—	Proof	10.00
	1981	1.230	—	1.00	2.00
	1982	1.080	—	1.00	2.00
	1983	.101	—	1.25	3.00
	1984	.170	—	1.00	2.00
	1985	.148	—	.65	1.25

Periwinkle

54	1985	.120	—	—	1.75
	1986	.120	—	—	1.75
	1987	.120	—	—	1.75

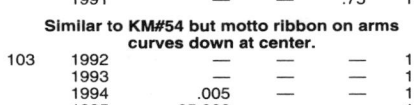

ALUMINUM-BRONZE

54b	1987	21.772	—	.75	1.50
	1988	59.332	—	.75	1.50
	1989	62.586	—	.75	1.50
	1990	37.608	—	.75	1.50
	1991	—	—	.75	1.50

Similar to KM#54 but motto ribbon on arms curves down at center.

103	1992	—	—	—	1.50
	1993	—	—	—	1.50
	1994	.005	—	—	1.50
	1995	65.000	—	—	1.50
	1996	—	—	—	1.50
	1997	—	—	—	1.50

5 DOLLARS

ALUMINUM-BRONZE center, COPPER-NICKEL ring
Vanda Miss Joaquim

KM#	Date	Mintage	VF	XF	Unc
104	1992		In mint sets only		12.00
	1993		In mint sets only		13.50
	1994		In mint sets only		13.50
	1995		In mint sets only		13.50
	1996		In mint sets only		12.00
	1997		In mint sets only		12.00

50th Anniversary - United Nations

138	1995	.500	—	—	9.50

SLOVAKIA

The Republic of Slovakia has an area of 18,923 sq. mi. (49,035 sq. km.) and a population of 4.9 million. Capital: Bratislava. Textiles, steel, and wood products are exported.

The Slovak lands were united with the Czechs and the Czechoslovak State came into existence on Oct. 28, 1918 upon the dissolution of Austrian-Hungarian Empire at the close of World War I. In March 1939, the German-influenced Slovak government proclaimed Slovakia independent and Germany incorporated the Czech lands into the Third Reich as the "Protectorate of Bohemia and Moravia". A Czechoslovak government-in-exile was set up in London in July 1940. The Soviet and USA forces liberated the area by May, 1945. At the close of World War II, Communist influence increased steadily while pressure for liberalization culminated in the overthrow of the Stalinist leader Antonin Novotn'y and his associates in 1968. The Communist Party then introduced far reaching reforms which received warnings from Moscow, followed by occcupation by Warsaw Pact forces resulting in stationing of Soviet forces. Mass civilian demonstrations for reform began in Nov. 1989 and the Federal Assembly abolished the Communist Party's sole right to govern. New governments followed on Dec. 3 and Dec. 10 and the Czech and Slovak Federal Republic was formed. The Movement for Democratic Slovakia was apparent in the June 1992 elections with the Slovak National Council adopting a declaration of sovereignty. Later, a constitution for an independent Slovakia with the Federal Assembly voting for the dissolution of the Republic came into effect on Dec. 31, 1992, and two new republics came into being on Jan. 1, 1993.

MINT MARK

Kremnica Mint

AUTONOMOUS REPUBLIC

MONETARY SYSTEM
100 Halierov = 1 Koruna

5 HALIEROV

ZINC

KM#	Date	Mintage	Fine	VF	XF	Unc
8	1942	1.000	1.50	3.00	7.50	20.00

10 HALIEROV

BRONZE

	1939	15.000	1.50	2.00	4.00	8.00
1	1942	7.000	1.50	4.00	4.00	8.00

20 HALIEROV

BRONZE

	1940	10.972	1.25	2.00	3.00	6.00
4	1941	4.028	1.25	2.00	3.00	6.00
	1942	6.474	1.25	3.00	5.00	9.00

ALUMINUM

	1942	5.000	1.00	1.50	2.00	4.50
4a	1943	15.000	1.00	1.50	2.00	4.50

NOTE: Varieties exist.

50 HALIEROV

COPPER-NICKEL

KM#	Date	Mintage	Fine	VF	XF	Unc
5	1940	—	30.00	45.00	60.00	125.00
	1941	8.000	1.00	2.00	3.00	6.00

ALUMINUM

	1943	4.400	1.00	1.50	2.50	5.00
5a	1944	2.621	1.25	2.00	4.00	7.00

KORUNA

COPPER-NICKEL

	1940	2.350	.75	1.25	2.25	6.00
6	1941	11.650	.50	1.00	2.00	5.00
	1942	6.000	.50	1.00	2.00	5.00
	1944	.884	1.50	2.50	4.50	10.00
	1945	3.321	.75	1.25	2.25	6.00

5 KORUN

NICKEL

2	1939	5.101	1.50	2.00	3.50	12.50

Approximately 2,000,000 pieces were melted down by the Czechoslovak National Bank in 1947.

10 KORUN

7.0000 g, .500 SILVER, .1125 oz ASW.
Pribina
Rev: Variety 1 - Cross atop church held by left figure.

9.1	1944	1.381	2.00	4.00	5.00	8.00

Rev: Variety 2 - W/o cross.

9.2	1944	Inc. Ab.	2.50	5.00	7.00	10.00

20 KORUN

15.0000 g, .500 SILVER, .2411 oz ASW
Dr. Joseph Tiso

3	1939	.200	5.00	10.00	15.00	30.00

St. Kyrill and St. Methodius
Rev: Variety 1 - Single bar cross in church at lower right.

7.1	1941	2.500	2.00	3.50	5.00	10.00

Rev: Variety 2 - Double bar cross.

7.2	1941	Inc. Ab.	4.00	6.50	9.00	15.00

---

50 KORUN

16.5000 g, .700 SILVER, .3713 oz ASW
5th Anniversary of Independence

KM#	Date	Mintage	Fine	VF	XF	Unc
10	1944	2.000	3.00	5.00	7.50	12.50

REPUBLIC

MONETARY SYSTEM
100 Haliers = 1 Slovak Koruna

10 HALIERS

ALUMINUM
Rev: Church steeple.

KM#	Date	Mintage	VF	XF	Unc
17	1993	—	—	—	.35
	1994	—	—	—	.35
	1995	—	—	—	.35
	1996	—	—	—	.35
	1997	—	—	—	.35
	1998	—	—	—	.35
	1999	—	—	—	.35

20 HALIERS

ALUMINUM
Rev: Mountain peak.

18	1993	—	—	—	.45
	1994	—	—	—	.45
	1995	—	—	—	.45
	1996	—	—	—	.45
	1997	—	—	—	.45
	1998	—	—	—	.45
	1999	—	—	—	.45

50 HALIERS

ALUMINUM
Rev: Watch tower.

15	1993	—	—	—	.55
	1994	—	—	—	.55
	1995	—	—	—	.55

COPPER PLATED STEEL
Rev: Watch tower.

35	1996	—	—	—	.60
	1997	—	—	—	.60
	1998	—	—	—	.60
	1999	—	—	—	.60

KORUNA

ALUMINUM - BRONZE

KM#	Date	Mintage	VF	XF	Unc
12	1993	—	—	—	.75

BRONZE CLAD STEEL

12a	1994	—	—	—	.75
	1995	—	—	—	.75
	1996	—	—	—	.75
	1997	—	—	—	.75
	1998	—	—	—	.75
	1999	—	—	—	.75

2 KORUNA

NICKEL CLAD STEEL

13	1993	—	—	—	.85
	1994	—	—	—	.85
	1995	—	—	—	.85
	1996	—	—	—	.85
	1997	—	—	—	.85
	1998	—	—	—	.85
	1999	—	—	—	.85

5 KORUN

NICKEL CLAD STEEL

14	1993	—	—	—	1.25
	1994	—	—	—	1.25
	1995	—	—	—	1.25
	1996	—	—	—	1.25
	1997	—	—	—	1.25
	1998	—	—	—	1.25

10 KORUNA

BRASS

11	1993	—	—	—	2.50
	1994	—	—	—	2.50
	1995	—	—	—	2.50
	1996	—	—	—	2.50
	1997	—	—	—	2.50
	1998	—	—	—	2.50
	1999	—	—	—	2.50

SLOVENIA

The Republic of Slovenia is located northwest of Yugoslavia in the valleys of the Danube River. It has an area of 7,819 sq. mi. and a population of *1.9 million. Capital: Ljubljana. Agriculture is the main industry with large amounts of hops and fodder crops grown as well as many varieties of fruit trees. Sheep raising, timber production and the mining of mercury from one of the country's oldest mines are also very important to their economy.

Slovenia was important as a land route between Europe and the eastern Mediterranean region. The Roman Catholic Austro-Hungarian Empire gained control of the area during the 14th century and retained its dominance until World War I. The United Kingdom of the Serbs, Croats and Slovenes (Yugoslavia) was founded in 1918 and consisted of various groups of South Slavs.

In 1929, King Alexander declared his assumption of power temporarily, however he was assassinated in 1934. His son Peter's regent, Prince Paul tried to settle internal problems, however, the Slovenes denounced the agreement he made. He resigned in 1941 and Peter assumed the throne. He was forced to flee when the invaders entered Yugoslavia. Slovenia was divided between Germany and Italy. Even though Yugoslavia attempted to remain neutral, the Nazis occupied the country and were resisted by guerilla armies, most notably Marshal Josif Broz Tito.

Under Marshal Tito, the Constitution of 1946 established 6 constituent republics which made up Yugoslavia. Each republic was permitted to fly their own flag, use their own language, control their judiciary system under supervision of the Communist Party and handle their local administration through its representative Peoples Assembly.

A legal opposition group, the Slovene League of Social Democrats, was formed in Jan. 1989. In Oct. 1989 the Slovene Assembly voted a constitutional amendment giving it the right to secede from Yugoslavia. On July 2, 1990 the Assembly adopted a ''declaration of sovereignty' and in Sept. proclaimed its control over the territorial defense force on its soil. A referendum on Dec. 23 resulted in a majority vote for independence, which was formally declared on Dec. 26.

In Feb. 1991 parliament ruled that henceforth Slovenian law took precedence over federal. On June 25 Slovenia declared independence, but agreed to suspend this for 3 months at peace talks sponsored by the EC. Federal troops moved into Slovenia on June 27 to secure Yugoslavia's external borders, but after some fighting finally withdrew by the end of July. The 3-month moratorium agreed at the EC having expired, Slovenia (and Croatia) declared their complete independence of the Yugoslav federation on Oct. 8, 1991. Currency was introduced on Oct. 12, 1991.

MINT MARKS
Based on last digit in date.
(K) - Kremnitz (Slovakia): open 4, upturned 5
(BP) - Budapest (Hungary): closed 4, downturned 5

MONETARY SYSTEM
100 Stotinov = 1 Tolar

10 STOTINOV

ALUMINUM
Salamandar - Larval Stage

KM#	Date	Mintage	VF	XF	Unc
7	1992	.500	—	—	.25
	1992	2,000	—	Proof	3.00
	1993	.500	—	—	.25
	1993	2,000	—	Proof	3.00
	1994	—	—	—	.25
	1994	—	—	Proof	3.00
	1995	—	—	—	.25
	1995	—	—	Proof	3.00

NOTE: Varieties exist.

20 STOTINOV

ALUMINUM
Obv: Similar to 10 Stotinov, KM#7.

Rev: Long eared owl.

KM#	Date	Mintage	VF	XF	Unc
8	1992	.500	—	—	.25
	1992	2,000	—	Proof	4.00
	1993	.500	—	—	.25
	1993	2,000	—	Proof	4.00
	1994	—	—	—	.25
	1994	—	—	Proof	4.00
	1995	—	—	—	.25
	1995	—	—	Proof	4.00

NOTE: Varieties exist.

50 STOTINOV

ALUMINUM
Bee

3	1992	4.999	—	.10	.35
	1992	1,000	—	Proof	6.00
	1993	18.299	—	.10	.35
	1993	1,000	—	Proof	6.00
	1994	—	—	.10	.35
	1994	—	—	Proof	6.00
	1995	—	—	.10	.35
	1995	—	—	Proof	6.00
	1995(K)	—	—	.10	.35
	1996	*.300	—	.10	.35
	1996	*3,000	—	Proof	6.00

NOTE: Varieties exist.

TOLAR

BRASS
3 Fish

4	1992	9,998	—	.20	.65
	1992	2,000	—	Proof	5.00
	1993	.030	—	.20	.65
	1993	2,000	—	Proof	5.00
	1994(K)	.010	—	—	.50
	1994(K)	—	—	Proof	5.00
	1994(BP)	5,000	—	—	.50
	1995	—	—	—	.50
	1995(K)	—	—	—	.50
	1995(K)	—	—	Proof	5.00
	1995(BP)	—	—	—	.50
	1996	*.300	—	—	.50
	1996	*3,000	—	Proof	5.00
	1997	—	—	—	.50

NOTE: Varieites exist.

2 TOLARJA

BRASS
Bird in Flight

5	1992	4,998	—	.25	.75
	1992	2,000	—	Proof	7.00
	1993	9,998	—	.25	.75
	1993	2,000	—	Proof	7.00
	1994(K)	.010	—	—	.65
	1994(K)	5,000	—	Proof	7.00
	1994(BP)	—	—	—	.65
	1995	—	—	—	.65
	1995(K)	—	—	—	.65
	1995(BP)	—	—	—	.65
	1996	*.300	—	—	.65
	1996	*3,000	—	Proof	7.00
	1997	—	—	—	.65

NOTE: Varieties exist.

5 TOLARJEV

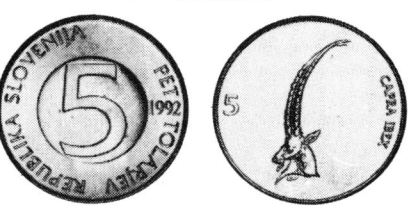

BRASS
Head and Horns of Ibex

6	1992	9,998	—	.35	1.00

KM#	Date	Mintage	VF	XF	Unc
6	1992	2,000	—	Proof	8.00
	1993	9,998	—	.35	1.00
	1993	2,000	—	Proof	8.00
	1994(K)	10,000	—	—	.85
	1994(K)	—	—	Proof	8.00
	1994 closed 4	—	—	—	.85
	1995	—	—	—	.85
	1996	—	—	—	.85
	1996	*3,000	—	Proof	8.00
	1997	—	—	—	.85

NOTE: Varieties exist.

Battle of Sisek

9	1993	.100	—	—	1.65

Operosorum Labacensium Academy

12	1993	.100	—	—	1.65

50th Anniversary - Slovenian Bank

15	1994	.100	—	—	1.65

1000th Anniversary - Glagolitic Alphabet

16	1994	.200	—	—	1.65

50th Anniversary - F.A.O.

21	1995	.500	—	—	1.65

50th Anniversary - Defeat of Facism

22	1995	.200	—	—	1.65

Aljazev Stolp

26	1995	.200	—	—	1.65

100th Anniversary - First Railway in Slovenia

KM#	Date	Mintage	VF	XF	Unc
29	1996	*.300	—	—	1.65
	1996	*3,000	—	Proof	8.00

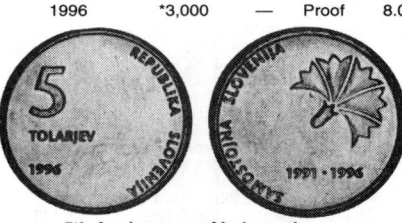

5th Anniversary of Independence
Rev: Stylized flower.

32	1996	—	—	—	1.65
	1996	—	—	Proof	8.00

Olympic Centennial - Gymnast

33	1996	*.300	—	—	1.65
	1996	*3,000	—	Proof	8.00

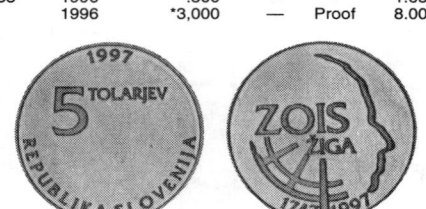

Ziga Zois
Obv: Denomination.

38	1997	—	—	—	1.65

SOLOMON ISLANDS

The Solomon Islands, located in the southwest Pacific east of Papua New Guinea, has an area of 10,983 sq. mi. (28,450 sq. km.) and a population of *324,000. Capital: Honiara. The most important islands of the Solomon chain are Guadalcanal (scene of some of the fiercest fighting of World War II), Malaitia, New Georgia, Florida, Vella Lavella, Choiseul, Rendova, San Cristobal, the Lord Howe group, the Santa Cruz islands, and the Duff group. Copra is the only important cash crop but it is hoped that timber will become an economic factor.

The Solomon Islands were discovered by Spanish navigator Alvaro de Mendana in 1567, and in 1569 he made an unsuccessful attempt to colonize them. European knowledge of the group would not be completed until the end of the 18th century. Germany declared a protectorate over the northern Solomons in 1885. The British protectorate over the southern Solomons was established in 1893. In 1899 Germany transferred its claim to all Solomon Islands except Buka and Bougainville to Great Britain in exchange for recognition of German claims in Western Samoa. Australia occupied the two German islands in 1914, and administered them after 1920.

The Japanese invaded the Solomons during 1942-43, but were driven out by an American counteroffensive after a series of bloody clashes.

Following World War II, the islands returned to the status of a British protectorate. In 1976 the protectorate was abolished, and the Solomons became a self-governing dependency. Full independence was achieved on July 7, 1978. Solomon Islands is a member of the Commonwealth of Nations. Queen Elizabeth II is Head of State, as Queen of the Solomon Islands.

RULERS

British, until 1978

MINT MARKS

FM - Franklin Mint, U.S.A.*

NOTE: From 1977-1985 the Franklin Mint produced coinage in up to 3 different qualities. Qualities of issue are designated in ( ) after each date and are defined as follows:

(M) MATTE - Normal circulation strike or a dull finish produced by sandblasting special uncirculated (polish finish) or proof quality dies.

(U) - SPECIAL UNCIRCULATED - Polished or proof-like in appearance without any frosted features.

(P) PROOF - The highest quality obtainable having mirror-like fields and frosted features.

MONETARY SYSTEM
100 Cents = 1 Dollar

CENT

BRONZE
F.A.O. Issue - Food Bowl

KM#	Date	Mintage	VF	XF	Unc
1	1977	1.828	—	.10	.20
	1977FM(M)	6,000	—	—	.50
	1977FM(U)	—	—	—	2.00
	1977FM(P)	.014	—	Proof	1.00
	1978FM(M)	6,000	—	—	.50
	1978FM(U)	544 pcs.	—	—	2.00
	1978FM(P)	5,122	—	Proof	1.00
	1979FM(M)	6,000	—	—	.50
	1979FM(U)	677 pcs.	—	—	2.00
	1979FM(P)	2,845	—	Proof	1.50
	1980FM(M)	6,000	—	—	.50
	1980FM(U)	624 pcs.	—	—	2.00
	1980FM(P)	1,031	—	Proof	1.50
	1981	—	—	—	.50
	1981FM(M)	6,000	—	—	.50
	1981FM(U)	212 pcs.	—	—	2.00
	1981FM(P)	448 pcs.	—	Proof	1.50
	1982FM(M)	—	—	—	2.00
	1982FM(P)	—	—	Proof	1.50
	1983FM(M)	—	—	—	.50
	1983FM(U)	200 pcs.	—	—	3.00
	1983FM(P)	—	—	Proof	1.50

BRONZE PLATED STEEL

1a	1985	—	—	—	.20

KM#	Date	Mintage	VF	XF	Unc
24	1987	—	—	—	.25

2 CENTS

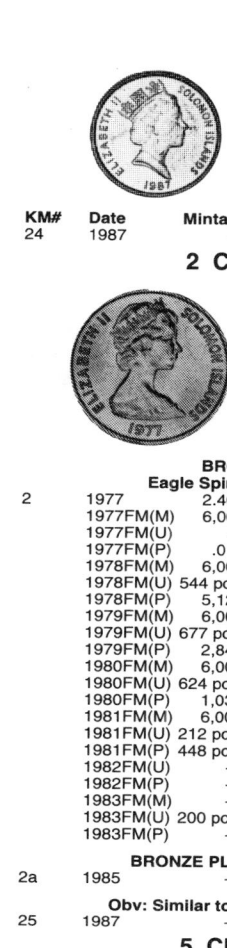

BRONZE
Eagle Spirit of Malaita

KM#	Date	Mintage	VF	XF	Unc
2	1977	2.400	—	.10	.25
	1977FM(M)	6,000	—	—	.75
	1977FM(U)	—	—	—	3.00
	1977FM(P)	.014	—	Proof	1.50
	1978FM(M)	6,000	—	—	.75
	1978FM(U)	544 pcs.	—	—	3.00
	1978FM(P)	5,122	—	Proof	1.50
	1979FM(M)	6,000	—	—	.75
	1979FM(U)	677 pcs.	—	—	3.00
	1979FM(P)	2,845	—	Proof	2.00
	1980FM(M)	6,000	—	—	.75
	1980FM(U)	624 pcs.	—	—	3.00
	1980FM(P)	1,031	—	Proof	2.00
	1981FM(M)	6,000	—	—	.75
	1981FM(U)	212 pcs.	—	—	3.00
	1981FM(P)	448 pcs.	—	Proof	2.00
	1982FM(U)	—	—	—	3.00
	1982FM(P)	—	—	Proof	2.00
	1983FM(M)	—	—	—	.75
	1983FM(U)	200 pcs.	—	—	3.00
	1983FM(P)	—	—	Proof	2.00

BRONZE PLATED STEEL

2a	1985	—	—	—	.25

Obv: Similar to 1 Cent, KM#24.

25	1987	—	—	—	.25

5 CENTS

COPPER-NICKEL
Santa Ysabel - Native Mask

KM#	Date	Mintage	VF	XF	Unc
3	1977	1.200	.10	.20	.40
	1977FM(U)	—	—	—	3.00
	1977FM(M)	6,000	—	—	1.50
	1977FM(P)	.014	—	Proof	2.00
	1978FM(M)	6,000	—	—	1.50
	1978FM(U)	544 pcs.	—	—	3.00
	1978FM(P)	5,122	—	Proof	2.00
	1979FM(M)	6,000	—	—	1.50
	1979FM(U)	677 pcs.	—	—	3.00
	1979FM(P)	2,845	—	Proof	2.50
	1980FM(M)	6,000	—	—	1.50
	1980FM(U)	624 pcs.	—	—	3.00
	1980FM(P)	1,031	—	Proof	2.50
	1981	—	—	—	—
	1981FM(M)	6,000	—	—	1.50
	1981FM(U)	212 pcs.	—	—	3.00
	1981FM(P)	448 pcs.	—	Proof	2.50
	1982FM(U)	—	—	—	3.00
	1982FM(P)	—	—	Proof	2.50
	1983FM(M)	—	—	—	1.50
	1983FM(U)	200 pcs.	—	—	4.00
	1983FM(P)	—	—	Proof	2.50
	1985	—	—	—	.30

Obv: Similar to 1 Cent, KM#24.

26	1988	—	—	—	.30
	1993	—	—	—	.30
	1996	—	—	—	.30

10 CENTS

COPPER-NICKEL
Ngorieru - Sea Spirit

KM#	Date	Mintage	VF	XF	Unc
4	1977	3.600	.15	.25	.50
	1977FM(M)	6,000	—	—	2.00
	1977FM(U)	—	—	—	5.00
	1977FM(P)	.014	—	Proof	3.00

KM#	Date	Mintage	VF	XF	Unc
4	1978FM(M)	6,000	—	—	2.00
	1978FM(U)	544 pcs.	—	—	5.00
	1978FM(P)	5,122	—	Proof	3.00
	1979FM(M)	6,000	—	—	2.00
	1979FM(U)	677 pcs.	—	—	5.00
	1979FM(P)	2,845	—	Proof	4.00
	1980FM(M)	6,000	—	—	2.00
	1980FM(U)	624 pcs.	—	—	5.00
	1980FM(P)	1,031	—	Proof	4.00
	1981FM(M)	6,000	—	—	2.00
	1981FM(U)	212 pcs.	—	—	5.00
	1981FM(P)	448 pcs.	—	Proof	4.00
	1982FM(U)	—	—	—	5.00
	1982FM(P)	—	—	Proof	4.00
	1983FM(M)	—	—	—	2.00
	1983FM(U)	200 pcs.	—	—	6.00
	1983FM(P)	—	—	Proof	4.00

27	1988	—	—	—	.50

NICKEL CLAD STEEL

27a	1990	—	—	—	.50
	1996	—	—	—	.50

20 CENTS

COPPER-NICKEL
Malaita Pendant Design

KM#	Date	Mintage	VF	XF	Unc
5	1977	3.000	.20	.35	.80
	1977FM(M)	5,000	—	—	3.00
	1977FM(P)	.014	—	Proof	4.00
	1978	.293	.25	.50	1.00
	1978FM(M)	5,000	—	—	3.00
	1978FM(U)	544 pcs.	—	—	5.50
	1978FM(P)	5,122	—	Proof	4.00
	1979FM(M)	5,000	—	—	3.00
	1979FM(U)	677 pcs.	—	—	5.00
	1979FM(P)	2,845	—	Proof	4.00
	1980FM(M)	5,000	—	—	3.00
	1980FM(U)	624 pcs.	—	—	5.00
	1980FM(P)	1,031	—	Proof	4.00
	1981FM(M)	5,000	—	—	3.00
	1981FM(U)	212 pcs.	—	—	6.00
	1981FM(P)	448 pcs.	—	Proof	4.00
	1982FM(U)	—	—	—	6.00
	1982FM(P)	—	—	Proof	4.00
	1983FM(M)	—	—	—	3.00
	1983FM(U)	200 pcs.	—	—	7.00
	1983FM(P)	—	—	Proof	4.00

NICKEL CLAD STEEL

28	1989	—	—	—	.75
	1996	—	—	—	.75

50 CENTS

COPPER-NICKEL
10th Anniversary of Independence

KM#	Date	Mintage	VF	XF	Unc
23	1988	—	—	—	2.50

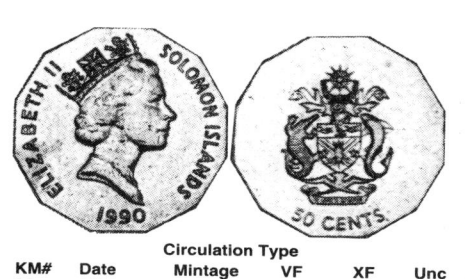

Circulation Type

KM#	Date	Mintage	VF	XF	Unc
29	1990	—	—	—	2.50
	1996	—	—	—	2.50

DOLLAR

COPPER-NICKEL
Nusu-Nusu Head - Sea Spirit

KM#	Date	Mintage	VF	XF	Unc
6	1977	1.500	1.00	1.50	2.50
	1977FM(M)	3,000	—	—	5.00
	1977FM(P)	.014	—	Proof	6.50
	1978FM(M)	3,000	—	—	5.00
	1978FM(U)	544 pcs.	—	—	9.00
	1978FM(P)	5,122	—	Proof	6.50
	1979FM(M)	3,000	—	—	5.00
	1979FM(U)	677 pcs.	—	—	9.00
	1979FM(P)	2,845	—	Proof	7.50
	1980FM(M)	3,000	—	—	5.00
	1980FM(U)	624 pcs.	—	—	9.00
	1980FM(P)	1,031	—	Proof	8.50
	1981FM(M)	3,000	—	—	5.00
	1981FM(U)	212 pcs.	—	—	10.00
	1981FM(P)	448 pcs.	—	Proof	8.50
	1982FM(U)	—	—	—	10.00
	1982FM(P)	—	—	Proof	8.50
	1983FM(M)	—	—	—	5.00
	1983FM(U)	200 pcs.	—	—	12.00
	1983FM(P)	—	—	Proof	8.50

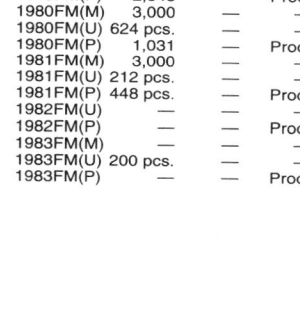

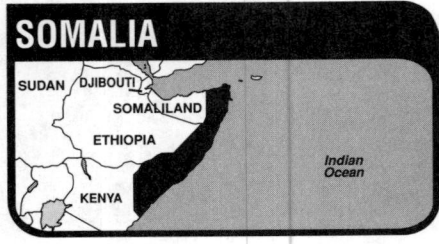

SOMALIA

SUDAN DJIBOUTI
SOMALILAND
ETHIOPIA
KENYA
Indian Ocean

The Somali Democratic Republic, comprised of the former Italian Somaliland, is located on the coast of the eastern projection of the African continent commonly referred to as the "Horn". It has an area of 178,201 sq. mi. (461,657 sq. km.) and a population of *8.2 million Capital: Mogadishu. The economy is pastoral and agricultural. Livestock, bananas and hides are exported.

The area of the British Somaliland Protectorate was known to the Egyptains at least 1,500 years B.C., and was occupied by the Arabs and Portuguese before British sea captains obtained trading and anchorage rights in 1827. The land of sandy clay and sporadic rainfall acquired a strategic importance with the opening of the Suez Canal in 1869. After negotiating treaties with the tribes, Britain declared the area a protectorate in 1888. Italy acquired Italian Somaliland in 1895 by purchase from the Sultan of Zanzibar. Britain occupied Italian Somaliland in 1941 and administered it until April 1, 1950, when it was returned to Italy as a U.N. trusteeship. The British Somaliland protectorate became independent on June 26, 1960. Five days later it joined with Italian Somaliland to form the Somali Republic. The country was under a revolutionary military regime installed Oct. 21, 1969. After 11 years of civil war rebel forces fought their way into the capital. A.M. Muhammad became president in Aug. 1991, but interfactional fighting continued. A UN-sponsored truce was signed in March 1992 and a peace plan and pact was signed Jan. 15, 1993.

The Northern Somali National Movement (SNM) declared a secession of the northwestern Somaliland Republic on May 17, 1991 which is not recognized by the Somali Democratic Republic.

RULERS

Italian, until 1941
British, until 1950

MINT MARKS

Az - Arezzo (Italy)
R - Rome

ITALIAN SOMALILAND

TITLES

الصومال الايطليانية

Al-Somal Al-Italiyaniya(t)

MONETARY SYSTEM

100 Bese = 1 Rupia

BESA

KM#	Date	Mintage	BRONZE Fine	VF	XF	Unc
1	1909R	2.000	10.00	20.00	40.00	135.00
	1910R	.500	10.00	20.00	40.00	135.00
	1913R	.200	15.00	30.00	80.00	265.00
	1921R	.500	12.50	22.50	45.00	160.00

2 BESE

2			BRONZE			
	1909R	.500	12.50	25.00	65.00	250.00
	1910R	.250	12.50	25.00	65.00	250.00
	1913R	.300	15.00	30.00	90.00	285.00
	1921R	.600	12.50	25.00	70.00	250.00
	1923R	1.500	12.50	22.50	60.00	230.00
	1924R	!nc. Ab.	12.50	20.00	55.00	220.00

4 BESE

KM#	Date	Mintage	BRONZE Fine	VF	XF	Unc
3	1909R	.250	18.00	35.00	85.00	200.00
	1910R	.250	18.00	35.00	85.00	210.00
	1913R	.050	35.00	85.00	225.00	475.00
	1921R	.200	20.00	40.00	90.00	215.00
	1923R	1.000	20.00	40.00	90.00	215.00
	1924R	Inc. Ab.	20.00	50.00	100.00	225.00

1/4 RUPIA

2.9160 g, .917 SILVER, .0859 oz ASW

4	1910R	.400	12.50	25.00	70.00	175.00
	1913R	.100	35.00	65.00	150.00	275.00

1/2 RUPIA

5.8319 g, .917 SILVER, .1719 oz ASW

5	1910R	.400	20.00	40.00	90.00	200.00
	1912R	.100	22.50	45.00	100.00	220.00
	1913R	.100	22.50	45.00	100.00	220.00
	1915R	.050	35.00	75.00	200.00	400.00
	1919R	.200	20.00	40.00	90.00	200.00

RUPIA

11.6638 g, .917 SILVER, .3437 oz ASW

6	1910R	.300	25.00	55.00	110.00	200.00
	1912R	.600	25.00	55.00	110.00	200.00
	1913R	.300	25.00	50.00	100.00	185.00
	1914R	.300	25.00	50.00	100.00	185.00
	1915R	.250	25.00	50.00	100.00	185.00
	1919R	.400	25.00	50.00	100.00	185.00
	1920R	1.300	500.00	900.00	2000.	3500.
	1921R	.940	950.00		2150.	3350.	5750.

MONETARY REFORM

100 Centesimi = 1 Lira

5 LIRE

6.0000 g, .835 SILVER, .1611 oz ASW

7	1925R	.400	65.00	125.00	225.00	350.00

10 LIRE

12.0000 g, .835 SILVER, .3221 oz ASW

KM#	Date	Mintage	Fine	VF	XF	Unc
8	1925R	.100	100.00	200.00	300.00	485.00

SOMALIA

TITLES

Al-Jumhuriya(t)as - Somaliya(t)

MONETARY SYSTEM

100 Centesimi = 1 Somalo

CENTESIMO

KM#	Date	Year	COPPER Mintage	VF	XF	Unc
1	AH1369	1950	4.000	.20	.50	1.50

5 CENTESIMI

2	AH1369	1950	COPPER 6.800	.25	.65	2.00

10 CENTESIMI

3	AH1369	1950	COPPER 7.400	.35	1.00	3.00

50 CENTESIMI

3.8000 g, .250 SILVER, .0305 oz ASW

4	AH1369	1950	1.800	1.25	3.75	9.00

SOMALO

7.6000 g, .250 SILVER, .0610 oz ASW

5	AH1369	1950	11.480	2.25	4.75	11.50

SOMALI REPUBLIC

TITLES

Al-Jumhuriya(t) ad -
Dimiqratiya(t) as-Somaliya(t)
Jumhuriya(t) as - Somal ad - Dimiqratiya(t)

MONETARY SYSTEM
100 Centesimi = 1 Somalo =
1 Scellino = 1 Shilling

5 CENTESIMI

BRASS

KM#	Date	Mintage	VF	XF	Unc
6	1967	10.000	—	.20	.60

10 CENTESIMI

BRASS

7	1967	15.000	.15	.25	.70

50 CENTESIMI

COPPER-NICKEL

8	1967	5.100	.50	1.00	2.50

SCELLINO
(Schilling)

COPPER-NICKEL

9	1967	8.150	1.00	3.00	6.00

MONETARY REFORM
100 Senti = 1 Shilling

5 SENTI

 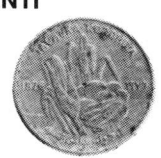

ALUMINUM
F.A.O. Issue

A24	1976	—	—	—	120.00

F.A.O. Issue

24	1976	18.500	.10	.20	.35

10 SENTI

ALUMINUM
F.A.O. Issue

25	1976	40.500	.10	.15	.35

50 SENTI

 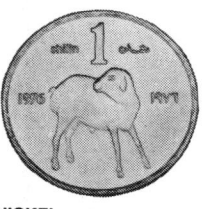

COPPER-NICKEL
F.A.O. Issue

KM#	Date	Mintage	VF	XF	Unc
26	1976	10.080	.15	.25	.75

NICKEL PLATED STEEL

26a	1984	—	1.00	2.00	5.00

SHILLING

COPPER-NICKEL
F.A.O. Issue

27	1976	20.040	.35	.65	2.25

NICKEL PLATED STEEL

27a	1984	—	2.00	4.00	10.00

SOMALILAND

The Somaliland Republic, comprising of the former British Somaliland Protectorate is located on the coast of the north-eastern projection of the African continent commonly referred to as the "Horn" on the southwestern end of the Gulf of Aden.

Bordered by Eritrea to the west, Ethiopia to west and south and Somalia to the east. It has an area of 68,000* sq. mi. (176,000* sq. km). Capital: Hargeysa. It is mostly arid and mountainous except for the gulf shoreline.

The Protectorate of British Somaliland was established in 1888 and from 1905 the territory was administered by a commissioner under the British Colonial Office. Italian Somaliland was administered as a colony from 1893 to 1941, when the territory was occupied by British forces. In 1950 the United Nations allowed Italy to resume control of Italian Somaliland under a trusteeship. In 1960 British and Italian Somaliland were united as Somalia, an independent republic outside the Commonwealth.

Civil war erupted in the late 1970's and continued until the capital of Somalia was taken in 1990. The United Nations provided aid and peacekeeping. A UN sponsored truce was signed in March 1992 and a peace plan and pact was signed Jan. 15, 1993. The northern Somali National Movement (SNM) declared a secession of the Somaliland Republic on May 17, 1991 which is not recognized by the Somali Democratic Republic.

The currency issued by the East African Currency Board was used in British Somaliland from 1945 to 1961, Somali currency was used later until 1995.

SHILLING

ALUMINUM
Obv: Bird. Rev: Denomination.

KM#	Date	Mintage	VF	XF	Unc
1	1994	—	—	—	1.85

SOUTH AFRICA

The Republic of South Africa, located at the southern tip of Africa, has an area, including the enclave of Walvis Bay, of 472,359 sq. mi. (1,221,040 sq. km.) and a population of *38.5 million. Capitals: Administrative, Pretoria; Legislative, Cape Town; Judicial, Bloemfontein. Manufacturing, mining and agriculture are the principal industries. Exports include wool, diamonds, gold, and metallic ores.

Portuguese navigator Bartholomew Diaz became the first European to sight the region of South Africa when he rounded the Cape of Good Hope in 1488, but throughout the 16th century the only white men to come ashore were the survivors of ships wrecked while attempting the stormy Cape passage. The first permanent settlement was established by Jan van Riebeeck of the Dutch East India Company in 1652. In subsequent decades additional Dutch and Germans and Huguenot refugees from France settled in the Cape area to form the Afrikaner segment of today's population.

Great Britain captured the Cape colony in 1795, and again in 1806, receiving permanent title in 1814. To escape British political rule and cultural dominance, many Afrikaner farmers (Boers) migrated northward (the Great Trek) beginning in 1836, and established the independent Boer Republics of the Transvaal (the South African Republic, Zuid Afrikaansche Republic) in 1852, and the Orange Free State in 1854. British political intrigues against the two republics, coupled with the discovery of diamonds and gold in the Boer-settled regions, led to the bitter Boer Wars (1880-81, 1899-1902) and the incorporation of the Boer republics into the British Empire.

On May 31, 1910, the two former Boer Republics (Transvaal and Orange Free State) were joined with the British colonies of Cape of Good Hope and Natal to form the Union of South Africa, a dominion of the British Empire. In 1934 the Union achieved status as a sovereign state within the British Empire.

Political integration of the various colonies did not still the conflict between the Afrikaners and the Englishspeaking groups, which continued to have a significant impact on political developments. A resurgence of Afrikaner nationalism in the 1940's and 1950's led to a referendum in the white community authorizing the relinquishment of dominion status and the establishment of a republic. The decision took effect on May 31, 1961. The Republic of South Africa withdrew from the British Commonwealth in Oct. 1961.

The apartheid era ended April 27, 1994 with the first democratic election for all people of South Africa. Nelson Mandela was inaugurated President May 10, 1994, and South Africa was readmitted to the Commonwealth of Nations.

South African coins and currency bear inscriptions in tribal languages, Afrikaans and English.

RULERS

British, until 1934

MONETARY SYSTEM

Until 1961

12 Pence = 1 Shilling
2 Shillings = 1 Florin
20 Shillings = 1 Pound (Pond)

Commencing 1961

100 Cents = 1 Rand

ZUID-AFRIKAANSCHE REPUBLIEK

MONETARY SYSTEM

12 Pence = 1 Shilling
20 Shillings = 1 Pond

EEN (1) POND

.999 GOLD
Veld-Boer War Siege Issue

KM#	Date	Mintage	Fine	VF	XF	Unc
11	1902	986 pcs.	550.00	1100.	2000.	3500.

UNION OF SOUTH AFRICA

MONETARY SYSTEM

12 Pence = 1 Shilling
2 Shillings = 1 Florin
20 Shillings = 1 Pound

1/4 PENNY FARTHING

BRONZE
Rev. denomination: 1/4 PENNY 1/4

KM#	Date	Mintage	Fine	VF	XF	Unc
12.1	1923	.033	2.00	5.00	10.00	20.00
	1923	1,402	—	—	Proof	30.00
	1924	.095	1.50	2.50	5.00	10.00

Rev. denomination: 1/4 PENNY

KM#	Date	Mintage	Fine	VF	XF	Unc
12.2	1926	16 pcs.	—	—	Proof	6000.
	1928	.064	1.50	3.00	5.00	12.50
	1930	6,560	30.00	60.00	120.00	200.00
	1930	14 pcs.		—	Proof	1200.
	1931	.154	1.00	1.50	4.00	6.00

Rev. denomination: 1/4 D

KM#	Date	Mintage	Fine	VF	XF	Unc
12.3	1931	Inc. Ab.	5.00	10.00	15.00	35.00
	1931	62 pcs.		—	Proof	200.00
	1932	.105	1.00	1.50	3.50	7.00
	1932	12 pcs.	—	—	Proof	375.00
	1933	76 pcs.	750.00	1450.	2200.	3250.
	1933	20 pcs.	—	—	Proof	4000.
	1934	52 pcs.	750.00	1450.	2200.	3250.
	1934	24 pcs.	—	—	Proof	3750.
	1935	.061	1.00	1.50	3.50	8.00
	1935	20 pcs.	—	—	Proof	3000.
	1936	43 pcs.	350.00	750.00	1100.	2000.
	1936	40 pcs.	—	—	Proof	3000.

KM#	Date	Mintage	Fine	VF	XF	Unc
23	1937	.038	1.50	3.00	6.00	12.50
	1937	116 pcs.	—	—	Proof	40.00
	1938	.051	1.00	2.00	4.00	8.00
	1938	44 pcs.	—	—	Proof	100.00
	1939	.102	.50	1.50	3.00	7.50
	1939	30 pcs.	—	—	Proof	125.00
	1941	.091	.50	1.50	3.00	7.50
	1942	3.756	.25	.50	1.00	2.00
	1943	9.918	.25	.50	.75	1.50
	1943	104 pcs.	—	—	Proof	40.00
	1944	4.468	.25	.50	.75	2.00
	1944	150 pcs.	—	—	Proof	35.00
	1945	5.297	.25	.50	1.50	3.00
	1945	150 pcs.	—	—	Proof	35.00
	1946	4.378	.25	.50	1.50	4.00
	1946	150 pcs.	—	—	Proof	35.00
	1947	3.895	.25	.50	1.50	4.00
	1947	2,600	—	—	Proof	4.00

KM#	Date	Mintage	Fine	VF	XF	Unc
32.1	1948	2.415	.25	.50	1.00	2.00
	1948	1,120	—	—	Proof	3.00
	1949	3.568	.25	.50	1.00	2.50
	1949	800 pcs.	—	—	Proof	5.00
	1950	8.694	.25	.50	.75	1.50
	1950	500 pcs.	—	—	Proof	8.00

Rev. leg. reversed: SUID AFRIKA-SOUTH AFRICA

KM#	Date	Mintage	Fine	VF	XF	Unc
32.2	1951	3.511	.15	.35	.75	2.50
	1951	2,000	—	—	Proof	2.00
	1952	2.805	.15	.35	.75	2.00
	1952	.016	—	—	Proof	2.00

KM#	Date	Mintage	Fine	VF	XF	Unc
44	1953	7.193	.15	.25	.50	1.50
	1953	5,000	—	—	Proof	2.00
	1954	6.568	.15	.25	.50	1.50
	1954	3,150	—	—	Proof	2.00
	1955	11.798	.15	.25	.50	1.50
	1955	2,850	—	—	Proof	2.00
	1956	1.287	.15	.25	.50	2.50
	1956	1,700	—	—	Proof	3.00
	1957	3.065	.15	.25	.50	1.50
	1957	1,130	—	—	Proof	4.00
	1958	5.452	.15	.25	.50	1.50
	1958	985 pcs.	—	—	Proof	5.00
	1959	1.567	.15	.25	.50	1.50
	1959	900 pcs.	—	—	Proof	6.00
	1960	1.023	.15	.25	.50	2.00
	1960	3,360	—	—	Proof	1.50

1/2 PENNY

BRONZE
Rev. denomination: 1/2 PENNY 1/2

KM#	Date	Mintage	Fine	VF	XF	Unc
13.1	1923	.012	25.00	40.00	70.00	100.00
	1923	1,402	—	—	Proof	100.00
	1924	.064	7.50	12.50	30.00	60.00
	1925	.069	7.50	12.50	30.00	80.00
	1926	.065	10.00	15.00	35.00	100.00

Rev. denomination: 1/2 PENNY

KM#	Date	Mintage	Fine	VF	XF	Unc
13.2	1928	.105	5.00	12.50	35.00	75.00
	1929	.272	2.50	5.00	15.00	35.00
	1930	.147	3.50	7.00	20.00	40.00
	1930	14 pcs.	—	—	Proof	400.00
	1930 w/o star after date					
		Inc. Ab.	4.00	8.00	25.00	50.00
	1931	.145	3.50	7.00	25.00	50.00

Rev. denomination: 1/2 D

KM#	Date	Mintage	Fine	VF	XF	Unc
13.3	1931	62 pcs.	—	—	Proof	1000.00
	1932	.106	5.00	10.00	30.00	75.00
	1932	12 pcs.	—	—	Proof	1000.00
	1933	.063	8.00	25.00	55.00	100.00
	1933	20 pcs.	—	—	Proof	500.00
	1934	.326	1.50	5.00	15.00	45.00
	1934	24 pcs.	—	—	Proof	500.00
	1935	.405	1.50	5.00	15.00	40.00
	1935	20 pcs.	—	—	Proof	500.00
	1936	.407	1.50	5.00	15.00	30.00
	1936	40 pcs.	—	—	Proof	200.00

KM#	Date	Mintage	Fine	VF	XF	Unc
24	1937	.638	1.00	2.00	9.00	15.00
	1937	116 pcs.	—	—	Proof	50.00
	1938	.560	1.00	2.00	6.00	15.00
	1938	44 pcs.	—	—	Proof	125.00
	1939	.271	2.50	5.00	10.00	20.00
	1939	30 pcs.	—	—	Proof	175.00
	1940	1.535	.30	.75	3.00	8.00
	1941	2.053	.30	.75	3.00	8.00
	1942	8.382	.25	.60	2.00	6.00
	1943	5.135	.25	.60	2.00	6.00
	1943	104 pcs.	—	—	Proof	45.00
	1944	3.920	.25	.75	3.00	8.00
	1944	150 pcs.	—	—	Proof	35.00
	1945	2.357	.25	.60	2.50	7.00
	1945	150 pcs.	—	—	Proof	35.00
	1946	1.022	.25	.75	3.00	9.00
	1946	150 pcs.	—	—	Proof	35.00
	1947	.258	1.00	3.00	6.00	17.50
	1947	2,600	—	—	Proof	10.00

KM#	Date	Mintage	Fine	VF	XF	Unc
33	1948	.685	.50	1.00	4.00	9.00
	1948	1,120	—	—	Proof	15.00
	1949	1.850	.25	.50	1.75	4.00
	1949	800 pcs.	—	—	Proof	15.00
	1950	2.186	.25	.50	1.50	3.00
	1950	500 pcs.	—	—	Proof	6.00
	1951	3.746	.25	.50	1.25	3.00
	1951	2,000	—	—	Proof	5.00
	1952	4.174	.25	.50	1.00	2.50
	1952	1,550	—	—	Proof	4.00

KM#	Date	Mintage	Fine	VF	XF	Unc
45	1953	5.572	.15	.35	1.00	3.00
	1953	5,000	—	—	Proof	4.00
	1954	.101	2.00	4.00	7.50	12.50
	1954	3,150	—	—	Proof	15.00
	1955	3.774	.15	.35	1.00	3.00
	1955	2,850	—	—	Proof	4.00
	1956	1.305	.15	.35	1.00	3.00
	1956	1,700	—	—	Proof	4.00
	1957	2.025	.15	.35	1.00	3.00
	1957	1,130	—	—	Proof	4.00
	1958	2.171	.15	.35	1.00	2.50
	1958	985 pcs.	—	—	Proof	5.00
	1959	2.397	.15	.25	.75	2.00
	1959	900 pcs.	—	—	Proof	6.00
	1960	2.552	.15	.25	.75	2.00
	1960	3,360	—	—	Proof	1.50

PENNY

BRONZE
Rev. denomination: 1 PENNY 1

KM#	Date	Mintage	Fine	VF	XF	Unc
14.1	1923	.091	3.00	7.00	17.50	35.00
	1923	1,402	—	—	Proof	50.00
	1924	.134	4.00	10.00	25.00	50.00

Rev. denomination: PENNY

KM#	Date	Mintage	Fine	VF	XF	Unc
14.2	1926	.393	3.00	10.00	40.00	100.00
	1926	16 pcs.	—	—	Proof	600.00
	1927	.285	3.00	10.00	40.00	90.00
	1928	.386	3.00	10.00	40.00	90.00
	1929	1.093	1.00	5.00	15.00	35.00
	1930	.754	1.00	5.00	20.00	40.00
	1930	14 pcs.	—	—	Proof	600.00

Rev. denomination: 1 D.

KM#	Date	Mintage	Fine	VF	XF	Unc
14.3	1931	.284	1.00	5.00	17.50	40.00
	1931	62 pcs.	—	—	Proof	400.00
	1932	.260	1.00	5.00	20.00	50.00
	1932	12 pcs.	—	—	Proof	800.00
	1933	.225	2.00	10.00	30.00	45.00
	1933	20 pcs.	—	—	Proof	500.00
	1933 w/o star after date					
		Inc. Ab.	4.00	10.00	30.00	50.00
	1934	2.090	.50	1.50	8.00	22.50
	1934	24 pcs.	—	—	Proof	600.00
	1935	2.295	.50	1.50	8.00	22.50
	1935	20 pcs.	—	—	Proof	600.00
	1936	1.819	.35	1.00	5.00	20.00
	1936	40 pcs.	—	—	Proof	300.00

KM#	Date	Mintage	Fine	VF	XF	Unc
25	1937	3.281	.50	1.50	10.00	25.00
	1937	116 pcs.	—	—	Proof	75.00
	1938	1.840	.50	1.50	8.00	30.00
	1938	44 pcs.	—	—	Proof	100.00
	1939	1.506	.50	1.50	10.00	25.00
	1939	30 pcs.	—	—	Proof	175.00
	1940	3.592	.35	1.00	4.00	10.00
	1940 w/o star after date					
		Inc. Ab.	1.50	3.00	6.00	15.00
	1941	7.871	.25	.75	2.50	7.00
	1942	14.428	.25	.75	2.00	6.00
	1942 w/o star after date					
		Inc. Ab.	3.00	6.00	12.50	30.00
	1943	4.010	.25	.75	2.50	6.00
	1943	104 pcs.	—	—	Proof	55.00
	1944	6.425	.25	.75	2.50	7.00
	1944	150 pcs.	—	—	Proof	45.00
	1945	4.810	.25	.75	2.50	7.00
	1945	150 pcs.	—	—	Proof	45.00
	1946	2.605	.25	.75	3.00	8.00
	1946	150 pcs.	—	—	Proof	45.00
	1947	.135	2.50	4.00	7.50	17.50
	1947	2,600	—	—	Proof	7.00

KM#	Date	Mintage	Fine	VF	XF	Unc
34.1	1948	2.398	.25	.75	2.50	6.00
	1948	1,120	—	—	Proof	5.00

KM#	Date	Mintage	Fine	VF	XF	Unc
34.1	1948 w/o star after date					
		Inc. Ab.	1.00	2.00	5.00	10.00
	1949	3.634	.25	.75	2.00	6.00
	1949	800 pcs.	—	—	Proof	12.00
	1950	4.890	.25	.75	2.00	5.00
	1950	500 pcs.	—	—	Proof	10.00

Rev. leg: SUID AFRIKA-SOUTH AFRICA

KM#	Date	Mintage	Fine	VF	XF	Unc
34.2	1951	3.787	.25	.75	1.50	4.00
	1951	2,000	—	—	Proof	5.00
	1952	12.674	.25	.50	1.00	2.50
	1952	.016	—	—	Proof	4.00

KM#	Date	Mintage	Fine	VF	XF	Unc
46	1953	5.491	.20	.35	.75	2.00
	1953	5,000	—	—	Proof	2.00
	1954	6.665	1.00	2.00	5.00	10.00
	1954	3,150	—	—	Proof	15.00
	1955	6.508	.20	.35	.75	3.00
	1955	2,850	—	—	Proof	3.00
	1956	4.390	.20	.35	1.00	4.00
	1956	1,700	—	—	Proof	3.00
	1957	3.973	.20	.35	.75	3.00
	1957	1,130	—	—	Proof	5.00
	1958	5.311	.20	.35	.75	3.00
	1958	985 pcs.	—	—	Proof	6.00
	1959	5.066	.20	.35	.75	2.00
	1959	900 pcs.	—	—	Proof	7.00
	1960	5.106	.20	.35	.75	2.00
	1960	3,360	—	—	Proof	2.00

3 PENCE

1.4100 g, .800 SILVER, .0362 oz ASW

KM#	Date	Mintage	Fine	VF	XF	Unc
15.1	1923	.302	4.00	8.00	20.00	45.00
	1923	1,402	—	—	Proof	50.00
	1924	.501	4.00	10.00	25.00	50.00
	1925	Inc. Bl	10.00	35.00	200.00	475.00

Rev. denomination: 3 PENCE

KM#	Date	Mintage	Fine	VF	XF	Unc
15.2	1925	.358	5.00	25.00	90.00	175.00
	1926	1.572	1.00	3.50	20.00	50.00
	1926	16 pcs.	—	—	Proof	2000.
	1927	2.285	1.00	2.50	15.00	45.00
	1928	.919	1.50	3.50	20.00	50.00
	1929	1.948	1.00	2.50	15.00	45.00
	1930	.981	1.00	3.50	20.00	50.00
	1930	14 pcs.	—	—	Proof	800.00

Rev. denomination: 3D

KM#	Date	Mintage	Fine	VF	XF	Unc
15.3	1931	66 pcs.	750.00	1000.	1750.	3500.
	1931	62 pcs.	—	—	—	3500.
	1932	2.622	1.00	2.50	15.00	30.00
	1932	12 pcs.	—	—	Proof	1000.
	1933	5.135	1.00	2.50	15.00	30.00
	1933	20 pcs.	—	—	Proof	1000.
	1934	2.357	1.00	2.50	15.00	30.00
	1934	24 pcs.	—	—	Proof	1000.
	1935	1.655	1.00	2.50	15.00	30.00
	1935	20 pcs.	—	—	Proof	1000.
	1936	1.095	1.00	2.50	15.00	35.00
	1936	40 pcs.	—	—	Proof	250.00

KM#	Date	Mintage	Fine	VF	XF	Unc
26	1937	3.576	.50	1.00	3.00	10.00
	1937	116 pcs.	—	—	Proof	80.00
	1938	2.394	.50	1.50	7.00	20.00
	1938	44 pcs.	—	—	Proof	100.00
	1939	3.224	.50	1.50	5.00	12.50
	1939	30 pcs.	—	—	Proof	250.00
	1940	4.887	.50	1.00	3.00	12.50
	1941	8.968	.50	1.00	3.00	9.00
	1942	8.056	.50	1.00	3.00	9.00
	1943	14.827	.50	1.00	2.50	6.00
	1943	104 pcs.	—	—	Proof	70.00
	1944	3.331	.50	1.00	3.00	9.00
	1944	150 pcs.	—	—	Proof	60.00
	1945/3	4.094	1.00	3.00	10.00	20.00
	1945	Inc. Ab.	.50	1.00	3.00	9.00
	1945	150 pcs.	—	—	Proof	60.00
	1946	2.219	.50	1.00	3.00	10.00
	1946	150 pcs.	—	—	Proof	65.00
	1947	1.127	.50	1.00	2.50	8.00
	1947	2,600	—	—	Proof	8.00

KM#	Date	Mintage	Fine	VF	XF	Unc
35.1	1948	2.720	.50	1.00	3.00	7.00
	1948	1,120	—	—	Proof	5.00
	1949	1.904	.50	1.00	3.00	7.00
	1949	800 pcs.	—	—	Proof	5.00
	1950	4.096	.50	1.00	2.50	5.00
	1950	500 pcs.	—	—	Proof	7.00

1.4100 g, .500 SILVER, .0226 oz ASW
Rev: Modified design.

KM#	Date	Mintage	Fine	VF	XF	Unc
35.2	1951	6.323	.25	.50	1.00	3.00
	1951	2,000	—	—	Proof	4.00
	1952	13.057	.25	.50	1.00	2.00
	1952	.016	—	—	Proof	2.00

NOTE: Many varieties exist of George VI 3 Pence.

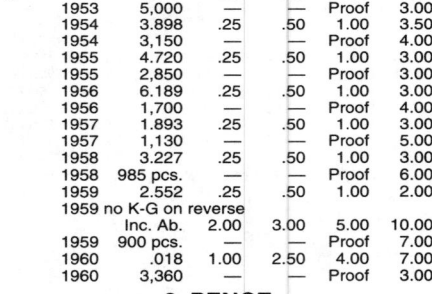

KM#	Date	Mintage	Fine	VF	XF	Unc
47	1953	5.483	.25	.50	1.00	3.00
	1953	5,000	—	—	Proof	3.00
	1954	3.898	.25	.50	1.00	3.50
	1954	3,150	—	—	Proof	4.00
	1955	4.720	.25	.50	1.00	3.00
	1955	2,850	—	—	Proof	3.00
	1956	6.189	.25	.50	1.00	3.00
	1956	1,700	—	—	Proof	4.00
	1957	1.893	.25	.50	1.00	3.00
	1957	1,130	—	—	Proof	5.00
	1958	3.227	.25	.50	1.00	3.00
	1958	985 pcs.	—	—	Proof	6.00
	1959	2.552	.25	.50	1.00	2.00
	1959 no K-G on reverse					
		Inc. Ab.	2.00	3.00	5.00	10.00
	1959	900 pcs.	—	—	Proof	7.00
	1960	.018	1.00	2.50	4.00	7.00
	1960	3,360	—	—	Proof	3.00

6 PENCE

2.8300 g, .800 SILVER, .0727 oz ASW

KM#	Date	Mintage	Fine	VF	XF	Unc
16.1	1923	.208	4.00	15.00	35.00	80.00
	1923	1,402	—	—	Proof	80.00
	1924	.326	3.50	12.50	30.00	70.00

Rev. denomination: 6 PENCE

KM#	Date	Mintage	Fine	VF	XF	Unc
16.2	1925	.079	5.00	20.00	60.00	125.00
	1926	.722	2.00	10.00	45.00	100.00
	1926	16 pcs.	—	—	Proof	3000.
	1927	1.548	1.50	4.00	25.00	50.00
16.2	1929	.784	2.00	8.00	30.00	60.00
	1930	.448	2.00	8.00	35.00	70.00
	1930	14 pcs.	—	—	Proof	1000.

Rev. denomination: 6 D

KM#	Date	Mintage	Fine	VF	XF	Unc
16.3	1931	4,743	75.00	150.00	250.00	550.00
	1931	62 pcs.	—	—	Proof	1000.
	1932	1.525	1.00	5.00	17.50	35.00
	1932	12 pcs.	—	—	Proof	1200.
	1933	2.819	1.00	5.00	17.50	35.00
	1933	20 pcs.	—	—	Proof	1200.
	1934	1.519	1.00	7.00	20.00	40.00
	1934	24 pcs.	—	—	Proof	1200.
	1935	.573	2.00	8.00	30.00	100.00
	1935	20 pcs.	—	—	Proof	1200.
	1936	.627	1.00	7.00	20.00	40.00
	1936	40 pcs.	—	—	Proof	275.00

KM#	Date	Mintage	Fine	VF	XF	Unc
27	1937	1.696	1.00	2.00	7.00	17.50
	1937	116 pcs.	—	—	Proof	90.00
	1938	1.725	1.00	2.00	7.00	17.50
	1938	44 pcs.	—	—	Proof	125.00
	1939	30 pcs.	—	—	Proof	3750.
	1940	1.629	1.00	1.50	5.00	10.00
	1941	2.263	1.00	1.50	5.00	10.00
	1942	4.936	.75	1.25	3.00	8.00
	1943	3.776	.75	1.25	3.00	8.00
	1943	104 pcs.	—	—	Proof	85.00
	1944	.228	2.00	7.00	15.00	30.00
	1944	150 pcs.	—	—	Proof	75.00
	1945	.420	1.00	5.00	15.00	35.00
	1945	150 pcs.	—	—	Proof	75.00
	1946	.290	1.00	6.00	15.00	30.00
	1946	150 pcs.	—	—	Proof	80.00
	1947	.577	1.00	1.50	5.00	10.00
	1947	2,600	—	—	Proof	10.00

KM#	Date	Mintage	Fine	VF	XF	Unc
36.1	1948	2.266	.75	1.25	2.50	6.00
	1948	1,120	—	—	Proof	10.00
	1949	.196	3.00	7.50	15.00	30.00
	1949	800 pcs.	—	—	Proof	15.00
	1950	2.122	.75	1.00	2.00	5.00
	1950	500 pcs.	—	—	Proof	15.00

2.8300 g, .500 SILVER, .0454 oz ASW

KM#	Date	Mintage	Fine	VF	XF	Unc
36.2	1951	2.602	.50	1.00	2.00	4.00
	1951	2,000	—	—	Proof	4.00
	1952	4.265	.50	.75	1.25	3.00
	1952	.016	—	—	Proof	2.00

KM#	Date	Mintage	Fine	VF	XF	Unc
48	1953	2.496	.50	.75	1.75	4.50
	1953	5,000	—	—	Proof	3.00
	1954	2.196	.50	1.00	2.00	4.50
	1954	3,150	—	—	Proof	4.00
	1955	1.969	.50	1.00	2.00	4.50
	1955	2,850	—	—	Proof	3.00
	1956	1.772	.50	1.00	2.00	5.00
	1956	1,700	—	—	Proof	4.00
	1957	3.288	.50	.75	1.75	4.50
	1957	1,130	—	—	Proof	6.00
	1958	1.172	.50	1.00	2.00	4.50
	1958	985 pcs.	—	—	Proof	6.00
	1959	.261	1.00	2.00	4.00	12.00
	1959	900 pcs.	—	—	Proof	8.00
	1960	1.587	.50	.75	1.25	2.50
	1960	3,360	—	—	Proof	2.50

SHILLING

5.6600 g, .800 SILVER, .1455 oz ASW
Rev. denomination: 1 SHILLING 1

KM#	Date	Mintage	Fine	VF	XF	Unc
17.1	1923	.808	4.00	15.00	35.00	75.00
	1923	1,402	—	—	Proof	80.00
	1924	1.269	3.50	12.50	30.00	75.00

Rev. denomination: SHILLING

KM#	Date	Mintage	Fine	VF	XF	Unc
17.2	1926	.238	15.00	75.00	400.00	1150.
	1926	16 pcs.	—	—	Proof	3000.
	1927	.488	10.00	25.00	150.00	375.00
	1928	.889	8.00	25.00	100.00	250.00
	1929	.926	5.00	10.00	30.00	175.00
	1930	.422	6.00	15.00	60.00	150.00
	1930	14 pcs.	—	—	Proof	1000.

KM#	Date	Mintage	Fine	VF	XF	Unc
17.3	1931	6,541	80.00	165.00	375.00	600.00
	1931	62 pcs.	—	—	Proof	1200.
	1932	2.537	2.50	5.00	15.00	30.00
	1932	12 pcs.	—	—	Proof	1400.
	1933	1.463	3.50	7.00	30.00	70.00
	1933	20 pcs.	—	—	Proof	1400.
	1934	.821	3.50	7.00	35.00	80.00
	1934	24 pcs.	—	—	Proof	1400.
	1935	.685	4.00	8.50	45.00	90.00
	1935	20 pcs.	—	—	Proof	1400.
	1936	.693	3.50	7.00	25.00	60.00
	1936	40 pcs.	—	—	Proof	500.00

KM#	Date	Mintage	Fine	VF	XF	Unc
28	1937	1.194	1.50	3.00	10.00	25.00
	1937	116 pcs.	—	—	Proof	120.00
	1938	1.160	1.50	3.00	10.00	25.00
	1938	44 pcs.	—	—	Proof	250.00
	1939	30 pcs.	—	—	Proof	4000.
	1940	1.365	1.50	2.50	7.50	17.50
	1941	1.826	1.50	2.50	7.50	17.50
	1942	3.867	1.50	2.50	7.50	17.50
	1943	4.188	1.00	2.00	5.00	10.00
	1943	104 pcs.	—	—	Proof	165.00
	1944	.048	8.00	20.00	45.00	80.00
	1944	160 pcs.	—	—	Proof	150.00
	1945	.054	8.00	20.00	45.00	80.00
	1945	150 pcs.	—	—	Proof	150.00
	1946	.027	10.00	30.00	60.00	120.00
	1946	150 pcs.	—	—	Proof	165.00
	1947	7,184	10.00	20.00	40.00	70.00
	1947	2,600	—	—	Proof	75.00

KM#	Date	Mintage	Fine	VF	XF	Unc
37.1	1948	4,974	10.00	20.00	40.00	70.00
	1948	1,120	—	—	Proof	75.00
	1949	800 pcs.	—	—	Proof	225.00
	1950	1.704	1.50	2.50	4.00	8.00
	1950	500 pcs.	—	—	Proof	40.00

5.6600 g, .500 SILVER, .0909 oz ASW
Rev. denomination: 1 S.

KM#	Date	Mintage	Fine	VF	XF	Unc
37.2	1951	2.405	1.00	1.50	4.00	8.00
	1951	2,000	—	—	Proof	4.00
	1952	1.934	1.00	1.50	3.50	7.00
	1952	1,550	—	—	Proof	3.00

49	1953	2.672	.75	1.25	2.50	5.50
	1953	5,000	—	—	Proof	4.00
	1954	3.576	.75	1.25	2.00	5.50
	1954	3,150	—	—	Proof	4.00
	1955	2.206	.75	1.25	2.50	5.50
	1955	2,850	—	—	Proof	5.50
	1956	2.142	.75	1.25	2.50	6.00
	1956	1,700	—	—	Proof	6.00
	1957	.791	1.00	2.00	5.00	10.00
	1957	1,130	—	—	Proof	6.00
	1958	4.067	.75	1.25	2.00	5.50
	1958	985 pcs.	—	—	Proof	8.00
	1959	.205	1.50	3.00	5.00	10.00
	1959	900 pcs.	—	—	Proof	10.00
	1960	2.187	.75	1.25	2.00	5.50
	1960	3,360	—	—	Proof	3.00

FLORIN

11.3100 g, .800 SILVER, .2909 oz ASW

18	1923	.695	5.00	20.00	40.00	80.00
	1923	1,402	—	—	Proof	125.00
	1924	1.513	4.00	15.00	40.00	150.00
	1925	.050	125.00	350.00	1000.	2200.
	1926	.324	7.50	40.00	250.00	650.00
	1927	.399	7.50	35.00	200.00	600.00
	1928	1.092	4.00	10.00	100.00	200.00
	1929	.648	5.00	15.00	120.00	225.00
	1930	.267	5.00	15.00	75.00	150.00
	1930	14 pcs.	—	—	Proof	1200.

2 SHILLINGS

11.3100 g, .800 SILVER, .2909 oz ASW
Rev. denomination: 2 SHILLINGS

22	1931	383 pcs.	250.00	450.00	700.00	950.00
	1931	62 pcs.	—	—	Proof	1500.
	1932	1.315	3.00	6.00	18.00	45.00
	1932	12 pcs.	—	—	Proof	2000.
	1933	.891	4.00	8.00	25.00	60.00
	1933	20 pcs.	—	—	Proof	2000.
	1934	.559	4.00	8.00	25.00	60.00
	1934	24 pcs.	—	—	Proof	1650.
	1935	.554	5.00	9.00	25.00	70.00
	1935	20 pcs.	—	—	Proof	1650.
	1936	.669	4.00	8.00	25.00	60.00
	1936	40 pcs.	—	—	Proof	650.00

KM#	Date	Mintage	Fine	VF	XF	Unc
29	1937	1.495	2.50	5.00	10.00	30.00
	1937	116 pcs.	—	—	Proof	150.00
	1938	.214	5.00	10.00	20.00	50.00
	1938	44 pcs.	—	—	Proof	325.00
	1939	.279	5.00	10.00	20.00	50.00
	1939	30 pcs.	—	—	Proof	1000.
	1940	2.600	2.50	3.50	8.00	20.00
	1941	1.764	2.50	3.50	8.00	20.00
	1942	2.847	2.00	3.00	5.00	10.00
	1943	3.125	2.00	3.00	5.00	10.00
	1943	104 pcs.	—	—	Proof	135.00
	1944	.225	3.50	7.00	17.50	40.00
	1945	.473	3.00	6.00	15.00	35.00
	1945	150 pcs.	—	—	Proof	120.00
	1946	.014	7.50	20.00	40.00	90.00
	1946	150 pcs.	—	—	Proof	135.00
	1947	2,892	15.00	25.00	40.00	75.00
	1947	2,600	—	—	Proof	85.00

38.1	1948	6,773	15.00	20.00	40.00	70.00
	1948	1,120	—	—	Proof	100.00
	1949	.203	5.00	10.00	15.00	35.00
	1949	800 pcs.	—	—	Proof	75.00
	1950	4,945	20.00	40.00	80.00	140.00
	1950	500 pcs.	—	—	Proof	175.00

11.3100 g, .500 SILVER, .1818 oz ASW
Rev. denomination: 2 S

38.2	1951	.730	2.00	3.00	5.00	10.00
	1951	2,000	—	—	Proof	15.00
	1952	3.570	1.50	2.00	3.00	6.50
	1952	.016	—	—	Proof	8.00

50	1953	3.274	1.50	2.25	4.00	8.50
	1953	5,000	—	—	Proof	9.00
	1954	5.866	1.50	2.25	3.00	7.00
	1954	3,150	—	—	Proof	8.00
	1955	3.745	1.50	2.25	3.00	7.50
	1955	2,850	—	—	Proof	8.00
	1956	2.549	1.50	2.25	4.00	9.00
	1956	1,700	—	—	Proof	10.00
	1957	2.507	1.50	2.25	4.00	10.00
	1957	1,130	—	—	Proof	11.00
	1958	2.821	1.50	2.25	4.00	10.00
	1958	985 pcs.	—	—	Proof	15.00
	1959	1.219	1.50	2.25	4.00	10.00
	1959	900 pcs.	—	—	Proof	20.00
	1960	1.951	1.50	2.25	3.00	5.00
	1960	3,360	—	—	Proof	4.00

2-1/2 SHILLINGS

14.1400 g, .800 SILVER, .3637 oz ASW
Rev. leg: ZUID-AFRICA,
denomination: 2-1/2 SHILLINGS 2-1/2

KM#	Date	Mintage	Fine	VF	XF	Unc
19.1	1923	1.227	4.00	15.00	35.00	70.00
	1923	1,402	—	—	Proof	125.00
	1924	2.556	3.50	10.00	50.00	120.00
	1925	.460	8.00	30.00	180.00	600.00

Rev. denomination: 2-1/2 SHILLINGS

19.2	1926	.205	10.00	40.00	250.00	650.00
	1926	16 pcs.	—	—	Proof	4000.
	1927	.194	10.00	40.00	350.00	850.00
	1928	.984	5.00	25.00	125.00	325.00
	1929	.617	5.00	25.00	175.00	350.00
	1930	.324	5.00	15.00	100.00	250.00
	1930	14 pcs.	—	—	Proof	1650.

Rev. leg: SUID. AFRICA

19.3	1931	790 pcs.	225.00	450.00	700.00	1000.
	1931	62 pcs.	—	—	Proof	1800.
	1932	1.029	4.00	6.00	22.50	40.00
	1932	12 pcs.	—	—	Proof	2400.
	1933	.136	8.00	40.00	185.00	300.00
	1933	20 pcs.	—	—	Proof	2400.
	1934	.416	4.00	8.00	30.00	100.00
	1934	24 pcs.	—	—	Proof	1650.
	1935	.345	5.00	12.50	32.50	100.00
	1935	20 pcs.	—	—	Proof	1650.
	1936	.553	4.00	8.00	25.00	70.00
	1936	40 pcs.	—	—	Proof	800.00

30	1937	1.154	3.00	5.00	15.00	32.50
	1937	116 pcs.	—	—	Proof	175.00
	1938	.534	4.00	8.00	20.00	60.00
	1938	44 pcs.	—	—	Proof	400.00
	1939	.133	6.00	15.00	40.00	80.00
	1939	30 pcs.	—	—	Proof	800.00
	1940	2.976	3.00	4.50	8.00	20.00
	1941	1.988	3.00	4.50	8.00	20.00
	1942	3.180	3.00	4.50	8.00	20.00
	1943	2.098	3.00	4.50	8.00	20.00
	1943	104 pcs.	—	—	Proof	150.00
	1944	1.360	3.00	5.00	10.00	25.00
	1944	150 pcs.	—	—	Proof	130.00
	1945	.183	3.50	7.00	25.00	60.00
	1945	150 pcs.	—	—	Proof	130.00
	1946	.011	15.00	30.00	50.00	90.00
	1946	150 pcs.	—	—	Proof	150.00
	1947	3,582	20.00	35.00	60.00	100.00
	1947	2,600	—	—	Proof	125.00

KM#	Date	Mintage	Fine	VF	XF	Unc
39.1	1948	1,600	30.00	50.00	80.00	100.00
	1948	1,120	—	—	Proof	110.00
	1949	1,891	30.00	50.00	80.00	120.00
	1949	800 pcs.	—	—	Proof	125.00
	1950	5,076	30.00	50.00	80.00	150.00
	1950	500 pcs.	—	—	Proof	200.00

14.1400 g, .500 SILVER, .2273 oz ASW
Rev. denomination: 2-1/2 S

39.2	1951	.783	3.00	4.50	6.00	15.00
	1951	2,000	—	—	Proof	9.00
	1952	1.996	2.00	3.00	4.00	8.50
	1952	.016	—	—	Proof	5.00

51	1953	2.513	2.00	3.00	4.00	8.50
	1953	6,000	—	—	Proof	6.00
	1954	4.249	2.00	3.00	4.00	8.50
	1954	3,150	—	—	Proof	9.00
	1955	3.863	2.00	3.00	4.00	8.50
	1955	2,850	—	—	Proof	8.00
	1956	2.437	2.00	3.00	4.00	8.50
	1956	1,700	—	—	Proof	13.00
	1957	2.137	2.00	3.00	4.00	8.50
	1957	1,130	—	—	Proof	14.00
	1958	2.260	2.00	3.00	4.50	9.00
	1958	985 pcs.	—	—	Proof	14.00
	1959	.046	2.50	4.00	6.00	12.00
	1959	900 pcs.	—	—	Proof	18.00
	1960	.012	3.00	5.00	7.50	12.50
	1960	3,360	—	—	Proof	5.00

5 SHILLINGS

28.2800 g, .800 SILVER, .7274 oz ASW
Royal Visit

31	1947	.300	BV	7.00	7.50	15.00
	1947	5,600	—	—	Proof	45.00

KM#	Date	Mintage	Fine	VF	XF	Unc
40.1	1948	.780	BV	6.00	7.50	15.00
	1948	1,000	—	—	P/L	20.00
	1948	1,120	—	—	Proof	25.00
	1949	.535	BV	6.00	7.50	15.00
	1949	2,000	—	—	P/L	35.00
	1949	800 pcs.	—	—	Proof	50.00
	1950	.083	BV	10.00	12.50	25.00
	1950	1,200	—	—	P/L	60.00
	1950	500 pcs.	—	—	Proof	75.00

28.2800 g, .500 SILVER, .4546 oz ASW
Rev. denomination: 5 S.

40.2	ND(1951)	.363	BV	5.00	7.00	15.00
	ND(1951)	1,483	—	—	P/L	25.00
	ND(1951)	2,000	—	—	Proof	35.00

300th Anniversary - Founding of Capetown

41	1952	1.698	BV	4.50	5.50	10.00
	1952	.012	—	—	P/L	12.50
	1952	.016	—	—	Proof	15.00

52	1953	.250	BV	5.00	7.00	12.00
	1953	8,000	—	—	P/L	15.00
	1953	5,000	—	—	Proof	20.00
	1953	—	—	—	Matte Proof	700.00
	1954	.010	BV	8.50	12.50	20.00
	1954	3,890	—	—	P/L	22.00
	1954	3,150	—	—	Proof	25.00
	1955	.040	BV	7.50	10.00	15.00
	1955	2,230	—	—	P/L	20.00
	1955	2,850	—	—	Proof	25.00
	1956	.100	BV	5.00	7.00	12.00
	1956	2,200	—	—	P/L	20.00
	1956	1,700	—	—	Proof	25.00
	1957	.154	BV	5.00	7.00	12.00
	1957	1,600	—	—	P/L	25.00
	1957	1,130	—	—	Proof	30.00
	1958	.233	BV	5.00	7.00	12.00
	1958	1,500	—	—	P/L	25.00
	1958	985 pcs.	—	—	Proof	30.00
	1959	2,989	20.00	35.00	65.00	100.00

KM#	Date	Mintage	Fine	VF	XF	Unc
52	1959	2,200	—	—	P/L	110.00
	1959	950 pcs.	—	—	Proof	125.00

50th Anniversary - South African Union

55	1960	.396	BV	4.50	5.50	6.50
	1960	.022	—	—	P/L	10.00
	1960	3,360	—	—	Proof	12.50

NOTE: Many varieties exist of letters HM below building.

1/2 SOVEREIGN

3.9940 g, .917 GOLD, .1177 oz AGW
British type w/Pretoria mint mark: SA

20	1923	655 pcs.	—	—	Proof	475.00
	1925	.947	55.00	65.00	75.00	100.00
	1926	.809	55.00	65.00	75.00	100.00

SOVEREIGN

7.9881 g, .917 GOLD, .2354 oz AGW
British type w/Pretoria mint mark: SA

21	1923	64 pcs.	200.00	300.00	400.00	500.00
	1923	655 pcs.	—	—	Proof	550.00
	1924	3,184	700.00	1350.	2250.	4000.
	1925	6.086	—	BV	110.00	125.00
	1926	11.108	—	BV	110.00	125.00
	1927	16.380	—	BV	110.00	125.00
	1928	18.235	—	BV	110.00	125.00

Obv: Modified effigy, slightly smaller bust.

A22	1929	12.024	—	BV	110.00	125.00
	1930	10.028	—	BV	110.00	125.00
	1931	8.512	—	BV	110.00	125.00
	1932	1.067	—	BV	110.00	145.00

REPUBLIC

MONETARY SYSTEM
100 Cents = 1 Rand

1/2 CENT

BRASS

KM#	Date	Mintage	VF	XF	Unc
56	1961	39.189	.15	.25	1.00
	1961	7,530	—	Proof	.75
	1962	17.895	.15	.25	1.00
	1962	3,844	—	Proof	.75
	1963	11.611	.15	.25	2.00
	1963	4,025	—	Proof	.75
	1964	9.258	.15	.25	1.00
	1964	.016	—	Proof	.65

BRONZE
Bilingual
Sparrows

81	1970	*57.721	.10	.25	.50
	1970	.010	—	Proof	2.50

KM#	Date	Mintage	VF	XF	Unc
81	1971	8,000	—	—	2.50
	1971	.012	—	Proof	2.50
	1972	8,000	—	—	2.50
	1972	.012	—	Proof	2.50
	1973	.020	.10	.20	2.50
	1973	.011	—	Proof	2.50
	1974	.020	.20	.40	2.50
	1974	.015	—	Proof	2.50
	1975	.020	.10	.20	2.50
	1975	.018	—	Proof	2.50
	1977	.020	.10	.20	2.50
	1977	.019	—	Proof	2.50
	1978	.018	.10	.20	2.50
	1978	.019	—	Proof	2.50
	1980	.015	—	Proof	2.50
	1981	.010	—	Proof	2.50
	1983	.014	—	Proof	2.50

*NOTE: Coins dated 1970 were also struck for circulation in 1971, 1972 and 1973.

President Fouche
Similar to 1 Cent, KM#91.

90	1976	.020	—	—	1.00
	1976	.021	—	Proof	1.50

President Diederichs

97	1979	.018	—	—	1.00
	1979	.017	—	Proof	1.50

CENT

BRASS

57	1961	52.266	.15	.40	1.50
	1961	7,530	—	Proof	.75
	1962	21.929	.15	.40	1.50
	1962	3,844	—	Proof	1.00
	1963	9.081	.15	.50	3.00
	1963	4,025	—	Proof	1.00
	1964	14.265	.15	.40	1.50
	1964	.016	—	Proof	2.00

BRONZE
Sparrows
English legend.

65.1	1965	.026	—	—	2.00
	1965	.025	—	Proof	2.50
	1966	50.157	—	.10	.50
	1967	21.114	—	.10	.50
	1969	10.196	—	.10	.50

Afrikaans legend.

65.2	1965	846 pcs.	100.00	200.00	300.00
	1965	185 pcs.	—	Proof	350.00
	1966	50.157	—	.10	.50
	1966	.025	—	Proof	1.00
	1967	21.114	—	.10	.50
	1967	.025	—	Proof	1.00
	1969	10.196	—	.10	.50
	1969	.012	—	Proof	1.50

President Charles Swart
English legend.

74.1	1968	6.000	—	.10	.30
	1968	.025	—	Proof	1.00

Afrikaans legend.

KM#	Date	Mintage	VF	XF	Unc
74.2	1968	6.000	—	.10	.30

Bilingual legend.

82	1970	37.072	—	—	.30
	1970	.010	—	Proof	1.00
	1971	34.053	—	—	.30
	1971	.012	—	Proof	1.00
	1972	35.662	—	—	.30
	1972	.010	—	Proof	1.00
	1973	35.898	.10	.20	.40
	1973	.011	—	Proof	1.00
	1974	54.940	—	—	.25
	1974	.015	—	Proof	1.00
	1975	62.982	—	—	.25
	1975	.018	—	Proof	1.00
	1977	72.444	—	—	.25
	1977	.019	—	Proof	1.00
	1978	70.152	—	—	.20
	1978	.017	—	Proof	.50
	1980	63.432	—	—	.20
	1980	.015	—	Proof	.50
	1981	63.444	—	—	.20
	1981	.010	—	Proof	.50
	1983	182.131	—	—	.20
	1983	.014	—	Proof	.50
	1984	107.155	—	—	.20
	1984	.011	—	Proof	.50
	1985	186.042	—	—	.20
	1985	9,859	—	Proof	.50
	1986	169.734	—	—	.20
	1986	7,000	—	Proof	.50
	1987	120.674	—	—	.20
	1987	6,781	—	Proof	.50
	1988	240.272	—	—	.20
	1988	7,250	—	Proof	.50
	1989	—	—	—	.20
	1989	—	—	Proof	.50

President Fouche

91	1976	91.860	—	.30	.50
	1976	.021	—	Proof	.75

President Diederichs

98	1979	63.432	—	.30	.50
	1979	.015	—	Proof	.75

President Vorster

109	1982	145.954	—	.30	.50
	1982	.012	—	Proof	.75

COPPER PLATED STEEL

132	1990	—	—	—	.25
	1990	—	—	Proof	.50
	1991	—	—	—	.25
	1991	—	—	Proof	.50
	1992	—	—	—	.25
	1993	—	—	—	.25
	1994	—	—	—	.25
	1995	—	—	—	.25
	1995	—	—	Proof	.50

Zulu Legend

KM#	Date	Mintage	VF	XF	Unc
158	1996	—	—	—	.25
	1996	.010	—	Proof	.50

Ndebele Legend - 2 Cape Sparrows

170	1997	—	—	—	.25
	1998	—	—	—	.25

2 CENTS

BRONZE
White-tailed Gnu
English legend.

66.1	1965	29.887	—	.10	.35
	1966	9.267	—	.10	.40
	1966	.025	—	Proof	.50
	1967	11.862	—	.10	.35
	1967	.025	—	Proof	.50
	1969	5.817	—	.10	.40
	1969	.012	—	Proof	.50

Afrikaans legend.

66.2	1965	29.887	—	.10	.35
	1965	.025	—	Proof	.50
	1966	9.267	—	.10	.35
	1967	11.862	—	.10	.35
	1969	5.817	—	.10	.40

President Charles Swart
English legend.

75.1	1968	5.500	—	.20	.50

Afrikaans legend.

75.2	1968	5.525	—	.20	.50
	1968	.025	—	Proof	1.00

Bilingual legend.

83	1970	35.217	—	.10	.35
	1970	.010	—	Proof	.50
	1971	24.093	—	.10	.35
	1971	.012	—	Proof	.50
	1972	7.304	—	.10	.35
	1972	.010	—	Proof	.50
	1973	18.685	—	.10	.35
	1973	.011	—	Proof	.50
	1974	25.301	—	.10	.35
	1974	.015	—	Proof	.50
	1975	24.982	—	.10	.35
	1975	.018	—	Proof	.50
	1977	45.116	—	.10	.35
	1977	.019	—	Proof	.50
	1978	50.527	—	.10	.35
	1978	.017	—	Proof	.50

KM#	Date	Mintage	VF	XF	Unc
83	1980	37.795	—	.10	.35
	1980	.015	—	Proof	.50
	1981	79.350	—	.10	.35
	1981	.010	—	Proof	.50
	1983	112.575	—	.10	.35
	1983	.014	—	Proof	.50
	1984	101.497	—	.10	.35
	1984	.011	—	Proof	.50
	1985	102.708	—	.10	.35
	1985	9,859	—	Proof	.50
	1986	683.294	—	.10	.35
	1986	7,100	—	Proof	.50
	1987	104.981	—	.10	.35
	1987	6,781	—	Proof	.50
	1988	182.036	—	.10	.35
	1988	7,250	—	Proof	.50
	1989	—	—	.10	.35
	1989	—	—	Proof	.50

President Fouche

92	1976	51.474	—	.25	.50
	1976	.021	—	Proof	.75

President Diederichs

99	1979	40.043	—	.25	.50
	1979	.015	—	Proof	.75

President Vorster

110	1982	53.962	—	.25	.50
	1982	.012	—	Proof	.75

COPPER PLATED STEEL

133	1990	—	—	—	1.50
	1990	—	—	Proof	2.00
	1991	—	—	—	1.50
	1992	—	—	—	.50
	1992	—	—	Proof	2.00
	1993	—	—	—	.50
	1994	—	—	—	.50
	1995	—	—	—	.50
	1995	—	—	Proof	2.00

Venda Legend

159	1996	—	—	—	.50
	1996	—	—	Proof	1.00
	1997	—	—	—	.50
	1998	—	—	—	.50

2-1/2 CENTS

1.4100 g, .500 SILVER, .0226 oz ASW

58	1961	.292	.50	1.00	2.00
	1961	7,530	—	Proof	4.00
	1962	8,745	2.00	4.00	8.00
	1962	3,844	—	Proof	8.00
	1963	.033	1.50	2.50	4.00
	1963	4,025	—	Proof	6.00

KM#	Date	Mintage	VF	XF	Unc
58	1964	.014	2.00	4.00	6.00
	1964	.016	—	Proof	4.00

5 CENTS

2.8300 g, .500 SILVER, .0454 oz ASW

59	1961	1.479	BV	.85	2.00
	1961	7,530	—	Proof	2.50
	1962	4.188	BV	.75	1.50
	1962	3,844	—	Proof	3.00
	1963	8.054	BV	.65	1.25
	1963	4,025	—	Proof	3.00
	1964	3.567	BV	.65	1.25
	1964	.016	—	Proof	1.50

NICKEL
Blue Crane
English legend.

67.1	1965	32.690	—	.15	.50
	1965	.025	—	Proof	.60
	1966	4.101	—	.15	.50
	1967	4.590	—	.15	.50
	1969	5.020	—	.15	.50

Afrikaans legend.

67.2	1965	32.690	—	.15	.50
	1966	4.101	—	.15	.50
	1966	.025	—	Proof	.60
	1967	4.590	—	.15	.50
	1967	.025	—	Proof	.60
	1969	5.020	—	.15	.50
	1969	.012	—	Proof	.60

President Charles Swart
English legend.

76.1	1968	6.000	—	.15	.60
	1968	.025	—	Proof	.60

Afrikaans legend.

76.2	1968	6.000	—	.15	.60

Bilingual legend.

84	1970	6.652	—	.15	.50
	1970	.010	—	Proof	.60
	1971	20.329	—	.15	.50
	1971	.012	—	Proof	.60
	1972	3.117	—	.15	.50
	1972	9,000	—	Proof	.60
	1973	17.092	—	.15	.50
	1973	.011	—	Proof	.60
	1974	19.978	—	.15	.50
	1974	.015	—	Proof	.60
	1975	21.982	—	.15	.50
	1975	.018	—	Proof	.60
	1977	51.729	—	.15	.50
	1977	.019	—	Proof	.60
	1978	30.036	—	.15	.50
	1978	.019	—	Proof	.60
	1980	46.665	—	.15	.50
	1980	.015	—	Proof	.60
	1981	40.351	—	.15	.50
	1981	.010	—	Proof	.60
	1983	57.487	—	.15	.50

KM#	Date	Mintage	VF	XF	Unc
84	1983	.014	—	Proof	.60
	1984	67.345	—	.15	.50
	1984	.011	—	Proof	.60
	1985	57.167	—	.15	.50
	1985	9,859	—	Proof	.60
	1986	54.226	—	.15	.50
	1986	7,100	—	Proof	.60
	1987	42.786	—	.15	.50
	1987	5,297	—	Proof	.60
	1988	110.164	—	.15	.50
	1988	7,250	—	Proof	.60
	1989	35.540	—	.25	.75
	1989	Inc. Ab.	—	Proof	1.50

President Fouche

93	1976	48.972	—	.30	.75
	1976	.019	—	Proof	1.50

President Diederichs

100	1979	17.533	—	.30	.75
	1979	.017	—	Proof	1.50

President Vorster

111	1982	47.236	—	.30	.75
	1982	.012	—	Proof	1.50

COPPER PLATED STEEL

134	1990	—	—	.15	.50
	1990	—	—	Proof	.60
	1991	—	—	.15	.50
	1992	—	—	.15	.50
	1992	—	—	Proof	.60
	1993	—	—	.15	.50
	1994	—	—	.15	.50
	1995	—	—	.15	.50
	1995	—	—	Proof	.60

Tsonga Legend

160	1996	—	—	.15	.50
	1996	—	—	Proof	.75
	1997	—	—	.15	.50
	1998	—	—	.15	.50

10 CENTS

5.6600 g, .500 SILVER, .0909 oz ASW

60	1961	1.136	BV	1.25	2.50
	1961	7,530	—	Proof	2.50
	1962	2.447	BV	1.25	2.50
	1962	3,844	—	Proof	3.50
	1963	3.327	BV	1.25	2.50
	1963	4,025	—	Proof	3.50
	1964	4.153	BV	1.25	2.00
	1964	.016	—	Proof	2.50

NICKEL
Aloe Plant
English legend.

KM#	Date	Mintage	VF	XF	Unc
68.1	1965	29.210	—	.10	.35
	1966	3.685	—	.10	.45
	1966	.025	—	Proof	.60
	1967	.050	—	—	1.00
	1967	.025	—	Proof	.60
	1969	.558	—	.10	.50
	1969	.012	—	Proof	1.00

Afrikaans legend.

KM#	Date	Mintage	VF	XF	Unc
68.2	1965	29.210	—	.10	.35
	1965	.025	—	Proof	.60
	1966	3.685	—	.10	.45
	1967	.050	—	—	1.00
	1969	.558	.10	.20	2.50

President Charles Swart
English legend.

KM#	Date	Mintage	VF	XF	Unc
77.1	1968	.050	—	—	2.00

Afrikaans legend.

KM#	Date	Mintage	VF	XF	Unc
77.2	1968	.050	—	—	1.50
	1968	.025	—	Proof	.60

Bilingual legend.

KM#	Date	Mintage	VF	XF	Unc
85	1970	7.598	—	.10	.35
	1970	.010	—	Proof	.60
	1971	6.440	—	.10	.35
	1971	.012	—	Proof	.60
	1972	10.028	—	.10	.35
	1972	.010	—	Proof	.60
	1973	1.760	—	.10	.35
	1973	.011	—	Proof	.60
	1974	9.897	—	.10	.35
	1974	.015	—	Proof	.60
	1975	12.982	—	.10	.35
	1975	.018	—	Proof	.60
	1977	28.851	—	.10	.35
	1977	.019	—	Proof	.60
	1978	25.008	—	.10	.35
	1978	.019	—	Proof	.60
	1980	5.040	—	.10	.35
	1980	.015	—	Proof	.60
	1981	9.604	—	.10	.35
	1981	.010	—	Proof	.60
	1983	26.495	—	.10	.35
	1983	.014	—	Proof	.60
	1984	35.465	—	.10	.35
	1984	.011	—	Proof	.60
	1985	29.270	—	.10	.35
	1985	9.859	—	Proof	.60
	1986	24.480	—	.10	.35
	1986	7.100	—	Proof	.60
	1987	43.234	—	.10	.35
	1987	6.781	—	Proof	.60
	1988	48.267	—	.10	.35
	1988	7.250	—	Proof	.60
	1989	—	—	—	.35
	1989	—	—	Proof	.60

President Fouche

KM#	Date	Mintage	VF	XF	Unc
94	1976	30.986	—	.40	1.00
	1976	.021	—	Proof	1.50

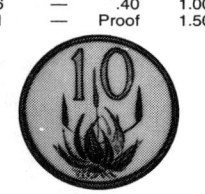

President Diederichs

KM#	Date	Mintage	VF	XF	Unc
101	1979	5.042	—	.40	1.00
	1979	.017	—	Proof	1.50

President Vorster

KM#	Date	Mintage	VF	XF	Unc
112	1982	15.806	—	.40	1.00
	1982	.012	—	Proof	1.50

BRASS PLATED STEEL

KM#	Date	Mintage	VF	XF	Unc
135	1990	—	—	—	.40
	1990	—	—	Proof	.60
	1991	—	—	—	.40
	1992	—	—	—	.40
	1992	—	—	Proof	.60
	1993	—	—	—	.40
	1994	—	—	—	.40
	1995	—	—	—	.40
	1995	—	—	Proof	.60

Obv: English legend above arms.

KM#	Date	Mintage	VF	XF	Unc
161	1996	—	—	—	.40
	1996	—	—	Proof	.75
	1997	—	—	—	.40
	1998	—	—	—	.40

20 CENTS

11.3100 g, .500 SILVER, .1818 oz ASW

KM#	Date	Mintage	VF	XF	Unc
61	1961	2.954	BV	1.50	2.50
	1961	7,530	—	Proof	3.50
	1962 sm.2	3.568	BV	1.50	2.50
	1962 lg.2	I.A.	—	—	—
	1962 sm.2	3,844	—	Proof	4.00
	1963	4.380	BV	1.50	2.50
	1963	4,025	—	Proof	4.00
	1964	4.335	BV	1.50	2.50
	1964	.016	—	Proof	2.50

NICKEL
Protea Cynaroides and Protea Repens
English legend.

KM#	Date	Mintage	VF	XF	Unc
69.1	1965	29.210	.15	.20	.40
	1965	.025	—	Proof	.60
	1966	4.049	.15	.20	.50
	1967	.058	—	—	1.00
	1969	9,952	—	—	10.00

Afrikaans legend.

KM#	Date	Mintage	VF	XF	Unc
69.2	1965	29.210	.15	.20	.40
	1966	4.049	.15	.20	.50
	1966	.025	—	Proof	.60
	1967	.058	—	—	1.00
	1967	.025	—	Proof	.60
	1969	9,952	—	—	6.00
	1969	.012	—	Proof	4.00

President Charles Swart
English legend.

KM#	Date	Mintage	VF	XF	Unc
78.1	1968	.050	—	—	3.00
	1968	.025	—	Proof	.60

Afrikaans legend.

KM#	Date	Mintage	VF	XF	Unc
78.2	1968	.050	—	—	3.50

Bilingual legend.

KM#	Date	Mintage	VF	XF	Unc
86	1970	.014	—	—	10.00
	1970	.010	—	Proof	1.50
	1971	5.893	.15	.25	.60
	1971	.012	—	Proof	1.50
	1972	9.069	.15	.25	.60
	1972	.010	—	Proof	1.50
	1973	.020	—	—	5.00
	1973	.011	—	Proof	1.50
	1974	2.436	.15	.35	.75
	1974	.015	—	Proof	1.50
	1975	12.982	—	.20	.60
	1975	.018	—	Proof	1.00
	1977	30.650	—	.20	.60
	1977	.019	—	Proof	.75
	1978	10.049	—	.20	.60
	1978	.019	—	Proof	.75
	1980	13.335	—	.20	.60
	1980	.015	—	Proof	.75
	1981	8.534	—	.20	.60
	1981	.010	—	Proof	.75
	1983	25.667	—	.20	.60
	1983	.014	—	Proof	.75
	1984	31.607	—	.20	.60
	1984	.011	—	Proof	.75
	1985	29.329	—	.20	.60
	1985	9.859	—	Proof	.75
	1986	11.408	—	.20	.60
	1986	7,100	—	Proof	.75
	1987	36.904	—	.20	.60
	1987	6,781	—	Proof	.75
	1988	43.115	—	.20	.60
	1988	7,250	—	Proof	.75
	1989	—	—	.20	.60
	1989	—	—	Proof	.75

NOTE: Varieties exist.

President Fouche

KM#	Date	Mintage	VF	XF	Unc
95	1976	18.826	—	.70	1.50
	1976	.021	—	Proof	2.50

President Diederichs

102	1979	5.032	—	.70	1.50
	1979	.015	—	Proof	2.50

President Vorster

113	1982	18.083	—	.70	1.50
	1982	.012	—	Proof	2.50

BRASS PLATED STEEL

136	1990	—	—	—	4.00
	1990	—	—	Proof	8.00
	1991	—	—	—	4.00
	1992	—	—	—	.60
	1992	—	—	Proof	8.00
	1993	—	—	—	.60
	1994	—	—	—	.60
	1995	—	—	—	.60
	1995	—	—	Proof	8.00

Obv: Tswana legend above arms.

162	1996	—	—	—	.60
	1996	—	—	Proof	4.00
	1997	—	—	—	.60
	1998	—	—	—	.60

50 CENTS

28.2800 g, .500 SILVER, .4546 oz ASW

KM#	Date	Mintage	VF	XF	Unc
62	1961	.026	BV	12.00	15.00
	1961	.020	—	P/L	15.00
	1961	8,530	—	Proof	25.00
	1962	.015	BV	12.00	15.00
	1962	6,024	—	P/L	22.00
	1962	3,844	—	Proof	40.00
	1963*	.143	BV	7.00	12.00
	1963	.010	—	P/L	17.50
	1963	4,025	—	Proof	30.00
	1964	.086	BV	7.50	12.50
	1964	.025	—	P/L	15.00
	1964	.016	—	Proof	15.00

NOTE: Varieties exist w/narrow, high relief and wide, low letters.

NICKEL
Zantedeschia Elliottiana
English legend.

70.1	1965	30 to 50 pcs.	—	Proof	3500.
	1966	8.056	—	.50	2.50
	1966	.025	—	Proof	4.00
	1967	.052	In sets only		1.50
	1967	.025	—	Proof	4.00
	1969	7,968	In sets only		10.00
	1969	.012	—	Proof	10.00

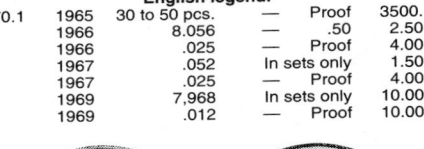

Afrikaans legend.

70.2	1965	.028	—	—	6.00
	1965	.025	—	Proof	6.00
	1966	8.056	—	.50	2.50
	1967	.052	In sets only		3.50
	1969	7,968	In sets only		15.00

President Charles Swart
English legend.

79.1	1968	.750	—	.50	1.50

 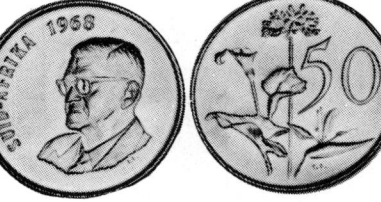

Afrikaans legend.

79.2	1968	.750	—	.50	2.00
	1968	.025	—	Proof	3.50

Bilingual legend.

KM#	Date	Mintage	VF	XF	Unc
87	1970	4.098	—	.50	1.50
	1970	.010	—	Proof	2.00
	1971	5.062	—	.50	1.50
	1971	.012	—	Proof	2.00
	1972	.771	—	.50	1.50
	1972	.010	—	Proof	2.00
	1973	1.043	—	.50	1.50
	1973	.011	—	Proof	2.00
	1974	1.942	—	.50	1.50
	1974	.015	—	Proof	2.00
	1975	4.888	—	.50	1.50
	1975	.018	—	Proof	2.00
	1977	10.196	—	.50	1.50
	1977	.019	—	Proof	2.00
	1978	5.071	—	.50	1.50
	1978	.017	—	Proof	2.00
	1980	4.268	—	.50	1.50
	1980	.015	—	Proof	2.00
	1981	5.681	—	.50	1.50
	1981	.010	—	Proof	2.00
	1983	5.150	—	.40	1.00
	1983	.014	—	Proof	1.50
	1984	9.687	—	.40	1.00
	1984	.011	—	Proof	1.50
	1985	13.339	—	.40	1.00
	1985	9,859	—	Proof	1.50
	1986	2.294	—	.40	1.00
	1986	7,100	—	Proof	1.50
	1987	19.071	—	.40	1.00
	1987	6,781	—	Proof	1.50
	1988	27.698	—	.40	1.00
	1988	7,250	—	Proof	1.50
	1989	—	—	.40	1.00
	1989	—	—	Proof	1.50
	1990	—	Reported, not confirmed		

NOTE: Varieties exist.

President Fouche

96	1976	9.632	.75	1.50	3.00
	1976	.021	—	Proof	5.00

President Diederichs

103	1979	5.051	.75	1.50	3.50
	1979	.015	—	Proof	5.00

President Vorster

114	1982	2.070	.75	1.50	3.50
	1982	.012	—	Proof	5.00

BRASS PLATED STEEL

KM#	Date	Mintage	VF	XF	Unc
137	1990	—	—	—	5.00
	1990	—	—	Proof	10.00
	1991	—	—	—	5.00
	1992	—	—	—	1.00
	1992	—	—	Proof	10.00
	1993	—	—	—	1.00
	1994	—	—	—	1.00
	1995	—	—	—	1.00
	1995	—	—	Proof	10.00

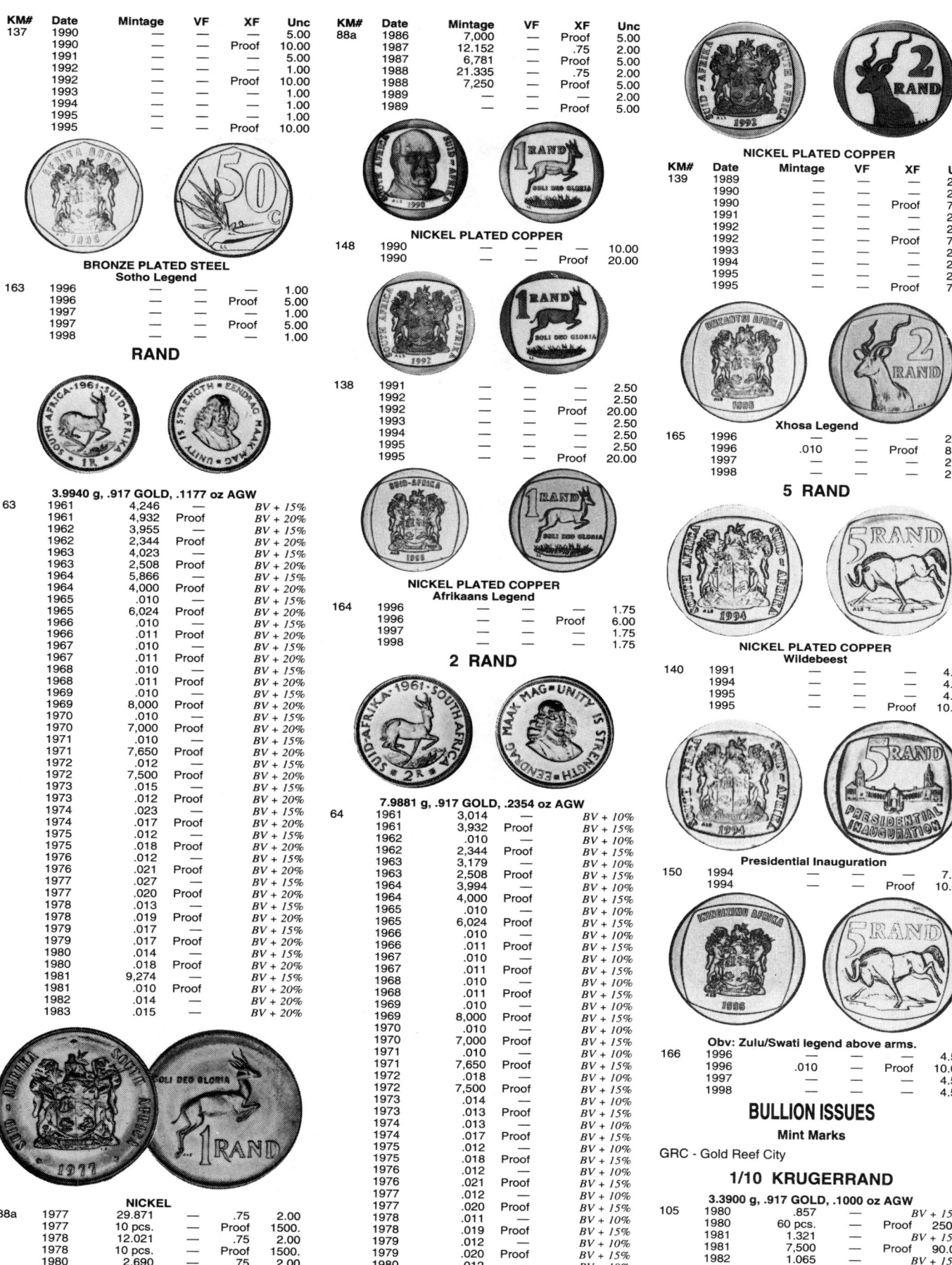

BRONZE PLATED STEEL
Sotho Legend

163	1996	—	—	—	1.00
	1996	—	—	Proof	5.00
	1997	—	—	—	1.00
	1997	—	—	Proof	5.00
	1998	—	—	—	1.00

RAND

3.9940 g, .917 GOLD, .1177 oz AGW

63	1961	4,246	—		BV + 15%
	1961	4,932	Proof		BV + 20%
	1962	3,955	—		BV + 15%
	1962	2,344	Proof		BV + 20%
	1963	4,023	—		BV + 15%
	1963	2,508	Proof		BV + 20%
	1964	5,866	—		BV + 15%
	1964	4,000	Proof		BV + 20%
	1965	.010	—		BV + 15%
	1965	6,024	Proof		BV + 20%
	1966	.010	—		BV + 15%
	1966	.011	Proof		BV + 20%
	1967	.010	—		BV + 15%
	1967	.011	Proof		BV + 20%
	1968	.010	—		BV + 15%
	1968	.011	Proof		BV + 20%
	1969	.010	—		BV + 15%
	1969	8,000	Proof		BV + 20%
	1970	.010	—		BV + 15%
	1970	7,000	Proof		BV + 20%
	1971	.010	—		BV + 15%
	1971	7,650	Proof		BV + 20%
	1972	.012	—		BV + 15%
	1972	7,500	Proof		BV + 20%
	1973	.015	—		BV + 15%
	1973	.012	Proof		BV + 20%
	1974	.023	—		BV + 15%
	1974	.017	Proof		BV + 20%
	1975	.012	—		BV + 15%
	1975	.018	Proof		BV + 20%
	1976	.012	—		BV + 15%
	1976	.021	Proof		BV + 20%
	1977	.027	—		BV + 15%
	1977	.020	Proof		BV + 20%
	1978	.013	—		BV + 15%
	1978	.019	Proof		BV + 20%
	1979	.017	—		BV + 15%
	1979	.017	Proof		BV + 20%
	1980	.014	—		BV + 15%
	1980	.018	Proof		BV + 20%
	1981	9,274	—		BV + 15%
	1981	.010	Proof		BV + 20%
	1982	.014	—		BV + 20%
	1983	.015	—		BV + 20%

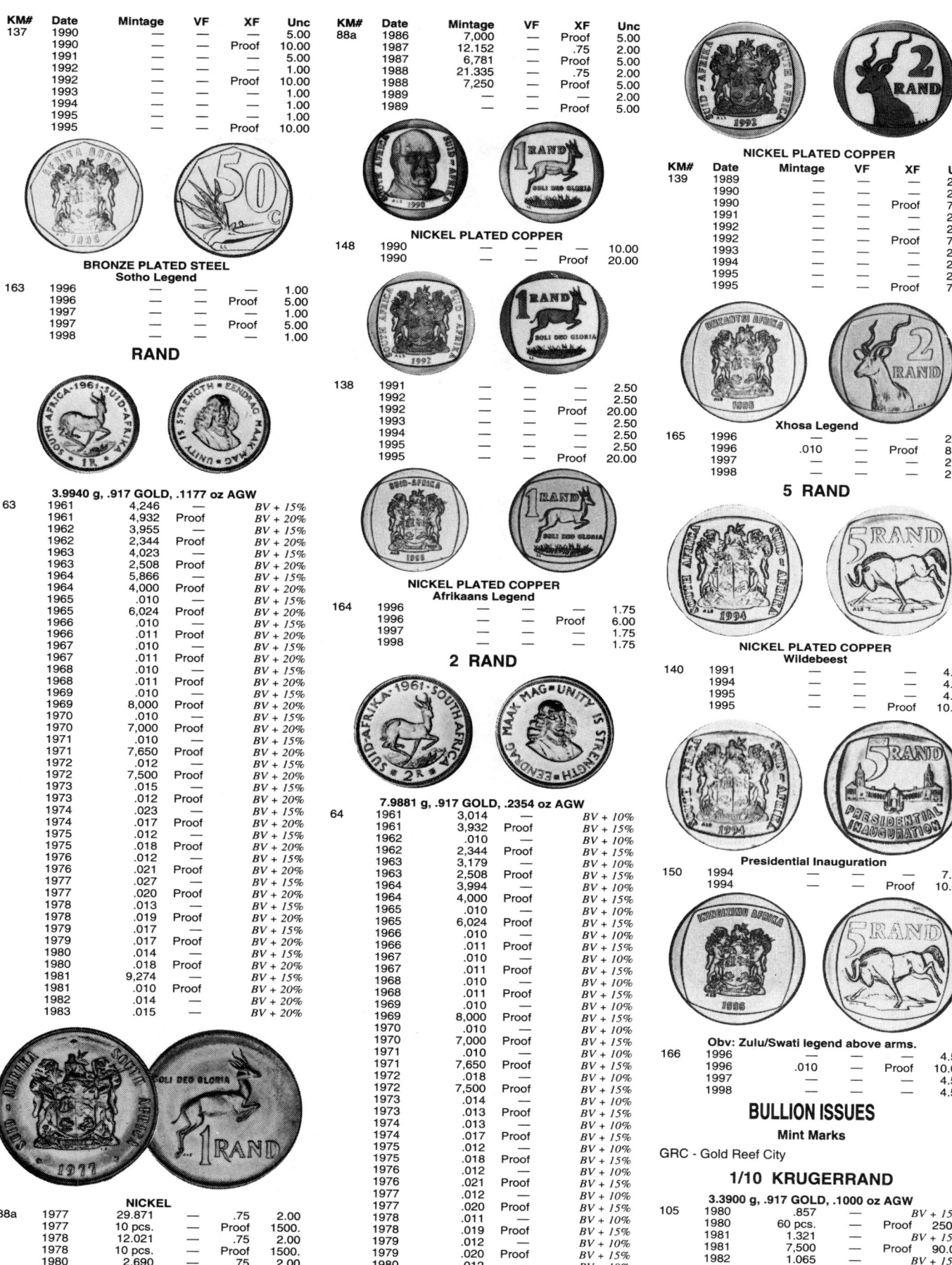

NICKEL

88a	1977	29.871	—	.75	2.00
	1977	10 pcs.	—	Proof	1500.
	1978	12.021	—	.75	2.00
	1978	10 pcs.	—	Proof	1500.
	1980	2.690	—	.75	2.00
	1981	2.035	—	.75	2.00
	1983	7.182	—	.75	2.00
	1983	10 pcs.	—	Proof	1500.
	1984	5.736	—	.75	2.00
	1984	.011	—	Proof	5.00
	1986	1.570	—	.75	2.00

KM#	Date	Mintage	VF	XF	Unc
88a	1986	7,000	—	Proof	5.00
	1987	12.152	—	.75	2.00
	1987	6,781	—	Proof	5.00
	1988	21.335	—	.75	2.00
	1988	7,250	—	Proof	5.00
	1989	—	—	—	2.00
	1989	—	—	Proof	5.00

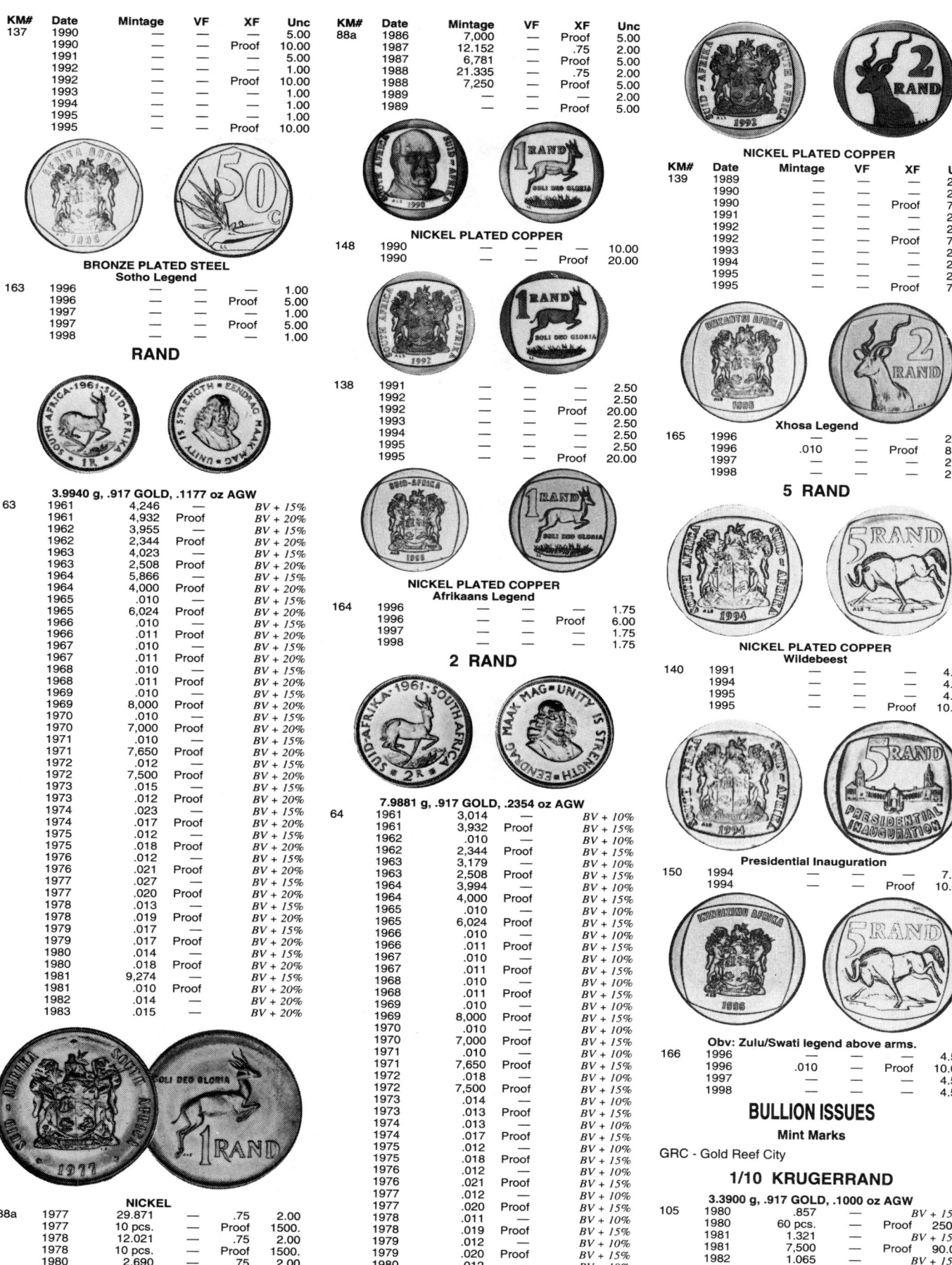

NICKEL PLATED COPPER

148	1990	—	—	—	10.00
	1990	—	—	Proof	20.00

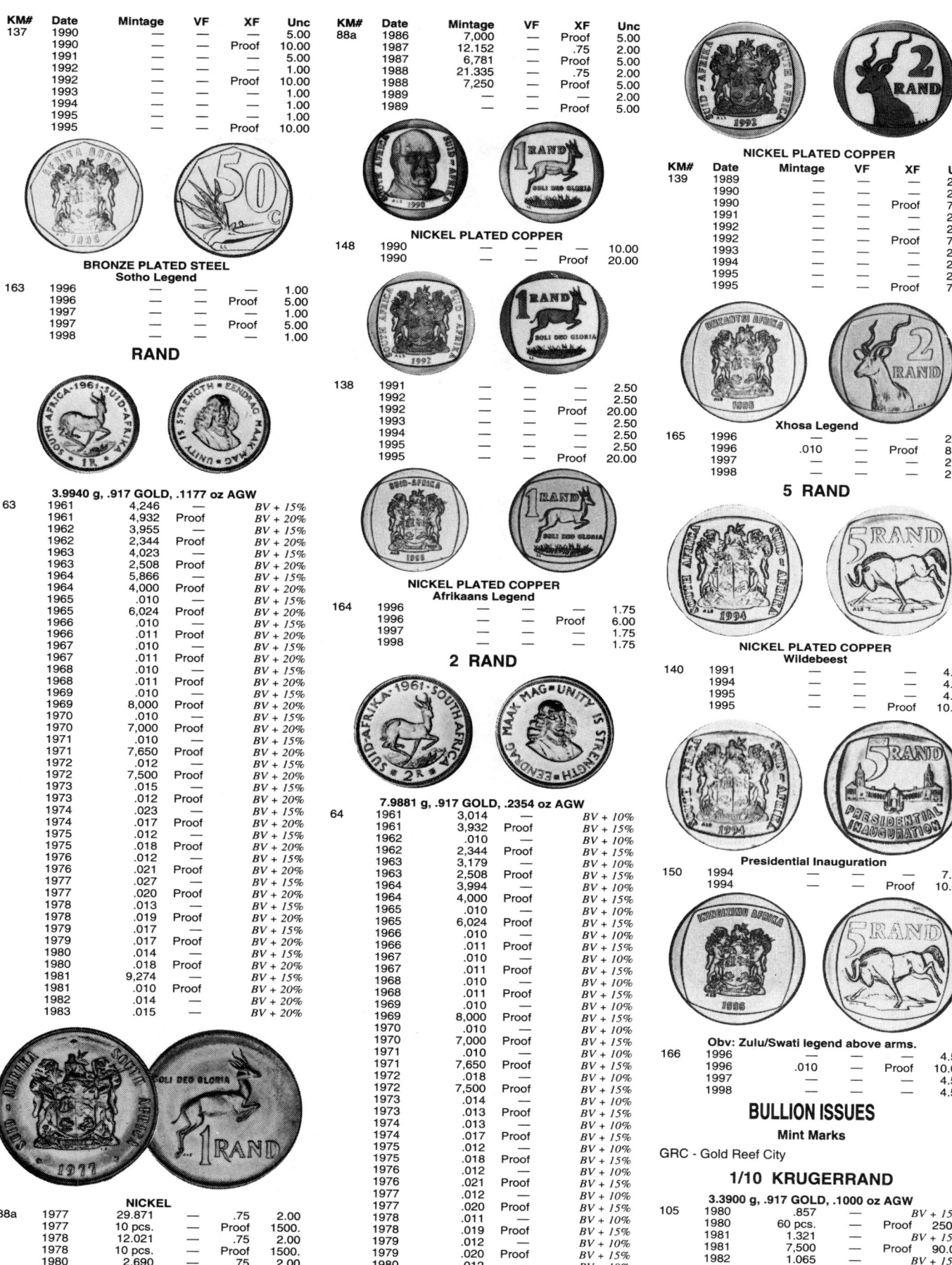

138	1991	—	—	—	2.50
	1992	—	—	—	2.50
	1992	—	—	Proof	20.00
	1993	—	—	—	2.50
	1994	—	—	—	2.50
	1995	—	—	—	2.50
	1995	—	—	Proof	20.00

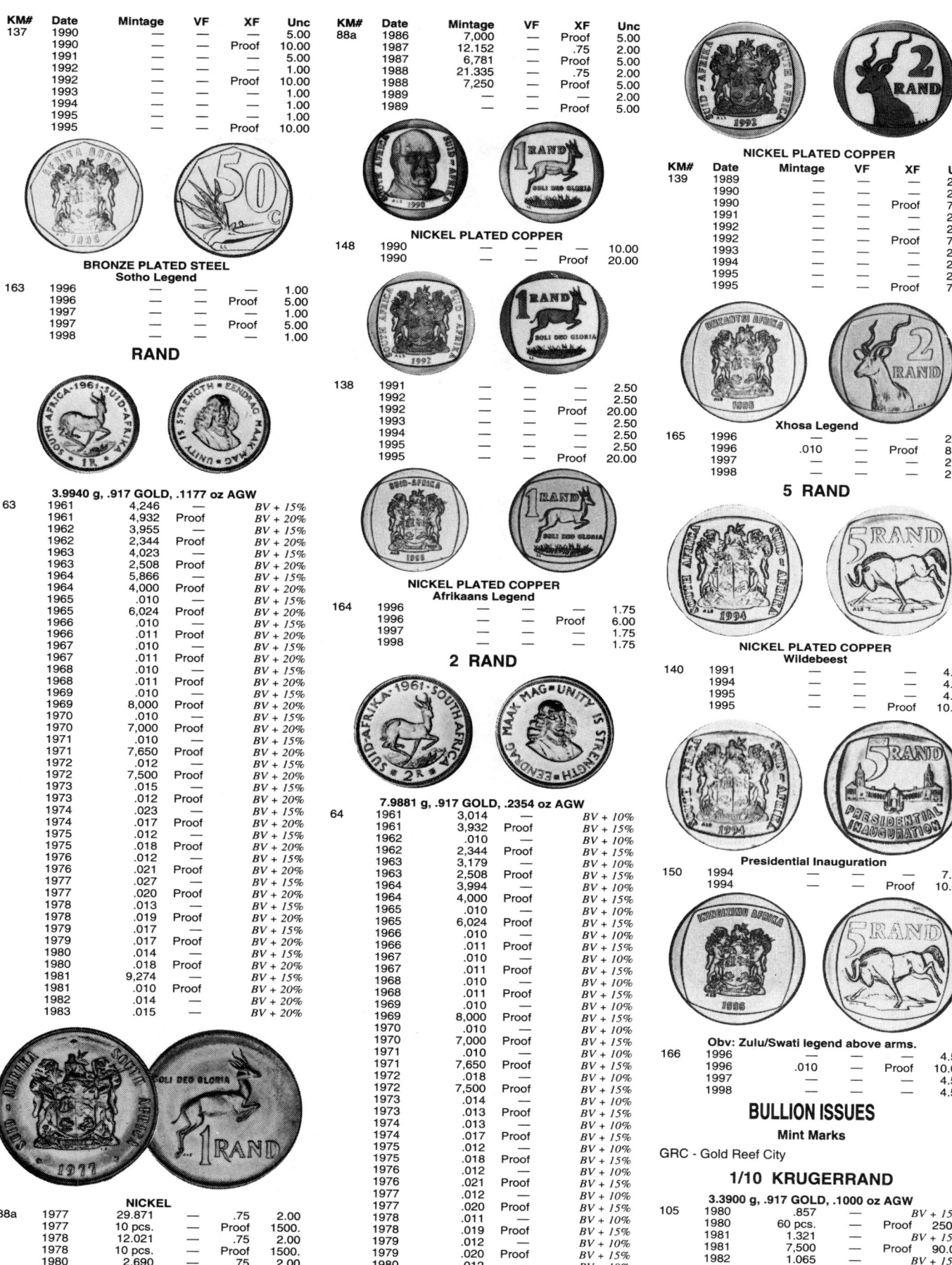

NICKEL PLATED COPPER
Afrikaans Legend

164	1996	—	—	—	1.75
	1996	—	—	Proof	6.00
	1997	—	—	—	1.75
	1998	—	—	—	1.75

2 RAND

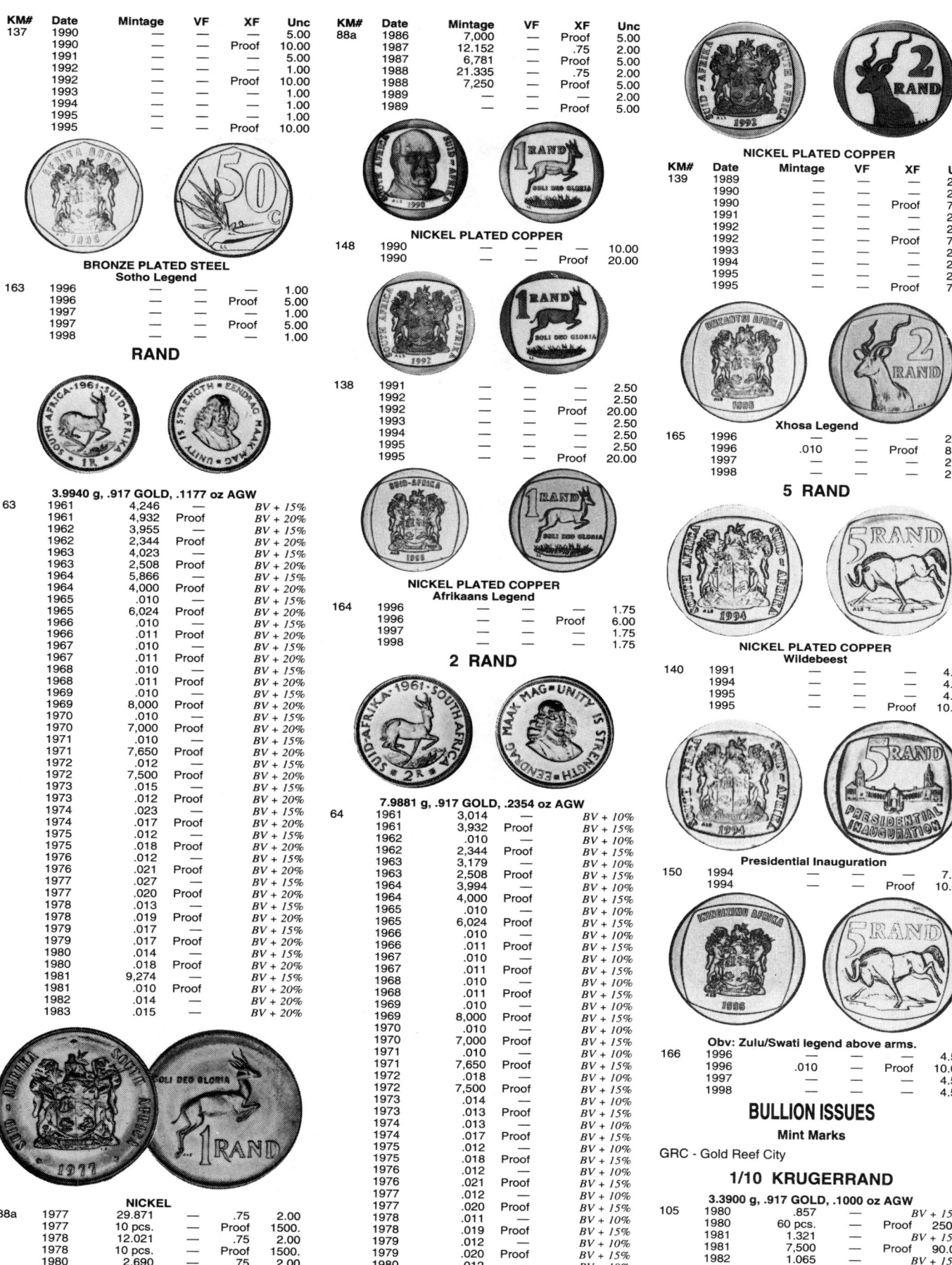

7.9881 g, .917 GOLD, .2354 oz AGW

64	1961	3,014	—		BV + 10%
	1961	3,932	Proof		BV + 15%
	1962	.010	—		BV + 10%
	1962	2,344	Proof		BV + 15%
	1963	3,179	—		BV + 10%
	1963	2,508	Proof		BV + 15%
	1964	3,994	—		BV + 10%
	1964	4,000	Proof		BV + 15%
	1965	.010	—		BV + 10%
	1965	6,024	Proof		BV + 15%
	1966	.010	—		BV + 10%
	1966	.011	Proof		BV + 15%
	1967	.010	—		BV + 10%
	1967	.011	Proof		BV + 15%
	1968	.010	—		BV + 10%
	1968	.011	Proof		BV + 15%
	1969	.010	—		BV + 10%
	1969	8,000	Proof		BV + 15%
	1970	.010	—		BV + 10%
	1970	7,000	Proof		BV + 15%
	1971	.010	—		BV + 10%
	1971	7,650	Proof		BV + 15%
	1972	.018	—		BV + 10%
	1972	7,500	Proof		BV + 15%
	1973	.014	—		BV + 10%
	1973	.013	Proof		BV + 15%
	1974	.013	—		BV + 10%
	1974	.017	Proof		BV + 15%
	1975	.012	—		BV + 10%
	1975	.018	Proof		BV + 15%
	1976	.012	—		BV + 10%
	1976	.021	Proof		BV + 15%
	1977	.012	—		BV + 10%
	1977	.020	Proof		BV + 15%
	1978	.011	—		BV + 10%
	1978	.019	Proof		BV + 15%
	1979	.012	—		BV + 10%
	1979	.020	Proof		BV + 15%
	1980	.012	—		BV + 10%
	1980	.018	Proof		BV + 15%
	1981	8,538	—		BV + 10%
	1981	.010	Proof		BV + 15%
	1982	2,030	—		BV + 15%
	1982	.012	Proof		BV + 15%
	1983	.015	—		BV + 15%

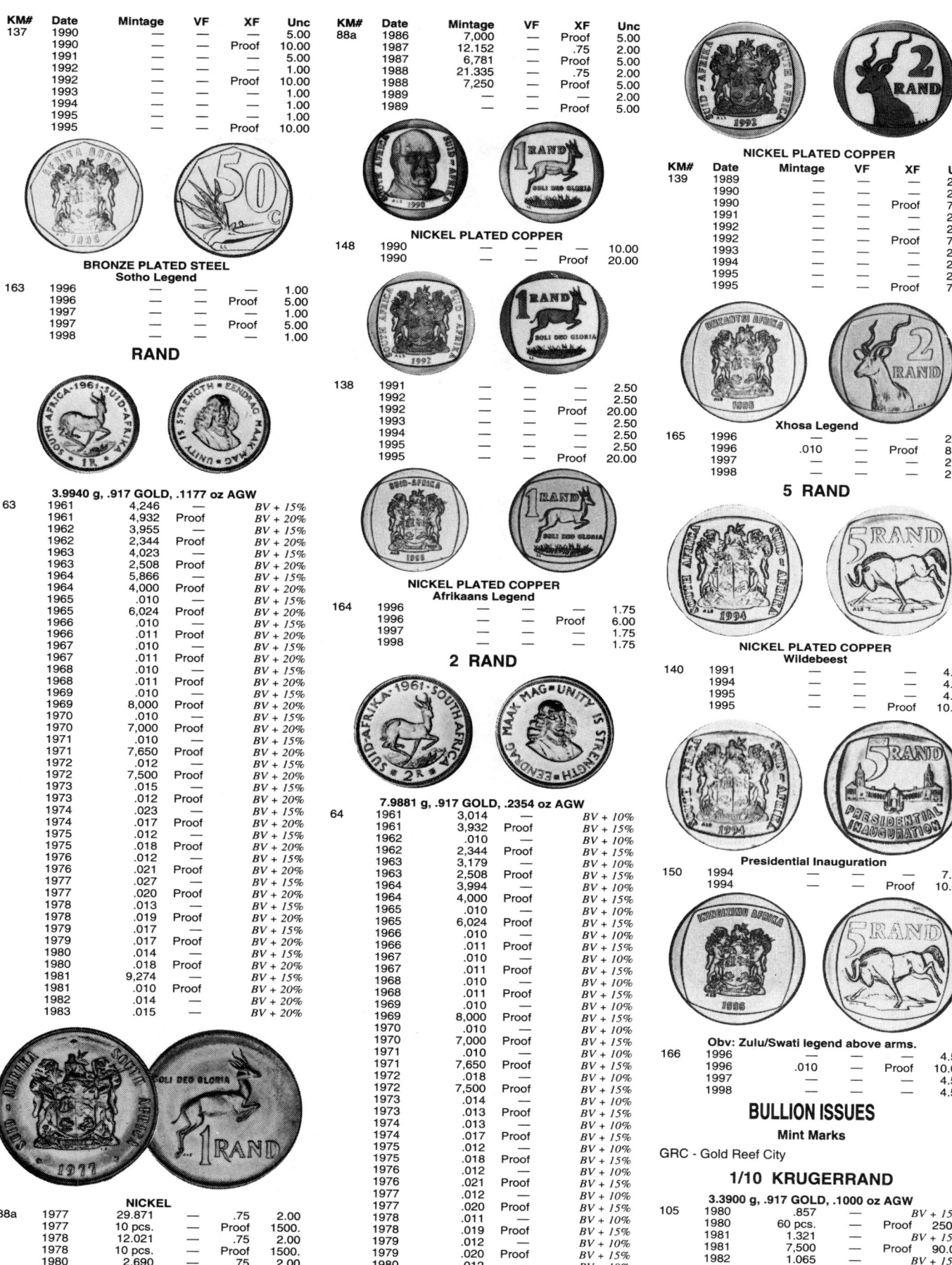

NICKEL PLATED COPPER

KM#	Date	Mintage	VF	XF	Unc
139	1989	—	—	—	2.00
	1990	—	—	—	2.00
	1990	—	—	Proof	7.50
	1991	—	—	—	2.00
	1992	—	—	—	2.00
	1992	—	—	Proof	7.50
	1993	—	—	—	2.00
	1994	—	—	—	2.00
	1995	—	—	—	2.00
	1995	—	—	Proof	7.50

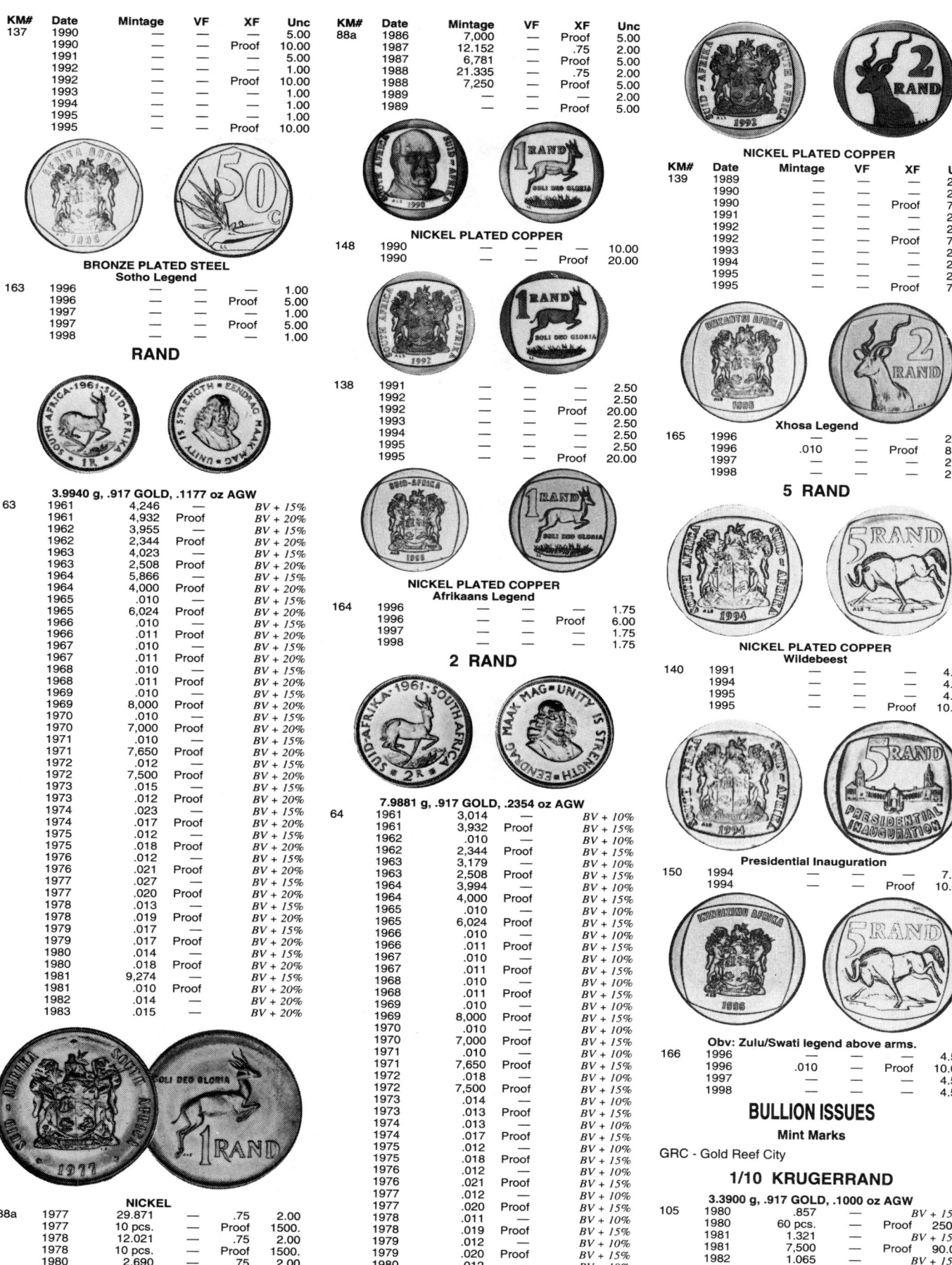

Xhosa Legend

165	1996	—	—	—	2.00
	1996	.010	—	Proof	8.00
	1997	—	—	—	2.00
	1998	—	—	—	2.00

5 RAND

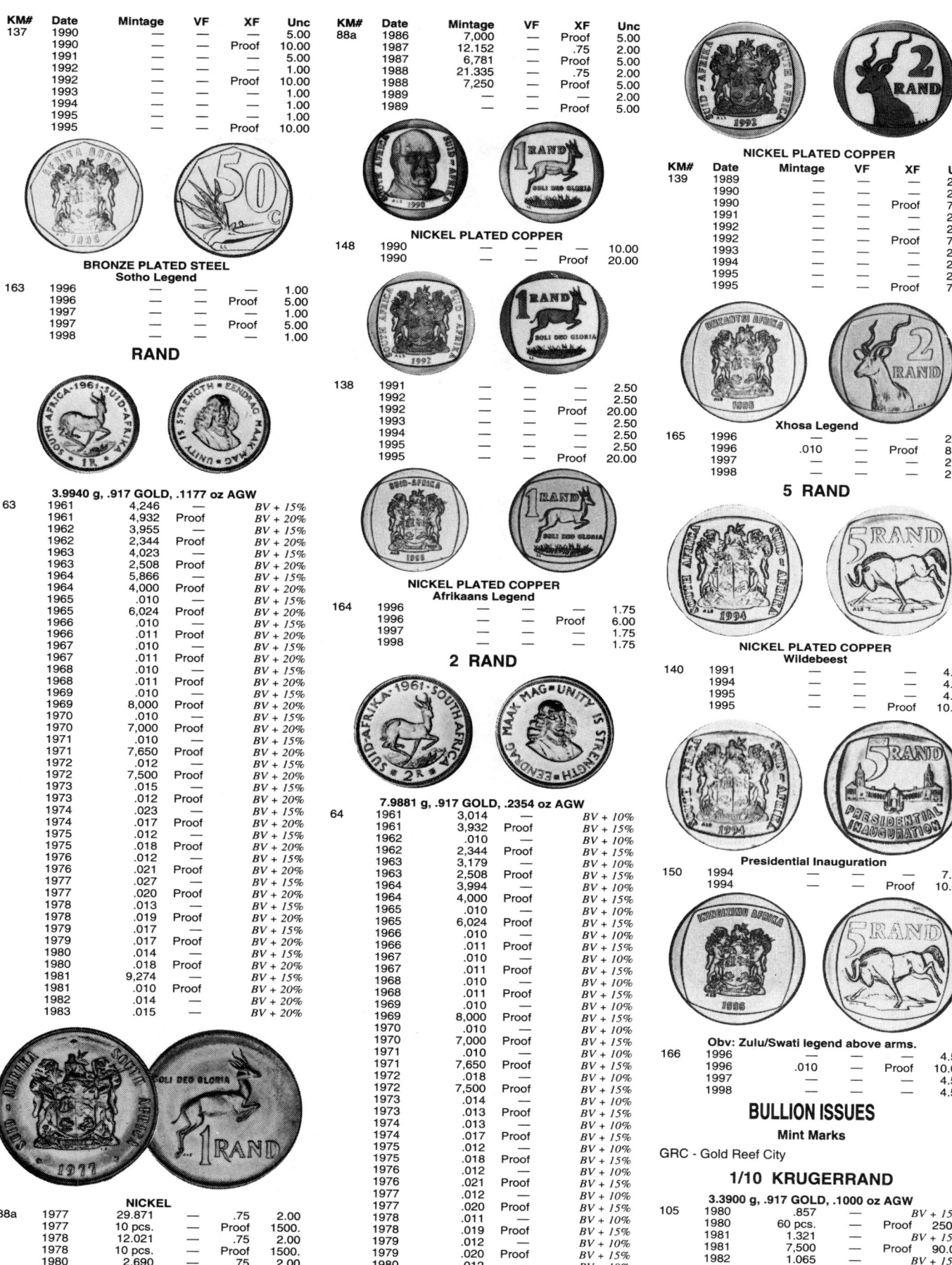

NICKEL PLATED COPPER
Wildebeest

140	1991	—	—	—	4.50
	1994	—	—	—	4.50
	1995	—	—	—	4.50
	1995	—	—	Proof	10.00

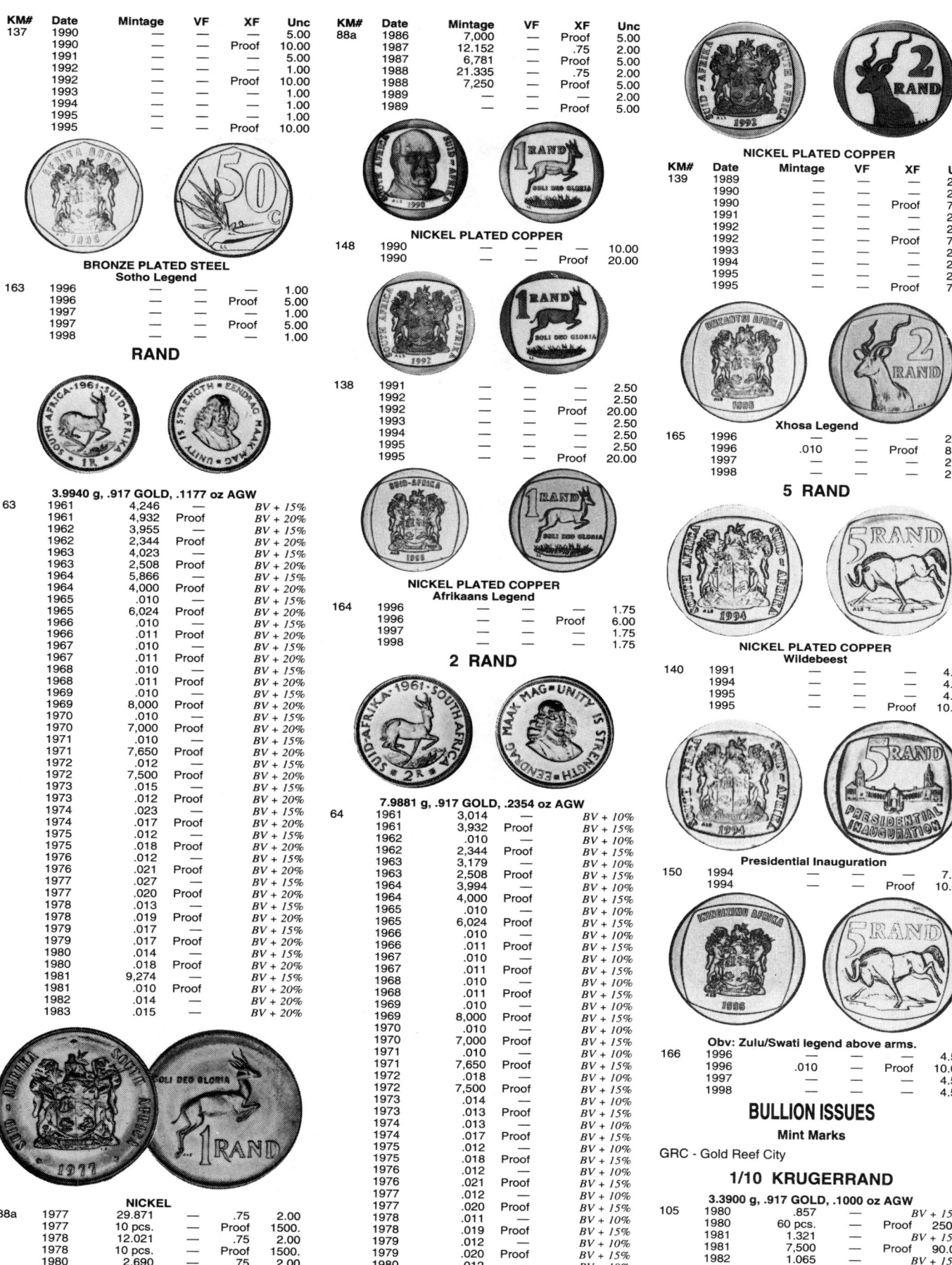

Presidential Inauguration

150	1994	—	—	—	7.50
	1994	—	—	Proof	10.00

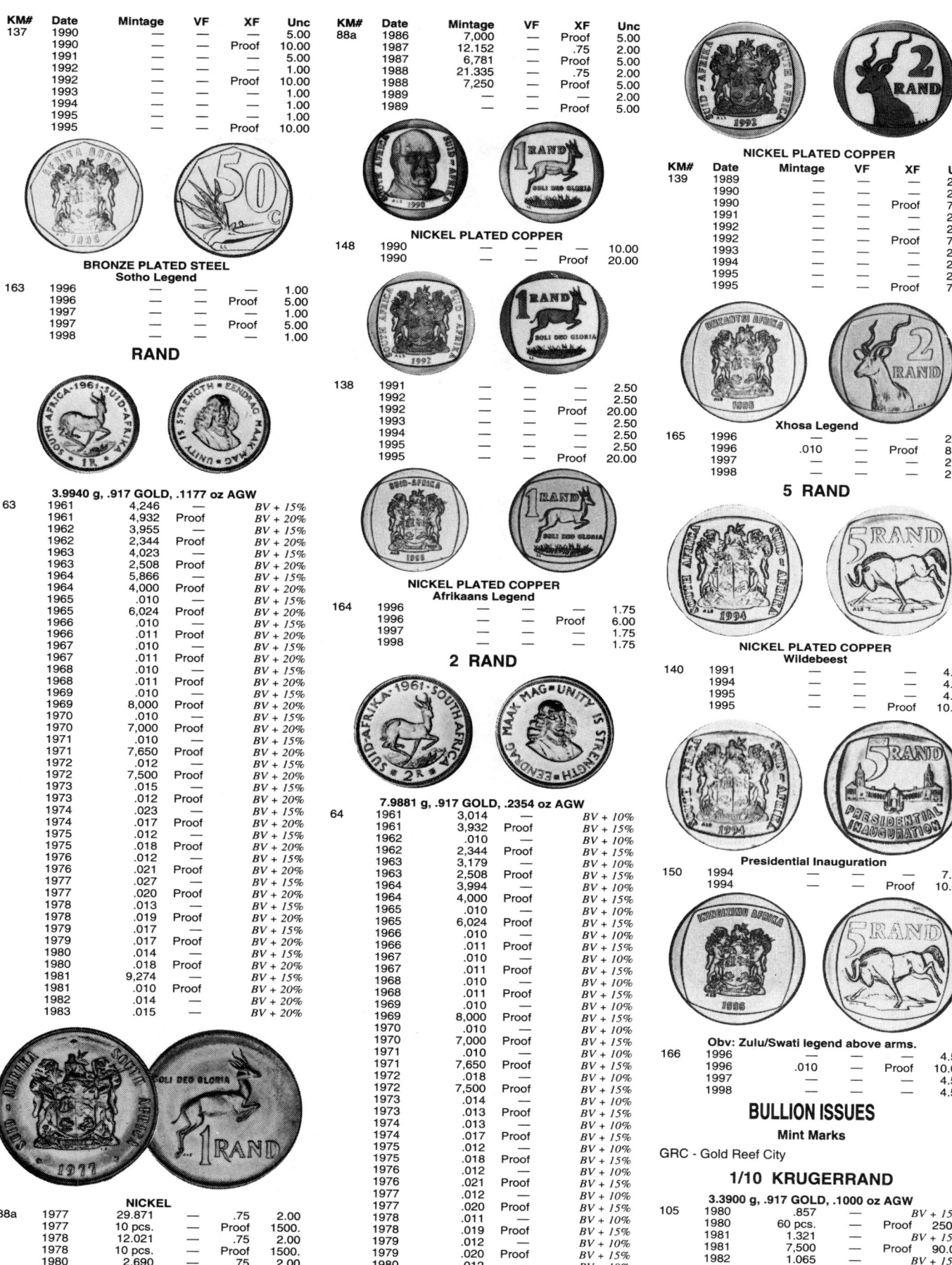

Obv: Zulu/Swati legend above arms.

166	1996	—	—	—	4.50
	1996	.010	—	Proof	10.00
	1997	—	—	—	4.50
	1998	—	—	—	4.50

BULLION ISSUES

Mint Marks

GRC - Gold Reef City

1/10 KRUGERRAND

3.3900 g, .917 GOLD, .1000 oz AGW

105	1980	.857	—		BV + 15%
	1980	60 pcs.	—	Proof	2500.
	1981	1.321	—		BV + 15%
	1981	7,500	—	Proof	90.00
	1982	1.065	—		BV + 15%
	1982	.011	—	Proof	90.00
	1983	.508	—		BV + 15%
	1983	.012	—	Proof	90.00
	1984	.898	—		BV + 15%
	1984	.013	—	Proof	90.00
	1985	.282	—		BV + 15%
	1985	6,700	—	Proof	90.00

KM#	Date	Mintage	VF	XF	Unc
105	1986	.087	—	BV + 15%	
	1986	8,001	—	Proof	90.00
	1987	.053	—	BV + 15%	
	1987	6,065	—	Proof	90.00
	1987 GRC	1,126	—	Proof	400.00
	1988	.087	—	BV + 15%	
	1988	2,056	—	Proof	90.00
	1988 GRC	949 pcs.	—	Proof	400.00
	1989	—	—	BV + 15%	
	1989	3,316	—	Proof	90.00
	1989 GRC	377 pcs.	—	Proof	1000.
	1990	—	—	BV + 15%	
	1990	3,459	—	Proof	90.00
	1990 GRC	1,096	—	Proof	275.00
	1991	3,524	—	Proof	90.00
	1991 GRC	426 pcs.	—	Proof	275.00
	1992	1,789	—	Proof	90.00
	1993	—	—	Proof	100.00
	1994	—	—	Proof	100.00
	1995	750 pcs.	—	Proof	175.00
	1996	4,000	—	Proof	90.00
	1998	—	—	Proof	90.00

1/4 KRUGERRAND

8.4800 g, .917 GOLD, .2500 oz AGW

KM#	Date	Mintage	VF	XF	Unc
106	1980	.534	—	BV + 10%	
	1980	60 pcs.	—	Proof	3000.
	1981	.726	—	BV + 10%	
	1981	7,500	—	Proof	175.00
	1982	1.269	—	BV + 10%	
	1982	.011	—	Proof	175.00
	1983	.064	—	BV + 10%	
	1983	.012	—	Proof	175.00
	1984	.503	—	BV + 10%	
	1984	.013	—	Proof	175.00
	1985	.594	—	BV + 10%	
	1985	6,700	—	Proof	175.00
	1986	8,001	—	Proof	175.00
	1987	6,050	—	Proof	175.00
	1987 GRC	1,121	—	Proof	500.00
	1988	5,946	—	BV + 10%	
	1988	2,056	—	Proof	175.00
	1988 GRC	835 pcs.	—	Proof	500.00
	1989	—	—	BV + 10%	
	1989	3,316	—	Proof	175.00
	1989 GRC	318 pcs.	—	Proof	1400.
	1990	—	—	BV + 10%	
	1990	2,750	—	Proof	175.00
	1990 GRC	1,066	—	Proof	400.00
	1991	1,626	—	Proof	175.00
	1991 GRC	426 pcs.	—	Proof	400.00
	1992	1,629	—	Proof	175.00
	1993	—	—	Proof	200.00
	1994	—	—	Proof	200.00
	1995	750 pcs.	—	Proof	250.00
	1996	3,000	—	Proof	175.00
	1998	—	—	Proof	175.00

1/2 KRUGERRAND

16.9700 g, .917 GOLD, .5000 oz AGW

KM#	Date	Mintage	VF	XF	Unc
107	1980	.374	—	BV + 8%	
	1980	60 pcs.	—	Proof	3500.
	1981	.178	—	BV + 8%	
	1981	9,000	—	Proof	300.00
	1982	.429	—	BV + 8%	
	1982	.013	—	Proof	300.00
	1983	.060	—	BV + 8%	
	1983	.014	—	Proof	300.00
	1984	.187	—	BV + 8%	
	1984	9,900	—	Proof	300.00
	1985	.104	—	BV + 8%	
	1985	5,945	—	Proof	300.00
	1986	8,002	—	Proof	300.00
	1987	5,389	—	Proof	300.00
	1987 GRC	1,186	—	Proof	800.00
	1988	5,454	—	BV + 8%	
	1988	2,282	—	Proof	300.00
	1988 GRC	1,026	—	Proof	800.00
	1989	—	—	BV + 8%	
	1989	3,727	—	Proof	300.00
	1989 GRC	399 pcs.	—	Proof	1500.
	1990	—	—	BV + 8%	
	1990	2,850	—	Proof	300.00
	1990 GRC	1,066	—	Proof	500.00
	1991	3,459	—	Proof	300.00
	1991 GRC	426 pcs.	—	Proof	500.00
	1992	1,501	—	Proof	300.00
	1993			Proof	300.00

KM#	Date	Mintage	VF	XF	Unc
107	1994	—	—	Proof	300.00
	1995	750 pcs.	—	Proof	400.00
	1996	3,000	—	Proof	300.00
	1998	—	—	Proof	300.00

KRUGERRAND

33.9305 g, .917 GOLD, 1.0000 oz AGW

KM#	Date	Mintage	VF	XF	Unc
73	1967	.040	—		BV + 5%
	1967	.010	—	Proof	525.00
	1968	.020	—		BV + 5%
	1968 frosted bust and frosted reverse				
	*5,000	—	Proof	1000.	
	1968	8,956	—	Proof	550.00
	1969	.020	—		BV + 5%
	1969	.010	—	Proof	525.00

*NOTE: In 1967-1969 superior quality specimens exhibiting proof-like surfaces are known. In addition, the following varieties are known: 1968 with normal mirror like obverse and reverse; 1968 with mirror like obverse and frosted reverse; 1969 with normal mirror like obverse and reverse; and 1969 with frosted bust and reverse frosted.

	Date	Mintage	VF	XF	Unc
	1970	.211	—		BV + 5%
	1970	.010	—	Proof	500.00
	1971	.550	—		BV + 5%
	1971	6,000	—	Proof	500.00
	1972	.544	—		BV + 5%
	1972	6,625	—	Proof	500.00
	1973	.859	—		BV + 5%
	1973	.010	—	Proof	500.00
	1974	3.204	—		BV + 5%
	1974	6,352	—	Proof	500.00
	1975	4.804	—		BV + 5%
	1975	5,600	—	Proof	500.00
	1976	3.005	—		BV + 5%
	1976	6,600	—	Proof	500.00
	1977 188 serrations on edge				
		3.331	—		BV + 5%
	1977 188 serrations on edge				
		8,500	—	Proof	500.00
	1977 220 serrations on edge				
	Inc. Ab.		—		BV + 5%
	1977 220 serrations on edge				
	Inc. Ab.		—	Proof	500.00
	1978	6.012	—		BV + 5%
	1978	.010	—	Proof	500.00
	1979	4.941	—		BV + 5%
	1979	.012	—	Proof	500.00
	1980	3.143	—		BV + 5%
	1980	.012	—	Proof	500.00
	1981	3.560	—		BV + 5%
	1981	.013	—	Proof	500.00
	1982	2.566	—		BV + 5%
	1982	.017	—	Proof	500.00
	1983	3.368	—		BV + 5%
	1983	.019	—	Proof	500.00
	1984	2.070	—		BV + 5%
	1984	.014	—	Proof	500.00
	1985	.875	—		BV + 5%
	1985	.010	—	Proof	500.00
	1986	.020	—	Proof	500.00
	1987	.011	—		BV + 5%
	1987	.011	—	Proof	500.00
	1987 GRC	1,160	—	Proof	1200.
	1988	.615	—		BV + 5%
	1988	4,268	—	Proof	500.00
	1988 GRC	1,220	—	Proof	1200.
	1989	—	—		BV + 5%
	1989	5,070	—	Proof	500.00
	1989 GRC	987 pcs.	—	Proof	1600.
	1990	—	—		BV + 5%
	1990	3,032	—	Proof	500.00
	1990 GRC	1,066	—	Proof	1600.
	1991	2,181	—	Proof	500.00
	1991 GRC	426 pcs.	—	Proof	1600.
	1992	2,067	—	Proof	500.00
	1995	750 pcs.	—	Proof	800.00
	1996	3,000	—	Proof	625.00
	1998	—	—	Proof	600.00

KM#	Date	Mintage	VF	XF	Unc
107	1994	—	—	Proof	300.00
	1995	750 pcs.	—	Proof	400.00
	1996	3,000	—	Proof	300.00
	1998	—	—	Proof	300.00

SPAIN

The Spanish State, forming the greater part of the Iberian Peninsula of southwest Europe, has an area of 195,988 sq. mi. (504,714 sq. km.) and a population of 39.4 million including the Balearic and the Canary Islands. Capital: Madrid. The economy is based on agriculture, industry and tourism. Machinery, fruit, vegetables and chemicals are exported.

It isn't known when man first came to the Iberian Peninsula - the Altamira caves off the Cantabrian coast approximately 50 miles west of Santander were fashioned in Palaeolithic times. Spain was a battleground for centuries before it became a united nation, fought for by Phoenicians, Carthaginians, Greeks, Celts, Romans, Vandals, Visigoths and Moors. Ferdinand and Isabella destroyed the last Moorish stronghold in 1492, freeing the national energy and resources for the era of discovery and colonization that would make Spain the most powerful country in Europe during the 16th century. After the destruction of the Spanish Armada, 1588, Spain never again played a major role in European politics. Forcing Ferdinand to give up his throne and placing him under military guard at Valencay in 1808, Napoleonic France ruled Spain until 1814. When the monarchy was restored in 1814 it continued, only interrupted by the short-lived republic of 1873-74, until the exile of Alfonso XIII in 1931 when the Second Republic was established.

The doomed republic was trapped in a tug-of-war between the right and left wing forces inevitably resulting in the Spanish Civil War of 1936-38. The leftist Republicans were supported by the USSR and the International Brigade, which consisted of mainly communist volunteers from all over the western world. The right wing Nationalists were supported by the Fascist governments of Italy and Germany. Under the leadership of Gen. Francisco Franco, the Nationalists emerged victorious and immediately embarked on a program of reconstruction and neutrality as dictated by the new "Caudillo" (leader) Franco.

The monarchy was reconstituted in 1947 under the regency of General Francisco Franco; the king designate to be crowned after Franco's death. Franco died on Nov. 20, 1975. Two days after his passing, Juan Carlos de Borbon, the grandson of Alfonso XIII, was proclaimed King of Spain.

RULERS

Alfonso XIII, 1886-1931
  2nd Republic and Civil War, 1931-1939
Francisco Franco, caudillo, 1939-1947
  Caudillo and regent, 1947-1975
Juan Carlos I, 1975-

NOTE: From 1868 to 1982, two dates may be found on most Spanish coinage. The larger date is the year of authorization and the smaller date incused on the two 6-pointed-stars found on most types is the year of issue. The latter appears in parentheses in these listings.

MINT MARKS

Until 1980

OM - Oeschger Mesdach & Co.
3-pointed star - Segovia after 1868
4-pointed star - Jubia
6-pointed star - Madrid
7-pointed star - Seville
8-pointed star - Barcelona
Letters after date are initials of mint officials.

After 1982

Crowned M - Madrid

THIRD DECIMAL COINAGE

100 Centimos = 1 Peseta

CENTIMO

BRONZE
Mint mark: 6-pointed star

KM#	Date	Mintage	Fine	VF	XF	Unc
726 (Y96)	1906(6) SL-V	7.500	.35	.75	1.50	4.00
	1906(6) SM-V	Inc. Ab.	100.00	200.00	350.00	700.00

KM#	Date	Mintage	Fine	VF	XF	Unc
731 (Y98)	1911(1) PC-V	1.462	3.50	7.00	20.00	50.00
	1912(2) PC-V	2.109	.75	1.00	2.00	7.50
	1913(3) PC-V	1.429	1.00	1.75	4.00	12.00

2 CENTIMOS

BRONZE
Mint mark: 6-pointed star

KM#	Date	Mintage	Fine	VF	XF	Unc
722 (Y97)	1904(04) SM-V	10.000	.35	.75	2.50	10.00
	1905(05) SM-V	5.000	.35	.75	2.50	10.00

KM#	Date	Mintage	Fine	VF	XF	Unc
732 (Y99)	1911(11) PC-V	2.284	.35	.75	2.50	10.00
	1912(12) PC-V	5.216	.35	.75	3.00	12.00

25 CENTIMOS

COPPER-NICKEL

KM#	Date	Mintage	Fine	VF	XF	Unc
740 (Y100)	1925 PC-S	8.001	.35	1.00	5.00	20.00
	1925	—	—	—	Proof	Rare

KM#	Date	Mintage	Fine	VF	XF	Unc
742 (Y101)	1927 PC-S	12.000	.35	1.00	2.00	15.00

50 CENTIMOS

2.5000 g, .835 SILVER, .0671 oz ASW

KM#	Date	Mintage	Fine	VF	XF	Unc
723 (Y92)	1904(04) SM-V	4.851	.75	2.25	5.00	15.00
	1904(10) PC-V	1.303	.75	2.25	5.00	16.00

KM#	Date	Mintage	Fine	VF	XF	Unc
730 (Y93)	1910(10) PC-V	4.526	.75	2.25	7.00	25.00

KM#	Date	Mintage	Fine	VF	XF	Unc
741 (Y102)	1926 PC-S	4.000	.75	2.00	3.00	10.00

PESETA

5.0000 g, .835 SILVER, .1342 oz ASW
Mint mark: 6-pointed star

KM#	Date	Mintage	Fine	VF	XF	Unc
706 (Y88)	1901(01) SM-V	8.449	2.00	6.00	20.00	80.00
	1902(02) SM-V	2.599	10.00	20.00	50.00	200.00

NOTE: Earlier dates (1896-1900) exist for this type. Prices are for coins with full star dates. Partial star dates sell for less. No star dates have limited collector appeal.

KM#	Date	Mintage	Fine	VF	XF	Unc
721 (Y94)	1903(03) SM-V	10.602	2.00	5.50	20.00	65.00
	1904(04) SM-V	5.294	2.00	6.00	25.00	75.00
	1905(05) SM-V	.492	30.00	70.00	280.00	800.00

2 PESETAS

10.0000 g, .835 SILVER, .2685 oz ASW
Mint mark: 6-pointed star

KM#	Date	Mintage	Fine	VF	XF	Unc
725 (Y95)	1905(05) SM-V	3.589	4.50	8.00	16.00	30.00

20 PESETAS

6.4516 g, .900 GOLD, .1867 oz AGW
Mint mark: 6-pointed star

KM#	Date	Mintage	Fine	VF	XF	Unc
724 (Y91)	1904(04) SM-V	3.814	1000.	2200.	2700.	4000.

REPUBLIC

1931-1939

5 CENTIMOS

IRON
Mint mark: 6-pointed star

KM#	Date	Mintage	Fine	VF	XF	Unc
752 (Y103)	1937	10.000	.35	.75	2.00	8.50

10 CENTIMOS

IRON

KM#	Date	Mintage	Fine	VF	XF	Unc
756 (Y-A103)	1938	1.000	350.00	650.00	1250.	2500.

25 CENTIMOS

COPPER-NICKEL

KM#	Date	Mintage	Fine	VF	XF	Unc
751 (Y107)	1934	12.272	.20	.50	2.00	10.00

Mint: Vienna

KM#	Date	Mintage	Fine	VF	XF	Unc
753 (Y109)	1937	42.000	.20	.40	1.00	3.00

NOTE: This coin was issued by way of decree April 5, 1938, by Franco and the Nationalist forces that controlled the majority of Spain by this point in time.

COPPER

KM#	Date	Mintage	Fine	VF	XF	Unc
757 (Y104)	1938	45.500	.75	2.00	4.00	9.00

50 CENTIMOS

COPPER
Mint mark: 6-pointed star
Rev: Border of dots.

KM#	Date	Mintage	Fine	VF	XF	Unc
754.1 (Y105)	1937(34)	50.000	.35	1.00	3.00	10.00
	1937(36)	1.000	.35	1.50	4.00	10.00
	1937 w/o stars Inc. Ab.		2.00	3.50	7.50	20.00

NOTE: Several varieties exist.

BRONZE

KM#	Date	Mintage	Fine	VF	XF	Unc
754.1a	1937(34)	—	—	—	—	—

COPPER
Rev: Border of rectangles.

KM#	Date	Mintage	Fine	VF	XF	Unc
754.2	1937(36)	Inc. Ab.	.40	1.75	5.00	12.50

PESETA

5.0000 g, .835 SILVER, .1342 oz ASW
Mint mark: 6-pointed star

KM#	Date	Mintage	Fine	VF	XF	Unc
750 (Y108)	1933(3-4)	2.000	2.00	5.00	10.00	20.00

NOTE: Several varieties exist.

BRASS

KM#	Date	Mintage	VF	XF	Unc	BU
755 (Y106)	1937	50.000	.50	1.00	2.00	5.00

NATIONALIST GOVERNMENT

1939-1947

5 CENTIMOS

NOTE: All Unc. and BU coins must have full strike including letters.

ALUMINUM
Mint mark: 6-pointed star

KM#	Date	Mintage	VF	XF	Unc	BU
765	1940	175.000	2.00	5.00	20.00	30.00
(Y110)	1941	202.107	.50	2.00	8.00	12.00
	1945	221.500	.25	1.00	5.00	10.00
	1953	31.573	10.00	20.00	40.00	50.00

10 CENTIMOS

ALUMINUM
Mint mark: 6-pointed star

KM#	Date	Mintage	VF	XF	Unc	BU
766	1940	225.000	1.50	5.00	20.00	25.00
(Y111)	1941	247.981	.25	2.00	8.00	12.00
	1945	250.000	.25	1.00	5.00	10.00
	1953	865.850	.10	.50	2.00	4.00

NOTE: Varieties exist.

PESETA

ALUMINUM-BRONZE
Mint mark: 6-pointed star

KM#	Date	Mintage	VF	XF	Unc	BU
767	1944	150.000	.25	5.00	10.00	20.00
(Y112)	1946(48)	—	—	—	Rare	—

KINGDOM

1949-

NOTE: The Madrid Mint has produced coinage in different qualities. Qualities of issue are designated in ( ) after each date as follows:

(M) MATTE - Normal circulation strike or a dull finish.

(U) SPECIAL UNCIRCULATED - Polished or proof-like in appearance without any frosted features.

10 CENTIMOS

ALUMINUM
Mint mark: 6-pointed star

KM#	Date	Mintage	VF	XF	Unc	BU
790	1959	900.000	—	—	.10	.15
(Y121)	1959	.101	—	—	Proof	1.50

50 CENTIMOS

NOTE: All 50 Centimos listed here are no longer legal tender.

COPPER-NICKEL
Mint mark: 6-pointed star
Rev: Arrows pointing down.

KM#	Date	Mintage	VF	XF	Unc	BU
776 (Y115)	1949(51)	.990	2.00	6.00	12.00	20.00

Rev: Arrows pointing up.

KM#	Date	Mintage	VF	XF	Unc	BU
777	1949(51)	8.010	.25	2.00	8.00	12.00
(Y116)	1949(E51)	*5,000	—	—	450.00	700.00
	1949(52)	18.567	.15	1.50	7.00	10.00
	1949(53)	17.500	.15	3.00	20.00	25.00
	1949(54)	37.000	.15	2.50	8.00	12.00
	1949(56)	38.000	.15	2.00	7.00	12.00
	1949(62)	31.000	.15	1.00	4.00	5.00
	1963(63)	4.000	.15	5.00	15.00	20.00
	1963(64)	20.000	.10	.25	1.50	2.00
	1963(65)	14.000	.10	.25	1.50	2.00

***NOTE:** Issued to commemorate a numismatic exposition December 2, 1951. An E replaces the 19 on the lower star.

ALUMINUM

KM#	Date	Mintage	VF	XF	Unc	BU
795	1966(67)	80.000	—	.10	.25	1.00
(Y124)	1966(68)	100.000	—	.10	.25	.50
	1966(69)	50.000	—	.10	1.00	2.00
	1966(70)	.023	—	—	Proof	80.00
	1966(71)	99.000	—	.10	.25	.50
	1966(72)	2.283	—	.10	1.00	2.00
	1966(72)	.023	—	—	Proof	4.00
	1966(73)	10.000	—	.10	.25	.50
	1966(73)	.028	—	—	Proof	1.00
	1966(74)	.025	—	—	Proof	25.00
	1966(75)	.075	—	—	Proof	5.00

COPPER-NICKEL

KM#	Date	Mintage	VF	XF	Unc	BU
805	1975(76)	4.060	—	.10	.25	.50
(Y126)	1975(76)	—	—	—	Proof	1.00

ALUMINUM
World Cup Soccer Games

KM#	Date	Mintage	VF	XF	Unc	BU
815 (Y132)	1980(80)	15.000	—	.10	.25	.50

PESETA

ALUMINUM-BRONZE
Mint mark: 6-pointed star

KM#	Date	Mintage	VF	XF	Unc	BU
775	1947(48)	15.000	1.00	5.00	25.00	50.00
(Y113)	1947(49)	27.600	.75	4.00	25.00	50.00
	1947(50)	4.000	4.00	10.00	75.00	150.00
	1947(51)	9.185	2.00	5.00	50.00	125.00
	1947(E51)	*5,000	—	—	450.00	700.00
	1947(52)	19.195	1.00	3.00	12.00	40.00
	1947(53)	34.000	.75	2.00	10.00	40.00
	1947(54)	50.000	.75	2.00	10.00	40.00
	1947(56)	—	10.00	30.00	100.00	200.00
	1953(54)	40.272	2.00	5.00	25.00	50.00
	1953(56)	118.000	.10	.25	2.00	3.00
	1953(60)	45.160	.10	3.00	10.00	25.00
	1953(61)	25.830	.10	2.00	8.00	20.00
	1953(62)	66.252	.10	.20	1.50	2.00
	1953(63)	37.000	.10	.75	3.00	5.00
	1963(63)	36.000	.10	.50	3.00	6.00
	1963(64)	80.000	.10	.20	.75	1.00
	1963(65)	70.000	.10	.20	.75	1.00
	1963(66)	63.000	.10	.20	1.00	2.00
	1963(67)	11.300	1.00	2.00	10.00	20.00

***NOTE:** Issued to commemorate a numismatic exposition December 2, 1951. An E replaces 19 on the lower star.

KM#	Date	Mintage	VF	XF	Unc	BU
796	1966(67)	59.000	.10	.20	1.00	2.00
(Y125)	1966(68)	120.000	.10	.20	1.00	2.00
	1966(69)	120.000	.10	.20	1.00	2.00
	1966(70)	75.000	.10	.20	1.00	2.00
	1966(71)	115.270	.10	.20	.75	1.00
	1966(72)	106.000	—	.10	.50	.75
	1966(72)	.023	—	—	Proof	1.50
	1966(73)	152.000	—	.10	.50	.75
	1966(73)	.028	—	—	Proof	1.00
	1966(74)	181.000	—	.10	.50	.75
	1966(74)	.025	—	—	Proof	1.00
	1966(75)	227.580	—	.10	.25	.35
	1966(75)	.025	—	—	Proof	.50

KM#	Date	Mintage	VF	XF	Unc	BU
806	1975(76)	170.380	—	.10	.25	.35
(Y127)	1975(76)	177.080	—	—	Proof	.75
	1975(77)	243.380	—	.10	.25	.35
	1975(77)	I.A.	—	—	Proof	.75
	1975(78)	*603.320	—	.10	.25	.35
	1975(79)	507.000	—	.10	.25	.35
	1975(79)	—	—	—	Proof	.75
	1975(80)	590.000	—	.10	.25	.35

***NOTE:** Two varieties of tilde size for the n in Espana exist of this date.

World Cup Soccer Games

KM#	Date	Mintage	VF	XF	Unc	BU
816	1980(80)	I.A.	—	.10	.20	.30
(Y133)	1980(81)	385.000	—	.10	.25	.35
	1980(82)	333.000	—	.10	.25	.35

ALUMINUM

KM#	Date	Mintage	VF	XF	Unc	BU
821	1982					
(Y140.1)		Inc. KM133	—	.10	.20	.35
	1983	52.000	—	.10	.50	1.00
	1984	131.000	—	.10	.20	.35
	1985	220.065	—	.10	.20	.35

KM#	Date	Mintage	VF	XF	Unc	BU
821	1986	299.960	—	.10	.20	.35
	1987	299.550	—	.10	.20	.35
	1988	223.460	—	.10	.20	.35
	1989	Inc. Be.	—	.10	.50	1.00

832	1989	198.415	—	.10	.20	.25
(Y165)	1990	197.700	—	.10	.20	.25
	1991	173.780	—	.10	.30	.50
	1992	168.870	—	.10	.20	.25
	1993	300.013	—	.10	.20	.25
	1994	162.860	—	.10	.20	.25
	1995	183.175	—	.10	.20	.25
	1996	101.885	—	.10	.20	.25
	1997	—	—	.10	.20	.25
	1998	—	—	.10	.20	.25

2 PESETAS

ALUMINUM

822	1982	—	—	.10	.25	.35
(Y141)	1984	47.650	—	.10	.30	.50

2-1/2 PESETAS

ALUMINUM-BRONZE

785	1953(54)	22.729	.25	1.00	2.00	4.00
(Y114)	1953(56)	30.322	.25	1.00	2.00	4.00
	1953(68)	1,000	—	In sets only		600.00
	1953(69)	2,000	—	In sets only		700.00
	1953(70)	6,000	—	In sets only		100.00
	1953(71)	10,000	—	In sets only		100.00

5 PESETAS

NICKEL

778	1949(49)	.612	1.00	5.00	10.00	15.00
(Y117)	1949(50)	21.000	.50	1.00	3.00	10.00
	1949(E51)	*6,000	—	—	725.00	1100.
	1949(51)	.145	—	—	—	4000.
	1949(52)	*.200	—	—	—	7000.

*NOTE: Issued to commemorate a numismatic exposition December 2, 1951. An E replaces the 19 on the lower star.

COPPER-NICKEL

786	1957(58)	13.000	.20	2.00	10.00	20.00
(Y118)	1957(BA)	*.043	35.00	75.00	100.00	150.00
	1957(59)					
		107.000	.10	1.00	5.00	8.00
	1957(60)	26.000	.10	.75	3.00	5.00
	1957(61)	78.992	.10	2.00	5.00	10.00
	1957(62)	40.963	.10	1.00	2.50	4.00
	1957(63)	50.000	.50	5.00	25.00	50.00
	1957(64)	51.000	.10	.75	5.00	10.00
	1957(65)	25.000	.10	.25	1.50	3.00
	1957(66)	28.000	.10	1.00	3.00	10.00
	1957(67)	30.000	.10	.25	1.00	2.00
	1957(68)	40.000	.10	.25	1.00	2.00
	1957(69)	40.000	.10	.25	1.00	2.00
	1957(70)	43.000	.10	.25	2.00	4.00
	1957(71)	77.000	.10	.25	1.00	2.00

KM#	Date	Mintage	VF	XF	Unc	BU
(Y118)	1957(72)	70.000	—	.10	1.00	2.00
	1957(72)	.023	—		Proof	5.00
	1957(73)	78.000	—	.10	.75	1.00
	1957(73)	.028	—		Proof	2.00
	1957(74)					
		100.000	—	.10	.25	.50
	1957(74)	.025	—		Proof	2.00
	1957(75)					
		139.047	—	.10	.25	.50
	1957(75)	.025	—		Proof	1.00

*NOTE: Issued to commemorate the 1958 Barcelona Exposition w/BA replacing the star on left side of rev.

807	1975(76)					
(Y128)		150.560	—	.10	.25	.35
	1975(76)	—	—		Proof	1.00
	1975(77)					
		154.982	—	.10	.25	.35
	1975(77)	I.A.	—		Proof	1.00
	1975(78)					
		412.610	—	.10	.50	1.00
	1975(79)					
		436.000	—	.10	.25	.35
	1975(79)	—	—		Proof	1.00
	1975(80)					
		322.000	—	.10	.50	1.00

World Cup Soccer Games

817	1980(80)	75.000	—	.10	.25	.35
(Y134)	1980(81)					
		294.000	—	.10	.25	.50
	1980(82)					
		291.000	—	.10	.25	.50

Mule. Obv: Y#128. Rev: Y#134 w/(80) star.

811	1975(80)	*.030	—	60.00	100.00	150.00
(Y138)						

Mint mark: Crowned M

823	1982					
(Y128a)		Inc. KM134	—	.10	.50	1.00
	1983	200.000	—	.10	.25	.50
	1984	169.000	—	.10	.35	.75
	1989	—	—	.10	.35	.75

ALUMINUM-BRONZE

833	1989	109.270	—	.10	.25	.40
(Y166)	1990	191.740	—	.10	.25	.50
	1991	313.820	—	.10	.25	.35
	1992	493.224	—	.10	.25	.35
	1998	—	—	.10	.25	.35

NICKEL-BRASS
Jacobeo

919	1993	372.746	—	—	.20	.35
(Y233)						

NOTE: Coins with extra metal in the denomination 5 sell for a premium.

Aragon

931	1994	199.678	—	—	.20	.35
(Y248)						

NOTE: Wide rim variety exists.

ALUMINUM-BRONZE
Asturias

KM#	Date	Mintage	VF	XF	Unc	BU
946	1995	301.756	—	—	.20	.35
(Y254)						

La Rioja

960	1996	199.091	—	—	.20	.35

BRASS
Balearic Islands - Horse and Rider
Obv: Stone monument.

981	1997	—	—	—	.20	.35

10 PESETAS

COPPER-NICKEL
Diez

827	1983	149.000	—	.25	.35	.40
(Y143)	1984	66.000	—	.25	.40	.50
	1985	45.706	—	.25	.50	.60

903	1992	51.820	—	.25	.30	.35
(Y235)	1998	—	—	.25	.30	.35

Juan Miro

918	1993	53.845	—	.25	.40	.65
(Y234)						

Musician P. Sarasate

932	1994	3.050	—	.25	.75	1.00
(Y245)						

Don Franco de Guebedo

947	1995	1.050	—	.25	1.00	2.00
(Y256)						

Emilia Pardo Bazan

961	1996	1.060	—	.25	.75	1.00

Seneca
Obv: Portrait. Rev: Castle gate.

KM#	Date	Mintage	VF	XF	Unc	BU
982	1997	—	—	—	.25	.75	1.00

25 PESETAS

COPPER-NICKEL

KM#	Date	Mintage	VF	XF	Unc	BU
787	1957(58)	8.635	.20	—	15.00	40.00
(Y119)	1957(BA)	*.043	25.00	45.00	85.00	100.00
	1957(59)	42.185	.20	1.00	10.00	20.00
	1957(61)	24.120	3.00	15.00	100.00	125.00
	1957(64)	42.200	.20	1.00	8.00	15.00
	1957(65)	20.000	.20	.75	4.00	6.00
	1957(66)	15.000	.20	1.00	5.00	8.00
	1957(67)	20.000	.20	2.00	8.00	15.00
	1957(68)	30.000	.20	.75	4.00	8.00
	1957(69)	24.000	.20	.50	1.25	3.00
	1957(70)	25.000	.20	.30	2.00	4.00
	1957(71)	7.800	1.00	3.00	20.00	30.00
	1957(72)	4.733	.20	.75	2.00	3.00
	1957(72)	.023	—	—	Proof	7.00
	1957(73)	.028	—	—	Proof	40.00
	1957(74)	5.000	.20	.30	2.00	3.00
	1957(74)	.025	—	—	Proof	6.00
	1957(75)	10.270	.20	.30	1.00	1.25
	1957(75)	.025	—	—	Proof	2.50

*NOTE: Issued to commemorate the 1958 Barcelona
Exposition w/BA replacing the star on left side of rev.

KM#	Date	Mintage	VF	XF	Unc	BU
808	1975(76)	35.707	.20	.25	.75	1.00
(Y129)	1975(76)	—	—	—	Proof	1.00
	1975(77)	46.690	.20	.25	.75	1.00
	1975(77)	I.A.	—	—	Proof	1.00
	1975(78)	97.555	.20	.25	2.00	3.00
	1975(79)	172.000	.20	.25	.75	1.00
	1975(79)	—	—	—	Proof	1.00
	1975(80)	136.000	.20	.25	2.00	3.00

World Cup Soccer Games

KM#	Date	Mintage	VF	XF	Unc	BU
818	1980(80)	35.000	.20	.30	.60	.75
(Y135)	1980(81)	117.000	.20	.30	.75	1.00
	1980(82)	100.000	.20	.30	1.00	2.00

Mint mark: Crowned M

824	1982	146.000	.20	.30	2.00	3.00
(Y129a)	1983	248.000	.20	.30	1.00	1.50
	1984	242.000	.20	.30	2.00	3.00

NICKEL-BRONZE
1992 Olympics - Discus Thrower

850	1990	150.000	.25	.35	.75	1.00
(Y170)	1991	Inc. Ab.	.25	.35	2.00	4.00

1992 Olympics - High Jumper

KM#	Date	Mintage	VF	XF	Unc	BU
851	1990	Inc. Ab.	—	—	1.00	1.50
(Y173)	1991	87.000	—	—	.75	1.00

Tower of Sevilla

904	1992	179.833	—	—	1.50	2.00
(Y230)						

Tower of Seville
Obv: Globe.

905	1992	Inc. Ab.	—	—	.75	1.25
(Y231)						

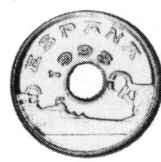 

Pais Vasco

920	1993	150.012	—	—	.60	1.00
(Y238)						

Canary Islands

933	1994	242.566	—	—	.60	1.00
(Y249)						

BRASS
Castilla & Leon

948	1995	221.963	—	—	.60	1.00
(Y255)						

NOTE: This coin was previously listed as KM#946, which
is incorrect.

COPPER-ZINC-NICKEL
Don Quixote

962	1996	37.403	—	—	.45	1.00

BRASS
Melilla
Obv: Two towered buildings.
Rev: Ancient amphora, dates.

983	1997	—	—	—	.45	1.00

COPPER-ZINC-NICKEL
Ceuta
Obv: Ornamented building corner.
Rev: Statue on wall shelf.

KM#	Date	Mintage	VF	XF	Unc	BU
990	1998	—	—	—	.45	1.00

50 PESETAS

COPPER-NICKEL

788	1957(58)	21.471	.50	1.00	3.00	4.00
(Y120)	1957(BA)	*.043	25.00	45.00	65.00	80.00
	1957(59)	28.000	.50	1.00	3.00	4.00
	1957(60)	24.800	.50	1.00	3.00	4.00
	1957(67)	.850	1.00	2.00	5.00	8.00
	1957(68)	1.000	—	In sets only	650.00
	1957(69)	1.200	—	In sets only	600.00
	1957(70)	.019	—	In sets only	150.00
	1957(71)	4.400	1.00	2.00	7.00	10.00
	1957(72)	.023	—	—	Proof	14.00
	1957(73)	.028	—	—	Proof	20.00
	1957(74)	.025	—	—	Proof	30.00
	1957(75)	.025	—	—	Proof	7.00

*NOTE: Issued to commemorate the 1958 Barcelona
Exposition w/BA replacing the star on left side of rev.
NOTE: Edge varieties exist.

809	1975(76)	4.400	.50	.75	1.00	1.50
(Y130)	1975(76)	—	—	—	Proof	2.00
	1975(78)	17.555	.50	.75	3.00	4.00
	1975(79)	33.000	.50	.60	1.00	1.50
	1975(79)	—	—	—	Proof	2.00
	1975(80)	34.000	.50	.60	4.00	5.00

World Cup Soccer Games

819	1980(80)	15.000	.50	.60	1.00	1.50
(Y136)	1980(81)	38.300	.50	.60	2.00	2.50
	1980(82)	30.950	.50	.60	2.50	3.00

Mint mark: Crowned M

825	1982	27.000	.50	1.00	3.00	5.00
(Y130a)	1983	93.000	.50	1.00	2.00	3.00
	1984	17.500	1.00	5.00	15.00	20.00

Expo '92 - Juan Carlos I

852	1990	25.234	—	—	1.00	1.50
(Y171)						

Expo '92 - City View

KM#	Date	Mintage	VF	XF	Unc	BU
853	1990	7.916	—	—	1.00	1.35
(Y174)						

1992 Olympics - Logo

906	1992	40.370	—	—	.75	1.25
(Y232)						

1992 Olympics - Cathedral

907	1992	Inc. Ab.	—	—	1.00	1.35
(Y247)						

Extremadura

921	1993	24.314	—	—	1.00	1.35
(Y239)						

Altamira Cave Paintings

934	1994	3.002	—	—	2.00	3.00
(Y246)						

949	1995	1.001	—	—	2.00	2.50
(Y257)						

Philip V

963	1996	.501	—	—	1.50	2.00

Juan De Herrera

985	1997	—	—	—	1.50	2.00

Obv: King Juan Carlos.

Rev: National arms and denomination.

KM#	Date	Mintage	VF	XF	Unc	BU
991	1998				1.50	2.00

100 PESETAS

19.0000 g, .800 SILVER, .4887 oz ASW

797	1966(66)	35.000	BV	3.00	5.00	6.00
(Y122)	1966(67)	15.000	BV	3.00	6.00	7.00
	1966(68)	24.000	BV	3.00	5.00	6.00
	1966(69) 69 w/straight 9 in star					
		1.000	—	100.00	200.00	250.00
	1966(69) 69 w/curved 9 in star					
		Inc. Ab.	—	50.00	100.00	125.00
	1966(70)	.995	4.00	6.00	10.00	20.00

NOTE: 1966(69) coins heavily altered. Authentication recommended.

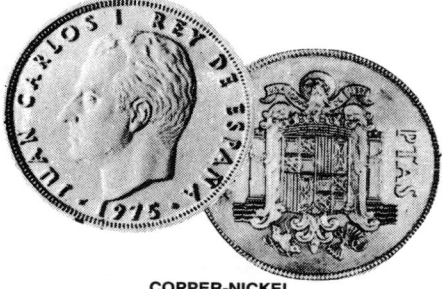

COPPER-NICKEL

810	1975(76)	4.400	—	.75	1.00	2.00
(Y131)	1975(76)		—	—	Proof	3.00

World Cup Soccer Games

820	1980(80)	20.000	—	.75	1.00	2.00
(Y137)						

ALUMINUM-BRONZE

826	1982	117.600	1.00	1.50	2.50	4.00
(Y139)	1982				Proof	5.00
	1983	—	1.00	1.50	6.00	20.00
	1984	208.000	1.00	1.50	3.00	6.00
	1985	118.000	1.00	1.50	5.00	10.00
	1986	160.000	1.00	1.50	2.50	3.00
	1988	125.674	1.00	1.50	3.00	5.00
	1989	80.877	1.00	1.50	2.50	3.00
	1990	25.636	1.00	1.50	2.00	4.00

NOTE: Varieties exist.

908	1992	22.661	—	—	2.00	3.00
(Y278)						

NOTE: Edge varieties exist w/positioning of fleur-de-lis.

NICKEL-BRASS
European Unity

KM#	Date	Mintage	VF	XF	Unc	BU
922	1993	39.723	—	—	2.00	3.00
(Y236)						

Museo del Prado

935	1994	24.853	—	—	2.00	3.00
(Y251)						

COPPER-NICKEL
F.A.O.

950	1995	71.957	—	—	1.75	2.75
(Y259)						

964	1996	21.466	—	—	1.50	2.75

COPPER-ZINC-NICKEL

Teatro Real
Obv: King.

984	1997	—	—	—	1.50	2.75

ALUMINUM-BRONZE
King Juan Carlos

989	1998	—	—	—	1.50	2.75

200 PESETAS

COPPER-NICKEL

829	1986	43.576	—	2.00	6.00	8.00
(Y146.1)						
	1987	66.718	—	2.00	7.00	10.00
	1988	37.190	—	2.00	6.00	9.00

KM#	Date	Mintage	VF	XF	Unc	BU
855 (Y172)	1990	*.019	—	—	5.00	6.00

Madrid - European Culture Capital

| 884 (Y228) | 1991 | *.038 | — | — | 2.50 | 4.50 |

Madrid - European Culture Capital - Equestrian

| 909 (Y260) | 1992 | Inc. Ab. | — | — | 2.50 | 4.50 |

Madrid - European Culture Capital - Bear By Tree

| 910 (Y261) | 1992 | Inc. Ab. | — | — | 2.00 | 3.50 |

Juan Luis Vives

| 923 (Y237) | 1993 | 2.811 | — | — | 6.00 | 7.00 |

Spanish "Old Masters" Paintings

| 936 (Y252) | 1994 | 2.997 | — | — | 3.00 | 4.50 |

Spanish Painters

| 951 (Y258) | 1995 | 1.022 | — | — | 4.00 | 5.50 |

Musicians

KM#	Date	Mintage	VF	XF	Unc	BU
965	1996	.417	—	—	3.00	4.50

Jacinto Benavente
Obv: Stylized books.
Rev: Portrait in inner circle.

| 986 | 1997 | — | — | — | 2.50 | 4.00 |

King Juan Carlos and Crown Prince
Rev: Denomination.

| 992 | 1998 | — | — | — | 2.50 | 4.00 |

500 PESETAS

COPPER-ALUMINUM-NICKEL
Juan Carlos and Sofia

831 (Y147)	1987	400.000	—	3.50	8.00	10.00
	1987	Inc. Ab.	—		Proof	10.00
	1988	81.309	—	3.50	8.00	10.00
	1989	103.861	—	3.50	4.50	5.00
	1990	28.372	—	3.50	8.00	9.00

924 (Y253)	1993	3.059	—	—	8.00	10.00
	1994	3.041	—	—	8.00	10.00
	1995	1.015	—	—	8.00	10.00
	1996	1.031	—	—	8.00	9.00
	1997	—	—	—	8.00	9.00
	1998	—	—	—	8.00	9.00

SRI (SHRI) LANKA

The Democratic Socialist Republic of Sri (Shri) Lanka (formerly Ceylon) situated in the Indian Ocean 18 miles (29 km.) southeast of India, has an area of 25,332 sq. mi. (65,610 sq. km.) and a population of *16.9 million. Capital: Colombo. The economy is chiefly agricultural. Tea, coconut products and rubber are exported.

The earliest known inhabitants of Ceylon, the Veddahs, were subjugated by the Sinhalese from northern India in the 6th century B.C. Sinhalese rule was maintained until 1408, after which the island was controlled by China for 30 years. The Portuguese came to Ceylon in 1505 and maintained control of the coastal area for 150 years. They were supplanted by the Dutch in 1658, who were in turn supplanted by the British who seized the Dutch colonies in 1796, and made them a Crown Colony in 1802. In 1815, the British conquered the independent Kingdom of Kandy in the central part of the island. Constitutional changes in 1931 and 1946 granted the Ceylonese a measure of autonomy and a parliamentary form of government. Britain granted Ceylon independence as a self-governing republic within the British Commonwealth on Feb. 4, 1948. On May 22, 1972, the Ceylonese adopted a new Constitution which declared Ceylon to be the Republic of Shri Lanka - 'Resplendent Island'. Shri Lanka is a member of the Commonwealth of Nations. The president is Chief of State. The prime minister is Head of Government. The present leaders of the country have reverted the country name back to Sri Lanka.

RULERS

British, 1796-1972

CEYLON

DECIMAL COINAGE

100 Cents = 1 Rupee

1/4 CENT

COPPER

KM#	Date	Mintage	Fine	VF	XF	Unc
90	1901	.216	1.50	3.00	5.00	12.00
	1901				Proof	100.00

NOTE: Earlier dates (1870-1898) exist for this type.

100	1904	.103	2.50	5.00	10.00	22.00
	1904	—	—	—	Proof	150.00

1/2 CENT

COPPER

91	1901	2.020	1.25	2.50	4.00	10.00

NOTE: Earlier dates (1870-1898) exist for this type.

101	1904	2.012	1.00	2.00	5.00	12.00
	1904	—	—	—	Proof	120.00
	1905	1.000	1.50	3.00	6.00	15.00
	1905	—	—	—	Proof	120.00
	1906	3.056	1.00	2.00	5.00	12.00
	1906	—	—	—	Proof	120.00
	1908	1.000	1.50	3.00	6.00	15.00
	1908	—	—	—	Proof	200.00
	1909	3.000	1.00	2.00	5.00	12.00
	1909	—	—	—	Proof	120.00

KM#	Date	Mintage	Fine	VF	XF	Unc
106	1912	5.008	1.25	2.75	4.00	10.00
	1912	—	—	—	Proof	120.00
	1914	2.000	1.25	2.75	6.00	12.00
	1914	—	—	—	Proof	120.00
	1917	2.000	1.50	3.00	6.00	12.00
	1917	—	—	—	Proof	120.00
	1926	5.000	.50	1.00	2.00	5.00
	1926	—	—	—	Proof	120.00

KM#	Date	Mintage	Fine	VF	XF	Unc
110	1937	3.026	.30	.85	1.50	3.50
	1937	—	—	—	Proof	175.00
	1940	5.080	.25	.65	1.25	3.00

CENT

COPPER

KM#	Date	Mintage	Fine	VF	XF	Unc
92	1901	1.014	2.50	5.00	10.00	22.00

NOTE: Earlier dates (1870-1900) exist for this type.

KM#	Date	Mintage	Fine	VF	XF	Unc
102	1904	2.529	1.00	2.00	4.00	8.00
	1904	—	—	—	Proof	125.00
	1905	1.509	1.25	2.25	5.00	10.00
	1905	—	—	—	Proof	125.00
	1906	1.751	1.25	2.25	5.00	10.00
	1906	—	—	—	Proof	125.00
	1908	—	1.00	2.00	4.00	8.00
	1908	—	—	—	Proof	225.00
	1909	2.500	1.00	2.00	4.00	8.00
	1909	—	—	—	Proof	125.00
	1910	8.236	.50	1.00	2.50	5.00
	1910	—	—	—	Proof	125.00

KM#	Date	Mintage	Fine	VF	XF	Unc
107	1912	5.855	.50	1.00	2.00	4.00
	1912	—	—	—	Proof	115.00
	1914	6.000	.50	1.00	2.25	5.00
	1914	—	—	—	Proof	115.00
	1917	1.000	1.00	1.75	3.00	8.00
	1917	—	—	—	Proof	115.00
	1920	2.000	.50	1.00	2.25	5.00
	1920	—	—	—	Proof	115.00
	1922	2.930	.50	1.00	2.25	5.00
	1922	—	—	—	Proof	115.00
	1923	2.500	.50	1.00	2.25	5.00
	1923	—	—	—	Proof	115.00
	1925	7.490	.35	.75	1.50	3.50
	1925	—	—	—	Proof	115.00
	1926	3.750	.35	.75	1.50	3.50
	1926	—	—	—	Proof	115.00
	1928	2.500	.35	.75	1.50	4.00
	1928	—	—	—	Proof	115.00
	1929	5.000	.35	.75	1.50	3.50
	1929	—	—	—	Proof	115.00

George VI
Obv: PM below bust, high relief.

KM#	Date	Mintage	Fine	VF	XF	Unc
111	1937	4.538	.25	.50	1.25	3.00
	1937	—	—	—	Proof	100.00
	1940	10.190	.15	.30	1.00	2.00
	1940	—	—	—	Proof	75.00
	1942	20.780	.15	.30	1.00	2.00

BRONZE
Obv: W/o initials, low relief, thin planchet.

KM#	Date	Mintage	Fine	VF	XF	Unc
111a	1942	Inc. Ab.	.15	.30	.75	1.75
	1942	—	—	—	Proof	75.00
	1943	43.705	.15	.30	.50	1.00
	1945	34.100	.15	.35	.60	1.20
	1945*	—	—	—	Proof	20.00

***NOTE:** These were restruck in quantity.

2 CENTS

NICKEL-BRASS

KM#	Date	Mintage	Fine	VF	XF	Unc
117	1944	30.165	.10	.25	.50	1.00

BRASS
Obv. leg: W/o EMPEROR OF INDIA.

KM#	Date	Mintage	Fine	VF	XF	Unc
119	1951	15.000	.10	.25	.75	1.50
	1951	—	—	—	Proof	20.00

KM#	Date	Mintage	Fine	VF	XF	Unc
124	1955	37.131	.10	.15	.25	.50
	1957	38.200	.10	.15	.25	.50
	1957	—	—	—	Proof	75.00

5 CENTS

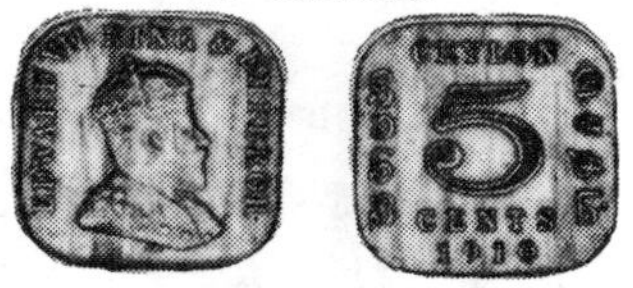

COPPER-NICKEL

KM#	Date	Mintage	Fine	VF	XF	Unc
103	1909	2.000	1.50	3.00	5.00	16.00
	1910	4.000	1.00	2.00	3.50	10.00

KM#	Date	Mintage	Fine	VF	XF	Unc
108	1912H	4.000	.75	1.50	3.00	8.00
	1920	6.000	.50	1.00	2.00	6.00
	1926	3.000	.75	1.50	4.00	10.00

NICKEL-BRASS

KM#	Date	Mintage	Fine	VF	XF	Unc
113.1	1942	12.752	.35	.75	1.50	4.00
	1942	—	—	—	Proof	50.00
	1943	Inc. Ab.	.35	.75	1.50	4.00
	1943	—	—	—	Proof	50.00

Thin planchet.

KM#	Date	Mintage	Fine	VF	XF	Unc
113.2	1944	18.064	.20	.35	.70	1.75
	1945	31.192	.15	.30	.60	1.50
	1945	—	—	—	Proof	60.00

NOTE: Varieties exist in bust, denomination and legend placement for 1945.

10 CENTS

1.1664 g, .800 SILVER, .0300 oz ASW

KM#	Date	Mintage	Fine	VF	XF	Unc
97	1902	1.000	1.00	2.50	6.00	20.00
	1902	—	—	—	Proof	150.00
	1903	1.000	1.00	2.50	6.00	20.00
	1903	—	—	—	Proof	150.00
	1907	.500	2.50	5.00	15.00	25.00
	1908	1.500	1.00	2.50	6.00	15.00
	1909	1.000	1.00	2.50	6.00	15.00
	1910	2.000	1.00	2.50	6.00	15.00

KM#	Date	Mintage	Fine	VF	XF	Unc
104	1911	1.000	1.00	1.75	5.00	12.00
	1912	1.000	1.25	2.00	6.00	15.00
	1913	2.000	1.00	1.50	4.00	10.00
	1914	2.000	1.00	1.50	4.00	10.00
	1914	—	—	—	Proof	150.00
	1917	.879	1.00	2.50	7.50	17.50
	1917	—	—	—	Proof	150.00

1.1664 g, .550 SILVER, .0206 oz ASW

KM#	Date	Mintage	Fine	VF	XF	Unc
104a	1919B	.750	1.50	3.50	10.00	20.00
	1919B	—	—	—	Proof	150.00
	1920B	3.059	1.00	2.50	6.00	15.00
	1920B	—	—	—	Proof	150.00
	1921B	1.583	.75	1.75	5.00	10.00
	1921B	—	—	—	Proof	150.00
	1922	.282	1.75	3.50	10.00	25.00
	1922	—	—	—	Proof	150.00
	1924	1.508	.75	1.75	4.00	10.00
	1924	—	—	—	Proof	150.00
	1925	1.500	.75	1.75	4.00	10.00
	1925	—	—	—	Proof	150.00
	1926	1.500	.75	1.75	4.00	10.00
	1926	—	—	—	Proof	150.00
	1927	1.500	.75	1.75	4.00	10.00
	1927	—	—	—	Proof	150.00
	1928	1.500	.75	1.75	4.00	10.00
	1928	—	—	—	Proof	150.00

1.1664 g, .800 SILVER, .0300 oz ASW

KM#	Date	Mintage	Fine	VF	XF	Unc
112	1941	16.271	.65	1.00	2.50	6.00

NICKEL-BRASS

KM#	Date	Mintage	Fine	VF	XF	Unc
118	1944	30.500	.25	.50	1.00	2.00
	1944	—	—	—	Proof	90.00

Obv. leg: W/o EMPEROR OF INDIA.

KM#	Date	Mintage	Fine	VF	XF	Unc
121	1951	34.760	.10	.20	.40	1.00
	1951	—	—	—	Proof	15.00
	1951	*3.000	—	Proof restrike		4.00

***NOTE:** Restrikes differ in the formation of native characters.

25 CENTS

2.9160 g, .800 SILVER, .0750 oz ASW

KM#	Date	Mintage	Fine	VF	XF	Unc
98	1902	.400	4.00	8.00	20.00	40.00
	1902	—	—	—	Proof	150.00
	1903	.400	4.00	8.00	20.00	40.00
	1903	—	—	—	Proof	150.00
	1907	.120	7.50	20.00	30.00	50.00

KM#	Date	Mintage	Fine	VF	XF	Unc
98	1908	.400	4.00	8.00	15.00	35.00
	1909	.400	4.00	8.00	15.00	35.00
	1910	.800	2.00	5.00	10.00	20.00
105	1911	.400	3.00	6.00	12.00	30.00
	1911	—	—	—	Proof	175.00
	1913	1.200	1.50	2.50	7.50	17.50
	1913	—	—	—	Proof	175.00
	1914	.400	3.00	6.00	12.00	25.00
	1914	—	—	—	Proof	175.00
	1917	.300	4.00	8.00	15.00	35.00
	1917	—	—	—	Proof	175.00

2.9160 g, .550 SILVER, .0516 oz ASW

KM#	Date	Mintage	Fine	VF	XF	Unc
105a	1919B	1.400	1.25	3.00	7.50	15.00
	1919B	—	—	—	Proof	150.00
	1920B	1.600	1.25	3.00	7.50	15.00
	1920B	—	—	—	Proof	150.00
	1921B	.600	3.50	7.50	15.00	30.00
	1921B	—	—	—	Proof	150.00
	1922	1.211	1.25	3.25	7.50	15.00
	1922	—	—	—	Proof	150.00
	1925	1.004	1.25	3.50	7.50	15.00
	1925	—	—	—	Proof	150.00
	1926	1.000	1.25	3.50	7.50	15.00
	1926	—	—	—	Proof	150.00

NICKEL-BRASS

KM#	Date	Mintage	Fine	VF	XF	Unc
115	1943	13.920	.25	.50	1.00	2.00

Obv. leg: W/o EMPEROR OF INDIA.

KM#	Date	Mintage	Fine	VF	XF	Unc
122	1951	25.940	.10	.30	.60	1.50
	1951	—	—	—	Proof	20.00
	1951	*2.500	—	Proof restrike		4.00

*NOTE: Numerals 9 and 5 differ on restrikes.

50 CENTS

5.8319 g, .800 SILVER, .1500 oz ASW

KM#	Date	Mintage	Fine	VF	XF	Unc
99	1902	.200	5.00	10.00	30.00	70.00
	1902	—	—	—	Proof	175.00
	1903	.800	3.00	8.00	18.00	35.00
	1903	—	—	—	Proof	175.00
	1910	.200	7.00	13.00	30.00	60.00
109	1913	.400	7.00	13.00	30.00	60.00
	1913	—	—	—	Proof	175.00
	1914	.200	5.00	15.00	30.00	60.00
	1914	—	—	—	Proof	175.00
	1917	1.073	2.50	5.00	10.00	20.00
	1917	—	—	—	Proof	175.00

5.8319 g, .550 SILVER, .1031 oz ASW

KM#	Date	Mintage	Fine	VF	XF	Unc
109a	1919B	.750	1.00	3.00	7.00	16.00
	1919B	—	—	—	Proof	120.00
	1920B	.800	1.00	3.00	7.00	16.00
	1920B	—	—	—	Proof	120.00
	1921B	.800	1.00	3.00	7.00	16.00
	1921B	—	—	—	Proof	120.00
	1922	1.040	1.00	3.00	7.00	16.00
	1922	—	—	—	Proof	120.00
	1924	1.010	1.00	3.00	7.00	16.00
	1924	—	—	—	Proof	120.00
	1925	.500	2.00	5.00	10.00	20.00
	1925	—	—	—	Proof	120.00
	1926	.500	2.00	5.00	10.00	20.00

KM#	Date	Mintage	Fine	VF	XF	Unc
109a	1926	—	—	—	Proof	120.00
	1927	.500	2.00	5.00	10.00	20.00
	1927	—	—	—	Proof	120.00
	1928	.500	2.00	5.00	10.00	20.00
	1928	—	—	—	Proof	120.00
	1929	.500	2.00	5.00	10.00	20.00
	1929	—	—	—	Proof	120.00

5.8319 g, .800 SILVER, .1500 oz ASW

KM#	Date	Mintage	Fine	VF	XF	Unc
114	1942	.662	2.00	4.00	8.00	17.50

NICKEL-BRASS

KM#	Date	Mintage	Fine	VF	XF	Unc
116	1943	8.600	.35	.75	1.50	3.00

Obv. leg: W/o EMPEROR OF INDIA.

KM#	Date	Mintage	Fine	VF	XF	Unc
123	1951	19.980	.20	.35	.75	1.50
	1951	—	—	—	Proof	20.00
	1951	*1.500	—	Proof restrike		5.00

*NOTE: Restrikes differ slightly in the formation of native inscriptions.

RUPEE

COPPER-NICKEL
2500 Years of Buddhism

KM#	Date	Mintage	Fine	VF	XF	Unc
125	1957	2.000	.50	1.00	2.00	3.00
	1957	1,800	—	—	Proof	12.00

5 RUPEES

28.2757 g, .925 SILVER, .8409 oz ASW
2500 Years of Buddhism

KM#	Date	Mintage	Fine	VF	XF	Unc
126	1957	.500	8.00	12.50	17.50	30.00
	1957	1,800	—	—	Proof	65.00

REPUBLIC
CENT

ALUMINUM

KM#	Date	Mintage	Fine	VF	XF	Unc
127	1963	33.000	—	—	—	.10
	1963	—	—	—	Proof	
	1965	12.000	—	—	.10	.15
	1967	10.000	—	—	.10	.15

KM#	Date	Mintage	Fine	VF	XF	Unc
127	1968	22.505	—	—	—	.10
	1969	10.000	—	—	—	.10
	1970	15.000	—	—	—	.10
	1971	55.000	—	—	—	.10
	1971	—	—	—	Proof	.50

2 CENTS

ALUMINUM

KM#	Date	Mintage	Fine	VF	XF	Unc
128	1963	26.000	—	—	.10	.15
	1963	—	—	—	Proof	
	1965	7.000	—	—	.10	.15
	1967	15.000	—	—	.10	.15
	1968	15.000	—	—	.10	.15
	1969	—	—	—	.10	.15
	1970	13.000	—	—	.10	.15
	1971	45.000	—	—	.10	.15
	1971	—	—	—	Proof	1.00

5 CENTS

NICKEL-BRASS

KM#	Date	Mintage	Fine	VF	XF	Unc
129	1963	16.000	—	.10	.15	.25
	1963	—	—	—	Proof	
	1965	9.000	—	.10	.15	.25
	1968	12.000	—	.10	.15	.25
	1968	—	—	—	Proof	3.00
	1969	2.500	—	.10	.20	.40
	1970	7.000	—	.10	.15	.25
	1971	32.000	—	.10	.15	.25
	1971	—	—	—	Proof	1.50

10 CENTS

NICKEL-BRASS

KM#	Date	Mintage	Fine	VF	XF	Unc
130	1963	14.000	—	.10	.15	.25
	1963	—	—	—	Proof	
	1965	3.000	—	.10	.15	.35
	1969	6.000	—	.10	.15	.25
	1970	—	—	.10	.15	.25
	1971	29.000	—	.10	.15	.20
	1971	—	—	—	Proof	1.25

25 CENTS

COPPER-NICKEL

KM#	Date	Mintage	Fine	VF	XF	Unc
131	1963	30.000	—	.10	.20	.40
	1963	—	—	—	Proof	
	1965	8.000	—	.10	.25	.50
	1968	—	—	.10	.25	.50
	1969	—	—	.10	.25	.50
	1970	—	—	.10	.25	.50
	1971	24.000	—	.10	.15	.30
	1971	—	—	—	Proof	1.50

50 CENTS

COPPER-NICKEL

KM#	Date	Mintage	Fine	VF	XF	Unc
132	1963	15.000	.10	.20	.35	.75
	1963	—	—	—	Proof	
	1965	7.000	.10	.20	.35	.75
	1968	—	.10	.20	.35	.75
	1969	—	.10	.20	.35	.75
	1970	—	.10	.20	.35	.75
	1971	4.000	.25	.50	.75	1.50
	1971	—	—	—	Proof	2.00
	1972	8.000	.10	.20	.35	.75

RUPEE

COPPER-NICKEL

KM#	Date	Mintage	Fine	VF	XF	Unc
133	1963	20.000	.10	.20	.40	1.00
	1963	—			Proof	—
	1965	5.000	.15	.25	.50	1.00
	1969	2.500	.15	.25	.50	1.50
	1970	—	.15	.25	.50	1.50
	1971	5.000	.15	.25	.50	1.25
	1971	—			Proof	3.00
	1972	7.000	.15	.25	.50	1.00

2 RUPEES

COPPER-NICKEL
F.A.O. Issue

KM#	Date	Mintage	VF	XF	Unc	
134	1968	.500	.50	1.50	2.25	3.00

SRI LANKA

100 Cents = 1 Rupee

CENT

ALUMINUM

KM#	Date	Mintage	VF	XF	Unc
137	1975	52.778	—	.10	.25
	1975	1,431	—	Proof	2.00
	1978	34.006	—	.10	.25
	1978	Inc. Ab.	—	Proof	2.00
	1989	—		.10	.25

2 CENTS

ALUMINUM

138	1975	62.503	—	.10	.25
	1975	1,431	—	Proof	2.50
	1977	2.500	—	.10	.25
	1978	23.425	—	.10	.25
	1978	Inc. Ab.	—	Proof	3.00

5 CENTS

NICKEL-BRASS

139	1975	19.584	—	.10	.25
	1975	1,431	—	Proof	2.50

ALUMINUM

139a	1978	272.308	—	.10	.25
	1978	Inc. Ab.	—	Proof	3.00
	1988	40.000	—	.10	.25
	1991	—		.10	.25

10 CENTS

NICKEL-BRASS

KM#	Date	Mintage	VF	XF	Unc
140	1975	10.800	—	.10	.25
	1975	1,431	—	Proof	4.25

ALUMINUM

140a	1978	188.820	—	.10	.25
	1978	Inc. Ab.	—	Proof	3.00
	1988	40.000	—	.10	.25
	1991	—		.10	.25

25 CENTS

COPPER-NICKEL
Security edge

141.1	1975	39.600	—	.10	.25
	1975	1,431	—	Proof	3.00
	1978	65.009	—	.10	.25
	1978	Inc. Ab.	—	Proof	3.00

Reeded edge

141.2	1982	90.000	—	.10	.25
	1982	Inc. Ab.	—	Proof	3.00
	1989	—		.10	.25
	1991	—		.10	.25
	1994	—		.10	.25
	1996	—		.10	.25

50 CENTS

COPPER-NICKEL
Security edge

135.1	1972	11.000	.15	.30	.60
	1975	34.000	.15	.30	.60
	1975	1,431	—	Proof	4.00
	1978	66.010	.15	.30	.60
	1978	Inc. Ab.	—	Proof	4.00

Reeded edge

135.2	1982	65.000	.10	.20	.50
	1982	Inc. Ab.	—	Proof	4.00
	1991	—	.10	.20	.50
	1994	—	.10	.20	.50

RUPEE

COPPER-NICKEL
Security edge

136.1	1972	5.000	.30	.60	1.25
	1975	31.500	.25	.50	1.00
	1975	1,431	—	Proof	6.50
	1978	37.018	.25	.50	1.00
	1978	Inc. Ab.	—	Proof	6.50

Reeded edge

136.2	1982	75.000	.25	.50	1.00
	1982	Inc. Ab.	—	Proof	5.00
	1994	—	.25	.50	1.00
	1996	—		.50	1.00

Inauguration of President Jayawardene

KM#	Date	Mintage	VF	XF	Unc
144	1978	1.997	.30	.60	1.25
	1978	2,600	—	Proof	8.00

3rd Anniversary - Induction of President

151	1992	—	—	—	1.25
	1992	—		Proof	8.00

50th Anniversary - UNICEF
Obv: Denomination.

157	1996	—	—	—	1.50

2 RUPEES

COPPER-NICKEL
Non-Aligned Nations Conference

142	1976	2.000	.50	1.00	1.50
	1976	1,000	—	Proof	6.00

Mahaweli Dam

145	1981	5.000	.25	.55	1.25

147	1984	25.000	.25	.50	1.00
	1993	—	.30	.60	1.35

50th Anniversary - F.A.O.

155	1995	—	—	—	1.75

5 RUPEES

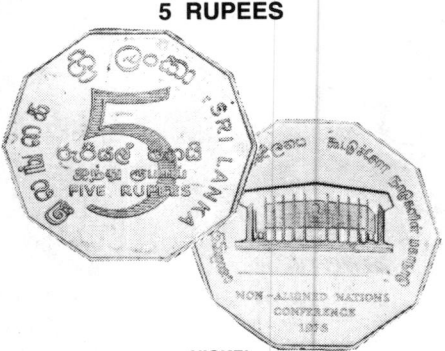

NICKEL
Non-Aligned Nations Conference

KM#	Date	Mintage	VF	XF	Unc
143	1976	1.000	.75	1.25	2.50
	1976	1,000	—	Proof	8.00

COPPER-NICKEL
50th Anniversary of Universal Adult Franchise

| 146 | 1981 | 2.000 | .50 | 1.00 | 2.25 |

ALUMINUM-BRONZE
Edge: CBC - Currency Board of Ceylon.

| 148.1 | 1984 | 25.000 | .35 | .75 | 2.25 |

Edge: CBSL - Currency Board of Sri Lanka.

148.2	1986	—	.35	.75	2.25
	1991	—	.35	.75	2.25
	1994	—	.35	.65	2.00

50th Anniversary - UN
Obv: Denomination.

| 156 | 1995 | — | — | — | 2.25 |

10 RUPEES

COPPER-NICKEL
I.Y.S.H.

| 149 | 1987 | 2.000 | — | — | 3.50 |

BRASS center in COPPER-NICKEL ring
50th Anniversary of Independence
Edge: CBSL, (4 times) reeded.

| 158 | 1998 | — | — | — | 4.00 |

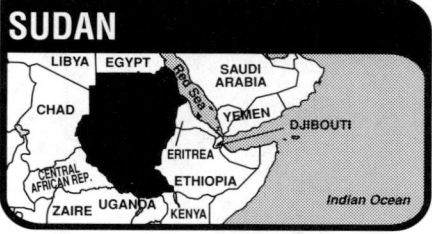

SUDAN

The Democratic Republic of the Sudan, located in northeast Africa on the Red Sea between Egypt and Ethiopia, has an area of 967,500 sq. mi. (2,505,810 sq. km.) and a population of *24.5 million. Capital: Khartoum. Agriculture and livestock raising are the chief occupations. Cotton, gum arabic and peanuts are exported.

The Sudan, site of the powerful Nubian kingdom of Roman times, was a collection of small independent states from the 14th century until 1820-22 when it was conquered and united by Mohammed Ali, Pasha of Egypt. Egyptian forces were driven from the area during the Mahdist revolt, 1881-98, but the Sudan was retaken by Anglo-Egyptian expeditions, 1896-98, and established as an Anglo-Egyptian condominium in 1899. Britain supplied the administrative apparatus and personnel, but the appearance of joint Anglo-Egyptian administration was continued until Jan. 9, 1954, when the first Sudanese self-government parliament was inaugurated. The Sudan achieved independence on Jan. 1, 1956 with the consent of the British and Egyptian government.

TITLES

جمهورية السودان

Jumhuriya(t) as-Sudan

الجمهورية توركية السودان الى ميقراطية

al-Jumhuriya(t) as-Sudan ad-Dimiqratiya(t)

MINTNAME

ام درمان

Omdurman

MONETARY SYSTEM

10 Millim (Milliemes) = 1 Ghirsh (Piastre)
100 Ghirsh (Piastre) = 1 Pound

MILLIM

BRONZE
Obv: Large legend and written denomination.

KM#	Date	Year	Mintage	VF	XF	Unc
29.1	AH1376	1956	5.000	—	.15	.30
	1379	1960	1.300	—	.15	.35
	1386	1966	—	—	Proof	
	1387	1967	—	—	.15	.30
	1388	1968	—	—	.15	.30
	1389	1969	—	—	.15	.30

Obv: New Arabic legend.

39	AH1390	1970	—	—	—	—
	1390	1970	1,646	—	Proof	1.00
	1391	1971	1,772	—	Proof	1.00

2 MILLIM

BRONZE
Obv: Large written denomination.

30.1	AH1376	1956	5.000	—	.15	.45
	1386	1966	—	—	Proof	1.00
	1387	1967	—	—	.15	.30
	1388	1968	—	—	.15	.30
	1389	1969	—	—	.15	.30

---

5 MILLIM

BRONZE
Obv: Thin legend and large denomination.

KM#	Date	Year	Mintage	VF	XF	Unc
31.1	AH1376	1956	30.000	.10	.20	.45
	1382	1962	6.000	.10	.20	.50
	1386	1966	4.000	.10	.15	.35
	1386	1966	—	—	Proof	
	1387	1967	4.000	.10	.15	.35
	1388	1968	—	.10	.15	.35
	1389	1969	—	.10	.15	.35

NOTE: Varieties of size of camel and rider exist.

Obv: New large Arabic legend and denomination.

| 41.1 | AH1390 | 1970 | — | .20 | .45 | 1.25 |
| | 1391 | 1971 | 3.000 | .20 | .45 | 1.25 |

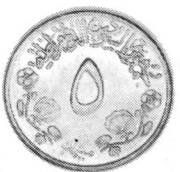

2nd Anniversary of Revolution

| 47 | AH1391 | 1971 | .500 | .15 | .25 | .50 |

F.A.O. Issue

| 53 | AH1392 | 1972 | 6.000 | — | .15 | .35 |
| | 1393 | 1973 | 9.000 | — | .15 | .35 |

Similar to 10 Millim, KM#55 but round.

| 54 | AH1392 | 1972 | — | — | .20 | .45 |

BRASS
Obv: Thick legend and written denomination.
Rev: Ribbon w/3 equal sections.

| 54a.1 | AH1395 | 1975 | 4.132 | — | .20 | .40 |
| | 1398 | 1978 | — | — | .20 | .40 |

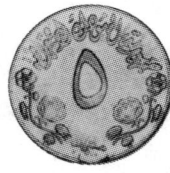

Rev: Ribbon w/long center section.

| 54a.2 | AH1398 | 1978 | — | — | .20 | .40 |

Obv: Small 5, crude lettering. Rev: Large eagle, ribbon w/long center section.

| 54a.4 | AH1403 | 1983 | — | — | — | — |

F.A.O. Issue

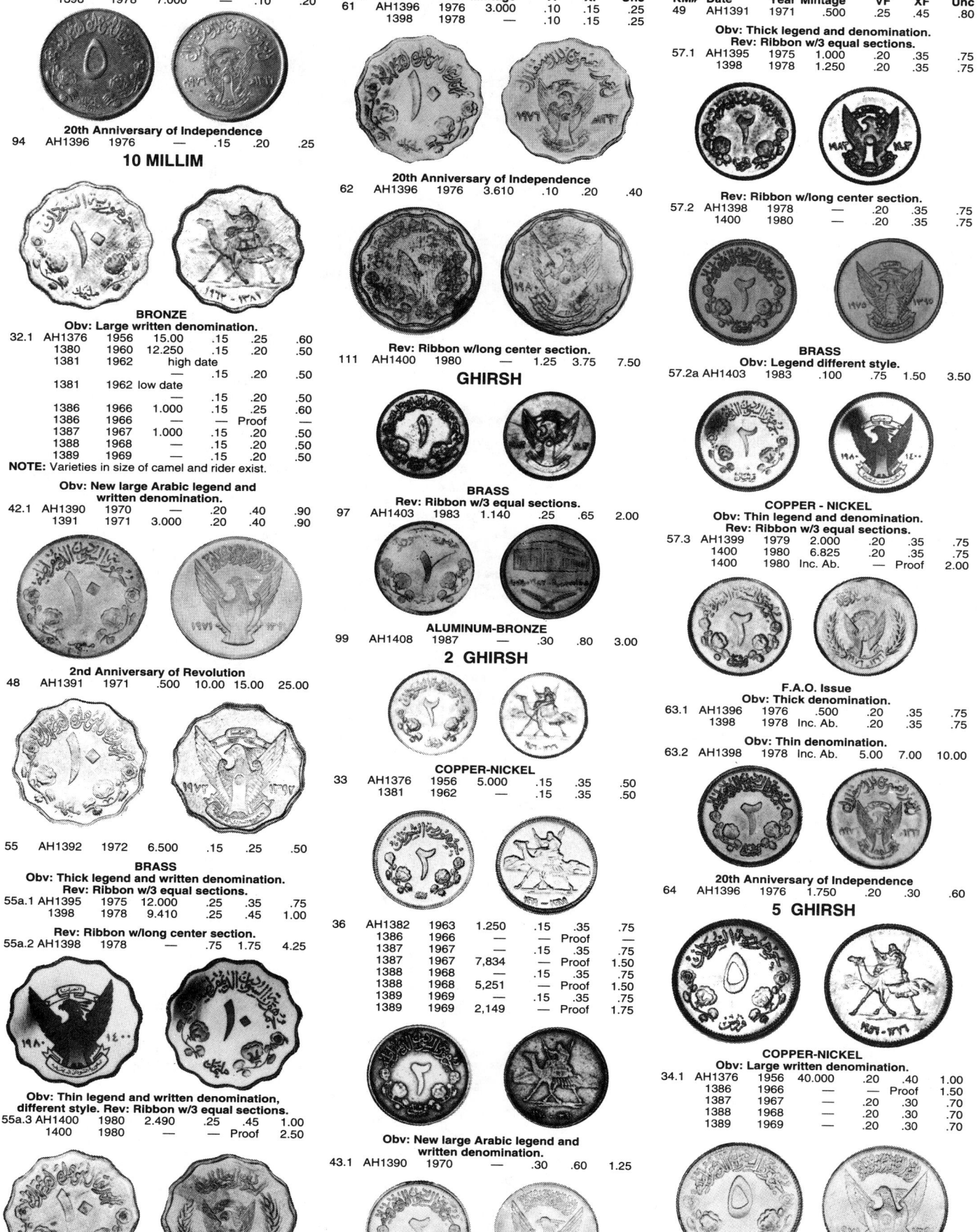

KM#	Date	Year	Mintage	VF	XF	Unc
60	AH1396	1976	7.868	—	.10	.20
	1398	1978	7.000	—	.10	.20

20th Anniversary of Independence

94	AH1396	1976	—	.15	.20	.25

10 MILLIM

BRONZE
Obv: Large written denomination.

32.1	AH1376	1956	15.00	.15	.25	.60
	1380	1960	12.250	.15	.20	.50
	1381	1962	high date			
			—	.15	.20	.50
	1381	1962	low date			
			—	.15	.20	.50
	1386	1966	1.000	.15	.25	.60
	1386	1966	—	—	Proof	—
	1387	1967	1.000	.15	.20	.50
	1388	1968	—	.15	.20	.50
	1389	1969	—	.15	.20	.50

NOTE: Varieties in size of camel and rider exist.

Obv: New large Arabic legend and written denomination.

42.1	AH1390	1970	—	.20	.40	.90
	1391	1971	3.000	.20	.40	.90

2nd Anniversary of Revolution

48	AH1391	1971	.500	10.00	15.00	25.00

55	AH1392	1972	6.500	.15	.25	.50

BRASS
Obv: Thick legend and written denomination. Rev: Ribbon w/3 equal sections.

55a.1	AH1395	1975	12.000	.25	.35	.75
	1398	1978	9.410	.25	.45	1.00

Rev: Ribbon w/long center section.

55a.2	AH1398	1978	—	.75	1.75	4.25

Obv: Thin legend and written denomination, different style. Rev: Ribbon w/3 equal sections.

55a.3	AH1400	1980	2.490	.25	.45	1.00
	1400	1980	—	—	Proof	2.50

F.A.O. Issue

KM#	Date	Year	Mintage	VF	XF	Unc
61	AH1396	1976	3.000	.10	.15	.25
	1398	1978	—	.10	.15	.25

20th Anniversary of Independence

62	AH1396	1976	3.610	.10	.20	.40

Rev: Ribbon w/long center section.

111	AH1400	1980	—	1.25	3.75	7.50

GHIRSH

BRASS
Rev: Ribbon w/3 equal sections.

97	AH1403	1983	1.140	.25	.65	2.00

ALUMINUM-BRONZE

99	AH1408	1987	—	.30	.80	3.00

2 GHIRSH

COPPER-NICKEL

33	AH1376	1956	5.000	.15	.35	.50
	1381	1962	—	.15	.35	.50

36	AH1382	1963	1.250	.15	.35	.75
	1386	1966	—	—	Proof	—
	1387	1967	—	.15	.35	.75
	1387	1967	7,834	—	Proof	1.50
	1388	1968	—	.15	.35	.75
	1388	1968	5,251	—	Proof	1.50
	1389	1969	—	.15	.35	.75
	1389	1969	2,149	—	Proof	1.75

Obv: New large Arabic legend and written denomination.

43.1	AH1390	1970	—	.30	.60	1.25

2nd Anniversary of Revolution

KM#	Date	Year	Mintage	VF	XF	Unc
49	AH1391	1971	.500	.25	.45	.80

Obv: Thick legend and denomination. Rev: Ribbon w/3 equal sections.

57.1	AH1395	1975	1.000	.20	.35	.75
	1398	1978	1.250	.20	.35	.75

Rev: Ribbon w/long center section.

57.2	AH1398	1978	—	.20	.35	.75
	1400	1980	—	.20	.35	.75

BRASS
Obv: Legend different style.

57.2a	AH1403	1983	.100	.75	1.50	3.50

COPPER - NICKEL
Obv: Thin legend and denomination. Rev: Ribbon w/3 equal sections.

57.3	AH1399	1979	2.000	.20	.35	.75
	1400	1980	6.825	.20	.35	.75
	1400	1980	Inc. Ab.	—	Proof	2.00

F.A.O. Issue
Obv: Thick denomination.

63.1	AH1396	1976	.500	.20	.35	.75
	1398	1978	Inc. Ab.	.20	.35	.75

Obv: Thin denomination.

63.2	AH1398	1978	Inc. Ab.	5.00	7.00	10.00

20th Anniversary of Independence

64	AH1396	1976	1.750	.20	.30	.60

5 GHIRSH

COPPER-NICKEL
Obv: Large written denomination.

34.1	AH1376	1956	40.000	.20	.40	1.00
	1386	1966	—	—	Proof	1.50
	1387	1967	—	.20	.30	.70
	1388	1968	—	.20	.30	.70
	1389	1969	—	.20	.30	.70

2nd Anniversary of Revolution

51	AH1391	1971	.500	.30	.60	1.20

Obv: Large legend and denomination.
Rev: Ribbon w/3 equal sections.

KM#	Date	Year	Mintage	VF	XF	Unc
58.1	AH1395	1975	1.600	.25	.45	.85

Obv: Small legend, different style.

KM#	Date	Year	Mintage	VF	XF	Unc
58.3	AH1397	1977	2.000	.25	.45	.85
	1398	1978	1.000	.25	.45	.85
	1400	1980	1.000	.25	.45	.85
	1400	1980	Inc. Ab.	—	Proof	3.00

Obv: Large legend style changed,
small denomination.
Rev: Ribbon w/long center section.

KM#	Date	Year		VF	XF	Unc
58.2	AH1400	1980				
			Inc. KM58.1	.25	.45	.85

NOTE: Edge varieties exist.

Obv: Large legend and small denomination,
style similar to KM#58.1.

KM#	Date	Year		VF	XF	Unc
58.4	AH1400	1980				
			Inc. KM58.1	.25	.45	.85

NOTE: Edge varieties exist.

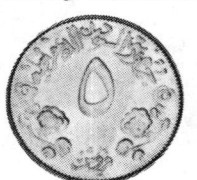 

F.A.O. Issue

KM#	Date	Year	Mintage	VF	XF	Unc
65	AH1396	1976	.500	.20	.30	.65
	1398	1978	—	.20	.30	.65

20th Anniversary of Independence

KM#	Date	Year	Mintage	VF	XF	Unc
66	AH1396	1976	3.940	.25	.50	1.00

Council of Arab Economic Unity

KM#	Date	Year	Mintage	VF	XF	Unc
74	AH1398	1978	5.040	.15	.25	.50

NOTE: Edge varieties exist.

 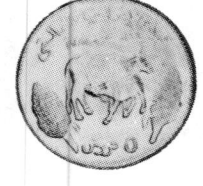

F.A.O. Issue

KM#	Date	Year	Mintage	VF	XF	Unc
84	AH1401	1981	1.000	.20	.40	.75

NOTE: Edge varieties exist.

BRASS
Obv: Large denomination.
Rev: Ribbon w/3 equal sections.

KM#	Date	Year		VF	XF	Unc
110.1	AH1403	1983		.25	.60	1.55

Obv: Small denomination, legend different style.

KM#	Date	Year		VF	XF	Unc
110.3	AH1403	1983	—	5.00	7.00	10.00

Rev: Ribbon w/long center section.

KM#	Date	Year		VF	XF	Unc
110.2	AH1403	1983	—	.50	1.25	2.25

Obv: Large denomination, legend
similar to KM#110.1.

KM#	Date	Year		VF	XF	Unc
110.4	AH1403	1983	—	1.50	4.50	7.50

ALUMINUM-BRONZE
Obv: Denomination.
Rev: The Central Bank Building.

KM#	Date	Year		VF	XF	Unc
100	AH1408	1987		.40	1.00	2.00

10 GHIRSH

COPPER-NICKEL
Obv: Large written denomination.

KM#	Date	Year	Mintage	VF	XF	Unc
35.1	AH1376	1956	15.000	.35	.75	2.00
	1386	1966	—	—	Proof	—
	1387	1967	—	.30	.60	1.50
	1388	1968	—	.30	.60	1.50
	1389	1969	—	.30	.60	1.50

Obv: New large Arabic legend and
written denomination.

KM#	Date	Year	Mintage	VF	XF	Unc
45.1	AH1390	1970	—	.60	1.25	2.50
	1391	1971	.385	.60	1.25	2.50

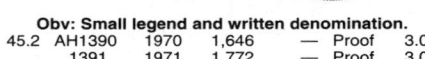

Obv: Small legend and written denomination.

KM#	Date	Year	Mintage	VF	XF	Unc
45.2	AH1390	1970	1,646	—	Proof	3.00
	1391	1971	1,772	—	Proof	3.00

2nd Anniversary of Revolution

KM#	Date	Year	Mintage	VF	XF	Unc
52	AH1391	1971	.500	.60	1.25	3.00

Obv: Thick legend.
Rev: Ribbon w/3 equal sections.

KM#	Date	Year	Mintage	VF	XF	Unc
59.1	AH1395	1975	1.000	.50	1.00	2.50

Obv: Thin legend, different style.

KM#	Date	Year	Mintage	VF	XF	Unc
59.5	AH1397	1977	1.000	.50	1.00	2.75
	1400	1980	2.965	.50	1.00	2.75
	1400	1980	—	—	Proof	4.50

Rev: Ribbon w/long center section.

KM#	Date	Year	Mintage	VF	XF	Unc
59.2	AH1400	1980	—	.50	1.00	2.50

NOTE: Edge varieties exist.

Reduced size.

KM#	Date	Year		VF	XF	Unc
59.3	AH1403	1983		.50	1.00	2.50

NOTE: Edge varieties exist.

Obv: Similar to KM#59.3.
Rev: Ribbon w/3 equal sections.

KM#	Date	Year	Mintage	VF	XF	Unc
59.4	AH1403	1983	1.100	7.00	10.00	20.00

F.A.O. Issue

KM#	Date	Year	Mintage	VF	XF	Unc
67	AH1396	1976	.500	.30	.65	1.50
	1398	1978	—	.30	.65	1.50

20th Anniversary of Independence

KM#	Date	Year	Mintage	VF	XF	Unc
68	AH1396	1976	5.540	.25	.60	1.25

NOTE: Edge varieties exist.

Council of Arab Economic Unity

KM#	Date	Year	Mintage	VF	XF	Unc
95	AH1398	1978	1.000	.60	1.25	2.50

NOTE: Edge varieties exist.

F.A.O. Issue

| 85 | AH1401 | 1981 | 1.000 | .60 | 1.25 | 2.50 |

NOTE: Edge varieties exist.

ALUMINUM-BRONZE
Obv: Denomination.
Rev: Central Bank Building.

| 107 | AH1408 | 1987 | — | .75 | 1.50 | 3.00 |

20 GHIRSH

| 98 | AH1403 | 1983 | .072 | — | — | 5.00 |

F.A.O. Issue

| 96 | AH1405 | 1985 | — | — | — | 3.00 |

ALUMINUM-BRONZE
Obv: Small denomination.
Rev: Central Bank Building.

| 101.1 | AH1408 | 1987 | — | .60 | 1.25 | 2.50 |

Obv: Large denomination.

| 101.2 | AH1408 | 1987 | — | .60 | 1.25 | 2.50 |

25 GHIRSH

COPPER-NICKEL
F.A.O. Issue

KM#	Date	Year	Mintage	VF	XF	Unc
38	AH1388	1968	.224	—	P/L	15.00

ALUMINUM-BRONZE
Obv: Denomination.
Rev: Central Bank Building.

| 102 | AH1408 | 1987 | — | .85 | 1.75 | 3.50 |

STAINLESS STEEL
Obv: Denomination.
Rev: Central Bank Building.

| 108 | AH1409 | 1989 | — | .50 | 1.00 | 2.25 |

50 GHIRSH

COPPER-NICKEL
F.A.O. Issue
Rev: Large design.

| 56.1 | AH1392 | 1972 | 1.000 | 1.50 | 3.00 | 6.50 |

Rev: Small design.

| 56.2 | AH1392 | 1972 | 30,000 | 5.00 | 10.00 | 20.00 |

NOTE: Struck in 1976.

Establishment of Arab Cooperative

| 69 | AH1396 | 1976 | | 1.00 | 2.25 | 4.50 |

8th Anniversary of 1969 Revolt
F.A.O. Issue

KM#	Date	Year	Mintage	VF	XF	Unc
73	AH1397	1977	.100	1.00	2.25	4.50

ALUMINUM-BRONZE
Obv: Denomination.
Central Bank Building.

| 103 | AH1408 | 1987 | — | .75 | 1.75 | 3.75 |

33rd Anniversary of Independence

| 105 | AH1409 | 1989 | — | .75 | 1.75 | 3.75 |

STAINLESS STEEL
Obv: Denomination.
Rev: Central Bank Building.

| 109 | AH1409 | 1989 | — | .65 | 1.25 | 2.75 |

POUND

COPPER-NICKEL
Rural Women and F.A.O. Issue

| 75 | AH1398 | 1978 | .456 | 2.50 | 4.00 | 8.00 |

ALUMINUM-BRONZE
Obv: Denomination.
Rev: Central Bank Building.

| 104 | AH1408 | 1987 | — | 2.00 | 3.00 | 7.00 |

STAINLESS STEEL
Obv: Denomination.
Rev: Central Bank Building.

| 106 | AH1409 | 1989 | — | .75 | 1.50 | 3.75 |

SURINAME

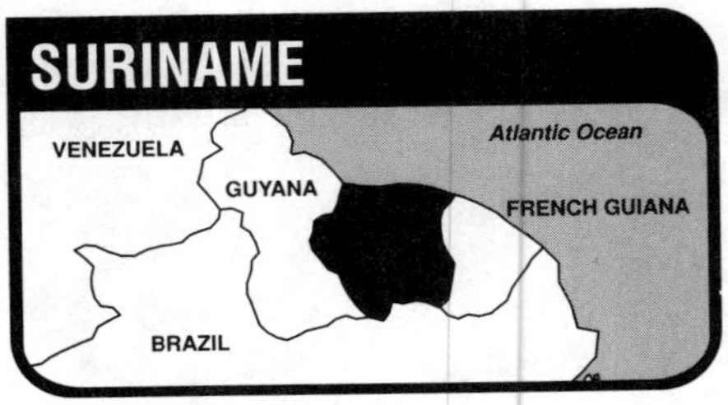

The Republic of Suriname also known as Dutch Guiana, located on the north central coast of South America between Guyana and French Guiana has an area of 63,037 sq. mi. (163,270 sq. km.) and a population of *401,000. Capital: Paramaribo. The country is rich in minerals and forests, and self-sufficient in rice, the staple food crop. The mining, processing and exporting of bauxite is the principal economic activity.

Lieutenants of Amerigo Vespucci sighted the Guiana coast in 1499. Spanish explorers of the 16th century, disappointed at finding no gold, departed leaving the area to be settled by the British in 1652. The colony prospered and the Netherlands acquired it in 1667 in exchange for the Dutch rights in Nieuw Nederland (state of New York). During the European wars of the 18th and 19th centuries, which were fought in part in the new world, Suriname was occupied by the British from 1781-1784 and 1796-1814. Surinam became an autonomous part of the Kingdom of the Netherlands on Dec. 15, 1954. Full independence was achieved on Nov. 25, 1975. In 1980, a coup installed a military government which has since been dissolved.

RULERS

Dutch, until 1975

MINT MARKS

(B) - British Royal Mint, no mint mark
FM - Franklin Mint, U.S.A.**
P - Philadelphia, U.S.A.
S - Sydney
(u) - Utrecht (privy marks only)

****NOTE:** From 1975-1985 the Franklin Mint produced coinage in up to 3 different qualities. Qualities of issue are designated in ( ) after each date and are defined as follows:

(M) MATTE - Normal circulation strike or a dull finish produced by sandblasting special uncirculated (polish finish) or proof quality dies.

(U) SPECIAL UNCIRCULATED - Polished or proof-like in appearance without any frosted features.

(P) PROOF - The highest quality obtainable having mirror-like fields and frosted features.

MONETARY SYSTEM

100 Cents = 1 Gulden (Guilders)

World War II Coinage

The 1942-43 issues following are homeland coinage types of the Netherlands - KM#152, KM#163 and KM#164 - were executed expressly for use in Suriname. Related issues produced for use in both Curacao and Suriname are listed under Curacao. They are distinguished by the presence of a palm tree (acorn on Homeland issues) and a mint mark (P-Philadelphia, D-Denver, S-San Francisco) flanking the date. Also see the Netherlands for similar issues.

CENT

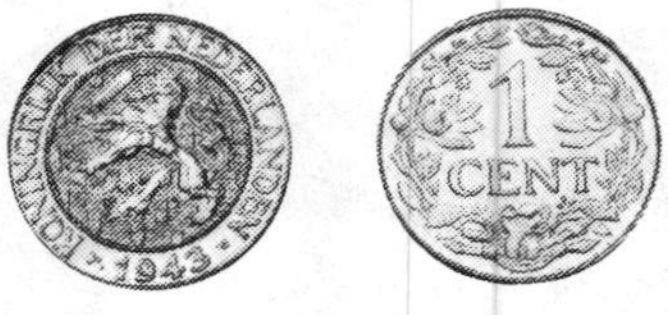

BRASS

KM#	Date	Mintage	Fine	VF	XF	Unc
10	1943P palm					
(2)		4.000	1.00	2.50	6.00	12.00

BRONZE

KM#	Date	Mintage	Fine	VF	XF	Unc
10a	1957(u)	1.200	.50	1.00	2.50	5.50
(2a)	1957(u)	—	—	—	Proof	27.50
	1959(u)	1.800	.50	1.00	2.50	5.50
	1959(u)	—	—	—	Proof	27.50
	1960(u)	1.200	.50	1.00	2.50	5.50
	1960(u)	—	—	—	Proof	30.00

NOTE: For similar coins dated 1942P see Netherlands Antilles (Curacao).

10 CENT

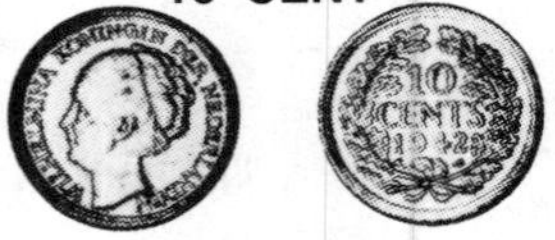

1.4000 g, .640 SILVER, .0288 oz ASW

KM#	Date	Mintage	Fine	VF	XF	Unc
9	1942P palm					
(1)		1.500	3.75	7.50	15.00	30.00

NOTE: For similar coins dated 1941P and 1943P see Netherlands Antilles (Curacao).

MODERN COINAGE

CENT

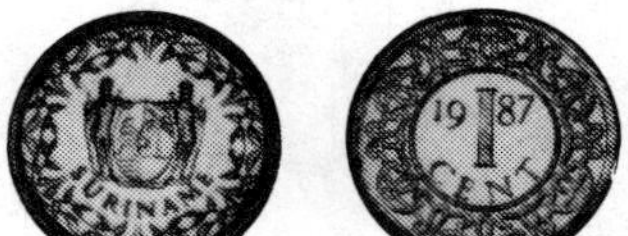

BRONZE

KM#	Date	Mintage	Fine	VF	XF	Unc
11	1962(u) fish					
(3)		6.000	—	.25	.75	1.25
	1962(u)S					
		650 pcs.	—	—	Proof	35.00
	1966(u)	6.500	—	.25	.75	1.25
	1966(u)	—	—	—	Proof	50.00
	1970(u) cock					
		5.000	—	.20	.60	1.00
	1972(u)	6.000	—	.20	.60	1.00

ALUMINUM

KM#	Date	Mintage	Fine	VF	XF	Unc
11a	1972	—	—	—	Proof	450.00
(3a)	1974(u)	1.000	—	.10	.25	.50
	1975(u)	1.000	—	.10	.25	.50
	1976(u)	3.000	—	.10	.25	.50
	1976	*10 pcs.	—	—	Proof	50.00
	1977(u)	10.000	—	—	.10	.25
	1978(u)	6.000	—	—	.10	.25
	1979(u)	10.000	—	—	.10	.25
	1980(u) cock and star privy marks					
		8.000	—	—	.10	.25
	1982(u) anvil					
		8.000	—	—	.10	.25
	1984	5.000	—	—	.10	.25
	1985	2.000	—	—	.10	.25
	1986	3.000	—	—	.10	.25

COPPER PLATED STEEL

KM#	Date	Mintage	Fine	VF	XF	Unc
11b	1987(B)	—	—	—	—	.10
(3b)	1988(B)	*1,500	—	—	Proof	2.00
	1989(B)	—	—	—	—	.10

5 CENT

For a 5 cent coin dated 1943 see Netherlands Antilles (Curacao).

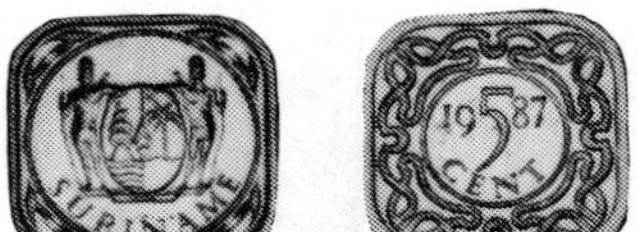

NICKEL-BRASS

KM#	Date	Mintage	Fine	VF	XF	Unc
12.1	1962(u) fish					
(4.1)		2.200	.20	.50	1.00	1.75
	1962(u)S					
		650 pcs.	—	—	Proof	25.00
	1966(u) privy marks					
		2.300	.20	.40	.75	1.50
	1966(u)	—	—	—	Proof	50.00
	1966 w/o privy marks					
		.400	.50	1.00	3.00	5.00
	1971(u) cock					
		.500	.20	.40	.75	1.50
	1972(u)	1.500	.20	.40	.75	1.50

Medal struck

KM#	Date	Mintage	Fine	VF	XF	Unc
12.2	1966(u)	—	3.00	7.50	15.00	30.00
(4.2)						

ALUMINUM

KM#	Date	Mintage	Fine	VF	XF	Unc
12.1a	1966(u)	—	—	—	Proof	450.00
(4.1a)	1976(u)	5.500	—	.15	.25	.60
	1976	*10 pcs.	—	—	Proof	75.00
	1978(u)	3.000	—	.15	.25	.60
	1979(u)	2.000	—	.15	.25	.60
	1980(u) cock and star privy marks					
		1.000	—	.15	.25	.60
	1982(u) anvil					
		1.000	—	.15	.25	.60
	1985(u)	1.000	—	.15	.25	.60
	1986(u)	1.500	—	.15	.25	.60

COPPER PLATED STEEL

KM#	Date	Mintage	Fine	VF	XF	Unc
12.1b	1987(B)	—	—	—	.10	.20
(4.1b)	1988(B)	—	—	—	.10	.20
	1988(B)	*1,500	—	—	Proof	2.00
	1989(B)	—	—	—	.10	.20

10 CENT

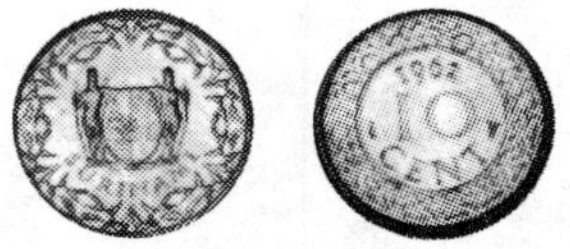

COPPER-NICKEL

KM#	Date	Mintage	Fine	VF	XF	Unc
13	1962(u) fish					
(5)		3.000	—	.50	1.00	2.00
	1962(u)S					
		650 pcs.	—	—	Proof	25.00
	1966(u)	2.500	—	.50	1.00	2.00
(5)	1966(u)	—	—	—	Proof	60.00
	1971(u) cock					
		.500	.40	1.00	3.75	6.00
	1972(u)	1.500	—	.35	.70	1.30
	1974(u)	1.500	—	.35	.70	1.30
	1976(u)	5.000	—	.10	.25	.60
	1976	*10 pcs.	—	—	Proof	100.00
	1978(u)	2.000	—	.10	.25	.60
	1979(u)	2.000	—	.10	.25	.60
	1982(u) anvil					
		1.000	—	.10	.25	.60
	1985(u)	1.000	—	.10	.25	.60
	1986(u)	1.500	—	.10	.25	.60

NICKEL PLATED STEEL

KM#	Date	Mintage	Fine	VF	XF	Unc
13a	1987(B)	—	—	.10	.25	.60
(5a)	1988(B)	*1,500	—	—	Proof	3.00
	1989(B)	—	—	.10	.25	.60

25 CENT

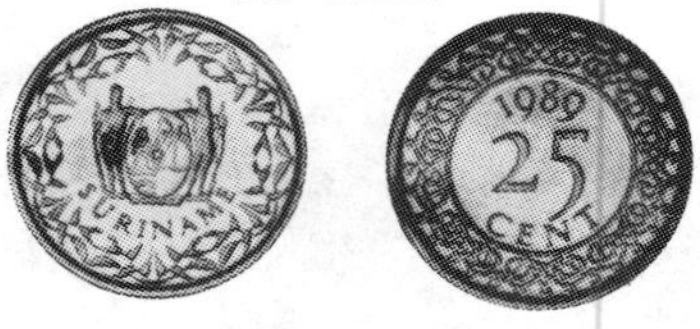

COPPER-NICKEL

KM#	Date	Mintage	Fine	VF	XF	Unc
14	1962(u) fish					
(6)		2.300	.25	.50	1.00	2.00
	1962(u)S					
		650 pcs.	—	—	Proof	25.00
	1966(u)	2.300	.25	.50	1.00	2.00
	1966(u)	—	—	—	Proof	60.00
	1972(u) cock					
		1.800	.25	.50	1.00	2.00
	1974(u)	1.500	.25	.50	1.00	2.00
	1976(u)	5.000	—	.20	.30	.65
	1976	*10 pcs.	—	—	Proof	125.00
	1979(u)	2.000	—	.20	.30	.65
	1982(u) anvil					
		2.000	—	.20	.30	.65
	1985(u)	1.000	—	.20	.30	.65
	1986(u)	1.500	—	.20	.30	.65

NICKEL PLATED STEEL

KM#	Date	Mintage	Fine	VF	XF	Unc
14a	1987(B)	—	—	.20	.30	.65
(6a)	1988(B)	—	—	.20	.30	.65
	1988(B)	*1,500	—	—	Proof	5.00
	1989(B)	—	—	.20	.30	.65

100 CENT

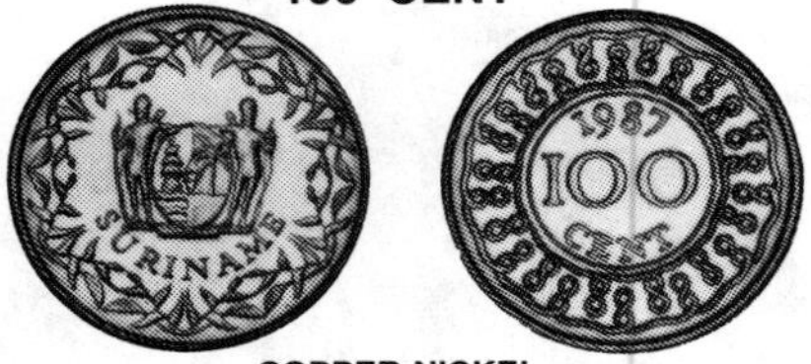

COPPER-NICKEL

KM#	Date	Mintage	Fine	VF	XF	Unc
23	1987(B)	—	—	—	.75	1.65
(15)	1988(B)	—	—	—	.75	1.65
	1988(B)	*1,500	—	—	Proof	12.00
	1989(B)	—	—	—	.75	1.65

250 CENT

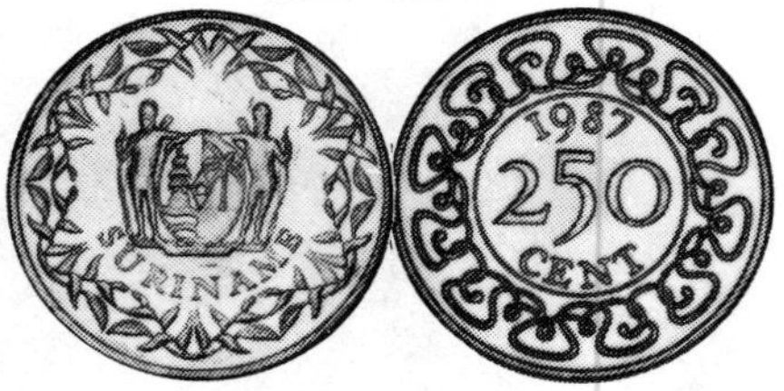

COPPER-NICKEL

KM#	Date	Mintage	Fine	VF	XF	Unc
24	1987(B)	—	—	—	1.75	3.75
(16)	1988(B)	*1,500	—	—	Proof	17.50
	1989(B)	—	—	—	1.75	3.75

GULDEN

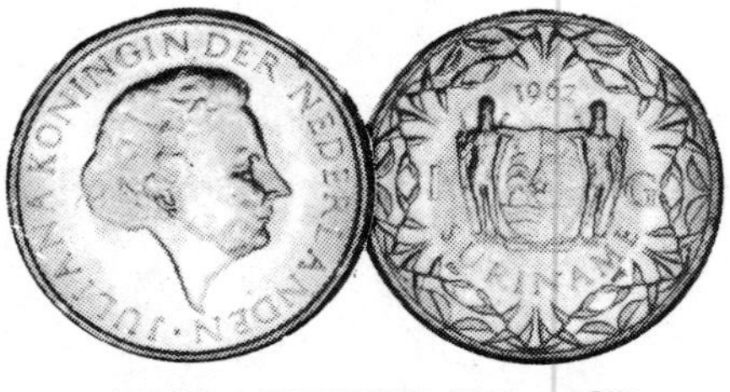

10.0000 g, .720 SILVER, .2315 oz ASW

KM#	Date	Mintage	Fine	VF	XF	Unc
15	1962(u)	.150	—	2.25	4.00	8.00
(7)	1962(u)S					
		650 pcs.	—	—	Proof	40.00
	1966(u)	*.100	10.00	25.00	50.00	100.00
	1966(u)	—	—	—	Proof	175.00

***NOTE:** Never officially released to circulation.

SWAZILAND

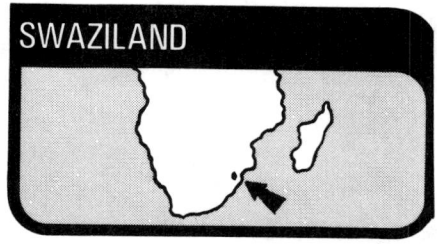

The Kingdom of Swaziland, located in south-eastern Africa, has an area of 6,704 sq. mi. (17,360 sq. km.) and a population of *756,000. Capital: Mbabane (administrative); Lobamba (legislative). The diversified economy includes mining, agriculture, and light industry. Asbestos, iron ore, wood pulp, and sugar are exported.

The people of the present Swazi nation established themselves in an area including what is now Swaziland in the early 1800s. The first Swazi contact with the British came early in the reign of the extremely able Swazi leader Mswati when he asked the British for aid against Zulu raids into Swaziland. The British and Transvaal responded by guaranteeing the independence of Swaziland, 1881. South Africa assumed the power of protection and adminstration in 1894 and Swaziland continued under this administration until the conquest of the Transvaal during the Anglo-Boer War, when administration was transferred to the British government. After World War II, Britain began to prepare Swaziland for independence, which was achieved on Sept. 6, 1968. The Kingdom is a member of the Commonwealth of Nations. King Mswati III is Head of State. The prime minister is Head of Government.

RULERS
Sobhuza II, 1968-1982
Queen Dzeliwe, Regent for
  Prince Makhosetive, 1982-1986
King Msawati III, 1986-

MONETARY SYSTEM
100 Cents = 1 Luhlanga
25 Luhlanga = 1 Lilangeni
  (plural - Emalangeni)

CENT

BRONZE
Ananas

KM#	Date	Mintage	VF	XF	Unc
7	1974	6.002	—	.10	.20
	1974	.013	—	Proof	.75
	1975	—	—	.10	.25
	1979	.500	—	.10	.25
	1979	.010	—	Proof	.75
	1982	—	—	.10	.25
	1983	1.100	—	.10	.25

F.A.O. Issue

21	1975	2.500	—	.10	.25

COPPER PLATED STEEL

39	1986	2.000	—	.10	.25
	1987	10.000	—	.10	.25

BRONZE

39a	1986	—	—	—	—

Obv: King's bust. Rev: Pineapple.

51	1995	—	—	—	.25

2 CENTS

BRONZE

KM#	Date	Mintage	VF	XF	Unc
8	1974	2.252	—	.15	.30
	1974	.013	—	Proof	.75
	1975	—	—	.15	.30
	1979	1.000	—	.15	.30
	1979	.010	—	Proof	1.00
	1982	.500	—	.15	.30

F.A.O. Issue

22	1975	1.500	—	.15	.30

5 CENTS

COPPER-NICKEL
Arum Lily

9	1974	1.252	.10	.20	.40
	1974	.013	—	Proof	1.00
	1975	1.500	.10	.20	.40
	1979	1.680	.10	.20	.40
	1979	.010	—	Proof	1.75

40.1	1986	—	.15	.25	.50

NICKEL PLATED STEEL

40.2	1992	—	.15	.25	.50

COPPER-NICKEL
King Msawati III

48	1995	—	—	—	.50
	1996	—	—	—	.50
	1998	—	—	—	.50

10 CENTS

COPPER-NICKEL
Sugar Cane

10	1974	.752	.15	.25	.50
	1974	.013	—	Proof	1.00
	1979	.500	.15	.25	.50
	1979	4,231	—	Proof	2.50

F.A.O. Issue

23	1975	1.500	.15	.25	.50

 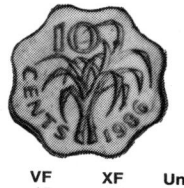

KM#	Date	Mintage	VF	XF	Unc
41.1	1986	—	.15	.25	.50
	1992	—	.15	.25	.50

King Msawati III

49	1995	—	—	—	.50
	1996	—	—	—	.50
	1998	—	—	—	.50

20 CENTS

COPPER-NICKEL

11	1974	.502	.35	.75	1.50
	1974	.013	—	Proof	3.00
	1975	1.000	.35	.75	1.50
	1979	—	.35	.75	1.50
	1979	.010	—	Proof	3.00
	1984	—	.35	.75	1.50

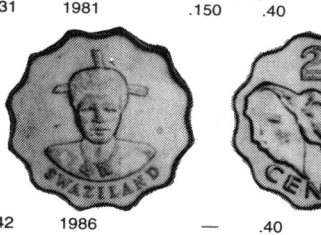

F.A.O. Issue

31	1981	.150	.40	.80	1.75

42	1986	—	.40	.80	1.75

King Msawati III

50	1996	—	—	—	1.25
	1998	—	—	—	1.25

50 CENTS

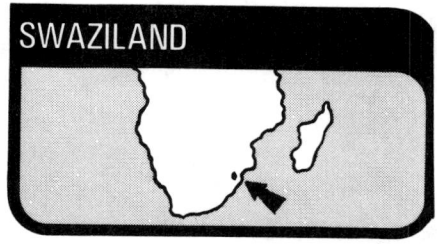

COPPER-NICKEL

12	1974	.252	1.00	1.50	2.75
	1974	.013	—	Proof	3.00
	1975	.500	1.00	1.50	2.75
	1979	—	.50	1.00	2.50

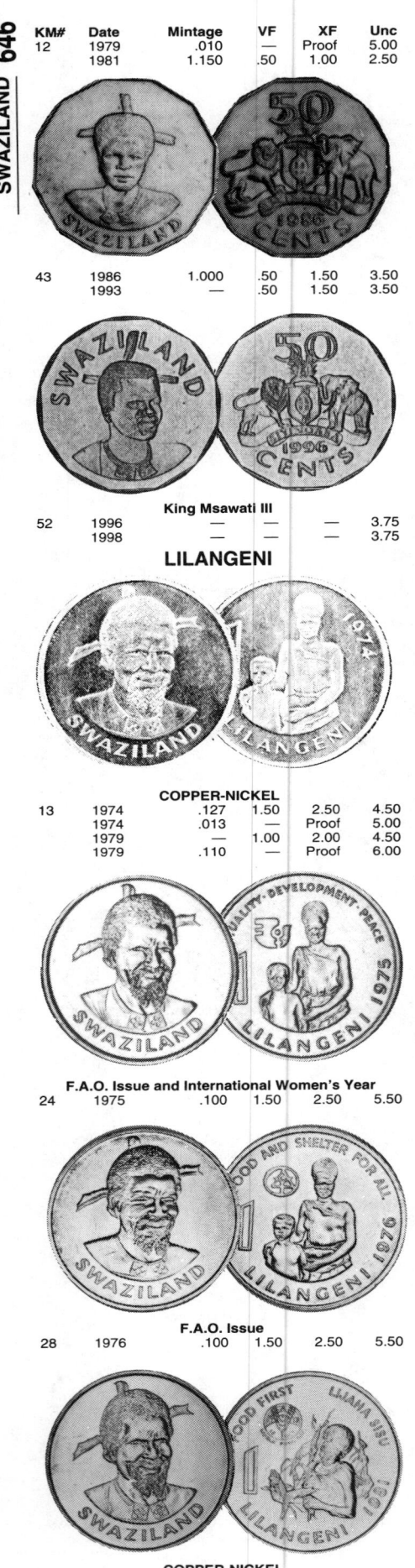

KM#	Date	Mintage	VF	XF	Unc
12	1979	.010	—	Proof	5.00
	1981	1.150	.50	1.00	2.50

| 43 | 1986 | 1.000 | .50 | 1.50 | 3.50 |
| | 1993 | — | .50 | 1.50 | 3.50 |

King Msawati III

| 52 | 1996 | — | — | — | 3.75 |
| | 1998 | — | — | — | 3.75 |

LILANGENI

COPPER-NICKEL

13	1974	.127	1.50	2.50	4.50
	1974	.013	—	Proof	5.00
	1979	—	1.00	2.00	4.50
	1979	.110	—	Proof	6.00

F.A.O. Issue and International Women's Year

| 24 | 1975 | .100 | 1.50 | 2.50 | 5.50 |

F.A.O. Issue

| 28 | 1976 | .100 | 1.50 | 2.50 | 5.50 |

COPPER-NICKEL
F.A.O. Issue

| 32 | 1981 | .871 | 1.50 | 3.00 | 7.00 |

NICKEL-BRASS

KM#	Date	Mintage	VF	XF	Unc
44.1	1986	1.025	—	2.00	4.00

NICKEL-BRASS PLATED STEEL

| 44.2 | 1992 | — | — | 1.50 | 3.50 |

BRASS

| 45 | 1995 | — | — | 1.50 | 3.50 |
| | 1998 | — | — | 1.50 | 3.50 |

2 EMALANGENI

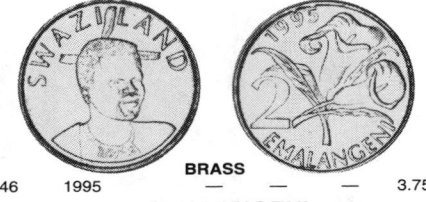

COPPER-NICKEL

| 33a | 1981 | .050 | 2.00 | 3.50 | 7.50 |

BRASS

| 46 | 1995 | — | — | — | 3.75 |

5 EMALANGENI

BRASS

| 47 | 1996 | — | — | — | 6.00 |

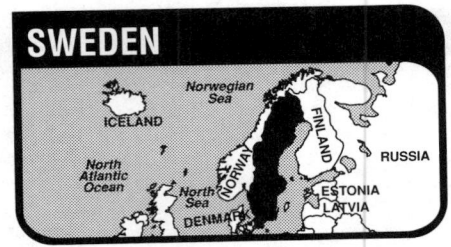

SWEDEN

The Kingdom of Sweden, a limited constitutional monarchy located in northern Europe between Norway and Finland, has an area of 173,732 sq. mi. (449,960 sq. km.) and a population of *8.5 million. Capital: Stockholm. Mining, lumbering and a specialized machine industry dominate the economy. Machinery, paper, iron and steel, motor vehicles and wood pulp are exported.

Sweden was founded as a Christian stronghold by Olaf Skottkonung late in the 10th century. After conquering Finland late in the 13th century, Sweden, together with Norway, came under the rule of Denmark, 1397-1523, in an association known as the Union of Kalmar. Modern Sweden had its beginning in 1523 when Gustaf Vasa drove the Danes out of Sweden and was himself chosen king. Under Gustaf Adolphus II and Charles XII, Sweden was one of the great powers of 17th century Europe - until Charles invaded Russia in 1708, and was defeated at the Battle of Pultowa in June, 1709. Early in the 18th century, a coalition of Russia, Poland and Denmark took away Sweden's Baltic empire and in 1809 Sweden was forced to cede Finland to Russia. Norway was ceded to Sweden by the Treaty of Kiel in January, 1814. The Norwegians resisted for a time but later signed the Act of Union at the Convention of Moss in August, 1814. The Union was dissolved in 1905 and Norway became independent. A new constitution which took effect on Jan. 1, 1975, restricts the function of the king largely to a ceremonial role.

RULERS

Oscar II, 1872-1907
Gustaf V, 1907-1950
Gustaf VI, 1950-1973
Carl XVI Gustaf, 1973-

MINTMASTERS INITIALS

Letter	Date	Name
AL	1898-1916	Adolf Lindberg, engraver
D	1986-	Bengt Dennis
EB	1876-1908	Emil Brusewitz
EL	1916-1944	Erik Lindberg, engraver
G	1927-1945	Alf Grabe
LH	1944-1974	Leo Holmberg, engraver
TS	1945-1961	Torsten Swensson
U	1961-1986	Benkt Ulvfot
W	1908-1927	Karl-August Wallroth

MONETARY SYSTEM

100 Ore = 1 Krona

ORE

BRONZE
Obv: Legend lengthened.

KM#	Date	Mintage	Fine	VF	XF	Unc
750	1901	3.075	.50	1.50	3.00	7.50
(528)	1902	2.685	.50	1.50	3.00	7.50
	1903	2.696	.50	1.50	3.00	7.50
	1904	2.033	.50	1.00	3.00	7.50
	1905	3.556	.50	1.00	2.00	6.00

NOTE: Earlier dates (1879-1900) exist for this type.

| 768 | 1906 | 1.783 | 3.00 | 7.50 | 12.50 | 30.00 |
| (543) | 1907 | 8.251 | .20 | .50 | 2.00 | 4.00 |

Obv: Small cross.

| 777.1 | 1909 | 3.810 | 6.00 | 8.00 | 17.50 | 85.00 |
| (552.1) | | | | | | |

Obv: Large cross.

777.2	1909	Inc. Ab.	2.00	3.00	7.50	25.00
(552.2)	1910	1.583	3.00	6.00	10.00	40.00
	1911	3.150	.75	1.50	3.00	12.50
	1912/1	3.170	7.50	20.00	40.00	200.00
	1912	Inc. Ab.	.75	1.50	3.00	12.50
	1913/12	3.197	3.50	10.00	20.00	100.00

KM#	Date	Mintage	Fine	VF	XF	Unc
(552.2)	1913	Inc. Ab.	.75	1.50	3.00	12.50
	1914 open 4					
		2.214	35.00	60.00	110.00	350.00
	1914 closed 4					
		Inc. Ab.	.75	1.50	4.50	25.00
	1915/3	4.471	2.00	6.00	10.00	30.00
	1915	Inc. Ab.	.25	.50	1.50	6.00

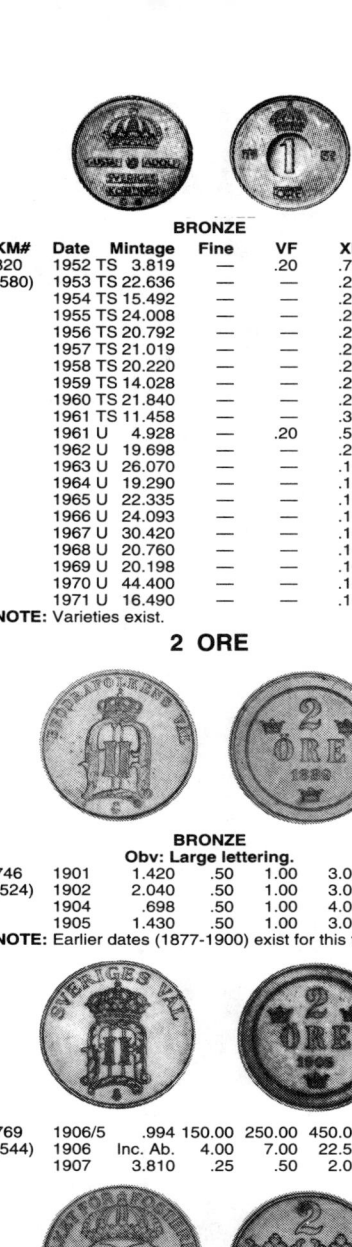

1916 short 6

		7.620	.25	.50	1.50	6.00

1916 long 6

		Inc. Ab.	.30	.75	2.00	9.00
	1920	5.548	.25	.50	1.00	4.00
	1921	7.442	.25	.50	1.00	4.00
	1922	1.166	2.00	4.00	6.00	25.00
	1923	4.512	.35	.75	1.50	6.00
	1924	2.579	.25	.75	1.50	7.00
	1925	4.715	.15	.35	.50	3.00
	1926	6.739	.15	.35	.50	3.00
	1927	3.601	.15	.35	.50	3.00
	1928	2.381	.25	.75	2.00	9.00
	1929 curved 2					
		6.091	.20	.35	.75	3.50
	1929 straight 2					
		Inc. Ab.	.40	.60	2.00	7.50
	1930	5.477	.20	.35	.75	3.50
	1931	5.680	.20	.35	.75	3.50
	1932	3.339	—	.45	1.50	6.00
	1933	3.427	—	.45	.75	5.00
	1934	6.121	—	.30	.50	3.00
	1935	4.600	—	.30	.50	3.00

1936 long 6

		6.116	.20	.45	1.00	3.50

1936 short 6

		Inc. Ab.	—	.25	.50	2.50
	1937	7.738	—	.20	.50	1.50
	1938	6.993	—	.20	.50	1.50
	1939	6.562	—	.20	.50	1.50
	1940	4.060	—	.20	.35	1.25
	1941	11.599	—	.20	.35	1.25
	1942	3.992	—	.20	.50	1.50
	1950	22.421	—	.20	.30	1.25

IRON
World War I Issues

KM#	Date	Mintage	Fine	VF	XF	Unc
789	1917	8.128	.75	1.50	4.00	25.00
(560)	1918	9.706	1.00	2.25	6.00	35.00
	1919	7.170	1.50	3.00	7.00	45.00

World War II Issues
Similar to KM#777.

810	1942	10.053	—	.20	.60	3.00
(572)	1943	10.714	—	.20	.75	4.00
	1944	8.699	—	.20	.60	4.00
	1945	9.527	—	.20	.60	4.00
	1945 serif 4					
		Inc. Ab.	3.00	6.00	12.50	22.50
	1946	6.611	—	.25	1.00	5.00
	1947	14.245	—	.20	.40	2.00
	1948	15.442	—	.20	.40	2.00
	1949	11.779	—	.20	.40	2.00
	1950	14.432	—	.20	.40	2.00

BRONZE

KM#	Date	Mintage	Fine	VF	XF	Unc
820	1952 TS	3.819	—	.20	.75	3.00
(580)	1953 TS	22.636	—	—	.25	2.00
	1954 TS	15.492	—	—	.25	2.00
	1955 TS	24.008	—	—	.25	2.00
	1956 TS	20.792	—	—	.25	2.00
	1957 TS	21.019	—	—	.25	2.00
	1958 TS	20.220	—	—	.25	2.00
	1959 TS	14.028	—	—	.25	2.00
	1960 TS	21.840	—	—	.20	2.00
	1961 TS	11.458	—	—	.30	2.25
	1961 U	4.928	—	.20	.50	4.00
	1962 U	19.698	—	—	.25	2.00
	1963 U	26.070	—	—	.10	.30
	1964 U	19.290	—	—	.10	.30
	1965 U	22.335	—	—	.10	.30
	1966 U	24.093	—	—	.10	.20
	1967 U	30.420	—	—	.10	.20
	1968 U	20.760	—	—	.10	.20
	1969 U	20.198	—	—	.10	.20
	1970 U	44.400	—	—	.10	.20
	1971 U	16.490	—	—	.10	.20

NOTE: Varieties exist.

2 ORE

BRONZE
Obv: Large lettering.

746	1901	1.420	.50	1.00	3.00	20.00
(524)	1902	2.040	.50	1.00	3.00	20.00
	1904	.698	.50	1.00	4.00	25.00
	1905	1.430	.50	1.00	3.00	20.00

NOTE: Earlier dates (1877-1900) exist for this type.

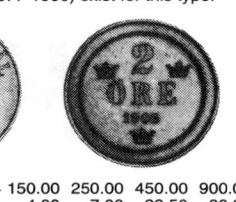

769	1906/5	.994	150.00	250.00	450.00	900.00
(544)	1906	Inc. Ab.	4.00	7.00	22.50	80.00
	1907	3.810	.25	.50	2.00	12.50

778	1909	1.580	.50	2.00	8.00	40.00
(553)	1910	.809	2.25	11.00	20.00	75.00
	1912	.446	4.75	16.00	30.00	85.00
	1913	.806	.25	2.00	10.00	40.00
	1914	1.200	.25	2.00	10.00	40.00
	1915/4	.814	4.00	12.50	35.00	85.00
	1915	Inc. Ab.	.25	2.00	10.00	40.00
	1916/5	2.820	3.00	9.00	25.00	75.00
	1916 short 6					
		Inc. Ab.	.25	.50	5.00	25.00
	1916 long 6					
		Inc. Ab.	.25	.50	5.00	25.00
	1919	1.203	.25	.50	4.00	20.00
	1920	3.465	.30	.50	2.00	10.00
	1921	2.958	.30	.50	2.00	10.00
	1922	.932	.80	1.50	6.00	30.00
	1923	.769	1.00	2.50	6.00	40.00
	1924	1.283	.25	.75	3.00	22.50
	1925	3.903	.20	.50	1.50	12.50
	1926	3.579	.20	.50	1.50	12.50
	1927	2.190	.20	.50	1.50	12.50
	1928	.832	.40	1.00	4.00	25.00
	1929	2.384	.20	.30	1.50	10.00
	1930	2.590	.20	.30	1.50	10.00
	1931	2.296	.20	.30	1.50	10.00
	1932	1.179	.30	.75	4.00	25.00
	1933	1.721	.20	.35	1.50	10.00
	1934	1.795	.20	.35	1.50	10.00
	1935	3.678	.20	.30	1.00	6.00
	1936 short 6					
		2.244	.10	.25	.75	5.00
	1936 long 6					
		Inc. Ab.	.75	1.25	3.00	15.00
	1937	2.981	.10	.25	1.00	5.00
	1938	3.225	.10	.25	.50	5.00
	1939	4.014	.10	.25	.50	4.00
	1940	3.305	.10	.25	.50	4.00

KM#	Date	Mintage	Fine	VF	XF	Unc
(553)	1941	7.337	.10	.25	.50	4.00
	1942	1.614	.30	.75	1.25	10.00
	1950	5.823	.10	.25	.50	4.00

IRON
World War I Issues
Similar to KM#553.

790	1917	4.576	2.00	3.50	8.00	40.00
(561)	1918	4.982	2.50	5.50	12.50	50.00
	1919	2.923	8.00	12.50	25.00	80.00
	1920	1 pc.	—	—	—	—

World War II Issues

811	1942	9.344	.15	.30	1.50	9.00
(573)	1943	6.999	.15	.30	1.50	9.00
	1944	6.126	.15	.30	1.50	9.00
	1945	4.773	.20	.40	1.50	10.00
	1946	5.854	.15	.30	1.50	9.00
	1947	9.536	.15	.30	.75	6.00
	1948	11.424	.15	.30	.75	6.00
	1949 long 9					
		10.600	.15	.30	.75	6.00
	1949 short 9					
		Inc. Ab.	.15	.30	.75	6.00
	1950	13.323	.15	.30	.75	6.00

BRONZE

821	1952 TS	3.011	.20	.50	.75	5.00
(581)	1953 TS	15.620	.10	.20	.75	4.00
	1954 TS	10.086	.10	.20	.75	4.00
	1955 TS	12.963	.10	.20	.75	4.00
	1956 TS	13.890	.10	.20	.75	4.00
	1957 TS	9.997	.10	.20	.75	4.00
	1958 TS	10.106	.10	.20	.75	4.00
	1959 TS	11.572	.10	.20	.75	4.00
	1960 TS	11.093	.10	.20	.75	4.00
	1961 TS	9.673	.10	.20	.75	4.00
	1961 U	1.075	.75	1.50	3.00	12.50
	1962 U	9.569	—	.10	.50	1.75
	1963 U	13.338	—	.10	.50	1.75
	1964 U	19.346	—	.10	.20	1.75
	1965 U	23.356	—	.10	.20	.75
	1966 U	18.278	—	.10	.20	.75
	1967 U	23.931	—	—	.10	.45
	1968 U	26.238	—	—	.10	.45
	1969 U	16.843	—	—	.10	.45
	1970 U	31.254	—	—	.10	.45
	1971 U	19.179	—	—	.10	.45

NOTE: Varieties exist.

5 ORE

BRONZE
Obv: Large lettering.

757	1901	.442	.75	4.00	10.00	45.00
(533)	1902	.652	.75	4.00	10.00	45.00
	1903	.243	1.50	5.00	15.00	55.00
	1904	.414	.75	4.00	10.00	35.00
	1905	.545	.75	4.00	12.50	45.00

NOTE: Earlier dates (1888-1900) exist for this type.
*NOTE: Varieties exist.

770	1906	.565	.50	3.00	10.00	35.00
(545)	1907	1.953	.35	1.50	5.00	20.00

Obv: Small cross.

KM#	Date	Mintage	Fine	VF	XF	Unc
779.1	1909	.917	1.50	6.00	30.00	160.00
(554.1)						

Obv: Large cross.

779.2	1909	Inc. Ab.	6.00	40.00	250.00	900.00
(554.2)	1910	.031	100.00	250.00	450.00	1150.
	1911	.778	.60	3.00	20.00	110.00
	1912	.547	.75	3.00	30.00	150.00
	1913	.762	.60	2.00	20.00	100.00
	1914	.400	2.00	5.00	35.00	175.00
	1915	1.222	.25	2.50	15.00	50.00
	1916/5	.955	10.00	20.00	35.00	135.00
	1916 short 6					
		Inc. Ab.	.25	2.50	12.50	55.00
	1916 long 6					
		Inc. Ab.	.25	2.50	12.50	55.00
	1917	1 pc.	—	—	—	—
	1919	1.129	.25	1.00	12.00	50.00
	1920	2.361	.25	1.00	8.00	30.00
	1921	1.879	.20	.75	10.00	40.00
	1922	.763	.20	2.50	25.00	95.00
	1923	.506	.75	4.50	60.00	195.00
	1924	.900	.25	1.50	17.50	70.00
	1925	1.944	.20	.75	9.00	40.00
	1926	1.742	.20	.75	9.00	40.00
	1927	.036	75.00	175.00	600.00	1250.
	1928	.987	.20	1.00	10.00	50.00
	1929	1.670	.20	.50	9.00	40.00
	1930	1.716	.20	.50	9.00	40.00
	1931	1.131	—	.50	9.00	40.00
	1932	1.165	—	.50	9.00	40.00
	1933	.574	.65	2.50	25.00	100.00
	1934	1.710	—	.35	5.00	30.00
	1935	1.682	—	.35	5.00	30.00
	1936 short 6					
		1.626	—	.35	6.00	30.00
	1936 long 6					
		Inc. Ab.	.25	.75	7.00	35.00
	1937	2.637	—	.30	4.00	20.00
	1938	2.354	—	.30	4.00	20.00
	1939	2.592	—	.45	6.00	25.00
	1940	2.730	—	.35	3.00	15.00
	1940 serif 4					
		Inc. Ab.	—	.35	3.00	15.00
	1941	2.055	—	.35	3.00	15.00
	1942	.395	2.25	4.75	25.00	95.00
	1950	12.559	—	.25	.75	5.00

NOTE: Varieties exist.

IRON

World War I Issues

Similar to KM#554.

791	1917	2.953	4.00	8.00	17.50	60.00
(562)	1918	2.458	9.00	20.00	30.00	125.00
	1919	2.302	9.00	20.00	30.00	100.00

World War II Issues

812	1942	4.343	.20	.75	4.00	22.50
(574)	1943	5.570	.20	.75	4.00	22.50
	1944	4.562	.20	.75	4.00	22.50
	1945	3.771	.20	.75	4.00	22.50
	1946	2.375	—	.50	3.00	15.00
	1947	6.035	—	.50	3.00	15.00
	1948	6.250	—	.50	3.00	15.00
	1949	7.840	—	.50	2.00	12.50
	1950	5.290	—	.50	2.00	12.50

BRONZE

KM#	Date	Mintage	Fine	VF	XF	Unc
822	1952 TS	3.065	.20	.50	1.50	9.00
(582)	1953 TS	12.329	.20	.50	1.75	9.00
	1954 TS	7.232	.20	.50	1.75	9.00
	1955 TS	8.465	.20	.50	1.50	9.00
	1956 TS	7.997	.20	.50	1.75	9.00
	1957 TS	6.276	.20	.50	1.75	9.00
	1958 TS	9.498	.20	.50	1.75	9.00
	1959 TS	8.370	.20	.50	1.75	9.00
	1960 TS	10.542	.20	.40	1.25	8.00
	1961 TS	3.909	.20	.40	1.25	8.00
	1961 U	2.452	.20	.50	1.25	9.00
	1962 U	22.306	—	.10	.50	3.00
	1963 U	17.156	—	.10	.50	3.00
	1964 U	10.923	—	.10	.75	7.00
	1964 U 50 in crown					
		Inc. Ab.	2.50	5.00	10.00	25.00
	1965 U	22.635	—	.10	.20	1.00
	1966 U	18.213	—	.10	.20	1.00
	1967 U	20.776	—	.10	.20	1.00
	1968 U	27.094	—	.10	.20	1.00
	1969 U	26.887	—	.10	.20	1.00
	1970 U	29.420	—	.10	.20	1.00
	1971 U	15.749	—	.10	.20	1.00

845	1972 U	107.894	—	—	.10	.20
(596)	1973 U	193.038	—	—	.10	.20

COPPER-TIN-ZINC

849	1976 U	4.672	—	—	.10	.35
(600)	1977 U	31.037	—	—	.10	.25
	1978 U	46.022	—	—	.10	.25
	1979 U	65.833	—	—	.10	.25
	1980 U	60.997	—	—	.10	.20
	1981 U	19.791	—	—	.10	.20

COPPER-ZINC

849a	1981 U	35.170	—	—	.10	.15
(600a)	1982 U	40.471	—	—	.10	.15
	1983 U	36.471	—	—	.10	.15
	1984 U	13.455	—	—	.10	.15

10 ORE

1.4500 g, .400 SILVER, .0186 oz ASW

Obv: Large lettering.

755	1902 EB	1.946	.75	2.50	10.00	25.00
(530)	1903 EB	1.509	.75	2.50	10.00	25.00
	1904 EB	3.280	.50	1.25	7.00	17.50

NOTE: Earlier dates (1880-1900) exist for this type.
NOTE: Varieties exist.

774	1907 EB	7.320	.40	1.00	4.50	16.00
(549)						

780	1909 W	1.610	1.25	4.00	12.50	50.00
(555)	1911 W	3.180	.35	2.00	7.50	22.50
	1913 W	1.581	1.00	2.50	10.00	35.00
	1914 W	1.571	.75	3.00	7.50	22.50
	1914 serif 4					
		Inc. Ab.	.75	2.50	10.00	35.00
	1915 W	1.547	.50	2.50	7.50	32.50

KM#	Date	Mintage	Fine	VF	XF	Unc
(555)	1916/5 W	3.035	2.50	7.50	20.00	75.00
	1916 W	Inc. Ab.	.75	1.75	6.00	22.50
	1917 W	4.996	.35	.75	2.50	12.50
	1918 W	4.114	.35	.75	2.50	12.50
	1919 W	5.740	.35	.75	2.50	12.50
	1927 W	2.510	.25	.60	2.50	15.00
	1928 G	2.901	.25	.60	2.50	15.00
	1929 G	5.505	.25	.60	1.75	8.00
	1930 G	3.223	.25	.60	1.75	8.00
	1931 G	4.272	.25	.60	1.75	8.00
	1933 G	1.948	.85	1.75	3.00	17.50
	1934 G	4.059	.25	.50	1.00	5.00
	1935 G	2.426	.25	.50	1.00	5.00
	1936 G short 6					
		5.097	1.75	4.00	16.00	45.00
	1936 G long 6					
		Inc. Ab.	.25	.45	1.25	6.50
	1937 G	5.117	.25	.40	.80	5.00
	1938 G	7.428	.25	.40	.80	5.00
	1938 G	—	—	—	Proof	12.50
	1939/29 G					
		2.021	3.50	7.50	16.50	40.00
	1939 G	Inc. Ab.	.25	.60	2.00	10.00
	1939 G	—	—	—	Proof	17.50
	1940 G	3.017	.25	.50	1.00	5.00
	1941 G	9.106	.25	.50	1.00	5.00
	1942 G	3.692	.25	.50	1.00	5.00

NICKEL-BRONZE

795	1920 W	3.612	.50	1.25	5.00	30.00
(563)	1920 lg. W	I.A.	12.50	25.00	50.00	225.00
	1921 W	2.270	.50	1.50	6.50	30.00
	1923 W	2.144	.50	1.50	7.50	35.00
	1924 W	1.600	.50	2.00	8.00	50.00
	1925 W	1.472	.75	3.50	15.00	65.00
	1940 G	3.374	.20	.50	2.00	12.00
	1941	.816	.75	1.50	4.00	22.50
	1946 TS	4.117	.10	.30	.75	5.00
	1947 TS	4.133	.10	.30	.75	5.00

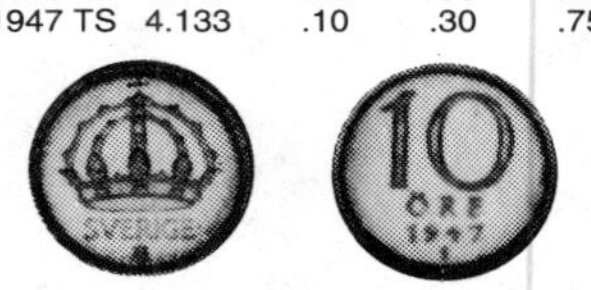

1.4400 g, .400 SILVER, .0185 oz ASW

813	1942 G	1.600	.25	.40	1.00	5.00
(575)	1942 G	—	—	—	Proof	35.00
	1943 G	7.661	.25	.40	1.00	5.00
	1944 G	12.277	.20	.35	.75	4.00
	1945 G	11.703	.20	.35	.75	4.00
	1945 TS	I.A.	.20	.35	.75	4.00
	1945 TS/G	I.A.	.20	.35	1.00	5.00
	1946/5 TS open 6					
		3.576	8.00	16.00	32.00	80.00
	1946 TS open 6					
		Inc. Ab.	.25	.75	2.50	20.00
	1946 TS closed 6					
		Inc. Ab.	.20	.35	1.25	10.00
	1947 TS	7.293	.20	.30	.75	4.00
	1948 TS	10.419	.20	.30	.60	4.00
	1949 TS	12.044	.20	.30	.60	4.00
	1950 TS	31.824	.20	.30	.60	3.00

NOTE: Varieties exist.

823	1952 TS	4.660	BV	.40	.75	4.00
(583)	1953 TS	28.484	BV	.15	.75	4.00
	1954 TS	15.913	BV	.15	.75	4.00
	1955 TS	16.687	BV	.15	.75	4.00
	1956 TS	21.986	BV	.15	.50	3.00
	1957 TS	21.294	BV	.15	.50	3.00
	1958 TS	19.605	BV	.15	.50	3.00
	1959 TS	18.523	BV	.15	.50	3.00
	1960 TS	16.605	BV	.15	.50	3.00
	1961 TS	8.284	BV	.15	.50	3.00
	1961 U	7.843	BV	.15	.50	3.00
	1962 U	8.619	BV	.15	.50	3.00

COPPER-NICKEL

835	1962 U	8.814	.10	.25	.50	3.00
(591)	1963 U	28.170	—	—	.10	.50
	1964 U	36.895	—	—	.10	.50
	1965 U	29.870	—	—	.10	.50
	1966 U	20.435	—	—	.10	.50
	1967 U	18.245	—	—	.10	.50
	1968 U	51.490	—	—	.10	.40
	1969 U	55.880	—	—	.10	.40
	1970 U	60.910	—	—	.10	.40
	1971 U	27.075	—	—	.10	.40

KM#	Date	Mintage	Fine	VF	XF	Unc
(591)	1972 U	36.750	—	—	.10	.20
	1973 U	160.740	—	—	.10	.20

KM#	Date	Mintage	Fine	VF	XF	Unc
850	1976 U	4.173	—	—	.15	.40
(601)	1977 U	44.517	—	—	.10	.30
	1978 U	74.342	—	—	.10	.30
	1979 U	75.306	—	—	.10	.15
	1980 U	108.294	—	—	.10	.15
	1981 U	102.454	—	—	.10	.15
	1982 U	103.906	—	—	.10	.15
	1983 U	77.315	—	—	.10	.15
	1984 U	122.100	—	—	.10	.15
	1985 U	74.222	—	—	.10	.15
	1986 U	83.193	—	—	.10	.15
	1986 D	17.205	—	—	.10	.15
	1987 D	146.877	—	—	.10	.15
	1988 D	194.986	—	—	.10	.15
	1989 D	245.181	—	—	.10	.15
	1990 D	139.238	—	—	.10	.15
	1991 D	5.177	—	—	.15	.35

25 ORE

2.4200 g, .600 SILVER, .0467 oz ASW
Obv: Large lettering.

KM#	Date	Mintage	Fine	VF	XF	Unc
739	1902 EB	1.259	1.00	2.50	10.00	55.00
(531)	1904 EB	.692	1.00	2.50	10.00	55.00
	1905 EB	.732	1.00	2.50	10.00	55.00

NOTE: Earlier dates (1874-1899) exist for this type.

KM#	Date	Mintage	Fine	VF	XF	Unc
775 (550)	1907 EB	3.223	.75	2.00	5.50	30.00

KM#	Date	Mintage	Fine	VF	XF	Unc
785	1910 W large cross					
(556)		2.044	.65	1.25	4.00	35.00
	1910 W small cross					
		Inc. Ab.	6.50	25.00	65.00	350.00
	1912 W	1.014	.65	2.00	12.00	50.00
	1914 W	3.719	.65	2.25	12.50	30.00
	1916 W	1.270	.65	2.00	12.00	50.00
	1917 W	1.657	.65	1.50	4.00	30.00
	1918 W small 8					
		2.365	.65	1.50	6.00	35.00
	1918 W wide 8					
		Inc. Ab.	.65	1.50	7.50	42.50
	1919 W	3.205	.65	1.00	3.50	25.00
	1927 W	1.688	.65	1.25	3.50	25.00
	1928 G	.837	.65	1.50	7.50	42.50
	1929 G	1.125	.65	1.25	4.50	30.00
	1930 G	3.490	.50	1.00	2.00	12.50
	1931 G	1.392	.50	1.00	2.00	12.50
	1932 G	1.133	.50	1.00	2.00	12.50
	1933 G	.964	.50	1.00	6.00	25.00
	1934 G	1.404	.50	1.00	2.00	8.00
	1936 G	1.852	.50	1.00	2.00	8.00
	1937 G small G					
		—	.50	1.25	3.00	12.50
	1937 G	—	—	—	Proof	20.00
	1937 G lg. G	—	.75	1.25	3.00	17.50
		I.A.	.60	1.00	2.50	12.50
	1938 G	3.679	.50	1.00	2.00	5.00
	1939 G	2.137	.30	.95	2.00	5.00
	1940 G	2.302	.30	.95	2.00	5.00
	1941 G	1.960	.30	.95	2.00	5.00

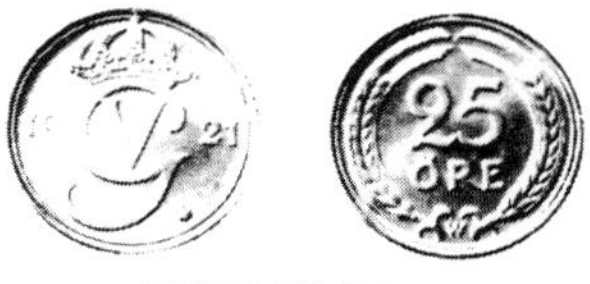

NICKEL-BRONZE

KM#	Date	Mintage	Fine	VF	XF	Unc
798	1921 W	1.355	2.00	3.50	12.50	65.00
(566)	1940 G	2.333	.15	.50	3.00	15.00
	1941 G	1.057	.15	.50	3.00	20.00
	1946 TS	2.066	.15	.25	1.00	6.00
	1947 TS	1.594	.15	.25	1.00	6.00

2.3200 g, .400 SILVER, .0298 oz ASW

KM#	Date	Mintage	Fine	VF	XF	Unc
816	1943 G	9.855	BV	.50	1.00	6.00
(578)	1944 G	9.532	BV	.50	1.00	6.00
	1945 G	5.363	BV	.50	1.00	6.00
	1945 TS	I.A.	.35	.75	2.00	9.00
	1945 G/TS	I.A.	BV	.60	3.00	12.00
	1946 TS	2.250	BV	.35	2.00	9.00
	1947 TS	5.633	BV	.35	1.00	4.00
	1948 TS	3.191	BV	.35	1.00	4.00
	1949 TS	5.812	BV	.35	1.00	4.00
	1950 TS	12.059	BV	.35	1.00	3.00

KM#	Date	Mintage	Fine	VF	XF	Unc
824	1952 TS	2.114	BV	.35	1.00	4.00
(584)	1953 TS	18.177	BV	.35	1.00	2.50
	1954 TS	9.492	BV	.35	1.00	2.50
	1955 TS	7.663	BV	.35	1.00	3.50
	1956 TS	10.931	BV	.35	1.00	3.00
	1957 TS	12.498	BV	.35	1.00	3.00
	1958 TS	6.884	BV	.35	1.00	3.00
	1959 TS	4.772	BV	.35	1.00	3.00
	1960 TS	4.374	BV	.50	2.00	9.00
	1961 TS	8.380	BV	.35	.75	3.00

COPPER-NICKEL

KM#	Date	Mintage	Fine	VF	XF	Unc
836	1962 U	4.426	—	.25	.75	3.00
(592)	1963 U	26.710	—	.20	.40	2.00
	1964 U	17.300	—	.20	.40	2.00
	1965 U	6.884	—	.20	.40	2.00
	1966 U	12.932	—	—	.20	1.00
	1967 U	28.038	—	—	.15	.50
	1968 U	14.366	—	—	.15	.50
	1969 U	20.214	—	—	.15	.50
	1970 U	23.780	—	—	.15	.50
	1971 U	8.606	—	—	.15	.50
	1972 U	13.270	—	—	.15	.50
	1973 U	76.993	—	—	.15	.35

KM#	Date	Mintage	Fine	VF	XF	Unc
851	1976 U	2.815	—	—	.15	.50
(602)	1977 U	5.509	—	—	.15	.40
	1978 U	54.593	—	—	.10	.25
	1979 U	48.423	—	—	.10	.25
	1980 U	38.889	—	—	.10	.25
	1981 U	46.371	—	—	.10	.25
	1982 U	43.218	—	—	.10	.25
	1983 U	28.954	—	—	.10	.25
	1984 U	7.302	—	—	.10	.25

50 ORE

5.0000 g, .600 SILVER, .0965 oz ASW

KM#	Date	Mintage	Fine	VF	XF	Unc
771	1906 EB	.319	2.00	7.50	30.00	140.00
(546)	1907 EB	.803	1.75	5.00	25.00	90.00

KM#	Date	Mintage	Fine	VF	XF	Unc
788	1911 W	.472	3.00	7.50	22.50	100.00
(559)	1912 W	.482	4.00	8.50	25.00	120.00
	1914 W	.378	4.00	8.50	25.00	120.00
	1916 W	.537	3.00	7.50	20.00	100.00
	1919 W	.458	3.00	7.50	22.50	85.00
	1927 W	.672	1.50	3.00	12.50	60.00
	1928 G	1.135	1.25	2.00	6.00	35.00

KM#	Date	Mintage	Fine	VF	XF	Unc
(559)	1929 G	.471	1.50	3.00	12.50	60.00
	1930 G	.548	1.50	3.00	12.50	55.00
	1931 G	.671	BV	2.00	10.00	40.00
	1933 G	.548	BV	2.00	10.00	40.00
	1934 G	.613	BV	2.00	6.00	30.00
	1935 G	.691	BV	2.00	6.00	30.00
	1936 G short 6					
		.823	BV	2.00	6.00	30.00
	1936 G long 6					
		Inc. Ab.	BV	3.50	10.00	50.00
	1938 G	.442	BV	1.25	3.75	20.00
	1939 G	.922	BV	1.00	2.50	12.00
	1939 G	—	—	—	Proof	35.00

NICKEL-BRONZE

KM#	Date	Mintage	Fine	VF	XF	Unc
796	1920 W oval 0					
(564)		.480	1.75	10.00	35.00	150.00
	1920 W round 0					
		Inc. Ab.	35.00	80.00	225.00	750.00
	1921 W	.215	4.00	35.00	120.00	480.00
	1924 W	.645	1.50	12.50	40.00	320.00
	1940 G	1.341	.25	1.00	4.00	27.50
	1946 TS	1.426	.25	1.00	3.00	17.50
	1947 TS	1.032	.25	1.00	3.00	17.50

NOTE: Varieties exist.

4.8000 g, .400 SILVER, .0617 oz ASW

KM#	Date	Mintage	Fine	VF	XF	Unc
817	1943 G	.785	1.50	3.25	8.00	40.00
(579)	1944 G	1.540	BV	1.00	2.00	10.00
	1945 G	2.585	BV	1.00	2.00	10.00
	1946 TS	1.091	BV	1.00	2.00	10.00
	1947 TS	1.771	BV	1.00	2.00	10.00
	1948 TS	1.731	BV	1.00	2.00	10.00
	1949 TS	1.883	BV	1.00	2.00	10.00
	1950 TS	3.354	BV	1.00	1.50	8.50

KM#	Date	Mintage	Fine	VF	XF	Unc
825	1952 TS	1.198	BV	.75	3.00	20.00
(585)	1953 TS	4.396	BV	.75	2.50	18.00
	1954 TS	5.779	BV	.75	2.50	18.00
	1955 TS	2.700	BV	.75	3.50	17.00
	1956 TS	7.057	BV	.75	2.00	10.00
	1957 TS	2.405	BV	.75	2.50	17.00
	1958 TS	1.660	BV	.75	2.50	17.00
	1961 TS	2.775	BV	.75	2.00	12.00

COPPER-NICKEL

KM#	Date	Mintage	Fine	VF	XF	Unc
837	1962 U	1.400	.50	.80	3.00	17.50
(593)	1963 U	5.808	.15	.25	1.00	10.00
	1964 U	5.325	.15	.25	1.00	10.00
	1965 U	6.453	.15	.25	.50	6.00
	1966 U	6.309	.15	.25	.40	5.00
	1967 U	7.890	.15	.25	.40	5.00
	1968 U	9.198	—	.15	.25	1.00
	1969 U	7.265	—	.15	.25	1.00
	1970 U	9.426	—	.15	.25	1.00
	1971 U	7.218	—	.15	.25	1.00
	1972 U	7.388	—	.15	.25	1.00
	1973 U	52.467	—	.15	.20	.60

KM#	Date	Mintage	Fine	VF	XF	Unc
855	1976 U	2.589	—	.15	.25	.70
(603)	1977 U	10.360	—	—	.15	.30
	1978 U	33.282	—	—	.15	.30
	1979 U	30.274	—	—	.15	.30
	1980 U	28.666	—	—	.15	.30

KM#	Date	Mintage	Fine	VF	XF	Unc
(603)	1981 U	15.516	—	—	.15	.30
	1982 U	14.778	—	—	.15	.30
	1983 U	17.530	—	—	.15	.30
	1984 U	27.541	—	—	.15	.30
	1985 U	14.062	—	—	.15	.30
	1986 U	.937	—	—	.20	.50
	1987 D	1.077	—	—	.20	.50
	1988 D	.532	—	—	.20	.50
	1989 D	.606	—	—	.20	.50
	1990 D	31.935	—	—	.10	.15
	1991 D	16.315	—	—	.10	.15

BRONZE

KM#	Date	Mintage	Fine	VF	XF	Unc
878 (625)	1992 D	39.531	—	—	.15	.30
	1993 D	.644	—	—	.20	.50
	1994 D	.518	—	—	.20	.50
	1995 D	.487	—	—	.10	.20
	1996 D	.248	—	—	.10	.20
	1997 D	.070	—	—	.10	.20
	1998 D	—	—	—	.10	.20

KRONA

7.5000 g, .800 SILVER, .1929 oz ASW
Obv: W/o initials below bust.

KM#	Date	Mintage	Fine	VF	XF	Unc
760 (535)	1901/898 EB	.271	8.00	30.00	125.00	500.00
	1901 EB	I.A.	6.50	27.50	110.00	400.00
	1903 EB	.473	5.50	25.00	75.00	300.00
	1904 EB	.564	8.00	15.00	75.00	350.00

NOTE: Earlier dates (1890-1898) exist for this type.

KM#	Date	Mintage	Fine	VF	XF	Unc
772 (547)	1906 EB	.427	5.00	17.50	65.00	320.00
	1907 EB	1.058	3.75	12.00	50.00	200.00

Obv: W/dots in date.

KM#	Date	Mintage	Fine	VF	XF	Unc
786.1 (557.1)	1.9.1.0 W	.643	3.00	12.50	40.00	140.00
	1.9.1.2 W	.303	8.00	22.50	90.00	360.00
	1.9.1.3 W	.353	3.50	12.50	40.00	150.00
	1.9.1.4 W	.622	3.00	12.50	35.00	140.00
	1.9.1.5. W	1.416	3.00	7.50	25.00	120.00
	1.9.1.6/5. W	1.139	4.00	14.00	50.00	180.00
	1.9.1.6 W	I.A.	3.00	12.00	35.00	150.00
	1.9.1.8 W	.258	3.00	6.00	27.00	160.00
	1.9.2.3 W	.746	2.00	8.00	25.00	120.00
	1.9.2.4 W	2.066	2.00	6.00	17.00	85.00

Obv: W/o dots in date.

KM#	Date	Mintage	Fine	VF	XF	Unc
786.2 (557.2)	1924 W	Inc. Ab.	1.50	5.00	20.00	80.00
	1925 W	.370	3.00	8.50	40.00	160.00
	1926 W	.465	2.50	7.50	25.00	110.00
	1927 G	.401	3.00	8.50	35.00	145.00
	1928 G	.739	1.50	4.00	20.00	70.00
	1929 G	1.346	1.25	3.00	12.00	40.00
	1930 G	1.744	1.25	2.50	6.00	30.00
	1931 G	1.008	1.25	2.50	6.00	30.00
	1932 G	1.036	1.25	2.50	6.00	30.00

KM#	Date	Mintage	Fine	VF	XF	Unc
(557.2)	1933 G	1.045	1.25	2.50	6.00	30.00
	1934 G	.586	1.25	2.50	12.00	50.00
	1935 G	1.604	1.00	2.00	3.00	12.00
	1936 G	3.223	1.00	2.00	3.00	10.00
	1937 G	2.667	1.00	2.00	3.00	10.00
	1938 G	1.911	1.00	2.00	3.00	10.00
	1938 G	—	—	—	Proof	25.00
	1939 G	7.589	1.00	2.00	3.00	5.00
	1940 G	6.917	1.00	2.00	3.00	5.00
	1941/4 G	2.183	4.00	8.00	17.50	45.00
	1941 G	Inc. Ab.	1.00	2.00	3.50	10.00
	1942 G	.240	35.00	65.00	150.00	400.00

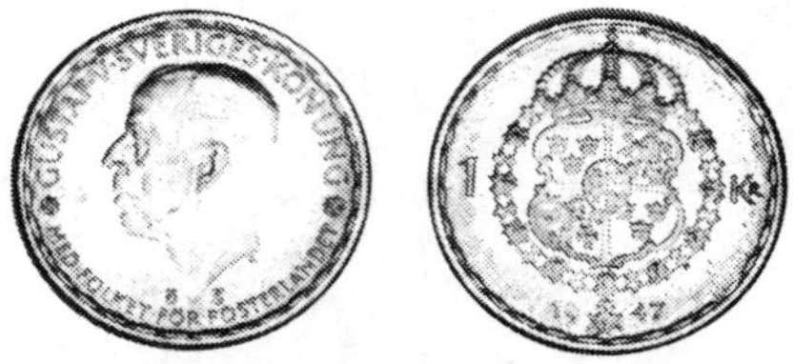

7.0000 g .400 SILVER, .0900 oz ASW

KM#	Date	Mintage	Fine	VF	XF	Unc
814 (576)	1942 G	5.650	BV	1.00	3.00	15.00
	1943 G plain 4	7.916	BV	1.00	3.00	15.00
	1943 G crosslet 4	Inc. Ab.	BV	1.00	3.00	15.00
	1944 G	7.423	BV	1.00	2.00	8.00
	1945 G	7.359	BV	1.00	2.00	8.00
	1945 TS	I.A.	BV	1.25	2.75	12.50
	1945 TS/G	I.A.	BV	1.50	3.00	17.50
	1946 TS	19.170	BV	1.00	1.75	6.00
	1947 TS	9.124	BV	1.00	1.75	6.00
	1948 TS	10.447	BV	1.00	1.75	6.00
	1949 TS	7.981	BV	1.00	1.75	6.00
	1950 TS	5.310	BV	1.00	1.50	8.00

KM#	Date	Mintage	Fine	VF	XF	Unc
826 (586)	1952 TS	1.102	BV	1.00	2.50	20.00
	1953/2 TS	I.A.	BV	1.50	5.00	25.00
	1953 TS	3.306	BV	1.00	2.50	17.50
	1954 TS	6.461	BV	1.00	2.50	12.50
	1955 TS	4.141	BV	1.00	2.50	12.50
	1956 TS	6.227	BV	1.00	2.50	8.00
	1957 TS	3.544	BV	1.00	2.50	9.00
	1958 TS	1.439	BV	1.50	3.50	17.50
	1959 TS	1.187	1.25	2.50	6.00	30.00
	1960 TS	4.085	BV	1.00	1.75	6.50
	1961 TS	4.283	BV	1.00	1.75	6.50
	1961 U	2.973	BV	1.25	2.50	17.50
	1962 U	6.839	BV	1.00	1.75	6.50
	1963 U	14.228	BV	BV	1.25	3.50
	1964 U	15.973	BV	BV	1.00	3.00
	1965 U	18.639	BV	BV	1.00	3.00
	1966 U	22.396	BV	BV	1.00	2.00
	1967 U	17.235	BV	BV	1.00	2.00
	1968 U	12.326	BV	BV	1.00	2.00

COPPER-NICKEL CLAD COPPER

KM#	Date	Mintage	Fine	VF	XF	Unc
826a (586a)	1968 U	5.177	—	.30	1.00	3.00
	1969 U	30.856	—	.30	.40	1.25
	1970 U	25.315	—	.30	.40	1.25
	1971 U	18.342	—	.30	.40	1.25
	1972 U	21.941	—	.30	.40	1.25
	1973 U	142.000	—	.30	.40	1.25
852 (604)	1976 U	4.321	—	.30	.50	1.25
	1977 U	80.478	—	.30	.40	.60
	1978 U	81.408	—	.30	.40	.60
	1979 U	47.450	—	.30	.40	.60
	1980 U	51.694	—	.30	.40	.60
	1981 U	62.079	—	.30	.40	.60

COPPER-NICKEL

KM#	Date	Mintage	Fine	VF	XF	Unc
852a (604a)	1982 U	24.837	—	—	.30	.50
	1983 U	23.530	—	—	.30	.50
	1984 U	37.805	—	—	.30	.50
	1985 U	4.893	—	—	.30	.55
	1986 U	.901	—	—	.40	.60
	1987 D	21.543	—	—	.30	.50
	1988 D	30.342	—	—	.30	.45
	1989 D	55.963	—	—	—	.25
	1990 D	54.470	—	—	—	.25
	1991 D	34.250	—	—	—	.25
	1992 D	16.771	—	—	—	.25
	1993 D	.407	—	.30	.50	.80
	1994 D	.547	—	.30	.50	.80

KM#	Date	Mintage	Fine	VF	XF	Unc
(604a)	1995 D	.500	—	.30	.50	.80
	1996 D	.324	—	—	—	.20
	1997 D	25.042	—	—	—	.20
	1998 D	—	—	—	—	.20

2 KRONOR

15.0000 g, .800 SILVER, .3858 oz ASW
Obv: W/o initials below bust.

KM#	Date	Mintage	Fine	VF	XF	Unc
761 (536)	1903 EB	.064	30.00	80.00	200.00	750.00
	1904 EB	.175	10.00	35.00	125.00	375.00

NOTE: Earlier dates (1890-1900) exist for this type.

KM#	Date	Mintage	Fine	VF	XF	Unc
773 (548)	1906 EB	.112	8.00	20.00	75.00	300.00
	1907 EB	.301	6.00	15.00	60.00	275.00

Golden Wedding Anniversary

KM#	Date	Mintage	Fine	VF	XF	Unc
776 (551)	1907 EB	.251	4.00	6.50	10.00	20.00

KM#	Date	Mintage	Fine	VF	XF	Unc
787 (558)	1910 W	.375	6.00	15.00	60.00	175.00
	1910 W mintmasters initial further from date	Inc. Ab.	35.00	100.00	325.00	800.00
	1912 W	.157	8.00	25.00	85.00	250.00
	1913 W	.305	5.00	12.00	50.00	175.00
	1914 W	.192	5.00	15.00	60.00	185.00
	1915 W	.156	7.00	17.50	65.00	200.00
	1922 W	.202	5.00	8.00	30.00	90.00
	1924 W	.199	5.00	8.00	30.00	95.00
	1926 W	.222	5.00	7.00	25.00	85.00
	1928 G	.160	5.00	8.00	30.00	140.00
	1929 G	.184	4.75	7.00	25.00	90.00
	1930 G	.178	4.75	7.00	25.00	80.00
	1931 G	.211	4.00	5.00	10.00	25.00
	1934 G	.273	3.00	5.00	10.00	25.00
	1935 G	.211	3.00	5.00	10.00	25.00
	1936 G	.491	2.25	5.00	8.00	16.00
	1937 G	.130	5.50	8.00	15.00	60.00
	1937 G	—	—	—	Proof	200.00
	1938 G	.639	BV	4.00	7.00	15.00
	1938 G	—	—	—	Proof	30.00
	1939 G	1.200	BV	4.00	7.00	12.00
	1939 G	—	—	—	Proof	30.00
	1940 G	.518	BV	4.00	7.00	12.00
	1940 G serif 4	Inc. Ab.	3.00	4.50	8.50	25.00

400th Anniversary of Political Liberty

KM#	Date	Mintage	Fine	VF	XF	Unc
799	1921 W	.265	3.00	5.00	8.00	18.00
(567)						

300th Anniversary - Death of Gustaf II Adolf

805	1932 G	.254	4.00	7.00	14.00	27.50
(569)						

300th Anniversary - Settlement of Delaware

807	1938 G	.509	3.00	5.50	10.00	20.00
(571)						

14.0000 g, .400 SILVER, .1800 oz ASW

815	1942 G	.200	2.00	3.50	6.00	27.50
(577)	1943 G	.272	3.00	6.00	12.50	60.00
	1944 G	.627	BV	2.00	4.00	16.00
	1945 G	.970	BV	2.00	4.00	16.00
	1945 G w/o dots in motto					
	Inc. Ab.	6.00	12.00	26.00	75.00
	1945 TS	I.A.	BV	2.00	4.00	16.00
	1945 TS/G	I.A.	2.00	4.00	8.00	30.00
	1946 TS	.978	BV	1.50	3.00	12.00
	1947 TS	1.466	BV	1.50	3.00	12.00
	1948 TS	.282	BV	2.00	4.00	16.00
	1949 TS	.332	BV	2.00	4.00	16.00
	1950/1 TS					
		3.727	BV	1.50	3.00	12.00
	1950 TS	I.A.	BV	1.50	3.00	9.00

827	1952 TS	.315	1.50	3.00	6.00	18.00
(587)	1953 TS	1.009	BV	1.50	3.00	9.00
	1954 TS	2.301	BV	1.50	3.00	9.00
	1955 TS	1.138	BV	1.50	3.00	9.00
	1956 TS	1.708	BV	1.50	3.00	9.00
	1957 TS	.689	BV	1.50	6.25	17.50
	1958 TS	1.104	BV	1.50	2.50	8.00
	1959 TS	.581	BV	2.00	6.25	18.00
	1961 TS	.534	BV	2.00	4.00	13.00
	1963 U	1.469	BV	BV	2.25	5.00
	1964 U	1.213	BV	BV	2.25	4.50
	1965 U	1.190	BV	BV	2.25	4.50
	1966 U	.989	BV	BV	2.25	5.00

COPPER-NICKEL

KM#	Date	Mintage	Fine	VF	XF	Unc
827a	1968 U	1.171	.50	.70	1.75	4.00
(587a)	1969 U	1.148	.50	.70	1.00	2.50
	1970 U	1.159	.50	.70	1.00	2.50
	1971 U	1.213	.50	.70	1.50	3.00

5 KRONOR

2.2402 g, .900 GOLD, .0648 oz AGW

766	1901 EB	.109	40.00	50.00	70.00	100.00
(541)						

797	1920 W	.103	40.00	50.00	70.00	100.00
(565)						

25.0000 g, .900 SILVER, .7234 oz ASW
500th Anniversary of Riksdag

806	1935 G	.664	5.00	7.00	10.00	17.50
(570)						

22.7000 g, .400 SILVER, .2920 oz ASW
70th Birthday of Gustaf VI Adolf

828	1952 TS	.219	6.50	11.50	16.50	28.00
(588)						

18.0000 g, .400 SILVER, .2315 oz ASW
Regular Issue

829	1954 TS	1.510	—	BV	3.00	6.00
(589)	1955 TS	3.569	—	BV	2.50	5.00
	1971 U	.713	—	BV	2.50	5.00

Constitution Sesquicentennial

830	1959 TS	.504	—	BV	4.00	7.00
(590)						

80th Birthday of Gustaf VI Adolf

KM#	Date	Mintage	Fine	VF	XF	Unc
838	1962 U	.256	—	9.00	15.00	30.00
(594)						

100th Anniversary of Constitution Reform

839	1966 U	1.024	—	BV	2.50	4.00
(595)						

COPPER-NICKEL CLAD NICKEL

846	1972 U	21.736	—	1.25	1.50	2.25
(597)	1973 U	1.139	—	1.25	1.50	4.00

COPPER-NICKEL

853	1976 U	2.253	—	—	1.25	3.50
(605)	1977 U	3.985	—	—	1.25	2.00
	1978 U	3.952	—	—	1.25	2.00
	1979 U	3.164	—	—	1.25	2.00
	1980 U	2.222	—	—	1.25	2.50
	1981 U	5.507	—	—	1.25	2.00
	1982 U	36.604	—	—	1.25	1.50
	1983 U	31.364	—	—	1.25	1.50
	1984 U	27.687	—	—	1.25	1.50
	1985 U	10.375	—	—	1.25	1.50
	1986 U	.714	—	—	1.25	4.00
	1987 D	15.117	—	—	1.25	1.50
	1988 D	18.644	—	—	1.25	1.50
	1989 D	.961	—	—	1.25	3.00
	1990 D	10.558	—	—	1.25	1.50
	1991 D	15.793	—	—	1.25	1.50
	1992 D	5.351	—	—	1.25	1.50

COPPER-NICKEL CLAD NICKEL

853a	1993 D	.275	—	—	—	1.50
(605a)	1994 D	.173	—	—	—	2.25
	1995 D	.187	—	—	—	.80
	1996 D	.180	—	—	—	.80
	1997 D	.174	—	—	—	.80
	1998 D		—	—	—	.80

50th Anniversary - United Nations

KM#	Date	Mintage	Fine	VF	XF	Unc
885 (630)	1995	.300	—	—	—	4.00

10 KRONOR

4.4803 g, .900 GOLD, .1296 oz AGW
Obv: Large head.

KM#	Date	Mintage	Fine	VF	XF	Unc
767	1901 EB	.213	40.00	65.00	95.00	135.00
(542)	1901 EB	I.A.	—	—	Proof	525.00

18.0000 g, .830 SILVER, .4803 oz ASW
90th Birthday of Gustaf VI Adolf

KM#	Date	Mintage	Fine	VF	XF	Unc
847 (598)	1972 U	2.000	—	BV	4.00	6.00

COPPER-ALUMINUM-ZINC

KM#	Date	Mintage	Fine	VF	XF	Unc
877	1991 D medal					
(620)		106.548	—	—	2.25	3.25
	1991 D coin					
		Inc. Ab.	22.50	40.00	55.00	100.00
	1992 D	42.507	—	—	—	1.75
	1993 D	201.107	—	—	—	1.75
	1994 D	.573	—	—	—	1.75
	1995 D	.524	—	—	—	1.75
	1996 D	.295	—	—	—	1.75
	1997 D	.332	—	—	—	1.75
	1998 D	.332	—	—	—	1.75

20 KRONOR

8.9606 g, .900 GOLD, .2593 oz AGW
Obv: Larger head.

KM#	Date	Mintage	Fine	VF	XF	Unc
765	1901 EB	.227	120.00	160.00	250.00	350.00
(540)	1902 EB	.114	125.00	160.00	300.00	400.00

NOTE: Earlier date (1900) exists for this type.

KM#	Date	Mintage	Fine	VF	XF	Unc
800 (568)	1925 W	.387	175.00	300.00	400.00	600.00

SWITZERLAND

The Swiss Confederation, located in central Europe north of Italy and south of Germany, has an area of 15,941 sq. mi. (41,290 sq. km.) and a population of *6.6 million. Capital: Bern. The economy centers about a well developed manufacturing industry. Machinery, chemicals, watches and clocks, and textiles are exported.

Switzerland, the habitat of lake dwellers in prehistoric times, was peopled by the Celtic Helvetians when Julius Caesar made it a part of the Roman Empire in 58 B.C. After the decline of Rome, Switzerland was invaded by Teutonic tribes, who established small temporal holdings which in the Middle Ages, became a federation of fiefs of the Holy Roman Empire. As a nation, Switzerland originated in 1291 when the districts of Nidwalden, Schwyz and Uri united to defeat Austria and attain independence as the Swiss Confederation. After acquiring new cantons in the 14th century, Switzerland was made independent from the Holy Roman Empire by the 1648 Treaty of Westphalia. The revolutionary armies of Napoleonic France occupied Switzerland and set up the Helvetian Republic, 1798-1803. After the fall of Napoleon, the Congress of Vienna, 1815, recognized the independence of Switzerland and guaranteed its neutrality. The Swiss Constitutions of 1848 and 1874 established a union modeled upon that of the United States.

MINT MARKS

B - Bern

NOTE: The coinage of Switzerland has been struck at the Bern Mint since 1853 with but a few exceptions. All coins minted there carry a 'B' mint mark through 1969, except for the 2-Centime and 2-Franc values where the mint mark was discontinued after 1968. In 1968 and 1969 some issues were struck at both Bern (B) and in London (no mint mark).

MONETARY SYSTEM

100 Rappen (Centimes) = 1 Franc

RAPPEN

BRONZE

KM#	Date	Mintage	VF	XF	Unc	BU
3	1902B	.950	45.00	80.00	140.00	190.00
	1903B	1.000	25.00	35.00	65.00	90.00
	1904B	1.000	25.00	35.00	60.00	85.00
	1905B	2.000	8.00	12.00	16.00	24.00
	1906B	1.000	17.50	30.00	40.00	54.00
	1907B	2.000	8.00	15.00	18.00	25.00
	1908B	3.000	2.50	6.00	12.00	18.00
	1909B	1.000	15.00	20.00	35.00	54.00
	1910B	.500	8.00	14.00	18.00	25.00
	1911B	.500	8.00	14.00	20.00	25.00
	1912B	2.000	2.50	5.00	14.00	21.50
	1913B	3.000	1.00	2.00	4.00	7.00
	1914B	3.500	1.50	3.50	7.00	12.00
	1915B	3.000	1.50	3.50	7.00	12.00
	1917B	2.000	3.50	6.00	18.00	30.00
	1918B	3.000	1.50	3.00	6.00	10.00
	1919B	3.000	1.50	3.00	6.00	10.00
	1920B	1.000	3.00	7.00	10.00	15.00
	1921B	3.000	1.50	3.00	5.00	8.00
	1924B	2.000	4.00	8.00	15.00	20.00
	1925/4B	2.500	4.50	10.00	20.00	30.00
	1925B	Inc. Ab.	2.00	4.00	6.00	10.00
	1926B	2.000	2.00	4.00	6.50	10.00
	1927B	1.500	3.00	6.00	11.00	15.00
	1928B	2.000	1.50	3.00	8.50	13.00
	1929B	4.000	.50	1.00	3.00	5.00
	1930B	2.500	1.50	3.50	5.00	8.00
	1931B	5.000	.50	1.25	3.00	6.00
	1932B	5.000	.50	1.00	3.00	6.00
	1933B	3.000	.75	1.50	3.00	6.00
	1934B	3.000	.50	1.00	3.00	6.00
	1936B	2.000	1.50	2.50	6.00	12.00
	1937B	2.400	.50	1.00	3.00	5.00
	1938B	5.300	.50	1.00	3.00	5.00
	1939B	.010	25.00	30.00	50.00	65.00
	1940B	3.027	1.00	1.50	6.00	9.00
	1941B	12.794	.25	.50	1.50	2.50

NOTE: Earlier dates (1850-1900) exist for this type.

ZINC

KM#	Date	Mintage	VF	XF	Unc	BU
3a	1942B	17.969	.50	1.00	3.50	6.00
	1943B	8.647	.75	1.25	3.50	6.00
	1944B	11.825	.50	1.00	3.50	6.00
	1945B	2.800	6.00	9.00	17.50	27.50
	1946B	12.063	.50	1.00	3.50	6.00

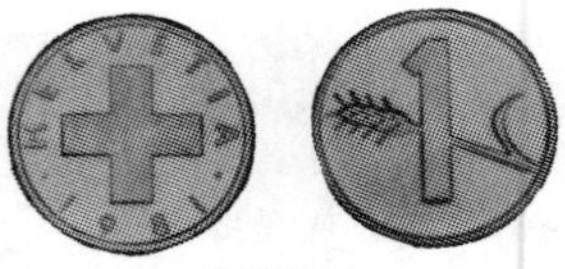

BRONZE

KM#	Date	Mintage	VF	XF	Unc	BU
46	1948B	10.500	.10	.50	1.50	3.00
	1949B	11.100	.10	.50	1.50	3.00
	1950B	3.610	.50	2.00	4.00	6.00
	1951B	22.624	.10	.30	1.00	2.00
	1952B	11.520	.10	.30	1.00	2.00
	1953B	5.947	.10	.30	1.00	2.00
	1954B	5.175	.10	.30	1.00	2.00
	1955B	5.282	.10	.60	1.25	2.00
	1956B	4.960	.10	.30	1.00	2.00
	1957B	15.226	.10	.15	.35	.50
	1958B	20.142	.10	.15	.35	.50
	1959B	5.582	.10	.15	.35	.50
	1962B	5.010	.10	.15	.35	.50
	1963B	15.920	—	.10	.25	.35
	1966B	5.030	—	.10	.25	.35
	1967B	3.020	—	.10	.25	.35
	1968B	4.920	—	.10	.25	.35
	1969B	4.810	—	.10	.25	.35
	1970	7.810	—	.10	.25	.35
	1971	5.030	—	.10	.25	.35
	1973	3.000	—	.10	.25	.35
	1974	3.007	—	.10	.25	.35
	1974	2,400	—	—	Proof	10.00
	1975	3.010	—	.10	.25	.35
	1975	.010	—	—	Proof	1.25
	1976	3.005	—	.10	.25	.35
	1976	5,130	—	—	Proof	1.50
	1977	2.007	—	.10	.25	.35
	1977	7,030	—	—	Proof	1.00
	1978	2.010	—	.10	.25	.35
	1978	.010	—	—	Proof	1.00
	1979	1.030	—	.10	.35	.50
	1979	.010	—	—	Proof	1.00
	1980	1.030	—	.10	.35	.50
	1980	.010	—	—	Proof	1.00
	1981	4.935	—	.10	.25	.35
	1981	.010	—	—	Proof	1.00
	1982	6.655	—	.10	.20	.30
	1982	.010	—	—	Proof	2.00
	1983	4.031	—	.10	.20	.30
	1983	.011	—	—	Proof	1.00
	1984	3.995	—	.10	.20	.30
	1984	.014	—	—	Proof	1.00
	1985	3.027	—	.10	.20	.30
	1985	.012	—	—	Proof	1.00
	1986B	2.031	—	.10	.20	.30
	1986B	.010	—	—	Proof	1.00
	1987B	1.028	—	.10	.35	.50
	1987B	8,800	—	—	Proof	1.25
	1988B	2.029	—	.10	.20	.30
	1988B	9,000	—	—	Proof	1.25
	1989B	2.032	—	.10	.20	.30
	1989B	8,800	—	—	Proof	1.25
	1990B	1.032	—	—	.20	.30
	1990B	8,900	—	—	Proof	1.25
	1991B	.536	—	—	.35	.50
	1991B	9,900	—	—	Proof	1.25
	1992B	.527	—	—	.35	.50
	1992B	7,450	—	—	Proof	1.00
	1993B	.522	—	—	.35	.50
	1993B	6,200	—	—	Proof	1.00
	1994B	2.000	—	—	.20	.35
	1994B	6,100	—	—	Proof	1.00
	1995B	6.024	—	—	.15	.25
	1995B	6,100	—	—	Proof	1.00
	1996B	1.000	—	—	.10	.20
	1996B	6,100	—	—	Proof	1.00
	1997B	1.000	—	—	.10	.20
	1997B	5,500	—	—	Proof	1.00
	1998B	—	—	—	.10	.20
	1998B	—	—	—	Proof	1.00

2 RAPPEN

BRONZE

KM#	Date	Mintage	VF	XF	Unc	BU
4	1902B	.500	24.00	35.00	60.00	90.00
	1903B	.500	24.00	30.00	50.00	75.00
	1904B	.500	22.00	30.00	50.00	75.00
	1906B	.500	22.00	30.00	50.00	75.00
	1907B	1.000	4.00	8.00	20.00	30.00
	1908B	1.000	3.00	5.00	12.00	18.00
	1909B	1.000	4.00	8.00	12.00	18.00
	1910B	.500	20.00	27.50	45.00	60.00
	1912B	1.000	4.50	7.00	17.50	30.00
	1913B	1.000	5.50	8.00	20.00	30.00
	1914B	1.000	5.50	8.00	20.00	30.00
	1915B	1.000	4.50	8.00	20.00	30.00
	1918B	1.000	4.00	5.00	12.50	20.00
	1919B	2.000	1.50	3.00	8.00	12.00
	1920B	.500	25.00	40.00	70.00	90.00
	1925B	1.250	1.00	3.00	8.00	12.00
	1926B	.750	17.50	30.00	40.00	60.00
	1927B	.500	25.00	35.00	50.00	75.00

KM#	Date	Mintage	VF	XF	Unc	BU
4	1928B	.500	25.00	35.00	50.00	75.00
	1929B	.750	7.50	12.00	18.00	25.00
	1930B	1.000	2.00	4.00	10.00	15.00
	1931B	1.288	3.00	6.00	10.00	15.00
	1932B	1.500	1.00	2.00	6.00	9.00
	1933B	1.000	3.00	6.00	10.00	15.00
	1934B	.500	12.50	22.50	40.00	55.00
	1936B	.500	5.00	9.00	15.00	24.00
	1937B	1.200	2.00	3.00	5.00	8.00
	1938B	1.369	2.00	4.00	8.00	12.00
	1941B	3.448	.75	1.50	3.00	6.00

NOTE: Earlier dates (1850-1900) exist for this type.

ZINC

KM#	Date	Mintage	VF	XF	Unc	BU
4a	1942B	8.954	.50	1.50	4.00	7.00
	1943B	4.499	.75	3.00	8.00	12.00
	1944B	8.086	.50	1.50	4.00	7.00
	1945B	3.640	2.00	6.00	16.00	22.50
	1946B	1.393	10.00	20.00	30.00	45.00

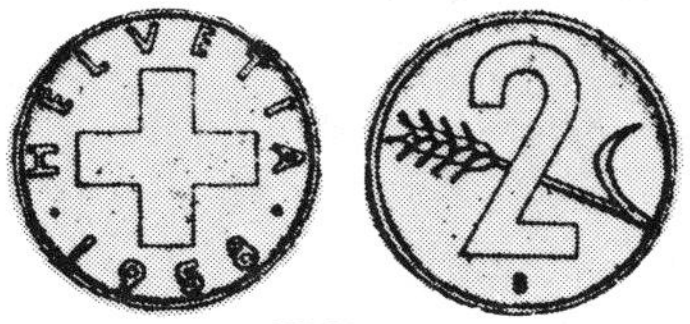

BRONZE

KM#	Date	Mintage	VF	XF	Unc	BU
47	1948B	10.197	.25	.50	4.00	6.00
	1951B	9.622	.25	.50	3.00	5.00
	1952B	1.915	.50	1.00	2.50	5.00
	1953B	2.006	.50	1.00	2.50	4.00
	1954B	2.539	.50	1.00	2.50	4.00
	1955B	2.493	.25	1.00	2.50	3.50
	1957B	8.099	.15	.25	1.25	2.00
	1958B	6.078	.15	.25	1.25	2.00
	1963B	10.065	.10	.15	.45	.75
	1966B	2.510	.10	.20	.45	.75
	1967B	1.510	.10	.20	.50	.75
	1968B	2.860	.10	.20	.45	.75
	1969	6.200	.10	.15	.45	.75
	1970	3.115	.10	.15	.45	.75
	1974	3.540	.10	.15	.45	.75
	1974	2,400	—	—	Proof	25.00

5 RAPPEN

COPPER-NICKEL

KM#	Date	Mintage	VF	XF	Unc	BU
26	1901B	3.000	1.50	10.00	27.50	42.00
	1902B	1.000	15.00	50.00	90.00	130.00
	1903B	2.000	2.50	15.00	40.00	60.00
	1904B	1.000	14.00	40.00	95.00	140.00
	1905B	1.000	12.00	22.50	75.00	110.00
	1906B	3.000	1.50	7.00	20.00	30.00
	1907B	5.000	1.00	4.00	10.00	15.00
	1908B	3.000	1.25	7.00	15.00	22.00
	1909B	2.000	1.50	8.00	20.00	27.00
	1910B	1.000	8.00	15.00	45.00	65.00
	1911B	2.000	1.50	6.00	12.50	18.00
	1912B	3.000	1.00	6.00	12.50	18.00
	1913B	3.000	1.00	6.00	14.00	20.00
	1914B	3.000	1.00	6.00	48.00	70.00
	1915B	3.000	1.00	10.00	120.00	175.00
	1917B	1.000	4.00	10.00	50.00	70.00
	1919B	6.000	.25	5.00	16.00	24.00
	1920B	5.000	.25	5.00	16.00	24.00
	1921B	3.000	.25	5.00	16.00	24.00
	1922B	4.000	.25	4.00	12.50	20.00
	1925B	3.000	.25	4.00	12.50	20.00
	1926B	3.000	.25	4.00	12.50	20.00
	1927B	2.000	.25	4.00	17.50	25.00
	1928B	2.000	.25	4.00	15.00	22.50
	1929B	2.000	.25	2.50	12.50	20.00
	1930B	3.000	.25	2.50	12.00	17.50
	1931B	5.037	.25	2.00	8.00	12.50
	1940B	1.416	.40	1.50	40.00	60.00
	1942B	5.078	.25	1.00	10.00	17.50
	1943B	6.591	.25	1.00	10.00	17.50
	1944B	9.981	.25	1.00	10.00	17.50
	1945B	.985	1.00	9.00	75.00	110.00
	1946B	6.179	.25	1.00	5.00	8.00
	1947B	5.125	.25	1.00	8.00	12.00
	1948B	4.710	.25	1.00	3.00	4.50
	1949B	4.589	.25	1.00	3.00	4.00
	1950B	.920	.50	1.00	2.00	3.00
	1951B	2.141	.50	1.00	16.00	24.00
	1952B	4.690	.20	.35	3.00	4.00
	1953B	9.131	.20	.35	2.00	3.00
	1954B	8.038	.20	.35	2.00	3.00
	1955B	19.943	.20	.35	1.50	2.25
	1957B	10.147	.20	.35	1.50	2.25
	1958B	10.217	.20	.35	1.50	2.25
	1959B	11.086	.20	.35	1.50	2.25
	1962B	23.840	.10	.20	50.00	75.00
	1963B	29.730	.10	.20	50.00	75.00
	1964B	17.080	.10	.20	50.00	75.00
	1965B	1.430	.10	.20	.75	1.25
	1966B	10.010	—	.15	.35	.50
	1967B	13.010	—	.15	.35	.50
	1968B	10.020	—	.15	.40	.65
	1969B	32.990	—	.10	.35	.50
	1970	34.800	—	.10	.30	.50
26	1971	40.020	—	.10	.30	.50
	1974	30.002	—	.10	.30	.50
	1974	2,400	—	—	Proof	20.00
	1975	34.005	—	.10	.30	.50
	1975	.010	—	—	Proof	2.00
	1976	12.005	—	.10	.30	.50
	1976	5,130	—	—	Proof	2.25
	1977	14.012	—	.10	.30	.50
	1977	7,030	—	—	Proof	1.75
	1978	16.415	—	.10	.30	.40
	1978	.010	—	—	Proof	1.00
	1979	27.010	—	.10	.30	.40
	1979	.010	—	—	Proof	1.00
	1980	15.500	—	.10	.30	.40
	1980	.010	—	—	Proof	1.00

NOTE: Earlier dates (1879-1900) exist for this type.

BRASS

KM#	Date	Mintage	VF	XF	Unc	BU
26a	1918B	6.000	12.50	20.00	25.00	35.00

NICKEL

KM#	Date	Mintage	VF	XF	Unc	BU
26b	1932B	6.000	.25	1.00	3.50	6.00
	1933B	3.000	.25	1.00	6.00	9.00
	1934B	4.000	.25	1.00	5.00	7.00
	1936B	1.000	.25	1.50	7.00	11.00
	1937B	2.000	.25	1.25	8.00	12.00
	1938B	1.000	.25	1.50	6.00	9.00
	1939B	10.048	.25	1.00	3.00	5.00
	1941B	3.030	2.00	4.00	25.00	35.00

ALUMINUM-BRASS

KM#	Date	Mintage	VF	XF	Unc	BU
26c	1981	79.020	—	—	.20	.30
	1981	.010	—	—	Proof	1.00
	1982	75.340	—	—	.20	.30
	1982	.010	—	—	Proof	1.50
	1983	92.746	—	—	.20	.30
	1983	.011	—	—	Proof	1.00
	1984	69.960	—	—	.20	.30
	1984	.014	—	—	Proof	1.00
	1985	60.032	—	—	.20	.30
	1985	.012	—	—	Proof	1.00
	1986B	55.041	—	—	.20	.30
	1986B	.010	—	—	Proof	1.00
	1987B	39.828	—	—	.20	.50
	1987B	8,800	—	—	Proof	1.25
	1988B	5.044	—	—	.20	.30
	1988B	9,000	—	—	Proof	1.25
	1989B	45.031	—	—	.20	.30
	1989B	8,800	—	—	Proof	1.25
	1990B	16.042	—	—	.20	.30
	1990B	8,900	—	—	Proof	1.25
	1991B	35.036	—	—	.20	.30
	1991B	9,900	—	—	Proof	1.25
	1992B	35.027	—	—	.20	.30
	1992B	7,450	—	—	Proof	1.00
	1993B	38.022	—	—	.20	.30
	1993B	6,200	—	—	Proof	1.25
	1994B	35.000	—	—	.20	.30
	1994B	6,100	—	—	Proof	1.25
	1995B	20.000	—	—	.20	.30
	1995B	6,100	—	—	Proof	1.25
	1996B	25.000	—	—	.20	.30
	1996B	6,100	—	—	Proof	1.25
	1997B	25.000	—	—	.20	.30
	1997B	5,500	—	—	Proof	1.25
	1998B	—	—	—	.20	.30
	1998B	—	—	—	Proof	1.25

10 RAPPEN

COPPER-NICKEL

KM#	Date	Mintage	VF	XF	Unc	BU
27	1901B	1.000	3.50	15.00	50.00	75.00
	1902B	1.000	3.50	12.00	50.00	72.00
	1903B	1.000	3.50	12.00	60.00	85.00
	1904B	1.000	3.50	10.00	115.00	160.00
	1906B	1.000	3.50	15.00	45.00	65.00
	1907B	2.000	1.50	7.00	25.00	36.00
	1908B	2.000	1.50	6.00	20.00	30.00
	1909B	2.000	1.50	7.00	20.00	30.00
	1911B	1.000	3.00	12.00	30.00	42.00
	1912B	1.500	1.00	5.00	40.00	55.00
	1913B	2.000	1.00	5.00	40.00	60.00
	1914B	2.000	1.00	7.00	50.00	70.00
	1915B	1.200	2.00	12.00	145.00	230.00
	1919B	3.000	.25	5.00	17.50	24.00
	1920B	3.500	.25	3.00	17.50	24.00
	1921B	3.000	.25	3.00	12.50	18.00
	1922B	2.000	.25	3.00	22.50	35.00
	1924B	2.000	.25	3.00	22.50	35.00
	1925B	3.000	.25	2.00	18.00	24.00
	1926B	3.000	.25	2.00	16.00	22.50
	1927B	2.000	.25	2.00	14.00	21.00
	1928B	2.000	.25	2.00	14.00	21.00
	1929B	2.000	.25	2.00	14.00	21.00
	1930B	2.000	.25	1.50	27.50	40.00
	1931B	2.244	.25	1.50	25.00	36.00
	1940B	2.000	.25	5.00	55.00	90.00
	1942B	2.110	.25	5.00	32.00	47.50
	1943B	3.176	.25	5.00	30.00	40.00
	1944B	6.133	.25	1.50	6.00	9.00
	1945B	.993	.75	5.00	60.00	85.00
	1946B	4.010	.25	1.50	25.00	36.00
	1947B	3.152	.25	1.50	19.00	27.00
27	1948B	1.000	.50	3.00	80.00	125.00
	1949B	2.269	.25	1.00	20.00	30.00
	1950B	3.200	.25	1.00	2.50	4.00
	1951B	3.430	.25	.75	6.00	9.00
	1952B	4.452	.25	.75	6.00	9.00
	1953B	6.149	.25	.75	4.00	6.00
	1954B	3.200	.25	1.00	15.00	22.50
	1955B	11.795	.20	.50	4.00	6.00
	1957B	10.092	.20	.50	4.00	6.00
	1958B	10.040	.20	.50	4.00	6.00
	1959B	13.053	.20	.50	6.00	10.00
	1960B	4.040	.20	.50	2.00	3.00
	1961B	7.949	.20	.35	1.25	2.00
	1962B	34.965	—	.20	.75	1.50
	1964B	16.340	—	.20	.75	1.50
	1965B	14.190	—	.20	.75	1.50
	1966B	4.025	—	.20	.75	1.50
	1967B	10.000	—	.20	.75	1.50
	1968B	14.065	—	.15	.50	.75
	1969B	28.855	—	.15	.50	.75
	1970	40.020	—	.15	.40	.75
	1972	7.877	—	.15	.30	.50
	1973	30.350	—	.15	.30	.50
	1974	30.007	—	.15	.30	.50
	1974	2,400	—	—	Proof	20.00
	1975	25.003	—	—	.30	.50
	1975	.010	—	—	Proof	2.00
	1976	19.013	—	—	.30	.50
	1976	5,130	—	—	Proof	2.50
	1977	10.007	—	—	.30	.50
	1977	7,030	—	—	Proof	1.50
	1978	19.958	—	—	.30	.50
	1978	.010	—	—	Proof	1.25
	1979	18.010	—	—	.30	.50
	1979	.010	—	—	Proof	1.25
	1980	18.005	—	—	.30	.50
	1980	.010	—	—	Proof	1.50
	1981	30.140	—	—	.30	.50
	1981	.010	—	—	Proof	1.50
	1982	50.110	—	—	.30	.50
	1982	.010	—	—	Proof	2.50
	1983	40.033	—	—	.30	.50
	1983	.011	—	—	Proof	1.50
	1984	22.022	—	—	.30	.50
	1984	.014	—	—	Proof	1.50
	1985	3.032	—	—	.50	.75
	1985	.012	—	—	Proof	1.50
	1986B	2.324	—	—	.50	.75
	1986B	.010	—	—	Proof	1.65
	1987B	5.028	—	—	.50	.75
	1987B	8,800	—	—	Proof	2.00
	1988B	5.029	—	—	.50	.75
	1988B	9,000	—	—	Proof	2.00
	1989B	41.031	—	—	.30	.50
	1989B	8,800	—	—	Proof	2.25
	1990B	40.032	—	—	.20	.50
	1990B	8,900	—	—	Proof	2.00
	1991B	35.046	—	—	.20	.40
	1991B	9,900	—	—	Proof	2.00
	1992B	18.027	—	—	.20	.40
	1992B	7,450	—	—	Proof	1.50
	1993B	27.022	—	—	.20	.40
	1993B	6,200	—	Proof		1.50
	1994B	18.000	—	—	.20	.40
	1994B	6,100	—	—	Proof	1.50
	1995B	5.024	—	—	.20	.40
	1995B	6,100	—	—	Proof	1.50
	1996B	18.000	—	—	.20	.40
	1996B	6,100	—	—	Proof	1.50
	1997B	15.000	—	—	.20	.40
	1997B	5,500	—	—	Proof	1.50
	1998B	—	—	—	.20	.40
	1998B	—	—	—	Proof	1.50

NOTE: Earlier dates (1879-1900) exist for this type.

BRASS

KM#	Date	Mintage	VF	XF	Unc	BU
27a	1918B	6.000	15.00	25.00	35.00	50.00
	1919B	3.000	60.00	45.00	130.00	175.00

NICKEL

KM#	Date	Mintage	VF	XF	Unc	BU
27b	1932B	3.500	.25	1.00	6.00	9.00
	1933B	2.000	.25	1.00	8.00	12.00
	1934B	3.000	.25	1.00	10.00	15.00
	1936B	1.500	.25	1.00	10.00	15.00
	1937B	1.000	.35	1.50	10.00	15.00
	1938B	1.000	.25	1.50	8.00	12.00
	1939B	10.022	.25	1.00	6.00	9.00

20 RAPPEN

NICKEL

KM#	Date	Mintage	VF	XF	Unc	BU
29	1901B	1.000	1.50	10.00	80.00	120.00
	1902B	1.000	1.50	10.00	45.00	65.00
	1903B	1.000	1.50	10.00	45.00	65.00
	1906B	1.000	1.50	10.00	45.00	65.00
	1907B	1.000	1.50	10.00	30.00	45.00
	1908B	1.500	.50	8.00	27.50	39.00
	1909B	2.000	.50	8.00	27.50	39.00
	1911B	1.000	1.00	8.00	50.00	75.00
	1912B	2.000	.50	8.00	30.00	45.00
	1913B	1.500	.50	8.00	30.00	45.00
	1919B	1.500	.50	6.00	27.50	42.50

KM#	Date	Mintage	VF	XF	Unc	BU
29	1920B	3.100	.35	4.00	16.00	24.00
	1921B	2.500	.35	4.00	16.00	24.00
	1924B	1.100	1.00	4.00	32.00	48.00
	1925B	1.500	.35	3.00	12.50	22.50
	1926B	1.500	.35	3.00	12.50	20.00
	1927B	.500	3.00	15.00	100.00	150.00
	1929B	2.000	.30	1.00	13.00	18.00
	1930B	2.000	.30	1.00	13.00	18.00
	1931B	2.250	.30	1.00	13.00	18.00
	1932B	2.000	.30	1.00	13.00	18.00
	1933B	1.500	.30	1.00	13.00	18.00
	1934B	2.000	.30	.50	13.00	18.00
	1936B	1.000	1.00	1.60	31.00	40.00
	1938B	2.805	.30	.60	28.00	37.00

NOTE: Earlier dates (1881-1900) exist for this type.

COPPER-NICKEL

KM#	Date	Mintage	VF	XF	Unc	BU
29a	1939B	8.100	.25	3.00	100.00	150.00
	1943B	10.173	.25	1.00	20.00	30.00
	1944B	7.139	.25	1.00	8.00	12.00
	1945B	1.992	.50	2.50	32.50	47.50
	1947B	5.131	.25	.50	17.00	24.00
	1950B	5.970	.25	.50	2.50	4.00
	1951B	3.640	.25	.50	7.00	12.00
	1952B	3.070	.25	.50	7.00	12.00
	1953B	6.958	.25	.50	4.00	6.00
	1954B	1.504	.50	1.00	30.00	50.00
	1955B	9.104	.25	.50	4.00	6.00
	1956B	5.111	.25	.50	4.00	6.00
	1957B	2.535	.35	2.50	28.00	60.00
	1958B	5.037	.25	.50	4.00	5.50
	1959B	10.136	—	.35	3.00	4.00
	1960B	15.467	—	.35	3.00	4.00
	1961B	8.234	—	.35	2.00	3.00
	1962B	30.145	—	.35	2.00	3.00
	1963B	9.020	—	.35	2.00	3.00
	1964B	14.370	—	.25	2.00	3.00
	1965B	15.005	—	.25	2.00	3.00
	1966B	10.785	—	.25	1.00	1.50
	1967B	8.995	—	.30	1.25	1.75
	1968B	10.540	—	.25	.50	1.00
	1969B	39.875	—	—	.40	.60
	1970	45.605	—	—	.40	.60
	1971	25.160	—	—	.40	.60
	1974	30.025	—	—	.40	.60
	1974	2,400	—	—	Proof	25.00
	1975	50.060	—	—	.40	.60
	1975	.010	—	—	Proof	2.50
	1976	23.150	—	—	.40	.60
	1976	5,130	—	—	Proof	3.50
	1977	14.012	—	—	.40	.60
	1977	7,030	—	—	Proof	2.25
	1978	14.815	—	—	.40	.60
	1978	.010	—	—	Proof	2.00
	1979	18.380	—	—	.40	.60
	1979	.010	—	—	Proof	2.00
	1980	24.560	—	—	.40	.60
	1980	.010	—	—	Proof	2.50
	1981	22.020	—	—	.40	.60
	1981	.010	—	—	Proof	2.50
	1982	25.035	—	—	.40	.60
	1982	.010	—	—	Proof	3.00
	1983	10.026	—	—	.40	.60
	1983	.011	—	—	Proof	2.00
	1984	22.055	—	—	.40	.60
	1984	.014	—	—	Proof	2.00
	1985	40.027	—	—	.40	.60
	1985	.012	—	—	Proof	2.00
	1986B	10.299	—	—	.40	.60
	1986B	.010	—	—	Proof	2.00
	1987B	10.028	—	—	.40	.60
	1987B	8,800	—	—	Proof	2.25
	1988B	25.029	—	—	.40	.60
	1988B	9,000	—	—	Proof	2.50
	1989B	20.031	—	—	.40	.60
	1989B	8,800	—	—	Proof	2.50
	1990B	6.534	—	—	.35	.50
	1990B	8,900	—	—	Proof	2.50
	1991B	48.076	—	—	.35	.50
	1991B	9,900	—	—	Proof	2.50
	1992B	12.627	—	—	.35	.50
	1992B	7,450	—	—	Proof	2.25
	1993B	32.522	—	—	.35	.50
	1993B	6,200	—	—	Proof	3.50
	1994B	20.000	—	—	.30	.40
	1994B	6,100	—	—	Proof	2.25
	1995B	8.024	—	—	.30	.40
	1995B	6,100	—	—	Proof	2.25
	1996B	4.000	—	—	.30	.40
	1996B	6,100	—	—	Proof	2.25
	1997B	6.000	—	—	.30	.40
	1997B	5,500	—	—	Proof	2.25
	1998B	—	—	—	.30	.40
	1998B	—	—	—	Proof	2.25

1/2 FRANC

2.5000 g, .835 SILVER, .0671 oz ASW

KM#	Date	Mintage	VF	XF	Unc	BU
23	1901B	.200	40.00	250.00	725.00	1100.
	1901B	—	—	—	P/L	3000.
	1903B	.800	3.00	25.00	80.00	125.00
	1903B	—	—	—	P/L	1000.
	1904B	.400	10.00	125.00	700.00	1050.
	1904B	—	—	—	P/L	3000.
	1905B	.600	3.50	40.00	110.00	165.00
	1905B	—	—	—	P/L	900.00
	1906B	1.000	2.00	40.00	140.00	210.00
	1906B	—	—	—	P/L	900.00
	1907B	1.200	2.00	30.00	100.00	150.00
	1907B	—	—	—	P/L	750.00
	1908B	.800	2.00	35.00	100.00	150.00
	1908B	—	—	—	P/L	750.00
	1909B	1.000	2.00	25.00	80.00	120.00
	1909B	—	—	—	P/L	750.00
	1910B	1.000	2.00	20.00	75.00	110.00
	1910B	—	—	—	P/L	750.00
	1913B	.800	2.00	15.00	75.00	110.00
	1913B	—	—	—	P/L	600.00
	1914B	2.000	2.00	7.50	30.00	45.00
	1914B	—	—	—	P/L	360.00
	1916B	.800	2.00	8.00	75.00	110.00
	1916B	—	—	—	P/L	450.00
	1920B	5.400	1.50	7.00	14.00	21.00
	1920B	—	—	—	P/L	150.00
	1921B	6.000	1.50	7.00	14.00	21.00
	1921B	—	—	—	P/L	150.00
	1928B	1.000	2.00	12.50	80.00	120.00
	1928B	—	—	—	P/L	300.00
	1929B	2.000	1.50	7.00	16.00	24.00
	1929B	—	—	—	P/L	180.00
	1931B	1.000	1.50	10.00	40.00	65.00
	1931B	—	—	—	P/L	240.00
	1932B	1.000	1.50	8.00	20.00	30.00
	1932B	—	—	—	P/L	240.00
	1934B	2.000	1.50	5.00	14.00	21.00
	1934B	—	—	—	P/L	120.00
	1936B	.400	2.00	10.00	32.50	50.00
	1936B	—	—	—	P/L	240.00
	1937B	1.000	1.25	5.00	14.00	21.00
	1937B	—	—	—	P/L	180.00
	1939B	1.001	1.25	5.00	14.00	21.00
	1939B	—	—	—	P/L	120.00
	1940B	2.002	1.25	4.00	12.00	18.00
	1940B	—	—	—	P/L	120.00
	1941B	.200	1.50	5.00	16.00	22.00
	1941B	—	—	—	P/L	90.00
	1942B	2.969	1.25	3.00	6.00	9.00
	1942B	—	—	—	P/L	90.00
	1943B	4.572	1.00	3.00	6.00	9.00
	1943B	—	—	—	P/L	90.00
	1944B	7.456	1.00	2.50	4.00	6.00
	1944B	—	—	—	P/L	90.00
	1945B	4.928	1.00	2.50	4.00	6.00
	1945B	—	—	—	P/L	90.00
	1946B	6.817	1.00	2.50	4.00	6.00
	1946B	—	—	—	P/L	90.00
	1948B	6.113	.75	1.50	2.50	4.00
	1948B	—	—	—	P/L	90.00
	1950B	7.148	.75	1.50	2.25	3.50
	1950B	—	—	—	P/L	90.00
	1951B	8.530	.65	1.50	2.25	3.50
	1951B	—	—	—	P/L	90.00
	1952B	14.023	.60	1.25	2.00	3.00
	1952B	—	—	—	P/L	75.00
	1953B	3.567	.65	1.25	3.00	4.25
	1953B	—	—	—	P/L	90.00
	1955B	1.320	.715	1.50	6.00	9.00
	1955B	—	—	—	P/L	110.00
	1956B	4.250	.60	1.00	2.25	3.25
	1956B	—	—	—	P/L	60.00
	1957B	12.085	.50	.85	2.00	3.00
	1957B	—	—	—	P/L	30.00
	1958B	11.558	.50	.85	2.00	3.00
	1958B	—	—	—	P/L	30.00
	1959B	12.581	.50	.85	2.00	3.00
	1959B	—	—	—	P/L	30.00
	1960B	14.528	.50	.85	2.00	3.00
	1960B	—	—	—	P/L	30.00
	1961B	6.906	.50	.85	2.00	3.00
	1961B	—	—	—	P/L	30.00
	1962B	18.272	.50	.75	1.50	2.25
	1962B	—	—	—	P/L	30.00
	1963B	25.168	.50	.75	1.50	2.25
	1963B	—	—	—	P/L	30.00
	1964B	22.720	.50	.75	1.50	2.25
	1964B	—	—	—	P/L	30.00
	1965B	17.920	.50	.75	1.50	2.25
	1965B	—	—	—	P/L	30.00
	1966B	10.008	.50	.75	1.50	2.25
	1966B	—	—	—	P/L	30.00
	1967B	16.096	.50	.75	1.50	2.25
	1967B	—	—	—	P/L	30.00

NOTE: Earlier dates (1875-1900) exist for this type.

NOTE: The P/L labels seen in this section are used to designate coins referred to in the market as Prooflike specimen strikes, specimen strikes or simply specimens.

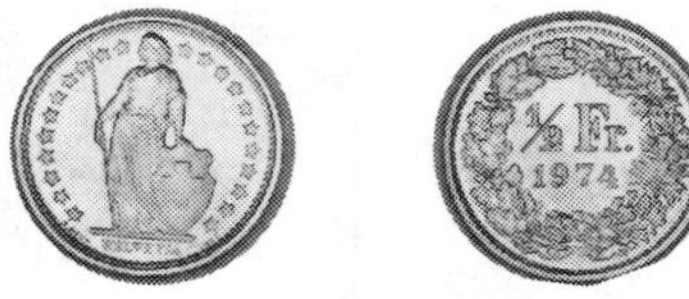

COPPER-NICKEL

KM#	Date	Mintage	VF	XF	Unc	BU
23a.1	1968	20.000	—	—	1.00	1.50
	1968B	44.920	—	—	1.00	1.50
	1969	31.400	—	—	.75	1.25
	1969B	51.704	—	—	.75	1.25
	1970	52.620	—	—	.75	1.25
	1971	34.472	—	—	.75	1.25
	1972	9.996	—	—	.75	1.25
	1973	5.000	—	—	.75	1.25
	1974	45.006	—	—	.75	1.25
	1974	2,400	—	—	Proof	35.00
	1975	27.234	—	—	.75	1.25
	1975	.010	—	—	Proof	3.50
	1976	10.009	—	—	.75	1.25
	1976	5,130	—	—	Proof	4.00
	1977	19.011	—	—	.75	1.25
	1977	7,030	—	—	Proof	3.00
	1978	20.818	—	—	.75	1.25
	1978	.010	—	—	Proof	2.50
	1979	27.010	—	—	.75	1.25
	1979	.010	—	—	Proof	2.50
	1980	31.064	—	—	.75	1.25
	1980	.010	—	—	Proof	3.00
	1981	30.155	—	—	.75	1.25
	1981	.010	—	—	Proof	3.00

Obv. and rev: Medallic alignment. Obv: 22 stars.

KM#	Date	Mintage	VF	XF	Unc	BU
23a.2	1982	30.151	—	—	.75	1.25
	1982	.010	—	—	Proof	6.00

Obv: 23 stars.

KM#	Date	Mintage	VF	XF	Unc	BU
23a.3	1983	22.020	—	—	.75	1.25
	1983	.011	—	—	Proof	3.00
	1984	22.036	—	—	.75	1.25
	1984	.014	—	—	Proof	2.75
	1985	6.026	—	—	.75	1.25
	1985	.012	—	—	Proof	2.75
	1986B	5.031	—	—	.75	1.25
	1986B	.010	—	—	Proof	3.00
	1987B	10.028	—	—	.75	1.25
	1987B	8,800	—	—	Proof	3.25
	1988B	5.029	—	—	.75	1.25
	1988B	9,000	—	—	Proof	3.25
	1989B	10.031	—	—	.75	1.25
	1989B	8,800	—	—	Proof	3.25
	1990B	20.032	—	—	.60	1.00
	1990B	8,900	—	—	Proof	3.25
	1991B	10.036	—	—	.60	1.00
	1991B	9,900	—	—	Proof	3.25
	1992B	30.027	—	—	.60	1.00
	1992B	7,450	—	—	Proof	3.00
	1993B	13.022	—	—	.60	1.00
	1993B	6,200	—	—	Proof	3.00
	1994B	15.000	—	—	.60	1.00
	1994B	6,100	—	—	Proof	3.50
	1995B	10.024	—	—	.60	1.00
	1995B	6,000	—	—	Proof	3.50
	1996B	8.000	—	—	.60	1.00
	1996B	6,100	—	—	Proof	3.50
	1997B	6.000	—	—	.60	1.00
	1997B	5,500	—	—	Proof	3.50
	1998B	—	—	—	.60	1.00
	1998B	—	—	—	Proof	3.50

FRANC

5.0000 g, .835 SILVER, .1342 oz ASW

KM#	Date	Mintage	VF	XF	Unc	BU
24	1901B	.400	12.00	250.00	575.00	850.00
	1901B	—	—	—	P/L	2400.
	1903B	1.000	5.00	40.00	140.00	210.00
	1903B	—	—	—	P/L	1200.
	1904B	.400	15.00	300.00	1000.	1500.
	1904B	—	—	—	P/L	4800.
	1905B	.700	5.00	45.00	200.00	275.00
	1905B	—	—	—	P/L	1200.
	1906B	.700	5.00	75.00	325.00	475.00
	1906B	—	—	—	P/L	1200.
	1907B	.800	5.00	75.00	300.00	425.00
	1907B	—	—	—	P/L	1200.
	1908B	1.200	5.00	40.00	125.00	200.00
	1908B	—	—	—	P/L	1200.
	1909B	.900	5.00	25.00	125.00	200.00
	1909B	—	—	—	P/L	1200.
	1910B	1.000	5.00	30.00	100.00	150.00
	1910B	—	—	—	P/L	1200.
	1911B	1.200	5.00	25.00	100.00	150.00
	1911B	—	—	—	P/L	900.00
	1912B	1.200	5.00	20.00	70.00	100.00
	1912B	—	—	—	P/L	750.00
	1913B	1.200	5.00	20.00	75.00	110.00
	1913B	—	—	—	P/L	900.00
	1914B	4.200	4.00	10.00	35.00	55.00
	1914B	—	—	—	P/L	600.00
	1916B	1.000	5.00	15.00	85.00	120.00
	1916B	—	—	—	P/L	1050.
	1920B	3.300	3.00	6.00	25.00	35.00
	1920B	—	—	—	P/L	180.00
	1921B	3.800	3.00	6.00	25.00	35.00
	1921B	—	—	—	P/L	180.00
	1928B	1.500	3.00	7.50	22.50	35.00
	1928B	—	—	—	P/L	240.00
	1931B	1.000	3.50	7.50	32.50	48.00
	1931B	—	—	—	P/L	240.00
	1932B	.500	4.00	15.00	75.00	110.00

KM#	Date	Mintage	VF	XF	Unc	BU
24	1932B	—	—	—	P/L	480.00
	1934B	.500	4.00	20.00	65.00	100.00
	1934B	—	—	—	P/L	480.00
	1936B	.500	4.00	15.00	55.00	80.00
	1936B	—	—	—	P/L	360.00
	1937B	1.000	3.00	5.00	25.00	36.00
	1937B	—	—	—	P/L	240.00
	1939B	2.106	2.00	3.00	10.00	15.00
	1939B	—	—	—	P/L	150.00
	1940B	2.003	2.00	3.00	9.00	12.50
	1940B	—	—	—	P/L	150.00
	1943B	3.526	1.50	3.00	6.00	9.00
	1943B	—	—	—	P/L	150.00
	1944B	6.225	1.50	3.00	4.50	6.50
	1944B	—	—	—	P/L	150.00
	1945B	7.794	1.50	3.00	5.00	7.50
	1945B	—	—	—	P/L	150.00
	1946B	2.539	1.50	3.00	7.00	10.00
	1946B	—	—	—	P/L	150.00
	1947B	.624	2.50	5.00	16.00	22.00
	1947B	—	—	—	P/L	150.00
	1952B	2.853	1.50	2.50	4.50	6.50
	1952B	—	—	—	P/L	120.00
	1953B	.786	3.00	5.00	17.50	24.00
	1953B	—	—	—	P/L	120.00
	1955B	.194	5.00	8.00	22.00	32.00
	1955B	—	—	—	P/L	120.00
	1956B	2.500	1.50	2.50	5.00	7.50
	1956B	—	—	—	P/L	90.00
	1957B	6.420	1.25	2.00	4.50	6.00
	1957B	—	—	—	P/L	45.00
	1958B	3.580	1.25	2.00	4.50	6.50
	1958B	—	—	—	P/L	45.00
	1959B	1.859	1.25	2.00	4.50	6.50
	1959B	—	—	—	P/L	45.00
	1960B	3.523	—	1.50	3.00	5.00
	1960B	—	—	—	P/L	45.00
	1961B	6.549	—	1.50	3.00	5.00
	1961B	—	—	—	P/L	45.00
	1962B	6.220	—	1.50	3.00	5.00
	1962B	—	—	—	P/L	45.00
	1963B	13.476	—	1.25	3.00	4.50
	1963B	—	—	—	P/L	45.00
	1964B	12.560	—	1.25	3.00	4.50
	1964B	—	—	—	P/L	45.00
	1965B	5.032	—	1.25	3.00	5.00
	1965B	—	—	—	P/L	45.00
	1966B	3.032	—	1.25	3.50	5.50
	1966B	—	—	—	P/L	45.00
	1967B	2.088	—	1.00	3.50	5.50
	1967B	—	—	—	P/L	45.00

NOTE: Earlier dates (1875-1900) exist for this type.

NOTE: The P/L labels seen in this section are used to designate coins referred to in the market as Prooflike specimen strikes, specimen strikes or simply specimens.

COPPER-NICKEL

KM#	Date	Mintage	VF	XF	Unc	BU
24a.1	1968	15.000	—	—	2.00	3.00
	1968B	40.864	—	—	2.00	3.00
	1969B	37.598	—	—	2.00	3.00
	1970	24.240	—	—	2.00	3.00
	1971	11.496	—	—	2.00	3.00
	1973	5.000	—	—	2.00	3.00
	1974	15.012	—	—	1.50	2.50
	1974	2,400	—	—	Proof	65.00
	1975	13.012	—	—	1.50	2.50
	1975	.010	—	—	Proof	5.00
	1976	5.009	—	—	2.00	3.00
	1976	5,130	—	—	Proof	6.50
	1977	6.019	—	—	2.00	3.00
	1977	7,030	—	—	Proof	4.00
	1978	13.548	—	—	1.50	2.50
	1978	.010	—	—	Proof	3.50
	1979	10.800	—	—	1.50	2.50
	1979	.010	—	—	Proof	3.50
	1980	11.002	—	—	1.50	2.50
	1980	.010	—	—	Proof	4.00
	1981	18.013	—	—	1.50	2.50
	1981	.010	—	—	Proof	4.00

Obv. and rev: Medallic alignment. Obv: 22 stars.

KM#	Date	Mintage	VF	XF	Unc	BU
24a.2	1982	15.039	—	—	2.00	3.00
	1982	.010	—	—	Proof	12.00

Obv: 23 stars.

KM#	Date	Mintage	VF	XF	Unc	BU
24a.3	1983	7.018	—	—	1.50	2.50
	1983	.011	—	—	Proof	4.00
	1984	3.028	—	—	2.00	3.00
	1984	.014	—	—	Proof	3.50
	1985	20.042	—	—	1.50	2.50
	1985	.012	—	—	Proof	3.50
	1986B	17.997	—	—	1.50	2.50
	1986B	.010	—	—	Proof	3.50
	1987B	17.028	—	—	1.50	2.50
	1987B	8,800	—	—	Proof	4.00
	1988B	18.029	—	—	1.50	2.50
	1988B	9,000	—	—	Proof	4.00
	1989B	15.031	—	—	1.50	2.50
	1989B	8,800	—	—	Proof	4.25
	1990B	2.032	—	—	1.50	2.50

KM#	Date	Mintage	VF	XF	Unc	BU
24a.3	1990B	8,900	—	—	Proof	4.00
	1991B	9.036	—	—	1.00	1.50
	1991B	9,900	—	—	Proof	4.00
	1992B	12.030	—	—	1.00	1.50
	1992B	7,450	—	—	Proof	3.50
	1993B	12.030	—	—	1.00	1.50
	1993B	6,200	—	—	Proof	3.50
	1994B	10.000	—	—	1.00	1.50
	1994B	6,100	—	—	Proof	4.00
	1995B	13,034	—	—	1.00	1.50
	1995B	6,100	—	—	Proof	4.00
	1996B	3.000	—	—	1.00	1.50
	1996B	6,100	—	—	Proof	4.00
	1997B	3.000	—	—	1.00	1.50
	1997B	5,500	—	—	Proof	4.00
	1998B	—	—	—	1.00	1.50
	1998B	—	—	—	Proof	4.00

2 FRANCS

10.0000 g, .835 SILVER, .2685 oz ASW

KM#	Date	Mintage	VF	XF	Unc	BU
21	1901B	.050	200.00	1250.	6500.	9000.
	1901B	—	—	—	P/L	Rare
	1903B	.300	10.00	80.00	600.00	850.00
	1903B	—	—	—	P/L	2700.
	1904B	.200	20.00	350.00	1200.	1750.
	1904B	—	—	—	P/L	5700.
	1905B	.300	10.00	75.00	475.00	650.00
	1905B	—	—	—	P/L	2700.
	1906B	.400	10.00	85.00	500.00	700.00
	1906B	—	—	—	P/L	3000.
	1907B	.300	12.50	145.00	725.00	1000.
	1907B	—	—	—	P/L	3000.
	1908B	.200	20.00	350.00	1400.	2000.
	1908B	—	—	—	P/L	5400.
	1909B	.300	9.00	75.00	275.00	400.00
	1909B	—	—	—	P/L	3900.
	1910B	.250	9.00	175.00	800.00	1200.
	1910B	—	—	—	P/L	4200.
	1911B	.400	7.50	40.00	180.00	275.00
	1911B	—	—	—	P/L	1800.
	1912B	.400	7.50	40.00	125.00	190.00
	1912B	—	—	—	P/L	1500.
	1913B	.300	7.50	40.00	160.00	250.00
	1913B	—	—	—	P/L	2100.
	1914B	1.000	5.00	25.00	100.00	150.00
	1914B	—	—	—	P/L	1200.
	1916B	.250	7.50	130.00	500.00	700.00
	1916B	—	—	—	P/L	2400.
	1920B	2.300	3.00	10.00	27.50	45.00
	1920B	—	—	—	P/L	450.00
	1921B	2.000	3.00	10.00	25.00	40.00
	1921B	—	—	—	P/L	450.00
	1922B	.400	3.00	35.00	160.00	225.00
	1922B	—	—	—	P/L	1200.
	1928B	.750	3.00	12.50	30.00	45.00
	1928B	—	—	—	P/L	450.00
	1931B	.500	3.00	12.50	40.00	60.00
	1931B	—	—	—	P/L	450.00
	1932B	.250	4.00	40.00	220.00	300.00
	1932B	—	—	—	P/L	1050.
	1936B	.250	4.00	35.00	110.00	165.00
	1936B	—	—	—	P/L	600.00
	1937B	.250	4.00	22.50	60.00	90.00
	1937B	—	—	—	P/L	450.00
	1939B	1.455	2.25	5.00	8.00	12.00
	1939B	—	—	—	P/L	600.00
	1940B	2.502	2.25	5.00	8.00	12.00
	1940B	—	—	—	P/L	180.00
	1941B	1.192	2.25	5.00	8.00	12.00
	1941B	—	—	—	P/L	180.00
	1943B	2.089	2.25	4.00	8.00	12.00
	1943B	—	—	—	P/L	180.00
	1944B	6.276	2.25	4.00	8.00	12.00
	1944B	—	—	—	P/L	180.00
	1945B	1.134	2.50	7.00	15.00	22.50
	1945B	—	—	—	P/L	180.00
	1946B	1.629	2.50	4.00	10.00	15.00
	1946B	—	—	—	P/L	180.00
	1947B	.500	4.00	8.00	22.00	32.00
	1947B	—	—	—	P/L	180.00
	1948B	.920	2.50	4.00	10.00	15.00
	1948B	—	—	—	P/L	180.00
	1953B	.438	3.00	6.00	20.00	30.00
	1953B	—	—	—	P/L	180.00
	1955B	1.032	2.50	3.50	6.00	9.00
	1955B	—	—	—	P/L	150.00
	1957B	2.298	2.00	3.00	4.00	6.00
	1957B	—	—	—	P/L	60.00
	1958B	.650	2.50	3.50	5.00	7.00
	1958B	—	—	—	P/L	60.00
	1959B	2.905	2.00	3.00	4.00	6.00
	1959B	—	—	—	P/L	60.00
	1960B	1.980	2.00	3.00	4.00	6.00
	1960B	—	—	—	P/L	60.00
	1961B	4.653	—	2.50	4.00	7.00
	1961B	—	—	—	P/L	60.00
	1963B	8.030	—	2.00	4.00	7.00

KM#	Date	Mintage	VF	XF	Unc	BU
21	1963B	—	—	—	P/L	60.00
	1964B	4.558	—	2.00	4.00	7.00
	1964B	—	—	—	P/L	60.00
	1965B	8.526	—	2.00	4.00	7.00
	1965B	—	—	—	P/L	60.00
	1967B	4.132	—	2.00	4.00	7.00
	1967B	—	—	—	P/L	60.00

NOTE: Earlier dates (1874-1896) exist for this type.

NOTE: The P/L labels seen in this section are used to designate coins referred to in the market as Prooflike specimen strikes, specimen strikes or simply specimens.

COPPER-NICKEL

KM#	Date	Mintage	VF	XF	Unc	BU
21a.1	1968	10.000	—	—	4.00	6.00
	1968B	31.588	—	—	4.00	6.00
	1969B	17.296	—	—	4.00	6.00
	1970	10.350	—	—	4.00	6.00
	1972	5.003	—	—	4.00	6.00
	1973	5.996	—	—	4.00	6.00
	1974	15.009	—	—	4.00	6.00
	1974	2,400	—	—	Proof	65.00
	1975	7.061	—	—	4.00	6.00
	1975	.010	—	—	Proof	9.00
	1976	5.011	—	—	4.00	6.00
	1976	5,130	—	—	Proof	10.00
	1977	2.010	—	—	4.00	6.00
	1977	7,030	—	—	Proof	9.00
	1978	12.812	—	—	3.00	4.00
	1978	.010	—	—	Proof	7.00
	1979	10.990	—	—	3.00	4.00
	1979	.010	—	—	Proof	7.00
	1980	10.001	—	—	3.00	4.00
	1980	.010	—	—	Proof	7.00
	1981	13.852	—	—	3.00	4.00
	1981	.010	—	—	Proof	7.00

Obv. and rev: Medal alignment. Obv: 22 stars.

KM#	Date	Mintage	VF	XF	Unc	BU
21a.2	1982	5.912	—	—	4.00	6.00
	1982	.010	—	—	Proof	15.00

Obv: 23 stars.

KM#	Date	Mintage	VF	XF	Unc	BU
21a.3	1983	3.023	—	—	3.00	4.00
	1983	.011	—	—	Proof	8.00
	1984	2.029	—	—	3.00	4.00
	1984	.014	—	—	Proof	8.00
	1985	3.022	—	—	3.00	4.00
	1985	.012	—	—	Proof	8.00
	1986B	3.032	—	—	3.00	4.00
	1986B	.010	—	—	Proof	8.00
	1987B	8.028	—	—	2.50	3.50
	1987B	8,800	—	—	Proof	7.50
	1988B	10.029	—	—	2.50	3.50
	1988B	9,000	—	—	Proof	7.50
	1989B	8.031	—	—	2.50	3.50
	1989B	8,800	—	—	Proof	7.50
	1990B	5.045	—	—	2.50	3.50
	1990B	8,900	—	—	Proof	7.50
	1991B	12.036	—	—	2.00	3.00
	1991B	9,900	—	—	Proof	7.50
	1992B	10.027	—	—	2.00	3.00
	1992B	7,450	—	—	Proof	7.00
	1993B	13.049	—	—	2.00	3.00
	1993B	6,200	—	—	Proof	7.00
	1994B	16.000	—	—	2.00	3.00
	1994B	6,100	—	—	Proof	7.00
	1995B	7.024	—	—	2.00	3.00
	1995B	6,100	—	—	Proof	7.00
	1996B	5.000	—	—	2.00	3.00
	1996B	6,100	—	—	Proof	7.00
	1997B	5.000	—	—	2.00	3.00
	1997B	5,500	—	—	Proof	7.00
	1998B	—	—	—	2.00	3.00
	1998B	—	—	—	Proof	7.00

5 FRANCS

25.0000 g, .900 SILVER, .7234 oz ASW

KM#	Date	Mintage	VF	XF	Unc	BU
34	1904B	.040	600.00	1000.	2000.	3000.
	1904B	—	—	—	P/L	7800.
	1907B	.277	125.00	300.00	600.00	900.00
	1907B	—	—	—	P/L	3600.
	1908B	.200	135.00	325.00	650.00	950.00

KM#	Date	Mintage	VF	XF	Unc	BU
34	1908B	—	—	—	P/L	3600.
	1909B	.120	175.00	350.00	650.00	950.00
	1909B	—	—	—	P/L	3600.
	1912B	.011	2750.	3500.	4500.	6000.
	1912B	—	—	—	P/L	12,000.
	1916B	.022	1000.	1500.	2000.	2750.
	1916B	—	—	—	P/L	6000.

NOTE: Earlier dates (1888-1900) exist for this type.

37	1922B	2.400	50.00	125.00	200.00	300.00
	1922B	—	—	—	P/L	1800.
	1923B	11.300	40.00	70.00	175.00	250.00
	1923B	—	—	—	P/L	3000.

38	1924B	.182	375.00	550.00	850.00	1250.
	1924B	—	—	—	P/L	2400.
	1925B	2.830	75.00	150.00	225.00	325.00
	1925B	—	—	—	P/L	1500.
	1926B	2.000	80.00	150.00	250.00	350.00
	1926B	—	—	—	P/L	1500.
	1928B	.024	7000.	9000.	12,500.	16,000.
	1928B	—	—	—	P/L	Rare

15.0000 g, .835 SILVER, .4027 oz ASW

NOTE: The several varieties of number KM#40, the 1931 and 1967 5 Francs, are distinguished by the relation of the edge lettering to the head of William Tell and in the amount of rotation of the reverse in relation to the obverse. Beginning above the head the normal sequence is:

a) PROVIDEBIT ******** *** DOMINUS**

A fairly common variety shows the lettering:
b) ******** *** DOMINUS PROVIDEBIT**

A somewhat rarer variety shows:
c) ******** PROVIDEBIT *** DOMINUS**

d) * DOMINUS ********** PROVIDEBIT**

The reverse of the regular issue is upset 180 degrees. There are varieties with:

e) The reverse rotated about 15 degrees to the left of the normal upset position.

f) The reverse rotated about 15 degrees to the right of the normal position.

Raised edge lettering.

40	1931B(a)	3.520	5.00	12.00	40.00	60.00
	1931B(a)	I.A.	—	—	P/L	900.00
	1931B(b)	I.A.	12.50	25.00	75.00	110.00
	1931B(c)	I.A.	35.00	90.00	200.00	300.00
	1931B(d)	I.A.	600.00	1000.	1400.	2100.
	1932B	10.580	4.00	7.50	12.00	20.00
	1932B	—	—	—	P/L	450.00
	1933B	5.900	5.00	9.00	14.00	21.00
	1933B	—	—	—	P/L	450.00
	1935B	3.000	6.00	10.00	17.50	27.50
	1935B	—	—	—	P/L	450.00
	1937B	.645	6.50	12.50	32.50	47.50
	1937B	—	—	—	P/L	900.00
	1939B	2.197	5.00	7.50	12.50	20.00
	1939B	—	—	—	P/L	450.00
	1940B	1.601	6.00	10.00	20.00	30.00

KM#	Date	Mintage	VF	XF	Unc	BU
40	1940B	—	—	—	P/L	600.00
	1948B	.416	6.50	13.00	30.00	45.00
	1948B	—	—	—	P/L	600.00
	1949B	.407	6.50	15.00	35.00	47.50
	1949B	—	—	—	P/L	600.00
	1950B	.482	6.50	10.00	30.00	45.00
	1950B	—	—	—	P/L	600.00
	1951B	1.196	5.00	10.00	20.00	30.00
	1951B	—	—	—	P/L	300.00
	1952B	.155	30.00	60.00	150.00	225.00
	1952B	—	—	—	P/L	750.00
	1953B	3.403	—	6.00	8.00	12.00
	1953B	—	—	—	P/L	150.00
	1954B	6.600	—	6.00	8.00	11.00
	1954B	—	—	—	P/L	150.00
	1965B	5.021	—	—	4.00	7.00
	1965B	—	—	—	P/L	120.00
	1966B	9.016	—	4.00	7.00	10.00
	1966B	—	—	—	P/L	120.00
	1967B (a)					
		13.817	—	4.00	7.00	10.00
	1967B (a)	—	—	—	P/L	120.00
	1967B (b)	—	50.00	80.00	110.00	155.00
	1967B (d)	—	400.00	750.00	1100.	1550.
	1969B	8.637	—	4.00	7.00	10.00
	1969B	—	—	—	P/L	120.00

NOTE: A few examples of the 1968B were struck in error on silver flans.

NOTE: The P/L labels seen in this section are used to designate coins referred to in the market as Prooflike specimen strikes, specimen strikes or simply specimens.

COPPER-NICKEL

40a.1	1968B	33.871	—	—	5.00	7.00
	1970	6.306	—	—	5.00	7.00
	1973	5.002	—	—	5.00	7.00
	1974	6.007	—	—	5.00	7.00
	1974	2,400	—	—	Proof	125.00
	1975	4.015	—	—	5.00	7.00
	1975	.010	—	—	Proof	12.00
	1976	3.007	—	—	5.00	7.00
	1976	5,130	—	—	Proof	14.00
	1977	2.009	—	—	5.00	7.00
	1977	7,030	—	—	Proof	12.00
	1978	4.411	—	—	5.00	7.00
	1978	.010	—	—	Proof	12.00
	1979	4.011	—	—	5.00	7.00
	1979	.010	—	—	Proof	12.00
	1980	4.026	—	—	5.00	7.00
	1980	.010	—	—	Proof	12.00
	1981	6.018	—	—	5.00	7.00
	1981	.010	—	—	Proof	12.00

Obv. and rev: Medallic alignment.

40a.2	1982	5.050	—	—	6.00	8.00
	1982	.010	—	—	Proof	18.00
	1983	4.033	—	—	6.00	8.00
	1983	.011	—	—	Proof	12.00
	1984	3.953	—	—	6.00	8.00
	1984	.014	—	—	Proof	11.00

Incuse edge lettering.

40a.3	1985	4.050	—	—	5.50	7.50
	1985	.012	—	—	Proof	10.00
	1986B	7.083	—	—	5.50	7.50
	1986B	.010	—	—	Proof	11.00
	1987B	7.028	—	—	5.50	7.50
	1987B	8,800	—	—	Proof	12.00
	1988B	7.029	—	—	5.50	7.50
	1988B	9,000	—	—	Proof	12.00
	1989B	5.031	—	—	5.50	7.50
	1989B	8,800	—	—	Proof	12.00
	1990B	1.049	—	—	6.00	8.00
	1990B	8,900	—	—	Proof	12.00
	1991B	.026	—	Mint sets only	110.00	
	1991B	9,900	—	—	Proof	120.00
	1992B	5.034	—	—	5.00	6.50
	1992B	7,450	—	—	Proof	12.00
	1993B	.016	—	Mint sets only	110.00	
	1993B	6,200	—	—	Proof	125.00
	1994B	12.000	—	—	5.00	6.50
	1994B	6,100	—	—	Proof	15.00
	1995B	12.000	—	—	5.00	6.50
	1995B	6,100	—	—	Proof	15.00
	1996B	12.000	—	—	5.00	6.50
	1996B	6,100	—	—	Proof	12.00
	1997B	9.000	—	—	5.00	6.50
	1997B	5,500	—	—	Proof	12.00
	1998B	—	—	—	5.00	6.50
	1998B	—	—	—	Proof	12.00

10 FRANCS

3.2258 g, .900 GOLD, .0933 oz AGW

36	1911B	.100	125.00	200.00	350.00	550.00
	1912B	.200	50.00	75.00	115.00	200.00
	1913B	.600	45.00	65.00	75.00	125.00
	1914B	.200	45.00	65.00	75.00	135.00
	1915B	.400	45.00	65.00	75.00	125.00
	1916B	.130	50.00	75.00	115.00	175.00
	1922B	1.020	45.00	60.00	75.00	100.00

20 FRANCS

6.4516 g, .900 GOLD, .1867 oz AGW

KM#	Date	Mintage	VF	XF	Unc	BU
35.1	1901B	.500	BV	75.00	90.00	110.00
	1902B	.600	BV	75.00	90.00	110.00
	1903B	.200	80.00	95.00	120.00	140.00
	1904B	.100	90.00	110.00	135.00	175.00
	1905B	.100	90.00	110.00	135.00	175.00
	1906B	.100	90.00	110.00	130.00	170.00
	1907B	.150	80.00	95.00	115.00	135.00
	1908B	.355	BV	75.00	95.00	115.00
	1909B	.400	BV	75.00	95.00	115.00
	1910B	.375	BV	75.00	95.00	115.00
	1911B	.350	BV	75.00	95.00	115.00
	1912B	.450	BV	75.00	95.00	115.00
	1913B	.700	BV	75.00	95.00	110.00
	1914B	.700	BV	75.00	95.00	110.00
	1915B	.750	BV	75.00	95.00	110.00
	1916B	.300	BV	75.00	95.00	110.00
	1922B	2.784	BV	65.00	80.00	95.00
	1925B	.400	BV	75.00	95.00	110.00
	1926B	.050	125.00	175.00	225.00	300.00
	1927B	5.015	BV	65.00	75.00	90.00
	1930B	3.372	BV	65.00	75.00	90.00
	1935B	.175	BV	80.00	95.00	110.00
	1935L-B**					
		20.009	—	BV	70.00	85.00

*NOTE: Struck of bright Valaisan gold from Gondo with a small cross punched in the center of the Swiss cross.

**NOTE: The 1935L-B issue was struck in 1945, 1946 and 1947.
NOTE: Earlier dates (1897-1900) exist for this type.

Edge: AD LEGEM ANNI MCMXXXI

35.2	1947B	9.200	BV	65.00	75.00	95.00
	1949B	10.000	BV	65.00	75.00	95.00

100 FRANCS

32.2581 g, .900 GOLD, .9334 oz AGW

39	1925B	5,000	3500.	4500.	6750.	8500.

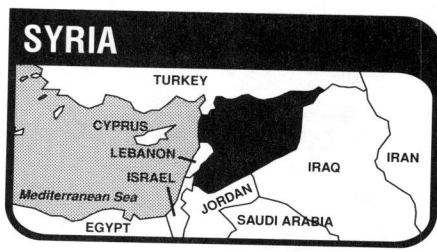

SYRIA

The Syrian Arab Republic, located in the Near East at the eastern end of the Mediterranean Sea, has an area of 71,498 sq. mi. (185,180 sq. km.) and a population of *12 million. Capital: Greater Damascus. Agriculture and animal breeding are the chief industries. Cotton, crude oil and livestock are exported.

Ancient Syria, a land bridge connecting Europe, Africa and Asia, has spent much of its history in thrall to the conqueror's whim. Its subjection by Egypt about 1500 B.C. was followed by successive conquests by the Hebrews, Phoenicians, Babylonians, Assyrians, Persians, Macedonians, Romans, Byzantines and finally, in 636 A.D., by the Moslems. The Arabs made Damascus, one of the oldest continuously inhabited cities of the world, the trade center and capital of an empire stretching from India to Spain. In 1516, following the total destruction of Damascus by the Mongols of Tamerlane, Syria fell to the Ottoman Turks and remained a part of Turkey until the end of World War I. The League of Nations gave France a mandate to the Levant states of Syria and Lebanon in 1920. In 1930, following a series of uprisings, France recognized Syria as an independent republic, but still subject to the mandate. Lebanon became fully independent on Nov. 22, 1943, and Syria on Jan. 1, 1944.

TITLES

الجمهورية السورية

al-Jumhuriya(t) al-Suriya(t)

الجمهورية لعربية السورية

al-Jumhuriya(t) al-Arabiya(t) as-Suriya(t)

RULERS

Ottoman, until 1918
Faysal, 1918-1920

MINT MARKS

(a) - Paris, privy marks only

MINTNAME

Damascus (Dimask)   د مشق

Halab (Aleppo)   حلب

MONETARY SYSTEM

100 Piastres (Qirsh) = 1 Pound (Lira)

FRENCH PROTECTORATE

1/2 PIASTRE

COPPER-NICKEL

KM#	Date	Mintage	Fine	VF	XF	Unc
68	1921(a)	4.000	.25	1.00	3.50	15.00

NICKEL-BRASS

75	1935(a)	.600	.75	2.50	10.00	40.00
	1936(a)	.800	.75	2.00	8.00	25.00

PIASTRE

NICKEL-BRASS

KM#	Date	Mintage	Fine	VF	XF	Unc
71	1929(a)	.750	.50	2.00	7.00	32.50
	1933(a)	.600	1.00	3.00	10.00	40.00
	1935(a)	1.950	.35	1.00	3.50	22.50
	1936(a)	1.400	.50	1.25	5.00	25.00

ZINC

71a	1940(a)	2.060	2.00	5.00	15.00	65.00

2 PIASTRES

ALUMINUM-BRONZE

69	1926(a)	.600	5.00	10.00	25.00	75.00
	1926 w/o privy marks		—	—	—	—

2-1/2 PIASTRES

ALUMINUM-BRONZE

76	1940(a)	2.000	1.25	2.50	6.00	15.00

5 PIASTRES

ALUMINUM-BRONZE

70	1926(a)	.300	.75	2.00	8.00	25.00
	1926 w/o privy marks					
		.400	.75	3.00	12.00	35.00
	1933(a)	1.200	.40	2.00	12.50	40.00
	1935(a)	2.000	.30	1.50	8.00	25.00
	1936(a)	.900	.50	2.00	10.00	30.00
	1940(a)	.500	.50	1.50	4.00	15.00

10 PIASTRES

2.0000 g, .680 SILVER .0437 oz ASW

72	1929	1.000	3.00	10.00	25.00	80.00

25 PIASTRES

5.0000 g, .680 SILVER .1093 oz ASW

73	1929	1.000	3.00	5.00	22.50	80.00
	1933(a)	.500	4.00	12.00	40.00	150.00
	1936(a)	.897	3.50	7.00	25.00	95.00
	1937(a)	.393	5.00	10.00	32.50	125.00

50 PIASTRES

 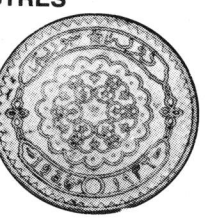

10.0000 g, .680 SILVER .2186 oz ASW

KM#	Date	Mintage	Fine	VF	XF	Unc
74	1929	.880	4.00	8.00	30.00	125.00
	1933(a)	.250	6.00	10.00	40.00	185.00
	1936(a)	.400	5.00	10.00	35.00	150.00
	1937(a) Inc. Ab.		7.00	12.00	45.00	200.00

WORLD WAR II
EMERGENCY COINAGE
PIASTRE

BRASS

77	ND		1.00	2.00	4.00	8.00

2-1/2 PIASTRES

ALUMINUM

78	ND		10.00	15.00	30.00	65.00

REPUBLIC
1944-1958

2-1/2 PIASTRES

COPPER-NICKEL

KM#	Date	Year	Mintage	VF	XF	Unc
81	AH1367	1948	2.500	.30	.60	2.00
	1375	1956	5.000	.25	.80	1.25

5 PIASTRES

COPPER-NICKEL

82	AH1367	1948	8.000	.50	1.00	2.50
	1375	1956	4.000	.35	.75	1.50

10 PIASTRES

COPPER-NICKEL

83	AH1367	1948	—	.60	1.00	2.50
	1375	1956	4.000	.40	.85	1.75

25 PIASTRES

2.5000 g, .600 SILVER .0482 oz ASW

79	AH1366	1947	6.300	2.50	5.00	20.00

50 PIASTRES

5.0000 g, .600 SILVER .0965 oz ASW

KM#	Date	Year	Mintage	VF	XF	Unc
80	AH1366	1947	4.500	3.50	7.00	22.50

1/2 POUND

3.3793 g, .900 GOLD, .0978 oz AGW

84	AH1369	1950	.100	55.00	65.00	110.00

LIRA

10.0000 g, .680 SILVER, .2186 oz ASW

85	AH1369	1950	7.000	5.00	7.50	25.00

POUND

6.7586 g, .900 GOLD .1956 oz AGW

86	AH1369	1950	.250	100.00	120.00	185.00

UNITED ARAB REPUBLIC
1958-1961
2-1/2 PIASTRES

ALUMINUM-BRONZE

90	AH1380	1960	1.100	.10	.20	.60

5 PIASTRES

ALUMINUM-BRONZE

91	AH1380	1960	4.240	.10	.20	.50

10 PIASTRES

ALUMINUM-BRONZE

92	AH1380	1960	2.800	.10	.25	.75

25 PIASTRES

2.5000 g, .600 SILVER, .0482 oz ASW

KM#	Date	Year	Mintage	VF	XF	Unc
87	AH1377	1958	2.300	1.50	2.00	6.00

50 PIASTRES

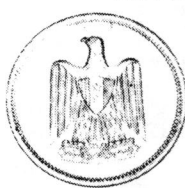 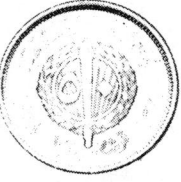

5.000 g, .600 SILVER, .0965 oz ASW

88	AH1377	1958	.120	3.00	6.50	18.00

1st Anniversary - Founding of United Arab Republic

89	AH1378	1959	1.500	3.00	4.50	12.00

SYRIAN ARAB REPUBLIC
1961-
2-1/2 PIASTRES

ALUMINUM-BRONZE

93	AH1382	1962	8.000	.10	.20	.50
	1385	1965	8.000	.10	.20	.50

104	AH1393	1973	10.000	.10	.15	.25

5 PIASTRES

ALUMINUM-BRONZE

94	AH1382	1962	7.000	.10	.15	.35
	1385	1965	18.000	.10	.15	.35

F.A.O. Issue

100	AH1391	1971	15.000	.10	.15	.25

105	AH1394	1974	—	.10	.15	.25

F.A.O. Issue

KM#	Date	Year	Mintage	VF	XF	Unc
110	AH1396	1976	2.000	.10	.15	.25

Similar to KM#94 but heavier neck feathers.

116	AH1399	1979	—	.10	.15	.25

10 PIASTRES

ALUMINUM-BRONZE

95	AH1382	1962	6.000	.10	.20	.45
	1385	1965	22.000	.10	.20	.45

106	AH1394	1974	—	.10	.15	.30

BRASS
F.A.O. Issue
Similar to 5 Piastres, KM#110.

111	AH1396	1976	.500	.10	.15	.25

ALUMINUM-BRONZE

117	AH1399	1979	—	.10	.15	.30

25 PIASTRES

NICKEL

96	AH1387	1968	15.000	.20	.30	.60

25th Anniversary - Al-Ba'ath Party

101	AH1392	1972	—	.15	.25	.60

107	AH1394	1974	—	.10	.25	.50

F.A.O. Issue

112	AH1396	1976	1.000	.10	.25	.50

COPPER-NICKEL

KM#	Date	Year	Mintage	VF	XF	Unc
118	AH1399	1979	—	.10	.25	.50

50 PIASTRES

NICKEL

97	AH1387	1968	10.000	.25	.50	.85

25th Anniversary Al-Ba'ath Party

102	AH1392	1972	—	.20	.30	.75
108	AH1394	1974	—	.20	.30	.75

F.A.O. Issue

113	AH1396	1976	1.000	.10	.20	.50

COPPER-NICKEL

119	AH1399	1979	—	.20	.30	.75

POUND

NICKEL

98	AH1387	1968	10.000	.30	.75	1.25
	1391	1971	10.000	.30	.75	1.25

F.A.O. Issue

KM#	Date	Year	Mintage	VF	XF	Unc
99	AH1388	1968	.500	.40	.85	1.65

25th Anniversary Al-Ba'ath Party

103	AH1392	1972	10.000	.30	.75	2.00
109	AH1394	1974	—	.30	.75	2.00

F.A.O. Issue
Similar to 5 Piastres, KM#110.

114	AH1396	1976	.500	.40	.85	1.65

Reelection of President

115	AH1398	1978	—	.65	1.25	3.00

COPPER-NICKEL

120.1	AH1399	1979	—	.30	.70	1.25

STAINLESS STEEL

120.2	AH1412	1991	—	.30	.70	1.25
121	AH1414	(1994)	—	.30	.70	1.25

2 POUNDS

STAINLESS STEEL
Obv: National emblem.
Rev: Ancient ruins.

KM#	Date	Year	Mintage	VF	XF	Unc
125	AH1416	1996	—	—	.75	1.50

5 POUNDS

COPPER-NICKEL
Rev: Palace.

123	AH1416	1996	—	—	.85	1.75

10 POUNDS

COPPER-NICKEL
Rev: Ancient ruins.

124	AH1416	1996	—	—	1.00	2.00

25 POUNDS

STAINLESS STEEL center in BRONZE ring
Obv: Heraldic eagle. Rev: President.

122	AH1416	1995	—	—	2.00	4.50

Obv: National emblem.
Rev: Large modern building.

126	AH1416	1996	—	—	2.00	4.50

TANZANIA

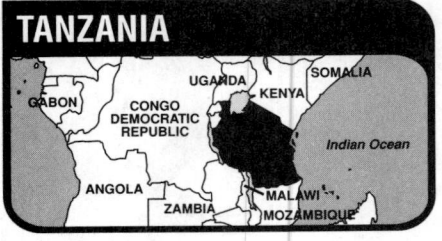

The United Republic of Tanzania, located on the east coast of Africa between Kenya and Mozambique, consists of Tanganyika and the islands of Zanzibar and Pemba. It has an area of 364,900 sq. mi. (945,090 sq. km.) and a population of *25.2 million. Capital: Dar es Salaam (Haven of Peace). The chief exports are cotton, coffee, diamonds, sisal, cloves, petroleum products, and cashew nuts.

Tanzania is a member of the Commonwealth of Nations. The President is Chief of State.

GERMAN EAST AFRICA

German East Africa (Tanganyika), located on the coast of east-central Africa between British East Africa (now Kenya) and Portuguese East Africa (now Mozambique), had an area of 362,284 sq. mi. (938,216 sq. km.) and a population of about 6 million. Capital: Dar es Salaam. Chief products prior to German control were ivory and slaves; after German control, sisal, coffee, and rubber. Germany acquired control of the area by treaties with coastal chiefs in 1884, established it as a protectorate in 1891, and proclaimed it the Colony of German East Africa in 1897. After World War I, Tanganyika was entrusted to Great Britain as a League of Nations mandate, and after World War II as a United Nations trust territory. Tanganyika became an independent nation within the British Commonwealth on Dec. 9, 1961.

Coins dated up until 1901 were issued by the German East Africa Company. From 1904 onwards, coins were issued by the government.

TITLES

شراكتة المانيا

Sharaka(t) Almania

RULERS

Wilhelm II, 1888-1918

MINT MARKS

A - Berlin
J - Hamburg
T - Tabora

MONETARY SYSTEM
Until 1904

64 Pesa = 1 Rupie
Commencing 1904
100 Heller = 1 Rupie

1/2 HELLER

BRONZE

KM#	Date	Mintage	Fine	VF	XF	Unc
6	1904A	1.201	1.25	3.50	6.50	28.00
	1905A	7.192	2.25	5.25	9.00	32.50
	1905J	4.000	2.25	5.25	9.00	32.50
	1906J	6.000	1.25	3.50	6.50	28.00
	1906J	—	—	—	Proof	150.00

HELLER

BRONZE

KM#	Date	Mintage	Fine	VF	XF	Unc
7	1904A	10.256	.75	2.25	4.00	20.00
	1904A	—	—	—	Proof	85.00
	1904J	2.500	.75	2.25	7.00	25.00
	1905A	3.760	.75	2.25	7.00	25.00
	1905A	—	—	—	Proof	85.00
	1905J	7.556	.75	2.25	4.00	20.00
	1906A	3.004	.75	2.25	7.00	25.00
	1906A	—	—	—	Proof	85.00
	1906J	1.962	.75	2.25	7.00	25.00
	1907J	17.790	.75	1.50	4.00	20.00
	1908J	12.205	.75	1.50	4.00	20.00
	1908J	—	—	—	Proof	95.00
	1909J	1.698	2.50	7.50	15.00	35.00
	1909J	—	—	—	Proof	95.00

KM#	Date	Mintage	Fine	VF	XF	Unc
7	1910J	5.096	.75	1.50	4.00	20.00
	1910J	—	—	—	Proof	95.00
	1911J	6.420	.75	1.50	4.00	20.00
	1911J	—	—	—	Proof	95.00
	1912J	7.012	.75	1.50	4.00	20.00
	1912J	—	—	—	Proof	95.00
	1913A	—	.75	1.50	4.00	20.00
	1913A	—	—	—	Proof	95.00
	1913J	5.186	.75	1.50	4.00	20.00
	1913J	—	—	—	Proof	125.00

5 HELLER

BRONZE

KM#	Date	Mintage	Fine	VF	XF	Unc
11	1908J	.600	15.00	30.00	70.00	450.00
	1908J	—	—	—	Proof	975.00
	1909J	.756	15.00	30.00	70.00	450.00
	1909J	60 pcs.	—	—	Proof	975.00

COPPER-NICKEL

KM#	Date	Mintage	Fine	VF	XF	Unc
13	1913A	1.000	6.00	15.00	25.00	55.00
	1913A	—	—	—	Proof	185.00
	1913J	1.000	6.00	15.00	25.00	50.00
	1913J	—	—	—	Proof	185.00
	1914J	1.000	5.00	12.00	22.00	50.00
	1914J	—	—	—	Proof	185.00

BRASS, 1 1/2-2mm thick
Obv: Oval base on crown.

KM#	Date	Mintage	Fine	VF	XF	Unc
14.1	1916T	.030	4.00	14.00	25.00	60.00

Obv: Flat base on crown, 1mm or less thick.

KM#	Date	Mintage	Fine	VF	XF	Unc
14.2	1916T	Inc. Ab.	4.00	12.00	20.00	50.00

10 HELLER

COPPER-NICKEL

KM#	Date	Mintage	Fine	VF	XF	Unc
12	1908J	—	5.00	15.00	30.00	90.00
	1908J	—	—	—	Proof	275.00
	1909J	1.990	3.00	10.00	20.00	60.00
	1909J	—	—	—	Proof	250.00
	1910J	.500	3.00	10.00	20.00	60.00

KM#	Date	Mintage	Fine	VF	XF	Unc
12	1910J	—	—	—	Proof	250.00
	1911A	.500	5.00	15.00	35.00	90.00
	1911A	—	—	—	Proof	260.00
	1914J	.200	5.00	15.00	35.00	90.00
	1914J	—	—	—	Proof	275.00

20 HELLER

**Obverse A
Large Crown**

**Obverse B
Small Crown**

**Reverse A
Curled Tip On Second L**

**Reverse B
Pointed Tips On L's**

**Reverse C
Curled Tips On L's**

COPPER

KM#	Date	Mintage	Fine	VF	XF	Unc
15	1916T obv. A & rev. A	.300	6.00	10.00	20.00	75.00
	1916T obv. A & rev. B Inc. Ab.	125.00	200.00	350.00	—	
	1916T obv. B & rev. A Inc. Ab.	60.00	85.00	140.00	—	
	1916T obv. B & rev. B Inc. Ab.	6.00	10.00	20.00	60.00	
	1916T obv. A & rev. C Inc. Ab.	—	—	Rare	—	
	1916T obv. B & rev. C Inc. Ab.	—	—	Rare	—	

BRASS

KM#	Date	Mintage	Fine	VF	XF	Unc
15a	1916T obv. A & rev. A	1.600	6.00	10.00	20.00	75.00
	1916T obv. A & rev. B Inc. Ab.	7.00	12.50	25.00	85.00	
	1916T obv. B & rev. A Inc. Ab.	7.00	12.50	25.00	85.00	
	1916T obv. B & rev. B Inc. Ab.	6.00	10.00	20.00	65.00	
	1916T obv. A & rev. C Inc. Ab.	10.00	30.00	45.00	125.00	
	1916T obv. B & rev. C Inc. Ab.	12.00	35.00	50.00	135.00	

1/4 RUPIE

2.9160 g, .917 SILVER, .0859 oz ASW

KM#	Date	Mintage	Fine	VF	XF	Unc
3	1901	.350	5.00	12.00	35.00	85.00

NOTE: Earlier dates (1891-1898) exist for this type.

KM#	Date	Mintage	Fine	VF	XF	Unc
8	1904A	.300	5.00	12.00	37.50	110.00
	1904A	—	—	—	Proof	250.00
	1906A	.300	5.00	12.00	37.50	110.00
	1906A	—	—	—	Proof	250.00
	1906J	.100	8.00	20.00	55.00	140.00
	1907J	.200	7.00	18.00	50.00	135.00
	1907J	—	—	—	Proof	300.00
	1909A	.300	6.00	13.50	40.00	120.00
	1910J	.600	5.00	12.00	37.50	110.00
	1910J	—	—	—	Proof	225.00
	1912J	.400	6.00	13.50	40.00	120.00
	1912J	—	—	—	Proof	225.00
	1913A	.200	6.50	14.50	42.50	125.00
	1913A	—	—	—	Proof	225.00
	1913J	.400	5.00	12.00	37.50	110.00
	1913J	—	—	—	Proof	225.00
	1914J	.200	6.50	14.50	42.50	125.00
	1914J	—	—	—	Proof	225.00

1/2 RUPIE

5.8319 g, .917 SILVER, .1719 oz ASW

4	1901	.215	12.50	25.00	65.00	175.00

NOTE: Earlier dates (1891-1897) exist for this type.

9	1904A	.400	12.50	25.00	65.00	185.00
	1904A	—	—	—	Proof	350.00
	1906A	.050	25.00	90.00	185.00	400.00
	1906A	—	—	—	Proof	600.00
	1906J	.050	25.00	90.00	185.00	400.00
	1907J	.140	14.00	40.00	90.00	185.00
	1907J	—	—	—	Proof	350.00
	1909A	.100	14.00	35.00	80.00	225.00
	1910J	.300	12.50	25.00	75.00	185.00
	1910J	—	—	—	Proof	325.00
	1912J	.200	12.50	25.00	75.00	185.00
	1913A	.100	14.00	35.00	80.00	220.00
	1913J	.200	12.50	25.00	75.00	185.00
	1914J	.100	14.00	35.00	85.00	220.00

RUPIE

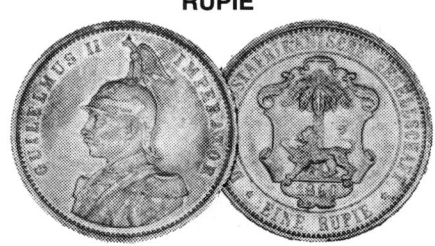

11.6638 g, .917 SILVER, .3437 oz ASW

2	1901	.319	12.50	25.00	55.00	185.00
	1902	.151	15.00	35.00	80.00	250.00

NOTE: Earlier dates (1890-1900) exist for this type.

10	1904A	1.000	11.50	22.50	45.00	125.00
	1904A	—	—	—	Proof	250.00
	1905A	.300	15.00	27.50	60.00	140.00
	1905A	—	—	—	Proof	300.00
	1905J	1.000	11.50	22.50	45.00	125.00
	1905J	—	—	—	Proof	275.00

KM#	Date	Mintage	Fine	VF	XF	Unc
10	1906A	.950	11.50	22.50	45.00	125.00
	1906J	.700	15.00	27.50	65.00	145.00
	1907J	.880	9.00	15.00	35.00	120.00
	1908J	.500	12.50	25.00	50.00	130.00
	1908J	—	—	—	Proof	300.00
	1909A	.200	15.00	27.50	60.00	155.00
	1910J	.270	9.00	15.00	35.00	120.00
	1911A	.300	12.50	25.00	50.00	130.00
	1911A	—	—	—	Proof	275.00
	1911J	1.400	9.00	15.00	35.00	120.00
	1911J	—	—	—	Proof	275.00
	1912J	.300	12.50	25.00	50.00	130.00
	1912J	—	—	—	Proof	300.00
	1913A	.400	12.50	25.00	50.00	130.00
	1913J	1.400	9.00	15.00	35.00	120.00
	1913J	—	—	—	Proof	275.00
	1914J	.500	11.50	22.50	45.00	125.00

15 RUPIEN

7.1680 g, .750 GOLD, .1728 oz AGW
Obv: Right arabesque ends below
T of OSTAFRIKA.

16.1	1916T	9,803	425.00	800.00	1200.	1750.

Obv: Right arabesque ends below
first A of OSTAFRIKA.

16.2	1916T	6,395	450.00	850.00	1250.	1800.

ZANZIBAR

The British protectorate of Zanzibar and adjacent small islands, located in the Indian Ocean 22 miles (35 km.) off the coast of Tanganyika, comprised a portion of British East Africa. Zanzibar was also the name of a sultanate which included the Zanzibar and Kenya protectorates. Zanzibar has an area of 637 sq. mi. (1,651 sq. km.). Chief city: Zanzibar. The islands are noted for their cloves, of which Zanzibar is the world's foremost producer.

Zanzibar came under Portuguese control in 1503, was conquered by the Omani Arabs in 1698, became independent of Oman in 1860, and (with Pemba) came under British control in 1890. Britain granted the protectorate self-government in 1961, and independence within the British Commonwealth on Dec. 19, 1963. On April 26, 1964, Tanganyika and Zanzibar (with Pemba) united to form the United Republic of Tanganyika and Zanzibar. The name of the country, which remained within the British Commonwealth was changed to Tanzania on Oct. 29, 1964.

TITLES

زنجباراه

Zanjibara

RULERS
Sultan Ali Bin Hamud, 1902-1911AD

MONETARY SYSTEM
100 Cents = 1 Rupee (to 1909)

CENT

BRONZE

8	1908	1.000	40.00	80.00	150.00	350.00

10 CENTS

BRONZE

KM#	Date	Mintage	Fine	VF	XF	Unc
9	1908	.100	75.00	140.00	285.00	550.00

20 CENTS

NICKEL

10	1908	.100	100.00	200.00	350.00	700.00

TANZANIA

MONETARY SYSTEM
100 Senti = 1 Shilingi

5 SENTI

BRONZE

KM#	Date	Mintage	VF	XF	Unc
1	1966	55.250	.10	.20	.50
	1966	5,500	—	Proof	1.00
	1971	5.000	.10	.20	.50
	1972	—	.10	.20	.50
	1973	20.000	.10	.20	.50
	1974	12.500	.10	.20	.50
	1975	—	.10	.20	.50
	1976	37.500	.10	.20	.50
	1977	10.000	.10	.20	.50
	1979	7.200	.10	.20	.50
	1980	10.000	.10	.20	.50
	1981	13.650	.10	.20	.50
	1982	—	.10	.20	.50
	1983	.018	.10	.20	.50
	1984	—	.10	.20	.50

10 SENTI

NICKEL-BRASS

11	1977	19.505	3.00	8.00	16.00
	1979	8.000	3.00	8.00	16.00
	1980	10.000	3.00	8.00	16.00
	1981	10.000	3.00	8.00	16.00
	1984	—	3.00	8.00	16.00

20 SENTI

NICKEL-BRASS

2	1966	26.500	.20	.40	1.50
	1966	5,500	—	Proof	1.50
	1970	5.000	.20	.40	1.50
	1973	20.100	.20	.40	1.50
	1975	—	.20	.40	1.50
	1976	10.000	.20	.40	1.50
	1977	10.000	.20	.40	1.50
	1979	10.000	.20	.40	1.50
	1980	10.000	.20	.40	1.50

KM#	Date	Mintage	VF	XF	Unc
2	1981	10.000	.20	.40	1.50
	1982	—	.20	.40	1.50
	1983	.050	.20	.40	1.50
	1984	—	.20	.40	1.50

50 SENTI

COPPER-NICKEL

3	1966	6.250	.20	.40	2.00
	1966	5,500	—	Proof	3.00
	1970	10.000	.20	.40	2.00
	1973	10.000	.25	.50	2.00
	1980	10.000	.25	.50	2.00
	1981	—	.25	.50	2.00
	1982	10.000	.25	.50	2.00
	1983	—	.25	.50	2.00
	1984	10.000	.25	.50	2.00

NICKEL CLAD STEEL
Rev: Rabbit.

26	1988	10.000	.50	1.00	2.50
	1989	—	.50	1.00	2.50
	1990	—	.50	1.00	2.50

SHILINGI

COPPER-NICKEL

4	1966	48.000	.25	.50	1.50
	1966	5,500	—	Proof	4.00
	1972	10.000	.25	.50	1.50
	1974	15.000	.30	.60	1.75
	1975	—	.30	.60	1.75
	1977	5,000	.30	.60	1.75
	1980	10.000	.25	.50	1.50
	1981	—	.30	.60	1.75
	1982	10.000	.30	.60	1.75
	1983	10.000	.30	.60	1.75
	1984	10.000	.30	.60	1.75

NICKEL CLAD STEEL

22	1987	5.000	.40	.80	1.85
	1988	10.000	.40	.80	1.85
	1989	—	.40	.80	1.85
	1990	—	.20	.40	1.00
	1991	—	.20	.40	1.00
	1992	—	.20	.40	1.00

5 SHILINGI

COPPER-NICKEL
F.A.O. Issue
10th Anniversary of Independence

5	ND(1971)	1.000	.75	1.50	2.50

F.A.O. Issue

KM#	Date	Mintage	VF	XF	Unc
6	1972	8.000	.75	1.50	2.50
	1973	5.000	.75	1.75	3.00
	1980	5.000	.75	1.75	3.00

10th Anniversary - Bank of Tanzania

10	ND(1976)	1.000	.75	1.50	3.25
	ND(1976)	200 pcs.	—	Proof	40.00

F.A.O. Regional Conference for Africa

12	1978	.050	.75	1.50	2.75
	1978	2,000	—	Proof	11.50

23	1987	5.000	.75	1.50	3.00
	1988	10.000	.75	1.50	3.00
	1989	—	.75	1.50	3.00

NICKEL CLAD STEEL

23a	1990	—	.60	1.20	1.85
	1991	—	.60	1.20	1.85
	1992	—	.50	1.00	1.50
	1993	—	.50	1.00	1.50

10 SHILINGI

COPPER-NICKEL

20	1987	10.000	1.00	1.50	3.25
	1988	10.000	1.00	1.50	3.25
	1989	—	1.00	1.50	3.25

NICKEL CLAD STEEL

20a	1990	—	1.00	1.50	2.25
	1991	—	1.00	1.50	2.25
	1992	—	.85	1.25	2.00
	1993	—	.85	1.25	2.00

---

20 SHILINGI

COPPER-NICKEL
20th Anniversary of Independence

KM#	Date	Mintage	VF	XF	Unc
13	ND(1981)	.997	3.00	6.00	12.00

COPPER-NICKEL
20th Anniversary of Central Bank

21	ND(1986)	—	4.00	10.00	20.00

NICKEL BONDED STEEL
Rev: Elephants.

27.1	1990	—	1.50	2.00	3.50
	1991	—	1.50	2.00	3.50

Reduced size: 31mm.

27.2	1992	—	1.25	1.75	3.25

50 SHILINGI

BRASS PLATED STEEL
Conservation - Mother Rhino and Calf

33	1996	—	—	—	3.25

100 SHILINGI

COPPER-NICKEL
Conservation - Elephant Mother and Calf

KM#	Date	Mintage	VF	XF	Unc
18	1986	—			6.50

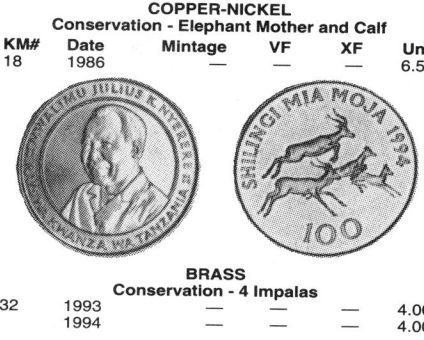

BRASS
Conservation - 4 Impalas

KM#	Date	Mintage	VF	XF	Unc
32	1993	—	—	—	4.00
	1994	—	—	—	4.00

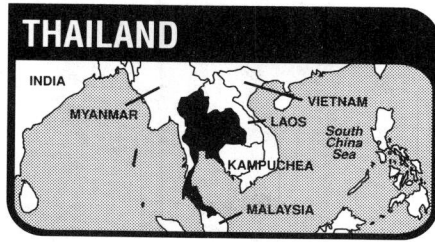

THAILAND

The Kingdom of Thailand (formerly Siam), a constitutional monarchy located in the center of mainland southeast Asia between Burma and Laos, has an area of 198,457 mi. (514,000 sq. km.) and a population of *55.5 million. Capital: Bangkok. The economy is based on agriculture and mining. Rubber, rice, teakwood, tin and tungsten are exported.

The history of The Kingdom of Siam, the only country in south and southeast Asia that was never colonized by an European power, dates from the 6th century A.D. when Thai people started to migrate into the area a process that accelerated with the Mongol invasion of China in the 13th century. After 400 years of sporadic warfare with the neighboring Burmese, King Taskin won the last battle in 1767. He founded a new capital, Dhonburi, on the west bank of the Chao Praya River. King Rama I moved the capital to Bangkok in 1782, thus initiating the so-called Bangkok Period of Siamese coinage characterized by Pot Duang money (bullet coins) stamped with regal symbols.

The Thai were introduced to the Western world by the Portuguese, who were followed by the Dutch, British and French. Rama III of the present ruling dynasty negotiated a treaty of friendship and commerce with Britain in 1826, and in 1896 the independence of the kingdom was guaranteed by an Anglo-French accord.

In 1909 Siam ceded to Great Britain its suzerain rights over the dependencies of Kedah, Kelantan, Trengganu and Perlis, Malay states situated in southern Siam just north of British Malaya which eliminated any British jurisdiction in Siam proper.

The absolute monarchy was changed into a constitutional monarchy in 1932.

On Dec. 8, 1941, after five hours of fighting, Thailand agreed to permit Japanese troops passage through the country to invade Northern British Malaysia. This eventually led to increased Japanese intervention and finally occupation of the country. On Jan. 25, 1942, Thailand declared war on Great Britain and the United States. A free Thai guerilla movement was soon organized to counteract the Japanese. In July 1943 Japan transferred the four northern Malay States back to Thailand. These were returned to Great Britain after peace treaties were signed in 1946.

RULERS

Rama V (Phra Maha Chulalongkorn),
   1868-1910
Rama VI (Phra Maha Vajiravudh),
   1910-1925
Rama VII (Phra Maha Prajadhipok),
   1925-1935
Rama VIII (Phra Maha Ananda Mahidol),
   1935-1946
Rama IX (Phra Maha Bhumifhol Adulyadej),
   1946-

MONETARY SYSTEM
Old currency system

2 Solos = 1 Att
2 Att = 1 Sio (Pai)
2 Sio = 1 Sik
2 Sik = 1 Fuang
2 Fuang = 1 Salung (not Sal'ung)
4 Salung = 1 Baht
4 Baht = 1 Tamlung
20 Tamlung = 1 Chang

UNITS OF OLD THAI CURRENCY

Chang =	ชั่ง	Sik =	ซีก
Tamlung =	ตำลึง	Sio (Pai) =	เสี้ยว
Baht =	บาท	Att =	อัฐ
Salung =	สลึง	Solos =	โสฬส
Fuang =	เฟื้อง		

MINT MARKS
H-Heaton Birmingham
DATING

Typical BE Dating

2480
2489

1238   1244

Typical CS Dating

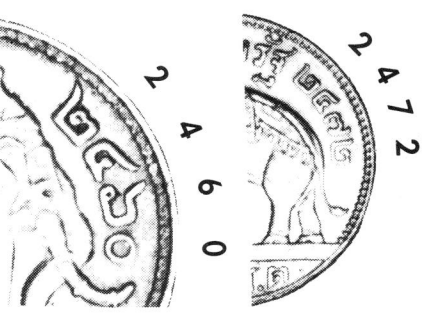

2460   2472

NOTE: Sometimes the era designator *BE* or *CS* will actually appear on the coin itself.

Denomination

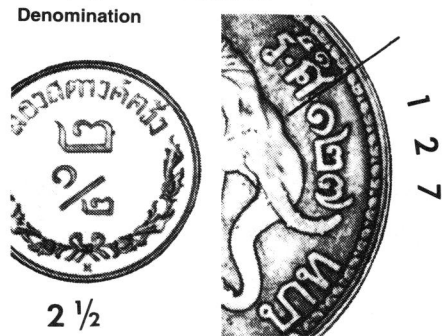

2 ½

2-1/2 (Satang)   **RS Dating**

127

2509

DATE CONVERSION TABLES
B.E. date - 543 = A.D. date
Ex: 2516 - 543 = 1973

R.S. date + 1781 = A.D. date
Ex: 127 + 1781 = 1908

C.S. date + 638 = A.D. date
Ex 1238 + 638 = 1876

1/2 ATT
(1 Solot)

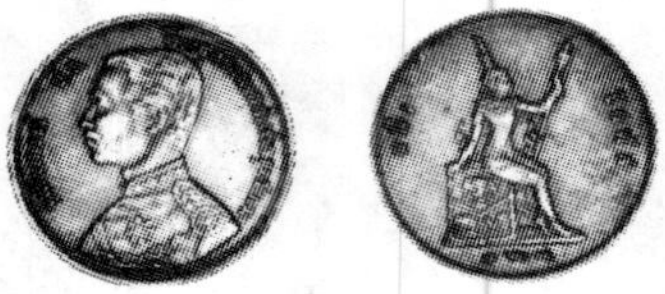

BRONZE

Y#	Date	Mintage	Fine	VF	XF	Unc
21	RS124(1905)	—	1.50	3.00	15.00	110.00

NOTE: Earlier dates (1887-1899) exist for this type.
NOTE: These coins were also minted in RS114, RS115, RS121, and RS122. The last year had a mintage of 5,120,000. Coins with these dates have not been observed and were probably additional mintings of coins dated RS109 and RS118. A nickel pattern dated RS114 does exist. Varieties in numeral size and rotated dies exist.

ATT
(1/64 Baht)

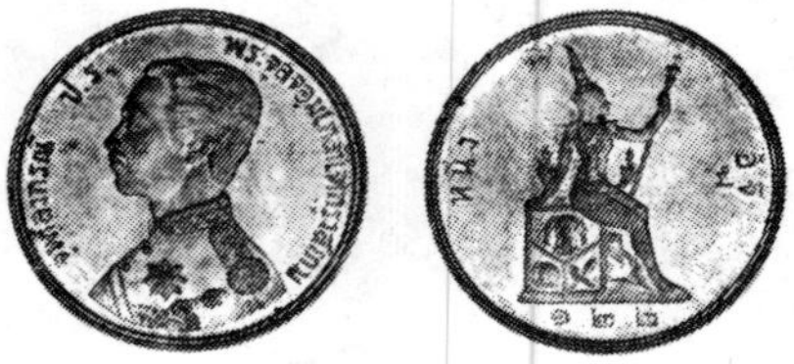

BRONZE

Y#	Date	Mintage	Fine	VF	XF	Unc
22	RS121(1902)	11.251	1.50	2.50	8.50	90.00
	122*(1903)	4.109	1.50	3.00	10.00	100.00
	124(1905)	—	1.50	3.00	10.00	100.00

NOTE: Earlier dates (1887-1899) exist for this type.
***NOTE:** RS114 and RS122 exist with large (greater than 1mm) and small (less than 1mm) numerals.
NOTE: Full red uncirculated coins of this type carry a substantial premium.

2 ATT
(1/32 Baht = 1 Sio)

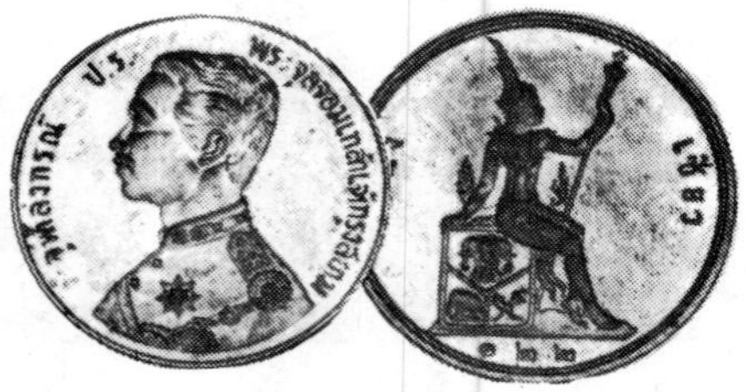

BRONZE

Y#	Date	Mintage	Fine	VF	XF	Unc
23	RS121(1902)	2.797	1.50	3.00	12.00	135.00
	122(1903)	2.323	1.50	3.00	12.00	135.00
	124(1905)	—	1.50	3.00	12.00	135.00

NOTE: Earlier dates (1887-1900) exist for this type.
NOTE: Varieties in numeral size and rotated dies exist.
NOTE: Full red uncirculated coins of this type carry a substantial premium.

FUANG
(1/8 Baht)

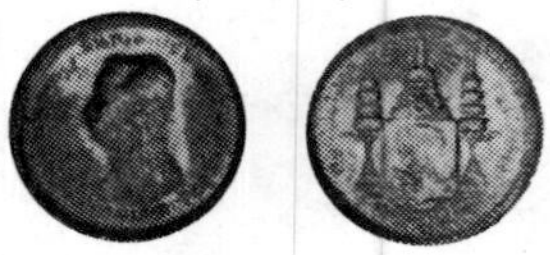

SILVER

Y#	Date	Mintage	Fine	VF	XF	Unc
32a	RS120(1901)	—	3.00	7.00	20.00	110.00
	121(1902)	.380	3.00	7.00	20.00	110.00
	122(1903)	.460	3.00	7.00	20.00	110.00
	123(1904)	.310	3.00	7.00	20.00	110.00
	124(1905)	.410	3.00	7.00	20.00	110.00
	125(1906)	—	3.00	7.00	20.00	110.00
	126(1907)	—	3.00	7.00	20.00	110.00
	127(1908)	.480	3.00	7.00	20.00	110.00

GOLD

Y#	Date	Mintage	Fine	VF	XF	Unc
32c	RS122(1903)	—	300.00	600.00	1250.	2250.
	123(1904)	—	300.00	600.00	1250.	2250.
	124(1905)	—	300.00	600.00	1250.	2250.
	125(1906)	—	300.00	600.00	1250.	2250.
	126(1907)	—	300.00	600.00	1250.	2250.
	127(1908)	—	300.00	600.00	1250.	2250.
	128(1909)	—	300.00	600.00	1250.	2250.
	129(1910)	—	300.00	600.00	1250.	2250.

SALUNG
(1/4 Baht)

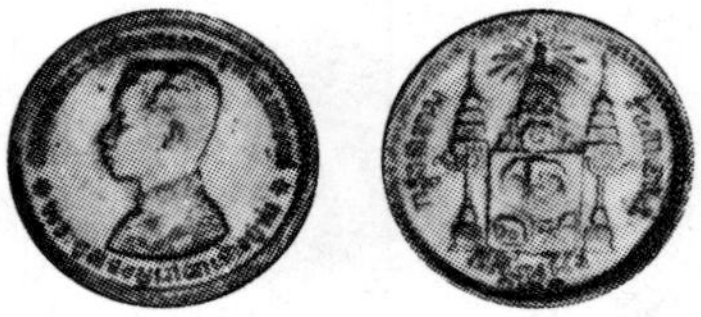

Y#	Date	Mintage	Fine	VF	XF	Unc
33a	RS120(1901)	—	4.50	10.00	30.00	275.00
	121(1902)	.560	3.00	8.00	25.00	165.00
	122(1903)	.340	3.00	8.00	25.00	165.00
	123(1904)	.190	3.00	8.00	25.00	165.00
	125(1906)	—	3.00	8.00	25.00	165.00
	126(1907)	—	3.00	8.00	25.00	165.00
	127(1908)	.270	3.00	8.00	25.00	200.00

BAHT

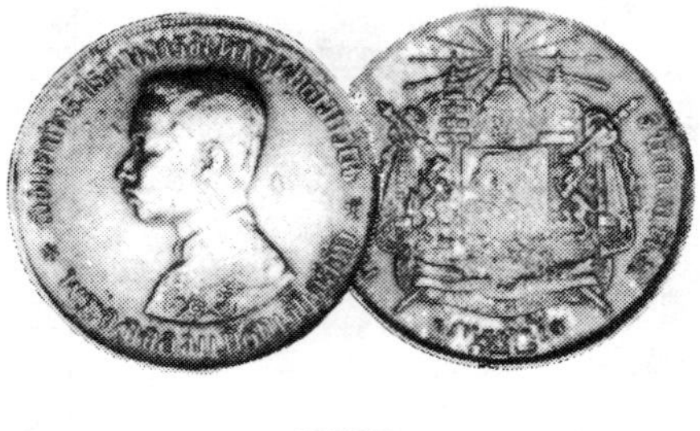

SILVER

Y#	Date	Mintage	Fine	VF	XF	Unc
34a	RS120(1901)	—	75.00	165.00	350.00	1600.
	121(1902)	*4.070	7.00	22.00	75.00	325.00
	122(1903)	19.150	6.00	20.00	60.00	300.00
	123(1904)	4.790	6.00	20.00	50.00	285.00
	124(1905)	6.770	6.00	20.00	50.00	285.00
	125(1906)	—	6.00	20.00	50.00	285.00
	126(1907)	—	15.00	35.00	100.00	375.00

***NOTE:** Because of a faulty die used the second 1 appears to be a 0 in some examples of this date.

DECIMAL COINAGE

100 Satang = 1 Baht
25 Satang = 1 Salung

1/2 SATANG

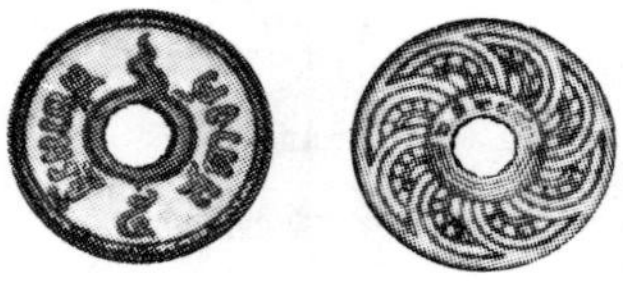

BRONZE

Y#	Date	Year	Mintage	VF	XF	Unc
50	(BE)2480	(1937)	—	.75	1.75	3.50

SATANG

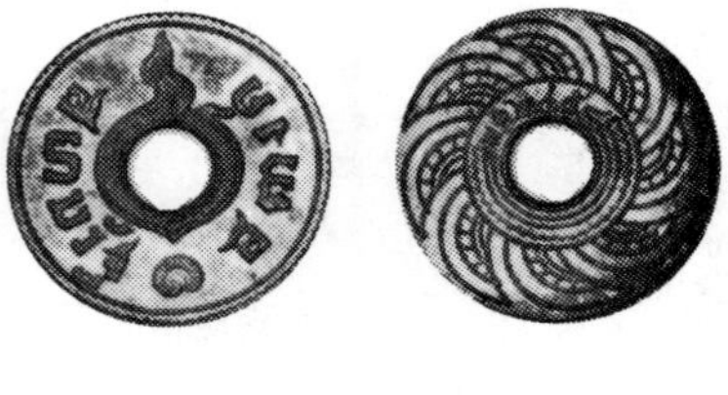

BRONZE

Y#	Date	Year	Mintage	VF	XF	Unc
35	RS127	(1908)	17.000	2.50	5.00	18.00
	128	(1909)	.150	3.50	10.00	28.00
	129	(1910)	9.000	1.50	3.50	18.00
	130	(1911)	30.000	1.50	3.50	12.50
	132	(1913)	—	—	Rare	—
	BE2456	(1913)	10.000	1.00	1.50	4.00
	2457	(1914)	1.000	2.00	4.00	12.50
	2458	(1915)	5.000	.75	1.00	2.75
	2461	(1918)	18.880	.65	1.25	3.00
	2462	(1919)	6.400	.65	1.00	2.75
	2463	(1920)	17.240	1.00	1.50	3.50
	2464	(1921)	6.360	15.00	25.00	40.00
	2466	(1923)	14.000	.75	1.00	2.75
	2467	(1924)	Inc. Ab.	1.00	1.50	3.50
	2469	(1926)	20.000	.50	.75	2.50
	2470	(1927)	—	.50	.75	2.50
	2472	(1929)	—	.50	1.00	2.75
	2478	(1935)	—	.50	.70	2.00
	2480	(1937)	—	.50	.70	2.00

NOTE: Variations in lettering exist.

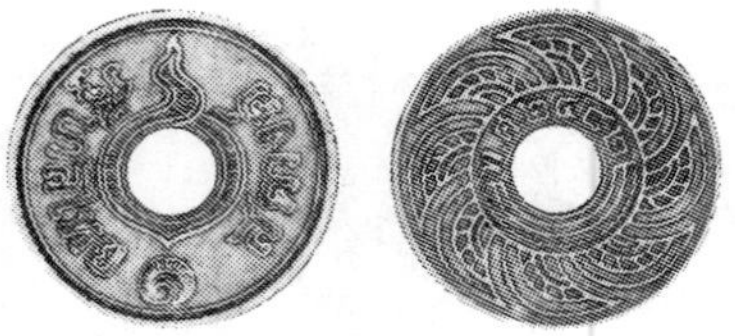

Y#	Date	Year	Mintage	VF	XF	Unc
51	BE2482	(1939)	24.400	1.50	3.00	6.00

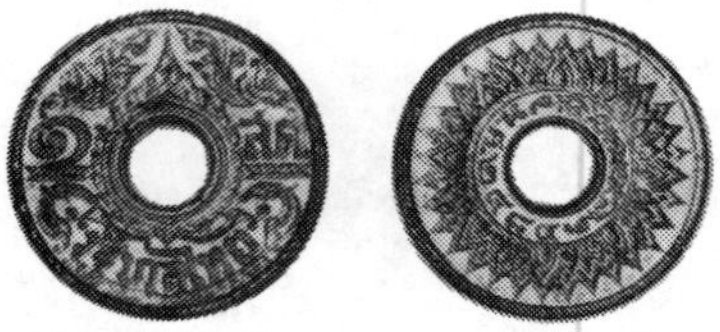

Y#	Date	Year	Mintage	VF	XF	Unc
54	BE2484	(1941)	—	.50	1.50	3.00

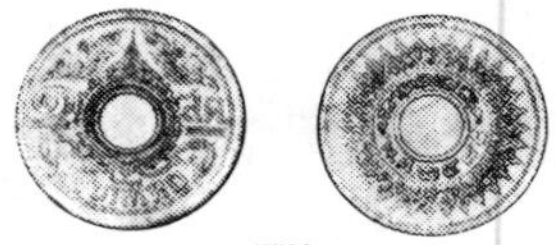

TIN

BE date & denomination in Thai numerals, w/o hole.

Y#	Date	Year	Mintage	VF	XF	Unc
57	BE2485	(1942)	20.700	.30	.50	1.00

NOTE: Approximately 790,000 coins were restruck for circulation 1967-73.

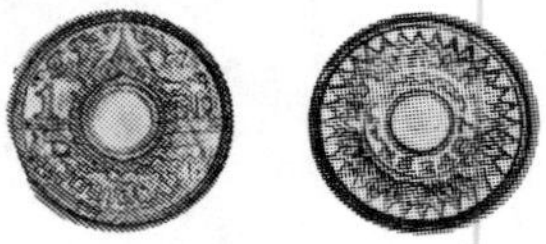

BE date and denomination in Western numerals, w/o hole.

Y#	Date	Year	Mintage	VF	XF	Unc
60	BE2487	—	.500	.10	.20	.50

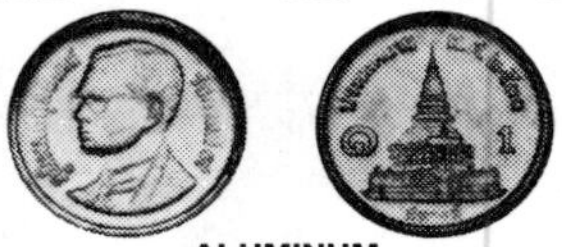

ALUMINUM

Y#	Date	Year	Mintage	VF	XF	Unc
186	BE2530	(1987)	.093	—	—	.10
	2531	(1988)	.200	—	—	.10
	2533	(1990)	—	—	—	.10
	2534	(1991)	—	—	—	.10
	2535	(1992)	—	—	—	.10
	2536	(1993)	—	—	—	.10
	2537	(1994)	—	—	—	.10

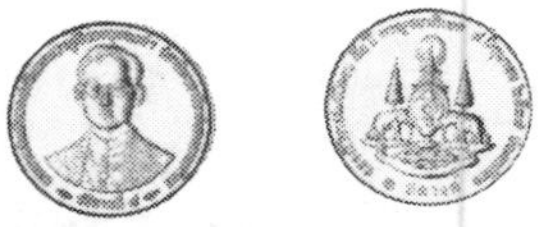

50th Anniversary - Reign of King Rama IX
Obv: King Rama IX.

Y#	Date	Year	Mintage	VF	XF	Unc
342	BE2539	(1996)	—	—	—	.15

5 SATANG

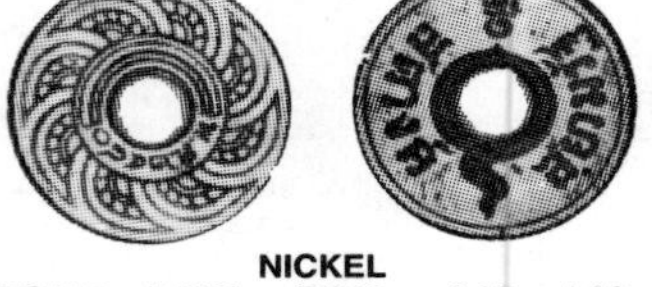

NICKEL

Y#	Date	Year	Mintage	VF	XF	Unc
36	RS127	(1908)	7.000	3.00	4.00	8.00
	128	(1909)	4.000	3.50	4.50	10.00
	129	(1910)	4.000	1.50	2.00	7.00
	131	(1912)	2.000	1.50	2.50	8.00
	132	(1913)	—	—	Rare	—
	BE2456	(1913)	2.000	1.50	2.50	6.00
	2457	(1914)	2.000	1.50	2.50	6.00
	2461	(1918)	2.000	1.50	2.50	6.00
	2462	(1919)	2.000	1.00	2.00	6.00
	2463	(1920)	9.900	1.00	1.50	4.50
	2464	(1921)	13.000	.60	1.25	3.00
	2469	(1926)	20.000	.60	1.25	3.00
	2478	(1935)	10.000	.60	1.25	3.00
	2480	(1937)	20.000	.60	1.25	3.00
	2482	(1939)	Reported, not confirmed			

NOTE: Variations in lettering exist.

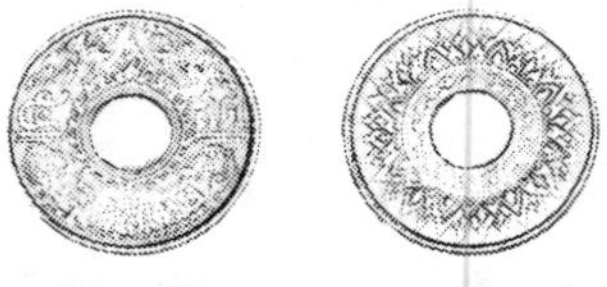

1.5000 g, .650 SILVER, .0313 oz ASW

Y#	Date	Year	Mintage	VF	XF	Unc
55	BE2484	(1941)	—	1.50	3.00	4.50

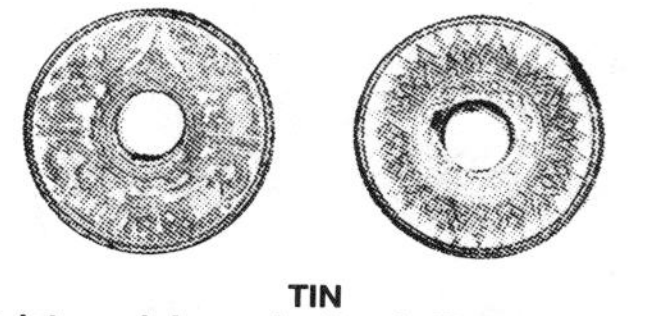

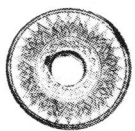

TIN
BE date and denomination in Thai numerals.

Y#	Date	Year	Mintage	VF	XF	Unc
58	BE2485	(1942)	—	.50	1.50	3.00

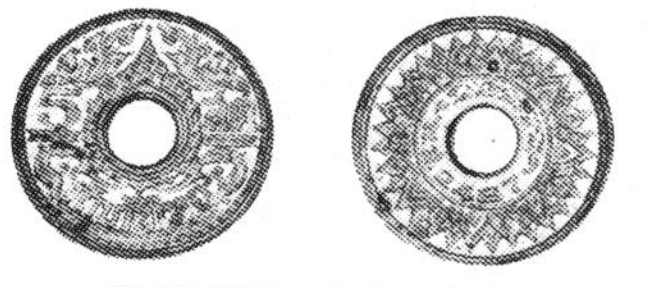

Thick (2.2mm) planchet.
BE date and denomination in Western numerals.

Y#	Date	Year	Mintage	VF	XF	Unc
61	BE2487	(1944)	—	.50	1.25	3.00
	2488	(1945)	—	.50	1.25	3.00

Medium planchet.

Y#	Date	Year	Mintage	VF	XF	Unc
61b	BE2488	(1945)	—	.50	1.25	3.00

Thin (2.0mm) planchet.

Y#	Date	Year	Mintage	VF	XF	Unc
61a	BE2488	(1945)	—	.50	1.25	3.00

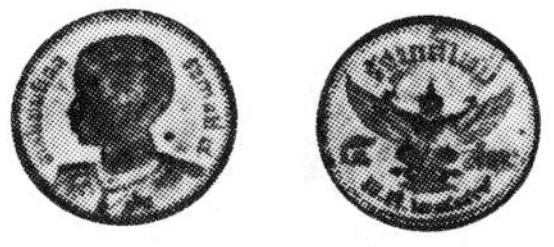

Obv: King Ananda, child head.

Y#	Date	Year	Mintage	VF	XF	Unc
64	BE2489	(1946)	—	.50	1.00	2.00

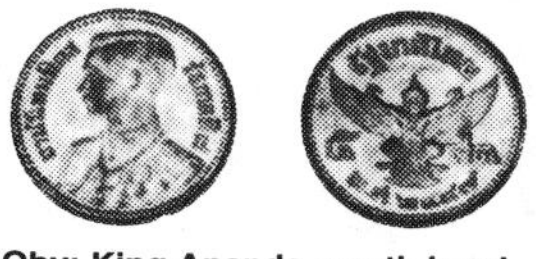

Obv: King Ananda, youth head.

Y#	Date	Year	Mintage	VF	XF	Unc
68	BE2489	(1946)	24.480	.15	.50	1.00

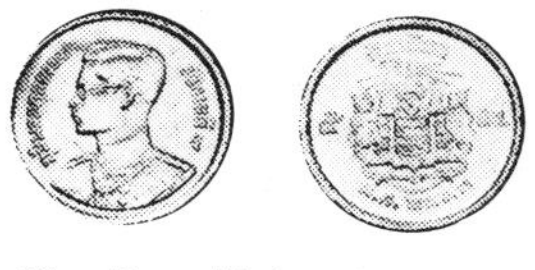

Obv: King Rama IX, 1 medal on uniform.

Y#	Date	Year	Mintage	VF	XF	Unc
72	BE2493	(1950)	*6.480	.50	.75	1.25

***NOTE:** Coins bearing this date were also struck in 1954, 58, 59, and 73. Mintages are included here.

ALUMINUM-BRONZE

Y#	Date	Year	Mintage	VF	XF	Unc
72a	BE2493	(1950)	15.500	.25	1.00	2.00

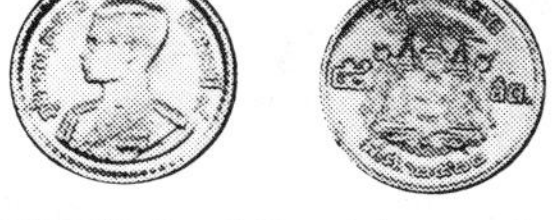

Obv: Smaller head, 3 medals on uniform.

Y#	Date	Year	Mintage	VF	XF	Unc
78	BE2500	(1957)	*46.440	—	.10	.25

***NOTE:** Current issues are minted without date change.

BRONZE

Y#	Date	Year	Mintage	VF	XF	Unc
78a	BE2500	(1957)	*6.240	.50	1.50	2.00

TIN

Y#	Date	Year	Mintage	VF	XF	Unc
78b	BE2500	(1957)	—	1.75	3.00	5.00

NOTE: The above coins were struck to replace Y#72 in mint sets.

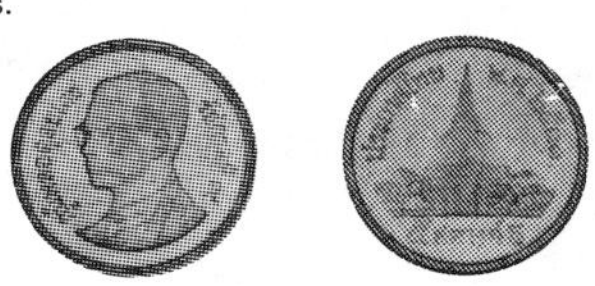

ALUMINUM

Y#	Date	Year	Mintage	VF	XF	Unc
208	BE2530	(1987)	—	—	—	20.00
	2531	(1988)	.704	—	—	.10
	2533	(1990)	—	—	—	.10
	2534	(1991)	—	—	—	.10
	2535	(1992)	—	—	—	.10
	2536	(1993)	—	—	—	.10
	2537	(1994)	—	—	—	.10

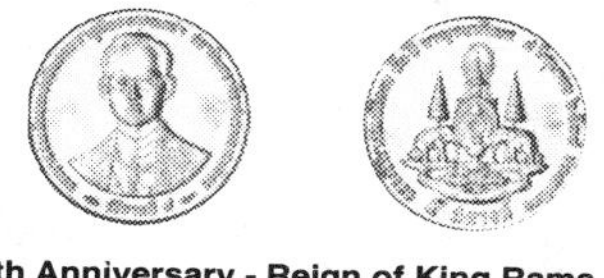

50th Anniversary - Reign of King Rama IX
Obv: King Rama IX.

Y#	Date	Year	Mintage	VF	XF	Unc
343	BE2539	(1996)	—	—	—	.25

10 SATANG

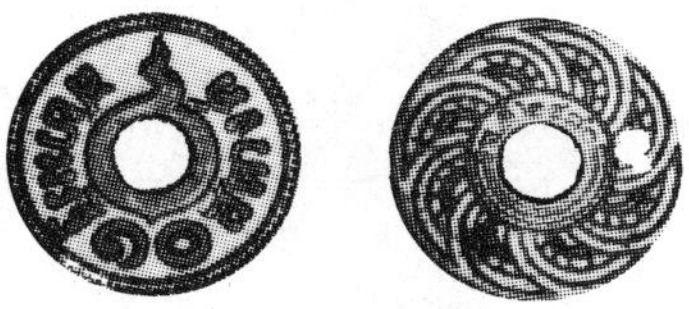

NICKEL

Y#	Date	Year	Mintage	VF	XF	Unc
37	RS127	(1908)	7.000	1.50	3.00	8.50
	129	(1910)	5.000	1.50	3.00	8.50
	130	(1911)	.500	2.00	5.00	12.00
	131	(1912)	1.500	1.50	3.00	10.00
	BE2456	(1913)	1.000	1.25	2.00	6.00
	2457	(1914)	1.000	1.25	2.00	6.00
	2461	(1918)	.770	2.50	3.50	9.00
	2462	(1919)	.774	1.25	1.50	3.50
	2463	(1920)	Inc. Ab.	1.25	1.50	3.50
	2464	(1921)	21.727	1.00	1.25	3.00
	2478	(1935)	5.000	1.00	1.25	3.00
	2480	(1937)	5.000	.75	1.00	2.50
	2482	(1939)	Reported, not confirmed			

NOTE: Variations in lettering exist.

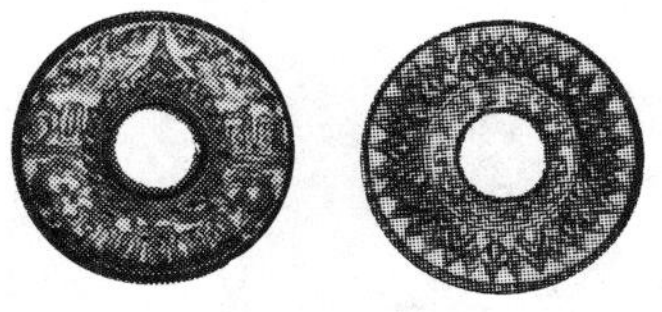

2.5000 g, .650 SILVER, .0522 oz ASW

Y#	Date	Year	Mintage	VF	XF	Unc
56	BE2484	(1941)	—	2.00	4.00	8.00

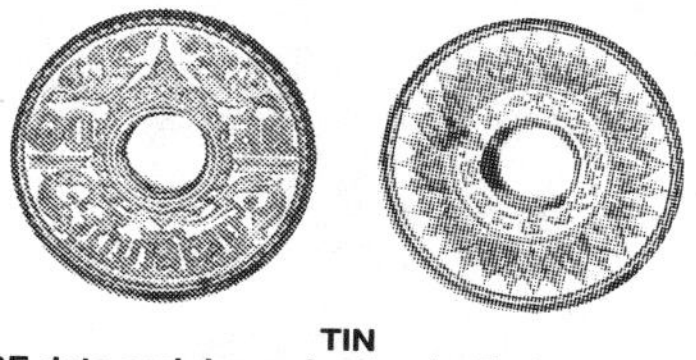

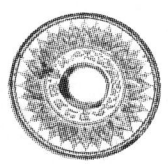

TIN
BE date and denomination in Thai numerals.

Y#	Date	Year	Mintage	VF	XF	Unc
59	BE2485	(1942)	.230	1.00	2.00	3.50

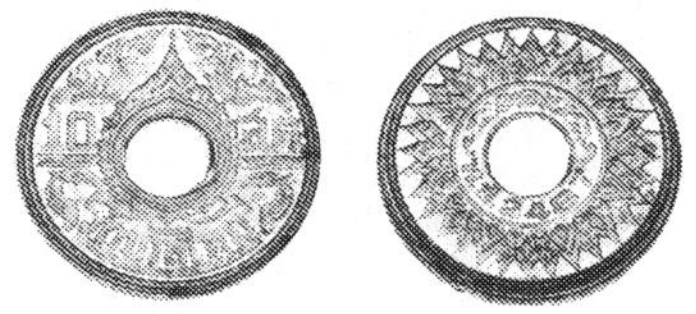

Thick (2.5mm) planchet.
BE date and denomination in Western numerals.

Y#	Date	Year	Mintage	VF	XF	Unc
62	BE2487	(1944)	—	1.00	2.00	3.50
	2488	(1945)	—	3.50	7.00	15.00

Thin (2.0mm) planchet.

Y#	Date	Year	Mintage	VF	XF	Unc
62a	BE2488	(1945)	—	1.00	2.50	4.00

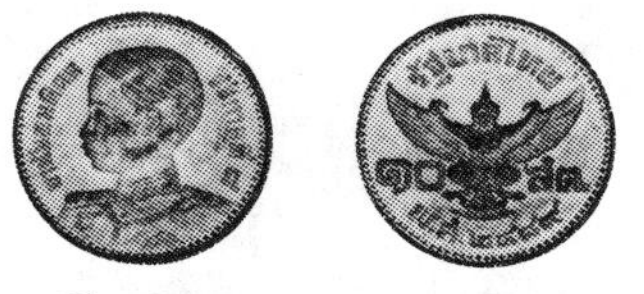

Obv: King Ananda, child head.

Y#	Date	Year	Mintage	VF	XF	Unc
65	BE2489	(1946)	—	.50	1.25	2.25

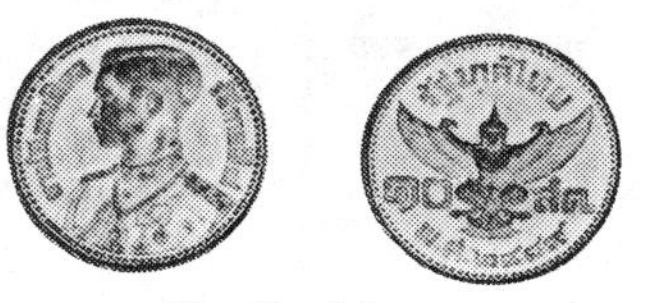

Obv: Youth head.

Y#	Date	Year	Mintage	VF	XF	Unc
69	BE2489	(1946)	40.470	.50	1.25	2.00

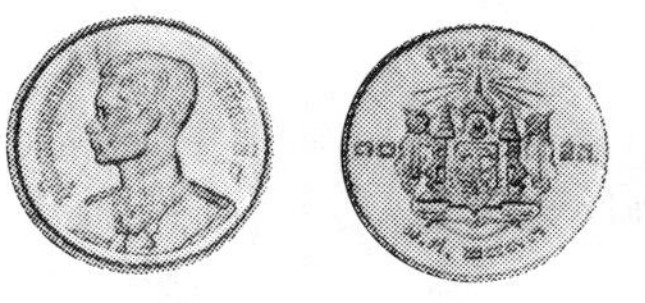

Obv: King Bhumiphol, 1 medal on uniform.

Y#	Date	Year	Mintage	VF	XF	Unc
73	BE2493	(1950)	*139.695	.40	1.00	1.50

***NOTE:** These coins were also struck in 1954-1973 and the mintages are also included here.

ALUMINUM-BRONZE

Y#	Date	Year	Mintage	VF	XF	Unc
73a	BE2493	(1950)	4.060	.75	1.50	2.50

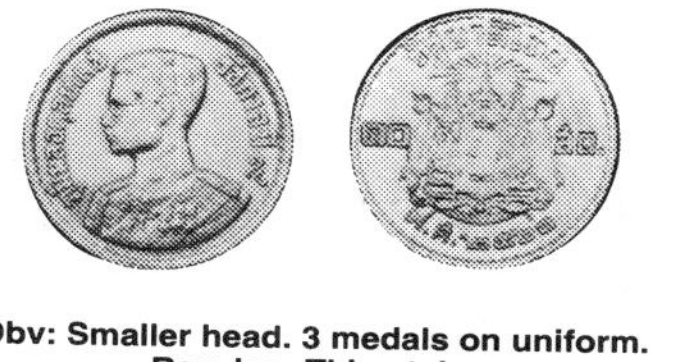

Obv: Smaller head. 3 medals on uniform.
Rev. leg: Thin style.

Y#	Date	Year	Mintage	VF	XF	Unc
79	BE2500	(1957)	*55.410	.10	.25	.50

***NOTE:** Current issues are minted without date change.

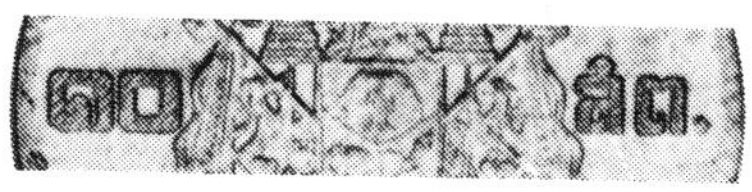

Rev. leg: Thick style.

Y#	Date	Year	Mintage	VF	XF	Unc
79d	BE2500	(1957)	—	.10	.25	.50

BRONZE
Rev. leg: Thick style.

Y#	Date	Year	Mintage	VF	XF	Unc
79a	BE2500	(1957)	*13.365	.25	.75	1.25
	2501	(1958)	—	.25	.75	1.25

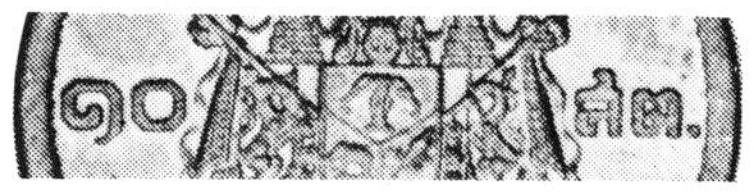

Rev. leg: Thin style.

Y#	Date	Year	Mintage	VF	XF	Unc
79c	BE2500	(1957)	Inc. Ab.	2.50	5.00	10.00

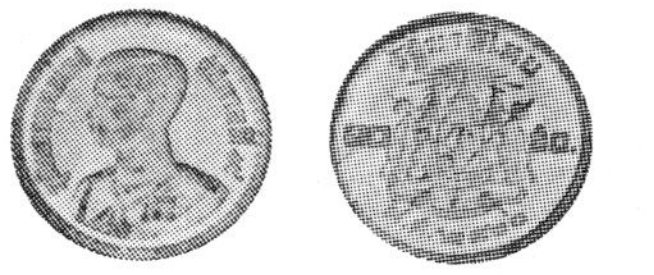

TIN

Y#	Date	Year	Mintage	VF	XF	Unc
79b	BE2500	(1957)	—	12.50	22.50	50.00

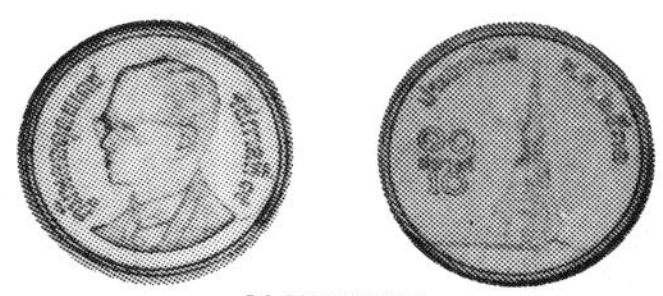

ALUMINUM

Y#	Date	Year	Mintage	VF	XF	Unc
209	BE2530	(1987)	—	—	—	20.00
	2531	(1988)	.900	—	—	.10
	2533	(1990)	—	—	—	.10
	2534	(1991)	—	—	—	.10
	2535	(1992)	—	—	—	.10
	2536	(1993)	—	—	—	.10
	2537	(1994)	—	—	—	.10

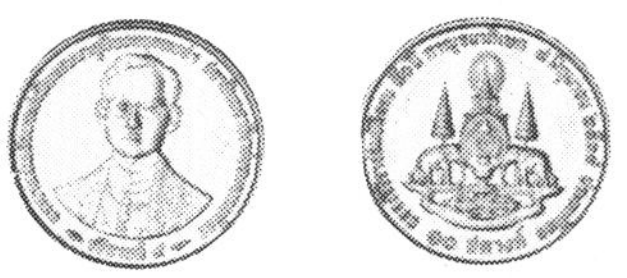

50th Anniversary - Reign of King Rama IX

Y#	Date	Year	Mintage	VF	XF	Unc
344	BE2539	(1996)	—	—	—	.35

20 SATANG

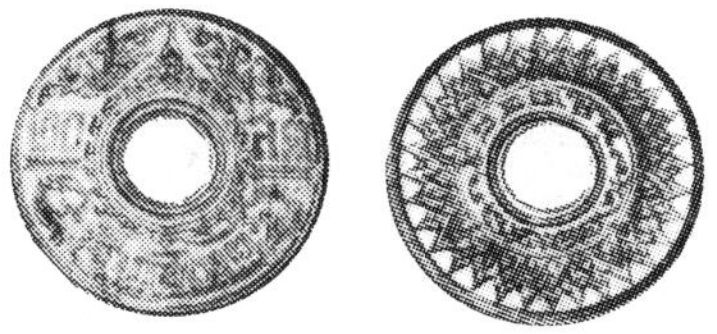

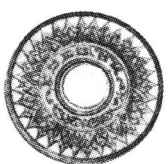

3.0000 g, .650 SILVER, .0627 oz ASW
BE date and denomination in Thai numerals.

Y#	Date	Year	Mintage	VF	XF	Unc
A56	BE2485	(1942)	—	3.00	6.00	12.00

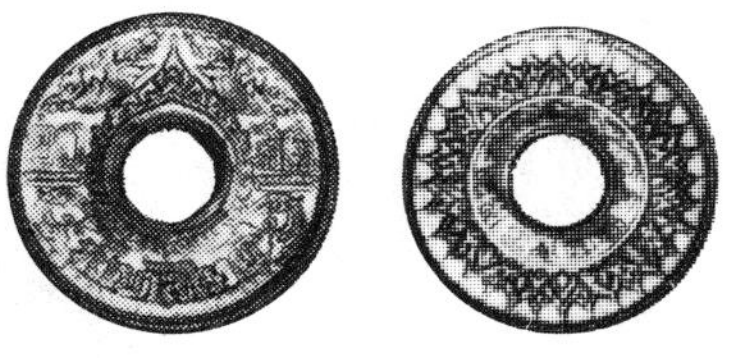

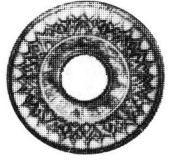

TIN
BE date and denomination in Western numerals.

Y#	Date	Year	Mintage	VF	XF	Unc
63	BE2488	(1945)	—	1.00	2.50	4.00

SALUNG = 1/4 BAHT

3.7500 g, .800 SILVER, .0965 oz ASW

Y#	Date	Year	Mintage	VF	XF	Unc
43	BE2458	(1915)	2.040	5.00	10.00	20.00

3.7500 g, .650 SILVER, .0784 oz ASW

43a	BE2460	(1917)	1.100	3.50	7.00	16.50
	2461	(1918)	2.170	3.50	7.00	16.50
	2462	(1919)	7.860	2.50	5.50	12.50
	2467	(1924)	2.100	3.50	7.00	18.50
	2468	(1925)	—	3.50	7.00	18.50

3.7500 g, .500 SILVER, .0603 oz ASW

| 43b | BE2462 | (1919) | dot after legend | | | |
| | | | Inc. Ab. | 50.00 | 85.00 | 125.00 |

25 SATANG = 1/4 BAHT

3.7500 g, .650 SILVER, .0784 oz ASW

| 48 | BE2472 | (1929) | — | 3.00 | 7.00 | 18.00 |

TIN
Obv: King Ananda, child's head.

| 66 | BE2489 | (1946) | — | 2.50 | 4.50 | 10.00 |

Obv: Youth's head.

| 70 | BE2489 | (1946) | *226.348 | .20 | .40 | .75 |

*NOTE: These coins were also struck 1954-64 and mintage figure is a total.

ALUMINUM-BRONZE
Obv: King Rama IX, 1 medal on uniform.

| 76 | BE2493 | (1950) | 23.170 | .75 | 1.75 | 3.00 |

Obv: Smaller head; 3 medals on uniform.

| 80 | BE2500 | (1957) | *620.480 | .10 | .15 | .25 |

*NOTE: Current issues are minted without date change and with and without reeded edges.

BRASS

| 109 | BE2520 | (1977) | 183.356 | — | .10 | .15 |

NOTE: Date varieties exist.

ALUMINUM-BRONZE

Y#	Date	Year	Mintage	VF	XF	Unc
187	BE2530	(1987)	5.108	—	—	.20
	2531	(1988)	42.096	—	—	.10
	2532	(1989)	—	—	—	.10
	2533	(1990)	—	—	—	.10
	2534	(1991)	—	—	—	.10
	2535	(1992)	—	—	—	.10
	2536	(1993)	—	—	—	.10
	2537	(1994)	—	—	—	.10
	2538	(1995)	—	—	—	.10

BRASS
Golden Jubilee - Reign of King Rama IX

| 345 | BE2539 | (1996) | — | — | — | .50 |

2 SALUNG = 1/2 BAHT

7.5000 g, .800 SILVER, .1929 oz ASW

| 44 | BE2458 | (1915) | 2.740 | 6.50 | 17.50 | 35.00 |

7.5000 g, .650 SILVER, .1568 oz ASW

44a	AH2462	(1919)	3.230	5.00	12.50	25.00
	2463	(1920)	4.970	5.00	12.50	25.00
	2464	(1921)	—	5.00	12.50	25.00

NOTE: Date varieties exist.

7.5000 g, .500 SILVER, .1206 oz ASW

44b	AH2462	(1919)	large dot after legend			
			Inc. Ab.	6.50	15.00	27.50
	2462	(1919)	small dot after legend			
			Inc. Ab.	6.50	15.00	27.50

50 SATANG = 1/2 BAHT

7.5000 g, .650 SILVER, .1567 oz ASW

| 49 | BE2472 | (1929) | 17.008 | 6.00 | 15.00 | 27.50 |

TIN
Obv: King Ananda, child's head.

| 67 | BE2489 | (1946) | — | 40.00 | 60.00 | 150.00 |

Obv: Youth's head.

| 71 | BE2489 | (1946) | *17.008 | .75 | 1.50 | 3.00 |

*NOTE: These coins were minted from 1954-57 and mintage figure is a total.

ALUMINUM-BRONZE
Obv: King Rama IX, 1 medal on uniform.

Y#	Date	Year	Mintage	VF	XF	Unc
77	BE2493	(1950)	20.710	.75	1.75	3.50

Obv: Smaller head; 3 medals on uniform.

| 81 | BE2500 | (1957) | *439.874 | .10 | .15 | .25 |

*NOTE: Current issues are minted without date change.

| 168 | BE2523 | (1980) | 122.260 | .10 | .15 | .25 |

BRASS

203	BE2531	(1988)	23.776	—	—	.10
	2530	(1987)	—	—	—	.10
	2532	(1989)	—	.20	.30	1.00
	2533	(1990)	—	—	—	.10
	2534	(1991)	—	—	—	.10
	2535	(1992)	—	—	—	.10
	2536	(1993)	—	—	—	.10
	2537	(1994)	—	—	—	.10
	2538	(1995)	—	—	—	.10

ALUMINUM-BRONZE
50th Year of Reign - King Rama IX

| 329 | BE2539 | (1996) | — | — | — | .35 |

BAHT

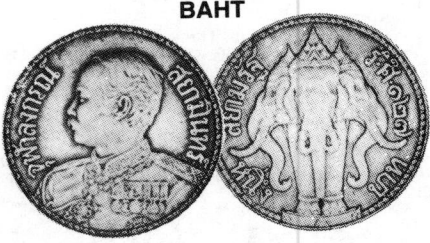

15.0000 g, .900 SILVER, .4340 oz ASW

| 39 | RS127 | (1908) | 1.037 | 3000. | 4000. | 7000. |

45	BE2456	(1913)	2.690	10.00	16.50	35.00
	2457	(1914)	.490	12.50	22.50	45.00
	2458	(1915)	5.000	10.00	16.50	35.00
	2459	(1916)	9.080	10.00	16.50	28.00
	2460	(1917)	14.340	10.00	16.50	28.00
	2461	(1918)	3.840	10.00	16.50	40.00

NOTE: BE2456 is often found weakly struck so it does appear similar to a counterfeit.

COPPER-NICKEL-SILVER-ZINC

Y#	Date	Year Mintage	VF	XF	Unc
82	BE2500 (1957)	*3.143	.75	1.50	6.00

***NOTE:** These coins were minted from 1958-60 and mintage figure is a total.*

COPPER-NICKEL
King Rama IX & Queen Sirikit

Y#	Date	Year Mintage	VF	XF	Unc
83	BE2504 (1961)	4.430	.40	.75	2.00

| 84 | BE2505 (1962) | | | | |
| | | *883.086 | .10 | .15 | .50 |

***NOTE:** These coins were minted from 1962-82 and mintage figure is a total.*

36th Birthday - King Rama IX

| 85 | ND | (1963) | 3.000 | .25 | .75 | 2.00 |

5th Asian Games

| 87 | BE2509 | 1966 | 9.000 | .25 | .75 | 3.00 |

6th Asian Games

| 91 | BE2513 | 1970 | 9.000 | .25 | .75 | 1.50 |

F.A.O. Issue

| 96 | BE2515 (1972) | 9.000 | .10 | .25 | .75 |

Prince Vajiralongkorn Investiture

Y#	Date	Year Mintage	VF	XF	Unc
97	BE2515 (1972)	9.000	.15	.40	1.00

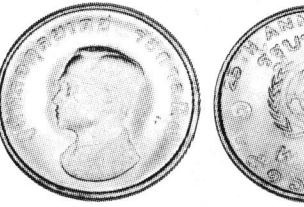

25th Anniversary - World Health Organization

| 99 | BE2516 | 1973 | 1.000 | .25 | .65 | 1.25 |

| 100 | BE2517 (1974) | 248.978 | .15 | .40 | 1.00 |

8th SEAP Games

| 105 | BE2518 | 1975 | 3.000 | .25 | .65 | 1.25 |

75th Birthday of Princess Mother

| 107 | BE2518 (1975) | 9.000 | .15 | .40 | 1.00 |

 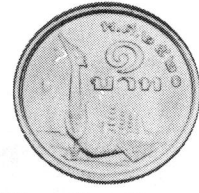

| 110 | BE2520 (1977) | 506.460 | | .10 | .20 | .50 |

F.A.O. Issue

| 112 | BE2520 (1977) | 2.000 | .15 | .40 | 1.00 |

Graduation of Princess Sirindhorn

Y#	Date	Year Mintage	VF	XF	Unc
114	BE2520 (1977)	8.998	.15	.40	1.00

BRONZE

| 114a | BE2520 (1977) | — | — | — | — |

COPPER-NICKEL
Investiture of Princess Sirindhorn

| 124 | BE2520 (1977) | 5.000 | .15 | .40 | 1.00 |

Graduation of Crown Prince Vijiralongkorn

| 127 | BE2521 (1978) | 5.000 | .10 | .20 | .50 |

8th Asian Games

| 130 | BE2521 | 1978 | 5.000 | .10 | .20 | .50 |

World Food Day

| 157 | BE2525 (1982) | 1.500 | .10 | .20 | .50 |

Obv: Large portrait w/collar touching hairline.

159.1	BE2525 (1982)	123.585	.10	.20	.50
	2525(27) (1984)	—	.10	.20	.50
	2525(28) (1985)	—	.10	.20	.50

NOTE: 2527 and 2528 are frozen dates, with the Thai numerals for 27 and 28 in the Finance Ministry decal at the bottom of the reverse.

Obv: Small portrait w/space between collar and lower hairline.

| 159.2 | BE2525 (1982) | Inc. Ab. | 2.50 | 5.00 | 10.00 |

Circulation Coinage

183	BE2529	(1986)	—	.20	.30	1.00
	2530	(1987)	325.271	—	—	.10
	2531	(1988)	391.442	—	—	.10
	2532	(1989)	—	—	—	.10
	2533	(1990)	—	—	—	.10
	2534	(1991)	—	—	—	.10
	2535	(1992)	—	—	—	.10
	2536	(1993)	—	—	—	.10
	2537	(1994)	—	—	—	.10
	2538	(1995)	—	—	—	.10
	2540	(1997)	—	—	—	.10

NOTE: Varieties exist.

50th Anniversary - Reign of King Rama IX

Y#	Date	Year Mintage	VF	XF	Unc
330	BE2539 (1996)	—	—	—	.35

2 BAHT

COPPER-NICKEL
Graduation of Princess Chulabhorn

134	BE2522 (1979)	5.000	.20	.40	1.00

COPPER-NICKEL CLAD COPPER
International Youth Year

176	BE2528 1985	10.000	.20	.40	1.00

XIII SEA Games

177	BE2528 1985	5.000	.20	.40	1.00

National Years of the Trees

178	ND (1986)	3.000	.50	1.00	3.50

Year of Peace

180	BE2529 1986	5.000	—	—	.50

Chulachomklao Royal Military Academy

188	BE2530 (1987)	3.000	—	—	.50

Princess Chulabhorn Awarded Einstein Medal

191	BE2529 (1986)	3.000	—	—	.50

60th Birthday - King Rama IX

Y#	Date	Year Mintage	VF	XF	Unc
194	BE2530 (1987)	.010	—	—	.50

72nd Anniversary of Thai Cooperatives

204	BE2531 (1988)	3.000	—	—	.50

42nd Anniversary - Reign of King Rama IX

210	BE2531 (1988)	5.000	—	—	.50

100th Anniversary of Siriraj Hospital

220	BE2531 (1988)	3.412	—	—	.50

Crown Prince's Birthday

222	BE2531 (1988)	2.000	—	—	.50

72nd Anniversary of Chulalongkorn University

225	BE2532 (1989)	3.000	—	—	.50

Centennial of First Medical College

230	BE2533 (1990)	1.000	—	—	.50

90th Birthday of Queen Mother

232	BE2533 (1990)	2.000	—	—	.50

100th Anniversary - Office of
the Comptroller General

235	BE2533 (1990)	1.000	—	—	.50

World Health Organization

Y#	Date	Year Mintage	VF	XF	Unc
243	BE2533 (1990)	2.000	—	—	1.00

36th Birthday of Princess Sirindhorn

237	BE2534 (1991)	2.300	—	—	.50

80th Anniversary of Thai Boy Scouts

240	BE2534 (1991)	2.000	—	—	1.50

Princess Sirindhorn's Magsaysay Foundation Award

255	BE2534 (1991)	12.000	—	—	.50

Centenary Celebration - Father of King Rama IX

248	BE2535 (1992)	2.308	—	—	.50

Ministry of Justice Centennial

251	BE2535 (1992)	1.500	—	—	.50

Ministry of Interior Centennial

253	1992	1.500	—	—	.50

Queen's 60th Birthday

259	BE2535 (1992)	1.700	—	—	.50

60th Anniversary of the National Assembly -
Anatasamakhom Throne Hall

268	BE2535 (1992)	—	—	—	.50

Ministry of Agriculture

Y#	Date	Year Mintage	VF	XF	Unc
270	BE2535 (1992)	1.000	—	—	.50

King's 64th Birthday

272	BE2535 (1992)	1.000			.50

Centennial of Thai Teacher Training - Emblem

276	BE2535 (1992)	1.200	—		.50

Centennial of Thai National Bank - Seated Figure

277	BE2535 (1992)	1.000			.50

Centennial of Attorney General's Office - Scale

278	BE2536 (1993)	1.000	—		.50

Centennial of Thai Red Cross - Symbols

279	BE2536 (1993)	1.200	—		.50

Treasury Department

282	BE2536 (1993)	1.200			.50

100th Anniversary of Rama VII

288	BE2536 (1993)	1.500	—		.50

60th Anniversary - Royal Institute

292	BE2537 (1994)	1.200			.50

120th Anniversary - Juridical Council

Y#	Date	Year Mintage	VF	XF	Unc
294	BE2537 (1994)	1.200	—	—	.50

60th Anniversary - Thammasat University

296	BE2537 (1994)	1.250			.50

F.A.O.

307	BE2538 (1995)	—	—	—	.65

Information Technology Year

313	BE2538 (1995)	—			.50

Asian Environment Year

315	BE2538 (1995)	—			.50

Siriraj Nursing and Midwifery School Centennial

317	BE2539 (1996)	—			.65

King's 50th Year of Reign

319	BE2539 (1996)	—	—		1.25

5 BAHT

COPPER-NICKEL

98	BE2515 (1972)	30.016	.30	.60	1.20

COPPER-NICKEL CLAD COPPER

Y#	Date	Year Mintage	VF	XF	Unc
111	BE2520 (1977)	27.257	.30	.60	1.20
	2522 (1979)	72.740	.30	.60	1.20

50th Birthday - King Rama IX
Obv. leg: *Prathet Thai.*

120	BE2520 (1977)	.500	.35	.75	1.50

Error: Obv. leg. *Siam Minta.*

121	BE2520 (1977)	—	7.00	15.00	30.00

8th Asian Games

131	BE2521 1978	.500	1.50	3.50	6.50

Royal Cradle Ceremony

132	BE2522 (1979)	1.000	.50	1.00	2.00

Queen's Anniversary and F.A.O. Ceres Medal

137	BE2523 (1980)	9.000	.25	.50	1.25

80th Birthday of King's Mother

Y#	Date	Year Mintage	VF	XF	Unc
140	BE2523	(1980)	3.504	.25	.50	1.25

Rama VII Constitutional Monarchy

144	BE2523	(1980)	2.113	.25	.50	1.25

Centennial - Birth of King Rama VI

142	BE2524	(1981)	2.222	.25	.50	1.25

Bicentennial of Bangkok

149	BE2525	(1982)	5.000	.25	.50	1.25

World Food Day

158	BE2525	(1982)	.400	.35	.75	1.50

160	BE2525	(1982)	.200	.50	1.00	2.00
	2525(28)	(1985)	—	.60	1.25	2.25
	2525(29)	(1986)	—	.60	1.25	2.25
		2526	(1983)	—	1.00	2.00	5.00
		2527	(1984)	—	5.00	10.00	25.00
		2528	(1985)	—	.20	.50	1.00
		2529	(1986)	—	.20	.50	1.00

NOTE: 2528 and 2529 are frozen dates, with the Thai numerals for 28 and 29 in the Finance Ministry decal at the bottom of the reverse.

75th Anniversary of Boy Scouts

Y#	Date	Year Mintage	VF	XF	Unc
161	BE2525	(1982)	.206	1.50	3.50	6.50

84th Birthday of Princess Mother

171	BE2527	(1984)	.600	1.00	2.00	4.50

200th Anniversary - Birth of Rama III

184	BE2530	(1987)	2.000	—	—	.75

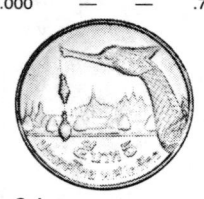

Circulation Coinage

185	BE2530	(1987)	14.000	—	—	.75
	2531	(1988)	—	—	—	.75

60th Birthday - King Rama IX

195	BE2530	(1987)	1.500	—	—	2.00

42nd Anniversary - Reign of King Rama IX

211	BE2531	(1988)	1.500	—	—	2.00

Circulation Coinage

219	BE2531	(1988)	—	—	—	.50
	2532	(1989)	—	—	—	.50
	2533	(1990)	—	—	—	.50
	2534	(1991)	—	—	—	.50
	2535	(1992)	—	—	—	.50
	2536	(1993)	—	—	—	.50
	2537	(1994)	—	—	—	.50
	2538	(1995)	—	—	—	.50

Queen's 60th Birthday

Y#	Date	Year Mintage	VF	XF	Unc
260	BE2535	(1992)	1.000	—	—	1.25

18th S.E.A. Games

306	BE2538	(1995)	—	—	—	1.25

King's 50th Year of Reign

320	BE2539	(1996)	—	—	—	1.50

10 BAHT

5.0000 g, .800 SILVER, .1286 oz ASW
25th Anniversary - Reign of King Rama IX

92	BE2514	(1971)	2.000	BV	2.00	4.50

NICKEL
Crown Prince Vajiralongkorn and
Princess Soamsawali Wedding

117	BE2520	(1977)	1.890	.50	1.00	2.50

Graduation of Princess Sirindhorn

115	BE2520	(1977)	2.097	.50	1.00	2.50

BRONZE

115a	BE2520	(1977)	—	—	—	20.00

NICKEL
Graduation of Princess Chulabhorn

135	BE2522	(1979)	1.196	.50	1.00	2.50

80th Birthday of King's Mother

Y#	Date	Year	Mintage	VF	XF	Unc
141	BE2523	(1980)	1.288	.50	1.00	2.50

30th Anniversary of Buddhist Fellowship

| 145 | BE2523 | (1980) | 1.035 | .50 | 1.00 | 2.50 |

King Rama IX Anniversary of Reign

| 146 | BE2524 | (1981) | 2.039 | .50 | 1.00 | 2.50 |

50th Birthday of Queen Sirikit

| 154 | BE2525 | (1982) | .500 | .75 | 1.50 | 3.50 |
| | 2525 | (1982) | 9,999 | — | Proof | 22.50 |

75th Anniversary of Boy Scouts
Similar to 5 Baht, Y#161.

| 162 | BE2525 | (1982) | .100 | 1.25 | 2.50 | 5.00 |
| | 2525 | (1982) | 1,500 | — | Proof | 45.00 |

100th Anniversary of Postal Service

| 163 | BE2526 | (1983) | .300 | .75 | 1.50 | 3.50 |
| | 2526 | (1983) | 5,000 | — | Proof | 25.00 |

700th Anniversary of Thai Alphabet

| 165 | BE2526 | (1983) | .500 | .75 | 1.50 | 3.50 |
| | 2526 | (1983) | 5,167 | — | Proof | 22.50 |

84th Birthday of Princess Mother
Similar to 5 Baht, Y#171.

Y#	Date	Year	Mintage	VF	XF	Unc
172	BE2527	(1984)	.200	1.25	2.50	5.50
	2527	(1984)	3,492	—	Proof	37.50

72nd Anniversary of Government Savings Bank

| 175 | BE2528 | (1985) | .500 | .50 | 1.00 | 2.50 |
| | 2528 | (1985) | 3,000 | — | Proof | 37.50 |

National Years of the Trees

| 179 | ND | (1986) | .100 | 1.50 | 3.00 | 6.50 |
| | ND | (1986) | 2,100 | — | Proof | 45.00 |

6th ASEAN Orchid Congress

| 181 | BE2529 | 1986 | .200 | — | — | 2.50 |
| | 2529 | 1986 | 3,000 | — | Proof | 37.50 |

Chulachomklao Royal Military Academy

| 189 | BE2530 | (1987) | .300 | — | — | 2.50 |
| | 2530 | (1987) | 2,060 | — | Proof | 45.00 |

Asian Institute of Technology

| 190 | BE2530 | (1987) | .300 | — | — | 2.50 |
| | 2530 | (1987) | 2,100 | — | Proof | 45.00 |

Princess Chulabhorn Awarded Einstein Medal

| 192 | BE2529 | (1986) | .200 | — | — | 2.50 |
| | 2529 | (1986) | 1,080 | — | Proof | 50.00 |

60th Birthday of King Rama IX

Y#	Date	Year	Mintage	VF	XF	Unc
196	BE2530	(1987)	.500	—	—	2.50
	2530	(1987)	5,000	—	Proof	30.00

72nd Anniversary of Thai Cooperatives

| 205 | BE2531 | (1988) | .143 | — | — | 2.50 |
| | 2530 | (1988) | 3,000 | — | Proof | 30.00 |

42nd Anniversary - Reign of King Rama IX

| 212 | BE2531 | (1988) | .500 | — | — | 2.50 |
| | 2531 | (1988) | 8,110 | — | Proof | 20.00 |

100th Anniversary of Siriraj Hospital

| 221 | BE2531 | (1988) | .290 | — | — | 2.50 |
| | 2531 | (1988) | 5,000 | — | Proof | 20.00 |

Crown Prince's Birthday

| 223 | BE2531 | (1988) | .200 | — | — | 2.50 |
| | 2531 | (1988) | 3,000 | — | Proof | 22.00 |

ALUMINUM-BRONZE center,
STAINLESS STEEL ring

227	BE2531	(1988)	.100	—	P/L	25.00
	2532	(1989)	200.000	—	—	2.25
	2534	(1991)	—	—	—	2.25
	2535	(1992)	—	—	—	2.25
	2536	(1993)	—	—	—	2.25
	2537	(1994)	—	—	—	3.00
	2538	(1995)	—	—	—	3.00
	2539	(1996)	—	—	—	3.00

NOTE: Varieties exist.
NOTE: The BE2531 (1988) pieces were not released to general circulation and are very scarce in the numismatic community.

NICKEL
Chulalongkorn University

Y#	Date	Year	Mintage	VF	XF	Unc
228	BE2532	(1989)	.500	—	—	2.00

COPPER-NICKEL
Centennial of First Medical College

231	BE2533	(1990)	.300	—	—	2.00
	2533	(1990)	3,772	—	Proof	32.50

90th Birthday of the Princess Mother

233	BE2533	(1990)	.500	—	—	2.50
	2533	(1990)	6,076	—	Proof	32.50

100th Anniversary - Office of Comptroller General

236	BE2533	(1990)	.300	—	—	2.50

World Health Organization

244	BE2533	(1990)	.800	—	—	3.00
	2533	(1990)	.034	—	Proof	20.00

36th Birthday of Princess Sirindhorn

Y#	Date	Year	Mintage	VF	XF	Unc
238	BE2534	(1991)	1.100	—	—	2.50
	2534	(1991)	3,300	—	Proof	30.00

80th Anniversary of Thai Boy Scouts

241	BE2534	(1991)	.650	—	—	3.00
	2534	(1991)	3,237	—	Proof	30.00

Princess Sirindhorn's Magsaysay Foundation Award

256	BE2534	(1991)	.800	—	—	2.50
	2534	(1991)	2,111	—	Proof	37.50

Centenary Celebration - Father of King Rama IX

249	BE2535	(1992)	.800	—	—	2.50
	2535	(1992)	5,314	—	Proof	22.50

Ministry of Justice Centennial

252	BE2535	(1992)	.800	—	—	2.50
	2535	(1992)		—	Proof	20.00

Ministry of Interior Centennial

254	BE2535	(1992)	.800	—	—	2.50
	2535	(1992)	.010	—	Proof	20.00

Queen's 60th Birthday

261	BE2535	(1992)	1.100	—	—	3.00
	2535	(1992)	.018	—	Proof	20.00

60th Anniversary of National Assembly

Y#	Date	Year	Mintage	VF	XF	Unc
269	BE2535	(1992)	.044	—	—	2.50

Ministry of Agriculture

271	BE2535	(1992)	.550	—	—	2.50
	2535	(1992)		—	Proof	22.50

King's 64th Birthday

273	BE2535	(1992)	.550	—	—	2.50
	2535	(1992)	3,711	—	Proof	25.00

Centennial of Thai Teacher Training - Emblem

284	BE2535	(1992)	.700	—	—	2.50

Centennial of Thai National Bank - Seated Figure

285	BE2535	(1992)	.700	—	—	2.50
	2535	(1992)	6,927	—	Proof	20.00

Centennial of Thai Red Cross - Symbols

280	BE2536	(1993)	.700	—	—	2.50
	2535	(1993)	.014	—	Proof	18.50

Treasury Department

Y#	Date	Year	Mintage	VF	XF	Unc
283	BE2536	(1993)	.600	—	—	2.50
	2535	(1993)	.010	—	Proof	18.50

Centennial of Attorney General's Office

286	BE2536	(1993)	.700	—	—	2.50

100th Anniversary of Rama VII

289	BE2536	(1993)	.800	—	—	2.50
	2536	(1993)	.010	—	Proof	18.50

60th Anniversary - Royal Institute

293	BE2537	(1994)	.700	—	—	2.50
	2537	(1994)	.010	—	Proof	18.50

120th Anniversary - Juridical Council

295	BE2537	(1994)	.800	—	—	2.50
	2537	(1994)	.012	—	Proof	18.50

60th Anniversary - Thammasat University

297	BE2537	(1994)	.800	—	—	2.50
	2537	(1994)	.012	—	Proof	18.50

50th Anniversary - Reign of King Rama IX and F.A.O. World Summit

Y#	Date	Year	Mintage	VF	XF	Unc
334	BE2539	(1996)	—	—	—	3.00

International Rice Award
Obv: King with camera. Rev: Rice plant.

339	BE2535	(1996)	—	—	—	3.00

50th Anniversary - Reign of King Rama IX
Obv: Small portrait does not contact inner ring.

328.1	BE2539	(1996)	—	—	—	2.50

50th Anniversary - Reign of King Rama IX
Obv: Large portrait contacts inner ring.

328.2	BE2539	(1996)	—	—	—	2.75

100th Anniversary of Chulalongkorn's European Tour

347	BE2540	(1997)	—	—	—	2.00

100th Anniversary - Central General Hospital - Medication Office

346	BE2541	(1998)	—	—	—	2.00

13th Asian Games - Symbols

348	BE2541	(1998)	10.000	—	—	2.00

19.6000 g, .750 SILVER, .4726 oz ASW
36th Birthday - King Rama IX

Y#	Date	Year	Mintage	VF	XF	Unc
86	ND	(1963)	1.000	—	5.00	10.00

COPPER-NICKEL
120th Anniversary - Ministry of Finance

298	BE2538	(1994)	.800	—	—	3.50
	2538	(1994)	1,920	—	Proof	28.00

108th Anniversary - Ministry of Defense

300	BE2538	(1994)	.800	—	—	3.50
	2538	(1994)	2,000	—	Proof	28.00

120th Anniversary - Ministry of Foreign Affairs

302	BE2538	(1994)	.800	—	—	3.50
	2538	(1994)	740 pcs.	—	Proof	55.00

72nd Birthday of Princess
Similar to 600 Baht, Y#305.

304	BE2538	(1995)	.800	—	—	3.50
	2538	(1995)	1,560	—	Proof	28.00

F.A.O.

308	BE2538	(1995)	.400	—	—	3.50
	2538	(1995)	—	—	Proof	20.00

80th Anniversary - Department of Revenue

Y#	Date	Year	Mintage	VF	XF	Unc
309	BE2538	(1995)	.800	—	—	3.50
	2538	(1995)		—	Proof	20.00

50th Anniversary - Reign of King Rama IX

Y#	Date	Year	Mintage	VF	XF	Unc
321.1	BE2539	(1996)		—	—	4.00
	2539	(1996)		—	Proof	25.00

50 Years of Peace

Y#	Date	Year	Mintage	VF	XF	Unc
338	ND	(1997)		—	—	3.50

120th Anniversary - Audit Council

311	BE2538	(1995)	.800	—	—	3.50
	2538	(1995)		—	Proof	20.00

Rev: Incomplete - missing the "Unalom" in center.

321.2	BE2539	(1996)		—	—	4.00
	2539	(1996)		—	Proof	25.00

50th Anniversary - Thai Veterans Organization

341	BE2541	(1998)		—	—	3.50
	2541	(1998)		—	Proof	12.50

Information Technology Year

314	BE2538	(1995)		—	—	3.50
	2538	(1995)		—	Proof	20.00

50th Anniversary - Reign of King Rama IX and F.A.O. World Food Summit

335	BE2539	(1996)		—	—	3.50

Asean Environment Year

316	BE2538	(1995)		—	—	3.50
	2538	(1995)		—	Proof	20.00

International Rice Award

340	BE2539	(1996)		—	—	3.50

Ministry of Commerce - Seal

331	BE2538	(1995)		—	—	4.00

100th Anniversary - Thai Railway

332	BE2540	(1997)		—	—	3.50
	2540	(1997)		—	Proof	30.00

Siriraj Nursing and Midwife School Centennial

318	BE2539	(1996)		—	—	3.50

84th Anniversary - Thai Savings Bank

333	BE2540	(1997)		—	—	3.50
	2540	(1997)		—	Proof	28.00

TIBET

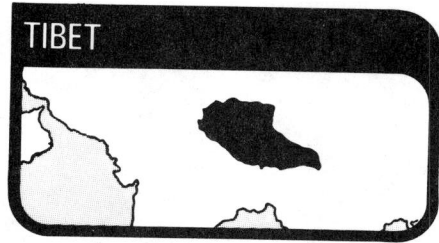

Tibet, an autonomous region of China located in central Asia between the Himalayan and Kunlun Mts. has an area of 471,660 sq. mi. (1,221,599 sq. km.) and a population of *1.9 million. Capital: Lhasa. The economy is based on agriculture and livestock raising. Wool, livestock, salt and hides are exported.

Lamaism, a form of Buddhism, developed in Tibet in the 8th century. From that time until the 1900s, the Tibetan rulers virtually isolated the country from the outside world. The British in India achieved some influence in the early 20th century, and encouraged Tibet to declare its independence from China in 1913. The Communist revolution in China marked a new era in Tibetan history. Chinese Communist troops invaded Tibet in Oct., 1950. After a token resistance, Tibet signed an agreement with China in which China recognized the spiritual and temporal leadership of the Dalai Lama, and Tibet recognized the suzerainty of Communist China. In 1959, a nationwide revolt triggered by Communist-initiated land reform broke out. The revolt was ruthlessly crushed. The Dalai Lama fled to India, and on Sept. 1, 1965, the Chinese made Tibet an autonomous region of China.

The first coins to circulate in Tibet were those of neighboring Nepal from about 1570. Shortly after 1720, the Nepalese government began striking specific issues for use in Tibet. These coins had a lower silver content than those struck for use in Nepal and were exchanged with the Tibetans for an equal weight in silver bullion. Around 1763 the Tibetans struck their own coins for the first time in history. The number of coins struck at that time must have been very small. Larger quantities of coins were struck by the Tibetan government mint which opened in 1791 with the permission of the Chinese. Operations of this mint however were suspended two years later. The Chinese opened a second mint in Lhasa in 1792. It produced a coinage until 1836. Shortly thereafter, the Tibetan mint was reopened and the government of Tibet continued to strike coins until 1953.

DATING
Based on the Tibetan calendar, Tibetan coins are dated by the cycle which contains 60 years. To calculate the western date use the following formula: Number of cycles -1, x 60 + number of years + 1026. Example 15th cycle 25th year = 1891 AD. Example: 15th cycle, 25th year 15 - 1 x 60 + 25 + 1026 = 1891AD.

13/30 = 1776	14/30 = 1836	15/30 = 1896
13/40 = 1786	14/40 = 1846	15/40 = 1906
13/50 = 1796	14/50 = 1856	15/50 = 1916
13/60 = 1806	14/60 = 1866	15/60 = 1926
14/10 = 1816	15/10 = 1876	16/10 = 1936
14/20 = 1826	15/20 = 1886	16/20 = 1946

Certain Sino-Tibetan issues are dated in the year of reign of the Emperor of China.

MONETARY SYSTEM
15 Skar = 1-1/2 Sho = 1 Tangka
10 Sho = 1 Srang

TANGKA
16(th)CYCLE 2(nd)YEAR = 1928AD

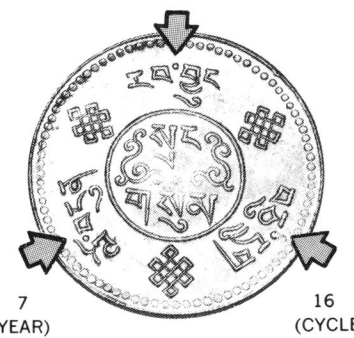

"CYCLE"

7 (YEAR)   16 (CYCLE)

16(th) CYCLE 7(th) YEAR = 1933AD

NUMERALS

1	༡	གཅིག
2	༢	གཉིས
3	༣	གསུམ
4	༤	བཞི
5	༥	ལྔ
6	༦	དྲུག
7	༧	བདུན
8	༨	བརྒྱད
9	༩	དགུ
10	༡༠	བཅུ or བཅུ་ཐམ་པ
11	༡༡	བཅུག or བཅུ་གཅིག
12	༡༢	བཅུས or བཅུ་གཉིས
13	༡༣	བཅུ ས or བཅུ་གསུམ
14	༡༤	བཅུ་བཞི
15	༡༥	བཅོ་ལྔ
16	༡༦	བཅུ་དྲུག
17	༡༧	བཅུ་བདུན
18	༡༨	བཅོ་བརྒྱད
19	༡༩	བཅུ་དགུ
20	༢༠	ཉི་ཤུ
21	༢༡	ཉི་ཤུ་ཅ་གཅིག or ཉེར་གཅིག
22	༢༢	ཉེར་གཉིས
23	༢༣	ཉེར་གསུམ
24	༢༤	ཉེར་བཞི
25	༢༥	ཉེར་ལྔ
26	༢༦	ཉེར་དྲུག
27	༢༧	ཉེར་བདུན
28	༢༨	ཉེར་བརྒྱད

SINO-TIBETAN COINAGE
RULERS
Hsuan T'ung, 1909-1911

In the name of Hsuan T'ung:

1/2 SKAR

COPPER, 3.10-3.60 g
Y#	Date	Mintage	Good	VG	Fine	VF
A4	(1910)	—	—	—	Rare	—

SKAR

COPPER, 5.40-6.60 g
Y#	Date	Mintage	Good	VG	Fine	VF
4	(1910)	—	40.00	50.00	80.00	160.00

SHO

SILVER, 3.30-4.10 g
| 5 | (1910) | — | 20.00 | 30.00 | 40.00 | 60.00 |

NOTE: A variety exists, having the inner circle of dots, on the Chinese side, connected by lines.

2 SHO

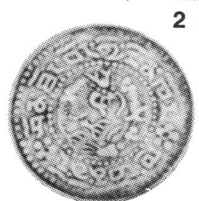 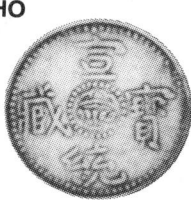

SILVER, 5.20-8.40 g
| 6 | (1910) | — | 25.00 | 40.00 | 80.00 | 150.00 |

NOTE: Varieties with different dragon claws exist.

TIBETAN COINAGE
Miscellaneous TANGKAS
(Size of Kong-par Tangka)

SILVER, ca. 5.40 g
C#	Date	Year	Good	VG	Fine	VF
27	15-40	(1906)	5.00	8.00	15.00	25.00
	15-46	(1912)	25.00	35.00	45.00	60.00

NOTE: Earlier dates (15/28-15/30 = 1894-1896) exist for this type.

NOTE: In addition to the above meaningful (probably) dates, the following meaningless ones exist: 13-16, 13-31, 13-92, 16-16, 16-61, 16-69, 16-92, 16-93, 92-39, 96-61 (sixes may be reversed threes and nines reversed ones). These are of billon, varying from 3.9 to 4.7 g.

NOTE: The legend appears to be in ornamental Lansa script and has yet to be deciphered. The type is a copy of the Nepalese issue: 'Cho-Tang'. Although struck unofficially, it was legal tender, due to an edict issued in 1881 ordering that no distinction be made between false and genuine coins!

NOTE: This type was cut in parts of 3, 4 and 5 petals to make change and the resulting fractions are occasionally encountered.

'Ga-den' TANGKA

SILVER, 3.90-5.20 g
Tip Arsenal Mint
Obv: 3 elongated dots on either side of lotus center and new arrangement of 8 symbols.

Y#	Date	Mintage	VG	Fine	VF	XF
13.2	ND(ca.1895-1901)	1.50		3.00	5.00	8.00

NOTE: 5 major varieties exist.

3.80-5.70 g
Similar to Y#13.3, but not uniform.

Y#	Date	Mintage	VG	Fine	VF	XF
13.4	ND(ca.1901-06)	1.00	2.50	4.50	7.00	

NOTE: 8 major varieties exist, including an error having the 8 symbols rotated one position clockwise.

3.80 g
Obv: 8mm circle around lotus, North and West symbols are similar.

13.5	ND(ca.1905)	—	20.00	30.00	50.00	100.00

3.00-5.60 g
Mint: Dode
Obv: 9 dots within lotus circle.

13.6	ND(ca.1906-12)	1.00	2.50	4.50	7.00

NOTE: 8 major varieties exist. See Y#13.9, 13.10 and 13.11 for other types, having 9 dots within lotus circle.

SILVER, 2.70-5.00 g
Obv. leg: *Gaden Palace, victorious in all directions.* **Rev: 8 Buddhist lucky symbols surround encircled symbols of sensuality.**

14	ND(ca.1909)	—	3.00	5.00	9.00	15.00

NOTE: Obverse varieties exist w/o or up to 2 dots inside flourishes enclosing the legend. Struck for presentation to monks.

BILLON, 3.30-5.88 g
Obv: 11 dots within lotus circle.

13.7	ND(ca.1912-23)	1.00	2.50	4.50	7.00

NOTE: 4 major varieties and numerous minor ones exist (40 to 78 dots compose outer circles).

Northeast symbol on obv:

3.00-5.00 g
Obv: 9 dots within lotus circle.

13.8	ND(ca.1914-23)	1.00	2.25	3.75	6.00

NOTE: 5 major and numerous minor varieties exist (35 to 68 dots compose outer circles).

Northeast symbol on obv:

3.30-4.60 g
Mint: Ser-Khang

Y#	Date	Mintage	VG	Fine	VF	XF
13.9	ND(ca.1920)	—	4.00	7.00	11.00	15.00

NOTE: Several other features are unique to this type.

3.80-4.30 g
Mint: Dode
Obv: 9 dots within lotus circle, uniform thickness (1.mm).

13.10	1929-30	—	7.00	10.00	15.00	25.00

NOTE: 2 minor die varieties exist.

SILVER, 3.10-5.30 g
Mint: Tapchi

31	ND(1946-48)	—	3.00	4.50	7.00	12.00

NOTE: This type was struck for presentation to monks.

2 TANGKA

BILLON, 7.80-10.50 g
Mint: Dode

15	ND(ca.1912)	—	100.00	150.00	200.00	300.00

NOTE: Struck in a collar. 2 varieties exist.

SHO-SRANG COINAGE
Size same as 'Kong-par' Tangka

1/8 SHO

COPPER
Mint: Dode

Y#	Date	Year	Good	VG	Fine	VF
A7	1	(1909)	35.00	50.00	90.00	150.00

NOTE: A silver striking of this type exists (rare), possibly a pattern. Varieties exist.

1/4 SHO

COPPER

Y#	Date	Year	Good	VG	Fine	VF
B7	1	(1909)	35.00	50.00	90.00	150.00

NOTE: The above coin struck in silver is a forgery.

2 1/2 SKAR

COPPER
Mint: Dode

10	15-43	(1909)	125.00	175.00	250.00	350.00

NOTE: Lion varieties exist.

23.5mm, 3.69-6.09 g
Obv: Lion crouching and looking upwards.

16	15-47	(1913)	4.00	8.00	20.00	40.00
	15-48	(1914)	4.00	8.00	20.00	40.00
	15-49	(1915)	10.00	20.00	35.00	60.00
	15-50	(1916)	8.00	15.00	28.00	50.00
	15-51	(1917)	6.00	12.00	25.00	45.00
	15-52	(1918)	4.00	8.00	20.00	40.00

NOTE: Varieties exist.

Mint: Mekyi
Obv: Lion standing and looking backwards.

16.1	15-48	(1914)	5.00	11.00	25.00	45.00

NOTE: Varieties exist.

 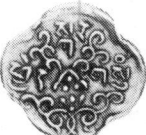

Mint: Dode

A19	15-52	(1918)	30.00	50.00	65.00	100.00
	15-53	(1919)	35.00	60.00	80.00	120.00
	15-55	(1921)	35.00	60.00	80.00	120.00

NOTE: Counterfeits dated 15-55 exist.

5 SKAR

COPPER
Mint: Dode

A10	15-43	(1909)	125.00	175.00	250.00	350.00

27mm
Obv: Lion looking upwards.

Y#	Date	Year	Good	VG	Fine	VF
17	15-47	(1913)	4.00	8.00	20.00	40.00
	15-48	(1914)	2.00	4.00	10.00	15.00
	15-49	(1915)	2.00	4.00	10.00	15.00
	15-50	(1916)	2.00	4.00	10.00	15.00
	15-51	(1917)	2.00	4.00	10.00	15.00
	15-52	(1918)	4.00	8.00	20.00	40.00

Mint: Mekyi
Obv: Lion looking backwards.

17.1	15-48	(1914)	2.00	4.00	9.00	22.00
	15-49	(1915)	1.50	3.50	8.50	10.00
	15-50	(1916)	1.50	3.50	8.50	10.00
	15-51	(1917)	1.50	3.50	8.50	10.00
	15-52	(1918)	1.50	3.50	8.50	10.00

NOTE: Varieties exist w/rotated reverse symbols. Lion varieties exist for 15-49 date strikes.

Obv: Lion looking backwards and upwards.

17.2	15-48	(1914)	4.00	8.00	20.00	30.00
	15-49	(1915)	6.00	15.00	35.00	50.00

Rev: Flower w/8 petals rather than wheel w/8 spokes.

17.3	15-48	(1914)	4.00	8.00	20.00	35.00

21mm
Mint: Lower Dode

19	15-52	(1918)	1.25	2.50	4.00	7.00
	15-53	(1919)	1.00	2.00	3.50	6.00
	15-54	(1920)	.75	1.50	3.00	5.00
	15-55	(1921)	.75	1.50	3.00	5.00
	15-56	(1922)	.75	1.50	3.00	5.00
56-15 (error)						
		(1922)	20.00	30.00	50.00	80.00

NOTE: Reverse inscription reads counterclockwise on error date coin.
NOTE: Varieties exist.

Mint: Upper Dode
Rev: Dot added above center.

19.1	15-55	(1921)	8.00	15.00	25.00	35.00
	15-56	(1922)	3.00	5.00	10.00	20.00

7 1/2 SKAR

COPPER
Mint: Dode

11	15-43	(1909)	125.00	175.00	250.00	350.00

 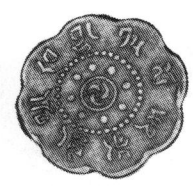

Y#	Date	Year	Good	VG	Fine	VF
20	15-52	(1918)	1.00	2.00	3.50	6.00
	15-53	(1919)	.80	1.75	3.00	5.00
	15-54	(1920)	.80	1.75	3.00	5.00
	15-55	(1921)	.80	1.75	3.00	5.00
	15-56	(1922)	.80	1.75	3.00	5.00
	15-60	(1926)	10.00	15.00	25.00	50.00

NOTE: Some 15-52, 15-53 and 15-55 specimens have the reverse central 'whirlwind' in a counterclockwise direction. Varieties exist.

SHO

COPPER, 25.6mm
Mint: Dode
Obv: Lion's head up. Rev: Central leg. horizontal.

21	15-52	(1918)	15.00	20.00	40.00	65.00

Obv: Lion looking back.

21b	15-52	(1918)	20.00	25.00	45.00	75.00

NOTE: 2 varieties exist (lion's head).

24mm, 3.95-7.13 g
Mint: Mekyi
Obv: Lion looking up, w/o dot.

21.1	15-52	(1918)	.80	1.50	3.00	6.50
	15-53	(1919)	.50	1.00	2.00	5.00
	15-54	(1920)	.50	1.00	2.00	5.00
	15-55	(1921)	.50	1.00	2.00	5.00
	15-56	(1922)	.50	1.00	2.00	5.00
	15-57	(1923)	.80	1.50	3.00	6.50
	15-58	(1924)	.50	1.00	2.00	5.00
	15-59	(1925)	.50	1.00	2.00	5.00
	15-60	(1926)	.50	1.00	2.00	5.00
	16-1	(1927)	.50	1.00	2.00	5.00
	16-2	(1928)	.50	1.00	2.00	5.00

NOTE: Varieties exist.

3.01-7.27 g
Mint: Ser-Khang
Obv: Lion looking up, w/dot.

21.2	15-54	(1920)	1.25	2.00	4.00	8.50
54-15(error)						
		(1920)	15.00	25.00	45.00	75.00
15/51-54(error)						
		(1920)	15.00	25.00	45.00	75.00
	15-55	(1921)	1.00	1.50	3.00	6.00
55-15 (error) 'year' and 'cycle' transposed						
		(1921)	15.00	25.00	45.00	75.00
	15-56/5	(1922)	.50	1.00	2.25	5.00
	15-56	(1922)	.50	1.00	2.25	5.00
	15-57	(1923)	.80	1.50	3.00	6.00
	15-58	(1924)	.50	1.00	2.25	5.00
	15-59	(1925)	.50	1.00	2.25	5.00
	15-60	(1926)	.50	1.00	2.25	5.00
16-1/15-60						
		(1927)	10.00	15.00	25.00	50.00

Y#	Date	Year	Good	VG	Fine	VF
21.2	16-1	(1927)	.50	1.00	2.25	4.50
	16-2/1	(1928)	.50	1.00	2.25	4.50
	16-2	(1928)	.50	1.00	2.25	4.50

NOTE: Specimens dated 15-54 may all be contemporary forgeries.
NOTE: Varieties of lion's head exist.

24mm, 3.43-4.73 g
Mint: Dode
Rev: Central leg. vertical.

Y#	Date	Year	VG	Fine	VF	XF
21a	15-56	(1922)	6.50	12.00	20.00	30.00
	15-57	(1923)	1.50	3.00	6.00	10.00
57-15 (error) year and cycle transposed						
	—		20.00	30.00	45.00	75.00
	15-58	(1924)	1.50	3.00	6.00	10.00
	15-59/8	(1925)	.75	2.00	4.00	8.00
15-60/59						
		(1926)	.75	2.00	4.00	8.00
	16-1	(1927)	.75	2.00	4.00	8.00
16-1 dot below O above denomination						
		(1927)	.75	2.00	4.00	8.00
(16-2/1)		(1927/8)	Reported, not confirmed			
	16-2	(1928)	1.50	3.00	6.00	10.00

NOTE: 2 varieties (lion) exist for each of the following dates: 15-56, 15-57, 15-58 & 16-2.

24mm, 4.02-6.09 g
Mint: Tapchi
The following marks are located in the position indicated by the arrow:

	a:	b:	c:	d:	e:	f:	g:			
23	16-6 (a)	(1932)	1.00	3.00	6.00	10.00
	16-7 (a)	(1933)	1.25	3.00	6.00	10.00
	16-8 (a)	(1934)	1.50	4.00	9.00	15.00
	16-9 (a)	(1935)	.75	2.00	4.00	7.00
	16-9 (b)	(1935)	.75	1.50	3.00	5.00
	16-10 (a)	(1936)	5.00	10.00	15.00	25.00
	16-10 (b)	(1936)	5.00	10.00	15.00	25.00
	16-10 (c)	(1936)	.75	1.50	3.00	5.00
	16-11 (a)	(1937)	1.50	4.00	9.00	15.00
	16-11 (b)	(1937)	5.00	10.00	15.00	25.00
	16-11 (c)	(1937)	1.50	4.00	9.00	15.00
	16-11 (d)	(1937)	1.50	4.00	9.00	15.00
	16-11 (e)	(1937)	.75	1.50	3.00	5.00
	16-11 (f)	(1937)	5.00	10.00	15.00	25.00
	16-11 (g)	(1937)	5.00	10.00	15.00	25.00
	16-12 (d)	(1938)	5.00	10.00	15.00	25.00
	16-12 (f)	(1938)	4.00	8.00	12.00	20.00
	16-12 (g)	(1938)	4.00	8.00	12.00	20.00

NOTE: Exist with thick and thin planchets and many obverse varieties.

3 SHO

COPPER
Single cloud line

27	16-20	(1946)	8.00	15.00	25.00	40.00

NOTE: 3 varieties of conch-shell on reverse.

Double cloud-line

27.1	16-20	(1946)	15.00	30.00	50.00	85.00

TIBET 678   5 SHO

SILVER

Y#	Date	Year	VG	Fine	VF	XF
8	1	(1909)	—	—	Rare	—

SRANG

COPPER, 29mm
Mint: Tapchi
Obv: 2 mountains w/two suns.

Y#	Date	Year	VG	Fine	VF	XF
28	16-21	(1947)	2.00	4.00	7.00	13.00

SILVER, 18.50 g
Mint: Dode

Y#	Date	Year	VG	Fine	VF	XF
9	1	(1909)	100.00	175.00	250.00	350.00

NOTE: 8 obverse varieties exist.

10.30 g
Mint: Dode
Obv: Lion looking upwards.

18	15-47	(1913)	25.00	40.00	65.00	100.00
	15-48	(1914)	22.50	35.00	55.00	85.00
	15-49	(1915)	22.50	35.00	55.00	85.00
	15-50	(1916)	22.50	35.00	55.00	85.00
	15-58	(1924)	—	—	Rare	—
	15-59	(1925)	35.00	65.00	100.00	140.00
	15-60	(1926)	35.00	65.00	100.00	140.00

NOTE: Two 15-50 varieties exist; small and large lions, or 14mm vs. 15mm lion-circle.

Obv: 3 mountains w/2 suns.

28.1	16-21	(1947)	.80	2.00	4.00	7.00
	16-22 dot after "cycle"					
		(1948)	.50	1.50	3.00	5.00
	16-22 dot after 16 and after "cycle"					
		(1948)	1.00	2.50	4.50	8.00
	16-22 dot after 6					
		(1948)	.40	1.00	2.50	5.00
	16-22	(1948)	.40	1.00	2.50	5.00
	16-23 12 sun rays left of sun					
		(1949)	.40	1.00	2.50	5.00
	16-23 sun rays right of sun					
		(1949)	.40	1.00	2.50	5.00
	16-23 dot after 16, 12 sun rays left of sun					
		(1949)	1.00	2.50	4.50	8.00
	89 9					
		(1949)	1.00	2.50	4.50	8.00
	16-24	(1950)	3.25	8.00	16.00	30.00
	16-24/23					
		(1950)	3.25	8.00	16.00	30.00

NOTE: Varieties exist.

NOTE: A modern medallic series dated 16-21 (1947) exists struck in copper, silver and gold which were authorized by the Dalai Lama while in exile. Refer to *Unusual World Coins,* 3rd edition, Krause Publications, 1992.

Plain edge.

12	15-43	(1909)	100.00	150.00	275.00	375.00

NOTE: Varieties exist.

Mint: Mekyi
Obv: Lion looking backwards.

18.1	15-49	(1915)	22.50	35.00	55.00	85.00
	15-50	(1916)	22.50	35.00	55.00	85.00
	15-51	(1917)	22.50	35.00	55.00	85.00
	15-52	(1918)	22.50	35.00	55.00	85.00
	15-53	(1919)	35.00	65.00	100.00	140.00
	15-56	(1922)	35.00	65.00	100.00	140.00
	15-59	(1925)	60.00	100.00	135.00	200.00
	15-60	(1926)	60.00	100.00	135.00	200.00
	16-1	(1927)	35.00	65.00	100.00	140.00

NOTE: Varieties exist.

COPPER

18.1a	15-53	(1919)	—	—	Rare	—

Obv: Lion looking upwards. Reeded edge.

A18	15-48	(1914)	250.00	450.00	650.00	800.00

COPPER
Obv: Cloud above middle mountain missing.

28.2	16-22	(1948)	20.00	50.00	90.00	125.00

Obv: Lion looking backwards.

A18.1	15-52	(1918)	100.00	200.00	350.00	500.00
	15-53	(1919)	125.00	250.00	400.00	550.00

1 1/2 SRANG

SILVER, 5.00 g
Mint: Tapchi

Y#	Date	Year	Fine	VF	XF	Unc
24	16-10	(1936)	3.00	6.00	10.00	20.00
	16-11	(1937)	2.50	5.00	9.00	17.00
	16-12	(1938)	3.00	6.00	10.00	20.00
	16-20	(1946)	11.00	20.00	30.00	40.00

SILVER
Mint: Dode

18.2	15-52	(1918)	40.00	75.00	125.00	200.00

32	ND	(1928-29)	—	—	Rare	—

Obv: Moon and sun above mountains.

28a	16-23	(1949)	3.00	8.00	15.00	25.00
	16-24 cloud merged w/middle mountain					
			4.00	9.00	20.00	30.00
	16-24	(1950)	.50	1.50	4.00	10.00
	16-24 moon cut above sun					
			3.00	5.00	9.00	20.00
	16-25/24		1.00	3.00	6.00	14.00
	16-25	(1951)	.50	1.50	4.00	10.00
	16-26	(1952)	1.50	4.00	9.00	20.00
	dot before 26		1.00	2.50	6.00	14.00
	16-27	(1953)	1.00	3.50	7.00	15.00
	16-27 (1953)					
	dots before 27 and after cycle					
			1.50	4.00	9.00	20.00
	16-27 (1953)					
	dot after cycle		1.50	4.00	9.00	20.00

NOTE: Edge varieties exist.

3 SRANG

SILVER, 11.30 g
Mint: Tapchi

Y#	Date	Year	Fine	VF	XF	Unc
25	16-7	(1933)	7.00	12.00	20.00	35.00
	16-8	(1934)	7.00	12.00	20.00	35.00

26	16-9	(1935)	6.00	10.00	18.00	30.00
	16-10	(1936)	5.00	9.00	15.00	25.00
	16-11	(1937)	5.00	9.00	15.00	25.00
	16-12	(1938)	5.00	9.00	15.00	25.00
	16-20	(1946)	20.00	25.00	30.00	40.00

NOTE: Dates for Y#24, 25 and 26 are written in words, not numerals. Obverse varieties exist.

5 SRANG

Except for a piece which is considered a pattern, no coins of this denomination are known to have been struck. Two Tanka types (Y#14 & 31, see under 'gaden' Tangkas) circulated briefly with this value and later with a value of 10 Srang.

10 SRANG

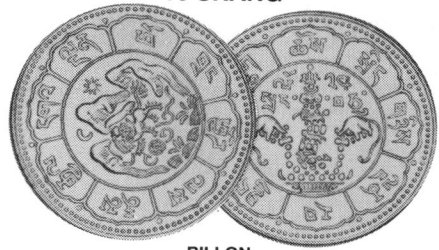

BILLON
Mint: Tapchi
Obv: 2 suns. Rev: Numerals for denomination.

29	16-22	(1948)	4.50	9.00	18.00	40.00

Rev: Word for denomination.

29.1	16-23/22					
		(1949)	12.00	20.00	35.00	70.00
	16-23 w/dot					
		(1949)	6.00	10.00	20.00	40.00
	16-23 w/o dot					
		(1949)	6.00	10.00	20.00	40.00

Obv: Moon and sun.

29a	16-23 w/dot					
		(1949)	20.00	45.00	100.00	175.00
	16-24/23 w/dot					
		(1950)	7.00	15.00	30.00	60.00
	16-24/22	(1950)	9.00	18.00	35.00	70.00

Y#	Date	Year	Fine	VF	XF	Unc
29a	16-24 moon cut above sun					
		(1950)	10.00	20.00	40.00	70.00
	16-24 w/dot					
		(1950)	12.00	22.00	50.00	90.00
	16-25/24 w/dot					
		(1951)	7.00	15.00	30.00	60.00
	16-25/24 w/o dot					
		(1951)	10.00	20.00	40.00	70.00
	16-25 w/dot					
		(1951)	7.00	15.00	30.00	60.00
	16-25 w/o dot					
		(1951)	7.00	15.00	30.00	60.00
	16-26/25 w/dot					
		(1952)	7.00	15.00	30.00	60.00
	16-26 w/dot					
		(1952)	7.00	15.00	30.00	60.00

*NOTE: The 'dot' is after the denomination. A modern medallic series dated 16-24 (1950) exist struck in copper-nickel, silver and gold which were authorized by the Dalai Lama while in exile. Refer to *Unusual World Coins*, 3rd edition, Krause Publications, 1992.

BILLON
Mint: Dogu

30	16-24	(1950)	6.00	12.00	25.00	55.00
	16-24 w/dot after date					
		(1950)	7.00	15.00	30.00	65.00
	16-25	(1951)	5.00	10.00	20.00	45.00

20 SRANG

GOLD
Mint: Ser-Khang
Obv: 8 Buddhist lucky symbols in outer circle.

22	15-52	(1918)	300.00	400.00	500.00	700.00
	15-53	(1919)	300.00	450.00	550.00	750.00
	15-54	(1920)	300.00	500.00	650.00	850.00
	15-55	(1921)	400.00	700.00	1000.	1500.

NOTE: Silver strikings for 15-53 and 15-54 exist and are believed to be forgeries.

TRADE COINAGE

MONETARY SYSTEM
1 Rupee = 3 Tangka

1/4 RUPEE

 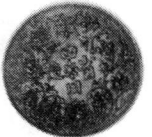

.935 SILVER, 2.80 g
Mint: Chengdu (Szechuan)

Y#	Date	Mintage	Fine	VF	XF	Unc
1	ND(1904-05,1912)					
		.120	30.00	55.00	90.00	150.00

NOTE: Varieties exist.

1/2 RUPEE

.935 SILVER, 5.60 g
Mint: Chengdu (Szechuan)

2	ND(1904,1905,1907,1912)					
		.130	40.00	75.00	125.00	200.00

NOTE: Varieties exist.

RUPEE

Lukuan (Kang Ting) City

SILVER

C#	Date	Year	Good	VG	Fine	VF
20	ND(1902-03)	—	250.00	350.00	500.00	850.00

NOTE: Struck in Kang Ting near the border of China Szechuan (Sichuan) and Tibet. It was meant to replace the Indian Rupee which was used in Eastern Tibet and western Szechuan (Sichuan) in the 19th century and is considered the forerunner of the Szechuan (Sichuan) Rupee. Chinese sources indicate it was struck in 1902 and 1903AD.

.935 SILVER, 11.40 g
Mint: Chengdu (Szechuan)
Obv: Small bust w/o collar. Rev: Vertical rosette.

Y#	Date	Mintage	Fine	VF	XF	Unc
3	ND(1902-11)	—	15.00	25.00	40.00	75.00

NOTE: 2 reverse varieties exist.

Rev: Horizontal rosette.

3.1	ND(1902-11)	—	25.00	40.00	60.00	100.00

NOTE: 2 reverse varieties exist.

.0935-.700 SILVER
Mint: Kangding (Taschieulu)
Obv: Small bust w/collar. Rev: Vertical rosette.

3.2	ND(1911-16,1930-33)	—	12.00	20.00	35.00	60.00

NOTE: 2 reverse varieties exist.

.650-.500 SILVER
Obv: Small bust w/flat nose, w/collar.
Rev: Vertical rosette.

3.4	ND(1933-39)	—	15.00	25.00	40.00	75.00

Rev: Horizontal rosette.

Y#	Date	Mintage	Fine	VF	XF	Unc
3.5	ND(1933-39)	—	25.00	35.00	60.00	100.00

.500 SILVER
Mint: Kanting (Tachienlu)
Obv: Large bust.

3.3	ND(1930-42)	—	25.00	40.00	75.00	125.00

DEBASED SILVER/BILLON

3a	ND(1939-42)	—	8.00	15.00	30.00	60.00

NOTE: Coins w/copper base and silver wash exist.
NOTE: Mintage figures are for 1900-1928 and do not include pieces struck between 1929-1938. Total mintage of the 1 Rupee between 1902 and 1942 was between 25.5 and 27.5 million according to Chinese sources. In addition to the types illustrated above, large quantities of the following coins also circulated in Tibet; China Dollars, Y#318a, 329 and 345 plus Szechuan issues Y#449 and 459 and India Rupees, KM#473, 492 and 508. Similar crown size pieces struck in silver and gold are fantasies. Refer to *Unusual World Coins*, 3rd edition.
NOTE: Rupees, due to their inscriptions and first mint also called Szechuan Rupees, were cut in half and quarter. They were in use as smaller denominations until 1934.
NOTE: Rupees exist with local merchant countermarks in Chinese, Tibetan and other scripts.

TOGO

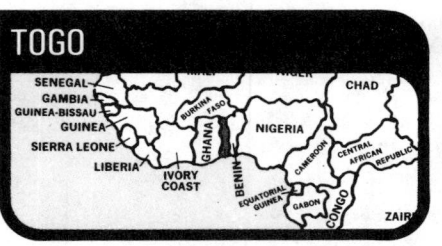

The Republic of Togo (formerly part of German Togoland), situated on the Gulf of Guinea in West Africa between Ghana and Dahomey, has an area of 21,622 sq. mi. (56,790 sq. km.) and a population of *3.4 million. Capital: Lome. Agriculture and herding, the production of dye-woods, and the mining of phosphates and iron ore are the chief industries. Copra, phosphates and coffee are exported.

Although Brazilians were the first traders to settle in Togo, Germany achieved possession, in 1884, by inducing coastal chiefs to place their territories under German protection. The German protectorate was extended international recognition at the Berlin conference of 1885 and its ultimate boundaries delimited by treaties with France in 1897 and with Britain in 1904. Togoland was occupied by Anglo-French forces in 1914, subsequently becoming a League of Nations mandate and a U.N. trusteeship divided, for administrative purpose, between Great Britain and France. The British portion voted in 1957 for incorporation with Ghana. The French portion became the independent Republic of Togo on April 27, 1960.

RULERS

German, 1884-1914
Anglo - French, 1914-1957
French, 1957-1960

MINT MARKS

(a) - Paris, privy marks only

MONETARY SYSTEM

100 Centimes = 1 Franc

50 CENTIMES

ALUMINUM-BRONZE

KM#	Date	Mintage	Fine	VF	XF	Unc
1	1924(a)	3.691	2.00	6.00	18.00	80.00
	1925(a)	2.064	2.50	7.00	20.00	90.00
	1926(a)	.445	7.00	20.00	75.00	250.00

FRANC

ALUMINUM-BRONZE

2	1924(a)	3.472	3.00	6.00	40.00	125.00
	1925(a)	2.768	3.50	7.00	45.00	140.00

ALUMINUM

4	1948(a)	5.000	2.00	6.00	20.00	50.00

2 FRANCS

ALUMINUM-BRONZE

3	1924(a)	.750	5.00	15.00	60.00	250.00
	1925(a)	.580	6.00	18.00	80.00	300.00

ALUMINUM
Similar to 1 Franc, KM#4.

5	1948(a)	5.000	3.00	8.00	25.00	55.00

5 FRANCS

ALUMINUM-BRONZE

6	1956(a)	10.000	1.50	3.00	6.00	12.50

TONGA

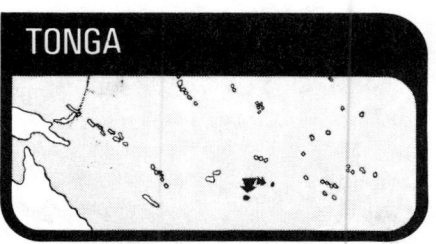

The Kingdom of Tonga (or Friendly Islands), a member of the British Commonwealth, is an archipelago situated in the southern Pacific Ocean south of Western Samoa and east of Fiji comprising 150 islands. Tonga has an area of 270 sq. mi. (748 sq. km.) and a population of *100,000. Capital: Nuku'alofa. Primarily agricultural, the kingdom exports bananas and copra.

Dutch navigators Willem Schouten and Jacob Lemaire were the first Europeans to visit Tonga in 1616. They were followed by the noted Dutch explorer Abel Tasman who visited the Tongatapu group in 1643. No further European contact was made until 1773 when British navigator Capt. James Cook arrived and, impressed by the peaceful deportment of the natives, named the islands the Friendly Islands. Within a few years of Cook's visit, Tonga was embroiled in a civil war that lasted until the great chief Taufa'ahau, who reigned as Siasoi Tupou I (1845-93), was converted to Christianity and brought unity and peace to the islands. Tonga became a self-governing protectorate of Great Britain in 1900 and a fully independent state on June 4, 1970. The monarchy is a member of the Commonwealth of Nations. King Taufa'ahau is Head of State and Government.

RULERS

Queen Salote, 1918-1965
King Taufa'ahau IV, 1967-

MONETARY SYSTEM

100 Seniti = 1 Pa'anga
100 Pa'anga = 1 Hau

SENITI

BRONZE
Giant Tortoise

KM#	Date	Mintage	VF	XF	Unc
4	1967	.500	.10	.15	1.00
	1967	—	—	Proof	2.00

27	1968	.500	.10	.15	1.00
	1968	—	—	Proof	2.00

BRASS

27a	1974	.500	.10	.15	1.00

BRONZE
F.A.O. Issue

42	1975	1.000	—	.10	.50
	1979	1.000	—	.10	.50

World Food Day

66	1981	1.544	—	.10	.50
	1990	—	—	.10	.50
	1991	—	—	.10	.50
	1994	.500	—	.10	.50
	1996	—	—	.10	.50

2 SENITI

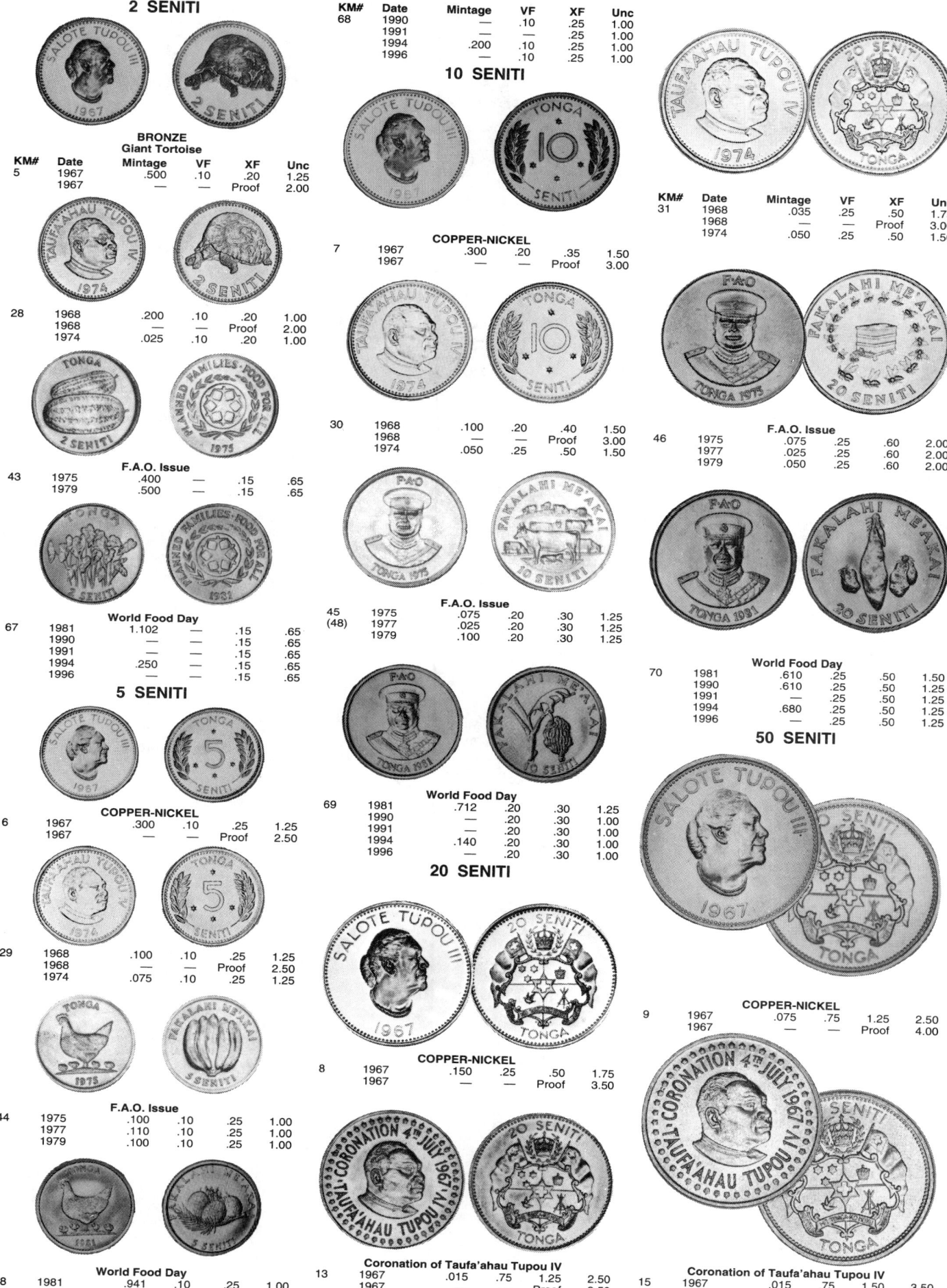

BRONZE
Giant Tortoise

KM#	Date	Mintage	VF	XF	Unc
5	1967	.500	.10	.20	1.25
	1967	—	—	Proof	2.00
28	1968	.200	.10	.20	1.00
	1968	—	—	Proof	2.00
	1974	.025	.10	.20	1.00

F.A.O. Issue

43	1975	.400	—	.15	.65
	1979	.500	—	.15	.65

World Food Day

67	1981	1.102	—	.15	.65
	1990	—	—	.15	.65
	1991	—	—	.15	.65
	1994	.250	—	.15	.65
	1996	—	—	.15	.65

5 SENITI

COPPER-NICKEL

6	1967	.300	.10	.25	1.25
	1967	—	—	Proof	2.50
29	1968	.100	.10	.25	1.25
	1968	—	—	Proof	2.50
	1974	.075	.10	.25	1.25

F.A.O. Issue

44	1975	.100	.10	.25	1.00
	1977	.110	.10	.25	1.00
	1979	.100	.10	.25	1.00

World Food Day

68	1981	.941	.10	.25	1.00

KM#	Date	Mintage	VF	XF	Unc
68	1990	—	.10	.25	1.00
	1991	—	—	.25	1.00
	1994	.200	.10	.25	1.00
	1996	—	—	.25	1.00

10 SENITI

COPPER-NICKEL

7	1967	.300	.20	.35	1.50
	1967	—	—	Proof	3.00
30	1968	.100	.20	.40	1.50
	1968	—	—	Proof	3.00
	1974	.050	.25	.50	1.50

F.A.O. Issue

45	1975	.075	.20	.30	1.25
(48)	1977	.025	.20	.30	1.25
	1979	.100	.20	.30	1.25

World Food Day

69	1981	.712	.20	.30	1.25
	1990	—	.20	.30	1.00
	1991	—	.20	.30	1.00
	1994	.140	.20	.30	1.00
	1996	—	.20	.30	1.00

20 SENITI

COPPER-NICKEL

8	1967	.150	.25	.50	1.75
	1967	—	—	Proof	3.50

Coronation of Taufa'ahau Tupou IV

13	1967	.015	.75	1.25	2.50
	1967	—	—	Proof	3.50

KM#	Date	Mintage	VF	XF	Unc
31	1968	.035	.25	.50	1.75
	1968	—	—	Proof	3.00
	1974	.050	.25	.50	1.50

F.A.O. Issue

46	1975	.075	.25	.60	2.00
	1977	.025	.25	.60	2.00
	1979	.050	.25	.60	2.00

World Food Day

70	1981	.610	.25	.50	1.50
	1990	.610	.25	.50	1.25
	1991	—	.25	.50	1.25
	1994	.680	.25	.50	1.25
	1996	—	.25	.50	1.25

50 SENITI

COPPER-NICKEL

9	1967	.075	.75	1.25	2.50
	1967	—	—	Proof	4.00

Coronation of Taufa'ahau Tupou IV

15	1967	.015	.75	1.50	3.50
	1967	—	—	Proof	4.50

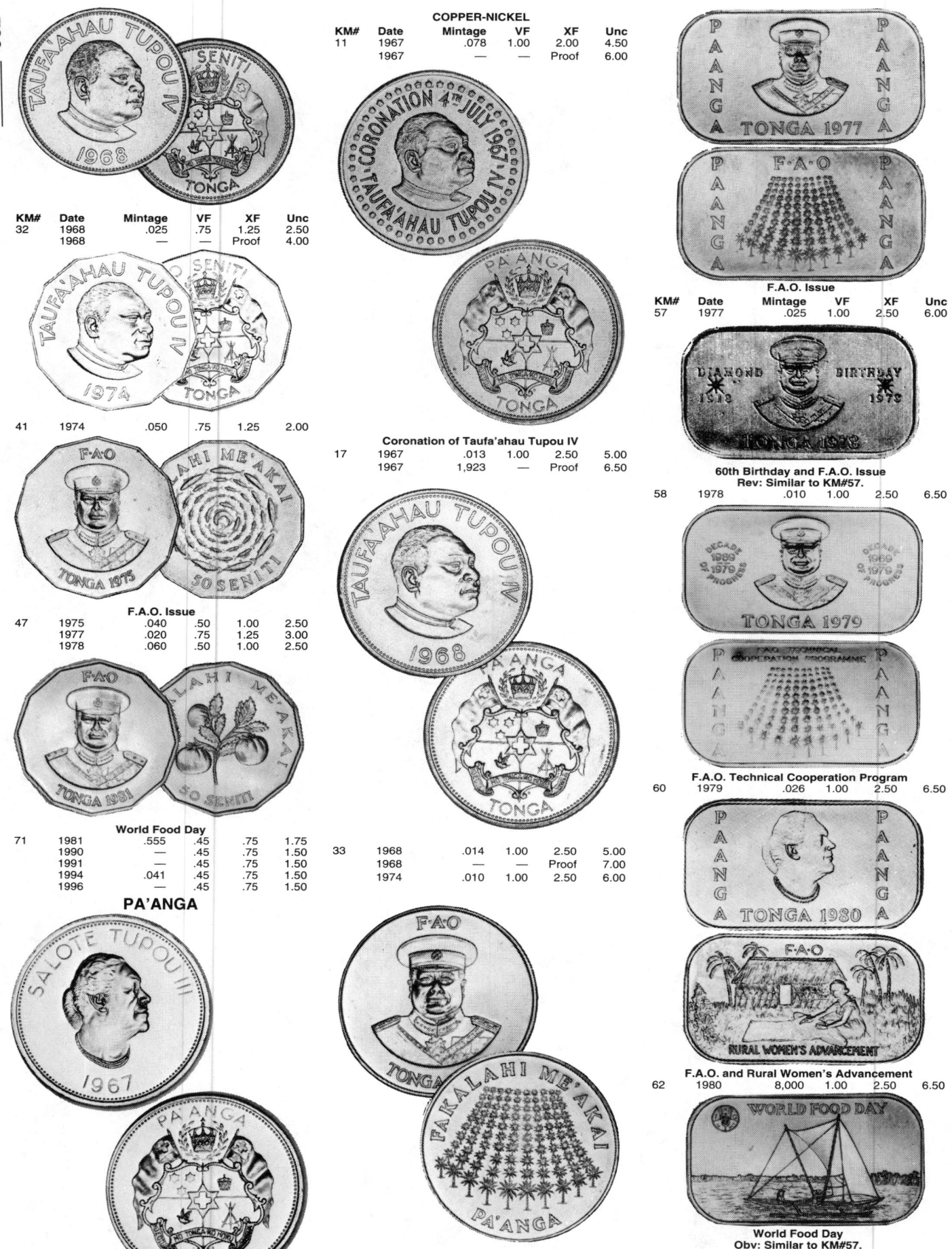

KM#	Date	Mintage	VF	XF	Unc
32	1968	.025	.75	1.25	2.50
	1968	—	—	Proof	4.00

| 41 | 1974 | .050 | .75 | 1.25 | 2.00 |

F.A.O. Issue

47	1975	.040	.50	1.00	2.50
	1977	.020	.75	1.25	3.00
	1978	.060	.50	1.00	2.50

World Food Day

71	1981	.555	.45	.75	1.75
	1990	—	.45	.75	1.50
	1991	—	.45	.75	1.50
	1994	.041	.45	.75	1.50
	1996	—	.45	.75	1.50

PA'ANGA

COPPER-NICKEL

KM#	Date	Mintage	VF	XF	Unc
11	1967	.078	1.00	2.00	4.50
	1967	—		Proof	6.00

Coronation of Taufa'ahau Tupou IV

| 17 | 1967 | .013 | 1.00 | 2.50 | 5.00 |
| | 1967 | 1,923 | — | Proof | 6.50 |

33	1968	.014	1.00	2.50	5.00
	1968	—	—	Proof	7.00
	1974	.010	1.00	2.50	6.00

F.A.O. Issue

| 48 | 1975 | .013 | 1.00 | 2.50 | 5.00 |

F.A.O. Issue

KM#	Date	Mintage	VF	XF	Unc
57	1977	.025	1.00	2.50	6.00

60th Birthday and F.A.O. Issue
Rev: Similar to KM#57.

| 58 | 1978 | .010 | 1.00 | 2.50 | 6.50 |

F.A.O. Technical Cooperation Program

| 60 | 1979 | .026 | 1.00 | 2.50 | 6.50 |

F.A.O. and Rural Women's Advancement

| 62 | 1980 | 8,000 | 1.00 | 2.50 | 6.50 |

World Food Day
Obv: Similar to KM#57.

| 72 | 1981 | .485 | 1.00 | 2.50 | 6.50 |

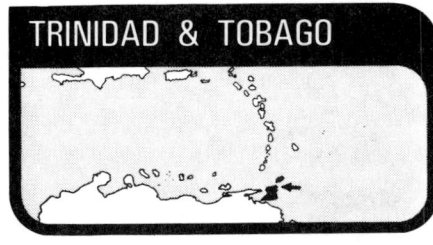

TRINIDAD & TOBAGO

The Republic of Trinidad and Tobago, a member of the British Commonwealth situated 7 miles (11 km.) off the coast of Venezuela, has an area of 1,981 sq. mi. (5,130 sq. km.) and a population of *1.2 million. Capital: Port-of-Spain. The island of Trinidad contains the world's largest natural asphalt bog. Birds of Paradise live on little Tobago, the only place outside of their native New Guinea where they can be found in a wild state. Petroleum and petroleum products are the mainstay of the economy. Petroleum products, crude oil and sugar are exported.

Trinidad and Tobago were discovered by Columbus in 1498. Trinidad remained under Spanish rule from the time of its settlement in 1592 until its capture by the British in 1797. It was ceded to the British in 1802. Tobago was occupied at various times by the French, Dutch and English before being ceded to Britain in 1814. Trinidad and Tobago were merged into a single colony in 1888. The colony was part of the Federation of the West Indies until Aug. 31, 1962, when it became an independent member of the Commonwealth of Nations. A new constitution establishing a republican form of government was adopted on Aug. 1, 1976. Trinidad and Tobago is a member of the Commonwealth of Nations. The President is Chief of State. The Prime Minister is Head of Government.

RULERS
British, until 1976

MINT MARKS
FM - Franklin Mint, U.S.A.*

*NOTE: From 1975-1985 the Franklin Mint produced coinage in up to 3 different qualities. Qualities of issue are designated in ( ) after each date and are defined as follows:

(M) MATTE - Normal circulation strike or a dull finish produced by sandblasting special uncirculated (polish finish) or proof quality dies.

(U) SPECIAL UNCIRCULATED - Polished or proof-like in appearance without any frosted features.

(P) PROOF - The highest quality obtainable having mirror-like fields and frosted features.

MONETARY SYSTEM
100 Cents = 1 Dollar

CENT

BRONZE

KM#	Date	Mintage	VF	XF	Unc
1	1966	24.500	—	—	.15
	1966	8,000	—	Proof	1.00
	1967	4.000	—	—	.15
	1968	5.000	—	—	.15
	1970	5.000	—	—	.15
	1970	2,104	—	Proof	1.50
	1971	10.600	—	—	.15
	1971FM(M)	.286	—	—	.20
	1971FM(P)	.012	—	Proof	.50
	1972	16.500	—	—	.15
	1973	10.000	—	—	.15

10th Anniversary of Independence

9	1972	5.000	—	.10	.15
	1972FM(M)	.125	—	—	.25
	1972FM(P)	.016	—	Proof	.50

17	1973FM(M)	.127	—	—	.50
	1973FM(P)	.020	—	Proof	.75

Balisier Hummingbird

KM#	Date	Mintage	VF	XF	Unc
25	1974FM(M)	.128	—	—	.25
	1974FM(P)	.014	—	Proof	.50
	1975	10.000	—	—	.15
	1975FM(M)	.125	—	—	.15
	1975FM(U)	1,111	—	—	1.25
	1975FM(P)	.024	—	Proof	.50
	1976	15.050	—	—	.15

5 CENTS

BRONZE

2	1966	7.500	—	.10	.25
	1966	8,000	—	Proof	1.25
	1967	3.000	—	.10	.25
	1970	2,104	—	Proof	1.75
	1971	2.400	—	.10	.25
	1971FM(M)	.057	—	—	.15
	1971FM(P)	.012	—	Proof	.75
	1972	2.250	—	.10	.20

10th Anniversary of Independence

10	1972	.015	—	—	.35
	1972FM(M)	.025	—	—	.25
	1972FM(P)	.016	—	Proof	.75

57	1973FM(M)	.027	—	—	.50
	1973FM(P)	.020	—	Proof	.75

Bird of Paradise

26	1974FM(M)	.028	—	—	.50
	1974FM(P)	.014	—	Proof	.75
	1975	1.500	—	.10	.20
	1975FM(M)	.025	—	—	.20
	1975FM(U)	1,111	—	—	1.50
	1975FM(P)	.024	—	Proof	.75
	1976	7.500	—	.10	.20

10 CENTS

COPPER-NICKEL

3	1966	7.800	—	.10	.30
	1966	8,000	—	Proof	1.50
	1967	4.000	—	.10	.30
	1970	2,104	—	Proof	2.00
	1971	—	—	.10	.30
	1971FM(M)	.029	—	—	.35
	1971FM(P)	.012	—	Proof	1.00
	1972	4.000	—	.10	.30

10th Anniversary of Independence

11	1972	.041	—	—	.40

11	1972FM(M)	.013	—	—	.60
	1972FM(P)	.016	—	Proof	1.00

58	1973FM(M)	.014	—	—	1.00
	1973FM(P)	.020	—	Proof	1.00

Flaming Hibiscus

27	1974FM(M)	.016	—	—	1.00
	1974FM(P)	.014	—	Proof	1.00
	1975	4.000	—	.10	.25
	1975FM(M)	.013	—	—	.50
	1975FM(U)	1,111	—	—	1.75
	1975FM(P)	.024	—	Proof	1.00
	1976	14.720	—	.10	.20

25 CENTS

 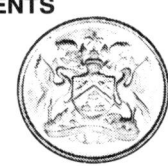

COPPER-NICKEL

4	1966	7.200	.10	.15	.35
	1966	8,000	—	Proof	1.75
	1967	1.800	.10	.15	.50
	1970	2,014	—	Proof	2.25
	1971	1.500	.10	.15	.50
	1971FM(M)	.011	—	—	.65
	1971FM(P)	.012	—	Proof	1.25
	1972	3.000	.10	.15	.35

10th Anniversary of Independence

12	1972	.014	—	—	.60
	1972FM(M)	5,000	—	—	1.50
	1972FM(P)	.016	—	Proof	1.25

59	1973FM(M)	6,575	—	—	2.25
	1973FM(P)	.020	—	Proof	1.25

Chaconia

28	1974FM(M)	8,258	—	—	1.75
	1974FM(P)	.014	—	Proof	1.25
	1975	3.000	.10	.15	.30
	1975FM(M)	5,000	—	—	1.50
	1975FM(U)	1,111	—	—	2.00
	1975FM(P)	.024	—	Proof	1.25
	1976	9.000	.10	.15	.30

50 CENTS

COPPER-NICKEL

5	1966	.975	.25	.50	1.25
	1966	8,000	—	Proof	2.00
	1967	.750	.25	.50	1.25
	1970	2,104	—	Proof	2.50

KM#	Date	Mintage	VF	XF	Unc
5	1971FM(M)	5,714	—	—	2.00
	1971FM(P)	.012	—	Proof	1.50

10th Anniversary of Independence

13	1972	.375	.50	.75	1.50
	1972FM(M)	2,500	—	—	5.00
	1972FM(P)	.016	—	Proof	1.50

Steel Band

22	1973FM(M)	4,075	—	—	2.50
	1973FM(P)	.020	—	Proof	1.50
	1974FM(M)	5,758	—	—	2.00
	1974FM(P)	.014	—	Proof	1.50
	1975FM(M)	2,500	—	—	3.75
	1975FM(U)	1,111	—	—	2.25
	1975FM(P)	.024	—	Proof	1.50
	1976	.750	.50	.75	1.50

DOLLAR

NICKEL
F.A.O. Issue

6	1969	.250	.50	1.00	2.00

7	1970	2,014	—	Proof	5.00

COPPER-NICKEL

7a	1971FM(M)	2,857	—	—	4.00
	1971FM(P)	.012	—	Proof	2.00

10th Anniversary of Independence

14	1972	9,700	—	—	4.00
	1972FM(M)	1,250	—	—	12.50
	1972FM(P)	.016	—	Proof	2.00

Coerico

KM#	Date	Mintage	VF	XF	Unc
23	1973FM(M)	2,825	—	—	3.00
	1973FM(P)	.020	—	Proof	2.00
	1974FM(M)	4,508	—	—	3.00
	1974FM(P)	.014	—	Proof	2.00
	1975FM(M)	1,250	—	—	5.00
	1975FM(U)	1,111	—	—	3.00
	1975FM(P)	.024	—	Proof	2.00

REPUBLIC
CENT

BRONZE

29	1976FM(M)	.150	—	—	.15
	1976FM(U)	582 pcs.	—	—	1.50
	1976FM(P)	.010	—	Proof	.50
	1977	25.000	—	—	.15
	1977FM(M)	.150	—	—	.15
	1977FM(U)	633 pcs.	—	—	1.50
	1977FM(P)	5,337	—	Proof	.50
	1978	12.500	—	—	.15
	1978FM(M)	.150	—	—	.15
	1978FM(U)	472 pcs.	—	—	1.50
	1978FM(P)	4,845	—	Proof	1.00
	1979	30.200	—	—	.15
	1979FM(M)	.150	—	—	.15
	1979FM(U)	518 pcs.	—	—	1.50
	1979FM(P)	3,270	—	Proof	.15
	1980	12.500	—	—	.10
	1980FM(M)	.075	—	—	.15
	1980FM(U)	796 pcs.	—	—	1.50
	1980FM(P)	2,393	—	Proof	1.00
	1981		—	—	.15
	1981FM(M)		—	—	.15
	1981FM(U)		—	—	1.50
	1981FM(P)		—	Proof	1.00
	1982		—	—	.15
	1983		—	—	.15
	1984		—	—	.15
	1985	25.400	—	—	.15
	1986	10.000	—	—	.15
	1987	10.000	—	—	.15
	1988	5.000	—	—	.15
	1989		—	—	.15
	1990		—	—	.15
	1991		—	—	.15
	1993		—	—	.15
	1994		—	—	.15
	1995		—	—	.15
	1997		—	—	.15

20th Anniversary of Independence
Obv: Coat of Arms.

42	1982FM(M)	—	—	—	.15
	1982FM(U)	—	—	—	1.50
	1982FM(P)	—	—	Proof	1.00

51	1983FM(M)	—	—	—	1.50
	1983FM(P)	—	—	Proof	1.00
	1984FM(P)	—	—	Proof	1.00

5 CENTS

BRONZE

KM#	Date	Mintage	VF	XF	Unc
30	1976FM(M)	.030	—	—	.20
	1976FM(U)	582 pcs.	—	—	1.75
	1976FM(P)	.010	—	Proof	.75
	1977	12.000	—	.10	.20
	1977FM(M)	.030	—	—	.20
	1977FM(U)	633 pcs.	—	—	1.75
	1977FM(P)	5,337	—	Proof	.75
	1978	1.500	—	.10	.20
	1978FM(M)	.030	—	—	.20
	1978FM(U)	472 pcs.	—	—	1.75
	1978FM(P)	4,845	—	Proof	1.25
	1979		—	.10	.20
	1979FM(M)	.030	—	—	.20
	1979FM(U)	518 pcs.	—	—	1.75
	1979FM(P)	3,270	—	Proof	1.25
	1980	15.000	—	.10	.20
	1980FM(M)	.015	—	—	.20
	1980FM(U)	796 pcs.	—	—	1.75
	1980FM(P)	2,393	—	Proof	1.25
	1981		—	.10	.20
	1981FM(M)		—	—	.20
	1981FM(U)		—	—	1.75
	1981FM(P)		—	Proof	1.25
	1983		—	.10	.20
	1984	4.095	—	.10	.20
	1988	20.000	—	.10	.20
	1990		—	.10	.20
	1992		—	.10	.20
	1995		—	.10	.20
	1996		—	.10	.20
	1997		—	.10	.20

20th Anniversary of Independence
Obv: Coat of Arms.

43	1982FM(M)	—	—	—	.35
	1982FM(U)	—	—	—	1.75
	1982FM(P)	—	—	Proof	1.25

Obv: Coat of Arms.

52	1983FM(M)	—	—	—	2.00
	1983FM(P)	—	—	Proof	1.25
	1984FM(P)	—	—	Proof	1.25

10 CENTS

COPPER-NICKEL

31	1976FM(M)	.015	—	—	.50
	1976FM(U)	582 pcs.	—	—	2.00
	1976FM(P)	.010	—	Proof	1.00
	1977	17.280	—	.10	.20
	1977FM(M)	.015	—	—	.50
	1977FM(U)	633 pcs.	—	—	2.00
	1977FM(P)	5,337	—	Proof	1.00
	1978	10.000	—	.10	.20
	1978FM(M)	.015	—	—	.50
	1978FM(U)	472 pcs.	—	—	2.00
	1978FM(P)	4,845	—	Proof	1.50
	1979	1.970	—	.10	.30
	1979FM(M)	.015	—	—	.50
	1979FM(U)	518 pcs.	—	—	2.00
	1979FM(P)	3,270	—	Proof	1.50
	1980	20.000	—	.10	.30
	1980FM(M)	7,500	—	—	.50
	1980FM(U)	796 pcs.	—	—	2.00
	1980FM(P)	2,393	—	Proof	1.50
	1981		—	.10	.30
	1981FM(M)		—	—	.50
	1981FM(U)		—	—	2.00
	1981FM(P)		—	Proof	1.50
	1990		—	.10	.30

20th Anniversary of Independence
Obv: Coat of Arms.

KM#	Date	Mintage	VF	XF	Unc
44	1982FM(M)	—	—	—	.50
	1982FM(U)	—	—	—	2.00
	1982FM(P)	—	—	Proof	1.50

Obv: Coat of Arms.

53	1983FM(M)	—	—	—	2.00
	1983FM(P)	—	—	Proof	1.50
	1984FM(P)	—	—	Proof	1.50

25 CENTS

COPPER-NICKEL

32	1976FM(M)	6,000	—	—	1.00
	1976FM(U)	582 pcs.	—	—	2.25
	1976FM(P)	.010	—	Proof	1.25
	1977	9.000	.10	.15	.30
	1977FM(M)	6,000	—	—	1.00
	1977FM(U)	633 pcs.	—	—	2.25
	1977FM(P)	5,337	—	Proof	1.25
	1978	5.470	.10	.15	.30
	1978FM(M)	6,000	—	—	1.00
	1978FM(U)	472 pcs.	—	—	2.25
	1978FM(P)	4,845	—	Proof	1.75
	1979	—	.10	.15	.40
	1979FM(M)	6,000	—	—	1.00
	1979FM(U)	518 pcs.	—	—	2.25
	1979FM(P)	3,270	—	Proof	1.75
	1980	15.000	.10	.15	.40
	1980FM(M)	3,000	—	—	1.00
	1980FM(U)	796 pcs.	—	—	2.25
	1980FM(P)	2,393	—	Proof	1.75
	1981	—	.10	.15	.40
	1981FM(M)	—	—	—	1.00
	1981FM(U)	—	—	—	2.25
	1981FM(P)	—	—	Proof	1.75
	1983	—	.10	.15	.40
	1983FM(M)	—	—	—	2.00
	1983FM(P)	—	—	Proof	1.75
	1984	—	.10	.15	.40
	1984	—	—	Proof	1.75
	1993	—	—	.15	.40
	1997	—	—	.15	.40

20th Anniversary of Independence
Obv: Coat of Arms.

45	1982FM(M)	—	—	—	1.00
	1982FM(U)	—	—	—	2.25
	1982FM(P)	—	—	Proof	1.75

50 CENTS

COPPER-NICKEL

33	1976FM(M)	3,000	—	—	3.25
	1976FM(U)	582 pcs.	—	—	2.50
	1976FM(P)	.010	—	Proof	1.50
	1977	1.500	.25	.50	1.00
	1977FM(M)	3,000	—	—	3.00
	1977FM(U)	633 pcs.	—	—	2.50
	1977FM(P)	5,337	—	Proof	1.50
	1978	.563	.50	.75	1.50
	1978FM(M)	3,000	—	—	3.00
	1978FM(U)	472 pcs.	—	—	2.50
	1978FM(P)	4,845	—	Proof	2.00
	1979	.750	.50	.75	1.50
	1979FM(M)	3,000	—	—	3.25

KM#	Date	Mintage	VF	XF	Unc
33	1979FM(U)	518 pcs.	—	—	2.50
	1979FM(P)	3,270	—	Proof	2.00
	1980	3.750	.25	.50	1.00
	1980FM(M)	1,500	—	—	3.00
	1980FM(U)	796 pcs.	—	—	2.50
	1980FM(P)	2,393	—	Proof	2.00
	1981FM(M)	—	—	—	3.00
	1981FM(U)	—	—	—	2.50
	1981FM(P)	—	—	Proof	2.00

20th Anniversary of Independence
Obv: Coat of Arms.

46	1982FM(M)	—	—	—	3.00
	1982FM(U)	—	—	—	2.50
	1982FM(P)	—	—	Proof	2.00

Obv: Coat of Arms.

54	1983FM(M)	—	—	—	4.00
	1983FM(P)	—	—	Proof	2.00
	1984FM(P)	—	—	Proof	2.00

DOLLAR

COPPER-NICKEL

34	1976FM(M)	1,500	—	—	5.00
	1976FM(U)	582 pcs.	—	—	3.00
	1976FM(P)	.010	—	Proof	2.00
	1977FM(M)	1,500	—	—	5.00
	1977FM(U)	633 pcs.	—	—	3.00
	1977FM(P)	5,337	—	Proof	2.00
	1978FM(M)	1,500	—	—	3.75
	1978FM(U)	472 pcs.	—	—	3.00
	1978FM(P)	4,845	—	Proof	2.50
	1979FM(M)	1,500	—	—	3.75
	1979FM(U)	518 pcs.	—	—	3.00
	1979FM(P)	3,270	—	Proof	2.50
	1980FM(M)	750 pcs.	—	—	5.00
	1980FM(U)	796 pcs.	—	—	3.00
	1980FM(P)	2,393	—	Proof	2.50
	1981FM(M)	—	—	—	5.00
	1981FM(U)	—	—	—	3.00
	1981FM(P)	—	—	Proof	2.50
	1983FM(M)	—	—	—	5.00
	1983FM(P)	—	—	Proof	2.50
	1984FM(P)	—	—	Proof	2.50

F.A.O. Issue

38	1979	—	.50	1.25	2.75

20th Anniversary of Independence
Obv: Coat of Arms.

KM#	Date	Mintage	VF	XF	Unc
47	1982FM(M)	—	—	—	7.00
	1982FM(U)	—	—	—	5.00
	1982FM(P)	—	—	Proof	4.50

50th Anniversary - F.A.O.

61	1995	—	—	—	1.75

TUNISIA

686

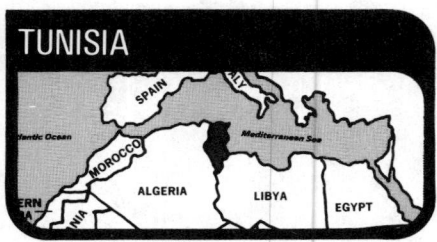

The Republic of Tunisia, located on the northern coast of Africa between Algeria and Libya, has an area of 63,170 sq. mi. (163,610 sq. km.) and a population of *7.9 million. Capital: Tunis. Agriculture is the backbone of the economy. Crude oil, phosphates, olive oil, and wine are exported.

Tunisia, settled by the Phoenicians in the 12th century B.C., was the center of the seafaring Carthaginian empire. After the total destruction of Carthage, Tunisia became part of Rome's African province. It remained a part of the Roman Empire (except for the 439-533 interval of Vandal conquest) until taken by the Arabs, 648, who administered it until the Turkish invasion of 1570. Under Turkish control, the public revenue was heavily dependent upon the piracy of Mediterranean shipping, an endeavor that wasn't abandoned until 1819 when a coalition of powers threatened appropriate reprisal. Deprived of its major source of income, Tunisia underwent a financial regression that ended in bankruptcy, enabling France to establish a protectorate over the country in 1881. National agitation and guerrilla fighting forced France to grant Tunisia internal autonomy in 1955 and to recognize Tunisian independence on March 20, 1956. Tunisia abolished the monarchy and established a republic on July 25, 1957.

TITLES

المملكة التونسية

al-Mamlaka(t) al-Tunisiya(t)

الجمهورية التونسية

al-Jumhuriya(t) al-Tunisiya(t)

MINT MARKS

A - Paris, AH1308/1891-AH1348/1928
(a) - Paris, privy marks,
AH1349/1929-AH1376/1957
FM - Franklin Mint, Franklin Center, PA
- Numismatica Italiana, Arezzo, Italy

TUNIS

Tunis, the capital and major seaport of Tunisia, existed in the Carthaginian era, but its importance dates only from the Moslem conquest, following which it became a major center of Arab power and prosperity. Spain seized it in 1535, lost it in 1564, retook it in 1573 and ceded it to the Turks in 1574. Thereafter the history of Tunis merged with that of Tunisia.

LOCAL RULERS

Ali Bey,
AH1299-1320/1882-1902AD
Muhammad Al-Hadi Bey,
AH1320-1324/1902-1906AD
Muhammad Al-Nasir Bey,
AH1324-1340/1906-1922AD
Muhammad Al-Habib Bey,
AH1340-1348/1922-1929AD
Ahmad Pasha Bey,
AH1348-1361/1929-1942AD
Muhammad Al-Munsif Bey,
AH1361-1362/1942-1943AD
Muhammad Al-Amin Bey,
AH1362-1376/1943-1957AD

NOTE: All coins struck until AH1298/1881AD bear the name of the Ottoman Sultan; the name of the Bey of Tunis was added in AH1272/1855AD. After AH1298, when the French established their protectorate, only the Bey's name appears on the coin until AH1376/1956AD.

TUNISIA

FRENCH PROTECTORATE

ALI BEY

AH1299-1320/AD1882-1902

MONETARY SYSTEM

100 Centimes = 1 Franc

NOTE: The following coins all bear French inscriptions on one side, Arabic on the other, and usually have both AH and AD dates. They are struck in the name of the Tunisian Bey.

5 CENTIMES

BRONZE
Obv. leg: *Muhammad al-Hadi.*

KM#	Date	Year	Mintage	VF	XF	Unc
228	AH1321	1903A	.500	6.00	10.00	25.00
	1322	1904A	1.000	5.50	8.00	20.00

Obv. leg: *Muhammad al-Nasir.*

235	AH1325	1907A	1.000	2.00	4.00	17.00
	1326	1908A	1.000	2.00	4.00	17.00
	1330	1912A	1.000	2.00	4.00	17.00
	1332	1914A	1.000	2.00	4.00	17.00
	1334	1916A	2.000	1.50	3.00	12.00
	1336	1917A	2.021	1.50	3.00	12.00

NICKEL BRONZE
Obv. leg: *Mohammed al-Nasir.*

242	AH1337	1918(a)	1.549	4.00	10.00	25.00
	1337	1919(a)	4.451	2.00	7.00	15.00
	1338/6					
		1920(a)	2.206	4.00	10.00	25.00
	1338/7					
		1920(a)	Inc. Ab.	4.00	10.00	25.00
	1338	1920(a)	Inc. Ab.	3.00	8.00	20.00
	1339	1920(a)	Inc. Ab.	2.00	7.00	15.00

Reduced Size

245	AH1339	1920(a)	1.794	20.00	40.00	75.00

Obv. leg: *Ahmad.*

258	AH1350	1931(a)	2.000	4.00	10.00	25.00
	1352	1933(a)	1.000	5.00	12.00	30.00
	1357	1938(a)	1.200	2.00	4.00	8.00

10 CENTIMES

BRONZE
Obv. leg: *Muhammad al-Hadi.*

229	AH1321	1903A	.250	10.00	20.00	30.00
	1322	1904A	.500	10.00	15.00	20.00

Obv. leg: *Muhammad al-Nasir.*

KM#	Date	Year	Mintage	VF	XF	Unc
236	AH1325	1907A	.500	3.00	6.00	20.00
	1326	1908A	.500	3.00	6.00	20.00
	1329	1911A	.500	3.00	6.00	20.00
	1330	1912A	.500	3.00	6.00	20.00
	1332	1914A	.500	3.00	6.00	20.00
	1334	1916A	1.000	3.00	6.00	20.00
	1336	1917A	1.050	3.00	6.00	20.00

NICKEL-BRONZE
Obv. leg: *Muhammed al-Nasir.*

243	AH1337	1918(a)	1.288	3.00	8.00	25.00
	1337	1919(a)	2.712	2.00	7.00	20.00
	1338	1920(a)	3.000	2.00	7.00	20.00

Obv. leg: *Muhammad al-Habib.*

254	AH1345	1926(a)	1.000	20.00	50.00	100.00

Obv. leg: *Ahmad.*

259	AH1350	1931(a)	.750	6.00	15.00	35.00
	1352	1933(a)	1.000	6.00	15.00	35.00
	1357	1938(a)	1.200	3.00	8.00	20.00

ZINC
Obv. leg: *Ahmad.*

267	AH1360	1941(a)	5.000	2.50	6.00	25.00
	1361	1942(a)	10.000	1.50	4.00	20.00

Obv. leg: *Muhammad al Amin.*

271	AH1364	1945(a)	10.000	20.00	40.00	70.00

NOTE: Most were probably melted.

20 CENTIMES

ZINC
Obv. leg: *Ahmad.*

268	AH1361	1942(a)	5.000	10.00	20.00	35.00

Obv. leg: *Muhammad al-Amin.*

272	AH1364	1945(a)	5.205	30.00	60.00	90.00

NOTE: A large quantity was remelted.

25 CENTIMES

NICKEL-BRONZE
Obv. leg: *Muhammad al-Nasir.*

KM#	Date	Year	Mintage	VF	XF	Unc
244	AH1337	1918(a)	—	4.00	12.00	35.00
	1337	1919(a)	2.000	3.00	10.00	25.00
	1338	1920(a)	2.000	3.00	10.00	25.00

Obv. leg: *Ahmad.*

KM#	Date	Year	Mintage	VF	XF	Unc
260	AH1350	1931(a)	.300	8.00	15.00	35.00
	1352	1933(a)	.400	8.00	15.00	35.00
	1357	1938(a)	.480	4.00	10.00	25.00

50 CENTIMES

2.5000 g, .835 SILVER, .0671 oz ASW
Obv. leg: *Ali.*

KM#	Date	Year	Mintage	VF	XF	Unc
223	AH1319	1901A	1,000	—	100.00	175.00
	1320	1902A	1,000	—	100.00	175.00

NOTE: Earlier dates (AH1308-1318) exist for this type.

Obv. leg: *Muhammad al-Hadi.*

KM#	Date	Year	Mintage	VF	XF	Unc
230	AH1321	1903A	1,003	—	150.00	250.00
	1322	1904A	1,003	—	150.00	250.00
	1323	1905A	1,003	—	150.00	250.00
	1324	1906A	1,003	—	150.00	250.00

Obv. leg: *Muhammad al-Nasir.*

KM#	Date	Year	Mintage	VF	XF	Unc
237	AH1325	1907A	.201	10.00	20.00	40.00
	1326	1908A	2,006	—	75.00	135.00
	1327	1909A	1,003	—	100.00	175.00
	1328	1910A	1,003	—	100.00	175.00
	1329	1911A	1,003	—	100.00	175.00
	1330	1912A	.201	10.00	20.00	40.00
	1331	1913A	1,003	—	100.00	175.00
	1332	1914A	.201	10.00	20.00	40.00
	1334	1915A	.707	8.00	15.00	30.00
	1334	1916A	3.614	7.00	12.00	25.00
	1335	1916A	Inc. Ab.	7.00	12.00	25.00
	1335	1917A	2.139	7.00	12.00	25.00
	1336	1917A	Inc. Ab.	7.00	12.00	25.00
	1337	1918A	1,003	—	100.00	175.00
	1338	1919A	1,003	—	100.00	175.00
	1339	1920A	1,003	—	100.00	175.00
	1340	1921A	1,003	—	100.00	175.00

ALUMINUM-BRONZE

KM#	Date	Year	Mintage	VF	XF	Unc
246	AH1340	1921(a)	4.000	1.00	7.00	20.00
	1345	1926(a)	1.000	3.00	10.00	25.00
	1352	1933(a)	.500	6.00	17.00	50.00
	1360	1941(a)	4.646	.35	1.50	10.00
	1364	1945(a)	11.180	.25	1.00	10.00

2.5000 g, .835 SILVER, .0671 oz ASW
Obv. leg: *Muhammad al-Habib.*

KM#	Date	Year	Mintage	VF	XF	Unc
249	AH1341	1922A	1,003	—	100.00	200.00
	1342	1923A	2,009	—	100.00	200.00
	1343	1924A	1,003	—	100.00	200.00
249	1344	1925A	1,003	—	100.00	200.00
	1345	1926A	1,003	—	100.00	200.00
	1346	1927A	1,003	—	100.00	200.00
	1347	1928A	1,003	—	100.00	200.00

FRANC

5.0000 g, .835 SILVER, .1342 oz ASW
Obv. leg: *Ali.*

KM#	Date	Year	Mintage	VF	XF	Unc
224	AH1319	1901A	700 pcs.	—	135.00	225.00
	1320	1902A	703 pcs.	—	135.00	225.00

NOTE: Earlier dates (AH1308-1318) exist for this type.

Obv. leg: *Muhammad al-Hadi.*

KM#	Date	Year	Mintage	VF	XF	Unc
231	AH1321	1903A	703 pcs.	—	135.00	225.00
	1322	1904A	.500	50.00	80.00	150.00
	1323	1905A	703 pcs.	—	135.00	225.00
	1324	1906A	703 pcs.	—	135.00	225.00

Obv. leg: *Muhammad al-Nasir.*

KM#	Date	Year	Mintage	VF	XF	Unc
238	AH1325	1907A	.301	10.00	20.00	35.00
	1326	1908A	.401	10.00	15.00	35.00
	1327	1909A	703 pcs.	—	135.00	225.00
	1328	1910A	703 pcs.	—	135.00	225.00
	1329	1911A	1.051	7.00	12.00	30.00
	1330	1912A	.501	8.00	15.00	30.00
	1331	1913A	703 pcs.	—	135.00	225.00
	1332	1914A	.201	8.00	15.00	25.00
	1333	1914A	I.A.	8.00	15.00	25.00
	1334	1915A	1.060	7.00	12.00	20.00
	1334	1916A	3.270	7.00	12.00	20.00
	1335	1916A	Inc. Ab.	7.00	12.00	20.00
	1335	1917A	1.628	7.00	12.00	20.00
	1336	1918A	.804	7.00	12.00	18.00
	1337	1918A	Inc. Ab.	7.00	12.00	18.00
	1338	1919A	703 pcs.	—	135.00	225.00
	1339	1920A	703 pcs.	—	135.00	225.00
	1340	1921A	703 pcs.	—	135.00	225.00

ALUMINUM-BRONZE

KM#	Date	Year	Mintage	VF	XF	Unc
247	AH1340	1921(a)	5.000	1.00	7.00	20.00
	1344	1926(a)	1.000	2.00	15.00	35.00
	1345	1926(a)	1.000	4.00	17.00	40.00
	1360	1941(a)	6.612	.50	2.00	10.00
	1364	1945(a)	10.699	.35	1.75	10.00

5.0000 g, .835 SILVER, .1342 oz ASW
Obv. leg: *Muhammad al-Habib.*

KM#	Date	Year	Mintage	VF	XF	Unc
250	AH1341	1922A	703 pcs.	—	135.00	275.00
	1342	1923A	1,409	—	100.00	250.00
	1343	1924A	703 pcs.	—	135.00	275.00
	1344	1925A	703 pcs.	—	135.00	275.00
	1345	1926A	703 pcs.	—	135.00	275.00
	1346	1927A	703 pcs.	—	135.00	275.00

5.5000 g, .835 SILVER, .1476 oz ASW

KM#	Date	Year	Mintage	VF	XF	Unc
250a	AH1347	1928A	703 pcs.	—	135.00	275.00

2 FRANCS

10.0000 g, .835 SILVER, .2685 oz ASW
Obv. leg: *Ali.*

KM#	Date	Year	Mintage	VF	XF	Unc
225	AH1319	1901A	300 pcs.	—	150.00	250.00
	1320	1902A	300 pcs.	—	150.00	250.00

NOTE: Earlier dates (AH1308-1318) exist for this type.

Obv. leg: *Muhammad al-Hadi.*

KM#	Date	Year	Mintage	VF	XF	Unc
232	AH1321	1903A	303 pcs.	—	150.00	250.00
	1322	1904A	.150	70.00	110.00	200.00
	1323	1905A	303 pcs.	—	150.00	250.00
	1324	1906A	303 pcs.	—	150.00	250.00

Obv. leg: *Muhammad al-Nasir.*

KM#	Date	Year	Mintage	VF	XF	Unc
239	AH1325	1907A	306 pcs.	—	150.00	250.00
	1326	1908A	.101	20.00	40.00	85.00
	1327	1909A	303 pcs.	—	150.00	250.00
	1328	1910A	303 pcs.	—	150.00	250.00
	1329	1911A	.475	15.00	25.00	40.00
	1330	1912A	.200	15.00	25.00	45.00
	1331	1913A	303 pcs.	—	150.00	250.00
	1332	1914A	.100	15.00	25.00	35.00
	1333	1914A	I.A.	15.00	25.00	35.00
	1334	1915A	.408	15.00	25.00	35.00
	1334	1916A	1.000	15.00	25.00	35.00
	1335	1916A	Inc. Ab.	15.00	25.00	35.00
	1336	1917A	303 pcs.	—	150.00	250.00
	1337	1918A	303 pcs.	—	150.00	250.00
	1338	1919A	303 pcs.	—	150.00	250.00
	1339	1920A	303 pcs.	—	150.00	250.00
	1340	1921A	303 pcs.	—	150.00	250.00

ALUMINUM-BRONZE

KM#	Date	Year	Mintage	VF	XF	Unc
248	AH1340	1921(a)	1.500	3.00	15.00	35.00
	1343	1924(a)	.500	8.00	20.00	50.00
	1345	1926(a)	.500	8.00	20.00	50.00
	1360	1941(a)	1.976	1.50	6.00	15.00
	1364	1945(a)	6.464	1.00	5.00	15.00

10.0000 g, .835 SILVER, .2685 oz ASW
Obv. leg: *Muhammad al-Habib.*

KM#	Date	Year	Mintage	VF	XF	Unc
251	AH1341	1922A	303 pcs.	—	150.00	325.00
	1342	1923A	690 pcs.	—	135.00	275.00
	1343	1924A	303 pcs.	—	150.00	325.00
	1344	1925A	303 pcs.	—	150.00	325.00
	1345	1926A	303 pcs.	—	150.00	325.00
	1346	1927A	303 pcs.	—	150.00	325.00
	1347	1928A	303 pcs.	—	150.00	325.00

5 FRANCS

5.0000 g, .680 SILVER, .1093 oz ASW
Obv. leg: *Ahmad.*

Y#	Date	Mintage	VF	XF	Unc
261	AH1353(a)	2.000	10.00	18.00	25.00
	1355(a)	2.000	10.00	18.00	25.00

KM#	Date	Year	Mintage	VF	XF	Unc
264	AH1358(a)	1939	1.600	10.00	18.00	25.00

ALUMINUM-BRONZE
Obv. leg: *Muhammad al-Amin.*

KM#	Date	Year	Mintage	VF	XF	Unc
273	AH1365(a)	1946	10.000	1.50	5.00	10.00

COPPER-NICKEL

KM#	Date	Year	Mintage	VF	XF	Unc
277	AH1373(a)	1954	18.000	.25	1.25	3.50
	1376(a)	1957	4.000	.50	1.25	3.00

10 FRANCS

3.2258 g, .900 GOLD, .0933 oz AGW
Obv. leg: *Ali.*

KM#	Date	Year	Mintage	VF	XF	Unc
226	AH1319	1901A	80 pcs.	—	450.00	850.00
	1320	1902A	83 pcs.	—	450.00	850.00

NOTE: Earlier dates (AH1308-1318) exist for this type.

Obv. leg: *Muhammad al-Hadi.*

233	AH1321	1903A	83 pcs.	—	450.00	900.00
	1322	1904A	83 pcs.	—	450.00	900.00
	1323	1905A	83 pcs.	—	450.00	900.00
	1324	1906A	83 pcs.	—	450.00	900.00

Obv. leg: *Muhammad al-Nasir.*

240	AH1325	1907A	36 pcs.	—	500.00	900.00
	1326	1908A	166 pcs.	—	300.00	500.00
	1327	1909A	83 pcs.	—	450.00	850.00
	1328	1910A	83 pcs.	—	450.00	850.00
	1329	1911A	83 pcs.	—	450.00	850.00
	1330	1912A	83 pcs.	—	450.00	850.00
	1331	1913A	83 pcs.	—	450.00	850.00
	1332	1914A	83 pcs.	—	450.00	850.00
	1334	1915A	83 pcs.	—	450.00	850.00
	1334	1916A	83 pcs.	—	450.00	850.00
	1336	1917A	83 pcs.	—	450.00	850.00
	1337	1918A	83 pcs.	—	450.00	850.00
	1338	1919A	83 pcs.	—	450.00	850.00
	1339	1920A	83 pcs.	—	450.00	850.00
	1340	1921A	83 pcs.	—	450.00	850.00

Obv. leg: *Muhammad al-Habib Bey.*

252	AH1341	1922A	83 pcs.	—	450.00	850.00
	1342	1923A	169 pcs.	—	300.00	500.00
	1343	1924A	83 pcs.	—	450.00	850.00
	1344	1925A	83 pcs.	—	450.00	850.00
	1345	1926A	83 pcs.	—	450.00	850.00
	1346	1927A	83 pcs.	—	450.00	850.00
	1347	1928A	83 pcs.	—	450.00	850.00

10.0000 g, .680 SILVER, .2186 oz ASW
Obv. leg: *Ahmad.*

255	AH1349	1930(a)	.060	35.00	60.00	110.00
	1350	1931(a)	1,103	150.00	250.00	350.00
	1351	1932(a)	.060	50.00	100.00	200.00
	1352	1933(a)	1,103	150.00	250.00	350.00
	1353	1934(a)	.030	30.00	50.00	90.00

KM#	Date	Mintage	VF	XF	Unc
262	AH1353(a)	1.501	4.50	9.00	15.00
	1354(a)	1,103	—	225.00	350.00
	1355(a)	2,006	—	225.00	350.00
	1356(a)	1,103	—	225.00	350.00
	1357	—	—	400.00	600.00
	1358	—	—	400.00	600.00

KM#	Date	Year	Mintage	VF	XF	Unc
265	AH1358	1939(a)	.501	6.00	15.00	35.00
	1359	1940(a)	—	—	225.00	350.00
	1360	1941(a)	1,103	—	225.00	350.00
	1361	1942(a)	1,103	—	225.00	350.00

Obv. leg: *Muhammad al-Amin.*

269	AH1363(a)	1943	1,503	—	225.00	350.00
	1364(a)	1944	2,206	—	200.00	300.00

20 FRANCS

6.4516 g, .900 GOLD, .1867 oz AGW
Obv. leg: *Ali.*

227	AH1319	1901A	.150	BV	80.00	110.00
	1320	1902A	20 pcs.	—	550.00	1000.

NOTE: Earlier dates (AH1308-1318) exist for this type.

Obv. leg: *Muhammad al-Hadi.*

234	AH1321	1903A	.300	BV	85.00	120.00
	1321	1904A	.600	BV	85.00	120.00
	1322	1904A	Inc. Ab.	BV	85.00	120.00
	1323	1905A	23 pcs.	—	550.00	1000.
	1324	1906A	23 pcs.	—	550.00	1000.

Obv. leg: *Muhammad al-Nasir.*

241	AH1325	1907A	26 pcs.	—	550.00	1000.
	1326	1908A	46 pcs.	—	450.00	850.00
	1327	1909A	23 pcs.	—	550.00	1000.
	1328	1910A	23 pcs.	—	550.00	1000.
	1329	1911A	23 pcs.	—	550.00	1000.
	1330	1912A	23 pcs.	—	550.00	1000.
	1331	1913A	23 pcs.	—	550.00	1000.
	1332	1914A	23 pcs.	—	550.00	1000.
	1334	1915A	23 pcs.	—	550.00	1000.
	1334	1916A	23 pcs.	—	550.00	1000.
	1336	1917A	23 pcs.	—	550.00	1000.
	1337	1918A	23 pcs.	—	550.00	1000.
	1338	1919A	23 pcs.	—	550.00	1000.
	1339	1920A	23 pcs.	—	550.00	1000.
	1340	1921A	23 pcs.	—	550.00	1000.

Obv. leg: *Muhammad al-Habib.*

253	AH1341	1922A	23 pcs.	—	550.00	1000.
	1342	1923A	49 pcs.	—	450.00	850.00
	1343	1924A	23 pcs.	—	550.00	1000.
	1344	1925A	23 pcs.	—	550.00	1000.
	1345	1926A	23 pcs.	—	550.00	1000.
	1346	1927A	23 pcs.	—	550.00	1000.
	1347	1928A	23 pcs.	—	550.00	1000.

20.0000 g, .680 SILVER, .4372 oz ASW
Obv. leg: *Ahmad.*

KM#	Date	Year	Mintage	VF	XF	Unc
256	AH1349	1930(a)	.020	60.00	100.00	175.00
	1350	1931(a)	53 pcs.	200.00	300.00	500.00
	1351	1932(a)	.020	75.00	150.00	275.00
	1352	1933(a)	53 pcs.	200.00	300.00	500.00
	1353	1934(a)	9,500	60.00	100.00	175.00

NOTE: It is believed that an additional number of coins dated AH1353/1934(a) were struck and included in mintage figures of KM#263 of the same date.

KM#	Date	Mintage	VF	XF	Unc
263	AH1353(a)	1.250	12.00	25.00	60.00
	1354(a)	53 pcs.	—	275.00	450.00
	1355(a)	106 pcs.	—	225.00	375.00
	1356(a)	53 pcs.	—	275.00	450.00

KM#	Date	Year	Mintage	VF	XF	Unc
266	AH1358	1939(a)	.100	20.00	40.00	90.00
	1359	1940(a)	Reported, not confirmed			
	1360	1941(a)	53 pcs.	—	275.00	450.00
	1361	1942(a)	53 pcs.	—	275.00	450.00

Obv. leg: *Muhammad al-Amin.*

270	AH1363(a)	1943	103 pcs.	—	300.00	500.00
	1364(a)	1944	106 pcs.	—	300.00	500.00

COPPER-NICKEL

274	AH1370	1950(a)	10.000	.60	2.25	6.50
	1376	1957(a)	4.000	.45	1.25	4.50

50 FRANCS

COPPER-NICKEL
Obv. leg: *Muhammad al-Amin.*

275	AH1370	1950(a)	5.000	.60	2.25	6.50
	1376	1957(a)	.600	1.25	2.75	6.50

100 FRANCS

6.5500 g, .900 GOLD, .1895 oz AGW
Obv. leg: *Ahmad.*

KM#	Date	Year	Mintage	VF	XF	Unc
257	AH1349	1930(a)	3,000	90.00	110.00	140.00
	1350	1931(a)	33 pcs.	—	500.00	900.00
	1351	1932(a)	3,000	90.00	110.00	140.00
	1352	1933(a)	33 pcs.	—	500.00	900.00
	1353	1934(a)	133 pcs.	—	300.00	400.00
	1354	1935(a)	3,000	90.00	110.00	140.00
	1355	1936(a)	33 pcs.	—	500.00	900.00
	1356	1937(a)	33 pcs.	—	500.00	900.00

COPPER-NICKEL
Obv. leg: *Muhammad al-Amin.*

	KM#	Date		Mintage	VF	XF	Unc
276	AH1370	1950(a)		8.000	2.25	5.50	11.50
	1376	1957(a)		1.000	2.25	4.50	10.00

REPUBLIC
1000 Millim = 1 Dinar

MILLIM

ALUMINUM

KM#	Date	Mintage	VF	XF	Unc
280	1960	—	—	.10	.25
	1983	—	—	.10	.25

2 MILLIM

ALUMINUM

281	1960	—	—	.10	.25
	1983	—	—	.10	.25

5 MILLIM

ALUMINUM

282	1960	—	—	.10	.25
	1983	—	—	.10	.25
	1993	—	—	.10	.25
	1996	—	—	.10	.25

Obv: Tree above dates. **Rev:** Denomination.

KM#	Date	Year	Mintage	VF	XF	Unc
348	AH1418	1997	—	—	—	.50

10 MILLIM

BRASS

KM#	Date	Year	Mintage	VF	XF	Unc
306	AH1380	1960	—	.15	.25	.50
	1403	1983		.15	.25	.50
	1414	1993		.15	.25	.50
	1416	1996		.15	.25	.50

20 MILLIM

BRASS

307	AH1380	1960	—	.30	.50	.80
	1403	1983		.30	.50	.80
	1414	1993		.30	.50	.80
	1416	1996		.30	.50	.80

50 MILLIM

BRASS

308	AH1380	1960	—	.65	.85	1.25
	1403	1983		.65	.85	1.25
	1414	1993		.65	.85	1.25
	1416	1996		.65	.85	1.25

100 MILLIM

BRASS

309	AH1380	1960	—	1.25	1.50	2.00
	1403	1983		1.25	1.50	2.00
	1414	1993		1.25	1.50	2.00
	1416	1996		1.25	1.50	2.00

1/2 DINAR

NICKEL

KM#	Date	Mintage	VF	XF	Unc
291	1968(a)	.500	1.00	2.00	4.00

COPPER-NICKEL
F.A.O. Issue

303	1976	—	1.50	3.50	7.50
	1983	—	1.50	3.50	7.50

NOTE: Varieties exist.

F.A.O. Issue

KM#	Date	Mintage	VF	XF	Unc
318	1988	—	1.00	3.00	6.50
	1990	—	1.00	3.00	6.50

Obv: National arms. **Rev:** Two hands
w/fruit and wheat stalk.

KM#	Date	Year	Mintage	VF	XF	Unc
346	AH1416	1996	—			4.50

TURKEY

a map of **The Mints of the Ottoman Empire**

The Republic of Turkey, a parliamentary democracy of the Near East located partially in Europe and partially in Asia between the Black and the Mediterranean Seas, has an area of 301,382 sq. mi. (780,580 sq. km.) and a population of *55.4 million. Capital: Ankara. Turkey exports cotton, hazelnuts, and tobacco, and enjoys a virtual monopoly in meerschaum.

The Ottoman Turks, a tribe from Central Asia, first appeared in the early 13th century, and by the 17th century had established the Ottoman Empire which stretched from the Persian Gulf to the southern frontier of Poland, and from the Caspian Sea to the Algerian plateau. The defeat of the Turkish navy by the Holy League in 1571, and of the Turkish forces besieging Vienna in 1683, began the steady decline of the Ottoman Empire which, accelerated by the rise of nationalism, contracted its European border, and by the end of World War I deprived it of its Arab lands. The present Turkish boundaries were largely fixed by the Treaty of Lausanne in 1923. The sultanate and caliphate, the political and spiritual ruling institutions of the old empire, were separated and the sultanate abolished in 1922. On Oct. 29, 1923, Turkey formally became a republic.

RULERS

Abdul Hamid II, AH1293-1327/
1876-1909AD
Muhammad V, AH1327-1336/
1909-1918AD
Muhammad VI, AH1336-1341/
1918-1923AD
Republic, AH1341/AD1923-

MINTNAMES

Constantinople قسطنطنية
(Qustantiniyah)

HONORIFIC TITLES

El Ghazi   *Reshat*

The first coinage of Abdul Hamid II has a flower right of the toughra while the second coinage has *el Ghazi* (The Victorious). The first coinage of Mohammad Reshat V has *Reshat* right of the toughra while his second coinage has *el Ghazi*.

MONETARY SYSTEM
1844-1923
40 Para = 1 Kurush (Piastre)
100 Kurush (Piastre) = 1 Lira

NOTE: The 20 Kurush coin was known as a Mecidi, after the name of Abdul Mejid, who established the currency reform in 1844. The entire series is sometimes called Mejidiye coinage.

ABDUL HAMID II

AH1293-1327/1876-1909AD

5 PARA

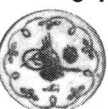 

1.0023 g, .100 SILVER, .0032 oz ASW
Accession date: AH1293
Mintname: *Qustantiniyah*

KM#	Year	Mintage	VG	Fine	VF	XF
743	25	3.336	.25	.50	1.25	4.00
	26	—	.25	.50	1.25	4.00
	27	—	.25	.50	1.25	4.00
	28	—	.50	1.00	3.00	12.00
	30	—	6.00	12.00	20.00	40.00

10 PARA

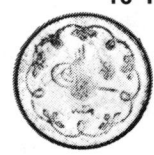 

2.0046 g, .100 SILVER, .0064 oz ASW
Accession date: AH1293
Mintname: *Qustantiniyah*

KM#	Year	Mintage	VG	Fine	VF	XF
744	25	3.492	.25	.50	1.00	4.00
	26	—	.25	.50	1.00	4.00
	27	—	.25	.50	1.00	4.00
	28	—	.25	.50	1.50	6.00
	30	—	1.00	2.00	5.00	15.00

NOTE: Varieties exist in size of regnal year 27.

KURUSH

1.2027 g, .830 SILVER, .0321 oz ASW
Accession date: AH1293
Mintname: *Qustantiniyah*
Obv: *el-Ghazi* right of toughra.

KM#	Year	Mintage	VG	Fine	VF	XF
735	25	.084	3.00	7.50	15.00	30.00
	26	.055	3.00	7.50	15.00	30.00
	27	9.945	1.00	2.00	3.00	5.00
	28	16.139	1.00	2.00	3.00	5.00
	29	7.076	1.00	2.00	3.00	5.00
	30	.707	1.00	2.00	3.00	5.00
	31	1.366	1.00	2.00	3.00	5.00
	32	1.140	1.00	2.00	3.00	5.00
	33	1.700	1.00	2.00	3.00	5.00
	34	—	40.00	60.00	115.00	225.00

NOTE: Earlier dates (Yr.8-24) exist for this type.
NOTE: Size of date & inscription varieties exist.

2 KURUSH

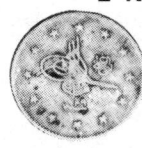 

2.4055 g, .830 SILVER, .0642 oz ASW
Accession date: AH1293
Mintname: *Qustantiniyah*
Obv: *el-Ghazi* right of toughra.

KM#	Year	Mintage	VG	Fine	VF	XF
736	25	.014	15.00	25.00	35.00	75.00
	26	.017	15.00	25.00	35.00	75.00
	27	4.689	1.50	2.00	4.00	7.00
	28	7.567	1.50	2.00	4.00	7.00
	29	7.775	1.50	2.00	4.00	7.00
	30	1.366	1.50	2.00	4.00	7.00
	31	3.014	1.50	2.00	4.00	7.00
	32	1.625	1.50	2.00	4.00	7.00
	33	2.173	1.50	2.00	4.00	7.00
	34	—	45.00	90.00	140.00	200.00

NOTE: Earlier dates (Yr.8-24) exist for this type.
NOTE: Varieties exist in size of toughra & date.

5 KURUSH

6.0130 g, .830 SILVER, .1605 oz ASW
Accession date: AH1293
Mintname: *Qustantiniyah*
Obv: *el-Ghazi* right of toughra.

KM#	Year	Mintage	VG	Fine	VF	XF
737	25	.013	15.00	30.00	45.00	75.00
	26	.008	15.00	30.00	45.00	75.00
	27	.016	15.00	30.00	45.00	75.00
	28	.006	15.00	30.00	45.00	75.00
	29	.007	15.00	30.00	45.00	75.00
	30	.038	5.00	10.00	15.00	30.00
	31/30	3.175	6.00	13.00	25.00	35.00
	31	Inc. Ab.	3.50	4.50	7.00	15.00
	32	3.334	2.00	3.25	4.50	9.50
	33	.907	2.00	3.50	6.00	11.50
	34	—	50.00	80.00	110.00	200.00

NOTE: Earlier dates (Yr.8-24) exist for this type.
NOTE: Varieties exist in size of toughra, inscription and date.

10 KURUSH

12.0270 g, .830 SILVER, .3210 oz ASW
Accession date: AH1293
Mintname: *Qustantiniyah*
Obv: *el-Ghazi* right of toughra.

KM#	Year	Mintage	VG	Fine	VF	XF
738	31	.051	20.00	40.00	75.00	125.00
	32	.575	7.50	12.50	15.00	25.00
	33	.273	6.00	10.00	12.50	20.00

NOTE: Earlier dates (Yr.12-20) exist for this type.

25 KURUSH

1.8040 g, .917 GOLD, .0532 oz AGW
Accession date: AH1293
Mintname: *Qustantiniyah*
Obv: *el-Ghazi* right of toughra.

KM#	Year	Mintage	VG	Fine	VF	XF
729	25	.057	BV	25.00	32.00	45.00
	26	—	BV	25.00	32.00	45.00
	27	—	BV	25.00	32.00	45.00
	28	—	BV	25.00	32.00	45.00
	29	—	BV	25.00	32.00	45.00
	30	—	BV	25.00	32.00	45.00
	31	—	BV	25.00	32.00	45.00
	32	—	BV	25.00	32.00	45.00
	33	—	BV	25.00	32.00	45.00
	34	—	BV	25.00	32.00	45.00

NOTE: Earlier dates (Yr.6-24) exist for this type.

50 KURUSH

3.6080 g, .917 GOLD, .1064 oz AGW
Accession date: AH1293
Mintname: *Qustantiniyah*
Obv: *el-Ghazi* right of toughra.

731	25	.013	BV	50.00	60.00	90.00
	26	—	BV	50.00	60.00	90.00
	27	—	BV	50.00	60.00	90.00
	28	—	BV	50.00	60.00	90.00
	29	—	BV	50.00	60.00	90.00
	30	—	BV	50.00	60.00	90.00
	31	—	BV	50.00	60.00	90.00
	32	—	BV	50.00	60.00	90.00
	33	—	BV	50.00	60.00	90.00
	34	—	BV	50.00	60.00	90.00

NOTE: Earlier dates (Yr.7-24) exist for this type.

100 KURUSH

7.2160 g, .917 GOLD, .2128 oz AGW
Accession date: AH1293
Mintname: *Qustantiniyah*
Obv: *el-Ghazi* right of toughra.

730	25	3,000	—	BV	100.00	115.00
	26	—	—	BV	100.00	115.00
	27	—	—	BV	100.00	115.00
	28	—	—	BV	100.00	115.00
	29	—	—	BV	100.00	115.00
	30	—	—	BV	100.00	115.00
	31	—	—	BV	100.00	115.00
	32	—	—	BV	100.00	115.00
	33	—	—	BV	100.00	115.00
	34	—	—	BV	100.00	115.00

NOTE: Earlier dates (Yr.6-24) exist for this type.

250 KURUSH

18.0400 g, .917 GOLD, .5319 oz AGW
Accession date: AH1293
Mintname: *Qustantiniyah*
Obv: *El Ghazi* right of toughra.

732	25	400 pcs.	BV	250.00	300.00	450.00
	26	—	BV	250.00	300.00	450.00
	27	—	BV	250.00	300.00	450.00
	28	—	BV	250.00	300.00	450.00
	29	—	BV	250.00	300.00	450.00
	30	—	BV	250.00	300.00	450.00
	31	—	BV	250.00	300.00	450.00
	32	—	BV	250.00	300.00	450.00
	33	—	BV	250.00	300.00	450.00
	34	—	BV	250.00	300.00	450.00

NOTE: Earlier dates (Yr.11-24) exist for this type.

500 KURUSH

36.0800 g, .917 GOLD, 1.0638 oz AGW
Accession date: AH1293
Mintname: *Qustantiniyah*
Obv: *El Ghazi* right of toughra.

KM#	Year	Mintage	VG	Fine	VF	XF
733	25	.011	BV	500.00	550.00	750.00
	26	—	BV	500.00	550.00	750.00
	27	—	BV	500.00	550.00	750.00
	28	—	BV	500.00	550.00	750.00
	29	—	BV	500.00	550.00	750.00
	30	—	BV	500.00	550.00	750.00
	31	—	BV	500.00	550.00	750.00
	32	—	BV	500.00	550.00	750.00
	33	—	BV	500.00	550.00	750.00
	34	—	BV	500.00	550.00	750.00

NOTE: Earlier dates (Yr.11-24) exist for this type.

MUHAMMAD V

AH1327-1336/1909-1918AD

5 PARA

NICKEL
Accession date: AH1327
Mintname: *Qustantiniyah*
Obv: *Reshat* right of toughra.

759	2	1.664	1.00	2.00	4.00	8.00
	3	21.760	.50	1.00	2.00	4.00
	4	21.392	.50	1.00	2.00	4.00
	5	30.579	.50	1.00	2.00	4.00
	6	15.751	.50	1.00	2.00	4.00
	7	2.512	15.00	35.00	60.00	100.00

Obv: *el-Ghazi* right of toughra.

767	7	.740	15.00	30.00	45.00	70.00

10 PARA

NICKEL
Accession date: AH1327
Mintname: *Qustantiniyah*
Obv: *Reshat* right of toughra.

760	2	2.576	.25	.50	2.00	5.00
	3	18.992	.15	.25	1.00	3.00
	4	18.576	.15	.25	1.00	3.00
	5	31.799	.15	.25	1.00	3.00
	6	17.024	.15	.25	1.00	3.00
	7	21.680	.30	.65	1.50	4.00

Obv: *el-Ghazi* right of toughra.

768	7	Inc. KM760	.30	.60	1.50	4.00
	8	7.590	.50	1.00	4.00	10.00

20 PARA

NICKEL

Accession date: AH1327
Mintname: *Qustantiniyah*
Obv: *Reshat* right of toughra.

KM#	Year	Mintage	VG	Fine	VF	XF
761	2	1.524	.25	.50	2.00	8.00
	3	11.418	.15	.35	1.50	6.00
	4	10.848	.15	.25	1.00	5.00
	5	24.350	.15	.25	1.00	5.00
	6	20.663	.15	.25	1.00	5.00
	7				Rare	
	W/o R.Y.	—	5.00	8.50	15.00	25.00

Obv: *el-Ghazi* at right of toughra.

769	7	—		—	Rare	—

40 PARA

NICKEL
Accession date: AH1327
Mintname: *Qustantiniyah*
Obv: *Reshat* right of toughra.

766	3	1.992	.50	1.00	3.00	10.00
	4	8.716	.15	.30	2.00	5.00
	5	9.248	.15	.30	2.00	5.00

COPPER-NICKEL
Obv: *el-Ghazi* right of toughra.

779	8	16.339	.15	.30	2.00	5.00
	9	3.034	1.00	2.00	10.00	25.00

KURUSH

1.2027 g, .830 SILVER, .0321 oz ASW
Accession date: AH1327
Mintname: *Qustantiniyah*

748	1	1.270	1.25	2.50	3.50	6.00
	2	8.770	1.00	2.00	3.00	5.00
	3	.840	1.50	3.00	6.00	12.50

2 KURUSH

2.4055 g, .830 SILVER, .0642 oz ASW
Accession date: AH1327
Mintname: *Qustantiniyah*
Obv: *Reshat* right of toughra.

749	1	5.157	1.75	2.25	3.50	7.50
	2	11.120	1.50	2.00	3.00	6.50
	3	6.110	1.50	2.00	3.00	6.50
	4	4.031	1.50	2.00	3.00	6.50
	5	.301	2.50	5.00	10.00	20.00
	6/2	1.884	2.00	2.50	4.00	8.00
	6	Inc. Ab.	2.00	2.50	4.00	8.00

NOTE: Varieties exist in size of date.

Obv: *el-Ghazi* right of toughra.

770	7	.017	12.50	25.00	40.00	75.00
	8	.398	20.00	30.00	50.00	100.00
	9	.008	60.00	100.00	200.00	350.00

5 KURUSH

6.0130 g, .830 SILVER, .1605 oz ASW
Accession date: AH1327
Mintname: *Qustantiniyah*
Obv: *Reshat* right of toughra.

750	1	1.558	BV	3.50	6.00	10.00
	2	1.886	BV	3.50	6.00	10.00
	3	1.273	BV	3.50	6.00	10.00
	4	1.635	BV	3.50	6.00	10.00
	5	.194	6.00	9.00	15.00	28.00
	6	.664	3.25	3.50	5.00	9.00
	7	.834	3.25	3.50	5.00	9.00

Obv: *el-Ghazi* right of toughra.

KM#	Year	Mintage	VG	Fine	VF	XF
771	7	Inc. KM750	3.50	4.50	7.00	10.00
	8	.648	4.00	7.00	10.00	20.00
	9	3,938	50.00	100.00	200.00	350.00

10 KURUSH

12.0270 g, .830 SILVER, .3210 oz ASW
Accession date: AH1327
Mintname: *Qustantiniyah*
Obv: *Reshat* right of toughra.

KM#	Year	Mintage	VG	Fine	VF	XF
751	1	.110	12.50	25.00	50.00	100.00
	2	Inc. Ab.	10.00	20.00	50.00	100.00
	3	8,000	150.00	250.00	500.00	1000.
	4	.096	3.50	7.50	15.00	25.00
	5	.034	10.00	20.00	50.00	100.00
	6	.081	7.50	12.50	17.50	30.00
	7	.582	5.00	10.00	16.50	32.00

Obv: *el-Ghazi* right of toughra.

KM#	Year	Mintage	VG	Fine	VF	XF
772	7	Inc. KM751	3.50	7.50	15.00	28.00
	8	.408	7.00	9.00	17.50	32.00
	9	.299	10.00	20.00	35.00	50.00
	10	.666	12.50	25.00	50.00	85.00

20 KURUSH

24.0550 g, .830 SILVER, .6419 oz ASW
Accession date: AH1327
Mintname: *Qustantiniyah*
Rev: Similar to KM#712.

KM#	Year	Mintage	VG	Fine	VF	XF
780	8	.713	9.00	12.00	20.00	35.00
	9	5.962	8.00	10.00	15.00	30.00
	10	11.025	9.00	12.00	20.00	35.00

25 KURUSH

1.8040 g, .917 GOLD, .0532 oz AGW
Accession date: AH1327
Mintname: *Qustantiniyah*
Obv: *Reshat* right of toughra.

KM#	Year		VG	Fine	VF	XF
752	1	—	BV	30.00	40.00	50.00
	2	—	BV	30.00	40.00	50.00
	3	—	BV	30.00	40.00	50.00
	4	—	BV	30.00	40.00	50.00
	5	—	BV	30.00	40.00	50.00
	6	—	BV	30.00	40.00	50.00

1.8040 g, .917 GOLD, .0532 oz AGW
Obv: *el-Ghazi* right of toughra.

KM#	Year	Mintage	VG	Fine	VF	XF
773	7	—	BV	35.00	45.00	55.00
	8	—	BV	35.00	45.00	55.00
	9	—	BV	35.00	45.00	55.00
	10	—	1000.	1500.	2000.	3000.

50 KURUSH

3.6080 g, .917 GOLD, .1064 oz AGW
Accession date: AH1327
Mintname: *Qustantiniyah*
Obv: *Reshat* right of toughra.

KM#	Year		VG	Fine	VF	XF
753	1	—	1000.	1500.	2000.	3000.
	2	—	BV	55.00	65.00	80.00
	3	—	BV	55.00	65.00	80.00
	4	—	BV	55.00	65.00	80.00
	5	—	BV	55.00	65.00	80.00
	6	—	BV	55.00	65.00	80.00

3.6080 g, .917 GOLD, .1064 oz AGW
Obv: *el-Ghazi* right of toughra.

KM#	Year		VG	Fine	VF	XF
775	7	—	60.00	75.00	150.00	250.00
	8	—	60.00	75.00	150.00	250.00
	9	—	60.00	75.00	150.00	250.00
	10	—	1000.	1500.	2000.	3000.

100 KURUSH

7.2160 g, .917 GOLD, .2128 oz AGW
Accession date: AH1327
Mintname: *Qustantiniyah*
Obv: *Reshat* right of toughra.

KM#	Year		VG	Fine	VF	XF
754	1	—	—	BV	100.00	135.00
	2	—	—	BV	100.00	135.00
	3	—	—	BV	100.00	135.00
	4	—	—	BV	100.00	135.00
	5	—	—	BV	100.00	135.00
	6	—	—	BV	100.00	135.00
	7	—	—	BV	100.00	135.00

7.2160 g, .917 GOLD, .2128 oz AGW
Obv: *el-Ghazi* right of toughra.

KM#	Year		VG	Fine	VF	XF
776	7	—	—	BV	110.00	150.00
	8	—	—	BV	110.00	150.00
	9	—	—	BV	110.00	150.00
	10	—	—	BV	110.00	150.00

250 KURUSH

18.0400 g, .917 GOLD, .5319 oz AGW
Accession date: AH1327
Mintname: *Qustantiniyah*
Obv: *Reshat* right of toughra.

KM#	Year		VG	Fine	VF	XF
756	1	—	—	BV	350.00	425.00
	2	—	—	BV	350.00	425.00
	3	—	—	BV	350.00	425.00
	4	—	—	BV	350.00	425.00
	5	—	—	BV	350.00	425.00
	6	—	—	BV	350.00	425.00

Obv: *el-Ghazi* right of toughra.

KM#	Year	Mintage	VG	Fine	VF	XF
777	7	30 pcs.	1250.	1750.	2800.	4000.
	8	21 pcs.	1750.	2500.	3500.	5000.
	9	28 pcs.	1750.	2500.	3500.	5000.

500 KURUSH

36.0800 g, .917 GOLD, 1.0638 oz AGW
Accession date: AH1327
Mintname: *Qustantiniyah*
Obv: *Reshat* right of toughra.

KM#	Year		VG	Fine	VF	XF
758	1	—	—	BV	525.00	650.00
	2	—	—	BV	525.00	650.00
	3	—	—	BV	525.00	650.00
	4	—	—	BV	525.00	650.00
	5	—	—	BV	525.00	650.00
	6	—	—	BV	525.00	650.00

Obv: *el-Ghazi* right of toughra.

KM#	Year	Mintage	VG	Fine	VF	XF
784	7	484 pcs.	1750.	2500.	3500.	5000.
	8	19 pcs.	1750.	2750.	4250.	6000.
	9	22 pcs.	1750.	2750.	4250.	6000.
	10	—	1750.	2500.	3500.	5000.

REPUBLIC

OLD MONETARY SYSTEM

100 PARA

ALUMINUM-BRONZE

KM#	Date	Mintage	Fine	VF	XF	Unc
830	AH1340	1.798	3.00	5.00	10.00	60.00
	1341	5.583	1.00	2.50	5.00	30.00
834	1926	4.388	1.00	2.50	6.00	32.00
	1928	—150.00	225.00	400.00	600.00	

5 KURUS

ALUMINUM-BRONZE

KM#	Date	Mintage	Fine	VF	XF	Unc
831	AH1340	5.023	1.00	2.50	7.00	32.00
	1341	23.545	1.00	2.50	7.00	32.00

KM#	Date	Mintage	Fine	VF	XF	Unc
835	1926	.356	1.00	2.50	7.00	32.00
	1928	—	175.00	250.00	500.00	700.00

10 KURUS

ALUMINUM-BRONZE

832	AH1340	4.836	1.50	3.00	8.00	35.00
	1341	14.223	1.50	3.00	8.00	35.00

NOTE: Varieties exist.

836	1926	.856	1.50	3.00	8.00	35.00
	1928	—	125.00	200.00	375.00	575.00

25 KURUS

NICKEL

833	AH1341	4.973	2.00	4.00	10.00	30.00
837	1926	.027	175.00	275.00	475.00	675.00
	1928	5.794	1.50	3.00	8.00	30.00

NOTE: Varieties exist.

DECIMAL COINAGE

Western numerals and Latin alphabet
MONETARY SYSTEM
40 Para = 1 Kurus
100 Kurus = 1 Lira

NOTE: Mintage figures of the 1930's and early 1940's may not be exact. It is suspected that in some cases, figures for a particular year may include quantities struck with the previous year's date.

10 PARA
(1/4 Kurus)

ALUMINUM-BRONZE

KM#	Date	Mintage	VG	Fine	VF	XF
868	1940	30.800	.25	.75	2.50	5.00
	1941	22.400	.25	.75	2.50	5.00
	1942	26.800	.25	.75	2.50	5.00

1/2 KURUS
(20 Para)

BRASS

KM#	Date	Mintage	Fine	VF	XF	Unc
884	1948	150 pcs.	—	300.00	550.00	

NOTE: Not released to circulation.

KURUS

COPPER-NICKEL

KM#	Date	Mintage	VG	Fine	VF	XF
861	1935	.784	2.00	4.00	6.00	15.00
	1936	5.300	.25	1.00	2.50	7.00
	1937	4.500	.25	1.00	2.50	7.00

867	1938	16.400	.25	.50	1.50	4.00
	1939	21.600	.25	.50	1.50	4.00
	1940	8.800	.50	1.00	2.00	8.00
	1941	6.700	.25	.75	1.75	5.00
	1942	10.800	.25	.50	1.50	4.00
	1943	4.000	.25	.75	1.75	5.00
	1944	6.000	.25	.75	1.75	5.00

BRASS

KM#	Date	Mintage	Fine	VF	XF	Unc
881	1947	.890	1.00	1.50	2.50	5.00
	1948	35.470	.15	.25	.50	1.50
	1949	29.530	.15	.25	.50	1.25
	1950	32.800	.15	.25	.50	1.25
	1951	6.310	.15	.30	.75	2.25

Olive Branch

895	1961	1.180	—	—	.10	.30
	1962	3.620	—	—	.10	.25
	1963	1.085	—	—	.10	.30

BRONZE

895a	1963	1.180	—	—	.10	.30
	1964	2.520	—	—	.10	.20
	1965	1.860	—	—	.10	.20
	1966	1.820	—	—	.10	.20
	1967	2.410	—	—	.10	.20
	1968	1.040	—	—	.10	.20
	1969	.900	—	—	.10	.20
	1970	1.960	—	—	.10	.20
	1971	2.940	—	—	.10	.20
	1972	.720	—	—	.10	.30
	1973	.540	—	—	.10	.30
	1974	.510	—	—	.10	.30

ALUMINUM

895b	1975	.690	—	.10	.25	1.00
	1976	.200	—	.10	.25	1.50
	1977	.108	—	.10	.25	1.75

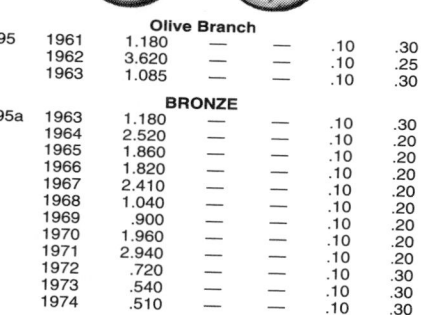

BRONZE
F.A.O. Issue

924	1979	.015	—	.25	1.00	3.00

ALUMINUM

924a	1979	.015	—	.25	1.00	3.00

2-1/2 KURUS

BRASS

		Mintage				
885	1948	24.720	.25	.50	1.00	3.00
	1949	23.720	.25	.50	1.00	3.00
	1950	11.560	.35	.65	1.25	4.00
	1951	2.000	2.00	5.00	12.00	40.00

5 KURUS

COPPER-NICKEL

KM#	Date	Mintage	VG	Fine	VF	XF
862	1935	.100	2.00	5.00	8.00	20.00
	1936	2.900	.50	1.00	2.00	8.00
	1937	4.060	.30	.75	1.50	8.00
	1938	13.380	.25	.50	1.00	5.00
	1939	12.520	.25	.50	1.00	5.00
	1940	4.340	.30	.75	1.50	5.00
	1942	10.160	.20	.40	1.00	5.00
	1943	15.360	.20	.40	1.00	5.00

BRASS

KM#	Date	Mintage	Fine	VF	XF	Unc
887	1949	4.500	.25	.50	1.00	4.00
	1950	45.900	.15	.35	.75	3.00
	1951	29.600	.15	.35	.75	3.00
	1955	15.300	.15	.35	.75	3.00
	1956	21.380	.15	.35	.75	3.00
	1957	3.320	.25	.50	1.00	4.00

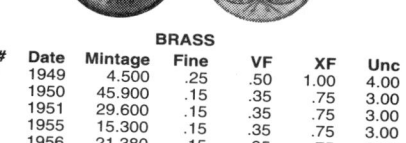

BRONZE, 2.50 g

890.1	1958	25.870	.10	.25	.50	1.50
	1959	21.580	—	—	.10	.30
	1960	17.150	—	—	.10	.30
	1961	11.110	—	—	.10	.20
	1962	15.280	—	—	.10	.30
	1963	17.680	—	—	.10	.20
	1964	18.190	—	—	.10	.30
	1965	19.170	—	—	.10	.20
	1966	19.840	—	—	.10	.30
	1967	16.170	—	—	.10	.30
	1968	26.050	—	—	.10	.30

Reduced weight, 2.00 g

890.2	1969	33.630	—	—	.10	.30
	1970	29.360	—	—	.10	.30
	1971	17.440	—	—	.10	.30
	1972	22.670	—	—	.10	.20
	1973	17.370	—	—	.10	.20

1.35 g

890.3	1974	13.540	—	—	.10	.20

NOTE: Varieties exist.

ALUMINUM

890a	1975	1.560	—	—	.10	.30
	1976	1.321	—	—	.10	.30
	1977	.190	—	.10	.20	1.00

F.A.O. Issue

906	1975	1.019	—	—	.50	1.50

F.A.O. Issue

907	1976	.017	—	.50	1.50	4.00

BRONZE
F.A.O. Issue

934	1980	.013	—	.25	.75	2.00

10 KURUS

COPPER-NICKEL

KM#	Date	Mintage	VG	Fine	VF	XF
863	1935	.060	2.00	5.00	8.00	20.00
	1936	3.580	.75	2.00	5.00	12.50
	1937	3.020	.50	1.00	4.00	8.00
	1938	6.610	.50	1.00	4.00	8.00
	1939	4.610	.50	1.00	2.50	5.00
	1940	6.960	.50	1.00	2.50	5.00

BRASS

KM#	Date	Mintage	Fine	VF	XF	Unc
888	1949	27.000	.10	.25	.75	3.00
	1951	6.200	.10	.25	.75	3.00
	1955	10.090	.10	.25	.75	3.00
	1956	9.910	.10	.25	.75	3.00

BRONZE, 4.00 g

KM#	Date	Mintage			XF	Unc
891.1	1958	14.770	—	.10	.25	1.50
	1959	11.160	—	—	.10	.40
	1960	9.450	—	—	.10	.40
	1961	5.370	—	—	.10	.40
	1962	9.250	—	—	.10	.40
	1963	10.390	—	—	.10	.40
	1964	9.890	—	—	.10	.40
	1965	10.480	—	—	.10	.40
	1966	12.200	—	—	.10	.40
	1967	11.410	—	—	.10	.40
	1968	1.862	—	—	.10	.40

Reduced weight, 3.50 g

891.2	1969	21.190	—	—	.10	.20
	1970	19.930	—	—	.10	.20
	1971	14.780	—	—	.10	.20
	1972	17.960	—	—	.10	.20
	1973	11.930	—	—	.10	.20

2.50 g

| 891.3 | 1974 | 9.280 | — | — | .10 | .20 |

NOTE: Varieties exist.

ALUMINUM

891a	1975	2.165	—	—	.10	.30
	1976	.559	—	.10	.20	.60
	1977	.106	—	.10	.50	1.00

BRONZE

F.A.O. Issue, 3.50 g

898.1	1971	.630	—	.10	.15	.75
	1972	.500	—	.10	.50	2.00
	1973	.010	—	4.00	10.00	30.00

2.50 g

| 898.2 | 1974 | .605 | — | .10 | .50 | 1.00 |

ALUMINUM

| 898a | 1975 | .517 | — | .10 | .25 | .75 |

F.A.O. Issue

| 908 | 1976 | .017 | — | .50 | 2.00 | 5.00 |

BRONZE

F.A.O. Issue

KM#	Date	Mintage	Fine	VF	XF	Unc
935	1980	.013	—	.25	1.00	2.50

25 KURUS

3.0000 g, .830 SILVER, .0801 oz ASW

KM#	Date	Mintage	VG	Fine	VF	XF
864	1935	.888	1.00	2.00	6.00	15.00
	1936	10.576	1.00	2.00	10.00	20.00
	1937	8.536	1.00	2.00	10.00	20.00

NICKEL-BRONZE

880	1944	20.000	.25	.50	1.00	2.50
	1945	5.328	.50	1.00	1.50	3.00
	1946	2.672	.50	1.25	2.00	4.00

BRASS

KM#	Date	Mintage	Fine	VF	XF	Unc
886	1948	18.000	.10	.20	.40	1.25
	1949	21.000	.10	.20	.40	1.25
	1951	2.000	.25	.50	2.50	10.00
	1955	9.624	.10	.20	.40	1.25
	1956	14.376	.10	.20	.40	1.25

STAINLESS STEEL, 5.0g
Obv: Smooth ground under woman's feet.

| 892.1 | 1959 | 21.864 | .10 | .15 | .30 | .75 |

Obv: Rough ground under woman's feet.

892.2	1960	14.778	—	.10	.15	.70
	1961	7.248	—	.10	.15	1.00
	1962	10.722	—	.10	.15	.80
	1963	11.016	—	.10	.15	.80
	1964	13.962	—	.10	.15	.70
	1965	9.816	—	.10	.15	.70
	1966	2.424	—	.10	.15	.80

Reduced weight, 4.00 g

892.3	1966	7.596	—	—	.10	.50
	1967	17.022	—	—	.10	.25
	1968	31.482	—	—	.10	.25
	1969	34.566	—	—	.10	.25
	1970	32.960	—	—	.10	.25
	1973	20.496	—	—	.10	.25
	1974	16.602	—	—	.10	.25
	1977	10.204	—	—	.10	.25
	1978	.185	.35	.75	1.25	2.00

---

50 KURUS

6.0000 g, .830 SILVER, .1601 oz ASW

KM#	Date	Mintage	VG	Fine	VF	XF
865	1935	.630	3.00	6.00	10.00	25.00
	1936	5.082	2.00	5.00	8.00	17.00
	1937	4.270	12.00	30.00	50.00	100.00

4.0000 g, .600 SILVER, .0772 oz ASW

KM#	Date	Mintage	Fine	VF	XF	Unc
882	1947	9.296	1.00	2.50	3.50	6.00
	1948	12.704	1.00	2.50	3.50	6.00

NOTE: Edge varieties exist.

STAINLESS STEEL

899	1971	16.756	—	.10	.15	.25
	1972	22.152	—	.10	.15	.25
	1973	18.928	—	.10	.15	.25
	1974	14.480	—	.10	.15	.25
	1975	27.714	—	.10	.15	.25
	1976	27.476	—	.10	.15	.25
	1977	5.062	—	.10	.15	.30
	1979	3.714	—	.10	.15	.30

F.A.O. Issue

| 913 | 1978 | .010 | — | .20 | .50 | 1.75 |

F.A.O. Issue

| 925 | 1979 | .020 | — | .20 | .50 | 1.75 |

F.A.O. Issue

| 936 | 1980 | .013 | — | .10 | .20 | 1.00 |

100 KURUS
(1 Lira)

12.0000 g, .830 SILVER, .3203 oz ASW
Obv: High star.

KM#	Date	Mintage	VG	Fine	VF	XF
860.1	1934	.718	15.00	30.00	40.00	75.00

Obv: Low star.

KM#	Date	Mintage	VG	Fine	VF	XF
860.2	1934	Inc. Ab.	10.00	20.00	30.00	50.00

LIRA

12.0000 g, .830 SILVER, .3203 oz ASW
Kemal Ataturk

	Date	Mintage	VG	Fine	VF	XF
866	1937	1.624	5.00	10.00	15.00	32.00
	1938	8.282	25.00	50.00	75.00	150.00
	1939	.376	5.00	10.00	15.00	32.00

Ismet Inonu

	Date	Mintage	VG	Fine	VF	XF
869	1940	.253	7.50	12.50	15.00	25.00
	1941	6.167	4.50	10.00	12.50	22.50

7.5000 g, .600 SILVER, .1447 oz ASW

KM#	Date	Mintage	Fine	VF	XF	Unc
883	1947	11.104	1.50	3.50	5.00	8.50
	1948	16.896	1.50	3.00	4.00	7.50

NOTE: Edge varieties exist.

COPPER-NICKEL

	Date	Mintage	Fine	VF	XF	Unc
889	1957	25.000	.25	.50	1.00	2.50

STAINLESS STEEL, 8.00g

	Date	Mintage	Fine	VF	XF	Unc
889a.1	1959	7.452	—	.10		.50
	1960	11.436	—	.10	.20	.50
	1961	2.100	—	.10	.20	1.00
	1962	4.228	—	.10	.20	.50
	1963	4.316	—	.10	.20	.50
	1964	4.976	—	.10	.20	.50
	1965	5.348	—	.10	.20	.50
	1966	8.040	—	.10	.20	.50
	1967	—	—	.10	.20	.50

Reduced weight, 7.00 g

KM#	Date	Mintage	Fine	VF	XF	Unc
889a.2	1967	10.444	—	.10	.20	.50
	1968	12.728	—	.10	.20	.50
	1969	6.612	—	.10	.20	.50
	1970	8.652	—	.10	.20	.50
	1971	10.504	—	.10	.20	.50
	1972	26.512	—	.10	.20	.50
	1973	12.596	—	.10	.20	.50
	1974	11.596	—	.10	.20	.50
	1975	20.348	—	.10	.20	.50
	1976	23.144	—	.10	.20	.50
	1977	30.244	—	.10	.20	.50
	1978	22.156	—	.10	.20	.50
	1979	9.289	—	.10	.20	.50
	1980	3.585	—	.10	.20	.50

F.A.O. Issue

914	1978	.020	—	.50	1.00	2.50

F.A.O. Issue
Similar to 50 Kurus, KM#925.

926	1979	.020	—	.50	1.00	2.50

F.A.O. Issue

937	1980	.013	—	.40	.75	2.00

ALUMINUM
Rev: Crescent opens left.

943	1981	14.432	—	—	.10	.25

Rev: Large (5mm) 1.

962.1	1984	.498	—	—	.10	.20

Rev: Small (3.5mm) 1.

962.2	1985	.712	—	—	.10	.20
	1986	.504	—	—	.10	.20
	1987	.500	—	—	.10	.20
	1988	.075	—	—	.10	.20
	1989	.010	—	—	.10	.20

NOTE: Varieties exist.

Obv: Similar to KM#943. Rev: Crescent opens right w/thin "1".

990	1982	.799	—	—	.10	.25

2-1/2 LIRA

STAINLESS STEEL, 12.00 g

893.1	1960	4.015	—	.25	1.00	3.00
	1961	1.222	—	.25	1.00	6.00
	1962	3.636	—	.25	1.00	3.00
	1963	3.108	—	.25	1.00	3.00
	1964	2.710	—	.25	1.00	3.00
	1965	1.246	—	.25	1.00	4.00
	1966	1.788	—	.25	1.00	3.00
	1967	5.333	—	.25	1.00	3.00
	1968	2.707	—	.25	1.00	3.00

Reduced weight, 9.00 g

893.2	1969	1.378	—	.15	.75	2.00
	1970	3.777	—	.15	.75	2.00

KM#	Date	Mintage	Fine	VF	XF	Unc
893.2	1971	2.170	—	.15	.75	2.00
	1972	9.147	—	.15	.50	2.00
	1973	4.348	—	.15	.50	3.00
	1974	3.816	—	.15	.50	3.00
	1975	9.811	—	.15	.50	2.50
	1976	3.952	—	.15	.50	2.50
	1977	21.473	—	.10	.25	.50
	1978	15.738	—	.10	.25	.50
	1979	6.074	—	.10	.25	.50
	1980	2.621	—	.10	.25	.75

NOTE: Varieties exist.

F.A.O. Issue

896	1970	.200	—	.10	.25	.75

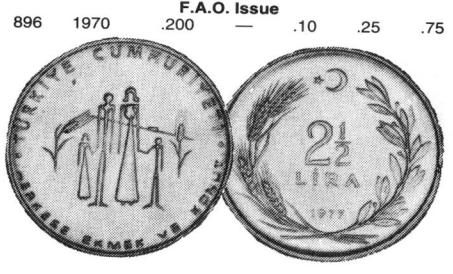

F.A.O. Issue

910	1977	.025	—	.25	.50	1.25

F.A.O. Issue

915	1978	.010	—	1.00	2.00	4.00

F.A.O. Issue

927	1979	.020	—	1.00	2.00	4.00

F.A.O. Issue

938	1980	.013	—	.50	1.50	3.50

5 LIRA

STAINLESS STEEL

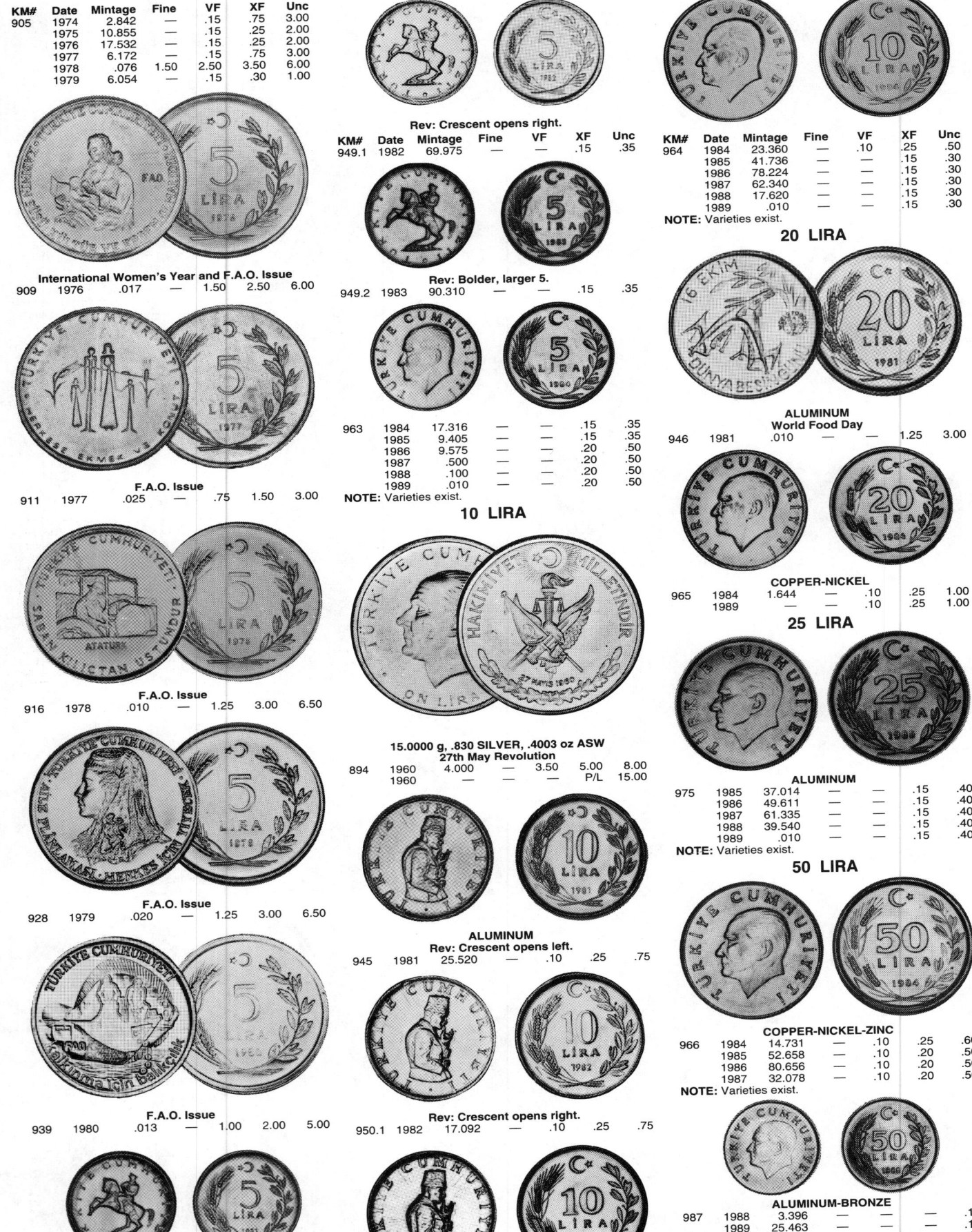

KM#	Date	Mintage	Fine	VF	XF	Unc
905	1974	2.842	—	.15	.75	3.00
	1975	10.855	—	.15	.25	2.00
	1976	17.532	—	.15	.25	2.00
	1977	6.172	—	.15	.75	3.00
	1978	.076	1.50	2.50	3.50	6.00
	1979	6.054	—	.15	.30	1.00

International Women's Year and F.A.O. Issue

909	1976	.017	—	1.50	2.50	6.00

F.A.O. Issue

911	1977	.025	—	.75	1.50	3.00

F.A.O. Issue

916	1978	.010	—	1.25	3.00	6.50

F.A.O. Issue

928	1979	.020	—	1.25	3.00	6.50

F.A.O. Issue

939	1980	.013	—	1.00	2.00	5.00

ALUMINUM
Rev: Crescent opens left.

944	1981	61.605	—	—	.15	.35

Rev: Crescent opens right.

KM#	Date	Mintage	Fine	VF	XF	Unc
949.1	1982	69.975	—	—	.15	.35

Rev: Bolder, larger 5.

949.2	1983	90.310	—	—	.15	.35

963	1984	17.316	—	—	.15	.35
	1985	9.405	—	—	.15	.35
	1986	9.575	—	—	.20	.50
	1987	.500	—	—	.20	.50
	1988	.100	—	—	.20	.50
	1989	.010	—	—	.20	.50

NOTE: Varieties exist.

10 LIRA

15.0000 g, .830 SILVER, .4003 oz ASW
27th May Revolution

894	1960	4.000	—	3.50	5.00	8.00
	1960		—	—	P/L	15.00

ALUMINUM
Rev: Crescent opens left.

945	1981	25.520	—	.10	.25	.75

Rev: Crescent opens right.

950.1	1982	17.092	—	.10	.25	.75

950.2	1983	2.228	—	.10	.25	.60

KM#	Date	Mintage	Fine	VF	XF	Unc
964	1984	23.360	—	.10	.25	.50
	1985	41.736	—	—	.15	.30
	1986	78.224	—	—	.15	.30
	1987	62.340	—	—	.15	.30
	1988	17.620	—	—	.15	.30
	1989	.010	—	—	.15	.30

NOTE: Varieties exist.

20 LIRA

ALUMINUM
World Food Day

946	1981	.010	—	—	1.25	3.00

COPPER-NICKEL

965	1984	1.644	—	.10	.25	1.00
	1989		—	.10	.25	1.00

25 LIRA

ALUMINUM

975	1985	37.014	—	—	.15	.40
	1986	49.611	—	—	.15	.40
	1987	61.335	—	—	.15	.40
	1988	39.540	—	—	.15	.40
	1989	.010	—	—	.15	.40

NOTE: Varieties exist.

50 LIRA

COPPER-NICKEL-ZINC

966	1984	14.731	—	.10	.25	.60
	1985	52.658	—	.10	.20	.50
	1986	80.656	—	.10	.20	.50
	1987	32.078	—	.10	.20	.50

NOTE: Varieties exist.

ALUMINUM-BRONZE

987	1988	3.396	—	—	—	.15
	1989	25.463	—	—	—	.15
	1990	.500	—	—	—	.15
	1991	.010	—	—	—	.15
	1992	.010	—	—	—	.15
	1993	5,000	—	—	—	.35
	1994	2,500	—	—	—	.50

NOTE: Varieties exist.

100 LIRA

COPPER-NICKEL-ZINC

KM#	Date	Mintage	Fine	VF	XF	Unc
967	1984	.758	—	.20	.40	.85
	1985	.866	—	.20	.40	.85
	1986	12.064	—	.20	.40	.85
	1987	91.400	—	.15	.25	.65
	1988	16.184	—	.15	.25	.65

NOTE: Varieties exist.

ALUMINUM-BRONZE

988	1988	10.000	—	—	—	.20
	1989	233.750	—	—	—	.20
	1990	152.230	—	—	—	.20
	1991	49.160	—	—	—	.20
	1992	22.930	—	—	—	.20
	1993	3.700	—	—	—	.20
	1994	2,500	—	—	—	.50

NOTE: Varieties exist.

500 LIRA

ALUMINUM-BRONZE

989	1989	141.813	—	—	—	.60
	1990	100.114	—	—	—	.60
	1991	30.006	—	—	—	.60
	1992	.010	—	—	—	.60
	1993	5,000	—	—	—	.75
	1994	2,500	—	—	—	.85
	1995	2,500	—	—	—	.85
	1996	.010	—	—	—	.60
	1997	—	—	—	—	.60

NOTE: Varieties exist.

1000 LIRA

COPPER-ZINC-NICKEL

997	1990	136.480	—	.15	.25	2.00
	1991	110.245	—	.15	.25	2.00
	1992	15.820	—	.15	.25	2.00
	1993	11.675	—	.15	.25	2.00
	1994	61.515	—	.15	.25	2.00

BRONZE CLAD BRASS

1028	1995	36.820	—	—	—	1.00
	1996	3.900	—	—	—	1.00
	1997	—	—	—	—	1.00

2500 LIRA

NICKEL-BRONZE

KM#	Date	Mintage	Fine	VF	XF	Unc
1015	1991	22.938	.10	.25	.50	3.00
	1992	48.784	.10	.25	.50	3.00
	1993	2.310	.10	.25	.50	3.00
	1994	2,500	.10	.25	.50	4.50
	1995	2,500	.10	.25	.50	4.50
	1996	.010	.10	.25	.50	3.00
	1997	—	.10	.25	.50	3.00

5000 LIRA

NICKEL-BRONZE

1025	1992	24.904	.10	.25	.50	3.00
	1992	—	—	—	Proof	6.50
	1993	15.872	.10	.25	.50	3.00
	1994	69.504	.10	.25	.50	3.00

BRASS

1029	1995 lg. dt.					
		69.550	—	—	—	1.50
	1995 sm. dt.					
	Inc. Ab.	—	—	—	—	.75
	1996	80.506	—	—	—	.75
	1997	—	—	—	—	.75

10 BIN LIRA

(10,000 Lira)

COPPER-NICKEL-ZINC, 9.75 g
Edge: Reeded with legend: TURKIYE CUMHURIYETI.

1027.1	1994	17.319	—	.10	.25	3.00
	1995	56.584	—	.10	.25	3.00
	1996	119.572	—	.10	.25	3.00
	1997	—	—	.10	.25	3.00

Thin planchet, 6.75 g
Edge: Lettered TC and dashes.

1027.2	1997		—	.10	.25	3.00

1994 Olympics

1042	1994	.500	—	—	—	3.75

25 BIN LIRA

(25,000 Lira)

COPPER-NICKEL-ZINC
Edge: Lettered TC and flower 5 times.

1041	1995	13.740	.20	.30	.50	3.00
	1996	59.742	.20	.30	.50	3.00
	1997	—	.20	.30	.50	3.00

Environmental Protection - 3 Human Heads

1043	1995	.500	—	—	—	4.50

TURKMENISTAN

The Turkmenistan Republic (formerly the Turkmen Soviet Socialist Republic) covers the territory of the Trans-Caspian Region of Turkestan, the Charjiui Vilayet of Bukhara and the part of Khiva located on the right bank of the Oxus. Bordered on the north by the Autonomous Kara-Kalpak Republic (a constituent of Uzbekistan), by Iran and Afghanistan on the south, by the Usbek Republic on the east and the Caspian Sea on the west. It has an area of 186,400 sq. mi. (488,100 sq. km.) and a population of 3.5 million. Capital: Ashkhabad (formerly Poltoratsk). Main occupation is agricultural products including cotton and maize. It is rich in minerals, oil, coal, sulphur and salt and is also famous for its carpets, Turkoman horses and Karakui sheep.

The Turkomans arrived in Trancaspia as nomadic Seluk Turks in the 11th century. It often became subjected to one of the neighboring states. Late in the 19th century the Czarist Russians invaded with their first victory at Kyzyl Arvat in 1877, arriving in Ashkhabad in 1882 resulting in submission of the Turkmen tribes. By Mar. 18, 1884 the Transcaspian province of Russian Turkestan was formed. During WW I the Czarist government tried to conscript the Turkmen; this led to a revolt in Oct. 1916 under the leadership of Aziz Chapykov. In 1918 the Turks captured Baku from the Red army and the British sent a constingent to Merv to prevent a German-Turkish offensive toward Afghanistan and India. In mid-1919 a Bureau of Turkistan Moslem Communist Organization was formed in Moscow hoping to develop one large republic including all surrounding Turkic areas within a Soviet federation. A Turkistan Autonomous Soviet Socialist Republic was formed and plans to partition Turkistan into five republics according to the principle of nationalities was quickly implemented by Joseph Stalin. On Oct. 27, 1924 Turkmenistan became a Soviet Socialist Republic and was accepted as a member of the U.S.S.R. on Jan. 29, 1925. The Bureau of T.M.C.O. was disbanded in 1934. In Aug. 1990 the Turkmen Supreme Soviet adopted a declaration of sovereignty followed by a declaration of independence in Oct. 1991 joining the Commonwealth of Independent States in Dec. A new constitution was adopted in 1992 providing for an executive presidency.

MONETARY SYSTEM
100 Tennesi = 1 Manat

TENNESI

COPPER PLATED STEEL
President Saparmyrat Nyyazow

KM#	Date	Mintage	VF	XF	Unc
1	1993	—	—	—	.25

5 TENNESI

COPPER PLATED STEEL
President Saparmyrat Nyyazow

2	1993	—	—	—	.35

10 TENNESI

COPPER PLATED STEEL
President Saparmyrat Nyyazow

3	1993	—	—	—	.60

20 TENNESI

NICKEL PLATED STEEL
President Saparmyrat Nyyazow

KM#	Date	Mintage	VF	XF	Unc
4	1993	—	—	—	1.00

50 TENNESI

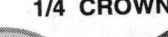

NICKEL PLATED STEEL
President Saparmyrat Nyyazow

5	1993	—	—	—	2.00

TURKS & CAICOS IS.

The Colony of the Turks and Caicos Islands, a British colony situated in the West Indies at the eastern end of the Bahama Islands, has an area of 166 sq. mi. (430 sq. km.) and a population of *10,000. Capital: Cockburn Town, on Grand Turk. The principal industry of the colony is the production of salt, which is gathered by raking. Salt, crayfish, and conch shells are exported.

The Turks and Caicos Islands were discovered by Juan Ponce de Leon in 1512, but were not settled until 1678 when Bermudians arrived to rake salt from the salt ponds. The British settlers were driven from the island by the Spanish in 1710, during the long War of the Spanish Succession. They returned and throughout the remaining years of the war repulsed repeated attacks by France and Spain. In 1799 the islands were granted representation in the Bahamian assembly, but in 1848, on petition of the inhabitants, they were made a separate colony under Jamaica. They were annexed by Jamaica in 1873 and remained a dependency until 1959 when they became a unit territory of the Federation of the West Indies. When the Federation was dissolved in 1962, the Turks and Caicos Islands became a separate Crown Colony.

RULERS

British

MONETARY SYSTEM

1 Crown = 1 Dollar U.S.A.

1/4 CROWN

COPPER-NICKEL

KM#	Date	Mintage	Fine	VF	XF	Unc
51	1981	—	—	—	—	1.50

1/2 CROWN

COPPER-NICKEL

52	1981	—	—	—	—	2.00

CROWN

COPPER-NICKEL

1	1969	.050	—	—	2.00	4.50
	1969	6,000	—	—	Proof	6.00

TUVALU

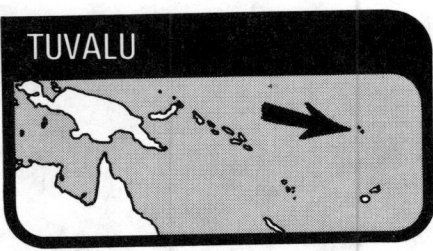

Tuvalu (formerly the Ellice or Lagoon Islands of the Gilbert and Ellice Islands), located in the South Pacific north of the Fiji Islands, has an area of 10 sq. mi. (26 sq. km.) and a population of *9,000. Capital: Funafuti. The independent state includes the islands of Nanumanga, Nanumea, Nui, Niutao, Viatupa, Funafuti, Nukufetau, Nukulailai and Nurakita. The latter four islands were claimed by the United States until relinquished by the Feb. 7, 1979, Treaty of Friendship signed by the United States and Tuvalu. The principal industries are copra production and phosphate mining.

The islands were discovered in 1764 by John Byron, a British navigator, and annexed by Britain in 1892. In 1915 they became part of the crown colony of the Gilbert and Ellice Islands. In 1974 the islanders voted to separate from the Gilberts, becoming on Jan. 1, 1976, the separate constitutional dependency of Tuvalu. Full independence was attained on Oct. 1, 1978. Tuvalu is a member of the Commonwealth of Nations. Elizabeth II is Head of State as Queen of Tuvalu.

RULERS

British, until 1978

MONETARY SYSTEM

100 Cents = 1 Dollar

CENT

BRONZE

KM#	Date	Mintage	Fine	VF	XF	Unc
1	1976	.093	—	—	.10	.25
	1976	.020	—	—	Proof	1.00
	1981	—	—	—	.10	.25
	1981	—	—	—	Proof	1.00
	1985	—	—	—	.10	.25

Obv: Queen's portrait. Rev: Sea shell.

26	1994	—	—	—	—	.35

2 CENTS

BRONZE

2	1976	.051	—	—	.10	.15	.30
	1976	.020	—	—	Proof	1.00
	1981	—	—	—	.10	.15	.30
	1981	—	—	—	Proof	1.00
	1985	—	—	—	.10	.15	.30

5 CENTS

COPPER-NICKEL

3	1976	.026	—	—	.10	.25	.75
	1976	.020	—	—	Proof	1.00
	1981	—	—	—	.10	.25	.75
	1981	—	—	—	Proof	1.00
	1985	—	—	—	.10	.25	.75

10 CENTS

COPPER-NICKEL
Crab

KM#	Date	Mintage	Fine	VF	XF	Unc
4	1976	.026	.15	.20	.30	.75
	1976	.020	—	—	Proof	2.00
	1981	—	.15	.20	.30	.75
	1981	—	—	—	Proof	2.00
	1985	—	.15	.20	.30	.75

20 CENTS

COPPER-NICKEL
Flying Fish

5	1976	.036	.30	.40	.50	1.00
	1976	.020	—	—	Proof	2.50
	1981	—	.30	.40	.50	1.00
	1981	—	—	—	Proof	2.50
	1985	—	.30	.40	.50	1.00

50 CENTS

COPPER-NICKEL
Octopus

6	1976	.019	.50	.75	1.00	4.00
	1976	.020	—	—	Proof	5.00
	1981	—	.50	.75	1.00	4.00
	1981	—	—	—	Proof	5.00
	1985	—	.50	.75	1.00	4.00

DOLLAR

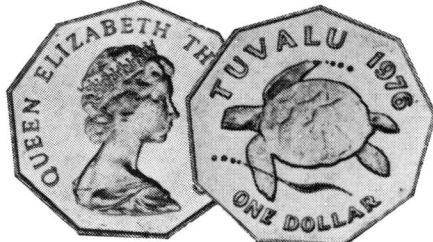

COPPER-NICKEL
Sea Turtle

7	1976	.021	1.00	1.50	2.00	5.00
	1976	.020	—	—	Proof	7.00
	1981	—	1.00	1.50	2.00	5.00
	1981	—	—	—	Proof	7.00
	1985	—	1.00	1.50	2.00	5.00

UGANDA

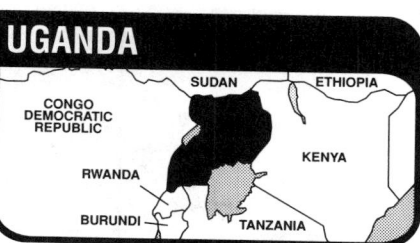

The Republic of Uganda, a former British protectorate located astride the equator in east-central Africa, has an area of 91,134 sq. mi. (236,040 sq. km.) and a population of *17 million. Capital: Kampala. Agriculture, including livestock, is the basis of the economy; there is some mining of copper, tin, gold and lead. Coffee, cotton, copper and tea are exported.

Uganda was first visited by Arab slavers in the 1830s. They were followed in the 1860s by British explorers searching for the headwaters of the Nile. The explorers, and the missionaries who followed them into the Lake Victoria region of south-central Africa in 1877-79, found well-developed African kingdoms dating back several centuries. In 1894 the local native Kingdom of Buganda was established as a British protectorate that was extended in 1896 to encompass an area substantially the same as the present Republic of Uganda. The protectorate was given a ministerial form of government in 1955, full internal self-government on March 1, 1962, and complete independence on Oct. 9, 1962. Uganda is a member of the Commonwealth of Nations. The president is Chief of State and Head of Government.

For earlier coinage refer to East Africa.

RULERS
British, until 1962

MONETARY SYSTEM
100 Cents = 1 Shilling

5 CENTS

BRONZE

KM#	Date	Mintage	VF	XF	Unc
1	1966	41.000	.10	.15	.30
	1966	—	—	Proof	1.00
	1974	10.000	.20	.30	.75
	1975	14.784	.20	.30	.75

COPPER PLATED STEEL

1a	1976	10.000	—	.30	.75

10 CENTS

BRONZE

2	1966	19.100	.10	.15	.35
	1966	—	—	Proof	1.00
	1968	20.000	.10	.15	.35
	1970	6.000	.20	.30	.75
	1972	5.000	.20	.30	.75
	1974	5.000	.20	.30	.75
	1975	14.110	.20	.30	.75

COPPER PLATED STEEL

2a	1976	10.000	.20	.30	.75

20 CENTS

BRONZE

3	1966	7.000	.30	.70	1.65
	1966	—	—	Proof	2.00
	1974	2.000	.50	1.00	2.25

---

50 CENTS

COPPER-NICKEL

KM#	Date	Mintage	VF	XF	Unc
4	1966	16.000	.20	.40	1.50
	1966	—	—	Proof	1.75
	1970	3.000	.25	.65	1.75
	1974	10.000	.25	.65	1.75

COPPER-NICKEL PLATED STEEL

4a	1976	10.000	.25	.65	1.75

NICKEL PLATED STEEL

4b	1986	—	.25	.65	1.75

SHILLING

COPPER-NICKEL

5	1966	24.500	.25	.50	2.00
	1966	—	—	Proof	3.00
	1968	10.000	.35	.85	2.25
	1972	—	.35	.85	2.25
	1975	15.540	.35	.85	2.25

COPPER-NICKEL PLATED STEEL

5a	1976	10.000	.35	.85	2.25
	1978	—	.35	.85	2.25

NICKEL PLATED STEEL

5b	1986	—	.35	.85	2.25

COPPER PLATED STEEL

27	1987	—	—	—	.25
	1987	—	—	Proof	2.50

2 SHILLINGS

COPPER-NICKEL

6	1966	4.000	1.00	2.00	4.00
	1966	—	—	Proof	6.00
	1970	Inc. Ab.	—	Proof	10.00

COPPER PLATED STEEL

28	1987	—	—	—	.50
	1987	—	—	Proof	4.00

5 SHILLINGS

COPPER-NICKEL
F.A.O. Issue

KM#	Date	Mintage	VF	XF	Unc
7	ND(1968)	.100	1.50	2.50	5.50
	ND(1968)	5,000	—	Proof	7.50

18	1972	*8.000	55.00	75.00	135.00

NOTE: Withdrawn from circulation. Almost entire mintage was melted.

STAINLESS STEEL

29	1987	—	—	—	1.50
	1987	—	—	Proof	6.50

10 SHILLINGS

STAINLESS STEEL

30	1987	—	—	—	2.50
	1987	—	—	Proof	12.50

UKRAINE

Ukraine (formerly the Ukrainian Soviet Socialist Republic) is bordered by Russia to the east, Russia and Belarus to the north, Poland, Slovakia and Hungary to the west, Romania and Moldova to the southwest and in the south by the Black Sea and the Sea of Azov. It has an area of 233,088 sq. mi. (603,700 sq. km.) and a population of 51.9 million. Capital: Kyiv (Kiev). Coal, grain, vegetables and heavy industrial machinery are major exports.

The territory of Ukraine has been inhabited for over 30,000 years. As the result of its location, Ukraine has served as the gateway to Europe for millennia and its early history has been recorded by Arabic, Greek, Roman, as well as Ukrainian historians.

Ukraine, which was known as *Rus'* until the sixteenth century (and from which the name Russia was derived in the 17th century) became the major political and cultural center of Eastern Europe in the 9th century. The Rus' Kingdom, under a dynasty of Varangian origin, due to its posistion on the intersection of the north-south Scandinavia to Byzantium and the east-west Orient to Europe trade routes, became a focal point of world trade. At its apex Rus' stretched from the Baltic to the Black Sea and from the upper Volga River in the east, almost to the Vistula River in the west. It has family ties to many European dynasties. In 988 knyaz (king) Volodymyr adopted Christianity from Byzantium. With it came church books written in the Cyrillic alphabet, which originated in Bulgaria. The Mongol invasion in 1240 brought an end to the might of the Rus' Kingdom.

In the seventeenth century, after almost four hundred years of Mongol, Lithuanian, Polish, and Turkish domination, the Cosack State under Hetman Bohdan Khmelnytsky regained Ukrainian independence. The Hetman State lasted until the mid-eighteenth century and was followed by a period of foreign rule. Eastern Ukraine was controlled by Russia, which enforced russification through introduction of the Russian language and prohibiting the use of the Ukrainian language in schools, books and public life. Western Ukraine came under relatively benign Austro-Hungarian rule.

With the disintegration of the Russian and Austro-Hungarian Empires in 1917 and 1918. Eastern Ukraine declared its full independence on January 22, 1918 and Western Ukraine followed suit on November 1 of that year. On January 22, 1919 both parts united into one state that had to defend itself on three fronts: from the "Red Bolsheviks" and their puppet Ukrainian Soviet Republic formed in Kharkiv, from the "White" czarist Russian forces, and from Poland. Ukraine lost the war. In 1920 Eastern Ukraine was occupied by the Bolsheviks and in 1922 was incorporated into the Soviet Union. There followed a brief resurgence of Ukrainian language and culture until Stalin suppressed it in 1928. The artificial famine-genocide of 1932-33 killed 7-10 million Ukrainians, and Stalinist purges in the mid-1930s took a heavy toll. Western Ukraine was partitioned between Poland, Romania, Hungary and Czechoslovakia.

On August 24, 1991 Ukraine once again declared its independence. On December 1, 1991 over 90% of Ukraine's electorate approved full independence from the Soviet Union. On December 5, 1991 the Ukrainian Parliament abrogated the 1922 treaty which incorporated Ukraine into the Soviet Union. Later, Leonid Kravchuk was elected president by a 65% majority.

Ukraine is a charter member of the United Nations and has inherited the third largest nuclear arsenal in the world. Ukraine was the site of the (Chernobyl) nuclear power station disaster in 1986.

Rulers

Russian, 1793-1917

MINT

w/o mm - Lugansk; Kiev (1997-1998)

MONETARY SYSTEM

100 Kopiyok = 1 Hryvnia

KOPIYKA

ALUMINUM

KM#	Date	Mintage	VF	XF	Unc
6	1992	—	—	6.50	12.50

STEEL

6a	1992	—	—	.15	.35
	1996	—	—	1.00	1.35

---

2 KOPIYKY

ALUMINUM

KM#	Date	Mintage	VF	XF	Unc
4	1992	—	.50	1.00	2.00
	1993	—	.50	1.00	2.00
	1994	—	.50	1.00	2.00
	1996	—	.50	1.50	3.00

BRASS

4a	1993	—	—	—	—

ALUMINUM-ZINC

4b	1993	—	—	—	—

5 KOPIJOK

WHITE BRASS

7	1992	—	—	7.50	15.00

STEEL

7a	1992	—	—	.35	.65
	1996	—	.50	1.50	3.00

10 KOPIYOK

BRASS
Rev: 5 dots right of final K in denomination.

1.1	1992	—	.50	1.00	2.25
	1993	—	.50	1.00	2.25
	1994	—	.50	1.00	2.25
	1995	—	.50	1.00	2.25
	1996	—	.60	1.25	2.50

NOTE: Varieties in edges exist with fine or coarse reeding.

Rev: 6 dots right of K.

1.2	1992	—	—	.50	1.00	2.25

Obv: Incuse shield.

1.3	1992	—	—	.60	1.25	2.50

15 KOPIYOK

BRASS

5	1992	—	—	15.00	30.00

BRONZE

5a	1992	—	—	15.00	30.00

ALUMINUM

5b (5a)	1993	—	—	12.50	25.00

25 KOPIYOK

BRASS

KM#	Date	Mintage	VF	XF	Unc
2.1	1992	—	.60	1.25	2.50
	1993	—	.60	1.25	2.50
	1994	—	.60	1.25	2.50
	1995	—	.60	1.25	2.50
	1996	—	.80	2.25	3.50

Rev: Berries w/dots inside.

2.2	1992	—	.60	1.25	2.50

Obv: Incuse shield.

2.3	1992	—	.70	1.50	3.00

ALUMINUM

2a	1996	—	—	—	—

50 KOPIYOK

BRASS
Edge: Reeded sections of 16 grooves each.
Rev: 5 dots grouped in wreath to right of final letter K in denomination.

3.1	1992	—	.85	1.75	3.50
	1994	—	.85	1.75	3.50

Edge: Reeded sections of 7 grooves each.
Rev: 4 dots grouped in wreath to right of final letter K in denomination.

3.2	1992	—	.85	1.75	3.50

Rev: 5 dots grouped in wreath to right of final letter K in denomination.

3.3	1992	—	.85	1.75	3.50
	1994	—	.85	1.75	3.50
	1996	—	.85	1.75	3.50

Obv: Incuse shield.

3.4	1992	—	1.00	2.00	4.00

HRYVNIA

BRASS

KM#	Date	Mintage	VF	XF	Unc
8	1992	—	—	10.00	20.00
	1995	—	—	3.50	6.50
	1996	—	—	2.50	4.50

COPPER-NICKEL
Modern Ukrainian Coinage
Obv: National arms.

30	1996	.200	—	—	8.50

UNITED ARAB EMIRATES

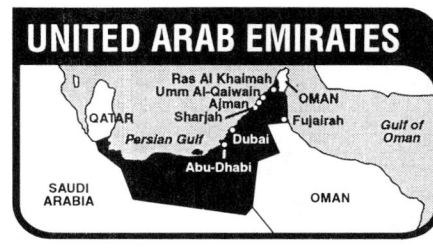

Ajman, al-Fujairah, Ras al-Khaimah, Sharjah and Umm al Qaiwain, five of the former Trucial States which comprise The United Arab Emirates, and which were formerly British treaty protectorates located along the southern shore of the Arabian Peninsula, have issued Non-Circulating Legal Tender Coins (NCLT). These coins have been declared legal tender by the issuing states but are not intended to circulate. No circulation strikes were minted, and none of the coins were available at face value.

RAS AL-KHAIMAH

Ras al-Khaimah is only one of the coin issuing emirates that was not one of the original members of the United Arab Emirates. It was a part of Sharjah. It has an estimated area of 650 sq. mi. (1700 sq. km.) and a population of 30,000. Ras al Khaimah is the only member of the United Arab Emirates that has agriculture as its principal industry.

TITLES

Ras al-Khaimah(t)   راس الخيمة

RULERS
Sultan bin Salim al-Qasimi, 1921-1948
Saqr Bin Muhammad al-Qasimi, 1948-

MONETARY SYSTEM
100 Dirhams = 1 Riyal

50 DIRHAMS

COPPER-NICKEL
Barbary Falcon

KM#	Date	Year Mintage	VF	XF	Unc
28	AH1390	1970	—	—	7.50

RIYAL

3.9500 g, .640 SILVER, .0812 oz ASW

1	AH1389	1969	—	—	12.50
	1389	1969	1,500	— Proof	22.50

2 RIYALS

6.4500 g, .835 SILVER, .1731 oz ASW

2	AH1389	1969	—	—	17.50
	1389	1969	1,500	— Proof	32.50

2 1/2 RIYALS

7.5000 g. .925 SILVER, .2231 oz ASW
Barbary Falcon

KM#	Date	Year Mintage	VF	XF	Unc
29	AH1390	1970 —			17.50

5 RIYALS

15.0000 g, .835 SILVER, .4027 oz ASW

3	AH1389	1969	—			25.00
	1389	1969	1,500		Proof	37.50

UNITED ARAB EMIRATES

The seven United Arab Emirates (formerly known as the Trucial Sheikhdoms or States), located along the southern shore of the Persian Gulf, are comprised of the Sheikhdoms of Abu Dhabi, Dubai, al-Sharjah, Ajman, Umm al Qaiwain, Ras al-Khaimah and al-Fujairah. They have a combined area of about 32,000 sq. mi. (83,600 sq. km.) and a population of *2.1 million. Capital: Abu Zaby (Abu Dhabi). Since the oil strikes of 1958-60, the economy has centered about petroleum.

The Trucial States came under direct British influence in 1892 when the Maritime Truce Treaty enacted after the supression of pirate activity along the Trucial Coast was enlarged to enjoin the states from disposing of any territory, or entering into any foreign agreements, without British consent in return for British protection from external aggression. In March of 1971 Britain reaffirmed its decision to terminate its treaty relationships with the Trucial Sheikhdoms, whereupon the seven states joined with Bahrain and Qatar in an effort to form a union of Arab Emirates under British protection. When the prospective members failed to agree on terms of union, Bahrain and Qatar declared their respective independence, Aug. and Sept. of 1971. Six of the sheikhdoms united to form the United Arab Emirates on Dec. 2, 1971. Ras al-Khaimah joined a few weeks later.

TITLES

الامارات العربية المتحدة

al-Imara(t) al-Arabiya(t) al-Muttahida(t)

MONETARY SYSTEM

Falus, Fulus   *Fals, Fils*   *Falsan*

100 Fils = 1 Dirham

FIL

BRONZE
F.A.O. Issue - Date Palms

1	AH1393	1973	4.000	.10	.15	.20
	1395	1975	—	.10	.15	.20
	1409	1989	—	.10	.15	.20

5 FILS

BRONZE
F.A.O. Issue - Mata Hari Fish

2.1	AH1393	1973	11.400	.10	.15	.25
	1402	1982	—	.10	.15	.25
	1407	1987	—	.10	.15	.25
	1408	1988	—	.10	.15	.25
	1409	1989	—	.10	.15	.25

Reduced size.

KM#	Date	Year Mintage	VF	XF	Unc
2.2	AH1416	1996	—	.10	.15	.25

10 FILS

BRONZE
Arab Dhow

3.1	AH1393	1973	6.400	.25	.40	.90
	1402	1982	—	.25	.40	.90
	1404	1984	—	.25	.40	.90
	1407	1987	—	.25	.40	.90
	1408	1988	—	.25	.40	.90
	1409	1989	—	.25	.40	.90

Reduced size.

3.2	1416	1996	—	.20	.30	.70

25 FILS

COPPER-NICKEL
Arab Dune Gazelle

4	AH1393	1973	10.400	.25	.35	.65
	1402	1982	—	.25	.35	.65
	1403	1983	—	.25	.35	.65
	1404	1984	—	.25	.35	.65
	1406	1986	—	.25	.35	.65
	1407	1987	—	.25	.35	.65
	1408	1988	—	.25	.35	.65
	1409	1989	—	.25	.35	.65
	1410	1990	—	.25	.35	.65
	1415	1995	—	.25	.35	.65

50 FILS

COPPER-NICKEL
Oil Derricks

5	AH1393	1973	8.400	.35	.50	1.50
	1402	1982	—	.35	.55	1.65
	1404	1984	—	.35	.55	1.65
	1407	1987	—	.35	.55	1.65
	1408	1988	—	.35	.55	1.65
	1409	1989	—	.35	.55	1.65

Reduced size, 7-sided coin.

16	AH1415	1995	—	.25	.45	1.35

DIRHAM

COPPER-NICKEL
Jug

KM#	Date	Year Mintage	VF	XF	Unc
6.1	AH1393	1973	13.000	.50	.75	2.00
	1402	1982	—	.50	.80	2.25
	1404	1984	—	.50	.80	2.25
	1406	1986	—	.50	.80	2.25
	1407	1987	—	.50	.80	2.25
	1408	1988	—	.50	.80	2.25
	1409	1989	—	.50	.80	2.25

Reduced size.

6.2	AH1415	1995	—	.35	.65	1.85

27th Chess Olympiad in Dubai

KM#	Date	Mintage	VF	XF	Unc
10	1986	—	2.00	4.50	9.00

25th Anniversary - Offshore Oil Drilling

11	ND(1987)	—	2.00	4.50	9.00

10th Anniversary - al-Ain University

14	ND(1987)	—	1.75	4.00	8.00

Soccer

15	ND(1990)	—	1.50	3.00	6.50

5 DIRHAMS

COPPER-NICKEL
1500th Anniversary - al-Hegira

KM#	Date	Year Mintage	VF	XF	Unc
9	AH1401	1981	—	2.00	3.50	7.00

UNITED STATES

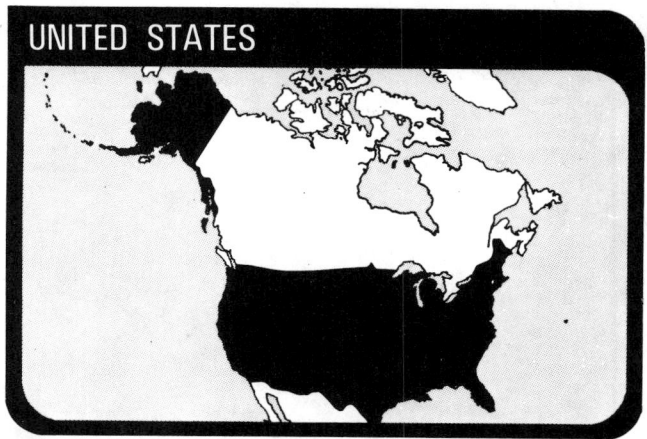

The United States of America as politically organized, under the Articles of Confederation consisted of the 13 original British-American colonies — New Hampshire, Massachusetts, Rhode Island, Connecticut, New York, New Jersey, Pennsylvania, Delaware, Virginia, North Carolina, South Carolina, Georgia and Maryland — clustered along the eastern seaboard of North American between the forests of Maine and the marshes of Georgia. Under the Article of Confederation, the United States had no national capital; Philadelphia, where the "United States in Congress Assembled" met, was the "seat of government." The population during this political phase of America's history (1781-1789) was about 3 million, most of whom lived on self-sufficient family farms. Fishing, lumbering and the production of grains for export were major economic endeavors. Rapid strides were also being made in industry and manufacturing by 1775, the (then) colonies were accounting for one-seventh of the world's production of raw iron.

On the basis of the voyage of John Cabot to the North American mainland in 1497, England claimed the entire continent. The first permanent English settlement was established at Jamestown, Virginia, in 1607. France and Spain also claimed extensive territory in North America. At the end of the French and Indian Wars (1763), England acquired all of the territory east of the Mississippi River, including East and West Florida. From 1776 to 1781, the States were governed by the Continental Congress. From 1781 to 1789, they were organized under the Articles of Confederation, during which period the individual States had the right to issue money. Independence from Great Britain was attained by the American Revolution in 1776. The Constitution which organized and governs the present United States was ratified on Nov. 21, 1788.

Small cents

Indian Head

Bronze composition

Weight: 3.11 grams. **Composition:** 95% copper, 5% tin and zinc.

Date	Mintage	G-4	VG-8	F-12	VF-20	XF-40	AU-50	MS-60	MS-65	Prf-65
1901	79,611,143	1.30	1.40	1.75	2.75	7.50	15.00	25.00	135.	390.
1902	87,376,722	1.30	1.40	1.75	2.75	7.50	15.00	25.00	135.	390.
1903	85,094,493	1.30	1.40	1.75	2.75	7.50	15.00	25.00	135.	400.
1904	61,328,015	1.30	1.40	1.75	2.75	7.50	15.00	25.00	135.	435.
1905	80,719,163	1.30	1.40	1.75	2.75	7.50	15.00	25.00	135.	435.
1906	96,022,255	1.30	1.40	1.70	2.75	7.50	15.00	25.00	135.	390.

Small cents

Date	Mintage	G-4	VG-8	F-12	VF-20	XF-40	AU-50	MS-60	MS-65	Prf-65
1907	108,138,618	1.30	1.40	1.70	2.75	7.50	15.00	25.00	135.	470.
1908	32,327,987	1.30	1.75	2.25	3.00	8.00	15.00	25.00	135.	375.
1908S	1,115,000	36.00	40.00	46.00	52.00	80.00	130.	195.	600.	—
1909	14,370,645	2.50	3.00	4.00	5.75	17.50	26.00	35.00	135.	425.
1909S	309,000	240.	275.	300.	345.	380.	430.	485.	1450.	—

NOTE: Earlier dates (1864-1900) exist for this type.

Lincoln

Wheat reverse   **"VDB"**   **Memorial reverse**

Wheat reverse, bronze composition

Designer: Victor D. Brenner. **Size:** 19 millimeters. **Weight** 3.11 grams. **Composition:** 95% copper, 5% tin and zinc. **Notes:** The 1909 "VDB" varieties have the designer's initials inscribed at the 6 o'clock position on the reverse. The initials were removed until 1918, when they were restored on the obverse.

Date	Mintage	G-4	VG-8	F-12	VF-20	XF-40	AU-50	MS-60	MS-65	Prf-65
1909	72,702,618	1.00	1.10	1.50	1.75	2.75	6.75	14.00	70.00	490.
1909VDB	27,995,000	2.50	2.60	2.75	2.90	4.25	6.00	9.00	43.00	3100.
1909S	1,825,000	38.00	43.00	52.00	68.00	95.00	110.	120.	425.	—
1909SVDB	484,000	350.	395.	435.	470.	510.	560.	660.	2250.	—
1910	146,801,218	.20	.25	.35	.60	2.50	6.00	14.50	75.00	470.
1910S	6,045,000	6.00	7.00	8.50	12.00	23.00	45.00	60.00	250.	—
1911	101,177,787	.25	.40	.75	1.95	4.50	7.50	18.00	125.	470.
1911D	12,672,000	4.50	5.00	7.00	12.00	35.00	55.00	72.00	750.	—
1911S	4,026,000	15.00	16.00	18.50	22.00	46.00	75.00	135.	1050.	—
1912	68,153,060	1.25	1.40	2.00	4.50	11.00	14.50	30.00	190.	625.
1912D	10,411,000	4.75	5.25	7.00	16.00	41.00	65.00	125.	790.	—
1912S	4,431,000	10.50	13.00	14.50	18.50	40.00	63.00	95.00	1200.	—
1913	76,532,352	.45	.60	1.60	3.50	13.00	17.00	29.00	190.	470.
1913D	15,804,000	2.25	2.40	3.50	8.00	26.00	50.00	80.00	925.	—
1913S	6,101,000	5.00	6.00	7.50	13.50	34.00	60.00	120.	1700.	—
1914	75,238,432	.35	.65	1.50	3.75	10.00	26.00	40.00	225.	500.
1914D	1,193,000	85.00	105.	135.	195.	450.	690.	1000.	7250.	—
1914S	4,137,000	10.00	11.00	13.00	20.00	42.50	95.00	195.	6500.	—
1915	29,092,120	1.10	1.20	4.00	12.00	44.00	65.00	80.00	475.	490.
1915D	22,050,000	1.10	1.20	2.00	3.50	12.00	25.00	49.00	450.	—
1915S	4,833,000	6.50	7.50	9.00	12.50	35.00	60.00	125.	2150.	—
1916	131,833,677	.15	.20	.45	1.25	4.00	6.50	12.00	100.	1250.
1916D	35,956,000	.35	.50	1.20	2.50	9.50	19.50	50.00	1350.	—
1916S	22,510,000	1.00	1.25	1.60	2.75	9.50	19.00	60.00	3000.	—
1917	196,429,785	.15	.20	.40	1.00	4.00	7.00	13.00	100.	—
1917D	55,120,000	.30	.40	1.00	2.50	9.00	17.00	55.00	850.	—
1917S	32,620,000	.45	.55	1.00	2.25	8.00	18.00	55.00	1800.	—
1918	288,104,634	.15	.20	.35	.90	4.00	7.00	12.00	165.	—
1918D	47,830,000	.30	.60	1.00	2.50	8.50	18.00	55.00	1050.	—
1918S	34,680,000	.35	.55	1.00	2.00	8.00	22.00	55.00	3900.	—
1919	392,021,000	.15	.20	.40	.65	2.00	5.00	9.00	75.00	—
1919D	57,154,000	.30	.40	.65	2.00	7.50	17.50	43.00	775.	—
1919S	139,760,000	.15	.25	1.25	1.50	3.50	13.50	33.00	1850.	—
1920	310,165,000	.15	.20	.30	.65	2.50	5.50	10.00	75.00	—
1920D	49,280,000	.25	.35	.95	2.50	8.75	17.00	50.00	680.	—
1920S	46,220,000	.25	.30	1.25	1.75	7.00	23.00	75.00	4200.	—
1921	39,157,000	.25	.35	.60	1.25	5.50	16.50	35.00	115.	—
1921S	15,274,000	1.00	1.10	1.75	3.75	16.50	60.00	85.00	3200.	—
1922D	7,160,000	7.00	8.50	10.00	12.50	23.00	42.00	65.00	600.	—
1922	Inc. Ab.	300.	350.	415.	540.	1250.	2500.	5200.	60,000.	—
1923	74,723,000	.20	.30	.40	1.25	4.50	7.00	11.50	185.	—
1923S	8,700,000	1.60	2.00	3.50	5.50	23.00	65.00	170.	2600.	—
1924	75,178,000	.20	.25	.45	1.25	4.50	10.00	20.00	100.	—
1924D	2,520,000	8.50	10.00	12.50	22.00	60.00	130.	225.	3700.	—
1924S	11,696,000	.85	1.10	2.00	3.00	12.00	50.00	95.00	5300.	—
1925	139,949,000	.20	.25	.40	1.00	3.00	6.00	9.00	70.00	—
1925D	22,580,000	.35	.70	1.00	2.00	9.00	22.50	45.00	1050.	—
1925S	26,380,000	.25	.35	.80	1.25	8.50	17.50	55.00	4450.	—
1926	157,088,000	.15	.20	.30	.80	2.00	5.50	8.00	45.00	—
1926D	28,020,000	.20	.40	.70	1.50	6.50	15.00	50.00	1200.	—
1926S	4,550,000	2.75	3.25	5.00	6.00	12.00	50.00	95.00	9500.	—
1927	144,440,000	.15	.20	.30	.80	2.00	5.00	8.00	85.00	—
1927D	27,170,000	.20	.25	.60	1.25	4.00	12.50	48.00	950.	—
1927S	14,276,000	.80	.95	1.50	3.00	10.00	18.00	60.00	2800.	—
1928	134,116,000	.15	.20	.30	.80	2.00	5.00	8.00	75.00	—
1928D	31,170,000	.20	.25	.50	1.00	3.50	10.00	25.00	375.	—
1928S	17,266,000	.60	.75	1.10	1.75	4.00	12.00	52.00	1150.	—
1929	185,262,000	.15	.20	.30	.80	1.50	5.00	6.00	70.00	—
1929D	41,730,000	.15	.20	.45	.90	3.50	7.50	15.00	170.	—
1929S	50,148,000	.15	.20	.35	.75	2.50	4.50	11.00	115.	—
1930	157,415,000	.10	.15	.20	.50	1.75	3.00	5.50	35.00	—
1930D	40,100,000	.15	.20	.45	.75	2.50	5.00	12.00	75.00	—
1930S	24,286,000	.20	.25	.35	.80	1.60	3.00	7.00	38.00	—
1931	19,396,000	.50	.60	1.00	1.35	2.00	7.00	16.50	80.00	—

Small cents

Date	Mintage	G-4	VG-8	F-12	VF-20	XF-40	AU-50	MS-60	MS-65	Prf-65
1931D	4,480,000	2.75	3.00	3.25	4.00	8.50	34.00	46.00	450.	—
1931S	866,000	34.00	35.00	40.00	42.00	44.00	49.00	59.00	250.	—
1932	9,062,000	1.50	1.80	2.25	2.50	3.50	9.50	17.00	60.00	—
1932D	10,500,000	1.00	1.25	1.40	1.50	2.75	7.00	14.00	57.00	—
1933	14,360,000	.90	1.15	1.50	1.90	3.50	9.00	16.00	59.00	—
1933D	6,200,000	1.75	2.25	3.00	3.20	5.00	11.00	16.00	50.00	—
1934	219,080,000	—	.15	.20	.25	.75	1.50	3.00	20.00	—
1934D	28,446,000	.15	.20	.25	.45	1.50	5.00	15.00	45.00	—
1935	245,338,000	—	.10	.15	.25	.75	1.00	1.50	20.00	—
1935D	11,011,000	—	.15	.20	.30	.95	2.50	4.50	9.00	—
1935S	38,702,000	.10	.20	.30	.40	1.00	3.00	10.00	44.00	—
1936	309,637,569	—	.10	.15	.25	.75	1.00	1.50	6.00	825.
1936D	40,620,000	—	.10	.15	.25	.75	1.50	2.50	8.00	—
1936S	29,130,000	.10	.15	.25	.35	.85	1.75	2.50	8.00	—
1937	309,179,320	—	.10	.15	.20	.70	.90	1.50	7.00	120.
1937D	50,430,000	—	.10	.15	.25	.70	1.00	2.25	9.00	—
1937S	34,500,000	—	.10	.15	.25	.60	1.25	1.75	8.00	—
1938	156,696,734	—	.10	.15	.20	.50	1.00	1.60	5.75	85.00
1938D	20,010,000	.20	.25	.35	.45	.75	1.50	2.50	8.00	—
1938S	15,180,000	.30	.35	.50	.70	.90	1.25	2.25	8.00	—
1939	316,479,520	—	.10	.15	.20	.30	.50	1.00	5.50	75.00
1939D	15,160,000	.30	.30	.35	.60	.85	1.90	2.25	8.00	—
1939S	52,070,000	—	.15	.20	.25	.45	.90	1.35	8.50	—
1940	586,825,872	—	.15	.20	.25	.30	.45	.95	5.50	65.00
1940D	81,390,000	—	.15	.20	.25	.35	.50	1.00	5.50	—
1940S	112,940,000	—	.15	.20	.25	.30	.75	1.00	5.50	—
1941	887,039,100	—	—	.10	.15	.25	.40	.85	5.50	65.00
1941D	128,700,000	—	—	.15	.20	.25	1.00	2.00	8.00	—
1941S	92,360,000	—	—	.15	.20	.25	1.25	2.25	11.00	—
1942	657,828,600	—	—	.10	.15	.20	.25	.50	4.50	70.00
1942D	206,698,000	—	—	.10	.15	.20	.30	.50	5.75	—
1942S	85,590,000	—	—	.10	.20	.30	1.50	3.50	14.00	—

Steel composition

Weight: 2.7 grams. **Composition:** steel coated with zinc.

Date	Mintage	G-4	VG-8	F-12	VF-20	XF-40	AU-50	MS-60	MS-65	Prf-65
1943	684,628,670	—	—	.25	.30	.50	.70	.85	4.50	—
1943D	217,660,000	—	—	.25	.35	.60	.65	1.00	6.00	—
1943S	191,550,000	—	.30	.35	.40	.70	1.00	1.75	8.50	—

Copper-zinc composition

Weight: 3.11 grams. **Composition:** 95% copper, 5% zinc. **Notes:** The 1995 "doubled die" has distinct doubling of the date and lettering on the obverse.

Date	Mintage	XF-40	MS-60	Prf-65
1944	1,435,400,000	.20	.50	—
1944D	430,578,000	.20	.45	—
1944D/S	—	150.	375.	—
1944S	282,760,000	.20	.45	—
1945	1,040,515,000	.20	.60	—
1945D	226,268,000	.20	.70	—
1945S	181,770,000	.20	.45	—
1946	991,655,000	.20	.35	—
1946D	315,690,000	.20	.50	—
1946S	198,100,000	.20	.50	—
1947	190,555,000	.20	.60	—
1947D	194,750,000	.20	.40	—
1947S	99,000,000	.20	.55	—
1948	317,570,000	.20	.50	—
1948D	172,637,000	.20	.45	—
1948S	81,735,000	.20	.65	—
1949	217,775,000	.20	.75	—
1949D	153,132,000	.20	.50	—
1949S	64,290,000	.25	1.00	—
1950	272,686,386	.20	.50	35.00
1950D	334,950,000	.20	.50	—
1950S	118,505,000	.20	.80	—
1951	295,633,500	.20	.90	30.00
1951D	625,355,000	.10	.50	—
1951S	136,010,000	.15	.75	—
1952	186,856,980	.10	.50	25.00
1952D	746,130,000	.10	.50	—
1952S	137,800,004	.15	1.00	—
1953	256,883,800	.10	.50	27.00
1953D	700,515,000	.10	.50	—
1953S	181,835,000	.15	.45	—
1954	71,873,350	.15	.75	15.00
1954D	251,552,500	.10	.35	—
1954S	96,190,000	.15	.35	—
1955	330,958,000	.10	.30	11.50
1955 doubled die	—	550.	1250.	—
1955D	563,257,500	.10	.30	—
1955S	44,610,000	.25	.60	—
1956	421,414,384	—	.30	2.50
1956D	1,098,201,100	—	.30	—
1957	283,787,952	—	.30	1.75
1957D	1,051,342,000	—	.30	—
1958	253,400,652	—	.30	2.50
1958D	800,953,300	—	.30	—

Small cents

Date	Mintage	XF-40	MS-65	Prf-65
1959	610,864,291	—	.50	1.50
1959D	1,279,760,000	—	.50	—
1960 small date	588,096,602	1.50	2.50	16.00
1960 large date Inc. Ab.		—	.30	1.00
1960D small date	1,580,884,000	—	.50	—
1960D large date Inc. Ab.		—	.30	—
1961	756,373,244	—	.30	.90
1961D	1,753,266,700	—	.30	—
1962	609,263,019	—	.30	.90
1962D	1,793,148,400	—	.30	—
1963	757,185,645	—	.30	.90
1963D	1,774,020,400	—	.30	—
1964	2,652,525,762	—	.30	.90
1964D	3,799,071,500	—	.30	—
1965	1,497,224,900	—	.30	—
1966	2,188,147,783	—	.30	—
1967	3,048,667,100	—	.30	—
1968	1,707,880,970	—	.30	—
1968D	2,886,269,600	—	.40	—
1968S	261,311,510	—	.40	.80
1969	1,136,910,000	—	.60	—
1969D	4,002,832,200	—	.40	—
1969S	547,309,631	—	.40	.80
1970	1,898,315,000	—	.40	—
1970D	2,891,438,900	—	.40	—
1970S	693,192,814	—	.40	.80
1970S small date	—	45.00	55.00	
1971	1,919,490,000	—	.35	—
1971D	2,911,045,600	—	.40	—
1971S	528,354,192	—	.20	.80
1972	2,933,255,000	—	.20	—
1972 doubled die	—	145.	400.	

1955 doubled die

1972 doubled die

Large date

Small date

Lincoln Memorial reverse

Reverse designer: Frank Gasparro. **Weight:** 3.11 grams. **Notes:** The dates were modified in 1960, 1970 and 1982, resulting in large-date and small-date varieties for those years. The 1972 "doubled die" shows doubling of "In God We Trust". The 1979-S and 1981-S Type II proofs have a clearer mintmark than the Type I proofs of those years. Some 1982 cents have the predominantly copper composition; others have the predominantly zinc composition. They can be distinguished by weight. The 1983 "doubled die reverse" shows doubling of "United States of America". The 1984 "doubled die" shows doubling of Lincoln's ear on the obverse.

Date	Mintage	XF-40	MS-65	Prf-65
1972D	2,665,071,400	—	.20	—
1972S	380,200,104	—	.20	.90
1973	3,728,245,000	—	.15	—
1973D	3,549,576,588	—	.15	—
1973S	319,937,634	—	.20	.80
1974	4,232,140,523	—	.15	—
1974D	4,235,098,000	—	.15	—
1974S	412,039,228	—	.20	.75
1975	5,451,476,142	—	.15	—
1975D	4,505,245,300	—	.15	—
1975S	(2,845,450)	—	—	5.50
1976	4,674,292,426	—	.20	—
1976D	4,221,592,455	—	.20	—
1976S	(4,149,730)	—	—	4.50
1977	4,469,930,000	—	.20	—
1977D	4,149,062,300	—	.20	—
1977S	(3,251,152)	—	—	4.00
1978	5,558,605,000	—	.20	—
1978D	4,280,233,400	—	.20	—
1978S	(3,127,781)	—	—	3.00
1979	6,018,515,000	—	.20	—
1979D	4,139,357,254	—	.20	—
1979S T-I	(3,677,175)	—	—	3.00
1979S T-II	(Inc. Ab.)	—	—	4.00
1980	7,414,705,000	—	.20	—
1980D	5,140,098,660	—	.20	—
1980S	(3,554,806)	—	—	2.25
1981	7,491,750,000	—	.20	—
1981D	5,373,235,677	—	.20	—
1981S T-I	(4,063,083)	—	—	3.00
1981S T-II	(Inc. Ab.)	—	—	50.00
1982 copper lg.dt.	10,712,525,000	—	.20	—
1982 copper sm.dt.		—	.20	—
1982 zinc lg.dt.		—	.50	—
1982 zinc sm.dt.		—	1.00	—
1982D copper lg.dt.	6,012,979,368	—	.20	—
1982D zinc lg.dt.		—	.30	—
1982D zinc sm.dt.		—	.20	—
1982S	(3,857,479)	—	—	3.00
1983	7,752,355,000	—	.20	—
1983 doubled die	—	400.	—	
1983D	6,467,199,428	—	.20	—
1983S	(3,279,126)	—	—	4.50
1984	8,151,079,000	—	.20	—
1984 doubled die	—	275.	—	
1984D	5,569,238,906	—	.70	—
1984S	(3,065,110)	—	—	3.50
1985	5,648,489,887	—	.25	—
1985D	5,287,399,926	—	.20	—
1985S	(3,362,821)	—	—	4.50
1986	4,491,395,493	—	.70	—
1986D	4,442,866,698	—	.20	—
1986S	(3,010,497)	—	—	7.50
1987	4,682,466,931	—	.20	—
1987D	4,879,389,514	—	.20	—
1987S	(4,227,728)	—	—	4.00
1988	6,092,810,000	—	.20	—
1988D	5,253,740,443	—	.20	—
1988S	(3,262,948)	—	—	2.75
1989	7,261,535,000	—	.20	—
1989D	5,345,467,111	—	.20	—
1989S	(3,220,194)	—	—	2.75
1990	6,851,765,000	—	.20	—
1990D	4,922,894,533	—	.20	—
1990S	(3,299,559)	—	—	5.75
1990 no S	—	—	1250.	
1991	5,165,940,000	—	.20	—
1991D	4,158,442,076	—	.20	—
1991S	(2,867,787)	—	—	7.50
1992	4,648,905,000	—	.20	—
1992D	4,448,673,300	—	.20	—
1992S	(4,176,560)	—	—	6.50
1993	5,684,705,000	—	.25	—
1993D	6,426,650,571	—	.25	—
1993S	(3,394,792)	—	—	9.50
1994	6,500,850,000	—	.20	—
1994D	7,131,765,000	—	.20	—
1994S	(3,269,923)	—	—	8.00
1995	6,411,440,000	—	.20	—
1995 doubled die	—	35.00	—	
1995D	7,128,560,000	—	.15	—
1995S		—	—	9.50
1996	6,612,465,000	—	.15	—
1996D	6,510,795,000	—	.15	—
1996S		—	—	6.50
1997	4,622,800,000	—	.15	—
1997D	4,576,555,000	—	.15	—
1997S	(1,975,000)	—	—	7.00
1998		—	.15	—
1998D		—	.15	—
1998S		—	—	5.50

Small date

Large date

Nickel five-cent

Liberty

Altered

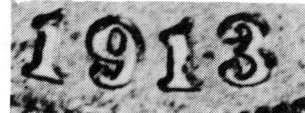
Authentic

Designer: Charles E. Barber. **Size:** 21.2 millimeters. **Weight:** 56 grams. **Composition:** 75% copper, 25% nickel.

Date	Mintage	G-4	VG-8	F-12	VF-20	XF-40	AU-50	MS-60	MS-65	Prf-65
1901	26,480,213	1.20	2.25	5.50	8.50	20.00	40.00	60.00	480.	450.
1902	31,480,579	1.20	2.25	4.25	8.00	19.00	40.00	60.00	480.	450.
1903	28,006,725	1.20	2.35	4.25	8.00	20.00	40.00	60.00	480.	450.
1904	21,404,984	1.20	1.50	4.25	9.00	21.00	40.00	60.00	480.	590.
1905	29,827,276	1.20	1.40	4.00	7.75	19.00	40.00	60.00	480.	490.
1906	38,613,725	1.20	1.40	4.00	7.75	20.00	40.00	60.00	490.	490.
1907	39,214,800	1.20	1.40	4.00	7.50	19.00	39.00	60.00	550.	550.
1908	22,686,177	1.20	1.40	4.50	8.00	20.00	38.00	60.00	600.	450.
1909	11,590,526	1.50	2.50	5.00	9.00	23.00	40.00	75.00	600.	490.
1910	30,169,353	1.20	1.40	4.00	7.50	19.00	40.00	60.00	550.	490.
1911	39,559,372	1.20	1.40	4.00	7.50	19.00	38.00	60.00	480.	490.
1912	26,236,714	1.20	1.40	4.00	7.50	19.00	38.00	60.00	480.	490.
1912D	8,474,000	1.40	1.75	6.00	18.00	48.00	125.	225.	900.	—
1912S	238,000	43.00	57.00	85.00	225.	450.	650.	800.	2250.	—

1913 Only 5 known, Eliasberg Sale, May 1996, Prf, $1,485,000.

NOTE: Earlier dates (1883-1900) exist for this type.

Buffalo

Mound type   **Line type**   **1918/17D**

Mound type

Designer: James Earle Fraser. **Size:** 21.2 millimeters. **Weight:** 5 grams. **Composition:** 75% copper, 25% nickel.

Date	Mintage	G-4	VG-8	F-12	VF-20	XF-40	AU-50	MS-60	MS-65	Prf-65
1913	30,993,520	5.50	6.00	6.50	8.00	14.00	21.00	32.00	110.	2000.
1913D	5,337,000	8.75	10.50	12.50	16.00	25.00	40.00	50.00	215.	—
1913S	2,105,000	15.00	17.00	22.00	30.00	45.00	59.00	65.00	600.	—

Line type

Notes: In 1913 the reverse design was modified so the ground under the buffalo was represented as a line rather than a mound. On the 1937-D 3-legged variety, the buffalo's right front leg is missing, the result of a damaged die.

Date	Mintage	G-4	VG-8	F-12	VF-20	XF-40	AU-50	MS-60	MS-65	Prf-65
1913	29,858,700	6.50	7.50	9.00	11.00	15.00	23.00	32.50	275.	1400.
1913D	4,156,000	49.00	60.00	70.00	80.00	90.00	110.	155.	800.	—
1913S	1,209,000	100.	140.	170.	185.	210.	260.	325.	2700.	—
1914	20,665,738	9.50	11.00	12.50	20.00	25.00	35.00	45.00	340.	1300.
1914D	3,912,000	45.00	55.00	70.00	80.00	120.	140.	195.	1400.	—
1914S	3,470,000	9.50	12.00	20.00	28.00	45.00	75.00	130.	1650.	—
1915	20,987,270	4.75	5.50	7.00	10.50	17.50	35.00	45.00	250.	1250.
1915D	7,569,500	12.50	15.50	29.00	39.00	70.00	90.00	190.	1850.	—
1915S	1,505,000	16.00	25.00	59.50	85.00	160.	260.	450.	2150.	—
1916	63,498,066	2.50	2.75	3.50	5.50	11.00	20.00	39.00	260.	2200.
1916/16	Inc. Ab.	1700.	3350.	5000.	8000.	11,500.	17,000.	28,000.	100,000.	—
1916D	13,333,000	8.50	11.00	16.50	28.00	58.00	80.00	130.	1600.	—
1916S	11,860,000	5.00	8.00	13.50	25.00	55.00	80.00	155.	2200.	—

Nickel five-cent

Date	Mintage	G-4	VG-8	F-12	VF-20	XF-40	AU-50	MS-60	MS-65	Prf-65
1917	51,424,029	2.40	3.00	5.00	9.00	17.50	35.00	48.00	475.	—
1917D	9,910,800	9.00	14.00	30.00	65.00	100.	160.	280.	2750.	—
1917S	4,193,000	10.00	15.00	33.00	70.00	120.	250.	340.	2900.	—
1918	32,086,314	1.90	3.25	5.50	12.50	28.00	45.00	85.00	1300.	—
1918/17D	8,362,314	390.	600.	1050.	2150.	4900.	8950.	13,000	215,000	—
1918D	Inc. Ab.	9.00	13.50	33.00	80.00	160.	255.	340.	4000.	—
1918S	4,882,000	9.00	16.00	30.00	79.00	160.	250.	390.	25,000.	—
1919	60,868,000	1.30	1.60	2.50	6.50	15.00	35.00	45.00	440.	—
1919D	8,006,000	10.00	16.50	38.00	89.00	175.	295.	475.	4400.	—
1919S	7,521,000	5.50	13.00	30.00	80.00	190.	310.	440.	10,000.	—
1920	63,093,000	1.00	1.50	2.25	7.00	15.00	35.00	45.00	650.	—
1920D	9,418,000	6.50	16.00	35.00	85.00	240.	300.	420.	4200.	—
1920S	9,689,000	3.50	6.50	18.50	75.00	175.	275.	360.	15,750.	—
1921	10,663,000	2.00	3.00	4.50	17.50	40.00	57.50	100.	620.	—
1921S	1,557,000	27.50	49.50	85.00	395.	725.	950.	1350.	5300.	—
1923	35,715,000	1.40	1.75	3.00	7.50	15.00	30.00	43.00	475.	—
1923S	6,142,000	3.00	6.00	16.50	90.00	250.	300.	385.	7500.	—
1924	21,620,000	1.25	1.90	3.00	8.00	20.00	35.00	62.00	600.	—
1924D	5,258,000	3.50	6.00	17.50	65.00	180.	250.	315.	3200.	—
1924S	1,437,000	7.00	16.00	69.50	400.	1100.	1375.	1850.	7600.	—
1925	35,565,100	2.25	2.50	3.50	8.00	15.00	36.00	40.00	500.	—
1925D	4,450,000	8.00	17.00	39.50	80.00	165.	245.	340.	3200.	—
1925S	6,256,000	3.00	9.00	17.50	69.00	175.	250.	340.	32,000.	—
1926	44,693,000	.75	.95	1.50	6.00	14.50	25.00	35.00	150.	—
1926D	5,638,000	4.00	9.50	29.00	85.00	160.	210.	240.	3050.	—
1926S	970,000	10.00	18.00	50.00	325.	700.	1350.	2650.	36,500.	—
1927	37,981,000	.80	1.00	1.50	5.00	12.50	25.00	30.00	190.	—
1927D	5,730,000	2.00	4.90	8.00	30.00	80.00	125.	160.	4000.	—
1927S	3,430,000	1.35	2.00	4.60	25.00	80.00	160.	450.	14,000.	—
1928	23,411,000	1.10	1.25	1.50	7.00	15.00	30.00	35.00	240.	—
1928D	6,436,000	1.35	2.50	6.00	17.50	35.00	45.00	49.00	600.	—
1928S	6,936,000	1.35	1.50	2.75	10.00	25.00	100.	200.	3500.	—
1929	36,446,000	.80	1.00	1.50	7.00	13.00	25.00	34.00	270.	—
1929D	8,370,000	1.25	1.25	2.00	8.00	35.00	45.00	55.00	1450.	—
1929S	7,754,000	.80	.90	1.25	3.00	12.00	30.00	45.00	375.	—
1930	22,849,000	.75	.85	1.50	4.00	9.00	20.00	27.00	125.	—
1930S	5,435,000	.85	1.00	2.00	4.00	10.00	30.00	43.00	450.	—
1931S	1,200,000	4.00	4.25	4.75	6.50	18.50	33.00	43.00	200.	—
1934	20,213,003	.70	.75	1.00	5.00	10.00	19.00	25.00	325.	—
1934D	7,480,000	.80	1.00	1.85	7.50	18.50	35.00	42.00	1000.	—
1935	58,264,000	.65	.80	1.00	2.75	4.50	9.50	17.00	100.	—
1935D	12,092,000	.70	.90	2.00	6.00	18.00	35.00	40.00	350.	—
1935S	10,300,000	.70	.80	1.00	2.90	5.50	15.00	30.00	150.	—
1936	119,001,420	.65	.75	.85	1.60	3.50	8.50	14.00	90.00	900.
1936D	24,814,000	.65	.75	.85	2.00	5.50	12.50	19.00	105.	—
1936S	14,930,000	.70	.75	.85	2.00	3.50	12.00	19.00	95.00	—
1937	79,485,769	.65	.75	.85	1.60	3.50	8.50	14.00	45.00	750.
1937D	17,826,000	.65	.75	.85	1.75	3.75	9.50	14.00	60.00	—
1937D 3 Leg.	Inc. Ab.	160.	225.	250.	295.	375.	575.	1150.	15,500.	—

1937D three-legged

Date	Mintage	G-4	VG-8	F-12	VF-20	XF-40	AU-50	MS-60	MS-65	Prf-65
1937S	5,635,000	.80	.90	1.00	1.90	3.75	9.00	14.00	55.00	—
1938D	7,020,000	1.40	1.50	1.75	3.00	4.50	9.00	13.00	35.00	—
1938 D/D		2.25	4.25	5.75	10.00	14.00	17.00	19.00	60.00	—
1938D/S	Inc. Ab.	6.00	8.00	10.00	15.00	19.00	32.00	40.00	165.	—

Jefferson

Wartime (note mintmark)

Pre-war composition

Designer: Felix Schlag. **Size:** 21.2 millimeters. **Weight:** 5 grams. **Composition:** 75% copper, 25% nickel. **Notes:** Some 1939 strikes have doubling of the word "Monticello" on the reverse.

Nickel five-cent

Date	Mintage	G-4	VG-8	F-12	VF-20	XF-40	MS-60	MS-65	Prf-65
1938	19,515,365	—	.25	.40	.80	1.25	3.50	7.00	60.00
1938D	5,376,000	.60	.90	1.00	1.25	1.75	4.25	8.00	—
1938S	4,105,000	1.25	1.35	1.50	1.75	2.25	3.75	8.50	—
1939	120,627,535	—	—	.20	.25	.30	1.75	3.50	55.00
1939 Doubled Monticello		—	20.00	30.00	45.00	75.00	200.	—	—
1939D	3,514,000	2.50	3.00	3.50	5.00	10.00	36.00	55.00	—
1939S	6,630,000	.40	.45	.60	1.50	2.75	13.00	30.00	—
1940	176,499,158	—	—	—	—	.25	1.00	1.25	53.00
1940D	43,540,000	—	—	.20	.30	.40	2.50	2.75	—
1940S	39,690,000	—	—	.20	.25	.50	2.75	5.00	—
1941	203,283,720	—	—	—	—	.20	.90	2.00	50.00
1941D	53,432,000	—	—	.20	.30	.50	2.50	5.00	—
1941S	43,445,000	—	—	.20	.30	.50	3.75	6.75	—
1942	49,818,600	—	—	—	—	.40	4.50	8.50	46.00
1942D	13,938,000	—	.30	.40	.60	2.00	17.00	35.00	—

Wartime composition

Composition: 56% copper, 35% silver (.0563 ounces), 9% manganese

Date	Mintage	G-4	VG-8	F-12	VF-20	XF-40	MS-60	MS-65	Prf-65
1942P	57,900,600	.40	.65	.85	1.00	1.75	7.00	12.50	85.00
1942S	32,900,000	.45	.70	1.00	1.10	1.75	5.00	8.50	—
1943P	271,165,000	.35	.50	.85	1.00	1.50	3.50	6.50	—
1943/2P	Inc. Ab.	20.00	30.00	45.00	60.00	75.00	250.	550.	—
1943D	15,294,000	.75	.90	1.20	1.50	1.75	2.75	5.50	—
1943S	104,060,000	.35	.55	.70	1.00	1.50	3.25	5.75	—
1944P	119,150,000	.35	.50	.70	1.00	1.50	4.50	8.50	—
1944D	32,309,000	.40	.60	.80	1.00	1.75	5.00	9.50	—
1944S	21,640,000	.40	.60	.80	1.15	1.75	3.50	7.00	—
1945P	119,408,100	.30	.50	.70	1.00	1.50	3.50	7.00	—
1945D	37,158,000	.40	.55	.75	1.00	1.50	3.50	7.00	—
1945S	58,939,000	.35	.50	.70	.80	.90	2.00	5.00	—

Pre-war composition resumed

Notes: The 1979-S and 1981-T Type II proofs have clearer mintmarks than the Type 1 proofs of those years.

Date	Mintage	G-4	VG-8	F-12	VF-20	XF-40	MS-60	MS-65	Prf-65
1946	161,116,000	—	—	—	.20	.25	.40	.75	—
1946D	45,292,200	—	—	—	.25	.35	.75	1.25	—
1946S	13,560,000	—	—	—	.30	.40	.50	1.00	—
1947	95,000,000	—	—	—	.20	.25	.75	2.00	—
1947D	37,822,000	—	—	—	.20	.30	.90	2.00	—
1947S	24,720,000	—	—	—	.20	.25	.70	2.00	—
1948	89,348,000	—	—	—	.20	.25	.40	1.50	—
1948D	44,734,000	—	—	—	.25	.35	1.20	2.75	—
1948S	11,300,000	—	—	—	.25	.50	1.00	2.25	—
1949	60,652,000	—	—	—	.25	.30	.80	2.50	—
1949D	36,498,000	—	—	—	.30	.40	1.00	2.50	—
1949D/S	Inc. Ab.	—	—	30.00	40.00	65.00	170.	325.	—
1949S	9,716,000	—	.25	.35	.45	.90	1.50	3.50	—
1950	9,847,386	—	.20	.30	.35	.75	1.50	3.50	33.00
1950D	2,630,030	—	5.00	5.15	5.25	5.50	6.50	9.00	—
1951	28,609,500	—	—	—	.40	.50	1.10	2.50	26.00
1951D	20,460,000	—	.25	.30	.40	.50	1.00	2.00	—
1951S	7,776,000	—	.30	.40	.50	1.10	1.75	4.00	—
1952	64,069,980	—	—	—	.20	.25	.85	3.00	26.00
1952D	30,638,000	—	—	—	.30	.45	1.50	3.50	—
1952S	20,572,000	—	—	—	.20	.25	.75	3.50	—
1953	46,772,800	—	—	—	.20	.25	.40	1.50	27.00
1953D	59,878,600	—	—	—	.20	.25	.40	1.50	—
1953S	19,210,900	—	—	—	.20	.25	.50	2.50	—
1954	47,917,350	—	—	—	—	—	.35	1.50	16.00
1954D	117,136,560	—	—	—	—	—	.35	1.00	—
1954S	29,384,000	—	—	—	—	.20	.35	2.50	—
1954S/D	Inc. Ab.	—	—	5.00	8.00	14.00	22.00	65.00	—
1955	8,266,200	—	.25	.35	.40	.45	.75	2.00	12.00
1955D	74,464,100	—	—	—	—	—	.30	1.00	—
1955D/S	Inc. Ab.	—	—	5.00	8.50	13.00	33.00	65.00	—
1956	35,885,384	—	—	—	—	—	.30	.70	2.50
1956D	67,222,940	—	—	—	—	—	.25	.60	—
1957	39,655,952	—	—	—	—	—	.25	.60	1.50
1957D	136,828,900	—	—	—	—	—	.25	.60	—
1958	17,963,652	—	—	—	.15	.20	.30	.65	2.50
1958D	168,249,120	—	—	—	—	—	.25	.60	—

Date	Mintage	MS-65	Prf-65	Date	Mintage	MS-65	Prf-65
1959	28,397,291	.65	1.25	1968D	91,227,880	.50	—
1959D	160,738,240	.55	—	1968S	103,437,510	.50	.60
1960	57,107,602	.55	1.00	1969	None minted	—	—
1960D	192,582,180	.55	—	1969D	202,807,500	.50	—
1961	76,668,244	.55	.70	1969S	123,099,631	.50	.60
1961D	229,342,760	.55	—	1970	None minted	—	—
1962	100,602,019	.55	.70	1970D	515,485,380	.50	—
1962D	280,195,720	.55	—	1970S	241,464,814	.50	.60
1963	178,851,645	.55	.70	1971	106,884,000	1.25	—
1963D	276,829,460	.55	—	1971D	316,144,800	.50	—
1964	1,028,622,762	.55	.70	1971S	—	—	1.50
1964D	1,787,297,160	.50	—	1972	202,036,000	.50	—
1965	136,131,380	.50	—	1972D	351,694,600	.50	—
1966	156,208,283	.50	—	1972S	—	—	1.50
1967	107,325,800	.50	—	1973	384,396,000	.50	—
1968	None minted	—	—	1973D	261,405,000	.50	—

Date	Mintage	MS-65	Prf-65	Date	Mintage	MS-65	Prf-65
1973S	—	—	1.60	1986D	361,819,140	2.00	—
1974	601,752,000	.50	—	1986S	—	—	6.50
1974D	277,373,000	.50	—	1987P	371,499,481	.75	—
1974S	—	—	2.00	1987D	410,590,604	.75	—
1975	181,772,000	.75	—	1987S	—	—	3.50
1975D	401,875,300	.50	—	1988P	771,360,000	.75	—
1975S	—	—	2.25	1988D	663,771,652	.75	—
1976	367,124,000	.75	—	1988S	—	—	4.50
1976D	563,964,147	.60	—	1989P	898,812,000	.75	—
1976S	—	—	2.00	1989D	570,842,474	.75	—
1977	585,376,000	.40	—	1989S	—	—	3.25
1977D	297,313,460	.55	—	1990P	661,636,000	.75	—
1977S	—	—	2.75	1990D	663,938,503	.75	—
1978	391,308,000	.40	—	1990S	—	—	4.75
1978D	313,092,780	.40	—	1991P	614,104,000	.75	—
1978S	—	—	1.75	1991D	436,496,678	.75	—
1979	463,188,000	.40	—	1991S	(2,867,787)	—	5.50
1979D	325,867,672	.40	—	1992P	399,552,000	1.10	—
1979S T-I	—	—	1.50	1992D	450,565,113	.75	—
1979S T-II	—	—	1.75	1992S	(4,176,560)	—	4.00
1980P	593,004,000	.40	—	1993P	412,076,000	.75	—
1980D	502,323,448	.40	—	1993D	406,084,135	.75	—
1980S	—	—	1.60	1993S	(3,394,792)	—	4.00
1981P	657,504,000	.40	—	1994P	722,160,000	.75	—
1981D	364,801,843	.40	—	1994D	715,762,110	.75	—
1981S T-I	—	—	2.00	1994S	(3,269,923)	—	4.50
1981S T-II	—	—	2.00	1995P	774,156,000	.75	—
1982P	292,355,000	2.50	—	1995D	888,112,000	.85	—
1982D	373,726,544	2.50	—	1995S	—	—	6.50
1982S	—	—	3.00	1996P	829,332,000	.75	—
1983P	561,615,000	3.00	—	1996D	817,736,000	.75	—
1983D	536,726,276	2.00	—	1996S	—	—	3.00
1983S	—	—	3.50	1997P	470,972,000	.75	—
1984P	746,769,000	3.00	—	1997D	466,640,000	.80	—
1984D	517,675,146	.85	—	1997S	(1,975,000)	—	4.75
1984S	—	—	5.00	1998P	—	.80	—
1985P	647,114,962	.75	—	1998D	—	.80	—
1985D	459,747,446	.75	—	1998S	—	—	4.75
1985S	—	—	3.50				
1986P	536,883,483	1.00	—				

Dimes

Barber

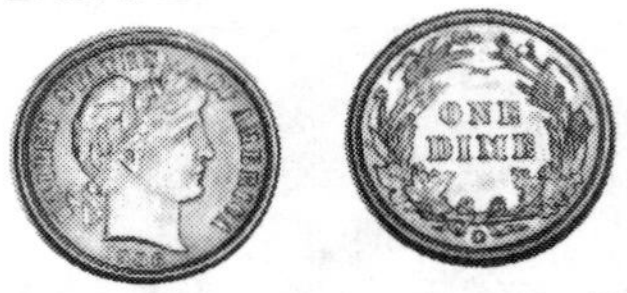

Designer: Charles E. Barber. **Size:** 17.9 millimeters. **Weight:** 2.5 grams. **Composition:** 90% silver (.0724 ounces), 10% copper.

Date	Mintage	G-4	VG-8	F-12	VF-20	XF-40	AU-50	MS-60	MS-65	Prf-65
1901	18,860,478	1.45	1.65	5.25	7.75	20.00	45.00	100.	1170.	1450.
1901O	5,620,000	2.75	4.50	12.00	18.00	42.00	115.	360.	2900.	—
1901S	593,022	39.00	64.00	280.	315.	380.	565.	790.	5000.	—
1902	21,380,777	1.30	1.75	4.50	6.75	21.00	52.00	91.00	540.	1450.
1902O	4,500,000	2.50	6.50	13.00	20.00	41.00	105.	325.	3350.	—
1902S	2,070,000	5.50	11.00	44.00	58.00	84.00	145.	325.	3600.	—
1903	19,500,755	1.30	1.75	4.50	7.15	20.00	52.00	91.00	1150.	1450.
1903O	8,180,000	2.00	3.00	8.75	13.00	26.00	91.00	240.	5050.	—
1903S	613,300	38.00	66.00	320.	415.	680.	855.	1050.	3800.	—
1904	14,601,027	1.30	1.75	5.50	9.00	20.00	52.00	105.	2100.	1450.
1904S	800,000	25.00	41.00	120.	155.	225.	430.	565.	4700.	—
1905	14,552,350	1.30	1.75	4.00	6.50	19.00	52.00	91.00	540.	1450.
1905O	3,400,000	2.50	5.75	30.00	43.00	58.00	105.	230.	2050.	—
1905S	6,855,199	2.25	4.75	7.75	16.50	30.00	72.00	210.	725.	—
1906	19,958,406	1.30	1.75	3.50	6.50	21.00	52.00	91.00	540.	1450.
1906D	4,060,000	2.25	3.75	9.00	14.00	27.00	72.00	155.	1950.	—
1906O	2,610,000	4.50	5.85	41.00	57.00	78.00	125.	180.	1250.	—
1906S	3,136,640	2.50	4.75	10.00	18.00	36.00	91.00	230.	1200.	—
1907	22,220,575	1.30	1.60	3.50	6.50	21.00	52.00	91.00	540.	1450.
1907D	4,080,000	2.75	4.75	9.00	15.00	32.00	91.00	260.	3550.	—
1907O	5,058,000	1.75	3.00	25.00	37.00	52.00	72.00	200.	1100.	—
1907S	3,178,470	2.25	5.00	9.75	18.00	41.00	100.	325.	2300.	—
1908	10,600,545	1.30	1.75	3.50	6.50	18.00	52.00	91.00	540.	1450.
1908D	7,490,000	1.75	2.25	6.50	9.50	26.00	59.00	125.	960.	—
1908O	1,789,000	2.75	5.50	39.00	52.00	72.00	130.	260.	1860.	—
1908S	3,220,000	2.75	4.50	9.00	14.00	32.00	145.	260.	2300.	—
1909	10,240,650	1.75	2.25	3.50	6.50	18.00	52.00	91.00	540.	1700.
1909D	954,000	3.25	9.00	58.00	85.00	105.	195.	390.	2300.	—
1909O	2,287,000	2.75	5.00	8.50	15.00	27.00	91.00	180.	1250.	—
1909S	1,000,000	4.00	11.00	78.00	110.	145.	295.	470.	3000.	—
1910	11,520,551	1.30	2.25	5.75	10.50	20.00	52.00	91.00	540.	1450.
1910D	3,490,000	2.75	4.75	7.75	15.00	34.00	91.00	195.	1800.	—
1910S	1,240,000	3.00	7.00	49.00	62.00	88.00	150.	350.	1925.	—
1911	18,870,543	1.30	1.75	3.00	6.50	18.00	52.00	91.00	540.	1700.
1911D	11,209,000	1.30	1.75	3.75	7.50	20.00	52.00	91.00	685.	—
1911S	3,520,000	1.75	2.75	7.75	15.00	31.00	85.00	145.	725.	—

Date	Mintage	G-4	VG-8	F-12	VF-20	XF-40	AU-50	MS-60	MS-65	Prf-65
1912	19,350,700	1.30	1.75	2.75	6.50	20.00	52.00	91.00	540.	1700.
1912D	11,760,000	1.30	1.75	3.75	7.50	18.00	52.00	91.00	720.	—
1912S	3,420,000	1.75	2.75	6.50	10.00	26.00	85.00	150.	1150.	—
1913	19,760,622	1.50	1.75	2.75	6.50	20.00	52.00	91.00	540.	1450.
1913S	510,000	8.00	13.00	67.00	100.	175.	260.	390.	1100.	—
1914	17,360,655	1.50	1.75	3.50	6.50	18.00	52.00	91.00	540.	1700.
1914D	11,908,000	1.50	1.75	3.50	6.75	18.00	52.00	91.00	540.	—
1914S	2,100,000	1.80	2.40	6.50	10.00	31.00	72.00	145.	1250.	—
1915	5,620,450	1.50	1.75	3.90	7.00	20.00	52.00	91.00	540.	2000.
1915S	960,000	2.40	4.40	29.00	39.00	52.00	125.	235.	1775.	—
1916	18,490,000	1.30	1.75	3.75	6.75	21.00	52.00	91.00	540.	—
1916S	5,820,000	1.50	2.25	4.75	6.50	20.00	52.00	91.00	780.	—

NOTE: Earlier dates (1892-1900) exist for this type.

Mercury

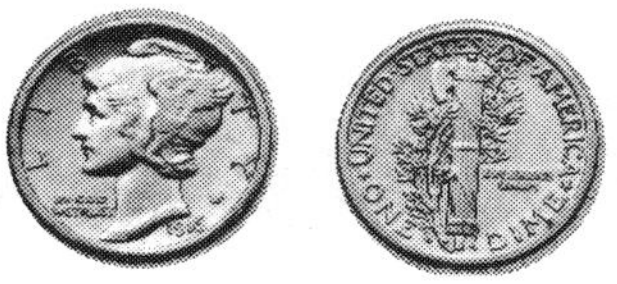

Designer: Adolph A. Weinman. **Size** 17.9 millimeters. **Weight:** 2.5 grams. **Composition:** 90% silver (.0724 ounces), 10% copper. **Notes:** "MS-65FSB" values are for coins with fully split and rounded horizontal bands around the faces on the reverse. The 1945-S "micro" variety has a smaller mintmark than the normal variety.

Date	Mintage	G-4	VG-8	F-12	VF-20	XF-40	MS-60	MS-65	-65FSB	Prf-65
1916	22,180,080	2.25	3.50	4.75	7.25	11.00	25.00	90.00	110.	—
1916D	264,000	475.	700.	1100.	1550.	2450.	4900.	18,000.	35,000.	—
1916S	10,450,000	3.50	4.50	5.75	9.75	16.50	34.00	195.	450.	—
1917	55,230,000	1.00	2.10	2.75	5.50	8.00	28.00	150.	340.	—
1917D	9,402,000	3.50	5.25	8.00	16.00	38.00	125.	1825.	5700.	—
1917S	27,330,000	1.25	2.35	3.25	6.00	9.50	49.00	585.	1690.	—
1918	26,680,000	1.50	3.00	4.25	11.00	25.00	70.00	390.	675.	—
1918D	22,674,800	2.25	3.00	4.00	9.50	23.00	105.	2200.	9750.	—
1918S	19,300,000	2.00	2.50	3.50	6.50	14.00	85.00	975.	6500.	—
1919	35,740,000	1.00	2.25	3.25	5.50	8.00	35.00	360.	550.	—
1919D	9,939,000	3.00	4.25	6.00	15.00	39.00	140.	1800.	18,000.	—
1919S	8,850,000	2.50	3.60	5.00	13.00	29.00	175.	1100.	10,500.	—
1920	59,030,000	1.00	2.10	2.75	5.00	7.00	27.00	230.	365.	—
1920D	19,171,000	2.25	3.25	4.25	7.00	15.00	100.	1250.	3050.	—
1920S	13,820,000	2.00	2.80	4.00	6.50	13.50	70.00	1175.	4875.	—
1921	1,230,000	20.00	32.00	70.00	160.	440.	945.	2850.	4000.	—
1921D	1,080,000	38.00	53.00	100.	210.	475.	1000.	2650.	5100.	—
1923	50,130,000	.90	1.40	2.25	4.25	7.00	25.00	115.	195.	—
1923S	6,440,000	2.25	3.50	4.25	11.00	29.00	135.	1500.	4000.	—
1924	24,010,000	1.00	1.60	2.75	5.00	9.00	38.00	170.	480.	—
1924D	6,810,000	2.25	3.25	5.50	10.00	29.00	155.	1275.	3300.	—
1924S	7,120,000	2.00	3.00	4.00	8.00	29.00	155.	1550.	10,500.	—
1925	25,610,000	1.00	1.60	2.75	4.25	7.50	28.00	195.	535.	
1925D	5,117,000	4.00	6.00	8.50	25.00	85.00	260.	1700.	5300.	
1925S	5,850,000	2.00	2.80	4.00	8.00	30.00	140.	2200.	4250.	—
1926	32,160,000	1.00	1.50	2.25	4.25	6.50	28.00	235.	560.	—
1926D	6,828,000	1.95	3.00	4.00	7.50	15.00	70.00	550.	2400.	—
1926S	1,520,000	6.00	9.50	15.00	34.00	190.	770.	3000.	4950.	—
1927	28,080,000	1.00	1.50	2.25	4.25	6.50	21.00	180.	325.	—
1927D	4,812,000	2.75	3.75	5.00	12.00	42.00	175.	1200.	8500.	—
1927S	4,770,000	1.90	2.65	3.75	5.50	11.00	240.	1625.	4550.	—
1928	19,480,000	1.00	1.50	2.25	4.25	6.50	21.00	115.	250.	—
1928D	4,161,000	3.00	4.25	6.00	15.00	30.00	135.	910.	2500.	—
1928S	7,400,000	1.75	2.35	3.25	5.00	12.00	70.00	495.	1500.	—
1929	25,970,000	1.00	1.40	2.35	3.75	5.00	19.50	58.00	180.	—
1929D	5,034,000	2.00	3.00	4.00	6.00	10.00	28.00	85.00	130.	—
1929S	4,730,000	1.65	1.90	2.25	4.25	5.50	34.00	120.	310.	—
1930	6,770,000	1.50	1.80	2.25	4.25	5.50	22.00	130.	275.	—
1930S	1,843,000	3.50	4.25	5.00	7.50	13.00	70.00	135.	260.	—
1931	3,150,000	2.60	3.00	3.75	5.00	11.00	35.00	155.	440.	—
1931D	1,260,000	6.00	8.00	11.00	18.00	30.00	77.00	210.	290.	—
1931S	1,800,000	3.50	4.00	5.00	7.50	13.00	63.00	210.	1900.	—
1934	24,080,000	1.00	1.45	1.75	3.00	5.00	15.00	32.00	100.	—
1934D	6,772,000	1.60	2.10	2.75	4.00	8.00	32.00	62.00	250.	—
1935	58,830,000	.80	1.00	1.50	2.15	4.25	11.00	30.00	45.00	—
1935D	10,477,000	1.50	2.00	3.00	4.75	9.25	32.00	60.00	425.	—
1935S	15,840,000	1.35	1.50	1.75	3.00	5.50	24.00	33.00	265.	—
1936	87,504,130	.80	1.00	1.50	2.25	3.50	8.50	24.00	60.00	875.
1936D	16,132,000	1.25	1.50	2.00	3.25	6.75	22.00	42.00	210.	—
1936S	9,210,000	1.25	1.50	1.75	2.75	4.75	17.00	28.00	50.00	—
1937	56,865,756	.80	1.00	1.50	2.00	3.25	10.00	24.00	36.00	300.
1937D	14,146,000	1.25	1.50	1.90	3.00	5.50	21.00	41.00	100.	—
1937S	9,740,000	1.25	1.50	1.90	3.00	5.50	18.00	31.00	160.	—
1938	22,198,728	.80	1.00	1.50	2.25	3.50	14.00	23.00	51.00	215.
1938D	5,537,000	1.75	2.00	2.25	3.75	6.00	15.00	26.00	41.00	—
1938S	8,090,000	1.35	1.55	1.85	2.35	3.75	16.00	31.00	110.	—
1939	67,749,321	.80	1.00	1.50	2.00	3.25	10.00	25.00	150.	210.
1939D	24,394,000	1.25	1.45	1.75	2.25	3.50	12.50	24.00	36.00	—
1939S	10,540,000	1.55	1.75	2.00	2.50	4.25	24.00	35.00	340.	—
1940	65,361,827	.60	.70	.90	1.10	2.50	6.50	23.00	33.00	185.
1940D	21,198,000	.60	.70	.90	1.10	1.50	8.50	23.00	33.00	—

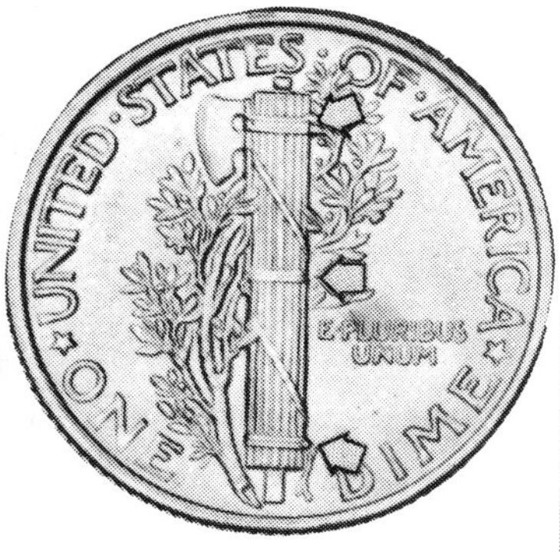

Fully split bands

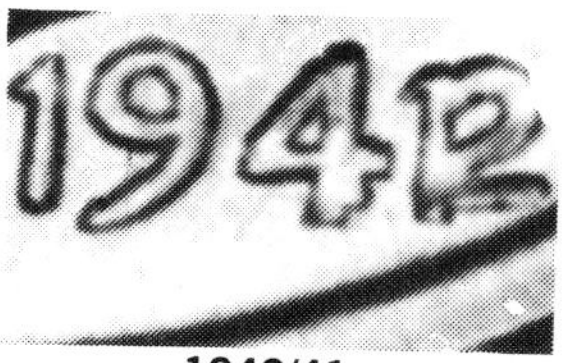

1942/41

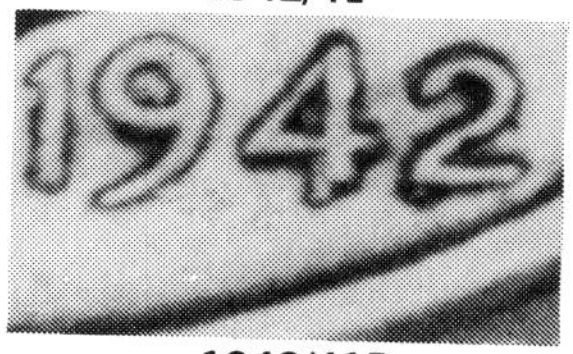

1942/41D

Date	Mintage	G-4	VG-8	F-12	VF-20	XF-40	MS-60	MS-65	-65FSB	Prf-65
1940S	21,560,000	.60	.70	.90	1.10	1.50	8.50	23.00	43.00	—
1941	175,106,557	.60	.70	.90	1.10	1.50	5.50	19.00	23.00	160.
1941D	45,634,000	.60	.70	.90	1.10	1.50	8.00	21.00	23.00	—
1941S	43,090,000	.60	.70	.90	1.10	1.50	10.00	19.00	30.00	—
1942	205,432,329	.60	.70	.90	1.10	1.50	5.50	20.00	36.00	160.
1942/41	Inc. Ab.	230.	280.	300.	320.	350.	1450.	6300.	9350.	—
1942D	60,740,000	.60	.70	.90	1.10	1.50	8.50	23.00	30.00	—
1942/41D	Inc. Ab.	260.	300.	320.	375.	490.	1600.	4850.	7300.	—
1942S	49,300,000	.60	.70	.90	1.10	1.50	10.00	23.00	61.00	—
1943	191,710,000	.60	.70	.90	1.10	1.50	6.50	19.00	23.00	—
1943D	71,949,000	.60	.70	.90	1.10	1.50	8.50	24.00	26.00	—
1943S	60,400,000	.60	.70	.90	1.10	1.50	10.00	20.00	32.00	—
1944	231,410,000	.60	.70	.90	1.10	1.50	5.50	20.00	39.00	—
1944D	62,224,000	.60	.70	.90	1.10	1.50	8.50	20.00	27.00	—
1944S	49,490,000	.60	.70	.90	1.10	1.50	10.00	20.00	30.00	—
1945	159,130,000	.60	.70	.90	1.10	1.50	5.50	22.00	3125.	—
1945D	40,245,000	.60	.70	.90	1.10	1.50	8.00	20.00	29.00	—
1945S	41,920,000	.60	.70	.90	1.10	1.50	8.50	20.00	85.00	—
1945S micro	Inc. Ab.	1.00	1.25	1.50	3.00	4.25	17.00	52.00	450.	—

Roosevelt

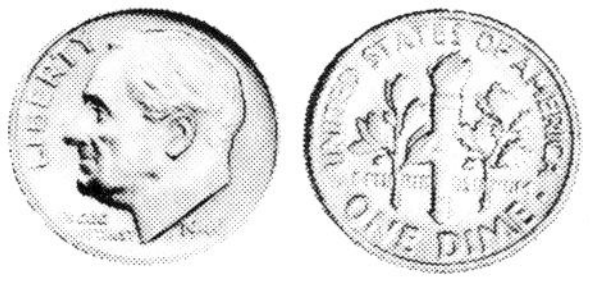

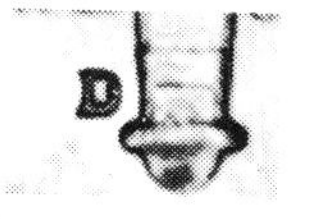

Reverse mintmark (1946-64)

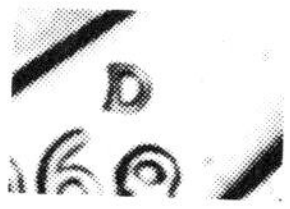

Obverse mintmark (1968-present)

Silver composition

Designer: John R. Sinnock. **Size:** 17.9 millimeters. **Weight:** 2.5 grams. **Composition:** 90% silver (.0724 ounces), 10% copper

Date	Mintage	G-4	VG-8	F-12	VF-20	XF-40	AU-50	MS-60	MS-65	Prf-65
1946	225,250,000	—	—	—	.50	.65	.95	1.05	2.50	—
1946D	61,043,500	—	—	—	.50	.65	1.10	1.25	4.50	—
1946S	27,900,000	—	—	—	.50	.65	1.10	2.00	5.25	—
1947	121,520,000	—	—	—	.50	.65	.95	1.00	4.75	—
1947D	46,835,000	—	—	—	.50	.95	1.20	1.40	10.00	—
1947S	34,840,000	—	—	—	.50	.95	1.10	1.35	5.50	—
1948	74,950,000	—	—	—	.50	.95	1.10	1.75	11.00	—
1948D	52,841,000	—	—	—	.50	1.20	1.50	2.00	10.00	—
1948S	35,520,000	—	—	—	.50	.95	1.10	1.35	9.00	—
1949	30,940,000	—	—	—	1.00	1.50	4.50	6.00	29.00	—
1949D	26,034,000	—	—	.60	.80	1.25	2.00	3.50	12.50	—
1949S	13,510,000	—	1.00	1.25	1.50	2.75	7.50	9.00	55.00	—
1950	50,181,500	—	—	—	.50	.95	1.10	1.35	4.60	37.00
1950D	46,803,000	—	—	—	.50	.65	.95	1.00	4.60	—
1950S	20,440,000	—	.85	1.00	1.10	1.25	5.00	7.00	35.00	—
1951	102,937,602	—	—	—	.50	.85	1.00	1.10	3.30	26.00
1951D	56,529,000	—	—	—	.50	.65	.95	1.00	3.50	—
1951S	31,630,000	—	—	—	1.00	1.05	2.75	3.25	24.00	—
1952	99,122,073	—	—	—	.50	.95	1.10	1.20	3.30	29.00
1952D	122,100,000	—	—	—	.50	.65	.95	1.00	3.80	—
1952S	44,419,500	—	—	—	1.00	1.05	1.10	1.35	7.00	—
1953	53,618,920	—	—	—	.50	.65	1.00	1.10	3.60	24.00
1953D	136,433,000	—	—	—	.50	.65	.95	1.00	3.50	—
1953S	39,180,000	—	—	—	.50	.95	1.10	2.00	2.75	—
1954	114,243,503	—	—	—	.50	.75	.90	1.00	2.15	11.00
1954D	106,397,000	—	—	—	.50	.65	.95	1.00	2.15	—
1954S	22,860,000	—	—	—	.50	.65	.80	.90	2.20	—
1955	12,828,381	—	—	—	.70	.80	.85	.95	3.00	15.00
1955D	13,959,000	—	—	—	.65	.75	.80	.90	2.25	—
1955S	18,510,000	—	—	—	.65	.75	.80	.90	2.00	—

Dimes

Date	Mintage	G-4	VG-8	F-12	VF-20	XF-40	AU-50	MS-60	MS-65	Prf-65
1956	109,309,384	—	—	—	.50	.65	.80	.90	2.00	2.50
1956D	108,015,100	—	—	—	.50	.65	.80	.90	1.65	—
1957	161,407,952	—	—	—	.50	.65	.80	.90	1.60	1.50
1957D	113,354,330	—	—	—	.50	.65	.80	.90	3.00	—
1958	32,785,652	—	—	—	.50	.65	.80	.90	1.80	2.00
1958D	136,564,600	—	—	—	.50	.65	.80	.90	1.50	—
1959	86,929,291	—	—	—	.50	.65	.80	.90	1.50	1.50
1959D	164,919,790	—	—	—	.50	.65	.80	.90	1.35	—
1960	72,081,602	—	—	—	.50	.65	.80	.90	1.40	1.40
1960D	200,160,400	—	—	—	.50	.65	.80	.90	1.35	—
1961	96,758,244	—	—	—	.50	.65	.80	.90	1.35	1.10
1961D	209,146,550	—	—	—	.50	.65	.80	.90	1.35	—
1962	75,668,019	—	—	—	.50	.65	.80	.90	1.35	1.10
1962D	334,948,380	—	—	—	.50	.65	.80	.90	1.35	—
1963	126,725,645	—	—	—	.50	.65	.80	.90	1.35	1.10
1963D	421,476,530	—	—	—	.50	.65	.80	.90	1.35	—
1964	933,310,762	—	—	—	.50	.65	.80	.90	1.35	1.00
1964D	1,357,517,180	—	—	—	.50	.65	.80	.90	1.35	—

Clad composition

Weight: 2.27 grams. **Composition:** clad layers of 75% copper and 25% nickel, bonded to a pure-copper core. **Notes:** The 1979-S and 1981-S Type II proofs have clearer mintmarks than the Type I proofs of those years. On the 1982 no-mintmark variety, the mintmark was inadvertently left off.

Date	Mintage	G-4	VG-8	F-12	VF-20	XF-40	AU-50	MS-60	MS-65	Prf-65
1965	1,652,140,570	—	—	—	—	—	—	—	.75	—
1966	1,382,734,540	—	—	—	—	—	—	—	.65	—
1967	2,244,007,320	—	—	—	—	—	—	—	.65	—
1968	424,470,000	—	—	—	—	—	—	—	.60	—
1968D	480,748,280	—	—	—	—	—	—	—	.60	—
1968S	—	—	—	—	—	—	—	—	—	.65
1969	145,790,000	—	—	—	—	—	—	—	.75	—
1969D	563,323,870	—	—	—	—	—	—	—	.75	—
1969S	—	—	—	—	—	—	—	—	—	.65
1970	345,570,000	—	—	—	—	—	—	—	.60	—
1970D	754,942,100	—	—	—	—	—	—	—	.60	—
1970S	—	—	—	—	—	—	—	—	—	.65
1971	162,690,000	—	—	—	—	—	—	—	.75	—
1971D	377,914,240	—	—	—	—	—	—	—	.60	—
1971S	—	—	—	—	—	—	—	—	—	.80
1972	431,540,000	—	—	—	—	—	—	—	.60	—
1972D	330,290,000	—	—	—	—	—	—	—	.60	—
1972S	—	—	—	—	—	—	—	—	—	.80
1973	315,670,000	—	—	—	—	—	—	—	.60	—
1973D	455,032,426	—	—	—	—	—	—	—	.50	—
1973S	—	—	—	—	—	—	—	—	—	.60
1974	470,248,000	—	—	—	—	—	—	—	.50	—
1974D	571,083,000	—	—	—	—	—	—	—	.50	—
1974S	—	—	—	—	—	—	—	—	—	1.25
1975	585,673,900	—	—	—	—	—	—	—	.60	—
1975D	313,705,300	—	—	—	—	—	—	—	.50	—
1975S	—	—	—	—	—	—	—	—	—	.60
1976	568,760,000	—	—	—	—	—	—	—	.60	—
1976D	695,222,774	—	—	—	—	—	—	—	.60	—
1976S	—	—	—	—	—	—	—	—	—	.75
1977	796,930,000	—	—	—	—	—	—	—	.50	—
1977D	376,607,228	—	—	—	—	—	—	—	.50	—
1977S	—	—	—	—	—	—	—	—	—	.60
1978	663,980,000	—	—	—	—	—	—	—	.50	—
1978D	282,847,540	—	—	—	—	—	—	—	.50	—
1978S	—	—	—	—	—	—	—	—	—	.60
1979	315,440,000	—	—	—	—	—	—	—	.50	—
1979D	390,921,184	—	—	—	—	—	—	—	.50	—
1979S T-I	—	—	—	—	—	—	—	—	—	.55
1979S T-II	—	—	—	—	—	—	—	—	—	1.25
1980P	735,170,000	—	—	—	—	—	—	—	.50	—
1980D	719,354,321	—	—	—	—	—	—	—	.50	—
1980S	—	—	—	—	—	—	—	—	—	.50
1981P	676,650,000	—	—	—	—	—	—	—	.50	—
1981D	712,284,143	—	—	—	—	—	—	—	.50	—
1981S T-I	—	—	—	—	—	—	—	—	—	.50
1981S T-II	—	—	—	—	—	—	—	—	—	4.00
1982P	519,475,000	—	—	—	—	—	—	—	1.50	—
1982 no mint mark				—	—	—	85.00	115.	220.	—
1982D	542,713,584	—	—	—	—	—	—	—	.60	—
1982S	—	—	—	—	—	—	—	—	—	.65
1983P	647,025,000	—	—	—	—	—	—	—	.75	—
1983D	730,129,224	—	—	—	—	—	—	—	.70	—
1983S	—	—	—	—	—	—	—	—	—	1.10
1984P	856,669,000	—	—	—	—	—	—	—	.50	—
1984D	704,803,976	—	—	—	—	—	—	—	.60	—
1984S	—	—	—	—	—	—	—	—	—	1.60
1985P	705,200,962	—	—	—	—	—	—	—	.60	—
1985D	587,979,970	—	—	—	—	—	—	—	.55	—
1985S	—	—	—	—	—	—	—	—	—	1.10
1986P	682,649,693	—	—	—	—	—	—	—	.70	—
1986D	473,326,970	—	—	—	—	—	—	—	.75	—
1986S	—	—	—	—	—	—	—	—	—	2.00
1987P	762,709,481	—	—	—	—	—	—	—	.50	—
1987D	653,203,402	—	—	—	—	—	—	—	.50	—
1987S	—	—	—	—	—	—	—	—	—	1.25
1988P	1,030,550,000	—	—	—	—	—	—	—	.50	—
1988D	962,385,488	—	—	—	—	—	—	—	.50	—
1988S	—	—	—	—	—	—	—	—	—	1.50
1989P	1,298,400,000	—	—	—	—	—	—	—	.50	—
1989D	896,535,597	—	—	—	—	—	—	—	.50	—
1989S	—	—	—	—	—	—	—	—	—	1.45
1990P	1,034,340,000	—	—	—	—	—	—	—	.50	—

Dimes

Date	Mintage	MS-65	Prf-65
1990D	839,995,824	.50	—
1990S	—	—	2.75
1991P	927,220,000	.50	—
1991D	601,241,114	.50	—
1991S	—	—	3.25
1992P	593,500,000	.50	—
1992D	616,273,932	.50	—
1992S	(2,858,981)	—	3.40
1992S	Silver proof	—	3.25
1993P	766,180,000	.50	—
1993D	750,110,166	.50	—
1993S	—	—	2.85
1993S	Silver proof	—	4.00
1994P	1,189,000,000	.50	—
1994D	1,303,268,110	.50	—
1994S	—	—	2.60
1994S	Silver proof	—	3.75
1995P	1,125,500,000	.50	—
1995D	1,274,890,000	.50	—
1995S	—	—	2.60
1995S	Silver proof	—	3.75
1996P	1,421,163,000	.50	—
1996D	1,400,300,000	.50	—
1996W	—	7.00	—
1996S	—	—	2.50
1996S	Silver proof	—	3.50
1997P	991,640,000	.50	—
1997D	979,810,000	.50	—
1997S	—	—	3.50
1997S	Silver proof	—	3.50
1998P	—	.50	—
1998D	—	.50	—
1998S	—	—	3.50
1998S	Silver proof	—	3.50

Quarters

Barber

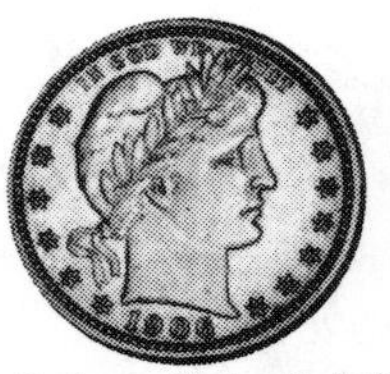
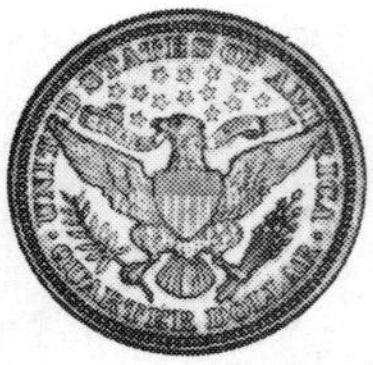
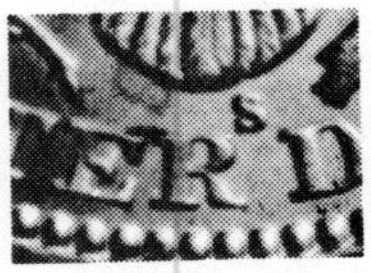

Mintmark

Designer: Charles E. Barber. **Size:** 24.3 millimeters. **Weight:** 6.25 grams. **Composition:** 90% silver (.1809 ounces), 10% copper.

Date	Mintage	G-4	VG-8	F-12	VF-20	XF-40	AU-50	MS-60	MS-65	Prf-65
1901	8,892,813	5.75	6.75	20.00	32.00	65.00	110.	170.	1900.	1900.
1901O	1,612,000	17.00	35.00	85.00	150.	275.	585.	750.	5750.	—
1901S	72,664	1750.	2800.	4500.	6500.	9500.	9650.	12,600.	40,500.	—
1902	12,197,744	3.25	4.25	19.00	30.00	65.00	110.	170.	1300.	2275.
1902O	4,748,000	4.75	8.50	35.00	54.00	100.	190.	360.	5700.	—
1902S	1,524,612	7.50	15.00	38.00	54.00	115.	190.	360.	3600.	—
1903	9,670,064	3.25	4.25	21.00	30.00	65.00	110.	170.	2600.	1600.
1903O	3,500,000	5.50	7.50	38.00	48.00	78.00	200.	275.	6800.	—
1903S	1,036,000	8.00	20.00	40.00	55.00	91.00	235.	360.	2100.	—
1904	9,588,813	3.25	5.00	21.00	30.00	65.00	110.	170.	1550.	1600.
1904O	2,456,000	6.00	11.00	48.00	70.00	160.	325.	675.	2750.	—
1905	4,968,250	3.75	5.00	24.00	35.00	65.00	110.	205.	1675.	1600.
1905O	1,230,000	6.00	10.00	36.00	75.00	130.	340.	450.	5700.	—
1905S	1,884,000	5.00	9.00	36.00	48.00	83.00	185.	295.	4100.	—
1906	3,656,435	3.50	5.00	21.00	30.00	65.00	110.	170.	1300.	1600.
1906D	3,280,000	4.00	5.25	28.00	39.00	65.00	150.	210.	3600.	—
1906O	2,056,000	4.25	5.25	32.00	39.00	77.00	180.	250.	1350.	—
1907	7,192,575	3.25	4.00	19.00	30.00	65.00	110.	170.	1300.	1600.
1907D	2,484,000	4.50	5.50	25.00	40.00	75.00	170.	295.	2650.	—
1907O	4,560,000	3.25	4.50	21.00	39.00	65.00	130.	235.	2750.	—
1907S	1,360,000	5.75	8.00	40.00	50.00	100.	200.	360.	3600.	—
1908	4,232,545	3.00	4.25	19.00	30.00	65.00	110.	205.	1300.	4050.
1908D	5,788,000	3.50	4.75	19.00	30.00	70.00	110.	215.	1500.	—
1908O	6,244,000	3.50	4.75	19.00	30.00	70.00	110.	205.	1300.	—
1908S	784,000	10.00	22.00	64.00	100.	215.	390.	650.	7200.	—
1909	9,268,650	2.75	4.00	19.00	30.00	65.00	110.	170.	1300.	1600.
1909D	5,114,000	3.00	4.50	19.00	30.00	65.00	165.	215.	1800.	—
1909O	712,000	10.00	24.00	75.00	125.	225.	360.	650.	7800.	—
1909S	1,348,000	3.50	5.50	28.00	36.00	65.00	175.	275.	3000.	—
1910	2,244,551	3.75	4.50	23.00	31.00	65.00	120.	175.	1425.	1600.
1910D	1,500,000	4.50	6.50	41.00	55.00	75.00	180.	280.	1400.	—
1911	3,720,543	3.25	4.00	21.00	30.00	72.00	110.	170.	1350.	1600.
1911D	933,600	5.00	8.00	65.00	125.	260.	425.	585.	5000.	—
1911S	988,000	5.00	8.50	45.00	75.00	115.	210.	295.	1425.	—
1912	4,400,700	3.25	4.00	19.00	30.00	65.00	110.	170.	1300.	1600.
1912S	708,000	6.00	8.00	43.00	51.00	90.00	210.	345.	3000.	—
1913	484,613	8.00	14.00	65.00	130.	370.	520.	1000.	4700.	2500.
1913D	1,450,800	5.50	6.50	30.00	42.00	70.00	145.	250.	1325.	—
1913S	40,000	415.	665.	1900.	2500.	3300.	4050.	4650.	10,000.	—
1914	6,244,610	3.25	4.00	16.00	30.00	65.00	110.	170.	1300.	2200.
1914D	3,046,000	3.25	4.00	17.00	29.00	65.00	110.	170.	1300.	—
1914S	264,000	50.00	75.00	130.	180.	370.	565.	865.	3250.	—
1915	3,480,450	3.25	4.00	17.00	28.00	65.00	110.	170.	1300.	2500.
1915D	3,694,000	3.25	4.00	17.00	28.00	65.00	110.	170.	1300.	—
1915S	704,000	4.00	6.00	28.00	36.00	88.00	180.	225.	1400.	—
1916	1,788,000	3.75	4.50	18.00	30.00	70.00	115.	170.	1300.	—
1916D	6,540,800	3.25	4.00	16.00	28.00	68.00	110.	170.	1300.	—

NOTE: Earlier dates (1892-1900) exist for this type.

Standing Liberty

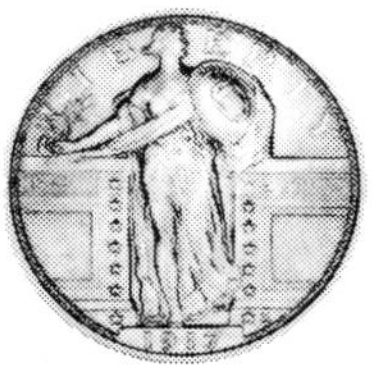

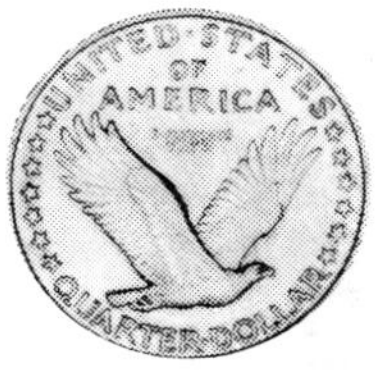

Type I

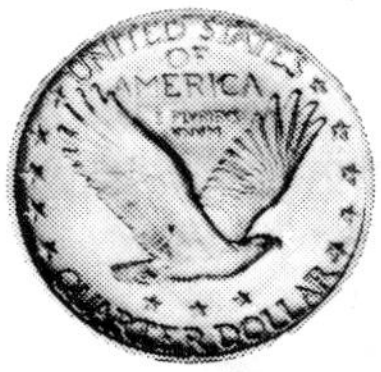

Type II

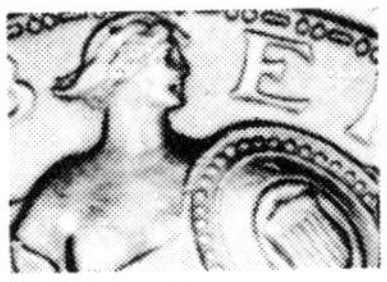

Type I

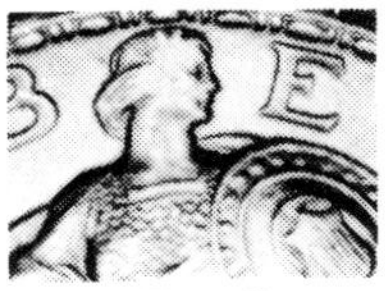

Type II

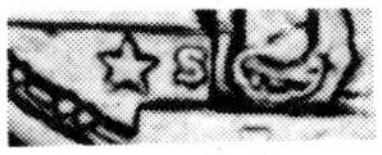

Mintmark

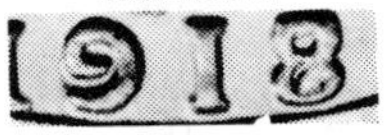

1918/17S

Type I

Designer: Hermon A. MacNeil. **Size** 24.3 millimeters. **Weight:** 6.5 grams. **Composition:** 90% silver (.1809 ounces), 10% copper. **Notes:** "MS-65FH" values are for coins that have full detail on Liberty's head.

Date	Mintage	G-4	VG-8	F-12	VF-20	XF-40	AU-50	MS-60	MS-65	-65FH
1916	52,000	1450.	1900.	2150.	2950.	3300.	4350.	5500.	17,500.	24,000.
1917	8,792,000	14.50	18.00	28.00	44.00	59.00	115.	175.	850.	1300.
1917D	1,509,200	16.50	20.00	27.00	55.00	85.00	140.	235.	975.	1600.
1917S	1,952,000	18.00	23.00	29.00	64.00	135.	190.	310.	1700.	2350.

Type II

Notes: In 1917 the obverse design was modified to cover Liberty's bare right breast.

Date	Mintage	G-4	VG-8	F-12	VF-20	XF-40	AU-50	MS-60	MS-65	-65FH
1917	13,880,000	13.50	17.00	21.00	26.00	48.00	75.00	125.	550.	900.
1917D	6,224,400	25.00	33.00	49.00	63.00	92.00	120.	175.	1450.	3500.
1917S	5,522,000	20.00	27.50	38.00	55.00	75.00	105.	175.	1100.	3500.
1918	14,240,000	14.00	18.00	22.00	33.00	47.00	78.00	150.	650.	1550.
1918D	7,380,000	28.00	34.00	43.00	65.00	95.00	140.	225.	1500.	5500.
1918S	11,072,000	15.00	21.00	28.00	35.00	45.00	89.00	190.	1500.	19,500.
1918/17S	Inc.Ab.	1200.	1450.	1950.	2800.	4900.	8950.	14,500.	85,000.	—
1919	11,324,000	29.00	35.00	43.00	53.00	67.50	95.00	150.	615.	1175.
1919D	1,944,000	68.00	100.	135.	190.	315.	495.	750.	2200.	24,000.
1919S	1,836,000	68.00	100.	135.	260.	380.	550.	895.	3000.	31,000.
1920	27,860,000	15.00	17.00	20.00	24.00	35.00	69.00	125.	500.	1700.
1920D	3,586,400	45.00	58.00	79.00	95.00	125.	180.	225.	1950.	5900.
1920S	6,380,000	17.00	22.00	28.00	39.00	59.00	92.50	250.	2300.	35,000.
1921	1,916,000	75.00	110.	145.	180.	280.	330.	450.	1650.	4000.
1923	9,716,000	15.00	17.00	22.00	28.00	40.00	65.00	125.	500.	3900.
1923S	1,360,000	145.	185.	250.	350.	450.	530.	695.	1975.	3750.
1924	10,920,000	16.00	18.00	24.00	28.00	35.00	65.00	125.	450.	1575.
1924D	3,112,000	38.00	43.00	51.00	73.00	95.00	135.	150.	465.	4900.
1924S	2,860,000	24.00	28.00	34.00	39.00	88.00	175.	350.	1975.	5900.
1925	12,280,000	2.50	3.00	6.30	15.00	25.00	59.00	110.	475.	850.
1926	11,316,000	2.50	3.00	6.30	15.00	26.00	57.00	110.	450.	1900.
1926D	1,716,000	6.50	9.00	14.00	29.00	65.00	95.00	110.	525.	30,000.
1926S	2,700,000	3.00	4.00	13.00	29.00	95.00	220.	350.	2100.	28,000.
1927	11,912,000	2.50	3.00	6.30	15.00	25.00	57.50	110.	450.	800.
1927D	976,400	7.00	12.00	19.00	45.00	95.00	120.	150.	450.	3500.
1927S	396,000	9.00	20.00	52.00	170.	1050.	3000.	3450.	9250.	110,000.
1928	6,336,000	2.50	3.00	6.30	15.00	25.00	57.50	110.	450.	1425.
1928D	1,627,600	4.00	6.00	8.00	23.00	39.00	83.00	145.	410.	7500.
1928S	2,644,000	3.50	4.25	6.75	15.00	33.00	68.00	135.	450.	750.
1929	11,140,000	3.50	4.00	6.30	15.00	30.00	50.00	110.	440.	675.
1929D	1,358,000	4.50	8.00	11.00	18.00	35.00	67.50	135.	480.	7500.
1929S	1,764,000	3.50	4.75	6.30	15.00	30.00	58.00	120.	430.	695.
1930	5,632,000	3.50	4.00	6.50	15.00	26.00	52.50	110.	450.	650.
1930S	1,556,000	3.50	4.25	6.30	15.00	30.00	59.50	115.	550.	995.

Washington

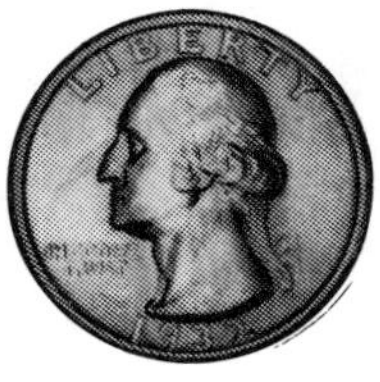

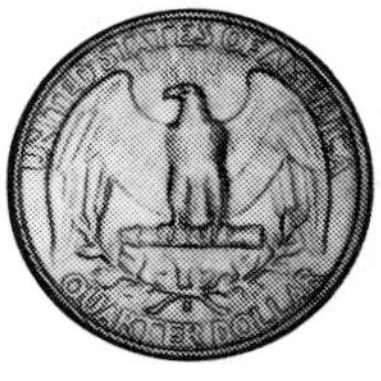

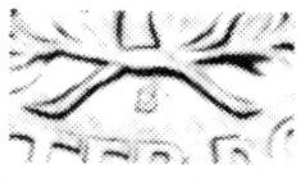

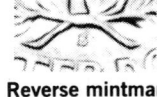

Reverse mintmark (1932-64)

Silver composition

Designer: John Flanagan. **Size** 24.3 millimeters. **Weight:** 6.25 grams. **Composition:** 90% silver (.1809 ounces), 10% copper

Date	Mintage	G-4	VG-8	F-12	VF-20	XF-40	AU-50	MS-60	MS-65	Prf-65
1932	5,404,000	3.50	4.50	5.00	7.50	9.00	13.00	21.00	195.	—
1932D	436,800	34.00	40.00	48.00	60.00	150.	325.	490.	5400.	—
1932S	408,000	38.00	40.00	42.00	45.00	72.00	175.	290.	2800.	—
1934	31,912,052	1.75	2.25	2.50	2.75	3.50	8.00	22.00	65.00	—
1934D	3,527,200	3.50	5.25	6.50	8.50	19.00	75.00	195.	1125.	—
1935	32,484,000	1.75	2.25	2.50	2.75	5.75	7.50	23.00	59.00	—
1935D	5,780,000	2.00	4.00	5.50	9.50	18.00	75.00	225.00	635.	—
1935S	5,660,000	2.00	3.00	4.50	5.00	15.00	32.00	66.00	180.	—
1936	41,303,837	1.75	2.25	2.50	2.75	6.00	7.50	20.00	52.00	1150.
1936D	5,374,000	2.80	3.50	4.50	15.00	42.00	165.	350.	650.	—
1936S	3,828,000	2.25	3.00	4.00	7.00	12.00	40.00	63.00	130.	—
1937	19,701,542	1.75	2.25	3.25	4.50	6.00	15.00	22.00	72.00	425.
1937D	7,189,600	1.80	3.00	4.00	5.50	12.00	28.00	44.00	78.00	—
1937S	1,652,000	2.00	3.50	5.50	12.00	21.00	68.00	110.	190.	—
1938	9,480,045	2.25	3.75	4.50	7.50	15.00	28.00	61.00	130.	260.
1938S	2,832,000	2.80	4.50	5.50	8.00	15.00	34.00	59.00	130.	—
1939	33,548,795	1.75	2.25	2.50	2.75	5.50	7.50	16.00	52.00	215.
1939D	7,092,000	2.00	2.50	3.75	4.50	7.50	16.00	35.00	72.00	—
1939S	2,628,000	3.25	3.50	4.50	6.50	14.00	36.00	62.00	125.	—
1940	35,715,246	1.50	2.25	3.00	3.25	4.50	8.25	15.00	42.00	225.
1940D	2,797,600	1.75	2.50	7.00	9.00	18.00	47.00	70.00	125.	—
1940S	8,244,000	1.75	2.50	4.25	5.00	7.00	12.00	16.00	44.00	—
1941	79,047,287	—	—	1.50	2.00	3.25	4.50	7.50	33.00	155.
1941D	16,714,800	—	—	1.50	2.00	3.25	6.50	30.00	50.00	—
1941S	16,080,000	—	—	1.50	2.00	3.25	6.50	20.00	70.00	—
1942	102,117,123	—	—	1.50	2.00	2.75	3.50	4.50	31.00	165.
1942D	17,487,200	—	—	1.50	2.00	3.25	7.00	11.00	36.00	—
1942S	19,384,000	—	—	1.50	2.00	4.50	17.00	50.00	100.	—
1943	99,700,000	—	—	1.50	2.00	2.25	2.75	5.00	36.00	—
1943D	16,095,600	—	—	1.50	2.00	3.25	10.00	17.50	39.00	—
1943S	21,700,000	—	—	1.50	2.00	5.50	11.50	26.00	43.00	—
1944	104,956,000	—	—	1.50	2.00	3.25	3.75	4.50	36.00	—
1944D	14,600,800	—	—	1.50	2.00	3.25	5.00	9.00	36.00	—
1944S	12,560,000	—	—	1.50	2.00	3.25	5.50	11.00	37.00	—
1945	74,372,000	—	—	1.50	2.00	3.25	4.00	5.00	36.00	—
1945D	12,341,600	—	—	1.50	2.00	3.25	5.00	7.50	36.00	—
1945S	17,004,001	—	—	1.50	2.00	3.25	4.50	6.00	36.00	—
1946	53,436,000	—	—	1.50	2.00	2.25	2.50	4.75	34.00	—
1946D	9,072,800	—	—	1.50	2.00	2.25	2.75	5.00	35.00	—
1946S	4,204,000	—	—	2.00	2.25	2.50	2.75	4.00	36.00	—
1947	22,556,000	—	—	1.50	2.00	3.00	4.50	6.50	35.00	—
1947D	15,338,400	—	—	1.50	2.00	3.00	4.00	5.00	36.00	—
1947S	5,532,000	—	—	1.50	2.00	2.25	2.50	5.00	35.00	—
1948	35,196,000	—	—	1.50	2.00	2.25	2.50	4.00	34.00	—
1948D	16,766,800	—	—	1.50	2.00	2.25	2.50	5.00	35.00	—
1948S	15,960,000	—	—	1.50	2.00	3.25	3.60	5.00	36.00	—
1949	9,312,000	—	—	1.50	2.50	3.50	14.00	19.00	36.00	—
1949D	10,068,400	—	—	1.50	2.00	4.00	5.00	9.00	42.00	—
1950	24,971,512	—	—	1.50	2.00	3.00	3.75	5.00	8.00	60.00
1950D	21,075,600	—	—	1.50	2.00	2.75	3.00	4.50	26.00	—
1950D/S	Inc. Ab.	21.00	25.00	36.00	60.00	150.	210.	275.	650.	—
1950S	10,284,004	—	—	1.50	2.50	3.25	5.75	7.25	20.00	—
1950S/D	Inc. Ab.	21.00	25.00	36.00	60.00	190.	315.	425.	715.	—
1951	43,505,602	—	—	1.40	1.75	2.00	2.25	4.75	16.00	46.00
1951D	35,354,800	—	—	1.40	1.75	2.00	2.25	3.25	20.00	—
1951S	9,048,000	—	—	1.40	1.75	4.25	8.25	15.00	20.00	—
1952	38,862,073	—	—	1.40	1.75	2.00	2.25	3.00	16.00	33.00
1952D	49,795,200	—	—	1.40	1.75	2.00	2.25	3.25	16.00	—
1952S	13,707,800	—	—	1.40	2.00	2.50	5.25	10.00	20.00	—
1953	18,664,920	—	—	1.40	1.75	2.00	2.50	3.25	20.00	26.00
1953D	56,112,400	—	—	—	1.25	1.50	1.75	2.25	16.00	—
1953S	14,016,000	—	—	1.40	1.75	2.25	2.75	4.00	16.00	—
1954	54,645,503	—	—	—	—	1.40	1.50	2.00	24.00	12.00
1954D	42,305,500	—	—	—	—	1.75	2.00	2.00	20.00	—
1954S	11,834,722	—	—	—	1.50	1.75	2.00	2.00	16.00	—
1955	18,558,381	—	—	—	1.50	1.75	2.00	2.00	13.00	12.00
1955D	3,182,400	—	—	—	1.75	2.00	2.75	3.00	16.00	—
1956	44,813,384	—	—	—	—	1.75	2.00	2.00	13.00	6.50
1956D	32,334,500	—	—	—	—	2.00	2.25	2.50	13.00	—
1957	47,779,952	—	—	—	—	1.40	2.00	2.75	16.00	3.50
1957D	77,924,160	—	—	—	—	1.40	1.75	2.00	16.00	—
1958	7,235,652	—	—	—	—	1.40	2.00	2.50	16.00	6.00
1958D	78,124,900	—	—	—	—	1.40	1.75	2.00	13.00	—
1959	25,533,291	—	—	—	—	1.40	1.75	2.00	13.00	4.25
1959D	62,054,232	—	—	—	—	1.40	1.75	2.00	13.00	—
1960	30,855,602	—	—	—	—	1.40	1.75	2.75	11.00	3.75
1960D	63,000,324	—	—	—	—	1.40	1.75	2.00	11.00	—
1961	40,064,244	—	—	—	—	1.40	1.50	1.75	13.00	3.50
1961D	83,656,928	—	—	—	—	1.40	1.50	1.75	13.00	—
1962	39,374,019	—	—	—	—	1.40	1.50	1.75	11.00	3.50
1962D	127,554,756	—	—	—	—	1.40	1.50	1.75	9.00	—
1963	77,391,645	—	—	—	—	1.40	1.50	1.75	9.00	3.50
1963D	135,288,184	—	—	—	—	1.40	1.50	1.75	9.00	—
1964	564,341,347	—	—	—	—	1.40	1.50	1.75	6.50	3.50
1964D	704,135,528	—	—	—	—	1.40	1.50	1.75	6.50	—

Quarters

Clad composition

Weight: 5.67 grams. **Composition:** clad layers of 75% copper and 25% nickel bonded to a pure-copper core.

Date	Mintage	MS-65	Prf-65	Date	Mintage	MS-65	Prf-65
1965	1,819,717,540	1.60	—	1971	109,284,000	1.00	—
1966	821,101,500	1.60	—	1971D	258,634,428	.70	—
1967	1,524,031,848	2.00	—	1971S	—	—	.95
1968	220,731,500	1.60	—	1972	215,048,000	1.00	—
1968D	101,534,000	2.00	—	1972D	311,067,732	1.00	—
1968S	—	—	1.00	1972S	—	—	.95
1969	176,212,000	2.00	—	1973	346,924,000	1.00	—
1969D	114,372,000	2.25	—	1973D	232,977,400	1.00	—
1969S	—	—	1.00	1973S	—	—	.95
1970	136,420,000	1.00	—	1974	801,456,000	1.00	—
1970D	417,341,364	1.00	—	1974D	353,160,300	1.00	—
1970S	—	—	.95	1974S	—	—	1.40

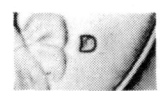

Obverse mintmark (1968-present)

Bicentennial reverse

Bicentennial reverse

Reverse designer: Jack L. Ahr.

Date	Mintage	G-4	VG-8	F-12	VF-20	XF-40	AU-50	MS-60	MS-65	Prf-65
1976	809,784,016	—	—	—	—	—	—	—	—	1.20
1976D	860,118,839	—	—	—	—	—	—	—	—	1.20
1976S	—	—	—	—	—	—	—	—	—	.90

Bicentennial reverse, silver composition

Weight: 5.75 grams. **Composition:** clad layers of 80% copper and 20% silver bonded to a core of 79.1% copper and 20.9% silver (.074 total ounces of silver).

Date	Mintage	G-4	VG-8	F-12	VF-20	XF-40	AU-50	MS-60	MS-65	Prf-65
1976S silver	11,000,000	—	—	—	—	—	—	—	2.00	1.95

Regular design resumed, clad composition

Notes: The 1979-S and 1981 Type II proofs have clearer mintmarks than the Type I proofs for those years.

Date	Mintage	MS-65	Prf-65	Date	Mintage	MS-65	Prf-65
1977	468,556,000	1.00	—	1989S	—	—	1.35
1977D	258,898,212	1.00	—	1990P	613,792,000	1.00	—
1977S	—	—	.95	1990D	927,638,181	1.00	—
1978	521,452,000	1.00	—	1990S	—	—	3.60
1978D	287,373,152	1.00	—	1991P	570,968,000	1.00	—
1978S	—	—	.95	1991D	630,966,693	1.00	—
1979	515,708,000	1.00	—	1991S	(2,867,787)	—	5.00
1979D	489,789,780	1.00	—	1992P	384,764,000	1.00	—
1979S T-I	—	—	.95	1992D	389,777,107	1.00	—
1979S T-II	—	—	1.45	1992S	(2,858,981)	—	4.00
1980P	635,832,000	1.00	—	1992S	Silver proof	—	4.00
1980D	518,327,487	1.00	—	1993P	639,276,000	1.00	—
1980S	—	—	.95	1993D	645,476,128	1.00	—
1981P	601,716,000	1.00	—	1993S	(2,633,439)	—	4.75
1981D	575,722,833	1.00	—	1993S	Silver proof	—	5.00
1981S T-I	—	—	.95	1994P	825,600,000	1.00	—
1981S T-II	—	—	3.00	1994D	880,034,110	1.00	—
1982P	500,931,000	2.00	—	1994S	(2,484,594)	—	3.25
1982D	480,042,788	2.00	—	1994S	Silver proof	—	4.50
1982S	—	—	2.25	1995P	1,004,336,000	1.00	—
1983P	673,535,000	4.00	—	1995D	1,103,216,000	1.00	—
1983D	617,806,446	3.50	—	1995S	(2,010,384)	—	3.00
1983S	—	—	1.75	1995S	Silver proof	—	4.75
1984P	676,545,000	1.75	—	1996P	925,040,000	1.00	—
1984D	546,483,064	2.00	—	1996D	906,868,000	1.00	—
1984S	—	—	1.60	1996S	—	—	3.00
1985P	775,818,962	2.50	—	1996S	Silver proof	—	4.75
1985D	519,962,888	3.25	—	1997P	595,740,000	1.00	—
1985S	—	—	1.25	1997D	599,680,000	1.00	—
1986P	551,199,333	4.00	—	1997S	(1,975,000)	—	3.00
1986D	504,298,660	2.75	—	1997S	Silver proof	—	4.75
1986S	—	—	2.00	1998P	—	1.00	—
1987P	582,499,481	1.00	—	1998D	—	1.00	—
1987D	655,594,696	1.00	—	1998S	—	—	3.00
1987S	—	—	1.10	1998S	Silver proof	—	4.75
1988P	562,052,000	1.50	—	1999P	Delaware	1.00	—
1988D	596,810,688	1.20	—				
1988S	—	—	1.25				
1989P	512,868,000	1.00	—				
1989D	896,535,597	1.00	—				

Half dollars

Barber

Mintmark

Designer: Charles I. Barber. **Size:** 30.6 millimeters. **Weight:** 12.5 grams. **Composition:** 90% silver (.3618 ounces), 10% copper.

Date	Mintage	G-4	VG-8	F-12	VF-20	XF-40	AU-50	MS-60	MS-65	Prf-65
1901	4,268,813	6.00	7.75	28.00	71.00	130.	300.	390.	4200.	3500.
1901O	1,124,000	8.00	13.00	53.00	115.	285.	450.	1250.	14,500.	—
1901S	847,044	17.00	28.00	110.	225.	500.	880.	1400.	12,500.	—
1902	4,922,777	5.85	7.75	28.00	71.00	130.	260.	390.	3400.	3700.
1902O	2,526,000	6.50	11.00	38.00	77.00	190.	350.	690.	9900.	—
1902S	1,460,670	8.00	13.00	48.00	87.00	200.	360.	585.	5500.	—
1903	2,278,755	7.50	10.00	37.00	78.00	165.	325.	500.	8000.	3825.
1903O	2,100,000	7.00	12.00	43.00	75.00	180.	325.	690.	9000.	—
1903S	1,920,772	7.00	12.00	43.00	75.00	210.	365.	565.	5900.	—
1904	2,992,670	5.85	8.00	28.00	71.00	130.	300.	390.	4200.	4100.
1904O	1,117,600	9.00	17.00	50.00	110.	300.	500.	1000.	9600.	—
1904S	553,038	16.00	27.00	135.00	325.	625.	950.	1800.	14,000.	—
1905	662,727	12.00	19.00	52.00	78.00	195.	300.	540.	5400.	3900.
1905O	505,000	15.00	29.00	80.00	130.	240.	415.	715.	6000.	—
1905S	2,494,000	6.75	11.00	38.00	79.00	190.	345.	550.	9000.	—
1906	2,638,675	5.50	7.50	27.00	71.00	130.	300.	390.	3400.	3300.
1906D	4,028,000	5.50	7.50	27.00	71.00	140.	300.	390.	4100.	—
1906O	2,446,000	5.50	7.50	35.00	74.00	165.	300.	585.	5400.	—
1906S	1,740,154	6.75	12.00	42.00	80.00	190.	300.	565.	5650.	—
1907	2,598,575	5.50	6.75	26.00	75.00	130.	300.	400.	2600.	4000.
1907D	3,856,000	5.50	8.25	27.00	75.00	150.	300.	390.	2600.	—
1907O	3,946,000	5.50	8.25	27.00	71.00	150.	300.	490.	3400.	—
1907S	1,250,000	6.50	12.00	73.00	125.00	300.	450.	850.	10,750.	—
1908	1,354,545	5.75	8.00	31.00	74.00	150.	300.	390.	3250.	4000.
1908D	3,280,000	5.50	7.50	28.00	71.00	145.	300.	480.	2600.	—
1908O	5,360,000	5.50	7.50	28.00	71.00	150.	300.	480.	2600.	—
1908S	1,644,828	7.00	13.00	42.00	82.00	190.	340.	750.	5200.	—
1909	2,368,650	5.50	7.50	26.00	60.00	130.	260.	390.	2600.	4000.
1909O	925,400	8.50	12.00	45.00	84.00	260.	475.	700.	4750.	—
1909S	1,764,000	5.75	8.50	28.00	71.00	175.	330.	550.	3350.	—
1910	418,551	10.00	15.00	64.00	115.	260.	415.	585.	3850.	4250.
1910S	1,948,000	5.50	8.25	28.00	71.00	175.	325.	625.	4300.	—
1911	1,406,543	5.50	6.75	28.00	60.00	130.	300.	390.	2600.	3300.
1911D	695,080	6.50	11.00	39.00	82.00	180.	260.	540.	2600.	—
1911S	1,272,000	5.50	8.25	31.00	74.00	165.	320.	550.	4900.	—
1912	1,550,700	5.50	7.50	26.00	60.00	150.	320.	390.	3700.	4000.
1912D	2,300,800	5.50	8.25	26.00	71.00	130.	300.	425.	2600.	—
1912S	1,370,000	5.50	8.25	29.00	71.00	165.	320.	500.	5300.	—
1913	188,627	20.00	25.00	100.	175.	345.	630.	880.	3800.	3800.
1913D	534,000	7.00	10.00	35.00	73.00	175.	285.	495.	4550.	—
1913S	604,000	7.50	11.00	44.00	80.00	190.	350.	585.	4000.	—
1914	124,610	30.00	45.00	160.	295.	460.	730.	915.	9200.	4300.
1914S	992,000	6.50	9.00	34.00	71.00	175.	345.	550.	3400.	—
1915	138,450	20.00	29.00	90.00	190.	350.	665.	945.	4550.	4250.
1915D	1,170,400	5.50	7.00	27.00	71.00	135.	260.	390.	2600.	—
1915S	1,604,000	5.50	7.00	27.00	71.00	145.	260.	470.	2600.	—

NOTE: Earlier dates (1892-1900) exist for this type.

Walking Liberty

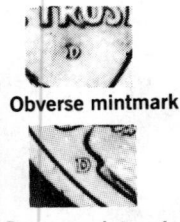

Obverse mintmark

Reverse mintmark

Mintmark on obverse

Designer: Adolph A. Weinman. **Size:** 30.6 millimeters. **Weight:** 12.5 grams. **Composition:** 90% silver (.3618 ounces), 10% copper

Half dollars

Date	Mintage	G-4	VG-8	F-12	VF-20	XF-40	AU-50	MS-60	MS-65	Prf-65
1916	608,000	25.00	29.00	57.00	120.	160.	210.	235.	1425.	—
1916D	1,014,400	19.00	21.00	30.00	70.00	145.	180.	260.	1800.	—
1916S	508,000	65.00	81.00	125.	285.	525.	600.	770.	4900.	—
1917D	765,400	12.00	18.00	39.00	84.00	165.	210.	550.	6500.	—
1917S	952,000	15.00	25.00	55.00	235.	665.	800.	1825.	19,000.	—

Mintmark on reverse

Date	Mintage	G-4	VG-8	F-12	VF-20	XF-40	AU-50	MS-60	MS-65	Prf-65
1917	12,292,000	4.00	7.00	10.50	20.00	35.00	63.00	100.	875.	—
1917D	1,940,000	8.50	11.00	21.00	59.00	230.	380.	650.	20,500.	—
1917S	5,554,000	5.00	8.00	13.50	25.00	55.00	120.	280.	9750.	—
1918	6,634,000	5.00	9.00	17.00	45.00	145.	245.	410.	3500.	—
1918D	3,853,040	8.00	9.50	22.00	51.00	155.	350.	750.	18,500.	—
1918S	10,282,000	5.00	8.00	14.00	27.00	56.00	135.	330.	14,250.	—
1919	962,000	10.50	15.00	30.00	140.	400.	595.	915.	4675.	—
1919D	1,165,000	9.50	12.00	48.00	150.	540.	875.	2600.	97,500.	—
1919S	1,552,000	8.50	10.00	30.00	135.	650.	1650.	2100.	11,000.	—
1920	6,372,000	5.00	8.00	11.00	23.00	56.00	91.00	220.	6800.	—
1920D	1,551,000	9.00	11.00	25.00	135.	350.	665.	1075.	9100.	—
1920S	4,624,000	5.00	8.00	14.00	45.00	160.	350.	650.	8050.	—
1921	246,000	73.00	105.	175.	540.	1350.	2500.	2850.	10,350.	—
1921D	208,000	115.	145.	230.	660.	2500.	2950.	3700.	11,000.	—
1921S	548,000	20.00	24.00	57.00	500.	5000.	6150.	8200.	60,000.	—
1923S	2,178,000	8.50	10.00	24.00	42.00	210.	525.	1100.	12,250.	—
1927S	2,392,000	5.00	7.75	11.00	25.00	90.00	265.	650.	8700.	—
1928S	1,940,000	5.00	7.25	12.50	30.00	90.00	250.	650.	4700.	—
1929D	1,001,200	6.25	8.00	14.00	35.00	80.00	155.	260.	2100.	—
1929S	1,902,000	4.00	6.75	10.00	16.00	68.00	170.	310.	2465.	—
1933S	1,786,000	5.00	7.00	10.00	11.50	45.00	170.	470.	3375.	—
1934	6,964,000	2.65	2.80	2.95	4.50	11.00	26.50	48.00	290.	—
1934D	2,361,400	3.25	4.00	5.50	7.50	25.00	56.00	125.	975.	—
1934S	3,652,000	3.00	3.50	4.50	6.00	25.00	77.00	250.	2700.	—
1935	9,162,000	2.65	2.80	2.95	4.50	9.00	22.00	44.00	265.	—
1935D	3,003,800	3.25	4.00	5.50	7.50	25.00	56.00	115.	1250.	—
1935S	3,854,000	3.10	3.50	4.50	5.50	25.00	70.00	125.	2000.	—
1936	12,617,901	2.50	2.80	3.50	4.50	9.00	21.00	36.00	130.	3250.
1936D	4,252,400	2.95	3.50	4.50	5.50	17.00	47.00	71.00	365.	—
1936S	3,884,000	3.00	3.50	4.50	5.50	17.00	50.00	115.	520.	—
1937	9,527,728	2.65	2.80	3.50	4.50	9.00	21.00	36.00	195.	850.
1937D	1,676,000	5.00	6.00	8.00	11.00	28.00	91.00	160.	500.	—
1937S	2,090,000	4.00	5.00	6.00	8.00	18.00	63.00	115.	515.	—
1938	4,118,152	3.00	3.50	4.50	6.50	11.00	42.00	65.00	260.	580.
1938D	491,600	22.00	25.00	28.00	34.00	90.00	240.	380.	915.	—
1939	6,820,808	2.65	2.80	3.50	4.50	10.00	21.00	39.00	140.	525.
1939D	4,267,800	2.95	3.50	4.50	5.50	10.50	24.00	39.00	140.	—
1939S	2,552,000	4.00	5.00	6.00	8.75	12.50	46.00	99.00	215.	—
1940	9,167,279	2.25	2.40	3.00	5.50	9.00	11.00	32.00	105.	450.
1940S	4,550,000	2.25	2.40	3.00	5.50	10.00	18.00	35.00	415.	—
1941	24,207,412	2.25	2.40	3.00	4.50	7.00	7.75	23.00	100.	375.
1941D	11,248,400	2.25	2.40	3.00	4.50	6.00	14.00	40.00	115.	—
1941S	8,098,000	2.25	2.40	3.00	4.75	7.00	24.00	71.00	1150.	—
1942	47,839,120	2.25	2.40	3.00	4.50	5.50	7.75	23.00	100.	375.
1942D	10,973,800	2.25	2.40	3.00	4.50	6.00	17.00	44.00	195.	—
1942S	12,708,000	2.25	2.40	3.00	4.75	7.00	21.00	34.00	415.	—
1943	53,190,000	2.25	2.40	3.00	4.50	5.50	7.75	23.00	100.	—
1943D	11,346,000	2.25	2.40	3.00	4.50	6.00	20.00	47.00	150.	—
1943S	13,450,000	2.25	2.40	3.00	4.75	6.00	21.00	33.00	325.	—
1944	28,206,000	2.25	2.40	3.00	4.50	5.50	7.75	32.00	105.	—
1944D	9,769,000	2.25	2.40	3.00	4.50	6.00	17.00	36.00	105.	—
1944S	8,904,000	2.25	2.40	3.00	4.75	6.25	21.00	36.00	605.	—
1945	31,502,000	2.25	2.40	3.00	4.50	5.50	7.75	23.00	100.	—
1945D	9,966,800	2.25	2.40	3.00	4.50	6.00	14.00	35.00	105.	—
1945S	10,156,000	2.25	2.40	3.00	4.75	6.00	17.00	34.00	145.	—
1946	12,118,000	2.25	2.40	3.00	4.50	5.50	12.50	32.00	130.	—
1946D	2,151,000	4.50	4.75	6.00	8.75	9.50	18.00	34.00	100.	—
1946S	3,724,000	2.65	2.80	3.50	5.00	5.50	15.00	33.00	105.	—
1947	4,094,000	2.65	3.15	3.50	5.00	7.00	18.00	34.00	170.	—
1947D	3,900,600	2.65	2.80	3.50	5.00	7.00	18.00	34.00	105.	—

Franklin

Mintmark

Designer: John R. Sinnock. **Size:** 30.6 millimeters. **Weight:** 12.5 grams. **Composition:** 90% (.3618 ounces), 10% copper. **Notes:** "MS-65FBL" values are for coins with full lines bell on the reverse.

Date	Mintage	VG-8	F-12	VF-20	XF-40	AU-50	MS-60	MS-65	-65FBL	Prf-65	-65CAM
1948	3,006,814	3.00	3.50	3.75	4.00	5.00	13.75	90.00	205.	—	—
1948D	122600.	3.00	3.25	3.50	3.75	5.00	9.50	195.	295.	—	—
1949	5,614,000	3.00	3.25	3.50	4.00	10.00	28.00	150.	290.	—	—
1949D	4,120,600	3.00	3.50	3.75	4.00	13.00	29.00	1050.	2200.	—	—

Half dollars

Date	Mintage	VG-8	F-12	VF-20	XF-40	AU-50	MS-60	MS-65	-65FBL	Prf-65	-65CAM
1949S	3,744,000	3.50	4.75	6.25	8.00	21.00	48.00	210.	725.	—	—
1950	7,793,509	—	3.00	3.50	6.00	7.00	20.00	150.	295.	275.	3700.
1950D	8,031,600	—	3.00	3.50	6.50	7.75	16.00	575.	1050.	—	—
1951	16,859,602	—	3.00	3.50	4.00	4.50	8.75	95.00	335.	200.	2200.
1951D	9,475,200	—	3.00	4.25	5.00	11.50	19.00	300.	500.	—	—
1951S	13,696,000	—	2.75	3.00	3.50	10.00	18.00	125.	695.	—	—
1952	21,274,073	—	2.50	2.75	3.00	4.00	7.00	90.00	290.	135.	1100.
1952D	25,395,600	—	2.50	2.75	3.00	4.00	6.25	250.	400.	—	—
1952S	5,526,000	—	2.50	3.25	3.75	17.00	33.00	135.	975.	—	—
1953	2,796,920	3.00	3.25	3.50	5.00	10.00	12.00	275.	950.	70.00	475.
1953D	20,900,400	—	2.25	3.50	4.00	4.25	6.00	250.	400.	—	—
1953S	4,148,000	—	2.60	4.25	4.75	8.50	11.00	70.00	7500.	—	—
1954	13,421,503	—	2.25	3.50	3.75	4.00	5.50	85.00	275.	55.00	225.
1954D	25,445,580	—	2.25	3.25	3.50	4.00	4.75	165.	250.	—	—
1954S	4,993,400	—	2.25	3.75	4.00	4.25	6.50	60.00	425.	—	—
1955	2,876,381	—	5.25	5.50	5.75	6.00	6.50	75.00	150.	40.00	175.
1956	4,701,384	—	2.50	3.00	3.50	4.25	5.00	50.00	120.	15.00	65.00
1957	6,361,952	—	2.50	2.75	3.00	3.75	4.00	50.00	120.	13.00	125.
1957D	19,966,850	—	—	2.10	2.25	2.50	3.50	50.00	105.	—	—
1958	4,917,652	—	2.25	2.50	2.75	3.00	3.75	50.00	135.	13.00	200.
1958D	23,962,412	—	—	2.25	2.50	2.75	3.25	50.00	105.	—	—
1959	7,349,291	—	—	2.25	2.50	2.75	3.75	150.	295.	12.00	400.
1959D	13,053,750	—	—	2.25	2.50	2.75	3.75	150.	275.	—	—
1960	7,715,602	—	—	2.25	2.50	2.75	2.80	175.	400.	12.00	75.00
1960D	18,215,812	—	—	2.25	2.50	2.75	3.50	750.	1450.	—	—
1961	11,318,244	—	—	2.25	2.50	2.75	3.25	275.	1550.	8.50	75.00
1961D	20,276,442	—	—	2.25	2.50	2.75	3.25	450.	1000.	—	—
1962	12,932,019	—	—	2.25	2.50	2.75	3.00	290.	2250.	8.50	50.00
1962D	35,473,281	—	—	2.25	2.50	2.75	3.00	400.	1000.	—	—
1963	25,239,645	—	—	—	2.50	2.75	3.00	90.00	925.	8.50	50.00
1963D	67,069,292	—	—	—	2.50	2.75	3.00	90.00	250.	—	—

Kennedy

Bicentennial reverse

90% silver composition

Designer: Gilroy Roberts and Frank Gasparro. **Size:** 30.6 millimeters. **Weight:** 12.5 grams. Composition: 90% silver (.3618 ounces), 10% copper

Date	Mintage	G-4	VG-8	F-12	VF-20	XF-40	AU-50	MS-60	MS-65	Prf-65
1964	277,254,766	—	—	—	—	—	2.25	2.50	3.50	8.00
1964D	156,205,446	—	—	—	—	—	2.25	2.50	3.50	—

40% silver composition

Weight: 11.5 grams. **Composition:** clad layers of 80% silver and 20% copper bonded to a core of 79.1% copper and 20.9% silver (.148 total ounces of silver).

Date	Mintage	G-4	VG-8	F-12	VF-20	XF-40	AU-50	MS-60	MS-65	Prf-65
1965	65,879,366	—	—	—	—	—	—	1.25	2.50	—
1966	108,984,932	—	—	—	—	—	—	1.20	2.40	—
1967	295,046,978	—	—	—	—	—	—	1.00	2.25	—
1968D	246,951,930	—	—	—	—	—	—	1.00	2.25	—
1968S	3,041,506	—	—	—	—	—	—	—	—	3.50
1969D	129,881,800	—	—	—	—	—	—	1.00	2.00	—
1969S	2,934,631	—	—	—	—	—	—	—	—	3.50
1970D	2,150,000	—	—	—	—	—	—	9.00	13.50	—
1970S	2,632,810	—	—	—	—	—	—	—	—	7.50

Clad composition

Weight: 11.34 grams. **Composition:** clad layers of 75% copper and 25% nickel bonded to a pure-copper core.

Date	Mintage	G-4	VG-8	F-12	VF-20	XF-40	AU-50	MS-60	MS-65	Prf-65
1971	155,640,000	—	—	—	—	—	—	1.50	2.50	—
1971D	302,097,424	—	—	—	—	—	—	1.00	1.50	—
1971S	3,244,183	—	—	—	—	—	—	—	—	2.75
1972	153,180,000	—	—	—	—	—	—	2.00	2.50	—
1972D	141,890,000	—	—	—	—	—	—	2.00	2.50	—
1972S	3,267,667	—	—	—	—	—	—	—	—	2.50
1973	64,964,000	—	—	—	—	—	—	1.35	2.50	—
1973D	83,171,400	—	—	—	—	—	—	—	2.50	—
1973S	—	—	—	—	—	—	—	—	—	1.75
1974	201,596,000	—	—	—	—	—	—	1.00	2.00	—
1974D	79,066,300	—	—	—	—	—	—	1.20	2.00	—
1974S	—	—	—	—	—	—	—	—	—	3.00

Half dollars

Bicentennial design, clad composition

Reverse designer: Seth Huntington.

Date	Mintage	G-4	VG-8	F-12	VF-20	XF-40	AU-50	MS-60	MS-65	Prf-65
1976	234,308,000	—	—	—	—	—	—	1.00	1.50	—
1976D	287,565,248	—	—	—	—	—	—	1.00	1.50	—
1976S	—	—	—	—	—	—	—	—	—	1.25

Bicentennial design, silver composition

Weight: 11.5 grams. **Composition:** 40% silver (.148 ounces), 60% copper.

Date	Mintage	G-4	VG-8	F-12	VF-20	XF-40	AU-50	MS-60	MS-65	Prf-65
1976S silver	11,000,000	—	—	—	—	—	—	—	6.00	5.75

Regular design resumed, clad composition

Notes: The 1979-S and 1981-S Type II proofs have clearer mintmarks than the Type I proofs of those years.

Date	Mintage	MS-60	MS-65	Prf-65	Date	Mintage	MS-60	MS-65	Prf-65
1979	68,312,000	—	1.50	—	1980D	33,456,449	—	2.00	—
1979D	15,815,422	—	1.25	—	1980S	—	—	—	1.25
1979S T-I	—	—	—	2.00	1981P	29,544,000	—	2.00	—
1979S T-II	—	—	—	14.00	1981D	27,839,533	—	2.00	—
1980P	44,134,000	—	1.75	—	1981S T-I	—	—	—	1.25

Half dollars

Date	Mintage	MS-60	MS-65	Prf-65	Date	Mintage	MS-60	MS-65	Prf-65
1981S T-II	—	—	—	14.50	1991S	(2,867,787)	—	—	15.00
1982P	10,819,000	—	1.50	—	1992P	17,628,000	—	1.50	—
1982D	13,140,102	—	2.00	—	1992D	17,000,106	—	1.50	—
1982S	—	—	—	3.50	1992S	(2,858,981)	—	—	16.00
1983P	34,139,000	—	1.50	—	1992S	Silver proof	—	—	13.50
1983D	32,472,244	—	1.50	—	1993P	15,510,000	—	1.50	—
1983S	—	—	—	3.00	1993D	15,000,006	—	1.50	—
1984P	26,029,000	—	1.50	—	1993S	(2,633,439)	—	—	14.00
1984D	26,262,158	—	1.50	—	1993S	Silver proof	—	—	14.75
1984S	—	—	—	6.50	1994P	23,718,000	—	1.50	—
1985P	18,706,962	—	1.50	—	1994D	23,828,110	—	1.50	—
1985D	19,814,034	—	1.50	—	1994S	(2,484,594)	—	—	9.75
1985S	—	—	—	4.50	1994S	Silver proof	—	—	13.00
1986P	13,107,633	—	2.00	—	1995P	26,496,000	—	1.50	—
1986D	15,336,145	—	1.50	—	1995D	26,288,000	—	1.50	—
1986S	—	—	—	15.00	1995S	(2,010,384)	—	—	13.00
1987P	2,890,758	—	3.00	—	1995S	Silver proof	—	—	13.00
1987D	2,890,758	—	3.00	—	1996P	24,442,000	—	1.50	—
1987S	—	—	—	3.50	1996D	24,744,000	—	1.50	—
1988P	13,626,000	—	2.50	—	1996S	—	—	—	13.00
1988D	12,000,096	—	2.50	—	1996S	Silver proof	—	—	13.00
1988S	—	—	—	7.25	1997P	20,882,000	—	1.50	—
1989P	24,542,000	—	2.50	—	1997D	19,876,000	—	1.50	—
1989D	23,000,216	—	2.50	—	1997S	(1,975,000)	—	—	13.00
1989S	—	—	—	3.50	1997S	Silver proof	—	—	13.00
1990P	22,780,000	—	1.50	—	1998P	—	—	1.50	—
1990D	20,096,242	—	1.50	—	1998D	—	—	1.50	—
1990S	—	—	—	9.75	1998S	—	—	—	5.00
1991P	14,874,000	—	1.50	—	1998S	Silver proof	—	—	13.00
1991D	15,054,678	—	1.50	—	1998S	Matte finish	—	150.00	—

Silver dollars

MORGAN DOLLARS

Designer: George T. Morgan. **Size:** 38.1 millimeters. **Weight:** 26.73 grams. **Composition:** 90% silver (.7736 ounces), 10% copper. **Notes:** "65DMPL" values are for coins grading MS-65 deep mirror prooflike.

Date	Mintage	VG-8	F-12	VF-20	XF-40	AU-50	MS-60	MS-63	MS-64	MS-65	65DMPL	Prf-60	Prf-63	Prf-65
1901	6,962,813	14.00	17.00	25.00	51.00	220.	1500.	16,000.	50,500.	189,000.	—	950.	1900.	8100.
1901O	13,320,000	11.00	11.50	12.00	13.00	15.00	22.00	32.00	48.00	180.	3800.	—	—	—
1901S	2,284,000	12.00	15.00	24.00	44.00	115.	265.	410.	790.	4150.	11,000.	—	—	—
1902	7,994,777	11.00	11.50	12.00	13.00	19.00	32.00	62.00	90.00	500.	15,750.	750.	1450.	5750.
1902O	8,636,000	11.00	11.50	12.00	13.00	15.00	21.00	28.00	50.00	150.	3800.	—	—	—
1902S	1,530,000	23.00	34.00	76.00	82.00	110.	175.	240.	500.	3150.	12,500.	—	—	—
1903	4,652,755	12.50	14.00	15.00	16.50	19.00	32.00	48.00	63.00	190.	9150.	750.	1450.	5500.
1903O	4,450,000	115.	120.	125.	135.	160.	180.	205.	230.	365.	5050.	—	—	—
1903S	1,241,000	14.00	23.00	63.00	250.	1075.	2650.	4450.	5250.	7900.	35,000.	—	—	—
1904	2,788,650	11.50	12.50	13.00	14.00	30.00	57.00	125.	440.	4200.	38,000.	750.	1450.	5500.
1904O	1138250.	11.00	12.00	13.00	14.00	16.00	21.00	29.00	50.00	120.	550.	—	—	—
1904S	2,304,000	13.00	20.00	38.00	175.	475.	950.	2000.	3000.	6100.	19,000.	—	—	—
1921	44,690,000	11.00	11.50	12.00	13.00	14.00	18.00	21.00	25.00	120.	8800.	—	—	—
1921D	20,345,000	11.00	11.50	12.00	13.00	14.00	32.00	34.00	53.00	260.	12,500.	—	—	—
1921S	21,695,000	11.00	11.50	12.00	13.00	14.00	22.00	45.00	125.	1600.	17,500.	—	—	—

NOTE: Earlier dates (1878-1900) exist for this type.

PEACE DOLLARS

Designer: Anthony DeFrancisci. **Size:** 38.1 millimeters. **Weight:** 26.73 grams. **Composition:** 90% silver (.7736 ounces), 10% copper.

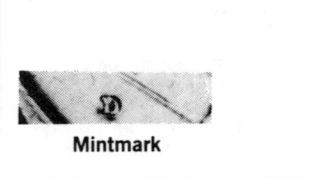

Mintmark

Date	Mintage	G-4	VG-8	F-12	VF-20	XF-40	AU-50	MS-60	MS-63	MS-64	MS-65
1921	1,006,473	16.00	35.00	38.00	40.00	50.00	76.00	135.	180.	450.	2250.
1922	51,737,000	8.00	10.50	11.00	11.50	12.00	13.00	14.00	20.00	53.00	145.
1922D	15,063,000	8.00	10.50	11.00	11.50	12.00	13.00	18.00	29.00	57.00	330.
1922S	17,475,000	8.00	10.50	11.00	11.50	12.00	13.00	18.00	45.00	245.	2150.
1923	30,800,000	8.00	10.50	11.00	11.50	12.00	13.00	14.00	20.00	53.00	145.
1923D	6,811,000	8.00	10.50	11.00	11.50	12.00	14.00	32.00	73.00	265.	1150.
1923S	19,020,000	8.00	10.50	11.00	11.50	12.00	13.00	18.00	57.00	215.	7000.
1924	11,811,000	8.00	10.50	11.00	11.50	12.00	13.00	14.00	20.00	53.00	155.

Silver dollars

Date	Mintage	G-4	VG-8	F-12	VF-20	XF-40	AU-50	MS-60	MS-63	MS-64	MS-65
1924S	1,728,000	9.00	12.00	13.00	14.00	20.00	48.00	160.	370.	1200.	8500.
1925	10,198,000	8.00	10.50	11.00	11.50	12.00	13.00	14.00	20.00	53.00	160.
1925S	1,610,000	8.50	10.50	11.00	11.50	13.50	25.00	50.00	100.	600.	21,000.
1926	1,939,000	8.00	10.50	11.00	11.50	12.00	15.00	21.00	38.00	73.00	280.
1926D	2,348,700	8.00	10.50	11.00	11.50	12.00	25.00	50.00	100.	210.	600.
1926S	6,980,000	8.00	10.50	11.00	11.50	12.00	17.00	32.00	55.00	145.	900.
1927	848,000	11.00	12.50	14.00	16.50	25.00	32.00	46.00	90.00	230.	2600.
1927D	1,268,900	8.00	11.00	14.00	17.00	22.00	63.00	125.	200.	525.	5350.
1927S	866,000	10.00	12.50	14.00	17.00	24.00	63.00	100.	225.	630.	9450.
1928	360,649	75.00	110.	120.	125.	140.	160.	175.	290.	600.	3150.
1928S	1,632,000	8.00	13.00	14.00	18.00	20.00	35.00	100.	285.	1650.	21,500.
1934	954,057	9.00	13.00	14.00	18.00	20.00	32.00	70.00	100.	280.	1150.
1934D	1,569,500	8.00	11.00	12.50	15.00	18.00	32.00	70.00	175.	600.	1900.
1934S	1,011,000	9.00	13.00	15.00	50.00	125.	440.	1000.	2500.	4400.	7500.
1935	1,576,000	8.00	10.50	12.50	13.50	15.00	22.00	49.00	63.00	140.	600.
1935S	1,964,000	8.00	10.50	12.50	13.50	20.00	63.00	120.	220.	380.	1100.

Clad dollars

Eisenhower

Designer: Frank Gasparro. **Size:** 38.1 millimeters. **Weight** 24.59 grams (silver issues) and 22.68 grams (copper-nickel issues). **Clad composition:** 75% copper and 25% nickel bonded to a pure copper core. Silver clad composition: clad layers of 80% silver and 20% copper bonded to a core of 79.1% copper and 20.9% silver (.3161 total ounces of silver).

Date	Mintage	(Proof)	MS-63	Prf-65
1971	47,799,000	—	2.50	—
1971D	68,587,424	—	2.50	—
1971S silver	6,868,530	(4,265,234)	4.60	5.00
1972	75,890,000	—	2.25	—
1972D	92,548,511	—	2.25	—
1972S silver	2,193,056	(1,811,631)	5.00	5.75
1973	2,000,056	—	3.50	—
1973D	2,000,000	—	3.50	—
1973S silver	1,833,140	(1,005,617)	5.00	17.00
1973S clad	—	2,769,624	—	5.50
1974	27,366,000	—	2.25	—
1974D	35,466,000	—	2.25	—
1974S silver	1,720,000	(1,306,579)	5.25	8.50
1974S clad	—	(2,617,350)	—	5.50

Type I Bicentennial reverse **Type II Bicentennial reverse**

Bicentennial design

Reverse designer: Dennis R. Williams. In 1976 the lettering on the reverse was changed to thinner letters, resulting in Type I and Type II varieties for that year.

Date	Mintage	(Proof)	MS-63	Prf-65
1976 Type I	117,337,000	—	3.25	—
1976 Type II	Inc. Ab.	—	2.00	—
1976D Type I	103,228,274	—	3.25	—
1976D Type II	Inc. Ab.	—	2.00	—
1976S cld Type I	—	(2,909,369)	—	5.60
1976S cld Type II	—	(4,149,730)	—	5.50
1976S silver	11,000,000	(4,000,000)	10.00	10.00

Regular design resumed

Date	Mintage	(Proof)	MS-63	Prf-65
1977	12,596,000	—	3.25	—
1977D	32,983,006	—	2.25	—
1977S clad	—	(3,251,152)	—	5.50
1978	25,702,000	—	2.25	—
1978D	33,012,890	—	3.30	—
1978S clad	—	(3,127,788)	—	5.50

Anthony

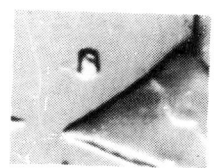

Mintmark

Designer: Frank Gasparro. **Size:** 26.5 millimeters. **Weight:** 8.1 grams. **Composition:** clad layers of 75% copper and 25% nickel bonded to a pure copper core. **Notes:** The 1979-S and 1981-S Type II coins have a clearer mintmark than the Type I varieties for those years.

Date	Mintage	MS-63	Date	Mintage	MS-63
1979P	360,222,000	1.30	1980S	20,422,000	1.30
1979P Near Date	Inc. Ab.	4.00	1980S Prf.	3,547,030	4.50
1979D	288,015,744	1.30	1981P	3,000,000	3.75
1979S	109,576,000	1.60	1981D	3,250,000	3.50
1979S Prf. Type I	3,677,175	4.50	1981S	3,492,000	3.50
1979S Prf. Type II	—	69.00	1981S Prf.Type I	4,063,083	5.50
1980P	27,610,000	1.40	1981S Prf. Type II	—	110.
1980D	41,628,708	1.30			

Gold $2.50 (Quarter eagle)

Coronet Head

Designer: Christian Gobrecht. **Size:** 18 millimeters. **Weight:** 4.18 grams. **Composition:** 90% gold (.121 ounces), 10% copper. Notes: Varieties for 1843 are distinguished by the size of the numerals in the date. One 1848 variety has "Cal." inscribed on the reverse, indicating it was made from California gold. The 1873 "closed 3" and "open 3" varieties are distinguished by the amount of space between the upper left and lower left serifs in the 3 in the date.

Date	Mintage	F-12	VF-20	XF-40	MS-60	Prf-65
1901	91,322	125.	130.	180.	275.	13,000.
1902	133,733	125.	130.	180.	275.	13,000.
1903	201,257	125.	130.	180.	275.	13,000.
1904	160,960	125.	130.	180.	275.	13,000.
1905	217,944	125.	130.	180.	275.	13,000.
1906	176,490	125.	130.	180.	275.	13,000.
1907	336,448	125.	130.	180.	275.	13,000.

NOTE: Earlier dates (1840-1900) exist for this type.

Indian Head

Mintmark

Designer: Bela Lyon Pratt. **Size:** 18 millimeters. **Weight:** 4.18 grams. **Composition:** 90% gold (.121 ounces), 10% copper.

Gold $2.50

Date	Mintage	VF-20	XF-40	AU-50	MS-60	MS-63	MS-65	Prf-65
1908	565,057	135.	175.	185.	210.	870.	2700.	15,000.
1909	441,899	135.	175.	185.	260.	930.	2700.	21,000.
1910	492,682	135.	175.	185.	255.	960.	5200.	18,000.
1911	704,191	135.	175.	185.	260.	600.	2700.	15,000.
1911D	55,680	700.	950.	1250.	2450.	7800.	36,000.	—
1912	616,197	135.	175.	185.	265.	960.	5200.	15,000.
1913	722,165	135.	175.	185.	270.	600.	2700.	15,000.
1914	240,117	135.	175.	210.	430.	2200.	13,750.	18,000.
1914D	448,000	135.	175.	185.	265.	1175.	19,000.	—
1915	606,100	135.	175.	185.	210.	600.	2700.	18,000.
1925D	578,000	135.	175.	185.	210.	600.	2700.	—
1926	446,000	135.	175.	185.	210.	600.	2700.	—
1927	388,000	135.	175.	185.	210.	600.	2700.	—
1928	416,000	135.	175.	185.	210.	600.	2700.	—
1929	532,000	135.	175.	185.	210.	600.	4800.	—

Gold $5 (Half eagle)

Coronet Head

Designer: Christian Gobrecht. **Size:** 21.6 millimeters. **Weight:** 8.359 grams. **Composition:** 90% gold (.242 ounces), 10% copper.

With motto

Notes: In 1866 the motto "In God We Trust" was added above the eagle on the reverse.

Date	Mintage	VF-20	XF-40	AU-50	MS-60	MS-65	Prf-65
1901	616,040	175.	210.	215.	240.	4400.	12,500.
1901S	3,648,000	175.	210.	215.	240.	4400.	—
1902	172,562	175.	210.	215.	240.	4400.	12,500.
1902S	939,000	175.	210.	215.	240.	4400.	—
1903	227,024	175.	210.	215.	240.	4400.	15,000.
1903S	1,855,000	175.	210.	215.	240.	4400.	—
1904	392,136	175.	210.	215.	240.	4400.	12,500.
1904S	97,000	195.	225.	300.	800.	11,000.	—
1905	302,308	175.	210.	215.	240.	7200.	12,500.
1905S	880,700	175.	225.	260.	900.	4400.	—
1906	348,820	175.	210.	215.	240.	4400.	12,500.
1906D	320,000	175.	210.	215.	240.	4400.	—
1906S	598,000	175.	210.	215.	275.	4400.	—
1907	626,192	175.	210.	215.	240.	4400.	20,000.
1907D	888,000	175.	210.	215.	240.	4400.	—
1908	421,874	175.	210.	215.	240.	4400.	—

NOTE: Earlier dates (1866-1900) exist for this type.

Indian Head

Designer: Bela Lyon Pratt. **Size:** 21.6 millimeters. **Weight:** 8.359 grams. **Composition:** 90% gold (.242 ounces), 10% copper.

Date	Mintage	VF-20	XF-40	AU-50	MS-60	MS-63	MS-65	Prf-65
1908	578,012	190.	225.	240.	280.	1400.	12,500.	21,500.
1908D	148,000	190.	225.	240.	280.	1400.	27,000.	—
1908S	82,000	225.	450.	540.	1100.	2600.	12,500.	—
1909	627,138	190.	225.	240.	325.	1400.	12,500.	26,500.
1909D	3,423,560	190.	225.	240.	280.	1400.	12,500.	—
1909O	34,200	600.	900.	1600.	5400.	30,000.	210,000.	—
1909S	297,200	215.	235.	275.	1175.	6600.	31,000.	—
1910	604,250	190.	225.	240.	280.	1700.	18,000.	23,000.
1910D	193,600	190.	225.	240.	350.	1700.	51,000.	—
1910S	770,200	190.	240.	260.	875.	7200.	49,000.	—
1911	915,139	190.	225.	240.	280.	1700.	12,500.	21,500.
1911D	72,500	350.	475.	600.	2850.	13,500.	130,000.	—
1911S	1,416,000	190.	240.	250.	425.	2900.	42,000.	—
1912	790,144	190.	225.	240.	280.	1700.	17,500.	21,500.
1912S	392,000	215.	240.	250.	1450.	9500.	74,000.	—

Gold $5

Date	Mintage	VF-20	XF-40	AU-50	MS-60	MS-63	MS-65	Prf-65
1913	916,099	190.	225.	240.	280.	1700.	14,500.	25,000.
1913S	408,000	250.	270.	340.	1200.	10,500.	115,000.	—
1914	247,125	190.	225.	240.	335.	1700.	14,500.	21,500.
1914D	247,000	190.	225.	240.	360.	1700.	42,000.	—
1914S	263,000	215.	235.	255.	1200.	8200.	57,000.	—
1915	588,075	190.	225.	240.	280.	1400.	12,500.	33,000.
1915S	164,000	300.	325.	425.	1850.	11,500.	75,000.	—
1916S	240,000	190.	250.	275.	515.	1700.	19,000.	—
1929	662,000	2000.	3500.	4200.	5400.	7500.	31,000.	—

Gold $10 (Eagle)

Coronet Head

New — style head, with motto

Designer: Christian Gobrecht. **Size:** 27 millimeters. **Weight:** 16.718 grams. **Composition:** 90% gold (.4839 ounces), 10% copper.

Date	Mintage	VF-20	XF-40	AU-50	MS-60	MS-65	Prf-65
1901	1,718,825	305.	310.	350.	375.	4350.	40,000.
1901O	72,041	310.	325.	400.	450.	13,500.	—
1901S	2,812,750	305.	310.	350.	375.	4500.	—
1902	82,513	305.	310.	350.	375.	12,500.	40,000.
1902S	469,500	305.	310.	350.	375.	6500.	—
1903	125,926	305.	325.	385.	425.	6500.	40,000.
1903O	112,771	305.	310.	375.	400.	6500.	—
1903S	538,000	305.	310.	350.	375.	6500.	—
1904	162,038	305.	310.	350.	375.	6500.	40,000.
1904O	108,950	305.	310.	375.	400.	6500.	—
1905	201,078	305.	310.	350.	375.	6500.	40,000.
1905S	369,250	305.	350.	425.	1300.	6500.	—
1906	165,497	305.	310.	350.	375.	6500.	40,000.
1906D	981,000	305.	310.	350.	375.	6500.	—
1906O	86,895	305.	325.	350.	750.	13,500.	—
1906S	457,000	305.	310.	325.	675.	6500.	—
1907	1,203,973	305.	310.	350.	375.	4350.	40,000.
1907D	1,030,000	305.	310.	350.	375.	4350.	—
1907S	210,500	305.	325.	375.	600.	6500.	—

NOTE: Earlier dates (1866-1900) exist for this type.

Indian Head

Reverse motto

No motto

Designer: Augustus Saint-Gaudens. **Size:** 27 millimeters. **Weight:** 16.718 grams. **Composition:** 90% gold (.4839 ounces), 10% copper. **Notes:** 1907 varieties are distinguished by whether the edge is rolled or wired, and whether the legend "E Pluribus Unum" has periods between each word.

Date	Mintage	VF-20	XF-40	AU-50	MS-60	MS-63	MS-65	Prf-65
1907 wire edge, periods before & after leg.								
	500		4500.	—	7800.	11,500.	36,000.	—
1907 same, without stars on edge								
	—	Unique	—	—	—	—	—	—
1907 rolled edge, periods								
	42	—	—	—	21,500.	34,000.	60,000.	—
1907 without periods								
	239,406	430.	450.	475.	490.	1750.	6000.	27,500.
1908 without motto								
	33,500	480.	525.	600.	780.	2500.	11,500.	—
1908D without motto								
	210,000	430.	440.	500.	720.	5650.	36,000.	—

Gold $10

With motto

Notes: In 1907 the motto "In God We Trust" was added on the reverse to the left of the eagle.

Date	Mintage	VF-20	XF-40	AU-50	MS-60	MS-63	MS-65	Prf-65
1908	341,486	310.	320.	340.	490.	1125.	6000.	27,500.
1908D	836,500	310.	320.	480.	650.	2800.	21,500.	—
1908S	59,850	310.	320.	600.	1450.	4800.	18,000.	—
1909	184,863	310.	320.	340.	510.	1400.	9000.	41,000.
1909D	121,540	310.	320.	340.	750.	2350.	42,000.	—
1909S	292,350	310.	320.	340.	590.	2050.	9600.	—
1910	318,704	310.	320.	340.	480.	930.	6000.	33,000.
1910D	2,356,640	310.	320.	340.	480.	925.	5150.	—
1910S	811,000	310.	320.	340.	725.	3100.	48,000.	—
1911	505,595	310.	320.	340.	490.	975.	5150.	35,000.
1911D	30,100	310.	550.	750.	3850.	11,000.	90,000.	—
1911S	51,000	310.	460.	650.	990.	3250.	8400.	—
1912	405,083	310.	320.	340.	480.	1050.	5500.	33,500.
1912S	300,000	310.	320.	340.	675.	2100.	45,000.	—
1913	442,071	310.	320.	340.	490.	1100.	5150.	36,000.
1913S	66,000	310.	650.	800.	3250.	20,000.	162,000.	—
1914	151,050	310.	320.	340.	500.	985.	6000.	30,000.
1914D	343,500	310.	320.	340.	510.	1100.	9000.	—
1914S	208,000	310.	320.	340.	750.	2900.	39,500.	—
1915	351,075	310.	320.	340.	500.	1100.	5150.	36,000.
1915S	59,000	310.	320.	340.	2500.	7800.	73,000.	—
1916S	138,500	310.	385.	400.	660.	2150.	12,000.	—
1920S	126,500	6500.	7500.	8000.	15,000.	33,000.	120,000.	—
1926	1,014,000	310.	320.	340.	400.	800.	4400.	—
1930S	96,000	3500.	5000.	7500.	8300.	9000.	23,500.	—
1932	4,463,000	310.	320.	340.	400.	800.	4400.	—
1933	312,500	—	—	—	—	264,000.	340,000.	—

Gold $20 (Double Eagle)

Coronet Head

Designer: James B. Longacre. **Size:** 34 millimeters. **Weight:** 33.436 grams. **Composition:** 90% gold (.9677 ounces), 10% copper.

Twenty Dollars with motto

Date	Mintage	VF-20	XF-40	AU-50	MS-60	MS-65	Prf-65
1901	111,526	530.	535.	545.	580.	7000.	—
1901S	1,596,000	530.	625.	650.	665.	—	—
1902	31,254	530.	535.	625.	975.	7200.	—
1902S	1,753,625	530.	535.	545.	580.	—	—
1903	287,428	530.	535.	545.	580.	4700.	62,000.
1903S	954,000	530.	535.	545.	580.	7200.	—
1904	6,256,797	530.	535.	545.	580.	3200.	67,500.
1904S	5,134,175	530.	535.	545.	580.	5550.	—
1905	59,011	530.	620.	650.	1200.	—	—
1905S	1,813,000	520.	575.	620.	635.	—	—
1906	69,690	585.	600.	615.	625.	6000.	67,500.
1906D	620,250	530.	535.	545.	580.	—	—
1906S	2,065,750	530.	535.	545.	580.	—	—
1907	1,451,864	530.	535.	545.	580.	9100.	—
1907D	842,250	530.	535.	545.	580.	3200.	—
1907S	2,165,800	530.	535.	545.	580.	—	—

NOTE: Earlier dates (1877-1900) exist for this type.

Saint-Gaudens

Designer: Augustus Saint-Gaudens. **Size:** 34 millimeters. **Weight:** 33.436 grams. **Composition:** 90% gold (.9677 ounces), 10% copper. **Notes:** The "Roman numerals" varieties for 1907 use Roman numerals for the date instead of Arabic numerals. The lettered-edge varieties have "E Pluribus Unum" on the edge, with stars between the words.

Gold $20

No motto

Date	Mintage	VF-20	XF-40	AU-50	MS-60	MS-63	MS-65	Prf-65
1907 extremely high relief, plain edge	—						Unique	
1907 extremely high relief, lettered edge								
Unrecorded			Prf-68 Private sale 1990 $1,500,000.			—	—	
1907 high relief, Roman numerals, plain edge					Unique - AU55 $150,000			
1907 high relief, Roman numerals, wire rim								
	11,250	2500.	4000.	4800.	7100.	11,000.	28,000.	—
1907 high relief, Roman numerals, flat rim								
	Inc. Ab.	3000.	4200.	5000.	7200.	11,000.	28,000.	—
1907 large letters on edge	—	—	—	—	—	Unique		
1907 small letters on edge								
	361,667	540.	615.	625.	650.	815.	2900.	—
1908	4,271,551	535.	540.	550.	575.	660.	1450.	—
1908D	663,750	500.	495.	565.	600.	815.	17,000.	—
1908	156,359	535.	575.	585.	685.	1125.	19,500.	40,500.
1908D	349,500	535.	540.	550.	650.	830.	3900.	—

Reverse motto

With motto

Notes: In 1908 the motto "In God We Trust" was added at the bottom of the reverse.

Date	Mintage	VF-20	XF-40	AU-50	MS-60	MS-63	MS-65	Prf-65
1908S	22,000	650.	1125.	1500.	3900.	10,500.	36,500.	—
1909/8	161,282	550.	640.	650.	1300.	5850.	45,500.	—
1909	Inc. Ab.	550.	615.	640.	875.	3150.	48,000.	58,000.
1909D	52,500	575.	685.	775.	1250.	3250.	36,000.	—
1909S	2,774,925	535.	540.	550.	575.	810.	4800.	—
1910	482,167	535.	540.	550.	575.	750.	5850.	58,000.
1910D	429,000	535.	540.	550.	575.	750.	2750.	—
1910S	2,128,250	550.	625.	640.	650.	850.	12,000.	—
1911	197,350	550.	625.	640.	650.	1175.	13,750.	41,000.
1911D	846,500	535.	540.	550.	575.	685.	1600.	—
1911S	775,750	535.	540.	550.	575.	715	4700.	—
1912	149,824	550.	600.	615.	700.	1250.	17,000.	36,000.
1913	168,838	550.	585.	600.	690.	1825.	22,500.	52,000.
1913D	393,500	535.	540.	550.	575.	880.	4600.	—
1913S	34,000	575.	715.	815.	1150.	3450.	39,500.	—
1914	95,320	535.	600.	625.	685.	1375.	13,750.	40,000.
1914D	453,000	535.	540.	550.	575.	730.	2350.	—
1914S	1,498,000	535.	540.	550.	575.	700.	2100.	—
1915	152,050	535.	540.	550.	680.	1450.	16,000.	52,000.
1915S	567,500	535.	540.	550.	575.	715.	2025.	—
1916S	796,000	535.	540.	550.	615.	710.	1900.	—
1920	228,250	535.	540.	550.	575.	780.	32,500.	—
1920S	558,000	4500.	8450.	15,000.	22,500.	62,000.	90,000.	—
1921	528,500	7200.	11,000.	12,500.	35,500.	61,000.	150,000.	—
1922	1,375,500	535.	540.	550.	575.	660.	3600.	—
1922S	2,658,000	535.	650.	715.	885.	1575.	36,000.	—
1923	566,000	535.	540.	550.	575.	660.	5850.	—
1923D	1,702,250	535.	540.	550.	575.	660.	1500.	—
1924	4,323,500	535.	540.	550.	575.	660.	1300.	—
1924D	3,049,500	700.	1150.	1350.	1800.	4950.	48,000.	—
1924S	2,927,500	700.	1050.	1175.	2200.	4950.	45,000.	—
1925	2,831,750	535.	540.	550.	575.	660.	1200.	—
1925D	2,938,500	875.	1300.	1800.	3000.	6800.	54,000.	—
1925S	3,776,500	875.	1250.	1625.	5200.	19,500.	75,000.	—
1926	816,750	535.	540.	550.	575.	660.	1400.	—
1926D	481,000	1250.	1950.	2400.	6150.	19,500.	57,500.	—
1926S	2,041,500	700.	1150.	1300.	1700.	3150.	36,000.	—
1927	2,946,750	535.	540.	550.	575.	660.	1200.	—
1927D	180,000	—	—	150,000.	265,000.	—	577,500.	—
1927S	3,107,000	2000.	3900.	4550.	11,750.	25,000.	90,000.	—
1928	8,816,000	535.	540.	550.	575.	660.	1200.	—
1929	1,779,750	4000.	6850.	7500.	9100.	13,000.	68,500.	—
1930S	74,000	6000.	9450.	10,500.	18,000.	45,500.	126,500.	—
1931	2,938,250	4250.	9100.	10,000.	13,000.	26,000.	66,000.	—
1931D	106,500	5500.	8450.	9100.	14,250.	23,000.	80,000.	—
1932	1,101,750	7000.	10,000.	11,750.	15,600.	22,500.	60,500.	—
1933	445,500			None placed in circulation				—

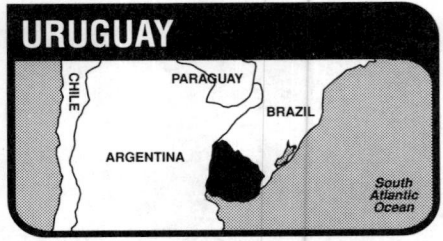

URUGUAY

The Oriental Republic of Uruguay (so called because of its location on the east bank of the Uruguay River) is situated on the Atlantic coast of South America between Argentina and Brazil. This most advanced of South American countries has an area of 68,536 sq. mi. (176,220 sq. km.) and a population of *3 million. Capital: Montevideo. Uruguay's chief economic asset is its rich, rolling grassy plains. Meat, wool, hides and skins are exported.

Uruguay was discovered in 1516 by Juan Diaz de Solis, a Spaniard, but settled by the Portuguese who founded Colonia in 1680. Spain contested Portuguese possession and, after a long struggle, gained control of the country in 1778. During the general South American struggle for independence, Uruguay 's first attempt was led by Gaucho soldier Jose Gervasio Artigas leading the Banda Oriental which was quelled by Spanish and Portuguese forces in 1811. The armistice was soon broken and Argentine force from Buenos Aires cast off the Spanish bond in the Plata region in 1814 only to be reconquered by the Portuguese from Brazil in the struggle of 1816-20. Revolt flared anew in 1825 and independence was reasserted in 1828 with the help of Argentina. The Uruguayan Republic was established in 1830.

MINT MARKS
A - Paris, Berlin, Vienna
(a) - Paris, privy marks only
D - Lyon (France)
H - Birmingham
Mx, Mo - Mexico City
(p) - Poissy, France
So - Santiago (Small O above S)
(u) - Utrecht

MONETARY SYSTEM
100 Centesimo = 1 Peso
1975-1993
1000 Old Pesos = 1 Nuevo (New) Peso
Commencing 1994
1000 Nuevos Pesos = 1 Peso Uruguayo

CENTESIMO

COPPER-NICKEL, 2.00 g

KM#	Date	Mintage	Fine	VF	XF	Unc
19	1901A	6.000	.45	.75	4.00	20.00
	1901A	—	—	—	Proof	225.00
	1909A	5.000	.45	.75	3.00	10.00
	1924(p)	3.000	.45	.75	2.50	8.50
	1936A	2.000	.50	1.00	3.00	12.50

1.50 g

32	1953	5.000	.15	.30	.50	1.00
	1953	—	—	—	Proof	60.00

2 CENTESIMOS

COPPER-NICKEL, 3.50 g

20	1901A	7.500	.50	1.25	3.50	16.00
	1909A	10.000	.50	1.00	2.75	7.00
	1924(p)	11.000	.50	1.00	2.75	7.00
	1936A	6.500	.50	1.25	3.50	10.00
	1941So	10.000	.50	1.00	2.75	7.00

COPPER, 3.50 g

20a	1943So	5.000	.25	.50	2.00	6.00
	1944So	3.500	.25	.50	2.00	6.00
	1945So	2.500	.25	.50	2.00	7.00
	1946So	2.500	.25	.50	2.00	7.50

KM#	Date	Mintage	Fine	VF	XF	Unc
20a	1947So	5.000	.25	.50	1.50	5.00
	1948So	7.500	.25	.50	1.00	4.00
	1949So	7.400	.25	.50	1.00	4.00
	1951So	12.500	.25	.50	1.00	3.00

COPPER-NICKEL, 2.50 g

33	1953	50.000	.15	.30	.50	1.25
	1953	—	—	—	Proof	65.00

NICKEL-BRASS, 2.00 g

37	1960	17.500	—	.15	.25	.50
	1960	—	—	—	Proof	40.00

5 CENTESIMOS

COPPER-NICKEL, 5.00 g

21	1901A	6.000	.25	.75	2.50	15.00
	1901A	—	—	—	Proof	325.00
	1909A	5.000	.25	.75	2.00	10.00
	1909A	—	—	—	Proof	125.00
	1924(p)	5.000	.35	1.00	3.50	9.00
	1936A	3.000	.35	1.00	3.00	9.00
	1941So	2.400	.25	.75	2.00	6.50
	1941S(O)	—	—	—	Proof	200.00

COPPER, 5.00 g

21a	1944So	4.000	.20	.65	1.50	7.50
	1946So	2.000	.20	.50	2.00	8.50
	1947So	2.000	.20	.50	2.00	8.50
	1948So	3.000	.20	.50	1.50	7.50
	1949So	2.800	.20	.50	1.50	7.50
	1951So	15.000	.20	.50	1.50	5.50

COPPER-NICKEL, 3.50 g

34	1953	17.500	.20	.30	.50	1.00
	1953	—	—	—	Proof	75.00

NICKEL-BRASS, 3.50 g

38	1960	88.000	—	.15	.25	.50
	1960	—	—	—	Proof	40.00

10 CENTESIMOS

ALUMINUM-BRONZE, 8.00 g
Constitution Centennial
Obv: MORLON behind neck.

25	1930(a)	5.000	1.00	2.50	7.50	18.50

6.00 g

KM#	Date	Mintage	Fine	VF	XF	Unc
28	1936A	2.000	1.50	3.50	8.50	20.00

COPPER-NICKEL, 4.50 g

35	1953	28.250	.15	.20	.30	.75
	1953	—	—	—	Proof	75.00
	1959	10.000	.20	.30	.50	1.50

NICKEL-BRASS, 4.50 g

39	1960	72.500	.15	.20	.30	.75

20 CENTESIMOS

5.0000 g, .800 SILVER, .1286 oz ASW

24	1920	2.500	2.00	4.00	9.00	22.00

Constitution Centennial
Obv: P. TURIN left of date.

26	1930(a)	2.500	2.00	3.50	8.00	20.00

3.0000 g, .720 SILVER, .0694 oz ASW

29	1942So	18.000	1.25	2.50	4.50	7.00

36	1954(u)	10.000	.75	1.50	2.50	4.50

ALUMINUM

44	1965So	40.000	.15	.20	.35	.60

25 CENTESIMOS

COPPER-NICKEL
Obv: HP below bust.

KM#	Date	Mintage	Fine	VF	XF	Unc
40	1960	48.000	.20	.35	.50	1.00
	1960	—	—	—	Proof	60.00

50 CENTESIMOS

12.5000 g, .900 SILVER, .3617 oz ASW

22	1916	.400	5.00	10.00	25.00	80.00
	1917	5.600	4.00	7.00	20.00	70.00

7.0000 g, .720 SILVER, .1620 oz ASW

31	1943So	10.800	BV	2.00	3.00	9.00

COPPER-NICKEL
Obv: HP below bust.

41	1960	18.000	.20	.40	.60	1.00
	1960	—	—	—	Proof	60.00

ALUMINUM

45	1965So	50.000	.15	.25	.40	.70

PESO

25.0000 g, .900 SILVER, .7235 oz ASW

23	1917	2.000	10.00	20.00	50.00	250.00

9.0000 g, .720 SILVER, .2083 oz ASW

KM#	Date	Mintage	Fine	VF	XF	Unc
30	1942So	9.000	BV	2.25	4.50	12.00

COPPER-NICKEL
Obv: HP below bust.

42	1960	8.000	.25	.50	.75	1.25
	1960	—	—	—	Proof	75.00

ALUMINUM-BRONZE

46	1965So	60.000	—	.15	.35	.60
	1965So	25 pcs.	—	—	Proof	65.00

NICKEL-BRASS
Ceibo - National Flower

49	1968So	103.200	—	—	.15	.30
	1968So	50 pcs.	—	—	Proof	50.00

ALUMINUM-BRONZE

52	1969So	51.800	—	—	.15	.30

5 PESOS

ALUMINUM-BRONZE

47	1965So	18.000	.20	.30	.50	1.00
	1965So	25 pcs.	—	—	Proof	75.00

NICKEL-BRASS
Ceibo - National Flower

50	1968So	42.680	.10	.20	.30	.40
	1968So	50 pcs.	—	—	Proof	65.00

ALUMINUM-BRONZE

53	1969So	42.320	—	—	.10	.30

---

10 PESOS

12.5000 g, .900 SILVER, .3617 oz ASW
Sesquicentennial of Revolution Against Spain

KM#	Date	Mintage	Fine	VF	XF	Unc
43	1961	3.000	—	BV	4.00	7.00
	1961	—	—	—	Proof	600.00

ALUMINUM-BRONZE

48	1965So	18.000	.15	.20	.35	1.00

NICKEL-BRASS
Ceibo - National Flower

51	1968So	90.000	.15	.20	.35	.65
	1968So	50 pcs.	—	—	Proof	80.00

ALUMINUM-BRONZE

54	1969So	10.000	.15	.20	.35	.65

20 PESOS

COPPER-NICKEL
Spears of Wheat

56	1970So	50.000	.15	.25	.40	.75
	1970So	—	—	—	Proof	80.00

50 PESOS

COPPER-NICKEL
Spears of Wheat

57	1970So	20.000	.20	.40	.60	1.50
	1970So	—	—	—	Proof	80.00

NICKEL-BRASS
Centennial - Birth of Rodo

KM#	Date	Mintage	Fine	VF	XF	Unc
58	1971So	15.000	.20	.50	1.00	2.00

100 PESOS

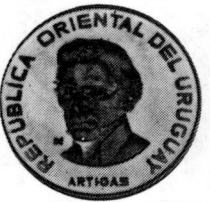 

COPPER-NICKEL

59	1973Mx	20.000	.25	.50	1.00	2.50

NOTE: Mx may be designer initials.

MONETARY REFORM

1000 Old Pesos = 1 Nuevo (New) Peso

CENTESIMO

ALUMINUM
Obv: Radiant sun.

71	1977So	10.000	—	—	.15	.25

3.7000 g, .900 SILVER, .1071 oz ASW

71a	1979So					
		202 pcs.	—	—	Proof	15.00

2 CENTESIMOS

ALUMINUM

72	1977So	17.000	—	—	.15	.25
	1978So	3.000	—	—	.15	.25

5 CENTESIMOS

ALUMINUM

73	1977So	11.000	—	—	.15	.45
	1978So	19.000	—	—	.15	.45

10 CENTESIMOS

ALUMINUM-BRONZE

66	1976So	127.400	—	—	.20	.70
	1977So	12.700	—	—	.25	.75
	1978So	19.900	—	—	.25	.75
	1981So	—	—	—	.25	.75

20 CENTESIMOS

ALUMINUM-BRONZE

KM#	Date	Mintage	Fine	VF	XF	Unc
67	1976So	40.000	—	—	.20	.45
	1977So	4.700	—	—	.20	.60
	1978So	15.300	—	—	.20	.45
	1981So	—	—	—	.20	.45

50 CENTESIMOS

ALUMINUM-BRONZE

68	1976So	30.000	—	—	.20	.50
	1977So	9.800	—	—	.20	.50
	1978So	.200	—	—	.20	.55
	1981So	—	—	—	.20	.50

NUEVO PESO

ALUMINUM-BRONZE

69	1976So	65.540	—	—	.30	.60
	1977So	7.360	—	—	.30	.65
	1978So	27.100	—	—	.30	.65

COPPER-NICKEL

74	1980So	50.000	—	.20	.35	.65
	1981So	—	—	.20	.35	.65

STAINLESS STEEL

95	1989		—	—	.15	.35

2 NUEVO PESOS

COPPER-NICKEL-ZINC
World Food Day

77	1981	95.000	—	.25	.50	1.00

5 NUEVO PESOS

COPPER-NICKEL-ALUMINUM
150th Anniversary - Revolutionary Movement

65	ND(1975)So					
		3.000	.50	.75	1.25	3.50

COPPER-ALUMINUM
250th Anniversary - Founding of Montevideo

KM#	Date	Mintage	Fine	VF	XF	Unc
70	1976So	.300	.75	1.00	1.50	4.00

COPPER-NICKEL

75	1980So	50.000	—	.20	.40	1.50
	1981So	—	—	.20	.40	1.50

STAINLESS STEEL

92	1989	65.000	—	—	.15	.35

10 NUEVO PESOS

COPPER-NICKEL

79	1981So		—	.20	.50	1.75

STAINLESS STEEL

93	1989	79.000	—	—	.20	.50

20 NUEVO PESOS

COPPER-NICKEL
World Fisheries Conference

86	1984	3,771	—	—	—	15.00

50 NUEVO PESOS

STAINLESS STEEL

94	1989		—	—	.20	.50

100 NUEVO PESOS

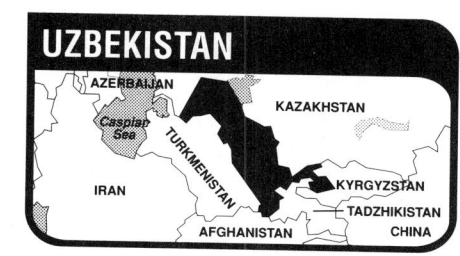

12.0000 g, .900 SILVER, .3472 oz ASW
Hydroelectric Dam

KM#	Date	Mintage	Fine	VF	XF	Unc
80	1981So	.025	—	—	—	6.50

STAINLESS STEEL
Gaucho Bust

96	1989		—	—	.35	.75

200 NUEVO PESOS

COPPER-NICKEL
Unchained Liberty

97	1989		—	—	—	1.50

500 NUEVO PESOS

COPPER-NICKEL
Artigas

98	1989		—	—	—	3.00

MONETARY REFORM
March, 1993 -

1,000 Nuevos Pesos = 1 Uruguayan Peso
100 Centesimos = 1 Uruguayan Peso (UYP)

10 CENTESIMOS

STAINLESS STEEL

102	1994		—	—	.25	.50

20 CENTESIMOS

STAINLESS STEEL

105	1994		—	—	.30	.60

50 CENTESIMOS

STAINLESS STEEL

106	1994		—	—	.35	.75

URUGUAYAN PESO

BRASS

KM#	Date	Mintage	Fine	VF	XF	Unc
103	1994		—	—	.50	1.00

2 URUGUAYAN PESOS

BRASS

104	1994		—	—	.75	1.50

The Republic of Uzbekistan (formerly the Uzbek S.S.R.), is bordered on the north by Kazakhstan, to the east by Kirghizia and Tajikistan, on the south by Afghanistan and on the west by Turkmenistan. The republic is comprised of the regions of Andizhan, Bukhara, Dzhizak, Ferghana, Kashkadar, Khorezm (Khiva), Namangan, Navoi, Samarkand, Surkhan-Darya, Syr-Darya, Tashkent and the Karakalpak Autonomous Republic. It has an area of 172,741 sq. mi. (447,400 sq. km.) and a population of 20.3 million. Capital: Tashkent.

Crude oil, natural gas, coal, copper, and gold deposits make up the chief resources, while intensive farming, based on artificial irrigation, provides an abundance of cotton.

On the eve of WW I, Khiva and Bukhara were enclaves within a Russian Turkestan divided into five provinces or oblasti. The czarist government did not attempt to Russify the indigenous Turkic or Tajik populations, preferring to keep them backward and illiterate. The revolution of March 1917 created a confused situation in the area. In Tashkent there was a Turkestan committee of the provisional government; a Communist-controlled council of workers', soldiers' and peasants' deputies; also a Moslem Turkic movement, Shuro-i-Islamiya, and a young Turkestan or Jaddidi (Renovation) party. The last named party claimed full political autonomy for Turkestan and the abolition of the emirate of Bukhara and the khanate of Khiva. After the Communist *coup d'etat* in Petrograd, the council of people's commissars on Nov. 24 (Dec. 7), 1917, published an appeal to "all toiling Moslems in Russia and in the east" proclaiming their right to build their national life "freely and unhindered". In response, the Moslem and Jaddidi organizations in Dec. 1917 convoked a national congress in Khokand which appointed a provisional government headed by Mustafa Chokayev (or Chokaigolu; 1890-1941) and resolved to elect a constituent assembly to decide whether Turkestan should remain within a Russian federal state or proclaim its independence. Khiva concluded a treaty of alliance with the Russian S.F.S.R. in Sept. 1920, and Bukhara followed suit in March 1921. Theoretically, a Turkestan Autonomous Soviet Socialist Republic had existed since May 1, 1918; in 1920 this "Turkrepublic", as it was called, was proclaimed part of the R.S.F.S.R. On Sept. 18, 1924, the Uzbek and Turkmen peoples were authorized to form S.S.R.'s of their own, and the Kazakhs, Kirghiz, and Tajiks to form autonomous S.S.R.'s. On Oct. 27, 1924, the Uzbek and Turkmen S.S.R. were officially constituted and the former was formally accepted on Jan. 15, 1925, as a member of the U.S.S.R. Tajikistan was an autonomous soviet republic within Uzbekistan until Dec. 5, 1929, when it became a S.S.R. On Dec. 5, 1936, Uzbekistan was territorially increased by incorporating into it the Kara-Kalpak A.S.S.R., which had belonged to Kazakhstan until 1930 and afterward had come under direct control of the R.S.F.S.R.

On June 20, 1990 the Uzbek Supreme Soviet adopted a declaration of sovereignty, and in Aug. 1991, following the unsuccessful coup, declared itself independent as the "Republic of Uzbekistan", which was confirmed by referendum in Dec. That same month Uzbekistan became a member of the CIS.

TIYIN

BRASS CLAD STEEL
Rev: Small denomination.

KM#	Date	Mintage	VF	XF	Unc
1.1	1994	—	—	—	.30

Rev: Large denomination.

1.2	1994	—	—	—	.30

3 TIYIN

BRASS PLATED STEEL
Rev: Small denomination.

KM#	Date	Mintage	VF	XF	Unc
2.1	1994	—	—	—	.40

Rev: Large denomination.

2.2	1994	—	—	—	.40

5 TIYIN

BRASS PLATED STEEL
Rev: Small denomination.

3.1	1994	—	—	—	.50

Rev: Large denomination.

3.2	1994	—	—	—	.50

10 TIYIN

NICKEL CLAD STEEL
Rev: Small denomination.

4.1	1994	—	—	—	.60

Rev: Large denomination.

4.2	1994	—	—	—	.60

20 TIYIN

NICKEL CLAD STEEL
Rev: Small denomination.

5.1	1994	—	—	—	.75

Rev: Large denomination.

5.2	1994	—	—	—	.75

50 TIYIN

NICKEL CLAD STEEL

6	1994	—	—	—	1.00

1 SOM

NICKEL CLAD STEEL
Rev: Denomination.

8	1997	—	—	—	.65

5 SOM

NICKEL CLAD STEEL
Rev: Denomination.

KM#	Date	Mintage	VF	XF	Unc
9	1997	—	—	—	.85

10 SOM

NICKEL CLAD STEEL
Rev: Denomination.

10	1997	—	—	—	1.25

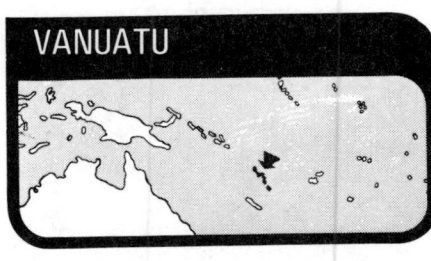

VANUATU

The Republic of Vanuatu, formerly New Hebrides Condominium, a group of islands located in the South Pacific 500 miles (800 km.) west of Fiji, were under the joint sovereignty of Great Britain and France. The islands have an area of 5,700 sq. mi. (14,760 sq. km.) and a population of 165,000, mainly Melanesians of mixed blood. Capital: Port-Vila. The volcanic and coral islands, while malarial and subject to frequent earthquakes, are extremely fertile, and produce copra, coffee, tropical fruits and timber for export.

The New Hebrides were discovered by Portuguese navigator Pedro de Quiros in 1606, visited by French explorer Bougainville in 1768, and named by British navigator Capt. James Cook in 1774. Ships of all nations converged on the islands to trade for sandalwood, prompting France and Britain to relinquish their individual claims and declare the islands a neutral zone in 1878. The New Hebrides were placed under the control of a mixed Anglo-French commission of naval officers during the native uprisings of 1887, and established as a condominium under the joint sovereignty of France and Great Britain in 1906.

Vanuatu became an independent republic within the Commonwealth in July 1980. A president is Head of State and the Prime Minister is Head of Government.

MINT MARKS
(a) - Paris, privy marks only

MONETARY SYSTEM
100 Centimes = 1 Franc

NEW HEBRIDES
FRANC

NICKEL-BRASS

KM#	Date	Mintage	VF	XF	Unc
4.1	1970(a)	.435	.25	.50	.75

Obv. leg: I.E.O.M. added.

4.2	1975(a)	.350	.20	.40	.60
	1978(a)	.200	.20	.40	.60
	1979(a)	.350	.20	.40	.60
	1982(a)	—	.20	.40	.60

2 FRANCS

NICKEL-BRASS

5.1	1970(a)	.264	.60	1.25	2.00

Obv. leg: I.E.O.M. added.

5.2	1973(a)	.200	.20	.40	.60
	1975(a)	.300	.20	.40	.60
	1978(a)	.150	.20	.40	.60
	1979(a)	.250	.20	.40	.60
	1982(a)	—	.20	.40	.60

5 FRANCS

NICKEL-BRASS

KM#	Date	Mintage	VF	XF	Unc
6.1	1970(a)	.375	.50	.75	1.50

Obv. leg: I.E.O.M. added.

6.2	1975(a)	.350	.30	.60	1.00
	1979(a)	.250	.30	.60	1.00
	1982(a)	—	.30	.60	1.00

10 FRANCS

NICKEL

2.1	1967(a)	.250	.30	.60	1.25
	1970(a)	.400	.30	.60	1.25

Obv. leg: I.E.O.M. added.

2.2	1973(a)	.200	.30	.60	1.25
	1975(a)	.300	.30	.60	1.25
	1977(a)	.200	.30	.60	1.25
	1979(a)	.400	.30	.60	1.25
	1982(a)	—	.30	.60	1.25

20 FRANCS

NICKEL

3.1	1967(a)	.250	.60	1.00	2.00
	1970(a)	.300	.60	1.00	2.00

Obv. leg: I.E.O.M. added.

3.2	1973(a)	.200	.60	1.00	2.00
	1975(a)	.150	.60	1.00	2.00
	1977(a)	.150	.60	1.00	2.00
	1979(a)	.300	.60	1.00	2.00
	1982(a)	—	.60	1.00	2.00

50 FRANCS

NICKEL

KM#	Date	Mintage	VF	XF	Unc
7	1972(a)	.200	1.50	2.50	3.50
	1979(a)	—	1.50	2.50	3.50

100 FRANCS

25.0000 g, .835 SILVER, .6712 oz ASW

1	1966(a)	.200	—	—	15.00
	1979(a)	—	—	—	20.00

VANUATU

VATU

NICKEL-BRASS

3	1983	—	—	.10	.35
	1983	—	—	Proof	1.50
	1990	—	—	.10	.35

2 VATU

NICKEL-BRASS

4	1983	—	—	.15	.50
	1983	—	—	Proof	2.00
	1990	—	—	.10	.45

5 VATU

NICKEL-BRASS

5	1983	—	—	.20	.75
	1983	—	—	Proof	2.50
	1990	—	—	.15	.60

10 VATU

COPPER-NICKEL
F.A.O. Issue

KM#	Date	Mintage	VF	XF	Unc
6	1983	—	—	.25	1.00
	1983	—	—	Proof	3.00
	1990	—	—	.25	1.00

20 VATU

COPPER-NICKEL
F.A.O. Issue

7	1983	—	—	.35	1.50
	1983	—	—	Proof	4.00
	1990	—	—	.35	1.50

50 VATU

NICKEL
1st Anniversary of Independence

1	1981	—	—	1.00	2.50

COPPER-NICKEL
F.A.O. Issue

8	1983	—	—	1.00	2.75
	1983	—	—	Proof	7.00
	1990	—	—	1.00	2.75

100 VATU

NICKEL-BRASS

9	1988	—	—	—	3.75

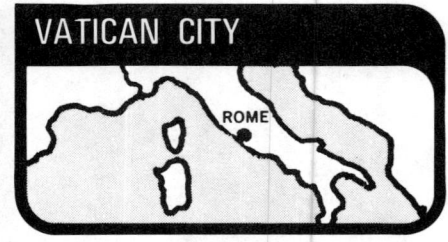

VATICAN CITY

The State of the Vatican City, a papal state on the right bank of the Tiber River within the boundaries of Rome, has an area of 0.17 sq. mi. (0.44 sq. km.) and a population of *775. Capital: Vatican City.

Vatican City State, comprising the Vatican, St. Peter's and extraterritorial right to Castel Gandolfo and 13 buildings in Rome, is all that remains of the extensive papal states over which the Pope exercised temporal power in central Italy. During the struggle for Italian unification, the papal states, including Rome, were forcibly incorporated into the Kingdom of Italy in 1870. The resultant confrontation of crozier and sword remained unresolved until the signing of the Lateran Treaty, Feb. 11, 1929, between the Vatican and the Kingdom of Italy which recognized the independence and sovereignty of the State of the Vatican City, defined the relationship between the government and the church within Italy, and financially compensated the Holy See for its territorial losses in 1870.

Today the Pope exercises supreme legislative, executive and judicial power within the Vatican City, and the State of the Vatican City is recognized by many nations as an independent sovereign state under the temporal jurisdiction of the Pope, even to the extent of ambassadorial exchange.

PONTIFFS

Pius XI, 1922-1939
   Sede Vacante, Feb. 10 - Mar. 2, 1939
Pius XII, 1939-1958
   Sede Vacante, Oct. 9 - 28, 1958
John XXIII, 1958-1963
   Sede Vacante, June 3 - 21, 1963
Paul VI, 1963-1978
   Sede Vacante, Aug. 6 - 26, 1978
John Paul I, Aug. 26 - Sept. 28, 1978
   Sede Vacante, Sept. 28 - Oct. 16, 1978
John Paul II, 1978-

MINT MARKS
Commencing 1981

R - Rome

MONETARY SYSTEM
100 Centesimi = 1 Lira

DATING
Most Vatican coins indicate the regnal year of the pope preceded by the word *Anno* (or an abbreviation), even if the anno domini date is omitted.

5 CENTESIMI

BRONZE

Y#	Date	Year	Mintage	VF	XF	Unc
1	1929	VIII	.010	5.00	7.50	16.00
	1930	IX	.100	2.50	4.00	6.00
	1931	X	.100	2.50	4.00	6.00
	1932	XI	.100	2.50	4.00	6.00
	1934	XIII	.100	2.50	4.00	6.00
	1935	XIV	.044	5.00	10.00	20.00
	1936	XV	.062	2.50	4.00	6.50
	1937	XVI	.062	2.50	4.00	6.50
	1938	XVII	—	—	Rare	—

Jubilee

11	1933-34	—	.100	5.00	10.00	20.00

ALUMINUM-BRONZE

Y#	Date	Year	Mintage	VF	XF	Unc
22	1939	I	.062	2.50	4.00	7.50
	1940	II	.062	2.50	4.00	7.50
	1941	III	5,000	7.50	15.00	27.00

BRASS
Pope Pius • XII

31	1942	IV	5,000	15.00	27.50	55.00
	1943	V	1,000	25.00	40.00	85.00
	1944	VI	1,000	25.00	40.00	85.00
	1945	VII	1,000	25.00	40.00	85.00
	1946	VIII	1,000	25.00	40.00	85.00

10 CENTESIMI

BRONZE

2	1929	VIII	.010	5.00	7.50	18.00
	1930	IX	.090	2.00	4.00	6.00
	1931	X	.090	2.00	4.00	6.00
	1932	XI	.090	2.00	4.00	6.00
	1934	XIII	.090	2.00	4.00	6.00
	1935	XIV	.090	2.00	4.00	6.00
	1936	XV	.081	2.00	4.00	8.00
	1937	XVI	.081	2.00	4.00	8.00
	1938	XVII	—	—	Rare	—

Jubilee

12	1933-34	—	.090	5.00	10.00	20.00

ALUMINUM-BRONZE

23	1939	I	.081	2.50	5.00	10.00
	1940	II	.081	2.50	5.00	10.00
	1941	III	7,500	7.50	15.00	27.00

BRASS
Pope Pius • XII

32	1942	IV	7,500	12.50	25.00	55.00
	1943	V	1,000	40.00	60.00	85.00
	1944	VI	1,000	40.00	60.00	85.00
	1945	VII	1,000	40.00	60.00	85.00
	1946	VIII	1,000	40.00	60.00	85.00

20 CENTESIMI

NICKEL
Pope Pius • XI

3	1929	VIII	.010	5.00	10.00	18.00
	1930	IX	.080	2.00	4.00	6.00
	1931	X	.080	2.00	4.00	6.00
	1932	XI	.080	2.00	4.00	6.00
	1934	XIII	.080	2.00	4.00	6.00

(20 CENTESIMI continued)

Y#	Date	Year	Mintage	VF	XF	Unc
3	1935	XIV	.011	25.00	50.00	75.00
	1936	XV	.064	2.00	4.00	6.00
	1937	XVI	.064	2.00	4.00	6.00

Jubilee

13	1933-34	—	.080	5.00	10.00	20.00

24	1939	I	.064	2.00	4.00	6.00

STAINLESS STEEL

24a	1940	II	.064	2.00	4.00	5.50
	1941	III	.125	2.00	3.00	4.50

33	1942	IV	.125	2.00	2.75	3.50
	1943	V	1,000	40.00	60.00	85.00
	1944	VI	1,000	40.00	60.00	85.00
	1945	VII	1,000	40.00	60.00	85.00
	1946	VIII	1,000	40.00	60.00	85.00

50 CENTESIMI

NICKEL

4	1929	VIII	.010	5.00	10.00	18.00
	1930	IX	.080	2.00	4.00	6.00
	1931	X	.080	2.00	4.00	6.00
	1932	XI	.080	2.00	4.00	6.00
	1934	XIII	.080	2.00	4.00	6.00
	1935	XIV	.014	6.00	12.00	25.00
	1936	XV	.052	2.00	4.00	6.00
	1937	XVI	.052	2.00	4.00	6.00

Jubilee

14	1933-34	—	.080	4.00	8.00	16.00

25	1939	I	.052	2.00	4.00	6.00

STAINLESS STEEL

25a	1940	II	.052	2.00	4.00	5.50
	1941	III	.180	2.00	3.50	5.00

ALUMINUM

Y#	Date	Year	Mintage	VF	XF	Unc
40	1947	IX	.120	1.00	2.00	4.00
	1948	X	.010	2.00	4.00	7.00
	1949	XI	.010	2.00	4.00	7.00

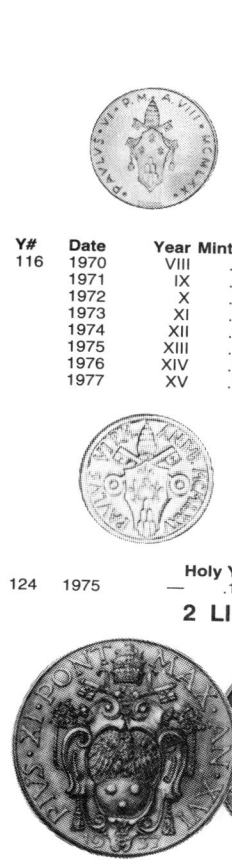

Y#	Date	Year	Mintage	VF	XF	Unc
116	1970	VIII	.100	.25	.50	1.00
	1971	IX	.110	.25	.50	1.00
	1972	X	.110	.25	.50	1.00
	1973	XI	.132	.25	.50	1.00
	1974	XII	.132	.25	.50	1.00
	1975	XIII	.150	.25	.50	1.00
	1976	XIV	.150	.25	.50	1.00
	1977	XV	.135	.25	.50	1.00

Y#	Date	Year	Mintage	VF	XF	Unc
34	1942	IV	.180	2.00	3.25	4.50
	1943	V	1,000	40.00	60.00	85.00
	1944	VI	1,000	40.00	60.00	85.00
	1945	VII	1,000	40.00	60.00	85.00
	1946	VIII	1,000	40.00	60.00	85.00

LIRA

Holy Year

Y#	Date		Mintage	VF	XF	Unc
44	1950	—	.050	1.00	2.00	3.50

NICKEL

Y#	Date	Year	Mintage	VF	XF	Unc
5	1929	VIII	.010	5.00	10.00	18.00
	1930	IX	.080	2.00	4.00	6.00
	1931	X	.080	2.00	4.00	6.00
	1932	XI	.080	2.00	4.00	6.00
	1934	XIII	.080	2.00	4.00	6.00
	1935	XIV	.040	2.00	4.00	6.00
	1936	XV	.040	2.00	4.00	6.00
	1937	XVI	.070	2.00	4.00	6.00

Y#	Date	Year	Mintage	VF	XF	Unc
49	1951	XIII	.400	.25	.50	1.50
	1952	XIV	.400	.25	.50	1.50
	1953	XV	.400	.25	.50	1.50
	1955	XVII	.010	1.50	3.00	6.00
	1956	XVIII	.010	1.50	3.00	6.00
	1957	XIX	.030	.75	2.00	3.50
	1958	XX	.030	.75	2.00	3.50

Holy Year

Y#	Date		Mintage	VF	XF	Unc
124	1975	—	.170	.25	.50	1.00

2 LIRE

Y#	Date	Year	Mintage	VF	XF	Unc
58	1959	I	.025	1.00	3.50	7.00
	1960	II	.025	1.00	2.00	4.00
	1961	III	.025	1.00	2.00	4.00
	1962	IV	.025	1.00	2.00	4.00

NICKEL

Y#	Date	Year	Mintage	VF	XF	Unc
6	1929	VIII	.010	5.00	10.00	18.00
	1930	IX	.050	2.00	4.00	5.50
	1931	X	.050	2.00	4.00	5.50
	1932	XI	.050	2.00	4.00	5.50
	1934	XIII	.050	2.00	4.00	5.50
	1935	XIV	.070	2.00	4.00	5.50
	1936	XV	.040	2.00	4.00	5.50
	1937	XVI	.070	2.00	4.00	5.50

2nd Ecumenical Council

Y#	Date	Year	Mintage	VF	XF	Unc
67	1962	IV	.050	1.00	1.50	3.00

Jubilee, enlargement of date area

Y#	Date		Mintage	VF	XF	Unc
15	1933-34	—	.080	5.00	10.00	20.00

Pope Paul VI

Y#	Date	Year	Mintage	VF	XF	Unc
76	1963	I	.060	.75	2.00	4.00
	1964	II	.060	.50	1.00	2.00
	1965	III	.060	.50	1.00	2.00

Jubilee

Y#	Date		Mintage	VF	XF	Unc
16	1933-34	—	.050	4.00	6.00	10.00

Y#	Date	Year	Mintage	VF	XF	Unc
84	1966	IV	.090	.25	.75	1.25

Y#	Date	Year	Mintage	VF	XF	Unc
26	1939	I	.070	3.00	5.00	10.00

STAINLESS STEEL

Y#	Date	Year	Mintage	VF	XF	Unc
26a	1940	II	.070	3.00	5.00	7.50
	1941	III	.284	1.00	2.00	4.50

Y#	Date	Year	Mintage	VF	XF	Unc
92	1967	V	.100	.25	.75	1.25

Y#	Date	Year	Mintage	VF	XF	Unc
27	1939	I	.040	3.00	5.00	10.00

STAINLESS STEEL

Y#	Date	Year	Mintage	VF	XF	Unc
27a	1940	II	.040	.75	1.50	4.00
	1941	III	.270	.50	1.00	3.00

Y#	Date	Year	Mintage	VF	XF	Unc
35	1942	IV	.284	1.00	1.75	3.50
	1943	V	1,000	40.00	60.00	85.00
	1944	VI	1,000	40.00	60.00	85.00
	1945	VII	1,000	40.00	60.00	85.00
	1946	VIII	1,000	40.00	60.00	85.00

F.A.O. Issue

Y#	Date	Year	Mintage	VF	XF	Unc
100	ND(1968)	VI	.100	.25	.75	1.25

Y#	Date	Year	Mintage	VF	XF	Unc
108	1969	VII	.100	.25	.75	1.25

Y#	Date	Year	Mintage	VF	XF	Unc
36	1942	IV	.270	.50	1.00	3.50
	1943	V	1,000	40.00	60.00	85.00
	1944	VI	1,000	40.00	60.00	85.00
	1945	VII	1,000	40.00	60.00	85.00
	1946	VIII	1,000	40.00	60.00	85.00

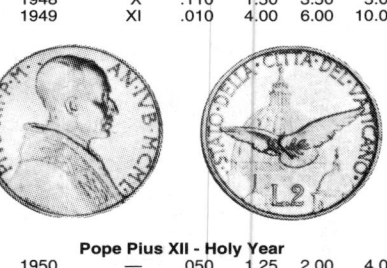

ALUMINUM

Y#	Date	Year	Mintage	VF	XF	Unc
41	1947	IX	.065	2.00	4.00	8.00
	1948	X	.110	1.50	3.50	5.00
	1949	XI	.010	4.00	6.00	10.00

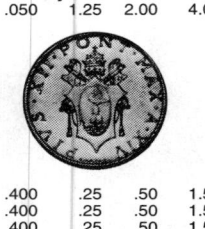

Pope Pius XII - Holy Year

Y#	Date	Year	Mintage	VF	XF	Unc
45	1950	—	.050	1.25	2.00	4.00

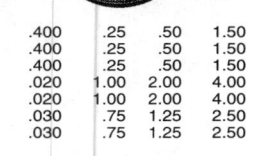

50	1951	XIII	.400	.25	.50	1.50
	1952	XIV	.400	.25	.50	1.50
	1953	XV	.400	.25	.50	1.50
	1955	XVII	.020	1.00	2.00	4.00
	1956	XVIII	.020	1.00	2.00	4.00
	1957	XIX	.030	.75	1.25	2.50
	1958	XX	.030	.75	1.25	2.50

59	1959	I	.025	1.50	4.00	7.00
	1960	II	.025	1.50	3.00	5.00
	1961	III	.025	1.50	3.00	5.00
	1962	IV	.025	1.50	3.00	5.00

2nd Ecumenical Council

68	1962	IV	.050	1.00	1.50	3.00

Pope Paul VI

77	1963	I	.060	.75	2.00	3.00
	1964	II	.060	.75	2.00	3.00
	1965	III	.060	.75	1.00	2.00

85	1966	IV	.090	.25	.75	1.25

93	1967	V	.100	.25	.75	1.25

F.A.O. Issue

Y#	Date	Year	Mintage	VF	XF	Unc
101	ND(1968)	VI	.100	.25	.75	1.50

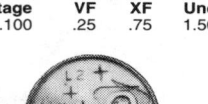

Pope Paul VI

109	1969	VII	.100	.25	.75	1.50

117	1970	VIII	.100	.25	.50	1.00
	1971	IX	.110	.25	.50	1.00
	1972	X	.110	.25	.50	1.00
	1973	XI	.132	.25	.50	1.00
	1974	XII	.132	.25	.50	1.00
	1975	XIII	.150	.25	.50	1.00
	1976	XIV	.150	.25	.50	1.00
	1977	XV	.135	.25	.50	1.00

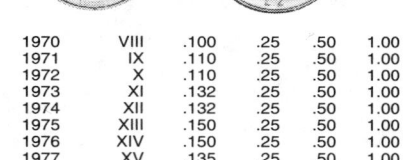

Holy Year

125	1975	—	.180	.25	.70	1.00

5 LIRE

5.0000 g, .835 SILVER, .1342 oz ASW
Pope Pius XI

7	1929	VIII	.010	7.50	15.00	30.00
	1930	IX	.050	5.00	9.00	20.00
	1931	X	.050	5.00	9.00	20.00
	1932	XI	.050	5.00	9.00	20.00
	1934	XIII	.030	5.00	10.00	20.00
	1935	XIV	.020	6.00	12.00	22.50
	1936	XV	.040	5.00	9.00	20.00
	1937	XVI	.040	5.00	9.00	20.00

Jubilee

17	1933-34	—	.050	5.00	10.00	20.00

Sede Vacante

20	1939	—	.040	7.50	15.00	25.00

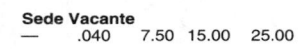

Pope Pius XII

Y#	Date	Year	Mintage	VF	XF	Unc
28	1939	I	.100	4.00	10.00	18.00
	1940	II	.100	4.00	10.00	18.00
	1941	III	4,000	25.00	35.00	65.00

37	1942	IV	4,000	25.00	40.00	65.00
	1943	V	1,000	50.00	75.00	100.00
	1944	VI	1,000	50.00	75.00	100.00
	1945	VII	1,000	50.00	75.00	100.00
	1946	VIII	1,000	50.00	75.00	100.00

ALUMINUM

42	1947	IX	.050	2.00	4.00	7.50
	1948	X	.074	2.00	4.00	7.50
	1949	XI	.074	2.00	4.00	7.50

Holy Year

46	1950	—	.050	3.00	5.00	7.50

51	1951	XIII	1.500	.25	.50	1.50
	1952	XIV	1.500	.25	.50	1.50
	1953	XV	1.500	.25	.50	1.50
	1955	XVII	.030	.50	.75	2.00
	1956	XVIII	.030	.50	.75	2.00
	1957	XIX	.030	.50	.75	2.00
	1958	XX	.030	.50	.75	2.00

Pope John XXIII

60	1959	I	.025	2.00	5.00	8.00
	1960	II	.025	2.00	5.00	8.00
	1961	III	.025	1.50	3.00	4.50
	1962	IV	.025	.50	1.00	2.50

2nd Ecumenical Council

69	1962	IV	.050	.40	.75	1.50

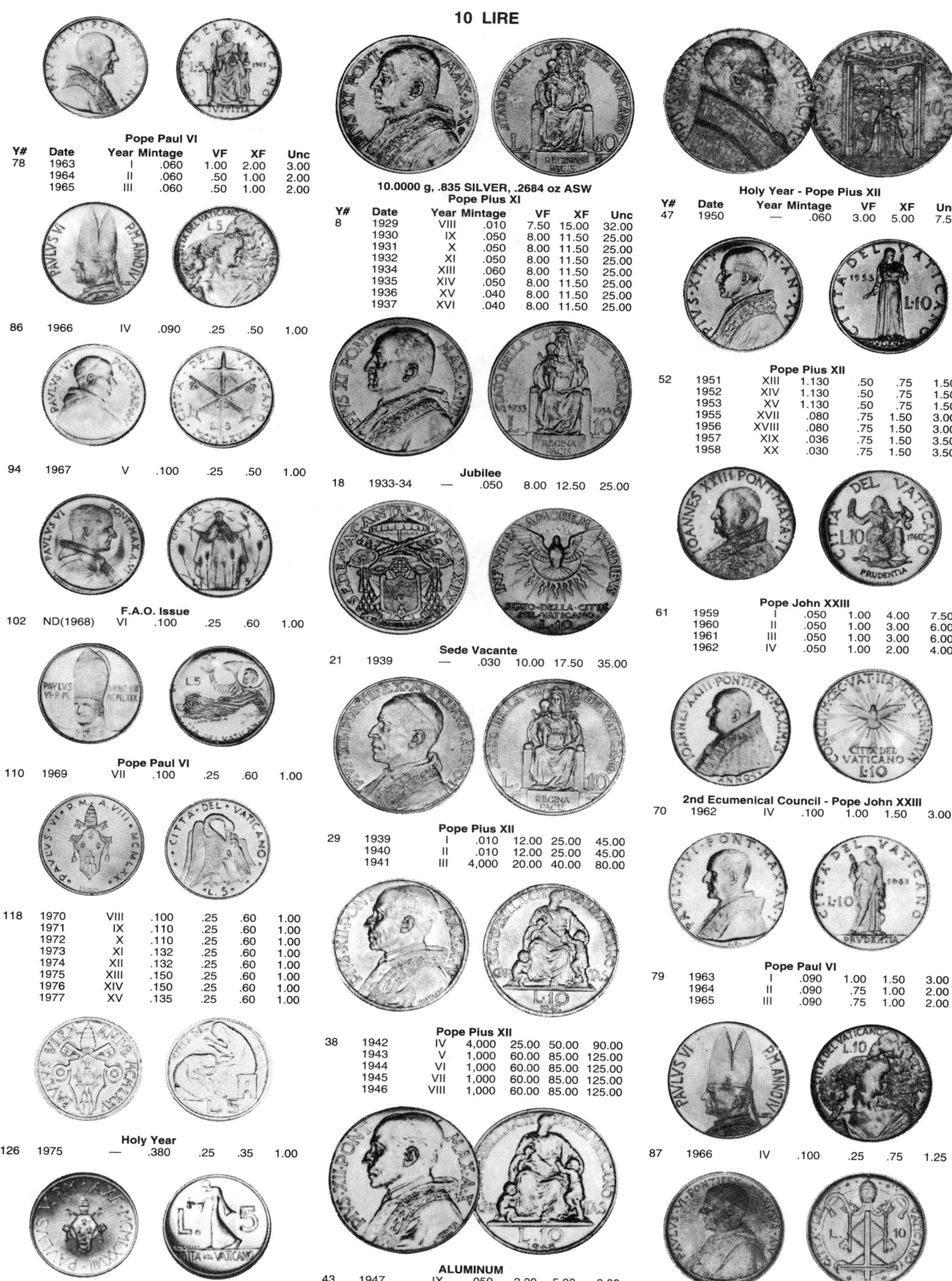

Pope Paul VI

Y#	Date	Year	Mintage	VF	XF	Unc
78	1963	I	.060	1.00	2.00	3.00
	1964	II	.060	.50	1.00	2.00
	1965	III	.060	.50	1.00	2.00
86	1966	IV	.090	.25	.50	1.00
94	1967	V	.100	.25	.50	1.00

F.A.O. Issue

| 102 | ND(1968) | VI | .100 | .25 | .60 | 1.00 |

Pope Paul VI

110	1969	VII	.100	.25	.60	1.00
118	1970	VIII	.100	.25	.60	1.00
	1971	IX	.110	.25	.60	1.00
	1972	X	.110	.25	.60	1.00
	1973	XI	.132	.25	.60	1.00
	1974	XII	.132	.25	.60	1.00
	1975	XIII	.150	.25	.60	1.00
	1976	XIV	.150	.25	.60	1.00
	1977	XV	.135	.25	.60	1.00

Holy Year

| 126 | 1975 | — | .380 | .25 | .35 | 1.00 |
| 133 | 1978 | XVI | .120 | .25 | .40 | 1.00 |

10 LIRE

10.0000 g, .835 SILVER, .2684 oz ASW

Pope Pius XI

Y#	Date	Year	Mintage	VF	XF	Unc
8	1929	VIII	.010	7.50	15.00	32.00
	1930	IX	.050	8.00	11.50	25.00
	1931	X	.050	8.00	11.50	25.00
	1932	XI	.050	8.00	11.50	25.00
	1934	XIII	.060	8.00	11.50	25.00
	1935	XIV	.050	8.00	11.50	25.00
	1936	XV	.040	8.00	11.50	25.00
	1937	XVI	.040	8.00	11.50	25.00

Jubilee

| 18 | 1933-34 | — | .050 | 8.00 | 12.50 | 25.00 |

Sede Vacante

| 21 | 1939 | — | .030 | 10.00 | 17.50 | 35.00 |

Pope Pius XII

29	1939	I	.010	12.00	25.00	45.00
	1940	II	.010	12.00	25.00	45.00
	1941	III	4,000	20.00	40.00	80.00

Pope Pius XII

38	1942	IV	4,000	25.00	50.00	90.00
	1943	V	1,000	60.00	85.00	125.00
	1944	VI	1,000	60.00	85.00	125.00
	1945	VII	1,000	60.00	85.00	125.00
	1946	VIII	1,000	60.00	85.00	125.00

ALUMINUM

43	1947	IX	.050	3.00	5.00	8.00
	1948	X	.060	3.00	5.00	8.00
	1949	XI	.060	3.00	5.00	8.00

Holy Year - Pope Pius XII

Y#	Date	Year	Mintage	VF	XF	Unc
47	1950	—	.060	3.00	5.00	7.50

Pope Pius XII

52	1951	XIII	1.130	.50	.75	1.50
	1952	XIV	1.130	.50	.75	1.50
	1953	XV	1.130	.50	.75	1.50
	1955	XVII	.080	.75	1.50	3.00
	1956	XVIII	.080	.75	1.50	3.00
	1957	XIX	.036	.75	1.50	3.50
	1958	XX	.030	.75	1.50	3.50

Pope John XXIII

61	1959	I	.050	1.00	4.00	7.50
	1960	II	.050	1.00	3.00	6.00
	1961	III	.050	1.00	3.00	6.00
	1962	IV	.050	1.00	2.00	4.00

2nd Ecumenical Council - Pope John XXIII

| 70 | 1962 | IV | .100 | 1.00 | 1.50 | 3.00 |

Pope Paul VI

79	1963	I	.090	1.00	1.50	3.00
	1964	II	.090	.75	1.00	2.00
	1965	III	.090	.75	1.00	2.00
87	1966	IV	.100	.25	.75	1.25
95	ND(1967)	V	.110	.25	.75	1.25

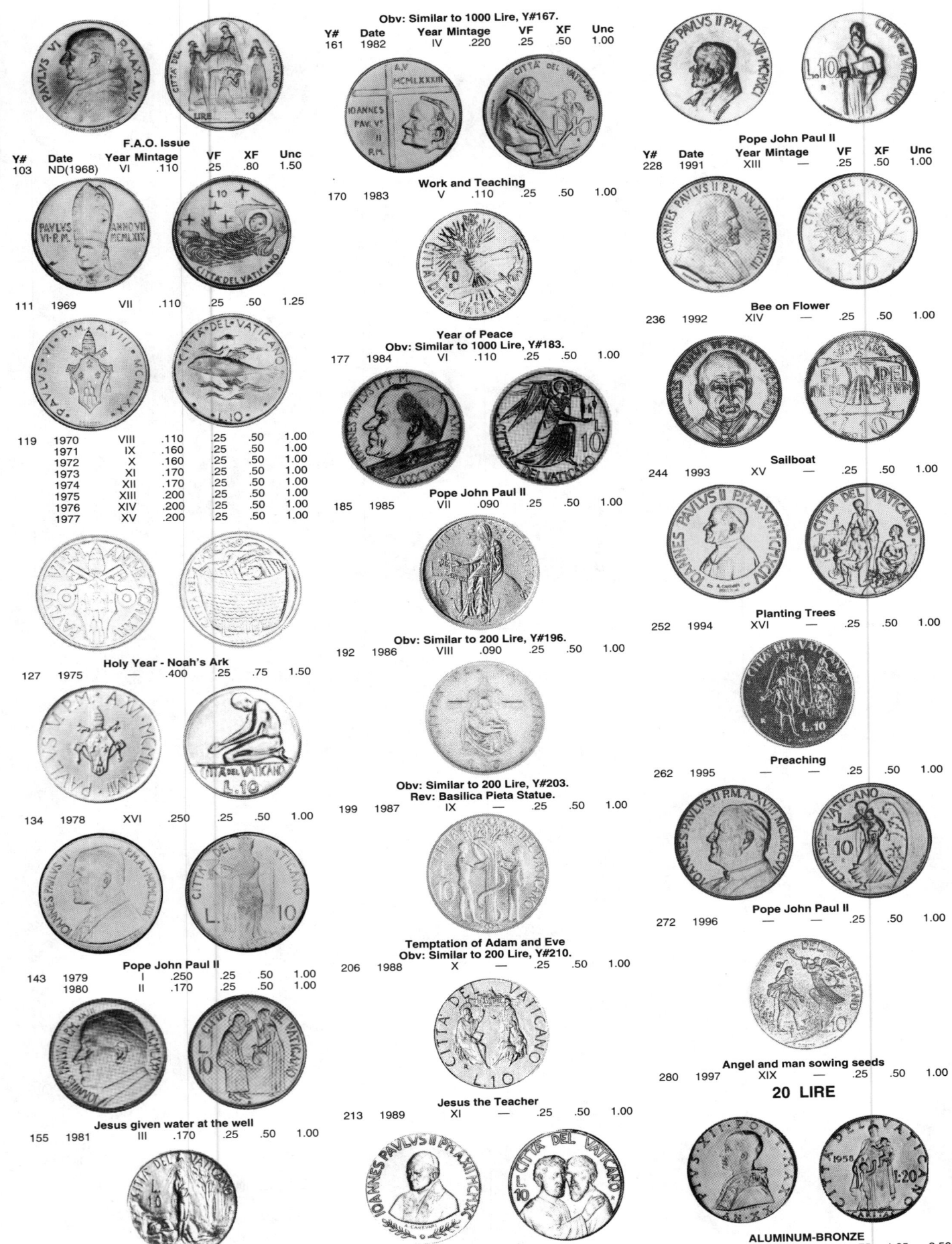

F.A.O. Issue

Y#	Date	Year	Mintage	VF	XF	Unc
103	ND(1968)	VI	.110	.25	.80	1.50

Y#	Date	Year	Mintage	VF	XF	Unc
111	1969	VII	.110	.25	.50	1.25

Y#	Date	Year	Mintage	VF	XF	Unc
119	1970	VIII	.110	.25	.50	1.00
	1971	IX	.160	.25	.50	1.00
	1972	X	.160	.25	.50	1.00
	1973	XI	.170	.25	.50	1.00
	1974	XII	.170	.25	.50	1.00
	1975	XIII	.200	.25	.50	1.00
	1976	XIV	.200	.25	.50	1.00
	1977	XV	.200	.25	.50	1.00

Holy Year - Noah's Ark

Y#	Date		Mintage	VF	XF	Unc
127	1975	—	.400	.25	.75	1.50

Y#	Date	Year	Mintage	VF	XF	Unc
134	1978	XVI	.250	.25	.50	1.00

Pope John Paul II

Y#	Date	Year	Mintage	VF	XF	Unc
143	1979	I	.250	.25	.50	1.00
	1980	II	.170	.25	.50	1.00

Jesus given water at the well

Y#	Date	Year	Mintage	VF	XF	Unc
155	1981	III	.170	.25	.50	1.00

Creation of Woman

Obv: Similar to 1000 Lire, Y#167.

Y#	Date	Year	Mintage	VF	XF	Unc
161	1982	IV	.220	.25	.50	1.00

Work and Teaching

Y#	Date	Year	Mintage	VF	XF	Unc
170	1983	V	.110	.25	.50	1.00

Year of Peace
Obv: Similar to 1000 Lire, Y#183.

Y#	Date	Year	Mintage	VF	XF	Unc
177	1984	VI	.110	.25	.50	1.00

Pope John Paul II

Y#	Date	Year	Mintage	VF	XF	Unc
185	1985	VII	.090	.50	1.00	

Obv: Similar to 200 Lire, Y#196.

Y#	Date	Year	Mintage	VF	XF	Unc
192	1986	VIII	.090	.50	1.00	

Obv: Similar to 200 Lire, Y#203.
Rev: Basilica Pieta Statue.

Y#	Date	Year	Mintage	VF	XF	Unc
199	1987	IX	—	.25	.50	1.00

Temptation of Adam and Eve
Obv: Similar to 200 Lire, Y#210.

Y#	Date	Year	Mintage	VF	XF	Unc
206	1988	X	—	.25	.50	1.00

Jesus the Teacher

Y#	Date	Year	Mintage	VF	XF	Unc
213	1989	XI	—	.25	.50	1.00

Saints Peter and Paul

Y#	Date	Year	Mintage	VF	XF	Unc
220	1990	XII	—	.25	.50	1.00

Pope John Paul II

Y#	Date	Year	Mintage	VF	XF	Unc
228	1991	XIII	—	.25	.50	1.00

Bee on Flower

Y#	Date	Year	Mintage	VF	XF	Unc
236	1992	XIV	—	.25	.50	1.00

Sailboat

Y#	Date	Year	Mintage	VF	XF	Unc
244	1993	XV	—	.25	.50	1.00

Planting Trees

Y#	Date	Year	Mintage	VF	XF	Unc
252	1994	XVI	—	.25	.50	1.00

Preaching

Y#	Date	Year	Mintage	VF	XF	Unc
262	1995		—	.25	.50	1.00

Pope John Paul II

Y#	Date	Year	Mintage	VF	XF	Unc
272	1996		—	.25	.50	1.00

Angel and man sowing seeds

Y#	Date	Year	Mintage	VF	XF	Unc
280	1997	XIX		.25	.50	1.00

20 LIRE

ALUMINUM-BRONZE

Y#	Date	Year	Mintage	VF	XF	Unc
A52	1957	XIX	.020	.75	1.25	2.50
	1958	XX	.060	.75	1.25	2.50

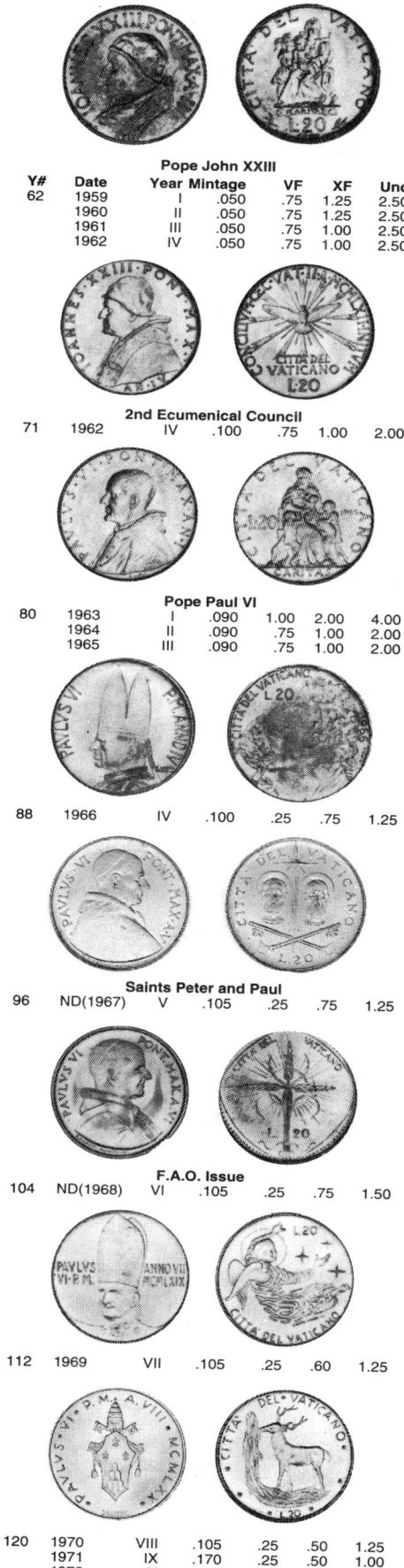

Pope John XXIII

Y#	Date	Year	Mintage	VF	XF	Unc
62	1959	I	.050	.75	1.25	2.50
	1960	II	.050	.75	1.25	2.50
	1961	III	.050	.75	1.00	2.50
	1962	IV	.050	.75	1.00	2.50

2nd Ecumenical Council

71	1962	IV	.100	.75	1.00	2.00

Pope Paul VI

80	1963	I	.090	1.00	2.00	4.00
	1964	II	.090	.75	1.00	2.00
	1965	III	.090	.75	1.00	2.00

88	1966	IV	.100	.25	.75	1.25

Saints Peter and Paul

96	ND(1967)	V	.105	.25	.75	1.25

F.A.O. Issue

104	ND(1968)	VI	.105	.25	.75	1.50

112	1969	VII	.105	.25	.60	1.25

120	1970	VIII	.105	.25	.50	1.25
	1971	IX	.170	.25	.50	1.00
	1972	X	.170	.25	.50	1.00
	1973	XI	—	.25	.50	1.00
	1974	XII	—	.25	.50	1.00
	1975	XIII	.250	.25	.50	1.00
	1976	XIV	.250	.25	.50	1.00
	1977	XV	.250	.25	.50	1.00

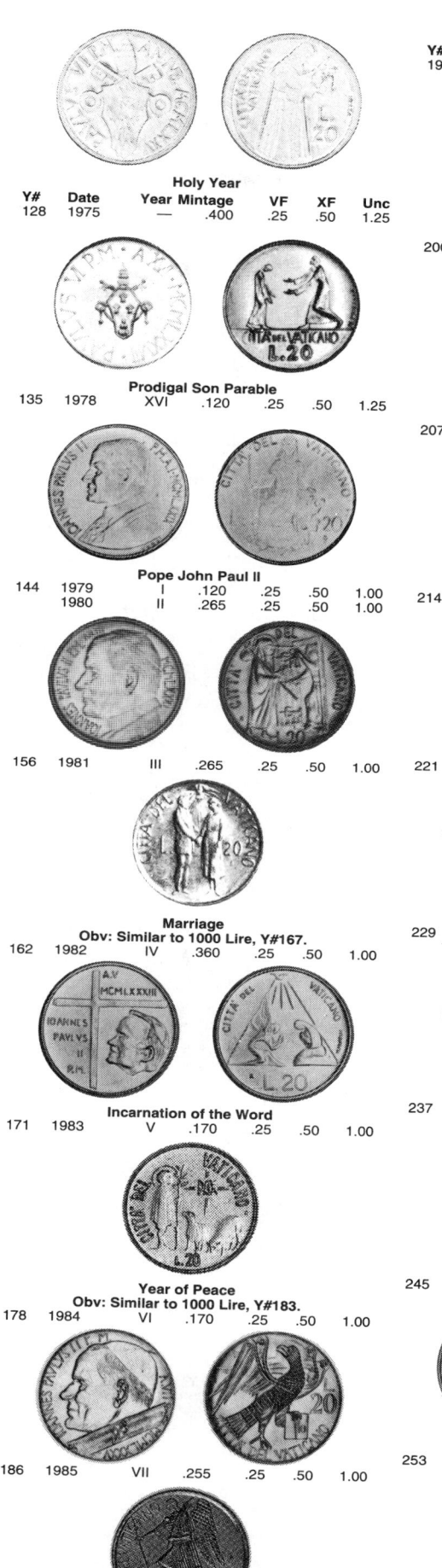

Holy Year

Y#	Date	Year	Mintage	VF	XF	Unc
128	1975	—	.400	.25	.50	1.25

Prodigal Son Parable

135	1978	XVI	.120	.25	.50	1.25

Pope John Paul II

144	1979	I	.120	.25	.50	1.00
	1980	II	.265	.25	.50	1.00

156	1981	III	.265	.25	.50	1.00

Marriage
Obv: Similar to 1000 Lire, Y#167.

162	1982	IV	.360	.25	.50	1.00

Incarnation of the Word

171	1983	V	.170	.25	.50	1.00

Year of Peace
Obv: Similar to 1000 Lire, Y#183.

178	1984	VI	.170	.25	.50	1.00

186	1985	VII	.255	.25	.50	1.00

Obv: Similar to 200 Lire, Y#196.

Y#	Date	Year	Mintage	VF	XF	Unc
193	1986	VIII	.100	.25	.50	1.00

Obv: Similar to 200 Lire, Y#203.
Rev: Assumption of Mother Mary into Heaven.

200	1987	IX	—	.25	.50	1.00

Temptation of Adam and Eve
Similar to 200 Lire, Y#210.

207	1988	X	—	.25	.50	1.00

The Harvest

214	1989	XI	—	.25	.50	1.00

Pope John Paul II and Eastern Rite Bishop

221	1990	XII	—	.25	.50	1.00

Crane and Buildings

229	1991	XIII	—	.25	.50	1.00

3 Children

237	1992	XIV	—	.25	.50	1.00

Crucifix

245	1993	XV	—	.25	.50	1.00

Hospital Patient With Visitors

253	1994	XVI	—	.25	.50	1.00

Euthanasia

263	1995	—	—	.25	.50	1.00

Parents praising child

Y#	Date	Year	Mintage	VF	XF	Unc
273	1996	—	—	.25	.50	1.00

Jesus teaching with book

281	1997	XIX	—	.25	.50	1.00

50 LIRE

STAINLESS STEEL
Pope Pius XII

54	1955	XVII	.180	1.00	1.50	3.00
	1956	XVIII	.180	1.00	1.50	3.00
	1957	XIX	.180	1.00	1.50	3.00
	1958	XX	.060	1.00	1.50	3.00

Pope John XXIII
Obv: Continuous legend.

63	1959	I	.100	1.00	2.50	7.00

Obv: Regnal year under bust.

63.1	1960	II	.100	1.00	2.50	7.50
	1961	III	.100	1.00	2.00	3.50
	1962	IV	.100	1.00	2.00	3.50

2nd Ecumenical Council

72	1962	IV	.200	.50	1.25	2.50

Spes - Hope

81	1963	I	.120	1.00	2.00	4.00
	1964	II	.120	.75	1.50	3.00
	1965	III	.120	.50	1.00	2.00

Y#	Date	Year	Mintage	VF	XF	Unc
89	1966	IV	.150	.50	1.00	2.00

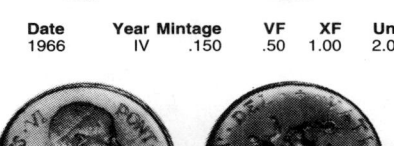

Conversion of Saint Paul

97	1967	V	.190	.50	1.00	2.00

F.A.O. Issue

105	ND(1968)	VI	.190	.50	1.00	2.00

113	1969	VII	.190	.50	1.00	2.00

121	1970	VIII	.190	.25	.75	1.75
	1971	IX	.700	.25	.75	1.50
	1972	X	.700	.25	.75	1.50
	1973	XI	.750	.25	.75	1.50
	1974	XII	.750	.25	.75	1.50
	1975	XIII	.600	.25	.75	1.50
	1976	XIV	.600	.25	.75	1.50

Holy Year

129	1975	—	.500	.40	.75	1.50

Wheat and grapes

A121	1977	XV	.600	.25	.35	1.25

16th Year

Y#	Date	Year	Mintage	VF	XF	Unc
136	1978	XVI	.223	.25	.50	1.25

Pope John Paul II

145	1979	I	.223	.25	.50	1.25
	1980	II	.250	.25	.50	1.25

157	1981	III	.240	.25	.50	1.25

Maternity
Obv: Similar to 1000 Lire, Y#167.

163	1982	IV	.400	.25	.50	1.25

Banishment of Adam and Eve

172	1983	V	.300	.25	.50	1.25

Year of Peace
Obv: Similar to 1000 Lire, Y#183.

179	1984	VI	.300	.25	.50	1.25

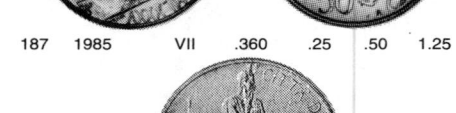

187	1985	VII	.360	.25	.50	1.25

Obv: Similar to 200 Lire, Y#196.

Y#	Date	Year	Mintage	VF	XF	Unc
194	1986	VIII	.100	.25	.50	1.25

Obv: Similar to 200 Lire, Y#203.
Rev: Mother Mary protecting kneeling sinners.

Y#	Date	Year	Mintage	VF	XF	Unc
201	1987	IX	—	.25	.50	1.25

Creation of Eve From Adam's Rib

Y#	Date	Year	Mintage	VF	XF	Unc
208	1988	X	—	.25	.50	1.25

Human Solidarity

Y#	Date	Year	Mintage	VF	XF	Unc
215	1989	XI	—	.25	.50	1.25

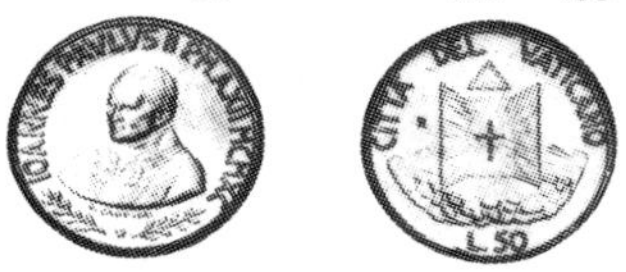

Radiant Cross in Open Door

Y#	Date	Year	Mintage	VF	XF	Unc
222	1990	XII	—	.25	.50	1.25

Baptism Scene

Y#	Date	Year	Mintage	VF	XF	Unc
230	1991	XIII	—	.25	.50	1.25

Cross as Balance Scale Between Agriculture and Industry

Y#	Date	Year	Mintage	VF	XF	Unc
238	1992	XIV	—	.25	.50	1.25

Chalice
Wheat and grapes

Y#	Date	Year	Mintage	VF	XF	Unc
246	1993	XV	—	.25	.50	1.25

Hands and Prison Bars

Y#	Date	Year	Mintage	VF	XF	Unc
254	1994	XVI	—	.25	.50	1.25

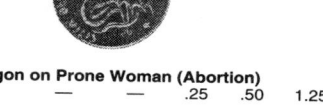

Dragon on Prone Woman (Abortion)

Y#	Date	Year	Mintage	VF	XF	Unc
264	1995	—	—	.25	.50	1.25

COPPER-NICKEL
Guardian angel protecting child

Y#	Date	Year	Mintage	VF	XF	Unc
274	1996	—	—	.25	.50	1.25

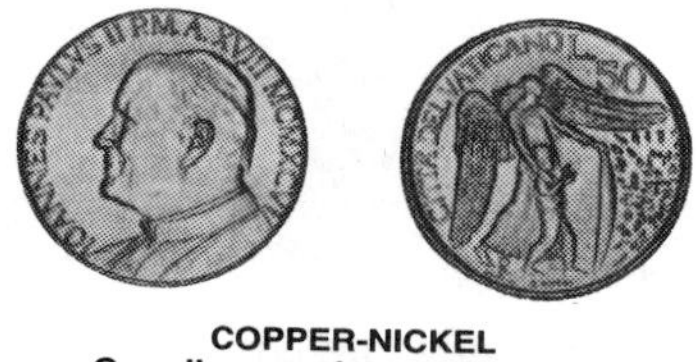

One man w/lowered sword, the other w/dove

Y#	Date	Year	Mintage	VF	XF	Unc
282	1997	XIX	—	.25	.50	1.25

100 LIRE

8.8000 g, .900 GOLD, .2546 oz AGW
Pope Pius XI

Y#	Date	Year	Mintage	VF	XF	Unc
9	1929	VIII	10,000	125.00	175.00	275.00
	1930	IX	2,621	300.00	650.00	1000.
	1931	X	3,343	175.00	325.00	500.00
	1932	XI	5,073	150.00	250.00	375.00
	1934	XIII	2,533	250.00	325.00	500.00
	1935	XIV	2,015	250.00	325.00	500.00

Jubilee

Y#	Date	Year	Mintage	VF	XF	Unc
19	1933-34	—	.023	125.00	175.00	245.00

5.1900 g, .900 GOLD, .1501 oz AGW

Y#	Date	Year	Mintage	VF	XF	Unc
10	1936	XV	8,239	175.00	220.00	275.00
	1937	XVI	2,000	1000.	2000.	3000.
	1938		6 pcs.	Rare	—	

Y#	Date	Year	Mintage	VF	XF	Unc
30	1939	I	2,700	165.00	200.00	350.00
	1940	II	2,000	175.00	250.00	375.00
	1941	III	2,000	175.00	250.00	375.00

Pope Pius • XII

Y#	Date	Year	Mintage	VF	XF	Unc
39	1942	IV	2,000	175.00	250.00	375.00
	1943	V	1,000	250.00	350.00	600.00
	1944	VI	1,000	250.00	350.00	600.00
	1945	VII	1,000	250.00	350.00	600.00
	1946	VIII	1,000	250.00	350.00	600.00
	1947	IX	1,000	250.00	350.00	600.00
	1948	X	5,000	150.00	200.00	275.00
	1949	XI	1,000	250.00	350.00	600.00

Holy Year

Y#	Date	Year	Mintage	VF	XF	Unc
48	1950	—	.020	150.00	200.00	275.00

Y#	Date	Year	Mintage	VF	XF	Unc
53	1951	XIII	1,000	250.00	350.00	625.00
	1952	XIV	1,000	250.00	350.00	625.00
	1953	XV	1,000	250.00	350.00	625.00
	1954	XVI	1,000	250.00	350.00	625.00
	1955	XVII	1,000	250.00	350.00	625.00
	1956	XVIII	1,000	250.00	350.00	625.00

STAINLESS STEEL

Y#	Date	Year	Mintage	VF	XF	Unc
55	1955	XVII	1,300	.50	1.00	2.00
	1956	XVIII	1,400	.50	1.00	2.00
	1957	XIX	.900	.50	1.00	2.00
	1958	XX	.852	.50	1.00	2.00

5.1900 g, .900 GOLD, .1501 oz AGW

Y#	Date	Year	Mintage	VF	XF	Unc
A53	1957	XIX	2,000	200.00	250.00	350.00
	1958	XX	3,000	200.00	250.00	325.00

Pope John XXIII

Y#	Date	Year	Mintage	VF	XF	Unc
66	1959	I	3,000	500.00	750.00	1250.

STAINLESS STEEL
Obv: Continuous legend.

Y#	Date	Year	Mintage	VF	XF	Unc
64	1959	I	.783	1.25	2.00	4.00

Obv: Regnal year under bust.

Y#	Date	Year	Mintage	VF	XF	Unc
64.1	1960	II	.783	1.75	3.00	7.50
	1961	III	.783	.75	1.00	2.50
	1962	IV	.783	.75	1.00	2.00

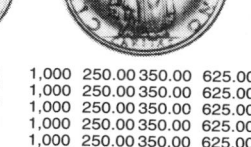

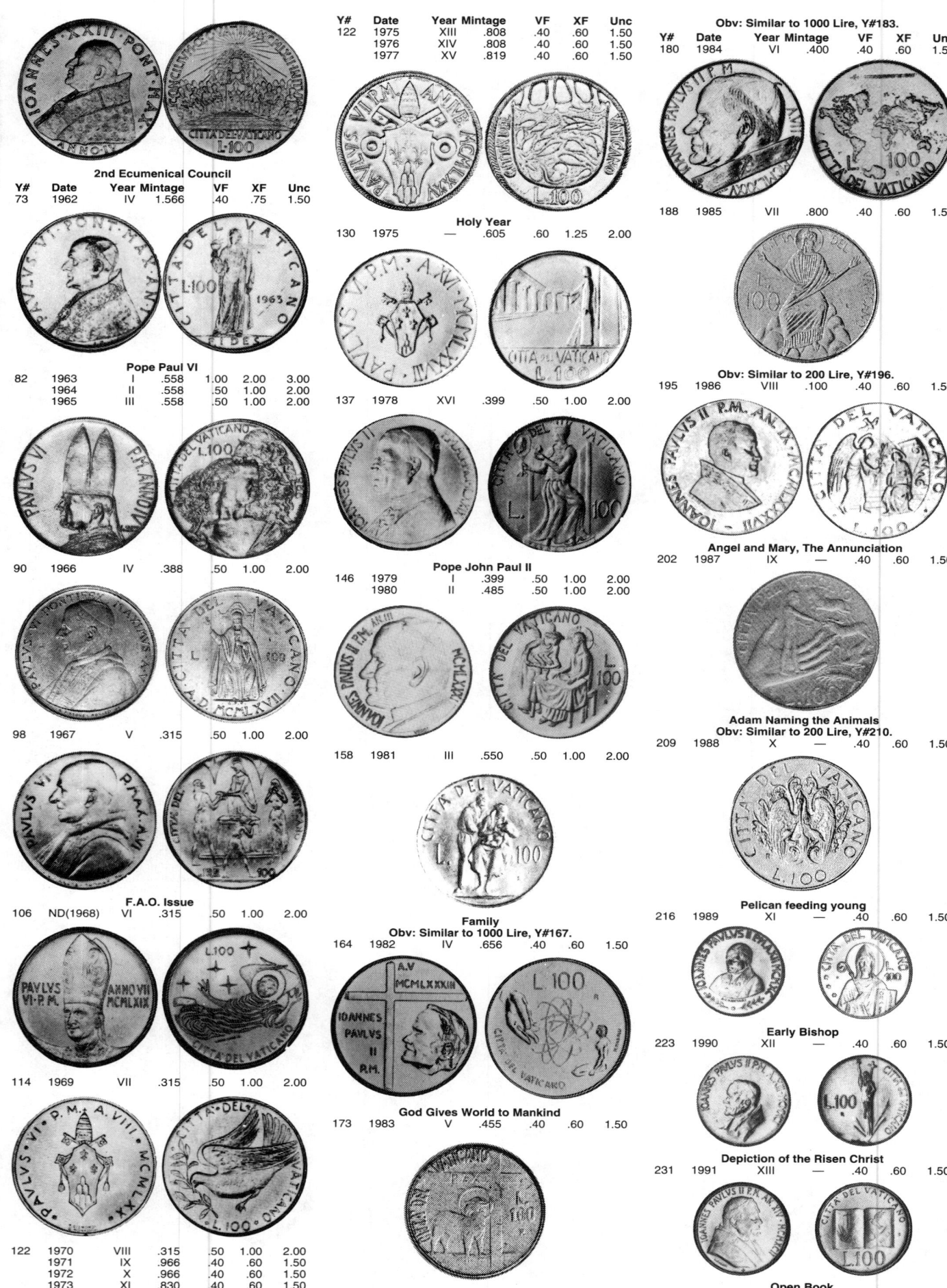

2nd Ecumenical Council

Y#	Date	Year	Mintage	VF	XF	Unc
73	1962	IV	1.566	.40	.75	1.50

Pope Paul VI

Y#	Date	Year	Mintage	VF	XF	Unc
82	1963	I	.558	1.00	2.00	3.00
	1964	II	.558	.50	1.00	2.00
	1965	III	.558	.50	1.00	2.00
90	1966	IV	.388	.50	1.00	2.00
98	1967	V	.315	.50	1.00	2.00

F.A.O. Issue

Y#	Date	Year	Mintage	VF	XF	Unc
106	ND(1968)	VI	.315	.50	1.00	2.00
114	1969	VII	.315	.50	1.00	2.00
122	1970	VIII	.315	.50	1.00	2.00
	1971	IX	.966	.40	.60	1.50
	1972	X	.966	.40	.60	1.50
	1973	XI	.830	.40	.60	1.50
	1974	XII	.830	.40	.60	1.50

Y#	Date	Year	Mintage	VF	XF	Unc
122	1975	XIII	.808	.40	.60	1.50
	1976	XIV	.808	.40	.60	1.50
	1977	XV	.819	.40	.60	1.50

Holy Year

Y#	Date	Year	Mintage	VF	XF	Unc
130	1975	—	.605	.60	1.25	2.00
137	1978	XVI	.399	.50	1.00	2.00

Pope John Paul II

Y#	Date	Year	Mintage	VF	XF	Unc
146	1979	I	.399	.50	1.00	2.00
	1980	II	.485	.50	1.00	2.00
158	1981	III	.550	.50	1.00	2.00

Family
Obv: Similar to 1000 Lire, Y#167.

Y#	Date	Year	Mintage	VF	XF	Unc
164	1982	IV	.656	.40	.60	1.50

God Gives World to Mankind

Y#	Date	Year	Mintage	VF	XF	Unc
173	1983	V	.455	.40	.60	1.50

Year of Peace

Obv: Similar to 1000 Lire, Y#183.

Y#	Date	Year	Mintage	VF	XF	Unc
180	1984	VI	.400	.40	.60	1.50
188	1985	VII	.800	.40	.60	1.50

Obv: Similar to 200 Lire, Y#196.

Y#	Date	Year	Mintage	VF	XF	Unc
195	1986	VIII	.100	.40	.60	1.50

Angel and Mary, The Annunciation

Y#	Date	Year	Mintage	VF	XF	Unc
202	1987	IX	—	.40	.60	1.50

Adam Naming the Animals
Obv: Similar to 200 Lire, Y#210.

Y#	Date	Year	Mintage	VF	XF	Unc
209	1988	X	—	.40	.60	1.50

Pelican feeding young

Y#	Date	Year	Mintage	VF	XF	Unc
216	1989	XI	—	.40	.60	1.50

Early Bishop

Y#	Date	Year	Mintage	VF	XF	Unc
223	1990	XII	—	.40	.60	1.50

Depiction of the Risen Christ

Y#	Date	Year	Mintage	VF	XF	Unc
231	1991	XIII	—	.40	.60	1.50

Open Book

Y#	Date	Year	Mintage	VF	XF	Unc
239	1992	XIV	—	.40	.60	1.50

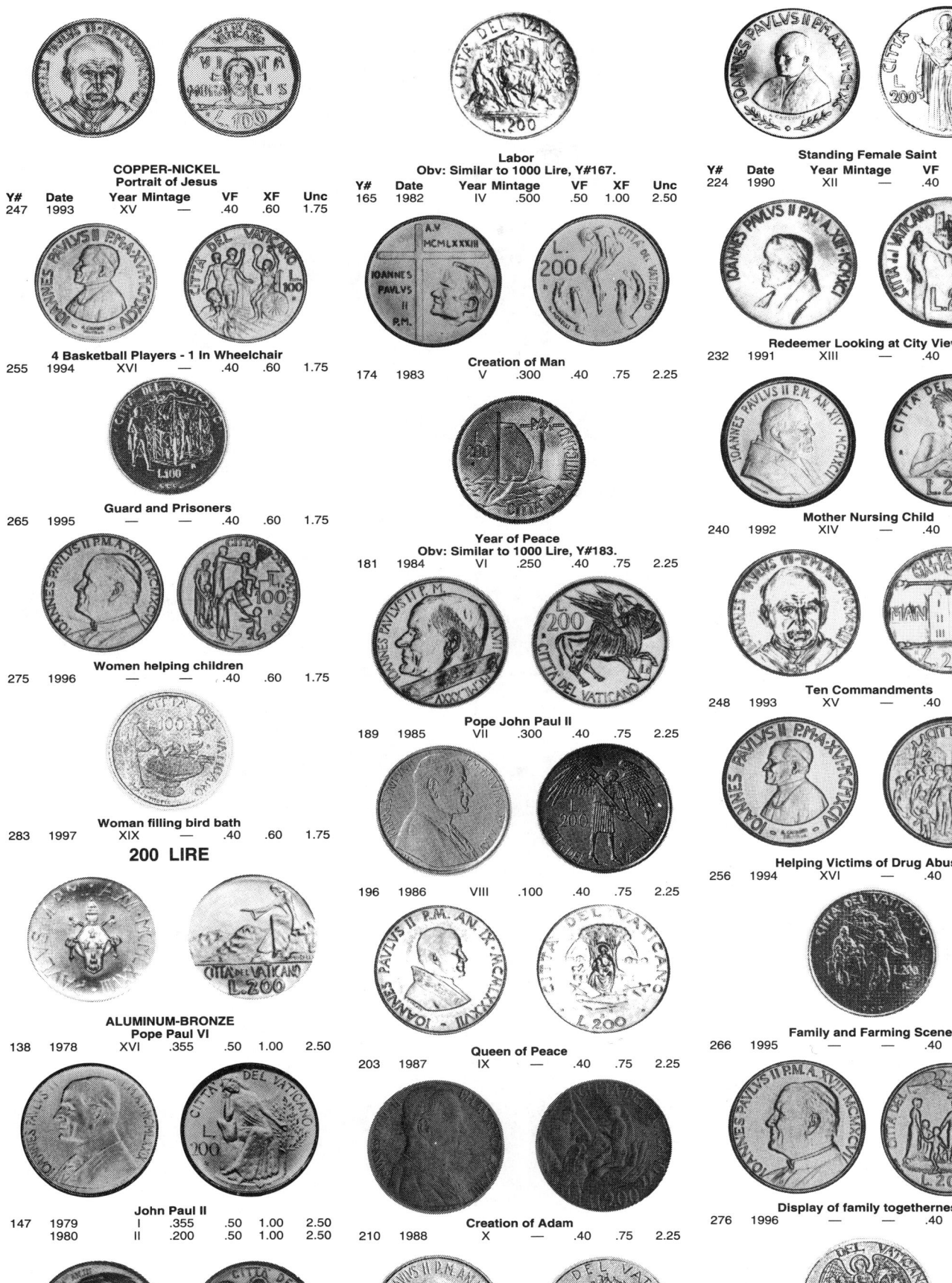

COPPER-NICKEL
Portrait of Jesus

Y#	Date	Year Mintage		VF	XF	Unc
247	1993	XV	—	.40	.60	1.75

4 Basketball Players - 1 In Wheelchair

| 255 | 1994 | XVI | — | .40 | .60 | 1.75 |

Guard and Prisoners

| 265 | 1995 | — | — | .40 | .60 | 1.75 |

Women helping children

| 275 | 1996 | — | — | .40 | .60 | 1.75 |

Woman filling bird bath

| 283 | 1997 | XIX | — | .40 | .60 | 1.75 |

200 LIRE

ALUMINUM-BRONZE
Pope Paul VI

| 138 | 1978 | XVI | .355 | .50 | 1.00 | 2.50 |

John Paul II

147	1979	I	.355	.50	1.00	2.50
	1980	II	.200	.50	1.00	2.50
159	1981	III	.170	.50	1.00	2.50

Labor
Obv: Similar to 1000 Lire, Y#167.

Y#	Date	Year Mintage		VF	XF	Unc
165	1982	IV	.500	.50	1.00	2.50

Creation of Man

| 174 | 1983 | V | .300 | .40 | .75 | 2.25 |

Year of Peace
Obv: Similar to 1000 Lire, Y#183.

| 181 | 1984 | VI | .250 | .40 | .75 | 2.25 |

Pope John Paul II

| 189 | 1985 | VII | .300 | .40 | .75 | 2.25 |
| 196 | 1986 | VIII | .100 | .40 | .75 | 2.25 |

Queen of Peace

| 203 | 1987 | IX | — | .40 | .75 | 2.25 |

Creation of Adam

| 210 | 1988 | X | — | .40 | .75 | 2.25 |

| 217 | 1989 | XI | — | .40 | .75 | 2.25 |

Standing Female Saint

Y#	Date	Year Mintage		VF	XF	Unc
224	1990	XII	—	.40	.75	2.25

Redeemer Looking at City Views

| 232 | 1991 | XIII | — | .40 | .75 | 2.25 |

Mother Nursing Child

| 240 | 1992 | XIV | — | .40 | .75 | 2.25 |

Ten Commandments

| 248 | 1993 | XV | — | .40 | .75 | 2.25 |

Helping Victims of Drug Abuse

| 256 | 1994 | XVI | — | .40 | .75 | 2.25 |

Family and Farming Scene

| 266 | 1995 | — | — | .40 | .75 | 2.25 |

Display of family togetherness

| 276 | 1996 | — | — | .40 | .75 | 2.25 |

Angel guiding 2 people

| 284 | 1997 | XIX | — | .40 | .75 | 2.25 |

500 LIRE

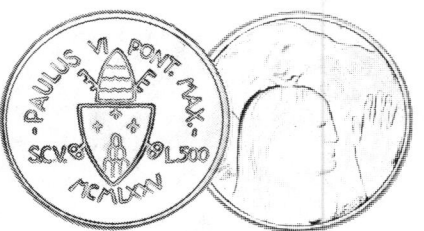

11.0000 g, .835 SILVER, .2953 oz ASW
Pope Pius XII

Y#	Date	Year	Mintage	VF	XF	Unc
56	1958	XX	.020	6.00	12.50	25.00

Sede Vacante

| 57 | 1958 | — | .100 | 4.00 | 6.00 | 10.00 |

Pope Paul VI

Y#	Date	Year	Mintage	VF	XF	Unc
83	1963	I	.070	8.00	16.00	32.00
	1964	II	.070	7.00	15.00	25.00
	1965	III	.070	6.00	9.00	20.00

Holy Year

Y#	Date	Year	Mintage	VF	XF	Unc
131	1975	—	.200	—	7.00	15.00

| 91 | 1966 | IV | .100 | 5.00 | 8.00 | 16.00 |

Book of the Evengelists

| 132 | 1977 | XV | .160 | — | 7.00 | 16.50 |

Pope John XXIII
Obv: Continuous legend.

| 65 | 1959 | I | .030 | 6.00 | 12.50 | 25.00 |

Saint Peter and Paul

| 99 | ND(1967) | V | .110 | 5.00 | 8.00 | 16.00 |

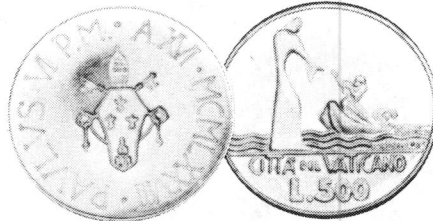

Jesus walking on water

| 139 | 1978 | XVI | .145 | — | 7.00 | 16.50 |

Obv: Regnal year under bust.

65.1	1960	II	.030	7.00	15.00	30.00
	1961	III	.030	6.00	12.50	25.00
	1962	IV	.030	6.00	12.50	25.00

F.A.O. Issue

| 107 | ND(1968) | VI | .110 | 4.50 | 7.50 | 15.00 |

First Sede Vacante

| 140 | 1978 | — | .500 | — | 8.00 | 17.50 |

2nd Ecumenical Council

| 74 | 1962 | IV | .060 | 6.00 | 12.50 | 25.00 |

| 115 | 1969 | VII | .110 | 4.50 | 7.50 | 15.00 |

Second Sede Vacante

| 141 | 1978 | — Inc.Y140 | — | 8.00 | 17.50 |

Pope John Paul II

| 148 | 1979 | I | .145 | — | 8.00 | 17.50 |
| | 1980 | II | .184 | — | 8.00 | 17.50 |

Wheat and grapes

123	1970	VIII	.110	—	6.00	12.00
	1971	IX	.125	—	6.00	12.00
	1972	X	.125	—	6.00	12.00
	1973	XI	.145	—	6.00	12.00
	1974	XII	.145	—	6.00	12.00
	1975	XIII	.162	—	6.00	12.00
	1976	XIV	.162	—	6.00	12.00

Sede Vacante

| 75 | 1963 | — | .200 | 4.00 | 6.00 | 10.00 |

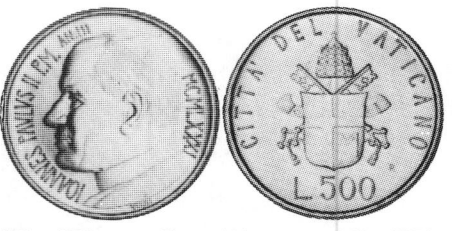

| 160 | 1981 | III | .184 | — | 8.00 | 17.50 |

**ALUMINUM-BRONZE center,
STAINLESS STEEL ring**
Education
Obv: Similar to 1000 Lire, Y#167.

Y#	Date	Year	Mintage	VF	XF	Unc
166	1982	IV	1.852	—	2.50	6.00

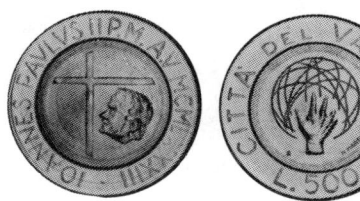

Creation of the Universe

175	1983	V		—	—	2.50	6.00

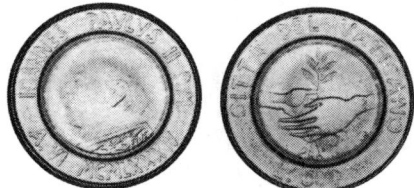

Year of Peace

182	1984	VI	.270	—	2.50	6.00

Saint Peter in boat

190	1985	VII	.300	—	2.00	4.00

197	1986	VIII	.300	—	2.00	4.00

Crucified Jesus

204	1987	IX		—	—	2.00	4.00

Holy Trinity

211	1988	X		—	—	2.00	4.00

Grape vine

Y#	Date	Year	Mintage	VF	XF	Unc
218	1989	XI		—	2.00	4.00

Jesus and 2 Kneeling Figures

225	1990	XII				4.00

Redeemer Sending Out Missionaries

233	1991	XIII		—	2.00	4.00

Hands holding bread loaf

241	1992	XIV		—	2.00	4.00

Thurible

249	1993	XV		—	2.00	4.00

People Meeting, Golgotha in Background

257	1994	XVI		—	2.00	4.00

Cain Slaying Abel

267	1995			—	2.00	4.00

Male figure protecting child from serpent

277	1996			—	2.00	4.00

One man freeing another from thorns

Y#	Date	Year	Mintage	VF	XF	Unc
285	1997	XIX		—	2.00	4.00

1000 LIRE

**ALUMINUM-BRONZE ring
STAINLESS STEEL center**
Obv: John Paul II.
Rev: Papal coat of arms.

286	1997	XIX		—	—	7.00

VENEZUELA

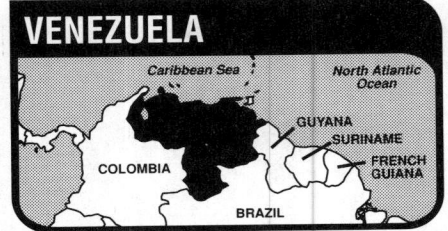

The Republic of Venezuela ("Little Venice"), located on the northern coast of South America between Colombia and Guyana, has an area of 352,145 sq. mi. (912,050 sq. km.) and a population of 20 million. Capital: Caracas. Petroleum and mining provide a significant portion of Venezuela's exports. Coffee, grown on 60,000 plantations, is the chief crop. Metalurgy, refining, oil, iron and steel production are the main employment industries.

Columbus discovered Venezuela on his third voyage in 1498. Initial exploration did not reveal Venezuela to be a land of great wealth. An active pearl trade operated on the off-shore islands and slavers raided the interior in search of Indians to be sold into slavery, but no significant mainland settlements were made before 1567 when Caracas was founded. Venezuela, the home of Bolivar, was among the first South American colonies to rebel against Spain in 1810. The declaration of Independence of Venezuela was signed by seven provinces which are represented by the seven stars of the Venezuelan flag. Coinage of Caracas and Margarita use the seven stars in their designs. These original provinces were: Barcelona, Barinas, Caracas, Cumana, Margarita, Merida and Trujillo. The Provinces of Coro, Guyana and Maracaibo were added to Venezuela during the Independence War. Independence was attained in 1821 but not recognized by Spain until 1845. Together with Ecuador, Panama and Colombia, Venezuela was part of "Gran Colombia" until 1830, when it became a sovereign and independent state.

RULERS
Republic, 1823-present

MINT MARKS
A - Paris
(a) - Paris, privy marks only
(aa) - Altena
(b) - Berlin
(bb) - Brussels
(cc) - Canada
(c) - Caracas
(d) - Denver
H, Heaton - Heaton, Birmingham
(l) - London
(m) - Madrid
(mm) - Mexico
(o) - Ontario
(p) - Philadelphia
(s) - San Francisco
(sc) - Schwerte - Vereinigte Deutsche Nickelwerke
(w) - Werdohl - Vereinigte Deutsche Metalwerke

MONETARY SYSTEM
100 Centimos = 1 Bolivar

5 CENTIMOS

COPPER-NICKEL

Y#	Date	Mintage	Fine	VF	XF	Unc
27	1915(p)	2.000	1.00	4.00	40.00	135.00
	1921(p)	2.000	.50	2.00	50.00	150.00
	1925(p)	2.000	.30	1.00	6.00	15.00
	1927(p)	2.000	.30	1.00	6.00	15.00
	1929(p)	2.000	.25	1.00	6.00	15.00
	1936(p)	5.000	.15	.50	4.00	10.00
	1938(p)	6.000	.10	.20	3.00	8.00

NOTE: Earlier date (1896) exists for this type.

BRASS

29	1944(d)	4.000	.50	1.00	4.50	20.00

COPPER-NICKEL

Y#	Date	Mintage	Fine	VF	XF	Unc
29a	1945(p)	12.000	.10	.20	.50	3.00
	1946(p)	12.000	.10	.20	.50	3.00
	1948(p)	18.000	.10	.20	.50	3.00

38	1958(p)	25.000	—	—	—	.75

38.1	1964(m)	40.000	—	—	—	.50
	1965(m)	60.000	—	—	—	.50
38.2	1971	40.000	—	—	—	.50

COPPER-CLAD STEEL

49	1974(w)	200.000	—	—	—	.15
	1976(w)	200.000	—	—	—	.15
	1977(l)	600.000	—	—	—	.15

NICKEL-CLAD STEEL

49a	1983(w)	600.000	—	—	—	.10

COPPER-NICKEL CLAD STEEL

49b	1986(w)	500.000	—	—	—	.10

10 CENTIMOS

COPPER-NICKEL

A40	1971(o)	60.000	—	—	.10	.25

12-1/2 CENTIMOS

COPPER-NICKEL

28	1925(p)	.800	2.50	6.50	45.00	150.00
	1927(p)	.800	1.00	2.00	12.00	60.00
	1929(p)	.800	.15	.50	5.00	35.00
	1936(p)	1.200	.15	.30	2.00	20.00
	1938(p)	1.600	.15	.30	1.00	10.00

NOTE: Earlier date (1896) exists for this type.
NOTE: Varieties exist.

BRASS

30	1944(d)	.800	2.50	4.50	9.00	60.00

COPPER-NICKEL

Y#	Date	Mintage	Fine	VF	XF	Unc
30a	1945(p)	11.200	.10	.20	.35	4.00
	1946(p)	9.200	.10	.20	.35	5.00
	1948(s)	6.000	.10	.20	.35	4.00

Rev: Knobbed 2.

39	1958(p)	10.000	—	—	.10	.50

Obv: Flat stars. Rev: Plain 2.

A39.1	1969(m)	1.500	—	—	100.00

Obv: Raised stars. Rev: Outlined stem ends.

A39.2	1969(m)	Inc. Ab.	—	—	100.00

Rev: Solid stem ends.

A39.3	1969(m)	Inc. Ab.	—	—	100.00

NOTE: 1969 dated strikes not released to circulate.

1/4 BOLIVAR

1.2500 g, .835 SILVER, .0336 oz ASW

Y#	Date	Mintage	Fine	VF	XF	Unc
20	1901(a)	.393	6.00	17.00	48.00	150.00
	1903(p)	.400	6.00	17.00	48.00	150.00
	1911(a)	.600	2.50	5.00	12.00	45.00
	1912(a)	.800	3.00	6.00	15.00	55.00
	1919(a)	.400	2.50	5.00	12.00	55.00
	1921(p) high 2					
		.800	2.00	4.00	10.00	40.00
	1921(p) low 2					
		Inc. Ab.	1.00	3.00	10.00	40.00
	1924(p)	.400	1.00	3.00	10.00	35.00
	1929(p)	1.200	—	BV	1.00	6.00
	1935(p)	3.400	—	BV	1.00	3.00
	1936(p)	2.800	—	BV	1.00	3.00
	1944(p)	1.800	—	BV	1.00	2.00
	1945(p)	8.000	—	—	BV	1.50
	1946(p)	8.000	—	—	BV	1.00
	1948(s)	8.638	—	—	BV	1.00

NOTE: Earlier dates (1894-1900) exist for this type.

25 CENTIMOS

1.2500 g, .835 SILVER, .0336 oz ASW

35	1954(p)	36.000	—	—	BV	1.00

35a	1960(a)	48.000	—	—	BV	.75

NICKEL

40	1965(l)	240.000	—	—	.10	.30

1.75 g, 1.18mm thick

50.1	1977(w)	240.000	—	—	.10	.20

1.50 g, thin

50.2	1977(w)	Inc. Ab.	—	—	.10	.20
	1978(w)	200.000	—	—	.10	.20
	1987	150.000	—	—	.10	.20

NOTE: Dies vary for each date.

NICKEL-CLAD STEEL, 1.50 g

Y#	Date	Mintage	Fine	VF	XF	Unc
50a	1989(sc)	510.000	—	—	.10	.20
	1990(mm)					
		400.000	—	—	.10	.20

NOTE: Varieties exist.

1/2 BOLIVAR

2.5000 g, .835 SILVER, .0671 oz ASW

Y#	Date	Mintage	Fine	VF	XF	Unc
21	1901(a)	.600	20.00	50.00	175.00	400.00
	1903(p)	.200	75.00	200.00	600.00	1200.
	1911(a)	.300	30.00	60.00	200.00	500.00
	1912(a)	1.920	5.00	10.00	25.00	100.00
	1919(p)	.400	6.00	12.00	40.00	150.00
	1921(p) normal date					
		.600	2.50	7.00	16.00	60.00
	1921(p) narrow date					
		Inc. Ab.	3.50	9.00	27.50	75.00
	1921(p) wide date					
		Inc. Ab.	3.50	9.00	27.50	75.00
	1924(p)	.800	2.50	7.00	16.00	60.00
	1929(p)	.400	1.00	2.00	6.00	20.00
	1935(p)	1.000	—	BV	1.00	7.00
	1936(p)	.600	BV	1.00	5.00	20.00

NOTE: Earlier dates (1879-1900) exist for this type.

Y#	Date	Mintage	Fine	VF	XF	Unc
21a	1944(d) accent in Bolivar					
		.500	1.00	3.00	5.00	15.00
	1944(d) w/o accent in Bolivar					
		Inc. Ab.	1.50	5.00	10.00	25.00
	1945(p)	4.000	—	BV	1.00	5.00
	1946(p)	2.500	—	BV	1.00	5.00

50 CENTIMOS

2.5000 g, .835 SILVER, .0671 OZ ASW

Y#	Date	Mintage	Fine	VF	XF	Unc
36	1954(p)	15.000	—	—	BV	3.00

Y#	Date	Mintage	Fine	VF	XF	Unc
36a	1960(a)	20.000	—	—	BV	2.00

NICKEL

Y#	Date	Mintage	Fine	VF	XF	Unc
41	1965(l)	180.000	—	.10	.15	.35
	1985(o)	50.000	—	.10	.15	.35

NICKEL CLAD STEEL, 3.2 g

Y#	Date	Mintage	Fine	VF	XF	Unc
41a	1988(w)	80.000	—	.10	.15	.35
	1989(w)	260.000	—	.10	.15	.35
	1990(l)	300.000	—	.10	.15	.35

NOTE: Die varieties exist for 1990 dated strikes.

BOLIVAR

5.0000 g, .835 SILVER, .1342 oz ASW

Y#	Date	Mintage	Fine	VF	XF	Unc
22	1901(a)	.323	20.00	40.00	120.00	400.00
	1903(p)	.800	5.00	15.00	90.00	260.00
	1911(a)	1.500	3.00	5.00	40.00	150.00
	1912(a) wide date					
		.820	6.00	16.50	75.00	250.00
	1912(a) narrow date					

Y#	Date	Mintage	Fine	VF	XF	Unc
22	1919	Inc. Ab.	6.00	16.50	75.00	250.00
	1921(p)	1.000	2.00	3.00	12.00	45.00
	1924(p)	1.500	2.00	3.00	12.00	40.00
	1926(p)	1.500	BV	2.00	6.00	30.00
	1929(p)	1.000	BV	2.00	6.00	30.00
	1935(p)	2.500	—	BV	1.50	8.00
	1936(p)	5.000	—	BV	1.50	5.00
		5.000	—	BV	1.50	5.00

NOTE: Earlier dates (1879-1900) exist for this type.

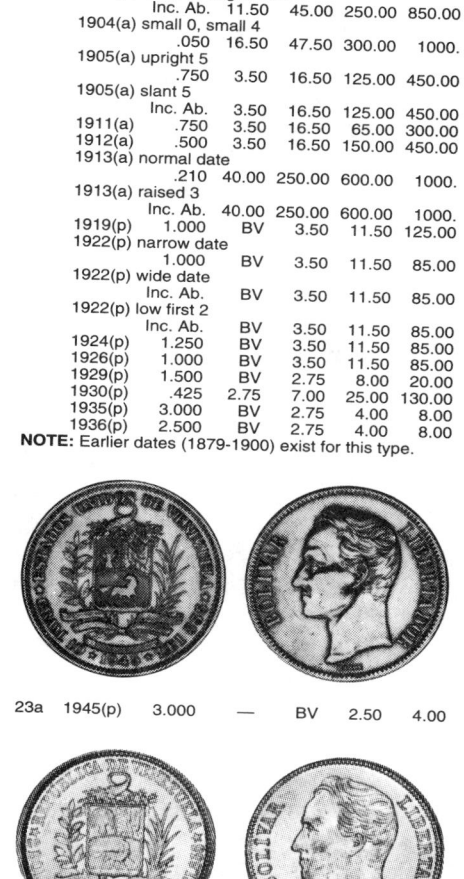

Y#	Date	Mintage	Fine	VF	XF	Unc
22a	1945(p)	8.000	—	—	BV	3.50

Y#	Date	Mintage	Fine	VF	XF	Unc
37	1954(p)	13.500	—	—	BV	2.50

Y#	Date	Mintage	Fine	VF	XF	Unc
37a	1960(a) thin letters					
		30.000	—	—	BV	1.50
	1960(a) thick letters					
		Inc. Ab.	—	—	BV	1.50
	1965(l)	20.000	—	—	BV	1.50

NICKEL

Y#	Date	Mintage	Fine	VF	XF	Unc
42	1967(l)	180.000	—	.10	.15	.75

Y#	Date	Mintage	Fine	VF	XF	Unc
52	1977(l)	200.000	—	.10	.15	.75
	1986(w)	200.000	—	.10	.15	.75
	1986(w)	50.000	—	—	P/L	25.00

NOTE: Dies vary for each date.

NICKEL-CLAD STEEL, 4.2 g
Obv. and rev: Small letters and date.

Y#	Date	Mintage	Fine	VF	XF	Unc
52a.1	1989(w)	370.000	—	—	—	.50

Obv. and rev: Large letters and date.

Y#	Date	Mintage	Fine	VF	XF	Unc
52a.2	1989(sc)	600.000	—	.10	.15	.50
	1990(mm)					
		600.000	—	.10	.15	.50

NOTE: Dies vary for each date.

2 BOLIVARES

10.0000 g, .835 SILVER, .2685 oz ASW

Y#	Date	Mintage	Fine	VF	XF	Unc
23	1902(p)	.500	11.50	45.00	250.00	800.00
	1903(p)	.500	11.50	25.00	150.00	500.00
	1904(a) large 0, small 4					
		.550	11.50	40.00	200.00	750.00
	1904(a) large 0, large 4					
		Inc. Ab.	11.50	40.00	200.00	750.00
	1904(a) small 0, large 4					
		Inc. Ab.	11.50	45.00	250.00	850.00

Y#	Date	Mintage	Fine	VF	XF	Unc
23	1904(a) small 0, large slant 4					
		Inc. Ab.	11.50	45.00	250.00	850.00
	1904(a) small 0, small 4					
		.050	16.50	47.50	300.00	1000.
	1905(a) upright 5					
		.750	3.50	16.50	125.00	450.00
	1905(a) slant 5					
		Inc. Ab.	3.50	16.50	125.00	450.00
	1911(a)	.750	3.50	16.50	65.00	300.00
	1912(a)	.500	3.50	16.50	150.00	450.00
	1913(a) normal date					
		.210	40.00	250.00	600.00	1000.
	1913(a) raised 3					
		Inc. Ab.	40.00	250.00	600.00	1000.
	1919(p)	1.000	BV	3.50	11.50	125.00
	1922(p) narrow date					
		1.000	BV	3.50	11.50	85.00
	1922(p) wide date					
		Inc. Ab.	BV	3.50	11.50	85.00
	1922(p) low first 2					
		Inc. Ab.	BV	3.50	11.50	85.00
	1924(p)	1.250	BV	3.50	11.50	85.00
	1926(p)	1.000	BV	3.50	11.50	85.00
	1929(p)	1.500	BV	2.75	8.00	20.00
	1930(p)	.425	2.75	7.00	25.00	130.00
	1935(p)	3.000	BV	2.75	4.00	8.00
	1936(p)	2.500	BV	2.75	4.00	8.00

NOTE: Earlier dates (1879-1900) exist for this type.

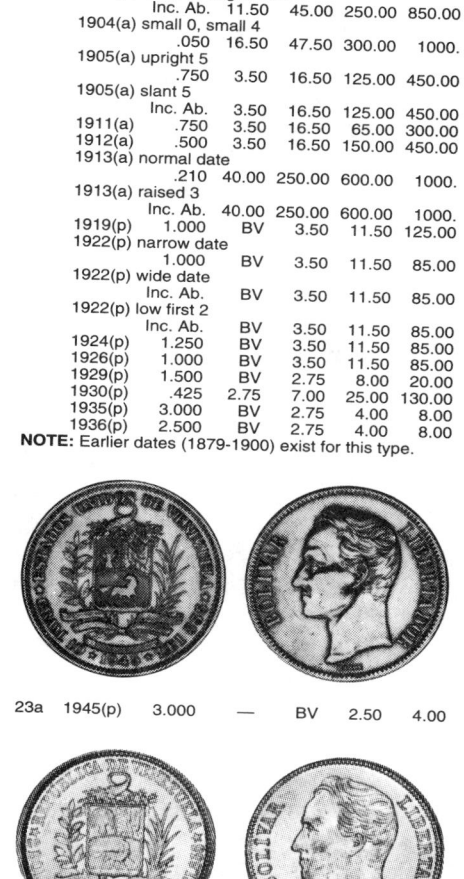

Y#	Date	Mintage	Fine	VF	XF	Unc
23a	1945(p)	3.000	—	BV	2.50	4.00

Y#	Date	Mintage	Fine	VF	XF	Unc
A37	1960(a)	4.000	—	—	BV	3.50
	1965(l)	7.170	—	—	BV	3.50

NICKEL

Y#	Date	Mintage	Fine	VF	XF	Unc
43	1967(l)	50.000	—	.15	.25	1.00
	1986(w)	50.000	—	.15	.25	1.00
	1986(w)	—	—	—	P/L	30.00
	1988(c)	80.000	—	.15	.25	1.00

NOTE: Die varieties exist for 1986 strikes. Dies vary for each date.

NICKEL CLAD STEEL, 7.50 g
Obv. and rev: Small letters.

Y#	Date	Mintage	Fine	VF	XF	Unc
43a.1	1989(sc)	200.000	—	.15	.25	1.00
	1990(c)	400.000	—	.15	.25	1.00

NOTE: Two varieties of 1990 exist.

Obv. and rev: Large letters.

Y#	Date	Mintage	Fine	VF	XF	Unc
43a.2	1989(w)	100.000	—	.15	.25	1.00
	1989(c)	95.000	—	.15	.25	1.00

5 BOLIVARES

25.0000 g, .900 SILVER, .7234 oz ASW
Obv: Date on ribbon right of arms
13 DE APRIL DE 1864.

Y#	Date	Mintage	Fine	VF	XF	Unc
24	1901(a)	.090	20.00	120.00	475.00	1500.
	1902(p) wide date	.500	9.00	16.00	120.00	700.00
	1902(p) narrow date					
	Inc. Ab.		9.00	16.00	120.00	700.00
	1903(p)	.200	9.00	16.00	120.00	700.00
	1904(a)	.200	9.00	16.00	150.00	1000.
	1905(a)	.300	9.00	16.00	120.00	650.00
	1910(a) oval 0	.400	9.00	16.00	85.00	450.00
	1910(a) round 0					
	Inc. Ab.		12.00	25.00	130.00	650.00
	1911(a) normal date	1.104	6.50	12.50	45.00	225.00
	1911(a) wide date					
	Inc. Ab.		6.50	12.50	45.00	225.00
	1911(a) narrow date					
	Inc. Ab.		6.50	12.50	45.00	225.00
	1912(a) normal date	.696	6.50	12.50	45.00	225.00
	1912(a) wide date					
	Inc. Ab.		6.50	12.50	45.00	225.00
	1912(a) narrow date					
	Inc. Ab.		6.50	12.50	45.00	225.00
	1919(p)	.400	6.50	12.50	30.00	175.00
	1921(p) wide date	.500	6.50	12.50	25.00	100.00
	1921(p) narrow date					
	Inc. Ab.		6.50	12.50	25.00	100.00
	1924(p) wide date	.500	6.50	12.50	25.00	100.00
	1924(p) narrow date					
	Inc. Ab.		6.50	12.50	25.00	100.00
	1924(p) low 9					
	Inc. Ab.		6.50	12.50	25.00	100.00
	1926(p)	.800	6.50	12.50	25.00	80.00
	1929(p) high 9	.800	6.50	12.50	22.00	60.00
	1929(p) low 9					
	Inc. Ab.		6.50	12.50	22.00	60.00
	1935(p)	1.600	BV	11.50	16.50	38.00
	1936(p) normal date	2.000	BV	11.50	16.50	38.00
	1936(p) high 3					
	Inc. Ab.		BV	11.50	16.50	38.00
	1936(p) low 3					
	Inc. Ab.		BV	11.50	16.50	38.00

NOTE: Earlier dates (1879-1900) exist for this type.

NICKEL

44	1973(m)	20.000	—	.50	.75	1.50

53	1977(m)	60.000	—	.25	.50	1.00
	1987(c)	25.000	—	.25	.50	1.00
	1987(c)	—	—	—	P/L	30.00
	1988(w)	20.000	—	.25	.50	1.00

NICKEL-CLAD STEEL, 13.3 g
Obv: Small letters. Rev: Large letters.

Y#	Date	Mintage	Fine	VF	XF	Unc
53a.1	1989(w)	55.000	—	.25	.50	1.00
	1989(w)	26.000	—	—	P/L	30.00

Obv: Large letters. Rev: Small letters.

53a.2	1989(sc)	100.000	—	.25	.50	1.00
	1990(c)	200.000	—	.25	.50	1.00

Obv. and rev. legends: Large letters.

53a.3	1990		—	.35	.65	1.50

10 BOLIVARES

3.2258 g, .900 GOLD, .0933 oz AGW

31	1930(p)	*.500	—	BV	40.00	70.00

NOTE: Only 10% of the total mintage was released. The balance remaining as part of the nation's gold reserve.

20 BOLIVARES

6.4516 g, .900 GOLD, .1867 oz AGW

32	1904(a)	.100	BV	70.00	80.00	100.00
	1905(a)	.100	BV	70.00	80.00	100.00
	1910(a)	.070	BV	70.00	80.00	100.00
	1911(a)	.080	BV	70.00	80.00	100.00
	1912(a)	.150	BV	70.00	80.00	100.00

NOTE: Earlier dates (1879-1888) exist for this type.
NOTE: Die varieties exist for dates 1910 and 1911 in the placement of dot between date and Lei, Type 1 is evenly spaced; Type 2 has dot close to L of Lei. Die varieties exist for 1912 with the placement of torch privy mark in relation to bust truncation. Type 1 is well below truncation, Type 2 is slightly below truncation and Type 3 is in line with truncation.

VIET NAM-ANNAM

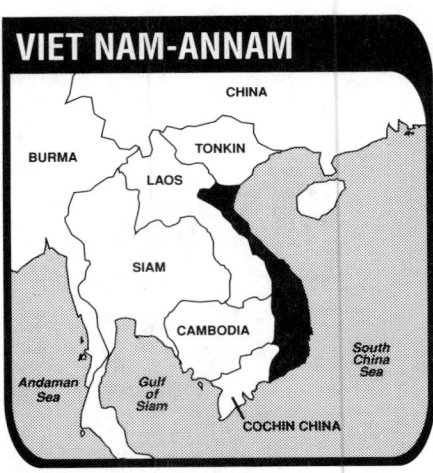

In 207 B.C. a Chinese general set up the Kingdom of Nam-Viet on the Red River. This kingdom was overthrown by the Chinese under the Han Dynasty in 111 B.C., whereupon the country became a Chinese province under the name of Giao-Chi, which was later changed to Annam or peaceful or pacified South. Chinese rule was maintained until 968, when the Vietnamese became independent until 1407 when China again invaded Viet Nam. The Chinese were driven out in 1428 and the country became independent and named Dai-Viet. Gia Long renamed the country Dai Nam in 1802.

After the French conquered Dai Nam, they split the country into three parts. The South became the Colony of Cochinchina; the North became the Protectorate of Tonkin; and the central became the Protectorate of Annam. The emperors were permitted to have their capital in Hue and to produce small quantities of their coins, presentation pieces, and bullion bars. Annam had an area of 57,840 sq. mi. (141,806 sq. km.) and a population of about 6 million. Chief products of the area are silk, cinnamon and rice. There are important mineral deposits in the mountainous inland.

Protectorate of Annam
EMPERORS

Thanh Thai, 1888-1907	成泰
Duy Tan, 1907-1916	維新
Khai Dinh, 1916-1925	啓定
Bao Dai, 1926-1945	保大

IDENTIFICATION

Khai 啓

Bao 寶

Dinh 定

通 *Thong*

通 *Thong*

Khai Dinh Thong Bao

The square holed cash coins of Annam are easily identified by reading the characters top-bottom (emperor's name) and right-left ("Thong Bao" general currency). The character at right will change with some emperors.

NUMERALS
Column A, conventional; Column B, formal.

NUMBER	CONVENTIONAL	FORMAL	COMMERCIAL
1	一 元	壹 弍	1
2	二	弍 貳	11
3	三	叁 弎	111
4	四	肆	X
5	五	伍	8
6	六	陸	上
7	七	柒	上
8	八	捌	三
9	九	玖	夊
10	十	拾 什	十
20	十 二 or 廿	拾貳	11十
25	五 十 二 or 五廿	伍拾貳	11十8
30	十 三 or 卅	拾叁	111十
100	百 一	佰壹	1百
1,000	千 一	仟壹	1千
10,000	萬 一	萬壹	1万
100,000	萬 十 億 一	萬拾 億壹	十万
1,000,000	萬 百 一	萬佰壹	一十万百

NOTE: This table has been adapted from *Chinese Bank Notes* by Ward Smith and Brian Matravers.

MONETARY SYSTEM
COPPER AND ZINC
10 Dong (zinc) = 1 Dong (copper)
600 Dong (zinc) = 1 Quan (string of cash)
Approx. 2600 Dong (zinc) = 1 Piastre

NOTE: Ratios between metals changed frequently, therefore the above is given as an approximate relationship.

COPPER, BRASS and ZINC 'CASH' COINAGE
(1 Phan)

CAST COPPER ALLOYS
Rev: Blank.

Y#	Date	Emperor	Good	VG	Fine	VF
1	(1888-1907)	Thanh Thai	2.00	3.50	5.50	9.00

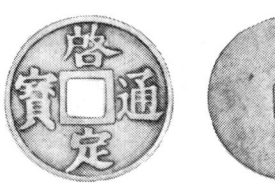

Similar to Y#5.1.

| 4 | (1916-25) | Khai Dinh | 5.50 | 9.00 | 15.00 | 25.00 |

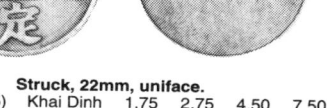

Struck, 22mm, uniface.

| 5.1 | (1916-25) | Khai Dinh | 1.75 | 2.75 | 4.50 | 7.50 |

 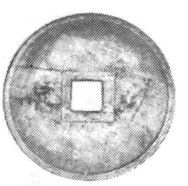

Larger size, characters slightly different.

Y#	Date	Emperor	Good	VG	Fine	VF
5.2	(1916-25)	Khai Dinh	2.00	3.50	6.00	10.00

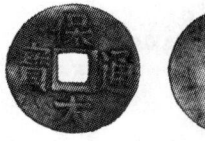

BRASS, struck 18mm

| 6 | (1926-45) | Bao Dai | 2.50 | 5.00 | 7.50 | 12.50 |

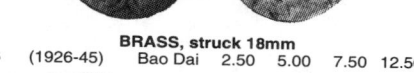

CAST BRASS, 24mm

| 6a | (1926-45) | Bao Dai | 2.50 | 5.00 | 7.50 | 12.50 |

NOTE: Later issues after the French colonial coinage was introduced in 1885 are considered awards for various services.

6 VAN

CAST COPPER ALLOYS, 24-26mm

| A2 | (1888-1907) | Thanh Thai | — | — | — | — |

NOTE: The above piece has been questioned by some authorities.

10 VAN

CAST COPPER ALLOYS
Rev: *Thap Van.*

| 2 | (1888-1907) | Thanh Thai | .50 | .75 | 1.25 | 2.50 |

CAST BRASS

| 3 | (1907-16) | Duy Tan | .50 | .75 | 1.25 | 2.50 |

| 7 | (1926-45) | Bao Dai | 2.00 | 3.50 | 7.50 | 12.50 |

NOTE: Later issues after the French colonial coinage was introduced in 1885 are considered awards for various services.

VIET NAM-TONKIN

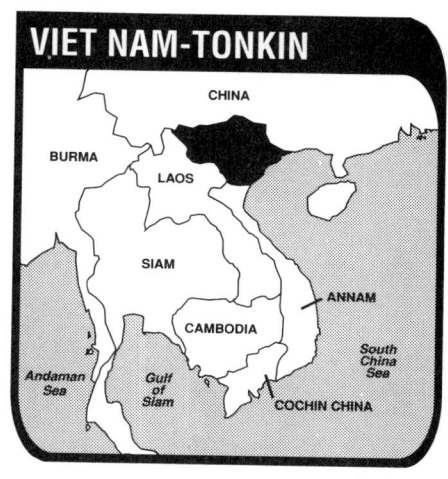

Tonkin, a former French protectorate in North IndoChina, comprises the greater part of present North Viet Nam. It had an area of 44,672 sq. mi. (75,700 sq. km.) and a population of about 4 million. Capital: Hanoi. The initial value of Tonkin to France was contained in the access it afforded to the trade of China's Yunnan province.

France established a protectorate over Annam and Tonkin by the treaties of Tientsin and Hue negotiated in 1884. Tonkin was incorporated in the independent state of Viet Nam (within the French Union) and upon the defeat of France by the Viet Minh became the body of North Viet Nam.

MINT MARKS
(a) - Paris, privy marks only

1/600 PIASTRE

ZINC

KM#	Date	Mintage	Fine	VF	XF	Unc
1	1905(a)	60.000	3.00	7.00	15.00	40.00

NOTE: About 0.9 mm thick and weighs 2.1 grams.

VIET NAM

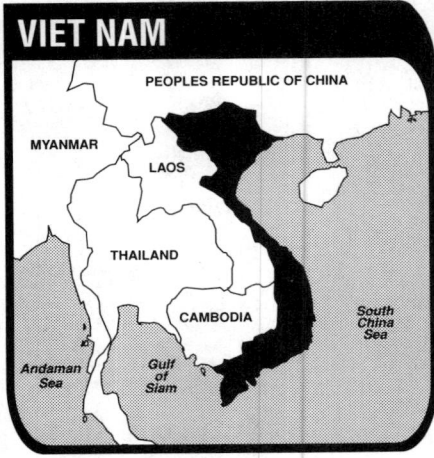

PEOPLES REPUBLIC OF CHINA
MYANMAR
LAOS
THAILAND
CAMBODIA
South China Sea
Andaman Sea
Gulf of Siam

The Socialist Republic of Viet Nam, located in Southeast Asia west of the South China Sea, has an area of 127,300 sq. mi. (329,560 sq. km.) and a population of *66.8 million. Capital: Hanoi. Agricultural products, coal, and mineral ores are exported.

At the start of World War II, Vietnamese Communists fled to China's Kwangsi provinces where Ho Chi Minh organized the Revolution to free Viet Nam of French rule. The Japanese occupied Viet Nam during World War II. As the end of the war drew near, they ousted the Vichy French administration and granted Viet Nam independence under a puppet government headed by Bao Dai, Emperor of Annam. The Bao Dai government collapsed at the end of the war, and on Sept. 2, 1945, Ho Chi Minh proclaimed the existence of an independent Viet Nam consisting of Cochin-China, Annam, and Tonkin, and set up a Communist government. France recognized the new government as a free state, but reneged and in 1949 reinstalled Bao Dai as Ruler of Viet Nam and extended the regime independence within the French Union. Ho Chi Minh led a guerrilla war, in the first Indochina war, against the French which raged on to the disastrous defeat of the French at Dien Bien Phu on May 7, 1954.

An agreement signed at Geneva on July 21, 1954, provided for a temporary division of Viet Nam at the 17th parallel of latitude, between a Communist-supported North and a U.S.-supported South. In Oct. 1955, South Viet Nam deposed Bao Dai by referendum and authorized the establishment of a republic with Ngo Dinh Diem as president. The Republic of South Viet Nam was proclaimed on Oct. 26, 1955, and was immediately recognized by some Western Powers.

The activities of Communists in South Viet Nam led to the second Indochina war which came to a brief halt in 1973 (when a cease-fire was arranged and U.S. forces withdrew), but it didn't end until April 30, 1975 when South Viet Nam surrendered unconditionally. The two Viet Nams were reunited as the Socialist Republic of Viet Nam on July 2, 1976.

For earlier coinage refer to French Indo-China.

MONETARY SYSTEM
10 Xu = 1 Hao
10 Hao = 1 Dong

20 XU

ALUMINUM

KM#	Date	Mintage	Fine	VF	XF	Unc
1	1945	—	40.00	125.00	175.00	200.00

5 HAO

ALUMINUM
Value in incuse lettering

2.1	1946	—	3.00	9.00	18.00	40.00

NOTE: Commonly encountered with rotated dies.

Value in raised lettering

KM#	Date	Mintage	Fine	VF	XF	Unc
2.2	1946	—	20.00	40.00	100.00	175.00

DONG

ALUMINUM

3	1946	—	45.00	85.00	165.00	250.00

2 DONG

BRONZE

4	1946	—	5.00	12.50	35.00	100.00

NOTE: Varieties exist.

NORTH VIET NAM

XU

ALUMINUM

5	1958	—	.65	1.25	2.00	3.50

2 XU

ALUMINUM

6	1958	—	.65	1.25	2.00	3.50

5 XU

ALUMINUM

7	1958	—	.75	1.50	2.50	4.50

STATE OF SOUTH VIET NAM

South Viet Nam (the former Republic of Viet Nam), located in the Southeast Asia, bounded by North Viet Nam on the north, Laos and Cambodia on the west, and the South China Sea on the east and south, had an area of 66,280 sq. mi. (171,665 sq. km.) and a population of 20 million. Capital: Saigon (now Ho Chi Minh City). The economy of the area is predominantly agricultural.

South Viet Nam, the direct successor of the French-dominated Emperor Bao Dai regime (also known as the State of Viet Nam), was created after the first Indo-China War (between the French and the Viet-Minh) by the Geneva agreement of 1954 which divided Viet Nam at the 17th parallel of latitude. The National Bank of Viet Nam, with headquarters in the old Bank of Indochina building in Saigon, came into being on Dec. 31, 1954. Elections which would have reunified North and South Viet Nam in 1956 never took place, and the North continued the war for unification of Viet Nam under the communist government of the Democratic Republic of Viet Nam begun at the close of World War II. South Viet Nam surrendered unconditionally on April 30, 1975. There followed a short period of coexistence of the two Viet Namese states, but the south was governed by the North through the Peoples' Revolutionary Government (PRG). On July 2, 1976, South and North Viet Nam joined to form the Socialist Republic of Viet Nam.

MINT MARKS
(a) - Paris, privy marks only

MONETARY SYSTEM
100 Xu (Su) = 1 Dong

10 SU

ALUMINUM
Rice Plant

KM#	Date	Mintage	Fine	VF	XF	Unc
1	1953(a)	20.000	.15	.25	.50	1.00

20 SU

ALUMINUM
Rice Plant

2	1953(a)	15.000	.30	.50	.85	1.75

50 XU

ALUMINUM

3	1953(a)	15.000	1.50	3.00	6.00	12.50

REPUBLIC OF VIET NAM

50 SU

ALUMINUM
Bamboo

4	1960	10.000	.25	.50	1.25	2.50
	1960				Proof	100.00

50 XU

ALUMINUM
Bamboo

KM#	Date	Mintage	Fine	VF	XF	Unc
6	1963	20.000	.20	.40	.75	1.50
	1963				Proof	100.00

DONG

COPPER-NICKEL
Bamboo

5	1960	105.000	.15	.50	1.25	2.50
	1960	—			Proof	100.00

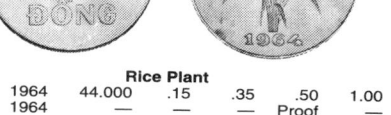

Rice Plant

7	1964	44.000	.15	.35	.50	1.00
	1964	—			Proof	—

NICKEL-CLAD STEEL

7a	1971	—	.10	.15	.35	1.00

ALUMINUM
F.A.O. Issue

12	1971	30.000	.10	.15	.25	.50

5 DONG

COPPER-NICKEL
Rice Plant

9	1966	100.000	.10	.35	.50	1.00

NICKEL-CLAD STEEL

9a	1971	15.000	.10	.25	.50	1.00

10 DONG

COPPER-NICKEL
Rice Plant

8	1964	15.000	.20	.40	.60	1.25

NICKEL-CLAD STEEL

8a	1968	30.000	.10	.20	.35	.75
	1970	50.000	.10	.20	.35	.75

BRASS-CLAD STEEL
F.A.O. Issue

KM#	Date	Mintage	Fine	VF	XF	Unc
13	1974	30.000	.10	.15	.30	.60

20 DONG

NICKEL—CLAD STEEL

10	1968		.25	.45	.85	1.85

F.A.O. Issue

11	1968	.500	.25	.50	1.00	2.00

50 DONG

NICKEL CLAD STEEL
F.A.O. Issue

14	1975	1.010	275.00	325.00	400.00	600.00

NOTE: It is reported that all but a few examples were "disposed of as scrap metal".

PROVISIONAL COINAGE

For use in occupied South Viet nam only.

XU

ALUMINUM

8	ND(1975)	—	.50	1.50	2.75	7.50

2 XU

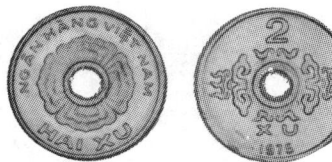

ALUMINUM

9	1975	—	.50	1.50	2.75	7.50

5 XU

ALUMINUM

KM#	Date	Mintage	Fine	VF	XF	Unc
10	ND(1975)	—	.50	1.50	2.75	7.50

VIET NAM
SOCIALIST REPUBLIC

MINT MARKS

(h) - Key - Havana, Cuba

HAO

ALUMINUM

11	1976	—	.25	.50	1.00	2.50

2 HAO

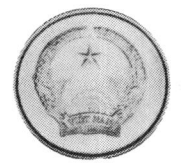 

ALUMINUM

12	1976	—	.35	.65	1.50	3.50

5 HAO

ALUMINUM

13	1976	—	.35	.65	1.50	3.50

DONG

ALUMINUM

14	1976	—	.65	1.35	3.50	7.50

WEST AFRICAN STATES

The West African States, a former federation of eight French colonial territories on the northwest coast of Africa, had area of 1,831,079 sq. mi. (4,742,495 sq. km.) and a population of about 17 million. Capital: Dakar. The constituent territories were Mauritania, Senegal, Dahomey, French Sudan, Ivory Coast, Upper Volta, Niger and French Guinea.

The members of the federation were overseas territories within the French Union until Sept. of 1958 when all but French Guinea approved the constitution of the Fifth French Republic, thereby electing to become autonomous members of the new French Community. French Guinea voted to become the fully independent Republic of Guinea. The other seven attained independence in 1960. The French West Africa territories were provided with a common currency, a practice which was continued as the monetary union of the West African States which provides a common currency to the autonomous republics of Dahomey (now Benin), Senegal, Upper Volta (now Burkina Faso), Ivory Coast, Mali, Togo and Niger.

For earlier coinage refer to Togo, and French West Africa.

MINT MARKS
(a) - Paris, privy marks only

MONETARY SYSTEM
100 Centimes = 1 Franc

FRANC

ALUMINUM

KM#	Date	Mintage	VF	XF	Unc
3.1	1961(a)	3.000	.15	.30	.60
	1964(a)	5.000	.15	.30	.60
	1965(a)	6.000	.15	.30	.60
	1967(a)	2.500	.15	.30	.60
	1970(a)	4.000	Reported, not confirmed		
	1971(a)	4.000	.15	.30	.60
	1972(a)	4.000	.15	.30	.60
	1973(a)	4.500	.15	.30	.60
	1974(a)	—	.15	.30	.60
	1975(a)	10.080	.15	.30	.60
	1976(a)	8.000	.15	.30	.60

Rev: Engraver general's name.
3.2	1962(a)	2.000	2.00	5.00	10.00
	1963(a)	4.500	1.50	4.00	7.00

STEEL
8	1976(a)	8.000	—	.10	.35
	1977(a)	14.700	—	.10	.35
	1978(a)	—	—	.10	.35
	1979(a)	—	—	.10	.35
	1980(a)	—	—	.10	.35
	1981(a)	—	—	.10	.35
	1982(a)	—	—	.10	.35
	1984(a)	—	—	.10	.35
	1985(a)	26.900	—	—	—
	1990(a)	—	—	.10	.35
	1991(a)	—	—	.10	.35
	1992(a)	—	—	.10	.35
	1995(a)	—	—	.10	.35

5 FRANCS

ALUMINUM-BRONZE
2	1960(a)	5.000	.20	.40	.70
	1962(a)	5.000	—	—	—
	1963(a)	—	—	—	—

ALUMINUM-NICKEL-BRONZE
2a	1965(a)	6.510	.20	.40	.70

KM#	Date	Mintage	VF	XF	Unc
2a	1966(a)	6.000	Reported, not confirmed		
	1967(a)	6.010	.20	.40	.70
	1968(a)	6.000	.20	.45	.75
	1969(a)	8.000	.20	.40	.70
	1970(a)	10.005	.20	.40	.70
	1971(a)	10.000	.20	.40	.70
	1972(a)	5.000	.20	.40	.70
	1973(a)	6.000	.20	.45	.75
	1974(a)	13.326	.10	.15	.30
	1975(a)	16.840	.20	.40	.70
	1976(a)	20.010	.20	.30	.60
	1977(a)	16.840	.20	.30	.60
	1978(a)	—	.20	.30	.60
	1979(a)	—	.10	.20	.40
	1980(a)	—	.10	.20	.40
	1981(a)	—	.10	.20	.40
	1982(a)	—	.10	.20	.40
	1984(a)	—	.10	.20	.40
	1985(a)	16.000	.10	.20	.40
	1986(a)	8.000	.10	.20	.40
	1987(a)	—	.10	.20	.40
	1988(a)	—	.10	.20	.40
	1989(a)	—	.10	.20	.40
	1990(a)	—	.10	.20	.40
	1991(a)	—	.10	.20	.40
	1992(a)	—	.10	.20	.40
	1994(a)	—	.10	.20	.40
	1996(a)	—	.10	.20	.40
	1997(a)	—	.10	.20	.40

10 FRANCS

ALUMINUM-BRONZE
1	1959(a)	10.000	.15	.30	.60
	1961(a)	—	—	—	—
	1962(a)	—	—	—	—
	1964(a)	10.000	.20	.40	.70

ALUMINUM-NICKEL-BRONZE
1a	1965(a)	6.000	Reported, not confirmed		
	1966(a)	6.000	.20	.40	.70
	1967(a)	3.500	.25	.50	.90
	1968(a)	6.000	.20	.40	.70
	1969(a)	7.000	.25	.50	.90
	1970(a)	7.000	.15	.30	.60
	1971(a)	8.000	.15	.30	.60
	1972(a)	5.500	.20	.40	.70
	1973(a)	3.000	.20	.40	.70
	1974(a)	10.000	.15	.30	.60
	1975(a)	17.000	.15	.30	.60
	1976(a)	18.000	.15	.30	.60
	1977(a)	9.050	.15	.25	.50
	1978(a)	—	.15	.25	.50
	1979(a)	—	.15	.25	.50
	1980(a)	—	.15	.25	.50
	1981(a)	—	.15	.25	.50

BRASS
F.A.O. Issue
10	1981(a)	—	.25	.50	1.25
	1982(a)	—	.25	.50	1.25
	1983(a)	—	.25	.50	1.25
	1984(a)	—	.25	.50	1.25
	1985(a)	5.000	.25	.50	1.25
	1986(a)	7.500	.25	.50	1.25
	1987(a)	—	.25	.50	1.25
	1989(a)	—	.25	.50	1.25
	1990(a)	—	.25	.50	1.25
	1991(a)	—	.25	.50	1.25
	1992(a)	—	.25	.50	1.25
	1994(a)	—	.25	.50	1.25
	1995(a)	—	.25	.50	1.25
	1996(a)	—	.25	.50	1.25
	1997(a)	—	.25	.50	1.25

25 FRANCS

ALUMINUM-BRONZE
5	1970(a)	7.000	.25	.45	.80

KM#	Date	Mintage	VF	XF	Unc
5	1971(a)	7.000	.50	.75	1.25
	1972(a)	2.000	1.00	1.50	3.00
	1975(a)	5.035	.25	.45	.80
	1976(a)	3.365	.25	.45	.80
	1977(a)	3.288	.25	.45	.80
	1978(a)	—	.25	.45	.80
	1979(a)	—	.25	.45	.80

F.A.O. Issue
9	1980(a)	—	.25	.75	1.75
	1981(a)	—	.25	.75	1.75
	1982(a)	—	.25	.75	1.75
	1984(a)	—	.25	.75	1.75
	1985(a)	8.587	—	—	—
	1987(a)	—	.25	.75	1.75
	1989(a)	—	.25	.75	1.75
	1990(a)	—	.25	.75	1.75
	1994(a)	—	.25	.75	1.75
	1996(a)	—	.25	.75	1.75
	1997(a)	—	.25	.75	1.75

50 FRANCS

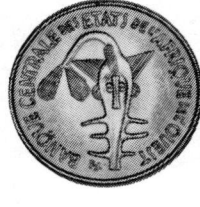

COPPER-NICKEL
F.A.O. Issue
6	1972(a)	20.000	.35	.50	1.25
	1974(a)	3.000	.50	.75	1.50
	1975(a)	9.000	.25	.40	1.00
	1976(a)	6.002	.35	.50	1.25
	1977(a)	4.832	.35	.50	1.25
	1978(a)	—	.35	.50	1.25
	1979(a)	—	.35	.50	1.25
	1980(a)	—	.35	.50	1.25
	1981(a)	—	.35	.50	1.25
	1982(a)	—	.35	.50	1.25
	1984(a)	—	.35	.50	1.25
	1985(a)	4.120	—	—	—
	1986(a)	—	.35	.50	1.25
	1987(a)	—	.35	.50	1.25
	1989(a)	—	.35	.50	1.25
	1990(a)	—	.35	.50	1.25
	1991(a)	—	.35	.50	1.25
	1992(a)	—	.35	.50	1.25
	1995(a)	—	.35	.50	1.25
	1996(a)	—	.35	.50	1.25
	1997(a)	—	.35	.50	1.25

100 FRANCS

NICKEL
4	1967(a)	—	.75	.90	2.00
	1968(a)	25.000	.75	.90	2.00
	1969(a)	25.000	.75	.90	2.00
	1970(a)	4.510	.80	.90	2.00
	1971(a)	12.000	.50	.75	1.75
	1972(a)	5.000	.60	.75	1.85
	1973(a)	5.000	.60	.75	1.85
	1974(a)	8.500	.60	.75	1.75
	1975(a)	16.000	.60	.75	1.75
	1976(a)	11.575	.60	.75	1.75
	1977(a)	9.355	.60	.75	1.75
	1978(a)	—	.60	.75	1.75
	1979(a)	—	.60	.75	1.85
	1980(a)	—	.60	.75	1.85
	1981(a)	—	.60	.75	1.85
	1982(a)	—	.60	.75	1.85
	1984(a)	—	.65	.85	2.00
	1985(a)	1.460	—	—	—
	1987(a)	—	.65	.85	2.00
	1989(a)	—	.65	.85	2.00
	1990(a)	—	.65	.85	2.00
	1991(a)	—	.65	.85	2.00
	1992(a)	—	.65	.85	2.00
	1996(a)	—	.65	.85	2.00
	1997(a)	—	.65	.85	2.00

250 FRANCS

BRASS center, COPPER-NICKEL ring

KM#	Date	Mintage	VF	XF	Unc
13	1992(a)	—	1.75	2.75	6.50
	1993(a)	—	1.75	2.75	6.00
	1996(a)	—	2.00	3.00	7.00

The Independent State of Western Samoa (formerly German Samoa), located in the Pacific Ocean 1,600 miles (2,574 km.) northeast of New Zealand, has an area of 1,097 sq. mi. (2,860 sq. km.) and a population of *182,000. Capital: Apia. The economy is based on agriculture, fishing and tourism. Copra, cocoa and bananas are exported.

The first European to sight the Samoan group of islands was the Dutch navigator Jacob Roggeveen in 1772. Great Britain, the United States and Germany established consular representation at Apia in 1847, 1853 and 1861 respectively. The conflicting interests of the three powers produced the Berlin agreement of 1889 which declared Samoa neutral and had the effect of establishing a tripartite protectorate over the islands. A further agreement, 1899, recognized the rights of the United States in those islands east of 171 deg. west longitude (American Samoa) and of Germany in the other islands (Western Samoa). New Zealand occupied Western Samoa at the start of World War I and administered it as a League of Nations mandate and U. N. trusteeship until Jan. 1, 1962, when it became an independent state.

Western Samoa is a member of the Commonwealth of Nations. The Chief Executive is Chief of State. The prime minister is the Head of Government. The present Head of State, Malietoa Tanumafili II, holds his position for life. Future Heads of State will be elected by the Legislative Assembly for 5-year terms.

Western Samoa, which had used New Zealand coinage, converted to a decimal coinage in 1967.

RULERS
British, until 1962
Malietoa Tanumafili II, 1962-

MONETARY SYSTEM
100 Sene = 1 Tala

SENE

BRONZE

KM#	Date	Mintage	VF	XF	Unc
1	1967	.915	.10	.15	.20
	1967	.015	—	Proof	.50
12	1974	3.380	—	.10	.15
	1987	—	—	.10	.15
	1988	—	—	.10	.15
	1996	—	—	.10	.15

2 SENE

BRONZE

KM#	Date	Mintage	VF	XF	Unc
2	1967	.465	.10	.15	.25
	1967	.015	—	Proof	.50
13	1974	1.640	.10	.15	.20
	1988	—	.10	.15	.20
	1996	—	.10	.15	.20

5 SENE

COPPER-NICKEL

KM#	Date	Mintage	VF	XF	Unc
3	1967	.495	.15	.25	.35
	1967	.015	—	Proof	1.00

14	1974	1.736	.10	.20	.30
	1987	—	.10	.20	.30
	1988	—	.10	.20	.30
	1993	—	.10	.20	.30
	1996	—	.10	.20	.30

10 SENE

COPPER-NICKEL

KM#	Date	Mintage	VF	XF	Unc
4	1967	.400	.20	.35	.50
	1967	.015	—	Proof	1.00

15	1974	1.580	.15	.30	.45
	1987	—	.15	.30	.45
	1988	—	.15	.30	.45
	1993	—	.15	.30	.45
	1996	—	.15	.30	.45

20 SENE

COPPER-NICKEL

KM#	Date	Mintage	VF	XF	Unc
5	1967	.400	.25	.50	1.00
	1967	.015	—	Proof	1.50

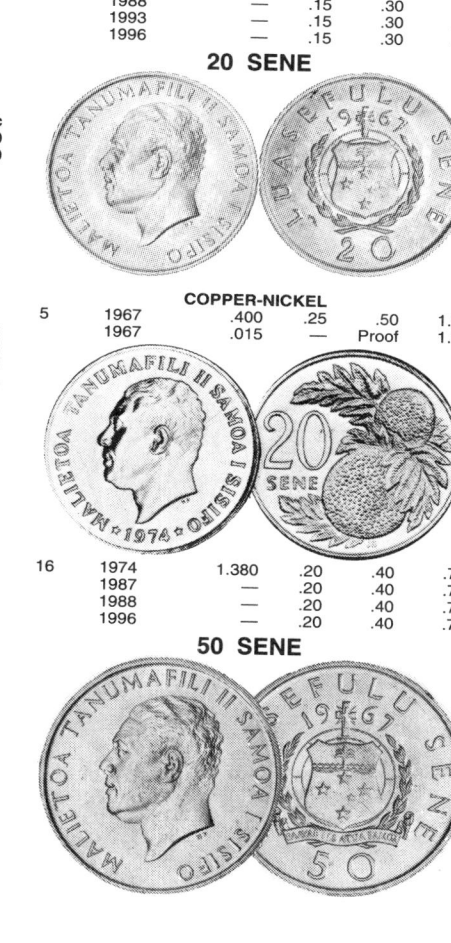

16	1974	1.380	.20	.40	.75
	1987	—	.20	.40	.75
	1988	—	.20	.40	.75
	1996	—	.20	.40	.75

50 SENE

COPPER-NICKEL

KM#	Date	Mintage	VF	XF	Unc
6	1967	.080	.75	1.25	1.75
	1967	.015	—	Proof	2.00

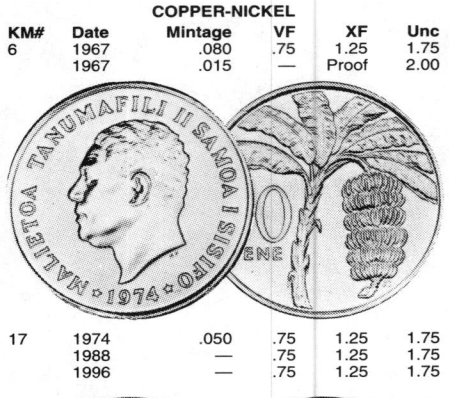

	1974				
17	1974	.050	.75	1.25	1.75
	1988	—	.75	1.25	1.75
	1996	—	.75	1.25	1.75

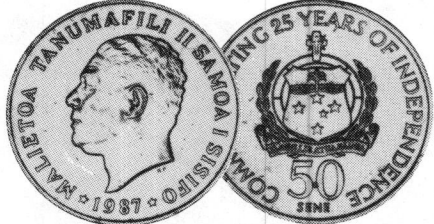

COPPER-NICKEL
25th Anniversary of Independence

80	1987				2.50

TALA

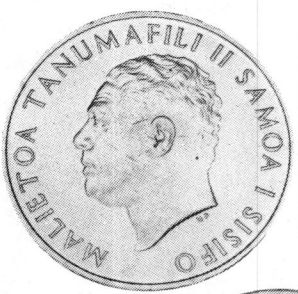

COPPER-NICKEL
Obv: Bust left.
Obv: Similar to 50 Sene, KM#6.

7	1967	.020	—	—	3.00
	1967	.015	—	Proof	7.50

ALUMINUM-BRONZE
Circulation Coinage

57	1984	1.000	.50	.75	1.00

YEMEN REPUBLIC

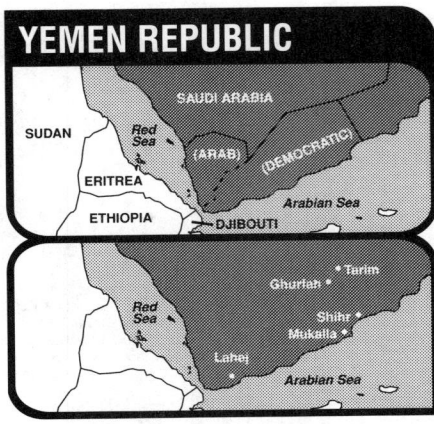

The Republic of Yemen, formerly Yemen Arab Republic and Peoples Republic of Yemen is located on the southern coast of the Arabian Peninsula. It has an area of 205,020 sq. mi. (531,000 sq. km.) and a population of 12 million. Capital: Sana'a. The port of Aden is the main commercial center and the area's most valuable natural resource. Recent oil and gas finds and a developing petroleum industry have improved their economic prospects. Agriculture and local handicrafts are the main industries. Cotton, fish, coffee, rock salt and hides are exported.

On May 22, 1990, the Yemen Arab Republic (North Yemen) and Peoples Democratic Republic of Yemen (South Yemen) merged into a unified Republic of Yemen.

TITLES

Dar al-Khilafa(t)

MONETARY SYSTEM
After Accession of Iman Yahya
AH1322/1904AD

1 Zalat = 1/160 Riyal
2 Zalat = 1 Halala = 1/80 Riyal
2 Halala = 1 Buqsha = 1/40 Riyal
40 Buqsha = 1 Riyal

BRONZE and ALUMINUM
Thumn ushr = 1/80 Riyal = 1/2 Buqsha = 1 Halala
Rub ushr = 1/40 Riyal = 1 Buqsha
SILVER
Nisf ushr = 1/20 Riyal = 2 Buqsha = 1/2 Bawlah
Nisf thumn = 1/16 Riyal = 2-1/2 Buqsha
Ushr = 1/10 Riyal = 4 Buqsha = 1 Bawlah
Thumn = 1/8 Riyal = 5 Buqsha
Rub = 1/4 Riyal = 10 Buqsha
Nisf = 1/2 Riyal = 20 Buqsha
1 Riyal (Imadi, Ahmadi) = 40 Buqsha

ARAB REPUBLIC
1/80 RIYAL
(1/2 Buqsha)

BRONZE

Y#	Date	Mintage	VF	XF	Unc
20	AH1382	—	.50	2.00	5.00

NOTE: Varieties exist.

	Rev: Full star.				
21.1	AH1382	—	2.00	6.00	15.00
	Rev: Outlined star.				
21.2	AH1382	—	2.00	6.00	15.00
	13882 (error)				

NOTE: Varieties exist.

1/2 BUQSHA

BRONZE

Y#	Date	Mintage	VF	XF	Unc
32	AH1382	—	3.00	5.00	9.00

NOTE: Varieties exist.

COPPER-ALUMINUM

Y#	Date	Year Mintage	VF	XF	Unc
26	AH1382	1963 10.000	.15	.20	.30

NOTE: Y#26-31 were struck at Cairo.

1/40 RIYAL
(1 Buqsha)

BRASS or BRONZE

Y#	Date	Mintage	VF	XF	Unc
22	AH1382	—	.75	1.00	2.25
	1383/282	—	—	—	—
	1383	—	1.50	2.25	6.00
	1384/284	—	—	—	—
	1384/3	—	—	—	—
	1384	—	4.00	7.50	20.00

NOTE: Dated both sides; AH1382, AH1383 and AH1384/3 are dated AH1382 on obverse, actual date on reverse; AH1384 and AH1384/284 dated AH1384 on both sides. There are varieties of date size and design.

BUQSHA

COPPER-ALUMINUM

Y#	Date	Year Mintage	VF	XF	Unc
27	AH1382	1963 10.377	.20	.30	.50

1/20 RIYAL
(2 Buqsha)

.720 SILVER
Thick variety, 1.10-1.60 g
Rev: 3 stones in top row of wall.

Y#	Date	Mintage	VF	XF	Unc
23.1	AH1382	—	6.00	10.00	30.00

Thin variety, 0.60-0.90 g
Rev: 2 stones in top row of wall.

23.2	AH1382	—	2.00	4.00	10.00

2 BUQSHA

COPPER-ALUMINUM

Y#	Date	Year Mintage	VF	XF	Unc
A27	AH1382	1963 —	.25	.60	.85

1/10 RIYAL
(4 Buqsha)

.720 SILVER
Thick variety, 2.40-3.00 g.
Rev: 3 or 4 stones in top row of wall within circle.

Y#	Date	Mintage	VF	XF	Unc
24.1	AH1382	—	5.00	10.00	20.00

Thin variety, 1.40-1.80 g.
Rev: 4 stones in top row of wall.

Y#	Date	Mintage	VF	XF	Unc
24.2	AH1382	—	2.00	4.00	10.00

NOTE: Edge varieties, varying number of stones in wall, exist.

5 BUQSHA

.720 SILVER

Y#	Date	Year	Mintage	VF	XF	Unc
28	AH1382	1963	1.600	1.25	1.50	2.50

2/10 RIYAL
(8 Buqsha)

.720 SILVER
Thick variety, 5.80-6.50 g.

Y#	Date	Mintage	VF	XF	Unc
25.1	AH1382	—	8.00	15.00	25.00

Thin variety, 4.90-5.10 g.

Y#	Date	Mintage	VF	XF	Unc
25.2	AH1382	—	60.00	100.00	150.00

1/4 RIYAL
(10 Buqsha)

.720 SILVER
Thick variety, 6.00-7.30 g.

Y#	Date	Mintage	VF	XF	Unc
A25.1	AH1382	—	40.00	65.00	150.00

Thin variety, 4.00-4.60 g.

Y#	Date	Mintage	VF	XF	Unc
A25.2	AH1382	—	40.00	65.00	150.00

NOTE: Overstrikes over earlier 1/4 Riyal coins exist.

10 BUQSHA

5.0000 g, .720 SILVER, .1157 oz ASW

Y#	Date	Year	Mintage	VF	XF	Unc
29	AH1382	1963	1.024	2.00	2.25	3.25

20 BUQSHA

9.8500 g, .720 SILVER, .2280 oz ASW

Y#	Date	Year	Mintage	VF	XF	Unc
30	AH1382	1963	1.016	4.00	5.00	7.00

RIYAL

19.7500 g, .720 SILVER, .4571 oz ASW

Y#	Date	Year	Mintage	VF	XF	Unc
31	AH1382	1963	4.614	5.00	6.00	9.00

DECIMAL COINAGE
MONETARY SYSTEM

Falus, Fulus   Fals, Fils   Falsan, Filsan
100 Fils = 1 Riyal

FILS

ALUMINUM

Y#	Date	Year	Mintage	VF	XF	Unc
33	AH1394	1974	*1.000	3.00	5.00	10.00
	1394	1974	5,024	—	Proof	1.50
	1400	1980	.010	—	Proof	1.50

***NOTE:** It is doubtful that the entire mintage was released to circulation.

F.A.O. Issue

Y#	Date	Year	Mintage	VF	XF	Unc
43	AH1398	1978	7,050	—	1.25	3.00

5 FILS

BRASS

Y#	Date	Year	Mintage	VF	XF	Unc
34	AH1394	1974	10.000	.50	1.00	2.50
	1394	1974	5,024	—	Proof	2.00
	1400	1980	.010	—	Proof	1.75

F.A.O. Issue

Y#	Date	Year	Mintage	VF	XF	Unc
38	AH1394	1974	.500	—	.10	.25

10 FILS

BRASS

---

25 FILS (continued — top)

Y#	Date	Year	Mintage	VF	XF	Unc
35	AH1394	1974	20.000	.50	1.00	2.50
	1394	1974	5,024	—	Proof	2.50
	1400	1980	.010	—	Proof	2.00

F.A.O. Issue

Y#	Date	Year	Mintage	VF	XF	Unc
39	AH1394	1974	.200	—	.10	.25

25 FILS

COPPER-NICKEL

Y#	Date	Year	Mintage	VF	XF	Unc
36	AH1394	1974	15.000	.25	.50	1.75
	1394	1974	5,024	—	Proof	3.00
	1399	1979	11.000	.25	.50	1.75
	1400	1980	.010	—	Proof	2.25

F.A.O. Issue

Y#	Date	Year	Mintage	VF	XF	Unc
40	AH1394	1974	.040	.20	.40	1.00

50 FILS

COPPER-NICKEL

Y#	Date	Year	Mintage	VF	XF	Unc
37	AH1394	1974	10.000	.35	.75	2.50
	1394	1974	5,024	—	Proof	3.50
	1399	1979	4.000	.35	.75	2.50
	1400	1980	.010	—	Proof	2.50
	1405	1985	—	.35	.75	2.50

F.A.O. Issue

Y#	Date	Year	Mintage	VF	XF	Unc
41	AH1394	1974	.025	.25	.50	1.25

RIYAL

12.0000 g, .925 SILVER, .3569 oz ASW
Qadhi Mohammed Mahmud Azzubairi Memorial

KM#	Date	Mintage	VF	XF	Unc
1	1969	3,200	—	Proof	12.50

COPPER-NICKEL

Y#	Date	Year	Mintage	VF	XF	Unc
42	AH1396	1976	7.800	.50	1.25	4.00

Y#	Date	Year	Mintage	VF	XF	Unc
42	1400	1980	—		Proof	5.00
	1405	1985	—	.50	1.25	4.00

F.A.O. Issue

44	AH1398	1978	7,050	—	2.00	5.00

REPUBLIC OF YEMEN
RIYAL

STAINLESS STEEL

KM#	Date	Year	Mintage	VF	XF	Unc
25	AH1414	1993	—	—	—	1.25

5 RIYALS

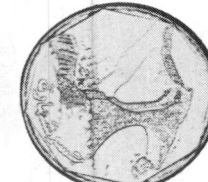

STAINLESS STEEL

26	AH1414	1993	—	—	—	1.75

10 RIYALS

STAINLESS STEEL
Bridge at Shaharah

27	AH1416	1995	—	—	—	2.75

SOUTH ARABIA

Fifteen of the sixteen Western Protectorate States, the Wahidi State of the Eastern Protectorate, and Aden Colony joined to form the Federation of South Arabia.

In 1959, Britain agreed to prepare South Arabia for full independence, which was achieved on Nov. 30, 1967, at which time South Arabia, including Aden, changed its name to the Peoples Republic of Southern Yemen. On Dec. 1, 1970, following the overthrow of the new government by the National Liberation Front, Southern Yemen changed its name to the Peoples Democratic Republic of Yemen.

TITLES
Al-Junubiya(t) al-Arabiya(t)
MONETARY SYSTEM
1000 Fils = 1 Dinar

FILS

ALUMINUM

KM#	Date	Mintage	VF	XF	Unc
1	1964	10.000	—	.10	.15
	1964			Proof	1.25

5 FILS

BRONZE

KM#	Date	Mintage	VF	XF	Unc
2	1964	10.000	.15	.25	.50
	1964			Proof	1.50

25 FILS

COPPER-NICKEL

3	1964	4.000	.25	.45	.85
	1964			Proof	2.00

50 FILS

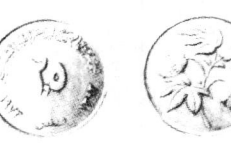

COPPER-NICKEL

4	1964	6.000	.45	.65	1.25
	1964		—	Proof	3.25

PEOPLES DEMOCRATIC REPUBLIC OF YEMEN
TITLES
Al-Jumhuriya(t) al-Yamaniya(t)
ad-Dimiqratiya(t) ash-Sha'biya(t)
MONETARY SYSTEM

Falus, Fulus   Fals, Fils   Falsan, Filsan
1000 Fils = 1 Dinar

2-1/2 FILS

ALUMINUM

KM#	Date	Year	Mintage	VF	XF	Unc
3	AH1393	1973	20.000	.25	.65	1.50

5 FILS

BRONZE

KM#	Date	Mintage	VF	XF	Unc
2	1971	2.000	.30	.60	1.00

5 FILS

ALUMINUM

KM#	Date	Year	Mintage	VF	XF	Unc
4	AH1393	1973	20.000	.15	.30	.60
	1404	1984	—	.15	.30	.60

10 FILS

ALUMINUM

KM#	Date	Mintage	VF	XF	Unc
9	1981	—	.35	.75	2.00

25 FILS

COPPER-NICKEL

5	1976	2.000	.25	.50	1.25
	1977	1.000	.25	.50	1.50
	1979	—	.25	.50	1.50
	1982	—	.25	.50	1.50
	1984	—	.25	.50	1.75

50 FILS

COPPER-NICKEL

6	1976	2.000	.35	.75	2.50
	1977	2.000	.35	.75	2.50
	1979	—	.35	.75	2.50
	1984	—	.35	.75	2.50

100 FILS

COPPER-NICKEL

10	1981	—	.50	1.00	3.00

250 FILS

COPPER-NICKEL

10th Anniversary of Independence

KM#	Date	Mintage	VF	XF	Unc
7	1977	.030	2.00	4.00	6.50

	1981	—	1.50	3.00	5.50
11					

YUGOSLAVIA

The Federal Republic of Yugoslavia, formerly the Socialist Federal Republic of Yugoslavia, a Balkan country located on the east shore of the Adriatic Sea, has an area of 39,450 sq. mi. (102,173 sq. km.) and a population of 10.5 million. Capital: Belgrade. The chief industries are agriculture, mining, manufacturing and tourism. Machinery, nonferrous metals, meat and fabrics are exported.

Yugoslavia was proclaimed on Dec. 1, 1918, after the union of the Kingdom of Serbia, Montenegro and the South Slav territories of Austria-Hungary; and changed its official name from the Kingdom of the Serbs, Croats and Slovenes to the Kingdom of Yugoslavia on Oct. 3, 1929. The republic was composed of six autonomous republics - Serbia, Croatia, Slovenia, Bosnia-Herzegovina, Macedonia and Montenegro - and two autonomous provinces within Serbia: Kosovo-Melohija and Vojvodina. The government of Yugoslavia attempted to remain neutral in World War II but, yielding to German pressure, aligned itself with the Axis powers in March of 1941; a few days later it was overthrown by revolutionary forces and its neutrality reasserted. The Nazis occupied the country on April 6, and throughout the remaining war years were resisted by a number of guerrilla armies, notably that of Marshal Josip Broz Tito. After the defeat of the Axis powers, a leftist coalition headed by Tito abolished the monarchy and, on Jan. 31, 1946, established a "People's Republic".

The collapse of the Federal Republic during 1991-1992 has resulted in the autonomous republics of Croatia, Slovenia, Bosnia-Herzegovina and Macedonia declaring their respective independence. Bosnia-Herzegovina is under military contest with the Serbian, Croat and Muslim populace opposing each other. Besides the remainder of the older Serbian sectors, a Serbian enclave in Knin located in southern Croatia has emerged called REPUBLIKE SRPSKE KRAJINE or Serbian Republic - Krajina whose capital is Knin and has also declared its independence in 1992 when the former Republics of Serbia and Montenegro became the Federal Republic of Yugoslavia.

The name Yugoslavia appears on the coinage in letters of the Cyrillic alphabet alone until formation of the Federated Peoples Republic of Yugoslavia in 1953, after which both the Cyrillic and Latin alphabets are employed. From 1965, the coin denomination appears in the 4 different languages of the federated republics in letters of both the Cyrillic and Latin alphabets.

DENOMINATIONS
Para ПАРА
Dinar ДИНАР, Dinara ДИНАРА
Dinari ДИНАРИ, Dinarjev

RULERS
Petar I, 1918-1921
Alexander I, 1921-1934
Petar II, 1934-1945

MINT MARKS
(a) - Paris, privy marks only
(b) - Brussels
(k) - КОВНИЦА, А.Д. = Kovnica, A.D.
 (Akcionarno Drustvo) Belgrade
(l) - London
(p) - Poissy (thunderbolt)
(v) - Vienna

MONETARY SYSTEM
100 Para = 1 Dinar

KINGDOM OF THE SERBS, CROATS AND SLOVENES

5 PARA

			ZINC			
KM#	Date	Mintage	Fine	VF	XF	Unc
1	1920(v)	3.826	3.00	7.50	15.00	40.00

10 PARA

			ZINC			
2	1920(v)	58.946		1.50	3.50	7.50	20.00

25 PARA

			NICKEL-BRONZE			
3	1920(v)	48.173		1.50	3.00	7.00	18.00

50 PARA

			NICKEL-BRONZE			
4	1925(b)	24.500	.50	1.00	2.00	6.00
	1925(p)	25.000	.50	1.50	3.00	7.00

DINAR

			NICKEL-BRONZE			
5	1925(b)	37.500	.50	1.00	2.00	6.00
	1925(p)	37.000	.75	1.50	3.00	7.00

2 DINARA

			NICKEL-BRONZE			
6	1925(b)	29.500	1.00	2.00	5.00	12.00
	1925(p)	25.004	1.00	2.50	5.50	14.00

20 DINARA

		6.4516 g, .900 GOLD, .1867 oz AGW			
7	1925(a)	1,000	125.00	150.00	185.00	240.00
	1925(a)	—	—	—	Proof	

KINGDOM OF YUGOSLAVIA

25 PARA

BRONZE

KM#	Date	Mintage	Fine	VF	XF	Unc
17	1938	40.000	1.25	2.00	4.00	12.00
	1938				Proof	

50 PARA

ALUMINUM-BRONZE

18	1938	100.000	.50	1.00	2.00	6.00

DINAR

ALUMINUM-BRONZE

19	1938	100.000	.50	.75	1.75	5.00
	1938				Proof	

2 DINARA

ALUMINUM-BRONZE, 14mm crown

20	1938	74.250	.50	1.00	2.50	7.00
	1938				Proof	

12mm crown

21	1938		.750	4.00	8.00	16.00	35.00
	1938					Proof	

10 DINARA

7.0000 g, .500 SILVER, .1125 oz ASW

10	1931(l)	16.000	2.00	4.00	8.00	17.50
	1931(l)				Proof	
	1931(a)	4.000	3.50	7.00	15.00	32.00
	1931(a)				Proof	

NICKEL

22	1938	25.000	.50	1.00	2.00	4.00

20 DINARA

14.0000 g, .500 SILVER, .2250 oz ASW

KM#	Date	Mintage	Fine	VF	XF	Unc
11	1931(k)	12.500	BV	6.00	12.00	32.00
	1931(k)	—	—	—	Proof	—

9.0000 g, .750 SILVER, .2170 oz ASW

23	1938	15.000	BV	2.50	4.50	10.00

50 DINARA

23.3300 g, .750 SILVER, .5626 oz ASW

16	1932(k)	5.500	10.00	22.00	45.00	175.00
	1932(l)	5.500	10.00	25.00	50.00	200.00
	1932(l)	—	—	—	Proof	2200.

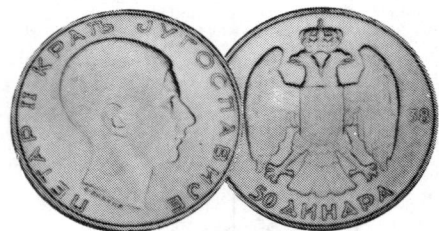

15.0000 g, .750 SILVER, .3617 oz ASW

24	1938	10.000	3.00	5.00	9.00	17.50

TRADE COINAGE

The Countermarks on these Trade issues were applied by the Yugoslav Control office for Noble Metals to confirm purity of the gold. The initial countermark displayed a sword but part way through the first year of production this was retired and the second countermark showing an ear of corn was put into use.

DUKAT

3.4900 g, .986 GOLD, .1106 oz AGW
c/m: Sword.
Obv. and rev: Small leg. w/ КОВНИЦА, А.Д. below head.

12.1	1931(k)	*.050	—	80.00	125.00	180.00
	1932(k) Inc. Be.				Rare	

NOTE: The 1932(k) examples with sword countermark are believed to be mint sports.

c/m: Ear of corn.
Obv. and rev: Small leg.

KM#	Date	Mintage	Fine	VF	XF	Unc
12.2	1931(k)	*.150	—	70.00	120.00	165.00
	1932(k)	*.070	—	80.00	125.00	175.00
	1933(k)	*.040	—	125.00	175.00	285.00
	1934(k)					
		*2,000	—	500.00	800.00	1200.

NOTE: Forgeries bearing no countermark exist for the 1932 and possibly other dates.

c/m: Sword.
Mule. Obv: KM#13.2. Rev: KM#12.1.

12.3	1931(k)	—	—	—	3000.	5000.

Obv. and rev: Large leg.

13.1	1931(k)	2,869	—	—	3500.	5500.

c/m: Sword.

13.2	1931(k) Inc. Ab.	—	—	—	4000.	6500.

NOTE: Large letter varieties bear the Kovnica, A.D. mint mark but were actually struck in Vienna.

4 DUKATA

13.9600 g, .986 GOLD, .4425 oz AGW
c/m: Sword.
Obv. and rev: Small leg.

14.1	1931(k)	*.010	—	450.00	750.00	950.00
	1932(k) Inc. Be.				Rare	

NOTE: The 1932(k) examples with sword countermark are believed to be mint sports.

c/m: Ear of corn.

14.2	1931(k)	*.015	—	450.00	750.00	950.00
	1932(k)	*.010	—	400.00	725.00	1000.
	1933(k)	*2,000	—	1000.	1600.	2500.
	1934(k)	—	—	2000.	3000.	4500.

Obv. and rev: W/o c/m.

14.3	1931(k)	—	—	—	Rare	—

NOTE: Only one genuine piece has been reported.

POST WAR COINAGE

1945-1946

50 PARA

ZINC

25	1945	40.000	.50	1.00	2.50	9.00

DINAR

KM#	Date	Mintage	Fine	VF	XF	Unc
26	1945	90.000	.50	1.00	2.50	7.00

ZINC

2 DINARA

ZINC						
27	1945	70.000	.50	1.25	3.00	9.00

5 DINARA

ZINC						
28	1945	50.000	.50	1.25	3.50	10.00

FEDERAL PEOPLES REPUBLIC

1946-1963

50 PARA

ALUMINUM						
29	1953	—	—	—	.10	.25

DINAR

ALUMINUM						
30	1953	—	—	.10	.15	.25

2 DINARA

ALUMINUM						
31	1953	—	—	.10	.20	.30

5 DINARA

ALUMINUM						
32	1953	—	.10	.25	.50	.75

10 DINARA

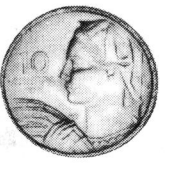

ALUMINUM-BRONZE						
KM#	Date	Mintage	Fine	VF	XF	Unc
33	1955		.15	.30	.75	1.50

20 DINARA

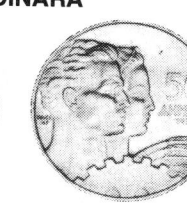

ALUMINUM-BRONZE						
34	1955		.25	.50	1.00	2.00

50 DINARA

ALUMINUM-BRONZE						
35	1955	—	.25	.50	1.50	3.00

SOCIALIST FEDERAL REPUBLIC

1963-1992

MONETARY SYSTEMS
Commencing 1964
100 Old Dinara = 1 New Dinara
Commencing 1990
10,000 Old Dinara = 1 New Dinara

5 PARA

COPPER-ZINC						
42	1965	23.839	—	.10	.20	.40

43	1965	16.200	—	—	.10	.20
	1973	36.384	—	—	.10	.15
	1974	3.628	—	—	.10	.25
	1975	20.272	—	—	.10	.15
	1976	30.490	—	—	.10	.15
	1977	10.270	—	—	.10	.15
	1978	12.000	—	—	.10	.15
	1979	20.414	—	—	.10	.15
	1980	22.412	—	—	.10	.15
	1981	.630	—	.10	.25	.50

10 PARA

COPPER-ZINC						
44	1965	15.400	—	—	.10	.20
	1973	16.647	—	—	.10	.20
	1974	60.139	—	—	.10	.20
	1975	36.954	—	—	.10	.15
	1976	36.111	—	—	.10	.15
	1977	40.451	—	—	.10	.15
	1978	50.129	—	—	.10	.15
	1979	89.738	—	—	.10	.15
	1980	90.111	—	—	.10	.15
	1981	14.090	—	—	.10	.15

KM#	Date	Mintage	Fine	VF	XF	Unc
139	1990	174.028	—	—	.10	.15
	1991	60.828	—	—	.15	.35

20 PARA

COPPER-ZINC						
45	1965	—	—	—	.10	.30
	1973	30.448	—	—	.10	.30
	1974	31.364	—	—	.10	.30
	1975	44.683	—	—	.10	.30
	1976	33.312	—	—	.10	.30
	1977	40.782	—	—	.10	.30
	1978	39.999	—	—	.10	.30
	1979	49.121	—	—	.10	.30
	1980	73.757	—	—	.10	.30
	1981	96.144	—	—	.10	.30

140	1990	41.353	—	.10	.20	.50
	1991	43.118	—	.10	.20	.50

25 PARA

BRONZE						
84	1982	185.316	—	—	.10	.25
	1983	65.290	—	—	.15	.30

50 PARA

COPPER-ZINC						
	Rev: Narrow 0 in denomination.					
46.1	1965	—	—	.10	.20	.65
	1973	23.739	—	.10	.20	.65
	1974	.033	1.00	1.50	2.50	5.00
	1975	10.220	—	.10	.20	.80
	1976	8.438	—	.10	.20	1.00
	1977	17.864	—	.10	.20	.75
	1978	40.177	—	.10	.20	.65
	1979	3.021	.50	1.00	2.00	5.00

	Rev: Wide 0 in denomination.					
46.2	1979	12.278	.20	.50	1.00	2.50
	1980	24.974	—	.10	.20	.65
	1981	40.319	—	.10	.20	.65

BRONZE						
85	1982	79.584	—	—	.10	.20
	1983	72.100	—	—	.10	.20
	1984	59.642	.25	.50	1.00	1.50

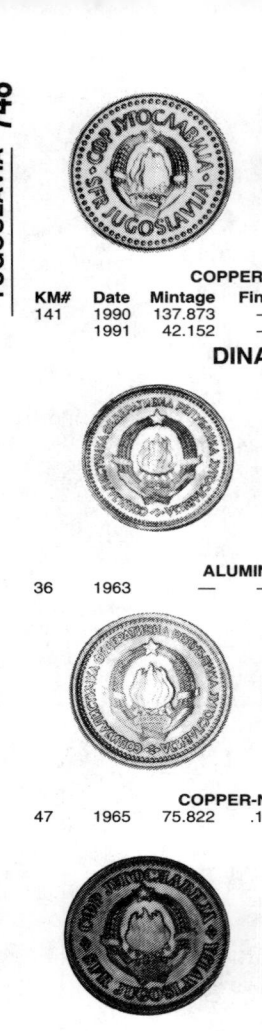

5 DINARA

COPPER-ZINC

KM#	Date	Mintage	Fine	VF	XF	Unc
141	1990	137.873	—	—	.10	.20
	1991	42.152	—	.20	.40	1.00

DINAR

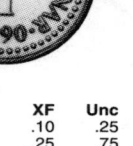

COPPER-NICKEL-ZINC

KM#	Date	Mintage	Fine	VF	XF	Unc
142	1990	172.105	—	—	.10	.25
	1991	79.549	—	.15	.25	.75

ALUMINUM

KM#	Date	Mintage	Fine	VF	XF	Unc
38	1963	—	.10	.20	.35	.50

COPPER-NICKEL-ZINC
F.A.O. Issue

56	1970	.500	.20	.50	1.00	2.00

ALUMINUM

36	1963	—	—	—	.10	.15

2 DINARA

ALUMINUM

37	1963	—	—	.10	.15	.25

COPPER-NICKEL

47	1965	75.822	.10	.15	.30	.60

COPPER-NICKEL-ZINC
F.A.O. Issue

55	1970	.500	—	.20	.40	1.00

Regular Issue

58	1971	10.224	.20	.40	.60	1.00
	1972	27.974	.10	.20	.35	.60
	1973	12.705	.20	.40	.60	1.00
	1974	6.054	.25	.50	1.00	2.00
	1975	12.533	.10	.20	.35	.60
	1976	4.965	.10	.25	.40	.80
	1977	.922	.30	.60	1.20	2.50
	1978	1.000	.10	.25	.50	1.50
	1979	3.000	.10	.25	.40	.80
	1980	9.977	.10	.20	.35	.60
	1981	15.450	.10	.20	.35	.60

48	1968	35.497	.10	.20	.40	.80

57	1971	10.413	—	.10	.30	.70
	1972	18.440	—	.10	.20	.50
	1973	31.848	—	.10	.20	.45
	1974	10.989	—	.10	.20	.50
	1975	.092	2.00	4.00	7.50	15.00
	1976	6.092	—	.10	.20	.50
	1977	19.335	—	.10	.20	.50
	1978	13.035	—	.10	.20	.50
	1979	20.069	—	.10	.20	.45
	1980	36.088	—	.10	.20	.45
	1981	42.599	—	.10	.20	.45

COPPER-NICKEL-ZINC

59	1973	18.974	—	.10	.15	.40
	1974	42.724	—	.10	.15	.35
	1975	30.260	—	.10	.15	.35
	1976	21.849	—	.10	.15	.35
	1977	30.468	—	.10	.15	.35
	1978	35.032	—	.10	.15	.35
	1979	39.848	—	.10	.15	.35
	1980	60.630	—	.10	.15	.35
	1981	56.650	—	.10	.15	.35

30th Anniversary of Nazi Defeat

60	1975	1.020	.25	.50	1.00	2.00

F.A.O. Issue

61	1976	.500	—	.10	.20	.50

NICKEL-BRASS

87	1982	40.632	—	.10	.15	.35
	1983	35.468	—	.10	.15	.35
	1984	51.500	—	.10	.15	.35
	1985	81.100	—	.10	.15	.35
	1986	50.453	—	.10	.15	.35

NICKEL-BRASS

88	1982	40.956	—	.10	.15	.50
	1983	40.156	—	.10	.15	.50
	1984	33.023	—	.10	.15	.50
	1985	94.422	—	.10	.15	.50
	1986	37.199	—	.10	.15	.50

NICKEL-BRASS

86	1982	70.105	—	—	.10	.30
	1983	114.180	—	—	.10	.20
	1984	172.185	—	—	.10	.20
	1985	64.436	—	—	.10	.25
	1986	122.643	—	—	.10	.20

COPPER-NICKEL-ZINC

143	1990	15.936	.15	.30	.60	2.00
	1991	32.836	—	.20	.40	1.00
	1992	—	2.50	3.50	7.00	12.50

COPPER-NICKEL-ZINC

144	1990	9.354	.25	.45	1.00	2.50
	1991	113.420	—	.25	.50	1.25
	1992	—	1.50	2.50	4.00	7.00

1990 Chess Olympiad - Logo

KM#	Date	Mintage	Fine	VF	XF	Unc
145	1990	.020	—	—	Proof	6.00

10 DINARA

ALUMINUM-BRONZE

39	1963	—	.15	.30	.75	1.25

COPPER-NICKEL

62	1976	10.550	.30	.60	.75	1.25
	1977	39.645	.30	.60	.75	1.00
	1978	29.834	.30	.60	.75	1.00
	1979	4.969	.30	.60	.75	1.00
	1980	10.139	.30	.60	.75	1.00
	1981	20.116	.30	.60	.75	1.00

COPPER-NICKEL-ZINC
F.A.O. Issue

63	1976	.500	.50	.75	1.00	2.50

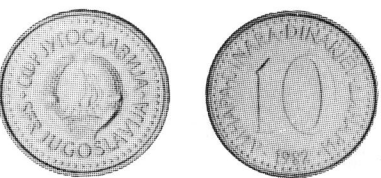

COPPER-NICKEL

89	1982	8.862	—	.10	.20	.80
	1983	42.400	—	.10	.20	.75
	1984	30.900	—	.10	.20	.75
	1985	31.647	—	.10	.20	.75
	1986	40.739	—	.10	.20	.75
	1987	104.988	—	.10	.20	.75
	1988	27.614	—	.10	.20	.75

40th Anniversary - Battle of Neretva River

96	1983	.900	—	1.00	1.50	3.00
	1983	.100	—	—	Proof	9.00

40th Anniversary - Battle of Sutjeska River

KM#	Date	Mintage	Fine	VF	XF	Unc
97.1	(1983)	.900	—	1.00	1.50	3.00
	(1983)	.100	—	—	Proof	9.00

Rev: W/o pathway in front of monument.

97.2	(1983)	—	—	3.00	6.00	10.00

BRASS

131	1988	35.992	—	—	.10	.25
	1989	75.000	—	—	.10	.25

20 DINARA

ALUMINUM-BRONZE

40	1963	—	.50	1.00	1.75	3.50

COPPER-ZINC-NICKEL

112	1985	5.000	—	.10	.15	.50
	1986	20.932	—	.10	.15	.35
	1987	39.514	—	.10	.15	.35

BRASS

132	1988	29.775	—	—	.10	.25
	1989	12.994	—	—	.10	.25

50 DINARA

ALUMINUM-BRONZE

41	1963	—	1.00	2.50	5.00	15.00

NOTE: Exists with filled letter in denomination.

COPPER-ZINC-NICKEL

113	1985	25.488	—	.10	.25	.75
	1986	20.353	—	.10	.25	.75
	1987	21.792	—	.10	.25	.75
	1988	28.370	—	.10	.25	.75

BRASS

KM#	Date	Mintage	Fine	VF	XF	Unc
133	1988	46.973	—	—	.10	.25
	1989	*2.999	—	.50	1.00	2.00

*NOTE: Currently not issued.

100 DINARA

COPPER-ZINC-NICKEL

KM#	Date	Mintage	VF	XF	Unc
114	1985	18.684	.25	.65	1.50
	1986	17.905	.20	.50	1.00
	1987	94.069	—	.40	.80
	1988	50.294	—	.40	.80

BRASS

134	1988	12.610	—	.15	.30
	1989	124.260	—	.15	.30

FEDERAL REPUBLIC

MONETARY SYSTEMS
1992-1993
10 Old Dinara = 1 New Dinar
1993
1 Million Old Dinara = 1 New Dinar
1.1.1994
1 Billion Old Dinara = 1 Novi (New) Dinar

PARA

BRASS

161	1994	25.350	—	—	.35

5 PARA

BRASS

164.1	1994	30.408	—	—	.50
	1995	3.400	—	—	.60

Reduced size, 17mm.

164.2	1996		—	—	.50

10 PARA

COPPER-NICKEL-ZINC

162.1	1994	52.161	—	—	.50
	1995	31.041	—	—	.50

BRASS

KM#	Date	Mintage	VF	XF	Unc
162.1a	1995	Inc. Ab.	—	—	.75

Reduced size.

162.2	1996		—	—	.65

Obv: Heraldic double eagle shield.
Rev: Denomination.

173	1996		—	—	.50
	1997		—	—	.50

50 PARA

COPPER-NICKEL-ZINC

163	1994	45.013	—	—	.75

BRASS

163a	1995	19.193	—	—	1.00

Obv: Heraldic double eagle shield.

174	1996		—	—	1.00
	1997		—	—	1.00

DINAR

COPPER-ZINC

149	1992	49.269	.10	.30	.60

COPPER-ZINC-NICKEL

154	1993	20.249	.10	.20	.50

BRASS

160	1994		—	—	1.00

NOVI DINAR

COPPER-NICKEL-ZINC

165	1994	47.755	—	—	1.00
	1995	10.359	—	—	1.25

Reduced size.

168	1996		—	—	1.00

2 DINARA

COPPER-ZINC

KM#	Date	Mintage	VF	XF	Unc
150	1992	10.571	.20	.40	1.00

COPPER-ZINC-NICKEL

155	1993	10.263	.10	.20	.50

5 DINARA

COPPER-ZINC

151	1992	26.658	.15	.30	.75

COPPER-ZINC-NICKEL

156	1993	10.135	.10	.20	.50

10 DINARA

COPPER-ZINC-NICKEL

152	1992	76.607	.10	.25	.60
157	1993	—	.15	.30	.70

50 DINARA

COPPER-ZINC-NICKEL

153	1992	50.571	.25	.50	1.00
158	1993	—	.20	.40	.80

100 DINARA

BRASS

KM#	Date	Mintage	VF	XF	Unc
159	1993		.25	.50	1.00

500 DINARA

BRASS

167	1993	20.475*	—	—	6.50

*NOTE: Reportedly all but 1,000 remelted. Not released for circulation.

MONTENEGRO

The former independent kingdom of Montenegro, now one of the nominally autonomous federated units of Yugoslavia, was located in southeastern Europe north of Albania. As a kingdom, it had an area of 5,333 sq. mi. (13,812 sq. km.) and a population of about 250,000. Capital: Podgorica.

Montenegro became an independent state in 1355 following the break-up of the Serb empire. During the Turkish invasion of Albania and Herzegovina in the 15th century, the Montenegrins moved their capital to the remote mountain village of Cetinje where they maintained their independence through two centuries of intermittent attack, emerging as the only one of the Balkan states not subjugated by the Turks. When World War I began, Montenegro joined with Serbia and was subsequently invaded and occupied by the Austrians. Austria withdrew upon the defeat of the Central Powers, permitting the Serbians to move in and maintain the occupation. Montenegro then joined the kingdom of the Serbs, Croats and Slovenes, which later became Yugoslavia.

The coinage, issued under the autocratic rule of Prince Nicholas, is obsolete.

RULERS
Nicholas I, as Prince, 1860-1910
   as King, 1910-1918

MINT MARKS
(a) - Paris, privy marks only

MONETARY SYSTEM
100 Para, ΠΑΡΑ = 1 Perper, ΠΕΡΠΕР

PARA

BRONZE

KM#	Date	Mintage	Fine	VF	XF	Unc
1	1906	.200	8.00	16.00	35.00	75.00

| 16 | 1913 | .100 | 12.50 | 25.00 | 60.00 | 125.00 |
| | 1914 | .200 | 6.00 | 12.00 | 25.00 | 70.00 |

2 PARE

BRONZE

2	1906	.600	4.00	8.00	18.00	35.00
	1908	.250	8.00	18.00	32.00	70.00

17	1913	.500	4.00	7.50	15.00	30.00
	1914	.400	4.50	9.00	18.00	45.00

10 PARA

NICKEL

3	1906	.750	2.50	5.00	12.00	25.00
	1908	.250	3.00	6.50	16.00	32.00

KM#	Date	Mintage	Fine	VF	XF	Unc
18	1913	.200	3.50	8.00	17.50	35.00
	1914	.800	2.50	5.00	12.00	25.00

20 PARA

NICKEL

4	1906	.600	3.00	6.00	12.00	25.00
	1908	.400	3.00	7.00	15.00	30.00

19	1913	.200	4.00	8.00	18.00	38.00
	1914	.800	3.00	6.00	12.00	25.00

PERPER

5.0000 g, .835 SILVER, .1342 oz ASW

5	1909(a)	*.500	10.00	20.00	40.00	90.00

***NOTE:** Approximately 30% melted.

14	1912	.520	8.00	14.00	30.00	80.00
	1914	.500	9.00	18.00	35.00	90.00

2 PERPERA

10.0000 g, .835 SILVER, .2685 oz ASW

7	1910	.300	15.00	30.00	65.00	160.00

20	1914	.200	15.00	35.00	75.00	170.00

5 PERPERA

24.0000 g, .900 SILVER, .6944 oz ASW

KM#	Date	Mintage	Fine	VF	XF	Unc
6	1909(a)	*.060	60.00	120.00	250.00	700.00

***NOTE:** Approximately 50% melted.

15	1912	.040	75.00	150.00	275.00	700.00
	1914	.020	85.00	160.00	300.00	950.00

SERBIA

Serbia, a former inland Balkan kingdom has an area of 34,116 sq. mi. (88,361 sq. km.). Capital: Belgrade.

Serbia emerged as a separate kingdom in the 12th century and attained its greatest expansion and political influence in the mid-14th century. After the Battle of Kosovo, 1389, Serbia became a vassal principality of Turkey and remained under Turkish suzerainty until it was re-established as an independent kingdom by the 1887 Treaty of Berlin. Following World War I, which had its immediate cause in the assassination of Austrian Archduke Francis Ferdinand by a Serbian nationalist, Serbia joined with the Croats and Slovenes to form the new Kingdom of the South Slavs with Peter I of Serbia as king. The name of the kingdom was later changed to Yugoslavia. Invaded by Germany during World War II, Serbia emerged as a constituent republic of the Socialist Federal Republic of Yugoslavia.

RULERS

Alexander I, 1889-1902
Peter I, 1903-1918

MINT MARKS

A - Paris
(a) - Paris, privy mark only
(g) - Gorham Mfg. Co., Providence, R.I.
H - Birmingham
V - Vienna
БП (BP) Budapest

MONETARY SYSTEM

100 Para = 1 Dinara

DENOMINATIONS

ПАРА = Para
ПАРЕ = Pare
ДИНАР = Dinar
ДИНАРА = Dinara

KINGDOM

2 PARE

BRONZE
Medal struck.

KM#	Date	Mintage	Fine	VF	XF	Unc
23	1904	12.500	2.00	5.00	14.00	35.00

5 PARA

COPPER-NICKEL
Medal struck.

18	1904*	8.000	1.00	2.50	5.00	12.00
	1904	Inc. Ab.	—	—	Proof	200.00
	1912*	10.000	.75	1.50	3.50	9.00
	1912	—	—	—	Proof	120.00
	1917(g)	5.000	5.00	10.00	20.00	32.00

NOTE: Earlier dates (1883-1884) exist for this type.

10 PARA

COPPER-NICKEL
Medal struck.

19	1904	—	—	—	Proof	350.00
	1912	7.700	.75	1.25	3.50	8.00
	1912	—	—	—	Proof	120.00
	1917(g)	5.000	1.00	2.50	7.00	22.00
	1917(g)	—	—	—	Proof	200.00

NOTE: Earlier dates (1883-1884) exist for this type.

20 PARA

COPPER-NICKEL
Medal struck.

KM#	Date	Mintage	Fine	VF	XF	Unc
20	1904	—	—	—	Proof	400.00
	1912	5.650	.75	2.00	4.50	9.00
	1912	—	—	—	Proof	125.00
	1917(g)	5.000	1.00	3.00	9.00	25.00

NOTE: Earlier dates (1883-1884) exist for this type.

50 PARA

2.5000 g, .835 SILVER, .0671 oz ASW
Obv: Designers signature below neck.
Medal struck.

24.1	1904	1.400	2.00	5.00	12.00	28.00
	1904	—	—	—	Proof	200.00
	1912	.800	2.50	6.00	15.00	30.00
	1915(a)	12.138	1.00	2.00	4.50	12.00

Obv: W/o designers signature.

24.2	1915(a)	1.862	5.00	10.00	25.00	85.00

DINAR

5.0000 g, .835 SILVER, .1342 oz ASW
Obv: Designers signature below neck.
Medal struck.

25.1	1904	.994	4.50	12.00	25.00	65.00
	1904	—	—	—	Proof	250.00
	1912	8.000	3.00	6.00	15.00	35.00
	1915(a)	10.688	2.00	4.00	8.00	18.00

Obv: W/o designers signature.

25.2	1915(a)	2.322	4.50	12.00	25.00	65.00

2 DINARA

10.0000 g, .835 SILVER, .2684 oz ASW
Obv: Designers signature below neck.
Medal struck.

26.1	1904	1.150	7.50	15.00	32.00	80.00
	1904	—	—	—	Proof	325.00
	1912	.800	8.00	16.00	35.00	85.00
	1915(a)	4.174	5.00	10.00	18.00	35.00

Obv: W/o designers signature.

26.2	1915(a)	.826	7.50	16.50	37.50	90.00

5 DINARA

25.0000 g, .900 SILVER, .7234 oz ASW
100th Anniversary - Karageorgevich Dynasty

Edge Type 1: БОГ*ЧУВА*СРБИЈУ***						
KM#	Date	Mintage	Fine	VF	XF	Unc
27	1904	.200	40.00	80.00	175.00	650.00
	1904	—	—	—	Proof	2000.
Edge Type 2: БОГ*СРБИЈУ*ЧУВА***						
28	1904	Inc. Ab.	150.00	250.00	425.00	1500.

GERMAN OCCUPATION WW II

50 PARA

ZINC

30	1942БП	—	2.00	4.50	10.00	18.00

DINAR

ZINC

31	1942БП	—	.50	1.50	5.00	13.00

2 DINARA

ZINC

32	1942БП	—	.50	1.50	6.00	15.00

10 DINARA

ZINC

33	1943БП	1.750	1.00	2.50	7.50	18.00

ZAMBIA

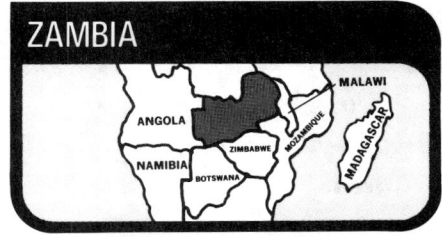

The Republic of Zambia (formerly Northern Rhodesia), a landlocked country in south-central Africa, has an area of 290,586 sq. mi. (752,610 sq. km.) and a population of *7.9 million. Capital: Lusaka. The economy of Zambia is based principally on copper, of which Zambia is the world's third largest producer. Copper, zinc, lead, cobalt and tobacco are exported.

The area that is now Zambia was brought within the British sphere of influence in 1888 by empire builder Cecil Rhodes, who obtained mining concessions in southcentral Africa from indigenous chiefs. The territory was ruled by the British South Africa Company, which Rhodes established, until 1924 when its administration was transferred to the British government as a protectorate. In 1953, Northern Rhodesia was joined with Nyasaland and the colony of Southern Rhodesia to form the Federation of Rhodesia and Nyasaland. Northern Rhodesia seceded from the Federation on Oct. 24, 1964, and became the independent Republic of Zambia. Zambia is a member of the Commonwealth of Nations. The president is Chief of State.

Zambia converted to a decimal coinage on January 16, 1969.

For earlier coinage refer to Rhodesia and Nyasaland.

RULERS

British, until 1964

MONETARY SYSTEM

12 Pence = 1 Shilling
20 Shillings = 1 Pound

PENNY

BRONZE

KM#	Date	Mintage	Fine	VF	XF	Unc
5	1966	7.200	.15	.35	.65	1.75
	1966	60 pcs.	—	—	Proof	—

SIXPENCE

COPPER-NICKEL-ZINC
Morning Glory

1	1964	3.500	.15	.30	.60	1.20
	1964	5,000	—	Proof		1.50

6	1966	7.200	.25	.50	1.00	2.00
	1966	60 pcs.	—	—	Proof	

SHILLING

COPPER-NICKEL
Crowned Hornbill

2	1964	3.510	.25	.50	1.00	2.00
	1964	5,000	—	—	Proof	2.50

KM#	Date	Mintage	Fine	VF	XF	Unc
7	1966	5.000	.35	.75	1.50	3.25
	1966	60 pcs.	—	—	Proof	

2 SHILLINGS

COPPER-NICKEL
Bohor Reedbuck

3	1964	3.770	.35	.75	1.50	3.00
	1964	5,000	—	—	Proof	3.50

8	1966	5.000	.45	1.00	2.25	4.50
	1966	60 pcs.	—	—	Proof	

5 SHILLINGS

COPPER-NICKEL
1st Anniversary of Independence

4	1965	.010	—	2.00	3.00	4.50
	1965	.020	—	—	Proof	6.50

DECIMAL COINAGE

100 Ngwee = 1 Kwacha

NGWEE

BRONZE
Aardvark

KM#	Date	Mintage	VF	XF	Unc
9	1968	8.000	.10	.20	.80
	1968	4,000	—	Proof	1.25
	1969	16.000	.10	.15	.75
	1972	21.000	.10	.15	.75
	1978	23.976	.10	.15	.75
	1978	.024	—	Proof	1.50

COPPER-CLAD-STEEL

KM#	Date	Mintage	VF	XF	Unc
9a	1982	10.000	.10	.20	.75
	1983	60.000	.10	.15	.65

2 NGWEE

BRONZE
Martial Eagle

10	1968	19.000	.10	.20	1.00
	1968	4,000	—	Proof	1.50
	1978	—	.15		1.25
	1978	.024	—	Proof	1.75

COPPER-CLAD-STEEL

10a	1982	7.500	.10	.20	1.00
	1983	60.000	.10	.15	.50

5 NGWEE

COPPER-NICKEL
Morning Glory

11	1968	12.000	.20	.30	.60
	1968	4,000	—	Proof	1.75
	1972	9.000	.20	.30	.60
	1978	1.976	.20	.30	.60
	1978	.024	—	Proof	2.00
	1982	12.000	.20	.30	.60
	1987	10.000	.20	.30	.60

10 NGWEE

COPPER-NICKEL-ZINC
Crowned Hornbill

12	1968	1.000	.40	.85	1.75
	1968	4,000	—	Proof	2.00
	1972	1.000	.30	.50	1.00
	1978	1.976	.30	.50	1.00
	1978	.024	—	Proof	2.25
	1982	8.000	.30	.50	1.00
	1983	2,500	.30	.50	1.00
	1987	6.000	.30	.50	1.00

20 NGWEE

COPPER-NICKEL
Bohor Reedbuck

13	1968	1.500	.75	1.50	2.50
	1968	4,000	—	Proof	2.75
	1972	7.500	.50	1.00	2.00
	1978	.024	—	Proof	3.00
	1983	.998	.75	1.50	2.50
	1987	—	.50	1.00	2.00
	1988	3.000	.50	1.00	2.00

World Food Day

22	1981	.970	.75	1.50	2.75

20th Anniversary - Bank of Zambia

KM#	Date	Mintage	VF	XF	Unc
23	1985	—	.50	1.00	1.50

25 NGWEE

NICKEL PLATED STEEL
Crowned Hornbill

29	1992	—	—	—	.75

50 NGWEE

COPPER-NICKEL
F.A.O. Issue

14	ND(1969)	.070	2.00	3.50	5.50

F.A.O. Issue

15	1972	.510	1.00	2.00	3.50

Second Republic 13th December 1972

16	1972	6.000	1.00	2.00	4.00
	1972	2,000	—	Proof	7.00
	1978	.024	—	Proof	5.00
	1983	.998	1.00	2.00	4.00

40th Anniversary of United Nations

24	1985	—	1.00	1.25	2.50

NICKEL PLATED STEEL
Kafue Lechwe

KM#	Date	Mintage	VF	XF	Unc
30	1992				1.00

KWACHA

NICKEL-BRASS

26	1989	8.000	.50	1.00	2.00

BRASS

38	1992	—	—	—	1.00

5 KWACHA

BRASS
Oryx

31	1992	—	—	—	1.50

10 KWACHA

BRASS
Rhinoceros

32	1992	—	—	—	2.00

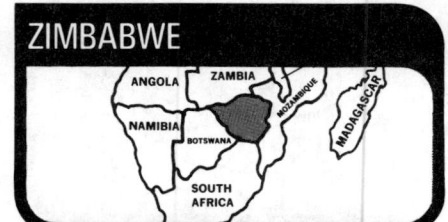

The Republic of Zimbabwe (formerly the Republic of Rhodesia or Southern Rhodesia), located in the east-central part of southern Africa, has an area of 150,804 sq. mi. (390,580 sq. km.) and a population of *10.1 million. Capital: Harare (formerly Salisbury). The economy is based on agriculture and mining. Tobacco, sugar, asbestos, copper, chrome, ore and coal are exported.

The Rhodesian area contains extensive evidence of the habitat of paleolithic man and earlier civilizations, notably the world-famous ruins of Zimbabwe, a gold-trading center that flourished about the 14th or 15th century A.D. The Portuguese of the 16th century were the first Europeans to attempt to develop south-central Africa, but it remained for Cecil Rhodes and the British South Africa Co. to open the hinterlands. Rhodes obtained a concession for mineral rights from local chiefs in 1888 and administered his African empire (named Southern Rhodesia in 1895) through the British South Africa Co. until 1923, when the British government annexed the area after the white settlers voted for existence as a separate entity, rather than for incorporation into the Union of South Africa. From Sept. of 1953 through 1963 Southern Rhodesia was joined with the British Protectorates of Northern Rhodesia and Nyasaland into a multiracial federation, known as the Federation of Rhodesia and Nyasaland. When the federation was dissolved at the end of 1963, Northern Rhodesia and Nyasaland became the independent states of Zambia and Malawi.

Britain was prepared to grant independence to Southern Rhodesia but declined to do so when the politically dominant white Rhodesians refused to give assurances of representative government. On Nov. 11, 1965, following two years of unsuccessful negotiation with the British government, Prime Minister Ian Smith issued an unilateral declaration of independence. Britain responded with economic sanctions supported by the United Nations. After further futile attempts to effect an accommodation, the Rhodesian Parliament severed all ties with Britain and on March 2, 1970, established the Republic of Rhodesia.

On March 3, 1978, Prime Minister Ian Smith and three moderate black nationalist leaders signed an agreement providing for black majority rule. The name of the country was changed to Zimbabwe Rhodesia. Following a conference in London in December 1979, the opposition government conceded and it was agreed that the British Government should resume control. A British Governor soon returned to Southern Rhodesia. One of his first acts was to affirm the nullification of the purported declaration of independence. On April 18, 1980 pursuant to an act of the British Parliament, the colony of Southern Rhodesia became independent within the Commonwealth as the Republic of Zimbabwe which remains a member of the British Commonwealth of Nations.

SOUTHERN RHODESIA

RULERS

British

MONETARY SYSTEM

12 Pence = 1 Shilling
2 Shillings = 1 Florin
5 Shillings = 1 Crown
20 Shillings = 1 Pound

1/2 PENNY

COPPER-NICKEL

KM#	Date	Mintage	Fine	VF	XF	Unc
6	1934	.240	1.00	2.00	8.00	22.50
	1934	—	—	—	Proof	125.00
	1936	.240	4.00	8.00	25.00	150.00
	1936	—	—	—	Proof	—

14	1938	.240	.75	1.75	6.50	20.00
	1938	—	—	—	Proof	—

KM#	Date	Mintage	Fine	VF	XF	Unc
14	1939	.480	1.00	2.00	9.00	60.00
	1939	—	—	—	Proof	—

BRONZE

KM#	Date	Mintage	Fine	VF	XF	Unc
14a	1942	.480	.60	1.50	3.50	25.00
	1942	—	—	—	Proof	—
	1943	.960	.35	.75	2.25	6.50
	1944	.960	.35	.75	2.50	8.00
	1944	—	—	—	Proof	—

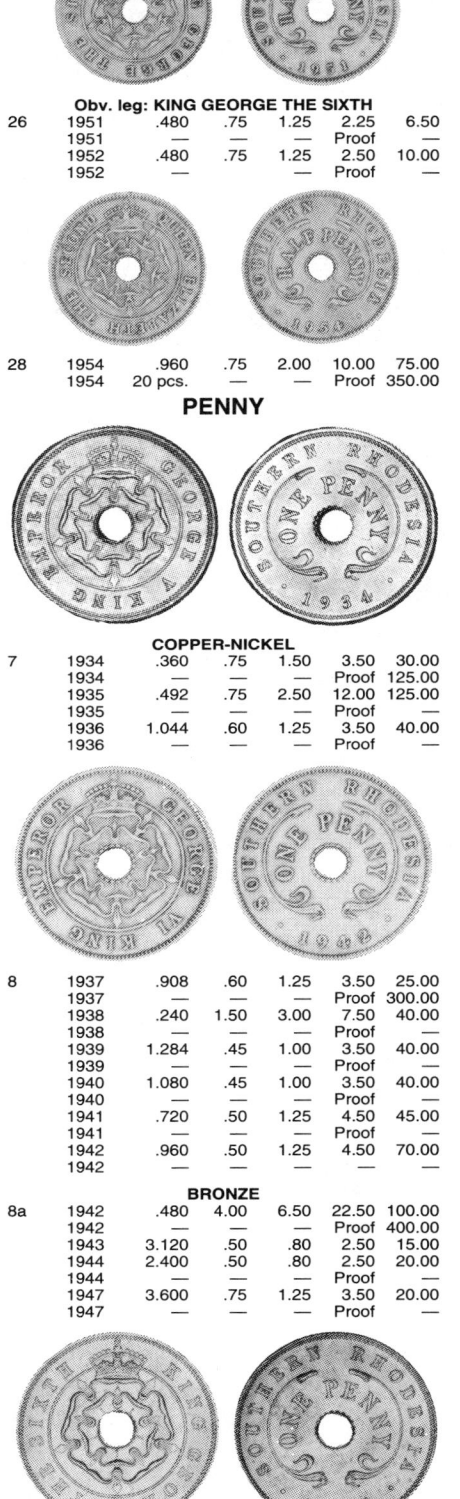

Obv. leg: KING GEORGE THE SIXTH

KM#	Date	Mintage	Fine	VF	XF	Unc
26	1951	.480	.75	1.25	2.25	6.50
	1951	—	—	—	Proof	—
	1952	.480	.75	1.25	2.50	10.00
	1952	—	—	—	Proof	—

KM#	Date	Mintage	Fine	VF	XF	Unc
28	1954	.960	.75	2.00	10.00	75.00
	1954	20 pcs.	—	—	Proof	350.00

PENNY

COPPER-NICKEL

KM#	Date	Mintage	Fine	VF	XF	Unc
7	1934	.360	.75	1.50	3.50	30.00
	1934	—	—	—	Proof	125.00
	1935	.492	.75	2.50	12.00	125.00
	1935	—	—	—	Proof	—
	1936	1.044	.60	1.25	3.50	40.00
	1936	—	—	—	Proof	—

KM#	Date	Mintage	Fine	VF	XF	Unc
8	1937	.908	.60	1.25	3.50	25.00
	1937	—	—	—	Proof	300.00
	1938	.240	1.50	3.00	7.50	40.00
	1938	—	—	—	Proof	—
	1939	1.284	.45	1.00	3.50	40.00
	1939	—	—	—	Proof	—
	1940	1.080	.45	1.00	3.50	40.00
	1940	—	—	—	Proof	—
	1941	.720	.50	1.25	4.50	45.00
	1941	—	—	—	Proof	—
	1942	.960	.50	1.25	4.50	70.00
	1942	—	—	—	Proof	—

BRONZE

KM#	Date	Mintage	Fine	VF	XF	Unc
8a	1942	.480	4.00	6.50	22.50	100.00
	1942	—	—	—	Proof	400.00
	1943	3.120	.50	.80	2.50	15.00
	1944	2.400	.50	.80	2.50	20.00
	1944	—	—	—	Proof	—
	1947	3.600	.75	1.25	3.50	20.00
	1947	—	—	—	Proof	—

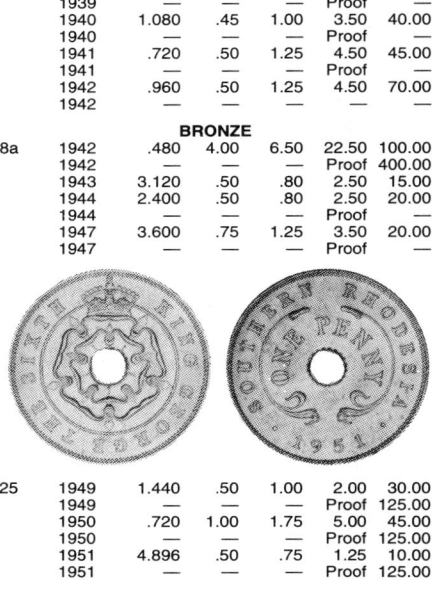

KM#	Date	Mintage	Fine	VF	XF	Unc
25	1949	1.440	.50	1.00	2.00	30.00
	1949	—	—	—	Proof	125.00
	1950	.720	1.00	1.75	5.00	45.00
	1950	—	—	—	Proof	125.00
	1951	4.896	.50	.75	1.25	10.00
	1951	—	—	—	Proof	125.00

KM#	Date	Mintage	Fine	VF	XF	Unc
25	1952	2.400	.50	.75	1.75	15.00
	1952	—	—	—	Proof	—

KM#	Date	Mintage	Fine	VF	XF	Unc
29	1954	.960	4.00	8.00	25.00	175.00
	1954	20 pcs.	—	—	Proof	500.00

3 PENCE

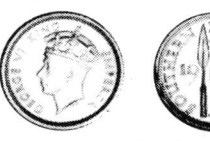

1.4100 g, .925 SILVER, .0419 oz ASW

KM#	Date	Mintage	Fine	VF	XF	Unc
1	1932	.688	.75	1.50	6.50	32.00
	1932	—	—	—	Proof	60.00
	1934	.628	.75	2.00	10.00	60.00
	1934	—	—	—	Proof	—
	1935	.840	.75	2.00	7.00	50.00
	1935	—	—	—	Proof	—
	1936	1.052	.75	2.00	7.00	50.00
	1936	—	—	—	Proof	—

KM#	Date	Mintage	Fine	VF	XF	Unc
9	1937	1.228	.75	2.00	6.00	30.00
	1937	—	—	—	Proof	250.00

Obv: KING moved behind head.

KM#	Date	Mintage	Fine	VF	XF	Unc
16	1939	.160	6.00	10.00	22.00	150.00
	1939	—	—	—	Proof	300.00
	1940	1.200	.75	2.00	7.00	40.00
	1940	—	—	—	Proof	—
	1941	.600	2.50	5.00	10.00	50.00
	1941	—	—	—	Proof	—
	1942	2.000	.50	1.50	6.50	30.00
	1942	—	—	—	Proof	—

1.4100 g, .500 SILVER, .0226 oz ASW

KM#	Date	Mintage	Fine	VF	XF	Unc
16a	1944	1.600	.50	1.50	10.00	65.00
	1945	.800	1.00	3.00	12.00	65.00
	1945	—	—	—	Proof	—
	1946	2.400	.50	1.50	7.00	35.00
	1946	—	—	—	Proof	—

COPPER-NICKEL

KM#	Date	Mintage	Fine	VF	XF	Unc
16b	1947	8.000	.40	.80	2.50	20.00
	1947	—	—	—	Proof	250.00

KM#	Date	Mintage	Fine	VF	XF	Unc
20	1948	2.000	.40	.80	3.50	30.00
	1948	—	—	—	Proof	—
	1949	4.000	.40	.80	3.00	25.00
	1949	—	—	—	Proof	150.00
	1951	5.600	.40	.80	2.50	20.00
	1951	—	—	—	Proof	—
	1952	4.800	.40	.80	2.50	30.00
	1952	—	—	—	Proof	150.00

6 PENCE

2.8300 g, .925 SILVER, .0841 oz ASW

KM#	Date	Mintage	Fine	VF	XF	Unc
2	1932	.544	2.00	3.50	10.00	60.00
	1932	—	—	—	Proof	75.00
	1934	.214	3.00	7.00	30.00	100.00
	1935	.380	2.00	6.00	30.00	100.00
	1935	—	—	—	Proof	—
	1936	.675	1.50	3.50	15.00	65.00
	1936	—	—	—	Proof	—

KM#	Date	Mintage	Fine	VF	XF	Unc
10	1937	.823	2.50	5.00	15.00	60.00
	1937	—	—	—	Proof	300.00

Obv: KING moved behind head.

KM#	Date	Mintage	Fine	VF	XF	Unc
17	1939	.200	3.00	7.00	45.00	200.00
	1939	—	—	—	Proof	450.00
	1940	.600	1.50	3.00	20.00	75.00
	1940	—	—	—	Proof	—
	1941	.300	2.00	4.00	15.00	65.00
	1941	—	—	—	Proof	—
	1942	1.200	1.00	2.00	7.50	55.00
	1942	—	—	—	Proof	200.00

2.8300 g, .500 SILVER, .0454 oz ASW

KM#	Date	Mintage	Fine	VF	XF	Unc
17a	1944	.800	1.25	2.50	15.00	90.00
	1945	.400	15.00	25.00	45.00	150.00
	1945	—	—	—	Proof	—
	1946	1.600	1.25	2.50	15.00	60.00
	1946	—	—	—	Proof	—

COPPER-NICKEL

KM#	Date	Mintage	Fine	VF	XF	Unc
17b	1947	5.000	.50	—	4.00	20.00
	1947	—	—	—	Proof	250.00

KM#	Date	Mintage	Fine	VF	XF	Unc
21	1948	1.000	.50	1.25	4.50	27.50
	1948	—	—	—	Proof	—
	1949	2.000	.50	1.00	3.50	30.00
	1949	—	—	—	Proof	250.00
	1950	2.000	.50	1.00	4.50	45.00
	1950	—	—	—	Proof	250.00
	1951	2.800	.50	1.00	2.50	22.50
	1951	—	—	—	Proof	—
	1952	1.200	.50	1.50	3.50	45.00
	1952	—	—	—	Proof	—

SHILLING

5.6600 g, .925 SILVER, .1683 oz ASW
Bird Sculpture

KM#	Date	Mintage	Fine	VF	XF	Unc
3	1932	.896	2.00	4.00	12.00	85.00
	1932	—	—	—	Proof	90.00
	1934	.333	4.00	8.00	35.00	175.00
	1935	.830	2.00	4.00	12.00	125.00
	1935	—	—	—	Proof	220.00
	1936	1.663	1.50	3.50	10.00	125.00
	1936	—	—	—	Proof	—

KM#	Date	Mintage	Fine	VF	XF	Unc
11	1937	1.700	2.00	4.00	12.00	90.00
	1937	—	—	—	Proof	300.00

Obv: KING moved behind head.

KM#	Date	Mintage	Fine	VF	XF	Unc
18	1939	.420	7.00	15.00	70.00	300.00
	1939	—	—	—	Proof	500.00
	1940	.750	5.50	12.00	50.00	175.00

KM#	Date	Mintage	Fine	VF	XF	Unc
18	1940	—	—	—	Proof	—
	1941	.800	6.50	12.00	45.00	150.00
	1941	—	—	—	Proof	—
	1942	2.100	2.00	4.00	15.00	55.00
	1942	—	—	—	Proof	—

5.6600 g, .500 SILVER, .0909 oz ASW

18a	1944	1.600	2.00	4.00	12.50	80.00
	1946	1.700	3.50	8.00	40.00	120.00
	1946	—	—	—	Proof	—

COPPER-NICKEL

18b	1947	8.000	.75	1.50	4.50	40.00
	1947	—	—	—	Proof	300.00

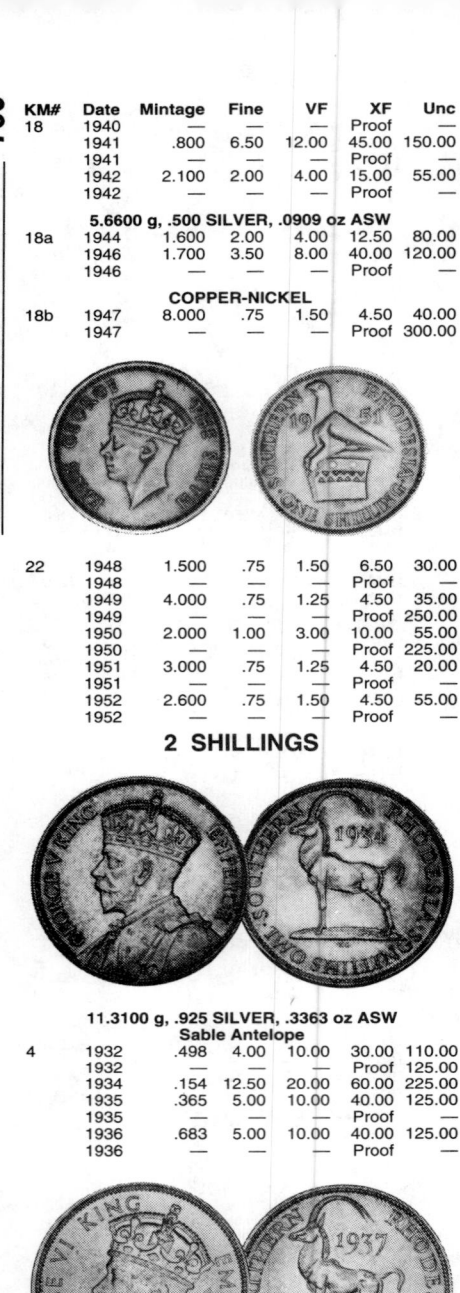

22	1948	1.500	.75	1.50	6.50	30.00
	1948	—	—	—	Proof	—
	1949	4.000	.75	1.25	4.50	35.00
	1949	—	—	—	Proof	250.00
	1950	2.000	1.00	3.00	10.00	55.00
	1950	—	—	—	Proof	225.00
	1951	3.000	.75	1.25	4.50	20.00
	1951	—	—	—	Proof	—
	1952	2.600	.75	1.50	4.50	55.00
	1952	—	—	—	Proof	—

2 SHILLINGS

11.3100 g, .925 SILVER, .3363 oz ASW
Sable Antelope

4	1932	.498	4.00	10.00	30.00	110.00
	1932	—	—	—	Proof	125.00
	1934	.154	12.50	20.00	60.00	225.00
	1935	.365	5.00	10.00	40.00	125.00
	1935	—	—	—	Proof	—
	1936	.683	5.00	10.00	40.00	125.00
	1936	—	—	—	Proof	—

12	1937	.552	7.50	20.00	45.00	135.00
	1937	—	—	—	Proof	400.00

Obv: KING moved behind head.

19	1939	.120	50.00	125.00	350.00	650.00
	1939	—	—	—	Proof	750.00
	1940	.525	8.00	16.00	75.00	250.00
	1940	—	—	—	Proof	—
	1941	.400	8.00	16.00	100.00	300.00
	1941	—	—	—	Proof	—
	1942	.850	4.00	8.00	25.00	90.00

11.3100 g, .500 SILVER, .1818 oz ASW

19a	1944	1.300	6.00	12.00	35.00	135.00
	1946	.700	100.00	200.00	300.00	650.00
	1946	—	—	—	Proof	—

COPPER-NICKEL

19b	1947	3.750	1.75	4.00	12.50	55.00
	1947	—	—	—	Proof	300.00

KM#	Date	Mintage	Fine	VF	XF	Unc
23	1948	.750	1.00	3.00	10.00	40.00
	1948	—	—	—	Proof	—
	1949	2.000	1.00	3.00	10.00	50.00
	1949	—	—	—	Proof	350.00
	1950	1.000	1.00	4.00	15.00	75.00
	1950	—	—	—	Proof	350.00
	1951	2.600	1.00	3.00	6.00	27.50
	1951	—	—	—	Proof	—
	1952	1.800	1.00	3.00	10.00	75.00
	1952	—	—	—	Proof	—

30	1954	.300	30.00	75.00	225.00	850.00
	1954	20 pcs.	—	—	Proof	1500.

1/2 CROWN

14.1400 g, .925 SILVER, .4205 oz ASW

5	1932	.634	5.00		30.00	100.00
	1932	—	—	—	Proof	125.00
	1934	.419	6.00	10.00	45.00	250.00
	1934	—	—	—	Proof	—
	1935	.512	5.00	8.00	32.50	175.00
	1935	—	—	—	Proof	—
	1936	.518	5.00	8.00	30.00	145.00
	1936	—	—	—	Proof	—

13	1937	1.174	4.50	8.00	30.00	135.00
	1937	—	—	—	Proof	350.00

15	1938	.400	5.00	8.50	32.00	150.00
	1938	—	—	—	Proof	—
	1939	.224	10.00	20.00	65.00	300.00
	1939	—	—	—	Proof	500.00
	1940	.800	5.00	8.50	27.50	80.00
	1940	—	—	—	Proof	—
	1941	1.240	3.00	6.00	15.00	65.00
	1941	—	—	—	Proof	—
	1942	2.008	3.00	6.00	15.00	70.00
	1942	—	—	—	Proof	—

14.1400 g, .500 SILVER, .2273 oz ASW

15a	1944	.800	4.00	8.00	22.50	80.00
	1946	1.400	4.00	10.00	27.50	150.00
	1946	—	—	—	Proof	—

COPPER-NICKEL

KM#	Date	Mintage	Fine	VF	XF	Unc
15b	1947	6.000	1.25	2.50	5.00	20.00
	1947	—	—	—	Proof	300.00

24	1948	.800	1.25	2.50	10.00	50.00
	1948	—	—	—	Proof	—
	1949	1.600	1.25	2.50	9.00	45.00
	1949	—	—	—	Proof	450.00
	1950	1.200	1.25	2.50	10.00	65.00
	1950	—	—	—	Proof	450.00
	1951	3.200	1.25	2.50	7.00	30.00
	1951	—	—	—	Proof	350.00
	1952	2.800	1.25	2.50	8.00	60.00
	1952	—	—	—	Proof	350.00

31	1954	1.200	10.00	17.50	45.00	85.00
	1954	20 pcs.	—	—	Proof	750.00

ZIMBABWE

MONETARY SYSTEM
100 Cents = 1 Dollar

CENT

BRONZE

KM#	Date	Mintage	VF	XF	Unc
1	1980	10.000	.10	.20	.40
	1980	.015	—	Proof	1.50
	1982	—	.10	.20	.40
	1983	—	.10	.20	.40
	1986	—	.10	.20	.40
	1988	—	.10	.20	.40
	1990	—	Reported, not confirmed		

BRONZE PLATED STEEL

1a	1989	—	.10	.20	.50
	1990	—	.10	.20	.50
	1991	—	.10	.20	.50
	1994	—	.10	.20	.50
	1995	—	.10	.20	.50
	1997	—	.10	.20	.50

5 CENTS

COPPER-NICKEL

2	1980	—	.15	.30	1.00
	1980	.015	—	Proof	1.50
	1982	—	.15	.30	1.00
	1983	—	.15	.30	1.00
	1988	—	.15	.30	1.00
	1989	—	.15	.30	1.00
	1990	—	.15	.30	1.00
	1991	—	.15	.30	1.00
	1995	—	.15	.30	1.00

10 CENTS

COPPER-NICKEL

KM#	Date	Mintage	VF	XF	Unc
3	1980	—	.15	.30	.75
	1980	.015	—	Proof	2.00
	1983	—	.15	.30	.75
	1987	—	.15	.30	.75
	1988	—	.15	.30	.75
	1989	—	.15	.30	.75
	1991	—	.15	.30	.75
	1994	—	.15	.30	.75

20 CENTS

COPPER-NICKEL

KM#	Date	Mintage	VF	XF	Unc
4	1980	—	.25	.50	1.50
	1980	.015	—	Proof	2.50
	1983	—	.25	.50	1.50
	1987	—	.20	.40	1.25
	1988	—	.20	.40	1.25
	1989	—	.20	.40	1.25
	1990	—	.20	.40	1.25
	1991	—	.20	.40	1.25
	1994	—	.20	.40	1.25
	1996	—	.20	.40	1.25

50 CENTS

COPPER-NICKEL

KM#	Date	Mintage	VF	XF	Unc
5	1980	—	.60	1.25	2.25
	1980	.015	—	Proof	4.50
	1988	—	.40	1.00	1.75
	1989	—	.40	1.00	1.75
	1990	—	.40	1.00	1.75
	1995	—	.40	1.00	1.75

DOLLAR

COPPER-NICKEL

KM#	Date	Mintage	VF	XF	Unc
6	1980	—	1.00	1.50	3.00
	1980	.015	—	Proof	6.50
	1993	—	1.00	1.50	3.00
	1997	—	1.00	1.50	3.00

2 DOLLARS

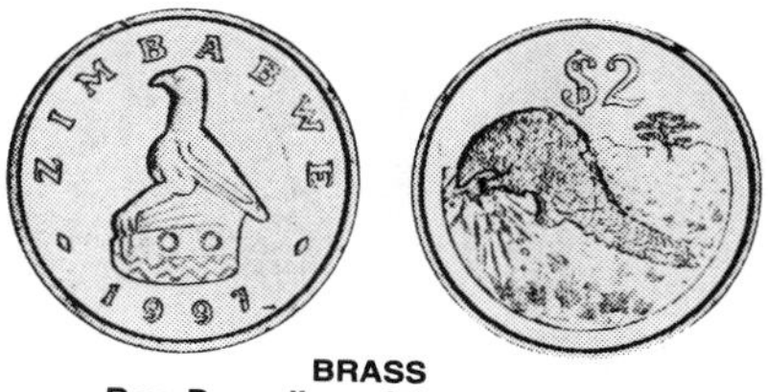

BRASS

Rev: Pangolin and denomination.

KM#	Date	Mintage	VF	XF	Unc
12	1997	—	—	—	5.00

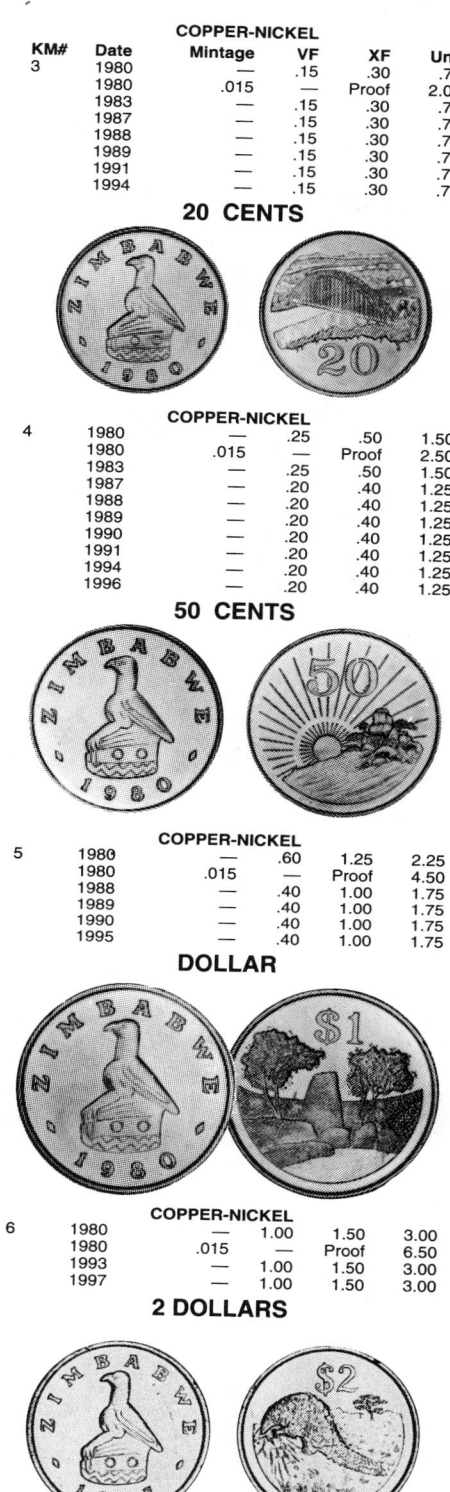

MONOGRAMS

MJ
Maximilian IV Joseph
Berg

CC99
Christian IX
Danish West Indies

V OC
Dutch East India
Co. (Indonesia)

CVII
Christian VII
Danish West Indies

CCX
Christian X
Danish West Indies

G
Georg
Mecklenburg-Strelitz

CWF
Carl Wilhelm
Ferdinand
Brunswick-
Wolfenbuttel

H7
Haakon VII
Norway

A
Albert I
Belgium

GRI
Georgius Rex
Imperator
New Guinea

L
Leopold II
Belgium

EAR
Ernest August Rex
Hannover

FRVI
Frederik VI Rex
Denmark

CX
Christian X
Denmark

A
Albert I
Belgium

AF
Adolph Friederich IV
Mecklenburg-Strelitz

B
Baudouin I
Belgium

C
Cayenne
French Guiana

CL
Carl & Louise
Saxe-Meiningen

CR
Christian VIII (Denmark)
Tranquebar

FW
Friedrich Wilhelm
Mecklenburg-Strelitz

C7
Christian VII
Tranquebar

C7
Christian VII
Denmark

CIX
Christian IX
Denmark

CCX
Christian X
Denmark

CCXIII
Charles XIII
Sweden

CLXIV
Carl XIV Johann
Norway

CXIV
Carl XIV Johann
Sweden

EP
Elizabeth-Philip
Great Britain

ERI
Edward Rex
Imperator
New Guinea

EIIR
Elizabeth II Regina
Cook Isl.

FA
Friedrich August
Lubeck Bishopric

FF
Friedrich Franz
Mecklenburg-
Schwerin

FJI
Franz Joseph I
Austria

O
Oscar I
Sweden

AFC
Alexius Friedrich
Christian
Anhalt-Bernburg

NII
Nicholas II
Russia

FRVII
Frederik VII Rex
Danish West Indies
Denmark

FC
Friedrich Christian
Brandenburg-
Bayreuth

AIII
Alexander III
Russia

W
William I
Netherlands

LLX
Ludwig X
Hesse-Darmstadt

MONOGRAMS

MJ
Maximilian IV Joseph
Berg

FI
Frederick IX & Ingrid
Denmark

F VI R
Fred. VI Denmark
Tranquebar

FVII
Frederick VII
Denmark

FF8
Frederick VIII
Denmark

F IX R
Frederick IX
Denmark

FVII
Ferdinand VII
Mexico

PI
Paul I
Russia

FVII
Ferdinand VII
Mexico

FW
Friedrich Wilhelm III
Prussia

GA IV
Gustav Adolf IV
Sweden

HI
Nicholas I
Russia

HC
Henri Christophe
Haiti

HVII
Haakon VII
Norway

HN
Hieronymus
Napoleon
Westphalia

J
Joachim (Murat)
Berg

E(K)I II
Katherine II
Russia

L
Ludwig
Hesse-Darmstadt

L
Leopold
Belgium

LL III
Leopold III
Belgium

LL
Louis XVIII
Antwerp

C XIVJ
Carl XIV Johann
Norway

M
Morelos
Revolutionary
Mexico

M 2 R
Margrethe II Regina
Denmark

NII
Nicholas II
Russia

NI
Nicholas I
Russia

NFP
Nicholas Friedrich
Peter
Oldenburg

OII
Oscar II
Norway

E
Ernest I
Saxe-Coburg-Gotha

O V
Olav V
Norway

P I
Paul I
Russia

P III
Peter III
Russia

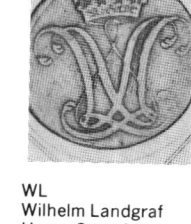

R
Rainier III
Monaco

WL
Wilhelm Landgraf
Hesse-Cassel

WR
William Rex
Hannover

PFA
Peter Friedrich
August
Oldenburg

OII
Oscar II
Sweden

GR
Georgius Rex
Hannover

FRVI
Frederik VI Rex
Tranquebar

PF
Paul Friedrich
Mecklenburg-
Schwerin

FII
Friedrich II
Wurttemberg

FER VII
Ferdinand VII
(Spain) Gerona

ILLUSTRATED GUIDE TO EASTERN MINT NAMES

PREPARED ESPECIALLY FOR THE **STANDARD CATALOG OF WORLD COINS** © 1999 KRAUSE PUBLICATIONS

Compiled by Harry S. Scherzer.
Scrip typeset by Ketab Corporation

Eastern mint names are basically composed of the Arabic alphabet which in fact covers a number of languages — Arabic is Semitic: Persian is Indo-European; and Malayan is in the Malayo-Polynesian group. Differences are not just of dialect, they are of basic structure. However, Arabic itself is the really important one, bearing a relationship to other Oriental languages not unlike that of Latin to the languages of Europe. Just as medieval European coins are inscribed in Latin, so are the majority of the coins of North African, Turkish, Persian, and Indian origin inscribed until very recent times in Arabic. A limited knowledge of Persian will also be necessary for unravelling the Persian poetic couplets found on Indian and Persian coins particularly during the seventeenth and eighteenth centuries A.D.

(Courtesy of Richard J. Plant)

"fi" (in)

"Zuriba" (was struck)

"Questentiniyah" Constantinople, Turkey

ANKARA
Turkey
انقره

AL-'ARAISH
"Larache", Morocco
العرايش

AL-'ARAISHAN
"Larache", Morocco
العرايشة

ABUSHAHR
"Bushire", Iran
ابو شهر

ADRANAH
"Edirne", Turkey
ادرنة

AFGHANISTAN
افغانستان

AHMADABAD
Bombay, India-British
احمد اباد

AHMADNAGAR-FARRUKHABAD
Afghanistan
احمدنكر فرخ اباد

AHMADPUR
See "Bahawalpur", Afghanistan
احمد پور

AHMADSHAHI
See "Ashraf Al-Bilad" and "Qandahar", Afghanistan
احمد شاهى

AJMAN
See "United Arab Emirates"
اجمان

AKSU
China-Sinkiang
اقصو

ALGERIA
See "Al-Jaza 'Iriyat"
—

BI-ANGLAND
"In England" (Birmingham) For Morocco
بانكلند

BI-ANGLAND
"In England" (London) For Morocco
بانكلند

DAULAT ANJAZANCHIYAH
"The State of Anjazanchiyah" See Comoros
دولة انجزنجية

ANWALA
"Aonla," Afghanistan
انوله

AL-ARABIYAT AS-SA'UDIYAT
"Saudi-Arabian", Saudi Arabia
العربية السعودية

ARDEBIL
Iran
اردبيل

ARKAT
"Arcot", India-French
اركات

ASHRAF AL-BILAD
"Most Noble of Cities" See "Ahmadshahi", Afghanistan
اشرف البلاد

ILLUSTRATED GUIDE TO EASTERN MINT NAMES

ASTARABAD
Iran

استراباد

ATCHEH
Indonesia

اجه

ATTOCK
Afghanistan

اتك

AZIMABAD
See "Patna", Bengal, India-British

عظیم اباد

BACAIM (no legends)
See "India-Portuguese"

—

BADAKHSHAN
See Afghanistan

بد خشان

BAGCHIH-SERAI
See "Krim"

باغجه سراي

BAGHDAD
Iraq

بغداد

BAHAWALPUR
See "Ahmadpur" and "Dar Es-Surur", Afghanistan

بها ولپور

BAHRAIN
See "El-Bahrain"

بحرین

EL-BAHRAIN
"Of the Two Seas", Bahrain

البحرین

BALKH
See "Umm Al-Bilad", Afghanistan

بلخ

BANARAS
"Awadh", Bengal, India-British

بنارس

BANDAR ABBAS
Iran

بندر عباس

BANJARMASIN
Indonesia

بنجرمسن

BARELI
Afghanistan

بریلي

BI BARIZ
"In Paris"
For Morocco

بباریز

BEHBEHAN
Iran

بهبهان

BERLIN
For Morocco

برلین

BHAKHAR
Afghanistan

بهکر

BOMBAY
See "Munbai", Bombay, India-British

—

BORUJERD
Iran

بروجرد

NEGRI BRUNEI
"State of Brunei", Brunei

نكري بروني

BRUSAH
"Bursa", Turkey

بروسة

BUKHARA
See Russian Turkestan

بخارا

BUSHIRE
See "Abushahr", Iran

—

CALCUTTA
See "Kalkatah", Bengal, India-British

كلكته

COCHIN
See India-Dutch and "V.O.C.", India-Dutch

—

COMOROS
See "Anjazanchiyah", "The Largest of the Islands", Comoros

كموز

DACCA
See "Jahangirnagar", Bengal, India-British

—

DAMAO (no legends)
See India-Portuguese

—

DAR AL-AMAN
"Abode of Security" (honorific)
See "Multan"

دار الامان

DAR AL-ISLAM
See Bahawalpur, India Princely States

دار الاسلام

DAR AL-MULK
"Abode of the King" (honorific)
See "Kabul"

دار الملك

DAR AL-NUSRAT
"Abode of the New (Town?)" (honorific)
See "Herat"

دار النصرت

DAR AL-KHILAFAT
"Abode of the Caliphate" (honorific)
See "Tehran" and "Yemen"

دار الخلافة

DAR AS-SALAM
"Abode of Peace" (honorific)
See "Ligkeh", Thailand

دار السلام

DAR AS-SULTANAT
"Abode of the Sultanate" (honorific)
See "Herat" and "Kabul", Afghanistan

دار السلطنة

DAR AS-SURUR
"Abode of Happiness" (honorific)
See "Bahawalpur", Afghanistan

دار السرور

DARBAND
Iran

دربند

ILLUSTRATED GUIDE TO EASTERN MINT NAMES

DARFUR
See "Al-Fasher", Sudan

دارفــرر

DEHLI
See "Shajahanabad", Afghanistan

دهلي

DELI
Indonesia

دلي

DERA
"Dera Ghazi Khan", Afghanistan

ديره

DERAJAT
"Dera Ishmael Khan", Afghanistan

ديره جات

DEZFUL
Iran

دزفول

DIU (no legends)
See India-Portuguese

—

DJIBOUTI
See "Jaibuti"

—

EDIRNE
See "Adranah", Turkey

—

EGYPT
See "Misr" and "Al-Misriyat"

—

ERAVAN
Iran

ايروان

FARRUKHABAD
Bengal, India-British

فرخ اباد

AL-FASHER
See "Darfur", Sudan

الفشير

FES
"Fez", Morocco

فاس

FERGANA
See "Khoqand",
Russian Turkestan

فرغانة

FILASTIN
"Palestine", Israel

فلسطين

AL-FUJAIRAH
See "United Arab Emirates"

الفجيره

GANJAH
Iran

گنجة

GERMAN EAST AFRICA
See "Sharakat Almaniyah",
Tanzania

شراكة المانية

GHAZNI
Afghanistan

غزني

GOA (no legends)
See India-Portuguese

—

HAIDARABAD SIND MINT
Afghanistan

حيدرآباد سند

HALEB
"Allepo", Syria

حلب

HAMADAN
Iran

يهمدان

AL-HARAR
Ethiopia-Eritrea

الهرر

AL-HEJAZ
Saudi Arabia-Hejaz

الحجاز

HERAT
See "Dar Al-Nushat" and "Dar As-Sultanat", Afghanistan

هرات

HERAT
Iran

يهرات

ILI
China-Sinkiang

الي

IRAN

ايران

AL-IRAQ
"Iraque"

العراق

AL-IRAQIYAT
"Iraqi," Iraq

العراقية

ISFAHAN
Iran

اصفهان

ISLAMBUL
Turkey

اسلامبول

ITALIAN SOMALILAND
See "Al-Somal Al-Italianiah",
Somalia

الصومال الايطاليانية

JAHANGIRNAGAR
See "Dacca", Bengal, India-British

جهانكيرنكر

BI-JAIBUTI
"In Djibouti", Djibouti

بجيبوتي

JAVA
Indonesia

جاوا

JAZA'IR
Algeria-Algiers

جزاير

AL-JAZA'IRIYAT
Algeria-Algiers

الجزايرة

JERING
"Jaring", Thailand

جريج

AL-JOMHURIYAT EL-IRAQIYAT
"The Iraqi Republic" Iraq

الجمهورية العرقية

AL-JOMHURIYAT EL-LUBNANIYAT
"The Lebanese Republic",
Lebanon

الجمهورية البنانية

ILLUSTRATED GUIDE TO EASTERN MINT NAMES

AL-JOMHURIYAT AL-MUTTAHIDAH AL-ARABIYAT
''United Arab Republic''
    See ''Egypt, Syria, Yemen''

الجمهورية المتحدة العربية

AL-JOMHURIYAT AS-SUDAN
''The Sudanese Republic'', Sudan

الجمهورية السودان

AL-JOMHURIYAT AS-SURIYAT
''The Syrian Republic'', Syria

الجمهورية السورية

AL-JOMHURIYAT AL-TUNISIAT
''The Tunisian Republic'', Tunisia

الجمهورية التونسية

AL-JOMHURIYAT AL-TURKIYAH
''The Turkish Republic'', Turkey

الجمهورية توركية

JORDAN
    See ''Al-Urduniyat'' and
    ''Al-Mamlakat, etc.,'' Jordan

———

KABUL
    See ''Dar Al-Mulk'' > AH1163 and
    ''Dar As-Sultanat'' >AH1164,
Afghanistan

كابل

KAFFA
    Krim, Russian Caucasia

كفه

KALKATAH
''Calcutta'', Bengal, India-British

كلكته

KASHAN
    Iran

كاشان

KASHMIR
    Afghanistan

كشمير

KASHQUAR
    China-Sinkiang

كشقر

KEDAH
    See ''Bilad Kedah'' and
    ''Bilad Al-Perlis Kedah'', Malaysia

كداه

KELANTAN
    See ''Khalifat Al-Mu'Minin'' and
    ''Negri Kelantin'', Malaysia

كلنتن

KEMASIN
    Malaysia

كماسن

KERMAN
    Iran

كرمان

KERMANSHAHAN
    See ''Kermanshah'', Iran

كرمانشاهان

KHALIFAT AL-MU'MININ
''Commander of the Faithful''
(honorific)
    See ''Kelantin'' and
    ''Trengganu''

خليفة المؤمنين

KHALIFAT AL-KARAM
''Noble Caliph'' (honorific)
    See ''Patani''

خليفة الكرم

KHANABAD
    Afghanistan

خان اباد

KHOQAND
    See Russian Turkestan

خوقند

KHUTAN
    China-Sinkiang

خوتن

KHUI
    See ''Khoy'', Iran

خوى

AL-KHURFAH
    See ''Yemen''

الخرفاه

KHWAREZM
    Russian Turkestan-Khiva

خوارزم

KOSOVAH
    Turkey

قوصوه

KOTSHA
    China-Sinkiang

كوتشر

AL-KUWAIT
    Kuwait

الكويت

LADAKH
    Afghanistan

لداخ

LAHEJ
    See ''Yemen''

لحج

LAHIJAN
    See ''Gilan'', Iran

لاهيجان

LAHORE
    Afghanistan

لاهور

LEBANON
    See ''Al-Lubnaniyat'' and
    ''Jomhuriyat, etc.''

———

AL-LIBIYAT
''Libyan'', Libya

اليبية

LIBYA
    See ''Al-Libyat'' and
    ''Mamlakat, etc.''

ليبيا

NEGRI LIGKEH
''State of Ligeh (or Ligor)''
    See ''Dar As-Salam'', Thialand

نكري لغكه

ILLUSTRATED GUIDE TO EASTERN MINT NAMES

AL-LUBNANIYAT
"Lebanese", Lebanon

النلنية

MACHHLIPATAN
See "Mazulipatam", India-French
"Masulipatam", India-Madras

مجهلي بتن

MACHHLIPATAN-BANDAR
See "Machhlipatan", India-Madras

مجهلي پتن بندر

AL-MAGHRIBIYAT
"Moroccan", Morocco

المغربية

TANAH MALAYU
"Land of the Malays"
See "Sumatra", Indonesia and
"Malacca", Malaysia

تانه ملايو

PULU MALAYU
"Island of the Malays"
See "Sumatra", Indonesia

قولو ملايو

MALUKA
Indonesia

ملوك

AL-MAMLAKAT AL-ARABIYAT
AL-SA'UDIYAT
"The Kingdom of Saudi Arabia"

المملكة
العربية السعودية

AL-MAMLAKAT AL-LIBIYAT
"The Kingdom of Libya"

المملكة الليبية

AL-MAMLAKAT AL-MAGHRIBIYAT
"The Kingdom of Morocco"

المملكة المغربية

AL-MAMLAKAT AL-MUTAWAKELIYAT
AL-YEMENIAT
"The Mutawakelite Kingdom of
Yemen"

المملكة
المتوكلية اليمنية

AL-MAMLAKAT AL-MISRIYAT
"The Kingdom of Egypt"

المملكة المصرية

AL-MAMLAKAT AL-URDUNIYAT
AL-HASHEMIYAT
"The Hashemite Kingdom of
Jordan"

المملكة
الاردنية الهاشمية

MANASTIR
Turkey

مناستر

MARAGHEH
Iran

مراغه

MARAKESH
"Marrakech", Morocco

مراكش

AL-MASCARA
Algeria-Algiers

المعسكر

MASH'HAD
Afghanistan

مشهد

MASH'HAD
Iran

مشهد

MASULIPATAM
See "Machhlipatan", India-Madras

——

MAZANDARAN
Iran

مازندران

MAZULIPATAM
See "Machhlipatan", India-French

——

MEDEA
Algeria-Algiers

مديه

MEKHA
"Mecca", Saudi-Arabia

مكة

MENANGKABAU
Indonesia

منفكابو

MIKNAS
"Meknes", Morocco

مكناس

MIKNASAH
"Meknes", Morocco

مكناسة

MISR
Egypt

مصر

AL-MISRIYAT
"Egptian", Egypt

المصرية

AL-MOHAMMEDIYAT ASH-SHERIFATE
"The Mohammedan Sherifate" or
"Empire Cherifien" (French), Morocco

المحمدية
الشريفة

MOMBASA
Kenya

ممباسه

MOROCCO
See "Al-Maghribyat" and
"Al-Mohammediyat Ash-Sherifate"

——

MOXOUDABAT
See "Murshidabad", India-French

——

MUBARAK
"Auspicious" (honorific)
See "Rikab"

مبارك

AL-MAKALA
"Mukalla"
See "Yemen"

المكلا

MULTAN
See "Dar Al-Aman", Afghanistan

ملتان

ILLUSTRATED GUIDE TO EASTERN MINT NAMES

MUNBAI
See "Bombay", India-British
منبي

MURADABAD
Afghanistan
مراد اباد

MURSHIDABAD
See "Moxoudabat", India-French
مرشد اباد

MURSHIDABAD
Bengal, India-British
مرشد اباد

MUSCAT
Oman
مسقط

NAJIBABAD
Afghanistan
نجيب اباد

NAKAPATTANAM (Tamil legends)
"Negapatnam", India-Dutch

NAKHCHAWAN
Iran
نخجوان

NEGAPATNAM
See "Nakappattanam"
———

NEJD
Saudi Arabia
نجد

NIHAWAND
Iran
نهاوند

NUKHWI
"Sheki", Iran
نخوى

NUKHWI
See "Sheki",
Russian Caucasia
نخوي

OMAN
عمان

OMDURMAN
Sudan
ام درمان

PAHANG
"Pahang Company", Malaysia
ڤاحغ

PAKISTAN
پاكستان

PALEMBANG
Indonesia
ڤلمبغ

PALESTINE
See "Filastin", Israel
———

PANA'HABAD
"Shusha"
See "Karabagh",
Russian Caucasia
پناه باد

AL-PATANI
See "Khalifat Al-Karam",
"Khalifat Al-Mu'Minin" and
"Bilad Al-Patani", Thailand
الفطاني

PATNA
See "Azimabad", Bengal,
India-British
پتنه

PULU PENANG
"Prince of Wales Island", Malaysia
ڤولو ڤنيغ

NEGRI PERAQ
"State of Perak", Malaysia
نڬري ڤيرق

PULU PERCHA
"Island of Sumatra", Indonesia
ڤولو فرج

PERLIS
See "Kedah", Malaysia
———

PESHAWAR
Afghanistan
پشاور

PHALICHERY
SEE "Pondichery", India-French
پهلجري

PONDICHERY
See "Phalichery", India-French
———

PONTIANAQ (no legends)
Indonesia
———

PULICAT (no legends)
See "India-Dutch"
———

QANDAHAR
See "Ashraf Al-Bilad" and
"Ahmadshahi", Afghanistan
قندهار

QATAR WA DUBAI
"Qatar and Dubai", Qatar
قطرودبي

DAULAT QATAR
"State of Qatar", Qatar
دولة قطر

QAZWIN
Iran
قزوين

QUAITI
Yemen
قيطي

QUM
Iran
قم

QUSANTINAT
"Constantine", Algeria-Algiers
قسنطينة

QUSTINTINIYAH
"Constantinople", Turkey
قسطنطينية

RA'NASH
Iran
رعنش

ILLUSTRATED GUIDE TO EASTERN MINT NAMES

RABAT
See "Rabat Al-Fath", Morocco

رباط

RABAT AL-FATH
"Rabat", Morocco

رباط الفتح

RAS AL-KHAIMA
See "United Arab Emirates"

راس الخيمه

RASHT
Iran

رشت

REHMAN
Thailand

رحمن

REZA'IYEH
See "Urumi", Iran

رظاعيه

RIKAB
See "Mubarak", Afghanistan

ركاب

RIKAB
Iran

ركاب

SA'UJBALAQ
Iran

ساوج بلاق

SAGAR
Bengal, India-British

ساگر

SAHRIND
Afghanistan

شهرند

AL-SAIWI
See "Bilad Al-Saiwi",
"Sai", "Saiburi" and
"Teluban", Thailand

السيوي

SAN'A
See "Yemen", Yemen
Republic

سنة

SARAKHS
Iran

سرخس

SARHIND
See "Sahrind", Afghanistan

——

SARI
Iran

ساري

SARI POL
Afghanistan

سربل

SAUDI ARABIA
"See "Al-Hejaz", "Nejd"
and "Al-Arabiyat As-Sa'udiya",
Saudi Arabia

——

NEGRI SELANGHUR
"State of Selangor", Malaysia

نكري سلاغور

SELANIK
"Salonika", Turkey

سلانيك

SHAJAHANABAD
See "Dehli", Afghanistan

شاجهان اباد

SHAMAKHI
Russian Caucasia

شماخ

SHAMAKHA
Russian Caucasia

شماخه

SHARAKAT ALMANIYAH
"German Company" or
"German East Africa", Tanzania

شراكتة المانيا

ES-SHARJAH
See "United Arab Emirates"

الشارجة

SHIRAZ
Iran

شيراز

SHUSHTAR
Iran

شوشتر

NEGRI SIAK
"State of Siak", Indonesia

نكري سيك

SIMNAN
Iran

سمنان

SIND
Afghanistan

سند

AL-SOMAL AL-ITALIANIYAH
"Italian Somaliland", Somalia

الصومال الايطليانية

SULTANABAD
Iran

سلطاناباد

SUMENEP
Indonesia

سمنف

SURAT
See "Surate", India-French

سورت

SURAT
Bombay, India-British

سورت

AS-SURIYAT
"Syrian", Syria

السورية

AL-SUWAIR
"Essaouira Mogador", Morocco

الصوير

AL-SUWAIRAH
"Essaouira Mogador", Morocco

الصويرة

SYRIA
See "Haleb", As-Suriyat",
"Jomhuriyat, etc.", Syria

——

TABARISTAN
Iran

طبرستان

TABRIZ
Iran

تبريز

ILLUSTRATED GUIDE TO EASTERN MINT NAMES

TANGIER
See "Tanjah", Morocco
—

TANJAH
"Tangier", Morocco
طنجة

TAQIDEMT
Algeria-Algiers
تاقدمت

TARABALUS GHARB
"Tripoli West", Libya
طرابلس غرب

TARIM
See "Yemen"
تريم

NEGRI TARUMON
"State of Tarumon", Indonesia
نكري ترومن

TASHQURGHAN
Afghanistan
تاش قورغان

TATTA
Afghanistan
تته

TEGNAPATAM (no legends)
"Fort St. David", Madras, India-British
—

TEHRAN
See "Dar Al-Khilafat", Iran
طهران

TELLICHERY
Bombay, India-British
تلچري

TETUAN
Morocco
تطوان

TIFLIS
See Russia, Georgia
تفليس

TRANQUEBAR (no legends)
See "India-Danish"
—

TRENGKANU
See "Khalifat Al-Mu'Minin", Malaysia
ترغكانو

TUNIS
Tunisia
تونس

TUNISIA
See "Tunis", "Al-Tunisiyat", "Jomhuriyat, etc."
—

AL-TUNISIYAT
"Tunisian," Tunisia
التونسية

TURKEY
See "Turkiyah", "Jomhuriyat, etc."
—

AL-TURKIYAH
"Turkish", Turkey
التوركية

TUTICORIN (degenerate Nagari legends)
See "India-Dutch"
—

TUYSERKAN
Iran
توى سركان

TANAH UGI
"Land of the Bugis", Indonesia
تانه اغيسى

UMM AL-BILAD
"Mother of Cities"
See "Balkh", Afghanistan
ام البلاد

UMM AL-QAIWAIN
See "United Arab Emirates"
ام القوين

UNITED ARAB EMIRATES
—

UNITED ARAB REPUBLIC
See "Al-Jomhuriyat Al-Arabiyat AL-Muttahidah
الامارات العربية المتحدة

AL-URDUNIYAT
"Jordanian", Jordan
الاردنية

URUMCHI
China-Sinkiang
ارومجي

URUMI
See "Reza'iyeh", Iran
ارومى

USHI
China-Sinkiang
اوش

WAN
"Van", Turkey
وان

YARKHAND
China-Sinkiang
يارقند

YARKHISSARMARAN
"Yanghissar"
China-Sinkiang
ياركسارمرن

YAZD
Iran
يزد

YEMEN
See "Sana", "Dar Al-Khilafat", Al-Yemeniyat", Mamlakat, etc."
—

AL-YEMENIYAT
"The Yemen"
اليمنية

ZANJAN
Iran
زنجان

ZANJIBARA
"Zanzibar", Tanzania
زنجباراه